UNIVERSITY CASEBOOK SERIES®

THE SUPREME COURT AND THE CONSTITUTION

ERNEST A. YOUNG

Alston & Bird Professor of Law

Duke University School of Law

FOUNDATION PRESS

University Casebook Series is a trademark registered in the U.S. Patent and Trademark Office.

© 2017 LEG, Inc. d/b/a West Academic
    444 Cedar Street, Suite 700
    St. Paul, MN 55101
    1-877-888-1330

Printed in the United States of America

ISBN: 978-1-62810-030-3

For Alex, Michael, and Caroline

INTRODUCTION

This volume is, in truth, the second edition to my earlier casebook, *The Supreme Court and the Constitutional Structure*. Because this edition significantly expands the coverage of individual rights, the old title no longer fits. As before, these materials are designed for an introductory, first-year course in Constitutional Law. The traditional course in this area was once comprehensive, covering both governmental structure and individual rights. Most Constitutional Law texts continue to attempt coverage of the entire subject, even though the course is rarely taught that way today. My impression is that most law schools now teach an introductory course that combines governmental structure—that is, judicial review, federalism, and separation of powers—with a more limited selection of individual rights. Most civil liberties issues are left to upper-level courses focusing on the First Amendment, race and the Constitution, privacy, and the like. The result is that most casebooks are at once too long and too short for the introductory course: they cover at length subjects generally not taught in the first year (for example, free speech), and their coverage of structural matters like separation of powers is often too abbreviated.

These materials seek to remedy that defect. They proceed in four parts. Part One is a brief introduction to the Constitution itself, a bit of constitutional theory, and the institution of judicial review—the courts' power to invalidate actions of the other branches of government on the ground that they are contrary to the Constitution. Part Two then undertakes a historical survey of the U.S. Supreme Court's exercise of that power. This portion of the course tries to kill two birds with one stone: it elaborates the structural role of the Court in the constitutional scheme, and—by canvassing some of the Court's most prominent civil liberties decisions—it provides some basic constitutional literacy on many individual rights issues that might not otherwise be covered in an introductory course. Notwithstanding the latter purpose, the arrangement of this Part is historical, rather than doctrinal, and the idea is to provide a sense of the development of the Court's role rather than an overview of constitutional law concerning individual rights. Part Two also introduces some basic issues of constitutional methodology, focusing on approaches to constitutional interpretation.

Part Three turns to the structural Constitution—specifically federalism and separation of powers. This portion of the course *is* doctrinal in its focus, and the emphasis is on current case law. On the federalism side, these materials focus on the "Federalist Revival" of the Rehnquist and Roberts Courts, in which the Court has taken at least some tentative steps toward enforceable limits on national power. Federal courts have always been far less reluctant to enforce limits on *state* power, and these materials offer reasonably extensive coverage of the "dormant" Commerce Clause and the doctrine of preemption. On the separation of powers side, I have stressed the theme that statutory law significantly complements constitutional principle in this area. That theme is most evident in the *Steel Seizure* case, which made presidential powers largely a function of congressional authorization or prohibition, but it also dominates discussion of legislative delegations to administrative agencies. I have long felt that it is misleading to teach the demise of the constitutional delegation doctrine after 1935 without also noting the degree to which the function of constitutional nondelegation review is now largely filled by statutory review under the Administrative Procedure Act. These materials thus offer a mini-introduction to Administrative Law, which will hopefully whet students' appetite for the upper level course in that subject. Finally, Part Three concludes with an extensive discussion of foreign affairs and military powers.

Part Four, which is new in this edition, adds extensive doctrinal coverage of the Due Process and Equal Protection Clauses. Most introductory courses seem to focus their coverage of individual rights in these areas. Individual chapters thus build on the introduction to these principles in Part Two by exploring contemporary doctrine. The Part concludes with a separate chapter-long case study of the Supreme Court's gay rights jurisprudence, which has combined both due process and equal principles, culminating in the *Obergefell* decision.

The addition of Part Four in the current edition affords considerable flexibility in shaping a syllabus. My own course (4.5 credit hours) is structure-heavy; it covers all of Parts One, Two, and Three and adds only the *Obergefell* case as a conclusion to Part Two. An instructor that wanted to retain the historical account in Part Two but balance structure and rights more evenly could cover Parts One, Two, and then draw evenly from Three and Four to round out the semester. Or, if one wanted to downplay the history and survey contemporary doctrine, one could teach Part One, excerpts of Part Two (perhaps *McCulloch*, *Brown* and *Roe*), and then most of Parts Three and Four. The current edition probably too long to teach in its entirety in most courses—although the glorious two-semester, six credit format that Villanova Law School employed in my first year of teaching could give it a shot—but it ought to offer far more options to instructors who do not share the author's obsession with constitutional structure.

Students often ask me to recommend historical works as background to the materials in this course. While I have attempted to include some historical background in the text, space permits relatively little detail and, in any event, I am not a professional historian. Outside reading can thus be a valuable supplement to these materials, particularly for those students coming to law school from a non-Liberal Arts background. The most critical periods are the Founding, Reconstruction, and the New Deal. The literature on each period, and on constitutional history in general, is vast. What follows are works that have been particularly helpful to me.

An excellent general history of the Supreme Court through each of these periods and up to the present, which I have at times assigned as a supplement to these materials, is ROBERT G. MCCLOSKEY, THE AMERICAN SUPREME COURT (4th ed., revised by Sanford Levinson 2005). LUCAS A. POWE, JR., THE SUPREME COURT AND THE AMERICAN ELITE (Harvard 2009) covers much of the same ground, but from a somewhat updated perspective that stresses the majoritarian character of the Court. On the Founding, the industry standards are JACK N. RAKOVE, ORIGINAL MEANINGS: POLITICS AND IDEAS IN THE MAKING OF THE CONSTITUTION (Knopf 1997), and GORDON S. WOOD, THE CREATION OF THE AMERICAN REPUBLIC, 1776–1787 (W.W. Norton 1969). The leading work on Reconstruction is ERIC FONER, RECONSTRUCTION: AMERICA'S UNFINISHED REVOLUTION 1863–1877 (Harper & Row 1988). For the New Deal, try DAVID M. KENNEDY, FREEDOM FROM FEAR: THE AMERICAN PEOPLE IN DEPRESSION AND WAR, 1929–1945 (Oxford 2001), or (considerably shorter) WILLIAM E. LEUCHTENBERG, THE SUPREME COURT REBORN: THE CONSTITUTIONAL REVOLUTION IN THE AGE OF ROOSEVELT (Oxford 1996). The only slightly less important Warren Court period is ably chronicled in LUCAS A. POWE, JR., THE WARREN COURT AND AMERICAN POLITICS (Belknap 2002). And the late Chief Justice's book, WILLIAM H. REHNQUIST, ALL THE LAWS BUT ONE: CIVIL LIBERTIES IN WARTIME (Vintage 2000), provides useful background to the various cases concerning national security. I do *not* recommend so-called "behind the scenes" accounts of the Supreme Court, its Justices, and its law clerks. These tend to be tendentious, self-serving, and riddled with inaccuracies. They also tend to distract attention from the Court's practice of issuing comprehensive written explanations for why it does what it does.

A number of works provide an accessible introduction to constitutional theory. These include ALEXANDER M. BICKEL, THE LEAST DANGEROUS BRANCH: THE SUPREME COURT AT THE BAR OF POLITICS (Yale 1962), JOHN HART ELY, DEMOCRACY AND DISTRUST: A THEORY OF JUDICIAL REVIEW (Harvard 1980), and ROBERT H. BORK, THE TEMPTING OF AMERICA: THE POLITICAL SEDUCTION OF THE LAW (Free Press 1997). A helpful overview of both theory and doctrine can be found in RICHARD H. FALLON, JR., THE DYNAMIC CONSTITUTION: AN INTRODUCTION TO AMERICAN CONSTITUTIONAL LAW (Cambridge 2004). The two leading treatises on Constitutional Law take quite different approaches. An extremely lucid and accessible summary is ERWIN CHEMERINSKY, CONSTITUTIONAL LAW: PRINCIPLES AND POLICIES (Aspen, 5th ed. 2015). Laurence Tribe's treatise provides a more opinionated guide. Only the first volume of the more recent edition is complete, LAURENCE TRIBE, AMERICAN CONSTITUTIONAL LAW (Foundation, 3d ed. 2000), but it covers most of the issues in this introductory course. For other issues, see the single-volume second edition, published in 1988.

For assistance in developing these materials, I am grateful to Chase Anderson, Johnson Atkinson, Kelli Baxter, Chris Berg, Gladys Bethea, Leah Brenner, Emily Borgen, Dawn Cronce, George Brell, Hillary Bunsow, David Coleman, Christine Couvillon, Ari Cuenin, Lee Czocher, Amelia DeGory, Jennifer Ferri, Rebecca Holljes, Elizabeth Hardy, Kalani Hawks, Jeffrey Lieberman, Shatanya McClure, Kerry Burns, Christine Wells, Karim Pirani, Daniel Rice, Adriana Rios, Hope Staneski, Francis Stapleton, Elle Stuart, Lauren Tanner, James Tian, Christine Umeh, and Tia Williams, as well as to my constitutional law students at Dartmouth College, Duke Law School, the University of Texas School of Law, and the Villanova University School of Law. I am also thankful for the unflagging support and wise counsel of my dean, David Levi, at Duke. I could not have undertaken this work without the benefit of great teachers and colleagues in this subject: Vincent Starzinger at Dartmouth, Richard Fallon, Charles Fried, Dan Meltzer, and Laurence Tribe at Harvard, Joseph Blocher, Curt Bradley, Guy Charles, and Neil Siegel at Duke, and, most important, my mentors at the University of Texas, Doug Laycock, Sandy Levinson, H.W. Perry, and Scot Powe. It is a privilege to labor in their vineyard.

Finally, no work of this magnitude reaches completion without incurring substantial debts at home. My wife Erin Blondel was a trusted critic and sounding board on matters of both style and substance. My sons Alex and Michael have inspired me as to the general interest of this work and also helped me to keep it in perspective. (Thanks for all those Founding Fathers bobbleheads, guys.) And my daughter Caroline, born during the revision of this book, has been both a delightful distraction and a reminder of the continuing importance of preserving our Constitution for the future.

ERNEST A. YOUNG
APEX, NORTH CAROLINA

June 2017

SUMMARY OF CONTENTS

TABLE OF CONTENTS

PART THREE. THE STRUCTURAL CONSTITUTION

TABLE OF CASES

The principal cases are in bold type.

UNIVERSITY CASEBOOK SERIES®

THE SUPREME COURT AND THE CONSTITUTION

PART ONE

THE CONSTITUTION AND JUDICIAL REVIEW

The American constitutional tradition is unusual, if not unique, both in the longevity of its founding document and the leading role it accords to courts in enforcing constitutional principles. This introductory Part focuses on both of these issues. The initial focus on courts is not, however, meant to downplay the critical role that other institutions—*e.g.*, Congress, the President, state governmental officials, and popular movements—play in constitutional interpretation. The role of non-judicial interpreters will come up throughout the course.

Chapter One introduces the Constitution itself as well as some basic issues of constitutional theory. The most important of these issues is the "Dead Hand Problem"—that is, why citizens of the contemporary United States should remain beholden to a document drafted by people long dead, who lived in a much different world. The recent case of *District of Columbia v. Heller*, which struck down the District of Columbia's handgun ban under the Second Amendment, illustrates this problem. If a democratically elected government concludes that public safety requires a ban on handguns, why should that conclusion be set aside on the basis of an ancient text drafted in ignorance of current conditions and imperatives? *Heller* also introduces two methods of constitutional interpretation: textualism and originalism. This book will highlight other important modalities of constitutional interpretation as they figure in other courses throughout the course.

Chapter Two turns to the role of the courts in enforcing the Constitution through their power of judicial review. The constitutional text does not explicitly recognize that power, and Chief Justice John Marshall's case for it in *Marbury v. Madison* remains controversial (as an academic matter, at least) even today. Under *Marbury*, the Supreme Court's power to "say what the law is" is an awesome one; the Court's interpretation of the Constitution may be overturned only by its own subsequent decision or by a constitutional amendment. But the power is not unlimited, and Chapter Two explores two important constraints on it: the "case or controversy" requirement of Article III and the political question doctrine. Other limits will emerge later in the course.

CHAPTER ONE

THE CONSTITUTION AND THE DEAD HAND

Unlike most courses in law school, Constitutional Law is built around a single canonical text. Notwithstanding that fact, the overwhelming majority of this book consists of constitutional decisions by the Supreme Court of the United States; indeed, many constitutional law texts place the document itself at the end in an appendix. This Chapter begins with the Constitution's text, because it is well to remember that the text remains primary to what the judges have said about it.

This course will also explore the relationship between the constitutional document and constitutional doctrine, theory, and history. By constitutional *doctrine*, we mean the operative rules of the Constitution—often developed by judges—that bear on the exercise of constitutional power and the resolution of constitutional disputes. Constitutional *theory*, on the other hand, includes a broad array of general principles and ideas concerning questions such as what values the Constitution embodies, why the Constitution binds us today, who should have authority to interpret the Constitution and how they should go about that task, and how constitutional doctrine should be formulated so as to secure the ends of constitutional law. Finally, constitutional *history* is important not only to provide context for the constitutional document and judicial decisions interpreting it, but also because historical understandings and practices often have binding force in constitutional law.

Three theoretical questions are central in this introductory chapter: What do constitutions *do*? Why do we continue to obey them long after the people who drafted and ratified them are dead? And what is the best methodology for interpreting constitutional meaning?

SECTION 1.1 CONSTITUTIONAL FUNCTIONS

Unlike many constitutions around the world, the U.S. Constitution can be read at one sitting. (The more recent constitutional treaty proposed for the European Union, by contrast, was over 300 pages in length, and one suspects that the French government's decision to send a copy of this door-stopper to every French citizen immediately prior to the vote on ratification in 2005 may not have been entirely helpful in rallying public support for the proposed document.[1]) Nonetheless, hardly

---

[1] The proposed constitutional treaty for the European Union is available online at http://europa.eu/eu-law/decisionmaking/treaties/pdf/treaty_establishing_a_constitution_for_

anyone reads the U.S. Constitution straight through anymore, and most attention tends to focus on a very few well-known provisions—*e.g.*, the First Amendment, the Commerce Clause, the first section of the Fourteenth Amendment.

As you read the *whole* document, consider the following questions:

1. Who is the intended audience for this document? Is it directed to lawyers? Or to the People at large?

2. What issues must a constitution address? What can be left for statutes and practice to fill in? Are there any issues missing that you think should be addressed in the document? Any subjects that don't belong?

3. The provisions of the original Constitution and the Bill of Rights reflect the preoccupations and concerns of its Framers in 1787 and 1791. What were they most worried about? To what extent are our present-day expectations of and concerns about government similar and dissimilar to theirs?

4. Look at the ratification dates of the amendments. They tend to cluster in particular historical periods. What explains these various bursts of amending activity, followed by long periods in which no formal changes were made to the document? What was going on in the country at these active times?

5. To what extent do the textual amendments really capture the basic changes over time in the structure of our government and the basic rights people have (or think they have)?

The Constitution of the United States of America

We the People of the United States, in Order to form a more perfect Union, establish Justice, insure domestic Tranquility, provide for the common defence, promote the general Welfare, and secure the Blessings of Liberty to ourselves and our Posterity, do ordain and establish this Constitution for the United States of America.

ARTICLE I

SECTION 1. All legislative Powers herein granted shall be vested in a Congress of the United States, which shall consist of a Senate and House of Representatives.

SECTION 2. [1] The House of Representatives shall be composed of Members chosen every second Year by the People of the several States,

---

europe/treaty_establishing_a_constitution_for_europe_en.pdf. That version failed after rejection by France and Dutch voters in 2005. The Lisbon Treaty, which contained many of the same reforms but was somewhat more modest in form, took effect on December 1, 2009.

and the Electors in each state shall have the Qualifications requisite for Electors of the most numerous Branch of the State Legislature.

[2] No Person shall be a Representative who shall not have attained to the Age of twenty five Years, and been seven Years a Citizen of the United States, and who shall not, when elected, be an Inhabitant of that State in which he shall be chosen.

[3] Representatives and direct Taxes shall be apportioned among the several States which may be included within this Union, according to their respective Numbers, which shall be determined by adding to the whole Number of free Persons, including those bound to Service for a Term of Years, and excluding Indians not taxed, three fifths of all other Persons. The actual Enumeration shall be made within three Years after the first Meeting of the Congress of the United States, and within every subsequent Term of ten Years, in such Manner as they shall by Law direct. The Number of Representatives shall not exceed one for every thirty Thousand, but each State shall have at Least one Representative; and until such enumeration shall be made, the State of New Hampshire shall be entitled to chuse three, Massachusetts eight, Rhode-Island and Providence Plantations one, Connecticut five, New York six, New Jersey four, Pennsylvania eight, Delaware one, Maryland six, Virginia ten, North Carolina five, South Carolina five, and Georgia three.

[4] When vacancies happen in the Representation from any State, the Executive Authority thereof shall issue Writs of Election to fill such Vacancies.

[5] The House of Representatives shall chuse their Speaker and other Officers; and shall have the sole Power of Impeachment.

SECTION 3. [1] The Senate of the United States shall be composed of two Senators from each State, chosen by the Legislature thereof, for six Years; and each Senator shall have one Vote.

[2] Immediately after they shall be assembled in Consequence of the first Election, they shall be divided as equally as may be into three Classes. The Seats of the Senators of the first Class shall be vacated at the Expiration of the second Year, of the second Class at the Expiration of the fourth Year, and the third Class at the Expiration of the sixth Year, so that one third may be chosen every second Year; and if Vacancies happen by Resignation, or otherwise, during the Recess of the Legislature of any State, the Executive thereof may make temporary Appointments until the next Meeting of the Legislature, which shall then fill such Vacancies.

[3] No Person shall be a Senator who shall not have attained to the Age of thirty Years, and been nine Years a Citizen of the United States, and who shall not, when elected, be an Inhabitant of that State for which he shall be chosen.

[4] The Vice President of the United States shall be President of the Senate, but shall have no Vote, unless they be equally divided.

[5]   The Senate shall chuse their other Officers, and also a President pro tempore, in the Absence of the Vice President, or when he shall exercise the Office of President of the United States.

[6]   The Senate shall have the sole Power to try all Impeachments. When sitting for that Purpose, they shall be on Oath or Affirmation. When the President of the United States is tried, the Chief Justice shall preside: And no Person shall be convicted without the Concurrence of two thirds of the Members present.

[7]   Judgment in Cases of Impeachment shall not extend further than to removal from Office, and disqualification to hold and enjoy any Office of honor, Trust or Profit under the United States: but the Party convicted shall nevertheless be liable and subject to Indictment, Trial, Judgment and Punishment, according to Law.

SECTION 4. [1] The Times, Places and Manner of holding Elections for Senators and Representatives, shall be prescribed in each State by the Legislature thereof; but the Congress may at any time by Law make or alter such Regulations, except as to the Places of chusing Senators.

[2]   The Congress shall assemble at least once in every Year, and such Meeting shall be on the first Monday in December, unless they shall by Law appoint a different Day.

SECTION 5. [1] Each House shall be the Judge of the Elections, Returns and Qualifications of its own Members, and a Majority of each shall constitute a Quorum to do Business; but a smaller Number may adjourn from day to day, and may be authorized to compel the Attendance of absent members, in such Manner, and under such Penalties as each House may provide.

[2]   Each House may determine the Rules of its Proceedings, punish its Members for disorderly Behaviour, and, with the Concurrence of two thirds, expel a Member.

[3]   Each House shall keep a Journal of its Proceedings, and from time to time publish the same, excepting such Parts as may in their Judgment require Secrecy; and the Yeas and Nays of the Members of either House on any question shall, at the Desire of one fifth of those Present, be entered on the Journal.

[4]   Neither House, during the Session of Congress, shall, without the Consent of the other, adjourn for more than three days, nor to any other place than that in which the two Houses shall be sitting.

SECTION 6. [1] The Senators and Representatives shall receive a Compensation for their Services, to be ascertained by Law, and paid out of the Treasury of the United States. They shall in all Cases, except Treason, Felony and Breach of the Peace, be privileged from Arrest during their Attendance at the Session of their respective Houses, and in going to and returning from the same; and for any Speech or Debate in either House, they shall not be questioned in any other Place.

[2] No Senator or Representative shall, during the Time for which he was elected, be appointed to any civil Office under the authority of the United States, which shall have been created, or the Emoluments whereof shall have been encreased during such time; and no Person holding any Office under the United States, shall be a Member of either House during his Continuance in Office.

SECTION 7. [1] All Bills for raising Revenue shall originate in the House of Representatives; but the Senate may propose or concur with Amendments as on other Bills.

[2] Every Bill which shall have passed the House of Representatives and the Senate, shall, before it become a Law, be presented to the President of the United States: If he approve he shall sign it, but if not he shall return it, with his Objections to that House in which it shall have originated, who shall enter the Objections at large on their Journal, and proceed to reconsider it. If after such Reconsideration two thirds of that House shall agree to pass the Bill, it shall be sent, together with the Objections, to the other House, by which it shall likewise be reconsidered, and if approved by two thirds of that House, it shall become a Law. But in all such Cases the Votes of both Houses shall be determined by Yeas and Nays, and the Names of the Persons voting for and against the Bill shall be entered on the Journal of each House respectively. If any Bill shall not be returned by the President within ten days (Sundays excepted) after it shall have been presented to him, the Same shall be a Law, in like Manner as if he had signed it, unless the Congress by their Adjournment prevent its Return, in which Case it shall not be a Law.

[3] Every Order, Resolution, or Vote to which the Concurrence of the Senate and House of Representatives may be necessary (except on a question of Adjournment) shall be presented to the President of the United States; and before the Same shall take Effect, shall be approved by him, or being disapproved by him, shall be repassed by two thirds of the Senate and House of Representatives, according to the Rules and Limitations prescribed in the Case of a Bill.

Section 8. [1] The Congress shall have Power To lay and collect Taxes, Duties, Imposts and Excises, to pay the Debts and provide for the common Defence and general Welfare of the United States; but all Duties, Imposts and Excises shall be uniform throughout the United States;

[2] To borrow Money on the credit of the United States;

[3] To regulate Commerce with foreign Nations, and among the several States, and with the Indian Tribes;

[4] To establish an uniform Rule of Naturalization, and uniform Laws on the subject of Bankruptcies throughout the United States;

[5] To coin Money, regulate the Value thereof, and of foreign Coin, and fix the Standard of Weights and Measures;

[6]   To provide for the Punishment of counterfeiting the Securities and current Coin of the United States;

[7]   To establish Post Offices and post Roads;

[8]   To promote the Progress of Science and useful Arts, by securing for limited Times to Authors and Inventors the exclusive Right to their respective Writings and Discoveries;

[9]   To constitute Tribunals inferior to the supreme Court;

[10] To define and punish Piracies and Felonies committed on the high Seas, and Offenses against the Law of Nations;

[11] To declare War, grant Letters of Marque and Reprisal, and make Rules concerning Captures on Land and Water;

[12] To raise and support Armies, but no Appropriation of Money to that Use shall be for a longer Term than two Years;

[13] To provide and maintain a Navy;

[14] To make Rules for the Government and Regulation of the land and naval Forces;

[15] To provide for calling forth the Militia to execute the Laws of the Union, suppress Insurrections and repel Invasions;

[16] To provide for organizing, arming, and disciplining, the Militia, and for governing such Part of them as may be employed in the Service of the United States, reserving to the States respectively, the Appointment of the Officers, and the Authority of training the Militia according to the discipline prescribed by Congress;

[17] To exercise exclusive Legislation in all Cases whatsoever, over such District (not exceeding ten Miles square) as may, by Cession of particular States, and the Acceptance of Congress, become the Seat of the Government of the United States, and to exercise like Authority over all Places purchased by the Consent of the Legislature of the State in which the Same shall be, for the Erection of Forts, Magazines, Arsenals, dock-Yards, and other needful Buildings;—And

[18] To make all Laws which shall be necessary and proper for carrying into Execution the foregoing Powers, and all other Powers vested by this Constitution in the Government of the United States, or in any Department or Officer thereof.

SECTION 9. [1] The Migration or Importation of such Persons as any of the States now existing shall think proper to admit, shall not be prohibited by the Congress prior to the Year one thousand eight hundred and eight, but a Tax or duty may be imposed on such Importation, not exceeding ten dollars for each Person.

[2]   The Privilege of the Writ of Habeas Corpus shall not be suspended, unless when in Cases of Rebellion or Invasion the public Safety may require it.

[3]   No Bill of Attainder or ex post facto Law shall be passed.

[4] No Capitation, or other direct, Tax shall be laid, unless in Proportion to the Census or Enumeration herein before directed to be taken.

[5] No Tax or Duty shall be laid on Articles exported from any State.

[6] No Preference shall be given by any Regulation of Commerce or Revenue to the Ports of one State over those of another; nor shall Vessels bound to, or from, one State, be obliged to enter, clear, or pay Duties in another.

[7] No Money shall be drawn from the Treasury, but in Consequence of Appropriations made by Law; and a regular Statement and Account of the Receipts and Expenditures of all public Money shall be published from time to time.

[8] No Title of Nobility shall be granted by the United States: And no Person holding any Office of Profit or Trust under them, shall, without the Consent of the Congress, accept of any present, Emolument, Office, or Title, of any kind whatever, from any King, Prince, or foreign State.

SECTION 10. [1] No State shall enter into any Treaty, Alliance, or Confederation; grant Letters of Marque and Reprisal; coin Money; emit Bills of Credit; make any Thing but gold and silver Coin a Tender in Payment of Debts; pass any Bill of Attainder, ex post facto Law, or Law impairing the Obligation of Contracts, or grant any Title of Nobility.

[2] No State shall, without the Consent of the Congress, lay any Imposts or Duties on Imports or Exports, except what may be absolutely necessary for executing it's inspection Laws: and the net Produce of all Duties and Imposts, laid by any State on Imports or Exports, shall be for the Use of the Treasury of the United States; and all such Laws shall be subject to the Revision and Controul of the Congress.

[3] No State shall, without the Consent of Congress, lay any Duty of Tonnage, keep Troops, or Ships of War in time of Peace, enter into any Agreement or Compact with another State, or with a foreign Power, or engage in War, unless actually invaded, or in such imminent Danger as will not admit of delay.

ARTICLE II

SECTION 1. [1] The executive Power shall be vested in a President of the United States of America. He shall hold his Office during the Term of four Years, and, together with the Vice President, chosen for the same Term, be elected, as follows:

[2] Each State shall appoint, in such Manner as the Legislature thereof may direct, a Number of Electors, equal to the whole Number of Senators and Representatives to which the State may be entitled in the Congress: but no Senator or Representative, or person holding an Office of Trust or Profit under the United States, shall be appointed an Elector.

[3] The Electors shall meet in their respective States, and vote by Ballot for two Persons, of whom one at least shall not be an Inhabitant of the same State with themselves. And they shall make a List of all the

Persons voted for, and of the Number of Votes for each; which List they shall sign and certify, and transmit sealed to the Seat of the Government of the United States, directed to the President of the Senate. The President of the Senate shall, in the Presence of the Senate and House of Representatives, open all the Certificates, and the Votes shall then be counted. The person having the greatest Number of Votes shall be the President, if such Number be a Majority of the whole Number of Electors appointed; and if there be more than one who have such Majority, and have an equal Number of Votes, then the House of Representatives shall immediately chuse by Ballot one of them for President; and if no Person have a Majority, then from the five highest on the List the said House shall in like Manner chuse the President. But in chusing the President, the Votes shall be taken by States, the Representation from each State having one Vote; A quorum for this Purpose shall consist of a Member or Members from two thirds of the States, and a Majority of all the States shall be necessary to a Choice. In every Case, after the Choice of the President, the Person having the greatest Number of Votes of the Electors shall be the Vice President. But if there should remain two or more who have equal votes, the Senate shall chuse from them by Ballot the Vice President.

[4]   The Congress may determine the Time of chusing the Electors, and the Day on which they shall give their Votes; which Day shall be the same throughout the United States.

[5]   No Person except a natural born Citizen, or a Citizen of the United States, at the time of the Adoption of this Constitution, shall be eligible to the Office of President; neither shall any Person be eligible to that Office who shall not have attained to the Age of thirty five Years, and been fourteen Years a Resident within the United States.

[6]   In Case of the Removal of the President from Office, or of his Death, Resignation, or Inability to discharge the Powers and Duties of the said Office, the Same shall devolve on the Vice President, and the Congress may by Law provide for the Case of Removal, Death, Resignation or Inability, both of the President and Vice President, declaring what Officer shall then act as President, and such Officer shall act accordingly, until the Disability be removed, or a President shall be elected.

[7]   The President shall, at stated Times, receive for his Services, a Compensation, which shall neither be encreased nor diminished during the Period for which he shall have been elected, and he shall not receive within that Period any other Emolument from the United States, or any of them.

[8]   Before he enter on the Execution of his Office, he shall take the following Oath or Affirmation:—"I do solemnly swear (or affirm) that I will faithfully execute the Office of President of the United States, and will to the best of my Ability, preserve, protect and defend the Constitution of the United States."

SECTION 2. [1] The President shall be Commander in Chief of the Army and Navy of the United States, and of the Militia of the several States, when called into the actual Service of the United States; he may require the Opinion, in writing, of the principal Officer in each of the executive Departments, upon any Subject relating to the Duties of their respective Offices, and he shall have Power to grant Reprieves and Pardons for Offences against the United States, except in Cases of Impeachment.

[2] He shall have Power, by and with the Advice and Consent of the Senate, to make Treaties, provided two thirds of the Senators present concur; and he shall nominate, and by and with the Advice and Consent of the Senate, shall appoint Ambassadors, other public Ministers and Consuls, Judges of the supreme Court, and all other Officers of the United States, whose Appointments are not herein otherwise provided for, and which shall be established by Law: but the Congress may by Law vest the Appointment of such inferior Officers, as they think proper, in the President alone, in the Courts of Law, or in the Heads of Departments.

[3] The President shall have Power to fill up all Vacancies that may happen during the Recess of the Senate, by granting Commissions which shall expire at the End of their next Session.

SECTION 3. He shall from time to time give to the Congress Information of the State of the Union, and recommend to their Consideration such Measures as he shall judge necessary and expedient; he may, on extraordinary Occasions, convene both Houses, or either of them, and in Case of Disagreement between them, with Respect to the Time of Adjournment, he may adjourn them to such Time as he shall think proper; he shall receive Ambassadors and other public Ministers; he shall take Care that the Laws be faithfully executed, and shall Commission all the Officers of the United States.

SECTION 4. The President, Vice President and all civil Officers of the United States, shall be removed from Office on Impeachment for, and Conviction of, Treason, Bribery, or other high Crimes and Misdemeanors.

ARTICLE III

SECTION 1. The judicial Power of the United States, shall be vested in one supreme Court, and in such inferior Courts as the Congress may from time to time ordain and establish. The Judges, both of the supreme and inferior Courts, shall hold their Offices during good Behaviour, and shall, at stated Times, receive for their Services, a Compensation, which shall not be diminished during their Continuance in Office.

SECTION 2. [1] The judicial Power shall extend to all Cases, in Law and Equity, arising under this Constitution, the Laws of the United States, and Treaties made, or which shall be made, under their Authority;—to all Cases affecting Ambassadors, other public Ministers and Consuls;—to all Cases of admiralty and maritime Jurisdiction;—to Controversies to which the United States shall be a Party;—to Controversies between two or more States;—between a State and Citizens of another State;—between Citizens of different States;—between Citizens of the same State claiming Lands under Grants of different States, and between a State, or the Citizens thereof, and foreign States, Citizens or Subjects.

[2] In all Cases affecting Ambassadors, other public Ministers and Consuls, and those in which a State shall be Party, the supreme Court shall have original Jurisdiction. In all the other Cases before mentioned, the supreme Court shall have appellate Jurisdiction, both as to Law and Fact, with such Exceptions, and under such Regulations as the Congress shall make.

[3] The Trial of all Crimes, except in Cases of Impeachment, shall be by Jury; and such Trial shall be held in the State where the said Crimes shall have been committed; but when not committed within any State, the Trial shall be at such Place or Places as the Congress may by Law have directed.

Section 3. [1] Treason against the United States, shall consist only in levying War against them, or in adhering to their Enemies, giving them Aid and Comfort. No Person shall be convicted of Treason unless on the Testimony of two Witnesses to the same overt Act, or on Confession in open Court.

[2] The Congress shall have Power to declare the Punishment of Treason, but no Attainder of Treason shall work Corruption of Blood, or Forfeiture except during the Life of the Person attained.

ARTICLE IV

SECTION 1. Full Faith and Credit shall be given in each State to the public Acts, Records, and judicial Proceedings of every other State. And the Congress may by general Laws prescribe the Manner in which such Acts, Records, and Proceedings shall be proved, and the Effect thereof.

SECTION 2. [1] The Citizens of each State shall be entitled to all Privileges and Immunities of Citizens in the several States.

[2] A Person charged in any State with Treason, Felony, or other Crime, who shall flee from Justice, and be found in another State, shall on Demand of the executive Authority of the State from which he fled, be delivered up, to be removed to the State having Jurisdiction of the Crime.

[3] No Person held to Service or Labour in one State, under the Laws thereof, escaping into another, shall, in Consequence of any Law or Regulation therein, be discharged from such Service or Labour, but shall be delivered up on Claim of the Party to whom such Service or Labour may be due.

SECTION 3. [1] New States may be admitted by the Congress into this Union; but no new State shall be formed or erected within the Jurisdiction of any other State; nor any State be formed by the Junction of two or more States, or Parts of States, without the Consent of the Legislatures of the States concerned as well as of the Congress.

[2] The Congress shall have Power to dispose of and make all needful Rules and Regulations respecting the Territory or other Property belonging to the United States; and nothing in this Constitution shall be so construed as to Prejudice any Claims of the United States, or of any particular State.

SECTION 4. The United States shall guarantee to every State in this Union a Republican Form of Government, and shall protect each of them against Invasion; and on Application of the Legislature, or of the Executive (when the Legislature cannot be convened) against domestic Violence.

ARTICLE V

The Congress, whenever two thirds of both Houses shall deem it necessary, shall propose Amendments to this Constitution, or, on the Application of the Legislatures of two thirds of the several States, shall call a Convention for proposing Amendments, which, in either Case, shall be valid to all Intents and Purposes, as Part of this Constitution, when ratified by the Legislatures of three fourths of the several States, or by Conventions in three fourths thereof, as the one or the other Mode of Ratification may be proposed by the Congress; Provided that no Amendment which may be made prior to the Year One thousand eight hundred and eight shall in any Manner affect the first and fourth Clauses in the Ninth Section of the first Article; and that no State, without its Consent, shall be deprived of its equal Suffrage in the Senate.

ARTICLE VI

[1] All Debts contracted and Engagements entered into, before the Adoption of this Constitution, shall be as valid against the United States under this Constitution, as under the Confederation.

[2] This Constitution, and the Laws of the United States which shall be made in Pursuance thereof; and all Treaties made, or which shall be made, under the Authority of the United States, shall be the supreme Law of the Land; and the Judges in every State shall be bound thereby, any Thing in the Constitution or Laws of any State to the Contrary notwithstanding.

[3] The Senators and Representatives before mentioned, and the Members of the several State Legislatures, and all executive and judicial Officers, both of the United States and of the several States, shall be bound by Oath or Affirmation, to support this Constitution; but no religious Test shall ever be required as a Qualification to any Office or public Trust under the United States.

ARTICLE VII

The Ratification of the Conventions of nine States, shall be sufficient for the Establishment of this Constitution between the States so ratifying the Same. Done in Convention by the Unanimous Consent of the States present the Seventeenth Day of September in the Year of our Lord one thousand seven hundred and Eighty seven and of the Independence of the United States of America the Twelfth.

AMENDMENT I (1791)

Congress shall make no law respecting an establishment of religion, or prohibiting the free exercise thereof; or abridging the freedom of speech, or of the press; or the right of the people peaceably to assemble, and to petition the Government for a redress of grievances.

AMENDMENT II (1791)

A well regulated Militia, being necessary to the security of a free State, the right of the people to keep and bear Arms, shall not be infringed.

AMENDMENT III (1791)

No Soldier shall, in time of peace be quartered in any house, without the consent of the Owner, nor in time of war, but in a manner to be prescribed by law.

AMENDMENT IV (1791)

The right of the people to be secure in their persons, houses, papers, and effects, against unreasonable searches and seizures, shall not be violated, and no Warrants shall issue, but upon probable cause, supported by Oath or affirmation, and particularly describing the place to be searched, and the persons or things to be seized.

AMENDMENT V (1791)

No person shall be held to answer for a capital, or otherwise infamous crime, unless on a presentment or indictment of a Grand Jury, except in cases arising in the land or naval forces, or in the Militia, when in actual service in time of War or public danger; nor shall any person be subject for the same offence to be twice put in jeopardy of life or limb; nor shall be compelled in any criminal case to be a witness against himself, nor be deprived of life, liberty, or property, without due process of law; nor shall private property be taken for public use, without just compensation.

AMENDMENT VI (1791)

In all criminal prosecutions, the accused shall enjoy the right to a speedy and public trial, by an impartial jury of the State and district wherein the crime shall have been committed, which district shall have been previously ascertained by law, and to be informed of the nature and cause of the accusation; to be confronted with the witnesses against him; to have compulsory process for obtaining witnesses in his favor, and to have the Assistance of Counsel for his defence.

AMENDMENT VII (1791)

In Suits at common law, where the value in controversy shall exceed twenty dollars, the right of trial by jury shall be preserved, and no fact tried by a jury, shall be otherwise re-examined in any Court of the United States, than according to the rules of the common law.

Amendment VIII (1791)

Excessive bail shall not be required, nor excessive fines imposed, nor cruel and unusual punishments inflicted.

Amendment IX (1791)

The enumeration in the Constitution, of certain rights, shall not be construed to deny or disparage others retained by the people.

Amendment X (1791)

The powers not delegated to the United States by the Constitution, nor prohibited by it to the states, are reserved to the States respectively, or to the people.

Amendment XI (1795)

The Judicial power of the United States shall not be construed to extend to any suit in law or equity, commenced or prosecuted against one of the United States by Citizens of another State, or by Citizens or Subjects of any Foreign State.

Amendment XII (1804)

The Electors shall meet in their respective states, and vote by ballot for President and Vice-President, one of whom, at least, shall not be an inhabitant of the same state with themselves; they shall name in their ballots the person voted for as President, and in distinct ballots the person voted for as Vice-President, and they shall make distinct lists of all persons voted for as President, and of all persons voted for as Vice-President, and of the number of votes for each, which lists they shall sign and certify, and transmit sealed to the seat of the government of the United States, directed to the President of the Senate;—The President of the Senate shall, in the presence of the Senate and House of Representatives, open all the certificates and the votes shall then be counted;—the person having the greatest number of votes for President, shall be the President, if such number be a majority of the whole number of Electors appointed; and if no person have such majority, then from the persons having the highest numbers not exceeding three on the list of those voted for as President, the House of Representatives shall choose immediately, by ballot, the President. But in choosing the President, the votes shall be taken by states, the representation from each state having one vote; a quorum for this purpose shall consist of a member or members from two-thirds of the states, and a majority of all the states shall be necessary to a choice. And if the House of Representatives shall not choose a President whenever the right of choice shall devolve upon them, before the fourth day of March next following, then the Vice-President shall act as President, as in the case of the death or other constitutional disability of the President.—The person having the greatest number of votes as Vice-President, shall be the Vice-President, if such number be a majority of the whole number of Electors appointed, and if no person have a majority, then from the two highest numbers on the list, the Senate shall choose the Vice-President; a quorum for the purpose shall consist of two-thirds of the whole number of Senators, and a majority of the whole number shall be necessary to a choice. But no person constitutionally ineligible to the office of President shall be eligible to that of Vice-President of the United States.

AMENDMENT XIII (1865)

SECTION 1. Neither slavery nor involuntary servitude, except as a punishment for crime whereof the party shall have been duly convicted, shall exist within the United States, or any place subject to their jurisdiction.

SECTION 2. Congress shall have power to enforce this article by appropriate legislation.

AMENDMENT XIV (1868)

SECTION 1. All persons born or naturalized in the United States, and subject to the jurisdiction thereof, are citizens of the United States and of the state wherein they reside. No State shall make or enforce any law which shall abridge the privileges or immunities of citizens of the United States; nor shall any State deprive any person of life, liberty, or property, without due process of law; nor deny to any person within its jurisdiction the equal protection of the laws.

SECTION 2. Representatives shall be apportioned among the several States according to their respective numbers, counting the whole number of persons in each state, excluding Indians not taxed. But when the right to vote at any election for the choice of electors for President and Vice President of the United States, Representatives in Congress, the Executive and Judicial officers of a state, or the members of the Legislature thereof, is denied to any of the male inhabitants of such State, being twenty-one years of age, and citizens of the United States, or in any way abridged, except for participation in rebellion, or other crime, the basis of representation therein shall be reduced in the proportion which the number of such male citizens shall bear to the whole number of male citizens twenty-one years of age in such State.

SECTION 3. No person shall be a Senator or Representative in Congress, or elector of President and Vice President, or hold any office, civil or military, under the United States, or under any State, who, having previously taken an oath, as a member of Congress, or as an officer of the United States, or as a member of any State legislature, or as an executive or judicial officer of any state, to support the Constitution of the United States, shall have engaged in insurrection or rebellion against the same, or given aid or comfort to the enemies thereof. But Congress may by a vote of two-thirds of each House, remove such disability.

SECTION 4. The validity of the public debt of the United States, authorized by law, including debts incurred for payment of pensions and bounties for services in suppressing insurrection or rebellion, shall not be questioned. But neither the United States nor any State shall assume or pay any debt or obligation incurred in aid of insurrection or rebellion against the United States, or any claim for the loss or emancipation of any slave; but all such debts, obligations and claims shall be held illegal and void.

SECTION 5. The Congress shall have power to enforce, by appropriate legislation, the provisions of this article.

AMENDMENT XV (1870)

SECTION 1. The right of citizens of the United States to vote shall not be denied or abridged by the United States or by any state on account of race, color, or previous condition of servitude.

SECTION 2. The Congress shall have power to enforce this article by appropriate legislation.

AMENDMENT XVI (1913)

The Congress shall have power to lay and collect taxes on incomes, from whatever source derived, without apportionment among the several States, and without regard to any census or enumeration.

AMENDMENT XVII (1913)

The Senate of the United States shall be composed of two Senators from each State, elected by the people thereof, for six years; and each Senator shall have one vote. The electors in each state shall have the qualifications requisite for electors of the most numerous branch of the State legislatures.

When vacancies happen in the representation of any State in the Senate, the executive authority of such State shall issue writs of election to fill such vacancies: Provided, That the legislature of any State may empower the executive thereof to make temporary appointments until the people fill the vacancies by election as the legislature may direct.

This amendment shall not be so construed as to affect the election or term of any Senator chosen before it becomes valid as part of the Constitution.

AMENDMENT XVIII (1919)

SECTION 1. After one year from the ratification of this article the manufacture, sale, or transportation of intoxicating liquors within, the importation thereof into, or the exportation thereof from the United States and all territory subject to the jurisdiction thereof for beverage purposes is hereby prohibited.

SECTION 2. The Congress and the several States shall have concurrent power to enforce this article by appropriate legislation.

SECTION 3. This article shall be inoperative unless it shall have been ratified as an amendment to the Constitution by the legislatures of the several States, as provided in the Constitution, within seven years from the date of the submission hereof to the States by the Congress.

AMENDMENT XIX (1920)

The right of citizens of the United States to vote shall not be denied or abridged by the United States or by any State on account of sex.

Congress shall have power to enforce this article by appropriate legislation.

AMENDMENT XX (1933)

SECTION 1. The terms of the President and Vice President shall end at noon on the 20th day of January, and the terms of Senators and Representatives at noon on the 3d day of January, of the years in which such terms would have ended if this article had not been ratified; and the terms of their successors shall then begin.

SECTION 2. The Congress shall assemble at least once in every year, and such meeting shall begin at noon on the 3d day of January, unless they shall by law appoint a different day.

SECTION 3. If, at the time fixed for the beginning of the term of the President, the President elect shall have died, the Vice President elect shall become President. If a President shall not have been chosen before the time fixed for the beginning of his term, or if the President elect shall have failed to qualify, then the Vice President elect shall act as President until a President shall have qualified; and the Congress may by law provide for the case wherein neither a President elect nor a Vice President elect shall have qualified, declaring who shall then act as President, or the manner in which one who is to act shall be selected, and such person shall act accordingly until a President or Vice President shall have qualified.

SECTION 4. The Congress may by law provide for the case of the death of any of the persons from whom the House of Representatives may choose a President whenever the right of choice shall have devolved upon them, and for the case of the death of any of the persons from whom the Senate may choose a Vice President whenever the right of choice shall have devolved upon them.

SECTION 5. Sections 1 and 2 shall take effect on the 15th day of October following the ratification of this article.

SECTION 6. This article shall be inoperative unless it shall have been ratified as an amendment to the Constitution by the legislatures of three-fourths of the several states within seven years from the date of its submission.

AMENDMENT XXI (1933)

SECTION 1. The eighteenth article of amendment to the Constitution of the United States is hereby repealed.

SECTION 2. The transportation or importation into any State, Territory, or possession of the United States for delivery or use therein of intoxicating liquors, in violation of the laws thereof, is hereby prohibited.

SECTION 3. This article shall be inoperative unless it shall have been ratified as an amendment to the Constitution by conventions in the several States, as provided in the Constitution, within seven years from the date of the submission hereof to the States by the Congress.

AMENDMENT XXII (1951)

SECTION 1. No person shall be elected to the office of the President more than twice, and no person who has held the office of President, or acted as President, for more than two years of a term to which some other person was elected President shall be elected to the office of the President more than once. But this Article shall not apply to any person holding the office of President when this Article was proposed by the Congress, and shall not prevent any person who may be holding the office of President, or acting as President, during the term within which this Article becomes operative from holding the office of President or acting as President during the remainder of such term.

SECTION 2. This article shall be inoperative unless it shall have been ratified as an amendment to the Constitution by the legislatures of three-fourths of the several States within seven years from the date of its submission to the States by the Congress.

AMENDMENT XXIII (1961)

SECTION 1. The District constituting the seat of Government of the United States shall appoint in such manner as the Congress may direct:

A number of electors of President and Vice President equal to the whole number of Senators and Representatives in Congress to which the District would be entitled if it were a State, but in no event more than the least populous State; they shall be in addition to those appointed by the States, but they shall be considered, for the purposes of the election of President and Vice President, to be electors appointed by a State; and they shall meet in the District and perform such duties as provided by the twelfth article of amendment.

SECTION 2. The Congress shall have power to enforce this article by appropriate legislation.

AMENDMENT XXIV (1964)

SECTION 1. The right of citizens of the United States to vote in any primary or other election for President or Vice President, for electors for President or Vice President, or for Senator or Representative in Congress, shall not be denied or abridged by the United States or any State by reason of failure to pay any poll tax or other tax.

SECTION 2. The Congress shall have power to enforce this article by appropriate legislation.

AMENDMENT XXV (1967)

SECTION 1. In case of the removal of the President from office or of his death or resignation, the Vice President shall become President.

SECTION 2. Whenever there is a vacancy in the office of the Vice President, the President shall nominate a Vice President who shall take office upon confirmation by a majority vote of both Houses of Congress.

SECTION 3. Whenever the President transmits to the President pro tempore of the Senate and the Speaker of the House of Representatives his written declaration that he is unable to discharge the powers and duties of his office, and until he transmits to them a written declaration to the contrary, such powers and duties shall be discharged by the Vice President as Acting President.

SECTION 4. Whenever the Vice President and a majority of either the principal officers of the executive departments or of such other body as Congress may by law provide, transmit to the President pro tempore of the Senate and the Speaker of the House of Representatives their written declaration that the President is unable to discharge the powers and duties of his office, the Vice President shall immediately assume the powers and duties of the office as Acting President.

Thereafter, when the President transmits to the President pro tempore of the Senate and the Speaker of the House of Representatives his written declaration that no inability exists, he shall resume the powers and duties of his office unless the Vice President and a majority of either the principal officers of the executive department or of such other body as Congress may by law provide, transmit within four days to the President pro tempore of the Senate and the Speaker of the House of Representatives their written declaration that the President is unable to discharge the powers and duties of his office. Thereupon Congress shall decide the issue, assembling within forty-eight hours for that purpose if not in session. If the Congress, within twenty-one days after receipt of the latter written declaration, or, if Congress is not in session, within twenty-one days after Congress is required to assemble, determines by two-thirds vote of both Houses that the President is unable to discharge the powers and duties of his office, the Vice President shall continue to discharge the same as Acting President; otherwise, the President shall resume the powers and duties of his office.

AMENDMENT XXVI (1971)

SECTION 1. The right of citizens of the United States, who are eighteen years of age or older, to vote, shall not be denied or abridged by the United States or any State on account of age.

SECTION 2. The Congress shall have the power to enforce this article by appropriate legislation.

AMENDMENT XXVII (1992)

No law, varying the compensation for the services of the Senators and Representatives, shall take effect, until an election of Representatives shall have intervened.

* * *

See also: Want to carry the Constitution with you everywhere you go? There's an app for that, of course. The Library of Congress has an annotated Constitution app for iPhones and iPads, *see* https://itunes. apple.com/us/app/u.s.-constitution-analysis/id692260032?mt=8, and similar products are available for Android. Better yet, you can have David Currie, one of the foremost constitutional scholars of his generation, read it to you in mp3 format. (Download from the University of Chicago at http://www.law.uchicago.edu/constitution/index.html.)

Having read what the Constitution *says*, it is worth pausing for a minute to think generally about what it *does*. Specifically, what are the functions of a constitution, and to what extent do these functions differ from the functions performed by ordinary law?

Joseph Raz, On the Authority and Interpretation of Constitutions: Some Preliminaries*

[T]he notion of a "constitution" is used in legal discourse sometimes in a thin sense and sometimes in a variety of thicker senses. In the thin sense, it is tautological that every legal system includes a constitution. For in that sense, the constitution is simply the law that establishes and regulates the main organs of government, their constitution and powers, and ipso facto it includes law that establishes the general principles under which the country is governed: democracy, if it establishes democratic organisms of government; federalism, if it establishes a federal structure; and so on.

The thick sense of a "constitution" is less clear, and there are probably several such senses in use in different legal cultures. For the purposes of the present discussion, I will regard constitutions as defined by a combination of seven features.

First, incorporating the thin sense, the constitution defines the constitution and powers of the main organs of the different branches of government. (This feature identifies the constitution as *constitutive* of the legal and political structure which is that legal system.)

Second, it is, and is meant to be, of long duration: It is meant to serve as a stable framework for the political and legal institutions of the country, to be adjusted and amended from time to time, but basically to preserve stability and continuity in the legal and political structure, and the basic principles that guide its institutions. (The constitution is *stable*, at least in aspiration.)

Third, it has a canonical formulation. That usually means that it is enshrined in one or a small number of written documents. It (they) is (are) commonly referred to as the constitution. (The constitution . . . is *written*.)

---

* Reprinted from LARRY ALEXANDER, ED., CONSTITUTIONALISM: PHILOSOPHICAL FOUNDATIONS 152, 153–54 (1998).

Fourth, it constitutes a superior law. This means that ordinary law which conflicts with the constitution is invalid or inapplicable. (The constitution is *superior law*.)

Fifth, there are judicial procedures to implement the superiority of the constitution, that is, judicial processes by which the compatibility of rules of law and of other legal acts with the constitution can be tested, and incompatible rules or legal acts can be declared inapplicable or invalid. (The constitution is *justiciable*.)

Sixth, while there usually are legal procedures for constitutional amendment, constitutional amendments are legally more difficult to secure than ordinary legislation. (The constitution is *entrenched*.)

Seventh, its provisions include principles of government (democracy, federalism, basic civil and political rights, etc.) that are generally held to express the common beliefs of the population about the way their society should be governed. It serves, you may say, not only as lawyers' law, but as the people's law. Its main provisions are generally known, command general consent, and are held to be the (or part of the) common ideology that governs public life in that country. (The constitution expresses a *common ideology*.)

NOTE ON CONSTITUTIONAL FUNCTIONS

1.   The list of constitutional functions compiled by Professor Raz (who is a British legal philosopher but seems to be thinking primarily of the American Constitution) is representative but hardly authoritative; other commentators would add or subtract entries or describe them differently. A different formulation would hold that most constitutions:

- **Constitute the government** by creating governmental institutions, conferring powers upon them, and setting the boundaries of their jurisdiction;

- **Confer rights on individuals** that limit the exercise of power by governmental institutions; and

- **Entrench** the institutions and rights thus created against future legal change.

The most controversial omission from this shorter list would be the notion that a Constitution should express society's fundamental values. Do you agree? Does the United States Constitution do that?

2.   The fundamental distinction between Professor Raz's "thin" constitution, which every legal system has, and a "thick" constitution, which only certain systems, like the United States, have, is twofold: a) the provisions of thick constitutions are collected together in one canonical document, and b) thick constitutions are entrenched against legal change through ordinary legislative processes. Compare, for example, the U.S. Constitution with the constitution of Great Britain. The British constitution is for the most part written down, but it is not collected in one canonical

document, and it can be changed by an ordinary Act of Parliament.[2] For example, when the Blair government decided to alter the composition of the House of Lords and to devolve certain governmental powers to Scotland, Wales, and Northern Ireland, it accomplished these changes through ordinary legislation.

How important is it for a constitution to be written down in one place? Does that make it easier for individual citizens, particularly non-lawyers, to discover what the Constitution means? Is it really possible to make much sense of the Constitution without also reading a bunch of Supreme Court opinions (or other materials)? If not, is that a problem? Is that problem realistically avoidable?

3.   To what extent is the United States government "constituted" by the document that you have just read? That document does not mention, for example, major national institutions like the federal administrative agencies (the Environmental Protection Agency, the Federal Communications Commission, the Social Security Administration, etc.), congressional committees, or our system of political parties. It does not resolve basic structural questions, like the entitlement to vote in national elections, the voting rules in Congress, or the structure of the lower federal courts. And many of the "rights" most valued by many Americans—for example, the right to public education, a clean environment, or financial security in old age— are completely missing. If Professor Raz is right that these constitutive issues are part of the basic function of a constitution, can it really be said that our "constitution" is collected in a single document?

4.   How important is it for a constitution to be *entrenched* against change through ordinary legislation? Different constitutions exhibit different degrees of entrenchment: the Texas Constitution, for example, can be amended whenever two-thirds of each House of the Legislature submits a proposal to the voters and a majority of the voters approves the proposal. As a result of this relatively easy procedure, the Texas Constitution has been amended over four hundred times since its adoption in 1876. Is that a good or a bad thing? Should the U.S. Constitution be easier to amend? Is it problematic that some of the basic changes to our governmental structure since the Founding Era—such as the rise of the national administrative state—are not reflected in any amendment to the Constitution's text?

5.   Does Professor Raz's fifth constitutional feature—that the constitution is *justiciable* (enforceable by courts through judicial review)— follow from the fourth (that the constitution is *superior law*), and the sixth (that the constitution is *entrenched*)? That will be John Marshall's argument in *Marbury v. Madison*, which we will read in Chapter Two, but many commentators have found the answer nonobvious.

See also: The argument suggested by the notes and questions above is developed at greater length in Ernest A. Young, *The Constitution Outside the Constitution*, 117 YALE L.J. 408 (2007). *See also* Karl N. Llewellyn, *The*

---

[2] This fact derives from the principle of "Parliamentary sovereignty," which holds that Parliament has "the right to make or unmake any law whatever." A.V. DICEY, INTRODUCTION TO THE STUDY OF THE LAW OF THE CONSTITUTION 3 (Liberty Classics 1982) (1885).

Constitution as an Institution, 34 COLUM. L. REV. 1 (1934); WILLIAM N. ESKRIDGE, JR. & JOHN A. FEREJOHN, A REPUBLIC OF STATUTES: THE NEW AMERICAN CONSTITUTION (2013). On the British Constitution, see ADAM TOMKINS, PUBLIC LAW (2003).

SECTION 1.2   THE DEAD HAND PROBLEM

The combination of the Constitution's status as supreme law and its entrenchment against easy legal change leads to the "Dead Hand Problem"—that is, the question why a diverse, democratic, and (most importantly) *living* society would consent to be ruled by a document penned by a small group of elites who are white, male, and (again, most importantly) *dead*. This is the basic question of constitutionalism. The answer we choose to that question—if there *is* a satisfactory answer—has important implications for how we interpret the Constitution's meaning.

Lest anyone think these matters are of merely theoretical importance, consider the Supreme Court's decision in *District of Columbia v. Heller*—a case in which the "dead hand" of the Framers significantly constrained contemporary policy on a matter of life and death. *Heller* also illustrates the need for courts to choose among various sources of constitutional meaning—for example, text, history, and precedent. As you read, consider how the justices handle these different sources of authority and resolve potential conflicts among them.

District of Columbia v. Heller

554 U.S. 570 (2008)

■ JUSTICE SCALIA delivered the opinion of the Court.

We consider whether a District of Columbia prohibition on the possession of usable handguns in the home violates the Second Amendment to the Constitution.

I

The District of Columbia generally prohibits the possession of handguns. It is a crime to carry an unregistered firearm, and the registration of handguns is prohibited. Wholly apart from that prohibition, no person may carry a handgun without a license, but the Chief of Police may issue licenses for one-year periods. District of Columbia law also requires residents to keep their lawfully-owned firearms, such as registered long guns, "unloaded and dissembled or bound by a trigger lock or similar device" unless they are located in a place of business or are being used for lawful recreational activities.

Respondent Dick Heller is a D.C. special police officer authorized to carry a handgun while on duty at the Federal Judicial Center. He applied for a registration certificate for a handgun that he wished to keep at home, but the District refused. He thereafter filed a lawsuit . . . seeking, on Second Amendment grounds, to enjoin the city from enforcing the bar on the registration of handguns, the licensing requirement insofar as it prohibits the carrying of a firearm in the home without a license, and the trigger-lock requirement insofar as it prohibits the use of "functional firearms within the home." The District Court dismissed respondent's complaint. The Court of Appeals for the District of Columbia Circuit . . . reversed. It held that the Second Amendment protects an individual right to possess firearms and that the city's total ban on handguns, as well as its requirement that firearms in the home be kept nonfunctional even when necessary for self-defense, violated that right. . . .

II

We turn first to the meaning of the Second Amendment.

A

The Second Amendment provides: "A well regulated Militia, being necessary to the security of a free State, the right of the people to keep and bear Arms, shall not be infringed." In interpreting this text, we are guided by the principle that the Constitution was written to be understood by the voters; its words and phrases were used in their normal and ordinary as distinguished from technical meaning. Normal meaning may of course include an idiomatic meaning, but it excludes secret or technical meanings that would not have been known to ordinary citizens in the founding generation.

The two sides in this case have set out very different interpretations of the Amendment. Petitioners and today's dissenting Justices believe that it protects only the right to possess and carry a firearm in connection with militia service. Respondent argues that it protects an individual right to possess a firearm unconnected with service in a militia, and to use that arm for traditionally lawful purposes, such as self-defense within the home.

The Second Amendment is naturally divided into two parts: its prefatory clause and its operative clause. The former does not limit the latter grammatically, but rather announces a purpose. . . . Logic demands that there be a link between the stated purpose and the command. . . . That requirement of logical connection may cause a prefatory clause to resolve an ambiguity in the operative clause. . . . But apart from that clarifying function, a prefatory clause does not limit or expand the scope of the operative clause. . . .

1. **Operative Clause.**

a. **"Right of the People."** The first salient feature of the operative clause is that it codifies a "right of the people." The unamended Constitution and the Bill of Rights use the phrase "right of the people" two other times, in the First Amendment's Assembly-and-Petition Clause and in the Fourth Amendment's Search-and-Seizure Clause. The Ninth Amendment uses very similar terminology. . . . All three of these instances unambiguously refer to individual rights, not "collective" rights, or rights that may be exercised only through participation in some corporate body. . . .

We start therefore with a strong presumption that the Second Amendment right is exercised individually and belongs to all Americans.

b. "Keep and Bear Arms." . . . Before addressing the verbs "keep" and "bear," we interpret their object: "Arms." The 18th-century meaning is no different from the meaning today. The 1773 edition of Samuel Johnson's dictionary defined "arms" as "weapons of offence, or armour of defence." . . . The term was applied, then as now, to weapons that were not specifically designed for military use and were not employed in a military capacity. . . .

Some have made the argument, bordering on the frivolous, that only those arms in existence in the 18th century are protected by the Second Amendment. We do not interpret constitutional rights that way. Just as the First Amendment protects modern forms of communications, and the Fourth Amendment applies to modern forms of search, the Second Amendment extends, prima facie, to all instruments that constitute bearable arms, even those that were not in existence at the time of the founding.

We turn to the phrases "keep arms" and "bear arms." Johnson defined "keep" as, most relevantly, "[t]o retain; not to lose," and "[t]o have in custody." [Noah] Webster defined it as "[t]o hold; to retain in one's power or possession." . . . Thus, the most natural reading of "keep Arms" in the Second Amendment is to "have weapons."

The phrase "keep arms" was not prevalent in the written documents of the founding period that we have found, but there are a few examples, all of which favor viewing the right to "keep Arms" as an individual right unconnected with militia service. William Blackstone, for example, wrote that Catholics convicted of not attending service in the Church of England suffered certain penalties, one of which was that they were not permitted to "keep arms in their houses." . . .

At the time of the founding, as now, to "bear" meant to "carry." When used with "arms," however, the term has a meaning that refers to carrying for a particular purpose—confrontation. . . . Although the phrase implies that the carrying of the weapon is for the purpose of "offensive or defensive action," it in no way connotes participation in a structured military organization.

From our review of founding-era sources, we conclude that this natural meaning was also the meaning that "bear arms" had in the 18th century. In numerous instances, "bear arms" was unambiguously used to refer to the carrying of weapons outside of an organized militia. The most prominent examples are those most relevant to the Second Amendment: Nine state constitutional provisions written in the 18th century or the first two decades of the 19th, which enshrined a right of citizens to "bear arms in defense of themselves and the state" or "bear arms in defense of himself and the state." It is clear from those formulations that "bear arms" did not refer only to carrying a weapon in an organized military unit. . . . That was also the interpretation of those state constitutional provisions adopted by pre-Civil War state courts. These provisions demonstrate—again, in the most analogous linguistic context—that "bear arms" was not limited to the carrying of arms in a militia.

The phrase "bear Arms" also had at the time of the founding an idiomatic meaning that was significantly different from its natural meaning: "to serve as a soldier, do military service, fight" or "to wage war." But it *unequivocally* bore that idiomatic meaning only when followed by the preposition "against," which was in turn followed by the target of the hostilities. (That is how, for example, our Declaration of Independence used the phrase: "He has constrained our fellow Citizens taken Captive on the high Seas to bear Arms against their Country. . . .") Every example given by petitioners' *amici* for the idiomatic meaning of "bear arms" from the founding period either includes the preposition "against" or is not clearly idiomatic. . . .

Petitioners justify their limitation of "bear arms" to the military context by pointing out the unremarkable fact that it was often used in that context. . . . It is especially unremarkable that the phrase was often used in a military context in the federal legal sources (such as records of congressional debate) that have been the focus of petitioners' inquiry. Those sources would have had little occasion to use it *except* in discussions about the standing army and the militia. And the phrases used primarily in those military discussions include not only "bear arms" but also "carry arms," "possess arms," and "have arms"—though no one thinks that those *other* phrases also had special military meanings. . . .

c. Meaning of the Operative Clause. Putting all of these textual elements together, we find that they guarantee the individual right to possess and carry weapons in case of confrontation. This meaning is strongly confirmed by the historical background of the Second Amendment. We look to this because it has always been widely understood that the Second Amendment, like the First and Fourth Amendments, codified a *pre-existing* right. The very text of the Second Amendment implicitly recognizes the pre-existence of the right and declares only that it "shall not be infringed." . . .

Between the Restoration and the Glorious Revolution, the Stuart Kings Charles II and James II succeeded in using select militias loyal to them to suppress political dissidents, in part by disarming their opponents. Under the auspices of the 1671 Game Act, for example, the Catholic James II had ordered general disarmaments of regions home to his Protestant enemies. These experiences caused Englishmen to be extremely wary of concentrated military forces run by the state and to be jealous of their arms. They accordingly obtained an assurance from William and Mary, in the Declaration of Right (which was codified as the English Bill of Rights), that Protestants would never be disarmed. . . .

This right has long been understood to be the predecessor to our Second Amendment. It was clearly an individual right, having nothing whatever to do with service in a militia. . . .

By the time of the founding, the right to have arms had become fundamental for English subjects. Blackstone, whose works . . . constituted the preeminent authority on English law for the founding generation, cited the arms provision of the Bill of Rights as one of the fundamental rights of Englishmen. His description of it cannot possibly be thought to tie it to militia or military service. It was, he said, "the natural right of resistance and self-preservation," and "the right of having and using arms for self-preservation and defence." Other contemporary authorities concurred. . . .

And, of course, what the Stuarts had tried to do to their political enemies, George III had tried to do to the colonists. In the tumultuous decades of the 1760's and 1770's, the Crown began to disarm the inhabitants of the most rebellious areas. That provoked polemical reactions by Americans invoking their rights as Englishmen to keep arms. A New York article of April 1769 said that "[i]t is a natural right which the people have reserved to themselves . . . to keep arms for their own defence." They understood the right to enable individuals to defend themselves. As the most important early American edition of Blackstone's Commentaries (by the law professor and former Antifederalist St. George Tucker) made clear in the notes to the description of the arms right, Americans understood the "right of self-preservation" as permitting a citizen to "repe[l] force by force" when "the intervention of society in his behalf, may be too late to prevent an injury."

There seems to us no doubt, on the basis of both text and history, that the Second Amendment conferred an individual right to keep and bear arms. Of course the right was not unlimited, just as the First Amendment's right of free speech was not. Thus, we do not read the Second Amendment to protect the right of citizens to carry arms for *any sort* of confrontation, just as we do not read the First Amendment to protect the right of citizens to speak for *any purpose*. Before turning to limitations upon the individual right, however, we must determine whether the prefatory clause of the Second Amendment comports with our interpretation of the operative clause.

2. Prefatory Clause.

The prefatory clause reads: "A well regulated Militia, being necessary to the security of a free State. . . ."

a. "Well-Regulated Militia." "[T]he Militia comprised all males physically capable of acting in concert for the common defense." That definition comports with founding-era sources. Petitioners take a seemingly narrower view of the militia, stating that "[m]ilitias are the state-and congressionally-regulated military forces described in the Militia Clauses (art. I, § 8, cls. 15–16)." Although we agree with petitioners' interpretive assumption that "militia" means the same thing in Article I and the Second Amendment, we believe that petitioners identify the wrong thing, namely, the organized militia. Unlike armies and navies, which Congress is given the power to create ("to raise . . . Armies"; "to provide . . . a Navy," Art. I, § 8, cls. 12–13), the militia is assumed by Article I already to be *in existence*. Congress is given the power to "provide for calling forth the militia," § 8, cl. 15; and the power not to create, but to "organiz[e]" it—and not to organize "a" militia, which is what one would expect if the militia were to be a federal creation, but to organize "the" militia, connoting a body already in existence. This is fully consistent with the ordinary definition of the militia as all able-bodied men. From that pool, Congress has plenary power to organize the units that will make up an effective fighting force. That is what Congress did in the first militia Act, which specified that "each and every free able-bodied white male citizen of the respective states, resident therein, who is or shall be of the age of eighteen years, and under the age of forty-five years (except as is herein after excepted) shall severally and respectively be enrolled in the militia." To be sure, Congress need not conscript every able-bodied man into the militia, because nothing in Article I suggests that in exercising its power to organize, discipline, and arm the militia, Congress must focus upon the entire body. Although the militia consists of all able-bodied men, the federally organized militia may consist of a subset of them.

Finally, the adjective "well-regulated" implies nothing more than the imposition of proper discipline and training.

b. "Security of a Free State." . . . It is true that the term "State" elsewhere in the Constitution refers to individual States, but the phrase "security of a free state" and close variations seem to have been terms of art in 18th-century political discourse, meaning a " 'free country' " or free polity. . . .

There are many reasons why the militia was thought to be "necessary to the security of a free state." First, of course, it is useful in repelling invasions and suppressing insurrections. Second, it renders large standing armies unnecessary—an argument that Alexander Hamilton made in favor of federal control over the militia. Third, when the able-bodied men of a nation are trained in arms and organized, they are better able to resist tyranny.

3. Relationship Between Prefatory Clause and Operative Clause.

We reach the question, then: Does the preface fit with an operative clause that creates an individual right to keep and bear arms? It fits perfectly, once one knows the history. . . . That history showed that the way tyrants had eliminated a militia consisting of all the able-bodied men was not by banning the militia but simply by taking away the people's arms, enabling a select militia or standing army to suppress political opponents. . . .

The debate with respect to the right to keep and bear arms . . . was not over whether it was desirable (all agreed that it was) but over whether it needed to be codified in the Constitution. During the 1788 ratification debates, the fear that the federal government would disarm the people in order to impose rule through a standing army or select militia was pervasive in Antifederalist rhetoric. John Smilie, for example, worried not only that Congress's "command of the militia" could be used to create a "select militia," or to have "no militia at all," but also, as a separate concern, that "[w]hen a select militia is formed; the people in general may be disarmed." Federalists responded that because Congress was given no power to abridge the ancient right of individuals to keep and bear arms, such a force could never oppress the people. It was understood across the political spectrum that the right helped to secure the ideal of a citizen militia, which might be necessary to oppose an oppressive military force if the constitutional order broke down.

It is therefore entirely sensible that the Second Amendment's prefatory clause announces the purpose for which the right was codified: to prevent elimination of the militia. The prefatory clause does not suggest that preserving the militia was the only reason Americans valued the ancient right; most undoubtedly thought it even more important for self-defense and hunting. But the threat that the new Federal Government would destroy the citizens' militia by taking away their arms was the reason that right . . . was codified in a written Constitution. . . .

Besides ignoring the historical reality that the Second Amendment was not intended to lay down a novel principle but rather codified a right inherited from our English ancestors, petitioners' interpretation does not even achieve the narrower purpose that prompted codification of the right. If, as they believe, the Second Amendment right is no more than the right to keep and use weapons as a member of an organized militia . . . it does not assure the existence of a "citizens' militia" as a safeguard against tyranny. For Congress retains plenary authority to organize the militia, which must include the authority to say who will belong to the organized force. . . . Thus, if petitioners are correct, the Second Amendment protects citizens' right to use a gun in an organization from which Congress has plenary authority to exclude them. It guarantees a select militia of the sort the Stuart kings found useful, but not the people's militia that was the concern of the founding generation.

B

Our interpretation is confirmed by analogous arms-bearing rights in state constitutions that preceded and immediately followed adoption of the Second Amendment. . . . The historical narrative that petitioners must endorse would thus treat the Federal Second Amendment as an odd outlier, protecting a right unknown in state constitutions or at English common law, based on little more than an overreading of the prefatory clause. . . .

D

We now address how the Second Amendment was interpreted from immediately after its ratification through the end of the 19th century. . . . As we will show, virtually all interpreters of the Second Amendment in the century after its enactment interpreted the amendment as we do.

1. Postratification Commentary

Three important founding-era legal scholars interpreted the Second Amendment in published writings. All three understood it to protect an individual right unconnected with militia service.

St. George Tucker's version of Blackstone's Commentaries . . . conceived of the Blackstonian arms right as necessary for self-defense. He equated that right, absent the religious and class-based restrictions, with the Second Amendment. . . . "This may be considered as the true palladium of liberty. . . . The right to self-defence is the first law of nature: in most governments it has been the study of rulers to confine the right within the narrowest limits possible. Wherever standing armies are kept up, and the right of the people to keep and bear arms is, under any colour or pretext whatsoever, prohibited, liberty, if not already annihilated, is on the brink of destruction." . . .

Antislavery advocates routinely invoked the right to bear arms for self-defense. Joel Tiffany, for example, citing Blackstone's description of the right, wrote that "the right to keep and bear arms, also implies the right to use them if necessary in self defence; without this right to use the guaranty would have hardly been worth the paper it consumed." In his famous Senate speech about the 1856 "Bleeding Kansas" conflict, Charles Sumner proclaimed:

> Never was [the rifle] more needed in just self-defence, than now in Kansas. . . . And yet . . . in defiance of the solemn guarantee . . . that "the right of the people to keep and bear arms shall not be infringed," the people of Kansas have been arraigned for keeping and bearing them . . . .

We have found only one early 19th-century commentator who clearly conditioned the right to keep and bear arms upon service in the militia—and he recognized that the prevailing view was to the contrary. . . .

2. Pre-Civil War Case Law

. . . Many early 19th-century state cases indicated that the Second Amendment right to bear arms was an individual right unconnected to militia service, though subject to certain restrictions. . . . In *Nunn v. State*, 1 Ga. 243, 251 (1846), the Georgia Supreme Court construed the Second Amendment as protecting the "*natural* right of self-defence" and therefore struck down a ban on carrying pistols openly. Its opinion perfectly captured the way in which the operative clause of the Second Amendment furthers the purpose announced in the prefatory clause, in continuity with the English right:

> The right of the whole people . . . and not militia only, to keep
> and bear *arms* of every description, and not *such* merely as are
> used by the *militia,* shall not be *infringed,* curtailed, or broken in
> upon, in the smallest degree; and all this for the important end
> to be attained: the rearing up and qualifying a well-regulated
> militia, so vitally necessary to the security of a free State. . . .

Likewise, in *State v. Chandler*, 5 La. Ann. 489, 490 (1850), the Louisiana
Supreme Court held that citizens had a right to carry arms openly: "This
is the right guaranteed by the Constitution of the United States, and
which is calculated to incite men to a manly and noble defence of
themselves, if necessary, and of their country. . . ." . . .

3.   Post-Civil War Legislation

In the aftermath of the Civil War, there was an outpouring of
discussion of the Second Amendment in Congress and in public discourse,
as people debated whether and how to secure constitutional rights for
newly free slaves. Since those discussions took place 75 years after the
ratification of the Second Amendment, they do not provide as much
insight into its original meaning as earlier sources. Yet those born and
educated in the early 19th century faced a widespread effort to limit arms
ownership by a large number of citizens; their understanding of the
origins and continuing significance of the Amendment is instructive.

Blacks were routinely disarmed by Southern States after the Civil
War. Those who opposed these injustices frequently stated that they
infringed blacks' constitutional right to keep and bear arms. Needless to
say, the claim was not that blacks were being prohibited from carrying
arms in an organized state militia. A Report of the Commission of the
Freedmen's Bureau in 1866 stated plainly: "[T]he civil law [of Kentucky]
prohibits the colored man from bearing arms. . . . Their arms are taken
from them by the civil authorities. . . . Thus, the right of the people to
keep and bear arms as provided in the Constitution is *infringed*." The
view expressed in these statements was widely reported and was
apparently widely held. . . .

Congress enacted the Freedmen's Bureau Act on July 16, 1866.
Section 14 stated:

> [T]he right . . . to have full and equal benefit of all laws and
> proceedings concerning personal liberty, personal security, and
> the acquisition, enjoyment, and disposition of estate, real and
> personal, including the constitutional right to bear arms, shall
> be secured to and enjoyed by all the citizens . . . without respect
> to race or color, or previous condition of slavery. . . .

The understanding that the Second Amendment gave freed blacks the
right to keep and bear arms was reflected in congressional discussion of
the bill, with even an opponent of it saying that the founding generation
"were for every man bearing his arms about him and keeping them in his
house, his castle, for his own defense."

Similar discussion attended the passage of the Civil Rights Act of 1871 and the Fourteenth Amendment. . . . With respect to the proposed Amendment, Senator Pomeroy described as one of the three "indispensable" "safeguards of liberty . . . under the Constitution" a man's "right to bear arms for the defense of himself and family and his homestead." . . . It was plainly the understanding in the post-Civil War Congress that the Second Amendment protected an individual right to use arms for self-defense.

4. Post-Civil War Commentators

Every late-19th-century legal scholar that we have read interpreted the Second Amendment to secure an individual right unconnected with militia service. The most famous was the judge and professor Thomas Cooley, who [concluded] that . . . [t]he Second Amendment . . . "was adopted with some modification and enlargement from the English Bill of Rights of 1688, where it stood as a protest against arbitrary action of the overturned dynasty in disarming the people." In a section entitled "The Right in General," he continued:

> It might be supposed from the phraseology of this provision that the right to keep and bear arms was only guaranteed to the militia; but this would be an interpretation not warranted by the intent. . . . The meaning of the provision undoubtedly is, that the people, from whom the militia must be taken, shall have the right to keep and bear arms; and they need no permission or regulation of law for the purpose. But this enables government to have a well-regulated militia; for to bear arms implies something more than the mere keeping; it implies the learning to handle and use them in a way that makes those who keep them ready for their efficient use; in other words, it implies the right to meet for voluntary discipline in arms, observing in doing so the laws of public order.

All other post-Civil War 19th-century sources we have found concurred with Cooley. . . .

E

We now ask whether any of our precedents forecloses the conclusions we have reached about the meaning of the Second Amendment. . . .

Justice Stevens places overwhelming reliance upon this Court's decision in *United States v. Miller,* 307 U.S. 174 (1939). . . . And what is, according to Justice Stevens, the holding of *Miller* . . . ? That the Second Amendment "protects the right to keep and bear arms for certain military purposes, but that it does not curtail the legislature's power to regulate the nonmilitary use and ownership of weapons." . . .

Miller did not hold that and cannot possibly be read to have held that. The judgment in the case upheld against a Second Amendment challenge two men's federal convictions for transporting an unregistered short-barreled shotgun in interstate commerce, in violation of the

National Firearms Act. It is entirely clear that the Court's basis for saying that the Second Amendment did not apply was *not* that the defendants were "bear[ing] arms" not "for . . . military purposes" but for "nonmilitary use". Rather, it was that the *type of weapon at issue* was not eligible for Second Amendment protection: "In the absence of any evidence tending to show that the possession or use of a [short-barreled shotgun] at this time has some reasonable relationship to the preservation or efficiency of a well regulated militia, we cannot say that the Second Amendment guarantees the right to keep and bear *such an instrument.*" "Certainly," the Court continued, "it is not within judicial notice that this weapon is any part of the ordinary military equipment or that its use could contribute to the common defense." Beyond that, the opinion provided no explanation of the content of the right.

This holding is not only consistent with, but positively suggests, that the Second Amendment confers an individual right to keep and bear arms (though only arms that "have some reasonable relationship to the preservation or efficiency of a well regulated militia"). Had the Court believed that the Second Amendment protects only those serving in the militia, it would have been odd to examine the character of the weapon rather than simply note that the two crooks were not militiamen. . . . The most Justice Stevens can plausibly claim for *Miller* is that it declined to decide the nature of the Second Amendment right, despite the Solicitor General's argument (made in the alternative) that the right was collective. *Miller* stands only for the proposition that the Second Amendment right, whatever its nature, extends only to certain types of weapons.

It is particularly wrongheaded to read *Miller* for more than what it said, because the case did not even purport to be a thorough examination of the Second Amendment. . . . The respondent made no appearance in the case, neither filing a brief nor appearing at oral argument; the Court heard from no one but the Government (reason enough, one would think, not to make that case the beginning and the end of this Court's consideration of the Second Amendment). . . . The Government's *Miller* brief thus provided scant discussion of the history of the Second Amendment—and the Court was presented with no counterdiscussion. As for the text of the Court's opinion itself, that discusses *none* of the history of the Second Amendment. . . . This is the mighty rock upon which the dissent rests its case.[24]

We conclude that nothing in our precedents forecloses our adoption of the original understanding of the Second Amendment. It should be unsurprising that such a significant matter has been for so long judicially

---

[24] As for the "hundreds of judges" who have relied on the view of the Second Amendment Justice Stevens claims we endorsed in *Miller*: If so, they overread *Miller*. And their erroneous reliance upon an uncontested and virtually unreasoned case cannot nullify the reliance of millions of Americans (as our historical analysis has shown) upon the true meaning of the right to keep and bear arms. In any event, it should not be thought that the cases decided by these judges would necessarily have come out differently under a proper interpretation of the right.

unresolved. For most of our history, the Bill of Rights was not thought applicable to the States, and the Federal Government did not significantly regulate the possession of firearms by law-abiding citizens. Other provisions of the Bill of Rights have similarly remained unilluminated for lengthy periods. This Court first held a law to violate the First Amendment's guarantee of freedom of speech in 1931, almost 150 years after the Amendment was ratified, and it was not until after World War II that we held a law invalid under the Establishment Clause. . . . It is demonstrably not true that, as Justice Stevens claims, "for most of our history, the invalidity of Second-Amendment-based objections to firearms regulations has been well settled and uncontroversial." For most of our history the question did not present itself.

III

Like most rights, the right secured by the Second Amendment is not unlimited. From Blackstone through the 19th-century cases, commentators and courts routinely explained that the right was not a right to keep and carry any weapon whatsoever in any manner whatsoever and for whatever purpose. For example, the majority of the 19th-century courts to consider the question held that prohibitions on carrying concealed weapons were lawful under the Second Amendment or state analogues. Although we do not undertake an exhaustive historical analysis today of the full scope of the Second Amendment, nothing in our opinion should be taken to cast doubt on longstanding prohibitions on the possession of firearms by felons and the mentally ill, or laws forbidding the carrying of firearms in sensitive places such as schools and government buildings, or laws imposing conditions and qualifications on the commercial sale of arms.

We also recognize another important limitation on the right to keep and carry arms. *Miller* said, as we have explained, that the sorts of weapons protected were those "in common use at the time." We think that limitation is fairly supported by the historical tradition of prohibiting the carrying of "dangerous and unusual weapons."

It may be objected that if weapons that are most useful in military service—M–16 rifles and the like—may be banned, then the Second Amendment right is completely detached from the prefatory clause. But as we have said, the conception of the militia at the time of the Second Amendment's ratification was the body of all citizens capable of military service, who would bring the sorts of lawful weapons that they possessed at home to militia duty. It may well be true today that a militia, to be as effective as militias in the 18th century, would require sophisticated arms that are highly unusual in society at large. Indeed, it may be true that no amount of small arms could be useful against modern-day bombers and tanks. But the fact that modern developments have limited the degree of fit between the prefatory clause and the protected right cannot change our interpretation of the right.

IV

We turn finally to the law at issue here. As we have said, the law totally bans handgun possession in the home. It also requires that any lawful firearm in the home be disassembled or bound by a trigger lock at all times, rendering it inoperable.

As the quotations earlier in this opinion demonstrate, the inherent right of self-defense has been central to the Second Amendment right. The handgun ban amounts to a prohibition of an entire class of "arms" that is overwhelmingly chosen by American society for that lawful purpose. The prohibition extends, moreover, to the home, where the need for defense of self, family, and property is most acute. Under any of the standards of scrutiny that we have applied to enumerated constitutional rights, banning from the home the most preferred firearm in the nation to 'keep' and use for protection of one's home and family, would fail constitutional muster.

Few laws in the history of our Nation have come close to the severe restriction of the District's handgun ban. And some of those few have been struck down. . . .

It is no answer to say, as petitioners do, that it is permissible to ban the possession of handguns so long as the possession of other firearms (*i.e.*, long guns) is allowed. It is enough to note, as we have observed, that the American people have considered the handgun to be the quintessential self-defense weapon. There are many reasons that a citizen may prefer a handgun for home defense: It is easier to store in a location that is readily accessible in an emergency; it cannot easily be redirected or wrestled away by an attacker; it is easier to use for those without the upper-body strength to lift and aim a long gun; it can be pointed at a burglar with one hand while the other hand dials the police. Whatever the reason, handguns are the most popular weapon chosen by Americans for self-defense in the home, and a complete prohibition of their use is invalid.

We must also address the District's requirement (as applied to respondent's handgun) that firearms in the home be rendered and kept inoperable at all times. This makes it impossible for citizens to use them for the core lawful purpose of self-defense and is hence unconstitutional. . . .

Justice Breyer . . . proposes . . . a judge-empowering "interest-balancing inquiry" that "asks whether the statute burdens a protected interest in a way or to an extent that is out of proportion to the statute's salutary effects upon other important governmental interests." . . . We know of no other enumerated constitutional right whose core protection has been subjected to a freestanding "interest-balancing" approach. The very enumeration of the right takes out of the hands of government— even the Third Branch of Government—the power to decide on a case-by-case basis whether the right is *really worth* insisting upon. A constitutional guarantee subject to future judges' assessments of its usefulness is no constitutional guarantee at all. Constitutional rights are enshrined with the scope they were understood to have when the people adopted them, whether or not future legislatures or (yes) even future judges think that scope too broad. We would not apply an "interest-balancing" approach to the prohibition of a peaceful neo-Nazi march through Skokie. . . . The Second Amendment is no different. Like the First, it is the very *product* of an interest-balancing by the people—which Justice Breyer would now conduct for them anew. And whatever else it leaves to future evaluation, it surely elevates above all other interests the right of law-abiding, responsible citizens to use arms in defense of hearth and home.

Justice Breyer chides us for leaving so many applications of the right to keep and bear arms in doubt. . . . But since this case represents this Court's first in-depth examination of the Second Amendment, one should not expect it to clarify the entire field. . . . In sum, we hold that the District's ban on handgun possession in the home violates the Second Amendment, as does its prohibition against rendering any lawful firearm in the home operable for the purpose of immediate self-defense. Assuming that Heller is not disqualified from the exercise of Second Amendment rights, the District must permit him to register his handgun and must issue him a license to carry it in the home.

* * *

We are aware of the problem of handgun violence in this country, and we take seriously the concerns raised by the many *amici* who believe that prohibition of handgun ownership is a solution. The Constitution leaves the District of Columbia a variety of tools for combating that problem, including some measures regulating handguns. But the enshrinement of constitutional rights necessarily takes certain policy choices off the table. These include the absolute prohibition of handguns held and used for self-defense in the home. Undoubtedly some think that the Second Amendment is outmoded in a society where our standing army is the pride of our Nation, where well-trained police forces provide personal security, and where gun violence is a serious problem. That is perhaps debatable, but what is not debatable is that it is not the role of this Court to pronounce the Second Amendment extinct.

We affirm the judgment of the Court of Appeals.

■ **JUSTICE STEVENS, with whom JUSTICE SOUTER, JUSTICE GINSBURG, and JUSTICE BREYER join, dissenting.**

The question presented by this case is not whether the Second Amendment protects a "collective right" or an "individual right." Surely it protects a right that can be enforced by individuals. But a conclusion that the Second Amendment protects an individual right does not tell us anything about the scope of that right.

Guns are used to hunt, for self-defense, to commit crimes, for sporting activities, and to perform military duties. The Second Amendment plainly does not protect the right to use a gun to rob a bank; it is equally clear that it *does* encompass the right to use weapons for certain military purposes. Whether it also protects the right to possess and use guns for nonmilitary purposes like hunting and personal self-defense is the question presented by this case. The text of the Amendment, its history, and our decision in *United States v. Miller,* 307 U.S. 174 (1939), provide a clear answer to that question.

The Second Amendment was adopted to protect the right of the people of each of the several States to maintain a well-regulated militia. It was a response to concerns raised during the ratification of the Constitution that the power of Congress to disarm the state militias and create a national standing army posed an intolerable threat to the sovereignty of the several States. Neither the text of the Amendment nor the arguments advanced by its proponents evidenced the slightest interest in limiting any legislature's authority to regulate private civilian uses of firearms. Specifically, there is no indication that the Framers of the Amendment intended to enshrine the common-law right of self-defense in the Constitution.

In 1934, Congress enacted the National Firearms Act, the first major federal firearms law. Upholding a conviction under that Act, this Court held that, "[i]n the absence of any evidence tending to show that possession or use of a 'shotgun having a barrel of less than eighteen inches in length' at this time has some reasonable relationship to the preservation or efficiency of a well regulated militia, we cannot say that the Second Amendment guarantees the right to keep and bear such an instrument." The view of the Amendment we took in *Miller*—that it protects the right to keep and bear arms for certain military purposes, but that it does not curtail the Legislature's power to regulate the nonmilitary use and ownership of weapons—is both the most natural reading of the Amendment's text and the interpretation most faithful to the history of its adoption.

Since our decision in *Miller,* hundreds of judges have relied on the view of the Amendment we endorsed there. . . .[2] The opinion the Court announces today fails to identify any new evidence supporting the view that the Amendment was intended to limit the power of Congress to regulate civilian uses of weapons. . . .

Even if the textual and historical arguments on both sides of the issue were evenly balanced, respect for the well-settled views of all of our predecessors on this Court, and for the rule of law itself, would prevent

---

[2]   Until the Fifth Circuit's decision in *United States v. Emerson,* 270 F.3d 203 (2001), every Court of Appeals to consider the question had understood *Miller* to hold that the Second Amendment does not protect the right to possess and use guns for purely private, civilian purposes. . . .

most jurists from endorsing such a dramatic upheaval in the law.[4] As Justice Cardozo observed years ago, the "labor of judges would be increased almost to the breaking point if every past decision could be reopened in every case, and one could not lay one's own course of bricks on the secure foundation of the courses laid by others who had gone before him." . . .

I

The text of the Second Amendment is brief. . . . Three portions of that text merit special focus: the introductory language defining the Amendment's purpose, the class of persons encompassed within its reach, and the unitary nature of the right that it protects.

"A well regulated Militia, being necessary to the security of a free State"

The preamble to the Second Amendment makes three important points. It identifies the preservation of the militia as the Amendment's purpose; it explains that the militia is necessary to the security of a free State; and it recognizes that the militia must be "well regulated." In all three respects it is comparable to provisions in several State Declarations of Rights that were adopted roughly contemporaneously with the Declaration of Independence. Those state provisions highlight the importance members of the founding generation attached to the maintenance of state militias; they also underscore the profound fear shared by many in that era of the dangers posed by standing armies. . . .

The parallels between the Second Amendment and these state declarations, and the Second Amendment's omission of any statement of purpose related to the right to use firearms for hunting or personal self-defense, is especially striking in light of the fact that the Declarations of Rights of Pennsylvania and Vermont did expressly protect such civilian uses at the time. . . . The contrast between those two declarations and the Second Amendment . . . confirms that the Framers' single-minded focus in crafting the constitutional guarantee "to keep and bear arms" was on military uses of firearms, which they viewed in the context of service in state militias.

The preamble thus both sets forth the object of the Amendment and informs the meaning of the remainder of its text. Such text should not be treated as mere surplusage. . . .

---

[4] See *Vasquez v. Hillery*, 474 U.S. 254, 265, 266 (1986) ("[*Stare decisis*] permits society to presume that bedrock principles are founded in the law rather than in the proclivities of individuals, and thereby contributes to the integrity of our constitutional system of government, both in appearance and in fact. While *stare decisis* is not an inexorable command, the careful observer will discern that any detours from the straight path of *stare decisis* in our past have occurred for articulable reasons, and only when the Court has felt obliged to bring its opinions into agreement with experience and with facts newly ascertained.").

"The right of the people"

. . . [T]he words "the people" in the Second Amendment refer back to the object announced in the Amendment's preamble. They remind us that it is the collective action of individuals having a duty to serve in the militia that the text directly protects and, perhaps more importantly, that the ultimate purpose of the Amendment was to protect the States' share of the divided sovereignty created by the Constitution. . . .

"To keep and bear Arms"

[T]hese words . . . describe a unitary right: to possess arms if needed for military purposes and to use them in conjunction with military activities. . . . The term "bear arms" is a familiar idiom; when used unadorned by any additional words, its meaning is "to serve as a soldier, do military service, fight." 1 Oxford English Dictionary 634 (2d ed. 1989). It is derived from the Latin *arma ferre,* which, translated literally, means "to bear *[ferre]* war equipment *[arma]."* One 18th-century dictionary defined "arms" as "weapons of offence, or armour of defence," and another contemporaneous source explained that "[b]y *arms,* we understand those instruments of offence generally made use of in war; such as firearms, swords, & c. By *weapons,* we more particularly mean instruments of other kinds (exclusive of fire-arms), made use of as offensive, on special occasions." Had the Framers wished to expand the meaning of the phrase "bear arms" to encompass civilian possession and use, they could have done so by the addition of phrases such as "for the defense of themselves," as was done in the Pennsylvania and Vermont Declarations of Rights. The *unmodified* use of "bear arms," by contrast, refers most naturally to a military purpose, as evidenced by its use in literally dozens of contemporary texts. . . .

The Amendment's use of the term "keep" in no way contradicts the military meaning conveyed by the phrase "bear arms" and the Amendment's preamble. To the contrary, a number of state militia laws in effect at the time of the Second Amendment's drafting used the term "keep" to describe the requirement that militia members store their arms at their homes, ready to be used for service when necessary. . . .

This reading is confirmed by the fact that the clause protects only one right, rather than two. It does not describe a right "to keep arms" and a separate right "to bear arms." Rather, the single right that it does describe is both a duty and a right to have arms available and ready for military service, and to use them for military purposes when necessary. . . .

When each word in the text is given full effect, the Amendment is most naturally read to secure to the people a right to use and possess arms in conjunction with service in a well-regulated militia. . . .

II

The proper allocation of military power in the new Nation was an issue of central concern for the Framers. . . . On the one hand, there was a widespread fear that a national standing Army posed an intolerable threat to individual liberty and to the sovereignty of the separate States. . . . On the other hand, the Framers recognized the dangers inherent in relying on inadequately trained militia members as the primary means of providing for the common defense; during the Revolutionary War, this force, though armed, was largely untrained, and its deficiencies were the subject of bitter complaint. In order to respond to those twin concerns, a compromise was reached: Congress would be authorized to raise and support a national Army and Navy, and also to organize, arm, discipline, and provide for the calling forth of "the Militia." U.S. Const., Art. I, § 8, cls. 12–16. The President, at the same time, was empowered as the "Commander in Chief of the Army and Navy of the United States, and of the Militia of the several States, when called into the actual Service of the United States." Art. II, § 2. But, with respect to the militia, a significant reservation was made to the States: Although Congress would have the power to call forth, organize, arm, and discipline the militia, as well as to govern "such Part of them as may be employed in the Service of the United States," the States respectively would retain the right to appoint the officers and to train the militia in accordance with the discipline prescribed by Congress. Art. I, § 8, cl. 16.

But the original Constitution's retention of the militia and its creation of divided authority over that body did not prove sufficient to allay fears about the dangers posed by a standing army. For it was perceived by some that Article I contained a significant gap: While it empowered Congress to organize, arm, and discipline the militia, it did not prevent Congress from providing for the militia's *dis*armament. . . .

This sentiment . . . was one of the primary objections to the original Constitution voiced by its opponents. . . . [A] number of States did propose to the first Federal Congress amendments reflecting a desire to ensure that the institution of the militia would remain protected under the new Government. . . . Madison, charged with the task of assembling the proposals for amendments sent by the ratifying States, was the principal draftsman of the Second Amendment. . . . [I]t is strikingly significant that Madison's first draft omitted any mention of nonmilitary use or possession of weapons. . . . [H]e considered and rejected formulations that would have unambiguously protected civilian uses of firearms. . . .

The history of the adoption of the Amendment thus describes an overriding concern about the potential threat to state sovereignty that a federal standing army would pose, and a desire to protect the States' militias as the means by which to guard against that danger. . . . The evidence plainly refutes the claim that the Amendment was motivated by the Framers' fears that Congress might act to regulate any civilian uses of weapons. . . .

III

Although it gives short shrift to the drafting history of the Second Amendment, the Court dwells at length on four other sources: the 17th-century English Bill of Rights; Blackstone's Commentaries on the Laws of England; postenactment commentary on the Second Amendment; and post-Civil War legislative history. All of these sources shed only indirect light on the question before us, and in any event offer little support for the Court's conclusion.

. . . Article VII of the 1689 English Bill of Rights . . . was enacted in response to different concerns from those that motivated the Framers of the Second Amendment, and . . . the guarantees of the two provisions were by no means coextensive. Moreover, the English text contained no preamble or other provision identifying a narrow, militia-related purpose. . . .

The Court's reliance on Blackstone's Commentaries . . . is unpersuasive for the same reason. . . . Blackstone's invocation of "the natural right of resistance and self-preservation," and "the right of having and using arms for self-preservation and defence", referred specifically to Article VII in the English Bill of Rights. The excerpt from Blackstone offered by the Court, therefore, is, like Article VII itself, of limited use in interpreting the very differently worded, and differently historically situated, Second Amendment. . . .

The Court also excerpts . . . commentary by a number of additional scholars, some near in time to the framing and others post-dating it by close to a century. Those scholars are for the most part of limited relevance. . . .

The most significant of these commentators was Joseph Story. Contrary to the Court's assertions . . . Story . . . began by tying the significance of the Amendment directly to the paramount importance of the militia. . . . There is not so much as a whisper . . . that Story believed that the right secured by the Amendment bore any relation to private use or possession of weapons for activities like hunting or personal self-defense. . . .

The Court suggests that by the post-Civil War period, the Second Amendment was understood to secure a right to firearm use and ownership for purely private purposes like personal self-defense. While it is true that some of the legislative history on which the Court relies supports that contention, . . . [a]ll of the statements the Court cites were made long after the framing of the Amendment and cannot possibly supply any insight into the intent of the Framers; and all were made during pitched political debates, so that they are better characterized as advocacy than good-faith attempts at constitutional interpretation. . . .

IV

. . . In 1792, the year after the Amendment was ratified, Congress passed a statute that purported to establish "an Uniform Militia throughout the United States." The statute commanded every able-bodied white male citizen between the ages of 18 and 45 to be enrolled therein and to "provide himself with a good musket or firelock" and other specified weaponry. The statute is significant, for it confirmed the way those in the founding generation viewed firearm ownership: as a duty linked to military service. The statute they enacted, however, "was virtually ignored for more than a century," and was finally repealed in 1901. . . .

In 1901 the President revitalized the militia by creating " 'the National Guard of the several States' "; meanwhile, the dominant understanding of the Second Amendment's inapplicability to private gun ownership continued well into the 20th century. . . . Indeed, the Second Amendment was not even mentioned in either full House of Congress during the legislative proceedings that led to the passage of the 1934 Act [prohibiting the possession of sawed-off shotguns and machine guns]. Yet enforcement of that law produced the judicial decision that confirmed the status of the Amendment as limited in reach to military usage. After reviewing many of the same sources that are discussed at greater length by the Court today, the *Miller* Court unanimously concluded that the Second Amendment did not apply to the possession of a firearm that did not have "some reasonable relationship to the preservation or efficiency of a well regulated militia."

The key to that decision did not, as the Court belatedly suggests, turn on the difference between muskets and sawed-off shotguns; it turned, rather, on the basic difference between the military and nonmilitary use and possession of guns. Indeed, if the Second Amendment were not limited in its coverage to military uses of weapons, why should the Court in *Miller* have suggested that some weapons but not others were eligible for Second Amendment protection? If use for self-defense were the relevant standard, why did the Court not inquire into the suitability of a particular weapon for self-defense purposes?

Perhaps in recognition of the weakness of its attempt to distinguish *Miller*, the Court argues in the alternative that *Miller* should be discounted because of its decisional history. It is true that the appellee in *Miller* did not file a brief or make an appearance, although the court below had held that the relevant provision of the National Firearms Act violated the Second Amendment (albeit without any reasoned opinion). But, as our decision in *Marbury v. Madison,* 5 U.S. (1 Cranch) 137, in which only one side appeared and presented arguments, demonstrates, the absence of adversarial presentation alone is not a basis for refusing to accord *stare decisis* effect to a decision of this Court. Of course, if it can be demonstrated that new evidence or arguments were genuinely not available to an earlier Court, that fact should be given special weight as we consider whether to overrule a prior case. But the Court does not make that claim, because it cannot. . . .

V

The Court concludes its opinion by declaring that it is not the proper role of this Court to change the meaning of rights "enshrine[d]" in the Constitution. But the right the Court announces was not "enshrined" in the Second Amendment by the Framers; it is the product of today's law-changing decision. . . .

Until today, it has been understood that legislatures may regulate the civilian use and misuse of firearms so long as they do not interfere with the preservation of a well-regulated militia. The Court's announcement of a new constitutional right to own and use firearms for private purposes upsets that settled understanding, but leaves for future cases the formidable task of defining the scope of permissible regulations. . . . I fear that the District's policy choice may well be just the first of an unknown number of dominoes to be knocked off the table. [T]oday's decision . . . will surely give rise to a far more active judicial role in making vitally important national policy decisions than was envisioned at any time in the 18th, 19th, or 20th centuries. . . .

For these reasons, I respectfully dissent.

■ JUSTICE BREYER, with whom JUSTICE STEVENS, JUSTICE SOUTER, and JUSTICE GINSBURG join, dissenting.

. . . The majority's conclusion is wrong for two independent reasons. The first reason is that set forth by Justice Stevens—namely, that the Second Amendment protects militia-related, not self-defense-related, interests. . . .

The second independent reason is that the protection the Amendment provides is not absolute. The Amendment permits government to regulate the interests that it serves. Thus, irrespective of what those interests are—whether they do or do not include an independent interest in self-defense—the majority's view cannot be correct unless it can show that the District's regulation is unreasonable or inappropriate in Second Amendment terms. This the majority cannot do. . . .

[A]lmost every gun-control regulation will seek to advance (as the one here does) a primary concern of every government—a concern for the safety and indeed the lives of its citizens. The Court has deemed that interest, as well as the Government's general interest in preventing crime, to be "compelling," and the Court has in a wide variety of constitutional contexts found such public-safety concerns sufficiently forceful to justify restrictions on individual liberties. . . .

The fact that important interests lie on both sides of the constitutional equation suggests that review of gun-control regulation is not a context in which a court should effectively presume either constitutionality . . . or unconstitutionality . . . Rather, where a law significantly implicates competing constitutionally protected interests in complex ways, the Court generally asks whether the statute burdens a protected interest in a way or to an extent that is out of proportion to the statute's salutary effects upon other important governmental interests. . . .

In applying this kind of standard the Court normally defers to a legislature's empirical judgment in matters where a legislature is likely to have greater expertise and greater institutional fact-finding capacity. Nonetheless, a court, not a legislature, must make the ultimate constitutional conclusion, exercising its independent judicial judgment in light of the whole record to determine whether a law exceeds constitutional boundaries. . . .

No one doubts the constitutional importance of the statute's basic objective, saving lives. But there is considerable debate about whether the District's statute helps to achieve that objective. I begin by reviewing the statute's tendency to secure that objective from the perspective of (1) the legislature (namely, the Council of the District of Columbia) that enacted the statute in 1976, and (2) a court that seeks to evaluate the Council's decision today.

First, consider the facts as the legislature saw them when it adopted the District statute. As stated by the local council committee that recommended its adoption, the major substantive goal of the District's handgun restriction is "to reduce the potentiality for gun-related crimes and gun-related deaths from occurring within the District of Columbia." The committee concluded, on the basis of "extensive public hearings" and "lengthy research," that "[t]he easy availability of firearms in the United States has been a major factor contributing to the drastic increase in gun-related violence and crime over the past 40 years." It reported to the Council "startling statistics" regarding gun-related crime, accidents, and deaths, focusing particularly on the relation between handguns and crime and the proliferation of handguns within the District. . . .

Next, consider the facts as a court must consider them looking at the matter as of today. Petitioners, and their *amici,* have presented us with more recent statistics that tell much the same story that the committee report told 30 years ago. . . .

From 1993 to 1997, there were 180,533 firearm-related deaths in the United States, an average of over 36,000 per year. Fifty-one percent were suicides, 44% were homicides, 1% were legal interventions, 3% were unintentional accidents, and 1% were of undetermined causes. Over that same period there were an additional 411,800 nonfatal firearm-related injuries treated in U.S. hospitals, an average of over 82,000 per year. Of these, 62% resulted from assaults, 17% were unintentional, 6% were suicide attempts, 1% were legal interventions, and 13% were of unknown causes.

The statistics are particularly striking in respect to children and adolescents. In over one in every eight firearm-related deaths in 1997, the victim was someone under the age of 20. . . . More male teenagers die from firearms than from all natural causes combined. . . .

Handguns are involved in a majority of firearm deaths and injuries in the United States. . . . [T]he linkage of handguns to firearms deaths and injuries appears to be much stronger in urban than in rural areas. . . .

Respondent and his many *amici* for the most part do not disagree about the *figures* set forth in the preceding subsection, but they do disagree strongly with the District's *predictive judgment* that a ban on handguns will help solve the crime and accident problems that those figures disclose. . . . First, they point out that, since the ban took effect, violent crime in the District has increased, not decreased. Indeed, a comparison with 49 other major cities reveals that the District's homicide rate is actually substantially *higher* relative to these other cities than it was before the handgun restriction went into effect. . . .

Second, respondent's *amici* point to a statistical analysis that regresses murder rates against the presence or absence of strict gun laws in 20 European nations. That analysis concludes that strict gun laws are correlated with *more* murders, not fewer. They also cite domestic studies, based on data from various cities, States, and the Nation as a whole, suggesting that a reduction in the number of guns does not lead to a reduction in the amount of violent crime. . . .

Third, they point to evidence indicating that firearm ownership does have a beneficial self-defense effect. Based on a 1993 survey, the authors of one study estimated that there were 2.2–to–2.5 million defensive uses of guns (mostly brandishing, about a quarter involving the actual firing of a gun) annually. . . . And additional evidence suggests that criminals are likely to be deterred from burglary and other crimes if they know the victim is likely to have a gun.

Fourth, respondent's *amici* argue that laws criminalizing gun possession are self-defeating, as evidence suggests that they will have the effect only of restricting law-abiding citizens, but not criminals, from acquiring guns. . . .

In the view of respondent's *amici*, this evidence shows that other remedies—such as *less* restriction on gun ownership, or liberal authorization of law-abiding citizens to carry concealed weapons—better fit the problem. They further suggest that at a minimum the District fails to show that its *remedy,* the gun ban, bears a reasonable relation to the crime and accident *problems* that the District seeks to solve.

These empirically-based arguments may have proved strong enough to convince many legislatures, as a matter of legislative policy, not to adopt total handgun bans. But the question here is whether they are strong enough to destroy judicial confidence in the reasonableness of a legislature that rejects them. And that they are not. For one thing, they can lead us more deeply into the uncertainties that surround any effort to reduce crime, but they cannot prove either that handgun possession diminishes crime or that handgun bans are ineffective. The statistics do show a soaring District crime rate. And the District's crime rate went up after the District adopted its handgun ban. But, as students of elementary logic know, *after it* does not mean *because of it*. What would the District's crime rate have looked like without the ban? Higher? Lower? The same? Experts differ; and we, as judges, cannot say. . . .

[T]he District and its *amici* support the District's handgun restriction with studies of their own. One in particular suggests that, statistically speaking, the District's law has indeed had positive life-saving effects. Others suggest that firearm restrictions as a general matter reduce homicides, suicides, and accidents in the home. Still others suggest that the defensive uses of handguns are not as great in number as respondent's *amici* claim. . . . The upshot is a set of studies and counterstudies that, at most, could leave a judge uncertain about the proper policy conclusion. But from respondent's perspective any such uncertainty is not good enough. That is because legislators, not judges, have primary responsibility for drawing policy conclusions from empirical fact. . . .

[D]eference to legislative judgment seems particularly appropriate here, where the judgment has been made by a local legislature, with particular knowledge of local problems and insight into appropriate local solutions. . . . For these reasons, I conclude that the District's statute properly seeks to further the sort of life-preserving and public-safety interests that the Court has called "compelling."

I next assess the extent to which the District's law burdens the interests that the Second Amendment seeks to protect. . . . The District's statute burdens the Amendment's first and primary objective hardly at all. [T]he principal (if not the only) purpose of the Second Amendment is . . . the preservation of a "well regulated Militia." [T]he present case has nothing to do with *actual* military service. . . .

The District's law does prevent a resident from keeping a loaded handgun in his home. And it consequently makes it more difficult for the householder to use the handgun for self-defense in the home against intruders, such as burglars. . . . To that extent the law burdens to some degree an interest in self-defense that for present purposes I have assumed the Amendment seeks to further.

In weighing needs and burdens, we must take account of the possibility that there are reasonable, but less restrictive alternatives. Are there *other* potential measures that might similarly promote the same goals while imposing lesser restrictions? Here I see none.

The reason there is no clearly superior, less restrictive alternative to the District's handgun ban is that the ban's very objective is to reduce significantly the number of handguns in the District, say, for example, by allowing a law enforcement officer immediately to assume that *any* handgun he sees is an *illegal* handgun. . . . [T]he very attributes that make handguns particularly useful for self-defense are also what make them particularly dangerous. That they are easy to hold and control means that they are easier for children to use. That they are maneuverable and permit a free hand likely contributes to the fact that they are by far the firearm of choice for crimes such as rape and robbery. That they are small and light makes them easy to steal and concealable.

This symmetry suggests that any measure less restrictive in respect to the use of handguns for self-defense will, to that same extent, prove less effective in preventing the use of handguns for illicit purposes. . . .

The upshot is that the District's objectives are compelling; its predictive judgments as to its law's tendency to achieve those objectives are adequately supported; the law does impose a burden upon any self-defense interest that the Amendment seeks to secure; and there is no clear less restrictive alternative. . . .

[A] contrary view, as embodied in today's decision, will have unfortunate consequences. The decision will encourage legal challenges to gun regulation throughout the Nation. Because it says little about the standards used to evaluate regulatory decisions, it will leave the Nation without clear standards for resolving those challenges. And litigation over the course of many years, or the mere specter of such litigation, threatens to leave cities without effective protection against gun violence and accidents during that time. As important, the majority's decision threatens severely to limit the ability of more knowledgeable, democratically-elected officials to deal with gun-related problems. . . .

The majority derides my approach as "judge-empowering." I take this criticism seriously, but I do not think it accurate. [T]his is an approach that the Court has taken in other areas of constitutional law. Application of such an approach, of course, requires judgment, but the very nature of the approach—requiring careful identification of the relevant interests and evaluating the law's effect upon them—limits the judge's choices; and the method's necessary transparency lays bare the judge's reasoning for all to see and to criticize. . . .

At the same time the majority ignores a more important question: Given the purposes for which the Framers enacted the Second Amendment, how should it be applied to modern-day circumstances that they could not have anticipated? Assume, for argument's sake, that the Framers did intend the Amendment to offer a degree of self-defense protection. Does that mean that the Framers also intended to guarantee a right to possess a loaded gun near swimming pools, parks, and playgrounds? That they would not have cared about the children who might pick up a loaded gun on their parents' bedside table? That they . . . would have lacked concern for the risk of accidental deaths or suicides that readily accessible loaded handguns in urban areas might bring? Unless we believe that they intended future generations to ignore such matters, answering questions such as the questions in this case requires judgment—judicial judgment exercised within a framework for constitutional analysis that guides that judgment and which makes its exercise transparent. . . .

The argument about method, however, is by far the less important argument surrounding today's decision. Far more important are the unfortunate consequences that today's decision is likely to spawn. Not least of these, as I have said, is the fact that the decision threatens to throw into doubt the constitutionality of gun laws throughout the United States. I can find no sound legal basis for launching the courts on so formidable and potentially dangerous a mission. In my view, there simply is no untouchable constitutional right guaranteed by the Second Amendment to keep loaded handguns in the house in crime-ridden urban areas. . . .

With respect, I dissent.

Michael W. McConnell, Textualism and the Dead Hand of the Past*

The first question any advocate of constitutionalism must answer is why Americans of today should be bound by the decisions of people some 212 years ago. The Framers and Ratifiers did not represent us, and in many cases did not even represent people like us, if we happen to be Catholic or Jewish, or female, or black, or poor. What is most devastating to any claim of authority on their part is that the Framers and Ratifiers are long dead. Why should their decisions prevent the people of today from governing ourselves as we see fit? This is commonly known as the "dead hand problem." Most often, the dead hand argument is aimed at originalism—the view that the Constitution should be interpreted as the people who enacted it would have understood it. But in truth, the dead hand argument, if accepted, is fatal to any form of constitutionalism. To whatever extent our present-day decisions are shaped or constrained by the Constitution—however interpreted—we are governed by the dead hand of the past. How can this be justified?

[T]he dead hand problem was recognized from the very beginning of the Republic. . . . "The earth belongs in usufruct to the living," Jefferson declared, and "the dead have neither powers nor rights over it." Jefferson accordingly thought that the Constitution (any constitution, indeed any law) should expire at the end of a generation, which he calculated to be nineteen years. Similarly, Tom Paine wrote that "every age and generation must be as free to act for itself, in all cases, as the ages and generations which preceded it," and Noah Webster declared that "the very attempt to make perpetual constitutions, is the assumption of a right to control the opinions of future generations; and to legislate for those over whom we have as little authority as we have over a nation in

---

*   Reprinted from 66 GEO. WASH. L. REV. 1127 (1998).

Asia." If these arguments are right, then the Founders' very attempt to "form a more perfect Union" for the benefit of "ourselves and our Posterity" was presumptuous and unjust. Likewise, fidelity to that Constitution on our part is profoundly misguided.

The dead hand problem thus raises the first question for constitutional theory. We cannot address the question of how to interpret the Constitution for the purpose of resolving present-day disputes without first understanding why we should consult the decisions of persons long dead for that purpose. Moreover, it turns out that our answer to the "why" question has implications for the "how" question. We can determine the method to interpret the Constitution only if we are first clear about why the Constitution is authoritative.

It is, of course, no answer to the dead hand problem to point out that the Constitution says it will govern the future, nor to prove that this was the Founders' intention. No document is authoritative because it says so. If the faculty of the George Washington University Law School drew up a "constitution" that purported to control the decisions of the rest of the world, no one would give it the slightest attention—no matter how explicit its assertions of its own authority might be. The answer to the dead hand problem, assuming there is an answer, must be found in the realm of political theory, and not in that of constitutional interpretation.

In principle, there might be any number of possible responses to the dead hand problem, but five strike me as the most common, the most plausible, and the most important to constitutional theory.

First, one might defend the authority of the Constitution on the ground that it expresses principles of political morality and organization that continue to command our assent and agreement. If the provisions of the Constitution were inefficient, evil, or unjust, we would be fully justified in scrapping it; it is only the happy contingency that the Framers, Ratifiers, and Amenders of our Constitution did such an excellent job on the merits that justifies constitutionalism today. In other words, the authority of the Constitution is attributable not to any authority the dead have over the living, but to the enduring validity of its principles.

Implicit in this answer is the notion that we should enforce only those portions of the Constitution that are valid, according to our present judgment, and we should modify or ignore those portions that are not. If the Contracts Clause has become an obstacle to salutary economic regulation in our modern economy, then the Contracts Clause should be left unenforced; if the idea of widespread gun ownership is scary in modern urban America, then the Second Amendment should be treated as a dead letter. Conversely, if the intrusive capabilities of government present more of a problem to us than they did to our forebears, or if sexual or other intimate forms of personal autonomy seem more essential to our post-Freudian sensibilities than they did to Americans steeped in Calvinist conceptions of the self, then we might conjure up a constitutional right of "privacy" whether it can be fairly located in the constitutional text or not. This approach to the text goes by the name of the "living Constitution."

Whatever the attractions of this approach to constitutional disputes, we should recognize that it is not an answer, but a capitulation to the dead hand argument. If the Constitution is authoritative only to the extent that it accords with our independent judgments about political morality and structure, then the Constitution itself is only a makeweight: what gives force to our conclusions is simply our beliefs about what is good, just, and efficient. Taken to its logical conclusion, this line of argument does not provide a reason for treating the Constitution as authoritative; it instructs us to disregard the Constitution whenever we disagree with it.

In practice, this approach to the dead hand problem could lead in two seemingly opposite directions, depending on which institutions are entitled to speak for "us" in determining which parts of the textual Constitution we should disregard or supplement. If "we" speak through our elected representatives in the political branches of government, then this interpretive approach prescribes democratic majoritarianism, with little or no role for judicial review. If "we" speak through the judiciary, however, as advocates of the "living Constitution" and its many cognates seem to assume, then the result is discretionary rule by judges. According to this latter view, the job of courts is to keep the Constitution contemporary, and the constitutional text and history will play little role in determining the outcome of hard cases. Neither of these polar opposites is recognizable as constitutionalism, if by "constitutionalism" we mean that the authoritative decisions of the past constrain (to at least some degree) the authority of government officials today. . . .

A second, more promising, answer to the dead hand problem is that . . . the legacy of the dead hand may be enabling rather than constraining. The rules of basketball do not merely constrain those who wish to play the game, but also make the game possible. If the rules were constantly up for grabs, players would be forced to spend their time in rulemaking rather than in playing basketball. Similarly, the rules of grammar do not merely constrain the speaker or writer, but make communication possible. For much the same reason, it is simplistic to treat constitutional rules solely as constraints on our ability to govern ourselves today: without constitutional rules, we would have no institutions through which self-government could take place. Rules such as the requirement of periodic elections, the separation of powers, and the freedom of political speech are necessary if democratic self-government is to work. In this sense . . . the dead do not govern the living but make it easier for the living to govern themselves.

To the extent that this response provides an answer to the dead hand problem, it implies a form of constitutional interpretation in which it matters more that issues be decided in a stable, consistent, and predictable fashion than that they be decided in accordance with any particular methodology. It therefore supports a strong doctrine of stare decisis and the view that the Supreme Court is supreme in its exposition of the Constitution (as opposed to the view that each branch of government has the responsibility to interpret the Constitution for itself, within the range of its own powers). But this response also suggests that constitutional law should be confined to essentially process-based issues such as election rules and government structure. It provides no justification for allowing the dead hand of the past to impose substantive limitations on policy—such as economic rights, privacy, criminal procedure, nonpolitical free speech, egalitarianism, or the like. There are, after all, relatively few issues that require constitutional pre-commitments to ensure democratic self-rule for ourselves and our posterity. Most of what we now think of as constitutional law lies outside this justification.

A third response to the dead hand problem is simply to defend the legitimacy of the dead hand. One may plausibly argue that a nation's right of self-determination includes its right to create lasting governmental institutions; accordingly, Jefferson, Paine, and Webster were wrong. Despite Jefferson's rhetoric, there is nothing troubling or unusual about the idea that today's generation is constrained, for better or worse, by the decisions and actions of people who came before. How could it be otherwise? It is the nature of people to make promises, and of groups of people to make promises that may apply not only to current members, but to future members as well (provided they avail themselves of the group's membership benefits). No one doubts the authority of a corporation to make binding commitments for the future—extending even beyond the expected lives of current shareholders. Parents can bequeath debts to their heirs—as long as the estate contains assets valuable enough that the heirs agree to accept them. By the same token, countries, as corporate bodies, can make commitments for the future, subject only to the power of future generations to change those rules in accordance with the procedures by which they were set in the first place. The Founders ordained and established the Constitution of 1787 first by fighting and winning a war of independence (which abrogated the prior British Constitution), and then by winning unanimous consent of the states for the new arrangements. The people of today could ordain and establish a new Constitution by means either of revolution or of the Article V amendment procedures. Indeed, I agree . . . that the people of today could create a new Constitution by any means that would command overwhelming popular consent, sufficient to establish a Union in fact. But until the people take such steps, the dead hands of Madison, Washington, Wilson, Hamilton, Pinckney, Morris, and the other Framers and Ratifiers continue, quite legitimately, to rule us from the grave.

This self-evidently was the view of the constitutional drafters themselves, most of whom had no qualms about establishing a perpetual union with onerous amendment procedures. It was the view of Chief Justice John Marshall, who declared as "the basis, on which the whole American fabric has been erected," the idea that "the people have an original right to establish, for their future government, such principles as, in their opinion, shall most conduce to their own happiness." Because the "exercise of this original right is a very great exertion," Marshall further explained, it cannot and ought not "be frequently repeated. The principles, therefore, so established, are deemed fundamental [and] . . . are designed to be permanent." This also is the view of democratic peoples all over the world, who are busily engaging in the task of constitutional draftsmanship as they emerge from Second or Third World tyranny. And it appears to be the view of the vast majority of the American people today, who revere the Constitution almost to the point of civil religion (without much knowledge of what it contains), and who seem utterly unaware that the ideal of constitutional government is subject to any problem of the dead hand.

This defense of the legitimacy of the dead hand underlies the perspective of constitutional positivism: All power stems from the sovereign people, and the authority of the Constitution comes from their act of sovereign will in creating it. It follows that the Constitution should be interpreted in accordance with their understanding. This is the theoretical foundation of originalism. If the Constitution is authoritative because the people of 1787 had an original right to establish a government for themselves and their posterity, the words they wrote should be interpreted—to the best of our ability—as they meant them.

A fourth answer to the dead hand problem lies in the notion of implied ratification. Under this view, the Constitution originally derived its authority from the will of the Framers and Ratifiers, but it derives its continued authority from the implicit consent of the people in each subsequent generation. For the claim of implicit consent to be persuasive, it must rest on more than the mere fact that the people have not often amended the Constitution through the Article V procedures. The Article V process is sufficiently onerous that the mere lack of amendments cannot, without more, be taken as proof of continued popular satisfaction with the Constitution. If there were persistent demands for significant constitutional amendment, backed by a majority of the people, but blocked by the two-level supermajority requirements of Article V, we would have a genuine crisis of legitimacy. In actuality, however, the American people venerate the Constitution, and even the more popular amendment proposals—school prayer, flag protection, and balanced budget—amount to tinkering around the edges. Americans whose predecessors were excluded from voting on the original Constitution— such as women and African-Americans—apparently venerate the Constitution no less ardently than propertied white males. For this reason, the oft-heard complaint that the Constitution has no legitimate claim of authority to bind us because blacks and women were excluded from the franchise in 1787, seems besides the point. No one now alive was represented in 1787, and blacks and women today are no more inclined than any other portions of the population to jettison the Constitution. If implicit consent is a valid basis for authority, our Constitution is surely valid.

This approach to the dead hand problem suggests a mode of constitutional interpretation that gives weight not only to constitutional principles as they were conceived at the founding, but also to those principles as they have been conceived by successive generations of Americans in the years since the founding. Those subsequent generations of Americans also "ratified" the Constitution, and their understandings should also count. In practical terms, that means the Constitution should be interpreted in accordance with the long-standing and evolving practices, experiences, and traditions of the nation. I refer to this constitutional methodology as "traditionalism." In recent years, it has been championed by the second Justice Harlan, revived by Justice Scalia, and adopted by the Supreme Court in *Washington v. Glucksberg.* Traditionalism is controversial because it assigns to courts the task of preserving continuity with the past, rather than fostering social change.

Jed Rubenfeld [has] propose[d] a fifth answer to the dead hand problem,* which might be seen as an amalgamation of the last two answers set forth above, but which might be better understood as an attempt to transcend the question. He argues that the dead hand problem, based on what he calls the "presentist ... conception of [democratic] self-government," is a misguided way to think about constitutional legitimacy. Thomas Jefferson's notion that each generation has the moral right to create a new constitutional order, Rubenfeld suggests, is simply an adolescent fantasy. It is the nature of human persons to conduct our lives through temporally extended projects, building upon what has come before us, building toward what will come after us. As Rubenfeld observes, "the freedom to act on nothing but present will is animal freedom." Living in the present may accord with some kind of nature, but it is not human nature.

It is no insult to Rubenfeld to say that Edmund Burke put the same point better, some 200 years ago. Burke's *Reflections on the Revolution in France*[30] is an extended critique of the notion that constitutional legitimacy is solely based on the will and choice of present-day majorities. Burke's target was precisely the doctrine of Jefferson, Rousseau, and Webster—and Richard Price—that Rubenfeld has called to our attention. Burke explained that if the presentist notion of legitimacy were accepted, "the whole chain and continuity of the commonwealth would be broken.

---

* [Editor's Note: Jed Rubenfeld, *The Moment and the Millennium*, 66 GEO. WASH. L. REV. 1085 (1998). Professor McConnell's essay was originally written as a response to Rubenfeld.]

[30] EDMUND BURKE, REFLECTIONS ON THE REVOLUTION IN FRANCE [1790] (J.G.A. Pocock ed., 1987).

No one generation could link with the other. Men would become little better than the flies of a summer."

Burke's image—"the flies of a summer"—is wonderfully apt. Flies are unburdened by the past or the future. Flies do not know their parents, and they do not know their descendants. No knowledge, no culture, no limits, no obligations are passed down from one generation to the next— only genetic material. Each generation of flies is "as free to act for itself, in all cases, as the ages and generations which preceded it."

That is not so with humans. We are born into families, communities, and nations not of our making and not of our choosing. Long before we can conceive of the possibility of freedom, we have been given a language and a set of cultural assumptions; we have accepted benefits and incurred obligations. We are not alone in the present, but part of a historically continuous community.

This is not to say that there is no freedom in the present. We are free to reject our inheritance. We can turn our backs on our parents. We can become traitors or revolutionaries. But we do not do these things, and cannot do these things morally, without a powerful reason. The inheritance must be tainted; our parents must be awful; our country must be evil. In Burke's words, "it is the first and supreme necessity only, a necessity that is not chosen but chooses, a necessity paramount to deliberation, that admits no discussion and demands no evidence, which alone can justify" the dissolution of the web of rights and obligations into which we were born.

Rubenfeld is also right to emphasize the inconsistency between Jeffersonian presentism and written constitutionalism. If Jefferson were right, there would be no point in talking about textualism or any of the competing approaches to constitutional interpretation, for it would all be illegitimate. It is important to understand why Jefferson may be wrong if we are to understand how to engage in a serious study of written constitutionalism. As Rubenfeld points out, "Jefferson lost the battle over the basic shape of American constitutionalism." The Constitution begins "We the People," claims the right to act on behalf of "ourselves and our Posterity," and "ordains and establishes" a Constitution designed to endure for the ages. Contrary to Jefferson, "constitutional law does not live in the moment—not in any moment, past, present, or hypothetical. It embodies a generation-spanning struggle—the historical struggle of a nation to be its own author." As Rubenfeld says, "written constitutionalism can only be properly understood, it can only claim legitimate authority, as an effort by a nation to achieve self-government over time." This concept of "self-government over time" does not refer to an ideal of governance at each successive moment by the will of the governed at that moment, nor to the imposition of one moment's democratic will on the rest of the nation's future, but rather to the nation's struggle to lay down temporally extended commitments and to honor those commitments over time. . . .

But what mode of constitutional interpretation follows from this response to the dead hand problem? One might think that once we are disabused of the dead hand problem, we would adopt some version of "textualism". . . . Textualists, like Justice Scalia, are committed to popular sovereignty—to rule by the people. . . . Constitutional law, as practiced by textualists like Justice Scalia, mediates between past and present—it allows us to recognize the legitimate claims of the past as well as the ongoing authority of the present. What Scalia rejects is the idea that the nation should be governed not by the will of the people over time, but by the opinions of judges, or of the legal elite.

Scalia is a textualist because he is a democratic positivist: "The text is the law, and it is the text that must be observed."[44] When a judge goes beyond the meaning of the words that were enacted—to the unexpressed intentions of the legislature, or to what the courts think would meet the needs and goals of society—the judge has no democratic warrant. The constitutional text is, therefore, the first and foremost consideration in judging. But the text is not always clear, and does not always provide answers to constitutional questions. Justice Scalia, therefore, interprets the text in light of three supplemental jurisprudential principles: originalism, traditionalism, and restraint. Originalism is the idea that the words of the Constitution must be understood as they were understood by the ratifying public at the time of enactment. Traditionalism is the idea that the words of the Constitution should be understood as they have been understood by the people over the course of our constitutional history, from enactment through the present. To accomplish this, the interpreter looks at what decentralized and representative bodies have done, over time, and treats their consensus as authoritative. Restraint is the idea that unless the text and history of the Constitution are tolerably clear, judges should defer to the decisions of present-day representative institutions.

Admittedly, these aspects of Justice Scalia's jurisprudence are sometimes in tension. It is not always clear when he believes judges should insist upon original meaning in the face of opposition by current democratic majorities; when judges should look to the unfolding interpretations of tradition instead of the meanings at the moments of enactment; or how much deference to give to the legislatures of today. Issues like the free exercise of religion and affirmative racial preferences highlight these tensions. I do not claim that Justice Scalia's resolution of those tensions is always satisfying or consistent. Maybe it is not possible to be entirely consistent. Maybe the task of constitutional law, in hard cases, is figuring out the relative weight that should be given to the founding, the tradition, and the present. . . .

---

[44] Antonin Scalia, *Common-Law Courts in a Civil-Law System: The Role of United States Federal Courts in Interpreting the Constitution and Laws*, in A MATTER OF INTERPRETATION: FEDERAL COURTS AND THE LAW 3 (Amy Gutmann ed., 1997).

What all three aspects of Scalia's jurisprudence have in common, however, is that all are dimensions of self-government. Originalism refers to the will of the people at the founding; traditionalism refers to the will of the people throughout the decades of our constitutional history; and restraint refers to the will of the people today. At no point does Scalia stand above the people, dictating that they should govern themselves according to a higher theory of justice, human dignity, or the common good. Scalia is committed to the idea of republican self-government over time. . . .

Written constitutionalism . . . can claim legitimate authority only as an effort by a nation to achieve self-government—meaning government of and by the people—over time. That means that the only legitimate sources for constitutional judgment are the will of the people at the beginning, the will of the people over time, and the will of the people in the present. In other words: originalism, traditionalism, and restraint.

See also: Anthony Kronman, *Precedent and Tradition*, 99 YALE L. J. 1029 (1990), develops Professor McConnell's Burkean argument for fidelity to the past in greater detail. For an attack on the dead hand, *see* Michael J. Klarman, *Antifidelity*, 70 S. CAL. L. REV. 381 (1997).

NOTE ON *HELLER* AND THE DEAD HAND

1.   On the morning after *Heller* came down, the *New York Times* ran an editorial asserting that "[t]his is a decision that will cost innocent lives, cause immeasurable pain and suffering and turn America into a more dangerous country. It will also diminish our standing in the world, sending yet another message that the United States values gun rights over human life."[3]

Assume, for the moment, that the *Heller* majority correctly construed the Second Amendment. And assume also that the *Times* is correct about the consequences, notwithstanding significant disagreement within the social science literature about the effects of gun laws on safety. Was the Court correct to enforce the Second Amendment in spite of the likelihood that, under contemporary conditions, such enforcement would make the country less safe? Whether or not a private right to bear arms made sense in 1791 (when the Bill of Rights was ratified), why should that decision bind us today in a very different world? Can any theory of obligation justify adherence to a centuries-old Constitution if such a decision "will cost innocent lives" today?

2.   In assessing the theoretical issues raised by *Heller*, it will help to distinguish between three kinds of constitutional theories:

- **Theories of *Obligation*** explain why we *obey* the Constitution. Professor McConnell's answers to the "dead hand" problem fall into this category. Arguments that we should follow the Constitution because it is morally sound, because constitutional constraints make collective government

---

[3]   *Lock and Load*, N.Y. TIMES, June 27, 2008.

possible, or because of the authority of the Framers are all examples of theories of obligation.

- **Theories of *Interpretation*** tell us how to figure out what the Constitution *means*. Examples include *textualism* (reliance on the plain meaning of the text); *originalism* (reliance on the original understanding of the text); *common law development* (reliance on precedent-setting interpretations of the Constitution's meaning over time); and *moral theory* (choosing the most morally satisfactory meaning of the Constitution).

- **Theories of *Judicial Review*** explain why *judges* are privileged to enforce the Constitution, as opposed to other governmental officials. Chief Justice Marshall offered a theory of judicial review in *Marbury v. Madison* based on the nature of judicial responsibility in a case raising a constitutional argument. Other commentators have suggested that the institutional independence and professional training of judges make them uniquely qualified to determine constitutional meaning.

Professor McConnell's various responses to the Dead Hand problem represent alternative theories of obligation. Which of those theories did you find the most persuasive?

Is it possible to defend some of the theories that McConnell criticizes? Could one argue, for example, that a theory of obligation predicated on the Constitution's normative appeal need not commit us to picking and choosing among the parts of the document that we do and don't like, because the Constitution's overall normative force might be best preserved if we all agree to take the document as a "package deal"? Alternatively, is McConnell wrong to dismiss the "rules of the game" account of constitutionalism—which we might also call "conventionalist"—as inapplicable to most of constitutional law? Isn't it fair to say that most constitutional law is, in fact, concerned with structures and procedures for democratic decisionmaking?

3.   The Constitution's entrenchment—and with it, the Dead Hand problem—arises from the extreme difficulty of amending our founding document. As already noted, the state constitutions are considerably easier to amend, as are many constitutions in other countries. The difficulty of amending the U.S. Constitution, however, stems not simply from the demanding institutional process specified in Article V but also from a strong cultural aversion to amendments. This aversion dates from the Founding era. As Professor McConnell notes, Thomas Jefferson and others thought that the Constitution ought to go up for general revision every generation. In Federalist 49, however, James Madison criticized his friend Thomas Jefferson's proposal for frequent constitutional amendments. Madison argued that "as every appeal to the people would carry an implication of some defect in the government, frequent appeals would in great measure deprive the government of that veneration, which time bestows on every thing, and without which perhaps the wisest and freest governments would not possess the requisite stability." Madison's notion that the Constitution should be

venerated rather than changed is evident throughout contemporary culture—for example, in the annual celebration of Constitution Day on September 17.

Has this veneration gone too far? Professor Sanford Levinson, for example, has argued that Americans should set aside veneration in favor of a reasoned critique of our Constitution's failure to provide a workable government. "We need a new constitutional convention," he writes, "one that could engage in a comprehensive overview of the U.S. Constitution and the utility of many of its provisions to twenty-first century Americans."[4] In a similar vein (but with quite different constitutional defects in mind), Texas Governor Jim Abbott called in early 2016 for a constitutional convention to consider amendments to the federal Constitution. He proposed nine amendments to achieve the following ends:

I.　Prohibit Congress from regulating activity that occurs wholly within one State.

II.　Require Congress to balance its budget.

III.　Prohibit administrative agencies—and the unelected bureaucrats that staff them—from creating federal law.

IV.　Prohibit administrative agencies—and the unelected bureaucrats that staff them—from preempting state law.

V.　Allow a two-thirds majority of the States to override a U.S. Supreme Court decision.

VI.　Require a seven-justice super-majority vote for U.S. Supreme Court decisions that invalidate a democratically enacted law.

VII.　Restore the balance of power between the federal and state governments by limiting the former to the powers expressly delegated to it in the Constitution.

VIII.　Give state officials the power to sue in federal court when federal officials overstep their bounds.

IX.　Allow a two-thirds majority of the States to override a federal law or regulation.[5]

These proposals, on their individual merits, raise a host of issues that we will address throughout the course. Taken together, they propose a radical reshaping of the current structure of American government—particularly the relationship between the Supreme Court and the political branches and between the national government and the states. (For proponents, however, the point is not so much as to radically change the original Constitution as to restore it in the wake of past departures.) Professor Levinson has proposed a quite different set of amendments, but both sets of proposals raise the same central question: How much change do we want? And in particular, would it

---

[4]　SANFORD LEVINSON, FRAMED: AMERICA'S 51 CONSTITUTIONS AND THE CRISIS OF GOVERNANCE 391 (2012).

[5]　GREG ABBOTT, RESTORING THE RULE OF LAW WITH STATES LEADING THE WAY 4 (2016), *available* at https://www.documentcloud.org/documents/2680556-Abbott-Constitutional-Proposals.html.

be a good idea to open up the possibility of broad amendments by calling a constitutional convention?

4.   Finally, to what extent does a theory of obligation—that is, that the Constitution binds future generations—imply that the Court has the power of judicial review? We consider that power in the next Chapter.

INTRODUCTORY NOTE ON INTERPRETIVE METHODOLOGY, WITH PARTICULAR EMPHASIS ON TEXTUALISM AND ORIGINALISM

1.   As Professor McConnell emphasizes, our choice of a particular theory of obligation usually has implications for the theory of interpretation that we adopt to determine the *meaning* of our constitutional obligations. Both these choices may, in turn, influence our account of judicial review and the extent to which we think courts should have primary responsibility for enforcing the Constitution. Theories of interpretation are deeply contested in our legal culture. The courts' response to the variety of contending interpretive theory has been eclectic; by and large, most judges have been reluctant to limit themselves to one particular method. Should they be more principled and consistent in this regard?

2.   This course will canvass a number of different interpretive approaches. Because of their prominence in *Heller*, we begin with textualism and originalism. As Professor McConnell's discussion indicates, the most prominent judicial proponent of textualist and originalist approaches in constitutional interpretation was Justice Antonin Scalia. Do you agree with McConnell and Scalia that the most plausible theories of constitutional obligation point toward textualism and originalism? If you prefer a "living constitution" approach to interpretation, what theory of *obligation* best supports that approach?

3.   Textualism and originalism are often combined but conceptually distinct. In *Heller*, the justices devote considerable attention to the wording and grammatical structure of the Second Amendment. What is the relationship between the Amendment's prefatory clause ("[a] well regulated Militia, being necessary to the security of a free State") and its operative clause ("the right of the people to keep and bear Arms, shall not be infringed")? Can the rules of grammar alone answer that question?

A central problem in textual interpretation concerns the extent to which the underlying purpose of a provision should limit its textual reach. For example, legal historians generally agree that the primary purpose of the First Amendment's protection for freedom of speech and press was to bar prior restraints on expression. But few argue today that the First Amendment's scope should be *limited* to that purpose. Would the opposite conclusion follow if the Amendment contained a prefatory clause, so that it read "*Prior restraints being inimical to public debate*, Congress shall make no law . . . abridging the freedom of speech, or of the press"? More generally, should we adopt rules of textual interpretation that make it more difficult for a textual provision to outlive the particular problem that gave rise to it?

4.   Originalism is an interpretive methodology that grounds constitutional meaning in the history of the era during which a given

constitutional provision was drafted and ratified. Although we will see different arguments for originalism later in the course, the most straightforward grounds it in the nature of the Constitution as law:

> Marshall said in *Marbury v. Madison* [that] (1) "[i]t is emphatically the province and duty of the judicial department to say what the law is," (2) "[i]f two laws conflict with each other, the courts must decide on the operation of each," and (3) "the constitution is to be considered, in court, as a paramount law." Central to that analysis, it seems to me, is the perception that the Constitution, though it has an effect superior to other laws, is in its nature the sort of "law" that is the business of the courts—an enactment that has a fixed meaning ascertainable through the usual devices familiar to those learned in the law. If the Constitution were not that sort of a "law," but a novel invitation to apply current societal values, what reason would there be to believe that the invitation was addressed to the courts rather than to the legislature? One simply cannot say, regarding that sort of novel enactment, that "[i]t is emphatically the province and duty of the judicial department" to determine its content. Quite to the contrary, the legislature would seem a much more appropriate expositor of social values, and its determination that a statute is compatible with the Constitution should, as in England, prevail.[6]

Is this rationale persuasive?

Early originalists focused on the *intentions* of the Constitution's framers. This focus on original intentions would ask whether the framers of the Second Amendment intended to protect individual rights to have and use firearms for self defense (in *Heller*), or whether the framers of the Fourteenth Amendment intended to desegregate the schools (in *Brown v. Board of Education*). Contemporary originalists, however, tend to combine originalism and textualism; they focus on the original *public meaning* of the words in the Constitution's text. Hence the focus in *Heller* on what people in the founding era would have understood words like "militia" and "to bear arms" to mean. What are the best arguments for choosing between "original intentions" and "original public meaning"? Does the answer depend on whether power to give legal force to the Constitution rested with its framers or its ratifiers? Can you think of cases in which the distinction might make a practical difference?

5.   Much of the critique of originalism can be divided into two strands, with the first emphasizing that the theory is unworkable on its own terms. This might true for several reasons:

a.   Originalism obviously depends heavily on the availability of evidence about the intentions of the Framers and/or the public understanding of terms in the constitutional text. Many of the questions in contemporary constitutional debate, however, involve subjects—e.g., the constitutionality of wiretapping—that the

---

[6]   Scalia, *Originalism: The Lesser Evil?*, 57 U. CIN. L. REV. 849, 854 (1989).

Framers simply had no occasion to consider. Moreover, the documentary record of the debates that did occur has all kinds of problems. These include the facts that Madison recorded only a relatively small fraction of the Philadelphia proceedings; that many of the ratification debates were recorded only by fervent partisans; and that even in the absence of partisanship many of the relevant records are simply unreliable.[7]

b.   Even if the documentary record for the Founding debates were similar in quality to modern collections of the legislative history behind contemporary statutes, we would still confront serious problems of *collective* intent. Political scientists have pointed out that "Congress is a they, not an it,"[8] and this is true in spades of the Philadelphia Convention and the ratification conventions in the several states. Different members of the critical majorities in each of these bodies may have had different intentions and understandings on key questions, and aggregating their intent may prove extremely difficult.

c.   What if the Framers themselves were not originalists? Professor H. Jefferson Powell has argued that, at the time the Constitution was adopted, "the 'intent' of [a legal] document . . . did not depend upon the subjective purposes of the author. . . . The modern practice of interpreting a law by reference to its legislative history was almost wholly nonexistent."[9] Should the Framers' own interpretive intentions—that is, their intentions about what method judges should employ in construing constitutional meaning—be dispositive? Does anything in Judge Bork's argument turn on the assumption that the Framers would have *wanted* us to be originalists?

d.   A narrower version of Professor Powell's argument is limited to some of the more open-ended clauses of the Constitution, such as the Due Process and Equal Protection Clauses. Many commentators have suggested that, while we may be able to determine the original intent or understanding of a relatively specific provision like the Establishment Clause or the Eleventh Amendment, phrases like "due process" or "equal protection" were intentionally left unspecified, so that they might evolve in response to the changing needs and circumstances of society. A plausible example is the Eighth Amendment's prohibition on "cruel and unusual" punishments, which at least plausibly suggests that a court applying the Amendment should measure a particular punishment against contemporary practice. If original meaning is

---

[7]   *See generally* James Hutson, *The Creation of the Constitution: The Integrity of the Documentary Record*, 65 TEXAS L. REV. 1 (1986).

[8]   *See* Kenneth Shepsle, *Congress is a "They," Not an "It": Legislative Intent as an Oxymoron*, 12 INT'L REV. of L. & ECON. 239 (1992).

[9]   H. Jefferson Powell, *The Original Understanding of Original Intent*, 98 HARV. L. REV. 885, 895–898 (1985).

not a guide to the interpretation of these provisions, to what should a court look?

6.   The second strand of critique argues that originalism is normatively undesirable. Again, several different arguments fall under this heading:

a.   Most critics of originalism argue that it fails to keep the Constitution "in tune with the times." Justice William Brennan, for example, argued that "the genius of the Constitution rests not in any static meaning it might have had in a world that is dead and gone, but in the adaptability of its great principles to cope with current problems and current needs."[10] If we concede that there must be some room to adapt our system of government to contemporary mores and circumstances, is it obvious that this is an appropriate role for *courts* in the exercise of judicial review? Isn't the reason that we *entrench* the Constitution precisely to keep certain aspects of it—e.g., respect for political dissent under the First Amendment—from changing with the times?

Moreover, if we accept "living constitutionalism" and allow constitutional principles to evolve, is there any reason to believe that those principles will always evolve in a progressive or more rights-protective direction? Could a living constitutionalist argue, for instance, that the unprecedented threat of nuclear and biological terrorism in the modern era requires that law enforcement be less constrained by constitutional liberties? Is there any difference between this sort of "dying constitutionalism" and the "living constitutionalism" advocated by Justice Brennan?

b.   A related line of argument accuses the originalists of excessive rationalism. One such critique argues that originalism is inconsistent with principles of classical Burkean conservatism,[11] which Professor McConnell discussed near the end of his essay. Burkeans objected to the French Revolutionaries' effort to reduce principles of political justice and good government to written charters:

A theory of written constitutions that precludes future adaptation . . . assumes a degree of rationality on the part of the Constitution's framers that Burke would have found unacceptable: it understands the Framers as great gamblers on the power of untested abstractions. Originalists must be similarly optimistic about the Framers' ability to overcome problems of textual indeterminacy and capture complex principles of government within clear written provisions. For Burke, however, no statesman, no matter how wise, could capture the infinite detail of society's needs or anticipate all future problems in a rigid system of formal rules. Instead, time

---

[10]   William J. Brennan, *The Constitution of the United States: Contemporary Ratification*, 27 S. TEX. L.J. 433, 438 (1986).

[11]   *See* EDMUND BURKE, REFLECTIONS ON THE REVOLUTION IN FRANCE (1791).

is essential to allow adaptation and compromise in light of unforeseen and changing circumstances.[12]

Does this conservative version of Justice Brennan's argument present a better answer for why adaptation and evolution cannot be left to the political branches of government?

    c.   A third problem has to do with the disruptive effects that seriously adopting an originalist approach would have on current constitutional law. Much of the relevant judicial precedent proceeds on non-originalist premises: A truly originalist court might have to overrule not only cases like *Griswold v. Connecticut* (recognizing an unenumerated right to privacy) and *Roe v. Wade*, (recognizing a constitutional right to abortion) but also much of contemporary free speech doctrine (the Framers arguably understood the First Amendment to forbid only prior restraints on publication), cases "incorporating" the Bill of Rights against the States, post-1937 understandings of the Commerce Clause, cases accepting the delegation of legislative and judicial authority to administrative agencies, and so on. Is this degree of radical legal change really "thinkable" for contemporary courts? If not, can originalism be taken seriously?

    7.   Much academic criticism of originalism plainly stems from the fact that the legal academy is overwhelmingly composed of political liberals, and originalism is identified with conservative outcomes in constitutional cases. Is this underlying political assumption really warranted? As Judge Robert Bork pointed out, "When the Supreme Court was dominated by conservative activists, prior to the coming of the New Deal Court, adherence to original understanding and judicial self-restraint was urged by liberals."[13] In any number of areas today, originalist outcomes may favor politically liberal results. The original understanding of the Establishment Clause, for example, arguably favors a rigorous prohibition on state support for religion that some have argued is out of step with modern conditions, in which the government supports, subsidizes, and is intertwined with a much broader range of private activity than it did in 1791.[14] Likewise, some have argued that in a modern world of terrorism and nuclear weapons, the President must have broader authority to act unilaterally to protect national security than the Framers may have originally understood him to possess. Moreover, the most rigorous originalist on the Rehnquist Court was arguably Justice David Souter, who also had one of the Court's most liberal voting records.[15]

    8.   How originalist was the majority's approach in *Heller*? Did the dissenters disagree about the proper methodology to employ? Did you find that the close analysis of text and history in the opinions meaningfully

---

[12] Ernest Young, *Rediscovering Conservatism: Burkean Political Theory and Constitutional Interpretation*, 72 N.C. L. REV. 619, 667–68 (1994).

[13] BORK, TEMPTING OF AMERICA, *supra*, at 177.

[14] *Cf.* Donald A. Gianella, *Religious Liberty, Nonestablishment, and Doctrinal Development, Part II. The Nonestablishment Principle*, 81 HARV. L. REV. 513 (1968).

[15] *See, e.g., Seminole Tribe of Florida v. Florida*, 517 U.S. 44, 100–185 (1996) (Souter, J., dissenting).

helped the Court reach an answer in the case? Or did the dueling opinions fight each other to a draw?

Heller illustrates several problems that different methods of constitutional interpretation raise. Much of the historical evidence suggests that the Second Amendment was drafted to protect the states from federal tyranny by ensuring the states could have armed, prepared militias. In the event insurrection were necessary (for example, if there were a coup that seized control of the government), the states could call upon the militia to resist. Further complicating matters, the Second Amendment does not simply guarantee the states the right to maintain a state militia. Instead, it arguably tries to ensure a functional militia (the prefatory clause) by giving "the people" the right to keep and bear arms. On this view, the Second Amendment gave people a right to have guns in case the need arose for a revolt against tyranny.[16]

At least two historical developments make it difficult to translate the Founders' commitment to modern times. First, the militia has largely ceased to exist as a decentralized military force. States no longer have organized militias, and the National Guard that has replaced them is subject to federal control. The result is that a federalism-based interpretation of the Second Amendment makes little sense today (and there is little chance the four *Heller* dissenters would have struck down, say, a President's decision to federalize the national guard on second amendment grounds). Second, the advent of a professional national military wielding advanced weaponry makes it unlikely that a grassroots handgun-wielding rebellion would succeed. Moreover, the Civil War did much to discredit the idea of armed insurrection against the federal government, and the Oklahoma City bombing and other terrorist threats have made many Americans profoundly suspicious of armed private groups.

Justice Scalia's opinion arguably reads a more contemporary purpose into the Second Amendment: a right to self-defense against private violence. His strongest historical evidence suggests that, by Reconstruction, Americans came to believe the Second Amendment protected an individual right to bear arms. On this account, the Reconstruction Congress intended for newly-freed blacks to rely on that right to protect themselves from white violence, particularly from the Ku Klux Klan.[17] Justice Scalia adopts an individual-right model that focuses on the right to possess guns primarily for self-defense (handguns) and perhaps for hunting (some rifles).

---

[16] *See* Sanford Levinson, *The Embarrassing Second Amendment*, 99 YALE L.J. 637 (1989). Or, as John Locke put it, "Whosoever uses force without right, as everyone does in society who does it without law, puts himself into a state of war with those against whom he uses it; and in that state all former ties are canceled, all other rights cease, and every one has a right to defend himself and resist the aggressor." JOHN LOCKE, THE SECOND TREATISE OF GOVERNMENT 130 [1690] (Thomas P. Peardon, ed., 1985).

[17] *See, e.g.*, AKHIL REED AMAR, THE BILL OF RIGHTS: CREATION AND RECONSTRUCTION 258–59 (1998) ("Reconstruction Republicans recast arms bearing as a core *civil* right, utterly divorced from the militia and other political rights and responsibilities. Arms were needed not as part of political and politicized militia service but to protect one's individual homestead. Everyone— even nonvoting, nonmilitia-serving women—had a right to a gun for self-protection.").

This approach reflects how Americans tend to practice and view gun ownership today: many accept private ownership of handguns or hunting rifles, and few Americans demand the right to arm themselves for insurrection. The self-defense model also avoids suggesting that Americans have a right to own bazookas in case they need to rise up against the federal government. But doesn't this "living constitution" analysis contradict Justice Scalia's avowed reliance on original meaning? Likewise, don't the dissenting justices—who frequently rely on evolutionary analyses in other individual rights cases but refused to acknowledge an evolving individual right to gun ownership in *Heller*—have a consistency problem of their own?

Is the fundamental problem with the dissent's analysis that it would render the Second Amendment largely a dead letter in today's world? Is it the Court's job to make sure that *all* constitutional provisions retain some contemporary relevance? What would that mean, for example, for the Third Amendment (banning quartering of soldiers in private homes)? More generally, what does *Heller* suggest about the desirability of an originalist or a more evolutionary approach to constitutional interpretation?

9.   Justice Scalia sometimes defended originalism on the ground that its critics have offered no principled alternative approaches to interpretation. As he points out, "You can't beat somebody with nobody."[18] Is he right? Does "living constitutionalism" offer a coherent methodological alternative? If you're against originalism as a method of constitutional interpretation, what are you *for*?[19]

See also: For a helpful (if somewhat dated) guide to the arguments for and against originalism, see Daniel A. Farber, *The Originalism Debate: A Guide for the Perplexed*, 49 OHIO ST. L.J. 1085 (1989); see also the entry on originalism at Lawrence Solum's ever-helpful "Legal Theory Lexicon," which is available at http://lsolum.typepad.com/legaltheory/2013/06/legal-theory-lexicon-originalism.html. One of the most coherent defenses of originalism is Richard S. Kay, *Adherence to the Original Intentions in Constitutional Adjudication: Three Objections and Responses*, 82 NW. U. L. REV. 226 (1988). For a liberal scholar's attempt to merge originalism and living constitutionalism, see Jack Balkin, *Abortion and Original Meaning*, 24 CONST. COMMENTARY 291 (2007).

INTRODUCTORY NOTE ON THE ROLE OF CONSTITUTIONAL DOCTRINE

1.   In addition to questions of constitutional obligation and interpretation, *Heller* also posed issues concerning the role of *doctrine* in constitutional law. Doctrine is distinct from the Constitution itself; it consists of settled judicial interpretations of the Constitution or judge-made principles that help implement the Constitution's provisions. When the Constitution does not specify particular tests and principles to implement its commands—which is most of the time—judges have considerable flexibility

---

[18]   Scalia, *Originalism, supra* note 6, at 855.

[19]   For a related argument that "we are all originalists now," see Randy Barnett, *An Originalism for Nonoriginalists*, 45 LOYOLA L. REV. 611 (1999).

in constructing those tests. For example, the Equal Protection Clause says that "No state shall . . . deny to any person within its jurisdiction the equal protection of the laws." The Clause says little about what would amount to a denial of equal protection; consequently, the courts have developed doctrinal tests to implement the Clause. The Supreme Court has thus said that governmental measures that discriminate on the basis of race "are constitutional only if they are narrowly tailored to further compelling governmental interests." [20] Note that this "strict scrutiny" test is not specified in the constitutional text; rather, it is a judicial judgment about what rules can best implement that text in particular cases.

The *Heller* majority does not say much about what its Second Amendment test will be—basically, Justice Scalia thinks the D.C. law is so draconian that it would fail *any* test. Was it appropriate to strike the law down without articulating a doctrinal standard for future cases? Are there advantages to proceeding gradually and waiting to see more Second Amendment litigation before developing a definitive test?

2.   A central question in the design of doctrine—perhaps *the* central question—concerns the degree of deference courts should accord to the decisions of other actors. Judicial *review* generally requires a court to examine an enactment or action by some other government actor, such as a law enacted by a legislature, a particular act by an executive official, or even a decision taken by a lower court. In each instance, the court must ask not whether it would have done the same thing, but whether the other actor's action was permissible under the relevant constitutional standard. In many instances, courts must *defer* to other actors' decisions even though they disagree with them, because the decision falls within a range of reasonable outcomes.

Dissenting in *Heller*, Justice Breyer advocated a doctrinal approach with two components: (a) a highly flexible balance of individual and governmental interests, and (b) a great deal of deference to legislative judgments in assessing the relevant interests. What do you think of this test? Typically this sort of deferential analysis is reserved for rights *not* considered fundamental, such as the right to be free of certain forms of economic regulation. The general thought has been that because fundamental rights are such important constraints on government action, courts should be less trusting of government actors when they seek to restrict those rights. Is Justice Breyer suggesting that *all* constitutional rights, like the right to criticize the government or the right to have an abortion, should trigger his more deferential standard of review? If not, is there a principled reason why some constitutional rights deserve this treatment and others do not?

3.   A related question concerns the deference that the Court owes to its prior decisions. Both Justice Scalia's majority opinion and Justice Stevens's dissent had to interpret not only the Second Amendment's text but also the Court's prior decision in *United States v. Miller,* 307 U.S. 174 (1939). The Justices debated not only precisely what *Miller* held but also how much respect *Miller* deserved, given the somewhat unusual circumstances of the

---

[20]   *Grutter v. Bollinger*, 539 U.S. 306, 326 (2003).

prior litigation. Suppose one were convinced that (a) Justice Scalia is right about the best interpretation of the Second Amendment's text, but (b) Justice Stevens is right that *Miller* held to the contrary. Which should prevail? The Constitution itself, or what the Justices said about it 150 years later in *Miller*? If you choose the former, is there any point in worrying about *Miller* at all? We will return to these questions about precedent, or *stare decisis*, when we consider the Court's abortion decision in *Planned Parenthood v. Casey*, 505 U.S. 833 (1992).

4.   Whatever your approach to constitutional interpretation, isn't it fair to say that the text of the Second Amendment and the relevant historical record are both significantly ambiguous? Isn't it also true that the questions of doctrinal design raised by *Heller* are difficult? Many commentators criticized both the majority and dissenting opinions in *Heller* for overstating the cases for their respective conclusions. If *Heller* is simply a hard case, should the opinions have acknowledged that and spoken less definitively? What are the costs—particularly in a landmark and controversial decision— of the justices admitting that some cases are just difficult and the right answer is sometimes uncertain? Might doing so undermine the legitimacy of a decision? Would public discourse be more open to reasonable disagreement if the justices less frequently suggested that law is clear and easy?

See also: For a sampling of contemporary Second Amendment scholarship, see Joseph Blocher & Darrell A. H. Miller, *What is Gun Control? Direct Burdens, Incidental Burdens, and the Boundaries of the Second Amendment*, 86 U. CHI. L. REV. 295 (2016); Sanford Levinson, *The Embarrassing Second Amendment*, 99 YALE L. J. 637 (1989). On the role of judge-made doctrine in constitutional law, see RICHARD H. FALLON, JR., IMPLEMENTING THE CONSTITUTION (2001); Akhil Reed Amar, *The Supreme Court, 1999 Term— Foreword: The Document and the Doctrine,* 114 HARV. L. REV. 26 (2000).

CHAPTER TWO

JUDICIAL REVIEW

"Judicial review" refers to the power of the judiciary to set aside actions—including statutes and executive actions—by the political branches of the national government and the states. Although courts may invalidate such actions on a variety of grounds, in this course "judicial review" generally means review for compliance with *constitutional* requirements. In other contexts, such as courses in administrative law, judicial review may also connote review of executive actions for consistency with statutory commands.

American-style judicial review is unusual. The English, until very recently, had no analogous practice; Parliament was supreme, so generally speaking there was no "higher law" to which a court might appeal in order to void an act of Parliament.[1] In the late twentieth century, a number of Western democracies adopted forms of judicial review, but they tended to centralize that power in a single "constitutional court" to which other courts would refer constitutional issues for decision. In the United States, by contrast, *any* court enjoys—in principle, and generally in practice—the authority to rule that a law or an executive action violates the Constitution. This institutional arrangement has allowed the judiciary to play a powerful role in the evolution of American constitutionalism.

Roughly half of this course concerns the development of the institution of judicial review. This chapter begins with the case for judicial review, as made first by Alexander Hamilton in the *Federalist Papers* and then by Chief Justice John Marshall in the landmark case of *Marbury v. Madison*. We then consider two important limits on judicial review: the requirement that courts may decide constitutional questions only in the context of a "case or controversy," and the doctrine that some controversies present nonjusticiable "political questions" resolvable only by the elected branches of government.

SECTION 2.1 THE CASE FOR JUDICIAL REVIEW

The Constitution makes no explicit provision for judicial review, although several of its provisions are arguably suggestive of that power. The historical record indicates that members of the Constitutional Convention assumed that the courts would have some power of judicial review, and that both supporters and critics of the Convention's product

---

[1] In recent years, English courts enjoyed a limited power to consider whether English law conflicts with the law of the European Union or the European Convention on Human Rights. *See* ANTHONY KING, THE BRITISH CONSTITUTION 96–100 (2007); *see also id.* at 115–149 (describing other, more domestic trends toward the expansion of judicial review in Britain).

likewise assumed that this would be so. Nonetheless, there was relatively little discussion of the issue. For the most fully-developed early defense of the judicial power in this regard, we turn to Alexander Hamilton's argument in Federalist No. 78.

The *Federalist Papers* were a series of newspaper essays—"op eds," in modern parlance—published anonymously by John Jay, James Madison, and Alexander Hamilton under the name "Publius." These essays appeared after the Philadelphia Convention had completed its draft Constitution and submitted that document to ratification conventions for ratification. Publius's work was intended to sway popular opinion in the State of New York in favor of ratification.[2] It is thus important to remember that, although the *Federalist Papers* are one of the most influential and original works in American political theory, they are also an exercise in spin control designed to "sell" the Constitution to a dubious public. The 78th essay, written by Hamilton, offers the Federalists' classic argument in favor of judicial review of the constitutionality of actions taken by the other departments of the government.

The Federalist, No. 78 (Alexander Hamilton)
May 28, 1788

We proceed now to an examination of the judiciary department of the proposed government. . . .

According to the plan of the convention, all judges who may be appointed by the United States are to hold their offices during good behavior. . . . The standard of good behavior for the continuance in office of the judicial magistracy . . . is the best expedient which can be devised in any government, to secure a steady, upright, and impartial administration of the laws.

Whoever attentively considers the different departments of power must perceive, that, in a government in which they are separated from each other, the judiciary, from the nature of its functions, will always be the least dangerous to the political rights of the Constitution; because it will be least in a capacity to annoy or injure them. The Executive not only dispenses the honors, but holds the sword of the community. The legislature not only commands the purse, but prescribes the rules by which the duties and rights of every citizen are to be regulated. The judiciary, on the contrary, has no influence over either the sword or the purse; no direction either of the strength or of the wealth of the society; and can take no active resolution whatever. It may truly be said to have

---

[2] For a sampling of the broader debate, with contributions both for and against ratification, see BERNARD BAILYN, ED., THE DEBATE ON THE CONSTITUTION (2 vols., Library of America 1993). The Antifederalist position is usefully explored in SAUL CORNELL, THE OTHER FOUNDERS: ANTI-FEDERALISM AND THE DISSENTING TRADITION IN AMERICA, 1788–1828 (1999).

neither force nor will, but merely judgment; and must ultimately depend upon the aid of the executive arm even for the efficacy of its judgments.

This simple view of the matter suggests several important consequences. It proves incontestably, that the judiciary is beyond comparison the weakest of the three departments of power; that it can never attack with success either of the other two; and that all possible care is requisite to enable it to defend itself against their attacks. It equally proves, that though individual oppression may now and then proceed from the courts of justice, the general liberty of the people can never be endangered from that quarter; I mean so long as the judiciary remains truly distinct from both the legislature and the Executive. For I agree [with Montesquieu], that "there is no liberty, if the power of judging be not separated from the legislative and executive powers." And it proves, in the last place, that as liberty can have nothing to fear from the judiciary alone, but would have every thing to fear from its union with either of the other departments; that as all the effects of such a union must ensue from a dependence of the former on the latter, notwithstanding a nominal and apparent separation; that as, from the natural feebleness of the judiciary, it is in continual jeopardy of being overpowered, awed, or influenced by its co-ordinate branches; and that as nothing can contribute so much to its firmness and independence as permanency in office, this quality may therefore be justly regarded as an indispensable ingredient in its constitution, and, in a great measure, as the citadel of the public justice and the public security.

The complete independence of the courts of justice is peculiarly essential in a limited Constitution. By a limited Constitution, I understand one which contains certain specified exceptions to the legislative authority; such, for instance, as that it shall pass no bills of attainder, no ex-post-facto laws, and the like. Limitations of this kind can be preserved in practice no other way than through the medium of courts of justice, whose duty it must be to declare all acts contrary to the manifest tenor of the Constitution void. Without this, all the reservations of particular rights or privileges would amount to nothing.

Some perplexity respecting the rights of the courts to pronounce legislative acts void, because contrary to the Constitution, has arisen from an imagination that the doctrine would imply a superiority of the judiciary to the legislative power. It is urged that the authority which can declare the acts of another void, must necessarily be superior to the one whose acts may be declared void. As this doctrine is of great importance in all the American constitutions, a brief discussion of the ground on which it rests cannot be unacceptable.

There is no position which depends on clearer principles, than that every act of a delegated authority, contrary to the tenor of the commission under which it is exercised, is void. No legislative act, therefore, contrary to the Constitution, can be valid. To deny this, would be to affirm, that the deputy is greater than his principal; that the servant is above his master; that the representatives of the people are superior to the people themselves; that men acting by virtue of powers, may do not only what their powers do not authorize, but what they forbid.

If it be said that the legislative body are themselves the constitutional judges of their own powers, and that the construction they put upon them is conclusive upon the other departments, it may be answered, that this cannot be the natural presumption, where it is not to be collected from any particular provisions in the Constitution. It is not otherwise to be supposed, that the Constitution could intend to enable the representatives of the people to substitute their will to that of their constituents. It is far more rational to suppose, that the courts were designed to be an intermediate body between the people and the legislature, in order, among other things, to keep the latter within the limits assigned to their authority. The interpretation of the laws is the proper and peculiar province of the courts. A constitution is, in fact, and must be regarded by the judges, as a fundamental law. It therefore belongs to them to ascertain its meaning, as well as the meaning of any particular act proceeding from the legislative body. If there should happen to be an irreconcilable variance between the two, that which has the superior obligation and validity ought, of course, to be preferred; or, in other words, the Constitution ought to be preferred to the statute, the intention of the people to the intention of their agents.

Nor does this conclusion by any means suppose a superiority of the judicial to the legislative power. It only supposes that the power of the people is superior to both; and that where the will of the legislature, declared in its statutes, stands in opposition to that of the people, declared in the Constitution, the judges ought to be governed by the latter rather than the former. They ought to regulate their decisions by the fundamental laws, rather than by those which are not fundamental.

This exercise of judicial discretion, in determining between two contradictory laws, is exemplified in a familiar instance. It not uncommonly happens, that there are two statutes existing at one time, clashing in whole or in part with each other, and neither of them containing any repealing clause or expression. In such a case, it is the province of the courts to liquidate and fix their meaning and operation. So far as they can, by any fair construction, be reconciled to each other, reason and law conspire to dictate that this should be done; where this is impracticable, it becomes a matter of necessity to give effect to one, in exclusion of the other. The rule which has obtained in the courts for determining their relative validity is, that the last in order of time shall be preferred to the first. But this is a mere rule of construction, not derived from any positive law, but from the nature and reason of the thing. It is a rule not enjoined upon the courts by legislative provision, but adopted by themselves, as consonant to truth and propriety, for the direction of their conduct as interpreters of the law. They thought it reasonable, that between the interfering acts of an equal authority, that which was the last indication of its will should have the preference.

But in regard to the interfering acts of a superior and subordinate authority, of an original and derivative power, the nature and reason of the thing indicate the converse of that rule as proper to be followed. They teach us that the prior act of a superior ought to be preferred to the subsequent act of an inferior and subordinate authority; and that accordingly, whenever a particular statute contravenes the Constitution, it will be the duty of the judicial tribunals to adhere to the latter and disregard the former.

It can be of no weight to say that the courts, on the pretense of a repugnancy, may substitute their own pleasure to the constitutional intentions of the legislature. This might as well happen in the case of two contradictory statutes; or it might as well happen in every adjudication upon any single statute. The courts must declare the sense of the law; and if they should be disposed to exercise WILL instead of JUDGMENT, the consequence would equally be the substitution of their pleasure to that of the legislative body. The observation, if it prove any thing, would prove that there ought to be no judges distinct from that body.

If, then, the courts of justice are to be considered as the bulwarks of a limited Constitution against legislative encroachments, this consideration will afford a strong argument for the permanent tenure of judicial offices, since nothing will contribute so much as this to that independent spirit in the judges which must be essential to the faithful performance of so arduous a duty.

This independence of the judges is equally requisite to guard the Constitution and the rights of individuals from the effects of those ill humors, which the arts of designing men, or the influence of particular conjunctures, sometimes disseminate among the people themselves, and which, though they speedily give place to better information, and more deliberate reflection, have a tendency, in the meantime, to occasion dangerous innovations in the government, and serious oppressions of the minor party in the community. Though I trust the friends of the proposed Constitution will never concur with its enemies, in questioning that fundamental principle of republican government, which admits the right of the people to alter or abolish the established Constitution, whenever they find it inconsistent with their happiness, yet it is not to be inferred from this principle, that the representatives of the people, whenever a momentary inclination happens to lay hold of a majority of their constituents, incompatible with the provisions in the existing Constitution, would, on that account, be justifiable in a violation of those provisions; or that the courts would be under a greater obligation to connive at infractions in this shape, than when they had proceeded wholly from the cabals of the representative body. Until the people have, by some solemn and authoritative act, annulled or changed the established form, it is binding upon themselves collectively, as well as individually; and no presumption, or even knowledge, of their sentiments, can warrant their representatives in a departure from it, prior to such an act. But it is easy to see, that it would require an uncommon portion of fortitude in the judges to do their duty as faithful guardians of the Constitution, where legislative invasions of it had been instigated by the major voice of the community.

But it is not with a view to infractions of the Constitution only, that the independence of the judges may be an essential safeguard against the effects of occasional ill humors in the society. These sometimes extend no farther than to the injury of the private rights of particular classes of citizens, by unjust and partial laws. Here also the firmness of the judicial magistracy is of vast importance in mitigating the severity and confining the operation of such laws. It not only serves to moderate the immediate mischiefs of those which may have been passed, but it operates as a check upon the legislative body in passing them; who, perceiving that obstacles to the success of iniquitous intention are to be expected from the scruples of the courts, are in a manner compelled, by the very motives of the injustice they meditate, to qualify their attempts. This is a circumstance calculated to have more influence upon the character of our governments, than but few may be aware of. The benefits of the integrity and moderation of the judiciary have already been felt in more States than one; and though they may have displeased those whose sinister expectations they may have disappointed, they must have commanded the esteem and applause of all the virtuous and disinterested. Considerate men, of every description, ought to prize whatever will tend to beget or fortify that temper in the courts: as no man can be sure that he may not be to-morrow the victim of a spirit of injustice, by which he may be a gainer to-day. And every man must now feel, that the inevitable tendency of such a spirit is to sap the foundations of public and private confidence, and to introduce in its stead universal distrust and distress.

That inflexible and uniform adherence to the rights of the Constitution, and of individuals, which we perceive to be indispensable in the courts of justice, can certainly not be expected from judges who hold their offices by a temporary commission. Periodical appointments, however regulated, or by whomsoever made, would, in some way or other, be fatal to their necessary independence. If the power of making them was committed either to the Executive or legislature, there would be danger of an improper complaisance to the branch which possessed it; if to both, there would be an unwillingness to hazard the displeasure of either; if to the people, or to persons chosen by them for the special purpose, there would be too great a disposition to consult popularity, to justify a reliance that nothing would be consulted but the Constitution and the laws.

There is yet a further and a weightier reason for the permanency of the judicial offices, which is deducible from the nature of the qualifications they require. It has been frequently remarked, with great propriety, that a voluminous code of laws is one of the inconveniences necessarily connected with the advantages of a free government. To avoid an arbitrary discretion in the courts, it is indispensable that they should be bound down by strict rules and precedents, which serve to define and point out their duty in every particular case that comes before them; and it will readily be conceived from the variety of controversies which grow out of the folly and wickedness of mankind, that the records of those precedents must unavoidably swell to a very considerable bulk, and must demand long and laborious study to acquire a competent knowledge of them. Hence it is, that there can be but few men in the society who will have sufficient skill in the laws to qualify them for the stations of judges. And making the proper deductions for the ordinary depravity of human nature, the number must be still smaller of those who unite the requisite integrity with the requisite knowledge. These considerations apprise us, that the government can have no great option between fit character; and that a temporary duration in office, which would naturally discourage such characters from quitting a lucrative line of practice to accept a seat on the bench, would have a tendency to throw the administration of justice into hands less able, and less well qualified, to conduct it with utility and dignity. In the present circumstances of this country, and in those in which it is likely to be for a long time to come, the disadvantages on this score would be greater than they may at first sight appear; but it must be confessed, that they are far inferior to those which present themselves under the other aspects of the subject.

Upon the whole, there can be no room to doubt that the convention acted wisely in copying from the models of those constitutions which have established good behavior as the tenure of their judicial offices, in point of duration; and that so far from being blamable on this account, their plan would have been inexcusably defective, if it had wanted this important feature of good government. The experience of Great Britain affords an illustrious comment on the excellence of the institution.

PUBLIUS.

NOTE ON HAMILTON'S ARGUMENT FOR JUDICIAL REVIEW

1.   As this essay is our first encounter with the *Federalist Papers*, it is worth pausing to consider what weight these essays should be accorded in constitutional interpretation. We know, for example, that the Philadelphia Convention had accorded Madison, Hamilton, and Jay no special dispensation to interpret the Convention's handiwork, that the *Federalist Papers* were seen by only a small fraction of the people who voted for ratification, and that the authors of the *Federalist Papers* later came to disagree amongst themselves on a number of fundamental points. Why do

courts nevertheless frequently treat these essays as authoritative expositions of constitutional meaning?[3]

2.   Why does Hamilton think that the judiciary is the "least dangerous" branch of the proposed federal government? Is he right? Does that assessment comport with the judiciary's role in contemporary government? Consider, in this regard, cases like *Bush v. Gore*,[4] *Roe v. Wade*,[5] or *Obergefell v. Hodges*.[6]

3.   Do you agree with Hamilton that judicial review encourages the political branches to adhere to the Constitution? Hamilton argues that the threat of having a law or executive action struck down in court will check the political branches. Has experience borne out this theory? Does judicial review actually enable unconstitutional actions by making the political branches feel less directly responsible for protecting the Constitution?

4.   It is important to Hamilton that judges be insulated from political pressure and popular opinion. Is this wise? Many state constitutions have taken a different tack, providing for popular election of judges. Would that approach be preferable? If you agree that judges should be insulated from the political process, how complete should that insulation be? Even if you believe that judges should be insulated from democratic forces, does it follow that they should hold their jobs *for life*?[7]

Professor Sanford Levinson, for example, has argued that life tenure may leave us with justices who are practically incapacitated by advanced age yet unwilling to leave the Court; that justices who serve too long are likely to be out of touch with values in the broader society; and that life tenure allows justices to time their own resignations in order to control the partisan affiliation of their successors. He points out, moreover, that virtually no other country in the world has thought it necessary to grant life tenure in order to assure the independence of its constitutional court.[8] On the other hand, it is not clear that any other country has a court as powerful and independent as ours. And other scholars have argued that our Supreme Court actually hews pretty close to public opinion over the medium to long term.[9]

---

[3]   For a thoughtful set of essays on the relevance of the *Federalist* to contemporary America, see SANFORD LEVINSON, AN ARGUMENT OPEN TO ALL: READING "THE FEDERALIST" IN THE 21ST CENTURY (2015).

[4]   531 U.S. 98 (2000) (effectively resolving the disputed presidential election of 2000).

[5]   410 U.S. 113 (1973) (proclaiming an unenumerated right to abortion).

[6]   135 S. Ct. 2584 (2015) (recognizing a fundamental right to marry for same-sex couples).

[7]   It may be relevant to this question that the average tenure of Supreme Court justices seems to have increased significantly over time, although there is considerable debate about exactly how much. *Compare, e.g.*, Steven G. Calabresi & James Lindgren, *Term Limits for the Supreme Court: Life Tenure Reconsidered*, 29 HARV. J. L. & PUB. POL'Y 769 (2006) (finding that average tenure was 15 years pre-1970, but jumps to 26 years since), *with* David R. Stras & Ryan W. Scott, *An Empirical Analysis of Life Tenure: A Response to Professors Calabresi & Lindgren*, 30 HARV. J. L. & PUB. POL'Y 791 (2007) (finding the increase to be considerably less dramatic).

[8]   SANFORD LEVINSON, OUR UNDEMOCRATIC CONSTITUTION: WHERE THE CONSTITUTION GOES WRONG (AND HOW WE THE PEOPLE CAN CORRECT IT) 129–39 (2006).

[9]   *See, e.g.*, BARRY FRIEDMAN, THE WILL OF THE PEOPLE: HOW PUBLIC OPINION HAS INFLUENCED THE SUPREME COURT AND SHAPED THE MEANING OF THE CONSTITUTION (2009).

What do you think: Should life tenure be replaced with a fixed judicial term? To what extent do attacks on life tenure simply reflect the critics' dissatisfaction with how the Court has ruled in prominent cases?

5.   One of Hamilton's arguments is that the law is complex and specialized, and only an elite few have the learning and integrity to be judges. This reflects the belief of many in the founding generation that a "natural aristocracy"—defined by education, experience, and talent rather than by birth—should take the lead in government. Hamilton himself was an example, having begun as an illegitimate orphan in the West Indies and risen, through sheer talent, hard work, and a little luck to become George Washington's closest advisor in the new Republic.[10] To what extent is Hamilton's elitism attractive? Do you see any problems with this view? Is some of Hamilton's conception of the unique training and expertise of lawyers—and the deference that ought to engender—inherent in current conceptions of the legal profession and legal education?

INTRODUCTORY NOTE ON *MARBURY V. MADISON*

As Federalist 78 indicates, the idea that the Supreme Court would have the authority to invalidate actions by other governmental actors that contravened limits the Constitution established was hardly unknown to the Framers and Ratifiers in 1789. All the same, there is no explicit textual mention of judicial review in the Constitution itself. Although the early Supreme Court decided a handful of cases presupposing the existence of the power,[11] the Court had little occasion to discuss the foundations of its power prior to its 1803 decision in *Marbury v. Madison*. Chief Justice John Marshall's argument for the existence of judicial review in *Marbury* has been frequently criticized, but the power itself has never been seriously questioned since. All of the cases that follow in these materials involve the exercise of this power recognized in *Marbury*. In that sense, *Marbury* is the case that makes the rest of the course possible.

The historical circumstances of *Marbury* are critical to an understanding of the case. *Marbury* arises out of the first partisan transition of power in U.S. history—from the Federalist administration of John Adams to the Republican administration of Thomas Jefferson. The Constitution itself makes no provision for political parties, and prior to the 1790s most politically minded men decried such political groupings as dangerous "factions." But although George Washington managed to attain the presidency as a nonpartisan, consensus candidate, political parties soon began to form around Jefferson, Washington's Secretary of State, and Alexander Hamilton, his Secretary of the Treasury. Although this split arose from a variety of issues, key disagreements concerned Hamilton's fiscal policy—especially the creation of a national bank and federal assumption of

---

[10] The hit musical *Hamilton* tells this story. For a compelling introduction, see this: https://www.youtube.com/watch?v=LBSuwa8mf9o.

[11] *See, e.g., Hylton v. United States*, 3 U.S. (3 Dall.) 171 (1796) (considering, but rejecting, a constitutional challenge to a federal tax on carriages).

the States' Revolutionary War debts—as well as the appropriate foreign policy concerning the war between Britain and revolutionary France.

The Federalist-Republican divide in the 1790s was both tied to and distinct from earlier debates between Federalists and Antifederalists over the Constitution itself. In that earlier debate, the Federalist proponents of the Constitution had been the advocates of a more centralized government that could defend the young Nation's interests in foreign affairs and develop its nascent economy at home. Antifederalists, on the other hand, had attacked the proposed Constitution from many perspectives but had generally been concerned about excessive centralization of power. In these earlier debates, James Madison, Alexander Hamilton, and even Thomas Jefferson had been united in support of the proposed Constitution (although Jefferson was largely absent in his role as ambassador to the French court).

Jefferson's Republicans in the 1790s were, in many ways, the intellectual heirs to the Antifederalists: they were wary of excessively centralized government, and they favored an agrarian republic of yeoman farmers rather than the industrial and financial development promoted by Hamilton's Department of the Treasury. But the Jeffersonians did not challenge the constitutional settlement of 1789; they simply interpreted it in a less centralized way and tended to opposed further consolidation of national power (certainly in theory, less consistently in practice). By this time, Madison—probably the most important of the Founding Generation's political theorists—had joined Jefferson in opposing his former *Federalist Papers* co-author, Hamilton.

The 1800 election was the first of many watershed elections in American politics. The atmosphere was charged: American political parties were in their infancy, and the idea of a "loyal opposition" was not yet firmly entrenched in public consciousness. As a result, "[e]ach party viewed the other not as a legitimate democratic alternative, but as a deep-dyed danger to the Constitution." [12] The unpopular Federalists lost control of the presidency and both houses of Congress. Jefferson defeated Adams only by a narrow margin, so narrow that it took over a month to count ballots and declare the Republicans the winner. But under the voting rules of the time, Jefferson and his running mate, Aaron Burr, were tied for the presidency. Federalists dominated the lame duck House of Representatives, which was responsible under Article II of the Constitution for settling disputed presidential elections. Some in the House sought to build support for a deal which would throw support to Burr in exchange for his support for Federalist policies, and the House deadlocked for three months. Though Jefferson was ultimately declared the president-elect, it was "as close as the nation would ever come to a coup, achieved in strict conformity to the forms of the Constitution."[13]

Fearful that the Republicans would undo all the nationalist gains of the previous twelve years, the defeated Federalists sought to retain a foothold in

---

[12] Michael W. McConnell, *The Story of* Marbury v. Madison*: Making Defeat Look Like Victory*, in MICHAEL C. DORF, ED., CONSTITUTIONAL LAW STORIES 13, 13 (2d ed. 2009).

[13] *Id.* at 14.

the judicial branch. In a new Judiciary Act passed in January of 1801, just before Jefferson took office, the Federalists created a large number of new federal judgeships, appointed reliable Federalists to those positions, and dramatically expanded the scope of federal jurisdiction. These "Midnight Judges," some of whom were appointed in the wee hours before Jefferson's inauguration, included Adams's Secretary of State, John Marshall, as Chief Justice and, fatefully, William Marbury as a Justice of the Peace for the District of Columbia. In the confusion of those waning hours of Federalist power, however, some of these appointments were not delivered to the appointees—including Marbury.

Unsurprisingly, the incoming Republicans did not see these last-minute moves as entirely legitimate. Jefferson complained that the Federalist regime "had retired into the judiciary, in a strong body where it lives on the treasury, & therefore cannot be starved out. While in possession of that ground it can check the popular current which runs against them, & seize the favorable occasion to promote reaction."[14] Thus the Republicans, upon finally taking office, moved aggressively against the Federalist judiciary. They immediately repealed the previous Congress's legislation expanding federal jurisdiction, abolished a number of the new federal judgeships, and took advantage of any opportunities—such as William Marbury's undelivered commission—to refuse to honor the new appointments. This repeal directly threatened the authority of the Supreme Court and the federal judiciary; in particular, Congress's elimination of already filled federal judgeships undermined the constitutional grant of life tenure. But if the Court held the repeal unconstitutional—an issue that was before the Court during the same Term as *Marbury*—the Court risked having the Republican political branches ignore it, revealing the Court as ineffectual and dependent on the other branches. Even more ominously, the Republicans began a program of impeaching Federalist judges perceived to be vulnerable. They even enacted legislation abolishing the 1801 term of the Supreme Court, to prevent that Court from hearing any immediate challenges to the new legislation.

In light of all this, it would have been understandable for the new Chief Justice to feel a bit under siege as the Court sat to hear *Marbury v. Madison.*[15] The Jefferson administration indicated its disdain for the proceeding by not appearing to contest Marbury's claim. *Marbury* was also awkward for Marshall because, as President Adams's secretary of state prior to Jefferson taking office, Marshall had been responsible for delivering these commissions. Marshall apparently trusted his brother, James, to deliver some of the commissions, including Marbury's. James's failure in this regard set the stage for the Court's first truly great case.

---

[14] Letter from Thomas Jefferson to James Monroe, March 3, 1801, quoted in LUCAS A. POWE, JR., THE SUPREME COURT AND THE AMERICAN ELITE, 1789–2008 at 43 (2009).

[15] For additional discussion of the political background to *Marbury*, see ROBERT G. MCCLOSKEY, THE AMERICAN SUPREME COURT ch. 2 (Sanford Levinson ed., 2005); *see also* James O'Fallon, *Marbury*, 44 STAN. L. REV. 219 (1992).

Marbury v. Madison

5 U.S. (1 Cranch) 137 (1803)

At the last term, viz. December term, 1801, William Marbury, Dennis Ramsay, Robert Townsend Hooe, and William Harper, by their counsel, Charles Lee, esq. late attorney general of the United States, severally moved the court for a rule to James Madison, secretary of state of the United States, to show cause why a mandamus should not issue commanding him to cause to be delivered to them respectively their several commissions as justices of the peace in the district of Columbia. This motion was supported by affidavits of the following facts; that notice of this motion had been given to Mr. Madison; that Mr. Adams, the late president of the United States, nominated the applicants to the senate for their advice and consent to be appointed justices of the peace of the district of Columbia; that the senate advised and consented to the appointments; that commissions in the due form were signed by the said president appointing them justices, & c. and that the seal of the United States was in due form affixed to the said commissions by the secretary of state; that the applicants have requested Mr. Madison to deliver them their said commissions, who has not complied with that request; and that their said commissions are withheld from them; that the applicants have made application to Mr. Madison as secretary of state of the United States at his office, for information whether the commissions were signed and sealed as aforesaid; that explicit and satisfactory information has not been given to that enquiry, either by the secretary of state or by any officer of the department of state; that application has been made to the secretary of the Senate for a certificate of the nomination of the applicants, and of the advice and consent of the senate, who has declined giving such a certificate; whereupon a rule was laid to show cause on the 4th day of this term. This rule having been duly served,

Afterwards, on the 24th of February the following opinion of the court was delivered by the chief justice. . . .

In the order in which the court has viewed this subject, the following questions have been considered and decided.

1st. Has the applicant a right to the commission he demands?

2dly. If he has a right, and that right has been violated, do the laws of his country afford him a remedy?

3dly. If they do afford him a remedy, is it a mandamus issuing from this court?

The first object of enquiry is,

1st. Has the applicant a right to the commission he demands? . . .

It is therefore decidedly the opinion of the court, that when a commission has been signed by the President, the appointment is made; and that the commission is complete, when the seal of the United States has been affixed to it by the secretary of state. . . .

Mr. Marbury, then, since his commission was signed by the President, and sealed by the secretary of state, was appointed; and as the law creating the office, gave the officer a right to hold for five years, independent of the executive, the appointment was not revocable; but vested in the officer legal rights, which are protected by the laws of his country.

To withhold his commission, therefore, is an act deemed by the court not warranted by law, but violative of a vested legal right.

This brings us to the second enquiry; which is,

2dly. If he has a right, and that right has been violated, do the laws of his country afford him a remedy?

The very essence of civil liberty certainly consists in the right of every individual to claim the protection of the laws, whenever he receives an injury. . . . Blackstone states . . . "it is a general and indisputable rule, that where there is a legal right, there is also a legal remedy by suit or action at law, whenever that right is invaded." . . .

The government of the United States has been emphatically termed a government of laws, and not of men. It will certainly cease to deserve this high appellation, if the laws furnish no remedy for the violation of a vested legal right.

If this obloquy is to be cast on the jurisprudence of our country, it must arise from the peculiar character of the case. It behooves us then to enquire whether there be in its composition any ingredient which shall exempt it from legal investigation, or exclude the injured party from legal redress. . . .

Is it in the nature of the transaction? Is the act of delivering or withholding a commission to be considered as a mere political act, belonging to the executive department alone, for the performance of which, entire confidence is placed by our constitution in the supreme executive; and for any misconduct respecting which, the injured individual has no remedy.

That there may be such cases is not to be questioned; but that every act of duty, to be performed in any of the great departments of government, constitutes such a case is not to be admitted. . . . Is it to be contended that where the law in precise terms, directs the performance of an act, in which an individual is interested, the law is incapable of securing obedience to its mandate?

Is it on account of the character of the person against whom the complaint is made? Is it to be contended that the heads of departments are not amenable to the laws of their country?

Whatever the practice on particular occasions may be, the theory of this principle will certainly never be maintained. No act of the legislature confers so extraordinary a privilege, nor can it derive countenance from the doctrines of the common law. . . .

It follows then that the question, whether the legality of an act of the head of a department be examinable in a court of justice or not, must always depend on the nature of that act. . . .

By the constitution of the United States, the President is invested with certain important political powers, in the exercise of which he is to use his own discretion, and is accountable only to his country in his political character, and to his own conscience. To aid him in the performance of these duties, he is authorized to appoint certain officers, who act by his authority and in conformity with his orders.

In such cases, their acts are his acts; and whatever opinion may be entertained of the manner in which executive discretion may be used, still there exists, and can exist, no power to control that discretion. The subjects are political. They respect the nation, not individual rights, and being entrusted to the executive, the decision of the executive is conclusive. The application of this remark will be perceived by adverting to the act of congress for establishing the department of foreign affairs. This office, as his duties were prescribed by that act, is to conform precisely to the will of the President. He is the mere organ by whom that will is communicated. The acts of such an officer, as an officer, can never be examinable by the courts.

But when the legislature proceeds to impose on that officer other duties; when he is directed peremptorily to perform certain acts; when the rights of individuals are dependent on the performance of those acts; he is so far the officer of the law; is amenable to the laws for his conduct; and cannot at his discretion sport away the vested rights of others.

The conclusion from this reasoning is, that where the heads of departments are the political or confidential agents of the executive, merely to execute the will of the President, or rather to act in cases in which the executive possesses a constitutional or legal discretion, nothing can be more perfectly clear than that their acts are only politically examinable. But where a specific duty is assigned by law, and individual rights depend upon the performance of that duty, it seems equally clear that the individual who considers himself injured, has a right to resort to the laws of his country for a remedy.

If this be the rule, let us enquire how it applies to the case under the consideration of the court.

The power of nominating to the senate, and the power of appointing the person nominated, are political powers, to be exercised by the President according to his own discretion. When he has made an appointment, he has exercised his whole power, and his discretion has been completely applied to the case. If, by law, the officer be removable at the will of the President, then a new appointment may be immediately made, and the rights of the officer are terminated. But as a fact which has existed cannot be made never to have existed, the appointment cannot be annihilated; and consequently if the officer is by law not removable at the will of the President; the rights he has acquired are protected by the law, and are not resumeable by the President. They cannot be extinguished by executive authority, and he has the privilege of asserting them in like manner as if they had been derived from any other source.

The question whether a right has vested or not, is, in its nature, judicial, and must be tried by the judicial authority. . . . So, if [Marbury] conceives that, by virtue of his appointment, he has a legal right, either to the commission which has been made out for him, or to a copy of that commission, it is equally a question examinable in a court, and the decision of the court upon it must depend on the opinion entertained of his appointment.

That question has been discussed, and the opinion is, that the latest point of time which can be taken as that at which the appointment was complete, and evidenced, was when, after the signature of the president, the seal of the United States was affixed to the commission.

It is then the opinion of the court,

1st. That by signing the commission of Mr. Marbury, the president of the United States appointed him a justice of peace, for the county of Washington in the district of Columbia; and that the seal of the United States, affixed thereto by the secretary of state, is conclusive testimony of the verity of the signature, and of the completion of the appointment; and that the appointment conferred on him a legal right to the office for the space of five years.

2dly. That, having this legal title to the office, he has a consequent right to the commission; a refusal to deliver which, is a plain violation of that right, for which the laws of his country afford him a remedy.

It remains to be enquired whether,

3dly. He is entitled to the remedy for which he applies. This depends on,

1st. The nature of the writ applied for, and,

2dly. The power of this court.

1st. The nature of the writ.

Blackstone . . . defines a mandamus to be, "a command issued in the King's name from the court of King's Bench, and directed to any person, corporation, or inferior court of judicature within the King's dominions, requiring them to do some particular thing therein specified, which appertains to their office and duty, and which the court of King's Bench has previously determined, or at least supposed, to be consonant to right and justice." . . . This writ, if awarded, would be directed to an officer of government, and its mandate to him would be, to use the words of Blackstone, "to do a particular thing therein specified, which appertains to his office and duty and which the court has previously determined, or at least supposes, to be consonant to right and justice." . . .

These circumstances certainly concur in this case. Still, to render the mandamus a proper remedy, the officer to whom it is directed, must be one to whom, on legal principles, such writ may be directed; and the person applying for it must be without any other specific and legal remedy.

1st. With respect to the officer to whom it would be directed. The intimate political relation, subsisting between the president of the United States and the heads of departments, necessarily renders any legal investigation of the acts of one of those high officers peculiarly irksome, as well as delicate; and excites some hesitation with respect to the propriety of entering into such investigation. Impressions are often received without much reflection or examination, and it is not wonderful that in such a case as this, the assertion, by an individual, of his legal claims in a court of justice; to which claims it is the duty of that court to attend; should at first view be considered by some, as an attempt to intrude into the cabinet, and to intermeddle with the prerogatives of the executive.

It is scarcely necessary for the court to disclaim all pretensions to such a jurisdiction. An extravagance, so absurd and excessive, could not have been entertained for a moment. The province of the court is, solely, to decide on the rights of individuals, not to enquire how the executive, or executive officers, perform duties in which they have a discretion. Questions, in their nature political, or which are, by the constitution and laws, submitted to the executive, can never be made in this court.

But, if this be not such a question; if so far from being an intrusion into the secrets of the cabinet, it respects a paper, which, according to law, is upon record . . . ; if it be no intermeddling with a subject, over which the executive can be considered as having exercised any control; what is there in the exalted station of the officer, which shall bar a citizen from asserting, in a court of justice, his legal rights, or shall forbid a court to listen to the claim; or to issue a mandamus, directing the performance of a duty, not depending on executive discretion, but on particular acts of congress and the general principles of law? . . .

It is not by the office of the person to whom the writ is directed, but the nature of the thing to be done that the propriety or impropriety of issuing a mandamus, is to be determined. Where the head of a department acts in a case, in which executive discretion is to be exercised; in which he is the mere organ of executive will; it is again repeated, that any application to a court to control, in any respect, his conduct, would be rejected without hesitation.

But where he is directed by law to do a certain act affecting the absolute rights of individuals, in the performance of which he is not placed under the particular direction of the President, and the performance of which, the President cannot lawfully forbid, and therefore is never presumed to have forbidden; as for example, to record a commission, or a patent for land, which has received all the legal solemnities; or to give a copy of such record; in such cases, it is not perceived on what ground the courts of the country are further excused from the duty of giving judgment, that right be done to an injured individual, than if the same services were to be performed by a person not the head of a department. . . .

This, then, is a plain case for a mandamus, either to deliver the commission, or a copy of it from the record; and it only remains to be enquired,

Whether it can issue from this court.

The act to establish the judicial courts of the United States authorizes the supreme court "to issue writs of mandamus, in cases warranted by the principles and usages of law, to any courts appointed, or persons holding office, under the authority of the United States."

The secretary of state, being a person holding an office under the authority of the United States, is precisely within the letter of the description; and if this court is not authorized to issue a writ of mandamus to such an officer, it must be because the law is unconstitutional, and therefore absolutely incapable of conferring the authority, and assigning the duties which its words purport to confer and assign.

The constitution vests the whole judicial power of the United States in one supreme court, and such inferior courts as congress shall, from time to time, ordain and establish. This power is expressly extended to all cases arising under the laws of the United States; and consequently, in some form, may be exercised over the present case; because the right claimed is given by a law of the United States.

In the distribution of this power it is declared that "the supreme court shall have original jurisdiction in all cases affecting ambassadors, other public ministers and consuls, and those in which a state shall be a party. In all other cases, the supreme court shall have appellate jurisdiction."

It has been insisted, at the bar, that as the original grant of jurisdiction, to the supreme and inferior courts, is general, and the clause, assigning original jurisdiction to the supreme court, contains no negative or restrictive words; the power remains to the legislature, to assign original jurisdiction to that court in other cases than those specified in the article which has been recited; provided those cases belong to the judicial power of the United States.

If it had been intended to leave it to the discretion of the legislature to apportion the judicial power between the supreme and inferior courts according to the will of that body, it would certainly have been useless to have proceeded further than to have defined the judicial powers, and the tribunals in which it should be vested. The subsequent part of the section is mere surplusage, is entirely without meaning, if such is to be the construction. If congress remains at liberty to give this court appellate jurisdiction, where the constitution has declared their jurisdiction shall be original; and original jurisdiction where the constitution has declared it shall be appellate; the distribution of jurisdiction, made in the constitution, is form without substance.

Affirmative words are often, in their operation, negative of other objects than those affirmed; and in this case, a negative or exclusive sense must be given to them or they have no operation at all.

It cannot be presumed that any clause in the constitution is intended to be without effect; and therefore such a construction is inadmissible, unless the words require it.

When an instrument organizing fundamentally a judicial system, divides it into one supreme, and so many inferior courts as the legislature may ordain and establish; then enumerates its powers, and proceeds so far to distribute them, as to define the jurisdiction of the supreme court by declaring the cases in which it shall take original jurisdiction, and that in others it shall take appellate jurisdiction; the plain import of the words seems to be, that in one class of cases its jurisdiction is original, and not appellate; in the other it is appellate, and not original. If any other construction would render the clause inoperative, that is an additional reason for rejecting such other construction, and for adhering to their obvious meaning.

To enable this court then to issue a mandamus, it must be shown to be an exercise of appellate jurisdiction, or to be necessary to enable them to exercise appellate jurisdiction. . . . It is the essential criterion of appellate jurisdiction, that it revises and corrects the proceedings in a cause already instituted, and does not create that cause. Although, therefore, a mandamus may be directed to courts, yet to issue such a writ to an officer for the delivery of a paper, is in effect the same as to sustain an original action for that paper, and therefore seems not to belong to appellate, but to original jurisdiction. Neither is it necessary in such a case as this, to enable the court to exercise its appellate jurisdiction.

The authority, therefore, given to the supreme court, by the act establishing the judicial courts of the United States, to issue writs of mandamus to public officers, appears not to be warranted by the constitution; and it becomes necessary to enquire whether a jurisdiction, so conferred, can be exercised.

The question, whether an act, repugnant to the constitution, can become the law of the land, is a question deeply interesting to the United States; but, happily, not of an intricacy proportioned to its interest. It seems only necessary to recognize certain principles, supposed to have been long and well established, to decide it.

That the people have an original right to establish, for their future government, such principles as, in their opinion, shall most conduce to their own happiness, is the basis, on which the whole American fabric has been erected. The exercise of this original right is a very great exertion; nor can it, nor ought it to be frequently repeated. The principles, therefore, so established, are deemed fundamental. And as the authority, from which they proceed, is supreme, and can seldom act, they are designed to be permanent.

This original and supreme will organizes the government, and assigns, to different departments, their respective powers. It may either stop here; or establish certain limits not to be transcended by those departments.

The government of the United States is of the latter description. The powers of the legislature are defined, and limited; and that those limits may not be mistaken, or forgotten, the constitution is written. To what purpose are powers limited, and to what purpose is that limitation committed to writing, if these limits may, at any time, be passed by those intended to be restrained? The distinction, between a government with limited and unlimited powers, is abolished, if those limits do not confine the persons on whom they are imposed, and if acts prohibited and acts allowed, are of equal obligation. It is a proposition too plain to be contested, that the constitution controls any legislative act repugnant to it; or, that the legislature may alter the constitution by an ordinary act.

Between these alternatives there is no middle ground. The constitution is either a superior, paramount law, unchangeable by ordinary means, or it is on a level with ordinary legislative acts, and like other acts, is alterable when the legislature shall please to alter it.

If the former part of the alternative be true, then a legislative act contrary to the constitution is not law: if the latter part be true, then written constitutions are absurd attempts, on the part of the people, to limit a power, in its own nature illimitable.

Certainly all those who have framed written constitutions contemplate them as forming the fundamental and paramount law of the nation, and consequently the theory of every such government must be, that an act of the legislature, repugnant to the constitution, is void.

This theory is essentially attached to a written constitution, and is consequently to be considered, by this court, as one of the fundamental principles of our society. It is not therefore to be lost sight of in the further consideration of this subject.

If an act of the legislature, repugnant to the constitution, is void, does it, notwithstanding its invalidity, bind the courts, and oblige them to give it effect? Or, in other words, though it be not law, does it constitute a rule as operative as if it was a law? This would be to overthrow in fact what was established in theory; and would seem, at first view, an absurdity too gross to be insisted on. It shall, however, receive a more attentive consideration.

It is emphatically the province and duty of the judicial department to say what the law is. Those who apply the rule to particular cases, must of necessity expound and interpret that rule. If two laws conflict with each other, the courts must decide on the operation of each.

So if a law be in opposition to the constitution; if both the law and the constitution apply to a particular case, so that the court must either decide that case conformably to the law, disregarding the constitution; or conformably to the constitution, disregarding the law; the court must determine which of these conflicting rules governs the case. This is of the very essence of judicial duty.

If then the courts are to regard the constitution; and the constitution is superior to any ordinary act of the legislature; the constitution, and not such ordinary act, must govern the case to which they both apply.

Those then who controvert the principle that the constitution is to be considered, in court, as a paramount law, are reduced to the necessity of maintaining that courts must close their eyes on the constitution, and see only the law.

This doctrine would subvert the very foundation of all written constitutions. It would declare that an act, which, according to the principles and theory of our government, is entirely void; is yet, in practice, completely obligatory. It would declare, that if the legislature shall do what is expressly forbidden, such act, notwithstanding the express prohibition, is in reality effectual. It would be giving to the legislature a practical and real omnipotence, with the same breath which professes to restrict their powers within narrow limits. It is prescribing limits, and declaring that those limits may be passed at pleasure.

That it thus reduces to nothing what we have deemed the greatest improvement on political institutions—a written constitution—would of itself be sufficient, in America, where written constitutions have been viewed with so much reverence, for rejecting the construction. But the peculiar expressions of the constitution of the United States furnish additional arguments in favor of its rejection.

The judicial power of the United States is extended to all cases arising under the constitution. Could it be the intention of those who gave this power, to say that, in using it, the constitution should not be looked into? That a case arising under the constitution should be decided without examining the instrument under which it arises? This is too extravagant to be maintained. In some cases then, the constitution must be looked into by the judges. And if they can open it at all, what part of it are they forbidden to read, or to obey?

There are many other parts of the constitution which serve to illustrate this subject. It is declared that "no tax or duty shall be laid on articles exported from any state." Suppose a duty on the export of cotton, of tobacco, or of flour; and a suit instituted to recover it. Ought judgment to be rendered in such a case? Ought the judges to close their eyes on the constitution, and only see the law.

The constitution declares that "no bill of attainder or ex post facto law shall be passed." If, however, such a bill should be passed and a person should be prosecuted under it; must the court condemn to death those victims whom the constitution endeavors to preserve?

"No person," says the constitution, "shall be convicted of treason unless on the testimony of two witnesses to the same overt act, or on confession in open court." Here the language of the constitution is addressed especially to the courts. It prescribes, directly for them, a rule of evidence not to be departed from. If the legislature should change that rule, and declare one witness, or a confession out of court, sufficient for conviction, must the constitutional principle yield to the legislative act?

From these, and many other selections which might be made, it is apparent, that the framers of the constitution contemplated that instrument, as a rule for the government of courts, as well as of the legislature.

Why otherwise does it direct the judges to take an oath to support it? This oath certainly applies, in an especial manner, to their conduct in their official character. How immoral to impose it on them, if they were to be used as the instruments, and the knowing instruments, for violating what they swear to support!

The oath of office, too, imposed by the legislature, is completely demonstrative of the legislative opinion on the subject. It is in these words, "I do solemnly swear that I will administer justice without respect to persons, and do equal right to the poor and to the rich; and that I will faithfully and impartially discharge all the duties incumbent on me as according to the best of my abilities and understanding, agreeably to the constitution, and laws of the United States."

Why does a judge swear to discharge his duties agreeably to the constitution of the United States, if that constitution forms no rule for his government? if it is closed upon him, and cannot be inspected by him? If such be the real state of things, this is worse than solemn mockery. To prescribe, or to take this oath, becomes equally a crime.

It is also not entirely unworthy of observation, that in declaring what shall be the supreme law of the land, the constitution itself is first mentioned; and not the laws of the United States generally, but those only which shall be made in pursuance of the constitution, have that rank.

Thus, the particular phraseology of the constitution of the United States confirms and strengthens the principle, supposed to be essential to all written constitutions, that a law repugnant to the constitution is void; and that courts, as well as other departments, are bound by that instrument.

The rule must be discharged.

NOTE ON *MARBURY* AND THE LEGITIMACY OF JUDICIAL REVIEW

1.   As already discussed, the Republican assault on the Judiciary left the Marshall Court in a precarious position. As Scot Powe puts it, "The Court had been dealt a terrible hand, one in which the Republicans held all the trumps." [16] To what extent did this political context constrain John Marshall's options as the Supreme Court sat to decide the case?

Professor Powe goes on to observe that "Marshall's genius—and make no mistake, it was genius—was that he found cards to play in such a losing hand."[17] Likewise, Robert McCloskey has said that *Marbury* and similar rulings show Marshall's genius for solidifying the judiciary's power by making political concessions in the short run while establishing much more important principles in the long run.[18] Professor McConnell, on the other hand, concludes that *Marbury*'s "bold, but empty, assertion of judicial power masked a quiet capitulation on all the issues that really mattered."[19] In support of the latter view, consider the Court's decision a week later in *Stuart v. Laird*, 5 U.S. (1 Cranch) 299 (1803), which upheld the Republican Congress's repeal of the 1801 Judiciary Act—including the 1802 Repeal Act's elimination of certain federal courts and its reimposition of circuit riding on the Justices. Although the issue in *Stuart* was potentially far more explosive than that in *Marbury*, John Marshall recused himself (he had decided the case on circuit), and Justice Paterson's terse opinion for the Court avoided stirring up any controversy by acquiescing in the Repeal Act's narrowing of judicial power. Is Professor McConnell right to think that *Stuart*'s "capitulation" was more important than the judiciary's victory in *Marbury*? In thinking about this question, consider also the fact that the Supreme Court would not actually *use* its asserted power to strike down a federal statute again until 1857, in *Dred Scott v. Sandford*, 60 U.S. (19 How.) 393 (1857).

2.   There are actually two important constitutional issues in *Marbury*. One concerns the power of the Court to order senior executive officials to comply with the law. Marbury has asked the Supreme Court for a writ of mandamus, directing Madison (Jefferson's Secretary of State) to deliver the commissions to Marbury and the other justices of the peace. A writ of mandamus is an order to perform a legal duty; the rub, of course, is that Madison disagreed with the Court as to what the law, properly construed, required him to do under the circumstances. The right of the courts to have their way in such situations was the difficult and controversial issue at the time that *Marbury* was decided; as Professor McConnell puts it, "[t]he real novelty of *Marbury* was its assertion of authority to issue affirmative commands to the executive."[20] Should the Court have even reached this issue, given its finding later in the opinion that it lacked jurisdiction over the case?

---

[16]   POWE, *supra* note 6, at 46.

[17]   *Id.* at 47.

[18]   MCCLOSKEY, *supra* note 7, at 28, 34.

[19]   McConnell, *supra* note 4, at 31.

[20]   *Id.* at 26.

Do you agree with Chief Justice Marshall's assertion of judicial authority in this regard? President Jefferson certainly did not; a few years later, Jefferson's Attorney General, Caesar Rodney, issued an opinion denying that federal courts may issue writs of mandamus to executive officers. Such a power, he argued, "would necessarily have the effect of transferring the powers vested in one department to another department," in violation of Article II of the Constitution's conferral of power on the president "to take care, that the laws be faithfully executed."[21] What limits on this power did the Court recognize in *Marbury*?

3.   The second constitutional issue—and the one for which *Marbury* is now famous—concerns the power of judicial review, that is, the judiciary's authority to declare statutes and other governmental actions unconstitutional. In any case in which a court exercises that power, it is important to identify both the challenged statute or government action and the provision or principle of the Constitution that the government's action is alleged to violate. Unfortunately, the constitutional question upon which the Court actually exercises its power of judicial review in *Marbury* is not presented in nearly so straightforward a manner as in many of the landmark cases later on.

By filing his suit in the Supreme Court, Marbury invoked the Supreme Court's *original* jurisdiction—the Court's jurisdiction over cases that are filed initially in the Supreme Court rather than a lower federal court. As Chief Justice Marshall points out, Article III recognizes two forms of Supreme Court jurisdiction, original and appellate. The Constitution specifies when a case may begin in the Supreme Court (for example, when one state sues another); it also provides that other cases may come to the Court on appeal from a lower federal court or state court.

In arguing that the Supreme Court had jurisdiction to hear his case, Marbury relied on a provision of the 1789 Judiciary Act that authorized the Court to issue writs of mandamus to federal officers. The constitutional issue, as Chief Justice Marshall saw it, was whether Congress could authorize original jurisdiction over mandamus cases if Article III does not list issuing writs of mandamus as a matter within the Court's original jurisdiction.

If Article III did not, in fact, authorize what the Judiciary Act permitted, then that would raise the more basic question of judicial review—that is, Does the Court have the power to set aside a statute that (the Court thinks) is contrary to the Constitution?

4.   Chief Justice Marshall's reasoning in *Marbury* has been criticized on any number of grounds. Consider the following lines of critique:

- Is Marshall's reading of the Judiciary Act as granting original jurisdiction to the Supreme Court in any case in which the plaintiff seeks a mandamus the most persuasive reading of the statute? Did the Act really do that? Should the Court have

---

[21]   Report of the Attorney General of the United States, July 15, 1808, quoted in McConnell, *supra* note 4, at 29.

favored an alternate reading of the statute that would have avoided the need to decide the constitutional questions in the case?

- Does it follow from the proposition that the Constitution trumps any other law inconsistent with its provisions that the *Court* is the one to say whether such an inconsistency exists? After all, the First Congress that drafted the Judiciary Act included many of the same people who drafted Article III in the first place. Why is the Court's interpretation more weighty than Congress's or the Executive's?

- If Marshall thinks the Court lacks jurisdiction to decide the case, should he be opining about the Court's power to issue orders to senior executive officials?

- Should John Marshall have recused himself in this case?[22]

The second of these criticisms is most salient for our present purposes. Legal experts generally agree that Article III does not explicitly create the power of judicial review. What sorts of arguments does Chief Justice Marshall make in support of his conclusion that courts must nonetheless be able to review the constitutionality of actions by the political branches (Congress and the Executive)? Which arguments do you find most persuasive?

5.   An important critique of judicial review generally proceeds from what Alexander Bickel called "the counter-majoritarian difficulty":

> The root difficulty is that judicial review is a counter-majoritarian force in our system. There are various ways of sliding over this ineluctable reality. Marshall did so when he spoke of enforcing, in behalf of "the people," the limits that they have ordained for the institutions of a limited government. . . . But the word "people" so used is an abstraction . . . obscuring the reality that when the Supreme Court declares unconstitutional a legislative act or the action of an elected executive, it thwarts the will of representatives of the actual people of the here and now; it exercises control, not in behalf of the prevailing majority, but against it. That, without mystic overtones, is what actually happens. . . . and it is the reason the charge can be made that judicial review is undemocratic.[23]

Professor Bickel sought to resolve this difficulty by pointing to the particular institutional characteristics of courts and judges:

> [C]ourts have certain capacities for dealing with matters of principle that legislatures and executives do not possess. Judges have, or should have, the leisure, the training, and the insulation to follow the ways of the scholar in pursuing the ends of government. This is crucial in sorting out the enduring values of a society, and it is not something that institutions can do well

---

[22]   For further development of these arguments, see William Van Alstyne, *A Critical Guide to* Marbury v. Madison, 1969 DUKE L.J. 1 (1969).

[23]   ALEXANDER BICKEL, THE LEAST DANGEROUS BRANCH: THE SUPREME COURT AT THE BAR OF POLITICS 16–17 (1962).

occasionally, while operating for the most part with a different set of gears. It calls for a habit of mind, and for undeviating institutional customs. Another advantage that courts have is that questions of principle never carry the same aspect for them as they did for the legislature or the executive. Statutes, after all, deal typically with abstract or dimly foreseen problems. The courts are concerned with the flesh and blood of an actual case. This tends to modify, perhaps to lengthen, everyone's view. It also provides an extremely salutary proving ground for all abstractions; it is conducive, in a phrase of [Justice Oliver Wendell] Holmes, to thinking things, not words, and thus to the evolution of principle by a process that tests as it creates.

Their insulation and the marvelous mystery of time give courts the capacity to appeal to men's better natures, to call forth their aspirations, which may have been forgotten in the moment's hue and cry. This is what Justice [Harlan] Stone called the opportunity for "the sober second thought." Hence it is that the courts, although they may somewhat dampen the people's and the legislatures' efforts to educate themselves, are also a great and highly effective educational institution.[24]

Do you agree with Professor Bickel's way of framing the problem? Would anyone besides a law professor think that judges must be able "to follow the ways of the scholar"? Is Bickel's defense of judicial review persuasive?

6.   *Marbury*'s holding that the Supreme Court has the power of judicial review does not spell out its implications for constitutional interpretation by *other* government officials, including the President and Members of Congress. We will return to the question of non-judicial constitutional interpretation in Chapter Six, but for now it suffices to say that other government officials will frequently confront issues of constitutional law. A legislator, for example, may need to decide whether a proposed measure is constitutional before she votes on it. Does judicial review tend to dissuade other government officials from taking their own constitutional obligations seriously? Consider the following famous argument made by Professor James Bradley Thayer around the turn of the Twentieth Century:

[T]he exercise of [judicial review], even when unavoidable, is always attended with a serious evil, namely, that the correction of legislative mistakes comes from the outside, and the people thus lose the political experience, and the moral education and stimulus that comes from fighting the question out in the ordinary way, and correcting their own errors. The tendency of a common and easy resort to this great function, now lamentably too common, is to dwarf the political capacity of the people, and to deaden its sense of moral responsibility. It is no light thing to do that.[25]

---

[24]   *Id.* at 25–26.
[25]   JAMES BRADLEY THAYER, JOHN MARSHALL 106–07 (1901).

To what extent are legislators and executive officials likely to worry less about whether what they are doing is constitutional because they expect the courts to sort the matter out? Is there a risk that judicial review will encourage people to think that the Constitution is something that belongs to the courts?

7.   Many commentators have observed that Chief Justice Marshall wanted to expand and entrench the power of the judiciary.[26] *Marbury's* declaration of the power of judicial review was an important step toward this goal. Are Marshall's arguments really a clever power grab? On the other hand, consider the alternative. Would it make more sense for the political branches to police themselves?

SECTION 2.2   CASES AND CONTROVERSIES

The power asserted by Chief Justice Marshall in *Marbury* is an awesome one. Professor McCloskey describes it (or what it would become) as "judicial sovereignty . . . the idea that a law may be held unconstitutional if the Court thinks it is, even though the case is not plain, and that the Court's opinion to this effect is binding on other branches of government."[27] As this power has developed, however, so too have important limits on that power.

Some limits on judicial power can be gleaned directly from the constitutional text. Most obviously, judges are "civil officers of the United States" and may be impeached for "treason, bribery, or other high crimes and misdemeanors" under Art. II, § 4. Impeachment was an important initial strategy in the struggle between the Jefferson administration and the Federalist-dominated federal courts, but this threat subsided after the Republicans failed to impeach Justice Samuel Chase. Numerous lower court judges have been impeached in the years since, generally for corruption, drunkenness, or similar offenses.[28] However, the convention seems relatively well established in modern practice that judges cannot be properly impeached simply on the ground that Congress disagrees with their rulings.[29]

The remainder of this chapter focuses on two additional limits on judicial review: Article III's limitation of judicial authority to "cases" and "controversies" and the doctrine of nonjusticiable "political questions." Many of these limits are covered in depth in upper-level Federal Courts and Administrative Law courses. This chapter offers a relatively brief overview.

Chief Justice Marshall's opinion in *Marbury* grounded the power of judicial review in the Court's duty to resolve the particular case before it.

---

[26] *See, e.g.*, MCCLOSKEY, *supra* note 7, at 25; G. EDWARD WHITE, THE AMERICAN JUDICIAL TRADITION: PROFILES OF LEADING AMERICAN JUDGES 9–10 (1976).

[27] MCCLOSKEY, *supra* note 7, at 19.

[28] The *Nixon* case in this chapter provides an example of a federal judge impeached for corruption.

[29] President Richard Nixon and House Minority Leader Gerald Ford tried to impeach liberal Justice William O. Douglas in 1970, but the movement failed after hearings on the issue.

That means that what counts as a "case" or "controversy" defines the scope of the Court's power. The most fundamental requirement is that the courts may only decide actual disputes between real parties; they may not simply weigh in with advice on the great questions of the day, in the absence of a litigated dispute. This prohibition on "advisory opinions" is the basic source of more specific doctrines of standing, ripeness, and mootness.

Correspondence of the Justices (1793)

The general rule against "advisory opinions" is often traced to an episode in 1793, when Thomas Jefferson, serving as President Washington's Secretary of State, wrote a letter to the justices of the Supreme Court asking their opinion on some thorny legal questions that might arise out of treaties with France concerning the rights and obligations of the United States in connection with France's war with Britain. Jefferson wrote as follows:

Gentlemen:

The war which has taken place among the powers of Europe produces frequent transactions within our ports and limits, on which questions arise of considerable difficulty, and of greater importance to the peace of the United States. These questions depend for their solution on the construction of our treaties, on the laws of nature and nations, and on the laws of the land, and are often presented under circumstances *which do not give a cognizance of them to the tribunals of the country*. Yet their decision is so little analogous to the ordinary functions of the executive, as to occasion much embarrassment and difficulty to them. The President therefore would be much relieved if he found himself free to refer questions of this description to the opinions of the judges of the Supreme Court of the United States, whose knowledge of the subject would secure us against errors dangerous to the peace of the United States, and their authority insure the respect of all parties. He has therefore asked the attendance of such of the judges as could be collected in time for the occasion, to know, in the first place, their opinion, whether the public may, with propriety, be availed of their *advice on these questions?* And if they may, to present, for their advice, the abstract questions which have already occurred, or may soon occur, from which they will themselves strike out such as any circumstances might, in their opinion, forbid them to pronounce on. I have the honour to be with sentiments of the most perfect respect, gentlemen,

YOUR MOST OBEDIENT AND
HUMBLE SERVANT,

THOS. JEFFERSON

Here are some of the 29 questions that the President's Cabinet agreed to present to the Court:

> 1.   Do the treaties between the United States and France give to France or her citizens a *right*, when at war with a power with whom the United States are at peace, to fit out originally and from the ports of the United States vessels armed for war, with or without commission? . . .
>
> 2.   Do the laws of neutrality . . . authorize the United States to permit France, her subjects, or citizens, the sale within their ports of prizes made of the subjects or property of a power at war with France, before they have been carried into some port of France and there condemned, refusing the like privilege to her enemy? . . .
>
> 20. To what distance, by the laws and usages of nations, may the United States exercise the right of prohibiting the hostilities of foreign powers at war with each other within rivers, bays, and arms of the sea, and upon the sea along the coasts of the United States? . . .
>
> 25. May we, within our own ports, sell ships to both parties, prepared merely for merchandise? May they be pierced for guns?
> . . .

The justices, however, politely refused to answer. Chief Justice Jay and the Associate Justices wrote:

> Sir:
>
> We have considered the previous question stated in a letter written to us by your direction by the Secretary of State on the 18th of last month. The lines of separation drawn by the Constitution between the three departments of the government—their being in certain respects checks upon each other—and our being judges of a court in the last resort—are considerations which afford strong arguments against the propriety of our extrajudicially deciding the questions alluded to; especially as the power given by the Constitution to the President of calling on the heads of departments for opinions, seems to have been *purposely* as well as expressly limited to the *executive* departments.[30]

NOTE ON ADVISORY OPINIONS

1.   Although the Court declined Jefferson's request concerning interpretation of the United States' rights and obligations vis-à-vis England and France, its practice on advice-giving was not uniform in the early

---

[30]   Both letters are available in 3 CORRESPONDENCE AND PUBLIC PAPERS OF JOHN JAY 486–89 (H. Johnston ed. 1893). The questions are in 10 SPARKS, WRITINGS OF WASHINGTON 542–45 (1836).

Republic. The Invalid Pensions Act of 1792 created a scheme for determining Revolutionary War veterans' eligibility for benefits, under which the federal courts were to process applications subject to review by the Secretary of War. Chief Justice Jay and Justice William Cushing wrote a letter to President Washington urging that the scheme was unconstitutional because it allowed the Secretary to sit "as a court of errors on the judicial acts or opinions of this court." [31] More broadly, federal judges in the early Republic routinely indulged in long-winded charges to federal grand juries; these wide-ranging speeches often offered opinions on a variety of legal issues not strictly before the court. And Jay had served as a presidential confidant on matters extending from the President's annual message to Congress to advice on questions of foreign policy.[32] Why do you think the justices chose to draw the line at Jefferson's request?

2. Chief Justice Jay's terse reply suggests three distinct rationales for declining to answer Jefferson's questions. One draws on the notion of "checks and balances" that is integral to the constitutional separation of powers. Is that rationale sufficient to bar *all* advisory opinions? Or simply those issued at the behest of the Executive?

3. The second rationale derives from the Court's reference to "extrajudicial" decisionmaking. What makes an advisory opinion "extrajudicial"? Is it the lack of a concrete case, based on real events, with concrete facts to ground decision of the abstract legal issues? Or is it the absence of two adversary parties before the Court, each with strong incentives to scrutinize the other side's factual and legal claims? Does the real problem stem from the lurking ambiguity with respect to whether President Washington would have been *bound* by the Court's answers to his questions, given that those answers would not have been embedded in a judgment that resolved a pending case?

Contemporary doctrine sometimes prevents federal courts from hearing a case if the parties are insufficiently adverse. In *United States v. Johnson*, for example, the Court dismissed a challenge to a federal rent control statute because the suit was a collusive one between a landlord and a tenant (whom the landlord had selected and provided with a lawyer).[33] Similarly, concerns about the finality of federal court judgments may render a case nonjusticiable. The Court decided early on that federal courts may not issue judgments that are subject to executive revision,[34] and it determined much more recently that Congress may not reopen federal court judgments once they have become final following the exhaustion of the parties' appeals.[35]

---

[31] Quoted in POWE, *supra* note 6, at 22.

[32] *See id.* at 23–24.

[33] *See also United States v. Windsor*, 133 S. Ct. 2675 (2013) (expressing concerns about adversariness where the United States agreed with a private plaintiff that the federal Defense of Marriage Act was unconstitutional, but finding those concerns overcome by the presence of the House of Representatives' "Bipartisan Legal Advisory Group," which had intervened in the suit to defend the law).

[34] *See Hayburn's Case*, 2 U.S. (2 Dall.) 408 (1792).

[35] *See Plaut v. Spendthrift Farm, Inc.*, 514 U.S. 211 (1995).

These justiciability doctrines are covered in greater detail in courses on Federal Courts.

4.　　The third rationale relies on Article II, § 2 of the Constitution, which empowers the President to "require the opinion, in writing, of the principal officer in each of the executive departments, upon any subject relating to the duties of their respective offices." Does this language really imply that the President *can't* ask other government officials for advice? That he cannot, for example, solicit the views of senior members of his party in Congress?

5.　　A year after the Correspondence, the Supreme Court answered one of the Cabinet's questions by holding that the French consul could not establish prize courts for disposing of captured English vessels within American cities.[36] Doesn't refusing to answer such questions in advance of an actual dispute increase the risk of disrupting the political branches' efforts to conduct foreign policy? Do the benefits of eschewing advisory opinions outweigh such risks?

6.　　Note that the general prohibition on advisory opinions has been identified with Article III, and many courts not bound by Article III—state courts and courts in other legal systems—often *do* have the power to issue advisory opinions. Nearly a dozen state high courts currently issue advisory opinions. And many civil law countries refer questions of constitutional law arising in lower courts to a central constitutional court, which generally issues an opinion on those particular questions rather than resolving the entire case.[37] These rulings are not typically "advisory" in the sense of being nonbinding, but they involve answering a question of law on a fairly abstract basis outside the context of a fully-litigated dispute.

By all accounts, the sky has not fallen in any of these state or foreign jurisdictions. Should the U.S. Supreme Court be more willing to issue advisory opinions? Would it have helped President George W. Bush in 2001, for example, to have a preliminary ruling on the constitutionality of trying suspected terrorists by military commission *before* constructing and engaging the whole machinery of military trials?[38] If, in that scenario, the Supreme Court had said such commissions were unconstitutional, would the President have been *bound* by that ruling not to undertake them?

7.　　The remainder of this section canvasses more specific doctrines that mark the boundaries of a "case or controversy" under Article III. First and foremost, a case does not exist unless the plaintiff has *standing to sue*. In *Marbury*, Marshall says that "[t]he province of the court is, solely, to decide on the rights of individuals." This idea has grown into the rule that the plaintiff must have a personal stake in the litigation in order to bring suit; hence, a plaintiff may not challenge unconstitutional government

---

[36]　*See Glass v. The Sloop Betsey*, 3 U.S. (3 Dall.) 6 (1794).

[37]　Likewise, when questions of European Union law arise in the course of ordinary litigation in national courts, they can make a "preliminary reference" of those questions to the European Court of Justice. That court will rule on the abstract questions presented, then send the case back to the national court for resolution of the remainder of the lawsuit.

[38]　For the Court's ultimate answer to this question, five years later, see *Hamdan v. Rumsfeld*, 548 U.S. 557 (2006), in Chapter Fourteen.

conduct unless he is personally injured by that conduct. Such harm need not be tangible—for instance, the feelings of inferiority produced in black schoolchildren by segregated schooling were sufficient to create standing in *Brown v. Board of Education*. But the injury must be specific to the plaintiff; again in *Brown*, an African-American citizen without children attending segregated schools would not have been allowed to sue on the ground that he found segregation offensive. The standing requirement has produced an extremely intricate body of law that is studied in more depth in courses on Federal Courts and Administrative Law.

Warth v. Seldin offers a good example of contemporary standing doctrine. As you read, it is important to keep straight the different plaintiffs in the case and the distinct sorts of injuries that they allege. The notes that follow add in two additional elements of justiciability: ripeness and mootness.

Warth v. Seldin
422 U.S. 490 (1975)

■ **MR. JUSTICE POWELL delivered the opinion of the Court.**

Petitioners, various organizations and individuals resident in the Rochester, N.Y., metropolitan area, brought this action in the District Court for the Western District of New York against the town of Penfield, an incorporated municipality adjacent to Rochester, and against members of Penfield's Zoning, Planning, and Town Boards. Petitioners claimed that the town's zoning ordinance, by its terms and as enforced by the defendant board members, respondents here, effectively excluded persons of low and moderate income from living in the town, in contravention of petitioners' First, Ninth, and Fourteenth Amendment rights. . . . The District Court dismissed the complaint. . . . The Court of Appeals for the Second Circuit affirmed, holding that none of the plaintiffs . . . had standing to prosecute the action. [W]e affirm.

I

Petitioners Metro-Act of Rochester, Inc., and eight individual plaintiffs, on behalf of themselves and all persons similarly situated, filed this action on January 24, 1972. . . . The complaint identified Metro-Act as a not-for-profit New York corporation, the purposes of which are "to alert ordinary citizens to problems of social concern; . . . to inquire into the reasons for the critical housing shortage for low and moderate income persons in the Rochester area and to urge action on the part of citizens to alleviate the general housing shortage for low and moderate income persons." Plaintiffs Vinkey, Reichert, Warth, and Harris were described as residents of the city of Rochester, all of whom owned real property in and paid property taxes to that city. Plaintiff Ortiz, "a citizen of Spanish/Puerto Rican extraction," also owned real property in and paid taxes to Rochester. Ortiz, however, resided in Wayland, N. Y., some 42 miles from Penfield where he was employed. The complaint described plaintiffs Broadnax, Reyes, and Sinkler as residents of Rochester and "persons fitting within the classification of low and moderate income as hereinafter defined. . . ." [T]he record shows that Broadnax, Reyes, and Sinkler are members of ethnic or racial minority groups: Reyes is of Puerto Rican ancestry; Broadnax and Sinkler are Negroes.

Petitioners' complaint alleged that Penfield's zoning ordinance, adopted in 1962, has the purpose and effect of excluding persons of low and moderate income from residing in the town. In particular, the ordinance allocates 98% of the town's vacant land to single-family detached housing, and allegedly by imposing unreasonable requirements relating to lot size, setback, floor area, and habitable space, the ordinance increases the cost of single-family detached housing beyond the means of persons of low and moderate income. Moreover, according to petitioners, only 0.3% of the land available for residential construction is allocated to multifamily structures (apartments, townhouses, and the like), and even on this limited space, housing for low-and moderate-income persons is not economically feasible because of low density and other requirements. Petitioners also alleged that "in furtherance of a policy of exclusionary zoning," the defendant members of Penfield's Town, Zoning, and Planning Boards had acted in an arbitrary and discriminatory manner: they had delayed action on proposals for low-and moderate-cost housing for inordinate periods of time; denied such proposals for arbitrary and insubstantial reasons; refused to grant necessary variances and permits, or to allow tax abatements; failed to provide necessary support services for low- and moderate-cost housing projects; and had amended the ordinance to make approval of such projects virtually impossible.

In sum, petitioners alleged that, in violation of their "rights, privileges and immunities secured by the Constitution and laws of the United States," the town and its officials had made "practically and economically impossible the construction of sufficient numbers of low and moderate income . . . housing in the Town of Penfield to satisfy the minimum housing requirements of both the Town of Penfield and the metropolitan Rochester area. . . ." Petitioners alleged, moreover, that by precluding low- and moderate-cost housing, the town's zoning practices also had the effect of excluding persons of minority racial and ethnic groups, since most such persons have only low or moderate incomes.

Petitioners further alleged certain harm to themselves. The Rochester property owners and taxpayers—Vinkey, Reichert, Warth, Harris, and Ortiz—claimed that because of Penfield's exclusionary practices, the city of Rochester had been forced to impose higher tax rates on them and others similarly situated than would otherwise have been necessary. The low- and moderate-income, minority plaintiffs—Ortiz, Broadnax, Reyes, and Sinkler—claimed that Penfield's zoning practices had prevented them from acquiring, by lease or purchase, residential property in the town, and thus had forced them and their families to reside in less attractive environments. To relieve these various harms, petitioners asked the District Court to declare the Penfield ordinance unconstitutional, to enjoin the defendants from enforcing the ordinance, to order the defendants to enact and administer a new ordinance designed to alleviate the effects of their past actions, and to award $750,000 in actual and exemplary damages.

On May 2, 1972, petitioner Rochester Home Builders Association, an association of firms engaged in residential construction in the Rochester metropolitan area, moved the District Court for leave to intervene as a party-plaintiff. In essence, Home Builders' intervenor complaint . . . claimed that [Penfield's zoning] practices arbitrarily and capriciously had prevented its member firms from building low- and moderate-cost housing in Penfield, and thereby had deprived them of potential profits. Home Builders prayed for equitable relief identical in substance to that requested by the original plaintiffs, and also for $750,000 in damages. On June 7, 1972, Metro-Act and the other original plaintiffs moved to join petitioner Housing Council in the Monroe County Area, Inc., as a party plaintiff. Housing Council is a not-for-profit New York corporation, its membership comprising some 71 public and private organizations interested in housing problems. An affidavit accompanying the motion stated that 17 of Housing Council's member groups were or hoped to be involved in the development of low- and moderate-cost housing, and that one of its members—the Penfield Better Homes Corp.—"is and has been actively attempting to develop moderate income housing" in Penfield, "but has been stymied by its inability to secure the necessary approvals. . . ."

[T]he District Court held that the original plaintiffs, Home Builders, and Housing Council lacked standing to prosecute the action. . . . The Court of Appeals affirmed, reaching only the standing questions.

II

We address first the principles of standing relevant to the claims asserted by the several categories of petitioners in this case. In essence the question of standing is whether the litigant is entitled to have the court decide the merits of the dispute or of particular issues. This inquiry involves both constitutional limitations on federal-court jurisdiction and prudential limitations on its exercise. In both dimensions it is founded in concern about the proper—and properly limited—role of the courts in a democratic society.

In its constitutional dimension, standing imports justiciability: whether the plaintiff has made out a "case or controversy" between himself and the defendant within the meaning of Art. III. This is the threshold question in every federal case, determining the power of the court to entertain the suit. As an aspect of justiciability, the standing question is whether the plaintiff has "alleged such a personal stake in the outcome of the controversy" as to warrant his invocation of federal-court jurisdiction and to justify exercise of the court's remedial powers on his behalf. The Art. III judicial power exists only to redress or otherwise to protect against injury to the complaining party, even though the court's judgment may benefit others collaterally. A federal court's jurisdiction therefore can be invoked only when the plaintiff himself has suffered "some threatened or actual injury resulting from the putatively illegal action. . . ."[10]

Apart from this minimum constitutional mandate, this Court has recognized other limits on the class of persons who may invoke the courts' decisional and remedial powers. First, the Court has held that when the asserted harm is a "generalized grievance" shared in substantially equal measure by all or a large class of citizens, that harm alone normally does not warrant exercise of jurisdiction. Second, even when the plaintiff has alleged injury sufficient to meet the "case or controversy" requirement, this Court has held that the plaintiff generally must assert his own legal rights and interests, and cannot rest his claim to relief on the legal rights or interests of third parties. Without such limitations closely related to Art. III concerns but essentially matters of judicial self-governance the courts would be called upon to decide abstract questions of wide public significance even though other governmental institutions may be more competent to address the questions and even though judicial intervention may be unnecessary to protect individual rights.

Although standing in no way depends on the merits of the plaintiff's contention that particular conduct is illegal, it often turns on the nature and source of the claim asserted. The actual or threatened injury required by Art. III may exist solely by virtue of "statutes creating legal rights, the invasion of which creates standing." Moreover, the source of the plaintiff's claim to relief assumes critical importance with respect to the prudential rules of standing that, apart from Art. III's minimum requirements, serve to limit the role of the courts in resolving public disputes. Essentially, the standing question in such cases is whether the constitutional or statutory provision on which the claim rests properly can be understood as granting persons in the plaintiff's position a right to judicial relief. . . .

One further preliminary matter requires discussion. For purposes of ruling on a motion to dismiss for want of standing, both the trial and reviewing courts must accept as true all material allegations of the complaint, and must construe the complaint in favor of the complaining party. At the same time, it is within the trial court's power to allow or to require the plaintiff to supply, by amendment to the complaint or by affidavits, further particularized allegations of fact deemed supportive of plaintiff's standing. If, after this opportunity, the plaintiff's standing does not adequately appear from all materials of record, the complaint must be dismissed.

---

[10] The standing question thus bears close affinity to questions of ripeness—whether the harm asserted has matured sufficiently to warrant judicial intervention—and of mootness—whether the occasion for judicial intervention persists.

III

With these general considerations in mind, we turn first to the claims of petitioners Ortiz, Reyes, Sinkler, and Broadnax, each of whom asserts standing as a person of low or moderate income and, coincidentally, as a member of a minority racial or ethnic group. We must assume, taking the allegations of the complaint as true, that Penfield's zoning ordinance and the pattern of enforcement by respondent officials have had the purpose and effect of excluding persons of low and moderate income, many of whom are members of racial or ethnic minority groups. We also assume, for purposes here, that such intentional exclusionary practices, if proved in a proper case, would be adjudged violative of the constitutional and statutory rights of the persons excluded.

But the fact that these petitioners share attributes common to persons who may have been excluded from residence in the town is an insufficient predicate for the conclusion that petitioners themselves have been excluded, or that the respondents' assertedly illegal actions have violated their rights. Petitioners must allege and show that they personally have been injured, not that injury has been suffered by other, unidentified members of the class to which they belong and which they purport to represent. Unless these petitioners can thus demonstrate the requisite case or controversy between themselves personally and respondents, "none may seek relief on behalf of himself or any other member of the class."

In their complaint, petitioners Ortiz, Reyes, Sinkler, and Broadnax alleged in conclusory terms that they are among the persons excluded by respondents' actions. None of them has ever resided in Penfield; each claims at least implicitly that he desires, or has desired, to do so. Each asserts, moreover, that he made some effort, at some time, to locate housing in Penfield that was at once within his means and adequate for his family's needs. Each claims that his efforts proved fruitless. We may assume, as petitioners allege, that respondents' actions have contributed, perhaps substantially, to the cost of housing in Penfield. But there remains the question whether petitioners' inability to locate suitable housing in Penfield reasonably can be said to have resulted, in any concretely demonstrable way, from respondents' alleged constitutional and statutory infractions. Petitioners must allege facts from which it reasonably could be inferred that, absent the respondents' restrictive zoning practices, there is a substantial probability that they would have been able to purchase or lease in Penfield and that, if the court affords the relief requested, the asserted inability of petitioners will be removed.

We find the record devoid of the necessary allegations. [N]one of these petitioners has a present interest in any Penfield property; none is himself subject to the ordinance's strictures; and none has ever been denied a variance or permit by respondent officials. Instead, petitioners claim that respondents' enforcement of the ordinance against third parties—developers, builders, and the like—has had the consequence of precluding the construction of housing suitable to their needs at prices they might be able to afford. The fact that the harm to petitioners may have resulted indirectly does not in itself preclude standing. When a governmental prohibition or restriction imposed on one party causes specific harm to a third party, harm that a constitutional provision or statute was intended to prevent, the indirectness of the injury does not necessarily deprive the person harmed of standing to vindicate his rights. But it may make it substantially more difficult to meet the minimum requirement of Art. III: to establish that, in fact, the asserted injury was the consequence of the defendants' actions, or that prospective relief will remove the harm.

Here, by their own admission, realization of petitioners' desire to live in Penfield always has depended on the efforts and willingness of third parties to build low- and moderate-cost housing. The record specifically refers to only two such efforts: that of Penfield Better Homes Corp., in late 1969, to obtain the rezoning of certain land in Penfield to allow the construction of subsidized cooperative townhouses that could be purchased by persons of moderate income; and a similar effort by O'Brien Homes, Inc., in late 1971. But the record is devoid of any indication that these projects, or other like projects, would have satisfied petitioners' needs at prices they could afford, or that, were the court to remove the obstructions attributable to respondents, such relief would benefit petitioners. Indeed, petitioners' descriptions of their individual financial situations and housing needs suggest precisely the contrary—that their inability to reside in Penfield is the consequence of the economics of the area housing market, rather than of respondents' assertedly illegal acts. In short, the facts alleged fail to support an actionable causal relationship between Penfield's zoning practices and petitioners' asserted injury.

In support of their position, petitioners refer to several decisions in the District Courts and Courts of Appeals, acknowledging standing in low-income, minority-group plaintiffs to challenge exclusionary zoning practices. In those cases, however, the plaintiffs challenged zoning restrictions as applied to particular projects that would supply housing within their means, and of which they were intended residents. The plaintiffs thus were able to demonstrate that unless relief from assertedly illegal actions was forthcoming, their immediate and personal interests would be harmed. Petitioners here assert no like circumstances. Instead, they rely on little more than the remote possibility, unsubstantiated by allegations of fact, that their situation might have been better had respondents acted otherwise, and might improve were the court to afford relief.

We hold only that a plaintiff who seeks to challenge exclusionary zoning practices must allege specific, concrete facts demonstrating that the challenged practices harm him, and that he personally would benefit in a tangible way from the court's intervention. Absent the necessary allegations of demonstrable, particularized injury, there can be no confidence of "a real need to exercise the power of judicial review" or that relief can be framed "no broader than required by the precise facts to which the court's ruling would be applied."

IV

The petitioners who assert standing on the basis of their status as taxpayers of the city of Rochester present a different set of problems. These "taxpayer-petitioners" claim that they are suffering economic injury consequent to Penfield's allegedly discriminatory and exclusionary zoning practices. Their argument, in brief, is that Penfield's persistent refusal to allow or to facilitate construction of low-and moderate-cost housing forces the city of Rochester to provide more such housing than it otherwise would do; that to provide such housing, Rochester must allow certain tax abatements; and that as the amount of tax-abated property increases, Rochester taxpayers are forced to assume an increased tax burden in order to finance essential public services.

"Of course, pleadings must be something more than an ingenious academic exercise in the conceivable." We think the complaint of the taxpayer-petitioners is little more than such an exercise. Apart from the conjectural nature of the asserted injury, the line of causation between Penfield's actions and such injury is not apparent from the complaint. Whatever may occur in Penfield, the injury complained of—increases in taxation—results only from decisions made by the appropriate Rochester authorities, who are not parties to this case.

But even if we assume that the taxpayer-petitioners could establish that Penfield's zoning practices harm them, their complaint nonetheless was properly dismissed. Petitioners do not, even if they could, assert any personal right under the Constitution or any statute to be free of action by a neighboring municipality that may have some incidental adverse effect on Rochester. On the contrary, the only basis of the taxpayer-petitioners' claim is that Penfield's zoning ordinance and practices violate the constitutional and statutory rights of third parties, namely, persons of low and moderate income who are said to be excluded from Penfield. In short the claim of these petitioners falls squarely within the prudential standing rule that normally bars litigants from asserting the rights or legal interests of others in order to obtain relief from injury to themselves. As we have observed above, this rule of judicial self-governance is subject to exceptions, the most prominent of which is that Congress may remove it by statute. Here, however, no statute expressly or by clear implication grants a right of action, and thus standing to seek relief, to persons in petitioners' position. . . . Nor do the taxpayer-petitioners show that their prosecution of the suit is necessary to insure protection of the rights asserted, as there is no indication that persons who in fact have been excluded from Penfield are disabled from asserting their own right in a proper case. In sum, we discern no justification for recognizing in the Rochester taxpayers a right of action on the asserted claim.

V

We turn next to the standing problems presented by the petitioner associations—Metro-Act of Rochester, Inc., . . . Housing Council in the Monroe County Area, Inc., . . . and Rochester Home Builders Association, Inc. . . . There is no question that an association may have standing in its own right to seek judicial relief from injury to itself and to vindicate whatever rights and immunities the association itself may enjoy. Moreover, in attempting to secure relief from injury to itself the association may assert the rights of its members, at least so long as the challenged infractions adversely affect its members' associational ties. With the limited exception of Metro-Act, however, none of the associational petitioners here has asserted injury to itself.

Even in the absence of injury to itself, an association may have standing solely as the representative of its members. . . . The association must allege that its members, or any one of them, are suffering immediate or threatened injury as a result of the challenged action of the sort that would make out a justiciable case had the members themselves brought suit. So long as this can be established, and so long as the nature of the claim and of the relief sought does not make the individual participation of each injured party indispensable to proper resolution of the cause, the association may be an appropriate representative of its members, entitled to invoke the court's jurisdiction.

A

Petitioner Metro-Act's claims to standing on its own behalf as a Rochester taxpayer, and on behalf of its members who are Rochester taxpayers or persons of low or moderate income, are precluded by our holdings in Parts III and IV, supra, as to the individual petitioners, and require no further discussion. Metro-Act also alleges, however, that 9% of its membership is composed of present residents of Penfield. It claims that, as a result of the persistent pattern of exclusionary zoning practiced by respondents and the consequent exclusion of persons of low and moderate income, those of its members who are Penfield residents are deprived of the benefits of living in a racially and ethnically integrated community. . . . Metro-Act argues that such deprivation is a sufficiently palpable injury to satisfy the Art. III case-or-controversy requirement, and that it has standing as the representative of its members to seek redress. . . .

Even if we assume, arguendo, that . . . the asserted harm to Metro-Act's Penfield members is sufficiently direct and personal to satisfy the case-or-controversy requirement of Art. III, prudential considerations strongly counsel against according them or Metro-Act standing to prosecute this action. We do not understand Metro-Act to argue that Penfield residents themselves have been denied any constitutional rights. . . . Instead, their complaint is that they have been harmed indirectly by the exclusion of others. This is an attempt to raise putative rights of third parties. . . . In these circumstances, we conclude that it is inappropriate to allow Metro-Act to invoke the judicial process.

B

Petitioner Home Builders . . . asserted standing to represent its member firms engaged in the development and construction of residential housing in the Rochester area, including Penfield. Home Builders alleged that the Penfield zoning restrictions, together with refusals by the town officials to grant variances and permits for the construction of low- and moderate-cost housing, had deprived some of its members of "substantial business opportunities and profits." Home Builders claimed damages of $750,000 and also joined in the original plaintiffs' prayer for declaratory and injunctive relief.

As noted above, to justify any relief the association must show that it has suffered harm, or that one or more of its members are injured. But, apart from this, whether an association has standing to invoke the court's remedial powers on behalf of its members depends in substantial measure on the nature of the relief sought. If in a proper case the association seeks a declaration, injunction, or some other form of prospective relief, it can reasonably be supposed that the remedy, if granted, will inure to the benefit of those members of the association actually injured. Indeed, in all cases in which we have expressly recognized standing in associations to represent their members, the relief sought has been of this kind.

The present case, however, differs significantly as here an association seeks relief in damages for alleged injuries to its members. Home Builders alleges no monetary injury to itself, nor any assignment of the damages claims of its members. No award therefore can be made to the association as such. Moreover, in the circumstances of this case, the damages claims are not common to the entire membership, nor shared by all in equal degree. To the contrary, whatever injury may have been suffered is peculiar to the individual member concerned, and both the fact and extent of injury would require individualized proof. Thus, to obtain relief in damages, each member of Home Builders who claims injury as a result of respondents' practices must be a party to the suit, and Home Builders has no standing to claim damages on his behalf.

Home Builders' prayer for prospective relief fails for a different reason. . . . The complaint refers to no specific project of any of its members that is currently precluded either by the ordinance or by respondents' action in enforcing it. There is no averment that any member has applied to respondents for a building permit or a variance with respect to any current project. Indeed, there is no indication that respondents have delayed or thwarted any project currently proposed by Home Builders' members, or that any of its members has taken advantage of the remedial processes available under the ordinance. In short, insofar as the complaint seeks prospective relief, Home Builders has failed to show the existence of any injury to its members of sufficient immediacy and ripeness to warrant judicial intervention.

A like problem is presented with respect to petitioner Housing Council. . . . [T]he Council includes in its membership "at least seventeen" groups that have been, are, or will be involved in the development of low- and moderate-cost housing. But, with one exception, the complaint does not suggest that any of these groups has focused its efforts on Penfield or has any specific plan to do so. Again with the same exception, neither the complaint nor any materials of record indicate that any member of Housing Council has taken any step toward building housing in Penfield, or has had dealings of any nature with respondents. The exception is the Penfield Better Homes Corp. As we have observed above, it applied to respondents in late 1969 for a zoning variance to allow construction of a housing project designed for persons of moderate income. The affidavit in support of the motion to join Housing Council refers specifically to this effort, and the supporting materials detail at some length the circumstances surrounding the rejection of Better Homes' application. It is therefore possible that in 1969, or within a reasonable time thereafter, Better Homes itself and possibly Housing Council as its representative would have had standing to seek review of respondents' action. The complaint, however, does not allege that the Penfield Better Homes project remained viable in 1972 when this complaint was filed, or that respondents' actions continued to block a then-current construction project. In short, neither the complaint nor the record supplies any basis from which to infer that the controversy between respondents and Better Homes, however vigorous it may once have been, remained a live, concrete dispute when this complaint was filed.

VI

The rules of standing, whether as aspects of the Art. III case-or-controversy requirement or as reflections of prudential considerations defining and limiting the role of the courts, are threshold determinants of the propriety of judicial intervention. It is the responsibility of the complainant clearly to allege facts demonstrating that he is a proper party to invoke judicial resolution of the dispute and the exercise of the court's remedial powers. We agree with the District Court and the Court of Appeals that none of the petitioners here has met this threshold requirement. Accordingly, the judgment of the Court of Appeals is

Affirmed.

■ MR. JUSTICE DOUGLAS, dissenting.

With all respect, I think that the Court reads the complaint and the record with antagonistic eyes. . . . Standing has become a barrier to access to the federal courts. . . . The mounting caseload of federal courts is well known. But cases such as this one reflect festering sores in our society; and the American dream teaches that if one reaches high enough and persists there is a forum where justice is dispensed. I would lower the technical barriers and let the courts serve that ancient need. They can in time be curbed by legislative or constitutional restraints if an emergency arises. . . .

■ MR. JUSTICE BRENNAN, with whom MR. JUSTICE WHITE and MR. JUSTICE MARSHALL join, dissenting.

. . . While the Court gives lip service to the principle . . . that "standing in no way depends on the merits of the plaintiff's contention that particular conduct is illegal," in fact the opinion, which tosses out of court almost every conceivable kind of plaintiff who could be injured by the activity claimed to be unconstitutional, can be explained only by an indefensible hostility to the claim on the merits. I can appreciate the Court's reluctance to adjudicate the complex and difficult legal questions involved in determining the constitutionality of practices which assertedly limit residence in a particular municipality to those who are white and relatively well off, and I also understand that the merits of this case could involve grave sociological and political ramifications. But courts cannot refuse to hear a case on the merits merely because they would prefer not to, and it is quite clear, when the record is viewed with dispassion, that at least three of the groups of plaintiffs have made allegations, and supported them with affidavits and documentary evidence, sufficient to survive a motion to dismiss for lack of standing.

I

. . . [T]he portrait which emerges from the allegations and affidavits is one of total, purposeful, intransigent exclusion of certain classes of people from the town, pursuant to a conscious scheme never deviated from. Because of this scheme, those interested in building homes for the excluded groups were faced with insurmountable difficulties, and those of the excluded groups seeking homes in the locality quickly learned that their attempts were futile. Yet, the Court turns the very success of the allegedly unconstitutional scheme into a barrier to a lawsuit seeking its invalidation. In effect, the Court tells the low-income minority and building company plaintiffs they will not be permitted to prove what they have alleged—that they could and would build and live in the town if changes were made in the zoning ordinance and its application—because they have not succeeded in breaching, before the suit was filed, the very barriers which are the subject of the suit.

II

Low-income and Minority Plaintiffs

As recounted above, plaintiffs Ortiz, Broadnax, Reyes, and Sinkler alleged that "as a result" of respondents' exclusionary practices, they were unable, despite attempts, to find the housing they desired in Penfield, and consequently have incurred high commuting expenses, received poorer municipal services, and, in some instances, have been relegated to live in substandard housing. The Court does not, as it could not, suggest that the injuries, if proved, would be insufficient to give petitioners the requisite "personal stake in the outcome of the controversy as to assure the concrete adverseness which sharpens the presentation of issues." Rather, it is abundantly clear that the harm alleged satisfies the "injury in fact, economic or otherwise," requirement which is prerequisite to standing in federal court. The harms claimed— consisting of out-of-pocket losses as well as denial of specifically enumerated services available in Penfield but not in these petitioners' present communities—are obviously more palpable and concrete than those held sufficient to sustain standing in other cases.

Instead, the Court insists that these petitioners' allegations are insufficient to show that the harms suffered were caused by respondents' allegedly unconstitutional practices, because "their inability to reside in Penfield [may be] the consequence of the economics of the area housing market, rather than of respondents' assertedly illegal acts."

True, this Court has held that to maintain standing, a plaintiff must not only allege an injury but must also assert a " 'direct' relationship between the alleged injury and the claim sought to be adjudicated,"—that is, "[t]he party who invokes [judicial] power must be able to show . . . that he has sustained or is immediately in danger of sustaining some direct injury as the result of [a statute's] enforcement." But as the allegations recited above show, these petitioners have alleged precisely what our cases require—that because of the exclusionary practices of respondents, they cannot live in Penfield and have suffered harm.

Thus, the Court's real holding is not that these petitioners have not alleged an injury resulting from respondents' action, but that they are not to be allowed to prove one, because "realization of petitioners' desire to live in Penfield always has depended on the efforts and willingness of third parties to build low- and moderate-cost housing," and "the record is devoid of any indication that . . . [any] projects, would have satisfied petitioners' needs at prices they could afford."

Certainly, this is not the sort of demonstration that can or should be required of petitioners at this preliminary stage. . . . Here, the very fact that, as the Court stresses, these petitioners' claim rests in part upon proving the intentions and capabilities of third parties to build in Penfield suitable housing which they can afford, coupled with the exclusionary character of the claim on the merits, makes it particularly inappropriate to assume that these petitioners' lack of specificity reflects a fatal weakness in their theory of causation. Obviously they cannot be expected, prior to discovery and trial, to know the future plans of building companies, the precise details of the housing market in Penfield, or everything which has transpired in 15 years of application of the Penfield zoning ordinance, including every housing plan suggested and refused. To require them to allege such facts is to require them to prove their case on paper in order to get into court at all, reverting to the form of fact pleading long abjured in the federal courts. This Court has not required such unachievable specificity in standing cases in the past, and the fact that it does so now can only be explained by an indefensible determination by the Court to close the doors of the federal courts to claims of this kind. Understandably, today's decision will be read as revealing hostility to breaking down even unconstitutional zoning barriers that frustrate the deep human yearning of low-income and minority groups for decent housing they can afford in decent surroundings.

III

Associations Including Building Concerns

Two of the petitioners are organizations among whose members are building concerns. Both of these organizations, Home Builders and Housing Council, alleged that these concerns have attempted to build in Penfield low- and moderate-income housing, but have been stymied by the zoning ordinance and refusal to grant individual relief therefrom.

Specifically, Home Builders, a trade association of concerns engaged in constructing and maintaining residential housing in the Rochester area, alleged that "[d]uring the past 15 years, over 80% of the private housing units constructed in the Town of Penfield have been constructed by [its] members." Because of respondents' refusal to grant relief from Penfield's restrictive housing statutes, members of Home Builders could not proceed with planned low- and moderate-income housing projects and thereby lost profits.

Housing Council numbers among its members at least 17 groups involved in the development and construction of low- and middle-income housing. In particular, one member, Penfield Better Homes, "is and has been actively attempting to develop moderate income housing in . . . Penfield" but has been unable to secure the necessary approvals.

The Court finds that these two organizations lack standing to seek prospective relief for basically the same reasons: none of their members is, as far as the allegations show, currently involved in developing a particular project. . . .

Again, the Court ignores the thrust of the complaints and asks petitioners to allege the impossible. According to the allegations, the building concerns' experience in the past with Penfield officials has shown any plans for low- and moderate-income housing to be futile for, again according to the allegations, the respondents are engaged in a purposeful, conscious scheme to exclude such housing. Particularly with regard to a low- or moderate-income project, the cost of litigating, with respect to any particular project, the legality of a refusal to approve it may well be prohibitive. And the merits of the exclusion of this or that project is not at the heart of the complaint; the claim is that respondents will not approve any project which will provide residences for low- and moderate-income people.

When this sort of pattern-and-practice claim is at the heart of the controversy, allegations of past injury, which members of both of these organizations have clearly made, and of a future intent, if the barriers are cleared, again to develop suitable housing for Penfield, should be more than sufficient. The past experiences, if proved at trial, will give credibility and substance to the claim of interest in future building activity in Penfield. These parties, if their allegations are proved, certainly have the requisite personal stake in the outcome of this controversy, and the Court's conclusion otherwise is only a conclusion that this controversy may not be litigated in a federal court.

I would reverse the judgment of the Court of Appeals.

NOTE ON THE JUSTICIABILITY DOCTRINES

1.   What is the point of the standing requirement? Imagine, for example, that a competent and exceptionally well-heeled public interest law firm sets out to bring litigation challenging unconstitutional government conduct wherever they can find it. Why should that firm have to dig up a plaintiff who suffered some specific injury before being able to challenge illegal government acts? Why shouldn't it be enough that the firm is in a position to bring such illegality to light?

One set of rationales for standing focuses on the need to *limit* courts. To what extent does the requirement of a particular plaintiff with an injury limit the power of judicial review? Can one argue that judicial review is more appropriately exercised on behalf of particular individuals than on behalf of diffuse groups or interests?

A second set of arguments suggests that standing requirements may *empower* courts. Specifically, these requirements may facilitate the court's consideration of the legal issues before it by grounding those issues in a concrete case. In what way would that grounding improve constitutional decisionmaking by courts?

2.   The constitutional "core" of the standing doctrine has three elements: the plaintiff must have a *concrete injury*; that injury must be *traceable* to the challenged conduct of the defendant; and the injury must be *redressable* if the court grants the plaintiff's requested relief. The latter two requirements both involve notions of causation. Traceability concerns the causal link running backward from the plaintiff's injury to the defendant's conduct. Redressability is causation running forward from issuance of the court's order in the case (assuming the plaintiff wins on the merits) to relief of the plaintiff's injury. To the extent that some of the claims in *Warth* fail on traceability or redressability grounds, what is it about those claims that render the relevant causal relationships suspect?

3.   The Court in *Warth*—and in many other cases—has distinguished between "constitutional" and "prudential" aspects of standing doctrine. As noted above, it has said that Article III itself requires a plaintiff to have a concrete injury-in-fact that is traceable to the challenged governmental conduct and redressable by the requested relief. Beyond this constitutional

minimum, however, the Court has also developed prudential rules barring plaintiff from (1) asserting a "generalized grievance," or (2) asserting the legal rights of third parties. (The Court has articulated some additional prudential requirements in more specialized contexts, such as judicial review of action by administrative agencies, but those doctrines are best reserved for upper-level classes in Federal Courts.) What sort of interests do these prudential rules protect?

The distinction between constitutional and prudential rules of justiciability will make a difference in at least two situations. The first is when Congress seeks to confer broad standing to sue in a particular statute. When Congress acts, it can override the prudential limitations on plaintiffs' standing, but not the constitutional ones.[39] The second situation concerns the Court's own flexibility in interpreting the justiciability rules. To the extent that those rules are prudential rather than constitutional in nature, the Court enjoys more flexibility in balancing the interests protected by those rules against other important interests that may be furthered, in particular situations, by allowing a broader class of plaintiffs to sue.

If the prudential standing doctrines aren't mandated by the Constitution, where does the Court's power to create them come from? The federal courts have long assumed a power to regulate proceedings before them in various ways—for instance, to sanction litigants who disobey court orders or to fill in gaps in the rules of procedure. In particular, federal courts have claimed a power to decline to exercise their jurisdiction in deference to other actors, such as Congress or the state courts. At the same time, the courts' exercise of discretion *not* to decide cases before them remains somewhat problematic. As Chief Justice Marshall observed in a somewhat different context, "[w]e have no more right to decline the exercise of jurisdiction which is given than to usurp that which is not given. The one or the other would be treason to the Constitution."[40] Are the prudential standing rules a wise and appropriate use of judicial discretion, or do they amount to "treason to the Constitution"?

4.   Although *Warth* rejected several plaintiffs' claims on the ground that they were asserting the constitutional rights of third parties, the prudential rule against third-party standing has many exceptions in practice. In *Griswold v. Connecticut*, 381 U.S. 479 (1965), for example, doctors prosecuted as accessories to the illegal use of contraceptives were allowed to assert the constitutional rights of the married couples to whom they had prescribed the contraceptives. Likewise, *Craig v. Boren*, 429 U.S. 190 (1976), which allowed a beer vendor third-party standing to challenge a restriction on the sale of alcohol to males (but not females) under the age of 21 on the ground that it violated the equal protection rights of his male

---

[39]   *Compare, e.g., Lujan v. Defenders of Wildlife*, 504 U.S. 555 (1992) (holding a citizen-suit provision of the Endangered Species Act unconstitutional insofar as it conferred a right to sue on plaintiffs who did not meet the Article III requirements), *with Federal Election Comm'n v. Akins*, 524 U.S. 11 (1998) (upholding a citizen suit provision of the Federal Election Campaign Act, even though it conferred rights to sue on a very broad class of persons, because the basic Article III requirements were met).

[40]   *Cohens v. Virginia*, 19 U.S. (6 Wheat.) 264, 404 (1821).

customers. Current doctrine suggests that "a party seeking third-party standing [must] make two additional showings. First . . . the party asserting the right [must have] a 'close' relationship with the person who possesses the right. Second . . . there [must be] a 'hindrance' to the possessor's ability to protect his own interests."[41] The Court noted in *Warth*, moreover, that "this Court has allowed standing to litigate the rights of third parties when enforcement of the challenged restriction against the litigant would result indirectly in the violation of third parties' rights." Was that true in *Griswold* and *Craig*? Is it clear that the *Warth* plaintiffs didn't meet this criterion?

5.   In *Lexmark International, Inc. v. Static Control Components*, 134 S. Ct. 1377 (2014), the Court seemed to question the very notion of prudential standing. *Lexmark* involved an aspect of prudential standing—the "zone of interests" test—usually covered in upper level courses in Federal Courts or Administrative Law. That test asks whether the plaintiff's injury falls within the "zone of interests" protected by the law under which the plaintiff sues. A competitor of the defendant business, for example, might not be able to assert claims that the defendant had violated a particular statute if Congress intended to protect only the interests of consumers. In *Lexmark*, Justice Scalia's unanimous opinion suggested that calling this requirement part of "prudential standing" is a "misnomer" because the question is simply whether "this particular class of persons has a right to sue under this substantive statute." That, in other words, is simply a substantive question of Congress's intent to be addressed as part of the merits, not a jurisdictional prerequisite governed by general principles of standing law.

Lexmark did not raise any questions under the more familiar aspects of prudential standing—that is, the bar to assertion of "generalized grievances" and to assertion of rights by third parties. In a footnote, however, Justice Scalia did suggest that "generalized grievances" raised constitutional questions, not prudential ones, and that the third party rule might derive from the same sorts of substantive questions about individual statutes as the zone of interests test. More generally, Justice Scalia observed that "a federal court's obligation to hear and decide cases within its jurisdiction is virtually unflagging"—suggesting that judge-made "prudential" rules of general applicability might *never* be appropriate. Do you agree that construction of prudential rules limiting access to the federal courts is an instance of judicial overreaching? Does it make any difference that Congress is free to (and sometimes does) override those rules by statute?

6.   Three of the petitioners in *Warth* were associations rather than natural persons. In *Hunt v. Washington Apple Advertising Comm'n*, 432 U.S. 333 (1977), the Court said that associations may sue on behalf of their members if three conditions are met:

(a)   At least one of the association's members would otherwise have standing in his own right;

(b)   The interests that the association seeks to protect in the suit are germane to the organization's purpose; and

---

[41]   *Kowalski v. Tesmer*, 543 U.S. 125, 130 (2004).

(c) Neither the claim asserted nor the relief requested requires the participation of individual members in the lawsuit.

Can you see why we might want to allow associations to stand in for their members as litigants in cases like *Warth*?

7. Do you agree with Justice Brennan that the majority's holding in *Warth* "can be explained only by an indefensible hostility to the claim on the merits"? Is it possible (or desirable) to separate the standing inquiry from the merits inquiry entirely?[42] The majority says, by contrast, that standing "often turns on the nature and source of the claim asserted. . . . Essentially, the standing question . . . is whether the constitutional or statutory provision on which the claim rests properly can be understood as granting persons in the plaintiff's position a right to judicial relief." Does the majority apply the standing rules to the *Warth* plaintiffs' claims in a principled way? What would it take to get a challenge to Penfield's zoning rules before a federal court?

8. Standing is only one of three important doctrines of justiciability derived from Article III's case and controversy requirement. The other two have to do with the timing of litigation. *Ripeness* asks whether the plaintiff has sued too soon—in essence, does he have an injury *yet*? Consider, for example, the facts of *United Public Workers v. Mitchell*, 330 U.S. 75 (1947). In *Mitchell*, government employees challenged the Hatch Act, which prohibits federal executive-branch employees from taking "any active part in political management or in political campaigns." The *Mitchell* plaintiffs wanted a court to rule on their challenge to this act under the First Amendment *before* they had actually violated the act. The Supreme Court held their claims were not ripe.

The plaintiffs in *Mitchell* had not violated the act, and the government had not, of course, prosecuted them under it. The lawsuit thus sought *pre-enforcement* review of the act's constitutionality. What is the alternative to pre-enforcement review? How else could one get the argument that the act is unconstitutional before a court? What are the pros and cons of the alternative? One issue in First Amendment law is the "chilling effect" of laws that restrict speech—that these laws might silence constitutionally protected speech before it is uttered. Does requiring the plaintiffs to risk losing their jobs before they can challenge the statute have a chilling effect on political speech?

What would the drawbacks of a pre-enforcement challenge be from the court's perspective? Would the timing of the suit affect the court's ability to decide the case? Assume that the government's interest supporting the law would be in avoiding political corruption and the coercion of government employees to help with their superiors' campaigns and that the relevant First Amendment doctrine would require the court to balance those interests against the interests of the employees in political expression. Because the *Mitchell* plaintiffs sought *pre*-enforcement review, they had not yet undertaken any specific form of political activity, and the Government had

---

[42] For a seminal argument that it is not, see William A. Fletcher, *The Structure of Standing*, 98 YALE L. J. 221 (1988).

not yet had the opportunity to determine whether and how it would enforce the act against them. Might having concrete facts on these matters help a court evaluate the constitutionality of the statute? Didn't the plaintiffs' lawsuit ask the court to imagine every possible application?

The Court's approach to ripeness under current law is quite flexible. Under the test announced in *Abbott Laboratories v. Gardner*, 387 U.S. 136 (1967), the federal courts will ask: (1) Are the issues "fit for judicial resolution"? and (2) Will the parties suffer hardship if judicial resolution is delayed? Can you see how these two inquiries map onto the concerns identified in *Mitchell*? In general, the Court has not applied the *Abbott Laboratories* test very strictly; as a result, according to one prominent commentator, pre-enforcement review has become "the norm" in challenging actions by government agencies (a particularly prominent category of ripeness cases). [43] Is there a risk that generous ripeness rules allow regulated entities to stymie regulatory reforms too easily through litigation?

9.   The third doctrine, also concerned with timing, is *mootness*. Henry Monaghan characterized mootness as "the doctrine of standing set in a time frame. The requisite personal interest that must exist at the commencement of the litigation (standing) must continue through its existence (mootness)."[44] Classic mootness problems include challenges to a criminal conviction after the prisoner has completed his sentence or challenges to a law after the law has been repealed. Consider, for example, a simplified version of the facts in *Friends of the Earth v. Laidlaw Environmental Services, Inc.*, 528 U.S. 167 (2000). In *Friends of the Earth*, an environmental group sued to enjoin a violation of the Clean Water Act by a factory owner. After suit was filed, the defendant ceased its polluting activities. The court of appeals held the case moot. Assuming that the plaintiffs were not entitled to any damages based on the defendant's past violations, would anything be gained by proceeding with the suit? Is there any drawback to dismissing the case at this point? The Supreme Court ultimately held that, because the defendant's cessation was purely voluntarily, the plaintiffs' claims were *not* moot. Can you see why?

One important exception to the mootness doctrine is for injuries that are "capable of repetition, yet evading review." In *Roe v. Wade*, 410 U.S. 113 (1973), for example, the plaintiff challenged the Texas abortion law as a violation of her right to privacy. At the time she brought the suit, of course, the plaintiff was pregnant and wished to secure an abortion. By the time the district court reached a decision, however, the record did not indicate that she was still pregnant. (The case was brought under a fictitious name to protect the plaintiff's privacy, and the record did not disclose *how* the pregnancy ended.) Ordinarily, the case would be moot, as Ms. Roe no longer needed an abortion by the time the appellate courts sat to decide the case. The Supreme Court held that "when, as here, pregnancy is a significant fact in the litigation, the normal 266-day human gestation period is so short that

---

[43] Jerry L. Mashaw, *Improving the Environment of Agency Rulemaking: An Essay on Management, Games, and Accountability*, 57 L. & CONTEMP. PROBS. 185, 235–36 (1994).

[44] Henry P. Monaghan, *Constitutional Adjudication: The Who and When*, 82 YALE L.J. 1363, 1384 (1973).

the pregnancy will come to term before the usual appellate process is complete. If that termination makes a case moot, pregnancy litigation seldom will survive much beyond the trial stage, and appellate review will be effectively denied. Our law should not be that rigid. Pregnancy often comes more than once to the same woman, and in the general population, if man is to survive, it will always be with us." Can you think of other situations in which this exception might be available? What does it tell you about the nature of the Constitution's mootness requirement? Is mootness more constitutional or prudential in nature?

SECTION 2.3 POLITICAL QUESTIONS

Chief Justice Marshall acknowledged in *Marbury* that "[q]uestions, in their nature political, or which are, by the constitution and laws, submitted to the executive, can never be made in this court." This statement is the font of the modern political question doctrine, which holds that some constitutional questions are committed to resolution to one or both of the political branches of the government and not subject to judicial review. Some lower courts and commentators have suggested, for example, that the question of who has the constitutional authority to initiate the use of military force must be resolved by Congress and the President, without judicial intervention. Depending on the scope of the doctrine, this principle could function as an important limit on the power of judicial review.

The seminal case on the political question doctrine is *Baker v. Carr*. The Court's holding that malapportionment of electoral districts is *not* a nonjusticiable "political question" opened the way for the Warren Court's "one-man, one-vote" revolution. The second case in this section, *Nixon v. United States*—no, not *that* Nixon—is a rare example of a case in which the Court *did* find a question nonjusticiable under *Baker*. In general, however, the Court has often proven willing to decide even extremely contentious political issues when they arise in suits that otherwise satisfy the "case or controversy" requirement. These include the legality of racial segregation in *Brown v. Board of Education* and abortion in *Roe v. Wade*, the disputed 2000 presidential election in *Bush v. Gore*, and the right to same-sex marriage in *Obergefell v. Hodges*. If the modern political question doctrine is *not* a tool to avoid politically-fraught cases that threaten the Court's legitimacy, then what is it for?

Baker v. Carr

369 U.S. 186 (1962)

■ MR. JUSTICE BRENNAN delivered the opinion of the Court.

This civil action was brought . . . to redress the alleged deprivation of federal constitutional rights. The complaint, alleging that by means of a 1901 statute of Tennessee apportioning the members of the General Assembly among the State's 95 counties, "these plaintiffs and others similarly situated, are denied the equal protection of the laws accorded them by the Fourteenth Amendment to the Constitution of the United States by virtue of the debasement of their votes," was dismissed by a three-judge court convened . . . in the Middle District of Tennessee. . . . We hold that the dismissal was error, and remand the cause to the District Court for trial and further proceedings consistent with this opinion.

The General Assembly of Tennessee consists of the Senate with 33 members and the House of Representatives with 99 members. . . . Tennessee's standard for allocating legislative representation among her counties is the total number of qualified voters resident in the respective counties, subject only to minor qualifications. . . . In 1901 the General Assembly abandoned separate enumeration in favor of reliance upon the Federal Census and passed the Apportionment Act here in controversy. In the more than 60 years since that action, all proposals in both Houses of the General Assembly for reapportionment have failed to pass.

Between 1901 and 1961, Tennessee has experienced substantial growth and redistribution of her population. In 1901 the population was 2,020,616, of whom 487,380 were eligible to vote. The 1960 Federal Census reports the State's population at 3,567,089, of whom 2,092,891 are eligible to vote. The relative standings of the counties in terms of qualified voters have changed significantly. It is primarily the continued application of the 1901 Apportionment Act to this shifted and enlarged voting population which gives rise to the present controversy. . . .

It is further alleged that "because of the population changes since 1900, and the failure of the legislature to reapportion itself since 1901," the 1901 statute became "unconstitutional and obsolete." Appellants also argue that, because of the composition of the legislature effected by the 1901 apportionment act, redress in the form of a state constitutional amendment to change the entire mechanism for reapportioning, or any other change short of that, is difficult or impossible.[14] The complaint concludes that "these plaintiffs and others similarly situated, are denied the equal protection of the laws accorded them by the Fourteenth Amendment to the Constitution of the United States by virtue of the debasement of their votes." They seek a declaration that the 1901 statute is unconstitutional and an injunction restraining the appellees from acting to conduct any further elections under it. They also pray that unless and until the General Assembly enacts a valid reapportionment, the district court should either decree a reapportionment by mathematical application of the Tennessee constitutional formulae to the most recent federal census figures, or direct the appellees to conduct legislative elections, primary and general, at large. . . .

---

[14] The appellants claim that no General Assembly constituted according to the 1901 Act will submit reapportionment proposals either to the people or to a Constitutional Convention. There is no provision for popular initiative in Tennessee. . . .

We hold that this challenge to an apportionment presents no nonjusticiable "political question." . . . Our discussion, even at the price of extending this opinion, requires review of a number of political question cases, in order to expose the attributes of the doctrine— attributes which, in various settings, diverge, combine, appear, and disappear in seeming disorderliness. . . . That review reveals that in the Guaranty Clause cases and in the other "political question" cases, it is the relationship between the judiciary and the coordinate branches of the Federal Government, and not the federal judiciary's relationship to the States, which gives rise to the "political question." . . .

The nonjusticiability of a political question is primarily a function of the separation of powers. Much confusion results from the capacity of the "political question" label to obscure the need for case-by-case inquiry. Deciding whether a matter has in any measure been committed by the Constitution to another branch of government, or whether the action of that branch exceeds whatever authority has been committed, is itself a delicate exercise in constitutional interpretation, and is a responsibility of this Court as ultimate interpreter of the Constitution. . . .

Foreign relations: There are sweeping statements to the effect that all questions touching foreign relations are political questions. Not only does resolution of such issues frequently turn on standards that defy judicial application, or involve the exercise of a discretion demonstrably committed to the executive or legislature; but many such questions uniquely demand single-voiced statement of the Government's views. Yet it is error to suppose that every case or controversy which touches foreign relations lies beyond judicial cognizance. Our cases in this field seem invariably to show a discriminating analysis of the particular question posed, in terms of the history of its management by the political branches, of its susceptibility to judicial handling in the light of its nature and posture in the specific case, and of the possible consequences of judicial action. For example, though a court will not ordinarily inquire whether a treaty has been terminated, since on that question "governmental action . . . must be regarded as of controlling importance," if there has been no conclusive "governmental action" then a court can construe a treaty and may find it provides the answer. . . .

Validity of enactments: In *Coleman v. Miller,* this Court held that the questions of how long a proposed amendment to the Federal Constitution remained open to ratification, and what effect a prior rejection had on a subsequent ratification, were committed to congressional resolution and involved criteria of decision that necessarily escaped the judicial grasp. Similar considerations apply to the enacting process: "The respect due to coequal and independent departments," and the need for finality and certainty about the status of a statute contribute to judicial reluctance to inquire whether, as passed, it complied with all requisite formalities. . . .

It is apparent that several formulations which vary slightly according to the settings in which the questions arise may describe a political question, although each has one or more elements which identify it as essentially a function of the separation of powers. Prominent on the surface of any case held to involve a political question is found a textually demonstrable constitutional commitment of the issue to a coordinate political department; or a lack of judicially discoverable and manageable standards for resolving it; or the impossibility of deciding without an initial policy determination of a kind clearly for nonjudicial discretion; or the impossibility of a court's undertaking independent resolution without expressing lack of the respect due coordinate branches of government; or an unusual need for unquestioning adherence to a political decision already made; or the potentiality of embarrassment from multifarious pronouncements by various departments on one question.

Unless one of these formulations is inextricable from the case at bar, there should be no dismissal for nonjusticiability on the ground of a political question's presence. The doctrine of which we treat is one of "political questions," not one of "political cases." . . .

But it is argued that this case shares the characteristics of decisions that constitute a category not yet considered, cases concerning the Constitution's guaranty, in Art. IV, § 4, of a republican form of government. . . . [T]he nonjusticiability of such claims has nothing to do with their touching upon matters of state governmental organization.

Republican form of government: *Luther v. Borden,* 48 U.S. (7 How.) 1 (1849), . . . was, as Daniel Webster said in opening the argument for the defense, "an unusual case." The defendants, admitting an otherwise tortious breaking and entering, sought to justify their action on the ground that they were agents of the established lawful government of Rhode Island, which State was then under martial law to defend itself from active insurrection; that the plaintiff was engaged in that insurrection; and that they entered under orders to arrest the plaintiff. The case arose "out of the unfortunate political differences which agitated the people of Rhode Island in 1841 and 1842," and which had resulted in a situation wherein two groups laid competing claims to recognition as the lawful government. The plaintiff's right to recover depended upon which of the two groups was entitled to such recognition. . . .

Clearly, several factors were thought by the Court in *Luther* to make the question there "political": the commitment to the other branches of the decision as to which is the lawful state government; the unambiguous action by the President, in recognizing the charter government as the lawful authority; the need for finality in the executive's decision; and the lack of criteria by which a court could determine which form of government was republican.

But the only significance that *Luther* could have for our immediate purposes is in its holding that the Guaranty Clause is not a repository of judicially manageable standards which a court could utilize independently in order to identify a State's lawful government. The Court has since refused to resort to the Guaranty Clause . . . as the source of a constitutional standard for invalidating state action. See *Taylor & Marshall v. Beckham (No. 1),* 178 U.S. 548 (1900) (claim that Kentucky's resolution of contested gubernatorial election deprived voters of republican government held nonjusticiable); *Pacific States Tel. Co. v. Oregon,* 223 U.S. 118 (1912) (claim that initiative and referendum negated republican government held nonjusticiable); ... *Highland Farms Dairy v. Agnew,* 300 U.S. 608 (1937) (claim that delegation to agency of power to control milk prices violated republican government, rejected). ...

We come, finally, to the ultimate inquiry whether our precedents as to what constitutes a nonjusticiable "political question" bring the case before us under the umbrella of that doctrine. A natural beginning is to note whether any of the common characteristics which we have been able to identify and label descriptively are present. We find none: The question here is the consistency of state action with the Federal Constitution. We have no question decided, or to be decided, by a political branch of government coequal with this Court. Nor do we risk embarrassment of our government abroad, or grave disturbance at home if we take issue with Tennessee as to the constitutionality of her action here challenged. Nor need the appellants, in order to succeed in this action, ask the Court to enter upon policy determinations for which judicially manageable standards are lacking. Judicial standards under the Equal Protection Clause are well developed and familiar, and it has been open to courts since the enactment of the Fourteenth Amendment to determine, if on the particular facts they must, that a discrimination reflects *no* policy, but simply arbitrary and capricious action.

This case does ... involve the allocation of political power within a State, and the appellants might conceivably have added a claim under the Guaranty Clause. ... But because any reliance on the Guaranty Clause could not have succeeded it does not follow that appellants may not be heard on the equal protection claim which in fact they tender. True, it must be clear that the Fourteenth Amendment claim is not so enmeshed with those political question elements which render Guaranty Clause claims nonjusticiable as actually to present a political question itself. But we have found that not to be the case here. ...

When challenges to state action respecting matters of "the administration of the affairs of the State and the officers through whom they are conducted" have rested on claims of constitutional deprivation which are amenable to judicial correction, this Court has acted upon its view of the merits of the claim. ...

We conclude that the complaint's allegations of a denial of equal protection present a justiciable constitutional cause of action upon which appellants are entitled to a trial and a decision. The right asserted is within the reach of judicial protection under the Fourteenth Amendment.

The judgment of the District Court is reversed and the cause is remanded for further proceedings consistent with this opinion.

■ **MR. JUSTICE FRANKFURTER, whom MR. JUSTICE HARLAN joins, dissenting.**

The Court today reverses a uniform course of decision established by a dozen cases, including one by which the very claim now sustained was unanimously rejected only five years ago. The impressive body of rulings thus cast aside reflected the equally uniform course of our political history regarding the relationship between population and legislative representation—a wholly different matter from denial of the franchise to individuals because of race, color, religion or sex. Such a massive repudiation of the experience of our whole past in asserting destructively novel judicial power demands a detailed analysis of the role of this Court in our constitutional scheme. Disregard of inherent limits in the effective exercise of the Court's "judicial Power" not only presages the futility of judicial intervention in the essentially political conflict of forces by which the relation between population and representation has time out of mind been and now is determined. It may well impair the Court's position as the ultimate organ of "the supreme Law of the Land" in that vast range of legal problems, often strongly entangled in popular feeling, on which this Court must pronounce. The Court's authority—possessed of neither the purse nor the sword—ultimately rests on sustained public confidence in its moral sanction. Such feeling must be nourished by the Court's complete detachment, in fact and in appearance, from political entanglements and by abstention from injecting itself into the clash of political forces in political settlements. . . .

In effect, today's decision empowers the courts of the country to devise what should constitute the proper composition of the legislatures of the fifty States. If state courts should for one reason or another find themselves unable to discharge this task, the duty of doing so is put on the federal courts or on this Court, if State views do not satisfy this Court's notion of what is proper districting. . . .

The Court has been particularly unwilling to intervene in matters concerning the structure and organization of the political institutions of the States. The abstention from judicial entry into such areas has been greater even than that which marks the Court's ordinary approach to issues of state power challenged under broad federal guarantees. We should be very reluctant to decide that we had jurisdiction in such a case, and thus in an action of this nature to supervise and review the political administration of a state government by its own officials and through its own courts. The jurisdiction of this court would only exist in case there had been . . . such a plain and substantial departure from the fundamental principles upon which our government is based that it could with truth and propriety be said that if the judgment were suffered to remain, the party aggrieved would be deprived of his life, liberty or property in violation of the provisions of the Federal Constitution. . . .

The present case involves all of the elements that have made the Guarantee Clause cases non-justiciable. It is, in effect, a Guarantee

Clause claim masquerading under a different label. But it cannot make the case more fit for judicial action that appellants invoke the Fourteenth Amendment rather than Art. IV, § 4, where, in fact, the gist of their complaint is the same—unless it can be found that the Fourteenth Amendment speaks with greater particularity to their situation. We have been admonished to avoid "the tyranny of labels." Art. IV, § 4, is not committed by express constitutional terms to Congress. It is the nature of the controversies arising under it, nothing else, which has made it judicially unenforceable. . . . But where judicial competence is wanting, it cannot be created by invoking one clause of the Constitution rather than another. . . .

What, then, is this question of legislative apportionment? Appellants invoke the right to vote and to have their votes counted. But they are permitted to vote and their votes are counted. They go to the polls, they cast their ballots, they send their representatives to the state councils. Their complaint is simply that the representatives are not sufficiently numerous or powerful—in short, that Tennessee has adopted a basis of representation with which they are dissatisfied. Talk of "debasement" or "dilution" is circular talk. One cannot speak of "debasement" or "dilution" of the value of a vote until there is first defined a standard of reference as to what a vote should be worth. What is actually asked of the Court in this case is to choose among competing bases of representation— ultimately, really, among competing theories of political philosophy—in order to establish an appropriate frame of government for the State of Tennessee and thereby for all the States of the Union. . . .

Manifestly, the Equal Protection Clause supplies no clearer guide for judicial examination of apportionment methods than would the Guarantee Clause itself. Apportionment, by its character, is a subject of extraordinary complexity, involving—even after the fundamental theoretical issues concerning what is to be represented in a representative legislature have been fought out or compromised— considerations of geography, demography, electoral convenience, economic and social cohesions or divergencies among particular local groups, communications, the practical effects of political institutions like the lobby and the city machine, ancient traditions and ties of settled usage, respect for proven incumbents of long experience and senior status, mathematical mechanics, censuses compiling relevant data, and a host of others. Legislative responses throughout the country to the reapportionment demands of the 1960 Census have glaringly confirmed that these are not factors that lend themselves to evaluations of a nature that are the staple of judicial determinations or for which judges are equipped to adjudicate by legal training or experience or native wit. And this is the more so true because in every strand of this complicated, intricate web of values meet the contending forces of partisan politics. The practical significance of apportionment is that the next election results may differ because of it. Apportionment battles are overwhelmingly party or intra-party contests. It will add a virulent source of friction and tension in federal-state relations to embroil the federal judiciary in them. . . .

Nixon v. United States

506 U.S. 224 (1993)

■ **CHIEF JUSTICE REHNQUIST delivered the opinion of the Court.**

Petitioner Walter L. Nixon, Jr., asks this Court to decide whether Senate Rule XI, which allows a committee of Senators to hear evidence against an individual who has been impeached and to report that evidence to the full Senate, violates the Impeachment Trial Clause, Art. I, § 3, cl. 6. That Clause provides that the "Senate shall have the sole Power to try all Impeachments." But before we reach the merits of such a claim, we must decide whether it is "justiciable," that is, whether it is a claim that may be resolved by the courts. We conclude that it is not.

Nixon, a former Chief Judge of the United States District Court for the Southern District of Mississippi, was convicted by a jury of two counts of making false statements before a federal grand jury and sentenced to prison. The grand jury investigation stemmed from reports that Nixon had accepted a gratuity from a Mississippi businessman in exchange for asking a local district attorney to halt the prosecution of the businessman's son. Because Nixon refused to resign from his office as a United States District Judge, he continued to collect his judicial salary while serving out his prison sentence.

On May 10, 1989, the House of Representatives adopted three articles of impeachment for high crimes and misdemeanors. The first two articles charged Nixon with giving false testimony before the grand jury and the third article charged him with bringing disrepute on the Federal Judiciary.

After the House presented the articles to the Senate, the Senate voted to invoke its own Impeachment Rule XI, under which the presiding officer appoints a committee of Senators to "receive evidence and take testimony." The Senate committee held four days of hearings, during which 10 witnesses, including Nixon, testified. Pursuant to Rule XI, the committee presented the full Senate with a complete transcript of the proceeding and a Report stating the uncontested facts and summarizing the evidence on the contested facts. Nixon and the House impeachment managers submitted extensive final briefs to the full Senate and delivered arguments from the Senate floor during the three hours set aside for oral argument in front of that body. Nixon himself gave a personal appeal, and several Senators posed questions directly to both parties. The Senate voted by more than the constitutionally required two-thirds majority to convict Nixon on the first two articles. The presiding officer then entered judgment removing Nixon from his office as United States District Judge.

Nixon thereafter commenced the present suit, arguing that Senate Rule XI violates the constitutional grant of authority to the Senate to "try" all impeachments because it prohibits the whole Senate from taking part in the evidentiary hearings. See Art. I, § 3, cl. 6. Nixon sought a declaratory judgment that his impeachment conviction was void and that his judicial salary and privileges should be reinstated. The District Court held that his claim was nonjusticiable, and the Court of Appeals for the District of Columbia Circuit agreed. We granted certiorari.

A controversy is nonjusticiable—*i.e.*, involves a political question—where there is "a textually demonstrable constitutional commitment of the issue to a coordinate political department; or a lack of judicially discoverable and manageable standards for resolving it. . . ." *Baker v. Carr*. But the courts must, in the first instance, interpret the text in question and determine whether and to what extent the issue is textually committed. As the discussion that follows makes clear, the concept of a textual commitment to a coordinate political department is not completely separate from the concept of a lack of judicially discoverable and manageable standards for resolving it; the lack of judicially manageable standards may strengthen the conclusion that there is a textually demonstrable commitment to a coordinate branch.

In this case, we must examine Art. I, § 3, cl. 6, to determine the scope of authority conferred upon the Senate by the Framers regarding impeachment. It provides:

> The Senate shall have the sole Power to try all Impeachments. When sitting for that Purpose, they shall be on Oath or Affirmation. When the President of the United States is tried, the Chief Justice shall preside: And no Person shall be convicted without the Concurrence of two thirds of the Members present.

The language and structure of this Clause are revealing. The first sentence is a grant of authority to the Senate, and the word "sole" indicates that this authority is reposed in the Senate and nowhere else. The next two sentences specify requirements to which the Senate proceedings shall conform: The Senate shall be on oath or affirmation, a two-thirds vote is required to convict, and when the President is tried the Chief Justice shall preside.

Petitioner argues that the word "try" in the first sentence imposes by implication an additional requirement on the Senate in that the proceedings must be in the nature of a judicial trial. From there petitioner goes on to argue that this limitation precludes the Senate from delegating to a select committee the task of hearing the testimony of witnesses, as was done pursuant to Senate Rule XI. . . .

There are several difficulties with this position which lead us ultimately to reject it. The word "try," both in 1787 and later, has considerably broader meanings than those to which petitioner would limit it. Older dictionaries define try as "to examine" or "to examine as a judge." In more modern usage the term has various meanings. . . . Based on the variety of definitions . . . we cannot say that the Framers used the word "try" as an implied limitation on the method by which the Senate might proceed in trying impeachments. . . .

The conclusion that the use of the word "try" in the first sentence of the Impeachment Trial Clause lacks sufficient precision to afford any judicially manageable standard of review of the Senate's actions is fortified by the existence of the three very specific requirements that the Constitution does impose on the Senate when trying impeachments: The Members must be under oath, a two-thirds vote is required to convict, and the Chief Justice presides when the President is tried. These limitations are quite precise, and their nature suggests that the Framers did not intend to impose additional limitations on the form of the Senate proceedings by the use of the word "try" in the first sentence. . . .

We think that the word "sole" is of considerable significance. Indeed, the word "sole" appears only one other time in the Constitution—with respect to the House of Representatives' "*sole* Power of Impeachment." Art. I, § 2, cl. 5 (emphasis added). . . . The commonsense meaning of the word "sole" is that the Senate alone shall have authority to determine whether an individual should be acquitted or convicted. . . . If the courts may review the actions of the Senate in order to determine whether that body "tried" an impeached official, it is difficult to see how the Senate would be "functioning . . . independently and without assistance or interference." . . .

Petitioner finally argues that even if significance be attributed to the word "sole" in the first sentence of the Clause, the authority granted is to the Senate, and this means that "the Senate—not the courts, not a lay jury, not a Senate Committee—shall try impeachments." It would be possible to read the first sentence of the Clause this way, but it is not a natural reading. Petitioner's interpretation would bring into judicial purview not merely the sort of claim made by petitioner, but other similar claims based on the conclusion that the word "Senate" has imposed by implication limitations on procedures which the Senate might adopt. . . .

The history and contemporary understanding of the impeachment provisions support our reading of the constitutional language. . . . The Framers labored over the question of where the impeachment power should lie. Significantly, in at least two considered scenarios the power was placed with the Federal Judiciary. . . . Despite these proposals, the Convention ultimately decided that the Senate would have "the sole Power to try all Impeachments." Art. I, § 3, cl. 6. According to Alexander Hamilton, the Senate was the "most fit depositary of this important trust" because its Members are representatives of the people. The Supreme Court was not the proper body because the Framers "doubted whether the members of that tribunal would, at all times, be endowed with so eminent a portion of fortitude as would be called for in the execution of so difficult a task" or whether the Court "would possess the degree of credit and authority" to carry out its judgment if it conflicted with the accusation brought by the Legislature—the people's representative. . . .

[J]udicial review would be inconsistent with the Framers' insistence that our system be one of checks and balances. In our constitutional system, impeachment was designed to be the *only* check on the Judicial Branch by the Legislature. . . . Judicial involvement in impeachment proceedings, even if only for purposes of judicial review, is counterintuitive because it would eviscerate the "important constitutional check" placed on the Judiciary by the Framers. Nixon's argument would place final reviewing authority with respect to impeachments in the hands of the same body that the impeachment process is meant to regulate. . . .

In addition to the textual commitment argument, we are persuaded that the lack of finality and the difficulty of fashioning relief counsel against justiciability. We agree with the Court of Appeals that opening the door of judicial review to the procedures used by the Senate in trying impeachments would "expose the political life of the country to months, or perhaps years, of chaos." This lack of finality would manifest itself most dramatically if the President were impeached. The legitimacy of any successor, and hence his effectiveness, would be impaired severely, not merely while the judicial process was running its course, but during any retrial that a differently constituted Senate might conduct if its first judgment of conviction were invalidated. Equally uncertain is the question of what relief a court may give other than simply setting aside the judgment of conviction. Could it order the reinstatement of a convicted federal judge, or order Congress to create an additional judgeship if the seat had been filled in the interim? . . .

We agree with Nixon that courts possess power to review either legislative or executive action that transgresses identifiable textual limits. As we have made clear, "whether the action of [either the Legislative or Executive Branch] exceeds whatever authority has been committed, is itself a delicate exercise in constitutional interpretation, and is a responsibility of this Court as ultimate interpreter of the Constitution." But we conclude, after exercising that delicate responsibility, that the word "try" in the Impeachment Trial Clause does not provide an identifiable textual limit on the authority which is committed to the Senate.

For the foregoing reasons, the judgment of the Court of Appeals is *Affirmed.*

■ **JUSTICE WHITE, with whom JUSTICE BLACKMUN joins, concurring in the judgment.**

. . . The Court is of the view that the Constitution forbids us even to consider [Nixon's] contention. I find no such prohibition and would therefore reach the merits of the claim. I concur in the judgment because the Senate fulfilled its constitutional obligation to "try" petitioner.

I

It should be said at the outset that, as a practical matter, it will likely make little difference whether the Court's or my view controls this case. This is so because the Senate has very wide discretion in specifying impeachment trial procedures and because it is extremely unlikely that the Senate would abuse its discretion and insist on a procedure that could not be deemed a trial by reasonable judges. Even taking a wholly practical approach, I would prefer not to announce an unreviewable discretion in the Senate to ignore completely the constitutional direction to "try" impeachment cases. When asked at oral argument whether that direction would be satisfied if, after a House vote to impeach, the Senate, without any procedure whatsoever, unanimously found the accused guilty of being "a bad guy," counsel for the United States answered that the Government's theory "leads me to answer that question yes." Especially in light of this advice from the Solicitor General, I would not issue an invitation to the Senate to find an excuse, in the name of other pressing business, to be dismissive of its critical role in the impeachment process. . . .

II

The majority states that the question raised in this case meets two of the criteria for political questions set out in *Baker v. Carr*. . . . Of course the issue in the political question doctrine is *not* whether the constitutional text commits exclusive responsibility for a particular governmental function to one of the political branches. There are numerous instances of this sort of textual commitment, *e. g.*, Art. I, § 8, and it is not thought that disputes implicating these provisions are non-justiciable. Rather, the issue is whether the Constitution has given one of the political branches final responsibility for interpreting the scope and nature of such a power.

Although *Baker* directs the Court to search for "a textually demonstrable constitutional commitment" of such responsibility, there are few, if any, explicit and unequivocal instances in the Constitution of this sort of textual commitment. . . . The courts therefore are usually left to infer the presence of a political question from the text and structure of the Constitution. In drawing the inference that the Constitution has committed final interpretive authority to one of the political branches, courts are sometimes aided by textual evidence that the Judiciary was not meant to exercise judicial review—a coordinate inquiry expressed in *Baker*'s "lack of judicially discoverable and manageable standards" criterion. *See, e.g., Coleman v. Miller*, 307 U.S. 433 (1939), where the Court refused to determine the life span of a proposed constitutional amendment given Art. V's placement of the amendment process with Congress and the lack of any judicial standard for resolving the question.

A

. . . In disagreeing with the Court, I note that the Solicitor General stated at oral argument that "we don't rest our submission on sole power to try." The Government was well advised in this respect. . . . That the word "sole" is found only in the House and Senate Impeachment Clauses demonstrates that its purpose is to emphasize the distinct role of each in the impeachment process. As the majority notes, the Framers, following English practice, were very much concerned to separate the prosecutorial from the adjudicative aspects of impeachment. Giving each House "sole" power with respect to its role in impeachments effected this division of labor. While the majority is thus right to interpret the term "sole" to indicate that the Senate ought to " 'function independently and without assistance or interference,' " *ante*, at 231, it wrongly identifies the Judiciary, rather than the House, as the source of potential interference with which the Framers were concerned when they employed the term "sole."

Even if the Impeachment Trial Clause is read without regard to its companion Clause, the Court's willingness to abandon its obligation to review the constitutionality of legislative acts merely on the strength of the word "sole" is perplexing. Consider, by comparison, the treatment of Art. I, § 1, which grants "All legislative powers" to the House and Senate. As used in that context "all" is nearly synonymous with "sole"—both connote entire and exclusive authority. Yet the Court has never thought it would unduly interfere with the operation of the Legislative Branch to entertain difficult and important questions as to the extent of the legislative power. . . .

The majority's review of the historical record . . . explains why the power to try impeachments properly resides with the Senate. It does not explain, however, the sweeping statement that the Judiciary was "not chosen to have any role in impeachments."[1] Not a single word in the historical materials cited by the majority addresses judicial review of the Impeachment Trial Clause. And a glance at the arguments surrounding the Impeachment Clauses negates the majority's attempt to infer nonjusticiability from the Framers' arguments in support of the Senate's power to try impeachments. . . .

The historical evidence reveals above all else that the Framers were deeply concerned about placing in any branch the "awful discretion, which a court of impeachments must necessarily have." Viewed against this history, the discord between the majority's position and the basic principles of checks and balances underlying the Constitution's separation of powers is clear. In essence, the majority suggests that the Framers' conferred upon Congress a potential tool of legislative dominance yet at the same time rendered Congress' exercise of that

---

[1] This latter contention is belied by the Impeachment Trial Clause itself, which designates the Chief Justice to preside over impeachment trials of the President.

power one of the very few areas of legislative authority immune from any judicial review. While the majority rejects petitioner's justiciability argument as espousing a view "inconsistent with the Framers' insistence that our system be one of checks and balances," it is the Court's finding of nonjusticiability that truly upsets the Framers' careful design. In a truly balanced system, impeachments tried by the Senate would serve as a means of controlling the largely unaccountable Judiciary, even as judicial review would ensure that the Senate adhered to a minimal set of procedural standards in conducting impeachment trials.

B

The majority also contends that the term "try" does not present a judicially manageable standard. . . . This argument comes in two variants. The first, which asserts that one simply cannot ascertain the sense of "try" which the Framers employed and hence cannot undertake judicial review, is clearly untenable. To begin with, one would intuitively expect that, in defining the power of a political body to conduct an inquiry into official wrongdoing, the Framers used "try" in its legal sense. That intuition is borne out by reflection on the alternatives. The third Clause of Art. I, § 3, cannot seriously be read to mean that the Senate shall "attempt" or "experiment with" impeachments. It is equally implausible to say that the Senate is charged with "investigating" impeachments given that this description would substantially overlap with the House of Representatives' "sole" power to draw up articles of impeachment. Art. I, § 2, cl. 5. . . .

The other variant of the majority position focuses not on which sense of "try" is employed in the Impeachment Trial Clause, but on whether the legal sense of that term creates a judicially manageable standard. . . . [T]he term "try" is hardly so elusive as the majority would have it. Were the Senate, for example, to adopt the practice of automatically entering a judgment of conviction whenever articles of impeachment were delivered from the House, it is quite clear that the Senate will have failed to "try" impeachments. Indeed in this respect, "try" presents no greater, and perhaps fewer, interpretive difficulties than some other constitutional standards that have been found amenable to familiar techniques of judicial construction, including, for example, "Commerce . . . among the several States," Art. I, § 8, cl. 3, and "due process of law," Amdt. 5.

III

The majority's conclusion that "try" is incapable of meaningful judicial construction is not without irony. One might think that if any class of concepts would fall within the definitional abilities of the Judiciary, it would be that class having to do with procedural justice. Examination of the remaining question—whether proceedings in accordance with Senate Rule XI are compatible with the Impeachment Trial Clause—confirms this intuition.

Petitioner bears the rather substantial burden of demonstrating that, simply by employing the word "try," the Constitution prohibits the Senate from relying on a factfinding committee. It is clear that the Framers were familiar with English impeachment practice and with that of the States employing a variant of the English model at the time of the Constitutional Convention. Hence there is little doubt that the term "try" as used in Art. I, § 3, cl. 6, meant that the Senate should conduct its proceedings in a manner somewhat resembling a judicial proceeding. Indeed, it is safe to assume that Senate trials were to follow the practice in England and the States, which contemplated a formal hearing on the charges, at which the accused would be represented by counsel, evidence would be presented, and the accused would have the opportunity to be heard.

Petitioner argues, however, that because committees were not used in state impeachment trials prior to the Convention, the word "try" cannot be interpreted to permit their use. It is, however, a substantial leap to infer from the absence of a particular device of parliamentary procedure that its use has been forever barred by the Constitution. And there is textual and historical evidence that undermines the inference sought to be drawn in this case.

The fact that Art. III, § 2, cl. 3, specifically exempts impeachment trials from the jury requirement provides some evidence that the Framers were anxious not to have additional specific procedural requirements read into the term "try." Contemporaneous commentary further supports this view. Hamilton, for example, stressed that a trial by so large a body as the Senate (which at the time promised to boast 26 members) necessitated that the proceedings not "be tied down to . . . strict rules, either in the delineation of the offence by the prosecutors, or in the construction of it by the Judges. . . ." The Federalist No. 65. . . .

It is also noteworthy that the delegation of factfinding by judicial and quasi-judicial bodies was hardly unknown to the Framers. . . . Federal courts likewise had appointed special masters and other factfinders "from the commencement of our Government." Particularly in light of the Constitution's grant to each House of the power to "determine the Rules of its Proceedings," see Art. I, § 5, cl. 2, the existence of legislative and judicial delegation strongly suggests that the Impeachment Trial Clause was not designed to prevent employment of a factfinding committee.

In short, textual and historical evidence reveals that the Impeachment Trial Clause was not meant to bind the hands of the Senate beyond establishing a set of minimal procedures. Without identifying the exact contours of these procedures, it is sufficient to say that the Senate's use of a fact-finding committee under Rule XI is entirely compatible with the Constitution's command that the Senate "try all impeachments." Petitioner's challenge to his conviction must therefore fail. . . .

■ **JUSTICE SOUTER, concurring in the judgment.**

I agree with the Court that this case presents a nonjusticiable political question. Because my analysis differs somewhat from the Court's, however, I concur in its judgment by this separate opinion.

As we cautioned in *Baker v. Carr,* "the 'political question' label" tends "to obscure the need for case-by-case inquiry." ... Whatever considerations feature most prominently in a particular case, the political question doctrine is "essentially a function of the separation of powers," existing to restrain courts "from inappropriate interference in the business of the other branches of Government," and deriving in large part from prudential concerns about the respect we owe the political departments. . . .

[T]he [Impeachment] Clause contemplates that the Senate may determine, within broad boundaries, such subsidiary issues as the procedures for receipt and consideration of evidence necessary to satisfy its duty to "try" impeachments. Other significant considerations confirm a conclusion that this case presents a nonjusticiable political question: the "unusual need for unquestioning adherence to a political decision already made," as well as "the potentiality of embarrassment from multifarious pronouncements by various departments on one question." As the Court observes, judicial review of an impeachment trial would under the best of circumstances entail significant disruption of government.

One can, nevertheless, envision different and unusual circumstances that might justify a more searching review of impeachment proceedings. If the Senate were to act in a manner seriously threatening the integrity of its results, convicting, say, upon a coin toss, or upon a summary determination that an officer of the United States was simply "a bad guy," judicial interference might well be appropriate. In such circumstances, the Senate's action might be so far beyond the scope of its constitutional authority, and the consequent impact on the Republic so great, as to merit a judicial response despite the prudential concerns that would ordinarily counsel silence. . . .

NOTE ON THE POLITICAL QUESTION DOCTRINE

1.   The various factors surveyed by Justice Brennan in *Baker* may be broken down into three categories:

- **The Textual Criterion:** Whether the issue is committed to another branch of government.

- **Functional Criteria:** Lack of judicially manageable standards; necessity of an initial policy determination. These go to the institutional *capacity* of the courts to decide the case.

- **Prudential Criteria:** Respect for coequal branches; need to adhere to a political decision already made; embarrassment

> from different branches reaching different conclusions. These
> go to the institutional *consequences* of an adjudication.

Which sort of criteria were most important to Justice Brennan? To Justice Frankfurter? Does Justice Souter's concurrence in *Nixon* suggest that the prudential approach still has some weight?

2.   Subsequent cases, such as *Nixon*, have made clear that the two most important of the *Baker* criteria are textual commitment of an issue to another branch of government and the lack of judicially manageable standards. Are these factors entirely independent of one another? What was the relationship between them in *Nixon*?

What does it mean to say that an issue is "textually committed" to another branch of government? Every governmental power conferred by the Constitution is "committed" to a particular branch by the Constitution's text; for example, Article I commits the power to regulate interstate commerce to Congress, while Article II commits the power to "take Care that the Laws be faithfully executed" to the President. Does this mean that whether a federal statute exceeds Congress's Commerce Power is a nonjusticiable political question, or that presidential enforcement of the law is not subject to judicial review? If not, how is the "textual commitment" to the Senate of the power to judge impeachments any different?

The concept of "judicially manageable standards" is equally ambiguous. Indeterminacy is a problem throughout constitutional law; justices have disagreed for centuries about the meaning of the Due Process Clause, for example. How is a court to assess whether some areas raise *unusually* severe problems of indeterminacy? There is also a problem of timing and experience. In *Baker*, the Court had to decide whether to venture into the "political thicket" of redistricting controversies. Because it had to make that decision at the outset, rather than after a series of decisions in the area, how could it know whether it would prove capable of developing "manageable standards"? As it happened, the Court developed a "one-man, one-vote" standard[45] that proved reasonably easy to apply. But was it obvious at the time the Court had to address the political question issue in *Baker* that this would prove to be the case?

More recently, the Court has been asked to impose a constitutional limit on the power of state legislatures to "gerrymander" congressional districts on the basis of party affiliation rather than race. Although established law requires these districts to be equal in population, sophisticated analysis of demographics and voting patterns permits drawing the lines in such a way as to virtually ensure that one party or the other will prevail within that district. Many have decried this practice as promoting political polarization (by drawing lopsided districts that send highly-partisan representatives to Congress, even where the state electorate is relatively balanced overall), but it is hard to derive any specific limits from the Constitution. Hence, in *Vieth v. Jubelirer*, 541 U.S. 267 (2004), a plurality of the Court held that political gerrymandering claims are nonjusticiable for lack of judicially manageable

---

[45]   *See Reynolds v. Sims*, 377 U.S. 533 (1964).

standards. Justice Kennedy concurred in the judgment, agreeing that the present case was nonjusticiable but holding out hope that the Court might discover workable standards in future cases. Despite this invitation to keep trying, such a standard continues to elude the Court.[46] If the Court can identify no workable standards, should it simply declare this category of cases nonjusticiable?[47]

3.   Is the political question doctrine consistent with *Marbury's* statement of the Court's authority and obligation to "say what the law is"? One way out of the dilemma would be to distinguish between a "strong" and a "weak" form of the doctrine:

- **Strong:** Even though there might be a constitutional violation, the Court is powerless to do anything about it because the question is committed to another branch.

- **Weak:** "Political question" is simply a way of explaining why there is no substantive violation, i.e., that the other branch has broad discretion to act in a particular area under the Constitution.

Consider, for example, a challenge to the President's decision to recognize the People's Republic of China, rather than Taiwan, as the legitimate government of China, pursuant to his Article II power to receive ambassadors. A court would likely dismiss such a suit as a political question. Which version of the doctrine, strong or weak, would best explain such a result?

The weak version raises no problem under *Marbury*, does it? Did the Court in *Nixon* apply a strong or a weak version of the doctrine?

4.   In a famous article,[48] Louis Henkin questioned whether there really is a "political question" doctrine at all. Professor Henkin argued that the Court's cases applications of the doctrine all reflected one of three situations:

- a)   The challenged governmental action was one committed by the Constitution to the discretion of a particular actor, such as the President's discretion whether to recognize a particular foreign government.

- b)   The act challenged was not entirely discretionary, but the Constitution imposes relatively few restrictions on it and those were not violated, such as the minimal requirements for "trial" under the Impeachment Clause.

- c)   The challenged act is subject to judicial review, but the plaintiffs have asked for an injunction and the case does not satisfy the traditional standards for equitable relief. These standards give the courts broad discretion to deny injunctive

---

[46]   *See League of United Latin American Citizens v. Perry*, 548 U.S. 399, 413–23 (2006) (rejecting various standards proposed to support a political gerrymandering claim).

[47]   On the general question of manageable standards, see Richard H. Fallon, Jr., *Judicially Manageable Standards and Constitutional Meaning*, 119 HARV. L. REV. 1274 (2006).

[48]   Louis Henkin, *Is There a "Political Question" Doctrine?* 85 YALE L.J. 597 (1976).

> relief where there is no workable way to fashion a remedy, for example, or where there is no pressing need for equitable relief.

Courts need invoke no special exception to judicial review in order to refrain from deciding cases in any of these situations. The first two entail decisions on the merits—there is simply no constitutional violation. And the third is a decision about remedies, not justiciability. What do you think of Henkin's argument? Does it fit *Nixon*? Is he simply arguing for a weak form of the political question doctrine? If Henkin is persuasive, why do the courts persist in speaking of a distinctive political question doctrine?

5. The Court recently revisited the political question doctrine in *Zivotofsky v. Clinton*, 566 U.S. 189 (2012), which addressed a statute that directed the State Department to allow Americans born in Jerusalem to list "Israel" as the country of birth on their passports. When the parents of a boy born in Jerusalem sought just that, the State Department refused, citing its policy against taking a position on Jerusalem's political status. The Zivotoskys sought a judicial ruling that the State Department must comply with the statute, but the district court characterized the suit as asking the courts "to decide the political status of Jerusalem." Both that court and the D.C. Circuit held that this was a political question upon which the courts could not intrude.

The Supreme Court reversed, rejecting this way of characterizing the case. Chief Justice Roberts wrote for the majority that "[t]he federal courts are not being asked to supplant a foreign policy decision of the political branches with the courts' own unmoored determination of what United States policy toward Jerusalem should be." Rather, "Zivotofsky requests that the courts enforce a specific statutory right. To resolve his claim, the Judiciary must decide if Zivotofsky's interpretation of the statute is correct, and whether the statute is constitutional. This is a familiar judicial exercise." Whether or the Constitution commits the power to recognize foreign claims to territory to the President, the Court reasoned, "there is, of course, no exclusive commitment to the Executive of the power to determine the constitutionality of a statute." The Court was thus responsible for resolving the boundary dispute between Congress's power and the President in this case. With respect to the existence of "judicially discoverable and manageable standards," the Court observed that the case was indistinguishable from other separation of powers disputes in which the courts must consult text, history, and precedent to resolve a matter of constitutional interpretation. "This," the Court concluded, "is what courts do."[49]

---

[49] The Court remanded the case to the D.C. Circuit to decide the constitutional issue on its merits. That court ruled against the Zivotofskys, holding that the passport statute intruded on the President's exclusive authority to recognize foreign governments' claims to territory. The Supreme Court affirmed that judgment in *Zivotofsky v. Kerry*, 135 S. Ct. 2076 (2015). We will turn to that opinion in Chapter Fourteen.

Does *Zivotofsky* suggest that the political question doctrine will never apply where the constitutionality of a statute is at issue? Would such a rule make sense?

6.   Has the Court given up too easily on any sort of prudential approach to the political question doctrine? Consider *Bush v. Gore*, 531 U.S. 98 (2000), in which the Court determined that the State of Florida was conducting its recount of ballots cast in the 2000 presidential election in a manner that violated the Equal Protection Clause. This ruling, in conjunction with the Court's order to stop the recount and accept the Florida Secretary of State's initial certification of George W. Bush as the winner of Florida's electoral votes, effectively decided the deadlocked election in Bush's favor. Some commentators have suggested that the Court should have avoided deciding the case by invoking the political question doctrine, although none of the dissenters made that claim. The most obvious argument for ruling the case nonjusticiable is that intervention in the election made the justices look political and hurt the credibility of the Court. Therefore, the argument goes, the Court should have protected its reputation by staying out.[50] Could such a ruling have been squared with *Baker*? If not, does that suggest that current doctrine should leave more leeway for the Court to avoid deciding particular disputes on prudential grounds?

On the other hand, if we took the prudential approach seriously, would the Court have decided the constitutionality of segregated schooling in *Brown v. Board of Education*? Would it have considered the issue of abortion in *Roe v. Wade*? Could a prudential-minded Court have possibly intervened in the national controversy over same-sex marriage in *Obergefell v. Hodges*? Which way do these examples cut?

7.   One reason that the contemporary Court decides so few political question doctrine cases is that, over the course of the Twentieth Century, Congress has gradually but steadily increased the Court's control over its own docket. That docket became almost entirely discretionary after 1988. The result is that, rather than having to hold an issue "nonjusticiable" under the political question doctrine in order to avoid deciding it, the Court can simply deny *certiorari*—a decision which ordinarily carries no expectation of an explanation. Perhaps for this reason, Justice Breyer's dissent in *Bush v. Gore* begins not with the political question doctrine but by asserting that "[t]he Court was wrong to take this case." Should it have simply denied *certiorari* and allowed the Florida Supreme Court's decision to stand?[51] More generally, does the option of simply denying *certiorari* mean that the Court no longer needs to designate disputes as "political questions" in order to

---

[50] For a bipartisan (and only a little schizophrenic) commentary rejecting the political question argument in *Bush v. Gore*, see Sanford Levinson & Ernest A. Young, *Who's Afraid of the Twelfth Amendment?* 29 FLA. ST. U. L. REV. 925 (2001).

[51] Note, however, that Justice Breyer's dissent also suggests that the Florida authorities may have been conducting the recount in a way that violated the Equal Protection Clause. Is it plausible to suggest (a) that the President may be being chosen in an unconstitutional fashion, but (b) that the Court has no business intervening?

avoid them on prudential grounds? Should it use that option more frequently than it does?[52]

NOTE ON OTHER LIMITS ON JUDICIAL REVIEW

1.   Several other important limits on the power of judicial review can receive only scant mention here; they are developed more fully in the upper level Federal Courts course. Another textual limit is in Art. III, § 2, which extends the Supreme Court's appellate jurisdiction over a wide variety of cases but "with such Exceptions, and under such Regulations as the Congress shall make." Similarly, because the Constitution leaves the question whether to establish lower federal courts (i.e., the federal circuit and district courts in our modern scheme) to Congress, the jurisdiction of those courts is likewise subject to Congress's Art. I, § 8 power "to constitute Tribunals inferior to the supreme Court."[53] Congress may thus prevent both the Supreme Court and the lower federal courts from exercising the power of judicial review in particular areas by narrowing the scope of federal jurisdiction. After the Civil War, Congress restricted the Supreme Court's appellate jurisdiction in order to preclude the Court from hearing constitutional challenges to Reconstruction, and the Court upheld that action in *Ex parte McCardle*, 74 U.S. 506 (1868). More recently, the Detainee Treatment Act of 2005 and the Military Commissions Act of 2006 limited the jurisdiction of federal courts, including the Supreme Court, to review certain cases involving suspected terrorists. Congress's power to limit federal jurisdiction is subject to certain limits,[54] but there is much disagreement among jurists and legal scholars about where those limits lie.

2.   Another limit comes from the persistent distinction between rights and remedies. Although Chief Justice Marshall's opinion in *Marbury* quoted William Blackstone to the effect that "where there is a legal right, there is also a legal remedy by suit or action at law, whenever that right is invaded," this maxim often falls down in practice. Although the Court has the power to decide that another governmental actor has violated the Constitution, it may struggle for legal instruments to force that actor to comply with its rulings. After the Court held racially-segregated public schools unconstitutional in *Brown v. Board of Education*, for example, it spent decades trying to come up with the proper legal remedies to actually bring black and white children together in the same schools. (We will return to this issue in Chapter Six.) To what extent are concerns about judicial remedies related to the finding of a political question in *Nixon*? If the Court had

---

[52] A key aspect of the *certiorari* power, however, is that this sort of discretion only belongs to the Supreme Court; lower courts must still decide the cases. The political question doctrine, by contrast, bars *any* federal court from considering the matter (and in some cases, it may bar *all* courts, state or federal).

[53] *See, e.g., Sheldon v. Sill*, 49 U.S. (8 How.) 441 (1850) (upholding a statutory restriction on the diversity jurisdiction on this ground).

[54] *See, e.g., Boumediene v. Bush*, 553 U.S. 723 (2008), in which the Supreme Court held that the Military Commissions Act's restriction on *habeas corpus* challenges brought by detainees at Guantanamo Bay, Cuba was unconstitutional under the Suspension Clause, Art. I, § 9, cl. 2.

accepted Judge Nixon's claim that his impeachment proceedings violated the Constitution, could it have forced the Senate to comply with its ruling?

3.   Although the political branches of the government cannot override Supreme Court interpretations of the Constitution through ordinary legislative processes, the Constitution can itself be amended. Four successful amendments to the U.S. Constitution were designed to overturn particular Supreme Court decisions: The Eleventh Amendment overturned *Chisholm v. Georgia*, 2 U.S. (2 Dall.) 419 (1793), by limiting the jurisdiction of the federal courts to hear damages suits by individual plaintiffs brought against state governments; the Fourteenth Amendment overruled *Dred Scott v. Sandford*, 60 U.S. 393 (1857), by rendering African Americans eligible to be U.S. citizens; the Sixteenth Amendment overruled *Pollock v. Farmers' Loan & Trust*, 157 U.S. 429 (1895), by permitting the federal income tax; and the Twenty-Sixth Amendment overruled *Oregon v. Mitchell*, 400 U.S. 112 (1970), by lowering the voting age to eighteen. Many other amendments have been proposed to overrule decisions such as *Roe v. Wade*, 410 U.S. 113 (1973) (recognizing a federal constitutional right to abortion), and the Court's several decisions banning prayer in public schools, *see, e.g., Engel v. Vitale*, 370 U.S. 421 (1962). How realistic a check on the Court is the threat of constitutional amendment? "As a practical matter," Sanford Levinson points out, "Article V makes it next to impossible to amend the Constitution with regard to genuinely controversial issues, even if substantial—and intense—majorities advocate amendment."[55] Should such amendments be easier than they are?

4.   Finally, those who are unhappy with the Supreme Court's exercise of judicial review on a given matter may seek to change the justices themselves. Finley Peter Dunne's famous character Mr. Dooley proclaimed, around the turn of the twentieth century, that "[no] matter whether th' constitution follows th' flag or not, th' supreme court follows th' ilection returns."[56] There are very few historical examples of the Supreme Court running against the strong course of popular opinion and government policy for an extended period of time, and this is in part because the ordinary turnover at the Court ensures that the elected branches of the government can select new justices more in tune with prevailing views. On the other hand, the extent to which either Presidents or Senators should impose "litmus tests" concerning prospective nominees' views on particular constitutional issues remains deeply controversial. Is it appropriate for the President and Senate to consider whether a potential Supreme Court nominee has views that reflect the prevailing current of public opinion?

See also: The literature on Congress's power to restrict federal court jurisdiction is voluminous and complex. A good place to start is RICHARD H. FALLON, JR., JOHN F. MANNING, DANIEL J. MELTZER, & DAVID L. SHAPIRO, HART AND WECHSLER'S THE FEDERAL COURTS AND THE FEDERAL SYSTEM ch. 4 (7th ed. 2015); for a shorter introduction, try Gerald Gunther,

---

[55] SANFORD LEVINSON, OUR UNDEMOCRATIC CONSTITUTION: WHERE THE CONSTITUTION GOES WRONG (AND HOW WE THE PEOPLE CAN CORRECT IT) 21 (2006).

[56] Finley Peter Dunne, *The Supreme Court's Decisions*, in MR. DOOLEY'S OPINIONS 26 (1900).

Congressional Power to Curtail Federal Court Jurisdiction: An Opinionated Guide to the Ongoing Debate, 36 STAN. L. REV. 895 (1984). The essays collected in SANFORD LEVINSON, ED., RESPONDING TO IMPERFECTION: THE THEORY AND PRACTICE OF CONSTITUTIONAL AMENDMENT (1995) provide a thoughtful introduction to constitutional amendment. And on the general relationship between popular opinion and the Supreme Court, see BARRY FRIEDMAN, THE WILL OF THE PEOPLE: HOW PUBLIC OPINION HAS INFLUENCED THE SUPREME COURT AND SHAPED THE MEANING OF THE CONSTITUTION (2009).

PART TWO

A History of Judicial Review

The first half of this course is devoted to the role of the Supreme Court (and to a lesser extent, the lower federal courts) in developing and enforcing constitutional principles. The arrangement of the materials is primarily chronological, beginning with the Marshall Court's decisions on federalism in the early 19th century and ending with the Burger and Rehnquist Court's cases on the unenumerated right to privacy at the end of the 20th century. The reason for this arrangement is that developments in one doctrinal area tend to influence developments in other doctrinal areas, both contemporaneously and down the line. One cannot understand the Court's decisions limiting national attempts to regulate the economy in the early 20th century under the Commerce Clause, for example, without knowing the cases decided at the same time limiting the *states'* regulatory powers under the Due Process Clause. Likewise, it is hard to understand the misgivings felt by many Rehnquist Court justices about aggressive judicial review in the areas of fundamental rights and federalism without knowing how overly-aggressive judicial review got the Court in trouble much earlier in the *Dred Scott* case and *Lochner v. New York*.

This chronological survey also serves a second purpose, which is to introduce a variety of doctrinal areas that might not otherwise be included in a first-year course that is oriented primarily toward issues of constitutional structure. *Brown v. Board of Education*, *Mapp v. Ohio*, and *Roe v. Wade* are included here for the light they shed on the development of the institution of judicial review, even though many first-year courses cannot undertake an in-depth study of racial equality, criminal procedure, or privacy. Some exposure to these landmarks, however, is important both as a matter of constitutional literacy and as an aid in charting one's course through the many different upper-level electives in the general field of constitutional law. For instructors wishing to focus on these areas, Part IV explores the contemporary doctrine in some depth.

Our central focus in the present Part, however, is on the institutional story of how Alexander Hamilton's "least dangerous branch" developed into the most powerful judicial tribunal in the world—one that can not only criticize presidents (*Marbury v. Madison*) but also make (*Bush v. Gore*) or break them (*United States v. Nixon*). This story has both a macro component, concerning the general relation between the Supreme Court and the other institutions of government, and a micro component, as the

Court experiments with different sorts of interpretive and doctrinal approaches to constitutional meaning.

Robert McCloskey's influential work on the history of the Supreme Court identifies three distinct ages of court history: "1789 to the close of the Civil War; 1865 to the 'Court revolution' of 1937; and 1937 to the present."[1] Professor McCloskey wrote in 1960, and it may be possible to distinguish a fourth era beginning in the last decade of the 20th century and continuing to the present, but McCloskey's framework is a helpful first cut at organizing the material. In the first era, from ratification of the Constitution to Appomattox, the Court's primary concern was with developing the authority of the national government and limiting the authority of the States. *McCulloch v. Maryland*, which recognized both a broad scope for Congress's legislative powers and the limitations that those powers imposed on state governments, might be taken as the paradigm case for this period.

The second period, encompassing the late 19th and early 20th century, saw the Court's focus shift to the scope and limits of governmental power to regulate the economy. The central case of this era is *Lochner v. New York*, in which the Court struck down a New York maximum hours law for bakers as an impermissible interference with the bakers' "freedom of contract"—a right that the Court grounded in the Due Process Clause of the Fourteenth Amendment. The Court also limited the national government's powers of economic regulation, both under the Fifth Amendment's Due Process Clause and by enforcing the limits of Congress's authority under the Commerce Clause. This era culminated in the Court's challenge to President Franklin Roosevelt's New Deal legislation, in response to which Roosevelt threatened to "pack" the Court with new and sympathetic justices. The Court backed down in 1937 by upholding key New Deal legislation, and it has not seriously interfered with government regulation of the economy since.

The third era, beginning after the New Deal crisis, brought a new focus on non-economic individual liberties. Particularly under the leadership of Chief Justice Earl Warren in the 1950s and 1960s, the Court dramatically expanded individual rights in areas such as criminal procedure, freedom of speech, and privacy. The paramount case of this period is *Brown v. Board of Education*, which ordered the desegregation of Southern schools and, in the process, brought the Court into bitter conflict with broad segments of society. Because these expansions of individual rights were aimed primarily at actions by *state* governments, and because the post-New Deal Court stopped enforcing limits on national action under the doctrine of enumerated powers, this era returned to the Marshall Court theme of limiting state autonomy. The most controversial issues, however, had to do with the Court's efforts to

---

[1]   Robert G. McCloskey, The American Supreme Court 15 (Sanford Levinson ed., 2005). Professor McCloskey's volume makes an outstanding companion to this section of the course.

achieve racial equality and, somewhat later, to develop a jurisprudence of unenumerated fundamental rights—e.g., the rights of privacy and abortion.

The issue of race cuts across all three of these eras, but it has manifested in ways that reflect the central preoccupations of each period. In the antebellum era, pro-slavery forces sought to wrap slavery in the mantle of "states' rights"; paradoxically, the decisions in *Prigg v. Pennsylvania* and *Dred Scott v. Sandford* would promote slavery by rejecting the authority of individual states to shield runaway slaves and define citizenship in their own terms. Race declined in salience at the Court between Reconstruction and the New Deal, but *Plessy v. Ferguson*'s doctrine of "separate but equal," which presumed that government could not and should not seek to remedy basic social inequalities, was consistent with the Court's approach to economic regulation. Finally, after the New Deal, race would be integral not simply to *Brown* but also to a host of free speech, criminal procedure, and voting cases. Many of the Warren Court's seminal speech cases, for example, involved protests that were part of the Civil Rights Movement, and many of that Court's criminal procedure reforms were directed at racially discriminatory justice systems in the Southern states.

Beginning with the consolidation of the Rehnquist Court's conservative majority in the early 1990s, the Court's focus shifted once again from issues of individual rights to those of constitutional structure. While the Court was largely unwilling to overrule its prior expansions of individual rights, such as the controversial right to an abortion recognized in *Roe v. Wade*, the Court likewise signaled—at least initially—that it was uninterested in dramatically expanding those rulings. On the structure side, a series of important but highly limited rulings revived some judicial enforcement of constitutional limits on national power; more recently, the War on Terror has forced the Court to confront the scope and limits of executive authority. We will consider these issues of federalism and separation of powers in depth in the third part of the course.

CHAPTER THREE

THE MARSHALL COURT AND THE FEDERAL BALANCE

John Marshall was not the first Chief Justice of the United States, but for all practical purposes the history of judicial review begins with the Marshall Court, over which he presided from 1801 to 1835. We have already considered Chief Justice Marshall's assertion of the power of judicial review in *Marbury v. Madison*. In this chapter, we focus on the Marshall Court's seminal treatment of the federal balance between national and state authority.

The most radical innovation in the new Constitution was its division of sovereignty between the Nation and the States. American federalism had little precedent in English law, which vested unitary sovereignty in Parliament, and political theorists had insisted for centuries that sovereign governmental power could not be coherently divided between different actors. Unsurprisingly, given the novelty of the American arrangement, the primary preoccupation of the Supreme Court in the years between the Founding and the Civil War concerned the proper allocation of authority between the national and state governments. The third part of this course will focus on federalism as a critical area of current constitutional doctrine; for present purposes, the emphasis is on the Marshall Court's federalism cases as part of the Supreme Court's own institutional development.

Much of the discussion of federalism in the early Republic is framed in terms of the ways in which the new Constitution altered the preexisting arrangement under the Articles of Confederation—the *first* "constitution" of the United States written after independence. The Articles created a very weak central authority with no centralized President or administrative apparatus; no power to raise its own revenues through taxation; no power to act directly on private actors, so that the national government depended on the States to enforce national laws; and quite limited enumerated powers. The Articles also established a clear principle of construction: "Each state retains its sovereignty, freedom, and independence, and every power, jurisdiction, and right, which is not by this Confederation expressly delegated to the United States, in Congress assembled." [1] All of the Framers of the new Constitution—including many Antifederalists—agreed that the Confederation was too decentralized, and that any new central government had to be much stronger and more independent of the States.

---

[1] Articles of Confederation, Art. II (1781). The full text of the Articles is available at http://www.usconstitution.net/articles.html.

But they disagreed about *how much* stronger and independent the new central government should be.

It is important to remember that the national and state governments did not start from a position of parity. The States had been fully sovereign under the Articles of Confederation, and they had experience as robust and, in many ways, autonomous governments as English colonies for decades before that. Many Americans had developed strong attachments to these state governments; the idea of Union, on the other hand, remained largely an abstraction to most people. The national government established by the new Constitution thus had to carve out its own authority and its claim on the citizenry in an environment of competition with state governments that enjoyed several decades' head start. In these circumstances, Chief Justice Marshall viewed the Court as an important force for both establishing the power of the national government and checking centrifugal impulses in the States; his court was plainly a *nationalizing* court.

McCulloch v. Maryland represents both parts of this task: By holding that Congress had implicit authority to establish the Bank of the United States, Chief Justice Marshall established that the powers of Congress would be interpreted generously. And by invalidating Maryland's attempt to tax the Bank, Marshall issued a sharp rebuke to state governmental efforts to interfere with national authority. *Gibbons v. Ogden* took this latter imperative of limiting state governmental action one step further by limiting state laws that less directly impinged on federal prerogatives. The final case in this chapter, *Willson v. Black Bird Creek Marsh Co.*, shows the limits of the Court's willingness to limit state action in the absence of activity by Congress.

INTRODUCTORY NOTE ON THE BANK OF THE UNITED STATES

The Bank of the United States, challenged in *McCulloch*, was one of the most controversial institutions of the early Republic. The Continental Congress had chartered a "Bank of North America" in 1781—despite an apparent lack of authority to do so under the Articles of Confederation—in order to help finance the Revolutionary War. In 1790, after the Constitution had been ratified, Secretary of the Treasury Alexander Hamilton submitted a plan for a new "Bank of the United States." Hamilton hoped that the Bank would strengthen the national government by issuing bank notes that could serve in the absence of a national paper currency, aiding in the collection of taxes and administration of public finances, and providing loans to the national government.

Both Houses of Congress adopted Hamilton's proposal, despite strong opposition from James Madison in the House of Representatives, who denounced the Bank as outside Congress's constitutional authority. Madison warned that "the essential characteristic of the government, as composed of limited and enumerated powers, would be destroyed: If instead of direct and incidental means, any means could be used, which . . . 'might be conceived to be conducive to the successful conducting of the finances.' " [2] President Washington was sufficiently concerned that he requested opinions on the constitutional issue from Hamilton, Attorney General Edmund Randolph, and Secretary of State Thomas Jefferson. These opinions—offered almost three decades before John Marshall's opinion in *McCulloch*—represent an important early example of constitutional interpretation outside the courts.

As Daniel Farber has observed, "Jefferson's vision of the American future was agrarian, and he was suspicious of manufacturing, commerce, and finance. Like most Southern planters, he was deeply hostile to banks."[3] Jefferson's opinion thus attacked the constitutionality of the bank proposal on the ground that it could not fit within any of the enumerated powers of Congress. "To take a single step beyond the boundaries thus specially drawn around the powers of Congress," he cautioned, "is to take possession of a boundless field of power, no longer susceptible of any definition."[4] Jefferson also specifically rejected the argument, grounded in the Necessary and Proper Clause, that John Marshall would later find persuasive in *McCulloch*; "the constitution," he concluded, "allows only the means which are 'necessary' not those which are merely 'convenient' for effecting the enumerated powers."[5] Attorney General Randolph likewise concluded that the Bank was unconstitutional.[6]

Hamilton, of course, defended the Bank as within Congress's implied powers. In his view, each of the enumerated powers necessarily included "a right to employ all the *means* requisite, and fairly *applicable* to the attainment of the *ends* of such power; and which are not precluded by restrictions & exceptions specified in the constitution; or not immoral, or not contrary to the essential ends of political society."[7] It was critical, moreover, to construe the enumerated powers themselves liberally, because the "means by which national exigencies are to be provided for, national inconveniencies obviated, national prosperity promoted, are of such infinite variety, extent and complexity, that there must, or necessity, be great latitude of discretion in the selection & application of those means."[8] Turning to the bank itself, Hamilton argued that it would facilitate payment of taxes by increasing the circulation of money, provide a source of emergency loans in wartime and other emergencies, and promote interstate commerce by supplying a medium

---

[2] James Madison, *Opinion on the Constitutionality of the Bill to Establish a National Bank* (Feb. 2, 1791), *in* CONTEXTS OF THE CONSTITUTION: A DOCUMENTARY COLLECTION ON PRINCIPLES OF AMERICAN CONSTITUTIONAL LAW 527, 531 (Neil H. Cogan ed., 1999) (quoting the preamble to the bank bill).

[3] Daniel A. Farber, *The Story of* McCulloch: *Banking on National Power*, *in* CONSTITUTIONAL LAW STORIES 33, 39 (MICHAEL C. DORF ed. 2d ed. 2009).

[4] Thomas Jefferson, *Opinion on the Constitutionality of the Bill to Establish a National Bank* (Feb. 15, 1791), *in* CONTEXTS OF THE CONSTITUTION, *supra* note 2, at 540, 541.

[5] *Id.* at 542.

[6] For Randolph's opinion, see Walter Dellinger & H. Jefferson Powell, *The Constitutionality of the Bank Bill: The Attorney General's First Constitutional Law Opinions*, 44 DUKE L.J. 110, 122–30 (1994).

[7] Alexander Hamilton, *Opinion on the Constitutionality of the Bill to Establish a National Bank* (Feb. 23, 1791), *in* CONTEXTS OF THE CONSTITUTION, *supra* note 2, at 544, 545.

[8] *Id.* at 549.

for trade.[9] President Washington sided with Hamilton, signing the act incorporating the Bank of the United States on February 25, 1791.

By the time the Bank's 20-year charter expired in 1811, congressional opposition from agrarians (opposed to the Bank's centralizing and commercializing tendencies) and the private banking community (opposed to competition from a quasi-public institution) was able to prevent renewal. It proved hard to do without the Bank over the ensuing four years, however, and Congress voted to establish a second Bank of the United States in 1815. President James Madison vetoed the renewal bill on policy grounds, but he explicitly put aside his former constitutional objections on the ground that "a concurrence of the general will of the nation" had accepted the Bank's constitutionality. By 1816, Madison had resolved his policy doubts as well, and he signed a renewal bill.

The Second Bank of the United States was a quasi-public entity: The U.S. government provided $7 million of the Bank's $35 million in capital (Hamilton's Bank had had a total capitalization of only $10 million) and the President appointed 5 of the Bank's 25 directors. The Bank served as the Government's primary fiscal agent: All public funds were deposited with the Bank by the Secretary of the Treasury, the Bank marketed the Treasury's securities to buyers all over the world, it handled virtually all foreign exchange transactions, and the Bank's notes were made legal tender for the payment of government debts. The Bank also policed the state-chartered banking system by serving as a creditor of state banks throughout the nation. The Bank would enjoy a love-hate relationship with the Federal Government, however, especially after Andrew Jackson became president in 1828.

McCulloch was decided against the backdrop of the Panic of 1819, which began with the bursting of a speculative bubble in cotton. Both foreign and domestic banks—including the Bank of the United States—responded by dramatically tightening credit, and this contraction rippled in turn through the state banking system. Investor confidence and land values plummeted, and demand for goods and services shriveled correspondingly. As one historian has pointed out, "[t]his was the first time that the American public had experienced collectively what would become a recurrent phenomenon, a sharp downward swing of the business cycle. Because it was the first time, people had no perspective from which to judge the events."[10] Many blamed the Bank—not entirely without reason, as the Bank's lax lending policies during the boom years and abrupt contraction of credit once the panic began had "certainly made matters worse than necessary."[11] The punitive state tax policies at issue in *McCulloch* were thus not simply a manifestation of anti-national sentiment, but also of more general resentment against the Bank's policies (as well, in Maryland, as a reaction against a massive embezzlement scandal involving McCulloch himself).

---

[9] *See* Farber, *supra* note 3, at 42 (summarizing Hamilton's arguments).

[10] DANIEL WALKER HOWE, WHAT HATH GOD WROUGHT: THE TRANSFORMATION OF AMERICA, 1815–1848, at 143 (2007).

[11] *Id.* at 144.

McCulloch v. Maryland

17 U.S. (4 Wheat.) 316 (1819)

ERROR to the Court of Appeals of the State of Maryland.

This was an action of debt brought by . . . the State of Maryland, in the County Court of Baltimore County, . . . against . . . McCulloch, to recover certain penalties under the act of the legislature of Maryland, hereafter mentioned. . . .

[T]here was passed on the 10th day of April, 1816, by the Congress of the United States, an act, entitled, "an act to incorporate the subscribers to the Bank of the United States;" and that there was passed, on the 11th day of February, 1818, by the General Assembly of Maryland, an act, entitled, "an act to impose a tax on all Banks, or branches thereof, in the State of Maryland, *not chartered by the legislature*[.]" . . . It is further admitted, that the President, Directors and Company of the Bank of the United States, incorporated by the act of Congress aforesaid, did organize themselves, and go into full operation in the City of Philadelphia, in the State of Pennsylvania, in pursuance of the said act, and that they did . . . establish a branch of the said Bank . . . in the city of Baltimore, in the state of Maryland, which has . . . ever since transacted and carried on business as a Bank . . . by issuing Bank notes and discounting promissory notes, and performing other operations usual and customary for Banks to do and perform. . . . It is further admitted, that the said President, Directors and Company of the said Bank, had no authority to establish the said branch . . . at the city of Baltimore, from the State of Maryland, otherwise than the said State having adopted the Constitution of the United States and composing one of the States of the Union. It is further admitted, that James William McCulloch, the defendant below, being the cashier of the said branch of office of discount and deposit, did . . . issue the said respective Bank notes . . . to a certain George Williams, in the city of Baltimore, in part payment of a promissory note of the said Williams, . . . which said respective Bank notes were not . . . so issued on stamped paper in the manner prescribed by the act of Assembly aforesaid. It is further admitted, that the said President, Directors and Company of the Bank of the United States, and the said branch . . . have not, nor has either of them, paid in advance, or otherwise, the sum of fifteen thousand dollars, to the Treasurer of the Western shore, for the use of the State of Maryland, before the issuing of the said notes. . . .

The question submitted to the Court for their decision in this case, is as to the validity of the said act of the General Assembly of Maryland, on the ground of its being repugnant to the constitution of the United States, and the act of Congress aforesaid, or to one of them. . . .

■ MR. CHIEF JUSTICE MARSHALL delivered the opinion of the Court.

In the case now to be determined, the defendant, a sovereign State, denies the obligation of a law enacted by the legislature of the Union, and the plaintiff, on his part, contests the validity of an act which has been passed by the legislature of that State. The constitution of our country, in its most interesting and vital parts, is to be considered; the conflicting powers of the government of the Union and of its members, as marked in that constitution, are to be discussed; and an opinion given, which may essentially influence the great operations of the government. No tribunal can approach such a question without a deep sense of its importance, and of the awful responsibility involved in its decision. But it must be decided peacefully, or remain a source of hostile legislation, perhaps of hostility of a still more serious nature; and if it is to be so decided, by this tribunal alone can the decision be made. On the Supreme Court of the United States has the constitution of our country devolved this important duty.

The first question made in the cause is, has Congress power to incorporate a bank?

It has been truly said, that this can scarcely be considered as an open question, entirely unprejudiced by the former proceedings of the nation respecting it. The principle now contested was introduced at a very early period of our history, has been recognised by many successive legislatures, and has been acted upon by the judicial department, in cases of peculiar delicacy, as a law of undoubted obligation.

It will not be denied, that a bold and daring usurpation might be resisted, after an acquiescence still longer and more complete than this. But it is conceived that a doubtful question, one on which human reason may pause . . . in the decision of which the great principles of liberty are not concerned, but the respective powers of those who are equally the representatives of the people, are to be adjusted; if not put at rest by the practice of the government, ought to receive a considerable impression from that practice. . . .

The power now contested was exercised by the first Congress elected under the present constitution. The bill for incorporating the bank of the United States did not steal upon an unsuspecting legislature, and pass unobserved. Its principle was completely understood, and was opposed with equal zeal and ability. After being resisted, first in the fair and open field of debate, and afterwards in the executive cabinet, with as much persevering talent as any measure has ever experienced, and being supported by arguments which convinced minds as pure and as intelligent as this country can boast, it became a law. The original act was permitted to expire; but a short experience of the embarrassments to which the refusal to revive it exposed the government, convinced those who were most prejudiced against the measure of its necessity, and induced the passage of the present law. It would require no ordinary share of intrepidity to assert that a measure adopted under these circumstances was a bold and plain usurpation, to which the constitution gave no countenance.

These observations . . . are not made under the impression that, were the question entirely new, the law would be found irreconcilable with the constitution.

In discussing this question, the counsel for the State of Maryland have deemed it of some importance, in the construction of the constitution, to consider that instrument not as emanating from the people, but as the act of sovereign and independent States. The powers of the general government, it has been said, are delegated by the States, who alone are truly sovereign; and must be exercised in subordination to the States, who alone possess supreme dominion.

It would be difficult to sustain this proposition. The Convention which framed the constitution was indeed elected by the State legislatures. But the instrument, when it came from their hands, was a mere proposal, without obligation, or pretensions to it. It was reported to the then existing Congress of the United States, with a request that it might "be submitted to a Convention of Delegates, chosen in each State by the people thereof, under the recommendation of its Legislature, for their assent and ratification." This mode of proceeding was adopted; and by the Convention, by Congress, and by the State Legislatures, the instrument was submitted to the people. They acted upon it in the only manner in which they can act safely, effectively, and wisely, on such a subject, by assembling in Convention. It is true, they assembled in their several States—and where else should they have assembled? No political dreamer was ever wild enough to think of breaking down the lines which separate the States, and of compounding the American people into one common mass. Of consequence, when they act, they act in their States. But the measures they adopt do not, on that account, cease to be the measures of the people themselves, or become the measures of the State governments.

From these Conventions the constitution derives its whole authority. The government proceeds directly from the people; is "ordained and established" in the name of the people; and is declared to be ordained, "in order to form a more perfect union, establish justice, ensure domestic tranquility, and secure the blessings of liberty to themselves and to their posterity." The assent of the States, in their sovereign capacity, is implied in calling a Convention, and thus submitting that instrument to the people. But the people were at perfect liberty to accept or reject it; and their act was final. It required not the affirmance, and could not be negatived, by the State governments. The constitution, when thus adopted, was of complete obligation, and bound the State sovereignties.

It has been said, that the people had already surrendered all their powers to the State sovereignties, and had nothing more to give. But, surely, the question whether they may resume and modify the powers granted to government does not remain to be settled in this country.

Much more might the legitimacy of the general government be doubted, had it been created by the States. The powers delegated to the State sovereignties were to be exercised by themselves, not by a distinct and independent sovereignty, created by themselves. To the formation of a league, such as was the confederation, the State sovereignties were certainly competent. But when, "in order to form a more perfect union," it was deemed necessary to change this alliance into an effective government, possessing great and sovereign powers, and acting directly on the people, the necessity of referring it to the people, and of deriving its powers directly from them, was felt and acknowledged by all.

The government of the Union, then, (whatever may be the influence of this fact on the case,) is, emphatically, and truly, a government of the people. In form and in substance it emanates from them. Its powers are granted by them, and are to be exercised directly on them, and for their benefit.

This government is acknowledged by all to be one of enumerated powers. The principle, that it can exercise only the powers granted to it, would seem too apparent to have required to be enforced by all those arguments which its enlightened friends, while it was depending before the people, found it necessary to urge. That principle is now universally admitted. But the question respecting the extent of the powers actually granted, is perpetually arising, and will probably continue to arise, as long as our system shall exist.

In discussing these questions, the conflicting powers of the general and State governments must be brought into view, and the supremacy of their respective laws, when they are in opposition, must be settled.

If any one proposition could command the universal assent of mankind, we might expect it would be this—that the government of the Union, though limited in its powers, is supreme within its sphere of action. This would seem to result necessarily from its nature. It is the government of all; its powers are delegated by all; it represents all, and acts for all. Though any one State may be willing to control its operations, no State is willing to allow others to control them. The nation, on those subjects on which it can act, must necessarily bind its component parts. But this question is not left to mere reason: the people have, in express terms, decided it, by saying, "this constitution, and the laws of the United States, which shall be made in pursuance thereof," "shall be the supreme law of the land," and by requiring that the members of the State legislatures, and the officers of the executive and judicial departments of the States, shall take the oath of fidelity to it.

The government of the United States, then, though limited in its powers, is supreme; and its laws, when made in pursuance of the constitution, form the supreme law of the land, "any thing in the constitution or laws of any State to the contrary notwithstanding."

Among the enumerated powers, we do not find that of establishing a bank or creating a corporation. But there is no phrase in the instrument which, like the articles of confederation, excludes incidental or implied powers; and which requires that every thing granted shall be expressly and minutely described. Even the 10th amendment, which was framed for the purpose of quieting the excessive jealousies which had been excited, omits the word "expressly," and declares only that the powers "not delegated to the United States, nor prohibited to the States, are reserved to the States or to the people;" thus leaving the question, whether the particular power which may become the subject of contest has been delegated to the one government, or prohibited to the other, to depend on a fair construction of the whole instrument. The men who drew and adopted this amendment had experienced the embarrassments resulting from the insertion of this word in the articles of confederation, and probably omitted it to avoid those embarrassments. A constitution, to contain an accurate detail of all the subdivisions of which its great powers will admit, and of all the means by which they may be carried into execution, would partake of the prolixity of a legal code, and could scarcely be embraced by the human mind. It would probably never be understood by the public. Its nature, therefore, requires, that only its great outlines should be marked, its important objects designated, and the minor ingredients which compose those objects be deduced from the nature of the objects themselves. That this idea was entertained by the framers of the American constitution, is not only to be inferred from the nature of the instrument, but from the language. Why else were some of the limitations, found in the ninth section of the 1st article, introduced? It is also, in some degree, warranted by their having omitted to use any restrictive term which might prevent its receiving a fair and just interpretation. In considering this question, then, we must never forget, that it is *a constitution* we are expounding.

Although, among the enumerated powers of government, we do not find the word "bank" or "incorporation," we find the great powers to lay and collect taxes; to borrow money; to regulate commerce; to declare and conduct a war; and to raise and support armies and navies. The sword and the purse, all the external relations, and no inconsiderable portion of the industry of the nation, are entrusted to its government. It can never be pretended that these vast powers draw after them others of inferior importance, merely because they are inferior. Such an idea can never be advanced. But it may with great reason be contended, that a government, entrusted with such ample powers, on the due execution of which the happiness and prosperity of the nation so vitally depends, must also be entrusted with ample means for their execution. The power being given, it is the interest of the nation to facilitate its execution. It can never be their interest, and cannot be presumed to have been their intention, to clog and embarrass its execution by withholding the most appropriate means. Throughout this vast republic, from the St. Croix to the Gulph of Mexico, from the Atlantic to the Pacific, revenue is to be collected and expended, armies are to be marched and supported. The exigencies of the nation may require that the treasure raised in the north should be transported to the south, that raised in the east conveyed to the west, or that this order should be reversed. Is that construction of the constitution to be preferred which would render these operations difficult, hazardous, and expensive? Can we adopt that construction, (unless the words imperiously require it,) which would impute to the framers of that instrument, when granting these powers for the public good, the intention of impeding their exercise by withholding a choice of means? If, indeed, such be the mandate of the constitution, we have only to obey; but that instrument does not profess to enumerate the means by which the powers it confers may be executed; nor does it prohibit the creation of a corporation, if the existence of such a being be essential to the beneficial exercise of those powers. It is, then, the subject of fair inquiry, how far such means may be employed.

It is not denied, that the powers given to the government imply the ordinary means of execution. That, for example, of raising revenue, and applying it to national purposes, is admitted to imply the power of conveying money from place to place, as the exigencies of the nation may require, and of employing the usual means of conveyance. But it is denied that the government has its choice of means; or, that it may employ the most convenient means, if, to employ them, it be necessary to erect a corporation.

On what foundation does this argument rest? On this alone: The power of creating a corporation, is one appertaining to sovereignty, and is not expressly conferred on Congress. This is true. But all legislative powers appertain to sovereignty. The original power of giving the law on any subject whatever, is a sovereign power; and if the government of the Union is restrained from creating a corporation, as a means for performing its functions, on the single reason that the creation of a corporation is an act of sovereignty; if the sufficiency of this reason be acknowledged, there would be some difficulty in sustaining the authority of Congress to pass other laws for the accomplishment of the same objects.

The government which has a right to do an act, and has imposed on it the duty of performing that act, must, according to the dictates of reason, be allowed to select the means; and those who contend that it may not select any appropriate means, that one particular mode of effecting the object is excepted, take upon themselves the burden of establishing that exception. . . .

But the constitution of the United States has not left the right of Congress to employ the necessary means, for the execution of the powers conferred on the government, to general reasoning. To its enumeration of powers is added that of making "all laws which shall be necessary and proper, for carrying into execution the foregoing powers, and all other powers vested by this constitution, in the government of the United States, or in any department thereof."

The counsel for the State of Maryland have urged various arguments, to prove that this clause, though in terms a grant of power, is not so in effect; but is really restrictive of the general right, which might otherwise be implied, of selecting means for executing the enumerated powers. . . . But the argument on which most reliance is placed, is drawn from the peculiar language of this clause. Congress is not empowered by it to make all laws, which may have relation to the powers conferred on the government, but such only as may be *"necessary and proper"* for carrying them into execution. The word *"necessary,"* is considered as controlling the whole sentence, and as limiting the right to pass laws for the execution of the granted powers, to such as are indispensable, and without which the power would be nugatory. That it excludes the choice of means, and leaves to Congress, in each case, that only which is most direct and simple.

Is it true, that this is the sense in which the word "necessary" is always used? Does it always import an absolute physical necessity . . . ? We think it does not. If reference be had to its use, in the common affairs of the world, or in approved authors, we find that it frequently imports no more than that one thing is convenient, or useful, or essential to another. To employ the means necessary to an end, is generally understood as employing any means calculated to produce the end, and not as being confined to those single means, without which the end would be entirely unattainable. Such is the character of human language, that no word conveys to the mind, in all situations, one single definite idea; and nothing is more common than to use words in a figurative sense. . . . It is essential to just construction, that many words which import something excessive, should be understood in a more mitigated sense. . . . The word "necessary" is of this description. It has not a fixed character peculiar to itself. It admits of all degrees of comparison; and is often connected with other words, which increase or diminish the impression the mind receives of the urgency it imports. A thing may be necessary, very necessary, absolutely or indispensably necessary. To no mind would the same idea be conveyed, by these several phrases. This comment on the word is well illustrated, by the passage cited at the bar, from the 10th section of the 1st article of the constitution. It is, we think, impossible to compare the sentence which prohibits a State from laying "imposts, or duties on imports or exports, except what may be *absolutely* necessary for executing its inspection laws," with that which authorizes Congress "to make all laws which shall be necessary and proper for carrying into execution" the powers of the general government, without feeling a conviction that the convention understood itself to change materially the meaning of the word "necessary," by prefixing the word "absolutely." This word, then, like others, is used in various senses; and, in its construction, the subject, the context, the intention of the person using them, are all to be taken into view.

Let this be done in the case under consideration. The subject is the execution of those great powers on which the welfare of a nation essentially depends. It must have been the intention of those who gave these powers, to insure, as far as human prudence could insure, their beneficial execution. This could not be done by confiding the choice of means to such narrow limits as not to leave it in the power of Congress to adopt any which might be appropriate, and which were conducive to the end. This provision is made in a constitution intended to endure for ages to come, and, consequently, to be adapted to the various *crises* of human affairs. To have prescribed the means by which government should, in all future time, execute its powers, would have been to change, entirely, the character of the instrument, and give it the properties of a legal code. It would have been an unwise attempt to provide, by immutable rules, for exigencies which, if foreseen at all, must have been seen dimly, and which can be best provided for as they occur. To have declared that the best means shall not be used, but those alone without which the power given would be nugatory, would have been to deprive the legislature of the capacity to avail itself of experience, to exercise its reason, and to accommodate its legislation to circumstances. If we apply this principle of construction to any of the powers of the government, we shall find it so pernicious in its operation that we shall be compelled to discard it. . . .

So, with respect to the whole penal code of the United States: whence arises the power to punish in cases not prescribed by the constitution? All admit that the government may, legitimately, punish any violation of its laws; and yet, this is not among the enumerated powers of Congress. . . .

Take, for example, the power "to establish post offices and post roads." This power is executed by the single act of making the establishment. But, from this has been inferred the power and duty of carrying the mail along the post road, from one post office to another. And, from this implied power, has again been inferred the right to punish those who steal letters from the post office, or rob the mail. It may be said, with some plausibility, that the right to carry the mail, and to punish those who rob it, is not indispensably necessary to the establishment of a post office and post road. This right is indeed essential to the beneficial exercise of the power, but not indispensably necessary to its existence. So, of the punishment of the crimes of stealing or falsifying a record or process of a Court of the United States, or of perjury in such Court. To punish these offences is certainly conducive to the due administration of justice. But courts may exist, and may decide the causes brought before them, though such crimes escape punishment.

The baneful influence of this narrow construction on all the operations of the government, and the absolute impracticability of maintaining it without rendering the government incompetent to its great objects, might be illustrated by numerous examples drawn from the constitution, and from our laws. The good sense of the public has pronounced, without hesitation, that the power of punishment appertains to sovereignty, and may be exercised whenever the sovereign has a right to act, as incidental to his constitutional powers. It is a means for carrying into execution all sovereign powers, and may be used, although not indispensably necessary. It is a right incidental to the power, and conducive to its beneficial exercise. . . .

In ascertaining the sense in which the word "necessary" is used in this clause of the constitution, we may derive some aid from that with which it is associated. Congress shall have power "to make all laws which shall be necessary and *proper* to carry into execution" the powers of the government. If the word "necessary" was used in that strict and rigorous sense for which the counsel for the State of Maryland contend, it would be an extraordinary departure from the usual course of the human mind, as exhibited in composition, to add a word, the only possible effect of which is to qualify that strict and rigorous meaning; to present to the mind the idea of some choice of means of legislation not straitened and compressed within the narrow limits for which gentlemen contend.

But the argument which most conclusively demonstrates the error of the construction contended for by the counsel for the State of Maryland, is founded on the intention of the Convention, as manifested in the whole clause. . . . This clause, as construed by the State of Maryland, would abridge, and almost annihilate this useful and necessary right of the legislature to select its means. That this could not be intended, is, we should think, had it not been already controverted, too apparent for controversy. We think so for the following reasons:

1st. The clause is placed among the powers of Congress, not among the limitations on those powers.

2nd. Its terms purport to enlarge, not to diminish the powers vested in the government. It purports to be an additional power, not a restriction on those already granted. No reason has been, or can be assigned for thus concealing an intention to narrow the discretion of the national legislature under words which purport to enlarge it. . . . If, then, their intention had been, by this clause, to restrain the free use of means which might otherwise have been implied, that intention would have been inserted in another place, and would have been expressed in terms resembling these. "In carrying into execution the foregoing powers, and all others," & c. "no laws shall be passed but such as are necessary and proper." Had the intention been to make this clause restrictive, it would unquestionably have been so in form as well as in effect.

The result of the most careful and attentive consideration bestowed upon this clause is, that if it does not enlarge, it cannot be construed to restrain the powers of Congress, or to impair the right of the legislature to exercise its best judgment in the selection of measures to carry into execution the constitutional powers of the government. If no other motive for its insertion can be suggested, a sufficient one is found in the desire to remove all doubts respecting the right to legislate on that vast mass of incidental powers which must be involved in the constitution, if that instrument be not a splendid bauble.

We admit, as all must admit, that the powers of the government are limited, and that its limits are not to be transcended. But we think the sound construction of the constitution must allow to the national legislature that discretion, with respect to the means by which the powers it confers are to be carried into execution, which will enable that body to perform the high duties assigned to it, in the manner most beneficial to the people. Let the end be legitimate, let it be within the scope of the constitution, and all means which are appropriate, which are plainly adapted to that end, which are not prohibited, but consist with the letter and spirit of the constitution, are constitutional.

That a corporation must be considered as a means not less usual, not of higher dignity, not more requiring a particular specification than other means, has been sufficiently proved. If we look to the origin of corporations, to the manner in which they have been framed in that government from which we have derived most of our legal principles and ideas, or to the uses to which they have been applied, we find no reason to suppose that a constitution . . . ought to have specified this. Had it been intended to grant this power as one which should be distinct and independent, to be exercised in any case whatever, it would have found a place among the enumerated powers of the government. But being considered merely as a means, to be employed only for the purpose of carrying into execution the given powers, there could be no motive for particularly mentioning it.

The propriety of this remark would seem to be generally acknowledged by the universal acquiescence in the construction which has been uniformly put on the 3rd section of the 4th article of the constitution. The power to "make all needful rules and regulations respecting the territory or other property belonging to the United States," is not more comprehensive, than the power "to make all laws which shall be necessary and proper for carrying into execution" the powers of the government. Yet all admit the constitutionality of a territorial government, which is a corporate body.

If a corporation may be employed indiscriminately with other means to carry into execution the powers of the government, no particular reason can be assigned for excluding the use of a bank, if required for its fiscal operations. To use one, must be within the discretion of Congress, if it be an appropriate mode of executing the powers of government. That it is a convenient, a useful, and essential instrument in the prosecution of its fiscal operations, is not now a subject of controversy. All those who have been concerned in the administration of our finances, have concurred in representing its importance and necessity; and so strongly have they been felt, that statesmen of the first class, whose previous opinions against it had been confirmed by every circumstance which can fix the human judgment, have yielded those opinions to the exigencies of the nation. . . .

But, were its necessity less apparent, none can deny its being an appropriate measure; and if it is, the degree of its necessity . . . is to be discussed in another place. Should Congress, in the execution of its powers, adopt measures which are prohibited by the constitution; or should Congress, under the pretext of executing its powers, pass laws for the accomplishment of objects not entrusted to the government; it would become the painful duty of this tribunal, should a case requiring such a decision come before it, to say that such an act was not the law of the land. But where the law is not prohibited, and is really calculated to effect any of the objects entrusted to the government, to undertake here to inquire into the degree of its necessity, would be to pass the line which circumscribes the judicial department, and to tread on legislative ground. This court disclaims all pretensions to such a power.

After this declaration, it can scarcely be necessary to say, that the existence of State banks can have no possible influence on the question. No trace is to be found in the constitution of an intention to create a dependence of the government of the Union on those of the States, for the execution of the great powers assigned to it. Its means are adequate to its ends; and on those means alone was it expected to rely for the accomplishment of its ends. To impose on it the necessity of resorting to means which it cannot control, which another government may furnish or withhold, would render its course precarious . . . and create a dependence on other governments, which might disappoint its most important designs, and is incompatible with the language of the constitution. But were it otherwise, the choice of means implies a right to choose a national bank in preference to State banks, and Congress alone can make the election.

After the most deliberate consideration, it is the unanimous and decided opinion of this Court, that the act to incorporate the Bank of the United States is a law made in pursuance of the constitution, and is a part of the supreme law of the land. . . .

It being the opinion of the Court, that the act incorporating the bank is constitutional; and that the power of establishing a branch in the State of Maryland might be properly exercised by the bank itself, we proceed to inquire—

2. Whether the State of Maryland may, without violating the constitution, tax that branch?

That the power of taxation is one of vital importance; that it is retained by the States; that it is not abridged by the grant of a similar power to the government of the Union; that it is to be concurrently exercised by the two governments: are truths which have never been denied. But, such is the paramount character of the constitution, that its capacity to withdraw any subject from the action of even this power, is admitted. The States are expressly forbidden to lay any duties on imports or exports, except what may be absolutely necessary for executing their inspection laws. If the obligation of this prohibition must be conceded— if it may restrain a State from the exercise of its taxing power on imports and exports; the same paramount character would seem to restrain, as it certainly may restrain, a State from such other exercise of this power, as is in its nature incompatible with, and repugnant to, the constitutional laws of the Union. A law, absolutely repugnant to another, as entirely repeals that other as if express terms of repeal were used.

On this ground the counsel for the bank place its claim to be exempted from the power of a State to tax its operations. There is no express provision for the case, but the claim has been sustained on a principle which so entirely pervades the constitution ... as to be incapable of being separated from it, without rending it into shreds.

This great principle is, that the constitution and the laws made in pursuance thereof are supreme; that they control the constitution and laws of the respective States, and cannot be controlled by them. From this, which may be almost termed an axiom, other propositions are deduced as corollaries, on the truth or error of which, and on their application to this case, the cause has been supposed to depend. These are, 1st. that a power to create implies a power to preserve. 2nd. That a power to destroy, if wielded by a different hand, is hostile to, and incompatible with these powers to create and to preserve. 3d. That where this repugnancy exists, that authority which is supreme must control, not yield to that over which it is supreme.

These propositions, as abstract truths, would, perhaps, never be controverted. Their application to this case, however, has been denied; and, both in maintaining the affirmative and the negative, a splendor of eloquence, and strength of argument, seldom, if ever, surpassed, have been displayed.

The power of Congress to create, and of course to continue, the bank, was the subject of the preceding part of this opinion; and is no longer to be considered as questionable.

That the power of taxing it by the States may be exercised so as to destroy it, is too obvious to be denied. But taxation is said to be an absolute power, which acknowledges no other limits than those expressly prescribed in the constitution, and like sovereign power of every other description, is trusted to the discretion of those who use it. But the very terms of this argument admit that the sovereignty of the State, in the article of taxation itself, is subordinate to, and may be controlled by the constitution of the United States. How far it has been controlled by that instrument must be a question of construction. In making this construction, no principle not declared, can be admissable, which would defeat the legitimate operations of a supreme government. It is of the very essence of supremacy to remove all obstacles to its action within its own sphere, and so to modify every power vested in subordinate governments, as to exempt its own operations from their own influence. This effect need not be stated in terms. It is so involved in the declaration of supremacy, so necessarily implied in it, that the expression of it could not make it more certain. We must, therefore, keep it in view while construing the constitution.

The argument on the part of the State of Maryland, is, not that the States may directly resist a law of Congress, but that they may exercise their acknowledged powers upon it, and that the constitution leaves them this right in the confidence that they will not abuse it.

Before we proceed to examine this argument, and to subject it to the test of the constitution, we must be permitted to bestow a few considerations on the nature and extent of this original right of taxation, which is acknowledged to remain with the States. It is admitted that the power of taxing the people and their property is essential to the very existence of government, and may be legitimately exercised on the objects to which it is applicable, to the utmost extent to which the government may chuse to carry it. The only security against the abuse of this power, is found in the structure of the government itself. In imposing a tax the legislature acts upon its constituents. This is in general a sufficient security against erroneous and oppressive taxation.

The people of a State, therefore, give to their government a right of taxing themselves and their property, and as the exigencies of government cannot be limited, they prescribe no limits to the exercise of this right, resting confidently on the interest of the legislator, and on the influence of the constituents over their representative, to guard then against its abuse. But the means employed by the government of the Union have no such security, nor is the right of a State to tax them sustained by the same theory. Those means are not given by the people of a particular State, not given by the constituents of the legislature, which claim the right to tax them, but by the people of all the States. They are given by all, for the benefit of all—and upon theory, should be subjected to that government only which belongs to all.

It may be objected to this definition, that the power of taxation is not confined to the people and property of a State. It may be exercised upon every object brought within its jurisdiction.

This is true. But to what source do we trace this right? It is obvious, that it is an incident of sovereignty, and is co-extensive with that to which it is an incident. All subjects over which the sovereign power of a State extends, are objects of taxation; but those over which it does not extend, are, upon the soundest principles, exempt from taxation. This proposition may almost be pronounced self-evident.

The sovereignty of a State extends to every thing which exists by its own authority, or is introduced by its permission; but does it extend to those means which are employed by Congress to carry into execution powers conferred on that body by the people of the United States? We think it demonstrable that it does not. Those powers are not given by the people of a single State. They are given by the people of the United States, to a government whose laws, made in pursuance of the constitution, are declared to be supreme. Consequently, the people of a single State cannot confer a sovereignty which will extend over them.

If we measure the power of taxation residing in a State, by the extent of sovereignty which the people of a single State possess, and can confer on its government, we have an intelligible standard, applicable to every case to which the power may be applied. We have a principle which leaves the power of taxing the people and property of a State unimpaired; which leaves to a State the command of all its resources, and which places beyond its reach, all those powers which are conferred by the people of the United States on the government of the Union, and all those means which are given for the purpose of carrying those powers into execution. We have a principle which is safe for the States, and safe for the Union. We are relieved, as we ought to be, from clashing sovereignty; from interfering powers; from a repugnancy between a right in one government to pull down what there is an acknowledged right in another to build up; from the incompatibility of a right in one government to destroy what there is a right in another to preserve. We are not driven to the perplexing inquiry, so unfit for the judicial department, what degree of taxation is the legitimate use, and what degree may amount to the abuse of the power. The attempt to use it on the means employed by the government of the Union, in pursuance of the constitution, is itself an abuse, because it is the usurpation of a power which the people of a single State cannot give.

We find, then, on just theory, a total failure of this original right to tax the means employed by the government of the Union, for the execution of its powers. The right never existed, and the question whether it has been surrendered, cannot arise.

But, waiving this theory for the present, let us resume the inquiry, whether this power can be exercised by the respective States, consistently with a fair construction of the constitution?

That the power to tax involves the power to destroy; that the power to destroy may defeat and render useless the power to create; that there is a plain repugnance, in conferring on one government a power to control the constitutional measures of another, which other, with respect to those very measures, is declared to be supreme over that which exerts the control, are propositions not to be denied. But all inconsistencies are to be reconciled by the magic of the word CONFIDENCE. Taxation, it is said, does not necessarily and unavoidably destroy. To carry it to the excess of destruction would be an abuse, to presume which, would banish that confidence which is essential to all government.

But is this a case of confidence? Would the people of any one State trust those of another with a power to control the most insignificant operations of their State government? We know they would not. Why, then, should we suppose that the people of any one State should be willing to trust those of another with a power to control the operations of a government to which they have confided their most important and most valuable interests? In the legislature of the Union alone, are all represented. The legislature of the Union alone, therefore, can be trusted by the people with the power of controlling measures which concern all, in the confidence that it will not be abused. This, then, is not a case of confidence, and we must consider it as it really is.

If we apply the principle for which the State of Maryland contends, to the constitution generally, we shall find it capable of changing totally the character of that instrument. We shall find it capable of arresting all the measures of the government, and of prostrating it at the foot of the States. The American people have declared their constitution, and the laws made in pursuance thereof, to be supreme; but this principle would transfer the supremacy, in fact, to the States.

If the States may tax one instrument, employed by the government in the execution of its powers, they may tax any and every other instrument. They may tax the mail; they may tax the mint; they may tax patent rights; they may tax the papers of the custom-house; they may tax judicial process; they may tax all the means employed by the government, to an excess which would defeat all the ends of government. This was not intended by the American people. They did not design to make their government dependent on the States.

Gentlemen say, they do not claim the right to extend State taxation to these objects. They limit their pretensions to property. But on what principle is this distinction made? Those who make it have furnished no reason for it, and the principle for which they contend denies it. They contend that the power of taxation has no other limit than is found in the 10th section of the 1st article of the constitution; that, with respect to every thing else, the power of the States is supreme, and admits of no control. If this be true, the distinction between property and other subjects to which the power of taxation is applicable, is merely arbitrary, and can never be sustained. This is not all. If the controling power of the States be established; if their supremacy as to taxation be acknowledged; what is to restrain their exercising this control in any shape they may please to give it? Their sovereignty is not confined to taxation. That is not the only mode in which it might be displayed. The question is, in truth, a question of supremacy; and if the right of the States to tax the means employed by the general government be conceded, the declaration that the constitution, and the laws made in pursuance thereof, shall be the supreme law of the land, is empty and unmeaning declamation. . . .

It has also been insisted, that, as the power of taxation in the general and State governments is acknowledged to be concurrent, every argument which would sustain the right of the general government to tax banks chartered by the States, will equally sustain the right of the States to tax banks chartered by the general government.

But the two cases are not on the same reason. The people of all the States have created the general government, and have conferred upon it the general power of taxation. The people of all the States, and the States themselves, are represented in Congress, and, by their representatives, exercise this power. When they tax the chartered institutions of the States, they tax their constituents; and these taxes must be uniform. But, when a State taxes the operations of the government of the United States, it acts upon institutions created, not by their own constituents, but by people over whom they claim no control. It acts upon the measures of a government created by others as well as themselves, for the benefit of others in common with themselves. The difference is that which always exists, and always must exist, between the action of the whole on a part, and the action of a part on the whole—between the laws of a government declared to be supreme, and those of a government which, when in opposition to those laws, is not supreme.

But if the full application of this argument could be admitted, it might bring into question the right of Congress to tax the State banks, and could not prove the right of the States to tax the Bank of the United States.

The Court has bestowed on this subject its most deliberate consideration. The result is a conviction that the States have no power, by taxation or otherwise, to retard, impede, burden, or in any manner control, the operations of the constitutional laws enacted by Congress to carry into execution the powers vested in the general government. This is, we think, the unavoidable consequence of that supremacy which the constitution has declared.

We are unanimously of opinion, that the law passed by the legislature of Maryland, imposing a tax on the Bank of the United States, is unconstitutional and void.

[Reversed.]

NOTE ON *MCCULLOCH* AND THE SCOPE OF NATIONAL POWER

1.   Scholars have suggested that *McCulloch* is "the single most important opinion in the Court's history."[12] Chief Justice Marshall asserts that the Supreme Court alone can decide the constitutionality of the Bank, and that "[o]n the Supreme Court of the United States has the constitution of our country devolved this important duty." This assertion has two critical dimensions. The first affirms *Marbury*'s conclusion that the Court has the authority to interpret the Constitution and strike down laws inconsistent with it. The second, raised for the first time in *McCulloch*, presents the Court

---

[12] Farber, *supra* note 3, at 33.

as the appropriate forum for resolving disputes between national and state authority—as the umpire, so to speak, for struggles within the federal system.

Does Marshall cite any constitutional provision for this authority? As already discussed, the debate over the Bank's constitutionality had begun within Congress and the executive branch over thirty years prior to the judiciary's involvement in *McCulloch*. As a result, Daniel Webster was able to argue to the Court that "the bank question had been fully explored in the early years of the republic, and that all three branches had been acting for over thirty years on the assumption that the bank was constitutional."[13] How do President Washington's extensive constitutional deliberations, not to mention's Congress's debates on the subject, fit into Chief Justice Marshall's assessment of constitutional interpretive authority? Why didn't Marshall even cite the opinions offered by Washington's cabinet? Does the fact that the Bank had been accepted for so long in practice have any bearing on the legal arguments before the Court in *McCulloch*?

2.　The textual arguments in *McCulloch* focus on the Necessary and Proper Clause and the Tenth Amendment. Textualism is often associated with simply ascertaining either the common or historical meanings of particular words. Can this sort of argument resolve the key questions in *McCulloch*? "Necessary," after all, is used—both nowadays and in the Founding era—in both the senses urged by the parties in *McCulloch*. Chief Justice Marshall thus has to take the textual method considerably further. What techniques does he employ to choose among the various plausible meanings that the critical words might have?

One way to resolve textual ambiguity is through default rules of construction. The early Republic featured vehement debates about whether the Constitution's words should be strictly or broadly construed. Recall that Thomas Jefferson had urged the former position, while Alexander Hamilton had argued for the latter. What argument does Marshall give for broad construction?

3.　The specific power at issue in *McCulloch* is the power to charter a corporation such as the Bank of the United States. The Court ultimately decided that Congress is so empowered, stating that Congress's choice to charter a corporation "must be within the discretion of Congress, if it be an appropriate mode of executing the powers of government." But the Framers, while debating whether to empower Congress to engineer canals, considered and rejected a measure that would have given Congress further power "to grant charters of incorporation where the interest of the U. S. might require & the legislative provisions of individual States may be incompetent." Jefferson's argument against the bank thus emphasized that "the very power now proposed *as a means*, was rejected *as an end*, by the very Convention which formed the constitution."[14] Should this history have counted more

---

[13]　*Id.* at 47; for Webster's argument, see 17 U.S. (4 Wheat.) at 371.

[14]　Jefferson, *supra* note 4, at 542.

strongly against the outcome of *McCulloch*? Can you think of a good reason *not* to rely on it?

4.   The key language concerning the scope of the "Necessary and Proper" power in *McCulloch* is this:

> [W]e think the sound construction of the constitution must allow to the national legislature that discretion, with respect to the means by which the powers it confers are to be carried into execution, which will enable that body to perform the high duties assigned to it, in the manner most beneficial to the people. Let the end be legitimate, let it be within the scope of the constitution, and all means which are appropriate, which are plainly adapted to that end, which are not prohibited, but consist with the letter and spirit of the constitution, are constitutional.

This test has two critical elements. First, it assesses the *end* to which the law is directed. This end must be both "legitimate" and "within the scope of the Constitution"—that is, enumerated. Second, the Court assesses the *fit* between the end pursued and the means that Congress has adopted to pursue it. Much of the debate in *McCulloch* focused on how close the fit between the unenumerated means and the enumerated end must be. How restrictive is test as it is applied in *McCulloch*? Is this? Is there anything Congress *can't* do?

Many of the doctrinal tests adopted by courts in various areas of constitutional law combine these two elements. For example, the "strict scrutiny" standard applicable to most racial discrimination or restrictions on the content of speech requires a "compelling" government interest (the *end*), and that the means adopted be "narrowly tailored" to that interest (the *fit*). Likewise, the much more lenient "rational basis" test applicable to government action that impacts no fundamental constitutional principle requires simply a "legitimate" interest and a "rational" relation between the means and that end. *McCulloch* is generally thought to be the origin of rational basis review. But can you see how the structure of more demanding tests like strict scrutiny still follows the basic outlines of Marshall's test?

5.   Not long after the language quoted in the previous note, Marshall observed that "should Congress, under the pretext of executing its powers, pass laws for the accomplishment of objects not entrusted to the government; it would become the painful duty of this tribunal, should a case requiring such a decision come before it, to say that such an act was not the law of the land." This sounds like an important limiting principle, but how is it to be enforced? Should the Court try to ascertain the motives behind legislation as a test of a law's validity? How would it do that? But if this is not a viable limiting principle, does the opinion contain any alternative limits?

6.   Even if Congress can incorporate a bank, why can't Maryland tax it? A key concept in the law of federalism concerns the difference between *exclusive* and *concurrent* governmental powers. In the next two cases, *Gibbons* and *Willson*, the Court seems to suggest that Congress's power to regulate interstate commerce is exclusive, not concurrent or shared with the States. In *McCulloch*, is the power to tax an exclusive or concurrent power?

7. Chief Justice Marshall's argument against the state tax rests principally on democratic theory:

> The people of all the States have created the general government, and have conferred upon it the general power of taxation. The people of all the States, and the States themselves, are represented in Congress, and, by their representatives, exercise this power. When they tax the chartered institutions of the States, they tax their constituents; and these taxes must be uniform. But, when a State taxes the operations of the government of the United States, it acts upon institutions created, not by their own constituents, but by people over whom they claim no control. It acts upon the measures of a government created by others as well as themselves, for the benefit of others in common with themselves. The difference is that which always exists, and always must exist, between the action of the whole on a part, and the action of a part on the whole.

This is an argument not so much about the supremacy of federal law but rather about the reliability of the political process that led to Maryland's tax. The implicit notion is that courts should exercise judicial review in such a way as to reinforce the representation of persons affected by a given law. You will see similar "representation reinforcement" arguments throughout the course. Is this a sound basis for judicial action invalidating a state law?

8. Much of Chief Justice Marshall's rhetoric in *McCulloch* suggests that States simply cannot tax or regulate federal entities. Is that proposition sustainable? Consider some hypothetical scenarios:

 a. A federal officer of the Social Security Administration, stopped for speeding by a state highway patrolman on his way to work.

 b. A teacher in a federal worker training program, whose salary is taxed under a generally-applicable state income tax.

 c. A national bank barred from opening a branch in a residential area under local zoning laws.

 d. A federal Marine recruiter barred from interviewing students at a state law school because the school opposes the military's policy discriminating against homosexuals.

Can state law apply in any of these instances under *McCulloch*? If your answer to any of them is "yes," what is the principle limiting the scope of *McCulloch*'s holding?

9. The *McCulloch* opinion addresses two distinct questions: a) Does Congress have the power to incorporate a bank? and b) Can Maryland legally tax the bank as a federal entity? But it also addressed a broader question about the nature of the Union. As Scot Powe has observed, "Marshall intended to use the case to slay the Virginia theology that the Constitution was just a compact among sovereign states."[15] That position, argued by

---

[15] LUCAS A. POWE, JR., THE SUPREME COURT AND THE AMERICAN ELITE, 1789–2008, at 69 (2009).

Maryland's Attorney General Luther Martin, would suggest both that Congress's enumerated powers should be construed narrowly vis-à-vis the States' reserved powers and that Maryland's sovereign right of taxation was on a par with any power that Congress enjoyed. Marshall's opinion emphatically rejected that notion, insisting that the Constitution derived its authority from its ratification by the People, and that although ratification did take place through state-level conventions, those bodies were wholly distinct from the established state legislatures. "The government of the Union, then, . . . is, emphatically, and truly, a government of the people. In form and in substance it emanates from them. Its powers are granted by them, and are to be exercised directly on them, and for their benefit." It followed that "the government of the Union, though limited in its powers, is supreme within its sphere of action."

One may doubt whether this political theorizing was really necessary to decide the question before the Court in *McCulloch*. But the dispute between the nationalist and compact views of the federal union had profound implications for the more fundamental conflicts—already brewing in 1819— about nullification, slavery, and secession. The Court itself would not take center stage in these conflicts until the *Dred Scott* decision in 1857. But *McCulloch* aroused protests in the South—particularly Virginia—precisely because it was understood to endorse a broad nationalist vision with implications for the impending sectional crisis.

See also: For an extensive case study of the Bank controversy, with excerpts from many of the original documents, see PAUL BREST, SANFORD LEVINSON, JACK M. BALKIN, AKHIL REED AMAR & REVA B. SIEGEL, PROCESSES OF CONSTITUTIONAL DECISIONMAKING: CASES AND MATERIALS 27–84 (5th ed. 2006).

Gibbons v. Ogden
22 U.S. (9 Wheat.) 1 (1824)

APPEAL from the Court for the Trial of Impeachments and Correction of Errors of the State of New York. Aaron Ogden filed his bill in the Court of Chancery of that State, against Thomas Gibbons, setting forth the several acts of the Legislature thereof, enacted for the purpose of securing to Robert R. Livingston and Robert Fulton, the exclusive navigation of all the waters within the jurisdiction of that State, with boats moved by fire or steam, for a term of years which has not yet expired; and authorizing the Chancellor to award an injunction, restraining any person whatever from navigating those waters with boats of that description. The bill stated an assignment from Livingston and Fulton to one John R. Livingston, and from him to the complainant, Ogden, of the right to navigate the waters between Elizabethtown, and other places in New-Jersey, and the city of New York; and that Gibbons, the defendant below, was in possession of two steam boats, called the Stoudinger and the Bellona, which were actually employed in running between New-York and Elizabethtown, in violation of the exclusive privilege conferred on the complainant, and praying an injunction to restrain the said Gibbons from using the said boats, or any other propelled by fire or steam, in navigating the waters within the territory of New-York. The injunction having been awarded, the answer of Gibbons was filed; in which he stated, that the boats employed by him were duly enrolled and licensed, to be employed in carrying on the coasting trade, under the act of Congress, passed the 18th of February, 1793, c. 3. entitled, "An act for enrolling and licensing ships and vessels to be employed in the coasting trade and fisheries, and for regulating the same." And the defendant insisted on his right, in virtue of such licenses, to navigate the waters between Elizabethtown and the city of New York, the said acts of the Legislature of the State of New York to the contrary notwithstanding. At the hearing, the Chancellor perpetuated the injunction, being of the opinion, that the said acts were not repugnant to the constitution and laws of the United States, and were valid. This decree was affirmed in the Court for the Trial of Impeachments and Correction of Errors, which is the highest Court of law and equity in the State, before which the cause could be carried, and it was thereupon brought to this Court by appeal.

■ **MR. CHIEF JUSTICE MARSHALL delivered the opinion of the Court, and, after stating the case, proceeded as follows:**

The appellant contends that this decree is erroneous, because the laws which purport to give the exclusive privilege it sustains, are repugnant to the constitution and laws of the United States.

They are said to be repugnant—

1st. To that clause in the constitution which authorizes Congress to regulate commerce. . . .

As preliminary to the very able discussions of the constitution, which we have heard from the bar . . . reference has been made to the political situation of these States, anterior to its formation. It has been said, that they were sovereign, were completely independent, and were connected with each other only by a league. This is true. But, when these allied sovereigns converted their league into a government, when they converted their Congress of Ambassadors, deputed to deliberate on their common concerns, and to recommend measures of general utility, into a Legislature, empowered to enact laws on the most interesting subjects, the whole character in which the States appear, underwent a change, the extent of which must be determined by a fair consideration of the instrument by which that change was effected.

This instrument contains an enumeration of powers expressly granted by the people to their government. It has been said, that these powers ought to be construed strictly. But why ought they to be so construed? Is there one sentence in the constitution which gives countenance to this rule? In the last of the enumerated powers, that which grants, expressly, the means for carrying all others into execution,

Congress is authorized "to make all laws which shall be necessary and proper" for the purpose. But this limitation on the means which may be used, is not extended to the powers which are conferred. . . .

What do gentlemen mean, by a strict construction? If they contend only against that enlarged construction, which would extend words beyond their natural and obvious import, we might question the application of the term, but should not controvert the principle. If they contend for that narrow construction which, in support of some theory not to be found in the constitution, would deny to the government those powers which the words of the grant, as usually understood, import, and which are consistent with the general views and objects of the instrument; for that narrow construction, which would cripple the government, and render it unequal to the object for which it is declared to be instituted, and to which the powers given, as fairly understood, render it competent; then we cannot perceive the propriety of this strict construction, nor adopt it as the rule by which the constitution is to be expounded.

As men, whose intentions require no concealment, generally employ the words which most directly and aptly express the ideas they intend to convey, the enlightened patriots who framed our constitution, and the people who adopted it, must be understood to have employed words in their natural sense, and to have intended what they have said. If, from the imperfection of human language, there should be serious doubts respecting the extent of any given power, it is a well settled rule, that the objects for which it was given, especially when those objects are expressed in the instrument itself, should have great influence in the construction. We know of no reason for excluding this rule from the present case. . . . We know of no rule for construing the extent of such powers, other than is given by the language of the instrument which confers them, taken in connexion with the purposes for which they were conferred.

The words are, "Congress shall have power to regulate commerce with foreign nations, and among the several States, and with the Indian tribes."

The subject to be regulated is commerce; and our constitution being, as was aptly said at the bar, one of enumeration, and not of definition, to ascertain the extent of the power, it becomes necessary to settle the meaning of the word. The counsel for the appellee would limit it to traffic, to buying and selling, or the interchange of commodities, and do not admit that it comprehends navigation. This would restrict a general term, applicable to many objects, to one of its significations. Commerce, undoubtedly, is traffic, but it is something more: it is intercourse. It describes the commercial intercourse between nations, and parts of nations, in all its branches, and is regulated by prescribing rules for carrying on that intercourse. The mind can scarcely conceive a system for regulating commerce between nations, which shall exclude all laws concerning navigation, which shall be silent on the admission of the vessels of the one nation into the ports of the other, and be confined to prescribing rules for the conduct of individuals, in the actual employment of buying and selling, or of barter.

If commerce does not include navigation, the government of the Union has no direct power over that subject, and can make no law prescribing what shall constitute American vessels, or requiring that they shall be navigated by American seamen. Yet this power has been exercised from the commencement of the government, has been exercised with the consent of all, and has been understood by all to be a commercial regulation. All America understands, and has uniformly understood, the word "commerce," to comprehend navigation. It was so understood, and must have been so understood, when the constitution was framed. The power over commerce, including navigation, was one of the primary objects for which the people of America adopted their government, and must have been contemplated in forming it. The convention must have used the word in that sense, because all have understood it in that sense; and the attempt to restrict it comes too late.

If the opinion that "commerce," as the word is used in the constitution, comprehends navigation also, requires any additional confirmation, that additional confirmation is, we think, furnished by the words of the instrument itself.

It is a rule of construction, acknowledged by all, that the exceptions from a power mark its extent; for it would be absurd, as well as useless, to except from a granted power, that which was not granted. . . .

The 9th section of the 1st article declares, that "no preference shall be given, by any regulation of commerce or revenue, to the ports of one State over those of another." This clause cannot be understood as applicable to those laws only which are passed for the purposes of revenue, because it is expressly applied to commercial regulations; and the most obvious preference which can be given to one port over another, in regulating commerce, relates to navigation. But the subsequent part of the sentence is still more explicit. It is, "nor shall vessels bound to or from one State, be obliged to enter, clear, or pay duties, in another." These words have a direct reference to navigation. . . .

The word used in the constitution, then, comprehends, and has been always understood to comprehend, navigation within its meaning; and a power to regulate navigation, is as expressly granted, as if that term had been added to the word "commerce."

To what commerce does this power extend? The constitution informs us, to commerce "with foreign nations, and among the several States, and with the Indian tribes."

It has, we believe, been universally admitted, that these words comprehend every species of commercial intercourse between the United States and foreign nations. . . . If this be the admitted meaning of the word, in its application to foreign nations, it must carry the same meaning throughout the sentence, and remain a unit, unless there be some plain intelligible cause which alters it.

The subject to which the power is next applied, is to commerce "among the several States." The word "among" means intermingled with. A thing which is among others, is intermingled with them. Commerce among the States, cannot stop at the external boundary line of each State, but may be introduced into the interior.

It is not intended to say that these words comprehend that commerce, which is completely internal, which is carried on between man and man in a State, or between different parts of the same State, and which does not extend to or affect other States. Such a power would be inconvenient, and is certainly unnecessary.

Comprehensive as the word "among" is, it may very properly be restricted to that commerce which concerns more States than one. . . . [T]he enumeration of the particular classes of commerce, to which the power was to be extended, would not have been made, had the intention been to extend the power to every description. The enumeration presupposes something not enumerated; and that something, if we regard the language or the subject of the sentence, must be the exclusively internal commerce of a State. The genius and character of the whole government seem to be, that its action is to be applied to all the external concerns of the nation, and to those internal concerns which affect the States generally; but not to those which are completely within a particular State, which do not affect other States, and with which it is not necessary to interfere, for the purpose of executing some of the general powers of the government. The completely internal commerce of a State, then, may be considered as reserved for the State itself.

But, in regulating commerce with foreign nations, the power of Congress does not stop at the jurisdictional lines of the several States. It would be a very useless power, if it could not pass those lines. The commerce of the United States with foreign nations, is that of the whole United States. Every district has a right to participate in it. The deep streams which penetrate our country in every direction, pass through the interior of almost every State in the Union, and furnish the means of exercising this right. If Congress has the power to regulate it, that power must be exercised whenever the subject exists. If it exists within the States, if a foreign voyage may commence or terminate at a port within a State, then the power of Congress may be exercised within a State.

This principle is, if possible, still more clear, when applied to commerce "among the several States." They either join each other, in which case they are separated by a mathematical line, or they are remote from each other, in which case other States lie between them. . . . Can a trading expedition between two adjoining States, commence and terminate outside of each? And if the trading intercourse be between two States remote from each other, must it not commence in one, terminate in the other, and probably pass through a third? Commerce among the States must, of necessity, be commerce within the States. . . . The power of Congress, then, whatever it may be, must be exercised within the territorial jurisdiction of the several States. . . .

We are now arrived at the inquiry—What is this power?

It is the power to regulate; that is, to prescribe the rule by which commerce is to be governed. This power, like all others vested in Congress, is complete in itself, may be exercised to its utmost extent, and acknowledges no limitations, other than are prescribed in the constitution. These are expressed in plain terms, and do not affect the questions which arise in this case, or which have been discussed at the bar. If, as has always been understood, the sovereignty of Congress, though limited to specified objects, is plenary as to those objects, the power over commerce with foreign nations, and among the several States, is vested in Congress as absolutely as it would be in a single government, having in its constitution the same restrictions on the exercise of the power as are found in the constitution of the United States. The wisdom and the discretion of Congress, their identity with the people, and the influence which their constituents possess at elections, are, in this, as in many other instances, as that, for example, of declaring war, the sole restraints on which they have relied, to secure them from its abuse. They are the restraints on which the people must often rely solely, in all representative governments.

The power of Congress, then, comprehends navigation, within the limits of every State in the Union; so far as that navigation may be, in any manner, connected with "commerce with foreign nations, or among the several States, or with the Indian tribes." It may, of consequence, pass the jurisdictional line of New-York, and act upon the very waters to which the prohibition now under consideration applies.

But it has been urged with great earnestness, that, although the power of Congress to regulate commerce with foreign nations, and among the several States, be co-extensive with the subject itself, and have no other limits than are prescribed in the constitution, yet the States may severally exercise the same power, within their respective jurisdictions. In support of this argument, it is said, that they possessed it as an inseparable attribute of sovereignty, before the formation of the constitution, and still retain it, except so far as they have surrendered it by that instrument; that this principle results from the nature of the government, and is secured by the tenth amendment; that an affirmative grant of power is not exclusive, unless in its own nature it be such that the continued exercise of it by the former possessor is inconsistent with the grant, and that this is not of that description.

The appellant, conceding these postulates, except the last, contends, that full power to regulate a particular subject, implies the whole power, and leaves no residuum; that a grant of the whole is incompatible with the existence of a right in another to any part of it. . . .

The grant of the power to lay and collect taxes is, like the power to regulate commerce, made in general terms, and has never been understood to interfere with the exercise of the same power by the States; and hence has been drawn an argument which has been applied to the question under consideration. But the two grants are not, it is conceived, similar in their terms or their nature. Although many of the powers formerly exercised by the States, are transferred to the government of the Union, yet the State governments remain, and constitute a most important part of our system. The power of taxation is indispensable to their existence, and is a power which, in its own nature, is capable of residing in, and being exercised by, different authorities at the same time. We are accustomed to see it placed, for different purposes, in different hands. Taxation is the simple operation of taking small portions from a perpetually accumulating mass, susceptible of almost infinite division; and a power in one to take what is necessary for certain purposes, is not, in its nature, incompatible with a power in another to take what is necessary for other purposes. Congress is authorized to lay and collect taxes, & c. to pay the debts, and provide for the common defence and general welfare of the United States. This does not interfere with the power of the States to tax for the support of their own governments; nor is the exercise of that power by the States, an exercise of any portion of the power that is granted to the United States. In imposing taxes for State purposes, they are not doing what Congress is empowered to do. Congress is not empowered to tax for those purposes which are within the exclusive province of the States. When, then, each government exercises the power of taxation, neither is exercising the power of the other. But, when a State proceeds to regulate commerce with foreign nations, or among the several States, it is exercising the very power that is granted to Congress, and is doing the very thing which Congress is authorized to do. There is no analogy, then, between the power of taxation and the power of regulating commerce.

In discussing the question, whether this power is still in the States, in the case under consideration, we may dismiss from it the inquiry, whether it is surrendered by the mere grant to Congress, or is retained until Congress shall exercise the power. We may dismiss that inquiry, because it has been exercised, and the regulations which Congress deemed it proper to make, are now in full operation. The sole question is, can a State regulate commerce with foreign nations and among the States, while Congress is regulating it?

The counsel for the respondent answer this question in the affirmative, and rely very much on the restrictions in the 10th section, as supporting their opinion. They say, very truly, that limitations of a power, furnish a strong argument in favour of the existence of that power, and that the section which prohibits the States from laying duties on imports or exports, proves that this power might have been exercised, had it not been expressly forbidden; and, consequently, that any other commercial regulation, not expressly forbidden, to which the original power of the State was competent, may still be made.

That this restriction shows the opinion of the Convention, that a State might impose duties on exports and imports, if not expressly forbidden, will be conceded; but that it follows as a consequence, from this concession, that a State may regulate commerce with foreign nations and among the States, cannot be admitted. . . .

These restrictions, then, are on the taxing power, not on that to regulate commerce; and presuppose the existence of that which they restrain, not of that which they do not purport to restrain.

But, the inspection laws are said to be regulations of commerce, and are certainly recognised in the constitution, as being passed in the exercise of a power remaining with the States.

That inspection laws may have a remote and considerable influence on commerce, will not be denied; but that a power to regulate commerce is the source from which the right to pass them is derived, cannot be admitted. The object of inspection laws, is to improve the quality of articles produced by the labour of a country; to fit them for exportation; or, it may be, for domestic use. They act upon the subject before it becomes an article of foreign commerce, or of commerce among the States, and prepare it for that purpose. They form a portion of that immense mass of legislation, which embraces every thing within the territory of a State, not surrendered to the general government: all which can be most advantageously exercised by the States themselves. Inspection laws, quarantine laws, health laws of every description, as well as laws for regulating the internal commerce of a State, and those which respect turnpike roads, ferries, & c., are component parts of this mass.

No direct general power over these objects is granted to Congress; and, consequently, they remain subject to State legislation. If the legislative power of the Union can reach them, it must be for national purposes; it must be where the power is expressly given for a special purpose, or is clearly incidental to some power which is expressly given. It is obvious, that the government of the Union, in the exercise of its express powers, that, for example, of regulating commerce with foreign nations and among the States, may use means that may also be employed by a State, in the exercise of its acknowledged powers; that, for example, of regulating commerce within the State. If Congress license vessels to sail from one port to another, in the same State, the act is supposed to be, necessarily, incidental to the power expressly granted to Congress, and implies no claim of a direct power to regulate the purely internal commerce of a State, or to act directly on its system of police. So, if a State, in passing laws on subjects acknowledged to be within its control, and with a view to those subjects, shall adopt a measure of the same character with one which Congress may adopt, it does not derive its authority from the particular power which has been granted, but from some other, which remains with the State, and may be executed by the same means. All experience shows that the same measures, or measures scarcely distinguishable from each other, may flow from distinct powers; but this does not prove that the powers themselves are identical. Although the means used in their execution may sometimes approach each other so nearly as to be confounded, there are other situations in which they are sufficiently distinct to establish their individuality.

In our complex system, presenting the rare and difficult scheme of one general government, whose action extends over the whole, but which possesses only certain enumerated powers; and of numerous State governments, which retain and exercise all powers not delegated to the Union, contests respecting power must arise. Were it even otherwise, the measures taken by the respective governments to execute their acknowledged powers, would often be of the same description, and might, sometimes, interfere. This, however, does not prove that the one is exercising, or has a right to exercise, the powers of the other.

The acts of Congress, passed in 1796 and 1799, empowering and directing the officers of the general government to conform to, and assist in the execution of the quarantine and health laws of a State, proceed, it is said, upon the idea that these laws are constitutional. It is undoubtedly true, that they do proceed upon that idea; and the constitutionality of such laws has never, so far as we are informed, been denied. But they do not imply an acknowledgment that a State may rightfully regulate commerce with foreign nations, or among the States; for they do not imply that such laws are an exercise of that power, or enacted with a view to it. On the contrary, they are treated as quarantine and health laws, are so denominated in the acts of Congress, and are considered as flowing from the acknowledged power of a State, to provide for the health of its citizens. . . .

These acts were cited at the bar for the purpose of showing an opinion in Congress, that the States possess, concurrently with the Legislature of the Union, the power to regulate commerce with foreign nations and among the States. Upon reviewing them, we think they do not establish the proposition they were intended to prove. They show the opinion, that the States retain powers enabling them to pass the laws to which allusion has been made, not that those laws proceed from the particular power which has been delegated to Congress.

It has been contended by the counsel for the appellant, that, as the word "to regulate" implies in its nature, full power over the thing to be regulated, it excludes, necessarily, the action of all others that would perform the same operation on the same thing. That regulation is designed for the entire result, applying to those parts which remain as they were, as well as to those which are altered. It produces a uniform whole, which is as much disturbed and deranged by changing what the regulating power designs to leave untouched, as that on which it has operated.

There is great force in this argument, and the Court is not satisfied that it has been refuted.

Since, however, in exercising the power of regulating their own purely internal affairs, whether of trading or police, the States may sometimes enact laws, the validity of which depends on their interfering with, and being contrary to, an act of Congress passed in pursuance of the constitution, the Court will enter upon the inquiry, whether the laws of New York, as expounded by the highest tribunal of that State, have, in their application to this case, come into collision with an act of Congress, and deprived a citizen of a right to which that act entitles him. Should this collision exist, it will be immaterial whether those laws were passed in virtue of a concurrent power "to regulate commerce with foreign nations and among the several States," or, in virtue of a power to regulate their domestic trade and police. In one case and the other, the acts of New-York must yield to the law of Congress; and the decision sustaining the privilege they confer, against a right given by a law of the Union, must be erroneous.

This opinion has been frequently expressed in this Court, and is founded, as well on the nature of the government as on the words of the constitution. In argument, however, it has been contended, that if a law passed by a State, in the exercise of its acknowledged sovereignty, comes into conflict with a law passed by Congress in pursuance of the constitution, they affect the subject, and each other, like equal opposing powers.

But the framers of our constitution foresaw this state of things, and provided for it, by declaring the supremacy not only of itself, but of the laws made in pursuance of it. The nullity of any act, inconsistent with the constitution, is produced by the declaration, that the constitution is the supreme law. The appropriate application of that part of the clause which confers the same supremacy on laws and treaties, is to such acts of the State Legislatures as do not transcend their powers, but, though enacted in the execution of acknowledged State powers, interfere with, or are contrary to the laws of Congress, made in pursuance of the constitution, or some treaty made under the authority of the United States. In every such case, the act of Congress, or the treaty, is supreme; and the law of the State, though enacted in the exercise of powers not controverted, must yield to it. . . .

In the exercise of this power, Congress has passed "an act for enrolling or licensing ships or vessels to be employed in the coasting trade and fisheries, and for regulating the same." . . . The first section declares, that vessels . . . having a [federal] license in force, as is by the act required, "and no others, shall be deemed ships or vessels of the United States, entitled to the privileges of ships of vessels employed in the coasting trade." . . .

The license must be understood to be what it purports to be, a legislative authority to the steamboat Bellona, "to be employed in carrying on the coasting trade, for one year from this date." . . . This act demonstrates the opinion of Congress, that steam boats may be enrolled and licensed, in common with vessels using sails. . . .

Powerful and ingenious minds, taking, as postulates, that the powers expressly granted to the government of the Union, are to be contracted by construction, into the narrowest possible compass, and that the original powers of the States are retained, if any possible construction will retain them, may, by a course of well digested, but refined and metaphysical reasoning, founded on these premises, explain away the constitution of our country, and leave it, a magnificent structure, indeed, to look at, but totally unfit for use. They may so entangle and perplex the understanding, as to obscure principles, which were before thought quite plain, and induce doubts where, if the mind were to pursue its own course, none would be perceived. In such a case, it is peculiarly necessary to recur to safe and fundamental principles to sustain those principles, and, when sustained, to make them the tests of the arguments to be examined.

Willson v. Black Bird Creek Marsh Co.

27 (2 Pet.) U.S. 245 (1829)

THIS was a writ of error to the high court of errors and appeals of the state of Delaware.

The Black Bird Creek Marsh Company were incorporated by an act of the general assembly of Delaware, passed in February 1822; and the owners and possessors of the marsh, cripple, and low grounds in Appoquinimink hundred, in New Castle county, and state of Delaware, lying on both sides of Black Bird Creek, below Mathews's landing, and extending to the river Delaware; were authorised and empowered to make and construct a good and sufficient dam across said creek, at such place as the managers or a majority of them shall find to be most suitable for the purpose; and also, to bank the said marsh, cripple, and low ground, & c.

After the passing of this act, the company proceeded to erect and place in the creek a dam, by which the navigation of the creek was obstructed; also embanking the creek, and carrying into execution all the purposes of their incorporation.

The defendants being the owners, & c. of a sloop called the Sally, of 95 9–95ths tons, regularly licensed and enrolled according to the navigation laws of the United States, broke and injured the dam so erected by the company; and thereupon an action of trespass, vi et armis, was instituted against them in the supreme court of the state of Delaware, in which damages were claimed amounting to $20,000. To the declaration filed in the supreme court, the defendants filed three pleas; the first only of which being noticed by the Court in their decision, the second and third are omitted.

This plea was in the following terms:

1.   That the place where the supposed trespass is alleged to have been committed, was, and still is, part and parcel of said Black Bird Creek, a public and common navigable creek, in the nature of a highway, in which the tides have always flowed and re-flowed; in which there was, and of right ought to have been, a certain common and public way, in the nature of a highway, for all the citizens of the state of Delaware and of the United States, with sloops or other vessels to navigate, sail, pass and repass, into, over, through, in, and upon the same, at all times of the year, at their own free will and pleasure.

Therefore the said defendants, being citizens of the state of Delaware and of the United States, with the said sloop, sailed in and upon the said creek, in which, & c. as they lawfully might for the cause aforesaid; and because the said gum piles, & c. bank and dam, in the said declaration mentioned, & c. had been wrongfully erected, and were there wrongfully continued standing, and being in and across said navigable creek, and obstructing the same, so that without pulling up, cutting, breaking, and destroying the said gum piles, & c. bank and dam respectively, the said defendants could not pass and repass with the said sloop, into, through, over, and along the said navigable creek. And that the defendants, in order to remove the said obstructions, pulled up, cut, broke, & c. as in the said declaration mentioned, doing no unnecessary damage to the said Black Bird Creek Marsh Company; which is the same supposed trespass, & c.

The plaintiffs, in the supreme court of the state, demurred generally to all the pleas; and the court sustained the demurrers, and gave judgment in their favour. This judgment was affirmed in the court of appeals, and the record remanded, for the purpose of having the damages assessed by a jury. Final judgment having been entered on the verdict of the jury, it was again carried to the court of appeals, where it was affirmed, and was now brought before this Court, by the defendants in that court, for its review.

■ MR. CHIEF JUSTICE MARSHALL **delivered the opinion of the Court.**

. . . The jurisdiction of the Court being established, the more doubtful question is to be considered, whether the act incorporating the Black Bird Creek Marsh Company is repugnant to the constitution, so far as it authorizes a dam across the creek. The plea states the creek to be navigable, in the nature of a highway, through which the tide ebbs and flows[.]

The act of assembly by which the plaintiffs were authorized to construct their dam, shows plainly that this is one of those many creeks, passing through a deep level marsh adjoining the Delaware, up which the tide flows for some distance. The value of the property on its banks must be enhanced by excluding the water from the marsh, and the health of the inhabitants probably improved. Measures calculated to produce these objects, provided they do not come into collision with the powers of the general government, are undoubtedly within those which are reserved to the states. But the measure authorised by this act stops a navigable creek, and must be supposed to abridge the rights of those who have been accustomed to use it. But this abridgement, unless it comes in conflict with the constitution or a law of the United States, is an affair between the government of Delaware and its citizens, of which this Court can take no cognizance.

The counsel for the plaintiffs in error insist that it comes in conflict with the power of the United States "to regulate commerce with foreign nations and among the several states."

If congress had passed any act which bore upon the case; any act in execution of the power to regulate commerce, the object of which was to control state legislation over those small navigable creeks into which the tide flows, and which abound throughout the lower country of the middle and southern states; we should feel not much difficulty in saying that a state law coming in conflict with such act would be void. But congress has passed no such act. The repugnancy of the law of Delaware to the constitution is placed entirely on its repugnancy to the power to regulate commerce with foreign nations and among the several states; a power which has not been so exercised as to affect the question.

We do not think that the act empowering the Black Bird Creek Marsh Company to place a dam across the creek, can, under all the circumstances of the case, be considered as repugnant to the power to regulate commerce in its dormant state, or as being in conflict with any law passed on the subject.

There is no error, and the judgment is affirmed.

NOTE ON THE COMMERCE CLAUSE AS A LIMIT ON STATE POWER

1.   James Madison noted in the preface to his Notes on Debates in the Federal Convention of 1787 that "want of a general power over Commerce led to an exercise of this power separately, by the States, which not only proved abortive, but engendered rival, conflicting and angry regulations." In light of these concerns, the Commerce Clause may be viewed as an effort to create both *economic* unity, in the form of a national market free of internal trade barriers, and *political* unity, based on the view that interstate trade wars would lead inevitably to political conflict. The European Union provides a modern example of the same dynamic: EU nations have worked to eliminate internal trade barriers not only as a means to economic development and prosperity following the devastation of World War II, but also as a means of minimizing *political* conflict in order to avoid a repeat of the wars of the first half of the Twentieth Century.

In modern times, the Commerce Clause has become a sort of "catch-all" power employed to justify a vast range of federal regulation and programs. It is not at all clear that the Founders attached the same significance to this power.[16] As we will see in Part III, however, modern debates about the scope of national power vis-à-vis the States are largely—if not exclusively—debates about the scope of the Commerce Clause.

2.   Like *McCulloch*, *Gibbons* is an important case about both the affirmative scope of Congress's own legislative powers and the limits that those powers impose on government action by the States. How does Chief Justice Marshall define the outer limit of Congress's affirmative commerce power in *Gibbons*? What sorts of action are reserved to the States under this definition? Is the line that *Gibbons* employs likely to prove workable in future cases?

3.   The original Constitution was primarily directed toward establishing and limiting the authority of the *national* government. The restrictions in the Bill of Rights, for example, applied only to the national government. *See infra* Section 4.2. The document did contain some explicit restrictions on state activity in Article I, Section 10—e.g., no granting titles of nobility, no ex post facto laws—but these were relatively minor and, with the exception of the Contracts Clause, seldom invoked. The most important constitutional limits on state governmental action derived from the original Constitution have been the two principles at issue in *Gibbons* and *Willson*: the implied or "dormant" aspect of Congress's legislative authority under the Commerce Clause; and the preemptive effect of affirmative legislation by Congress on conflicting state law under the Supremacy Clause. We will study both of these principles in depth in the second part of the course, but it will be helpful to consider both concepts briefly here.

a.   *The Dormant Commerce Clause.* Marshall notes the possibility that the Commerce Power is exclusive—i.e., *only* Congress may regulate commerce among the several states. If so, then the Commerce Clause would restrain state regulation even where Congress's authority is unexercised or "dormant." Does the Court actually adopt this argument in *Gibbons*? How does Marshall avoid striking down useful state measures like quarantine laws, if Congress's power over interstate commerce is exclusive?

b.   *Preemption of State Law by Federal Action.* The dormant Commerce Clause operates where Congress has not itself acted by passing regulatory legislation. Where Congress *has* acted, the resulting laws are supreme under the Supremacy Clause and any state laws in conflict with federal law are invalid. What is the effect, then, of Gibbons's federal license to operate steamboats?

4.   For most of the Nineteenth Century, the Commerce Clause cases that came to the Court were cases like *Gibbons* and *Willson*—that is, cases that focused not on the validity of national legislation but rather on

---

[16]   *See, e.g.*, CALVIN H. JOHNSON, RIGHTEOUS ANGER AT THE WICKED STATES: THE MEANING OF THE FOUNDERS' CONSTITUTION 190 (2005) ("In the constitutional debates . . . 'regulation of commerce,' was a synonym for a set of mercantilist programs that would restrict imports or grant monopoly privileges.").

challenges to *state* legislation under the dormant Commerce Clause. This is because Congress simply didn't enact much regulatory legislation in the first century of its existence; state and local regulation, on the other hand, was more extensive early on. [17] This would all change near the end of the Nineteenth Century, with the passage of the Interstate Commerce Act in 1887, the Sherman Anti-Trust Act in 1890, and similar legislation. We will revisit the scope of the Commerce Clause in Part III, *infra*.

The important point for present purposes is that both affirmative and dormant Commerce Clause cases prior to 1937 relied on dividing the world of commercial regulation into two distinct and exclusive spheres. This approach is known as "dual federalism," and it entails "two mutually exclusive, reciprocally limiting fields of power—that of the national government and of the States. The two authorities confront each other as equals across a precise constitutional line, defining their respective jurisdictions." [18] Under this regime, the national government had the exclusive right to regulate commerce "among the several states"; the States, by the same token, had the sole authority to regulate intrastate commerce. Can you see how *Gibbons* contributed to this vision of the federal structure? The alternative to dual federalism is a regime of *concurrent* jurisdiction, in which national and state governments share jurisdiction over the same subject matter. As we will see in Chapters Five and Nine, this latter model much better describes our current federal arrangement.

5.   The problem with dual federalism, of course, is that from the beginning the various parts of the economy, as well as the realms of commercial and other forms of regulation, have been highly interrelated. As early as 1791, Alexander Hamilton asked "what regulation of trade between the States, but must affect the internal trade of every State?"[19] The Court struggled mightily to keep the state and national spheres distinct; it went through three different doctrinal frameworks between *Gibbons* and 1937:

- *"Commerce" vs. "Police" Regulation*: The Marshall Court suggested in *Gibbons* and *Willson* that Congress's power over "commerce" regulation might be exclusive, but that the States retained authority to engage in "police" regulation. The Court's task was thus to assess which category any given regulatory measure fell into. But don't many "police" regulations regulate commercial activity?

- *"Local" vs. "National"*: The Taney Court held that federal and state powers are concurrent with respect to some issues, but that states have exclusive reserved powers over "local" issues, and federal power is exclusive over "[w]hatever subjects of this power are in their nature national, or admit only of one uniform system, [may] justly be said to be of such a nature as

---

[17]   *See, e.g.*, WILLIAM J. NOVAK, THE PEOPLE'S WELFARE: LAW & REGULATION IN NINETEENTH-CENTURY AMERICA (1996).

[18]   Alpheus Thomas Mason, *The Role of the Court*, in FEDERALISM: INFINITE VARIETY IN THEORY AND PRACTICE 8, 24–25 (Valerie A. Earle ed., 1968).

[19]   Hamilton, *supra* note 7, at 564.

to require exclusive legislation by Congress."[20] How easy is it to tell the difference?

- *Direct vs. Indirect*: Between the late 19th century and the New Deal, the Court applied a direct/indirect distinction. For example, the States could regulate things that had an indirect effect on interstate commerce, but not a direct one; likewise, Congress could regulate things having an indirect effect on *intra*state commerce, but not a direct one. But isn't this simply a difference of degree? How much guidance does the Constitution give as to where to draw the line?

Do any of these tests strike you as particularly workable?

6.   One critical observer of the Court's nineteenth century Commerce Clause jurisprudence was Professor Felix Frankfurter, who would later become an important Supreme Court justice in his own right. Frankfurter observed that a central concern of the Court was to formulate its doctrinal tests in a way that would avoid the appearance of "judicial policy-making."[21] Professor Lawrence Lessig later elaborated on the "Frankfurter constraint" in the construction and application of judicial doctrine:

> Whatever else defines a successful judicial system, one dimension of its success is its ability to deliver consistent rulings in cases that appear to be the same. . . . To the extent that results of a particular rule appear consistent, it is easier for the legal culture to view this rule as properly judicial, and its results as properly judicial. . . . To the extent, however, that the results appear inconsistent, this pedigree gets questioned; it becomes easier for observers to view these results as determined, or influenced, by factors external to the rule—in particular, factors considered political. [For this reason] a rule is an inferior rule if, in its application, it appears to be political, in the sense of appearing to allow extra-legal factors to control its application.[22]

The Frankfurter constraint focuses on the *determinacy* of legal doctrine: If doctrine is insufficiently precise to yield clear answers to the questions presented by constitutional cases, then people will begin to think that the results are driven by the political preferences of the judges—e.g., their biases in favor of one steamboat operator over another, or in favor of bridge building or against riverboat companies—rather than by the law. On this analysis, the Court kept shifting its approach to the Commerce Clause because each formula it came up with—e.g., commercial vs. police regulation or local vs. national—was insufficiently determinate to avoid the appearance that the Court was exercising political discretion. The crucial question in federalism doctrine is whether *any* formula is sufficiently determinate to provide a principled basis for judges to restrict the exercise of national or state power.

---

[20]   *Cooley v. Board of Wardens*, 53 U.S. (12 How.) 299 (1852).

[21]   FELIX FRANKFURTER, THE COMMERCE CLAUSE UNDER MARSHALL, TANEY AND WAITE 54 (1937).

[22]   Lawrence Lessig, *Translating Federalism: United States v. Lopez*, 1995 SUP. CT. REV. 125, 170–71, 174.

The Frankfurter constraint represents a central dilemma in constitutional law, not just with respect to federalism but also relating to separation of powers and individual rights. Recall that both Hamilton and Marshall justified judicial review on the ground that the judges would be enforcing the *law*, not their own views of sound policy. The Legal Realist and Critical Legal Studies movements in American legal scholarship, on the other hand, have argued that all law is indeterminate, and that the doctrinal explanations in opinions are simply façades constructed to mask the judges' political preference for a particular result. These indictments may be overstated, but throughout this course you should ask yourself whether the doctrinal arguments are really driving the results in the cases. The problem is particularly acute in the slavery cases in the next section.

CHAPTER FOUR

SLAVERY, CIVIL WAR, AND RECONSTRUCTION

Slavery is the original sin of American constitutionalism. Although the word does not appear in our founding document, the original Constitution acknowledges the institution in three places:

- The "Slave Trade" Clause, Art. I, § 9, cl.1: "The Migration or Importation of such Persons as any of the States now existing shall think proper to admit, shall not be prohibited by the Congress prior to the Year one thousand eight hundred and eight, but a Tax or duty may be imposed on such Importation, not exceeding ten dollars for each Person."

- The Fugitive Slave Clause, Art. IV, § 2, cl. 3: "No Person held to Service or Labour in one State, under the Laws thereof, escaping into another, shall, in Consequence of any Law or Regulation therein, be discharged from such Service or Labour, but shall be delivered up on Claim of the Party to whom such Service or Labour may be due."

- The "Three-Fifths" Clause, Art. I, § 2, cl. 3: "Representatives and direct Taxes shall be apportioned among the several States . . . according to their respective Numbers, which shall be determined by adding to the whole Number of free Persons, including those bound to Service for a Term of Years, and excluding Indians not taxed, three fifths of all other Persons."

These affirmative provisions, as well as the more basic omission—that the Framers of our basic charter of liberties did nothing to remedy the most profound injustice existing in their midst—raise a basic normative question: Is the Constitution *good*? Does it deserve our allegiance? If it does now, did it always?

The Supreme Court's engagement with slavery and the continuing issues of racial equality that sprang from it has been a persistent theme of the Court's institutional life. The cases in this section raise troubling questions concerning the judicial role. Was the Court right to try—at the urging of both Congress and the President—to resolve the slavery debate in *Dred Scott*? Was Justice Story, a committed abolitionist, right to decide *Prigg* the way he did? And did the Court's Reconstruction cases construing the Fourteenth Amendment remain faithful to the meaning of the War and the amendments that it gave rise to?

SECTION 4.1   THE TANEY COURT AND SLAVERY

Marbury v. Madison was the first time that the Supreme Court held an Act of Congress unconstitutional. The second time was 54 years later, in *Dred Scott v. Sandford*, which not only held that free blacks could not be U.S. citizens but also that the Missouri Compromise, which barred slavery in the Louisiana Territory north of 36°30′ N latitude, was unconstitutional. (In the interim, the Court had struck a number of *state* laws, but it had largely avoided confrontations with the national political branches.) The Court's efforts to maintain slavery would tarnish its prestige for generations. Although we are accustomed today to view the federal courts as primary protectors of individual rights, that role during the Civil War and Reconstruction was filled by the President and, even more broadly, the Congress.

National controversies over slavery were driven primarily by the process of westward expansion. National politicians could put off the general question of slavery's legality by classifying it as a matter for the States; Congress could not avoid, however, the question of slavery's legality in the territories, which were governed by federal law until such time as they could be admitted to the Union as States. The first territorial legislation enacted by Congress—the Northwest Ordinance of 1787—had prohibited slavery, but the territories it covered were generally considered to be unsuitable for slave-intensive agriculture in any event. As the United States acquired more southerly territories in which slavery might flourish if permitted, the issue of federal legislation on the subject became more sensitive.

Likewise, the steady admission of new States to the Union kept the slavery issue constantly before the nation, on account of admitting new states as either slave or free. Slavery in the new states affected not only the expansion of the South's "peculiar institution" itself, but also the balance of power between slave and free States in Congress. The admissions of Oregon and Texas, which involved complicated foreign relations issues of their own, thus became inextricably bound to the ongoing contest between North and South over Slavery.

The statesmen of the antebellum Republic—including such giants of the Senate as Henry Clay, Daniel Webster, John C. Calhoun, and Stephen Douglas—dealt with these issues through a series of grand "compromises" enacted between 1820 and the 1850s. The Missouri Compromise of 1820 admitted Missouri as a slave state and partitioned the remainder of the Louisiana purchase—still governed as federal territories—along the line at latitude 36°30′ north. Slavery would be permitted south of this line, and prohibited to its north. The Compromise of 1850, engineered primarily by Clay and Douglas, similarly sought to give something to each side: admission of California as a free state and abolition of slavery in the District of Columbia, on the one hand, and imposition of a stronger Fugitive Slave Law, on the other.

Prigg and *Dred Scott* concern key elements of these compromises. *Prigg* addressed the scope and enforcement of the Fugitive Slave Act— an act which must be evaluated not only on its own moral merits, but also in connection with its role in preserving the Union in 1850.[1] *Dred Scott* concerned not only the question of Mr. Scott's citizenship, but also the constitutional authority of Congress to prohibit slavery in the territories (and, possibly, in the States as well). If Congress were found to lack that power, its ability to enforce compromises of the sort that saved the Union in 1820 and 1850 might well be undermined.

In an important sense, the Taney Court's slavery cases continued the Marshall Court's theme of national consolidation. *Prigg* rigorously enforced Congress's power to provide for the return of fugitive slaves against Northern states that had sought to regulate and even impede that process. And *Dred Scott* itself affirmed that control over eligibility for national citizenship remained with the national government, not with the States. But these cases also foreshadow the Court's preoccupation, in the Twentieth Century, with issues of equality and individual rights.

Prigg v. Pennsylvania
41 U.S. 539 (1842)

■ **MR. JUSTICE STORY delivered the opinion of the Court.**

This is a writ of error to the Supreme Court of Pennsylvania . . . in a case involving the construction of the Constitution and laws of the United States.

The facts are briefly these: The plaintiff in error was indicted in the Court of Oyer and Terminer for York county, for having, with force and violence, taken and carried away from that county to the state of Maryland, a certain negro woman, named Margaret Morgan, with a design and intention of selling and disposing of, and keeping her as a slave or servant for life, contrary to a statute of Pennsylvania, passed on the 26th of March, 1826. That statute in the first section, in substance, provides, that if any person or persons shall from and after the passing of the act, by force and violence take and carry away, or cause to be taken and carried away, and shall by fraud or false pretense, or shall attempt to take, carry away, or seduce any negro or mulatto from any part of that commonwealth, with a design and intention of selling and disposing of, or causing to be sold, or of keeping and detaining, or of causing to be kept and detained, such negro or mulatto as a slave or servant for life, or for any term whatsoever; every such person or persons, his or their aiders or abettors, shall, on conviction thereof, be deemed guilty of a felony, and shall forfeit and pay a sum not less than five hundred, nor more than one thousand dollars; and moreover, shall be sentenced to undergo a

---

[1]   *Prigg*, decided in 1842, involved the somewhat less draconian version of that law enacted in 1793.

servitude for any term or terms of years, not less than seven years nor exceeding twenty-one years; and shall be confined and kept to hard labour. . . .

The plaintiff in error pleaded not guilty to the indictment; and at the trial the jury found . . . that the negro woman, Margaret Morgan, was a slave for life, and held to labour and service under and according to the laws of Maryland, to a certain Margaret Ashmore, a citizen of Maryland; that the slave escaped and fled from Maryland into Pennsylvania in 1832; that the plaintiff in error, being legally constituted the agent and attorney of the said Margaret Ashmore, in 1837, caused the said negro woman to be taken and apprehended as a fugitive from labour by a state constable, under a warrant from a Pennsylvania magistrate; that the said negro woman was thereupon brought before the said magistrate, who refused to take further cognisance of the case; and thereupon the plaintiff in error did remove, take, and carry away the said negro woman and her children out of Pennsylvania into Maryland, and did deliver the said negro woman and her children into the custody and possession of the said Margaret Ashmore. The special verdict further finds, that one of the children was born in Pennsylvania, more than a year after the said negro woman had fled and escaped from Maryland.

Upon this special verdict, the Court of Oyer and Terminer of York County, adjudged that the plaintiff in error was guilty of the offence charged in the indictment. A writ of error was brought from that judgment to the Supreme Court of Pennsylvania, where the judgment was, pro forma, affirmed. From this latter judgment, the present writ of error has been brought to this Court. . . .

1.   The question arising in the case, as to the constitutionality of the statute of Pennsylvania, has been most elaborately argued at the bar. The counsel for the plaintiff in error have contended that the statute of Pennsylvania is unconstitutional; first, because Congress has the exclusive power of legislation upon the subject-matter under the Constitution of the United States, and under the act of the 12th of February, 1793, ch. 51, (7), which was passed in pursuance thereof; secondly, that if this power is not exclusive in Congress, still the concurrent power of the state legislatures is suspended by the actual exercise of the power by Congress; and thirdly, that if not suspended, still the statute of Pennsylvania, in all its provisions applicable to this case, is in direct collision with the act of Congress, and therefore is unconstitutional and void. The counsel for Pennsylvania maintain the negative of all these points.

Few questions which have ever come before this Court involve more delicate and important considerations. . . .

There are two clauses in the Constitution upon the subject of fugitives, which stand in juxtaposition with each other, and have been thought mutually to illustrate each other. They are both contained in the second section of the fourth article, and are in the following words: "A person charged in any state with treason, felony, or other crime, who shall flee from justice, and be found in another state, shall, on demand of the executive authority of the state from which he fled, be delivered up, to be removed to the state having jurisdiction of the crime."

"No person held to service or labour in one state under the laws thereof, escaping into another, shall in consequence of any law or regulation therein, be discharged from such service or labour; but shall be delivered up, on claim of the party to whom such service or labour may be due."

The last clause is that, the true interpretation whereof is directly in judgment before us. Historically, it is well known, that the object of this clause was to secure to the citizens of the slaveholding states the complete right and title of ownership in their slaves, as property, in every state in the Union into which they might escape from the state where they were held in servitude. The full recognition of this right and title was indispensable to the security of this species of property in all the slaveholding states; and, indeed, was so vital to the preservation of their domestic interests and institutions . . . that it constituted a fundamental article, without the adoption of which the Union could not have been formed. Its true design was to guard against the doctrines and principles prevalent in the non-slaveholding states, by preventing them from intermeddling with, or obstructing, or abolishing the rights of the owners of slaves. . . .

How, then, are we to interpret the language of the clause? The true answer is, in such a manner, as, consistently with the words, shall fully and completely effectuate the whole objects of it. If by one mode of interpretation the right must become shadowy and unsubstantial, and without any remedial power adequate to the end; and by another mode it will attain its just end and secure its manifest purpose; it would seem, upon principles of reasoning, absolutely irresistible, that the latter ought to prevail: No Court of justice can be authorized so to construe any clause of the Constitution as to defeat its obvious ends, when another construction, equally accordant with the words and sense thereof, will enforce and protect them.

The clause manifestly contemplates the existence of a positive, unqualified right on the part of the owner of the slave, which no state law or regulation can in any way qualify, regulate, control, or restrain. The slave is not to be discharged from service or labour, in consequence of any state law or regulation. Now, certainly, . . . any state law or state regulation, which interrupts, limits, delays, or postpones the right of the owner to the immediate possession of the slave, and the immediate command of his service and labour, operates, *pro tanto*, a discharge of the slave therefrom. . . . The question is not one of quantity or degree, but of withholding, or controlling the incidents of a positive and absolute right. . . .

Upon this ground we have not the slightest hesitation in holding, that, under and in virtue of the Constitution, the owner of a slave is clothed with entire authority, in every state in the Union, to seize and recapture his slave, whenever he can do it without any breach of the peace, or any illegal violence. In this sense, and to this extent this clause of the Constitution may properly be said to execute itself; and to require no aid from legislation, state or national.

But the clause of the Constitution does not stop here; nor indeed, consistently with its professed objects, could it do so. Many cases must arise in which, if the remedy of the owner were confined to the mere right of seizure and recaption, he would be utterly without any adequate redress. He may not be able to lay his hands upon the slave. He may not be able to enforce his rights against persons who either secrete or conceal, or withhold the slave. He may be restricted by local legislation as to the mode of proofs of his ownership; as to the Courts in which he shall sue, and as to the actions which he may bring; or the process he may use to compel the delivery of the slave. Nay, the local legislation may be utterly inadequate to furnish the appropriate redress. . . .

If, therefore, the clause of the Constitution had stopped at the mere recognition of the right, without providing or contemplating any means by which it might be established and enforced in cases where it did not execute itself, it is plain that it would have, in a great variety of cases, a delusive and empty annunciation. . . .

And this leads us to the consideration of the other part of the clause, which implies at once a guaranty and duty. It says, "But he (the slave) shall be delivered up on claim of the party to whom such service or labour may be due." Now, we think it exceedingly difficult, if not impracticable, to read this language and not to feel that it contemplated some farther remedial redress than that which might be administered at the hands of the owner himself. . . .

These, and many other questions, will readily occur upon the slightest attention to the clause; and it is obvious that they can receive but one satisfactory answer. They require the aid of legislation to protect the right, to enforce the delivery, and to secure the subsequent possession of the slave. If, indeed, the Constitution guarantees the right, and if it requires the delivery upon the claim of the owner, (as cannot well be doubted,) the natural inference certainly is, that the national government is clothed with the appropriate authority and functions to enforce it. The fundamental principle applicable to all cases of this sort, would seem to be, that where the end is required, the means are given; and where the duty is enjoined, the ability to perform it is contemplated to exist on the part of the functionaries to whom it is entrusted. The clause is found in the national Constitution, and not in that of any state. It does not point out any state functionaries, or any state action to carry its provisions into effect. The states cannot, therefore, be compelled to enforce them; and it might well be deemed an unconstitutional exercise of the power of interpretation, to insist that the states are bound to provide means to carry into effect the duties of the national government, nowhere delegated or intrusted to them by the Constitution. On the contrary, the natural, if not the necessary conclusion is, that the national government, in the absence of all positive provisions to the contrary, is bound, through its own proper departments . . . as the case may require, to carry into effect all the rights and duties imposed upon it by the Constitution. . . .

Congress has taken this very view of the power and duty of the national government. As early as the year 1791, the attention of Congress was drawn to it. . . . The result of their deliberations, was the passage of the act of the 12th of February, 1793, which . . . proceeds . . . to provide, that when a person held to labour or service in any of the United States, shall escape into any other of the states or territories, the person to whom such labour or service may be due, his agent or attorney, is hereby empowered to seize or arrest such fugitive from labour, and take him or her before any judge of the Circuit or District Courts of the United States, residing or being within the state, or before any magistrate of a county, city, or town corporate, wherein such seizure or arrest shall be made; and upon proof to the satisfaction of such judge or magistrate, either by oral evidence or affidavit, & c., that the person so seized or arrested, doth, under the laws of the state or territory from which he or she fled, owe service or labour to the person claiming him or her, it shall be the duty of such judge or magistrate, to give a certificate thereof to such claimant . . . which shall be sufficient warrant for removing the said fugitive from labour, to the state or territory from which he or she fled. The fourth section provides a penalty against any person who shall knowingly and willingly obstruct or hinder such claimant, his agent, or attorney, in so seizing or arresting such fugitive from labour, or rescue such fugitive from the claimant, or his agent, or attorney when so arrested, or who shall harbour or conceal such fugitive after notice that he is such; and it also saves to the person claiming such labour or service, his right of action for or on account of such injuries. . . .

But it has been argued, that the act of Congress is unconstitutional, because it does not fall within the scope of any of the enumerated powers of legislation confided to that body; and therefore it is void. Stripped of its artificial and technical structure, the argument comes to this, that although rights are exclusively secured by, or duties are exclusively imposed upon the national government, yet, unless the power to enforce these rights, or to execute these duties can be found among the express powers of legislation enumerated in the Constitution, they remain without any means of giving them effect by any act of Congress; and they must operate solely *proprio vigore*, however, defective may be their operation; nay, even although, in a practical sense, they may become a nullity from the want of a proper remedy to enforce them, or to provide against their violation.

If this be the true interpretation of the Constitution, it must, in a great measure, fail to attain many of its avowed and positive objects as a security of rights, and a recognition of duties. Such a limited construction of the Constitution has never yet been adopted as correct. . . . No one has ever supposed that Congress could, constitutionally, by its legislation, exercise powers, or enact laws beyond the powers delegated to it by the Constitution; but it has, on various occasions, exercised powers which were necessary and proper as means to carry into effect rights expressly given, and duties expressly enjoined thereby. The end being required, it has been deemed a just and necessary implication, that the means to accomplish it are given also; or, in other words, that the power flows as a necessary means to accomplish the end. . . .

We hold the Act to be clearly constitutional in all its leading provisions, and, indeed, with the exception of that part which confers authority upon state magistrates, to be free from reasonable doubt and difficulty upon the grounds already stated. As to the authority so conferred upon state magistrates, while a difference of opinion has existed, and may exist still on the point, in different states, whether state magistrates are bound to act under it; none is entertained by this Court that state magistrates may, if they choose, exercise that authority, unless prohibited by state legislation.

The remaining question is, whether the power of legislation upon this subject is exclusive in the national government, or concurrent in the states, until it is exercised by Congress. In our opinion it is exclusive. . . . The doctrine stated by this Court, in *Sturgis v. Crowninshield*, 4 Wheat. Rep. 122, 193 . . . is applicable to this particular subject. "Wherever," said Mr. Chief Justice Marshall, in delivering the opinion of the Court, "the terms in which a power is granted to Congress, or the nature of the power require that it should be exercised exclusively by Congress, the subject is as completely taken from the state legislatures, as if they had been forbidden to act." . . .

In the first place, . . . the right to seize and retake fugitive slaves, and the duty to deliver them up, in whatever state of the Union they may be found, and of course the corresponding power in Congress to use the appropriate means to enforce the right and duty, derive their whole validity and obligation exclusively from the Constitution of the United States; and are there, for the first time, recognised and established in that peculiar character. . . . It is, therefore, in a just sense a new and positive right, independent of comity, confined to no territorial limits, and bounded by no state institutions or policy. The natural inference . . . is in the absence of any positive delegation of power to the state legislatures, that it belongs to the legislative department of the national government, to which it owes its origin and establishment. . . .

In the next place, the nature of the provision and the objects to be attained by it, require that it should be controlled by one and the same will, and act uniformly by the same system of regulations throughout the

Union. If, then, the states have a right, in the absence of legislation by Congress, to act upon the subject, each state is at liberty to prescribe just such regulations as suit its own policy, local convenience, and local feelings. The legislation of one state may not only be different from, but utterly repugnant to and incompatible with that of another. The time, and mode, and limitation of the remedy; the proofs of the title, and all other incidents applicable thereto, may be prescribed in one state, which are rejected or disclaimed in another. . . . The right, therefore, would never, in a practical sense be the same in all the states. It would have no unity of purpose, or uniformity of operation. The duty might be enforced in some states; retarded, or limited in others; and denied, as compulsory in many, if not in all. Consequences like these must have been foreseen as very likely to occur in the non-slaveholding states; where legislation, if not silent on the subject, and purely voluntary, could scarcely be presumed to be favourable to the exercise of the rights of the owner.

It is scarcely conceivable that the slaveholding states would have been satisfied with leaving to the legislation of the non-slaveholding states, a power of regulation, in the absence of that of Congress, which would or might practically amount to a power to destroy the rights of the owner. If the argument, therefore, of a concurrent power in the states to act upon the subject-matter in the absence of legislation by Congress, be well founded; then, if Congress had never acted at all; or if the act of Congress should be repealed without providing a substitute, there would be a resulting authority in each of the states to regulate the whole subject at its pleasure; and to dole out its own remedial justice, or withhold it at its pleasure and according to its own views of policy and expediency. Surely such a state of things never could have been intended, under such a solemn guarantee of right and duty. On the other hand, construe the right of legislation as exclusive in Congress, and every evil, and every danger vanishes. The right and the duty are then co-extensive and uniform in remedy and operation throughout the whole Union. The owner has the same security, and the same remedial justice, and the same exemption from state regulation and control, through however many states he may pass with his fugitive slave in his possession, . . . to his own domicile. . . . [T]he nature and objects of the provision imperiously require, that, to make it effectual, it should be construed to be exclusive of state authority. . . .

Upon these grounds, we are of opinion that the act of Pennsylvania upon which this indictment is founded, is unconstitutional and void. . . .

■ [CHIEF JUSTICE TANEY and JUSTICES THOMPSON and DANIEL filed partial dissents, all arguing various permutations of the position that the federal law did not preempt all state legislation in *aid* of recovering fugitives.]

■ **MR. JUSTICE MCLEAN, dissenting.**

. . . I cannot perceive how any one can doubt that the remedy given in the Constitution, if indeed it give any remedy without legislation, was designed to be a peaceful one; a remedy sanctioned by judicial authority; a remedy guarded by the forms of law. But the inquiry is reiterated, is not the master entitled to his property? I answer that he is. His right is guaranteed by the Constitution, and the most summary means for its enforcement is found in the act of Congress. And neither the state nor its citizens can obstruct the prosecution of this right.

The slave is found in a state where every man, black or white, is presumed to be free; and this state, to preserve the peace of its citizens, and its soil and jurisdiction from acts of violence, has prohibited the forcible abduction of persons of colour. Does this law conflict with the Constitution? It clearly does not, in its terms. . . .

It is a most important police regulation. And if the master violate it, is he not amenable? The offence consists in the abduction of a person of colour. And this is attempted to be justified upon the simple ground that the slave is property. That a slave is property must be admitted. The state law is not violated by the seizure of the slave by the master, for this is authorized by the act of Congress; but by removing him out of the state by force, and without proof of right, which the act does not authorize. Now, is not this an act which a state may prohibit? The presumption in a non-slaveholding state is against the right of the master, and in favour of the freedom of the person he claims. This presumption may be rebutted, but until it is rebutted by the proof required in the act of 1793, and also, in my judgment, by the Constitution, must not the law of the state be respected and obeyed? . . .

The important point is, shall the presumption of right set up by the master, unsustained by any proof, or the presumption which arises from the laws and institutions of the state, prevail. This is the true issue. The sovereignty of the state is on one side, and the asserted interest of the master on the other. . . .

The presumption of the state that the coloured person is free may be erroneous in fact; and if so, there can be no difficulty in proving it. But may not the assertion of the master be erroneous also; and if so, how is his act of force to be remedied? The coloured person is taken, and forcibly conveyed beyond the jurisdiction of the state. This force, not being authorized by the act of Congress nor by the Constitution, may be prohibited by the state. . . .

This view respects the rights of the master and the rights of the state. It neither jeopardizes nor retards the reclamation of the slave. It removes all state action prejudicial to the rights of the master; and recognises in the state a power to guard and protect its own jurisdiction, and the peace of its citizens. . . .

NOTE ON *PRIGG* AND THE RELATION BETWEEN SLAVERY AND FEDERALISM

1.   Most people associate "states' rights" with the defense of slavery. In *Prigg*, however, a pro-slavery policy at the national level, embodied in the Fugitive Slave Law, confronted efforts by individual states to deviate from national policy by according additional due process to persons accused of being escaped slaves. Looking back on the antebellum period, Henry Adams offered the following assessment:

> Between the slave power and states' rights there was no necessary connection. The slave power, when in control, was a centralizing influence, and all the most considerable encroachments on states' rights were its acts. . . . Whenever a question arose of extending or protecting slavery, the slaveholders became friends of centralized power. . . . Slavery in fact required centralization in order to maintain and protect itself. . . . Thus, in truth, states' rights were the protection of the free states, and as a matter of fact, during the domination of the slave power, Massachusetts appealed to this protecting principle as often and almost as loudly as South Carolina.[2]

Do you agree that "there was no necessary connection" between slavery and states' rights? In addition to the Fugitive Slave Acts, the national House of Representatives imposed an imfamous "gag rule" on considering antislavery petitions, and federal officials cooperated in the suppression of abolitionist literature sent into the South via the U.S. mail. Does the national government's promotion of slavery prior to the Civil War undermine contemporary assumptions about the relation between federalism and civil rights?

2.   Much like *Gibbons*, *Prigg* is a case about the displacement of state law by federal legislative authority. Once again, there are two distinct arguments: (a) a "dormant" argument that federal authority to regulate fugitive slaves, whether or not Congress has actually acted, is exclusive, and (b) a preemption argument that Pennsylvania's liberty law was in actual conflict with the federal Fugitive Slave Act. Does it make sense, however, to read the constitutional provision as barring all state legislation on the subject, whether it hindered or assisted the slavecatcher? And is there anything in either the Fugitive Slave Clause or the congressional statute implementing the Clause's mandate to suggest states were barred from regulating the prior issue of how fugitive status should be determined? Should the Court have been more jealous of state prerogatives to protect the rights of persons who might be kidnapped within their jurisdiction?

3.   Justice Story, the author of the majority opinion in *Prigg*, was both a strong abolitionist and a committed nationalist. Did he make the right choice when those views came into conflict in *Prigg*? Is his resolution of the case best explained as resting on the simple duty of the judge to follow the law, or on a more pragmatic view that only a strong national government

---

[2]   HENRY ADAMS, JOHN RANDOLPH (1882).

could ultimately resolve the slavery question in a just way? Are either of those justifications morally appealing?

4.   Justice Story thought that, notwithstanding the primary holding of *Prigg* that the Fugitive Slave Law preempted Pennsylvania's liberty law, he had saved his abolitionist soul by also holding that the national government could not require state officials to participate in the enforcement of the federal law. This holding is the forerunner of the modern "anti-commandeering doctrine," which we will explore in Chapter Ten. Why did Story think the participation of state officers was such a critical point?

5.   As Scot Powe has observed, "[t]he consequences of *Prigg* were potentially enormous. All Negroes in the North, whether free or escaped, were placed at risk of being taken South."[3] Moreover, the spectacle of Southern slave catchers seeking to apprehend allegedly escaped slaves in Northern cities, often in the teeth of abolitionist crowds, exacerbated sectional tensions. Nonetheless, many on both sides of the deepening divide continued to look to the Supreme Court to resolve the slavery issue once and for all. As attention focused on the issue of slavery in the territories, "[s]eemingly everyone thought that a judicial decision on [that issue] offered the best opportunity for the republic. Politicians as diverse as James Polk, Stephen Douglas, Jefferson Davis, and Henry Clay had favored it."[4] Even Abraham Lincoln affirmed in 1856 that "the Supreme Court of the United States is the tribunal to decide such questions, and we will submit to its decisions."[5] As you consider the Court's foray into this tragic dispute, keep in mind that it did not enter the field uninvited.

Dred Scott v. Sandford
60 U.S. 393 (1857)

■ **MR. CHIEF JUSTICE TANEY delivered the opinion of the court.**

. . . There are two leading questions presented by the record:

1.   Had the Circuit Court of the United States jurisdiction to hear and determine the case between these parties? And

2.   If it had jurisdiction, is the judgment it has given erroneous or not?

The plaintiff in error, who was also the plaintiff in the court below, was, with his wife and children, held as slaves by the defendant, in the State of Missouri; and he brought this action in the Circuit Court of the United States for that district, to assert the title of himself and his family to freedom.

The declaration . . . contains the averment necessary to give the court jurisdiction; that he and the defendant are citizens of different

---

[3]   LUCAS A. POWE, JR., THE SUPREME COURT AND THE AMERICAN ELITE, 1789–2008, at 98 (2009).

[4]   *Id.* at 105.

[5]   Quoted in POWE, *supra* note 2, at 105.

States; that is, that he is a citizen of Missouri, and the defendant a citizen of New York.

The defendant pleaded in abatement to the jurisdiction of the court, that the plaintiff was not a citizen of the State of Missouri, as alleged in his declaration, being a negro of African descent, whose ancestors were of pure African blood, and who were brought into this country and sold as slaves. . . .

The question is simply this: Can a negro, whose ancestors were imported into this country, and sold as slaves, become a member of the political community formed and brought into existence by the Constitution of the United States, and as such become entitled to all the rights, and privileges, and immunities, guaranteed by that instrument to the citizen? One of which rights is the privilege of suing in a court of the United States in the cases specified in the Constitution. . . .

We think they are not, and that they are not included, and were not intended to be included, under the word "citizens" in the Constitution, and can therefore claim none of the rights and privileges which that instrument provides for and secures to citizens of the United States. On the contrary, they were at that time considered as a subordinate and inferior class of beings, who had been subjugated by the dominant race, and, whether emancipated or not, yet remained subject to their authority, and had no rights or privileges but such as those who held the power and the Government might choose to grant them.

It is not the province of the court to decide upon the justice or injustice, the policy or impolicy, of these laws. The decision of that question belonged to the political or law-making power; to those who formed the sovereignty and framed the Constitution. The duty of the court is, to interpret the instrument they have framed, with the best lights we can obtain on the subject, and to administer it as we find it, according to its true intent and meaning when it was adopted.

In discussing this question, we must not confound the rights of citizenship which a State may confer within its own limits, and the rights of citizenship as a member of the Union. It does not by any means follow, because he has all the rights and privileges of a citizen of a State, that he must be a citizen of the United States. . . . For, previous to the adoption of the Constitution of the United States, every State had the undoubted right to confer on whomsoever it pleased the character of citizen, and to endow him with all its rights. . . . Nor have the several States surrendered the power of conferring these rights and privileges by adopting the Constitution of the United States. Each State may still confer them upon an alien, or any one it thinks proper, or upon any class or description of persons; yet he would not be a citizen in the sense in which that word is used in the Constitution of the United States, nor entitled to sue as such in one of its courts, nor to the privileges and immunities of a citizen in the other States. The rights which he would acquire would be restricted to the State which gave them. The

Constitution has conferred on Congress the right to establish an uniform rule of naturalization, and this right is evidently exclusive, and has always been held by this court to be so. . . .

It is very clear, therefore, that no State can, by any act or law of its own, passed since the adoption of the Constitution, introduce a new member into the political community created by the Constitution of the United States. It cannot make him a member of this community by making him a member of its own. And for the same reason it cannot introduce any person, or description of persons, who were not intended to be embraced in this new political family, which the Constitution brought into existence, but were intended to be excluded from it.

The question then arises, whether the provisions of the Constitution, in relation to the personal rights and privileges to which the citizen of a State should be entitled, embraced the negro African race . . . who had then or should afterwards be made free in any State; and to put it in the power of a single State to make him a citizen of the United States, and endue him with the full rights of citizenship in every other State without their consent? Does the Constitution of the United States act upon him whenever he shall be made free under the laws of a State, and raised there to the rank of a citizen, and immediately clothe him with all the privileges of a citizen in every other State, and in its own courts?

The court thinks the affirmative of these propositions cannot be maintained. And if it cannot, the plaintiff in error could not be a citizen of the State of Missouri, within the meaning of the Constitution of the United States, and, consequently, was not entitled to sue in its courts.

It is true, every person, and every class and description of persons, who were at the time of the adoption of the Constitution recognized as citizens in the several States, became also citizens of this new political body; but none other; it was formed by them, and for them and their posterity, but for no one else. And the personal rights and privileges guaranteed to citizens of this new sovereignty were intended to embrace those only who were then members of the several State communities. . . .

It becomes necessary, therefore, to determine who were citizens of the several States when the Constitution was adopted. . . . In the opinion of the court, the legislation and histories of the times, and the language used in the Declaration of Independence, show, that neither the class of persons who had been imported as slaves, nor their descendants, whether they had become free or not, were then acknowledged as a part of the people, nor intended to be included in the general words used in that memorable instrument.

It is difficult at this day to realize the state of public opinion in relation to that unfortunate race, which prevailed in the civilized and enlightened portions of the world at the time of the Declaration of Independence, and when the Constitution of the United States was framed and adopted. But the public history of every European nation displays it in a manner too plain to be mistaken.

They had for more than a century before been regarded as beings of an inferior order, and altogether unfit to associate with the white race, either in social or political relations; and so far inferior, that they had no rights which the white man was bound to respect; and that the negro might justly and lawfully be reduced to slavery for his benefit. He was bought and sold, and treated as an ordinary article of merchandise and traffic, whenever a profit could be made by it. This opinion was at that time fixed and universal in the civilized portion of the white race. It was regarded as an axiom in morals as well as in politics, which no one thought of disputing, or supposed to be open to dispute; and men in every grade and position in society daily and habitually acted upon it in their private pursuits, as well as in matters of public concern, without doubting for a moment the correctness of this opinion.

And in no nation was this opinion more firmly fixed or more uniformly acted upon than by the English Government and English people. They . . . were far more extensively engaged in this commerce than any other nation in the world.

The opinion thus entertained and acted upon in England was naturally impressed upon the colonies they founded on this side of the Atlantic. And, accordingly, a negro of the African race was regarded by them as an article of property, and held, and bought and sold as such, in every one of the thirteen colonies which united in the Declaration of Independence, and afterwards formed the Constitution of the United States. The slaves were more or less numerous in the different colonies, as slave labor was found more or less profitable. But no one seems to have doubted the correctness of the prevailing opinion of the time.

The legislation of the different colonies furnishes positive and indisputable proof of this fact.

It would be tedious, in this opinion, to enumerate the various laws they passed upon this subject. It will be sufficient, as a sample of the legislation which then generally prevailed throughout the British colonies, to give the laws of two of them; one being still a large slaveholding State, and the other the first State in which slavery ceased to exist.

The province of Maryland, in 1717, passed a law declaring "that if any free negro or mulatto intermarry with any white woman, or if any white man shall intermarry with any negro or mulatto woman, such negro or mulatto shall become a slave during life, excepting mulattoes born of white women, who, for such intermarriage, shall only become servants for seven years, to be disposed of as the justices of the county court, where such marriage so happens, shall think fit; to be applied by them towards the support of a public school within the said county. And any white man or white woman who shall intermarry as aforesaid, with any negro or mulatto, such white man or white woman shall become servants during the term of seven years, and shall be disposed of by the justices as aforesaid, and be applied to the uses aforesaid."

The other colonial law to which we refer was passed by Massachusetts in 1705. It is entitled "An act for the better preventing of a spurious and mixed issue," & c.; and it provides . . . "that none of her Majesty's English or Scottish subjects, nor of any other Christian nation, within this province, shall contract matrimony with any negro or mulatto; nor shall any person, duly authorized to solemnize marriage, presume to join any such in marriage, on pain of forfeiting the sum of fifty pounds. . . ."

We give both of these laws in the words used by the respective legislative bodies, because the language in which they are framed, as well as the provisions contained in them, show, too plainly to be misunderstood, the degraded condition of this unhappy race. They were still in force when the Revolution began, and are a faithful index to the state of feeling towards the class of persons of whom they speak, and of the position they occupied throughout the thirteen colonies, in the eyes and thoughts of the men who framed the Declaration of Independence and established the State Constitutions and Governments. They show that a perpetual and impassable barrier was intended to be erected between the white race and the one which they had reduced to slavery, and governed as subjects with absolute and despotic power, and which they then looked upon as so far below them in the scale of created beings, that intermarriages between white persons and negroes or mulattoes were regarded as unnatural and immoral, and punished as crimes, not only in the parties, but in the person who joined them in marriage. And no distinction in this respect was made between the free negro or mulatto and the slave, but this stigma, of the deepest degradation, was fixed upon the whole race.

We refer to these historical facts for the purpose of showing the fixed opinions concerning that race, upon which the statesmen of that day spoke and acted. It is necessary to do this, in order to determine whether the general terms used in the Constitution of the United States, as to the rights of man and the rights of the people, was intended to include them, or to give to them or their posterity the benefit of any of its provisions.

The language of the Declaration of Independence is equally conclusive. . . . "We hold these truths to be self-evident: that all men are created equal; that they are endowed by their Creator with certain unalienable rights; that among them is life, liberty, and the pursuit of happiness; that to secure these rights, Governments are instituted, deriving their just powers from the consent of the governed."

The general words above quoted would seem to embrace the whole human family, and if they were used in a similar instrument at this day would be so understood. But it is too clear for dispute, that the enslaved African race were not intended to be included, and formed no part of the people who framed and adopted this declaration; for if the language, as understood in that day, would embrace them, the conduct of the distinguished men who framed the Declaration of Independence would have been utterly and flagrantly inconsistent with the principles they asserted. . . .

Yet the men who framed this declaration were great men . . . high in their sense of honor, and incapable of asserting principles inconsistent with those on which they were acting. They perfectly understood the meaning of the language they used, and how it would be understood by others; and they knew that it would not in any part of the civilized world be supposed to embrace the negro race, which, by common consent, had been excluded from civilized Governments and the family of nations, and doomed to slavery. They spoke and acted according to the then established doctrines and principles, and in the ordinary language of the day, no one misunderstood them. The unhappy black race . . . were never thought of or spoken of except as property, and when the claims of the owner or the profit of the trader were supposed to need protection.

This state of public opinion had undergone no change when the Constitution was adopted, as is equally evident from its provisions and language. . . . [T]here are two clauses in the Constitution which point directly and specifically to the negro race as a separate class of persons, and show clearly that they were not regarded as a portion of the people or citizens of the Government then formed.

One of these clauses reserves to each of the thirteen States the right to import slaves until the year 1808, if it thinks proper. And the importation which it thus sanctions was unquestionably of persons of the race of which we are speaking. . . . And by the other provision the States pledge themselves to each other to maintain the right of property of the master, by delivering up to him any slave who may have escaped from his service, and be found within their respective territories. . . . [T]hese two provisions show, conclusively, that neither the description of persons therein referred to, not their descendants, were embraced in any of the other provisions of the Constitution; for certainly these two clauses were not intended to confer on them or their posterity the blessings of liberty, or any of the personal rights so carefully provided for the citizen.

No one of that race had ever migrated to the United States voluntarily; all of them had been brought here as articles of merchandise. The number that had been emancipated at that time were but few in comparison with those held in slavery; and they were identified in the public mind with the race to which they belonged, and regarded as a part of the slave population rather than the free. It is obvious that they were not even in the minds of the framers of the Constitution when they were conferring special rights and privileges upon the citizens of a State in every other part of the Union.

Indeed, when we look to the condition of this race in the several States at the time, it is impossible to believe that these rights and privileges were intended to be extended to them.

It is very true, that in that portion of the Union where the labor of the negro race was found to be unsuited to the climate and unprofitable to the master, but few slaves were held at the time of the Declaration of Independence; and when the Constitution was adopted, it had entirely worn out in one of them, and measures had been taken for its gradual abolition in several others. But this change had not been produced by any change of opinion in relation to this race; but because it was discovered, from experience, that slave labor was unsuited to the climate and productions of these States: for some of the States, where it had ceased or nearly ceased to exist, were actively engaged in the slave trade, procuring cargoes on the coast of Africa, and transporting them for sale to those parts of the Union where their labor was found to be profitable, and suited to the climate and productions. And this traffic was openly carried on. . . . And it can hardly be supposed that, in the States where it was then countenanced in its worst form—that is, in the seizure and transportation—the people could have regarded those who were emancipated as entitled to equal rights with themselves.

And we may here again refer, in support of this proposition, to the plain and unequivocal language of the laws of the several States, some passed after the Declaration of Independence and before the Constitution was adopted, and some since the Government went into operation.

We need not refer, on this point, particularly to the laws of the present slaveholding States. Their statute books are full of provisions in relation to this class, in the same spirit with the Maryland law which we have before quoted. They have continued to treat them as an inferior class, and to subject them to strict police regulations, drawing a broad line of distinction between the citizen and the slave races, and legislating in relation to them upon the same principle which prevailed at the time of the Declaration of Independence. As related to these States . . . they have never been regarded as a part of the people or citizens of the State, nor supposed to possess any political rights which the dominant race might not withhold or grant at their pleasure. And as long ago as 1822, the Court of Appeals of Kentucky decided that free negroes and mulattoes were not citizens within the meaning of the Constitution of the United States. . . .

And if we turn to the legislation of the States where slavery had worn out, or measures taken for its speedy abolition, we shall find the same opinions and principles equally fixed and equally acted upon.

Thus, Massachusetts, [t]he law of 1786 . . . forbids the marriage of any white person with any negro, Indian, or mulatto, and inflicts a penalty of fifty pounds upon any one who shall join them in marriage; and declares all such marriages absolutely null and void, and degrades thus the unhappy issue of the marriage by fixing upon it the stain of bastardy. And this mark of degradation was renewed [in] their revised code published in 1836. This code forbids any person from joining in marriage any white person with any Indian, negro, or mulatto, and subjects the party who shall offend in this respect, to imprisonment . . . or to hard labor, and to a fine . . . [and] declares the marriage to be absolutely null and void. . . .

So, too, in Connecticut [which] was not only among the first to put an end to slavery within its own territory, but was the first to fix a mark of reprobation upon the African slave trade. . . . [I]n the same statute passed in 1774, which prohibited the further importation of slaves into the State, there is also a provision by which any negro, Indian, or mulatto servant, who was found wandering out of the town or place to which he belonged, without a written pass . . . was made liable to be seized by any one, and taken before the next authority to be examined and delivered up to his master. . . . And this law was in full operation when the Constitution of the United States was adopted, and was not repealed till 1797. So that up to that time free negroes and mulattoes were associated with servants and slaves in the police regulations established by the laws of the State.

And again, in 1833, Connecticut passed another law, which made it penal to set up or establish any school in that State for the instruction of persons of the African race not inhabitants of the State. . . . And it appears by the case of *Crandall v. The State*, that upon an information filed against Prudence Crandall for a violation of this law, one of the points raised in the defence was, that the law was a violation of the Constitution of the United States; and that the persons instructed, although of the African race, were citizens of other States, and therefore entitled to the rights and privileges of citizens in the State of Connecticut. But Chief Justice Dagget, before whom the case was tried, held, that persons of that description were not citizens of a State, within the meaning of the word citizen in the Constitution of the United States, and were not therefore entitled to the privileges and immunities of citizens in other States. . . .

We have made this particular examination into the legislative and judicial action of Connecticut, because, from the early hostility it displayed to the slave trade on the coast of Africa, we may expect to find the laws of that State as lenient and favorable to the subject race as those of any other State in the Union; and if we find that at the time the Constitution was adopted, they were not even there raised to the rank of citizens, but were still held and treated as property, and the laws relating to them passed with reference altogether to the interest and convenience of the white race, we shall hardly find them elevated to a higher rank anywhere else.

A brief notice of the laws of two other States, and we shall pass on to other considerations.

By the laws of New Hampshire, collected and finally passed in 1815, no one was permitted to be enrolled in the militia of the State, but free white citizens; and the same provision is found in a subsequent collection of the laws, made in 1855. Nothing could more strongly mark the entire repudiation of the African race. The alien is excluded, because, being born in a foreign country, he cannot be a member of the community until he is naturalized. But why are the African race, born in the State, not permitted to share in one of the highest duties of the citizen? The answer is obvious; he is not, by the institutions and laws of the State, numbered among its people. He forms no part of the sovereignty of the State, and is not therefore called on to uphold and defend it.

Again, in 1822, Rhode Island, in its revised code, passed a law forbidding persons who were authorized to join persons in marriage, from joining in marriage any white person with any negro, Indian, or mulatto, under the penalty of two hundred dollars, and declaring all such marriages absolutely null and void; and the same law was again re-enacted in its revised code of 1844. So that, down to the last-mentioned period, the strongest mark of inferiority and degradation was fastened upon the African race in that State.

It would be impossible to enumerate and compress in the space usually allotted to an opinion of a court, the various laws, marking the condition of this race, which were passed from time to time after the Revolution, and before and since the adoption of the Constitution of the United States. In addition to those already referred to, it is sufficient to say, that Chancellor Kent, whose accuracy and research no one will question, states in the sixth edition of his Commentaries, (published in 1848) that in no part of the country except Maine, did the African race, in point of fact, participate equally with the whites in the exercise of civil and political rights.

The legislation of the States therefore shows, in a manner not to be mistaken, the inferior and subject condition of that race at the time the Constitution was adopted, and long afterwards, throughout the thirteen States by which that instrument was framed; and it is hardly consistent with the respect due to these States, to suppose that they regarded at that time, as fellow-citizens and members of the sovereignty, a class of beings whom they had thus stigmatized. . . . More especially, it cannot be believed that the large slaveholding States regarded them as included in the word citizens, or would have consented to a Constitution which might compel them to receive them in that character from another State. For if they were so received, and entitled to the privileges and immunities of citizens, it would exempt them from the operation of the special laws and from the police regulations which they considered to be necessary for their own safety. It would give to persons of the negro race, who were recognized as citizens in any one State of the Union, the right to enter every other State whenever they pleased, singly or in companies, without pass or passport, and without obstruction, to sojourn there as long as they pleased, to go where they pleased at every hour of the day or night without molestation, unless they committed some violation of law for which a white man would be punished; and it would give them the full liberty of speech in public and in private upon all subjects upon which its own citizens might speak; to hold public meetings upon political affairs, and to keep and carry arms wherever they went. And all of this would be done in the face of the subject race of the same color, both free and slaves, and inevitably producing discontent and insubordination among them, and endangering the peace and safety of the State.

It is impossible, it would seem, to believe that the great men of the slaveholding States, who took so large a share in framing the Constitution of the United States, and exercised so much influence in procuring its adoption, could have been so forgetful or regardless of their own safety and the safety of those who trusted and confided in them.

Besides, this want of foresight and care would have been utterly inconsistent with the caution displayed in providing for the admission of new members into this political family. For, when they gave to the citizens of each State the privileges and immunities of citizens in the several States, they at the same time took from the several States the power of naturalization, and confined that power exclusively to the Federal Government. No State was willing to permit another State to determine who should or should not be admitted as one of its citizens, and entitled to demand equal rights and privileges with their own people, within their own territories. The right of naturalization was therefore, with one accord, surrendered by the States, and confided to the Federal Government. . . .

To all this mass of proof we have still to add, that Congress has repeatedly legislated upon the same construction of the Constitution that we have given. Three laws, two of which were passed almost immediately after the Government went into operation, will be abundantly sufficient to show this. The two first are particularly worthy of notice, because many of the men who assisted in framing the Constitution . . . were then in the halls of legislation, and certainly understood what they meant when they used the words "people of the United States" and "citizen" in that well-considered instrument.

The first of these acts is the naturalization law, which was passed at the second session of the first Congress, March 26, 1790, and confines the right of becoming citizens "to aliens being free white persons."

Now, the Constitution does not limit the power of Congress in this respect to white persons. And they may, if they think proper, authorize the naturalization of any one, of any color, who was born under allegiance to another Government. But the language of the law above quoted, shows that citizenship at that time was perfectly understood to be confined to the white race; and that they alone constituted the sovereignty in the Government. . . .

Another of the early laws of which we have spoken, is the first militia law, which was passed in 1792, at the first session of the second Congress. The language of this law is equally plain and significant with the one just mentioned. It directs that every "free able-bodied white male citizen" shall be enrolled in the militia. The word white is evidently used to exclude the African race, and the word "citizen" to exclude unnaturalized foreigners; the latter forming no part of the sovereignty, owing it no allegiance, and therefore under no obligation to defend it. The African race, however, born in the country, did owe allegiance to the Government, whether they were slave or free; but it is repudiated, and rejected from the duties and obligations of citizenship in marked language.

The third act to which we have alluded is even still more decisive; it was passed as late as 1813, and it provides: "That from and after the termination of the war in which the United States are now engaged with Great Britain, it shall not be lawful to employ, on board of any public or private vessels of the United States, any person or persons except citizens of the United States, or persons of color, natives of the United States."

Here the line of distinction is drawn in express words: Persons of color, in the judgment of Congress, were not included in the word citizens, and they are described as another and different class of persons, and authorized to be employed, if born in the United States. . . .

The conduct of the Executive Department of the Government has been in perfect harmony upon this subject with this course of legislation. The question was brought officially before the late William Wirt, when he was the Attorney General of the United States, in 1821, and he decided that the words "citizens of the United States" were used in the acts of Congress in the same sense as in the Constitution; and that free persons of color were not citizens, within the meaning of the Constitution and laws; and this opinion has been confirmed by that of the late Attorney General, Caleb Cushing, in a recent case, and acted upon by the Secretary of State, who refused to grant passports to them as "citizens of the United States."

But it is said that a person may be a citizen, and entitled to that character, although he does not possess all the rights which may belong to other citizens; as, for example, the right to vote, or to hold particular offices; and that yet, when he goes into another State, he is entitled to be recognized there as a citizen, although the State may measure his rights by the rights which it allows to persons of a like character or class resident in the State, and refuse to him the full rights of citizenship.

This argument overlooks the language of the provision in the Constitution of which we are speaking. Undoubtedly, a person may be a citizen, that is, a member of the community who form the sovereignty, although he exercises no share of the political power, and is incapacitated from holding particular offices. Women and minors, who form a part of the political family, cannot vote; and when a property qualification is required to vote or hold a particular office, those who have not the necessary qualification cannot vote or hold the office, yet they are citizens.

So, too, a person may be entitled to vote by the law of the State, who is not a citizen even of the State itself. And in some of the States of the Union foreigners not naturalized are allowed to vote. And the State may give the right to free negroes and mulattoes, but that does not make them citizens of the State, and still less of the United States. And the provision in the Constitution giving privileges and immunities in other States, does not apply to them. . . .

This case, however, strikingly illustrates the consequences that would follow the construction of the Constitution which would give the power contended for to a State. It would in effect give it also to an individual. For if the father of young Darnall had manumitted him in his lifetime, and sent him to reside in a State which recognized him as a citizen, he might have visited and sojourned in Maryland when he pleased, and as long as he pleased, as a citizen of the United States; and the States officers and tribunals would be compelled, by the paramount authority of the Constitution, to receive him and treat him as one of its citizens, exempt from the laws and police of the State in relation to a person of that description, and allow him to enjoy all the rights and privileges of citizenship, without respect to the laws of Maryland, although such laws were deemed by it absolutely essential to its own safety.

The only two provisions which point to them and include them, treat them as property, and make it the duty of the Government to protect it; no other power, in relation to this race, is to be found in the Constitution; and as it is a Government of special, delegated, powers, no authority beyond these two provisions can be constitutionally exercised. The Government of the United States had no right to interfere for any other purpose but that of protecting the rights of the owner, leaving it altogether with the several States to deal with this race, whether emancipated or not, as each State may think justice, humanity, and the interests and safety of society, require. The States evidently intended to reserve this power exclusively to themselves.

No one, we presume, supposes that any change in public opinion or feeling, in relation to this unfortunate race, in the civilized nations of Europe or in this country, should induce the court to give to the words of the Constitution a more liberal construction in their favor than they were intended to bear when the instrument was framed and adopted. Such an argument would be altogether inadmissible in any tribunal called on to interpret it. If any of its provisions are deemed unjust, there is a mode prescribed in the instrument itself by which it may be amended; but while it remains unaltered, it must be construed now as it was understood at the time of its adoption. It is not only the same in words, but the same in meaning, and delegates the same powers to the

Government, and reserves and secures the same rights and privileges to the citizen; and as long as it continues to exist in its present form, it speaks not only in the same words, but with the same meaning and intent with which it spoke when it came from the hands of its framers, and was voted on and adopted by the people of the United States. Any other rule of construction would abrogate the judicial character of this court, and make it the mere reflex of the popular opinion or passion of the day. This court was not created by the Constitution for such purposes. Higher and graver trusts have been confided to it, and it must not falter in the path of duty.

What the construction was at that time, we think can hardly admit of doubt. We have the language of the Declaration of Independence and of the Articles of Confederation, in addition to the plain words of the Constitution itself; we have the legislation of the different States, before, about the time, and since, the Constitution was adopted; we have the legislation of Congress, from the time of its adoption to a recent period; and we have the constant and uniform action of the Executive Department, all concurring together, and leading to the same result. And if anything in relation to the construction of the Constitution can be regarded as settled, it is that which we now give to the word "citizen" and the word "people."

And upon a full and careful consideration of the subject, the court is of opinion, that, upon the facts stated in the plea in abatement, Dred Scott was not a citizen of Missouri within the meaning of the Constitution of the United States, and not entitled as such to sue in its courts; and, consequently, that the Circuit Court had no jurisdiction of the case, and that the judgment on the plea in abatement is erroneous. . . .

We proceed, therefore, to inquire whether the facts relied on by the plaintiff entitled him to his freedom. The case, as he himself states it, on the record brought here by his writ of error, it this:

The plaintiff was a negro slave, belonging to Dr. Emerson, who was a surgeon in the army of the United States. In the year 1834, he took the plaintiff from the State of Missouri to the military post at Rock Island, in the State of Illinois, and held him there as a slave until the month of April or May, 1836. At the time last mentioned, said Dr. Emerson removed the plaintiff from said military post at Rock Island to the military post at Fort Snelling, situate on the west bank of the Mississippi river, in the Territory known as Upper Louisiana, acquired by the United States of France, and situate north of the latitude of thirty-six degrees thirty minutes north, and north of the State of Missouri. Said Dr. Emerson held the plaintiff in slavery at said Fort Snelling, from said last-mentioned date until the year 1838.

In the year 1835, Harriet, who is named in the second count of the plaintiff's declaration, was the negro slave of Major Taliaferro, who belonged to the army of the United States. In that year, 1835, said Major Taliaferro took said Harriet to said Fort Snelling, a military post, situated as hereinbefore stated, and kept her there as a slave until the year 1836, and then sold and delivered her as a slave, at said Fort Snelling, unto the said Dr. Emerson hereinbefore named. Said Dr. Emerson held said Harriet in slavery at said Fort Snelling until the year 1838.

In the year 1836, the plaintiff and Harriet intermarried, at Fort Snelling, with the consent of Dr. Emerson, who then claimed to be their master and owner. Eliza and Lizzie, named in the third count of the plaintiff's declaration, are the fruit of that marriage. Eliza is about fourteen years old, and was born on board the steamboat Gipsey, north of the north line of the State of Missouri, and upon the river Mississippi. Lizzie is about seven years old, and was born in the State of Missouri, at the military post called Jefferson Barracks.

In the year 1838, said Dr. Emerson removed the plaintiff and said Harriet, and their said daughter Eliza, from said Fort Snelling to the State of Missouri, where they have ever since resided.

Before the commencement of this suit, said Dr. Emerson sold and conveyed the plaintiff, and Harriet, Eliza, and Lizzie, to the defendant, as slaves, and the defendant has ever since claimed to hold them, and each of them, as slaves.

In considering this part of the controversy, two questions arise: 1. Was he, together with his family, free in Missouri by reason of the stay in the territory of the United States hereinbefore mentioned? And 2. If they were not, is Scott himself free by reason of his removal to Rock Island, in the State of Illinois, as stated in the above admissions?

We proceed to examine the first question.

The act of Congress, upon which the plaintiff relies, declares that slavery and involuntary servitude, except as a punishment for crime, shall be forever prohibited in all that part of the territory ceded by France, under the name of Louisiana, which lies north of thirty-six degrees thirty minutes north latitude, and not included within the limits of Missouri. And the difficulty which meets us at the threshold of this part of the inquiry is, whether Congress was authorized to pass this law under any of the powers granted to it by the Constitution. . . .

But the power of Congress over the person or property of a citizen can never be a mere discretionary power under our Constitution and form of Government. The powers of the Government and the rights and privileges of the citizen are regulated and plainly defined by the Constitution itself. And when the Territory becomes a part of the United States, the Federal Government enters into possession . . . with its powers over the citizen strictly defined, and limited by the Constitution, from which it derives its own existence, and by virtue of which alone it continues to exist and act as a Government and sovereignty. . . .

For example, no one, we presume, will contend that Congress can make any law in a Territory respecting that establishment of religion, or the free exercise thereof, or abridging the freedom of speech or of the press, or the right of the people of the Territory peaceably to assemble, and to petition the Government for the redress of grievances. . . .

These powers, and others, in relation to rights of person, which it is not necessary here to enumerate, are, in express and positive terms, denied to the General Government; and the rights of private property have been guarded with equal care. Thus the rights of property are united with the rights of person, and placed on the same ground by the fifth amendment to the Constitution, which provides that no person shall be deprived of life, liberty, and property, without due process of law. And an act of Congress which deprives a citizen of the United States of his liberty or property, merely because he came himself or brought his property into a particular Territory of the United States, and who had committed no offence against the laws, could hardly be dignified with the name of due process of law. . . .

It seems, however, to be supposed, that there is a difference between property in a slave and other property, and that different rules may be applied to it in expounding the Constitution of the United States. . . .

Now, as we have already said in an earlier part of this opinion, upon a different point, the right of property in a slave is distinctly and expressly affirmed in the Constitution. The right to traffic in it, like an ordinary article of merchandise and property, was guaranteed to the citizens of the United States, in every State that might desire it, for twenty years. And the Government in express terms is pledged to protect it in all future time, if the slave escapes from his owner. This is done in plain words—too plain to be misunderstood. And no word can be found in the Constitution which gives Congress a greater power over slave property, or which entitles property of that kind to less protection than property of any other description. The only power conferred is the power coupled with the duty of guarding and protecting the owner in his rights.

Upon these considerations, it is the opinion of the court that the act of Congress which prohibited a citizen from holding and owning property of this kind in the territory of the United States north of the line therein mentioned, is not warranted by the Constitution, and is therefore void; and that neither Dred Scott himself, nor any of his family, were made free by being carried into this territory; even if they had been carried there by the owner, with the intention of becoming a permanent resident.

■ MR. JUSTICE MCLEAN dissenting.

. . . Slavery is emphatically a State institution. . . . In the formation of the Federal Constitution, care was taken to confer no power on the Federal Government to interfere with this institution in the States. In the provision respecting the slave trade, in fixing the ratio of representation, and providing for the reclamation of fugitives from labor, slaves were referred to as persons, and in no other respect are they considered in the Constitution.

We need not refer to the mercenary spirit which introduced the infamous traffic in slaves, to show the degradation of negro slavery in our country. This system was imposed upon our colonial settlements by the mother country, and it is due to truth to say that the commercial colonies and States were chiefly engaged in the traffic. But we know as a historical fact, that James Madison, that great and good man, a leading member in the Federal Convention, was solicitous to guard the language of that instrument so as not to convey the idea that there could be property in man.

I prefer the lights of Madison, Hamilton, and Jay, as a means of construing the Constitution in all its bearings, rather than to look behind that period, into a traffic which is now declared to be piracy, and punished with death by Christian nations. I do not like to draw the sources of our domestic relations from so dark a ground. Our independence was a great epoch in the history of freedom; and while I admit the Government was not made especially for the colored race, yet many of them were citizens of the New England States, and exercised the rights of suffrage when the Constitution was adopted, and it was not doubted by any intelligent person that its tendencies would greatly ameliorate their condition.

Many of the States, on the adoption of the Constitution, or shortly afterward, took measures to abolish slavery within their respective jurisdictions; and it is a well-known fact that a belief was cherished by the leading men, South as well as North, that the institution of slavery would gradually decline, until it would become extinct. The increased value of slave labor, in the culture of cotton and sugar, prevented the realization of this expectation. Like all other communities and States, the South were influenced by what they considered to be their own interests.

But if we are to turn our attention to the dark ages of the world, why confine our view to colored slavery? On the same principles, white men were made slaves. All slavery has its origin in power, and is against right.

The power of Congress to establish Territorial Governments, and to prohibit the introduction of slavery therein, is the next point to be considered. . . . If Congress should deem slaves or free colored persons injurious to the population of a free Territory, as conducing to lessen the value of the public lands, or on any other ground connected with the public interest, they have the power to prohibit them from becoming settlers in it. This can be sustained on the ground of a sound national policy . . .

A slave is not a mere chattel. He bears the impress of his Maker, and is amenable to the laws of God and man; and he is destined to an endless existence. . . .

I think the judgment of the court below should be reversed.

■ **MR. JUSTICE CURTIS dissenting.**

. . . To determine whether any free persons, descended from Africans held in slavery, were citizens of the United States under the Confederation, and consequently at the time of the adoption of the Constitution of the United States, it is only necessary to know whether any such persons were citizens of either of the States under the Confederation, at the time of the adoption of the Constitution.

Of this there can be no doubt. At the time of the ratification of the Articles of Confederation, all free native-born inhabitants of the States of New Hampshire, Massachusetts, New York, New Jersey, and North Carolina, though descended from African slaves, were not only citizens of those States, but such of them as had the other necessary qualifications possessed the franchise of electors, on equal terms with other citizens. . . .

Did the Constitution of the United States deprive them or their descendants of citizenship?

That Constitution was ordained and established by the people of the United States, through the action, in each State, of those persons who were qualified by its laws to act thereon, in behalf of themselves and all other citizens of that State. In some of the States, as we have seen, colored persons were among those qualified by law to act on this subject. These colored persons were not only included in the body of "the people of the United States," by whom the Constitution was ordained and established, but in at least five of the States they had the power to act, and doubtless did act, by their suffrages, upon the question of its adoption. It would be strange, if we were to find in that instrument anything which deprived of their citizenship any part of the people of the United States who were among those by whom it was established.

I can find nothing in the Constitution which, *proprio vigore*, deprives of their citizenship any class of persons who were citizens of the United States at the time of its adoption, or who should be native-born citizens of any State after its adoption; nor any power enabling Congress to disfranchise persons born on the soil of any State, and entitled to citizenship of such State by its Constitution and laws. And my opinion is, that, under the Constitution of the United States, every free person born on the soil of a State, who is a citizen of that State by force of its Constitution or laws, is also a citizen of the United States. . . .

It has been often asserted that the Constitution was made exclusively by and for the white race. It has already been shown that in five of the thirteen original States, colored persons then possessed the elective franchise, and were among those by whom the Constitution was ordained and established. If so, it is not true, in point of fact, that the Constitution was made exclusively by the white race. And that it was made exclusively for the white race is, in my opinion, not only an assumption not warranted by anything in the Constitution, but contradicted by its opening declaration, that it was ordained and established by the people of the United States, for themselves and their posterity. And as free colored persons were then citizens of at least five States, and so in every sense part of the people of the United States, they were among those for whom and whose posterity the Constitution was ordained and established.

Again, it has been objected, that if the Constitution has left to the several States the rightful power to determine who of their inhabitants shall be citizens of the United States, the States may make aliens citizens.

The answer is obvious. The Constitution has left to the States the determination what persons, born within their respective limits, shall acquire by birth citizenship of the United States; it has not left to them any power to prescribe any rule for the removal of the disabilities of alienage. This power is exclusively in Congress.

It has been further objected, that if free colored persons, born within a particular State, and made citizens of that State by its Constitution and laws, are thereby made citizens of the United States, then, under the second section of the fourth article of the Constitution, such persons would be entitled to all the privileges and immunities of citizens in the several States; and if so, then colored persons could vote, and be eligible to not only Federal offices, but offices even in those States whose Constitutions and laws disqualify colored persons from voting or being elected to office.

But this position rests upon an assumption which I deem untenable. Its basis is, that no one can be deemed a citizen of the United States who is not entitled to enjoy all the privileges and franchises which are conferred on any citizen. That this is not true, under the Constitution of the United States, seems to me clear.

A naturalized citizen cannot be President of the United States, nor a Senator till after the lapse of nine years, nor a Representative till after the lapse of seven years, from his naturalization. Yet, as soon as naturalized, he is certainly a citizen of the United States. Nor is any inhabitant of the District of Columbia, or of either of the Territories, eligible to the office of Senator or Representative in Congress, though they may be citizens of the United States. So, in all the States, numerous persons, though citizens, cannot vote, or cannot hold office, either on account of their age, or sex, or the want of the necessary legal qualifications. The truth is, that citizenship, under the Constitution of the United States, is not dependent on the possession of any particular political or even of all civil rights; and any attempt so to define it must lead to error. To what citizens the elective franchise shall be confided, is a question to be determined by each State, in accordance with its own views of the necessities or expediencies of its condition. . . .

[T]his clause of the Constitution does not confer on the citizens of one State, in all other States, specific and enumerated privileges and immunities. They are entitled to such as belong to citizenship, but not to such as belong to particular citizens attended by other qualifications. Privileges and immunities which belong to certain citizens of a State, by reason of the operation of causes other than mere citizenship, are not conferred. Thus, if the laws of a State require, in addition to citizenship of the State, some qualification for office, or the exercise of the elective franchise, citizens of all other States, coming thither to reside, and not possessing those qualifications, cannot enjoy those privileges, not because they are not to be deemed entitled to the privileges of citizens of the State in which they reside, but because they, in common with the native-born citizens of that State, must have the qualifications prescribed by law for the enjoyment of such privileges, under its Constitution and laws. . . .

It has sometimes been urged that colored persons are shown not to be citizens of the United States by the fact that the naturalization laws apply only to white persons. But whether a person born in the United States be or be not a citizen, cannot depend on laws which refer only to aliens, and do not affect the status of persons born in the United States. The utmost effect which can be attributed to them is, to show that Congress has not deemed it expedient generally to apply the rule to colored aliens. That they might do so, if thought fit, is clear. . . .

I do not deem it necessary to review at length the legislation of Congress having more or less bearing on the citizenship of colored persons. It does not seem to me to have any considerable tendency to prove that it has been considered by the legislative department of the Government, that no such persons are citizens of the United States. Undoubtedly they have been debarred from the exercise of particular rights or privileges extended to white persons, but, I believe, always in terms which, by implication, admit they may be citizens. Thus the act of May 17, 1792, for the organization of the militia, directs the enrolment of "every free, able-bodied, white male citizen." An assumption that none but white persons are citizens, would be as inconsistent with the just import of this language, as that all citizens are able-bodied, or males. . . .

I dissent, therefore, from that part of the opinion of the majority of the court, in which it is held that a person of African descent cannot be a citizen of the United States; and I regret I must go further, and dissent both from what I deem their assumption of authority to examine the constitutionality of the act of Congress commonly called the Missouri compromise act, and the grounds and conclusions announced in their opinion. . . .

If, then, [the Constitution] does contain a power to legislate respecting the territory, what are the limits of that power?

To this I answer, that, in common with all the other legislative powers of Congress, it finds limits in the express prohibitions on

Congress not to do certain things; that, in the exercise of the legislative power, Congress cannot pass an ex post facto law or bill of attainder; and so in respect to each of the other prohibitions contained in the Constitution.

Besides this, the rules and regulations must be needful. But undoubtedly the question whether a particular rule or regulation be needful, must be finally determined by Congress itself. Whether a law be needful, is a legislative or political, not a judicial, question. Whatever Congress deems needful is so, under the grant of power. . . .

Looking at the power of Congress over the Territories as of the extent just described, what positive prohibition exists in the Constitution, which restrained Congress from enacting a law in 1820 to prohibit slavery north of thirty-six degrees thirty minutes north latitude?

The only one suggested is that clause in the fifth article of the amendments of the Constitution which declares that no person shall be deprived of his life, liberty, or property, without due process of law. I will now proceed to examine the question, whether this clause is entitled to the effect thus attributed to it. . . .

Is it conceivable that the Constitution has conferred the right on every citizen to become a resident on the territory of the United States with his slaves, and there to hold them as such, but has neither made nor provided for any municipal regulations which are essential to the existence of slavery?

Is it not more rational to conclude that they who framed and adopted the Constitution were aware that persons held to service under the laws of a State are property only to the extent and under the conditions fixed by those laws; that they must cease to be available as property, when their owners voluntarily place them permanently within another jurisdiction, where no municipal laws on the subject of slavery exist; and that, being aware of these principles, and having said nothing to interfere with or displace them, or to compel Congress to legislate in any particular manner on the subject, and having empowered Congress to make all needful rules and regulations respecting the territory of the United States, it was their intention to leave to the discretion of Congress what regulations, if any, should be made concerning slavery therein? Moreover, if the right exists, what are its limits, and what are its conditions? If citizens of the United States have the right to take their slaves to a Territory, and hold them there as slaves, without regard to the laws of the Territory, I suppose this right is not to be restricted to the citizens of slaveholding States. A citizen of a State which does not tolerate slavery can hardly be denied the power of doing the same thing. And what law of slavery does either take with him to the Territory? If it be said to be those laws respecting slavery which existed in the particular State from which each slave last came, what an anomaly is this? Where else can we find, under the law of any civilized country, the power to introduce and permanently continue diverse systems of foreign municipal law, for holding persons in slavery? . . .

Nor, in my judgment, will the position, that a prohibition to bring slaves into a Territory deprives any one of his property without due process of law, bear examination.

It must be remembered that this restriction on the legislative power is not peculiar to the Constitution of the United States; it was borrowed from Magna Charta; was brought to America by our ancestors, as part of their inherited liberties, and has existed in all the States, usually in the very words of the great charter. It existed in every political community in America in 1787, when the ordinance prohibiting slavery north and west of the Ohio was passed.

And if a prohibition of slavery in a Territory in 1820 violated this principle of Magna Charta, the ordinance of 1787* also violated it; and what power had, I do not say the Congress of the Confederation alone, but the Legislature of Virginia, or the Legislature of any or all the States of the Confederacy, to consent to such a violation? The people of the States had conferred no such power. I think I may at least say, if the Congress did then violate Magna Charta by the ordinance, no one discovered that violation. Besides, if the prohibition upon all persons, citizens as well as others, to bring slaves into a Territory, and a declaration that if brought they shall be free, deprives citizens of their property without due process of law, what shall we say of the legislation of many of the slaveholding States which have enacted the same prohibition?

As early as October, 1778, a law was passed in Virginia, that thereafter no slave should be imported into that Commonwealth by sea or by land, and that every slave who should be imported should become free. A citizen of Virginia purchased in Maryland a slave who belonged to another citizen of Virginia, and removed with the slave to Virginia. The slave sued for her freedom, and recovered it; as may be seen in *Wilson v. Isabel*, (5 Call's R., 425). See also *Hunter v. Fulcher*, (1 Leigh, 172); and a similar law has been recognised as valid in Maryland, in *Stewart v. Oaks*, (5 Har. and John., 107). I am not aware that such laws, though they exist in many States, were ever supposed to be in conflict with the principle of Magna Charta incorporated into the State Constitutions. It was certainly understood by the Convention which framed the Constitution, and has been so understood ever since, that, under the power to regulate commerce, Congress could prohibit the importation of slaves; and the exercise of the power was restrained till 1808. A citizen of the United States owns slaves in Cuba, and brings them to the United States, where they are set free by the legislation of

---

* [Editor's Note] The Northwest Ordinance, enacted by the Confederation Congress and later confirmed by the First Congress after ratification of the Constitution, provided a structure of government for U.S. territory not incorporated into the original states. It prohibited slavery in the relevant territory.

Congress. Does this legislation deprive him of his property without due process of law? If so, what becomes of the laws prohibiting the slave trade? If not, how can a similar regulation respecting a Territory violate the fifth amendment of the Constitution? . . .

For these reasons, I am of opinion that so much of the several acts of Congress as prohibited slavery and involuntary servitude within that part of the Territory of Wisconsin lying north of thirty-six degrees thirty minutes north latitude, and west of the river Mississippi, were constitutional and valid laws. . . .

In my opinion, the judgment of the Circuit Court should be reversed, and the cause remanded for a new trial.

Sanford Levinson, Pledging Faith in the Civil Religion, or, Would You Sign the Constitution?[*]

The principal exhibit commemorating the bicentennial of the Constitution is located in Philadelphia, in the Second Bank of the United States. Called "Miracle at Philadelphia," it is designed not only to inform, but also, inevitably, to establish a mood suitable to contact with the miraculous. One suspects, for example, that the letters from George Washington and the original notebook of James Madison function for most viewers as sacred relics rather than as sources of information.

As the exhibit reaches the culminating event of September 17, viewers are presented with an invitation to become a latter-day signatory of the Constitution. The exhibit in fact takes ample note of the controversy surrounding both the signing and the subsequent ratification. Yet it is hard to believe that most viewers will not interpret the invitation as a suggested transformation of the visit from a mere remembrance of times past to a renewed dedication to the Constitution . . . as an ever-living presence that is vital to the establishment of a more perfect Union committed above all to the realization of justice and the blessings of liberty. Every participant in the exhibit is thus asked to make a choice—to sign or not to sign, to ratify or to reject, the Constitution of the United States.

I have now visited the exhibit twice, and I commend it to all who have not yet seen it. I have not yet accepted the invitation to sign, however, and I want to devote my remarks not only to explaining my own indecision about signing—for that is probably a better term, at least so far, than "decision not to sign"—but also to indicating why I believe that the question is of some general import and worth our collective attention. . . .

---

[*]   Reprinted from 29 WM. & MARY L. REV. 113 (1987).

The . . . invitation to sign . . . raises the possibility of challenging [the Constitution's] authority. . . . So please join me in an imaginative trip to the Second Bank as we place ourselves in front of the scrolls. . . .

Much more serious [than the lack of a Bill of Rights] is the brooding omnipresence of . . . race and, more precisely, slavery. Now one can immediately try to evade the slavery issue in somewhat the same way one evades the lack of a Bill of Rights in the 1787 Constitution. That is, just as one can in effect stipulate that the document one is signing is that supplemented by the 1791 amendments, so can one announce that he or she is signing the post-1868 Constitution. But that is scarcely a satisfactory resolution to the context of the Philadelphia exhibit. . . . For surely we must decide what our stance . . . is toward the specific work of Madison, Wilson, the Morrises, and others.

We can, of course, . . . say that it is absurd to try to place ourselves within the context of 1787 and decide whether we would have endorsed the Constitution then. . . . I am sympathetic to that argument, given that I do not believe we can shed our historically located skin. . . . But is not the bicentennial predicated on the notion that we are celebrating something that is recognizable as a continuing part of our own lives and political culture. . . . Does not the same predication of endurance through many generations, uniting the living, the dead, and the yet unborn, undergird in substantial ways the presentation of the standard constitutional law course, in which we often view ourselves as linked in discourse with John Marshall, and perhaps even Madison? . . .

So let us return to what is surely one of the most difficult problems presented those who would celebrate the Constitution—chattel slavery. An ever-present temptation revealed, among other places, in the contents of most casebooks on constitutional law is basically to ignore chattel slavery as a constitutionally legitimized presence in American history. To put it mildly, that does not seem to be a satisfactory solution. . . .

What, for example, should we expect the black visitor to Philadelphia to do when invited to sign the Constitution? Many of us remember well Barbara Jordan's impassioned pronouncement, just before she cast her vote to impeach Richard Nixon, that "[m]y faith in the Constitution is whole, it is complete, it is total, and I am not going to sit here and be an idle spectator to the diminution, the subversion of the Constitution." Could she possibly have made the same speech in regard to the Constitution of 200 years ago? Might she not have joined William Lloyd Garrison in describing it as a "covenant with death and an agreement with hell," with its subversion therefore becoming the heartfelt duty of a moral being? . . .

I suppose that one option open to us—and especially to those of us identified with what are perceived to be free-wheeling approaches to constitutional interpretation—is the adoption of an argument like that which Frederick Douglass made in 1860, when he labeled the Constitution, correctly understood, as in fact antislavery. "I undertake to say," stated Douglass, "that the constitutionality of slavery can be made out only by disregarding the plain and common-sense reading of the Constitution itself. . . . [T]he Constitution will afford slavery no protection when it shall cease to be administered by slaveholders." . . .

Douglass's central move, of course, was a radical one: to split off the Constitution from decisions of the Supreme Court, which he recognized as recurrently protective of slavery. I personally have no problem with this, although the recent response to a similar move by Attorney General Meese certainly indicates a great deal of disquiet with such arguments.* In any case, acceptance of Douglass's view of the Constitution presumably allows an opponent of slavery to sign even the 1787 Constitution with a clear heart, the only price being the necessity to embrace some especially controversial theories of constitutional interpretation.

Assume, however, that the potential signer . . . is unwilling to pay that price or, at the very least, is unable to agree with Douglass's reading of the Constitution and accepts instead the more standard reading of the document as significantly protective of slaveholder interests. What follows? One might, for example, adopt Justice Story's view that abominations like the Fugitive Slave Clause, not to mention the guaranteed protection of the international slave trade for twenty years and the added representation given to the South because of its slaves, were necessary in order to form the Union. At this point the inquiry could branch off into at least two directions. The first assumes the desirability of union and then asks whether in fact achievement of that end required the means chosen in Philadelphia and therefore our retrospective, albeit reluctant, ratification. To ask the question this way, of course, inevitably gives greatest weight to the historical record as it actually developed and to the justifications offered at the time, for it indeed seems tendentious to deny the efficacy of the compromises offered to attaining the goal of creating a strengthened United States. We may, however, ask a second question: Do we in fact share the commitment to union that justifies the compromises? . . .

[O]f course, the central problem with "disunionist" thinking . . . is that it focused more on the immorality of collaboration with slavery than on the question of how one most quickly could bring slavery to an end. We know that with ratification of the thirteenth amendment, chattel slavery ended by 1865. Is there good reason to believe that it would have ended earlier if the Constitution had not been ratified and balkanization

---

    * [Editor's Note] Edwin Meese, who was Attorney General under President Reagan, stirred considerable controversy by denying that the Constitution and judicial decisions interpreting it are synonymous. Meese argued that such decisions "bind[ ] the parties in a case and also the executive branch for whatever enforcement is necessary. But such a decision does not establish a 'supreme Law of the Land' that is binding on all persons and parts of government, henceforth and forevermore." Edwin Meese, *The Law of the Constitution*, 61 TUL. L. REV. 979 (1987). Meese was thinking of *Roe v. Wade*, and he was roundly condemned by liberals. But Abraham Lincoln took much the same position with regard to *Dred Scott. See infra* Section 6.2.

had followed instead? I suspect not. But the important point is surely this: Can one who believes that the ratification of the Constitution did enhance the prospects and the actuality of chattel slavery still sign the Constitution? What precisely is the value of the Constitution and of the concomitant nation that would justify even an extra week's slavery? What precisely is the omelet that justified breaking those particular eggs?

[O]ne might try to finesse these difficult, if not excruciating, questions by focusing on what some have called the "second" Constitution; that is, the post Civil War document distinguished by the addition of the thirteenth, fourteenth and fifteenth amendments. That allows a solution to the chattel slavery problem, though not necessarily other kinds of slavery such as wage slavery, and it might justify the decision of many blacks to add their signatures to the reformed document. But could Barbara Jordan necessarily sign even the 1868 Constitution? After all, the standard reading of that Constitution is that it did not guarantee women the right to vote. Women were not given this most basic attribute of community membership until 1920 and the nineteenth amendment. Some partisans of the Equal Rights Amendment would deny that women have been granted full rights of membership even today. . . .

But what of today's Constitution? Is it sufficiently "perfect" that signing is not problematic? For example, what might persons mired in poverty have to say to a Constitution that is seemingly indifferent, at least under the "orthodox" views articulated by the Court and taught in most law school classrooms, to their plight? Protection of "negative" liberties are precious, but that does not make any less pressing the need for "affirmative" access to food, shelter, medical care, education, and the like. Should we expect the homeless victims of a literally careless political economy to sign the Constitution?

Even the well-off need hardly believe that the Constitution is sufficiently perfect to merit their unequivocal endorsement. I assume that no one need believe that it is truly perfect in order to sign; the question is what deviation from perfection is tolerable, justifying inevitable compromises. Consider, in this context, the recent report by Lloyd Cutler and other distinguished citizens suggesting that the vaunted system of separation of powers and checks and balances is in fact a recipe for immobilism and a government incapacitated from effective action or, what is worse, a government tempted to achieve "effectiveness" by the surreptitious practices carried to new heights—or depths—by the current administration. The answer, according to these analyses, lies in such practices as tightening the connection between presidential and congressional elections, allowing members of Congress to serve in the Cabinet, and, most radical of all, allowing the calling of new elections should President and Congress be hopelessly deadlocked.

Perhaps one way of testing whether these truly would be "fundamental" changes in our constitutional system would be by asking whether a person who shares the premises of this analysis will sign the Constitution. An affirmative answer could well have two aspects. First, even with the defects of the present system of governance, it is still sufficiently protective of liberty and helpful to achieving justice that it deserves our support. Second, one could emphasize as key to the Constitution the existence of article V, the amending clause. Article V is the best possible evidence for the proposition that the framers themselves did not believe that they had created a perfect document and that future changes were completely legitimate, at least so long as the changes arose through article V procedures.

Article V can become the great source of consensus—paradoxically, insofar as it appears to legitimize radical dissents. That is, so long as we do not believe that the Constitution is absolutely terrible, then presumably we can sign it by saying that we will strive to bring it more in line with our favorite vision of the polity through an article V amendment. But this emphasis on article V itself raises some profound problems. . . .

I have been engaging in a process of repeated deferral, indicating the various ramifications of the question without indicating my own answers. . . . I shall be in Philadelphia on May 25, which, not entirely by coincidence, is the 200th anniversary of the opening of the Convention. It will be easy enough to stop by the Second Bank once more. Will I add my signature to the scroll this time?

I can honestly say that I did not know what the answer would be when I began thinking about this paper, or even when I began writing it. No doubt there was a temptation to say no, whether to indicate a symbolic solidarity with the victims of the American Constitution— including but not limited to slaves—or simply to manifest a certain kind of iconoclasm. That opinion, however, just doesn't write, at least for me, though I do regard it as a genuine possibility for others.

The Constitution is a linguistic system, what some among us might call a discourse. It has helped to generate a uniquely American form of political rhetoric that allows one to grapple with every important political issue imaginable. As Jeff Powell has written, it provides "a common language with which to carry on debate about the distribution and use of power in our society." The fact that its teachings are, according to some of us, indeterminate, is quite beside the point, for so is any system of language. . . . If the orthodox language of the Constitution promotes a stingy, "negative"-rights oriented view of the polity, there are alternate sentences available . . . that can promote a socialist vision. The key point is that one need not learn a "new language" in order to promote one's favored vision of the polity.

Obviously one can learn new languages, just as it is helpful to try to become less parochial about the so-called American way of doing things, but it is a radical step indeed when a person consciously repudiates an old language, and the renunciation and abjuration of that language almost always are accompanied by special circumstances. I have been told that there are some Afrikaaner writers who have chosen to stop writing in that language as a sign of their revulsion against the terrible culture linked with it; presumably, some writers did the same with German some fifty years ago. For a writer, no more magnificent, or terrible, gesture can be imagined.

In preparing these remarks, I have come to realize my refusal to sign the Constitution would require a much deeper alienation from American life and politics than I can genuinely feel, or, indeed, have ever felt. The Constitution . . . has in some of its manifestations incarnated what is worst about the United States; but, of course, it captures as well what is best about this country. . . . [C]onstitutionalist discourse can be a valuable way of addressing crucial public issues, and I am not sure that any competing rhetoric is likely to prove more productive, not to mention all the costs attached to learning the new language of any such rhetoric.

[There is] a sense of . . . fluidity [to] the Constitution, its resistance to any kind of fixity or closure, even though some would seek it either in the text or in the pronouncements of an authoritative institution like the Supreme Court. For me, signing the Constitution commits one not to closure but only to a process of becoming, and to taking responsibility for constructing the political vision toward which I, joined, I hope, with others, strive. It is less a series of propositional utterances . . . than a commitment to taking political conversation seriously. . . .

There is, undoubtedly, little that is surprising in this conclusion. "Well-off law professor supports Constitution" is scarcely a headline likely to sell newspapers. . . . I am willing to add my signature to the Constitution, secure mainly in the belief that a refusal to do so would be not only a far more hostile gesture than I am capable of, but also a yet further step toward the end of conversation itself. . . . I take it that most of us prefer to believe that some kind of dialogue remains more or less possible, the question being, of course, whether we can find a common language in which to speak and ask our questions.

In any event, I have tried to sketch out what constitutes my Constitution, and why I am willing to sign it and even to celebrate its presence in our culture. What is your Constitution, and are you willing to sign it?

NOTE ON SLAVERY AND THE CONSTITUTION

1. There are two issues in *Dred Scott*: a) Can free blacks be "citizens" within the meaning of the Constitution? and b) Was the Missouri Compromise, barring slavery in certain parts of the western territories, constitutional? Was the Court's decision right or wrong on each of these two issues?

2.   How does the federalism issue cut on each of the issues in *Dred Scott*? More generally, if the slave question had been decided at the national level in 1789, rather than being reserved to the States, which way do you think it would have come out?

3.   In *McCulloch*, Chief Justice Marshall relied primarily on textual and structural arguments. *Dred Scott* is an example of two additional methodologies: originalism (the reliance on the understanding of constitutional meaning at the time that the relevant constitutional provisions were drafted and ratified), and the identification of unenumerated fundamental rights. Chief Justice Taney's opinion on the citizenship question, as well as the dissents disputing that question, was highly originalist. What sort of evidence did they employ to determine the original understanding of the Constitution with respect to citizenship of free blacks? Did the majority or the dissent have the better of the historical argument? Suppose we reject originalism as a method of interpretation and instead interpret the Constitution in light of an evolving moral consensus. Do you think that a moral consensus existed in 1857 that free blacks were entitled to U.S. citizenship? If the society is deeply divided on a question, how should the Court decide?

When Chief Justice Taney turned to the validity of the Missouri Compromise, however, he struck it down based on a fundamental right (to property in slaves) that is hard to locate in the constitutional text or in specific historical evidence. Because this sort of right is grounded in the notion that the Fifth Amendment's Due Process Clause protects not only procedural but substantive entitlements, it is often called "substantive due process." In this sense, *Dred Scott* is the forerunner of cases like *Lochner v. New York*, *Griswold v. Connecticut*, and *Roe v. Wade*. One may certainly criticize Taney's refusal to apply this more generous approach to personal liberty in the *first* part of the opinion—that is, to Dred Scott's right to liberty and recognition as a citizen. But granting that the Court should be consistent, which part of Taney's opinion provides the better model? In answering this question, keep in mind that the Court's decision to strike down the Missouri Compromise arguably had the more destructive consequences for the nation.

4.   Chief Justice Taney strongly believed that the Supreme Court had to resolve the slavery question before it tore the country apart. His hope was that, if the resolution could be grounded in the Constitution, the partisans of both North and South would accept the Court's resolution as definitive and let the matter rest. We now know that things didn't quite work out that way: Over 600,000 Americans died resolving the question in the Civil War. *Dred Scott* plainly didn't prevent this tragedy, and it may have made it more likely by suggesting that the Court would strike down future attempts at legislative compromise just as it had struck down the Missouri Compromise. Is the problem that *Dred Scott* sought to resolve the slavery question in the wrong direction (in favor of slavery) or that a *court* thought that it could resolve the issue at all?

What would have happened if *Dred Scott* had gone the other way in 1857? Scott Powe suggests that "to appease its subsequent critics, the Court would have had to sustain the Missouri Compromise line and free the Scotts. . . . As a result of that hypothetical . . . decision, the South would likely have abandoned the Union under [President] Buchanan—and with impunity. Although Buchanan believed that secession was illegal, he also believed that the national government could not prevent it by force." Professor Powe thus concludes that "[i]f *Dred Scott* had been decided the other way and the South seceded, the United States as we know it would not exist."[6] Do—or should—considerations like this have any bearing on a court's approach to a case like *Dred Scott*? On our later assessments of the Court's work?

If the problem with *Dred Scott* is instead that a *court* should never have tried to resolve the bitter dispute over slavery, what does that tell you about the Court's efforts to resolve divisive contemporary social issues like abortion, gay rights, or affirmative action? In answering that question, it is important to know that "Congress had repeatedly tried to pass the responsibility on to the courts" to determine the extent of Congress's constitutional power over slavery.[7] A number of the statutory compromise measures included explicit provisions seeking to expedite judicial review of the question of Congress's authority to prohibit slavery. *Dred Scott* did not arise pursuant to these statutes, but these provisions do reflect an earnest desire for judicial resolution. Should the Court have ignored the country's call for a judicial resolution?

5.   Because of its tolerance of slavery, William Lloyd Garrison said that "the compact which exists between the North and the South"—that is, the Constitution—"is a covenant with death and an agreement with hell—involving both parties in atrocious criminality—and should be immediately annulled." A similar sentiment obviously informs Professor Levinson's ambivalence about symbolically signing the Constitution at its bicentennial celebration. Would you sign?

Levinson's question is of particular significance for lawyers. Admission to the Bar typically requires prospective attorneys to take an oath similar to the following one, administered in Texas:

> I, _____ do solemnly swear that I will support the constitution of the United States, and of this State; that I will honestly demean myself in the practice of the law, and will discharge my duties to my clients to the best of my ability. So help me God.

Other states impose similar requirements. Can you honestly take the oath today? Could you have done so prior to Emancipation and the Reconstruction Amendments?

See also: The leading account of *Dred Scott* is DON E. FEHRENBACHER, THE *DRED SCOTT* CASE: ITS SIGNIFICANCE IN AMERICAN LAW AND POLITICS (1978). For an affirmative response to Professor Levinson's question, from a prominent African-American law professor, *see* Randall Kennedy, *Afro-American Faith in the Civil Religion, or, Yes, I Would Sign the Constitution*,

---

[6]   POWE, *supra* note 2, at 109.
[7]   DAVID M. POTTER, THE IMPENDING CRISIS, 1848–1861, at 271 (1976).

29 WM. & MARY L. REV. 163 (1987). Professor Levinson has since concluded that the Constitution is even worse than he previously thought. *See* SANFORD LEVINSON, OUR UNDEMOCRATIC CONSTITUTION: WHERE THE CONSTITUTION GOES WRONG (AND HOW WE THE PEOPLE CAN CORRECT IT) (2006).

SECTION 4.2   RECONSTRUCTION AND THE FOURTEENTH AMENDMENT

Slavery died at Appomattox, but it quickly became apparent that extirpating its social and legal legacy, particularly in the face of efforts by Southern whites to maintain their system of racial supremacy, would be a considerably more difficult undertaking. This effort gave rise to the most significant set of constitutional amendments since the Bill of Rights. The Thirteenth formally abolished slavery; the Fourteenth conferred individual rights of citizenship, due process, and equal protection of the laws (it also included provisions designed to root out the political order of the Confederacy); and the Fifteenth barred racial discrimination with respect to voting. Each provision included not only substantive provisions susceptible to judicial enforcement but also broad grants of power to Congress to enforce those provisions through legislation. This feature reflected the strong sense of the amendment's framers that, while the Supreme Court remained the institution that had inflicted *Dred Scott* on the country, the Reconstruction Congress (dominated by Abraham Lincoln's Republican party) was the most reliable protector of the rights of the freedmen.

Although the Reconstruction Amendments incorporated this separation-of-powers shift from judicial to legislative enforcement, the more important shift was along the dimension of federalism. Many Americans in the Founding Era had viewed the new national government as novel and dangerous, while the States were established and trusted; hence, the Bill of Rights was directed at limiting the authority of the national government with relatively little thought to the States as a threat to civil liberties. The crisis of the Civil War, however, cast the States as the threat to liberty and the national government as liberty's champion. The Reconstruction Amendments thus created individual rights against state governmental action and empowered the national government to enforce those rights. Congress used its new powers both to enact substantive civil rights legislation and to expand the role of the federal courts in enforcing federal rights. The primary federal civil rights statute providing for judicial remedies against state and local officials, 42 U.S.C. § 1983, dates from this period. More broadly, the Civil War both required a considerable expansion of national governmental capacity and engendered a profound sense of national identity—at least on the victorious Northern side.

As the cases in this section demonstrate, however, the Supreme Court quickly moved to protect the traditional federal balance against more radical interpretations of this shift. In order to understand the shift in rights enforcement—and to assess the extent to which Reconstruction may have shifted the federal balance more generally—we need to back up and consider the posture of the Bill of Rights prior to the Civil War. Our story thus begins with John Marshall's last constitutional case. We then fast-forward to two landmark decisions limiting the scope of the Reconstruction Amendments.

Barron v. Baltimore
32 U.S. 243 (1833)

[Barron owned a wharf in Baltimore harbor. He claimed that street construction work conducted by the City had diverted the flow of streams and deposited "large masses of sand and earth" near his wharf, making the wharf inaccessible for most vessels. His suit alleged a "taking" of private property without just compensation in violation of the Fifth Amendment.]

■ MR. CHIEF JUSTICE MARSHALL delivered the opinion of the Court.

. . . The plaintiff in error contends that [this case] comes within that clause in the fifth amendment to the constitution, which inhibits the taking of private property for public use, without just compensation. He insists that this amendment, being in favour of the liberty of the citizen, ought to be so construed as to restrain the legislative power of a state, as well as that of the United States. If this proposition be untrue, the court can take no jurisdiction of the cause.

The question thus presented is, we think, of great importance, but not of much difficulty. The constitution was ordained and established by the people of the United States for themselves, for their own government, and not for the government of the individual states. Each state established a constitution for itself, and, in that constitution, provided such limitations and restrictions on the powers of its particular government as its judgment dictated. The people of the United States framed such a government for the United States as they supposed best adapted to their situation, and best calculated to promote their interests. The powers they conferred on this government were to be exercised by itself; and the limitations on power, if expressed in general terms, are naturally, and, we think, necessarily applicable to the government created by the instrument. They are limitations of power granted in the instrument itself; not of distinct governments, framed by different persons and for different purposes.

If these propositions be correct, the fifth amendment must be understood as restraining the power of the general government, not as applicable to the states. In their several constitutions they have imposed such restrictions on their respective governments as their own wisdom suggested; such as they deemed most proper for themselves. It is a subject on which they judge exclusively, and with which others interfere no farther than they are supposed to have a common interest.

The counsel for the plaintiff in error insists that the constitution was intended to secure the people of the several states against the undue exercise of power by their respective state governments; as well as against that which might be attempted by their general government. In support of this argument he relies on the inhibitions contained in the tenth section of the first article.

We think that section affords a strong if not a conclusive argument in support of the opinion already indicated by the court.

The preceding section contains restrictions which are obviously intended for the exclusive purpose of restraining the exercise of power by the departments of the general government. Some of them use language applicable only to congress: others are expressed in general terms. The third clause, for example, declares that "no bill of attainder or ex post facto law shall be passed." No language can be more general; yet the demonstration is complete that it applies solely to the government of the United States. In addition to the general arguments furnished by the instrument itself, some of which have been already suggested, the succeeding section, the avowed purpose of which is to restrain state legislation, contains in terms the very prohibition. It declares that "no state shall pass any bill of attainder or ex post facto law." This provision, then, of the ninth section, however comprehensive its language, contains no restriction on state legislation.

The ninth section having enumerated, in the nature of a *bill of rights*, the limitations intended to be imposed on the powers of the general government, the tenth proceeds to enumerate those which were to operate on the state legislatures. These restrictions are brought together in the same section, and are by express words applied to the states. "No state shall enter into any treaty," & c. Perceiving that in a constitution framed by the people of the United States for the government of all, no limitation of the action of government on the people would apply to the state government, unless expressed in terms; the restrictions contained in the tenth section are in direct words so applied to the states.

It is worthy of remark, too, that these inhibitions generally restrain state legislation on subjects entrusted to the general government, or in which the people of all the states feel an interest.

A state is forbidden to enter into any treaty, alliance or confederation. If these compacts are with foreign nations, they interfere with the treaty making power which is conferred entirely on the general government; if with each other, for political purposes, they can scarcely fail to interfere with the general purpose and intent of the constitution. To grant letters of marque and reprisal, would lead directly to war; the power of declaring which is expressly given to congress. To coin money is also the exercise of a power conferred on congress. It would be tedious to recapitulate the several limitations on the powers of the states which are contained in this section. They will be found, generally, to restrain state legislation on subjects entrusted to the government of the union, in which the citizens of all the states are interested. In these alone were the whole people concerned. The question of their application to states is not left to construction. It is averred in positive words.

If the original constitution, in the ninth and tenth sections of the first article, draws this plain and marked line of discrimination between the limitations it imposes on the powers of the general government, and on those of the states; if in every inhibition intended to act on state power, words are employed which directly express that intent; some strong reason must be assigned for departing from this safe and judicious course in framing the amendments, before that departure can be assumed.

We search in vain for that reason. Had the people of the several states . . . required changes in their constitutions; had they required additional safeguards to liberty from the apprehended encroachments of their particular governments: the remedy was in their own hands, and would have been applied by themselves. A convention would have been assembled by the discontented state, and the required improvements would have been made by itself. The unwieldy and cumbrous machinery of procuring a recommendation from two-thirds of congress, and the assent of three-fourths of their sister states, could never have occurred to any human being as a mode of doing that which might be effected by the state itself. Had the framers of these amendments intended them to be limitations on the powers of the state governments, they would have imitated the framers of the original constitution, and have expressed that intention. Had congress engaged in the extraordinary occupation of improving the constitutions of the several states by affording the people additional protection from the exercise of power by their own governments in matters which concerned themselves alone, they would have declared this purpose in plain and intelligible language.

But it is universally understood, it is a part of the history of the day, that the great revolution which established the constitution of the United States, was not effected without immense opposition. Serious fears were extensively entertained that those powers which the patriot statesmen, who then watched over the interests of our country, deemed essential to union, and to the attainment of those invaluable objects for which union was sought, might be exercised in a manner dangerous to liberty. In almost every convention by which the constitution was adopted, amendments to guard against the abuse of power were recommended. These amendments demanded security against the apprehended encroachments of the general government—not against those of the local governments.

In compliance with a sentiment thus generally expressed, to quiet fears thus extensively entertained, amendments were proposed by the required majority in congress, and adopted by the states. These amendments contain no expression indicating an intention to apply them to the state governments. This court cannot so apply them.

We are of opinion that the provision in the fifth amendment to the constitution, declaring that private property shall not be taken for public use without just compensation, is intended solely as a limitation on the exercise of power by the government of the United States, and is not applicable to the legislation of the states. We are therefore of opinion that there is no repugnancy between the several acts of the general assembly of Maryland, given in evidence by the defendants at the trial of this cause, in the court of that state, and the constitution of the United States. This court, therefore, has no jurisdiction of the cause; and it is dismissed. . . .

Slaughter-House Cases

83 U.S. 36 (1873)

■ **MR. JUSTICE MILLER delivered the opinion of the court.**

These cases . . . arise out of the efforts of the butchers of New Orleans to resist the Crescent City Live-Stock Landing and Slaughter-House Company in the exercise of certain powers conferred by the charter which created it, and which was granted by the legislature of that State.

The cases . . . were all decided by the Supreme Court of Louisiana in favor of the Slaughter-House Company. . . .

[The Act conferred a monopoly of the slaughterhouse business on the Crescent City company and forbade all other persons from slaughtering animals for food within the City of New Orleans.]

It is . . . both the right and the duty of the legislative body . . . to prescribe and determine the localities where the business of slaughtering for a great city may be conducted. To do this effectively it is indispensable that all persons who slaughter animals for food shall do it in those places and nowhere else.

The statute under consideration defines these localities and forbids slaughtering in any other. It does not, as has been asserted, prevent the butcher from doing his own slaughtering. . . . [B]ut he is required to slaughter at a specified place and to pay a reasonable compensation for the use of the accommodations furnished him at that place.

The wisdom of the monopoly granted by the legislature may be open to question, but it is difficult to see a justification for the assertion that the butchers are deprived of the right to labor in their occupation, or the people of their daily service in preparing food, or how this statute, with the duties and guards imposed upon the company, can be said to destroy the business of the butcher, or seriously interfere with its pursuit.

The power here exercised by the legislature of Louisiana is, in its essential nature, one which has been . . . always conceded to belong to the States. . . . This is called the police power; and it is . . . much easier to perceive and realize the existence and sources of it than to mark its boundaries, or prescribe limits to its exercise.

This power is, and must be from its very nature, incapable of any very exact definition or limitation. Upon it depends the security of social order, the life and health of the citizen, the comfort of an existence in a thickly populated community, the enjoyment of private and social life, and the beneficial use of property. . . .

The regulation of the place and manner of conducting the slaughtering of animals, and the business of butchering within a city, and the inspection of the animals to be killed for meat, and of the meat afterwards, are among the most necessary and frequent exercises of this power. . . .

It cannot be denied that the statute under consideration is aptly framed to remove from the more densely populated part of the city, the noxious slaughter-houses, and large and offensive collections of animals necessarily incident to the slaughtering business of a large city, and to locate them where the convenience, health, and comfort of the people require they shall be located. And it must be conceded that the means adopted by the act for this purpose are appropriate, are stringent, and effectual. . . .

It may, therefore, be considered as established, that the authority of the legislature of Louisiana to pass the present statute is ample, unless some restraint in the exercise of that power be found in the constitution of that State or in the amendments to the Constitution of the United States, adopted since the date of the decisions we have already cited. . . .

The plaintiffs in error accepting this issue, allege that the statute is a violation of the Constitution of the United States in these several particulars:

That it creates an involuntary servitude forbidden by the thirteenth article of amendment;

That it abridges the privileges and immunities of citizens of the United States;

That it denies to the plaintiffs the equal protection of the laws; and,

That it deprives them of their property without due process of law; contrary to the provisions of the first section of the fourteenth article of amendment.

This court is thus called upon for the first time to give construction to these articles. We do not conceal from ourselves the great responsibility which this duty devolves upon us. . . .

Twelve articles of amendment were added to the Federal Constitution soon after the original organization of the government [in] 1789. Of these all but the last were adopted so soon afterwards as to justify the statement that they were practically contemporaneous with the adoption of the original; and the twelfth, adopted in eighteen hundred and three, was so nearly so as to have become, like all the others, historical and of another age. But within the last eight years three other articles of amendment of vast importance have been added by the voice of the people to that now venerable instrument.

The most cursory glance at these articles discloses a unity of purpose, when taken in connection with the history of the times, which cannot fail to have an important bearing on any question of doubt concerning their true meaning. Nor can such doubts . . . be safely and rationally solved without a reference to that history; for in it is found the occasion and the necessity for recurring again to the great source of power in this country, the people of the States, for additional guarantees of human rights; additional powers to the Federal government; additional restraints upon those of the States. Fortunately that history is fresh within the memory of us all, and its leading features, as they bear upon the matter before us, free from doubt.

The institution of African slavery, as it existed in about half the States of the Union, and the contests pervading the public mind for many years, between those who desired its curtailment and ultimate extinction and those who desired additional safeguards for its security and perpetuation, culminated in the effort, on the part of most of the States in which slavery existed, to separate from the Federal government, and to resist its authority. This constituted the war of the rebellion, and whatever auxiliary causes may have contributed to bring about this war, undoubtedly the overshadowing and efficient cause was African slavery.

In that struggle slavery, as a legalized social relation, perished. It perished as a necessity of the bitterness and force of the conflict. When the armies of freedom found themselves upon the soil of slavery they could do nothing less than free the poor victims whose enforced servitude was the foundation of the quarrel. And when hard pressed in the contest these men (for they proved themselves men in that terrible crisis) offered their services and were accepted by thousands to aid in suppressing the unlawful rebellion, slavery was at an end wherever the Federal government succeeded in that purpose. The proclamation of President Lincoln expressed an accomplished fact as to a large portion of the insurrectionary districts, when he declared slavery abolished in them all. But the war being over, those who had succeeded in re-establishing the authority of the Federal government were not content to permit this great act of emancipation to rest on the actual results of the contest or the proclamation of the Executive. . . . Hence the thirteenth article of amendment of that instrument. Its two short sections seem hardly to admit of construction, so vigorous is their expression and so appropriate to the purpose we have indicated.

> 1. Neither slavery nor involuntary servitude, except as a punishment for crime, whereof the party shall have been duly convicted, shall exist within the United States or any place subject to their jurisdiction.

2.   Congress shall have power to enforce this article by appropriate legislation.

. . . The process of restoring to their proper relations with the Federal government and with the other States those which had sided with the rebellion, undertaken under the proclamation of President Johnson in 1865, and before the assembling of Congress, developed the fact that, notwithstanding the formal recognition by those States of the abolition of slavery, the condition of the slave race would, without further protection of the Federal government, be almost as bad as it was before. Among the first acts of legislation adopted by several of the States in the legislative bodies which claimed to be in their normal relations with the Federal government, were laws which imposed upon the colored race onerous disabilities and burdens, and curtailed their rights in the pursuit of life, liberty, and property to such an extent that their freedom was of little value, while they had lost the protection which they had received from their former owners from motives both of interest and humanity.

They were in some States forbidden to appear in the towns in any other character than menial servants. They were required to reside on and cultivate the soil without the right to purchase or own it. They were excluded from many occupations of gain, and were not permitted to give testimony in the courts in any case where a white man was a party. It was said that their lives were at the mercy of bad men, either because the laws for their protection were insufficient or were not enforced.

These circumstances . . . forced upon the statesmen who had conducted the Federal government in safety through the crisis of the rebellion, and who supposed that by the thirteenth article of amendment they had secured the result of their labors, the conviction that something more was necessary in the way of constitutional protection to the unfortunate race who had suffered so much. They accordingly passed through Congress the proposition for the fourteenth amendment, and they declined to treat as restored to their full participation in the government of the Union the States which had been in insurrection, until they ratified that article by a formal vote of their legislative bodies. . . .

A few years' experience satisfied the thoughtful men who had been the authors of the other two amendments that, notwithstanding the restraints of those articles on the States, and the laws passed under the additional powers granted to Congress, these were inadequate for the protection of life, liberty, and property, without which freedom to the slave was no boon. They were in all those States denied the right of suffrage. The laws were administered by the white man alone. It was urged that a race of men distinctively marked as was the negro, living in the midst of another and dominant race, could never be fully secured in their person and their property without the right of suffrage.

Hence the fifteenth amendment, which declares that "the right of a citizen of the United States to vote shall not be denied or abridged by any State on account of race, color, or previous condition of servitude." The negro having, by the fourteenth amendment, been declared to be a citizen of the United States, is thus made a voter in every State of the Union.

We repeat, then, in the light of this recapitulation of events, almost too recent to be called history, but which are familiar to us all; and on the most casual examination of the language of these amendments, no one can fail to be impressed with the one pervading purpose found in them all, lying at the foundation of each, and without which none of them would have been even suggested; we mean the freedom of the slave race, the security and firm establishment of that freedom, and the protection of the newly-made freeman and citizen from the oppressions of those who had formerly exercised unlimited dominion over him. It is true that only the fifteenth amendment, in terms, mentions the negro by speaking of his color and his slavery. But it is just as true that each of the other articles was addressed to the grievances of that race, and designed to remedy them as the fifteenth.

We do not say that no one else but the negro can share in this protection. Both the language and spirit of these articles are to have their fair and just weight in any question of construction. Undoubtedly while negro slavery alone was in the mind of the Congress which proposed the thirteenth article, it forbids any other kind of slavery, now or hereafter. If Mexican peonage or the Chinese coolie labor system shall develop slavery of the Mexican or Chinese race within our territory, this amendment may safely be trusted to make it void. And so if other rights are assailed by the States which properly and necessarily fall within the protection of these articles, that protection will apply, though the party interested may not be of African descent. But what we do say, and what we wish to be understood is, that in any fair and just construction of any section or phrase of these amendments, it is necessary to look to the purpose which we have said was the pervading spirit of them all, the evil which they were designed to remedy, and the process of continued addition to the Constitution, until that purpose was supposed to be accomplished, as far as constitutional law can accomplish it.

The first section of the fourteenth article, to which our attention is more specially invited, opens with a definition of citizenship—not only citizenship of the United States, but citizenship of the States. No such definition was previously found in the Constitution, nor had any attempt been made to define it by act of Congress. It had been the occasion of much discussion in the courts, by the executive departments, and in the public journals. . . . But it had been held by this court, in the celebrated *Dred Scott* case, only a few years before the outbreak of the civil war, that a man of African descent, whether a slave or not, was not and could not be a citizen of a State or of the United States. This decision, while it met the condemnation of some of the ablest statesmen and constitutional lawyers of the country, had never been overruled. . . .

To remove this difficulty primarily, and to establish a clear and comprehensive definition of citizenship which should declare what should constitute citizenship of the United States, and also citizenship of a State, the first clause of the first section was framed.

> All persons born or naturalized in the United States, and subject to the jurisdiction thereof, are citizens of the United States and of the State wherein they reside.

The first observation we have to make on this clause is, that . . . its main purpose was to establish the citizenship of the negro can admit of no doubt. . . .

The next observation is more important in view of the arguments of counsel in the present case. It is, that the distinction between citizenship of the United States and citizenship of a State is clearly recognized and established. Not only may a man be a citizen of the United States without being a citizen of a State, but an important element is necessary to convert the former into the latter. He must reside within the State to make him a citizen of it, but it is only necessary that he should be born or naturalized in the United States to be a citizen of the Union.

It is quite clear, then, that there is a citizenship of the United States, and a citizenship of a State, which are distinct from each other, and which depend upon different characteristics or circumstances in the individual.

We think this distinction and its explicit recognition in this amendment of great weight in this argument, because the next paragraph of this same section, which is the one mainly relied on by the plaintiffs in error, speaks only of privileges and immunities of citizens of the United States, and does not speak of those of citizens of the several States. The argument, however, in favor of the plaintiffs rests wholly on the assumption that the citizenship is the same, and the privileges and immunities guaranteed by the clause are the same.

The language is, "No State shall make or enforce any law which shall abridge the privileges or immunities of citizens of the United States." It is a little remarkable, if this clause was intended as a protection to the citizen of a State against the legislative power of his own State, that the word citizen of the State should be left out when it is so carefully used, and used in contradistinction to citizens of the United States, in the very sentence which precedes it. It is too clear for argument that the change in phraseology was adopted understandingly and with a purpose.

Of the privileges and immunities of the citizen of the United States, and of the privileges and immunities of the citizen of the State, and what they respectively are, we will presently consider; but we wish to state here that it is only the former which are placed by this clause under the protection of the Federal Constitution, and that the latter, whatever they may be, are not intended to have any additional protection by this paragraph of the amendment. . . .

The first occurrence of the words "privileges and immunities" in our constitutional history, is to be found in the fourth of the articles of the old Confederation. It declares "that the better to secure and perpetuate mutual friendship and intercourse among the people of the different States in this Union, the free inhabitants of each of these States, paupers, vagabonds, and fugitives from justice excepted, shall be entitled to all the privileges and immunities of free citizens in the several States; and the people of each State shall have free ingress and regress to and from any other State, and shall enjoy therein all the privileges of trade and commerce, subject to the same duties, impositions, and restrictions as the inhabitants thereof respectively."

In the Constitution of the United States, which superseded the Articles of Confederation, the corresponding provision is found in section two of the fourth article, in the following words: "The citizens of each State shall be entitled to all the privileges and immunities of citizens of the several States."

There can be but little question that the purpose of both these provisions is the same, and that the privileges and immunities intended are the same in each. In the article of the Confederation we have some of these specifically mentioned, and enough perhaps to give some general idea of the class of civil rights meant by the phrase.

Fortunately we are not without judicial construction of this clause of the Constitution. The first and the leading case on the subject is that of *Corfield v. Coryell*, 6 Fed. Cas. 546, decided by Mr. Justice Washington in the Circuit Court for the District of Pennsylvania in 1823.

"The inquiry," he says, "is, what are the privileges and immunities of citizens of the several States? We feel no hesitation in confining these expressions to those privileges and immunities which are fundamental; which belong of right to the citizens of all free governments, and which have at all times been enjoyed by citizens of the several States which compose this Union, from the time of their becoming free, independent, and sovereign. What these fundamental principles are, it would be more tedious than difficult to enumerate. They may all, however, be comprehended under the following general heads: protection by the government, with the right to acquire and possess property of every kind, and to pursue and obtain happiness and safety, subject, nevertheless, to such restraints as the government may prescribe for the general good of the whole."

This definition of the privileges and immunities of citizens of the States is adopted in the main by this court embrac[ing] nearly every civil right for the establishment and protection of which organized government is instituted. They are, in the language of Judge Washington, those rights which are fundamental. Throughout his opinion, they are spoken of as rights belonging to the individual as a citizen of a State. . . .

The constitutional provision there alluded to did not create those rights, which it called privileges and immunities of citizens of the States.

It threw around them in that clause no security for the citizen of the State in which they were claimed or exercised. Nor did it profess to control the power of the State governments over the rights of its own citizens.

Its sole purpose was to declare to the several States, that whatever those rights, as you grant or establish them to your own citizens, or as you limit or qualify, or impose restrictions on their exercise, the same, neither more nor less, shall be the measure of the rights of citizens of other States within your jurisdiction.

[U]p to the adoption of the recent amendments, no claim or pretence was set up that those rights depended on the Federal government for their existence or protection, beyond the very few express limitations which the Federal Constitution imposed upon the States—such, for instance, as the prohibition against ex post facto laws, bills of attainder, and laws impairing the obligation of contracts. But with the exception of these and a few other restrictions, the entire domain of the privileges and immunities of citizens of the States, as above defined, lay within the constitutional and legislative power of the States, and without that of the Federal government. Was it the purpose of the fourteenth amendment, by the simple declaration that no State should make or enforce any law which shall abridge the privileges and immunities of citizens of the United States, to transfer the security and protection of all the civil rights which we have mentioned, from the States to the Federal government? And where it is declared that Congress shall have the power to enforce that article, was it intended to bring within the power of Congress the entire domain of civil rights heretofore belonging exclusively to the States?

All this and more must follow, if the proposition of the plaintiffs in error be sound. For not only are these rights subject to the control of Congress whenever in its discretion any of them are supposed to be abridged by State legislation, but that body may also pass laws in advance, limiting and restricting the exercise of legislative power by the States, in their most ordinary and usual functions, as in its judgment it may think proper on all such subjects. And still further, such a construction followed by the reversal of the judgments of the Supreme Court of Louisiana in these cases, would constitute this court a perpetual censor upon all legislation of the States, on the civil rights of their own citizens, with authority to nullify such as it did not approve as consistent with those rights, as they existed at the time of the adoption of this amendment. The argument we admit is not always the most conclusive which is drawn from the consequences urged against the adoption of a particular construction of an instrument.

But when, as in the case before us, these consequences are so serious, so far-reaching and pervading, so great a departure from the structure and spirit of our institutions; when the effect is to fetter and degrade the State governments by subjecting them to the control of Congress, in the exercise of powers heretofore universally conceded to them of the most ordinary and fundamental character; when in fact it radically changes the whole theory of the relations of the State and Federal governments to each other and of both these governments to the people; the argument has a force that is irresistible, in the absence of language which expresses such a purpose too clearly to admit of doubt.

We are convinced that no such results were intended by the Congress which proposed these amendments, nor by the legislatures of the States which ratified them.

Having shown that the privileges and immunities relied on in the argument are those which belong to citizens of the States as such, and that they are left to the State governments for security and protection, and not by this article placed under the special care of the Federal government, we may hold ourselves excused from defining the privileges and immunities of citizens of the United States which no State can abridge, until some case involving those privileges may make it necessary to do so.

But lest it should be said that no such privileges and immunities are to be found if those we have been considering are excluded, we venture to suggest some which owe their existence to the Federal government, its National character, its Constitution, or its laws.

One of these is . . . the right of the citizen of this great country . . . "to come to the seat of government to assert any claim he may have upon that government, to transact any business he may have with it, to seek its protection, to share its offices, to engage in administering its functions. He has the right of free access to its seaports, through which all operations of foreign commerce are conducted, to the subtreasuries, land offices, and courts of justice in the several States." . . .

Another privilege of a citizen of the United States is to demand the care and protection of the Federal government over his life, liberty, and property when on the high seas or within the jurisdiction of a foreign government. Of this there can be no doubt, nor that the right depends upon his character as a citizen of the United States. The right to peaceably assemble and petition for redress of grievances, the privilege of the writ of habeas corpus, are rights of the citizen guaranteed by the Federal Constitution. The right to use the navigable waters of the United States, however they may penetrate the territory of the several States, all rights secured to our citizens by treaties with foreign nations, are dependent upon citizenship of the United States, and not citizenship of a State. One of these privileges is conferred by the very article under consideration. It is that a citizen of the United States can, of his own volition, become a citizen of any State of the Union by a bona fide residence therein, with the same rights as other citizens of that State. To these may be added the rights secured by the thirteenth and fifteenth articles of amendment, and by the other clause of the fourteenth, next to be considered.

But it is useless to pursue this branch of the inquiry, since we are of opinion that the rights claimed by these plaintiffs in error, if they have any existence, are not privileges and immunities of citizens of the United States within the meaning of the clause of the fourteenth amendment under consideration. . . .

The argument has not been much pressed in these cases that the defendant's charter deprives the plaintiffs of their property without due process of law, or that it denies to them the equal protection of the law. The first of these paragraphs has been in the Constitution since the adoption of the fifth amendment, as a restraint upon the Federal power. It is also to be found in some form of expression in the constitutions of nearly all the States, as a restraint upon the power of the States. This law then, has practically been the same as it now is during the existence of the government, except so far as the present amendment may place the restraining power over the States in this matter in the hands of the Federal government.

We are not without judicial interpretation, therefore, both State and National, of the meaning of this clause. And it is sufficient to say that under no construction of that provision that we have ever seen, or any that we deem admissible, can the restraint imposed by the State of Louisiana upon the exercise of their trade by the butchers of New Orleans be held to be a deprivation of property within the meaning of that provision.

"Nor shall any State deny to any person within its jurisdiction the equal protection of the laws." In the light of the history of these amendments, and the pervading purpose of them, which we have already discussed, it is not difficult to give a meaning to this clause. The existence of laws in the States where the newly emancipated negroes resided, which discriminated with gross injustice and hardship against them as a class, was the evil to be remedied by this clause, and by it such laws are forbidden.

If, however, the States did not conform their laws to its requirements, then by the fifth section of the article of amendment Congress was authorized to enforce it by suitable legislation. We doubt very much whether any action of a State not directed by way of discrimination against the negroes as a class, or on account of their race, will ever be held to come within the purview of this provision. It is so clearly a provision for that race and that emergency, that a strong case would be necessary for its application to any other. . . .

In the early history of the organization of the government, its statesmen seem to have divided on the line which should separate the powers of the National government from those of the State governments, and though this line has never been very well defined in public opinion, such a division has continued from that day to this.

The adoption of the first eleven amendments to the Constitution so soon after the original instrument was accepted, shows a prevailing sense of danger at that time from the Federal power. And it cannot be denied that such a jealousy continued to exist with many patriotic men until the breaking out of the late civil war. It was then discovered that the true danger to the perpetuity of the Union was in the capacity of the State organizations to combine and concentrate all the powers of the State, and of contiguous States, for a determined resistance to the General Government.

Unquestionably this has given great force to the argument, and added largely to the number of those who believe in the necessity of a strong National government. But, however pervading this sentiment, and however it may have contributed to the adoption of the amendments we have been considering, we do not see in those amendments any purpose to destroy the main features of the general system. Under the pressure of all the excited feeling growing out of the war, our statesmen have still believed that the existence of the States with powers for domestic and local government, including the regulation of civil rights— the rights of person and of property—was essential to the perfect working of our complex form of government, though they have thought proper to impose additional limitations on the States, and to confer additional power on that of the Nation.

But whatever fluctuations may be seen in the history of public opinion on this subject during the period of our national existence, we think it will be found that this court, so far as its functions required, has always held with a steady and an even hand the balance between State and Federal power, and we trust that such may continue to be the history of its relation to that subject so long as it shall have duties to perform which demand of it a construction of the Constitution, or of any of its parts.

The judgments of the Supreme Court of Louisiana in these cases are

AFFIRMED.

■ MR. JUSTICE FIELD, dissenting:

. . . It is contended in justification for the act in question that it was adopted in the interest of the city, to promote its cleanliness and protect its health, and was the legitimate exercise of what is termed the police power of the State. That power undoubtedly extends to all regulations affecting the health, good order, morals, peace, and safety of society, and is exercised on a great variety of subjects, and in almost numberless ways. All sorts of restrictions and burdens are imposed under it, and when these are not in conflict with any constitutional prohibitions, or fundamental principles, they cannot be successfully assailed in a judicial tribunal. With this power of the State and its legitimate exercise I shall not differ from the majority of the court. But under the pretence of prescribing a police regulation the State cannot be permitted to encroach upon any of the just rights of the citizen, which the Constitution intended to secure against abridgment.

In the law in question there are only two provisions which can properly be called police regulations—the one which requires the landing and slaughtering of animals below the city of New Orleans, and the other which requires the inspection of the animals before they are slaughtered. When these requirements are complied with, the sanitary purposes of the act are accomplished. In all other particulars the act is a mere grant to a corporation created by it of special and exclusive privileges by which the health of the city is in no way promoted. It is plain that if the corporation can, without endangering the health of the public, carry on the business of landing, keeping, and slaughtering cattle within a district below the city embracing an area of over a thousand square miles, it would not endanger the public health if other persons were also permitted to carry on the same business within the same district under similar conditions as to the inspection of the animals.

The health of the city might require the removal from its limits and suburbs of all buildings for keeping and slaughtering cattle, but no such object could possibly justify legislation removing such buildings from a large part of the State for the benefit of a single corporation. The pretence of sanitary regulations for the grant of the exclusive privileges is a shallow one, which merits only this passing notice.

It is also sought to justify the act in question on the same principle that exclusive grants for ferries, bridges, and turnpikes are sanctioned. But it can find no support there. Those grants are of franchises of a public character appertaining to the government. Their use usually requires the exercise of the sovereign right of eminent domain. It is for the government to determine when one of them shall be granted, and the conditions upon which it shall be enjoyed. It is the duty of the government to provide suitable roads, bridges, and ferries for the convenience of the public, and if it chooses to devolve this duty to any extent, or in any locality, upon particular individuals or corporations, it may of course stipulate for such exclusive privileges connected with the franchise as it may deem proper, without encroaching upon the freedom or the just rights of others. The grant, with exclusive privileges, of a right thus appertaining to the government, is a very different thing from a grant, with exclusive privileges, of a right to pursue one of the ordinary trades or callings of life, which is a right appertaining solely to the individual. . . .

The act of Louisiana presents the naked case, unaccompanied by any public considerations, where a right to pursue a lawful and necessary calling, previously enjoyed by every citizen, and in connection with which a thousand persons were daily employed, is taken away and vested exclusively for twenty-five years, for an extensive district and a large population, in a single corporation, or its exercise is for that period restricted to the establishment of the corporation, and there allowed only upon onerous conditions.

If exclusive privileges of this character can be granted to a corporation of seventeen persons, they may, in the discretion of the legislature, be equally granted to a single individual. If they may be granted for twenty-five years they may be equally granted for a century, and in perpetuity. If they may be granted for the landing and keeping of animals intended for sale or slaughter they may be equally granted for the landing and storing of grain and other products of the earth, or for any article of commerce. If they may be granted for structures in which animal food is prepared for market they may be equally granted for structures in which farinaceous or vegetable food is prepared. They may be granted for any of the pursuits of human industry, even in its most simple and common forms. Indeed, upon the theory on which the exclusive privileges granted by the act in question are sustained, there is no monopoly, in the most odious form, which may not be upheld.

The question presented is, therefore, one of the gravest importance, not merely to the parties here, but to the whole country. It is nothing less than the question whether the recent amendments to the Federal Constitution protect the citizens of the United States against the deprivation of their common rights by State legislation. In my judgment the fourteenth amendment does afford such protection, and was so intended by the Congress which framed and the States which adopted it. . . .

The amendment does not attempt to confer any new privileges or immunities upon citizens, or to enumerate or define those already existing. It assumes that there are such privileges and immunities which belong of right to citizens as such, and ordains that they shall not be abridged by State legislation. If this inhibition has no reference to privileges and immunities of this character, but only refers, as held by the majority of the court in their opinion, to such privileges and immunities as were before its adoption specially designated in the Constitution or necessarily implied as belonging to citizens of the United States, it was a vain and idle enactment, which accomplished nothing, and most unnecessarily excited Congress and the people on its passage. With privileges and immunities thus designated or implied no State could ever have interfered by its laws, and no new constitutional provision was required to inhibit such interference. The supremacy of the Constitution and the laws of the United States always, controlled any State legislation of that character. But if the amendment refers to the natural and inalienable rights which belong to all citizens, the inhibition has a profound significance and consequence.

What, then, are the privileges and immunities which are secured against abridgment by State legislation?

In the first section of the Civil Rights Act Congress . . . has stated some of the rights which, in its judgment, these terms include; it has there declared that they include the right "to make and enforce contracts, to sue, be parties and give evidence, to inherit, purchase, lease, sell, hold, and convey real and personal property, and to full and equal benefit of all laws and proceedings for the security of person and property." That act, it is true, was passed before the fourteenth amendment, but the amendment was adopted, as I have already said, to obviate objections to the act, or, speaking more accurately, I should say, to obviate objections to legislation of a similar character, extending the protection of the National government over the common rights of all citizens of the United States. Accordingly, after its ratification, Congress re-enacted the act under the belief that whatever doubts may have previously existed of its validity, they were removed by the amendment.

The terms, privileges and immunities, are not new in the amendment; they were in the Constitution before the amendment was adopted. They are found in the second section of the fourth article, which declares that "the citizens of each State shall be entitled to all privileges and immunities of citizens in the several States," and they have been the subject of frequent consideration in judicial decisions [citing *Corfield v. Coryell*]. . . . In the discussions in Congress upon the passage of the Civil Rights Act repeated reference was made to this language of Mr. Justice Washington. . . .

The privileges and immunities designated in the second section of the fourth article of the Constitution are, then, according to the decision cited, those which of right belong to the citizens of all free governments, and they can be enjoyed under that clause by the citizens of each State in the several States upon the same terms and conditions as they are enjoyed by the citizens of the latter States. No discrimination can be made by one State against the citizens of the States in their enjoyment, nor can any greater imposition be levied than such as is laid upon its own citizens. It is a clause which insures equality in the enjoyment of these rights between citizens of the several States whilst in the same State. . . .

Now, what the clause in question does for the protection of citizens of one State against the creation of monopolies in favor of citizens of other States, the fourteenth amendment does for the protection of every citizen of the United States against the creation of any monopoly whatever. The privileges and immunities of citizens of the United States, of every one of them, is secured against abridgment in any form by any State. The fourteenth amendment places them under the guardianship of the National authority. All monopolies in any known trade or manufacture are an invasion of these privileges, for they encroach upon the liberty of citizens to acquire property and pursue happiness, and were held void at common law. . . .

This equality of right, with exemption from all disparaging and partial enactments, in the lawful pursuits of life, throughout the whole country, is the distinguishing privilege of citizens of the United States. To them, everywhere, all pursuits, all professions, all avocations are open without other restrictions than such as are imposed equally upon all others of the same age, sex, and condition. The State may prescribe such regulations for every pursuit and calling of life as will promote the public health, secure the good order and advance the general prosperity of society, but when once prescribed, the pursuit or calling must be free to be followed by every citizen who is within the conditions designated, and will conform to the regulations. This is the fundamental idea upon which our institutions rest; and unless adhered to in the legislation of the country our government will be a republic only in name. The fourteenth amendment, in my judgment, makes it essential to the validity of the legislation of every State that this equality of right should be respected. How widely this equality has been departed from, how entirely rejected and trampled upon by the act of Louisiana, I have already shown. And it is to me a matter of profound regret that its validity is recognized by a majority of this court, for by it the right of free labor, one of the most sacred and imprescriptible rights of man, is violated.[39] . . .

I am authorized by the CHIEF JUSTICE, MR. JUSTICE SWAYNE, and MR. JUSTICE BRADLEY, to state that they concur with me in this dissenting opinion.

■ **MR. JUSTICE BRADLEY, also dissenting:**

I concur in the opinion which has just been read by Mr. Justice Field; but desire to add a few observations. . . .

The right of a State to regulate the conduct of its citizens is undoubtedly a very broad and extensive one, and not to be lightly restricted. But there are certain fundamental rights which this right of regulation cannot infringe. . . .

The people of this country brought with them to its shores the rights of Englishmen; the rights which had been wrested from English sovereigns at various periods of the nation's history. One of these fundamental rights was expressed in these words, found in Magna Charta: "No freeman shall be taken or imprisoned, or be disseized of his freehold or liberties or free customs, or be outlawed or exiled, or any otherwise destroyed; nor will we pass upon him or condemn him but by lawful judgment of his peers or by the law of the land." English constitutional writers expound this article as rendering life, liberty, and property inviolable, except by due process of law. This is the very right which the plaintiffs in error claim in this case. Another of these rights was that of habeas corpus, or the right of having any invasion of personal liberty judicially examined into, at once, by a competent judicial

---

[39] "The property which every man has in his own labor," says Adam Smith, "as it is the original foundation of all other property, so it is the most sacred and inviolable. The patrimony of the poor man lies in the strength and dexterity of his own hands; and to hinder him from employing this strength and dexterity in what manner he thinks proper, without injury to his neighbor, is a plain violation of this most sacred property. It is a manifest encroachment upon the just liberty both of the workman and of those who might be disposed to employ him. As it hinders the one from working at what he thinks proper, so it hinders the others from employing whom they think proper." (Smith's Wealth of Nations, b. 1, ch. 10, part 2.)

magistrate. Blackstone classifies these fundamental rights under three heads, as the absolute rights of individuals, to wit: the right of personal security, the right of personal liberty, and the right of private property. And of the last he says: "The third absolute right, inherent in every Englishman, is that of property, which consists in the free use, enjoyment, and disposal of all his acquisitions, without any control or diminution save only by the laws of the land." . . .

[T]he Declaration of Independence, which was the first political act of the American people in their independent sovereign capacity, lays the foundation of our National existence upon this broad proposition: "That all men are created equal; that they are endowed by their Creator with certain inalienable rights; that among these are life, liberty, and the pursuit of happiness." Here again we have the great threefold division of the rights of freemen, asserted as the rights of man. Rights to life, liberty, and the pursuit of happiness are equivalent to the rights of life, liberty, and property. These are the fundamental rights which can only be taken away by due process of law, and which can only be interfered with, or the enjoyment of which can only be modified, by lawful regulations necessary or proper for the mutual good of all; and these rights, I contend, belong to the citizens of every free government. . . .

But we are not bound to resort to implication, or to the constitutional history of England, to find an authoritative declaration of some of the most important privileges and immunities of citizens of the United States. It is in the Constitution itself. The Constitution, it is true, as it stood prior to the recent amendments, specifies, in terms, only a few of the personal privileges and immunities of citizens, but they are very comprehensive in their character. The States were merely prohibited from passing bills of attainder, ex post facto laws, laws impairing the obligation of contracts, and perhaps one or two more. But others of the greatest consequence were enumerated, although they were only secured, in express terms, from invasion by the Federal government; such as the right of habeas corpus, the right of trial by jury, of free exercise of religious worship, the right of free speech and a free press, the right peaceably to assemble for the discussion of public measures, the right to be secure against unreasonable searches and seizures, and above all, and including almost all the rest, the right of not being deprived of life, liberty, or property, without due process of law. These, and still others are specified in the original Constitution, or in the early amendments of it, as among the privileges and immunities of citizens of the United States, or, what is still stronger for the force of the argument, the rights of all persons, whether citizens or not.

But even if the Constitution were silent, the fundamental privileges and immunities of citizens, as such, would be no less real and no less inviolable than they now are. It was not necessary to say in words that the citizens of the United States should have and exercise all the privileges of citizens; the privilege of buying, selling, and enjoying property; the privilege of engaging in any lawful employment for a livelihood; the privilege of resorting to the laws for redress of injuries, and the like. Their very citizenship conferred these privileges, if they did not possess them before. And these privileges they would enjoy whether they were citizens of any State or not. Inhabitants of Federal territories and new citizens ... lay claim to every one of the privileges and immunities which have been enumerated; and among these none is more essential and fundamental than the right to follow such profession or employment as each one may choose, subject only to uniform regulations equally applicable to all. . . .

If my views are correct with regard to what are the privileges and immunities of citizens, it follows conclusively that any law which establishes a sheer monopoly, depriving a large class of citizens of the privilege of pursuing a lawful employment, does abridge the privileges of those citizens.

The amendment also prohibits any State from depriving any person (citizen or otherwise) of life, liberty, or property, without due process of law. In my view, a law which prohibits large class of citizens from adopting a lawful employment, or from following a lawful employment previously adopted, does deprive them of liberty as well as property, without due process of law. Their right of choice is a portion of their liberty; their occupation is their property. Such a law also deprives those citizens of the equal protection of the laws, contrary to the last clause of the section. . . .

It is futile to argue that none but persons of the African race are intended to be benefited by this amendment. They may have been the primary cause of the amendment, but its language is general, embracing all citizens, and I think it was purposely so expressed.

The mischief to be remedied was not merely slavery and its incidents and consequences; but that spirit of insubordination and disloyalty to the National government which had troubled the country for so many years in some of the States, and that intolerance of free speech and free discussion which often rendered life and property insecure, and led to much unequal legislation. The amendment was an attempt to give voice to the strong National yearning for that time and that condition of things, in which American citizenship should be a sure guaranty of safety, and in which every citizen of the United States might stand erect on every portion of its soil, in the full enjoyment of every right and privilege belonging to a freeman, without fear of violence or molestation.

But great fears are expressed that this construction of the amendment will lead to enactments by Congress interfering with the internal affairs of the States, and establishing therein civil and criminal codes of law for the government of the citizens, and thus abolishing the State governments in everything but name; or else, that it will lead the Federal courts to draw to their cognizance the supervision of State tribunals on every subject of judicial inquiry, on the plea of ascertaining whether the privileges and immunities of citizens have not been abridged.

In my judgment no such practical inconveniences would arise. Very little, if any, legislation on the part of Congress would be required to carry the amendment into effect. Like the prohibition against posing a law impairing the obligation of a contract, it would execute itself. The point would be regularly raised, in a suit at law, and settled by final reference to the Federal court. As the privileges and immunities protected are only those fundamental ones which belong to every citizen, they would soon become so far defined as to cause but a slight accumulation of business in the Federal courts. Besides, the recognized existence of the law would prevent its frequent violation. But even if the business of the National courts should be increased, Congress could easily supply the remedy by increasing their number and efficiency. The great question is, What is the true construction of the amendment? When once we find that, we shall find the means of giving it effect. The argument from inconvenience ought not to have a very controlling influence in questions of this sort. The National will and National interest are of far greater importance.

In my opinion the judgment of the Supreme Court of Louisiana ought to be reversed.

Civil Rights Cases
109 U.S. 3 (1883)

These cases were all founded on the first and second sections of the Act of Congress, known as the Civil Rights Act, passed March 1st, 1875, entitled "An Act to protect all citizens in their civil and legal rights." Two of the cases, those against Stanley and Nichols, were indictments for denying to persons of color the accommodations and privileges of an inn or hotel; two of them, those against Ryan and Singleton, were . . . for denying to individuals the privileges and accommodations of a theatre, the information against Ryan being for refusing a colored person a seat in the dress circle of Maguire's theatre in San Francisco; and the indictment against Singleton was for denying to another person, whose color was not stated, the full enjoyment of the accommodations of the theatre known as the Grand Opera House in New York, "said denial not being made for any reasons by law applicable to citizens of every race and color, and regardless of any previous condition of servitude."

The case of Robinson and wife against the Memphis & Charleston R.R. Company was an action brought in the Circuit Court of the United States for the Western District of Tennessee, to recover the penalty of five hundred dollars given by the second section of the act; and the gravamen was the refusal by the conductor of the railroad company to allow the wife to ride in the ladies' car, for the reason, as stated in one of the counts, that she was a person of African descent. The jury rendered a verdict for the defendants in this case upon the merits. . . . The case was tried on the assumption by both parties of the validity of the act of Congress; and the principal point made by the exceptions was, that the judge allowed evidence to go to the jury tending to show that the conductor had reason to suspect that the plaintiff, the wife, was an improper person, because she was in company with a young man whom he supposed to be a white man, and on that account inferred that there was some improper connection between them; and the judge charged the jury, in substance, that if this was the conductor's bona fide reason for excluding the woman from the car, they might take it into consideration on the question of the liability of the company. The case was brought here by writ of error at the suit of the plaintiffs. . . .

■ MR. JUSTICE BRADLEY delivered the opinion of the court.

It is obvious that the primary and important question in all the cases is the constitutionality of the law: for if the law is unconstitutional none of the prosecutions can stand.

The sections of the law referred to provide as follows:

"SEC. 1. That all persons within the jurisdiction of the United States shall be entitled to the full and equal enjoyment of the accommodations, advantages, facilities, and privileges of inns, public conveyances on land or water, theatres, and other places of public amusement; subject only to the conditions and limitations established by law, and applicable alike to citizens of every race and color, regardless of any previous condition of servitude.

"SEC. 2. That any person who shall violate the foregoing section by denying to any citizen, except for reasons by law applicable to citizens of every race and color, and regardless of any previous condition of servitude, the full enjoyment of any of the accommodations, advantages, facilities, or privileges in said section enumerated, or by aiding or inciting such denial, shall for every such offence forfeit and pay the sum of five hundred dollars to the person aggrieved thereby, to be recovered in an action of debt, with full costs; and shall also, for every such offence, be deemed guilty of a misdemeanor, and, upon conviction thereof, shall be fined not less than five hundred nor more than one thousand dollars, or shall be imprisoned not less than thirty days nor more than one year. . . ."

The essence of the law is, not to declare broadly that all persons shall be entitled to the full and equal enjoyment of the accommodations, advantages, facilities, and privileges of inns, public conveyances, and theatres; but that such enjoyment shall not be subject to any conditions applicable only to citizens of a particular race or color, or who had been in a previous condition of servitude. In other words, it is the purpose of the law to declare that, in the enjoyment of the accommodations and privileges of inns, public conveyances, theatres, and other places of public amusement, no distinction shall be made between citizens of different race or color, or between those who have, and those who have not, been slaves. Its effect is to declare, that in all inns, public conveyances, and places of amusement, colored citizens, whether formerly slaves or not, and citizens of other races, shall have the same accommodations and privileges in all inns, public conveyances, and places of amusement as are enjoyed by white citizens; and vice versa. The second section makes it a penal offence in any person to deny to any citizen of any race or color, regardless of previous servitude, any of the accommodations or privileges mentioned in the first section.

Has Congress constitutional power to make such a law? Of course, no one will contend that the power to pass it was contained in the Constitution before the adoption of the last three amendments. The power is sought, first, in the Fourteenth Amendment, and the views and arguments of distinguished Senators, advanced whilst the law was under consideration, claiming authority to pass it by virtue of that amendment, are the principal arguments adduced in favor of the power. . . .

The first section of the Fourteenth Amendment (which is the one relied on), after declaring who shall be citizens of the United States, and of the several States, is prohibitory in its character, and prohibitory upon the States. It declares that:

> "No State shall make or enforce any law which shall abridge the privileges or immunities of citizens of the United States; nor shall any State deprive any person of life, liberty, or property without due process of law; nor deny to any person within its jurisdiction the equal protection of the laws."

It is State action of a particular character that is prohibited. Individual invasion of individual rights is not the subject-matter of the amendment. It has a deeper and broader scope. It nullifies and makes void all State legislation, and State action of every kind, which impairs the privileges and immunities of citizens of the United States, or which injures them in life, liberty or property without due process of law, or which denies to any of them the equal protection of the laws. It not only does this, but . . . the last section of the amendment invests Congress with power to enforce it by appropriate legislation. To enforce what?

To enforce the prohibition. To adopt appropriate legislation for correcting the effects of such prohibited State laws and State acts, and thus to render them effectually null, void, and innocuous. This is the legislative power conferred upon Congress, and this is the whole of it. It does not invest Congress with power to legislate upon subjects which are within the domain of State legislation; but to provide modes of relief against State legislation, or State action, of the kind referred to. It does not authorize Congress to create a code of municipal law for the regulation of private rights; but to provide modes of redress against the operation of State laws, and the action of State officers executive or judicial, when these are subversive of the fundamental rights specified in the amendment. Positive rights and privileges are undoubtedly secured by the Fourteenth Amendment; but they are secured by way of prohibition against State laws and State proceedings affecting those rights and privileges, and by power given to Congress to legislate for the purpose of carrying such prohibition into effect: and such legislation must necessarily be predicated upon such supposed State laws or State proceedings, and be directed to the correction of their operation and effect. . . .

And so in the present case, until some State law has been passed, or some State action through its officers or agents has been taken, adverse to the rights of citizens sought to be protected by the Fourteenth Amendment, no legislation of the United States under said amendment, nor any proceeding under such legislation, can be called into activity: for the prohibitions of the amendment are against State laws and acts done under State authority. Of course, legislation may, and should be, provided in advance to meet the exigency when it arises; but it should be adapted to the mischief and wrong which the amendment was intended to provide against; and that is, State laws, or State action of some kind, adverse to the rights of the citizen secured by the amendment. Such legislation cannot properly cover the whole domain of rights appertaining to life, liberty and property, defining them and providing for their vindication. That would be to establish a code of municipal law regulative of all private rights between man and man in society. It would be to make Congress take the place of the State legislatures and to supersede them.

It is absurd to affirm that, because the rights of life, liberty and property (which include all civil rights that men have), are by the amendment sought to be protected against invasion on the part of the State without due process of law, Congress may therefore provide due process of law for their vindication in every case; and that, because the denial by a State to any persons, of the equal protection of the laws, is prohibited by the amendment, therefore Congress may establish laws for their equal protection. In fine, the legislation which Congress is authorized to adopt in this behalf is not general legislation upon the rights of the citizen, but corrective legislation, that is, such as may be necessary and proper for counteracting such laws as the States may adopt or enforce, and which, by the amendment, they are prohibited from making or enforcing, or such acts and proceedings as the States may commit or take, and which, by the amendment, they are prohibited from committing or taking. It is not necessary for us to state, if we could, what legislation would be proper for Congress to adopt. It is sufficient for us to examine whether the law in question is of that character.

An inspection of the law shows that it makes no reference whatever to any supposed or apprehended violation of the Fourteenth Amendment on the part of the States. It is not predicated on any such view. It proceeds *ex directo* to declare that certain acts committed by individuals shall be deemed offences, and shall be prosecuted and punished by proceedings in the courts of the United States. It does not profess to be corrective of any constitutional wrong committed by the States; it does not make its operation to depend upon any such wrong committed. It applies equally to cases arising in States which have the justest laws respecting the personal rights of citizens, and whose authorities are ever ready to enforce such laws, as to those which arise in States that may have violated the prohibition of the amendment. In other words, it steps into the domain of local jurisprudence, and lays down rules for the conduct of individuals in society towards each other, and imposes sanctions for the enforcement of those rules, without referring in any manner to any supposed action of the State or its authorities.

If this legislation is appropriate for enforcing the prohibitions of the amendment, it is difficult to see where it is to stop. Why may not Congress with equal show of authority enact a code of laws for the enforcement and vindication of all rights of life, liberty, and property? If it is supposable that the States may deprive persons of life, liberty, and property without due process of law (and the amendment itself does suppose this), why should not Congress proceed at once to prescribe due process of law for the protection of every one of these fundamental rights, in every possible case, as well as to prescribe equal privileges in inns, public conveyances, and theatres?

The truth is, that the implication of a power to legislate in this manner is based upon the assumption that if the States are forbidden to legislate or act in a particular way on a particular subject, and power is conferred upon Congress to enforce the prohibition, this gives Congress power to legislate generally upon that subject, and not merely power to provide modes of redress against such State legislation or action. The assumption is certainly unsound. It is repugnant to the Tenth Amendment of the Constitution, which declares that powers not delegated to the United States by the Constitution, nor prohibited by it to the States, are reserved to the States respectively or to the people.

We have not overlooked the fact that the fourth section of the act now under consideration has been held by this court to be constitutional. That section declares "that no citizen, possessing all other qualifications which are or may be prescribed by law, shall be disqualified for service as grand or petit juror in any court of the United States, or of any State, on account of race, color, or previous condition of servitude; and any officer or other person charged with any duty in the selection or summoning of jurors who shall exclude or fail to summon any citizen for the cause aforesaid, shall, on conviction thereof, be deemed guilty of a misdemeanor, and be fined not more than five thousand dollars."

In *Ex parte Virginia*, 100 U.S. 339, it was held that an indictment against a State officer under this section for excluding persons of color from the jury list is sustainable. But a moment's attention to its terms will show that the section is entirely corrective in its character. Disqualifications for service on juries are only created by the law, and the first part of the section is aimed at certain disqualifying laws, namely, those which make mere race or color a disqualification; and the second clause is directed against those who, assuming to use the authority of the State government, carry into effect such a rule of disqualification. In the Virginia case, the State, through its officer, enforced a rule of disqualification which the law was intended to abrogate and counteract. Whether the statute book of the State actually laid down any such rule of disqualification, or not, the State, through its officer, enforced such a rule: and it is against such State action, through its officers and agents, that the last clause of the section is directed. This aspect of the law was deemed sufficient to divest it of any unconstitutional character, and makes it differ widely from the first and second sections of the same act which we are now considering.

These sections, in the objectionable features before referred to, are different also from the law ordinarily called the "Civil Rights Bill," originally passed April 9th, 1866, and re-enacted with some modifications in . . . the Enforcement Act, passed May 31st, 1870. That law, as re-enacted, after declaring that all persons within the jurisdiction of the United States shall have the same right in every State and Territory to make and enforce contracts, to sue, be parties, give evidence, and to the full and equal benefit of all laws and proceedings for the security of persons and property as is enjoyed by white citizens, and shall be subject to like punishment, pains, penalties, taxes, licenses and exactions of every kind, and none other, any law, statute, ordinance, regulation or custom to the contrary notwithstanding, proceeds to enact, that any person who, under color of any law, statute, ordinance, regulation or custom, shall subject, or cause to be subjected, any inhabitant of any State or Territory to the deprivation of any rights secured or protected by the preceding section (above quoted), or to different punishment, pains, or penalties, on account of such person being an alien, or by reason of his color or race, than is prescribed for the punishment of citizens, shall be deemed guilty of a misdemeanor, and subject to fine and imprisonment as specified in the act. This law is clearly corrective in its character, intended to counteract and furnish redress against State laws and proceedings, and customs having the force of law, which sanction the wrongful acts specified . . .

In this connection it is proper to state that civil rights, such as are guaranteed by the Constitution against State aggression, cannot be impaired by the wrongful acts of individuals, unsupported by State authority in the shape of laws, customs, or judicial or executive proceedings. The wrongful act of an individual, unsupported by any such authority, is simply a private wrong, or a crime of that individual; an invasion of the rights of the injured party, it is true, whether they affect his person, his property, or his reputation; but if not sanctioned in some way by the State, or not done under State authority, his rights remain in full force, and may presumably be vindicated by resort to the laws of the

State for redress. An individual cannot deprive a man of his right to vote, to hold property, to buy and sell, to sue in the courts, or to be a witness or a juror; he may, by force or fraud, interfere with the enjoyment of the right in a particular case; he may commit an assault against the person, or commit murder, or use ruffian violence at the polls, or slander the good name of a fellow citizen; but, unless protected in these wrongful acts by some shield of State law or State authority, he cannot destroy or injure the right; he will only render himself amenable to satisfaction or punishment; and amenable therefor to the laws of the State where the wrongful acts are committed.

Hence, in all those cases where the Constitution seeks to protect the rights of the citizen against discriminative and unjust laws of the State by prohibiting such laws, it is not individual offences, but abrogation and denial of rights, which it denounces, and for which it clothes the Congress with power to provide a remedy. This abrogation and denial of rights, for which the States alone were or could be responsible, was the great seminal and fundamental wrong which was intended to be remedied. And the remedy to be provided must necessarily be predicated upon that wrong. It must assume that in the cases provided for, the evil or wrong actually committed rests upon some State law or State authority for its excuse and perpetration.

Of course, these remarks do not apply to those cases in which Congress is clothed with direct and plenary powers of legislation over the whole subject, accompanied with an express or implied denial of such power to the States, as in the regulation of commerce with foreign nations, among the several States, and with the Indian tribes, the coining of money, the establishment of post offices and post reads, the declaring of war, etc. In these cases Congress has power to pass laws for regulating the subjects specified in every detail, and the conduct and transactions of individuals in respect thereof. But where a subject is not submitted to the general legislative power of Congress . . . and any legislation by Congress in the matter must necessarily be corrective in its character, adapted to counteract and redress the operation of such prohibited State laws or proceedings of State officers.

If the principles of interpretation which we have laid down are correct, as we deem them to be . . . it is clear that the law in question cannot be sustained by any grant of legislative power made to Congress by the Fourteenth Amendment. . . . The law in question, without any reference to adverse State legislation on the subject, declares that all persons shall be entitled to equal accommodations and privileges of inns, public conveyances, and places of public amusement, and imposes a penalty upon any individual who shall deny to any citizen such equal accommodations and privileges. This is not corrective legislation; it is primary and direct; it takes immediate and absolute possession of the subject of the right of admission to inns, public conveyances, and places of amusement. It supersedes and displaces State legislation on the same subject, or only allows it permissive force. . . . Whether it would not have been a more effective protection of the rights of citizens to have clothed Congress with plenary power over the whole subject, is not now the question. What we have to decide is, whether such plenary power has been conferred upon Congress by the Fourteenth Amendment; and, in our judgment, it has not. . . .

But the power of Congress to adopt direct and primary, as distinguished from corrective legislation, on the subject in hand, is sought, in the second place, from the Thirteenth Amendment, which abolishes slavery. This amendment declares "that neither slavery, nor involuntary servitude, except as a punishment for crime, whereof the party shall have been duly convicted, shall exist within the United States, or any place subject to their jurisdiction;" and it gives Congress power to enforce the amendment by appropriate legislation.

This amendment, as well as the Fourteenth, is undoubtedly self-executing without any ancillary legislation, so far as its terms are applicable to any existing state of circumstances. By its own unaided force and effect it abolished slavery, and established universal freedom. Still, legislation may be necessary and proper to meet all the various cases and circumstances to be affected by it, and to prescribe proper modes of redress for its violation in letter or spirit. And such legislation may be primary and direct in its character; for the amendment is not a mere prohibition of State laws establishing or upholding slavery, but an absolute declaration that slavery or involuntary servitude shall not exist in any part of the United States. . . .

[I]t is assumed, that the power vested in Congress to enforce the article by appropriate legislation, clothes Congress with power to pass all laws necessary and proper for abolishing all badges and incidents of slavery in the United States: and upon this assumption it is claimed, that this is sufficient authority for declaring by law that all persons shall have equal accommodations and privileges in all inns, public conveyances, and places of amusement; the argument being, that the denial of such equal accommodations and privileges is, in itself, a subjection to a species of servitude within the meaning of the amendment. Conceding the major proposition to be true, that Congress has a right to enact all necessary and proper laws for the obliteration and prevention of slavery with all its badges and incidents, is the minor proposition also true, that the denial to any person of admission to the accommodations and privileges of an inn, a public conveyance, or a theatre, does subject that person to any form of servitude, or tend to fasten upon him any badge of slavery? If it does not, then power to pass the law is not found in the Thirteenth Amendment. . . .

It may be that by the Black Code (as it was called), in the times when slavery prevailed, the proprictors of inns and public conveyances were forbidden to receive persons of the African race, because it might assist slaves to escape from the control of their masters. This was merely a means of preventing such escapes, and was no part of the servitude itself. A law of that kind could not have any such object now, however justly it might be deemed an invasion of the party's legal right as a citizen, and amenable to the prohibitions of the Fourteenth Amendment.

The long existence of African slavery in this country gave us very distinct notions of what it was, and what were its necessary incidents. Compulsory service of the slave for the benefit of the master, restraint of his movements except by the master's will, disability to hold property, to make contracts, to have a standing in court, to be a witness against a white person, and such like burdens and incapacities, were the inseparable incidents of the institution. Severer punishments for crimes were imposed on the slave than on free persons guilty of the same offences. Congress, as we have seen, by the Civil Rights Bill of 1866, passed in view of the Thirteenth Amendment, before the Fourteenth was adopted, undertook to wipe out these burdens and disabilities, the necessary incidents of slavery, constituting its substance and visible form; and to secure to all citizens of every race and color, and without regard to previous servitude, those fundamental rights which are the essence of civil freedom, namely, the same right to make and enforce contracts, to sue, be parties, give evidence, and to inherit, purchase, lease, sell and convey property, as is enjoyed by white citizens. Whether this legislation was fully authorized by the Thirteenth Amendment alone, without the support which it afterward received from the Fourteenth Amendment, after the adoption of which it was re-enacted with some additions, it is not necessary to inquire. It is referred to for the purpose of showing that at that time (in 1866) Congress did not assume, under the authority given by the Thirteenth Amendment, to adjust what may be called the social rights of men and races in the community; but only to declare and vindicate those fundamental rights which appertain to the essence of citizenship, and the enjoyment or deprivation of which constitutes the essential distinction between freedom and slavery.

We must not forget that the province and scope of the Thirteenth and Fourteenth amendments are different; the former simply abolished slavery: the latter prohibited the States from abridging the privileges or immunities of citizens of the United States; from depriving them of life, liberty, or property without due process of law, and from denying to any the equal protection of the laws. The amendments are different, and the powers of Congress under them are different. What Congress has power to do under one, it may not have power to do under the other. Under the Thirteenth Amendment, it has only to do with slavery and its incidents. Under the Fourteenth Amendment, it has power to counteract and render nugatory all State laws and proceedings which have the effect to abridge any of the privileges or immunities of citizens of the United States, or to deprive them of life, liberty or property without due process of law, or to deny to any of them the equal protection of the laws. Under the Thirteenth Amendment, the legislation, so far as necessary or proper to eradicate all forms and incidents of slavery and involuntary servitude, may be direct and primary, operating upon the acts of individuals, whether sanctioned by State legislation or not; under the Fourteenth, as we have already shown, it must necessarily be, and can only be, corrective in its character, addressed to counteract and afford relief against State regulations or proceedings.

The only question under the present head, therefore, is, whether the refusal to any persons of the accommodations of an inn, or a public conveyance, or a place of public amusement, by an individual, and without any sanction or support from any State law or regulation, does inflict upon such persons any manner of servitude, or form of slavery, as those terms are understood in this country? ... The Thirteenth Amendment has respect, not to distinctions of race, or class, or color, but to slavery. . . .

After giving to these questions all the consideration which their importance demands, we are forced to the conclusion that such an act of refusal has nothing to do with slavery or involuntary servitude, and that if it is violative of any right of the party, his redress is to be sought under the laws of the State; or if those laws are adverse to his rights and do not protect him, his remedy will be found in the corrective legislation which Congress has adopted, or may adopt, for counteracting the effect of State laws, or State action, prohibited by the Fourteenth Amendment. It would be running the slavery argument into the ground to make it apply to every act of discrimination which a person may see fit to make as to the guests he will entertain, or as to the people he will take into his coach or cab or car, or admit to his concert or theatre, or deal with in other matters of intercourse or business. Innkeepers and public carriers, by the laws of all the States, so far as we are aware, are bound, to the extent of their facilities, to furnish proper accommodation to all unobjectionable persons who in good faith apply for them. If the laws themselves make any unjust discrimination, amenable to the prohibitions of the Fourteenth Amendment, Congress has full power to afford a remedy under that amendment and in accordance with it.

When a man has emerged from slavery, and by the aid of beneficent legislation has shaken off the inseparable concomitants of that state, there must be some stage in the progress of his elevation when he takes the rank of a mere citizen, and ceases to be the special favorite of the laws, and when his rights as a citizen, or a man, are to be protected in the ordinary modes by which other men's rights are protected. There were thousands of free colored people in this country before the abolition of slavery, enjoying all the essential rights of life, liberty and property the same as white citizens; yet no one, at that time, thought that it was any invasion of his personal status as a freeman because he was not admitted to all the privileges enjoyed by white citizens, or because he was subjected to discriminations in the enjoyment of accommodations in inns, public conveyances and places of amusement. Mere discriminations on account of race or color were not regarded as badges of slavery. . . .

On the whole we are of opinion, that no countenance of authority for the passage of the law in question can be found in either the Thirteenth or Fourteenth Amendment of the Constitution; and no other ground of authority for its passage being suggested, it must necessarily be declared void, at least so far as its operation in the several States is concerned. . . .

■ MR. JUSTICE HARLAN dissenting.

The opinion in these cases proceeds, it seems to me, upon grounds entirely too narrow and artificial. I cannot resist the conclusion that the substance and spirit of the recent amendments of the Constitution have been sacrificed by a subtle and ingenious verbal criticism. "It is not the words of the law but the internal sense of it that makes the law: the letter of the law is the body; the sense and reason of the law is the soul." Constitutional provisions, adopted in the interest of liberty, and for the purpose of securing, through national legislation, if need be, rights inhering in a state of freedom, and belonging to American citizenship, have been so construed as to defeat the ends the people desired to accomplish, which they attempted to accomplish, and which they supposed they had accomplished by changes in their fundamental law. By this I do not mean that the determination of these cases should have been materially controlled by considerations of mere expediency or policy. I mean only, in this form, to express an earnest conviction that the court has departed from the familiar rule requiring, in the interpretation of constitutional provisions, that full effect be given to the intent with which they were adopted. . . .

The Thirteenth Amendment, it is conceded, did something more than to prohibit slavery as an institution, resting upon distinctions of race, and upheld by positive law. My brethren admit that it established and decreed universal civil freedom throughout the United States. But did the freedom thus established involve nothing more than exemption from actual slavery? Was nothing more intended than to forbid one man from owning another as property? Was it the purpose of the nation simply to destroy the institution, and then remit the race, theretofore held in bondage, to the several States for such protection, in their civil rights, necessarily growing out of freedom, as those States, in their discretion, might choose to provide? Were the States against whose protest the institution was destroyed, to be left free, so far as national interference was concerned, to make or allow discriminations against that race, as such, in the enjoyment of those fundamental rights which by universal concession, inhere in a state of freedom? Had the Thirteenth Amendment stopped with the sweeping declaration, in its first section, against the existence of slavery and involuntary servitude, except for crime, Congress would have had the power, by implication, according to the doctrines of *Prigg v. Commonwealth of Pennsylvania* . . . to protect the freedom established, and consequently, to secure the enjoyment of such civil rights as were fundamental in freedom. That it can exert its authority to that extent is made clear, and was intended to be made clear, by the express grant of power contained in the second section of the Amendment.

That there are burdens and disabilities which constitute badges of slavery and servitude, and that the power to enforce by appropriate legislation the Thirteenth Amendment may be exerted by legislation of a direct and primary character, for the eradication, not simply of the institution, but of its badges and incidents, are propositions which ought to be deemed indisputable. They lie at the foundation of the Civil Rights Act of 1866. . . .

I do not contend that the Thirteenth Amendment invests Congress with authority, by legislation, to define and regulate the entire body of the civil rights which citizens enjoy, or may enjoy, in the several States. But I hold that since slavery, as the court has repeatedly declared, *Slaughter-house Cases,* 16 Wall. 36, was the moving or principal cause of the adoption of that amendment, and since that institution rested wholly upon the inferiority, as a race, of those held in bondage, their freedom necessarily involved immunity from, and protection against, all discrimination against them, because of their race, in respect of such civil rights as belong to freemen of other races. Congress, therefore, under its express power to enforce that amendment, by appropriate legislation, may enact laws to protect that people against the deprivation, because of their race, of any civil rights granted to other freemen in the same State; and such legislation may be of a direct and primary character, operating upon States, their officers and agents, and, also, upon, at least, such individuals and corporations as exercise public functions and wield power and authority under the State. . . .

It remains now to inquire what are the legal rights of colored persons in respect of the accommodations, privileges and facilities of public conveyances, inns and places of public amusement?

First, as to public conveyances on land and water. . . . [T]his court [has] said that a common carrier is "in the exercise of a sort of public office, and has public duties to perform, from which he should not be permitted to exonerate himself without the assent of the parties concerned." . . . [We have also] ruled that railroads are public highways, established by authority of the State for the public use; . . . that it is a part of the function of government to make and maintain highways for the convenience of the public; that no matter who is the agent, or what is the agency, the function performed is that of the State; that although the owners may be private companies, they may be compelled to permit the public to use these works in the manner in which they can be used; that, upon these grounds alone, have the courts sustained the investiture of railroad corporations with the State's right of eminent domain, or the right of municipal corporations, under legislative authority, to assess, levy and collect taxes to aid in the construction of railroads. . . .

Such being the relations these corporations hold to the public, it would seem that the right of a colored person to use an improved public highway, upon the terms accorded to freemen of other races, is as fundamental, in the state of freedom established in this country, as are any of the rights which my brethren concede to be so far fundamental as to be deemed the essence of civil freedom. "Personal liberty consists," says Blackstone, "in the power of locomotion, of changing situation, or removing one's person to whatever places one's own inclination may direct, without restraint, unless by due course of law." But of what value is this right of locomotion, if it may be clogged by such burdens as Congress intended by the act of 1875 to remove? They are burdens which lay at the very foundation of the institution of slavery as it once existed. . . . The Thirteenth Amendment alone obliterated the race line, so far as all rights fundamental in a state of freedom are concerned.

Second, as to inns. The same general observations which have been made as to railroads are applicable to inns. . . . These authorities are sufficient to show that a keeper of an inn is in the exercise of a quasi public employment. The law gives him special privileges and he is charged with certain duties and responsibilities to the public. The public nature of his employment forbids him from discriminating against any person asking admission as a guest on account of the race or color of that person.

Third. As to places of public amusement. . . . The authority to establish and maintain them comes from the public. The colored race is a part of that public. . . . A license from the public to establish a place of public amusement, imports, in law, equality of right, at such places, among all the members of that public. This must be so, unless it be— which I deny—that the common municipal government of all the people may, in the exertion of its powers, . . . discriminate or authorize discrimination against a particular race, solely because of its former condition of servitude. . . .

In the *Munn* case the question was whether the State of Illinois could fix, by law, the maximum of charges for the storage of grain in certain warehouses in that State—the private property of individual citizens. . . . [T]he court says:

> Property does become clothed with a public interest when used in a manner to make it of public consequence and affect the community at large. When, therefore, one devotes his property to a use in which the public has an interest, he, in effect, grants to the public an interest in that use, and must submit to be controlled by the public for the common good, to the extent of the interest he has thus created. He may withdraw his grant by discontinuing the use, but, so long as he maintains the use, he must submit to the control. . . .

Congress has not, in these matters, entered the domain of State control and supervision. It does not, as I have said, assume to prescribe the general conditions and limitations under which inns, public conveyances, and places of public amusement, shall be conducted or managed. It simply declares, in effect, that since the nation has established universal freedom in this country, for all time, there shall be no discrimination, based merely upon race or color, in respect of the accommodations and advantages of public conveyances, inns, and places of public amusement.

I am of the opinion that such discrimination practised by corporations and individuals in the exercise of their public or quasi-public functions is a badge of servitude the imposition of which Congress may prevent under its power, by appropriate legislation, to enforce the Thirteenth Amendment; and, consequently, without reference to its enlarged power under the Fourteenth Amendment, the act of March 1, 1875, is not, in my judgment, repugnant to the Constitution.

It remains now to consider these cases with reference to the power Congress has possessed since the adoption of the Fourteenth Amendment. Much that has been said as to the power of Congress under the Thirteenth Amendment is applicable to this branch of the discussion, and will not be repeated.

Before the adoption of the recent amendments, it had become, as we have seen, the established doctrine of this court that negroes, whose ancestors had been imported and sold as slaves, could not become citizens of a State, or even of the United States, with the rights and privileges guaranteed to citizens by the national Constitution; further, that one might have all the rights and privileges of a citizen of a State without being a citizen in the sense in which that word was used in the national Constitution, and without being entitled to the privileges and immunities of citizens of the several States. Still, further, between the adoption of the Thirteenth Amendment and the proposal by Congress of the Fourteenth Amendment, on June 16, 1866, the statute books of several of the States, as we have seen, had become loaded down with enactments which, under the guise of Apprentice, Vagrant, and Contract regulations, sought to keep the colored race in a condition, practically, of servitude. It was openly announced that whatever might be the rights which persons of that race had, as freemen, under the guarantees of the national Constitution, they could not become citizens of a State, with the privileges belonging to citizens, except by the consent of such State; consequently, that their civil rights, as citizens of the State, depended entirely upon State legislation. To meet this new peril to the black race, that the purposes of the nation might not be doubted or defeated, and by way of further enlargement of the power of Congress, the Fourteenth Amendment was proposed for adoption.

Remembering that this court, in the *Slaughter-House Cases*, declared that the one pervading purpose found in all the recent amendments, lying at the foundation of each, and without which none of them would have been suggested—was "the freedom of the slave race, the security and firm establishment of that freedom, and the protection of the newly-made freeman and citizen from the oppression of those who had formerly exercised unlimited dominion over him"—that each amendment was addressed primarily to the grievances of that race—let us proceed to consider the language of the Fourteenth Amendment. . . .

The Fourteenth Amendment presents the first instance in our history of the investiture of Congress with affirmative power, by legislation, to enforce an express prohibition upon the States. . . .

The assumption that this amendment consists wholly of prohibitions upon State laws and State proceedings in hostility to its provisions, is unauthorized by its language. The first clause of the first section—"All persons born or naturalized in the United States, and subject to the jurisdiction thereof, are citizens of the United States, and of the State wherein they reside"—is of a distinctly affirmative character. In its application to the colored race, previously liberated, it created and granted, as well citizenship of the United States, as citizenship of the State in which they respectively resided. It introduced all of that race, whose ancestors had been imported and sold as slaves, at once, into the political community known as the "People of the United States." They became, instantly, citizens of the United States, and of their respective States. Further, they were brought, by this supreme act of the nation, within the direct operation of that provision of the Constitution which declares that "the citizens of each State shall be entitled to all privileges and immunities of citizens in the several States." Art. 4, § 2.

The citizenship thus acquired, by that race, in virtue of an affirmative grant from the nation, may be protected, not alone by the judicial branch of the government, but by congressional legislation of a primary direct character; this, because the power of Congress is not restricted to the enforcement of prohibitions upon State laws or State action. It is, in terms distinct and positive, to enforce "the provisions of this article" of amendment; not simply those of a prohibitive character, but . . . all of the provisions[,] affirmative and prohibitive, of the amendment. . . . If any right was created by that amendment, the grant of power, through appropriate legislation, to enforce its provisions, authorizes Congress, by means of legislation, operating throughout the entire Union, to guard, secure, and protect that right. . . .

But what was secured to colored citizens of the United States—as between them and their respective States—by the national grant to them of State citizenship? With what rights, privileges, or immunities did this grant invest them? There is one, if there be no other—exemption from race discrimination in respect of any civil right belonging to citizens of the white race in the same State. That, surely, is their constitutional privilege when within the jurisdiction of other States. And such must be their constitutional right, in their own State, unless the recent amendments be splendid baubles, thrown out to delude those who deserved fair and generous treatment at the hands of the nation.

Citizenship in this country necessarily imports at least equality of civil rights among citizens of every race in the same State. . . .

If, then, exemption from discrimination, in respect of civil rights, is a new constitutional right, secured by the grant of State citizenship to colored citizens of the United States . . . why may not the nation, by means of its own legislation of a primary direct character, guard, protect and enforce that right? It is a right and privilege which the nation conferred. It did not come from the States in which those colored citizens reside. It has been the established doctrine of this court during all its history, accepted as essential to the national supremacy, that Congress, in the absence of a positive delegation of power to the State legislatures, may, by its own legislation, enforce and protect any right derived from or created by the national Constitution. It was so declared in *Prigg v. Commonwealth of Pennsylvania*. . . .

This court has always given a broad and liberal construction to the Constitution, so as to enable Congress, by legislation, to enforce rights secured by that instrument. . . . [I]t is for Congress, not the judiciary, to say that legislation is appropriate . . . to the end to be attained. . . . "The sound construction of the Constitution," said Chief Justice Marshall, "must allow to the national legislature that discretion, with respect to the means by which the powers it confers are to be carried into execution, which will enable that body to perform the high duties assigned to it in the manner most beneficial to the people. Let the end be legitimate, let it be within the scope of the Constitution, and all means which are appropriate, which are plainly adapted to that end, which are not prohibited, but consist with the letter and spirit of the Constitution, are constitutional." *McCulloch v. Maryland*. . . .

In view of the circumstances under which the recent amendments were incorporated into the Constitution, and especially in view of the peculiar character of the new rights they created and secured, it ought not to be presumed that the general government has abdicated its authority, by national legislation, direct and primary in its character, to guard and protect privileges and immunities secured by that instrument. Such an interpretation of the Constitution ought not to be accepted if it be possible to avoid it. Its acceptance would lead to this anomalous result: that whereas, prior to the amendments, Congress, with the sanction of this court, passed the most stringent laws—operating directly and primarily upon States and their officers and agents, as well as upon individuals—in vindication of slavery and the right of the master, it may not now, by legislation of a like primary and direct character, guard, protect, and secure the freedom established, and the most essential right of the citizenship granted, by the constitutional amendments. . . . I insist that the national legislature may . . . do for human liberty and the fundamental rights of American citizenship, what it did, with the sanction of this court, for the protection of slavery and the rights of the masters of fugitive slaves. . . .

But if it were conceded that the power of Congress could not be brought into activity until the rights specified in the act of 1875 had been abridged or denied by some State law or State action, I maintain that the decision of the court is erroneous. There has been adverse State action within the Fourteenth Amendment as heretofore interpreted by this court. . . .

In every material sense applicable to the practical enforcement of the Fourteenth Amendment, railroad corporations, keepers of inns, and managers of places of public amusement are agents or instrumentalities of the State, because they are charged with duties to the public, and are amenable, in respect of their duties and functions, to governmental regulation. It seems to me that . . . a denial, by these instrumentalities of the State, to the citizen, because of his race, of that equality of civil rights secured to him by law, is a denial by the State, within the meaning of the Fourteenth Amendment. If it be not, then that race is left, in respect of the civil rights in question, practically at the mercy of corporations and individuals wielding power under the States. . . .

For the reasons stated I feel constrained to withhold my assent to the opinion of the court.

NOTE ON THE EFFECT AND INTERPRETATION OF THE RECONSTRUCTION AMENDMENTS

1.   We are used to thinking of the Bill of Rights as a general charter of individual liberties, applicable to all American governmental actors. As *Barron* makes clear, however, the Bill of Rights was originally understood as a set of restrictions on the *national* government. It was not until the Supreme Court interpreted the Fourteenth Amendment's Due Process Clause to "incorporate" most provisions of the Bill of Rights and render them applicable to the States that the Bill of Rights became universal. (We will cover incorporation in Section 6.3, *infra*.) This hardly means that, prior to incorporation, *no* rights-based restrictions constrained state governments. The states had their own constitutions, after all, that imposed important limits on state government action. [8] Moreover, the United States Constitution imposed some limits on states; most importantly, it prohibited them from impairing the obligation of contracts.[9] But these provisions are admittedly sparse compared to the restrictions on the national government in the Bill of Rights. What does the failure to include more rights provisions directed at the States in the original Constitution suggest about how the Founding Generation viewed the respective state and national governments? How does this view change after the Civil War?

2.   The primary debate in the *Slaughter-House Cases* concerned the meaning of the Privileges or Immunities Clause of the Fourteenth

---

[8]   Contemporary scholarship has begun to recover a rich constitutional tradition in the states. *See, e.g.,* EMILY ZACKIN, LOOKING FOR RIGHTS IN ALL THE WRONG PLACES: WHY STATE CONSTITUTIONS CONTAIN AMERICA'S POSITIVE RIGHTS (2013).

[9]   *See* U.S. CONST. art. I, § 10, cl. 1.

Amendment. The privileges and immunities protected by the Fourteenth Amendment and by Article IV of the original Constitution, respectively, are not the same. The majority holds that the privileges and immunities of *national* citizenship (protected by the Fourteenth Amendment) are distinct from and considerably narrower than the privileges and immunities of *state* citizenship (protected by Article IV). What are some examples of each? Although the issue was not directly presented in *Slaughter-House*, the majority's interpretation of the Fourteenth Amendment excluded the possibility that the privileges and immunities of national citizenship include the protections of the Bill of Rights. Would this have been a more plausible textual basis for incorporation than the Due Process Clause?[10] More broadly, is the majority's narrow view of the privileges and immunities of national citizenship consistent with the history and purpose of the Fourteenth Amendment? In particular, is it consistent with the historic shift to the national government as the primary guarantor of individual rights?

On its face, the Fourteenth Amendment's general protection for "privileges and immunities" of national citizenship offers a plausible textual home for a broad array of unenumerated rights—not only the right to pursue a profession asserted in *Slaughter-House*, but perhaps also the freedom of contract recognized in cases like *Lochner v. New York* and the right to privacy recognized in *Griswold v. Connecticut* and *Roe v. Wade*. *Slaughter-House* largely put an end to this possibility, and that aspect of the decision has never really been revisited; instead, attention has shifted to the Due Process Clause of the Fourteenth Amendment as the textual hook for unenumerated rights. Justice Miller's majority opinion in *Slaughter-House* gave the due process argument the back of the hand, but Justice Bradley's dissent on this point would prove prophetic in *Lochner* and other cases down the line. As we move through the Twentieth Century unenumerated rights cases, ask yourself whether it would have been better to pursue that line of enquiry under the Privileges or Immunities Clause.

3.   Was the decision in the *Slaughter-House Cases* about federalism or about individual rights? The two issues are closely linked by Section Five of the Fourteenth Amendment, which gives Congress a new enumerated power to legislate in order to "enforce" the rights provisions contained in Section One. (Similar provisions are included in the Thirteenth and Fifteenth Amendments as well.) The upshot is that expanding the rights protected under Section One necessarily expands Congress's legislative authority under Section Five. What is the majority's concern about the interpretation of Section One offered by the plaintiffs? Do the dissenters adequately address this concern? In particular, do they offer a limiting principle to constrain

---

[10]   In *McDonald v. City of Chicago*, 561 U.S. 742 (2010), the plaintiffs argued that the right to bear arms recognized in *District of Columbia v. Heller*, 554 U.S. 570 (2008), should also bind state and local governments. The plaintiffs chose to ground their primary argument in the Privileges or Immunities Clause of the Fourteenth Amendment, contending that it provided a better basis for incorporation of the Second Amendment than did the Due Process Clause. They persuaded Justice Thomas that privileges and immunites offered "a more straightforward path" to incorporation, *id.* at 805 (Thomas, J., concurring in part and in the judgment), and that the due process approach was fraught with textual and historical difficulties. Nonetheless, the majority refused to reconsider its precedents and held that the Second Amendment bound state and local governments through the Fourteenth Amendment's Due Process Clause.

Congress's power if their view of Section One were accepted? To the extent that the majority opinion construes the Fourteenth Amendment as not having fundamentally altered the relationship between the Nation and the States, is that consistent with the underlying history of the Civil War and Reconstruction?

4.   Why did the Court refuse to apply constitutional restrictions to private actors in *Civil Rights Cases*? This "state action" requirement applies both when particular actions are challenged in court as violating the Constitution, and when Congress seeks to legislate to bar particular practices under Section Five of the Fourteenth Amendment. Is the Court's reasoning equally compelling in each of these two contexts? Given the strong historical evidence that Congress proposed the Fourteenth Amendment in order to ensure the constitutionality of the Civil Rights Act, is the Court's construction of the Amendment in the *Civil Rights Cases* too restrictive? If it is, is there any way to construe the Amendment short of junking the state action requirement altogether or turning the Amendment into an overly broad grant of legislative authority?

Most state action cases concern whether actions by private or quasi-private actors have a sufficient connection to governmental action to bring constitutional requirements into play. Justice Harlan's dissent, for example, argues that proprietors of public accommodations—theaters, railroads, restaurants, etc.—all exercise a public function. Why would this be true? Is it plausible to treat all these entities as state actors?

Confusion persists concerning what sorts of entities should be treated as state actors. Recent cases have struggled, for instance, with whether interscholastic athletic associations, which often include both state-run and private schools, count as the government so that their actions may be challenged on constitutional grounds.[11] Others have considered whether judicial enforcement of discriminatory provisions in private contracts can violate the Fourteenth Amendment,[12] as well as the extent to which public licensing or authorization transforms private entities into state actors.[13] The ins and outs of this doctrine are complex and outside the scope of this text. But it is important to know a) that the state action requirement exists as a basic limit on the scope of constitutional rights, and b) that private actors are sometimes sufficiently linked to governmental action that the Constitution may apply to them.[14]

---

[11] *See, e.g., Brentwood Academy v. Tennessee Secondary School Athletic Assn.*, 531 U.S. 288 (2001) (holding that a statewide organization of public and private secondary schools was a state actor because of its "pervasive entwinement" of private and public institutions).

[12] *Shelley v. Kraemer*, 334 U.S. 1 (1948) (it can).

[13] *See, e.g., Moose Lodge No. 107 v. Irvis*, 407 U.S. 163 (1972) (holding that a local fraternal organization did not become a state actor, so that exclusion of blacks would violate the Equal Protection Clause, simply because it had been licensed by the State to serve liquor).

[14] The Court reaffirmed the *Civil Rights Cases* in *United States v. Morrison*, 529 U.S. 598 (2000), holding that the Violence Against Women Act's provision for civil suits against private actors who commit gender-motivated violence could not be sustained under Congress's power to enforce the Fourteenth Amendment. The Court reasoned that the Act's provisions were directed against persons who were not themselves state actors and therefore beyond the Fourteenth Amendment's reach.

5.   The one provision of the Constitution that applies to public and private actors alike is the Thirteenth Amendment, which simply bans slavery whether sponsored by the State or simply practiced by private individuals. The scope of the Thirteenth Amendment is an important issue in both the *Slaughter-House Cases* and the *Civil Rights Cases*. There is general agreement that the Thirteenth Amendment covers not only the formal practice of slavery but also its "badges and incidents"; the question is how broadly this category of practices associated with slavery extends. Does it include all forms of racial discrimination? If so, does that make the Fourteenth Amendment superfluous? On the other hand, can the majority in the *Civil Rights Cases* plausibly deny that discrimination against black people in places of public accommodation is a vestige of slavery?

6.   Reconstruction came to an abrupt end after the presidential election of 1876. Calling themselves "Redeemers," white Southerners were already striving to regain control of their state governments, both overtly through the Democratic party and covertly through a campaign of terrorism and assassination waged by the Klu Klux Klan. Reconstructed Republican governments in the South thus depended on the support of the Union Army to maintain their grip on power. Unfortunately, that support waned with the fortunes of the Republican party in the North, which had been hurt by corruption scandals in the Grant administration as well as the economic Panic of 1873.

Much like the election of 2000, early returns for the election of 1876 showed a virtual tie. Democrat Samuel Tilden clearly won the popular vote, but initial returns gave Republican Rutherford B. Hayes a one-vote margin in the Electoral College. Alleging fraud in several Southern states still controlled by Republicans, Democrats challenged the results. Congress created a fifteen-man electoral commission to review ballots from Florida, Louisiana, Mississippi, and Oregon. The Commission included five members of the House, five senators, and four Supreme Court justices—all split evenly by party. The four justices were to name a fifth, who turned out to be Joseph P. Bradley, the author of the *Civil Rights Cases* but a dissenter in *Slaughter-House*. Despite having been appointed as the most balanced of the justices not already on the commission (all were Republicans), Bradley voted with the other Republicans on every contested issue. A series of straight party-line votes thus awarded the election to Hayes.

Democrats did not accept the legitimacy of this result, however, without further concessions. The most important was the withdrawal of federal troops from the South, with the result that Republican state governments and the black voters that supported them were left to the not-so-tender mercies of the Redeemers. As Professor Powe recounts, "[s]ome three thousand freedmen and their white allies were murdered, often brutally, to overthrow the most democratic governments the South had ever seen. Through terror, voter fraud, and a Northern electorate weary of policing the South and depressed by economic woes, plus administration scandals, the South was 'redeemed.' "[15]

---

[15] POWE, *supra* note 2, at 140.

See also: The leading history of Reconstruction is ERIC FONER, RECONSTRUCTION: AMERICA'S UNFINISHED REVOLUTION, 1863–1877 (2002). On the relation between Reconstruction and federalism, see MICHAEL LES BENEDICT, PRESERVING THE CONSTITUTION: ESSAYS ON POLITICS AND THE CONSTITUTION IN THE RECONSTRUCTION ERA (2006).

CHAPTER FIVE

THE *LOCHNER* ERA AND THE NEW DEAL CRISIS

Robert McCloskey wrote that "as war and Reconstruction recede into the past, the Court's history becomes a history of response to the advance of what was later to be called 'the general-welfare state.' "[1] Federalism would remain an important issue in this second epoch, but it would not be so much an end in itself as one instrument among several for checking the growth of the regulatory state. That growth occurred at both the federal and state levels at the end of the Nineteenth Century, and while federal legislation could often be limited under the Commerce Clause, the Court turned to the Due Process Clause of the Fourteenth Amendment for the primary limit on analogous state regulation. These two constitutional provisions—the Commerce Clause and the Due Process Clause—are quite distinct doctrinally, but they are inextricably linked as a historical matter between the turn of the Twentieth Century and the New Deal Crisis in 1937. For a time, they served as complementary instruments for defending the free market economy, until the Court essentially abandoned constitutional review of economic legislation under pressure from President Franklin Delano Roosevelt's "court-packing" plan. It is impossible to understand one stream of cases without knowledge of the other.

The arc of judicial review over the course of the period discussed in this Chapter is in part a story about the Court's response to external pressures: The Court responded to increasingly aggressive regulation (which was in turn driven by the increasingly apparent social costs of industrialization) by engaging in increasingly aggressive judicial review. *Lochner v. New York* and *Hammer v. Dagenhart* are key examples of this development. The New Deal's radical expansion of the welfare state in response to the Depression brought matters to a head. When the Court struck down several key pieces of New Deal legislation in cases like *A.L.A. Schechter Poultry Corp. v. United States*, President Roosevelt proposed to "pack" the Court with more sympathetic justices. The conventional historical account holds that this existential threat to the Court's independence caused the Court to back off in 1937. In particular, Justice Owen Roberts—the crucial fifth vote in economic regulation cases during this period—changed sides in *West Coast Hotel Co. v. Parrish* and *NLRB v. Jones & Laughlin Steel Corp.*—the "switch in time that saved

---

[1]   ROBERT G. MCCLOSKEY, THE AMERICAN SUPREME COURT 81 (Sanford Levinson, ed, 4th ed. 2005).

nine." After 1937, the Court never again engaged in aggressive judicial review of economic regulation.

There is also, however, a parallel story internal to the Court and its doctrines.[2] Although the fact is frequently overlooked, the Court upheld at least as many regulatory statutes as it struck down between 1900 and 1937. The *Shreveport Rate Cases*, for example, represented a fairly generous interpretation of Congress's commerce power, and *Nebbia v. New York* displayed an equally generous view of the government's ability to restrict freedom of contract. The opinions revealed a continuing struggle to draw workable lines between permissible and impermissible forms of regulation. On this view, what happened in 1937 is that the doctrinal distinctions that had driven judicial review in this area collapsed of their own weight, leaving the Court with no alternative but to get out of the business of reviewing economic regulation entirely.[3]

Lochner v. New York, the 1905 case that struck down a state law regulating the hours of bakers, remains the great cautionary tale of Twentieth Century judicial review. Contemporary debates about judicial review in the areas of abortion, property rights, federalism, and even election law frequently come down to accusations that one side or the other is repeating the mistakes of *Lochner*. "Lochner" has become not simply a case name but a pejorative verb: "To *Lochner*" is to exceed the bounds of legitimate judicial review, and early twentieth-century criticisms of the *Lochner* court from the political Left find their contemporary echo in conservative critiques of judges who "legislate from the bench." Figuring out precisely *why Lochner* was wrong—if it was—is thus a predicate to developing a viable modern view about the appropriate role of the courts in enforcing the Constitution. Likewise, the vast regulatory state that the *Lochner* Court opposed has become the central reality with which contemporary debates about federalism and separation of powers must grapple.

SECTION 5.1 FREEDOM OF CONTRACT

Although the *Slaughter-House Cases* rejected the notion that the Due Process Clause prohibits economic regulation such as the New Orleans butcher monopoly, the idea did not stay buried for long. As economic regulation increased at both the federal and state level at the end of the Nineteenth Century, the Court fastened on the Due Process Clause's principle of "liberty" as protecting basic economic freedoms. The most important of these—the freedom of parties to a contract to agree on

---

[2] For an account emphasizing the internal dimension, see BARRY CUSHMAN, RETHINKING THE NEW DEAL COURT: THE STRUCTURE OF A CONSTITUTIONAL REVOLUTION (1998).

[3] Recall Chapter Three's discussion of the "Frankfurter constraint," which holds that the Court cannot successfully enforce a constitutional principle unless it can reduce that principle to a relatively determinate form.

terms without state interference—was first recognized in *Allgeyer v. Louisiana*:[4]

> The liberty mentioned in [the 14th] amendment means not only the right of the citizen to be free from the mere physical restraint of his person . . . [but] the right of the citizen to be free in the enjoyment of all his faculties; to be free to use them in all lawful ways; to live and work where he will; to earn his livelihood by any lawful calling; to pursue any livelihood or avocation, and for that purpose to enter into all contracts which may be proper, necessary and essential to his carrying out to a successful conclusion the purposes above mentioned.

The author of this language, Justice Rufus Peckham, would also pen the definitive freedom of contract opinion eight years later in *Lochner v. New York*.

Lochner v. New York
198 U.S. 45 (1905)

■ **MR. JUSTICE PECKHAM delivered the opinion of the court.**

The indictment . . . charges that the plaintiff in error violated the . . . labor law of the State of New York, in that he wrongfully and unlawfully required and permitted an employee working for him to work more than sixty hours in one week. . . . There is no pretense in any of the opinions that the statute was intended to meet a case of involuntary labor in any form. . . . The mandate of the statute that "no employee shall be required or permitted to work," is the substantial equivalent of an enactment that "no employee shall contract or agree to work," more than ten hours per day, and as there is no provision for special emergencies the statute is mandatory in all cases. . . . The employee may desire to earn the extra money, which would arise from his working more than the prescribed time, but this statute forbids the employer from permitting the employee to earn it.

The statute necessarily interferes with the right of contract between the employer and employees, concerning the number of hours in which the latter may labor in the bakery of the employer. The general right to make a contract in relation to his business is part of the liberty of the individual protected by the Fourteenth Amendment of the Federal Constitution. *Allgeyer v. Louisiana.* Under that provision no State can deprive any person of life, liberty or property without due process of law. The right to purchase or to sell labor is part of the liberty protected by this amendment. . . . There are, however, certain powers, existing in the sovereignty of each State in the Union, somewhat vaguely termed police powers. . . . Those powers, broadly stated . . . relate to the safety, health, morals and general welfare of the public. Both property and liberty are

---

4   165 U.S. 578 (1897).

held on such reasonable conditions as may be imposed by the governing power of the State in the exercise of those powers, and with such conditions the Fourteenth Amendment was not designed to interfere. . . .

This court has recognized the existence and upheld the exercise of the police powers of the States in many cases which might fairly be considered as border ones. . . . Among the later cases where the state law has been upheld by this court is that of *Holden v. Hardy,* 169 U.S. 366 (1898). A provision in the act of the legislature of Utah was there under consideration, the act limiting the employment of workmen in all underground mines or workings, to eight hours per day, "except in cases of emergency, where life or property is in imminent danger." . . . The act was held to be a valid exercise of the police powers of the State. . . . [T]he kind of employment, mining, smelting, etc., and the character of the employees in such kinds of labor, were such as to make it reasonable and proper for the State to interfere to prevent the employees from being constrained by the rules laid down by the proprietors in regard to labor. . . .

It must, of course, be conceded that there is a limit to the valid exercise of the police power by the State. . . . Otherwise the Fourteenth Amendment would have no efficacy and the legislatures of the States would have unbounded power. . . . In every case that comes before this court, therefore, where legislation of this character is concerned and where the protection of the Federal Constitution is sought, the question necessarily arises: Is this a fair, reasonable and appropriate exercise of the police power of the State, or is it an unreasonable, unnecessary and arbitrary interference with the right of the individual to his personal liberty or to enter into those contracts in relation to labor which may seem to him appropriate or necessary for the support of himself and his family? Of course the liberty of contract relating to labor includes both parties to it. The one has as much right to purchase as the other to sell labor.

This is not a question of substituting the judgment of the court for that of the legislature. If the act be within the power of the State it is valid, although the judgment of the court might be totally opposed to the enactment of such a law. But the question would still remain: Is it within the police power of the State? And that question must be answered by the court.

The question whether this act is valid as a labor law, pure and simple, may be dismissed in a few words. There is no reasonable ground for interfering with the liberty of person or the right of free contract, by determining the hours of labor, in the occupation of a baker. There is no contention that bakers as a class are not equal in intelligence and capacity to men in other trades or manual occupations, or that they are not able to assert their rights and care for themselves without the protecting arm of the State, interfering with their independence of judgment and of action. They are in no sense wards of the State. Viewed in the light of a purely labor law, with no reference whatever to the question of health, we think that a law like the one before us involves neither the safety, the morals nor the welfare of the public, and that the interest of the public is not in the slightest degree affected by such an act. The law must be upheld, if at all, as a law pertaining to the health of the individual engaged in the occupation of a baker. It does not affect any other portion of the public than those who are engaged in that occupation. Clean and wholesome bread does not depend upon whether the baker works but ten hours per day or only sixty hours a week. The limitation of the hours of labor does not come within the police power on that ground. . . .

The mere assertion that the subject relates though but in a remote degree to the public health does not necessarily render the enactment valid. The act must have a more direct relation, as a means to an end, and the end itself must be appropriate and legitimate, before an act can be held to be valid which interferes with the general right of an individual to be free in his person and in his power to contract in relation to his own labor. . . .

We think the limit of the police power has been reached and passed in this case. There is, in our judgment, no reasonable foundation for holding this to be necessary or appropriate as a health law to safeguard the public health or the health of the individuals who are following the trade of a baker. If this statute be valid, and if, therefore, a proper case is made out in which to deny the right of an individual . . . as employer or employee, to make contracts for the labor of the latter under the protection of the provisions of the Federal Constitution, there would seem to be no length to which legislation of this nature might not go. . . .

We think that there can be no fair doubt that the trade of a baker, in and of itself, is not an unhealthy one to that degree which would authorize the legislature to interfere with the right to labor, and with the right of free contract. . . . In looking through statistics regarding all trades and occupations, it may be true that the trade of a baker does not appear to be as healthy as some other trades, and is also vastly more healthy than still others. To the common understanding the trade of a baker has never been regarded as an unhealthy one. Very likely physicians would not recommend the exercise of that or of any other trade as a remedy for ill health. . . . It might be safely affirmed that almost all occupations more or less affect the health. . . . But are we all, on that account, at the mercy of legislative majorities? . . .

It is also urged . . . that it is to the interest of the State that its population should be strong and robust, and therefore any legislation which may be said to tend to make people healthy must be valid as health laws, enacted under the police power. If this be a valid argument and a justification for this kind of legislation, it follows that the protection of the Federal Constitution from undue interference with liberty of person and freedom of contract is visionary, wherever the law is sought to be justified as a valid exercise of the police power. Scarcely any law but might find shelter under such assumptions, and conduct, properly so called, as well as contract, would come under the restrictive sway of the legislature. Not only the hours of employees, but the hours of employers, could be regulated, and doctors, lawyers, scientists, all professional men, as well as athletes and artisans, could be forbidden to fatigue their brains and bodies by prolonged hours of exercise, lest the fighting strength of the State be impaired. We mention these extreme cases because the contention is extreme. . . . The act is not, within any fair meaning of the term, a health law, but is an illegal interference with the rights of individuals, both employers and employees, to make contracts regarding labor upon such terms as they may think best, or which they may agree upon with the other parties to such contracts. Statutes of the nature of that under review, limiting the hours in which grown and intelligent men may labor to earn their living, are mere meddlesome interferences with the rights of the individual, and they are not saved from condemnation by the claim that they are passed in the exercise of the police power and upon the subject of the health of the individual whose rights are interfered with, unless there be some fair ground, reasonable in and of itself, to say that there is material danger to the public health or to the health of the employees, if the hours of labor are not curtailed. . . .

All that [the State] could properly do has been done by it with regard to the conduct of bakeries, as provided for in the other sections of the act. . . . These several sections provide for the inspection of the premises where the bakery is carried on, with regard to furnishing proper wash-rooms and water-closets, apart from the bake-room, also with regard to providing proper drainage, plumbing and painting; the sections, in addition, provide for the height of the ceiling, the cementing or tiling of floors, where necessary in the opinion of the factory inspector, and for other things of that nature; alterations are also provided for and are to be made where necessary in the opinion of the inspector, in order to comply with the provisions of the statute. These various sections may be wise and valid regulations, and they certainly go to the full extent of providing for the cleanliness and the healthiness, so far as possible, of the quarters in which bakeries are to be conducted. Adding to all these requirements, a prohibition to enter into any contract of labor in a bakery for more than a certain number of hours a week, is, in our judgment, so wholly beside the matter of a proper, reasonable and fair provision, as to run counter to that liberty of person and of free contract provided for in the Federal Constitution.

It was further urged on the argument that restricting the hours of labor in the case of bakers was valid because it tended to cleanliness on the part of the workers, as a man was more apt to be cleanly when not overworked, and if cleanly then his "output" was also more likely to be so. . . . We do not admit the reasoning to be sufficient to justify the claimed right of such interference. The State in that case would assume the position of a supervisor, or *pater familias*, over every act of the individual, and its right of governmental interference with his hours of labor, his hours of exercise, the character thereof, and the extent to which it shall be carried would be recognized and upheld. In our judgment it is not possible in fact to discover the connection between the number of hours a baker may work in the bakery and the healthful quality of the bread made by the workman. The connection, if any exists, is too shadowy and thin to build any argument for the interference of the legislature. . . . This, we think, is unreasonable and entirely arbitrary. . . .

It is impossible for us to shut our eyes to the fact that many of the laws of this character, while passed under what is claimed to be the police power for the purpose of protecting the public health or welfare, are, in reality, passed from other motives. [F]rom the character of the law and the subject upon which it legislates, it is apparent that the public health or welfare bears but the most remote relation to the law. The purpose of a statute must be determined from the natural and legal effect of the language employed; and whether it is or is not repugnant to the Constitution of the United States must be determined from the natural effect of such statutes when put into operation, and not from their proclaimed purpose. The court looks beyond the mere letter of the law in such cases. . . .

It seems to us that the real object and purpose were simply to regulate the hours of labor between the master and his employees . . . in a private business, not dangerous in any degree to morals or in any real and substantial degree, to the health of the employees. Under such circumstances the freedom of master and employee to contract with each other in relation to their employment . . . cannot be prohibited or interfered with, without violating the Federal Constitution. . . .

Reversed.

■ MR. JUSTICE HARLAN, with whom MR. JUSTICE WHITE and MR. JUSTICE DAY concurred, dissenting.

While this court has not attempted to mark the precise boundaries of . . . the police power of the State, the existence of the power has been uniformly recognized, both by the Federal and state courts. All the cases agree that this power extends at least to the protection of the lives, the health and the safety of the public against the injurious exercise by any citizen of his own rights. . . .

I take it to be firmly established that what is called the liberty of contract may, within certain limits, be subjected to regulations designed and calculated to promote the general welfare or to guard the public health, the public morals or the public safety. "The liberty secured by the Constitution of the United States to every person within its jurisdiction does not import," this court has recently said, "an absolute right in each person to be, at all times and in all circumstances, wholly freed from restraint. There are manifold restraints to which every person is necessarily subject for the common good." . . .

[W]hat are the conditions under which the judiciary may declare such regulations to be in excess of legislative authority and void? Upon this point there is no room for dispute; for, the rule is universal that a legislative enactment, Federal or state, is never to be disregarded or held invalid unless it be, beyond question, plainly and palpably in excess of legislative power. . . . If there be doubt as to the validity of the statute, that doubt must therefore be resolved in favor of its validity, and the courts must keep their hands off, leaving the legislature to meet the responsibility for unwise legislation. If the end which the legislature seeks to accomplish be one to which its power extends, and if the means employed to that end, although not the wisest or best, are yet not plainly and palpably unauthorized by law, then the court cannot interfere. In other words, when the validity of a statute is questioned, the burden of proof, so to speak, is upon those who assert it to be unconstitutional. *McCulloch v. Maryland.*

Let these principles be applied to the present case. . . . It is plain that this statute was enacted in order to protect the physical well-being of those who work in bakery and confectionery establishments. It may be that the statute had its origin, in part, in the belief that employers and employees in such establishments were not upon an equal footing, and that the necessities of the latter often compelled them to submit to such exactions as unduly taxed their strength. Be this as it may, the statute must be taken as expressing the belief of the people of New York that, as a general rule, and in the case of the average man, labor in excess of sixty hours during a week in such establishments may endanger the health of those who thus labor. Whether or not this be wise legislation it is not the province of the court to inquire. Under our systems of government the courts are not concerned with the wisdom or policy of legislation. So that in determining the question of power to interfere with liberty of contract, the court may inquire whether the means devised by the State are germane to an end which may be lawfully accomplished and have a real or substantial relation to the protection of health, as involved in the daily work of the persons, male and female, engaged in bakery and confectionery establishments. But when this inquiry is entered upon I find it impossible, in view of common experience, to say that there is here no real or substantial relation between the means employed by the State and the end sought to be accomplished by its legislation. Nor can I say that the statute has no appropriate or direct connection with that protection to health which each State owes to her citizens, or that it is not promotive of the health of the employees in question, or that the regulation prescribed by the State is utterly unreasonable and extravagant or wholly arbitrary. . . . Therefore I submit that this court will transcend its functions if it assumes to annul the statute of New York. . . .

Professor Hirt in his treatise on the "Diseases of the Workers" has said: "The labor of the bakers is among the hardest and most laborious imaginable, because it has to be performed under conditions injurious to the health of those engaged in it. It is hard, very hard work, not only because it requires a great deal of physical exertion in an overheated workshop and during unreasonably long hours, but more so because of the erratic demands of the public, compelling the baker to perform the greater part of his work at night thus depriving him of an opportunity to enjoy the necessary rest and sleep, a fact which is highly injurious to his health." Another writer says: "The constant inhaling of flour dust causes inflammation of the lungs and of the bronchial tubes. The eyes also suffer through this dust, which is responsible for the many cases of running eyes among the bakers. The long hours of toil to which all bakers are subjected produce rheumatism, cramps and swollen legs. The intense heat in the workshops induces the workers to resort to cooling drinks, which together with their habit of exposing the greater part of their bodies to the change in the atmosphere, is another source of a number of diseases of various organs. Nearly all bakers are pale-faced and of more delicate health than the workers of other crafts, which is chiefly due to their hard work and their irregular and unnatural mode of living, whereby the power of resistance against disease is greatly diminished. The average age of a baker is below that of other workmen; they seldom live over their fiftieth year, most of them dying between the ages of forty and fifty. During periods of epidemic diseases the bakers are generally the first to succumb to the disease, and the number swept away during such periods far exceeds the number of other crafts in comparison to the men employed in the respective industries. When, in 1720, the plague visited the city of Marseilles, France, every baker in the city succumbed to the epidemic, which caused considerable excitement in the neighboring cities and resulted in measures for the sanitary protection of the bakers."

In the Eighteenth Annual Report by the New York Bureau of Statistics of Labor it is stated that among the occupations involving exposure to conditions that interfere with nutrition is that of a baker. In that Report it is also stated that "[s]horter hours of work, by allowing higher standards of comfort and purer family life, promise to enhance the industrial efficiency of the wage-working class-improved health, longer life, more content and greater intelligence and inventiveness". . . .

We judicially know that the question of the number of hours during which a workman should continuously labor has been, for a long period, and is yet, a subject of serious consideration among civilized peoples, and by those having special knowledge of the laws of health. . . . What is the true ground for the State to take between legitimate protection, by legislation, of the public health and liberty of contract is not a question easily solved, nor one in respect of which there is or can be absolute certainty. There are very few, if any, questions in political economy about which entire certainty may be predicated. . . .

We also judicially know that the number of hours that should constitute a day's labor in particular occupations involving the physical strength and safety of workmen has been the subject of enactments by Congress and by nearly all of the States. Many, if not most, of those enactments fix eight hours as the proper basis of a day's labor.

I do not stop to consider whether any particular view of this economic question presents the sounder theory. What the precise facts are it may be difficult to say. It is enough for the determination of this case, and it is enough for this court to know, that the question is one about which there is room for debate and for an honest difference of opinion. There are many reasons of a weighty, substantial character, based upon the experience of mankind, in support of the theory that, all things considered, more than ten hours' steady work each day, from week to week, in a bakery or confectionery establishment, may endanger the health, and shorten the lives of the workmen, thereby diminishing their physical and mental capacity to serve the State, and to provide for those dependent upon them.

If such reasons exist that ought to be the end of this case, for the State is not amenable to the judiciary, in respect of its legislative enactments, unless such enactments are plainly, palpably, beyond all question, inconsistent with the Constitution of the United States. We are not to presume that the State of New York has acted in bad faith. Nor can we assume that its legislature acted without due deliberation, or that it did not determine this question upon the fullest attainable information, and for the common good. . . . Let the State alone in the management of its purely domestic affairs, so long as it does not appear beyond all question that it has violated the Federal Constitution. This view necessarily results from the principle that the health and safety of the people of a State are primarily for the State to guard and protect.

[T]he New York statute, in the particulars here involved, cannot be held to be in conflict with the Fourteenth Amendment, without enlarging the scope of the Amendment far beyond its original purpose and without bringing under the supervision of this court matters which have been supposed to belong exclusively to the legislative departments of the several States when exerting their conceded power to guard the health and safety of their citizens by such regulations as they in their wisdom deem best. Health laws of every description constitute, said Chief Justice Marshall, a part of that mass of legislation which "embraces everything within the territory of a State, not surrendered to the General Government; all which can be most advantageously exercised by the States themselves." *Gibbons v. Ogden.* A decision that the New York statute is void under the Fourteenth Amendment . . . would seriously cripple the inherent power of the States to care for the lives, health and well-being of their citizens. . . . The preservation of the just powers of the States is quite as vital as the preservation of the powers of the General Government. . . .

The judgment in my opinion should be affirmed.

■ **MR. JUSTICE HOLMES dissenting.**

. . . This case is decided upon an economic theory which a large part of the country does not entertain. If it were a question whether I agreed with that theory I should desire to study it further and long before making up my mind. But I do not conceive that to be my duty, because I strongly believe that my agreement or disagreement has nothing to do with the right of a majority to embody their opinions in law. It is settled by various decisions of this court that state constitutions and state laws may regulate life in many ways which we as legislators might think as injudicious or if you like as tyrannical as this, and which equally with this interfere with the liberty to contract. Sunday laws and usury laws are ancient examples. A more modern one is the prohibition of lotteries. The liberty of the citizen to do as he likes so long as he does not interfere with the liberty of others to do the same, which has been a shibboleth for some well-known writers, is interfered with by school laws, by the Post Office, by every state or municipal institution which takes his money for purposes thought desirable, whether he likes it or not. The Fourteenth Amendment does not enact Mr. Herbert Spencer's Social Statics. The other day we sustained the Massachusetts vaccination law. *Jacobson v. Massachusetts*. United States and state statutes and decisions cutting down the liberty to contract by way of combination are familiar to this court. Two years ago we upheld the prohibition of sales of stock on margins or for future delivery in the constitution of California. *Otis v. Parker*. The decision sustaining an eight hour law for miners is still recent. *Holden v. Hardy*. Some of these laws embody convictions or prejudices which judges are likely to share. Some may not. But a constitution is not intended to embody a particular economic theory, whether of paternalism and the organic relation of the citizen to the State or of *laissez faire*. It is made for people of fundamentally differing views, and the accident of our finding certain opinions natural and familiar or novel and even shocking ought not to conclude our judgment upon the question whether statutes embodying them conflict with the Constitution of the United States.

General propositions do not decide concrete cases. The decision will depend on a judgment or intuition more subtle than any articulate major premise. But I think that the proposition just stated, if it is accepted, will carry us far toward the end. Every opinion tends to become a law. I think that the word liberty in the Fourteenth Amendment is perverted when it is held to prevent the natural outcome of a dominant opinion, unless it can be said that a rational and fair man necessarily would admit that the statute proposed would infringe fundamental principles as they have been understood by the traditions of our people and our law. It does not need research to show that no such sweeping condemnation can be passed upon the statute before us. A reasonable man might think it a proper measure on the score of health. Men whom I certainly could not pronounce unreasonable would uphold it as a first installment of a general regulation of the hours of work. Whether in the latter aspect it would be open to the charge of inequality I think it unnecessary to discuss.

NOTE ON *LOCHNER* AND JUDICIAL REVIEW OF ECONOMIC REGULATION

1.   Substantive due process can be traced all the way back to the founding era. The most important case is *Calder v. Bull*, 3 Dall. (3 U.S.) 386 (1798), in which the Connecticut legislature had enacted a statute effectively setting aside a prior probate court decree rejecting a will. The statute required a new hearing, in which the court approved the will. The parties who would have inherited if the will had been rejected claimed that this was an *ex post facto* law—a claim the Supreme Court rejected on grounds that the clause applied only to criminal matters—and also made arguments based on natural law. Justice Chase accepted the latter argument, insisting that "an Act of the Legislature . . . contrary to the great first principles of the social compact, cannot be considered a rightful exercise of legislative authority." Likewise, the Marshall Court's landmark decision in *Fletcher v. Peck*, 6 Cranch (10 U.S.) 87 (1810), [5] hinted at recognizing some unenumerated protection for property rights. And *Dred Scott* explicitly relied on the Due Process Clause to hold that the Missouri Compromise could not lawfully deprive a slaveholder of his property.

The notion of unenumerated restrictions on government interference with private interests has always been controversial, however. In *Calder*, for example, Justice Iredell insisted that a court can strike down legislative acts only based on an explicit constitutional provision. Iredell rejected the natural law approach on the ground that it was too indeterminate and controversial. "The ideas of natural justice are regulated by no fixed standard," he wrote, "[and] the ablest and the purest men have differed upon the subject." Most of the Marshall Court decisions, as well, relied on express constitutional provisions and not natural law. Does *Marbury*'s reasoning, which relies heavily on the idea that courts are enforcing a *written* constitution, make the notion of unenumerated rights problematic?

2.   The *Lochner* Court analyzed the New York law by asking whether (1) there is a legitimate state interest at stake, and (2) the law is a reasonable means of furthering that interest. Recall that Chief Justice Marshall applied a similar test in *McCulloch v. Maryland*—that is, analyzing the legitimacy of the end, and the fit between the means and the end. These sorts of tests can be deployed with varying means of rigor, however. How would you characterize the standard of review in each case? Note that Justice Harlan cited *McCulloch* in his dissent. To the extent that the *Lochner* majority employed a more rigorous standard, was that justified?

---

[5]   *Fletcher* was primarily a Contracts Clause case invalidating Georgia's effort to revoke a land grant. But Chief Justice Marshall invoked "general principles" as an alternative ground.

3.   New York asserted two ends for the maximum hour legislation in *Lochner*: First, it defended the statute as a "labor law" designed to equalize bargaining power between the bakers and their employers.

The majority's reaction to the labor law justification suggests that it saw the statute as "class legislation," although the Court did not use the term. In an essay published a decade earlier, Justice Henry Brown had defined class legislation as based on "the desire of one class to better itself at the expense of the other."[6] Such legislation went against a broad consensus, at least among political elites of the time, that "the sole valid goal of legislation was to be of general applicability and to promote the general welfare by being neutral among classes."[7] Is this a valid principle? Isn't it similar to contemporary criticisms of "special interest" legislation?

If the New York legislature thought that bakers lacked the ability to bargain on a level playing field with their employers for a shorter work week, would intervention to impose fairer terms amount to class legislation? Consider David Bernstein's account of the origins of the New York legislation:

> By the mid-1890s, bakers in large bakeries rarely worked more than ten hours per day, sixty hours per week. However, these bakers were concerned that their improved situation was endangered by competition from small, old-fashioned bakeries, especially those that employed Italian, French, and Jewish immigrants. . . . Workers in such bakeries often worked far more than ten hours a day.[8]

Professor Bernstein points out that the bakers' union that pushed for the maximum hours law was dominated by bakers of German descent working in the newer and larger bakeries, who sought to disadvantage their competitors in the old-fashioned bakeries.[9] Seen in this light, does the New York law begin to look more like rent-seeking by special interests? If one group is able to use the political process to disadvantage another, less powerful group, should courts step in to invalidate the laws that result?

Justice Holmes thought courts plainly should *not* step in under these circumstances. His dissent in *Lochner* is one of the most famous dissents in the U.S. Reports. His remark that "[t]he Fourteenth Amendment does not enact Mr. Herbert Spencer's Social Statics" is the source of the widespread perception that the Court was simply imposing its own free market, *laissez faire* ideology on a more progressively-minded legislature—in Archibald Cox's words, a "willful defense of wealth and power."[10] Is that a fair characterization?

---

[6]   Henry Brown, *The Distribution of Property*, 27 AM. L. REV. 656, 660 (1893).

[7]   LUCAS A. POWE, JR., THE SUPREME COURT AND THE AMERICAN ELITE, 1789–2008, at 150 (2009).

[8]   David E. Bernstein, *The Story of* Lochner v. New York: *Impediment to the Growth of the Regulatory State*, in MICHAEL C. DORF, ED., CONSTITUTIONAL LAW STORIES 299, 303 (2d ed. 2009).

[9]   *See id.* at 303–05.

[10]   ARCHIBALD COX, THE COURT AND THE CONSTITUTION 135 (1987).

More broadly, what did Justice Holmes mean when he said that "I think that the word liberty in the Fourteenth Amendment is perverted when it is held to prevent the natural outcome of a dominant opinion, unless it can be said that a rational and fair man necessarily would admit that the statute proposed would infringe fundamental principles as they have been understood by the traditions of our people and our law"? Is that, as Scot Powe has suggested, "the cry of judicial abdication"?[11] As we will see, many have read *Lochner* as a general cautionary tale against rigorous judicial review in *any* context. Do you agree?

4.   New York also argued that its law promoted health—both of the bakers themselves, and of consumers of the bread that the bakers produce. How did the Court analyze each of these justifications? Rejecting the bakers' health rationale, the *Lochner* majority acknowledged that the Court's earlier decision in *Holden v. Hardy*, 169 U.S. 366 (1898), had upheld maximum hour legislation where necessary to protect those engaged in "dangerous or unhealthful employments." The debate about the health justification thus turned on a factual disagreement. Justice Harlan's dissent cited a medical treatise for the proposition that baking is in fact "unhealthful," and Justice Peckham's majority opinion relied (albeit without citation) on scientific evidence pointing in the other direction collected in Mr. Lochner's brief. How should courts review the constitutionality of legislation in the face of such disagreements about the facts? Who should have the burden of proof? The challenger, on the ground that he is challenging the judgment of the people's elected representatives? Or the State, on the ground that it is seeking to limit the rights of individuals?

The state's other health justification sought to protect consumers of the bread produced by overworked bakers. As already noted, the New York law fell most heavily on small, old-fashioned bakeries, and these bakeries were characterized not only by long hours but also by unsanitary conditions. One inspector reported:

> Cockroaches and other insects . . . abounded, and as chance willed became part of the salable products. Rats, which seemed not to fear the human denizens of these catacombs, ran back and forth between the piled up bread and their holes.[12]

Although *Lochner* focused on the maximum hours provisions of the state law, the statute also included sanitary regulations; moreover, because bakers working long hours in small bakeries tended to live on the premises, thereby creating additional sanitation problems,[13] the law's hours and sanitation provisions were arguably interlinked. Should the Court have taken the public health rationale more seriously?

---

[11] POWE, *supra* note 5, at 169.

[12] Tenth Annual Report of the Factory Inspectors of the State of New York (1896), quoted in David E. Bernstein, *The Story of* Lochner v. New York: *Impediment to the Growth of the Regulatory State*, in MICHAEL C. DORF, ED., CONSTITUTIONAL LAW STORIES 299, 306 (2d ed. 2009).

[13] *See generally* Bernstein, *supra* note 6, at 305–08.

5.   The Court would not strike down another statute on freedom of contract grounds until the 1920s; hence, "for almost two decades *Lochner* turned out to be an aberration."[14] That intervening period saw the Court uphold a wide variety of social and economic legislation. After four conservative appointments by President Warren G. Harding, however, the Court took a more aggressive stance. *Adkins v. Children's Hospital*, 261 U.S. 525 (1923), for example, involved a District of Columbia law establishing a minimum wage law for women. A hospital, as well as a 21-year-old woman working as an elevator operator in a hotel, argued that the law violated their freedom of contract.

The Court agreed in a decision similar to *Lochner*. The District defended the law as necessary to preserve the health and morals of the workers. The Court, however, found that the regulation was too blunt an instrument for achieving those goals. It found no relation between the fixed minimum wage and the value of particular work or the needs of particular women in particular circumstance. Chief Justice Taft wrote a dissent, similar to Justice Harlan's in *Lochner*, accepting the general notion of freedom of contract but finding the case indistinguishable from prior decisions upholding maximum hour laws. Justice Holmes, on the other hand, again expressed skepticism of the very notion of freedom of contract.

Three additional aspects of *Adkins* are worth noting. The first is that, unlike *Lochner*, *Adkins* involved a *federal* statute rather than a state law. The Court's decision thus signaled that federal laws would get no more deference than state ones under the freedom of contract doctrine, although— as we explore in the next section—most successful challenges to federal regulation during this era continued to be brought under the Commerce Clause.

Second, the majority opinion provided a useful catalog of regulatory laws that had been *upheld* against freedom of contract challenges. These included:

- regulations setting rates for businesses impressed with a public interest;

- regulation of the terms for performance of government contracts;

- wage regulations other than amount (i.e., methods for time & payment); and

- maximum hour laws for workers in particularly hazardous lines of work, and also for women.

Can you think of principled distinctions between the sorts of laws the Court upheld and those it struck down?

Finally, *Adkins* raised an issue which has sparked disagreement among feminists. In *Muller v. Oregon*, 208 U.S. 412 (1908), the Court upheld a maximum hours law that regulated women working in laundries. It did so in large part of Louis Brandeis's famous "Brandeis brief," which marshalled

---

[14]   Bernstein, *supra* note 6, at 323.

empirical evidence about the debilitating effects of long hours on female workers. The *Muller* Court was willing to accept that women were less able to look out for their own interests, and were more vulnerable to debilitating work conditions. In *Adkins*, however, the majority was unwilling to extend *Muller*'s reasoning to a minimum wage law, citing recent strides that women had taken toward equality. Which stance toward women—*Muller*'s view that women need special protection, or *Adkins*'s view that should be treated in parity with men—should a feminist prefer?

Nebbia v. New York

291 U.S. 502 (1934)

■ MR. JUSTICE ROBERTS delivered the opinion of the Court.

The Legislature of New York established . . . a Milk Control Board with power, among other things, to "fix minimum and maximum . . . retail prices to be charged by . . . stores to consumers for consumption off the premises where sold." The Board fixed nine cents as the price to be charged by a store for a quart of milk. Nebbia, the proprietor of a grocery store in Rochester, sold two quarts and a five cent loaf of bread for eighteen cents; and was convicted for violating the Board's order. At his trial he asserted the statute and order contravene the equal protection clause and the due process clause of the Fourteenth Amendment, and renewed the contention in successive appeals to the county court and the Court of Appeals. Both overruled his claim and affirmed the conviction.

The question for decision is whether the Federal Constitution prohibits a state from so fixing the selling price of milk. We first inquire as to the occasion for the legislation and its history.

During 1932 the prices received by farmers for milk were much below the cost of production. The decline in prices during 1931 and 1932 was much greater than that of prices generally. The situation of the families of dairy producers had become desperate and called for state aid similar to that afforded the unemployed, if conditions should not improve.

On March 10, 1932, the senate and assembly resolved "That a joint Legislative committee is hereby created . . . to investigate the causes of the decline of the price of milk to producers and the resultant effect of the low prices upon the dairy industry and the future supply of milk to the cities of the State; to investigate the cost of distribution of milk and its relation to prices paid to milk producers, to the end that the consumer may be assured of an adequate supply of milk at a reasonable price, both to producer and consumer." The committee organized May 6, 1932, and its activities lasted nearly a year. It held 13 public hearings at which 254 witnesses testified and 2350 typewritten pages of testimony were taken. Numerous exhibits were submitted. Under its direction an extensive research program was prosecuted by experts and official bodies and employees of the state and municipalities, which resulted in the assembling of much pertinent information. Detailed reports were received from over 100 distributors of milk, and these were collated and the information obtained analyzed. As a result of the study of this material, a report covering 473 closely printed pages, embracing the conclusions and recommendations of the committee, was presented to the legislature April 10, 1933. This document included detailed findings, with copious references to the supporting evidence; appendices outlining the nature and results of prior investigations of the milk industry of the state, briefs upon the legal questions involved, and forms of bills recommended for passage. The conscientious effort and thoroughness exhibited by the report lend weight to the committee's conclusions.

In part those conclusions are:

Milk is an essential item of diet. It cannot long be stored. It is an excellent medium for growth of bacteria. These facts necessitate safeguards in its production and handling for human consumption which greatly increase the cost of the business. Failure of producers to receive a reasonable return for their labor and investment over an extended period threaten a relaxation of vigilance against contamination.

The production and distribution of milk is a paramount industry of the state, and largely affects the health and prosperity of its people. Dairying yields fully one-half of the total income from all farm products. Dairy farm investment amounts to approximately $1,000,000,000. Curtailment or destruction of the dairy industry would cause a serious economic loss to the people of the state.

In addition to the general price decline, other causes for the low price of milk include: a periodic increase in the number of cows and in milk production; the prevalence of unfair and destructive trade practices in the distribution of milk, leading to a demoralization of prices in the metropolitan area and other markets; and the failure of transportation and distribution charges to be reduced in proportion to the reduction in retail prices for milk and cream.

The fluid milk industry is affected by factors of instability peculiar to itself which call for special methods of control. . . .

Various remedies were suggested, amongst them united action by producers, the fixing of minimum prices for milk and cream by state authority, and the imposition of certain graded taxes on milk dealers proportioned so as to equalize the cost of milk and cream to all dealers and so remove the cause of price-cutting.

The legislature adopted Chapter 158 as a method of correcting the evils, which the report of the committee showed could not be expected to right themselves through the ordinary play of the forces of supply and demand, owing to the peculiar and uncontrollable factors affecting the industry. . . .

Section 312(e), on which the prosecution in the present case is founded, provides: "After the board shall have fixed prices to be charged or paid for milk in any form . . . it shall be unlawful for a milk dealer to sell or buy or offer to sell or buy milk at any price less or more than such price . . . , and no method or device shall be lawful whereby milk is bought or sold . . . at a price less or more than such price. . . ." . . .

The more serious question is whether, in the light of the conditions disclosed, the enforcement of § 312 (e) denied the appellant the due process secured to him by the Fourteenth Amendment.

Save the conduct of railroads, no business has been so thoroughly regimented and regulated by the State of New York as the milk industry. Legislation controlling it in the interest of the public health was adopted in 1862 and subsequent statutes have been carried into the general codification known as the Agriculture and Markets Law. A perusal of these statutes discloses that the milk industry has been progressively subjected to a larger measure of control. . . . In addition there is a large volume of legislation intended to promote cleanliness and fair trade practices, affecting all who are engaged in the industry. The challenged amendment of 1933 carried regulation much farther than the prior enactments. Appellant insists that it went beyond the limits fixed by the Constitution.

Under our form of government the use of property and the making of contracts are normally matters of private and not of public concern. The general rule is that both shall be free of governmental interference. But neither property rights nor contract rights are absolute; for government cannot exist if the citizen may at will use his property to the detriment of his fellows, or exercise his freedom of contract to work them harm. Equally fundamental with the private right is that of the public to regulate it in the common interest. As Chief Justice Marshall said, speaking specifically of inspection laws, such laws form "a portion of that immense mass of legislation, which embraces everything within the territory of a State . . . all which can be most advantageously exercised by the States themselves. Inspection laws, quarantine laws, health laws of every description, as well as laws for regulating the internal commerce of a State, . . . are component parts of this mass." . . .

Thus has this court from the early days affirmed that the power to promote the general welfare is inherent in government. . . . These correlative rights, that of the citizen to exercise exclusive dominion over property and freely to contract about his affairs, and that of the state to regulate the use of property and the conduct of business, are always in collision. No exercise of the private right can be imagined which will not in some respect, however slight, affect the public; no exercise of the legislative prerogative to regulate the conduct of the citizen which will not to some extent abridge his liberty or affect his property. But subject only to constitutional restraint the private right must yield to the public need.

The Fifth Amendment, in the field of federal activity, and the Fourteenth, as respects state action, do not prohibit governmental regulation for the public welfare. They merely condition the exertion of the admitted power, by securing that the end shall be accomplished by methods consistent with due process. And the guaranty of due process, as has often been held, demands only that the law shall not be unreasonable, arbitrary or capricious, and that the means selected shall have a real and substantial relation to the object sought to be attained. It results that a regulation valid for one sort of business, or in given circumstances, may be invalid for another sort, or for the same business under other circumstances, because the reasonableness of each regulation depends upon the relevant facts. . . .

The court has repeatedly sustained curtailment of enjoyment of private property, in the public interest. The owner's rights may be subordinated to the needs of other private owners whose pursuits are vital to the paramount interests of the community. The state may control the use of property in various ways; may prohibit advertising bill boards except of a prescribed size and location, or their use for certain kinds of advertising; may in certain circumstances authorize encroachments by party walls in cities; may fix the height of buildings, the character of materials, and methods of construction, the adjoining area which must be left open, and may exclude from residential sections offensive trades, industries and structures likely injuriously to affect the public health or safety; or may establish zones within which certain types of buildings or businesses are permitted and others excluded. And although the Fourteenth Amendment extends protection to aliens as well as citizens, a state may for adequate reasons of policy exclude aliens altogether from the use and occupancy of land.

Laws passed for the suppression of immorality, in the interest of health, to secure fair trade practices, and to safeguard the interests of depositors in banks, have been found consistent with due process. These measures not only affected the use of private property, but also interfered with the right of private contract. Other instances are numerous where valid regulation has restricted the right of contract, while less directly affecting property rights.

The Constitution does not guarantee the unrestricted privilege to engage in a business or to conduct it as one pleases. Certain kinds of business may be prohibited; and the right to conduct a business, or to pursue a calling, may be conditioned. Regulation of a business to prevent waste of the state's resources may be justified. And statutes prescribing the terms upon which those conducting certain businesses may contract, or imposing terms if they do enter into agreements, are within the state's competency.

Legislation concerning sales of goods, and incidentally affecting prices, has repeatedly been held valid. In this class fall laws forbidding unfair competition by the charging of lower prices in one locality than those exacted in another, by giving trade inducements to purchasers, and by other forms of price discrimination. The public policy with respect to free competition has engendered state and federal statutes prohibiting monopolies, which have been upheld. On the other hand, where the policy of the state dictated that a monopoly should be granted, statutes having that effect have been held inoffensive to the constitutional guarantees. Moreover, the state or a municipality may itself enter into business in competition with private proprietors, and thus effectively although indirectly control the prices charged by them.

The milk industry in New York has been the subject of long-standing and drastic regulation in the public interest. The legislative investigation of 1932 was persuasive of the fact that for this and other reasons unrestricted competition aggravated existing evils, and the normal law of supply and demand was insufficient to correct maladjustments detrimental to the community. The inquiry disclosed destructive and demoralizing competitive conditions and unfair trade practices which resulted in retail price-cutting and reduced the income of the farmer below the cost of production. We do not understand the appellant to deny that in these circumstances the legislature might reasonably consider further regulation and control desirable for protection of the industry and the consuming public. That body believed conditions could be improved by preventing destructive price-cutting by stores which, due to the flood of surplus milk, were able to buy at much lower prices than the larger distributors and to sell without incurring the delivery costs of the latter. In the order of which complaint is made the Milk Control Board fixed a price of ten cents per quart for sales by a distributor to a consumer, and nine cents by a store to a consumer, thus recognizing the lower costs of the store, and endeavoring to establish a differential which would be just to both. In the light of the facts the order appears not to be unreasonable or arbitrary, or without relation to the purpose to prevent ruthless competition from destroying the wholesale price structure on which the farmer depends for his livelihood, and the community for an assured supply of milk. . . .

We may as well say at once that the dairy industry is not, in the accepted sense of the phrase, a public utility. We think the appellant is also right in asserting that there is in this case no suggestion of any monopoly or monopolistic practice. It goes without saying that those engaged in the business are in no way dependent upon public grants or franchises for the privilege of conducting their activities. But if, as must be conceded, the industry is subject to regulation in the public interest, what constitutional principle bars the state from correcting existing maladjustments by legislation touching prices? We think there is no such principle. The due process clause makes no mention of sales or of prices any more than it speaks of business or contracts or buildings or other incidents of property. The thought seems nevertheless to have persisted that there is something peculiarly sacrosanct about the price one may charge for what he makes or sells, and that, however able to regulate other elements of manufacture or trade, with incidental effect upon price, the state is incapable of directly controlling the price itself. This view was negatived many years ago. *Munn v. Illinois*, 94 U.S. 113 (1877). The appellant's claim is, however, that this court, in there sustaining a statutory prescription of charges for storage by the proprietors of a grain elevator, limited permissible legislation of that type to businesses affected with a public interest, and he says no business is so affected except it have one or more of the characteristics he enumerates. But this is a misconception. Munn and Scott held no franchise from the state. . . . Their enterprise could not fairly be called a monopoly, although it was referred to in the decision as a "virtual monopoly." This meant only that their elevator was strategically situated and that a large portion of the public found it highly inconvenient to deal with others. This court concluded the circumstances justified the legislation as an exercise of the governmental right to control the business in the public interest; that is, as an exercise of the police power. . . . Thus understood, "affected with a public interest" is the equivalent of "subject to the exercise of the police power"; and it is plain that nothing more was intended by the expression. . . .

Many other decisions show that the private character of a business does not necessarily remove it from the realm of regulation of charges or prices. The usury laws fix the price which may be exacted for the use of money, although no business more essentially private in character can be imagined than that of loaning one's personal funds. Insurance agents' compensation may be regulated, though their contracts are private, because the business of insurance is considered one properly subject to public control. Statutes prescribing in the public interest the amounts to be charged by attorneys for prosecuting certain claims, a matter ordinarily one of personal and private nature, are not a deprivation of due process. A stockyards corporation, "while not a common carrier, nor engaged in any distinctively public employment, is doing a work in which the public has an interest," and its charges may be controlled. Private contract carriers, who do not operate under a franchise, and have no monopoly of the carriage of goods or passengers, may, since they use the highways to compete with railroads, be compelled to charge rates not lower than those of public carriers for corresponding services, if the state, in pursuance of a public policy to protect the latter, so determines.

It is clear that there is no closed class or category of businesses affected with a public interest, and the function of courts in the application of the Fifth and Fourteenth Amendments is to determine in each case whether circumstances vindicate the challenged regulation as a reasonable exertion of governmental authority or condemn it as arbitrary or discriminatory. The phrase "affected with a public interest" can, in the nature of things, mean no more than that an industry, for adequate reason, is subject to control for the public good. . . .

So far as the requirement of due process is concerned, and in the absence of other constitutional restriction, a state is free to adopt whatever economic policy may reasonably be deemed to promote public welfare, and to enforce that policy by legislation adapted to its purpose. The courts are without authority either to declare such policy, or, when it is declared by the legislature, to override it. If the laws passed are seen to have a reasonable relation to a proper legislative purpose, and are neither arbitrary nor discriminatory, the requirements of due process are satisfied. . . . With the wisdom of the policy adopted, with the adequacy or practicability of the law enacted to forward it, the courts are both incompetent and unauthorized to deal. . . .

Tested by these considerations we find no basis in the due process clause of the Fourteenth Amendment for condemning the provisions of the Agriculture and Markets Law here drawn into question.

The judgment is *Affirmed*.

■ MR. JUSTICE MCREYNOLDS, dissenting.

. . . The power . . . to regulate private business can be invoked only under special circumstances. It may be so invoked when the Legislature is dealing with a paramount industry upon which the prosperity of the entire State in large measure depends. It may not be invoked when we are dealing with an ordinary business, essentially private in its nature. . . .

If validity of the enactment depends upon emergency, then to sustain this conviction we must be able to affirm that an adequate one has been shown by competent evidence of essential facts. The asserted right is federal. Such rights may demand and often have received affirmation and protection here. They do not vanish simply because the power of the State is arrayed against them. Nor are they enjoyed in subjection to mere legislative findings. . . .

It is argued that the report of the Legislative Committee, dated April 10th, 1933, disclosed the essential facts. May one be convicted of crime upon such findings? Are federal rights subject to extinction by reports of committees? Heretofore, they have not been. Apparently the Legislature acted upon this report. . . . We have no basis for determining whether the findings of the committee or legislature are correct or otherwise. . . .

The exigency is of the kind which inevitably arises when one set of men continue to produce more than all others can buy. The distressing result to the producer followed his ill-advised but voluntary efforts. Similar situations occur in almost every business. If here we have an emergency sufficient to empower the Legislature to fix sales prices, then whenever there is too much or too little of an essential thing—whether of milk or grain or pork or coal or shoes or clothes—constitutional provisions may be declared inoperative and the "anarchy and despotism" . . . are at the door. . . .

Is the milk business so affected with public interest that the Legislature may prescribe prices for sales by stores? This Court has approved the contrary view; has emphatically declared that a State lacks power to fix prices in similar private businesses. *Adkins v. Children's Hospital.* . . .

Regulation to prevent recognized evils in business has long been upheld as permissible legislative action. But fixation of the price at which "A," engaged in an ordinary business, may sell, in order to enable "B," a producer, to improve his condition, has not been regarded as within legislative power. This is not regulation, but management, control, dictation—it amounts to the deprivation of the fundamental right which one has to conduct his own affairs honestly and along customary lines. The argument advanced here would support general prescription of prices for farm products, groceries, shoes, clothing, all the necessities of modern civilization, as well as labor, when some legislature finds and declares such action advisable and for the public good. This Court has declared that a State may not by legislative fiat convert a private business into a public utility. And if it be now ruled that one dedicates his property to public use whenever he embarks on an enterprise which the Legislature may think it desirable to bring under control, this is but to declare that rights guaranteed by the Constitution exist only so long as supposed public interest does not require their extinction. To adopt such a view, of course, would put an end to liberty under the Constitution. . . .

But plainly, I think, this Court must have regard to the wisdom of the enactment. At least, we must inquire concerning its purpose and decide whether the means proposed have reasonable relation to something within legislative power—whether the end is legitimate, and the means appropriate. If a statute to prevent conflagrations should require householders to pour oil on their roofs as a means of curbing the spread of fire when discovered in the neighborhood, we could hardly uphold it. Here, we find direct interference with guaranteed rights defended upon the ground that the purpose was to promote the public welfare by increasing milk prices at the farm. Unless we can affirm that the end proposed is proper and the means adopted have reasonable relation to it, this action is unjustifiable.

The court below has not definitely affirmed this necessary relation; it has not attempted to indicate how higher charges at stores to impoverished customers when the output is excessive and sale prices by producers are unrestrained, can possibly increase receipts at the farm. The Legislative Committee pointed out as the obvious cause of decreased consumption, notwithstanding low prices, the consumers' reduced buying power. Higher store prices will not enlarge this power; nor will they decrease production. Low prices will bring less cows only after several years. The prime causes of the difficulties will remain. Nothing indicates early decreased output. Demand at low prices being wholly insufficient, the proposed plan is to raise and fix higher minimum prices at stores and thereby aid the producer whose output and prices remain unrestrained! It is not true as stated that "the State seeks to protect the producer by fixing a minimum price for his milk." She carefully refrained from doing this; but did undertake to fix the price after the milk had passed to other owners. Assuming that the views and facts reported by the Legislative Committee are correct, it appears to me wholly unreasonable to expect this legislation to accomplish the proposed end—increase of prices at the farm. We deal only with Order No. 5 as did the court below. It is not merely unwise; it is arbitrary and unduly oppressive. Better prices may follow but it is beyond reason to expect them as the consequent of that order. The Legislative Committee reported—"It is recognized that the dairy industry of the State cannot be placed upon a profitable basis without a decided rise in the general level of commodity prices."

Not only does the statute interfere arbitrarily with the rights of the little grocer to conduct his business according to standards long accepted . . . but it takes away the liberty of twelve million consumers to buy a necessity of life in an open market. It imposes direct and arbitrary burdens upon those already seriously impoverished with the alleged immediate design of affording special benefits to others. To him with less than nine cents it says—You cannot procure a quart of milk from the grocer although he is anxious to accept what you can pay and the demands of your household are urgent! A superabundance; but no child can purchase from a willing storekeeper below the figure appointed by three men at headquarters! And this is true although the storekeeper himself may have bought from a willing producer at half that rate and must sell quickly or lose his stock through deterioration. The fanciful scheme is to protect the farmer against undue exactions by prescribing the price at which milk disposed of by him at will may be resold!

The statement by the court below that "[d]oubtless the statute before us would be condemned by an earlier generation as a temerarious interference with the rights of property and contract" . . . is obviously correct. But another, that "statutes aiming to stimulate the production of a vital food product by fixing living standards of prices for the producer, are to be interpreted with that degree of liberality which is essential to the attainment of the end in view," conflicts with views of Constitutional rights accepted since the beginning. An end although apparently desirable cannot justify inhibited means. . . . The Legislature cannot lawfully destroy guaranteed rights of one man with the prime purpose of enriching another, even if for the moment, this may seem advantageous to the public. And the adoption of any "concept of jurisprudence" which permits facile disregard of the Constitution as long interpreted and respected will inevitably lead to its destruction. Then, all rights will be subject to the caprice of the hour; government by stable laws will pass.

The judgment of the court below should be reversed.

MR. JUSTICE VAN DEVANTER, MR. JUSTICE SUTHERLAND, and MR. JUSTICE BUTLER authorize me to say that they concur in this opinion.

NOTE ON *NEBBIA* AND THE SCOPE OF SUBSTANTIVE DUE PROCESS UNDER *LOCHNER*

1.   *Nebbia* is an important example of the fact that the Court upheld many economic regulations against due process challenges, even before the "switch in time" of 1937. By the time of *Nebbia*, the key distinction that had emerged in the cases was between those industries or businesses that were "affected with a public interest" and those that were not. Under this principle, for example, the public interest in the operation of a public power utility warranted much more extensive regulation than that which would be permitted of ordinary contracts. Much of the debate had thus come to focus on which businesses implicated this public interest. How does the majority in *Nebbia* define that category? Is Justice McReynolds's dissent correct to accuse the majority of lacking a viable limiting principle?

2.   The Court's expansive reading of the Due Process Clause during this period didn't include only economic rights like freedom of contract. Recall that Justice Peckham's definition of "liberty" in *Allgeyer* was basically all those freedoms which make it possible for an individual to choose their own vision of the good life. That broad reading was borne out in two critical cases during the *Lochner* period involving non-economic rights.

In *Meyer v. Nebraska*, 262 U.S. 390 (1923), the Court struck down a state law forbidding the teaching of foreign languages to young children. Justice McReynolds used the case to announce a very broad view of "liberty" as including

> not merely freedom from bodily restraint but also the right of the individual to contract, to engage in any of the common occupations of life, to acquire useful knowledge, to marry, establish a home and bring up children, to worship God according to the dictates of his own conscience, and generally to enjoy those privileges long recognized at common law as essential to the orderly pursuit of happiness by free men.

The foreign language rule was invalid because it interfered with "the opportunity of pupils to acquire knowledge, and with the power of parents to control the education of their own."

Similarly, in *Pierce v. Society of Sisters*, 268 U.S. 510 (1925), the Court struck down a law mandating that children attend public schools. The Court said that "[t]he fundamental theory of liberty upon which all governments in this Union repose excludes any general power of the state to standardize its children by forcing them to accept instruction from public teachers only. The child is not the mere creature of the state; those who nurture him and direct his destiny have the right, coupled with the high duty, to recognize and prepare him for additional obligations."

Pierce and *Meyer* are important precursors for more recent decisions recognizing rights of family privacy and reproductive choice. Those cases, including *Griswold v. Connecticut*, [15] *Roe v. Wade*, [16] and *Obergefell v. Hodges*, [17] enjoy widespread support today notwithstanding *Lochner's* ignominy. Is their principle distinguishable from that in *Lochner*? If one thinks that *Lochner* was wrong, must *Meyer* and *Pierce* go, too?

3.   The result in *Nebbia*, decided in 1934, suggests that the deepening Depression—and perhaps the Democratic victories in the 1932 election— pushed moderates on the Court toward accepting a broader role for government economic regulation. Another such sign occurred in *Home Building & Loan Association v. Blaisdell*, 290 U.S. 398 (1934), which rejected a Contracts Clause challenge to the Minnesota Mortgage Moratorium law. That law extended the time available to mortgagees (especially farmers) to redeem their mortgages from foreclosure, essentially for the duration of the Depression as determined by the state courts. In so doing, the law altered the terms of the contracts to which the lenders and debtors had agreed— precisely the sort of state debtor-relief legislation that had given rise to the Contracts Clause in the first place. The state courts had upheld the law as temporary legislation to deal with the economic emergency, and while Chief Justice Hughes insisted that "[e]mergency does not create power," he nonetheless upheld the State's power to "safeguard the vital interests of its people."

Many commentators point to *Blaisdell* as a key step in abandoning the Constitution's protection for economic liberties. Richard Epstein, for example, has argued that "*Blaisdell* trumpeted a false liberation from the constitutional text that has paved the way for massive government intervention that undermines the security of private transactions. Today the police power exception has come to eviscerate the contracts clause."[18] As Professor Epstein points out, the Contracts Clause differs from *Lochner's* "freedom of contract" in that the former is actually in the constitutional text. Was the Court right to gut that protection in *Blaisdell*?

4.   *Nebbia* and *Blaisdell* suggested that the Court would tolerate emergency regulatory measures to deal with the Depression. But as President Roosevelt's New Deal programs gathered steam, the Court instead became increasingly confrontational.[19] This hardening of the Court's stance toward economic regulation occurred across all areas of doctrine, including even the Contracts Clause that *Blaisdell* had seemed to inter.

SECTION 5.2   FEDERALISM IN THE *LOCHNER* ERA

As *Adkins* indicates, the Court occasionally employed economic substantive due process against national legislation as well as state

---

[15]   381 U.S. 479 (1965) (recognizing a right of privacy that protects use of contraceptives).

[16]   410 U.S. 113 (1973) (recognizing a substantive due process right to abortion).

[17]   135 S. Ct. 2584 (2015) (recognizing a due process right to same-sex marriage).

[18]   Richard A. Epstein, *Toward a Revitalization of the Contracts Clause*, 51 U. CHI. L. REV. 703, 738 (1984).

[19]   *See, e.g.*, POWE, *supra* note 5, at 205 (observing that "the Court went on a rampage against the New Deal that was without precedent in American history, striking down ten federal statutes—including the National Industrial Recovery Act (NIRA), which Roosevelt deemed the most important statute in American history—in just two years").

regulatory measures. But the more frequent instrument for fending off national regulation of the market was the Commerce Clause, which the Court tended to enforce vigorously during the first part of the Twentieth Century. In the preceding century, most Commerce Clause litigation had involved *dormant* challenges to state regulation—cases like *Gibbons* and *Willson*—and the Court continued to enforce the dormant aspects of the Commerce Clause rigorously throughout the *Lochner* era. The cases in the present section, by contrast, present the flip side of *Gibbons* and *Willson*: They concern the scope of Congress's legislative authority over interstate commerce, not the extent of the states' own *intra*-state sphere. But both dormant and affirmative Commerce Clause cases focus on the location of the boundary between these two supposedly exclusive spheres. Both, in other words, were part of the regime of "dual federalism." This section traces the arc of the Court's Commerce Clause jurisprudence, which traveled a route largely parallel to the freedom of contract decisions.

United States v. E.C. Knight Co.

156 U.S. 1 (1895)

■ MR. CHIEF JUSTICE FULLER, after stating the case, delivered the opinion of the court.

By the purchase of the stock of the four Philadelphia refineries, with shares of its own stock, the American Sugar Refining Company acquired nearly complete control of the manufacture of refined sugar within the United States. The bill charged that the contracts under which these purchases were made constituted combinations in restraint of trade, and that in entering into them the defendants combined and conspired to restrain the trade and commerce in refined sugar among the several States and with foreign nations, contrary to the [Sherman Antitrust Act] of July 2, 1890. . . .

[T]he monopoly and restraint denounced by the act are the monopoly and restraint of interstate and international trade or commerce, while the conclusion to be assumed on this record is that the result of the transaction complained of was the creation of a monopoly in the manufacture of a necessary of life. . . . The fundamental question is, whether conceding that the existence of a monopoly in manufacture is established by the evidence, that monopoly can be directly suppressed under the act of Congress in the mode attempted by this bill.

It cannot be denied that the power of a State to protect the lives, health, and property of its citizens, and to preserve good order and the public morals, "the power to govern men and things within the limits of its dominion," is a power originally and always belonging to the States, not surrendered by them to the general government, nor directly restrained by the Constitution of the United States, and essentially exclusive. The relief of the citizens of each State from the burden of monopoly and the evils resulting from the restraint of trade among such citizens was left with the States to deal with, and this court has recognized their possession of that power even to the extent of holding that an employment or business carried on by private individuals . . . when it becomes a practical monopoly . . . is subject to regulation by state legislative power. On the other hand, the power of Congress to regulate commerce among the several States is also exclusive. The Constitution does not provide that interstate commerce shall be free, but, by the grant of this exclusive power to regulate it, it was left free except as Congress might impose restraints. Therefore it has been determined that the failure of Congress to exercise this exclusive power in any case is an expression of its will that the subject shall be free from restrictions or impositions upon it by the several States, and if a law passed by a State in the exercise of its acknowledged powers comes into conflict with that will, the Congress and the State cannot occupy the position of equal opposing sovereignties, because the Constitution declares its supremacy and that of the laws passed in pursuance thereof; and that which is not supreme must yield to that which is supreme. "Commerce, undoubtedly, is traffic," said Chief Justice Marshall, "but it is something more; it is intercourse. It describes the commercial intercourse between nations and parts of nations in all its branches, and is regulated by prescribing rules for carrying on that intercourse." That which belongs to commerce is within the jurisdiction of the United States, but that which does not belong to commerce is within the jurisdiction of the police power of the State. . . .

The argument is that the power to control the manufacture of refined sugar is a monopoly over a necessary of life, to the enjoyment of which by a large part of the population of the United States interstate commerce is indispensable, and that, therefore, the general government in the exercise of the power to regulate commerce may repress such monopoly directly and set aside the instruments which have created it. But this argument cannot be confined to necessaries of life merely, and must include all articles of general consumption. Doubtless the power to control the manufacture of a given thing involves in a certain sense the control of its disposition, but this is a secondary and not the primary sense; and although the exercise of that power may result in bringing the operation of commerce into play, it does not control it, and affects it only incidentally and indirectly. Commerce succeeds to manufacture, and is not a part of it. . . .

It will be perceived how far-reaching the proposition is that the power of dealing with a monopoly directly may be exercised by the general government whenever interstate or international commerce may be ultimately affected. The regulation of commerce applies to the subjects of commerce and not to matters of internal police. Contracts to buy, sell, or exchange goods to be transported among the several States, the transportation and its instrumentalities, and articles bought, sold, or exchanged for the purposes of such transit among the States, or put in the way of transit, may be regulated, but this is because they form part of interstate trade or commerce. The fact that an article is manufactured for export to another State does not of itself make it an article of interstate commerce, and the intent of the manufacturer does not determine the time when the article or product passes from the control of the State and belongs to commerce. . . .

Mr. Justice Lamar remarked: "No distinction is more popular to the common mind, or more clearly expressed in economic and political literature, than that between manufacture and commerce. Manufacture is transformation—the fashioning of raw materials into a change of form for use. The functions of commerce are different. The buying and selling and the transportation incidental thereto constitute commerce; and the regulation of commerce in the constitutional sense embraces the regulation at least of such transportation. . . . If it be held that the term includes the regulation of all such manufactures as are intended to be the subject of commercial transactions in the future, it is impossible to deny that it would also include all productive industries that contemplate the same thing. The result would be that Congress would be invested, to the exclusion of the States, with the power to regulate, not only manufactures, but also agriculture, horticulture, stock raising, domestic fisheries, mining—in short, every branch of human industry. For is there one of them that does not contemplate, more or less clearly, an interstate or foreign market? Does not the wheat grower of the Northwest or the cotton planter of the South, plant, cultivate, and harvest his crop with an eye on the prices at Liverpool, New York, and Chicago? The power being vested in Congress and denied to the States, it would follow as an inevitable result that the duty would devolve on Congress to regulate all of these delicate, multiform and vital interests—interests which in their nature are and must be local in all the details of their successful management. . . . The demands of such a supervision would require, not uniform legislation generally applicable throughout the United States, but a swarm of statutes only locally applicable and utterly inconsistent. Any movement toward the establishment of rules of production in this vast country, with its many different climates and opportunities, could only be at the sacrifice of the peculiar advantages of a large part of the localities in it, if not of every one of them. . . ." [*Kidd v. Pearson*, 128 U.S. 1, 20–22 (1888).]

Contracts, combinations, or conspiracies to control domestic enterprise in manufacture, agriculture, mining, production in all its forms, or to raise or lower prices or wages, might unquestionably tend to restrain external as well as domestic trade, but the restraint would be an indirect result, however inevitable and whatever its extent, and such result would not necessarily determine the object of the contract, combination, or conspiracy.

. . . Slight reflection will show that if the national power extends to all contracts and combinations in manufacture, agriculture, mining, and other productive industries, whose ultimate result may affect external commerce, comparatively little of business operations and affairs would be left for state control.

It was in the light of well-settled principles that the act of July 2, 1890, was framed. Congress did not attempt thereby to assert the power to deal with monopoly directly as such; or to limit and restrict the rights of corporations created by the States or the citizens of the States in the acquisition, control, or disposition of property; or to regulate or prescribe the price or prices at which such property or the products thereof should be sold; or to make criminal the acts of persons in the acquisition and control of property which the States of their residence or creation sanctioned or permitted. . . . [W]hat the law struck at was combinations, contracts, and conspiracies to monopolize trade and commerce among the several States or with foreign nations; but the contracts and acts of the defendants related exclusively to the acquisition of the Philadelphia refineries and the business of sugar refining in Pennsylvania, and bore no direct relation to commerce between the States or with foreign nations. The object was manifestly private gain in the manufacture of the commodity, but not through the control of interstate or foreign commerce. It is true that the bill alleged that the products of these refineries were sold and distributed among the several States, and that all the companies were engaged in trade or commerce with the several States and with foreign nations; but this was no more than to say that trade and commerce served manufacture to fulfill its function. Sugar was refined for sale, and sales were probably made at Philadelphia for consumption, and undoubtedly for resale by the first purchasers throughout Pennsylvania and other States, and refined sugar was also forwarded by the companies to other States for sale. Nevertheless it does not follow that an attempt to monopolize, or the actual monopoly of, the manufacture was an attempt, whether executory or consummated, to monopolize commerce, even though, in order to dispose of the product, the instrumentality of commerce was necessarily invoked. There was nothing in the proofs to indicate any intention to put a restraint upon trade or commerce, and the fact, as we have seen, that trade or commerce might be indirectly affected was not enough to entitle complainants to a decree. . . .

Decree affirmed.

■ MR. JUSTICE HARLAN, dissenting.

Prior to the 4th day of March, 1892, the American Sugar Refining Company, a corporation organized under a general statute of New Jersey for the purpose of buying, manufacturing, refining, and selling sugar in different parts of the country, had obtained the control of all the sugar refineries in the United States except five, of which four were owned and operated by Pennsylvania corporations—the E.C. Knight Company, the

Franklin Sugar Refining Company, Spreckels' Sugar Refining Company, and the Delaware Sugar House—and the other, by the Revere Sugar Refinery of Boston. These five corporations were all in active competition with the American Sugar Refining Company and with each other. The product of the Pennsylvania companies was about thirty-three per cent, and that of the Boston company about two per cent, of the entire quantity of sugar refined in the United States.

In March, 1892, by means of contracts or arrangements with stockholders of the four Pennsylvania companies, the New Jersey corporation—using for that purpose its own stock—purchased the stock of those companies, and thus obtained absolute control of the entire business of sugar refining in the United States except that done by the Boston company, which is too small in amount to be regarded in this discussion. . . .

In its consideration of the important constitutional question presented, this court assumes on the record before us that the result of the transactions disclosed by the pleadings and proof was the creation of a monopoly in the manufacture of a necessary of life. If this combination, so far as its operations necessarily or directly affect interstate commerce, cannot be restrained or suppressed under some power granted to Congress, it will be cause for regret that the patriotic statesmen who framed the Constitution did not foresee the necessity of investing the national government with power to deal with gigantic monopolies holding in their grasp, and injuriously controlling in their own interest, the entire trade among the States in food products that are essential to the comfort of every household in the land.

The court holds it to be vital in our system of government to recognize and give effect to both the commercial power of the nation and the police powers of the States, to the end that the Union be strengthened and the autonomy of the States preserved. In this view I entirely concur. . . . But it is equally true that the preservation of the just authority of the General Government is essential as well to the safety of the States as to the attainment of the important ends for which that government was ordained by the People of the United States; and the destruction of that authority would be fatal to the peace and well-being of the American people. The Constitution which enumerates the powers committed to the nation for objects of interest to the people of all the States should not, therefore, be subjected to an interpretation so rigid, technical, and narrow, that those objects cannot be accomplished. . . .

[T]here is a trade among the several States which is distinct from that carried on within the territorial limits of a State. The regulation and control of the former is committed by the national Constitution to Congress. Commerce among the States, as this court has declared, is a unit, and in respect of that commerce this is one country, and we are one people. It may be regulated by rules applicable to every part of the United States, and state lines and state jurisdiction cannot interfere with the enforcement of such rules. The jurisdiction of the general government extends over every foot of territory within the United States. Under the power with which it is invested, Congress may remove unlawful obstructions, of whatever kind, to the free course of trade among the States. In so doing it would not interfere with the "autonomy of the States," because the power thus to protect interstate commerce is expressly given by the people of all the States. . . . Any combination, therefore, that disturbs or unreasonably obstructs freedom in buying and selling articles manufactured to be sold to persons in other States or to be carried to other States—a freedom that cannot exist if the right to buy and sell is fettered by unlawful restraints that crush out competition— affects, not incidentally, but directly, the people of all the States; and the remedy for such an evil is found only in the exercise of powers confided to a government which, this court has said, was the government of all, exercising powers delegated by all, representing all, acting for all. *McCulloch v. Maryland.* . . .

It is said that manufacture precedes commerce and is not a part of it. But it is equally true that when manufacture ends, that which has been manufactured becomes a subject of commerce; that buying and selling succeed manufacture, come into existence after the process of manufacture is completed, precede transportation, and are as much commercial intercourse, where articles are bought to be carried from one State to another, as is the manual transportation of such articles after they have been so purchased. The distinction was recognized by this court in *Gibbons v. Ogden*, where the principal question was whether commerce included navigation. Both the court and counsel recognized buying and selling or barter as included in commerce. Chief Justice Marshall said that the mind can scarcely conceive a system for regulating commerce, which was "confined to prescribing rules for the conduct of individuals in the actual employment of buying and selling, or of barter." . . .

In committing to Congress the control of commerce with foreign nations and among the several States, the Constitution did not define the means that may be employed to protect the freedom of commercial intercourse and traffic established for the benefit of all the people of the Union. It wisely forbore to impose any limitations upon the exercise of that power except those arising from the general nature of the government, or such as are embodied in the fundamental guarantees of liberty and property. It gives to Congress, in express words, authority to enact all laws necessary and proper for carrying into execution the power to regulate commerce; and whether an act of Congress, passed to accomplish an object to which the general government is competent, is within the power granted, must be determined by the rule announced through Chief Justice Marshall three-quarters of a century ago, and which has been repeatedly affirmed by this court. That rule is: "The sound construction of the Constitution must allow to the national legislature the discretion with respect to the means by which the powers it confers are to be carried into execution, which will enable that body to perform the high duties assigned to it in the manner most beneficial to the people. Let the end be legitimate, let it be within the scope of the Constitution, and all means which are appropriate, which are plainly adapted to that end, which are not prohibited, but consistent with the letter and spirit of the Constitution, are constitutional." *McCulloch v. Maryland.*

The end proposed to be accomplished by the act of 1890 is the protection of trade and commerce among the States against unlawful restraints. Who can say that that end is not legitimate or is not within the scope of the Constitution? The means employed are the suppression, by legal proceedings, of combinations, conspiracies, and monopolies, which by their inevitable and admitted tendency, improperly restrain trade and commerce among the States. Who can say that such means are not appropriate to attain the end of freeing commercial intercourse among the States from burdens and exactions imposed upon it by combinations which, under principles long recognized in this country as well as at the common law, are illegal and dangerous to the public welfare? What clause of the Constitution can be referred to which prohibits the means thus prescribed in the act of Congress? . . .

While the opinion of the court in this case does not declare the act of 1890 to be unconstitutional, it defeats the main object for which it was passed. For it is, in effect, held that the statute would be unconstitutional if interpreted as embracing such unlawful restraints upon the purchasing of goods in one State to be carried to another State as necessarily arise from the existence of combinations formed for the purpose and with the effect, not only of monopolizing the ownership of all such goods in every part of the country, but of controlling the prices for them in all the States. This view of the scope of the act leaves the public, so far as national power is concerned, entirely at the mercy of combinations which arbitrarily control the prices of articles purchased to be transported from one State to another State. I cannot assent to that view. In my judgment, the general government is not placed by the Constitution in such a condition of helplessness that it must fold its arms and remain inactive while capital combines, under the name of a corporation, to destroy competition, not in one State only, but throughout the entire country, in the buying and selling of articles—especially the necessaries of life—that go into commerce among the States. The doctrine of the autonomy of the States cannot properly be invoked to justify a denial of power in the national government to meet such an emergency, involving as it does that freedom of commercial intercourse among the States which the Constitution sought to attain. . . .

For the reasons stated I dissent from the opinion and judgment of the court.

The Shreveport Rate Cases*
234 U.S. 342 (1914)

■ MR. JUSTICE HUGHES delivered the opinion of the court.

These suits were brought in the Commerce Court by the Houston, East & West Texas Railway Company, and the Houston & Shreveport Railroad Company, and by the Texas & Pacific Railway Company, respectively, to set aside an order of the Interstate Commerce Commission, dated March 11, 1912, upon the ground that it exceeded the Commission's authority. . . .

The order of the Interstate Commerce Commission was made in a proceeding initiated in March, 1911, by the Railroad Commission of Louisiana. The complaint was that the appellants, and other interstate carriers, maintained unreasonable rates from Shreveport, Louisiana, to various points in Texas, and, further, that these carriers in the adjustment of rates over their respective lines unjustly discriminated in favor of traffic within the State of Texas and against similar traffic between Louisiana and Texas. . . .

The gravamen of the complaint, said the Interstate Commerce Commission, was that the carriers made rates out of Dallas and other Texas points into eastern Texas which were much lower than those which they extended into Texas from Shreveport. The situation may be briefly described: Shreveport, Louisiana, is about 40 miles from the Texas state line, and 231 miles from Houston, Texas, on the line of the Houston, East & West Texas and Houston & Shreveport Companies (which are affiliated in interest); it is 189 miles from Dallas, Texas, on the line of the Texas & Pacific. Shreveport competes with both cities for the trade of the intervening territory. The rates on these lines from Dallas and Houston, respectively, eastward to intermediate points in Texas were much less, according to distance, than from Shreveport westward to the same points. It is undisputed that the difference was substantial and injuriously affected the commerce of Shreveport. . . .

The Interstate Commerce Commission found that the interstate class rates out of Shreveport to named Texas points were unreasonable, and it established maximum class rates for this traffic. These rates, we understand, were substantially the same as the class rates fixed by the Railroad Commission of Texas, and charged by the carriers, for transportation for similar distances in that State. The Interstate Commerce Commission also found that the carriers maintained "higher rates from Shreveport to points in Texas" than were in force "from cities in Texas to such points under substantially similar conditions and circumstances," and that thereby "an unlawful and undue preference and advantage" was given to the Texas cities and a "discrimination" that was

---

* [Editor's Note: Houston, East & West Texas Railway Co. v. United States; Texas & Pacific Railway Co. v. United States.]

"undue and unlawful" was effected against Shreveport. In order to correct this discrimination, the carriers were directed to desist from charging higher rates for the transportation of any commodity from Shreveport to Dallas and Houston, respectively, and intermediate points, than were contemporaneously charged for the carriage of such commodity from Dallas and Houston toward Shreveport for equal distances. . . .

The point of the objection to the order is that, as the discrimination found by the Commission to be unjust arises out of the relation of intrastate rates, maintained under state authority, to interstate rates that have been upheld as reasonable, its correction was beyond the Commission's power. . . . The invalidity of the order in this aspect is challenged upon [the ground that] Congress is impotent to control the intrastate charges of an interstate carrier even to the extent necessary to prevent injurious discrimination against interstate traffic. . . .

It is unnecessary to repeat what has frequently been said by this court with respect to the complete and paramount character of the power confided to Congress to regulate commerce among the several States. It is of the essence of this power that, where it exists, it dominates. Interstate trade was not left to be destroyed or impeded by the rivalries of local governments. The purpose was to make impossible the recurrence of the evils which had overwhelmed the Confederation and to provide the necessary basis of national unity by insuring 'uniformity of regulation against conflicting and discriminating state legislation.' By virtue of the comprehensive terms of the grant, the authority of Congress is at all times adequate to meet the varying exigencies that arise and to protect the national interest by securing the freedom of interstate commercial intercourse from local control. . . .

Congress['s] . . . authority, extending to these interstate carriers as instruments of interstate commerce, necessarily embraces the right to control their operations in all matters having such a close and substantial relation to interstate traffic that the control is essential or appropriate to the security of that traffic, to the efficiency of the interstate service, and to the maintenance of conditions under which interstate commerce may be conducted upon fair terms and without molestation or hindrance. As it is competent for Congress to legislate to these ends, unquestionably it may seek their attainment by requiring that the agencies of interstate commerce shall not be used in such manner as to cripple, retard or destroy it. The fact that carriers are instruments of intrastate commerce, as well as of interstate commerce, does not derogate from the complete and paramount authority of Congress over the latter or preclude the Federal power from being exerted to prevent the intrastate operations of such carriers from being made a means of injury to that which has been confided to Federal care. Wherever the interstate and intrastate transactions of carriers are so related that the government of the one involves the control of the other, it is Congress, and not the State, that is entitled to prescribe the final and dominant rule, for otherwise Congress would be denied the exercise of its constitutional authority and the State, and not the Nation, would be supreme within the national field. . . .

In *Baltimore & Ohio Railroad Co. v. Interstate Commerce Commission,* the argument against the validity of the Hours of Service Act involved the consideration that the interstate and intrastate transactions of the carriers were so interwoven that it was utterly impracticable for them to divide their employees so that those who were engaged in interstate commerce should be confined to that commerce exclusively. Employees dealing with the movement of trains were employed in both sorts of commerce; but the court held that this fact did not preclude the exercise of Federal power. As Congress could limit the hours of labor of those engaged in interstate transportation, it necessarily followed that its will could not be frustrated by prolonging the period of service through other requirements of the carriers or by the commingling of duties relating to interstate and intrastate operations. Again, in *Southern Railway Co. v. United States*, the question was presented whether the amendment to the Safety Appliance Act was within the power of Congress in view of the fact that the statute was not confined to vehicles that were used in interstate traffic but also embraced those used in intrastate traffic. The court answered affirmatively, because there was such a close relation between the two classes of traffic moving over the same railroad as to make it certain that the safety of the interstate traffic, and of those employed in its movement, would be promoted in a real and substantial sense by applying the requirements of the act to both classes of vehicles. . . .

While these decisions sustaining the Federal power relate to measures adopted in the interest of the safety of persons and property, they illustrate the principle that Congress in the exercise of its paramount power may prevent the common instrumentalities of interstate and intrastate commercial intercourse from being used in their intrastate operations to the injury of interstate commerce. This is not to say that Congress possesses the authority to regulate the internal commerce of a State, as such, but that it does possess the power to foster and protect interstate commerce, and to take all measures necessary or appropriate to that end, although intrastate transactions of interstate carriers may thereby be controlled.

This principle is applicable here. We find no reason to doubt that Congress is entitled to keep the highways of interstate communication open to interstate traffic upon fair and equal terms. That an unjust discrimination in the rates of a common carrier, by which one person or locality is unduly favored as against another under substantially similar conditions of traffic, constitutes an evil is undeniable; and where this evil consists in the action of an interstate carrier in unreasonably discriminating against interstate traffic over its line, the authority of Congress to prevent it is equally clear. It is immaterial, so far as the protecting power of Congress is concerned, that the discrimination arises from intrastate rates as compared with interstate rates. The use of the instrument of interstate commerce in a discriminatory manner so as to inflict injury upon that commerce, or some part thereof, furnishes abundant ground for Federal intervention. Nor can the attempted exercise of state authority alter the matter, where Congress has acted, for a State may not authorize the carrier to do that which Congress is entitled to forbid and has forbidden. . . .

Affirmed.

■ MR. JUSTICE LURTON and MR. JUSTICE PITNEY dissent.

Hammer v. Dagenhart
247 U.S. 251 (1918)

■ MR. JUSTICE DAY delivered the opinion of the court.

A bill was filed in the United States District Court for the Western District of North Carolina by a father in his own behalf and as next friend of his two minor sons, one under the age of fourteen years and the other between the ages of fourteen and sixteen years, employees in a cotton mill at Charlotte, North Carolina, to enjoin the enforcement of the act of Congress intended to prevent interstate commerce in the products of child labor. The District Court held the act unconstitutional and entered a decree enjoining its enforcement. This appeal brings the case here. . . .

The controlling question for decision is: Is it within the authority of Congress in regulating commerce among the States to prohibit the transportation in interstate commerce of manufactured goods, the product of a factory in which, within thirty days prior to their removal therefrom, children under the age of fourteen have been employed or permitted to work, or children between the ages of fourteen and sixteen years have been employed or permitted to work more than eight hours in any day, or more than six days in any week, or after the hour of 7 o'clock P.M. or before the hour of 6 o'clock A.M.?

The power essential to the passage of this act, the Government contends, is found in the commerce clause of the Constitution which authorizes Congress to regulate commerce with foreign nations and among the States.

In *Gibbons v. Ogden,* Chief Justice Marshall, . . . defining the extent and nature of the commerce power, said, "It is the power to regulate; that is, to prescribe the rule by which commerce is to be governed." In other words, the power is one to control the means by which commerce is carried on, which is directly the contrary of the assumed right to forbid commerce from moving and thus destroy it as to particular commodities. But it is insisted that adjudged cases in this court establish the doctrine that the power to regulate given to Congress incidentally includes the authority to prohibit the movement of ordinary commodities and therefore that the subject is not open for discussion. The cases demonstrate the contrary. They rest upon the character of the particular subjects dealt with and the fact that the scope of governmental authority, state or national, possessed over them is such that the authority to prohibit is as to them but the exertion of the power to regulate.

The first of these cases is *Champion v. Ames*, 188 U.S. 321, the so-called *Lottery Case*, in which it was held that Congress might pass a law having the effect to keep the channels of commerce free from use in the transportation of tickets used in the promotion of lottery schemes. In *Hipolite Egg Co. v. United States*, 220 U.S. 45, this court sustained the power of Congress to pass the Pure Food and Drug Act which prohibited the introduction into the States by means of interstate commerce of impure foods and drugs. In *Hoke v. United States*, 227 U.S. 308, this court sustained the constitutionality of the so-called "White Slave Traffic Act" whereby the transportation of a woman in interstate commerce for the purpose of prostitution was forbidden. . . .

In *Caminetti v. United States*, 242 U.S. 470, we held that Congress might prohibit the transportation of women in interstate commerce for the purposes of debauchery and kindred purposes. In *Clark Distilling Co. v. Western Maryland Ry. Co.*, 242 U.S. 311, the power of Congress over the transportation of intoxicating liquors was sustained. . . .

In each of these instances the use of interstate transportation was necessary to the accomplishment of harmful results. In other words, although the power over interstate transportation was to regulate, that could only be accomplished by prohibiting the use of the facilities of interstate commerce to effect the evil intended.

This element is wanting in the present case. The thing intended to be accomplished by this statute is the denial of the facilities of interstate commerce to those manufacturers in the States who employ children within the prohibited ages. The act in its effect does not regulate transportation among the States, but aims to standardize the ages at which children may be employed in mining and manufacturing within the States. The goods shipped are of themselves harmless. The act permits them to be freely shipped after thirty days from the time of their removal from the factory. When offered for shipment, and before transportation begins, the labor of their production is over, and the mere fact that they were intended for interstate commerce transportation does not make their production subject to federal control under the commerce power.

Commerce "consists of intercourse and traffic . . . and includes the transportation of persons and property, as well as the purchase, sale and exchange of commodities." The making of goods and the mining of coal are not commerce, nor does the fact that these things are to be afterwards shipped or used in interstate commerce, make their production a part thereof. Over interstate transportation, or its incidents, the regulatory power of Congress is ample, but the production of articles, intended for interstate commerce, is a matter of local regulation. . . .

It is further contended that the authority of Congress may be exerted to control interstate commerce in the shipment of child-made goods because of the effect of the circulation of such goods in other States where the evil of this class of labor has been recognized by local legislation, and the right to thus employ child labor has been more rigorously restrained than in the State of production. In other words, that the unfair competition, thus engendered, may be controlled by closing the channels of interstate commerce to manufacturers in those States where the local laws do not meet what Congress deems to be the more just standard of other States.

There is no power vested in Congress to require the States to exercise their police power so as to prevent possible unfair competition. Many causes may cooperate to give one State, by reason of local laws or conditions, an economic advantage over others. The Commerce Clause was not intended to give to Congress a general authority to equalize such conditions. In some of the States laws have been passed fixing minimum wages for women, in others the local law regulates the hours of labor of women in various employments. Business done in such States may be at an economic disadvantage when compared with States which have no such regulations; surely, this fact does not give Congress the power to deny transportation in interstate commerce to those who carry on business where the hours of labor and the rate of compensation for women have not been fixed by a standard in use in other States and approved by Congress. . . .

The grant of authority over a purely federal matter was not intended to destroy the local power always existing and carefully reserved to the States in the Tenth Amendment to the Constitution. Police regulations relating to the internal trade and affairs of the States have been uniformly recognized as within such control. . . .

That there should be limitations upon the right to employ children in mines and factories in the interest of their own and the public welfare, all will admit. That such employment is generally deemed to require regulation is shown by the fact that . . . every State in the Union has a law upon the subject, limiting the right to thus employ children. In North Carolina, the State wherein is located the factory in which the employment was had in the present case, no child under twelve years of age is permitted to work. It may be desirable that such laws be uniform, but our Federal Government is one of enumerated powers. . . .

A statute must be judged by its natural and reasonable effect. The control by Congress over interstate commerce cannot authorize the exercise of authority not entrusted to it by the Constitution. . . .

We have neither authority nor disposition to question the motives of Congress in enacting this legislation. The purposes intended must be attained consistently with constitutional limitations and not by an invasion of the powers of the States. This court has no more important function than that which devolves upon it the obligation to preserve inviolate the constitutional limitations upon the exercise of authority, federal and state, to the end that each may continue to discharge, harmoniously with the other, the duties entrusted to it by the Constitution.

In our view the necessary effect of this act is, by means of a prohibition against the movement in interstate commerce of ordinary commercial commodities, to regulate the hours of labor of children in factories and mines within the States, a purely state authority. Thus the act in a twofold sense is repugnant to the Constitution. It not only transcends the authority delegated to Congress over commerce but also exerts a power as to a purely local matter to which the federal authority does not extend. The far reaching result of upholding the act cannot be more plainly indicated than by pointing out that if Congress can thus regulate matters entrusted to local authority by prohibition of the movement of commodities in interstate commerce, all freedom of commerce will be at an end, and the power of the States over local matters may be eliminated, and thus our system of government be practically destroyed.

For these reasons we hold that this law exceeds the constitutional authority of Congress. It follows that the decree of the District Court must be

Affirmed.

■ **MR. JUSTICE HOLMES, dissenting.**

. . . [I]f an act is within the powers specifically conferred upon Congress, it seems to me that it is not made any less constitutional because of the indirect effects that it may have, however obvious it may be that it will have those effects, and that we are not at liberty upon such grounds to hold it void.

The first step in my argument is to make plain what no one is likely to dispute—that the statute in question is within the power expressly given to Congress if considered only as to its immediate effects and that if invalid it is so only upon some collateral ground. The statute confines itself to prohibiting the carriage of certain goods in interstate or foreign commerce. Congress is given power to regulate such commerce in unqualified terms. It would not be argued today that the power to regulate does not include the power to prohibit. Regulation means the prohibition of something, and when interstate commerce is the matter to be regulated I cannot doubt that the regulation may prohibit any part of such commerce that Congress sees fit to forbid. . . .

The question then is narrowed to whether the exercise of its otherwise constitutional power by Congress can be pronounced unconstitutional because of its possible reaction upon the conduct of the States in a matter upon which I have admitted that they are free from direct control. I should have thought that that matter had been disposed of so fully as to leave no room for doubt. I should have thought that most conspicuous decisions of this Court had made it clear that the power to regulate commerce and other constitutional powers could not be cut down or qualified by the fact that it might interfere with the carrying out of the domestic policy of any State. . . .

But if there is any matter upon which civilized countries have agreed . . . it is the evil of premature and excessive child labor. I should have thought that if we were to introduce our own moral conceptions where in my opinion they do not belong, this was preeminently a case for upholding the exercise of all its powers by the United States.

But I had thought that the propriety of the exercise of a power admitted to exist in some cases was for the consideration of Congress alone and that this Court always had disavowed the right to intrude its judgment upon questions of policy or morals. It is not for this Court to pronounce when prohibition is necessary to regulation if it ever may be necessary—to say that it is permissible as against strong drink but not as against the product of ruined lives.

The act does not meddle with anything belonging to the States. They may regulate their internal affairs and their domestic commerce as they like. But when they seek to send their products across the state line they are no longer within their rights. If there were no Constitution and no Congress their power to cross the line would depend upon their neighbors. Under the Constitution such commerce belongs not to the States but to Congress to regulate. It may carry out its views of public policy whatever indirect effect they may have upon the activities of the States. Instead of being encountered by a prohibitive tariff at her boundaries the State encounters the public policy of the United States which it is for Congress to express. The public policy of the United States is shaped with a view to the benefit of the nation as a whole. If, as has been the case within the memory of men still living, a State should take a different view of the propriety of sustaining a lottery from that which generally prevails, I cannot believe that the fact would require a different decision from that reached in *Champion v. Ames*. Yet in that case it would be said with quite as much force as in this that Congress was attempting to intermeddle with the State's domestic affairs. The national welfare as understood by Congress may require a different attitude within its sphere from that of some self-seeking State. It seems to me entirely constitutional for Congress to enforce its understanding by all the means at its command.

■ MR. JUSTICE MCKENNA, MR. JUSTICE BRANDEIS, and MR. JUSTICE CLARKE concur in this opinion.

A.L.A. Schechter Poultry Corp. v. United States

295 U.S. 495 (1935)

■ MR. CHIEF JUSTICE HUGHES delivered the opinion of the Court.

Petitioners . . . were convicted in the District Court of the United States for the Eastern District of New York on eighteen counts of an indictment charging violations of what is known as the "Live Poultry Code," and on an additional count for conspiracy to commit such violations. By demurrer to the indictment and appropriate motions on the trial, the defendants contended (1) that the Code had been adopted pursuant to an unconstitutional delegation by Congress of legislative power; (2) that it attempted to regulate intrastate transactions which lay outside the authority of Congress; and (3) that in certain provisions it was repugnant to the due process clause of the Fifth Amendment. . . .

New York City is the largest live-poultry market in the United States. Ninety-six per cent of the live poultry there marketed comes from other States. Three-fourths of this amount arrives by rail and is consigned to commission men or receivers. Most of these freight shipments (about 75 per cent.) come in at the Manhattan Terminal of the New York Central Railroad, and the remainder at one of the four terminals in New Jersey serving New York City. The commission men . . . sell to slaughterhouse operators who are also called market-men.

The defendants are slaughterhouse operators of the latter class. A. L. A. Schechter Poultry Corporation and Schechter Live Poultry Market are corporations conducting wholesale poultry slaughterhouse markets in Brooklyn, New York City. . . . Defendants ordinarily purchase their live poultry from commission men at the West Washington Market in New York City or at the railroad terminals serving the City, but occasionally they purchase from commission men in Philadelphia. They buy the poultry for slaughter and resale. After the poultry is trucked to their slaughterhouse markets in Brooklyn, it is there sold, usually within twenty-four hours, to retail poultry dealers and butchers who sell directly to consumers. The poultry purchased from defendants is immediately slaughtered, prior to delivery, by shochtim* in defendants' employ. Defendants do not sell poultry in interstate commerce.

The "Live Poultry Code" was promulgated under § 3 of the National Industrial Recovery Act. . . . Its divisions indicate its nature and scope. The Code has eight articles entitled (1) purposes, (2) definitions, (3) hours, (4) wages, (5) general labor provisions, (6) administration, (7) trade practice provisions, and (8) general.

The declared purpose is "To effect the policies of title I of the National Industrial Recovery Act." The Code is established as "a code of

---

* [Editor's Note] "Shochtim are the only persons qualified to slaughter poultry in accordance with Jewish dietary laws." Local 167 of the Int'l Brotherhood of Teamsters v. United States, 291 U.S. 293, 294 (1934).

fair competition for the live poultry industry of the metropolitan area in and about the City of New York." That area is described as embracing the five boroughs of New York City, the counties of Rockland, Westchester, Nassau and Suffolk in the State of New York, the counties of Hudson and Bergen in the State of New Jersey, and the county of Fairfield in the State of Connecticut. . . .

The Code fixes the number of hours for work-days. It provides that no employee, with certain exceptions, shall be permitted to work in excess of forty (40) hours in any one week, and that no employee, save as stated, "shall be paid in any pay period less than at the rate of fifty (50) cents per hour." The article containing "general labor provisions" prohibits the employment of any person under sixteen years of age, and declares that employees shall have the right of "collective bargaining," and freedom of choice with respect to labor organizations, in the terms of § 7 (a) of the Act. The minimum number of employees, who shall be employed by slaughterhouse operators, is fixed, the number being graduated according to the average volume of weekly sales. . . .

Of the eighteen counts of the indictment upon which the defendants were convicted, aside from the count for conspiracy, two counts charged violation of the minimum wage and maximum hour provisions of the Code, and ten counts were for violation of the requirement (found in the "trade practice provisions") of "straight killing." This requirement was really one of "straight" selling. The term "straight killing" was defined in the Code as "the practice of requiring persons purchasing poultry for resale to accept the run of any half coop, coop, or coops, as purchased by slaughterhouse operators, except for culls." The charges in the ten counts, respectively, were that the defendants in selling to retail dealers and butchers had permitted "selections of individual chickens taken from particular coops and half coops." . . .

First. . . . We are told that the provision of the statute authorizing the adoption of codes must be viewed in the light of the grave national crisis with which Congress was confronted. Undoubtedly, the conditions to which power is addressed are always to be considered when the exercise of power is challenged. Extraordinary conditions may call for extraordinary remedies. But the argument necessarily stops short of an attempt to justify action which lies outside the sphere of constitutional authority. Extraordinary conditions do not create or enlarge constitutional power. The Constitution established a national government with powers deemed to be adequate, as they have proved to be both in war and peace, but these powers of the national government are limited by the constitutional grants. Those who act under these grants are not at liberty to transcend the imposed limits because they believe that more or different power is necessary. Such assertions of extra-constitutional authority were anticipated and precluded by the explicit terms of the Tenth Amendment,—"The powers not delegated to the United States by the Constitution, nor prohibited by it to the States, are reserved to the States respectively, or to the people."

[The Court held that the statute violated the constitutional prohibition on delegation of legislative power by delegating complete discretion to formulate codes of fair competition to the Executive Branch.]

Third. The question of the application of the provisions of the Live Poultry Code to intrastate transactions. Although the validity of the codes (apart from the question of delegation) rests upon the commerce clause of the Constitution, § 3(a) is not in terms limited to interstate and foreign commerce. From the generality of its terms, and from the argument of the Government at the bar, it would appear that § 3(a) was designed to authorize codes without that limitation. But under § 3(f) penalties are confined to violations of a code provision "in any transaction in or affecting interstate or foreign commerce." This aspect of the case presents the question whether the particular provisions of the Live Poultry Code, which the defendants were convicted for violating and for having conspired to violate, were within the regulating power of Congress.

These provisions relate to the hours and wages of those employed by defendants in their slaughterhouses in Brooklyn and to the sales there made to retail dealers and butchers.

(1) Were these transactions *"in"* interstate commerce? Much is made of the fact that almost all the poultry coming to New York is sent there from other States. But the code provisions, as here applied, do not concern the transportation of the poultry from other States to New York, or the transactions of the commission men or others to whom it is consigned, or the sales made by such consignees to defendants. When defendants had made their purchases, whether at the West Washington Market in New York City or at the railroad terminals serving the City, or elsewhere, the poultry was trucked to their slaughterhouses in Brooklyn for local disposition. The interstate transactions in relation to that poultry then ended. Defendants held the poultry at their slaughterhouse markets for slaughter and local sale to retail dealers and butchers who in turn sold directly to consumers. Neither the slaughtering nor the sales by defendants were transactions in interstate commerce.

The undisputed facts thus afford no warrant for the argument that the poultry handled by defendants at their slaughterhouse markets was in a *"current"* or *"flow"* of interstate commerce and was thus subject to congressional regulation. The mere fact that there may be a constant flow of commodities into a State does not mean that the flow continues after the property has arrived and has become commingled with the mass of property within the State and is there held solely for local disposition and use. So far as the poultry here in question is concerned, the flow in interstate commerce had ceased. The poultry had come to a permanent rest within the State. It was not held, used, or sold by defendants in relation to any further transactions in interstate commerce and was not destined for transportation to other States. Hence, decisions which deal with a stream of interstate commerce—where goods come to rest within a State temporarily and are later to go forward in interstate commerce—and with the regulations of transactions involved in that practical continuity of movement, are not applicable here.

Did the defendants' transactions directly *"affect"* interstate commerce so as to be subject to federal regulation? The power of Congress extends not only to the regulation of transactions which are part of interstate commerce, but to the protection of that commerce from injury. It matters not that the injury may be due to the conduct of those engaged in intrastate operations. Thus, Congress may protect the safety of those employed in interstate transportation "no matter what may be the source of the dangers which threaten it." . . . We have held that, in dealing with common carriers engaged in both interstate and intrastate commerce, the dominant authority of Congress necessarily embraces the right to control their intrastate operations in all matters having such a close and substantial relation to interstate traffic that the control is essential or appropriate to secure the freedom of that traffic from interference or unjust discrimination and to promote the efficiency of the interstate service. *The Shreveport Case.*

In determining how far the federal government may go in controlling intrastate transactions upon the ground that they "affect" interstate commerce, there is a necessary and well-established distinction between direct and indirect effects. The precise line can be drawn only as individual cases arise, but the distinction is clear in principle. Direct effects are illustrated by the railroad cases we have cited, as *e.g.,* the effect of failure to use prescribed safety appliances on railroads which are the highways of both interstate and intrastate commerce, injury to an employee engaged in interstate transportation by the negligence of an employee engaged in an intrastate movement, the fixing of rates for intrastate transportation which unjustly discriminate against interstate commerce. But where the effect of intrastate transactions upon interstate commerce is merely indirect, such transactions remain within the domain of state power. If the commerce clause were construed to reach all enterprises and transactions which could be said to have an indirect effect upon interstate commerce, the federal authority would embrace practically all the activities of the people and the authority of the State over its domestic concerns would exist only by sufferance of the federal government. Indeed, on such a theory, even the development of the State's commercial facilities would be subject to federal control. As we said in the *Minnesota Rate Cases,* 230 U.S. 352, 410: "In the intimacy of commercial relations, much that is done in the superintendence of local matters may have an indirect bearing upon interstate commerce. The development of local resources and the extension of local facilities may have a very important effect upon communities less favored and to an appreciable degree alter the course of trade. The freedom of local trade may stimulate interstate commerce, while restrictive measures within the police power of the State enacted exclusively with respect to internal business, as distinguished from interstate traffic, may in their reflex or indirect influence diminish the latter and reduce the volume of articles transported into or out of the State." . . .

[T]he distinction between direct and indirect effects of intrastate transactions upon interstate commerce must be recognized as a fundamental one, essential to the maintenance of our constitutional system. Otherwise, as we have said, there would be virtually no limit to the federal completely centralized government. We must consider the provisions here in question in the light of this distinction.

The question of chief importance relates to the provisions of the Code as to the hours and wages of those employed in defendants' slaughterhouse markets. It is plain that these requirements are imposed in order to govern the details of defendants' management of their local business. The persons employed in slaughtering and selling in local trade are not employed in interstate commerce. Their hours and wages have no direct relation to interstate commerce. The question of how many hours these employees should work and what they should be paid differs in no essential respect from similar questions in other local businesses which handle commodities brought into a State and there dealt in as a part of its internal commerce. This appears from an examination of the considerations urged by the Government with respect to conditions in the poultry trade. Thus, the Government argues that hours and wages affect prices; that slaughterhouse men sell at a small margin above operating costs; that labor represents 50 to 60 per cent. of these costs; that a slaughterhouse operator paying lower wages or reducing his cost by exacting long hours of work, translates his saving into lower prices; that this results in demands for a cheaper grade of goods; and that the cutting of prices brings about a demoralization of the price structure. Similar conditions may be adduced in relation to other businesses. The argument of the Government proves too much. If the federal government may determine the wages and hours of employees in the internal commerce of a State, because of their relation to cost and prices and their indirect effect upon interstate commerce, it would seem that a similar control might be exerted over other elements of cost, also affecting prices, such as the number of employees, rents, advertising, methods of doing business, etc. All the processes of production and distribution that enter into cost could likewise be controlled. If the cost of doing an intrastate business is in itself the permitted object of federal control, the extent of the regulation of cost would be a question of discretion and not of power.

The Government also makes the point that efforts to enact state legislation establishing high labor standards have been impeded by the belief that unless similar action is taken generally, commerce will be diverted from the States adopting such standards, and that this fear of diversion has led to demands for federal legislation on the subject of wages and hours. The apparent implication is that the federal authority under the commerce clause should be deemed to extend to the establishment of rules to govern wages and hours in intrastate trade and industry generally throughout the country, thus overriding the authority of the States to deal with domestic problems arising from labor conditions in their internal commerce.

It is not the province of the Court to consider the economic advantages or disadvantages of such a centralized system. It is sufficient to say that the Federal Constitution does not provide for it. Our growth and development have called for wide use of the commerce power of the federal government in its control over the expanded activities of interstate commerce, and in protecting that commerce from burdens, interferences, and conspiracies to restrain and monopolize it. But the authority of the federal government may not be pushed to such an extreme as to destroy the distinction, which the commerce clause itself establishes, between commerce "among the several States" and the internal concerns of a State. The same answer must be made to the contention that is based upon the serious economic situation which led to the passage of the Recovery Act, the fall in prices, the decline in wages and employment, and the curtailment of the market for commodities. Stress is laid upon the great importance of maintaining wage distributions which would provide the necessary stimulus in starting "the cumulative forces making for expanding commercial activity." Without in any way disparaging this motive, it is enough to say that the recuperative efforts of the federal government must be made in a manner consistent with the authority granted by the Constitution.

We are of the opinion that the attempt through the provisions of the Code to fix the hours and wages of employees of defendants in their intrastate business was not a valid exercise of federal power. . . . In view of these conclusions, we find it unnecessary to discuss other questions which have been raised as to the validity of certain provisions of the Code under the due process clause of the Fifth Amendment.

On both the grounds we have discussed, the attempted delegation of legislative power, and the attempted regulation of intrastate transactions which affect interstate commerce only indirectly, we hold the code provisions here in question to be invalid and that the judgment of conviction must be reversed.

■ MR. JUSTICE CARDOZO, concurring.

. . . If this code had been adopted by Congress itself, and not by the President on the advice of an industrial association, it would even then be void unless authority to adopt it is included in the grant of power "to regulate commerce with foreign nations and among the several states."

I find no authority in that grant for the regulation of wages and hours of labor in the intrastate transactions that make up the defendants' business. As to this feature of the case little can be added to the opinion of the court. There is a view of causation that would obliterate the distinction between what is national and what is local in the activities of commerce. Motion at the outer rim is communicated perceptibly, though minutely, to recording instruments at the center. A society such as ours "is an elastic medium which transmits all tremors throughout its territory; the only question is of their size." Per Learned Hand, J., in the court below. The law is not indifferent to considerations of degree. Activities local in their immediacy do not become interstate and national because of distant repercussions. What is near and what is distant may at times be uncertain. There is no penumbra of uncertainty obscuring judgment here. To find immediacy or directness here is to find it almost everywhere. If centripetal forces are to be isolated to the exclusion of the forces that opposed and counteract them, there will be an end to our federal system. . . .

I am authorized to state that MR. JUSTICE STONE joins in this opinion.

NOTE ON DUAL FEDERALISM IN THE *LOCHNER* ERA

1.   As discussed in Chapter Three, the theory of federalism that largely prevailed between 1789 and 1937 was called "dual federalism." Edward Corwin defined that theory in terms of four postulates:

- "The national government is one of enumerated powers only;

- Also, the purposes which it may constitutionally promote are few;

- Within their respective spheres the two centers of government are 'sovereign' and hence 'equal';

- The relation of the two centers with each other is one of tension rather than collaboration."[20]

This approach to federalism obviously put a great deal of pressure on the Court's ability to define the boundary between the state and federal spheres of authority in a principled and precise way. How did the Court define the limits of Congress's Commerce Clause authority in *Knight, Hammer* and *Schechter*? Do the limits relied upon seem principled and workable to you? Do they pass the test of the "Frankfurter constraint"? Or do the results in these cases, like *Lochner* perhaps, seem born of hostility to economic regulation?

2.   The *E.C. Knight* Court framed the question before it not as whether the Sherman Act was unconstitutional, but rather as whether the Act should be construed to reach manufacturing and similar activities in addition to interstate business transaction. The Court strongly suggested, however, that if the Act *were* construed to reach such activity then it would be unconstitutional. *E.C. Knight* is thus an instance of the doctrine of *constitutional avoidance*. That doctrine holds that when a court confronts an ambiguous statute with two or more plausible readings, and one of those readings would avoid constitutional difficulties while others would be

---

[20]   Edward S. Corwin, *The Passing of Dual Federalism*, 36 VA. L. REV. 1, 4 (1950).

constitutionally problematic, the court should "avoid" the constitutional question by adopting the clearly constitutional reading. This avoidance doctrine is one way in which constitutional principles exert considerable influence on non-constitutional cases—that is, cases where the disputed issue is the meaning of a statute or some other form of "ordinary" law. Is the avoidance doctrine legitimate? If the Court thought that Congress probably intended to reach mergers like the sugar merger in *Knight*, should it have construed the statute more broadly and confronted the question whether the statute was constitutional? Does the opinion leave any doubt as to what the result would have been?

3.   Like *Nebbia* in the previous section, the *Shreveport Rate Cases* are an example of the many instances in which the Supreme Court *upheld* national legislation against Commerce Clause challenge during this period. Other important examples are noted in both the majority and dissenting opinions in *Hammer*. *Champion v. Ames*, 188 U.S. 321 (1903), in which Congress had passed a law prohibiting the transportation of lottery tickets from one state to another, is a paradigm case. The Court held that, although Congress would have no authority to regulate lotteries within a particular state, it could nonetheless prohibit interstate transport of lottery tickets. Similar cases prohibited the interstate transport of impure food and drugs,[21] and the interstate transport of women for purposes of prostitution.[22] How does *Hammer* distinguish these cases?

4.   It may help to divide the pre-New Deal federalism cases into two distinct categories.

- *Economic Regulation* cases, in which Congress's purpose relates to the interstate economy, but it is trying to regulate somewhat more broadly than strictly commercial transactions involving more than one state. The classic examples include *E.C. Knight* (regulation of manufacturing activities antecedent to sale of a product) and the *Shreveport Rate Cases* (regulation of *intra*state railroad routes that affect *inter*state routes). In these cases, regulating interstate commerce is an *end*.

- *Social Regulation* cases, in which Congress is trying to achieve certain social or moral ends—not economic ones—through banning interstate transportation of certain people or goods. *See, e.g., Champion v. Ames* (regulating interstate shipment of lottery tickets in order to suppress lotteries on moral grounds); *Hammer v. Dagenhart* (regulating interstate shipment of goods produced by child labor in order to suppress child labor). In these cases, regulating commerce is a *means* to a non-commercial end.

Note that the Court goes both ways within both categories over the course of the period surveyed in this section, upholding some national measures and striking down others. Should Congress's intent—that is, whether the

---

[21] *Hipolite Egg Co. v. United States*, 220 U.S. 45 (1911).

[22] *Hoke v. United States*, 227 U.S. 308 (1913).

Commerce Power is employed for an economic purpose—matter to the resolution of these cases? Should Congress's power be broader when it is legislating for economic ends? How does *McCulloch* bear on these questions?

5.   The pre-1937 federalism cases are good examples of the difference between "formalism" and "realism" as approaches to constructing legal rules. "Formalism" has many different definitions, but for present purposes it describes an approach where the court examines the statute and the regulated activity to determine whether certain objective criteria are met. Actual economic effects or legislative motive—neither of which is apparent on the face of the statute—are unimportant. [23] "Realism" is likewise a complicated concept, but here we mean simply that the court focuses not simply on the formal character of the law but on "real world" circumstances, such as the actual economic impact of the regulation or the actual motivation of Congress.

The *Lochner*-era Court is often accused of excessive formalism. In *E.C. Knight*, for example, the Court focused exclusively on the fact that the activity challenged under the Sherman Act involved monopolization of manufacturing facilities, not interstate commercial transactions—a formal aspect of the regulation at issue. It did not give weight to (although it was certainly aware of) the "realistic" certainty that a monopoly over manufacturing would profoundly alter the interstate market for sugar sales to consumers. The formalist approach to the Commerce Clause thus tended to constrain Congress's power more severely than a realist approach would have done.

The situation is more complicated, however, than this easy equation of formalism with narrow national power would suggest. In the social regulation cases, for example, the issue is whether Congress may use its power over interstate transport to pursue ends that have little to do with commerce, such as the suppression of lotteries. (This sort of regulation seems to violate *McCulloch*'s prohibition on *pretextual* uses of the enumerated powers, doesn't it?) Justice Holmes's dissent in *Hammer* gives a formalist answer: As long as what the federal law formally does is restrict interstate transport, we don't ask what the motive was or whether the law would have a regulatory effect *within* the state. The majority's more realist approach, on the other hand, is more restrictive of federal power precisely because the Court broadens its focus to take in what actually happens in the world.

How important is it for a court to be consistent in taking a formalist or realist approach to the law? Which approach do you prefer?

6.   Finally, pay attention to the voting line-ups in each of the cases. For much of the pre-1937 period, the Court's conservative "Four Horsemen" (McReynolds, Sutherland, Van Devanter, and Butler) were joined by one or both of the two more moderate justices (Hughes and Roberts) in reining in national power, while the more liberal justices (especially Brandeis and Cardozo) voted for a broader construction of Congress's authority. But notice that in *Schechter*—a case that caused a political firestorm by striking down

---

[23] For a helpful discussion, see http://legaltheorylexicon.blogspot.com/2005/05/legal-theory-lexicon-043-formalism-and.html.

a key piece of early New Deal legislation—the Court is unanimous in saying that Congress had gone too far. This demonstrates that, unlike the situation on the contemporary Supreme Court, *all* the justices were committed to the idea that the national government is one of enumerated powers only and judges should enforce the limits of those powers with a fair degree of rigor.

SECTION 5.3   THE JUDICIAL REVOLUTION OF 1937

Conflict between the Supreme Court and the national political branches intensified after the election of President Franklin Delano Roosevelt in 1932. With the support of large Democratic majorities in Congress, Roosevelt launched "a New Deal for the American People," consisting of a sweeping expansion of government regulation and benefits designed to ameliorate and bring an end to the effects of the economic Depression that had begun in 1929. The Court blocked a number of these initiatives, particularly on grounds of the commerce clause and non-delegation—the two grounds that are uniquely concerned with *federal* legislation. (We will discuss the nondelegation doctrine, which holds that Congress may not delegate authority to make legal rules to other actors, such as administrative agencies, in Chapter Thirteen.)

This Section is concerned primarily with the battle between the Court and the President over the New Deal's constitutional validity and the Court's right to decide that question. But it is worth pausing a moment to consider the New Deal itself, as Roosevelt's legislative program changed the broader "constitution" of American government and society in ways that the relevant judicial opinions only dimly reflect. David Kennedy has noted that "[i]nto the five years of the New Deal was crowded more social and institutional change than into virtually any comparable compass of time in the nation's past."[24] Professor Kennedy summarizes the pattern of New Deal reform "in a single word: security— security for vulnerable individuals, to be sure . . . but security for capitalists and consumers, for workers and employers, for corporations and farms and homeowners and bankers and builders as well. Job security, life-cycle security, financial security, market security—however it might be defined, achieving security was the leitmotif of virtually everything the New Deal attempted."[25]

Hence the New Deal sought to stabilize financial markets through the Glass-Steagall Banking Act of 1933, which stopped "runs" on banks by insuring their deposits, and the Securities Exchange Acts of 1933 and 1934, which protected investors. It stabilized the housing sector as well by providing uniform appraisal and construction standards, insuring home loans, and creating a market for resale of mortgages. In other sectors, like agriculture, the New Deal applied blunter instruments of

---

[24]   DAVID KENNEDY, FREEDOM FROM FEAR: THE AMERICAN PEOPLE IN DEPRESSION AND WAR, 1929–1945, at 363 (2005).

[25]   *Id.* at 365.

subsidies and limits on competition; hence, the Civil Aeronautics Board, Interstate Commerce Commission, Federal Communications Commission, Federal Power Commission, and Federal Trade Commissions all sought to manage, i.e., limit, destructive competition in the industries under their jurisdiction. In the labor market, the Government prohibited child labor, guaranteed a minimum wage, and promoted labor peace by protecting unions and establishing an orderly forum, in the National Labor Relations Board, for resolving labor disputes. It also directly provided millions of out-of-work Americans with jobs through the Civilian Conservation Corps, the Works Progress Administration, and other agencies. And of course the Social Security Act, which one Roosevelt biographer described as "the most important single piece of social legislation in all American history,"[26] provided security to millions more Americans confronting old age. One result was that "ever after, Americans assumed that the federal government had not merely a role, but a major responsibility, in ensuring the health of the economy and the welfare of citizens. That simple but momentous shift in perception was the newest thing in all the New Deal, and the most consequential too."[27] It would have a profound effect on constitutional law.

One of the key decisions invalidating New Deal legislation was *Schechter Poultry*, included in the last assignment, which struck down the National Industrial Recovery Act. The Court followed *Schechter* with *Carter v. Carter Coal Co.*,[28] which struck down the Bituminous Coal Conservation Act of 1935—a far more important statute than the NIRA— on Commerce Clause grounds. The Court likewise invalidated the Agricultural Adjustment Act of 1933 as outside Congress's *taxing* power in *United States v. Butler*,[29] and the reasoning of the opinion suggested that the Social Security Act of 1935—a centerpiece of the New Deal program—might also be in danger.

On the Due Process or Freedom of Contract side, decisions like *Nebbia v. New York* had seemed to suggest a more tolerant judicial stance toward economic regulation. But two years later, in *Morehead v. New York ex rel. Tipaldo*,[30] the Court reaffirmed its hard-line freedom of contract stance from *Adkins* by invalidating New York's minimum wage law for women. President Roosevelt remarked that, by precluding the states from doing what the Court's Commerce Clause had already forbidden Congress to do, *Tipaldo* effectively marked off a "no man's land where no Government—State or Federal—can function." [31] As one

---

[26] Quoted in *id.* at 273.

[27] KENNEDY, *supra* note 17, at 377.

[28] 298 U.S. 238 (1936).

[29] 297 U.S. 1 (1936).

[30] 298 U.S. 587 (1936).

[31] Quoted in WILLIAM E. LEUCHTENBERG, THE SUPREME COURT REBORN: THE CONSTITUTIONAL REVOLUTION IN THE AGE OF ROOSEVELT 106 (1995).

academic put it, "[t]he New York Minimum Wage decision . . . convinced even the most reverent that five stubborn old men had planted themselves squarely in the path of progress."[32]

After his sweeping re-election victory in 1936, President Roosevelt unveiled a plan to overcome the Supreme Court's resistance to his program by appointing a raft of justices friendly to the New Deal.

Franklin Delano Roosevelt, Fireside Chat on Reorganization of the Judiciary
March 9, 1937

My friends, last Thursday I described in detail certain economic problems which everyone admits now face the nation. For the many messages which have come to me after that speech, and which it is physically impossible to answer individually, I take this means of saying thank you. Tonight, sitting at my desk in the White House, I make my first radio report to the people in my second term of office. . . .

In 1933 you and I knew that we must never let our economic system get completely out of joint again—that we could not afford to take the risk of another Great Depression. We also became convinced that the only way to avoid a repetition of those dark days was to have a government with power to prevent and to cure the abuses and the inequalities which had thrown that system out of joint. We then began a program of remedying those abuses and inequalities-to give balance and stability to our economic system, to make it bomb-proof against the causes of 1929. . . . To complete our program of protection in time . . . we cannot delay one moment in making certain that our national government has power to carry through. . . .

The American people have learned from the depression. For in the last three national elections an overwhelming majority of them voted a mandate that the Congress and the president begin the task of providing that protection—not after long years of debate, but now.

The courts, however, have cast doubts on the ability of the elected Congress to protect us against catastrophe by meeting squarely our modern social and economic conditions. We are at a crisis, a crisis in our ability to proceed with that protection. It is a quiet crisis. There are no lines of depositors outside closed banks. But to the farsighted it is far-reaching in its possibilities of injury to America.

I want to talk with you very simply tonight about the need for present action in this crisis—the need to meet the unanswered challenge of one-third of a nation ill-nourished, ill-clad, ill-housed. . . .

I hope that you have re-read the Constitution of the United States in these past few weeks. Like the Bible, it ought to be read again and

---

[32] ALPHEUS T. MASON, HARLAN FISKE STONE: PILLAR OF THE LAW 438 (1956).

again. It is an easy document to understand when you remember that it was called into being because the Articles of Confederation . . . showed the need of a national government with power enough to handle national problems. In its Preamble, the Constitution states that it was intended to form a more perfect union and promote the general welfare; and the powers given to the Congress to carry out those purposes can best be described by saying that they were all the powers needed to meet each and every problem which then had a national character and which could not be met by merely local action.

But the framers of the Constitution went further. Having in mind that in succeeding generations many other problems then undreamed of would become national problems, they gave to the Congress the ample broad powers "to levy taxes . . . and provide for the common defense and general welfare of the United States." That, my friends, is what I honestly believe to have been the clear and underlying purpose of the patriots who wrote a federal Constitution to create a national government with national power, intended as they said, "to form a more perfect union . . . for ourselves and our posterity."

For nearly twenty years there was no conflict between the Congress and the Court. Then in 1803 Congress passed a statute which the Court said violated an express provision of the Constitution. The Court claimed the power to declare it unconstitutional and did so declare it. But a little later the Court itself admitted that it was an extraordinary power to exercise and through Mr. Justice Washington laid down this limitation upon it: he said, "It is but a decent respect due to the wisdom, the integrity and the patriotism of the legislative body, by which any law is passed, to presume in favor of its validity until its violation of the Constitution is proved beyond all reasonable doubt."

But since the rise of the modern movement for social and economic progress through legislation, the Court has more and more often and more and more boldly asserted a power to veto laws passed by the Congress and by state legislatures in complete disregard of this original limitation which I have just read. In the last four years the sound rule of giving statutes the benefit of all reasonable doubt has been cast aside. The Court has been acting not as a judicial body, but as a policymaking body.

When the Congress has sought to stabilize national agriculture, to improve the conditions of labor, to safeguard business against unfair competition, to protect our national resources, and in many other ways, to serve our clearly national needs, the majority of the Court has been assuming the power to pass on the wisdom of these acts of the Congress— and to approve or disapprove the public policy written into these laws.

That is not only my accusation. It is the accusation of most distinguished justices of the present Supreme Court. I have not the time to quote to you all the language used by dissenting justices in many of these cases. But in the case holding the Railroad Retirement Act unconstitutional, for instance, Chief Justice Hughes said in a dissenting opinion that the majority opinion was "a departure from sound principles," and placed "an unwarranted limitation upon the commerce clause." And three other justices agreed with him.

In the case of holding the AAA unconstitutional, Justice Stone said of the majority opinion that it was a "tortured construction of the Constitution." And two other justices agreed with him. In the case holding the New York minimum wage law unconstitutional, Justice Stone said that the majority were actually reading into the Constitution their own "personal economic predilections," and that if the legislative power is not left free to choose the methods of solving the problems of poverty, subsistence, and health of large numbers in the community, then "government is to be rendered impotent." And two other justices agreed with him.

In the face of these dissenting opinions, there is no basis for the claim made by some members of the Court that something in the Constitution has compelled them regretfully to thwart the will of the people. In the face of such dissenting opinions, it is perfectly clear that, as Chief Justice Hughes has said, "We are under a Constitution, but the Constitution is what the judges say it is."

The Court in addition to the proper use of its judicial functions has improperly set itself up as a third house of the Congress—a super-legislature, as one of the justices has called it—reading into the Constitution words and implications which are not there, and which were never intended to be there. We have, therefore, reached the point as a nation where we must take action to save the Constitution from the Court and the Court from itself. We must find a way to take an appeal from the Supreme Court to the Constitution itself. We want a Supreme Court which will do justice under the Constitution and not over it. In our courts we want a government of laws and not of men.

I want—as all Americans want—an independent judiciary as proposed by the framers of the Constitution. That means a Supreme Court that will enforce the Constitution as written, that will refuse to amend the Constitution by the arbitrary exercise of judicial power—in other words by judicial say-so. It does not mean a judiciary so independent that it can deny the existence of facts which are universally recognized.

How then could we proceed to perform the mandate given us? It was said in last year's Democratic platform, and here are the words, "if these problems cannot be effectively solved within the Constitution, we shall seek such clarifying amendments as will assure the power to enact those laws, adequately to regulate commerce, protect public health and safety, and safeguard economic security." In their words, we said we would seek an amendment only if every other possible means by legislation were to fail.

When I commenced to review the situation with the problem squarely before me, I came by a process of elimination to the conclusion that, short of amendments, the only method which was clearly constitutional, and would at the same time carry out other much needed reforms, was to infuse new blood into all our courts. We must have men worthy and equipped to carry out impartial justice. But, at the same time, we must have judges who will bring to the courts a present-day sense of the Constitution—judges who will retain in the courts the judicial functions of a court, and reject the legislative powers which the courts have today assumed.

It is well for us to remember that in forty-five out of the forty-eight states of the Union, judges are chosen not for life but for a period of years. In many states judges must retire at the age of seventy. Congress has provided financial security by offering life pensions at full pay for federal judges on all courts who are willing to retire at seventy. In the case of Supreme Court justices, that pension is $20,000 a year. But all federal judges, once appointed, can, if they choose, hold office for life, no matter how old they may get to be.

What is my proposal? It is simply this: whenever a judge or justice of any federal court has reached the age of seventy and does not avail himself of the opportunity to retire on a pension, a new member shall be appointed by the president then in office, with the approval, as required by the Constitution, of the Senate of the United States.

That plan has two chief purposes. By bringing into the judicial system a steady and continuing stream of new and younger blood, I hope, first, to make the administration of all federal justice, from the bottom to the top, speedier and, therefore, less costly; secondly, to bring to the decision of social and economic problems younger men who have had personal experience and contact with modern facts and circumstances under which average men have to live and work. This plan will save our national Constitution from hardening of the judicial arteries. The number of judges to be appointed would depend wholly on the decision of present judges now over seventy, or those who would subsequently reach the age of seventy. . . .

There is nothing novel or radical about this idea. It seeks to maintain the federal bench in full vigor. It has been discussed and approved by many persons of high authority ever since a similar proposal passed the House of Representatives in 1869.

Why was the age fixed at seventy? Because the laws of many states, and the practice of the civil service, the regulations of the Army and Navy, and the rules of many of our universities and of almost every great private business enterprise, commonly fix the retirement age at seventy years or less. . . .

Those opposing this plan have sought to arouse prejudice and fear by crying that I am seeking to "pack" the Supreme Court and that a baneful precedent will be established. What do they mean by the words "packing the Supreme Court?" Let me answer this question with a bluntness that will end all honest misunderstanding of my purposes.

If by that phrase "packing the Court" it is charged that I wish to place on the bench spineless puppets who would disregard the law and would decide specific cases as I wished them to be decided, I make this answer: that no president fit for his office would appoint, and no Senate of honorable men fit for their office would confirm, that kind of appointees to the Supreme Court.

But if by that phrase the charge is made that I would appoint and the Senate would confirm justices worthy to sit beside present members of the Court, who understand modern conditions, that I will appoint justices who will not undertake to override the judgment of the Congress on legislative policy, that I will appoint justices who will act as justices and not as legislators—if the appointment of such justices can be called "packing the Courts," then I say that I and with me the vast majority of the American people favor doing just that thing—now.

Is it a dangerous precedent for the Congress to change the number of the justices? The Congress has always had, and will have, that power. The number of justices has been changed several times before, in the administrations of John Adams and Thomas Jefferson—both of them signers of the Declaration of Independence—in the administrations of Andrew Jackson, Abraham Lincoln, and Ulysses S. Grant. I suggest only the addition of justices to the bench in accordance with a clearly defined principle relating to a clearly defined age limit. Fundamentally, if in the future, America cannot trust the Congress it elects to refrain from abuse of our constitutional usages, democracy will have failed far beyond the importance to democracy of any kind of precedent concerning the judiciary. . . .

It is the clear intention of our public policy to provide for a constant flow of new and younger blood into the judiciary. . . . Until my first term practically every president of the United States in our history had appointed at least one member of the Supreme Court. . . . But chance and the disinclination of individuals to leave the Supreme bench have now given us a Court in which five justices will be over seventy-five years of age before next June and one over seventy. Thus a sound public policy has been defeated. . . .

[W]e cannot yield our constitutional destiny to the personal judgment of a few men who, being fearful of the future, would deny us the necessary means of dealing with the present. This plan of mine is no attack on the Court; it seeks to restore the Court to its rightful and historic place in our system of constitutional government and to have it resume its high task of building anew on the Constitution "a system of living law." The Court itself can best undo what the Court has done.

I have thus explained to you the reasons that lie behind our efforts to secure results by legislation within the Constitution. I hope that thereby the difficult process of constitutional amendment may be rendered unnecessary. But let us examine that process.

There are many types of amendment proposed. Each one is radically different from the other. But there is no substantial group within the Congress or outside the Congress who are agreed on any single amendment. I believe that it would take months or years to get substantial agreement upon the type and language of an amendment. It would take months and years thereafter to get a two-thirds majority in favor of that amendment in both houses of the Congress.

Then would come the long course of ratification by three-quarters of all the states. No amendment which any powerful economic interests or the leaders of any powerful political party have had reason to oppose has ever been ratified within anything like a reasonable time. And remember that thirteen states which contain only 5 percent of the voting population can block ratification even though the thirty-five states with 95 percent of the population are in favor of it. . . .

And remember one thing more. Even if an amendment were passed, and even if in the years to come it were to be ratified, its meaning would depend upon the kind of justices who would be sitting on the Supreme Court bench. For an amendment, like the rest of the Constitution, is what the justices say it is rather than what its framers or you might hope it is.

This proposal of mine will not infringe in the slightest upon the civil or religious liberties so dear to every American. My record as governor and as president proves my devotion to those liberties. You who know me can have no fear that I would tolerate the destruction by any branch of government of any part of our heritage of freedom. . . .

I am in favor of action through legislation: First, because I believe it can be passed at this session of the Congress. Second, because it will provide a reinvigorated, liberal-minded judiciary necessary to furnish quicker and cheaper justice from bottom to top. Third, because it will provide a series of federal courts willing to enforce the Constitution as written, and unwilling to assert legislative powers by writing into it their own political and economic policies.

During the past half-century the balance of power between the three great branches of the federal government has been tipped out of balance by the courts in direct contradiction of the high purposes of the framers of the Constitution. It is my purpose to restore that balance. You who know me will accept my solemn assurance that in a world in which democracy is under attack, I seek to make American democracy succeed. You and I will do our part.

NOTE ON COURT-PACKING AND THE "SWITCH IN TIME"

1.   President Roosevelt's court-packing plan ignited a firestorm of criticism, notwithstanding FDR's popularity and the general *un*popularity of the Court's resistance to the New Deal. What do you think of the scheme? As he noted, it would not have been the first time that Congress altered the size of the Supreme Court; Presidents Adams, Jefferson, Jackson, Lincoln, and Grant all did so in the past. At least some of those earlier alterations were designed to influence the results of future decisions. Is this sort of action a necessary check on the broad power of judicial review or an illegitimate threat to judicial independence?

Many prominent Democrats at the time agreed with FDR that something needed to be done about the Court, but found the President's proposal disingenuous, both because it was originally pitched as a "neutral" effort to help the aging justices cope with their workload and because it proceeded by way of ordinary legislation. These opponents of court-packing proposed a variety of constitutional amendments as alternatives to the President's bill. Some amendments would have required decisions striking down national legislation to be reached by six-vote majorities; others would have allowed the Congress to overrule such decisions by a supermajority vote. Would these amendment options have been preferable to the President's approach?

2.   Before Congress could vote on the court-packing plan, the Court took the wind out of its sails. First, Chief Justice Hughes (a respected moderate who generally voted to uphold economic regulation) sent a letter to the Senate Judiciary Committee noting that the Court was fully abreast of its work—thereby giving the lie to FDR's claim that the aging Court needed an infusion of fresh blood to help it keep up. Justices Van Devanter and Brandeis—the respective leaders of the Court's conservative and liberal wings—co-signed the letter. More importantly, a week after the Hughes letter the Court began issuing a series of landmark rulings abandoning its opposition to the New Deal and state economic regulation.

In *West Coast Hotel v. Parrish*, the Court overruled *Adkins* and upheld a state minimum wage law against a Due Process challenge. Next, in *National Labor Relations Board v. Jones & Laughlin Steel Corp.*, the Court rejected a Commerce Clause challenge to the National Labor Relations Act, a centerpiece of the New Deal. Finally, in *Steward Machine Co. v. Davis*, 301 U.S. 548 (1937), the Court upheld the unemployment compensation provisions of the Social Security Act of 1935, rejecting an argument under *United States v. Butler* that the law exceeded Congress's power to tax. In each of these cases, Justice Owen Roberts—who had voted with the Four Horsemen in the key 1935 decisions challenging the New Deal—switched to a pro-regulatory stance. This would prove to be the famous "switch in time that saved nine."

Although FDR continued to press the court-packing legislation, the Senate Judiciary Committee issued a scathing report calling the bill "a needless, futile and utterly dangerous abandonment of constitutional principle . . . without precedent or justification."[33] All hope for the bill vanished when the bill's floor manager, Senate Majority Leader Joseph Robinson, was found dead of a heart attack in his apartment. The Senate rejected the proposal a week later. FDR ultimately got his justices, however. Willis Van Devanter had announced his retirement in May, and the rest of the Horsemen were gone by 1940—as were Cardozo and Brandeis, with Hughes following in 1941. Roosevelt ultimately appointed nine justices to the Court—all committed New Dealers.

Just as the defeat of FDR's court-packing plan masked a victory on the substantive law, however, that victory also had its Pyrrhic element. As Henry Wallace, FDR's second vice president, observed, "the whole New Deal really went up in smoke as a result of the Supreme Court fight."[34] The President had expended so much legislative capital on the court-packing plan, and aroused so much distrust, that he would enjoy only one more major legislative victory (the Fair Labor Standards Act, with its minimum wage and maximum hours provisions) after the plan's defeat.

3.   The issues raised by FDR's court-packing scheme are very much still with us. In 2004, a Republican Congressman from Kentucky introduced HR 3920, the Congressional Accountability for Judicial Activism Act of 2004, which would have allowed Congress to override Supreme Court decisions holding an Act of Congress unconstitutional by a 2/3 vote of each house. (It is unlikely this act, if passed, would have been constitutional, but similar measures have been proposed as constitutional amendments.) Even more recently, a leading biographer of John Marshall proposed that a future Democratic administration should consider packing the Supreme Court to prevent the Court from drifting to the Right under Chief Justice John Roberts:

> If the current five-man majority persists in thumbing its nose at popular values, the election of a Democratic president and Congress could provide a corrective. It requires only a majority vote in both houses to add a justice or two. Chief Justice John Roberts and his conservative colleagues might do well to bear in mind that the roll call of presidents who have used this option includes not just Roosevelt but also Adams, Jefferson, Jackson, Lincoln and Grant.[35]

Are these sorts of proposals sensible? Legitimate?

Most lawyers, judges, academics, and even politicians would probably say "no." But that fact is interesting in itself, isn't it? After all, court-packing is rather clearly permitted by the constitutional text, and there are no clear judicial precedents against it. Does the general sense that court-packing is illegitimate suggest that our history has given rise to certain "conventions"

---

[33] Senate Committee on the Judiciary, *Reorganization of the Federal Judiciary*, S. Rep. No. 711, 75th Congress, 1st Session, 1 (1937).

[34] Quoted in POWE, *supra* note 5, at 213.

[35] Jean Edward Smith, *Stacking the Court*, N.Y. TIMES, July 26, 2007, at A19.

that restrain political actors from doing things that the text plainly allows?[36] Other examples might include the general sense that Article III judges may not be impeached based on disagreement with their rulings, and the unwritten rule—followed until FDR broke it in 1940—that a President should not run for a third term. How do such conventions arise? What happens if they are violated?

West Coast Hotel Co. v. Parrish

300 U.S. 379 (1937)

■ MR. CHIEF JUSTICE HUGHES delivered the opinion of the Court.

This case presents the question of the constitutional validity of the minimum wage law of the State of Washington. The Act, entitled "Minimum Wages for Women," authorizes the fixing of minimum wages for women and minors. Further provisions required the Commission to ascertain the wages and conditions of labor of women and minors within the State. Public hearings were to be held. If after investigation the Commission found that in any occupation, trade or industry the wages paid to women were "inadequate to supply them necessary cost of living and to maintain the workers in health," the Commission was empowered to call a conference of representatives of employers and employees together with disinterested persons representing the public. The conference was to recommend to the Commission, on its request, an estimate of a minimum wage adequate for the purpose above stated, and on the approval of such a recommendation it became the duty of the Commission to issue an obligatory order fixing minimum wages. . . .

The appellant conducts a hotel. The appellee Elsie Parrish was employed as a chambermaid and (with her husband) brought this suit to recover the difference between the wages paid her and the minimum wage fixed pursuant to the state law. The minimum wage was $14.50 per week of 48 hours. The appellant challenged the act as repugnant to the due process clause of the Fourteenth Amendment of the Constitution of the United States. The Supreme Court of the State, reversing the trial court, sustained the statute and directed judgment for the plaintiffs. The case is here on appeal.

The appellant relies upon . . . *Adkins v. Children's Hospital*, which held invalid the District of Columbia Minimum Wage Act . . . under the due process clause of the Fifth Amendment. On the argument at bar, counsel for the appellees attempted to distinguish the *Adkins* case upon the ground that the appellee was employed in a hotel and that the business of an innkeeper was affected with a public interest. That effort at distinction is obviously futile. . . .

---

[36] *See generally* Curtis A. Bradley & Neil Siegel, *Historical Gloss, Constitutional Conventions, and the Judicial Separation of Powers*, 105 GEO. L. J. 255 (2017).

We are of the opinion that this ruling of the state court demands on our part a reexamination of the *Adkins* case. The importance of the question, in which many States having similar laws are concerned, the close division by which the decision in the *Adkins* case was reached, and the economic conditions which have supervened, . . . make it not only appropriate, but we think imperative, that in deciding the present case the subject should receive fresh consideration. . . .

In each case the violation alleged by those attacking minimum wage regulation for women is deprivation of freedom of contract. What is this freedom? The Constitution does not speak of freedom of contract. It speaks of liberty and prohibits the deprivation of liberty without due process of law. In prohibiting that deprivation the Constitution does not recognize an absolute and uncontrollable liberty. . . . [T]he liberty safeguarded is liberty in a social organization which requires the protection of law against the evils which menace the health, safety, morals and welfare of the people. Liberty under the Constitution is thus necessarily subject to the restraints of due process, and regulation which is reasonable in relation to its subject and is adopted in the interests of the community is due process. . . .

This power under the Constitution to restrict freedom of contract has had many illustrations. That it may be exercised in the public interest with respect to contracts between employer and employee is undeniable. Thus statutes have been sustained limiting employment in underground mines and smelters to eight hours a day (*Holden v. Hardy*); in requiring redemption in cash of store orders or other evidences of indebtedness issued in the payment of wages (*Knoxville Iron Co. v. Harbison,* 183 U.S. 13); in forbidding the payment of seamen's wages in advance (*Patterson v. Bark Eudora,* 190 U.S. 169); in making it unlawful to contract to pay miners employed at quantity rates upon the basis of screened coal instead of the weight of the coal as originally produced in the mine (*McLean v. Arkansas,* 211 U.S. 539); in prohibiting contracts limiting liability for injuries to employees (*Chicago, B. & Q. R. Co. v. McGuire,* 219 U.S. 549); in limiting hours of work of employees in manufacturing establishments (*Bunting v. Oregon,* 243 U.S. 426); and in maintaining workmen's compensation laws (*New York Central R. Co. v. White,* 243 U.S. 188; *Mountain Timber Co. v. Washington,* 243 U.S. 219). In dealing with the relation of employer and employed, the legislature has necessarily a wide field of discretion in order that there may be suitable protection of health and safety, and that peace and good order may be promoted through regulations designed to insure wholesome conditions of work and freedom from oppression.

The point that has been strongly stressed that adult employees should be deemed competent to make their own contracts was decisively met nearly forty years ago in *Holden v. Hardy,* where we pointed out the inequality in the footing of the parties. We said:

"The legislature has also recognized the fact, which the experience of legislators in many States has corroborated, that the proprietors of these establishments and their operatives do not stand upon an equality, and that their interests are, to a certain extent, conflicting. The former naturally desire to obtain as much labor as possible from their employees, while the latter are often induced by the fear of discharge to conform to regulations which their judgment, fairly exercised, would pronounce to be detrimental to their health or strength. In other words, the proprietors lay down the rules and the laborers are practically constrained to obey them. In such cases self-interest is often an unsafe guide, and the legislature may properly interpose its authority." . . .

It is manifest that this established principle is peculiarly applicable in relation to the employment of women in whose protection the State has a special interest. That phase of the subject received elaborate consideration in *Muller v. Oregon* 208 U.S. 412 (1908), where the constitutional authority of the State to limit the working hours of women was sustained. . . .

The minimum wage to be paid under the Washington statute is fixed after full consideration by representatives of employers, employees and the public. It may be assumed that the minimum wage is fixed in consideration of the services that are performed in the particular occupations under normal conditions. . . . The statement of Mr. Justice Holmes in the *Adkins* case is pertinent: "This statute does not compel anybody to pay anything. It simply forbids employment at rates below those fixed as the minimum requirement of health and right living. It is safe to assume that women will not be employed at even the lowest wages allowed unless they earn them, or unless the employer's business can sustain the burden." . . .

We think that the views thus expressed are sound and that the decision in the *Adkins* case was a departure from the true application of the principles governing the regulation by the State of the relation of employer and employed. Those principles have been reenforced by our subsequent decisions [citing *Nebbia v. New York*] . . .

[W]e find it impossible to reconcile [*Adkins*] with these well-considered declarations. What can be closer to the public interest than the health of women and their protection from unscrupulous and overreaching employers? And if the protection of women is a legitimate end of the exercise of state power, how can it be said that the requirement of the payment of a minimum wage fairly fixed in order to meet the very necessities of existence is not an admissible means to that end? The legislature of the State was clearly entitled to consider the situation of women in employment, the fact that they are in the class receiving the least pay, that their bargaining power is relatively weak, and that they are the ready victims of those who would take advantage of their necessitous circumstances. The legislature was entitled to adopt measures to reduce the evils of the "sweating system," the exploiting of workers at wages so low as to be insufficient to meet the bare cost of living, thus making their very helplessness the occasion of a most injurious competition. . . . The adoption of similar requirements by many States evidences a deepseated conviction both as to the presence of the evil and as to the means adapted to check it. . . . Even if the wisdom of the policy be regarded as debatable and its effects uncertain, still the legislature is entitled to its judgment.

There is an additional and compelling consideration which recent economic experience has brought into a strong light. The exploitation of a class of workers . . . is not only detrimental to their health and well being but casts a direct burden for their support upon the community. What these workers lose in wages the taxpayers are called upon to pay. The bare cost of living must be met. We may take judicial notice of the unparalleled demands for relief which arose during the recent period of depression and still continue to an alarming extent despite the degree of economic recovery which has been achieved. It is unnecessary to cite official statistics to establish what is of common knowledge through the length and breadth of the land. . . . The community is not bound to provide what is in effect a subsidy for unconscionable employers. . . .

Our conclusion is that the case of *Adkins v. Children's Hospital* should be, and it is, overruled. The judgment of the Supreme Court of the State of Washington is

Affirmed.

■ MR. JUSTICE SUTHERLAND, dissenting:

MR. JUSTICE VAN DEVANTER, MR. JUSTICE MCREYNOLDS, MR. JUSTICE BUTLER and I think the judgment of the court below should be reversed. . . .

[W]here the written Constitution . . . is the supreme law, some agency, of necessity, must have the power to say the final word as to the validity of a statute assailed as unconstitutional. The Constitution makes it clear that the power has been entrusted to this court when the question arises in a controversy within its jurisdiction; and so long as the power remains there, its exercise cannot be avoided without betrayal of the trust.

[T]he meaning of the Constitution does not change with the ebb and flow of economic events. . . . [T]o say, if that be intended, that the words of the Constitution mean today what they did not mean when written . . . is to rob that instrument of the essential element which continues it in force as the people have made it until they, and not their official agents, have made it otherwise. . . . If the Constitution, intelligently and reasonably construed in the light of these principles, stands in the way of desirable legislation, the blame must rest upon that instrument, and not upon the court for enforcing it according to its terms. The remedy in that situation . . . is to amend the Constitution. . . .

In support of minimum-wage legislation it has been urged, on the one hand, that great benefits will result in favor of underpaid labor, and, on the other hand, that the danger of such legislation is that the minimum will tend to become the maximum and thus bring down the earnings of the more efficient toward the level of the less-efficient employees. But with these speculations we have nothing to do. We are concerned only with the question of constitutionality.

That the clause of the Fourteenth Amendment which forbids a state to deprive any person of life, liberty or property without due process of law includes freedom of contract is so well settled as to be no longer open to question. Nor reasonably can it be disputed that contracts of employment of labor are included in the rule. . . .

[M]inimum-wage legislation such as that here involved does not deal with any business charged with a public interest, or with public work, or with a temporary emergency, or with the character, methods or periods of wage payments, or with hours of labor, or with the protection of persons under legal disability, or with the prevention of fraud. It is, simply and exclusively, a law fixing wages for adult women who are legally as capable of contracting for themselves as men, and cannot be sustained unless upon principles apart from those involved in cases already decided by the court. . . .

The Washington statute, like the one for the District of Columbia [in *Adkins*], fixes minimum wages for adult women. Adult men and their employers are left free to bargain as they please; and it is a significant and an important fact that all state statutes to which our attention has been called are of like character. The common-law rules restricting the power of women to make contracts have, under our system, long since practically disappeared. Women today stand upon a legal and political equality with men. There is no longer any reason why they should be put in different classes in respect of their legal right to make contracts; nor should they be denied, in effect, the right to compete with men for work paying lower wages which men may be willing to accept. And it is an arbitrary exercise of the legislative power to do so. . . .

National Labor Relations Board v. Jones & Laughlin Steel Corp.

301 U.S. 1 (1937)

■ MR. CHIEF JUSTICE HUGHES delivered the opinion of the Court.

In a proceeding under the National Labor Relations Act of 1935, the National Labor Relations Board found that the respondent, Jones & Laughlin Steel Corporation, had violated the Act by engaging in unfair labor practices affecting commerce. The proceeding was instituted by the

Beaver Valley Lodge No. 200, affiliated with the Amalgamated Association of Iron, Steel and Tin Workers of America, a labor organization. The unfair labor practices charged were that the corporation was discriminating against members of the union with regard to hire and tenure of employment, and was coercing and intimidating its employees in order to interfere with their self-organization. The discriminatory and coercive action alleged was the discharge of certain employees.

The National Labor Relations Board, sustaining the charge, ordered the corporation to cease and desist from such discrimination and coercion, to offer reinstatement to ten of the employees named, to make good their losses in pay, and to post for thirty days notices that the corporation would not discharge or discriminate against members, or those desiring to become members, of the labor union. As the corporation failed to comply, the Board petitioned the Circuit Court of Appeals to enforce the order. The court denied the petition, holding that the order lay beyond the range of federal power. We granted certiorari.

The scheme of the National Labor Relations Act . . . may be briefly stated. The first section sets forth findings with respect to the injury to commerce resulting from the denial by employers of the right of employees to organize and from the refusal of employers to accept the procedure of collective bargaining. There follows a declaration that it is the policy of the United States to eliminate these causes of obstruction to the free flow of commerce. The Act then . . . creates the National Labor Relations Board and prescribes its organization. It sets forth the right of employees to self-organization and to bargain collectively through representatives of their own choosing. It defines "unfair labor practices." It lays down rules as to the representation of employees for the purpose of collective bargaining. The Board is empowered to prevent the described unfair labor practices affecting commerce and the Act prescribes the procedure to that end. . . .

[T]he respondent argues (1) that the Act is in reality a regulation of labor relations and not of interstate commerce; [and] (2) that the Act can have no application to the respondent's relations with its production employees because they are not subject to regulation by the federal government. . . .

The facts as to the nature and scope of the business of the Jones & Laughlin Steel Corporation . . . are not in dispute. The Labor Board has found: The corporation is organized under the laws of Pennsylvania and has its principal office at Pittsburgh. It is engaged in the business of manufacturing iron and steel in plants situated in Pittsburgh and nearby Aliquippa, Pennsylvania. It [is] the fourth largest producer of steel in the United States. With its subsidiaries . . . it is a completely integrated enterprise, owning and operating ore, coal and limestone properties, lake and river transportation facilities and terminal railroads located at its manufacturing plants. It owns or controls mines in Michigan and

Minnesota. It operates four ore steamships on the Great Lakes, used in the transportation of ore to its factories. It owns coal mines in Pennsylvania. It operates towboats and steam barges used in carrying coal to its factories. It owns limestone properties in various places in Pennsylvania and West Virginia. It owns the Monongahela connecting railroad which connects the plants of the Pittsburgh works and forms an interconnection with the Pennsylvania, New York Central and Baltimore and Ohio Railroad systems. It owns the Aliquippa and Southern Railroad Company which connects the Aliquippa works with the Pittsburgh and Lake Erie, part of the New York Central system. Much of its product is shipped to its warehouses in Chicago, Detroit, Cincinnati and Memphis,—to the last two places by means of its own barges and transportation equipment. In Long Island City, New York, and in New Orleans it operates structural steel fabricating shops in connection with the warehousing of semi-finished materials sent from its works. Through one of its wholly-owned subsidiaries it owns, leases and operates stores, warehouses and yards for the distribution of equipment and supplies for drilling and operating oil and gas wells and for pipe lines, refineries and pumping stations. It has sales offices in twenty cities in the United States and a wholly-owned subsidiary which is devoted exclusively to distributing its product in Canada. Approximately 75 per cent. of its product is shipped out of Pennsylvania.

[T]he Labor Board concluded that the works in Pittsburgh and Aliquippa "might be likened to the heart of a self-contained, highly integrated body. They draw in the raw materials from Michigan, Minnesota, West Virginia, Pennsylvania in part through arteries and by means controlled by the respondent; they transform the materials and then pump them out to all parts of the nation through the vast mechanism which the respondent has elaborated."

To carry on the activities of the entire steel industry, 33,000 men mine ore, 44,000 men mine coal, 4,000 men quarry limestone, 16,000 men manufacture coke, 343,000 men manufacture steel, and 83,000 men transport its product. Respondent has about 10,000 employees in its Aliquippa plant, which is located in a community of about 30,000 persons. . . .

[T]he employees in the Aliquippa plant whose discharge was the subject of the complaint . . . were active leaders in the labor union. . . . Two of the employees were motor inspectors; one was a tractor driver; three were crane operators; one was a washer in the coke plant; and three were laborers. . . . [T]he evidence supports the findings of the Board that respondent discharged these men "because of their union activity and for the purpose of discouraging membership in the union." We turn to the questions of law which respondent urges in contesting the validity and application of the Act.

First. The scope of the Act. The Act is challenged in its entirety as an attempt to regulate all industry, thus invading the reserved powers of the States over their local concerns. It is asserted that the references in the Act to interstate and foreign commerce are colorable at best; that the Act is not a true regulation of such commerce or of matters which directly affect it but on the contrary has the fundamental object of placing under the compulsory supervision of the federal government all industrial labor relations within the nation. . . .

If this conception of terms, intent and consequent inseparability were sound, the Act would necessarily fall by reason of the limitation upon the federal power which inheres in the constitutional grant, as well as because of the explicit reservation of the Tenth Amendment. *Schechter Corp. v. United States.* The authority of the federal government may not be pushed to such an extreme as to destroy the distinction, which the commerce clause itself establishes, between commerce "among the several States" and the internal concerns of a State. That distinction between what is national and what is local in the activities of commerce is vital to the maintenance of our federal system. . . .

We think it clear that the National Labor Relations Act may be construed so as to operate within the sphere of constitutional authority. The jurisdiction conferred upon the Board, and invoked in this instance, is found in § 10 (a), which . . . limits . . . the Board's authority [to] labor practices . . . "affecting commerce." . . . There can be no question that the commerce thus contemplated by the Act . . . is interstate and foreign commerce in the constitutional sense. The Act also defines the term "affecting commerce":

The term 'affecting commerce' means in commerce, or burdening or obstructing commerce or the free flow of commerce, or having led or tending to lead to a labor dispute burdening or obstructing commerce or the free flow of commerce.

This definition is one of exclusion as well as inclusion. The grant of authority to the Board does not purport to extend to the relationship between all industrial employees and employers. . . . It purports to reach only what may be deemed to burden or obstruct [interstate or foreign] commerce and, thus qualified, it must be construed as contemplating the exercise of control within constitutional bounds. It is a familiar principle that acts which directly burden or obstruct interstate or foreign commerce, or its free flow, are within the reach of the congressional power. Acts having that effect are not rendered immune because they grow out of labor disputes. It is the effect upon commerce, not the source of the injury, which is the criterion. Whether or not particular action does affect commerce in such a close and intimate fashion as to be subject to federal control, and hence to lie within the authority conferred upon the Board, is left by the statute to be determined as individual cases arise. We are thus to inquire whether in the instant case the constitutional boundary has been passed. . . .

Third. The application of the Act to employees engaged in production. . . . Respondent says that whatever may be said of employees engaged in interstate commerce, the industrial relations and activities in the manufacturing department of respondent's enterprise are not subject to federal regulation. The argument rests upon the proposition that manufacturing in itself is not commerce. *Schechter Corp. v. United States*; *Carter v. Carter Coal Co.*

The Government distinguishes these cases. . . . It is urged that [Respondents's] activities constitute a "stream" or "flow" of commerce, of which the Aliquippa manufacturing plant is the focal point, and that industrial strife at that point would cripple the entire movement. . . .

The congressional authority to protect interstate commerce from burdens and obstructions is not limited to transactions which can be deemed to be an essential part of a "flow" of interstate or foreign commerce. Burdens and obstructions may be due to injurious action springing from other sources. The fundamental principle is that the power to regulate commerce is the power to enact "all appropriate legislation" for "its protection and advancement"; to adopt measures "to promote its growth and insure its safety"; "to foster, protect, control and restrain." That power is plenary and may be exerted to protect interstate commerce "no matter what the source of the dangers which threaten it." Although activities may be intrastate in character when separately considered, if they have such a close and substantial relation to interstate commerce that their control is essential or appropriate to protect that commerce from burdens and obstructions, Congress cannot be denied the power to exercise that control. Undoubtedly the scope of this power must be considered in the light of our dual system of government and may not be extended so as to embrace effects upon interstate commerce so indirect and remote that to embrace them, in view of our complex society, would effectually obliterate the distinction between what is national and what is local and create a completely centralized government. The question is necessarily one of degree. "Whatever amounts to more or less constant practice, and threatens to obstruct or unduly to burden the freedom of interstate commerce is within the regulatory power of Congress under the commerce clause and it is primarily for Congress to consider and decide the fact of the danger and meet it."

That intrastate activities, by reason of close and intimate relation to interstate commerce, may fall within federal control is demonstrated in the case of carriers who are engaged in both interstate and intrastate transportation. There federal control has been found essential to secure the freedom of interstate traffic from interference or unjust discrimination and to promote the efficiency of the interstate service. *Shreveport Rate Cases.* . . .

The close and intimate effect which brings the subject within the reach of federal power may be due to activities in relation to productive industry although the industry when separately viewed is local. . . . It is thus apparent that the fact that the employees here concerned were engaged in production is not determinative. The question remains as to the effect upon interstate commerce of the labor practice involved. In the *Schechter* case, we found that the effect there was so remote as to be beyond the federal power. To find "immediacy or directness" there was to find it "almost everywhere," a result inconsistent with the maintenance of our federal system. In the *Carter* case, the Court was of the opinion that the provisions of the statute relating to production were invalid upon several grounds,—that there was improper delegation of legislative power, and that the requirements not only went beyond any sustainable measure of protection of interstate commerce but were also inconsistent with due process. These cases are not controlling here.

Fourth. Effects of the unfair labor practice in respondent's enterprise. . . . [T]he stoppage of [respondent's] operations by industrial strife would have a most serious effect upon interstate commerce. In view of respondent's far-flung activities, it is idle to say that the effect would be indirect or remote. It is obvious that it would be immediate and might be catastrophic. We are asked to shut our eyes to the plainest facts of our national life and to deal with the question of direct and indirect effects in an intellectual vacuum. Because there may be but indirect and remote effects upon interstate commerce in connection with a host of local enterprises throughout the country, it does not follow that other industrial activities do not have such a close and intimate relation to interstate commerce as to make the presence of industrial strife a matter of the most urgent national concern. When industries organize themselves on a national scale, making their relation to interstate commerce the dominant factor in their activities, how can it be maintained that their industrial labor relations constitute a forbidden field into which Congress may not enter when it is necessary to protect interstate commerce from the paralyzing consequences of industrial war? . . . [I]nterferences with that commerce must be appraised by a judgment that does not ignore actual experience.

Experience has abundantly demonstrated that the recognition of the right of employees to self-organization and to have representatives of their own choosing for the purpose of collective bargaining is often an essential condition of industrial peace. Refusal to confer and negotiate has been one of the most prolific causes of strife. This is such an outstanding fact in the history of labor disturbances that it is a proper subject of judicial notice and requires no citation of instances. . . .

These questions have frequently engaged the attention of Congress and have been the subject of many inquiries. The steel industry is one of the great basic industries of the United States, with ramifying activities affecting interstate commerce at every point. . . . [R]espondent's enterprise . . . presents in a most striking way the close and intimate relation which a manufacturing industry may have to interstate commerce and we have no doubt that Congress had constitutional authority to safeguard the right of respondent's employees to self-organization and freedom in the choice of representatives for collective bargaining.

Fifth. The means which the Act employs. Questions under the due process clause and other constitutional restrictions. Respondent asserts its right to conduct its business in an orderly manner without being subjected to arbitrary restraints. What we have said points to the fallacy in the argument. Employees have their correlative right to organize for the purpose of securing the redress of grievances and to promote agreements with employers relating to rates of pay and conditions of work. Restraint for the purpose of preventing an unjust interference with that right cannot be considered arbitrary or capricious . . .

Our conclusion is that the order of the Board was within its competency and that the Act is valid as here applied. . . .

Reversed.

■ **MR. JUSTICE MCREYNOLDS delivered the following dissenting opinion in the cases preceding:**

MR. JUSTICE VAN DEVANTER, MR. JUSTICE SUTHERLAND, MR. JUSTICE BUTLER and I are unable to agree with the decisions just announced. . . .

The Court, as we think, departs from well-established principles followed in *Schechter Corp. v. United States* and *Carter v. Carter Coal Co.* . . . No decision or judicial opinion to the contrary has been cited, and we find none. Every consideration brought forward to uphold the Act before us was applicable to support the Acts held unconstitutional in causes decided within two years. And the lower courts rightly deemed them controlling. . . .

The precise question for us to determine is whether in the circumstances disclosed Congress has power to authorize what the Labor Board commanded the respondents to do. . . . The record in Nos. 422–23—a typical case—plainly presents [the] essentials and we may properly base further discussion upon the circumstances there disclosed.

A relatively small concern caused raw material to be shipped to its plant at Richmond, Virginia, converted this into clothing, and thereafter shipped the product to points outside the state. A labor union sought members among the employees at the plant and obtained some. The Company's management opposed this effort, and in order to discourage it discharged eight who had become members. The business of the Company is so small that to close its factory would have no direct or material effect upon the volume of interstate commerce in clothing. The number of operatives who joined the union is not disclosed; the wishes of other employees are not shown; probability of a strike is not found.

The argument in support of the Board affirms: "Thus the validity of any specific application of the preventive measures of this Act depends upon whether industrial strife resulting from the practices in the particular enterprise under consideration would be of the character which Federal power could control if it occurred. If strife in that enterprise could be controlled, certainly it could be prevented."

Manifestly that view of Congressional power would extend it into almost every field of human industry. With striking lucidity, fifty years ago, *Kidd v. Pearson* declared: "If it be held that the term [commerce with foreign nations and among the several states] includes the regulation of all such manufactures as are intended to be the subject of commercial transactions in the future, it is impossible to deny that it would also include all productive industries that contemplate the same thing. The result would be that Congress would be invested, to the exclusion of the States, with the power to regulate, not only manufactures, but also agriculture, horticulture, stock raising, domestic fisheries, mining—in short, every branch of human industry." This doctrine found full approval in *United States v. E. C. Knight Co.*; *Schechter Poultry Corp. v. United States*, and *Carter v. Carter Coal Co.* . . .

Any effect on interstate commerce by the discharge of employees shown here, would be indirect and remote in the highest degree, as consideration of the facts will show. In No. 419 ten men out of ten thousand were discharged; in the other cases only a few. The immediate effect in the factory may be to create discontent among all those employed and a strike may follow, which, in turn, may result in reducing production, which ultimately may reduce the volume of goods moving in interstate commerce. By this chain of indirect and progressively remote events we finally reach the evil with which it is said the legislation under consideration undertakes to deal. A more remote and indirect interference with interstate commerce or a more definite invasion of the powers reserved to the states is difficult, if not impossible, to imagine.

The Constitution still recognizes the existence of states with indestructible powers; the Tenth Amendment was supposed to put them beyond controversy. . . .

There is no ground on which reasonably to hold that refusal by a manufacturer, whose raw materials come from states other than that of his factory and whose products are regularly carried to other states, to bargain collectively with employees in his manufacturing plant, directly affects interstate commerce. In such business, there is not one but two distinct movements or streams in interstate transportation. The first brings in raw material and there ends. Then follows manufacture, a separate and local activity. Upon completion of this, and not before, the second distinct movement or stream in interstate commerce begins and the products go to other states. Such is the common course for small as well as large industries. It is unreasonable and unprecedented to say the commerce clause confers upon Congress power to govern relations between employers and employees in these local activities. In *Schechter's* case we condemned as unauthorized by the commerce clause assertion of federal power in respect of commodities which had come to rest after interstate transportation. And, in *Carter's* case, we held Congress lacked power to regulate labor relations in respect of commodities before interstate commerce has begun.

It is gravely stated that experience teaches that if an employer discourages membership in "any organization of any kind" "in which employees participate, and which exists for the purpose in whole or in part of dealing with employers concerning grievances, labor disputes, wages, rates of pay, hours of employment or conditions of work," discontent may follow and this in turn may lead to a strike, and as the outcome of the strike there may be a block in the stream of interstate commerce. Therefore Congress may inhibit the discharge! Whatever effect any cause of discontent may ultimately have upon commerce is far too indirect to justify Congressional regulation. Almost anything— marriage, birth, death—may in some fashion affect commerce. . . .

The right to contract is fundamental and includes the privilege of selecting those with whom one is willing to assume contractual relations. This right is [also] unduly abridged by the Act now upheld. A private owner is deprived of power to manage his own property by freely selecting those to whom his manufacturing operations are to be entrusted. We think this cannot lawfully be done in circumstances like those here disclosed.

It seems clear to us that Congress has transcended the powers granted.

Wickard v. Filburn
317 U.S. 111 (1942)

■ MR. JUSTICE JACKSON delivered the opinion of the Court.

The appellee filed his complaint against the Secretary of Agriculture of the United States [and other officials]. He sought to enjoin enforcement against himself of the marketing penalty imposed by the amendment of May 26, 1941, to the Agricultural Adjustment Act of 1938, upon that part of his 1941 wheat crop which was available for marketing in excess of the marketing quota established for his farm. He also sought a declaratory judgment that the wheat marketing quota provisions of the Act as amended and applicable to him were unconstitutional because not sustainable under the Commerce Clause or consistent with the Due Process Clause of the Fifth Amendment. . . .

The appellee for many years past has owned and operated a small farm in Montgomery County, Ohio, maintaining a herd of dairy cattle, selling milk, raising poultry, and selling poultry and eggs. It has been his practice to raise a small acreage of winter wheat, sown in the Fall and harvested in the following July; to sell a portion of the crop; to feed part to poultry and livestock on the farm, some of which is sold; to use some in making flour for home consumption; and to keep the rest for the following seeding. The intended disposition of the crop here involved has not been expressly stated.

In July of 1940, pursuant to the Agricultural Adjustment Act of 1938, as then amended, there were established for the appellee's 1941 crop a wheat acreage allotment of 11.1 acres and a normal yield of 20.1 bushels of wheat an acre. He was given notice of such allotment in July of 1940, before the Fall planting of his 1941 crop of wheat, and again in July of 1941, before it was harvested. He sowed, however, 23 acres, and harvested from his 11.9 acres of excess acreage 239 bushels, which under the terms of the Act as amended on May 26, 1941, constituted farm marketing excess, subject to a penalty of 49 cents a bushel, or $117.11 in all. The appellee has not paid the penalty and he has not postponed or avoided it by storing the excess under regulations of the Secretary of Agriculture, or by delivering it up to the Secretary. The Committee, therefore, refused him a marketing card, which was, under the terms of Regulations promulgated by the Secretary, necessary to protect a buyer from liability to the penalty and upon its protecting lien.

The general scheme of the Agricultural Adjustment Act of 1938 as related to wheat is to control the volume moving in interstate and foreign commerce in order to avoid surpluses and shortages and the consequent abnormally low or high wheat prices and obstructions to commerce. Within prescribed limits and by prescribed standards the Secretary of Agriculture is directed to ascertain and proclaim each year a national acreage allotment for the next crop of wheat, which is then apportioned to the states and their counties, and is eventually broken up into allotments for individual farms. Loans and payments to wheat farmers are authorized in stated circumstances. . . .

II

It is urged that under the Commerce Clause of the Constitution, Congress does not possess the power it has in this instance sought to exercise. . . . [T]his Act extends federal regulation to production not intended in any part for commerce but wholly for consumption on the farm. The Act includes a definition of "market" and its derivatives, so that as related to wheat, in addition to its conventional meaning, it also means to dispose of "by feeding (in any form) to poultry or livestock which, or the products of which, are sold, bartered, or exchanged, or to be so disposed of." Hence, marketing quotas not only embrace all that may be sold without penalty but also what may be consumed on the premises. Wheat produced on excess acreage is designated as "available for marketing" as so defined, and the penalty is imposed thereon. Penalties do not depend upon whether any part of the wheat, either within or without the quota, is sold or intended to be sold. The sum of this is that the Federal Government fixes a quota including all that the farmer may harvest for sale or for his own farm needs, and declares that wheat produced on excess acreage may neither be disposed of nor used except upon payment of the penalty, or except it is stored as required by the Act or delivered to the Secretary of Agriculture.

Appellee says that this is a regulation of production and consumption of wheat. Such activities are, he urges, beyond the reach of Congressional power under the Commerce Clause, since they are local in character, and their effects upon interstate commerce are at most "indirect." In answer the Government argues that the statute regulates neither production nor consumption, but only marketing; and, in the alternative, that if the Act does go beyond the regulation of marketing it is sustainable as a "necessary and proper" implementation of the power of Congress over interstate commerce.

The Government's concern lest the Act be held to be a regulation of production or consumption, rather than of marketing, is attributable to a few dicta and decisions of this Court which might be understood to lay it down that activities such as "production," "manufacturing," and "mining" are strictly "local" and, except in special circumstances which are not present here, cannot be regulated under the commerce power because their effects upon interstate commerce are, as matter of law, only "indirect." Even today, when this power has been held to have great latitude, there is no decision of this Court that such activities may be regulated where no part of the product is intended for interstate commerce or intermingled with the subjects thereof. We believe that a review of the course of decision under the Commerce Clause will make plain, however, that questions of the power of Congress are not to be decided by reference to any formula which would give controlling force to nomenclature such as "production" and "indirect" and foreclose consideration of the actual effects of the activity in question upon interstate commerce.

At the beginning Chief Justice Marshall described the federal commerce power with a breadth never yet exceeded. *Gibbons v. Ogden.* He made emphatic the embracing and penetrating nature of this power by warning that effective restraints on its exercise must proceed from political rather than from judicial processes.

For nearly a century, however, decisions of this Court under the Commerce Clause dealt rarely with questions of what Congress might do in the exercise of its granted power under the Clause, and almost entirely with the permissibility of state activity which it was claimed discriminated against or burdened interstate commerce. During this period there was perhaps little occasion for the affirmative exercise of the commerce power, and the influence of the Clause on American life and law was a negative one, resulting almost wholly from its operation as a restraint upon the powers of the states. In discussion and decision the point of reference, instead of being what was "necessary and proper" to the exercise by Congress of its granted power, was often some concept of sovereignty thought to be implicit in the status of statehood. Certain activities such as "production," "manufacturing," and "mining" were occasionally said to be within the province of state governments and beyond the power of Congress under the Commerce Clause.

It was not until 1887, with the enactment of the Interstate Commerce Act, that the interstate commerce power began to exert positive influence in American law and life. This first important federal resort to the commerce power was followed in 1890 by the Sherman Anti-Trust Act and, thereafter, mainly after 1903, by many others. These statutes ushered in new phases of adjudication, which required the Court to approach the interpretation of the Commerce Clause in the light of an actual exercise by Congress of its power thereunder.

When it first dealt with this new legislation, the Court adhered to its earlier pronouncements, and allowed but little scope to the power of Congress. *United States v. E.C. Knight Co.* These earlier pronouncements also played an important part in several of the five cases in which this Court later held that Acts of Congress under the Commerce Clause were in excess of its power.

Even while important opinions in this line of restrictive authority were being written, however, other cases called forth broader interpretations of the Commerce Clause destined to supersede the earlier ones, and to bring about a return to the principles first enunciated by Chief Justice Marshall in *Gibbons v. Ogden.* . . .

In the *Shreveport Rate Cases*, the Court held that railroad rates of an admittedly intrastate character and fixed by authority of the state might, nevertheless, be revised by the Federal Government because of the economic effects which they had upon interstate commerce. The opinion of Mr. Justice Hughes found federal intervention constitutionally authorized because of "matters having such a close and substantial relation to interstate traffic that the control is essential or appropriate to the security of that traffic, to the efficiency of the interstate service, and to the maintenance of conditions under which interstate commerce may be conducted upon fair terms and without molestation or hindrance."

The Court's recognition of the relevance of the economic effects in the application of the Commerce Clause, exemplified by this statement, has made the mechanical application of legal formulas no longer feasible. Once an economic measure of the reach of the power granted to Congress in the Commerce Clause is accepted, questions of federal power cannot be decided simply by finding the activity in question to be "production," nor can consideration of its economic effects be foreclosed by calling them "indirect." The present Chief Justice has said in summary of the present state of the law: "The commerce power is not confined in its exercise to the regulation of commerce among the states. It extends to those activities intrastate which so affect interstate commerce, or the exertion of the power of Congress over it, as to make regulation of them appropriate means to the attainment of a legitimate end, the effective execution of the granted power to regulate interstate commerce. . . . The power of Congress over interstate commerce is plenary and complete in itself, may be exercised to its utmost extent, and acknowledges no limitations other than are prescribed in the Constitution. . . . It follows that no form of state activity can constitutionally thwart the regulatory power granted by the commerce clause to Congress. Hence the reach of that power extends to those intrastate activities which in a substantial way interfere with or obstruct the exercise of the granted power."

Whether the subject of the regulation in question was "production," "consumption," or "marketing" is, therefore, not material for purposes of deciding the question of federal power before us. That an activity is of local character may help in a doubtful case to determine whether Congress intended to reach it. The same consideration might help in determining whether in the absence of Congressional action it would be permissible for the state to exert its power on the subject matter, even though in so doing it to some degree affected interstate commerce. But even if appellee's activity be local and though it may not be regarded as commerce, it may still, whatever its nature, be reached by Congress if it exerts a substantial economic effect on interstate commerce, and this irrespective of whether such effect is what might at some earlier time have been defined as "direct" or "indirect."

The parties have stipulated a summary of the economics of the wheat industry. Commerce among the states in wheat is large and important. Although wheat is raised in every state but one, production in most states is not equal to consumption. Sixteen states on average have had a surplus of wheat above their own requirements for feed, seed, and food. Thirty-two states and the District of Columbia, where production has been below consumption, have looked to these surplus-producing states for their supply as well as for wheat for export and carry-over.

The wheat industry has been a problem industry for some years. Largely as a result of increased foreign production and import restrictions, annual exports of wheat and flour from the United States during the ten-year period ending in 1940 averaged less than 10 per cent of total production, while during the 1920's they averaged more than 25 per cent. The decline in the export trade has left a large surplus in production which, in connection with an abnormally large supply of wheat and other grains in recent years, caused congestion in a number of markets; tied up railroad cars; and caused elevators in some instances to turn away grains, and railroads to institute embargoes to prevent further congestion. . . .

In the absence of regulation, the price of wheat in the United States would be much affected by world conditions. During 1941, producers who cooperated with the Agricultural Adjustment program received an average price on the farm of about $1.16 a bushel, as compared with the world market price of 40 cents a bushel. . . .

The effect of consumption of home-grown wheat on interstate commerce is due to the fact that it constitutes the most variable factor in the disappearance of the wheat crop. Consumption on the farm where grown appears to vary in an amount greater than 20 per cent of average production. The total amount of wheat consumed as food varies but relatively little, and use as seed is relatively constant.

. . . The effect of the statute before us is to restrict the amount which may be produced for market and the extent as well to which one may forestall resort to the market by producing to meet his own needs. That appellee's own contribution to the demand for wheat may be trivial by itself is not enough to remove him from the scope of federal regulation where, as here, his contribution, taken together with that of many others similarly situated, is far from trivial.

It is well established by decisions of this Court that the power to regulate commerce includes the power to regulate the prices at which commodities in that commerce are dealt in and practices affecting such prices. One of the primary purposes of the Act in question was to increase the market price of wheat, and to that end to limit the volume thereof that could affect the market. It can hardly be denied that a factor of such volume and variability as home-consumed wheat would have a substantial influence on price and market conditions. This may arise because being in marketable condition such wheat overhangs the market and, if induced by rising prices, tends to flow into the market and check price increases. But if we assume that it is never marketed, it supplies a need of the man who grew it which would otherwise be reflected by purchases in the open market. Home-grown wheat in this sense competes with wheat in commerce. The stimulation of commerce is a use of the regulatory function quite as definitely as prohibitions or restrictions thereon. This record leaves us in no doubt that Congress may properly have considered that wheat consumed on the farm where grown, if wholly outside the scheme of regulation, would have a substantial effect in defeating and obstructing its purpose to stimulate trade therein at increased prices.

It is said, however, that this Act, forcing some farmers into the market to buy what they could provide for themselves, is an unfair promotion of the markets and prices of specializing wheat growers. It is of the essence of regulation that it lays a restraining hand on the self-interest of the regulated and that advantages from the regulation commonly fall to others. The conflicts of economic interest between the regulated and those who advantage by it are wisely left under our system to resolution by the Congress under its more flexible and responsible legislative process. Such conflicts rarely lend themselves to judicial determination. And with the wisdom, workability, or fairness, of the plan of regulation we have nothing to do. . . .

Reversed.

NOTE ON THE CONSTITUTIONAL REVOLUTION OF 1937

1.   Scholars still debate whether FDR's court-packing proposal caused the Court's "switch in time." There is evidence, for example, that the justices had already voted in conference to uphold the Washington minimum wage law in *West Coast Hotel* prior to announcement of FDR's proposal. Chief Justice Hughes thus wrote that "[t]he President's proposal had not the slightest effect on our decision."[37] On the other hand, the vote occurred after FDR's landslide re-election, which may have put more general pressure on the Court not to continue to oppose policies endorsed by the People. If you think the justices bowed to political pressure, was that appropriate?[38]

Does the opinion in *West Coast Hotel* help answer this question? That opinion, after all, emphasizes the inconsistency of *Adkins* (and, implicitly, *Lochner*) with the Court's other precedents. On the other hand, isn't it hard to read language questioning the very existence of a freedom of contract as anything other than a departure?

2.   The majority opinion in *Jones & Laughlin* emphasized the vast scope of the particular entity before the Court, the Jones & Laughlin Steel Corp., and the impact on the national economy that a labor strike at the company's plant might have. In other words, the particular activity regulated in Jones & Laughlin—unfair labor practices at a massive and fully-integrated steel company—was likely *itself* to affect interstate commerce. But as the dissent makes clear, the Court also had before it NLRB orders issued to much smaller entities whose activities, in and of themselves, could not plausibly be said to affect commerce among the several states. On the Court's reasoning in *Jones & Laughlin*, was the NLRA constitutional as applied to these smaller instances of enforcement?

Wickard v. Filburn deals with this problem head on. That case, after all, involved the small-scale operation of one farmer. Recognizing that "appellee's own contribution to the demand for wheat may be trivial by itself," the Court said that this "is not enough to remove him from the scope of federal regulation where, as here, his contribution, taken together with that of many others similarly situated, is far from trivial." This "aggregation principle" represented a significant step beyond the rationale of *Jones & Laughlin*, and it permits Congress to regulate minute activities of individuals, so long as those activities, as a class, have a substantial effect on interstate commerce. Did *Wickard* go too far? Can you think of *any* activity that Congress could not regulate under this standard?

3.   A third landmark Commerce Clause decision, *United States v. Darby*, 312 U.S. 100 (1941), cemented the turn in the Court's jurisprudence after 1937. *Darby* involved the federal Fair Labor Standards Act (FLSA), which set national standards for wages and hours. The FLSA enforced those standards in two ways. First, it prohibited interstate shipment of goods made by workers not complying with the federal wage and hour requirements.

---

[37] Quoted in MARIAN C. McKENNA, FRANKLIN ROOSEVELT AND THE GREAT CONSTITUTIONAL WAR: THE COURT-PACKING CRISIS OF 1937, at 419 (2002).

[38] For an overview of the historical debate, see Laura Kalman, *The Constitution, the Supreme Court, and the New Deal*, 110 AMERICAN HIST. REV. 1052 (Oct. 2005).

Second, it imposed those wage and hour requirements directly on workers engaged in making goods for interstate commerce. In upholding the ban on interstate shipment, the Court overruled *Hammer v. Dagenhart* and returned to the more permissive rule of *Champion v. Ames*. With respect to the direct regulation of wages and hours, the Court upheld the statute on two alternative grounds: that regulating wages and hours was a necessary and proper means to facilitate the interstate shipment ban; and that wages and hours themselves have a substantial effect on interstate commerce.

The first ground is clearly bootstrapping, isn't it? It upholds an unenumerated means (regulating intra-state transactions) to an unenumerated end (worker welfare). Can that be defended without abandoning the reasoning of *McCulloch*? On the other hand, can the Court's second ground be more readily defended?

4.   *Jones & Laughlin*, *Wickard*, and *Darby* remain largely good law today concerning the scope of Congress's regulatory powers under the Commerce Clause. In the wake of those decisions, Edward Corwin penned an assessment of the "dual federalism" regime that had dominated constitutional law for the first 150 years of the Republic. "This entire system of constitutional interpretation touching the Federal System is today in ruins," he announced.

> [B]y the constitutional revolution . . . of the "New Deal" . . . American federalism has been converted into an instrument for the achievement of peace abroad and economic security for "the common man" at home. In the process of remolding the Federal System for these purposes, however, the instrument has been overwhelmed and submerged in the objectives sought, so that today the question faces us whether the constituent States of the System can be saved for any useful purpose, and thereby saved as the vital cells that they have been heretofore of democratic sentiment, impulse, and action.[39]

What's left, after *Jones & Laughlin* and *Wickard*, of the pre-1937 limited Commerce Clause? Is Professor Corwin's assessment accurate? If he is correct, is that a good or a bad thing?

5.   Similar things could be said of the disappearance of economic rights like freedom of contract after *West Coast Hotel*. The next section deals with the disparity between the Court's willingness to enforce economic rights after 1937 and its emerging interest in aggressive enforcement of *non*economic rights.

SECTION 5.4   JUDICIAL DEFERENCE AND THE DOUBLE STANDARD

After 1937, the Supreme Court largely swore off the sorts of judicial review that it had engaged in during the *Lochner* era. Scot Powe has thus observed that "the Court-packing plan gave FDR the Constitution just

---

[39]   Edward S. Corwin, *The Passing of Dual Federalism*, 36 VA. L. REV. 1, 23 (1950).

the way he wanted."[40] As the cases in the next Chapter demonstrate, however, the Court was shortly to take up a new role as protector of a new set of liberties in areas such as criminal procedure, personal privacy, and racial justice. The Court's reluctance to engage in some forms of judicial review while pushing aggressively ahead with others is often described as the "double standard" in constitutional law. Henry Abraham, for example, observed "a double standard of judicial attitude, whereby governmental economic experimentation is accorded all but *carte blanche* by the courts, but alleged violations of individual civil rights are given meticulous judicial attention."[41] This divide is one of the central organizing themes of modern constitutional law—and of this course.

The readings in this assignment explore Professor Abraham's "double standard" and the mechanisms of judicial deference that dominate the post-1937 caselaw concerning economic regulation. *Carolene Products* and *Lee Optical* both demonstrate the Justices' retreat from review of economic legislation under the Due Process Clause, while the former opinion's famous Footnote Four looks ahead to the expansion of judicial review in other areas under the Warren Court. (Chapters Six and Seven explore some of the areas of that expansion.) Footnote Four turns out to be an incomplete account of where and why the Court engages in more or less deferential review, however. These materials thus grapple with various definitions of and justifications for this "double standard."

United States v. Carolene Products
304 U.S. 144 (1938)

■ **MR. JUSTICE STONE delivered the opinion of the Court.**

The question for decision is whether the "Filled Milk Act" of Congress of March 4, 1923, which prohibits the shipment in interstate commerce of skimmed milk compounded with any fat or oil other than milk fat, so as to resemble milk or cream, transcends the power of Congress to regulate interstate commerce or infringes the Fifth Amendment.

Appellee was indicted in the district court for southern Illinois for violation of the Act by the shipment in interstate commerce of certain packages of "Milnut," a compound of condensed skimmed milk and coconut oil made in imitation or semblance of condensed milk or cream. The indictment states, in the words of the statute, that Milnut "is an adulterated article of food, injurious to the public health." . . .

---

[40] POWE, *supra* note 5, at 213.

[41] HENRY J. ABRAHAM, FREEDOM AND THE COURT: CIVIL RIGHTS AND LIBERTIES IN THE UNITED STATES 10 (4th ed. 1982).

Appellee assails the statute as beyond the power of Congress over interstate commerce, and hence an invasion of a field of action said to be reserved to the states by the Tenth Amendment. Appellee also complains that the statute denies to it equal protection of the laws and, in violation of the Fifth Amendment, deprives it of its property without due process of law, particularly in that the statute purports to make binding and conclusive upon appellee the legislative declaration that appellee's product "is an adulterated article of food injurious to the public health and its sale constitutes a fraud on the public."

First. The power to regulate commerce is the power "to prescribe the rule by which commerce is to be governed," *Gibbons v. Ogden*, and extends to the prohibition of shipments in such commerce. *Lottery Case*, 188 U.S. 321. The power "is complete in itself, may be exercised to its utmost extent and acknowledges no limitations other than are prescribed by the Constitution." *Gibbons, supra*. Hence Congress is free to exclude from interstate commerce articles whose use in the states for which they are destined it may reasonably conceive to be injurious to the public health, morals or welfare, *Lottery Case; Hipolite Egg Co. v. United States*, 220 U.S. 45, or which contravene the policy of the state of their destination. Such regulation is not a forbidden invasion of state power either because its motive or its consequence is to restrict the use of articles of commerce within the states of destination, and is not prohibited unless by the due process clause of the Fifth Amendment. . . . The prohibition of the shipment of filled milk in interstate commerce is a permissible regulation of commerce, subject only to the restrictions of the Fifth Amendment.

Second. The prohibition of shipment of appellee's product in interstate commerce does not infringe the Fifth Amendment. . . . [E]vidence has steadily accumulated of the danger to the public health from the general consumption of foods which have been stripped of elements essential to the maintenance of health. The Filled Milk Act was adopted by Congress after committee hearings, in the course of which eminent scientists and health experts testified. An extensive investigation was made of the commerce in milk compounds in which vegetable oils have been substituted for natural milk fat, and of the effect upon the public health of the use of such compounds as a food substitute for milk. The conclusions drawn from evidence presented at the hearings were embodied in reports of the House Committee on Agriculture and the Senate Committee on Agriculture and Forestry. Both committees concluded, as the statute itself declares, that the use of filled milk as a substitute for pure milk is generally injurious to health and facilitates fraud on the public.

There is nothing in the Constitution which compels a legislature, either national or state, to ignore such evidence, nor need it disregard the other evidence which amply supports the conclusions of the Congressional Committees that the danger is greatly enhanced where an inferior product, like appellee's, is indistinguishable from a valuable food of almost universal use, thus making fraudulent distribution easy and protection of the consumer difficult.

Here the prohibition of the statute is inoperative unless the product is "in imitation or semblance of milk, cream, or skimmed milk, whether or not condensed." Whether in such circumstances the public would be adequately protected by the prohibition of false labels and false branding imposed by the Pure Food and Drugs Act, or whether it was necessary to go farther and prohibit a substitute food product thought to be injurious to health if used as a substitute when the two are not distinguishable, was a matter for the legislative judgment and not that of courts. . . .

Appellee raises no valid objection to the present statute by arguing that its prohibition has not been extended to oleomargarine or other butter substitutes in which vegetable fats or oils are substituted for butter fat. The Fifth Amendment has no equal protection clause, and even that of the Fourteenth, applicable only to the states, does not compel their legislatures to prohibit all like evils, or none. A legislature may hit at an abuse which it has found, even though it has failed to strike at another. . . .

Third. We may assume for present purposes that no pronouncement of a legislature can forestall attack upon the constitutionality of the prohibition which it enacts by applying opprobrious epithets to the prohibited act, and that a statute would deny due process which precluded the disproof in judicial proceedings of all facts which would show or tend to show that a statute depriving the suitor of life, liberty or property had a rational basis.

But such we think is not the purpose or construction of the statutory characterization of filled milk as injurious to health and as a fraud upon the public. There is no need to consider it here as more than a declaration of the legislative findings deemed to support and justify the action taken as a constitutional exertion of the legislative power, aiding informed judicial review, as do the reports of legislative committees, by revealing the rationale of the legislation. Even in the absence of such aids the existence of facts supporting the legislative judgment is to be presumed, for regulatory legislation affecting ordinary commercial transactions is not to be pronounced unconstitutional unless in the light of the facts made known or generally assumed it is of such a character as to preclude the assumption that it rests upon some rational basis within the knowledge and experience of the legislators.[4] . . .

---

[4] There may be narrower scope for operation of the presumption of constitutionality when legislation appears on its face to be within a specific prohibition of the Constitution, such as those of the first ten amendments, which are deemed equally specific when held to be embraced within the Fourteenth.

It is unnecessary to consider now whether legislation which restricts those political processes which can ordinarily be expected to bring about repeal of undesirable legislation, is to be subjected to more exacting judicial scrutiny under the general prohibitions of the Fourteenth Amendment than are most other types of legislation. On restrictions upon the right to vote, see

Where the existence of a rational basis for legislation whose constitutionality is attacked depends upon facts beyond the sphere of judicial notice, such facts may properly be made the subject of judicial inquiry, and the constitutionality of a statute predicated upon the existence of a particular state of facts may be challenged by showing to the court that those facts have ceased to exist. Similarly we recognize that the constitutionality of a statute, valid on its face, may be assailed by proof of facts tending to show that the statute as applied to a particular article is without support in reason because the article, although within the prohibited class, is so different from others of the class as to be without the reason for the prohibition, though the effect of such proof depends on the relevant circumstances of each case, as for example the administrative difficulty of excluding the article from the regulated class. But by their very nature such inquiries, where the legislative judgment is drawn in question, must be restricted to the issue whether any state of facts either known or which could reasonably be assumed affords support for it. Here the demurrer challenges the validity of the statute on its face and it is evident from all the considerations presented to Congress, and those of which we may take judicial notice, that the question is at least debatable whether commerce in filled milk should be left unregulated, or in some measure restricted, or wholly prohibited. As that decision was for Congress, neither the finding of a court arrived at by weighing the evidence, nor the verdict of a jury can be substituted for it.

The prohibition of shipment in interstate commerce of appellee's product, as described in the indictment, is a constitutional exercise of the power to regulate interstate commerce. As the statute is not unconstitutional on its face the demurrer should have been overruled and the judgment will be

Reversed.

■ MR. JUSTICE BLACK concurs in the result and in all of the opinion except the part marked *"Third."*

■ MR. JUSTICE MCREYNOLDS thinks that the judgment should be affirmed.

Nixon v. Herndon, 273 U.S. 536; *Nixon v. Condon,* 286 U.S. 73; on restraints upon the dissemination of information, see *Near v. Minnesota ex rel. Olson,* 283 U.S. 697; *Grosjean v. American Press Co.,* 297 U.S. 233; *Lovell v. Griffin, supra;* on interferences with political organizations, see *Stromberg, supra; Fiske v. Kansas,* 274 U.S. 380; *Whitney v. California,* 274 U.S. 357; *Herndon v. Lowry,* 301 U.S. 242; and see Holmes, J., in *Gitlow v. New York,* 268 U.S. 652; as to prohibition of peaceable assembly, see *De Jonge v. Oregon,* 299 U.S. 353.

Nor need we enquire whether similar considerations enter into the review of statutes directed at particular religious, *Pierce v. Society of Sisters,* 268 U.S. 510, or national, *Meyer v. Nebraska,* 262 U.S. 390; or racial minorities, *Nixon v. Herndon, supra; Nixon v. Condon, supra:* whether prejudice against discrete and insular minorities may be a special condition, which tends seriously to curtail the operation of those political processes ordinarily to be relied upon to protect minorities, and which may call for a correspondingly more searching judicial inquiry. Compare *McCulloch v. Maryland,* 4 Wheat. 316, 428.

■ MR. JUSTICE CARDOZO and MR. JUSTICE REED took no part in the consideration or decision of this case.

■ [MR. JUSTICE BUTLER concurred in the result, arguing that the statute would be unconstitutional if it were construed not to provide the defendant with an opportunity to prove at trial that his goods were not harmful.]

Williamson v. Lee Optical of Oklahoma, Inc.
348 U.S. 483 (1955)

■ MR. JUSTICE DOUGLAS delivered the opinion of the Court.

This suit was instituted in the District Court to have an Oklahoma law declared unconstitutional and to enjoin state officials from enforcing it . . . The District Court held unconstitutional portions of three sections of the Act. First, it held invalid under the Due Process Clause of the Fourteenth Amendment the portions of § 2 which make it unlawful for any person not a licensed optometrist or ophthalmologist to fit lenses to a face or to duplicate or replace into frames lenses or other optical appliances, except upon written prescriptive authority of an Oklahoma licensed ophthalmologist or optometrist. . . .

An ophthalmologist is a duly licensed physician who specializes in the care of the eyes. An optometrist examines eyes for refractive error, recognizes (but does not treat) diseases of the eye, and fills prescriptions for eyeglasses. The optician is an artisan qualified to grind lenses, fill prescriptions, and fit frames.

The effect of § 2 is to forbid the optician from fitting or duplicating lenses without a prescription from an ophthalmologist or optometrist. In practical effect, it means that no optician can fit old glasses into new frames or supply a lens, whether it be a new lens or one to duplicate a lost or broken lens, without a prescription. The District Court conceded that it was in the competence of the police power of a State to regulate the examination of the eyes. But it rebelled at the notion that a State could require a prescription from an optometrist or ophthalmologist "to take old lenses and place them in new frames and then fit the completed spectacles to the *face* of the eyeglass wearer." It held that such a requirement was not "reasonably and rationally related to the health and welfare of the people." The court found that through mechanical devices and ordinary skills the optician could take a broken lens or a fragment thereof, measure its power, and reduce it to prescriptive terms. The court held that "Although on this precise issue of duplication, the legislature in the instant regulation was dealing with a matter of public interest, the particular means chosen are neither reasonably necessary nor reasonably related to the end sought to be achieved." It was, accordingly, the opinion of the court that this provision of the law violated the Due Process Clause by arbitrarily interfering with the optician's right to do business. . . .

The Oklahoma law may exact a needless, wasteful requirement in many cases. But it is for the legislature, not the courts, to balance the advantages and disadvantages of the new requirement. It appears that in many cases the optician can easily supply the new frames or new lenses without reference to the old written prescription. It also appears that many written prescriptions contain no directive data in regard to fitting spectacles to the face. But in some cases the directions contained in the prescription are essential, if the glasses are to be fitted so as to correct the particular defects of vision or alleviate the eye condition. The legislature might have concluded that the frequency of occasions when a prescription is necessary was sufficient to justify this regulation of the fitting of eyeglasses. Likewise, when it is necessary to duplicate a lens, a written prescription may or may not be necessary. But the legislature might have concluded that one was needed often enough to require one in every case. Or the legislature may have concluded that eye examinations were so critical, not only for correction of vision but also for detection of latent ailments or diseases, that every change in frames and every duplication of a lens should be accompanied by a prescription from a medical expert. To be sure, the present law does not require a new examination of the eyes every time the frames are changed or the lenses duplicated. For if the old prescription is on file with the optician, he can go ahead and make the new fitting or duplicate the lenses. But the law need not be in every respect logically consistent with its aims to be constitutional. It is enough that there is an evil at hand for correction, and that it might be thought that the particular legislative measure was a rational way to correct it.

The day is gone when this Court used the Due Process Clause of the Fourteenth Amendment to strike down state laws, regulatory of business and industrial conditions, because they may be unwise, improvident, or out of harmony with a particular school of thought. See *Nebbia v. New York*; *West Coast Hotel Co. v. Parrish*. We emphasize again what Chief Justice Waite said in *Munn v. Illinois*: "For protection against abuses by legislatures the people must resort to the polls, not to the courts."

Secondly, the District Court held that it violated the Equal Protection Clause of the Fourteenth Amendment to subject opticians to this regulatory system and to exempt . . . all sellers of ready-to-wear glasses. The problem of legislative classification is a perennial one, admitting of no doctrinaire definition. Evils in the same field may be of different dimensions and proportions, requiring different remedies. Or so the legislature may think. Or the reform may take one step at a time, addressing itself to the phase of the problem which seems most acute to the legislative mind. The legislature may select one phase of one field and apply a remedy there, neglecting the others. The prohibition of the Equal Protection Clause goes no further than the invidious discrimination. We cannot say that that point has been reached here. For all this record shows, the ready-to-wear branch of this business may not loom large in

Oklahoma or may present problems of regulation distinct from the other branch. . . .

Affirmed in part and reversed in part.

■ MR. JUSTICE HARLAN **took no part in the consideration or decision of these cases.**

NOTE ON THE "DOUBLE STANDARD" AFTER 1937

1.   The cases in this section illustrate the pervasive importance of standards of review. In many contexts—including most constitutional cases—courts are not making a decision or creating a rule in the first instance, but rather reviewing the decision of some other actor—a legislature, an executive officer, a lower court. In these situations, the question before the court is not simply what to do, but whether the other actor's decision should be struck down as invalid. In adjudicating a constitutional challenge to a law enacted by a state legislature, for example, a court will typically apply one of the three different standards of review:

- *Rational Basis Review:* The law will be upheld if it is rationally related to a legitimate state interest.

- *Intermediate Scrutiny:* The law will be upheld if it is closely related to an important state interest.

- *Strict Scrutiny:* The law will be upheld only if it is narrowly tailored to a compelling state interest.

These are not the only standards of review by any means, but most other tests can be better understood by considering their relationship to these three standards. *Carolene Products* and *Lee Optical* illustrate the permissive nature of rational basis review. At the other end of the spectrum, the Court has virtually never been willing to uphold government discrimination on the basis of race or restrictions on political speech, both of which get strict scrutiny. The differences generally have to do with a) the sort of justifications or interests that may be taken into account, and b) the closeness of "fit" required between the ends to be promoted and the means chosen to pursue those ends. In particular, strict scrutiny generally requires that the restriction on constitutional rights be the *least restrictive alternative* that can fulfill the compelling governmental interest.

Although the basic contours of rational basis review are often traced all the way back to *McCulloch v. Maryland*, these tiers of scrutiny are a fairly contemporary concept. The Court itself did not begin using terms like "strict scrutiny" with any consistency until the 1970s, although the label aptly describes the analysis in at least some cases that predate the terminology. It is also possible, as the cases in Chapter Seventeen suggest, that the tiers of scrutiny are of declining importance in contemporary constitutional law. At present, however, they retain helpful descriptive and predictive force. Pay attention to the standard of review, whether explicit or implicit, in the cases in the remainder of this Part.

2.   Here is a contemporary statement of the rational basis standard:

On rational-basis review, a classification in a statute . . . comes to us bearing a strong presumption of validity and those attacking the rationality of the legislative classification have the burden to negative every conceivable basis which might support it. Moreover, because we never require a legislature to articulate its reasons for enacting a statute, it is entirely irrelevant for constitutional purposes whether the conceived reason for the challenged distinction actually motivated the legislature. Thus, the absence of legislative facts explaining the distinction on the record, has no significance in rational-basis analysis. In other words, a legislative choice is not subject to courtroom fact-finding and may be based on rational speculation unsupported by evidence or empirical data. Only by faithful adherence to this guiding principle of judicial review of legislation is it possible to preserve to the legislative branch its rightful independence and its ability to function.[42]

This statement makes explicit some of the elements of rational basis review on display in *Carolene Products* and *Lee Optical*. The first is a *strong presumption in favor of legislative factfinding*. As the *Carolene Products* Court puts it, courts should uphold legislation if "any state of facts either known or which could reasonably be assumed" supports the law, or if the question "is at least debatable." Can this deference really be defended on the ground that legislatures are institutionally better-suited to investigate facts than courts?

A second element is the Court's willingness to accept *hypothetical rationales and facts*. Consider, for example, the Court's supposition in *Lee Optical* that the Oklahoma law, which effectively forced patients to return to the ophthalmologist or optometrist more often than they otherwise would, might benefit the health of those patients. Was there any evidence that the Oklahoma legislature actually had this rationale in mind? That the state's lawyers argued it to the Court? Should a rationale concocted by the justices themselves (or their law clerks) be sufficient to uphold a law against constitutional challenge?

Isn't it more likely that the Oklahoma law reflected a struggle for business between different classes of optical care-givers, and that the ophthalmologists prevailed? Should legislation require a better rationale than the brute fact that one interest group had better lobbyists than its competitors? On the other hand, do we really want courts to pry into the actual, behind-the-scenes workings of the legislative process?

3.   One of the most influential constitutional theorists of the late nineteenth century, James Bradley Thayer, argued that something much like the rational basis standard should apply across the board. Professor Thayer insisted that courts should hold laws unconstitutional only "when those who have the right to make laws have not merely made a mistake, but have made a very clear one—so clear that it is not open to rational

---

[42] *FCC v. Beach Communications, Inc.*, 508 U.S. 307, 314–15 (1993) (citations omitted).

question." [43] But as Professor Abraham's notion of a "double standard" suggests, the Court has *not* adopted Thayer's approach in all constitutional cases.

Assessing this double standard involves two distinct questions, one descriptive and one normative. The descriptive question is to map exactly which constitutional principles fall on each side of the divide. We must ask, in other words, "A double standard between what and what?" [44] The normative issue, one the other hand, concerns whether and how such a bifurcated approach can be justified. At least three different kinds of normative justifications for the double standard have been advanced: (1) that it reserves judicial review for norms that courts are *institutionally competent* to enforce; (2) that it reserves judicial intervention for situations in which it is most *necessary*, because the political process is unlikely to correct its own mistakes; or (3) that it focuses judicial review on those constitutional principles that are most *normatively appealing*. [45]

Isn't the very idea of a "double standard" suspect? Douglas Laycock has insisted that "we should take the whole Constitution seriously. We cannot legitimately pick and choose the clauses we want enforced." [46] Is that what the Court is doing—picking and choosing which clauses to enforce?

4.   Footnote Four in *Carolene Products* is often called the most important footnote in constitutional law. While the text of the opinion is extremely deferential to the challenged government regulation, the footnote lays out a theory for when such deference may not be appropriate. John Hart Ely argued that Footnote Four provided the most persuasive account of the Warren Court's jurisprudence expanding protection for individual rights on a number of fronts, notwithstanding the Court's more deferential approach in many areas after 1947. [47] Hence, Footnote Four may offer a helpful first cut at both describing and justifying Professor Abraham's "double standard."

Begin with the footnote's first paragraph, which states that "[t]here may be narrower scope for operation of the presumption of constitutionality when legislation appears on its face to be within a specific prohibition of the Constitution, such as those of the first ten amendments, which are deemed equally specific when held to be embraced within the Fourteenth." Descriptively speaking, does the double standard track a distinction between textual and non-textual principles? Lynn Baker and Ernest Young are skeptical:

> The appeal of this textual distinction seems superficial at best. As Professor Abraham acknowledges, the "categorical" language of the First Amendment has not led us to adopt the absolutist position of

---

[43]   James Bradley Thayer, *The Origin and Scope of the American Doctrine of Constitutional Law*, 7 HARV. L. REV. 129, 150 (1893).

[44]   Lynn A. Baker & Ernest A. Young, *Federalism and the Double Standard of Judicial Review*, 51 DUKE L. J. 75, 80 (2001).

[45]   *See id.* at 85–86.

[46]   Douglas Laycock, *Equal Citizens of Equal and Territorial States: The Constitutional Foundations of Choice of Law*, 92 COLUM. L. REV. 249, 267 (1992).

[47]   *See generally* JOHN HART ELY, DEMOCRACY AND DISTRUST (1980).

Justice Hugo Black. The wondrous complexity of free speech doctrine—endless distinctions between "commercial" and "political" speech, or among "viewpoint-based," "content-based," and "time, place, and manner" restrictions—is no more derivable from the text of the First Amendment than "freedom of contract" is derivable from the text of the Due Process Clause. More importantly, the Constitution contains protections for economic rights which are no less explicit than the strictures of the Bill of Rights. The textually explicit nature of the Contract Clause, for example, has not saved that provision from exile. [*See Home Building & Loan Ass'n v. Blaisdell,* 290 U.S. 398, 447–48 (1934) (holding that a Minnesota act that extended time for recovery of property from foreclosure did not violate the Contract Clause).] And of course the Court aggressively has protected areas of noneconomic due process that are every bit as textually suspect as the repudiated doctrine of *Lochner v. New York.* [*See, e.g., Roe v. Wade,* 410 U.S. 113, 166 (1973) (recognizing a woman's right to an abortion); *Griswold v. Connecticut,* 381 U.S. 479, 485–86 (1965) (recognizing a right to birth control devices for married couples).][48]

From a normative standpoint, *should* courts be more deferential when constitutional challenges to government action cannot be firmly grounded in the constitutional text? Is it more difficult for courts to develop determinate doctrines—and therefore, to demonstrate that their rulings rest on law, not politics—when they venture into the realm of unenumerated constitutional principles?

5.   John Hart Ely's famous "representation reinforcement" theory of judicial review rests primarily on the second and third paragraphs of Footnote Four. Like the Founders themselves, Professor Ely was centrally concerned with the tyranny of the majority:

[T]he document of 1789 and 1791, though at no point explicitly invoking the concept of equality, did strive by at least two strategies to protect the interests of minorities from the potentially destructive will of some majority coalition. The more obvious one may be the "list" strategy employed by the Bill of Rights, itemizing things that cannot be done to anyone, at least by the federal government (though even here the safeguards turn out to be mainly procedural). The original Constitution's more pervasive strategy, however, can be loosely styled a strategy of pluralism, one of structuring the government, and to a limited extent society generally, so that a variety of voices would be guaranteed their say and no majority coalition could dominate.[49]

Ely was unwilling to limit courts to enforcing the first of these strategies— that is, the Constitution's explicit textual guarantees. After all, he said, "No finite list of entitlements can possibly cover all the ways majorities can

---

[48]   Baker & Young, *supra* note 44, at 81–82. The examples cited in the original footnotes have been incorporated into the quoted text.

[49]   ELY, *supra* note 47, at 79–80.

tyrannize minorities, and the informal and more formal mechanisms of pluralism cannot always be counted on either."[50] On the other hand, he also rejected the notion that courts should supplement the constitutional text by declaring additional "fundamental values," such as a right to privacy; "the claim that appointed and life-tenured judges are better reflectors of conventional values than elected representatives," he argued, was "unacceptab[le]."[51]

Instead, Professor Ely articulated an approach that is "akin to what might be called an 'antitrust' as opposed to a 'regulatory' orientation to economic affairs—rather than dictate substantive results it intervenes only when the 'market,' in our case the political market, is systemically malfunctioning."[52] He explained:

> Our government cannot fairly be said to be "malfunctioning" simply because it sometimes generates outcomes with which we disagree, however strongly (and claims that it is reaching results with which "the people" really disagree—or would "if they understood"—are likely to be little more than self-deluding projections). In a representative democracy value determinations are to be made by our elected representatives, and if in fact most of us disapprove we can vote them out of office. Malfunction occurs when the *process* is undeserving of trust, when (1) the ins are choking off the channels of political change to ensure that they will stay in and the outs will stay out, or (2) though no one is actually denied a voice or a vote, representatives beholden to an effective majority are systematically disadvantaging some minority out of simple hostility or a prejudiced refusal to recognize commonalities of interest, and thereby denying that minority the protection afforded other groups by a representative system.[53]

Can you see how these two types of malfunction map onto the second and third paragraphs of the *Carolene Products* footnote? What sort of actions would amount to "choking off the channels of political change"? What sorts of laws might "systematically disadvantage[e]" minorities? Ely thought judges were particularly well-suited to address these malfunctions in the political process:

> Obviously our elected representatives are the last persons we should trust with identification of either of these situations. Appointed judges, however, are comparative outsiders in our governmental system, and need worry about continuance in office only very obliquely. This does not give them some special pipeline to the genuine values of the American people: in fact it goes far to ensure that they won't have one. It does, however, put them in a position objectively to assess claims—though no one could suppose the evaluation won't be full of judgment calls—that either by

---

[50] *Id.* at 81.

[51] *Id.* at 102.

[52] *Id.* at 102–03.

[53] *Id.* at 103.

clogging the channels of change or by acting as accessories to majority tyranny, our elected representatives in fact are not representing the interests of those whom the system presupposes they are.[54]

Ultimately, Ely's theory is a theory of judicial review. Do you find it more persuasive than those advanced by John Marshall or Alexander Bickel?

6.   How does Professor Ely's theory fare as a descriptive account of the post-1937 double standard? Professors Baker and Young have argued that it doesn't fare very well:

> [T]he Court's decisions frequently fail to track the divide that such a theory would suggest. Decisions like *Griswold v. Connecticut*, [381 U.S. 479, 485–86 (1965) (striking down a state restriction on the use of contraceptives by married couples),] *Roe v. Wade*, [410 U.S. 113, 166 (1973) (striking down a state law infringing upon a woman's right to an abortion),] and *United States v. Virginia*, [518 U.S. 515, 558 (1996) (holding that Virginia could not exclude women from a public military academy),] involve aggressive judicial review on behalf of interests that are well represented within contemporary political processes; perhaps even more striking, cases like *Board of Education of Kiryas Joel Village School District v. Grumet*, [512 U.S. 687, 709–10 (1994) (striking down, as a violation of the Establishment Clause, the New York legislature's attempt to accommodate the distinctive culture of the Satmar Hasidim by creating a separate public school district made up primarily of members of the sect),] and B*oy Scouts of America v. Dale*, [530 U.S. 640, 659 (2000) (holding that a New Jersey statute barring discrimination against gays in public accommodations violated the Boy Scouts' freedom of (non)association),] have struck down majority attempts to benefit particular minority groups. And in many cases, the Court has been reluctant to protect minorities from economic or social legislation that imposes disproportionate burdens on members of minority groups. [*See, e.g., Employment Div. v. Smith*, 494 U.S. 872, 890 (1990) (holding that the Free Exercise Clause did not require an exemption from state narcotics laws for religious peyote users); *McCleskey v. Kemp*, 481 U.S. 279, 319 (1987) (rejecting a challenge to a capital sentencing scheme alleged to have disproportionately resulted in the execution of black defendants); *Washington v. Davis*, 426 U.S. 229, 248 (1976) (rejecting a challenge to a police officer qualification exam based on claims that higher percentages of blacks than whites failed the test).][55]

Do Baker and Young understate the many areas—such as Free Speech and Equal Protection doctrine—in which Ely's account fits rather better? Does Ely's theory fare better as a *normative* justification for a more double

---

[54] *Id.*

[55] Baker & Young, *supra* note 44, at 83–84.

standard based on representation reinforcement, even if the Court has so far not followed his prescription?

7.   Perhaps a more straightforward account is in order. Professors Baker and Young suggest that "[p]erhaps the double standard simply separates economic regulation from all other sorts of government action":

> Certainly this seems to have been the basic aim of the judicial revolution of 1937—that is, to facilitate and legitimate the government's expanded regulatory authority over the economy embodied in the New Deal. But even here there are problems. Judicial review of state economic legislation under the dormant Commerce Clause, for example, has continued to be considerably more aggressive than the Court's modern treatment of economic substantive due process. And the gradually expanding protection of commercial speech similarly has required more searching judicial review of economic regulation than conventional views of the double standard would prescribe. These two lines of cases reflect the fact that economic regulation may affect constitutional values— e.g., national unity, individual autonomy—with an importance transcending the economic sphere.[56]

Are Baker and Young thus right to conclude "that the double standard may not be reducible to a single coherent formulation and that it may derive more from history than from principle"? [57] Robert McCloskey, for example, speculated that the double standard "was never really thought through. It seems to have been a kind of reflex, arising out of indignation against the excesses of the Old Court, and resting on the vague, uncritical idea that 'personal rights' are 'O.K.' but economic rights are 'Not O.K.' "[58] If this assessment is correct, then how much respect do contemporary courts owe to prior decisions reflecting this double standard?

8.   Was the Court wrong to abandon economic substantive due process and limited national government after 1937? Writing about the nondelegation doctrine—another constitutional principle left largely unenforced after 1937, Judge Douglas Ginsburg observed that "for 60 years the nondelegation doctrine has existed only as part of the Constitution-in-exile, along with the doctrines of enumerated powers, unconstitutional conditions, and substantive due process, and their textual cousins, the Necessary and Proper, Contracts, Takings, and Commerce Clauses. The memory of these ancient exiles, banished for standing in opposition to unlimited government, is kept alive by a few scholars who labor on in the hope of a restoration, a second coming of the Constitution of liberty—even if perhaps not in their own lifetimes."[38] Around the turn of the twenty-first century, liberal commentators accused conservatives of plotting to restore this "Constitution in Exile" with horrific results:

---

[56] *Id.* at 84–85 (citations omitted).

[57] *Id.* at 85.

[58] Robert G. McCloskey, *Economic Due Process and the Supreme Court: An Exhumation and Reburial*, 1962 SUP. CT. REV. 34, 54.

[38] Douglas Ginsburg, *Delegation Running Riot*, 1 REGULATION 83, 83–84 (1995).

In the last few years, right-wing activists have become far more ambitious. There is a great deal of talk about restoration of the "Constitution in Exile"—the Constitution as it existed in 1932, before President Franklin Delano Roosevelt's New Deal. Under this Constitution, the powers of the national government were sharply limited. The National Labor Relations Act of 1935, not to mention the Civil Rights Act of 1964, would have been impermissible. Under the Constitution in Exile, rights to have recourse against discrimination, and to protection of privacy, were minimal. A far more significant right was freedom of contract, which threw minimum-wage legislation into constitutional doubt. The Supreme Court tends to move slowly, and under a second Bush term, it would not adopt the Constitution of 1932; but it would probably move in that direction.[39]

It is worth noting that, even after a re-elected President Bush in fact appointed two conservative justices, it remains hard to identify any movement toward restoring any sort of "constitution in exile." Would a restoration of the pre-1937 view of the Constitution be desirable? Possible? Would abandoning the double standard necessarily entail abandoning the Court's post-1937 guardianship of non-economic liberties?[59]

9. An alternative to reviving notions of economic rights as fundamental would be to simply make the general test applicable to most constitutional challenges—the rational basis test—less deferential. Even under current law, litigants still occasionally challenge state or federal economic regulation on due process or equal protection grounds, as in *Carolene Produces* or *Lee Optical*. Sometimes they even win. In *Merrifield v. Lockyer*, 547 F.3d 978 (9th Cir. 2008), the owner of a "non-pesticide animal damage prevention and bird control" company challenged a California law requiring that he obtain a state license. The Ninth Circuit rejected Merrifield's privileges and immunities and due process arguments, but it struck down the statute under the Equal Protection Clause. The problem was that the statute exempted from the licensing requirement persons engaged in the non-pesticide-based control of "bats, raccoons, skunks, and squirrels," but did *not* exempt non-pesticide-based controllers of "mice, rats, and pigeons." Although the parties conceded that rational basis review applied, the Court of Appeals found that this distinction lacked such a basis. Judge Hawkins, in dissent, argued that California enjoyed essentially unreviewable discretion to "determine which type of service providers should face a testing or licensing requirement and which should not." What do you think of the decision in *Merrifield*? Is it a sensible rejection of an unusually silly law, or a return to the bad old days of *Lochner*?[60]

---

[39] Cass R. Sunstein, *Hoover's Court Rides Again*, WASH. MONTHLY, Sept. 2004.

[59] For an introduction to the controversy, see the debate between Cass Sunstein and Randy Barnett at Legal Affairs Debate Club, May 2, 2005 (available at http://www.legalaffairs.org/web exclusive/debateclub_cie0505.msp).

[60] For discussion and a tentative defense of the legislature's distinction, see http://volokh. com/posts/1221601821.shtml.

CHAPTER SIX

CIVIL RIGHTS AND THE WARREN COURT

The "double standard" examined in the last Chapter speaks to a shift from judicial review of economic legislation to judicial review focused on protecting individual non-economic rights. That shift is embodied most dramatically in the Warren Court, which expanded judicial protection of rights of free speech, privacy, criminal procedure, and racial equality. Based on these rulings, journalist Anthony Lewis called the Warren Court "a second American Constitutional Convention."[1] The central case, of course, is *Brown v. Board of Education*, which helped ignite the Civil Rights revolution by striking down segregated schooling under the Equal Protection Clause of the Fourteenth Amendment. A comprehensive account of the Warren Court would require its own course, but the next two chapters hope to give a flavor of that Court's approach to judicial review and some familiarity with some of the most salient doctrinal areas.

The first two sections deal with the problem of racial segregation. The cases continue the story of the Supreme Court's difficult struggle with race begun in *Prigg* and *Dred Scott*. But they also raise three more general sets of questions:

- **Principle:** Critics of the *Lochner* Court's assault on governmental regulation of the economy accused the Court of substituting its own political preferences for the law. Are we any more confident about the Court's ability to distinguish between law and politics when we *like* what it's doing than when we don't? Here the critical readings are Herbert Wechsler's landmark article on "Neutral Principles in Constitutional Law" and Charles Black's effort to explain why *Brown* was, in fact, principled.

- **Interpretive Authority:** Is the Court the last word on what the Constitution means? Do its rulings bind other government officials who are not parties to the case? This is the question in *Cooper v. Aaron*, the Little Rock case, but we will reach back for other examples involving the Bank of the United States and the *Dred Scott* decision.

- **Efficacy:** We will also question the conventional wisdom that *Brown* made a big difference, practically speaking, out in the world. Gerald Rosenberg's book *The Hollow Hope* argues that nothing changed in the South following the

---

[1]   Quoted in LUCAS A. POWE, JR., THE WARREN COURT AND AMERICAN POLITICS 485 (2000).

Brown decision until over a decade later when the national political branches decided to force the South to end segregation. Professor Rosenberg has made similar arguments that judicial review made little difference in other areas, such as abortion rights. This material takes us back to the distinction between right and remedy, and asks whether *judicial* remedies are really that meaningful.

Finally, don't forget about the continuing question of the double standard. If judicial activism was wrong in opposition to the New Deal, is it right in opposition to racial segregation? If so, what is the best way to characterize and defend the difference?

The final section of this chapter turns to another central concern of the Warren Court: criminal procedure and the rights of the accused. Although substantively quite distinct from matters of race, in practice the two areas were significantly related. Many of the Warren Court's criminal procedure decisions, after all, were motivated in significant part by the mistreatment of African Amerians in the criminal justice system, particularly in the South. The Court's concern for the rights of the accused came to transcend race and region however. Although the incorporation of the Bill of Rights' criminal procedure provisions against the States through the Due Process Clause of the Fourteenth Amendment did not begin with the Warren Court, that Court's decisions effectively nationalized the law of criminal procedure. This chapter takes that body of law as an opportunity to discuss the general issue of incorporation as well as the implications of incorporation for federalism.

SECTION 6.1 *BROWN* AND THE PROBLEM OF RACIAL SEGREGATION

To pick up the story of racial segregation and civil rights, we jump back to 1896, just thirteen years after the *Civil Rights Cases* and nine years before *Lochner*. Racial segregation had *not* generally been part of slavery; as historian C. Vann Woodward has observed, "[i]n most aspects of slavery as practiced in the ante-bellum South, . . . segregation would have been an inconvenience and an obstruction to the functioning of the system."[2] The "Jim Crow" system of segregation grew up in the South toward the end of the Nineteenth Century, beginning with segregation in railroad cars (as in *Plessy*) and not extending much to other avenues of life until after the turn of the Twentieth Century. The subsequent "mushroom growth" of the segregation codes "lent the sanction of law to a racial ostracism that extended to churches and schools, to housing and jobs, to eating and drinking. Whether by law or by custom, that ostracism extended to virtually all forms of public transportation, to sports and

---

[2]   C. VANN WOODWARD, THE STRANGE CAREER OF JIM CROW 12 (1974).

recreations, to hospitals, orphanages, prisons, and asylums, and ultimately to funeral homes, morgues, and cemeteries."[3]

Unlike the *Civil Rights Cases*, *Plessy v. Ferguson* involves a challenge to government-mandated discrimination between persons on the basis of race. *Plessy*'s endorsement of a "separate but equal" standard would set the terms of debate for half a century, until the Court's watershed decision to reconsider *Plessy* in *Brown v. Board of Education*.

Plessy v. Ferguson
163 U.S. 537 (1896)

■ **MR. JUSTICE BROWN . . . delivered the opinion of the court.**

This case turns upon the constitutionality of an act of the General Assembly of the State of Louisiana, passed in 1890, providing for separate railway carriages for the white and colored races. The first section of the statute enacts "that all railway companies carrying passengers in their coaches in this State, shall provide equal but separate accommodations for the white, and colored races, by providing two or more passenger coaches for each passenger train, or by dividing the passenger coaches by a partition so as to secure separate accommodations: Provided, That this section shall not be construed to apply to street railroads. No person or persons, shall be admitted to occupy seats in coaches, other than the ones assigned to them on account of the race they belong to."

By the second section it was enacted "that the officers of such passenger trains shall have power and are hereby required to assign each passenger to the coach or compartment used for the race to which such passenger belongs; any passenger insisting on going into a coach or compartment to which by race he does not belong, shall be liable to a fine of twenty-five dollars, or in lieu thereof to imprisonment for a period of not more than twenty days in the parish prison, and any officer of any railroad insisting on assigning a passenger to a coach or compartment other than the one set aside for the race to which said passenger belongs, shall be liable to a fine of twenty-five dollars, or in lieu thereof to imprisonment for a period of not more than twenty days in the parish prison; and should any passenger refuse to occupy the coach or compartment to which he or she is assigned by the officer of such railway, said officer shall have power to refuse to carry such passenger on his train, and for such refusal neither he nor the railway company which he represents shall be liable for damages in any of the courts of this State."

. . .

The information filed in the criminal District Court charged in substance that Plessy, being a passenger between two stations within the State of Louisiana, was assigned by officers of the company to the coach

---

[3]   *Id.* at 7, 98.

used for the race to which he belonged, but he insisted upon going into a coach used by the race to which he did not belong. Neither in the information nor plea was his particular race or color averred.

The petition for the writ of prohibition averred that petitioner was seven eighths Caucasian and one eighth African blood; that the mixture of colored blood was not discernible in him, and that he was entitled to every right, privilege and immunity secured to citizens of the United States of the white race; and that, upon such theory, he took possession of a vacant seat in a coach where passengers of the white race were accommodated, and was ordered by the conductor to vacate said coach and take a seat in another assigned to persons of the colored race, and having refused to comply with such demand he was forcibly ejected with the aid of a police officer, and imprisoned in the parish jail to answer a charge of having violated the above act.

The constitutionality of this act is attacked upon the ground that it conflicts both with the Thirteenth Amendment of the Constitution, abolishing slavery, and the Fourteenth Amendment, which prohibits certain restrictive legislation on the part of the States.

1.   That it does not conflict with the Thirteenth Amendment, which abolished slavery and involuntary servitude, except as a punishment for crime, is too clear for argument. Slavery implies involuntary servitude— a state of bondage; the ownership of mankind as a chattel, or at least the control of the labor and services of one man for the benefit of another, and the absence of a legal right to the disposal of his own person, property and services. . . .

2.   By the Fourteenth Amendment, all persons born or naturalized in the United States, and subject to the jurisdiction thereof, are made citizens of the United States and of the State wherein they reside; and the States are forbidden from making or enforcing any law which shall abridge the privileges or immunities of citizens of the United States, or shall deprive any person of life, liberty or property without due process of law, or deny to any person within their jurisdiction the equal protection of the laws. . . .

The object of the amendment was undoubtedly to enforce the absolute equality of the two races before the law, but in the nature of things it could not have been intended to abolish distinctions based upon color, or to enforce social, as distinguished from political equality, or a commingling of the two races upon terms unsatisfactory to either. Laws permitting, and even requiring, their separation in places where they are liable to be brought into contact do not necessarily imply the inferiority of either race to the other, and have been generally, if not universally, recognized as within the competency of the state legislatures in the exercise of their police power. The most common instance of this is connected with the establishment of separate schools for white and colored children, which has been held to be a valid exercise of the legislative power even by courts of States where the political rights of the colored race have been longest and most earnestly enforced. . . .

Similar laws have been enacted by Congress under its general power of legislation over the District of Columbia, as well as by the legislatures of many of the States, and have been generally, if not uniformly, sustained by the courts. . . .

Laws forbidding the intermarriage of the two races may be said in a technical sense to interfere with the freedom of contract, and yet have been universally recognized as within the police power of the State. . . .

In this connection, it is also suggested . . . that the same argument that will justify the state legislature in requiring railways to provide separate accommodations for the two races will also authorize them to require separate cars to be provided for people whose hair is of a certain color, or who are aliens, or who belong to certain nationalities, or to enact laws requiring colored people to walk upon one side of the street, and white people upon the other, or requiring white men's houses to be painted white, and colored men's black, or their vehicles or business signs to be of different colors, upon the theory that one side of the street is as good as the other, or that a house or vehicle of one color is as good as one of another color. The reply to all this is that every exercise of the police power must be reasonable, and extend only to such laws as are enacted in good faith for the promotion for the public good, and not for the annoyance or oppression of a particular class. Thus in *Yick Wo v. Hopkins*, 118 U.S. 356 (1886), it was held by this court that a municipal ordinance of the city of San Francisco, to regulate the carrying on the public laundries within the limits of the municipality, violated the provisions of the Constitution of the United States, if it conferred upon the municipal authorities arbitrary power, at their own will, and without regard to discretion, in the legal sense of the term, to give or withhold consent as to persons or places, without regard to the competency of the persons applying, or the propriety of the places selected for the carrying on the business. It was held to be a covert attempt on the part of the municipality to make an arbitrary and unjust discrimination against the Chinese race. . . .

So far, then, as a conflict with the Fourteenth Amendment is concerned, the case reduces itself to the question whether the statute of Louisiana is a reasonable regulation, and with respect to this there must necessarily be a large discretion on the part of the legislature. In determining the question of reasonableness it is at liberty to act with reference to the established usages, customs and traditions of the people, and with a view to the promotion of their comfort, and the preservation of the public peace and good order. Gauged by this standard, we cannot say that a law which authorizes or even requires the separation of the two races in public conveyances is unreasonable, or more obnoxious to the Fourteenth Amendment than the acts of Congress requiring separate schools for colored children in the District of Columbia, the constitutionality of which does not seem to have been questioned, or the corresponding acts of state legislatures.

We consider the underlying fallacy of the plaintiff's argument to consist in the assumption that the enforced separation of the two races stamps the colored race with a badge of inferiority. If this be so, it is not by reason of anything found in the act, but solely because the colored race chooses to put that construction upon it. . . . The argument also assumes that social prejudices may be overcome by legislation, and that equal rights cannot be secured to the negro except by an enforced commingling of the two races. We cannot accept this proposition. If the two races are to meet upon terms of social equality, it must be the result of natural affinities, a mutual appreciation of each other's merits and a voluntary consent of individuals. As was said by the Court of Appeals of New York in *People v. Gallagher*, 93 N.Y. 438, 448 (1883), "this end can neither be accomplished nor promoted by laws which conflict with the general sentiment of the community upon whom they are designed to operate. When the government, therefore, has secured to each of its citizens equal rights before the law and equal opportunities for improvement and progress, it has accomplished the end for which it was organized and performed all of the functions respecting social advantages with which it is endowed." Legislation is powerless to eradicate racial instincts or to abolish distinctions based upon physical differences, and the attempt to do so can only result in accentuating the difficulties of the present situation. If the civil and political rights of both races be equal one cannot be inferior to the other civilly or politically. If one race be inferior to the other socially, the Constitution of the United States cannot put them upon the same plane. . . .

The judgment of the court below is, therefore, Affirmed.

■ **MR. JUSTICE HARLAN dissenting.**

. . . I deny that any legislative body or judicial tribunal may have regard to the race of citizens when the civil rights of those citizens are involved. Indeed, such legislation, as that here in question, is inconsistent not only with that equality of rights which pertains to citizenship, National and State, but with the personal liberty enjoyed by every one within the United States.

The Thirteenth Amendment does not permit the withholding or the deprivation of any right necessarily inhering in freedom. It not only struck down the institution of slavery as previously existing in the United States, but it prevents the imposition of any burdens or disabilities that constitute badges of slavery or servitude. It decreed universal civil freedom in this country. This court has so adjudged. But that amendment having been found inadequate to the protection of the rights of those who had been in slavery, it was followed by the Fourteenth Amendment, which added greatly to the dignity and glory of American citizenship, and to the security of personal liberty, by declaring that "all persons born or naturalized in the United States, and subject to the jurisdiction thereof, are citizens of the United States and of the State wherein they reside," and that "no State shall make or enforce any law which shall abridge the privileges or immunities of citizens of the United States; nor shall any State deprive any person of life, liberty or property without due process of law, nor deny to any person within its jurisdiction the equal protection of the laws." These two amendments, if enforced according to their true intent and meaning, will protect all the civil rights that pertain to freedom and citizenship. Finally, and to the end that no citizen should be denied, on account of his race, the privilege of participating in the political control of his country, it was declared by the Fifteenth Amendment that "the right of citizens of the United States to vote shall not be denied or abridged by the United States or by any State on account of race, color or previous condition of servitude."

These notable additions to the fundamental law were welcomed by the friends of liberty throughout the world. They removed the race line from our governmental systems. They had, as this court has said, a common purpose, namely, to secure "to a race recently emancipated, a race that through many generations have been held in slavery, all the civil rights that the superior race enjoy." They declared, in legal effect, this court has further said, "that the law in the States shall be the same for the black as for the white; that all persons, whether colored or white, shall stand equal before the laws of the States, and, in regard to the colored race, for whose protection the amendment was primarily designed, that no discrimination shall be made against them by law because of their color." We also said: "The words of the amendment, it is true, are prohibitory, but they contain a necessary implication of a positive immunity, or right, most valuable to the colored race—the right to exemption from unfriendly legislation against them distinctively as colored—exemption from legal discriminations, implying inferiority in civil society, lessening the security of their enjoyment of the rights which others enjoy, and discriminations which are steps towards reducing them to the condition of a subject race." It was, consequently, adjudged that a state law that excluded citizens of the colored race from juries, because of their race and however well qualified in other respects to discharge the duties of jurymen, was repugnant to the Fourteenth Amendment. *Strauder v. West Virginia*, 100 U.S. 303, 306, 307 (1880). At the present term, referring to the previous adjudications, this court declared that "underlying all of those decisions is the principle that the Constitution of the United States, in its present form, forbids, so far as civil and political rights are concerned, discrimination by the General Government or the States against any citizen because of his race. All citizens are equal before the law." *Gibson v. Mississippi*, 162 U.S. 565 (1896). . . .

It was said in argument that the statute of Louisiana does not discriminate against either race, but prescribes a rule applicable alike to white and colored citizens. But this argument does not meet the difficulty. Every one knows that the statute in question had its origin in the purpose, not so much to exclude white persons from railroad cars occupied by blacks, as to exclude colored people from coaches occupied by or assigned to white persons. Railroad corporations of Louisiana did not make discrimination among whites in the matter of accommodation for travelers. The thing to accomplish was, under the guise of giving equal accommodation for whites and blacks, to compel the latter to keep to themselves while traveling in railroad passenger coaches. No one would be so wanting in candor as to assert the contrary. The fundamental objection, therefore, to the statute is that it interferes with the personal freedom of citizens. "Personal liberty," it has been well said, "consists in the power of locomotion, of changing situation, or removing one's person to whatsoever places one's own inclination may direct, without imprisonment or restraint, unless by due course of law." 1 Blackstone's Commentaries *134. If a white man and a black man choose to occupy the same public conveyance on a public highway, it is their right to do so, and no government, proceeding alone on grounds of race, can prevent it without infringing the personal liberty of each. . . .

The white race deems itself to be the dominant race in this country. And so it is, in prestige, in achievements, in education, in wealth and in power. So, I doubt not, it will continue to be for all time, if it remains true to its great heritage and holds fast to the principles of constitutional liberty. But in view of the Constitution, in the eye of the law, there is in this country no superior, dominant, ruling class of citizens. There is no caste here. Our Constitution is color-blind, and neither knows nor tolerates classes among citizens. In respect of civil rights, all citizens are equal before the law. The humblest is the peer of the most powerful. The law regards man as man, and takes no account of his surroundings or of his color when his civil rights as guaranteed by the supreme law of the land are involved. It is, therefore, to be regretted that this high tribunal, the final expositor of the fundamental law of the land, has reached the conclusion that it is competent for a State to regulate the enjoyment by citizens of their civil rights solely upon the basis of race.

In my opinion, the judgment this day rendered will, in time, prove to be quite as pernicious as the decision made by this tribunal in the *Dred Scott* case. It was adjudged in that case that the descendants of Africans who were imported into this country and sold as slaves were not included nor intended to be included under the word "citizens" in the Constitution, and could not claim any of the rights and privileges which that instrument provided for and secured to citizens of the United States; that at the time of the adoption of the Constitution they were "considered as a subordinate and inferior class of beings, who had been subjugated by the dominant race, and, whether emancipated or not, yet remained subject to their authority, and had no rights or privileges but such as those who held the power and the government might choose to grant them." The recent amendments of the Constitution, it was supposed, had eradicated these principles from our institutions. But it seems that we have yet, in some of the States, a dominant race—a superior class of citizens, which assumes to regulate the enjoyment of civil rights, common to all citizens, upon the basis of race. The present decision, it may well be apprehended, will not only stimulate aggressions, more or less brutal and irritating, upon the admitted rights of colored citizens, but will encourage the belief that it is possible, by means of state enactments, to defeat the beneficent purposes which the people of the United States had in view when they adopted the recent amendments of the Constitution, by one of which the blacks of this country were made citizens of the United States and of the States in which they respectively reside, and whose privileges and immunities, as citizens, the States are forbidden to abridge. Sixty millions of whites are in no danger from the presence here of eight millions of blacks. The destinies of the two races, in this country, are indissolubly linked together, and the interests of both require that the common government of all shall not permit the seeds of race hate to be planted under the sanction of law. What can more certainly arouse race hate, what more certainly create and perpetuate a feeling of distrust between these races, than state enactments, which, in fact, proceed on the ground that colored citizens are so inferior and degraded that they cannot be allowed to sit in public coaches occupied by white citizens? That, as all will admit, is the real meaning of such legislation as was enacted in Louisiana.

The sure guarantee of the peace and security of each race is the clear, distinct, unconditional recognition by our governments, National and State, of every right that inheres in civil freedom, and of the equality before the law of all citizens of the United States without regard to race. State enactments, regulating the enjoyment of civil rights, upon the basis of race, and cunningly devised to defeat legitimate results of the war, under the pretence of recognizing equality of rights, can have no other result than to render permanent peace impossible, and to keep alive a conflict of races, the continuance of which must do harm to all concerned. This question is not met by the suggestion that social equality cannot exist between the white and black races in this country. That argument, if it can be properly regarded as one, is scarcely worthy of consideration; for social equality no more exists between two races when traveling in a passenger coach or a public highway than when members of the same races sit by each other in a street car or in the jury box, or stand or sit with each other in a political assembly, or when they use in common the streets of a city or town, or when they are in the same room for the purpose of having their names placed on the registry of voters, or when they approach the ballot-box in order to exercise the high privilege of voting.

There is a race so different from our own that we do not permit those belonging to it to become citizens of the United States. Persons belonging to it are, with few exceptions, absolutely excluded from our country. I allude to the Chinese race. But by the statute in question, a Chinaman can ride in the same passenger coach with white citizens of the United States, while citizens of the black race in Louisiana, many of whom, perhaps, risked their lives for the preservation of the Union, who are entitled, by law, to participate in the political control of the State and nation, who are not excluded, by law or by reason of their race, from public stations of any kind, and who have all the legal rights that belong to white citizens, are yet declared to be criminals, liable to imprisonment, if they ride in a public coach occupied by citizens of the white race. It is scarcely just to say that a colored citizen should not object to occupying a public coach assigned to his own race. He does not object, nor, perhaps, would he object to separate coaches for his race, if his rights under the law were recognized. But he objects, and ought never to cease objecting to the proposition, that citizens of the white and black races can be adjudged criminals because they sit, or claim the right to sit, in the same public coach on a public highway.

The arbitrary separation of citizens, on the basis of race, while they are on a public highway, is a badge of servitude wholly inconsistent with the civil freedom and the equality before the law established by the Constitution. It cannot be justified upon any legal grounds.

If evils will result from the commingling of the two races upon public highways established for the benefit of all, they will be infinitely less than those that will surely come from state legislation regulating the enjoyment of civil rights upon the basis of race. We boast of the freedom enjoyed by our people above all other peoples. But it is difficult to reconcile that boast with a state of the law which, practically, puts the brand of servitude and degradation upon a large class of our fellow-citizens, our equals before the law. The thin disguise of "equal" accommodations for passengers in railroad coaches will not mislead any one, nor atone for the wrong this day done. . . .

I am of opinion that the statute of Louisiana is inconsistent with the personal liberty of citizens, white and black, in that State, and hostile to both the spirit and letter of the Constitution of the United States. If laws of like character should be enacted in the several States of the Union, the effect would be in the highest degree mischievous. Slavery, as an institution tolerated by law would, it is true, have disappeared from our country, but there would remain a power in the States, by sinister legislation, to interfere with the full enjoyment of the blessings of freedom; to regulate civil rights, common to all citizens, upon the basis of race; and to place in a condition of legal inferiority a large body of American citizens, now constituting a part of the political community called the People of the United States, for whom, and by whom through representatives, our government is administered. . . .

For the reasons stated, I am constrained to withhold my assent from the opinion and judgment of the majority.

NOTE ON THE APPLICATION OF "SEPARATE BUT EQUAL"

1.   What limits is Justice Brown's majority opinion willing to impose on segregation in *Plessy*? What is the standard of review for this sort of law? Where have you seen that standard before?

2.   Justice Harlan's famous dissent in *Plessy* is the origin of the notion that the Constitution is "color-blind." (Did Harlan actually think blacks were *equal* to whites?) While surely a great advance over the social conditions of Harlan's day, "colorblindness" is now a controversial way of thinking about racial equality. Chapter Fifteen considers, for example, how the principle of "colorblindness" bears on affirmative action programs meant to benefit racial minorities. Should Harlan have chosen a different organizing principle?

The colorblindness idea is sometime fleshed out as an "antidiscrimination principle" of equal protection doctrine. This principle would bar government action that classifies persons according to race. The principal alternative to that view is generally expressed as an "antisubjugation" or "antisubordination" principle. That principle might be summed up as one that "aims to break down legally created or legally reinforced systems of subordination that treat some people as second-class citizens."[4] According to Professor Tribe,

> The antidiscrimination principle harbors a fundamental gap because it identifies but one mechanism of subjugation: the purposeful, affirmative adoption or use of rules that disadvantage the target group. . . . This overlooks the fact that minorities can also be injured when the government is "only" indifferent to their suffering or "merely" blind to how prior official discrimination contributed to it and how current official acts will perpetuate it.[5]

The anti-subjugation principle thus leads to the conclusion "that race may be taken into account by a government body at least for the purpose of remedying past racial discrimination reasonably believed, by that body, to have distorted the situation that would otherwise confront."[6] Is the anti-subjugation principle a better way than colorblindness to think about "equal protection of the laws"?

3.   The *Plessy* majority criticizes the dissent for "assum[ing] that social prejudices may be overcome by legislation," and suggests that "[i]f one race be inferior to the other socially, the Constitution of the United States cannot put them upon the same plane." Is the majority right to be pessimistic about the capacity of courts and constitutional law to effect major social change? We will return to this question in Section 6.2, *infra*.

4.   *Plessy* stated the law of the land for over half a century. Near the end of this period, however, the Court was confronted with a series of increasingly difficult cases applying the "separate but equal" doctrine in the context of education. These cases laid an important foundation for *Brown v.*

---

[4]   LAURENCE TRIBE, AMERICAN CONSTITUTIONAL LAW § 16–21, at 1515 (2d ed. 1988).

[5]   *Id.* at 1518.

[6]   *Id.* at § 16–22, p. 1525.

Board of Education, which ultimately struck down the practice of segregated schooling.

a.   *Missouri ex rel. Gaines v. Canada*, 305 U.S. 337 (1938), struck down Missouri's law school system, which required segregated education for whites and blacks. The all-white University of Missouri provided a law school, while the black university, Lincoln University, did not. Missouri law provided for sending black residents to law schools in neighboring states and paying their tuition there. The Court ruled that the State must provide equal facilities within the state. Why was it so important to provide facilities in-state?

b.   In *Sweatt v. Painter*, 339 U.S. 629 (1950), the Court required the University of Texas law school to admit a black student, because the black law school was not in fact equal. Importantly, the Court took into account intangible factors like reputation and networking in assessing "equality" of facilities: According to Chief Justice Vinson's majority opinion, "the University of Texas Law School possesses to a far greater degree those qualities which are incapable of objective measurement but which make for greatness in a law school." (You have recently chosen a law school: How important were intangible factors like faculty quality and reputation in your choice?) If intangibles count, how is a court to measure them in assessing the equality of separate facilities?

c.   *McLaurin v. Oklahoma State Regents*, 339 U.S. 637 (1950), decided the same term as *Sweatt*, addressed the University of Texas's arch-rival: the University of Oklahoma. [7] The University allowed Mr. McLaurin, a graduate student in education, to attend the white university, but required him to sit in a special seat, prohibited him from dining with other students in the cafeteria, and made him sit at a special table in the library. The Court held that these restrictions "[impaired] and [inhibited] his ability to study, to engage in discussion and exchange views with other students, and, in general, to learn his profession." Here, of course, the facilities, faculty, and curriculum were clearly equal—they were, in fact, the *very same* facilities, faculty, and curriculum that the white students were getting. What was being denied to McLaurin?

These decisions are a good case study in how a doctrine that seems fairly determinate can nonetheless fall apart when it comes in contact with the real world. How much is left of "separate but equal," practically speaking, after these cases? If a state wanted to set up a segregated university system in "good faith" compliance with *Plessy*, how would it do so?

---

[7]   In a fourth case, decided two years prior to *Sweatt* and *McLaurin*, the Court had ordered the admission to the University of Oklahoma's law school of a black student excluded solely on the basis of race. *Sipuel v. Board of Regents*, 332 U.S. 631 (1948). The Court's brief *per curiam* opinion relied solely on a citation to *Gaines*.

Note also that all three of these earlier cases involved graduate education; two involved law schools. Can you see the importance of the context and sequencing of these cases in mounting a challenge to *Plessy*? In answering this question, keep in mind that the Supreme Court has only limited control over its own agenda, and the sequence of decisions is also a function of strategic decisions by civil rights attorneys—especially Thurgood Marshall and the National Association for the Advancement of Colored People's Legal Defense Fund. (Marshall argued both *Sweatt* and *McLaurin*, as well as *Brown* itself.) Why do you think the NAACP chose to focus on education in general, and (initially) legal education in particular?

Brown v. Board of Education (Brown I)
347 U.S. 483 (1954)

■ MR. CHIEF JUSTICE WARREN **delivered the opinion of the Court.**

These cases come to us from the States of Kansas, South Carolina, Virginia, and Delaware. They are premised on different facts and different local conditions, but a common legal question justifies their consideration together in this consolidated opinion.

In each of the cases, minors of the Negro race, through their legal representatives, seek the aid of the courts in obtaining admission to the public schools of their community on a nonsegregated basis. In each instance, they had been denied admission to schools attended by white children under laws requiring or permitting segregation according to race. This segregation was alleged to deprive the plaintiffs of the equal protection of the laws under the Fourteenth Amendment. In each of the cases other than the Delaware case, a three-judge federal district court denied relief to the plaintiffs on the so-called "separate but equal" doctrine announced by this Court in *Plessy v. Ferguson*. Under that doctrine, equality of treatment is accorded when the races are provided substantially equal facilities, even though these facilities be separate. In the Delaware case, the Supreme Court of Delaware adhered to that doctrine, but ordered that the plaintiffs be admitted to the white schools because of their superiority to the Negro schools.

The plaintiffs contend that segregated public schools are not "equal" and cannot be made "equal," and that hence they are deprived of the equal protection of the laws. Because of the obvious importance of the question presented, the Court took jurisdiction. Argument was heard in the 1952 Term, and reargument was heard this Term on certain questions propounded by the Court.

Reargument was largely devoted to the circumstances surrounding the adoption of the Fourteenth Amendment in 1868. It covered exhaustively consideration of the Amendment in Congress, ratification by the states, then existing practices in racial segregation, and the views of proponents and opponents of the Amendment. This discussion and our own investigation convince us that, although these sources cast some light, it is not enough to resolve the problem with which we are faced. At best, they are inconclusive. The most avid proponents of the post-War Amendments undoubtedly intended them to remove all legal distinctions among "all persons born or naturalized in the United States." Their opponents, just as certainly, were antagonistic to both the letter and the spirit of the Amendments and wished them to have the most limited effect. What others in Congress and the state legislatures had in mind cannot be determined with any degree of certainty.

An additional reason for the inconclusive nature of the Amendment's history, with respect to segregated schools, is the status of public education at that time. In the South, the movement toward free common schools, supported by general taxation, had not yet taken hold. Education of white children was largely in the hands of private groups. Education of Negroes was almost nonexistent, and practically all of the race were illiterate. In fact, any education of Negroes was forbidden by law in some states. Today, in contrast, many Negroes have achieved outstanding success in the arts and sciences as well as in the business and professional world. It is true that public school education at the time of the Amendment had advanced further in the North, but the effect of the Amendment on Northern States was generally ignored in the congressional debates. Even in the North, the conditions of public education did not approximate those existing today. The curriculum was usually rudimentary; ungraded schools were common in rural areas; the school term was but three months a year in many states; and compulsory school attendance was virtually unknown. As a consequence, it is not surprising that there should be so little in the history of the Fourteenth Amendment relating to its intended effect on public education.

In the first cases in this Court construing the Fourteenth Amendment, decided shortly after its adoption, the Court interpreted it as proscribing all state-imposed discriminations against the Negro race. The doctrine of "separate but equal" did not make its appearance in this Court until 1896 in the case of *Plessy v. Ferguson,* involving not education but transportation. American courts have since labored with the doctrine for over half a century. In this Court, there have been six cases involving the "separate but equal" doctrine in the field of public education. In *Cumming v. County Board of Education*, 175 U.S. 528 (1899), and *Gong Lum v. Rice*, 275 U.S. 78 (1927), the validity of the doctrine itself was not challenged. In more recent cases, all on the graduate school level, inequality was found in that specific benefits enjoyed by white students were denied to Negro students of the same educational qualifications. *Missouri ex rel. Gaines v. Canada*, 305 U.S. 337 (1938); *Sipuel v. Oklahoma*, 332 U.S. 631 (1948); *Sweatt v. Painter*, 339 U.S. 629 (1950); *McLaurin v. Oklahoma State Regents*, 339 U.S. 637 (1950). In none of these cases was it necessary to re-examine the doctrine to grant relief to the Negro plaintiff. And in *Sweatt v. Painter*, the Court expressly reserved decision on the question whether *Plessy v. Ferguson* should be held inapplicable to public education.

In the instant cases, that question is directly presented. Here, unlike *Sweatt v. Painter*, there are findings below that the Negro and white schools involved have been equalized, or are being equalized, with respect to buildings, curricula, qualifications and salaries of teachers, and other "tangible" factors. Our decision, therefore, cannot turn on merely a comparison of these tangible factors in the Negro and white schools involved in each of the cases. We must look instead to the effect of segregation itself on public education.

In approaching this problem, we cannot turn the clock back to 1868 when the Amendment was adopted, or even to 1896 when *Plessy v. Ferguson* was written. We must consider public education in the light of its full development and its present place in American life throughout the Nation. Only in this way can it be determined if segregation in public schools deprives these plaintiffs of the equal protection of the laws.

Today, education is perhaps the most important function of state and local governments. Compulsory school attendance laws and the great expenditures for education both demonstrate our recognition of the importance of education to our democratic society. It is required in the performance of our most basic public responsibilities, even service in the armed forces. It is the very foundation of good citizenship. Today it is a principal instrument in awakening the child to cultural values, in preparing him for later professional training, and in helping him to adjust normally to his environment. In these days, it is doubtful that any child may reasonably be expected to succeed in life if he is denied the opportunity of an education. Such an opportunity, where the state has undertaken to provide it, is a right which must be made available to all on equal terms.

We come then to the question presented: Does segregation of children in public schools solely on the basis of race, even though the physical facilities and other "tangible" factors may be equal, deprive the children of the minority group of equal educational opportunities? We believe that it does.

In *Sweatt v. Painter,* in finding that a segregated law school for Negroes could not provide them equal educational opportunities, this Court relied in large part on "those qualities which are incapable of objective measurement but which make for greatness in a law school." In *McLaurin v. Oklahoma State Regents*, the Court, in requiring that a Negro admitted to a white graduate school be treated like all other students, again resorted to intangible considerations: ". . . his ability to study, to engage in discussions and exchange views with other students, and, in general, to learn his profession." Such considerations apply with added force to children in grade and high schools. To separate them from others of similar age and qualifications solely because of their race generates a feeling of inferiority as to their status in the community that may affect their hearts and minds in a way unlikely ever to be undone. The effect of this separation on their educational opportunities was well stated by a finding in the Kansas case by a court which nevertheless felt compelled to rule against the Negro plaintiffs:

> Segregation of white and colored children in public schools has a detrimental effect upon the colored children. The impact is greater when it has the sanction of the law; for the policy of separating the races is usually interpreted as denoting the inferiority of the negro group. A sense of inferiority affects the motivation of a child to learn. Segregation with the sanction of law, therefore, has a tendency to [retard] the educational and mental development of negro children and to deprive them of some of the benefits they would receive in a racial[ly] integrated school system.

Whatever may have been the extent of psychological knowledge at the time of *Plessy v. Ferguson*, this finding is amply supported by modern authority.[11] Any language in *Plessy v. Ferguson* contrary to this finding is rejected.

We conclude that in the field of public education the doctrine of "separate but equal" has no place. Separate educational facilities are inherently unequal. Therefore, we hold that the plaintiffs and others similarly situated for whom the actions have been brought are, by reason of the segregation complained of, deprived of the equal protection of the laws guaranteed by the Fourteenth Amendment. This disposition makes unnecessary any discussion whether such segregation also violates the Due Process Clause of the Fourteenth Amendment.

Because these are class actions, because of the wide applicability of this decision, and because of the great variety of local conditions, the formulation of decrees in these cases presents problems of considerable complexity. On reargument, the consideration of appropriate relief was necessarily subordinated to the primary question—the constitutionality of segregation in public education. We have now announced that such segregation is a denial of the equal protection of the laws. In order that we may have the full assistance of the parties in formulating decrees, the cases will be restored to the docket, and the parties are requested to present further argument. . . . The Attorney General of the United States is again invited to participate. The Attorneys General of the states

---

[11] K. B. CLARK, EFFECT OF PREJUDICE AND DISCRIMINATION ON PERSONALITY DEVELOPMENT (MIDCENTURY WHITE HOUSE CONFERENCE ON CHILDREN AND YOUTH, 1950); Witmer and Kotinsky, Personality in the Making (1952), c. VI; Deutscher and Chein, *The Psychological Effects of Enforced Segregation: A Survey of Social Science Opinion*, 26 J. PSYCHOL. 259 (1948); Chein, *What are the Psychological Effects of Segregation Under Conditions of Equal Facilities?*, 3 INT. J. OPINION AND ATTITUDE RES. 229 (1949); BRAMELD, EDUCATIONAL COSTS, IN DISCRIMINATION AND NATIONAL WELFARE (MacIver, ed., 1949), 44–48; Frazier, The Negro in the United States (1949), 674–681. And *see generally* MYRDAL, AN AMERICAN DILEMMA (1944).

requiring or permitting segregation in public education will also be permitted to appear as *amici curiae* upon request to do so. . . .

Bolling v. Sharpe

347 U.S. 497 (1954)

■ MR. CHIEF JUSTICE WARREN **delivered the opinion of the Court.**

This case challenges the validity of segregation in the public schools of the District of Columbia. The petitioners, minors of the Negro race, allege that such segregation deprives them of due process of law under the Fifth Amendment. They were refused admission to a public school attended by white children solely because of their race. They sought the aid of the District Court for the District of Columbia in obtaining admission. That court dismissed their complaint. The Court granted a writ of certiorari before judgment in the Court of Appeals because of the importance of the constitutional question presented.

We have this day held that the Equal Protection Clause of the Fourteenth Amendment prohibits the states from maintaining racially segregated public schools. The legal problem in the District of Columbia is somewhat different, however. The Fifth Amendment, which is applicable in the District of Columbia, does not contain an equal protection clause as does the Fourteenth Amendment which applies only to the states. But the concepts of equal protection and due process, both stemming from our American ideal of fairness, are not mutually exclusive. The "equal protection of the laws" is a more explicit safeguard of prohibited unfairness than "due process of law," and, therefore, we do not imply that the two are always interchangeable phrases. But, as this Court has recognized, discrimination may be so unjustifiable as to be violative of due process.

Classifications based solely upon race must be scrutinized with particular care, since they are contrary to our traditions and hence constitutionally suspect. As long ago as 1896, this Court declared the principle "that the Constitution of the United States, in its present form, forbids, so far as civil and political rights are concerned, discrimination by the General Government, or by the States, against any citizen because of his race." *Gibson v. Mississippi*, 162 U.S. 565. And in *Buchanan v. Warley*, 245 U.S. 60 (1917), the Court held that a statute which limited the right of a property owner to convey his property to a person of another race was, as an unreasonable discrimination, a denial of due process of law.

Although the Court has not assumed to define "liberty" with any great precision, that term is not confined to mere freedom from bodily restraint. Liberty under law extends to the full range of conduct which the individual is free to pursue, and it cannot be restricted except for a proper governmental objective. Segregation in public education is not reasonably related to any proper governmental objective, and thus it imposes on Negro children of the District of Columbia a burden that constitutes an arbitrary deprivation of their liberty in violation of the Due Process Clause.

In view of our decision that the Constitution prohibits the states from maintaining racially segregated public schools, it would be unthinkable that the same Constitution would impose a lesser duty on the Federal Government. We hold that racial segregation in the public schools of the District of Columbia is a denial of the due process of law guaranteed by the Fifth Amendment to the Constitution. . . .

NOTE ON THE SCHOOL SEGREGATION DECISIONS

1.   Historians of the Court often suggest that *Brown* was initially held over for reargument not simply to get more information about the history of the Fourteenth Amendment, but also to gain time to rally the justices behind a single, unanimous opinion. (Note also that the composition of the Court changed between the term of the initial argument and the term of ultimate decision: Chief Justice Vinson died and was replaced by Chief Justice Earl Warren.) How important is it that the Court speak with one voice in a case like this? If—as is also widely believed—Chief Justice Warren's eventual opinion sacrificed clarity and coherence for unanimity, was that a trade-off worth making?

2.   What was the Court's rationale in *Brown I*? How dependent was the Court's decision on social science data concerning the impact of segregation on black children? Was that reliance wise? Subsequent commentators have criticized the methodology of the particular studies involved; if later studies disproved some of the early empirical conclusions, would *Brown I* need to be reconsidered?

How important to the rationale is the fact this case concerned public education? Subsequent cases that reached the Court shortly after *Brown* concerned segregation in other areas of life, but the Court prohibited segregation in a series of unsigned *per curiam* opinions that simply cited to *Brown*.[8] If *Brown* was about education, can one defend its extension to courts and restaurants?

3.   What is the harm of segregation? Is it unequal treatment by the state, or is it the actual division of society along racial lines? The question is important in particular for issues of remedy considered in the next assignment. It is one thing to tell the state to stop segregating, and quite another to actually undo the social results of two centuries of slavery and segregation. Is the end of formal, *de jure* segregation sufficient to satisfy the Constitution?

4.   We will discuss precedent and *stare decisis* in Section 7.3, *infra*, but the sequence of *Gaines*, *Sipuel*, *Sweatt*, and *McLaurin* illustrate one important consideration relevant to overruling precedent—that is, the

---

[8]   *See, e.g.*, *Johnson v. Virginia*, 373 U.S. 61 (1963) (*per curiam*) (invalidating segregation of courtroom seating); *Turner v. City of Memphis*, 369 U.S. 350 (1962) (*per curiam*) (enjoining segregation in an airport restaurant).

"workability" of the rule articulated in the prior decision. Do these cases suggest that *Plessy* had become unworkable? Was *Brown* a big break with prior trends?

5. Historians have noted that "[n]ot only were the Court's new opinions favorable for attacking separate but equal, but so were trends in society as well":

> After World War II, Jackie Robinson integrated major league baseball, the undisputed national past-time; the Democrats at their 1948 convention joined the Republicans in including a strong civil rights plank; Truman had ordered an end to segregation in the armed forces. Additionally, and significantly, the imperatives of the cold war, in which both the United States and the Soviet Union were trying to woo recently independent nations into their respective orbits, made segregation a huge problem for the State Department, and the Justice Department so informed the Court in a friend of the Court brief.[9]

How important do you think these broader social trends were to the Justices in *Brown* and *Bolling*?

6. Is *Bolling* a harder case than *Brown I*? If equal protection and due process are really the same thing, why does the Fourteenth Amendment bother with both? Traditional incorporation doctrine applies the provisions of the Bill of Rights to the States through the medium of the Due Process Clause of the Fourteenth Amendment. That argument can draw upon at least some historical evidence that the Framers of the Fourteenth Amendment looked back to the Bill of Rights. But is it really possible to justify on similar grounds the "reverse incorporation" of the Equal Protection Clause to apply to the federal government through the Due Process Clause of the *Fifth* Amendment? Doesn't the timing pose a problem for this sort of argument?

More generally, do you find the Court's explanation of the result in *Bolling* adequate? If not, can you come up with a better one? The Court's incorporation cases, discussed in Section 6.3, *infra*, posit that the Due Process Clause protects elements of "fundamental fairness"—an interpretation that presumably applies to the Fifth Amendment as well as the Fourteenth. Is it fair to say that, with *Brown* in the books, desegregation had to be considered an element of "fundamental fairness"? In any event, could the Court really have gone the other way in *Bolling*? What would have happened if it had?

Despite any misgivings we may have about *Bolling*'s reasoning, however, the principle is now firmly established that principles of equal protection apply to the federal government as well as to the states. Indeed, despite occasional suggestions to the contrary, the Court has largely treated federal and state equal protection cases interchangeably. Even if one accepts

---

[9] LUCAS A. POWE, JR., THE SUPREME COURT AND THE AMERICAN ELITE, 1789–2008, at 241–42 (2009); *see also* MARY L. DUDZIAK, COLD WAR CIVIL RIGHTS: RACE AND THE IMAGE OF AMERICAN DEMOCRACY (2d ed. 2011).

some degree of "reverse incorporation," does it follow that the federal government and the states should be treated exactly the same in this regard?

7. Some contemporary observers of the Court who were profoundly sympathetic to the result in *Brown I* nonetheless had misgivings about the Court's action. The most prominent example was Columbia's Herbert Wechsler, one of the leading legal scholars of his generation. Professor Wechsler articulated his misgivings about *Brown* in a famous Holmes Lecture at Harvard Law School. These materials reproduce excerpts both of Wechsler's critique and the most influential response, by Professor Charles Black of Yale.

Herbert Wechsler, Toward Neutral Principles in Constitutional Law*

. . . If courts cannot escape the duty of deciding whether actions of the other branches of the government are consistent with the Constitution, when a case is properly before them . . . , you will not doubt the relevancy and importance of demanding what, if any, are the standards to be followed in interpretation. Are there, indeed, any criteria that both the Supreme Court and those who undertake to praise or to condemn its judgments are morally and intellectually obligated to support?

. . . Even to put the problem is, of course, to raise an issue no less old than our culture. Those who perceive in law only the element of fiat, in whose conception of the legal cosmos reason has no meaning or no place, will not join gladly in the search for standards of the kind I have in mind. . . . So too must I anticipate dissent from those . . . who . . . frankly or covertly make the test of virtue in interpretation whether its result in the immediate decision seems to hinder or advance the interests or the values they support. . . .

The man who simply lets his judgment turn on the immediate result may not, however, realize that his position implies that the courts are free to function as a naked power organ, that it is an empty affirmation to regard them, as ambivalently he so often does, as courts of law. If he may know he disapproves of a decision when all he knows is that it has sustained a claim put forward by a labor union or a taxpayer, a Negro or a segregationist, a corporation or a Communist—he acquiesces in the proposition that a man of different sympathy but equal information may no less properly conclude that he approves.

You will not charge me with exaggeration if I say that this type of *ad hoc* evaluation is, as it has always been, the deepest problem of our constitutionalism, not only with respect to judgments of the courts but also in the wider realm in which conflicting constitutional positions have played a part in our politics.

---

* Reprinted from 73 HARV. L. REV. 1 (1959). This paper was delivered on April 7, 1959, as the Oliver Wendell Holmes Lecture at the Harvard Law School.

Did not New England challenge the embargo [imposed by the Madison administration on Britain prior to the War of 1812] that the South supported on the very ground on which the South was to resist New England's demand for a protective tariff? Was not Jefferson in the Louisiana Purchase forced to rest on an expansive reading of the clauses granting national authority of the very kind that he had steadfastly opposed in his attacks upon the Bank? Can you square his disappointment about Burr's acquittal on the treason charge and his subsequent request for legislation with the attitude towards freedom and repression most enduringly associated with his name? Were the abolitionists who rescued fugitives and were acquitted in defiance of the evidence able to distinguish their view of the compulsion of a law of the United States from that advanced by South Carolina in the [nullification] ordinance that they despised? . . .

All I have said, you may reply, is something no one will deny, that principles are largely instrumental as they are employed in politics, instrumental in relation to results that a controlling sentiment demands at any given time. Politicians recognize this fact of life and are obliged to trim and shape their speech and votes accordingly, unless perchance they are prepared to step aside. . . .

[W]hether you are tolerant, perhaps more tolerant than I, of the *ad hoc* in politics, with principle reduced to a manipulative tool, are you not also ready to agree that something else is called for from the courts? I put it to you that the main constituent of the judicial process is precisely that it must be genuinely principled, resting with respect to every step that is involved in reaching judgment on analysis and reasons quite transcending the immediate result that is achieved. To be sure, the courts decide, or should decide, only the case they have before them. But must they not decide on grounds of adequate neutrality and generality, tested not only by the instant application but by others that the principles imply? Is it not the very essence of judicial method to insist upon attending to such other cases, preferably those involving an opposing interest, in evaluating any principle avowed?

Here too I do not think that I am stating any novel or momentous insight. But now, as Holmes said long ago . . . we "need education in the obvious." We need it more particularly now respecting constitutional interpretation, since it has become a commonplace to grant what many for so long denied: that courts in constitutional determinations face issues that are inescapably "political" . . . in that they involve a choice among competing values or desires, a choice reflected in the legislative or executive action in question, which the court must either condemn or condone.

I should be the last to argue otherwise. . . . But what is crucial, I submit, is not the nature of the question but the nature of the answer that may validly be given by the courts. No legislature or executive is obligated by the nature of its function to support its choice of values by the type of reasoned explanation that I have suggested is intrinsic to judicial action—however much we may admire such a reasoned exposition when we find it in those other realms. . . .

Is there not, in short, a vital difference between legislative freedom to appraise the gains and losses in projected measures and the kind of principled appraisal, in respect of values that can reasonably be asserted to have constitutional dimension, that alone is in the province of the courts? Does not the difference yield a middle ground between a judicial House of Lords and the abandonment of any limitation on the other branches—a middle ground consisting of judicial action that embodies what are surely the main qualities of law, its generality and its neutrality? This must, it seems to me, have been in Mr. Justice Jackson's mind when in his chapter on the Supreme Court "as a political institution" he wrote in words that I find stirring, "Liberty is not the mere absence of restraint, it is not a spontaneous product of majority rule, it is not achieved merely by lifting underprivileged classes to power, nor is it the inevitable by-product of technological expansion. It is achieved only by a rule of law." Is it not also what Mr. Justice Frankfurter must mean in calling upon judges for "allegiance to nothing except the effort, amid tangled words and limited insights, to find the path through precedent, through policy, through history, to the best judgment that fallible creatures can reach in that most difficult of all tasks: the achievement of justice between man and man, between man and state, through reason called law"?

You will not understand my emphasis upon the role of reason and of principle in the judicial . . . appraisal of conflicting values to imply that I depreciate the duty of fidelity to the text of the Constitution, when its words may be decisive—though I would certainly remind you of the caution stated by Chief Justice Hughes: "Behind the words of the constitutional provisions are postulates which limit and control." Nor will you take me to deny that history has weight in the elucidation of the text, though it is surely subtle business to appraise it as a guide. Nor will you even think that I deem precedent without importance, for we surely must agree with Holmes that "imitation of the past, until we have a clear reason for change, no more needs justification than appetite." But after all, it was Chief Justice Taney who declared his willingness "that it be regarded hereafter as the law of this court, that its opinion upon the construction of the Constitution is always open to discussion when it is supposed to have been founded in error, and that its judicial authority should hereafter depend altogether on the force of the reasoning by which it is supported." Would any of us have it otherwise, given the nature of the problems that confront the courts?

At all events, is not the relative compulsion of the language of the Constitution, of history and precedent—where they do not combine to make an answer clear—itself a matter to be judged, so far as possible, by neutral principles—by standards that transcend the case at hand? I know, of course, that it is common to distinguish, as Judge Hand did, clauses like "due process," cast "in such sweeping terms that their history does not elucidate their contents," from other provisions of the Bill of Rights addressed to more specific problems. But the contrast, as it seems to me, often implies an overstatement of the specificity or the immutability these other clauses really have—at least when problems under them arise. . . .

Let me repeat what I have thus far tried to say. The courts have both the title and the duty when a case is properly before them to review the actions of the other branches in the light of constitutional provision, even though the action involves value choices, as invariably action does. In doing so, however, they are bound to function otherwise than as a naked power organ; they participate as courts of law. This calls for facing how determinations of this kind can be asserted to have any legal quality. The answer, I suggest, inheres primarily in that they are—or are obliged to be—entirely principled. A principled decision, in the sense I have in mind, is one that rests on reasons with respect to all the issues in the case, reasons that in their generality and their neutrality transcend any immediate result that is involved. When no sufficient reasons of this kind can be assigned for overturning value choices of the other branches of the Government or of a state, those choices must, of course, survive. Otherwise, as Holmes said in his first opinion for the Court, "a constitution, instead of embodying only relatively fundamental rules of right . . . would become the partisan of a particular set of ethical or economical opinions. . . ."

The virtue or demerit of a judgment turns, therefore, entirely on the reasons that support it and their adequacy to maintain any choice of values it decrees, or, it is vital that we add, to maintain the rejection of a claim that any given choice should be decreed. The critic's role . . . is the sustained, disinterested, merciless examination of the reasons that the courts advance, measured by standards of the kind I have attempted to describe. . . .

Lastly, I come to the school decision, which for one of my persuasion stirs the deepest conflict I experience in testing the thesis I propose. Yet I would surely be engaged in playing Hamlet without Hamlet if I did not try to state the problems that appear to me to be involved.

The problem for me, I hardly need to say, is not that the Court departed from its earlier decisions holding or implying that the equality of public educational facilities demanded by the Constitution could be met by separate schools. I stand with the long tradition of the Court that previous decisions must be subject to reexamination when a case against their reasoning is made. Nor is the problem that the Court disturbed the settled patterns of a portion of the country; even that must be accepted as a lesser evil than nullification of the Constitution. Nor is it that history does not confirm that an agreed purpose of the fourteenth amendment was to forbid separate schools or that there is important evidence that many thought the contrary; the words are general and leave room for expanding content as time passes and conditions change. Nor is it that the Court may have miscalculated the extent to which its judgment would be honored or accepted; it is not a prophet of the strength of our national commitment to respect the judgments of the courts. Nor is it even that the Court did not remit the issue to the Congress, acting under the enforcement clause of the amendment. That was a possible solution, to be sure, but . . . it would merely have evaded the claims made.

The problem inheres strictly in the reasoning of the opinion, an opinion which is often read with less fidelity by those who praise it than by those by whom it is condemned. The Court did not declare, as many wish it had, that the fourteenth amendment forbids all racial lines in legislation, though subsequent per curiam decisions may . . . now go that far. Rather, as Judge Hand observed, the separate-but-equal formula was not overruled "in form" but was held to have "no place" in public education on the ground that segregated schools are "inherently unequal," with deleterious effects upon the colored children in implying their inferiority, effects which retard their educational and mental development. So, indeed, the district court had found as a fact in the Kansas case, a finding which the Supreme Court embraced, citing some further "modern authority" in its support.

Does the validity of the decision turn then on the sufficiency of evidence or of judicial notice to sustain a finding that the separation harms the Negro children who may be involved? There were, indeed, some witnesses who expressed that opinion in the Kansas case, as there were also witnesses in the companion Virginia case, including Professor Garrett of Columbia, whose view was to the contrary. Much depended on the question that the witness had in mind, which rarely was explicit. Was he comparing the position of the Negro child in a segregated school with his position in an integrated school where he was happily accepted and regarded by the whites; or was he comparing his position under separation with that under integration where the whites were hostile to his presence and found ways to make their feelings known? And if the harm that segregation worked was relevant, what of the benefits that it entailed: sense of security, the absence of hostility? Were they irrelevant? Moreover, was the finding in Topeka applicable without more to Clarendon County, South Carolina, with 2,799 colored students and only 295 whites? Suppose that more Negroes in a community preferred separation than opposed it? Would that be relevant to whether they were hurt or aided by segregation as opposed to integration? Their fates would be governed by the change of system quite as fully as those of the students who complained.

I find it hard to think the judgment really turned upon the facts. Rather, it seems to me, it must have rested on the view that racial segregation is, in principle, a denial of equality to the minority against whom it is directed; that is, the group that is not dominant politically and, therefore, does not make the choice involved. For many who support the Court's decision this assuredly is the decisive ground. But this position also presents problems. Does it not involve an inquiry into the motive of the legislature, which is generally foreclosed to the courts? Is it alternatively defensible to make the measure of validity of legislation the way it is interpreted by those who are affected by it? In the context of a charge that segregation *with equal facilities* is a denial of equality, is there not a point in *Plessy* in the statement that if "enforced separation stamps the colored race with a badge of inferiority" it is solely because its members choose "to put that construction upon it"? Does enforced separation of the sexes discriminate against females merely because it may be the females who resent it and it is imposed by judgments predominantly male? Is a prohibition of miscegenation a discrimination against the colored member of the couple who would like to marry?

For me, assuming equal facilities, the question posed by state-enforced segregation is not one of discrimination at all. Its human and its constitutional dimensions lie entirely elsewhere, in the denial by the state of freedom to associate, a denial that impinges in the same way on any groups or races that may be involved. I think, and I hope not without foundation, that the Southern white also pays heavily for segregation, not only in the sense of guilt that he must carry but also in the benefits he is denied. In the days when I was joined with Charles H. Houston in a litigation in the Supreme Court, before the present building was constructed, he did not suffer more than I in knowing that we had to go to Union Station to lunch together during the recess. Does not the problem of miscegenation show most clearly that it is the freedom of association that at bottom is involved, the only case, I may add, where it is implicit in the situation that association is desired by the only individuals involved? . . .

But if the freedom of association is denied by segregation, integration forces an association upon those for whom it is unpleasant or repugnant. Is this not the heart of the issue involved, a conflict in human claims of high dimension. . . . Given a situation where the state must practically choose between denying the association to those individuals who wish it or imposing it on those who would avoid it, is there a basis in neutral principles for holding that the Constitution demands that the claims for association should prevail? I should like to think there is, but I confess that I have not yet written the opinion. To write it is for me the challenge of the school-segregation cases.

Having said what I have said, I certainly should add that I offer no comfort to anyone who claims legitimacy in defiance of the courts. This is the ultimate negation of all neutral principles, to take the benefits accorded by the constitutional system, including the national market and common defense, while denying it allegiance when a special burden is imposed. That certainly is the antithesis of law. . . .

Charles Black, The Lawfulness
of the Segregation Decisions[*]

If the cases outlawing segregation were wrongly decided, then they ought to be overruled. . . . There is pragmatic meaning then, there is call for action, in the suggestion that the segregation cases cannot be justified.[3] In the long run, as a corollary, there is practical and not merely intellectual significance in the question whether these cases were rightly decided. I think they were rightly decided, by overwhelming weight of reason, and I intend here to say why I hold this belief.

My liminal difficulty is rhetorical—or, perhaps more accurately, one of fashion. Simplicity is out of fashion, and the basic scheme of reasoning on which these cases can be justified is awkwardly simple. First, the equal protection clause of the fourteenth amendment should be read as saying that the Negro race, as such, is not to be significantly disadvantaged by the laws of the states. Secondly, segregation is a massive intentional disadvantaging of the Negro race, as such, by state law. No subtlety at all. Yet I cannot disabuse myself of the idea that that is really all there is to the segregation cases. . . .

As a general thing, the first of these propositions has so far as I know never been controverted in a holding of the Supreme Court. I rest here on the solid sense of *The Slaughterhouse Cases* and of *Strauder v. West Virginia,* where Mr. Justice Strong said of the fourteenth amendment:

> . . . What is this but declaring that the law in the States shall be the same for the black as for the white; that all persons, whether colored or white, shall stand equal before the laws of the States, and, in regard to the colored race, for whose protection the amendment was primarily designed, that no discrimination shall be made against them by law because of their color? The words of the amendment, it is true, are prohibitory, but they contain a necessary implication of a positive immunity, or right, most valuable to the colored race— the right to exemption from unfriendly legislation against them distinctively as colored—exemption from legal discriminations, implying inferiority in civil society, lessening the security of their enjoyment of the rights which others enjoy, and discriminations which are steps towards reducing them to the condition of a subject race.[6]

If *Plessy v. Ferguson* be thought a faltering from this principle, I step back to the principle itself. But the *Plessy* Court clearly conceived it to be its task to show that segregation did not really disadvantage the Negro, except through his own choice. There is in this no denial of the

---

[*]   Reprinted from 69 YALE L.J. 421 (1960).

[3]   See Herbert L. Wechsler, *Toward Neutral Principles of Constitutional Law,* 73 HARV. L. REV. 1, 34 (1959).

[6]   100 U.S. 303, 307–08 (1880).

Slaughterhouse and *Strauder* principle; the fault of *Plessy* is in the psychology and sociology of its minor premise. . . .

What the fourteenth amendment, in its historical setting, must be read to say is that the Negro is to enjoy equal protection of the laws, and that the fact of his being a Negro is not to be taken to be a good enough reason for denying him this equality, however "reasonable" that might seem to some people. All possible arguments, however convincing, for discriminating against the Negro, were finally rejected by the fourteenth amendment. . . .

Then does segregation offend against equality? Equality, like all general concepts, has marginal areas where philosophic difficulties are encountered. But if a whole race of people finds itself confined within a system which is set up and continued for the very purpose of keeping it in an inferior station, and if the question is then solemnly propounded whether such a race is being treated "equally," I think we ought to exercise one of the sovereign prerogatives of philosophers—that of laughter. The only question remaining (after we get our laughter under control) is whether the segregation system answers to this description.

Here I must confess to a tendency to start laughing all over again. I was raised in the South, in a Texas city where the pattern of segregation was firmly fixed. I am sure it never occurred to anyone, white or colored, to question its meaning. The fiction of "equality" is just about on a level with the fiction of "finding" in the action of trover. I think few candid southerners deny this. Northern people may be misled by the entirely sincere protestations of many southerners that segregation is "better" for the Negroes, is not intended to hurt them. But I think a little probing would demonstrate that what is meant is that it is better for the Negroes to accept a position of inferiority, at least for the indefinite future.

But the subjectively obvious, if queried, must be backed up by more public materials. What public materials assure me that my reading of the social meaning of segregation is not a mere idiosyncrasy?

First, of course, is history. Segregation in the South comes down in apostolic succession from slavery and the *Dred Scott* case. The South fought to keep slavery, and lost. Then it tried the Black Codes, and lost. Then it looked around for something else and found segregation. The movement for segregation was an integral part of the movement to maintain and further "white supremacy"; its triumph . . . represented a triumph of extreme racialist over moderate sentiment about the Negro. It is now defended very largely on the ground that the Negro as such is not fit to associate with the white.

History, too, tells us that segregation was imposed on one race by the other race; consent was not invited or required. Segregation in the South grew up and is kept going because and only because the white race has wanted it that way—an incontrovertible fact which in itself hardly consorts with equality. This fact perhaps more than any other confirms the picture which a casual or deep observer is likely to form of the life of a southern community—a picture not of mutual separation of whites and Negroes, but of one in-group enjoying full normal communal life and one out-group that is barred from this life and forced into an inferior life of its own. . . . When you are in Leeville and hear someone say "Leeville High," you know he has reference to the white high school; the Negro school will be called something else—Carver High, perhaps, or Lincoln High to our shame. That is what you would expect when one race forces a segregated position on another, and that is what you get. Segregation is historically and contemporaneously associated in a functioning complex with practices which are indisputably and grossly discriminatory. I have in mind especially the long-continued and still largely effective exclusion of Negroes from voting. Here we have two things. First, a certain group of people is "segregated." Secondly, at about the same time, the very same group of people, down to the last man and woman, is barred, or sought to be barred, from the common political life of the community—from all political power. Then we are solemnly told that segregation is not intended to harm the segregated race, or to stamp it with the mark of inferiority. How long must we keep a straight face?

Here it may be added that, generally speaking, segregation is the pattern of law in communities where the extralegal patterns of discrimination against Negroes are the tightest, where Negroes are subjected to the strictest codes of "unwritten law" as to job opportunities, social intercourse, patterns of housing, going to the back door, being called by the first name, saying "Sir," and all the rest of the whole sorry business. Of course these things, in themselves, need not and usually do not involve "state action," and hence the fourteenth amendment cannot apply to them. But they can assist us in understanding the meaning and assessing the impact of state action.

"Separate but equal" facilities are almost never really equal. Sometimes this concerns small things—if the "white" men's room has mixing hot and cold taps, the "colored" men's room will likely have separate taps; it is always the back of the bus for the Negroes; "Lincoln Beach" will rarely if ever be as good as the regular beach. Sometimes it concerns the most vital matters—through the whole history of segregation, colored schools have been so disgracefully inferior to white schools that only ignorance can excuse those who have remained acquiescent members of a community that lived the Molochian child-destroying lie that put them forward as "equal."

Attention is usually focused on these inequalities as things in themselves, correctible by detailed decrees. I am more interested in their very clear character as *evidence* of what segregation means to the people who impose it and to the people who are subjected to it. This evidentiary character cannot be erased by one-step-ahead-of-the-marshal correction. Can a system which, in all that can be measured, has practiced the grossest inequality, actually have been "equal" in intent, in total social

meaning and impact? "Thy speech maketh thee manifest ...";
segregation, in all visible things, speaks only haltingly any dialect but
that of inequality.

Further arguments could be piled on top of one another, for we have
here to do with the most conspicuous characteristic of a whole regional
culture. It is actionable defamation in the South to call a white man a
Negro. A small proportion of Negro "blood" puts one in the inferior race
for segregation purposes; this is the way in which one deals with a taint,
such as a carcinogen in cranberries.

The various items I have mentioned differ in weight; not every one
would suffice in itself to establish the character of segregation. Taken
together they are of irrefragable strength. The society that has just lost
the Negro as a slave, that has just lost out in an attempt to put him under
quasi-servile "Codes," the society that views his blood as a contamination
and his name as an insult, the society that extra-legally imposes on him
every humiliating mark of low caste and that until yesterday kept him in
line by lynching—this society, careless of his consent, moves by law, first
to exclude him from voting, and secondly to cut him off from mixing in
the general public life of the community. The Court that refused to see
inequality in this cutting off would be making the only kind of law that
can be warranted outrageous in advance—law based on self-induced
blindness, on flagrant contradiction of known fact. I have stated all these
points shortly because they are matters of common notoriety, matters not
so much for judicial notice as for the background knowledge of educated
men who live in the world. A court may advise itself of them as it advises
itself of the facts that we are a "religious people," that the country is more
industrialized than in Jefferson's day, that children are the natural
objects of fathers' bounty, that criminal sanctions are commonly thought
to deter, that steel is a basic commodity in our economy, that the
imputation of unchastity is harmful to a woman. Such judgments, made
on such a basis, are in the foundations of all law, decisional as well as
statutory; it would be the most unneutral of principles, improvised *ad
hoc*, to require that a court faced with the present problem refuse to note
a plain fact about the society of the United States—the fact that the social
meaning of segregation is the putting of the Negro in a position of walled-
off inferiority—or the other equally plain fact that such treatment is
hurtful to human beings. Southern courts, on the basis of just such a
judgment, have held that the placing of a white person in a Negro
railroad car is an actionable humiliation; must a court pretend not to
know that the Negro's situation there is humiliating?

I think that some of the artificial mist of puzzlement called into being
around this question originates in a single fundamental mistake. The
issue is seen in terms of what might be called the metaphysics of
sociology: "Must Segregation Amount to Discrimination?" That is an
interesting question; someday the methods of sociology may be adequate
to answering it. But it is not our question. Our question is whether

discrimination inheres in that segregation which is imposed by law in the twentieth century in certain specific states in the American Union. And that question has meaning and can find an answer only on the ground of history and of common knowledge about the facts of life in the times and places aforesaid.

Now I need not and do not maintain that the evidence is all one way; it never is on issues of burning, fighting concern. Let us not question here the good faith of those who assert that segregation represents no more than an attempt to furnish a wholesome opportunity for parallel development of the races; let us rejoice at the few scattered instances they can bring forward to support their view of the matter. But let us then ask which balance-pan flies upward.

The case seems so one-sided that it is hard to make out what is being protested against when it is asked, rhetorically, how the Court can possibly advise itself of the real character of the segregation system. It seems that what is being said is that, while no actual doubt exists as to what segregation is for and what kind of societal pattern it supports and implements, there is no ritually sanctioned way in which the Court, as a Court, can permissibly learn what is obvious to everybody else and to the Justices as individuals. But surely, confronted with such a problem, legal acumen has only one proper task—that of developing ways to make it permissible for the Court to use what it knows; any other counsel is of despair. And, equally surely, the fact that the Court has assumed as true a matter of common knowledge in regard to broad societal patterns, is (to say the very least) pretty far down the list of things to protest against.

I conclude, then, that the Court had the soundest reasons for judging that segregation violates the fourteenth amendment. These reasons make up the simple syllogism with which I began: The fourteenth amendment commands equality, and segregation as we know it is inequality. . . .

Finally it is doubtless true that the School Segregation Cases, and perhaps others of the cases on segregation, represented a choice between two kinds of freedom of association. Freedom from the massive wrong of segregation entails a corresponding loss of freedom on the part of the whites who must now associate with Negroes on public occasions, as we all must on such occasions associate with many persons we had rather not associate with. It is possible to state the competing claims in symmetry, and to ask whether there are constitutional reasons for preferring the Negroes' desire for merged participation public life to the white man's desire to live a public life without Negroes in proximity.

The question must be answered, but I would approach it in a way which seems to me more normal—the way in which we more usually approach comparable symmetries that might be stated as to all other asserted rights. The fourteenth amendment forbids inequality, forbids the disadvantaging of the Negro race by law. It was surely anticipated that the following of this directive would entail some disagreeableness for some white southerners. The disagreeableness might take many forms; the white man, for example, might dislike having a Negro neighbor in the exercise of the latter's equal right to own a home, or dislike serving on a jury with a Negro, or dislike having Negroes on the streets with him after ten o'clock. When the directive of equality cannot be followed without displeasing the white, then something that can be called a "freedom" of the white must be impaired. If the fourteenth amendment commands equality, and if segregation violates equality, then the status of the reciprocal "freedom" is automatically settled.

I find reinforcement here, at least as a matter of spirit, in the fourteenth amendment command that Negroes shall be "citizens" of their States. It is hard for me to imagine in what operative sense a man could be a "citizen" without his fellow citizens' once in a while having to associate with him. If, for example, his "citizenship" results in his election to the School Board, the white members may (as recently in Houston) put him off to one side of the room, but there is still some impairment of their freedom "not to associate." That freedom, in fact, exists only at home; in public, we have to associate with anybody who has a right to be there. The question of our right not to associate with him is concluded when we decide whether he has a right to be there.

I am not really apologetic for the simplicity of my ideas on the segregation cases. The decisions call for mighty diastrophic change. We ought to call for such change only in the name of a solid reasoned simplicity that takes law out of artfulness into art. Only such grounds can support the nation in its resolve to uphold the law declared by its Court; only such grounds can reconcile the white South to what must be. *Elegantia juris* and conceptual algebra have here no place. Without pretending either to completeness or to definitiveness of statement, I have tried here to show reasons for believing that we as lawyers can without fake or apology present to the lay community, and to ourselves, a rationale of the segregation decisions that rises to the height of the great argument.

These judgments, like all judgments, must rest on the rightness of their law and the truth of their fact. Their law is right if the equal protection clause in the fourteenth amendment is to be taken as stating, without arbitrary exceptions, a broad principle of practical equality for the Negro race, inconsistent with any device that in fact relegates the Negro race to a position of inferiority. Their facts are true if it is true that the segregation system is actually conceived and does actually function as a means of keeping the Negro in a status of inferiority. I dare say at this time that in the end, the decisions will be accepted by the profession on just that basis. Opinions composed under painful stresses may leave much to be desired;[25] it may be that the per curiam device has been

---

[25] I do not mean here to join the hue and cry against the *Brown* opinion. The charge that it is "sociological" is either a truism or a canard—a truism if it means that the Court, precisely like the *Plessy* Court, and like innumerable other courts facing innumerable other issues of law,

unwisely used. But the judgments, in law and in fact, are as right and true as any that ever was uttered.

NOTE ON NEUTRAL PRINCIPLES AND THE SEGREGATION DECISIONS

1.   Although *Brown* is well-accepted today, Professor Wechsler's idea of "Neutral Principles" has been highly influential. Do you agree with Wechsler that principles of constitutional law must be "neutral"? What does he mean by that? Isn't Wechsler right to say that the tendency to judge constitutional positions and decisions on their immediate political valence, rather than on the underlying principles involved, is "the deepest problem of our constitutionalism"? Consider these examples from other constitutional contexts:

- In *Employment Division v. Smith*, 494 U.S. 872 (1990), the Supreme Court held that the Free Exercise Clause did not exempt members of the Native American Church, who wished to smoke the narcotic peyote in religious rituals, from generally-applicable drug laws. In *Burwell v. Hobby Lobby Stores, Inc.*, 134 S. Ct. 2751 (2014), the Court held that the Religious Freedom Restoration Act (passed in response to *Smith*) *did* exempt companies objecting on religious grounds from a federal requirement that employer-provided health insurance plans cover certain contraceptives. Political liberals were generally sympathetic to the Native Americans in *Smith*, while political conservatives tended to side with the religious objectors in *Hobby Lobby*. The cases are legally reconcilable, because *Smith* interpreted the First Amendment while *Hobby Lobby* interpreted a federal statute. But shouldn't one nonetheless have a consistent position as to whether the principle of religious liberty requires exemptions from generally-applicable laws?

- Political liberals, including President Obama, have been highly critical of the Court's decision in *Citizens United v. Federal Election Comm'n*, 558 U.S. 310 (2010), often on the ground that it recognized constitutional free speech rights for corporations, which of course are not real persons. Can this view be squared with approval of cases like *National Association for the Advancement of Colored People v. Button*, 371 U.S. 415 (1963), in which the Warren Court enforced the

---

had to resolve and did resolve a question about social fact, a canard if it means that anything like principal reliance was placed on the formally "scientific" authorities, which are relegated to a footnote and treated as merely corroboratory of common sense. It seems to me that the venial fault of the opinion consists in its not spelling out that segregation, for reasons of the kind I have brought forward in this Article, is perceptibly a means of ghettoizing the imputedly inferior race. (I would conjecture that the motive for this omission was reluctance to go into the distasteful details of the southern caste system.) That such treatment is generally not good for children needs less talk than the Court gives it.

free speech rights of the NAACP—a corporation organized in 1911 under the laws of New York?

- Political conservatives have argued that President Obama's 2014 executive action deferring deportation for millions of undocumented immigrants exceeded the President's unilateral authority under the Constitution.[10] However, many conservatives defended President George W. Bush's use of executive authority to establish a program of warrantless surveillance of Americans by the National Security Agency. Is it principled to take both these positions?

Each of these examples raises complexities that lie beyond the scope of our discussion here, and it may be possible to distinguish between superficially similar examples on narrower, but still principled, grounds. Nonetheless, Wechsler's point is that one can't applaud the results in *Smith* and *Hobby Lobby* because one likes broad enforcement of the drug laws but opposes use of certain contraceptives; one can't condemn *Citizens United* and support *Button* simply because one worries about corporations pursuing a pro-business agenda but favors civil rights; and one can't oppose broad executive powers for Republican Presidents but not Democratic ones.

More broadly, it should worry you if your judgments about the application of constitutional principles tend to line up with your political preferences as to the results in particular disputes. The widespread belief that judges' rulings are a function of their political leanings—and the not-infrequent confirmation of that belief by the Justices' own voting behavior in high-profile cases—has made the judicial confirmation process a high-stakes political battleground. Is it naive to hope, with Wechsler, that judges can demonstrate, through restraint and reason-giving, a compelling distinction between law and politics?

2.   Does the Court's reasoning in *Brown I* pass Professor Wechsler's test of neutrality? Wechsler's problem seems to be that separate but equal is accepted in any number of contexts (e.g., gender-segregated public bathrooms), but condemned when particular groups complain about it. Does Professor Black (who grew up in Austin, Texas during the period of segregation) successfully refute Wechsler's concerns? When Black says that "the fourteenth amendment, in its setting, must be read to say . . . that the Negro is to enjoy equal protection of the laws," isn't he walking right into Wechsler's idea that constitutional principles cannot turn off and on according to whether they would benefit a favored group? On the other hand, surely the Framers of the Fourteenth Amendment, recognizing the need to overcome centuries of oppressive laws and practices directed toward a particular group, could target their amendment to remedying harms to that group. Is the anti-subordination reading of equal protection a neutral principle?

Unless one thinks the Constitution makes no value choices at all, there will be some situations in which constitutional principles will favor certain

---

[10]   *See Texas* v. *United States*, 809 F.3d 134 (5th Cir. 2015) (enjoining implementation of the President's program), *aff'd by an equally divided court*, 2016 WL 3434401 (June 23, 2016).

values or groups over others. By protecting property in the Takings and Due Process Clauses, for example, the Constitution favors capitalists over communists. By locking in certain institutions against easy change, the Constitution favors conservatives over revolutionaries. These realities make it difficult to pin down what Wechsler means by a "neutral principle." At the same time, however, isn't there something to his insistence that courts give "reasons that in their generality and their neutrality transcend any immediate result that is involved" in a case?

3.   Do you agree with Professor Wechsler that it is "hard to think [*Brown*] really turned upon the facts"? For Professor Black, the facts are everything: whether or not separate but equal might be defensible in certain contexts, it was obvious that "the institution [of segregation] as it prevails in the American South today" was a system of oppression. Does the difference between the two scholars really come down to a question of *evidence*? Wechsler confines himself to the admittedly shaky (and contradicted) facts in the *Brown* litigation's evidentiary record, while Black invokes "matters of common notoriety, matters not so much for judicial notice as for the background knowledge of educated men who live in the world." Isn't Black right that courts cannot turn a blind eye to obvious social reality, even if it is hard to point to a specific piece of record evidence confirming a fact? But isn't Wechsler also right to suggest, implicitly, that one of the virtues of the judicial process is that it subjects widespread intuitions and assumptions to a more rigorous test of truth?

4.   How should an originalist deal with *Brown*? Here is what Judge Bork had to say on that subject in the *Neutral Principles* article:

> A court required to decide *Brown* would perceive two crucial facts about the history of the fourteenth amendment. First, the men who put the amendment in the Constitution intended that the Supreme Court should secure against government action some large measure of racial equality. That is certainly the core meaning of the amendment. Second, those same men were not agreed about what the concept of racial equality requires. Many or most of them had not even thought the matter through. . . . The Court cannot conceivably know how these long-dead men would have resolved these issues had they considered, debated and voted on each of them. Perhaps it was precisely because they could not resolve them that they took refuge in the majestic and ambiguous formula: the equal protection of the laws.

> But one thing the Court does know: it was intended to enforce a core idea of black equality against governmental discrimination. And the Court, because it must be neutral, cannot pick and choose between competing gratifications and, likewise, cannot write the detailed code the framers omitted, requiring equality in this case but not in another. The Court must, for that reason, choose a general principle of equality that applies to all cases. For the same reason, the Court cannot decide that physical equality is important but psychological equality is not. Thus, the no-state-enforced-discrimination rule of *Brown* must overturn and replace the

separate-but-equal doctrine of *Plessy v. Ferguson*. The same result might be reached on an alternative ground. If the Court found that it was incapable as an institution of policing the issue of the physical equality of separate facilities, the variables being insufficiently comparable and the cases too many, it might fashion a no-segregation rule as the only feasible means of assuring even physical equality.

> In either case, the value choice ... of the fourteenth amendment is fleshed out and made into a legal rule—not by moral precept, not by a determination that claims for association prevail over claims for separation as a general matter, still less by consideration of psychological test results, but on purely juridical grounds.[11]

Is this a plausible account? Michael McConnell has made a similar argument, suggesting that the Framers of the Fourteenth Amendment understood it to guarantee equality with respect to basic civil rights.[12] Professor McConnell concedes that those Framers might not have regarded public education as such a right in 1868, but he argues that it *had* come to be so perceived by 1954, when *Brown* was decided. Would it be fair to say that both Bork and McConnell may have shown that originalism is not necessarily *inconsistent* with *Brown*, but that originalist interpretation alone is hardly capable of doing all the work necessary to reach *Brown*'s result?[13]

SECTION 6.2   SEGREGATION REMEDIES AND THE JUDICIAL ROLE

Deciding that segregation was wrong was the easy part; the hard part was determining what to do about it. At the end of the opinion in *Brown I*, the Court ordered the case set for reargument on the question of remedy—that is, the precise shape that the judicial order resolving the case should take. The immediate disposition of that question occurred in *Brown II*. But *Brown II* fell far short of resolving the issue, as the ensuing decade's lack of progress toward desegregation, followed by vigorous debates over more aggressive remedial measures such as busing, would demonstrate. These remedial disputes raised not only difficult questions of social policy (e.g., Is it more important to give black children a quality education or an education with whites?), but also fundamental questions about the allocation of authority to interpret the Constitution among different institutions of the government and the basic efficacy of judicial efforts to effect social change.

We begin with the Court's remedial decision in *Brown II*, then shift focus to Southern resistance to desegregation remedies in the Little Rock

---

[11] Robert H. Bork, *Neutral Principles and Some First Amendment Problems*, 47 IND. L. J. 1, 14–15 (1971).

[12] *See* Michael W. McConnell, *Originalism and the Desegregation Decisions*, 81 VA. L. REV. 947 (1995).

[13] *See, e.g.*, Michael Klarman, *Antifidelity*, 70 S. CAL. L. REV. 371, 409–11 (1997).

crisis. The Court's opinion addressing that crisis, *Cooper v. Aaron*, asserted judicial primacy in constitutional interpretation—a position disputed not only by Arkansas Governor Orval Faubus but also by a long list of U.S. Presidents, including Thomas Jefferson, Andrew Jackson, Abraham Lincoln, and Franklin Roosevelt. As the views of these other presidents suggest, this question of interpretive authority is important not just for desegregation cases, but for any issue as to which different governmental actors may disagree about the appropriate interpretation of the Constitution.

We then turn to the practical efficacy of judicial decisions interpreting and enforcing the Constitution, focusing on Gerald Rosenberg's empirical study of the results of judicial desegregation orders after *Brown*. The sobering findings of that study call into question whether courts alone can ever bring social conditions into line with constitutional principle.

Brown v. Board of Education (Brown II)
349 U.S. 294 (1955)

■ MR. CHIEF JUSTICE WARREN delivered the opinion of the Court.

These cases were decided on May 17, 1954. The opinions of that date, declaring the fundamental principle that racial discrimination in public education is unconstitutional, are incorporated herein by reference. All provisions of federal, state, or local law requiring or permitting such discrimination must yield to this principle. There remains for consideration the manner in which relief is to be accorded.

Because these cases arose under different local conditions and their disposition will involve a variety of local problems, we requested further argument on the question of relief.[2] In view of the nationwide importance

---

[2]   Further argument was requested on the following questions previously propounded by the Court:

4. Assuming it is decided that segregation in public schools violates the Fourteenth Amendment

(*a*) would a decree necessarily follow providing that, within the limits set by normal geographic school districting, Negro children should forthwith be admitted to schools of their choice, or

(*b*) may this Court, in the exercise of its equity powers, permit an effective gradual adjustment to be brought about from existing segregated systems to a system not based on color distinctions?

5. On the assumption on which questions 4 (*a*) and (*b*) are based, and assuming further that this Court will exercise its equity powers to the end described in question 4 (*b*),

(*a*)   should this Court formulate detailed decrees in these cases;

(*b*)   if so, what specific issues should the decrees reach;

(*c*)   should this Court appoint a special master to hear evidence with a view to recommending specific terms for such decrees;

(*d*)   should this Court remand to the courts of first instance with directions to frame decrees in these cases, and if so what general directions should the decrees

of the decision, we invited the Attorney General of the United States and the Attorneys General of all states requiring or permitting racial discrimination in public education to present their views on that question. The parties, the United States, and the States of Florida, North Carolina, Arkansas, Oklahoma, Maryland, and Texas filed briefs and participated in the oral argument.

These presentations were informative and helpful to the Court in its consideration of the complexities arising from the transition to a system of public education freed of racial discrimination. The presentations also demonstrated that substantial steps to eliminate racial discrimination in public schools have already been taken, not only in some of the communities in which these cases arose, but in some of the states appearing as *amici curiae*, and in other states as well. Substantial progress has been made in the District of Columbia and in the communities in Kansas and Delaware involved in this litigation. The defendants in the cases coming to us from South Carolina and Virginia are awaiting the decision of this Court concerning relief.

Full implementation of these constitutional principles may require solution of varied local school problems. School authorities have the primary responsibility for elucidating, assessing, and solving these problems; courts will have to consider whether the action of school authorities constitutes good faith implementation of the governing constitutional principles. Because of their proximity to local conditions and the possible need for further hearings, the courts which originally heard these cases can best perform this judicial appraisal. Accordingly, we believe it appropriate to remand the cases to those courts.

In fashioning and effectuating the decrees, the courts will be guided by equitable principles. Traditionally, equity has been characterized by a practical flexibility in shaping its remedies and by a facility for adjusting and reconciling public and private needs. These cases call for the exercise of these traditional attributes of equity power. At stake is the personal interest of the plaintiffs in admission to public schools as soon as practicable on a nondiscriminatory basis. To effectuate this interest may call for elimination of a variety of obstacles in making the transition to school systems operated in accordance with the constitutional principles set forth in our May 17, 1954, decision. Courts of equity may properly take into account the public interest in the elimination of such obstacles in a systematic and effective manner. But it should go without saying that the vitality of these constitutional principles cannot be allowed to yield simply because of disagreement with them.

While giving weight to these public and private considerations, the courts will require that the defendants make a prompt and reasonable

---

of this Court include and what procedures should the courts of first instance follow in arriving at the specific terms of more detailed decrees?

start toward full compliance with our May 17, 1954, ruling. Once such a start has been made, the courts may find that additional time is necessary to carry out the ruling in an effective manner. The burden rests upon the defendants to establish that such time is necessary in the public interest and is consistent with good faith compliance at the earliest practicable date. To that end, the courts may consider problems related to administration, arising from the physical condition of the school plant, the school transportation system, personnel, revision of school districts and attendance areas into compact units to achieve a system of determining admission to the public schools on a nonracial basis, and revision of local laws and regulations which may be necessary in solving the foregoing problems. They will also consider the adequacy of any plans the defendants may propose to meet these problems and to effectuate a transition to a racially nondiscriminatory school system. During this period of transition, the courts will retain jurisdiction of these cases.

The judgments below, except that in the Delaware case, are accordingly reversed and the cases are remanded to the District Courts to take such proceedings and enter such orders and decrees consistent with this opinion as are necessary and proper to admit to public schools on a racially nondiscriminatory basis with all deliberate speed the parties to these cases. The judgment in the Delaware case—ordering the immediate admission of the plaintiffs to schools previously attended only by white children—is affirmed on the basis of the principles stated in our May 17, 1954, opinion, but the case is remanded to the Supreme Court of Delaware for such further proceedings as that Court may deem necessary in light of this opinion.

NOTE ON DESEGREGATION REMEDIES

1. Two aspects of the *Brown II* opinion are critical:

a. The first is the Court's statement that segregation remedies are to be governed by *equitable* principles. The English legal system, and its successors in the early American republic, was divided into two systems of courts: the courts of law, and the courts of equity. The equity courts tended to focus on achieving fairness in a particular situation, rather than adhering to the strict and general principles of the common law. They also specialized in "prospective" relief—that is, relief operating into the future by injunctions to parties to do or refrain from doing something, or declarations of rights, as opposed to retrospective relief in the form of money damages. The American legal system combined the law and equity courts into one jurisdiction in the Twentieth Century, but we still speak in terms of a contrast between "legal" and "equitable" relief. The *Brown II* Court's reference to "equitable principles" thus indicates that individual district judges would be accorded flexibility in fitting their decrees to the circumstances of individual communities.

b.   The second component is the *Brown II* Court's obvious tolerance for some delay in achieving desegregation. The Court called only for a "prompt and reasonable start toward compliance" with *Brown I*, and it stated that desegregation should proceed with "all deliberate speed."

Did the Court place too much power in the hands of federal district judges in the South, many of whom came from the same segregationist establishment that would shortly be engaged in "massive resistance" to the *Brown* decision? Was it too respectful of the administrative difficulties, both real and imagined, that stood in the way of desegregation? Should the Court have demanded full desegregation, right away?

2.   How far should courts be willing to go to achieve desegregation? It's easy enough to order segregation laws deleted from the statute books. But patterns of residential segregation arising from an array of state and private practices stretching back decades mean that even a student assignment plan based on a "neutral" criterion like geographic proximity to the school will yield a highly disproportionate racial mix at any given school. Should courts require busing to overcome such difficulties? What about the problem of "white flight" from public to private schools? Should the courts try to make the public schools more attractive, for example by mandating the construction of "magnet" schools or even by ordering local districts to raise taxes to pay for better schools? And what should courts do if it becomes apparent that the disruption occasioned by the remedies themselves—long hours on buses, hostile receptions for black students in predominantly white schools—is actually undermining the education of the children?

3.   In the wake of *Brown II*, many Southern communities engaged in a strategy of "massive resistance" to the Court's rulings. Some of the South's anger at the Court is captured in the "Southern Manifesto," signed by eleven Senators and seventy-seven Members of the House of Representatives and submitted to the Senate on March 12, 1956:

- We regard the decisions of the Supreme Court in the school cases as a clear abuse of judicial power. It climaxes a trend in the Federal Judiciary undertaking to legislate, in derogation of the authority of Congress, and to encroach upon the reserved rights of the States and the people. . . .

- In the case of *Plessy v. Ferguson* in 1896 the Supreme Court expressly declared that under the 14th Amendment no person was denied any of his rights if the States provided separate but equal facilities. . . . This interpretation, restated time and again, became a part of the life of the people of many of the States and confirmed their habits, traditions, and way of life. It is founded on elemental humanity and commonsense, for parents should not be deprived by Government of the right to direct the lives and education of their own children.

- Though there has been no constitutional amendment or act of Congress changing this established legal principle almost a century old, the Supreme Court of the United States, with no legal basis for such action, undertook to exercise their naked judicial power and substituted their personal political and social ideas for the established law of the land.

- This unwarranted exercise of power by the Court, contrary to the Constitution, is creating chaos and confusion in the States principally affected. It is destroying the amicable relations between the white and Negro races that have been created through 90 years of patient effort by the good people of both races. It has planted hatred and suspicion where there has been heretofore friendship and understanding. . . .

- We reaffirm our reliance on the Constitution as the fundamental law of the land.

- We decry the Supreme Court's encroachment on the rights reserved to the States and to the people, contrary to established law, and to the Constitution.

- We commend the motives of those States which have declared the intention to resist forced integration by any lawful means. . . .

- We pledge ourselves to use all lawful means to bring about a reversal of this decision which is contrary to the Constitution and to prevent the use of force in its implementation.

- In this trying period, as we all seek to right this wrong, we appeal to our people not to be provoked by the agitators and troublemakers invading our States and to scrupulously refrain from disorder and lawless acts.[14]

What do you think of this statement? Assuming a good faith disagreement on the governing law, is it legitimate for legislative officials to call for resistance to implementing the orders of the Supreme Court? How would you have felt about a "Northern Manifesto" in response to *Prigg* or *Dred Scott*?

4.   Notwithstanding the Southern Manifesto's call to "refrain from disorder and lawless acts," such acts occurred on a large scale as at least some district courts sought to enforce the *Brown* mandate. One of the worst situations developed in Little Rock, Arkansas, where the Governor of the state, Orval Faubus, employed the National Guard to prevent black students from entering the Central High School. The ensuing events gave rise to one of the Supreme Court's strongest statements ever concerning not only the principle of *Brown* but also the broader issue of the Court's supremacy in constitutional interpretation.

---

[14] *Congressional Record*, 84th Congress Second Session. Vol. 102, part 4, at 4459–4460 (March 12, 1956).

Cooper v. Aaron

358 U.S. 1 (1958)

■ **Opinion of the Court by THE CHIEF JUSTICE, MR. JUSTICE BLACK, MR. JUSTICE FRANKFURTER, MR. JUSTICE DOUGLAS, MR. JUSTICE BURTON, MR. JUSTICE CLARK, MR. JUSTICE HARLAN, MR. JUSTICE BRENNAN, AND MR. JUSTICE WHITTAKER.**

As this case reaches us it raises questions of the highest importance to the maintenance of our federal system of government. It necessarily involves a claim by the Governor and Legislature of a State that there is no duty on state officials to obey federal court orders resting on this Court's considered interpretation of the United States Constitution. Specifically it involves actions by the Governor and Legislature of Arkansas upon the premise that they are not bound by our holding in *Brown v. Board of Education.* That holding was that the Fourteenth Amendment forbids States to use their governmental powers to bar children on racial grounds from attending schools where there is state participation through any arrangement, management, funds or property. We are urged to uphold a suspension of the Little Rock School Board's plan to do away with segregated public schools in Little Rock until state laws and efforts to upset and nullify our holding in *Brown v. Board of Education* have been further challenged and tested in the courts. We reject these contentions.

The case was argued before us on September 11, 1958. On the following day we unanimously affirmed the judgment of the Court of Appeals for the Eighth Circuit, which had reversed a judgment of the District Court for the Eastern District of Arkansas. The District Court had granted the application of the petitioners, the Little Rock School Board and School Superintendent, to suspend for two and one-half years the operation of the School Board's court-approved desegregation program. In order that the School Board might know, without doubt, its duty in this regard before the opening of school, which had been set for the following Monday, September 15, 1958, we immediately issued the judgment, reserving the expression of our supporting views to a later date. This opinion of all of the members of the Court embodies those views.

The following are the facts and circumstances so far as necessary to show how the legal questions are presented.

On May 17, 1954, this Court decided that enforced racial segregation in the public schools of a State is a denial of the equal protection of the laws enjoined by the Fourteenth Amendment. The Court postponed, pending further argument, formulation of a decree to effectuate this decision. That decree was rendered May 31, 1955. In the formulation of that decree the Court recognized that good faith compliance with the principles declared in *Brown* might in some situations "call for elimination of a variety of obstacles in making the transition to school systems operated in accordance with the constitutional principles set forth in our May 17, 1954, decision." . . .

Under such circumstances, the District Courts were directed to require "a prompt and reasonable start toward full compliance," and to take such action as was necessary to bring about the end of racial segregation in the public schools "with all deliberate speed." Of course, in many locations, obedience to the duty of desegregation would require the immediate general admission of Negro children, otherwise qualified as students for their appropriate classes, at particular schools. On the other hand, a District Court, after analysis of the relevant factors (which, of course, excludes hostility to racial desegregation), might conclude that justification existed for not requiring the present nonsegregated admission of all qualified Negro children. In such circumstances, however, the courts should scrutinize the program of the school authorities to make sure that they had developed arrangements pointed toward the earliest practicable completion of desegregation, and had taken appropriate steps to put their program into effective operation. It was made plain that delay in any guise in order to deny the constitutional rights of Negro children could not be countenanced, and that only a prompt start, diligently and earnestly pursued, to eliminate racial segregation from the public schools could constitute good faith compliance. State authorities were thus duty bound to devote every effort toward initiating desegregation and bringing about the elimination of racial discrimination in the public school system.

On May 20, 1954, three days after the first *Brown* opinion, the Little Rock District School Board adopted, and on May 23, 1954, made public, a statement of policy entitled "Supreme Court Decision—Segregation in Public Schools." In this statement the Board recognized that

> It is our responsibility to comply with Federal Constitutional
> Requirements and we intend to do so when the Supreme Court
> of the United States outlines the method to be followed.

Thereafter the Board undertook studies of the administrative problems confronting the transition to a desegregated public school system at Little Rock. It instructed the Superintendent of Schools to prepare a plan for desegregation, and approved such a plan on May 24, 1955, seven days before the second *Brown* opinion. The plan provided for desegregation at the senior high school level (grades 10 through 12) as the first stage. Desegregation at the junior high and elementary levels was to follow. It was contemplated that desegregation at the high school level would commence in the fall of 1957, and the expectation was that complete desegregation of the school system would be accomplished by 1963. Following the adoption of this plan, the Superintendent of Schools discussed it with a large number of citizen groups in the city. As a result of these discussions, the Board reached the conclusion that "a large majority of the residents" of Little Rock were of "the belief . . . that the Plan, although objectionable in principle," from the point of view of those supporting segregated schools, "was still the best for the interests of all pupils in the District."

Upon challenge by a group of Negro plaintiffs desiring more rapid completion of the desegregation process, the District Court upheld the School Board's plan. The Court of Appeals affirmed. Review of that judgment was not sought here.

While the School Board was thus going forward with its preparation for desegregating the Little Rock school system, other state authorities, in contrast, were actively pursuing a program designed to perpetuate in Arkansas the system of racial segregation which this Court had held violated the Fourteenth Amendment. First came, in November 1956, an amendment to the State Constitution flatly commanding the Arkansas General Assembly to oppose "in every Constitutional manner the Unconstitutional desegregation decisions of May 17, 1954 and May 31, 1955 of the United States Supreme Court," and, through the initiative, a pupil assignment law. Pursuant to this state constitutional command, a law relieving school children from compulsory attendance at racially mixed schools, and a law establishing a State Sovereignty Commission, were enacted by the General Assembly in February 1957.

The School Board and the Superintendent of Schools nevertheless continued with preparations to carry out the first stage of the desegregation program. Nine Negro children were scheduled for admission in September 1957 to Central High School, which has more than two thousand students. Various administrative measures, designed to assure the smooth transition of this first stage of desegregation, were undertaken.

On September 2, 1957, the day before these Negro students were to enter Central High, the school authorities were met with drastic opposing action on the part of the Governor of Arkansas who dispatched units of the Arkansas National Guard to the Central High School grounds and placed the school "off limits" to colored students. As found by the District Court in subsequent proceedings, the Governor's action had not been requested by the school authorities, and was entirely unheralded. The findings were these:

> Up to this time [September 2], no crowds had gathered about Central High School and no acts of violence or threats of violence in connection with the carrying out of the plan had occurred. Nevertheless, out of an abundance of caution, the school authorities had frequently conferred with the Mayor and Chief of Police of Little Rock about taking appropriate steps by the Little Rock police to prevent any possible disturbances or acts of violence in connection with the attendance of the 9 colored students at Central High School. The Mayor considered that the Little Rock police force could adequately cope with any incidents which might arise at the opening of school. The Mayor, the Chief of Police, and the school authorities made no request to the

Governor or any representative of his for State assistance in maintaining peace and order at Central High School. Neither the Governor nor any other official of the State government consulted with the Little Rock authorities about whether the Little Rock police were prepared to cope with any incidents which might arise at the school, about any need for State assistance in maintaining peace and order, or about stationing the Arkansas National Guard at Central High School.

The Board's petition for postponement in this proceeding states: "The effect of that action [of the Governor] was to harden the core of opposition to the Plan and cause many persons who theretofore had reluctantly accepted the Plan to believe there was some power in the State of Arkansas which, when exerted, could nullify the Federal law and permit disobedience of the decree of this [District] Court, and from that date hostility to the Plan was increased and criticism of the officials of the [School] District has become more bitter and unrestrained." The Governor's action caused the School Board to request the Negro students on September 2 not to attend the high school "until the legal dilemma was solved." The next day, September 3, 1957, the Board petitioned the District Court for instructions, and the court, after a hearing, found that the Board's request of the Negro students to stay away from the high school had been made because of the stationing of the military guards by the state authorities. The court determined that this was not a reason for departing from the approved plan, and ordered the School Board and Superintendent to proceed with it.

On the morning of the next day, September 4, 1957, the Negro children attempted to enter the high school but, as the District Court later found, units of the Arkansas National Guard "acting pursuant to the Governor's order, stood shoulder to shoulder at the school grounds and thereby forcibly prevented the 9 Negro students . . . from entering," as they continued to do every school day during the following three weeks.

That same day, September 4, 1957, the United States Attorney for the Eastern District of Arkansas was requested by the District Court to begin an immediate investigation in order to fix responsibility for the interference with the orderly implementation of the District Court's direction to carry out the desegregation program. Three days later, September 7, the District Court denied a petition of the School Board and the Superintendent of Schools for an order temporarily suspending continuance of the program.

Upon completion of the United States Attorney's investigation, he and the Attorney General of the United States, at the District Court's request, entered the proceedings and filed a petition on behalf of the United States, as *amicus curiae*, to enjoin the Governor of Arkansas and officers of the Arkansas National Guard from further attempts to prevent obedience to the court's order. After hearings on the petition, the District

Court found that the School Board's plan had been obstructed by the Governor through the use of National Guard troops, and granted a preliminary injunction on September 20, 1957, enjoining the Governor and the officers of the Guard from preventing the attendance of Negro children at Central High School, and from otherwise obstructing or interfering with the orders of the court in connection with the plan. The National Guard was then withdrawn from the school.

The next school day was Monday, September 23, 1957. The Negro children entered the high school that morning under the protection of the Little Rock Police Department and members of the Arkansas State Police. But the officers caused the children to be removed from the school during the morning because they had difficulty controlling a large and demonstrating crowd which had gathered at the high school. On September 25, however, the President of the United States dispatched federal troops to Central High School and admission of the Negro students to the school was thereby effected. Regular army troops continued at the high school until November 27, 1957. They were then replaced by federalized National Guardsmen who remained throughout the balance of the school year. Eight of the Negro students remained in attendance at the school throughout the school year.

We come now to the aspect of the proceedings presently before us. On February 20, 1958, the School Board and the Superintendent of Schools filed a petition in the District Court seeking a postponement of their program for desegregation. Their position in essence was that because of extreme public hostility, which they stated had been engendered largely by the official attitudes and actions of the Governor and the Legislature, the maintenance of a sound educational program at Central High School, with the Negro students in attendance, would be impossible. The Board therefore proposed that the Negro students already admitted to the school be withdrawn and sent to segregated schools, and that all further steps to carry out the Board's desegregation program be postponed for a period later suggested by the Board to be two and one-half years.

After a hearing the District Court granted the relief requested by the Board. Among other things the court found that the past year at Central High School had been attended by conditions of "chaos, bedlam and turmoil"; that there were "repeated incidents of more or less serious violence directed against the Negro students and their property"; that there was "tension and unrest among the school administrators, the class-room teachers, the pupils, and the latter's parents, which inevitably had an adverse effect upon the educational program"; that a school official was threatened with violence; that a "serious financial burden" had been cast on the School District; that the education of the students had suffered "and under existing conditions will continue to suffer"; that the Board would continue to need "military assistance or its equivalent"; that the local police department would not be able "to detail enough men to afford the necessary protection"; and that the situation was "intolerable."

The District Court's judgment was dated June 20, 1958. The Negro respondents appealed to the Court of Appeals for the Eighth Circuit and also sought there a stay of the District Court's judgment. At the same time they filed a petition for certiorari in this Court asking us to review the District Court's judgment without awaiting the disposition of their appeal to the Court of Appeals, or of their petition to that court for a stay. That we declined to do. The Court of Appeals did not act on the petition for a stay, but, on August 18, 1958, after convening in special session on August 4 and hearing the appeal, reversed the District Court. On August 21, 1958, the Court of Appeals stayed its mandate to permit the School Board to petition this Court for certiorari. . . . Recognizing the vital importance of a decision of the issues in time to permit arrangements to be made for the 1958–1959 school year, we convened in Special Term on August 28, 1958, and heard oral argument on the respondents' motions, and also argument of the Solicitor General who, by invitation, appeared for the United States as *amicus curiae*, and asserted that the Court of Appeals' judgment was clearly correct on the merits, and urged that we vacate its stay forthwith. . . . On September 12, 1958 . . . we unanimously affirmed the judgment of the Court of Appeals. . . .

In affirming the judgment of the Court of Appeals which reversed the District Court we have accepted without reservation the position of the School Board, the Superintendent of Schools, and their counsel that they displayed entire good faith in the conduct of these proceedings and in dealing with the unfortunate and distressing sequence of events which has been outlined. We likewise have accepted the findings of the District Court as to the conditions at Central High School during the 1957–1958 school year, and also the findings that the educational progress of all the students, white and colored, of that school has suffered and will continue to suffer if the conditions which prevailed last year are permitted to continue.

The significance of these findings, however, is to be considered in light of the fact, indisputably revealed by the record before us, that the conditions they depict are directly traceable to the actions of legislators and executive officials of the State of Arkansas, taken in their official capacities, which reflect their own determination to resist this Court's decision in the *Brown* case and which have brought about violent resistance to that decision in Arkansas. In its petition for certiorari filed in this Court, the School Board itself describes the situation in this language: "The legislative, executive, and judicial departments of the state government opposed the desegregation of Little Rock schools by enacting laws, calling out troops, making statements vilifying federal law and federal courts, and failing to utilize state law enforcement agencies and judicial processes to maintain public peace."

One may well sympathize with the position of the Board in the face of the frustrating conditions which have confronted it, but, regardless of the Board's good faith, the actions of the other state agencies responsible for those conditions compel us to reject the Board's legal position. Had Central High School been under the direct management of the State itself, it could hardly be suggested that those immediately in charge of the school should be heard to assert their own good faith as a legal excuse for delay in implementing the constitutional rights of these respondents, when vindication of those rights was rendered difficult or impossible by the actions of other state officials. The situation here is in no different posture because the members of the School Board and the Superintendent of Schools are local officials; from the point of view of the Fourteenth Amendment, they stand in this litigation as the agents of the State.

The constitutional rights of respondents are not to be sacrificed or yielded to the violence and disorder which have followed upon the actions of the Governor and Legislature. As this Court said some 41 years ago in a unanimous opinion in a case involving another aspect of racial segregation: "It is urged that this proposed segregation will promote the public peace by preventing race conflicts. Desirable as this is, and important as is the preservation of the public peace, this aim cannot be accomplished by laws or ordinances which deny rights created or protected by the Federal Constitution." *Buchanan v. Warley*, 245 U.S. 60 (1917). Thus law and order are not here to be preserved by depriving the Negro children of their constitutional rights. The record before us clearly establishes that the growth of the Board's difficulties to a magnitude beyond its unaided power to control is the product of state action. Those difficulties, as counsel for the Board forthrightly conceded on the oral argument in this Court, can also be brought under control by state action.

The controlling legal principles are plain. The command of the Fourteenth Amendment is that no "State" shall deny to any person within its jurisdiction the equal protection of the laws. "A State acts by its legislative, its executive, or its judicial authorities. It can act in no other way. The constitutional provision, therefore, must mean that no agency of the State, or of the officers or agents by whom its powers are exerted, shall deny to any person within its jurisdiction the equal protection of the laws. Whoever, by virtue of public position under a State government . . . denies or takes away the equal protection of the laws, violates the constitutional inhibition; and as he acts in the name and for the State, and is clothed with the State's power, his act is that of the State. This must be so, or the constitutional prohibition has no meaning." *Ex parte Virginia*, 100 U.S. 339 (1879). Thus the prohibitions of the Fourteenth Amendment extend to all action of the State denying equal protection of the laws; whatever the agency of the State taking the action, or whatever the guise in which it is taken. In short, the constitutional rights of children not to be discriminated against in school admission on grounds of race or color declared by this Court in the *Brown* case can neither be nullified openly and directly by state legislators or state executive or judicial officers, nor nullified indirectly by them through evasive schemes for segregation whether attempted "ingeniously or ingenuously."

What has been said, in the light of the facts developed, is enough to dispose of the case. However, we should answer the premise of the actions of the Governor and Legislature that they are not bound by our holding in the *Brown* case. It is necessary only to recall some basic constitutional propositions which are settled doctrine.

Article VI of the Constitution makes the Constitution the "supreme Law of the Land." In 1803, Chief Justice Marshall, speaking for a unanimous Court, referring to the Constitution as "the fundamental and paramount law of the nation," declared in the notable case of *Marbury v. Madison*, that "It is emphatically the province and duty of the judicial department to say what the law is." This decision declared the basic principle that the federal judiciary is supreme in the exposition of the law of the Constitution, and that principle has ever since been respected by this Court and the Country as a permanent and indispensable feature of our constitutional system. It follows that the interpretation of the Fourteenth Amendment enunciated by this Court in the *Brown* case is the supreme law of the land, and Art. VI of the Constitution makes it of binding effect on the States "any Thing in the Constitution or Laws of any State to the Contrary notwithstanding." Every state legislator and executive and judicial officer is solemnly committed by oath taken pursuant to Art. VI, cl. 3, "to support this Constitution." Chief Justice Taney, speaking for a unanimous Court in 1859, said that this requirement reflected the framers' "anxiety to preserve it [the Constitution] in full force, in all its powers, and to guard against resistance to or evasion of its authority, on the part of a State. . . ." *Ableman v. Booth*, 21 How. 506 (1859).

No state legislator or executive or judicial officer can war against the Constitution without violating his undertaking to support it. Chief Justice Marshall spoke for a unanimous Court in saying that: "If the legislatures of the several states may, at will, annul the judgments of the courts of the United States, and destroy the rights acquired under those judgments, the constitution itself becomes a solemn mockery. . . ." *United States v. Peters*, 5 Cranch 115 (1809). A Governor who asserts a power to nullify a federal court order is similarly restrained. If he had such power, said Chief Justice Hughes, in 1932, also for a unanimous Court, "it is manifest that the fiat of a state Governor, and not the Constitution of the United States, would be the supreme law of the land; that the restrictions of the Federal Constitution upon the exercise of state power would be but impotent phrases. . . ." *Sterling v. Constantin*, 287 U.S. 378.

It is, of course, quite true that the responsibility for public education is primarily the concern of the States, but it is equally true that such responsibilities, like all other state activity, must be exercised consistently with federal constitutional requirements as they apply to state action. The Constitution created a government dedicated to equal justice under law. The Fourteenth Amendment embodied and emphasized that ideal. State support of segregated schools through any arrangement, management, funds, or property cannot be squared with the Amendment's command that no State shall deny to any person within its jurisdiction the equal protection of the laws. The right of a student not to be segregated on racial grounds in schools so maintained is indeed so fundamental and pervasive that it is embraced in the concept of due process of law. *Bolling v. Sharpe*. The basic decision in *Brown* was unanimously reached by this Court only after the case had been briefed and twice argued and the issues had been given the most serious consideration. Since the first *Brown* opinion three new Justices have come to the Court. They are at one with the Justices still on the Court who participated in that basic decision as to its correctness, and that decision is now unanimously reaffirmed. The principles announced in that decision and the obedience of the States to them, according to the command of the Constitution, are indispensable for the protection of the freedoms guaranteed by our fundamental charter for all of us. Our constitutional ideal of equal justice under law is thus made a living truth.

NOTE ON *COOPER* AND THE ALLOCATION OF AUTHORITY TO INTERPRET THE CONSTITUTION

1. The school board argued in *Cooper* that the pandemonium surrounding desegregation efforts in Little Rock was making it impossible for the public schools to perform their basic educational mission. To what extent should such considerations provide a reason for delaying implementation of a segregation decree? Was the Court's ruling in *Cooper* too indifferent to the welfare of the children involved? If such arguments *were* taken into account, would that make it impossible to achieve real desegregation?

2. Governor Faubus's argument in *Cooper* was that, as a public official who had taken his own oath to uphold the Constitution, he had the same authority and obligation to interpret the Constitution as the justices of the Supreme Court. Is this a crazy position? Suppose that there were no *Brown* decision, and the Governor were asked to sign a bill providing for segregated schools. Wouldn't his oath obligate him to determine for himself whether there were any valid constitutional objections to the bill? To what extent does the existence of a Supreme Court decision on point change that obligation?

Is it significant that the state government of Arkansas was not a party to either the *Brown* case or the Little Rock desegregation litigation? This is a question of the general law of judgments, not simply of constitutional law. Consider, for example, a suit arising out of an auto accident in which the injured driver claims that the car was defective. She sues the dealer who sold her the car and gets a judgment in her favor. Would that judgment, rendered between the driver and the dealer, also obligate the *manufacturer* to concede the existence of a defect and pay part of the damages? Or would the manufacturer be entitled to its own day in court to contest whether its product was defective? On the other hand, were the Governor's actions in *Cooper* entirely unrelated to the federal desegregation litigation?

3.   The Court's opinion in *Cooper*, signed by all nine Justices, emphatically reaffirmed the Court's commitment to the principles of *Brown* even in the face of "massive resistance" from Southern whites. While the result in *Cooper* is no longer controversial, the following language remains a focus for criticism and debate:

> In 1803, Chief Justice Marshall . . . declared in the notable case of *Marbury v. Madison* that "It is emphatically the province and duty of the judicial department to say what the law is." This decision declared the basic principle that the federal judiciary is supreme in the exposition of the law of the Constitution, and that principle has ever since been respected by this Court and the Country as a permanent and indispensable feature of our constitutional system. It follows that the interpretation of the Fourteenth Amendment enunciated by this Court in the *Brown* case is the supreme law of the land, and Art. VI of the Constitution makes it of binding effect on the States "any Thing in the Constitution or Laws of any State to the Contrary notwithstanding."

It is one thing to say that a state official like Governor Faubus has no authority to interfere with the enforcement of a federal court order. Isn't it quite another to say that the *Brown* decision—i.e., the Court's interpretation of the Constitution—has the same authority as the Constitution itself? The Court relies on *Marbury* for this proposition. Does *Marbury* say that?

4.   The debate over the allocation of interpretive authority between the Supreme Court and the other institutions of government has gone on since the beginning of the Republic. It may help to break the question down into two related issues:

- Does the effect of the Court's judgment in a constitutional case extend beyond the parties to the litigation?

- To what extent can other actors in the other branches of government implement their own interpretations of the Constitution when they disagree with the Court?

In addressing these questions, it may help to look at statements by several presidents who have had rather profound disagreements with the Supreme Court:

> a.   *Thomas Jefferson*: President Jefferson pardoned several individuals who had been convicted, during the Adams administration, of violating the Sedition Act of 1798 by criticizing federal officials. In a letter to Abigail Adams, Jefferson responded to criticism that he had no right to issue a pardon on the ground that he thought the Sedition Act unconstitutional, when the courts had never so held:

> You seem to think it devolved on the judges to decide on the validity of the sedition law. But nothing in the Constitution has given them a right to decide for the Executive, more than the Executive to decide for them. Both magistracies are entirely independent in the sphere of action assigned to them. The judges, believing the law constitutional, had a right to pass a sentence of fine and imprisonment; because that power was placed in their hands by the Constitution. But the Executive, believing the law to be unconstitutional, was bound to remit the execution of it; because that power has been confided to him by the Constitution. That instrument meant that its co-ordinate branches should be checks on each other. But the opinion which gives to the judges the right to decide what laws are constitutional, and what not, not only for themselves in their own sphere of action, but for the Legislature & Executive also, in their spheres, would make the judiciary a despotic branch.[15]

b.   *Andrew Jackson*: President Jackson vetoed a bill to recharter the Bank of the United States, on the ground that he thought the Bank unconstitutional. Jackson explained:

> It is maintained by the advocates of the bank that its constitutionality in all its features ought to be considered as settled by precedent and by the decision of the Supreme Court [in *McCulloch*]. To this conclusion I can not assent. Mere precedent is a dangerous source of authority, and should not be regarded as deciding questions of constitutional power except where the acquiescence of the people and the States can be considered as well settled. [Even if] the opinion of the Supreme Court covered the whole ground of this act, it ought not to control the coordinate authorities of this Government. . . .

> [Under] the decision of the Supreme Court, [it] is the exclusive province of Congress and the President to decide whether the particular features of this act are *necessary* and *proper* in order to enable the bank to perform conveniently and efficiently the public duties assigned to it as a fiscal agent, and therefore constitutional, or *unnecessary* and *improper*, and therefore unconstitutional. . . . [M]any of the powers and privileges conferred on [the Bank] can not be supposed necessary for the purpose for which it is proposed to be created, and are not, therefore . . . justified by the Constitution.[16]

c.   *Abraham Lincoln*: As an opponent of slavery, Abraham Lincoln was a staunch opponent of the *Dred Scott* decision. He

---

[15] Letter to Abigail Adams, Sept. 11, 1804, 8 THE WRITINGS OF THOMAS JEFFERSON 310 (Ford. ed. 1897).

[16] Veto Message, July 10, 1832, in 2 MESSAGES AND PAPERS OF THE PRESIDENTS 576, 581–83 (Richardson ed., 1896).

explained his view of the decision's authority while running for the Senate in 1858:

> We oppose the *Dred Scott* decision in a certain way. [We] do not propose that when Dred Scott has been decided to be a slave by the court, we, as a mob, will decide him to be free. We do not propose that, when any other one, or one thousand, shall be decided by that court to be slaves, we will in any violent way disturb the rights of property thus settled; but we nevertheless do oppose that decision as a political rule which shall be binding on the voter, to vote for nobody who thinks it wrong, which shall be binding on the members of Congress or the President to favor no measure that does not actually concur with the principles of that decision. [We] propose so resisting it as to have it reversed if we can, and a new judicial rule established upon this subject.[17]

d.   *Franklin D. Roosevelt*: Shortly after the Court's decision in *Schechter Poultry* invalidating the National Industrial Recovery Act, President Roosevelt nevertheless pressed Congress to adopt legislation governing the coal industry that was closely modeled on the NIRA. In a letter to a congressman, he urged leaving any constitutional doubts to the courts to resolve:

> Manifestly, no one is in a position to give assurance that the proposed act will withstand constitutional tests. [But] the situation is so urgent and the benefits of the legislation so evident that all doubts should be resolved in favor of the bill, leaving to the courts, in an orderly fashion, the ultimate question of constitutionality. A decision by the Supreme Court relative to this measure would be helpful as indicating [the] constitutional limits within which this Government must operate. [I] hope your committee will not permit doubts as to constitutionality, however reasonable, to block the suggested legislation.[18]

5.   As Professor Walter Murphy has noted, the Constitution contains language suggesting that each of the branches has an obligation and authority to interpret the Constitution. Article I, § 8 suggests that Congress must determine, in the first instance, what means are "necessary and proper" to the accomplishment of constitutional ends, and similar language occurs in the enforcement provisions of the Thirteenth, Fourteenth, Fifteenth, Nineteenth, Twenty-third, Twenty-fourth, and Twenty-sixth amendments. Article II confers on the President the power to "take care that the laws be faithfully executed," and it requires him to swear an oath to "preserve, protect, and defend the constitution." And Article III extends the "judicial power" "to all cases . . . arising under this Constitution." As Murphy

---

[17] Speech During the Lincoln-Douglas Senatorial Campaign, October 1858, in 3 THE COLLECTED WORKS OF ABRAHAM LINCOLN 255 (Basler ed., 1953).

[18] Letter to Congressman Hill, July 6, 1935, in 4 THE PUBLIC PAPERS AND ADDRESSES OF FRANKLIN D. ROOSEVELT 297–98 (1938).

points out, however, "there is not a word in these clauses about whose views should prevail if the branches disagree."[19]

Professor Murphy identified three leading theories of interpretive authority:

a. *Judicial Supremacy*. In *Cooper*, the Court declared that "the federal judiciary is supreme in the exposition of the law of the Constitution." Murphy traces this idea back to Justice Story's *Commentaries*, which held that the judiciary's interpretation of the constitution "becomes obligatory and conclusive upon all the departments of the federal government and upon the whole people, so far as their rights and duties are derived from, or affected by that constitution."[20] Although often derived from *Marbury* (as in *Cooper*), this theory is also bolstered by practical advantages: it allows the judiciary to function as an umpire by issuing uniform interpretations that bind the other branches; it plays to the particular legal interpretive expertise of courts; and buttresses the judiciary's role as a protector of individual liberties against intrusions by the "political" branches of government. As the presidential views quoted above demonstrate, however, judicial supremacy has always been contested by the other branches of government.

b. *Legislative Supremacy*. This theory has had relatively few defenders, although it probably describes the views of the Radical Republicans who dominated Congress during Reconstruction and the early Jeffersonians who sought to impeach Federalist justices. The best argument for this position "rests on legislators' connections to the people"; "[o]n the other hand, constitutionalism is wary of arguments that allow popularly elected officials final authority to define substantive rights. . . . One does not, as the Italian proverb goes, make the goat one's gardener."[21]

c. *Departmentalism*. This theory holds that each department of the Government—e.g., the President, Congress, and the courts— has the authority to construe the Constitution for itself in the course of performing its constitutionally-appointed functions. For example, Members of Congress may refuse to support, or a President may veto, a bill on constitutional grounds, even if the courts have already taken the position that such a measure would be constitutionally permissible. But when, as in *Marbury*, the courts must decide a case involving a constitutional issue, they too must interpret the Constitution for themselves and need not defer to the views of the other branches. The great advantage of this theory is that it replicates, for purposes of constitutional

---

[19] Walter F. Murphy, *Who Shall Interpret? The Quest for the Ultimate Constitutional Intepreter*, 48 Review of Politics 401, 405 (1986).

[20] 1 Joseph Story, Commentaries on the Constitution of the United States § 383 (1st ed. 1833).

[21] Murphy, *supra* note 16, at 411.

interpretation, the division of mutually-checking powers that characterizes the constitutional separation of powers generally.

Departmentalism works fine for instances in which a particular branch exercises sole authority, and can act for any reason or no reason at all. These instances include a legislator's decision to support a bill or the President's choice to exercise his veto. But what about actions by the political branches that are subsequently subject to challenge in litigation before the courts? A departmentalist may say that a Member of Congress must interpret the Constitution for herself in determining to vote for a bill, but if the bill passes and it is enforced against an individual in a court, that court will then have to judge—as part of *its* departmental responsibility—the constitutionality of the bill. Since the judiciary will typically act last in time, does this not make the courts *effectively* supreme in constitutional interpretation even if we accept departmentalist premises? Is anything left of the departmental independence of the other branches?

NOTE ON THE EFFICACY OF JUDICIAL DECISIONS

1.   Assuming that courts have the authority both to interpret the Constitution's commands and to issue orders to other actors enforcing those interpretations, we must still ask whether judicial decisions make any practical difference in the real world. This question is particularly pressing in contexts like racial equality, where the courts have often been ahead of other institutions in society in seeking to promote social change. The successful plaintiffs in *Brown*, for example, took an exceptionally optimistic view of what they had won. Their lawyer, Thurgood Marshall, predicted it would only take "up to five years" to eliminate segregated schooling throughout the country, and that all forms of segregation would be eliminated by the 100th anniversary of the Emancipation Proclamation in 1963.[22]

Political scientist Gerald Rosenberg notes that "[i]n the last several decades movements and groups advocating what I will shortly define as significant social reform have turned increasingly to the courts."[23] *Brown* is generally the poster-child for judicially-driven social reform. As such, it stands for what Professor Rosenberg calls the "Dynamic Court" model of the judiciary, which "sees courts as powerful, vigorous, and potent proponents of change."[24] The alternative model, tracing its lineage back to Alexander Hamilton's description of the judiciary as the "least dangerous branch," posits a "Constrained Court" that "can do little more than point out how actions have fallen short of constitutional or legislative requirements and hope that appropriate action is taken."[25]

In an important recent study, Professor Rosenberg sought out empirical evidence that might demonstrate which of these two descriptive models is

---

[22] Quoted in GERALD ROSENBERG, THE HOLLOW HOPE: CAN COURTS BRING ABOUT SOCIAL CHANGE? 43 (1991).

[23] *Id.* at 2.

[24] *Id.*

[25] *Id.* at 3.

more accurate. As he explains, the history of public school desegregation in the South presents something of a natural experiment:

> The decade from 1954 to 1964 provides close to an ideal setting for measuring the contribution of the courts vis-à-vis Congress and the executive branch in desegregating public schools. For ten years the court spoke forcefully while Congress and the executive did little. Then, in 1964, Congress and the executive branch entered the battle with the most significant piece of civil rights legislation in nearly ninety years. In 1965, the enactment of [the Elementary and Secondary Education Act] made a billion dollars in federal funds available to school districts that, in accord with Title VI, did not discriminate. This history allows one to isolate the contribution of the courts. If the courts were effective in desegregating public schools the results should show up before 1964. However, if it was Congress and the executive branch, through the 1964 Civil Rights Act and 1965 ESEA, that made the real difference, then change would occur only in the years after 1964 or 1965.[26]

Rosenberg's findings strongly favor the Constrained Court model. In the border states (Delaware, Kentucky, Maryland, Missouri, Oklahoma, and West Virginia) and the District of Columbia, the amount of desegregation[27] increased 15.2 percent between 1956 and 1964—the period in which the courts acted alone. It increased 22 percent in those jurisdictions in the eight school years following passage of the 1964 Act. Rosenberg thus concludes that "the Court made a major contribution to desegregation of the public schools in the border states," but that "the rate of desegregation noticeably increased" after Congress got involved.[28] What happened in the eleven southern states, however, is truly remarkable:

> For ten years, 1954–64, virtually *nothing happened*. Ten years after *Brown* only 1.2 percent of black schoolchildren in the South attended school with whites. . . . Despite the unanimity and forcefulness of the *Brown* opinion, the Supreme Court's reiteration of its position and its steadfast refusal to yield, its decree was flagrantly disobeyed. After ten years of Court-ordered desegregation, in the eleven Southern states barely 1 out of every 100 black children attended school with whites. The Court ordered an end to segregation and segregation was not ended. As Judge Wisdom put it . . . *"the courts acting alone have failed."* The numbers show that the Supreme Court contributed virtually *nothing* to ending segregation of the public schools in the Southern States in the decade following *Brown*.[29]

---

[26] *Id.* at 49.

[27] Rosenberg defined desegregation as the percentage of black school children who attended school with at least some whites. He acknowledged that this probably overstates the amount of meaningful desegregation, but the important point is the change in desegregation rates—not their absolute magnitude. *See id.* at 50.

[28] *Id.* at 51.

[29] *Id.* at 52.

After Congress and the Executive (which gained authority to file desegregation suits in the 1964 Act) joined in, however, things changed significantly:

> [D]esegregation took off after 1964, reaching 91.3 percent in 1972 .... In the first year of the act, 1964–65, nearly as much desegregation was achieved as during all the preceding years of Supreme Court action. In just the few months between the end of the 1964–65 school year and the start of the 1965–66 year, nearly three times as many black students entered desegregated schools as had in the preceding decade of Court action. And the years following showed significant increases. While much segregation still existed, and still exists, the change after 1964 is as extraordinary as is the utter lack of impact of the Supreme Court prior to 1964. The actions of the Supreme Court appear irrelevant to desegregation from *Brown* to the enactment of the 1964 Civil Rights Act and 1965 ESEA. Only after the passage of these acts was there any desegregation of public schools in the South.[30]

Rosenberg thus concludes that "*Brown* and its progeny stand for the proposition that courts are impotent to produce significant social reform."[31] Do you find Professor Rosenberg's account of the judicial role in the history of desegregation persuasive? Depressing? If Rosenberg is right, what follows for our sense of the role of the courts in effecting social change in other areas, such as gay rights or abortion?

2.   Professor Rosenberg's argument is primarily *descriptive*—he seeks to accurately show the effect of Supreme Court decisions on issues like segregation. He does not take much of a *normative* position—that is, a position on how large a role the courts *should* have in promoting social change. Which vision of the courts' role—the Dynamic or Constrained Court—do you find more normatively attractive? If you think the court should play a larger role, what institutional reforms could bring about that result?

3.   If you think Professor Rosenberg's account is descriptively accurate, does that conclusion take some of the pressure off of Alexander Bickel's "countermajoritarian difficulty"? In other words, if the courts can't really move the country without the concurrence and assistance of the democratically-elected branches, is it easier to accept the courts' own lack of a democratic mandate?

4.   One possible rejoinder to Professor Rosenberg's account would be that judicial actions—particularly the *Brown* decision—play a catalytic role by inspiring social movements and spurring other governmental actors to action. Historian David Garrow has written, for example, of "the direct influence of *Brown* on the instigation of the 1955 Montgomery [bus] boycott. Almost every significant black Montgomery activist of that time has without

---

[30] *Id.*

[31] *Id.* at 71.

prompting spoken of Brown's importance for the bus protesters."[32] The Montgomery boycott brought Dr. Martin Luther King, the 26-year-old pastor of a local Baptist church, into the civil rights movement. Without underestimating the critical role civil rights movement's role as the most proximate cause of Congress's civil rights legislation and the national Executive's increased involvement in the fight against segregation, isn't it likely that the Supreme Court's holdings played an important role in mobilizing that movement?

5.   It is also possible that judicial decisions play a more central role in particular settings—for example, in defending reformers from attacks and, more generally, in protecting the sorts of political freedoms that make reform possible. For example, *New York Times, Inc. v. Sullivan*, 376 U.S. 254 (1964), foreclosed segregationists' efforts to use libel litigation to deter coverage of the civil rights movement by news organizations by holding that the First Amendment requires a high standard for libel suits. Likewise, *Garner v. Louisiana*, 368 U.S. 157 (1961), overturned convictions of civil rights protesters involved in lunch counter sit-ins on due process grounds. Rather than mandating social change directly, these decisions and others like them helped create and maintain the conditions for social protest.

In each of these scenarios, however, judges played a supporting role to non-judicial actors, particularly broad social movements, that pursued their constitutional vision primarily outside the courts. Vigorous debate persists concerning the extent to which judicial decisions matter out in the world, but hardly anyone believes anymore that constitutionalism *inside* the courts can go it alone. We will return to this issue in Chapter Seventeen, which considers the extraordinary role of the courts in recognizing gay rights.

SECTION 6.3   INCORPORATION AND THE
NATIONALIZATION OF CRIMINAL PROCEDURE

The Warren Court's efforts to expand constitutional protection for individual rights proceeded on a number of fronts. One, as we have already seen, was the issue of segregation and racial equality. Another was an effort to nationalize the law of criminal procedure, primarily by extending the procedural safeguards in the Bill of Rights to state prosecutions—a category that has encompassed by far the larger proportion of criminal law enforcement throughout our history. Although conceptually distinct, history bound the two fronts closely together. As Kenneth Pye observed,

> The Court's concern with criminal procedure can be understood only in the context of the struggle for civil rights. . . . It is hard to conceive of a Court that would accept the challenge of guaranteeing the rights of Negroes and other disadvantaged

---

[32]   David Garrow, *Hopelessly Hollow History: Revisionist Devaluing of* Brown v. Board of Education, 80 VA. L. REV. 151, 152–53 (1994). *But see* Michael J. Klarman, Brown, *Racial Change, and the Civil Rights Movement*, 80 VA. L. REV. 7, 82 n. 353 (1994) (concluding that "the *Brown* decision was a relatively unimportant motivating factor for the civil rights movement").

groups to equality before the law and at the same time do nothing to ameliorate the invidious discrimination between rich and poor which existed in the criminal process. It would have been equally anomalous for such a Court to ignore the clear evidence that members of disadvantaged groups generally bore the brunt of most unlawful police activity.[33]

This linkage between racial equality and issues of policing and criminal justice echoes in contemporary concerns over the use of force by (and against) police officers.

Although courses in criminal law typically cover the Bill of Rights' criminal procedure provisions, developments in this area are also important to more general debates in constitutional law for several reasons. First, the "criminal procedure revolution" in the mid-Twentieth Century is an important element of the Supreme Court's developing role in this period. Second, incorporation of the Bill of Rights through the Due Process Clause of the Fourteenth Amendment is an aspect of "substantive due process"—albeit a generally uncontroversial one, nowadays—and thus important to debates over other due process rights, such as the right to privacy. Finally, the effective nationalization of criminal procedure by way of the Court's incorporation decisions may well be as important to the development of American federalism as the Court's expansion of Congress's regulatory authority under the Commerce Clause in cases like *Jones & Laughlin* and *Wickard*.

Notwithstanding the *Slaughterhouse Cases'* narrow interpretation of the Fourteenth Amendment, the Court began "incorporating" individual aspects of the Bill of Rights to apply against the States early in the Twentieth Century. For example, the Court incorporated the Takings Clause against the States as early as 1897,[34] and the speech, press, and religion provisions of the First Amendment by the middle of the 20th Century. [35] During this period, the Court divided over the proper approach to incorporation. *Adamson v. California* is a good example of the pre-Warren Court debate, and it sets out the two sharply contrasting approaches advocated by Justices Frankfurter (and later Harlan), on the one hand, and Justice Black. The second case in this section, *Duncan v. Louisiana*, exemplifies the Warren Court's compromise between these approaches, under which virtually all the provisions of the Bill of Rights were eventually incorporated.

---

[33] A. Kenneth Pye, *The Warren Court and Criminal Procedure*, in THE WARREN COURT: A CRITICAL ANALYSIS 58, 65 (Richard H. Sayler, Barry B. Boyer, & Robert E. Gooding, Jr., eds. 1968).

[34] Chicago, B. & Q. R. Co. v. Chicago, 166 U.S. 226 (1897).

[35] Fiske v. Kansas, 274 U.S. 380 (1927) (speech); Near v. Minnesota, 283 U.S. 697 (1931) (press); Cantwell v. Connecticut, 310 U.S. 296 (1940) (free exercise of religion); Everson v. Board of Education, 330 U.S. 1 (1947) (establishment of religion).

Adamson v. California

332 U.S. 46 (1947)

■ MR. JUSTICE REED delivered the opinion of the Court.

The appellant, Adamson . . . was convicted, without recommendation for mercy, by a jury in a Superior Court of the State of California of murder in the first degree. After considering the same objections to the conviction that are pressed here, the sentence of death was affirmed by the Supreme Court of the state. . . . The provisions of California law which were challenged in the state proceedings . . . permit the failure of a defendant to explain or to deny evidence against him to be commented upon by court and by counsel and to be considered by court and jury. The defendant did not testify. As the trial court gave its instructions and the District Attorney argued the case in accordance with the constitutional and statutory provisions just referred to, we have for decision the question of their constitutionality in these circumstances under the limitations of § 1 of the Fourteenth Amendment. . . .

In the first place, appellant urges that the provision of the Fifth Amendment that no person "shall be compelled in any criminal case to be a witness against himself" is a fundamental national privilege or immunity protected against state abridgment by the Fourteenth Amendment or a privilege or immunity secured, through the Fourteenth Amendment, against deprivation by state action because it is a personal right, enumerated in the federal Bill of Rights.

Secondly, appellant relies upon the due process of law clause of the Fourteenth Amendment to invalidate the provisions of the California law. . . .

We shall assume, but without any intention thereby of ruling upon the issue, that permission by law to the court, counsel and jury to comment upon and consider the failure of defendant "to explain or to deny by his testimony any evidence or facts in the case against him" would infringe defendant's privilege against self-incrimination under the Fifth Amendment if this were a trial in a court of the United States under a similar law. Such an assumption does not determine appellant's rights under the Fourteenth Amendment. It is settled law that the clause of the Fifth Amendment, protecting a person against being compelled to be a witness against himself, is not made effective by the Fourteenth Amendment as a protection against state action on the ground that freedom from testimonial compulsion is a right of national citizenship, or because it is a personal privilege or immunity secured by the Federal Constitution as one of the rights of man that are listed in the Bill of Rights.

The reasoning that leads to those conclusions starts with the unquestioned premise that the Bill of Rights, when adopted, was for the protection of the individual against the federal government and its provisions were inapplicable to similar actions done by the states. *Barron v. Baltimore*. With the adoption of the Fourteenth Amendment, it was suggested that the dual citizenship recognized by its first sentence secured for citizens federal protection for their elemental privileges and immunities of state citizenship. The *Slaughter-House Cases* decided, contrary to the suggestion, that these rights, as privileges and immunities of state citizenship, remained under the sole protection of the state governments. . . . The power to free defendants in state trials from self-incrimination was specifically determined to be beyond the scope of the privileges and immunities clause of the Fourteenth Amendment in *Twining v. New Jersey*, 211 U.S. 78 (1908). . . . The *Twining* case likewise disposed of the contention that freedom from testimonial compulsion, being specifically granted by the Bill of Rights, is a federal privilege or immunity that is protected by the Fourteenth Amendment against state invasion. This Court held that the inclusion in the Bill of Rights of this protection against the power of the national government did not make the privilege a federal privilege or immunity secured to citizens by the Constitution against state action. [See also] *Palko v. Connecticut*, 302 U.S. 319 (1937). After declaring that state and national citizenship coexist in the same person, the Fourteenth Amendment forbids a state from abridging the privileges and immunities of citizens of the United States. As a matter of words, this leaves a state free to abridge, within the limits of the due process clause, the privileges and immunities flowing from state citizenship. This reading of the Federal Constitution has heretofore found favor with the majority of this Court as a natural and logical interpretation. It accords with the constitutional doctrine of federalism by leaving to the states the responsibility of dealing with the privileges and immunities of their citizens except those inherent in national citizenship. It is the construction placed upon the amendment by justices whose own experience had given them contemporaneous knowledge of the purposes that led to the adoption of the Fourteenth Amendment. This construction has become embedded in our federal system as a functioning element in preserving the balance between national and state power. We reaffirm the conclusion of the *Twining* and *Palko* cases that protection against self-incrimination is not a privilege or immunity of national citizenship.

Appellant secondly contends that if the privilege against self-incrimination is not a right protected by the privileges and immunities clause of the Fourteenth Amendment against state action, this privilege, to its full scope under the Fifth Amendment, inheres in the right to a fair trial. A right to a fair trial is a right admittedly protected by the due process clause of the Fourteenth Amendment. Therefore, appellant argues, the due process clause of the Fourteenth Amendment protects his privilege against self-incrimination. The due process clause of the Fourteenth Amendment, however, does not draw all the rights of the federal Bill of Rights under its protection. That contention was made and rejected in *Palko*. . . . Nothing has been called to our attention that either the framers of the Fourteenth Amendment or the states that adopted intended its due process clause to draw within its scope the earlier amendments to the Constitution. *Palko* held that such provisions of the Bill of Rights as were "implicit in the concept of ordered liberty" became secure from state interference by the clause. But it held nothing more.

Specifically, the due process clause does not protect, by virtue of its mere existence, the accused's freedom from giving testimony by compulsion in state trials that is secured to him against federal interference by the Fifth Amendment. For a state to require testimony from an accused is not necessarily a breach of a state's obligation to give a fair trial. . . .

Generally, comment on the failure of an accused to testify is forbidden in American jurisdictions. This arises from state constitutional or statutory provisions similar in character to the federal provisions. California, however, is one of a few states that permits limited comment upon a defendant's failure to testify.[16] That permission is narrow. . . .

It is true that if comment were forbidden, an accused in this situation could remain silent and avoid evidence of former crimes and comment upon his failure to testify. We are of the view, however, that a state may control such a situation in accordance with its own ideas of the most efficient administration of criminal justice. The purpose of due process is not to protect an accused against a proper conviction but against an unfair conviction. When evidence is before a jury that threatens conviction, it does not seem unfair to require him to choose between leaving the adverse evidence unexplained and subjecting himself to impeachment through disclosure of former crimes. Indeed, this is a dilemma with which any defendant may be faced. If facts, adverse to the defendant, are proven by the prosecution, there may be no way to explain them favorably to the accused except by a witness who may be vulnerable to impeachment on cross-examination. The defendant must then decide whether or not to use such a witness. The fact that the witness may also be the defendant makes the choice more difficult but a denial of due process does not emerge from the circumstances. . . .

We find no other error that gives ground for our intervention in California's administration of criminal justice.

Affirmed.

■ **MR. JUSTICE FRANKFURTER, concurring.**

. . . To suggest that it is inconsistent with a truly free society to begin prosecutions without an indictment, to try petty civil cases without the paraphernalia of a common law jury, to take into consideration that one who has full opportunity to make a defense remains silent is, in de Tocqueville's phrase, to confound the familiar with the necessary.

The short answer to the suggestion that the provision of the Fourteenth Amendment, which ordains "nor shall any State deprive any

---

[16] New Jersey, Ohio and Vermont permit comment. . . .

person of life, liberty, or property, without due process of law," was a way of saying that every State must thereafter initiate prosecutions through indictment by a grand jury, must have a trial by a jury of twelve in criminal cases, and must have trial by such a jury in common law suits where the amount in controversy exceeds twenty dollars, is that it is a strange way of saying it. It would be extraordinarily strange for a Constitution to convey such specific commands in such a roundabout and inexplicit way. After all, an amendment to the Constitution should be read in a " 'sense most obvious to the common understanding at the time of its adoption.' . . . For it was for public adoption that it was proposed." Those reading the English language with the meaning which it ordinarily conveys, those conversant with the political and legal history of the concept of due process, those sensitive to the relations of the States to the central government as well as the relation of some of the provisions of the Bill of Rights to the process of justice, would hardly recognize the Fourteenth Amendment as a cover for the various explicit provisions of the first eight Amendments. Some of these are enduring reflections of experience with human nature, while some express the restricted views of Eighteenth-Century England regarding the best methods for the ascertainment of facts. The notion that the Fourteenth Amendment was a covert way of imposing upon the States all the rules which it seemed important to Eighteenth Century statesmen to write into the Federal Amendments, was rejected by judges who were themselves witnesses of the process by which the Fourteenth Amendment became part of the Constitution. Arguments that may now be adduced to prove that the first eight Amendments were concealed within the historic phrasing of the Fourteenth Amendment were not unknown at the time of its adoption. A surer estimate of their bearing was possible for judges at the time than distorting distance is likely to vouchsafe. Any evidence of design or purpose not contemporaneously known could hardly have influenced those who ratified the Amendment. Remarks of a particular proponent of the Amendment, no matter how influential, are not to be deemed part of the Amendment. What was submitted for ratification was his proposal, not his speech. Thus, at the time of the ratification of the Fourteenth Amendment the constitutions of nearly half of the ratifying States did not have the rigorous requirements of the Fifth Amendment for instituting criminal proceedings through a grand jury. It could hardly have occurred to these States that by ratifying the Amendment they uprooted their established methods for prosecuting crime and fastened upon themselves a new prosecutorial system.

Indeed, the suggestion that the Fourteenth Amendment incorporates the first eight Amendments as such is not unambiguously urged. Even the boldest innovator would shrink from suggesting to more than half the States that they may no longer initiate prosecutions without indictment by grand jury, or that thereafter all the States of the Union must furnish a jury of twelve for every case involving a claim above twenty dollars. There is suggested merely a selective incorporation of the first eight Amendments into the Fourteenth Amendment. Some are in and some are out, but we are left in the dark as to which are in and which are out. Nor are we given the calculus for determining which go in and which stay out. If the basis of selection is merely that those provisions of the first eight Amendments are incorporated which commend themselves to individual justices as indispensable to the dignity and happiness of a free man, we are thrown back to a merely subjective test. The protection against unreasonable search and seizure might have primacy for one judge, while trial by a jury of twelve for every claim above twenty dollars might appear to another as an ultimate need in a free society. In the history of thought "natural law" has a much longer and much better founded meaning and justification than such subjective selection of the first eight Amendments for incorporation into the Fourteenth. If all that is meant is that due process contains within itself certain minimal standards which are "of the very essence of a scheme of ordered liberty," *Palko v. Connecticut*, putting upon this Court the duty of applying these standards from time to time, then we have merely arrived at the insight which our predecessors long ago expressed. . . . As judges charged with the delicate task of subjecting the government of a continent to the Rule of Law we must be particularly mindful that it is "a *constitution* we are expounding," so that it should not be imprisoned in what are merely legal forms even though they have the sanction of the Eighteenth Century. . . .

The [Fourteenth] Amendment neither comprehends the specific provisions by which the founders deemed it appropriate to restrict the federal government nor is it confined to them. The Due Process Clause of the Fourteenth Amendment has an independent potency, precisely as does the Due Process Clause of the Fifth Amendment in relation to the Federal Government. It ought not to require argument to reject the notion that due process of law meant one thing in the Fifth Amendment and another in the Fourteenth. The Fifth Amendment specifically prohibits prosecution of an "infamous crime" except upon indictment; it forbids double jeopardy; it bars compelling a person to be a witness against himself in any criminal case; it precludes deprivation of "life, liberty, or property, without due process of law. . . ." Are Madison and his contemporaries in the framing of the Bill of Rights to be charged with writing into it a meaningless clause? To consider "due process of law" as merely a shorthand statement of other specific clauses in the same amendment is to attribute to the authors and proponents of this Amendment ignorance of, or indifference to, a historic conception which was one of the great instruments in the arsenal of constitutional freedom which the Bill of Rights was to protect and strengthen.

A construction which gives to due process no independent function but turns it into a summary of the specific provisions of the Bill of Rights would, as has been noted, tear up by the roots much of the fabric of law in the several States, and would deprive the States of opportunity for reforms in legal process designed for extending the area of freedom. It would assume that no other abuses would reveal themselves in the course of time than those which had become manifest in 1791. Such a view not only disregards the historic meaning of "due process." It leads inevitably to a warped construction of specific provisions of the Bill of Rights to bring within their scope conduct clearly condemned by due process but not easily fitting into the pigeon-holes of the specific provisions. It seems pretty late in the day to suggest that a phrase so laden with historic meaning should be given an improvised content consisting of some but not all of the provisions of the first eight Amendments, selected on an undefined basis, with improvisation of content for the provisions so selected.

And so, when, as in a case like the present, a conviction in a State court is here for review under a claim that a right protected by the Due Process Clause of the Fourteenth Amendment has been denied, the issue is not whether an infraction of one of the specific provisions of the first eight Amendments is disclosed by the record. The relevant question is whether the criminal proceedings which resulted in conviction deprived the accused of the due process of law to which the United States Constitution entitled him. Judicial review of that guaranty of the Fourteenth Amendment inescapably imposes upon this Court an exercise of judgment upon the whole course of the proceedings in order to ascertain whether they offend those canons of decency and fairness which express the notions of justice of English-speaking peoples even toward those charged with the most heinous offenses. These standards of justice are not authoritatively formulated anywhere as though they were prescriptions in a pharmacopoeia. But neither does the application of the Due Process Clause imply that judges are wholly at large. The judicial judgment in applying the Due Process Clause must move within the limits of accepted notions of justice and is not to be based upon the idiosyncrasies of a merely personal judgment. The fact that judges among themselves may differ whether in a particular case a trial offends accepted notions of justice is not disproof that general rather than idiosyncratic standards are applied. An important safeguard against such merely individual judgment is an alert deference to the judgment of the State court under review.

■ MR. JUSTICE BLACK, dissenting.

. . . This decision reasserts a constitutional theory spelled out in *Twining v. New Jersey* that this Court is endowed by the Constitution with boundless power under "natural law" periodically to expand and contract constitutional standards to conform to the Court's conception of what at a particular time constitutes "civilized decency" and "fundamental liberty and justice." Invoking this *Twining* rule, the Court concludes that although comment upon testimony in a federal court would violate the Fifth Amendment, identical comment in a state court does not violate today's fashion in civilized decency and fundamentals and is therefore not prohibited by the Federal Constitution as amended.

The *Twining* case was the first, as it is the only, decision of this Court which has squarely held that states were free, notwithstanding the Fifth and Fourteenth Amendments, to extort evidence from one accused of crime. I agree that if *Twining* be reaffirmed, the result reached might appropriately follow. But I would not reaffirm the *Twining* decision. I think that decision and the "natural law" theory of the Constitution upon which it relies degrade the constitutional safeguards of the Bill of Rights and simultaneously appropriate for this Court a broad power which we are not authorized by the Constitution to exercise. . . .

My study of the historical events that culminated in the Fourteenth Amendment, and the expressions of those who sponsored and favored, as well as those who opposed its submission and passage, persuades me that one of the chief objects that the provisions of the Amendment's first section, separately, and as a whole, were intended to accomplish was to make the Bill of Rights, applicable to the states. With full knowledge of the import of the *Barron* decision, the framers and backers of the Fourteenth Amendment proclaimed its purpose to be to overturn the constitutional rule that case had announced. This historical purpose has never received full consideration or exposition in any opinion of this Court interpreting the Amendment. . . .

For this reason, I am attaching to this dissent an appendix which contains a resume, by no means complete, of the Amendment's history. In my judgment that history conclusively demonstrates that the language of the first section of the Fourteenth Amendment, taken as a whole, was thought by those responsible for its submission to the people, and by those who opposed its submission, sufficiently explicit to guarantee that thereafter no state could deprive its citizens of the privileges and protections of the Bill of Rights. Whether this Court ever will, or whether it now should, in the light of past decisions, give full effect to what the Amendment was intended to accomplish is not necessarily essential to a decision here. However that may be, our prior decisions, including *Twining*, do not prevent our carrying out that purpose, at least to the extent of making applicable to the states, not a mere part, as the Court has, but the full protection of the Fifth Amendment's provision against compelling evidence from an accused to convict him of crime. And I further contend that the "natural law" formula which the Court uses to reach its conclusion in this case should be abandoned as an incongruous excrescence on our Constitution. I believe that formula to be itself a violation of our Constitution, in that it subtly conveys to courts, at the expense of legislatures, ultimate power over public policies in fields where no specific provision of the Constitution limits legislative power. And my belief seems to be in accord with the views expressed by this Court, at least for the first two decades after the Fourteenth Amendment was adopted. . . .

Thus, up to and for some years after 1873, when *Munn v. Illinois* was decided, this Court steadfastly declined to invalidate states' legislative regulation of property rights or business practices under the Fourteenth Amendment unless there were racial discrimination involved in the state law challenged. . . . [I]n 1896, in *Chicago, B. & Q. R. Co. v. Chicago*, 166 U.S. 226, this Court [held], under the new due process-natural law formula, that the Fourteenth Amendment forbade a state from taking private property for public use without payment of just compensation.[9] . . .

Following the pattern of the new doctrine . . . the Court in 1896 applied the due process clause to strike down a state statute which had forbidden certain types of contracts. *Allgeyer v. Louisiana*, 165 U.S. 578. In doing so, it substantially adopted the rejected argument of counsel in the *Slaughter-House* cases, that the Fourteenth Amendment guarantees the liberty of all persons under "natural law" to engage in their chosen business or vocation. . . .

The foregoing constitutional doctrine, judicially created and adopted by expanding the previously accepted meaning of "due process," marked a complete departure from the *Slaughter-House* philosophy of judicial tolerance of state regulation of business activities. Conversely, the new formula contracted the effectiveness of the Fourteenth Amendment as a protection from state infringement of individual liberties enumerated in the Bill of Rights. . . .

At the same time that the *Twining* decision held that the states need not conform to the specific provisions of the Bill of Rights, it consolidated the power that the Court had assumed under the due process clause by laying even broader foundations for the Court to invalidate state and even federal regulatory legislation. For under the *Twining* formula, which includes non-regard for the first eight amendments, what are "fundamental rights" and in accord with "canons of decency," as the Court said in *Twining*, and today reaffirms, is to be independently "ascertained from time to time by judicial action. . . ." . . .

In *Palko v. Connecticut,* a case which involved former jeopardy only, this Court re-examined the path it had traveled in interpreting the Fourteenth Amendment since the *Twining* opinion was written. In *Twining* the Court had declared that none of the rights enumerated in the first eight amendments were protected against state invasion because they were incorporated in the Bill of Rights. But the Court in *Palko* answered a contention that all eight applied with the more guarded statement . . . that "there is no such general rule." Implicit in this statement, and in the cases decided in the interim between *Twining* and *Palko* and since, is the understanding that some of the eight amendments do apply by their very terms. Thus the Court said in the *Palko* case that the Fourteenth Amendment may make it unlawful for a state to abridge by its statutes the "freedom of speech which the First Amendment

---

[9]   This case . . . apparently was the first decision of this Court which brought in a Bill of Rights provision under the due process clause.

safeguards against encroachment by the Congress . . . or the like freedom of the press . . . or the free exercise of religion . . . or the right of peaceable assembly . . . or the right of one accused of crime to the benefit of counsel. . . . In these and other situations immunities that are valid as against the federal government by force of the specific pledges of particular amendments have been found to be implicit in the concept of ordered liberty, and thus, through the Fourteenth Amendment, become valid as against the states." . . .

The Court's opinion in *Twining*, and the dissent in that case, made it clear that the Court intended to leave the states wholly free to compel confessions, so far as the Federal Constitution is concerned. Yet in a series of cases since *Twining* this Court has held that the Fourteenth Amendment does bar all American courts, state or federal, from convicting people of crime on coerced confessions. *Chambers v. Florida*, 309 U.S. 227 (1940). Federal courts cannot do so because of the Fifth Amendment. And state courts cannot do so because the principles of the Fifth Amendment are made applicable to the States through the Fourteenth by one formula or another. And taking note of these cases, the Court is careful to point out in its decision today that coerced confessions violate the Federal Constitution if secured "by fear of hurt, torture or exhaustion." Nor can a state, according to today's decision, constitutionally compel an accused to testify against himself by "any other type of coercion that falls within the scope of due process." Thus the Court itself destroys or at least drastically curtails the very *Twining* decision it purports to reaffirm. It repudiates the foundation of that opinion, which presented much argument to show that compelling a man to testify against himself does not "violate" a "fundamental" right or privilege. . . .

I cannot consider the Bill of Rights to be an outworn 18th Century "strait jacket" as the *Twining* opinion did. Its provisions may be thought outdated abstractions by some. And it is true that they were designed to meet ancient evils. But they are the same kind of human evils that have emerged from century to century wherever excessive power is sought by the few at the expense of the many. In my judgment the people of no nation can lose their liberty so long as a Bill of Rights like ours survives and its basic purposes are conscientiously interpreted, enforced and respected so as to afford continuous protection against old, as well as new, devices and practices which might thwart those purposes. I fear to see the consequences of the Court's practice of substituting its own concepts of decency and fundamental justice for the language of the Bill of Rights as its point of departure in interpreting and enforcing that Bill of Rights. If the choice must be between the selective process of the *Palko* decision applying some of the Bill of Rights to the States, or the *Twining* rule applying none of them, I would choose the *Palko* selective process. But rather than accept either of these choices, I would follow what I believe was the original purpose of the Fourteenth Amendment—to extend to all the people of the nation the complete protection of the Bill of Rights. To hold that this Court can determine what, if any, provisions of the Bill of Rights will be enforced, and if so to what degree, is to frustrate the great design of a written Constitution. . . .

It is an illusory apprehension that literal application of some or all of the provisions of the Bill of Rights to the States would unwisely increase the sum total of the powers of this Court to invalidate state legislation. . . . It must be conceded, of course, that the natural-law-due-process formula, which the Court today reaffirms, has been interpreted to limit substantially this Court's power to prevent state violations of the individual civil liberties guaranteed by the Bill of Rights. But this formula also has been used in the past, and can be used in the future, to license this Court, in considering regulatory legislation, to roam at large in the broad expanses of policy and morals and to trespass, all too freely, on the legislative domain of the States as well as the Federal Government. . . .

■ MR. JUSTICE DOUGLAS joins in this opinion.

■ MR. JUSTICE MURPHY, with whom MR. JUSTICE RUTLEDGE concurs, dissenting.

While in substantial agreement with the views of MR. JUSTICE BLACK, I have one reservation and one addition to make. I agree that the specific guarantees of the Bill of Rights should be carried over intact into the first section of the Fourteenth Amendment. But I am not prepared to say that the latter is entirely and necessarily limited by the Bill of Rights. Occasions may arise where a proceeding falls so far short of conforming to fundamental standards of procedure as to warrant constitutional condemnation in terms of a lack of due process despite the absence of a specific provision in the Bill of Rights.

Duncan v. Louisiana
391 U.S. 145 (1968)

■ MR. JUSTICE WHITE delivered the opinion of the Court.

Appellant, Gary Duncan, was convicted of simple battery in the Twenty-fifth Judicial District Court of Louisiana. Under Louisiana law simple battery is a misdemeanor, punishable by a maximum of two years' imprisonment and a $300 fine. Appellant sought trial by jury, but because the Louisiana Constitution grants jury trials only in cases in which capital punishment or imprisonment at hard labor may be imposed, the trial judge denied the request. Appellant was convicted and sentenced to serve 60 days in the parish prison and pay a fine of $150. Appellant . . . sought review in this Court, alleging that the Sixth and Fourteenth Amendments to the United States Constitution secure the right to jury trial in state criminal prosecutions where a sentence as long as two years may be imposed.

Appellant was 19 years of age when tried. While driving on Highway 23 in Plaquemines Parish on October 18, 1966, he saw two younger cousins engaged in a conversation by the side of the road with four white boys. Knowing his cousins, Negroes who had recently transferred to a formerly all-white high school, had reported the occurrence of racial incidents at the school, Duncan stopped the car, got out, and approached the six boys. At trial the white boys and a white onlooker testified, as did appellant and his cousins. The testimony was in dispute on many points, but the witnesses agreed that appellant and the white boys spoke to each other, that appellant encouraged his cousins to break off the encounter and enter his car, and that appellant was about to enter the car himself for the purpose of driving away with his cousins. The whites testified that just before getting in the car appellant slapped Herman Landry, one of the white boys, on the elbow. The Negroes testified that appellant had not slapped Landry, but had merely touched him. The trial judge concluded that the State had proved beyond a reasonable doubt that Duncan had committed simple battery, and found him guilty.

I

The Fourteenth Amendment denies the States the power to "deprive any person of life, liberty, or property, without due process of law." In resolving conflicting claims concerning the meaning of this spacious language, the Court has looked increasingly to the Bill of Rights for guidance; many of the rights guaranteed by the first eight Amendments to the Constitution have been held to be protected against state action by the Due Process Clause of the Fourteenth Amendment. That clause now protects the right to compensation for property taken by the State; the rights of speech, press, and religion covered by the First Amendment; the Fourth Amendment rights to be free from unreasonable searches and seizures and to have excluded from criminal trials any evidence illegally seized; the right guaranteed by the Fifth Amendment to be free of compelled self-incrimination; and the Sixth Amendment rights to counsel, to a speedy and public trial, to confrontation of opposing witnesses, and to compulsory process for obtaining witnesses.

The test for determining whether a right extended by the Fifth and Sixth Amendments with respect to federal criminal proceedings is also protected against state action by the Fourteenth Amendment has been phrased in a variety of ways in the opinions of this Court. The question has been asked whether a right is among those "fundamental principles of liberty and justice which lie at the base of all our civil and political institutions"; whether it is "basic in our system of jurisprudence"; and whether it is "a fundamental right, essential to a fair trial." The claim before us is that the right to trial by jury guaranteed by the Sixth Amendment meets these tests. . . . Because we believe that trial by jury in criminal cases is fundamental to the American scheme of justice, we hold that the Fourteenth Amendment guarantees a right of jury trial in all criminal cases which—were they to be tried in a federal court—would come within the Sixth Amendment's guarantee.[14] Since we consider the appeal before us to be such a case, we hold that the Constitution was violated when appellant's demand for jury trial was refused.

The history of trial by jury in criminal cases has been frequently told. It is sufficient for present purposes to say that by the time our Constitution was written, jury trial in criminal cases had been in existence in England for several centuries and carried impressive credentials traced by many to Magna Carta. . . .

Jury trial came to America with English colonists, and received strong support from them. Royal interference with the jury trial was deeply resented. . . . The Declaration of Independence stated solemn objections to the King's . . . "depriving us in many cases, of the benefits of Trial by Jury," and to his "transporting us beyond Seas to be tried for pretended offenses." The Constitution itself, in Art. III, § 2, commanded:

> The Trial of all Crimes, except in Cases of Impeachment, shall be by Jury; and such Trial shall be held in the State where the said Crimes shall have been committed.

Objections to the Constitution because of the absence of a bill of rights were met by the immediate submission and adoption of the Bill of Rights. Included was the Sixth Amendment which, among other things, provided:

> In all criminal prosecutions, the accused shall enjoy the right to a speedy and public trial, by an impartial jury of the State and district wherein the crime shall have been committed.

---

[14] In one sense recent cases applying provisions of the first eight Amendments to the States represent a new approach to the "incorporation" debate. Earlier the Court can be seen as having asked, when inquiring into whether some particular procedural safeguard was required of a State, if a civilized system could be imagined that would not accord the particular protection. For example, *Palko v. Connecticut* stated: "The right to trial by jury and the immunity from prosecution except as the result of an indictment may have value and importance. Even so, they are not of the very essence of a scheme of ordered liberty. . . . Few would be so narrow or provincial as to maintain that a fair and enlightened system of justice would be impossible without them." The recent cases, on the other hand, have proceeded upon the valid assumption that state criminal processes are not imaginary and theoretical schemes but actual systems bearing virtually every characteristic of the common-law system that has been developing contemporaneously in England and in this country. The question thus is whether given this kind of system a particular procedure is fundamental—whether, that is, a procedure is necessary to an Anglo-American regime of ordered liberty. It is this sort of inquiry that can justify the conclusions that state courts must exclude evidence seized in violation of the Fourth Amendment, *Mapp v. Ohio*, 367 U.S. 643 (1961); that state prosecutors may not comment on a defendant's failure to testify, *Griffin v. California*, 380 U.S. 609 (1965); and that criminal punishment may not be imposed for the status of narcotics addiction, *Robinson v. California*, 370 U.S. 660 (1962). Of immediate relevance for this case are the Court's holdings that the States must comply with certain provisions of the Sixth Amendment, specifically that the States may not refuse a speedy trial, confrontation of witnesses, and the assistance, at state expense if necessary, of counsel. . . .

A criminal process which was fair and equitable but used no juries is easy to imagine. It would make use of alternative guarantees and protections which would serve the purposes that the jury serves in the English and American systems. Yet no American State has undertaken to construct such a system. . . .

The constitutions adopted by the original States guaranteed jury trial. Also, the constitution of every State entering the Union thereafter in one form or another protected the right to jury trial in criminal cases.

Even such skeletal history is impressive support for considering the right to jury trial in criminal cases to be fundamental to our system of justice, an importance frequently recognized in the opinions of this Court. . . .

Jury trial continues to receive strong support. The laws of every State guarantee a right to jury trial in serious criminal cases; no State has dispensed with it; nor are there significant movements underway to do so. . . .

The guarantees of jury trial in the Federal and State Constitutions reflect a profound judgment about the way in which law should be enforced and justice administered. A right to jury trial is granted to criminal defendants in order to prevent oppression by the Government. Those who wrote our constitutions knew from history and experience that it was necessary to protect against unfounded criminal charges brought to eliminate enemies and against judges too responsive to the voice of higher authority. The framers of the constitutions strove to create an independent judiciary but insisted upon further protection against arbitrary action. Providing an accused with the right to be tried by a jury of his peers gave him an inestimable safeguard against the corrupt or overzealous prosecutor and against the compliant, biased, or eccentric judge. If the defendant preferred the common-sense judgment of a jury to the more tutored but perhaps less sympathetic reaction of the single judge, he was to have it. Beyond this, the jury trial provisions in the Federal and State Constitutions reflect a fundamental decision about the exercise of official power—a reluctance to entrust plenary powers over the life and liberty of the citizen to one judge or to a group of judges. Fear of unchecked power, so typical of our State and Federal Governments in other respects, found expression in the criminal law in this insistence upon community participation in the determination of guilt or innocence. The deep commitment of the Nation to the right of jury trial in serious criminal cases as a defense against arbitrary law enforcement qualifies for protection under the Due Process Clause of the Fourteenth Amendment, and must therefore be respected by the States. . . .

II

Louisiana's final contention is that even if it must grant jury trials in serious criminal cases, the conviction before us is valid and constitutional because here the petitioner was tried for simple battery and was sentenced to only 60 days in the parish prison. We are not persuaded. It is doubtless true that there is a category of petty crimes or offenses which is not subject to the Sixth Amendment jury trial provision and should not be subject to the Fourteenth Amendment jury trial requirement here applied to the States. Crimes carrying possible penalties up to six months do not require a jury trial if they otherwise qualify as petty offenses. But the penalty authorized for a particular crime is of major relevance in determining whether it is serious or not and may in itself, if severe enough, subject the trial to the mandates of the Sixth Amendment. . . . In the case before us the Legislature of Louisiana has made simple battery a criminal offense punishable by imprisonment for up to two years and a fine. The question, then, is whether a crime carrying such a penalty is an offense which Louisiana may insist on trying without a jury.

We think not. So-called petty offenses were tried without juries both in England and in the Colonies and have always been held to be exempt from the otherwise comprehensive language of the Sixth Amendment's jury trial provisions. There is no substantial evidence that the Framers intended to depart from this established common-law practice, and the possible consequences to defendants from convictions for petty offenses have been thought insufficient to outweigh the benefits to efficient law enforcement and simplified judicial administration resulting from the availability of speedy and inexpensive nonjury adjudications. These same considerations compel the same result under the Fourteenth Amendment. Of course the boundaries of the petty offense category have always been ill-defined, if not ambulatory. In the absence of an explicit constitutional provision, the definitional task necessarily falls on the courts, which must either pass upon the validity of legislative attempts to identify those petty offenses which are exempt from jury trial or, where the legislature has not addressed itself to the problem, themselves face the question in the first instance. In either case it is necessary to draw a line in the spectrum of crime, separating petty from serious infractions. This process, although essential, cannot be wholly satisfactory, for it requires attaching different consequences to events which, when they lie near the line, actually differ very little.

In determining whether the length of the authorized prison term or the seriousness of other punishment is enough in itself to require a jury trial, we . . . refer to objective criteria, chiefly the existing laws and practices in the Nation. In the federal system, petty offenses are defined as those punishable by no more than six months in prison and a $500 fine. In 49 of the 50 States crimes subject to trial without a jury, which occasionally include simple battery, are punishable by no more than one year in jail. Moreover, in the late 18th century in America crimes triable without a jury were for the most part punishable by no more than a six-month prison term, although there appear to have been exceptions to this rule. We need not, however, settle in this case the exact location of the line between petty offenses and serious crimes. It is sufficient for our purposes to hold that a crime punishable by two years in prison is, based on past and contemporary standards in this country, a serious crime and not a petty offense. Consequently, appellant was entitled to a jury trial and it was error to deny it.

The judgment below is reversed and the case is remanded for proceedings not inconsistent with this opinion.

■ **MR. JUSTICE BLACK, with whom MR. JUSTICE DOUGLAS joins, concurring.**

. . . I am very happy to support this selective process through which our Court has since the *Adamson* case held most of the specific Bill of Rights' protections applicable to the States to the same extent they are applicable to the Federal Government. Among these are the right to trial by jury decided today, the right against compelled self-incrimination, the right to counsel, the right to compulsory process for witnesses, the right to confront witnesses, the right to a speedy and public trial, and the right to be free from unreasonable searches and seizures.

All of these holdings making Bill of Rights' provisions applicable as such to the States mark, of course, a departure from the *Twining* doctrine holding that none of those provisions were enforceable as such against the States. The dissent in this case, however, makes a spirited and forceful defense of that now discredited doctrine. I do not believe that it is necessary for me to repeat the historical and logical reasons for my challenge to the *Twining* holding contained in my *Adamson* dissent and Appendix to it. . . .

[JUSTICE HARLAN's] dissent states that "the great words of the four clauses of the first section of the Fourteenth Amendment would have been an exceedingly peculiar way to say that 'The rights heretofore guaranteed against federal intrusion by the first eight Amendments are henceforth guaranteed against state intrusion as well.'" In response to this I can say only that the words "No State shall make or enforce any law which shall abridge the privileges or immunities of citizens of the United States" seem to me an eminently reasonable way of expressing the idea that henceforth the Bill of Rights shall apply to the States. What more precious "privilege" of American citizenship could there be than that privilege to claim the protections of our great Bill of Rights? I suggest that any reading of "privileges or immunities of citizens of the United States" which excludes the Bill of Rights' safeguards renders the words of this section of the Fourteenth Amendment meaningless. Senator Howard, who introduced the Fourteenth Amendment for passage in the Senate, certainly read the words this way. . . .

> Such is the character of the privileges and immunities spoken of in the second section of the fourth article of the Constitution [the Senator had just read from the old opinion of *Corfield v. Coryell*, 6 Fed. Cas. 546 (No. 3,230) (E.D. Pa. 1825)]. To these privileges and immunities, whatever they may be—for they are not and cannot be fully defined in their entire extent and precise nature—to these should be added the personal rights guaranteed and secured by the first eight amendments of the Constitution. . . .

> The great object of the first section of this amendment is,
> therefore, to restrain the power of the States and compel them
> at all times to respect these great fundamental guarantees.

From this I conclude, contrary to my Brother HARLAN, that if anything, it is "exceedingly peculiar" to read the *Fourteenth Amendment* differently from the way I do.

While I do not wish at this time to discuss at length my disagreement with Brother HARLAN's forthright and frank restatement of the now discredited *Twining* doctrine, I do want to point out what appears to me to be the basic difference between us. His view, as was indeed the view of *Twining*, is that "due process is an evolving concept" and therefore that it entails a "gradual process of judicial inclusion and exclusion" to ascertain those "immutable principles . . . of free government which no member of the Union may disregard." Thus the Due Process Clause is treated as prescribing no specific and clearly ascertainable constitutional command that judges must obey in interpreting the Constitution, but rather as leaving judges free to decide at any particular time whether a particular rule or judicial formulation embodies an "immutable principl[e] of free government" or is "implicit in the concept of ordered liberty," or whether certain conduct "shocks the judge's conscience" or runs counter to some other similar, undefined and undefinable standard. Thus due process, according to my Brother HARLAN, is to be a phrase with no permanent meaning, but one which is found to shift from time to time in accordance with judges' predilections and understandings of what is best for the country. If due process means this, the Fourteenth Amendment, in my opinion, might as well have been written that "no person shall be deprived of life, liberty or property except by laws that the judges of the United States Supreme Court shall find to be consistent with the immutable principles of free government." It is impossible for me to believe that such unconfined power is given to judges in our Constitution that is a written one in order to limit governmental power.

Another tenet of the *Twining* doctrine as restated by my Brother HARLAN is that "due process of law requires only fundamental fairness." But the "fundamental fairness" test is one on a par with that of shocking the conscience of the Court. Each of such tests depends entirely on the particular judge's idea of ethics and morals instead of requiring him to depend on the boundaries fixed by the written words of the Constitution. Nothing in the history of the phrase "due process of law" suggests that constitutional controls are to depend on any particular judge's sense of values. . . .

Finally I want to add that I am not bothered by the argument that applying the Bill of Rights to the States, "according to the same standards that protect those personal rights against federal encroachment," interferes with our concept of federalism in that it may prevent States from trying novel social and economic experiments. I have never believed that under the guise of federalism the States should be able to experiment with the protections afforded our citizens through the Bill of Rights. As Justice Goldberg said . . .

> to deny to the States the power to impair a fundamental constitutional right is not to increase federal power, but, rather, to limit the power of both federal and state governments in favor of safeguarding the fundamental rights and liberties of the individual. In my view this promotes rather than undermines the basic policy of avoiding excess concentration of power in government, federal or state, which underlies our concepts of federalism.

It seems to me totally inconsistent to advocate, on the one hand, the power of this Court to strike down any state law or practice which it finds "unreasonable" or "unfair" and, on the other hand, urge that the States be given maximum power to develop their own laws and procedures. Yet the due process approach of my Brothers HARLAN and FORTAS does just that since in effect it restricts the States to practices which a majority of this Court is willing to approve on a case-by-case basis. . . .

In closing I want to emphasize that I believe as strongly as ever that the Fourteenth Amendment was intended to make the Bill of Rights applicable to the States. I have been willing to support the selective incorporation doctrine, however, as an alternative, although perhaps less historically supportable than complete incorporation. The selective incorporation process, if used properly, does limit the Supreme Court in the Fourteenth Amendment field to specific Bill of Rights' protections only and keeps judges from roaming at will in their own notions of what policies outside the Bill of Rights [are] desirable and what are not. And, most importantly for me, the selective incorporation process has the virtue of having already worked to make most of the Bill of Rights' protections applicable to the States.

■ **MR. JUSTICE HARLAN, whom MR. JUSTICE STEWART joins, dissenting.**

Every American jurisdiction provides for trial by jury in criminal cases. The question before us is not whether jury trial is an ancient institution, which it is; nor whether it plays a significant role in the administration of criminal justice, which it does; nor whether it will endure, which it shall. The question in this case is whether the State of Louisiana, which provides trial by jury for all felonies, is prohibited by the Constitution from trying charges of simple battery to the court alone. In my view, the answer to that question, mandated alike by our constitutional history and by the longer history of trial by jury, is clearly "no."

The States have always borne primary responsibility for operating the machinery of criminal justice within their borders, and adapting it to their particular circumstances. In exercising this responsibility, each State is compelled to conform its procedures to the requirements of the

Federal Constitution. The Due Process Clause of the Fourteenth Amendment requires that those procedures be fundamentally fair in all respects. It does not, in my view, impose or encourage nationwide uniformity for its own sake; it does not command adherence to forms that happen to be old; and it does not impose on the States the rules that may be in force in the federal courts except where such rules are also found to be essential to basic fairness.

The Court's approach to this case is an uneasy and illogical compromise among the views of various Justices on how the Due Process Clause should be interpreted. The Court does not say that those who framed the Fourteenth Amendment intended to make the Sixth Amendment applicable to the States. And the Court concedes that it finds nothing unfair about the procedure by which the present appellant was tried. Nevertheless, the Court reverses his conviction: it holds, for some reason not apparent to me, that the Due Process Clause incorporates the particular clause of the Sixth Amendment that requires trial by jury in federal criminal cases—including, as I read its opinion, the sometimes trivial accompanying baggage of judicial interpretation in federal contexts. I have raised my voice many times before against the Court's continuing undiscriminating insistence upon fastening on the States federal notions of criminal justice, and I must do so again in this instance. With all respect, the Court's approach and its reading of history are altogether topsy-turvy.

I

I believe I am correct in saying that every member of the Court for at least the last 135 years has agreed that our Founders did not consider the requirements of the Bill of Rights so fundamental that they should operate directly against the States. They were wont to believe rather that the security of liberty in America rested primarily upon the dispersion of governmental power across a federal system. The Bill of Rights was considered unnecessary by some but insisted upon by others in order to curb the possibility of abuse of power by the strong central government they were creating.

The Civil War Amendments dramatically altered the relation of the Federal Government to the States. The first section of the Fourteenth Amendment imposes highly significant restrictions on state action. But the restrictions are couched in very broad and general terms: citizenship; privileges and immunities; due process of law; equal protection of the laws. Consequently, for 100 years this Court has been engaged in the difficult process Professor Jaffe has well called "the search for intermediate premises." The question has been, Where does the Court properly look to find the specific rules that define and give content to such terms as "life, liberty, or property" and "due process of law"?

A few members of the Court have taken the position that the intention of those who drafted the first section of the Fourteenth Amendment was simply, and exclusively, to make the provisions of the first eight Amendments applicable to state action. This view has never been accepted by this Court. In my view, often expressed elsewhere, the first section of the Fourteenth Amendment was meant neither to incorporate, nor to be limited to, the specific guarantees of the first eight Amendments. The overwhelming historical evidence marshalled by Professor Fairman demonstrates, to me conclusively, that the Congressmen and state legislators who wrote, debated, and ratified the Fourteenth Amendment did not think they were "incorporating" the Bill of Rights[9] and the very breadth and generality of the Amendment's provisions suggest that its authors did not suppose that the Nation would always be limited to mid-19th century conceptions of "liberty" and "due process of law" but that the increasing experience and evolving conscience of the American people would add new "intermediate premises." In short, neither history, nor sense, supports using the Fourteenth Amendment to put the States in a constitutional straitjacket with respect to their own development in the administration of criminal or civil law.

Although I therefore fundamentally disagree with the total incorporation view of the Fourteenth Amendment, it seems to me that such a position does at least have the virtue, lacking in the Court's selective incorporation approach, of internal consistency: we look to the Bill of Rights, word for word, clause for clause, precedent for precedent because, it is said, the men who wrote the Amendment wanted it that way. For those who do not accept this "history," a different source of "intermediate premises" must be found. The Bill of Rights is not necessarily irrelevant to the search for guidance in interpreting the Fourteenth Amendment, but the reason for and the nature of its relevance must be articulated.

Apart from the approach taken by the absolute incorporationists, I can see only one method of analysis that has any internal logic. That is to start with the words "liberty" and "due process of law" and attempt to define them in a way that accords with American traditions and our system of government. This approach, involving a much more discriminating process of adjudication than does "incorporation," is, albeit difficult, the one that was followed throughout the 19th and most of the present century. It entails a "gradual process of judicial inclusion and exclusion," seeking, with due recognition of constitutional tolerance for state experimentation and disparity, to ascertain those "immutable principles . . . of free government which no member of the Union may disregard." Due process was not restricted to rules fixed in the past, for that "would be to deny every quality of the law but its age, and to render it incapable of progress or improvement." Nor did it impose nationwide uniformity in details. . . .

---

[9] Fairman, *Does the Fourteenth Amendment Incorporate the Bill of Rights? The Original Understanding*, 2 STAN. L. REV. 5 (1949). . . .

The relationship of the Bill of Rights to this "gradual process" seems to me to be twofold. In the first place it has long been clear that the Due Process Clause imposes some restrictions on state action that parallel Bill of Rights restrictions on federal action. Second, and more important than this accidental overlap, is the fact that the Bill of Rights is evidence, at various points, of the content Americans find in the term "liberty" and of American standards of fundamental fairness. . . .

If the problem is to discover and articulate the rules of fundamental fairness in criminal proceedings, there is no reason to assume that the whole body of rules developed in this Court constituting Sixth Amendment jury trial must be regarded as a unit. The requirement of trial by jury in federal criminal cases has given rise to numerous subsidiary questions respecting the exact scope and content of the right. It surely cannot be that every answer the Court has given, or will give, to such a question is attributable to the Founders; or even that every rule announced carries equal conviction of this Court; still less can it be that every such subprinciple is equally fundamental to ordered liberty.

Examples abound. I should suppose it obviously fundamental to fairness that a "jury" means an "impartial jury." I should think it equally obvious that the rule, imposed long ago in the federal courts, that "jury" means "jury of exactly twelve," is not fundamental to anything: there is no significance except to mystics in the number 12. Again, trial by jury has been held to require a unanimous verdict of jurors in the federal courts, although unanimity has not been found essential to liberty in Britain, where the requirement has been abandoned.

One further example is directly relevant here. The co-existence of a requirement of jury trial in federal criminal cases and a historic and universally recognized exception for "petty crimes" has compelled this Court, on occasion, to decide whether a particular crime is petty, or is included within the guarantee. Individual cases have been decided without great conviction and without reference to a guiding principle. The Court today holds, for no discernible reason, that if and when the line is drawn its exact location will be a matter of such fundamental importance that it will be uniformly imposed on the States. This Court is compelled to decide such obscure borderline questions in the course of administering federal law. This does not mean that its decisions are demonstrably sounder than those that would be reached by state courts and legislatures, let alone that they are of such importance that fairness demands their imposition throughout the Nation. . . .

II

. . . The argument that jury trial is not a requisite of due process is quite simple. The central proposition of *Palko*, a proposition to which I would adhere, is that "due process of law" requires only that criminal trials be fundamentally fair. . . . If due process of law requires only fundamental fairness, then the inquiry in each case must be whether a state trial process was a fair one. The Court has held, properly I think, that in an adversary process it is a requisite of fairness, for which there is no adequate substitute, that a criminal defendant be afforded a right to counsel and to cross-examine opposing witnesses. But it simply has not been demonstrated, nor, I think, can it be demonstrated, that trial by jury is the only fair means of resolving issues of fact.

The jury is of course not without virtues. It affords ordinary citizens a valuable opportunity to participate in a process of government, an experience fostering, one hopes, a respect for law. It eases the burden on judges by enabling them to share a part of their sometimes awesome responsibility. A jury may, at times, afford a higher justice by refusing to enforce harsh laws (although it necessarily does so haphazardly, raising the questions whether arbitrary enforcement of harsh laws is better than total enforcement, and whether the jury system is to be defended on the ground that jurors sometimes disobey their oaths). And the jury may, or may not, contribute desirably to the willingness of the general public to accept criminal judgments as just.

It can hardly be gainsaid, however, that the principal original virtue of the jury trial—the limitations a jury imposes on a tyrannous judiciary—has largely disappeared. We no longer live in a medieval or colonial society. Judges enforce laws enacted by democratic decision, not by regal fiat. They are elected by the people or appointed by the people's elected officials, and are responsible not to a distant monarch alone but to reviewing courts, including this one.

The jury system can also be said to have some inherent defects, which are multiplied by the emergence of the criminal law from the relative simplicity that existed when the jury system was devised. It is a cumbersome process, not only imposing great cost in time and money on both the State and the jurors themselves, but also contributing to delay in the machinery of justice. Untrained jurors are presumably less adept at reaching accurate conclusions of fact than judges, particularly if the issues are many or complex. And it is argued by some that trial by jury, far from increasing public respect for law, impairs it: the average man, it is said, reacts favorably neither to the notion that matters he knows to be complex are being decided by other average men, nor to the way the jury system distorts the process of adjudication.

That trial by jury is not the only fair way of adjudicating criminal guilt is well attested by the fact that it is not the prevailing way, either in England or in this country. . . . Parliament generally provides that new statutory offenses, unless they are of "considerable gravity" shall be tried to judges; consequently, summary offenses now outnumber offenses for which jury trial is afforded by more than six to one. Then, within the latter category, 84% of all cases are in fact tried to the court. Over all, "the ratio of defendants actually tried by jury becomes in some years little more than 1 per cent."

In the United States, where it has not been as generally assumed that jury waiver is permissible, the statistics are only slightly less revealing. Two experts have estimated that, of all prosecutions for crimes triable to a jury, 75% are settled by guilty plea and 40% of the remainder are tried to the court. In one State, Maryland, which has always provided for waiver, the rate of court trial appears in some years to have reached 90%. . . .

I therefore see no reason why this Court should reverse the conviction of appellant, absent any suggestion that his particular trial was in fact unfair, or compel the State of Louisiana to afford jury trial in an as yet unbounded category of cases that can, without unfairness, be tried to a court.

Indeed, even if I were persuaded that trial by jury is a fundamental right in some criminal cases, I could see nothing fundamental in the rule, not yet formulated by the Court, that places the prosecution of appellant for simple battery within the category of "jury crimes" rather than "petty crimes." Trial by jury is ancient, it is true. [However,] through the long course of British and American history, summary procedures have been used in a varying category of lesser crimes as a flexible response to the burden jury trial would otherwise impose. . . .

The reason for the historic exception for relatively minor crimes is the obvious one: the burden of jury trial was thought to outweigh its marginal advantages. Exactly why the States should not be allowed to make continuing adjustments, based on the state of their criminal dockets and the difficulty of summoning jurors, simply escapes me. . . .

This Court, other courts, and the political process are available to correct any experiments in criminal procedure that prove fundamentally unfair to defendants. That is not what is being done today: instead, and quite without reason, the Court has chosen to impose upon every State one means of trying criminal cases; it is a good means, but it is not the only fair means, and it is not demonstrably better than the alternatives States might devise.

I would affirm the judgment of the Supreme Court of Louisiana.

NOTE ON INCORPORATION OF THE BILL OF RIGHTS INTO THE FOURTEENTH AMENDMENT

1.   The opinions in *Adamson* and *Duncan* reflect three distinct approaches to incorporation:

    a.   *Fundamental Fairness:* This approach, which came to be associated with Justice Frankfurter and later Justice Harlan, incorporated only a limited set of "fundamental" rights. Formulations varied, but the Court would generally inquire whether a given requirement was "implicit in the concept of ordered liberty,"[36] or represented a "principle of justice so rooted in the traditions and conscience of our people as to be

---

[36]   Palko v. Connecticut, 302 U.S. 319, 325 (1937).

ranked as fundamental."[37] As Justice White noted in *Duncan*, the earlier form of the theory suggested that rights worthy of incorporation were those that were so fundamental that one could not conceive of a civilized system of government without them. As the theory evolved, the Court began focusing on the history and tradition of the United States as a source of what rights the People considered to be fundamental, eschewing more abstract appeals to Natural Law and the ideal ordered society. Importantly, inclusion of a given principle in the Bill of Rights was neither *necessary* nor *sufficient* to meet this requirement.

b. *Total Incorporation:* Justice Black's preferred approach would have incorporated the Bill of Rights—no more, no less. It was never adopted by a majority of the Court, but its influence was such that almost all of the Bill of Rights provisions were eventually incorporated.

c. *Selective Incorporation:* The Warren Court, led by Justice Brennan, used the language of fundamental fairness to incorporate almost all of the Bill of Rights, as well as various extra-textual requirements such as the proof of guilt beyond a reasonable doubt in criminal trials. The majority opinion in *Duncan* reflects this approach.

What are the advantages and disadvantages of each approach? Do you agree with the course that the Court ultimately took?

2.   The contemporary Supreme Court continues to wrestle with issues of incorporation. In *McDonald v. City of Chicago*, 561 U.S. 742 (2010), the Court considered whether the Fourteenth Amendment incorporated the Second Amendment's right to bear arms. *McDonald* involved several Chicago firearms laws that effectively banned handgun possession by most private citizens residing within the city limits. In *District of Columbia v. Heller*, 554 U.S. 570 (2008), the Court held that the right to possess a firearm in the home is protected by the Second Amendment. Resting heavily on the history and tradition of firearm ownership within American society and the popular understanding of the Fourteenth Amendment at the time of ratification, *McDonald* held that the Second Amendment right as recognized in *Heller* was a fundamental right that applies equally to the States.

Given *Heller*, the decision in *McDonald* follows naturally from a total incorporation perspective. Justice Stevens's dissent, however, urged that under a selective incorporation approach, the right to bear arms did not warrant application to the States. For him, the decision in *Heller* "sheds no light on the meaning of the Due Process Clause of the Fourteenth Amendment"; rather, that clause "stands . . . on its own bottom." Moreover, "[t]he rights protected against state infringement by the Fourteenth Amendment's Due Process Clause need not be identical in shape or scope to the rights protected against Federal Government infringement by the

---

[37]   Snyder v. Massachusetts, 291 U.S. 97, 105 (1934).

various provisions of the Bill of Rights." From this perspective, Stevens argued that the right to bear arms was not "fundamental" under the Fourteenth Amendment. This was true for several reasons: (1) "firearms have a fundamentally ambivalent relationship to liberty," because they can undermine the rights and safety of others; (2) the right to possess a firearm "is different in kind" from the liberty interests recognized in prior cases; (3) other countries do not recognize an expansive right to gun ownership; (4) unlike other incorporated amendments, the Second Amendment "is a federalism provision"; and (5) "the States have a long and unbroken history of regulating firearms." Are these persuasive reasons to distinguish the Second Amendment from other provisions of the Bill of Rights, or do they amount to an attempt to re-litigate *Heller*? Does the room that selective incorporation leaves for such argument demonstrate the subjectivity of that approach?

3.   After *McDonald*, the following provisions of the Bill of Rights remain unincorporated (at least by the Supreme Court):

- the Third Amendment prohibition of the quartering of soldiers;[38]

- the Fifth Amendment's requirement of grand jury indictment;[39]

- the Sixth Amendment's requirement of a unanimous jury verdict in criminal trials;[40]

- the Seventh Amendment's guarantee of a jury trial in civil cases;[41] and

- the Eighth Amendment's prohibition on excessive fines.[42]

On the other hand, the Court has held that the Fourteenth Amendment's Due Process Clause also may incorporate rights not explicitly mentioned in the Bill of Rights. The leading example is *In re Winship*, 397 U.S. 358 (1970), which held that the Fourteenth Amendment requires that criminal charges be proven beyond a reasonable doubt. Nonetheless, the Court has more recently insisted that "beyond the specific guarantees enumerated in the Bill of Rights, the Due Process Clause has limited operation."[43]

4.   We have already seen an example of *reverse* incorporation. In *Bolling v. Sharpe*, 347 U.S. 497 (1954), the Court effectively "incorporated" the Equal Protection Clause of the Fourteenth Amendment—which applies only to the States—into the Due Process Clause of the *Fifth* Amendment in order to strike down segregated schooling in the District of Columbia. Are the historical and textual arguments for reverse incorporation easier or harder than they are in the standard incorporation case? Is it somehow

---

[38]   *But see Engblom v. Carey*, 677 F.2d 957, 961 (2d Cir. 1982) (holding, as a matter of first impression, that the Fourteenth Amendment incorporates the Third Amendment).

[39]   *See Hurtado v. California*, 110 U.S. 516 (1884).

[40]   *See Johnson v. Louisiana*, 406 U.S. 356 (1972).

[41]   *See Minneapolis & St. Louis R. Co. v. Bombolis*, 241 U.S. 211 (1916).

[42]   *See Browning Ferris Industries of Vt., Inc. v. Kelco Disposal, Inc.*, 492 U.S. 257, 276 n.22 (1989) (declining to decide whether the excessive fines provision applies to the States).

[43]   *Medina v. California*, 505 U.S. 437, 443 (1992) (quoting *Dowling v. United States*, 493 U.S. 342, 352 (1990)).

illegitimate, in our contemporary legal culture, to have individual rights that apply to some but not all governments? Are there any other constitutional provisions applicable only to the States that ought to be reverse-incorporated?

5.   Although incorporation is an issue that cuts across virtually all the Constitution's rights provisions, it proved most controversial in criminal procedure. The most prominent example is *Mapp v. Ohio*, 367 U.S. 643 (1961), which applied to the States the "exclusionary rule" remedy for illegal searches and seizures under the Fourth Amendment. *Mapp* did not invent the exclusionary rule; the Court had held nearly a half-century earlier that in federal prosecutions, courts must exclude evidence obtained by an illegal search.[44] And in *Wolf v. Colorado*, 338 U.S. 25 (1949), the Court held that the Fourth Amendment's prohibition of unreasonable searches and seizures was "basic to a free society" and therefore binding on the States. But *Wolf* was unwilling to say that the exclusionary remedy for Fourth Amendment violations was equally fundamental; instead, it held that the proper remedy for illegal searches was something upon which reasonable States could disagree. *Mapp*, on the other hand, found the exclusion of illegally-obtained evidence to be the "most important constitutional privilege" conferred by the Fourth Amendment. The Court thus overruled *Wolf* and held that not only the Fourth Amendment, but also its exclusionary remedy, was incorporated into the Due Process Clause of the Fourteenth Amendment.

Abe Fortas, who would join the Court as a justice in 1965, called *Mapp* "the most radical decision in recent times."[45] Practically speaking, *Mapp* was radical because it adopted a controversial constitutional remedy that had been rejected by half the states, and that struck home in an area—crime and punishment—of particular public sensitivity. The doctrinal radicalism of *Mapp*, on the other hand, was that it seemed to elevate the judge-made exclusionary rule to the status of constitutional law. In so doing, *Mapp* represented an important extension of the judiciary's traditional power over legal remedies.

The Fourth Amendment says simply that "[t]he right of the people to be secure in their persons, houses, papers, and effects, against unreasonable searches and seizures, shall not be violated"; it does not say how such violations are to be prevented. The exclusionary rule seeks to deter violations by eliminating the police's ordinary incentive (securing a conviction) to search and seize. Other remedial mechanisms include authorizing victims of unconstitutional searches to sue the offending officers for damages or imposing disciplinary sanctions against such officers within the police department. The important point for present purposes is that the Constitution does not explicitly choose among these alternatives. That might mean, as the Court had earlier held in *Wolf*, that the states are free to experiment about remedies; in *Mapp*, however, the Court made the choice for them.

---

[44]   *See Weeks v. United States*, 232 U.S. 383 (1914).

[45]   Quoted in POWE, *supra* note 1, at 195.

The question, as put by Henry Monaghan in a famous article, is this: "Can the Court . . . create a sub-order of 'quasi-constitutional' law—of a remedial, substantive, and procedural character—to vindicate constitutional liberties?"[46] Professor Monaghan argued that it can:

> [T]he affirmative case for recognizing a constitutional common law of individual liberties is a strong one. The Court's history and its institutional role in our scheme of government, in which it defines the constitutionally compelled limits of governmental power, make it a singularly appropriate institution to fashion many of the details as well as the framework of the constitutional guarantees. . . . As a general matter, it does not appear appropriate that federally guaranteed rights, particularly when their basis is constitutional, should have materially different dimensions in each of the states when both the source of the right and any ultimate interpretation is unitary.[47]

On this view, the exclusionary rule is a form of "constitutional common law"—not the same as the Constitution itself, but a legitimate part of the machinery for implementing constitutional rights. Do you agree that the Court should have the power to fashion rules of this kind?

6. Another signature Warren Court criminal procedure decision, *Miranda v. Arizona*, 384 U.S. 436 (1966), may also be best described as an instance of constitutional common law. *Miranda* was a set of consolidated cases all raising the issue of confessions obtained by interrogations of suspects in police custody. The Fifth Amendment simply requires that any confession be voluntary. Prior to *Miranda*, the voluntariness of a confession was evaluated by looking to the "totality of the circumstances"—that is, all the facts bearing on whether the confession was rendered of the suspect's own free will. The *Miranda* Court, however, undertook a general survey of state police practices, focusing on the proverbial "third degree" of physical and psychological intimidation of suspects. In order to offset the effects of such intimidation, the Court said that suspects must be warned of their rights before they are interrogated; moreover, it provided a specific list of minimum warnings necessary to satisfy the Court's mandate.

These famous warnings—"You have the right to remain silent. Anything you say can and will be used against you in a court of law. You have the right to an attorney . . ."—are obviously not part of the Fifth Amendment's text, nor did the *Miranda* Court purport to say that they are the *only* way that the Constitution's general requirement of voluntary confessions can be satisfied. They are a "prophylactic rule," designed to prevent involuntary confessions by providing police with specific rules of conduct to implement the constitutional requirement. Professor Monaghan explains that "[a] prophylactic rule might be constitutionally compelled when it is necessary to overprotect a constitutional right because a narrow, theoretically more discriminating rule may not work in practice. This may happen where, for

---

[46] Henry P. Monaghan, *The Supreme Court, 1974 Term—Foreword: Constitutional Common Law*, 89 HARV. L. REV. 1, 9 (1975).

[47] *Id.* at 19.

example, there is a substantial danger that a more finely tuned rule may be subverted in its administration by unsympathetic courts, juries, or public officials." Because there may be other equally effective means of protecting Fifth Amendment rights, however, he acknowledges that such rules "are admittedly not integral parts of the Constitution and . . . go beyond its minimum requirements."[48]

How far does the judicial power extend to fashion prophylactic rules, like the *Miranda* warnings, or other constitutional remedies, like *Mapp*'s exclusionary rule, to protect constitutional rights? Can decisions like *Mapp* and *Miranda* be justified under the conception of judicial review defended in *Marbury*—that is, as a function of a court's need to resolve conflicts among different rules of law in order to decide the case before it, and in so doing to give primacy to the Constitution over ordinary laws? Similar issues arise in the segregation contexts covered in the last assignment. Does the power to declare segregated schooling unconstitutional, for example, necessarily imply the power to mandate cross-town busing of school children to attain racial balance?

7. *Mapp* addressed not only *which* rights should be incorporated against the States, but also *in what manner* those rights should apply. As a matter of theory, it is not obvious that just because a particular constitutional provision is incorporated, all of the doctrine developed under that provision in cases involving federal action automatically applies to the States. For example, *Duncan* recognized, but did not appear to resolve, the question whether all the details of the Sixth Amendment's jury trial right, developed for the administration of the federal courts, should now bind the States.[49] Subsequently the Court has said that although federal trials require a twelve-member jury, six members is sufficient to satisfy due process in a state trial.[50]

The *Mapp* Court, however, seemed to think that if the Fourth Amendment were incorporated against the States, it necessarily followed that it must be "enforceable against them by the same sanction of exclusion as is used against the Federal Government." Notwithstanding some wavering on the size of juries, the Court has generally held that incorporated rights apply to the States "jot for jot"—that is, in exactly the same way that they apply to the federal government. In *Malloy v. Hogan,* 378 U.S. 1, 10–11 (1964), for example, the Court rejected "the notion that the Fourteenth

---

[48] *Id.* at 21, 23. Perhaps taking a similar view to Professor Monaghan that the *Miranda* warnings were not constitutionally compelled, Congress tried to overrule *Miranda* by statute in 1968. It enacted 18 U.S.C. § 3501, which effectively sought to return to the pre-*Miranda* totality of the circumstances standard for admissibility of confessions in federal trials. Federal prosecutors only rarely relied on this statute, however, and its constitutionality did not come before the Supreme Court until 2000. In *Dickerson v. United States,* 530 U.S. 428 (2000), the Court held § 3501 unconstitutional. The trouble with the statute, however, was that it ignored *Miranda*'s injunction that a totality of the circumstances approach to evaluating voluntariness is unconstitutional. The Court certainly did *not* hold that the Fifth Amendment mandates the particular warnings that *Miranda* prescribed.

[49] An aversion to imposing all the details of federal procedure on state courts probably best explains why the Fifth Amendment's requirement of grand jury indictment remains unincorporated.

[50] *See Williams v. Florida,* 399 U.S. 78 (1970).

Amendment applies to the States only a watered-down, subjective version of the individual guarantees of the Bill of Rights." Is this consistent with the Court's supposed reliance on "fundamental fairness" as the criterion? If the exclusionary rule's ability to deter illegal searches remains fairly debatable, for example, can one say that "fundamental fairness" requires it? Does it make sense to eliminate state experimentation as to remedies for constitutional violations?

8.   As the experimentation point suggests, the incorporation cases are about government structure as well as individual rights. After all, when the Court applies an aspect of the Bill of Rights to the States, it constrains state-by-state variation and innovation with respect to the rights in question. Justice Harlan, dissenting in *Mapp*, emphasized that "[t]he specifics of trial procedure, which in every mature legal system will vary greatly in detail, are within the sole competence of the States." Hence, "[t]he preservation of a proper balance between state and federal responsibility in the administration of criminal justice demands patience on the part of those who might like to see things move faster among the States in this respect." Harlan's point underscores the extent to which the Warren Court's decisions expanding the rights of the accused and incorporating them to apply to the States through the Fourteenth Amendment effectively nationalized much of American criminal procedure.

Was this nationalization of an area previously reserved to the States well-advised? Was it consistent with the federal structure mandated by the Constitution? In assessing this federalism dimension of the Warren Court, it is important to recognize that, as Scot Powe has pointed out, the Court did not generally impose reform on the country as a whole; rather, it tended simply to nationalize best practices prevalent at the federal level or in most of the States, effectively requiring laggard jurisdictions to catch up to national norms.[51] The exclusionary rule, for example, had been imposed in federal prosecutions for half a century and voluntarily adopted in many states by the time *Mapp* was decided. Is this "harmonization" role an appropriate one for the Court? Would it be fair to say that federalism only makes sense if it rests on a uniform floor of basic human rights?

9.   Many of the Warren Court's criminal procedure decisions were highly unpopular. Law enforcement officials complained loudly; Los Angeles Mayor Sam Yorty, for example, claimed that *Miranda* was "another set of handcuffs on the police department."[52] Crime had emerged as a major issue by the presidential election of 1968. Presidential candidate Richard Nixon ran on a platform of "law and order," claiming that "some of our courts have gone too far in weakening the peace forces as against the criminal forces."[53]

After his victory, President Nixon was able to make four quick appointments to the Supreme Court, including Warren Burger—a leading critic of the Warren Court—as chief justice. And yet the Burger Court has

---

[51] *See* POWE, *supra* note 1, at 492.

[52] Quoted in *id.*, at 399.

[53] Quoted in *id.*, at 266.

been famously described as "The Counter-Revolution That Wasn't."[54] In the criminal procedure area, "[t]he Court steadfastly refused to extend Warren Court decisions, and it carved out many exceptions to those decisions but wouldn't overrule them."[55] That trend has largely continued through the Rehnquist and Roberts Courts.

In one important area, the Burger Court not only refused to reverse liberal precedents but proved willing to extend them significantly. That area—a newfound "right to privacy" under the Due Process Clause—is the focus of the next chapter.

---

[54] *See* VINCENT BLASI, ED., THE BURGER COURT: THE COUNTER-REVOLUTION THAT WASN'T (1986).

[55] POWE, *supra* note 1, at 294.

CHAPTER SEVEN

THE REBIRTH OF SUBSTANTIVE DUE PROCESS

Although the race and criminal procedure decisions of the Warren Court illustrate the Court's turn from matters of economic regulation to questions of non-economic rights, nothing so vividly signifies the post-1937 "double standard" as the Court's revival of substantive due process protections—this time for rights of personal privacy. No area of the Court's jurisprudence in the last quarter of the Twentieth Century has been more controversial than its recognition of a "fundamental" right to privacy—and in particular, its extension of that right to cover the practice of abortion.

This chapter begins with the first "official" recognition of the right to privacy in *Griswold v. Connecticut*. *Griswold* struck down a Connecticut law that prohibited the use of contraceptives, even by married couples and even in the privacy of their own homes. Like many of the decisions that followed, *Griswold*'s privacy principle protected activities that many Americans had long assumed were none of the government's business; the lack of any explicit grounding in constitutional text, however, rendered the generally uncontroversial *results* of these cases highly debatable as a matter of constitutional principle.

The rest of the Chapter deals with the right to abortion—first *Roe v. Wade* itself, then its reaffirmation in *Planned Parenthood v. Casey*. Abortion poses difficult legal, moral, and policy issues in its own right. But because abortion is so controversial, it has also become a leading battleground upon which broader issues of constitutional theory have been fought out. Hence, *Roe* is a central case for advocates of a "living" or "unwritten" constitution, and it provides an occasion to consider the significant historical and precedential support for that position. *Casey*, on the other hand, relied heavily on notions of *stare decisis*, and in connection with that decision we consider the important role of precedent and common law development in constitutional law.

Because the right to privacy potentially extends to a wide variety of personal activities and decisions, litigants frequently have asked the Court to recognize additional fundamental privacy rights. Chapters Fifteen through Seventeen take up that story and survey current Due Process doctrine. As in the earlier Chapters in the current Part, our focus here remains on the development of the Supreme Court's institutional role.

The laws at issue in these cases raise fundamental questions of personal morality and social cohesion. When the courts intervene to evaluate such laws, they raise a further institutional question concerning the proper relationship between judicial review and majoritarian democracy. Hopefully, the preceding chapters have put you in a position to address this latter question in terms of the Supreme Court's historical experience. In particular, you should ask whether the new substantive due process cases manage persuasively to avoid the pitfalls that led the Court to abandon economic substantive due process in *West Coast Hotel*.

SECTION 7.1   THE RIGHT TO PRIVACY

We have already canvassed two precursors to the right of privacy recognized in *Griswold*: *Meyer v. Nebraska*[1] struck down a state law forbidding the teaching of foreign languages to young children, and *Pierce v. Society of Sisters*[2] invalidated a law mandating that children attend public schools. Both these cases were decided under a *Lochner* rationale, extending that case's freedom of contract reasoning to a broader right to make decisions about private matters, including the education of one's children.

A third case, *Skinner v. Oklahoma*,[3] came even closer to the question of reproductive freedom at issue in *Griswold*. *Skinner* involved a challenge to Oklahoma's Habitual Criminal Sterilization Act, which mandated sterilization of persons who had three or more convictions for "felonies involving moral turpitude." The Court struck down the law under the Equal Protection Clause, citing various arbitrary distinctions—e.g., grand larcenists were at risk for sterilization, but embezzlers were not. But in the course of its discussion, the Court said that the case "involves one of the basic civil rights of man. Marriage and procreation are fundamental to the very existence and survival of the race." The Warren Court expanded this principle in *Griswold*.

Griswold v. Connecticut

381 U.S. 479 (1965)

■ MR. JUSTICE DOUGLAS delivered the opinion of the Court.

Appellant Griswold is Executive Director of the Planned Parenthood League of Connecticut. Appellant Buxton is a licensed physician and a professor at the Yale Medical School who served as Medical Director for the League at its Center in New Haven—a center open and operating from November 1 to November 10, 1961, when appellants were arrested.

They gave information, instruction, and medical advice to *married persons* as to the means of preventing conception. They examined the wife and prescribed the best contraceptive device or material for her use. Fees were usually charged, although some couples were serviced free.

---

[1]   262 U.S. 390 (1923).

[2]   268 U.S. 510 (1925).

[3]   316 U.S. 535 (1942).

The statutes whose constitutionality is involved in this appeal are §§ 53–32 and 54–196 of the General Statutes of Connecticut. The former provides:

> "Any person who uses any drug, medicinal article or instrument for the purpose of preventing conception shall be fined not less than fifty dollars or imprisoned not less than sixty days nor more than one year or be both fined and imprisoned."

Section 54–196 provides:

> "Any person who assists, abets, counsels, causes, hires or commands another to commit any offense may be prosecuted and punished as if he were the principal offender."

The appellants were found guilty as accessories and fined $100 each, against the claim that the accessory statute as so applied violated the Fourteenth Amendment. The Appellate Division of the Circuit Court affirmed. The Supreme Court of Errors affirmed that judgment. . . .

Coming to the merits, we are met with a wide range of questions that implicate the Due Process Clause of the Fourteenth Amendment. Overtones of some arguments suggest that *Lochner v. New York* should be our guide. But we decline that invitation as we did in *West Coast Hotel Co. v. Parrish* [and] *Williamson v. Lee Optical Co.* We do not sit as a super-legislature to determine the wisdom, need, and propriety of laws that touch economic problems, business affairs, or social conditions. This law, however, operates directly on an intimate relation of husband and wife and their physician's role in one aspect of that relation.

The association of people is not mentioned in the Constitution nor in the Bill of Rights. The right to educate a child in a school of the parents' choice—whether public or private or parochial—is also not mentioned. Nor is the right to study any particular subject or any foreign language. Yet the First Amendment has been construed to include certain of those rights.

By *Pierce v. Society of Sisters*, the right to educate one's children as one chooses is made applicable to the States by the force of the First and Fourteenth Amendments. By *Meyer v. Nebraska,* the same dignity is given the right to study the German language in a private school. In other words, the State may not, consistently with the spirit of the First Amendment, contract the spectrum of available knowledge. The right of freedom of speech and press includes not only the right to utter or to print, but the right to distribute, the right to receive, the right to read and freedom of inquiry, freedom of thought, and freedom to teach— indeed the freedom of the entire university community. Without those peripheral rights the specific rights would be less secure. And so we reaffirm the principle of the *Pierce* and the *Meyer* cases.

In *NAACP v. Alabama*, 357 U.S. 449 (1958), we protected the "freedom to associate and privacy in one's associations," noting that freedom of association was a peripheral First Amendment right.

Disclosure of membership lists of a constitutionally valid association, we held, was invalid "as entailing the likelihood of a substantial restraint upon the exercise by petitioner's members of their right to freedom of association." In other words, the First Amendment has a penumbra where privacy is protected from governmental intrusion. In like context, we have protected forms of "association" that are not political in the customary sense but pertain to the social, legal, and economic benefit of the members. . . .

Those cases involved more than the "right of assembly"—a right that extends to all irrespective of their race or ideology. The right of "association," like the right of belief, is more than the right to attend a meeting; it includes the right to express one's attitudes or philosophies by membership in a group or by affiliation with it or by other lawful means. Association in that context is a form of expression of opinion; and while it is not expressly included in the First Amendment its existence is necessary in making the express guarantees fully meaningful.

The foregoing cases suggest that specific guarantees in the Bill of Rights have penumbras, formed by emanations from those guarantees that help give them life and substance. Various guarantees create zones of privacy. The right of association contained in the penumbra of the First Amendment is one, as we have seen. The Third Amendment in its prohibition against the quartering of soldiers "in any house" in time of peace without the consent of the owner is another facet of that privacy. The Fourth Amendment explicitly affirms the "right of the people to be secure in their persons, houses, papers, and effects, against unreasonable searches and seizures." The Fifth Amendment in its Self-Incrimination Clause enables the citizen to create a zone of privacy which government may not force him to surrender to his detriment. The Ninth Amendment provides: "The enumeration in the Constitution, of certain rights, shall not be construed to deny or disparage others retained by the people."

The Fourth and Fifth Amendments [have been] described . . . as protection against all governmental invasions "of the sanctity of a man's home and the privacies of life." We recently referred in *Mapp v. Ohio*, 367 U.S. 643 (1961), to the Fourth Amendment as creating a "right to privacy, no less important than any other right carefully and particularly reserved to the people."

We have had many controversies over these penumbral rights of "privacy and repose." These cases bear witness that the right of privacy which presses for recognition here is a legitimate one.

The present case, then, concerns a relationship lying within the zone of privacy created by several fundamental constitutional guarantees. And it concerns a law which, in forbidding the *use* of contraceptives rather than regulating their manufacture or sale, seeks to achieve its goals by means having a maximum destructive impact upon that relationship. Such a law cannot stand in light of the familiar principle, so often applied by this Court, that a "governmental purpose to control or prevent activities constitutionally subject to state regulation may not be achieved by means which sweep unnecessarily broadly and thereby invade the area of protected freedoms." Would we allow the police to search the sacred precincts of marital bedrooms for telltale signs of the use of contraceptives? The very idea is repulsive to the notions of privacy surrounding the marriage relationship.

We deal with a right of privacy older than the Bill of Rights—older than our political parties, older than our school system. Marriage is a coming together for better or for worse, hopefully enduring, and intimate to the degree of being sacred. It is an association that promotes a way of life, not causes; a harmony in living, not political faiths; a bilateral loyalty, not commercial or social projects. Yet it is an association for as noble a purpose as any involved in our prior decisions.

Reversed.

■ **MR. JUSTICE GOLDBERG, whom THE CHIEF JUSTICE and MR. JUSTICE BRENNAN join, concurring.**

I agree with the Court that Connecticut's birth-control law unconstitutionally intrudes upon the right of marital privacy, and I join in its opinion and judgment. Although I have not accepted the view that "due process" as used in the Fourteenth Amendment incorporates all of the first eight Amendments, I do agree that the concept of liberty protects those personal rights that are fundamental, and is not confined to the specific terms of the Bill of Rights. . . . In reaching the conclusion that the right of marital privacy is protected, as being within the protected penumbra of specific guarantees of the Bill of Rights, the Court refers to the Ninth Amendment. I add these words to emphasize the relevance of that Amendment to the Court's holding. . . .

The language and history of the Ninth Amendment reveal that the Framers of the Constitution believed that there are additional fundamental rights, protected from governmental infringement, which exist alongside those fundamental rights specifically mentioned in the first eight constitutional amendments.

The Ninth Amendment reads, "The enumeration in the Constitution, of certain rights, shall not be construed to deny or disparage others retained by the people." The Amendment is almost entirely the work of James Madison. It was introduced in Congress by him and passed the House and Senate with little or no debate and virtually no change in language. It was proffered to quiet expressed fears that a bill of specifically enumerated rights could not be sufficiently broad to cover all essential rights and that the specific mention of certain rights would be interpreted as a denial that others were protected.

In presenting the proposed Amendment, Madison said:

It has been objected also against a bill of rights, that, by enumerating particular exceptions to the grant of power, it would disparage those rights which were not placed in that enumeration; and it might follow by implication, that those rights which were not singled out, were intended to be assigned into the hands of the General Government, and were consequently insecure. This is one of the most plausible arguments I have ever heard urged against the admission of a bill of rights into this system; but, I conceive, that it may be guarded against. I have attempted it, as gentlemen may see by turning to the last clause of the fourth resolution [the Ninth Amendment].

. . . These statements of Madison and [others] make clear that the Framers did not intend that the first eight amendments be construed to exhaust the basic and fundamental rights which the Constitution guaranteed to the people.

While this Court has had little occasion to interpret the Ninth Amendment, "it cannot be presumed that any clause in the constitution is intended to be without effect." *Marbury v. Madison.* In interpreting the Constitution, "real effect should be given to all the words it uses." The Ninth Amendment to the Constitution may be regarded by some as a recent discovery and may be forgotten by others, but since 1791 it has been a basic part of the Constitution which we are sworn to uphold. To hold that a right so basic and fundamental and so deep-rooted in our society as the right of privacy in marriage may be infringed because that right is not guaranteed in so many words by the first eight amendments to the Constitution is to ignore the Ninth Amendment and to give it no effect whatsoever. Moreover, a judicial construction that this fundamental right is not protected by the Constitution because it is not mentioned in explicit terms by one of the first eight amendments or elsewhere in the Constitution would violate the Ninth Amendment, which specifically states that "the enumeration in the Constitution, of certain rights, shall not be *construed* to deny or disparage others retained by the people." . . .

In determining which rights are fundamental, judges are not left at large to decide cases in light of their personal and private notions. Rather, they must look to the "traditions and [collective] conscience of our people" to determine whether a principle is "so rooted [there] . . . as to be ranked as fundamental." The inquiry is whether a right involved "is of such a character that it cannot be denied without violating those 'fundamental principles of liberty and justice which lie at the base of all our civil and political institutions'. . . ." "Liberty" also "gains content from the emanations of . . . specific [constitutional] guarantees" and "from experience with the requirements of a free society." . . .

Although the Constitution does not speak in so many words of the right of privacy in marriage, I cannot believe that it offers these fundamental rights no protection. The fact that no particular provision of the Constitution explicitly forbids the State from disrupting the traditional relation of the family—a relation as old and as fundamental as our entire civilization—surely does not show that the Government was meant to have the power to do so. Rather, as the Ninth Amendment expressly recognizes, there are fundamental personal rights such as this one, which are protected from abridgment by the Government though not specifically mentioned in the Constitution. . . .

Finally, it should be said of the Court's holding today that it in no way interferes with a State's proper regulation of sexual promiscuity or misconduct. As my Brother HARLAN so well stated in his dissenting opinion in *Poe v. Ullman*:

> Adultery, homosexuality and the like are sexual intimacies which the State forbids . . . but the intimacy of husband and wife is necessarily an essential and accepted feature of the institution of marriage, an institution which the State not only must allow, but which always and in every age it has fostered and protected. It is one thing when the State exerts its power either to forbid extra-marital sexuality . . . or to say who may marry, but it is quite another when, having acknowledged a marriage and the intimacies inherent in it, it undertakes to regulate by means of the criminal law the details of that intimacy. . . .

■ **MR. JUSTICE HARLAN, concurring in the judgment.**

I fully agree with the judgment of reversal, but find myself unable to join the Court's opinion. . . . In my view, the proper constitutional inquiry in this case is whether this Connecticut statute infringes the Due Process Clause of the Fourteenth Amendment because the enactment violates basic values "implicit in the concept of ordered liberty," *Palko v. Connecticut*, 302 U.S. 319 (1937). For reasons stated at length in my dissenting opinion in *Poe v. Ullman*, 367 U.S. 497, 522–55 (1961), I believe that it does. While the relevant inquiry may be aided by resort to one or more of the provisions of the Bill of Rights, it is not dependent on them or any of their radiations. The Due Process Clause of the Fourteenth Amendment stands, in my opinion, on its own bottom.

A further observation seems in order respecting the justification of my Brothers BLACK and STEWART for their "incorporation" approach to this case. Their approach does not rest on historical reasons, which are of course wholly lacking. . . . but on the thesis that by limiting the content of the Due Process Clause of the Fourteenth Amendment to the protection of rights which can be found elsewhere in the Constitution, in this instance in the Bill of Rights, judges will thus be confined to "interpretation" of specific constitutional provisions, and will thereby be restrained from introducing their own notions of constitutional right and wrong into the "vague contours of the Due Process Clause."

While I could not more heartily agree that judicial "self restraint" is an indispensable ingredient of sound constitutional adjudication, I do submit that the formula suggested for achieving it is more hollow than real. "Specific" provisions of the Constitution, no less than "due process," lend themselves as readily to "personal" interpretations by judges whose constitutional outlook is simply to keep the Constitution in supposed "tune with the times". Need one go further than to recall last Term's reapportionment cases, *Wesberry v. Sanders*, 376 U.S. 1 (1964), and *Reynolds v. Sims*, 377 U.S. 533 (1964), where a majority of the Court "interpreted" "by the People" (Art. I, § 2) and "equal protection" (Amdt. 14) to command "one person, one vote," an interpretation that was made in the face of irrefutable and still unanswered history to the contrary?

Judicial self-restraint will not, I suggest, be brought about in the "due process" area by the historically unfounded incorporation formula long advanced by my Brother BLACK, and now in part espoused by my Brother STEWART. It will be achieved in this area, as in other constitutional areas, only by continual insistence upon respect for the teachings of history, solid recognition of the basic values that underlie our society, and wise appreciation of the great roles that the doctrines of federalism and separation of powers have played in establishing and preserving American freedoms. Adherence to these principles will not, of course, obviate all constitutional differences of opinion among judges, nor should it. Their continued recognition will, however, go farther toward keeping most judges from roaming at large in the constitutional field than will the interpolation into the Constitution of an artificial and largely illusory restriction on the content of the Due Process Clause.

■ **MR. JUSTICE WHITE, concurring in the judgment.**

In my view this Connecticut law as applied to married couples deprives them of "liberty" without due process of law, as that concept is used in the Fourteenth Amendment. I therefore concur in the judgment of the Court reversing these convictions under Connecticut's aiding and abetting statute. . . .

An examination of the justification offered, however, cannot be avoided by saying that the Connecticut anti-use statute invades a protected area of privacy and association or that it demeans the marriage relationship. The nature of the right invaded is pertinent, to be sure, for statutes regulating sensitive areas of liberty do, under the cases of this Court, require "strict scrutiny," *Skinner v. Oklahoma*, 316 U.S. 535 (1942), and "must be viewed in the light of less drastic means for achieving the same basic purpose." "Where there is a significant encroachment upon personal liberty, the State may prevail only upon showing a subordinating interest which is compelling." But such statutes, if reasonably necessary for the effectuation of a legitimate and substantial state interest, and not arbitrary or capricious in application, are not invalid under the Due Process Clause.

As I read the opinions of the Connecticut courts and the argument of Connecticut in this Court, the State claims but one justification for its anti-use statute. There is no serious contention that Connecticut thinks the use of artificial or external methods of contraception immoral or unwise in itself, or that the anti-use statute is founded upon any policy of promoting population expansion. Rather, the statute is said to serve the State's policy against all forms of promiscuous or illicit sexual relationships, be they premarital or extramarital, concededly a permissible and legitimate legislative goal.

Without taking issue with the premise that the fear of conception operates as a deterrent to such relationships in addition to the criminal proscriptions Connecticut has against such conduct, I wholly fail to see how the ban on the use of contraceptives by married couples in any way reinforces the State's ban on illicit sexual relationships. Connecticut does not bar the importation or possession of contraceptive devices; they are not considered contraband material under state law, and their availability in that State is not seriously disputed. The only way Connecticut seeks to limit or control the availability of such devices is through its general aiding and abetting statute whose operation in this context has been quite obviously ineffective and whose most serious use has been against birth-control clinics rendering advice to married, rather than unmarried, persons. Indeed, after over 80 years of the State's proscription of use, the legality of the sale of such devices to prevent disease has never been expressly passed upon, although it appears that sales have long occurred and have only infrequently been challenged. This "undeviating policy . . . throughout all the long years . . . bespeaks more than prosecutorial paralysis." Moreover, it would appear that the sale of contraceptives to prevent disease is plainly legal under Connecticut law.

In these circumstances one is rather hard pressed to explain how the ban on use by married persons in any way prevents use of such devices by persons engaging in illicit sexual relations and thereby contributes to the State's policy against such relationships. Neither the state courts nor the State before the bar of this Court has tendered such an explanation. It is purely fanciful to believe that the broad proscription on use facilitates discovery of use by persons engaging in a prohibited relationship or for some other reason makes such use more unlikely and thus can be supported by any sort of administrative consideration. Perhaps the theory is that the flat ban on use prevents married people from possessing contraceptives and without the ready availability of such devices for use in the marital relationship, there will be no or less temptation to use them in extramarital ones. This reasoning rests on the premise that married people will comply with the ban in regard to their marital relationship, notwithstanding total nonenforcement in this context and apparent nonenforcibility, but will not comply with criminal statutes prohibiting extramarital affairs and the anti-use statute in respect to illicit sexual relationships, a premise whose validity has not been demonstrated and whose intrinsic validity is not very evident. At most the broad ban is of marginal utility to the declared objective. A statute limiting its prohibition on use to persons engaging in the prohibited relationship would serve the end posited by Connecticut in the same way, and with the same effectiveness, or ineffectiveness, as the broad anti-use statute under attack in this case. I find nothing in this record justifying the sweeping scope of this statute, with its telling effect on the freedoms of married persons, and therefore conclude that it deprives such persons of liberty without due process of law.

■ MR. JUSTICE BLACK, with whom MR. JUSTICE STEWART joins, dissenting.

I agree with my Brother STEWART'S dissenting opinion. And like him I do not to any extent whatever base my view that this Connecticut law is constitutional on a belief that the law is wise or that its policy is a good one. In order that there may be no room at all to doubt why I vote as I do, I feel constrained to add that the law is every bit as offensive to me as it is to my Brethren of the majority and my Brothers HARLAN, WHITE and GOLDBERG who, reciting reasons why it is offensive to them, hold it unconstitutional. There is no single one of the graphic and eloquent strictures and criticisms fired at the policy of this Connecticut law either by the Court's opinion or by those of my concurring Brethren to which I cannot subscribe—except their conclusion that the evil qualities they see in the law make it unconstitutional. . . .

The Court talks about a constitutional "right of privacy" as though there is some constitutional provision or provisions forbidding any law ever to be passed which might abridge the "privacy" of individuals. But there is not. There are, of course, guarantees in certain specific constitutional provisions which are designed in part to protect privacy at certain times and places with respect to certain activities. Such, for example, is the Fourth Amendment's guarantee against "unreasonable searches and seizures." But I think it belittles that Amendment to talk about it as though it protects nothing but "privacy." . . . The average man would very likely not have his feelings soothed any more by having his property seized openly than by having it seized privately and by stealth. He simply wants his property left alone. And a person can be just as much, if not more, irritated, annoyed and injured by an unceremonious public arrest by a policeman as he is by a seizure in the privacy of his office or home.

One of the most effective ways of diluting or expanding a constitutionally guaranteed right is to substitute for the crucial word or words of a constitutional guarantee another word or words, more or less flexible and more or less restricted in meaning. This fact is well illustrated by the use of the term "right of privacy" as a comprehensive substitute for the Fourth Amendment's guarantee against "unreasonable searches and seizures." "Privacy" is a broad, abstract and ambiguous concept which can easily be shrunken in meaning but which can also, on the other hand, easily be interpreted as a constitutional ban against many things other than searches and seizures. I have expressed the view many times that First Amendment freedoms, for example, have suffered from a failure of the courts to stick to the simple language of the First Amendment in construing it, instead of invoking multitudes of words substituted for those the Framers used. For these reasons I get nowhere in this case by talk about a constitutional "right of privacy" as an emanation from one or more constitutional provisions.[1] I like my privacy as well as the next one, but I am nevertheless compelled to admit that government has a right to invade it unless prohibited by some specific constitutional provision. For these reasons I cannot agree with the Court's judgment and the reasons it gives for holding this Connecticut law unconstitutional.

This brings me to the arguments made by my Brothers HARLAN, WHITE and GOLDBERG for invalidating the Connecticut law. . . . I think that if properly construed neither the Due Process Clause nor the Ninth Amendment, nor both together, could under any circumstances be a proper basis for invalidating the Connecticut law. I discuss the due process and Ninth Amendment arguments together because on analysis they turn out to be the same thing—merely using different words to claim for this Court and the federal judiciary power to invalidate any legislative act which the judges find irrational, unreasonable or offensive.

The due process argument which my Brothers HARLAN and WHITE adopt here is based . . . on the premise that this Court is vested with power to invalidate all state laws that it considers to be arbitrary, capricious, unreasonable, or oppressive, or on this Court's belief that a particular state law under scrutiny has no "rational or justifying" purpose, or is offensive to a "sense of fairness and justice." If these formulas based on "natural justice," or others which mean the same thing, are to prevail, they require judges to determine what is or is not constitutional on the basis of their own appraisal of what laws are unwise or unnecessary. The power to make such decisions is of course that of a legislative body. Surely it has to be admitted that no provision of the Constitution specifically gives such blanket power to courts to exercise such a supervisory veto over the wisdom and value of legislative policies and to hold unconstitutional those laws which they believe unwise or dangerous. I readily admit that no legislative body, state or national,

---

[1] The phrase "right to privacy" appears first to have gained currency from an article written by Messrs. Warren and (later Mr. Justice) Brandeis in 1890 which urged that States should give some form of tort relief to persons whose private affairs were exploited by others. *The Right to Privacy*, 4 HARV. L. REV. 193. Largely as a result of this article, some States have passed statutes creating such a cause of action, and in others state courts have done the same thing by exercising their powers as courts of common law. Thus the Supreme Court of Georgia, in granting a cause of action for damages to a man whose picture had been used in a newspaper advertisement without his consent, said that "A right of privacy in matters purely private is . . . derived from natural law" and that "The conclusion reached by us seems to be . . . thoroughly in accord with natural justice, with the principles of the law of every civilized nation, and especially with the elastic principles of the common law. . . ." *Pavesich v. New England Life Ins. Co.*, 50 S. E. 68 (Ga. 1905). Observing that "the right of privacy . . . presses for recognition here," today this Court, which I did not understand to have power to sit as a court of common law, now appears to be exalting a phrase which Warren and Brandeis used in discussing grounds for tort relief, to the level of a constitutional rule which prevents state legislatures from passing any law deemed by this Court to interfere with "privacy."

should pass laws that can justly be given any of the invidious labels invoked as constitutional excuses to strike down state laws. But perhaps it is not too much to say that no legislative body ever does pass laws without believing that they will accomplish a sane, rational, wise and justifiable purpose. . . . I do not believe that we are granted power by the Due Process Clause or any other constitutional provision or provisions to measure constitutionality by our belief that legislation is arbitrary, capricious or unreasonable, or accomplishes no justifiable purpose, or is offensive to our own notions of "civilized standards of conduct." Such an appraisal of the wisdom of legislation is an attribute of the power to make laws, not of the power to interpret them. . . .

My Brother GOLDBERG has adopted the recent discovery that the Ninth Amendment as well as the Due Process Clause can be used by this Court as authority to strike down all state legislation which this Court thinks violates "fundamental principles of liberty and justice," or is contrary to the "traditions and [collective] conscience of our people." He also states, without proof satisfactory to me, that in making decisions on this basis judges will not consider "their personal and private notions." One may ask how they can avoid considering them. Our Court certainly has no machinery with which to take a Gallup Poll. And the scientific miracles of this age have not yet produced a gadget which the Court can use to determine what traditions are rooted in the "[collective] conscience of our people." Moreover, one would certainly have to look far beyond the language of the Ninth Amendment to find that the Framers vested in this Court any such awesome veto powers over lawmaking, either by the States or by the Congress. Nor does anything in the history of the Amendment offer any support for such a shocking doctrine. The whole history of the adoption of the Constitution and Bill of Rights points the other way, and the very material quoted by my Brother GOLDBERG shows that the Ninth Amendment was intended to protect against the idea that "by enumerating particular exceptions to the grant of power" to the Federal Government, "those rights which were not singled out, were intended to be assigned into the hands of the General Government [the United States], and were consequently insecure." That Amendment was passed, not to broaden the powers of this Court or any other department of "the General Government," but, as every student of history knows, to assure the people that the Constitution in all its provisions was intended to limit the Federal Government to the powers granted expressly or by necessary implication. If any broad, unlimited power to hold laws unconstitutional because they offend what this Court conceives to be the "[collective] conscience of our people" is vested in this Court by the Ninth Amendment, the Fourteenth Amendment, or any other provision of the Constitution, it was not given by the Framers, but rather has been bestowed on the Court by the Court. This fact is perhaps responsible for the peculiar phenomenon that for a period of a century and a half no serious suggestion was ever made that the Ninth Amendment, enacted to protect state powers against federal invasion, could be used as a weapon of federal power to prevent state legislatures from passing laws they consider appropriate to govern local affairs. Use of any such broad, unbounded judicial authority would make of this Court's members a day-to-day constitutional convention. . . .

I realize that many good and able men have eloquently spoken and written . . . about the duty of this Court to keep the Constitution in tune with the times. . . . For myself, I must with all deference reject that philosophy. The Constitution makers knew the need for change and provided for it. Amendments suggested by the people's elected representatives can be submitted to the people or their selected agents for ratification. . . . The Due Process Clause with an "arbitrary and capricious" or "shocking to the conscience" formula was liberally used by this Court to strike down economic legislation in the early decades of this century, threatening, many people thought, the tranquility and stability of the Nation. See, *e.g., Lochner v. New York*. That formula . . . is no less dangerous when used to enforce this Court's views about personal rights than those about economic rights. I had thought that we had laid that formula, as a means for striking down state legislation, to rest once and for all in cases like *West Coast Hotel Co. v. Parrish*. . . .

So far as I am concerned, Connecticut's law as applied here is not forbidden by any provision of the Federal Constitution as that Constitution was written, and I would therefore affirm.

■ MR. JUSTICE STEWART, whom MR. JUSTICE BLACK joins, dissenting.

Since 1879 Connecticut has had on its books a law which forbids the use of contraceptives by anyone. I think this is an uncommonly silly law. As a practical matter, the law is obviously unenforceable, except in the oblique context of the present case. As a philosophical matter, I believe the use of contraceptives in the relationship of marriage should be left to personal and private choice, based upon each individual's moral, ethical, and religious beliefs. As a matter of social policy, I think professional counsel about methods of birth control should be available to all, so that each individual's choice can be meaningfully made. But we are not asked in this case to say whether we think this law is unwise, or even asinine. We are asked to hold that it violates the United States Constitution. And that I cannot do.

In the course of its opinion the Court refers to no less than six Amendments to the Constitution: the First, the Third, the Fourth, the Fifth, the Ninth, and the Fourteenth. But the Court does not say which of these Amendments, if any, it thinks is infringed by this Connecticut law.

We *are* told that the Due Process Clause of the Fourteenth Amendment is not, as such, the "guide" in this case. With that much I agree. There is no claim that this law, duly enacted by the Connecticut Legislature, is unconstitutionally vague. There is no claim that the appellants were denied any of the elements of procedural due process at their trial, so as to make their convictions constitutionally invalid. And, as the Court says, the day has long passed since the Due Process Clause was regarded as a proper instrument for determining "the wisdom, need, and propriety" of state laws. Compare *Lochner v. New York* with *Ferguson v. Skrupa*. My Brothers HARLAN and WHITE to the contrary, "we have returned to the original constitutional proposition that courts do not substitute their social and economic beliefs for the judgment of legislative bodies, who are elected to pass laws."

As to the First, Third, Fourth, and Fifth Amendments, I can find nothing in any of them to invalidate this Connecticut law, even assuming that all those Amendments are fully applicable against the States. . . . [T]here is not involved here any abridgment of "the freedom of speech, or of the press; or the right of the people peaceably to assemble, and to petition the Government for a redress of grievances." No soldier has been quartered in any house. There has been no search, and no seizure. Nobody has been compelled to be a witness against himself.

The Court also quotes the Ninth Amendment, and my Brother GOLDBERG's concurring opinion relies heavily upon it. But to say that the Ninth Amendment has anything to do with this case is to turn somersaults with history. The Ninth Amendment, like its companion the Tenth . . . was framed by James Madison and adopted by the States simply to make clear that the adoption of the Bill of Rights did not alter the plan that the *Federal* Government was to be a government of express and limited powers, and that all rights and powers not delegated to it were retained by the people and the individual States. Until today no member of this Court has ever suggested that the Ninth Amendment meant anything else, and the idea that a federal court could ever use the Ninth Amendment to annul a law passed by the elected representatives of the people of the State of Connecticut would have caused James Madison no little wonder.

What provision of the Constitution, then, does make this state law invalid? The Court says it is the right of privacy "created by several fundamental constitutional guarantees." With all deference, I can find no such general right of privacy in the Bill of Rights, in any other part of the Constitution, or in any case ever before decided by this Court.

At the oral argument in this case we were told that the Connecticut law does not "conform to current community standards." But it is not the function of this Court to decide cases on the basis of community standards. We are here to decide cases "agreeably to the Constitution and laws of the United States." It is the essence of judicial duty to subordinate our own personal views, our own ideas of what legislation is wise and what is not. If, as I should surely hope, the law before us does not reflect the standards of the people of Connecticut, the people of Connecticut can freely exercise their true Ninth and Tenth Amendment rights to persuade their elected representatives to repeal it. That is the constitutional way to take this law off the books.

NOTE ON *GRISWOLD*, THE RIGHT TO PRIVACY, AND NEUTRAL PRINCIPLES

1. John Hart Ely said that, textually speaking, "substantive due process" is a "contradiction in terms—sort of like green pastel redness."[4] Do you agree? Can you accept his position that there's no such thing as substantive due process and still believe in incorporation of the Bill of Rights against the States? In the "reverse-incorporation" of the Equal Protection Clause against the Federal Government?

As discussed in Section 5.4, *supra*, Professor Ely developed his "representation reinforcement" approach to judicial review largely as a means of justifying the work of the Warren Court, and he built that approach around the famous "footnote four" in *Carolene Products*. Does the right to privacy recognized in *Griswold* fit the *Carolene Products* criteria for more aggressive judicial review? In this connection, consider Justice Stewart's position that Connecticut's statute was "an uncommonly silly law" but that such laws must be repealed by the legislature, not the courts. Why do you think the good people of Connecticut had failed to repeal the contraception statute? Are there circumstances in which we can't count on legislatures to take care of problems like this? Does it make a difference that the State of Connecticut chose almost never to enforce the anti-contraception statute? Which way does that fact cut?

2. What are the differences between the approaches of Justice Douglas, Justice Goldberg, and Justice Harlan in *Griswold*? Which do you find the most persuasive?

a. Why was Justice Douglas unwilling to rely upon the Due Process Clause? Many commentators have made fun of his "penumbra" theory of the Bill of Rights in *Griswold*, but one way of framing it is to say that the specific provisions of the Bill of Rights provide *examples* of individual liberty rather than an exhaustive list of individual rights. If we accept that much, is it crazy to say that we can extrapolate from the specific rights protected in the text to identify other protected liberties?

b. Justice Goldberg relied instead on the Ninth Amendment, which seems to invite the recognition of unenumerated rights. But does the Ninth Amendment mean that *courts* should identify and protect additional rights, or does it simply recognize that legislatures may well choose to protect additional rights by statute? After all, we protect any number of critical rights—e.g., rights to public education, health care, retirement security—by statute. Is the Ninth Amendment, in any event, too vague to be applied by courts? Can a court answer "yes" to the immediately preceding

---

4 JOHN HART ELY, DEMOCRACY AND DISTRUST: A THEORY OF JUDICIAL REVIEW 18 (1980).

question without effectively reading the Ninth Amendment out of the Constitution?[5]

c.   Justice Harlan did frankly rest upon the Due Process Clause in his concurring opinion. That opinion drew heavily upon his dissent in *Poe v. Ullman*, 367 U.S. 497 (1961), a prior challenge to the Connecticut contraception law that the majority rejected on jurisdictional grounds. Harlan's *Poe* dissent laid out his theory of evolving unenumerated rights in considerably greater detail; you will see extensive reliance on this opinion by the plurality in *Planned Parenthood v. Casey*, 505 U.S. 833 (1992), which reaffirmed the right to an abortion recognized in *Roe v. Wade*, 410 U.S. 113 (1973). *See infra* Section 7.3. Isn't the big problem with Harlan's position, however, that he must rely on a substantive reading of the Due Process Clause while still explaining how he is not repeating the mistakes of *Lochner*?

3.   Does *Griswold* satisfy Professor Wechsler's criteria for "neutral principles" necessary to support legitimate judicial action? In an influential article,[6] Professor Robert Bork (who later became a prominent federal circuit judge whom President Reagan unsuccessfully sought to place on the high court) argued that *Griswold* was *not* neutral. In so doing, Bork fleshed out an important aspect of Wechsler's theory of neutrality. Recall that Wechsler defined "[a] principled decision" as "one that rests on reasons with respect to all the issues in a case, reasons that in their generality and their neutrality transcend any immediate result that is involved."[7] This formulation emphasizes neutrality in the *application* of principle—that is, a judge must be willing to apply the principle consistently even in cases where he does not relish the result.

Professor Bork argued, however, that neutrality in *application* is not enough. "If judges are to avoid imposing their own values upon the rest of us," he wrote, "they must be neutral as well in the *definition* and the *derivation* of principles."[8] Consider, for example, two possible ways of formulating the principle adopted by the Court in *Griswold*:

(a)   The government may not interfere with acts done in private.

(b)   The government may not prohibit the use of contraceptives by married couples.

Principle (a) fails the test of neutral application, right? As the majority pointed out, it was not prepared to protect acts of incest or adultery, whether or not done in private. But principle (b) has no such problem, does it? The Court can simply say that adultery and incest fall outside the scope of its

---

[5]   *See, e.g.*, Randy Barnett, *The 9th Amendment: It Means What It Says*, 85 TEX. L. REV. 1, 1 (2006) ("The [Ninth] Amendment is what it appears to be: a meaningful check on federal power and a significant guarantee of individual liberty.").

[6]   Robert H. Bork, *Neutral Principles and Some First Amendment Problems*, 47 IND. L. J. 1 (1971).

[7]   Herbert L. Wechsler, *Toward Neutral Principles of Constitutional Law*, 73 HARV. L. REV. 1, 19 (1959).

[8]   Bork, *supra* note 6, at 7.

principle. But wouldn't the Court have avoided the neutral application problem with (a) simply by formulating its principle so narrowly that it only applies to the precise circumstances before it in *Griswold*? The question, of course, is how the Court can derive that specific principle from the Constitution. In other words, a court must be able to show that it derived and defined its principle in a neutral way. As Bork put it, "a legitimate Court must be controlled by principles exterior to the will of the Justices."[9]

Do you agree with Professor Bork that the *Griswold* majority could point to no neutrally-derived basis for the right to privacy? Is each of the various approaches to that right discussed in Note (2), *supra*, equally vulnerable to that criticism?

4.   Professor Bork believed that a neutral derivation requirement ruled out "a Supreme Court that 'chooses fundamental values' because a Court that makes rather than implements value choices cannot be squared with the presuppositions of a democratic society."[10] But if a Court relies on what it believes to be objective principles of morality—as it sometimes does in Eighth Amendment cases, for example—is it fair to say that those principles are not "exterior to the will of the Justices"? Would one have to deny that objective principles of morality exist at all to say that? Likewise, if the Court relies on a current or emerging moral consensus in American society, as it seemed to do in the same-sex marriage cases, isn't that "exterior" to the Justices' will?

Is the problem with such appeals to morality or social consensus rather that they fall outside the legitimate responsibilities of judges in our system? Why would we expect courts to be better at moral reasoning or evaluating the *zeitgeist* than other institutions, such as state legislatures or Congress?[11] Professor Bork derived his argument from our system's need to accommodate the antidemocratic nature of judicial review with the democratic principle of majority rule. "[T]he Court's power is legitimate," he said, "only if it has, and can demonstrate in reasoned opinions that it has, a valid theory, derived from the Constitution, or the respective spheres of majority and minority freedom."[12] Hence, "[w]here constitutional materials do not clearly specify the value to be preferred, there is no principled way to prefer any claimed human value to any other. The judge must stick close to the text and the history, and their fair implications, and not construct new rights."[13]

Professor Bork's later work went on to argue that originalism is the only theory of interpretation that can meet the test of neutral derivation and definition:

---

[9]   *Id.* at 6.

[10]   *Id.*

[11]   *See also* Antonin Scalia, *Originalism: The Lesser Evil?*, 57 U. CIN. L. REV. 849, 854 (1989) (suggesting "the legislature would seem a much more appropriate expositor of social values," and that if such values are the basic criterion of constitutionality, then the legislature's "determination that a statute is compatible with the Constitution should, as in England, prevail").

[12]   Bork, *supra* note 6, at 3.

[13]   *Id.* at 8.

> The philosophy of original understanding is capable of supplying neutrality in all three respects—in deriving, defining, and applying principle. When a judge finds his principle in the Constitution as originally understood, the problem of the neutral derivation of principle is solved. The judge accepts the ratifier's definition of the appropriate ranges of majority and minority freedom. The Madisonian dilemma is resolved in the way that the founders resolved it, and the judge accepts the fact that he is bound by that resolution as law. He need not, and must not, make unguided value judgments of his own. This means, of course, that a judge, no matter on what court he sits, may never create new constitutional rights or destroy old ones. . . .[14]

Recall that in Chapter One, we distinguished between theories of constitutional *obligation, interpretation,* and *judicial review.* Originalism is a theory of interpretation, and it is often derived from particular theories of constitutional obligation that stress the nature of the Constitution as law, to be interpreted in line with the authoritative will of its adopters.[15] Bork's analysis comes to originalism from another direction entirely, doesn't it? His originalism rests on a theory of judicial review, which postulates originalism as the only interpretive approach sufficiently neutral to legitimate judicial authority. Do you agree? Is this a better justification for originalism than one that rests on the authority of our (dead) Founders? Is it really true that originalism is the only method that can neutrally derive constitutional principles?

5.   On the other hand, are we really prepared to accept a theory of neutral principles that constrains courts from recognizing new fundamental rights like privacy? Robert Bork's "Neutral Principles" article was portrayed as highly radical in the debate over his nomination by President Ronald Reagan to the Supreme Court. Senator Edward Kennedy, for example, asserted that Bork's originalism would have dire consequences for the country:

> Robert Bork's America is a land in which women would be forced into back-alley abortions, blacks would sit at segregated lunch counters, rogue police could break down citizens' doors in midnight raids, schoolchildren could not be taught about evolution, writers and artists could be censored at the whim of the Government, and the doors of the Federal courts would be shut on the fingers of millions of citizens.[16]

---

[14] ROBERT H. BORK, THE TEMPTING OF AMERICA: THE POLITICAL SEDUCTION OF THE LAW 146–47 (1990).

[15] *See, e.g.,* Michael W. McConnell, *Textualism and the Dead Hand of the Past,* 66 GEO. WASH. L. REV. 1127, 1132 (1998) (excerpted in Section 1.2, *supra*) (emphasizing that because the Constitution's authority stems from the sovereign power of the people who adopted it, "[i]t follows that the Constitution should be interpreted in accordance with their understanding"); Scalia, *supra* note 11, at 854 (stressing that "the Constitution, though it has an effect superior to other laws, is . . . an enactment that has a fixed meaning ascertainable through the usual devices familiar to those learned in the law").

[16] Quoted in James Reston, *Washington; Kennedy and Bork,* N.Y. TIMES, July 5, 1987.

Is this a fair assessment? Wasn't Bork's point instead that new rights should have to be recognized by political actors rather than courts? But without judicial innovation in cases like *Griswold* (or *Mapp* or *Roe* or *Brown*), wouldn't we still be closer to Senator Kennedy's dire vision?[17] Would that be the Court's fault—or the fault of Congress and state legislatures?

6.   How broad a privacy right did *Griswold* actually support? The opinions in *Griswold* relied heavily on two bases for the right of married couples to use contraception:

a)   traditional respect for the privacy of the marital relationship, and

b)   the constitutional protection of activities that take place in the home, as evidenced by the Third and Fourth Amendment.

Given the centrality of these elements in *Griswold*, would the Court's reasoning, for example, support striking down a law barring use of contraceptives by unmarried persons? How about *sales* of contraceptives, which take place not in the marital bedroom but in the convenience store on the street corner?

The Court confronted the first of these questions in *Eisenstadt v. Baird*, 405 U.S. 438 (1972), which involved a Massachusetts statute prohibiting distribution of contraceptives to unmarried persons. The Court, in an opinion by Justice Brennan, held that the statute violated the Equal Protection Clause because it discriminated against unmarried persons. Although the Court purported to ask whether the statutory distinction between married and unmarried person was "rational," it nonetheless rejected all three justifications that Massachusetts put forward for the law. Justice Brennan noted that two of those justifications—that contraceptives pose health risks and the some people view contraception as inherently immoral—applied to use by *any* persons, married or unmarried. A third justification—the desire to deter premarital sex—was more targeted to unmarried persons, but the Court was skeptical that this was the actual purpose of the law. "It would be plainly unreasonable to assume," Justice Brennan wrote, "that Massachusetts has prescribed pregnancy and the birth of an unwanted child as punishment for fornication." The Court also noted that "in making contraceptives available to married persons without regard to their intended use," Massachusetts have not attempted "to deter married persons engaging in illicit sexual relations with unmarried persons." Are these criticisms of the statute's rationale consistent with the deferential standard of rational basis review in cases like *Carolene Products* and *Lee Optical*?

Eisenstadt has generally been read as extending the privacy right of contraception to unmarried persons, notwithstanding *Griswold*'s strong emphasis on the importance of marriage. On this point, Justice Brennan wrote:

> It is true that in *Griswold* the right of privacy in question inhered in the marital relationship. Yet the marital couple is not an independent entity with a mind and heart of its own, but an

---

[17]   For Professor Bork's own defense of *Brown*, see *supra* Section 6.1.

association of two individuals each with a separate intellectual and emotional makeup. If the right of privacy means anything, it is the right of the *individual*, married or single, to be free from unwarranted governmental intrusion into matters so fundamentally affecting a person as the decision whether to bear or beget a child.

Can this expansion be justified?

On the other hand, if we take *Eisenstadt* seriously as a case about equal protection rather than the scope of the substantive due process right to privacy, the case reveals a potentially powerful doctrinal dynamic. The line of argument seems to proceed as follows:

a)   the Due Process Clause guarantees *married* persons the right to use contraceptives;

b)   the Equal Protection Clause requires the State to treat *unmarried* persons the same as married persons (absent a good reason not to);

therefore

c)   unmarried persons have a right to use contraceptives.

This combination of due process and equal protection is extremely powerful. Due Process, as conceived in *Griswold*, requires the courts to protect *traditional* rights; the Equal Protection Clause, by contrast, is an avowedly *anti*-traditional provision in that it breaks up traditional social and political distinctions between persons.[18] Can you make an argument for same-sex marriage similar in structure to the argument in *Eisenstadt*?[19]

Does extension of a traditional right to a non-traditional group or context vitiate the ability to derive that right from tradition in the first place? For instance, is the traditional right of marital intimacy in *Griswold* defined in important part by the web of rights and obligations that married status creates? If not, is *Eisenstadt's* extension of *Griswold* a bridge too far?

7.   A third case on contraceptives, decided five years after *Eisenstadt*, is *Carey v. Population Services International*, 431 U.S. 678 (1977). In *Carey*, the Court struck down a New York law prohibiting any person other than a licensed pharmacist from distributing contraceptives. Justice Brennan wrote for the majority that "*Griswold* may no longer be read as holding only that a State may not prohibit a married couple's use of contraceptives. Read in light of its progeny, the teaching of *Griswold* is that the Constitution protects individual decisions in matters of childbearing from unjustified intrusion by the State." Notably, the Court subjected the statute to *strict scrutiny*, rather than the rational basis review purportedly applied in *Eisenstadt*. Do you think the Court has adequately explained each incremental advance, between *Griswold* and *Carey*, in the scope of the privacy right and the level of scrutiny applied to restrictions upon that right?

---

[18]   *See generally* Cass R. Sunstein, *Sexual Orientation and the Constitution: A Note on the Relationship Between Due Process and Equal Protection*, 55 U. CHI. L. REV. 1161 (1988).

[19]   For more on same-sex marriage, see Section 17.3, *infra*.

SECTION 7.2   THE RIGHT OF ABORTION

The Burger Court is often called "the revolution that wasn't." Despite expectations of a sharp conservative turn following President Nixon's four appointments, retreats from Warren Court liberalism (primarily in the area of criminal procedure) occurred mostly around the edges. And in some areas, the Burger Court forged boldly ahead. The most dramatic advances occurred in the area of privacy rights. We have just seen how the Burger Court began, in *Eisenstadt v. Baird*, by expanding the right to use contraception announced in *Griswold v. Connecticut* to circumstances and persons beyond the scope of that prior decision. The most controversial step, of course, occurred a year later in *Roe v. Wade*.

Roe v. Wade
410 U.S. 113 (1973)

■ **MR. JUSTICE BLACKMUN delivered the opinion of the Court.**

This Texas federal appeal and its Georgia companion, *Doe v. Bolton,* present constitutional challenges to state criminal abortion legislation. The Texas statutes under attack here are typical of those that have been in effect in many States for approximately a century. The Georgia statutes, in contrast, have a modern cast and are a legislative product that, to an extent at least, obviously reflects the influences of recent attitudinal change, of advancing medical knowledge and techniques, and of new thinking about an old issue.

We forthwith acknowledge our awareness of the sensitive and emotional nature of the abortion controversy, of the vigorous opposing views, even among physicians, and of the deep and seemingly absolute convictions that the subject inspires. One's philosophy, one's experiences, one's exposure to the raw edges of human existence, one's religious training, one's attitudes toward life and family and their values, and the moral standards one establishes and seeks to observe, are all likely to influence and to color one's thinking and conclusions about abortion.

In addition, population growth, pollution, poverty, and racial overtones tend to complicate and not to simplify the problem.

Our task, of course, is to resolve the issue by constitutional measurement, free of emotion and of predilection. We seek earnestly to do this, and, because we do, we have inquired into, and in this opinion place some emphasis upon, medical and medical-legal history and what that history reveals about man's attitudes toward the abortion procedure over the centuries. We bear in mind, too, Mr. Justice Holmes' admonition in his now-vindicated dissent in *Lochner v. New York*, 198 U.S. 45, 76 (1905):

> [The Constitution] is made for people of fundamentally differing views, and the accident of our finding certain opinions natural

and familiar or novel and even shocking ought not to conclude our judgment upon the question whether statutes embodying them conflict with the Constitution of the United States.

I

The Texas statutes . . . make it a crime to "procure an abortion," . . . or to attempt one, except with respect to "an abortion procured or attempted by medical advice for the purpose of saving the life of the mother." Similar statutes are in existence in a majority of the States.

Texas first enacted a criminal abortion statute in 1854. This was soon modified into language that has remained substantially unchanged to the present time. . . .

II

Jane Roe,[4] a single woman who was residing in Dallas County, Texas, instituted this federal action in March 1970 against the District Attorney of the county. She sought a declaratory judgment that the Texas criminal abortion statutes were unconstitutional on their face, and an injunction restraining the defendant from enforcing the statutes.

Roe alleged that she was unmarried and pregnant; that she wished to terminate her pregnancy by an abortion "performed by a competent, licensed physician, under safe, clinical conditions"; that she was unable to get a "legal" abortion in Texas because her life did not appear to be threatened by the continuation of her pregnancy; and that she could not afford to travel to another jurisdiction in order to secure a legal abortion under safe conditions. She claimed that the Texas statutes were unconstitutionally vague and that they abridged her right of personal privacy, protected by the First, Fourth, Fifth, Ninth, and Fourteenth Amendments. By an amendment to her complaint Roe purported to sue "on behalf of herself and all other women" similarly situated. . . .

V

The principal thrust of appellant's attack on the Texas statutes is that they improperly invade a right, said to be possessed by the pregnant woman, to choose to terminate her pregnancy. Appellant would discover this right in the concept of personal "liberty" embodied in the Fourteenth Amendment's Due Process Clause; or in personal, marital, familial, and sexual privacy said to be protected by the Bill of Rights or its penumbras, see *Griswold v. Connecticut*, 381 U.S. 479 (1965); *Eisenstadt v. Baird*, 405 U.S. 438 (1972); or among those rights reserved to the people by the Ninth Amendment, *Griswold v. Connecticut*, 381 U.S., at 486 (Goldberg, J., concurring). Before addressing this claim, we feel it desirable briefly to survey, in several aspects, the history of abortion, for such insight as that history may afford us, and then to examine the state purposes and interests behind the criminal abortion laws.

---

[4]   The name is a pseudonym.

VI

It perhaps is not generally appreciated that the restrictive criminal abortion laws in effect in a majority of States today are of relatively recent vintage. Those laws, generally proscribing abortion or its attempt at any time during pregnancy except when necessary to preserve the pregnant woman's life, are not of ancient or even of common-law origin. Instead, they derive from statutory changes effected, for the most part, in the latter half of the 19th century.

1. *Ancient attitudes.* These are not capable of precise determination. We are told that at the time of the Persian Empire abortifacients were known and that criminal abortions were severely punished. We are also told, however, that abortion was practiced in Greek times as well as in the Roman Era, and that "it was resorted to without scruple." . . .

3. *The common law.* It is undisputed that at common law, abortion performed *before* "quickening"—the first recognizable movement of the fetus *in utero*, appearing usually from the 16th to the 18th week of pregnancy—was not an indictable offense. . . .

Whether abortion of a *quick* fetus was a felony at common law, or even a lesser crime, is still disputed. . . .

4. *The English statutory law.* England's first criminal abortion statute, Lord Ellenborough's Act, came in 1803. It made abortion of a quick fetus, § 1, a capital crime, but in § 2 it provided lesser penalties for the felony of abortion before quickening, and thus preserved the "quickening" distinction. . . . It disappeared, however, together with the death penalty, in 1837, and did not reappear in the Offenses Against the Person Act of 1861 that formed the core of English anti-abortion law until the liberalizing reforms of 1967. In 1929, the Infant Life (Preservation) Act came into being. Its emphasis was upon the destruction of "the life of a child capable of being born alive." It made a willful act performed with the necessary intent a felony. It contained a proviso that one was not to be found guilty of the offense "unless it is proved that the act which caused the death of the child was not done in good faith for the purpose only of preserving the life of the mother." . . .

Recently, Parliament enacted a new abortion law. This is the Abortion Act of 1967. The Act permits a licensed physician to perform an abortion where two other licensed physicians agree (a) "that the continuance of the pregnancy would involve risk to the life of the pregnant woman, or of injury to the physical or mental health of the pregnant woman or any existing children of her family, greater than if the pregnancy were terminated," or (b) "that there is a substantial risk that if the child were born it would suffer from such physical or mental abnormalities as to be seriously handicapped." The Act also provides that, in making this determination, "account may be taken of the pregnant woman's actual or reasonably foreseeable environment." It also permits a physician, without the concurrence of others, to terminate a pregnancy where he is of the good-faith opinion that the abortion "is immediately necessary to save the life or to prevent grave permanent injury to the physical or mental health of the pregnant woman."

5.   *The American law.* In this country, the law in effect in all but a few States until mid-19th century was the pre-existing English common law. . . . It was not until after the War Between the States that legislation began generally to replace the common law. Most of these initial statutes dealt severely with abortion after quickening but were lenient with it before quickening. Most punished attempts equally with completed abortions. While many statutes included the exception for an abortion thought by one or more physicians to be necessary to save the mother's life, that provision soon disappeared and the typical law required that the procedure actually be necessary for that purpose.

Gradually, in the middle and late 19th century the quickening distinction disappeared from the statutory law of most States and the degree of the offense and the penalties were increased. By the end of the 1950's, a large majority of the jurisdictions banned abortion, however and whenever performed, unless done to save or preserve the life of the mother. The exceptions, Alabama and the District of Columbia, permitted abortion to preserve the mother's health. Three States permitted abortions that were not "unlawfully" performed or that were not "without lawful justification," leaving interpretation of those standards to the courts. In the past several years, however, a trend toward liberalization of abortion statutes has resulted in adoption, by about one-third of the States, of less stringent laws. . . .

It is thus apparent that at common law, at the time of the adoption of our Constitution, and throughout the major portion of the 19th century, abortion was viewed with less disfavor than under most American statutes currently in effect. Phrasing it another way, a woman enjoyed a substantially broader right to terminate a pregnancy than she does in most States today. At least with respect to the early stage of pregnancy, and very possibly without such a limitation, the opportunity to make this choice was present in this country well into the 19th century. Even later, the law continued for some time to treat less punitively an abortion procured in early pregnancy.

6.   *The position of the American Medical Association.* The anti-abortion mood prevalent in this country in the late 19th century was shared by the medical profession. Indeed, the attitude of the profession may have played a significant role in the enactment of stringent criminal abortion legislation during that period. . . .

In 1970, after the introduction of a variety of proposed resolutions, and of a report from its Board of Trustees, a reference committee noted "polarization of the medical profession on this controversial issue"; division among those who had testified; a difference of opinion among AMA councils and committees; "the remarkable shift in testimony" in six months, felt to be influenced "by the rapid changes in state laws and by the judicial decisions which tend to make abortion more freely available"; and a feeling "that this trend will continue." On June 25, 1970, the House of Delegates adopted preambles and most of the resolutions proposed by the reference committee. The preambles emphasized "the best interests of the patient," "sound clinical judgment," and "informed patient consent," in contrast to "mere acquiescence to the patient's demand." The resolutions asserted that abortion is a medical procedure that should be performed by a licensed physician in an accredited hospital only after consultation with two other physicians and in conformity with state law, and that no party to the procedure should be required to violate personally held moral principles. Proceedings of the AMA House of Delegates 220 (June 1970). The AMA Judicial Council rendered a complementary opinion.

7. *The position of the American Public Health Association.* In October 1970, the Executive Board of the APHA adopted Standards for Abortion Services. These were five in number:

a. Rapid and simple abortion referral must be readily available through state and local public health departments, medical societies, or other nonprofit organizations.

b. An important function of counseling should be to simplify and expedite the provision of abortion services; it should not delay the obtaining of these services.

c. Psychiatric consultation should not be mandatory. As in the case of other specialized medical services, psychiatric consultation should be sought for definite indications and not on a routine basis.

d. A wide range of individuals from appropriately trained, sympathetic volunteers to highly skilled physicians may qualify as abortion counselors.

e. Contraception and/or sterilization should be discussed with each abortion patient. Recommended Standards for Abortion Services, 61 Am. J. Pub. Health 396 (1971).

Among factors pertinent to life and health risks associated with abortion were three that "are recognized as important":

a. the skill of the physician,

b. the environment in which the abortion is performed, and above all

c. the duration of pregnancy, as determined by uterine size and confirmed by menstrual history. *Id.,* at 397. . . .

8. *The position of the American Bar Association.* At its meeting in February 1972 the ABA House of Delegates approved, with 17 opposing votes, the Uniform Abortion Act that had been drafted and approved the preceding August by the Conference of Commissioners on Uniform State

Laws. We set forth the Act in full in the margin.[40] The Conference has appended an enlightening Prefatory Note.[41]

VII

Three reasons have been advanced to explain historically the enactment of criminal abortion laws in the 19th century and to justify their continued existence.

It has been argued occasionally that these laws were the product of a Victorian social concern to discourage illicit sexual conduct. Texas, however, does not advance this justification in the present case, and it appears that no court or commentator has taken the argument seriously. The appellants and *amici* contend, moreover, that this is not a proper state purpose at all and suggest that, if it were, the Texas statutes are overbroad in protecting it since the law fails to distinguish between married and unwed mothers.

A second reason is concerned with abortion as a medical procedure. When most criminal abortion laws were first enacted, the procedure was a hazardous one for the woman. This was particularly true prior to the development of antisepsis. Antiseptic techniques, of course, were based on discoveries by Lister, Pasteur, and others first announced in 1867, but were not generally accepted and employed until about the turn of the century. Abortion mortality was high. Even after 1900, and perhaps until as late as the development of antibiotics in the 1940's, standard modern techniques such as dilation and curettage were not nearly so safe as they are today. Thus, it has been argued that a State's real concern in enacting a criminal abortion law was to protect the pregnant woman, that is, to

---

[40] UNIFORM ABORTION ACT

SECTION 1. [Abortion Defined; When Authorized.]

"(a) 'Abortion' means the termination of human pregnancy with an intention other than to produce a live birth or to remove a dead fetus.

"(b) An abortion may be performed in this state only if it is performed:

"(1) by a physician licensed to practice medicine [or osteopathy] in this state or by a physician practicing medicine [or osteopathy] in the employ of the government of the United States or of this state, [and the abortion is performed [in the physician's office or in a medical clinic, or] in a hospital approved by the [Department of Health] or operated by the United States, this state, or any department, agency, or political subdivision of either;] or by a female upon herself upon the advice of the physician; and

"(2) within [20] weeks after the commencement of the pregnancy [or after [20] weeks only if the physician has reasonable cause to believe (i) there is a substantial risk that continuance of the pregnancy would endanger the life of the mother or would gravely impair the physical or mental health of the mother, (ii) that the child would be born with grave physical or mental defect, or (iii) that the pregnancy resulted from rape or incest, or illicit intercourse with a girl under the age of 16 years].

"SECTION 2. [*Penalty.*] Any person who performs or procures an abortion other than authorized by this Act is guilty of a [felony] and, upon conviction thereof, may be sentenced to pay a fine not exceeding [$1,000] or to imprisonment [in the state penitentiary] not exceeding [5 years], or both." . . .

[41] "This Act is based largely upon the New York abortion act following a review of the more recent laws on abortion in several states and upon recognition of a more liberal trend in laws on this subject. Recognition was given also to the several decisions in state and federal courts which show a further trend toward liberalization of abortion laws, especially during the first trimester of pregnancy."

restrain her from submitting to a procedure that placed her life in serious jeopardy.

Modern medical techniques have altered this situation. Appellants and various *amici* refer to medical data indicating that abortion in early pregnancy, that is, prior to the end of the first trimester, although not without its risk, is now relatively safe. Mortality rates for women undergoing early abortions, where the procedure is legal, appear to be as low as or lower than the rates for normal childbirth. Consequently, any interest of the State in protecting the woman from an inherently hazardous procedure, except when it would be equally dangerous for her to forgo it, has largely disappeared. Of course, important state interests in the areas of health and medical standards do remain. The State has a legitimate interest in seeing to it that abortion, like any other medical procedure, is performed under circumstances that insure maximum safety for the patient. This interest obviously extends at least to the performing physician and his staff, to the facilities involved, to the availability of after-care, and to adequate provision for any complication or emergency that might arise. The prevalence of high mortality rates at illegal "abortion mills" strengthens, rather than weakens, the State's interest in regulating the conditions under which abortions are performed. Moreover, the risk to the woman increases as her pregnancy continues. Thus, the State retains a definite interest in protecting the woman's own health and safety when an abortion is proposed at a late stage of pregnancy.

The third reason is the State's interest—some phrase it in terms of duty—in protecting prenatal life. Some of the argument for this justification rests on the theory that a new human life is present from the moment of conception. The State's interest and general obligation to protect life then extends, it is argued, to prenatal life. Only when the life of the pregnant mother herself is at stake, balanced against the life she carries within her, should the interest of the embryo or fetus not prevail. Logically, of course, a legitimate state interest in this area need not stand or fall on acceptance of the belief that life begins at conception or at some other point prior to live birth. In assessing the State's interest, recognition may be given to the less rigid claim that as long as at least *potential* life is involved, the State may assert interests beyond the protection of the pregnant woman alone. . . .

It is with these interests, and the weight to be attached to them, that this case is concerned.

VIII

The Constitution does not explicitly mention any right of privacy. In a line of decisions, however, going back perhaps as far as *Union Pacific R. Co. v. Botsford*, 141 U.S. 250 (1891), the Court has recognized that a right of personal privacy, or a guarantee of certain areas or zones of privacy, does exist under the Constitution. In varying contexts, the Court or individual Justices have, indeed, found at least the roots of that right in the First Amendment, *Stanley v. Georgia*, 394 U.S. 557 (1969); in the Fourth and Fifth Amendments, *Terry v. Ohio*, 392 U.S. 1 (1968), *Katz v. United* States, 389 U.S. 347 (1967), *Boyd v. United States*, 116 U.S. 616 (1886), see *Olmstead v. United States*, 277 U.S. 438 (1928) (Brandeis, J., dissenting); in the penumbras of the Bill of Rights, *Griswold v. Connecticut*; in the Ninth Amendment, *id.* (Goldberg, J., concurring); or in the concept of liberty guaranteed by the first section of the Fourteenth Amendment, see *Meyer v. Nebraska*, 262 U.S. 390 (1923). These decisions make it clear that only personal rights that can be deemed "fundamental" or "implicit in the concept of ordered liberty," *Palko v. Connecticut*, 302 U.S. 319 (1937), are included in this guarantee of personal privacy. They also make it clear that the right has some extension to activities relating to marriage, *Loving v. Virginia*, 388 U.S. 1 (1967); procreation, *Skinner v. Oklahoma*, 316 U.S. 535 (1942); contraception, *Eisenstadt v. Baird*; family relationships, *Prince v. Massachusetts*, 321 U.S. 158 (1944); and child rearing and education, *Pierce v. Society of Sisters*, 268 U.S. 510 (1925), *Meyer v. Nebraska, supra.*

This right of privacy, whether it be founded in the Fourteenth Amendment's concept of personal liberty and restrictions upon state action, as we feel it is, or, as the District Court determined, in the Ninth Amendment's reservation of rights to the people, is broad enough to encompass a woman's decision whether or not to terminate her pregnancy. The detriment that the State would impose upon the pregnant woman by denying this choice altogether is apparent. Specific and direct harm medically diagnosable even in early pregnancy may be involved. Maternity, or additional offspring, may force upon the woman a distressful life and future. Psychological harm may be imminent. Mental and physical health may be taxed by child care. There is also the distress, for all concerned, associated with the unwanted child, and there is the problem of bringing a child into a family already unable, psychologically and otherwise, to care for it. In other cases, as in this one, the additional difficulties and continuing stigma of unwed motherhood may be involved. All these are factors the woman and her responsible physician necessarily will consider in consultation.

On the basis of elements such as these, appellant and some *amici* argue that the woman's right is absolute and that she is entitled to terminate her pregnancy at whatever time, in whatever way, and for whatever reason she alone chooses. With this we do not agree. Appellant's arguments that Texas either has no valid interest at all in regulating the abortion decision, or no interest strong enough to support any limitation upon the woman's sole determination, are unpersuasive. The Court's decisions recognizing a right of privacy also acknowledge that some state regulation in areas protected by that right is appropriate. As noted above, a State may properly assert important interests in safeguarding health, in maintaining medical standards, and in protecting potential life. At some point in pregnancy, these respective interests become sufficiently compelling to sustain regulation of the factors that govern the abortion decision. The privacy right involved, therefore, cannot be said to be absolute. In fact, it is not clear to us that the claim asserted by some *amici* that one has an unlimited right to do with one's body as one pleases bears a close relationship to the right of privacy previously articulated in the Court's decisions. The Court has refused to recognize an unlimited right of this kind in the past. *Jacobson v. Massachusetts*, 197 U.S. 11 (1905) (vaccination); *Buck v. Bell*, 274 U.S. 200 (1927) (sterilization).

We, therefore, conclude that the right of personal privacy includes the abortion decision, but that this right is not unqualified and must be considered against important state interests in regulation. . . .

Where certain "fundamental rights" are involved, the Court has held that regulation limiting these rights may be justified only by a "compelling state interest," and that legislative enactments must be narrowly drawn to express only the legitimate state interests at stake. *Griswold v. Connecticut*, 381 U.S., at 485. . . .

IX

. . . A. The appellee and certain *amici* argue that the fetus is a "person" within the language and meaning of the Fourteenth Amendment. . . . If this suggestion of personhood is established, the appellant's case, of course, collapses, for the fetus' right to life would then be guaranteed specifically by the Amendment. The appellant conceded as much on reargument. On the other hand, the appellee conceded on reargument that no case could be cited that holds that a fetus is a person within the meaning of the Fourteenth Amendment.

The Constitution does not define "person" in so many words. Section 1 of the Fourteenth Amendment contains three references to "person." The first, in defining "citizens," speaks of "persons born or naturalized in the United States." The word also appears both in the Due Process Clause and in the Equal Protection Clause. "Person" is used in other places in the Constitution: in the listing of qualifications for Representatives and Senators, Art. I, § 2, cl. 2, and § 3, cl. 3; in the Apportionment Clause, Art. I, § 2, cl. 3;[53] in the Migration and Importation provision, Art. I, § 9, cl. 1; in the Emolument Clause, Art. I, § 9, cl. 8; in the Electors provisions, Art. II, § 1, cl. 2, and the superseded cl. 3; in the provision outlining qualifications for the office of President, Art. II, § 1, cl. 5; in the Extradition provisions, Art. IV, § 2, cl. 2, and the superseded Fugitive Slave Clause 3; and in the Fifth, Twelfth, and Twenty-second Amendments, as well as in §§ 2 and 3 of the Fourteenth Amendment. But in nearly all these instances, the use of the word is such that it has application only postnatally. None indicates, with any assurance, that it has any possible pre-natal application.

---

[53] We are not aware that in the taking of any census under this clause, a fetus has ever been counted.

All this, together with our observation, *supra*, that throughout the major portion of the 19th century prevailing legal abortion practices were far freer than they are today, persuades us that the word "person," as used in the Fourteenth Amendment, does not include the unborn. . . .

B. The pregnant woman cannot be isolated in her privacy. She carries an embryo and, later, a fetus. . . . The situation therefore is inherently different from marital intimacy, or bedroom possession of obscene material, or marriage, or procreation, or education, with which *Eisenstadt* and *Griswold, Stanley, Loving, Skinner*, and *Pierce* and *Meyer* were respectively concerned. As we have intimated above, it is reasonable and appropriate for a State to decide that at some point in time another interest, that of health of the mother or that of potential human life, becomes significantly involved. The woman's privacy is no longer sole and any right of privacy she possesses must be measured accordingly.

Texas urges that, apart from the Fourteenth Amendment, life begins at conception and is present throughout pregnancy, and that, therefore, the State has a compelling interest in protecting that life from and after conception. We need not resolve the difficult question of when life begins. When those trained in the respective disciplines of medicine, philosophy, and theology are unable to arrive at any consensus, the judiciary, at this point in the development of man's knowledge, is not in a position to speculate as to the answer.

It should be sufficient to note briefly the wide divergence of thinking on this most sensitive and difficult question. There has always been strong support for the view that life does not begin until live birth. This was the belief of the Stoics. It appears to be the predominant, though not the unanimous, attitude of the Jewish faith. It may be taken to represent also the position of a large segment of the Protestant community, insofar as that can be ascertained; organized groups that have taken a formal position on the abortion issue have generally regarded abortion as a matter for the conscience of the individual and her family. As we have noted, the common law found greater significance in quickening. Physicians and their scientific colleagues have regarded that event with less interest and have tended to focus either upon conception, upon live birth, or upon the interim point at which the fetus becomes "viable," that is, potentially able to live outside the mother's womb, albeit with artificial aid. Viability is usually placed at about seven months (28 weeks) but may occur earlier, even at 24 weeks. The Aristotelian theory of "mediate animation," that held sway throughout the Middle Ages and the Renaissance in Europe, continued to be official Roman Catholic dogma until the 19th century, despite opposition to this "ensoulment" theory from those in the Church who would recognize the existence of life from the moment of conception. The latter is now, of course, the official belief of the Catholic Church. As one brief *amicus* discloses, this is a view strongly held by many non-Catholics as well, and by many physicians. Substantial problems for precise definition of this view are posed, however, by new embryological data that purport to indicate that conception is a "process" over time, rather than an event, and by new medical techniques such as menstrual extraction, the "morning-after" pill, implantation of embryos, artificial insemination, and even artificial wombs.

In areas other than criminal abortion, the law has been reluctant to endorse any theory that life, as we recognize it, begins before live birth or to accord legal rights to the unborn except in narrowly defined situations and except when the rights are contingent upon live birth. For example, the traditional rule of tort law denied recovery for prenatal injuries even though the child was born alive. That rule has been changed in almost every jurisdiction. In most States, recovery is said to be permitted only if the fetus was viable, or at least quick, when the injuries were sustained, though few courts have squarely so held. In a recent development, generally opposed by the commentators, some States permit the parents of a stillborn child to maintain an action for wrongful death because of prenatal injuries. Such an action, however, would appear to be one to vindicate the parents' interest and is thus consistent with the view that the fetus, at most, represents only the potentiality of life. Similarly, unborn children have been recognized as acquiring rights or interests by way of inheritance or other devolution of property, and have been represented by guardians *ad litem*. Perfection of the interests involved, again, has generally been contingent upon live birth. In short, the unborn have never been recognized in the law as persons in the whole sense.

X

In view of all this, we do not agree that, by adopting one theory of life, Texas may override the rights of the pregnant woman that are at stake. We repeat, however, that the State does have an important and legitimate interest in preserving and protecting the health of the pregnant woman, whether she be a resident of the State or a nonresident who seeks medical consultation and treatment there, and that it has still *another* important and legitimate interest in protecting the potentiality of human life. These interests are separate and distinct. Each grows in substantiality as the woman approaches term and, at a point during pregnancy, each becomes "compelling."

With respect to the State's important and legitimate interest in the health of the mother, the "compelling" point, in the light of present medical knowledge, is at approximately the end of the first trimester. This is so because of the now-established medical fact . . . that until the end of the first trimester mortality in abortion may be less than mortality in normal childbirth. It follows that, from and after this point, a State may regulate the abortion procedure to the extent that the regulation reasonably relates to the preservation and protection of maternal health. Examples of permissible state regulation in this area are requirements as to the qualifications of the person who is to perform the abortion; as to the licensure of that person; as to the facility in which the procedure is to be performed, that is, whether it must be a hospital or may be a clinic or some other place of less-than-hospital status; as to the licensing of the facility; and the like.

This means, on the other hand, that, for the period of pregnancy prior to this "compelling" point, the attending physician, in consultation with his patient, is free to determine, without regulation by the State, that, in his medical judgment, the patient's pregnancy should be terminated. If that decision is reached, the judgment may be effectuated by an abortion free of interference by the State.

With respect to the State's important and legitimate interest in potential life, the "compelling" point is at viability. This is so because the fetus then presumably has the capability of meaningful life outside the mother's womb. State regulation protective of fetal life after viability thus has both logical and biological justifications. If the State is interested in protecting fetal life after viability, it may go so far as to proscribe abortion during that period, except when it is necessary to preserve the life or health of the mother.

Measured against these standards, Art. 1196 of the Texas Penal Code, in restricting legal abortions to those "procured or attempted by medical advice for the purpose of saving the life of the mother," sweeps too broadly. The statute makes no distinction between abortions performed early in pregnancy and those performed later, and it limits to a single reason, "saving" the mother's life, the legal justification for the procedure. The statute, therefore, cannot survive the constitutional attack made upon it here. . . .[67]

XI

. . . This holding, we feel, is consistent with the relative weights of the respective interests involved, with the lessons and examples of medical and legal history, with the lenity of the common law, and with the demands of the profound problems of the present day. The decision leaves the State free to place increasing restrictions on abortion as the period of pregnancy lengthens, so long as those restrictions are tailored to the recognized state interests. The decision vindicates the right of the physician to administer medical treatment according to his professional judgment up to the points where important state interests provide compelling justifications for intervention. Up to those points, the abortion decision in all its aspects is inherently, and primarily, a medical decision, and basic responsibility for it must rest with the physician. If an

---

[67] Neither in this opinion nor in *Doe v. Bolton,* do we discuss the father's rights, if any exist in the constitutional context, in the abortion decision. No paternal right has been asserted in either of the cases, and the Texas and the Georgia statutes on their face take no cognizance of the father. We are aware that some statutes recognize the father under certain circumstances. North Carolina, for example, requires written permission for the abortion from the husband when the woman is a married minor, that is, when she is less than 18 years of age; if the woman is an unmarried minor, written permission from the parents is required. We need not now decide whether provisions of this kind are constitutional. [relocated footnote]

individual practitioner abuses the privilege of exercising proper medical judgment, the usual remedies, judicial and intra-professional, are available. . . .

■ **MR. JUSTICE REHNQUIST, dissenting.**

II

. . . I have difficulty in concluding, as the Court does, that the right of "privacy" is involved in this case. Texas, by the statute here challenged, bars the performance of a medical abortion by a licensed physician on a plaintiff such as Roe. A transaction resulting in an operation such as this is not "private" in the ordinary usage of that word. Nor is the "privacy" that the Court finds here even a distant relative of the freedom from searches and seizures protected by the Fourth Amendment to the Constitution, which the Court has referred to as embodying a right to privacy.

If the Court means by the term "privacy" no more than that the claim of a person to be free from unwanted state regulation of consensual transactions may be a form of "liberty" protected by the Fourteenth Amendment, there is no doubt that similar claims have been upheld in our earlier decisions on the basis of that liberty. I agree with the statement of MR. JUSTICE STEWART in his concurring opinion that the "liberty," against deprivation of which without due process the Fourteenth Amendment protects, embraces more than the rights found in the Bill of Rights. But that liberty is not guaranteed absolutely against deprivation, only against deprivation without due process of law. The test traditionally applied in the area of social and economic legislation is whether or not a law such as that challenged has a rational relation to a valid state objective. *Williamson v. Lee Optical Inc.*, 348 U.S. 483 (1955). The Due Process Clause of the Fourteenth Amendment undoubtedly does place a limit, albeit a broad one, on legislative power to enact laws such as this. If the Texas statute were to prohibit an abortion even where the mother's life is in jeopardy, I have little doubt that such a statute would lack a rational relation to a valid state objective under the test stated in *Williamson, supra.* But the Court's sweeping invalidation of any restrictions on abortion during the first trimester is impossible to justify under that standard, and the conscious weighing of competing factors that the Court's opinion apparently substitutes for the established test is far more appropriate to a legislative judgment than to a judicial one. . . .

While the Court's opinion quotes from the dissent of Mr. Justice Holmes in *Lochner v. New York*, 198 U.S. 45 (1905), the result it reaches is more closely attuned to the majority opinion of Mr. Justice Peckham in that case. As in *Lochner* and similar cases applying substantive due process standards to economic and social welfare legislation, the adoption of the compelling state interest standard will inevitably require this Court to examine the legislative policies and pass on the wisdom of these policies in the very process of deciding whether a particular state interest put forward may or may not be "compelling." The decision here to break pregnancy into three distinct terms and to outline the permissible restrictions the State may impose in each one, for example, partakes more of judicial legislation than it does of a determination of the intent of the drafters of the Fourteenth Amendment.

The fact that a majority of the States reflecting, after all, the majority sentiment in those States, have had restrictions on abortions for at least a century is a strong indication, it seems to me, that the asserted right to an abortion is not "so rooted in the traditions and conscience of our people as to be ranked as fundamental," *Snyder v. Massachusetts*, 291 U.S. 97 (1934). Even today, when society's views on abortion are changing, the very existence of the debate is evidence that the "right" to an abortion is not so universally accepted as the appellant would have us believe.

To reach its result, the Court necessarily has had to find within the scope of the Fourteenth Amendment a right that was apparently completely unknown to the drafters of the Amendment. As early as 1821, the first state law dealing directly with abortion was enacted by the Connecticut Legislature. By the time of the adoption of the Fourteenth Amendment in 1868, there were at least 36 laws enacted by state or territorial legislatures limiting abortion. While many States have amended or updated their laws, 21 of the laws on the books in 1868 remain in effect today. Indeed, the Texas statute struck down today was, as the majority notes, first enacted in 1857 and "has remained substantially unchanged to the present time."

There apparently was no question concerning the validity of this provision or of any of the other state statutes when the Fourteenth Amendment was adopted. The only conclusion possible from this history is that the drafters did not intend to have the Fourteenth Amendment withdraw from the States the power to legislate with respect to this matter. . . .

For all of the foregoing reasons, I respectfully dissent.

NOTE ON *ROE V. WADE* AND THE "LIVING CONSTITUTION"

1.   How does Justice Blackmun go about justifying the abortion right recognized in *Roe*? How does his reasoning compare to the different approaches in *Griswold*? Does *Roe* follow from *Griswold*? From *Eisenstadt*? Consider the following argument from John Hart Ely:

> [The] Court in *Griswold* stressed that it was invalidating only that portion of the Connecticut law that proscribed the use, as opposed to the manufacture, sale, or other distribution of contraceptives. That distinction [makes] sense [only] if the case is rationalized on the ground that [enforcement of the challenged provision] *would have been virtually impossible without* the most outrageous sort of governmental prying into the privacy of the home. [No] such

rationalization is [possible in *Roe*], for whatever else may be involved, it is not a case about governmental snooping.[20]

Do you agree that there is no real "privacy" interest at stake in Roe? Does *Roe* fit into the categories justifying close judicial scrutiny in the famous *Carolene Products* footnote?

2.   What is the import of Justice Blackmun's extensive canvass of the historical background of abortion regulation? Which way does this material cut? And how relevant should the positions of the American Medical Association and the American Bar Association be?

3.   The woman's right to choose in *Roe* raises similar questions to the right of contraception in *Griswold* and *Eisenstadt*: It is an unenumerated right, and it does not fit all that easily into traditional legal protections. But what makes *Roe* much harder is a second question: Even assuming that the pregnant woman has a strong privacy right, doesn't the State have a strong interest in protecting the unborn child? How does Justice Blackmun deal with that question? Is his reasoning persuasive?

4.   Does the *Roe* Court really remain agnostic on when life begins? Can it avoid that question in deciding the case? The Court at least has to decide, doesn't it, when a "person" acquires a right to "life" within the meaning of the Due Process Clause of the Fourteenth Amendment? Do you find Justice Blackmun's discussion of that issue persuasive?

Some commentators have maintained that the woman's right to choose should prevail even if we assume the fetus is a full-fledged person. The philosopher Judith Jarvis Thomson proposed a famous thought experiment involving an "unconscious violinist."[21] Basically, imagine that you wake up to find yourself strapped to a hospital bed and connected through various tubes and medical apparatus to an unconscious man in the next bed. It turns out that the man is a world-famous violinist with a life-threatening condition, and the only way to save him is to connect him to a healthy person. You've been kidnapped by a band of music lovers and impressed into this service. Do you have a right to pull the plug?

Professor Thomson thought the answer was clearly yes, notwithstanding that the violinist is plainly a full-fledged person. Her hypothetical powerfully illustrates the proposition that no person has a moral obligation to keep another person alive by sacrificing their own autonomy. If you agree, does the argument work best for involuntary pregnancies, such as those resulting from rape or incest? And is there a distinction between letting the violinist die and affirmatively killing a fetus through the abortion procedure? In any event, is Thomson's principle of autonomy best employed as a moral argument addressed to a legislature or as an interpretation of the Due Process Clause of the Fourteenth Amendment?

---

[20]   John Hart Ely, *The Wages of Crying Wolf: A Comment on* Roe v. Wade, 82 YALE L.J. 920, 930 (1973).

[21]   Judith Jarvis Thomson, *A Defense of Abortion*, 1 PHIL. & PUBLIC AFFAIRS 47 (Autumn 1971).

5.   The Court sets out the following framework for permissible abortion regulation:

- First Trimester: No regulation, period.

- Second Trimester: States may regulate abortion procedures in ways that are reasonably related to maternal health.

- Third Trimester: State may regulate or forbid abortion except when necessary to preserve the life or health of the mother.

Where does this framework come from? Does it strike you as more like a statute than a test for abortion regulation derived from the Constitution? Is it flexible enough to stand up to advances in medical technology and practice over time?

6.   Some scholars, particularly then-Professor Ruth Bader Ginsburg, have argued that *Roe* should have been grounded in the Equal Protection Clause—as protecting gender equality—rather than the Due Process Clause. Professor Laurence Tribe, for example, has argued that

> [A]lthough current law nowhere forces *men* to sacrifice their bodies and restructure their lives even in those tragic situations . . . where nothing less will permit their children to survive, those who would outlaw abortion . . . would rely upon . . . physiological circumstances . . . to conscript women . . . as involuntary incubators. . . . [A] right to end pregnancy might be seen more plausibly as a matter of resisting sexual . . . domination than as a matter of shielding from public control "private" transactions between patients and physicians.[22]

Is this a better rationale for abortion rights? Are women really similarly situated to men with respect to pregnancy? Would relying on an equality argument allow the Court to avoid the problem of the fetus's status? Would deriving the woman's right to choose from principles of equality make it any easier to weigh that right against the state's interest in protecting unborn life?

A related problem may lurk in the assumption that the only relevant discrimination in *Roe* is between women and men. Consider Professor Ely's argument that this is not the case:

> Compared with men, very few women sit in our legislatures, a fact I believe should bear some relevance . . . to the appropriate standard of review for legislation that favors men over women. But no fetuses sit in our legislatures. Of course they have their champions, but so have women. . . . [I]t is at least arguable that, constitutional directive or not, the Court should throw its weight on the side of a minority demanding in court more than it was able to achieve politically. But [this] should be reserved for those interests which, as compared with the interests to which they have been subordinated, constitute minorities unusually incapable of protecting themselves. Compared with men, women

---

[22]   LAURENCE TRIBE, CONSTITUTIONAL CHOICES 243 (1985).

may constitute such a "minority"; compared with the unborn, they do not. I'm not sure I'd know a discrete and insular minority if I saw one, but confronted with a multiple choice question requiring me to designate (a) women or (b) fetuses as one, I'd expect no credit for the former answer.[23]

Ely's argument suggests that an equality-based argument works only if we reject the notion *Roe*'s recognition of a right to an abortion itself subjects fetuses to discrimination. Does that mean one can justify *Roe* on equality grounds only if one has already concluded that the fetus is not a person?

7. One of the most influential defenses of the expansive model of judicial review in *Roe* and *Griswold* is Thomas Grey's article, *Do We Have an Unwritten Constitution?*[24] Professor Grey argued that in most major constitutional cases, "reference to and analysis of the constitutional text plays a minor role. The dominant norms of decision are those large conceptions of governmental structure and individual rights that are at best referred to, and whose content is scarcely at all specified, in the written Constitution—dual federalism, vested rights, fair procedure, equality before the law." For Grey, "[t]he broad textual provisions . . . sources of legitimacy for judicial development and explication of basic shared national values":

> These values may be seen as permanent and universal features of human social arrangements—natural law principles—as they typically were in the 18th and 19th centuries. Or they may be seen as relative to our particular civilization, and subject to growth and change, as they typically are today. Our characteristic contemporary metaphor is "the living Constitution"—a constitution with provisions suggesting restraints on government in the name of basic rights, yet sufficiently unspecific to permit the judiciary to elucidate the development and change in the content of those rights over time.

This "living Constitution," Grey thought, had a solid grounding in the original understanding of the Constitution and the development of judicial review:

> For the generation that framed the Constitution, the concept of a "higher law," protecting "natural rights," and taking precedence over ordinary positive law as a matter of political obligation, was widely shared and deeply felt. An essential element of American constitutionalism was the reduction to written form— and hence to positive law—of some of the principles of natural rights. But at the same time, it was generally recognized that written Constitution could not completely codify the higher law. Thus in the framing of the original American constitutions it was widely accepted that there remained unwritten but still binding principles of higher law. The ninth amendment is the textual expression of this idea in the federal Constitution.

---

[23] Ely, *Crying Wolf, supra* note 20, at 933–35.
[24] 27 STAN. L. REV. 703 (1975).

As it came to be accepted that the judiciary had the power to enforce the commands of the written Constitution when these conflicted with ordinary law, it was also widely assumed that judges would enforce as constitutional restraints the unwritten natural rights as well. The practice of the Marshall Court and of many of its contemporary state courts, and the writings of the leading constitutional commentators through the first generation of our national life, confirm this understanding.

A parallel development during the first half of the 19th century was the frequent attachment of unwritten constitutional principles to the vaguer and more general clauses of the state and federal constitutions. Natural-rights reasoning in constitutional adjudication persisted up to the Civil War, particularly with respect to property and contract rights, and increasingly involving "due process" and "law of the land" clauses in constitutional texts. At the same time, an important wing of the antislavery movement developed a natural-rights constitutional theory, built around the concepts of due process, of national citizenship and its rights, and of the human equality proclaimed in the Declaration of Independence.

Though this latter movement had little direct effect on pre-Civil War judicial decisions, it was the formative theory underlying the due process, equal protection, and privileges and immunities clauses of the 14th amendment. Section I of the 14th amendment is thus properly seen as a reaffirmation and reenactment in positive law of the principle that fundamental human rights have constitutional status.

Although Grey acknowledged a backlash against unenumerated rights based on opposition to the *Lochner* Court, he rightly notes that other forms of expansive and atextual judicial review quickly became accepted after the New Deal, including the incorporation and privacy cases. He thus concluded that *Roe* "is the modern offspring, in a direct and traceable line of legitimate descent, of the natural-rights tradition that is so deeply embedded in our constitutional origins."

Do you find Professor Grey's argument persuasive? Should an originalist be for unenumerated rights?

8.   Professor Grey divided his "unwritten constitution" cases into three helpful categories:

First are those instances where the courts have created (or found) independent constitutional rights with almost no textual guidance. Examples are the contemporary right of privacy, and the older liberty of contract.

Second are those instances where the courts have given general application to norms that the constitutional text explicitly applies in a more limited way. Examples are the application of equal protection and contract clause principles to the federal government, and the application of the Bill of Rights to the states—"under" the conveniently all-embracing due process clauses.

The third type is the extension or broadening of principles stated in the Constitution beyond the normative content intended for them by the framers. Examples are the School Segregation Cases, and the extension of the fourth amendment to cover eavesdropping.[25]

As Grey noted, these categories are not equally controversial. Do they each raise the same legitimacy problems? Given the breadth of these categories, and their inclusion of such well-accepted notions as incorporation of the Bill of Rights against the States, isn't Grey correct that "an extraordinarily radical purge of established constitutional doctrine would be required if we candidly and consistently applied the pure [textualist/originalist] model"?

9.   Although Professor Grey acknowledged that "[a]rguments about institutional competence and the general propensities of judges" are relevant to assessing the unwritten constitution, his discussion—like most discussions of living constitutionalism—was notably fuzzy on the constraints guiding judges in identifying and cabining "unwritten" principles. Recall, for example, Justice Iredell's concern in *Calder v. Bull* that "[t]he ideas of natural justice are regulated by no fixed standard, [and] the ablest and the purest men have differed upon the subject."[26] How can a court reassure outside observers that it is engaged in law rather than politics when it discovers and expounds unwritten principles of a "living" constitution?

SECTION 7.3 ABORTION AND STARE DECISIS

Despite the dissent in *Roe*, the opinions in that case provided relatively little clue as to how divisive the abortion issue would become, both for the Court and for the nation. The next twenty years brought a steady stream of abortion cases to the Court. These cases generally did not challenge the abortion right directly, but rather involved important collateral issues. For example, *City of Akron v. Akron Center for Reproductive Health, Inc.*[27] challenged state regulation of the procedures and facilities involved in abortions, including requirements that information be provided to women seeking an abortion and mandatory waiting periods. The Court invalidated each of those provisions. *Planned Parenthood of Central Missouri v. Danforth*[28] invalidated a state statute requiring spousal consent to an abortion unless the procedure was necessary to protect the life of the mother. The Court also tackled the question of whether the Government has a constitutional obligation to *fund* abortions for poor persons, concluding that there was no such constitutional demand.[29] The opinions in these cases reflected a highly

---

[25] *Id.* at 713 n.46.

[26] 3 Dall. (3 U.S.) 386, 399 (1798).

[27] 462 U.S. 416 (1983).

[28] 428 U.S. 52 (1976).

[29] *See Harris v. McRae*, 448 U.S. 297 (1980).

divided court, some members of which remained committed to overruling *Roe* in its entirety.

Meanwhile, the confirmation process for new justices became dominated by the abortion issue. By the time *Casey* came to the Court, the Reagan and (first) Bush administrations had appointed five new justices to the Court—Sandra Day O'Connor, Antonin Scalia, Anthony Kennedy, David Souter, and Clarence Thomas—and most conservatives were counting on these new additions to swing the Court in favor of overruling *Roe*. *Casey* thus raised not only the issue of *Roe*'s correctness, but also the broader question of *stare decisis* in constitutional adjudication—that is, would a Court composed largely of justices who might not have recognized a fundamental right to abortion in the first place nonetheless adhere to *Roe* as an established precedent?

Planned Parenthood of Southeastern Pennsylvania v. Casey

505 U.S. 833 (1992)

■ **JUSTICE O'CONNOR, JUSTICE KENNEDY, and JUSTICE SOUTER announced the judgment of the Court and delivered the opinion of the Court with respect to Parts I, II, III, V–A, V–C, and VI, an opinion with respect to Part V–E, in which JUSTICE STEVENS joins, and an opinion with respect to Parts IV, V–B, and V–D.**

I

Liberty finds no refuge in a jurisprudence of doubt. Yet 19 years after our holding that the Constitution protects a woman's right to terminate her pregnancy in its early stages, *Roe v. Wade*, that definition of liberty is still questioned. Joining the respondents as *amicus curiae*, the United States, as it has done in five other cases in the last decade, again asks us to overrule *Roe*. . . .

At issue in these cases are five provisions of the Pennsylvania Abortion Control Act of 1982, as amended in 1988 and 1989. . . . The Act requires that a woman seeking an abortion give her informed consent prior to the abortion procedure, and specifies that she be provided with certain information at least 24 hours before the abortion is performed. For a minor to obtain an abortion, the Act requires the informed consent of one of her parents, but provides for a judicial bypass option if the minor does not wish to or cannot obtain a parent's consent. Another provision of the Act requires that, unless certain exceptions apply, a married woman seeking an abortion must sign a statement indicating that she has notified her husband of her intended abortion. The Act exempts compliance with these three requirements in the event of a "medical emergency". . . . In addition to the above provisions regulating the performance of abortions, the Act imposes certain reporting requirements on facilities that provide abortion services.

Before any of these provisions took effect, the petitioners, who are five abortion clinics and one physician representing himself as well as a class of physicians who provide abortion services, brought this suit seeking declaratory and injunctive relief. Each provision was challenged as unconstitutional on its face. The District Court entered a preliminary injunction against the enforcement of the regulations, and, after a 3-day bench trial, held all the provisions at issue here unconstitutional, entering a permanent injunction against Pennsylvania's enforcement of them. The Court of Appeals for the Third Circuit affirmed in part and reversed in part, upholding all of the regulations except for the husband notification requirement. We granted certiorari. . . .

After considering the fundamental constitutional questions resolved by *Roe*, principles of institutional integrity, and the rule of *stare decisis*, we are led to conclude this: the essential holding of *Roe v. Wade* should be retained and once again reaffirmed.

It must be stated at the outset and with clarity that *Roe's* essential holding, the holding we reaffirm, has three parts. First is a recognition of the right of the woman to choose to have an abortion before viability and to obtain it without undue interference from the State. Before viability, the State's interests are not strong enough to support a prohibition of abortion or the imposition of a substantial obstacle to the woman's effective right to elect the procedure. Second is a confirmation of the State's power to restrict abortions after fetal viability, if the law contains exceptions for pregnancies which endanger the woman's life or health. And third is the principle that the State has legitimate interests from the outset of the pregnancy in protecting the health of the woman and the life of the fetus that may become a child. These principles do not contradict one another; and we adhere to each.

II

Constitutional protection of the woman's decision to terminate her pregnancy derives from the Due Process Clause of the Fourteenth Amendment. It declares that no State shall "deprive any person of life, liberty, or property, without due process of law." The controlling word in the cases before us is "liberty." Although a literal reading of the Clause might suggest that it governs only the procedures by which a State may deprive persons of liberty, for at least 105 years, since *Mugler v. Kansas*, 123 U.S. 623 (1887), the Clause has been understood to contain a substantive component as well, one "barring certain government actions regardless of the fairness of the procedures used to implement them." As Justice Brandeis (joined by Justice Holmes) observed, "despite arguments to the contrary which had seemed to me persuasive, it is settled that the due process clause of the Fourteenth Amendment applies to matters of substantive law as well as to matters of procedure. Thus all fundamental rights comprised within the term liberty are protected by the Federal Constitution from invasion by the States." *Whitney v. California*, 274 U.S. 357 (1927) (concurring opinion). "The guaranties of due process, though having their roots in Magna Carta's *'per legem terrae'* and considered as procedural safeguards 'against executive usurpation and tyranny,' have in this country 'become bulwarks also against arbitrary legislation.'" *Poe v. Ullman*, 367 U.S. 497 (1961) (Harlan, J., dissenting from dismissal on jurisdictional grounds).

The most familiar of the substantive liberties protected by the Fourteenth Amendment are those recognized by the Bill of Rights. We have held that the Due Process Clause of the Fourteenth Amendment incorporates most of the Bill of Rights against the States. *See, e.g., Duncan v. Louisiana*, 391 U.S. 145 (1968). It is tempting, as a means of curbing the discretion of federal judges, to suppose that liberty encompasses no more than those rights already guaranteed to the individual against federal interference by the express provisions of the first eight Amendments to the Constitution. See *Adamson v. California*, 332 U.S. 46 (1947) (Black, J., dissenting). But of course this Court has never accepted that view. . . .

Neither the Bill of Rights nor the specific practices of States at the time of the adoption of the Fourteenth Amendment marks the outer limits of the substantive sphere of liberty which the Fourteenth Amendment protects. See U.S. Const., Amdt. 9. As the second Justice Harlan recognized:

> The full scope of the liberty guaranteed by the Due Process Clause cannot be found in or limited by the precise terms of the specific guarantees elsewhere provided in the Constitution. This 'liberty' is not a series of isolated points pricked out in terms of the taking of property; the freedom of speech, press, and religion; the right to keep and bear arms; the freedom from unreasonable searches and seizures; and so on. It is a rational continuum which, broadly speaking, includes a freedom from all substantial arbitrary impositions and purposeless restraints . . . and which also recognizes . . . that certain interests require particularly careful scrutiny of the state needs asserted to justify their abridgment.

Justice Harlan wrote these words in addressing an issue the full Court did not reach in *Poe v. Ullman*, but the Court adopted his position four Terms later in *Griswold v. Connecticut*. In *Griswold*, we held that the Constitution does not permit a State to forbid a married couple to use contraceptives. That same freedom was later guaranteed, under the Equal Protection Clause, for unmarried couples. See *Eisenstadt v. Baird*. Constitutional protection was extended to the sale and distribution of contraceptives in *Carey v. Population Services International*. It is settled now . . . that the Constitution places limits on a State's right to interfere with a person's most basic decisions about family and parenthood, see *Carey*; *Moore v. East Cleveland*, 431 U.S. 494 (1977); *Eisenstadt v. Baird*; *Loving v. Virginia*; *Griswold v. Connecticut*; *Skinner v. Oklahoma*, 316 U.S. 535 (1942); *Pierce v. Society of Sisters*; *Meyer v. Nebraska*, as well as bodily integrity, *see, e. g., Washington v. Harper*, 494 U.S. 210 (1990); *Winston v. Lee*, 470 U.S. 753; *Rochin v. California*, 342 U.S. 165 (1952).

The inescapable fact is that adjudication of substantive due process claims may call upon the Court in interpreting the Constitution to exercise that same capacity which by tradition courts always have exercised: reasoned judgment. Its boundaries are not susceptible of expression as a simple rule. That does not mean we are free to invalidate state policy choices with which we disagree; yet neither does it permit us to shrink from the duties of our office. As Justice Harlan observed:

> Due process has not been reduced to any formula; its content cannot be determined by reference to any code. The best that can be said is that through the course of this Court's decisions it has represented the balance which our Nation, built upon postulates of respect for the liberty of the individual, has struck between that liberty and the demands of organized society. If the supplying of content to this Constitutional concept has of necessity been a rational process, it certainly has not been one where judges have felt free to roam where unguided speculation might take them. The balance of which I speak is the balance struck by this country, having regard to what history teaches are the traditions from which it developed as well as the traditions from which it broke. That tradition is a living thing. A decision of this Court which radically departs from it could not long survive, while a decision which builds on what has survived is likely to be sound. No formula could serve as a substitute, in this area, for judgment and restraint.

Men and women of good conscience can disagree, and we suppose some always shall disagree, about the profound moral and spiritual implications of terminating a pregnancy, even in its earliest stage. Some of us as individuals find abortion offensive to our most basic principles of morality, but that cannot control our decision. Our obligation is to define the liberty of all, not to mandate our own moral code. The underlying constitutional issue is whether the State can resolve these philosophic questions in such a definitive way that a woman lacks all choice in the matter, except perhaps in those rare circumstances in which the pregnancy is itself a danger to her own life or health, or is the result of rape or incest. . . .

Our law affords constitutional protection to personal decisions relating to marriage, procreation, contraception, family relationships, child rearing, and education. Our cases recognize "the right of the *individual*, married or single, to be free from unwarranted governmental intrusion into matters so fundamentally affecting a person as the decision whether to bear or beget a child." *Eisenstadt v. Baird*. Our precedents "have respected the private realm of family life which the state cannot enter." These matters, involving the most intimate and personal choices a person may make in a lifetime, choices central to personal dignity and autonomy, are central to the liberty protected by the Fourteenth Amendment. At the heart of liberty is the right to define one's own concept of existence, of meaning, of the universe, and of the mystery of human life. Beliefs about these matters could not define the attributes of personhood were they formed under compulsion of the State.

These considerations begin our analysis of the woman's interest in terminating her pregnancy but cannot end it, for this reason: though the abortion decision may originate within the zone of conscience and belief, it is more than a philosophic exercise. Abortion is a unique act. It is an act fraught with consequences for others: for the woman who must live with the implications of her decision; for the persons who perform and assist in the procedure; for the spouse, family, and society which must confront the knowledge that these procedures exist, procedures some deem nothing short of an act of violence against innocent human life; and, depending on one's beliefs, for the life or potential life that is aborted. Though abortion is conduct, it does not follow that the State is entitled to proscribe it in all instances. That is because the liberty of the woman is at stake in a sense unique to the human condition and so unique to the law. The mother who carries a child to full term is subject to anxieties, to physical constraints, to pain that only she must bear. That these sacrifices have from the beginning of the human race been endured by woman with a pride that ennobles her in the eyes of others and gives to the infant a bond of love cannot alone be grounds for the State to insist she make the sacrifice. Her suffering is too intimate and personal for the State to insist, without more, upon its own vision of the woman's role, however dominant that vision has been in the course of our history and our culture. The destiny of the woman must be shaped to a large extent on her own conception of her spiritual imperatives and her place in society.

It should be recognized, moreover, that in some critical respects the abortion decision is of the same character as the decision to use contraception, to which *Griswold*, *Eisenstadt*, and *Carey* afford constitutional protection. We have no doubt as to the correctness of those decisions. They . . . involve personal decisions concerning not only the meaning of procreation but also human responsibility and respect for it. As with abortion, reasonable people will have differences of opinion about these matters. One view is based on such reverence for the wonder of creation that any pregnancy ought to be welcomed and carried to full term no matter how difficult it will be to provide for the child and ensure its well-being. Another is that the inability to provide for the nurture and care of the infant is a cruelty to the child and an anguish to the parent. These are intimate views with infinite variations, and their deep, personal character underlay our decisions in *Griswold*, *Eisenstadt*, and *Carey*. The same concerns are present when the woman confronts the reality that, perhaps despite her attempts to avoid it, she has become pregnant. . . .

While we appreciate the weight of the arguments made on behalf of the State in the cases before us ... the reservations any of us may have in reaffirming the central holding of *Roe* are outweighed by the explication of individual liberty we have given combined with the force of *stare decisis*. We turn now to that doctrine.

III

A

The obligation to follow precedent begins with necessity, and a contrary necessity marks its outer limit. With Cardozo, we recognize that no judicial system could do society's work if it eyed each issue afresh in every case that raised it. Indeed, the very concept of the rule of law underlying our own Constitution requires such continuity over time that a respect for precedent is, by definition, indispensable. At the other extreme, a different necessity would make itself felt if a prior judicial ruling should come to be seen so clearly as error that its enforcement was for that very reason doomed.

... [I]t is common wisdom that the rule of *stare decisis* is not an "inexorable command," and certainly it is not such in every constitutional case.... Rather, when this Court reexamines a prior holding, its judgment is customarily informed by a series of prudential and pragmatic considerations designed to test the consistency of overruling a prior decision with the ideal of the rule of law, and to gauge the respective costs of reaffirming and overruling a prior case. Thus, for example, we may ask whether the rule has proven to be intolerable simply in defying practical workability; whether the rule is subject to a kind of reliance that would lend a special hardship to the consequences of overruling and add inequity to the cost of repudiation; whether related principles of law have so far developed as to have left the old rule no more than a remnant of abandoned doctrine; or whether facts have so changed, or come to be seen so differently, as to have robbed the old rule of significant application or justification. . . .

1

Although *Roe* has engendered opposition, it has in no sense proven "unworkable," representing as it does a simple limitation beyond which a state law is unenforceable. While *Roe* has, of course, required judicial assessment of state laws affecting the exercise of the choice guaranteed against government infringement, and although the need for such review will remain as a consequence of today's decision, the required determinations fall within judicial competence.

2

The inquiry into reliance counts the cost of a rule's repudiation as it would fall on those who have relied reasonably on the rule's continued application. [T]he classic case for weighing reliance heavily in favor of following the earlier rule occurs in the commercial context ... where advance planning of great precision is most obviously a necessity. . . .

Abortion is customarily chosen as an unplanned response to the consequence of unplanned activity or to the failure of conventional birth control, and except on the assumption that no intercourse would have occurred but for *Roe's* holding, such behavior may appear to justify no reliance claim. . . .

To eliminate the issue of reliance that easily, however, one would need to limit cognizable reliance to specific instances of sexual activity. But to do this would be simply to refuse to face the fact that for two decades of economic and social developments, people have organized intimate relationships and made choices that define their views of themselves and their places in society, in reliance on the availability of abortion in the event that contraception should fail. The ability of women to participate equally in the economic and social life of the Nation has been facilitated by their ability to control their reproductive lives. The Constitution serves human values, and while the effect of reliance on *Roe* cannot be exactly measured, neither can the certain cost of overruling *Roe* for people who have ordered their thinking and living around that case be dismissed.

3

No evolution of legal principle has left *Roe's* doctrinal footings weaker than they were in 1973. . . . *Roe* stands at an intersection of two lines of decisions. . . . The *Roe* Court itself placed its holding in the succession of cases most prominently exemplified by *Griswold v. Connecticut*. [S]ubsequent constitutional developments have neither disturbed, nor do they threaten to diminish, the scope of recognized protection accorded to the liberty relating to intimate relationships, the family, and decisions about whether or not to beget or bear a child.

Roe, however, may be seen . . . as a rule . . . of personal autonomy and bodily integrity, with doctrinal affinity to cases recognizing limits on governmental power to mandate medical treatment or to bar its rejection. If so, our cases since *Roe* accord with *Roe's* view that a State's interest in the protection of life falls short of justifying any plenary override of individual liberty claims. . . .

Finally, one could classify *Roe* as *sui generis*. If the case is so viewed, then there clearly has been no erosion of its central determination. The original holding resting on the concurrence of seven Members of the Court in 1973 was expressly affirmed by a majority of six in 1983, see *Akron v. Akron Center for Reproductive Health, Inc.*, 462 U.S. 416, and by a majority of five in 1986, see *Thornburgh v. American College of Obstetricians and Gynecologists*, 476 U.S. 747, expressing adherence to the constitutional ruling despite legislative efforts in some States to test its limits. More recently, in *Webster v. Reproductive Health Services*, 492 U.S. 490 (1989), although two of the present authors questioned the trimester framework in a way consistent with our judgment today, a majority of the Court either decided to reaffirm or declined to address the constitutional validity of the central holding of *Roe*. . . .

4

We have seen how time has overtaken some of *Roe's* factual assumptions: advances in maternal health care allow for abortions safe to the mother later in pregnancy than was true in 1973, and advances in neonatal care have advanced viability to a point somewhat earlier. But these facts go only to the scheme of time limits on the realization of competing interests, and the divergences from the factual premises of 1973 have no bearing on the validity of *Roe's* central holding, that viability marks the earliest point at which the State's interest in fetal life is constitutionally adequate to justify a legislative ban on nontherapeutic abortions. The soundness or unsoundness of that constitutional judgment in no sense turns on whether viability occurs at approximately 28 weeks, as was usual at the time of *Roe*, at 23 to 24 weeks, as it sometimes does today, or at some moment even slightly earlier in pregnancy, as it may if fetal respiratory capacity can somehow be enhanced in the future. Whenever it may occur, the attainment of viability may continue to serve as the critical fact, just as it has done since *Roe* was decided; which is to say that no change in *Roe's* factual underpinning has left its central holding obsolete, and none supports an argument for overruling it.

5

The sum of the precedential enquiry to this point shows *Roe's* underpinnings unweakened in any way affecting its central holding. . . . [T]he stronger argument is for affirming *Roe's* central holding, with whatever degree of personal reluctance any of us may have, not for overruling it.

B

In a less significant case, *stare decisis* analysis could, and would, stop at the point we have reached. But the sustained and widespread debate *Roe* has provoked calls for some comparison between that case and others of comparable dimension that have responded to national controversies and taken on the impress of the controversies addressed. . . .

The first example is that line of cases identified with *Lochner v. New York*, which imposed substantive limitations on legislation limiting economic autonomy in favor of health and welfare regulation, adopting, in Justice Holmes' view, the theory of laissez-faire. The *Lochner* decisions were exemplified by *Adkins v. Children's Hospital of District of Columbia*, in which this Court held it to be an infringement of constitutionally protected liberty of contract to require the employers of adult women to satisfy minimum wage standards. Fourteen years later, *West Coast Hotel Co. v. Parrish* signaled the demise of *Lochner* by overruling *Adkins*. In the meantime, the Depression had come and, with it, the lesson that seemed unmistakable to most people by 1937, that the interpretation of contractual freedom protected in *Adkins* rested on fundamentally false factual assumptions about the capacity of a relatively unregulated market to satisfy minimal levels of human welfare. As Justice Jackson wrote of the constitutional crisis of 1937 shortly before he came on the bench: "The older world of *laissez faire* was recognized everywhere outside the Court to be dead." The facts upon which the earlier case had premised a constitutional resolution of social controversy had proven to be untrue, and history's demonstration of their untruth not only justified but required the new choice of constitutional principle that *West Coast Hotel* announced. Of course, it was true that the Court lost something by its misperception, or its lack of prescience, and the Court-packing crisis only magnified the loss; but the clear demonstration that the facts of economic life were different from those previously assumed warranted the repudiation of the old law.

The second comparison that 20th century history invites is with the cases employing the separate-but-equal rule for applying the Fourteenth Amendment's equal protection guarantee. They began with *Plessy v. Ferguson*, holding that legislatively mandated racial segregation in public transportation works no denial of equal protection, rejecting the argument that racial separation enforced by the legal machinery of American society treats the black race as inferior. . . . [T]his understanding of the implication of segregation was the stated justification for the Court's opinion. But this understanding of the facts and the rule it was stated to justify were repudiated in *Brown v. Board of Education*. . . .

The Court in *Brown* . . . observ[ed] that whatever may have been the understanding in *Plessy's* time of the power of segregation to stigmatize those who were segregated with a "badge of inferiority," it was clear by 1954 that legally sanctioned segregation had just such an effect, to the point that racially separate public educational facilities were deemed inherently unequal. Society's understanding of the facts upon which a constitutional ruling was sought in 1954 was thus fundamentally different from the basis claimed for the decision in 1896. While we think *Plessy* was wrong the day it was decided, we must also recognize that the *Plessy* Court's explanation for its decision was so clearly at odds with the facts apparent to the Court in 1954 that the decision to reexamine *Plessy* was on this ground alone not only justified but required.

West Coast Hotel and *Brown* each rested on facts, or an understanding of facts, changed from those which furnished the claimed justifications for the earlier constitutional resolutions. Each case was comprehensible as the Court's response to facts that the country could understand, or had come to understand already, but which the Court of an earlier day . . . had not been able to perceive. As the decisions were thus comprehensible they were also defensible, not merely as the victories of one doctrinal school over another by dint of numbers . . . but as applications of constitutional principle to facts as they had not been seen by the Court before. In constitutional adjudication as elsewhere in life, changed circumstances may impose new obligations, and the thoughtful part of the Nation could accept each decision to overrule a prior case as a response to the Court's constitutional duty.

Because the cases before us present no such occasion it could be seen as no such response. Because neither the factual underpinnings of *Roe's* central holding nor our understanding of it has changed (and because no other indication of weakened precedent has been shown), the Court could not pretend to be reexamining the prior law with any justification beyond a present doctrinal disposition to come out differently from the Court of 1973. To overrule prior law for no other reason than that would run counter to the view repeated in our cases, that a decision to overrule should rest on some special reason over and above the belief that a prior case was wrongly decided. *See, e. g., Mitchell v. W. T. Grant Co.*, 416 U.S. 600, 636 (1974) (Stewart, J., dissenting) ("A basic change in the law upon a ground no firmer than a change in our membership invites the popular misconception that this institution is little different from the two political branches of the Government. No misconception could do more lasting injury to this Court and to the system of law which it is our abiding mission to serve.").

C

The examination of the conditions justifying the repudiation of *Adkins* by *West Coast Hotel* and *Plessy* by *Brown* is enough to suggest the terrible price that would have been paid if the Court had not overruled as it did. In the present cases, however . . . the terrible price would be paid for overruling. Our analysis would not be complete, however, without explaining why overruling *Roe's* central holding would not only reach an unjustifiable result under principles of *stare decisis*, but would seriously weaken the Court's capacity to exercise the judicial power and to function as the Supreme Court of a Nation dedicated to the rule of law. . . .

The root of American governmental power is revealed most clearly in the instance of the power conferred by the Constitution upon the Judiciary of the United States and specifically upon this Court. . . . [T]he Court cannot buy support for its decisions by spending money and, except to a minor degree, it cannot independently coerce obedience to its decrees. The Court's power lies, rather, in its legitimacy, a product of substance and perception that shows itself in the people's acceptance of the Judiciary as fit to determine what the Nation's law means and to declare what it demands.

The underlying substance of this legitimacy is of course the warrant for the Court's decisions in the Constitution and the lesser sources of legal principle on which the Court draws. That substance is expressed in the Court's opinions, and our contemporary understanding is such that a decision without principled justification would be no judicial act at all. . . . The Court must take care to speak and act in ways that allow people to accept its decisions on the terms the Court claims for them, as grounded truly in principle, not as compromises with social and political pressures having, as such, no bearing on the principled choices that the Court is obliged to make. Thus, the Court's legitimacy depends on making legally principled decisions under circumstances in which their principled character is sufficiently plausible to be accepted by the Nation.

The need for principled action to be perceived as such is implicated to some degree whenever this, or any other appellate court, overrules a prior case. This is not to say, of course, that this Court cannot give a perfectly satisfactory explanation in most cases. People understand that some of the Constitution's language is hard to fathom and that the Court's Justices are sometimes able to perceive significant facts or to understand principles of law that eluded their predecessors and that justify departures from existing decisions. However upsetting it may be to those most directly affected when one judicially derived rule replaces another, the country can accept some correction of error without necessarily questioning the legitimacy of the Court.

In two circumstances, however, the Court would almost certainly fail to receive the benefit of the doubt in overruling prior cases. There is, first, a point beyond which frequent overruling would overtax the country's belief in the Court's good faith. Despite the variety of reasons that may inform and justify a decision to overrule, we cannot forget that such a decision is usually perceived (and perceived correctly) as, at the least, a statement that a prior decision was wrong. There is a limit to the amount of error that can plausibly be imputed to prior Courts. If that limit should be exceeded, disturbance of prior rulings would be taken as evidence that justifiable reexamination of principle had given way to drives for particular results in the short term. The legitimacy of the Court would fade with the frequency of its vacillation.

That first circumstance can be described as hypothetical; the second is to the point here and now. Where, in the performance of its judicial duties, the Court decides a case in such a way as to resolve the sort of intensely divisive controversy reflected in *Roe* and those rare, comparable cases, its decision has a dimension that the resolution of the normal case does not carry. It is the dimension present whenever the Court's interpretation of the Constitution calls the contending sides of a national controversy to end their national division by accepting a common mandate rooted in the Constitution.

The Court is not asked to do this very often, having thus addressed the Nation only twice in our lifetime, in the decisions of *Brown* and *Roe*. But when the Court does act in this way, its decision requires an equally rare precedential force to counter the inevitable efforts to overturn it and to thwart its implementation. Some of those efforts may be mere unprincipled emotional reactions; others may proceed from principles worthy of profound respect. But whatever the premises of opposition may be, only the most convincing justification under accepted standards of precedent could suffice to demonstrate that a later decision overruling the first was anything but a surrender to political pressure, and an unjustified repudiation of the principle on which the Court staked its authority in the first instance. So to overrule under fire in the absence of the most compelling reason to reexamine a watershed decision would subvert the Court's legitimacy beyond any serious question.

The country's loss of confidence in the Judiciary would be underscored by an equally certain and equally reasonable condemnation for another failing in overruling unnecessarily and under pressure. Some cost will be paid by anyone who approves or implements a constitutional decision where it is unpopular. . . . An extra price will be paid by those who themselves disapprove of the decision's results when viewed outside of constitutional terms, but who nevertheless struggle to accept it, because they respect the rule of law. To all those who will be so tested by following, the Court implicitly undertakes to remain steadfast, lest in the end a price be paid for nothing. The promise of constancy, once given, binds its maker for as long as the power to stand by the decision survives and the understanding of the issue has not changed so fundamentally as to render the commitment obsolete. From the obligation of this promise this Court cannot and should not assume any exemption when duty requires it to decide a case in conformance with the Constitution. A willing breach of it would be nothing less than a breach of faith. . . .

It is true that diminished legitimacy may be restored, but only slowly. . . . Like the character of an individual, the legitimacy of the Court must be earned over time. So, indeed, must be the character of a Nation of people who aspire to live according to the rule of law. Their belief in themselves as such a people is not readily separable from their understanding of the Court invested with the authority to decide their constitutional cases and speak before all others for their constitutional ideals. If the Court's legitimacy should be undermined, then, so would the country be in its very ability to see itself through its constitutional ideals. The Court's concern with legitimacy is not for the sake of the Court, but for the sake of the Nation to which it is responsible.

The Court's duty in the present cases is clear. In 1973, it confronted the already-divisive issue of governmental power to limit personal choice to undergo abortion, for which it provided a new resolution based on the due process guaranteed by the Fourteenth Amendment. Whether or not a new social consensus is developing on that issue, its divisiveness is no less today than in 1973, and pressure to overrule the decision, like pressure to retain it, has grown only more intense. A decision to overrule *Roe's* essential holding under the existing circumstances would address error, if error there was, at the cost of both profound and unnecessary damage to the Court's legitimacy, and to the Nation's commitment to the rule of law. It is therefore imperative to adhere to the essence of *Roe's* original decision, and we do so today.

IV

From what we have said so far it follows that it is a constitutional liberty of the woman to have some freedom to terminate her pregnancy.

We conclude that the basic decision in *Roe* was based on a constitutional analysis which we cannot now repudiate. The woman's liberty is not so unlimited, however, that from the outset the State cannot show its concern for the life of the unborn, and at a later point in fetal development the State's interest in life has sufficient force so that the right of the woman to terminate the pregnancy can be restricted.

That brings us, of course, to the point where much criticism has been directed at *Roe*, a criticism that always inheres when the Court draws a specific rule from what in the Constitution is but a general standard. We conclude, however, that the urgent claims of the woman to retain the ultimate control over her destiny and her body, claims implicit in the meaning of liberty, require us to perform that function. Liberty must not be extinguished for want of a line that is clear. And it falls to us to give some real substance to the woman's liberty to determine whether to carry her pregnancy to full term.

We conclude the line should be drawn at viability, so that before that time the woman has a right to choose to terminate her pregnancy. We adhere to this principle for two reasons. First, as we have said, is the doctrine of *stare decisis*. Any judicial act of line-drawing may seem somewhat arbitrary, but *Roe* was a reasoned statement, elaborated with great care. We have twice reaffirmed it in the face of great opposition. . . .

The second reason is that the concept of viability, as we noted in *Roe*, is the time at which there is a realistic possibility of maintaining and nourishing a life outside the womb, so that the independent existence of the second life can in reason and all fairness be the object of state protection that now overrides the rights of the woman. Consistent with other constitutional norms, legislatures may draw lines which appear arbitrary without the necessity of offering a justification. But courts may not. We must justify the lines we draw. And there is no line other than viability which is more workable. To be sure, as we have said, there may be some medical developments that affect the precise point of viability, but this is an imprecision within tolerable limits. . . . The viability line also has, as a practical matter, an element of fairness. In some broad sense it might be said that a woman who fails to act before viability has consented to the State's intervention on behalf of the developing child. . . .

On the other side of the equation is the interest of the State in the protection of potential life. The *Roe* Court recognized the State's "important and legitimate interest in protecting the potentiality of human life." The weight to be given this state interest, not the strength of the woman's interest, was the difficult question faced in *Roe*. We do not need to say whether each of us, had we been Members of the Court when the valuation of the state interest came before it as an original matter, would have concluded, as the *Roe* Court did, that its weight is insufficient to justify a ban on abortions prior to viability even when it is subject to certain exceptions. The matter is not before us in the first instance, and coming as it does after nearly 20 years of litigation in *Roe's* wake we are satisfied that the immediate question is not the soundness of *Roe's* resolution of the issue, but the precedential force that must be accorded to its holding. And we have concluded that the essential holding of *Roe* should be reaffirmed.

Yet it must be remembered that *Roe v. Wade* speaks with clarity in establishing not only the woman's liberty but also the State's "important and legitimate interest in potential life." That portion of the decision in *Roe* has been given too little acknowledgment and implementation by the Court in its subsequent cases. Those cases decided that any regulation touching upon the abortion decision must survive strict scrutiny, to be sustained only if drawn in narrow terms to further a compelling state interest. Not all of the cases decided under that formulation can be reconciled with the holding in *Roe* itself that the State has legitimate interests in the health of the woman and in protecting the potential life within her. In resolving this tension, we choose to rely upon *Roe*, as against the later cases.

Roe established a trimester framework to govern abortion regulations. Under this elaborate but rigid construct, almost no regulation at all is permitted during the first trimester of pregnancy; regulations designed to protect the woman's health, but not to further the State's interest in potential life, are permitted during the second trimester; and during the third trimester, when the fetus is viable, prohibitions are permitted provided the life or health of the mother is not at stake. . . .

Though the woman has a right to choose to terminate or continue her pregnancy before viability, it does not at all follow that the State is prohibited from taking steps to ensure that this choice is thoughtful and informed. Even in the earliest stages of pregnancy, the State may enact rules and regulations designed to encourage her to know that there are philosophic and social arguments of great weight that can be brought to bear in favor of continuing the pregnancy to full term and that there are procedures and institutions to allow adoption of unwanted children as well as a certain degree of state assistance if the mother chooses to raise the child herself. "'The Constitution does not forbid a State or city, pursuant to democratic processes, from expressing a preference for normal childbirth.'" It follows that States are free to enact laws to provide a reasonable framework for a woman to make a decision that has such profound and lasting meaning. This, too, we find consistent with *Roe's* central premises, and indeed the inevitable consequence of our holding that the State has an interest in protecting the life of the unborn.

We reject the trimester framework, which we do not consider to be part of the essential holding of *Roe*. . . . Measures aimed at ensuring that a woman's choice contemplates the consequences for the fetus do not necessarily interfere with the right recognized in *Roe*, although those measures have been found to be inconsistent with the rigid trimester framework announced in that case. . . . The trimester framework suffers from these basic flaws: in its formulation it misconceives the nature of the pregnant woman's interest; and in practice it undervalues the State's interest in potential life, as recognized in *Roe*.

As our jurisprudence relating to all liberties save perhaps abortion has recognized, not every law which makes a right more difficult to exercise is, *ipso facto*, an infringement of that right. . . . The fact that a law which serves a valid purpose, one not designed to strike at the right itself, has the incidental effect of making it more difficult or more expensive to procure an abortion cannot be enough to invalidate it. Only where state regulation imposes an undue burden on a woman's ability to make this decision does the power of the State reach into the heart of the liberty protected by the Due Process Clause. . . .

For the most part, the Court's early abortion cases adhered to this view. . . . [I]t is an overstatement to describe [the abortion right] as a right to decide whether to have an abortion "without interference from the State." All abortion regulations interfere to some degree with a woman's ability to decide whether to terminate her pregnancy. . . . [T]he trimester framework has led to the striking down of some abortion regulations which in no real sense deprived women of the ultimate decision. Those decisions went too far because the right recognized by *Roe* is a right "to be free from unwarranted governmental intrusion into matters so fundamentally affecting a person as the decision whether to bear or beget a child." Not all governmental intrusion is of necessity unwarranted; and that brings us to the other basic flaw in the trimester framework: even in *Roe's* terms, in practice it undervalues the State's interest in the potential life within the woman. . . . In our view, the undue burden standard is the appropriate means of reconciling the State's interest with the woman's constitutionally protected liberty. . . .

A finding of an undue burden is a shorthand for the conclusion that a state regulation has the purpose or effect of placing a substantial obstacle in the path of a woman seeking an abortion of a nonviable fetus. . . . What is at stake is the woman's right to make the ultimate decision, not a right to be insulated from all others in doing so. Regulations which do no more than create a structural mechanism by which the State, or the parent or guardian of a minor, may express profound respect for the life of the unborn are permitted, if they are not a substantial obstacle to the woman's exercise of the right to choose. Unless it has that effect on her right of choice, a state measure designed to persuade her to choose childbirth over abortion will be upheld if reasonably related to that goal. Regulations designed to foster the health of a woman seeking an abortion are valid if they do not constitute an undue burden. . . .

We give this summary:

(a) To protect the central right recognized by *Roe v. Wade* while at the same time accommodating the State's profound interest in potential life, we will employ the undue burden analysis as explained in this opinion. An undue burden exists, and therefore a provision of law is invalid, if its purpose or effect is to place a substantial obstacle in the path of a woman seeking an abortion before the fetus attains viability.

(b) We reject the rigid trimester framework of *Roe v. Wade*. To promote the State's profound interest in potential life, throughout pregnancy the State may take measures to ensure that the woman's choice is informed, and measures designed to advance this interest will not be invalidated as long as their purpose is to persuade the woman to choose childbirth over abortion. These measures must not be an undue burden on the right.

(c) As with any medical procedure, the State may enact regulations to further the health or safety of a woman seeking an abortion. Unnecessary health regulations that have the purpose or effect of presenting a substantial obstacle to a woman seeking an abortion impose an undue burden on the right.

(d) Our adoption of the undue burden analysis does not disturb the central holding of *Roe v. Wade*, and we reaffirm that holding. Regardless of whether exceptions are made for particular circumstances, a State may not prohibit any woman from making the ultimate decision to terminate her pregnancy before viability.

(e) We also reaffirm *Roe's* holding that "subsequent to viability, the State in promoting its interest in the potentiality of human life may, if it chooses, regulate, and even proscribe, abortion except where it is necessary, in appropriate medical judgment, for the preservation of the life or health of the mother."

These principles control our assessment of the Pennsylvania statute, and we now turn to the issue of the validity of its challenged provisions.

V

A

. . . We . . . conclude that, as construed by the Court of Appeals, the medical emergency definition imposes no undue burden on a woman's abortion right.

B

We next consider the informed consent requirement. . . . To the extent *Akron I* and *Thornburgh* find a constitutional violation when the government requires, as it does here, the giving of truthful, nonmisleading information about the nature of the procedure, the attendant health risks and those of childbirth, and the "probable gestational age" of the fetus, those cases go too far, are inconsistent with *Roe's* acknowledgment of an important interest in potential life, and are overruled. . . .

We also see no reason why the State may not require doctors to inform a woman seeking an abortion of the availability of materials relating to the consequences to the fetus, even when those consequences have no direct relation to her health. . . .

The Pennsylvania statute also requires us to reconsider the holding in *Akron I* that the State may not require that a physician, as opposed to a qualified assistant, provide information relevant to a woman's informed consent. . . . The idea that important decisions will be more informed and deliberate if they follow some period of reflection . . . does not strike us as unreasonable. . . .

Whether the mandatory 24-hour waiting period is nonetheless invalid because in practice it is a substantial obstacle to a woman's choice to terminate her pregnancy is a closer question. . . . [T]he District Court found that for those women who have the fewest financial resources, those who must travel long distances, and those who have difficulty explaining their whereabouts to husbands, employers, or others, the 24-hour waiting period will be "particularly burdensome." These findings are troubling in some respects, but they do not demonstrate that the waiting period constitutes an undue burden. . . .

C

. . . Pennsylvania's abortion law provides, except in cases of medical emergency, that no physician shall perform an abortion on a married woman without receiving a signed statement from the woman that she has notified her spouse that she is about to undergo an abortion. The woman has the option of providing an alternative signed statement certifying that her husband is not the man who impregnated her; that her husband could not be located; that the pregnancy is the result of spousal sexual assault which she has reported; or that the woman believes that notifying her husband will cause him or someone else to inflict bodily injury upon her. A physician who performs an abortion on a married woman without receiving the appropriate signed statement will have his or her license revoked, and is liable to the husband for damages. . . .

[M]illions of women in this country . . . are the victims of regular physical and psychological abuse at the hands of their husbands. Should these women become pregnant, they may have very good reasons for not wishing to inform their husbands of their decision to obtain an abortion. . . . The spousal notification requirement is thus likely to prevent a significant number of women from obtaining an abortion. . . .

We recognize that a husband has a "deep and proper concern and interest . . . in his wife's pregnancy and in the growth and development of the fetus she is carrying." With regard to the children he has fathered and raised, the Court has recognized his "cognizable and substantial" interest in their custody. . . .

Before birth, however, the issue takes on a very different cast. It is an inescapable biological fact that state regulation with respect to the child a woman is carrying will have a far greater impact on the mother's

liberty than on the father's. . . . The Court has held that "when the wife
and the husband disagree on this decision, the view of only one of the two
marriage partners can prevail. Inasmuch as it is the woman who
physically bears the child and who is the more directly and immediately
affected by the pregnancy, as between the two, the balance weighs in her
favor." . . .

D

We next consider the parental consent provision. Except in a medical
emergency, an unemancipated young woman under 18 may not obtain an
abortion unless she and one of her parents (or guardian) provides
informed consent as defined above. If neither a parent nor a guardian
provides consent, a court may authorize the performance of an abortion
upon a determination that the young woman is mature and capable of
giving informed consent and has in fact given her informed consent, or
that an abortion would be in her best interests.

We have been over most of this ground before. Our cases establish,
and we reaffirm today, that a State may require a minor seeking an
abortion to obtain the consent of a parent or guardian, provided that
there is an adequate judicial bypass procedure. . . . Under these
precedents, in our view, the one-parent consent requirement and judicial
bypass procedure are constitutional. . . .

E

. . . In *Danforth,* we held that recordkeeping and reporting provisions
"that are reasonably directed to the preservation of maternal health and
that properly respect a patient's confidentiality and privacy are
permissible." We think that under this standard, all the provisions at
issue here, except that relating to spousal notice, are constitutional. . . .

VI

Our Constitution is a covenant running from the first generation of
Americans to us and then to future generations. It is a coherent
succession. Each generation must learn anew that the Constitution's
written terms embody ideas and aspirations that must survive more ages
than one. We accept our responsibility not to retreat from interpreting
the full meaning of the covenant in light of all of our precedents. We
invoke it once again to define the freedom guaranteed by the
Constitution's own promise, the promise of liberty. . . .

■ **JUSTICE STEVENS, concurring in part and dissenting in part.**

The portions of the Court's opinion that I have joined are more
important than those with which I disagree. I shall therefore first
comment on significant areas of agreement, and then explain the limited
character of my disagreement. . . .

Weighing the State's interest in potential life and the woman's
liberty interest, I agree with the joint opinion that the State may "express
a preference for normal childbirth," that the State may take steps to

ensure that a woman's choice "is thoughtful and informed," and that "States are free to enact laws to provide a reasonable framework for a woman to make a decision that has such profound and lasting meaning." Serious questions arise, however, when a State attempts to "persuade the woman to choose childbirth over abortion." Decisional autonomy must limit the State's power to inject into a woman's most personal deliberations its own views of what is best. The State may promote its preferences by funding childbirth, by creating and maintaining alternatives to abortion, and by espousing the virtues of family; but it must respect the individual's freedom to make such judgments. . . .

Under these principles, §§ 3205(a)(2)(i)–(iii) of the Pennsylvania statute are unconstitutional. Those sections require a physician or counselor to provide the woman with a range of materials clearly designed to persuade her to choose not to undergo the abortion. While the Commonwealth is free . . . to produce and disseminate such material, the Commonwealth may not inject such information into the woman's deliberations just as she is weighing such an important choice.

Under this same analysis, §§ 3205(a)(1)(i) and (iii) . . . are constitutional. Those sections, which require the physician to inform a woman of the nature and risks of the abortion procedure and the medical risks of carrying to term, are neutral requirements comparable to those imposed in other medical procedures. Those sections indicate no effort by the Commonwealth to influence the woman's choice in any way. If anything, such requirements *enhance*, rather than skew, the woman's decisionmaking.

III

The 24-hour waiting period required by . . . the Pennsylvania statute raises even more serious concerns. . . . Part of the constitutional liberty to choose is the equal dignity to which each of us is entitled. A woman who decides to terminate her pregnancy is entitled to the same respect as a woman who decides to carry the fetus to term. The mandatory waiting period denies women that equal respect.

Accordingly, while I disagree with Parts IV, V–B, and V–D of the joint opinion, I join the remainder of the Court's opinion.

■ JUSTICE BLACKMUN, concurring in part, concurring in the judgment in part, and dissenting in part.

I join Parts I, II, III, V–A, V–C, and VI of the joint opinion of JUSTICES O'CONNOR, KENNEDY, and SOUTER, *ante.*

I

Make no mistake, the joint opinion of JUSTICES O'CONNOR, KENNEDY, and SOUTER is an act of personal courage and constitutional principle. In contrast to previous decisions in which JUSTICES O'CONNOR and KENNEDY postponed reconsideration of *Roe v. Wade*, the authors of the joint opinion today join JUSTICE STEVENS and me in concluding that "the essential holding of *Roe v. Wade* should be retained and once again reaffirmed." In brief, five Members of this Court today recognize that "the Constitution protects a woman's right to terminate her pregnancy in its early stages." . . .

II

Today, no less than yesterday, the Constitution and decisions of this Court require that a State's abortion restrictions be subjected to the strictest judicial scrutiny. Our precedents and the joint opinion's principles require us to subject all non-*de-minimis* abortion regulations to strict scrutiny. Under this standard, the Pennsylvania statute's provisions requiring content-based counseling, a 24-hour delay, informed parental consent, and reporting of abortion-related information must be invalidated.

A

The Court today reaffirms the long recognized rights of privacy and bodily integrity. . . . State restrictions on abortion violate a woman's right of privacy in two ways. First, compelled continuation of a pregnancy infringes upon a woman's right to bodily integrity by imposing substantial physical intrusions and significant risks of physical harm. . . . Further, when the State restricts a woman's right to terminate her pregnancy, it deprives a woman of the right to make her own decision about reproduction and family planning—critical life choices that this Court long has deemed central to the right to privacy. . . .

A State's restrictions on a woman's right to terminate her pregnancy also implicate constitutional guarantees of gender equality. State restrictions on abortion compel women to continue pregnancies they otherwise might terminate. By restricting the right to terminate pregnancies, the State conscripts women's bodies into its service, forcing women to continue their pregnancies, suffer the pains of childbirth, and in most instances, provide years of maternal care. The State does not compensate women for their services; instead, it assumes that they owe this duty as a matter of course. This assumption—that women can simply be forced to accept the "natural" status and incidents of motherhood—appears to rest upon a conception of women's role that has triggered the protection of the Equal Protection Clause. The joint opinion recognizes that these assumptions about women's place in society "are no longer consistent with our understanding of the family, the individual, or the Constitution."

B

The Court has held that limitations on the right of privacy are permissible only if they survive "strict" constitutional scrutiny—that is, only if the governmental entity imposing the restriction can demonstrate that the limitation is both necessary and narrowly tailored to serve a compelling governmental interest. *Griswold v. Connecticut.* We have applied this principle specifically in the context of abortion regulations. . . .

In my view, application of this analytical framework is no less warranted than when it was approved by seven Members of this Court in *Roe*. Strict scrutiny of state limitations on reproductive choice still offers the most secure protection of the woman's right to make her own reproductive decisions, free from state coercion. No majority of this Court has ever agreed upon an alternative approach. The factual premises of the trimester framework have not been undermined, and the *Roe* framework is far more administrable, and far less manipulable, than the "undue burden" standard adopted by the joint opinion. . . .

The final, and more genuine, criticism of the trimester framework is that it fails to find the State's interest in potential human life compelling throughout pregnancy. No Member of this Court—nor for that matter, the Solicitor General—has ever questioned our holding in *Roe* that an abortion is not "the termination of life entitled to Fourteenth Amendment protection." Accordingly, a State's interest in protecting fetal life is not grounded in the Constitution. Nor, consistent with our Establishment Clause, can it be a theological or sectarian interest. It is, instead, a legitimate interest grounded in humanitarian or pragmatic concerns. But while a State has "legitimate interests from the outset of the pregnancy in protecting the health of the woman and the life of the fetus that may become a child," legitimate interests are not enough. To overcome the burden of strict scrutiny, the interests must be compelling. . . .

In sum, *Roe's* requirement of strict scrutiny as implemented through a trimester framework should not be disturbed. . . .

C

Application of the strict scrutiny standard results in the invalidation of all the challenged provisions. Indeed, as this Court has invalidated virtually identical provisions in prior cases, *stare decisis* requires that we again strike them down. . . .

III

At long last, THE CHIEF JUSTICE and those who have joined him admit it. Gone are the contentions that the issue need not be (or has not been) considered. There, on the first page, for all to see, is what was expected: "We believe that *Roe* was wrongly decided, and that it can and should be overruled consistently with our traditional approach to *stare decisis* in constitutional cases." If there is much reason to applaud the advances made by the joint opinion today, there is far more to fear THE CHIEF JUSTICE's opinion.

THE CHIEF JUSTICE's criticism of *Roe* follows from his stunted conception of individual liberty. While recognizing that the Due Process Clause protects more than simple physical liberty, he then goes on to construe this Court's personal-liberty cases as establishing only a laundry list of particular rights, rather than a principled account of how these particular rights are grounded in a more general right of privacy. This constricted view is reinforced by THE CHIEF JUSTICE's exclusive reliance on tradition as a source of fundamental rights. He argues that the record in favor of a right to abortion is no stronger than the record in *Michael H. v. Gerald D.*, 491 U.S. 110 (1989), where the plurality found no fundamental right to visitation privileges by an adulterous father, or in *Bowers v. Hardwick*, 478 U.S. 186 (1986), where the Court found no fundamental right to engage in homosexual sodomy, or in a case involving the " 'firing [of] a gun . . . into another person's body.' " In THE CHIEF JUSTICE's world, a woman considering whether to terminate a pregnancy is entitled to no more protection than adulterers, murderers, and so-called sexual deviates. Given THE CHIEF JUSTICE's exclusive reliance on tradition, people using contraceptives seem the next likely candidate for his list of outcasts. . . .

IV

In one sense, the Court's approach is worlds apart from that of THE CHIEF JUSTICE and JUSTICE SCALIA. And yet, in another sense, the distance between the two approaches is short—the distance is but a single vote.

I am 83 years old. I cannot remain on this Court forever, and when I do step down, the confirmation process for my successor well may focus on the issue before us today. That, I regret, may be exactly where the choice between the two worlds will be made.

■ **CHIEF JUSTICE REHNQUIST, with whom JUSTICE WHITE, JUSTICE SCALIA, and JUSTICE THOMAS join, concurring in the judgment in part and dissenting in part.**

The joint opinion, following its newly minted variation on *stare decisis*, retains the outer shell of *Roe v. Wade*, but beats a wholesale retreat from the substance of that case. We believe that *Roe* was wrongly decided, and that it can and should be overruled consistently with our traditional approach to *stare decisis* in constitutional cases. We would . . . uphold the challenged provisions of the Pennsylvania statute in their entirety.

I

 . . . [O]ur decision in *Roe* is not directly implicated by the Pennsylvania statute, which does not prohibit, but simply regulates, abortion. But . . . the state of our post-*Roe* decisional law dealing with the regulation of abortion is confusing and uncertain, indicating that a reexamination of that line of cases is in order. . . . [T]he reexamination undertaken today leaves the Court no less divided than beforehand. Although they reject the trimester framework that formed the underpinning of *Roe*, JUSTICES O'CONNOR, KENNEDY, and SOUTER adopt a revised undue burden standard to analyze the challenged regulations. We conclude, however, that such an outcome is an unjustified constitutional compromise, one which leaves the Court in a position to closely scrutinize all types of abortion regulations despite the fact that it lacks the power to do so under the Constitution.

In *Roe v. Wade*, the Court recognized a "guarantee of personal privacy" which "is broad enough to encompass a woman's decision whether or not to terminate her pregnancy." We are now of the view that, in terming this right fundamental, the Court in *Roe* read the earlier opinions upon which it based its decision much too broadly. Unlike marriage, procreation, and contraception, abortion "involves the purposeful termination of a potential life." The abortion decision must therefore "be recognized as *sui generis*, different in kind from the others that the Court has protected under the rubric of personal or family privacy and autonomy." One cannot ignore the fact that a woman is not isolated in her pregnancy, and that the decision to abort necessarily involves the destruction of a fetus.

Nor do the historical traditions of the American people support the view that the right to terminate one's pregnancy is "fundamental." The common law which we inherited from England made abortion after "quickening" an offense. At the time of the adoption of the Fourteenth Amendment, statutory prohibitions or restrictions on abortion were commonplace; in 1868, at least 28 of the then-37 States and 8 Territories had statutes banning or limiting abortion. By the turn of the century virtually every State had a law prohibiting or restricting abortion on its books. By the middle of the present century, a liberalization trend had set in. But 21 of the restrictive abortion laws in effect in 1868 were still in effect in 1973 when *Roe* was decided, and an overwhelming majority of the States prohibited abortion unless necessary to preserve the life or health of the mother. On this record, it can scarcely be said that any deeply rooted tradition of relatively unrestricted abortion in our history supported the classification of the right to abortion as "fundamental" under the Due Process Clause of the Fourteenth Amendment.

We think, therefore, both in view of this history and of our decided cases dealing with substantive liberty under the Due Process Clause, that the Court was mistaken in *Roe* when it classified a woman's decision to terminate her pregnancy as a "fundamental right" that could be abridged only in a manner which withstood "strict scrutiny." In so concluding, we repeat the observation made in *Bowers v. Hardwick*, 478 U.S. 186 (1986):

> Nor are we inclined to take a more expansive view of our authority to discover new fundamental rights imbedded in the Due Process Clause. The Court is most vulnerable and comes nearest to illegitimacy when it deals with judge-made constitutional law having little or no cognizable roots in the language or design of the Constitution.

We believe that the sort of constitutionally imposed abortion code of the type illustrated by our decisions following *Roe* is inconsistent "with the notion of a Constitution cast in general terms, as ours is, and usually speaking in general principles, as ours does." The Court in *Roe* reached too far when it analogized the right to abort a fetus to the rights involved in *Pierce*, *Meyer*, *Loving*, and *Griswold*, and thereby deemed the right to abortion fundamental.

II

The joint opinion of JUSTICES O'CONNOR, KENNEDY, and SOUTER cannot bring itself to say that *Roe* was correct as an original matter. . . . [T]he opinion therefore contains an elaborate discussion of *stare decisis*. This discussion of the principle of *stare decisis* appears to be almost entirely dicta, because the joint opinion does not apply that principle in dealing with *Roe*. *Roe* decided that a woman had a fundamental right to an abortion. The joint opinion rejects that view. *Roe* decided that abortion regulations were to be subjected to "strict scrutiny" and could be justified only in the light of "compelling state interests." The joint opinion rejects that view. *Roe* analyzed abortion regulation under a rigid trimester framework, a framework which has guided this Court's decisionmaking for 19 years. The joint opinion rejects that framework. . . .

Roe continues to exist, but only in the way a storefront on a western movie set exists: a mere facade to give the illusion of reality. Decisions following *Roe*, such as *Akron* and *Thornburgh*, are frankly overruled in part under the "undue burden" standard expounded in the joint opinion.

In our view, authentic principles of *stare decisis* do not require that any portion of the reasoning in *Roe* be kept intact. "*Stare decisis* is not . . . a universal, inexorable command," especially in cases involving the interpretation of the Federal Constitution. Erroneous decisions in such constitutional cases are uniquely durable, because correction through legislative action, save for constitutional amendment, is impossible. It is therefore our duty to reconsider constitutional interpretations that "depart from a proper understanding" of the Constitution. . . .

The joint opinion discusses several *stare decisis* factors which, it asserts, point toward retaining a portion of *Roe*. Two of these factors are that the main "factual underpinning" of *Roe* has remained the same, and that its doctrinal foundation is no weaker now than it was in 1973. Of course, what might be called the basic facts which gave rise to *Roe* have remained the same—women become pregnant, there is a point somewhere, depending on medical technology, where a fetus becomes viable, and women give birth to children. But this is only to say that the same facts which gave rise to *Roe* will continue to give rise to similar cases. . . . The opinion frankly concludes that *Roe* and its progeny were wrong in failing to recognize that the State's interests in maternal health and in the protection of unborn human life exist throughout pregnancy. . . .

The joint opinion also points to the reliance interests involved in this context in its effort to explain why precedent must be followed for precedent's sake. . . . But, as the joint opinion apparently agrees, any traditional notion of reliance is not applicable here. The Court today cuts back on the protection afforded by *Roe*, and no one claims that this action defeats any reliance interest in the disavowed trimester framework. . . .

The joint opinion thus turns to what can only be described as an unconventional—and unconvincing—notion of reliance, a view based on the surmise that the availability of abortion since *Roe* has led to "two decades of economic and social developments" that would be undercut if the error of *Roe* were recognized. The joint opinion's assertion of this fact is undeveloped and totally conclusory. In fact, one cannot be sure to what economic and social developments the opinion is referring. Surely it is dubious to suggest that women have reached their "places in society" in reliance upon *Roe*, rather than as a result of their determination to obtain higher education and compete with men in the job market, and of society's increasing recognition of their ability to fill positions that were previously thought to be reserved only for men.

In the end, having failed to put forth any evidence to prove any true reliance, the joint opinion's argument is based solely on generalized assertions about the national psyche, on a belief that the people of this country have grown accustomed to the *Roe* decision over the last 19 years and have "ordered their thinking and living around" it. . . . [A]t various points in the past, the same could have been said about this Court's erroneous decisions that the Constitution allowed "separate but equal" treatment of minorities, see *Plessy v. Ferguson*, or that "liberty" under the Due Process Clause protected "freedom of contract," see *Lochner v. New York*. . . .

[T]he joint opinion goes on to state that when the Court "resolves the sort of intensely divisive controversy reflected in *Roe* and those rare, comparable cases," its decision is exempt from reconsideration under established principles of *stare decisis* in constitutional cases. . . . This is a truly novel principle, one which is contrary to both the Court's historical practice and to the Court's traditional willingness to tolerate criticism of its opinions. Under this principle, when the Court has ruled on a divisive issue, it is apparently prevented from overruling that decision for the sole reason that it was incorrect, *unless opposition to the original decision has died away.*

The first difficulty with this principle lies in its assumption that cases that are "intensely divisive" can be readily distinguished from those that are not. . . . The joint opinion picks out and discusses two prior Court rulings [*Lochner v. New York*, *supra*, and *Plessy v. Ferguson*] that it believes are of the "intensely divisive" variety, and concludes that they are of comparable dimension to *Roe*. It appears to us very odd indeed that the joint opinion chooses as benchmarks two cases in which the Court chose *not* to adhere to erroneous constitutional precedent, but instead enhanced its stature by acknowledging and correcting its error, apparently in violation of the joint opinion's "legitimacy" principle. See *West Coast Hotel Co. v. Parrish; Brown v. Board of Education.* . . .

The joint opinion acknowledges that the Court improved its stature by overruling *Plessy* in *Brown* on a deeply divisive issue. And our decision in *West Coast Hotel*, which overruled *Adkins v. Children's Hospital* and *Lochner*, was rendered at a time when Congress was considering President Franklin Roosevelt's proposal to "reorganize" this Court and enable him to name six additional Justices in the event that any Member of the Court over the age of 70 did not elect to retire. It is difficult to imagine a situation in which the Court would face more intense opposition to a prior ruling than it did at that time, and, under the general principle proclaimed in the joint opinion, the Court seemingly should have responded to this opposition by stubbornly refusing to re-examine the *Lochner* rationale, lest it lose legitimacy by appearing to "overrule under fire."

The joint opinion . . . contends that the Court was entitled to overrule *Plessy* and *Lochner* . . . only because both the Nation and the Court had learned new lessons in the interim. This is at best a feebly supported, *post hoc* rationalization for those decisions.

For example, the opinion asserts that the Court could justifiably overrule its decision in *Lochner* only because the Depression had convinced "most people" that constitutional protection of contractual freedom contributed to an economy that failed to protect the welfare of all. Surely the joint opinion does not mean to suggest that people saw this Court's failure to uphold minimum wage statutes as the cause of the Great Depression! In any event, the *Lochner* Court did not base its rule upon the policy judgment that an unregulated market was fundamental to a stable economy; it simple believed, erroneously, that "liberty" under the Due Process Clause protected the "right to make a contract." Nor is it the case that the people of this Nation only discovered the dangers of extreme laissez-faire economics because of the Depression. State laws regulating maximum hours and minimum wages were in existence well before that time. . . .

When the Court finally recognized its error in *West Coast Hotel*, it did not engage in the *post hoc* rationalization that the joint opinion attributes to it today; it did not state that *Lochner* had been based on an economic view that had fallen into disfavor, and that it therefore should be overruled. Chief Justice Hughes in his opinion for the Court simply recognized what Justice Holmes had previously recognized in his *Lochner* dissent, that "the Constitution does not speak of freedom of contract." Although the Court did acknowledge in the last paragraph of its opinion the state of affairs during the then-current Depression, the theme of the opinion is that the Court had been mistaken as a matter of constitutional law when it embraced "freedom of contract" 32 years previously.

The joint opinion also agrees that the Court acted properly in rejecting the doctrine of "separate but equal" in *Brown*. In fact, the opinion lauds *Brown* in comparing it to *Roe*. This is strange, in that under the opinion's "legitimacy" principle the Court would seemingly have been forced to adhere to its erroneous decision in *Plessy* because of its "intensely divisive" character. To us, adherence to *Roe* today under the guise of "legitimacy" would seem to resemble more closely adherence to *Plessy* on the same ground. Fortunately, the Court did not choose that option in *Brown*, and instead frankly repudiated *Plessy*. The joint opinion concludes that such repudiation was justified only because of newly discovered evidence that segregation had the effect of treating one race as inferior to another. But it can hardly be argued that this was not urged upon those who decided *Plessy*, as Justice Harlan observed in his dissent that the law at issue "puts the brand of servitude and degradation upon a large class of our fellow-citizens, our equals before the law." It is clear that the same arguments made before the Court in *Brown* were made in *Plessy* as well. . . . The rule of *Brown* is not tied to popular opinion about the evils of segregation; it is a judgment that the Equal Protection Clause does not permit racial segregation, no matter whether the public might come to believe that it is beneficial. On that ground it stands, and on that ground alone the Court was justified in properly concluding that the *Plessy* Court had erred.

There is also a suggestion in the joint opinion that the propriety of overruling a "divisive" decision depends in part on whether "most people" would now agree that it should be overruled. . . . How such agreement would be ascertained, short of a public opinion poll, the joint opinion does not say. But surely even the suggestion is totally at war with the idea of "legitimacy" in whose name it is invoked. The Judicial Branch derives its legitimacy, not from following public opinion, but from deciding by its best lights whether legislative enactments of the popular branches of Government comport with the Constitution. . . .

In assuming that the Court is perceived as "surrendering to political pressure" when it overrules a controversial decision, the joint opinion forgets that there are two sides to any controversy. . . . The decision in *Roe* has engendered large demonstrations, including repeated marches on this Court and on Congress, both in opposition to and in support of that opinion. A decision either way on *Roe* can therefore be perceived as favoring one group or the other. But this perceived dilemma arises only if one assumes, as the joint opinion does, that the Court should make its decisions with a view toward speculative public perceptions. If one assumes instead, as the Court surely did in both *Brown* and *West Coast Hotel*, that the Court's legitimacy is enhanced by faithful interpretation of the Constitution irrespective of public opposition, such self-engendered difficulties may be put to one side. . . .

The end result of the joint opinion's paeans of praise for legitimacy is the enunciation of a brand new standard for evaluating state regulation of a woman's right to abortion—the "undue burden" standard. . . . [T]he "undue burden" standard . . . is created largely out of whole cloth by the authors of the joint opinion. It is a standard which even today does not command the support of a majority of this Court. . . .

In that this standard is based even more on a judge's subjective determinations than was the trimester framework, the standard will do nothing to prevent "judges from roaming at large in the constitutional field" guided only by their personal views. Because the undue burden standard is plucked from nowhere, the question of what is a "substantial obstacle" to abortion will undoubtedly engender a variety of conflicting views. For example, in the very matter before us now, the authors of the joint opinion would uphold Pennsylvania's 24-hour waiting period, concluding that a "particular burden" on some women is not a substantial obstacle. But the authors would at the same time strike down Pennsylvania's spousal notice provision, after finding that in a "large fraction" of cases the provision will be a substantial obstacle. And, while the authors conclude that the informed consent provisions do not constitute an "undue burden," JUSTICE STEVENS would hold that they do.

Furthermore, while striking down the spousal *notice* regulation, the joint opinion would uphold a parental *consent* restriction that certainly places very substantial obstacles in the path of a minor's abortion choice. The joint opinion is forthright in admitting that it draws this distinction based on a policy judgment that parents will have the best interests of their children at heart, while the same is not necessarily true of husbands as to their wives. This may or may not be a correct judgment, but it is quintessentially a legislative one. . . . Despite the efforts of the joint opinion, the undue burden standard presents nothing more workable than the trimester framework which it discards today. . . .

We have stated above our belief that the Constitution does not subject state abortion regulations to heightened scrutiny. Accordingly, we think that the correct analysis is that . . . [a] woman's interest in having an abortion is a form of liberty protected by the Due Process Clause, but States may regulate abortion procedures in ways rationally related to a legitimate state interest. *Williamson v. Lee Optical of Oklahoma, Inc.* With this rule in mind, we examine each of the challenged provisions.

III

C

Section 3209 of the Act contains the spousal notification provision. . . . Petitioners contend [that] many notified husbands will prevent abortions through physical force, psychological coercion, and other types of threats. But Pennsylvania has incorporated exceptions in the notice provision in an attempt to deal with these problems. . . .

The question before us is therefore whether the spousal notification requirement rationally furthers any legitimate state interests. We conclude that it does. First, a husband's interests in procreation within marriage and in the potential life of his unborn child are certainly substantial ones. . . . The State itself has legitimate interests both in protecting these interests of the father and in protecting the potential life of the fetus, and the spousal notification requirement is reasonably related to advancing those state interests. . . .

The State also has a legitimate interest in promoting "the integrity of the marital relationship." . . . In our view, the spousal notice requirement is a rational attempt by the State to improve truthful communication between spouses and encourage collaborative decisionmaking, and thereby fosters marital integrity. . . . The Pennsylvania Legislature was in a position to weigh the likely benefits of the provision against its likely adverse effects, and presumably concluded, on balance, that the provision would be beneficial. Whether this was a wise decision or not, we cannot say that it was irrational. We therefore conclude that the spousal notice provision comports with the Constitution. . . .

IV

For the reasons stated, we therefore would hold that each of the challenged provisions of the Pennsylvania statute is consistent with the Constitution. . . .

■ JUSTICE SCALIA, with whom THE CHIEF JUSTICE, JUSTICE WHITE, and JUSTICE THOMAS, concurring in the judgment in part and dissenting in part.

. . . [This] is, quite simply, the issue in these cases: not whether the power of a woman to abort her unborn child is a "liberty" in the absolute sense; or even whether it is a liberty of great importance to many women. Of course it is both. The issue is whether it is a liberty protected by the Constitution of the United States. I am sure it is not. I reach that conclusion not because of anything so exalted as my views concerning the "concept of existence, of meaning, of the universe, and of the mystery of human life." Rather, I reach it . . . because of two simple facts: (1) the Constitution says absolutely nothing about it, and (2) the longstanding traditions of American society have permitted it to be legally proscribed.

. . . The Court's statement that it is "tempting" to acknowledge the authoritativeness of tradition in order to "curb the discretion of federal judges," is of course rhetoric rather than reality; no government official is "tempted" to place restraints upon his own freedom of action, which is why Lord Acton did not say "Power tends to purify." The Court's temptation is in the quite opposite and more natural direction—towards systematically eliminating checks upon its own power; and it succumbs.

Beyond that brief summary of the essence of my position, I will not swell the United States Reports with repetition of what I have said before; and applying the rational basis test, I would uphold the Pennsylvania statute in its entirety. I must, however, respond to a few of the more outrageous arguments in today's opinion, which it is beyond human nature to leave unanswered. I shall discuss each of them under a quotation from the Court's opinion to which they pertain.

"The inescapable fact is that adjudication of substantive due process claims may call upon the Court in interpreting the Constitution to exercise that same capacity which by tradition courts always have exercised: reasoned judgment."

. . . Today's opinion describes the methodology of *Roe*, quite accurately, as weighing against the woman's interest the State's "important and legitimate interest in protecting the potentiality of human life." But "reasoned judgment" does not begin by begging the question, as *Roe* and subsequent cases unquestionably did by assuming that what the State is protecting is the mere "potentiality of human life." . . . The whole argument of abortion opponents is that what the Court calls the fetus and what others call the unborn child *is a human life*. Thus, whatever answer *Roe* came up with after conducting its "balancing" is bound to be wrong, unless it is correct that the human fetus is in some critical sense merely potentially human. There is of course no way to determine that as a legal matter; it is in fact a value judgment. . . .

The emptiness of the "reasoned judgment" that produced *Roe* is displayed in plain view by the fact that, after more than 19 years of effort by some of the brightest (and most determined) legal minds in the country, after more than 10 cases upholding abortion rights in this Court . . . the best the Court can do to explain how it is that the word "liberty" *must* be thought to include the right to destroy human fetuses is to rattle off a collection of adjectives that simply decorate a value judgment and conceal a political choice. The right to abort, we are told, inheres in "liberty" because it is among "a person's most basic decisions"; it involves a "most intimate and personal choice"; it is "central to personal dignity and autonomy"; it "originates within the zone of conscience and belief"; it is "too intimate and personal" for state interference; it reflects "intimate views" of a "deep, personal character"; it involves "intimate relationships" and notions of "personal autonomy and bodily integrity"; and it concerns a particularly "important decision." But it is obvious to anyone applying "reasoned judgment" that the same adjectives can be applied to many forms of conduct that this Court has held are *not* entitled to constitutional protection. . . . Those adjectives might be applied, for example, to homosexual sodomy, polygamy, adult incest, and suicide, all of which are equally "intimate" and "deeply personal" decisions involving "personal autonomy and bodily integrity," and all of which can constitutionally be proscribed because it is our unquestionable constitutional tradition that they are proscribable. It is not reasoned judgment that supports the Court's decision; only personal predilection. . . .

"Liberty finds no refuge in a jurisprudence of doubt."

One might have feared to encounter this august and sonorous phrase in an opinion defending the real *Roe v. Wade*, rather than the revised version fabricated today by the authors of the joint opinion. The shortcomings of *Roe* did not include lack of clarity: Virtually all regulation of abortion before the third trimester was invalid. But to come across this phrase in the joint opinion—which calls upon federal district judges to apply an "undue burden" standard as doubtful in application as it is unprincipled in origin—is really more than one should have to bear.

The joint opinion frankly concedes that the amorphous concept of "undue burden" has been inconsistently applied by the Members of this Court in the few brief years since that "test" was first explicitly propounded by JUSTICE O'CONNOR in her dissent in *Akron I*. Because the three Justices now wish to "set forth a standard of general application," the joint opinion announces that "it is important to clarify what is meant by an undue burden." I certainly agree with that, but I do not agree that the joint opinion succeeds in the announced endeavor. To the contrary, its efforts at clarification make clear only that the standard is inherently manipulable and will prove hopelessly unworkable in practice. . . .

Reason finds no refuge in this jurisprudence of confusion. . . .

"Where, in the performance of its judicial duties, the Court decides a case in such a way as to resolve the sort of intensely divisive controversy reflected in *Roe*. . . , its decision has a dimension that the resolution of the normal case does not carry. It is the dimension present whenever the Court's interpretation of the Constitution calls the contending sides of a national controversy to end their national division by accepting a common mandate rooted in the Constitution."

The Court's description of the place of *Roe* in the social history of the United States is unrecognizable. Not only did *Roe* not . . . *resolve* the deeply divisive issue of abortion; it did more than anything else to nourish it, by elevating it to the national level where it is infinitely more difficult to resolve. National politics were not plagued by abortion protests, national abortion lobbying, or abortion marches on Congress before *Roe v. Wade* was decided. Profound disagreement existed among our citizens over the issue—as it does over other issues, such as the death penalty—but that disagreement was being worked out at the state level. As with many other issues, the division of sentiment within each State was not as closely balanced as it was among the population of the Nation as a whole, meaning not only that more people would be satisfied with the results of state-by-state resolution, but also that those results would be more stable. Pre-*Roe*, moreover, political compromise was possible.

Roe's mandate for abortion on demand destroyed the compromises of the past, rendered compromise impossible for the future, and required the entire issue to be resolved uniformly, at the national level. At the same time, *Roe* created a vast new class of abortion consumers and abortion proponents by eliminating the moral opprobrium that had attached to the act. ("If the Constitution *guarantees* abortion, how can it be bad?"—not an accurate line of thought, but a natural one.) Many favor all of those developments, and it is not for me to say that they are wrong. But to portray *Roe* as the statesmanlike "settlement" of a divisive issue . . . is nothing less than Orwellian. *Roe* fanned into life an issue that has inflamed our national politics in general, and has obscured with its smoke the selection of Justices to this Court in particular, ever since. And by keeping us in the abortion-umpiring business, it is the perpetuation of that disruption, rather than of any *Pax Roeana*, that the Court's new majority decrees.

> **"To overrule under fire . . . would subvert the Court's legitimacy. . . .**
>
> **". . . To all those who will be . . . tested by following, the Court implicitly undertakes to remain stead-fast. . . . The promise of constancy, once given, binds its maker for as long as the power to stand by the decision survives and . . . the commitment [is not] obsolete. . . .**
>
> **"[The American people's] belief in themselves as . . . a people [who aspire to live according to the rule of law] is not readily separable from their understanding of the Court invested with the authority to decide their constitutional cases and speak before all others for their constitutional ideals. If the Court's legitimacy should be undermined, then, so would the country be in its very ability to see itself through its constitutional ideals."**

The Imperial Judiciary lives. It is instructive to compare this Nietzschean vision of us unelected, life-tenured judges—leading a Volk who will be "tested by following," and whose very "belief in themselves" is mystically bound up in their "understanding" of a Court that "speaks before all others for their constitutional ideals"—with the somewhat more modest role envisioned for these lawyers by the Founders.

> The judiciary . . . has . . . no direction either of the strength or of the wealth of the society, and can take no active resolution whatever. It may truly be said to have neither Force nor Will, but merely judgment. . . . The Federalist No. 78.

Or, again, to compare this ecstasy of a Supreme Court in which there is, especially on controversial matters, no shadow of change or hint of alteration ("There is a limit to the amount of error that can plausibly be imputed to prior Courts"), with the more democratic views of a more humble man:

> The candid citizen must confess that if the policy of the Government upon vital questions affecting the whole people is to be irrevocably fixed by decisions of the Supreme Court, . . . the people will have ceased to be their own rulers, having to that extent practically resigned their Government into the hands of that eminent tribunal. A. Lincoln, First Inaugural Address (Mar. 4, 1861).

It is particularly difficult, in the circumstances of the present decision, to sit still for the Court's lengthy lecture upon the virtues of "constancy," of "remaining steadfast," and adhering to "principle." Among the five Justices who purportedly adhere to *Roe*, at most three agree upon the *principle* that constitutes adherence (the joint opinion's "undue burden" standard)—and that principle is inconsistent with *Roe*. To make matters worse, two of the three, in order thus to remain steadfast, had to abandon previously stated positions. . . . It is beyond me how the Court expects these accommodations to be accepted "as grounded truly in principle, not as compromises with social and political pressures. . . ." The only principle the Court "adheres" to, it seems to me, is the principle that the Court must be seen as standing by *Roe*. That is not a principle of law . . . but a principle of *Realpolitik*—and a wrong one at that.

I cannot agree with, indeed I am appalled by, the Court's suggestion that the decision whether to stand by an erroneous constitutional decision must be strongly influenced—*against* overruling, no less—by the substantial and continuing public opposition the decision has generated. . . . In my history book, the Court was covered with dishonor and deprived of legitimacy by *Dred Scott v. Sandford*, an erroneous (and widely opposed) opinion that it did not abandon, rather than by *West Coast Hotel Co. v. Parrish*, which produced the famous "switch in time" from the Court's erroneous (and widely opposed) constitutional opposition to the social measures of the New Deal. (Both *Dred Scott* and one line of the cases resisting the New Deal rested upon the concept of "substantive due process" that the Court praises and employs today. Indeed, *Dred Scott* was "very possibly the first application of substantive due process in the Supreme Court, the original precedent for *Lochner v. New York* and *Roe v. Wade*.")

But whether it would "subvert the Court's legitimacy" or not, the notion that we would decide a case differently from the way we otherwise would have in order to show that we can stand firm against public disapproval is frightening. . . .

Of course, as THE CHIEF JUSTICE points out, we have been subjected to what the Court calls " 'political pressure' " by *both* sides of this issue. Maybe today's decision *not* to overrule *Roe* will be seen as buckling to pressure from *that* direction. Instead of engaging in the hopeless task of predicting public perception—a job not for lawyers but for political campaign managers—the Justices should do what is *legally* right by asking two questions: (1) Was *Roe* correctly decided? (2) Has *Roe* succeeded in producing a settled body of law? If the answer to both questions is no, *Roe* should undoubtedly be overruled.

In truth, I am as distressed as the Court is . . . about the "political pressure" directed to the Court: the marches, the mail, the protests aimed at inducing us to change our opinions. How upsetting it is, that so many of our citizens . . . think that we Justices should properly take into account their views, as though we were engaged not in ascertaining an objective law but in determining some kind of social consensus. The Court would profit, I think, from giving less attention to the *fact* of this distressing phenomenon, and more attention to the *cause* of it. That cause permeates today's opinion: a new mode of constitutional adjudication that relies not upon text and traditional practice to determine the law, but upon what the Court calls "reasoned judgment," which turns out to be nothing but philosophical predilection and moral intuition. . . .

What makes all this relevant to the bothersome application of "political pressure" against the Court are the twin facts that the American people love democracy and the American people are not fools. As long as this Court thought (and the people thought) that we Justices were doing essentially lawyers' work up here—reading text and discerning our society's traditional understanding of that text—the public pretty much left us alone. Texts and traditions are facts to study, not convictions to demonstrate about. But if in reality our process of constitutional adjudication . . . rests primarily on value judgments, then a free and intelligent people's attitude towards us can be expected to be (*ought* to be) quite different. The people know that their value judgments are quite as good as those taught in any law school—maybe better. If, indeed, the "liberties" protected by the Constitution are, as the Court says, undefined and unbounded, then the people *should* demonstrate, to protest that we do not implement *their* values instead of *ours*. Not only that, but confirmation hearings for new Justices *should* deteriorate into question-and-answer sessions in which Senators go through a list of their constituents' most favored and most disfavored alleged constitutional rights, and seek the nominee's commitment to support or oppose them. Value judgments, after all, should be voted on, not dictated. . . .

There is a poignant aspect to today's opinion. Its length, and what might be called its epic tone, suggest that its authors believe they are bringing to an end a troublesome era in the history of our Nation and of our Court. "It is the dimension" of authority, they say, to "call the contending sides of national controversy to end their national division by accepting a common mandate rooted in the Constitution."

There comes vividly to mind a portrait by Emanuel Leutze that hangs in the Harvard Law School: Roger Brooke Taney, painted in 1859, the 82d year of his life, the 24th of his Chief Justiceship, the second after his opinion in *Dred Scott*. He is all in black, sitting in a shadowed red armchair, left hand resting upon a pad of paper in his lap, right hand hanging limply, almost lifelessly, beside the inner arm of the chair. He sits facing the viewer and staring straight out. There seems to be on his face, and in his deep-set eyes, an expression of profound sadness and disillusionment. Perhaps he always looked that way, even when dwelling upon the happiest of thoughts. But those of us who know how the lustre of his great Chief Justiceship came to be eclipsed by *Dred Scott* cannot help believing that he had that case—its already apparent consequences for the Court and its soon-to-be-played-out consequences for the Nation—burning on his mind. I expect that two years earlier he, too, had thought himself "calling the contending sides of national controversy to end their national division by accepting a common mandate rooted in the Constitution."

It is no more realistic for us in this litigation, than it was for him in that, to think that an issue of the sort they both involved—an issue involving life and death, freedom and subjugation—can be "speedily and finally settled" by the Supreme Court, as President James Buchanan in his inaugural address said the issue of slavery in the territories would be. Quite to the contrary, by foreclosing all democratic outlet for the deep passions this issue arouses, by banishing the issue from the political forum that gives all participants, even the losers, the satisfaction of a fair hearing and an honest fight, by continuing the imposition of a rigid national rule instead of allowing for regional differences, the Court merely prolongs and intensifies the anguish.

We should get out of this area, where we have no right to be, and where we do neither ourselves nor the country any good by remaining.

NOTE ON *CASEY*, THE ABORTION DEBATE, AND COMMON LAW CONSTITUTIONALISM

1.   Both sides of the abortion debate were disappointed with the result in *Planned Parenthood v. Casey*. Pro-lifers were obviously unhappy that the Court had rejected their pleas to overrule *Roe*. Pro-choicers, on the other hand, were furious that the Court had rejected strict scrutiny and upheld most of the Pennsylvania abortion law. Which group do you think had better cause to be upset? Is it fair to say that if both sides were upset, then the Court might be doing something right?

2.   Although the Court's opinion in *Roe v. Wade* did not specify the level of scrutiny that it used to invalidate the Texas and Georgia abortion laws, subsequent decisions prior to *Casey* applied strict scrutiny to laws restricting abortions. The plurality opinion in *Casey*, however, rejected that standard and instead adopted an "undue burden" standard:

> A finding of an undue burden is a shorthand for the conclusion that a state regulation has the purpose or effect of placing a substantial obstacle in the path of a woman seeking an abortion of a nonviable fetus. A statute with this purpose is invalid because the means chosen by the State to further the interest in potential life must be calculated to inform the woman's free choice, not hinder it. And a statute which, while furthering the interest in potential life or some other valid state interest, has the effect of placing a substantial obstacle in the path of a woman's choice cannot be considered a permissible means of serving its legitimate ends.[30]

---

[30]   505 U.S. at 877 (plurality opinion).

This test seems to have two aspects: purpose and effect. But both aspects are at least somewhat ambiguous. For example, an abortion regulation may not have the purpose of "hindering" a woman's choice, but it *can* be "designed to persuade her to choose childbirth over abortion." And the plurality also made clear that "[t]he fact that a law which serves a valid purpose . . . has the incidental effect of making it more difficult or more expensive to procure an abortion cannot be enough to invalidate it." It thus seems unlikely that laws meant to discourage abortion cannot be described as serving a more permissible purpose, such as "[e]xpress[ing] profound respect for the life of the unborn." And the precise degree of interference that constitutes an impermissible effect remains murky.

Is undue burden simply a form of intermediate scrutiny, requiring a somewhat less compelling state interest and a less precise fit between means and ends than would be necessary for a law to withstand strict scrutiny? Or is it a different sort of test altogether? Consider that strict scrutiny typically applies in contexts where we are happy to wholly prohibit certain sorts of government actions. Where government censorship of speech or discrimination based on race are at issue, for instance, we are generally content for judicial scrutiny to be "strict in theory but fatal in fact." Society can generally get by, in other words, if the government simply cannot regulate in these particular ways. But not all rights are like that. Consider property rights, for example, which are plainly protected by the Takings and Due Process Clauses but have never been held to require strict scrutiny of all property regulations. That is because civilized society could hardly exist if all persons could use their property in any way they saw fit, free of government regulation. Moreover, some regulation of property rights may well be necessary to ensure that others can fully enjoy *their* property rights at the same time.

Is abortion similar? It is, after all, a potentially dangerous procedure. No one questions the necessity or legitimacy of certain basic regulations to ensure that practitioners have at least some medical training or that the procedure is performed under sanitary conditions. Strict scrutiny of all abortion regulations might make it very difficult to provide these sorts of regulations that are necessary to make abortion a meaningful and viable right for women. Other regulations, however, may be designed to deter or defeat the exercise of that right. The undue burden test seems intended to distinguish between these two different kinds of abortion regulations—those designed to *facilitate* the exercise of the right, and those meant to *deter or impede* the exercise of that right. Can you think of other constitutional rights that might benefit from this sort of treatment? Would it make sense, for example, to analyze free speech challenges to restrictions on expenditures by political campaigns in this way?

Did the plurality apply the undue burden test faithfully in *Casey* itself? Does the result there—upholding the majority of Pennsylvania's restrictions—suggest that the test is too lenient?

3. The Court grappled with the meaning of the undue burden standard most recently in *Whole Woman's Health v. Hellerstedt*, 136 S. Ct. 2292 (2016). That case involved a Texas law imposing two new requirements

on abortion providers. First, physicians performing abortions were required to have admitting privileges at a hospital located within 30 miles of the location where the abortion was to be performed. Second, abortion facilities were required to meet the minimum standards under state law for ambulatory surgical centers. After a bench trial, the district court concluded that both of these requirements would have virtually no medical benefit, given the general safety of existing abortion procedures, and that the new law had caused many abortion providers in Texas to go out of business. According to the district court, abortion facilities would remain only in Houston, Austin, San Antonio, and the Dallas/Fort Worth area; these facilities, the court found, would likely be unable to handle the resulting increase in demand for abortion services (a finding the court of appeals rejected as clearly erroneous in light of the record).

In a 5–3 decision, the Supreme Court ruled the Texas law unconstitutional. Justice Breyer's majority opinion (joined by Justices Kennedy, Ginsburg, Sotomayor, and Kagan) determined that the undue burden standard "requires that courts consider the burdens a law imposes on abortion access together with the benefits those laws confer." Moreover, it held that the court of appeals' position that "legislatures, and not courts, must resolve questions of medical uncertainty is . . . inconsistent with this Court's case law." Instead, it was appropriate for courts to evaluate the benefits and burdens of the law based on evidence in the judicial record. Rejecting the court of appeals' view of the record, the Court agreed with the trial court that the Texas law did not advance the state's interest in protecting women's health, and that it placed a substantial obstacle in the path of a woman's choice.

In dissent, Justice Thomas argued that "the majority radically rewrites the undue-burden test in three ways":

> First, today's decision requires courts to "consider the burdens a law imposes on abortion access together with the benefits those laws confer." Second, today's opinion tells the courts that, when the law's justifications are medically uncertain, they need not defer to the legislature, and must instead assess medical justifications for abortion restrictions by scrutinizing the record themselves. Finally, even if a law imposes no "substantial obstacle" to women's access to abortions, the law now must have more than a "reasonabl[e] relat[ion] to . . . a legitimate state interest." These precepts are nowhere to be found in *Casey* or its successors, and transform the undue-burden test to something much more akin to strict scrutiny.

Assuming Thomas's is a fair reading of the majority's analysis, is that analysis in fact consistent with *Casey*? Does the approach of simply balancing burdens vs benefits give a court too much freedom in evaluating abortion restrictions? If there are disputed medical—or other factual—questions, should courts defer to the legislature? (Does the fact that the court of appeals reached a different conclusion about the factual record than did the district court and the Supreme Court majority trouble you in this regard?) To what extent does the majority's approach to undue burden analysis revive the risks associated with *Lochner*'s reasonableness review?

On the other hand, wouldn't more deferential review make it easy for legislatures to undermine abortion rights?

4.   According to the joint opinion, *Roe* was a case in which "the Court's interpretation of the Constitution call[ed] the contending sides of a national controversy to end their national division by accepting a common mandate rooted in the Constitution." Is Justice Scalia right that this is exactly what Justice Taney thought he was doing in *Dred Scott*? Would it also be fair to say that it's what the Court was trying to do in *Brown*? How good is the Court at "settling" divisive social controversies through the medium of constitutional law? Should it stop trying?

A column published on the thirtieth anniversary of *Roe* compared the court-driven abortion debate in this country and the political resolution of the same debate in Europe:

> Why does abortion remain so much more controversial in America than in the other countries that have legalised it? The fundamental reason is the way the Americans went about legalisation. European countries did so through legislation and, occasionally, referenda. This allowed abortion opponents to vent their objections and legislators to adjust the rules to local tastes. Above all, it gave legalisation the legitimacy of majority support.
>
> Most European countries provide abortion free. But they have also hedged the practice with all sorts of qualifications. They justify abortion on the basis of health rather than rights. Many European countries impose a 12-week limit (America, by contrast, allows abortion up to about 24 weeks and beyond, and many abortion-rights advocates seem to oppose any restrictions.) Frances Kissling, head of Catholics for a Free Choice, also points out that the Europeans have been careful to preserve a patina of disapproval. Even in England, the country with the most liberal abortion laws in Europe, women have to get permission from two doctors.
>
> America went down the alternative route of declaring abortion a constitutional right. (The only other country that has done anything comparable is South Africa.) . . . It would be hard to design a way of legalising abortion that could be better calculated to stir up controversy. Abortion opponents were furious about being denied their say. Abortion supporters had to rely on the precarious balance of power on the Supreme Court. Legalisation did not have the legitimacy of majority support. Instead, it rested on a highly controversial interpretation of the constitution. . . . By going down the legislative road, the Europeans managed to neutralise the debate; by relying on the hammer-blow of a Supreme Court decision, the Americans institutionalised it.[31]

Do you agree that a legislative resolution of the abortion debate would have been more likely to achieve social peace on the issue? Should that resolution have taken place at the federal or the state level?

---

[31] *The War that Never Ends*, ECONOMIST, Jan. 16, 2003.

The *Economist* piece also noted some basic social differences between the U.S. and Europe—in particular, high levels of religious belief in the U.S. and a lesser willingness to cede hard questions to elites. (It also suggested that both major political parties have a stake in perpetuating the abortion debate in order to mobilize their respective supporters.) Do these factors foreclose a moderate, European-style resolution in the U.S.?

5.   Of the nine justices that sat to hear *Planned Parenthood v. Casey*, only one (Justice White, who dissented) was a Democratic appointee. And of the five appointed by Republican presidents after 1980, by which time abortion had become a central issue related to Supreme Court appointments, three (O'Connor, Kennedy, and Souter) voted to reaffirm the "central holding" of *Roe v. Wade*. What does this tell you about the ability of presidents to predict how their nominees will rule on "litmus test" issues? Or to predict what the litmus test issues will even *be*, a decade or more down the line? Recall, in this connection, that President Franklin Roosevelt appointed Hugo Black, Robert Jackson, Felix Frankfurter, and William O. Douglas because they all agreed on the constitutionality of the New Deal— the most salient constitutional issue at the time of their appointment. But these justices came to disagree sharply once attention shifted to matters of individual non-economic rights under the Warren Court.[32]

6.   Do you think that Justices O'Connor, Kennedy, and Souter would have voted with Justice Blackmun in *Roe*? To what extent is the result in *Casey* driven by imperatives of *stare decisis* rather than by agreement with *Roe*'s reasoning? Doesn't *Casey* suggest that, in vetting future supreme court nominees, it is at least as important to ask them about their views on precedent as it is to inquire into their substantive views?

> Can the authors of the joint opinion argue *stare decisis* with a straight face, given the extent to which they're willing to depart from *Roe*? After all, that opinion junks *Roe*'s trimester framework, and it abandons the strict scrutiny test for abortion regulations that developed shortly after *Roe*. Hence the Court's decision to uphold almost all the regulations on abortions that Pennsylvania had imposed. Did the Court reaffirm *Roe* in name only?

7.   The essence of *stare decisis* is that a prior decision has some degree of authoritative weight that is independent of whether a later court thinks the prior decision was right or wrong on the merits. In other words, it is insufficient to argue that a prior decision should be overruled simply on the ground that it was wrongly decided. Something more is required. The *Casey* opinions do a good job of elaborating what this "something more" entails. The Court asks:

a)   whether the rule established by the prior decision has proven *workable*;

b)   whether people have *relied* on that prior rule;

---

[32] *See generally* NOAH FELDMAN, SCORPIONS: THE BATTLES AND TRIUMPHS OF FDR'S GREAT SUPREME COURT JUSTICES (2011).

c)   whether *factual circumstances* have changed since the prior decision in a way that undermines the old rule; and

d)   whether related *legal developments* have undermined the old rule.

How helpful are these criteria? Who has the better argument as to how they play out in *Casey*? Keep in mind that these factors are not unique to the abortion context, or even to constitutional law; rather, they afford a template for *stare decisis* arguments generally.

What *is* unique in *Casey* is the joint opinion's addition of a fifth factor, relating to the special weight of *stare decisis* in "watershed" cases. In order to analyze this factor, the Court undertakes to compare *Roe* to other watershed cases. (One useful thing about the *stare decisis* debate in *Casey* is thus that it affords a review of much of the material that we've covered so far in the course.) Is the joint opinion's analysis of *Plessy* and *Lochner* persuasive? Did the Court really overrule those cases because factual circumstances had changed? Do *Brown* and *West Coast Hotel* show that the Court endangers its legitimacy by overruling prior precedent? Or do they demonstrate that sometimes overruling a prior decision can *enhance* the Court's legitimacy?

8.   Given the centrality of *stare decisis* to the plurality's analysis, it seems fair to consider *Casey* as an example of a "common law" approach to constitutional interpretation, based on incremental, case-by-case development of legal principles in much the same way as one sees in the fields of contracts or torts. A few years after *Casey*, Justice Antonin Scalia wrote a famous essay contrasting this approach with a "civil law" approach, based on the Continental legal tradition.[33] In that tradition, there is no strong doctrine of judicial precedent, and judges are exhorted simply to apply their own best interpretation of the relevant statutory or constitutional text. It follows that the meaning of the governing statutes is not supposed to evolve through judicial interpretations. Each successive judicial application of the statute looks back to the original text, not to what courts have said about that text.[34] The Anglo-American legal tradition, by contrast, features a heavy reliance on "common law"—that is, incremental development of legal principles through judicial decisions in individual cases, which then become part of the enduring law through *stare decisis*. Consider, for example, the evolution of tort, contract, and property law, which has occurred mostly through judicial elaboration with relatively little intervention by legislatures.

Justice Scalia's argument was that although American judges— particularly *state* judges—have common law powers in many areas, constitutional law is not supposed to be one of them. Constitutional law, in

---

[33] Antonin Scalia, *Common Law Courts in a Civil-Law System*, in ANTONIN SCALIA, A MATTER OF INTERPRETATION: FEDERAL COURTS AND THE LAW 37–47 (Amy Gutmann ed., 1997).

[34] *But see* JOHN HENRY MERRYMAN & ROGELIO PÉREZ-PERDOMO, THE CIVIL LAW TRADITION: AN INTRODUCTION TO THE LEGAL SYSTEMS OF WESTERN EUROPE AND LATIN AMERICA 47 (3d ed. 2007) ("Although there is no formal rule of *stare decisis*, the practice is for judges to be influenced by prior decisions.").

his view, is meant to be a *civil law* system, based upon an authoritative text and giving no law*making* authority to judges. What binds judges, in other words, is the Constitution—not what judges have said about it. [35] Some commentators have taken this argument even further to say that, to the extent *stare decisis* requires a judge to adhere to a prior judicial decision rather than his own best judgment as to what the constitutional text itself means, the doctrine of *stare decisis* is unconstitutional. Consider this argument by Professor Gary Lawson:

> Suppose ... that a court is faced with a conflict between the Constitution on the one hand and a prior judicial decision on the other. Is there any doubt that, under the reasoning of *Marbury*, the court must choose the Constitution over the prior decision? ... If the Constitution says X and a prior judicial decision says Y, a court has not merely the power, but the obligation, to prefer the Constitution. [36]

If you disagree with Professor Lawson, where precisely can you fault his argument? More generally, do you agree with Justice Scalia that the Court over-emphasizes prior decisions as a means of determining the meaning of the Constitution?

9. Other commentators have defended the role of the courts in elaborating constitutional meaning. Lawrence Sager, for example, has urged that judges are full "partners" with the constitutional Founders in elaborating constitutional meaning:

> The justice-seeking account [of constitutionalism] sees a transtemporal partnership at the heart of our constitutional practice. One partner consists of those persons in the founding or amending generations who participate in the utterance of the Constitution's text. The other partner consists of the judges who participate in the judicial interpretation of that text. Key is the idea of *partnership* as opposed to *agency*: Judges are not merely or even primarily instruction-takers; their independent normative judgment is expected and welcomed. The object of this partnership is the project of bringing our political community better into conformity with fundamental requirements of political justice.

> The partnership at the center of our justice-seeking constitutional practice has a characteristic structure: At least with regard to the liberty bearing provisions of the Constitution, the popular constitutional decision-maker typically speaks at a high level of generality and of moral abstraction. The job of the constitutional judiciary thus becomes applying very general constitutional commitments to concrete cases, with the concomitant obligations of generating case-spanning doctrine and

---

[35] *But see Cooper v. Aaron*, 358 U.S. 1, 18 (1958) ("[T]he interpretation of the Fourteenth Amendment enunciated by this Court in the *Brown* case is the supreme law of the land.").

[36] Gary Lawson, *The Constitutional Case Against Precedent*, 17 HARV. J.L. & PUB. POL'Y 23, 28 (1994).

> moral understandings which choose among competing accounts of the Constitution's lofty norms. . . .
>
> Obviously, on this view, judges are not merely taking instructions in some mechanical sense. . . . Justice-seeking constitutionalism . . . welcomes the independent judgmental role of judges as well-suited to the enterprise that is its namesake.[37]

Is this view of the judges' role persuasive? Does it presume that judges will "seek justice" in a particular way—for example, by advancing "progressive" versions of morality? On the other hand, if judges cannot seek justice, what is the point of making them independent?

Does the institutional independence of judges alone warrant the assumption that judges will be better at making moral choices than elected officials? Does this perspective provide any basis for criticizing Chief Justice Taney in *Dred Scott* or Justice Peckham in *Lochner*? That is, can they not say that, by injecting their own values into the Due Process Clause, they were simply "partnering" with the Framers? One answer would be to say that Taney and Peckham simply advanced the *wrong* values. But can that response be squared with Justice Holmes' insistence in his *Lochner* dissent that "a constitution . . . is made for people of fundamentally differing views"?

10. A more modest defense of a judicial role in the evolution of common law meaning might embrace the common law method that Justice Scalia decries. Thomas Grey, for instance, argued that "[i]f common law development is an appropriate judicial function, falling within the traditionally accepted judicial role, is not the functionally similar case-by-case development of constitutional norms appropriate as well?"[38] The question, of course, is what constrains judicial discretion in a common-law constitution?

> In a jurisprudence of *doctrine*, the primary tool of constitutional interpretation will be judicial precedent rather than originalist history or abstract moral theory. This approach mirrors the reality of constitutional advocacy. . . . [A]dherence to precedent . . . takes account of a constitutional provision's line of growth from the original period down to the present. When used as a means of divining the present meaning of a constitutional provision as it has evolved over time, precedent itself functions as a tool of interpretation; rather than offering a reason to adhere to an incorrect interpretation under the doctrine of *stare decisis*, the force of precedent enters into the initial determination of what the correct interpretation *is*. Use of precedent in this way allows the judge to tap into a cumulative wisdom that transcends his own rationality. As Dean Brest observes, "a doctrine that survives over a period of time has the approval of a court composed, in effect, of all the judges who have ever had occasion to consider and apply it." More generally, a heavy reliance on precedent acknowledges the

---

[37] LAWRENCE G. SAGER, JUSTICE IN PLAINCLOTHES: A THEORY OF AMERICAN CONSTITUTIONAL PRACTICE 76–77 (2004).

[38] Grey, *supra* note 25, at 715.

fact that "no judicial system could do society's work if it eyed each issue afresh in every case that raised it."

When specific precedents cannot directly determine a result, judges pursuing the common-law model are nonetheless constrained to some extent by the conventions of legal argument and reasoning. These considerations confine the range of arguments presented to courts by advocates. . . . [T]his shared sense of what is relevant in a situation sharply reduces the number of considerations that might otherwise be thought germane and makes it much more than merely idealistic to talk about treating like cases alike. An important part of this shared vision of what it means to argue like a lawyer is a commitment to the method of analogical reasoning. . . . According to [Cass] Sunstein, the doctrine of stare decisis means that a certain number of outcomes must be respected as starting points for further reasoning; as a result, "[w]ithin the legal culture, analogical reasoning imposes a certain discipline" that can help courts to reach determinate results even in the absence of "widespread moral or political consensus."

Similarly, judges may also be constrained by norms and procedures inherent in the judicial process . . . including "dedication to analyzing the record of the case, a refusal to twist the historical truth to reach a desired result, a respect for adjacent institutions, and a vision of a judicial opinion as a ruling tailored to address the specific legal issues presented to the Court in a given case." These norms, of course, can hardly decide cases, and judges pursuing them may certainly find ways to impose their own subjective preferences. Nonetheless, a judge who approaches a dispute feeling that he is bound to certain norms of craft regardless of his substantive predispositions is already a long way from the attitude of a court that is nothing but a "naked power organ." . . . The individual discretionary power of any given judge is further constrained by the fact that, at the appellate levels at least, judicial decisionmaking is a collective process. The need to convince others of potentially differing views provides an incentive to confine discussion to the more common ground of distinctly "legal" modes of analysis, an incentive which strengthens the already "deeply internalized role constraints" of most judges, who tend to insist that "judgment is not politics." Even good faith commitment to the norms of legal reasoning, of course, cannot entirely prevent substantive moral and political views from intruding into adjudication. The need for consensus, however, will substantially constrain the range of possible outcomes.[39]

Is this "common law" approach really any more constrained than Dean Sager's "partnership" approach? Is Justice Scalia right to think that *any*

---

[39] Ernest Young, *Rediscovering Conservatism: Burkean Political Theory and Constitutional Interpretation*, 72 N.C. L. REV. 619, 691–93 (1994).

evolutionary position will dissolve the crucial distinction between law and politics?

11.   Perhaps the real danger of common law constitutionalism lies in the other direction, however. Rather than making judges too powerful, Justice Scalia worried that "evolutionary" forms of interpretation would empower majorities:

> In the last analysis, however, it probably does not matter what principle, among the innumerable possibilities, the evolutionist proposes to determine in what direction The Living Constitution will grow. Whatever he might propose, at the end of the day an evolving constitution will evolve the way the majority wishes. . . . The American people have been converted to belief in The Living Constitution, a "morphing" document that means, from age to age, what it ought to mean. And with that conversion has inevitably come the new phenomenon of selecting and confirming federal judges, at all levels, on the basis of their views regarding a whole series of proposals for constitutional evolution. If the courts are free to write the Constitution anew, they will, by God, write it the way the majority wants; the appointment and confirmation process will see to that. This, of course, is the end of the Bill of Rights, whose meaning will be committed to the very body it was meant to protect against: the majority. By trying to make the Constitution do everything that needs doing from age to age, we shall have caused it to do nothing at all.[40]

Is Justice Scalia right that "living constitutionalism" may threaten constitutionalism itself?

---

[40]   Scalia, *supra* note 33, at 46.

PART THREE

THE STRUCTURAL CONSTITUTION

We turn now from rights to structure, and from history to doctrine. It is worth bearing in mind that the original Constitution of 1789 had relatively little to say about individual rights. The primary means by which the Framers proposed to secure individual liberty was by limiting and dividing the powers of government. Although they were quickly persuaded to add a Bill of Rights to the original Constitution, for much of our history the principal "action" in Constitutional Law concerned the structural principles of federalism and separation of powers. This has again been true in recent years. Between the Rehnquist Court's "revival" of constitutional federalism, the early Roberts Court's preoccupation with executive power in the War on Terror, and broad-based federalism-based challenges to national policy on healthcare, immigration, and drug enforcement, structural issues once again occupy the foreground of Constitutional Law.

Prior to 1789, the conventional wisdom in political theory was that "sovereignty"—ultimate political authority—must reside at some unitary point in every political system. According to the historian Bernard Bailyn, the Framers believed that "there must reside somewhere in every political unit a single, undivided, final power, higher in legal authority than any other power, subject to no law, a law unto itself."[1] In monarchical systems, this point was the king or queen; in parliamentary systems like Britain, it was "the King in Parliament," that is, the Crown and Parliament working together. The people who fought the Revolution, however, had had enough of unitary sovereigns with the power to make or unmake any law they pleased. The Framers thus paid only lip service to the traditional principle that sovereignty must be unitary, reposing that ultimate, undivided authority in the People at large. Alexander Hamilton reflected the general view when he wrote in Federalist 22 that the People were "that pure original fountain of all legitimate authority."[2]

The People, of course, are something of an abstraction most of the time. As a practical matter, the Framers' political theory divided sovereignty between multiple government institutions. As James Wilson explained, the People "can distribute one portion of power to the more contracted circle called State governments; they can also furnish another

---

[1] BERNARD BAILYN, THE IDEOLOGICAL ORIGINS OF THE AMERICAN REVOLUTION 198 (2d ed. 1992).

[2] THE FEDERALIST No. 22 (Alexander Hamilton), at 146 (Cooke ed. 1982).

proportion to the government of the United States."[3] The American Founders thus "split the atom of sovereignty" by dividing ultimate power along constitutional lines.[4] This third part of the course explores the contours and implications of that division.

The American Constitution divides sovereignty in two ways: between the Nation and the States, and among the three branches of the federal government. (The States' portion of sovereignty is also divided among different branches of government, but that division is reflected in *state* constitutions.) We call the vertical division "federalism" and the horizontal division "separation of powers", but it is important to remember that both principles reflect the Framers' commitment to separated and divided power. The first chapters of this Part deal with federalism; the latter sections deal with separation of powers. It will become apparent, however, that many different connections link these two sets of issues.

---

[3]   1 PENNSYLVANIA AND THE FEDERAL CONSTITUTION, 1787–1788, at 302 (J. McMaster & F. Stone eds. 1888) (quoting James Wilson).

[4]   *United States Term Limits v. Thornton*, 514 U.S. 779, 838 (1995) (Kennedy, J., concurring).

CHAPTER EIGHT

THE FEDERAL SYSTEM

Writing in *New York v. United States*,[1] Justice O'Connor described the appropriate division of authority between the States and the Nation as "the oldest question of constitutional law." It is critical to remember that, in 1787, the "United States" was a new creation but the States were not, having existed not only as independent and robust entities since 1776 but also as largely autonomous colonies for many decades under British rule. The American colonies and the early states were not only politically autonomous but also considerably more ethnically, culturally, and religiously distinctive than the states we know today.

American federalism was thus in part a concession to political and social reality: The States would not surrender their independence lightly, and appeals over their heads to "the People" would encounter firmly rooted loyalties to the existing state governments. These loyalties were much stronger than most Americans would feel today, in an age when most citizens pay most of their attention to national politics. Robert E. Lee's decision to decline the offer of command of the Union Army in 1861 and cast his lot with Virginia, for example, likely seems incomprehensible to most of us today. It would have seemed quite natural to John Jay, however, who resigned his post as Chief Justice of the United States in 1795 in order to take what he regarded as a better job as Governor of the State of New York.

This Chapter offers an introductory overview of American constitutional federalism. Chapters Nine, Ten, and Eleven then cover particular aspects of federalism doctrine. Section 8.1 begins with two key essays from the Federalist Papers, which lay out the Framers' theories of the extended republic and of institutionally-divided powers. We then turn to the *Term Limits* case, which explored in depth the Framers' theory of sovereignty and democratic representation in a federal system. The Section concludes with an overview of the underlying values—e.g., efficiency, democratic participation, protection of liberty—at stake in choosing between state and national power.

Section 8.2 addresses the relation between judicial review and the political dynamics of federalism. In particular, we consider a widely held view that judicial enforcement of federalism is relatively unnecessary because the States are protected from national encroachments by the structure and composition of Congress itself. This argument was advanced most famously by Professor Herbert Wechsler in the 1950's, but it can be traced back to James Madison in Federalist Nos. 45 and 46. We will examine this claim about the "political safeguards of federalism"

---

[1] *New York v. United States*, 505 U.S. 144, 149 (1992).

in the context of a line of cases concerning Congress's power to subject the institutions of state government themselves to federal regulation. In considering the propriety of judicial review in federalism cases, however, you should recall the Supreme Court's experience in that area chronicled in Part Two.

SECTION 8.1   THE FEDERAL SYSTEM AND DUAL SOVEREIGNTY

Most of the Founding Generation believed that republican government—that is, government by active and virtuous citizens committed to the common good—was realistically possible only in relatively small political communities, like the city states of ancient Greece. They regarded the national Leviathan proposed by the Philadelphia Convention with a great deal of suspicion, afraid that it would become a distant and unaccountable empire on the Roman or British model. Federalists and Antifederalists alike thus agreed that the new national entity must share power with the smaller state governments, which were closer to the People.

The essays from the Federalist Papers that follow address this problem of how to maintain a republican government in the new circumstances of America. In particular, these essays consider the problem of "faction"—that is, special interests that seek to use government to pursue their own selfish ends rather than the public good. Federalist 10 and 51 propose distinct strategies to deal with faction: Federalist 10 argues that the *size* of the new nation is a help, not a hindrance to republican government, and Federalist 51 contends that selfish interests can be harnessed to serve the public good through a system of checks and balances. These two essays form the core of the political theory defended in the Federalist and embodied in the proposed Constitution.

The notion of "dual sovereignty" was central to the Federalists' political theory, although it is not the focus of Federalist 10 or 51. The Founders acknowledged the conventional wisdom that sovereignty must be unitary by positing that supreme power "resides in the PEOPLE, as the fountain of government."[2] But in practice, they held that the People *delegated* this sovereignty to different agents for different purposes. With respect to the enumerated powers delegated to the national government in the Constitution, that national government would be "sovereign"; with respect to those powers reserved to the States, on the other hand, each State government would wield sovereign authority. As a practical matter, then, the sovereign authority was split in two. In such a system, of course, it is terribly important to identify and police the boundary between the powers of each potentially sovereign government; hence the recurrent

---

[2]   1 PENNSYLVANIA AND THE FEDERAL CONSTITUTION, 1787–1788, at 302 (J. McMaster & f. Stone eds. 1888) (quoting leading Federalist James Wilson).

litigation over the line between inter- and intra-state commerce in cases like *Gibbons v. Ogden*, *Hammer v. Dagenhart*, and *Wickard v. Filburn*.

Although the concepts are sometimes blurred or confused, these materials distinguish sharply between "dual sovereignty," used here to signify simply the division of ultimate political authority between two levels of government, and "dual federalism," connoting one strategy (among many) for drawing the boundary between the authority of the national sovereign and the States. Under dual federalism, as exemplified by cases like *U. S. v. E.C. Knight* and *Hammer v. Dagenhart*, the Nation and the States have separate and exclusive spheres of authority. That is one way to implement the notion of dual *sovereignty*, but as subsequent assignments will make clear, it is not the only one. We will take up that boundary question again shortly in defining the powers of Congress. The current assignment, however, focuses on the implications of dual sovereignty for the Framers' theory of representation—a question debated by the Justices in the *Term Limits* case.

Finally, this assignment lays some groundwork for the remainder of the unit by exploring some of the values associated with national action, as well as the values associated with leaving certain matters to the States. These values will frequently undergird disputes about the scope and limits of national and state power.

Federalist No. 10 (James Madison)

To the People of the State of New York:

Among the numerous advantages promised by a well constructed Union, none deserves to be more accurately developed than its tendency to break and control the violence of faction. The friend of popular governments never finds himself so much alarmed for their character and fate, as when he contemplates their propensity to this dangerous vice. He will not fail, therefore, to set a due value on any plan which, without violating the principles to which he is attached, provides a proper cure for it. The instability, injustice, and confusion introduced into the public councils, have, in truth, been the mortal diseases under which popular governments have everywhere perished; as they continue to be the favorite and fruitful topics from which the adversaries to liberty derive their most specious declamations. The valuable improvements made by the American [state] constitutions on the popular models, both ancient and modern, cannot certainly be too much admired; but it would be an unwarrantable partiality, to contend that they have as effectually obviated the danger on this side, as was wished and expected. Complaints are everywhere heard from our most considerate and virtuous citizens, equally the friends of public and private faith, and of public and personal liberty, that our governments are too unstable, that the public good is disregarded in the conflicts of rival parties, and that measures are too often decided, not according to the rules of justice and the rights of the minor party, but by the superior force of an interested and overbearing majority. However anxiously we may wish that these complaints had no foundation, the evidence of known facts will not permit us to deny that they are in some degree true. It will be found, indeed, on a candid review of our situation, that some of the distresses under which we labor have been erroneously charged on the operation of our governments; but it will be found, at the same time, that other causes will not alone account for many of our heaviest misfortunes; and, particularly, for that prevailing and increasing distrust of public engagements, and alarm for private rights, which are echoed from one end of the continent to the other. These must be chiefly, if not wholly, effects of the unsteadiness and injustice with which a factious spirit has tainted our public administrations.

By a faction, I understand a number of citizens, whether amounting to a majority or a minority of the whole, who are united and actuated by some common impulse of passion, or of interest, adverse to the rights of other citizens, or to the permanent and aggregate interests of the community.

There are two methods of curing the mischiefs of faction: the one, by removing its causes; the other, by controlling its effects.

There are again two methods of removing the causes of faction: the one, by destroying the liberty which is essential to its existence; the other, by giving to every citizen the same opinions, the same passions, and the same interests.

It could never be more truly said than of the first remedy, that it was worse than the disease. Liberty is to faction what air is to fire, an aliment without which it instantly expires. But it could not be less folly to abolish liberty, which is essential to political life, because it nourishes faction, than it would be to wish the annihilation of air, which is essential to animal life, because it imparts to fire its destructive agency.

The second expedient is as impracticable as the first would be unwise. As long as the reason of man continues fallible, and he is at liberty to exercise it, different opinions will be formed. As long as the connection subsists between his reason and his self-love, his opinions and his passions will have a reciprocal influence on each other; and the former will be objects to which the latter will attach themselves. The diversity in the faculties of men, from which the rights of property originate, is not less an insuperable obstacle to a uniformity of interests. The protection of these faculties is the first object of government. From the protection of different and unequal faculties of acquiring property, the possession of different degrees and kinds of property immediately results; and from the influence of these on the sentiments and views of the respective proprietors, ensues a division of the society into different interests and parties.

The latent causes of faction are thus sown in the nature of man; and we see them everywhere brought into different degrees of activity, according to the different circumstances of civil society. A zeal for different opinions concerning religion, concerning government, and many other points, as well of speculation as of practice; an attachment to different leaders ambitiously contending for pre-eminence and power; or to persons of other descriptions whose fortunes have been interesting to the human passions, have, in turn, divided mankind into parties, inflamed them with mutual animosity, and rendered them much more disposed to vex and oppress each other than to co-operate for their common good. So strong is this propensity of mankind to fall into mutual animosities, that where no substantial occasion presents itself, the most frivolous and fanciful distinctions have been sufficient to kindle their unfriendly passions and excite their most violent conflicts. But the most common and durable source of factions has been the various and unequal distribution of property. Those who hold and those who are without property have ever formed distinct interests in society. Those who are creditors, and those who are debtors, fall under a like discrimination. A landed interest, a manufacturing interest, a mercantile interest, a moneyed interest, with many lesser interests, grow up of necessity in civilized nations, and divide them into different classes, actuated by different sentiments and views. The regulation of these various and interfering interests forms the principal task of modern legislation, and involves the spirit of party and faction in the necessary and ordinary operations of the government.

No man is allowed to be a judge in his own cause, because his interest would certainly bias his judgment, and, not improbably, corrupt his integrity. With equal, nay with greater reason, a body of men are unfit to be both judges and parties at the same time; yet what are many of the most important acts of legislation, but so many judicial determinations, not indeed concerning the rights of single persons, but concerning the rights of large bodies of citizens? And what are the different classes of legislators but advocates and parties to the causes which they determine? Is a law proposed concerning private debts? It is a question to which the creditors are parties on one side and the debtors on the other. Justice ought to hold the balance between them. Yet the parties are, and must be, themselves the judges; and the most numerous party, or, in other words, the most powerful faction must be expected to prevail. Shall domestic manufactures be encouraged, and in what degree, by restrictions on foreign manufactures? are questions which would be differently decided by the landed and the manufacturing classes, and probably by neither with a sole regard to justice and the public good. The apportionment of taxes on the various descriptions of property is an act which seems to require the most exact impartiality; yet there is, perhaps, no legislative act in which greater opportunity and temptation are given to a predominant party to trample on the rules of justice. Every shilling with which they overburden the inferior number, is a shilling saved to their own pockets.

It is in vain to say that enlightened statesmen will be able to adjust these clashing interests, and render them all subservient to the public good. Enlightened statesmen will not always be at the helm. Nor, in many cases, can such an adjustment be made at all without taking into view indirect and remote considerations, which will rarely prevail over the immediate interest which one party may find in disregarding the rights of another or the good of the whole.

The inference to which we are brought is, that the CAUSES of faction cannot be removed, and that relief is only to be sought in the means of controlling its EFFECTS.

If a faction consists of less than a majority, relief is supplied by the republican principle, which enables the majority to defeat its sinister views by regular vote. It may clog the administration, it may convulse the society; but it will be unable to execute and mask its violence under the forms of the Constitution. When a majority is included in a faction, the form of popular government, on the other hand, enables it to sacrifice to its ruling passion or interest both the public good and the rights of other citizens. To secure the public good and private rights against the danger of such a faction, and at the same time to preserve the spirit and the form of popular government, is then the great object to which our inquiries are directed. Let me add that it is the great desideratum by which this form of government can be rescued from the opprobrium under which it has so long labored, and be recommended to the esteem and adoption of mankind.

By what means is this object attainable? Evidently by one of two only. Either the existence of the same passion or interest in a majority at the same time must be prevented, or the majority, having such coexistent passion or interest, must be rendered, by their number and local situation, unable to concert and carry into effect schemes of oppression. If the impulse and the opportunity be suffered to coincide, we well know that neither moral nor religious motives can be relied on as an adequate control. They are not found to be such on the injustice and violence of individuals, and lose their efficacy in proportion to the number combined together, that is, in proportion as their efficacy becomes needful.

From this view of the subject it may be concluded that a pure democracy, by which I mean a society consisting of a small number of citizens, who assemble and administer the government in person, can admit of no cure for the mischiefs of faction. A common passion or interest will, in almost every case, be felt by a majority of the whole; a communication and concert result from the form of government itself; and there is nothing to check the inducements to sacrifice the weaker party or an obnoxious individual. Hence it is that such democracies have ever been spectacles of turbulence and contention; have ever been found incompatible with personal security or the rights of property; and have in general been as short in their lives as they have been violent in their deaths. Theoretic politicians, who have patronized this species of government, have erroneously supposed that by reducing mankind to a perfect equality in their political rights, they would, at the same time, be perfectly equalized and assimilated in their possessions, their opinions, and their passions.

A republic, by which I mean a government in which the scheme of representation takes place, opens a different prospect, and promises the cure for which we are seeking. Let us examine the points in which it varies from pure democracy, and we shall comprehend both the nature of the cure and the efficacy which it must derive from the Union.

The two great points of difference between a democracy and a republic are: first, the delegation of the government, in the latter, to a small number of citizens elected by the rest; secondly, the greater number of citizens, and greater sphere of country, over which the latter may be extended.

The effect of the first difference is, on the one hand, to refine and enlarge the public views, by passing them through the medium of a chosen body of citizens, whose wisdom may best discern the true interest of their country, and whose patriotism and love of justice will be least likely to sacrifice it to temporary or partial considerations. Under such a regulation, it may well happen that the public voice, pronounced by the representatives of the people, will be more consonant to the public good than if pronounced by the people themselves, convened for the purpose. On the other hand, the effect may be inverted. Men of factious tempers, of local prejudices, or of sinister designs, may, by intrigue, by corruption, or by other means, first obtain the suffrages, and then betray the interests, of the people. The question resulting is, whether small or extensive republics are more favorable to the election of proper guardians of the public weal; and it is clearly decided in favor of the latter by two obvious considerations:

In the first place, it is to be remarked that, however small the republic may be, the representatives must be raised to a certain number, in order to guard against the cabals of a few; and that, however large it may be, they must be limited to a certain number, in order to guard against the confusion of a multitude. Hence, the number of representatives in the two cases not being in proportion to that of the two constituents, and being proportionally greater in the small republic, it follows that, if the proportion of fit characters be not less in the large than in the small republic, the former will present a greater option, and consequently a greater probability of a fit choice.

In the next place, as each representative will be chosen by a greater number of citizens in the large than in the small republic, it will be more difficult for unworthy candidates to practice with success the vicious arts by which elections are too often carried; and the suffrages of the people being more free, will be more likely to centre in men who possess the most attractive merit and the most diffusive and established characters.

It must be confessed that in this, as in most other cases, there is a mean, on both sides of which inconveniences will be found to lie. By enlarging too much the number of electors, you render the representatives too little acquainted with all their local circumstances and lesser interests; as by reducing it too much, you render him unduly attached to these, and too little fit to comprehend and pursue great and national objects. The federal Constitution forms a happy combination in this respect; the great and aggregate interests being referred to the national, the local and particular to the State legislatures.

The other point of difference is, the greater number of citizens and extent of territory which may be brought within the compass of republican than of democratic government; and it is this circumstance principally which renders factious combinations less to be dreaded in the former than in the latter. The smaller the society, the fewer probably will be the distinct parties and interests composing it; the fewer the distinct parties and interests, the more frequently will a majority be found of the same party; and the smaller the number of individuals composing a majority, and the smaller the compass within which they are placed, the more easily will they concert and execute their plans of oppression. Extend the sphere, and you take in a greater variety of parties and interests; you make it less probable that a majority of the whole will have a common motive to invade the rights of other citizens; or if such a common motive exists, it will be more difficult for all who feel it to discover their own strength, and to act in unison with each other. Besides other impediments, it may be remarked that, where there is a consciousness of unjust or dishonorable purposes, communication is always checked by distrust in proportion to the number whose concurrence is necessary.

Hence, it clearly appears, that the same advantage which a republic has over a democracy, in controlling the effects of faction, is enjoyed by a large over a small republic, is enjoyed by the Union over the States composing it. Does the advantage consist in the substitution of representatives whose enlightened views and virtuous sentiments render them superior to local prejudices and schemes of injustice? It will not be denied that the representation of the Union will be most likely to possess these requisite endowments. Does it consist in the greater security afforded by a greater variety of parties, against the event of any one party being able to outnumber and oppress the rest? In an equal degree does the increased variety of parties comprised within the Union, increase this security. Does it, in fine, consist in the greater obstacles opposed to the concert and accomplishment of the secret wishes of an unjust and interested majority? Here, again, the extent of the Union gives it the most palpable advantage.

The influence of factious leaders may kindle a flame within their particular States, but will be unable to spread a general conflagration through the other States. A religious sect may degenerate into a political faction in a part of the Confederacy; but the variety of sects dispersed over the entire face of it must secure the national councils against any danger from that source. A rage for paper money, for an abolition of debts, for an equal division of property, or for any other improper or wicked project, will be less apt to pervade the whole body of the Union than a particular member of it; in the same proportion as such a malady is more likely to taint a particular county or district, than an entire State.

In the extent and proper structure of the Union, therefore, we behold a republican remedy for the diseases most incident to republican government. And according to the degree of pleasure and pride we feel in being republicans, ought to be our zeal in cherishing the spirit and supporting the character of Federalists.

PUBLIUS.

Federalist No. 51 (James Madison)

To the People of the State of New York:

To what expedient, then, shall we finally resort, for maintaining in practice the necessary partition of power among the several departments, as laid down in the Constitution? The only answer that can be given is, that as all these exterior provisions are found to be inadequate, the defect must be supplied, by so contriving the interior structure of the government as that its several constituent parts may, by their mutual relations, be the means of keeping each other in their proper places. Without presuming to undertake a full development of this important idea, I will hazard a few general observations, which may perhaps place it in a clearer light, and enable us to form a more correct judgment of the principles and structure of the government planned by the convention.

In order to lay a due foundation for that separate and distinct exercise of the different powers of government, which to a certain extent is admitted on all hands to be essential to the preservation of liberty, it is evident that each department should have a will of its own; and consequently should be so constituted that the members of each should have as little agency as possible in the appointment of the members of the others. Were this principle rigorously adhered to, it would require that all the appointments for the supreme executive, legislative, and judiciary magistracies should be drawn from the same fountain of authority, the people, through channels having no communication whatever with one another. Perhaps such a plan of constructing the several departments would be less difficult in practice than it may in contemplation appear. Some difficulties, however, and some additional expense would attend the execution of it. Some deviations, therefore, from the principle must be admitted. In the constitution of the judiciary department in particular, it might be inexpedient to insist rigorously on the principle: first, because peculiar qualifications being essential in the members, the primary consideration ought to be to select that mode of choice which best secures these qualifications; secondly, because the permanent tenure by which the appointments are held in that department, must soon destroy all sense of dependence on the authority conferring them.

It is equally evident, that the members of each department should be as little dependent as possible on those of the others, for the emoluments annexed to their offices. Were the executive magistrate, or the judges, not independent of the legislature in this particular, their independence in every other would be merely nominal.

But the great security against a gradual concentration of the several powers in the same department, consists in giving to those who administer each department the necessary constitutional means and personal motives to resist encroachments of the others. The provision for defense must in this, as in all other cases, be made commensurate to the danger of attack. Ambition must be made to counteract ambition. The interest of the man must be connected with the constitutional rights of the place. It may be a reflection on human nature, that such devices should be necessary to control the abuses of government. But what is government itself, but the greatest of all reflections on human nature? If men were angels, no government would be necessary. If angels were to govern men, neither external nor internal controls on government would be necessary. In framing a government which is to be administered by men over men, the great difficulty lies in this: you must first enable the government to control the governed; and in the next place oblige it to control itself. A dependence on the people is, no doubt, the primary control on the government; but experience has taught mankind the necessity of auxiliary precautions.

This policy of supplying, by opposite and rival interests, the defect of better motives, might be traced through the whole system of human affairs, private as well as public. We see it particularly displayed in all the subordinate distributions of power, where the constant aim is to divide and arrange the several offices in such a manner as that each may be a check on the other that the private interest of every individual may be a sentinel over the public rights. These inventions of prudence cannot be less requisite in the distribution of the supreme powers of the State.

But it is not possible to give to each department an equal power of self-defense. In republican government, the legislative authority necessarily predominates. The remedy for this inconveniency is to divide the legislature into different branches; and to render them, by different modes of election and different principles of action, as little connected with each other as the nature of their common functions and their common dependence on the society will admit. It may even be necessary to guard against dangerous encroachments by still further precautions. As the weight of the legislative authority requires that it should be thus divided, the weakness of the executive may require, on the other hand, that it should be fortified. An absolute negative on the legislature appears, at first view, to be the natural defense with which the executive magistrate should be armed. But perhaps it would be neither altogether safe nor alone sufficient. On ordinary occasions it might not be exerted with the requisite firmness, and on extraordinary occasions it might be perfidiously abused. May not this defect of an absolute negative be supplied by some qualified connection between this weaker department and the weaker branch of the stronger department, by which the latter may be led to support the constitutional rights of the former, without being too much detached from the rights of its own department?

If the principles on which these observations are founded be just, as I persuade myself they are, and they be applied as a criterion to the several State constitutions, and to the federal Constitution it will be found that if the latter does not perfectly correspond with them, the former are infinitely less able to bear such a test.

There are, moreover, two considerations particularly applicable to the federal system of America, which place that system in a very interesting point of view.

First. In a single republic, all the power surrendered by the people is submitted to the administration of a single government; and the usurpations are guarded against by a division of the government into distinct and separate departments. In the compound republic of America, the power surrendered by the people is first divided between two distinct governments, and then the portion allotted to each subdivided among distinct and separate departments. Hence a double security arises to the rights of the people. The different governments will control each other, at the same time that each will be controlled by itself.

Second. It is of great importance in a republic not only to guard the society against the oppression of its rulers, but to guard one part of the society against the injustice of the other part. Different interests necessarily exist in different classes of citizens. If a majority be united by a common interest, the rights of the minority will be insecure. There are but two methods of providing against this evil: the one by creating a will in the community independent of the majority that is, of the society itself; the other, by comprehending in the society so many separate descriptions of citizens as will render an unjust combination of a majority of the whole very improbable, if not impracticable. The first method prevails in all governments possessing an hereditary or self-appointed authority. This, at best, is but a precarious security; because a power independent of the society may as well espouse the unjust views of the major, as the rightful interests of the minor party, and may possibly be turned against both parties. The second method will be exemplified in the federal republic of the United States. Whilst all authority in it will be derived from and dependent on the society, the society itself will be broken into so many parts, interests, and classes of citizens, that the rights of individuals, or of the minority, will be in little danger from interested combinations of the majority. In a free government the security for civil rights must be the same as that for religious rights. It consists in the one case in the multiplicity of interests, and in the other in the multiplicity of sects. The degree of security in both cases will depend on the number of interests and sects; and this may be presumed to depend on the extent of country and number of people comprehended under the same government. This view of the subject must particularly recommend a proper federal system to all the sincere and considerate friends of republican government, since it shows that in exact proportion as the territory of the Union may be formed into more circumscribed Confederacies, or States oppressive combinations of a majority will be facilitated: the best security, under the republican forms, for the rights of every class of citizens, will be diminished: and consequently the stability and independence of some member of the government, the only other security, must be proportionately increased.

Justice is the end of government. It is the end of civil society. It ever has been and ever will be pursued until it be obtained, or until liberty be lost in the pursuit. In a society under the forms of which the stronger faction can readily unite and oppress the weaker, anarchy may as truly be said to reign as in a state of nature, where the weaker individual is not secured against the violence of the stronger; and as, in the latter state, even the stronger individuals are prompted, by the uncertainty of their condition, to submit to a government which may protect the weak as well as themselves; so, in the former state, will the more powerful factions or parties be gradually induced, by a like motive, to wish for a government which will protect all parties, the weaker as well as the more powerful.

It can be little doubted that if the State of Rhode Island was separated from the Confederacy and left to itself, the insecurity of rights under the popular form of government within such narrow limits would be displayed by such reiterated oppressions of factious majorities that some power altogether independent of the people would soon be called for by the voice of the very factions whose misrule had proved the necessity of it. In the extended republic of the United States, and among the great variety of interests, parties, and sects which it embraces, a coalition of a majority of the whole society could seldom take place on any other principles than those of justice and the general good; whilst there being thus less danger to a minor from the will of a major party, there must be less pretext, also, to provide for the security of the former, by introducing into the government a will not dependent on the latter, or, in other words, a will independent of the society itself. It is no less certain than it is important, notwithstanding the contrary opinions which have been entertained, that the larger the society, provided it lie within a practical sphere, the more duly capable it will be of self-government. And happily for the REPUBLICAN CAUSE, the practicable sphere may be carried to a very great extent, by a judicious modification and mixture of the FEDERAL PRINCIPLE.

PUBLIUS.

NOTE ON THE POLITICAL THEORY OF THE FEDERALIST

1. The *Federalist Papers* were penned by John Jay, James Madison, and Alexander Hamilton and published as individual "op-eds" in newspapers in order to influence the debate over ratification in the State of New York. They can be read on at least two levels—as advocacy, designed to persuade ordinary people to take a particular political action, and as high political theory. There is evidence that the *Federalist* essays were not all that widely read at the time of their original publication. [3] Should that matter in assessing their importance? Nevertheless, later courts, scholars, and lawyers treat them almost as an "owner's manual" for the Constitution. What accounts for their influence?

2. Political theorists, from Plato and Aristotle to the present day, have often started out with a basic view of human nature—that is, of whether people are basically good or bad, rational or irrational. What is Madison's view on this question? How does he allow for the basic proclivities of human nature in constructing his theory of government?

3. The Constitution itself makes no provision for political parties. Federalist 10 indicates why: A "political party" is simply another term for a *faction*, and in the Federalists' view, an important purpose of constitution-making was to minimize the influence of such self-interested groupings of persons. Contemporary political scientists, by contrast, often take the view that "the only way collective responsibility has ever existed, and can exist, given our institutions, is through the agency of the political party; in American politics, responsibility requires cohesive parties."[4] The two-party system is a pervasive aspect of our governmental structure, notwithstanding its absence from the constitutional text.

Throughout our study of constitutional structure, it will be important to consider the impact of contemporary party politics on the structures that the anti-faction Federalists established. For example, shared partisan loyalties may account for the willingness of congressional majorities to cede power to the President, notwithstanding Federalist 51's expectation that each institution would zealously guard its own power.

Is it possible to reconcile strong parties with Federalist 10 if the parties themselves are "extended spheres" comprising many diverse interests? For much of the twentieth century, for example, both the Republican and Democratic parties were ideologically diverse, with each including both liberal and conservative wings. It seems plausible that political parties contribute to political stability when both major parties are ideologically heterogeneous and inter-party competition takes the form of appeals to the undecided political center (the median voter).

---

[3] *See* Larry D. Kramer, *Madison's Audience*, 112 HARV. L. REV. 611 (1999).

[4] Morris P. Fiorina, *The Decline of Collective Responsibility in American Politics*, 109 DAEDALUS 25, 26 (1980).

It is also worth considering, however, whether the benign view of partisan competition that pervaded American political science in the twentieth century adequately describes our current politics, which is dominated by a high degree of partisan polarization.[5] In recent years, however, both the Republican and Democratic parties have become ideologically homogeneous; there are virtually no more Rockefeller (liberal) Republicans or Blue Dog (conservative) Democrats.[6] And electoral competition has increasingly become a matter of maximizing turnout of partisans by mobilizing each party's "base"—that is, the most ideologically-committed members of the party. Hence one sees less appeals to moderates and greater demonization of the other party. Under these conditions, is it fair to say that American parties have become more like the factions that the authors of the Federalist dreaded?

4.   Is Madison's argument in Federalist 10 based on the *relative* size of the Nation and the individual States, or is it based on their *absolute* sizes? To see why this distinction might matter, consider the following observation:

> Madison's argument has . . . been undermined by the maturation of the states themselves into large political communities by the standards of Madison's day. The total United States population in 1790 was around 3.9 million. In 2000, the State of California alone boasted 33.8 million inhabitants. The United States in 1790 had slightly more people than the State of Oregon (the 28th most populous state) today. The largest state in 1790—Madison's own Virginia, with approximately three-quarters of a million people-was about the size of the city of San Francisco or Indianapolis today.[7]

What do these changes in absolute size for each level of government—national, state, and local—mean for Madison's argument? Can a medium-sized state like Oregon now capture all the advantages of Madison's "extended sphere"? On the other hand, do advances in communications and social media allow much larger groups to operate as if they were smaller?

5.   Contemporary political scientists have criticized Madison's "failure to appreciate the disproportionate influence that can be wielded on a national level by certain groups that may be relatively small in numbers but that are cohesive and can avoid the problem of too many free riders."[8] This literature suggests that "the diffusion of power among a multiplicity of [state] governments may increase the difficulties such groups experience in realizing their objectives."[9] For example, the coal industry probably finds it easier to lobby one government (Congress) against strict CO_2 emissions

---

[5] *See generally* ALAN I. ABRAMOWITZ, THE POLARIZED PUBLIC? WHY AMERICAN GOVERNMENT IS SO DYSFUNCTIONAL (2013).

[6]   *See, e.g.,* Cristina Marcos, *Blue Dog Ranks Dwindle Further*, THE HILLE, Nov. 5, 2014, available at http://thehill.com/blogs/ballot-box/house-races/223069-blue-dog-ranks-to-shrink-in-next-congress.

[7]   Ernest A. Young, *Making Federalism Doctrine: Fidelity, Institutional Competence, and Compensating Adjustments*, 46 WM. & MARY L. REV. 1733, 1791 n.232 (2005) (citations omitted).

[8]   DAVID L. SHAPIRO, FEDERALISM: A DIALOGUE 79 (1995).

[9]   *Id.*

controls than it would to lobby in fifty different state capitols. If we must guard against *both* tyrannical majorities *and* cohesive minorities, can we still accept Madison's argument for the superiority of the "extended sphere"?

6.   In Federalist 51, federalism and separation of powers work together to form a "double security" for liberty:

> In the compound republic of America, the power surrendered by the people is first divided between two distinct governments, and then the portion allotted to each subdivided among distinct and separate departments. Hence a double security arises to the rights of the people. The different governments will control each other, at the same time that each will be controlled by itself.

Doesn't this arrangement safeguard liberty at the expense of efficient and effective governance? How helpful is the "double security" of a "compound republic" if, for example, multiple levels of government must coordinate their responses to a disaster like Hurricane Katrina? Can we afford to guard liberty by immobilizing government in our present day and age?

7.   We know from Hamilton's essay in Federalist 78 that the authors of the *Federalist Papers* contemplated a role for judicial review in enforcing constitutional guarantees. But given that Federalist 10 and 51 form the heart of the Federalists' structural theory, how important do you think that judicial role really is? Does Madison even mention it?

> Neither Federalist 10 nor 51 has much to say about representation or dual sovereignty. The Framers' views on that question emerge, however, from the evidence discussed in *Term Limits*. Consider, as you read, which Justice paints the most persuasive picture of the Framers' theory.

See also: For a contemporary take on the Federalist essays, see SANFORD LEVINSON, AN ARGUMENT OPEN TO ALL: READING "THE FEDERALIST" IN THE 21ST CENTURY (2015).

U.S. Term Limits, Inc. v. Thornton

514 U.S. 779 (1995)

■ JUSTICE STEVENS delivered the opinion of the Court.

The Constitution sets forth qualifications for membership in the Congress of the United States. Article I, § 2, cl. 2, which applies to the House of Representatives, provides:

> No Person shall be a Representative who shall not have attained to the Age of twenty five Years, and been seven Years a Citizen of the United States, and who shall not, when elected, be an Inhabitant of that State in which he shall be chosen.

Article I, § 3, cl. 3, which applies to the Senate, similarly provides:

> No Person shall be a Senator who shall not have attained to the Age of thirty Years, and been nine Years a Citizen of the United

States, and who shall not, when elected, be an Inhabitant of that State for which he shall be chosen.

Today's cases present a challenge to an amendment to the Arkansas State Constitution that prohibits the name of an otherwise-eligible candidate for Congress from appearing on the general election ballot if that candidate has already served three terms in the House of Representatives or two terms in the Senate. The Arkansas Supreme Court held that the amendment violates the Federal Constitution. We agree with that holding. Such a state-imposed restriction is contrary to the "fundamental principle of our representative democracy," embodied in the Constitution, that "the people should choose whom they please to govern them." Allowing individual States to adopt their own qualifications for congressional service would be inconsistent with the Framers' vision of a uniform National Legislature representing the people of the United States. If the qualifications set forth in the text of the Constitution are to be changed, that text must be amended.

I

At the general election on November 3, 1992, the voters of Arkansas adopted Amendment 73 to their State Constitution. Proposed as a "Term Limitation Amendment," its preamble stated:

> The people of Arkansas find and declare that elected officials who remain in office too long become preoccupied with reelection and ignore their duties as representatives of the people. Entrenched incumbency has reduced voter participation and has led to an electoral system that is less free, less competitive, and less representative than the system established by the Founding Fathers. Therefore, the people of Arkansas, exercising their reserved powers, herein limit the terms of elected officials.

The limitations in Amendment 73 apply to three categories of elected officials. Section 1 provides that no elected official in the executive branch of the state government may serve more than two 4-year terms. Section 2 applies to the legislative branch of the state government; it provides that no member of the Arkansas House of Representatives may serve more than three 2-year terms and no member of the Arkansas Senate may serve more than two 4-year terms. Section 3, the provision at issue in these cases, applies to the Arkansas Congressional Delegation. It provides:

(a) Any person having been elected to three or more terms as a member of the United States House of Representatives from Arkansas shall not be certified as a candidate and shall not be eligible to have his/her name placed on the ballot for election to the United States House of Representatives from Arkansas.

(b) Any person having been elected to two or more terms as a member of the United States Senate from Arkansas shall not be certified as a candidate and shall not be eligible to have his/her name placed on the ballot for election to the United States Senate from Arkansas.

... On November 13, 1992, respondent Bobbie Hill, on behalf of herself, similarly situated Arkansas "citizens, residents, taxpayers and registered voters," and the League of Women Voters of Arkansas, filed a complaint in the Circuit Court for Pulaski County, Arkansas, seeking a declaratory judgment that § 3 of Amendment 73 is "unconstitutional and void." ... Several proponents of the amendment ... intervened, including petitioner U.S. Term Limits, Inc.

On cross-motions for summary judgment, the Circuit Court held that § 3 of Amendment 73 violated Article I of the Federal Constitution. With respect to that holding ... the Arkansas Supreme Court affirmed. ... We now affirm.

II

[T]he constitutionality of Amendment 73 depends critically on the resolution of two distinct issues. The first is whether the Constitution forbids States to add to or alter the qualifications specifically enumerated in the Constitution. The second is, if the Constitution does so forbid, whether the fact that Amendment 73 is formulated as a ballot access restriction rather than as an outright disqualification is of constitutional significance. Our resolution of these issues draws upon our prior resolution of a related but distinct issue: whether Congress has the power to add to or alter the qualifications of its Members.

Twenty-six years ago, in *Powell v. McCormack,* 395 U.S. 486 (1969), we reviewed the history and text of the Qualifications Clauses in a case involving an attempted exclusion of a duly elected Member of Congress. The principal issue was whether the power granted to each House in Art. I, § 5, cl. 1, to judge the "Qualifications of its own Members"[3] includes the power to impose qualifications other than those set forth in the text of the Constitution. In an opinion by Chief Justice Warren for eight Members of the Court, we held that it does not. ...

The Issue in Powell

In November 1966, Adam Clayton Powell, Jr., was elected from a District in New York to serve in the United States House of Representatives for the 90th Congress. Allegations that he had engaged in serious misconduct while serving as a committee chairman during the 89th Congress led to the appointment of a Select Committee to determine his eligibility to take his seat. That committee found that Powell met the age, citizenship, and residency requirements set forth in Art. I, § 2, cl. 2. The committee also found, however, that Powell had wrongfully diverted House funds for the use of others and himself and had made false reports

---

[3]   Art. I, § 5, cl. 1, provides in part: "Each House shall be the Judge of the Elections, Returns and Qualifications of its own Members. . . ."

on expenditures of foreign currency. Based on those findings, the House after debate adopted House Resolution 278, excluding Powell from membership in the House, and declared his seat vacant.

Powell and several voters of the district from which he had been elected filed suit seeking a declaratory judgment that the House Resolution was invalid because Art. I, § 2, cl. 2, sets forth the exclusive qualifications for House membership. We ultimately accepted that contention, concluding that the House of Representatives has no "authority to *exclude* any person, duly elected by his constituents, who meets all the requirements for membership expressly prescribed in the Constitution." In reaching that conclusion, we undertook a detailed historical review to determine the intent of the Framers. Though recognizing that the Constitutional Convention debates themselves were inconclusive, we determined that the "relevant historical materials" reveal that Congress has no power to alter the qualifications in the text of the Constitution.

Powell's Reliance on History

We started our analysis in *Powell* by examining the British experience with qualifications for membership in Parliament, focusing in particular on the experience of John Wilkes. While serving as a member of Parliament, Wilkes had published an attack on a peace treaty with France. This literary endeavor earned Wilkes a conviction for seditious libel and a 22-month prison sentence. In addition, Parliament declared Wilkes ineligible for membership and ordered him expelled. Despite (or perhaps because of) these difficulties, Wilkes was reelected several times. Parliament, however, persisted in its refusal to seat him. After several years of Wilkes' efforts, the House of Commons voted to expunge the resolutions that had expelled Wilkes and had declared him ineligible, labeling those prior actions "subversive of the rights of the whole body of electors of this kingdom." After reviewing Wilkes' "long and bitter struggle for the right of the British electorate to be represented by men of their own choice," we concluded in *Powell* that "on the eve of the Constitutional Convention, English precedent stood for the proposition that the law of the land had regulated the qualifications of members to serve in parliament' and those qualifications were 'not occasional but fixed.'"

Against this historical background, we viewed the Convention debates as manifesting the Framers' intent that the qualifications in the Constitution be fixed and exclusive. We found particularly revealing the debate concerning a proposal made by the Committee of Detail that would have given Congress the power to add property qualifications. James Madison argued that such a power would vest "an improper & dangerous power in the Legislature," by which the Legislature "can by degrees subvert the Constitution." 2 Records of the Federal Convention of 1787, pp. 249–250 (M. Farrand ed. 1911). Madison continued: "A Republic may be converted into an aristocracy or oligarchy as well by limiting the number capable of being elected, as the number authorized to elect." We expressly noted that the "parallel between Madison's arguments and those made in Wilkes' behalf is striking." . . .

We also recognized in *Powell* that the post-Convention ratification debates confirmed that the Framers understood the qualifications in the Constitution to be fixed and unalterable by Congress. For example, we noted that in response to the antifederalist charge that the new Constitution favored the wealthy and well born, Alexander Hamilton wrote:

> The truth is that there is no method of securing to the rich the preference apprehended but by prescribing qualifications of property either for those who may elect or be elected. But this forms no part of the power to be conferred upon the national government. . . . *The qualifications of the persons who may choose or be chosen, as has been remarked upon other occasions, are defined and fixed in the Constitution, and are unalterable by the legislature.*

We thus attached special significance to "Hamilton's express reliance on the immutability of the qualifications set forth in the Constitution." Moreover, we reviewed the debates at the state conventions and found that they "also demonstrate the Framers' understanding that the qualifications for members of Congress had been fixed in the Constitution."

The exercise by Congress of its power to judge the qualifications of its Members further confirmed this understanding. We concluded that, during the first 100 years of its existence, "Congress strictly limited its power to judge the qualifications of its members to those enumerated in the Constitution."

As this elaborate summary reveals, our historical analysis in *Powell* was both detailed and persuasive. We thus conclude now, as we did in *Powell*, that history shows that, with respect to Congress, the Framers intended the Constitution to establish fixed qualifications.[9]

Powell's Reliance on Democratic Principles

In *Powell*, of course, we did not rely solely on an analysis of the historical evidence, but instead complemented that analysis with "an examination of the basic principles of our democratic system." We noted that allowing Congress to impose additional qualifications would violate

---

[9] The text of the Qualifications Clauses also supports the result we reached in *Powell*. John Dickinson of Delaware observed that the enumeration of a few qualifications "would by implication tie up the hands of the Legislature from supplying omissions." Justice Story made the same point: "It would seem but fair reasoning upon the plainest principles of interpretation, that when the constitution established certain qualifications, as necessary for office, it meant to exclude all others, as prerequisites. . . ." 1 J. Story, Commentaries on the Constitution of the United States § 625 (3d ed. 1858). . . .

that "fundamental principle of our representative democracy . . . 'that the people should choose whom they please to govern them.' ' "

Our opinion made clear that this broad principle incorporated at least two fundamental ideas.[10] First, we emphasized the egalitarian concept that the opportunity to be elected was open to all. We noted in particular Madison's statement in The Federalist [No. 52] that "under these reasonable limitations [enumerated in the Constitution], the door of this part of the federal government is open to merit of every description, whether native or adoptive, whether young or old, and without regard to poverty or wealth, or to any particular profession of religious faith." . . .

Second, we recognized the critical postulate that sovereignty is vested in the people, and that sovereignty confers on the people the right to choose freely their representatives to the National Government. For example, we noted that "Robert Livingston . . . endorsed this same fundamental principle: 'The people are the best judges who ought to represent them. To dictate and control them, to tell them whom they shall not elect, is to abridge their natural rights.' " . . .

Powell thus establishes two important propositions: first, that the "relevant historical materials" compel the conclusion that, at least with respect to qualifications imposed by Congress, the Framers intended the qualifications listed in the Constitution to be exclusive; and second, that that conclusion is equally compelled by an understanding of the "fundamental principle of our representative democracy . . . 'that the people should choose whom they please to govern them.' " . . .

III

Our reaffirmation of *Powell* does not necessarily resolve the specific questions presented in these cases. For petitioners argue that whatever the constitutionality of additional qualifications for membership imposed by Congress, the historical and textual materials discussed in *Powell* do not support the conclusion that the Constitution prohibits additional qualifications imposed by States. In the absence of such a constitutional prohibition, petitioners argue, the Tenth Amendment and the principle of reserved powers require that States be allowed to add such qualifications. . . . We disagree for two independent reasons. First, we conclude that the power to add qualifications is not within the "original powers" of the States, and thus is not reserved to the States by the Tenth Amendment. Second, even if States possessed some original power in this area, we conclude that the Framers intended the Constitution to be the

---

[10] The principle also incorporated the more practical concern that reposing the power to adopt qualifications in Congress would lead to a self perpetuating body to the detriment of the new Republic. See, *e.g.,* 2 Farrand 250 (Madison) ("If the Legislature could regulate [the qualification of electors or elected], it can by degrees subvert the Constitution. A Republic may be converted into an aristocracy or oligarchy as well by limiting the number capable of being elected, as the number authorized to elect.")

exclusive source of qualifications for Members of Congress, and that the Framers thereby "divested" States of any power to add qualifications.

The "plan of the convention" as illuminated by the historical materials, our opinions, and the text of the Tenth Amendment draws a basic distinction between the powers of the newly created Federal Government and the powers retained by the pre-existing sovereign States. . . . Hamilton[ ] reason[ed] in The Federalist No. 32 that the plan of the Constitutional Convention did not contemplate "an entire consolidation of the States into one complete national sovereignty," but only a partial consolidation in which "the State governments would clearly retain all the rights of sovereignty which they before had, and which were not, by that act, *exclusively* delegated to the United States." The text of the Tenth Amendment unambiguously confirms this principle:

> The powers not delegated to the United States by the Constitution, nor prohibited by it to the States, are reserved to the States respectively, or to the people.

As we have frequently noted, "the States unquestionably do retain a significant measure of sovereign authority. They do so, however, *only to the extent that the Constitution has not divested them of their original powers* and transferred those powers to the Federal Government." *Garcia v. San Antonio Metropolitan Transit Authority,* 469 U.S. 528 (1985).

Source of the Power

Contrary to petitioners' assertions, the power to add qualifications is not part of the original powers of sovereignty that the Tenth Amendment reserved to the States. [T]hat Amendment could only "reserve" that which existed before. As Justice Story recognized, "the states can exercise no powers whatsoever, which exclusively spring out of the existence of the national government, which the constitution does not delegate to them. . . . No state can say, that it has reserved, what it never possessed." . . .

With respect to setting qualifications for service in Congress, no such right existed before the Constitution was ratified. . . . [T]he Framers envisioned a uniform national system, rejecting the notion that the Nation was a collection of States, and instead creating a direct link between the National Government and the people of the United States. . . . In that National Government, representatives owe primary allegiance not to the people of a State, but to the people of the Nation. As Justice Story observed, each Member of Congress is "an officer of the union, deriving his powers and qualifications from the constitution, and neither created by, dependent upon, nor controllable by, the states. . . . Those officers owe their existence and functions to the united voice of the whole, not of a portion, of the people." . . .

We believe that the Constitution reflects the Framers' general agreement with the approach later articulated by Justice Story. For example, Art. I, § 5, cl. 1, provides: "Each House shall be the Judge of the Elections, Returns and Qualifications of its own Members." The text of the Constitution thus gives the representatives of all the people the final say in judging the qualifications of the representatives of any one State. . . .

In short, as the Framers recognized, electing representatives to the National Legislature was a new right, arising from the Constitution itself. The Tenth Amendment thus provides no basis for concluding that the States possess reserved power to add qualifications to those that are fixed in the Constitution. Instead, any state power to set the qualifications for membership in Congress must derive not from the reserved powers of state sovereignty, but rather from the delegated powers of national sovereignty. In the absence of any constitutional delegation to the States of power to add qualifications to those enumerated in the Constitution, such a power does not exist.

The Preclusion of State Power

Even if we believed that States possessed as part of their original powers some control over congressional qualifications, the text and structure of the Constitution, the relevant historical materials, and, most importantly, the "basic principles of our democratic system" all demonstrate that the Qualifications Clauses were intended to preclude the States from exercising any such power and to fix as exclusive the qualifications in the Constitution. . . .

The Convention and Ratification Debates

The available affirmative evidence indicates the Framers' intent that States have no role in the setting of qualifications. In Federalist Paper No. 52, dealing with the House of Representatives, Madison addressed the "qualifications of the electors and the elected." Madison first noted the difficulty in achieving uniformity in the qualifications for electors, which resulted in the Framers' decision to require only that the qualifications for federal electors be the same as those for state electors. . . . Madison then explicitly contrasted the state control over the qualifications of electors with the lack of state control over the qualifications of the elected:

> The qualifications of the elected, being less carefully and properly defined by the State constitutions, and being at the same time more susceptible of uniformity, have been very properly considered and regulated by the convention. A representative of the United States must be of the age of twenty-five years; must have been seven years a citizen of the United States; must, at the time of his election be an inhabitant of the State he is to represent; and, during the time of his service must be in no office under the United States. Under these reasonable limitations, the door of this part of the federal government is open to merit of every description, whether native or adoptive,

whether young or old, and without regard to poverty or wealth, or to any particular profession of religious faith.

Madison emphasized this same idea in The Federalist No. 57:

Who are to be the objects of popular choice? Every citizen whose merit may recommend him to the esteem and confidence of his country. *No qualification of wealth, of birth, of religious faith, or of civil profession is permitted to fetter the judgment or disappoint the inclination of the people.* (emphasis added).

The provisions in the Constitution governing federal elections confirm the Framers' intent that States lack power to add qualifications. The Framers feared that the diverse interests of the States would undermine the National Legislature, and thus they adopted provisions intended to minimize the possibility of state interference with federal elections. For example, to prevent discrimination against federal electors, the Framers required in Art. I, § 2, cl. 1, that the qualifications for federal electors be the same as those for state electors. As Madison noted, allowing States to differentiate between the qualifications for state and federal electors "would have rendered too dependent on the State governments that branch of the federal government which ought to be dependent on the people alone." Similarly, in Art. I, § 4, cl. 1, though giving the States the freedom to regulate the "Times, Places and Manner of holding Elections," the Framers created a safeguard against state abuse by giving Congress the power to "by Law make or alter such Regulations." . . .

The Framers' discussion of the salary of representatives reveals similar concerns. . . . The Convention ultimately agreed to vest in Congress the power to set its own compensation. See Art. I, § 6.[20]

In light of the Framers' evident concern that States would try to undermine the National Government, they could not have intended States to have the power to set qualifications. Indeed, one of the more anomalous consequences of petitioners' argument is that it accepts federal supremacy over the procedural aspects of determining the times, places, and manner of elections while allowing the States *carte blanche* with respect to the substantive qualifications for membership in Congress. . . .

In our view, it is inconceivable that the Framers would provide a specific constitutional provision to ensure that federal elections would be held while at the same time allowing States to render those elections meaningless by simply ensuring that no candidate could be qualified for office. Given the Framers' wariness over the potential for state abuse, we must conclude that the specification of fixed qualifications in the constitutional text was intended to prescribe uniform rules that would preclude modification by either Congress or the States.

---

[20] The Framers' decision to reject a proposal allowing for States to recall their own representatives reflects these same concerns.

We find further evidence of the Framers' intent in Art. 1, § 5, cl. 1, which provides: "Each House shall be the Judge of the Elections, Returns and Qualifications of its own Members." That Art. I, § 5, vests a federal tribunal with ultimate authority to judge a Member's qualifications is fully consistent with the understanding that those qualifications are fixed in the Federal Constitution, but not with the understanding that they can be altered by the States. . . .

We also find compelling the complete absence in the ratification debates of any assertion that States had the power to add qualifications. In those debates, the question whether to require term limits, or "rotation," was a major source of controversy. The draft of the Constitution that was submitted for ratification contained no provision for rotation.[22] In arguments that echo in the preamble to Arkansas' Amendment 73, opponents of ratification condemned the absence of a rotation requirement, noting that "there is no doubt that senators will hold their office perpetually; and in this situation, they must of necessity lose their dependence, and their attachments to the people." Even proponents of ratification expressed concern about the "abandonment in every instance of the necessity of rotation in office." At several ratification conventions, participants proposed amendments that would have required rotation.

The Federalists' responses to those criticisms and proposals addressed the merits of the issue, arguing that rotation was incompatible with the people's right to choose. . . .

Regardless of which side has the better of the debate over rotation, it is most striking that nowhere in the extensive ratification debates have we found any statement by either a proponent or an opponent of rotation that the draft constitution would permit States to require rotation for the representatives of their own citizens. If the participants in the debate had believed that the States retained the authority to impose term limits, it is inconceivable that the Federalists would not have made this obvious response to the arguments of the pro-rotation forces. . . .

Congressional Experience

. . . In *Powell*, we . . . noted that during the first 100 years of its existence, "Congress strictly limited its power to judge the qualifications of its members to those enumerated in the Constitution." Congress first confronted the issue in 1807 when it faced a challenge to the qualifications of William McCreery, a Representative from Maryland who allegedly did not satisfy a residency requirement imposed by that State. In recommending that McCreery be seated, the Report of the House Committee on Elections noted:

> The committee proceeded to examine the Constitution, with relation to the case submitted to them, and find that

---

[22] A proposal requiring rotation for Members of the House was proposed at the Convention but was defeated unanimously. There is no record of any debate on either occasion.

qualifications of members are therein determined, without reserving any authority to the State Legislatures to change, add to, or diminish those qualifications; and that, by that instrument, Congress is constituted the sole judge of the qualifications prescribed by it, and are obliged to decide agreeably to the Constitutional rules. . . .

The Chairman of the House Committee on Elections elaborated during debate:

> The Committee of Elections considered the qualifications of members to have been unalterably determined by the Federal Convention, unless changed by an authority equal to that which framed the Constitution at first; that neither the State nor the Federal Legislatures are vested with authority to add to those qualifications, so as to change them.

As we noted in *Powell*, the congressional debate over the committee's recommendation tended to focus on the "narrow issue of the power of the States to add to the standing qualifications set forth in the Constitution." The whole House, however, did not vote on the committee's report, and instead voted only on a simple resolution: "*Resolved*, That William McCreery is entitled to his seat in this House." That resolution passed by a vote of 89 to 18.

Though the House Debate may be inconclusive, commentators at the time apparently viewed the seating of McCreery as confirmation of the States' lack of power to add qualifications. For example . . . Thomas Jefferson noted the argument that "to add new qualifications to those of the Constitution would be as much an alteration as to detract from them"; he then added: "And so I think the House of Representatives of Congress decided in some case; I believe that of a member from Baltimore."

Similarly, for over 150 years prior to *Powell*, commentators viewed the seating of McCreery as an expression of the view of the House that States could not add to the qualifications established in the Constitution. . . .

The Senate experience with state-imposed qualifications further supports our conclusions. In 1887, for example, the Senate seated Charles Faulkner of West Virginia, despite the fact that a provision of the West Virginia Constitution purported to render him ineligible to serve. . . . We recognize, as we did in *Powell*, that "congressional practice has been erratic" and that the precedential value of congressional exclusion cases is "quite limited." Nevertheless, those incidents lend support to the result we reach today.

Democratic Principles

Our conclusion that States lack the power to impose qualifications vindicates the same "fundamental principle of our representative democracy" that we recognized in *Powell*, namely, that "the people should choose whom they please to govern them."

[A]n egalitarian ideal—that election to the National Legislature should be open to all people of merit—provided a critical foundation for the constitutional structure. This egalitarian theme echoes throughout the constitutional debates. . . . Additional qualifications pose the same obstacle to open elections whatever their source. The egalitarian ideal, so valued by the Framers, is thus compromised to the same degree by additional qualifications imposed by States as by those imposed by Congress.

Similarly, we believe that state-imposed qualifications, as much as congressionally imposed qualifications, would undermine the second critical idea recognized in *Powell:* that an aspect of sovereignty is the right of the people to vote for whom they wish. Again, the source of the qualification is of little moment in assessing the qualification's restrictive impact.

Finally, state-imposed restrictions, unlike the congressionally imposed restrictions at issue in *Powell*, violate a third idea central to this basic principle: that the right to choose representatives belongs not to the States, but to the people. From the start, the Framers recognized that the "great and radical vice" of the Articles of Confederation was "the principle of LEGISLATION for STATES or GOVERNMENTS, in their CORPORATE or COLLECTIVE CAPACITIES, and as contradistinguished from the INDIVIDUALS of whom they consist." The Federalist No. 15 (Hamilton). Thus the Framers, in perhaps their most important contribution, conceived of a Federal Government directly responsible to the people, possessed of direct power over the people, and chosen directly, not by States, but by the people. The Framers implemented this ideal most clearly in the provision, extant from the beginning of the Republic, that calls for the Members of the House of Representatives to be "chosen every second Year by the People of the several States." Art. I, § 2, cl. 1. Following the adoption of the Seventeenth Amendment in 1913, this ideal was extended to elections for the Senate. The Congress of the United States, therefore, is not a confederation of nations in which separate sovereigns are represented by appointed delegates, but is instead a body composed of representatives of the people. . . .

The Framers deemed this principle critical when they discussed qualifications. For example, during the debates on residency requirements, [Robert] Morris noted that in the House, *"the people at large,* not the *States,* are represented." Similarly, George Read noted that the Framers "were forming a *National* Government and such a regulation would correspond little with the idea that we were one people." James Wilson "enforced the same consideration."

Consistent with these views, the constitutional structure provides for a uniform salary to be paid from the national treasury, allows the States but a limited role in federal elections, and maintains strict checks on state interference with the federal election process. The Constitution also provides that the qualifications of the representatives of each State will be judged by the representatives of the entire Nation. The Constitution thus creates a uniform national body representing the interests of a single people.

Permitting individual States to formulate diverse qualifications for their representatives would result in a patchwork of state qualifications, undermining the uniformity and the national character that the Framers envisioned and sought to ensure. . . . Such a patchwork would also sever the direct link that the Framers found so critical between the National Government and the people of the United States.[32]

State Practice

Petitioners attempt to overcome this formidable array of evidence against the States' power to impose qualifications by arguing that the practice of the States immediately after the adoption of the Constitution demonstrates their understanding that they possessed such power. One may properly question the extent to which the States' own practice is a reliable indicator of the contours of restrictions that the Constitution imposed on States, especially when no court has ever upheld a state-imposed qualification of any sort. But petitioners' argument is unpersuasive even on its own terms. At the time of the Convention, "almost all the State Constitutions required members of their Legislatures to possess considerable property." Despite this near uniformity, only one State, Virginia, placed similar restrictions on Members of Congress, requiring that a representative be, *inter alia*, a "freeholder." Just 15 years after imposing a property qualification, Virginia replaced that requirement with a provision requiring that representatives be only "qualified according to the constitution of the United States." Moreover, several States, including New Hampshire, Georgia, Delaware, and South Carolina, revised their Constitutions at around the time of the Federal Constitution. In the revised Constitutions, each State retained property qualifications for its own state elected officials yet placed no property qualification on its congressional representatives.

The contemporaneous state practice with respect to term limits is similar. At the time of the Convention, States widely supported term limits in at least some circumstances. The Articles of Confederation contained a provision for term limits. As we have noted, some members of the Convention had sought to impose term limits for Members of Congress. In addition, many States imposed term limits on state officers, four placed limits on delegates to the Continental Congress, and several

---

[32] There is little significance to the fact that Amendment 73 was adopted by a popular vote, rather than as an act of the state legislature. In fact, none of the petitioners argues that the constitutionality of a state law would depend on the method of its adoption. This is proper, because the voters of Arkansas, in adopting Amendment 73, were acting as citizens of the State of Arkansas, and not as citizens of the National Government. The people of the State of Arkansas have no more power than does the Arkansas Legislature to supplement the qualifications for service in Congress. . . .

States voiced support for term limits for Members of Congress. Despite this widespread support, no State sought to impose any term limits on its own federal representatives. Thus . . . contemporaneous state practice provides further persuasive evidence of a general understanding that the qualifications in the Constitution were unalterable by the States.[41]

In sum, the available historical and textual evidence, read in light of the basic principles of democracy underlying the Constitution and recognized by this Court in *Powell*, reveal the Framers' intent that neither Congress nor the States should possess the power to supplement the exclusive qualifications set forth in the text of the Constitution. . . .

V

The merits of term limits, or "rotation," have been the subject of debate since the formation of our Constitution, when the Framers unanimously rejected a proposal to add such limits to the Constitution. The cogent arguments on both sides of the question that were articulated during the process of ratification largely retain their force today. . . . It is not our province to resolve this longstanding debate.

We are, however, firmly convinced that allowing the several States to adopt term limits for congressional service would effect a fundamental change in the constitutional framework. Any such change must come not by legislation adopted either by Congress or by an individual State, but rather . . . through the amendment procedures set forth in Article V. The Framers decided that the qualifications for service in the Congress of the United States be fixed in the Constitution and be uniform throughout the Nation. That decision reflects the Framers' understanding that Members of Congress are chosen by separate constituencies, but that they become, when elected, servants of the people of the United States. They are not merely delegates appointed by separate, sovereign States; they occupy offices that are integral and essential components of a single National Government. In the absence of a properly passed constitutional amendment, allowing individual States to craft their own qualifications

---

[41] Petitioners and the dissent also point out that Georgia, Maryland, Massachusetts, Virginia, and North Carolina added district residency requirements. . . . They rely on these facts to show that the States believed they had the power to add qualifications. We again are unpersuaded. . . . [I]t seems to us that States may simply have viewed district residency requirements as the necessary analog to state residency requirements. Thus, state practice with respect to residency requirements does not necessarily indicate that States believed that they had a broad power to add restrictions. Finally, we consider the number of state-imposed qualifications to be remarkably small. Despite the array of property, religious, and other qualifications that were contained in state constitutions, petitioners and the dissent can point to only one instance of a state-imposed property qualification on candidates for Congress, and five instances of district residency requirements. The state practice seems to us notable for its restraint, and thus supports the conclusion that States did not believe that they generally had the power to add qualifications.

Nor are we persuaded by the more recent state practice involving qualifications such as those that bar felons from being elected. As we have noted, the practice of States is a poor indicator of the effect of restraints on the States, and no court has ever upheld one of these restrictions. Moreover, as one moves away from 1789, it seems to us that state practice is even less indicative of the Framers' understanding of state power. . . .

for Congress would thus erode the structure envisioned by the Framers, a structure that was designed, in the words of the Preamble to our Constitution, to form a "more perfect Union."

The judgment is affirmed.

■ **JUSTICE KENNEDY, concurring.**

I join the opinion of the Court.

The majority and dissenting opinions demonstrate the intricacy of the question whether or not the Qualifications Clauses are exclusive. In my view, however, it is well settled that the whole people of the United States asserted their political identity and unity of purpose when they created the federal system. The dissent's course of reasoning suggesting otherwise might be construed to disparage the republican character of the National Government, and it seems appropriate to add these few remarks to explain why that course of argumentation runs counter to fundamental principles of federalism.

Federalism was our Nation's own discovery. The Framers split the atom of sovereignty. It was the genius of their idea that our citizens would have two political capacities, one state and one federal, each protected from incursion by the other. The resulting Constitution created a legal system unprecedented in form and design, establishing two orders of government, each with its own direct relationship, its own privity, its own set of mutual rights and obligations to the people who sustain it and are governed by it. It is appropriate to recall these origins, which instruct us as to the nature of the two different governments created and confirmed by the Constitution.

A distinctive character of the National Government, the mark of its legitimacy, is that it owes its existence to the act of the whole people who created it. . . . As James Madison explained, the House of Representatives "derive[s] its powers from the people of America," and "the operation of the government on the people in their individual capacities" makes it "a national government," not merely a federal one. The Court confirmed this principle in *McCulloch v. Maryland*, when it said: "The government of the Union, then . . . is, emphatically, and truly, a government of the people. In form and in substance it emanates from them. Its powers are granted by them, and are to be exercised directly on them, and for their benefit." . . .

In one sense it is true that "the people of each State retained their separate political identities," for the Constitution takes care both to preserve the States and to make use of their identities and structures at various points in organizing the federal union. It does not at all follow from this that the sole political identity of an American is with the State of his or her residence. It denies the dual character of the Federal Government which is its very foundation to assert that the people of the United States do not have a political identity as well, one independent of, though consistent with, their identity as citizens of the State of their residence. It must be recognized that "for all the great purposes for which the Federal government was formed, we are one people, with one common country." . . .

The political identity of the entire people of the Union is reinforced by the proposition, which I take to be beyond dispute, that, though limited as to its objects, the National Government is, and must be, controlled by the people without collateral interference by the States. *McCulloch* affirmed this proposition as well, when the Court rejected the suggestion that States could interfere with federal powers. "This was not intended by the American people. They did not design to make their government dependent on the States." The States have no power, reserved or otherwise, over the exercise of federal authority within its proper sphere. . . . That the States may not invade the sphere of federal sovereignty is as incontestable, in my view, as the corollary proposition that the Federal Government must be held within the boundaries of its own power when it intrudes upon matters reserved to the States.

Of course, because the Framers recognized that state power and identity were essential parts of the federal balance, the Constitution is solicitous of the prerogatives of the States, even in an otherwise sovereign federal province. The Constitution uses state boundaries to fix the size of congressional delegations, Art. I, § 2, cl. 3, ensures that each State shall have at least one representative, grants States certain powers over the times, places, and manner of federal elections (subject to congressional revision), Art. I, § 4, cl. 1, requires that when the President is elected by the House of Representatives, the delegations from each State have one vote, Art. II, § 1, cl. 3, and Amdt. 12, and allows States to appoint electors for the President, Art. II, § 1, cl. 2. Nothing in the Constitution or The Federalist Papers, however, supports the idea of state interference with the most basic relation between the National Government and its citizens, the selection of legislative representatives. Indeed, even though the Constitution uses the qualifications for voters of the most numerous branch of the States' own legislatures to set the qualifications of federal electors, Art. I, § 2, cl. 1, when these electors vote, we have recognized that they act in a federal capacity and exercise a federal right. . . .

There can be no doubt, if we are to respect the republican origins of the Nation and preserve its federal character, that there exists a federal right of citizenship, a relationship between the people of the Nation and their National Government, with which the States may not interfere. Because the Arkansas enactment intrudes upon this federal domain, it exceeds the boundaries of the Constitution.

■ JUSTICE THOMAS, with whom THE CHIEF JUSTICE, JUSTICE O'CONNOR, and JUSTICE SCALIA join, dissenting.

It is ironic that the Court bases today's decision on the right of the people to "choose whom they please to govern them." Under our Constitution, there is only one State whose people have the right to "choose whom they please" to represent Arkansas in Congress. The Court holds, however, that neither the elected legislature of that State nor the people themselves (acting by ballot initiative) may prescribe any qualifications for those representatives. The majority therefore defends the right of the people of Arkansas to "choose whom they please to govern them" by invalidating a provision that won nearly 60% of the votes cast in a direct election and that carried every congressional district in the State.

I dissent. Nothing in the Constitution deprives the people of each State of the power to prescribe eligibility requirements for the candidates who seek to represent them in Congress. The Constitution is simply silent on this question. And where the Constitution is silent, it raises no bar to action by the States or the people.

I

Because the majority fundamentally misunderstands the notion of "reserved" powers, I start with some first principles. Contrary to the majority's suggestion, the people of the States need not point to any affirmative grant of power in the Constitution in order to prescribe qualifications for their representatives in Congress, or to authorize their elected state legislators to do so.

A

Our system of government rests on one overriding principle: All power stems from the consent of the people. To phrase the principle in this way, however, is to be imprecise about something important to the notion of "reserved" powers. The ultimate source of the Constitution's authority is the consent of the people of each individual State, not the consent of the undifferentiated people of the Nation as a whole.

The ratification procedure erected by Article VII makes this point clear. The Constitution took effect once it had been ratified by the people gathered in convention in nine different States. But the Constitution went into effect only "between the States so ratifying the same," Art. VII; it did not bind the people of North Carolina until they had accepted it. In Madison's words, the popular consent upon which the Constitution's authority rests was "given by the people, not as individuals composing one entire nation, but as composing the distinct and independent States to which they respectively belong." . . .[1]

When they adopted the Federal Constitution, of course, the people of each State surrendered some of their authority to the United States (and hence to entities accountable to the people of other States as well as to themselves). They affirmatively deprived their States of certain powers, see, *e.g.*, Art. I, § 10, and they affirmatively conferred certain powers upon the Federal Government, see, *e.g.*, Art. I, § 8. Because the people of the several States are the only true source of power, however, the Federal

---

[1]   The ringing initial words of the Constitution—"We the People of the United States"—convey something of the same idea. (In the Constitution, after all, "the United States" is consistently a plural noun.) . . .

Government enjoys no authority beyond what the Constitution confers: The Federal Government's powers are limited and enumerated. In the words of Justice Black: "The United States is entirely a creature of the Constitution. Its power and authority have no other source."

In each State, the remainder of the people's powers—"the powers not delegated to the United States by the Constitution, nor prohibited by it to the States," Amdt. 10—are either delegated to the state government or retained by the people. The Federal Constitution does not specify which of these two possibilities obtains; it is up to the various state constitutions to declare which powers the people of each State have delegated to their state government. As far as the Federal Constitution is concerned, then, the States can exercise all powers that the Constitution does not withhold from them. The Federal Government and the States thus face different default rules: Where the Constitution is silent about the exercise of a particular power—that is, where the Constitution does not speak either expressly or by necessary implication—the Federal Government lacks that power and the States enjoy it.

These basic principles are enshrined in the Tenth Amendment, which declares that all powers neither delegated to the Federal Government nor prohibited to the States "are reserved to the States respectively, or to the people." With this careful last phrase, the Amendment avoids taking any position on the division of power between the state governments and the people of the States: It is up to the people of each State to determine which "reserved" powers their state government may exercise. But the Amendment does make clear that powers reside at the state level except where the Constitution removes them from that level. All powers that the Constitution neither delegates to the Federal Government nor prohibits to the States are controlled by the people of each State. . . .

The Constitution simply does not recognize any mechanism for action by the undifferentiated people of the Nation. Thus, the amendment provision of Article V calls for amendments to be ratified not by a convention of the national people, but by conventions of the people in each State or by the state legislatures elected by those people. Likewise, the Constitution calls for Members of Congress to be chosen State by State, rather than in nationwide elections. Even the selection of the President . . . is accomplished by an electoral college made up of delegates chosen by the various States, and candidates can lose a Presidential election despite winning a majority of the votes cast in the Nation as a whole. See also Art. II, § 1, cl. 3 (providing that when no candidate secures a majority of electoral votes, the election of the President is thrown into the House of Representatives, where "the Votes shall be taken by States, the Representatives from each State having one Vote"); Amdt. 12 (same).

In short, the notion of popular sovereignty that undergirds the Constitution does not erase state boundaries, but rather tracks them. The people of each State obviously did trust their fate to the people of the several States when they consented to the Constitution; not only did they empower the governmental institutions of the United States, but they also agreed to be bound by constitutional amendments that they themselves refused to ratify. See Art. V (providing that proposed amendments shall take effect upon ratification by three-quarters of the States). At the same time, however, the people of each State retained their separate political identities. As Chief Justice Marshall put it, "no political dreamer was ever wild enough to think of breaking down the lines which separate the States, and of compounding the American people into one common mass." *McCulloch v. Maryland.* . . .

B

1

The majority begins by announcing an enormous and untenable limitation on the principle expressed by the Tenth Amendment. According to the majority, the States possess only those powers that the Constitution affirmatively grants to them or that they enjoyed before the Constitution was adopted; the Tenth Amendment "could only 'reserve' that which existed before." From the fact that the States had not previously enjoyed any powers over the particular institutions of the Federal Government established by the Constitution, the majority derives a rule precisely opposite to the one that the Amendment actually prescribes: " 'The states can exercise no powers whatsoever, which exclusively spring out of the existence of the national government, which the constitution does not delegate to them.' " (Quoting Justice Story).

The majority's essential logic is that the state governments could not "reserve" any powers that they did not control at the time the Constitution was drafted. . . . The Tenth Amendment's use of the word "reserved" does not help the majority's position. If someone says that the power to use a particular facility is reserved to some group, he is not saying anything about whether that group has previously used the facility. He is merely saying that the people who control the facility have designated that group as the entity with authority to use it. The Tenth Amendment is similar: The people of the States, from whom all governmental powers stem, have specified that all powers not prohibited to the States by the Federal Constitution are reserved "to the States respectively, or to the people."

The majority is therefore quite wrong to conclude that the people of the States cannot authorize their state governments to exercise any powers that were unknown to the States when the Federal Constitution was drafted. . . .

[T]he only true support for [the majority's] view of the Tenth Amendment comes from Joseph Story's 1833 treatise on constitutional law. Justice Story was a brilliant and accomplished man, and one cannot casually dismiss his views. On the other hand, he was not a member of the Founding generation, and his Commentaries on the Constitution were written a half century after the framing. Rather than representing the original understanding of the Constitution, they represent only his own understanding. In a range of cases concerning the federal/state relation, moreover, this Court has deemed positions taken in Story's commentaries to be more nationalist than the Constitution warrants. See also 1 Life and Letters of Joseph Story 296 (W. Story ed. 1851) ("I hold . . . that the Government of the United States is intrinsically too weak, and the powers of the State Governments too strong"). In this case too, Story's position that the only powers reserved to the States are those that the States enjoyed before the framing conflicts with both the plain language of the Tenth Amendment and the underlying theory of the Constitution.

2

The majority also sketches out what may be an alternative (and narrower) argument. Again citing Story, the majority suggests that it would be inconsistent with the notion of "national sovereignty" for the States or the people of the States to have any reserved powers over the selection of Members of Congress. . . .

From the framing to the present, however, the *selection* of the Representatives and Senators from each State has been left entirely to the people of that State or to their state legislature. See Art. I, § 2, cl. 1 (providing that Members of the House of Representatives are chosen "by the People of the several States"); Art. I, § 3, cl. 1 (originally providing that the Senators from each State are "chosen by the Legislature thereof"); Amdt. 17 (amending § 3 to provide that the Senators from each State are "elected by the people thereof"). The very name "congress" suggests a coming together of representatives from distinct entities.[7] In keeping with the complexity of our federal system, once the representatives chosen by the people of each State assemble in Congress, they form a national body and are beyond the control of the individual States until the next election. But the selection of representatives in Congress is indisputably an act of the people of each State, not some abstract people of the Nation as a whole.

The concurring opinion suggests that this cannot be so, because it is the Federal Constitution that guarantees the right of the people of each State (so long as they are qualified electors under state law) to take part in choosing the Members of Congress from that State. But the presence of a federally guaranteed right hardly means that the selection of those

---

[7]   See 1 S. Johnson, A Dictionary of the English Language 393 (4th ed. 1773) (defining "congress" as "an appointed meeting for settlement of affairs between different nations: as, the *congress* of Cambray"); T. Sheridan, A Complete Dictionary of the English Language (6th ed. 1796) ("an appointed meeting for settlement of affairs between different nations; the assembly which governs the United States of America").

representatives constitutes "the exercise of federal authority." When the people of Georgia pick their representatives in Congress, they are acting as the people of Georgia, not as the corporate agents for the undifferentiated people of the Nation as a whole. *See In re Green*, 134 U.S. 377 (1890) ("Although [Presidential] electors are appointed and act under and pursuant to the Constitution of the United States, they are no more officers or agents of the United States than are the members of the state legislatures when acting as electors of federal senators, or the people of the States when acting as electors of representatives in Congress"). The concurring opinion protests that the exercise of "reserved" powers in the area of congressional elections would constitute "state interference with the most basic relation between the National Government and its citizens, the selection of legislative representatives." But when one strips away its abstractions, the concurring opinion is simply saying that the people of Arkansas cannot be permitted to inject themselves into the process by which they themselves select Arkansas' representatives in Congress. . . .

In short, while the majority is correct that the Framers expected the selection process to create a "direct link" between Members of the House of Representatives and the people, the link was between the Representatives from each State and the people of that State; the people of Georgia have no say over whom the people of Massachusetts select to represent them in Congress. This arrangement must baffle the majority, whose understanding of Congress would surely fit more comfortably within a system of nationwide elections. But the fact remains that when it comes to the selection of Members of Congress, the people of each State have retained their independent political identity. As a result, there is absolutely nothing strange about the notion that the people of the States or their state legislatures possess "reserved" powers in this area.

The majority seeks support from the Constitution's specification that Members of Congress "shall receive a Compensation for their Services, to be ascertained by Law, and paid out of the Treasury of the United States." Art. I, § 6, cl. 1. But the fact that Members of Congress draw a federal salary once they have assembled hardly means that the people of the States lack reserved powers over the selection of their representatives. Indeed, the historical evidence about the compensation provision suggests that the States' reserved powers may even extend beyond the selection stage. The majority itself indicates that if the Constitution had made no provision for congressional compensation, this topic would have been "left to state legislatures." Accord 1 Farrand 215–216 (remarks of James Madison and George Mason). Likewise, Madison specifically indicated that even with the compensation provision in place, the individual States still enjoyed the reserved power to supplement the federal salary. 3 *id.*, at 315 (remarks at the Virginia ratifying convention). . . .

In fact, the Constitution's treatment of Presidential elections actively contradicts the majority's position. While the individual States have no "reserved" power to set qualifications for the office of President, we have long understood that they do have the power (as far as the Federal Constitution is concerned) to set qualifications for their Presidential electors—the delegates that each State selects to represent it in the electoral college that actually chooses the Nation's chief executive. Even respondents do not dispute that the States may establish qualifications for their delegates to the electoral college, as long as those qualifications pass muster under other constitutional provisions (primarily the First and Fourteenth Amendments). As the majority cannot argue that the Constitution affirmatively grants this power, the power must be one that is "reserved" to the States. It necessarily follows that the majority's understanding of the Tenth Amendment is incorrect, for the position of Presidential elector surely " 'spring[s] out of the existence of the national government.' "

3

In a final effort to deny that the people of the States enjoy "reserved" powers over the selection of their representatives in Congress, the majority suggests that the Constitution expressly delegates to the States certain powers over congressional elections. Such delegations of power, the majority argues, would be superfluous if the people of the States enjoyed reserved powers in this area.

Only one constitutional provision—the Times, Places and Manner Clause of Article I, § 4—even arguably supports the majority's suggestion. It reads:

> The Times, Places and Manner of holding Elections for Senators and Representatives, shall be prescribed in each State by the Legislature thereof; but the Congress may at any time by Law make or alter such Regulations, except as to the Places of choosing Senators.

Contrary to the majority's assumption, however, this Clause does not delegate any authority to the States. Instead, it simply imposes a duty upon them. The majority gets it exactly right: By specifying that the state legislatures "shall" prescribe the details necessary to hold congressional elections, the Clause "expressly requires action by the States." This command meshes with one of the principal purposes of Congress' "make or alter" power: to ensure that the States hold congressional elections in the first place, so that Congress continues to exist. . . . Constitutional provisions that impose affirmative duties on the States are hardly inconsistent with the notion of reserved powers.

Of course, the second part of the Times, Places and Manner Clause does grant a power rather than impose a duty. As its contrasting uses of the words "shall" and "may" confirm, however, the Clause grants power exclusively to Congress, not to the States. If the Clause did not exist at all, the States would still be able to prescribe the times, places, and manner of holding congressional elections; the deletion of the provision would simply deprive Congress of the power to override these state regulations. . . .

II

I take it to be established, then, that the people of Arkansas do enjoy "reserved" powers over the selection of their representatives in Congress. Purporting to exercise those reserved powers, they have agreed among themselves that the candidates covered by § 3 of Amendment 73—those whom they have already elected to three or more terms in the House of Representatives or to two or more terms in the Senate—should not be eligible to appear on the ballot for reelection, but should nonetheless be returned to Congress if enough voters are sufficiently enthusiastic about their candidacy to write in their names. Whatever one might think of the wisdom of this arrangement, we may not override the decision of the people of Arkansas unless something in the Federal Constitution deprives them of the power to enact such measures.

The majority settles on "the Qualifications Clauses" as the constitutional provisions that Amendment 73 violates. . . . In my view, the historical evidence is simply inadequate to warrant the majority's conclusion that the Qualifications Clauses mean anything more than what they say.

A

The provisions that are generally known as the Qualifications Clauses read as follows:

> No Person shall be a Representative who shall not have attained to the age of twenty five Years, and been seven Years a Citizen of the United States, and who shall not, when elected, be an Inhabitant of that State in which he shall be chosen. Art. I, § 2, cl. 2.

> No Person shall be a Senator who shall not have attained to the Age of thirty Years, and been nine Years a Citizen of the United States, and who shall not, when elected, be an Inhabitant of that State for which he shall be chosen. Art. I, § 3, cl. 3.

Later in Article I, the "Ineligibility Clause" imposes another nationwide disqualification from congressional office: "No Person holding any Office under the United States, shall be a Member of either House during his Continuance in Office." § 6, cl. 2. . . .

[These clauses] merely establish *minimum* qualifications. They are quite different from an *exclusive* formulation, such as the following:

> Every Person who shall have attained to the age of twenty five Years, and been seven Years a Citizen of the United States, and who shall, when elected, be an Inhabitant of that State in which he shall be chosen, shall be eligible to be a Representative.

At least on their face, then, the Qualifications Clauses do nothing to prohibit the people of a State from establishing additional eligibility requirements for their own representatives.

Joseph Story thought that such a prohibition was nonetheless implicit in the constitutional list of qualifications, because "from the very nature of such a provision, the affirmation of these qualifications would seem to imply a negative of all others." This argument rests on the maxim *expressio unius est exclusio alterius*. When the Framers decided which qualifications to include in the Constitution, they also decided not to include any other qualifications in the Constitution. In Story's view, it would conflict with this latter decision for the people of the individual States to decide, as a matter of state law, that they would like their own representatives in Congress to meet additional eligibility requirements.

To spell out the logic underlying this argument is to expose its weakness. . . . Story's application of the *expressio unius* maxim takes no account of federalism. At most, the specification of certain nationwide disqualifications in the Constitution implies the negation of other *nationwide* disqualifications; it does not imply that individual States or their people are barred from adopting their own disqualifications on a state-by-state basis. Thus, the one delegate to the Philadelphia Convention who voiced anything approaching Story's argument said only that a recital of qualifications in the Constitution would imply that *Congress* lacked any qualification-setting power.

The Qualifications Clauses do prevent the individual States from abolishing all eligibility requirements for Congress. This restriction on state power reflects the fact that when the people of one State send immature, disloyal, or unknowledgeable representatives to Congress, they jeopardize not only their own interests but also the interests of the people of other States. Because Congress wields power over all the States, the people of each State need some guarantee that the legislators elected by the people of other States will meet minimum standards of competence. The Qualifications Clauses provide that guarantee: They list the requirements that the Framers considered essential to protect the competence of the National Legislature.

If the people of a State decide that they would like their representatives to possess additional qualifications, however, they have done nothing to frustrate the policy behind the Qualifications Clauses. . . .

This conclusion is buttressed by our reluctance to read constitutional provisions to preclude state power by negative implication. The very structure of the Constitution counsels such hesitation. After all, § 10 of Article I contains a brief list of *express* prohibitions on the States. Many of the prohibitions listed in § 10, moreover, might have been thought to be implicit in other constitutional provisions or in the very nature of our federal system. The fact that the Framers nonetheless made these prohibitions express confirms that one should not lightly read provisions like the Qualifications Clauses as implicit deprivations of state power. . . .

The majority responds that "a patchwork of state qualifications" would "undermine the uniformity and the national character that the Framers envisioned and sought to ensure." Yet the Framers thought it perfectly consistent with the "national character" of Congress for the Senators and Representatives from each State to be chosen by the legislature or the people of that State. The majority never explains why Congress' fundamental character permits this state-centered system, but nonetheless prohibits the people of the States and their state legislatures from setting any eligibility requirements for the candidates who seek to represent them.

As for the majority's related assertion that the Framers intended qualification requirements to be uniform, this is a conclusion, not an argument. Indeed, it is a conclusion that the Qualifications Clauses themselves contradict. At the time of the framing, and for some years thereafter, the Clauses' citizenship requirements incorporated laws that varied from State to State. Thus, the Qualifications Clauses themselves made it possible that a person would be qualified to represent State *A* in Congress even though a similarly situated person would not be qualified to represent State *B*.

To understand this point requires some background. Before the Constitution was adopted, citizenship was controlled entirely by state law, and the different States established different criteria. Even after the Constitution gave Congress the power to "establish an uniform Rule of Naturalization . . . throughout the United States," Art. I, § 8, cl. 4, Congress was under no obligation to do so, and the Framers surely expected state law to continue in full force unless and until Congress acted. . . . Accordingly, the constitutional requirement that Members of Congress be United States citizens meant different things in different States. The very first contested election case in the House of Representatives, which involved the citizenship of a would-be Congressman from South Carolina, illustrates this principle. As Representative James Madison told his colleagues, "I take it to be a clear point, that we are to be guided, in our decision, by the laws and constitution of South Carolina, so far as they can guide us; and where the laws do not expressly guide us, we must be guided by principles of a general nature." . . .

Even if the Qualifications Clauses had not themselves incorporated nonuniform requirements, of course, there would still be no basis for the assertion of the plurality below that they mandate "uniformity in qualifications." The Clauses wholly omit the exclusivity provision that, according to both the plurality below and today's majority, was their central focus. In fact, neither the text nor the apparent purpose of the Qualifications Clauses does anything to refute Thomas Jefferson's elegant legal analysis:

Had the Constitution been silent, nobody can doubt but that the right to prescribe all the qualifications and disqualifications of those they would send to represent them, would have belonged to the State. So also the Constitution might have prescribed the whole, and excluded all others. It seems to have preferred the middle way. It has exercised the power in part, by declaring some disqualifications. . . . But it does not declare, itself, that the member shall not be a lunatic, a pauper, a convict of treason, of murder, of felony, or other infamous crime, or a non-resident of his district; nor does it prohibit to the State the power of declaring these, or any other disqualifications which its particular circumstances may call for; and these may be different in different States. Of course, then, by the tenth amendment, the power is reserved to the State.

B

Although the Qualifications Clauses neither state nor imply the prohibition that it finds in them, the majority infers from the Framers' "democratic principles" that the Clauses must have been generally understood to preclude the people of the States and their state legislatures from prescribing any additional qualifications for their representatives in Congress. But the majority's evidence on this point establishes only two more modest propositions: (1) the Framers did not want the Federal Constitution itself to impose a broad set of disqualifications for congressional office, and (2) the Framers did not want the Federal Congress to be able to supplement the few disqualifications that the Constitution does set forth. The logical conclusion is simply that the Framers did not want the people of the States and their state legislatures to be constrained by too many qualifications imposed at the national level. The evidence does not support the majority's more sweeping conclusion that the Framers intended to bar the people of the States and their state legislatures from adopting additional eligibility requirements to help narrow their own choices. . . .

One reason why the Framers decided not to let Congress prescribe the qualifications of its own Members was that incumbents could have used this power to perpetuate themselves or their ilk in office. As Madison pointed out at the Philadelphia Convention, Members of Congress would have an obvious conflict of interest if they could determine who may run against them. But neither the people of the States nor the state legislatures would labor under the same conflict of interest when prescribing qualifications for Members of Congress, and so the Framers would have had to use a different calculus in determining whether to deprive them of this power. . . .

Congressional power over qualifications would have enabled the representatives from some States, acting collectively in the National Legislature, to prevent the people of another State from electing their preferred candidates. The John Wilkes episode in 18th-century England illustrates the problems that might result. As the majority mentions, Wilkes' district repeatedly elected him to the House of Commons, only to have a majority of the representatives of other districts frustrate their will by voting to exclude him. Americans who remembered these events might well have wanted to prevent the National Legislature from fettering the choices of the people of any individual State (for the House of Representatives) or their state legislators (for the Senate).

. . . Indeed, the invocation of democratic principles to invalidate Amendment 73 seems particularly difficult in the present case, because Amendment 73 remains fully within the control of the people of Arkansas. If they wanted to repeal it (despite the 20-point margin by which they enacted it less than three years ago), they could do so by a simple majority vote. See Ark. Const., Amdt. 7.

The majority appears to believe that restrictions on eligibility for office are inherently undemocratic. But the Qualifications Clauses themselves prove that the Framers did not share this view; eligibility requirements to which the people of the States consent are perfectly consistent with the Framers' scheme. . . . When the people of a State themselves decide to restrict the field of candidates whom they are willing to send to Washington as their representatives, they simply have not violated the principle that "the people should choose whom they please to govern them." . . .

In seeking ratification of the Constitution, James Madison did assert that "under these reasonable limitations [set out in the House Qualifications Clause], the door of this part of the federal government is open to merit of every description. . . ." The majority stresses this assertion, and others to the same effect, in support of its "egalitarian concept." But there is no reason to interpret these statements as anything more than claims that the Constitution itself imposes relatively few disqualifications for congressional office. . . .

C

3

In discussing the ratification period, the majority stresses two principal data. One of these pieces of evidence is no evidence at all—literally. The majority devotes considerable space to the fact that the recorded ratification debates do not contain any affirmative statement that the States can supplement the constitutional qualifications. For the majority, this void is "compelling" evidence that "unquestionably reflects the Framers' common understanding that States lacked that power." . . .

But the majority's argument cuts both ways. The recorded ratification debates also contain no affirmative statement that the States *cannot* supplement the constitutional qualifications. While ratification was being debated, the existing rule in America was that the States could prescribe eligibility requirements for their delegates to Congress, even though the Articles of Confederation gave Congress itself no power to impose such qualifications. If the Federal Constitution had been understood to deprive the States of this significant power, one might well have expected its opponents to seize on this point in arguing against ratification.

The fact is that arguments based on the absence of recorded debate at the ratification conventions are suspect, because the surviving records of those debates are fragmentary. We have no records at all of the debates in several of the conventions, and only spotty records from most of the others.

If one concedes that the absence of relevant records from the ratification debates is not strong evidence for either side, then the majority's only significant piece of evidence from the ratification period is The Federalist No. 52. Contrary to the majority's assertion, however, this essay simply does not talk about "the lack of state control over the qualifications of the elected," whether "explicitly" or otherwise. . . .

In fact, the constitutional text supports the contrary inference. . . . [A]t the time of the framing some States also imposed religious qualifications on state legislators. The Framers evidently did not want States to impose such qualifications on federal legislators, for the Constitution specifically provides that "no religious Test shall ever be required as a Qualification to any Office or public Trust under the United States." Art. VI, cl. 3. Both the context and the plain language of the Clause show that it bars the States as well as the Federal Government from imposing religious disqualifications on federal offices. But the only reason for extending the Clause to the States would be to protect Senators and Representatives from state-imposed religious qualifications. . . . If the *expressio unius* maxim cuts in any direction in this case, then, it undermines the majority's position: The Framers' prohibition on state-imposed religious disqualifications for Members of Congress suggests that other types of state-imposed disqualifications are permissible.

4

. . . [S]tate practice immediately after the ratification of the Constitution refutes the majority's suggestion that the Qualifications Clauses were commonly understood as being exclusive. Five States supplemented the constitutional disqualifications in their very first election laws, and the surviving records suggest that the legislatures of these States considered and rejected the interpretation of the Constitution that the majority adopts today. . . .

[T]he first Virginia election law erected a property qualification for Virginia's contingent in the Federal House of Representatives. What is more, while the Constitution merely requires representatives to be inhabitants of their State, the legislatures of five of the seven States that divided themselves into districts for House elections added that representatives also had to be inhabitants of the district that elected them. Three of these States adopted durational residency requirements too, insisting that representatives have resided within their districts for at least a year (or, in one case, three years) before being elected. . . .

The majority's argument also fails to account for the durational element of the residency requirements adopted in Georgia, North Carolina, and Virginia (and soon thereafter in Tennessee). These States obliged Congressmen not only to be district residents when elected but also to have been district residents for at least a year before then. . . .

[W]e are left only with state treatment of property qualifications. It is true that nine of the state constitutions in effect at the time of the framing required members of the lower house of the state legislature to possess some property, and that four of these constitutions were revised shortly after the framing but continued to impose such requirements. Only one State, by contrast, established a property qualification for the Federal House of Representatives. But the fact that more States did not adopt congressional property qualifications does not mean that the Qualifications Clauses were commonly understood to be exclusive; there are a host of other explanations for the relative liberality of state election laws. And whatever the explanation, the fact remains that five of the election laws enacted immediately after ratification of the Constitution imposed additional qualifications that would clearly be unconstitutional under today's holding. . . .

5

[T]he final category of historical evidence discussed by the majority [is] controversies in the House and the Senate over seating candidates who were duly elected but who arguably failed to satisfy qualifications imposed by state law.

As the majority concedes, "congressional practice has been erratic" and is of limited relevance anyway. Actions taken by a single House of Congress in 1887 or in 1964 shed little light on the original understanding of the Constitution. Presumably for that reason, the majority puts its chief emphasis on the 1807 debate in the House of Representatives about whether to seat Maryland's William McCreery. I agree with the majority that this debate might lend some support to the majority's position if it had transpired as reported in *Powell v. McCormack*. But the Court's discussion—both in *Powell* and today—is misleading.

A Maryland statute dating from 1802 had created a district entitled to send two representatives to the House, one of whom had to be a resident of Baltimore County and the other of whom had to be a resident of Baltimore City. McCreery was elected to the Ninth Congress as a resident of Baltimore City. After his reelection to the Tenth Congress, however, his qualifications were challenged on the ground that because he divided his time between his summer estate in Baltimore County and his residence in Washington, D. C., he was no longer a resident of Baltimore City at all.

As the majority notes, a report of the House Committee of Elections recommended that McCreery be seated on the ground that state legislatures have no authority to add to the qualifications set forth in the Constitution. But the committee's submission of this initial report sparked a heated debate. . . . Finally, a large majority of the House voted to recommit the report to the Committee of Elections. The committee thereupon deleted all references to the constitutional issue and issued a revised report that focused entirely on the factual question whether McCreery satisfied the state residency requirement. After receiving the new report, the House seated McCreery with a resolution simply saying: "*Resolved*, That William McCreery is entitled to his seat in this House." By overwhelming majorities, the House rejected both a proposal to specify that McCreery possessed "the qualifications required by the law of Maryland" and a proposal to declare only that he was "duly qualified, agreeably to the constitution of the United States." Far from supporting the majority's position, the McCreery episode merely demonstrates that the [House] was deeply divided over whether state legislatures may add to the qualifications set forth in the Constitution.

The majority needs more than that. The prohibition that today's majority enforces is found nowhere in the text of the Qualifications Clauses. In the absence of evidence that the Clauses nonetheless were generally understood at the time of the framing to imply such a prohibition, we may not use the Clauses to invalidate the decisions of a State or its people.

III

It is radical enough for the majority to hold that the Constitution implicitly precludes the people of the States from prescribing any eligibility requirements for the congressional candidates who seek their votes. This holding, after all, does not stop with negating the term limits that many States have seen fit to impose on their Senators and Representatives. Today's decision also means that no State may disqualify congressional candidates whom a court has found to be mentally incompetent, see, *e.g.*, Fla. Stat. §§ 97.041(2), 99.021(1)(a), who are currently in prison, see, *e.g.*, Ill. Comp. Stat. Ann., ch. 10, §§ 5/3–5, 5/7–10, 5/10–5, or who have past vote-fraud convictions, see, *e. g.*, Ga. Code Ann. §§ 21–2–2(25), 21–2–8. . . . I do not mean to suggest that States have unbridled power to handicap particular classes of candidates, even when those candidates enjoy federally conferred advantages that may threaten to skew the electoral process. But laws that allegedly have the purpose and effect of handicapping a particular class of candidates traditionally are reviewed under the First and Fourteenth Amendments rather than the Qualifications Clauses. . . .

To analyze such laws under the Qualifications Clauses may open up whole new vistas for courts. If it is true that "the current congressional campaign finance system . . . has created an electoral system so stacked against challengers that in many elections voters have no real choices," are the Federal Election Campaign Act Amendments of 1974 unconstitutional under (of all things) the Qualifications Clauses? If it can be shown that nonminorities are at a significant disadvantage when they seek election in districts dominated by minority voters, would the intentional creation of "majority-minority districts" violate the Qualifications Clauses even if it were to survive scrutiny under the Fourteenth Amendment? . . . More generally, if "district lines are rarely neutral phenomena" and if "districting inevitably has and is intended to have substantial political consequences," *Gaffney v. Cummings,* 412 U.S. 735 (1973), will plausible Qualifications Clause challenges greet virtually every redistricting decision? . . .

The majority's opinion may not go so far, although it does not itself suggest any principled stopping point. No matter how narrowly construed, however, today's decision reads the Qualifications Clauses to impose substantial implicit prohibitions on the States and the people of the States. I would not draw such an expansive negative inference from the fact that the Constitution requires Members of Congress to be a certain age, to be inhabitants of the States that they represent, and to have been United States citizens for a specified period. Rather, I would read the Qualifications Clauses to do no more than what they say. I respectfully dissent.

NOTE ON SOVEREIGNTY, REPRESENTATION, AND THE *TERM LIMITS* CASE

1.   Do the history-driven opinions in *Term Limits* suggest that we are all originalists now? Given the controversy among scholars (*compare, e.g.,* Thomas Grey and Robert Bork in Chapter Seven), why is there no controversy among the justices in *Term Limits* as to the correct theory of interpretation? Should there be? The opinions are the historian's equivalent of the Battle of the Somme: a massive, grinding slugfest over the meaning of every inch of the relevant historical terrain. Can anyone win a debate like that? Do you come away with the impression that one opinion is "right" and the other "wrong"? Who has the better of the historical argument? If the answer is "no one," what does that tell you about the merits of originalism as an approach to constitutional interpretation?

2.   Under the Articles of Confederation, the States were "sovereign"; moreover, only the States were represented in Congress, and only the States could act directly upon individuals. The Confederation Congress was thus dependent upon the States both to provide it with funding to meet national needs and to enact and implement legislation that Congress judged necessary to further the national interest. Proponents of the new Constitution judged this arrangement to be highly unsatisfactory, and the new government enjoyed powers to both tax and regulate the people directly.

Part of the debate in *Term Limits* concerns the extent to which the new Constitution displaced the old state-centered order. Justice Thomas contends that the new Constitution remained an act of the States themselves, whereas Justice Stevens argues that it was an act of the People acting in a collective, national capacity. Each of these positions has implications for a theory of representation: For Thomas, federal representatives remain fundamentally ambassadors from the States, and the States can control the qualifications of those ambassadors. For Stevens (and Justice Kennedy), by contrast, federal representatives are agents of the People of the United States, and the States are no party to that relationship. Who has the better of this argument?

3.   Another important aspect of the *Term Limits* debate concerns the concept of reserved powers and default rules. The Qualifications Clauses, like many constitutional provisions, are ambiguous as to important aspects of their application—specifically, they do not say whether the qualifications listed in the text are meant to be exclusive or not. In such cases of ambiguity, a default rule—e.g., the states can do anything not specifically forbidden in the Constitution—can be a helpful guide to decision. In *Term Limits*, the choice of the correct default rule turns on the interpretation of the Tenth Amendment, which "reserves" to the States all powers not granted to the National Government.

Justice Stevens takes the position that a power that the States could not have exercised (or simply did not exercise) before ratification of the Constitution cannot be "reserved" to them. Does this mean that the States have no "reserved" powers to issue drivers' licenses for automobiles? To regulate the safety of nuclear power plants? To operate public schools? Might he nonetheless be right to say, more narrowly, that power to determine the federal government's own rules of composition should not be subject to the same default rule as general regulatory powers?

4.   The questions in *Term Limits* go to the foundational political theory of our federal union. Linda Greenhouse, for example, asserted that "it is only a slight exaggeration to say that the dissent brought the Court a single vote shy of reinstalling the Articles of Confederation." [10] A less breathless assessment described *Term Limits* as "a confrontation . . . over the basic structural principles of the federal union: are we one people insofar as we constitute the federal government, as the majority held, or rather, as the dissent would have it, irreducibly the peoples of the several states?"[11] Does it surprise you that these questions were still being vigorously debated in 1995—and that they are still being debated today?

---

[10]   Linda Greenhouse, *Focus on Federal Power*, N.Y. TIMES, May 24, 1995.

[11]   Kathleen M. Sullivan, *Dueling Sovereignties*: U.S. Term Limits, Inc. v. Thornton, 109 HARV. L. REV. 78, 80 (1995).

NOTE ON THE VALUES OF FEDERALISM

1. At the outset of our unit on federalism, it will be helpful briefly to outline the values often served by both national and state action. Here are some of the leading values often associated with action by the States:

- **Public Participation and Accountability:** State governments are closer to the people. It's easier to get involved on the state level, and your voice counts for more. Hence, prominent national politicians from Abraham Lincoln to Barack Obama have gotten their start at the state level, and political movements from abolitionism to progressive "good government" reform have likewise focused initially on state government.

- **Diversity:** If political or policy preferences are not distributed evenly across the geographic regions of the country, then allowing majorities of voters in individual states to have their own way will tend to please more of the people more of the time. For example, if Massachusetts voters favor same-sex marriage by 70% to 30%, but Texans oppose it by the same margin, then state variation will allow 70% of the voters in each state to have their way. A national rule in either direction, by contrast, would displease 70% of the voters in one of the two states. Moreover, to the extent that an issue is important and citizens are mobile, then state differences allow people to vote with their feet.

- **State Competition:** States have an incentive to constantly reform and improve in order to lure more citizens and businesses. States wishing to attract new citizens and industry have incentives, for example, to provide good public education and low taxes.

- **State Experimentation:** Justice Louis Brandeis famously observed that "[i]t is one of the happy incidents of the federal system that a single courageous State may, if its citizens choose, serve as a laboratory; and try novel social and economic experiments without risk to the rest of the country."[12] The national welfare reforms of the mid-1990s, for example, were based in part on innovative approaches developed in Wisconsin and other states, and California has more recently pioneered legislation to reduce greenhouse gas emissions.

- **Administrative Efficiency:** States can tailor regulation to local conditions—they do not have to use a one size fits all approach. In order to achieve the same levels of ambient air quality, for example, we may have to undertake quite different measures in Southern California than in upstate New York.

---

[12] *New State Ice Co. v. Liebmann*, 285 U.S. 262, 311 (1932) (Brandeis, J., dissenting).

- **Diffusion of Power:** The Framers divided sovereignty precisely to keep any one part of the government from becoming too powerful. The existence of the States always provides some power base for resisting federal measures. When the Federalist Congress enacted the Alien and Sedition Acts, for example, the primary opposition came in the form of resolutions adopted by the Virginia and Kentucky legislatures arguing that the Acts were unconstitutional.

2.   Here are some of the leading values often associated with action by the National Government:

- **Legal Uniformity:** Businesses that must operate in many states hate having to comply with fifty different sets of rules. Consider, for instance, the plight of an auto manufacturer trying to meet fifty different sets of auto safety and fuel efficiency standards.

- **Externalities and Spillover Effects:** Decisions made in one state may have consequences in other states. Or residents of the state may not bear the full costs of activity carried on inside the state. In such cases, we can't count on the state's own political processes to adequately address the problem. If Ohio allows factories with very tall smokestacks, it does not bear the cost of the acid rain that falls on New Hampshire; Granite State voters, on the other hand, are powerless to regulate the production of pollution outside their borders. In this scenario, only the national legislature represents both the producers of the pollution and those affected by it.

- **Race to the Bottom:** Jurisdictional competition may be a harm as well as a help; failure to regulate in one jurisdiction may make it harder to regulate in another, due to the mobility of jobs and capital. In *Hammer v. Dagenhart*, for example, we saw arguments that no individual state could afford to prohibit child labor, for fear that industry would relocate to more permissive jurisdictions.

- **Administrative Efficiency and Concentration of Expertise:** Having multiple levels of government with authority over the same activity inevitably leads to jurisdictional disputes and delays. This was evident, for example, in the response to Hurricane Katrina. Moreover, there is no need to have 50 different environmental protection agencies doing research on the health effects of dioxin in the water.

- **Mitigation of Faction:** Madison's idea in Federalist 10 is that factions have a harder time taking control of a larger government. Tobacco farmers in North Carolina, for example, may be able to block anti-smoking legislation in the North Carolina General Assembly for a long time; they are less likely to dominate the "extended sphere" of the national legislature.

- **Protection of Individual Rights:** Following the Civil War, the national government came to be seen as the primary guarantor of human rights. Likewise, for much of our history, the most important way in which States struggled to be "different," and to resist federal encroachment on their power, was in preserving slavery and segregation. The question is whether this relationship is somehow inherent in national and state action, or whether these are simply contingent facts of our history.

3. To what extent is it possible to generalize about these competing values of state and national action? Is it meaningful to say that one is "better" than the other in a general way? Or can that judgment only be made by reference to particular issues or circumstances? Recall, for example, that the enactment of personal liberty laws in states like Pennsylvania prior to the Civil War produced the "externality" or "spillover effect" of undermining slavery in Maryland. Likewise, another prominent example of state-centered dissent is the South's "massive resistance" to *Brown*.

To what extent can these underlying values associated with state and national power be employed directly as criteria for allocating power in a federal system? Professors Robert Cooter and Neil Siegel recently proposed that Congress's power vis-à-vis the States should be defined largely by reference to the underlying values of federalism.[13] In particular, they argue that national action under the Commerce Clause and other provisions of Article I is constitutional if it solves a collective action problem among the States. Although they offer this criterion primarily as a guide for legislative action, they also suggest that courts should apply it to the extent they engage in judicial review of federalism issues at all. Hence, if federal action is *not* necessary to overcome interstate externalities or some other difficulty foreclosing collective action among the states, the national law must be struck down.[14] It is fairly unusual to recommend this sort of approach as a basis for judicial review. Why *don't* courts typically proceed in this way?[15]

Constitutional provisions and legal doctrines typically seek to further certain values, but there is often a conceptual gap between the underlying values and the provisions or doctrines that further them. Reviewing courts thus rarely ask directly whether a federal or state law furthers the values associated with federalism. Nonetheless, the values of federalism may be relevant in at least two ways. First, the constitutional limitations on national and state action can often be construed either broadly or narrowly. Which

---

[13] Robert D. Cooter & Neil S. Siegel, *Collective Action Federalism: A General Theory of Article I, Section 8*, 63 STAN. L. REV. 115 (2010).

[14] *Id.* at 119.

[15] *Compare, e.g.*, Donald H. Regan, *How to Think About the Federal Commerce Power and Incidentally Rewrite* United States v. Lopez, 94 MICH. L. REV. 554, 557 (1995) ("[I]n thinking about whether the federal government has the power to do something or other, we should ask what special reason there is for the federal government to have that power. What reason is there to think the states are incapable or untrustworthy?"), *with* Ernest A. Young, *Making Federalism Doctrine: Fidelity, Institutional Competence, and Compensating Adjustments*, 46 WM. & MARY L. REV. 1733, 1846 (2005) (arguing that direct value-application is indeterminate and indistinguishable from legislative policy judgments).

approach one takes may well be influenced by perceptions of the values served by national or state action in a given context. Second, it will become apparent that our basic structure is now one of *concurrent powers*—that is, on most matters both state and national governments have constitutional authority to act, and the choice between them will manifest as an issue of policy. That policy question will often turn on forthright assessment of the values associated with national or state action.

4.   Some critics of constitutional federalism have drawn a sharp distinction between "federalism" and "decentralization."[16] Professors Rubin and Feeley define "decentralization" as "a managerial concept: it refers to the delegation of centralized authority to subordinate units of either a geographic or functional character." This delegation of authority exists purely for purposes of efficiency, and it may be withdrawn at the discretion of the centralized authority. "Federalism," by contrast, is a constitutionally-guaranteed form of decentralization: "[I]n a federal system, the subordinate units possess prescribed areas of jurisdiction that cannot be invaded by the central authority, and leaders of the subordinate units draw their power from sources independent of that central authority."[17]

Rubin and Feeley's central argument is that virtually all of the virtues of state action cited above stem from decentralization, not federalism. In other words, efficiency, experimentation, public participation, and the like can all be achieved simply by delegating authority to the States on a discretionary basis; it is unnecessary, and often undesirable, to entrench that delegation of authority as a constitutional principle. The sole exception is the value of the states as a bulwark against centralized tyranny, but Rubin and Feeley doubt that the States really serve that purpose in a modern society. They conclude that "decentralization is the only purpose states serve, and that they do not embody any important normative principle at this juncture in our history. The Supreme Court should never invoke federalism as a reason for invalidating a federal statute or as a principle for interpreting it."[18]

What do you think of this argument? Is it clear that the States would do as good a job at policy experimentation or fostering public participation in government if, rather than being permanent, constitutionally-entrenched political communities with over a century (in most cases) of autonomous existence, they were instead simply administrative sub-units of the national government with no guaranteed measure of independence? And can we really trust national authorities to make optimal judgments about decentralization when their own prerogatives are at stake?

5.   Many of the Founders' arguments that states would help to preserve liberty and check centralized tyranny seem to have expected the states to provide a military counterweight to the national government. That

---

[16] *See* Edward Rubin & Malcolm Feeley, *Federalism: Some Notes on a National Neurosis*, 41 UCLA L. REV. 903 (1994). (Incidentally, is it conducive to civil debate to label proponents of the opposing view "neurotic"?)

[17] *Id.* at 911.

[18] *Id.* at 909.

seems unlikely in the twenty-first century. To what extent, and in what ways, do the States continue to protect liberty today? The contemporary literature on federalism offers several possible answers:

First, one key aspect of liberty is the ability to choose the laws under which one lives. Preserving state autonomy to make divergent regulatory choices maintains citizens' option of *exit*: If one finds a given state's regime oppressive, one can move someplace else. And because it is generally easier to participate in politics at the state and local levels, states also preserve the option of *voice*—that is, citizens may more readily influence political outcomes when decisions are made closer to home.[19]

Second, states sometimes serve as *rallying points for dissent*.[20] Much as Virginia and Kentucky rallied opposition to the Alien and Sedition Acts in the early Republic, Texas led opposition to President Obama's relaxation of immigration enforcement, while Washington, Minnesota, and Virginia have taken early stands against President Trump's executive order excluding certain aliens from the country.

Third, states have the ability not just to speak out or challenge federal actions in court, but also to *dissent by deciding*.[21] That is, states that take a view rejected at the national level can often implement their dissenting view as a matter of state policy. California, for instance, has not only criticized successive national administrations for not doing enough to combat air pollution and climate change; it has also enacted and enforced considerably stricter regulations as a matter of state law. This sort of dissent may be uniquely persuasive, because it offers the minority a viewpoint a chance to demonstrate the soundness of its dissenting view in practice to a skeptical national audience.

Finally, the availability of states as alternative power centers may help *preserve partisan competition* in the wider country.[22] Because the partisan makeup of many states diverges sharply from the national average, a party that has been run out of power in Washington, D.C., can hunker down in the states it still controls and plot its return to power. The Republican party, for example, was able to recover from losing all three branches of the national government in 2008 in part because it remained strong in a large number of states. It is no surprise that four of the last seven presidents had served as governors in their states during a period when their party was out of power at the national level.

---

[19] *See generally* ALBERT O. HIRSCHMAN, EXIT, VOICE, AND LOYALTY: RESPONSES TO DECLINE IN FIRMS, ORGANIZATIONS, AND STATES (1970); *see also* Ernest A. Young, *Exit, Voice, and Loyalty as Federalism Strategies: Lessons from the Same-Sex Marriage Debate*, 85 U. COLO. L. REV. 1133 (2014).

[20] *See, e.g.*, The Federalist No. 26, at 169 (J.E. Cooke ed., 1961) (Alexander Hamilton) (observing that "the state Legislature . . . will constantly have their attention awake to the conduct of the national rulers and will be ready enough, if any thing improper appears, to sound the alarm to the people and not only to be the VOICE but if necessary the ARM of their discontent"); *see also* Daniel Francis, *Litigation as a Political Safeguard*, unpublished manuscript, 10/24/2016.

[21] *See generally* Heather K. Gerken, *Dissenting by Deciding*, 57 STAN. L. REV. 1745 (2005).

[22] *See generally* Jessica Bulman-Pozen, *Partisan Federalism*, 127 HARV. L. REV. 1077 (2014) (discussing the states generally as fora for, and instruments of, partisan competition).

Keep in mind, however, that each of these federalism dynamics simply preserves a *different* view from the one prevailing at the national level—not necessarily a *better* or even a more libertarian one. States helped rally opposition to *Brown* as well as to the Alien and Sedition Acts. Is this observation about federalism any different from the fact that most constitutional liberties protect *negative* freedoms—that is, they protect autonomy of choice without any guarantee that the subject will make *good* choices?

6.   How strong a personal connection do you feel to your State? In another essay, Professor Rubin argued that there is no point to protecting federalism if the States are no longer highly-distinctive political communities that constitute an important aspect of their citizens' personal identity.[23] Federalism might thus make sense within the European Union, for example, where people still identify as German or French or Czech, or in the post-Saddam Hussein government of Iraq, where federalism might accommodate clashing Shiite, Sunni, and Kurdish identities. However, in Rubin's view, it makes no sense to retain a federal structure in contemporary America, where you can find a Starbucks on every corner whether you are in Boston or Austin. Do you agree? Is federalism only valuable in divided societies?

How strong are state identities these days? If we accept that nowadays it would be virtually inconceivable for an American to choose his state allegiance over his national one, as Robert E. Lee did in 1861, are there nonetheless people who meaningfully self-identify as Texans or Carolinians or Vermonters? Although many law professors take national homogeneity for granted, scholars of political science,[24] history,[25] and cultural geography[26] frequently emphasize the continuing diversity of states and regions and the impact of that diversity on political culture. Suppose, however, that the long-term tendency is toward ever looser attachments to the states. What impact would you expect that to have on constitutional federalism? If a significant decline in citizens' identification with their states might undermine the federal structure, is there any means to preserve or restore a sense of strong identity in the states?

7.   Is there an argument to be made that we should seek to preserve the federal balance—that is, that we should limit national power and protect state autonomy from federal encroachment—irrespective of whether state action serves any particular policy values? If the Constitution can be shown

---

[23] *See* Edward L. Rubin, *Puppy Federalism and the Blessings of America*, 574 ANNALS AM. ACAD. POL. & SOC. SCI. 37 (2001).

[24] *See, e.g.*, ANDREW GELMAN, RED STATE, BLUE STATE, RICH STATE, POOR STATE: WHY AMERICANS VOTE THE WAY THEY DO 21–22 (2008); ROBERT S. ERIKSON, GERALD C. WRIGHT, & JOHN P. MCIVER, STATEHOUSE DEMOCRACY: PUBLIC OPINION AND POLICY IN THE AMERICAN STATES 47 (1993).

[25] *See, e.g.*, DAVID HACKETT FISCHER, ALBION'S SEED: FOUR BRITISH FOLKWAYS IN AMERICA (1989); COLIN WOODARD, AMERICAN NATIONS: A HISTORY OF THE ELEVEN RIVAL REGIONAL CULTURES OF NORTH AMERICA (2011).

[26] *See, e.g.*, WILBUR ZELINSKY, NOT YET A PLACELESS LAND: TRACKING AN EVOLVING AMERICAN GEOGRAPHY (2011); *see also* STATE BY STATE: A PANORAMIC PORTRAIT OF AMERICA xiv (Matt Weiland & Sean Wilsey, eds. 2009)

to presuppose and/or embody a principle of meaningful balance between national and state authority, would that impose an independent obligation of fidelity to that structural arrangement? In other words, are we bound to uphold federalism simply because it's in the Constitution, whether or not it's actually a good thing?

See also: For a more extended discussion of the values associated with both state and national action, see DAVID L. SHAPIRO, FEDERALISM: A DIALOGUE (1995); Barry Friedman, *Valuing Federalism*, 82 MINN. L. REV. 317 (1997).

SECTION 8.2   JUDICIAL AND POLITICAL SAFEGUARDS OF FEDERALISM

It is plain from Federalist 10 and 51 that the Framers of the Constitution relied primarily on structural and political safeguards, rather than judicial review, in order to protect liberty in the new republic. The question, however, is whether that reliance should be primary or *exclusive* when it comes to protecting the federal structure itself. In other words, should courts attempt to enforce limits on national authority, or should they leave those limits to be protected by institutional and political mechanisms?

This may seem like an odd question. We do not, after all, generally view judicial review as superfluous in other areas—e.g., separation of powers, individual rights—simply because the branches of the federal government or individual rightholders have non-judicial means of protecting their interests. On the other hand, the point of theories like John Hart Ely's "representation reinforcement" approach is that the *level* or intensity of judicial review ought to reflect the extent to which ordinary political processes can be relied upon to safeguard the right in question. This is the way that Professor Herbert Wechsler framed his influential argument about the "political safeguards of federalism."[27] Wechsler noted that the Senate, in which all states are equally represented, "cannot fail to function as the guardian of state interests as such," and that "[f]ederalist considerations [e.g., the allocation of electoral votes by state] play an important role even in the selection of the President." He therefore concluded that "the Court is on weakest ground when it opposes its interpretation of the Constitution to that of Congress in the interests of the states, whose representatives control the legislative process and, by hypothesis, have broadly acquiesced in sanctioning the challenged Act of Congress."[28]

Other scholars have taken Wechsler's argument further, however, so as not to counsel merely deferential judicial review but to foreclose judicial review of federalism questions *at all*. Jesse Choper, for example, has argued that the Supreme Court has limited political capital to spend

---

[27] *See* Herbert L. Wechsler, *The Political Safeguards of Federalism: The Role of the States in the Composition and Selection of the National Government*, 54 COLUM. L. REV. 543 (1954).

[28] *Id.* at 548, 557, 559.

in striking down acts of the political branches, and that it should conserve that capital for cases involving individual rights.[29] Dean Choper thus proposed that "the constitutional issue of whether federal action is beyond the authority of the central government and thus violates 'states' rights' should be treated as nonjusticiable, final resolution being relegated to the political branches."[30] Although Dean Choper's is the most extreme version of the argument, the basic point can be traced back all the way to James Madison's essays in Federalist Nos. 45 and 46.

The political safeguards debate came to a head at the Supreme Court in a somewhat odd context. Most of the federalism litigation thus far in the course has concerned the scope of Congress's power under the Commerce Clause—an issue to which we will return in the next assignment. Between 1937 and 1995, the Supreme Court did not strike down a single Act of Congress as exceeding the commerce power. In 1976, however, the Court formulated an unenumerated right of state governments not to be the *subject* of regulation, in certain circumstances, by the federal government. In *National League of Cities v. Usery*,[31] the Supreme Court considered a challenge to amendments to the Fair Labor Standards Act (FLSA) that subjected state governments themselves to federal wage and hour regulation. It is important to note that in *United States v. Darby*,[32] the Supreme Court had already upheld the FLSA against a challenge that regulating wages and hours of employees fell outside its commerce powers. *National League of Cities* left *Darby* intact and instead held that state governments have a special, unenumerated constitutional immunity from federal regulation, at least when they are performing traditional state governmental functions.

The test for this immunity, as stated in a later case, had four parts:

1. the challenged statute must regulate "the States as States";

2. the federal regulation must address matters that are indisputably "attribute[s] of state sovereignty";

3. the States' compliance with the federal law must directly impair their ability "to structure integral operations in areas of traditional governmental functions"; and

4. there must not be any overriding federal interest advanced by the regulation.[33]

The *National League of Cities* Court was deeply divided, however, and it struggled to apply the test in subsequent cases. Nine years later, in the *Garcia* case, the Court asked for reargument on the question whether

---

[29] *See* JESSE H. CHOPER, JUDICIAL REVIEW AND THE NATIONAL POLITICAL PROCESS: A FUNCTIONAL RECONSIDERATION OF THE ROLE OF THE SUPREME COURT (1980).

[30] *Id.* at 175–84.

[31] 426 U.S. 833 (1976).

[32] 312 U.S. 100 (1941).

[33] Hodel v. Virginia Surface Mining & Reclamation Ass'n, 452 U.S. 264, 287–88 & n. 29 (1981).

National League of Cities should be overruled. The "political safeguards" arguments advanced by Professor Wechsler and others would play a central role in the ensuing decision.

Garcia v. San Antonio Metropolitan Transit Authority
469 U.S. 528 (1985)

■ JUSTICE BLACKMUN delivered the opinion of the Court.

We revisit in these cases an issue raised in *National League of Cities v. Usery,* 426 U.S. 833 (1976) . . . . In the present cases, a Federal District Court concluded that municipal ownership and operation of a mass-transit system is a traditional governmental function and thus, under *National League of Cities*, is exempt from the obligations imposed by the FLSA. Faced with the identical question, three Federal Courts of Appeals and one state appellate court have reached the opposite conclusion.

Our examination of this "function" standard applied in these and other cases over the last eight years now persuades us that the attempt to draw the boundaries of state regulatory immunity in terms of "traditional governmental function" is not only unworkable but is also inconsistent with established principles of federalism and, indeed, with those very federalism principles on which *National League of Cities* purported to rest. That case, accordingly, is overruled.

I

The history of public transportation in San Antonio, Tex., is characteristic of the history of local mass transit in the United States generally. Passenger transportation for hire within San Antonio originally was provided on a private basis by a local transportation company. . . . The city continued to rely on such publicly regulated private mass transit until 1959, when it purchased the privately owned San Antonio Transit Company and replaced it with a public authority known as the San Antonio Transit System (SATS). SATS operated until 1978, when the city transferred its facilities and equipment to appellee San Antonio Metropolitan Transit Authority (SAMTA), a public mass-transit authority organized on a countywide basis. SAMTA currently is the major provider of transportation in the San Antonio metropolitan area; between 1978 and 1980 alone, its vehicles traveled over 26 million route miles and carried over 63 million passengers. . . .

The present controversy concerns the extent to which SAMTA may be subjected to the minimum-wage and overtime requirements of the FLSA. When the FLSA was enacted in 1938, its wage and overtime provisions did not apply to local mass-transit employees or, indeed, to employees of state and local governments. In 1961, Congress extended minimum-wage coverage to employees of any private mass-transit carrier whose annual gross revenue was not less than $1 million. Five years later, Congress extended FLSA coverage to state and local-government employees for the first time by withdrawing the minimum-wage and overtime exemptions from public hospitals, schools, and mass-transit carriers whose rates and services were subject to state regulation. At the same time, Congress eliminated the overtime exemption for all mass-transit employees other than drivers, operators, and conductors. The application of the FLSA to public schools and hospitals was ruled to be within Congress' power under the Commerce Clause. *Maryland v. Wirtz,* 392 U.S. 183 (1968).

The FLSA obligations of public mass-transit systems like SATS were expanded in 1974 when Congress provided for the progressive repeal of the surviving overtime exemption for mass-transit employees. Congress simultaneously brought the States and their subdivisions further within the ambit of the FLSA by extending FLSA coverage to virtually all state and local-government employees. SATS complied with the FLSA's overtime requirements until 1976, when this Court, in *National League of Cities*, overruled *Maryland v. Wirtz*, and held that the FLSA could not be applied constitutionally to the "traditional governmental functions" of state and local governments. Four months after *National League of Cities* was handed down, SATS informed its employees that the decision relieved SATS of its overtime obligations under the FLSA.

Matters rested there until September 17, 1979, when the Wage and Hour Administration of the Department of Labor issued an opinion that SAMTA's operations "are not constitutionally immune from the application of the Fair Labor Standards Act" under *National League of Cities*. On November 21 of that year, SAMTA filed this action against the Secretary of Labor in the United States District Court for the Western District of Texas. It sought a declaratory judgment that, contrary to the Wage and Hour Administration's determination, *National League of Cities* precluded the application of the FLSA's overtime requirements to SAMTA's operations. The Secretary counterclaimed . . . for enforcement of the overtime and recordkeeping requirements of the FLSA. On the same day that SAMTA filed its action, appellant Garcia and several other SAMTA employees brought suit against SAMTA in the same District Court for overtime pay under the FLSA. . . .

After initial argument, the cases were restored to our calendar for reargument, and the parties were requested to brief and argue the following additional question:

> Whether or not the principles of the Tenth Amendment as set forth in *National League of Cities v. Usery* should be reconsidered? . . .

II

Appellees have not argued that SAMTA is immune from regulation under the FLSA on the ground that it is a local transit system engaged in intrastate commercial activity. In a practical sense, SAMTA's operations might well be characterized as "local." Nonetheless, it long has been settled that Congress' authority under the Commerce Clause extends to intrastate economic activities that affect interstate commerce. See, *e.g., Wickard v. Filburn*. . . . Any constitutional exemption from the requirements of the FLSA therefore must rest on SAMTA's status as a governmental entity rather than on the "local" nature of its operations.

[U]nder *National League of Cities* . . . four conditions must be satisfied before a state activity may be deemed immune from a particular federal regulation under the Commerce Clause. First, it is said that the federal statute at issue must regulate "the 'States as States.' " Second, the statute must "address matters that are indisputably '[attributes] of state sovereignty.' " Third, state compliance with the federal obligation must "directly impair [the States'] ability 'to structure integral operations in areas of traditional governmental functions.' " Finally, the relation of state and federal interests must not be such that "the nature of the federal interest . . . justifies state submission."

The controversy in the present cases has focused on the third . . . requirement—that the challenged federal statute trench on "traditional governmental functions." The District Court voiced a common concern: "Despite the abundance of adjectives, identifying which particular state functions are immune remains difficult." Just how troublesome the task has been is revealed by the results reached in other federal cases. Thus, courts have held that regulating ambulance services . . . licensing automobile drivers . . . operating a municipal airport . . . performing solid waste disposal . . . and operating a highway authority . . . are functions *protected* under *National League of Cities*. At the same time, courts have held that issuance of industrial development bonds . . . regulation of intrastate natural gas sales . . . regulation of traffic on public roads . . . regulation of air transportation . . . operation of a telephone system . . . leasing and sale of natural gas . . . operation of a mental health facility . . . and provision of in-house domestic services for the aged and handicapped . . . are *not* entitled to immunity. We find it difficult, if not impossible, to identify an organizing principle that places each of the cases in the first group on one side of a line and each of the cases in the second group on the other side. The constitutional distinction between licensing drivers and regulating traffic, for example, or between operating a highway authority and operating a mental health facility, is elusive at best.

Thus far, this Court itself has made little headway in defining the scope of the governmental functions deemed protected under *National League of Cities*. In that case the Court set forth examples of protected and unprotected functions but provided no explanation of how those examples were identified. The only other case in which the Court has had occasion to address the problem is [*United Transportation Union v. Long Island Railroad Co.*, 455 U.S. 678 (1982)]. . . . We relied in large part there on "the *historical reality* that the operation of railroads is not among the functions *traditionally* performed by state and local governments," but we simultaneously disavowed "a static historical view of state functions generally immune from federal regulation." We held that the inquiry into a particular function's "traditional" nature was merely a means of determining whether the federal statute at issue unduly handicaps "basic state prerogatives," but we did not offer an explanation of what makes one state function a "basic prerogative" and another function not basic. Finally, having disclaimed a rigid reliance on the historical pedigree of state involvement in a particular area, we nonetheless found it appropriate to emphasize the extended historical record of *federal* involvement in the field of rail transportation.

Many constitutional standards involve "[undoubted] . . . gray areas," and . . . it normally might be fair to venture the assumption that case-by-case development would lead to a workable standard for determining whether a particular governmental function should be immune from federal regulation under the Commerce Clause. A further cautionary note is sounded, however, by the Court's experience in the related field of state immunity from federal taxation. . . .

If these tax-immunity cases had any common thread, it was in the attempt to distinguish between "governmental" and "proprietary" functions. To say that the distinction between "governmental" and "proprietary" proved to be stable, however, would be something of an overstatement. In 1911, for example, the Court declared that the provision of a municipal water supply "is no part of the essential governmental functions of a State." Twenty-six years later, without any intervening change in the applicable legal standards, the Court simply rejected its earlier position and decided that the provision of a municipal water supply *was* immune from federal taxation as an essential governmental function, even though municipal waterworks long had been operated for profit by private industry. At the same time that the Court was holding a municipal water supply to be immune from federal taxes, it had held that a state-run commuter rail system was *not* immune. . . . It was this uncertainty and instability that led the Court shortly thereafter, in *New York v. United States*, 326 U.S. 572 (1946), unanimously to conclude that the distinction between "governmental" and "proprietary" functions was "untenable" and must be abandoned. . . .

Even during the heyday of the governmental/proprietary distinction in intergovernmental tax-immunity doctrine the Court never explained the constitutional basis for that distinction. . . . Although the need to reconcile state and federal interests obviously demanded that state immunity have some limiting principle, the Court did not try to justify the particular result it reached; it simply concluded that a "line [must] be drawn," and proceeded to draw that line. . . . This inability to give principled content to the distinction between "governmental" and "proprietary," no less significantly than its unworkability, led the Court to abandon the distinction in *New York v. United States*.

The distinction the Court discarded as unworkable in the field of tax immunity has proved no more fruitful in the field of regulatory immunity under the Commerce Clause. Neither do any of the alternative standards that might be employed to distinguish between protected and unprotected governmental functions appear manageable. . . . The most obvious defect of a historical approach to state immunity is that it prevents a court from accommodating changes in the historical functions of States, changes that have resulted in a number of once-private functions like education being assumed by the States and their subdivisions. At the same time, the only apparent virtue of a rigorous historical standard, namely, its promise of a reasonably objective measure for state immunity, is illusory. . . . [C]ourts would have to decide by fiat precisely how longstanding a pattern of state involvement had to be for federal regulatory authority to be defeated.[10]

A nonhistorical standard for selecting immune governmental functions is likely to be just as unworkable as is a historical standard. The goal of identifying "uniquely" governmental functions, for example, has been rejected by the Court in the field of government tort liability in part because the notion of a "uniquely" governmental function is unmanageable. Another possibility would be to confine immunity to "necessary" governmental services, that is, services that would be provided inadequately or not at all unless the government provided them. The set of services that fits into this category, however, may well be negligible. . . . It also is open to question how well equipped courts are to make this kind of determination about the workings of economic markets.

We believe, however, that there is a more fundamental problem at work here. . . . [N]either the governmental/proprietary distinction nor any other that purports to separate out important governmental functions can be faithful to the role of federalism in a democratic society. The essence of our federal system is that within the realm of authority left open to them under the Constitution, the States must be equally free to engage in any activity that their citizens choose for the common weal, no matter how unorthodox or unnecessary anyone else . . . deems state involvement to be. Any rule of state immunity that looks to the "traditional," "integral," or "necessary" nature of governmental functions inevitably invites an unelected federal judiciary to make decisions about which state policies it favors and which ones it dislikes. "The science of government . . . is the science of experiment," and the States cannot serve as laboratories for social and economic experiment if they must pay an

---

[10] For much the same reasons, the existence *vel non* of a tradition of *federal* involvement in a particular area does not provide an adequate standard for state immunity. Most of the Federal Government's current regulatory activity originated less than 50 years ago with the New Deal, and a good portion of it has developed within the past two decades. The recent vintage of this regulatory activity does not diminish the strength of the federal interest in applying regulatory standards to state activities, nor does it affect the strength of the States' interest in being free from federal supervision. . . .

added price when they meet the changing needs of their citizenry by taking up functions that an earlier day and a different society left in private hands. . . .

We therefore now reject, as unsound in principle and unworkable in practice, a rule of state immunity from federal regulation that turns on a judicial appraisal of whether a particular governmental function is "integral" or "traditional." Any such rule leads to inconsistent results at the same time that it disserves principles of democratic self-governance, and it breeds inconsistency precisely because it is divorced from those principles. If there are to be limits on the Federal Government's power to interfere with state functions—as undoubtedly there are—we must look elsewhere to find them. We accordingly return to the underlying issue that confronted this Court in *National League of Cities*—the manner in which the Constitution insulates States from the reach of Congress' power under the Commerce Clause.

III

The central theme of *National League of Cities* was that the States occupy a special position in our constitutional system and that the scope of Congress' authority under the Commerce Clause must reflect that position. Of course, the Commerce Clause by its specific language does not provide any special limitation on Congress' actions with respect to the States. It is equally true, however, that the text of the Constitution provides the beginning rather than the final answer to every inquiry into questions of federalism, for "[behind] the words of the constitutional provisions are postulates which limit and control." *National League of Cities* reflected the general conviction that the Constitution precludes "the National Government [from] [devouring] the essentials of state sovereignty." . . .

What has proved problematic is not the perception that the Constitution's federal structure imposes limitations on the Commerce Clause, but rather the nature and content of those limitations. . . . We doubt that courts ultimately can identify principled constitutional limitations on the scope of Congress' Commerce Clause powers over the States merely by relying on *a priori* definitions of state sovereignty. In part, this is because of the elusiveness of objective criteria. . . . There is, however, a more fundamental reason: the sovereignty of the States is limited by the Constitution itself. A variety of sovereign powers, for example, are withdrawn from the States by Article I, § 10. Section 8 of the same Article works an equally sharp contraction of state sovereignty by authorizing Congress to exercise a wide range of legislative powers and (in conjunction with the Supremacy Clause of Article VI) to displace contrary state legislation. . . . Finally, the developed application, through the Fourteenth Amendment, of the greater part of the Bill of Rights to the States limits the sovereign authority that States otherwise would possess to legislate with respect to their citizens and to conduct their own affairs.

The States unquestionably do "[retain] a significant measure of sovereign authority." They do so, however, only to the extent that the Constitution has not divested them of their original powers and transferred those powers to the Federal Government. In the words of James Madison to the Members of the First Congress: "Interference with the power of the States was no constitutional criterion of the power of Congress. If the power was not given, Congress could not exercise it; if given, they might exercise it, although it should interfere with the laws, or even the Constitution of the States." . . .

As a result, to say that the Constitution assumes the continued role of the States is to say little about the nature of that role. . . . With rare exceptions, like the guarantee, in Article IV, § 3, of state territorial integrity, the Constitution does not carve out express elements of state sovereignty that Congress may not employ its delegated powers to displace. . . . In short, we have no license to employ freestanding conceptions of state sovereignty when measuring congressional authority under the Commerce Clause.

When we look for the States' "residuary and inviolable sovereignty," The Federalist No. 39 (J. Madison), in the shape of the constitutional scheme rather than in predetermined notions of sovereign power, a different measure of state sovereignty emerges. Apart from the limitation on federal authority inherent in the delegated nature of Congress' Article I powers, the principal means chosen by the Framers to ensure the role of the States in the federal system lies in the structure of the Federal Government itself. . . . [T]he composition of the Federal Government was designed in large part to protect the States from overreaching by Congress.[11] The Framers thus gave the States a role in the selection both of the Executive and the Legislative Branches of the Federal Government. The States were vested with indirect influence over the House of Representatives and the Presidency by their control of electoral qualifications and their role in Presidential elections. U.S. Const., Art. I, § 2, and Art. II, § 1. They were given more direct influence in the Senate, where each State received equal representation and each Senator was to be selected by the legislature of his State. Art. I, § 3. The significance attached to the States' equal representation in the Senate is underscored by the prohibition of any constitutional amendment divesting a State of equal representation without the State's consent. Art. V.

The extent to which the structure of the Federal Government itself was relied on to insulate the interests of the States is evident in the views of the Framers. James Madison explained that the Federal Government "will partake sufficiently of the spirit [of the States], to be disinclined to

---

[11] See, e. g., J. Choper, *Judicial Review and the National Political Process 175–184 (1980);* Wechsler, *The Political Safeguards of Federalism: The Role of the States in the Composition and Selection of the National Government,* 54 COLUM. L. REV. 543 (1954); La Pierre, *The Political Safeguards of Federalism Redux: Intergovernmental Immunity and the States as Agents of the Nation,* 60 WASH. U. L. Q. 779 (1982).

invade the rights of the individual States, or the prerogatives of their governments." Similarly, James Wilson observed that "it was a favorite object in the Convention" to provide for the security of the States against federal encroachment and that the structure of the Federal Government itself served that end. Madison placed particular reliance on the equal representation of the States in the Senate, which he saw as "at once a constitutional recognition of the portion of sovereignty remaining in the individual States, and an instrument for preserving that residuary sovereignty." He further noted that "the residuary sovereignty of the States [is] implied *and secured* by that principle of representation in one branch of the [federal] legislature." In short, the Framers chose to rely on a federal system in which special restraints on federal power over the States inhered principally in the workings of the National Government itself, rather than in discrete limitations on the objects of federal authority. State sovereign interests, then, are more properly protected by procedural safeguards inherent in the structure of the federal system than by judicially created limitations on federal power.

The effectiveness of the federal political process in preserving the States' interests is apparent even today in the course of federal legislation. On the one hand, the States have been able to direct a substantial proportion of federal revenues into their own treasuries in the form of general and program-specific grants in aid. The federal role in assisting state and local governments is a longstanding one; Congress provided federal land grants to finance state governments from the beginning of the Republic, and direct cash grants were awarded as early as 1887 under the Hatch Act. In the past quarter century alone, federal grants to States and localities have grown from $7 billion to $96 billion. As a result, federal grants now account for about one-fifth of state and local government expenditures. The States have obtained federal funding for such services as police and fire protection, education, public health and hospitals, parks and recreation, and sanitation. Moreover, at the same time that the States have exercised their influence to obtain federal support, they have been able to exempt themselves from a wide variety of obligations imposed by Congress under the Commerce Clause. For example, the Federal Power Act, the National Labor Relations Act, the Labor-Management Reporting and Disclosure Act, the Occupational Safety and Health Act, the Employee Retirement Income Security Act, and the Sherman Act all contain express or implied exemptions for States and their subdivisions. The fact that some federal statutes such as the FLSA extend general obligations to the States cannot obscure the extent to which the political position of the States in the federal system has served to minimize the burdens that the States bear under the Commerce Clause.[17]

---

[17] Even as regards the FLSA, Congress incorporated special provisions concerning overtime pay for law enforcement and firefighting personnel when it amended the FLSA in 1974 in order to take account of the special concerns of States and localities with respect to these

We realize that changes in the structure of the Federal Government have taken place since 1789, not the least of which has been the substitution of popular election of Senators by the adoption of the Seventeenth Amendment in 1913, and that these changes may work to alter the influence of the States in the federal political process. Nonetheless, against this background, we are convinced that the fundamental limitation that the constitutional scheme imposes on the Commerce Clause to protect the "States as States" is one of process rather than one of result. Any substantive restraint on the exercise of Commerce Clause powers must find its justification in the procedural nature of this basic limitation, and it must be tailored to compensate for possible failings in the national political process rather than to dictate a "sacred province of state autonomy."

Insofar as the present cases are concerned, then, we need go no further than to state that we perceive nothing in the overtime and minimum-wage requirements of the FLSA, as applied to SAMTA, that is destructive of state sovereignty or violative of any constitutional provision. SAMTA faces nothing more than the same minimum-wage and overtime obligations that hundreds of thousands of other employers, public as well as private, have to meet.

In these cases, the status of public mass transit simply underscores the extent to which the structural protections of the Constitution insulate the States from federally imposed burdens. . . . In short, Congress has not simply placed a financial burden on the shoulders of States and localities that operate mass-transit systems, but has provided substantial countervailing financial assistance as well. . . . Congress' treatment of public mass transit reinforces our conviction that the national political process systematically protects States from the risk of having their functions in that area handicapped by Commerce Clause regulation.[21]

IV

This analysis makes clear that Congress' action in affording SAMTA employees the protections of the wage and hour provisions of the FLSA contravened no affirmative limit on Congress' power under the Commerce Clause. The judgment of the District Court therefore must be reversed. . . .

We do not lightly overrule recent precedent. We have not hesitated, however, when it has become apparent that a prior decision has departed from a proper understanding of congressional power under the Commerce Clause. . . . *National League of Cities v. Usery* is overruled.

---

positions. Congress also declined to impose any obligations on state and local governments with respect to policymaking personnel who are not subject to civil service laws.

[21] Our references to UMTA are not meant to imply that regulation under the Commerce Clause must be accompanied by countervailing financial benefits under the Spending Clause. The application of the FLSA to SAMTA would be constitutional even had Congress not provided federal funding under UMTA.

The judgment of the District Court is reversed, and these cases are remanded to that court for further proceedings consistent with this opinion.

■ JUSTICE POWELL, with whom THE CHIEF JUSTICE, JUSTICE REHNQUIST, and JUSTICE O'CONNOR join, dissenting.

. . . Because I believe this decision substantially alters the federal system embodied in the Constitution, I dissent.

I

. . . Whatever effect the Court's decision may have in weakening the application of *stare decisis*, it is likely to be less important than what the Court has done to the Constitution itself. A unique feature of the United States is the *federal* system of government guaranteed by the Constitution and implicit in the very name of our country. Despite some genuflecting in the Court's opinion to the concept of federalism, today's decision effectively reduces the Tenth Amendment to meaningless rhetoric when Congress acts pursuant to the Commerce Clause. . . .

To leave no doubt about its intention, the Court renounces its decision in *National League of Cities* because it "inevitably invites an unelected federal judiciary to make decisions about which state policies its favors and which ones it dislikes." In other words, the extent to which the States may exercise their authority, when Congress purports to act under the Commerce Clause, henceforth is to be determined from time to time by political decisions made by members of the Federal Government, decisions the Court says will not be subject to judicial review. I note that it does not seem to have occurred to the Court that *it*—an unelected majority of five Justices—today rejects almost 200 years of the understanding of the constitutional status of federalism. . . .

II

A

Much of the Court's opinion is devoted to arguing that it is difficult to define *a priori* "traditional governmental functions." *National League of Cities* neither engaged in, nor required, such a task. . . . *National League of Cities* adopted a familiar type of balancing test for determining whether Commerce Clause enactments transgress constitutional limitations imposed by the federal nature of our system of government. . . .

Our subsequent decisions also adopted this approach of weighing the respective interests of the States and Federal Government.[5] In *EEOC v.*

---

[5] In undertaking such balancing, we have considered, on the one hand, the strength of the federal interest in the challenged legislation and the impact of exempting the States from its reach. Central to our inquiry into the federal interest is how closely the challenged action implicates the central concerns of the Commerce Clause, viz., the promotion of a national economy and free trade among the States. . . . Similarly, we have considered whether exempting States from federal regulation would undermine the goals of the federal program. . . . On the

Wyoming, 460 U.S. 226 (1983), for example, the Court stated that "[the] principle of immunity articulated in *National League of Cities* is a functional doctrine . . . whose ultimate purpose is not to create a sacred province of state autonomy, but to ensure that the unique benefits of a federal system . . . not be lost through undue federal interference in certain core state functions." In overruling *National League of Cities*, the Court incorrectly characterizes the mode of analysis established therein and developed in subsequent cases.

Moreover, the statute at issue in this case, the FLSA, is the identical statute that was at issue in *National League of Cities*. Although JUSTICE BLACKMUN's concurrence noted that he was "not untroubled by certain possible implications of the Court's opinion" in *National League of Cities*, it also stated that "the result with respect to the statute under challenge here [the FLSA] is *necessarily correct*." His opinion for the Court today does not discuss the statute, nor identify any changed circumstances that warrant the conclusion today that *National League of Cities* is *necessarily wrong*.

B

Today's opinion does not explain how the States' role in the electoral process guarantees that particular exercises of the Commerce Clause power will not infringe on residual state sovereignty.[7] Members of Congress are elected from the various States, but once in office they are Members of the Federal Government.[8] Although the States participate in the Electoral College, this is hardly a reason to view the President as a representative of the States' interest against federal encroachment. We noted recently "[the] hydraulic pressure inherent within each of the separate Branches to exceed the outer limits of its power. . . ." *INS v. Chadha,* 462 U.S. 919 (1983). The Court offers no reason to think that this pressure will not operate when Congress seeks to invoke its powers under the Commerce Clause, notwithstanding the electoral role of the States.[9]

---

other hand, we have also assessed the injury done to the States if forced to comply with federal Commerce Clause enactments.

[7] Late in its opinion, the Court suggests that after all there may be some "affirmative limits the constitutional structure might impose on federal action affecting the States under the Commerce Clause." . . . The Court's failure to specify the "affirmative limits" on federal power, or when and how these limits are to be determined, may well be explained by the transparent fact that any such attempt would be subject to precisely the same objections on which it relies to overrule *National League of Cities*.

[8] One can hardly imagine this Court saying that because Congress is composed of individuals, individual rights guaranteed by the Bill of Rights are amply protected by the political process. Yet, the position adopted today is indistinguishable in principle. The Tenth Amendment also is an essential part of the Bill of Rights.

[9] At one time in our history, the view that the structure of the Federal Government sufficed to protect the States might have had a somewhat more practical, although not a more logical, basis. Professor Wechsler, whose seminal article in 1954 proposed the view adopted by the Court today, predicated his argument on assumptions that simply do not accord with current reality. Professor Wechsler wrote: "National action has . . . always been regarded as exceptional in our polity, an intrusion to be justified by some necessity, the special rather than the ordinary case." Not only is the premise of this view clearly at odds with the proliferation of national

The Court apparently thinks that the States' success at obtaining federal funds for various projects and exemptions from the obligations of some federal statutes is indicative of the "effectiveness of the federal political process in preserving the States' interests. . . ." But such political success is not relevant to the question whether the political *processes* are the proper means of enforcing constitutional limitations.[11] The fact that Congress generally does not transgress constitutional limits on its power to reach state activities does not make judicial review any less necessary to rectify the cases in which it does do so.[12] The States' role in our system of government is a matter of constitutional law, not of legislative grace. "The powers not delegated to the United States by the Constitution, nor prohibited by it to the States, are reserved to the States, respectively, or to the people." U.S. Const., Amdt. 10.

More troubling . . . is the result of [the Court's] holding, *i.e.*, that federal political officials, invoking the Commerce Clause, are the sole judges of the limits of their own power. This result is inconsistent with the fundamental principles of our constitutional system. At least since *Marbury v. Madison,* it has been the settled province of the federal judiciary "to say what the law is" with respect to the constitutionality of Acts of Congress. . . .

III

A

In our federal system, the States have a major role that cannot be pre-empted by the National Government. As contemporaneous writings and the debates at the ratifying conventions make clear, the States' ratification of the Constitution was predicated on this understanding of

---

legislation over the past 30 years, but "a variety of structural and political changes occurring in this century have combined to make Congress particularly *insensitive* to state and local values." The adoption of the Seventeenth Amendment (providing for direct election of Senators), the weakening of political parties on the local level, and the rise of national media, among other things, have made Congress increasingly less representative of state and local interests, and more likely to be responsive to the demands of various national constituencies. As one observer explained: "As Senators and members of the House develop independent constituencies among groups such as farmers, businessmen, laborers, environmentalists, and the poor, each of which generally supports certain national initiatives, their tendency to identify with state interests and the positions of state officials is reduced." Kaden, Federalism in the Courts: Agenda for the 1980s, in ACIR, The Future of Federalism in the 1980s, p. 97 (1981). Thus, even if one were to ignore the numerous problems with the Court's position in terms of constitutional theory, there would remain serious questions as to its factual premises.

[11] Apparently in an effort to reassure the States, the Court identifies several major statutes that thus far have not been made applicable to state governments. . . . The Court does not suggest that this restraint will continue after its decision here. . . .

[12] This Court has never before abdicated responsibility for assessing the constitutionality of challenged action on the ground that affected parties theoretically are able to look out for their own interests through the electoral process. As the Court noted in *National League of Cities,* a much stronger argument as to inherent structural protections could have been made in either *Buckley v. Valeo,* 424 U.S. 1 (1976), or *Myers v. United States,* 272 U.S. 52 (1926), than can be made here. In these cases, the President signed legislation that limited his authority with respect to certain appointments and thus arguably "it was . . . no concern of this Court that the law violated the Constitution." The Court nevertheless held the laws unconstitutional because they infringed on Presidential authority, the President's consent notwithstanding. The Court does not address this point; nor does it cite any authority for its contrary view.

federalism. Indeed, the Tenth Amendment was adopted specifically to ensure that the important role promised the States by the proponents of the Constitution was realized.

Much of the initial opposition to the Constitution was rooted in the fear that the National Government would be too powerful and eventually would eliminate the States as viable political entities. This concern was voiced repeatedly until proponents of the Constitution made assurances that a Bill of Rights, including a provision explicitly reserving powers in the States, would be among the first business of the new Congress. Samuel Adams argued, for example, that if the several States were to be joined in "one entire Nation, under one Legislature, the Powers of which shall extend to every Subject of Legislation, and its Laws be supreme & controul the whole, the Idea of Sovereignty in these States must be lost." Likewise, George Mason feared that "the general government being paramount to, and in every respect more powerful than the state governments, the latter must give way to the former."

Antifederalists raised these concerns in almost every state ratifying convention. As a result, eight States voted for the Constitution only after proposing amendments to be adopted after ratification. All eight of these included among their recommendations some version of what later became the Tenth Amendment. So strong was the concern that the proposed Constitution was seriously defective without a specific bill of rights, including a provision reserving powers to the States, that in order to secure the votes for ratification, the Federalists eventually conceded that such provisions were necessary. . . .

This history, which the Court simply ignores, documents the integral role of the Tenth Amendment in our constitutional theory. It exposes as well, I believe, the fundamental character of the Court's error today. Far from being "unsound in principle," judicial enforcement of the Tenth Amendment is essential to maintaining the federal system so carefully designed by the Framers and adopted in the Constitution. . . .

D

In contrast, the Court today propounds a view of federalism that pays only lip service to the role of the States. . . . Indeed, the Court's view of federalism appears to relegate the States to precisely the trivial role that opponents of the Constitution feared they would occupy.

In *National League of Cities*, we spoke of fire prevention, police protection, sanitation, and public health as "typical of [the services] performed by state and local governments in discharging their dual functions of administering the public law and furnishing public services." Not only are these activities remote from any normal concept of interstate commerce, they are also activities that epitomize the concerns of local, democratic self-government. In emphasizing the need to protect traditional governmental functions, we identified the kinds of activities engaged in by state and local governments that affect the everyday lives of citizens. These are services that people are in a position to understand and evaluate, and in a democracy, have the right to oversee.[18] We recognized that "it is functions such as these which governments are created to provide . . ." and that the States and local governments are better able than the National Government to perform them.

The Court maintains that the standard approved in *National League of Cities* "disserves principles of democratic self-governance." In reaching this conclusion, the Court looks myopically only to persons elected to positions in the Federal Government. It disregards entirely the far more effective role of democratic self-government at the state and local levels. One must compare realistically the operation of the state and local governments with that of the Federal Government. Federal legislation is drafted primarily by the staffs of the congressional committees. In view of the hundreds of bills introduced at each session of Congress and the complexity of many of them, it is virtually impossible for even the most conscientious legislators to be truly familiar with many of the statutes enacted. Federal departments and agencies customarily are authorized to write regulations. Often these are more important than the text of the statutes. As is true of the original legislation, these are drafted largely by staff personnel. The administration and enforcement of federal laws and regulations necessarily are largely in the hands of staff and civil service employees. These employees may have little or no knowledge of the States and localities that will be affected by the statutes and regulations for which they are responsible. In any case, they hardly are as accessible and responsive as those who occupy analogous positions in state and local governments.

In drawing this contrast, I imply no criticism of these federal employees or the officials who are ultimately in charge. . . . My point is simply that members of the immense federal bureaucracy are not elected, know less about the services traditionally rendered by States and localities, and are inevitably less responsive to recipients of such services, than are state legislatures, city councils, boards of supervisors, and state and local commissions, boards, and agencies. It is at these state and local levels—not in Washington as the Court so mistakenly thinks—that "democratic self-government" is best exemplified. . . .

---

[18] The Framers recognized that the most effective democracy occurs at local levels of government, where people with firsthand knowledge of local problems have more ready access to public officials responsible for dealing with them. This is as true today as it was when the Constitution was adopted. "Participation is likely to be more frequent, and exercised at more different stages of a governmental activity at the local level, or in regional organizations, than at the state and federal levels. [Additionally,] the proportion of people actually involved from the total population tends to be greater, the lower the level of government, and this, of course, better approximates the citizen participation ideal."

Moreover, we have witnessed in recent years the rise of numerous special interest groups that engage in sophisticated lobbying, and make substantial campaign contributions to some Members of Congress. These groups are thought to have significant influence in the shaping and enactment of certain types of legislation. Contrary to the Court's view, a "political process" that functions in this way is unlikely to safeguard the sovereign rights of States and localities.

V

Although the Court's opinion purports to recognize that the States retain some sovereign power, it does not identify even a single aspect of state authority that would remain when the Commerce Clause is invoked to justify federal regulation. . . .

As I view the Court's decision today as rejecting the basic precepts of our federal system and limiting the constitutional role of judicial review, I dissent.

■ **JUSTICE REHNQUIST, dissenting.**

I join both JUSTICE POWELL's and JUSTICE O'CONNOR's thoughtful dissents. JUSTICE POWELL's reference to the "balancing test" approved in *National League of Cities* is not identical with the language in that case, which recognized that Congress could not act under its commerce power to infringe on certain fundamental aspects of state sovereignty that are essential to "the States' separate and independent existence." Nor is either test, or JUSTICE O'CONNOR's suggested approach, precisely congruent with JUSTICE BLACKMUN's views in 1976, when he spoke of a balancing approach which did not outlaw federal power in areas "where the federal interest is demonstrably greater." But under any one of these approaches the judgment in these cases should be affirmed, and I do not think it incumbent on those of us in dissent to spell out further the fine points of a principle that will, I am confident, in time again command the support of a majority of this Court.

■ **JUSTICE O'CONNOR, with whom JUSTICE POWELL and JUSTICE REHNQUIST join, dissenting.**

The Court today surveys the battle scene of federalism and sounds a retreat. Like JUSTICE POWELL, I would prefer to hold the field and, at the very least, render a little aid to the wounded. I join JUSTICE POWELL's opinion. I also write separately to note my fundamental disagreement with the majority's views of federalism and the duty of this Court. . . .

In my view, federalism cannot be reduced to the weak "essence" distilled by the majority today. There is more to federalism than the nature of the constraints that can be imposed on the States in the realm of authority left open to them by the Constitution. The central issue of federalism, of course, is whether any realm *is* left open to the States by the Constitution—whether any area remains in which a State may act free of federal interference. The issue . . . is whether the federal system has any *legal* substance, any core of constitutional right that courts will enforce. The true "essence" of federalism is that the States *as States* have legitimate interests which the National Government is bound to respect even though its laws are supreme. If federalism . . . is to remain meaningful, this Court cannot abdicate its constitutional responsibility to oversee the Federal Government's compliance with its duty to respect the legitimate interests of the States.

Due to the emergence of an integrated and industrialized national economy, this Court has been required to examine and review a breathtaking expansion of the powers of Congress. In doing so the Court correctly perceived that the Framers of our Constitution intended Congress to have sufficient power to address national problems. . . . Just as surely . . . they also envisioned a republic whose vitality was assured by the diffusion of power not only among the branches of the Federal Government, but also between the Federal Government and the States. In the 18th century these intentions did not conflict because technology had not yet converted every local problem into a national one. A conflict has now emerged, and the Court today retreats rather than reconcile the Constitution's dual concerns for federalism and an effective commerce power. . . .

In the view of the Framers . . . the powers delegated to the United States, after all, were "few and defined." . . . The States were to retain authority over those local concerns of greatest relevance and importance to the people. . . .

Of course, one of the "few and defined" powers delegated to the National Congress was the power "To regulate Commerce with foreign Nations, and among the several States, and with the Indian Tribes." U.S. Const., Art. I, § 8, cl. 3. . . . In an era when interstate commerce represented a tiny fraction of economic activity and most goods and services were produced and consumed close to home, the interstate commerce power left a broad range of activities beyond the reach of Congress.

In the decades since ratification of the Constitution, interstate economic activity has steadily expanded. Industrialization, coupled with advances in transportation and communications, has created a national economy in which virtually every activity occurring within the borders of a State plays a part. . . . This Court has been increasingly generous in its interpretation of the commerce power of Congress, primarily to assure that the National Government would be able to deal with national economic problems. Most significantly, the Court in *NLRB v. Jones & Laughlin Steel Corp.* and *United States v. Darby* rejected its previous interpretations of the commerce power which had stymied New Deal legislation. . . .

Incidental to this expansion of the commerce power, Congress has been given an ability it lacked prior to the emergence of an integrated national economy. Because virtually every *state* activity, like virtually every activity of a private individual, arguably "affects" interstate commerce, Congress can now supplant the States from the significant sphere of activities envisioned for them by the Framers. It is in this context that recent changes in the workings of Congress, such as the direct election of Senators and the expanded influence of national interest groups, become relevant. These changes may well have lessened the weight Congress gives to the legitimate interests of States as States.

As a result, there is now a real risk that Congress will gradually erase the diffusion of power between State and Nation on which the Framers based their faith in the efficiency and vitality of our Republic.

It would be erroneous, however, to conclude that the Supreme Court was blind to the threat to federalism when it expanded the commerce power.... Thus many of this Court's decisions acknowledge that the means by which national power is exercised must take into account concerns for state autonomy. See, *e.g., NLRB v. Jones & Laughlin Steel Corp.* ("Undoubtedly, the scope of this [commerce] power must be considered in the light of our dual system of government and may not be extended so as to embrace effects upon interstate commerce so indirect and remote that to embrace them, in view of our complex society, would effectually obliterate the distinction between what is national and what is local and create a completely centralized government"). For example, Congress might rationally conclude that the location a State chooses for its capital may affect interstate commerce, but the Court has suggested that Congress would nevertheless be barred from dictating that location because such an exercise of a delegated power would undermine the state sovereignty inherent in the Tenth Amendment. *Coyle v. Oklahoma,* 221 U.S. 559 (1911).... The operative language of these cases varies, but the underlying principle is consistent: state autonomy is a relevant factor in assessing the means by which Congress exercises its powers.

This principle requires the Court to enforce affirmative limits on federal regulation of the States to complement the judicially crafted expansion of the interstate commerce power. *National League of Cities v. Usery* represented an attempt to define such limits. The Court today rejects *National League of Cities* and washes its hands of all efforts to protect the States. In the process, the Court opines that unwarranted federal encroachments on state authority are and will remain " 'horrible possibilities that never happen in the real world.' " There is ample reason to believe to the contrary.

The last two decades have seen an unprecedented growth of federal regulatory activity, as the majority itself acknowledges. In 1954, one could still speak of a "burden of persuasion on those favoring national intervention" in asserting that "National action has ... always been regarded as exceptional in our polity, an intrusion to be justified by some necessity, the special rather than the ordinary case." Wechsler, *The Political Safeguards of Federalism: The Role of the States in the Composition and Selection of the National Government,* 54 Colum. L. Rev. 543 (1954). Today, as federal legislation and coercive grant programs have expanded to embrace innumerable activities that were once viewed as local, the burden of persuasion has surely shifted, and the extraordinary has become ordinary. For example, recently the Federal Government has, with this Court's blessing, undertaken to tell the States the age at which they can retire their law enforcement officers, and the regulatory standards, procedures, and even the agenda which their utilities commissions must consider and follow. *See EEOC v. Wyoming*, 460 U.S. 226 (1983); *FERC v. Mississippi*, 456 U.S. 742 (1982). The political process has not protected against these encroachments on state activities, even though they directly impinge on a State's ability to make and enforce its laws. With the abandonment of *National League of Cities*, all that stands between the remaining essentials of state sovereignty and Congress is the latter's underdeveloped capacity for self-restraint.

The problems of federalism in an integrated national economy are capable of more responsible resolution than holding that the States as States retain no status apart from that which Congress chooses to let them retain. The proper resolution, I suggest, lies in weighing state autonomy as a factor in the balance when interpreting the means by which Congress can exercise its authority on the States as States. It is insufficient, in assessing the validity of congressional regulation of a State pursuant to the commerce power, to ask only whether the same regulation would be valid if enforced against a private party. That reasoning, embodied in the majority opinion, is inconsistent with the spirit of our Constitution. It remains relevant that a *State* is being regulated, as *National League of Cities* and every recent case have recognized. As far as the Constitution is concerned, a State should not be equated with any private litigant. Instead, the autonomy of a State is an essential component of federalism. If state autonomy is ignored in assessing the means by which Congress regulates matters affecting commerce, then federalism becomes irrelevant simply because the set of activities remaining beyond the reach of such a commerce power "may well be negligible."

It has been difficult for this Court to craft bright lines defining the scope of the state autonomy protected by *National League of Cities*. Such difficulty is to be expected whenever constitutional concerns as important as federalism and the effectiveness of the commerce power come into conflict. Regardless of the difficulty, it is and will remain the duty of this Court to reconcile these concerns in the final instance. That the Court shuns the task today by appealing to the "essence of federalism" can provide scant comfort to those who believe our federal system requires something more than a unitary, centralized government. I would not shirk the duty acknowledged by *National League of Cities* and its progeny, and I share JUSTICE REHNQUIST's belief that this Court will in time again assume its constitutional responsibility.

I respectfully dissent.

Federalist No. 45 (James Madison)

To the People of the State of New York:

Having shown that no one of the powers transferred to the federal government is unnecessary or improper, the next question to be considered is, whether the whole mass of them will be dangerous to the portion of authority left in the several States.

The adversaries to the plan of the convention, instead of considering in the first place what degree of power was absolutely necessary for the purposes of the federal government, have exhausted themselves in a secondary inquiry into the possible consequences of the proposed degree of power to the governments of the particular States. But if the Union, as has been shown, be essential to the security of the people of America against foreign danger; if it be essential to their security against contentions and wars among the different States; if it be essential to guard them against those violent and oppressive factions which embitter the blessings of liberty, and against those military establishments which must gradually poison its very fountain; if, in a word, the Union be essential to the happiness of the people of America, is it not preposterous, to urge as an objection to a government, without which the objects of the Union cannot be attained, that such a government may derogate from the importance of the governments of the individual States? Was, then, the American Revolution effected, was the American Confederacy formed, was the precious blood of thousands spilt, and the hard-earned substance of millions lavished, not that the people of America should enjoy peace, liberty, and safety, but that the government of the individual States, that particular municipal establishments, might enjoy a certain extent of power, and be arrayed with certain dignities and attributes of sovereignty? We have heard of the impious doctrine in the Old World, that the people were made for kings, not kings for the people. Is the same doctrine to be revived in the New, in another shape that the solid happiness of the people is to be sacrificed to the views of political institutions of a different form? It is too early for politicians to presume on our forgetting that the public good, the real welfare of the great body of the people, is the supreme object to be pursued; and that no form of government whatever has any other value than as it may be fitted for the attainment of this object. Were the plan of the convention adverse to the public happiness, my voice would be, Reject the plan. Were the Union itself inconsistent with the public happiness, it would be, Abolish the Union. In like manner, as far as the sovereignty of the States cannot be reconciled to the happiness of the people, the voice of every good citizen must be, Let the former be sacrificed to the latter. How far the sacrifice is necessary, has been shown. How far the unsacrificed residue will be endangered, is the question before us.

Several important considerations have been touched in the course of these papers, which discountenance the supposition that the operation of the federal government will by degrees prove fatal to the State governments. The more I revolve the subject, the more fully I am persuaded that the balance is much more likely to be disturbed by the preponderancy of the last than of the first scale.

We have seen, in all the examples of ancient and modern confederacies, the strongest tendency continually betraying itself in the members, to despoil the general government of its authorities, with a very ineffectual capacity in the latter to defend itself against the encroachments. Although, in most of these examples, the system has been so dissimilar from that under consideration as greatly to weaken any inference concerning the latter from the fate of the former, yet, as the States will retain, under the proposed Constitution, a very extensive portion of active sovereignty, the inference ought not to be wholly disregarded. In the Achaean league it is probable that the federal head had a degree and species of power, which gave it a considerable likeness to the government framed by the convention. The Lycian Confederacy, as far as its principles and form are transmitted, must have borne a still greater analogy to it. Yet history does not inform us that either of them ever degenerated, or tended to degenerate, into one consolidated government. On the contrary, we know that the ruin of one of them proceeded from the incapacity of the federal authority to prevent the dissensions, and finally the disunion, of the subordinate authorities. These cases are the more worthy of our attention, as the external causes by which the component parts were pressed together were much more numerous and powerful than in our case; and consequently less powerful ligaments within would be sufficient to bind the members to the head, and to each other.

In the feudal system, we have seen a similar propensity exemplified. Notwithstanding the want of proper sympathy in every instance between the local sovereigns and the people, and the sympathy in some instances between the general sovereign and the latter, it usually happened that the local sovereigns prevailed in the rivalship for encroachments. Had no external dangers enforced internal harmony and subordination, and particularly, had the local sovereigns possessed the affections of the people, the great kingdoms in Europe would at this time consist of as many independent princes as there were formerly feudatory barons.

The State government will have the advantage of the Federal government, whether we compare them in respect to the immediate dependence of the one on the other; to the weight of personal influence which each side will possess; to the powers respectively vested in them; to the predilection and probable support of the people; to the disposition and faculty of resisting and frustrating the measures of each other.

The State governments may be regarded as constituent and essential parts of the federal government; whilst the latter is nowise essential to the operation or organization of the former. Without the intervention of the State legislatures, the President of the United States cannot be elected at all. They must in all cases have a great share in his appointment, and will, perhaps, in most cases, of themselves determine it. The Senate will be elected absolutely and exclusively by the State legislatures. Even the House of Representatives, though drawn immediately from the people, will be chosen very much under the influence of that class of men, whose influence over the people obtains for themselves an election into the State legislatures. Thus, each of the principal branches of the federal government will owe its existence more or less to the favor of the State governments, and must consequently feel a dependence, which is much more likely to beget a disposition too obsequious than too overbearing towards them. On the other side, the component parts of the State governments will in no instance be indebted for their appointment to the direct agency of the federal government, and very little, if at all, to the local influence of its members.

The number of individuals employed under the Constitution of the United States will be much smaller than the number employed under the particular States. There will consequently be less of personal influence on the side of the former than of the latter. The members of the legislative, executive, and judiciary departments of thirteen and more States, the justices of peace, officers of militia, ministerial officers of justice, with all the county, corporation, and town officers, for three millions and more of people, intermixed, and having particular acquaintance with every class and circle of people, must exceed, beyond all proportion, both in number and influence, those of every description who will be employed in the administration of the federal system. Compare the members of the three great departments of the thirteen States, excluding from the judiciary department the justices of peace, with the members of the corresponding departments of the single government of the Union; compare the militia officers of three millions of people with the military and marine officers of any establishment which is within the compass of probability, or, I may add, of possibility, and in this view alone, we may pronounce the advantage of the States to be decisive. If the federal government is to have collectors of revenue, the State governments will have theirs also. And as those of the former will be principally on the seacoast, and not very numerous, whilst those of the latter will be spread over the face of the country, and will be very numerous, the advantage in this view also lies on the same side. It is true, that the Confederacy is to possess, and may exercise, the power of collecting internal as well as external taxes throughout the States; but it is probable that this power will not be resorted to, except for supplemental purposes of revenue; that an option will then be given to the States to supply their quotas by previous collections of their own; and that the eventual collection, under the immediate authority of the Union, will generally be made by the officers, and according to the rules, appointed by the several States. Indeed it is extremely probable, that in other instances, particularly in the organization of the judicial power, the officers of the States will be clothed with the correspondent authority of the Union. Should it happen, however, that separate collectors of internal revenue should be appointed under the federal government, the influence of the whole number would not bear a comparison with that of the multitude of State officers in the opposite scale. Within every district to which a federal collector would be allotted, there would not be less than thirty or forty, or even more, officers of different descriptions, and many of them persons of character and weight, whose influence would lie on the side of the State.

The powers delegated by the proposed Constitution to the federal government are few and defined. Those which are to remain in the State governments are numerous and indefinite. The former will be exercised principally on external objects, as war, peace, negotiation, and foreign commerce; with which last the power of taxation will, for the most part, be connected. The powers reserved to the several States will extend to all the objects which, in the ordinary course of affairs, concern the lives, liberties, and properties of the people, and the internal order, improvement, and prosperity of the State.

The operations of the federal government will be most extensive and important in times of war and danger; those of the State governments, in times of peace and security. As the former periods will probably bear a small proportion to the latter, the State governments will here enjoy another advantage over the federal government. The more adequate, indeed, the federal powers may be rendered to the national defense, the less frequent will be those scenes of danger which might favor their ascendancy over the governments of the particular States.

If the new Constitution be examined with accuracy and candor, it will be found that the change which it proposes consists much less in the addition of NEW POWERS to the Union, than in the invigoration of its ORIGINAL POWERS. The regulation of commerce, it is true, is a new power; but that seems to be an addition which few oppose, and from which no apprehensions are entertained. The powers relating to war and peace, armies and fleets, treaties and finance, with the other more considerable powers, are all vested in the existing Congress by the articles of Confederation. The proposed change does not enlarge these powers; it only substitutes a more effectual mode of administering them. The change relating to taxation may be regarded as the most important; and yet the present Congress have as complete authority to REQUIRE of the States indefinite supplies of money for the common defense and general welfare, as the future Congress will have to require them of individual citizens; and the latter will be no more bound than the States themselves have been, to pay the quotas respectively taxed on them. Had the States complied punctually with the articles of Confederation, or could their compliance have been enforced by as peaceable means as may be used with success towards single persons, our past experience is very far from countenancing an opinion, that the State governments would have lost their constitutional powers, and have gradually undergone an entire consolidation. To maintain that such an event would have ensued, would be to say at once, that the existence of the State governments is incompatible with any system whatever that accomplishes the essential purposes of the Union.

PUBLIUS.

Federalist No. 46 (James Madison)

To the People of the State of New York:

Resuming the subject of the last paper, I proceed to inquire whether the federal government or the State governments will have the advantage with regard to the predilection and support of the people. Notwithstanding the different modes in which they are appointed, we must consider both of them as substantially dependent on the great body of the citizens of the United States. I assume this position here as it respects the first, reserving the proofs for another place. The federal and State governments are in fact but different agents and trustees of the people, constituted with different powers, and designed for different purposes. The adversaries of the Constitution seem to have lost sight of the people altogether in their reasonings on this subject; and to have viewed these different establishments, not only as mutual rivals and enemies, but as uncontrolled by any common superior in their efforts to usurp the authorities of each other. These gentlemen must here be reminded of their error. They must be told that the ultimate authority, wherever the derivative may be found, resides in the people alone, and that it will not depend merely on the comparative ambition or address of the different governments, whether either, or which of them, will be able to enlarge its sphere of jurisdiction at the expense of the other. Truth, no less than decency, requires that the event in every case should be supposed to depend on the sentiments and sanction of their common constituents.

Many considerations, besides those suggested on a former occasion, seem to place it beyond doubt that the first and most natural attachment of the people will be to the governments of their respective States. Into the administration of these a greater number of individuals will expect to rise. From the gift of these a greater number of offices and emoluments will flow. By the superintending care of these, all the more domestic and personal interests of the people will be regulated and provided for. With the affairs of these, the people will be more familiarly and minutely conversant. And with the members of these, will a greater proportion of the people have the ties of personal acquaintance and friendship, and of family and party attachments; on the side of these, therefore, the popular bias may well be expected most strongly to incline.

Experience speaks the same language in this case. The federal administration, though hitherto very defective in comparison with what may be hoped under a better system, had, during the war, and particularly whilst the independent fund of paper emissions was in credit, an activity and importance as great as it can well have in any future circumstances whatever. It was engaged, too, in a course of measures which had for their object the protection of everything that was dear, and the acquisition of everything that could be desirable to the people at large. It was, nevertheless, invariably found, after the transient enthusiasm for the early Congresses was over, that the attention and attachment of the people were turned anew to their own particular governments; that the federal council was at no time the idol of popular favor; and that opposition to proposed enlargements of its powers and importance was the side usually taken by the men who wished to build their political consequence on the prepossessions of their fellow-citizens.

If, therefore, as has been elsewhere remarked, the people should in future become more partial to the federal than to the State governments, the change can only result from such manifest and irresistible proofs of a better administration, as will overcome all their antecedent propensities. And in that case, the people ought not surely to be precluded from giving most of their confidence where they may discover it to be most due; but even in that case the State governments could have little to apprehend, because it is only within a certain sphere that the federal power can, in the nature of things, be advantageously administered.

The remaining points on which I propose to compare the federal and State governments, are the disposition and the faculty they may respectively possess, to resist and frustrate the measures of each other.

It has been already proved that the members of the federal will be more dependent on the members of the State governments, than the latter will be on the former. It has appeared also, that the prepossessions of the people, on whom both will depend, will be more on the side of the State governments, than of the federal government. So far as the disposition of each towards the other may be influenced by these causes, the State governments must clearly have the advantage. But in a distinct and very important point of view, the advantage will lie on the same side. The prepossessions, which the members themselves will carry into the federal government, will generally be favorable to the States; whilst it will rarely happen, that the members of the State governments will carry into the public councils a bias in favor of the general government. A local spirit will infallibly prevail much more in the members of Congress, than a national spirit will prevail in the legislatures of the particular States. Every one knows that a great proportion of the errors committed by the State legislatures proceeds from the disposition of the members to sacrifice the comprehensive and permanent interest of the State, to the particular and separate views of the counties or districts in which they reside. And if they do not sufficiently enlarge their policy to embrace the collective welfare of their particular State, how can it be imagined that they will make the aggregate prosperity of the Union, and the dignity and respectability of its government, the objects of their affections and consultations? For the same reason that the members of the State legislatures will be unlikely to attach themselves sufficiently to national objects, the members of the federal legislature will be likely to attach themselves too much to local objects. The States will be to the latter what counties and towns are to the former. Measures will too often be decided according to their probable effect, not on the national prosperity and happiness, but on the prejudices, interests, and pursuits of the governments and people of the individual States.

What is the spirit that has in general characterized the proceedings of Congress? A perusal of their journals, as well as the candid acknowledgments of such as have had a seat in that assembly, will inform us, that the members have but too frequently displayed the character, rather of partisans of their respective States, than of impartial guardians of a common interest; that where on one occasion improper sacrifices have been made of local considerations, to the aggrandizement of the federal government, the great interests of the nation have suffered on a hundred, from an undue attention to the local prejudices, interests, and views of the particular States. I mean not by these reflections to insinuate, that the new federal government will not embrace a more enlarged plan of policy than the existing government may have pursued; much less, that its views will be as confined as those of the State legislatures; but only that it will partake sufficiently of the spirit of both, to be disinclined to invade the rights of the individual States, or the prerogatives of their governments. The motives on the part of the State governments, to augment their prerogatives by defalcations from the federal government, will be overruled by no reciprocal predispositions in the members.

Were it admitted, however, that the Federal government may feel an equal disposition with the State governments to extend its power beyond the due limits, the latter would still have the advantage in the means of defeating such encroachments. If an act of a particular State, though unfriendly to the national government, be generally popular in that State and should not too grossly violate the oaths of the State officers, it is executed immediately and, of course, by means on the spot and depending on the State alone. The opposition of the federal government, or the interposition of federal officers, would but inflame the zeal of all parties on the side of the State, and the evil could not be prevented or repaired, if at all, without the employment of means which must always be resorted to with reluctance and difficulty. On the other hand, should an unwarrantable measure of the federal government be unpopular in particular States, which would seldom fail to be the case, or even a warrantable measure be so, which may sometimes be the case, the means of opposition to it are powerful and at hand. The disquietude of the people; their repugnance and, perhaps, refusal to co-operate with the officers of the Union; the frowns of the executive magistracy of the State; the embarrassments created by legislative devices, which would often be added on such occasions, would oppose, in any State, difficulties not to be despised; would form, in a large State, very serious impediments; and where the sentiments of several adjoining States happened to be in unison, would present obstructions which the federal government would hardly be willing to encounter.

But ambitious encroachments of the federal government, on the authority of the State governments, would not excite the opposition of a single State, or of a few States only. They would be signals of general alarm. Every government would espouse the common cause. A correspondence would be opened. Plans of resistance would be concerted. One spirit would animate and conduct the whole. The same combinations, in short, would result from an apprehension of the federal, as was produced by the dread of a foreign, yoke; and unless the projected innovations should be voluntarily renounced, the same appeal to a trial of force would be made in the one case as was made in the other. But what degree of madness could ever drive the federal government to such an extremity. In the contest with Great Britain, one part of the empire was employed against the other. The more numerous part invaded the rights of the less numerous part. The attempt was unjust and unwise; but it was not in speculation absolutely chimerical. But what would be the contest in the case we are supposing? Who would be the parties? A few representatives of the people would be opposed to the people themselves; or rather one set of representatives would be contending against thirteen sets of representatives, with the whole body of their common constituents on the side of the latter.

The only refuge left for those who prophesy the downfall of the State governments is the visionary supposition that the federal government may previously accumulate a military force for the projects of ambition. The reasonings contained in these papers must have been employed to little purpose indeed, if it could be necessary now to disprove the reality of this danger. That the people and the States should, for a sufficient period of time, elect an uninterrupted succession of men ready to betray both; that the traitors should, throughout this period, uniformly and systematically pursue some fixed plan for the extension of the military establishment; that the governments and the people of the States should silently and patiently behold the gathering storm, and continue to supply the materials, until it should be prepared to burst on their own heads, must appear to every one more like the incoherent dreams of a delirious jealousy, or the misjudged exaggerations of a counterfeit zeal, than like the sober apprehensions of genuine patriotism. Extravagant as the supposition is, let it however be made. Let a regular army, fully equal to the resources of the country, be formed; and let it be entirely at the devotion of the federal government; still it would not be going too far to say, that the State governments, with the people on their side, would be able to repel the danger. The highest number to which, according to the best computation, a standing army can be carried in any country, does not exceed one hundredth part of the whole number of souls; or one twenty-fifth part of the number able to bear arms. This proportion would not yield, in the United States, an army of more than twenty-five or thirty thousand men. To these would be opposed a militia amounting to near half a million of citizens with arms in their hands, officered by men chosen from among themselves, fighting for their common liberties, and united and conducted by governments possessing their affections and confidence. It may well be doubted, whether a militia thus circumstanced could ever be conquered by such a proportion of regular troops. Those who are best acquainted with the last successful resistance of this country against the British arms, will be most inclined to deny the possibility of it.

Besides the advantage of being armed, which the Americans possess over the people of almost every other nation, the existence of subordinate governments, to which the people are attached, and by which the militia officers are appointed, forms a barrier against the enterprises of ambition, more insurmountable than any which a simple government of any form can admit of. Notwithstanding the military establishments in the several kingdoms of Europe, which are carried as far as the public resources will bear, the governments are afraid to trust the people with arms. And it is not certain, that with this aid alone they would not be able to shake off their yokes. But were the people to possess the additional advantages of local governments chosen by themselves, who could collect the national will and direct the national force, and of officers appointed out of the militia, by these governments, and attached both to them and to the militia, it may be affirmed with the greatest assurance, that the throne of every tyranny in Europe would be speedily overturned in spite of the legions which surround it. Let us not insult the free and gallant citizens of America with the suspicion, that they would be less able to defend the rights of which they would be in actual possession, than the debased subjects of arbitrary power would be to rescue theirs from the hands of their oppressors. Let us rather no longer insult them with the supposition that they can ever reduce themselves to the necessity of making the experiment, by a blind and tame submission to the long train of insidious measures which must precede and produce it.

The argument under the present head may be put into a very concise form, which appears altogether conclusive. Either the mode in which the federal government is to be constructed will render it sufficiently dependent on the people, or it will not. On the first supposition, it will be restrained by that dependence from forming schemes obnoxious to their constituents. On the other supposition, it will not possess the confidence of the people, and its schemes of usurpation will be easily defeated by the State governments, who will be supported by the people.

On summing up the considerations stated in this and the last paper, they seem to amount to the most convincing evidence, that the powers proposed to be lodged in the federal government are as little formidable to those reserved to the individual States, as they are indispensably necessary to accomplish the purposes of the Union; and that all those alarms which have been sounded, of a meditated and consequential annihilation of the State governments, must, on the most favorable interpretation, be ascribed to the chimerical fears of the authors of them.

PUBLIUS.

NOTE ON THE POLITICAL, JUDICIAL, AND PROCEDURAL SAFEGUARDS OF FEDERALISM

1.   One way to view Justice Blackmun's argument in *Garcia* is as a manifestation of the "double standard" of judicial review after 1937. *Garcia*, after all, overruled the most significant exception to the Court's failure to enforce any meaningful limits on Congress's power vis-à-vis the States after *Jones & Laughlin* and *Wickard*. Does the Footnote 4 framework discussed in Chapter Five offer any guidance about the appropriate level of judicial review in federalism cases?

As we have already seen, the New Deal Court retreated from its restrictive jurisprudence under the Due Process and Commerce Clauses in part because of its felt inability to draw principled lines between permissible and impermissible government action. The *Garcia* Court made clear that it was overruling *National League of Cities* for much the same reason: the doctrinal formula developed to define "traditional state governmental functions" that were immune from federal regulation were simply unworkable. (Note that the joint opinion in *Planned Parenthood v. Casey* cited *Garcia* and *National League of Cities* as an example of when it is appropriate to overrule an unworkable prior decision.) Do you see an affinity between Justice O'Connor's rejection of this conclusion in *Garcia* and her willingness to muddle through with a somewhat ambiguous "undue burden" standard in abortion cases? What do you think about the Justices (Blackmun, Stevens) who were uncomfortable with judicial discretion to define and apply unenumerated constitutional principles in *Garcia* but embraced it in *Casey*? What about Justice Rehnquist's converse acceptance of an ill-defined standard in *Garcia* and his complaints about judicial discretion in *Casey*? Are the two areas of federalism and privacy distinguishable as an *institutional* matter—that is, in terms of whether the relevant lines should be drawn by legislatures or courts?

2.   As noted in the introduction to this section, *Garcia* largely adopted an academic theory propounded by Professor Herbert Wechsler in 1954. (*Garcia* was thus a brief, shining instance in which the Court actually paid attention to legal scholarship.) Was *Garcia*'s adoption of Professor Wechsler's theory consistent with *Term Limits*? What is the concept of representation that undergirds Justice Blackmun's (and Professor Wechsler's) "political safeguards" argument? Doesn't that argument see federal representatives as representing their *states*, not simply the people of those states? *Term Limits*, on the other hand, firmly rejected that notion. It forbade states to set qualifications for Congress precisely because Congress represents the People, *not* the States. Justice Stevens was in the majority in both *Garcia* and *Term Limits*, and in other cases he frequently reaffirmed his belief in the "political safeguards of federalism." Was he consistent?

3.   Do federal representatives represent state institutions or interests within states? Do you see why the answer matters? Consider the following not-so-hypothetical: Large numbers of politically-mobilized voters and donors of campaign funds are concerned about the state of public education, which has traditionally been viewed as a concern of state and local government. You are a U.S. senator, seeking both the political support of your constituents and the financial support of your donors. You need an issue to mobilize that support (and channel it to *you*). Are you content to allow state and local officials to deal with the problem of education, or would you prefer to propose a federal solution that you can get enacted at the national level? If state and local politicians have their own proposals in this area, do you view those politicians as allies, whose institutional prerogatives you should defend against federal incursions, or as competitors for the support of the same donors and constituents? If the latter, are you inclined to play the role of guardian of state institutional interests that Justice Blackmun and Professor Wechsler envisioned by opposing federal intervention in public education?

4.   Many contemporary scholars have criticized the *Garcia*/Wechsler version of the political safeguards argument, often along the lines suggested in the preceding note and in Justice Powell's dissent in *Garcia*.[34] Professor Kramer, however, has sought to rehabilitate Wechsler's argument by suggesting two alternative political mechanisms that protect state prerogatives. The most important is political parties, which "protect[ ] the states by making national officials politically dependent upon state and local party organizations."[35] Similarly, Kramer also emphasizes the interlocking structure of administrative bureaucracies at the federal and state level, which must cooperate in the enforcement of many federal programs. "[T]he federal government depends . . . heavily on state officials to help administer its programs. . . . and this mutual dependency guarantees state officials a voice in the process."[36] Other scholars have questioned these arguments.[37] What happens when party loyalty encourages members of a political party to sacrifice their concerns about state prerogatives in order to achieve a particular party policy goal?[38] Or when state bureaucratic officials become so invested in enforcing federal law that they find themselves at odds with state elected officials? More recently, some scholars have argued that there are other effective political safeguards of state interests, including the

---

[34]   *See, e.g.*, Larry D. Kramer, *Putting the Politics Back into the Political Safeguards of Federalism*, 100 COLUM. L. REV. 215 (2000); Saikrishna B. Prakash & John C. Yoo, *The Puzzling Persistence of Process-Based Federalism Theories*, 79 TEXAS L. REV. 1459 (2001).

[35]   Kramer, *supra* note 34, at 278.

[36]   Larry Kramer, *Understanding Federalism*, 47 VAND. L. REV. 1485, 1544 (1994). *See also* Jessica Bulman-Pozen & Heather K. Gerken, *Uncooperative Federalism*, 118 YALE L.J. 1256, 1286 (2009).

[37]   *See* Prakash & Yoo, *supra* note 24, at 1480–89; Lynn A. Baker, *Putting the Safeguards Back into the Political Safeguards of Federalism*, 46 VILL. L. REV. 951 (2001).

[38]   *See, e.g.*, Note, *No Child Left Behind and the Political Safeguards of Federalism*, 119 HARV. L. REV. 885 (2006) (concluding that Republicans in Congress who would ordinarily resist federal inroads into education policy voted for a vast expansion of federal authority in order to support their President as the leader of the party).

uniform-laws process, intergovernmental lobbying, and states' strategic use of administrative discretion when implementing federal policy.[39]

Are you persuaded that adequate safeguards exist for states in the national political process? Does it matter that none of the "modern" political safeguards are constitutionally entrenched, and their salience and structure have changed significantly over time?

5.   In thinking about the political dynamics of federalism, it may help to distinguish between "vertical" and "horizontal" aggrandizement. In the familiar vertical scenario, the national government itself seeks to increase its power at the expense of the States. This was the situation in *National League of Cities* and *Garcia*. Horizontal aggrandizement, on the other hand, involves the propensity of a powerful group of states to use the national government as an instrument to impose their policy preferences on another group of states. The federal fugitive slave law in *Prigg*, which the Southern states demanded over the objection of Northern states opposed to slavery, illustrates this phenomenon. Do the "political safeguards" of federalism guard against horizontal aggrandizement? Isn't the representation of the States in Congress the very *mechanism* by which horizontal aggrandizement occurs? If we are, in fact, concerned about both vertical and horizontal incursions on state autonomy, what should that concern imply for judicial review in federalism cases?

6.   Does Justice Blackmun's view preclude judicial review entirely? The Court cited *Coyle v. Oklahoma*, 221 U.S. 559 (1911), which held that Congress could not require a State to choose a particular location for its capitol. Does this suggest that there are certain sovereign decisions that are committed to the States and immune from federal interference? How are those decisions to be identified? Do you think the category is confined to scenarios, like *Coyle*, that seem unlikely to arise under current conditions?

Justice Blackmun also suggested "that the fundamental limitation that the constitutional scheme imposes on the Commerce Clause to protect the 'States as States' is one of process rather than one of result. Any substantive restraint on the exercise of Commerce Clause powers must find its justification in the procedural nature of this basic limitation, and it must be tailored to compensate for possible failings in the national political process rather than to dictate a 'sacred province of state autonomy.'" Can you imagine "process" limits on national power that judges adhering to *Garcia* might be inclined to enforce? Do you see an affinity between this "process federalism" version of "states' rights" and John Hart Ely's argument that the Court should intervene to protect *individual* rights when it discerns a malfunction in the political process?

7.   Why doesn't the political safeguards argument apply—in spades—to judicial review of *state* regulation under the Dormant Commerce Clause? Surely Congress is more than capable of looking out for itself; after all, it can preempt any offending state regulation of interstate commerce simply by enacting a federal statute. And yet, the federal courts continue to rigorously

---

[39] *See* JOHN D. NUGENT, SAFEGUARDING FEDERALISM: HOW STATES PROTECT THEIR INTERESTS IN NATIONAL POLICYMAKING (2009).

review state laws challenged on the ground that they intrude on Congress's commerce authority. Can this aspect of the "double standard" possibly be justified? We will return to the Dormant Commerce Clause in Chapter Eleven.

8.   Is it relevant that constitutional courts in other federal systems around the world enforce limits on central authority? For example, the European Court of Justice has long played a leading role in defining the balance between the European Union and its Member States. Although for much of its history, the ECJ worked primarily to consolidate the Community's authority, it recently held that a Community directive exceeded the competence granted to the Community under its constitutive treaties.[40] The constitutional courts of Germany, Canada, and Australia enjoy similar powers. Some international commentators have even suggested that judicial enforcement is central to the very *definition* of federalism.[41] Given that the U.S. Supreme Court's propensity to look to foreign law in other contexts, why shouldn't it pay attention to foreign practice recognizing the importance of judicial review in federalism cases?

9.   In addition to the "political safeguards" discussed in *Garcia*, the States also benefit from *procedural* safeguards of federalism derived from the difficulty of making federal law. Even where Congress enjoys constitutional authority to act, it must still navigate the exceptionally difficult lawmaking process set forth in Article I. Not many legislative proposals successfully run this gauntlet, and to that extent the States remain free to act on their own free from federal preemption or interference.[42] On this view, the primary threats to state autonomy are those mechanisms of federal lawmaking, such as delegation of authority to federal administrative agencies, that make it considerably *easier* to make federal law.[43]

From this perspective, the most important federalism decisions of the Twentieth Century was *Erie Railroad v. Tompkins*, 304 U.S. 64 (1938)—a case ordinarily taught in Civil Procedure rather than Constitutional Law.[44] *Erie* held that, unless Congress has supplied a federal rule of decision by enacting a statute, federal courts must apply state law. Federal courts, in other words, have no authority to add to the body of supreme federal law by exercising general common lawmaking powers. Although there are limited exceptions to this principle, it stands as a critical limit on the scope and quantity of federal law. If federal courts could make law on their own outside the legislative process—as state courts generally have the power to do—then

---

[40] *See* Case C–376/98, Germany v. Parliament and Council (Tobacco Advertising), 2000 E.C.R. I–8419, [2000] C.M.L.R. 1175 (2000).

[41] *See, e.g.*, Koen Lenaerts, *Constitutionalism and the Many Faces of Federalism*, 38 AM. J. COMP. L. 205, 263 (1990) ("Federalism is present whenever a divided sovereign is guaranteed by a national or supranational constitution and umpired by the supreme court of the common legal order.").

[42] *See generally* Bradford R. Clark, *Separation of Powers as a Safeguard of Federalism*, 79 TEXAS L. REV. 1321 (2001).

[43] *See also* Scott A. Keller, *How Courts Can Protect State Autonomy from Federal Administrative Encroachment*, 82 S. CAL. L. REV. 45 (2008) (arguing that current doctrines in administrative law inadequately safeguards state autonomy).

[44] If your Civil Procedure professor didn't cover *Erie* (some don't), ask for your money back.

rigorous congressional lawmaking procedures and the states' political representation in Congress would not be nearly as effective limits on federal authority.[45]

Unfortunately, *Erie* did not address the other, more pervasive non-legislative form of federal lawmaking—the vast lawmaking authority of federal administrative agencies. As Justice Powell pointed out in his *Garcia* dissent, federal agencies make most federal law nowadays—and they do it outside the process of state representation in Congress upon which the "political safeguards of federalism" argument so critically relies.

10. Finally, consider the affinities between the *Garcia*/Wechsler argument and James Madison's own account of the "political safeguards of federalism" in Federalist Nos. 45 and 46. Madison viewed federalism as a dynamic competition between the two constitutional levels of government for the loyalties of the People. He thought the States would enjoy a number of important natural advantages in this competition, the most important being that they would tend to provide the relevant regulation and services on matters most dear to the hearts of people in their everyday lives—e.g., schools, sewers, property rights, etc. Does this suggest that courts should be particularly concerned about federal legislation that undermines this advantage by intruding into these critical areas? Should courts try to undermine what Wechsler identified as a national "mood" in the hopes of reviving a "federal culture" where citizens identify with both state and federal government?[46]

In Madison's version of the argument, to what extent do the "political safeguards" of federalism substitute for judicial review? Madison stressed that the powers of the national government were "few and defined"; does this mean that courts should stand ready to enforce the limits of those powers? At the same time, it bears noting that Madison stresses other means of keeping the national government within bounds, including military resistance.

Madison made a number of assumptions about the relative salience of federal and state responsibilities. He argued in No. 45, for example, that "[t]he operations of the federal government will be most extensive and important in times of war and danger; those of the State governments, in times of peace and security," and that "the former periods will probably bear a small proportion to the latter." Has the history of the Twentieth and the Twenty-first centuries born out that prediction? To what extent does the advent of apparently permanent threats of nuclear attack and terrorism affect the appropriate balance between national and state authority, as well as the political dynamics that may maintain or undermine that balance?

Madison also likely assumed that people would continue to identify primarily with their states, rather than with the nation. To what extent do the political safeguards of federalism depend on the people involved—

---

[45] *See generally* Ernest A. Young, *A General Defense of Erie Railroad Co. v. Tompkins*, 10 J. L., ECON. & POL'Y 17, 112–21 (2013).

[46] *See* JENNA BEDNAR, THE ROBUST FEDERATION: PRINCIPLES OF DESIGN 186–91 (2009) (discussing cultural aspects of federalism).

Members of Congress, state officials, ordinary citizens—feeling some meaningful attachment to their states? If those attachments are declining, are the political safeguards in trouble?

CHAPTER NINE

THE POWERS OF CONGRESS

In *McCulloch v. Maryland*, Chief Justice Marshall wrote that "[t]his government is acknowledged by all to be one of enumerated powers." By this he meant that the federal government may exercise only those powers affirmatively conferred upon it by the Constitution; all other powers, as the Tenth Amendment makes clear, are reserved to the States. Other federal systems have sometimes employed different principles of allocation. In Canada, for example, the national government enjoys a general power to preserve "peace, order, and good government," while specific enumerated powers are reserved to the provinces.[1] In America, however, the residual powers belong to the states, and every national action must be tied to some power enumerated in the Constitution. Hence, as Marshall predicted, "the question respecting the extent of the powers actually granted, is perpetually arising, and will probably continue to arise, as long as our system shall exist."

Structurally speaking, limits on national power vis-à-vis the states take both "internal" and "external" forms. *National League of Cities*, for example, recognized a freestanding principle of state sovereignty that prevented federal regulation of the activities of state governments, even when such regulation—wage and hour regulation, in the case of the Fair Labor Standards Act—would otherwise be within the scope of the Commerce Clause. A limit like that functions much like the individual rights guarantees of the Bill of Rights: Even though Congress would have the power under the Commerce Clause to ban the interstate shipment of newspapers, that power would be "trumped" by the freedom of the press enumerated in the First Amendment. We will return to other federalism-based external limits on national power, such as the "anti-commandeering" doctrine of *New York v. United States*, in Chapter Ten.

"Internal" limits, on the other hand, are inherent in the constitutional power grants to Congress themselves. The Commerce Power, for instance, is obviously limited by the definition of "Commerce . . . among the several states."[2] Congress's power "to lay and collect Taxes, Duties, Imposts and Excises" is qualified by the requirement that "all Duties, Imposts and Excises shall be uniform throughout the United States"[3]; its power to create additional federal courts is subject to the restriction that those courts be "inferior to the supreme Court."[4] This

---

[1]   *See* Constitution Act, 1867, §§ 91, 92; *see also* Allen Linden, *Flexible Federalism: The Canadian Way*, in PATTERNS OF REGIONALISM AND FEDERALISM: LESSONS FOR THE UK 17, 25 (Jorg Fedtke & Basil Markesinis eds., 2006).

[2]   Art. I, § 8, cl. 3.

[3]   Art. I, § 8, cl. 1.

[4]   Art. I, § 8, cl. 9.

Chapter explores the Court's construction of the extent and limits of the three most important enumerated powers granted to Congress: the Commerce Power, the power to enforce the Reconstruction Amendments, and the Spending Power. We consider another key congressional power—to declare war—in Chapter Fourteen.

SECTION 9.1 THE COMMERCE POWER

The scope of Congress's power to regulate commerce "among the several states" has been a fertile ground of controversy at least since *Gibbons v. Ogden*.[5] We have already traced the Court's use of that power to impose "dormant" limits on *state* regulation, as in *Willson v. Black Bird Creek Marsh Co.*, and to limit national regulation of the economy, as in *Hammer v. Dagenhart*. We have also seen the origins of the modern affirmative Commerce Clause doctrine in the "switch-in-time" cases— *NLRB v. Jones & Laughlin Steel Corp.* and *Wickard v. Filburn*—which announced an extremely expansive view of Congress's regulatory authority. After *Jones & Laughlin*, the Court did not strike down another federal statute on the ground that it exceeded the limits of the Commerce Power for 58 years. The conventional wisdom among most scholars and lawyers was that the Commerce Clause imposed *no* limits on congressional authority—or at least that the courts were completely unwilling to enforce any such limits.

That all changed in 1995, as a result of the Court's decision in *United States v. Lopez*. By seeming to signal that courts might once again enforce constitutional limits on national power, *Lopez* ignited an explosion of interest in federalism and aroused fears that a conservative court was about to embark on a reactionary campaign against the national administrative state. As you read the case, consider the extent to which it represents a departure from the jurisprudence of *Jones & Laughlin* and *Wickard* and, if so, how far the Court is likely to go.

United States v. Lopez
514 U.S. 549 (1995)

■ **CHIEF JUSTICE REHNQUIST delivered the opinion of the Court.**

In the Gun-Free School Zones Act of 1990, Congress made it a federal offense "for any individual knowingly to possess a firearm at a place that the individual knows, or has reasonable cause to believe, is a school zone." 18 U.S.C. § 922(q)(1)(A). The Act neither regulates a commercial activity nor contains a requirement that the possession be connected in any way to interstate commerce. We hold that the Act exceeds the

---

[5]   There are actually *three* commerce powers: In addition to commerce "among the several states," Congress also has power to regulate commerce "with foreign nations" and "with the Indian tribes." Art. I, § 8, cl. 3. This chapter focuses on the interstate commerce power, although we shall discuss the foreign commerce power briefly in Chapter Eleven.

authority of Congress "to regulate Commerce . . . among the several States. . . ." U.S. Const., Art. I, § 8, cl. 3.

On March 10, 1992, respondent, who was then a 12th-grade student, arrived at Edison High School in San Antonio, Texas, carrying a concealed .38 caliber handgun and five bullets. Acting upon an anonymous tip, school authorities confronted respondent, who admitted that he was carrying the weapon. He was arrested and charged under Texas law with firearm possession on school premises. The next day, the state charges were dismissed after federal agents charged respondent by complaint with violating the Gun-Free School Zones Act of 1990.[1] . . . Respondent moved to dismiss his federal indictment on the ground that § 922(q) "is unconstitutional as it is beyond the power of Congress to legislate control over our public schools." The District Court denied the motion . . . conducted a bench trial, found him guilty of violating § 922(q), and sentenced him to six months' imprisonment and two years' supervised release. . . . The Court of Appeals for the Fifth Circuit . . . reversed respondent's conviction. . . . [W]e now affirm.

We start with first principles. The Constitution creates a Federal Government of enumerated powers. See Art. I, § 8. As James Madison wrote, "the powers delegated by the proposed Constitution to the federal government are few and defined. Those which are to remain in the State governments are numerous and indefinite." This constitutionally mandated division of authority "was adopted by the Framers to ensure protection of our fundamental liberties." "Just as the separation and independence of the coordinate branches of the Federal Government serve to prevent the accumulation of excessive power in any one branch, a healthy balance of power between the States and the Federal Government will reduce the risk of tyranny and abuse from either front." . . .

The Court . . . first defined the nature of Congress' commerce power in *Gibbons v. Ogden*:

> Commerce . . . describes the commercial intercourse between nations, and parts of nations, in all its branches, and is regulated by prescribing rules for carrying on that intercourse.

> [However,] it is not intended to say that these words comprehend that commerce, which is completely internal, which is carried on between man and man in a State, or between different parts of the same State, and which does not extend to or affect other States. Such a power would be inconvenient, and is certainly unnecessary.

> Comprehensive as the word 'among' is, it may very properly be restricted to that commerce which concerns more States than

---

[1] The term "school zone" is defined as "in, or on the grounds of a public, parochial or private school" or "within a distance of 1,000 feet from the grounds of a public, parochial or private school."

one. . . . The enumeration presupposes something not enumerated; and that something . . . must be the exclusively internal commerce of a State.

For nearly a century thereafter, the Court's Commerce Clause decisions dealt but rarely with the extent of Congress' power, and almost entirely with the Commerce Clause as a limit on state legislation that discriminated against interstate commerce. . . . Under this line of precedent, the Court held that certain categories of activity such as "production," "manufacturing," and "mining" were within the province of state governments, and thus were beyond the power of Congress under the Commerce Clause.

In 1887, Congress enacted the Interstate Commerce Act, and in 1890, Congress enacted the Sherman Antitrust Act. These laws ushered in a new era of federal regulation under the commerce power. When cases involving these laws first reached this Court, we imported from our negative Commerce Clause cases the approach that Congress could not regulate activities such as "production," "manufacturing," and "mining." See, *e.g., United States v. E. C. Knight Co.* Simultaneously, however, the Court held that, where the interstate and intrastate aspects of commerce were so mingled together that full regulation of interstate commerce required incidental regulation of intrastate commerce, the Commerce Clause authorized such regulation. See, *e g., Shreveport Rate Cases.*

In *A.L.A. Schechter Poultry Corp. v. United States*, the Court struck down regulations that fixed the hours and wages of individuals employed by an intrastate business because the activity being regulated related to interstate commerce only indirectly. In doing so, the Court characterized the distinction between direct and indirect effects of intrastate transactions upon interstate commerce as "a fundamental one, essential to the maintenance of our constitutional system." . . . The justification for this formal distinction was rooted in the fear that otherwise "there would be virtually no limit to the federal power and for all practical purposes we should have a completely centralized government."

Two years later, in the watershed case of *NLRB v. Jones & Laughlin Steel Corp.*, the Court upheld the National Labor Relations Act against a Commerce Clause challenge, and in the process, departed from the distinction between "direct" and "indirect" effects on interstate commerce. The Court held that intrastate activities that "have such a close and substantial relation to interstate commerce that their control is essential or appropriate to protect that commerce from burdens and obstructions" are within Congress' power to regulate.

In *United States v. Darby*, 312 U.S. 100 (1941), the Court upheld the Fair Labor Standards Act, stating:

The power of Congress over interstate commerce is not confined to the regulation of commerce among the states. It extends to those activities intrastate which so affect interstate commerce or the exercise of the power of Congress over it as to make regulation of them appropriate means to the attainment of a legitimate end, the exercise of the granted power of Congress to regulate interstate commerce.

In *Wickard v. Filburn*, the Court upheld the application of amendments to the Agricultural Adjustment Act of 1938 to the production and consumption of homegrown wheat. The *Wickard* Court explicitly rejected earlier distinctions between direct and indirect effects on interstate commerce, stating:

> Even if appellee's activity be local and though it may not be regarded as commerce, it may still, whatever its nature, be reached by Congress if it exerts a substantial economic effect on interstate commerce, and this irrespective of whether such effect is what might at some earlier time have been defined as 'direct' or 'indirect.'

The *Wickard* Court emphasized that although Filburn's own contribution to the demand for wheat may have been trivial by itself, that was not "enough to remove him from the scope of federal regulation where, as here, his contribution, taken together with that of many others similarly situated, is far from trivial."

Jones & Laughlin Steel, Darby, and *Wickard* ushered in an era of Commerce Clause jurisprudence that greatly expanded the previously defined authority of Congress under that Clause. In part, this was a recognition of the great changes that had occurred in the way business was carried on in this country. Enterprises that had once been local or at most regional in nature had become national in scope. But the doctrinal change also reflected a view that earlier Commerce Clause cases artificially had constrained the authority of Congress to regulate interstate commerce.

But even these modern-era precedents which have expanded congressional power under the Commerce Clause confirm that this power is subject to outer limits. In *Jones & Laughlin Steel*, the Court warned that the scope of the interstate commerce power "must be considered in the light of our dual system of government and may not be extended so as to embrace effects upon interstate commerce so indirect and remote that to embrace them, in view of our complex society, would effectually obliterate the distinction between what is national and what is local and create a completely centralized government." Since that time, the Court has heeded that warning and undertaken to decide whether a rational basis existed for concluding that a regulated activity sufficiently affected interstate commerce.

Consistent with this structure, we have identified three broad categories of activity that Congress may regulate under its commerce power. First, Congress may regulate the use of the channels of interstate commerce. Second, Congress is empowered to regulate and protect the instrumentalities of interstate commerce, or persons or things in interstate commerce, even though the threat may come only from intrastate activities. Finally, Congress' commerce authority includes the power to regulate those activities . . . that substantially affect interstate commerce. . . .

We now turn to consider the power of Congress . . . to enact § 922(q). The first two categories of authority may be quickly disposed of: § 922(q) is not a regulation of the use of the channels of interstate commerce, nor is it an attempt to prohibit the interstate transportation of a commodity through the channels of commerce; nor can § 922(q) be justified as a regulation by which Congress has sought to protect an instrumentality of interstate commerce or a thing in interstate commerce. Thus, if § 922(q) is to be sustained, it must be under the third category as a regulation of an activity that substantially affects interstate commerce.

First, we have upheld a wide variety of congressional Acts regulating intrastate economic activity where we have concluded that the activity substantially affected interstate commerce. Examples include the regulation of intrastate coal mining, *Hodel v. Virginia Surface Mining & Reclamation Assn., Inc.*, 452 U.S. 264 (1981), intrastate extortionate credit transactions, *Perez v. United States*, 402 U.S. 146 (1971), restaurants utilizing substantial interstate supplies, *Katzenbach v. McClung*, 379 U.S. 294 (1964), inns and hotels catering to interstate guests, *Heart of Atlanta Motel, Inc. v. United States*, 379 U.S. 241 (1964), and production and consumption of homegrown wheat, *Wickard*. These examples are by no means exhaustive, but the pattern is clear. Where economic activity substantially affects interstate commerce, legislation regulating that activity will be sustained.

Even *Wickard*, which is perhaps the most far reaching example of Commerce Clause authority over intrastate activity, involved economic activity in a way that the possession of a gun in a school zone does not. . . . [T]he Agricultural Adjustment Act of 1938 . . . was designed to regulate the volume of wheat moving in interstate and foreign commerce in order to avoid surpluses and shortages, and concomitant fluctuation in wheat prices, which had previously obtained. . . .

Section 922(q) is a criminal statute that by its terms has nothing to do with "commerce" or any sort of economic enterprise, however broadly one might define those terms.[3] Section 922(q) is not an essential part of a larger regulation of economic activity, in which the regulatory scheme could be undercut unless the intrastate activity were regulated. It cannot, therefore, be sustained under our cases upholding regulations of activities that arise out of or are connected with a commercial transaction, which viewed in the aggregate, substantially affects interstate commerce.

---

[3] Under our federal system, the " 'States possess primary authority for defining and enforcing the criminal law.' " *Brecht v. Abrahamson*, 507 U.S. 619, 635 (1993).

Second, § 922(q) contains no jurisdictional element which would ensure, through case-by-case inquiry, that the firearm possession in question affects interstate commerce. For example, in *United States v. Bass*, 404 U.S. 336 (1971), the Court interpreted former 18 U.S.C. § 1202(a), which made it a crime for a felon to "receive, posses[s], or transport in commerce or affecting commerce . . . any firearm." . . . The *Bass* Court set aside the conviction because although the Government had demonstrated that Bass had possessed a firearm, it had failed "to show the requisite nexus with interstate commerce." . . . Unlike the statute in *Bass*, § 922(q) has no express jurisdictional element which might limit its reach to a discrete set of firearm possessions that additionally have an explicit connection with or effect on interstate commerce.

Although as part of our independent evaluation of constitutionality under the Commerce Clause we of course consider legislative findings, and indeed even congressional committee findings, regarding effect on interstate commerce, the Government concedes that "neither the statute nor its legislative history contain[s] express congressional findings regarding the effects upon interstate commerce of gun possession in a school zone." We agree with the Government that Congress normally is not required to make formal findings as to the substantial burdens that an activity has on interstate commerce. But to the extent that congressional findings would enable us to evaluate the legislative judgment that the activity in question substantially affected interstate commerce, even though no such substantial effect was visible to the naked eye, they are lacking here. . . .

The Government's essential contention, *in fine*, is that we may determine here that § 922(q) is valid because possession of a firearm in a local school zone does indeed substantially affect interstate commerce. The Government argues that possession of a firearm in a school zone may result in violent crime and that violent crime can be expected to affect the functioning of the national economy in two ways. First, the costs of violent crime are substantial, and, through the mechanism of insurance, those costs are spread throughout the population. Second, violent crime reduces the willingness of individuals to travel to areas within the country that are perceived to be unsafe. The Government also argues that the presence of guns in schools poses a substantial threat to the educational process by threatening the learning environment. A handicapped educational process, in turn, will result in a less productive citizenry. That, in turn, would have an adverse effect on the Nation's economic well-being. As a result, the Government argues that Congress could rationally have concluded that § 922(q) substantially affects interstate commerce.

We pause to consider the implications of the Government's arguments. The Government admits, under its "costs of crime" reasoning, that Congress could regulate not only all violent crime, but all activities that might lead to violent crime, regardless of how tenuously they relate to interstate commerce. Similarly, under the Government's "national productivity" reasoning, Congress could regulate any activity that it found was related to the economic productivity of individual citizens: family law (including marriage, divorce, and child custody), for example. Under the theories that the Government presents in support of § 922(q), it is difficult to perceive any limitation on federal power, even in areas such as criminal law enforcement or education where States historically have been sovereign. Thus, if we were to accept the Government's arguments, we are hard pressed to posit any activity by an individual that Congress is without power to regulate.

Although JUSTICE BREYER argues that acceptance of the Government's rationales would not authorize a general federal police power, he is unable to identify any activity that the States may regulate but Congress may not. JUSTICE BREYER posits that there might be some limitations on Congress' commerce power, such as family law or certain aspects of education. These suggested limitations, when viewed in light of the dissent's expansive analysis, are devoid of substance.

JUSTICE BREYER focuses, for the most part, on the threat that firearm possession in and near schools poses to the educational process and the potential economic consequences flowing from that threat. Specifically, the dissent reasons that (1) gun-related violence is a serious problem; (2) that problem, in turn, has an adverse effect on classroom learning; and (3) that adverse effect on classroom learning, in turn, represents a substantial threat to trade and commerce. This analysis would be equally applicable, if not more so, to subjects such as family law and direct regulation of education.

For instance, if Congress can, pursuant to its Commerce Clause power, regulate activities that adversely affect the learning environment, then, *a fortiori*, it also can regulate the educational process directly. Congress could determine that a school's curriculum has a "significant" effect on the extent of classroom learning. As a result, Congress could mandate a federal curriculum for local elementary and secondary schools because what is taught in local schools has a significant "effect on classroom learning," and that, in turn, has a substantial effect on interstate commerce. . . .

Admittedly, a determination whether an intrastate activity is commercial or noncommercial may in some cases result in legal uncertainty. But, so long as Congress' authority is limited to those powers enumerated in the Constitution, and so long as those enumerated powers are interpreted as having judicially enforceable outer limits, congressional legislation under the Commerce Clause always will engender "legal uncertainty." The Constitution mandates this uncertainty by withholding from Congress a plenary police power that would authorize enactment of every type of legislation. See Art. I, § 8. Congress has operated within this framework of legal uncertainty ever since this Court determined that it was the Judiciary's duty "to say what the law is." *Marbury v. Madison.* Any possible benefit from eliminating this "legal uncertainty" would be at the expense of the Constitution's system of enumerated powers.

In *Jones & Laughlin Steel,* we held that the question of congressional power under the Commerce Clause "is necessarily one of degree." . . . These are not precise formulations, and in the nature of things they cannot be. But we think they point the way to a correct decision of this case. The possession of a gun in a local school zone is in no sense an economic activity that might, through repetition elsewhere, substantially affect any sort of interstate commerce. Respondent was a local student at a local school; there is no indication that he had recently moved in interstate commerce, and there is no requirement that his possession of the firearm have any concrete tie to interstate commerce.

To uphold the Government's contentions here, we would have to pile inference upon inference in a manner that would bid fair to convert congressional authority under the Commerce Clause to a general police power of the sort retained by the States. Admittedly, some of our prior cases have taken long steps down that road, giving great deference to congressional action. The broad language in these opinions has suggested the possibility of additional expansion, but we decline here to proceed any further. To do so would require us to conclude that the Constitution's enumeration of powers does not presuppose something not enumerated, cf. *Gibbons v. Ogden,* and that there never will be a distinction between what is truly national and what is truly local, cf. *Jones & Laughlin Steel.* This we are unwilling to do.

For the foregoing reasons the judgment of the Court of Appeals is *Affirmed.*

■ **JUSTICE KENNEDY, with whom JUSTICE O'CONNOR joins, concurring.**

The history of the judicial struggle to interpret the Commerce Clause during the transition from the economic system the Founders knew to the single, national market still emergent in our own era counsels great restraint before the Court determines that the Clause is insufficient to support an exercise of the national power. That history gives me some pause about today's decision, but I join the Court's opinion with these observations on what I conceive to be its necessary though limited holding. . . .

The history of our Commerce Clause decisions contains at least two lessons of relevance to this case. The first, as stated at the outset, is the imprecision of content-based boundaries used without more to define the limits of the Commerce Clause. The second . . . is that the Court as an institution and the legal system as a whole have an immense stake in the stability of our Commerce Clause jurisprudence as it has evolved to this point. *Stare decisis* operates with great force in counseling us not to call in question the essential principles now in place respecting the congressional power to regulate transactions of a commercial nature. That fundamental restraint on our power forecloses us from reverting to an understanding of commerce that would serve only an 18th-century economy . . . ; it also mandates against returning to the time when congressional authority to regulate undoubted commercial activities was limited by a judicial determination that those matters had an insufficient connection to an interstate system. Congress can regulate in the commercial sphere on the assumption that we have a single market and a unified purpose to build a stable national economy. . . .

It does not follow, however, that in every instance the Court lacks the authority and responsibility to review congressional attempts to alter the federal balance. . . .

Of the various structural elements in the Constitution, separation of powers, checks and balances, judicial review, and federalism, only concerning the last does there seem to be much uncertainty respecting the existence, and the content, of standards that allow the Judiciary to play a significant role in maintaining the design contemplated by the Framers. Although the resolution of specific cases has proved difficult, we have derived from the Constitution workable standards to assist in preserving separation of powers and checks and balances. These standards are by now well accepted. Judicial review is also established beyond question, and though we may differ when applying its principles, its legitimacy is undoubted. Our role in preserving the federal balance seems more tenuous.

There is irony in this, because of the four structural elements in the Constitution just mentioned, federalism was the unique contribution of the Framers to political science and political theory. Though on the surface the idea may seem counter-intuitive, it was the insight of the Framers that freedom was enhanced by the creation of two governments, not one. . . .

The theory that two governments accord more liberty than one requires for its realization two distinct and discernable lines of political accountability: one between the citizens and the Federal Government; the second between the citizens and the States. If, as Madison expected, the Federal and State Governments are to control each other, see The Federalist No. 51, and hold each other in check by competing for the affections of the people, see The Federalist No. 46, those citizens must have some means of knowing which of the two governments to hold accountable for the failure to perform a given function. . . . Were the Federal Government to take over the regulation of entire areas of traditional state concern, areas having nothing to do with the regulation of commercial activities, the boundaries between the spheres of federal and state authority would blur and political responsibility would become illusory. The resultant inability to hold either branch of the government answerable to the citizens is more dangerous even than devolving too much authority to the remote central power.

To be sure, one conclusion that could be drawn from The Federalist Papers is that the balance between national and state power is entrusted in its entirety to the political process. Madison's observation that "the people ought not surely to be precluded from giving most of their confidence where they may discover it to be most due" can be interpreted to say that the essence of responsibility for a shift in power from the State to the Federal Government rests upon a political judgment, though he added assurance that "the State governments could have little to apprehend, because it is only within a certain sphere that the federal power can, in the nature of things, be advantageously administered." Whatever the judicial role, it is axiomatic that Congress does have substantial discretion and control over the federal balance.

For these reasons, it would be mistaken and mischievous for the political branches to forget that the sworn obligation to preserve and protect the Constitution in maintaining the federal balance is their own in the first and primary instance. . . .

At the same time, the absence of structural mechanisms to require those officials to undertake this principled task, and the momentary political convenience often attendant upon their failure to do so, argue against a complete renunciation of the judicial role. Although it is the obligation of all officers of the Government to respect the constitutional design, the federal balance is too essential a part of our constitutional structure and plays too vital a role in securing freedom for us to admit inability to intervene when one or the other level of Government has tipped the scales too far. . . .

Our ability to preserve this principle under the Commerce Clause has presented a much greater challenge. . . . But as the branch whose distinctive duty it is to declare "what the law is," we are often called upon to resolve questions of constitutional law not susceptible to the mechanical application of bright and clear lines. The substantial element of political judgment in Commerce Clause matters leaves our institutional capacity to intervene more in doubt than when we decide cases, for instance, under the Bill of Rights even though clear and bright lines are often absent in the latter class of disputes. But our cases do not teach that we have no role at all in determining the meaning of the Commerce Clause.

Our position in enforcing the dormant Commerce Clause is instructive. The Court's doctrinal approach in that area has likewise "taken some turns." Yet in contrast to the prevailing skepticism that surrounds our ability to give meaning to the explicit text of the Commerce Clause, there is widespread acceptance of our authority to enforce the dormant Commerce Clause, which we have but inferred from the constitutional structure as a limitation on the power of the States. . . .

The statute before us upsets the federal balance to a degree that renders it an unconstitutional assertion of the commerce power, and our intervention is required. As THE CHIEF JUSTICE explains, unlike the earlier cases to come before the Court here neither the actors nor their conduct have a commercial character, and neither the purposes nor the design of the statute have an evident commercial nexus. The statute makes the simple possession of a gun within 1,000 feet of the grounds of the school a criminal offense. In a sense any conduct in this interdependent world of ours has an ultimate commercial origin or consequence, but we have not yet said the commerce power may reach so far. If Congress attempts that extension, then at the least we must inquire whether the exercise of national power seeks to intrude upon an area of traditional state concern.

An interference of these dimensions occurs here, for it is well established that education is a traditional concern of the States. The proximity to schools, including of course schools owned and operated by the States or their subdivisions, is the very premise for making the conduct criminal. In these circumstances, we have a particular duty to ensure that the federal-state balance is not destroyed.

While it is doubtful that any State, or indeed any reasonable person, would argue that it is wise policy to allow students to carry guns on school premises, considerable disagreement exists about how best to accomplish that goal. In this circumstance, the theory and utility of our federalism are revealed, for the States may perform their role as laboratories for experimentation to devise various solutions where the best solution is far from clear.

If a State or municipality determines that harsh criminal sanctions are necessary and wise to deter students from carrying guns on school premises, the reserved powers of the States are sufficient to enact those measures. Indeed, over 40 States already have criminal laws outlawing the possession of firearms on or near school grounds.

Other, more practicable means to rid the schools of guns may be thought by the citizens of some States to be preferable for the safety and welfare of the schools those States are charged with maintaining. These might include inducements to inform on violators where the information leads to arrests or confiscation of the guns, programs to encourage the voluntary surrender of guns with some provision for amnesty, penalties imposed on parents or guardians for failure to supervise the child, laws providing for suspension or expulsion of gun-toting students, or programs for expulsion with assignment to special facilities.

The statute now before us forecloses the States from experimenting and exercising their own judgment in an area to which States lay claim by right of history and expertise, and it does so by regulating an activity beyond the realm of commerce in the ordinary and usual sense of that term. The tendency of this statute to displace state regulation in areas of traditional state concern is evident from its territorial operation. There are over 100,000 elementary and secondary schools in the United States. Each of these now has an invisible federal zone extending 1,000 feet beyond the (often irregular) boundaries of the school property. In some communities no doubt it would be difficult to navigate without infringing on those zones. Yet throughout these areas, school officials would find their own programs for the prohibition of guns in danger of displacement by the federal authority unless the State chooses to enact a parallel rule. . . . Absent a stronger connection or identification with commercial concerns that are central to the Commerce Clause, that interference contradicts the federal balance the Framers designed and that this Court is obliged to enforce.

For these reasons, I join in the opinion and judgment of the Court.

■ **JUSTICE THOMAS, concurring.**

The Court today properly concludes that the Commerce Clause does not grant Congress the authority to prohibit gun possession within 1,000 feet of a school, as it attempted to do in the Gun-Free School Zones Act of 1990. Although I join the majority, I write separately to observe that our case law has drifted far from the original understanding of the Commerce Clause. In a future case, we ought to temper our Commerce Clause jurisprudence in a manner that both makes sense of our more recent case law and is more faithful to the original understanding of that Clause.

We have said that Congress may regulate not only "Commerce . . . among the several States," U.S. Const., Art. I, § 8, cl. 3, but also anything that has a "substantial effect" on such commerce. This test, if taken to its logical extreme, would give Congress a "police power" over all aspects of American life. Unfortunately, we have never come to grips with this implication of our substantial effects formula. Although we have supposedly applied the substantial effects test for the past 60 years, we *always* have rejected readings of the Commerce Clause and the scope of federal power that would permit Congress to exercise a police power; our cases are quite clear that there are real limits to federal power. . . .

At the time the original Constitution was ratified, "commerce" consisted of selling, buying, and bartering, as well as transporting for these purposes. See 1 S. Johnson, A Dictionary of the English Language 361 (4th ed. 1773) (defining commerce as "Intercour[s]e; exchange of one thing for another; interchange of any thing; trade; traffick"); N. Bailey, An Universal Etymological English Dictionary (26th ed. 1789) ("trade or traffic"); T. Sheridan, A Complete Dictionary of the English Language (6th ed. 1796) ("Exchange of one thing for another; trade, traffick"). This understanding finds support in the etymology of the word, which literally means "with merchandise." In fact, when Federalists and Anti-Federalists discussed the Commerce Clause during the ratification period, they often used trade (in its selling/bartering sense) and commerce interchangeably. See The Federalist No. 4 (Jay) (asserting that countries will cultivate our friendship when our "trade" is prudently regulated by Federal Government); No. 7 (Hamilton) (discussing "competitions of commerce" between States resulting from state "regulations of trade"); No. 40 (Madison) (asserting that it was an "acknowledged object of the Convention . . . that the regulation of trade should be submitted to the general government").

As one would expect, the term "commerce" was used in contradistinction to productive activities such as manufacturing and agriculture. Alexander Hamilton, for example, repeatedly treated commerce, agriculture, and manufacturing as three separate endeavors. See, *e.g.*, The Federalist No. 36 (referring to "agriculture, commerce, manufactures"); No. 21 (distinguishing commerce, arts, and industry); No. 12 (asserting that commerce and agriculture have shared interests). The same distinctions were made in the state ratification conventions. See, *e. g.*, 2 Debates in the Several State Conventions on the Adoption of the Federal Constitution 57 (J. Elliot ed. 1836) (T. Dawes at Massachusetts convention); *id.*, at 336 (M. Smith at New York convention). . . .

The Constitution not only uses the word "commerce" in a narrower sense than our case law might suggest, it also does not support the proposition that Congress has authority over all activities that "substantially affect" interstate commerce. . . . Clearly, the Framers could have drafted a Constitution that contained a "substantially affects interstate commerce" Clause had that been their objective.

In addition to its powers under the Commerce Clause, Congress has the authority to enact such laws as are "necessary and proper" to carry into execution its power to regulate commerce among the several States. U.S. Const., Art. I, § 8, cl. 18. But on this Court's understanding of congressional power under these two Clauses, many of Congress' other enumerated powers under Art. I, § 8, are wholly superfluous. After all, if Congress may regulate all matters that substantially affect commerce, there is no need for the Constitution to specify that Congress may enact bankruptcy laws, cl. 4, or coin money and fix the standard of weights and measures, cl. 5, or punish counterfeiters of United States coin and securities, cl. 6. Likewise, Congress would not need the separate authority to establish post offices and post roads, cl. 7, or to grant patents and copyrights, cl. 8, or to "punish Piracies and Felonies committed on the high Seas," cl. 10. It might not even need the power to raise and support an Army and Navy, cls. 12 and 13, for fewer people would engage in commercial shipping if they thought that a foreign power could expropriate their property with ease. Indeed, if Congress could regulate matters that substantially affect interstate commerce, there would have been no need to specify that Congress can regulate international trade and commerce with the Indians. As the Framers surely understood, these other branches of trade substantially affect interstate commerce.

Put simply, much if not all of Art. I, § 8 (including portions of the Commerce Clause itself), would be surplusage if Congress had been given authority over matters that substantially affect interstate commerce. An interpretation of cl. 3 that makes the rest of § 8 superfluous simply cannot be correct. Yet this Court's Commerce Clause jurisprudence has endorsed just such an interpretation: The power we have accorded Congress has swallowed Art. I, § 8. . . .

Our construction of the scope of congressional authority has the additional problem of coming close to turning the Tenth Amendment on its head. Our case law could be read to reserve to the United States all powers not expressly *prohibited* by the Constitution. Taken together, these fundamental textual problems should, at the very least, convince us that the "substantial effects" test should be reexamined. . . .

In short, the Founding Fathers were well aware of what the principal dissent calls " 'economic . . . realities.' " Even though the boundary between commerce and other matters may ignore "economic reality" and thus seem arbitrary or artificial to some, we must nevertheless respect a constitutional line that does not grant Congress power over all that substantially affects interstate commerce. . . .

This extended discussion of the original understanding and our first century and a half of case law does not necessarily require a wholesale abandonment of our more recent opinions.[8] It simply reveals that our substantial effects test is far removed from both the Constitution and from our early case law and that the Court's opinion should not be viewed as "radical" or another "wrong turn" that must be corrected in the future.[9]
. . .

At an appropriate juncture, I think we must modify our Commerce Clause jurisprudence. Today, it is easy enough to say that the Clause certainly does not empower Congress to ban gun possession within 1,000 feet of a school. . . .

■ **JUSTICE SOUTER, dissenting.**

In reviewing congressional legislation under the Commerce Clause, we defer to what is often a merely implicit congressional judgment that its regulation addresses a subject substantially affecting interstate commerce "if there is any rational basis for such a finding." *Hodel v. Virginia Surface Mining & Reclamation Assn., Inc.*, 452 U.S. 264 (1981). If that congressional determination is within the realm of reason, "the only remaining question for judicial inquiry is whether 'the means chosen by Congress [are] reasonably adapted to the end permitted by the Constitution.' "

---

[8] Although I might be willing to return to the original understanding, I recognize that many believe that it is too late in the day to undertake a fundamental reexamination of the past 60 years. Consideration of *stare decisis* and reliance interests may convince us that we cannot wipe the slate clean.

[9] Nor can the majority's opinion fairly be compared to *Lochner v. New York*. Unlike *Lochner* and our more recent "substantive due process" cases, today's decision enforces only the Constitution and not "judicial policy judgments." . . .

The practice of deferring to rationally based legislative judgments "is a paradigm of judicial restraint." In judicial review under the Commerce Clause, it reflects our respect for the institutional competence of the Congress on a subject expressly assigned to it by the Constitution and our appreciation of the legitimacy that comes from Congress's political accountability in dealing with matters open to a wide range of possible choices. See *United States v. Carolene Products Co.*; cf. *Williamson v. Lee Optical of Okla., Inc.*

It was not ever thus, however, as even a brief overview of Commerce Clause history during the past century reminds us. The modern respect for the competence and primacy of Congress in matters affecting commerce developed only after one of this Court's most chastening experiences, when it perforce repudiated an earlier and untenably expansive conception of judicial review in derogation of congressional commerce power. A look at history's sequence will serve to show how today's decision tugs the Court off course, leading it to suggest opportunities for further developments that would be at odds with the rule of restraint to which the Court still wisely states adherence.

I

Notwithstanding the Court's recognition of a broad commerce power in *Gibbons v. Ogden*, Congress saw few occasions to exercise that power prior to Reconstruction, and it was really the passage of the Interstate Commerce Act of 1887 that opened a new age of congressional reliance on the Commerce Clause for authority to exercise general police powers at the national level. Although the Court upheld a fair amount of the ensuing legislation as being within the commerce power, see, *e.g.*, *Shreveport Rate Cases*, the period from the turn of the century to 1937 is better noted for a series of cases applying highly formalistic notions of "commerce" to invalidate federal social and economic legislation, see, *e.g.*, *A.L.A. Schechter Poultry Corp. v. United States*; *Hammer v. Dagenhart*.

These restrictive views of commerce subject to congressional power complemented the Court's activism in limiting the enforceable scope of state economic regulation. It is most familiar history that during this same period the Court routinely invalidated state social and economic legislation under an expansive conception of Fourteenth Amendment substantive due process. See, *e. g.*, *Lochner v. New York*. The fulcrums of judicial review in these cases were the notions of liberty and property characteristic of laissez-faire economics, whereas the Commerce Clause cases turned on what was ostensibly a structural limit of federal power, but under each conception of judicial review the Court's character for the first third of the century showed itself in exacting judicial scrutiny of a legislature's choice of economic ends and of the legislative means selected to reach them.

It was not merely coincidental, then, that sea changes in the Court's conceptions of its authority under the Due Process and Commerce Clauses occurred virtually together, in 1937. . . . In *West Coast Hotel*, the

Court's rejection of a due process challenge to a state law fixing minimum wages for women and children marked the abandonment of its expansive protection of contractual freedom. Two weeks later, *Jones & Laughlin* affirmed congressional commerce power to authorize NLRB injunctions against unfair labor practices. The Court's finding that the regulated activity had a direct enough effect on commerce has since been seen as beginning the abandonment, for practical purposes, of the formalistic distinction between direct and indirect effects.

In the years following these decisions, deference to legislative policy judgments on commercial regulation became the powerful theme under both the Due Process and Commerce Clauses, and in due course that deference became articulate in the standard of rationality review. In due process litigation, the Court's statement of a rational basis test came quickly. See *United States v. Carolene Products Co;* see also *Williamson v. Lee Optical Co.* The parallel formulation of the Commerce Clause test came later, only because complete elimination of the direct/indirect effects dichotomy and acceptance of the cumulative effects doctrine, *Wickard v.* Filburn, so far settled the pressing issues of congressional power over commerce as to leave the Court for years without any need to phrase a test explicitly deferring to rational legislative judgments. The moment came, however . . . when the Court simply made explicit what the earlier cases had implied: "where we find that the legislators, in light of the facts and testimony before them, have a rational basis for finding a chosen regulatory scheme necessary to the protection of commerce, our investigation is at an end." *Katzenbach v. McClung,* 379 U.S. 294, 303–04 (1964). Thus, under commerce, as under due process, adoption of rational basis review expressed the recognition that the Court had no sustainable basis for subjecting economic regulation as such to judicial policy judgments, and for the past half century the Court has no more turned back in the direction of formalistic Commerce Clause review (as in deciding whether regulation of commerce was sufficiently direct) than it has inclined toward reasserting the substantive authority of *Lochner* due process (as in the inflated protection of contractual autonomy).

II

There is today, however, a backward glance at both the old pitfalls, as the Court treats deference under the rationality rule as subject to gradation according to the commercial or noncommercial nature of the immediate subject of the challenged regulation. The distinction between what is patently commercial and what is not looks much like the old distinction between what directly affects commerce and what touches it only indirectly. And the act of calibrating the level of deference by drawing a line between what is patently commercial and what is less purely so will probably resemble the process of deciding how much interference with contractual freedom was fatal. Thus, it seems fair to ask whether the step taken by the Court today does anything but portend a return to the untenable jurisprudence from which the Court extricated itself almost 60 years ago. The answer is not reassuring. . . . [T]here is no reason to hope that the Court's qualification of rational basis review will be any more successful than the efforts at substantive economic review made by our predecessors as the century began. Taking the Court's opinion on its own terms, JUSTICE BREYER has explained both the hopeless porosity of "commercial" character as a ground of Commerce Clause distinction in America's highly connected economy, and the inconsistency of this categorization with our rational basis precedents from the last 50 years.

Further glosses on rationality review, moreover, may be in the offing. Although this case turns on commercial character, the Court gestures toward two other considerations that it might sometime entertain in applying rational basis scrutiny (apart from a statutory obligation to supply independent proof of a jurisdictional element): does the congressional statute deal with subjects of traditional state regulation, and does the statute contain explicit factual findings supporting the otherwise implicit determination that the regulated activity substantially affects interstate commerce? Once again, any appeal these considerations may have depends on ignoring the painful lesson learned in 1937, for neither of the Court's suggestions would square with rational basis scrutiny. . . .

III

Because JUSTICE BREYER's opinion demonstrates beyond any doubt that the Act in question passes the rationality review that the Court continues to espouse, today's decision may be seen as only a misstep, its reasoning and its suggestions not quite in gear with the prevailing standard, but hardly an epochal case. I would not argue otherwise, but I would raise a caveat. Not every epochal case has come in epochal trappings. *Jones & Laughlin* did not reject the direct-indirect standard in so many words; it just said the relation of the regulated subject matter to commerce was direct enough. But we know what happened.

I respectfully dissent.

■ **JUSTICE BREYER, with whom JUSTICE STEVENS, JUSTICE SOUTER, and JUSTICE GINSBURG join, dissenting.**

II

[W]e must ask whether Congress could have had a *rational basis* for finding a significant (or substantial) connection between gun-related school violence and interstate commerce. . . . Could Congress rationally have found that "violent crime in school zones," through its effect on the "quality of education," significantly (or substantially) affects "interstate" or "foreign commerce"? As long as one views the commerce connection, not as a "technical legal conception," but as "a practical one," the answer to this question must be yes. Numerous reports and studies—generated both inside and outside government—make clear that Congress could reasonably have found the empirical connection that its law, implicitly or explicitly, asserts. . . .

For one thing, reports, hearings, and other readily available literature make clear that the problem of guns in and around schools is widespread and extremely serious. These materials report, for example, that four percent of American high school students (and six percent of inner-city high school students) carry a gun to school at least occasionally; that 12 percent of urban high school students have had guns fired at them; that 20 percent of those students have been threatened with guns; and that, in any 6-month period, several hundred thousand schoolchildren are victims of violent crimes in or near their schools. And, they report that this widespread violence in schools throughout the Nation significantly interferes with the quality of education in those schools. Based on reports such as these, Congress obviously could have thought that guns and learning are mutually exclusive. Congress could therefore have found a substantial educational problem—teachers unable to teach, students unable to learn—and concluded that guns near schools contribute substantially to the size and scope of that problem.

Having found that guns in schools significantly undermine the quality of education in our Nation's classrooms, Congress could also have found, given the effect of education upon interstate and foreign commerce, that gun-related violence in and around schools is a commercial, as well as a human, problem. Education, although far more than a matter of economics, has long been inextricably intertwined with the Nation's economy. . . . Scholars estimate that nearly a quarter of America's economic growth in the early years of this century is traceable directly to increased schooling; that investment in "human capital" (through spending on education) exceeded investment in "physical capital" by a ratio of almost two to one; and that the economic returns to this investment in education exceeded the returns to conventional capital investment.

In recent years the link between secondary education and business has strengthened, becoming both more direct and more important. Scholars on the subject report that technological changes and innovations in management techniques have altered the nature of the workplace so that more jobs now demand greater educational skills. There is evidence that "service, manufacturing or construction jobs are being displaced by technology that requires a better-educated worker or, more likely, are being exported overseas"; that "workers with truly few skills by the year 2000 will find that only one job out of ten will remain"; and that

> over the long haul the best way to encourage the growth of high-wage jobs is to upgrade the skills of the work force. . . . Better-trained workers become more productive workers, enabling a company to become more competitive and expand.

Increasing global competition also has made primary and secondary education economically more important. The portion of the American economy attributable to international trade nearly tripled between 1950 and 1980, and more than 70 percent of American-made goods now compete with imports. Yet, lagging worker productivity has contributed to negative trade balances and to real hourly compensation that has fallen below wages in 10 other industrialized nations. At least some significant part of this serious productivity problem is attributable to students who emerge from classrooms without the reading or mathematical skills necessary to compete with their European or Asian counterparts. Indeed, Congress has said, when writing other statutes, that "functionally or technologically illiterate" Americans in the work force "erode" our economic "standing in the international marketplace," and that "our Nation is . . . paying the price of scientific and technological illiteracy, with our productivity declining, our industrial base ailing, and our global competitiveness dwindling".

Finally, there is evidence that, today more than ever, many firms base their location decisions upon the presence, or absence, of a work force with a basic education. . . . [I]t is no surprise that half of the Nation's manufacturers have become involved with setting standards and shaping curricula for local schools, that 88 percent think this kind of involvement is important, that more than 20 States have recently passed educational reforms to attract new business, and that business magazines have begun to rank cities according to the quality of their schools.

The economic links I have just sketched seem fairly obvious. Why then is it not equally obvious, in light of those links, that a widespread, serious, and substantial physical threat to teaching and learning *also* substantially threatens the commerce to which that teaching and learning is inextricably tied? That is to say, guns in the hands of six percent of inner-city high school students and gun-related violence throughout a city's schools must threaten the trade and commerce that those schools support. The only question, then, is whether the latter threat is (to use the majority's terminology) "substantial." The evidence of (1) the *extent* of the gun-related violence problem, (2) the *extent* of the resulting negative effect on classroom learning, and (3) the *extent* of the consequent negative commercial effects, when taken together, indicate a threat to trade and commerce that is "substantial." At the very least, Congress could rationally have concluded that the links are "substantial." . . .

To hold this statute constitutional is not to "obliterate" the "distinction between what is national and what is local," nor is it to hold that the Commerce Clause permits the Federal Government to "regulate any activity that it found was related to the economic productivity of individual citizens," to regulate "marriage, divorce, and child custody," or to regulate any and all aspects of education. First, this statute is aimed at curbing a particularly acute threat to the educational process. . . . Second, the immediacy of the connection between education and the national economic well-being is documented by scholars and accepted by society at large in a way and to a degree that may not hold true for other social institutions. It must surely be the rare case, then, that a statute strikes at conduct that (when considered in the abstract) seems so removed from commerce, but which (practically speaking) has so significant an impact upon commerce.

In sum, a holding that the particular statute before us falls within the commerce power would not expand the scope of that Clause. Rather, it simply would apply pre-existing law to changing economic circumstances. . . .

III

The majority's holding—that § 922 falls outside the scope of the Commerce Clause—creates three serious legal problems. First, the majority's holding runs contrary to modern Supreme Court cases that have upheld congressional actions despite connections to interstate or foreign commerce that are less significant than the effect of school violence. . . .

The second legal problem the Court creates comes from its apparent belief that it can reconcile its holding with earlier cases by making a critical distinction between "commercial" and noncommercial "transaction[s]." That is to say, the Court believes the Constitution would distinguish between two local activities, each of which has an identical effect upon interstate commerce, if one, but not the other, is "commercial" in nature. As a general matter, this approach fails to heed this Court's earlier warning not to turn "questions of the power of Congress" upon "formula[s]" that would give "controlling force to nomenclature such as 'production' and 'indirect' and foreclose consideration of the actual effects of the activity in question upon interstate commerce." *Wickard.* Moreover, the majority's test is not consistent with what the Court saw as the point of the cases that the majority now characterizes. Although the majority today attempts to categorize *Perez, McClung*, and *Wickard* as involving intrastate "economic activity," the Courts that decided each of those cases did *not* focus upon the economic nature of the activity regulated. Rather, they focused upon whether that activity *affected* interstate or foreign commerce. In fact, the *Wickard* Court expressly held that Filburn's consumption of homegrown wheat, *"though it may not be regarded as commerce,"* could nevertheless be regulated—*"whatever its nature"*—so long as "it exerts a substantial economic effect on interstate commerce." . . .

Regardless, if there is a principled distinction that could work both here and in future cases, Congress (even in the absence of vocational classes, industry involvement, and private management) could rationally conclude that schools fall on the commercial side of the line. In 1990, the year Congress enacted the statute before us, primary and secondary schools spent $230 billion—that is, nearly a quarter of a trillion dollars—which accounts for a significant portion of our $5.5 trillion gross domestic product for that year. The business of schooling requires expenditure of these funds on student transportation, food and custodial services, books, and teachers' salaries. These expenditures enable schools to provide a valuable service—namely, to equip students with the skills they need to survive in life and, more specifically, in the workplace. Certainly, Congress has often analyzed school expenditure as if it were a commercial investment, closely analyzing whether schools are efficient, whether they justify the significant resources they spend, and whether they can be restructured to achieve greater returns. Why could Congress, for Commerce Clause purposes, not consider schools as roughly analogous to commercial investments from which the Nation derives the benefit of an educated work force?

The third legal problem created by the Court's holding is that it threatens legal uncertainty in an area of law that, until this case, seemed reasonably well settled. Congress has enacted many statutes (more than 100 sections of the United States Code), including criminal statutes (at least 25 sections), that use the words "affecting commerce" to define their scope, see, *e.g.*, 18 U.S.C. § 844(i) (destruction of buildings used in activity affecting interstate commerce), and other statutes that contain no jurisdictional language at all, see, *e.g.*, 18 U.S.C. § 922(*o*)(1) (possession of machineguns). Do these, or similar, statutes regulate noncommercial activities? . . . However these questions are eventually resolved, the legal uncertainty now created will restrict Congress' ability to enact criminal laws aimed at criminal behavior that . . . seriously threatens the economic, as well as social, well-being of Americans.

IV

In sum, to find this legislation within the scope of the Commerce Clause would permit "Congress . . . to act in terms of economic . . . realities." It would interpret the Clause as this Court has traditionally interpreted it. . . . Upholding this legislation would do no more than simply recognize that Congress had a "rational basis" for finding a significant connection between guns in or near schools and (through their effect on education) the interstate and foreign commerce they threaten. For these reasons, I would reverse the judgment of the Court of Appeals. Respectfully, I dissent.

NOTE ON *LOPEZ* AND THE "FEDERALIST REVIVAL"

1.   Unlike many areas of federal law, federal criminal law ordinarily does not preempt or otherwise supplant state criminal law; rather, "[f]ederal law has simply been layered over existing state law to produce dual jurisdiction."[6] Why did Congress make it a federal crime to possess a gun

---

[6]   Sara Sun Beale, *Too Many and Yet Too Few: New Principles to Define the Proper Limits For Federal Criminal Jurisdiction*, 46 HASTINGS L. J. 979, 997 (1995).

near a school when the act was already illegal under most states' laws? Why did prosecutors "take Lopez federal" by charging him under the federal statute rather than the state law? The Gun-Free School Zones Act is one example of what an American Bar Association task force called the "federalization of criminal law." [7] The task force reported that "Congressional activity making essentially local conduct a federal crime has accelerated greatly"; indeed, "[m]ore than 40% of the federal criminal provisions enacted since the Civil War have been enacted since 1970."[8] Both the task force and other scholars have concluded that this expansion generally responds to short-term political imperatives, such as the need for Congress to seem responsive to highly-publicized incidents, rather than any sort of principled allocation of responsibility between the federal government and the states.[9] Likewise, critics of federalization worry that it undermines the effectiveness of the federal courts.[10] Other scholars are less troubled, however, arguing that despite the proliferation of federal criminal statutes, most of these laws are rarely enforced and the relative proportion of criminal prosecutions brought under federal law has remained largely static.[11]

One potentially troubling aspect of federalization is the discretion that it gives to federal prosecutors, who may choose to handle crimes federally or leave them to state authorities. As Professor Sara Beale points out, "[t]he sentences available in a federal prosecution are generally higher than those available in state court—often ten or even twenty times higher."[12] The result is "a kind of cruel lottery, in which a small minority of the persons who commit a particular offense is selected for federal prosecution and subjected to much harsher sentences—and often to significantly less favorable procedural or substantive standards—than persons prosecuted for parallel state offenses."[13] Is this sort of prosecutorial discretion appropriate? On the other hand, does federal/state redundancy allow federal prosecutors to serve as a valuable backstop in situations where, for example, local political considerations make it hard for state authorities to pursue certain defendants?

If over-federalization is a concern in this area, would it best be addressed by regulating prosecutorial discretion, congressional review to prune back the criminal provisions of the U.S. Code, or more decisions like *Lopez* limiting Congress's authority to criminalize activities traditionally regulated by the states?

---

[7] American Bar Ass'n, *The Federalization of Criminal Law* (1998), available at http://www.americanbar.org/content/dam/aba/publications/criminaljustice/Federalization_of_Criminal_Law.authcheckdam.pdf.

[8] *Id.* at 5, 7.

[9] *Id.* at 14–17; *see also* William J. Stuntz, *The Pathological Politics of Criminal Law*, 100 MICH. L. REV. 505 (2001).

[10] See, e.g., Sara Sun Beale, Federalizing Crime: Assessing the Impact on the Federal Courts, 543 ANNALS AM. ACAD. POL. & SOC. SCI. 39 (1996).

[11] *See* Susan R. Klein & Ingrid B. Grobey, *Debunking Claims of Over-Federalization of Crime*, 62 EMORY L. J. 1 (2012).

[12] Beale, *New Principles, supra* note [1], at 998.

[13] *Id.* at 997; *see also* Steven D. Clymer, *Unequal Justice: The Federalization of Criminal Law*, 70 S. CAL. L. REV. 643 (1997).

2.   Much of legal academia greeted *Lopez* as a Sign of the Apocalypse. Charles Ares, for example, opined that

> Chief Justice Rehnquist in *Lopez* has . . . opened the floodgates just by saying that there are limits on the commerce power, draping the opinion in references to things traditionally local, and then leaving it to the lower courts to begin the process of dismantling what they regard as offending intrusions on 'our federalism.'[3]

Contrary to these expectations, however, the lower courts acted like nothing at all had changed.[14] Other observers saw *Lopez* "less as a fundamental recasting of relations between nation and state than as a warning shot across the bow—to remind Congress that there may be a price to pay when it cavalierly fails to make out even a minimally plausible case for utilizing the commerce power to undergird a new regulatory scheme, especially one that deals with problems historically regarded as chiefly of state and local concern."[15] Who's right? Is *Lopez* revolutionary?

3.   *Lopez* was decided roughly contemporaneously with several other cases, in related doctrinal areas, that also limited national power in favor of state autonomy. These include *Gregory v. Ashcroft*, 501 U.S. 452 (1991), which seemed to cut back on *Garcia* by holding that, if Congress wishes to regulate the institutions of state government, it must clearly state its intention to do so in the relevant statute; *New York v. United States*, 505 U.S. 144 (1992), which held that Congress may not "commandeer" the institutions of state government by requiring them to implement federal law; and *Seminole Tribe v. Florida*, 517 U.S. 44 (1996), which held that Congress may not subject state governments to federal lawsuits seeking money damages for violations of federal law. These and other related cases have been viewed as signifying a "federalist revival" by the Rehnquist Court—that is, a general effort to roll back national power and expand constitutional protections for state authority. Indeed, most commentators suggested, following Chief Justice Rehnquist's death, that the most important jurisprudential legacy of his Court will be this renewal of interest in constitutional federalism. We will read *Gregory*, *New York*, and similar cases later in this unit. A recurring question will be, How significant is this "federalist revival"?

4.   The Court said in *Hodel v. Virginia Surface Mining & Reclamation Assn., Inc.*, 452 U.S. 264, 276 (1981), that it would defer to what is often a merely implicit congressional judgment that its regulation addresses a subject substantially affecting interstate commerce "if there is any rational basis for such a finding." Although the *Lopez* majority cites *Hodel* positively, saying that "the Court has heeded [the] warning and undertaken to decide whether a rational basis existed for concluding that a regulated activity

---

[3]   Charles E. Ares, Lopez *and the Future Constitutional Crisis*, 38 ARIZ. L. REV. 825, 825–26 (1996).

[14]   *See* Glenn H. Reynolds & Brannon P. Denning, *Lower Court Readings of* Lopez, *or What if the Supreme Court Held a Constitutional Revolution and Nobody Came?* 2000 WIS. L. REV. 369 (finding, after five years, that the lower courts had largely ignored *Lopez*).

[15]   Daniel J. Meltzer, *The* Seminole *Decision and State Sovereign Immunity*, 1996 SUP. CT. REV. 1, 63.

sufficiently affected interstate commerce," Justice Souter argues in his dissent that the rational basis test of *Hodel* has been ignored. Does the majority *de facto* overrule the basic rational basis test of *Hodel*? Or does the majority simply confine the scope of that test to a particular portion of the commerce clause analysis? On the latter view, the courts would determine for themselves whether the regulated activity was "commercial" in nature; if so, then it would defer to Congress's judgment that that activity substantially affects interstate commerce so long as that judgment had a rational basis. Is that a sensible way of proceeding?

5.   What is the importance, in *Lopez*, of Congress's inclusion (or failure to include) in the statute a "jurisdictional element"—for example, a requirement, as an element of the federal crime, that the gun involved have "traveled in interstate commerce" or that the possession of the gun somehow "affected interstate commerce"? Likewise, what is the importance of "findings" by Congress that the activity being regulated has a substantial effect on interstate commerce? One can argue that jurisdictional elements and congressional findings are ways of enlisting one of the other branches to consider the "substantial effect" question in the first instance. Jurisdictional elements (sometimes) require the federal prosecutor—a representative of the Executive branch—to demonstrate a connection to interstate commerce as part of his proof to the jury. Findings, on the other hand, demonstrate that Congress has considered whether the proposed regulation fits within the scope of its constitutional powers.

The exercise of having another branch consider the relation to commerce in the first interest might be important for either of two reasons: First, the presentation of evidence regarding the connection to interstate commerce, either to a jury or to a congressional committee, generates an evidentiary record that may assist the courts when they ultimately have to decide, for themselves, whether such a connection exists. Second, jurisdictional elements and findings requirements might be seen as a "process" requirement, rather than a substantive restriction on congressional action. Recall that, in *Garcia*, the Court emphasized that "the fundamental limitation that the constitutional scheme imposes on the Commerce Clause to protect the 'States as States' is one of process rather than one of result." Is there any independent value to making Congress jump through hoops in order to legislate under the Commerce Clause?

6.   Justice Souter plainly saw *Lopez* as a return to the "bad old days" of the *Lochner* era. Is that fair? Were the *Lochner* era commerce clause and freedom of contract cases equally troubling? Was the trouble in all these cases inherent in the judicial effort to draw lines between permissible and impermissible exercises of government authority? Or was the Court trying to draw the line in the wrong place?

Is Justice Souter's position that *Lochner*ism must be avoided in federalism cases, even at the cost of abandoning any attempt to enforce the constitutional structure, consistent with his enthusiastic embrace of substantive due process in cases like *Casey* and his endorsement of "reasoned judgment," even in the face of doctrinal indeterminacy, in *Glucksberg*?[16] Is there something about federalism or the Commerce Clause that makes a court's exercise of "reasoned judgment" particularly illegitimate?

7.   The Court lent some support to those who saw *Lopez* as a significant shift by its decision, five years later, in *United States v. Morrison*, 529 U.S. 598 (2000). *Morrison* involved the Violence Against Women Act (VAWA), a federal statute that took a number of steps to address an apparent lack of adequate remedies at the state level for female victims of violence. After a particularly ugly rape by football players at Virginia Tech, Christy Brzonkala sued her attackers under a VAWA provision for federal civil rights suits, in federal court, against perpetrators of gender-motivated violence. When the defendants challenged the VAWA's constitutionality, the United States defended the constitutionality of this provision on the ground that violence against women substantially affects interstate commerce. One key difference from *Lopez* was that Congress had held extensive hearings on the VAWA and made detailed findings that "[g]ender-based violence bars its most likely targets—women—from full participation in the national economy." Further, Congress found that domestic violence and sexual assault imposed billions of dollars' worth of costs on the national economy each year, not to mention the long-term productivity costs associated with victimized women who are afraid to travel to certain areas, work outside the home, etc.

Nonetheless, the *Morrison* Court struck down this provision of the VAWA by a 5–4 vote, with the same alignment of justices as in *Lopez*. Chief Justice Rehnquist's majority opinion made clear that references to the importance of legislative findings in *Lopez* were not central to the result in that case, and it also downplayed the importance of including a "jurisdictional element" in the statute. For the majority, the VAWA's findings were irrelevant to the central issue: whether the regulated activity is commercial or noncommercial in nature. Determining that violence against women is *not* commercial activity, the Court found that it lay outside the ambit of Congress's commerce power. Do you agree that the VAWA did not regulate commercial activity? If so, was the Court right to make this factor dispositive?

A second important development in *Morrison* was the explicit adoption by the dissenters of the *Garcia*/Wechsler position that federalism should be protected by "political safeguards" rather than judicial review. According to Justice Souter's dissent, the Court should not enforce the limits of the Commerce Power because "the Constitution remits them to politics." Much of the debate about this proposition focused on the following passage from *Gibbons*, which Justice Souter took to represent Chief Justice Marshall's adoption of the "political safeguards" argument:

> This [commerce] power, like all others vested in Congress, is complete in itself, may be exercised to its utmost extent, and acknowledges no limitations, other than are prescribed in the

---

[16] On this question, *see generally* Lynn A. Baker & Ernest A. Young, *Federalism and the Double Standard of Judicial Review*, 51 DUKE L. J. 75, 87–100 (2001).

constitution. These are expressed in plain terms, and do not affect the questions which arise in this case, or which have been discussed at the bar. If, as has always been understood, the sovereignty of Congress, though limited to specified objects, is plenary as to those objects, the power over commerce with foreign nations, and among the several States, is vested in Congress as absolutely as it would be in a single government, having in its constitution the same restrictions on the exercise of the power as are found in the constitution of the United States. *The wisdom and the discretion of Congress, their identity with the people, and the influence which their constituents possess at elections, are, in this, as in many other instances, as that, for example, of declaring war, the sole restraints on which they have relied, to secure them from its abuse.* They are the restraints on which the people must often rely solely, in all representative governments.[17]

Was Justice Souter right to read Marshall as rejecting judicial review in federalism cases? Or was Marshall's view that political safeguards are the only restrictions on national action that operate *within* the "limitations . . . prescribed in the constitution"? Would Marshall's position foreclose judicial enforcement of the outer bounds of the commerce power itself?

8. How viable is the commercial/noncommercial distinction at the heart of *Lopez* and *Morrison*? Notice that in drawing the line here, the Court seems to be abandoning any attempt to distinguish between commerce that *inter*state and that which is *intra*state. By abandoning that line, the Court seems to accept the integration of the national economy. At that point, however, is there any point in distinguishing between commercial and noncommercial activity? What values associated with federalism would *that* distinction serve? Is state-by-state policy diversity, for example, any less important with respect to commercial activities than noncommercial ones?

Equally important, is the commercial/noncommercial line one that will pass the Frankfurter Constraint—that is, is it a line that courts can draw and enforce in a principled, law-like way? Or is Justice Breyer right that the majority is simply replicating the direct/indirect distinction from *Hammer*, *E.C. Knight*, and similar cases?

9. One can plausibly argue that both the Gun Free School Zones Act and the provision of the VAWA struck down in *Morrison* were largely symbolic federal statutes, with relatively little practical importance.[18] Federal prosecutions were rarely brought under either statute. In the next case, however, the Court encountered a Commerce Clause challenge to one of the mainstay statutes of federal criminal law enforcement.

---

[17] 22 U.S. (9 Wheat.) 1, 196–97 (1824) (emphasis added).

[18] In his *Morrison* dissent, Justice Souter noted that "I and other Members of this Court appearing before Congress have repeatedly argued against the federalization of traditional state crimes and the extension of federal remedies to problems for which the States have historically taken responsibility and may deal with today," and that "[t]he Judicial Conference of the United States originally opposed the [VAWA]" in particular. 529 U.S. at 636 n.10.

Gonzales v. Raich

545 U.S. 1 (2005)

■ **JUSTICE STEVENS delivered the opinion of the Court.**

California is one of at least nine States that authorize the use of marijuana for medicinal purposes. The question presented in this case is whether the power vested in Congress by Article I, § 8, of the Constitution "to make all Laws which shall be necessary and proper for carrying into Execution" its authority to "regulate Commerce with foreign Nations, and among the several States" includes the power to prohibit the local cultivation and use of marijuana in compliance with California law.

I

California has been a pioneer in the regulation of marijuana. In 1913, California was one of the first States to prohibit the sale and possession of marijuana, and at the end of the century, California became the first State to authorize limited use of the drug for medicinal purposes. In 1996, California voters passed Proposition 215, now codified as the Compassionate Use Act of 1996. The proposition was designed to ensure that "seriously ill" residents of the State have access to marijuana for medical purposes, and to encourage Federal and State Governments to take steps towards ensuring the safe and affordable distribution of the drug to patients in need. The Act creates an exemption from criminal prosecution for physicians, as well as for patients and primary caregivers who possess or cultivate marijuana for medicinal purposes with the recommendation or approval of a physician. A "primary caregiver" is a person who has consistently assumed responsibility for the housing, health, or safety of the patient.

Respondents Angel Raich and Diane Monson are California residents who suffer from a variety of serious medical conditions and have sought to avail themselves of medical marijuana pursuant to the terms of the Compassionate Use Act. They are being treated by licensed, board-certified family practitioners, who have concluded, after prescribing a host of conventional medicines to treat respondents' conditions and to alleviate their associated symptoms, that marijuana is the only drug available that provides effective treatment. Both women have been using marijuana as a medication for several years pursuant to their doctors' recommendation, and both rely heavily on cannabis to function on a daily basis. Indeed, Raich's physician believes that forgoing cannabis treatments would certainly cause Raich excruciating pain and could very well prove fatal.

Respondent Monson cultivates her own marijuana, and ingests the drug in a variety of ways including smoking and using a vaporizer. Respondent Raich, by contrast, is unable to cultivate her own, and thus relies on two caregivers . . . to provide her with locally grown marijuana at no charge. These caregivers also process the cannabis into hashish or keif, and Raich herself processes some of the marijuana into oils, balms, and foods for consumption.

On August 15, 2002, county deputy sheriffs and agents from the federal Drug Enforcement Administration (DEA) came to Monson's home. After a thorough investigation, the county officials concluded that her use of marijuana was entirely lawful as a matter of California law. Nevertheless, after a 3-hour standoff, the federal agents seized and destroyed all six of her cannabis plants.

Respondents thereafter brought this action against the Attorney General of the United States and the head of the DEA seeking injunctive and declaratory relief prohibiting the enforcement of the federal Controlled Substances Act (CSA), 21 U.S.C. § 801 et seq., to the extent it prevents them from possessing, obtaining, or manufacturing cannabis for their personal medical use. . . . Respondents claimed that enforcing the CSA against them would violate the Commerce Clause, the Due Process Clause of the Fifth Amendment, the Ninth and Tenth Amendments of the Constitution, and the doctrine of medical necessity. . . .

The question before us . . . is not whether it is wise to enforce the statute in these circumstances; rather, it is whether Congress' power to regulate interstate markets for medicinal substances encompasses the portions of those markets that are supplied with drugs produced and consumed locally. Well-settled law controls our answer. The CSA is a valid exercise of federal power, even as applied to the troubling facts of this case. . . .

II

Shortly after taking office in 1969, President Nixon declared a national "war on drugs." As the first campaign of that war, Congress set out to enact legislation that would consolidate various drug laws on the books into a comprehensive statute, provide meaningful regulation over legitimate sources of drugs to prevent diversion into illegal channels, and strengthen law enforcement tools against the traffic in illicit drugs. That effort culminated in the passage of the Comprehensive Drug Abuse Prevention and Control Act of 1970. . . .

Title II of that Act, the CSA, repealed most of the earlier antidrug laws in favor of a comprehensive regime to combat the international and interstate traffic in illicit drugs. The main objectives of the CSA were to conquer drug abuse and to control the legitimate and illegitimate traffic in controlled substances.[20] Congress was particularly concerned with the need to prevent the diversion of drugs from legitimate to illicit channels.

---

[20] In particular, Congress made the following findings:

(1) Many of the drugs included within this subchapter have a useful and legitimate medical purpose and are necessary to maintain the health and general welfare of the American people.

To effectuate these goals, Congress devised a closed regulatory system making it unlawful to manufacture, distribute, dispense, or possess any controlled substance except in a manner authorized by the CSA. The CSA categorizes all controlled substances into five schedules. The drugs are grouped together based on their accepted medical uses, the potential for abuse, and their psychological and physical effects on the body. Each schedule is associated with a distinct set of controls regarding the manufacture, distribution, and use of the substances listed therein. The CSA and its implementing regulations set forth strict requirements regarding registration, labeling and packaging, production quotas, drug security, and recordkeeping.

In enacting the CSA, Congress classified marijuana as a Schedule I drug. . . . Schedule I drugs are categorized as such because of their high potential for abuse, lack of any accepted medical use, and absence of any accepted safety for use in medically supervised treatment. . . . Schedule II substances also have a high potential for abuse which may lead to severe psychological or physical dependence, but unlike Schedule I drugs, they have a currently accepted medical use. By classifying marijuana as a Schedule I drug, as opposed to listing it on a lesser schedule, the manufacture, distribution, or possession of marijuana became a criminal offense. . . .

The CSA provides for the periodic updating of schedules and delegates authority to the Attorney General, after consultation with the Secretary of Health and Human Services, to add, remove, or transfer

---

(2) The illegal importation, manufacture, distribution, and possession and improper use of controlled substances have a substantial and detrimental effect on the health and general welfare of the American people.

(3) A major portion of the traffic in controlled substances flows through interstate and foreign commerce. Incidents of the traffic which are not an integral part of the interstate or foreign flow, such as manufacture, local distribution, and possession, nonetheless have a substantial and direct effect upon interstate commerce because—

(A) after manufacture, many controlled substances are transported in interstate commerce,

(B) controlled substances distributed locally usually have been transported in interstate commerce immediately before their distribution, and

(C) controlled substances possessed commonly flow through interstate commerce immediately prior to such possession.

(4) Local distribution and possession of controlled substances contribute to swelling the interstate traffic in such substances.

(5) Controlled substances manufactured and distributed intrastate cannot be differentiated from controlled substances manufactured and distributed interstate. Thus, it is not feasible to distinguish, in terms of controls, between controlled substances manufactured and distributed interstate and controlled substances manufactured and distributed intrastate.

6) Federal control of the intrastate incidents of the traffic in controlled substances is essential to the effective control of the interstate incidents of such traffic.

21 U.S.C. §§ 801(1)–(6).

substances to, from, or between schedules. Despite considerable efforts to reschedule marijuana, it remains a Schedule I drug.[23]

III

Respondents in this case do not dispute that passage of the CSA, as part of the Comprehensive Drug Abuse Prevention and Control Act, was well within Congress' commerce power. Nor do they contend that any provision or section of the CSA amounts to an unconstitutional exercise of congressional authority. Rather, respondents' challenge is actually quite limited; they argue that the CSA's categorical prohibition of the manufacture and possession of marijuana as applied to the intrastate manufacture and possession of marijuana for medical purposes pursuant to California law exceeds Congress' authority under the Commerce Clause. . . .

Our case law firmly establishes Congress' power to regulate purely local activities that are part of an economic "class of activities" that have a substantial effect on interstate commerce. As we stated in *Wickard*, "even if appellee's activity be local and though it may not be regarded as commerce, it may still, whatever its nature, be reached by Congress if it exerts a substantial economic effect on interstate commerce." We have never required Congress to legislate with scientific exactitude. When Congress decides that the total incidence of a practice poses a threat to a national market, it may regulate the entire class. In this vein, we have reiterated that when "a general regulatory statute bears a substantial relation to commerce, the *de minimis* character of individual instances arising under that statute is of no consequence." *Lopez*.

Our decision in *Wickard* . . . establishes that Congress can regulate purely intrastate activity that is not itself "commercial," in that it is not produced for sale, if it concludes that failure to regulate that class of activity would undercut the regulation of the interstate market in that commodity.

The similarities between this case and *Wickard* are striking. Like the farmer in *Wickard*, respondents are cultivating, for home consumption, a fungible commodity for which there is an established, albeit illegal, interstate market. Just as the Agricultural Adjustment Act was designed "to control the volume [of wheat] moving in interstate and foreign commerce in order to avoid surpluses . . . " and consequently control the market price, a primary purpose of the CSA is to control the supply and demand of controlled substances in both lawful and unlawful drug markets. In *Wickard*, we had no difficulty concluding that Congress had a rational basis for believing that, when viewed in the aggregate,

---

[23] Starting in 1972, the National Organization for the Reform of Marijuana Laws (NORML) began its campaign to reclassify marijuana. . . . The DEA Administrator . . . has routinely denied petitions to reschedule the drug, most recently in 2001. The Court of Appeals for the District of Columbia Circuit has reviewed the petition to reschedule marijuana on five separate occasions over the course of 30 years, ultimately upholding the Administrator's final order.

leaving home-consumed wheat outside the regulatory scheme would have a substantial influence on price and market conditions. Here too, Congress had a rational basis for concluding that leaving home-consumed marijuana outside federal control would similarly affect price and market conditions.

More concretely, one concern prompting inclusion of wheat grown for home consumption in the 1938 Act was that rising market prices could draw such wheat into the interstate market, resulting in lower market prices. The parallel concern making it appropriate to include marijuana grown for home consumption in the CSA is the likelihood that the high demand in the interstate market will draw such marijuana into that market. While the diversion of homegrown wheat tended to frustrate the federal interest in stabilizing prices by regulating the volume of commercial transactions in the interstate market, the diversion of homegrown marijuana tends to frustrate the federal interest in eliminating commercial transactions in the interstate market in their entirety. In both cases, the regulation is squarely within Congress' commerce power because production of the commodity meant for home consumption, be it wheat or marijuana, has a substantial effect on supply and demand in the national market for that commodity.[29]

Nonetheless, respondents suggest that *Wickard* differs from this case in three respects: (1) the Agricultural Adjustment Act, unlike the CSA, exempted small farming operations; (2) *Wickard* involved a "quintessential economic activity"—a commercial farm—whereas respondents do not sell marijuana; and (3) the *Wickard* record made it clear that the aggregate production of wheat for use on farms had a significant impact on market prices. Those differences, though factually accurate, do not diminish the precedential force of this Court's reasoning.

. . . That the Secretary of Agriculture elected to exempt even smaller farms from regulation does not speak to his power to regulate all those whose aggregated production was significant, nor did that fact play any role in the Court's analysis. Moreover, even though Wickard was indeed a commercial farmer, the activity he was engaged in—the cultivation of wheat for home consumption—was not treated by the Court as part of his commercial farming operation. And while it is true that the record in the *Wickard* case itself established the causal connection between the production for local use and the national market, we have before us findings by Congress to the same effect.

Findings in the introductory sections of the CSA explain why Congress deemed it appropriate to encompass local activities within the scope of the CSA. The submissions of the parties and the numerous *amici*

---

[29] To be sure, the wheat market is a lawful market that Congress sought to protect and stabilize, whereas the marijuana market is an unlawful market that Congress sought to eradicate. This difference, however, is of no constitutional import. It has long been settled that Congress' power to regulate commerce includes the power to prohibit commerce in a particular commodity.

all seem to agree that the national, and international, market for marijuana has dimensions that are fully comparable to those defining the class of activities regulated by the Secretary pursuant to the 1938 statute.[31] Respondents nonetheless insist that the CSA cannot be constitutionally applied to their activities because Congress did not make a specific finding that the intrastate cultivation and possession of marijuana for medical purposes based on the recommendation of a physician would substantially affect the larger interstate marijuana market. Be that as it may, we have never required Congress to make particularized findings in order to legislate, absent a special concern such as the protection of free speech. While congressional findings are certainly helpful in reviewing the substance of a congressional statutory scheme, particularly when the connection to commerce is not self-evident, and while we will consider congressional findings in our analysis when they are available, the absence of particularized findings does not call into question Congress' authority to legislate.[32]

In assessing the scope of Congress' authority under the Commerce Clause, we stress that the task before us is a modest one. We need not determine whether respondents' activities, taken in the aggregate, substantially affect interstate commerce in fact, but only whether a "rational basis" exists for so concluding. Given the enforcement difficulties that attend distinguishing between marijuana cultivated locally and marijuana grown elsewhere, and concerns about diversion into illicit channels, we have no difficulty concluding that Congress had a rational basis for believing that failure to regulate the intrastate manufacture and possession of marijuana would leave a gaping hole in the CSA. Thus, as in *Wickard*, when it enacted comprehensive legislation to regulate the interstate market in a fungible commodity, Congress was acting well within its authority to "make all Laws which shall be necessary and proper" to "regulate Commerce . . . among the several States." U.S. Const., Art. I, § 8. That the regulation ensnares some purely intrastate activity is of no moment. As we have done many times before, we refuse to excise individual components of that larger scheme.

IV

To support their contrary submission, respondents rely heavily on two of our more recent Commerce Clause cases. . . . Those two cases, of course, are *Lopez* and *Morrison*. As an initial matter, the statutory challenges at issue in those cases were markedly different from the challenge respondents pursue in the case at hand. Here, respondents ask

---

[31] The Executive Office of the President has estimated that in 2000 American users spent $10.5 *billion* on the purchase of marijuana.

[32] Moreover . . . Congress did make findings regarding the effects of intrastate drug activity on interstate commerce. . . . The dissenters, however, would impose a new and heightened burden on Congress (unless the litigants can garner evidence sufficient to cure Congress' perceived "inadequacies")—that legislation must contain detailed findings proving that each activity regulated within a comprehensive statute is essential to the statutory scheme. Such an exacting requirement is not only unprecedented, it is also impractical. . . .

us to excise individual applications of a concededly valid statutory scheme. In contrast, in both *Lopez* and *Morrison*, the parties asserted that a particular statute or provision fell outside Congress' commerce power in its entirety. This distinction is pivotal for we have often reiterated that "where the class of activities is regulated and that class is within the reach of federal power, the courts have no power 'to excise, as trivial, individual instances' of the class."

At issue in *Lopez,* was the validity of the Gun-Free School Zones Act of 1990, which was a brief, single-subject statute making it a crime for an individual to possess a gun in a school zone. The Act did not regulate any economic activity and did not contain any requirement that the possession of a gun have any connection to past interstate activity or a predictable impact on future commercial activity. . . .

The statutory scheme that the Government is defending in this litigation is at the opposite end of the regulatory spectrum. As explained above, the CSA, enacted in 1970 as part of the Comprehensive Drug Abuse Prevention and Control Act, was a lengthy and detailed statute creating a comprehensive framework for regulating the production, distribution, and possession of five classes of "controlled substances." . . . Our opinion in *Lopez* casts no doubt on the validity of such a program.

Nor does this Court's holding in *Morrison*. The Violence Against Women Act of 1994 created a federal civil remedy for the victims of gender-motivated crimes of violence. . . . Despite congressional findings that such crimes had an adverse impact on interstate commerce, we held the statute unconstitutional because, like the statute in *Lopez*, it did not regulate economic activity. . . .

Unlike those at issue in *Lopez* and *Morrison*, the activities regulated by the CSA are quintessentially economic. "Economics" refers to "the production, distribution, and consumption of commodities." Webster's Third New International Dictionary 720 (1966). The CSA is a statute that regulates the production, distribution, and consumption of commodities for which there is an established, and lucrative, interstate market. Prohibiting the intrastate possession or manufacture of an article of commerce is a rational (and commonly utilized) means of regulating commerce in that product. . . .

The Court of Appeals was able to conclude otherwise only by isolating a "separate and distinct" class of activities that it held to be beyond the reach of federal power, defined as "the intrastate, noncommercial cultivation, possession and use of marijuana for personal medical purposes on the advice of a physician and in accordance with state law." The court characterized this class as "different in kind from drug trafficking." The differences between the members of a class so defined and the principal traffickers in Schedule I substances might be sufficient to justify a policy decision exempting the narrower class from the coverage of the CSA. The question, however, is whether Congress' contrary policy judgment, *i.e.*, its decision to include this narrower "class of activities" within the larger regulatory scheme, was constitutionally deficient. We have no difficulty concluding that Congress acted rationally in determining that none of the characteristics making up the purported class, whether viewed individually or in the aggregate, compelled an exemption from the CSA; rather, the subdivided class of activities defined by the Court of Appeals was an essential part of the larger regulatory scheme.

First, the fact that marijuana is used "for personal medical purposes on the advice of a physician" cannot itself serve as a distinguishing factor. The CSA designates marijuana as contraband for *any* purpose; in fact, by characterizing marijuana as a Schedule I drug, Congress expressly found that the drug has no acceptable medical uses. . . .

More fundamentally, if, as the principal dissent contends, the personal cultivation, possession, and use of marijuana for medicinal purposes is beyond the " 'outer limits' of Congress' Commerce Clause authority," it must also be true that such personal use of marijuana (or any other homegrown drug) for recreational purposes is also beyond those " 'outer limits,' " whether or not a State elects to authorize or even regulate such use. JUSTICE THOMAS' separate dissent suffers from the same sweeping implications. That is, the dissenters' rationale logically extends to place *any* federal regulation (including quality, prescription, or quantity controls) of *any* locally cultivated and possessed controlled substance for *any* purpose beyond the " 'outer limits' " of Congress' Commerce Clause authority. One need not have a degree in economics to understand why a nationwide exemption for the vast quantity of marijuana (or other drugs) locally cultivated for personal use (which presumably would include use by friends, neighbors, and family members) may have a substantial impact on the interstate market for this extraordinarily popular substance. The congressional judgment that an exemption for such a significant segment of the total market would undermine the orderly enforcement of the entire regulatory scheme is entitled to a strong presumption of validity. . . .

Second, limiting the activity to marijuana possession and cultivation "in accordance with state law" cannot serve to place respondents' activities beyond congressional reach. The Supremacy Clause unambiguously provides that if there is any conflict between federal and state law, federal law shall prevail. It is beyond peradventure that federal power over commerce is superior to that of the States to provide for the welfare or necessities of their inhabitants, however legitimate or dire those necessities may be. Just as state acquiescence to federal regulation cannot expand the bounds of the Commerce Clause, so too state action cannot circumscribe Congress' plenary commerce power. See *United States v. Darby*, 312 U.S. 100 (1941) ("That power can neither be enlarged nor diminished by the exercise or non-exercise of state power").[38]

Respondents acknowledge this proposition, but nonetheless contend that their activities were not "an essential part of a larger regulatory scheme" because they had been "isolated by the State of California, and [are] policed by the State of California," and thus remain "entirely separated from the market." The dissenters fall prey to similar reasoning. The notion that California law has surgically excised a discrete activity that is hermetically sealed off from the larger interstate marijuana market is a dubious proposition, and, more importantly, one that Congress could have rationally rejected.

Indeed, that the California exemptions will have a significant impact on both the supply and demand sides of the market for marijuana is . . . readily apparent. The exemption for physicians provides them with an economic incentive to grant their patients permission to use the drug. In contrast to most prescriptions for legal drugs, which limit the dosage and duration of the usage, under California law the doctor's permission to recommend marijuana use is open-ended. The authority to grant permission whenever the doctor determines that a patient is afflicted with "any other illness for which marijuana provides relief," is broad enough to allow even the most scrupulous doctor to conclude that some recreational uses would be therapeutic. And our cases have taught us that there are some unscrupulous physicians who overprescribe when it is sufficiently profitable to do so.

The exemption for cultivation by patients and caregivers can only increase the supply of marijuana in the California market. The likelihood that all such production will promptly terminate when patients recover or will precisely match the patients' medical needs during their convalescence seems remote; whereas the danger that excesses will satisfy some of the admittedly enormous demand for recreational use seems obvious. Moreover, that the national and international narcotics trade has thrived in the face of vigorous criminal enforcement efforts suggests that no small number of unscrupulous people will make use of the California exemptions to serve their commercial ends whenever it is feasible to do so. Taking into account the fact that California is only one of at least nine States to have authorized the medical use of marijuana . . . Congress could have rationally concluded that the aggregate impact on the national market of all the transactions exempted from federal supervision is unquestionably substantial. . . .

[T]the case for the exemption comes down to the claim that a locally cultivated product that is used domestically rather than sold on the open

---

[38] That is so even if California's current controls (enacted eight years after the Compassionate Use Act was passed) are "effective," as the dissenters would have us blindly presume. California's decision (made 34 years after the CSA was enacted) to impose "strict controls" on the "cultivation and possession of marijuana for medical purposes," cannot retroactively divest Congress of its authority under the Commerce Clause. . . . .

market is not subject to federal regulation. Given the findings in the CSA and the undisputed magnitude of the commercial market for marijuana, our decisions in *Wickard v. Filburn* and the later cases endorsing its reasoning foreclose that claim.

V

Respondents also raise a substantive due process claim and seek to avail themselves of the medical necessity defense. These theories of relief were set forth in their complaint but were not reached by the Court of Appeals. We therefore do not address the question whether judicial relief is available to respondents on these alternative bases.* We do note, however, the presence of another avenue of relief. As the Solicitor General confirmed during oral argument, the statute authorizes procedures for the reclassification of Schedule I drugs. But perhaps even more important than these legal avenues is the democratic process, in which the voices of voters allied with these respondents may one day be heard in the halls of Congress. Under the present state of the law, however, the judgment of the Court of Appeals must be vacated. . . .

■ **JUSTICE SCALIA, concurring in the judgment.**

I agree with the Court's holding that the Controlled Substances Act (CSA) may validly be applied to respondents' cultivation, distribution, and possession of marijuana for personal, medicinal use. I write separately because my understanding of the doctrinal foundation on which that holding rests is, if not inconsistent with that of the Court, at least more nuanced. . . .

[U]nlike the channels, instrumentalities, and agents of interstate commerce, activities that substantially affect interstate commerce are not themselves part of interstate commerce, and thus the power to regulate them cannot come from the Commerce Clause alone. Rather . . . Congress's regulatory authority over intrastate activities that are not themselves part of interstate commerce (including activities that have a substantial effect on interstate commerce) derives from the Necessary and Proper Clause. . . .

I

Our cases show that the regulation of intrastate activities may be necessary to and proper for the regulation of interstate commerce in two general circumstances. Most directly, the commerce power permits Congress not only to devise rules for the governance of commerce between States but also to facilitate interstate commerce by eliminating potential obstructions, and to restrict it by eliminating potential stimulants. That is why the Court has repeatedly sustained congressional legislation on the ground that the regulated activities had a substantial effect on interstate commerce. See, *e.g.*, *Hodel* (surface coal

---

* The Ninth Circuit rejected these arguments on remand. *See Raich v. Gonzales*, 500 F.3d 850 (9th Cir. 2007). [Editor's Note].

mining); *Katzenbach* (discrimination by restaurants); *Heart of Atlanta Motel, Inc. v. United States*, 379 U.S. 241 (1964) (discrimination by hotels); *Mandeville Island Farms v. American Crystal Sugar Co.*, 334 U.S. 219 (1948) (intrastate price-fixing). . . .

This principle is not without limitation. In *Lopez* and *Morrison*, the Court—conscious of the potential of the "substantially affects" test to "obliterate the distinction between what is national and what is local"—rejected the argument that Congress may regulate *noneconomic* activity based solely on the effect that it may have on interstate commerce through a remote chain of inferences. "If we were to accept [such] arguments," the Court reasoned in *Lopez*, "we are hard pressed to posit any activity by an individual that Congress is without power to regulate." . . .

As we implicitly acknowledged in *Lopez*, however, Congress's authority to enact laws necessary and proper for the regulation of interstate commerce is not limited to laws directed against economic activities that have a substantial effect on interstate commerce. Though the conduct in *Lopez* was not economic, the Court nevertheless recognized that it could be regulated as "an essential part of a larger regulation of economic activity, in which the regulatory scheme could be undercut unless the intrastate activity were regulated." This statement referred to those cases permitting the regulation of intrastate activities "which in a substantial way interfere with or obstruct the exercise of the granted power." . . . [W]here Congress has the authority to enact a regulation of interstate commerce, "it possesses every power needed to make that regulation effective."

Although this power "to make . . . regulation effective" commonly overlaps with the authority to regulate economic activities that substantially affect interstate commerce,[2] and may in some cases have been confused with that authority, the two are distinct. The regulation of an intrastate activity may be essential to a comprehensive regulation of interstate commerce even though the intrastate activity does not itself "substantially affect" interstate commerce. Moreover . . . Congress may regulate even noneconomic local activity if that regulation is a necessary part of a more general regulation of interstate commerce. The relevant question is simply whether the means chosen are "reasonably adapted" to the attainment of a legitimate end under the commerce power. . . .

As the Court said in the *Shreveport Rate Cases*, the Necessary and Proper Clause does not give "Congress . . . the authority to regulate the internal commerce of a State, as such," but it does allow Congress "to

---

[2] *Wickard v. Filburn* presented such a case. Because the unregulated production of wheat for personal consumption diminished demand in the regulated wheat market, the Court said, it carried with it the potential to disrupt Congress's price regulation by driving down prices in the market. This potential disruption of Congress's interstate regulation, and not only the effect that personal consumption of wheat had on interstate commerce, justified Congress's regulation of that conduct.

take all measures necessary or appropriate to" the effective regulation of the interstate market, "although intrastate transactions . . . may thereby be controlled."

II

Today's principal dissent objects that, by permitting Congress to regulate activities necessary to effective interstate regulation, the Court reduces *Lopez* and *Morrison* to "little more than a drafting guide." I think that criticism unjustified. Unlike the power to regulate activities that have a substantial effect on interstate commerce, the power to enact laws enabling effective regulation of interstate commerce can only be exercised in conjunction with congressional regulation of an interstate market, and it extends only to those measures necessary to make the interstate regulation effective. . . . Congress may regulate noneconomic intrastate activities only where the failure to do so "could . . . undercut" its regulation of interstate commerce. . . .

Lopez and *Morrison* affirm that Congress may not regulate certain "purely local" activity within the States based solely on the attenuated effect that such activity may have in the interstate market. But those decisions do not declare noneconomic intrastate activities to be categorically beyond the reach of the Federal Government. Neither case involved the power of Congress to exert control over intrastate activities in connection with a more comprehensive scheme of regulation; *Lopez* expressly disclaimed that it was such a case, and *Morrison* did not even discuss the possibility that it was. . . . To dismiss this distinction as "superficial and formalistic," is to misunderstand the nature of the Necessary and Proper Clause, which empowers Congress to enact laws in effectuation of its enumerated powers that are not within its authority to enact in isolation.

And there are other restraints upon the Necessary and Proper Clause authority. As Chief Justice Marshall wrote in *McCulloch v. Maryland*, even when the end is constitutional and legitimate, the means must be "appropriate" and "plainly adapted" to that end. Moreover, they may not be otherwise "prohibited" and must be "consistent with the letter and spirit of the constitution." These phrases are not merely hortatory. For example, cases such as *Printz v. United States*, 521 U.S. 898 (1997), and *New York v. United States*, 505 U.S. 144 (1992), affirm that a law is not " '*proper* for carrying into Execution the Commerce Clause' " "when [it] violates [a constitutional] principle of state sovereignty."

III

The application of these principles to the case before us is straightforward. In the CSA, Congress has undertaken to extinguish the interstate market in Schedule I controlled substances, including marijuana. The Commerce Clause unquestionably permits this. The power to regulate interstate commerce "extends not only to those regulations which aid, foster and protect the commerce, but embraces those which prohibit it." To effectuate its objective, Congress has prohibited almost all intrastate activities related to Schedule I substances—both economic activities (manufacture, distribution, possession with the intent to distribute) and noneconomic activities (simple possession). That simple possession is a noneconomic activity is immaterial to whether it can be prohibited as a necessary part of a larger regulation. Rather, Congress's authority to enact all of these prohibitions of intrastate controlled-substance activities depends only upon whether they are appropriate means of achieving the legitimate end of eradicating Schedule I substances from interstate commerce.

By this measure, I think the regulation must be sustained. Not only is it impossible to distinguish "controlled substances manufactured and distributed intrastate" from "controlled substances manufactured and distributed interstate," but it hardly makes sense to speak in such terms. Drugs like marijuana are fungible commodities. As the Court explains, marijuana that is grown at home and possessed for personal use is never more than an instant from the interstate market—and this is so whether or not the possession is for medicinal use or lawful use under the laws of a particular State.[3] Congress need not accept on faith that state law will be effective in maintaining a strict division between a lawful market for "medical" marijuana and the more general marijuana market. "To impose on [Congress] the necessity of resorting to means which it cannot control, which another government may furnish or withhold, would render its course precarious, the result of its measures uncertain, and create a dependence on other governments, which might disappoint its most important designs, and is incompatible with the language of the constitution." *McCulloch*. . . .

I thus agree with the Court that, however the class of regulated activities is subdivided, Congress could reasonably conclude that its objective of prohibiting marijuana from the interstate market "could be undercut" if those activities were excepted from its general scheme of regulation. That is sufficient to authorize the application of the CSA to respondents.

---

[3]   The principal dissent claims that, if this is sufficient to sustain the regulation at issue in this case, then it should also have been sufficient to sustain the regulation at issue in *United States v. Lopez*. This claim founders upon the shoals of *Lopez* itself, which made clear that the statute there at issue was "*not* an essential part of a larger regulation of economic activity." On the dissent's view of things, that statement is inexplicable. Of course it is in addition difficult to imagine what intelligible scheme of regulation of the interstate market in guns could have as an appropriate means of effectuation the prohibition of guns within 1000 feet of schools (and nowhere else). The dissent points to a federal law, 18 U.S.C. § 922(b)(1), barring licensed dealers from selling guns to minors, but the relationship between the regulatory scheme of which § 922(b)(1) is a part (requiring all dealers in firearms that have traveled in interstate commerce to be licensed) and the statute at issue in *Lopez* approaches the nonexistent—which is doubtless why the Government did not attempt to justify the statute on the basis of that relationship.

■ **JUSTICE O'CONNOR, with whom THE CHIEF JUSTICE and JUSTICE THOMAS join as to all but Part III, dissenting.**

We enforce the "outer limits" of Congress' Commerce Clause authority not for their own sake, but to protect historic spheres of state sovereignty from excessive federal encroachment and thereby to maintain the distribution of power fundamental to our federalist system of government. One of federalism's chief virtues, of course, is that it promotes innovation by allowing for the possibility that "a single courageous State may, if its citizens choose, serve as a laboratory; and try novel social and economic experiments without risk to the rest of the country." *New State Ice Co. v. Liebmann*, 285 U.S. 262, 311 (1932) (Brandeis, J., dissenting).

This case exemplifies the role of States as laboratories. The States' core police powers have always included authority to define criminal law and to protect the health, safety, and welfare of their citizens. Exercising those powers, California . . . has come to its own conclusion about the difficult and sensitive question of whether marijuana should be available to relieve severe pain and suffering. Today the Court sanctions an application of the federal Controlled Substances Act that extinguishes that experiment, without any proof that the personal cultivation, possession, and use of marijuana for medicinal purposes, if economic activity in the first place, has a substantial effect on interstate commerce and is therefore an appropriate subject of federal regulation. In so doing, the Court announces a rule that gives Congress a perverse incentive to legislate broadly pursuant to the Commerce Clause—nestling questionable assertions of its authority into comprehensive regulatory schemes—rather than with precision. That rule and the result it produces in this case are irreconcilable with our decisions in *Lopez,* and *Morrison*. Accordingly I dissent. . . .

II

A

What is the relevant conduct subject to Commerce Clause analysis in this case? The Court takes its cues from Congress, applying the [*Lopez*] considerations to the activity regulated by the Controlled Substances Act (CSA) in general. The Court's decision rests on two facts about the CSA: (1) Congress chose to enact a single statute providing a comprehensive prohibition on the production, distribution, and possession of all controlled substances, and (2) Congress did not distinguish between various forms of intrastate noncommercial cultivation, possession, and use of marijuana. Today's decision suggests that the federal regulation of local activity is immune to Commerce Clause challenge because Congress chose to act with an ambitious, all-encompassing statute, rather than piecemeal. In my view, allowing Congress to set the terms of the constitutional debate in this way, *i.e.*, by packaging regulation of local activity in broader schemes, is tantamount to removing meaningful limits on the Commerce Clause.

The Court's principal means of distinguishing *Lopez* from this case is to observe that the Gun-Free School Zones Act of 1990 was a "brief, single-subject statute," whereas the CSA is "a lengthy and detailed statute creating a comprehensive framework for regulating the production, distribution, and possession of five classes of 'controlled substances.'" Thus, according to the Court, it was possible in *Lopez* to evaluate in isolation the constitutionality of criminalizing local activity (there gun possession in school zones), whereas the local activity that the CSA targets (in this case cultivation and possession of marijuana for personal medicinal use) cannot be separated from the general drug control scheme of which it is a part.

Today's decision allows Congress to regulate intrastate activity without check, so long as there is some implication by legislative design that regulating intrastate activity is [necessary] to the interstate regulatory scheme.... If the Court is right, then *Lopez* stands for nothing more than a drafting guide: Congress should have described the relevant crime as "transfer or possession of a firearm anywhere in the nation"—thus including commercial and noncommercial activity, and clearly encompassing some activity with assuredly substantial effect on interstate commerce. Had it done so, the majority hints, we would have sustained its authority to regulate possession of firearms in school zones....

I cannot agree that our decision in *Lopez* contemplated such evasive or overbroad legislative strategies with approval.... If the Court always defers to Congress as it does today, little may be left to the notion of enumerated powers.

The hard work for courts, then, is to identify objective markers for confining the analysis in Commerce Clause cases. Here, respondents challenge the constitutionality of the CSA as applied to them and those similarly situated. I agree with the Court that we must look beyond respondents' own activities. Otherwise, individual litigants could always exempt themselves from Commerce Clause regulation merely by pointing to the obvious—that their personal activities do not have a substantial effect on interstate commerce. The task is to identify a mode of analysis that allows Congress to regulate more than nothing (by declining to reduce each case to its litigants) and less than everything (by declining to let Congress set the terms of analysis)....

A number of objective markers are available to confine the scope of constitutional review here. Both federal and state legislation—including the CSA itself, the California Compassionate Use Act, and other state medical marijuana legislation—recognize that medical and nonmedical (*i.e.*, recreational) uses of drugs are realistically distinct and can be segregated, and regulate them differently. Respondents challenge only the application of the CSA to medicinal use of marijuana. Moreover, because fundamental structural concerns about dual sovereignty animate our Commerce Clause cases, it is relevant that this case involves the interplay of federal and state regulation in areas of criminal law and social policy, where "States lay claim by right of history and expertise." . . . To ascertain whether Congress' encroachment is constitutionally justified in this case, then, I would focus here on the personal cultivation, possession, and use of marijuana for medicinal purposes.

B

Having thus defined the relevant conduct, we must determine whether, under our precedents, the conduct is economic and, in the aggregate, substantially affects interstate commerce. . . .

The Court's definition of economic activity is breathtaking. It defines as economic any activity involving the production, distribution, and consumption of commodities. And it appears to reason that when an interstate market for a commodity exists, regulating the intrastate manufacture or possession of that commodity is constitutional either because that intrastate activity is itself economic, or because regulating it is a rational part of regulating its market. Putting to one side the problem endemic to the Court's opinion—the shift in focus from the activity at issue in this case to the entirety of what the CSA regulates— the Court's definition of economic activity for purposes of Commerce Clause jurisprudence threatens to sweep all of productive human activity into federal regulatory reach.

The Court uses a dictionary definition of economics to skirt the real problem of drawing a meaningful line between "what is national and what is local." It will not do to say that Congress may regulate noncommercial activity simply because it may have an effect on the demand for commercial goods, or because the noncommercial endeavor can, in some sense, substitute for commercial activity. Most commercial goods or services have some sort of privately producible analogue. Home care substitutes for daycare. Charades games substitute for movie tickets. Backyard or windowsill gardening substitutes for going to the supermarket. To draw the line wherever private activity affects the demand for market goods is to draw no line at all, and to declare everything economic. We have already rejected the result that would follow—a federal police power.

In *Lopez* and *Morrison*, we suggested that economic activity usually relates directly to commercial activity. The homegrown cultivation and personal possession and use of marijuana for medicinal purposes has no apparent commercial character. Everyone agrees that the marijuana at issue in this case was never in the stream of commerce, and neither were the supplies for growing it. . . . *Lopez* makes clear that possession is not itself commercial activity. And respondents have not come into possession by means of any commercial transaction; they have simply grown, in their own homes, marijuana for their own use, without acquiring, buying, selling, or bartering a thing of value.

The Court suggests that *Wickard* . . . established federal regulatory power over any home consumption of a commodity for which a national market exists. I disagree. *Wickard* involved a challenge to the Agricultural Adjustment Act of 1938 (AAA), which directed the Secretary of Agriculture to set national quotas on wheat production, and penalties for excess production. The AAA itself confirmed that Congress made an explicit choice not to reach—and thus the Court could not possibly have approved of federal control over—small-scale, noncommercial wheat farming. In contrast to the CSA's limitless assertion of power, Congress provided an exemption within the AAA for small producers. When Filburn planted the wheat at issue in *Wickard*, the statute exempted plantings less than 200 bushels (about six tons), and when he harvested his wheat it exempted plantings less than six acres. *Wickard,* then, did not extend Commerce Clause authority to something as modest as the home cook's herb garden. This is not to say that Congress may never regulate small quantities of commodities possessed or produced for personal use, or to deny that it sometimes needs to enact a zero tolerance regime for such commodities. It is merely to say that *Wickard* did not hold or imply that small-scale production of commodities is always economic, and automatically within Congress' reach.

Even assuming that economic activity is at issue in this case, the Government has made no showing in fact that the possession and use of homegrown marijuana for medical purposes, in California or elsewhere, has a substantial effect on interstate commerce. Similarly, the Government has not shown that regulating such activity is necessary to an interstate regulatory scheme. Whatever the specific theory of "substantial effects" at issue . . . a concern for dual sovereignty requires that Congress' excursion into the traditional domain of States be justified.

That is why characterizing this as a case about the Necessary and Proper Clause does not change the analysis significantly. Congress must exercise its authority under the Necessary and Proper Clause in a manner consistent . . . with the notion of enumerated powers—a structural principle that is as much part of the Constitution as the Tenth Amendment's explicit textual command. Accordingly, something more than mere assertion is required when Congress purports to have power over local activity whose connection to an intrastate market is not self-evident. Otherwise, the Necessary and Proper Clause will always be a back door for unconstitutional federal regulation. Indeed, if it were enough in "substantial effects" cases for the Court to supply conceivable justifications for intrastate regulation related to an interstate market, then we could have surmised in *Lopez* that guns in school zones are "never more than an instant from the interstate market" in guns already subject to extensive federal regulation, recast *Lopez* as a Necessary and Proper Clause case, and thereby upheld the Gun-Free School Zones Act of 1990. (According to the Court's and the concurrence's logic, for example, the *Lopez* court should have reasoned that the prohibition on gun possession in school zones could be an appropriate means of effectuating a related prohibition on "selling" or "delivering" firearms or ammunition to "any individual who the licensee knows or has reasonable cause to believe is less than eighteen years of age." 18 U.S.C. § 922(b)(1).)

There is simply no evidence that homegrown medicinal marijuana users constitute, in the aggregate, a sizable enough class to have a discernable, let alone substantial, impact on the national illicit drug market—or otherwise to threaten the CSA regime. Explicit evidence is helpful when substantial effect is not "visible to the naked eye." And here, in part because common sense suggests that medical marijuana users may be limited in number and that California's Compassionate Use Act and similar state legislation may well isolate activities relating to medicinal marijuana from the illicit market, the effect of those activities on interstate drug traffic is not self-evidently substantial.

In this regard, again, this case is readily distinguishable from *Wickard*. To decide whether the Secretary could regulate local wheat farming, the Court looked to "the actual effects of the activity in question upon interstate commerce." Critically, the Court was able to consider "actual effects" because the parties had "stipulated a summary of the economics of the wheat industry." After reviewing in detail the picture of the industry provided in that summary, the Court explained that consumption of homegrown wheat was the most variable factor in the size of the national wheat crop, and that on-site consumption could have the effect of varying the amount of wheat sent to market by as much as 20 percent. With real numbers at hand, the *Wickard* Court could easily conclude that "a factor of such volume and variability as home-consumed wheat would have a substantial influence on price and market conditions" nationwide.

The Court recognizes that "the record in the *Wickard* case itself established the causal connection between the production for local use and the national market" and argues that "we have before us findings by Congress *to the same effect*." The Court refers to a series of declarations in the introduction to the CSA saying that (1) local distribution and possession of controlled substances causes "swelling" in interstate traffic; (2) local production and distribution cannot be distinguished from interstate production and distribution; (3) federal control over intrastate incidents "is essential to effective control" over interstate drug trafficking. These bare declarations . . . amount to nothing more than a legislative insistence that the regulation of controlled substances must be absolute. They are asserted without any supporting evidence— descriptive, statistical, or otherwise. "Simply because Congress may conclude a particular activity substantially affects interstate commerce does not necessarily make it so." Indeed, if declarations like these suffice to justify federal regulation, and if the Court today is right about what passes rationality review before us, then our decision in *Morrison* should have come out the other way. . . .

In particular, the CSA's introductory declarations are too vague and unspecific to demonstrate that the federal statutory scheme will be undermined if Congress cannot exert power over individuals like respondents. The declarations are not even specific to marijuana. . . . Because here California, like other States, has carved out a limited class of activity for distinct regulation, the inadequacy of the CSA's findings is especially glaring. The California Compassionate Use Act exempts from other state drug laws patients and their caregivers "who possess or cultivate marijuana for the *personal* medical purposes of the patient upon the written or oral recommendation of a physician" to treat a list of serious medical conditions. The Act specifies that it should not be construed to supersede legislation prohibiting persons from engaging in acts dangerous to others, or to condone the diversion of marijuana for nonmedical purposes. To promote the Act's operation and to facilitate law enforcement, California recently enacted an identification card system for qualified patients. We generally assume States enforce their laws, and have no reason to think otherwise here.

The Government has not overcome empirical doubt that the number of Californians engaged in personal cultivation, possession, and use of medical marijuana, or the amount of marijuana they produce, is enough to threaten the federal regime. Nor has it shown that Compassionate Use Act marijuana users have been or are realistically likely to be responsible for the drug's seeping into the market in a significant way. The Government does cite one estimate that there were over 100,000 Compassionate Use Act users in California in 2004, but does not explain, in terms of proportions, what their presence means for the national illicit drug market. It also provides anecdotal evidence about the CSA's enforcement. The Court also offers some arguments about the effect of the Compassionate Use Act on the national market. It says that the California statute might be vulnerable to exploitation by unscrupulous physicians, that Compassionate Use Act patients may overproduce, and that the history of the narcotics trade shows the difficulty of cordoning off any drug use from the rest of the market. These arguments are plausible; if borne out in fact they could justify prosecuting Compassionate Use Act patients under the federal CSA. But, without substantiation, they add little to the CSA's conclusory statements about diversion, essentiality, and market effect. Piling assertion upon assertion does not, in my view, satisfy the substantiality test of *Lopez* and *Morrison*.

III

We would do well to recall how James Madison . . . described our system of joint sovereignty to the people of New York: "The powers delegated by the proposed constitution to the federal government are few and defined. Those which are to remain in the State governments are numerous and indefinite. . . . The powers reserved to the several States will extend to all the objects which, in the ordinary course of affairs, concern the lives, liberties, and properties of the people, and the internal order, improvement, and prosperity of the State."

Relying on Congress' abstract assertions, the Court has endorsed making it a federal crime to grow small amounts of marijuana in one's own home for one's own medicinal use. This overreaching stifles an express choice by some States, concerned for the lives and liberties of their people, to regulate medical marijuana differently. If I were a California citizen, I would not have voted for the medical marijuana ballot initiative; if I were a California legislator I would not have supported the Compassionate Use Act. But whatever the wisdom of California's experiment with medical marijuana, the federalism principles that have driven our Commerce Clause cases require that room for experiment be protected in this case. For these reasons I dissent.

■ JUSTICE THOMAS, dissenting.

. . . Even assuming the CSA's ban on locally cultivated and consumed marijuana is "necessary," that does not mean it is also "proper." The means selected by Congress to regulate interstate commerce cannot be "prohibited" by, or inconsistent with the "letter and spirit" of, the Constitution. *McCulloch*. . . . If the Federal Government can regulate growing a half-dozen cannabis plants for personal consumption . . . then Congress' Article I powers—as expanded by the Necessary and Proper Clause—have no meaningful limits. . . .

The majority's treatment of the substantial effects test is malleable, because the majority expands the relevant conduct. . . .

The substantial effects test is easily manipulated for another reason. This Court has never held that Congress can regulate noneconomic activity that substantially affects interstate commerce. To evade even that modest restriction on federal power, the majority defines economic activity in the broadest possible terms as the "'the production, distribution, and consumption of commodities.'" (quoting Webster's Third New International Dictionary 720 (1966) (hereinafter Webster's 3d). . . . [E]ven a Court interested more in the modern than the original understanding of the Constitution ought to resolve cases based on the meaning of words that are actually in the document. Congress is authorized to regulate "Commerce," and respondents' conduct does not qualify under any definition of that term. The majority's opinion only illustrates the steady drift away from the text of the Commerce Clause. There is an inexorable expansion from "'commerce,'" to "commercial" and "economic" activity, and finally to all "production, distribution, and consumption" of goods or services for which there is an "established . . . interstate market." Federal power expands, but never contracts, with each new locution. The majority is not interpreting the Commerce Clause, but rewriting it.

The majority's rewriting of the Commerce Clause seems to be rooted in the belief that, unless the Commerce Clause covers the entire web of human activity, Congress will be left powerless to regulate the national economy effectively. The interconnectedness of economic activity is not a modern phenomenon unfamiliar to the Framers. Moreover, the Framers understood what the majority does not appear to fully appreciate: There is a danger to concentrating too much, as well as too little, power in the Federal Government. This Court has carefully avoided stripping Congress of its ability to regulate *inter*state commerce, but it has casually allowed the Federal Government to strip States of their ability to regulate *intra*state commerce—not to mention a host of local activities, like mere drug possession, that are not commercial.

One searches the Court's opinion in vain for any hint of what aspect of American life is reserved to the States. Yet this Court knows that " 'the Constitution created a Federal Government of limited powers.' " That is why today's decision will add no measure of stability to our Commerce Clause jurisprudence: This Court is willing neither to enforce limits on federal power, nor to declare the Tenth Amendment a dead letter. If stability is possible, it is only by discarding the stand-alone substantial effects test and revisiting our definition of "Commerce among the several States." . . .

Our federalist system, properly understood, allows California and a growing number of other States to decide for themselves how to safeguard the health and welfare of their citizens. I would affirm the judgment of the Court of Appeals. I respectfully dissent.

NOTE ON *RAICH* AND THE FUTURE OF THE COMMERCE CLAUSE

1.   One frequent criticism of *Lopez* and *Morrison* was that a politically-conservative majority (Rehnquist, O'Connor, Scalia, Kennedy, and Thomas) was striking down politically-liberal federal laws (gun control, protecting women from violence and sexual assault). It is, of course, possible to quibble with this description: For example, query whether a conservative like Justice O'Connor is even plausibly "pro" violence against women. But this hypothesis that the Rehnquist Court's Commerce Clause decisions were really a mask for the majority's conservative political preferences received a boost in *Gonzales v. Raich*, when the Court did an about-face and upheld a federal law shutting down a politically liberal social experiment with medical marijuana. Does this prove that the political charge is true? Does it matter, in considering this question, whether you think of "the Court" in the aggregate or evaluate the stand of individual justices?[19]

---

[19]   On the significance of *Raich* and the possibility that the Court's federalism decisions are motivated by political preferences, *compare* Peter J. Smith, *Federalism, Instrumentalism, and the Legacy of the Rehnquist Court*, 74 GEO. WASH. L. REV. 906 (2006) (spreading the heresy that it's all politics), *with* Ernest A. Young, *Just Blowing Smoke? Politics, Doctrine, and the Federalist Revival after* Gonzales v. Raich, 2005 SUP. CT. REV. 1 (keeping the faith).

More fundamentally, is it ever really possible to disentangle views about federalism from views about the underlying policy? Is it realistic, for instance, to expect people to oppose a federal law doing something they favor, simply because it is being done at the federal level? Should we expect controversies over Congress's power to regulate guns or marijuana to always reduce to views about those policy issues, not about the Commerce Clause?[20]

2.   Part of the debate among the justices in *Raich* involves the important distinction between "facial" and "as-applied" challenges. This distinction plays an important role throughout constitutional law. A "facial" challenge to a law contends that the law is unconstitutional in its entirety— that is, that there are no circumstances in which the law might be applied in a way that did not violate the Constitution. An "as-applied" challenge contends only that the law is unconstitutional under the particular circumstances of the case before the court; it does not ask the court to take a position on whether the law might be unconstitutional in other circumstances. Consider, for example, a general law against setting fires. That statute might be unconstitutional as applied to someone torching an American flag as part of a political protest; it is easy to imagine, however, that many—surely, most—of the law's applications to other acts of arson would raise no constitutional objections whatsoever. The law would therefore survive a *facial* challenge even if it could not survive an as-applied challenge brought by the flag-burner.

The Justices have sometimes disagreed about the proper standard for resolving facial challenge, but it is clear that facial challenges are difficult to win. The reason is that a facial challenge must show that *all*, or at least a very large proportion, of a statute's applications are unconstitutional, whereas an as-applied challenge must prove simply that the statute is unconstitutional in its application to the case before the court. In *Raich*, it is easy to see why the Controlled Substances Act would survive a *facial* challenge under the Commerce Clause: On any view of that Clause's scope, applying the CSA to interstate, for-profit drug sales would be clearly constitutional.

The harder question is whether the *Raich* plaintiffs should be allowed to challenge the CSA as applied only to the particular activity in which they are engaged—that is, the non-commercial, home-grown production and consumption of marijuana for medicinal purposes inside a single state. The majority rejects that view of the matter, refusing to "carve out" particular subsets of the broad class of activities that Congress chose to regulate in the CSA. Can this refusal be justified? After all, as the dissenters point out, the Court generally prefers to evaluate as-applied claims rather than facial ones, because the latter ordinarily require the Court to consider hypothetical situations and applications of the challenged law that are not actually before the Court. Would allowing plaintiffs to challenge Commerce Clause statutes as applied to their own particular conduct resolve one of the central

---

[20] For an effort to answer this question empirically, see Robert A. Mikos & Cindy D. Kam, *Do Citizens Care About Federalism? An Experimental Test*, 4 J. EMP. LEG. STUD. 589 (2007) (finding that preferences for national or state action *do* make a difference to many people).

difficulties in *Raich*, which was determining the correct level of generality at which to define the activity being regulated?

3.   In *Lopez*, the majority noted that the Gun Free School Zones Act was "not an essential part of a larger regulation of economic activity, in which the regulatory scheme could be undercut unless the intrastate activity were regulated." This language became a central focus of debate in *Raich*, because the Government claimed that regulating non-commercial production and consumption of marijuana was an "essential part" of the larger regulation of the commercial market. What is the constitutional basis for national regulation that extends beyond interstate commerce? In *Raich*, Justice Scalia thought such regulation best justified under the Necessary and Proper Clause. To what extent should the Government's assertion that some noncommercial regulation is "necessary" to facilitate commercial regulation itself be subject to judicial review? Should the Court have required the Government to introduce actual evidence to support that point? Or should it apply a mere rationality standard? If it takes the latter course, is there any means left for the Court to prevent the complete erosion of limits on the Commerce Power?

4.   The Court's decision in *Raich* did not prevent a large number of states from following California in legalizing medicinal marijuana use. As of late 2016, twenty-six states permitted such states, with three more preparing to follow suit in the wake of ballot measures approved in the most recent election. Even more strikingly, Colorado legalized *recreational* marijuana use in 2012, and since then Alaska, California, Maine, Massachusetts, Nevada, Oregon, Washington, and the District of Columbia have all adopted similar measures.[21] These changes to state law cannot, of course, change the fact that marijuana remains illegal under the federal Controlled Substances Act. Nonetheless, legalization for purposes of state law has been terribly important as a practical matter:

> [S]tate marijuana laws provide the basis for nearly every marijuana arrest in the country. Since the CSA's implementation more than 40 years ago, nearly all marijuana enforcement in the United States has taken place at the state level. For example, of the nearly 900,000 marijuana arrests in 2012, arrests made at the state and local level dwarfed those made by federal officials by a ratio of 109 to 1.[22]

These enforcement patterns—and the limitations on federal enforcement resources they reflect—mean that individual users, at least, can most likely treat marijuana as legal in states that have repealed state-level prohibitions, even though federal prohibitions remain in force. That is because, under the anti-commandeering doctrine, the Constitution prohibits Congress from requiring state officials to force federal law. *See* Section 10.2, *infra*. Does this state of affairs allow states like Colorado to effectively nullify

---

[21] Whether the local government of the District of Columbia has the power to legalize marijuana in the teeth of opposition from Congress—which has plenary power to govern D.C. under Art. I, § 8, cl. 17—remains contested as this edition goes to press.

[22] Erwin Chemerinsky, Jolene Forman, Allen Hopper, & Sam Kamin, *Cooperative Federalism and Marijuana Regulation*, 62 UCLA L. REV. 74, 84 (2015).

federal law, much as South Carolina tried to nullify the federal tariff in the early nineteenth century?

The situation is more complicated for people and businesses who wish to produce and distribute marijuana in legalizing states. These persons may remain a worthwhile target for limited federal enforcement resources. However, the Obama Justice Department issued a series of memoranda indicating that it would generally forbear enforcement activities against persons engaged in the marijuana business so long as they were in compliance with state law. [23] Was this an appropriate exercise of prosecutorial discretion, given Congress's failure to amend the Controlled Substances Act? Is it appropriate to have federal criminal laws that are enforced in some states but not others? Or do the federal executive waivers reflect appropriate deference to political choices made by the States? More generally, what do these post-*Raich* developments tell you about the importance of political pressure and federal resource constraints as safeguards of federalism?[24]

5.   The Court revisited the Necessary and Proper Clause in *United States v. Comstock*, 560 U.S. 126 (2010), which considered a provision of the Adam Walsh Child Safety and Protection Act of 2006. The Act allowed a district court to order the civil commitment of a mentally ill, sexually dangerous federal prisoner beyond the date he would otherwise be released. The Court of Appeals had held that Congress lacked any enumerated power to hold someone after they had finished their sentence for violating some other federal law, simply because the person was sexually dangerous. Justice Breyer's opinion for the Court rejected that reasoning based on "five considerations":

> (1)   the breadth of the Necessary and Proper Clause, (2) the long history of federal involvement in this arena, (3) the sound reasons for the statute's enactment in light of the Government's custodial interest in safeguarding the public from dangers posed by those in federal custody, (4) the statute's accommodation of state interests, and (5) the statute's narrow scope. Taken together, these considerations lead us to conclude that the statute is a "necessary and proper" means of exercising the federal authority that permits Congress to create federal criminal laws, to punish their violation, to imprison violators, to provide appropriately for those imprisoned, and to maintain the security of those who are not imprisoned but who may be affected by the federal imprisonment of others.

Justices Kennedy and Alito both wrote separately to stress that the Constitution requires a substantial link between an enumerated end and the unenumerated means Congress employs to reach that end and that the courts should review that connection with some care.

---

[23] *See* James M. Cole, Deputy Attorney General, U.S. Department of Justice, *Memorandum for All United States Attorneys: Guidance Regarding Marijuana Enforcement* (August 29, 2013).

[24] On the issues canvassed in this note, *see generally Symposium: Marijuana, Federal Power and the States*, 65 CASE W. RES. L. REV. 505 (2015).

What is the line beyond which the link between a statutory means and a constitutionally prescribed end becomes too attenuated? Is it even possible to draw such a line? Consider, for instance, that Congress has the power to create certain criminal offenses (e.g., mail fraud) under its Commerce Power. It then relies on the Necessary and Proper Clause to create federal prosecutors to prosecute such offenses, and federal prisons to house those convicted. The question in *Comstock* was whether Congress could take the additional step of preventing persons released from federal custody from harming the public. How many steps past the initial enumerated end are too many?

Was Justice Thomas right, dissenting in *Comstock*, to say that "the Court endorses the precise abuse of power Article I is designed to prevent— the use of a limited grant of authority as a 'pretext . . . for the accomplishment of objects not intrusted to the government'"? (citing *McCulloch*).

6.   In *National Federation of Independent Business v. Sebelius*, 567 U.S. 519 (2012), the Court upheld a provision of the federal Patient Protection and Affordable Care Act (ACA) requiring most Americans to purchase health insurance. Chief Justice Roberts, joined on this point by Justices Ginsburg, Breyer, Sotomayor, and Kagan, upheld this "individual mandate" as a valid exercise of Congress's *taxing* power. *See infra* Section 9.3. But the Chief Justice, now supported by Justices Scalia, Kennedy, Thomas, and Alito, rejected attempts to justify the mandate under the Commerce and Necessary and Proper Clauses.

The Government argued that the mandate addressed two problems raised by the ACA's effort to ensure near-universal health insurance coverage for Americans. First, because federal law requires hospitals to provide care even to the uninsured, individuals have incentives to "free ride" on this provision by not buying insurance of their own. Second, because the ACA required insurance companies to offer health insurance to all without regard to preexisting health conditions and to charge the same premiums to healthy and unhealthy individuals, insurers would suffer unacceptable losses unless healthy individuals could be induced to be part of the risk pool by buying insurance. Accepting the soundness of these policy arguments, the Chief Justice nonetheless rejected the notion that they supported Congress's authority:

> The individual mandate . . . does not regulate existing commercial activity. It instead compels individuals to become active in commerce by purchasing a product, on the ground that their failure to do so affects interstate commerce. . . . Allowing Congress to justify federal regulation by pointing to the effect of inaction on commerce would bring countless decisions an individual could potentially make within the scope of federal regulation, and— under the Government's theory—empower Congress to make those decisions for him.

In dissent on this point, Justice Ginsburg found the Chief's argument "difficult to fathom." "Requiring individuals to obtain insurance," she observed, "unquestionably regulates the interstate health-insurance and health-care markets, both of them in existence well before the enactment of the ACA." She also rejected "the activity versus inactivity line," noting that "[t]his Court's former endeavors to impose categorical limits on the commerce power have not fared well." And she suggested that "[a]t bottom, the Chief Justice's and the joint dissenters' view that an individual cannot be subject to Commerce Clause regulation absent voluntary, affirmative acts that enter him or her into, or affect, the interstate market expresses a concern for individual liberty that [is] more redolent of Due Process Clause arguments." Is Justice Ginsburg right that the Chief Justice's distinction between activity and inactivity is incoherent and unworkable? Is it really a *Lochner*-esque economic liberty argument in disguise—e.g., a freedom *not* to contract? On the other hand, can Ginsburg offer a good limiting principle on Congress's power to *create* commerce as a predicate to regulating it?

The Chief Justice and the four dissenting conservatives likewise rejected the argument that the individual mandate, if not a valid regulation of commerce in itself, was necessary and proper to Congress's broader regulatory scheme. That broader scheme, after all, regulated the purchase and sale of health insurance—unquestionably a commercial activity. Quoting *McCulloch*, the Chief Justice noted that "[a]lthough the [Necessary and Proper] Clause gives Congress authority to 'legislate on that vast mass of incidental powers which must be involved in the constitution,' it does not license the exercise of any 'great substantive and independent power[s]' beyond those specifically enumerated." The mandate involved the latter sort of power because it was not "narrow in scope" or " 'incidental' to the exercise of the commerce power." If the mandate was valid, moreover, Congress could reach beyond the natural limit of its authority and draw within its regulatory scope those who otherwise would be outside of it." Hence, "[e]ven if the individual mandate is 'necessary' to the Act's insurance reforms, such an expansion of federal power is not a 'proper' means for making those reforms effective."

Justice Ginsburg responded that the Court had never previously held a federal statute "improper," outside the narrow context of the anti-commandeering doctrine.[25] And she noted that the Court had upheld very broad instances of implied powers, such as the "power to enact criminal laws; the power to imprison, including civil imprisonment; and the power to create a national bank." Further, Ginsburg observed that the mandate "addresses the very sort of interstate problem that made the commerce power essential in our federal system. The crisis created by the large number of U.S. residents who lack health insurance is one of national dimension that States are separately incompetent to handle."[26]

Does McCulloch support Chief Justice Roberts' effort to tighten up the Necessary and Proper analysis? Can that be done without threatening a vast array of federal laws and programs? If, on the other hand, Justice Ginsburg

---

[25] *See* Section 10.2, *infra*.

[26] On this point, see Neil S. Siegel, *Free-Riding on Benevolence: Collective Action Federalism and the Minimum Coverage Provision*, 75 L. & CONTEMP. PROBS 29 (2012).

is right that federal action is "proper" anytime one can identify a collective action problem impeding action by individual states, is there any limit to federal power?

More broadly, how important is the holding of the Chief Justice plus the four conservative dissenters on the Commerce and Necessary and Proper Clauses? Although the Chief Justice argued that resolving these questions was necessary in order to reach his holding on the Taxing Power,[27] should his discussion be regarded as dictum since the Court went on to uphold the individual mandate? Moreover, given the rarity of federal mandates requiring unwilling individuals to participate in commerce, is the holding on this point likely to affect many other federal laws?

7.   Do the limits of Congress's enumerated powers, and the corresponding reserved powers of the States, operate indirectly when federal legislation is challenged on the ground that it violates constitutional principles of individual rights? Consider the federal Defense of Marriage Act (DOMA), enacted by Congress in 1996, which defined marriage as exclusively between a man and a woman for purposes of federal law. *United States v. Windsor*, 133 S. Ct. 2675 (2013), involved an equal protection challenge to DOMA by Edith Windsor, the widow of Thea Spyer, whom she had married in Toronto in 2007. The couple lived in New York, which recognized same-sex marriages solemnized in other jurisdictions; later on, New York explicitly legalized same-sex marriage by statute. But when Spyer died in 2009, the federal Internal Revenue Service refused to acknowledge Windsor as a surviving spouse entitled to exemption from federal estate tax, assessing an estate tax of $363,053.

The Supreme Court struck down the DOMA on equal protection grounds, as applicable to the United States by way of the Fifth Amendment's Due Process Clause. But Justice Kennedy's opinion, joined by Justices Ginsburg, Breyer, Sotomayor, and Kagan, heavily emphasized principles of federalism. He began his analysis by noting that "regulation of domestic relations is an area that has long been regarded as a virtually exclusive province of the States, and "[t]he definition of marriage is the foundation of the State's broader authority to regulate the subject of domestic relations with respect to the protection of offspring, property interests, and the enforcement of marital responsibilities." Critically, the Court said that New York's decision to recognize same-sex couples' right to marry "conferred upon them a dignity and status of immense import. When the State used its historic and essential authority to define the marital relation in this way, its role and its power in making the decision enhanced the recognition, dignity, and protection of the class in their own community."

Did *Windsor* hold that, whether or not same-sex marriage is a fundamental right in some abstract sense, state law had the power to make it so for purposes of equal protection analysis? Would that be so different from the states' ability to define property rights, which in turn trigger

---

[27]   *See infra* Section 9.3.

heightened protection under the Fourth Amendment and the Due Process Clause? Is there any limit to the state's power to "fundamentalize" rights?

The Windsor Court also rejected arguments, tendered by DOMA's defenders, that "the federal government has the same latitude as the states to adopt its own definition of marriage for federal-law purposes." Justice Kennedy treated this alleged interest as illegitimate, suggesting that Congress may not "put a thumb on the scales and influence a state's decision as to how to shape its own marriage laws." Ordinarily, federal law takes state family law as it finds it; it recognizes whatever marriages state law permits. Do you see how a specific *federal* definition of marriage might interfere with the state's own administration of its marriage laws? Is the asserted federal interest illegitimate because Congress lacks power to simply establish a nationally-uniform definition of marriage? What about the immigration anti-fraud statute, which refuses to recognize—for purposes of admitting persons to the country—marriages entered into solely for the purposes of immigration? Is that provision similarly vulnerable? Does the Court's invocation of marriage as a traditional area of state authority harken back to the old pre-1937 regime of "dual federalism"?[28]

See also: For recent analyses of the Commerce Clause and the scope of Congress's Article I, § 8 powers generally, see respectively Jack M. Balkin, *Commerce*, 109 MICH. L. REV. 1 (2010), and Robert D. Cooter & Neil S. Siegel, *Collective Action Federalism: A General Theory of Article I, Section 8*, 63 STAN. L. REV. 115 (2010).

SECTION 9.2   CONGRESS'S POWER TO ENFORCE THE RECONSTRUCTION AMENDMENTS

We have already explored how the Reconstruction Congress was suspicious of judicial power and, accordingly, entrusted itself with the primary authority to enforce the Thirteenth, Fourteenth, and Fifteenth Amendments. The *Civil Rights Cases*, in Chapter Four, involved one important limit on that enforcement power: Because the Fourteenth and Fifteenth Amendments apply only to state action, Congress's enforcement authority is likewise limited to addressing action by public authorities.

The cases that follow involve another aspect of Congress's enforcement power: the scope of that power when Congress and the Court disagree about the meaning of the Fourteenth Amendment's rights provisions. In *Katzenbach v. Morgan*, Congress sought to ban literacy tests for voting even though the Supreme Court had already held that such tests do not violate the Equal Protection Clause. In *City of Boerne v. Flores*, Congress sought to restore a high standard of justification for laws burdening the free exercise of religion, notwithstanding that the Court had overruled that test in a recent case. These cases implicate

---

[28] On the federalism arguments in *Windsor*, *see generally* Ernest A. Young & Erin C. Blondel, *Federalism, Liberty, and Equality in* United States v. Windsor, 2012 CATO SUP. CT. REV. 117 (2013).

longstanding debates about the allocation of interpretive authority that we began exploring in connection with *Cooper v. Aaron* in Chapter Six. As you read the opinions here, consider the extent to which the theories of judicial supremacy, legislative supremacy, and departmentalism might bear on the Section Five debate.

Katzenbach v. Morgan
384 U.S. 641 (1966)

■ MR. JUSTICE BRENNAN delivered the opinion of the Court.

These cases concern the constitutionality of § 4(e) of the Voting Rights Act of 1965. That law, in the respects pertinent in these cases, provides that no person who has successfully completed the sixth primary grade in a public school in, or a private school accredited by, the Commonwealth of Puerto Rico in which the language of instruction was other than English shall be denied the right to vote in any election because of his inability to read or write English. Appellees, registered voters in New York City, brought this suit to challenge the constitutionality of § 4(e) insofar as it *pro tanto* prohibits the enforcement of the election laws of New York requiring an ability to read and write English as a condition of voting. Under these laws many of the several hundred thousand New York City residents who have migrated there from the Commonwealth of Puerto Rico had previously been denied the right to vote, and appellees attack § 4(e) insofar as it would enable many of these citizens to vote. . . . We hold that, in the application challenged in these cases, § 4(e) is a proper exercise of the powers granted to Congress by § 5 of the Fourteenth Amendment. . . .

Under the distribution of powers effected by the Constitution, the States establish qualifications for voting for state officers, and the qualifications established by the States for voting for members of the most numerous branch of the state legislature also determine who may vote for United States Representatives and Senators. But, of course, the States have no power to grant or withhold the franchise on conditions that are forbidden by the Fourteenth Amendment, or any other provision of the Constitution. . . .

The Attorney General of the State of New York argues that an exercise of congressional power under § 5 of the Fourteenth Amendment that prohibits the enforcement of a state law can only be sustained if the judicial branch determines that the state law is prohibited by the provisions of the Amendment that Congress sought to enforce. More specifically, he urges that § 4(e) cannot be sustained as appropriate legislation to enforce the Equal Protection Clause unless the judiciary decides . . . that the application of the English literacy requirement prohibited by § 4(e) is forbidden by the Equal Protection Clause itself. We disagree. Neither the language nor history of § 5 supports such a construction. As was said with regard to § 5 in *Ex parte Virginia*, 100

U.S. 339 (1880), "It is the power of Congress which has been enlarged. Congress is authorized to *enforce* the prohibitions by appropriate legislation. Some legislation is contemplated to make the amendments fully effective." A construction of § 5 that would require a judicial determination that the enforcement of the state law precluded by Congress violated the Amendment, as a condition of sustaining the congressional enactment, would depreciate both congressional resourcefulness and congressional responsibility for implementing the Amendment. It would confine the legislative power in this context to the insignificant role of abrogating only those state laws that the judicial branch was prepared to adjudge unconstitutional . . . .

Thus our task in this case is not to determine whether the New York English literacy requirement as applied to deny the right to vote to a person who successfully completed the sixth grade in a Puerto Rican school violates the Equal Protection Clause. Accordingly, our decision in *Lassiter v. Northampton Election Bd.*, 360 U.S. 45 (1959), sustaining the North Carolina English literacy requirement as not in all circumstances prohibited by the first sections of the Fourteenth and Fifteenth Amendments, is inapposite. . . . *Lassiter* did not present the question before us here: Without regard to whether the judiciary would find that the Equal Protection Clause itself nullifies New York's English literacy requirement as so applied, could Congress prohibit the enforcement of the state law by legislating under § 5 of the Fourteenth Amendment? In answering this question, our task is limited to determining whether such legislation is, as required by § 5, appropriate legislation to enforce the Equal Protection Clause.

By including § 5 the draftsmen sought to grant to Congress, by a specific provision applicable to the Fourteenth Amendment, the same broad powers expressed in the Necessary and Proper Clause, Art. I, § 8, cl. 18.[9] The classic formulation of the reach of those powers was established by Chief Justice Marshall in *McCulloch v. Maryland:*

> Let the end be legitimate, let it be within the scope of the constitution, and all means which are appropriate, which are plainly adapted to that end, which are not prohibited, but consist with the letter and spirit of the constitution, are constitutional.

Ex parte Virginia, decided 12 years after the adoption of the Fourteenth Amendment, held that congressional power under § 5 had this same broad scope:

> Whatever legislation is appropriate, that is, adapted to carry out the objects the amendments have in view, whatever tends to

---

[9] In fact, earlier drafts of the proposed Amendment employed the "necessary and proper" terminology to describe the scope of congressional power under the Amendment. The substitution of the "appropriate legislation" formula was never thought to have the effect of diminishing the scope of this congressional power.

enforce submission to the prohibitions they contain, and to secure to all persons the enjoyment of perfect equality of civil rights and the equal protection of the laws against State denial or invasion, if not prohibited, is brought within the domain of congressional power.

. . . Thus the *McCulloch v. Maryland* standard is the measure of what constitutes "appropriate legislation" under § 5 of the Fourteenth Amendment. Correctly viewed, § 5 is a positive grant of legislative power authorizing Congress to exercise its discretion in determining whether and what legislation is needed to secure the guarantees of the Fourteenth Amendment.

We therefore proceed to the consideration whether § 4(e) is "appropriate legislation" to enforce the Equal Protection Clause, that is . . . whether § 4(e) may be regarded as an enactment to enforce the Equal Protection Clause, whether it is "plainly adapted to that end" and whether it is not prohibited by but is consistent with "the letter and spirit of the constitution."[10]

There can be no doubt that § 4(e) may be regarded as an enactment to enforce the Equal Protection Clause. Congress explicitly declared that it enacted § 4 (e) "to secure the rights under the fourteenth amendment of persons educated in American-flag schools in which the predominant classroom language was other than English." The persons referred to include those who have migrated from the Commonwealth of Puerto Rico to New York and who have been denied the right to vote because of their inability to read and write English, and the Fourteenth Amendment rights referred to include those emanating from the Equal Protection Clause. More specifically, § 4(e) may be viewed as a measure to secure for the Puerto Rican community residing in New York nondiscriminatory treatment by government—both in the imposition of voting qualifications and the provision or administration of governmental services, such as public schools, public housing and law enforcement.

Section 4(e) may be readily seen as "plainly adapted" to furthering these aims of the Equal Protection Clause. The practical effect of § 4(e) is to prohibit New York from denying the right to vote to large segments of its Puerto Rican community. Congress has thus prohibited the State from denying to that community the right that is "preservative of all rights." . . . It was for Congress . . . to assess and weigh the various conflicting considerations—the risk or pervasiveness of the discrimination in governmental services, the effectiveness of eliminating the state

---

[10]   Contrary to the suggestion of the dissent, § 5 does not grant Congress power to exercise discretion in the other direction and to enact "statutes so as in effect to dilute equal protection and due process decisions of this Court." We emphasize that Congress' power under § 5 is limited to adopting measures to enforce the guarantees of the Amendment; § 5 grants Congress no power to restrict, abrogate, or dilute these guarantees. Thus, for example, an enactment authorizing the States to establish racially segregated systems of education would not be—as required by § 5—a measure "to enforce" the Equal Protection Clause since that clause of its own force prohibits such state laws.

restriction on the right to vote as a means of dealing with the evil, the adequacy or availability of alternative remedies, and the nature and significance of the state interests that would be affected . . . . It is not for us to review the congressional resolution of these factors. It is enough that we be able to perceive a basis upon which the Congress might resolve the conflict as it did. . . .

The result is no different if we confine our inquiry to the question whether § 4(e) was merely legislation aimed at the elimination of an invidious discrimination in establishing voter qualifications. We are told that New York's English literacy requirement originated in the desire to provide an incentive for non-English speaking immigrants to learn the English language and in order to assure the intelligent exercise of the franchise. Yet Congress might well have questioned, in light of the many exemptions provided, and some evidence suggesting that prejudice played a prominent role in the enactment of the requirement, whether these were actually the interests being served. Congress might have also questioned whether denial of a right deemed so precious and fundamental in our society was a necessary or appropriate means of encouraging persons to learn English, or of furthering the goal of an intelligent exercise of the franchise.

Finally, Congress might well have concluded that as a means of furthering the intelligent exercise of the franchise, an ability to read or understand Spanish is as effective as ability to read English for those to whom Spanish-language newspapers and Spanish-language radio and television programs are available to inform them of election issues and governmental affairs. Since Congress undertook to legislate so as to preclude the enforcement of the state law, and did so in the context of a general appraisal of literacy requirements for voting, to which it brought a specially informed legislative competence, it was Congress' prerogative to weigh these competing considerations. Here again, it is enough that we perceive a basis upon which Congress might predicate a judgment that the application of New York's English literacy requirement to deny the right to vote to a person with a sixth grade education in Puerto Rican schools in which the language of instruction was other than English constituted an invidious discrimination in violation of the Equal Protection Clause. . . .

We therefore conclude that § 4(e), in the application challenged in this case, is appropriate legislation to enforce the Equal Protection Clause and that the judgment of the District Court must be and hereby is

Reversed.

■ MR. JUSTICE HARLAN, whom MR. JUSTICE STEWART joins, dissenting.

. . . The Court declares that since § 5 of the Fourteenth Amendment gives to the Congress power to "enforce" the prohibitions of the

Amendment by "appropriate" legislation, the test for judicial review of any congressional determination in this area is simply one of rationality; that is, in effect, was Congress acting rationally in declaring that the New York statute is irrational? Although § 5 most certainly does give to the Congress wide powers in the field of devising remedial legislation to effectuate the Amendment's prohibition on arbitrary state action, I believe the Court has confused the issue of how much enforcement power Congress possesses under § 5 with the distinct issue of what questions are appropriate for congressional determination and what questions are essentially judicial in nature.

When recognized state violations of federal constitutional standards have occurred, Congress is of course empowered by § 5 to take appropriate remedial measures to redress and prevent the wrongs. But it is a judicial question whether the condition with which Congress has thus sought to deal is in truth an infringement of the Constitution, something that is the necessary prerequisite to bringing the § 5 power into play at all. Thus, in *Ex parte Virginia,* involving a federal statute making it a federal crime to disqualify anyone from jury service because of race, the Court first held as a matter of constitutional law that "the Fourteenth Amendment secures, among other civil rights, to colored men, when charged with criminal offences against a State, an impartial jury trial, by jurors indifferently selected or chosen without discrimination against such jurors because of their color." Only then did the Court hold that to enforce this prohibition upon state discrimination, Congress could enact a criminal statute of the type under consideration. . . .

Section 4(e), however, presents a significantly different type of congressional enactment. The question here is not whether the statute is appropriate remedial legislation to cure an established violation of a constitutional command, but whether there has in fact been an infringement of that constitutional command, that is, whether a particular state practice or, as here, a statute is so arbitrary or irrational as to offend the command of the Equal Protection Clause of the Fourteenth Amendment. That question is one for the judicial branch ultimately to determine. Were the rule otherwise, Congress would be able to qualify this Court's constitutional decisions under the Fourteenth and Fifteenth Amendments, let alone those under other provisions of the Constitution, by resorting to congressional power under the Necessary and Proper Clause. In view of this Court's holding in *Lassiter,* that an English literacy test is a permissible exercise of state supervision over its franchise, I do not think it is open to Congress to limit the effect of that decision as it has undertaken to do by § 4(e). In effect the Court reads § 5 of the Fourteenth Amendment as giving Congress the power to define the *substantive* scope of the Amendment. If that indeed be the true reach of § 5, then I do not see why Congress should not be able as well to exercise its § 5 "discretion" by enacting statutes so as in effect to dilute equal protection and due process decisions of this Court. In all such cases there is room for reasonable men to differ as to whether or not a denial of equal protection or due process has occurred, and the final decision is one of judgment. Until today this judgment has always been one for the judiciary to resolve.

I do not mean to suggest in what has been said that a legislative judgment of the type incorporated in § 4(e) is without any force whatsoever. Decisions on questions of equal protection and due process are based not on abstract logic, but on empirical foundations. To the extent "legislative facts" are relevant to a judicial determination, Congress is well equipped to investigate them, and such determinations are of course entitled to due respect. In *South Carolina v. Katzenbach,* 383 U.S. 301 (1966), such legislative findings were made to show that racial discrimination in voting was actually occurring. Similarly, in *Heart of Atlanta Motel, Inc. v. United States,* 379 U.S. 241 (1964), and *Katzenbach v. McClung,* 379 U.S. 294 (1964), this Court upheld Title II of the Civil Rights Act of 1964 under the Commerce Clause. There again the congressional determination that racial discrimination in a clearly defined group of public accommodations did effectively impede interstate commerce was based on "voluminous testimony," which had been put before the Congress and in the context of which it passed remedial legislation.

But no such factual data provide a legislative record supporting § 4(e) by way of showing that Spanish-speaking citizens are fully as capable of making informed decisions in a New York election as are English-speaking citizens. Nor was there any showing whatever to support the Court's alternative argument that § 4(e) should be viewed as but a remedial measure designed to cure or assure against unconstitutional discrimination of other varieties, *e.g.,* in "public schools, public housing and law enforcement," to which Puerto Rican minorities might be subject in such communities as New York. There is simply no legislative record supporting such hypothesized discrimination of the sort we have hitherto insisted upon when congressional power is brought to bear on constitutionally reserved state concerns.

Thus, we have here not a matter of giving deference to a congressional estimate, based on its determination of legislative facts, bearing upon the validity *vel non* of a statute, but rather what can at most be called a legislative announcement that Congress believes a state law to entail an unconstitutional deprivation of equal protection. Although this kind of declaration is of course entitled to the most respectful consideration, coming as it does from a concurrent branch and one that is knowledgeable in matters of popular political participation, I do not believe it lessens our responsibility to decide the fundamental issue of whether in fact the state enactment violates federal constitutional rights.

In assessing the deference we should give to this kind of congressional expression of policy, it is relevant that the judiciary has always given to congressional enactments a presumption of validity. However, it is also a canon of judicial review that state statutes are given a similar presumption. Whichever way this case is decided, one statute will be rendered inoperative in whole or in part, and although it has been suggested that this Court should give somewhat more deference to Congress than to a state legislature, such a simple weighing of presumptions is hardly a satisfying way of resolving a matter that touches the distribution of state and federal power in an area so sensitive as that of the regulation of the franchise. Rather it should be recognized that while the Fourteenth Amendment is a "brooding omnipresence" over all state legislation, the substantive matters which it touches are all within the primary legislative competence of the States. Federal authority, legislative no less than judicial, does not intrude unless there has been a denial by state action of Fourteenth Amendment limitations, in this instance a denial of equal protection. At least in the area of primary state concern a state statute that passes constitutional muster under the judicial standard of rationality should not be permitted to be set at naught by a mere contrary congressional pronouncement unsupported by a legislative record justifying that conclusion.

To deny the effectiveness of this congressional enactment is not of course to disparage Congress' exertion of authority in the field of civil rights; it is simply to recognize that the Legislative Branch like the other branches of federal authority is subject to the governmental boundaries set by the Constitution. To hold, on this record, that § 4(e) overrides the New York literacy requirement seems to me tantamount to allowing the Fourteenth Amendment to swallow the State's constitutionally ordained primary authority in this field. For if Congress by what, as here, amounts to mere *ipse dixit* can set that otherwise permissible requirement partially at naught I see no reason why it could not also substitute its judgment for that of the States in other fields of their exclusive primary competence as well.

I would affirm the judgments in each of these cases.

City of Boerne v. Flores
521 U.S. 507 (1997)

■ JUSTICE KENNEDY delivered the opinion of the Court.[*]

A decision by local zoning authorities to deny a church a building permit was challenged under the Religious Freedom Restoration Act of 1993 (RFRA), 42 U.S.C. § 2000bb et seq. The case calls into question the authority of Congress to enact RFRA. We conclude the statute exceeds Congress' power.

---

[*]   JUSTICE SCALIA joins all but Part III-A-1 of this opinion.

I

Situated on a hill in the city of Boerne, Texas, some 28 miles northwest of San Antonio, is St. Peter Catholic Church. Built in 1923, the church's structure replicates the mission style of the region's earlier history. The church seats about 230 worshippers, a number too small for its growing parish. Some 40 to 60 parishioners cannot be accommodated at some Sunday masses. In order to meet the needs of the congregation the Archbishop of San Antonio gave permission to the parish to plan alterations to enlarge the building.

A few months later, the Boerne City Council passed an ordinance authorizing the city's Historic Landmark Commission to prepare a preservation plan with proposed historic landmarks and districts. Under the ordinance, the Commission must preapprove construction affecting historic landmarks or buildings in a historic district.

Soon afterwards, the Archbishop applied for a building permit so construction to enlarge the church could proceed. City authorities, relying on the ordinance and the designation of a historic district (which, they argued, included the church), denied the application. The Archbishop brought this suit challenging the permit denial in the United States District Court for the Western District of Texas.

. . . The Archbishop relied upon RFRA as one basis for relief from the refusal to issue the permit. The District Court concluded that by enacting RFRA Congress exceeded the scope of its enforcement power under § 5 of the Fourteenth Amendment. The court certified its order for interlocutory appeal and the Fifth Circuit reversed, finding RFRA to be constitutional. We granted certiorari and now reverse.

II

Congress enacted RFRA in direct response to the Court's decision in *Employment Div., Dept. of Human Resources of Ore. v. Smith,* 494 U.S. 872 (1990). There we considered a Free Exercise Clause claim brought by members of the Native American Church who were denied unemployment benefits when they lost their jobs because they had used peyote. Their practice was to ingest peyote for sacramental purposes, and they challenged an Oregon statute of general applicability which made use of the drug criminal. In evaluating the claim, we declined to apply the balancing test set forth in *Sherbert v. Verner,* 374 U.S. 398 (1963), under which we would have asked whether Oregon's prohibition substantially burdened a religious practice and, if it did, whether the burden was justified by a compelling government interest. We stated:

> Government's ability to enforce generally applicable prohibitions of socially harmful conduct . . . cannot depend on measuring the effects of a governmental action on a religious objector's spiritual development. To make an individual's obligation to obey such a law contingent upon the law's coincidence with his religious beliefs, except where the State's

interest is 'compelling' ... contradicts both constitutional tradition and common sense.

The application of the *Sherbert* test, the *Smith* decision explained, would have produced an anomaly in the law, a constitutional right to ignore neutral laws of general applicability. The anomaly would have been accentuated, the Court reasoned, by the difficulty of determining whether a particular practice was central to an individual's religion. We explained, moreover, that it "is not within the judicial ken to question the centrality of particular beliefs or practices to a faith, or the validity of particular litigants' interpretations of those creeds." ...

Four Members of the Court disagreed. They argued the law placed a substantial burden on the Native American Church members so that it could be upheld only if the law served a compelling state interest and was narrowly tailored to achieve that end. JUSTICE O'CONNOR concluded Oregon had satisfied the test, while Justice Blackmun, joined by Justice Brennan and Justice Marshall, could see no compelling interest justifying the law's application to the members.

These points of constitutional interpretation were debated by Members of Congress in hearings and floor debates. Many criticized the Court's reasoning, and this disagreement resulted in the passage of RFRA. Congress announced:

(1)   The framers of the Constitution, recognizing free exercise of religion as an unalienable right, secured its protection in the First Amendment to the Constitution;

(2)   laws 'neutral' toward religion may burden religious exercise as surely as laws intended to interfere with religious exercise;

(3)   governments should not substantially burden religious exercise without compelling justification;

(4)   in *Employment Division v. Smith*, 494 U.S. 872 (1990), the Supreme Court virtually eliminated the requirement that the government justify burdens on religious exercise imposed by laws neutral toward religion; and

(5)   the compelling interest test as set forth in prior Federal court rulings is a workable test for striking sensible balances between religious liberty and competing prior governmental interests."

The Act's stated purposes are:

(1)   to restore the compelling interest test as set forth in *Sherbert v. Verner*, 374 U.S. 398 (1963) and *Wisconsin v. Yoder*, 406 U.S. 205 (1972) and to guarantee its application in all cases where free exercise of religion is substantially burdened; and

(2) to provide a claim or defense to persons whose religious exercise is substantially burdened by government.

RFRA prohibits "government" from "substantially burdening" a person's exercise of religion even if the burden results from a rule of general applicability unless the government can demonstrate the burden "(1) is in furtherance of a compelling governmental interest; and (2) is the least restrictive means of furthering that compelling governmental interest." The Act's mandate applies to any "branch, department, agency, instrumentality, and official (or other person acting under color of law) of the United States," as well as to any "State, or . . . subdivision of a State." The Act's universal coverage is confirmed in § 2000bb–3(a), under which RFRA "applies to all Federal and State law, and the implementation of that law, whether statutory or otherwise, and whether adopted before or after [RFRA's enactment]." In accordance with RFRA's usage of the term, we shall use "state law" to include local and municipal ordinances.

III

A

Under our Constitution, the Federal Government is one of enumerated powers. The judicial authority to determine the constitutionality of laws, in cases and controversies, is based on the premise that the "powers of the legislature are defined and limited; and that those limits may not be mistaken, or forgotten, the constitution is written." *Marbury v. Madison.*

Congress relied on its Fourteenth Amendment enforcement power in enacting the most far reaching and substantial of RFRA's provisions, those which impose its requirements on the States. . . . The parties disagree over whether RFRA is a proper exercise of Congress' § 5 power "to enforce" by "appropriate legislation" the constitutional guarantee that no State shall deprive any person of "life, liberty, or property, without due process of law" nor deny any person "equal protection of the laws."

In defense of the Act respondent contends, with support from the United States as *amicus*, that RFRA is permissible enforcement legislation. Congress, it is said, is only protecting by legislation one of the liberties guaranteed by the Fourteenth Amendment's Due Process Clause, the free exercise of religion, beyond what is necessary under *Smith.* It is said the congressional decision to dispense with proof of deliberate or overt discrimination and instead concentrate on a law's effects accords with the settled understanding that § 5 includes the power to enact legislation designed to prevent as well as remedy constitutional violations. It is further contended that Congress' § 5 power is not limited to remedial or preventive legislation.

All must acknowledge that § 5 is "a positive grant of legislative power" to Congress. . . . Legislation which deters or remedies constitutional violations can fall within the sweep of Congress' enforcement power even if in the process it prohibits conduct which is not itself unconstitutional and intrudes into "legislative spheres of autonomy previously reserved to the States." For example, the Court upheld a suspension of literacy tests and similar voting requirements under Congress' parallel power to enforce the provisions of the Fifteenth Amendment, as a measure to combat racial discrimination in voting, *South Carolina v. Katzenbach*, 383 U.S. 301 (1966), despite the facial constitutionality of the tests under *Lassiter v. Northampton County Bd. of Elections*, 360 U.S. 45 (1959). We have also concluded that other measures protecting voting rights are within Congress' power to enforce the Fourteenth and Fifteenth Amendments, despite the burdens those measures placed on the States. *Katzenbach v. Morgan* (upholding ban on literacy tests that prohibited certain people schooled in Puerto Rico from voting); *Oregon v. Mitchell*, 400 U.S. 112 (1970) (upholding 5-year nationwide ban on literacy tests and similar voting requirements for registering to vote); *City of Rome v. United States*, 446 U.S. 156, 161 (1980) (upholding 7-year extension of the Voting Rights Act's requirement that certain jurisdictions preclear any change to a " 'standard, practice, or procedure with respect to voting' ").

It is also true, however, that "as broad as the congressional enforcement power is, it is not unlimited." In assessing the breadth of § 5's enforcement power, we begin with its text. Congress has been given the power "to enforce" the "provisions of this article." We agree with respondent, of course, that Congress can enact legislation under § 5 enforcing the constitutional right to the free exercise of religion. The "provisions of this article," to which § 5 refers, include the Due Process Clause of the Fourteenth Amendment. Congress' power to enforce the Free Exercise Clause follows from our holding in *Cantwell v. Connecticut*, 310 U.S. 296 (1940), that the "fundamental concept of liberty embodied in [the Fourteenth Amendment's Due Process Clause] embraces the liberties guaranteed by the First Amendment."

Congress' power under § 5, however, extends only to "enforcing" the provisions of the Fourteenth Amendment. The Court has described this power as "remedial." The design of the Amendment and the text of § 5 are inconsistent with the suggestion that Congress has the power to decree the substance of the Fourteenth Amendment's restrictions on the States. Legislation which alters the meaning of the Free Exercise Clause cannot be said to be enforcing the Clause. Congress does not enforce a constitutional right by changing what the right is. It has been given the power "to enforce," not the power to determine what constitutes a constitutional violation. Were it not so, what Congress would be enforcing would no longer be, in any meaningful sense, the "provisions of [the Fourteenth Amendment]."

While the line between measures that remedy or prevent unconstitutional actions and measures that make a substantive change in the governing law is not easy to discern, and Congress must have wide latitude in determining where it lies, the distinction exists and must be observed. There must be a congruence and proportionality between the injury to be prevented or remedied and the means adopted to that end. Lacking such a connection, legislation may become substantive in operation and effect. History and our case law support drawing the distinction, one apparent from the text of the Amendment.

1

The Fourteenth Amendment's history confirms the remedial, rather than substantive, nature of the Enforcement Clause. The Joint Committee on Reconstruction of the 39th Congress began drafting what would become the Fourteenth Amendment in January 1866. The objections to the Committee's first draft of the Amendment, and the rejection of the draft, have a direct bearing on the central issue of defining Congress' enforcement power. In February, Republican Representative John Bingham of Ohio reported the following draft amendment to the House of Representatives on behalf of the Joint Committee:

> The Congress shall have power to make all laws which shall be necessary and proper to secure to the citizens of each State all privileges and immunities of citizens in the several States, and to all persons in the several States equal protection in the rights of life, liberty, and property.

The proposal encountered immediate opposition, which continued through three days of debate. Members of Congress from across the political spectrum criticized the Amendment, and the criticisms had a common theme: The proposed Amendment gave Congress too much legislative power at the expense of the existing constitutional structure. Democrats and conservative Republicans argued that the proposed Amendment would give Congress a power to intrude into traditional areas of state responsibility, a power inconsistent with the federal design central to the Constitution. Typifying these views, Republican Representative Robert Hale of New York labeled the Amendment "an utter departure from every principle ever dreamed of by the men who framed our Constitution," and warned that under it "all State legislation, in its codes of civil and criminal jurisprudence and procedures . . . may be overridden, may be repealed or abolished, and the law of Congress established instead." Senator William Stewart of Nevada likewise stated the Amendment would permit "Congress to legislate fully upon all subjects affecting life, liberty, and property," such that "there would not be much left for the State Legislatures," and would thereby "work an entire change in our form of government." Some radicals, like their brethren "unwilling that Congress shall have any such power . . . to establish uniform laws throughout the United States upon . . . the protection of life, liberty, and property," also objected that giving Congress primary responsibility for enforcing legal equality would place power in the hands of changing congressional majorities.

As a result of these objections having been expressed from so many different quarters, the House voted to table the proposal until April. The congressional action was seen as marking the defeat of the proposal. The measure was defeated "chiefly because many members of the legal profession saw in [it] . . . a dangerous centralization of power," The Nation, at 291, and "many leading Republicans of the House [of Representatives] would not consent to so radical a change in the Constitution," Cong. Globe, 42d Cong., 1st Sess., App., at 151 (statement of Rep. Garfield). The Amendment in its early form was not again considered. Instead, the Joint Committee began drafting a new article of Amendment, which it reported to Congress on April 30, 1866.

Section 1 of the new draft Amendment imposed self-executing limits on the States. Section 5 prescribed that "the Congress shall have power to enforce, by appropriate legislation, the provisions of this article." Under the revised Amendment, Congress' power was no longer plenary but remedial. Congress was granted the power to make the substantive constitutional prohibitions against the States effective. Representative Bingham said the new draft would give Congress "the power . . . to protect by national law the privileges and immunities of all the citizens of the Republic . . . whenever the same shall be abridged or denied by the unconstitutional acts of any State." Representative Stevens described the new draft Amendment as "allowing Congress to correct the unjust legislation of the States." The revised Amendment proposal did not raise the concerns expressed earlier regarding broad congressional power to prescribe uniform national laws with respect to life, liberty, and property. After revisions not relevant here, the new measure passed both Houses and was ratified in July 1868 as the Fourteenth Amendment. . . .

The design of the Fourteenth Amendment has proved significant also in maintaining the traditional separation of powers between Congress and the Judiciary. The first eight Amendments to the Constitution set forth self-executing prohibitions on governmental action, and this Court has had primary authority to interpret those prohibitions. The Bingham draft, some thought, departed from that tradition by vesting in Congress primary power to interpret and elaborate on the meaning of the new Amendment through legislation. Under it, "Congress, and not the courts, was to judge whether or not any of the privileges or immunities were not secured to citizens in the several States." While this separation of powers aspect did not occasion the widespread resistance which was caused by the proposal's threat to the federal balance, it nonetheless attracted the attention of various Members. As enacted, the Fourteenth Amendment confers substantive rights against the States which, like the provisions of the Bill of Rights, are self-executing. The power to interpret the Constitution in a case or controversy remains in the Judiciary.

2

The remedial and preventive nature of Congress' enforcement power, and the limitation inherent in the power, were confirmed in our earliest cases on the Fourteenth Amendment. In the *Civil Rights Cases*, the Court invalidated sections of the Civil Rights Act of 1875 which prescribed criminal penalties for denying to any person "the full enjoyment of" public accommodations and conveyances, on the grounds that it exceeded Congress' power by seeking to regulate private conduct. The Enforcement Clause, the Court said, did not authorize Congress to pass "general legislation upon the rights of the citizen, but corrective legislation; that is, such as may be necessary and proper for counteracting such laws as the States may adopt or enforce, and which, by the amendment, they are prohibited from making or enforcing. . . ." The power to "legislate generally upon" life, liberty, and property, as opposed to the "power to provide modes of redress" against offensive state action, was "repugnant" to the Constitution. Although the specific holdings of these early cases might have been superseded or modified, their treatment of Congress' § 5 power as corrective or preventive, not definitional, has not been questioned.

Recent cases have continued to revolve around the question of whether § 5 legislation can be considered remedial. In *South Carolina v. Katzenbach,* we emphasized that "the constitutional propriety of [legislation adopted under the Enforcement Clause] must be judged with reference to the historical experience . . . it reflects." There we upheld various provisions of the Voting Rights Act of 1965, finding them to be "remedies aimed at areas where voting discrimination has been most flagrant," and necessary to "banish the blight of racial discrimination in voting, which has infected the electoral process in parts of our country for nearly a century." We noted evidence in the record reflecting the subsisting and pervasive discriminatory—and therefore unconstitutional—use of literacy tests. The Act's new remedies, which used the administrative resources of the Federal Government, included the suspension of both literacy tests and, pending federal review, all new voting regulations in covered jurisdictions, as well as the assignment of federal examiners to list qualified applicants enabling those listed to vote. The new, unprecedented remedies were deemed necessary given the ineffectiveness of the existing voting rights laws, and the slow costly character of case-by-case litigation.

After *South Carolina v. Katzenbach,* the Court continued to acknowledge the necessity of using strong remedial and preventive measures to respond to the widespread and persisting deprivation of constitutional rights resulting from this country's history of racial discrimination. See *Oregon v. Mitchell* ("In enacting the literacy test ban . . . Congress had before it a long history of the discriminatory use of literacy tests to disfranchise voters on account of their race") (opinion of Black, J.); *id.* ("There is no question but that Congress could legitimately have concluded that the use of literacy tests anywhere within the United States has the inevitable effect of denying the vote to members of racial minorities whose inability to pass such tests is the direct consequence of previous governmental discrimination in education") (opinion of Brennan, J.).

3

Any suggestion that Congress has a substantive, non-remedial power under the Fourteenth Amendment is not supported by our case law. . . . There is language in our opinion in *Katzenbach v. Morgan* which could be interpreted as acknowledging a power in Congress to enact legislation that expands the rights contained in § 1 of the Fourteenth Amendment. This is not a necessary interpretation, however, or even the best one. In *Morgan*, the Court considered the constitutionality of § 4(e) of the Voting Rights Act of 1965, which provided that no person who had successfully completed the sixth primary grade in a public school in, or a private school accredited by, the Commonwealth of Puerto Rico in which the language of instruction was other than English could be denied the right to vote because of an inability to read or write English. New York's Constitution, on the other hand, required voters to be able to read and write English. The Court provided two related rationales for its conclusion that § 4(e) could "be viewed as a measure to secure for the Puerto Rican community residing in New York nondiscriminatory treatment by government." Under the first rationale, Congress could prohibit New York from denying the right to vote to large segments of its Puerto Rican community, in order to give Puerto Ricans "enhanced political power" that would be "helpful in gaining nondiscriminatory treatment in public services for the entire Puerto Rican community." Section 4(e) thus could be justified as a remedial measure to deal with "discrimination in governmental services." The second rationale, an alternative holding, did not address discrimination in the provision of public services but "discrimination in establishing voter qualifications." The Court perceived a factual basis on which Congress could have concluded that New York's literacy requirement "constituted an invidious discrimination in violation of the Equal Protection Clause." Both rationales for upholding § 4(e) rested on unconstitutional discrimination by New York and Congress' reasonable attempt to combat it. As Justice Stewart explained in *Oregon v. Mitchell*, interpreting *Morgan* to give Congress the power to interpret the Constitution "would require an enormous extension of that decision's rationale."

If Congress could define its own powers by altering the Fourteenth Amendment's meaning, no longer would the Constitution be "superior paramount law, unchangeable by ordinary means." It would be "on a level with ordinary legislative acts, and, like other acts . . . alterable when the legislature shall please to alter it." *Marbury v. Madison*. Under this approach, it is difficult to conceive of a principle that would limit congressional power. Shifting legislative majorities could change the

Constitution and effectively circumvent the difficult and detailed amendment process contained in Article V.

We now turn to consider whether RFRA can be considered enforcement legislation under § 5 of the Fourteenth Amendment.

B

Respondent contends that RFRA is a proper exercise of Congress' remedial or preventive power. The Act, it is said, is a reasonable means of protecting the free exercise of religion as defined by *Smith*. It prevents and remedies laws which are enacted with the unconstitutional object of targeting religious beliefs and practices. To avoid the difficulty of proving such violations, it is said, Congress can simply invalidate any law which imposes a substantial burden on a religious practice unless it is justified by a compelling interest and is the least restrictive means of accomplishing that interest. . . .

While preventive rules are sometimes appropriate remedial measures, there must be a congruence between the means used and the ends to be achieved. The appropriateness of remedial measures must be considered in light of the evil presented. Strong measures appropriate to address one harm may be an unwarranted response to another, lesser one.

A comparison between RFRA and the Voting Rights Act is instructive. In contrast to the record which confronted Congress and the judiciary in the voting rights cases, RFRA's legislative record lacks examples of modern instances of generally applicable laws passed because of religious bigotry. The history of persecution in this country detailed in the hearings mentions no episodes occurring in the past 40 years. The absence of more recent episodes stems from the fact that, as one witness testified, "deliberate persecution is not the usual problem in this country." House Hearings 334 (statement of Douglas Laycock). See also House Report 2 ("Laws directly targeting religious practices have become increasingly rare"). Rather, the emphasis of the hearings was on laws of general applicability which place incidental burdens on religion. Much of the discussion centered upon anecdotal evidence of autopsies performed on Jewish individuals and Hmong immigrants in violation of their religious beliefs, and on zoning regulations and historic preservation laws (like the one at issue here), which as an incident of their normal operation, have adverse effects on churches and synagogues. It is difficult to maintain that they are examples of legislation enacted or enforced due to animus or hostility to the burdened religious practices or that they indicate some widespread pattern of religious discrimination in this country. Congress' concern was with the incidental burdens imposed, not the object or purpose of the legislation. This lack of support in the legislative record, however, is not RFRA's most serious shortcoming. Judicial deference, in most cases, is based not on the state of the legislative record Congress compiles but "on due regard for the decision of the body constitutionally appointed to decide." As a general matter, it is for Congress to determine the method by which it will reach a decision.

Regardless of the state of the legislative record, RFRA cannot be considered remedial, preventive legislation, if those terms are to have any meaning. RFRA is so out of proportion to a supposed remedial or preventive object that it cannot be understood as responsive to, or designed to prevent, unconstitutional behavior. It appears, instead, to attempt a substantive change in constitutional protections. Preventive measures prohibiting certain types of laws may be appropriate when there is reason to believe that many of the laws affected by the congressional enactment have a significant likelihood of being unconstitutional. Remedial legislation under § 5 "should be adapted to the mischief and wrong which the [Fourteenth] Amendment was intended to provide against." *Civil Rights Cases.*

RFRA is not so confined. Sweeping coverage ensures its intrusion at every level of government, displacing laws and prohibiting official actions of almost every description and regardless of subject matter. RFRA's restrictions apply to every agency and official of the Federal, State, and local Governments. RFRA applies to all federal and state law, statutory or otherwise, whether adopted before or after its enactment. RFRA has no termination date or termination mechanism. Any law is subject to challenge at any time by any individual who alleges a substantial burden on his or her free exercise of religion.

The reach and scope of RFRA distinguish it from other measures passed under Congress' enforcement power, even in the area of voting rights. In *South Carolina v. Katzenbach,* the challenged provisions were confined to those regions of the country where voting discrimination had been most flagrant, and affected a discrete class of state laws, *i.e.,* state voting laws. Furthermore, to ensure that the reach of the Voting Rights Act was limited to those cases in which constitutional violations were most likely (in order to reduce the possibility of overbreadth), the coverage under the Act would terminate "at the behest of States and political subdivisions in which the danger of substantial voting discrimination has not materialized during the preceding five years." The provisions restricting and banning literacy tests, upheld in *Katzenbach v. Morgan* and *Oregon v. Mitchell,* attacked a particular type of voting qualification, one with a long history as a "notorious means to deny and abridge voting rights on racial grounds." In *City of Rome,* the Court rejected a challenge to the constitutionality of a Voting Rights Act provision which required certain jurisdictions to submit changes in electoral practices to the Department of Justice for preimplementation review. The requirement was placed only on jurisdictions with a history of intentional racial discrimination in voting. [T]his provision permitted a covered jurisdiction to avoid preclearance requirements under certain conditions and, moreover, lapsed in seven years. This is not to say, of course, that § 5 legislation requires termination dates, geographic restrictions or egregious predicates. Where, however, a congressional enactment pervasively prohibits constitutional state action in an effort to remedy or to prevent unconstitutional state action, limitations of this kind tend to ensure Congress' means are proportionate to ends legitimate under § 5.

The stringent test RFRA demands of state laws reflects a lack of proportionality or congruence between the means adopted and the legitimate end to be achieved. If an objector can show a substantial burden on his free exercise, the State must demonstrate a compelling governmental interest and show that the law is the least restrictive means of furthering its interest. Claims that a law substantially burdens someone's exercise of religion will often be difficult to contest. Requiring a State to demonstrate a compelling interest and show that it has adopted the least restrictive means of achieving that interest is the most demanding test known to constitutional law. If " 'compelling interest' really means what it says . . . many laws will not meet the test. . . . [The test] would open the prospect of constitutionally required religious exemptions from civic obligations of almost every conceivable kind." Laws valid under *Smith* would fall under RFRA without regard to whether they had the object of stifling or punishing free exercise. We make these observations not to reargue the position of the majority in *Smith* but to illustrate the substantive alteration of its holding attempted by RFRA. Even assuming RFRA would be interpreted in effect to mandate some lesser test, say one equivalent to intermediate scrutiny, the statute nevertheless would require searching judicial scrutiny of state law with the attendant likelihood of invalidation. This is a considerable congressional intrusion into the States' traditional prerogatives and general authority to regulate for the health and welfare of their citizens.

The substantial costs RFRA exacts, both in practical terms of imposing a heavy litigation burden on the States and in terms of curtailing their traditional general regulatory power, far exceed any pattern or practice of unconstitutional conduct under the Free Exercise Clause as interpreted in *Smith*. Simply put, RFRA is not designed to identify and counteract state laws likely to be unconstitutional because of their treatment of religion. In most cases, the state laws to which RFRA applies are not ones which will have been motivated by religious bigotry. If a state law disproportionately burdened a particular class of religious observers, this circumstance might be evidence of an impermissible legislative motive. RFRA's substantial burden test, however, is not even a discriminatory effects or disparate impact test. It is a reality of the modern regulatory state that numerous state laws, such as the zoning regulations at issue here, impose a substantial burden on a large class of individuals. When the exercise of religion has been burdened in an incidental way by a law of general application, it does not follow that the persons affected have been burdened any more than other citizens, let alone burdened because of their religious beliefs. In addition, the Act imposes in every case a least restrictive means requirement—a requirement that was not used in the pre-*Smith* jurisprudence RFRA purported to codify—which also indicates that the legislation is broader than is appropriate if the goal is to prevent and remedy constitutional violations.

When Congress acts within its sphere of power and responsibilities, it has not just the right but the duty to make its own informed judgment on the meaning and force of the Constitution. This has been clear from the early days of the Republic. In 1789, when a Member of the House of Representatives objected to a debate on the constitutionality of legislation based on the theory that "it would be officious" to consider the constitutionality of a measure that did not affect the House, James Madison explained that "it is incontrovertibly of as much importance to this branch of the Government as to any other, that the constitution should be preserved entire. It is our duty." Were it otherwise, we would not afford Congress the presumption of validity its enactments now enjoy.

Our national experience teaches that the Constitution is preserved best when each part of the government respects both the Constitution and the proper actions and determinations of the other branches. When the Court has interpreted the Constitution, it has acted within the province of the Judicial Branch, which embraces the duty to say what the law is. *Marbury v. Madison*. When the political branches of the Government act against the background of a judicial interpretation of the Constitution already issued, it must be understood that in later cases and controversies the Court will treat its precedents with the respect due them under settled principles, including *stare decisis*, and contrary expectations must be disappointed. RFRA was designed to control cases and controversies, such as the one before us; but as the provisions of the federal statute here invoked are beyond congressional authority, it is this Court's precedent, not RFRA, which must control. . . .

It is for Congress in the first instance to "determine whether and what legislation is needed to secure the guarantees of the Fourteenth Amendment," and its conclusions are entitled to much deference. Congress' discretion is not unlimited, however, and the courts retain the power, as they have since *Marbury v. Madison*, to determine if Congress has exceeded its authority under the Constitution. Broad as the power of Congress is under the Enforcement Clause of the Fourteenth Amendment, RFRA contradicts vital principles necessary to maintain separation of powers and the federal balance. The judgment of the Court of Appeals sustaining the Act's constitutionality is reversed.[*]

---

[*]   Justices O'Connor, Souter, and Breyer dissented on the ground that they thought *Smith* should be reconsidered, without reaching the question of whether—assuming *Smith*'s validity— the RFRA would be a valid statute. [Editor's Note]

NOTE ON THE SECTION FIVE POWER

1. As Justice Kennedy noted in *Boerne*, there were two alternative grounds in *Morgan*, and the second had two alternative readings. It is important to sort these positions out:

The first ground was that Congress could have chosen to protect Puerto Ricans' right to vote as a *remedy* for other forms of unconstitutional discrimination against that group. If Puerto Ricans are a powerful voting bloc, after all, the ordinary political process should correct for discrimination against them. This theory relies on the relatively uncontested proposition that Congress has broader freedom to devise remedies for unconstitutional state action than a court might enjoy in framing an injunction. The Voting Rights Act, for example, creates an elaborate institutional mechanism by which southern jurisdictions that had historically excluded black people from voting must "pre-clear" any changes in their electoral systems with the Justice Department. This mechanism is designed to prevent clever electoral schemes that would have the effect of diluting black electoral power without formally discriminating on the basis of race. It seems unlikely that a court, wielding traditional equitable powers, could have implemented a remedy of this kind; Congress, however, is understood to have considerably broader remedial authority once unconstitutional action is present.

The second ground in *Morgan* relied on the proposition that voter literacy tests themselves are a form of unconstitutional racial discrimination. The problem with that proposition, of course, is that the Court had already rejected it in the *Lassiter* case. One answer to this has to do with the fact that the Court has traditionally declined to apply strict scrutiny to cases of disparate impact discrimination—that is, cases in which state action is neutral on its face (everyone must pass a literacy test to vote) but tends to impact one racial group more than another (blacks fail the literacy test at a much higher rate than whites, perhaps because it is administered in a discriminatory way).[29] The Court has explained this aspect of the doctrine by noting that it is hard for courts, as an institution, to investigate the motives behind such practices so as to determine whether the Government has acted out of unconstitutional racial bias. Congress, however, may have a greater institutional capacity to investigate these issues and draw valid conclusions. Hence, the *Morgan* majority deferred to Congress's judgment, embodied in the Voting Rights Act, that most jurisdictions have adopted literacy tests for the purpose of excluding members of racial minorities (such as the Puerto Ricans) from voting. Essentially, Congress's superior fact-finding ability enabled it to discover a constitutional violation that the Court was unable to detect. As Justice Harlan pointed out, however, there was no legislative record indicating that Congress had made such an investigation in *Morgan*. Should Congress get deference if it has not in fact done its homework?

The alternative, and considerably more controversial, reading of *Morgan* starts by recognizing that the issue of whether literacy tests are

---

[29] *See, e.g., Washington v. Davis,* 426 U.S. 229 (1976).

unconstitutional is a close question on the law. Where reasonable people can disagree, the argument goes, Congress may adopt its own interpretation of the Fourteenth Amendment, even if the Supreme Court has already adopted a contrary reading (as it had in *Lassiter*). *City of Boerne* clearly rejects that interpretation of *Morgan*—as an interpretation both of what *Morgan* held and of what Section Five permits—and affirms the judiciary's ultimate authority "to say what the law is." (citing *Marbury*) Should the *Boerne* Court have been more respectful of Congress's authority to interpret the Constitution in close cases?

2.   Suppose we were to adopt the alternate reading of *Morgan*'s second ground and say that the Court must defer to Congress's reading of the Fourteenth Amendment when Congress exercises its Section Five power. Justice Harlan, dissenting in *Morgan*, worried that this approach would allow Congress to adopt narrower or more restrictive interpretations of the rights protected by the Fourteenth Amendment. Did Justice Brennan have a good answer to this concern? Brennan insisted in footnote 10 of the majority opinion that Congress can only *expand* rights, but why would this be true? How would this "one-way ratchet" theory deal with rights that may press in opposite directions in the same case, such as the right to free exercise of religion and the right to be free from religious establishments? And how would it deal with the fact that constitutional rights often trade off with other constitutional values, such as state autonomy? Vigorous enforcement of the Fifteenth Amendment right to vote, for example, frequently impinges on the States' constitutionally-conferred power to regulate their own electorates.

3.   *City of Boerne* holds that the Court's interpretation of the Fourteenth Amendment is binding on Congress. But it does not entirely reject the proposition that Congress may legislate somewhat more broadly. In particular, the Court accepts the possibility of prophylactic remedies to prevent or deter constitutional violation. For example, the Court endorses Congress' findings that literacy tests are almost always motivated by a desire to suppress voting by racial minorities and, therefore, almost always unconstitutional. Based on this finding, however, the Court has upheld statutes that ban *all* literacy tests, even though that category surely contains some such tests (think about tests administered in areas without a significant minority population) that do not have any such unconstitutional purpose. The Voting Rights Act, therefore, sweeps somewhat more broadly than does the Equal Protection Clause itself. The reason is that it is hard for courts to tell an unconstitutional literacy test from a constitutional one on a case by case basis, and so the only way to adequately prevent unconstitutional tests is to prophylactically ban them all.[30]

What are the limits on Congress's authority to create prophylactic remedies for constitutional violations? In *Boerne*, the Court says that such remedies must be "congruent and proportional" to the constitutional violation. What does Justice Kennedy mean by that? In connection with this question, consider the Court's post-*Boerne* decision in *Trustees of the Univ. of Alabama v. Garrett*, 531 U.S. 356 (2001). The Americans With Disabilities

---

[30]   Recall the similar prophylactic quality of the warnings in *Miranda*, Section 6.3.

Act bars discrimination against the disabled; any disability-based classifications, such as a test excluding the disabled from a certain form of employment, must meet a very high burden of justification. Under the Equal Protection Clause, however, the Court has held that the disabled are not a "suspect class" and, therefore, that state discrimination against them is subject only to rational basis review.[31] *Garrett* held that a portion of the ADA barring discrimination against the disabled by state governments was not valid Section Five legislation.[32] How would you expect the level of scrutiny accorded to disability classifications under the Equal Protection Clause to bear on the congruence and proportionality question? *Garrett* strongly suggested that Congress may only employ the Section Five power to prohibit forms of discrimination that trigger some form of heightened equal protection scrutiny. Does that make sense?

4.   How much power would Congress enjoy if *Garrett* had gone the other way? Recall that *any* state-imposed classification is subject to challenge under the Equal Protection Clause on the ground that it is not rationally related to a legitimate state purpose; moreover, *any* government action is also subject to challenge on the ground that it is arbitrary under the Due Process Clause. *See Williamson v. Lee Optical.* Courts have been very deferential to state policies in such cases. But what if Congress determined that a particular state law was arbitrary? Could it enact legislation under Section 5 preempting that law, based on its own judgment that the law lacked a rational basis? Would any state law be safe from preemption on this ground? What would prevent Congress from simply using such a theory to invalidate any state law with which it disagreed?

5.   As already noted, the conventional reading of the second ground in *Morgan* relied heavily on Congress's superior fact-finding ability. Similarly, language in *City of Boerne* emphasizes the importance of congressional *findings* and the legislative record—usually in the form of evidence presented at hearings—before Congress. (But note Justice Harlan's argument, dissenting in *Morgan*, that Congress had not actually *exercised* its superior fact-finding capabilities.) We have already discussed such findings in connection with *Lopez*. What purpose do such findings serve in *Boerne*?

6.   *United States v. Morrison*, 529 U.S. 598 (2000), raised another important question concerning the reach of Congress's Section Five power. As we have already noted,[33] *Morrison* was a case under the federal Violence Against Women Act (VAWA), which provided a federal private right of action

---

[31]   *City of Cleburne v. Cleburne Living Ctr.*, 473 U.S. 432 (1985).

[32]   The Court did not question that the ADA would be constitutional, even as applied to state governments, under the Commerce Clause. The Section Five issue arose for the purpose of determining whether the States could be made subject to private lawsuits for money damages. The Eleventh Amendment, and the broader principle of state sovereign immunity for which it stands, ordinarily bars such suits when Congress authorizes them pursuant to its Article I powers. *See Seminole Tribe v. Florida*, 517 U.S. 44 (1996). But the Court has long recognized an exception when Congress acts pursuant to its power to enforce the Reconstruction Amendments. *See Fitzpatrick v. Bitzer*, 427 U.S. 445 (1976). This topic is explored in much greater depth in the upper level course in Federal Courts.

[33]   *See supra* Section 9.1.

for victims of gender-related violence to sue their attackers for damages. The Court rejected efforts to justify this aspect of the VAWA under both the Commerce Clause and Section Five of the Fourteenth Amendment. The Section Five argument was predicated on the argument that the failure of state governments to protect women from violence denied those women the equal protection of the laws:

> Petitioners' § 5 argument is founded on an assertion that there is pervasive bias in various state justice systems against victims of gender-motivated violence. This assertion is supported by a voluminous congressional record. Specifically, Congress received evidence that many participants in state justice systems are perpetuating an array of erroneous stereotypes and assumptions. Congress concluded that these discriminatory stereotypes often result in insufficient investigation and prosecution of gender-motivated crime, inappropriate focus on the behavior and credibility of the victims of that crime, and unacceptably lenient punishments for those who are actually convicted of gender-motivated violence. Petitioners contend that this bias denies victims of gender-motivated violence the equal protection of the laws and that Congress therefore acted appropriately in enacting a private civil remedy against the perpetrators of gender-motivated violence to both remedy the States' bias and deter future instances of discrimination in the state courts.

The *Morrison* majority rejected this claim on the authority of the *Civil Rights Cases*,[34] which held that there can be no constitutional violation—and hence no predicate for "enforcement" of the Constitution—in the absence of state action. Antonio Morrison, the defendant in Christie Brzonkala's VAWA suit for sexual assault, was not a state actor. Hence, the Section Five power could not support a law providing for redress against a defendant not subject to the Fourteenth Amendment's strictures. Mr. Morrison's deeds were morally reprehensible, and likely punishable under state tort or criminal law, but not *unconstitutional*.

Is the private nature of Morrison's conduct a complete answer to the Government's effort to ground the VAWA in Section Five? The argument in favor of the statute, after all, was that the *Commonwealth* of Virginia—and many other states, too—had failed to provide equal protection of the laws by failing to deal adequately with the pervasive problem of gender-motivated violence. Should Congress's power to remedy such a failure be limited to laws that act directly on the state government—a federal requirement, for instance, that states enact certain procedures for investigating gender-related violence? Or should Congress simply be able to provide a substitute remedy under federal law where state laws are inadequate? How would *Boerne*'s "congruence and proportionality" test apply to such an effort?

7.   Can a federal statute that is a valid exercise of Congress's power to enforce the Reconstruction Amendments at the time of its enactment become unconstitutional with the passage of time? Section Four of the Voting Rights

---

[34]   *See supra* Section 4.2.

Act of 1965 prohibit states and their political subdivisions from imposing any test or device "for the purpose or with the effect of denying or abridging the right to vote on account of race or color." 79 Stat. 438. Section Five then requires governments seeking to change their voting procedures in any way to "preclear" those procedures by seeking the approval of either the Justice Department or a special three-judge federal court. This requirement applies, however, only to "covered" jurisdictions—mostly in the South—that Congress had found to have engaged in unconstitutional voting discrimination in the past. The Supreme Court upheld this regime in *South Carolina v. Katzenbach*, 383 U.S. 301 (1966), as a valid exercise of Congress's power to enforce the Fifteenth Amendment.

Congress initially included a "sunset" provision in the Voting Rights Act under which Sections Four and Five would expire after five years. It reauthorized the Act for another five years in 1970, seven years in 1975, and twenty-five years in both 1982 and 2006. In 2009, all nine justices expressed serious doubts about the constitutionality of these provisions, noting that they both intrude on the States' basic autonomy to structure their own governments and offended "our historic tradition that all the States enjoy equal sovereignty." *Northwest Austin Municipal Util. Dist. No. One v. Holder*, 557 U.S. 193, 202 (2009) ("*NAMUDNO*"). The Court noted, moreover, that "[t]hings have changed in the South. Voter turnout and registration rates now approach parity. Blatantly discriminatory evasions of federal decrees are rare. And minority candidates hold office at unprecedented levels." The *NAMUDNO* Court was able to avoid deciding whether the Act was unconstitutional by construing it to allow the plaintiff to avoid the preclearance requirement, but the Court strongly suggested that the Act's distinctions between covered and non-covered jurisdictions, enacted nearly a half century before, no longer fit current realities.

The Court confronted another challenge to Sections Four and Five just four years later in *Shelby County, Alabama v. Holder*, 133 S. Ct. 2612 (2013), and this time the Court had no choice but to reach the constitutional question. The Court focused not on the validity of Section Five's preclearance requirement itself, but rather on Section Four's coverage formula, which imposed preclearance on some states and political subdivisions but not others:

> The Government falls back to the argument that because the formula was relevant in 1965, its continued use is permissible so long as any discrimination remains in the States Congress identified back then—regardless of how that discrimination compares to discrimination in States unburdened by coverage. . . . But history did not end in 1965. By the time the Act was reauthorized in 2006, there had been 40 more years of it. In assessing the current need for a preclearance system that treats States differently from one another today, that history cannot be ignored. During that time, largely because of the Voting Rights Act, voting tests were abolished, disparities in voter registration and turnout due to race were erased, and African-Americans attained political office in record numbers. And yet the coverage formula

that Congress reauthorized in 2006 ignores these developments, keeping the focus on decades-old data relevant to decades-old problems, rather than current data reflecting current needs.[35]

The Court thus struck down the coverage formula as invalid. The majority conceded that, in reauthorizing the Act in 2006, Congress had reviewed considerable evidence that discrimination in voting persists in this country. The problem, however, was that "Congress did not use the record it compiled to shape a coverage formula grounded in current conditions. It instead reenacted a formula based on 40-year-old facts having no logical relation to the present day."[36]

Does the Court's decision in *Shelby County* indicate that it will demand a closer fit than *Morgan* did between remedial measures and the underlying evidence of unconstitutional state action considered by Congress? Or was the problem that although Congress in 2006 did consider considerable contemporary evidence concerning racial discrimination, it did not alter the coverage formula *at all* to reflect that evidence? If a statute may be constitutional when enacted but become unconstitutional as the underlying circumstances change, how often should Congress have to revisit its legislation? Does it depend on how intrusive the legislation is on state prerogatives?

8.   To what extent should we view Congress's power to enforce the Reconstruction Amendments as its *exclusive* tool for vindicating basic human rights? Recall that the Reconstruction Congress proposed Section Five of the Fourteenth Amendment primarily as a vehicle for enacting statutes like the 1866 Civil Rights Act, which (among other things) banned private discrimination on the basis of race in access to public accommodations. The *Civil Rights Cases* stymied that effort by holding that the Section Five power could reach only state action, and subsequent civil rights statutes governing private conduct—like the 1964 Civil Rights Act—have relied on the *Commerce* Power instead. Both supporters and opponents of such laws have sometimes criticized reliance on the Commerce Power in this context as an illegitimate pretext, since the Government's purpose is to vindicate equal rights rather than regulate the economy.

The Court upheld use of the Commerce Clause to support civil rights legislation in *Heart of Atlanta Motel, Inc. v. United States*, 379 U.S. 241 (1964) (upholding Title II of the 1964 Act as applied to accommodations at a hotel in Atlanta, Georgia), and *Katzenbach v. McClung*, 379 U.S. 294 (1964) (holding that mandating equal access to Ollie's Barbecue in Birmingham, Alabama, fell within the Commerce Power). Should the Court have struck down use of the Commerce Power in this context as pretextual?

SECTION 9.3   THE TAXING AND SPENDING POWERS

The first clause of Article I, Section 8, which collects the primary enumerated powers of Congress, provides that "The Congress shall have

---

[35]   133 S. Ct. at 2628–29.

[36]   *Id.* at 2629.

Power To lay and collect Taxes, Duties, Imposts and Excises, to pay the Debts and provide for the common Defence and general Welfare of the United States. . . ." This "pay the Debts" language is typically relied upon as the basis of Congress's spending power.[37] Although this power has existed since 1789, it became considerably more important after ratification of the Sixteenth Amendment in 1913. That Amendment conferred on Congress "power to lay and collect taxes on incomes, from whatever source derived, without apportionment among the several States, and without regard to any census or enumeration." The income tax amendment significantly expanded national financial resources by conferring access to what has become Congress's primary source of revenue.

If one looks at federal systems around the world, it is obvious that a key variable determining the relative power of national and subnational units—whatever the formal distribution of governmental powers—is the allocation of financial resources. This unit will explore one particularly thorny aspect of that allocation: the ability of Congress to tax and spend in order to determine policy on matters that it might not be able to reach by direct regulation. Typically, Congress does this through the imposition of conditions on funds that it grants to the States for various purposes. In *South Dakota v. Dole*, for example, Congress required, as a condition on the receipt of federal highway construction funds, that the States raise their drinking age to twenty-one years. The question, still much-debated after *Dole*, is whether such a condition could ever be found to violate the Constitution.

The Supreme Court's decision in *National Federation of Independent Business v. Sebelius (NFIB)* was the Court's most important statement in decades on the scope of the federal government's financial powers. It addressed two critical questions relevant to this section: First, when should an act of Congress that exacts money from citizens be treated as an exercise of the taxing power? And second, what are the limits of Congress's authority under the spending power to condition the states' receipt of federal monies on compliance with federal directives?[38] We begin with the first of these questions as an explication of Congress's power to tax. We then cover the spending aspect of *NFIB* immediately following the Court's earlier conditional spending decision in *South Dakota v. Dole*.

---

[37] The spending power is also occasionally grounded in the Property Clause, Art. IV, § 3, cl. 2, which provides that "The Congress shall have Power to dispose of and make all needful Rules and Regulations respecting the Territory or other Property belonging to the United States. . . ." Money in the national coffers is, after all, "property belonging to the United States."

[38] The Court also addressed whether the individual mandate could be justified as an exercise of Congress's powers under the Commerce and Necessary and Proper Clauses. That aspect of *NFIB* is considered in Section 9.1.

National Federation of Independent Business v. Sebelius

567 U.S. 519 (2012)

■ CHIEF JUSTICE ROBERTS announced the judgment of the Court and delivered the opinion of the Court with respect to Parts I, II, and III-C, an opinion with respect to Part IV, in which JUSTICE BREYER and JUSTICE KAGAN join, and an opinion with respect to Parts III-A, III-B, and III-D.

Today we resolve constitutional challenges to two provisions of the Patient Protection and Affordable Care Act of 2010: the individual mandate, which requires individuals to purchase a health insurance policy providing a minimum level of coverage; and the Medicaid expansion, which gives funds to the States on the condition that they provide specified health care to all citizens whose income falls below a certain threshold. We do not consider whether the Act embodies sound policies. That judgment is entrusted to the Nation's elected leaders. We ask only whether Congress has the power under the Constitution to enact the challenged provisions. . . .

This case concerns two powers that the Constitution does grant the Federal Government, but which must be read carefully to avoid creating a general federal authority akin to the police power. The Constitution authorizes Congress to "regulate Commerce with foreign Nations, and among the several States, and with the Indian Tribes." Art. I, § 8, cl. 3. . . . Congress may also "lay and collect Taxes, Duties, Imposts and Excises, to pay the Debts and provide for the common Defence and general Welfare of the United States." U.S. Const., Art. I, § 8, cl. 1. Put simply, Congress may tax and spend. This grant gives the Federal Government considerable influence even in areas where it cannot directly regulate. The Federal Government may enact a tax on an activity that it cannot authorize, forbid, or otherwise control. And in exercising its spending power, Congress may offer funds to the States, and may condition those offers on compliance with specified conditions. These offers may well induce the States to adopt policies that the Federal Government itself could not impose. See, e.g., *South Dakota v. Dole*, 483 U.S. 203 (1987) (conditioning federal highway funds on States raising their drinking age to 21). . . .

Our permissive reading of these powers is explained in part by a general reticence to invalidate the acts of the Nation's elected leaders. . . . [P]olicy judgments . . . are entrusted to our Nation's elected leaders, who can be thrown out of office if the people disagree with them. It is not our job to protect the people from the consequences of their political choices.

Our deference in matters of policy cannot, however, become abdication in matters of law. "The powers of the legislature are defined and limited; and that those limits may not be mistaken, or forgotten, the constitution is written." *Marbury v. Madison*, 5 U.S. 137, 1 Cranch 137,

176 (1803). Our respect for Congress's policy judgments thus can never extend so far as to disavow restraints on federal power that the Constitution carefully constructed. . . .

I

In 2010, Congress enacted the Patient Protection and Affordable Care Act. The Act aims to increase the number of Americans covered by health insurance and decrease the cost of health care. The Act's 10 titles stretch over 900 pages and contain hundreds of provisions. This case concerns constitutional challenges to two key provisions, commonly referred to as the individual mandate and the Medicaid expansion. The individual mandate requires most Americans to maintain "minimum essential" health insurance coverage. . . . Many individuals will receive the required coverage through their employer, or from a government program such as Medicaid or Medicare. But for individuals who are not exempt and do not receive health insurance through a third party, the means of satisfying the requirement is to purchase insurance from a private company.

Beginning in 2014, those who do not comply with the mandate must make a "[s]hared responsibility payment" to the Federal Government. That payment, which the Act describes as a "penalty," is calculated as a percentage of household income, subject to a floor based on a specified dollar amount and a ceiling based on the average annual premium the individual would have to pay for qualifying private health insurance. In 2016, for example, the penalty will be 2.5 percent of an individual's household income, but no less than $695 and no more than the average yearly premium for insurance that covers 60 percent of the cost of 10 specified services (e.g., prescription drugs and hospitalization). The Act provides that the penalty will be paid to the Internal Revenue Service with an individual's taxes, and "shall be assessed and collected in the same manner" as tax penalties, such as the penalty for claiming too large an income tax refund. The Act, however, bars the IRS from using several of its normal enforcement tools, such as criminal prosecutions and levies. And some individuals who are subject to the mandate are nonetheless exempt from the penalty—for example, those with income below a certain threshold and members of Indian tribes.

On the day the President signed the Act into law, Florida and 12 other States filed a complaint in the Federal District Court for the Northern District of Florida. Those plaintiffs—who are both respondents and petitioners here, depending on the issue—were subsequently joined by 13 more States, several individuals, and the National Federation of Independent Business. The plaintiffs alleged, among other things, that the individual mandate provisions of the Act exceeded Congress's powers under Article I of the Constitution. The District Court agreed, holding that Congress lacked constitutional power to enact the individual mandate. The District Court determined that the individual mandate could not be severed from the remainder of the Act, and therefore struck down the Act in its entirety.

The Court of Appeals for the Eleventh Circuit affirmed in part and reversed in part. The court affirmed the District Court's holding that the individual mandate exceeds Congress's power. The panel unanimously agreed that the individual mandate did not impose a tax, and thus could not be authorized by Congress's power to "lay and collect Taxes." . . .

III

A

[Chief Justice Roberts, writing only for himself, concluded that the individual mandate could not be justified under the Commerce or the Necessary and Proper Clause. The four dissenting justices (Scalia, Kennedy, Thomas, and Alito) agreed with this holding and reasoning, although they did not formally join the Chief's opinion. Justice Ginsburg, joined by Justices Breyer, Sotomayor, and Kagan, dissented on this point. *See* Section 9.1, *supra*.]

B

That is not the end of the matter. Because the Commerce Clause does not support the individual mandate, it is necessary to turn to the Government's second argument: that the mandate may be upheld as within Congress's enumerated power to "lay and collect Taxes." The Government's tax power argument asks us to view the statute differently than we did in considering its commerce power theory. In making its Commerce Clause argument, the Government defended the mandate as a regulation requiring individuals to purchase health insurance. The Government does not claim that the taxing power allows Congress to issue such a command. Instead, the Government asks us to read the mandate not as ordering individuals to buy insurance, but rather as imposing a tax on those who do not buy that product. . . .

[I]t is well established that if a statute has two possible meanings, one of which violates the Constitution, courts should adopt the meaning that does not do so. Justice Story said that 180 years ago: "No court ought, unless the terms of an act rendered it unavoidable, to give a construction to it which should involve a violation, however unintentional, of the constitution." *Parsons v. Bedford*, 28 U.S. 433, 3 Pet. 433, 448–449 (1830). . . .

The most straightforward reading of the mandate is that it commands individuals to purchase insurance. After all, it states that individuals "shall" maintain health insurance. Congress thought it could enact such a command under the Commerce Clause, and the Government primarily defended the law on that basis. But, for the reasons explained above, the Commerce Clause does not give Congress that power. Under our precedent, it is therefore necessary to ask whether the Government's alternative reading of the statute—that it only imposes a tax on those without insurance—is a reasonable one.

Under the mandate, if an individual does not maintain health insurance, the only consequence is that he must make an additional payment to the IRS when he pays his taxes. That, according to the Government, means the mandate can be regarded as establishing a condition—not owning health insurance—that triggers a tax—the required payment to the IRS. Under that theory, the mandate is not a legal command to buy insurance. Rather, it makes going without insurance just another thing the Government taxes, like buying gasoline or earning income. And if the mandate is in effect just a tax hike on certain taxpayers who do not have health insurance, it may be within Congress's constitutional power to tax.

The question is not whether that is the most natural interpretation of the mandate, but only whether it is a "fairly possible" one. . . . The Government asks us to interpret the mandate as imposing a tax, if it would otherwise violate the Constitution. Granting the Act the full measure of deference owed to federal statutes, it can be so read, for the reasons set forth below.

C

The exaction the Affordable Care Act imposes on those without health insurance looks like a tax in many respects. The "[s]hared responsibility payment," as the statute entitles it, is paid into the Treasury by "taxpayer[s]" when they file their tax returns. It does not apply to individuals who do not pay federal income taxes because their household income is less than the filing threshold in the Internal Revenue Code. For taxpayers who do owe the payment, its amount is determined by such familiar factors as taxable income, number of dependents, and joint filing status. The requirement to pay is found in the Internal Revenue Code and enforced by the IRS, which . . . must assess and collect it "in the same manner as taxes." This process yields the essential feature of any tax: it produces at least some revenue for the Government. *United States v. Kahriger*, 345 U.S. 22, 28, n. 4 (1953). Indeed, the payment is expected to raise about $4 billion per year by 2017.

It is of course true that the Act describes the payment as a "penalty," not a "tax." But [that label] does not determine whether the payment may be viewed as an exercise of Congress's taxing power. . . . We have . . . held that exactions not labeled taxes nonetheless were authorized by Congress's power to tax. In the *License Tax Cases*, for example, we held that federal licenses to sell liquor and lottery tickets—for which the licensee had to pay a fee—could be sustained as exercises of the taxing power. 72 U.S., 5 Wall., 462, 471 (1866). And in *New York v. United States* we upheld as a tax a "surcharge" on out-of-state nuclear waste shipments, a portion of which was paid to the Federal Treasury. 505 U.S. 144, 171 (1992). We thus ask whether the shared responsibility payment falls within Congress's taxing power, "[d]isregarding the designation of the exaction, and viewing its substance and application." *United States v. Constantine*, 296 U.S. 287, 294 (1935); cf. *Quill Corp. v. North Dakota*, 504 U.S. 298, 310 (1992) ("[M]agic words or labels" should not "disable an otherwise constitutional levy").

Our cases confirm this functional approach. For example, in *Drexel Furniture*, we focused on three practical characteristics of the so-called tax on employing child laborers that convinced us the "tax" was actually a penalty. First, the tax imposed an exceedingly heavy burden—10 percent of a company's net income—on those who employed children, no matter how small their infraction. Second, it imposed that exaction only on those who knowingly employed underage laborers. Such scienter requirements are typical of punitive statutes, because Congress often wishes to punish only those who intentionally break the law. Third, this "tax" was enforced in part by the Department of Labor, an agency responsible for punishing violations of labor laws, not collecting revenue.

The same analysis here suggests that the shared responsibility payment may for constitutional purposes be considered a tax, not a penalty: First, for most Americans the amount due will be far less than the price of insurance, and, by statute, it can never be more. It may often be a reasonable financial decision to make the payment rather than purchase insurance, unlike the "prohibitory" financial punishment in *Drexel Furniture*. Second, the individual mandate contains no scienter requirement. Third, the payment is collected solely by the IRS through the normal means of taxation—except that the Service is not allowed to use those means most suggestive of a punitive sanction, such as criminal prosecution. The reasons the Court in *Drexel Furniture* held that what was called a "tax" there was a penalty support the conclusion that what is called a "penalty" here may be viewed as a tax.

None of this is to say that the payment is not intended to affect individual conduct. Although the payment will raise considerable revenue, it is plainly designed to expand health insurance coverage. But taxes that seek to influence conduct are nothing new. Some of our earliest federal taxes sought to deter the purchase of imported manufactured goods in order to foster the growth of domestic industry. Cf. 2 J. Story, Commentaries on the Constitution of the United States § 962, p. 434 (1833) ("the taxing power is often, very often, applied for other purposes, than revenue"). Today, federal and state taxes can compose more than half the retail price of cigarettes, not just to raise more money, but to encourage people to quit smoking. And we have upheld such obviously regulatory measures as taxes on selling marijuana and sawed-off shotguns. See *United States v. Sanchez*, 340 U.S. 42, 44–45 (1950); *Sonzinsky v. United States*, 300 U.S. 506, 513 (1937). Indeed, "[e]very tax is in some measure regulatory. To some extent it interposes an economic impediment to the activity taxed as compared with others not taxed." *Sonzinsky, supra*, at 513. That § 5000A seeks to shape decisions about whether to buy health insurance does not mean that it cannot be a valid exercise of the taxing power.

In distinguishing penalties from taxes, this Court has explained that "if the concept of penalty means anything, it means punishment for an unlawful act or omission." *United States v. Reorganized CF&I Fabricators of Utah, Inc.*, 518 U.S. 213, 224 (1996). While the individual mandate clearly aims to induce the purchase of health insurance, it need not be read to declare that failing to do so is unlawful. Neither the Act nor any other law attaches negative legal consequences to not buying health insurance, beyond requiring a payment to the IRS. The Government agrees with that reading, confirming that if someone chooses to pay rather than obtain health insurance, they have fully complied with the law.

Indeed, it is estimated that four million people each year will choose to pay the IRS rather than buy insurance. . . .

The plaintiffs contend that Congress's choice of language—stating that individuals "shall" obtain insurance or pay a "penalty"—requires reading § 5000A as punishing unlawful conduct, even if that interpretation would render the law unconstitutional. We have rejected a similar argument before. . . .

The joint dissenters argue that we cannot uphold § 5000A as a tax because Congress did not "frame it as such." In effect, they contend that even if the Constitution permits Congress to do exactly what we interpret this statute to do, the law must be struck down because Congress used the wrong labels. An example may help illustrate why labels should not control here. Suppose Congress enacted a statute providing that every taxpayer who owns a house without energy efficient windows must pay $50 to the IRS. The amount due is adjusted based on factors such as taxable income and joint filing status, and is paid along with the taxpayer's income tax return. Those whose income is below the filing threshold need not pay. The required payment is not called a "tax," a "penalty," or anything else. No one would doubt that this law imposed a tax, and was within Congress's power to tax. That conclusion should not change simply because Congress used the word "penalty" to describe the payment. . . .

Our precedent demonstrates that Congress had the power to impose the exaction in § 5000A under the taxing power, and that § 5000A need not be read to do more than impose a tax. That is sufficient to sustain it. The "question of the constitutionality of action taken by Congress does not depend on recitals of the power which it undertakes to exercise." *Woods v. Cloyd W. Miller Co.*, 333 U.S. 138, 144 (1948). . . .

Even if only a tax, the payment under § 5000A(b) remains a burden that the Federal Government imposes for an omission, not an act. If it is troubling to interpret the Commerce Clause as authorizing Congress to regulate those who abstain from commerce, perhaps it should be similarly troubling to permit Congress to impose a tax for not doing something.

Three considerations allay this concern. First, and most importantly, it is abundantly clear the Constitution does not guarantee that individuals may avoid taxation through inactivity. A capitation, after all, is a tax that everyone must pay simply for existing, and capitations are expressly contemplated by the Constitution. The Court today holds that our Constitution protects us from federal regulation under the Commerce Clause so long as we abstain from the regulated activity. But from its creation, the Constitution has made no such promise with respect to taxes. See Letter from Benjamin Franklin to M. Le Roy (Nov. 13, 1789) ("Our new Constitution is now established . . . but in this world nothing can be said to be certain, except death and taxes").

Whether the mandate can be upheld under the Commerce Clause is a question about the scope of federal authority. Its answer depends on whether Congress can exercise what all acknowledge to be the novel course of directing individuals to purchase insurance. Congress's use of the Taxing Clause to encourage buying something is, by contrast, not new. Tax incentives already promote, for example, purchasing homes and professional educations. . . .

Second, Congress's ability to use its taxing power to influence conduct is not without limits. A few of our cases policed these limits aggressively, invalidating punitive exactions obviously designed to regulate behavior otherwise regarded at the time as beyond federal authority. *See, e.g., United States v. Butler*, 297 U.S. 1 (1936); *Bailey v. Drexel Furniture Co.*, 259 U.S. 20 (1922). More often and more recently we have declined to closely examine the regulatory motive or effect of revenue-raising measures. See *Kahriger*, 345 U.S., at 27–31 (collecting cases). We have nonetheless maintained that " 'there comes a time in the extension of the penalizing features of the so-called tax when it loses its character as such and becomes a mere penalty with the characteristics of regulation and punishment." *Dept. of Revenue v. Kurth Ranch*, 511 U.S. 767, 779 (1994).

We have already explained that the shared responsibility payment's practical characteristics pass muster as a tax under our narrowest interpretations of the taxing power. Because the tax at hand is within even those strict limits, we need not here decide the precise point at which an exaction becomes so punitive that the taxing power does not authorize it. It remains true, however, that the "power to tax is not the power to destroy while this Court sits." *Oklahoma Tax Comm'n v. Texas Co.*, 336 U.S. 342, 364 (1949).

Third, although the breadth of Congress's power to tax is greater than its power to regulate commerce, the taxing power does not give Congress the same degree of control over individual behavior. Once we recognize that Congress may regulate a particular decision under the Commerce Clause, the Federal Government can bring its full weight to bear. Congress may simply command individuals to do as it directs. An individual who disobeys may be subjected to criminal sanctions. Those sanctions can include not only fines and imprisonment, but all the attendant consequences of being branded a criminal: deprivation of otherwise protected civil rights, such as the right to bear arms or vote in elections; loss of employment opportunities; social stigma; and severe disabilities in other controversies, such as custody or immigration disputes.

By contrast, Congress's authority under the taxing power is limited to requiring an individual to pay money into the Federal Treasury, no more. If a tax is properly paid, the Government has no power to compel or punish individuals subject to it. We do not make light of the severe burden that taxation—especially taxation motivated by a regulatory purpose—can impose. But imposition of a tax nonetheless leaves an individual with a lawful choice to do or not do a certain act, so long as he is willing to pay a tax levied on that choice.

The Affordable Care Act's requirement that certain individuals pay a financial penalty for not obtaining health insurance may reasonably be characterized as a tax. Because the Constitution permits such a tax, it is not our role to forbid it, or to pass upon its wisdom or fairness. . . .

JUSTICE GINSBURG, with whom JUSTICE SOTOMAYOR joins, and with whom JUSTICE BREYER and JUSTICE KAGAN join as to Parts I, II, III, and IV, concurring in part, concurring in the judgment in part, and dissenting in part.

I agree with The Chief Justice that . . . the minimum coverage provision is a proper exercise of Congress' taxing power. I therefore join Parts I, II, and III-C of The Chief Justice's opinion. Unlike The Chief Justice, however, I would hold, alternatively, that the Commerce Clause authorizes Congress to enact the minimum coverage provision. I would also hold that the Spending Clause permits the Medicaid expansion exactly as Congress enacted it. . . .

JUSTICE SCALIA, JUSTICE KENNEDY, JUSTICE THOMAS, and JUSTICE ALITO, dissenting.

What is absolutely clear, affirmed by the text of the 1789 Constitution, by the Tenth Amendment ratified in 1791, and by innumerable cases of ours in the 220 years since, is that there are structural limits upon federal power—upon what it can prescribe with respect to private conduct, and upon what it can impose upon the sovereign States. Whatever may be the conceptual limits upon the Commerce Clause and upon the power to tax and spend, they cannot be such as will enable the Federal Government to regulate all private conduct and to compel the States to function as administrators of federal programs. . . .

II
The Taxing Power

The Government contends, however, as expressed in the caption to Part II of its brief, that "THE MINIMUM COVERAGE PROVISION IS INDEPENDENTLY AUTHORIZED BY CONGRESS'S TAXING POWER." The phrase "independently authorized" suggests the existence of a creature never hitherto seen in the United States Reports: A penalty for constitutional purposes that is also a tax for constitutional purposes. In all our cases the two are mutually exclusive. The provision challenged under the Constitution is either a penalty or else a tax. Of course in many cases what was a regulatory mandate enforced by a penalty could have been imposed as a tax upon permissible action; or what was imposed as a tax upon permissible action could have been a regulatory mandate enforced by a penalty. But we know of no case, and the Government cites none, in which the imposition was, for constitutional purposes, both. . . . It is important to bear this in mind in evaluating the tax argument of the Government and of those who support it: The issue is not whether Congress had the power to frame the minimum-coverage provision as a tax, but whether it did so.

In answering that question we must, if fairly possible, construe the provision to be a tax rather than a mandate-with-penalty, since that would render it constitutional rather than unconstitutional . . . . But we cannot rewrite the statute to be what it is not. "[A]lthough this Court will often strain to construe legislation so as to save it against constitutional attack, it must not and will not carry this to the point of perverting the purpose of a statute . . . or judicially rewriting it." *Commodity Futures Trading Comm'n v. Schor*, 478 U.S. 833, 841 (1986). In this case, there is simply no way, without doing violence to the fair meaning of the words used, to escape what Congress enacted: a mandate that individuals maintain minimum essential coverage, enforced by a penalty.

Our cases establish a clear line between a tax and a penalty: "[A] tax is an enforced contribution to provide for the support of government; a penalty . . . is an exaction imposed by statute as punishment for an unlawful act." *United States v. Reorganized CF&I Fabricators of Utah, Inc.*, 518 U.S. 213, 224 (1996). In a few cases, this Court has held that a "tax" imposed upon private conduct was so onerous as to be in effect a penalty. But we have never held—never—that a penalty imposed for violation of the law was so trivial as to be in effect a tax. We have never held that any exaction imposed for violation of the law is an exercise of Congress' taxing power—even when the statute calls it a tax, much less when (as here) the statute repeatedly calls it a penalty. When an act "adopt[s] the criteria of wrongdoing" and then imposes a monetary penalty as the "principal consequence on those who transgress its standard," it creates a regulatory penalty, not a tax. *Child Labor Tax Case*, 259 U.S. 20, 38 (1922).

So the question is, quite simply, whether the exaction here is imposed for violation of the law. It unquestionably is. The minimum-coverage provision is found in 26 U.S.C. § 5000A, entitled "*Requirement to maintain minimum essential coverage.*" (emphasis added.) It commands that every "applicable individual *shall* . . . ensure that the individual . . . is covered under minimum essential coverage." Ibid. (emphasis added). And the immediately following provision states that, "[i]f . . . an applicable individual . . . fails to meet the *requirement* of subsection (a) . . . there is hereby imposed . . . a penalty." § 5000A(b) (emphasis added). And several of Congress' legislative "findings" with regard to § 5000A confirm that it sets forth a legal requirement and constitutes the assertion of regulatory power, not mere taxing power. See 42 U.S.C. § 18091(2)(A) ("The requirement regulates activity . . ."); § 18091(2)(C) ("The requirement . . . will add millions of new consumers to the health insurance market . . ."); § 18091(2)(D) ("The requirement achieves near-universal coverage"); 18091(2)(H) ("The requirement is an essential part of this larger regulation of economic activity, and the absence of the requirement would undercut Federal regulation of the health insurance market"); § 18091(3) ("[T]he Supreme Court of the United States ruled that insurance is interstate commerce subject to Federal regulation"). . . .

Quite separately, the fact that Congress (in its own words) "imposed . . . a penalty," 26 U.S.C. § 5000A(b)(1), for failure to buy insurance is alone sufficient to render that failure unlawful. It is one of the canons of interpretation that a statute that penalizes an act makes it unlawful: "[W]here the statute inflicts a penalty for doing an act, although the act itself is not expressly prohibited, yet to do the act is unlawful, because it cannot be supposed that the Legislature intended that a penalty should be inflicted for a lawful act." *Powhatan Steamboat Co. v. Appomattox R. Co.*, 65 U.S. 247, 24 How. 247, 252 (1861). . . .

We never have classified as a tax an exaction imposed for violation of the law, and so too, we never have classified as a tax an exaction described in the legislation itself as a penalty. . . . Eighteen times in § 5000A itself and elsewhere throughout the Act, Congress called the exaction in § 5000A(b) a "penalty."

That § 5000A imposes not a simple tax but a mandate to which a penalty is attached is demonstrated by the fact that some are exempt from the tax who are not exempt from the mandate—a distinction that would make no sense if the mandate were not a mandate. Section 5000A(d) exempts three classes of people from the definition of "applicable individual" subject to the minimum coverage requirement: Those with religious objections or who participate in a "health care sharing ministry," § 5000A(d)(2); those who are "not lawfully present" in the United States, § 5000A(d)(3); and those who are incarcerated, § 5000A(d)(4). Section 5000A(e) then creates a separate set of exemptions, excusing from liability for the penalty certain individuals who are subject to the minimum coverage requirement: Those who cannot afford coverage, § 5000A(e)(1); who earn too little income to require filing a tax return, § 5000A(e)(2); who are members of an Indian tribe, § 5000A(e)(3); who experience only short gaps in coverage, § 5000A(e)(4); and who, in the judgment of the Secretary of Health and Human Services, "have suffered a hardship with respect to the capability to obtain coverage," § 5000A(e)(5). If § 5000A were a tax, these two classes of exemption would make no sense; there being no requirement, all the exemptions would attach to the penalty (renamed tax) alone.

In the face of all these indications of a regulatory requirement accompanied by a penalty, the Solicitor General assures us that "neither the Treasury Department nor the Department of Health and Human Services interprets Section 5000A as imposing a legal obligation," and that "[i]f [those subject to the Act] pay the tax penalty, they're in compliance with the law." These self-serving litigating positions are entitled to no weight. What counts is what the statute says, and that is entirely clear. It is worth noting, moreover, that these assurances contradict the Government's position in related litigation. Shortly before the Affordable Care Act was passed, the Commonwealth of Virginia enacted Va. Code Ann. § 38.2–3430.1:1 (Lexis Supp. 2011), which states, "No resident of [the] Commonwealth . . . shall be required to obtain or maintain a policy of individual insurance coverage except as required by a court or the Department of Social Services". In opposing Virginia's assertion of standing to challenge § 5000A based on this statute, the Government said that "if the minimum coverage provision is unconstitutional, the [Virginia] statute is unnecessary, and if the minimum coverage provision is upheld, the state statute is void under the Supremacy Clause." Brief for Appellant in No. 11–1057 etc. (CA4), p. 29. But it would be void under the Supremacy Clause only if it was contradicted by a federal "require[ment] to obtain or maintain a policy of individual insurance coverage."

Against the mountain of evidence that the minimum coverage requirement is what the statute calls it—a requirement—and that the penalty for its violation is what the statute calls it—a penalty—the Government brings forward the flimsiest of indications to the contrary. It notes that "[t]he minimum coverage provision amends the Internal Revenue Code to provide that a non-exempted individual . . . will owe a monetary penalty, in addition to the income tax itself," and that "[t]he [Internal Revenue Service (IRS)] will assess and collect the penalty in the same manner as assessable penalties under the Internal Revenue Code." The manner of collection could perhaps suggest a tax if IRS penalty-collection were unheard-of or rare. It is not. See, e.g., 26 U.S.C. § 527(j) (2006 ed.) (IRS-collectible penalty for failure to make campaign finance disclosures); § 5761(c) (IRS-collectible penalty for domestic sales of tobacco products labeled for export); § 9707 (IRS-collectible penalty for failure to make required health-insurance premium payments on behalf of mining employees). In *United States v. Reorganized CF&I Fabricators of Utah, Inc.*, 518 U.S. 213 (1996), we held that an exaction not only enforced by the Commissioner of Internal Revenue but even called a "tax" was in fact a penalty. "[I]f the concept of penalty means anything," we said, "it means punishment for an unlawful act or omission." Id., at 224. Moreover, while the penalty is assessed and collected by the IRS, § 5000A is administered both by that agency and by the Department of Health and Human Services (and also the Secretary of Veteran Affairs), which is responsible for defining its substantive scope—a feature that would be quite extraordinary for taxes.

The Government points out that "[t]he amount of the penalty will be calculated as a percentage of household income for federal income tax purposes, subject to a floor and [a] ca[p]," and that individuals who earn so little money that they "are not required to file income tax returns for the taxable year are not subject to the penalty" (though they are, as we discussed earlier, subject to the mandate). But varying a penalty according to ability to pay is an utterly familiar practice. See, e.g., 33 U.S.C. § 1319(d) (2006 ed., Supp. IV) ("In determining the amount of a civil penalty the court shall consider . . . the economic impact of the penalty on the violator") . . . .

The last of the feeble arguments in favor of petitioners that we will address is the contention that what this statute repeatedly calls a penalty is in fact a tax because it contains no scienter requirement. The presence of such a requirement suggests a penalty—though one can imagine a tax imposed only on willful action; but the absence of such a requirement does not suggest a tax. Penalties for absolute-liability offenses are commonplace. . . .

And the nail in the coffin is that the mandate and penalty are located in Title I of the Act, its operative core, rather than where a tax would be found—in Title IX, containing the Act's "Revenue Provisions." In sum, "the terms of [the] act rende[r] it unavoidable," *Parsons v. Bedford*, 28 U.S. 433, 3 Pet. 433, 448 (1830), that Congress imposed a regulatory penalty, not a tax.

For all these reasons, to say that the Individual Mandate merely imposes a tax is not to interpret the statute but to rewrite it. Judicial tax-writing is particularly troubling. Taxes have never been popular, see, e.g., Stamp Act of 1765, and in part for that reason, the Constitution requires tax increases to originate in the House of Representatives. See Art. I, § 7, cl. 1. That is to say, they must originate in the legislative body most accountable to the people . . . . We have no doubt that Congress knew precisely what it was doing when it rejected an earlier version of this legislation that imposed a tax instead of a requirement-with-penalty. Imposing a tax through judicial legislation inverts the constitutional scheme, and places the power to tax in the branch of government least accountable to the citizenry. . . .

NOTE ON THE TAXING POWER

1.   As Chief Justice Roberts' discussion in *NFIB* makes clear, the Taxing Power is independent of Congress's other enumerated powers; it is not limited, for instance, to taxing commercial activities. The danger, of course, is that Congress will use the taxing power to extend its regulatory reach far beyond what would otherwise be permissible. For instance, could Congress impose a tax on anyone bringing a gun within 1000 feet of a school? And could it, as a necessary and proper incident to its taxing authority, imprison any person who possessed a gun on school grounds and failed to pay the tax?

Such a statute might run afoul of a venerable—albeit informal— legal principle, the "Neat Trick Rule." That rule holds that legal strategies that allow the complete evasion of an otherwise-constraining principle are themselves invalid: if it's too neat a trick, it doesn't (or at least shouldn't) work. Prior to the Court's decision in *NFIB*, many observers greeted the Government's taxing power argument for the individual mandate with considerable skepticism for precisely this reason—that is, it seemed to offer a "neat trick" to evade the limits on Congress's Commerce Power. Does Chief Justice Roberts' opinion suggest that the "Neat Trick Rule" has been repealed?

2.   If the Taxing Power is not to offer a general work-around for the limits on Congress's other enumerated powers, then there must be some sort of limit on Congress's power to tax. One possibility would be to distinguish between taxes that are intended to raise revenue and those that are meant to regulate—that is, to influence private behavior. But as the Chief points out, *most* taxes are also meant to influence behavior. Should provisions like cigarette taxes or the mortgage interest deduction have to pass muster under some other federal enumerated power? Should it be enough as long as a tax generates "some revenue for the government"?

An alternative approach would be to insist that Congress openly designate statutes enacted pursuant to the Taxing Power as "taxes." This approach would rely primarily on *political* checks on excessively broad use of this federal power. After all, the label "tax" is toxic in contemporary politics. When asked in a televised interview whether the ACA's individual mandate was a tax, for example, President Obama angrily denied the suggestion.[39] And Congress, of course, was careful not to call the "shared responsibility payment" a tax in the ACA itself. Should the Government be able to have it both ways? Would insisting that taxes be labeled as such provide a sufficient check against abuse of the Taxing Power's breadth?

On the other hand, Chief Justice Roberts is correct in noting that Congress ordinarily does not have to formally designate the powers upon which it relies; part of the deference that courts pay to the legislature is that they will uphold federal laws so long as they can be justified under *any* of Congress's enumerated powers. There is, however, at least one exception to

---

[39]   *See* ABC News, *Obama: Mandate is Not a Tax*, Sept. 20, 2009, available at http://abc news.go.com/blogs/politics/2012/06/obama-in-2009-its-not-a-tax/ ("I absolutely reject that notion.").

this rule; in *Gregory v. Ashcroft*, 502 U.S. 452, 469 (1992), the Court imposed a clear statement rule for statutes justified under Congress's power to enforce the Fourteenth Amendment: "Because such legislation imposes congressional policy on a State involuntarily, and because it often intrudes on traditional state authority, we should not quickly attribute to Congress an unstated intent to act under its authority to enforce the Fourteenth Amendment." Would a similar rule be appropriate for the taxing power? If not, are there other viable limiting principles available?

3. If Chief Justice Roberts thought that the individual mandate in the ACA was valid as a tax, does that make his discussion of the Commerce and Necessary and Proper Clauses dictum? Was Justice Ginsburg right to argue that these portions of his opinion should have been left out? What precedential value do they have?

South Dakota v. Dole

483 U.S. 203 (1987)

■ **CHIEF JUSTICE REHNQUIST delivered the opinion of the Court.**

Petitioner South Dakota permits persons 19 years of age or older to purchase beer containing up to 3.2% alcohol. In 1984 Congress enacted 23 U. S. C. § 158, which directs the Secretary of Transportation to withhold a percentage of federal highway funds otherwise allocable from States "in which the purchase or public possession . . . of any alcoholic beverage by a person who is less than twenty-one years of age is lawful." The State sued in United States District Court seeking a declaratory judgment that § 158 violates the constitutional limitations on congressional exercise of the spending power and violates the Twenty-first Amendment to the United States Constitution. The District Court rejected the State's claims, and the Court of Appeals for the Eighth Circuit affirmed. . . .

Relying on our statement in *California Retail Liquor Dealers Assn. v. Midcal Aluminum, Inc.,* 445 U.S. 97 (1980), that the "Twenty-first Amendment grants the States virtually complete control over whether to permit importation or sale of liquor and how to structure the liquor distribution system," South Dakota asserts that the setting of minimum drinking ages is clearly within the "core powers" reserved to the States under § 2 of the Amendment.[15] Section 158, petitioner claims, usurps that core power. The Secretary in response asserts that the Twenty-first Amendment is simply not implicated by § 158; the plain language of § 2 confirms the States' broad power to impose restrictions on the sale and distribution of alcoholic beverages but does not confer on them any power to *permit* sales that Congress seeks to *prohibit*. That Amendment, under this reasoning, would not prevent Congress from affirmatively enacting

---

[15] Section 2 of the Twenty-first Amendment provides: "The transportation or importation into any State, Territory, or possession of the United States for delivery or use therein of intoxicating liquors, in violation of the laws thereof, is hereby prohibited."

a national minimum drinking age more restrictive than that provided by the various state laws; and it would follow *a fortiori* that the indirect inducement involved here is compatible with the Twenty-first Amendment.

These arguments present questions of the meaning of the Twenty-first Amendment, the bounds of which have escaped precise definition. . . . [H]owever, we need not decide in this case whether that Amendment would prohibit an attempt by Congress to legislate directly a national minimum drinking age. Here, Congress has acted indirectly under its spending power to encourage uniformity in the States' drinking ages. As we explain below, we find this legislative effort within constitutional bounds even if Congress may not regulate drinking ages directly.

The Constitution empowers Congress to "lay and collect Taxes, Duties, Imposts, and Excises, to pay the Debts and provide for the common Defence and general Welfare of the United States." Art. I, § 8, cl. 1. Incident to this power, Congress may attach conditions on the receipt of federal funds, and has repeatedly employed the power "to further broad policy objectives by conditioning receipt of federal moneys upon compliance by the recipient with federal statutory and administrative directives." The breadth of this power was made clear in *United States v. Butler*, 297 U.S. 1 (1936), where the Court, resolving a longstanding debate over the scope of the Spending Clause, determined that "the power of Congress to authorize expenditure of public moneys for public purposes is not limited by the direct grants of legislative power found in the Constitution." Thus, objectives not thought to be within Article I's "enumerated legislative fields," may nevertheless be attained through the use of the spending power and the conditional grant of federal funds.

The spending power is of course not unlimited. . . . The first . . . limitation[ ] is derived from the language of the Constitution itself: the exercise of the spending power must be in pursuit of "the general welfare." In considering whether a particular expenditure is intended to serve general public purposes, courts should defer substantially to the judgment of Congress.[16] Second, we have required that if Congress desires to condition the States' receipt of federal funds, it "must do so unambiguously . . . , enabl[ing] the States to exercise their choice knowingly, cognizant of the consequences of their participation." Third, our cases have suggested (without significant elaboration) that conditions on federal grants might be illegitimate if they are unrelated "to the federal interest in particular national projects or programs." Finally, we have noted that other constitutional provisions may provide an independent bar to the conditional grant of federal funds.

---

[16] The level of deference to the congressional decision is such that the Court has more recently questioned whether "general welfare" is a judicially enforceable restriction at all.

South Dakota does not seriously claim that § 158 is inconsistent with any of the first three restrictions mentioned above. We can readily conclude that the provision is designed to serve the general welfare, especially in light of the fact that "the concept of welfare or the opposite is shaped by Congress. . . ." Congress found that the differing drinking ages in the States created particular incentives for young persons to combine their desire to drink with their ability to drive, and that this interstate problem required a national solution. The means it chose to address this dangerous situation were reasonably calculated to advance the general welfare. The conditions upon which States receive the funds, moreover, could not be more clearly stated by Congress. And . . . the condition imposed by Congress is directly related to one of the main purposes for which highway funds are expended—safe interstate travel. This goal of the interstate highway system had been frustrated by varying drinking ages among the States. A Presidential commission . . . concluded that the lack of uniformity in the States' drinking ages created "an incentive to drink and drive" because "young persons commut[e] to border States where the drinking age is lower." . . .

The remaining question about the validity of § 158 . . . is whether the Twenty-first Amendment constitutes an "independent constitutional bar" to the conditional grant of federal funds. Petitioner, relying on its view that the Twenty-first Amendment prohibits *direct* regulation of drinking ages by Congress, asserts that "Congress may not use the spending power to regulate that which it is prohibited from regulating directly under the Twenty-first Amendment." But our cases show that this "independent constitutional bar" limitation on the spending power is not of the kind petitioner suggests. *United States v. Butler,* for example, established that the constitutional limitations on Congress when exercising its spending power are less exacting than those on its authority to regulate directly. . . .

[T]he "independent constitutional bar" limitation on the spending power is not, as petitioner suggests, a prohibition on the indirect achievement of objectives which Congress is not empowered to achieve directly. Instead, we think that the language in our earlier opinions stands for the unexceptionable proposition that the power may not be used to induce the States to engage in activities that would themselves be unconstitutional. Thus, for example, a grant of federal funds conditioned on invidiously discriminatory state action or the infliction of cruel and unusual punishment would be an illegitimate exercise of the Congress' broad spending power. But no such claim can be or is made here. Were South Dakota to succumb to the blandishments offered by Congress and raise its drinking age to 21, the State's action in so doing would not violate the constitutional rights of anyone.

Our decisions have recognized that in some circumstances the financial inducement offered by Congress might be so coercive as to pass the point at which "pressure turns into compulsion." Here, however,

Congress has directed only that a State desiring to establish a minimum drinking age lower than 21 lose a relatively small percentage of certain federal highway funds. Petitioner contends that the coercive nature of this program is evident from the degree of success it has achieved. We cannot conclude, however, that a conditional grant of federal money of this sort is unconstitutional simply by reason of its success in achieving the congressional objective.

When we consider, for a moment, that all South Dakota would lose if she adheres to her chosen course as to a suitable minimum drinking age is 5% of the funds otherwise obtainable under specified highway grant programs, the argument as to coercion is shown to be more rhetoric than fact. As we said a half century ago in *Steward Machine Co. v. Davis*, 301 U.S. 548 (1937):

> Every rebate from a tax when conditioned upon conduct is in some measure a temptation. But to hold that motive or temptation is equivalent to coercion is to plunge the law in endless difficulties. The outcome of such a doctrine is the acceptance of a philosophical determinism by which choice becomes impossible. Till now the law has been guided by a robust common sense which assumes the freedom of the will as a working hypothesis in the solution of its problems.

Here Congress has offered relatively mild encouragement to the States to enact higher minimum drinking ages than they would otherwise choose. But the enactment of such laws remains the prerogative of the States not merely in theory but in fact. Even if Congress might lack the power to impose a national minimum drinking age directly, we conclude that encouragement to state action found in § 158 is a valid use of the spending power. Accordingly, the judgment of the Court of Appeals is

Affirmed.

■ JUSTICE BRENNAN, dissenting.

I agree with JUSTICE O'CONNOR that regulation of the minimum age of purchasers of liquor falls squarely within the ambit of those powers reserved to the States by the Twenty-first Amendment. Since States possess this constitutional power, Congress cannot condition a federal grant in a manner that abridges this right. The Amendment, itself, strikes the proper balance between federal and state authority. I therefore dissent.

■ JUSTICE O'CONNOR, dissenting.

The Court today upholds the National Minimum Drinking Age Amendment, 23 U. S. C. § 158, as a valid exercise of the spending power conferred by Article I, § 8. But § 158 is not a condition on spending reasonably related to the expenditure of federal funds and cannot be justified on that ground. Rather, it is an attempt to regulate the sale of liquor, an attempt that lies outside Congress' power to regulate commerce because it falls within the ambit of § 2 of the Twenty-first Amendment.

My disagreement with the Court is relatively narrow on the spending power issue: it is a disagreement about the application of a principle rather than a disagreement on the principle itself. I agree with the Court that Congress may attach conditions on the receipt of federal funds to further "the federal interest in particular national projects or programs." I also subscribe to the established proposition that the reach of the spending power "is not limited by the direct grants of legislative power found in the Constitution." *United States v. Butler*, 297 U.S. 1 (1936). Finally, I agree that there are four separate types of limitations on the spending power: the expenditure must be for the general welfare, the conditions imposed must be unambiguous, they must be reasonably related to the purpose of the expenditure, and the legislation may not violate any independent constitutional prohibition. Insofar as two of those limitations are concerned, the Court is clearly correct that § 158 is wholly unobjectionable. Establishment of a national minimum drinking age certainly fits within the broad concept of the general welfare and the statute is entirely unambiguous. I am also willing to assume, *arguendo*, that the Twenty-first Amendment does not constitute an "independent constitutional bar" to a spending condition.

But the Court's application of the requirement that the condition imposed be reasonably related to the purpose for which the funds are expended is cursory and unconvincing. . . .

[T]he Court asserts the reasonableness of the relationship between the supposed purpose of the expenditure—"safe interstate travel"—and the drinking age condition. The Court reasons that Congress wishes that the roads it builds may be used safely, that drunken drivers threaten highway safety, and that young people are more likely to drive while under the influence of alcohol under existing law than would be the case if there were a uniform national drinking age of 21. It hardly needs saying, however, that if the purpose of § 158 is to deter drunken driving, it is far too over-and under-inclusive. It is over-inclusive because it stops teenagers from drinking even when they are not about to drive on interstate highways. It is under-inclusive because teenagers pose only a small part of the drunken driving problem in this Nation. See, *e. g.*, 130 Cong. Rec. 18648 (1984) (remarks of Sen. Humphrey) ("Eighty-four percent of all highway fatalities involving alcohol occur among those whose ages exceed 21"); *id.*, at 18651 (remarks of Sen. McClure) ("Certainly, statistically, if you use that one set of statistics, then the mandatory drinking age ought to be raised at least to 30"); *ibid.* (remarks of Sen. Symms) ("Most of the studies point out that the drivers of age 21– 24 are the worst offenders").

When Congress appropriates money to build a highway, it is entitled to insist that the highway be a safe one. But it is not entitled to insist as a condition of the use of highway funds that the State impose or change regulations in other areas of the State's social and economic life because of an attenuated or tangential relationship to highway use or safety. Indeed, if the rule were otherwise, the Congress could effectively regulate almost any area of a State's social, political, or economic life on the theory that use of the interstate transportation system is somehow enhanced. If, for example, the United States were to condition highway moneys upon moving the state capital, I suppose it might argue that interstate transportation is facilitated by locating local governments in places easily accessible to interstate highways—or, conversely, that highways might become overburdened if they had to carry traffic to and from the state capital. In my mind, such a relationship is hardly more attenuated than the one which the Court finds supports § 158. Cf. Tr. of Oral Arg. 39 (counsel for the United States conceding that to condition a grant upon adoption of a unicameral legislature would violate the "germaneness" requirement).

There is a clear place at which the Court can draw the line between permissible and impermissible conditions on federal grants. It is the line identified in the Brief for the National Conference of State Legislatures et al. as *Amici Curiae*:

> Congress has the power to *spend* for the general welfare, it has the power to *legislate* only for delegated purposes. . . .

> The appropriate inquiry, then, is whether the spending requirement or prohibition is a condition on a grant or whether it is regulation. The difference turns on whether the requirement specifies in some way how the money should be spent, so that Congress' intent in making the grant will be effectuated. Congress has no power under the Spending Clause to impose requirements on a grant that go beyond specifying how the money should be spent. A requirement that is not such a specification is not a condition, but a regulation, which is valid only if it falls within one of Congress' delegated regulatory powers.

This approach harks back to *United States v. Butler*, 297 U.S. 1 (1936), the last case in which this Court struck down an Act of Congress as beyond the authority granted by the Spending Clause. There the Court wrote that "there is an obvious difference between a statute stating the conditions upon which moneys shall be expended and one effective only upon assumption of a contractual obligation to submit to a regulation which otherwise could not be enforced." The *Butler* Court saw the Agricultural Adjustment Act for what it was—an exercise of regulatory, not spending, power. The error in *Butler* was not the Court's conclusion that the Act was essentially regulatory, but rather its crabbed view of the extent of Congress' regulatory power under the Commerce Clause. The Agricultural Adjustment Act was regulatory but it was regulation that today would likely be considered within Congress' commerce power. See, *e.g., Wickard v. Filburn*.

While *Butler*'s authority is questionable insofar as it assumes that Congress has no regulatory power over farm production, its discussion of the spending power and its description of both the power's breadth and its limitations remain sound. The Court's decision in *Butler* also properly recognizes the gravity of the task of appropriately limiting the spending power. If the spending power is to be limited only by Congress' notion of the general welfare, the reality, given the vast financial resources of the Federal Government, is that the Spending Clause gives "power to the Congress to tear down the barriers, to invade the states' jurisdiction, and to become a parliament of the whole people, subject to no restrictions save such as are self-imposed." This, of course, as *Butler* held, was not the Framers' plan and it is not the meaning of the Spending Clause. . . .

[A] condition that a State will raise its drinking age to 21 cannot fairly be said to be reasonably related to the expenditure of funds for highway construction. The only possible connection, highway safety, has nothing to do with how the funds Congress has appropriated are expended. Rather than a condition determining how federal highway money shall be expended, it is a regulation determining who shall be able to drink liquor. As such it is not justified by the spending power.

Of the other possible sources of congressional authority for regulating the sale of liquor only the commerce power comes to mind. But in my view, the regulation of the age of the purchasers of liquor, just as the regulation of the price at which liquor may be sold, falls squarely within the scope of those powers reserved to the States by the Twenty-first Amendment. . . .

The immense size and power of the Government of the United States ought not obscure its fundamental character. It remains a Government of enumerated powers. *McCulloch v. Maryland.* Because 23 U. S. C. § 158 cannot be justified as an exercise of any power delegated to the Congress, it is not authorized by the Constitution. The Court errs in holding it to be the law of the land, and I respectfully dissent.

National Federation of Independent Business v. Sebelius

567 U.S. 519 (2012)

■ **CHIEF JUSTICE ROBERTS announced the judgment of the Court and delivered the opinion of the Court with respect to Parts I, II, and III-C, an opinion with respect to Part IV, in which JUSTICE BREYER and JUSTICE KAGAN join, and an opinion with respect to Parts III-A, III-B, and III-D.**

The second provision of the Affordable Care Act directly challenged here is the Medicaid expansion. Enacted in 1965, Medicaid offers federal funding to States to assist pregnant women, children, needy families, the blind, the elderly, and the disabled in obtaining medical care. In order to receive that funding, States must comply with federal criteria governing matters such as who receives care and what services are provided at what cost. By 1982 every State had chosen to participate in Medicaid. Federal funds received through the Medicaid program have become a substantial part of state budgets, now constituting over 10 percent of most States' total revenue.

The Affordable Care Act expands the scope of the Medicaid program and increases the number of individuals the States must cover. For example, the Act requires state programs to provide Medicaid coverage to adults with incomes up to 133 percent of the federal poverty level, whereas many States now cover adults with children only if their income is considerably lower, and do not cover childless adults at all. The Act increases federal funding to cover the States' costs in expanding Medicaid coverage, although States will bear a portion of the costs on their own. If a State does not comply with the Act's new coverage requirements, it may lose not only the federal funding for those requirements, but all of its federal Medicaid funds.

Along with their challenge to the individual mandate, the state plaintiffs in the Eleventh Circuit argued that the Medicaid expansion exceeds Congress's constitutional powers. The Court of Appeals unanimously held that the Medicaid expansion is a valid exercise of Congress's power under the Spending Clause. . . .

IV

A

The States . . . contend that the Medicaid expansion exceeds Congress's authority under the Spending Clause. They claim that Congress is coercing the States to adopt the changes it wants by threatening to withhold all of a State's Medicaid grants, unless the State accepts the new expanded funding and complies with the conditions that come with it. This, they argue, violates the basic principle that the "Federal Government may not compel the States to enact or administer a federal regulatory program." *New York v. United States*, 505 U.S. 144, 188 (1992).

There is no doubt that the Act dramatically increases state obligations under Medicaid. The current Medicaid program requires States to cover only certain discrete categories of needy individuals— pregnant women, children, needy families, the blind, the elderly, and the disabled. There is no mandatory coverage for most childless adults, and the States typically do not offer any such coverage. The States also enjoy considerable flexibility with respect to the coverage levels for parents of needy families. On average States cover only those unemployed parents who make less than 37 percent of the federal poverty level, and only those employed parents who make less than 63 percent of the poverty line.

The Medicaid provisions of the Affordable Care Act, in contrast, require States to expand their Medicaid programs by 2014 to cover all individuals under the age of 65 with incomes below 133 percent of the federal poverty line. The Act also establishes a new "[e]ssential health benefits" package, which States must provide to all new Medicaid recipients—a level sufficient to satisfy a recipient's obligations under the individual mandate. The Affordable Care Act provides that the Federal Government will pay 100 percent of the costs of covering these newly eligible individuals through 2016. In the following years, the federal payment level gradually decreases, to a minimum of 90 percent. In light of the expansion in coverage mandated by the Act, the Federal Government estimates that its Medicaid spending will increase by approximately $100 billion per year, nearly 40 percent above current levels.

The Spending Clause grants Congress the power "to pay the Debts and provide for the . . . general Welfare of the United States." U.S. Const., Art. I, § 8, cl. 1. We have long recognized that Congress may use this power to grant federal funds to the States, and may condition such a grant upon the States' "taking certain actions that Congress could not require them to take." *College Savings Bank v. Florida Prepaid Postsecondary Ed. Expense Bd.*, 527 U.S. 666, 686 (1999). Such measures "encourage a State to regulate in a particular way, [and] influenc[e] a State's policy choices." *New York, supra*, at 166. The conditions imposed by Congress ensure that the funds are used by the States to "provide for the . . . general Welfare" in the manner Congress intended.

At the same time, our cases have recognized limits on Congress's power under the Spending Clause to secure state compliance with federal objectives. We have repeatedly characterized . . . Spending Clause legislation as 'much in the nature of a contract. The legitimacy of Congress's exercise of the spending power "thus rests on whether the State voluntarily and knowingly accepts the terms of the 'contract.'" *Pennhurst State Sch. & Hosp. v. Halderman*, 451 U.S. 1, 17 (1981). Respecting this limitation is critical to ensuring that Spending Clause legislation does not undermine the status of the States as independent sovereigns in our federal system. . . . "[T]he Constitution has never been understood to confer upon Congress the ability to require the States to govern according to Congress' instructions." *New York*, supra, at 162. Otherwise the two-government system established by the Framers would give way to a system that vests power in one central government, and individual liberty would suffer.

That insight has led this Court to strike down federal legislation that commandeers a State's legislative or administrative apparatus for federal purposes. *See, e.g., Printz v. United States*, 521 U.S. 898, 933 (1997) (striking down federal legislation compelling state law enforcement officers to perform federally mandated background checks on handgun purchasers); *New York, supra*, at 174–175 (invalidating provisions of an Act that would compel a State to either take title to nuclear waste or enact particular state waste regulations). It has also led us to scrutinize Spending Clause legislation to ensure that Congress is not using financial inducements to exert a "power akin to undue influence." *Steward Machine Co. v. Davis*, 301 U.S. 548, 590 (1937). Congress may use its spending power to create incentives for States to act in accordance with federal policies. But when "pressure turns into compulsion," *ibid.*, the legislation runs contrary to our system of federalism. . . .

Permitting the Federal Government to force the States to implement a federal program would threaten the political accountability key to our federal system. "[W]here the Federal Government directs the States to regulate, it may be state officials who will bear the brunt of public disapproval, while the federal officials who devised the regulatory program may remain insulated from the electoral ramifications of their decision." *New York, supra,* at 169. Spending Clause programs do not pose this danger when a State has a legitimate choice whether to accept the federal conditions in exchange for federal funds. In such a situation, state officials can fairly be held politically accountable for choosing to accept or refuse the federal offer. But when the State has no choice, the Federal Government can achieve its objectives without accountability, just as in *New York* and *Printz*. Indeed, this danger is heightened when Congress acts under the Spending Clause, because Congress can use that power to implement federal policy it could not impose directly under its enumerated powers. . . .

Congress may attach appropriate conditions to federal taxing and spending programs to preserve its control over the use of federal funds. In the typical case we look to the States to defend their prerogatives by adopting the simple expedient of not yielding to federal blandishments when they do not want to embrace the federal policies as their own. The States are separate and independent sovereigns. Sometimes they have to act like it.

The States, however, argue that the Medicaid expansion is far from the typical case. They object that Congress has "crossed the line distinguishing encouragement from coercion," *New York, supra,* at 175, in the way it has structured the funding: Instead of simply refusing to grant the new funds to States that will not accept the new conditions, Congress has also threatened to withhold those States' existing Medicaid funds. The States claim that this threat serves no purpose other than to force unwilling States to sign up for the dramatic expansion in health care coverage effected by the Act. Given the nature of the threat and the programs at issue here, we must agree. We have upheld Congress's authority to condition the receipt of funds on the States' complying with restrictions on the use of those funds, because that is the means by which Congress ensures that the funds are spent according to its view of the "general Welfare." Conditions that do not here govern the use of the funds, however, cannot be justified on that basis. When, for example, such conditions take the form of threats to terminate other significant independent grants, the conditions are properly viewed as a means of pressuring the States to accept policy changes.

In *South Dakota v. Dole*, we considered a challenge to a federal law that threatened to withhold five percent of a State's federal highway funds if the State did not raise its drinking age to 21. The Court found that the condition was "directly related to one of the main purposes for which highway funds are expended—safe interstate travel." At the same time, the condition was not a restriction on how the highway funds—set aside for specific highway improvement and maintenance efforts—were to be used.

We accordingly asked whether "the financial inducement offered by Congress" was "so coercive as to pass the point at which 'pressure turns into compulsion.' " By "financial inducement" the Court meant the threat of losing five percent of highway funds; no new money was offered to the States to raise their drinking ages. We found that the inducement was not impermissibly coercive, because Congress was offering only "relatively mild encouragement to the States." We observed that "all South Dakota would lose if she adheres to her chosen course as to a suitable minimum drinking age is 5%" of her highway funds. In fact, the federal funds at stake constituted less than half of one percent of South Dakota's budget at the time. . . .

In this case, the financial "inducement" Congress has chosen is much more than "relatively mild encouragement"—it is a gun to the head. Section 1396c of the Medicaid Act provides that if a State's Medicaid plan does not comply with the Act's requirements, the Secretary of Health and Human Services may declare that "further payments will not be made to the State." A State that opts out of the Affordable Care Act's expansion in health care coverage thus stands to lose not merely "a relatively small percentage" of its existing Medicaid funding, but all of it. Medicaid spending accounts for over 20 percent of the average State's total budget, with federal funds covering 50 to 83 percent of those costs. The Federal Government estimates that it will pay out approximately $3.3 trillion between 2010 and 2019 in order to cover the costs of pre-expansion Medicaid. In addition, the States have developed intricate statutory and administrative regimes over the course of many decades to implement their objectives under existing Medicaid. It is easy to see how the *Dole* Court could conclude that the threatened loss of less than half of one percent of South Dakota's budget left that State with a "prerogative" to reject Congress's desired policy, "not merely in theory but in fact." The threatened loss of over 10 percent of a State's overall budget, in contrast, is economic dragooning that leaves the States with no real option but to acquiesce in the Medicaid expansion.[12]

---

[12]   Justice Ginsburg observes that state Medicaid spending will increase by only 0.8 percent after the expansion. That not only ignores increased state administrative expenses, but also assumes that the Federal Government will continue to fund the expansion at the current statutorily specified levels. It is not unheard of, however, for the Federal Government to increase

Justice Ginsburg claims that *Dole* is distinguishable because here "Congress has not threatened to withhold funds earmarked for any other program." But that begs the question: The States contend that the expansion is in reality a new program and that Congress is forcing them to accept it by threatening the funds for the existing Medicaid program. We cannot agree that existing Medicaid and the expansion dictated by the Affordable Care Act are all one program simply because "Congress styled" them as such. If the expansion is not properly viewed as a modification of the existing Medicaid program, Congress's decision to so title it is irrelevant.

Here, the Government claims that the Medicaid expansion is properly viewed merely as a modification of the existing program because the States agreed that Congress could change the terms of Medicaid when they signed on in the first place. The Government observes that the Social Security Act, which includes the original Medicaid provisions, contains a clause expressly reserving "[t]he right to alter, amend, or repeal any provision" of that statute. 42 U.S.C. § 1304. So it does. But "if Congress intends to impose a condition on the grant of federal moneys, it must do so unambiguously." *Pennhurst*, 451 U.S. at 17. A State confronted with statutory language reserving the right to "alter" or "amend" the pertinent provisions of the Social Security Act might reasonably assume that Congress was entitled to make adjustments to the Medicaid program as it developed. Congress has in fact done so, sometimes conditioning only the new funding, other times both old and new.

The Medicaid expansion, however, accomplishes a shift in kind, not merely degree. The original program was designed to cover medical services for four particular categories of the needy: the disabled, the blind, the elderly, and needy families with dependent children. Previous amendments to Medicaid eligibility merely altered and expanded the boundaries of these categories. Under the Affordable Care Act, Medicaid is transformed into a program to meet the health care needs of the entire nonelderly population with income below 133 percent of the poverty level. It is no longer a program to care for the neediest among us, but rather an element of a comprehensive national plan to provide universal health insurance coverage.[14]

---

requirements in such a manner as to impose unfunded mandates on the States. More importantly, the size of the new financial burden imposed on a State is irrelevant in analyzing whether the State has been coerced into accepting that burden. "Your money or your life" is a coercive proposition, whether you have a single dollar in your pocket or $500.

[14] Justice Ginsburg suggests that the States can have no objection to the Medicaid expansion, because "Congress could have repealed Medicaid [and,] [t]hereafter . . . could have enacted Medicaid II, a new program combining the pre-2010 coverage with the expanded coverage required by the ACA." But it would certainly not be that easy. Practical constraints would plainly inhibit, if not preclude, the Federal Government from repealing the existing program and putting every feature of Medicaid on the table for political reconsideration. Such a massive undertaking would hardly be "ritualistic." The same is true of Justice Ginsburg's suggestion that Congress could establish Medicaid as an exclusively federal program.

Indeed, the manner in which the expansion is structured indicates that while Congress may have styled the expansion a mere alteration of existing Medicaid, it recognized it was enlisting the States in a new health care program. Congress created a separate funding provision to cover the costs of providing services to any person made newly eligible by the expansion. While Congress pays 50 to 83 percent of the costs of covering individuals currently enrolled in Medicaid once the expansion is fully implemented Congress will pay 90 percent of the costs for newly eligible persons. The conditions on use of the different funds are also distinct. Congress mandated that newly eligible persons receive a level of coverage that is less comprehensive than the traditional Medicaid benefit package.

As we have explained, "[t]hough Congress' power to legislate under the spending power is broad, it does not include surprising participating States with postacceptance or 'retroactive' conditions." *Pennhurst, supra,* at 25. A State could hardly anticipate that Congress's reservation of the right to "alter" or "amend" the Medicaid program included the power to transform it so dramatically. . . .

The Court in *Steward Machine* did not attempt to "fix the outermost line" where persuasion gives way to coercion. The Court found it "[e]nough for present purposes that wherever the line may be, this statute is within it." We have no need to fix a line either. It is enough for today that wherever that line may be, this statute is surely beyond it. Congress may not simply "conscript state [agencies] into the national bureaucratic army," *FERC v. Mississippi*, 456 U.S. 742, 775 (1982) (O'Connor, J., concurring in judgment in part and dissenting in part), and that is what it is attempting to do with the Medicaid expansion.

B

Nothing in our opinion precludes Congress from offering funds under the Affordable Care Act to expand the availability of health care, and requiring that States accepting such funds comply with the conditions on their use. What Congress is not free to do is to penalize States that choose not to participate in that new program by taking away their existing Medicaid funding. Section 1396c gives the Secretary of Health and Human Services the authority to do just that. It allows her to withhold all "further [Medicaid] payments . . . to the State" if she determines that the State is out of compliance with any Medicaid requirement, including those contained in the expansion. In light of the Court's holding, the Secretary cannot apply § 1396c to withdraw existing Medicaid funds for failure to comply with the requirements set out in the expansion.

That fully remedies the constitutional violation we have identified. The chapter of the United States Code that contains § 1396c includes a severability clause confirming that we need go no further. That clause specifies that "[i]f any provision of this chapter, or the application thereof to any person or circumstance, is held invalid, the remainder of the chapter, and the application of such provision to other persons or circumstances shall not be affected thereby." § 1303. Today's holding does not affect the continued application of § 1396c to the existing Medicaid program. Nor does it affect the Secretary's ability to withdraw funds provided under the Affordable Care Act if a State that has chosen to participate in the expansion fails to comply with the requirements of that Act. . . .

The judgment of the Court of Appeals for the Eleventh Circuit is affirmed in part and reversed in part.

It is so ordered.

JUSTICE GINSBURG, with whom JUSTICE SOTOMAYOR joins, and with whom JUSTICE BREYER and JUSTICE KAGAN join as to Parts I, II, III, and IV, concurring in part, concurring in the judgment in part, and dissenting in part.

I would . . . hold that the Spending Clause permits the Medicaid expansion exactly as Congress enacted it. . . .

V

. . . The spending power conferred by the Constitution, the Court has never doubted, permits Congress to define the contours of programs financed with federal funds. And to expand coverage, Congress could have recalled the existing legislation, and replaced it with a new law making Medicaid as embracive of the poor as Congress chose.

The question posed by the 2010 Medicaid expansion, then, is essentially this: To cover a notably larger population, must Congress take the repeal/reenact route, or may it achieve the same result by amending existing law? The answer should be that Congress may expand by amendment the classes of needy persons entitled to Medicaid benefits. A ritualistic requirement that Congress repeal and reenact spending legislation in order to enlarge the population served by a federally funded program would advance no constitutional principle and would scarcely serve the interests of federalism. To the contrary, such a requirement would rigidify Congress' efforts to empower States by partnering with them in the implementation of federal programs.

Medicaid is a prototypical example of federal-state cooperation in serving the Nation's general welfare. Rather than authorizing a federal agency to administer a uniform national health-care system for the poor, Congress offered States the opportunity to tailor Medicaid grants to their particular needs, so long as they remain within bounds set by federal law. In shaping Medicaid, Congress did not endeavor to fix permanently the terms participating states must meet; instead, Congress reserved the "right to alter, amend, or repeal" any provision of the Medicaid Act. States, for their part, agreed to amend their own Medicaid plans consistent with changes from time to time made in the federal law. And from 1965 to the present, States have regularly conformed to Congress' alterations of the Medicaid Act.

The Chief Justice acknowledges that Congress may "condition the receipt of [federal] funds on the States' complying with restrictions on the use of those funds," but nevertheless concludes that the 2010 expansion is unduly coercive. His conclusion rests on three premises, each of them essential to his theory. First, the Medicaid expansion is, in The Chief Justice's view, a new grant program, not an addition to the Medicaid program existing before the ACA's enactment. Congress, The Chief Justice maintains, has threatened States with the loss of funds from an old program in an effort to get them to adopt a new one. Second, the expansion was unforeseeable by the States when they first signed on to Medicaid. Third, the threatened loss of funding is so large that the States have no real choice but to participate in the Medicaid expansion. The Chief Justice therefore—*for the first time ever*—finds an exercise of Congress' spending power unconstitutionally coercive.

Medicaid, as amended by the ACA, however, is not two spending programs; it is a single program with a constant aim—to enable poor persons to receive basic health care when they need it. Given past expansions, plus express statutory warning that Congress may change the requirements participating States must meet, there can be no tenable claim that the ACA fails for lack of notice. Moreover, States have no entitlement to receive any Medicaid funds; they enjoy only the opportunity to accept funds on Congress' terms. Future Congresses are not bound by their predecessors' dispositions; they have authority to spend federal revenue as they see fit. The Federal Government, therefore, is not, as The Chief Justice charges, threatening States with the loss of "existing" funds from one spending program in order to induce them to opt into another program. Congress is simply requiring States to do what States have long been required to do to receive Medicaid funding: comply with the conditions Congress prescribes for participation. . . .

A

Expansion has been characteristic of the Medicaid program. Akin to the ACA in 2010, the Medicaid Act as passed in 1965 augmented existing federal grant programs jointly administered with the States. States were not required to participate in Medicaid. But if they did, the Federal Government paid at least half the costs. To qualify for these grants, States had to offer a minimum level of health coverage to beneficiaries of four federally funded, state-administered welfare programs: Aid to Families with Dependent Children; Old Age Assistance; Aid to the Blind; and Aid to the Permanently and Totally Disabled. At their option, States could enroll additional "medically needy" individuals; these costs, too, were partially borne by the Federal Government at the same, at least 50%, rate.

Since 1965, Congress has amended the Medicaid program on more than 50 occasions, sometimes quite sizably. Most relevant here, between 1988 and 1990, Congress required participating States to include among their beneficiaries pregnant women with family incomes up to 133% of the federal poverty level, children up to age 6 at the same income levels, and children ages 6 to 18 with family incomes up to 100% of the poverty level. These amendments added millions to the Medicaid-eligible population. Between 1966 and 1990, annual federal Medicaid spending grew from $631.6 million to $42.6 billion; state spending rose to $31 billion over the same period. And between 1990 and 2010, federal spending increased to $269.5 billion. Enlargement of the population and services covered by Medicaid, in short, has been the trend.

Compared to past alterations, the ACA is notable for the extent to which the Federal Government will pick up the tab. Medicaid's 2010 expansion is financed largely by federal outlays. In 2014, federal funds will cover 100% of the costs for newly eligible beneficiaries; that rate will gradually decrease before settling at 90% in 2020. By comparison, federal contributions toward the care of beneficiaries eligible pre-ACA range from 50% to 83%, and averaged 57% between 2005 and 2008.

Nor will the expansion exorbitantly increase state Medicaid spending. The Congressional Budget Office (CBO) projects that States will spend 0.8% more than they would have, absent the ACA. Whatever the increase in state obligations after the ACA, it will pale in comparison to the increase in federal funding.

Finally, any fair appraisal of Medicaid would require acknowledgment of the considerable autonomy States enjoy under the Act. Far from "conscript[ing] state agencies into the national bureaucratic army," Medicaid is designed to advance cooperative federalism. Subject to its basic requirements, the Medicaid Act empowers States to "select dramatically different levels of funding and coverage, alter and experiment with different financing and delivery modes, and opt to cover (or not to cover) a range of particular procedures and therapies. States have leveraged this policy discretion to generate a myriad of dramatically different Medicaid programs over the past several decades." Ruger, *Of Icebergs and Glaciers*, 75 Law & Contemp. Probs. 215, 233 (2012). The ACA does not jettison this approach. States, as first-line administrators, will continue to guide the distribution of substantial resources among their needy populations.

The alternative to conditional federal spending, it bears emphasis, is not state autonomy but state marginalization. In 1965, Congress elected to nationalize health coverage for seniors through Medicare. It could similarly have established Medicaid as an exclusively federal program. Instead, Congress gave the States the opportunity to partner in the program's administration and development. Absent from the nationalized model, of course, is the state-level policy discretion and experimentation that is Medicaid's hallmark; undoubtedly the interests of federalism are better served when States retain a meaningful role in the implementation of a program of such importance.[17]

Although Congress "has no obligation to use its Spending Clause power to disburse funds to the States," *College Sav. Bank v. Florida Prepaid Postsecondary Ed. Expense Bd.*, 527 U.S. 666, 686 (1999), it has provided Medicaid grants notable for their generosity and flexibility. "[S]uch funds," we once observed, "are gifts," *id.*, and so they have remained through decades of expansion in their size and scope.

B

. . . To ensure that federal funds granted to the States are spent "to 'provide for the . . . general Welfare' in the manner Congress intended," Congress must of course have authority to impose limitations on the States' use of the federal dollars. This Court, time and again, has respected Congress' prescription of spending conditions, and has required States to abide by them. . . .

Congress' authority to condition the use of federal funds is not confined to spending programs as first launched. The legislature may, and often does, amend the law, imposing new conditions grant recipients henceforth must meet in order to continue receiving funds.

Yes, there are federalism-based limits on the use of Congress' conditional spending power. In the leading decision in this area, *South Dakota v. Dole*, 483 U.S. 203 (1987), the Court identified four criteria. The conditions placed on federal grants to States must (a) promote the "general welfare," (b) "unambiguously" inform States what is demanded of them, (c) be germane "to the federal interest in particular national projects or programs," and (d) not "induce the States to engage in activities that would themselves be unconstitutional."

The Court in *Dole* mentioned, but did not adopt, a further limitation . . . In "some circumstances," Congress might be prohibited from offering a "financial inducement . . . so coercive as to pass the point at which pressure turns into compulsion." Prior to today's decision, however, the Court has never ruled that the terms of any grant crossed the indistinct line between temptation and coercion. . . .

This case does not present the concerns that led the Court in *Dole* even to consider the prospect of coercion. . . . The ACA . . . relates solely to the federally funded Medicaid program; if States choose not to comply, Congress has not threatened to withhold funds earmarked for any other program. Nor does the ACA use Medicaid funding to induce States to take action Congress itself could not undertake. The Federal Government

---

[17]   The Chief Justice and the joint dissenters perceive in cooperative federalism a "threa[t]" to "political accountability." By that, they mean voter confusion: Citizens upset by unpopular government action, they posit, may ascribe to state officials blame more appropriately laid at Congress' door. But no such confusion is apparent in this case: Medicaid's status as a federally funded, state-administered program is hardly hidden from view.

undoubtedly could operate its own health-care program for poor persons, just as it operates Medicare for seniors' health care.

That is what makes this such a simple case, and the Court's decision so unsettling. Congress, aiming to assist the needy, has appropriated federal money to subsidize state health-insurance programs that meet federal standards. . . . Enforcing that prescription ensures that federal funds will be spent on health care for the poor in furtherance of Congress' present perception of the general welfare.

C

1

The starting premise on which The Chief Justice's coercion analysis rests is that the ACA did not really "extend" Medicaid; instead, Congress created an entirely new program to co-exist with the old. The Chief Justice calls the ACA new, but in truth, it simply reaches more of America's poor than Congress originally covered. . . .

Congress styled and clearly viewed the Medicaid expansion as an amendment to the Medicaid Act, not as a "new" health-care program. To the four categories of beneficiaries for whom coverage became mandatory in1965, and the three mandatory classes added in the late 1980's, the ACA adds an eighth: individuals under 65 with incomes not exceeding 133% of the federal poverty level. The expansion is effectuated by § 2001 of the ACA, aptly titled: "Medicaid Coverage for the Lowest Income Populations." That section amends Title 42, Chapter 7, Subchapter XIX: Grants to States for Medical Assistance Programs. Commonly known as the Medicaid Act, Subchapter XIX filled some 278 pages in 2006. Section 2001 of the ACA would add approximately three pages.

Congress has broad authority to construct or adjust spending programs to meet its contemporary understanding of "the general Welfare." *Helvering v. Davis*, 301 U.S. 619, 640–641 (1937). Courts owe a large measure of respect to Congress' characterization of the grant programs it establishes. Even if courts were inclined to second-guess Congress' conception of the character of its legislation, how would reviewing judges divine whether an Act of Congress, purporting to amend a law, is in reality not an amendment, but a new creation? At what point does an extension become so large that it "transforms" the basic law? . . .

Consider also that Congress could have repealed Medicaid. Thereafter, Congress could have enacted Medicaid II, a new program combining the pre-2010 coverage with the expanded coverage required by the ACA. By what right does a court stop Congress from building up without first tearing down?

2

The Chief Justice finds the Medicaid expansion vulnerable because it took participating States by surprise. . . . For the notion that States must be able to foresee, when they sign up, alterations Congress might make later on, the Chief Justice cites only one case: *Pennhurst State School and Hospital v. Halderman*, 451 U.S. 1(1981). . . . *Pennhurst* . . . instructs that "if Congress intends to impose a condition on the grant of federal moneys, it must do so unambiguously." That requirement is met in this case. Section 2001 does not take effect until 2014. The ACA makes perfectly clear what will be required of States that accept Medicaid funding after that date: They must extend eligibility to adults with incomes no more than 133% of the federal poverty line.

The Chief Justice appears to find in *Pennhurst* a requirement that, when spending legislation is first passed, or when States first enlist in the federal program, Congress must provide clear notice of conditions it might later impose. If I understand his point correctly, it was incumbent on Congress, in 1965, to warn the States clearly of the size and shape potential changes to Medicaid might take. And absent such notice, sizable changes could not be made mandatory. Our decisions do not support such a requirement.

In *Bennett v. New Jersey*, 470 U.S. 632 (1985), the Secretary of Education sought to recoup Title I funds based on the State's noncompliance, from 1970 to 1972, with a 1978 amendment to Title I. Relying on *Pennhurst*, we rejected the Secretary's attempt to recover funds based on the States' alleged violation of a rule that did not exist when the State accepted and spent the funds. When amendment of an existing grant program has no such retroactive effect, however, we have upheld Congress' instruction. In *Bennett v. Kentucky Dep't of Education*, 470 U.S. 656 (1985), the Secretary sued to recapture Title I funds based on the Commonwealth's 1974 violation of a spending condition Congress added to Title I in 1970. Rejecting Kentucky's argument pinned to *Pennhurst*, we held that the Commonwealth suffered no surprise after accepting the federal funds. Kentucky was therefore obliged to return the money. The conditions imposed were to be assessed as of 1974, in light of "the legal requirements in place when the grants were made," not as of 1965, when Title I was originally enacted.

As these decisions show, *Pennhurst's* rule demands that conditions on federal funds be unambiguously clear at the time a State receives and uses the money—not at the time, perhaps years earlier, when Congress passed the law establishing the program. *See also Dole*, 483 U.S., at 208 (finding *Pennhurst* satisfied based on the clarity of the Federal Aid Highway Act as amended in 1984, without looking back to 1956, the year of the Act's adoption).

In any event, from the start, the Medicaid Act put States on notice that the program could be changed: "The right to alter, amend, or repeal any provision of [Medicaid]," the statute has read since 1965, "is hereby reserved to the Congress." 42 U.S.C. § 1304. . . .

In fact, no State proceeded on that understanding [that Congress could not make major alterations to Medicaid]. In compliance with Medicaid regulations, each State expressly undertook to abide by future

Medicaid changes. Whenever a State notifies the Federal Government of a change in its own Medicaid program, the State certifies both that it knows the federally set terms of participation may change, and that it will abide by those changes as a condition of continued participation.

The Chief Justice insists that the most recent expansion, in contrast to its predecessors, "accomplishes a shift in kind, not merely degree." But why was Medicaid altered only in degree, not in kind, when Congress required States to cover millions of children and pregnant women? . . .

3

. . . The Chief Justice sees no need to "fix the outermost line where persuasion gives way to coercion." Neither do the joint dissenters. . . . When future Spending Clause challenges arrive, as they likely will in the wake of today's decision, how will litigants and judges assess whether "a State has a legitimate choice whether to accept the federal conditions in exchange for federal funds"? Are courts to measure the number of dollars the Federal Government might withhold for noncompliance? The portion of the State's budget at stake?

And which State's—or States'—budget is determinative: the lead plaintiff, all challenging States (26 in this case, many with quite different fiscal situations), or some national median? Does it matter that Florida, unlike most States, imposes no state income tax, and therefore might be able to replace foregone federal funds with new state revenue? Or that the coercion state officials in fact fear is punishment at the ballot box for turning down a politically popular federal grant? The coercion inquiry, therefore, appears to involve political judgments that defy judicial calculation. *See Baker v. Carr*, 369 U.S. 186, 217 (1962). Even commentators sympathetic to robust enforcement of *Dole*'s limitations have concluded that conceptions of "impermissible coercion" premised on States' perceived inability to decline federal funds "are just too amorphous to be judicially administrable." Baker & Berman, *Getting off the Dole*, 78 Ind. L. J. 459, 521, 522, n. 307 (2003).

At bottom, my colleagues' position is that the States' reliance on federal funds limits Congress' authority to alter its spending programs. This gets things backwards: Congress, not the States, is tasked with spending federal money in service of the general welfare. And each successive Congress is empowered to appropriate funds as it sees fit. When the 110th Congress reached a conclusion about Medicaid funds that differed from its predecessors' view, it abridged no State's right to "existing," or "pre-existing," funds. For, in fact, there are no such funds. There is only money States *anticipate* receiving from future Congresses.

JUSTICE SCALIA, JUSTICE KENNEDY, JUSTICE THOMAS, and JUSTICE ALITO, dissenting.

The second question is whether the congressional power to tax and spend, U.S. Const., Art. I, § 8, cl. 1, permits the conditioning of a State's continued receipt of all funds under a massive state-administered federal welfare program upon its acceptance of an expansion to that program. Several of our opinions have suggested that the power to tax and spend cannot be used to coerce state administration of a federal program, but we have never found a law enacted under the spending power to be coercive. Those questions are difficult. . . .

Monetary grants, so-called grants-in-aid, became more frequent during the 1930's, and by 1950 they had reached $20 billion or 11.6% of state and local government expenditures from their own sources. By 1970 this number had grown to $123.7 billion or 29.1% of state and local government expenditures from their own sources. As of 2010, federal outlays to state and local governments came to over $608 billion or 37.5% of state and local government expenditures. . . .

This formidable power, if not checked in any way, would present a grave threat to the system of federalism created by our Constitution. . . .

Amici who support the Government argue that forcing state employees to implement a federal program is more respectful of federalism than using federal workers to implement that program. They note that Congress, instead of expanding Medicaid, could have established an entirely federal program to provide coverage for the same group of people. By choosing to structure Medicaid as a cooperative federal-state program, they contend, Congress allows for more state control.

This argument reflects a view of federalism that our cases have rejected—and with good reason. When Congress compels the States to do its bidding, it blurs the lines of political accountability. If the Federal Government makes a controversial decision while acting on its own, "it is the Federal Government that makes the decision in full view of the public, and it will be federal officials that suffer the consequences if the decision turns out to be detrimental or unpopular." *New York*, 505 U.S., at 168. But when the Federal Government compels the States to take unpopular actions, "it may be state officials who will bear the brunt of public disapproval, while the federal officials who devised the regulatory program may remain insulated from the electoral ramifications of their decision." *Id.*, at 169. For this reason, federal officeholders may view this "departur[e] from the federal structure to be in their personal interests . . . as a means of shifting responsibility for the eventual decision." *New York*, 505 U.S., at 182–183. And even state officials may favor such a "departure from the constitutional plan," since uncertainty concerning responsibility may also permit them to escape accountability. *Id.*, at 182. If a program is popular, state officials may claim credit; if it is unpopular, they may protest that they were merely responding to a federal directive.

Once it is recognized that spending-power legislation cannot coerce state participation, two questions remain: (1) What is the meaning of coercion in this context? (2) Is the ACA's expanded Medicaid coverage coercive? . . .

The answer to the first of these questions—the meaning of coercion in the present context—is straightforward. . . . [I]f States really have no choice other than to accept the package, the offer is coercive, and the conditions cannot be sustained under the spending power. And as our decision in *South Dakota v. Dole* makes clear, theoretical voluntariness is not enough. . . .

The Federal Government's argument in this case at best pays lip service to the anticoercion principle. The Federal Government suggests that it is sufficient if States are "free, as a matter of law, to turn down" federal funds. According to the Federal Government, neither the amount of the offered federal funds nor the amount of the federal taxes extracted from the taxpayers of a State to pay for the program in question is relevant in determining whether there is impermissible coercion.

This argument ignores reality. When a heavy federal tax is levied to support a federal program that offers large grants to the States, States may, as a practical matter, be unable to refuse to participate in the federal program and to substitute a state alternative. Even if a State believes that the federal program is ineffective and inefficient, withdrawal would likely force the State to impose a huge tax increase on its residents, and this new state tax would come on top of the federal taxes already paid by residents to support subsidies to participating States.[13]

Acceptance of the Federal Government's interpretation of the anticoercion rule would permit Congress to dictate policy in areas traditionally governed primarily at the state or local level. Suppose, for example, that Congress enacted legislation offering each State a grant equal to the State's entire annual expenditures for primary and secondary education. Suppose also that this funding came with conditions governing such things as school curriculum, the hiring and tenure of teachers, the drawing of school districts, the length and hours of the school day, the school calendar, a dress code for students, and rules for student discipline. As a matter of law, a State could turn down that offer, but if it did so, its residents would not only be required to pay the federal taxes needed to support this expensive new program, but they would also be forced to pay an equivalent amount in state taxes. And if the State gave in to the federal law, the State and its subdivisions would surrender their traditional authority in the field of education. Asked at oral argument whether such a law would be allowed under the spending power, the Solicitor General responded that it would. . . .

Whether federal spending legislation crosses the line from enticement to coercion is often difficult to determine, and courts should not conclude that legislation is unconstitutional on this ground unless

---

[13]   Justice Ginsburg argues that "[a] State . . . has no claim on the money its residents pay in federal taxes." This is true as a formal matter. . . . But unless Justice Ginsburg thinks that there is no limit to the amount of money that can be squeezed out of taxpayers, heavy federal taxation diminishes the practical ability of States to collect their own taxes.

the coercive nature of an offer is unmistakably clear. In this case, however, there can be no doubt. In structuring the ACA, Congress unambiguously signaled its belief that every State would have no real choice but to go along with the Medicaid Expansion. If the anticoercion rule does not apply in this case, then there is no such rule. . . .

In crafting the ACA, Congress clearly expressed its informed view that no State could possibly refuse the offer that the ACA extends.

The stated goal of the ACA is near-universal health care coverage. To achieve this goal, the ACA mandates that every person obtain a minimum level of coverage. It attempts to reach this goal in several different ways. . . . [F]or low-income individuals who are simply not able to obtain insurance, Congress expanded Medicaid, transforming it from a program covering only members of a limited list of vulnerable groups into a program that provides at least the requisite minimum level of coverage for the poor. This design was intended to provide at least a specified minimum level of coverage for all Americans, but the achievement of that goal obviously depends on participation by every single State. . . .

If Congress had thought that States might actually refuse to go along with the expansion of Medicaid, Congress would surely have devised a backup scheme so that the most vulnerable groups in our society, those previously eligible for Medicaid, would not be left out in the cold. But nowhere in the over 900-page Act is such a scheme to be found. By contrast, because Congress thought that some States might decline federal funding for the operation of a "health benefit exchange," Congress provided a backup scheme; if a State declines to participate in the operation of an exchange, the Federal Government will step in and operate an exchange in that State. . . .

These features of the ACA convey an unmistakable message: Congress never dreamed that any State would refuse to go along with the expansion of Medicaid. Congress well understood that refusal was not a practical option.

The Federal Government does not dispute the inference that Congress anticipated 100% state participation, but it argues that this assumption was based on the fact that ACA's offer was an "exceedingly generous" gift. . . .

This characterization of the ACA's offer raises obvious questions. If that offer is "exceedingly generous," as the Federal Government maintains, why have more than half the States brought this lawsuit, contending that the offer is coercive? And why did Congress find it necessary to threaten that any State refusing to accept this "exceedingly generous" gift would risk losing all Medicaid funds? . . . It is true that the Federal Government will bear most of the initial costs associated with the Medicaid Expansion . . . But that is just part of the picture. Participating States will be forced to shoulder substantial costs as well, because after 2019 the Federal Government will cover only 90% of the costs associated with the Expansion, with state spending projected to increase by at least $20 billion by 2020 as a consequence. After 2019, state spending is expected to increase at a faster rate; the CBO estimates new state spending at $60 billion through 2021. And these costs may increase in the future because of the very real possibility that the Federal Government will change funding terms and reduce the percentage of funds it will cover. . . . Finally, after 2015, the States will have to pick up the tab for 50% of all administrative costs associated with implementing the new program, costs that could approach $12 billion between fiscal years 2014 and 2020.

In sum, it is perfectly clear from the goal and structure of the ACA that the offer of the Medicaid Expansion was one that Congress understood no State could refuse. The Medicaid Expansion therefore exceeds Congress' spending power and cannot be implemented. . . .

Seven Members of the Court agree that the Medicaid Expansion, as enacted Congress, is unconstitutional. Because the Medicaid Expansion is unconstitutional, the question of remedy arises. The most natural remedy would be to invalidate the Medicaid Expansion. However, the government proposes . . . preserving the Expansion. Under its proposal, States would receive the additional Medicaid funds if they expand eligibility, but States would keep their pre-existing Medicaid funds if they do not expand eligibility. We cannot accept the Government's suggestion.

The reality that States were given no real choice but to expand Medicaid was not an accident. Congress assumed States would have no choice, and the ACA depends on States' having no choice, because its Mandate requires low-income individuals to obtain insurance many of them can afford only through the Medicaid Expansion. Furthermore, a State's withdrawal might subject everyone in the State to much higher insurance premiums. That is because the Medicaid Expansion will no longer offset the cost to the insurance industry imposed by the ACA's insurance regulations and taxes . . . To make the Medicaid Expansion optional despite the ACA's structure and design would be to make a new law, not to enforce an old one. This is no part of our duty. . . .

NOTE ON THE SPENDING POWER

1.   The nature of the spending power was a bone of contention between James Madison and Alexander Hamilton in the early Republic. Madison's view, as summarized by the Court in *United States v. Butler*, 297 U.S. 1, 65 (1936), was that the Spending Clause "amounted to no more than a reference to the other powers enumerated in the subsequent clauses of the same section; that, as the United States is a government of limited and enumerated powers, the grant of power to tax and spend for the general national welfare must be confined to the enumerated legislative fields committed to the Congress." In other words, Congress can use the

enumerated means—spending—only for enumerated ends. Hamilton, on the other hand, maintained that "the power of Congress to authorize expenditure of public moneys for public purposes is not limited by the direct grants of legislative power found in the Constitution"; rather, "its confines are set in the clause which confers it. . . ."[40] For Hamilton, then, the only limit on the purposes for which Congress may spend money are that they have to implicate the common defense or the general welfare.

As the *Dole* opinions make clear, the Court has long since adopted Hamilton's view of the spending power. This confirms the relationship between enumerated means and ends suggested by Chief Justice Marshall in *McCulloch*.

- Principle of Unenumerated Means: When Congress legislates in furtherance of an enumerated end—e.g., regulation of the interstate economy—it may use any necessary and proper means whether or not that means is an enumerated power. See McCulloch.

- Principle of Unenumerated Ends: When Congress employs an enumerated power or means—e.g., spending money—it may do so for any purpose whether or not it is an enumerated end. See Butler (adopting Hamilton over Madison).

In other words, as long as *either* the goal that Congress is pursuing or the *means* Congress is using is specifically set forth in the Constitution, the law will be constitutional. (This is subject, as always, to the proviso that no *affirmative* constitutional limitation, such as a provision of the Bill of Rights, is implicated.)

This analysis has two important corollaries:

- Corollary #1: Congress's necessary and proper authority doesn't extend to unenumerated ends. In other words, if the goal isn't in the Constitution, Congress is stuck with the limited means that the Constitution explicitly gives it.

- Corollary #2: Unenumerated ends do not themselves have the force of federal law—i.e., they have no preemptive effect. States are free to legislate in pursuit of contradictory goals.

For instance, Congress can withhold federal education funds from state schools that refuse to ban handguns (principle of unenumerated ends), but it can't regulate guns in schools directly in order to facilitate the purpose of handgun safety (Corollary #1), and the federal policy embodied in Congress's denial of funds to non-gun-free schools would not itself preempt, under the Supremacy Clause, a state's decision to issue handguns to teachers (Corollary #2).[41]

2. The constitutionality of conditions on federal grants of money to the states is an important instance of a general problem in modern constitutional

---

[40] Alexander Hamilton, *Report on Manufactures to the House of Representatives*, 3 WORKS OF ALEXANDER HAMILTON 372 (Lodge ed. 1885).

[41] On these principles, see generally David Engdahl, *The Spending Power*, 44 DUKE L. J. 1 (1994).

law. In the early Republic, neither the national government nor the state did much in the way of providing government benefits—e.g., welfare benefits, access to public education, public employment—to individuals. But the modern state does this on a vast scale, with the upshot that most individuals and many corporate entities are dependent in important ways on governmental largesse. (Consider, for example, the proportion of the law school class that has received a federal student loan.) These benefits, which we do not generally think of as constitutional entitlements, give the government a great deal of leverage over private persons. Sometimes the government exerts this leverage to induce individuals or entities to waive important constitutional rights. Many of these waivers are eminently sensible and unproblematic: While it might well be unconstitutional for the government to require individuals to attend graduate school, it is hardly unreasonable to make graduate school attendance a precondition for receipt of a federal graduate student loan. On the other hand, a condition that required the recipient of a federal student loan to refrain from criticizing the federal government would be considerably more troubling. This is the general problem of "unconstitutional conditions," and it is one of the most intractable problems in constitutional law.

For much of our history, courts viewed conditions requiring the waiver of constitutional rights as unproblematic. In *McAuliffe v. Mayor of New Bedford*, 155 Mass. 216, 220 (1892), for example, Justice Oliver Wendell Holmes rejected a free speech claim by a police officer who had been discharged on account of his political views: "The petitioner may have a constitutional right to talk politics, but he has no constitutional right to be a policeman. . . . The servant cannot complain, as he takes the employment on the terms that are offered him." Later cases have rejected this categorical view and accepted that, at least sometimes, conditions on the receipt of a benefit may impermissibly burden constitutional rights, even though there is no such right to receive the benefit in the first place. For example, in *FCC v. League of Women Voters*, 468 U.S. 364 (1984), the Court struck down a condition on grants of federal monies from the Corporation on Public Broadcasting that the recipient broadcasting stations must refrain from "editorializing." However, the "unconstitutional conditions doctrine" is not so much a doctrine—that is, a set of relatively determinate rules—as an acknowledgment that conditions on governmental benefits will sometimes be constitutionally problematic. The rules for how far such conditions can go have been left to be worked out differently in different doctrinal contexts.[42]

3.   *South Dakota v. Dole* poses one particular instance of the unconstitutional conditions problem. In *Dole*, the State is assumed to have the "right" to regulate alcohol consumption without federal interference; it is asked to waive that right, however, as a condition on the receipt of federal highway funds. Is this problem any different from that of the policeman in *McAuliffe*, who is asked to suppress his own political views, protected by the First Amendment, as a condition of continued public employment? Does this parallel structure of the spending power problem in *Dole* and the individual

---

[42]   *See* Cass. R. Sunstein, *Why the Unconstitutional Conditions Doctrine is an Anachronism (With Particular Reference to Religion, Speech, and Abortion)*, 70 B.U. L. REV. 593 (1990).

rights problem in cases like *McAuliffe* or *League of Women Voters* explain why Justice Brennan, ordinarily no crusader for "states' rights," joined Justice O'Connor's dissent in *Dole*? Does it make sense to treat individuals and states the same in this context? Isn't it a lot harder to coerce South Dakota than Officer McAuliffe?

On the other hand, the amount of federal financial leverage on the States is vast. Lynn Baker noted in 1995 that "[o]ver the past fifty years, federal grants to states and localities have increased nearly 20,000%, growing from $991 million in 1943 to $18.173 billion in 1968 and 195.201 billion in 1993."[43] Moreover, "these federal grants have constituted an increasingly large proportion of total state and local revenues, increasing from 10.8% in 1950, to nearly twice that—19.9%—in 1991."[44] More recent state financial woes may have increased this dependence even further.[45] Should the Court in *Dole* have been more concerned about the coercive effect of federal spending conditions?

4. In the leading treatment of the unconstitutional conditions problem under the Spending Clause, Lynn Baker acknowledges that "the Constitution does not guarantee the states any federal funds"; moreover, "the Court has never questioned that Congress can seek indirectly, through conditions on federal funds it offers the states, any regulatory objective that it could also achieve directly."[46] This latter point means that any analysis of a spending condition must begin by asking whether Congress could simply have imposed the condition as a direct mandate. Because Congress's direct regulatory powers are so broad, many spending power claims will stop at this point.

Cases like *United States v. Lopez*, however, do put certain things beyond Congress's power to mandate directly. Professor Baker notes that "[t]hree days after the Court's ruling in *Lopez*, President Clinton proclaimed that he was 'determined to keep guns out of our schools,' and contended that Congress would not run afoul of the Constitution if it now chose to 'encourage states to ban guns from school zones by linking Federal funds to enactment of school-zone gun bans.' "[47] The concern, of course, is that "if the Spending Clause is . . . interpreted to permit Congress to seek otherwise forbidden regulatory aims indirectly through a conditional offer of federal funds to the states, the notion of 'a federal government of enumerated powers' will have no meaning."[48] Would President Clinton's proposal, if upheld as a valid exercise of the spending power, effectively allow the Congress to overrule *Lopez*?

NFIB dealt with a somewhat different problem. Congress likely has power to enact a Medicaid-type program of social insurance without state

---

[43] Lynn A. Baker, *Conditional Federal Spending after* Lopez, 95 COLUM. L. REV. 1911, 1918 n.24 (1995).

[44] *Id.*

[45] *See, e.g.*, Meredith Whitney, *State Bailouts? They've Already Begun*, WALL ST. J., Nov. 3, 2010.

[46] Baker, *supra* note 43, at 1923.

[47] *Id.* at 1913.

[48] *Id.* at 1920.

participation. However, it lacks power to *require* state governments to participate in implementing such a program. *See, e.g., New York v. United States*, 505 U.S. 144 (1992) (holding that Congress may not "commandeer" state officials by forcing them to implement federal law).[49] The Medicaid expansion's constitutionality thus depended on the proposition that the ACA left states a meaningful choice whether or not to participate.

5.   The Court's analysis in *Dole* combines several different doctrinal approaches to limiting the use of conditional spending:

- General Welfare: Spending can only be undertaken if in pursuit of the general welfare.

- Clear Statement: The condition on federal grants must be clearly stated in the legislation creating the grant.

- Germaneness: There must be some degree of "fit" between the condition and the purpose of the grant itself.

- Coercion: At some point, the condition might be such as to render the State's compliance involuntary.

To what extent is each of these methods a helpful approach to the unconstitutional conditions problem under the spending power? Consider, in addressing this question, both the extent to which each avenue would impose a meaningful limit on federal power and the extent to which each approach could be readily enforced by a court.

6.   To what extent is Justice O'Connor's approach different from that of Chief Justice Rehnquist? Professor Baker has proposed a variant on Justice O'Connor's approach:

> [T]hose offers of federal funds to the states which, if accepted, would regulate the states in ways that Congress could not directly mandate, will be presumed invalid. This presumption will be rebutted upon a determination that the offer of funds constitutes 'reimbursement spending' rather than 'regulatory spending.' 'Reimbursement spending' legislation specifies the purpose for which the states are to spend the offered federal funds and simply reimburses the states, in whole or in part, for their expenditures for that purpose.[50]

She illustrates the application of her criterion by comparing two hypothetical offers of federal funds that implement President Clinton's suggestion that the States be encouraged to enact school-zone gun bans:

> (A) Any state receiving federal Safe School funds must have a Gun-Free School Zones Act . . . which makes it a criminal offense for any individual knowingly to possess a firearm at a place that the individual knows, or has reasonable cause to believe, is a school zone; participating states shall receive Safe School funds in the amount of their demonstrated costs of prosecuting offenders under the state's Act.

---

[49]   *See* Section 10.2, *infra.*

[50]   Baker, *supra* note 43, at 1962–63.

(B) Any state receiving federal Education funds must apply them toward the cost of providing a free education to children in grades K through 12 residing in the state, and must have a Gun-Free School Zones Act, which makes it a criminal offense for any individual knowingly to possess a firearm at a place that the individual knows, or has reasonable cause to believe, is a school zone; participating states shall receive Education funds in the amount of $100 per student enrolled in grades K through 12 of the state's public schools.[51]

How should Professor Baker's proposed test apply to these two hypothetical offers of federal funds? Is this a better approach than the Court's multipart test in *Dole*? Is it too restrictive?

7.   Although the Supreme Court had occasionally found that spending conditions were not sufficiently clear under *Dole*, *NFIB* was the first time that the Court invalidated a spending condition as coercive.[52] Although most public attention at the time focused on the debate over the validity of the individual mandate, is it fair to say that the Court's invalidation of the Medicaid expansion is more doctrinally significant? *NFIB* is also the first time in the post-*Lopez* era that any of the liberal justices have joined in invalidating a federal statute on federalism grounds. What do you make of Justices Breyer's and Kagan's decision to join the Chief Justice on the spending point?

8.   The Chief Justice's opinion in *NFIB* emphasizes two aspects of the Medicaid expansion as problematic: First, Congress threatened to take away "old money" if the states did not agree to expand Medicaid, and second, the Medicaid program is incredibly large and represents a striking proportion of state budgets. What is the relationship between these two factors? Is either sufficient to invalidate a spending condition?

Consider the "old money" point first. This argument arises not only from *Dole*'s coercion language, but also from its requirement that spending conditions be clear and evident when states accept federal money. States originally signing up for Medicaid in 1965 could not have known that they would be required to participate in an expansion of the program four decades down the line. On the other hand, as a formal matter, Congress appropriates Medicaid funds—and the states agree to accept them—each year. In this sense, it's all "new money." Should this be dispositive, as Justice Ginsburg suggests? Or does it matter that the states have participated in Medicaid for years and established complex programs of their own under its aegis, so that it would be exceptionally difficult to start over now? If we credit this sort of argument, how much reliance does there have to be before a spending condition is invalid? Once Congress establishes a federal program involving spending conditions, is it eternally locked into the program's original form?

---

[51] *Id.* at 1963.

[52] *But see* New York v. United States, 505 U.S. 144 (1992), in Section 10.2, *infra* (finding a provision of a federal conditional *preemption* regime to be coercive and therefore unconstitutional).

What about the size of Medicaid? Given the extraordinary dependence of the states on Medicaid funding, how likely is it that any other federal spending conditions will be found coercive?

9.   Does Justice Ginsburg's dissent seriously grapple with the problem of finding workable doctrinal limits on Congress's conditional spending power? Can you imagine a spending condition that she would be willing to invalidate? Should she instead be understood as arguing, as the dissenters did in *Morrison* with respect to the Commerce Clause, that courts should defer entirely to the political process on these questions? By citing *Baker v. Carr*, is she implying that spending cases present nonjusticiable political questions?

Alternatively, could she be suggesting that states are simply better off when they *can* be coerced into implementing federal programs, because their very participation in those programs is an important aspect of state autonomy?[53] After all, state officials will have a much greater say in how healthcare policy proceeds if they participate under the ACA than if they stand aside and force Congress to create purely federal bureaucracies. Are the states better off participating in "cooperative federalism" ventures like Medicaid? How likely is it that decisions like *NFIB* will actually prevent such participation?

10.   The Chief Justice, joined by Justice Ginsburg's bloc on this point, concludes that assuming Congress may not condition the states' existing Medicaid funding on acceptance of the ACA's expansion in coverage, the Court need not strike down the entire expansion; instead, it is sufficient to order the Secretary administering Medicaid to permit the states to decline participation in the expansion without forfeiting the entirety of their Medicaid funds. Are the dissenters right that this resolution creates a new Medicaid program different from the one that Congress authorized?

The problem is one of "severability," and it arises whenever a court finds part—but not all—of a statutory scheme unconstitutional. The question is, Can the remainder of the statute survive—can it be "severed"—if the unconstitutional part is excised? The Court has generally treated this as a question of legislative intent, asking whether Congress would have enacted the constitutional portion of the statute even if it had known it could not have the unconstitutional portion. Hence, the question under the ACA is whether Congress would have wanted to expand Medicaid at all if it had known that states would be allowed to continue to be part of the program but not participate in the expansion. The answer is not obvious, is it?

As an example of a strong argument for nonseverability, consider the situation if the Court had struck down the individual mandate. This would have left intact the ACA's provisions requiring insurers to offer insurance to all comers regardless of their preexisting medical conditions and at a uniform price that did not reflect relative health risks. But absent the individual mandate, insurers' losses on having to insure unhealthy individuals at uniform rates would not have been offset by the mandatory inclusion of

---

[53]   For an argument along those lines, see Jessica Bulman-Pozen & Heather K. Gerken, *Uncooperative Federalism*, 118 YALE L. J. 1256 (2009).

healthy individuals in the risk pool. This would have created a situation in the insurance market far different from the one Congress envisioned. In that situation, would the Court have been forced to strike down the entire ACA?

See also: The literature on the unconstitutional conditions doctrine is vast. For a taste, see Richard A. Epstein, *The Supreme Court, 1987 Term— Foreword: Unconstitutional Conditions, State Power, and the Limits of Consent*, 102 HARV. L. REV. 4 (1988); Seth F. Kreimer, *Allocational Sanctions: The Problem of Negative Rights in a Positive State*, 132 U. PA. L. REV. 1293 (1984); Kathleen M. Sullivan, *Unconstitutional Conditions*, 102 HARV. L. REV. 1413 (1989); William W. Van Alstyne, *The Demise of the Right-Privilege Distinction in Constitutional Law*, 81 HARV. L. REV. 1439 (1968*)*.

CHAPTER TEN

EXTERNAL LIMITS ON NATIONAL POWER

"External" limits on congressional power operate in circumstances that are acknowledged to fall within the scope of Congress's enumerated powers.[1] We have already considered one external limit on Congress's enumerated powers—the failed doctrine of *National League of Cities*. The next two assignments consider two external limits that are very much alive and well.

The first such limit is the use of "clear statement" rules in construing the scope of federal statutes. In the clear statement cases, the question is not the constitutional validity of the federal statute, but rather the statute's *meaning*. Because federal statutes are often ambiguous as to their precise scope, constitutional values may come into play in resolving disputes about the extent to which the statute intrudes on state prerogatives. The second limit, the "anti-commandeering" doctrine, goes to the means that Congress may employ in exercising its enumerated powers. In particular, the question is whether Congress may require the institutions of *state* government—state legislatures, executive officials, and courts—to implement federal law.

The Constitution's text does not prescribe rules of statutory construction, and it does not specifically address state implementation of federal policy. All of these cases thus raise the broader issue of judicial creativity in fashioning doctrines designed to maintain the federal balance. As you read, compare the debates about judicial creativity in these cases with similar debates about judicial identification of unenumerated individual rights.

SECTION 10.1 CLEAR STATEMENT RULES

It is hard to find a perfectly unambiguous statute. Even if the law's text seems clear on its face, cases are bound to arise in which the proper application of the law is unclear. Consider, for example, H.L.A. Hart's famous example of a local ordinance that forbids "vehicles" in a public park: "Plainly this forbids an automobile, but what about bicycles, roller skates, toy automobiles? . . . Are these, as we say, to be called 'vehicles' for the purpose of the rule or not?"[2] One might think that, despite some ambiguous cases around the edges, a rule like this nonetheless has a

---

[1] Recall that "internal" limits, by contrast, concern the scope of those powers themselves. *E.g.*, the Commerce Power is limited to regulating "commercial" activities.

[2] H.L.A. Hart, *Positivism and the Separation of Law and Morals*, 71 HARV. L. REV. 593, 607 (1958).

clear "core." But ambiguity may exist even here. Notwithstanding Professor Hart's suggestion that "[p]lainly this forbids an automobile," would it forbid a military truck that was incorporated into a war memorial? [3] Courts thus inevitably confront uncertainties about statutory meaning. And although statutes may be more readily amended than constitutions to resolve ambiguities and deal with unforeseen circumstances, such amendment is in fact often difficult: Congress has a very limited agenda, relatively small constituencies have many opportunities to block statutory change, and even successful amendments may take a great deal of time. Statutory interpretation thus raises many of the same methodological problems that we have already encountered in interpreting the constitutional text.

When confronted with an ambiguous statutory text, judges often fall back upon default rules or "canons" of statutory construction. These rules generally fall into two categories. The first sort are sometimes called "descriptive" canons—they attempt to describe the legislature's usual preferences. The dominant paradigm in American statutory interpretation is that judges are to be "faithful agents" of the legislature. The idea, in other words, is to resolve statutory ambiguities by imagining what the enacting legislature would have wanted. Many canons of statutory construction thus reflect judicial judgments about likely legislative preferences. An example is the rule that "the specific controls the general"—that is, that when two statutory provisions are potentially applicable to the same situation, the one that deals more specifically with the situation will apply. [4] This reflects a judgment that when a legislature has dealt with a situation in a detailed way, it generally will not mean to set that aside without making some specific provision to that effect.

Some rules of construction, however, are based not so much on a view of likely legislative intent but rather on the desire to promote certain normative values. These "normative" canons seek to push interpretation in a particular direction in order to serve some purpose that the court feels is valuable for its own sake—e.g., protection of individual rights or general principles of fairness—whether or not the legislature had that value in mind in drafting this particular statute. The rule that "repeals by implication are disfavored," [5] for example, promotes a norm of continuity in the law which is considered independently valuable, whether or not the legislature actually favors such continuity.

In each of the next three cases, federal statutes arguably intrude significantly on state autonomy, but the extent of that intrusion is somewhat ambiguous. The Court has, in recent years, developed a set of federalism-protecting canons of statutory construction that tend to

---

[3]   *See Lon L. Fuller, Positivism and Fidelity to Law—A Reply to Professor Hart*, 71 HARV. L. REV. 630, 663 (1958) (offering this example).

[4]   *See, e.g., Kepner v. United States*, 195 U.S. 100, 123 (1904).

[5]   *See, e.g., Morton v. Mancari*, 417 U.S. 535, 549–50 (1974).

resolve such ambiguities in ways that minimize the degree of federal intrusion. As *Jones v. United States* shows, these canons rely in part on the notion of avoiding constructions that raise a constitutional doubt. In *Gregory v. Ashcroft*, however, it is unclear what the constitutional "problem" in *Gregory* would be. The canon of avoiding constitutional doubt is also in play in *Solid Waste Authority v. U.S. Army Corps of Engineers*, and again it is unclear whether even a broad reading of the statute in question would be unconstitutional. *Solid Waste* adds an additional element, moreover, which is the role of a federal administrative agency in interpreting the federal statutes it enforces.

Each of these cases adopts a variant of a pro-federalism "clear statement" rule—that is, a canon of construction that reads ambiguous federal statutes to minimize their intrusion on the States. One might account for such a rule in either descriptive or normative terms: We might think, as a general matter, that Congress generally cares about the States and intends to respect their authority unless it clearly says otherwise, or we might view federalism as independently important and interpret federal statutes narrowly as a means of serving that goal, whether or not that is what Congress would have intended if asked. As you read each case, ask yourself whether the clear statement rule that the Court applies is descriptive or normative in nature, and whether imposing such a rule is consistent with the Court's job in interpreting federal statutes.

Jones v. United States
529 U.S. 848 (2000)

■ JUSTICE GINSBURG **delivered the opinion of the Court.**

It is a federal crime under 18 U.S.C. § 844(i) to damage or destroy, "by means of fire or an explosive, any . . . property used in interstate or foreign commerce or in any activity affecting interstate or foreign commerce." This case presents the question whether arson of an owner-occupied private residence falls within § 844(i)'s compass. Construing the statute's text, we hold that an owner-occupied residence not used for any commercial purpose does not qualify as property "used in" commerce or commerce-affecting activity; arson of such a dwelling, therefore, is not subject to federal prosecution under § 844(i). Our construction of § 844(i) is reinforced by the Court's opinion in *United States v. Lopez* and the interpretive rule that constitutionally doubtful constructions should be avoided where possible.

I

On February 23, 1998, petitioner Dewey Jones tossed a Molotov cocktail through a window into a home in Fort Wayne, Indiana, owned and occupied by his cousin. No one was injured in the ensuing fire, but the blaze severely damaged the home. A federal grand jury returned a three-count indictment charging Jones with arson; using a destructive device during and in relation to a crime of violence (the arson); and making an illegal destructive device. Jones was tried under that indictment in the Northern District of Indiana and convicted by a jury on all three counts. The District Court sentenced him . . . to a total prison term of 35 years, to be followed by five years of supervised release. The court also ordered Jones to pay $77,396.87 to the insurer of the damaged home as restitution for its loss. Jones appealed, and the Court of Appeals for the Seventh Circuit affirmed the judgment of the District Court.

Jones unsuccessfully urged, both before the District Court and on appeal to the Seventh Circuit, that § 844(i), when applied to the arson of a private residence, exceeds the authority vested in Congress under the Commerce Clause of the Constitution, Art. I, § 8, cl. 3. . . . Satisfied that § 844(i) does not reach an owner-occupied residence that is not used for any commercial purpose, we reverse the Court of Appeals' judgment.

II

Congress enacted 18 U.S.C. § 844(i) as part of Title XI of the Organized Crime Control Act of 1970, "because of the need 'to curb the use, transportation, and possession of explosives.'" The word "fire," which did not appear in § 844(i) as originally composed, was introduced by statutory amendment in 1982. As now worded, § 844(i) reads in relevant part:

> Whoever maliciously damages or destroys, or attempts to damage or destroy, by means of fire or an explosive, any building, vehicle, or other real or personal property used in interstate or foreign commerce or in any activity affecting interstate or foreign commerce shall be imprisoned for not less than 5 years and not more than 20 years, fined under this title, or both. . . .

In support of its argument that § 844(i) reaches the arson of an owner-occupied private residence, the Government relies principally on the breadth of the statutory term "affecting . . . commerce," words that, when unqualified, signal Congress' intent to invoke its full authority under the Commerce Clause. But § 844(i) contains the qualifying words "used in" a commerce-affecting activity. The key word is "used." Congress did not define the crime described in § 844(i) as the explosion of a building whose damage or destruction might affect interstate commerce. . . . Congress required that the damaged or destroyed property must itself have been used in commerce or in an activity affecting commerce. The proper inquiry . . . is into the function of the building itself, and then a determination of whether that function affects interstate commerce.

The Government urges that the Fort Wayne, Indiana residence into which Jones tossed a Molotov cocktail was constantly "used" in at least three "activities affecting commerce." First, the homeowner "used" the dwelling as collateral to obtain and secure a mortgage from an Oklahoma lender; the lender, in turn, "used" the property as security for the home loan. Second, the homeowner "used" the residence to obtain a casualty insurance policy from a Wisconsin insurer. . . . Third, the homeowner "used" the dwelling to receive natural gas from sources outside Indiana.

The Government correctly observes that § 844(i) excludes no particular type of building (it covers "any building"); the provision does, however, require that the building be "used" in an activity affecting commerce. That qualification is most sensibly read to mean active employment for commercial purposes, and not merely a passive, passing, or past connection to commerce. Although variously defined, the word "use," in legislation as in conversation, ordinarily signifies "active employment."

It surely is not the common perception that a private, owner-occupied residence is "used" in the "activity" of receiving natural gas, a mortgage, or an insurance policy. The Government does not allege that the Indiana residence involved in this case served as a home office or the locus of any commercial undertaking. The home's only "active employment," so far as the record reveals, was for the everyday living of Jones's cousin and his family. . . .

Were we to adopt the Government's expansive interpretation of § 844(i), hardly a building in the land would fall outside the federal statute's domain. Practically every building in our cities, towns, and rural areas is constructed with supplies that have moved in interstate commerce, served by utilities that have an interstate connection, financed or insured by enterprises that do business across state lines, or bears some other trace of interstate commerce. If such connections sufficed to trigger § 844(i), the statute's limiting language, "used in" any commerce-affecting activity, would have no office. Judges should hesitate . . . to treat statutory terms in any setting as surplusage, and resistance should be heightened when the words describe an element of a criminal offense.

III

Our reading of § 844(i) is in harmony with the guiding principle that where a statute is susceptible of two constructions, by one of which grave and doubtful constitutional questions arise and by the other of which such questions are avoided, our duty is to adopt the latter. In *Lopez,* this Court invalidated the Gun-Free School Zones Act, former 18 U.S.C. § 922(q), which made it a federal crime to possess a firearm within 1,000 feet of a school. . . . Holding that the Act exceeded Congress' power to regulate commerce, the Court stressed that the area was one of traditional state concern, and that the legislation aimed at activity in which "neither the actors nor their conduct has a commercial character."

Given the concerns brought to the fore in *Lopez,* it is appropriate to avoid the constitutional question that would arise were we to read § 844(i) to render the traditionally local criminal conduct in which petitioner Jones engaged a matter for federal enforcement. Our comprehension of § 844(i) is additionally reinforced by other interpretive guides. We have instructed that ambiguity concerning the ambit of criminal statutes should be resolved in favor of lenity, *Rewis v. United States*, 401 U.S. 808, 812 (1971), and that when choice has to be made between two readings of what conduct Congress has made a crime, it is appropriate, before we choose the harsher alternative, to require that Congress should have spoken in language that is clear and definite. *United States v. Universal C.I.T. Credit Corp.*, 344 U.S. 218, 221–22 (1952). We have cautioned, as well, that unless Congress conveys its purpose clearly, it will not be deemed to have significantly changed the federal-state balance in the prosecution of crimes. *United States v. Bass*, 404 U.S. 336, 350 (1971). To read § 844(i) as encompassing the arson of an owner-occupied private home would effect such a change, for arson is a paradigmatic common-law state crime.

IV

We conclude that § 844(i) is not soundly read to make virtually every arson in the country a federal offense. We hold that the provision covers only property currently used in commerce or in an activity affecting commerce. The home owned and occupied by petitioner Jones's cousin was not so used—it was a dwelling place used for everyday family living. As we read § 844(i), Congress left cases of this genre to the law enforcement authorities of the States. . . .

Accordingly, the judgment of the Court of Appeals is reversed, and the case is remanded for further proceedings consistent with this opinion.

■ **JUSTICE STEVENS, with whom JUSTICE THOMAS joins, concurring.**

Part II of the Court's opinion convincingly explains why its construction of 18 U.S.C. § 844(i) better fits the text and context of the provision than the Government's expansive reading. It also seems appropriate, however, to emphasize the kinship between our well-established presumption against federal pre-emption of state law, *Ray v. Atlantic Richfield Co.*, 435 U.S. 151, 157 (1978), and our reluctance to believe Congress intended to authorize federal intervention in local law enforcement in a marginal case such as this. The fact that petitioner received a sentence of 35 years in prison when the maximum penalty for the comparable state offense was only 10 years illustrates how a criminal law like this may effectively displace a policy choice made by the State. Even when Congress has undoubted power to pre-empt local law, we have wisely decided that "unless Congress conveys its purpose clearly, it will not be deemed to have significantly changed the federal-state balance." *United States v. Bass*, 404 U.S. 336 (1971). For this reason, I reiterate my firm belief that we should interpret narrowly federal criminal laws that overlap with state authority unless congressional intention to assert its jurisdiction is plain.

Gregory v. Ashcroft

501 U.S. 452 (1991)

■ JUSTICE O'CONNOR delivered the opinion of the Court.

Article V, § 26, of the Missouri Constitution provides that "all judges other than municipal judges shall retire at the age of seventy years." We consider whether this mandatory retirement provision violates the federal Age Discrimination in Employment Act of 1967 (ADEA), and whether it comports with the federal constitutional prescription of equal protection of the laws.

I

Petitioners are Missouri state judges. Judge Ellis Gregory, Jr., is an associate circuit judge for the Twenty-first Judicial Circuit. Judge Anthony P. Nugent, Jr., is a judge of the Missouri Court of Appeals, Western District. Both are subject to the § 26 mandatory retirement provision. Petitioners were appointed to office by the Governor of Missouri. . . . Each has, since his appointment, been retained in office by means of a retention election in which the judge ran unopposed, subject only to a "yes or no" vote.

Petitioners and two other state judges filed suit against John D. Ashcroft, the Governor of Missouri . . . challenging the validity of the mandatory retirement provision. The judges alleged that the provision violated both the ADEA and the Equal Protection Clause of the Fourteenth Amendment to the United States Constitution. The Governor filed a motion to dismiss.

The District Court granted the motion, holding that Missouri's appointed judges are not protected by the ADEA because they are "appointees . . . 'on a policymaking level' " and therefore are excluded from the Act's definition of "employee." The court held also that the mandatory retirement provision does not violate the Equal Protection Clause because there is a rational basis for the distinction between judges and other state officials to whom no mandatory retirement age applies.

The United States Court of Appeals for the Eighth Circuit affirmed the dismissal. . . . We . . . now affirm.

II

The ADEA makes it unlawful for an "employer" "to discharge any individual" who is at least 40 years old "because of such individual's age." The term "employer" is defined to include "a State or political subdivision of a State." Petitioners work for the State of Missouri. They contend that the Missouri mandatory retirement requirement for judges violates the ADEA.

A

As every schoolchild learns, our Constitution establishes a system of dual sovereignty between the States and the Federal Government. This Court also has recognized this fundamental principle. In *Tafflin v. Levitt,* 493 U.S. 455 (1990), "we beg[a]n with the axiom that, under our federal system, the States possess sovereignty concurrent with that of the Federal Government, subject only to limitations imposed by the Supremacy Clause." Over 120 years ago, the Court described the constitutional scheme of dual sovereigns:

> The people of each State compose a State, having its own government, and endowed with all the functions essential to separate and independent existence. . . . Not only . . . can there be no loss of separate and independent autonomy to the States, through their union under the Constitution, but . . . the preservation of the States, and the maintenance of their governments, are as much within the design and care of the Constitution as the preservation of the Union and the maintenance of the National government. The Constitution . . . looks to an indestructible Union, composed of indestructible States. *Texas v. White,* 74 U.S. (7 Wall.) 700 (1869).

The Constitution created a Federal Government of limited powers. "The powers not delegated to the United States by the Constitution, nor prohibited by it to the States, are reserved to the States respectively, or to the people." U.S. Const., Amdt. 10. The States thus retain substantial sovereign authority under our constitutional system. . . .

This federalist structure of joint sovereigns preserves to the people numerous advantages. It assures a decentralized government that will be more sensitive to the diverse needs of a heterogenous society; it increases opportunity for citizen involvement in democratic processes; it allows for more innovation and experimentation in government; and it makes government more responsive by putting the States in competition for a mobile citizenry.

Perhaps the principal benefit of the federalist system is a check on abuses of government power. The constitutionally mandated balance of power between the States and the Federal Government was adopted by the Framers to ensure the protection of 'our fundamental liberties. Just as the separation and independence of the coordinate branches of the Federal Government serve to prevent the accumulation of excessive power in any one branch, a healthy balance of power between the States and the Federal Government will reduce the risk of tyranny and abuse from either front. Alexander Hamilton explained to the people of New York, perhaps optimistically, that the new federalist system would suppress completely "the attempts of the government to establish a tyranny":

... Power being almost always the rival of power, the general government will at all times stand ready to check the usurpations of the state governments, and these will have the same disposition towards the general government. The people, by throwing themselves into either scale, will infallibly make it preponderate. If their rights are invaded by either, they can make use of the other as the instrument of redress.

... One fairly can dispute whether our federalist system has been quite as successful in checking government abuse as Hamilton promised, but there is no doubt about the design. If this "double security" is to be effective, there must be a proper balance between the States and the Federal Government. These twin powers will act as mutual restraints only if both are credible. In the tension between federal and state power lies the promise of liberty.

The Federal Government holds a decided advantage in this delicate balance: the Supremacy Clause. U.S. Const., Art. VI, cl. 2. As long as it is acting within the powers granted it under the Constitution, Congress may impose its will on the States. Congress may legislate in areas traditionally regulated by the States. This is an extraordinary power in a federalist system. It is a power that we must assume Congress does not exercise lightly.

The present case concerns a state constitutional provision through which the people of Missouri establish a qualification for those who sit as their judges. This provision goes beyond an area traditionally regulated by the States; it is a decision of the most fundamental sort for a sovereign entity. Through the structure of its government, and the character of those who exercise government authority, a State defines itself as a sovereign. It is obviously essential to the independence of the States, and to their peace and tranquility, that their power to prescribe the qualifications of their own officers ... should be exclusive, and free from external interference, except so far as plainly provided by the Constitution of the United States.

Congressional interference with this decision of the people of Missouri, defining their constitutional officers, would upset the usual constitutional balance of federal and state powers. For this reason, it is incumbent upon the federal courts to be certain of Congress' intent before finding that federal law overrides this balance. We explained recently:

> If Congress intends to alter the usual constitutional balance
> between the States and the Federal Government, it must make
> its intention to do so unmistakably clear in the language of the
> statute. ... Congress should make its intention clear and
> manifest if it intends to pre-empt the historic powers of the
> States. ... In traditionally sensitive areas, such as legislation
> affecting the federal balance, the requirement of clear statement
> assures that the legislature has in fact faced, and intended to
> bring into issue, the critical matters involved in the judicial

decision. *Will v. Mich. Dept. of State Police*, 491 U.S. 58, 65 (1989).

This plain statement rule is nothing more than an acknowledgment that the States retain substantial sovereign powers under our constitutional scheme, powers with which Congress does not readily interfere. . . .

[T]he authority of the people of the States to determine the qualifications of their most important government officials. . . . is an authority that lies at "the heart of representative government." It is a power reserved to the States under the Tenth Amendment and guaranteed them by that provision of the Constitution under which the United States "guarantee[s] to every State in this Union a Republican Form of Government." U.S. Const., Art. IV, § 4.

The authority of the people of the States to determine the qualifications of their government officials is, of course, not without limit. Other constitutional provisions, most notably the Fourteenth Amendment, proscribe certain qualifications. . . . Here, we must decide what Congress did in extending the ADEA to the States, pursuant to its powers under the Commerce Clause. See *EEOC v. Wyoming*, 460 U.S. 226 (1983) (the extension of the ADEA to employment by state and local governments was a valid exercise of Congress' powers under the Commerce Clause). As against Congress' powers "to regulate Commerce . . . among the several States," U.S. Const., Art. I, § 8, cl. 3, the authority of the people of the States to determine the qualifications of their government officials may be inviolate.

We are constrained in our ability to consider the limits that the state-federal balance places on Congress' powers under the Commerce Clause. See *Garcia v. San Antonio Metropolitan Transit Authority* (declining to review limitations placed on Congress' *Commerce Clause* powers by our federal system). But there is no need to do so if we hold that the ADEA does not apply to state judges. Application of the plain statement rule thus may avoid a potential constitutional problem. Indeed, inasmuch as this Court in *Garcia* has left primarily to the political process the protection of the States against intrusive exercises of Congress' Commerce Clause powers, we must be absolutely certain that Congress intended such an exercise. "To give the state-displacing weight of federal law to mere congressional *ambiguity* would evade the very procedure for lawmaking on which *Garcia* relied to protect states' interests." L. TRIBE, AMERICAN CONSTITUTIONAL LAW § 6–25, p. 480 (2d ed. 1988).

B

In 1974, Congress extended the substantive provisions of the ADEA to include the States as employers. At the same time, Congress amended the definition of "employee" to exclude all elected and most high-ranking government officials. Under the Act, as amended:

The term 'employee' means an individual employed by any employer except that the term 'employee' shall not include any person elected to public office in any State or political subdivision of any State by the qualified voters thereof, or any person chosen by such officer to be on such officer's personal staff, or an appointee on the policymaking level or an immediate adviser with respect to the exercise of the constitutional or legal powers of the office. 29 U. S. C. § 630(f).

Governor Ashcroft contends that the § 630(f) exclusion of certain public officials also excludes judges, like petitioners, who are appointed to office by the Governor and are then subject to retention election. The Governor points to two passages in § 630(f). First, he argues, these judges are selected by an elected official and, because they make policy, are "appointee[s] on the policymaking level."

Petitioners counter that judges merely resolve factual disputes and decide questions of law; they do not make policy. Moreover, petitioners point out that the policymaking-level exception is part of a trilogy, tied closely to the elected-official exception. Thus, the Act excepts elected officials and: (1) "any person chosen by such officer to be on such officer's personal staff"; (2) "an appointee on the policymaking level"; and (3) "an immediate advisor with respect to the exercise of the constitutional or legal powers of the office." Applying the maxim of statutory construction *noscitur a sociis*—that a word is known by the company it keeps—petitioners argue that since (1) and (3) refer only to those in close working relationships with elected officials, so too must (2). Even if it can be said that judges may make policy, petitioners contend, they do not do so at the behest of an elected official.

Governor Ashcroft relies on the plain language of the statute: It exempts persons appointed "at the policymaking level." The Governor argues that state judges, in fashioning and applying the common law, make policy. Missouri is a common law state. See Mo. Rev. Stat. § 1.010 (adopting "the common law of England" consistent with federal and state law). The common law, unlike a constitution or statute, provides no definitive text; it is to be derived from the interstices of prior opinions and a well-considered judgment of what is best for the community. As Justice Holmes put it:

The very considerations which judges most rarely mention, and always with an apology, are the secret root from which the law draws all the juices of life. I mean, of course, considerations of what is expedient for the community concerned. Every important principle which is developed by litigation is in fact and at bottom the result of more or less definitely understood views of public policy; most generally, to be sure, under our practice and traditions, the unconscious result of instinctive preferences and inarticulate convictions, but nonetheless traceable to views of public policy in the last analysis.

Governor Ashcroft contends that Missouri judges make policy in other ways as well. The Missouri Supreme Court and Courts of Appeals have supervisory authority over inferior courts. The Missouri Supreme Court has the constitutional duty to establish rules of practice and procedure for the Missouri court system, and inferior courts exercise policy judgment in establishing local rules of practice. The state courts have supervisory powers over the state bar, with the Missouri Supreme Court given the authority to develop disciplinary rules.

The Governor stresses judges' policymaking responsibilities, but it is far from plain that the statutory exception requires that judges actually make policy. The statute refers to appointees "on the policymaking level," not to appointees "who make policy." It may be sufficient that the appointee is in a position requiring the exercise of discretion concerning issues of public importance. This certainly describes the bench, regardless of whether judges might be considered policymakers in the same sense as the executive or legislature.

Nonetheless, "appointee at the policymaking level," particularly in the context of the other exceptions that surround it, is an odd way for Congress to exclude judges; a plain statement that judges are not "employees" would seem the most efficient phrasing. But in this case we are not looking for a plain statement that judges are excluded. We will not read the ADEA to cover state judges unless Congress has made it clear that judges are *included*. This does not mean that the Act must mention judges explicitly, though it does not. Rather, it must be plain to anyone reading the Act that it covers judges. In the context of a statute that plainly excludes most important state public officials, "appointee on the policymaking level" is sufficiently broad that we cannot conclude that the statute plainly covers appointed state judges. Therefore, it does not. . . .

C

The extension of the ADEA to employment by state and local governments was a valid exercise of Congress' powers under the Commerce Clause. *EEOC v. Wyoming*, 460 U.S. 226 (1983). In *Wyoming*, we reserved the questions whether Congress might also have passed the ADEA extension pursuant to its powers under § 5 of the Fourteenth Amendment, and whether the extension would have been a valid exercise of that power. We noted, however, that the principles of federalism that constrain Congress' exercise of its Commerce Clause powers are attenuated when Congress acts pursuant to its powers to enforce the Civil War Amendments. This is because those "Amendments were specifically designed as an expansion of federal power and an intrusion on state sovereignty." One might argue, therefore, that if Congress passed the ADEA extension under its § 5 powers, the concerns about federal intrusion into state government that compel the result in this case might carry less weight.

By its terms, the Fourteenth Amendment contemplates interference with state authority: "No State shall . . . deny to any person within its jurisdiction the equal protection of the laws." U.S. Const., Amdt. 14. But this Court has never held that the Amendment may be applied in complete disregard for a State's constitutional powers. Rather, the Court has recognized that the States' power to define the qualifications of their officeholders has force even as against the proscriptions of the Fourteenth Amendment. . . .

Of particular relevance here is *Pennhurst State School and Hospital v. Halderman*, 451 U.S. 1 (1981). . . . The Court was required to consider the "appropriate test for determining when Congress intends to enforce" the guarantees of the Fourteenth Amendment. We adopted a rule fully cognizant of the traditional power of the States: "Because such legislation imposes congressional policy on a State involuntarily, and because it often intrudes on traditional state authority, we should not quickly attribute to Congress an unstated intent to act under its authority to enforce the Fourteenth Amendment." Because Congress nowhere stated its intent to impose mandatory obligations on the States under its § 5 powers, we concluded that Congress did not do so.

The *Pennhurst* rule looks much like the plain statement rule we apply today. . . . *Pennhurst* established a rule of statutory construction to be applied where statutory intent is ambiguous. In light of the ADEA's clear exclusion of most important public officials, it is at least ambiguous whether Congress intended that appointed judges nonetheless be included. In the face of such ambiguity, we will not attribute to Congress an intent to intrude on state governmental functions regardless of whether Congress acted pursuant to its Commerce Clause powers or § 5 of the Fourteenth Amendment.

III

[The Court also held that the Missouri constitutional provision did not violate the federal Equal Protection Clause.]

IV

The people of Missouri have established a qualification for those who would be their judges. It is their prerogative as citizens of a sovereign State to do so. Neither the ADEA nor the Equal Protection Clause prohibits the choice they have made. Accordingly, the judgment of the Court of Appeals is

Affirmed.

■ JUSTICE WHITE, with whom JUSTICE STEVENS joins, concurring in part, dissenting in part, and concurring in the judgment.

I agree with the majority that neither the Age Discrimination in Employment Act of 1967 (ADEA) nor the Equal Protection Clause prohibits Missouri's mandatory retirement provision as applied to petitioners, and I therefore concur in the judgment and in Parts I and III of the majority's opinion. I cannot agree, however, with the majority's reasoning in Part II of its opinion, which ignores several areas of well-established precedent and announces a rule that is likely to prove both unwise and infeasible. That the majority's analysis in Part II is completely unnecessary to the proper resolution of this case makes it all the more remarkable.

I

. . . The majority . . . holds that whether or not the ADEA can fairly be read to exclude state judges from its scope, "we will not read the ADEA to cover state judges unless Congress has made it clear that judges are *included*." I cannot agree with this "plain statement" rule because it is unsupported by the decisions upon which the majority relies, contrary to our Tenth Amendment jurisprudence, and fundamentally unsound. . . .

In 1974, Congress amended the definition of "employer" in the ADEA to include "a State or political subdivision of a State." With that amendment, "there is no doubt what the intent of Congress was: to extend the application of the ADEA to the States." *EEOC v. Wyoming*, 460 U.S. 226, 244 (1983). The dispute in this case therefore is not whether Congress has outlawed age discrimination by the States. It clearly has. The only question is whether petitioners fall within the definition of "employee" in the Act, which contains exceptions for elected officials and certain appointed officials. If petitioners *are* "employee[s]," Missouri's mandatory retirement provision clearly conflicts with the antidiscrimination provisions of the ADEA. . . . Pre-emption therefore is automatic, since "state law is pre-empted to the extent that it actually conflicts with federal law." The majority's federalism concerns are irrelevant to such "actual conflict" pre-emption. "The relative importance to the State of its own law is not material when there is a conflict with a valid federal law, for the Framers of our Constitution provided that the federal law must prevail." *Fidelity Fed. Sav. & Loan Ass'n v. De la Cuesta*, 458 U.S. 141, 153 (1982).

While acknowledging this principle of federal legislative supremacy, the majority nevertheless imposes upon Congress a "plain statement" requirement. . . . Congress has expressly extended the coverage of the ADEA to the States and their employees. Its intention to regulate age discrimination by States is thus "unmistakably clear in the language of the statute." The only dispute is over the precise details of the statute's application. We have never extended the plain statement approach that far, and the majority offers no compelling reason for doing so. . . .

The majority's plain statement rule is not only unprecedented, it directly contravenes our decisions in *Garcia v. San Antonio Metropolitan Transit Authority* and *South Carolina v. Baker*, 485 U.S. 505 (1988). In those cases we made it clear "that States must find their protection from congressional regulation through the national political process, not through judicially defined spheres of unregulable state activity." *Id.* at 512. We also rejected as "unsound in principle and unworkable in practice" any test for state immunity that requires a judicial determination of which state activities are " 'traditional,' " " 'integral,' " or " 'necessary.' " *Garcia.* The majority disregards those decisions in its attempt to carve out areas of state activity that will receive special protection from federal legislation.

The majority's approach is also unsound because it will serve only to confuse the law. First, the majority fails to explain the scope of its rule. Is the rule limited to federal regulation of the qualifications of state officials? Or does it apply more broadly to the regulation of any "state governmental functions"? Second, the majority does not explain its requirement that Congress' intent to regulate a particular state activity be "plain to anyone reading [the federal statute]." Does that mean that it is now improper to look to the purpose or history of a federal statute in determining the scope of the statute's limitations on state activities? If so, the majority's rule is completely inconsistent with our pre-emption jurisprudence. The vagueness of the majority's rule undoubtedly will lead States to assert that various federal statutes no longer apply to a wide variety of state activities if Congress has not expressly referred to those activities in the statute. Congress, in turn, will be forced to draft long and detailed lists of which particular state functions it meant to regulate. . . .

The majority asserts that its plain statement rule is helpful in avoiding a "potential constitutional problem." It is far from clear, however, why there would be a constitutional problem if the ADEA applied to state judges, in light of our decisions in *Garcia* and *Baker*, discussed above. . . . There is no claim in this case that the political process by which the ADEA was extended to state employees was inadequate to protect the States from being "unduly burdened" by the Federal Government. In any event . . . a straightforward analysis of the ADEA's definition of "employee" reveals that the ADEA does not apply here. Thus, even if there were potential constitutional problems in extending the ADEA to state judges, the majority's proposed plain statement rule would not be necessary to avoid them in this case. . . .

II

[Justice White found that the ADEA did not cover state judges under normal principles of statutory construction.]

I join Parts I and III of the Court's opinion and concur in its judgment.

■ **JUSTICE BLACKMUN, with whom JUSTICE MARSHALL joins, dissenting.**

I agree entirely with the cogent analysis contained in Part I of JUSTICE WHITE's opinion. . . . I part company with JUSTICE WHITE, however, in his determination that appointed state judges fall within the narrow exclusion from ADEA coverage that Congress created for an "appointee on the policymaking level." . . .

For two reasons, I do not accept the notion that an appointed state judge is an "appointee on the policymaking level." First, even assuming that judges may be described as policymakers in certain circumstances, the structure and legislative history of the policymaker exclusion make clear that judges are not the kind of policymakers whom Congress intended to exclude from the ADEA's broad reach. Second, whether or not a plausible argument may be made for judges' being policymakers, I would defer to the EEOC's reasonable construction of the ADEA as covering appointed state judges. . . .

I dissent.

Solid Waste Agency of Northern Cook County v. United States Army Corps of Engineers

531 U.S. 159 (2001)

■ **Chief Justice Rehnquist delivered the opinion of the Court.**

Section 404(a) of the Clean Water Act (CWA) regulates the discharge of dredged or fill material into "navigable waters." The United States Army Corps of Engineers (Corps), has interpreted § 404(a) to confer federal authority over an abandoned sand and gravel pit in northern Illinois which provides habitat for migratory birds. We are asked to decide whether the provisions of § 404(a) may be fairly extended to these waters, and, if so, whether Congress could exercise such authority consistent with the Commerce Clause, U.S. Const., Art. I, § 8, cl. 3. We answer the first question in the negative and therefore do not reach the second.

Petitioner, the Solid Waste Agency of Northern Cook County (SWANCC), is a consortium of 23 suburban Chicago cities and villages that united in an effort to locate and develop a disposal site for baled nonhazardous solid waste. The Chicago Gravel Company informed the municipalities of the availability of a 533-acre parcel, bestriding the Illinois counties Cook and Kane, which had been the site of a sand and gravel pit mining operation for three decades up until about 1960. Long since abandoned, the old mining site eventually gave way to a successional stage forest, with its remnant excavation trenches evolving into a scattering of permanent and seasonal ponds of varying size (from under one-tenth of an acre to several acres) and depth (from several inches to several feet).

The municipalities decided to purchase the site for disposal of their baled nonhazardous solid waste. By law, SWANCC was required to file for various permits from Cook County and the State of Illinois before it could begin operation of its balefill project. In addition, because the operation called for the filling of some of the permanent and seasonal ponds, SWANCC contacted federal respondents (hereinafter respondents), including the Corps, to determine if a federal landfill permit was required under § 404(a) of the CWA.

Section 404(a) grants the Corps authority to issue permits "for the discharge of dredged or fill material into the navigable waters at specified disposal sites." The term "navigable waters" is defined under the Act as "the waters of the United States, including the territorial seas." The Corps has issued regulations defining the term "waters of the United States" to include

> waters such as intrastate lakes, rivers, streams (including intermittent streams), mudflats, sandflats, wetlands, sloughs, prairie potholes, wet meadows, playa lakes, or natural ponds, the use, degradation or destruction of which could affect interstate or foreign commerce. . . .

In 1986, in an attempt to "clarify" the reach of its jurisdiction, the Corps stated that § 404(a) extends to intrastate waters:

a. Which are or would be used as habitat by birds protected by Migratory Bird Treaties; or

b. Which are or would be used as habitat by other migratory birds which cross state lines; or

c. Which are or would be used as habitat for endangered species; or

d. Used to irrigate crops sold in interstate commerce.

This last promulgation has been dubbed the "Migratory Bird Rule."

The Corps initially concluded that it had no jurisdiction over the site because it contained no "wetlands," or areas which support "vegetation typically adapted for life in saturated soil conditions." However, after the Illinois Nature Preserves Commission informed the Corps that a number of migratory bird species had been observed at the site, the Corps reconsidered and ultimately asserted jurisdiction over the balefill site pursuant to subpart (b) of the "Migratory Bird Rule." The Corps found that approximately 121 bird species had been observed at the site, including several known to depend upon aquatic environments for a significant portion of their life requirements. Thus, on November 16, 1987, the Corps formally "determined that the seasonally ponded, abandoned gravel mining depressions located on the project site, while not wetlands, did qualify as 'waters of the United States' . . . based upon the following criteria: (1) the proposed site had been abandoned as a gravel mining operation; (2) the water areas and spoil piles had developed a natural character; and (3) the water areas are used as habitat by migratory bird [*sic*] which cross state lines."

During the application process, SWANCC made several proposals to mitigate the likely displacement of the migratory birds and to preserve a great blue heron rookery located on the site. Its balefill project ultimately received the necessary local and state approval. . . . Despite SWANCC's securing the required water quality certification from the Illinois Environmental Protection Agency, the Corps refused to issue a § 404(a) permit. The Corps found that SWANCC had not established that its proposal was the "least environmentally damaging, most practicable alternative" for disposal of nonhazardous solid waste; that SWANCC's failure to set aside sufficient funds to remediate leaks posed an "unacceptable risk to the public's drinking water supply"; and that the impact of the project upon area-sensitive species was "unmitigatable since a landfill surface cannot be redeveloped into a forested habitat."

Petitioner filed suit under the Administrative Procedure Act . . . challenging both the Corps' jurisdiction over the site and the merits of its denial of the § 404(a) permit. The District Court granted summary judgment to respondents on the jurisdictional issue, and petitioner abandoned its challenge to the Corps' permit decision. [The Court of Appeals affirmed.] We granted certiorari, and now reverse.

Congress passed the CWA for the stated purpose of "restoring and maintaining the chemical, physical, and biological integrity of the Nation's waters." In so doing, Congress chose to "recognize, preserve, and protect the primary responsibilities and rights of States to prevent, reduce, and eliminate pollution, to plan the development and use (including restoration, preservation, and enhancement) of land and water resources, and to consult with the Administrator in the exercise of his authority under this chapter." Relevant here, § 404(a) authorizes respondents to regulate the discharge of fill material into "navigable waters," which the statute defines as "the waters of the United States, including the territorial seas." Respondents have interpreted these words to cover the abandoned gravel pit at issue here because it is used as habitat for migratory birds. We conclude that the "Migratory Bird Rule" is not fairly supported by the CWA.

This is not the first time we have been called upon to evaluate the meaning of § 404(a). In *United States v. Riverside Bayview Homes, Inc.*, 474 U.S. 121 (1985), we held that the Corps had § 404(a) jurisdiction over wetlands that actually abutted on a navigable waterway. In so doing, we noted that the term "navigable" is of "limited import" and that Congress evidenced its intent to "regulate at least some waters that would not be deemed 'navigable' under the classical understanding of that term." But our holding was based in large measure upon Congress' unequivocal acquiescence to, and approval of, the Corps' regulations interpreting the CWA to cover wetlands adjacent to navigable waters. We found that Congress' concern for the protection of water quality and aquatic ecosystems indicated its intent to regulate wetlands "inseparably bound up with the 'waters' of the United States." . . .

In order to rule for respondents here, we would have to hold that the jurisdiction of the Corps extends to ponds that are *not* adjacent to open water. But we conclude that the text of the statute will not allow this.

Indeed, the Corps' *original* interpretation of the CWA, promulgated two years after its enactment, is inconsistent with that which it espouses here. Its 1974 regulations defined § 404(a)'s "navigable waters" to mean "those waters of the United States which are subject to the ebb and flow of the tide, and/or are presently, or have been in the past, or may be in the future susceptible for use for purposes of interstate or foreign commerce." The Corps emphasized that "it is the water body's capability of use by the public for purposes of transportation or commerce which is the determinative factor." Respondents put forward no persuasive evidence that the Corps mistook Congress' intent in 1974.

Respondents next contend that whatever its original aim in 1972, Congress charted a new course five years later when it approved the more expansive definition of "navigable waters" found in the Corps' 1977 regulations. . . .

Although we have recognized congressional acquiescence to administrative interpretations of a statute in some situations, we have done so with extreme care. "Failed legislative proposals are 'a particularly dangerous ground on which to rest an interpretation of a prior statute.'" A bill can be proposed for any number of reasons, and it can be rejected for just as many others. The relationship between the actions and inactions of the 95th Congress and the intent of the 92d Congress in passing § 404(a) is also considerably attenuated. Because "subsequent history is less illuminating than the contemporaneous evidence," respondents face a difficult task in overcoming the plain text and import of § 404(a).

We conclude that respondents have failed to make the necessary showing that the failure of the 1977 House bill demonstrates Congress' acquiescence to the Corps' regulations or the "Migratory Bird Rule," which, of course, did not first appear until 1986. . . .

Section 404(g) is equally unenlightening. In *Riverside Bayview Homes* we recognized that Congress intended the phrase "navigable waters" to include "at least some waters that would not be deemed 'navigable' under the classical understanding of that term." But § 404(g) gives no intimation of what those waters might be; it simply refers to them as "other . . . waters." Respondents conjecture that "other . . . waters" must incorporate the Corps' 1977 regulations, but it is also plausible, as petitioner contends, that Congress simply wanted to include all waters adjacent to "navigable waters," such as nonnavigable tributaries and streams. The exact meaning of § 404(g) is not before us and we express no opinion on it, but for present purposes it is sufficient to say . . . that "§ 404(g)(1) does not conclusively determine the construction to be placed on the use of the term 'waters' elsewhere in the Act. . . ."

We thus decline respondents' invitation to take what they see as the next ineluctable step after *Riverside Bayview Homes*: holding that isolated ponds, some only seasonal, wholly located within two Illinois counties, fall under § 404(a)'s definition of "navigable waters" because they serve as habitat for migratory birds. . . . We cannot agree that Congress' separate definitional use of the phrase "waters of the United

States" constitutes a basis for reading the term "navigable waters" out of the statute. . . .

Respondents . . . contend that, at the very least, it must be said that Congress did not address the precise question of § 404(a)'s scope with regard to nonnavigable, isolated, intrastate waters, and that, therefore, we should give deference to the "Migratory Bird Rule." See, *e.g.*, *Chevron U.S.A. Inc. v. Natural Resources Defense Council, Inc.*, 467 U.S. 837 (1984). We find § 404(a) to be clear, but even were we to agree with respondents, we would not extend *Chevron* deference here.

Where an administrative interpretation of a statute invokes the outer limits of Congress' power, we expect a clear indication that Congress intended that result. This requirement stems from our prudential desire not to needlessly reach constitutional issues and our assumption that Congress does not casually authorize administrative agencies to interpret a statute to push the limit of congressional authority. This concern is heightened where the administrative interpretation alters the federal-state framework by permitting federal encroachment upon a traditional state power. See *United States v. Bass*, 404 U.S. 336 (1971) ("Unless Congress conveys its purpose clearly, it will not be deemed to have significantly changed the federal-state balance"). Thus, where an otherwise acceptable construction of a statute would raise serious constitutional problems, the Court will construe the statute to avoid such problems unless such construction is plainly contrary to the intent of Congress.

Twice in the past six years we have reaffirmed the proposition that the grant of authority to Congress under the Commerce Clause, though broad, is not unlimited. See *United States v. Morrison*, 529 U.S. 598 (2000); *United States v. Lopez*, 514 U.S. 549 (1995). Respondents argue that the "Migratory Bird Rule" falls within Congress' power to regulate intrastate activities that "substantially affect" interstate commerce. They note that the protection of migratory birds is a "national interest of very nearly the first magnitude," *Missouri v. Holland*, 252 U.S. 416 (1920), and that, as the Court of Appeals found, millions of people spend over a billion dollars annually on recreational pursuits relating to migratory birds. These arguments raise significant constitutional questions. For example, we would have to evaluate the precise object or activity that, in the aggregate, substantially affects interstate commerce. This is not clear, for although the Corps has claimed jurisdiction over petitioner's land because it contains water areas used as habitat by migratory birds, respondents now . . . focus upon the fact that the regulated activity is petitioner's municipal landfill, which is "plainly of a commercial nature." But this is a far cry, indeed, from the "navigable waters" and "waters of the United States" to which the statute by its terms extends.

These are significant constitutional questions raised by respondents' application of their regulations, and yet we find nothing approaching a clear statement from Congress that it intended § 404(a) to reach an abandoned sand and gravel pit such as we have here. Permitting respondents to claim federal jurisdiction over ponds and mudflats falling within the "Migratory Bird Rule" would result in a significant impingement of the States' traditional and primary power over land and water use. Rather than expressing a desire to readjust the federal-state balance in this manner, Congress chose to "recognize, preserve, and protect the primary responsibilities and rights of States . . . to plan the development and use . . . of land and water resources. . . ." We thus read the statute as written to avoid the significant constitutional and federalism questions raised by respondents' interpretation, and therefore reject the request for administrative deference.[8]

We hold that 33 CFR § 328.3(a)(3), as clarified and applied to petitioner's balefill site pursuant to the "Migratory Bird Rule," exceeds the authority granted to respondents under § 404(a) of the CWA. The judgment of the Court of Appeals for the Seventh Circuit is therefore reversed.

■ JUSTICE STEVENS, with whom JUSTICE SOUTER, JUSTICE GINSBURG, and JUSTICE BREYER join, dissenting.

In 1969, the Cuyahoga River in Cleveland, Ohio, coated with a slick of industrial waste, caught fire. Congress responded to that dramatic event, and to others like it, by enacting the Federal Water Pollution Control Act (FWPCA) Amendments of 1972, commonly known as the Clean Water Act (CWA). The Act proclaimed the ambitious goal of ending water pollution by 1985. The Court's past interpretations of the CWA have been fully consistent with that goal. Although Congress' vision of zero pollution remains unfulfilled, its pursuit has unquestionably retarded the destruction of the aquatic environment. Our Nation's waters no longer burn. Today, however, the Court takes an unfortunate step that needlessly weakens our principal safeguard against toxic water. . . .

[In a detailed analysis of the statute and legislative history, Justice Stevens found the Corps' interpretation of the Clean Water Act to be correct.]

III

Although it might have appeared problematic on a "linguistic" level for the Corps to classify "lands" as "waters" in *Riverside Bayview,* we squarely held that the agency's construction of the statute that it was charged with enforcing was entitled to deference under *Chevron U.S.A. Inc. v. Natural Resources Defense Council, Inc.,* 467 U.S. 837 (1984). Today, however, the majority refuses to extend such deference to the same agency's construction of the same statute. This refusal is unfaithful to both *Riverside Bayview* and *Chevron.* For it is the majority's reading,

---

[8] Because violations of the CWA carry criminal penalties, petitioner invokes the rule of lenity as another basis for rejecting the Corps' interpretation of the CWA. We need not address this alternative argument.

not the agency's, that does violence to the scheme Congress chose to put into place.

Contrary to the Court's suggestion, the Corps' interpretation of the statute does not "encroach" upon "traditional state power" over land use. . . . The CWA is not a land-use code; it is a paradigm of environmental regulation. Such regulation is an accepted exercise of federal power. . . . The Corps' interpretation of the statute as extending beyond navigable waters, tributaries of navigable waters, and wetlands adjacent to each is manifestly reasonable and therefore entitled to deference.

IV

Because I am convinced that the Court's miserly construction of the statute is incorrect, I shall comment briefly on petitioner's argument that Congress is without power to prohibit it from filling any part of the 31 acres of ponds on its property in Cook County, Illinois. The Corps' exercise of its § 404 permitting power over "isolated" waters that serve as habitat for migratory birds falls well within the boundaries set by this Court's Commerce Clause jurisprudence.

In *United States v. Lopez*, 514 U.S. 549 (1995), this Court identified "three broad categories of activity that Congress may regulate under its commerce power": (1) channels of interstate commerce; (2) instrumentalities of interstate commerce, or persons and things in interstate commerce; and (3) activities that "substantially affect" interstate commerce. The migratory bird rule at issue here is properly analyzed under the third category. In order to constitute a proper exercise of Congress' power over intrastate activities that "substantially affect" interstate commerce, it is not necessary that each individual instance of the activity substantially affect commerce; it is enough that, taken in the aggregate, the *class of activities* in question has such an effect. *Wickard v. Filburn.*

The activity being regulated in this case (and by the Corps' § 404 regulations in general) is the discharge of fill material into water. The Corps did not assert jurisdiction over petitioner's land simply because the waters were "used as habitat by migratory birds." It asserted jurisdiction because petitioner planned to *discharge fill* into waters "used as habitat by migratory birds." Had petitioner intended to engage in some other activity besides discharging fill (*i.e.*, had there been no activity to regulate), or, conversely, had the waters not been habitat for migratory birds (*i.e.*, had there been no basis for federal jurisdiction), the Corps would never have become involved in petitioner's use of its land. There can be no doubt that, unlike the class of activities Congress was attempting to regulate in *Morrison* ("gender-motivated crimes") and *Lopez* (possession of guns near school property), the discharge of fill material into the Nation's waters is almost always undertaken for economic reasons. See V. Albrecht & B. Goode, Wetland Regulation in the Real World, Exh. 3 (Feb. 1994) (demonstrating that the overwhelming majority of acreage for which § 404 permits are sought is intended for commercial, industrial, or other economic use).

Moreover, no one disputes that the discharge of fill into "isolated" waters that serve as migratory bird habitat will, in the aggregate, adversely affect migratory bird populations. See, *e.g.*, 1 Secretary of the Interior, Report to Congress, The Impact of Federal Programs on Wetlands: The Lower Mississippi Alluvial Plain and the Prairie Pothole Region 79–80 (Oct. 1988) (noting that "isolated," phase 3 waters "are among [the] most important and also the most threatened ecosystems in the United States" because "they are prime nesting grounds for many species of North American waterfowl . . ." and provide "up to 50 percent of the [U.S.] production of migratory waterfowl"). Nor does petitioner dispute that the particular waters it seeks to fill are home to many important species of migratory birds, including the second-largest breeding colony of Great Blue Herons in northeastern Illinois, and several species of waterfowl protected by international treaty and Illinois endangered species laws.

In addition to the intrinsic value of migratory birds, it is undisputed that literally millions of people regularly participate in birdwatching and hunting and that those activities generate a host of commercial activities of great value.[17] The causal connection between the filling of wetlands and the decline of commercial activities associated with migratory birds is not "attenuated"; it is direct and concrete.

Finally, the migratory bird rule does not blur the "distinction between what is truly national and what is truly local." Justice Holmes cogently observed in *Missouri v. Holland* that the protection of migratory birds is a textbook example of a *national* problem. The destruction of aquatic migratory bird habitat, like so many other environmental problems, is an action in which the benefits (*e.g.*, a new landfill) are disproportionately local, while many of the costs (*e.g.*, fewer migratory birds) are widely dispersed and often borne by citizens living in other States. In such situations, described by economists as involving "externalities," federal regulation is both appropriate and necessary. Identifying the Corps' jurisdiction by reference to waters that serve as habitat for birds that migrate over state lines also satisfies this Court's expressed desire for some "jurisdictional element" that limits federal activity to its proper scope.

The power to regulate commerce among the several States necessarily and properly includes the power to preserve the natural resources that generate such commerce. Migratory birds, and the waters

---

[17] In 1984, the U.S. Congress Office of Technology Assessment found that, in 1980, 5.3 million Americans hunted migratory birds, spending $638 million. More than 100 million Americans spent almost $14.8 billion in 1980 to watch and photograph fish and wildlife. Of 17.7 million birdwatchers, 14.3 million took trips in order to observe, feed, or photograph waterfowl, and 9.5 million took trips specifically to view other water-associated birds, such as herons like those residing at petitioner's site.

on which they rely, are such resources. Moreover, the protection of migratory birds is a well-established federal responsibility. As Justice Holmes noted in *Missouri v. Holland*, the federal interest in protecting these birds is of "the first magnitude." Because of their transitory nature, they "can be protected only by national action."

Whether it is necessary or appropriate to refuse to allow petitioner to fill those ponds is a question on which we have no voice. Whether the Federal Government has the power to require such permission, however, is a question that is easily answered. . . . There is no merit in petitioner's constitutional argument. . . .

I respectfully dissent.

NOTE ON THE CLEAR STATEMENT CASES

1.   One frequent justification for the Court's federalism-protecting clear statement rules is that they are just particular instances of the general canon of avoiding constitutional doubts. Justice Brandeis famously wrote that "[w]hen the validity of an act of the Congress is drawn in question, and even if a serious doubt of constitutionality is raised, it is a cardinal principle that this Court will first ascertain whether a construction of the statute is fairly possible by which the question may be avoided." *Ashwander v. Tennessee Valley Authority*, 297 U.S. 288, 348 (1936) (Brandeis, J., concurring). How plausible are such constitutional "doubts" in *Jones*, *Gregory*, and *Solid Waste*?

- In *Jones*, why is the Court unanimous? Do the nationalist justices—Ginsburg (who writes the majority), as well as Stevens, Souter, and Breyer—really think that the statute would be unconstitutional if it covered private residences? If not, what is the justification for going along with the clear statement rule?

- In *Gregory*, it is well established that statutes like the ADEA fall within the Commerce Power. What, then, is the source of any constitutional doubt? Is it *National League of Cities*? But wasn't that case overruled?

- In *Solid Waste*, the nationalists do reject application of the clear statement rule and insist that a broad reading of the statute would be constitutional. Are they right about that?[6] If they are, can the majority's use of the clear statement canon still be defended?

Each of these cases raises a similar set of issues: Are the federalism "clear statement" rules simply a particular case of the canon of avoiding

---

[6]   In particular, was Justice Stevens right that "[t]he power to regulate commerce among the several States necessarily and properly includes the power to preserve the natural resources that generate such commerce"? Is there any sort of environmental or land use regulation that could not fit under this rationale? And isn't it a bit of an exaggeration to say that migratory birds pose a federal interest "of the first magnitude"? Are birds comparable, say, to protecting civil rights or preventing nuclear proliferation?

constitutional doubts? Or are they something different—perhaps simply a normative canon designed to protect federalism values? If the latter is true, then what justifies the Courts' creation of new canons to limit national power in this fashion?

2.   Was Justice White right to say that the Court's prior decision in *Garcia* foreclosed *Gregory*'s clear statement rule?[7] Or can *Gregory* be seen as the natural consequence of *Garcia*'s notion of process federalism? In what ways do "clear statement" rules promote or enhance the political safeguards of federalism?

Even if clear statement rules make sense in the abstract, doesn't *Gregory* raise serious line-drawing problems? The old *National League of Cities* doctrine forbade federal regulation of "traditional state functions," but *Garcia* abandoned that doctrine on the ground that it was impossible to identify those functions. Doesn't *Gregory*'s clear statement rule turn on the same criteria? Is a fuzzy line less troubling when it simply triggers a clear statement requirement rather than requiring invalidation of a federal law?

3.   One issue in *Solid Waste* concerns deference to interpretations of federal statutes by federal administrative agencies that enforce those statutes. (Likewise, in *Gregory*, Justice Blackmun urged deference to the Equal Employment Opportunity Commission's interpretation of the ADEA.) The opinions cite *Chevron U.S.A. Inc. v. Natural Resources Defense Council, Inc.*, 467 U.S. 837 (1984), an immensely important case in the field of administrative law. *Chevron* held that, if a statute is ambiguous, courts must defer to the interpretation of that statute by the federal agency that administers the statute, so long as the agency's interpretation is reasonable. This doctrine places considerable power to determine the meaning of federal law in the hands of administrative agencies, notwithstanding *Marbury*'s injunction that the *judiciary* holds the power "to say what the law is." In *Solid Waste*, the agency's interpretation of the Clean Water Act was embodied in the Migratory Bird Rule, which arguably extends the scope of the CWA.

Our discussion of the "procedural safeguards of federalism" in Section 8.2 touched on the importance of the difficulty of the federal lawmaking process, and the fact that federal lawmaking by administrative agencies— like the Migratory Bird Rule—need not go through that difficult process. Agency-created rules likewise undermine the *political* safeguards of federalism, since the States enjoy no special representation at the Army Corps of Engineers or other federal agencies.[8] By refusing to defer to the Corps' rule, the *Solid Waste* majority suggested that federal law made by administrative agencies would not get the same broad leeway under the Commerce Power that a federal statute might under cases like *Wickard* and *Raich*. Is this distinction appropriate, especially in an age in which *most* federal law is made by administrative agencies?

---

[7]   *See* Section 8.2.

[8]   *See generally* Bradford R. Clark, *Separation of Powers as a Safeguard of Federalism*, 79 TEXAS L. REV. 1321 (2001); Ernest A. Young, *Executive Preemption*, 102 NW. U. L. REV. 869 (2008).

4.   Ordinarily, canons of statutory construction apply only when a court finds an ambiguity in the meaning of the statutory text. Can the values underlying a canon—such as the federalism principles articulated in cases like *Gregory*—actually *create* the ambiguity in the first place? In *Bond v. United States*, 134 S. Ct. 2077 (2014), for example, the Court considered a federal statute, enacted to implement an international chemical weapons treaty, that imposed criminal penalties for using a broadly defined class of chemicals to harm another. The question was whether this statute covered an enraged Pennsylvania woman's attempt to poison her next-door neighbor, whom she had discovered to be pregnant with her husband's child. Although it was clear that Bond had committed the statutorily prohibited act, the majority doubted—citing *Jones*, *Gregory*, and *Solid Waste*—whether a law aimed at chemical weapons and implementing an international treaty should be read to cover this sort of domestic dispute. The Court concluded that Congress had not clearly expressed a desire to readjust the balance of state and federal authority concerning every-day intrastate crimes. Does the result in *Bond* logically follow from the Court's decision in *Jones*? Or, as Justice Scalia pointed out in dissent, was the majority engaging in "result-driven antitextualism" to create an ambiguity from the fact the statute has a broad reach? If federalism concerns can *create* an ambiguity where the statutory text is otherwise clear, wouldn't that radically expand the scope of the Court's clear statement rules?

5.   The cases in this section illustrate the broad extent to which the boundary between state and national authority is set, not by the provisions of the Constitution themselves, but by the terms of federal statutes. How those statutes are interpreted, especially in cases of ambiguity, thus becomes a central concern of federalism doctrine. If we think of "constituting" the governmental structure as a central constitutional function, [9] then the interpretation of statutes that structure federal-state relations is an important *constitutional* question.

A striking illustration of this point occurred in *Gonzales v. Oregon*, 546 U.S. 243 (2006). *Gonzales* considered whether Oregon's Death with Dignity Act, which allowed physician-assisted suicide in certain cases involving terminally ill patients, had been successfully preempted by a regulation issued by U.S. Attorney General John Ashcroft under the federal Controlled Substances Act. A straight-up Commerce Clause challenge to the federal regulation would almost surely have failed in the wake of *Gonzales v. Raich*. The Court nonetheless held that Congress did not intend the CSA to extend to the right-to-die issue, so that the Ashcroft directive was invalid under the statute. In so holding, the Court relied significantly on "clear statement" rules disfavoring interpretations of ambiguous federal statutes that alter the traditional relationship between federal and state governments.

---

[9]   *See* Section 1.1, *supra*.

Does the juxtaposition of *Gonzales v. Oregon* and *Gonzales v. Raich* suggest that issues of statutory construction will eclipse traditional constitutional law in determining the federal balance?[10]

See also: On the role of canons of construction in statutory interpretation, one might start with Karl Llewellyn's famous argument that for every canon there is an equal and opposite counter-canon. *See* Karl N. Llewellyn, *Remarks on the Theory of Appellate Decision and the Rules or Canons About How Statutes Are to Be Construed*, 3 VAND. L. REV. 395 (1950). More recent (and balanced) treatments include David L. Shapiro, *Continuity and Change in Statutory Interpretation*, 67 N.Y.U. L. REV. 921 (1992), and Stephen F. Ross, *Where Have You Gone, Karl Llewellyn? Should Congress Turn Its Lonely Eyes to You?* 45 VAND. L. REV. 561 (1992). For the debate over federalism-based clear statement rules, see William N. Eskridge, Jr., & Philip P. Frickey, *Quasi-Constitutional Law: Clear Statement Rules as Constitutional Lawmaking*, 45 VAND. L. REV. 593 (1992); John F. Manning, *Federalism and the Generality Problem in Constitutional Interpretation*, 122 HARV. L. REV. 2003 (2009); and Ernest A. Young, *The Continuity of Statutory and Constitutional Interpretation: An Essay for Phil Frickey*, 98 CAL. L. REV. 1371 (2010).

SECTION 10.2   THE ANTI-COMMANDEERING DOCTRINE

Much federal law is in fact implemented and enforced by the States. The Clean Air Act, for instance, requires the federal Environmental Protection Agency to set ambient air quality standards for various pollutants, but it authorizes the States to submit implementation plans choosing among alternative means to reach the federal standards. If approved by the EPA, those plans are then enforced by state-level agencies (with EPA supervision). Many other federal programs are structured in a similar manner. It is fair to say that many familiar federal welfare and regulatory programs could not operate without state implementation.

These "cooperative federalism" regimes, however, generally involve a voluntary choice by the States to participate, with the alternative being direct federal implementation. Sometimes Congress induces state participation by imposing conditions on large grants of federal funding. For example, Congress secured state participation in the No Child Left Behind education program in this way. Given the large national revenue base permitted by the Sixteenth Amendment (authorizing a federal income tax), as well as the Supreme Court's reluctance to constrain Congress's spending power, Congress can generally persuade the States to cooperate by administering federal programs.

The cases that follow involve efforts by Congress to *mandate* state implementation and enforcement. (These requirements are sometimes called "unfunded mandates," although in principle Congress could

---

[10]   *See generally* Ernest A. Young, *The Constitution Outside the Constitution*, 117 YALE L.J. 408, 429–36 (2007) (discussing *Oregon* and *Raich* in this regard).

attempt to *require* state participation while still providing some funding to cover the costs.) The first case, *New York v. United States*, struck down federal mandates requiring action by the state legislature. The second, *Printz v. United States*, rejected mandatory enforcement of a federal program by state executive officers. A third case, *Testa v. Katt*, is discussed in both *New York* and *Printz*. Contrary to *New York* and *Printz*, *Testa* held that state *courts* can often be required to implement federal law by hearing federal causes of action.

Taken together, *New York* and *Printz* stand for an "anticommandeering doctrine": Congress may not "commandeer" state legislatures or executive officials and require them to enforce federal law. Unlike the "clear statement" cases, the anti-commandeering cases involve statutes that undoubtedly fall within Congress's Commerce Power. What, then, is the basis for the doctrine?

New York v. United States
505 U.S. 144 (1992)

■ JUSTICE O'CONNOR delivered the opinion of the Court.

These cases implicate one of our Nation's newest problems of public policy and perhaps our oldest question of constitutional law. The public policy issue involves the disposal of radioactive waste: In these cases, we address the constitutionality of three provisions of the Low-Level Radioactive Waste Policy Amendments Act of 1985. The constitutional question is as old as the Constitution: It consists of discerning the proper division of authority between the Federal Government and the States. We conclude that while Congress has substantial power under the Constitution to encourage the States to provide for the disposal of the radioactive waste generated within their borders, the Constitution does not confer upon Congress the ability simply to compel the States to do so. We therefore find that only two of the Act's three provisions at issue are consistent with the Constitution's allocation of power to the Federal Government.

I

We live in a world full of low level radioactive waste. Radioactive material is present in luminous watch dials, smoke alarms, measurement devices, medical fluids, research materials, and the protective gear and construction materials used by workers at nuclear power plants. Low level radioactive waste is generated by the Government, by hospitals, by research institutions, and by various industries. The waste must be isolated from humans for long periods of time, often for hundreds of years. Millions of cubic feet of low level radioactive waste must be disposed of each year. . . .

Faced with the possibility that the Nation would be left with no disposal sites for low level radioactive waste, Congress responded by enacting the Low-Level Radioactive Waste Policy Act. Relying largely on a report submitted by the National Governors' Association, Congress declared a federal policy of holding each State "responsible for providing for the availability of capacity either within or outside the State for the disposal of low-level radioactive waste generated within its borders," and found that such waste could be disposed of "most safely and efficiently . . . on a regional basis." The 1980 Act authorized States to enter into regional compacts that, once ratified by Congress, would have the authority beginning in 1986 to restrict the use of their disposal facilities to waste generated within member States. The 1980 Act included no penalties for States that failed to participate in this plan.

By 1985, only three approved regional compacts had operational disposal facilities; not surprisingly, these were the compacts formed around South Carolina, Nevada, and Washington, the three sited States. The following year, the 1980 Act would have given these three compacts the ability to exclude waste from nonmembers, and the remaining 31 States would have had no assured outlet for their low level radioactive waste. With this prospect looming, Congress once again took up the issue of waste disposal. The result was the legislation challenged here, the Low-Level Radioactive Waste Policy Amendments Act of 1985.

The 1985 Act was again based largely on a proposal submitted by the National Governors' Association. In broad outline, the Act embodies a compromise among the sited and unsited States. The sited States agreed to extend for seven years the period in which they would accept low level radioactive waste from other States. In exchange, the unsited States agreed to end their reliance on the sited States by 1992.

The mechanics of this compromise are intricate. The Act directs: "Each State shall be responsible for providing, either by itself or in cooperation with other States, for the disposal of . . . low-level radioactive waste generated within the State," with the exception of certain waste generated by the Federal Government. The Act authorizes States to "enter into such [interstate] compacts as may be necessary to provide for the establishment and operation of regional disposal facilities for low-level radioactive waste." For an additional seven years beyond the period contemplated by the 1980 Act, from the beginning of 1986 through the end of 1992, the three existing disposal sites "shall make disposal capacity available for low-level radioactive waste generated by any source," with certain exceptions not relevant here. But the three States in which the disposal sites are located are permitted to exact a graduated surcharge for waste arriving from outside the regional compact—in 1986–1987, $10 per cubic foot; in 1988–1989, $20 per cubic foot; and in 1990–1992, $40 per cubic foot. After the 7-year transition period expires, approved regional compacts may exclude radioactive waste generated outside the region.

The Act provides three types of incentives to encourage the States to comply with their statutory obligation to provide for the disposal of waste generated within their borders.

1.   *Monetary incentives.* One quarter of the surcharges collected by the sited States must be transferred to an escrow account held by the Secretary of Energy. The Secretary then makes payments from this account to each State that has complied with a series of deadlines. By July 1, 1986, each State was to have ratified legislation either joining a regional compact or indicating an intent to develop a disposal facility within the State. By January 1, 1988, each unsited compact was to have identified the State in which its facility would be located, and each compact or stand-alone State was to have developed a siting plan and taken other identified steps. By January 1, 1990, each State or compact was to have filed a complete application for a license to operate a disposal facility, or the Governor of any State that had not filed an application was to have certified that the State would be capable of disposing of all waste generated in the State after 1992. The rest of the account is to be paid out to those States or compacts able to dispose of all low level radioactive waste generated within their borders by January 1, 1993. Each State that has not met the 1993 deadline must either take title to the waste generated within its borders or forfeit to the waste generators the incentive payments it has received.

2.   *Access incentives.* The second type of incentive involves the denial of access to disposal sites. States that fail to meet the July 1986 deadline may be charged twice the ordinary surcharge for the remainder of 1986 and may be denied access to disposal facilities thereafter. States that fail to meet the 1988 deadline may be charged double surcharges for the first half of 1988 and quadruple surcharges for the second half of 1988, and may be denied access thereafter. States that fail to meet the 1990 deadline may be denied access. Finally, States that have not filed complete applications by January 1, 1992, for a license to operate a disposal facility, or States belonging to compacts that have not filed such applications, may be charged triple surcharges.

3.   *The take title provision.* The third type of incentive is the most severe. The Act provides:

> If a State . . . in which low-level radioactive waste is generated is unable to provide for the disposal of all such waste generated within such State or compact region by January 1, 1996, each State in which such waste is generated, upon the request of the generator or owner of the waste, shall take title to the waste, be obligated to take possession of the waste, and shall be liable for all damages directly or indirectly incurred by such generator or owner as a consequence of the failure of the State to take possession of the waste as soon after January 1, 1996, as the generator or owner notifies the State that the waste is available for shipment.

These three incentives are the focus of petitioners' constitutional challenge.

In the seven years since the Act took effect, Congress has approved nine regional compacts, encompassing 42 of the States. All six unsited compacts and four of the unaffiliated States have met the first three statutory milestones.

New York, a State whose residents generate a relatively large share of the Nation's low level radioactive waste, did not join a regional compact. Instead, the State complied with the Act's requirements by enacting legislation providing for the siting and financing of a disposal facility in New York. The State has identified five potential sites, three in Allegany County and two in Cortland County. Residents of the two counties oppose the State's choice of location.

Petitioners—the State of New York and the two counties—filed this suit against the United States in 1990. They sought a declaratory judgment that the Act is inconsistent with the Tenth and Eleventh Amendments to the Constitution, with the Due Process Clause of the Fifth Amendment, and with the Guarantee Clause of Article IV of the Constitution. The District Court dismissed the complaint. The Court of Appeals affirmed. Petitioners have abandoned their due process and Eleventh Amendment claims on their way up the appellate ladder; as the cases stand before us, petitioners claim only that the Act is inconsistent with the Tenth Amendment and the Guarantee Clause.

II

A

. . . Congress exercises its conferred powers subject to the limitations contained in the Constitution. Thus, for example, under the Commerce Clause Congress may regulate publishers engaged in interstate commerce, but Congress is constrained in the exercise of that power by the First Amendment. The Tenth Amendment likewise restrains the power of Congress, but this limit is not derived from the text of the Tenth Amendment itself, which . . . is essentially a tautology. Instead, the Tenth Amendment confirms that the power of the Federal Government is subject to limits that may, in a given instance, reserve power to the States. The Tenth Amendment thus directs us to determine . . . whether an incident of state sovereignty is protected by a limitation on an Article I power.

The benefits of this federal structure have been extensively cataloged elsewhere, but they need not concern us here. Our task would be the same even if one could prove that federalism secured no advantages to anyone. . . . This framework has been sufficiently flexible over the past two centuries to allow for enormous changes in the nature of government. The Federal Government undertakes activities today that would have been unimaginable to the Framers in two senses; first, because the Framers would not have conceived that *any* government would conduct such activities; and second, because the Framers would not have believed that the *Federal* Government, rather than the States, would assume such responsibilities. Yet the powers conferred upon the Federal Government by the Constitution were phrased in language broad enough to allow for the expansion of the Federal Government's role. . . .

In the end, just as a cup may be half empty or half full, it makes no difference whether one views the question at issue in these cases as one of ascertaining the limits of the power delegated to the Federal Government under the affirmative provisions of the Constitution or one of discerning the core of sovereignty retained by the States under the Tenth Amendment. Either way, we must determine whether any of the three challenged provisions of the Low-Level Radioactive Waste Policy Amendments Act of 1985 oversteps the boundary between federal and state authority.

B

Petitioners do not contend that Congress lacks the power to regulate the disposal of low level radioactive waste. Space in radioactive waste disposal sites is frequently sold by residents of one State to residents of another. Regulation of the resulting interstate market in waste disposal is therefore well within Congress' authority under the Commerce Clause. Petitioners likewise do not dispute that under the Supremacy Clause Congress could, if it wished, pre-empt state radioactive waste regulation. Petitioners contend only that the Tenth Amendment limits the power of Congress to regulate in the way it has chosen. Rather than addressing the problem of waste disposal by directly regulating the generators and disposers of waste, petitioners argue, Congress has impermissibly directed the States to regulate in this field.

Most of our recent cases interpreting the Tenth Amendment have concerned the authority of Congress to subject state governments to generally applicable laws. The Court's jurisprudence in this area has traveled an unsteady path. This litigation presents no occasion to apply or revisit the holdings of any of these cases, as this is not a case in which Congress has subjected a State to the same legislation applicable to private parties.

This litigation instead concerns the circumstances under which Congress may use the States as implements of regulation; that is, whether Congress may direct or otherwise motivate the States to regulate in a particular field or a particular way. Our cases have established a few principles that guide our resolution of the issue.

1

As an initial matter, Congress may not simply "commandeer the legislative processes of the States by directly compelling them to enact and enforce a federal regulatory program." *Hodel v. Virginia Surface Mining & Reclamation Assn., Inc.*, 452 U.S. 264 (1981). In *Hodel*, the Court upheld the Surface Mining Control and Reclamation Act of 1977 precisely because it did *not* "commandeer" the States into regulating mining. The Court found that "the States are not compelled to enforce the steep-slope standards, to expend any state funds, or to participate in the federal regulatory program in any manner whatsoever. If a State does not wish to submit a proposed permanent program that complies with the Act and implementing regulations, the full regulatory burden will be borne by the Federal Government."

The Court reached the same conclusion the following year in *FERC v. Mississippi*, 456 U.S. 742 (1982). At issue in *FERC* was the Public Utility Regulatory Policies Act of 1978, a federal statute encouraging the States in various ways to develop programs to combat the Nation's energy crisis. We observed that "this Court never has sanctioned explicitly a federal command to the States to promulgate and enforce laws and regulations." As in *Hodel*, the Court upheld the statute at issue because it did not view the statute as such a command. The Court emphasized: "Titles I and III of [the Public Utility Regulatory Policies Act of 1978 (PURPA)] require *only consideration* of federal standards. And if a State has no utilities commission, or simply stops regulating in the field, it need not even entertain the federal proposals." Because "there was nothing in PURPA 'directly compelling' the States to enact a legislative program," the statute was not inconsistent with the Constitution's division of authority between the Federal Government and the States.

These statements in *FERC* and *Hodel* were not innovations. While Congress has substantial powers to govern the Nation directly, including in areas of intimate concern to the States, the Constitution has never been understood to confer upon Congress the ability to require the States to govern according to Congress' instructions. The Court has been explicit about this distinction. "Both the States and the United States existed before the Constitution. The people, through that instrument, established a more perfect union by substituting a national government, acting, with ample power, *directly upon the citizens*, instead of the Confederate government, which acted with powers, greatly restricted, only upon the States." *Lane Cty. v. Oregon*, 74 U.S. (7 Wall.) 71, 76 (1868). The Court has made the same point with more rhetorical flourish, although perhaps with less precision, on a number of occasions. In Chief Justice Chase's much-quoted words, "the preservation of the States, and the maintenance of their governments, are as much within the design and care of the Constitution as the preservation of the Union and the maintenance of the National government. The Constitution, in all its provisions, looks to an indestructible Union, composed of indestructible States." *Texas v. White*, 74 U.S. (7 Wall.) 700, 725 (1869).

Indeed, the question whether the Constitution should permit Congress to employ state governments as regulatory agencies was a topic of lively debate among the Framers. Under the Articles of Confederation, Congress lacked the authority in most respects to govern the people directly. In practice, Congress could not directly tax or legislate upon individuals; it had no explicit legislative or governmental power to make binding law enforceable as such.

The inadequacy of this governmental structure was responsible in part for the Constitutional Convention. Alexander Hamilton observed: "The great and radical vice in the construction of the existing Confederation is in the principle of LEGISLATION for STATES or GOVERNMENTS, in their CORPORATE or COLLECTIVE CAPACITIES, and as contradistinguished from the INDIVIDUALS of whom they consist." As Hamilton saw it, "we must resolve to incorporate into our plan those ingredients which may be considered as forming the characteristic difference between a league and a government; we must extend the authority of the Union to the persons of the citizens—the only proper objects of government." The new National Government "must carry its agency to the persons of the citizens. It must stand in need of no intermediate legislations. . . . The government of the Union, like that of each State, must be able to address itself immediately to the hopes and fears of individuals." The Federalist, No. 16.

The Convention generated a great number of proposals for the structure of the new Government, but two quickly took center stage. Under the Virginia Plan, as first introduced by Edmund Randolph, Congress would exercise legislative authority directly upon individuals, without employing the States as intermediaries. Under the New Jersey Plan, as first introduced by William Paterson, Congress would continue to require the approval of the States before legislating, as it had under the Articles of Confederation. These two plans underwent various revisions as the Convention progressed, but they remained the two primary options discussed by the delegates. One frequently expressed objection to the New Jersey Plan was that it might require the Federal Government to coerce the States into implementing legislation. As Randolph explained the distinction, "the true question is whether we shall adhere to the federal plan [*i.e.*, the New Jersey Plan], or introduce the national plan. The insufficiency of the former has been fully displayed. . . . There are but two modes, by which the end of a General Government can be attained: the 1st is by coercion as proposed by Mr. Paterson's plan[, the 2nd] by real legislation as proposed by the other plan. Coercion [is] *impracticable, expensive, cruel to individuals. . . .* We must resort therefore to a national *Legislation over individuals.*" Madison echoed this view: "The practicability of making laws, with coercive sanctions, for the States as political bodies, had been exploded on all hands."

Under one preliminary draft of what would become the New Jersey Plan, state governments would occupy a position relative to Congress similar to that contemplated by the Act at issue in these cases: "The laws of the United States ought, as far as may be consistent with the common interests of the Union, to be carried into execution by the judiciary and executive officers of the respective states, wherein the execution thereof is required." This idea apparently never even progressed so far as to be debated by the delegates, as contemporary accounts of the Convention do not mention any such discussion. The delegates' many descriptions of the Virginia and New Jersey Plans speak only in general terms about whether Congress was to derive its authority from the people or from the States, and whether it was to issue directives to individuals or to States.

In the end, the Convention opted for a Constitution in which Congress would exercise its legislative authority directly over individuals rather than over States; for a variety of reasons, it rejected the New Jersey Plan in favor of the Virginia Plan. This choice was made clear to the subsequent state ratifying conventions. Oliver Ellsworth, a member of the Connecticut delegation in Philadelphia, explained the distinction to his State's convention: "This Constitution does not attempt to coerce sovereign bodies, states, in their political capacity. . . . But this legal coercion singles out the . . . individual." Charles Pinckney, another delegate at the Constitutional Convention, emphasized to the South Carolina House of Representatives that in Philadelphia "the necessity of having a government which should at once operate upon the people, and not upon the states, was conceived to be indispensable by every delegation present." Rufus King, one of Massachusetts' delegates, returned home to support ratification by recalling the Commonwealth's unhappy experience under the Articles of Confederation and arguing: "Laws, to be effective, therefore, must not be laid on states, but upon individuals." At New York's convention, Hamilton (another delegate in Philadelphia) exclaimed: "But can we believe that one state will ever suffer itself to be used as an instrument of coercion? The thing is a dream; it is impossible. Then we are brought to this dilemma—either a federal standing army is to enforce the requisitions, or the federal treasury is left without supplies, and the government without support. What, sir, is the cure for this great evil? Nothing, but to enable the national laws to operate on individuals, in the same manner as those of the states do." At North Carolina's convention, Samuel Spencer recognized that "all the laws of the Confederation were binding on the states in their political capacities . . . but now the thing is entirely different. The laws of Congress will be binding on individuals."

In providing for a stronger central government, therefore, the Framers explicitly chose a Constitution that confers upon Congress the power to regulate individuals, not States. As we have seen, the Court has consistently respected this choice. We have always understood that even where Congress has the authority under the Constitution to pass laws requiring or prohibiting certain acts, it lacks the power directly to compel the States to require or prohibit those acts. The allocation of power contained in the Commerce Clause, for example, authorizes Congress to regulate interstate commerce directly; it does not authorize Congress to regulate state governments' regulation of interstate commerce.

2

This is not to say that Congress lacks the ability to encourage a State to regulate in a particular way, or that Congress may not hold out incentives to the States as a method of influencing a State's policy choices. Our cases have identified a variety of methods, short of outright coercion, by which Congress may urge a State to adopt a legislative program consistent with federal interests. Two of these methods are of particular relevance here.

First, under Congress' spending power, "Congress may attach conditions on the receipt of federal funds." *South Dakota v. Dole*. Such conditions must (among other requirements) bear some relationship to the purpose of the federal spending; otherwise, of course, the spending power could render academic the Constitution's other grants and limits of federal authority. Where the recipient of federal funds is a State, as is not unusual today, the conditions attached to the funds by Congress may influence a State's legislative choices. . . .

Second, where Congress has the authority to regulate private activity under the Commerce Clause, we have recognized Congress' power to offer States the choice of regulating that activity according to federal standards or having state law pre-empted by federal regulation. *Hodel*. This arrangement, which has been termed "a program of cooperative federalism," is replicated in numerous federal statutory schemes. These include the Clean Water Act, the Occupational Safety and Health Act of 1970, the Resource Conservation and Recovery Act of 1976, and the Alaska National Interest Lands Conservation Act.

By either of these methods . . . the residents of the State retain the ultimate decision as to whether or not the State will comply. If a State's citizens view federal policy as sufficiently contrary to local interests, they may elect to decline a federal grant. If state residents would prefer their government to devote its attention and resources to problems other than those deemed important by Congress, they may choose to have the Federal Government rather than the State bear the expense of a federally mandated regulatory program, and they may continue to supplement that program to the extent state law is not pre-empted. Where Congress encourages state regulation rather than compelling it, state governments remain responsive to the local electorate's preferences; state officials remain accountable to the people.

By contrast, where the Federal Government compels States to regulate, the accountability of both state and federal officials is diminished. If the citizens of New York, for example, do not consider that making provision for the disposal of radioactive waste is in their best interest, they may elect state officials who share their view. That view can always be pre-empted under the Supremacy Clause if it is contrary to the national view, but in such a case it is the Federal Government that makes the decision in full view of the public, and it will be federal officials that suffer the consequences if the decision turns out to be detrimental or unpopular. But where the Federal Government directs the States to regulate, it may be state officials who will bear the brunt of public disapproval, while the federal officials who devised the regulatory program may remain insulated from the electoral ramifications of their decision. Accountability is thus diminished when, due to federal coercion, elected state officials cannot regulate in accordance with the views of the local electorate in matters not pre-empted by federal regulation.

With these principles in mind, we turn to the three challenged provisions of the Low-Level Radioactive Waste Policy Amendments Act of 1985.

III

. . . Construed as a whole, the Act comprises three sets of "incentives" for the States to provide for the disposal of low level radioactive waste generated within their borders. We consider each in turn.

A

The first set of incentives works in three steps. First, Congress has authorized States with disposal sites to impose a surcharge on radioactive waste received from other States. Second, the Secretary of Energy collects a portion of this surcharge and places the money in an escrow account. Third, States achieving a series of milestones receive portions of this fund.

The first of these steps is an unexceptionable exercise of Congress' power to authorize the States to burden interstate commerce. While the Commerce Clause has long been understood to limit the States' ability to discriminate against interstate commerce, that limit may be lifted, as it has been here, by an expression of the "unambiguous intent" of Congress. Whether or not the States would be permitted to burden the interstate transport of low level radioactive waste in the absence of Congress' approval, the States can clearly do so *with* Congress' approval, which is what the Act gives them.

The second step, the Secretary's collection of a percentage of the surcharge, is no more than a federal tax on interstate commerce, which petitioners do not claim to be an invalid exercise of either Congress' commerce or taxing power.

The third step is a conditional exercise of Congress' authority under the Spending Clause: Congress has placed conditions—the achievement of the milestones—on the receipt of federal funds. Petitioners do not contend that Congress has exceeded its authority in any of the four respects our cases have identified. *South Dakota v. Dole.* The expenditure is for the general welfare; the States are required to use the money they receive for the purpose of assuring the safe disposal of radioactive waste. The conditions imposed are unambiguous; the Act informs the States exactly what they must do and by when they must do it in order to obtain a share of the escrow account. The conditions imposed are reasonably related to the purpose of the expenditure; both the conditions and the payments embody Congress' efforts to address the pressing problem of radioactive waste disposal. Finally, petitioners do not claim that the conditions imposed by the Act violate any independent constitutional prohibition. . . .

The Act's first set of incentives, in which Congress has conditioned grants to the States upon the States' attainment of a series of milestones, is thus well within the authority of Congress under the Commerce and Spending Clauses. . . .

B

In the second set of incentives, Congress has authorized States and regional compacts with disposal sites gradually to increase the cost of access to the sites, and then to deny access altogether, to radioactive waste generated in States that do not meet federal deadlines. As a simple regulation, this provision would be within the power of Congress to authorize the States to discriminate against interstate commerce. Where federal regulation of private activity is within the scope of the Commerce Clause, we have recognized the ability of Congress to offer States the choice of regulating that activity according to federal standards or having state law pre-empted by federal regulation.

This is the choice presented to nonsited States by the Act's second set of incentives: States may either regulate the disposal of radioactive waste according to federal standards by attaining local or regional self-sufficiency, or their residents who produce radioactive waste will be subject to federal regulation authorizing sited States and regions to deny access to their disposal sites. The affected States are not compelled by Congress to regulate, because any burden caused by a State's refusal to regulate will fall on those who generate waste and find no outlet for its disposal, rather than on the State as a sovereign. A State whose citizens do not wish it to attain the Act's milestones may devote its attention and its resources to issues its citizens deem more worthy; the choice remains at all times with the residents of the State, not with Congress. The State need not expend any funds, or participate in any federal program, if local residents do not view such expenditures or participation as worth-while. Nor must the State abandon the field if it does not accede to federal direction; the State may continue to regulate the generation and disposal of radioactive waste in any manner its citizens see fit.

The Act's second set of incentives thus represents a conditional exercise of Congress' commerce power, along the lines of those we have held to be within Congress' authority. As a result, the second set of incentives does not intrude on the sovereignty reserved to the States by the Tenth Amendment.

C

The take title provision is of a different character. This third so-called "incentive" offers States, as an alternative to regulating pursuant to Congress' direction, the option of taking title to and possession of the low level radioactive waste generated within their borders and becoming liable for all damages waste generators suffer as a result of the States' failure to do so promptly. In this provision, Congress has crossed the line distinguishing encouragement from coercion. . . .

The take title provision offers state governments a "choice" of either accepting ownership of waste or regulating according to the instructions of Congress. Respondents do not claim that the Constitution would authorize Congress to impose either option as a freestanding requirement. On one hand, the Constitution would not permit Congress simply to transfer radioactive waste from generators to state governments. Such a forced transfer, standing alone, would in principle be no different than a congressionally compelled subsidy from state governments to radioactive waste producers. The same is true of the provision requiring the States to become liable for the generators' damages. Standing alone, this provision would be indistinguishable from an Act of Congress directing the States to assume the liabilities of certain state residents. Either type of federal action would "commandeer" state governments into the service of federal regulatory purposes, and would for this reason be inconsistent with the Constitution's division of authority between federal and state governments. On the other hand, the second alternative held out to state governments—regulating pursuant to Congress' direction—would, standing alone, present a simple command to state governments to implement legislation enacted by Congress. As we have seen, the Constitution does not empower Congress to subject state governments to this type of instruction.

Because an instruction to state governments to take title to waste, standing alone, would be beyond the authority of Congress, and because a direct order to regulate, standing alone, would also be beyond the authority of Congress, it follows that Congress lacks the power to offer the States a choice between the two. Unlike the first two sets of incentives, the take title incentive does not represent the conditional exercise of any congressional power enumerated in the Constitution. In this provision, Congress has not held out the threat of exercising its spending power or its commerce power; it has instead held out the threat, should the States not regulate according to one federal instruction, of simply forcing the States to submit to another federal instruction. A choice between two unconstitutionally coercive regulatory techniques is no choice at all. Either way, the Act commandeers the legislative processes of the States by directly compelling them to enact and enforce a federal regulatory program, an outcome that has never been understood to lie within the authority conferred upon Congress by the Constitution. . . .

The take title provision appears to be unique. No other federal statute has been cited which offers a state government no option other than that of implementing legislation enacted by Congress. Whether one views the take title provision as lying outside Congress' enumerated powers, or as infringing upon the core of state sovereignty reserved by the Tenth Amendment, the provision is inconsistent with the federal structure of our Government established by the Constitution.

IV

A

The United States proposes three alternative views of the constitutional line separating state and federal authority. . . . First, the United States argues that the Constitution's prohibition of congressional directives to state governments can be overcome where the federal interest is sufficiently important to justify state submission. . . . But whether or not a particularly strong federal interest enables Congress to bring state governments within the orbit of generally applicable *federal* regulation, no Member of the Court has ever suggested that such a federal interest would enable Congress to command a state government to enact *state* regulation. No matter how powerful the federal interest involved, the Constitution simply does not give Congress the authority to require the States to regulate. The Constitution instead gives Congress the authority to regulate matters directly and to pre-empt contrary state regulation. Where a federal interest is sufficiently strong to cause Congress to legislate, it must do so directly; it may not conscript state governments as its agents.

Second, the United States argues that the Constitution does, in some circumstances, permit federal directives to state governments. Various cases are cited for this proposition, but none support it. Some of these cases discuss the well established power of Congress to pass laws enforceable in state courts. See *Testa v. Katt*, 330 U.S. 386 (1947). These cases involve no more than an application of the Supremacy Clause's provision that federal law "shall be the supreme Law of the Land," enforceable in every State. More to the point, all involve congressional regulation of individuals, not congressional requirements that States regulate. Federal statutes enforceable in state courts do, in a sense, direct state judges to enforce them, but this sort of federal "direction" of state judges is mandated by the text of the Supremacy Clause. No comparable constitutional provision authorizes Congress to command state legislatures to legislate.

Additional cases cited by the United States discuss the power of federal *courts* to order state officials to comply with federal law. See *Cooper v. Aaron*; *Brown v. Board of Education*. Again, however, the text of the Constitution plainly confers this authority on the federal courts, the "judicial Power" of which "shall extend to all Cases, in Law and Equity, arising under this Constitution, [and] the Laws of the United States . . . ; [and] to Controversies between two or more States; [and] between a State and Citizens of another State." U.S. Const., Art. III, § 2. The Constitution contains no analogous grant of authority to Congress. Moreover, the Supremacy Clause makes federal law paramount over the contrary positions of state officials; the power of federal courts to enforce federal law thus presupposes some authority to order state officials to comply.

In sum, the cases relied upon by the United States hold only that federal law is enforceable in state courts and that federal courts may in proper circumstances order state officials to comply with federal law, propositions that by no means imply any authority on the part of Congress to mandate state regulation.

Third, the United States, supported by the three sited regional compacts as *amici*, argues that the Constitution envisions a role for Congress as an arbiter of interstate disputes. The United States observes that federal courts, and this Court in particular, have frequently resolved conflicts among States. Many of these disputes have involved the allocation of shared resources among the States, a category perhaps broad enough to encompass the allocation of scarce disposal space for radioactive waste. The United States suggests that if the Court may resolve such interstate disputes, Congress can surely do the same under the Commerce Clause. . . .

While the Framers no doubt endowed Congress with the power to regulate interstate commerce in order to avoid further instances of the interstate trade disputes that were common under the Articles of Confederation, the Framers did *not* intend that Congress should exercise that power through the mechanism of mandating state regulation. The Constitution established Congress as "a superintending authority over the reciprocal trade" among the States by empowering Congress to regulate that trade directly, not by authorizing Congress to issue trade-related orders to state governments. As Madison and Hamilton explained, "a sovereignty over sovereigns, a government over governments, a legislation for communities, as contradistinguished from individuals, as it is a solecism in theory, so in practice it is subversive of the order and ends of civil polity."

B

The sited state respondents . . . correctly observe that public officials representing the State of New York lent their support to the Act's enactment. . . . Respondents note that the Act embodies a bargain among the sited and unsited States, a compromise to which New York was a willing participant and from which New York has reaped much benefit. Respondents then pose what appears at first to be a troubling question: How can a federal statute be found an unconstitutional infringement of state sovereignty when state officials consented to the statute's enactment?

The answer follows from an understanding of the fundamental purpose served by our Government's federal structure. The Constitution does not protect the sovereignty of States for the benefit of the States or state governments as abstract political entities, or even for the benefit of the public officials governing the States. To the contrary, the

Constitution divides authority between federal and state governments for the protection of individuals. State sovereignty is not just an end in itself: Rather, federalism secures to citizens the liberties that derive from the diffusion of sovereign power. . . .

Where Congress exceeds its authority relative to the States, therefore, the departure from the constitutional plan cannot be ratified by the "consent" of state officials. An analogy to the separation of powers among the branches of the Federal Government clarifies this point. The Constitution's division of power among the three branches is violated where one branch invades the territory of another, whether or not the encroached-upon branch approves the encroachment. In *Buckley v. Valeo*, 424 U.S. 1 (1976), for instance, the Court held that Congress had infringed the President's appointment power, despite the fact that the President himself had manifested his consent to the statute that caused the infringement by signing it into law. In *INS v. Chadha*, 462 U.S. 919 (1983), we held that the legislative veto violated the constitutional requirement that legislation be presented to the President, despite Presidents' approval of hundreds of statutes containing a legislative veto provision. The constitutional authority of Congress cannot be expanded by the "consent" of the governmental unit whose domain is thereby narrowed, whether that unit is the Executive Branch or the States.

State officials thus cannot consent to the enlargement of the powers of Congress beyond those enumerated in the Constitution. Indeed, the facts of these cases raise the possibility that powerful incentives might lead both federal and state officials to view departures from the federal structure to be in their personal interests. Most citizens recognize the need for radioactive waste disposal sites, but few want sites near their homes. As a result, while it would be well within the authority of either federal or state officials to choose where the disposal sites will be, it is likely to be in the political interest of each individual official to avoid being held accountable to the voters for the choice of location. If a federal official is faced with the alternatives of choosing a location or directing the States to do it, the official may well prefer the latter, as a means of shifting responsibility for the eventual decision. If a state official is faced with the same set of alternatives—choosing a location or having Congress direct the choice of a location—the state official may also prefer the latter, as it may permit the avoidance of personal responsibility. The interests of public officials thus may not coincide with the Constitution's intergovernmental allocation of authority. Where state officials purport to submit to the direction of Congress in this manner, federalism is hardly being advanced. . . .

VII

Some truths are so basic that, like the air around us, they are easily overlooked. Much of the Constitution is concerned with setting forth the form of our government, and the courts have traditionally invalidated measures deviating from that form. The result may appear "formalistic" in a given case to partisans of the measure at issue, because such measures are typically the product of the era's perceived necessity. But the Constitution protects us from our own best intentions: It divides power among sovereigns and among branches of government precisely so that we may resist the temptation to concentrate power in one location as an expedient solution to the crisis of the day. The shortage of disposal sites for radioactive waste is a pressing national problem, but a judiciary that licensed extraconstitutional government with each issue of comparable gravity would, in the long run, be far worse.

States are not mere political subdivisions of the United States. State governments are neither regional offices nor administrative agencies of the Federal Government. The positions occupied by state officials appear nowhere on the Federal Government's most detailed organizational chart. The Constitution instead leaves to the several States a residuary and inviolable sovereignty reserved explicitly to the States by the Tenth Amendment.

Whatever the outer limits of that sovereignty may be, one thing is clear: The Federal Government may not compel the States to enact or administer a federal regulatory program. . . . While there may be many constitutional methods of achieving regional self-sufficiency in radioactive waste disposal, the method Congress has chosen is not one of them. The judgment of the Court of Appeals is accordingly.

Affirmed in part and reversed in part.

■ JUSTICE WHITE, with whom JUSTICE BLACKMUN and JUSTICE STEVENS join, concurring in part and dissenting in part.

I

. . . The Low-Level Radioactive Waste Policy Act of 1980, and its amendatory 1985 Act, resulted from the efforts of state leaders to achieve a state-based set of remedies to the waste problem. They sought not federal pre-emption or intervention, but rather congressional sanction of interstate compromises they had reached. . . .

A movement thus arose to achieve a compromise between the sited and the unsited States, in which the sited States agreed to continue accepting waste in exchange for the imposition of stronger measures to guarantee compliance with the unsited States' assurances that they would develop alternative disposal facilities. As Representative Derrick explained, the compromise 1985 legislation "gives nonsited States more time to develop disposal sites, but also establishes a very firm timetable and sanctions for failure to live up [to] the agreement." Representative Markey added that "this compromise became the basis for our amendments to the Low-Level Radioactive Waste Policy Act of 1980. In the process of drafting such amendments, various concessions have been made by all sides in an effort to arrive at a bill which all parties could accept." The bill that in large measure became the 1985 Act "represented the diligent negotiating undertaken by" the National Governors'

Association and "embodied" the "fundamentals of their settlement." (statement of Rep. Udall). In sum, the 1985 Act was very much the product of cooperative federalism, in which the States bargained among themselves to achieve compromises for Congress to sanction. . . .

Unlike legislation that directs action from the Federal Government to the States, the 1980 and 1985 Acts reflected hard-fought agreements among States as refereed by Congress. The distinction is key, and the Court's failure properly to characterize this legislation ultimately affects its analysis of the take title provision's constitutionality.

II

. . . Curiously absent from the Court's analysis is any effort to place the take title provision within the overall context of the legislation. . . . Congress could have pre-empted the field by directly regulating the disposal of this waste pursuant to its powers under the Commerce and Spending Clauses, but instead it *unanimously* assented to the States' request for congressional ratification of agreements to which they had acceded. As the floor statements of Members of Congress reveal, the States wished to take the lead in achieving a solution to this problem and agreed among themselves to the various incentives and penalties implemented by Congress to ensure adherence to the various deadlines and goals. The chief executives of the States proposed this approach, and I am unmoved by the Court's vehemence in taking away Congress' authority to sanction a recalcitrant unsited State now that New York has reaped the benefits of the sited States' concessions.

A

In my view, New York's actions subsequent to enactment of the 1980 and 1985 Acts fairly indicate its approval of the interstate agreement process embodied in those laws within the meaning of Art. I, § 10, cl. 3, of the Constitution, which provides that "no State shall, without the Consent of Congress . . . enter into any Agreement or Compact with another State." First, the States—including New York—worked through their Governors to petition Congress for the 1980 and 1985 Acts. . . . Second, New York acted in compliance with the requisites of both statutes in key respects, thus signifying its assent to the agreement achieved among the States as codified in these laws. After enactment of the 1980 Act and pursuant to its provision in § 4(a)(2), New York entered into compact negotiations with several other northeastern States before withdrawing from them to "go it alone." Indeed, in 1985, as the January 1, 1986, deadline crisis approached and Congress considered the 1985 legislation that is the subject of this lawsuit, the Deputy Commissioner for Policy and Planning of the New York State Energy Office testified before Congress that "New York State supports the efforts of Mr. Udall and the members of this Subcommittee to resolve the current impasse over Congressional consent to the proposed LLRW compacts and provide interim access for states and regions without sites. *New York State has been participating with the National Governors' Association and the other large states and compact commissions in an effort to further refine the recommended approach in HR 1083 and reach a consensus between all groups.*" (emphasis added). . . .

The State should be estopped from asserting the unconstitutionality of a provision that seeks merely to ensure that, after deriving substantial advantages from the 1985 Act, New York in fact must live up to its bargain. . . .

B

Even were New York not to be estopped from challenging the take title provision's constitutionality, I am convinced that, seen as a term of an agreement entered into between the several States, this measure proves to be less constitutionally odious than the Court opines. First, the practical effect of New York's position is that because it is unwilling to honor its obligations to provide in-state storage facilities for its low-level radioactive waste, *other* States with such plants *must accept* New York's waste, whether they wish to or not. Otherwise, the many economically and socially beneficial producers of such waste in the State would have to cease their operations. The Court's refusal to force New York to accept responsibility for its own problem inevitably means that some other State's sovereignty will be impinged by it being forced, for public health reasons, to accept New York's low-level radioactive waste. I do not understand the principle of federalism to impede the National Government from acting as referee among the States to prohibit one from bullying another. . . .

III

The Court announces that it has no occasion to revisit such decisions as *Garcia v. San Antonio Metropolitan Transit Authority* and *National League of Cities v. Usery* because "this is not a case in which Congress has subjected a State to the same legislation applicable to private parties." . . .

The Court's distinction between a federal statute's regulation of States and private parties for general purposes, as opposed to a regulation solely on the activities of States, is unsupported by our recent Tenth Amendment cases. In no case has the Court rested its holding on such a distinction. . . . An incursion on state sovereignty hardly seems more constitutionally acceptable if the federal statute that "commands" specific action also applies to private parties. . . .

In *Garcia*, we stated the proper inquiry: "We are convinced that the fundamental limitation that the constitutional scheme imposes on the Commerce Clause to protect the 'States as States' is one of process rather than one of result. Any substantive restraint on the exercise of Commerce Clause powers must find its justification in the procedural nature of this basic limitation, and it must be tailored to compensate for possible failings in the national political process rather than to dictate a sacred province of state autonomy." Where it addresses this aspect of respondents' argument, the Court tacitly concedes that a failing of the political process cannot be shown in these cases because it refuses to rebut the unassailable arguments that the States were well able to look after themselves in the legislative process that culminated in the 1985 Act's passage. Indeed, New York acknowledges that its "congressional delegation participated in the drafting and enactment of both the 1980 and the 1985 Acts." . . .

Ultimately, I suppose, the entire structure of our federal constitutional government can be traced to an interest in establishing checks and balances to prevent the exercise of tyranny against individuals. But these fears seem extremely far distant to me in a situation such as this. We face a crisis of national proportions in the disposal of low-level radioactive waste, and Congress has acceded to the wishes of the States by permitting local decisionmaking rather than imposing a solution from Washington. . . . For me, the Court's civics lecture has a decidedly hollow ring at a time when action, rather than rhetoric, is needed to solve a national problem.[3] . . .

V

The ultimate irony of the decision today is that in its formalistically rigid obeisance to "federalism," the Court gives Congress fewer incentives to defer to the wishes of state officials in achieving local solutions to local problems. . . . The States urged the National Legislature not to impose from Washington a solution to the country's low-level radioactive waste management problems. Instead, they sought a reasonable level of local and regional autonomy consistent with Art. I, § 10, cl. 3, of the Constitution. By invalidating the measure designed to ensure compliance for recalcitrant States, such as New York, the Court upsets the delicate compromise achieved among the States and forces Congress to erect several additional formalistic hurdles to clear before achieving exactly

---

[3] With selective quotations from the era in which the Constitution was adopted, the majority attempts to bolster its holding that the take title provision is tantamount to federal "commandeering" of the States. In view of the many Tenth Amendment cases decided over the past two decades in which resort to the kind of historical analysis generated in the majority opinion was not deemed necessary, I do not read the majority's many invocations of history to be anything other than elaborate window dressing. Certainly nowhere does the majority announce that its rule is compelled by an understanding of what the Framers may have thought about statutes of the type at issue here. Moreover, I would observe that, while its quotations add a certain flavor to the opinion, the majority's historical analysis has a distinctly wooden quality. One would not know from reading the majority's account, for instance, that the nature of federal-state relations changed fundamentally after the Civil War. That conflict produced in its wake a tremendous expansion in the scope of the Federal Government's law-making authority, so much so that the persons who helped to found the Republic would scarcely have recognized the many added roles the National Government assumed for itself. Moreover, the majority fails to mention the New Deal era, in which the Court recognized the enormous growth in Congress' power under the Commerce Clause. While I believe we should not be blind to history, neither should we read it so selectively as to restrict the proper scope of Congress' powers under Article I, especially when the history not mentioned by the majority fully supports a more expansive understanding of the legislature's authority than may have existed in the late 18th century. . . .

the same objective. Because the Court's justifications for undertaking this step are unpersuasive to me, I respectfully dissent.

Printz v. United States
521 U.S. 898 (1997)

■ JUSTICE SCALIA delivered the opinion of the Court.

The question presented in these cases is whether certain interim provisions of the Brady Handgun Violence Prevention Act, commanding state and local law enforcement officers to conduct background checks on prospective handgun purchasers and to perform certain related tasks, violate the Constitution.

I

The Gun Control Act of 1968 (GCA) establishes a detailed federal scheme governing the distribution of firearms. It prohibits firearms dealers from transferring handguns to any person under 21, not resident in the dealer's State, or prohibited by state or local law from purchasing or possessing firearms. It also forbids possession of a firearm by, and transfer of a firearm to, convicted felons, fugitives from justice, unlawful users of controlled substances, persons adjudicated as mentally defective or committed to mental institutions, aliens unlawfully present in the United States, persons dishonorably discharged from the Armed Forces, persons who have renounced their citizenship, and persons who have been subjected to certain restraining orders or been convicted of a misdemeanor offense involving domestic violence.

In 1993, Congress amended the GCA by enacting the Brady Act. The Act requires the Attorney General to establish a national instant background check system by November 30, 1998, and immediately puts in place certain interim provisions until that system becomes operative. Under the interim provisions, a firearms dealer who proposes to transfer a handgun must first: (1) receive from the transferee a statement (the Brady Form) containing the name, address and date of birth of the proposed transferee along with a sworn statement that the transferee is not among any of the classes of prohibited purchasers; (2) verify the identity of the transferee by examining an identification document; and (3) provide the "chief law enforcement officer" (CLEO) of the transferee's residence with notice of the contents (and a copy) of the Brady Form. With some exceptions, the dealer must then wait five business days before consummating the sale, unless the CLEO earlier notifies the dealer that he has no reason to believe the transfer would be illegal. . . .

When a CLEO receives the required notice of a proposed transfer from the firearms dealer, the CLEO must "make a reasonable effort to ascertain within 5 business days whether receipt or possession would be in violation of the law, including research in whatever State and local recordkeeping systems are available and in a national system designated by the Attorney General." The Act does not require the CLEO to take any particular action if he determines that a pending transaction would be unlawful; he may notify the firearms dealer to that effect, but is not required to do so. If, however, the CLEO notifies a gun dealer that a prospective purchaser is ineligible to receive a handgun, he must, upon request, provide the would-be purchaser with a written statement of the reasons for that determination. Moreover, if the CLEO does not discover any basis for objecting to the sale, he must destroy any records in his possession relating to the transfer, including his copy of the Brady Form. Under a separate provision of the GCA, any person who "knowingly violates [the section of the GCA amended by the Brady Act] shall be fined under this title, imprisoned for no more than 1 year, or both."

Petitioners Jay Printz and Richard Mack, the CLEOs for Ravalli County, Montana, and Graham County, Arizona, respectively, filed separate actions challenging the constitutionality of the Brady Act's interim provisions. In each case, the District Court held that the provision requiring CLEOs to perform background checks was unconstitutional, but concluded that that provision was severable from the remainder of the Act, effectively leaving a voluntary background-check system in place. A divided panel of the Court of Appeals for the Ninth Circuit reversed, finding none of the Brady Act's interim provisions to be unconstitutional. . . .

II

From the description set forth above, it is apparent that the Brady Act purports to direct state law enforcement officers to participate, albeit only temporarily, in the administration of a federally enacted regulatory scheme. . . . The petitioners here object to being pressed into federal service, and contend that congressional action compelling state officers to execute federal laws is unconstitutional.

Because there is no constitutional text speaking to this precise question, the answer to the CLEOs' challenge must be sought in historical understanding and practice, in the structure of the Constitution, and in the jurisprudence of this Court. . . .

Petitioners contend that compelled enlistment of state executive officers for the administration of federal programs is, until very recent years at least, unprecedented. The Government contends, to the contrary, that "the earliest Congresses enacted statutes that required the participation of state officials in the implementation of federal laws." The Government's contention demands our careful consideration, since early congressional enactments "provide 'contemporaneous and weighty evidence' of the Constitution's meaning." Indeed, such "contemporaneous legislative exposition of the Constitution . . . acquiesced in for a long term of years, fixes the construction to be given its provisions." Conversely if, as petitioners contend, earlier Congresses avoided use of this highly attractive power, we would have reason to believe that the power was thought not to exist.

The Government observes that statutes enacted by the first Congresses required state courts to record applications for citizenship, Act of Mar. 26, 1790, to transmit abstracts of citizenship applications and other naturalization records to the Secretary of State, Act of June 18, 1798, and to register aliens seeking naturalization and issue certificates of registry, Act of Apr. 14, 1802. It may well be, however, that these requirements applied only in States that authorized their courts to conduct naturalization proceedings. See Act of Mar. 26, 1790; *Holmgren v. United States,* 217 U.S. 509 (1910) (explaining that the Act of March 26, 1790 "conferred authority upon state courts to admit aliens to citizenship" and refraining from addressing the question "whether the States can be required to enforce such naturalization laws against their consent"). Other statutes of that era apparently or at least arguably required state courts to perform functions unrelated to naturalization, such as resolving controversies between a captain and the crew of his ship concerning the seaworthiness of the vessel, Act of July 20, 1790, hearing the claims of slave owners who had apprehended fugitive slaves and issuing certificates authorizing the slave's forced removal to the State from which he had fled, Act of Feb. 12, 1793, taking proof of the claims of Canadian refugees who had assisted the United States during the Revolutionary War, Act of Apr. 7, 1798, and ordering the deportation of alien enemies in times of war, Act of July 6, 1798.

These early laws establish, at most, that the Constitution was originally understood to permit imposition of an obligation on state *judges* to enforce federal prescriptions, insofar as those prescriptions related to matters appropriate for the judicial power. That assumption was perhaps implicit in one of the provisions of the Constitution, and was explicit in another. In accord with the so-called Madisonian Compromise, Article III, § 1, established only a Supreme Court, and made the creation of lower federal courts optional with the Congress—even though it was obvious that the Supreme Court alone could not hear all federal cases throughout the United States. And the Supremacy Clause, Art. VI, cl. 2, announced that "the Laws of the United States . . . shall be the supreme Law of the Land; and the Judges in every State shall be bound thereby." It is understandable why courts should have been viewed distinctively in this regard; unlike legislatures and executives, they applied the law of other sovereigns all the time. . . .

For these reasons, we do not think the early statutes imposing obligations on state courts imply a power of Congress to impress the state executive into its service. Indeed, it can be argued that the numerousness of these statutes, contrasted with the utter lack of statutes imposing obligations on the States' executive (notwithstanding the attractiveness of that course to Congress), suggests an assumed *absence* of such power. The only early federal law the Government has brought to our attention that imposed duties on state executive officers is the Extradition Act of 1793, which required the "executive authority" of a State to cause the arrest and delivery of a fugitive from justice upon the request of the executive authority of the State from which the fugitive had fled. That was in direct implementation, however, of the Extradition Clause of the Constitution itself, see Art. IV, § 2.

Not only do the enactments of the early Congresses, as far as we are aware, contain no evidence of an assumption that the Federal Government may command the States' executive power in the absence of a particularized constitutional authorization, they contain some indication of precisely the opposite assumption. On September 23, 1789—the day before its proposal of the Bill of Rights—the First Congress enacted a law aimed at obtaining state assistance of the most rudimentary and necessary sort for the enforcement of the new Government's laws: the holding of federal prisoners in state jails at federal expense. Significantly, the law issued not a command to the States' executive, but a recommendation to their legislatures. Congress "recommended to the legislatures of the several States to pass laws, making it expressly the duty of the keepers of their gaols, to receive and safe keep therein all prisoners committed under the authority of the United States," and offered to pay 50 cents per month for each prisoner. Act of Sept. 23, 1789. Moreover, when Georgia refused to comply with the request, Congress's only reaction was a law authorizing the marshal in any State that failed to comply with the Recommendation of September 23, 1789, to rent a temporary jail until provision for a permanent one could be made, see Resolution of Mar. 3, 1791.

In addition to early legislation, the Government . . . points to portions of The Federalist which reply to criticisms that Congress's power to tax will produce two sets of revenue officers—for example, "Brutus's" assertion in his letter to the New York Journal of December 13, 1787, that the Constitution "opens a door to the appointment of a swarm of revenue and excise officers to prey upon the honest and industrious part of the community, eat up their substance, and riot on the spoils of the country". "Publius" responded that Congress will probably "make use of the State officers and State regulations, for collecting" federal taxes, The Federalist No. 36 (A. Hamilton), and predicted that "the eventual collection [of internal revenue] under the immediate authority of the Union, will generally be made by the officers, and according to the rules, appointed by the several States," *id.*, No. 45 (J. Madison). The Government also invokes the Federalist's more general observations that the Constitution would "enable the [national] government to employ the ordinary magistracy of each [State] in the execution of its laws," *id.*, No. 27 (A. Hamilton), and that it was "extremely probable that in other instances, particularly in the organization of the judicial power, the officers of the States will be clothed in the correspondent authority of the Union," *id.*, No. 45 (J. Madison). But none of these statements necessarily implies—what is the critical point here—that Congress could impose these responsibilities *without the consent of the States*. They appear to rest on the natural assumption that the States would consent to allowing their officials to assist the Federal Government, an assumption proved correct by the extensive mutual assistance the States and Federal Government voluntarily provided one another in the early days of the Republic, including voluntary *federal implementation of state law*, see, *e.g.*, Act of Apr. 2, 1790 (directing federal tax collectors and customs officers to assist in enforcing state inspection laws). . . .

To complete the historical record, we must note that there is not only an absence of executive-commandeering statutes in the early Congresses, but there is an absence of them in our later history as well, at least until very recent years. The Government points to the Act of August 3, 1882, which enlisted state officials "to take charge of the local affairs of immigration in the ports within such State, and to provide for the support and relief of such immigrants therein landing as may fall into distress or need of public aid"; to inspect arriving immigrants and exclude any person found to be a "convict, lunatic, idiot," or indigent; and to send convicts back to their country of origin "without compensation." The statute did not, however, *mandate* those duties, but merely empowered the Secretary of the Treasury "to *enter into contracts* with such State . . . officers as *may be designated* for that purpose *by the governor* of any State." (Emphasis added.)

The Government cites the World War I selective draft law that authorized the President "to utilize the service of any or all departments and any or all officers or agents of the United States *and of the several States*, Territories, and the District of Columbia, and subdivisions thereof, in the execution of this Act," and made any person who refused to comply with the President's directions guilty of a misdemeanor. Act of May 18, 1917 (emphasis added). However, it is far from clear that the authorization "to utilize the service" of state officers was an authorization to *compel* the service of state officers; and the misdemeanor provision surely applied only to refusal to comply with the President's *authorized* directions, which might not have included directions to officers of States whose governors had not volunteered their services. It is interesting that in implementing the Act President Wilson did not commandeer the services of state officers, but instead requested the assistance of the States' governors, obtained the consent of each of the governors, and left it to the governors to issue orders to their subordinate state officers. It is impressive that even with respect to a wartime measure the President should have been so solicitous of state independence. . . .

III

The constitutional practice we have examined above tends to negate the existence of the congressional power asserted here, but is not conclusive. We turn next to consideration of the structure of the Constitution, to see if we can discern among its "essential postulates," a principle that controls the present cases.

A

It is incontestible that the Constitution established a system of "dual sovereignty." Although the States surrendered many of their powers to the new Federal Government, they retained "a residuary and inviolable sovereignty," The Federalist No. 39 (J. Madison). This is reflected throughout the Constitution's text, including (to mention only a few examples) the prohibition on any involuntary reduction or combination of a State's territory, Art. IV, § 3; the Judicial Power Clause, Art. III, § 2, and the Privileges and Immunities Clause, Art. IV, § 2, which speak of the "Citizens" of the States; the amendment provision, Article V, which requires the votes of three-fourths of the States to amend the Constitution; and the Guarantee Clause, Art. IV, § 4, which "presupposes the continued existence of the states and . . . those means and instrumentalities which are the creation of their sovereign and reserved rights." Residual state sovereignty was also implicit, of course, in the Constitution's conferral upon Congress of not all governmental powers, but only discrete, enumerated ones, Art. I, § 8, which implication was rendered express by the Tenth Amendment's assertion that "the powers not delegated to the United States by the Constitution, nor prohibited by it to the States, are reserved to the States respectively, or to the people."

The Framers' experience under the Articles of Confederation had persuaded them that using the States as the instruments of federal governance was both ineffectual and provocative of federal-state conflict. Preservation of the States as independent political entities being the price of union, and "the practicality of making laws, with coercive sanctions, for the States as political bodies" having been, in Madison's words, "exploded on all hands," 2 Records of the Federal Convention of 1787, p. 9 (M. Farrand ed., 1911), the Framers rejected the concept of a central government that would act upon and through the States, and instead designed a system in which the state and federal governments would exercise concurrent authority over the people—who were, in Hamilton's words, "the only proper objects of government," The Federalist No. 15. We have set forth the historical record in more detail elsewhere, see *New York v. United States*, and need not repeat it here. It suffices to repeat the conclusion: "The Framers explicitly chose a Constitution that confers upon Congress the power to regulate individuals, not States."[10] The great innovation of this design was that "our citizens would have two political capacities, one state and one federal, each protected from incursion by the other"—"a legal system unprecedented in form and design, establishing two orders of

---

[10] The dissent maintains that the Constitution merely *augmented* the pre-existing power under the Articles to issue commands to the States with the additional power to make demands directly on individuals. That argument, however, was squarely rejected by the Court in *New York*, and with good reason. Many of Congress's powers under Art. I, § 8, were copied almost verbatim from the Articles of Confederation, indicating quite clearly that "where the Constitution intends that our Congress enjoy a power once vested in the Continental Congress, it specifically grants it."

government, each with its own direct relationship, its own privity, its own set of mutual rights and obligations to the people who sustain it and are governed by it." *U.S. Term Limits, Inc. v. Thornton*, 514 U.S. 779, 838 (1995) (Kennedy, J., concurring). The Constitution thus contemplates that a State's government will represent and remain accountable to its own citizens. As Madison expressed it: "The local or municipal authorities form distinct and independent portions of the supremacy, no more subject, within their respective spheres, to the general authority than the general authority is subject to them, within its own sphere." The Federalist No. 39.[11]

This separation of the two spheres is one of the Constitution's structural protections of liberty. . . . To quote Madison once again:

> In the compound republic of America, the power surrendered by the people is first divided between two distinct governments, and then the portion allotted to each subdivided among distinct and separate departments. Hence a double security arises to the rights of the people. The different governments will control each other, at the same time that each will be controlled by itself. The Federalist No. 51.

The power of the Federal Government would be augmented immeasurably if it were able to impress into its service—and at no cost to itself—the police officers of the 50 States. . . .

C

The dissent of course resorts to the last, best hope of those who defend *ultra vires* congressional action, the Necessary and Proper Clause. It reasons that the power to regulate the sale of handguns under the Commerce Clause, coupled with the power to "make all Laws which shall

---

11 JUSTICE BREYER'S dissent would have us consider the benefits that other countries, and the European Union, believe they have derived from federal systems that are different from ours. We think such comparative analysis inappropriate to the task of interpreting a constitution, though it was of course quite relevant to the task of writing one. The Framers were familiar with many federal systems, from classical antiquity down to their own time; they are discussed in Nos. 18–20 of The Federalist. Some were (for the purpose here under discussion) quite similar to the modern "federal" systems that JUSTICE BREYER favors. Madison's and Hamilton's opinion of such systems could not be clearer. Federalist No. 20, after an extended critique of the system of government established by the Union of Utrecht for the United Netherlands, concludes:

> I make no apology for having dwelt so long on the contemplation of these federal precedents. Experience is the oracle of truth; and where its responses are unequivocal, they ought to be conclusive and sacred. The important truth, which it unequivocally pronounces in the present case, is that a sovereignty over sovereigns, a government over governments, a legislation for communities, as contradistinguished from individuals, as it is a solecism in theory, so in practice it is subversive of the order and ends of civil polity.

Antifederalists, on the other hand, pointed specifically to Switzerland—and its then-400 years of success as a "confederate republic"—as proof that the proposed Constitution and its federal structure was unnecessary. See Patrick Henry, Speeches given before the Virginia Ratifying Convention, 4 and 5 June, 1788. The fact is that our federalism is not Europe's. It is "the unique contribution of the Framers to political science and political theory." *United States v. Lopez*, 514 U.S. 549, 575 (1995) (Kennedy, J., concurring).

be necessary and proper for carrying into Execution the foregoing Powers," Art. I, § 8, conclusively establishes the Brady Act's constitutional validity, because the Tenth Amendment imposes no limitations on the exercise of *delegated* powers but merely prohibits the exercise of powers "*not* delegated to the United States." What destroys the dissent's Necessary and Proper Clause argument, however, is not the Tenth Amendment but the Necessary and Proper Clause itself.[13] When a "Law . . . for carrying into Execution" the Commerce Clause violates the principle of state sovereignty reflected in the various constitutional provisions we mentioned earlier, it is not a "Law . . . *proper* for carrying into Execution the Commerce Clause," and is thus, in the words of The Federalist, "merely [an] act of usurpation" which "deserves to be treated as such." The Federalist No. 33 (A. Hamilton). We in fact answered the dissent's Necessary and Proper Clause argument in *New York*: "Even where Congress has the authority under the Constitution to pass laws requiring or prohibiting certain acts, it lacks the power directly to compel the States to require or prohibit those acts. . . . The Commerce Clause, for example, authorizes Congress to regulate interstate commerce directly; it does not authorize Congress to regulate state governments' regulation of interstate commerce."

The dissent perceives a simple answer in that portion of Article VI which requires that "all executive and judicial Officers, both of the United States and of the several States, shall be bound by Oath or Affirmation, to support this Constitution," arguing that by virtue of the Supremacy Clause this makes "not only the Constitution, but every law enacted by Congress as well," binding on state officers, including laws requiring state-officer enforcement. The Supremacy Clause, however, makes "Law of the Land" only "Laws of the United States which shall be made in Pursuance [of the Constitution]"; so the Supremacy Clause merely brings us back to the question discussed earlier, whether laws conscripting state officers violate state sovereignty and are thus not in accord with the Constitution.

IV

Finally, and most conclusively in the present litigation, we turn to the prior jurisprudence of this Court. . . . At issue in *New York v. United States*, 505 U.S. 144 (1992), were the so-called "take title" provisions of the Low-Level Radioactive Waste Policy Amendments Act of 1985, which required States either to enact legislation providing for the disposal of radioactive waste generated within their borders, or to take title to, and

---

[13] This argument also falsely presumes that the Tenth Amendment is the exclusive textual source of protection for principles of federalism. Our system of dual sovereignty is reflected in numerous constitutional provisions, and not only those, like the Tenth Amendment, that speak to the point explicitly. It is not at all unusual for our resolution of a significant constitutional question to rest upon reasonable implications. See, *e.g.*, *Myers v. United States*, 272 U.S. 52 (1926) (finding by implication from Art. II, §§ 1, 2, that the President has the exclusive power to remove executive officers); *Plaut v. Spendthrift Farm, Inc.*, 514 U.S. 211 (1995) (finding that Article III implies a lack of congressional power to set aside final judgments).

possession of the waste—effectively requiring the States either to legislate pursuant to Congress's directions, or to implement an administrative solution. We concluded that Congress could constitutionally require the States to do neither. "The Federal Government," we held, "may not compel the States to enact or administer a federal regulatory program."

The Government contends that *New York* is distinguishable on the following ground: unlike the "take title" provisions invalidated there, the background-check provision of the Brady Act does not require state legislative or executive officials to make policy, but instead issues a final directive to state CLEOs. It is permissible, the Government asserts, for Congress to command state or local officials to assist in the implementation of federal law so long as "Congress itself devises a clear legislative solution that regulates private conduct" and requires state or local officers to provide only "limited, non-policymaking help in enforcing that law." "The constitutional line is crossed only when Congress compels the States to make law in their sovereign capacities."

The Government's distinction between "making" law and merely "enforcing" it, between "policymaking" and mere "implementation," is an interesting one. It is perhaps not meant to be the same as, but it is surely reminiscent of, the line that separates proper congressional conferral of Executive power from unconstitutional delegation of legislative authority for federal separation-of-powers purposes. See *A.L.A. Schechter Poultry Corp. v. United States*, 295 U.S. 495, 530 (1935). This Court has not been notably successful in describing the latter line; indeed, some think we have abandoned the effort to do so. We are doubtful that the new line the Government proposes would be any more distinct. Executive action that has utterly no policymaking component is rare, particularly at an executive level as high as a jurisdiction's chief law-enforcement officer. Is it really true that there is no policymaking involved in deciding, for example, what "reasonable efforts" shall be expended to conduct a background check? It may well satisfy the Act for a CLEO to direct that (a) no background checks will be conducted that divert personnel time from pending felony investigations, and (b) no background check will be permitted to consume more than one-half hour of an officer's time. But nothing in the Act *requires* a CLEO to be so parsimonious; diverting at least *some* felony-investigation time, and permitting at least *some* background checks beyond one-half hour would certainly not be *un*reasonable. Is this decision whether to devote maximum "reasonable efforts" or minimum "reasonable efforts" not preeminently a matter of policy? It is quite impossible, in short, to draw the Government's proposed line at "no policymaking," and we would have to fall back upon a line of "not too much policymaking." How much is too much is not likely to be answered precisely; and an imprecise barrier against federal intrusion upon state authority is not likely to be an effective one.

Even assuming, moreover, that the Brady Act leaves no "policymaking" discretion with the States, we fail to see how that improves rather than worsens the intrusion upon state sovereignty. Preservation of the States as independent and autonomous political entities is arguably less undermined by requiring them to make policy in certain fields than . . . by reducing [them] to puppets of a ventriloquist Congress. It is an essential attribute of the States' retained sovereignty that they remain independent and autonomous within their proper sphere of authority. It is no more compatible with this independence and autonomy that their officers be "dragooned" . . . into administering federal law, than it would be compatible with the independence and autonomy of the United States that its officers be impressed into service for the execution of state laws.

The Government purports to find support for its proffered distinction of *New York* in our decision[ ] in *Testa v. Katt*, 330 U.S. 386 (1947). . . . *Testa* stands for the proposition that state courts cannot refuse to apply federal law—a conclusion mandated by the terms of the Supremacy Clause ("the Judges in every State shall be bound [by federal law]"). As we have suggested earlier, that says nothing about whether state executive officers must administer federal law.

The Government also maintains that requiring state officers to perform discrete, ministerial tasks specified by Congress does not violate the principle of *New York* because it does not diminish the accountability of state or federal officials. This argument fails even on its own terms. By forcing state governments to absorb the financial burden of implementing a federal regulatory program, Members of Congress can take credit for "solving" problems without having to ask their constituents to pay for the solutions with higher federal taxes. And even when the States are not forced to absorb the costs of implementing a federal program, they are still put in the position of taking the blame for its burdensomeness and for its defects. Under the present law, for example, it will be the CLEO and not some federal official who stands between the gun purchaser and immediate possession of his gun. And it will likely be the CLEO, not some federal official, who will be blamed for any error (even one in the designated federal database) that causes a purchaser to be mistakenly rejected. . . .

Finally, the Government puts forward a cluster of arguments that can be grouped under the heading: "The Brady Act serves very important purposes, is most efficiently administered by CLEOs during the interim period, and places a minimal and only temporary burden upon state officers." There is considerable disagreement over the extent of the burden, but we need not pause over that detail. Assuming *all* the mentioned factors were true, they might be relevant if we were evaluating whether the incidental application to the States of a federal law of general applicability excessively interfered with the functioning of state governments. See, *e.g., National League of Cities v. Usery,* 426 U.S.

833, 853 (1976) (overruled by *Garcia v. San Antonio Metropolitan Transit Authority*, 469 U.S. 528 (1985)). But where, as here, it is the whole *object* of the law to direct the functioning of the state executive, and hence to compromise the structural framework of dual sovereignty, such a "balancing" analysis is inappropriate. It is the very *principle* of separate state sovereignty that such a law offends, and no comparative assessment of the various interests can overcome that fundamental defect. We expressly rejected such an approach in *New York*. . . . We adhere to that principle today, and conclude categorically, as we concluded categorically in *New York*: "The Federal Government may not compel the States to enact or administer a federal regulatory program." The mandatory obligation imposed on CLEOs to perform background checks on prospective handgun purchasers plainly runs afoul of that rule.

V

. . . We held in *New York* that Congress cannot compel the States to enact or enforce a federal regulatory program. Today we hold that Congress cannot circumvent that prohibition by conscripting the State's officers directly. The Federal Government may neither issue directives requiring the States to address particular problems, nor command the States' officers, or those of their political subdivisions, to administer or enforce a federal regulatory program. . . . Accordingly, the judgment of the Court of Appeals for the Ninth Circuit is reversed.

■ **JUSTICE STEVENS, with whom JUSTICE SOUTER, JUSTICE GINSBURG, and JUSTICE BREYER join, dissenting.**

When Congress exercises the powers delegated to it by the Constitution, it may impose affirmative obligations on executive and judicial officers of state and local governments as well as ordinary citizens. This conclusion is firmly supported by the text of the Constitution, the early history of the Nation, decisions of this Court, and a correct understanding of the basic structure of the Federal Government.

These cases do not implicate the more difficult questions associated with congressional coercion of state legislatures addressed in *New York v. United States*, 505 U.S. 144 (1992). Nor need we consider the wisdom of relying on local officials rather than federal agents to carry out aspects of a federal program, or even the question whether such officials may be required to perform a federal function on a permanent basis. The question is whether Congress, acting on behalf of the people of the entire Nation, may require local law enforcement officers to perform certain duties during the interim needed for the development of a federal gun control program. It is remarkably similar to the question, heavily debated by the Framers of the Constitution, whether the Congress could require state agents to collect federal taxes. Or the question whether Congress could impress state judges into federal service to entertain and decide cases that they would prefer to ignore.

Indeed, since the ultimate issue is one of power, we must consider its implications in times of national emergency. Matters such as the enlistment of air raid wardens, the administration of a military draft, the mass inoculation of children to forestall an epidemic, or perhaps the threat of an international terrorist, may require a national response before federal personnel can be made available to respond. If the Constitution empowers Congress and the President to make an appropriate response, is there anything in the Tenth Amendment, in historical understanding and practice, in the structure of the Constitution, [or] in the jurisprudence of this Court, that forbids the enlistment of state officers to make that response effective? More narrowly, what basis is there in any of those sources for concluding that it is the Members of this Court, rather than the elected representatives of the people, who should determine whether the Constitution contains the unwritten rule that the Court announces today?

Perhaps today's majority would suggest that no such emergency is presented by the facts of these cases. But such a suggestion is itself an expression of a policy judgment. And Congress' view of the matter is quite different from that implied by the Court today.

The Brady Act was passed in response to what Congress described as an "epidemic of gun violence." The Act's legislative history notes that 15,377 Americans were murdered with firearms in 1992, and that 12,489 of these deaths were caused by handguns. Congress expressed special concern that "the level of firearm violence in this country is, by far, the highest among developed nations." The partial solution contained in the Brady Act, a mandatory background check before a handgun may be purchased, has met with remarkable success. Between 1994 and 1996, approximately 6,600 firearm sales each month to potentially dangerous persons were prevented by Brady Act checks; over 70% of the rejected purchasers were convicted or indicted felons. Whether or not the evaluation reflected in the enactment of the Brady Act is correct as to the extent of the danger and the efficacy of the legislation, the congressional decision surely warrants more respect than it is accorded in today's unprecedented decision.

I

The text of the Constitution provides a sufficient basis for a correct disposition of this case. Article I, § 8, grants the Congress the power to regulate commerce among the States. . . . [T]here can be no question that that provision adequately supports the regulation of commerce in handguns effected by the Brady Act. Moreover, the additional grant of authority in that section of the Constitution "to make all Laws which shall be necessary and proper for carrying into Execution the foregoing Powers" is surely adequate to support the temporary enlistment of local police officers in the process of identifying persons who should not be entrusted with the possession of handguns. In short, the affirmative delegation of power in Article I provides ample authority for the congressional enactment.

Unlike the First Amendment, which prohibits the enactment of a category of laws that would otherwise be authorized by Article I, the Tenth Amendment imposes no restriction on the exercise of delegated powers. . . . The Amendment confirms the principle that the powers of the Federal Government are limited to those affirmatively granted by the Constitution, but it does not purport to limit the scope or the effectiveness of the exercise of powers that are delegated to Congress. Thus, the Amendment provides no support for a rule that immunizes local officials from obligations that might be imposed on ordinary citizens.[2] Indeed, it would be more reasonable to infer that federal law may impose greater duties on state officials than on private citizens because another provision of the Constitution requires that "all executive and judicial Officers, both of the United States and of the several States, shall be bound by Oath or Affirmation, to support this Constitution." U.S. Const., Art. VI, cl. 3.

It is appropriate for state officials to make an oath or affirmation to support the Federal Constitution because, as explained in The Federalist, they "have an essential agency in giving effect to the federal Constitution."[3] The Federalist No. 44 (J. Madison). There can be no conflict between their duties to the State and those owed to the Federal Government because Article VI unambiguously provides that federal law "shall be the supreme Law of the Land," binding in every State. U.S. Const., Art. VI, cl. 2. Thus, not only the Constitution, but every law enacted by Congress as well, establishes policy for the States just as firmly as do laws enacted by state legislatures. . . .

There is not a clause, sentence, or paragraph in the entire text of the Constitution of the United States that supports the proposition that a local police officer can ignore a command contained in a statute enacted

---

[2] Recognizing the force of the argument, the Court suggests that this reasoning is in error because . . . it does not answer the possibility that the Court's holding can be rooted in a "principle of state sovereignty" mentioned nowhere in the constitutional text. As a ground for invalidating important federal legislation, this argument is remarkably weak. The majority's further claim that, while the Brady Act may be legislation "necessary" to Congress' execution of its undisputed Commerce Clause authority to regulate firearms sales, it is nevertheless not "proper" because it violates state sovereignty, is wholly circular and provides no traction for its argument. Moreover, this reading of the term "proper" gives it a meaning directly contradicted by Chief Justice Marshall in *McCulloch v. Maryland*, 17 U.S. 316, 4 Wheat. 316 (1819). As the Chief Justice explained, the Necessary and Proper Clause by "its terms purports to enlarge, not to diminish the powers vested in the government. It purports to be an additional power, not a restriction on those already granted." . . .

[3] "It has been asked why it was thought necessary, that the State magistracy should be bound to support the federal Constitution, and unnecessary that a like oath should be imposed on the officers of the United States, in favor of the State constitutions. Several reasons might be assigned for the distinction. I content myself with one, which is obvious and conclusive. The members of the federal government will have no agency in carrying the State constitutions into effect. The members and officers of the State governments, on the contrary, will have an essential agency in giving effect to the federal Constitution." The Federalist No. 44 (J. Madison).

by Congress pursuant to an express delegation of power enumerated in Article I.

II

Under the Articles of Confederation the National Government had the power to issue commands to the several sovereign states, but it had no authority to govern individuals directly. Thus, it raised an army and financed its operations by issuing requisitions to the constituent members of the Confederacy, rather than by creating federal agencies to draft soldiers or to impose taxes.

That method of governing proved to be unacceptable, not because it demeaned the sovereign character of the several States, but rather because it was cumbersome and inefficient. Indeed, a confederation that allows each of its members to determine the ways and means of complying with an overriding requisition is obviously more deferential to state sovereignty concerns than a national government that uses its own agents to impose its will directly on the citizenry. The basic change in the character of the government that the Framers conceived was designed to enhance the power of the national government, not to provide some new, unmentioned immunity for state officers. Because indirect control over individual citizens ("the only proper objects of government") was ineffective under the Articles of Confederation, Alexander Hamilton explained that "we must *extend* the authority of the Union to the persons of the citizens." The Federalist No. 15 (emphasis added).

Indeed, the historical materials strongly suggest that the Founders intended to enhance the capacity of the federal government by empowering it . . . to act through local officials. Hamilton made clear that the new Constitution, "by extending the authority of the federal head to the individual citizens of the several States, will enable the government to employ the ordinary magistracy of each, in the execution of its laws." The Federalist No. 27. Hamilton's meaning was unambiguous; the federal government was to have the power to demand that local officials implement national policy programs. . . .

More specifically, during the debates concerning the ratification of the Constitution, it was assumed that state agents would act as tax collectors for the federal government. Opponents of the Constitution had repeatedly expressed fears that the new federal government's ability to impose taxes directly on the citizenry would result in an overbearing presence of federal tax collectors in the States. Federalists rejoined that this problem would not arise because, as Hamilton explained, "the United States . . . will make use of the State officers and State regulations for collecting" certain taxes. The Federalist No. 36. Similarly, Madison made clear that the new central government's power to raise taxes directly from the citizenry would "not be resorted to, except for supplemental purposes of revenue . . . and that the eventual collection, under the immediate authority of the Union, will generally be made by the officers . . . appointed by the several States." *Id.*, No. 45.

The Court's response to this powerful historical evidence is weak. The majority suggests that "none of these statements necessarily implies . . . Congress could impose these responsibilities without the consent of the States." No fair reading of these materials can justify such an interpretation. . . .

This point is made especially clear in Hamilton's statement that "the legislatures, courts, and magistrates, of the respective members, will be incorporated into the operations of the national government as far as its *just and constitutional authority extends*; and *will be rendered auxiliary to the enforcement of its laws*." *Ibid.* (second emphasis added). It is hard to imagine a more unequivocal statement that state judicial and executive branch officials may be required to implement federal law where the National Government acts within the scope of its affirmative powers. . . .

Bereft of support in the history of the founding, the Court rests its conclusion on the claim that there is little evidence the National Government actually exercised such a power in the early years of the Republic. This reasoning is misguided in principle and in fact. While we have indicated that the express consideration and resolution of difficult constitutional issues by the First Congress in particular "provides 'contemporaneous and weighty evidence' of the Constitution's meaning since many of [its] Members . . . 'had taken part in framing that instrument,'" we have never suggested that the failure of the early Congresses to address the scope of federal power in a particular area or to exercise a particular authority was an argument against its existence. That position, if correct, would undermine most of our post-New Deal Commerce Clause jurisprudence. As JUSTICE O'CONNOR quite properly noted in *New York*, "the Federal Government undertakes activities today that would have been unimaginable to the Framers."

More importantly, the fact that Congress did elect to rely on state judges and the clerks of state courts to perform a variety of executive functions is surely evidence of a contemporary understanding that their status as state officials did not immunize them from federal service. . . .

For example, statutes of the early Congresses required in mandatory terms that state judges and their clerks perform various executive duties with respect to applications for citizenship. . . . Similarly, the First Congress enacted legislation requiring state courts to serve, functionally, like contemporary regulatory agencies in certifying the seaworthiness of vessels. Act of July 20, 1790. The majority casts this as an adjudicative duty, but that characterization is misleading. . . .

The Court's evaluation of the historical evidence, furthermore, fails to acknowledge the important difference between policy decisions that may have been influenced by respect for state sovereignty concerns, and decisions that are compelled by the Constitution.[12] Thus, for example, the decision by Congress to give President Wilson the authority to utilize the services of state officers in implementing the World War I draft, surely indicates that the national legislature saw no constitutional impediment to the enlistment of state assistance during a federal emergency. The fact that the President was able to implement the program by respectfully "requesting" state action, rather than bluntly commanding it, is evidence that he was an effective statesman, but surely does not indicate that he doubted either his or Congress' power to use mandatory language if necessary. . . .

Indeed, the majority's opinion consists almost entirely of arguments *against* the substantial evidence weighing in opposition to its view; the Court's ruling is strikingly lacking in affirmative support. Absent even a modicum of textual foundation for its judicially crafted constitutional rule, there should be a presumption that if the Framers had actually intended such a rule, at least one of them would have mentioned it.

III

The Court's "structural" arguments are not sufficient to rebut that presumption. The fact that the Framers intended to preserve the sovereignty of the several States simply does not speak to the question whether individual state employees may be required to perform federal obligations, such as registering young adults for the draft, creating state emergency response commissions designed to manage the release of hazardous substances, collecting and reporting data on underground storage tanks that may pose an environmental hazard, and reporting traffic fatalities and missing children to a federal agency.

As we explained in *Garcia v. San Antonio Metropolitan Transit Authority*, 469 U.S. 528 (1985): "The principal means chosen by the Framers to ensure the role of the States in the federal system lies in the structure of the Federal Government itself. . . ." Given the fact that the Members of Congress are elected by the people of the several States, . . . [i]t is . . . reasonable to presume that their decisions to impose modest burdens on state officials from time to time reflect a considered judgment that the people in each of the States will benefit therefrom. . . .

Recent developments demonstrate that the political safeguards protecting Our Federalism are effective. The majority expresses special concern that were its rule not adopted the Federal Government would be able to avail itself of the services of state government officials "at no cost to itself." But this specific problem of federal actions that have the effect of imposing so-called "unfunded mandates" on the States has been

---

[12] Indeed, an entirely appropriate concern for the prerogatives of state government readily explains Congress' sparing use of this otherwise "highly attractive" power. Congress' discretion, contrary to the majority's suggestion, indicates not that the power does not exist, but rather that the interests of the States are more than sufficiently protected by their participation in the National Government.

identified and meaningfully addressed by Congress in recent legislation.[18] See Unfunded Mandates Reform Act of 1995.

The statute was designed "to end the imposition, in the absence of full consideration by Congress, of Federal mandates on State . . . governments without adequate Federal funding, in a manner that may displace other essential State . . . governmental priorities." It functions, *inter alia*, by permitting Members of Congress to raise an objection by point of order to a pending bill that contains an "unfunded mandate," as defined by the statute, of over $50 million.[19] The mandate may not then be enacted unless the Members make an explicit decision to proceed anyway. Whatever the ultimate impact of the new legislation, its passage demonstrates that unelected judges are better off leaving the protection of federalism to the political process in all but the most extraordinary circumstances. . . .

By limiting the ability of the Federal Government to enlist state officials in the implementation of its programs, the Court creates incentives for the National Government to aggrandize itself. In the name of State's rights, the majority would have the Federal Government create vast national bureaucracies to implement its policies. This is exactly the sort of thing that the early Federalists promised would not occur, in part as a result of the National Government's ability to rely on the magistracy of the states. . . .

IV

. . . *New York v. United States*. . . clearly did not decide the question presented here, whether state executive officials—as opposed to state legislators—may in appropriate circumstances be enlisted to implement federal policy. The "take title" provision at issue in *New York* was beyond Congress' authority to enact because it was "in principle . . . no different than a congressionally compelled subsidy from state governments to radioactive waste producers," almost certainly a legislative act.

---

[18] The majority also makes the more general claim that requiring state officials to carry out federal policy causes states to "take the blame" for failed programs. . . . This concern is vastly overstated. Unlike state legislators, local government executive officials routinely take action in response to a variety of sources of authority: local ordinance, state law, and federal law. . . . [A]ffected citizens must look past the official before them to find the true cause of their grievance. But the majority's rule neither creates nor alters this basic truth.

The problem is of little real consequence in any event, because to the extent that a particular action proves politically unpopular, we may be confident that elected officials charged with implementing it will be quite clear to their constituents where the source of the misfortune lies. These cases demonstrate the point. Sheriffs Printz and Mack have made public statements . . . denouncing the Brady Act. Indeed, Sheriff Mack has written a book discussing his views on the issue. See R. Mack & T. Walters, From My Cold Dead Fingers: Why America Needs Guns (1994). Moreover, we can be sure that CLEOs will inform disgruntled constituents who have been denied permission to purchase a handgun about the origins of the Brady Act requirements. . . .

[19] Unlike the majority's judicially crafted rule, the statute excludes from its coverage bills in certain subject areas, such as emergency matters, legislation prohibiting discrimination, and national security measures.

The majority relies upon dictum in *New York* to the effect that "the Federal Government may not compel the States to enact *or administer* a federal regulatory program" (emphasis added). But that language was wholly unnecessary to the decision of the case. . . . To the extent that [this dictum] has any substance at all . . . it is hard to characterize the minimal requirement that CLEOs perform background checks as one involving the exercise of substantial policymaking discretion on that essentially legislative scale. . . .

Finally, the majority provides an incomplete explanation of our decision in *Testa v. Katt*, 330 U.S. 386 (1947), and demeans its importance. In that case the Court unanimously held that state courts of appropriate jurisdiction must occupy themselves adjudicating claims brought by private litigants under the federal Emergency Price Control Act of 1942, regardless of how otherwise crowded their dockets might be with state law matters. . . . As *Testa* held, because the "Laws of the United States . . . [are] the supreme Law of the Land," state courts of appropriate jurisdiction must hear federal claims whenever a federal statute, such as the Emergency Price Control Act, requires them to do so.

Hence, the Court's textual argument is quite misguided. The majority focuses on the [Supremacy] Clause's specific attention to the point that "Judges in every State shall be bound." That language commands state judges to "apply federal law" in cases that they entertain, but it is not the source of their duty to accept jurisdiction of federal claims that they would prefer to ignore. Our opinions in *Testa* . . . rested generally on the language of the Supremacy Clause, without any specific focus on the reference to judges. . . .

Throughout our history judges, state as well as federal, have merited as much respect as executive agents. The notion that the Framers would have had no reluctance to "press state judges into federal service" against their will but would have regarded the imposition of a similar—indeed, far lesser—burden on town constables as an intolerable affront to principles of state sovereignty, can only be considered perverse. . . .

The provision of the Brady Act that crosses the Court's newly defined constitutional threshold is more comparable to a statute requiring local police officers to report the identity of missing children to the Crime Control Center of the Department of Justice than to an offensive federal command to a sovereign state. If Congress believes that such a statute will benefit the people of the Nation, and serve the interests of cooperative federalism better than an enlarged federal bureaucracy, we should respect both its policy judgment and its appraisal of its constitutional power.

Accordingly, I respectfully dissent.

■ **JUSTICE BREYER, with whom JUSTICE STEVENS joins, dissenting.**

I would add to the reasons JUSTICE STEVENS sets forth the fact that the United States is not the only nation that seeks to reconcile the practical need for a central authority with the democratic virtues of more local control. At least some other countries, facing the same basic problem, have found that local control is better maintained through application of a principle that is the direct opposite of the principle the majority derives from the silence of our Constitution. The federal systems of Switzerland, Germany, and the European Union, for example, all provide that constituent states, not federal bureaucracies, will themselves implement many of the laws, rules, regulations, or decrees enacted by the central "federal" body. They do so in part because they believe that such a system interferes less, not more, with the independent authority of the "state," member nation, or other subsidiary government, and helps to safeguard individual liberty as well.

Of course, we are interpreting our own Constitution, not those of other nations, and there may be relevant political and structural differences between their systems and our own. *Cf.* The Federalist No. 20 (J. Madison and A. Hamilton) (rejecting certain aspects of European federalism). But their experience may nonetheless cast an empirical light on the consequences of different solutions to a common legal problem— in this case the problem of reconciling central authority with the need to preserve the liberty-enhancing autonomy of a smaller constituent governmental entity. *Cf. id.*, No. 42 (J. Madison) (looking to experiences of European countries); *id.*, No. 43 (J. Madison) (same). And that experience here offers empirical confirmation of the implied answer to a question JUSTICE STEVENS asks: Why, or how, would what the majority sees as a constitutional alternative—the creation of a new federal gun-law bureaucracy, or the expansion of an existing federal bureaucracy— better promote either state sovereignty or individual liberty? . . .

For these reasons and those set forth in JUSTICE STEVENS' opinion, I join his dissent.

NOTE ON THE ANTI-COMMANDEERING DOCTRINE

1.   The *New York* case arose in unusual circumstances: The States themselves had initiated the effort to organize a solution to the problem of siting radioactive waste sites, and Congress acted in its capacity as a referee to lend binding force to the solution negotiated among the States. In these circumstances, was Justice White right to suggest that the Court should put aside any concerns about state autonomy? Doesn't the federal role in these circumstances *enable* state autonomy, much as the Constitution itself enables We the People to make binding precommitments? If you agree with Justice White, however, to what extent would his objection apply to more run-of-the-mill instances of commandeering?

2.   The Court advances two main arguments for the anti-commandeering doctrine in *New York* and *Printz*. One is historical, As the Court explained in *Term Limits*, ratification of the Constitution changed the interaction between "the people" and the national government. Under the Articles of Confederation, States served as intermediaries. The people

elected their state governments, which in turn sent representatives to the Confederation Congress. And that Congress issued regulatory directives and funding requests to States, which retained exclusive authority to regulate and tax the people. The 1789 Constitution, however, established a direct relationship—parallel to the one between the people and their States—between "the people" to the national government. This meant both that the people directly elected (most) national officials, *see Term Limits*, and that Congress could both tax and regulate the people directly.

Do *New York* and *Printz* follow from *Term Limits*? In *Term Limits*, the Court found that the Framers' view of *representation* required a direct link between the People and their federal representatives, with the states not a party to that relationship. In *Printz*, the majority views the exercise of governmental power in the same way. Justice Stevens's dissent in *Printz* says that empowering Congress to regulate directly does not logically foreclose leaving it with the *option* to commandeer state officials as intermediaries, much as it had done under the Articles? But does Stevens, who wrote the majority opinion in *Term Limits* but dissented in *New York* and *Printz*, have a valid ground for distinguishing his earlier opinion? In any event, doesn't the tenor of many of the Founders' statements expressing dissatisfaction with the Articles suggest that commandeering had proven counterproductive and "subversive of . . . order"?

How much weight should history get in deciding how to structure present governmental institutions? Note Justice White's statement, in a long footnote in his *New York* dissent, that "I do not read the majority's many invocations of history to be anything other than elaborate window dressing." In cases like *Heller*, *Term Limits*, and *Printz*, both majority and dissent have implicitly agreed that the original understanding of the Constitution is relevant and even potentially determinative, although they have disagreed as to what that understanding was. It is not surprising that Justice White, a Kennedy appointee and the last holdover from the Warren Court, should be the one to question the use of history *per se*. Should the Court eschew the sorts of intricate historical debates we see in these cases?

Even if you find the Court's view of the Founding-era history compelling in *New York* and *Printz*, what do you make of Justice White's point that both Reconstruction and the New Deal profoundly altered the structure of American federalism? Should Reconstruction be viewed as altering the constitutional structure insofar as the Reconstruction *Amendments* specifically provided? Should the New Deal—which after all added no amendments to the Constitution's text—be irrelevant? Or should both epochs be seen from a more practical perspective, as having profoundly altered the constitutive arrangements of our federal republic?

3.   *New York* and *Printz* also rely on a functional argument about political accountability. Federal commandeering of state officials, the Court suggests, obfuscates for the general public who is ultimately responsible for the action or regulation. Because we rely on political safeguards as a main check for federalism, such a blurring of accountability is unacceptable. On this view, *Garcia's* political safeguards require a certain degree of governmental transparency. But does the majority have a good answer to

Justice Stevens's point that state officials forced to implement unpopular federal mandates can simply publicize the fact that they are acting under federal duress?

The concern for political transparency, however, may not exhaust the functional justifications for the anti-commandeering doctrine.

> Federal power often is limited not simply by political disapproval of national actions, but also by limits on federal governmental resources. Federal resources, while vast, only extend so far, and many federal initiatives that might otherwise encroach on state regulatory authority are defeated by the lack of federal resources to carry them out. This check only works, however, if the federal government must internalize the costs of its actions. If Congress can expand the scope of federal regulation while shifting the enforcement costs of such regulation onto other actors, for example, then an important limit on federal activity has been circumvented.[11]

This perspective views the transparency argument in both *New York* and *Printz* as a requirement that Congress internalize the *political* costs of its actions rather than shift them to state actors. But resource costs are also significant and lie at the heart of the debate over "unfunded mandates." Congress's power would be much extended if it could make the states carry out (and pay for) expensive federal regulation. Justice Stevens points out that Congress has itself restricted such actions in the Unfunded Mandates Reform Act, which raised certain procedural hurdles to such legislation. How effective a check is that likely to be?

Finally, it is important to note that resource constraints can impose *political* checks on national action:

> In a world of finite resources, the prioritization of resources can be politically charged even if individual goals are not politically controversial. Forcing the federal government to internalize the costs of its policies—thereby forcing difficult decisions about resource allocation—is thus likely to sharpen the functioning of the political safeguards of federalism. Governmental actors that oppose particular programs on state autonomy grounds are likely, in these circumstances, to find allies among those who oppose those programs based on a different set of priorities, with the net effect that legislation encroaching on state autonomy becomes more difficult to enact.[12]

Do you agree that the political safeguards of federalism are more likely to work well when the national government must pay its own way?

4.   Nothing in *New York* or *Printz* purports to forbid Congress from employing state officials to implement federal law so long as they do so voluntarily. And in fact most broad federal benefit programs—including Medicaid, Social Security, and unemployment compensation—and

---

[11]   Ernest A. Young, *Two Cheers for Process Federalism*, 46 VILL. L. REV. 1349, 1360 (2001).

[12]   *Id.* at 1361.

regulatory regimes—such as the Clean Air Act, the 1996 Telecom Act, and the Affordable Care Act—build in a role for state implementation.[13] Each of these federal programs operates through either conditional spending or conditional preemption; states choosing *not* to participate either forego federal funds or the chance to tailor federal policy to their own preferences and objectives. *New York* and *Printz* dealt with the relatively rare instance in which Congress fails to offer states a meaningful choice.

Most federalism scholars have seen cooperative federalism as a threat to the states' autonomy.[14] But others have suggested that the states' role in implementing federal law is itself an important safeguard for federalism. Heather Gerken and Jessica Bulman-Pozen, for example, have argued that "power also resides with states when they play the role of federal servants." This power stems from the "dependence" of the federal government on state officials to administer federal programs, which gives state officials both "leverage" and "discretion in choosing how to accomplish [their] tasks and which tasks to prioritize." State officials also derive power from their "integration" into federal regulatory schemes; "[w]hen an actor is embedded in a larger system," Bulman-Pozen and Gerken argue, "a web of connective tissues binds higher- and lower-level decisionmakers. Regular interactions generate trust and give lower-level decisionmakers the knowledge and relationships they need to work the system." Finally, Bulman-Pozen and Gerken note that state officials "serve two masters" in the sense that although they are implementing federal policy, "their constituencies are based within the state." This gives state officials both the incentive and the power to challenge federal officials, because they are not beholden to federal officials for their positions and have alternative sources of resources.[15] A number of political scientists have confirmed these insights and documented the mechanisms by which state officials can work their own preferences and priorities into federal governmental regimes.[16]

Does the anti-commandeering doctrine facilitate or undermine the dynamics of "uncooperative federalism" identified by Professors Gerken and Bulman-Pozen? They suggest the latter, because the doctrine permits states to refuse to participate in cooperative federalism schemes altogether, leaving the field to exclusively federal bureaucracies in which states have little input.[17] In this vein, Justice Stevens argued in *Printz* that "[b]y limiting the ability of the Federal Government to enlist state officials in the implementation of its programs, the Court creates incentives for the National Government to aggrandize itself. In the name of State's rights, the

---

[13] *See, e.g.,* Philip J. Weiser, *Towards a Constitutional Architecture for Cooperative Federalism,* 79 N.C. L. REV. 663 (2001).

[14] *See, e.g.,* JOSEPH F. ZIMMERMAN, CONTEMPORARY AMERICAN FEDERALISM: THE GROWTH OF NATIONAL POWER (1992).

[15] Jessica Bulman-Pozen & Heather K. Gerken, *Uncooperative Federalism,* 118 YALE L.J. 1256, 1265–71 (2009).

[16] *See, e.g.,* JOHN D. NUGENT, SAFEGUARDING FEDERALISM: HOW STATES PROTECT THEIR INTERESTS IN NATIONAL POLICYMAKING (2009); JOHN J. DIIULIO, JR. & DONALD F. KETTL, FINE PRINT: THE CONTRACT WITH AMERICA, DEVOLUTION, AND THE ADMINISTRATIVE REALITIES OF AMERICAN FEDERALISM 18 (1995).

[17] *See* Bulman-Pozen & Gerken, *supra* note 15, at 1297–99.

majority would have the Federal Government create vast national bureaucracies to implement its policies." One possible example of this phenomenon is *Prigg v. Pennsylvania* in Chapter Four. In that early anti-commandeering case, Justice Story probably hoped to effectively nullify the federal fugitive slave law by forbidding federal authorities to require state officials to assist them in apprehending and repatriating fugitive slaves. Instead, Congress created one of the earliest federal enforcement bureaucracies to catch fugitive slaves—just as Justice Stevens might have predicted.

On the other hand, it is not at all clear that Congress's inability to *require* state officials to implement contemporary federal regulatory statutes has effectively impeded Congress's ability to enlist them voluntarily. Very few federal statutes have attempted to commandeer state officials; instead, most employ either conditional spending or conditional preemption as incentives for voluntary state cooperation. Arguably, the anti-commandeering doctrine simply enhances the states' bargaining position concerning the terms of their participation in federal legislative schemes. Shouldn't this enhance state officials' ability to be "uncooperative federalists" when circumstances require?

5.   Even if the anti-commandeering doctrine makes sense from a process standpoint, isn't it, well . . . made up? Isn't Justice Stevens right to say that "[t]here is not a clause, sentence, or paragraph in the entire text of the Constitution of the United States that supports the proposition"? Is there any way to justify this sort of doctrinal creativity? Consider, for example, the Court's willingness to create new individual rights protections in cases like *Griswold*, and the plurality's defense of that practice in *Casey*. Should the Court be less willing to imply limitations on government power when those limitations protect states than when they protect individuals? Isn't the ultimate point of limiting national power in federalism cases also to protect individual liberty?

6.   Shouldn't the majorities in *Printz* and *New York* be more worried about the consequences of applying the anti-commandeering doctrine to a truly important federal need? As Justice Stevens points out, "[m]atters such as the enlistment of air raid wardens, the administration of a military draft, the mass inoculation of children to forestall an epidemic, or perhaps the threat of an international terrorist, may require a national response before federal personnel can be made available to respond." Can we really afford, for example, a constitutional doctrine that would allow state and local officials to refuse to participate in a federal effort to locate a terrorist cell hiding a nuclear bomb in New York City?

On the other hand, how likely is it—politically speaking—that state or local authorities would refuse to assist federal officials in responding to a credible terrorist threat? Is this point generalizable—that is, are there "political safeguards of *national* power" that ensure state cooperation even when the states are immune from federal command? *Cf. Garcia.* Do such political dynamics mitigate the effects of doctrines like the anti-commandeering rule?

7.   Two recent and ongoing political controversies do involve the unwillingness of states to enforce federal law. The first concerns those states that have legalized the use of marijuana, whether for medicinal purposes only or for recreational use as well.[18] For decades, although marijuana was illegal as a matter of both state and federal law, federal authorities relied almost entirely on state officials to enforce prohibitions against personal use. Now some states have decriminalized the drug under state law, and *Printz* prevents Congress from compelling state and local police to enforce the remaining federal prohibition. Given limited federal enforcement resources, this means that marijuana use is—practically speaking—permitted in some states despite its continuing illegality under federal statutes. Is that a fair or sustainable state of affairs?

The second area of current controversy arises from vows by some state attorneys general and mayors of so-called "sanctuary cities" to resist the enforcement of the Trump Administration's immigration policies. A number of cities, including New York Los Angeles, and Chicago, have prohibited their own law enforcement personnel from cooperating in various ways with federal enforcement of the immigration laws.[19] Some of these policies may run afoul of a federal statute, 8 U.S.C. § 1373, which provides as follows:

> Notwithstanding any other provision of Federal, State, or local law, a Federal, State, or local government entity or official may not prohibit, or in any way restrict, any government entity or official from sending to, or receiving from, the Immigration and Naturalization Service information regarding the citizenship or immigration status, lawful or unlawful, of any individual.

Is this statute constitutional in light of *Printz*? Could the statute constitutionally bar cities from prohibiting their policy from *asking* persons about their immigration status in the first place? Would it require a city to notify federal officials when an undocumented immigrant is released from city custody? President Trump has threatened to cut off all federal funding to sanctuary cities.[20] Assuming that most such funding is not expressly conditioned on cooperation with federal immigration efforts, would carrying out that threat be constitutional under *Dole* and *NFIB*?

8.   What do you make of the tiff between Justice Scalia and Justice Breyer in *Printz* over the value of comparative constitutional analysis? In the European Union, for example, the central EU institutions have very little in the way of enforcement institutions; instead, they issue "directives" to the Member States, which then legislate and enforce in a manner consistent with the central command. Arguably, the Member States' control over enforcement is an important check on central power, rather than a sign of

---

[18] *See supra* Section 9.1.

[19] *See, e.g.*, Henry Grabar, *Not in Our Town: Can American Cities Stop Trump from Deporting Millions?* SLATE, Nov. 20, 2016, available at http://www.slate.com/articles/news_and_politics/cover_story/2016/11/how_cities_could_thwart_donald_trump_s_deportation_plan.html.

[20] *See* Henry Grabar, *The Siege of Sanctuary Cities Has Begun*, SLATE, Jan. 25, 2017, available at http://www.slate.com/articles/business/metropolis/2017/01/trump_s_siege_of_sanctuary_cities_has_begun.html.

the erosion of their sovereignty. Does this tell us anything useful about how our own system should be structured?[21]

The relevance of foreign constitutional law and practice has become an important issue across a variety of areas in constitutional law. Most of the dispute has focused on references to foreign law that may shape the interpretation of individual constitutional rights. *Roper v. Simmons*, 543 U.S. 551 (2005), for example, held that the Eighth Amendment prohibits capital punishment for crimes committed by a 17-year-old. In so holding, Justice Kennedy's majority opinion relied in part on "the stark reality that the United States is the only country in the world that continues to give official sanction to the juvenile death penalty."[22] Justice Scalia's dissent, on the other hand, insisted that "the basic premise of the Court's argument— that American law should conform to the laws of the rest of the world—ought to be rejected out of hand."[23] Discussion has focused on a number of different considerations:

- Do American judges have *authority* to look to any provisions of law other than the domestic provisions that they are interpreting? Where would such authority come from?

- Do American judges (and their law clerks) have the *expertise* to research and accurately assess the laws of other countries?

- Given that there are so many different foreign jurisdictions to choose from, how should judges decide *which* foreign laws are relevant? On the issue of gay rights, for instance, what principle dictates that American judges look to Europe rather than to the Islamic world?

Are these issues more or less difficult when the question before the court is one of constitutional structure rather than of individual rights?

See also: For varying perspectives on the anti-commandeering doctrine, see Vicki C. Jackson, *Federalism and the Uses and Limits of Law:* Printz *and Principle?* 111 HARV. L. REV. 2180 (1998) (cautiously endorsing *Printz*'s goals but preferring a more flexible approach), Saikrishna Bangalore Prakash, *Field Office Federalism*, 79 VA. L. REV. 1957 (1993) (exploring the historical evidence), and Neil S. Siegel, *Commandeering and Its Alternatives: A Federalism Perspective*, 69 VAND. L. REV. 1629 (2006) (considering whether commandeering is worse for states than the alternative of federal preemption). For a sample of the broad debate over whether American courts should look to foreign law in constitutional interpretation, see Comment, *The Debate Over Foreign Law in* Roper v. Simmons, 119 HARV. L. REV. 103–67

---

[21] For a thoughtful analysis, concluding that Justice Breyer overlooks important aspects of the European structure that call its direct relevance into question, see Daniel Halberstam, *Comparative Federalism and the Issue of Commandeering, in* THE FEDERAL VISION: LEGITIMACY AND LEVELS OF GOVERNANCE IN THE UNITED STATES AND THE EUROPEAN UNION 213–51 (Kalypso Nicolaidis & Robert Howse, eds., 2001); *see also* Vicki C. Jackson, *Narratives of Federalism: Of Continuities and Comparative Constitutional Experience*, 51 DUKE L.J. 223 (2001) (discussing the difficulties of comparing structural constitutional arrangements across different legal systems).

[22] *Roper*, 543 U.S. at 575.

[23] *Id.* at 624 (Scalia, J., dissenting).

(2005) (collecting brief essays by three scholars of divergent views); Sarah H. Cleveland, *Our International Constitution*, 31 YALE J. INT'L L. 1 (2006) (pointing out that the Supreme Court has looked to foreign law in some contexts for much of our history); Jed Rubenfeld, *Unilateralism and Constitutionalism,* 79 N.Y.U. L. REV. 1971 (2004) (questioning the legitimacy of looking to foreign law based on basic divergences between the United States and Europe over the nature of constitutionalism).

CHAPTER ELEVEN

LIMITS ON STATE POWER

"Federalism" connotes not only limits on the power of central governments, but also corresponding limits on the authority of subnational units. Although the former sort of limits are often primary in conceptual discussions of federalism, American courts have been considerably more successful in articulating and enforcing the latter— that is, courts have acted more frequently and vigorously to limit the authority of state governments than they have to check central power. Despite the controversy arising from judicial efforts to limit national power in cases like *Lopez* and *Printz*, it is fair to say that the federal courts have tended to be a *centralizing* force in our polity.

This chapter focuses on federalism-based limits on *state* authority. These limits are of four basic kinds:

- The **Dormant Commerce Clause**—that is, the negative implication of Congress's power over interstate commerce— limits the States' corresponding authority over that commerce.

- The **Privileges and Immunities Clause of Art. IV, § 2**, restricts the ability of states to confer some "privileges or immunities" on their own citizens—like the right to work in the state—without granting similar privileges to out-of-staters.

- The **Equal Protection Clause** of the Fourteenth Amendment forbids some forms of state discrimination against out-of-staters in favor of in-staters.

- The **Supremacy Clause** provides that federal statutes trump inconsistent state laws.

Of these, the first and last kinds of limit are by far the most important. The Privileges and Immunities and Equal Protection Clauses, by contrast, impose only modest constraints on state regulation of economic matters. It is useful to canvass these two clauses, however, as an introduction to the strategic questions that arise for lawyers when multiple constitutional approaches are available to challenge the same forms of governmental conduct.

Section 11.1 of this Chapter lays out the basic structure of contemporary Dormant Commerce Clause doctrine. Section 11.2 adds a few wrinkles to this basic structure; in particular, it deals with the primary *defense* to Dormant Commerce Clause claims—the "market participant" doctrine—and introduces alternative routes for challenging state discrimination against out-of-staters under the Privileges and Immunities and Equal Protection Clauses. Section 11.3 then turns to the pervasive phenomenon of federal statutes that may *preempt* state law under the Supremacy Clause. As both the breadth and depth of affirmative federal regulation have increased since the New Deal, preemption has arguably become the paramount issue of constitutional federalism.

SECTION 11.1   THE DORMANT COMMERCE CLAUSE

We have already discussed the early dormant commerce cases—e.g., *Gibbons, Willson*—in the first part of the course. Although the Commerce Clause by its terms simply grants regulatory authority to Congress, it has long been understood to impliedly limit state authority over interstate commerce. That implication derives in part from the importance of economic unity in the early Republic: the Framers were concerned that a patchwork of beggar-thy-neighbor trade policies in the States would both stifle the nascent national economy and lead to political (and possibly even military) conflict among jurisdictions.

The overwhelming majority of Commerce Clause litigation in the Nineteenth Century involved "dormant" challenges to state regulation. The doctrine, unfortunately, proved somewhat unstable. At least three different approaches can be discerned in the Nineteenth and early Twentieth Century cases:

- The Marshall Court tried, in cases like *Gibbons* and *Willson v. Black Bird Creek Marsh Co.,* to distinguish between commerce and "police" regulation.

- The Taney Court, starting with *Cooley v. Board of Wardens*,[1] tried to distinguish between inherently national and inherently local activities.

- Later on, the Court used the same direct/indirect effects test that it used in the affirmative Commerce Clause cases like *E.C. Knight.*

Each of these approaches assumed that the spheres of authority allocated to national and state power were each *exclusive*—that is, whatever the states could regulate was off limits to Congress, and vice versa. Each was thus part of the "dual federalism" regime discussed in Chapter Five. This notion of separate and exclusive spheres was replaced after 1937 with a paradigm of *concurrent* regulatory authority. That change had the important effect not only of expanding the reach of national authority, but also of removing a significant constraint on *state* regulation. In this sense, the New Deal Court expanded the authority of both national and state governments.[2]

---

[1]   12 How. (53 U.S.) 299 (1851).

[2]   *See generally* Stephen A. Gardbaum, *New Deal Constitutionalism and the Unshackling of the States*, 64 U. CHI. L. REV. 483 (1997).

In this world of concurrent power, dormant Commerce Clause doctrine necessarily had to assume a considerably different form. The two tracks of the modern doctrine are reflected in *Philadelphia v. New Jersey* and *Kassel*, respectively. The first track deals with state laws that *discriminate* against out-of-staters. The second addresses neutral state laws—that is, laws that treat in-staters and out-of-staters alike—that impose a *burden* on interstate commerce. As you read, ask yourself whether each of these two forms of the doctrine is equally necessary, and which is likely to be more easily applied by courts.

Philadelphia v. New Jersey
437 U.S. 617 (1978)

■ **MR. JUSTICE STEWART delivered the opinion of the Court.**

A New Jersey law prohibits the importation of most "solid or liquid waste which originated or was collected outside the territorial limits of the State. . . ." In this case we are required to decide whether this statutory prohibition violates the Commerce Clause of the United States Constitution.

I

The statutory provision in question is ch. 363 of 1973 N. J. Laws, which took effect in early 1974. In pertinent part it provides:

> No person shall bring into this State any solid or liquid waste which originated or was collected outside the territorial limits of the State, except garbage to be fed to swine in the State of New Jersey, until the commissioner [of the State Department of Environmental Protection] shall determine that such action can be permitted without endangering the public health, safety and welfare and has promulgated regulations permitting and regulating the treatment and disposal of such waste in this State.

. . . Apart from [some] narrow exceptions, . . . New Jersey closed its borders to all waste from other States.

Immediately affected by these developments were the operators of private landfills in New Jersey, and several cities in other States that had agreements with these operators for waste disposal. They brought suit against New Jersey and its Department of Environmental Protection in state court, attacking the statute and regulations on a number of state and federal grounds. In an oral opinion granting the plaintiffs' motion for summary judgment, the trial court declared the law unconstitutional because it discriminated against interstate commerce. The New Jersey Supreme Court . . . found that ch. 363 advanced vital health and environmental objectives with no economic discrimination against, and with little burden upon, interstate commerce, and that the law was therefore permissible under the Commerce Clause of the Constitution. . . .

The dispositive question . . . is whether the law is constitutionally permissible in light of the Commerce Clause of the Constitution. . . .

III

A

Although the Constitution gives Congress the power to regulate commerce among the States, many subjects of potential federal regulation under that power inevitably escape congressional attention "because of their local character and their number and diversity." *South Carolina State Highway Dept. v. Barnwell Bros., Inc.*, 303 U.S. 177, 185 (1938). In the absence of federal legislation, these subjects are open to control by the States so long as they act within the restraints imposed by the Commerce Clause itself. The bounds of these restraints appear nowhere in the words of the Commerce Clause, but have emerged gradually in the decisions of this Court giving effect to its basic purpose. That broad purpose was well expressed by Mr. Justice Jackson:

> This principle that our economic unit is the Nation, which alone has the gamut of powers necessary to control of the economy, including the vital power of erecting customs barriers against foreign competition, has as its corollary that the states are not separable economic units. . . . [W]hat is ultimate is the principle that one state in its dealings with another may not place itself in a position of economic isolation.

The opinions of the Court through the years have reflected an alertness to the evils of "economic isolation" and protectionism, while at the same time recognizing that incidental burdens on interstate commerce may be unavoidable when a State legislates to safeguard the health and safety of its people. Thus, where simple economic protectionism is effected by state legislation, a virtually *per se* rule of invalidity has been erected. The clearest example of such legislation is a law that overtly blocks the flow of interstate commerce at a State's borders. But where other legislative objectives are credibly advanced and there is no patent discrimination against interstate trade, the Court has adopted a much more flexible approach, the general contours of which were outlined in *Pike v. Bruce Church, Inc.*, 397 U.S. 137 (1970):

> Where the statute regulates evenhandedly to effectuate a legitimate local public interest, and its effects on interstate commerce are only incidental, it will be upheld unless the burden imposed on such commerce is clearly excessive in relation to the putative local benefits. . . . If a legitimate local purpose is found, then the question becomes one of degree. And the extent of the burden that will be tolerated will of course depend on the nature of the local interest involved, and on

whether it could be promoted as well with a lesser impact on interstate activities.

. . . The crucial inquiry, therefore, must be directed to determining whether ch. 363 is basically a protectionist measure, or whether it can fairly be viewed as a law directed to legitimate local concerns, with effects upon interstate commerce that are only incidental.

B

The purpose of ch. 363 is set out in the statute itself as follows:

> The Legislature finds and determines that . . . the volume of solid and liquid waste continues to rapidly increase, that the treatment and disposal of these wastes continues to pose an even greater threat to the quality of the environment of New Jersey, that the available and appropriate land fill sites within the State are being diminished, that the environment continues to be threatened by the treatment and disposal of waste which originated or was collected outside the State, and that the public health, safety and welfare require that the treatment and disposal within this State of all wastes generated outside of the State be prohibited.

The New Jersey Supreme Court . . . additionally found that New Jersey's existing landfill sites will be exhausted within a few years; that to go on using these sites or to develop new ones will take a heavy environmental toll, both from pollution and from loss of scarce open lands; that new techniques to divert waste from landfills to other methods of disposal and resource recovery processes are under development, but that these changes will require time; and finally, that "the extension of the lifespan of existing landfills, resulting from the exclusion of out-of-state waste, may be of crucial importance in preventing further virgin wetlands or other undeveloped lands from being devoted to landfill purposes." Based on these findings, the court concluded that ch. 363 was designed to protect, not the State's economy, but its environment, and that its substantial benefits outweigh its "slight" burden on interstate commerce.

The appellants strenuously contend that ch. 363, "while outwardly cloaked 'in the currently fashionable garb of environmental protection,' . . . is actually no more than a legislative effort to suppress competition and stabilize the cost of solid waste disposal for New Jersey residents. . . ." They cite passages of legislative history suggesting that the problem addressed by ch. 363 is primarily financial: Stemming the flow of out-of-state waste into certain landfill sites will extend their lives, thus delaying the day when New Jersey cities must transport their waste to more distant and expensive sites.

The appellees, on the other hand, deny that ch. 363 was motivated by financial concerns or economic protectionism. In the words of their brief, "[no] New Jersey commercial interests stand to gain advantage over competitors from outside the state as a result of the ban on dumping out-of-state waste." Noting that New Jersey landfill operators are among the plaintiffs, the appellee's brief argues that "[the] complaint is not that New Jersey has forged an economic preference for its own commercial interests, but rather that it has denied a small group of its entrepreneurs an economic opportunity to traffic in waste in order to protect the health, safety and welfare of the citizenry at large."

This dispute about ultimate legislative purpose need not be resolved, because its resolution would not be relevant to the constitutional issue to be decided in this case. Contrary to the evident assumption of the state court and the parties, the evil of protectionism can reside in legislative means as well as legislative ends. Thus, it does not matter whether the ultimate aim of ch. 363 is to reduce the waste disposal costs of New Jersey residents or to save remaining open lands from pollution, for we assume New Jersey has every right to protect its residents' pocketbooks as well as their environment. And it may be assumed as well that New Jersey may pursue those ends by slowing the flow of *all* waste into the State's remaining landfills, even though interstate commerce may incidentally be affected. But whatever New Jersey's ultimate purpose, it may not be accomplished by discriminating against articles of commerce coming from outside the State unless there is some reason, apart from their origin, to treat them differently. Both on its face and in its plain effect, ch. 363 violates this principle of nondiscrimination.

The Court has consistently found parochial legislation of this kind to be constitutionally invalid, whether the ultimate aim of the legislation was to assure a steady supply of milk by erecting barriers to allegedly ruinous outside competition, or to create jobs by keeping industry within the State, or to preserve the State's financial resources from depletion by fencing out indigent immigrants. In each of these cases, a presumably legitimate goal was sought to be achieved by the illegitimate means of isolating the State from the national economy.

Also relevant here are the Court's decisions holding that a State may not accord its own inhabitants a preferred right of access over consumers in other States to natural resources located within its borders. These cases stand for the basic principle that a "State is without power to prevent privately owned articles of trade from being shipped and sold in interstate commerce on the ground that they are required to satisfy local demands or because they are needed by the people of the State."

The New Jersey law at issue in this case falls squarely within the area that the Commerce Clause puts off limits to state regulation. On its face, it imposes on out-of-state commercial interests the full burden of conserving the State's remaining landfill space. It is true that in our previous cases the scarce natural resource was itself the article of commerce, whereas here the scarce resource and the article of commerce are distinct. But that difference is without consequence. In both instances, the State has overtly moved to slow or freeze the flow of commerce for protectionist reasons. It does not matter that the State has shut the article of commerce inside the State in one case and outside the State in the other. What is crucial is the attempt by one State to isolate itself from a problem common to many by erecting a barrier against the movement of interstate trade.

The appellees argue that not all laws which facially discriminate against out-of-state commerce are forbidden protectionist regulations. In particular, they point to quarantine laws, which this Court has repeatedly upheld even though they appear to single out interstate commerce for special treatment. In the appellees' view, ch. 363 is analogous to such health-protective measures, since it reduces the exposure of New Jersey residents to the allegedly harmful effects of landfill sites.

It is true that certain quarantine laws have not been considered forbidden protectionist measures, even though they were directed against out-of-state commerce. But those quarantine laws banned the importation of articles such as diseased livestock that required destruction as soon as possible because their very movement risked contagion and other evils. Those laws thus did not discriminate against interstate commerce as such, but simply prevented traffic in noxious articles, whatever their origin.

The New Jersey statute is not such a quarantine law. There has been no claim here that the very movement of waste into or through New Jersey endangers health, or that waste must be disposed of as soon and as close to its point of generation as possible. The harms caused by waste are said to arise after its disposal in landfill sites, and at that point, as New Jersey concedes, there is no basis to distinguish out-of-state waste from domestic waste. If one is inherently harmful, so is the other. Yet New Jersey has banned the former while leaving its landfill sites open to the latter. The New Jersey law blocks the importation of waste in an obvious effort to saddle those outside the State with the entire burden of slowing the flow of refuse into New Jersey's remaining landfill sites. That legislative effort is clearly impermissible under the Commerce Clause of the Constitution.

Today, cities in Pennsylvania and New York find it expedient or necessary to send their waste into New Jersey for disposal, and New Jersey claims the right to close its borders to such traffic. Tomorrow, cities in New Jersey may find it expedient or necessary to send their waste into Pennsylvania or New York for disposal, and those States might then claim the right to close their borders. The Commerce Clause will protect New Jersey in the future, just as it protects her neighbors now, from efforts by one State to isolate itself in the stream of interstate commerce from a problem shared by all. The judgment is

Reversed.

■ MR. JUSTICE REHNQUIST, with whom THE CHIEF JUSTICE joins, dissenting.

A growing problem in our Nation is the sanitary treatment and disposal of solid waste. For many years, solid waste was incinerated. Because of the significant environmental problems attendant on incineration, however, this method of solid waste disposal has declined in use in many localities, including New Jersey. "Sanitary" landfills have replaced incineration as the principal method of disposing of solid waste. In ch. 363 of the 1973 N. J. Laws, the State of New Jersey legislatively recognized the unfortunate fact that landfills also present extremely serious health and safety problems. First, in New Jersey, "virtually all sanitary landfills can be expected to produce leachate, a noxious and highly polluted liquid which is seldom visible and frequently pollutes . . . ground and surface waters." The natural decomposition process which occurs in landfills also produces large quantities of methane and thereby presents a significant explosion hazard. Landfills can also generate "health hazards caused by rodents, fires and scavenger birds" and, "needless to say, do not help New Jersey's aesthetic appearance nor New Jersey's noise or water or air pollution problems."

The health and safety hazards associated with landfills present appellees with a currently unsolvable dilemma. Other, hopefully safer, methods of disposing of solid wastes are still in the development stage and cannot presently be used. But appellees obviously cannot completely stop the tide of solid waste that its citizens will produce in the interim. For the moment, therefore, appellees must continue to use sanitary landfills to dispose of New Jersey's own solid waste despite the critical environmental problems thereby created.

The question presented in this case is whether New Jersey must also continue to receive and dispose of solid waste from neighboring States, even though these will inexorably increase the health problems discussed above. The Court answers this question in the affirmative. New Jersey must either prohibit *all* landfill operations, leaving itself to cast about for a presently nonexistent solution to the serious problem of disposing of the waste generated within its own borders, or it must accept waste from every portion of the United States, thereby multiplying the health and safety problems which would result if it dealt only with such wastes generated within the State. Because past precedents establish that the Commerce Clause does not present appellees with such a Hobson's choice, I dissent.

The Court recognizes that States can prohibit the importation of items " 'which, on account of their existing condition, would bring in and spread disease, pestilence, and death, such as rags or other substances infected with the germs of yellow fever or the virus of small-pox, or cattle or meat or other provisions that are diseased or decayed, or otherwise, from their condition and quality, unfit for human use or consumption.' " As the Court points out, such "quarantine laws have not been considered forbidden protectionist measures, even though they were directed against out-of-state commerce."

In my opinion, these cases are dispositive of the present one. Under them, New Jersey may require germ-infected rags or diseased meat to be disposed of as best as possible within the State, but at the same time prohibit the *importation* of such items for disposal at the facilities that are set up within New Jersey for disposal of such material generated *within* the State. The physical fact of life that New Jersey must somehow dispose of its own noxious items does not mean that it must serve as a depository for those of every other State. Similarly, New Jersey should be free under our past precedents to prohibit the importation of solid waste because of the health and safety problems that such waste poses to its citizens. The fact that New Jersey continues to, and indeed must continue to, dispose of its own solid waste does not mean that New Jersey may not prohibit the importation of even more solid waste into the State. I simply see no way to distinguish solid waste, on the record of this case, from germ-infected rags, diseased meat, and other noxious items.

The Court's effort to distinguish these prior cases is unconvincing. It first asserts that the quarantine laws which have previously been upheld "banned the importation of articles such as diseased livestock that required destruction as soon as possible because their very movement risked contagion and other evils." According to the Court, the New Jersey law is distinguishable from these other laws, and invalid, because the concern of New Jersey is not with the *movement* of solid waste but with the present inability to safely *dispose* of it once it reaches its destination. But I think it far from clear that the State's law has as limited a focus as the Court imputes to it: Solid waste which is a health hazard when it reaches its destination may in all likelihood be an equally great health hazard in transit.

Even if the Court is correct in its characterization of New Jersey's concerns, I do not see why a State may ban the importation of items whose movement risks contagion, but cannot ban the importation of items which, although they may be transported into the State without undue hazard, will then simply pile up in an ever increasing danger to the public's health and safety. The Commerce Clause was not drawn with a view to having the validity of state laws turn on such pointless distinctions.

Second, the Court implies that the challenged laws must be invalidated because New Jersey has left its landfills open to domestic waste. But, as the Court notes, this Court has repeatedly upheld quarantine laws "even though they appear to single out interstate commerce for special treatment." The fact that New Jersey has left its landfill sites open for domestic waste does not, of course, mean that solid waste is not innately harmful. Nor does it mean that New Jersey prohibits importation of solid waste for reasons other than the health and safety of its population. New Jersey must out of sheer necessity treat and dispose of its solid waste in some fashion, just as it must treat New Jersey cattle suffering from hoof-and-mouth disease. It does not follow that New Jersey must, under the Commerce Clause, accept solid waste or diseased cattle from outside its borders and thereby exacerbate its problems.

The Supreme Court of New Jersey expressly found that ch. 363 was passed "to preserve the health of New Jersey residents by keeping their exposure to solid waste and landfill areas to a minimum." The Court points to absolutely no evidence that would contradict this finding by the New Jersey Supreme Court. Because I find no basis for distinguishing the laws under challenge here from our past cases upholding state laws that prohibit the importation of items that could endanger the population of the State, I dissent.

Kassel v. Consolidated Freightways Corp.

450 U.S. 662 (1981)

■ JUSTICE POWELL announced the judgment of the Court and delivered an opinion, in which JUSTICE WHITE, JUSTICE BLACKMUN, and JUSTICE STEVENS joined.

The question is whether an Iowa statute that prohibits the use of certain large trucks within the State unconstitutionally burdens interstate commerce.

I

Appellee Consolidated Freightways Corporation of Delaware (Consolidated) is one of the largest common carriers in the country. It offers service in 48 States under a certificate of public convenience and necessity issued by the Interstate Commerce Commission. Among other routes, Consolidated carries commodities through Iowa on Interstate 80, the principal east-west route linking New York, Chicago, and the west coast, and on Interstate 35, a major north-south route.

Consolidated mainly uses two kinds of trucks. One consists of a three-axle tractor pulling a 40-foot two-axle trailer. This unit, commonly called a single, or "semi," is 55 feet in length overall. Such trucks have long been used on the Nation's highways. Consolidated also uses a two-axle tractor pulling a single-axle trailer which, in turn, pulls a single-axle dolly and a second single-axle trailer. This combination, known as a double, or twin, is 65 feet long overall. Many trucking companies, including Consolidated, increasingly prefer to use doubles to ship certain kinds of commodities. Doubles have larger capacities, and the trailers can be detached and routed separately if necessary. Consolidated would like to use 65-foot doubles on many of its trips through Iowa.

The State of Iowa, however, by statute restricts the length of vehicles that may use its highways. Unlike all other States in the West and Midwest, Iowa generally prohibits the use of 65-foot doubles within its borders. Instead, most truck combinations are restricted to 55 feet in length. Doubles,[2] mobile homes, trucks carrying vehicles such as tractors and other farm equipment, and singles hauling livestock, are permitted to be as long as 60 feet. Notwithstanding these restrictions, Iowa's statute permits cities abutting the state line by local ordinance to adopt the length limitations of the adjoining State. Where a city has exercised this option, otherwise oversized trucks are permitted within the city limits and in nearby commercial zones.

Iowa also provides for two other relevant exemptions. An Iowa truck manufacturer may obtain a permit to ship trucks that are as large as 70 feet. Permits also are available to move oversized mobile homes, provided that the unit is to be moved from a point within Iowa or delivered for an Iowa resident.[7]

Because of Iowa's statutory scheme, Consolidated cannot use its 65-foot doubles to move commodities through the State. Instead, the company must do one of four things: (i) use 55-foot singles; (ii) use 60-foot doubles; (iii) detach the trailers of a 65-foot double and shuttle each through the State separately; or (iv) divert 65-foot doubles around Iowa.

Dissatisfied with these options, Consolidated filed this suit in the District Court averring that Iowa's statutory scheme unconstitutionally burdens interstate commerce. Iowa defended the law as a reasonable safety measure enacted pursuant to its police power. The State asserted that 65-foot doubles are more dangerous than 55-foot singles and, in any event, that the law promotes safety and reduces road wear within the State by diverting much truck traffic to other States.

In a 14-day trial, both sides adduced evidence on safety, and on the burden on interstate commerce imposed by Iowa's law. On the question of safety, the District Court found that the "evidence clearly establishes that the twin is as safe as the semi." For that reason,

> there is no valid safety reason for barring twins from Iowa's highways because of their configuration. The evidence convincingly, if not overwhelmingly, establishes that the 65 foot twin is as safe as, if not safer than, the 60 foot twin and the 55 foot semi. . . . Twins and semis have different characteristics. Twins are more maneuverable, are less sensitive to wind, and create less splash and spray. However, they are more likely than semis to jackknife or upset. They can be backed only for a short distance. The negative characteristics are not such that they

---

[2] The 60-foot double is not commonly used anywhere except in Iowa. It consists of a tractor pulling a large trailer, which in turn pulls a dolly attached to a small trailer. The odd-sized trailer used in the 60-foot double is not compatible for interchangeable use in other trailer combinations.

[7] The parochial restrictions in the mobile home provision were enacted after Governor Ray vetoed a bill that would have permitted the interstate shipment of all mobile homes through Iowa. Governor Ray commented, in his veto message:

> This bill . . . would make Iowa a bridge state as these oversized units are moved into Iowa after being manufactured in another state and sold in a third. None of this activity would be of particular economic benefit to Iowa.

render the twin less safe than semis overall. Semis are more stable but are more likely to 'rear end' another vehicle.

In light of these findings, the District Court . . . concluded that the state law impermissibly burdened interstate commerce. . . . The Court of Appeals for the Eighth Circuit affirmed. . . . Iowa appealed, and we . . . now affirm.

II

. . . The Commerce Clause does not, of course, invalidate all state restrictions on commerce. . . . The extent of permissible state regulation is not always easy to measure. It may be said with confidence, however, that a State's power to regulate commerce is never greater than in matters traditionally of local concern. For example, regulations that touch upon safety—especially highway safety—are those that "the Court has been most reluctant to invalidate." Indeed, "if safety justifications are not illusory, the Court will not second-guess legislative judgment about their importance in comparison with related burdens on interstate commerce." Those who would challenge such bona fide safety regulations must overcome a "strong presumption of validity."

But the incantation of a purpose to promote the public health or safety does not insulate a state law from Commerce Clause attack. Regulations designed for that salutary purpose nevertheless may further the purpose so marginally, and interfere with commerce so substantially, as to be invalid under the Commerce Clause. In the Court's recent unanimous decision in *Raymond Motor Transportation, Inc. v. Rice*, we declined to "accept the State's contention that the inquiry under the Commerce Clause is ended without a weighing of the asserted safety purpose against the degree of interference with interstate commerce." This "weighing" by a court requires . . . "a sensitive consideration of the weight and nature of the state regulatory concern in light of the extent of the burden imposed on the course of interstate commerce."

III

Applying these general principles, we conclude that the Iowa truck-length limitations unconstitutionally burden interstate commerce.

In *Raymond*, the Court held that a Wisconsin statute that precluded the use of 65-foot doubles violated the Commerce Clause. This case is *Raymond* revisited. Here, as in *Raymond*, the State failed to present any persuasive evidence that 65-foot doubles are less safe than 55-foot singles. Moreover, Iowa's law is now out of step with the laws of all other Midwestern and Western States. Iowa thus substantially burdens the interstate flow of goods by truck. In the absence of congressional action to set uniform standards,[11] some burdens associated with state safety regulations must be tolerated. But where, as here, the State's safety

---

[11] The Senate last year passed a bill that would have pre-empted the field of truck lengths by setting a national limit of 65 feet. See S. 1390, 96th Cong., 2d Sess. (1980). The House took no action before adjournment.

interest has been found to be illusory, and its regulations impair significantly the federal interest in efficient and safe interstate transportation, the state law cannot be harmonized with the Commerce Clause.

A

Iowa made a more serious effort to support the safety rationale of its law than did Wisconsin in *Raymond*, but its effort was no more persuasive. As noted above, the District Court found that the "evidence clearly establishes that the twin is as safe as the semi." The record supports this finding.

The trial focused on a comparison of the performance of the two kinds of trucks in various safety categories. The evidence showed, and the District Court found, that the 65-foot double was at least the equal of the 55-foot single in the ability to brake, turn, and maneuver. The double, because of its axle placement, produces less splash and spray in wet weather.[13] And, because of its articulation in the middle, the double is less susceptible to dangerous "off-tracking,"[14] and to wind.

None of these findings is seriously disputed by Iowa. Indeed, the State points to only three ways in which the 55-foot single is even arguably superior: singles take less time to be passed and to clear intersections; they may back up for longer distances; and they are somewhat less likely to jackknife. The first two of these characteristics are of limited relevance on modern interstate highways. . . . In any event, no evidence suggested any difference in backing capability between the 60-foot doubles that Iowa permits and the 65-foot doubles that it bans. Similarly, although doubles tend to jackknife somewhat more than singles, 65-foot doubles actually are less likely to jackknife than 60-foot doubles.

Statistical studies supported the view that 65-foot doubles are at least as safe overall as 55-foot singles and 60-foot doubles. One such study, which the District Court credited, reviewed Consolidated's comparative accident experience in 1978 with its own singles and doubles. Each kind of truck was driven 56 million miles on identical routes. The singles were involved in 100 accidents resulting in 27 injuries and one fatality. The 65-foot doubles were involved in 106 accidents resulting in 17 injuries and one fatality. Iowa's expert statistician admitted that this study provided "moderately strong evidence" that singles have a higher injury rate than doubles. Another study, prepared by the Iowa Department of Transportation at the request of the state

---

[13] Twin trailers have single axles; semis, by contrast, have tandem axles. The axle configuration of the semi aggravates splash and spray. The forward tire creates upward wind currents in the same place that the rear tire creates downward wind currents. The confluence of these currents occurs at a point just above and between the tandem axles. The resulting turbulence then is blasted outward, carrying spray with it.

[14] "Off-tracking" refers to the extent to which the rear wheels of a truck deviate from the path of the front wheels while turning.

legislature, concluded that "[sixty-five] foot twin trailer combinations have *not* been shown by experiences in other states to be less safe than 60 foot twin trailer combinations *or* conventional tractor-semitrailers." Numerous insurance company executives, and transportation officials from the Federal Government and various States, testified that 65-foot doubles were at least as safe as 55-foot singles. Iowa concedes that it can produce no study that establishes a statistically significant difference in safety between the 65-foot double and the kinds of vehicles the State permits. Nor, as the District Court noted, did Iowa present a single witness who testified that 65-foot doubles were more dangerous overall than the vehicles permitted under Iowa law. . . .

B

Consolidated, meanwhile, demonstrated that Iowa's law substantially burdens interstate commerce. Trucking companies that wish to continue to use 65-foot doubles must route them around Iowa or detach the trailers of the doubles and ship them through separately. Alternatively, trucking companies must use the smaller 55-foot singles or 60-foot doubles permitted under Iowa law. Each of these options engenders inefficiency and added expense. The record shows that Iowa's law added about $12.6 million each year to the costs of trucking companies. Consolidated alone incurred about $2 million per year in increased costs.

In addition to increasing the costs of the trucking companies (and, indirectly, of the service to consumers), Iowa's law may aggravate, rather than ameliorate, the problem of highway accidents. Fifty-five foot singles carry less freight than 65-foot doubles. Either more small trucks must be used to carry the same quantity of goods through Iowa, or the same number of larger trucks must drive longer distances to bypass Iowa. In either case, as the District Court noted, the restriction requires more highway miles to be driven to transport the same quantity of goods. Other things being equal, accidents are proportional to distance traveled. Thus, if 65-foot doubles are as safe as 55-foot singles, Iowa's law tends to *increase* the number of accidents, and to shift the incidence of them from Iowa to other States.

IV

Perhaps recognizing the weakness of the evidence supporting its safety argument, and the substantial burden on commerce that its regulations create, Iowa urges the Court simply to "defer" to the safety judgment of the State. It argues that the length of trucks is generally, although perhaps imprecisely, related to safety. The task of drawing a line is one that Iowa contends should be left to its legislature.

The Court normally does accord "special deference" to state highway safety regulations. This traditional deference "derives in part from the assumption that where such regulations do not discriminate on their face against interstate commerce, their burden usually falls on local economic interests as well as other States' economic interests, thus insuring that a State's own political processes will serve as a check against unduly burdensome regulations." Less deference to the legislative judgment is due, however, where the local regulation bears disproportionately on out-of-state residents and businesses. Such a disproportionate burden is apparent here. Iowa's scheme, although generally banning large doubles from the State, nevertheless has several exemptions that secure to Iowans many of the benefits of large trucks while shunting to neighboring States many of the costs associated with their use.[19]

At the time of trial there were two particularly significant exemptions. First, singles hauling livestock or farm vehicles were permitted to be as long as 60 feet. [T]his provision undoubtedly was helpful to local interests. Second, cities abutting other States were permitted to enact local ordinances adopting the larger length limitation of the neighboring State. This exemption offered the benefits of longer trucks to individuals and businesses in important border cities without burdening Iowa's highways with interstate through traffic.

The origin of the "border cities exemption" also suggests that Iowa's statute may not have been designed to ban dangerous trucks, but rather to discourage interstate truck traffic. In 1974, the legislature passed a bill that would have permitted 65-foot doubles in the State. Governor Ray vetoed the bill. He said:

> I find sympathy with those who are doing business in our state and whose enterprises could gain from increased cargo carrying ability by trucks. However, with this bill, the Legislature has pursued a course that would benefit only a few Iowa-based companies while providing a great advantage for out-of-state trucking firms and competitors at the expense of our Iowa citizens.

After the veto, the "border cities exemption" was immediately enacted and signed by the Governor.

It is thus far from clear that Iowa was motivated primarily by a judgment that 65-foot doubles are less safe than 55-foot singles. Rather, Iowa seems to have hoped to limit the use of its highways by deflecting some through traffic. In the District Court and Court of Appeals, the State explicitly attempted to justify the law by its claimed interest in keeping trucks out of Iowa. . . . The Court of Appeals correctly concluded that a State cannot constitutionally promote its own parochial interests by requiring safe vehicles to detour around it.

V

In sum, the statutory exemptions, their history, and the arguments Iowa has advanced in support of its law in this litigation, all suggest that

---

[19] As the District Court noted, diversion of traffic benefits Iowa by holding down (i) accidents in the State, (ii) auto insurance premiums, (iii) police staffing needs, and (iv) road wear.

the deference traditionally accorded a State's safety judgment is not warranted. The controlling factors thus are the findings of the District Court . . . with respect to the relative safety of the types of trucks at issue, and the substantiality of the burden on interstate commerce.

Because Iowa has imposed this burden without any significant countervailing safety interest, its statute violates the Commerce Clause. The judgment of the Court of Appeals is affirmed.

■ JUSTICE BRENNAN, with whom JUSTICE MARSHALL joins, concurring in the judgment.

. . . For me, analysis of Commerce Clause challenges to state regulations must take into account three principles: (1) The courts are not empowered to second-guess the empirical judgments of lawmakers concerning the utility of legislation. (2) The burdens imposed on commerce must be balanced against the local benefits actually sought to be achieved by the State's lawmakers, and not against those suggested after the fact by counsel. (3) Protectionist legislation is unconstitutional under the Commerce Clause, even if the burdens and benefits are related to safety rather than economics.

I

Both the opinion of my Brother POWELL and the opinion of my Brother REHNQUIST are predicated upon the supposition that the constitutionality of a state regulation is determined by the factual record created by the State's lawyers in trial court. But that supposition cannot be correct, for it would make the constitutionality of state laws and regulations depend on the vagaries of litigation rather than on the judgments made by the State's lawmakers.

In considering a Commerce Clause challenge to a state regulation, the judicial task is to balance the burden imposed on commerce against the local benefits sought to be achieved by the State's lawmakers. See *Pike v. Bruce Church, Inc.,* 397 U.S. 137 (1970). In determining those benefits, a court should focus ultimately on the regulatory purposes identified by the lawmakers and on the evidence before or available to them that might have supported their judgment. Since the court must confine its analysis to the purposes the lawmakers had for maintaining the regulation, the only relevant evidence concerns whether the lawmakers could rationally have believed that the challenged regulation would foster those purposes. It is not the function of the court to decide whether *in fact* the regulation promotes its intended purpose, so long as an examination of the evidence before or available to the lawmaker indicates that the regulation is not wholly irrational in light of its purposes.

II

. . . [A]lthough Iowa's lawyers in this litigation have defended the truck-length regulation on the basis of the safety advantages of 55-foot singles and 60-foot doubles over 65-foot doubles, Iowa's actual rationale for maintaining the regulation had nothing to do with these purported differences. Rather, Iowa sought to discourage interstate truck traffic on Iowa's highways. Thus, the safety advantages and disadvantages of the types and lengths of trucks involved in this case are irrelevant to the decision.

My Brother POWELL concedes that "[it] is . . . far from clear that Iowa was motivated primarily by a judgment that 65-foot doubles are less safe than 55-foot singles. Rather, Iowa seems to have hoped to limit the use of its highways by deflecting some through traffic." This conclusion is more than amply supported by the record and the legislative history of the Iowa regulation. . . .

In 1974, the Iowa Legislature again voted to increase the permissible length of trucks to conform to uniform standards then in effect in most other States. This legislation, House Bill 671, would have increased the maximum length of twin trailer trucks operable in Iowa from 60 to 65 feet. But Governor Ray broke from prior state policy, and vetoed the legislation. The legislature did not override the veto, and the present regulation was thus maintained. In his veto, Governor Ray did not rest his decision on the conclusion that 55-foot singles and 60-foot doubles are any safer than 65-foot doubles, or on any other safety consideration inherent in the type or size of the trucks. Rather, his principal concern was that to allow 65-foot doubles would "basically [open] our state to literally thousands and thousands more trucks per year." This increase in interstate truck traffic would, in the Governor's estimation, greatly increase highway maintenance costs, which are borne by the citizens of the State, and increase the number of accidents and fatalities within the State. The legislative response was not to override the veto, but to accede to the Governor's action, and in accord with his basic premise, to enact a "border cities exemption." This permitted cities within border areas to allow 65-foot doubles while otherwise maintaining the 60-foot limit throughout the State to discourage interstate truck traffic.

Although the Court has stated that "[in] no field has . . . deference to state regulation been greater than that of highway safety," it has declined to go so far as to presume that size restrictions are inherently tied to public safety. The Court has emphasized that the "strong presumption of validity" of size restrictions "cannot justify a court in closing its eyes to uncontroverted evidence of record,"—here the obvious fact that the safety characteristics of 65-foot doubles did not provide the motivation for either legislators or Governor in maintaining the regulation.

III

Though my Brother POWELL recognizes that the State's actual purpose in maintaining the truck-length regulation was "to limit the use of its highways by deflecting some through traffic," he fails to recognize that this purpose, being *protectionist* in nature, is *impermissible* under the Commerce Clause. The Governor admitted that he blocked legislative efforts to raise the length of trucks because the change "would benefit only a few Iowa-based companies while providing a great advantage for out-of-state trucking firms and competitors at the expense of our Iowa citizens." . . .

Iowa may not shunt off its fair share of the burden of maintaining interstate truck routes, nor may it create increased hazards on the highways of neighboring States in order to decrease the hazards on Iowa highways. Such an attempt has all the hallmarks of the "simple . . . protectionism" this Court has condemned in the economic area. *Philadelphia v. New Jersey.* Just as a State's attempt to avoid interstate competition in economic goods may damage the prosperity of the Nation as a whole, so Iowa's attempt to deflect interstate truck traffic has been found to make the Nation's highways as a whole more hazardous. That attempt should therefore be subject to "a virtually *per se* rule of invalidity."

This Court's heightened deference to the judgments of state lawmakers in the field of safety is largely attributable to a judicial disinclination to weigh the interests of safety against other societal interests, such as the economic interest in the free flow of commerce. Thus, "if safety justifications are not illusory, the Court will not second-guess legislative judgment about their importance *in comparison with related burdens on interstate commerce." Raymond Motor Transportation, Inc. v. Rice* (BLACKMUN, J., concurring) (emphasis added). Here, the decision of Iowa's lawmakers to promote *Iowa's* safety and other interests at the direct expense of the safety and other interests of neighboring States merits no such deference. No special judicial acuity is demanded to perceive that this sort of parochial legislation violates the Commerce Clause. As Justice Cardozo has written, the Commerce Clause "was framed upon the theory that the peoples of the several states must sink or swim together, and that in the long run prosperity and salvation are in union and not division."

I therefore concur in the judgment.

■ JUSTICE REHNQUIST, with whom THE CHIEF JUSTICE and JUSTICE STEWART join, dissenting.

The result in this case suggests, to paraphrase Justice Jackson, that the only state truck-length limit "that is valid is one which this Court has not been able to get its hands on." Although the plurality opinion and the opinion concurring in the judgment strike down Iowa's law by different routes, I believe the analysis in both opinions oversteps our "limited authority to review state legislation under the commerce clause," and seriously intrudes upon the fundamental right of the States to pass laws to secure the safety of their citizens. Accordingly, I dissent.

I

. . . Iowa's action in limiting the length of trucks which may travel on its highways is in no sense unusual. Every State in the Union regulates the length of vehicles permitted to use the public roads. Nor is Iowa a renegade in having length limits which operate to exclude the 65-foot doubles favored by Consolidated. These trucks are prohibited in other areas of the country as well, some 17 States and the District of Columbia, including all of New England and most of the Southeast. . . . In short, the persistent effort in the plurality opinion to paint Iowa as an oddity standing alone to block commerce carried in 65-foot doubles is simply not supported by the facts. . . .

II

The Commerce Clause is . . . a grant of authority to Congress, not to the courts. Although the Court when it interprets the "dormant" aspect of the Commerce Clause will invalidate unwarranted state intrusion, such action is a far cry from simply undertaking to regulate when Congress has not because we believe such regulation would facilitate interstate commerce.

It is also well established that "the Court has been most reluctant to invalidate under the Commerce Clause 'state legislation in the field of safety where the propriety of local regulation has long been recognized.' " . . . The Court very recently reaffirmed the longstanding view that "[in] no field has . . . deference to state regulation been greater than that of highway safety." Those challenging a highway safety regulation must overcome a "strong presumption of validity," particularly when, as here, Congress has not acted in the area and the claim is that "the bare possession of power by Congress" invalidates the state legislation.[3]

A determination that a state law is a rational safety measure does not end the Commerce Clause inquiry. A "sensitive consideration" of the safety purpose in relation to the burden on commerce is required. . . . [T]he Court does not directly compare safety benefits to commerce costs and strike down the legislation if the latter can be said in some vague sense to "outweigh" the former. Such an approach would make an empty gesture of the strong presumption of validity accorded state safety measures, particularly those governing highways. It would also arrogate to this Court functions of forming public policy, functions which, in the absence of congressional action, were left by the Framers of the Constitution to state legislatures. . . . These admonitions are peculiarly apt when, as here, the question involves the difficult comparison of financial losses and "the loss of lives and limbs of workers and people using the highways."[4]

---

[3] Congress has considered the question of regulating truck length several times but has consistently left the matter for state regulation.

[4] It should not escape notice that a majority of the Court goes on record today as agreeing that courts in Commerce Clause cases do not sit to weigh safety benefits against burdens on commerce when the safety benefits are not illusory. Even the plurality gives lipservice to this principle. I do not agree with my Brother BRENNAN, however, that only those safety benefits somehow articulated by the legislature as *the* motivation for the challenged statute can be considered in supporting the state law.

The purpose of the "sensitive consideration" referred to above is rather to determine if the asserted safety justification, although rational, is merely a pretext for discrimination against interstate commerce. We will conclude that it is if the safety benefits from the regulation are demonstrably trivial while the burden on commerce is great. . . . The nature of the inquiry is perhaps best illustrated by examining those cases in which state safety laws have been struck down on Commerce Clause grounds. In *Southern Pacific* a law regulating train lengths was viewed by the Court as having "at most slight and dubious advantage, if any, over unregulated train lengths"; the lower courts concluded the law actually tended to *increase* the number of accidents by increasing the number of trains. In *Bibb* the contoured mudguards required by Illinois, alone among the States, had *no* safety advantages over conventional mudguards and, as in *Southern Pacific*, actually *increased* hazards. . . . The cases thus demonstrate that the safety benefits of a state law must be slight indeed before it will be struck down under the dormant Commerce Clause.

III

. . . There can be no doubt that the challenged statute is a valid highway safety regulation and thus entitled to the strongest presumption of validity. . . . [A]ll 50 States regulate the length of trucks which may use their highways. The American Association of State Highway and Transportation Officials has consistently recommended length as well as other limits on vehicles. The Iowa Supreme Court has long viewed the provision in question as intended to promote highway safety, and "[this] Court has also had occasion to point out that the sizes and weights of automobiles have an important relation to the safe and convenient use of the highways, which are matters of state control." There can also be no question that the particular limit chosen by Iowa—60 feet—is rationally related to Iowa's safety objective. Most truck limits are between 55 and 65 feet, and Iowa's choice is thus well within the widely accepted range.

Iowa adduced evidence supporting the relation between vehicle length and highway safety. The evidence indicated that longer vehicles take greater time to be passed, thereby increasing the risks of accidents, particularly during the inclement weather not uncommon in Iowa. . . . Longer trucks are more likely to clog intersections, and although there are no intersections on the Interstate Highways, the order below went beyond the highways themselves and the concerns about greater length at intersections would arise "[at] every trip origin, every trip destination, every intermediate stop for picking up trailers, reconfiguring loads, change of drivers, eating, refueling—every intermediate stop would generate this type of situation." The Chief of the Division of Patrol in the Iowa Department of Public Safety testified that longer vehicles pose greater problems at the scene of an accident. For example, trucks involved in accidents often must be unloaded at the scene, which would take longer the bigger the load.

In rebuttal of Consolidated's evidence on the relative safety of 65-foot doubles to trucks permitted on Iowa's highways, Iowa introduced evidence that doubles are more likely than singles to jackknife or upset. The District Court concluded that this was so and that singles are more stable than doubles. Iowa also introduced evidence from Consolidated's own records showing that Consolidated's overall accident rate for doubles exceeded that of semis for three of the last four years, and that some of Consolidated's own drivers expressed a preference for the handling characteristics of singles over doubles.

In addition Iowa elicited evidence undermining the probative value of Consolidated's evidence. For example, Iowa established that the more experienced drivers tended to drive doubles, because they have seniority and driving doubles is a higher paying job than driving singles. Since the leading cause of accidents was driver error, Consolidated's evidence of the relative safety record of doubles may have been based in large part not on the relative safety of the vehicles themselves but on the experience of the drivers. Although the District Court, the Court of Appeals, and the plurality all fail to recognize the fact, Iowa also negated much of Consolidated's evidence by establishing that it considered the relative safety of doubles to singles, and not the question of length alone. Consolidated introduced much evidence that its doubles were as safe as singles. Such evidence is beside the point. The trucks which Consolidated wants to run in Iowa are prohibited because of their length, not their configuration. Doubles are allowed in Iowa, up to a length of 60 feet, and Consolidated in fact operates 60-foot doubles in Iowa. Consolidated's experts were often forced to admit that they could draw no conclusions about the relative safety of 65-foot doubles and 60-foot doubles, as opposed to doubles and singles. Conclusions that the double configuration is as safe as the single do not at all mean the 65-foot double is as safe as the 60-foot double, or that length is not relevant to vehicle safety. For example, one of Consolidated's experts testified that doubles "off track" better than singles, because of their axle placement, but conceded on cross-examination that a 60-foot double would off-track better than a 65-foot double. In sum, there was sufficient evidence presented at trial to support the legislative determination that length is related to safety, and nothing in Consolidated's evidence undermines this conclusion.

The District Court approached the case as if the question were whether Consolidated's 65-foot trucks were as safe as others permitted on Iowa highways, and the Court of Appeals as if its task were to determine if the District Court's factual findings in this regard were "clearly erroneous." The question, however, is whether the Iowa Legislature has acted rationally in regulating vehicle lengths and whether the safety benefits from this regulation are more than slight or problematical. "The classification of the traffic for the purposes of regulation . . . is a legislative, not a judicial, function. Its merits are not to be weighed in the judicial balance and the classification rejected merely because the weight of the evidence in court appears to favor a different standard." . . .

The answering of the relevant question is not appreciably advanced by comparing trucks slightly over the length limit with those at the length limit. It is emphatically not our task to balance any incremental safety benefits from prohibiting 65-foot doubles as opposed to 60-foot doubles against the burden on interstate commerce. Lines drawn for safety purposes will rarely pass muster if the question is whether a slight increment can be permitted without sacrificing safety. As Justice Holmes put it:

> When a legal distinction is determined, as no one doubts that it may be, between night and day, childhood and maturity, or any other extremes, a point has to be fixed or a line has to be drawn, or gradually picked out by successive decisions, to mark where the change takes place. Looked at by itself without regard to the necessity behind it the line or point seems arbitrary. It might as well or nearly as well be a little more to one side or the other. But when it is seen that a line or point there must be, and that there is no mathematical or logical way of fixing it precisely, the decision of the legislature must be accepted unless we can say that it is very wide of any reasonable mark.

The question is rather whether it can be said that the benefits flowing to Iowa from a rational truck-length limitation are "slight or problematical." The particular line chosen by Iowa—60 feet—is relevant only to the question whether the limit is a rational one. Once a court determines that it is, it considers the overall safety benefits *from the regulation* against burdens on interstate commerce, and not any marginal benefits from the scheme the State established as opposed to that the plaintiffs desire.

The difficulties with the contrary approach are patent. While it may be clear that there are substantial safety benefits from a 55-foot truck as compared to a 105-foot truck, these benefits may not be discernible in 5-foot jumps. Appellee's approach would permit what could not be accomplished in one lawsuit to be done in 10 separate suits, each challenging an additional five feet.

Any direct balancing of marginal safety benefits against burdens on commerce would make the burdens on commerce the sole significant factor, and make likely the odd result that similar state laws enacted for identical safety reasons might violate the Commerce Clause in one part of the country but not another. For example, Mississippi and Georgia prohibit trucks over 55 feet. Since doubles are not operated in the Southeast, the demonstrable burden on commerce may not be sufficient to strike down these laws, while Consolidated maintains that it is in this case, even though the doubles here are given an additional five feet. On the other hand, if Consolidated were to win this case it could shift its 65-foot doubles to routes leading into Mississippi or Georgia (both States border States in which 65-foot trucks are permitted) and claim the same constitutional violation it claims in this case. Consolidated Freightways, and not this Court, would become the final arbiter of the Commerce Clause. . . .

Forcing Iowa to yield to the policy choices of neighboring States perverts the primary purpose of the Commerce Clause, that of vesting power to regulate interstate commerce in Congress, where all the States are represented. In *Barnwell Brothers*, the Court upheld a South Carolina width limit of 90 inches even though "all other states permit a width of 96 inches, which is the standard width of trucks engaged in interstate commerce." Then Justice Stone, writing for the Court, stressed:

> The fact that many states have adopted a different standard is not persuasive. . . . The legislature, being free to exercise its own judgment, is not bound by that of other legislatures. It would hardly be contended that if all the states had adopted a single standard none, in the light of its own experience and in the exercise of its judgment upon all the complex elements which enter into the problem, could change it.

Nor is Iowa's policy preempted by Consolidated's decision to invest in 65-foot trucks, particularly since this was done when Iowa's 60-foot limit was on the books.[9] . . .

My Brother BRENNAN argues that the Court should consider only *the* purpose the Iowa legislators *actually* sought to achieve by the length limit, and not the purposes advanced by Iowa's lawyers in defense of the statute. . . . The argument has been consistently rejected by the Court in other contexts. . . . The problems with [such] a view . . . are apparent. To name just a few, it assumes that individual legislators are motivated by one discernible "actual" purpose, and ignores the fact that different legislators may vote for a single piece of legislation for widely different reasons. How, for example, would a court adhering to the views expressed in the opinion concurring in the judgment approach a statute, the legislative history of which indicated that 10 votes were based on safety considerations, 10 votes were based on protectionism, and the statute passed by a vote of 40–20? What would the *actual* purpose of the *legislature* have been in that case? This Court has wisely "never insisted that a legislative body articulate its reasons for enacting a statute."

Both the plurality and the concurrence attach great significance to the Governor's veto of a bill passed by the Iowa Legislature permitting 65-foot doubles. Whatever views one may have about the significance of legislative motives, it must be emphasized that the law which the Court

---

[9]   The extent to which the assertion of a violation of the Commerce Clause is simply an effort to compel Iowa to yield to the decisions of its neighbors is clearest if one asks whether Iowa's law would violate the Commerce Clause if the 17 States which currently prohibit Consolidated's 65-foot doubles were not in the East and Southeast but rather surrounded Iowa.

strikes down today was not passed to achieve the protectionist goals the plurality and the concurrence ascribe to the Governor. Iowa's 60-foot length limit was established in 1963, at a time when very few States permitted 65-foot doubles. Striking down legislation on the basis of asserted legislative motives is dubious enough, but the plurality and concurrence strike down the legislation involved in this case because of asserted impermissible motives for *not* enacting *other* legislation, motives which could not possibly have been present when the legislation under challenge here was considered and passed. Such action is, so far as I am aware, unprecedented in this Court's history.

Furthermore, the effort in both the plurality and the concurrence to portray the legislation involved here as protectionist is in error. Whenever a State enacts more stringent safety measures than its neighbors, in an area which affects commerce, the safety law will have the incidental effect of deflecting interstate commerce to the neighboring States. Indeed, the safety and protectionist motives cannot be separated: The whole purpose of safety regulation of vehicles is to *protect* the State from unsafe vehicles. If a neighboring State chooses *not* to protect its citizens from the danger discerned by the enacting State, that is its business, but the enacting State should not be penalized when the vehicles it considers unsafe travel through the neighboring State. . . .

The true problem with today's decision is that it gives no guidance whatsoever to these States as to whether their laws are valid or how to defend them. For that matter, the decision gives no guidance to Consolidated or other trucking firms either. Perhaps, after all is said and done, the Court today neither says nor does very much at all. We know only that Iowa's law is invalid and that the jurisprudence of the "negative side" of the Commerce Clause remains hopelessly confused.

NOTE ON THE "DORMANT" COMMERCE CLAUSE

1.   As noted in the introduction to this Chapter, modern dormant Commerce Clause doctrine proceeds along two tracks. Laws that *discriminate* against out-of-staters are subject to strict scrutiny and almost never upheld. *See Philadelphia v. New Jersey*. Those laws that regulate evenhandedly but impose *burdens* on interstate commerce, on the other hand, are subject to a balancing test that weighs the interests behind the law against its impact on commerce. *See Kassel*. Notwithstanding the result in *Kassel*, these evenhanded laws are generally upheld. There are many twists on this basic framework, as economic regulation takes a bewildering variety of forms and the Court has decided a vast number of cases in this area. This unit undertakes only to analyze the basic rules.

It is worth asking at the outset, however, why the Court applies the Commerce Clause to limit state regulation *at all*. There is some textual support for such a notion if one reads the affirmative grant of power to Congress to regulate interstate commerce as *exclusive*. But this reading became untenable once the Court construed Congress's Commerce Power to reach the entire economy after 1937. (Can you see why?) After *Garcia*, moreover, one may fairly ask why we rely on "political safeguards" to protect the States from national encroachments, but think that Congress is so helpless as to require judicial assistance in limiting state encroachments on the national union. Is there any answer to this criticism?

2.   What is the best justification for the strong antidiscrimination rule applied in *Philadelphia v. New Jersey*? Commentary on the dormant Commerce Clause emphasizes at least three different rationales:

- **Political and economic unity:** Justice Cardozo said that the Constitution "was framed upon the theory that the peoples of the several states must sink or swim together, and that in the long run prosperity and salvation are in union and not division."[3]

- **Social welfare:** Protectionist legislation may be inefficient by impeding the free flow of goods and discouraging production by those jurisdictions that can produce them at the lowest cost.

- **Representation reinforcement:** The burdens imposed by protectionist laws fall primarily upon out-of-staters, who are not represented in the state political process.

Are there any answers to these arguments for strict scrutiny?

3.   As in many other areas of constitutional law, "strict scrutiny" under the dormant Commerce Clause is generally "fatal in fact." A prominent counter-example is *Maine v. Taylor*, 477 U.S. 131 (1986), in which the state prohibited the importation of live baitfish. Evidence at trial indicated that out-of-state baitfish had parasites not found in Maine baitfish, and that those parasites could damage Maine's population of wild fish. The trial court also found that there was no satisfactory way to inspect imported baitfish for parasites or commingled species. The Court held, in an opinion by Justice Blackmun, that the state law was constitutional notwithstanding that it discriminated and was therefore subject to strict scrutiny. Maine's interest in guarding its marine ecosystem against ecological risks was compelling, and there was no evidence that nondiscriminatory alternatives were available. There was also no evidence of protectionist intent.

4.   Sometimes the Court has struck down facially-neutral laws that are discriminatory in either purpose or effect.[4] *Hunt v. Washington State Apple Advertising Comm'n*, 432 U.S. 333 (1977), for example, considered a North Carolina statute requiring that containers of apples sold or shipped into the State bear "no grade other than the applicable U.S. grade or standard." The State of Washington—the country's largest producer of apples—had its own well-established system of testing and grading apples, and its standard was generally considered to be superior to that adopted by the U.S. Department of Agriculture. The Court found that the North Carolina law was directed at helping the in-state apple industry by stripping its primary competitors—Washington apple growers—of an important

---

[3]   *Baldwin v. G. A. F. Seelig, Inc.*, 294 U.S. 511, 523 (1935).

[4]   *See, e.g., Bacchus Imports, Ltd. v. Dias*, 468 U.S. 263 (1984).

competitive advantage. "[B]y prohibiting Washington growers and dealers from marketing apples under their State's grades, the statute has a leveling effect which insidiously operates to the advantage of local apple producers." The Court thus treated the North Carolina law as discriminatory and struck it down under heightened scrutiny.

It is not easy to derive a clear rule distinguishing between the laws that are struck down on these grounds and the ones that upheld.[5] Professor Chemerinsky offers three factors that are likely to persuade courts to find a law to be discriminatory where it imposes a disparate impact on out-of-staters:

- "[A] law is likely to be found discriminatory if its effect is to exclude virtually all out-of-staters from a particular state market, but not if it only excludes one group of out-of-staters."

- "[A] law is likely to be found discriminatory if it imposes costs on out-of-staters that in-staters would not have to bear."

- "[T]he Court is more likely to find discrimination if it believes that a law is motivated by a protectionist purpose, helping in-staters at the expense of out-of-staters."[6]

It must be acknowledged, however, that these are tendencies rather than rules, and the caselaw in this area does not follow a particularly determinate pattern.

5.   The classic formulation of the balancing test for nondiscriminatory statutes that *burden* interstate commerce comes from *Pike v. Bruce Church, Inc.*, 397 U.S. 137 (1970): "Where the statute regulates even-handedly to effectuate a legitimate local public interest, and its effects on interstate commerce are only incidental, it will be upheld unless the burden imposed on such commerce is clearly excessive in relation to the putative local benefits." Are courts likely to be good at weighing interests in this way? Is there any distinction between the policy judgments required by the *Pike* test and those involved in *Lochner v. New York*? How persuasive is the Court's treatment of the various interests in *Kassel*? Isn't it odd to see the Supreme Court giving a detailed disquisition on the mechanics of wind currents and axle placements as they may influence truck safety? *See, e.g.*, note 13 in *Kassel*. Are courts better than legislatures at these sorts of decisions?

Consistent with his general preference for bright-line rules, Justice Scalia has been a vocal critic of the *Pike* test. He argues that, in balancing, "the scale analogy is not really appropriate, since the interests on both sides are incommensurate. It is more like judging whether a particular line is longer than a particular rock is heavy."[7] Is this a fair criticism? Is there any way to avoid the incommensurability problem? Look again at the various

---

[5]   *See, e.g., Exxon Corp. v. Governor of Maryland*, 437 U.S. 117 (1978) (upholding a state law as nondiscriminatory, even though there was evidence that the law's impact fell more heavily on out-of-state companies).

[6]   ERWIN CHEMERINSKY, CONSTITUTIONAL LAW: PRINCIPLES AND POLICIES § 5.3.4, at 436 (3d ed. 2006).

[7]   *Bendix Autolite Corp. v. Midwesco Enters,, Inc.*, 486 U.S. 888 (1988) (Scalia, J., concurring).

opinions in *Kassel*. Do they actually balance the weights of the interests involved? Or do they find ways to avoid actually balancing the relevant interests?

6.　It is important to remember that *Kassel* is an outlier—both in its result and the heightened level of scrutiny the Supreme Court seems to apply. In the vast majority of cases where a state statute—although imposing a burdensome regulation on interstate commerce—is not facially discriminatory and is applied evenhandedly to those within and without the state, the Court upholds the state legislation as a valid exercise of the state's police power.[8] Do you think the Court is too permissive with respect to nondiscriminatory state regulation that nonetheless throws sand into the gears of the interstate market?

7.　The dormant Commerce Clause has always been viewed as a "free trade" principle, and it is not surprising that efforts to protect free trade at the international level raise many of the same issues that we encounter in the domestic dormant commerce cases. The World Trade Organization (WTO) agreement and the North American Free Trade Agreement (NAFTA), for example, contain broad restrictions on protectionist regulation that arguably could be interpreted to impose a "burden" principle like that applied in *Kassel* or, in the alternative, simply a "nondiscrimination" principle like that in *Philadelphia v. New Jersey*. What does your experience with these issues in the domestic context suggest about how supranational WTO and NAFTA tribunals should approach this choice? Can you think of any relevant differences in the international context? Does the fact that recently-formed federations like the European Union have tended to *start* with a principle of economic union and free trade strengthen the case for reading such a principle into the Commerce Clause?

See also: For a critique of the Dormant Commerce Clause jurisprudence, see Julian N. Eule, *Laying the Dormant Commerce Clause to Rest*, 99 YALE L. J. 425 (1982). For a discussion of the relationship between that jurisprudence and international trade law, see John O. McGinnis & Mark L. Movsesian, *The World Trade Constitution*, 114 HARV. L. REV. 511 (2000).

SECTION 11.2　CONGRESSIONAL CONSENT, MARKET PARTICIPANTS, AND ALTERNATE CONSTRAINTS ON DISCRIMINATION AGAINST OUT-OF-STATERS

This second assignment on the dormant Commerce Clause develops two important wrinkles on the basic constitutional prohibition of discriminatory or burdensome state regulation of interstate commerce. The first is the notion of congressional *consent*—that is, that because the constraint on state regulation stems from the negative implication of

---

[8]　See, e.g., *Am. Trucking Associations, Inc. v. Michigan Pub. Serv. Com'n*, 545 U.S. 429 (2005) (upholding Michigan's imposition of a flat $100 annual fee on trucks engaging in intrastate commercial hauling); *United Haulers Ass'n, Inc. v. Oneida-Herkimer Solid Waste Mgmt. Auth.*, 550 U.S. 330 (2007) (upholding central New York county flow control ordinances that favored state-created public benefit corporation by requiring all businesses, whether in or out of state, to bring waste to that corporation's facilities).

Congress's own power over interstate commerce, that constraint is in turn waivable by congressional action. In a number of areas, such as banking and insurance regulation, Congress has explicitly authorized state regulation that would otherwise violate the dormant commerce principle.[9] The second wrinkle is the *market participant* defense, which shields state activities from dormant commerce scrutiny where the State is acting as a participant in a market rather than a regulator of that market. Not surprisingly, drawing the participant/regulator line turns out to be a bit tricky. Both the consent and market participant issues are on display in the first case of this section, *South-Central Timber*.

The remaining two cases deal with alternative constitutional theories for addressing the same basic problem—state discrimination against out-of-staters—at issue in the dormant commerce cases. *United Building & Construction Trades Council v. City of Camden* deals with the Privileges and Immunities Clause of Article IV, a provision that we first encountered in the *Slaughter-House Cases*. *Metropolitan Life v. Ward*, on the other hand, addresses state discrimination through the lens of the Equal Protection Clause of the Fourteenth Amendment. Each of these theories has certain advantages and disadvantages, from a litigant's standpoint, as a vehicle for addressing state discrimination. This material thus offers a chance to "think like a plaintiff's lawyer" who must frame a complaint in anticipation of certain defenses and burdens of proof.

South-Central Timber Development, Inc. v. Wunnicke

467 U.S. 82 (1984)

■ JUSTICE WHITE announced the judgment of the Court and delivered the opinion of the Court with respect to Parts I and II, and an opinion with respect to Parts III and IV, in which JUSTICE BRENNAN, JUSTICE BLACKMUN, and JUSTICE STEVENS joined.

We granted certiorari in this case to review a decision of the Court of Appeals for the Ninth Circuit that held that Alaska's requirement that timber taken from state lands be processed within the State prior to export was "implicitly authorized" by Congress and therefore does not violate the Commerce Clause. We hold that it was not authorized and reverse the judgment of the Court of Appeals.

I

In September 1980, the Alaska Department of Natural Resources published a notice that it would sell approximately 49 million board-feet

---

[9]   Recall from the last chapter that in *New York v. United States*, Congress authorized states that were in compliance with deadlines under the Low Level Radioactive Waste Amendments Act to exclude from their disposal sites waste from states that were *not* in compliance. Absent congressional consent, such discrimination against out-of-state waste would have been unconstitutional under *Philadelphia v. New Jersey*.

of timber in the area of Icy Cape, Alaska, on October 23, 1980. The notice of sale, the prospectus, and the proposed contract for the sale all provided . . . that "[primary] manufacture within the State of Alaska will be required as a special provision of the contract." Under the primary-manufacture requirement, the successful bidder must partially process the timber prior to shipping it outside of the State. The requirement is imposed by contract and does not limit the export of unprocessed timber not owned by the State. The stated purpose of the requirement is to "protect existing industries, provide for the establishment of new industries, derive revenue from all timber resources, and manage the State's forests on a sustained yield basis." When it imposes the requirement, the State charges a significantly lower price for the timber than it otherwise would.

The major method of complying with the primary-manufacture requirement is to convert the logs into *cants*, which are logs slabbed on at least one side. In order to satisfy the Alaska requirement, cants must be either sawed to a maximum thickness of 12 inches or squared on four sides along their entire length.

Petitioner, South-Central Timber Development, Inc., is an Alaska corporation engaged in the business of purchasing standing timber, logging the timber, and shipping the logs into foreign commerce, almost exclusively to Japan.[4] It does not operate a mill in Alaska and customarily sells unprocessed logs. When it learned that the primary-manufacture requirement was to be imposed on the Icy Cape sale, it brought an action in Federal District Court seeking an injunction, arguing that the requirement violated the negative implications of the Commerce Clause.[5] The District Court agreed. . . . The Court of Appeals for the Ninth Circuit reversed, finding it unnecessary to reach the question whether, standing alone, the requirement would violate the Commerce Clause, because it found implicit congressional authorization in the federal policy of imposing a primary-manufacture requirement on timber taken from federal land in Alaska.

We must first decide whether the court was correct in concluding that Congress has authorized the challenged requirement. If Congress has not, we must respond to respondents' submission that we should affirm the judgment on two grounds not reached by the Court of Appeals: (1) whether in the absence of congressional approval Alaska's requirement is permissible because Alaska is acting as a market

---

[4]   Apparently, there is virtually no interstate market in Alaska timber because of the high shipping costs associated with shipment between American ports. Consequently, over 90% of Alaska timber is exported to Japan.

[5]   Although it would appear at first blush that it would be economically more efficient to have the primary processing take place within Alaska, that is apparently not the case. Material appearing in the record suggests that the slabs removed from the log in the process of making cants are often quite valuable, but apparently cannot be used and are burned. It appears that because of the wasted wood, cants are actually worth *less* than the unprocessed logs. . . .

participant, rather than as a market regulator; and (2), if not, whether the local-processing requirement is forbidden by the Commerce Clause.

II

Although the Commerce Clause is by its text an affirmative grant of power to Congress to regulate interstate and foreign commerce, the Clause has long been recognized as a self-executing limitation on the power of the States to enact laws imposing substantial burdens on such commerce. It is equally clear that Congress may "redefine the distribution of power over interstate commerce" by "[permitting] the states to regulate the commerce in a manner which would otherwise not be permissible." *Southern Pacific Co. v. Arizona*, 325 U.S. 761, 769 (1945). . . . The Court of Appeals held that Congress had done just that by consistently endorsing primary-manufacture requirements on timber taken from *federal* land.

Alaska argues that federal statutes and regulations demonstrate an affirmative expression of approval of its primary-manufacture requirement for three reasons: (1) federal timber export policy has, since 1928, treated federal timber land in Alaska differently from that in other States; (2) the Federal Government has specifically tailored its policies to ensure development of wood-processing capacity for utilization of timber from the National Forests; and (3) the regulation forbidding without prior approval the export from Alaska of unprocessed timber or its shipment to other States demonstrates that it is the Alaska wood-processing industry in particular, not the domestic wood-processing industry generally, that has been the object of federal concern.

Acceptance of Alaska's three factual propositions does not mandate acceptance of its conclusion. Neither South-Central nor the United States[6] challenges the existence of a federal policy to restrict the out-of-state shipment of unprocessed Alaska timber from federal lands. They challenge only the derivation from that policy of an affirmative expression of federal approval of a parallel policy with respect to state timber. They argue that our cases dealing with congressional authorization of otherwise impermissible state interference with interstate commerce have required an "express" statement of such authorization, and that no such authorization may be implied.

It is true that most of our cases have looked for an express statement of congressional policy prior to finding that state regulation is permissible. For example, in *Sporhase v. Nebraska ex rel. Douglas,* the Court declined to find congressional authorization for state-imposed burdens on interstate commerce in ground water despite 37 federal statutes and a number of interstate compacts that demonstrated Congress' deference to state water law. We noted that on those occasions in which consent has been found, congressional intent and policy to

---

[6]   The United States appears as *amicus curiae* in support of the position of South-Central.

insulate state legislation from Commerce Clause attack have been "expressly stated." . . .

[T]he phrase "expressly stated," however[,] merely states one way of meeting the requirement that for a state regulation to be removed from the reach of the dormant Commerce Clause, congressional intent must be unmistakably clear. . . . The Commerce Clause was designed "to avoid the tendencies toward economic Balkanization that had plagued relations among the Colonies and later among the States under the Articles of Confederation." Unrepresented interests will often bear the brunt of regulations imposed by one State having a significant effect on persons or operations in other States. Thus, "when the regulation is of such a character that its burden falls principally upon those without the state, legislative action is not likely to be subjected to those political restraints which are normally exerted on legislation where it affects adversely some interests within the state." On the other hand, when Congress acts, all segments of the country are represented, and there is significantly less danger that one State will be in a position to exploit others. . . . A rule requiring a clear expression of approval by Congress ensures that there is, in fact, such a collective decision and reduces significantly the risk that unrepresented interests will be adversely affected by restraints on commerce.

The fact that the state policy in this case appears to be consistent with federal policy—or even that state policy furthers the goals we might believe that Congress had in mind—is an insufficient indicium of congressional intent. Congress acted only with respect to federal lands; we cannot infer from that fact that it intended to authorize a similar policy with respect to state lands. Accordingly, we reverse the contrary judgment of the Court of Appeals.

III

We now turn to the issues left unresolved by the Court of Appeals. The first of these issues is whether Alaska's restrictions on export of unprocessed timber from state-owned lands are exempt from Commerce Clause scrutiny under the "market-participant doctrine."

Our cases make clear that if a State is acting as a market participant, rather than as a market regulator, the dormant Commerce Clause places no limitation on its activities. The precise contours of the market-participant doctrine have yet to be established, however, the doctrine having been applied in only three cases of this Court to date.

The first of the cases, *Hughes v. Alexandria Scrap Corp.*, 426 U.S. 794 (1976), involved a Maryland program designed to reduce the number of junked automobiles in the State. A "bounty" was established on Maryland-licensed junk cars, and the State imposed more stringent documentation requirements on out-of-state scrap processors than on in-state ones. The Court rejected a Commerce Clause attack on the program, although it noted that under traditional Commerce Clause analysis the program might well be invalid because it had the effect of reducing the flow of goods in interstate commerce. The Court concluded that Maryland's action was not "the kind of action with which the Commerce Clause is concerned" because "[nothing] in the purposes animating the Commerce Clause prohibits a State, in the absence of congressional action, from participating in the market and exercising the right to favor its own citizens over others."

In *Reeves, Inc. v. Stake*, 447 U.S. 429 (1980), the Court upheld a South Dakota policy of restricting the sale of cement from a state-owned plant to state residents, declaring that "[the] basic distinction drawn in *Alexandria Scrap* between States as market participants and States as market regulators makes good sense and sound law." The Court relied upon " 'the long recognized right of trader or manufacturer, engaged in an entirely private business, freely to exercise his own independent discretion as to parties with whom he will deal.' " In essence, the Court recognized the principle that the Commerce Clause places no limitations on a State's refusal to deal with particular parties when it is participating in the interstate market in goods.

The most recent of this Court's cases developing the market-participant doctrine is *White v. Massachusetts Council of Construction Employers, Inc.*, 460 U.S. 204 (1983), in which the Court sustained against a Commerce Clause challenge an executive order of the Mayor of Boston that required all construction projects funded in whole or in part by city funds or city-administered funds to be performed by a work force of at least 50% city residents. The Court rejected the argument that the city was not entitled to the protection of the doctrine because the order had the effect of regulating employment contracts between public contractors and their employees. Recognizing that "there are some limits on a state or local government's ability to impose restrictions that reach beyond the immediate parties with which the government transacts business," the Court found it unnecessary to define those limits because "[everyone] affected by the order [was], in a substantial if informal sense, 'working for the city.' " The fact that the employees were "working for the city" was "crucial" to the market-participant analysis in *White*.

The State of Alaska contends that its primary-manufacture requirement fits squarely within the market-participant doctrine, arguing that "Alaska's entry into the market may be viewed as precisely the same type of subsidy to local interests that the Court found unobjectionable in *Alexandria Scrap*." However, when Maryland became involved in the scrap market it was as a purchaser of scrap; Alaska, on the other hand, participates in the timber market, but imposes conditions downstream in the timber-processing market. Alaska is not merely subsidizing local timber processing in an amount "roughly equal to the difference between the price the timber would fetch in the absence of such a requirement and the amount the state actually receives." If the State directly subsidized the timber-processing industry by such an amount, the purchaser would retain the option of taking advantage of the subsidy by processing timber in the State or forgoing the benefits of the subsidy and exporting unprocessed timber. Under the Alaska requirement, however, the choice is made for him: if he buys timber from the State he is not free to take the timber out of state prior to processing.

The State also would have us find *Reeves* controlling. It states that "*Reeves* made it clear that the Commerce Clause imposes no limitation on Alaska's power to choose the terms on which it will sell its timber." Such an unrestrained reading of *Reeves* is unwarranted. Although the Court in *Reeves* did strongly endorse the right of a State to deal with whomever it chooses when it participates in the market, it did not . . . sanction the imposition of any terms that the State might desire. For example, the Court expressly noted in *Reeves* that "Commerce Clause scrutiny may well be more rigorous when a restraint on foreign commerce is alleged"; that a natural resource "like coal, timber, wild game, or minerals," was not involved, but instead the cement was "the end product of a complex process whereby a costly physical plant and human labor act on raw materials"; and that South Dakota did not bar resale of South Dakota cement to out-of-state purchasers. In this case, all three of the elements that were not present in *Reeves*—foreign commerce, a natural resource, and restrictions on resale—are present.

Finally, Alaska argues that since . . . *White* upheld a requirement that reached beyond "the boundary of formal privity of contract," then, *a fortiori*, the primary-manufacture requirement is permissible, because the State is not regulating contracts for resale of timber or regulating the buying and selling of timber, but is instead "a seller of timber, pure and simple." Yet it is clear that the State is more than merely a seller of timber. In the commercial context, the seller usually has no say over, and no interest in, how the product is to be used after sale; in this case, however, . . . despite the fact that the purchaser has taken delivery of the timber and has paid for it, he cannot do with it as he pleases. Instead, he is obligated to deal with a stranger to the contract after completion of the sale.

That privity of contract is not always the outer boundary of permissible state activity does not necessarily mean that the Commerce Clause has no application within the boundary of formal privity. The market-participant doctrine permits a State to influence "a discrete, identifiable class of economic activity in which [it] is a major participant." Contrary to the State's contention, the doctrine is not *carte blanche* to impose any conditions that the State has the economic power to dictate, and does not validate any requirement merely because the State imposes it upon someone with whom it is in contractual privity.

The limit of the market-participant doctrine must be that it allows a State to impose burdens on commerce within the market in which it is a participant, but allows it to go no further. The State may not impose conditions, whether by statute, regulation, or contract, that have a substantial regulatory effect outside of that particular market. Unless the "market" is relatively narrowly defined, the doctrine has the potential of swallowing up the rule that States may not impose substantial burdens on interstate commerce even if they act with the permissible state purpose of fostering local industry.

At the heart of the dispute in this case is disagreement over the definition of the market. Alaska contends that it is participating in the processed timber market, although it acknowledges that it participates in no way in the actual processing. South-Central argues, on the other hand, that although the State may be a participant in the timber market, it is using its leverage in that market to exert a regulatory effect in the processing market, in which it is not a participant. We agree with the latter position.

There are sound reasons for distinguishing between a State's preferring its own residents in the initial disposition of goods when it is a market participant and a State's attachment of restrictions on dispositions subsequent to the goods coming to rest in private hands. First, . . . a state market participant has a greater interest as a "private trader" in the immediate transaction than it has in what its purchaser does with the goods after the State no longer has an interest in them. The common law recognized such a notion in the doctrine of restraints on alienation. Similarly, the antitrust laws place limits on vertical restraints. It is no defense in an action charging vertical trade restraints that the same end could be achieved through vertical integration; if it were, there would be virtually no antitrust scrutiny of vertical arrangements. We reject the contention that a State's action as a market regulator may be upheld against Commerce Clause challenge on the ground that the State could achieve the same end as a market participant. We therefore find it unimportant for present purposes that the State could support its processing industry by selling only to Alaska processors, by vertical integration, or by direct subsidy.

Second, downstream restrictions have a greater regulatory effect than do limitations on the immediate transaction. Instead of merely choosing its own trading partners, the State is attempting to govern the private, separate economic relationships of its trading partners; that is, it restricts the post-purchase activity of the purchaser, rather than merely the purchasing activity. In contrast to . . . *White*, this restriction on private economic activity takes place after the completion of the parties' direct commercial obligations, rather than during the course of an ongoing commercial relationship in which the city retained a continuing proprietary interest in the subject of the contract.[11] In sum, the State may not avail itself of the market-participant doctrine to

---

[11] This is not to say that the State could evade the reasoning of this opinion by merely including a provision in its contract that title does not pass until the processing is complete. It is the substance of the transaction, rather than the label attached to it, that governs Commerce Clause analysis.

immunize its downstream regulation of the timber-processing market in which it is not a participant.

IV

Finally, the State argues that even if we find that Congress did not authorize the processing restriction, and even if we conclude that its actions do not qualify for the market-participant exception, the restriction does not substantially burden interstate or foreign commerce under ordinary Commerce Clause principles. We need not labor long over that contention.

Viewed as a naked restraint on export of unprocessed logs, there is little question that the processing requirement cannot survive scrutiny. . . . Because of the protectionist nature of Alaska's local-processing requirement and the burden on commerce resulting therefrom, we conclude that it falls within the rule of virtual *per se* invalidity of laws that "[block] the flow of interstate commerce at a State's borders." *Philadelphia v. New Jersey.*

We are buttressed in our conclusion that the restriction is invalid by the fact that foreign commerce is burdened by the restriction. It is a well-accepted rule that state restrictions burdening foreign commerce are subjected to a more rigorous and searching scrutiny. It is crucial to the efficient execution of the Nation's foreign policy that "the Federal Government . . . speak with one voice when regulating commercial relations with foreign governments." In light of the substantial attention given by Congress to the subject of export restrictions on unprocessed timber, it would be peculiarly inappropriate to permit state regulation of the subject.

The judgment of the Court of Appeals is reversed, and the case is remanded for proceedings consistent with the opinion of this Court.[*]

■ **JUSTICE REHNQUIST, with whom JUSTICE O'CONNOR joins, dissenting.**

In my view, the line of distinction drawn in the plurality opinion between the State as market participant and the State as market regulator is both artificial and unconvincing. The plurality draws this line "simply as a matter of intuition," but then seeks to bolster its intuition through a series of remarks more appropriate to antitrust law than to the Commerce Clause.[a1] For example, the plurality complains

---

[*]   Justice Marshall took no part in this decision. Justice Brennan wrote a short concurrence suggesting that the market participant doctrine should be abandoned altogether. Justice Powell (joined by Chief Justice Burger) concurred in the judgment but suggested that the case should be remanded to the court of appeals to determine the issues other than Congressional consent (which the court of appeals did not reach the first time around) [Editor's Note].

[a1]   The plurality does offer one other reason for its demarcation of the boundary between these two concepts. "[Downstream] restrictions have a greater regulatory effect than do limitations on the immediate transaction." . . . But, of course, this is not a "reason" at all, but merely a restatement of the conclusion. The line between participation and regulation is what

that the State is using its "leverage" in the timber market to distort consumer choice in the timber-processing market, a classic example of a tying arrangement. And the plurality cites the common-law doctrine of restraints on alienation and the antitrust limits on vertical restraints in dismissing the State's claim that it could accomplish exactly the same result in other ways. . . .

The contractual term at issue here no more transforms Alaska's sale of timber into "regulation" of the processing industry than the resident-hiring preference imposed by the city of Boston in *White v. Massachusetts Council of Construction Employers, Inc.* constituted regulation of the construction industry. Alaska is merely paying the buyer of the timber indirectly, by means of a reduced price, to hire Alaska residents to process the timber. Under existing precedent, the State could accomplish that same result in any number of ways. For example, the State could choose to sell its timber only to those companies that maintain active primary-processing plants in Alaska. *Reeves, Inc. v. Stake.* Or the State could directly subsidize the primary-processing industry within the State. *Hughes v. Alexandria Scrap Corp.* The State could even pay to have the logs processed and then enter the market only to sell processed logs. It seems to me unduly formalistic to conclude that the one path chosen by the State as best suited to promote its concerns is the path forbidden it by the Commerce Clause.

For these reasons, I would affirm the judgment of the Court of Appeals.

United Building & Construction Trades Council v. Mayor and Council of the City of Camden
465 U.S. 208 (1984)

■ JUSTICE REHNQUIST delivered the opinion of the Court.

A municipal ordinance of the city of Camden, New Jersey, requires that at least 40% of the employees of contractors and subcontractors working on city construction projects be Camden residents. Appellant, the United Building and Construction Trades Council of Camden County and Vicinity, challenges that ordinance as a violation of the Privileges and Immunities Clause, Art. IV, § 2, cl. 1. . . . The Supreme Court of New Jersey rejected appellant's privileges and immunities attack on the ground that the ordinance discriminates on the basis of *municipal*, not state, residency. The court "[declined] to apply the Privileges and Immunities Clause in the context of a municipal ordinance that has identical effects upon out-of-state citizens and New Jersey citizens not residing in the locality." We conclude that the challenged ordinance is properly subject to the strictures of the Clause. We therefore reverse the

---

we are trying to determine. To invoke that very distinction in support of the line drawn is merely to fall back again on intuition.

judgment of the Supreme Court of New Jersey and remand the case for a determination of the validity of the ordinance under the appropriate constitutional standard.

I

On August 28, 1980, the Camden City Council, acting pursuant to a statewide affirmative-action program, adopted an ordinance setting minority hiring "goals" on all public works contracts. The ordinance also created a hiring preference for Camden residents, with a separate 1-year residency requirement triggering eligibility for that preference. As subsequently amended, the ordinance requires that on all construction projects funded by the city:

> The developer/contractor, in hiring for jobs, shall make every effort to employ persons residing within the City of Camden but, in no event, shall less than forty percent (40%) of the entire labor force be residents of the City of Camden.

The contractor is also obliged to ensure that any subcontractors working on such projects adhere to the same requirement.

The amended ordinance was submitted for approval to the Chief Affirmative Action Officer of the New Jersey Treasury Department in November 1980. Following brief administrative proceedings, the ordinance was designated as a state-approved affirmative-action construction program. Appellant, an association of labor organizations representing private employees in the building and construction trades in various New Jersey counties[4] . . . challenged state approval of the resident-hiring quota as ultra vires, and as unconstitutional under the Commerce Clause and the Privileges and Immunities Clause of Art. IV . . . and under the Fourteenth Amendment's Equal Protection Clause. The New Jersey court sustained the Treasurer's action as consistent both with state law and the Federal Constitution. Citing *Reeves, Inc. v. Stake* and *Hughes v. Alexandria Scrap Corp.*, the court held that the resident quota was not subject to challenge under the Commerce Clause because the State was acting as a market participant rather than as a market regulator. The court also held that the quota did not violate the Privileges and Immunities Clause because it was not aimed primarily at out-of-state residents. "It almost certainly affects more New Jersey residents not living in Camden than it does out-of-state residents. Because the Camden ordinance does not affect 'the States['] . . . treatment of each other's residents,' . . . it does not violate any privilege of state citizenship." . . .

Appellant then filed this appeal raising the same three constitutional challenges to the resident-hiring quota. We noted probable jurisdiction. Since the Council filed its appeal, however, there have been two significant changes in the posture of the case. First, the Court

---

4   The Council has at least some members who reside outside New Jersey.

decided *White v. Massachusetts Council of Construction Employers, Inc.,* which held that an executive order of the Mayor of Boston, requiring that at least 50% of all jobs on construction projects funded in whole or in part by city funds be filled by bona fide city residents, was immune from scrutiny under the Commerce Clause because Boston was acting as a market participant rather than as a market regulator. In light of the decision in *White,* appellant has abandoned its Commerce Clause challenge to the Camden ordinance.

Second, in July 1983 Camden amended its affirmative-action plan. . . . Because of these changes, the only question left for our consideration is whether the Camden ordinance, as now written, violates the Privileges and Immunities Clause.[7] We first address the argument, accepted by the Supreme Court of New Jersey, that the Clause does not even apply to a *municipal* ordinance such as this. Two separate contentions are advanced in support of this position: first, that the Clause only applies to laws passed by a *state* and, second, that the Clause only applies to laws that discriminate on the basis of *state* citizenship.

The first argument can be quickly rejected. The fact that the ordinance in question is a municipal, rather than a state, law does not somehow place it outside the scope of the Privileges and Immunities Clause. First of all, one cannot easily distinguish municipal from state action in this case: the municipal ordinance would not have gone into effect without express approval by the State Treasurer. . . . More fundamentally, a municipality is merely a political subdivision of the State from which its authority derives. . . . [W]hat would be unconstitutional if done directly by the State can no more readily be accomplished by a city deriving its authority from the State. Thus, even if the ordinance had been adopted solely by Camden, and not pursuant to a state program or with state approval, the hiring preference would still have to comport with the Privileges and Immunities Clause.

The second argument merits more consideration. The New Jersey Supreme Court concluded that the Privileges and Immunities Clause does not apply to an ordinance that discriminates solely on the basis of *municipal* residency. The Clause is phrased in terms of *state* citizenship and was designed "to place the citizens of each State upon the same footing with citizens of other States, so far as the advantages resulting from citizenship in those States are concerned."

> The primary purpose of this clause, like the clauses between which it is located—those relating to full faith and credit and to interstate extradition of fugitives from justice—was to help fuse into one Nation a collection of independent, sovereign States. It was designed to insure to a citizen of State A who ventures into

---

[7] In *White v. Massachusetts Council of Construction Employers, Inc.* we specifically declined to pass on the merits of a privileges and immunities challenge to the Mayor's executive order because the court below did not reach the issue.

State B the same privileges which the citizens of State B enjoy. For protection of such equality the citizen of State A was not to be restricted to the uncertain remedies afforded by diplomatic processes and official retaliation.

Municipal residency classifications, it is argued, simply do not give rise to the same concerns.

We cannot accept this argument. We have never read the Clause so literally as to apply it only to distinctions based on state citizenship. . . . [D]espite some initial uncertainty, it is now established that the terms "citizen" and "resident" are "essentially interchangeable" for purposes of analysis of most cases under the Privileges and Immunities Clause. A person who is not residing in a given State is *ipso facto* not residing in a city within that State. Thus, whether the exercise of a privilege is conditioned on state residency or on municipal residency he will just as surely be excluded.

Given the Camden ordinance, an out-of-state citizen who ventures into New Jersey will not enjoy the same privileges as the New Jersey citizen residing in Camden. It is true that New Jersey citizens not residing in Camden will be affected by the ordinance as well as out-of-state citizens. And it is true that the disadvantaged New Jersey residents have no claim under the Privileges and Immunities Clause. *Slaughter-House Cases*. But New Jersey residents at least have a chance to remedy at the polls any discrimination against them. Out-of-state citizens have no similar opportunity, and they must not "be restricted to the uncertain remedies afforded by diplomatic processes and official retaliation."[9] We conclude that Camden's ordinance is not immune from constitutional review at the behest of out-of-state residents merely because some instate residents are similarly disadvantaged.

Application of the Privileges and Immunities Clause to a particular instance of discrimination against out-of-state residents entails a two-step inquiry. As an initial matter, the Court must decide whether the ordinance burdens one of those privileges and immunities protected by

---

[9] The dissent suggests that New Jersey citizens not residing in Camden will adequately protect the interests of out-of-state residents and that the scope of the Privileges and Immunities Clause should be measured in light of this political reality. What the dissent fails to appreciate is that the Camden ordinance at issue in this case was adopted pursuant to a comprehensive, statewide program applicable in all New Jersey cities. The Camden resident-preference ordinance has already received state sanction and approval, and every New Jersey city is free to adopt a similar protectionist measure. Some have already done so. Thus, it is hard to see how New Jersey residents living outside Camden will protect the interests of out-of-state citizens.

More fundamentally, the dissent's proposed blanket exemption for all classifications that are less than statewide would provide States with a simple means for evading the strictures of the Privileges and Immunities Clause. Suppose, for example, that California wanted to guarantee that all employees of contractors and subcontractors working on construction projects funded in whole or in part by state funds are state residents. Under the dissent's analysis, the California Legislature need merely divide the State in half, providing one resident-hiring preference for northern Californians on all such projects taking place in northern California, and one for southern Californians on all projects taking place in southern California. . . .

the Clause. Not all forms of discrimination against citizens of other States are constitutionally suspect.

> Some distinctions between residents and nonresidents merely reflect the fact that this is a Nation composed of individual States, and are permitted; other distinctions are prohibited because they hinder the formation, the purpose, or the development of a single Union of those States. Only with respect to those 'privileges' and 'immunities' bearing upon the vitality of the Nation as a single entity must the State treat all citizens, resident and nonresident, equally.

As a threshold matter, then, we must determine whether an out-of-state resident's interest in employment on public works contracts in another State is sufficiently "fundamental" to the promotion of interstate harmony so as to "fall within the purview of the Privileges and Immunities Clause."

> Certainly, the pursuit of a common calling is one of the most fundamental of those privileges. . . . Many, if not most, of our cases expounding the Privileges and Immunities Clause have dealt with this basic and essential activity. Public employment, however, is qualitatively different from employment in the private sector; it is a subspecies of the broader opportunity to pursue a common calling. We have held that there is no fundamental right to government employment for purposes of the Equal Protection Clause. And in *White,* we held that for purposes of the Commerce Clause everyone employed on a city public works project is, "in a substantial if informal sense, 'working for the city.' "

> It can certainly be argued that for purposes of the Privileges and Immunities Clause everyone affected by the Camden ordinance is also "working for the city" and, therefore, has no grounds for complaint when the city favors its own residents. But we decline to transfer mechanically into this context an analysis fashioned to fit the Commerce Clause. Our decision in *White* turned on a distinction between the city acting as a market participant and the city acting as a market regulator. The question whether employees of contractors and subcontractors on public works projects were or were not, in some sense, working for the city was crucial to that analysis. The question had to be answered in order to chart the boundaries of the distinction. But the distinction between market participant and market regulator relied upon in *White* to dispose of the Commerce Clause challenge is not dispositive in this context. The two Clauses have different aims and set different standards for state conduct.

> The Commerce Clause acts as an implied restraint upon state regulatory powers. Such powers must give way before the superior authority of Congress to legislate on (or leave unregulated) matters involving interstate commerce. When the State acts solely as a market participant, no conflict between state *regulation* and federal regulatory authority can arise. The Privileges and Immunities Clause, on the other hand, imposes a direct restraint on state action in the interests of

interstate harmony. This concern with comity cuts across the market regulator-market participant distinction that is crucial under the Commerce Clause. It is discrimination against out-of-state residents on matters of fundamental concern which triggers the Clause, not regulation affecting interstate commerce. Thus, the fact that Camden is merely setting conditions on its expenditures for goods and services in the marketplace does not preclude the possibility that those conditions violate the Privileges and Immunities Clause.

In *Hicklin v. Orbeck,* 437 U.S. 518 (1978), we struck down as a violation of the Privileges and Immunities Clause an "Alaska Hire" statute containing a resident-hiring preference for all employment related to the development of the State's oil and gas resources. Alaska argued in that case that "because the oil and gas that are the subject of Alaska Hire are *owned* by the State, this ownership, of itself, is sufficient justification for the Act's discrimination against nonresidents, and takes the Act totally without the scope of the Privileges and Immunities Clause." We concluded, however, that the State's interest in controlling those things it claims to own is not absolute. "Rather than placing a statute completely beyond the Clause, a State's ownership of the property with which the statute is concerned is a factor—although often the crucial factor—to be considered in evaluating whether the statute's discrimination against noncitizens violates the Clause." Much the same analysis, we think, is appropriate to a city's efforts to bias private employment decisions in favor of its residents on construction projects funded with public moneys. The fact that Camden is expending its own funds or funds it administers in accordance with the terms of a grant is certainly a factor—perhaps the crucial factor—to be considered in evaluating whether the statute's discrimination violates the Privileges and Immunities Clause. But it does not remove the Camden ordinance completely from the purview of the Clause.

In sum, Camden may, without fear of violating the Commerce Clause, pressure private employers engaged in public works projects funded in whole or in part by the city to hire city residents. But that same exercise of power to bias the employment decisions of private contractors and subcontractors against out-of-state residents may be called to account under the Privileges and Immunities Clause. A determination of whether a privilege is "fundamental" for purposes of that Clause does not depend on whether the employees of private contractors and subcontractors engaged in public works projects can or cannot be said to be "working for the city." The opportunity to seek employment with such private employers is "sufficiently basic to the livelihood of the Nation," as to fall within the purview of the Privileges and Immunities Clause even though the contractors and subcontractors are themselves engaged in projects funded in whole or part by the city.

The conclusion that Camden's ordinance discriminates against a protected privilege does not, of course, end the inquiry. We have stressed in prior cases that "[like] many other constitutional provisions, the privileges and immunities clause is not an absolute." It does not preclude discrimination against citizens of other States where there is a "substantial reason" for the difference in treatment. "[The] inquiry in each case must be concerned with whether such reasons do exist and whether the degree of discrimination bears a close relation to them." As part of any justification offered for the discriminatory law, nonresidents must somehow be shown to "constitute a peculiar source of the evil at which the statute is aimed."

The city of Camden contends that its ordinance is necessary to counteract grave economic and social ills. Spiraling unemployment, a sharp decline in population, and a dramatic reduction in the number of businesses located in the city have eroded property values and depleted the city's tax base. The resident-hiring preference is designed, the city contends, to increase the number of employed persons living in Camden and to arrest the "middle-class flight" currently plaguing the city. The city also argues that all non-Camden residents employed on city public works projects, whether they reside in New Jersey or Pennsylvania, constitute a "source of the evil at which the statute is aimed." That is, they "live off" Camden without "living in" Camden. Camden contends that the scope of the discrimination practiced in the ordinance, with its municipal residency requirement, is carefully tailored to alleviate this evil without unreasonably harming nonresidents, who still have access to 60% of the available positions.

Every inquiry under the Privileges and Immunities Clause "must . . . be conducted with due regard for the principle that the States should have considerable leeway in analyzing local evils and in prescribing appropriate cures." This caution is particularly appropriate when a government body is merely setting conditions on the expenditure of funds it controls. The Alaska Hire statute at issue in *Hicklin v. Orbeck* swept within its strictures not only contractors and subcontractors dealing directly with the State's oil and gas; it also covered suppliers who provided goods and services to those contractors and subcontractors. We invalidated the Act as "an attempt to force virtually all businesses that benefit in some way from the economic ripple effect of Alaska's decision to develop its oil and gas resources to bias their employment practices in favor of the State's residents." No similar "ripple effect" appears to infect the Camden ordinance. It is limited in scope to employees working directly on city public works projects.

Nonetheless, we find it impossible to evaluate Camden's justification on the record as it now stands. No trial has ever been held in the case. No findings of fact have been made. The Supreme Court of New Jersey certified the case for direct appeal after the brief administrative proceedings that led to approval of the ordinance by the State Treasurer. It would not be appropriate for this Court either to make factual determinations as an initial matter or to take judicial notice of Camden's decay. We, therefore, deem it wise to remand the case to the New Jersey Supreme Court. That court may decide, consistent with state procedures, on the best method for making the necessary findings.

The judgment of the Supreme Court of New Jersey is reversed, and the case is remanded for proceedings not inconsistent with this opinion.

■ **JUSTICE BLACKMUN, dissenting.**

. . . Today . . . the Court casually extends the scope of the [Privileges and Immunities] Clause by holding that it applies to laws that discriminate *among* state residents on the basis of *municipal* residence, simply because discrimination on the basis of municipal residence disadvantages citizens of other States *"ipso facto."* . . . Because I believe that the Privileges and Immunities Clause was not intended to apply to the kind of municipal discrimination presented by this case, I would affirm the judgment of the Supreme Court of New Jersey.[3]

I

The historical underpinnings of the Privileges and Immunities Clause are not in serious dispute. The Clause was derived from the fourth Article of Confederation[4] and was designed to carry forward that provision's prescription of interstate comity. Both the text of the Clause and the historical record confirm that the Framers meant to foreclose any one State from denying citizens of other States the same "privileges and immunities" accorded its own citizens. James Madison complained during the Constitutional Convention of "Acts of Virginia. & Maryland which give a preference to their own citizens in cases where the Citizens [of other States] are entitled to equality of privileges by the Articles of Confederation." Alexander Hamilton, who deemed the Privileges and Immunities Clause "the basis of the Union," expressly linked the Clause with the concern over state parochialism that gave rise to the federal courts' diversity jurisdiction under Article III. . . .

While the Framers thus conceived of the Privileges and Immunities Clause as an instrument for frustrating discrimination based on state citizenship, there is no evidence of any sort that they were concerned by intrastate discrimination based on municipal residence. The most obvious reason for this is also the most simple one: by the time the Constitution was enacted, such discrimination was rarely practiced and even more rarely successful. Even had attempts to practice the kind of economic localism at issue here been more widespread, moreover, there

---

[3] I agree with the Court that the Camden ordinance is not insulated from scrutiny under the Privileges and Immunities Clause merely because it is a municipal ordinance rather than a state statute. . . .

[4] "The better to secure and perpetuate mutual friendship and intercourse among the people of the different States in this Union, the free inhabitants of each of these States, paupers, vagabonds and fugitives from justice excepted, shall be entitled to all privileges and immunities of free citizens in the several States; and the people of each State shall have free ingress and regress to and from any other State, and shall enjoy therein all the privileges of trade and commerce, subject to the same duties, impositions and restrictions as the inhabitants thereof respectively. . . ." Articles of Confederation, Art. 4, 1 Stat. 4.

is little reason to believe that the Framers would have devoted their limited institutional resources to bringing such conduct within the ambit of the Privileges and Immunities Clause. . . . [T]he Framers had every reason to believe that intrastate discrimination based on municipal residence could and would be dealt with by the States themselves in those instances where it persisted.

In light of the historical context in which the Privileges and Immunities Clause was adopted, it hardly is surprising that none of this Court's intervening decisions has suggested that the Clause applies to discrimination on the basis of municipal residence. . . . The Court's decision clashes with other Privileges and Immunities Clause precedents as well. The Court recognizes, as it must, that the Privileges and Immunities Clause does not afford state residents any protection against their own State's laws. When this settled rule is combined with the Court's newly fashioned rule concerning municipal discrimination, however, it has the perverse effect of vesting non-New Jersey residents with constitutional privileges that are not enjoyed by most New Jersey residents themselves. This result is directly contrary to the Court's longstanding position that the Privileges and Immunities Clause does not give nonresidents "higher and greater privileges than are enjoyed by the citizens of the state itself." . . .

Finally, the Court fails to attend to the functional considerations that underlie the Privileges and Immunities Clause. The Clause has been a necessary limitation on state autonomy not simply because of the self-interest of individual States, but because state parochialism is likely to go unchecked by state political processes when those who are disadvantaged are by definition disenfranchised as well. The Clause remedies this breakdown in the representative process by requiring state residents to bear the same burdens that they choose to place on nonresidents; "by constitutionally tying the fate of outsiders to the fate of those possessing political power, the framers insured that their interests would be well looked after." J. ELY, DEMOCRACY AND DISTRUST 83 (1980). As a practical matter, therefore, the scope of the Clause may be measured by asking whether failure to link the interests of those who are disadvantaged with the interests of those who are preferred will consign the former group to "the uncertain remedies afforded by diplomatic processes and official retaliation."

Contrary to the Court's tacit assumption, discrimination on the basis of municipal residence is substantially different in this regard from discrimination on the basis of state citizenship. The distinction is simple but fundamental: discrimination on the basis of municipal residence penalizes persons within the State's political community as well as those without. The Court itself points out that while New Jersey citizens who reside outside Camden are not protected by the Privileges and Immunities Clause, they may resort to the State's political processes to protect themselves. What the Court fails to appreciate is that this avenue of relief for New Jersey residents works to protect residents of other States as well; disadvantaged state residents who turn to the state legislature to displace ordinances like Camden's further the interests of nonresidents as well as their own. Nor is this mechanism for relief merely a theoretical one; in the past decade several States, including California and Georgia, have repealed or forbidden protectionist ordinances like the one at issue here. In short, discrimination on the basis of municipal residence simply does not consign residents of other States to "the uncertain remedies afforded by diplomatic processes and official retaliation." The Court thus has applied the Privileges and Immunities Clause without regard for the political ills that it was designed to cure. . . .

II

. . . [T]he issue before us is not the desirability of the ordinance but its constitutionality . . . under the Privileges and Immunities Clause.[16] Because I believe that the Clause does not apply to discrimination based on municipal residence, I dissent.

Metropolitan Life Ins. Co. v. Ward

470 U.S. 869 (1985)

■ JUSTICE POWELL delivered the opinion of the Court.

This case presents the question whether Alabama's domestic preference tax statute, that taxes out-of-state insurance companies at a higher rate than domestic insurance companies, violates the Equal Protection Clause.

I

Since 1955, the State of Alabama has granted a preference to its domestic insurance companies by imposing a substantially lower gross premiums tax rate on them than on out-of-state (foreign) companies.[2] Under the current statutory provisions, foreign life insurance companies pay a tax on their gross premiums received from business conducted in Alabama at a rate of three percent, and foreign companies selling other types of insurance pay at a rate of four percent. All domestic insurance companies, in contrast, pay at a rate of only one percent on all types of insurance premiums. As a result, a foreign insurance company doing the same type and volume of business in Alabama as a domestic company generally will pay three to four times as much in gross premiums taxes as its domestic competitor.

---

[16] I argued without success last Term that, absent congressional authorization, ordinances like Camden's violate the dormant Commerce Clause. *White v. Massachusetts Council of Construction Employers, Inc.,* 460 U.S. 204 (1983).

[2] For domestic preference tax purposes, Alabama defines a domestic insurer as a company that both is incorporated in Alabama and has its principal office and chief place of business within the State. A corporation that does not meet both of these criteria is characterized as a foreign insurer.

Alabama's domestic preference tax statute does provide that foreign companies may reduce the differential in gross premiums taxes by investing prescribed percentages of their worldwide assets in specified Alabama assets and securities. By investing 10 percent or more of its total assets in Alabama investments, for example, a foreign life insurer may reduce its gross premiums tax rate from 3 to 2 percent. Similarly, a foreign property and casualty insurer may reduce its tax rate from four to three percent. Smaller tax reductions are available based on investment of smaller percentages of a company's assets. Regardless of how much of its total assets a foreign company places in Alabama investments, it can never reduce its gross premiums tax rate to the same level paid by comparable domestic companies. These are entitled to the one-percent tax rate even if they have no investments in the State. Thus, the investment provision permits foreign insurance companies to reduce, but never to eliminate, the discrimination inherent in the domestic preference tax statute.

II

Appellants, a group of insurance companies incorporated outside of the State of Alabama, filed claims with the Alabama Department of Insurance . . . contending that the domestic preference tax statute, as applied to them, violated the Equal Protection Clause. . . . The Commissioner of Insurance denied all of their claims. . . .

Appellants appealed to the Circuit Court for Montgomery County . . . [which held] that the Alabama statute did not violate the Equal Protection Clause because it served "at least two purposes, in addition to raising revenue: (1) encouraging the formation of new insurance companies in Alabama, and (2) encouraging capital investment by foreign insurance companies in the Alabama assets and governmental securities set forth in the statute." The court also found that the distinction the statute created between foreign and domestic companies was rationally related to those two purposes. . . . We now reverse.

III

. . . Because appellants waived their right to an evidentiary hearing on the issue whether the classification in the Alabama domestic preference tax statute bears a rational relation to the two purposes upheld by the Circuit Court, the only question before us is whether those purposes are legitimate.

A

(1)

The first of the purposes found by the trial court to be a legitimate reason for the statute's classification between foreign and domestic corporations is that it encourages the formation of new domestic insurance companies in Alabama. . . . Alabama asks us to approve its purpose of promoting the business of its domestic insurers *in Alabama* by penalizing foreign insurers who also want to do business in the

State. . . . Alabama's aim to promote domestic industry is purely and completely discriminatory, designed only to favor domestic industry within the State, no matter what the cost to foreign corporations also seeking to do business there. Alabama's purpose constitutes the very sort of parochial discrimination that the Equal Protection Clause was intended to prevent. . . . [T]his Court always has held that the Equal Protection Clause forbids a State to discriminate in favor of its own residents solely by burdening "the residents of other state members of our federation." Unlike [a] retaliatory tax . . . which only burdens residents of a State that imposes its own discriminatory tax on outsiders, the domestic preference tax gives the "home team" an advantage by burdening *all* foreign corporations seeking to do business within the State, no matter what they or their States do.

The validity of the view that a State may not constitutionally favor its own residents by taxing foreign corporations at a higher rate solely because of their residence is confirmed by a long line of this Court's cases so holding. As the Court stated . . . with respect to general tax burdens on business, "the foreign corporation stands equal, and is to be classified with domestic corporations of the same kind." In all of these cases, the discriminatory tax was imposed by the State on foreign corporations doing business within the State solely because of their residence, presumably to promote domestic industry within the State. . . .

(2)

The State argues nonetheless that it is impermissible to view a discriminatory tax such as the one at issue here as violative of the Equal Protection Clause. This approach, it contends, amounts to no more than "Commerce Clause rhetoric in equal protection clothing." The State maintains that because Congress, in enacting the McCarran-Ferguson Act, intended to authorize States to impose taxes that burden interstate commerce in the insurance field, the tax at issue here must stand. Our concerns are much more fundamental than as characterized by the State. Although the McCarran-Ferguson Act exempts the insurance industry from Commerce Clause restrictions, it does not purport to limit in any way the applicability of the Equal Protection Clause. [O]ur opinion in *Western & Southern* expressly reaffirmed the viability of equal protection restraints on discriminatory taxes in the insurance context.

Moreover, the State's view ignores the differences between Commerce Clause and equal protection analysis and the consequent different purposes those two constitutional provisions serve. Under Commerce Clause analysis, the State's interest, if legitimate, is weighed against the burden the state law would impose on interstate commerce. In the equal protection context, however, if the State's purpose is found to be legitimate, the state law stands as long as the burden it imposes is found to be rationally related to that purpose, a relationship that is not difficult to establish.

The two constitutional provisions perform different functions in the analysis of the permissible scope of a State's power—one protects interstate commerce, and the other protects persons[9] from unconstitutional discrimination by the States. The effect of the statute at issue here is to place a discriminatory tax burden on foreign insurers who desire to do business within the State, thereby also incidentally placing a burden on interstate commerce. Equal protection restraints are applicable even though the *effect* of the discrimination in this case is similar to the type of burden with which the Commerce Clause also would be concerned. We reaffirmed the importance of the Equal Protection Clause in the insurance context . . . and see no reason now for reassessing that view.

In whatever light the State's position is cast, acceptance of its contention that promotion of domestic industry is always a legitimate state purpose under equal protection analysis would eviscerate the Equal Protection Clause in this context. A State's natural inclination frequently would be to prefer domestic business over foreign. If we accept the State's view here, then any discriminatory tax would be valid if the State could show it reasonably was intended to benefit domestic business.[10] A discriminatory tax would stand or fall depending primarily on how a State framed its purpose—as benefiting one group or as harming another. This is a distinction without a difference. . . . We hold that under the circumstances of this case, promotion of domestic business by discriminating against nonresident competitors is not a legitimate state purpose.

B

The second purpose found by the courts below to be legitimate was the encouragement of capital investment in the Alabama assets and governmental securities specified in the statute. We do not agree that this is a legitimate state purpose when furthered by discrimination. Domestic insurers remain entitled to the more favorable rate of tax regardless of whether they invest in Alabama assets. Moreover, the investment incentive provision of the Alabama statute does not enable foreign insurance companies to eliminate the discriminatory effect of the statute. No matter how much of their assets they invest in Alabama, foreign insurance companies are still required to pay a higher gross premiums tax than domestic companies. The State's investment incentive provision therefore does not cure, but reaffirms, the statute's impermissible classification based solely on residence. We hold that

---

[9] It is well established that a corporation is a "person" within the meaning of the Fourteenth Amendment.

[10] Indeed, under the State's analysis, *any* discrimination subject to the rational relation level of scrutiny could be justified simply on the ground that it favored one group at the expense of another. This case does not involve or question, as the dissent suggests, the broad authority of a State to promote and regulate its own economy. We hold only that such regulation may not be accomplished by imposing discriminatorily higher taxes on nonresident corporations solely because they are nonresidents.

encouraging investment in Alabama assets and securities in this plainly discriminatory manner serves no legitimate state purpose.

IV

We conclude that neither of the two purposes furthered by the Alabama domestic preference tax statute . . . is legitimate under the Equal Protection Clause to justify the imposition of the discriminatory tax at issue here. The judgment of the Alabama Supreme Court accordingly is reversed, and the case is remanded for further proceedings not inconsistent with this opinion.

■ JUSTICE O'CONNOR, with whom JUSTICE BRENNAN, JUSTICE MARSHALL, and JUSTICE REHNQUIST join, dissenting.

This case presents a simple question: Is it legitimate for a State to use its taxing power to promote a domestic insurance industry and to encourage capital investment within its borders? In a holding that can only be characterized as astonishing, the Court determines that these purposes are illegitimate. This holding is unsupported by precedent and subtly distorts the constitutional balance, threatening the freedom of both state and federal legislative bodies to fashion appropriate classifications in economic legislation. Because I disagree with both the Court's method of analysis and its conclusion, I respectfully dissent.

I

. . . Appellants rely on the Equal Protection Clause because, as corporations, they are not "citizens" protected by the Privileges and Immunities Clauses of the Constitution. Similarly, they cannot claim Commerce Clause protection because Congress in the McCarran-Ferguson Act explicitly suspended Commerce Clause restraints on state taxation of insurance and placed insurance regulation firmly within the purview of the several States.

Our precedents impose a heavy burden on those who challenge local economic regulation solely on Equal Protection Clause grounds. In this context, our long-established jurisprudence requires us to defer to a legislature's judgment if the classification is rationally related to a legitimate state purpose. Yet the Court evades this careful framework for analysis, melding the proper two-step inquiry regarding the State's purpose and the classification's relationship to that purpose into a single unarticulated judgment. This tactic enables the Court to characterize state goals that have been legitimated by Congress itself as improper solely because it disagrees with the concededly rational means of differential taxation selected by the legislature. This unorthodox approach leads to further error. The Court gives only the most cursory attention to the factual and legal bases supporting the State's purposes and ignores both precedent and significant evidence in the record establishing their legitimacy. Most troubling, the Court discovers in the Equal Protection Clause an implied prohibition against classifications whose purpose is to give the "home team" an advantage over interstate competitors even where Congress has authorized such advantages.

The Court overlooks the unequivocal language of our prior decisions. "Unless a classification trammels fundamental personal rights or is drawn upon inherently suspect distinctions such as race, religion, or alienage, our decisions presume the constitutionality of the statutory discriminations and require only that the classification challenged be rationally related to a legitimate state interest." *New Orleans v. Dukes*, 427 U.S. 297, 303 (1976). Judicial deference is strongest where a tax classification is alleged to infringe the right to equal protection. "[In] taxation, even more than in other fields, legislatures possess the greatest freedom in classification." "Where the public interest is served one business may be left untaxed and another taxed, in order to promote the one or to restrict or suppress the other." As the Court emphatically noted in *Allied Stores of Ohio, Inc. v. Bowers*, 358 U.S. 522 (1959):

> [It] has repeatedly been held and appears to be entirely settled that a statute which encourages the location within the State of needed and useful industries by exempting them, though not also others, from its taxes is not arbitrary and does not violate the Equal Protection Clause of the Fourteenth Amendment. Similarly, it has long been settled that a classification, though discriminatory, is not arbitrary or violative of the Equal Protection Clause of the Fourteenth Amendment if any state of facts reasonably can be conceived that would sustain it.

Appellants waived their right to an evidentiary hearing and conceded that Alabama's classification was rationally related to its purposes of encouraging the formation of domestic insurance companies and bringing needed services and capital to the State. Thus the only issue in dispute is the legitimacy of these purposes. Yet it is obviously legitimate for a State to seek to promote local business and attract capital investment, and surely those purposes animate a wide range of legislation in all 50 States. . . .

Appellees claim that Alabama's insurance tax, in addition to raising revenue and promoting investment, promotes the formation of new domestic insurance companies and enables them to compete with the many large multistate insurers that currently occupy some 75% to 85% of the Alabama insurance market. Economic studies submitted by the State document differences between the two classes of insurers that are directly relevant to the well-being of Alabama's citizens. Foreign insurers typically concentrate on affluent, high volume, urban markets and offer standardized national policies. In contrast, domestic insurers such as intervenors American Educators Life Insurance Company and Booker T. Washington Life Insurance Company are more likely to serve Alabama's rural areas, and to write low-cost industrial and burial policies not offered by the larger national companies.[1] Additionally, appellees argue persuasively that Alabama can more readily regulate domestic insurers and more effectively safeguard their solvency than that of insurers domiciled and having their principal places of business in other States.

Ignoring these policy considerations, the Court insists that Alabama seeks only to benefit local business, a purpose the Court labels invidious. Yet if the classification chosen by the State can be shown *actually* to promote the public welfare, this is strong evidence of a legitimate state purpose. . . .

II

The policy of favoring local concerns in state regulation and taxation of insurance, which the majority condemns as illegitimate, is not merely a recent invention of the States. The States initiated regulation of the business of insurance as early as 1851. In 1944, however, this Court overruled a long line of cases holding that the business of insurance was an intrastate activity beyond the scope of the Commerce Clause. "The decision provoked widespread concern that the States would no longer be able to engage in taxation and effective regulation of the insurance industry. Congress moved quickly, enacting the McCarran-Ferguson Act within a year of the decision . . . ."

The drafters of the Act were sensitive to the same concerns Alabama now vainly seeks to bring to this Court's attention: the greater responsiveness of local insurance companies to local conditions, the different insurance needs of rural and industrial States, the special advantages and constraints of state-by-state regulation, and the importance of insurance license fees and taxes as a major source of state revenues. "As this Court observed shortly afterward, '[obviously] Congress' purpose was broadly to give support to the existing and future state systems for regulating and taxing the business of insurance.' " . . .

The majority opinion correctly notes that Congress did not intend the McCarran-Ferguson Act to give the States any power to tax or regulate the insurance industry other than they already possessed. But the . . . Court fails to mention that at the time the Act was under consideration the taxing schemes of Alabama, Arizona, Arkansas, Illinois, Kansas, Kentucky, Maine, Michigan, Mississippi, Ohio, Oklahoma, Oregon, South Dakota, Tennessee, Texas, Washington, and Wisconsin all incorporated tax differentials favoring domestic insurers. . . .

The contemporary realities of insurance regulation and taxation continue to justify a uniquely local perspective. Insurance regulation and

---

[1] "Industrial insurance" is the trade term for a low face-value policy typically sold door-to-door and maintained through home collection of monthly or weekly premiums. Alabama currently has more industrial insurance in force than any other State. Burial insurance is another form of insurance popular in rural Alabama that is offered exclusively by local insurers. By contrast, Metropolitan Life, like many multistate insurers, has discontinued writing even whole-life policies with face values below $15,000.

taxation must serve local social policies including assuring the solvency and reliability of companies doing business in the State and providing special protection for those who might be denied insurance in a free market, such as the urban poor, small businesses, and family farms. . . .

State insurance commissions vary widely in manpower and expertise. In practice, the State of incorporation exercises primary oversight of the solvency of its insurers. Even the State of incorporation's efforts to regulate a multistate insurer may be seriously hampered by the difficulty of gaining access to records and assets in 49 other States. Thus the security of Alabama's citizens who purchase insurance from out-of-state companies may depend in part on the diligence of another State's insurance commissioner, over whom Alabama has no authority and limited influence. In the event of financial failure of a foreign insurer the State may have difficulty levying on out-of-state assets. . . .

Many have sharply criticized this piecemeal system, but Congress has resisted suggestions that it modify the McCarran-Ferguson Act to permit greater federal intervention. This Court cannot ignore the exigencies of contemporary insurance regulation outlined above simply because it might prefer uniform federal regulation. Given the distinctions in ease of regulation and services rendered by foreign and domestic insurers, we cannot dismiss as illegitimate the State's goal of promoting a healthy local insurance industry sensitive to regional differences and composed of companies that agree to subordinate themselves to the Alabama Commissioner's control and to maintain a principal place of business within Alabama's borders. . . .

III

Despite abundant evidence of a legitimate state purpose, the majority condemns Alabama's tax as "purely and completely discriminatory" and "the very sort of parochial discrimination that the Equal Protection Clause was intended to prevent." Apparently, the majority views any favoritism of domestic commercial entities as inherently suspect. The majority ignores a long line of our decisions. In the past this Court has not hesitated to apply the rational basis test to regulatory classifications that distinguish between domestic and out-of-state corporations or burden foreign interests to protect local concerns. The Court has always recognized that there are certain legitimate restrictions or policies in which, "[by] definition, discrimination against nonresidents would inhere." For example, where State of incorporation or principal place of business affect the State's ability to regulate or exercise its jurisdiction, a State may validly discriminate between foreign and domestic entities. . . .

The majority's attempts to distinguish these precedents are unconvincing. First the majority suggests that a state purpose might be legitimate for purposes of the Commerce Clause but somehow illegitimate for purposes of the Equal Protection Clause. No basis is advanced for this theory because no basis exists. . . .

IV

Because Alabama's classification bears a rational relationship to a legitimate purpose, our precedents demand that it be sustained. . . . Instead the Court engrafts its own economic values on the Equal Protection Clause. Beyond guarding against arbitrary or irrational discrimination, as interpreted by the Court today this Clause now prohibits the effectuation of economic policies, even where sanctioned by Congress, that elevate local concerns over interstate competition. "But a constitution is not intended to embody a particular economic theory. . . . It is made for people of fundamentally differing views." *Lochner v. New York* (Holmes, J., dissenting). In the heyday of economic due process, Justice Holmes warned:

> Courts should be careful not to extend [the express] prohibitions [of the Constitution] beyond their obvious meaning by reading into them conceptions of public policy that the particular Court may happen to entertain.

Ignoring the wisdom of this observation, the Court fashions its own brand of economic equal protection. In so doing, it supplants a legislative policy endorsed by both Congress and the individual States that explicitly sanctioned the very parochialism in regulation and taxation of insurance that the Court's decision holds illegitimate. . . .

V

Today's opinion charts an ominous course. I can only hope this unfortunate adventure away from the safety of our precedents will be an isolated episode. . . . I respectfully dissent.

NOTE ON THE LITIGANT'S TOOLKIT IN CHALLENGES TO STATE ECONOMIC REGULATION

1. The first case recognizing the market participant doctrine, *Hughes v. Alexandria Scrap Corp.*, 426 U.S. 794 (1976), was decided on the same day as *National League of Cities v. Usery*. Do you see a connection between *National League of Cities*' protection for the traditional governmental functions of state governments and the market participant doctrine? Does the Court's effort to parse *Alexandria Scrap* and its subsequent cases—e.g., *Reeves, White*—suggest that the market participant doctrine is comparably difficult to define and enforce in a principled way?

2. In *South-Central Timber*, Justice White states that "state restrictions burdening foreign commerce are subjected to a more rigorous and searching scrutiny. It is crucial to the efficient execution of the Nation's foreign policy that 'the Federal Government . . . speak with one voice when regulating commercial relations with foreign governments.'" What form would such "more rigorous and searching scrutiny" take? (What's "stricter" than strict scrutiny, which already applies to discriminatory legislation? Or is the suggestion that there should either be (a) strict scrutiny for *neutral* state legislation that burdens foreign commerce as in *Kassel*, or (b) no market

participant defense at all in foreign commerce cases?) In a world of globalizing economic relationships, how practicable is it to distinguish between domestic and international commerce? Would this be similar to trying to distinguish between intrastate and interstate commerce? Justice Breyer's dissent in *Lopez*, after all, demonstrated that bringing a gun to school impacts not only the interstate economy but the *international* one as well.

3. Recall that in *Corfield v. Coryell*, 6 F. Cas. 546, 551–52 (1823), Justice Bushrod Washington offered a compendious definition of the privileges and immunities of state citizenship:

> We feel no hesitation in confining these expressions to those privileges and immunities which are fundamental; which belong of right to the citizens of all free governments, and which have at all times been enjoyed by citizens of the several States which compose this Union, from the time of their becoming free, independent, and sovereign. What these fundamental principles are, it would be more tedious than difficult to enumerate. They may all, however, be comprehended under the following general heads: protection by the government, with the right to acquire and possess property of every kind, and to pursue and obtain happiness and safety, subject, nevertheless, to such restraints as the government may prescribe for the general good of the whole.

We have relatively few cases fleshing this out. In *Supreme Court of New Hampshire v. Piper*, 470 U.S. 274 (1985), the Court struck down a New Hampshire law that restricted bar admission to local residents. It held that practicing law is a "privilege" because of the lawyer's role in the national economy and the noncommercial role in representing persons with unpopular federal claims. Privileges and immunities also come up in the right to travel cases. These cases are frequently decided on equal protection grounds, but in *Edwards v. California*, 314 U.S. 160 (1941), some concurring justices suggested that privileges and immunities might be a sounder basis. What other rights should be included?

4. What are the advantages and disadvantages, from a litigant's standpoint, of pleading a challenge to state regulation that discriminates against out-of-staters under the Commerce Clause, the Privileges and Immunities Clause, and the Equal Protection Clause, respectively? Consider, by way of example, the following situations:

a. An out-of-state student at a public university challenging preferential tuition rates for in-state students.

b. An out-of-state bank challenging favorable treatment for in-state banks, arguably authorized by federal banking legislation.

c. An out-of-state funeral home company challenging state legislation restricting mortuary licenses to companies incorporated within the state.

5. As we finish our survey of the dormant Commerce Clause, it is worth stopping to ask whether this entire area of law can be justified. One

might argue that it cannot on at least two grounds. First, the same "political safeguards" arguments against judicial review in federalism cases seeking to limit national power might be made against dormant Commerce Clause review. Second, one might simply think that the dormant Commerce clause doctrine has proven unworkable. Justice Scalia has said that "to the extent that we have gone beyond guarding against rank discrimination against citizens of other states . . . the Court for over a century has engaged in an enterprise that it has been unable to justify by textual support or even coherent nontextual theory, that it was almost certainly not intended to undertake, and that it has not undertaken very well."[10] More recently, in *Camps Newfound/Owatonna v. Town of Harrison*, 520 U.S. 564 (1997), Justice Thomas called for abolishing the dormant Commerce Clause doctrine altogether. Would that be a good thing?

SECTION 11.3   FEDERAL PREEMPTION OF STATE LAW

The most important constraint on state authority is not the "dormant" preemptive effect of Congress's unexercised authority, but rather the preemptive effective of the laws that Congress actually enacts. After 1937, federal and state regulatory authority is largely concurrent— most subjects are within the reach of both federal and state legislation. Since federal legislation is supreme in the event of a conflict, the bounds of permissible state regulation are defined largely by the actual scope of federal legislation and the extent to which that legislation is intended to foreclose state measures.

In assessing this dynamic, it may help to begin with a summary of the relationship between state and federal law included in an influential textbook published in 1953:

> Federal law is generally interstitial in its nature. It rarely occupies a legal field completely, totally excluding all participation by the legal systems of the states. This was plainly true in the beginning when the federal legislative product (including the Constitution) was extremely small. It is significantly true today, despite the volume of Congressional enactments, and even within areas where Congress has been very active. Federal legislation, on the whole, has been conceived and drafted on an *ad hoc* basis to accomplish limited objectives. It builds upon legal relationships established by the states, altering or supplanting them only so far as necessary for the special purpose. Congress acts, in short, against the background of the total *corpus juris* of the states in much the same way that a state legislature acts against the background

---

[10]   *Tyler Pipe Indus., Inc. v. Washington State Dept. of Revenue*, 483 U.S. 232, 265 (1987) (Scalia, J., concurring in part and dissenting in part).

of the common law, assumed to govern unless changed by legislation.[11]

This description summarizes the state of affairs after the New Deal, but before the Civil Rights revolution and Lyndon Johnson's "Great Society." The current edition of the same textbook offers the following caveat:

> In the fifty years since the First Edition was published, the expansion of federal legislation and administrative regulation . . . has accelerated; today one finds many more instances in which federal enactments . . . wholly occupy a particular field. . . . Thus, at present federal law appears to be more primary than interstitial in numerous areas. Nonetheless, consider . . . whether the First Edition's thesis does not remain accurate over an extremely broad range of applications.[12]

This way of thinking about the relationship between state and federal law has a number of important implications (many of which are played out in the upper level course in Federal Courts), but two are critical for present purposes. The first is that the boundary between state and federal authority is defined largely by the terms of federal statutes—not by the Constitution itself. And the second is that the location of this boundary changes over time as Congress enacts (and sometimes repeals) federal laws. Preemption—the subject of this section—represents the impact on state law of these changes.

Preemption is a constitutional issue to the extent that a state law that conflicts with federal legislation is unconstitutional under the Supremacy Clause. But the difficult questions in preemption cases tend to focus on the interpretation of the federal and state legislation at issue. These cases thus focus on issues of statutory construction, much like the "clear statement" cases in the previous chapter. The cases that follow should give you some sense of the complexity of the statutory schemes at issue in modern preemption litigation, as well as the practical importance of the policy issues at stake.

Pacific Gas & Electric Co. v. State Energy Resources Conservation & Development Comm'n

461 U.S. 190 (1983)

■ JUSTICE WHITE delivered the opinion of the Court.

The turning of swords into plowshares has symbolized the transformation of atomic power into a source of energy in American society. To facilitate this development the Federal Government relaxed

---

[11] HENRY M. HART, JR. & HERBERT WECHSLER, THE FEDERAL COURTS AND THE FEDERAL SYSTEM (1st ed. 1953); see also Henry M. Hart, Jr., The Relations Between State and Federal Law, 54 COLUM. L. REV. 489 (1954).

[12] RICHARD H. FALLON, JR., JOHN F. MANNING, DANIEL J. MELTZER, & DAVID L. SHAPIRO, HART AND WECHSLER'S THE FEDERAL COURTS AND THE FEDERAL SYSTEM 459–60 (6th ed. 2009).

its monopoly over fissionable materials and nuclear technology, and in its place, erected a complex scheme to promote the civilian development of nuclear energy, while seeking to safeguard the public and the environment from the unpredictable risks of a new technology. Early on, it was decided that the States would continue their traditional role in the regulation of electricity production. The interrelationship of federal and state authority in the nuclear energy field has not been simple; the federal regulatory structure has been frequently amended to optimize the partnership.

This case emerges from the intersection of the Federal Government's efforts to ensure that nuclear power is safe with the exercise of the historic state authority over the generation and sale of electricity. At issue is whether provisions in the 1976 amendments to California's Warren-Alquist Act, which condition the construction of nuclear plants on findings by the State Energy Resources Conservation and Development Commission that adequate storage facilities and means of disposal are available for nuclear waste, are pre-empted by the Atomic Energy Act of 1954.

I

A nuclear reactor must be periodically refueled and the "spent fuel" removed. This spent fuel is intensely radioactive and must be carefully stored. The general practice is to store the fuel in a water-filled pool at the reactor site. For many years, it was assumed that this fuel would be reprocessed. . . . As expectations for reprocessing remained unfulfilled, the spent fuel accumulated in the storage pools, creating the risk that nuclear reactors would have to be shut down. . . . Government studies indicate that a number of reactors could be forced to shut down in the near future due to the inability to store spent fuel. . . .

[P]ermanent disposal is needed because the wastes will remain radioactive for thousands of years. . . . Problems of how and where to store nuclear wastes has engendered considerable scientific, political, and public debate. There are both safety and economic aspects to the nuclear waste issue: first, if not properly stored, nuclear wastes might leak and endanger both the environment and human health; second, the lack of a long-term disposal option increases the risk that the insufficiency of interim storage space for spent fuel will lead to reactor shutdowns, rendering nuclear energy an unpredictable and uneconomical adventure.

The California laws at issue here are responses to these concerns. In 1974, California adopted the Warren-Alquist State Energy Resources Conservation and Development Act. The Act requires that a utility seeking to build in California any electric power generating plant, including a nuclear powerplant, must apply for certification to the State Energy Resources Conservation and Development Commission. The Warren-Alquist Act was amended in 1976 to provide additional state regulation of new nuclear powerplant construction.

Two sections of these amendments are before us. Section 25524.1(b) provides that before additional nuclear plants may be built, the Energy Commission must determine on a case-by-case basis that there will be "adequate capacity" for storage of a plant's spent fuel rods "at the time such nuclear facility requires such . . . storage." The law also requires that each utility provide continuous, on-site, "full core reserve storage capacity" in order to permit storage of the entire reactor core if it must be removed to permit repairs of the reactor. In short, § 25524.1(b) addresses the interim storage of spent fuel.

Section 25524.2 deals with the long-term solution to nuclear wastes. This section imposes a moratorium on the certification of new nuclear plants until the Energy Commission "finds that there has been developed and that the United States through its authorized agency has approved and there exists a demonstrated technology or means for the disposal of high-level nuclear waste." "Disposal" is defined as a "method for the permanent and terminal disposition of high-level nuclear waste. . . ." Such a finding must be reported to the state legislature, which may nullify it.

In 1978, petitioners Pacific Gas & Electric Co. and Southern California Edison Co. filed this action in the United States District Court, requesting a declaration that numerous provisions of the Warren-Alquist Act, including the two sections challenged here, are invalid under the Supremacy Clause because they are pre-empted by the Atomic Energy Act. The District Court held . . . that the two provisions are void because they are pre-empted by and in conflict with the Atomic Energy Act.

The Court of Appeals for the Ninth Circuit . . . held that the nuclear moratorium provisions of § 25524.2 were not pre-empted because §§ 271 and 274(k) of the Atomic Energy Act, constitute a congressional authorization for States to regulate nuclear powerplants "for purposes other than protection against radiation hazards."[11] . . .

III

It is well established that within constitutional limits Congress may pre-empt state authority by so stating in express terms. Absent explicit pre-emptive language, Congress' intent to supersede state law altogether may be found from a " 'scheme of federal regulation . . . so pervasive as to make reasonable the inference that Congress left no room for the

---

[11] Section 271 . . . provides:

Nothing in this chapter shall be construed to affect the authority or regulations of any Federal, State or local agency with respect to the generation, sale, or transmission of electric power produced through the use of nuclear facilities licensed by the Commission: *Provided*, That this section shall not be deemed to confer upon any Federal, State or local agency any authority to regulate, control, or restrict any activities of the Commission.

Section 274(k) . . . provides:

Nothing in this section shall be construed to affect the authority of any State or local agency to regulate activities for purposes other than protection against radiation hazards.

States to supplement it,' because 'the Act of Congress may touch a field in which the federal interest is so dominant that the federal system will be assumed to preclude enforcement of state laws on the same subject,' or because 'the object sought to be obtained by the federal law and the character of obligations imposed by it may reveal the same purpose.' " Even where Congress has not entirely displaced state regulation in a specific area, state law is pre-empted to the extent that it actually conflicts with federal law. Such a conflict arises when "compliance with both federal and state regulations is a physical impossibility," or where state law "stands as an obstacle to the accomplishment and execution of the full purposes and objectives of Congress."

Petitioners . . . present three major lines of argument as to why § 25524.2 is pre-empted. First, they submit that the statute—because it regulates construction of nuclear plants and because it is allegedly predicated on safety concerns—ignores the division between federal and state authority created by the Atomic Energy Act, and falls within the field that the Federal Government has preserved for its own exclusive control. Second, the statute, and the judgments that underlie it, conflict with decisions concerning the nuclear waste disposal issue made by Congress and the Nuclear Regulatory Commission. Third, the California statute frustrates the federal goal of developing nuclear technology as a source of energy. We consider each of these contentions in turn.

A

Even a brief perusal of the Atomic Energy Act reveals that, despite its comprehensiveness, it does not at any point expressly require the States to construct or authorize nuclear powerplants or prohibit the States from deciding, as an absolute or conditional matter, not to permit the construction of any further reactors. Instead, petitioners argue that the Act is intended to preserve the Federal Government as the sole regulator of all matters nuclear, and that § 25524.2 falls within the scope of this impliedly pre-empted field. But as we view the issue, Congress, in passing the 1954 Act and in subsequently amending it, intended that the Federal Government should regulate the radiological safety aspects involved in the construction and operation of a nuclear plant, but that the States retain their traditional responsibility in the field of regulating electrical utilities for determining questions of need, reliability, cost, and other related state concerns.

Need for new power facilities, their economic feasibility, and rates and services, are areas that have been characteristically governed by the States. Justice Brandeis once observed that the "franchise to operate a public utility . . . is a special privilege which . . . may be granted or withheld at the pleasure of the State." . . . With the exception of the broad authority of the Federal Power Commission, now the Federal Energy Regulatory Commission, over the need for and pricing of electrical power transmitted in interstate commerce, these economic aspects of electrical generation have been regulated for many years and in great detail by the

States. . . . Thus, "Congress legislated here in a field which the States have traditionally occupied. . . . So we start with the assumption that the historic police powers of the States were not to be superseded by the Federal Act unless that was the clear and manifest purpose of Congress." *Rice v. Santa Fe Elevator Corp.*, 331 U.S. 218 (1947).

The Atomic Energy Act must be read, however, against another background. Enrico Fermi demonstrated the first nuclear reactor in 1942, and Congress authorized civilian application of atomic power in 1946, at which time the Atomic Energy Commission (AEC) was created. Until 1954, however, the use, control, and ownership of nuclear technology remained a federal monopoly. The Atomic Energy Act of 1954 grew out of Congress' determination that the national interest would be best served if the Government encouraged the private sector to become involved in the development of atomic energy for peaceful purposes under a program of federal regulation and licensing. The Act implemented this policy decision by providing for licensing of private construction, ownership, and operation of commercial nuclear power reactors. The AEC, however, was given exclusive jurisdiction to license the transfer, delivery, receipt, acquisition, possession, and use of nuclear materials. Upon these subjects, no role was left for the States.

The Commission, however, was not given authority over the generation of electricity itself, or over the economic question whether a particular plant should be built. We observed ... that "[the] Commission's prime area of concern in the licensing context ... is national security, public health, and safety." The Nuclear Regulatory Commission (NRC), which now exercises the AEC's regulatory authority, does not purport to exercise its authority based on economic considerations, and has recently repealed its regulations concerning the financial qualifications and capabilities of a utility proposing to construct and operate a nuclear powerplant. In its notice of rule repeal, the NRC stated that utility financial qualifications are only of concern to the NRC if related to the public health and safety. It is almost inconceivable that Congress would have left a regulatory vacuum; the only reasonable inference is that Congress intended the States to continue to make these judgments. Any doubt that ratemaking and plant-need questions were to remain in state hands was removed by § 271, which provided:

> Nothing in this chapter shall be construed to affect the authority or regulations of any Federal, State or local agency with respect to the generation, sale, or transmission of electric power produced through the use of nuclear facilities licensed by the Commission.

[S]tatements on the floor of Congress confirm that while the safety of nuclear technology was the exclusive business of the Federal Government, state power over the production of electricity was not otherwise displaced.

The 1959 Amendments reinforced this fundamental division of authority. In 1959, Congress amended the Atomic Energy Act in order to "clarify the respective responsibilities ... of the States and the Commission with respect to the regulation of byproduct, source, and special nuclear materials." The authority of the States over the planning for new powerplants and ratemaking were not at issue. Indeed, the point of the 1959 Amendments was to heighten the States' role. Section 274(b) authorized the NRC, by agreements with state governors to discontinue its regulatory authority over certain nuclear materials under limited conditions.[20] State programs permitted under the amendment were required to be "coordinated and compatible" with that of the NRC. The subject matters of those agreements were also limited by § 274(c), which states

> [The] Commission shall retain authority and responsibility with respect to regulation of—
>
> (1) the construction and operation of any production or utilization facility; ...
>
> (4) the disposal of such ... byproduct, source, or special nuclear material as the Commission determines ... should, because of the hazards or potential hazards thereof, not be so disposed of without a license from the Commission.

Although the authority reserved by § 274(c) was exclusively for the Commission to exercise, Congress made clear that the section was not intended to cut back on pre-existing state authority outside the NRC's jurisdiction.[21] Section 274(k) states:

> Nothing in this section shall be construed to affect the authority of any State or local agency to regulate activities for purposes other than protection against radiation hazards.

Section 274(k), by itself, limits only the pre-emptive effect of "this section," that is, § 274, and does not represent an affirmative grant of power to the States. But Congress, by permitting regulation "for purposes other than protection against radiation hazards" underscored the distinction drawn in 1954 between the spheres of activity left respectively to the Federal Government and the States. ...

This account indicates that from the passage of the Atomic Energy Act in 1954, through several revisions, and to the present day, Congress has preserved the dual regulation of nuclear-powered electricity generation: the Federal Government maintains complete control of the safety and "nuclear" aspects of energy generation; the States exercise their traditional authority over the need for additional generating

---

[20] ... California has signed a § 274 agreement.

[21] In addition to § 274(k), § 274(*l*) created an advisory role for the States respecting activities exclusively within the NRC's jurisdiction, and § 274(g) directs the Commission to cooperate with the States even in the formulation of standards for regulation against radiation hazards.

capacity, the type of generating facilities to be licensed, land use, ratemaking, and the like.

The above is not particularly controversial. But deciding how § 25524.2 is to be construed and classified is a more difficult proposition. At the outset, we emphasize that the statute does not seek to regulate the construction or operation of a nuclear powerplant. It would clearly be impermissible for California to attempt to do so, for such regulation, even if enacted out of nonsafety concerns, would nevertheless directly conflict with the NRC's exclusive authority over plant construction and operation. Respondents appear to concede as much. Respondents do broadly argue, however, that although safety regulation of nuclear plants by States is forbidden, a State may completely prohibit new construction until its safety concerns are satisfied by the Federal Government. We reject this line of reasoning. State safety regulation is not pre-empted only when it conflicts with federal law. Rather, the Federal Government has occupied the entire field of nuclear safety concerns, except the limited powers expressly ceded to the States.[25] When the Federal Government completely occupies a given field or an identifiable portion of it, as it has done here, the test of pre-emption is whether "the matter on which the State asserts the right to act is in any way regulated by the Federal Act." A state moratorium on nuclear construction grounded in safety concerns falls squarely within the prohibited field. Moreover, a state judgment that nuclear power is not safe enough to be further developed would conflict directly with the countervailing judgment of the NRC that nuclear construction may proceed notwithstanding extant uncertainties as to waste disposal. A state prohibition on nuclear construction for safety reasons would also be in the teeth of the Atomic Energy Act's objective to insure that nuclear technology be safe enough for widespread development and use—and would be pre-empted for that reason.

That being the case, it is necessary to determine whether there is a nonsafety rationale for § 25524.2. California has maintained, and the Court of Appeals agreed, that § 25524.2 was aimed at economic problems, not radiation hazards. The California Assembly Committee on Resources, Land Use, and Energy, which proposed a package of bills including § 25524.2, reported that the waste disposal problem was "largely economic or the result of poor planning, *not* safety related." The Committee explained that the lack of a federally approved method of waste disposal created a "clog" in the nuclear fuel cycle. Storage space was limited while more nuclear wastes were continuously produced. Without a permanent means of disposal, the nuclear waste problem could become critical, leading to unpredictably high costs to contain the problem or, worse, shutdowns in reactors. "Waste disposal *safety*," the Reassessment Report notes, "is not directly addressed by the bills, which

---

[25]   In addition to the opportunity to enter into agreements with the NRC under § 274(c), Congress has specifically authorized the States to regulate radioactive air pollutants from nuclear plants, and to impose certain siting and land-use requirements for nuclear plants.

ask only that a method [of waste disposal] be chosen and accepted by the federal government." . . .

Although these specific indicia of California's intent in enacting § 25524.2 are subject to varying interpretation, there are two further reasons why we should not become embroiled in attempting to ascertain California's true motive. First, inquiry into legislative motive is often an unsatisfactory venture. What motivates one legislator to vote for a statute is not necessarily what motivates scores of others to enact it. Second, it would be particularly pointless for us to engage in such inquiry here when it is clear that the States have been allowed to retain authority over the need for electrical generating facilities easily sufficient to permit a State so inclined to halt the construction of new nuclear plants by refusing on economic grounds to issue certificates of public convenience in individual proceedings. In these circumstances, it should be up to Congress to determine whether a State has misused the authority left in its hands.

Therefore, we accept California's avowed economic purpose as the rationale for enacting § 25524.2. Accordingly, the statute lies outside the occupied field of nuclear safety regulation.

B

Petitioners' second major argument concerns federal regulation aimed at the nuclear waste disposal problem itself. It is contended that § 25524.2 conflicts with federal regulation of nuclear waste disposal, with the NRC's decision that it is permissible to continue to license reactors, notwithstanding uncertainty surrounding the waste disposal problem, and with Congress' recent passage of legislation directed at that problem.

Pursuant to its authority under the Act, the AEC, and later the NRC, promulgated extensive and detailed regulations concerning the operation of nuclear facilities and the handling of nuclear materials. The following provisions are relevant to the spent fuel and waste disposal issues in this case. To receive an NRC operating license, one must submit a safety analysis report, which includes a "radioactive waste handling [system]." The regulations specify general design criteria and control requirements for fuel storage and handling and radioactive waste to be stored at the reactor site. In addition, the NRC has promulgated detailed regulations governing storage and disposal away from the reactor. NRC has also promulgated procedural requirements covering license applications for disposal of high-level radioactive waste in geologic repositories.

Congress gave the Department of Energy the responsibility for "the establishment of temporary and permanent facilities for storage, management, and ultimate disposal of nuclear wastes." No such permanent disposal facilities have yet been licensed, and the NRC and the Department of Energy continue to authorize the storage of spent fuel at reactor sites in pools of water. In 1977, the NRC was asked by the Natural Resources Defense Council to halt reactor licensing until it had determined that there was a method of permanent disposal for high-level waste. The NRC concluded that, given the progress toward the development of disposal facilities and the availability of interim storage, it could continue to license new reactors.

The NRC's imprimatur, however, indicates only that it is safe to proceed with such plants, not that it is economically wise to do so. Because the NRC order does not and could not compel a utility to develop a nuclear plant, compliance with both it and § 25524.2 is possible. Moreover, because the NRC's regulations are aimed at insuring that plants are safe, not necessarily that they are economical, § 25524.2 does not interfere with the objective of the federal regulation.

Nor has California sought through § 25524.2 to impose its own standards on nuclear waste disposal. The statute accepts that it is the federal responsibility to develop and license such technology. As there is no attempt on California's part to enter this field, one which is occupied by the Federal Government, we do not find § 25524.2 pre-empted any more by the NRC's obligations in the waste disposal field than by its licensing power over the plants themselves. . . .

C

Finally, it is strongly contended that § 25524.2 frustrates the Atomic Energy Act's purpose to develop the commercial use of nuclear power. It is well established that state law is pre-empted if it "stands as an obstacle to the accomplishment and execution of the full purposes and objectives of Congress."

There is little doubt that a primary purpose of the Atomic Energy Act was, and continues to be, the promotion of nuclear power. The Act itself states that it is a program "to encourage widespread participation in the development and utilization of atomic energy for peaceful purposes to the maximum extent consistent with the common defense and security and with the health and safety of the public." . . .

The Court of Appeals is right, however, that the promotion of nuclear power is not to be accomplished "at all costs." The elaborate licensing and safety provisions and the continued preservation of state regulation in traditional areas belie that. Moreover, Congress has allowed the States to determine—as a matter of economics—whether a nuclear plant vis-a-vis a fossil fuel plant should be built. The decision of California to exercise that authority does not, in itself, constitute a basis for pre-emption. Therefore, while the argument of petitioners and the United States has considerable force, the legal reality remains that Congress has left sufficient authority in the States to allow the development of nuclear power to be slowed or even stopped for economic reasons. Given this statutory scheme, it is for Congress to rethink the division of regulatory authority in light of its possible exercise by the States to undercut a federal objective. The courts should not assume the role which our system assigns to Congress.

IV

The judgment of the Court of Appeals is *Affirmed*.

■ JUSTICE BLACKMUN, with whom JUSTICE STEVENS joins, concurring in part and concurring in the judgment.

I join the Court's opinion, except to the extent it suggests that a State may not prohibit the construction of nuclear powerplants if the State is motivated by concerns about the safety of such plants. . . . The Atomic Energy Act's twin goals were to promote the development of a technology and to ensure the safety of that technology. Although that Act reserves to the NRC decisions about how to build and operate nuclear plants, the Court reads too much into the Act in suggesting that it also limits the States' traditional power to decide what types of electric power to utilize. . . . In my view, a ban on construction of nuclear powerplants would be valid even if its authors were motivated by fear of a core meltdown or other nuclear catastrophe.

Lorillard Tobacco Co. v. Reilly

533 U.S. 525 (2001)

■ JUSTICE O'CONNOR delivered the opinion of the Court.

In January 1999, the Attorney General of Massachusetts promulgated comprehensive regulations governing the advertising and sale of cigarettes, smokeless tobacco, and cigars. Petitioners, a group of cigarette, smokeless tobacco, and cigar manufacturers and retailers, filed suit in Federal District Court claiming that the regulations violate federal law and the United States Constitution. In large measure, the District Court determined that the regulations are valid and enforceable. The United States Court of Appeals for the First Circuit affirmed in part and reversed in part, concluding that the regulations are not pre-empted by federal law and do not violate the First Amendment. The first question presented for our review is whether certain cigarette advertising regulations are pre-empted by the Federal Cigarette Labeling and Advertising Act (FCLAA). The second question presented is whether certain regulations governing the advertising and sale of tobacco products violate the First Amendment.

I

In November 1998, Massachusetts, along with over 40 other States, reached a landmark agreement with major manufacturers in the cigarette industry. The signatory States settled their claims against these companies in exchange for monetary payments and permanent injunctive relief. At the press conference covering Massachusetts' decision to sign the agreement, then-Attorney General Scott Harshbarger announced that as one of his last acts in office, he would create consumer protection regulations to restrict advertising and sales practices for tobacco products. He explained that the regulations were necessary in order to "close holes" in the settlement agreement and "to stop Big Tobacco from recruiting new customers among the children of Massachusetts."

In January 1999, pursuant to his authority to prevent unfair or deceptive practices in trade, the Massachusetts Attorney General promulgated regulations governing the sale and advertisement of cigarettes, smokeless tobacco, and cigars. The purpose of the cigarette and smokeless tobacco regulations is "to eliminate deception and unfairness in the way cigarettes and smokeless tobacco products are marketed, sold and distributed in Massachusetts in order to address the incidence of cigarette smoking and smokeless tobacco use by children under legal age. . . [and] in order to prevent access to such products by underage consumers." The similar purpose of the cigar regulations is "to eliminate deception and unfairness in the way cigars and little cigars are packaged, marketed, sold and distributed in Massachusetts [so that] . . . consumers may be adequately informed about the health risks associated with cigar smoking, its addictive properties, and the false perception that cigars are a safe alternative to cigarettes . . . [and so that] the incidence of cigar use by children under legal age is addressed . . . in order to prevent access to such products by underage consumers." The regulations have a broader scope than the master settlement agreement, reaching advertising, sales practices, and members of the tobacco industry not covered by the agreement. The regulations place a variety of restrictions on outdoor advertising, point-of-sale advertising, retail sales transactions, transactions by mail, promotions, sampling of products, and labels for cigars.

The cigarette and smokeless tobacco regulations being challenged before this Court provide:

> (2) Retail Outlet Sales Practices. Except as otherwise provided in [§ 21.04(4)], it shall be an unfair or deceptive act or practice for any person who sells or distributes cigarettes or smokeless tobacco products through a retail outlet located within Massachusetts to engage in any of the following retail outlet sales practices: . . .

> (c) Using self-service displays of cigarettes or smokeless tobacco products;

> (d) Failing to place cigarettes and smokeless tobacco products out of the reach of all consumers, and in a location accessible only to outlet personnel.

> (5) Advertising Restrictions. Except as provided in [§ 21.04(6)], it shall be an unfair or deceptive act or practice for any manufacturer, distributor or retailer to engage in any of the following practices:

> (a) Outdoor advertising, including advertising in enclosed stadiums and advertising from within a retail establishment

that is directed toward or visible from the outside of the establishment, in any location that is within a 1,000 foot radius of any public playground, playground area in a public park, elementary school or secondary school;

(b) Point-of-sale advertising of cigarettes or smokeless tobacco products any portion of which is placed lower than five feet from the floor of any retail establishment which is located within a one thousand foot radius of any public playground, playground area in a public park, elementary school or secondary school, and which is not an adult-only retail establishment.

. . . The term "advertisement" is defined as:

any oral, written, graphic, or pictorial statement or representation, made by, or on behalf of, any person who manufactures, packages, imports for sale, distributes or sells within Massachusetts [tobacco products], the purpose or effect of which is to promote the use or sale of the product. Advertisement includes, without limitation, any picture, logo, symbol, motto, selling message, graphic display, visual image, recognizable color or pattern of colors, or any other indicia of product identification identical or similar to, or identifiable with, those used for any brand of [tobacco product]. This includes, without limitation, utilitarian items and permanent or semi-permanent fixtures with such indicia of product identification such as lighting fixtures, awnings, display cases, clocks and door mats, but does not include utilitarian items with a volume of 200 cubic inches or less.

Before the effective date of the regulations, February 1, 2000, members of the tobacco industry sued the Attorney General in the United States District Court for the District of Massachusetts. Four cigarette manufacturers (Lorillard Tobacco Company, Brown & Williamson Tobacco Corporation, R. J. Reynolds Tobacco Company, and Philip Morris Incorporated), a maker of smokeless tobacco products (U.S. Smokeless Tobacco Company), and several cigar manufacturers and retailers claimed that many of the regulations violate the Commerce Clause, the Supremacy Clause, [and] the First and Fourteenth Amendments.

II

Before reaching the First Amendment issues, we must decide to what extent federal law pre-empts the Attorney General's regulations. The cigarette petitioners contend that the FCLAA pre-empts the Attorney General's cigarette advertising regulations.

A

Article VI of the United States Constitution commands that the laws of the United States "shall be the supreme Law of the Land; . . . any Thing in the Constitution or Laws of any State to the Contrary notwithstanding." Art. VI, cl. 2. See also *McCulloch v. Maryland* ("It is of the very essence of supremacy, to remove all obstacles to its action within its own sphere, and so to modify every power vested in subordinate governments"). This relatively clear and simple mandate has generated considerable discussion in cases where we have had to discern whether Congress has pre-empted state action in a particular area. State action may be foreclosed by express language in a congressional enactment, by implication from the depth and breadth of a congressional scheme that occupies the legislative field, or by implication because of a conflict with a congressional enactment.

In the FCLAA, Congress has crafted a comprehensive federal scheme governing the advertising and promotion of cigarettes. The FCLAA's pre-emption provision provides:

(a) Additional statements

No statement relating to smoking and health, other than the statement required by section 1333 of this title, shall be required on any cigarette package.

(b) State regulations

No requirement or prohibition based on smoking and health shall be imposed under State law with respect to the advertising or promotion of any cigarettes the packages of which are labeled in conformity with the provisions of this chapter.

The FCLAA's pre-emption provision does not cover smokeless tobacco or cigars.

In this case, our task is to identify the domain expressly pre-empted, because "an express definition of the pre-emptive reach of a statute . . . supports a reasonable inference . . . that Congress did not intend to pre-empt other matters." *Freightliner Corp. v. Myrick*, 514 U.S. 280, 288 (1995). Congressional purpose is the "ultimate touchstone" of our inquiry. Because "federal law is said to bar state action in [a] field of traditional state regulation," namely, advertising, *see Packer Corp. of Utah*, 285 U.S. 105, 108 (1932), we "work on the assumption that the historic police powers of the States are not to be superseded by the Federal Act unless that [is] the clear and manifest purpose of Congress." *California Div. of Labor Stands Enforcement v. Dillingham Constr., N.A., Inc.*, 519 U.S. 316, 325 (1997).

Our analysis begins with the language of the statute. In the pre-emption provision, Congress unequivocally precludes the requirement of any additional statements on cigarette packages beyond those provided in § 1333. Congress further precludes States or localities from imposing any requirement or prohibition based on smoking and health with respect to the advertising and promotion of cigarettes. Without question, the second clause is more expansive than the first; it employs far more sweeping language to describe the state action that is pre-empted. We must give meaning to each element of the pre-emption provision. We are aided in our interpretation by considering the predecessor pre-emption provision and the circumstances in which the current language was adopted.

In 1964, the groundbreaking Report of the Surgeon General's Advisory Committee on Smoking and Health concluded that "cigarette smoking is a health hazard of sufficient importance in the United States to warrant appropriate remedial action." In 1965, Congress enacted the FCLAA as a proactive measure in the face of impending regulation by federal agencies and the States. The purpose of the FCLAA was twofold: to inform the public adequately about the hazards of cigarette smoking, and to protect the national economy from interference due to diverse, nonuniform, and confusing cigarette labeling and advertising regulations with respect to the relationship between smoking and health. The FCLAA prescribed a label for cigarette packages: "Caution: Cigarette Smoking May Be Hazardous to Your Health." The FCLAA also required the Secretary of Health, Education, and Welfare (HEW) and the Federal Trade Commission (FTC) to report annually to Congress about the health consequences of smoking and the advertising and promotion of cigarettes.

Section 5 of the FCLAA included a pre-emption provision in which "Congress spoke precisely and narrowly." Subsection 5(a) prohibited any requirement of additional statements on cigarette packaging. Subsection 5(b) provided that "no statement relating to smoking and health shall be required in the advertising of any cigarettes the packages of which are labeled in conformity with the provisions of this Act." Section 10 of the FCLAA set a termination date of July 1, 1969 for these provisions. As we have previously explained, "on their face, [the pre-emption] provisions merely prohibited state and federal rulemaking bodies from mandating particular cautionary statements on cigarette labels [subsection (a)] or in cigarette advertisements [subsection (b)]."

The FCLAA was enacted with the expectation that Congress would reexamine it in 1969 in light of the developing information about cigarette smoking and health. In the intervening years, Congress received reports and recommendations from the HEW Secretary and the FTC. The HEW Secretary recommended that Congress strengthen the warning, require the warning on all packages and in advertisements, and publish tar and nicotine levels on packages and in advertisements. The FTC made similar and additional recommendations. The FTC sought a complete ban on radio and television advertising, a requirement that broadcasters devote time for health hazard announcements concerning smoking, and increased funding for public education and research about smoking. The FTC urged Congress not to continue to prevent federal agencies from regulating cigarette advertising. In addition, the Federal Communications Commission (FCC) had concluded that advertising which promoted the use of cigarettes created a duty in broadcast stations to provide information about the hazards of cigarette smoking.

In 1969, House and Senate committees held hearings about the health effects of cigarette smoking and advertising by the cigarette industry. The bill that emerged from the House of Representatives strengthened the warning and maintained the pre-emption provision. The Senate amended that bill, adding the ban on radio and television advertising, and changing the pre-emption language to its present form.

The final result was the Public Health Cigarette Smoking Act of 1969, in which Congress, following the Senate's amendments, made three significant changes to the FCLAA. First, Congress drafted a new label that read: "Warning: The Surgeon General Has Determined That Cigarette Smoking Is Dangerous to Your Health." Second, Congress declared it unlawful to advertise cigarettes on any medium of electronic communication subject to the jurisdiction of the FCC. Finally, Congress enacted the current pre-emption provision, which proscribes any "requirement or prohibition based on smoking and health . . . imposed under State law with respect to the advertising or promotion" of cigarettes. § 5(b). The new subsection 5(b) did not pre-empt regulation by federal agencies, freeing the FTC to impose warning requirements in cigarette advertising. The new pre-emption provision, like its predecessor, only applied to cigarettes, and not other tobacco products.

In 1984, Congress again amended the FCLAA in the Comprehensive Smoking Education Act. The purpose of the Act was to "provide a new strategy for making Americans more aware of any adverse health effects of smoking, to assure the timely and widespread dissemination of research findings and to enable individuals to make informed decisions about smoking." The Act established a series of warnings to appear on a rotating basis on cigarette packages and in cigarette advertising, and directed the Health and Human Services Secretary to create and implement an educational program about the health effects of cigarette smoking.

The FTC has continued to report on trade practices in the cigarette industry. In 1999, the first year since the master settlement agreement, the FTC reported that the cigarette industry expended $8.24 billion on advertising and promotions, the largest expenditure ever. . . . Congress and federal agencies continue to monitor advertising and promotion practices in the cigarette industry.

The scope and meaning of the current pre-emption provision become clearer once we consider the original pre-emption language and the amendments to the FCLAA. Without question, "the plain language of the pre-emption provision in the 1969 Act is much broader." Rather than preventing only "statements," the amended provision reaches all "requirements or prohibitions . . . imposed under State law." And, although the former statute reached only statements "in the advertising," the current provision governs "with respect to the advertising or promotion" of cigarettes. Congress expanded the pre-emption provision with respect to the States, and at the same time, it allowed the FTC to regulate cigarette advertising. Congress also prohibited cigarette advertising in electronic media altogether. Viewed in light of the context in which the current pre-emption provision was adopted, we must determine whether the FCLAA pre-empts Massachusetts' regulations governing outdoor and point-of-sale advertising of cigarettes.

B

The Court of Appeals acknowledged that the FCLAA pre-empts any "requirement or prohibition based on smoking and health . . . with respect to the advertising or promotion of . . . cigarettes," but concluded that the FCLAA does not nullify Massachusetts' cigarette advertising regulations. The court concentrated its analysis on whether the regulations are "with respect to" advertising and promotion, relying on two of its sister Circuits to conclude that the FCLAA only pre-empts regulations of the content of cigarette advertising. The Court of Appeals also reasoned that the Attorney General's regulations are a form of zoning, a traditional area of state power; therefore the presumption against pre-emption applied.

The cigarette petitioners maintain that the Court of Appeals' "with respect to" analysis is inconsistent with the FCLAA's statutory text and legislative history, and gives the States license to prohibit almost all cigarette advertising. Petitioners also maintain that there is no basis for construing the pre-emption provision to prohibit only content-based advertising regulations.

Although they support the Court of Appeals' result, the Attorney General and United States as *amicus curiae* do not fully endorse that court's textual analysis of the pre-emption provision. Instead, they assert that the cigarette advertising regulations are not pre-empted because they are not "based on smoking and health." The Attorney General and the United States also contend that the regulations are not pre-empted because they do not prescribe the content of cigarette advertising and they fall squarely within the State's traditional powers to control the location of advertising and to protect the welfare of children.

Turning first to the language in the pre-emption provision relied upon by the Court of Appeals, we reject the notion that the Attorney General's cigarette advertising regulations are not "with respect to" advertising and promotion. Here . . . there is no question about an indirect relationship between the regulations and cigarette advertising because the regulations expressly target cigarette advertising.

Before this Court, the Attorney General focuses on a different phrase in the pre-emption provision: "based on smoking and health." The Attorney General argues that the cigarette advertising regulations are not "based on smoking and health," because they do not involve health-related content in cigarette advertising but instead target youth exposure to cigarette advertising. To be sure, Members of this Court have debated the precise meaning of "based on smoking and health," but we cannot agree with the Attorney General's narrow construction of the phrase.

As Congress enacted the current pre-emption provision, Congress did not concern itself solely with health warnings for cigarettes. In the 1969 amendments, Congress not only enhanced its scheme to warn the public about the hazards of cigarette smoking, but also sought to protect the public, including youth, from being inundated with images of cigarette smoking in advertising. In pursuit of the latter goal, Congress banned electronic media advertising of cigarettes. And to the extent that Congress contemplated additional targeted regulation of cigarette advertising, it vested that authority in the FTC.

The context in which Congress crafted the current pre-emption provision leads us to conclude that Congress prohibited state cigarette advertising regulations motivated by concerns about smoking and health. Massachusetts has attempted to address the incidence of underage cigarette smoking by regulating advertising, much like Congress' ban on cigarette advertising in electronic media. At bottom, the concern about youth exposure to cigarette advertising is intertwined with the concern about cigarette smoking and health. Thus the Attorney General's attempt to distinguish one concern from the other must be rejected.

The Attorney General next claims that the State's outdoor and point-of-sale advertising regulations for cigarettes are not pre-empted because they govern the location, and not the content, of advertising. This is also JUSTICE STEVENS' main point with respect to pre-emption.

The content versus location distinction has some surface appeal. The pre-emption provision immediately follows the section of the FCLAA that prescribes warnings. The pre-emption provision itself refers to cigarettes "labeled in conformity with" the statute. But the content/location distinction cannot be squared with the language of the pre-emption provision, which reaches *all* "requirements" and "prohibitions" "imposed under State law." A distinction between the content of advertising and the location of advertising in the FCLAA also cannot be reconciled with Congress' own location-based restriction, which bans advertising in electronic media, but not elsewhere. We are not at liberty to pick and choose which provisions in the legislative scheme we will consider, but must examine the FCLAA as a whole.

Moreover, any distinction between the content and location of cigarette advertising collapses once the implications of that approach are fully considered. At oral argument, the Attorney General was pressed to explain what types of state regulations of cigarette advertising, in his view, are pre-empted by the FCLAA. The Attorney General maintained that a state law that required cigarette retailers to remove the word "tobacco" from advertisements, or required cigarette billboards to be blank, would be pre-empted if it were a regulation of "health-related content." The Attorney General also maintained, however, that a complete ban on all cigarette advertising would not be pre-empted because Congress did not intend to invade local control over zoning. The latter position clearly follows from the factual distinction between content and location, but it finds no support in the text of the FCLAA's pre-emption provision. We believe that Congress wished to ensure that "a State could not do through negative mandate (*e.g.*, banning all cigarette advertising) that which it already was forbidden to do through positive mandate (*e.g.*, mandating particular cautionary statements)."

JUSTICE STEVENS maintains that Congress did not intend to displace state regulation of the location of cigarette advertising. There is a critical distinction, however, between generally applicable zoning regulations, and regulations targeting cigarette advertising. The latter type of regulation, which is inevitably motivated by concerns about smoking and health, squarely contradicts the FCLAA. The FCLAA's comprehensive warnings, advertising restrictions, and pre-emption provision would make little sense if a State or locality could simply target and ban all cigarette advertising.

JUSTICE STEVENS finds it ironic that we conclude that "federal law precludes States and localities from protecting children from dangerous products within 1,000 feet of a school," in light of our prior conclusion that the "Federal Government lacks the constitutional authority to impose a similarly-motivated ban" in *United States v. Lopez*. Our holding is not as broad as the dissent states; we hold only that the FCLAA pre-empts state regulations targeting cigarette advertising. States remain free to enact generally applicable zoning regulations, and to regulate conduct with respect to cigarette use and sales. The reference to *Lopez* is also inapposite. In *Lopez*, we held that Congress exceeded the limits of its Commerce Clause power in the Gun-Free School Zones Act of 1990, which made it a federal crime to possess a firearm in a school zone. This case, by contrast, concerns the Supremacy Clause and the doctrine of pre-emption as applied in a case where Congress expressly precluded certain state regulations of cigarette advertising. Massachusetts did not raise a constitutional challenge to the FCLAA, and we are not confronted with whether Congress exceeded its constitutionally delegated authority in enacting the FCLAA.

In sum, we fail to see how the FCLAA and its pre-emption provision permit a distinction between the specific concern about minors and cigarette advertising and the more general concern about smoking and health in cigarette advertising, especially in light of the fact that Congress crafted a legislative solution for those very concerns. We also conclude that a distinction between state regulation of the location as opposed to the content of cigarette advertising has no foundation in the text of the pre-emption provision. Congress pre-empted state cigarette advertising regulations like the Attorney General's because they would upset federal legislative choices to require specific warnings and to impose the ban on cigarette advertising in electronic media in order to address concerns about smoking and health. Accordingly, we hold that the Attorney General's outdoor and point-of-sale advertising regulations targeting cigarettes are pre-empted by the FCLAA.

C

Although the FCLAA prevents States and localities from imposing special requirements or prohibitions "based on smoking and health" "with respect to the advertising or promotion" of cigarettes, that language still leaves significant power in the hands of States to impose generally applicable zoning regulations and to regulate conduct. As we [have] noted . . . "each phrase within [the provision] limits the universe of [state action] pre-empted by the statute."

For instance, the FCLAA does not restrict a State or locality's ability to enact generally applicable zoning restrictions. We have recognized that state interests in traffic safety and esthetics may justify zoning regulations for advertising. . . .

The FCLAA also does not foreclose all state regulation of conduct as it relates to the sale or use of cigarettes. The FCLAA's pre-emption provision explicitly governs state regulations of "advertising or promotion." Accordingly, the FCLAA does not pre-empt state laws prohibiting cigarette sales to minors. To the contrary, there is an established congressional policy that supports such laws; Congress has required States to prohibit tobacco sales to minors as a condition of receiving federal block grant funding for substance abuse treatment activities.

In Massachusetts, it is illegal to sell or distribute tobacco products to persons under the age of 18. Having prohibited the sale and distribution of tobacco products to minors, the State may prohibit common inchoate offenses that attach to criminal conduct, such as solicitation, conspiracy, and attempt. . . . States and localities also have at their disposal other means of regulating conduct to ensure that minors do not obtain cigarettes. . . .

III

By its terms, the FCLAA's pre-emption provision only applies to cigarettes. Accordingly, we must evaluate the smokeless tobacco and cigar petitioners' First Amendment challenges to the State's outdoor and point-of-sale advertising regulations. The cigarette petitioners did not raise a pre-emption challenge to the sales practices regulations. Thus, we must analyze the cigarette as well as the smokeless tobacco and cigar petitioners' claim that certain sales practices regulations for tobacco products violate the First Amendment.

[The Court struck down the majority of the smokeless tobacco regulations.]

■ JUSTICE STEVENS, with whom JUSTICES SOUTER, GINSBURG and BREYER join, concurring in the judgment in part, and dissenting in part.

. . . Because I strongly disagree with the Court's conclusion that the Federal Cigarette Labeling and Advertising Act of 1965, precludes States and localities from regulating the location of cigarette advertising, I dissent from Parts II-A and II-B of the Court's opinion. . . .

I

As the majority acknowledges, under prevailing principles, any examination of the scope of a preemption provision must " 'start with the assumption that the historic police powers of the States [are] not to be superseded by . . . Federal Act unless that [is] the clear and manifest purpose of Congress.' " As the regulations at issue in this suit implicate two powers that lie at the heart of the States' traditional police power— the power to regulate land usage and the power to protect the health and safety of minors—our precedents require that the Court construe the preemption provision "narrowly." If Congress' intent to preempt a particular category of regulation is ambiguous, such regulations are not preempted.

The text of the preemption provision must be viewed in context, with proper attention paid to the history, structure, and purpose of the regulatory scheme in which it appears. An assessment of the scope of a preemption provision must give effect to a "reasoned understanding of the way in which Congress intended the statute and its surrounding regulatory scheme to affect business, consumers, and the law."

This task, properly performed, leads inexorably to the conclusion that Congress did not intend to preempt state and local regulations of the location of cigarette advertising when it adopted the provision at issue in this suit. In both 1965 and 1969, Congress made clear the purposes of its regulatory endeavor, explaining with precision the federal policies motivating its actions. According to the acts, Congress adopted a "comprehensive Federal program to deal with cigarette labeling and advertising with respect to any relationship between smoking and health," for two reasons: (1) to inform the public that smoking may be hazardous to health and (2) to ensure that commerce and the interstate economy not be "impeded by diverse, nonuniform, and confusing cigarette labeling and advertising regulations with respect to any relationship between smoking and health."

In order to serve the second purpose it was necessary to preempt state regulation of the content of both cigarette labels and cigarette advertising. If one State required the inclusion of a particular warning on the package of cigarettes while another State demanded a different formulation, cigarette manufacturers would have been forced into the difficult and costly practice of producing different packaging for use in different States. To foreclose the waste of resources that would be entailed by such a patchwork regulatory system, Congress expressly precluded other regulators from requiring the placement on cigarette packaging of any "statement relating to smoking and health." Similar concerns applied to cigarette advertising. If different regulatory bodies required that different warnings or statements be used when cigarette manufacturers advertised their products, the text and layout of a company's ads would have had to differ from locale to locale. The resulting costs would have come with little or no health benefit. Moreover, given the nature of publishing, it might well have been the case that cigarette companies would not have been able to advertise in national publications without violating the laws of some jurisdictions. In response to these concerns, Congress adopted a parallel provision preempting state and local regulations requiring inclusion in cigarette advertising of any "statement relating to smoking and health."

There was, however, no need to interfere with state or local zoning laws or other regulations prescribing limitations on the location of signs or billboards. Laws prohibiting a cigarette company from hanging a billboard near a school in Boston in no way conflict with laws permitting the hanging of such a billboard in other jurisdictions. Nor would such laws even impose a significant administrative burden on would-be advertisers, as the great majority of localities impose general restrictions on signage, thus requiring advertisers to examine local law before posting signs whether or not cigarette-specific laws are preempted. Hence, it is unsurprising that Congress did not include any provision in the 1965 Act preempting location restrictions.

The Public Health Cigarette Smoking Act of 1969 made two important changes in the preemption provision. First, it limited the applicability of the advertising prong to States and localities, paving the way for further federal regulation of cigarette advertising. Second, it expanded the scope of the advertising preemption provision. Where previously States were prohibited from requiring particular statements in cigarette advertising based on health concerns, they would henceforth be prohibited from imposing any "requirement or prohibition based on smoking and health . . . with respect to the advertising or promotion" of cigarettes.

Ripped from its context, this provision could theoretically be read as a breathtaking expansion of the limitations imposed by the 1965 Act. However, both our precedents and common sense require us to read statutory provisions—and, in particular, preemption clauses—in the context of both their neighboring provisions and of the history and purpose of the statutory scheme. When so viewed, it is quite clear that the 1969 amendments were intended to expand the provision to capture a narrow set of content regulations that would have escaped preemption under the prior provision, not to fundamentally reorder the division of regulatory authority between the Federal and State Governments.

All signs point inescapably to the conclusion that Congress only intended to preempt content regulations in the 1969 Act. It is of crucial importance that, in making modifications of the preemption provision, Congress did not alter the statement laying out the federal policies the provision was intended to serve. To this day, the stated federal policies in this area are (1) to inform the public of the dangers of cigarette smoking and (2) to protect the cigarette companies from the burdens of confusing and contradictory state regulations of their labels and advertisements. The retention of this provision unchanged is strong evidence that Congress' only intention in expanding the preemption clause was to capture forms of content regulation that had fallen through the cracks of the prior provision—for example, state laws prohibiting cigarette manufacturers from making particular claims in their advertising or requiring them to utilize specified layouts or include particular graphics in their marketing.

The legislative history of the provision also supports such a reading. The record does not contain any evidence that Congress intended to expand the scope of preemption beyond content restrictions. To the contrary, the Senate Report makes it clear that the changes merely "clarified" the scope of the original provision. Even as amended, Congress perceived the provision as "narrowly phrased" and emphasized that its purpose is to "avoid the chaos created by a multiplicity of conflicting regulations." According to the Senate Report, the changes "in no way affect the power of any state or political subdivision of any state with respect to . . . the sale of cigarettes to minors . . . or similar police regulations." . . .

I am firmly convinced that, when Congress amended the preemption provision in 1969, it did not intend to expand the application of the provision beyond content regulations. I, therefore, find the conclusion inescapable that the zoning regulation at issue in this suit is not a "requirement or prohibition . . . with respect to . . . advertising" within the meaning of the 1969 Act. Even if I were not so convinced, however, I would still dissent from the Court's conclusion with regard to preemption, because the provision is, at the very least, ambiguous. The historical record simply does not reflect that it was Congress' 'clear and manifest purpose' to preempt attempts by States to utilize their traditional zoning authority to protect the health and welfare of minors. Absent such a manifest purpose, Massachusetts and its sister States retain their traditional police powers.[8] . . .

---

[8] The Court's holding that federal law precludes States and localities from protecting children from dangerous products within 1,000 feet of a school is particularly ironic given the Court's conclusion six years ago that the Federal Government lacks the constitutional authority to impose a similarly-motivated ban. See *United States v. Lopez*, 514 U.S. 549 (1995). Despite the absence of any identified federal interest in creating "an invisible federal zone extending 1,000 feet beyond the (often irregular) boundaries of the school property," as the majority construes it today, the "statute now before us forecloses the States from experimenting and exercising their own judgment in an area to which States lay claim by right of history and expertise," *id.* (KENNEDY, J., concurring). I wonder why a Court sensitive to federalism

NOTE ON FEDERAL PREEMPTION OF STATE LAW

1.   The *Pacific Gas & Electric* opinion discusses three distinct kinds of preemption:

- *Express* preemption in the statutory text.

- *Field* preemption where the scheme of federal regulation is so pervasive that we infer Congress intended no state supplementation.

- *Conflict* preemption where compliance with both federal and state regulations is a "physical impossibility," or where state law "stands as an obstacle to the accomplishment and execution of the full purposes and objectives of Congress."

Note that there is a significant difference between "impossibility" conflicts and "obstacle" conflicts. Some opinions suggest that there is a fourth kind of preemption:

- *Frustration* preemption occurs where state law does not conflict directly with a federal statute, but it would unduly frustrate the purposes of that statute to permit concurrent state regulation.

Such "frustration" preemption may simply be a form of conflict preemption. It is absolutely critical to remember that under modern doctrine, these different categories are simply aids in answering the critical question: Did Congress *intend* to preempt state law?

2.   The "presumption against preemption" is a close family relative of the pro-federalism "clear statement" rules discussed in Section 10.1, *supra*. The canonical citation is to *Rice v. Santa Fe Elevator Corp.*, 331 U.S. 218 (1947). [13] In a helpful historical treatment, Stephen Gardbaum has demonstrated that prior to the 1930s, preemption of state authority followed virtually *automatically* whenever the Federal Government regulated in a particular field. This broad approach to preemption changed, however, as the *scope* of national regulatory power expanded:

> By the 1930s, a second and greater movement to extend national powers was under way. In this new context, the preemption power was qualified by replacing its automatic element with a new requirement that a federal statute would be considered to have taken over a given field only if Congress clearly manifested its intent to do so. Thus, at a time of radical increases in the general power of Congress at the expense of the states, it is perhaps paradoxical that Congress's preemptive power was seemingly curtailed.

> This new requirement of intent was, however, a logical result of the restructuring of American federalism that began with the New Deal in 1933 and that was judicially affirmed in 1937. The greatly

---

concerns would adopt such a strange construction of statutory language whose quite different purpose Congress took pains to explain.

[13] *See also Mintz v. Baldwin*, 289 U.S. 346 (1933).

enlarged power granted to Congress by the new interpretation of the Commerce Clause took from the states their previously sacrosanct exclusive power over intrastate commerce. Henceforth, no area of intrastate commerce would be open to the states to regulate which at the same time is constitutionally closed to Congress; no such area remained fully protected from the threat of congressional intervention.

In this context of a revolutionary extension of federal legislative competence, the consequence of the preexisting preemption doctrine (established while there were still significant areas of exclusive state jurisdiction) would have been to threaten vast areas of state regulation of seemingly local matters with extinction. Instead, the new constitutional strategy replaced a strict division of powers version of federalism with a new version embodying the presumption that state powers, though no longer constitutionally guaranteed, survive unless clearly ended by Congress. Preemption doctrine was thus modified to reflect this new presumption, and thereafter, Congress was affirmatively required to manifest an intent to preempt.[14]

Does it make sense to view the *Rice* presumption against preemption as a "compensating adjustment" by the Court, designed to offset its decision to expand the scope of Congress's Commerce Power in cases like *NLRB v. Jones & Laughlin* and *Wickard v. Filburn*?[15]

    3.   *Rice*'s presumption against preemption has also been defended in terms of the "process federalism" approach suggested in *Garcia*. Justice Stevens has explained that

> The signal virtues of this presumption are its placement of the power of pre-emption squarely in the hands of Congress, which is far more suited than the Judiciary to strike the appropriate state/federal balance (particularly in areas of traditional state regulation), and its requirement that Congress speak clearly when exercising that power. In this way, the structural safeguards inherent in the normal operation of the legislative process operate to defend state interests from undue infringement.[16]

Is this process-based approach more attractive than the substantive limits on Congress's power that the Court has sought to impose in cases like *Lopez*?[17]

---

[14] Stephen A. Gardbaum, *The Nature of Preemption*, 79 CORNELL L. REV. 767, 806 (1994).

[15] *Compare, e.g.*, Caleb Nelson, *Preemption*, 86 VA. L. REV. 225 (2000) (arguing that the *Rice* presumption is contrary to the original understanding of the Supremacy Clause), *with* Ernest A. Young, *Making Federalism Doctrine: Fidelity, Institutional Competence, and Compensating Adjustments*, 46 WM. & MARY L. REV. 1733, 1848–50 (2005) (defending the presumption as a legitimate compensating adjustment).

[16] *Geier v. American Honda Motor Co.*, 529 U.S. 861, 907 (2000) (Stevens, J., dissenting) (citing *Garcia*).

[17] *See generally* Thomas W. Merrill, *Rescuing Federalism After* Raich: *The Case for Clear Statement Rules*, 9 LEWIS & CLARK L. REV. 823 (2005).

4.   One important continuing dispute concerns the *scope* of the *Rice* presumption. The Court has occasionally suggested that this clear statement rule applies only when Congress intervenes in areas of "traditional state regulation." In *United States v. Locke*, 529 U.S. 89 (2000), for example, the Court considered whether federal statutes and regulations imposing certain safety requirements on oil tankers operating in navigable waters preempted the State of Washington's effort to impose more stringent safety rules on tankers operating in Puget Sound and other critical state waters. (Washington tightened its requirements in the wake of the *Exxon Valdez* disaster in 1989.) In considering the preemptive effect of the relevant federal laws, Justice Kennedy's opinion for a unanimous court rejected any presumption against preemption: "The state laws now in question bear upon national and international maritime commerce, and in this area there is no beginning assumption that concurrent regulation by the State is a valid exercise of its police powers."

Is this distinction between areas of traditionally federal and traditionally state regulation a workable one? Recall the difficulty in defining "traditional state functions" noted by the Court in *Garcia*. Does the distinction even hold up in the context of *Locke* itself? The Court concludes that historic federal authority over navigable waters takes the case outside the *Rice* presumption, but does not the case *also* involve the State's "historic" concern with pollution, safety, and the economic well-being of the state in the event of a catastrophic spill? Is it really possible to define separate and exclusive spheres of national and state regulatory concern? Isn't this the same mistake that the pre-1937 Court made in trying to define the limits of Congress's enumerated powers?

The Court has gone back and forth on the scope question. *Rice* itself emphasized that the federal statute in question existed "in a field which the States have traditionally occupied." 331 U.S. at 230. On the other hand, in *Medtronic, Inc. v. Lohr*, 518 U.S. 470, 485 (1996), the Court said that *Rice* applies "[i]n all pre-emption cases." *Locke* did not address *Medtronic*, a case decided just four years earlier, and it seems unlikely that the Court has definitively resolved this question.

5.   A second important question under *Rice* concerns how the presumption may be applied in cases where the relevant federal law emanates from a federal administrative agency rather than directly from Congress. Agency action is problematic from a *Garcia*-esque "political safeguards" perspective; as Justice Stevens has explained, "[u]nlike Congress, administrative agencies are clearly not designed to represent the interests of States, yet with relative ease they can promulgate comprehensive and detailed regulations that have broad pre-emption ramifications for state law."[18] The problem of agency preemption has two distinct dimensions.[19]

Sometimes, a federal statute is ambiguous as to whether it preempts state law, but the federal agency has interpreted that statute to have

---

[18] *Geier*, 529 U.S. at 908 (Stevens, J., dissenting).

[19] *See generally* Ernest A. Young, *Executive Preemption*, 102 Nw. U. L. Rev. 869 (2008).

preemptive effect. This was the case in *Geier*, in which federal statutory law set certain safety standards for automobiles, but did not say whether state tort law could hold manufacturers to an even higher standard. The federal agency charged with administering the federal regulatory regime concluded that state tort suits are preempted. Ordinarily, agency interpretations of an ambiguous federal statute are entitled to some degree of deference from courts under *Chevron* and similar doctrines,[20] as we saw in *Solid Waste Agency of Northern Cook County v. United States Army Corps of Engineers*, in Chapter Ten. But where the agency finds preemption, a presumption in favor of the agency's interpretation will run counter to the *Rice* presumption, which says that ambiguous federal statutes should be read *not* to preempt state law. In *Geier*, the majority gave some degree of deference to agency's preemptive reading, but did not appear to give it as much deference as such agency interpretations get in ordinary administrative law cases. It seems fair to say that the conflict between *Rice* and *Chevron* remains largely unresolved.[21]

The second situation arises when a federal statute does not itself preempt state law, but it does authorize an administrative agency to promulgate regulations or take other actions, and these actions are themselves said to preempt state law. This was the case in the *Solid Waste* litigation.[22] In that case, the Government argued that Cook County's plan to build a landfill was preempted not by the Clean Water Act itself but by the Army Corps of Engineers' "Migratory Bird Rule"—a regulation promulgated by the agency acting pursuant to its delegated authority under the Act. The same issue arose in *Locke*, where the Coast Guard promulgated regulations for oil tankers that arguably preempted the State of Washington's rules. Should federal agencies have the same preemptive powers as Congress?

The Supreme Court seemed to equate administrative regulations and federal statutes for preemption purposes in *Fidelity Federal Savings & Loan Ass'n v. de la Cuesta*, 458 U.S. 141, 153 (1982), stating that "[f]ederal regulations have no less pre-emptive effect than federal statutes." But the Court immediately turned its focus back to Congress by noting that "Congress has directed [the] administrator to exercise his discretion" and that the administrator's actions were "subject to judicial review . . . to determine whether he has exceeded his statutory authority."[23] Nothing in *de la Cuesta* suggests that agency actions have preemptive force apart from underlying congressional action.

The Roberts Court rejected broad preemption arguments based on federal administrative agency action in two recent cases, *Wyeth v. Levine*, 555 U.S. 555 (2009) (holding that neither the federal Food, Drug, and

---

[20] *See Chevron U.S.A. Inc. v. Natural Resources Defense Council, Inc.*, 467 U.S. 837 (1984) (holding that, if a statute is ambiguous, courts must defer to the interpretation of that statute by the federal agency that administers the statute, so long as the agency's interpretation is reasonable).

[21] *See generally* Nina A. Mendelson, Chevron *and Preemption*, 102 MICH. L. REV. 737 (2004).

[22] 531 U.S. 159 (2001).

[23] *De la Cuesta*, 458 U.S. at 152 ("The pre-emption doctrine, which has its roots in the Supremacy Clause, requires us to examine congressional intent.").

Cosmetic Act nor agency regulations promulgated under that Act preempted state tort actions concerning drugs approved by the Food and Drug Administration), and *Altria Group, Inc. v. Good*, 555 U.S. 70 (2008) (holding that neither the Federal Cigarette Labeling and Advertising Act nor actions by the Federal Trade Commission enforcing that act preempted state law suits for fraudulent advertising). Neither case, however, purported to comprehensively define the preemptive powers of federal agencies.[24]

6.   Federal *courts* are similar to federal agencies in that (a) they are not structured in such a way as to represent the states, and (b) they operate outside the procedural constraints of the Article I lawmaking process. Judge-made federal law, which is also generally considered supreme for preemption purposes, thus raises similar problems to those just discussed regarding federal agency action.[25] Of course, *Erie Railroad v. Tompkins*, 304 U.S. 64 (1938), held that "[e]xcept in matters governed by the Federal Constitution or by Acts of Congress, the law to be applied in any case is the law of the State . . . . There is no federal general common law." Can you see why this is arguably the most important pro-federalism holding of the Twentieth Century? On the other hand, federal judicial authority to formulate rules of federal common law *is* recognized in certain areas.[26] The precise scope of federal common lawmaking authority remains controversial.

7.   What do you make of the voting line-up in *Lorillard*? In particular, note Justice Stevens' final footnote, which points out that

> The Court's holding that federal law precludes States and localities from protecting children from dangerous products within 1,000 feet of a school is particularly ironic given the Court's conclusion six years ago that the Federal Government lacks the constitutional authority to impose a similarly-motivated ban. See *United States v. Lopez*.

In *Lorillard*, all five justices who had voted in the *Lopez* majority found preemption; all four *Lopez* dissenters argued in favor of state autonomy. What explains this curious alignment? Although the voting lineup in other preemption cases does not always fit this stark 5–4 pattern, it is demonstrably true that the "nationalist" justices in cases about the Commerce Clause, anti-commandeering doctrine, etc., tend to vote *against* preemption of state law more often than the justices in the *Lopez* and *Printz* majorities. Is it possible that the nationalist justices are not really

---

[24] For an exchange on the role of federal administrative agencies in preemption cases, compare Brian Galle & Mark Seidenfeld, *Administrative Law's Federalism: Preemption, Delegation, and Agencies at the Edge of Federal Power*, 57 DUKE L. J. 1933 (2008), and Gillian E. Metzger, *Administrative Law as the New Federalism*, 57 DUKE L. J. 2023 (2008) (both embracing a primary role for administrative agencies in preemption cases), with Stuart Minor Benjamin & Ernest A. Young, *Tennis with the Net Down: Administrative Federalism Without Congress*, 57 DUKE L. J. 2111 (2008) (insisting that the preemptive force of federal law can derive only from Congress).

[25] *See, e.g.*, Ernest A. Young, *Preemption at Sea*, 67 GEO. WASH. L. REV. 273 (1999).

[26] *See generally* Henry J. Friendly, *In Praise of* Erie—*And of the New Federal Common Law*, 39 N.Y.U. L. REV. 383 (1964).

nationalist, but simply have a different view of how federalism should be protected?[27]

8.   Some commentators who are quite concerned about the values of constitutional federalism have nevertheless rejected the *Rice* presumption as a mechanism for protecting state autonomy. Professor Viet Dinh, for example, has argued that "[r]edefining the proper balance of legislative powers between Congress and the states is better accomplished directly, through an insistence on the limits of Congress's enumerated and limited powers under Article I, rather than circuitously and ineffectually through some vague and ill-conceived presumption against preemption under the Supremacy Clause."[28] Do you agree? Are the prospects for meaningful limits on the commerce power sufficiently rosy to make Professor Dinh's strategy viable, especially after *Raich*?

9.   Dissenting in an obscure preemption case under the Employee Retirement Income Security Act, Justice Breyer expressed a much different view from Professor Dinh's:

> In today's world, filled with legal complexity, the true test of federalist principle may lie, not in the occasional effort to trim Congress's commerce power at its edges, . . . or to protect a State's treasury from a private damages action, . . . but rather in those many statutory cases where courts interpret the mass of technical detail that is the ordinary diet of the law.[29]

Is Justice Breyer right? From the perspective of someone concerned about state regulatory autonomy, would you rather win *Lopez* or *Lorillard*? *Printz* or *Locke*?

Consider, in this regard, the Court's decision in *AT & T Corp. v. Iowa Utilities Board*, 525 U.S. 366 (1999). The original federal Communications Act, enacted in the 1930s, explicitly restricted the regulatory authority of the Federal Communications Commission to *interstate* telephone service and reserved authority over intrastate or local phone service to state regulators. The 1996 Telecommunications Act changed the regulatory regime *substantively* by seeking to introduce competition in the local telephone market; it was ambiguous, however, as to whether the new rules for local competition were to be developed by the FCC or by state utility commissions. The Court held that the Act implicitly shifted this vast regulatory authority to the FCC, rejecting the argument that the *Rice* presumption ought to favor the continuance of local control. In dissent, Justice Breyer wrote that

> Two Terms ago the Court held that Congress could not constitutionally require a state sheriff to fill out a form providing background information about a buyer of a gun. *Printz v. United States,* 521 U.S. 898 (1997). Dissenters in that case noted that the law deprived the States of a power that had little practical

---

[27]   *See generally* Ernest A. Young, *The Rehnquist Court's Two Federalisms*, 83 TEXAS L. REV. 1 (2004) (arguing that they do).

[28]   Viet D. Dinh, *Reassessing the Law of Preemption*, 88 GEO. L. J. 2085, 2117 (2000).

[29]   *Egelhoff v. Egelhoff,* 532 U.S. 141, 160–61 (2001) (Breyer, J., dissenting).

significance. Today's decision does deprive the States of practically significant power, a camel compared with *Printz*'s gnat.

Do you agree?

Finally, in assessing the importance of preemption to federalism doctrine generally, consider that the Supreme Court tends to hear at least two or three major preemption cases every year, as opposed to five major Commerce Clause cases (*Lopez, Morrison, Raich, Comstock,* and *NFIB*) over the past twenty-two years. Should the Court's putatively pro-States conservative justices place more emphasis on preemption cases? Does the willingness of "nationalist" justices to protect the States in preemption cases offer some hope for federalism after decisions like *Raich*?

See also: On the preemption debate generally, see the essays collected in RICHARD A. EPSTEIN & MICHAEL S. GREVE, FEDERAL PREEMPTION: STATES' POWERS, NATIONAL INTERESTS (2007). On the Court's more recent cases, see Ernest A. Young, *"The Ordinary Diet of the Law": The Presumption Against Preemption in the Roberts Court,* 2011 SUP. CT. REV. 253 (2012).

CHAPTER TWELVE

THE SEPARATION OF POWERS

The Framers of the Constitution divided power not only between the national government and the States, but also among the national government's three branches. Although this division is reflected in the organization of the Constitutional text—the first three Articles correspond, respectively, to the legislative, executive, and judicial authority—the text is less clear on the precise contours of the division of power. Edward Corwin's famous description of the constitutional allocation of authority over foreign affairs as an "invitation to struggle"[1] may be fairly applied to the separation of powers in general. The remainder of this Part takes up this invitation.

Although America's structural separation of powers had antecedents in the political theory of Montesquieu and other enlightenment thinkers,[2] it had few precursors in practice. The British Constitution had evolved organically from a classical monarchy to a "mixed government" reflecting the Aristotelian division of power between "the one" (the Monarch), "the few" (the aristocracy, represented in the House of Lords), and "the many" (the Commons). Mixed government was a division of governing influence among the different "interests" of society, and it reflected certain institutional strengths of each interest: the "one" can act decisively, the elite "few" have education and independent judgment, the "many" confer democratic legitimacy. But British government did not seek to divide governmental functions among different governing institutions in anything like the ways that we associate with modern American separation of powers.

Montesquieu's influential idea was that liberty could be best secured by separating the law-making, law-interpreting, and law-enforcing functions among different institutional actors. This idea had gained such currency in America by 1787 that James Madison's central concern in Federalist 47 and 48 was to defend the proposed constitution against charges that it impermissibly blurred these functions by giving each branch a hand in the others' responsibilities. Madison thus introduces the idea of "checks and balances" as a counterpoint to "separated powers." Much of modern separation of powers doctrine arises out of this tension.

This Chapter offers a general introduction to separation of powers. It begins with the Founders' political theory, then turns to the *Steel Seizure Case*, which continues to frame much of the law in this area. Chapter Thirteen addresses the structure of the political branches—in

---

[1] EDWARD CORWIN, THE PRESIDENT, OFFICE AND POWERS, 1787–1957, at 171 (1957).

[2] *See generally* CHARLES DE SECONDAT, BARON DE MONTESQUIEU, THE SPIRIT OF THE LAWS (1748).

particular, the delegation of legislative authority to executive agencies, efforts to alter the congressional lawmaking process by statutory means, the "unitary" integrity of the executive branch, and the privileges and immunities of executive officials. Chapter Fourteen concludes our discussion of separation of powers by exploring executive authority in foreign and military affairs.

Federalist No. 47 (James Madison)

To the People of the State of New York:

Having reviewed the general form of the proposed government and the general mass of power allotted to it, I proceed to examine the particular structure of this government, and the distribution of this mass of power among its constituent parts.

One of the principal objections inculcated by the more respectable adversaries to the Constitution, is its supposed violation of the political maxim, that the legislative, executive, and judiciary departments ought to be separate and distinct. In the structure of the federal government, no regard, it is said, seems to have been paid to this essential precaution in favor of liberty. The several departments of power are distributed and blended in such a manner as at once to destroy all symmetry and beauty of form, and to expose some of the essential parts of the edifice to the danger of being crushed by the disproportionate weight of other parts.

No political truth is certainly of greater intrinsic value, or is stamped with the authority of more enlightened patrons of liberty, than that on which the objection is founded. The accumulation of all powers, legislative, executive, and judiciary, in the same hands, whether of one, a few, or many, and whether hereditary, self appointed, or elective, may justly be pronounced the very definition of tyranny. Were the federal Constitution, therefore, really chargeable with the accumulation of power, or with a mixture of powers, having a dangerous tendency to such an accumulation, no further arguments would be necessary to inspire a universal reprobation of the system. I persuade myself, however, that it will be made apparent to every one, that the charge cannot be supported, and that the maxim on which it relies has been totally misconceived and misapplied. In order to form correct ideas on this important subject, it will be proper to investigate the sense in which the preservation of liberty requires that the three great departments of power should be separate and distinct.

The oracle who is always consulted and cited on this subject is the celebrated Montesquieu. If he be not the author of this invaluable precept in the science of politics, he has the merit at least of displaying and recommending it most effectually to the attention of mankind. Let us endeavor, in the first place, to ascertain his meaning on this point.

The British Constitution was to Montesquieu what Homer has been to the didactic writers on epic poetry. As the latter have considered the work of the immortal bard as the perfect model from which the principles and rules of the epic art were to be drawn, and by which all similar works were to be judged, so this great political critic appears to have viewed the Constitution of England as the standard or . . . the mirror of political liberty. . . . That we may be sure, then, not to mistake his meaning in this case, let us recur to the source from which the maxim was drawn.

On the slightest view of the British Constitution, we must perceive that the legislative, executive, and judiciary departments are by no means totally separate and distinct from each other. The executive magistrate forms an integral part of the legislative authority. He alone has the prerogative of making treaties with foreign sovereigns, which, when made, have, under certain limitations, the force of legislative acts. All the members of the judiciary department are appointed by him, can be removed by him on the address of the two Houses of Parliament, and form, when he pleases to consult them, one of his constitutional councils. One branch of the legislative department forms also a great constitutional council to the executive chief, as, on another hand, it is the sole depositary of judicial power in cases of impeachment, and is invested with the supreme appellate jurisdiction in all other cases. The judges, again, are so far connected with the legislative department as often to attend and participate in its deliberations, though not admitted to a legislative vote.

From these facts, . . . it may clearly be inferred that, in saying "There can be no liberty where the legislative and executive powers are united in the same person, or body of magistrates," or, "if the power of judging be not separated from the legislative and executive powers," [Montesquieu] did not mean that these departments ought to have no PARTIAL AGENCY in, or no CONTROL over, the acts of each other. His meaning . . . can amount to no more than this, that where the WHOLE power of one department is exercised by the same hands which possess the WHOLE power of another department, the fundamental principles of a free constitution are subverted. This would have been the case in the constitution examined by him, if the king, who is the sole executive magistrate, had possessed also the complete legislative power, or the supreme administration of justice; or if the entire legislative body had possessed the supreme judiciary, or the supreme executive authority. This, however, is not among the vices of that constitution. . . .

The reasons on which Montesquieu grounds his maxim are a further demonstration of his meaning. "When the legislative and executive powers are united in the same person or body," says he, "there can be no liberty, because apprehensions may arise lest THE SAME monarch or senate should ENACT tyrannical laws to EXECUTE them in a tyrannical manner." Again: "Were the power of judging joined with the legislative, the life and liberty of the subject would be exposed to arbitrary control, for THE JUDGE would then be THE LEGISLATOR. Were it joined to the executive power, THE JUDGE might behave with all the violence of AN

OPPRESSOR." Some of these reasons are more fully explained in other passages; but briefly stated as they are here, they sufficiently establish the meaning which we have put on this celebrated maxim of this celebrated author.

If we look into the constitutions of the several States, we find that, notwithstanding the emphatical and, in some instances, the unqualified terms in which this axiom has been laid down, there is not a single instance in which the several departments of power have been kept absolutely separate and distinct. New Hampshire, whose constitution was the last formed, seems to have been fully aware of the impossibility and inexpediency of avoiding any mixture whatever of these departments, and has qualified the doctrine by declaring "that the legislative, executive, and judiciary powers ought to be kept as separate from, and independent of, each other AS THE NATURE OF A FREE GOVERNMENT WILL ADMIT; OR AS IS CONSISTENT WITH THAT CHAIN OF CONNECTION THAT BINDS THE WHOLE FABRIC OF THE CONSTITUTION IN ONE INDISSOLUBLE BOND OF UNITY AND AMITY." Her constitution accordingly mixes these departments in several respects. . . .

The constitution of Massachusetts has observed a sufficient though less pointed caution, in expressing this fundamental article of liberty. It declares "that the legislative department shall never exercise the executive and judicial powers, or either of them; the executive shall never exercise the legislative and judicial powers, or either of them; the judicial shall never exercise the legislative and executive powers, or either of them." This declaration corresponds precisely with the doctrine of Montesquieu . . . and is not in a single point violated by the plan of the convention. It goes no farther than to prohibit any one of the entire departments from exercising the powers of another department. In the very Constitution to which it is prefixed, a partial mixture of powers has been admitted. The executive magistrate has a qualified negative on the legislative body, and the Senate, which is a part of the legislature, is a court of impeachment for members both of the executive and judiciary departments. The members of the judiciary department, again, are appointable by the executive department, and removable by the same authority on the address of the two legislative branches. Lastly, a number of the officers of government are annually appointed by the legislative department. As the appointment to offices, particularly executive offices, is in its nature an executive function, the compilers of the Constitution have, in this last point at least, violated the rule established by themselves. . . .

The language of Virginia is still more pointed on this subject. Her constitution declares, "that the legislative, executive, and judiciary departments shall be separate and distinct; so that neither exercise the powers properly belonging to the other; nor shall any person exercise the powers of more than one of them at the same time, except that the justices of county courts shall be eligible to either House of Assembly." Yet we find not only this express exception, with respect to the members of the inferior courts, but that the chief magistrate, with his executive council, are appointable by the legislature; that two members of the latter are triennially displaced at the pleasure of the legislature; and that all the principal offices, both executive and judiciary, are filled by the same department. The executive prerogative of pardon, also, is in one case vested in the legislative department. . . .

In citing these cases, in which the legislative, executive, and judiciary departments have not been kept totally separate and distinct, I wish not to be regarded as an advocate for the particular organizations of the several State governments. I am fully aware that among the many excellent principles which they exemplify, they carry strong marks of the haste, and still stronger of the inexperience, under which they were framed. It is but too obvious that in some instances the fundamental principle under consideration has been violated by too great a mixture, and even an actual consolidation, of the different powers; and that in no instance has a competent provision been made for maintaining in practice the separation delineated on paper. What I have wished to evince is, that the charge brought against the proposed Constitution, of violating the sacred maxim of free government, is warranted neither by the real meaning annexed to that maxim by its author, nor by the sense in which it has hitherto been understood in America. This interesting subject will be resumed in the ensuing paper.

PUBLIUS.

Federalist No. 48 (James Madison)

To the People of the State of New York:

IT WAS shown in the last paper that the political apothegm there examined does not require that the legislative, executive, and judiciary departments should be wholly unconnected with each other. I shall undertake, in the next place, to show that unless these departments be so far connected and blended as to give to each a constitutional control over the others, the degree of separation which the maxim requires, as essential to a free government, can never in practice be duly maintained.

It is agreed on all sides, that the powers properly belonging to one of the departments ought not to be directly and completely administered by either of the other departments. It is equally evident, that none of them ought to possess, directly or indirectly, an overruling influence over the others, in the administration of their respective powers. It will not be denied, that power is of an encroaching nature, and that it ought to be effectually restrained from passing the limits assigned to it. After discriminating, therefore, in theory, the several classes of power, as they may in their nature be legislative, executive, or judiciary, the next and most difficult task is to provide some practical security for each, against the invasion of the others. What this security ought to be, is the great problem to be solved.

Will it be sufficient to mark, with precision, the boundaries of these departments, in the constitution of the government, and to trust to these parchment barriers against the encroaching spirit of power? This is the security which appears to have been principally relied on by the compilers of most of the American constitutions. But experience assures us, that the efficacy of the provision has been greatly overrated; and that some more adequate defense is indispensably necessary for the more feeble, against the more powerful, members of the government. The legislative department is everywhere extending the sphere of its activity, and drawing all power into its impetuous vortex.

The founders of our republics have so much merit for the wisdom which they have displayed, that no task can be less pleasing than that of pointing out the errors into which they have fallen. A respect for truth, however, obliges us to remark, that they seem never for a moment to have turned their eyes from the danger to liberty from the overgrown and all-grasping prerogative of an hereditary magistrate, supported and fortified by an hereditary branch of the legislative authority. They seem never to have recollected the danger from legislative usurpations, which, by assembling all power in the same hands, must lead to the same tyranny as is threatened by executive usurpations.

In a government where numerous and extensive prerogatives are placed in the hands of an hereditary monarch, the executive department is very justly regarded as the source of danger.... But in a representative republic, where the executive magistracy is carefully limited; both in the extent and the duration of its power; and where the legislative power is exercised by an assembly, which is inspired, by a supposed influence over the people, with an intrepid confidence in its own strength; which is sufficiently numerous to feel all the passions which actuate a multitude, yet not so numerous as to be incapable of pursuing the objects of its passions . . . it is against the enterprising ambition of this department that the people ought to indulge all their jealousy and exhaust all their precautions.

The legislative department derives a superiority in our governments from other circumstances. Its constitutional powers being at once more extensive, and less susceptible of precise limits, it can, with the greater facility, mask, under complicated and indirect measures, the encroachments which it makes on the co-ordinate departments. It is not unfrequently a question of real nicety in legislative bodies, whether the operation of a particular measure will, or will not, extend beyond the legislative sphere. On the other side, the executive power being restrained within a narrower compass, and being more simple in its nature, and the judiciary being described by landmarks still less uncertain, projects of usurpation by either of these departments would immediately betray and defeat themselves. Nor is this all: as the legislative department alone has access to the pockets of the people, and has in some constitutions full discretion, and in all a prevailing influence, over the pecuniary rewards of those who fill the other departments, a dependence is thus created in the latter, which gives still greater facility to encroachments of the former.

I have appealed to our own experience for the truth of what I advance on this subject. Were it necessary to verify this experience by particular proofs, they might be multiplied without end. I might find a witness in every citizen who has shared in, or been attentive to, the course of public administrations. I might collect vouchers in abundance from the records and archives of every State in the Union. But as a more concise, and at the same time equally satisfactory, evidence, I will refer to the example of two States, attested by two unexceptionable authorities.

The first example is that of Virginia, a State which, as we have seen, has expressly declared in its constitution, that the three great departments ought not to be intermixed. The authority in support of it is Mr. Jefferson, who . . . was himself the chief magistrate of [the state]. In order to convey fully the ideas with which his experience had impressed him on this subject, it will be necessary to quote a passage of some length from his very interesting "Notes on the State of Virginia." "All the powers of government, legislative, executive, and judiciary, result to the legislative body. The concentrating these in the same hands, is precisely the definition of despotic government. It will be no alleviation, that these powers will be exercised by a plurality of hands, and not by a single one. One hundred and seventy-three despots would surely be as oppressive as one. . . . As little will it avail us, that they are chosen by ourselves. An ELECTIVE DESPOTISM was not the government we fought for; but one which should not only be founded on free principles, but in which the powers of government should be so divided and balanced among several bodies of magistracy, as that no one could transcend their legal limits, without being effectually checked and restrained by the others. For this reason, that convention which passed the ordinance of government, laid its foundation on this basis, that the legislative, executive, and judiciary departments should be separate and distinct, so that no person should exercise the powers of more than one of them at the same time. BUT NO BARRIER WAS PROVIDED BETWEEN THESE SEVERAL POWERS. The judiciary and the executive members were left dependent on the legislative for their subsistence in office, and some of them for their continuance in it. If, therefore, the legislature assumes executive and judiciary powers, no opposition is likely to be made; nor, if made, can be effectual. . . . [The legislators] have accordingly, IN MANY instances, DECIDED RIGHTS which should have been left to JUDICIARY CONTROVERSY, and THE DIRECTION OF THE EXECUTIVE . . . IS BECOMING HABITUAL AND FAMILIAR."

The other State which I shall take for an example is Pennsylvania; and the other authority, the Council of Censors, which assembled in the years 1783 and 1784. A part of the duty of this body, as marked out by the constitution, was "to inquire whether the constitution had been preserved inviolate in every part; and whether the legislative and executive branches of government had performed their duty as guardians of the people, or assumed to themselves, or exercised, other or greater powers than they are entitled to by the constitution." In the execution of this trust, the council were necessarily led to a comparison of both the legislative and executive proceedings, with the constitutional powers of these departments; and from the facts enumerated, and to the truth of most of which both sides in the council subscribed, it appears that the constitution had been flagrantly violated by the legislature in a variety of important instances. . . .

The conclusion which I am warranted in drawing from these observations is, that a mere demarcation on parchment of the constitutional limits of the several departments, is not a sufficient guard against those encroachments which lead to a tyrannical concentration of all the powers of government in the same hands.

PUBLIUS.

NOTE ON SEPARATION OF POWERS AND POLITICAL THEORY

1.   Madison proposed an explicit separation of powers provision as part of the Bill of Rights:

> The powers delegated by this constitution, are appropriated to the departments to which they are respectively distributed: so that the legislative department shall never exercise the powers vested in the executive or judicial; nor the executive exercise the powers vested in the legislative or judicial; nor the judicial exercise the powers vested in the legislative or executive departments.

This proposal was never adopted, although several state constitutions feature similar provisions. We are left, instead, with the "vesting" clauses in each of the first three Articles, vesting legislative, executive, and judicial power in each respective branch, as well as certain specific enumerated powers conferred on each branch. Constitutional separation of powers doctrine, like federalism doctrine, has thus struggled to give life to broad theoretical principles that are only vaguely and incompletely realized in the constitutional text. And just as in the federalism context, many of the important demarcations of authority among the branches occur in statutory enactments and other forms of "ordinary law." Would it be better if the Constitution specified more detail concerning the separation of powers at the national level?

2.   Many in the Founding generation associated separation of powers with a sharp division of labor among the various departments of the government, with stringent safeguards to prevent interference of one department in the discharge of the functions of another. Such an approach is evident in Madison's proposed provision and even now reflected in some state constitutions:

Indiana Constitution, Art. 3, § 1: Three departments.

The powers of the Government are divided into three separate departments; the Legislative, the Executive including the Administrative, and the Judicial; and no person, charged with official duties under one of these departments, shall exercise any of the functions of another, except as in this Constitution expressly provided.

Notwithstanding Madison's failed textual proposal, his discussion in Federalist Nos. 47 and 48 argues that separated powers must be tempered by a second principle: checks and balances. The latter requires that each branch must have some input into the functions of the others, so as to exercise a check on those other branches. For example, the President participates in legislation by way of the veto, the Congress participates in execution of the laws by confirming executive officials, and so on. Checks and balances is thus not synonymous with separated powers; instead, it presupposes some degree of *overlap* among the functions of each branch.

3.   The tension between separated powers and checks and balances is reflected, to a degree, in the different forms taken by constitutional doctrine in this area. The Court's decisions have frequently veered back and forth between "formalism" and "functionalism." *Formalism* emphasizes the idea of separated powers. The key is to draw bright lines between the functions of each branch. To do that, we ask two questions:

- What sort of power is being exercised—legislative, executive, or judicial?

- Who is exercising that power? If it's the wrong branch, or a branch is exercising power outside the means constitutionally prescribed for that branch, a court is likely to strike the act down.

Departures from separated powers are thus confined strictly to those authorized in the constitutional text itself. This approach will frequently invalidate institutional innovations, such as the legislative veto.

Functionalism, on the other hand, puts greater emphasis on the idea of checks and balances. It is acceptable for one branch to have its fingers in another branch's function. The critical question is simply whether a particular governmental arrangement undermines the independence and core functions of one of the other branches. Three sorts of problems are typically identified:

- *Aggrandizement:* A particular measure *increases* the power of one branch vis-à-vis the others.

- *Encroachment:* A particular measure *decreases* the power or autonomy of one branch vis-à-vis the others.

- *Dilution:* Conferring a power or function on one branch renders that branch less able to do the job it's supposed to do.

These functional problems are often evaluated through a relatively open-ended balancing-type analysis. Unsurprisingly, this approach tends to be considerably more tolerant of institutional innovations that arguably depart from the constitutional norm.[3]

4.   The ebb and flow of separation of powers law reflects historical shifts in preoccupation: Many of the discussions and cases reflect a general intuition about the direction of "threat" at any particular time. The Declaration of Independence, for example, reflects a preoccupation with the abuse of executive power by George III. Hence, after the Revolution, the first wave of State constitutions sharply limited executive authority and placed virtually all power in the legislature. Madison says in Federalist No. 48 that the legislatures turned out to be almost as bad about abusing their power as King George had been. The experience under the Articles of Confederation also showed, at the national level, that the country could not get along without a relatively strong executive. Hence the Constitution of 1789 reflects a concern with restoring a strong executive and checking the power of the legislature.

By the 20th century the power of the presidency had expanded, especially after World War II, to the point of reviving a primary preoccupation with executive power. That concern was evident, for example, in discussions of "the Imperial Presidency."[4] Fear of executive authority seemed to fade a bit after Watergate, under a succession of less threatening presidents. But concerns about executive power have returned in the Twenty-first Century with the War on Terror and the broad claims by the second Bush Administration of unilateral executive authority to conduct that conflict. More recently, concerns about "gridlock" arising from divided partisan control of the legislative and executive branches led both the George W. Bush and Obama administrations to assert very broad claims of authority to act unilaterally. As the next case illustrates, however, those sorts of claims are hardly new.

Youngstown Sheet & Tube Co. v. Sawyer
343 U.S. 579 (1952)

[The Korean War began on June 25, 1950, when North Korea's armed forces crossed the 38th parallel and invaded South Korea. Soon after, the United Nations passed a resolution condemning North Korea's actions and authorizing the use of military force in response. Pursuant to this resolution, President Truman sent U.S. troops to South Korea. Truman did not ask Congress for a declaration of war on North Korea.

U.S. involvement in the war spurred heavy inflation. To counter its harmful effects, the President, under the Defense Production Act of 1950, sought to stabilize wages and implement price ceilings. Under the Act, the President created the Wage Stabilization Board (WSB) and Director of Price Stabilization (DPS) to advise him and help him implement the

---

[3]   On the distinction between formalism and functionalism, *see generally* Peter L. Strauss, *Formal and Functional Approaches to Separation-of-Powers Questions: A Foolish Inconsistency?* 72 CORNELL L. REV. 488 (1987).

[4]   *See* ARTHUR M. SCHLESINGER, JR., THE IMPERIAL PRESIDENCY (1973).

Act's provisions. Though the President established price controls on the industry, the United Steelworkers of America believed the profits of the steel companies to be unduly great, and the union threatened to strike if the wages of its members were not increased. Negotiations between the President (with the help of the WSB and DPS), the union, and the steel companies proved futile, as the companies refused to increase wages without a substantial increase in the price of steel. As a result, the union announced that a strike would begin at midnight on April 9, 1952.

President Truman, worried about the effects that a shortage of steel would have on the domestic economy and war efforts in Korea, issued Executive Order 10340 directing the Secretary of Commerce to seize the steel mills and keep them operating under federal control. The President sent two messages to Congress reporting what he had done, but Congress took no action. The steel companies, however, brought suit against the Secretary of Commerce in federal court.]

■ **MR. JUSTICE BLACK delivered the opinion of the Court.**

We are asked to decide whether the President was acting within his constitutional power when he issued an order directing the Secretary of Commerce to take possession of and operate most of the Nation's steel mills. . . .

Obeying the Secretary's orders under protest, the companies brought proceedings against him in the District Court. Their complaints charged that the seizure was not authorized by an act of Congress or by any constitutional provisions. The District Court was asked to declare the orders of the President and the Secretary invalid and to issue preliminary and permanent injunctions restraining their enforcement. Opposing the motion for preliminary injunction, the United States asserted that a strike disrupting steel production for even a brief period would so endanger the well-being and safety of the Nation that the President had "inherent power" to do what he had done. . . . Holding against the Government on all points, the District Court on April 30 issued a preliminary injunction restraining the Secretary from "continuing the seizure and possession of the plants. . . ." On the same day the Court of Appeals stayed the District Court's injunction. Deeming it best that the issues raised be promptly decided by this Court, we granted certiorari on May 3 and set the cause for argument on May 12. . . .

II

The President's power, if any, to issue the order must stem either from an act of Congress or from the Constitution itself. There is no statute that expressly authorizes the President to take possession of property as he did here. Nor is there any act of Congress to which our attention has been directed from which such a power can fairly be implied. Indeed, we do not understand the Government to rely on statutory authorization for this seizure. There are two statutes which do authorize the President to take both personal and real property under certain conditions.[2] However, the Government admits that these conditions were not met and that the President's order was not rooted in either of the statutes. The Government refers to the seizure provisions of one of these statutes (§ 201(b) of the Defense Production Act) as "much too cumbersome, involved, and time-consuming for the crisis which was at hand."

Moreover, the use of the seizure technique to solve labor disputes in order to prevent work stoppages was not only unauthorized by any congressional enactment; prior to this controversy, Congress had refused to adopt that method of settling labor disputes. When the Taft-Hartley Act was under consideration in 1947, Congress rejected an amendment which would have authorized such governmental seizures in cases of emergency. Apparently it was thought that the technique of seizure, like that of compulsory arbitration, would interfere with the process of collective bargaining. Consequently, the plan Congress adopted in that Act did not provide for seizure under any circumstances. Instead, the plan sought to bring about settlements by use of the customary devices of mediation, conciliation, investigation by boards of inquiry, and public reports. In some instances temporary injunctions were authorized to provide cooling-off periods. All this failing, unions were left free to strike after a secret vote by employees as to whether they wished to accept their employers' final settlement offer.

It is clear that if the President had authority to issue the order he did, it must be found in some provision of the Constitution. And it is not claimed that express constitutional language grants this power to the President. The contention is that presidential power should be implied from the aggregate of his powers under the Constitution. Particular reliance is placed on provisions in Article II which say that "The executive Power shall be vested in a President . . ."; that "he shall take Care that the Laws be faithfully executed"; and that he "shall be Commander in Chief of the Army and Navy of the United States."

The order cannot properly be sustained as an exercise of the President's military power as Commander in Chief of the Armed Forces. The Government attempts to do so by citing a number of cases upholding broad powers in military commanders engaged in day-to-day fighting in a theater of war. Such cases need not concern us here. Even though "theater of war" be an expanding concept, we cannot with faithfulness to our constitutional system hold that the Commander in Chief of the Armed Forces has the ultimate power as such to take possession of private property in order to keep labor disputes from stopping production. This is a job for the Nation's lawmakers, not for its military authorities.

---

[2]   The Selective Service Act of 1948; the Defense Production Act of 1950.

Nor can the seizure order be sustained because of the several constitutional provisions that grant executive power to the President. In the framework of our Constitution, the President's power to see that the laws are faithfully executed refutes the idea that he is to be a lawmaker. The Constitution limits his functions in the lawmaking process to the recommending of laws he thinks wise and the vetoing of laws he thinks bad. And the Constitution is neither silent nor equivocal about who shall make laws which the President is to execute. The first section of the first article says that "All legislative Powers herein granted shall be vested in a Congress of the United States. . . ." After granting many powers to the Congress, Article I goes on to provide that Congress may "make all Laws which shall be necessary and proper for carrying into Execution the foregoing Powers, and all other Powers vested by this Constitution in the Government of the United States, or in any Department or Officer thereof."

The President's order does not direct that a congressional policy be executed in a manner prescribed by Congress—it directs that a presidential policy be executed in a manner prescribed by the President. The preamble of the order itself, like that of many statutes, sets out reasons why the President believes certain policies should be adopted, proclaims these policies as rules of conduct to be followed, and again, like a statute, authorizes a government official to promulgate additional rules and regulations consistent with the policy proclaimed and needed to carry that policy into execution. The power of Congress to adopt such public policies as those proclaimed by the order is beyond question. It can authorize the taking of private property for public use. It can make laws regulating the relationships between employers and employees, prescribing rules designed to settle labor disputes, and fixing wages and working conditions in certain fields of our economy. The Constitution does not subject this lawmaking power of Congress to presidential or military supervision or control. . . .

The Founders of this Nation entrusted the lawmaking power to the Congress alone in both good and bad times. It would do no good to recall the historical events, the fears of power and the hopes for freedom that lay behind their choice. Such a review would but confirm our holding that this seizure order cannot stand.

The judgment of the District Court is *Affirmed.*

■ MR. JUSTICE FRANKFURTER, concurring.

Before the cares of the White House were his own, President Harding is reported to have said that government after all is a very simple thing. He must have said that, if he said it, as a fleeting inhabitant of fairyland. . . .

[Our Founders] rested the structure of our central government on the system of checks and balances. For them the doctrine of separation of powers was not mere theory; it was a felt necessity. Not so long ago it was fashionable to find our system of checks and balances obstructive to effective government. It was easy to ridicule that system as outmoded— too easy. The experience through which the world has passed in our own day has made vivid the realization that the Framers of our Constitution were not inexperienced doctrinaires. These long-headed statesmen had no illusion that our people enjoyed biological or psychological or sociological immunities from the hazards of concentrated power. It is absurd to see a dictator in a representative product of the sturdy democratic traditions of the Mississippi Valley. The accretion of dangerous power does not come in a day. It does come, however slowly, from the generative force of unchecked disregard of the restrictions that fence in even the most disinterested assertion of authority. . . .

Marshall's admonition that "it is *a constitution* we are expounding" is especially relevant when the Court is required to give legal sanctions to an underlying principle of the Constitution—that of separation of powers. "The great ordinances of the Constitution do not establish and divide fields of black and white." Holmes, J., dissenting in *Springer v. Philippine Islands*, 277 U.S. 189 (1928).

The issue before us can be met, and therefore should be, without attempting to define the President's powers comprehensively. I shall not attempt to delineate what belongs to him by virtue of his office beyond the power even of Congress to contract; what authority belongs to him until Congress acts; what kind of problems may be dealt with either by the Congress or by the President or by both; what power must be exercised by the Congress and cannot be delegated to the President. It is as unprofitable to lump together in an undiscriminating hotch-potch past presidential actions . . . as it is to conjure up hypothetical future cases. The judiciary may, as this case proves, have to intervene in determining where authority lies as between the democratic forces in our scheme of government. But in doing so we should be wary and humble. . . .

The question before the Court comes in this setting. Congress has frequently—at least 16 times since 1916—specifically provided for executive seizure of production, transportation, communications, or storage facilities. In every case it has qualified this grant of power with limitations and safeguards. This body of enactments . . . demonstrates that Congress deemed seizure so drastic a power as to require that it be carefully circumscribed whenever the President was vested with this extraordinary authority. The power to seize has uniformly been given only for a limited period or for a defined emergency, or has been repealed after a short period. Its exercise has been restricted to particular circumstances such as "time of war or when war is imminent," the needs of "public safety" or of "national security or defense," or "urgent and impending need." The period of governmental operation has been limited, as, for instance, to "sixty days after the restoration of productive efficiency." Seizure statutes usually make executive action dependent on detailed conditions: for example, (a) failure or refusal of the owner of a plant to meet governmental supply needs or (b) failure of voluntary negotiations with the owner for the use of a plant necessary for great public ends. Congress often has specified the particular executive agency which should seize or operate the plants or whose judgment would appropriately test the need for seizure. Congress also has not left to implication that just compensation be paid; it has usually legislated in detail regarding enforcement of this litigation-breeding general requirement.

Congress in 1947 was again called upon to consider whether governmental seizure should be used to avoid serious industrial shutdowns. Congress decided against conferring such power generally and in advance, without special Congressional enactment to meet each particular need. Under the urgency of telephone and coal strikes in the winter of 1946, Congress addressed itself to the problems raised by "national emergency" strikes and lockouts.[1] The termination of wartime seizure powers on December 31, 1946, brought these matters to the attention of Congress with vivid impact. A proposal that the President be given powers to seize plants to avert a shutdown where the "health or safety" of the Nation was endangered, was thoroughly canvassed by Congress and rejected. No room for doubt remains that the proponents as well as the opponents of the bill which became the Labor Management Relations Act of 1947 clearly understood that as a result of that legislation the only recourse for preventing a shutdown in any basic industry, after failure of mediation, was Congress. Authorization for seizure as an available remedy for potential dangers was unequivocally put aside. The Senate Labor Committee, through its Chairman, explicitly reported to the Senate that a general grant of seizure powers had been considered and rejected in favor of reliance on *ad hoc* legislation, as a particular emergency might call for it. An amendment presented in the House providing that, where necessary "to preserve and protect the public health and security," the President might seize any industry in which there is an impending curtailment of production, was voted down after debate, by a vote of more than three to one. . . .

In any event, nothing can be plainer than that Congress made a conscious choice of policy in a field full of perplexity and peculiarly within legislative responsibility for choice. In formulating legislation for dealing with industrial conflicts, Congress could not more clearly and emphatically have withheld authority than it did in 1947. Perhaps as much so as is true of any piece of modern legislation, Congress acted with full consciousness of what it was doing and in the light of much recent history. . . . The President could not ignore the specific limitations of

---

[1] The power to seize plants under the War Labor Disputes Act ended with the termination of hostilities, proclaimed on Dec. 31, 1946, . . . and the power to operate previously seized plants ended on June 30, 1947, only a week after the enactment of the Labor Management Relations Act over the President's veto.

prior seizure statutes. No more could he act in disregard of the limitation put upon seizure by the 1947 Act.

It cannot be contended that the President would have had power to issue this order had Congress explicitly negated such authority in formal legislation. Congress has expressed its will to withhold this power from the President as though it had said so in so many words. . . . By the Labor Management Relations Act of 1947, Congress said to the President, "You may not seize. Please report to us and ask for seizure power if you think it is needed in a specific situation." This of course calls for a report on the unsuccessful efforts to reach a voluntary settlement, as a basis for discharge by Congress of its responsibility—which it has unequivocally reserved—to fashion further remedies than it provided. . . .

The utmost that the Korean conflict may imply is that it may have been desirable to have given the President further authority, a freer hand in these matters. Absence of authority in the President to deal with a crisis does not imply want of power in the Government. Conversely the fact that power exists in the Government does not vest it in the President. The need for new legislation does not enact it. Nor does it repeal or amend existing law. . . .

Apart from his vast share of responsibility for the conduct of our foreign relations, the embracing function of the President is that "he shall take Care that the Laws be faithfully executed. . . ." Art. II, § 3. The nature of that authority has for me been comprehensively indicated by Mr. Justice Holmes. "The duty of the President to see that the laws be executed is a duty that does not go beyond the laws or require him to achieve more than Congress sees fit to leave within his power." The powers of the President are not as particularized as are those of Congress. But unenumerated powers do not mean undefined powers. The separation of powers built into our Constitution gives essential content to undefined provisions in the frame of our government.

To be sure, the content of the three authorities of government is not to be derived from an abstract analysis. The areas are partly interacting, not wholly disjointed. The Constitution is a framework for government. Therefore the way the framework has consistently operated fairly establishes that it has operated according to its true nature. Deeply embedded traditional ways of conducting government cannot supplant the Constitution or legislation, but they give meaning to the words of a text or supply them. It is an inadmissibly narrow conception of American constitutional law to confine it to the words of the Constitution and to disregard the gloss which life has written upon them. In short, a systematic, unbroken, executive practice, long pursued to the knowledge of the Congress and never before questioned, engaged in by Presidents who have also sworn to uphold the Constitution, making as it were such exercise of power part of the structure of our government, may be treated as a gloss on "executive Power" vested in the President by § 1 of Art. II. . . .

Down to the World War II period, then, the record is barren of instances comparable to the one before us. Of twelve seizures by President Roosevelt prior to the enactment of the War Labor Disputes Act in June, 1943, three were sanctioned by existing law, and six others were effected after Congress, on December 8, 1941, had declared the existence of a state of war. In this case, reliance on the powers that flow from declared war has been commendably disclaimed by the Solicitor General. Thus the list of executive assertions of the power of seizure in circumstances comparable to the present reduces to three in the six-month period from June to December of 1941. We need not split hairs in comparing those actions to the one before us, though much might be said by way of differentiation. . . . [I]t suffices to say that these three isolated instances do not add up, either in number, scope, duration or contemporaneous legal justification, to [a consistent] executive construction of the Constitution. . . . Nor do they come to us sanctioned by long-continued acquiescence of Congress giving decisive weight to a construction by the Executive of its powers.

A scheme of government like ours no doubt at times feels the lack of power to act with complete, all-embracing, swiftly moving authority. No doubt a government with distributed authority, subject to be challenged in the courts of law, at least long enough to consider and adjudicate the challenge, labors under restrictions from which other governments are free. It has not been our tradition to envy such governments. In any event our government was designed to have such restrictions. The price was deemed not too high in view of the safeguards which these restrictions afford. . . .

■ **MR. JUSTICE DOUGLAS, concurring.**

There can be no doubt that the emergency which caused the President to seize these steel plants was one that bore heavily on the country. But the emergency did not create power; it merely marked an occasion when power should be exercised. And the fact that it was necessary that measures be taken to keep steel in production does not mean that the President, rather than the Congress, had the constitutional authority to act. The Congress, as well as the President, is trustee of the national welfare. The President can act more quickly than the Congress. The President with the armed services at his disposal can move with force as well as with speed. All executive power—from the reign of ancient kings to the rule of modern dictators—has the outward appearance of efficiency.

Legislative power, by contrast, is slower to exercise. There must be delay while the ponderous machinery of committees, hearings, and debates is put into motion. That takes time; and while the Congress slowly moves into action, the emergency may take its toll in wages, consumer goods, war production, the standard of living of the people, and perhaps even lives. Legislative action may indeed often be cumbersome, time-consuming, and apparently inefficient. But as Mr. Justice Brandeis stated in his dissent in *Myers v. United States*, 272 U.S. 52 (1926):

> The doctrine of the separation of powers was adopted by the Convention of 1787, not to promote efficiency but to preclude the exercise of arbitrary power. The purpose was, not to avoid friction, but, by means of the inevitable friction incident to the distribution of the governmental powers among three departments, to save the people from autocracy.

We therefore cannot decide this case by determining which branch of government can deal most expeditiously with the present crisis. The answer must depend on the allocation of powers under the Constitution. . . .

The legislative nature of the action taken by the President seems to me to be clear. When the United States takes over an industrial plant to settle a labor controversy, it is condemning property. The seizure of the plant is a taking in the constitutional sense. . . . [T]hough the seizure is only for a week or a month, the condemnation is complete and the United States must pay compensation for the temporary possession. . . . I have no doubt but that condemnation of a plant, factory, or industry in order to promote industrial peace would be constitutional. But there is a duty to pay for all property taken by the Government. . . .

The President has no power to raise revenues. That power is in the Congress by Article I, Section 8 of the Constitution. The President might seize and the Congress by subsequent action might ratify the seizure. But until and unless Congress acted, no condemnation would be lawful. The branch of government that has the power to pay compensation for a seizure is the only one able to authorize a seizure or make lawful one that the President has effected. That seems to me to be the necessary result of the condemnation provision in the Fifth Amendment. It squares with the theory of checks and balances expounded by MR. JUSTICE BLACK in the opinion of the Court in which I join.

If we sanctioned the present exercise of power by the President, we would be expanding Article II of the Constitution and rewriting it to suit the political conveniences of the present emergency. . . . Article II, Section 2 makes the Chief Executive the Commander in Chief of the Army and Navy. But our history and tradition rebel at the thought that the grant of military power carries with it authority over civilian affairs. . . .

Stalemates may occur when emergencies mount and the Nation suffers for lack of harmonious, reciprocal action between the White House and Capitol Hill. That is a risk inherent in our system of separation of powers. The tragedy of such stalemates might be avoided by allowing the President the use of some legislative authority. The Framers with memories of the tyrannies produced by a blending of executive and legislative power rejected that political arrangement. . . .

We pay a price for our system of checks and balances. . . . It is a price that today may seem exorbitant to many. Today a kindly President uses the seizure power to effect a wage increase and to keep the steel furnaces in production. Yet tomorrow another President might use the same power to prevent a wage increase, to curb trade-unionists, to regiment labor as oppressively as industry thinks it has been regimented by this seizure.

■ **Mr. Justice Jackson, concurring in the judgment and opinion of the Court.**

. . . A judge, like an executive adviser, may be surprised at the poverty of really useful and unambiguous authority applicable to concrete problems of executive power as they actually present themselves. Just what our forefathers did envision, or would have envisioned had they foreseen modern conditions, must be divined from materials almost as enigmatic as the dreams Joseph was called upon to interpret for Pharaoh. A century and a half of partisan debate and scholarly speculation yields no net result but only supplies more or less apt quotations from respected sources on each side of any question. They largely cancel each other. And court decisions are indecisive because of the judicial practice of dealing with the largest questions in the most narrow way. . . .

While the Constitution diffuses power the better to secure liberty, it also contemplates that practice will integrate the dispersed powers into a workable government. It enjoins upon its branches separateness but interdependence, autonomy but reciprocity. Presidential powers are not fixed but fluctuate, depending upon their disjunction or conjunction with those of Congress. We may well begin by a somewhat over-simplified grouping of practical situations in which a President may doubt, or others may challenge, his powers, and by distinguishing roughly the legal consequences of this factor of relativity.

1.   When the President acts pursuant to an express or implied authorization of Congress, his authority is at its maximum, for it includes all that he possesses in his own right plus all that Congress can delegate. In these circumstances, and in these only, may he be said (for what it may be worth) to personify the federal sovereignty. If his act is held unconstitutional under these circumstances, it usually means that the Federal Government as an undivided whole lacks power. A seizure executed by the President pursuant to an Act of Congress would be supported by the strongest of presumptions and the widest latitude of judicial interpretation, and the burden of persuasion would rest heavily upon any who might attack it.

2.   When the President acts in absence of either a congressional grant or denial of authority, he can only rely upon his own independent powers, but there is a zone of twilight in which he and Congress may have concurrent authority, or in which its distribution is uncertain. Therefore, congressional inertia, indifference or quiescence may sometimes, at least as a practical matter, enable, if not invite, measures

on independent presidential responsibility. In this area, any actual test of power is likely to depend on the imperatives of events and contemporary imponderables rather than on abstract theories of law.

3.   When the President takes measures incompatible with the expressed or implied will of Congress, his power is at its lowest ebb, for then he can rely only upon his own constitutional powers minus any constitutional powers of Congress over the matter. Courts can sustain exclusive presidential control in such a case only by disabling the Congress from acting upon the subject. Presidential claim to a power at once so conclusive and preclusive must be scrutinized with caution, for what is at stake is the equilibrium established by our constitutional system.

Into which of these classifications does this executive seizure of the steel industry fit? It is eliminated from the first by admission, for it is conceded that no congressional authorization exists for this seizure. . . .

Can it then be defended under flexible tests available to the second category? It seems clearly eliminated from that class because Congress has not left seizure of private property an open field but has covered it by three statutory policies inconsistent with this seizure. In cases where the purpose is to supply needs of the Government itself, two courses are provided: one, seizure of a plant which fails to comply with obligatory orders placed by the Government;[6] another, condemnation of facilities, including temporary use under the power of eminent domain.[7] The third is applicable where it is the general economy of the country that is to be protected rather than exclusive governmental interests.[8] None of these were invoked. In choosing a different and inconsistent way of his own, the President cannot claim that it is necessitated or invited by failure of Congress to legislate upon the occasions, grounds and methods for seizure of industrial properties.

This leaves the current seizure to be justified only by the severe tests under the third grouping, where it can be supported only by any remainder of executive power after subtraction of such powers as Congress may have over the subject. In short, we can sustain the President only by holding that seizure of such strike-bound industries is within his domain and beyond control by Congress. . . .

The Solicitor General seeks the power of seizure in three clauses of the Executive Article, the first reading, "The executive Power shall be vested in a President of the United States of America." Lest I be thought to exaggerate, I quote the interpretation which his brief puts upon it: "In our view, this clause constitutes a grant of all the executive powers of which the Government is capable." If that be true, it is difficult to see

---

[6]   Selective Service Act of 1948.

[7]   Defense Production Act of 1950. . . .

[8]   Labor Management Relations Act, 1947, §§ 206–210. . . .

why the forefathers bothered to add several specific items, including some trifling ones.[9]

The example of such unlimited executive power that must have most impressed the forefathers was the prerogative exercised by George III, and the description of its evils in the Declaration of Independence leads me to doubt that they were creating their new Executive in his image. Continental European examples were no more appealing. And if we seek instruction from our own times, we can match it only from the executive powers in those governments we disparagingly describe as totalitarian. I cannot accept the view that this clause is a grant in bulk of all conceivable executive power but regard it as an allocation to the presidential office of the generic powers thereafter stated.

The clause on which the Government next relies is that "The President shall be Commander in Chief of the Army and Navy of the United States. . . ." These cryptic words have given rise to some of the most persistent controversies in our constitutional history. Of course, they imply something more than an empty title. But just what authority goes with the name has plagued presidential advisers who would not waive or narrow it by nonassertion yet cannot say where it begins or ends. It undoubtedly puts the Nation's armed forces under presidential command. Hence, this loose appellation is sometimes advanced as support for any presidential action, internal or external, involving use of force, the idea being that it vests power to do anything, anywhere, that can be done with an army or navy.

That seems to be the logic of an argument tendered at our bar—that the President having, on his own responsibility, sent American troops abroad derives from that act "affirmative power" to seize the means of producing a supply of steel for them. . . . I cannot foresee all that it might entail if the Court should indorse this argument. Nothing in our Constitution is plainer than that declaration of a war is entrusted only to Congress. Of course, a state of war may in fact exist without a formal declaration. But no doctrine that the Court could promulgate would seem to me more sinister and alarming than that a President whose conduct of foreign affairs is so largely uncontrolled, and often even is unknown, can vastly enlarge his mastery over the internal affairs of the country by his own commitment of the Nation's armed forces to some foreign venture. . . .

The Constitution expressly places in Congress power "to raise and *support* Armies" and "to *provide* and *maintain* a Navy." (Emphasis supplied.) This certainly lays upon Congress primary responsibility for supplying the armed forces. Congress alone controls the raising of

---

[9] "[H]e may require the Opinion, in writing, of the principal Officer in each of the executive Departments, upon any Subject relating to the Duties of their respective Offices. . . ." U.S. Const., Art. II, § 2. He ". . . shall Commission all the Officers of the United States." U.S. Const., Art. II, § 3. Matters such as those would seem to be inherent in the Executive if anything is.

revenues and their appropriation and may determine in what manner and by what means they shall be spent for military and naval procurement. . . .

[T]he Constitution did not contemplate that the title Commander in Chief *of the Army and Navy* will constitute him also Commander in Chief of the country, its industries and its inhabitants. He has no monopoly of "war powers," whatever they are. While Congress cannot deprive the President of the command of the army and navy, only Congress can provide him an army or navy to command. . . .

We should not use this occasion to circumscribe, much less to contract, the lawful role of the President as Commander in Chief. I should indulge the widest latitude of interpretation to sustain his exclusive function to command the instruments of national force, at least when turned against the outside world for the security of our society. But, when it is turned inward, not because of rebellion but because of a lawful economic struggle between industry and labor, it should have no such indulgence. His command power is not such an absolute as might be implied from that office in a militaristic system but is subject to limitations consistent with a constitutional Republic whose law and policy-making branch is a representative Congress. The purpose of lodging dual titles in one man was to insure that the civilian would control the military, not to enable the military to subordinate the presidential office. No penance would ever expiate the sin against free government of holding that a President can escape control of executive powers by law through assuming his military role. What the power of command may include I do not try to envision, but I think it is not a military prerogative, without support of law, to seize persons or property because they are important or even essential for the military and naval establishment. . . .

The Solicitor General lastly grounds support of the seizure upon nebulous, inherent powers . . . to deal with a crisis or an emergency according to the necessities of the case, the unarticulated assumption being that necessity knows no law.

Loose and irresponsible use of adjectives colors all nonlegal and much legal discussion of presidential powers. "Inherent" powers, "implied" powers, "incidental" powers, "plenary" powers, "war" powers and "emergency" powers are used, often interchangeably and without fixed or ascertainable meanings.

The appeal, however, that we declare the existence of inherent powers *ex necessitate* to meet an emergency asks us to do what many think would be wise, although it is something the forefathers omitted. They knew what emergencies were, knew the pressures they engender for authoritative action, knew, too, how they afford a ready pretext for usurpation. We may also suspect that they suspected that emergency powers would tend to kindle emergencies. Aside from suspension of the privilege of the writ of habeas corpus in time of rebellion or invasion, when the public safety may require it,[18] they made no express provision for exercise of extraordinary authority because of a crisis. I do not think we rightfully may so amend their work, and, if we could, I am not convinced it would be wise to do so. . . .

In the practical working of our Government we already have evolved a technique within the framework of the Constitution by which normal executive powers may be considerably expanded to meet an emergency. Congress may and has granted extraordinary authorities which lie dormant in normal times but may be called into play by the Executive in war or upon proclamation of a national emergency. . . .

In view of the ease, expedition and safety with which Congress can grant and has granted large emergency powers, certainly ample to embrace this crisis, I am quite unimpressed with the argument that we should affirm possession of them without statute. Such power either has no beginning or it has no end. If it exists, it need submit to no legal restraint. I am not alarmed that it would plunge us straightway into dictatorship, but it is at least a step in that wrong direction.

As to whether there is imperative necessity for such powers, it is relevant to note the gap that exists between the President's paper powers and his real powers. The Constitution does not disclose the measure of the actual controls wielded by the modern presidential office. . . . Vast accretions of federal power, eroded from that reserved by the States, have magnified the scope of presidential activity. . . .

Executive power has the advantage of concentration in a single head in whose choice the whole Nation has a part, making him the focus of public hopes and expectations. In drama, magnitude and finality his decisions so far overshadow any others that almost alone he fills the public eye and ear. No other personality in public life can begin to compete with him in access to the public mind through modern methods of communications. By his prestige as head of state and his influence upon public opinion he exerts a leverage upon those who are supposed to check and balance his power which often cancels their effectiveness.

Moreover, rise of the party system has made a significant extraconstitutional supplement to real executive power. No appraisal of his necessities is realistic which overlooks that he heads a political system as well as a legal system. Party loyalties and interests, sometimes more binding than law, extend his effective control into branches of government other than his own and he often may win, as a political leader, what he cannot command under the Constitution. . . .

But I have no illusion that any decision by this Court can keep power in the hands of Congress if it is not wise and timely in meeting its problems. A crisis that challenges the President equally, or perhaps primarily, challenges Congress. If not good law, there was worldly

---

[18]   U.S. Const., Art. I, § 9, cl. 2.

wisdom in the maxim attributed to Napoleon that "The tools belong to the man who can use them." We may say that power to legislate for emergencies belongs in the hands of Congress, but only Congress itself can prevent power from slipping through its fingers. . . .

The executive action we have here originates in the individual will of the President and represents an exercise of authority without law. No one, perhaps not even the President, knows the limits of the power he may seek to exert in this instance and the parties affected cannot learn the limit of their rights. . . . With all its defects, delays and inconveniences, men have discovered no technique for long preserving free government except that the Executive be under the law, and that the law be made by parliamentary deliberations.

Such institutions may be destined to pass away. But it is the duty of the Court to be last, not first, to give them up. . . .

■ **MR. CHIEF JUSTICE VINSON, with whom MR. JUSTICE REED and MR. JUSTICE MINTON join, dissenting.**

I

. . . Those who suggest that this is a case involving extraordinary powers should be mindful that these are extraordinary times. A world not yet recovered from the devastation of World War II has been forced to face the threat of another and more terrifying global conflict. . . .

In 1950, when the United Nations called upon member nations "to render every assistance" to repel aggression in Korea, the United States furnished its vigorous support. For almost two full years, our armed forces have been fighting in Korea, suffering casualties of over 108,000 men. Hostilities have not abated. The "determination of the United Nations to continue its action in Korea to meet the aggression" has been reaffirmed. Congressional support of the action in Korea has been manifested by provisions for increased military manpower and equipment and for economic stabilization, as hereinafter described.

Further efforts to protect the free world from aggression are found in the congressional enactments of the Truman Plan for assistance to Greece and Turkey and the Marshall Plan for economic aid needed to build up the strength of our friends in Western Europe. In 1949, the Senate approved the North Atlantic Treaty under which each member nation agrees that an armed attack against one is an armed attack against all. Congress immediately implemented the North Atlantic Treaty by authorizing military assistance to nations dedicated to the principles of mutual security under the United Nations Charter. The concept of mutual security recently has been extended by treaty to friends in the Pacific. . . .

The President has the duty to execute the foregoing legislative programs. Their successful execution depends upon continued production of steel and stabilized prices for steel. Accordingly, when the collective bargaining agreements between the Nation's steel producers and their employees, represented by the United Steel Workers, were due to expire on December 31, 1951, and a strike shutting down the entire basic steel industry was threatened, the President acted to avert a complete shutdown of steel production. . . .

One is not here called upon even to consider the possibility of executive seizure of a farm, a corner grocery store or even a single industrial plant. Such considerations arise only when one ignores the central fact of this case—that the Nation's entire basic steel production would have shut down completely if there had been no Government seizure. Even ignoring for the moment whatever confidential information the President may possess as "the Nation's organ for foreign affairs," the uncontroverted affidavits in this record amply support the finding that "a work stoppage would immediately jeopardize and imperil our national defense."

Plaintiffs do not remotely suggest any basis for rejecting the President's finding that *any* stoppage of steel production would immediately place the Nation in peril. . . . At the time of seizure there was not, and there is not now, the slightest evidence to justify the belief that any strike will be of short duration. . . . Plaintiffs' counsel tells us that "sooner or later" the mills will operate again. . . . But our soldiers and our allies will hardly be cheered with the assurance that the ammunition upon which their lives depend will be forthcoming—"sooner or later," or, in other words, "too little and too late."

Accordingly, if the President has any power under the Constitution to meet a critical situation in the absence of express statutory authorization, there is no basis whatever for criticizing the exercise of such power in this case.

II

The steel mills were seized for a public use. The power of eminent domain, invoked in this case, is an essential attribute of sovereignty and has long been recognized as a power of the Federal Government. Plaintiffs cannot complain that any provision in the Constitution prohibits the exercise of the power of eminent domain in this case. The Fifth Amendment provides: "nor shall private property be taken for public use, without just compensation." It is no bar to this seizure for, if the taking is not otherwise unlawful, plaintiffs are assured of receiving the required just compensation.

Admitting that the Government could seize the mills, plaintiffs claim that the implied power of eminent domain can be exercised only under an Act of Congress. . . . Under this view, the President is left powerless at the very moment when the need for action may be most pressing and when no one, other than he, is immediately capable of action. Under this view, he is left powerless because a power not expressly given to Congress is nevertheless found to rest exclusively with Congress. . . .

[T]he Presidency was deliberately fashioned as an office of power and independence. Of course, the Framers created no autocrat capable of arrogating any power unto himself at any time. But neither did they create an automaton impotent to exercise the powers of Government at a time when the survival of the Republic itself may be at stake.

In passing upon the grave constitutional question presented in this case, we must never forget, as Chief Justice Marshall admonished, that the Constitution is "intended to endure for ages to come, and, consequently, to be adapted to the various *crises* of human affairs," and that "its means are adequate to its ends." Cases do arise presenting questions which could not have been foreseen by the Framers. . . . But we are not called upon today to expand the Constitution to meet a new situation. For, in this case, we need only look to history and time-honored principles of constitutional law. . . .

III

A review of executive action demonstrates that our Presidents have on many occasions exhibited the leadership contemplated by the Framers when they made the President Commander in Chief, and imposed upon him the trust to "take Care that the Laws be faithfully executed." With or without explicit statutory authorization, Presidents have at such times dealt with national emergencies by acting promptly and resolutely to enforce legislative programs, at least to save those programs until Congress could act. Congress and the courts have responded to such executive initiative with consistent approval. . . .

When the national revenue laws were openly flouted in some sections of Pennsylvania, President Washington, without waiting for a call from the state government, summoned the militia and took decisive steps to secure the faithful execution of the laws. When international disputes engendered by the French revolution threatened to involve this country in war, and while congressional policy remained uncertain, Washington issued his Proclamation of Neutrality. Hamilton, whose defense of the Proclamation has endured the test of time, invoked the argument that the Executive has the duty to do that which will preserve peace until Congress acts and, in addition, pointed to the need for keeping the Nation informed of the requirements of existing laws and treaties as part of the faithful execution of the laws. . . .

Jefferson's initiative in the Louisiana Purchase, the Monroe Doctrine, and Jackson's removal of Government deposits from the Bank of the United States further serve to demonstrate by deed what the Framers described by word when they vested the whole of the executive power in the President.

Without declaration of war, President Lincoln took energetic action with the outbreak of the War Between the States. He summoned troops and paid them out of the Treasury without appropriation therefor. He proclaimed a naval blockade of the Confederacy and seized ships violating that blockade. Congress, far from denying the validity of these acts, gave them express approval. The most striking action of President Lincoln was the Emancipation Proclamation, issued in aid of the successful prosecution of the War Between the States, but wholly without statutory authority. . . .

During World War I, President Wilson established a War Labor Board without awaiting specific direction by Congress. . . . [T]he Board had as its purpose the prevention of strikes and lockouts interfering with the production of goods needed to meet the emergency. Effectiveness of War Labor Board decision was accomplished by Presidential action, including seizure of industrial plants. Seizure of the Nation's railroads was also ordered by President Wilson.

Beginning with the Bank Holiday Proclamation and continuing through World War II, executive leadership and initiative were characteristic of President Franklin D. Roosevelt's administration. In 1939, upon the outbreak of war in Europe, the President proclaimed a limited national emergency for the purpose of strengthening our national defense. In May of 1941, the danger from the Axis belligerents having become clear, the President proclaimed "an unlimited national emergency" calling for mobilization of the Nation's defenses to repel aggression. The President took the initiative in strengthening our defenses by acquiring rights from the British Government to establish air bases in exchange for overage destroyers. . . .

This is but a cursory summary of executive leadership. But it amply demonstrates that Presidents have taken prompt action to enforce the laws and protect the country whether or not Congress happened to provide in advance for the particular method of execution. . . . [T]he fact that Congress and the courts have consistently recognized and given their support to such executive action indicates that such a power of seizure has been accepted throughout our history. . . .

IV

. . . Much of the argument in this case has been directed at straw men. We do not now have before us the case of a President acting solely on the basis of his own notions of the public welfare. Nor is there any question of unlimited executive power in this case. The President himself closed the door to any such claim when he sent his Message to Congress stating his purpose to abide by any action of Congress, whether approving or disapproving his seizure action. Here, the President immediately made sure that Congress was fully informed of the temporary action he had taken only to preserve the legislative programs from destruction until Congress could act.

The absence of a specific statute authorizing seizure of the steel mills as a mode of executing the laws—both the military procurement program and the anti-inflation program—has not until today been thought to prevent the President from executing the laws. Unlike an administrative commission confined to the enforcement of the statute under which it was created, or the head of a department when administering a particular statute, the President is a constitutional officer charged with taking care that a "mass of legislation" be executed. Flexibility as to mode of execution to meet critical situations is a matter of practical necessity. . . .

There is no statute prohibiting seizure as a method of enforcing legislative programs. . . .

Whatever the extent of Presidential power on more tranquil occasions . . . the single Presidential purpose disclosed on this record is to faithfully execute the laws by acting in an emergency to maintain the status quo, thereby preventing collapse of the legislative programs until Congress could act. . . . In his Message to Congress immediately following the seizure, the President explained the necessity of his action in executing the military procurement and anti-inflation legislative programs and expressed his desire to cooperate with any legislative proposals approving, regulating or rejecting the seizure of the steel mills. Consequently, there is no evidence whatever of any Presidential purpose to defy Congress or act in any way inconsistent with the legislative will. . . .

V

. . . [A]s of December 22, 1951, the President had a choice between alternate procedures for settling the threatened strike in the steel mills: one route created to deal with peacetime disputes; the other route specially created to deal with disputes growing out of the defense and stabilization program. There is no question of by-passing a statutory procedure because both of the routes available to the President in December were based upon statutory authorization. Both routes were available in the steel dispute. The Union, by refusing to abide by the defense and stabilization program, could have forced the President to invoke Taft-Hartley at that time to delay the strike a maximum of 80 days. Instead, the Union agreed to cooperate with the defense program and submit the dispute to the Wage Stabilization Board.

Plaintiffs had no objection whatever at that time to the President's choice of the WSB route. As a result, the strike was postponed, a WSB panel held hearings and reported the position of the parties and the WSB recommended the terms of a settlement which it found were fair and equitable. Moreover, the WSB performed a function which the board of inquiry contemplated by Taft-Hartley could not have accomplished when it checked the recommended wage settlement against its own wage stabilization regulations issued pursuant to its stabilization functions under Title IV of the Defense Production Act. Thereafter, the parties bargained on the basis of the WSB recommendation.

When the President acted on April 8, he had exhausted the procedures for settlement available to him. Taft-Hartley was a route parallel to, not connected with, the WSB procedure. The strike had been delayed 99 days as contrasted with the maximum delay of 80 days under Taft-Hartley. There had been a hearing on the issues in dispute and bargaining which promised settlement up to the very hour before seizure had broken down. Faced with immediate national peril through stoppage in steel production on the one hand and faced with destruction of the wage and price legislative programs on the other, the President took temporary possession of the steel mills as the only course open to him consistent with his duty to take care that the laws be faithfully executed.

Plaintiffs' property was taken and placed in the possession of the Secretary of Commerce to prevent any interruption in steel production. It made no difference whether the stoppage was caused by a union-management dispute over terms and conditions of employment, a union-Government dispute over wage stabilization or a management-Government dispute over price stabilization. The President's action has thus far been effective, not in settling the dispute, but in saving the various legislative programs at stake from destruction until Congress could act in the matter.

VI

The diversity of views expressed in the six opinions of the majority, the lack of reference to authoritative precedent, the repeated reliance upon prior dissenting opinions, the complete disregard of the uncontroverted facts showing the gravity of the emergency and the temporary nature of the taking all serve to demonstrate how far afield one must go to affirm the order of the District Court.

The broad executive power granted by Article II to an officer on duty 365 days a year cannot, it is said, be invoked to avert disaster. Instead, the President must confine himself to sending a message to Congress recommending action. Under this messenger-boy concept of the Office, the President cannot even act to preserve legislative programs from destruction so that Congress will have something left to act upon. There is no judicial finding that the executive action was unwarranted because there was in fact no basis for the President's finding of the existence of an emergency for, under this view, the gravity of the emergency and the immediacy of the threatened disaster are considered irrelevant as a matter of law.

Seizure of plaintiffs' property is not a pleasant undertaking. Similarly unpleasant to a free country are the draft which disrupts the home and military procurement which causes economic dislocation and compels adoption of price controls, wage stabilization and allocation of materials. The President informed Congress that even a temporary Government operation of plaintiffs' properties was "thoroughly distasteful" to him, but was necessary to prevent immediate paralysis of the mobilization program. Presidents have been in the past, and any man worthy of the Office should be in the future, free to take at least interim action necessary to execute legislative programs essential to survival of the Nation. A sturdy judiciary should not be swayed by the unpleasantness or unpopularity of necessary executive action. . . .

As the District Judge stated, this is no time for "timorous" judicial action. But neither is this a time for timorous executive action. Faced with the duty of executing the defense programs which Congress had enacted and the disastrous effects that any stoppage in steel production would have on those programs, the President acted to preserve those programs by seizing the steel mills. There is no question that the possession was other than temporary in character and subject to congressional direction—either approving, disapproving or regulating the manner in which the mills were to be administered and returned to the owners. The President immediately informed Congress of his action and clearly stated his intention to abide by the legislative will. No basis for claims of arbitrary action, unlimited powers or dictatorial usurpation of congressional power appears from the facts of this case. On the contrary, judicial, legislative and executive precedents throughout our history demonstrate that in this case the President acted in full conformity with his duties under the Constitution. Accordingly, we would reverse the order of the District Court.

NOTE ON THE *STEEL SEIZURE* CASE

1.   President Truman had several options for dealing with the possibility of a strike at the steel mills that might imperil critical military production:

- Wage Stabilization Board Proceedings: Three-way negotiations between the administration, labor, and management, leading to recommendations on wage and price increases by the Wage Stabilization Board (WSB).

- Taft-Hartley Act Injunction: Where a strike imperils national health or safety, the President can appoint a board of inquiry to report on the underlying facts; if the report doesn't induce agreement, the Attorney General may seek an injunction barring a strike for eighty days. At the end of eighty days, the President reports to Congress with recommendations.

- Seizure under the Selective Service Act: When producers fail to fill orders for goods required by the armed forces, the President may seize the facilities subject to an obligation to pay compensation.

- Condemnation under the Defense Production Act: The President may seize property when necessary for national defense, provided that the Government pays 75% of just compensation up front.

- Submit the Problem to Congress.

- Seize the Mills under the President's own Executive Power.

The Administration proceeded initially under the WSB, but those negotiations failed to produce a settlement. Following that failure, why do you think President Truman chose the last option?

2.   Recall the discussion of formalism and functionalism in the preceding Note. Which approach does Justice Black take? Justice Frankfurter? Justice Jackson? Which approach do you think is most sensible here?

Formalist approaches generally require the courts to characterize governmental actions as "executive," "legislative," or "judicial" in character. In *Youngstown*, Justices Black and Douglas saw seizure of the steel mills as a legislative action, while Chief Justice Vinson characterized it as executive. These views influenced the justices' analyses and ultimately led them to reach different conclusions as to the legality of President Truman's actions. Which justice was correct? In cases such as this one, where the nature of an act is not obvious, is there any way to truly determine whether the action is executive, legislative, or judicial in nature? Does the difficulty of such characterizations suggest a fundamental problem with the formalist approach?

3.   Justice Jackson's *Youngstown* concurrence is probably the most important separation of powers opinion in the U.S. Reports. Jackson's approach makes presidential authority largely a function of congressional action:

I. Congress Authorizes Presidential Action	II. Presidential Action/Congressional Silence	III. Presidential Action Contrary to Congressional Directive
Presidential authority is "at its maximum." Action can be struck down only if the federal government as a whole lacks power. "Strongest presumption" in favor of such actions.	"Zone of twilight"; President must rely on his independent powers alone. Case-by-case inquiry.	Presidential power is "at its lowest ebb." President can rely only on his own power *minus* whatever power Congress has. President can act only if Congress *lacks* power; his action must be "scrutinized with caution."

How helpful is Jackson's tripartite framework?

Under Justice Jackson's (and Justice Frankfurter's) approach, courts look at the totality of legislative action to determine whether Congress has authorized or forbidden the action in question. The Youngstown majority concluded that Congress not only failed to grant, but also denied, the seizure power to the President. For evidence of this denial, the concurring justices pointed to the text and legislative history of the Taft-Hartley Act. The Act set out specific procedures for dealing with labor disputes, and Congress had denied a proposed amendment to the Act that would have granted seizure power in times of emergency. Do you agree that Congress denied this power to the President?

Although Justices Jackson and Frankfurter found no constitutional or statutory support for the President's actions, Chief Justice Vinson argued that seizing the mills was necessary for the President to fulfill his constitutional duty to "take care that the laws be faithfully executed." In particular, Vinson was able to point to the NATO treaty, acts acknowledging obligations to the United Nations, the Marshall Plan, and other measures as committing the country to come to the aid of South Korea; the steel seizure, Vinson argued, was in furtherance of these obligations. Who was correct? If Vinson is correct that Truman's use of the seizure power to execute these general obligations was constitutional, is there anything the president could not do in support of these sorts of legislative directives?

Under Justice Jackson's framework, if Congress does not address a specific power, that power falls under the second box. Does the Youngstown case belong in the "zone of twilight"? Jackson offers little guidance as to how courts should approach analysis in this category. Should courts treat congressional silence as neither authorization nor denial, and ask whether the President's constitutional powers, on their own, authorize the action? If so, do the President's constitutional powers support this kind of action?[5]

One might, on the other hand, effectively dissolve the "twilight" category by interpreting congressional silence as denial. Article II, after all, explicitly confers relatively few powers on the President; most executive actions are taken pursuant to legislative authorization. Does that structure suggest a default rule that everything not authorized is forbidden? Given the inherent unpredictability of events, on the other hand, is it simply unrealistic to expect Congress to anticipate future needs for executive action? Would that difficulty actually lead to a *broadening* of executive authority by encouraging Congress to enact very broad and open-ended delegations of power?

4.   In *Dames & Moore v. Regan*, 453 U.S. 654 (1981), a unanimous Court adopted Justice Jackson's analysis from *Youngstown*, although Justice Rehnquist's opinion allowed as how the three categories might be better viewed as a continuum of congressional authorization to prohibition. *Dames & Moore* upheld President Reagan's suspension of private legal claims against the government of Iran as part of a deal to free the American hostages taken by that country. Although there was no express statutory authorization for that action, the Court found it to be consistent with the general tenor of related congressional legislation, most importantly the International Emergency Economic Powers Act, which allowed the President to take related measures in order to settle economic disputes with foreign nations.

---

[5] For an argument that courts should use cases of congressional silence to explore and define the limits of executive power under the Constitution, but have thus far failed to do so, see Patricia Bellia, *The Story of the Steel Seizure Case*, in PRESIDENTIAL POWER STORIES 273–75 (Christopher Schroeder & Curtis A. Bradley eds., 2008).

As in *Youngstown*, Congress had authorized similar measures—but not the particular measure that the President elected to take. Nonetheless, the Court treated Congress's silence as acquiescence, not prohibition. While this was a plausible reading of the tenor of political discourse concerning the hostage agreement at the time, it nonetheless illustrates the difficulty of drawing a line between Justice Jackson's categories. For a case upholding presidential action that clearly did fall within the third category, see *Zivotofsky v. Kerry, infra* Section 14.2.

5. Should courts not become involved at all in cases like the *Steel Seizure Case* and instead allow the political branches to function without interference? Courts might simply declare interbranch disputes to be nonjusticiable political questions. Congress, after all, has a number of weapons at its disposal in disputes with the President, including its power of the purse and control over the appointments process. What recourse would Congress have in a case like this one if the President acted unilaterally and the courts refused to intervene? Can one make an argument, similar to the *Garcia*/Wechsler "political safeguards of federalism" position, that judicial review is unnecessary in this area?

Any assessment of judicial deference to "political remedies," however, should consider the form that those remedies are likely to take. Congress rarely has the ability to override a presidential veto; as a result, its "weapons" are generally negative in character. They include:

- refusing to fund (and thus shutting down) government operations;

- refusing to approve other financial measures (such as raising the legal debt ceiling);

- blocking confirmation of Presidential appointees.

Other, non-negative political remedies open to Congress include congressional investigations of executive conduct and impeachment of executive officials (including the President.) Recent years have seen recourse to each of these options. Don't these "political remedies" carry risks of their own? Does it make sense to risk the credit of the United States, for example, by refusing to raise the debt ceiling in retaliation for executive actions on unrelated issues? Is it clear that judicial resolution of interbranch disputes would be worse for the country than resort to such remedies?

"Political safeguards" also protect executive authority from encroachment by Congress. Near the end of his concurrence, Justice Jackson notes the difference between the President's "paper powers" and the practical advantages of his office. The latter include:

- the unity of the office;

- its capacity for secrecy and dispatch;

- its superior sources of information;

- its easy access to the media;

- the President's role as head of his political party; and

- the fact that the President is always in session.

What is the relevance of these functional advantages to interpretation of the President's *constitutional* powers?

At the close of his opinion, Justice Jackson remarked, "only Congress itself can prevent power from slipping through its fingers." Does this observation suggest that, whatever role the courts assume in principle, in practice judicial review will not be a sufficient check to stop significant shifts in the balance of power among the political branches? Are such shifts likely to always move in the direction of greater executive authority? Or are worries about an "Imperial Presidency" historically contingent?

6.   The current War on Terror has revived the debate in *Youngstown* about emergency powers. The Constitution explicitly provides for one emergency power—the suspension of *habeas corpus* in cases of invasion or rebellion. See Art. I, § 9.[6] Do you agree with the majority's dismissal of the need for additional *implied* emergency powers? This debate is in part a manifestation of the admitted inefficiency of the separation of powers that the majority finds in the Constitution. That inefficiency may well have been an acceptable cost for a minimalist government with relatively few responsibilities, largely buffered from hostile forces by oceans and wilderness, in an age when communications and armies both moved relatively slowly. Is such inefficiency still tolerable today?

It is also worth remembering that, while the Constitution does not provide the President with explicit emergency powers, Congress can delegate such powers by statute (as long as such powers do not purport to override other constitutional principles). For example, the International Emergency Economic Powers Act (IEEPA), 50 U.S.C. §§ 1701 *et seq.*, confers certain economic powers upon the President to deal with foreign policy crises. And, of course, the various seizure laws canvassed in *Youngstown* conferred extraordinary powers upon the President in a variety of circumstances. Should the lack of power to seize the steel mills in *Youngstown* be viewed as a failure of constitutional foresight, or as a failure by the Executive to persuade Congress that it needed and deserved broader authority?

7.   The recent struggle against fascism during World War II, as well as the ongoing Cold War against Soviet totalitarianism, looms over all of the opinions in *Youngstown*. Justice Jackson, for instance, had served as one of the U.S. prosecutors at the Nuremberg trials. The fear of a "slippery slope" thus runs throughout the opinions. For example, Justice Frankfurter admits that "[i]t is absurd to see a dictator in a representative product of the sturdy democratic traditions of the Mississippi Valley"—e.g., in Harry Truman— but warns that "[t]he accretion of dangerous power does not come in a day." Are the justices in the majority too paranoid about Executive usurpations?

There is also a discernable note of melancholy in Justice Jackson's concluding musings about the Constitution's separation of powers: "Such institutions may be destined to pass away. But it is the duty of the Court to be last, not first, to give them up." From the perspective of today, it is easy to forget how impressive the performance of fascist and communist political

---

[6]   That power was held to belong to *Congress*, not the President, in *Ex parte Merryman*, *infra* Section 14.4.

systems seemed in the 1950s, and how Americans of that time may have harbored real doubts about the competitive prospects of governments constrained with firm constitutional limits. As we debate emergency powers again in the wake of financial crises and the War on Terror, what conclusions can you draw on this point from the experience of the intervening decades? And wholly apart from crises and emergencies, does the general gridlock prevailing in Washington, D.C. make you more sympathetic to Justice Jackson's pessimism?

CHAPTER THIRTEEN

STRUCTURE OF THE POLITICAL BRANCHES

Early advocates of separating the various functions of government hoped that such separation would increase government efficiency by dividing labor and promoting institutional specialization. Experience has largely frustrated those hopes. As the debate in *Youngstown* suggests, the constitutional separation of powers is now generally seen as undermining governmental efficiency, and the question is whether we are willing to pay that price in exchange for maintaining protections for liberty. The price has been perceived as particularly exorbitant in the area of lawmaking, and American government has accordingly developed extensive mechanisms for circumventing the frequently-cumbersome lawmaking process described in Article I.

The most important of these mechanisms is the delegation of legislative authority to administrative agencies. Section 13.1 describes the main constitutional constraint on such delegation, as well as its eventual replacement by judicial review of agency compliance with delegating statutes. This area is a classic instance of "the Constitution Outside the Constitution," where constitutional values of separation of powers are now served by a framework of administrative law constructed largely of statutory, regulatory, and common-law materials.

Section 13.2 turns to congressional efforts to alter the Article I lawmaking process itself, both by retaining post-enactment authority to oversee administrative lawmaking and by ceding additional veto authority to the Executive in order to overcome collective action problems in the legislature. One question that arises is whether the Court's highly formalistic approach to this second set of cases can be squared with the modern Court's pragmatic or functional approach to nondelegation.

Section 13.3 concerns executive privileges and immunities. Our main focus is on the famous Watergate tapes case and the doctrine of "executive privilege," which shields confidential presidential communications from outside scrutiny. We also consider the President's broader immunity from civil liability, which the Court has recognized for official acts but denied for unofficial ones. All of these cases seek to strike a balance between the need to protect the President's ability to do his job for the public welfare and the imperative, central to our history since the revolt against George III, to subject executive authority to the rule of law.

Finally, Section 13.4 surveys the problem of appointing and removing executive officers. This set of issues implicates the general principle of a "unitary" executive—that is, that the entire "executive power" is vested in one President, who alone in the executive branch is directly accountable to the people. This principle, which has been highly influential but never adopted in its purest form, has important implications for congressional attempts to insulate particular governmental officials from executive control.

SECTION 13.1 NONDELEGATION AND THE ADMINISTRATIVE STATE

Most federal law is made not by Congress but by federal administrative agencies. The primary constitutional constraint on this state of affairs is the nondelegation doctrine, which purportedly prohibits Congress from delegating actual legislative authority—as opposed to authority to implement or "flesh out" federal statutes—to agencies. The Court has actually employed that doctrine to strike down an Act of Congress only twice, including in the *Schechter* case below. While the doctrine may still foreclose extremely broad delegations like that in *Schechter*—"delegation running riot," in Justice Cardozo's memorable phrase—it is generally not enforced with much rigor anymore.

This is not to say, however, that federal agencies now operate unchecked. Constitutional review under the nondelegation doctrine has largely been replaced by judicial review of agency action. Such review, which generally proceeds under the Administrative Procedure Act (APA), takes three primary forms: (1) substantive review of the agency's legal determinations; (2) substantive review of fact and policy questions under a very deferential "arbitrary and capricious" standard; and (3) review of the agency's compliance with procedural requirements imposed by the APA and other statutes. Courts review agency determinations of law deferentially under the *Chevron* doctrine, which requires that where a federal statute is ambiguous, courts must defer to the administering agency's interpretation so long as that interpretation is reasonable. The *American Trucking* case demonstrates that, although courts generally accord agencies considerable deference—especially under *Chevron*—they will rein agencies in when they have exceeded the bounds of their statutory authority. Judicial enforcement of statutory mandates against agencies is thus meant to ensure that Congress retains ultimate control over federal lawmaking.

As you read these cases, consider whether the Court gave up too easily on the constitutional nondelegation doctrine, whether that doctrine could feasibly be revived, and whether statutory review is an adequate substitute for protecting the structural values that the old doctrine served.

A.L.A. Schechter Poultry Corp. v. United States

295 U.S. 495 (1935)

■ MR. CHIEF JUSTICE HUGHES delivered the opinion of the Court.

Petitioners . . . were convicted [of] violations of . . . the "Live Poultry Code". . . . [T]he defendants contended (1) that the Code had been adopted pursuant to an unconstitutional delegation by Congress of legislative power; (2) that it attempted to regulate intrastate transactions which lay outside the authority of Congress; and (3) that in certain provisions it was repugnant to the due process clause of the Fifth Amendment.

The Circuit Court of Appeals sustained the conviction[s]. . . .

A. L. A. Schechter Poultry Corporation and Schechter Live Poultry Market are corporations conducting wholesale poultry slaughterhouse markets in Brooklyn, New York City. . . .

The "Live Poultry Code" was promulgated under § 3 of the National Industrial Recovery Act. That section . . . authorizes the President to approve "codes of fair competition." Such a code may be approved for a trade or industry, upon application by one or more trade or industrial associations or groups, if the President finds (1) that such associations or groups "impose no inequitable restrictions on admission to membership therein and are truly representative," and (2) that such codes are not designed "to promote monopolies or to eliminate or oppress small enterprises and will not operate to discriminate against them, and will tend to effectuate the policy" of Title I of the Act. Such codes "shall not permit monopolies or monopolistic practices." As a condition of his approval, the President may "impose such conditions . . . for the protection of consumers, competitors, employees, and others, and in furtherance of the public interest, and may provide such exceptions to and exemptions from the provisions of such code as the President in his discretion deems necessary to effectuate the policy herein declared." Where such a code has not been approved, the President may prescribe one. . . . Violation of any provision of a code (so approved or prescribed) "in any transaction in or affecting interstate or foreign commerce" is made a misdemeanor punishable by a fine of not more than $500 for each offense. . . .

The "Live Poultry Code" was approved by the President on April 13, 1934. Its divisions indicate its nature and scope. The Code has eight articles entitled (1) purposes, (2) definitions, (3) hours, (4) wages, (5) general labor provisions, (6) administration, (7) trade practice provisions, and (8) general.

The declared purpose is "To effect the policies of title I of the National Industrial Recovery Act." The Code is established as "a code of fair competition for the live poultry industry of the metropolitan area in and about the City of New York." . . . The "industry" is defined as including "every person engaged in the business of selling, purchasing for resale, transporting, or handling and/or slaughtering live poultry . . ." and such "related branches" as may from time to time be included by amendment. Employers are styled "members of the industry," and the term employee is defined to embrace "any and all persons engaged in the industry, however compensated," except "members."

The Code fixes the number of hours for work-days. It provides that no employee, with certain exceptions, shall be permitted to work in excess of forty (40) hours in any one week, and that no employee, save as stated, "shall be paid in any pay period less than at the rate of fifty (50) cents per hour." The article containing "general labor provisions" prohibits the employment of any person under sixteen years of age, and declares that employees shall have the right of "collective bargaining," and freedom of choice with respect to labor organizations. . . . The minimum number of employees, who shall be employed by slaughterhouse operators, is fixed, the number being graduated according to the average volume of weekly sales.

Provision is made for administration through an "industry advisory committee," to be selected by trade associations and members of the industry, and a "code supervisor" to be appointed, with the approval of the committee, by agreement between the Secretary of Agriculture and the Administrator for Industrial Recovery. The expenses of administration are to be borne by the members of the industry proportionately upon the basis of volume of business, or such other factors as the advisory committee may deem equitable, "subject to the disapproval of the Secretary and/or Administrator."

The seventh article, containing "trade practice provisions," prohibits various practices which are said to constitute "unfair methods of competition." The final article provides for verified reports . . . "(1) for the protection of consumers, competitors, employees, and others, and in furtherance of the public interest, and (2) for the determination by the Secretary or Administrator of the extent to which the declared policy of the act is being effectuated by this code." . . .

The President approved the Code by an executive order in which he found that the application for his approval had been duly made in accordance with the provisions of Title I of the National Industrial Recovery Act, that there had been due notice and hearings, that the Code constituted "a code of fair competition" as contemplated by the Act and complied with its pertinent provisions . . . and that the Code would tend "to effectuate the policy of Congress as declared in section 1 of Title I." The executive order also recited that the Secretary of Agriculture and the Administrator of the National Industrial Recovery Act had rendered separate reports as to the provisions within their respective jurisdictions. The Secretary of Agriculture reported that the provisions of the Code "establishing standards of fair competition (a) are regulations of transactions in or affecting the current of interstate and/or foreign commerce and (b) are reasonable," and also that the Code would tend to effectuate the policy declared in Title I of the Act, as set forth in § 1. The report of the Administrator for Industrial Recovery dealt with wages, hours of labor and other labor provisions.

Of the eighteen counts of the indictment upon which the defendants were convicted . . . ten counts were for violation of the requirement (found in the "trade practice provisions") of "straight killing." . . . The term "straight killing" was defined in the Code as "the practice of requiring persons purchasing poultry for resale to accept the run of any half coop, coop, or coops, as purchased by slaughterhouse operators, except for culls." The charges . . . were that the defendants in selling to retail dealers and butchers had permitted "selections of individual chickens taken from particular coops and half coops." . . .

Second. The question of the delegation of legislative power. . . . The Constitution provides that "All legislative powers herein granted shall be vested in a Congress of the United States, which shall consist of a Senate and House of Representatives." Art I, § 1. And the Congress is authorized "To make all laws which shall be necessary and proper for carrying into execution" its general powers. Art. I, § 8. The Congress is not permitted to abdicate or to transfer to others the essential legislative functions with which it is thus vested. We have repeatedly recognized the necessity of adapting legislation to complex conditions involving a host of details with which the national legislature cannot deal directly. [T]he Constitution has never been regarded as denying to Congress the necessary resources of flexibility and practicality, which will enable it to perform its function in laying down policies and establishing standards, while leaving to selected instrumentalities the making of subordinate rules within prescribed limits and the determination of facts to which the policy as declared by the legislature is to apply. But we said that the constant recognition of the necessity and validity of such provisions, and the wide range of administrative authority which has been developed by means of them, cannot be allowed to obscure the limitations of the authority to delegate, if our constitutional system is to be maintained.

Accordingly, we look to the statute to see whether Congress has overstepped these limitations—whether Congress in authorizing "codes of fair competition" has itself established the standards of legal obligation, thus performing its essential legislative function, or, by the failure to enact such standards, has attempted to transfer that function to others. . . .

What is meant by "fair competition" as the term is used in the Act? Does it refer to a category established in the law, and is the authority to make codes limited accordingly? Or is it used as a convenient designation for whatever set of laws the formulators of a code for a particular trade or industry may propose and the President may approve . . . ?

The Act does not define "fair competition." "Unfair competition," as known to the common law, is a limited concept. Primarily, and strictly, it relates to the palming off of one's goods as those of a rival trader. In recent years, its scope has been extended. . . . But it is evident that in its widest range, "unfair competition," as it has been understood in the law, does not reach the objectives of the codes which are authorized by the National Industrial Recovery Act. The codes may, indeed, cover conduct which existing law condemns, but they are not limited to conduct of that sort. The Government does not contend that the Act contemplates such a limitation. . . .

The Federal Trade Commission Act (§ 5) introduced the expression "unfair methods of competition," which were declared to be unlawful. That was an expression new in the law. . . . We have said that the substituted phrase has a broader meaning, that it does not admit of precise definition, its scope being left to judicial determination as controversies arise. What are "unfair methods of competition" are thus to be determined in particular instances, upon evidence, in the light of particular competitive conditions and of what is found to be a specific and substantial public interest. To make this possible, Congress set up a special procedure. A Commission, a quasi-judicial body, was created. Provision was made for formal complaint, for notice and hearing, for appropriate findings of fact supported by adequate evidence, and for judicial review to give assurance that the action of the Commission is taken within its statutory authority.

In providing for codes, the National Industrial Recovery Act dispenses with this administrative procedure and with any administrative procedure of an analogous character. But the difference between the code plan of the Recovery Act and the scheme of the Federal Trade Commission Act lies not only in procedure but in subject matter. We cannot regard the "fair competition" of the codes as antithetical to the "unfair methods of competition" of the Federal Trade Commission Act. The "fair competition of the codes has a much broader range and a new significance. The Recovery Act provides that it shall not be construed to impair the powers of the Federal Trade Commission, but, when a code is approved, its provisions are to be the "standards of fair competition" for the trade or industry concerned, and any violation of such standards in any transaction in or affecting interstate or foreign commerce is to be deemed "an unfair method of competition" within the meaning of the Federal Trade Commission Act. § 3(b).

For a statement of the authorized objectives and content of the "codes of fair competition" we are referred repeatedly to the "Declaration of Policy" in section one of Title I of the Recovery Act. Thus, the approval of a code by the President is conditioned on his finding that it "will tend to effectuate the policy of this title." The President is authorized to impose such conditions "for the protection of consumers, competitors, employees, and others, and in furtherance of the public interest, and may provide such exceptions to and exemptions from the provisions of such code as the President in his discretion deems necessary to effectuate the policy herein declared." The "policy herein declared" is manifestly that set forth in section one. . . . It is there declared to be "the policy of Congress"

> to remove obstructions to the free flow of interstate and foreign commerce which tend to diminish the amount thereof; and to provide for the general welfare by promoting the organization of industry for the purpose of cooperative action among trade groups, to induce and maintain united action of labor and management under adequate governmental sanctions and supervision, to eliminate unfair competitive practices, to promote the fullest possible utilization of the present productive capacity of industries, to avoid undue restriction of production (except as may be temporarily required), to increase the consumption of industrial and agricultural products by increasing purchasing power, to reduce and relieve unemployment, to improve standards of labor, and otherwise to rehabilitate industry and to conserve natural resources.

Under § 3, whatever "may tend to effectuate" these general purposes may be included in the "codes of fair competition." We think the conclusion is inescapable that the authority sought to be conferred by § 3 was not merely to deal with "unfair competitive practices" which offend against existing law, and could be the subject of judicial condemnation without further legislation, or to create administrative machinery for the application of established principles of law to particular instances of violation. Rather, the purpose is clearly disclosed to authorize new and controlling prohibitions through codes of laws which would embrace what the formulators would propose, and what the President would approve, or prescribe, as wise and beneficient measures for the government of trades and industries in order to bring about their rehabilitation, correction and development, according to the general declaration of policy in section one. . . .

We find no real controversy upon this point . . . . As the Government candidly says in its brief: "The words 'policy of this title' clearly refer to the 'policy' which Congress declared in the section entitled 'Declaration of Policy'—§ 1. All of the policies there set forth point toward a single goal—the rehabilitation of industry and the industrial recovery which unquestionably was the major policy of Congress in adopting the National Industrial Recovery Act." . . .

The Government urges that the codes will "consist of rules of competition deemed fair for each industry by representative members of that industry—by the persons most vitally concerned and most familiar with its problems." Instances are cited in which Congress has availed itself of such assistance; as *e.g.,* in the exercise of its authority over the public domain, with respect to the recognition of local customs or rules of miners as to mining claims, or, in matters of a more or less technical nature, as in designating the standard height of drawbars. But would it be seriously contended that Congress could delegate its legislative authority to trade or industrial associations or groups so as to empower them to enact the laws they deem to be wise and beneficent for the rehabilitation and expansion of their trade or industries? Could trade or industrial associations or groups be constituted legislative bodies for that purpose because such associations or groups are familiar with the problems of their enterprises? And, could an effort of that sort be made valid by such a preface of generalities as to permissible aims as we find in section 1 of title I? The answer is obvious. Such a delegation of legislative power is unknown to our law and is utterly inconsistent with the constitutional prerogatives and duties of Congress.

The question, then, turns upon the authority which § 3 of the Recovery Act vests in the President to approve or prescribe. If the codes have standing as penal statutes, this must be due to the effect of the executive action. But Congress cannot delegate legislative power to the President to exercise an unfettered discretion to make whatever laws he thinks may be needed or advisable for the rehabilitation and expansion of trade or industry.

Accordingly we turn to the Recovery Act to ascertain what limits have been set to the exercise of the President's discretion. *First,* the President, as a condition of approval, is required to find that the trade or industrial associations or groups which propose a code, "impose no inequitable restrictions on admission to membership" and are "truly representative." That condition, however, relates only to the status of the initiators of the new laws and not to the permissible scope of such laws. *Second,* the President is required to find that the code is not "designed to promote monopolies or to eliminate or oppress small enterprises and will not operate to discriminate against them." And, to this is added a proviso that the code "shall not permit monopolies or monopolistic practices." But these restrictions leave virtually untouched the field of policy envisaged by section one, and, in that wide field of legislative possibilities, the proponents of a code, refraining from monopolistic designs, may roam at will and the President may approve or disapprove their proposals as he may see fit. That is the precise effect of the further finding that the President is to make—that the code "will tend to effectuate the policy of this title." While this is called a finding, it is really but a statement of an opinion as to the general effect upon the promotion of trade or industry of a scheme of laws. These are the only findings which Congress has made essential in order to put into operation a legislative code having the aims described in the "Declaration of Policy."

Nor is the breadth of the President's discretion left to the necessary implications of this limited requirement as to his findings. As already noted, the President in approving a code may impose his own conditions, adding to or taking from what is proposed, as "in his discretion" he thinks necessary "to effectuate the policy" declared by the Act . . . .

Such a sweeping delegation of legislative power finds no support in the decisions upon which the Government especially relies. By the Interstate Commerce Act, Congress has itself provided a code of laws regulating the activities of the common carriers subject to the Act, in order to assure the performance of their services upon just and reasonable terms, with adequate facilities and without unjust discrimination. . . . To facilitate the application of the standards prescribed by the Act, Congress has provided an expert body. That administrative agency, in dealing with particular cases, is required to act upon notice and hearing, and its orders must be supported by findings of fact which in turn are sustained by evidence. When the Commission is authorized to issue, for the construction, extension or abandonment of lines, a certificate of "public convenience and necessity," or to permit the acquisition by one carrier of the control of another, if that is found to be "in the public interest," we have pointed out that these provisions are not left without standards to guide determination. The authority conferred has direct relation to the standards prescribed for the service of common carriers and can be exercised only upon findings, based upon evidence, with respect to particular conditions of transportation.

Similarly, we have held that the Radio Act of 1927 established standards to govern radio communications and, in view of the limited number of available broadcasting frequencies, Congress authorized allocation and licenses. The Federal Radio Commission was created as the licensing authority, in order to secure a reasonable equality of opportunity in radio transmission and reception. The authority of the Commission to grant licenses "as public convenience, interest or necessity requires" was limited by the nature of radio communications, and by the scope, character and quality of the services to be rendered and the relative advantages to be derived through distribution of facilities. . . . .

In *Hampton & Co. v. United States,* 276 U.S. 394 (1928), the question related to the "flexible tariff provision" of the Tariff Act of 1922. We held that Congress had described its plan "to secure by law the imposition of customs duties on articles of imported merchandise which should equal the difference between the cost of producing in a foreign country the articles in question and laying them down for sale in the United States, and the cost of producing and selling like or similar articles in the United States." As the differences in cost might vary from time to time, provision was made for the investigation and determination of these differences by the executive branch so as to make "the adjustments necessary to conform the duties to the standard underlying that policy and plan." The Court found the same principle to be applicable in fixing customs duties as that which permitted Congress to exercise its rate-making power in interstate commerce, "by declaring the rule which shall prevail in the legislative fixing of rates" and then remitting "the fixing of such rates" in accordance with its provisions "to a rate-making body." . . .

To summarize and conclude . . . Section 3 of the Recovery Act is without precedent. It supplies no standards for any trade, industry or activity. It does not undertake to prescribe rules of conduct to be applied to particular states of fact determined by appropriate administrative procedure. Instead of prescribing rules of conduct, it authorizes the making of codes to prescribe them. For that legislative undertaking, § 3 sets up no standards, aside from the statement of the general aims of rehabilitation, correction and expansion described in section one. . . . [T]he discretion of the President in approving or prescribing codes, and thus enacting laws for the government of trade and industry throughout the country, is virtually unfettered. We think that the code-making authority thus conferred is an unconstitutional delegation of legislative power. . . .

On both the grounds we have discussed, the attempted delegation of legislative power, and the attempted regulation of intrastate transactions which affect interstate commerce only indirectly, we hold the code provisions here in question to be invalid and that the judgment of conviction must be reversed.

■ **MR. JUSTICE CARDOZO, concurring.**

The delegated power of legislation which has found expression in this code is not canalized within banks that keep it from overflowing. It is unconfined and vagrant. . . . This court has held that delegation may be unlawful though the act to be performed is definite and single, if the necessity, time and occasion of performance have been left in the end to the discretion of the delegate. *Panama Refining Co. v. Ryan,* 293 U.S. 388 (1935). I thought that ruling went too far. I pointed out in an opinion that there had been "no grant to the Executive of any roving commission to inquire into evils and then, upon discovering them, do anything he pleases." Choice, though within limits, had been given him "as to the occasion, but none whatever as to the means." Here, in the case before us, is an attempted delegation not confined to any single act nor to any class or group of acts identified or described by reference to a standard. Here in effect is a roving commission to inquire into evils and upon discovery correct them.

I have said that there is no standard, definite or even approximate, to which legislation must conform. Let me make my meaning more precise. If codes of fair competition are codes eliminating "unfair" methods of competition ascertained upon inquiry to prevail in one industry or another, there is no unlawful delegation of legislative functions when the President is directed to inquire into such practices and denounce them when discovered. For many years a like power has been committed to the Federal Trade Commission with the approval of this court in a long series of decisions. Delegation in such circumstances is born of the necessities of the occasion. The industries of the country are too many and diverse to make it possible for Congress, in respect of matters such as these, to legislate directly with adequate appreciation of varying conditions. Nor is the substance of the power changed because the President may act at the instance of trade or industrial associations having special knowledge of the facts. Their function is strictly advisory; it is the *imprimatur* of the President that begets the quality of law. When the task that is set before one is that of cleaning house, it is prudent as well as usual to take counsel of the dwellers.

But there is another conception of codes of fair competition, their significance and function, which leads to very different consequences, though it is one that is struggling now for recognition and acceptance. By this other conception a code is not to be restricted to the elimination of business practices that would be characterized by general acceptation as oppressive or unfair. It is to include whatever ordinances may be desirable or helpful for the well-being or prosperity of the industry affected. In that view, the function of its adoption is not merely negative, but positive; the planning of improvements as well as the extirpation of abuses. What is fair, as thus conceived, is not something to be contrasted with what is unfair or fraudulent or tricky. The extension becomes as wide as the field of industrial regulation. If that conception shall prevail, anything that Congress may do within the limits of the commerce clause for the betterment of business may be done by the President upon the recommendation of a trade association by calling it a code. This is delegation running riot. No such plenitude of power is susceptible of transfer. The statute, however, aims at nothing less . . . .

I am authorized to state that MR. JUSTICE STONE joins in this opinion.

Whitman v. American Trucking Assn's, Inc.

531 U.S. 457 (2001)

■ JUSTICE SCALIA delivered the opinion of the Court.

These cases present the following questions: (1) Whether § 109(b)(1) of the Clean Air Act (CAA) delegates legislative power to the Administrator of the Environmental Protection Agency (EPA). (2) Whether the Administrator may consider the costs of implementation in setting national ambient air quality standards (NAAQS) under § 109(b)(1). (3) Whether the Court of Appeals had jurisdiction to review the EPA's interpretation of Part D of Title I of the CAA with respect to implementing the revised ozone NAAQS. (4) If so, whether the EPA's interpretation of that part was permissible.

I

Section 109(a) of the CAA requires the Administrator of the EPA to promulgate NAAQS for each air pollutant for which "air quality criteria" have been issued under § 108. Once a NAAQS has been promulgated, the Administrator must review the standard (and the criteria on which it is based) "at five-year intervals" and make "such revisions . . . as may be appropriate." These cases arose when, on July 18, 1997, the Administrator revised the NAAQS for particulate matter (PM) and ozone. American Trucking Associations, Inc., and its co-respondents . . .—which include, in addition to other private companies, the States of Michigan, Ohio, and West Virginia—challenged the new standards in the Court of Appeals for the District of Columbia Circuit. . . .

The District of Columbia Circuit accepted some of the challenges and rejected others. It agreed with the respondents that § 109(b)(1) delegated legislative power to the Administrator in contravention of the United States Constitution, Art. I, § 1, because it found that the EPA had interpreted the statute to provide no "intelligible principle" to guide the agency's exercise of authority. The court thought, however, that the EPA could perhaps avoid the unconstitutional delegation by adopting a restrictive construction of § 109(b)(1), so instead of declaring the section unconstitutional the court remanded the NAAQS to the agency. . . . On the second issue that the Court of Appeals addressed, it unanimously rejected respondents' argument that the court should depart from the rule . . . that the EPA may not consider the cost of implementing a NAAQS in setting the initial standard. It also rejected respondents' argument that the implementation provisions for ozone found in Part D, Subpart 2, of Title I of the CAA were so tied to the existing ozone standard that the EPA lacked the power to revise the standard. The court held that although Subpart 2 constrained the agency's method of implementing the new standard, it did not prevent the EPA from revising the standard and designating areas of the country as "nonattainment areas" by reference to it. . . .

The Administrator and the EPA petitioned this Court for review of the first, third, and fourth questions described in the first paragraph of this opinion. Respondents conditionally cross-petitioned for review of the second question. We granted certiorari on both petitions . . . .

II

In *Lead Industries Assn., Inc. v. EPA*, 647 F.2d 1130 (CADC 1980), the District of Columbia Circuit held that "economic considerations [may] play no part in the promulgation of ambient air quality standards under Section 109" of the CAA. . . . Respondents argue that [this was] incorrect. We disagree; and since the first step in assessing whether a statute delegates legislative power is to determine what authority the statute confers, we address that issue of interpretation first and reach respondents' constitutional arguments in Part III.

Section 109(b)(1) instructs the EPA to set primary ambient air quality standards "the attainment and maintenance of which . . . are requisite to protect the public health" with "an adequate margin of safety." Were it not for the hundreds of pages of briefing respondents have submitted on the issue, one would have thought it fairly clear that this text does not permit the EPA to consider costs in setting the standards. The language, as one scholar has noted, "is absolute." The

EPA, "based on" the information about health effects contained in the technical "criteria" documents compiled under § 108(a)(2), is to identify the maximum airborne concentration of a pollutant that the public health can tolerate, decrease the concentration to provide an "adequate" margin of safety, and set the standard at that level. Nowhere are the costs of achieving such a standard made part of that initial calculation.

Against this most natural of readings, respondents make a lengthy, spirited, but ultimately unsuccessful attack. . . . The 1970 Congress . . . not only anticipated that compliance costs could injure the public health, but provided for that precise exigency. Section 110(f)(1) of the CAA permitted the Administrator to waive the compliance deadline for stationary sources if, *inter alia,* sufficient control measures were simply unavailable and "the continued operation of such sources is *essential . . . to the public health* or welfare." Other provisions explicitly permitted or required economic costs to be taken into account in implementing the air quality standards. . . . Subsequent amendments to the CAA have added many more provisions directing, in explicit language, that the Administrator consider costs in performing various duties. We have therefore refused to find implicit in ambiguous sections of the CAA an authorization to consider costs that has elsewhere, and so often, been expressly granted.

Accordingly, to prevail in their present challenge, respondents must show a textual commitment of authority to the EPA to consider costs in setting NAAQS under § 109(b)(1). And because § 109(b)(1) and the NAAQS for which it provides are the engine that drives nearly all of Title I of the CAA, that textual commitment must be a clear one. Congress, we have held, does not alter the fundamental details of a regulatory scheme in vague terms or ancillary provisions—it does not, one might say, hide elephants in mouseholes. Respondents' textual arguments ultimately founder upon this principle.

Their first claim is that § 109(b)(1)'s terms "adequate margin" and "requisite" leave room to pad health effects with cost concerns. . . . [W]e find it implausible that Congress would give to the EPA through these modest words the power to determine whether implementation costs should moderate national air quality standards. . . .

Respondents point, finally, to a number of provisions in the CAA that *do* require attainment cost data to be generated. Section 108(b)(1), for example, instructs the Administrator to "issue to the States," simultaneously with the criteria documents, "information on air pollution control techniques, which information shall include data relating to the cost of installation and operation." . . . Respondents argue that these provisions make no sense unless costs are to be considered in setting the NAAQS. That is not so. These provisions enable the Administrator to assist the States in carrying out their statutory role as primary *implementers* of the NAAQS. It is to the States that the Act assigns initial and primary responsibility for deciding what emissions reductions will be required from which sources. See 42 U.S.C. §§ 7407(a), 7410 (giving States the duty of developing implementation plans). It would be impossible to perform that task intelligently without considering which abatement technologies are most efficient, and most economically feasible—which is why we have said that "the most important forum for consideration of claims of economic and technological infeasibility is before the state agency formulating the implementation plan.". . .

The text of § 109(b), interpreted in its statutory and historical context and with appreciation for its importance to the CAA as a whole, unambiguously bars cost considerations from the NAAQS-setting process, and thus ends the matter for us as well as the EPA. We therefore affirm the judgment of the Court of Appeals on this point.

III

Section 109(b)(1) of the CAA instructs the EPA to set "ambient air quality standards the attainment and maintenance of which in the judgment of the Administrator, based on [the] criteria [documents of § 108] and allowing an adequate margin of safety, are requisite to protect the public health." The Court of Appeals held that this section as interpreted by the Administrator did not provide an "intelligible principle" to guide the EPA's exercise of authority in setting NAAQS. "[The] EPA," it said, "lacked any determinate criteria for drawing lines. It has failed to state intelligibly how much is too much." The court hence found that the EPA's interpretation (but not the statute itself) violated the nondelegation doctrine. We disagree.

In a delegation challenge, the constitutional question is whether the statute has delegated legislative power to the agency. Article I, § 1, of the Constitution vests "all legislative Powers herein granted . . . in a Congress of the United States." This text permits no delegation of those powers, so we repeatedly have said that when Congress confers decisionmaking authority upon agencies Congress must "lay down by legislative act an intelligible principle to which the person or body authorized to [act] is directed to conform." *J. W. Hampton, Jr., & Co. v. United States,* 276 U.S. 394 (1928). We have never suggested that an agency can cure an unlawful delegation of legislative power by adopting in its discretion a limiting construction of the statute. . . . The idea that an agency can cure an unconstitutionally standardless delegation of power by declining to exercise some of that power seems to us internally contradictory. The very choice of which portion of the power to exercise—that is to say, the prescription of the standard that Congress had omitted—would *itself* be an exercise of the forbidden legislative authority. Whether the statute delegates legislative power is a question for the courts, and an agency's voluntary self-denial has no bearing upon the answer.

We agree with the Solicitor General that the text of § 109(b)(1) of the CAA at a minimum requires that "for a discrete set of pollutants and based on published air quality criteria that reflect the latest scientific knowledge, [the] EPA must establish uniform national standards at a level that is requisite to protect public health from the adverse effects of the pollutant in the ambient air." Requisite, in turn, "means sufficient, but not more than necessary." These limits on the EPA's discretion are strikingly similar to the ones we approved in *Touby v. United States,* 500 U.S. 160 (1991), which permitted the Attorney General to designate a drug as a controlled substance for purposes of criminal drug enforcement if doing so was "necessary to avoid an imminent hazard to the public safety." They also resemble the Occupational Safety and Health Act provision requiring the agency to "set the standard which most adequately assures, to the extent feasible, on the basis of the best available evidence, that no employee will suffer any impairment of health"—which the Court upheld in *Industrial Union Dept., AFL-CIO v. American Petroleum Institute,* 448 U.S. 607 (1980) . . . .

The scope of discretion § 109(b)(1) allows is in fact well within the outer limits of our nondelegation precedents. In the history of the Court we have found the requisite "intelligible principle" lacking in only two statutes, one of which provided literally no guidance for the exercise of discretion, and the other of which conferred authority to regulate the entire economy on the basis of no more precise a standard than stimulating the economy by assuring "fair competition." See *Panama Refining Co. v. Ryan,* 293 U.S. 388 (1935); *A. L. A. Schechter Poultry Corp. v. United States.* We have, on the other hand, upheld the validity of § 11(b)(2) of the Public Utility Holding Company Act of 1935, which gave the Securities and Exchange Commission authority to modify the structure of holding company systems so as to ensure that they are not "unduly or unnecessarily complicated" and do not "unfairly or inequitably distribute voting power among security holders." *American Power & Light Co. v. SEC,* 329 U.S. 90 (1946). We have approved the wartime conferral of agency power to fix the prices of commodities at a level that "will be generally fair and equitable and will effectuate the [in some respects conflicting] purposes of the Act." *Yakus v. United States,* 321 U.S. 414 (1944). And we have found an "intelligible principle" in various statutes authorizing regulation in the "public interest." See, *e.g., National Broadcasting Co. v. United States,* 319 U.S. 190 (1943) (FCC's power to regulate airwaves); *New York Central Securities Corp. v. United States,* 287 U.S. 12 (1932) (ICC's power to approve railroad consolidations). In short, we have "almost never felt qualified to second-guess Congress regarding the permissible degree of policy judgment that can be left to those executing or applying the law." *Mistretta v. United States,* 488 U.S. 361 (1989) (Scalia, J., dissenting); *see id.* (majority opinion).

It is true enough that the degree of agency discretion that is acceptable varies according to the scope of the power congressionally conferred. While Congress need not provide any direction to the EPA regarding the manner in which it is to define "country elevators," which are to be exempt from new-stationary-source regulations governing grain elevators, it must provide substantial guidance on setting air standards that affect the entire national economy. But even in sweeping regulatory schemes we have never demanded, as the Court of Appeals did here, that statutes provide a "determinate criterion" for saying "how much [of the regulated harm] is too much." In *Touby*, for example, we did not require the statute to decree how "imminent" was too imminent, or how "necessary" was necessary enough, or even—most relevant here—how "hazardous" was too hazardous. . . . It is therefore not conclusive for delegation purposes that, as respondents argue, ozone and particulate matter are "nonthreshold" pollutants that inflict a continuum of adverse health effects at any airborne concentration greater than zero, and hence require the EPA to make judgments of degree. A certain degree of discretion, and thus of lawmaking, inheres in most executive or judicial action. Section 109(b)(1) of the CAA, which to repeat we interpret as requiring the EPA to set air quality standards at the level that is "requisite"—that is, not lower or higher than is necessary—to protect the public health with an adequate margin of safety, fits comfortably within the scope of discretion permitted by our precedent.

We therefore reverse the judgment of the Court of Appeals remanding for reinterpretation that would avoid a supposed delegation of legislative power. . . .

IV

The final two issues on which we granted certiorari concern the EPA's authority to implement the revised ozone NAAQS in areas whose ozone levels currently exceed the maximum level permitted by that standard. The CAA designates such areas "nonattainment," § 107(d)(1), and it exposes them to additional restrictions over and above the implementation requirements imposed generally by § 110 of the CAA. These additional restrictions are found in the five substantive subparts of Part D of Title I. Subpart 1 contains general nonattainment regulations that pertain to every pollutant for which a NAAQS exists. Subparts 2 through 5 contain rules tailored to specific individual pollutants. Subpart 2, added by the Clean Air Act Amendments of 1990, addresses ozone. The dispute before us here, in a nutshell, is whether Subpart 1 alone (as the agency determined), or rather Subpart 2 or some combination of Subparts 1 and 2, controls the implementation of the revised ozone NAAQS in nonattainment areas. . . .

B

Our approach to the merits of the parties' dispute is the familiar one of *Chevron U.S.A. Inc. v. Natural Resources Defense Council, Inc.*, 467 U.S. 837 (1984). If the statute resolves the question whether Subpart 1 or Subpart 2 (or some combination of the two) shall apply to revised ozone NAAQS, then "that is the end of the matter." But if the statute is "silent or ambiguous" with respect to the issue, then we must defer to a "reasonable interpretation made by the administrator of an agency." We cannot agree with the Court of Appeals that Subpart 2 clearly controls the implementation of revised ozone NAAQS because we find the statute to some extent ambiguous. We conclude, however, that the agency's interpretation goes beyond the limits of what is ambiguous and contradicts what in our view is quite clear. We therefore hold the implementation policy unlawful.

The text of Subpart 1 at first seems to point the way to a clear answer to the question, which Subpart controls? Two sections of Subpart 1 contain switching provisions stating that if the classification of ozone nonattainment areas is "specifically provided [for] under other provisions of [Part D]," then those provisions will control instead of Subpart 1's. Thus it is true but incomplete to note, as the Administrator does, that the substantive language of Subpart 1 is broad enough to apply to revised ozone standards. To determine whether that language *does* apply one must resolve the further textual issue whether some *other* provision, namely Subpart 2, provides for the classification of ozone nonattainment areas. If it does, then according to the switching provisions of Subpart 1 it will control.

So, does Subpart 2 provide for classifying nonattainment ozone areas under the revised standard? It unquestionably does. The backbone of the subpart is Table 1 . . . which defines five categories of ozone nonattainment areas and prescribes attainment deadlines for each. Section 7511(a)(1) funnels all nonattainment areas into the table for classification, declaring that "each area designated nonattainment for ozone . . . shall be classified at the time of such designation, under table 1, by operation of law." And once an area has been classified, "the primary standard attainment date for ozone shall be as expeditiously as practicable but not later than the date provided in table 1." The EPA argues that this text is not as clear or comprehensive as it seems, because the title of § 7511(a) reads "Classification and attainment dates for 1989 nonattainment areas," which suggests that Subpart 2 applies only to areas that were in nonattainment in 1989, and not to areas later designated nonattainment under a revised ozone standard. The suggestion must be rejected, however, because § 7511(b)(1) specifically provides for the classification of areas that *were* in attainment in 1989 but have subsequently slipped into nonattainment. It thus makes clear that Subpart 2 is *not* limited solely to 1989 nonattainment areas. This eliminates the interpretive role of the title, which may only "shed light on some ambiguous word or phrase in the statute itself."

It may well be, as the EPA argues . . . that some provisions of Subpart 2 are ill fitted to implementation of the revised standard. Using the old 1-hour averages of ozone levels, for example, as Subpart 2 requires, would produce at best an inexact estimate of the new 8-hour averages. Also, to the extent that the new ozone standard is stricter than the old one, the classification system of Subpart 2 contains a gap, because it fails to classify areas whose ozone levels are greater than the new standard (and thus nonattaining) but less than the approximation of the old standard codified by Table 1. And finally, Subpart 2's method for calculating attainment dates—which is simply to count forward a certain number of years from November 15, 1990 (the date the 1990 CAA Amendments took force), depending on how far out of attainment the area started—seems to make no sense for areas that are first classified under a new standard after November 15, 1990. If, for example, areas were classified in the year 2000, many of the deadlines would already have expired at the time of classification.

These gaps in Subpart 2's scheme prevent us from concluding that Congress clearly intended Subpart 2 to be the exclusive, permanent means of enforcing a revised ozone standard in nonattainment areas. The statute is in our view ambiguous concerning the manner in which Subpart 1 and Subpart 2 interact with regard to revised ozone standards, and we would defer to the EPA's reasonable resolution of that ambiguity. We cannot defer, however, to the interpretation the EPA has given.

Whatever effect may be accorded the gaps in Subpart 2 as implying some limited applicability of Subpart 1, they cannot be thought to render Subpart 2's carefully designed restrictions on EPA discretion utterly nugatory once a new standard has been promulgated, as the EPA has concluded. The principal distinction between Subpart 1 and Subpart 2 is that the latter eliminates regulatory discretion that the former allowed. While Subpart 1 permits the EPA to establish classifications for nonattainment areas, Subpart 2 classifies areas as a matter of law based on a table. Whereas the EPA has discretion under Subpart 1 to extend attainment dates for as long as 12 years, under Subpart 2 it may grant no more than 2 years' extension. Whereas Subpart 1 gives the EPA considerable discretion to shape nonattainment programs, Subpart 2 prescribes large parts of them by law. Yet according to the EPA, Subpart 2 was simply Congress's "approach to the implementation of the [old] 1-hour" standard, and so there was no reason that "the new standard could not simultaneously be implemented under . . . subpart 1." To use a few apparent gaps in Subpart 2 to render its textually explicit applicability to nonattainment areas under the new standard utterly inoperative is to go over the edge of reasonable interpretation. The EPA may not construe the statute in a way that completely nullifies textually applicable provisions meant to limit its discretion.

The EPA's interpretation making Subpart 2 abruptly obsolete is all the more astonishing because Subpart 2 was obviously written to govern implementation for some time. Some of the elements required to be included in [state implementation plans] under Subpart 2 were not to take effect until many years after the passage of the Act. A plan reaching so far into the future was not enacted to be abandoned the next time the EPA reviewed the ozone standard—which Congress knew could happen at any time, since the technical staff papers had already been completed in late 1989. Yet nothing in the EPA's interpretation would have prevented the agency from aborting Subpart 2 the day after it was enacted. Even now, if the EPA's interpretation were correct, some areas of the country could be required to meet the new, more stringent ozone standard in *at most* the same time that Subpart 2 had allowed them to meet the old standard. Los Angeles, for instance, "would be required to attain the revised NAAQS under Subpart 1 no later than the same year that marks the outer time limit for attaining Subpart 2's one-hour ozone standard." An interpretation of Subpart 2 so at odds with its structure and manifest purpose cannot be sustained.

We therefore find the EPA's implementation policy to be unlawful, though not in the precise respect determined by the Court of Appeals. After our remand, and the Court of Appeals' final disposition of this case, it is left to the EPA to develop a reasonable interpretation of the nonattainment implementation provisions insofar as they apply to revised ozone NAAQS. . . .

To summarize our holdings in these unusually complex cases: (1) The EPA may not consider implementation costs in setting primary and secondary NAAQS under § 109(b) of the CAA. (2) Section 109(b)(1) does not delegate legislative power to the EPA in contravention of Art. I, § 1, of the Constitution. (3) The Court of Appeals had jurisdiction to review the EPA's interpretation of Part D of Title I of the CAA, relating to the implementation of the revised ozone NAAQS. (4) The EPA's interpretation of that Part is unreasonable.

The judgment of the Court of Appeals is affirmed in part and reversed in part, and the cases are remanded for proceedings consistent with this opinion.

■ JUSTICE THOMAS, concurring.

I agree with the majority that § 109's directive to the agency is no less an "intelligible principle" than a host of other directives that we have approved. I also agree that the Court of Appeals' remand to the agency to make its own corrective interpretation does not accord with our understanding of the delegation issue. I write separately, however, to express my concern that there may nevertheless be a genuine constitutional problem with § 109, a problem which the parties did not address.

The parties to this case who briefed the constitutional issue wrangled over constitutional doctrine with barely a nod to the text of the Constitution. Although this Court since 1928 has treated the "intelligible principle" requirement as the only constitutional limit on congressional grants of power to administrative agencies, see *J. W. Hampton, Jr., & Co. v. United States*, 276 U.S. 394 (1928), the Constitution does not speak of "intelligible principles." Rather, it speaks in much simpler terms: "*All* legislative Powers herein granted shall be vested in a Congress." U.S. Const., Art. 1, § 1. I am not convinced that the intelligible principle doctrine serves to prevent all cessions of legislative power. I believe that there are cases in which the principle is intelligible and yet the significance of the delegated decision is simply too great for the decision to be called anything other than "legislative."

As it is, none of the parties to this case has examined the text of the Constitution or asked us to reconsider our precedents on cessions of legislative power. On a future day, however, I would be willing to address the question whether our delegation jurisprudence has strayed too far from our Founders' understanding of separation of powers.

■ JUSTICE STEVENS, with whom JUSTICE SOUTER joins, concurring in part and concurring in the judgment.

Section 109(b)(1) delegates to the Administrator of the Environmental Protection Agency the authority to promulgate national ambient air quality standards. In Part III of its opinion, the Court convincingly explains why the Court of Appeals erred when it concluded that § 109 effected "an unconstitutional delegation of legislative power." I wholeheartedly endorse the Court's result and endorse its explanation of its reasons, albeit with the following caveat.

The Court has two choices. We could choose to articulate our ultimate disposition of this issue by frankly acknowledging that the power delegated to the EPA is "legislative" but nevertheless conclude that the delegation is constitutional because adequately limited by the terms of the authorizing statute. Alternatively, we could pretend, as the Court does, that the authority delegated to the EPA is somehow not "legislative power." . . . [I]t would be both wiser and more faithful to what we have actually done in delegation cases to admit that agency rulemaking authority is "legislative power."[2]

The proper characterization of governmental power should generally depend on the nature of the power, not on the identity of the person exercising it. See Black's Law Dictionary 899 (6th ed. 1990) (defining "legislation" as, *inter alia*, "formulation of rules for the future"); 1 K. Davis & R. Pierce, Administrative Law Treatise § 2.3, p. 37 (3d ed. 1994) ("If legislative power means the power to make rules of conduct that bind everyone based on resolution of major policy issues, scores of agencies exercise legislative power routinely by promulgating what are candidly called 'legislative rules' "). If the NAAQS that the EPA promulgated had been prescribed by Congress, everyone would agree that those rules would be the product of an exercise of "legislative power." The same

---

[2]   See *Mistretta v. United States*, 488 U.S. 361 (1989) ("Our jurisprudence has been driven by a practical understanding that in our increasingly complex society . . . Congress simply cannot do its job absent an ability to delegate power . . ."). See also *Loving v. United States*, 517 U.S. 748 (1996) ("[The nondelegation] principle does not mean . . . that only Congress can make a rule of prospective force"); 1 K. Davis & R. Pierce, Administrative Law Treatise § 2.6, p. 66 (3d ed. 1994) ("Except for two 1935 cases, the Court has never enforced its frequently announced prohibition on congressional delegation of legislative power").

characterization is appropriate when an agency exercises rulemaking authority pursuant to a permissible delegation from Congress.

My view is not only more faithful to normal English usage, but is also fully consistent with the text of the Constitution. In Article I, the Framers vested "All legislative Powers" in the Congress, Art. I., § 1, just as in Article II they vested the "executive Power" in the President, Art. II, § 1. Those provisions do not purport to limit the authority of either recipient of power to delegate authority to others. Surely the authority granted to members of the Cabinet and federal law enforcement agents is properly characterized as "Executive" even though not exercised by the President.

It seems clear that an executive agency's exercise of rulemaking authority pursuant to a valid delegation from Congress is "legislative." As long as the delegation provides a sufficiently intelligible principle, there is nothing inherently unconstitutional about it. Accordingly, while I join Parts I, II, and IV of the Court's opinion, and agree with almost everything said in Part III, I would hold that when Congress enacted § 109, it effected a constitutional delegation of legislative power to the EPA.

■ [JUSTICE BREYER also concurred in part and in the judgment.]

NOTE ON JUDICIAL REVIEW OF AGENCIES EXERCISING DELEGATED AUTHORITY

1.   Why does Congress delegate authority to administrative agencies? Federalist 51 predicted that officials in different governmental institutions would jealously guard their own authority, not voluntarily cede it to others. Congress has nonetheless been willing to broadly shift lawmaking authority to federal administrative bureaucracies. One reason is that, because political parties operate *across* branches, legislators may have strong incentives to delegate to executive officials controlled by a President of the same party. Nonetheless, broad delegations also occur during periods of divided government. Three additional reasons are typically suggested to explain the phenomenon of widespread delegation:

- **Expertise:** Especially in technical areas such as environmental protection or telecommunications, administrative agencies are seen as having the expertise necessary to determine the details of government policy.

- **Flexibility:** Conditions in many regulated areas may change over time—sometimes very quickly. And it's sometimes difficult to enact a new law because of legislative inertia. Delegation allows an agency to adapt the original law to changed conditions.

- **Avoiding Political Costs:** In many cases, there may be broad political consensus in favor of some goal, but bitter disputes over how to pursue it. Congress can take credit for pursuing the general goal—like air quality—without taking the blame for deciding whose ox will be gored.

- Does Congress's willingness to cede power call into question the basic theory of Federalist 51? Are these reasons for delegating authority to be encouraged and facilitated or resisted? What are the *costs* of broad delegations?

2.   The basic requirement in delegation cases is that Congress lay down an "intelligible principle" for the agency to follow in exercising its delegated authority. What were the possible sources of such a principle in *Schechter*? What was the intelligible principle in *American Trucking*? Note that the intelligible principle need not appear in the statute itself. In *Schechter*, for example, it would have been sufficient if the statutory reference to "unfair competition" had invoked a set of more particular meanings embodied in common law decisions applying that principle.

The nondelegation doctrine and its "intelligible principle" requirement sought to ensure that the right branch was exercising the right power. The thought was that doing so would both make agencies more accountable and their actions more predictable. Do you think that having an intelligible principle would accomplish these goals? How important are these goals to begin with?

3.   The Court's nondelegation holding in *Schechter* is frequently considered part-and-parcel of the Court's general resistance to economic regulation during the *Lochner* era. The National Industrial Recovery Act, partially struck down in *Schechter*, was a centerpiece of the Roosevelt Administration's early approach to the economic crisis of the 1930s. The Court struck down a second portion of the NIRA in *Panama Refining Co. v. Ryan*, 293 U.S. 388 (1935), on grounds similar to those in *Schechter*, although the delegation at issue in *Ryan* covered a considerably narrower subject matter and Justice Cardozo would have upheld it on that ground. Is it fair to characterize nondelegation as part of the *Lochner* era's excesses? Do you agree that the inquiry into whether legislation sets forth an "intelligible principle" is so open-ended that judges will end up simply imposing their policy preferences? Does delegation belong on the "do not resuscitate" side of the Court's post-1937 "double standard," along with freedom of contract and the limited Commerce Clause?

Schechter and *Ryan* were not only the *last* time that the Court struck down a statute on straight-up nondelegation grounds—they were also the *first* time. For that reason, commentators have observed that the nondelegation doctrine "has had one good year, and 211 bad ones (and counting)."[1] Many observers expected that the Rehnquist Court would seize the opportunity presented by *American Trucking* to perform a revival of the nondelegation doctrine akin to the Court's revival of the Commerce Clause in *Lopez*. Of course, the Court did nothing of the kind. Was *American Trucking* analogous to *Lopez* in the sense that, if the Court upheld the provision of the Clean Air Act at issue, it would be forced to admit that *no*

---

[1]   Cass R. Sunstein, *Nondelegation Canons*, 67 U. CHI. L. REV. 315, 322 (2000).

delegation could be unconstitutional? Would the *American Trucking* Court have reached a different result in *Schechter* itself? *Should* the Court have revived the nondelegation doctrine in *American Trucking*? Should it seize the opportunity to do so in a future case?

4.   Unlike *American Trucking*, *Schechter* involved a delegation of lawmaking authority not only to the Executive, but also to private industry. *Schechter*'s firm rejection of private delegations is still generally thought to be good law. But note the crucial distinction: It is generally permissible to adopt a rule proposed or drafted by private parties, but it is *not* acceptable to endow a private entity with authority to say what the law is in the future. Congress might require, for example, that all federally-funded construction projects conform to the most recent building specifications promulgated by the American Association of General Contractors. But it could not say that, in the future, whatever specifications that association promulgates will be binding federal law governing all federally-funded projects.

Are private delegations inherently more troubling than delegations to federal agencies? What about those cases—not unheard-of—in which Congress delegates authority to state governments?

5.   Some commentators have suggested that, although the Court no longer strikes down statutory delegations as unconstitutional, it continues to enforce nondelegation principles through the means of statutory construction. In several cases, the Supreme Court has interpreted statutory delegations narrowly in order to avoid raising delegation concerns.[2] And in areas where the exercise of delegated authority by an agency may infringe on other constitutional concerns, such as individual rights or federalism, the courts have frequently interpreted the scope of such authority narrowly. The *Solid Waste* case in Section 10.1, in which the Court refused to construe the Clean Water Act as authorizing the Corps of Engineers to promulgate a rule that would press the bounds of the Commerce Power, demonstrates this approach.

6.   The most important checks on agency discretion are twofold. First, Congress exercises considerable oversight over agency action. This oversight takes place through a number of mechanisms:

- Oversight Hearings: Congress can call executive officials before it to explain their actions publicly.

- Confirmation of Officers: The Senate can often exercise a check and extract concessions when confirming nominees to executive departments.

- Budgetary Controls: Congress can use control of funding for agencies to control agency action.

How important are these sorts of checks? Do they depend on the Executive's willingness—which has often been lacking in recent administrations—to provide information to Congress concerning its activities?

---

[2]   *See, e.g.*, *Industrial Union Dept. v. American Petroleum Inst.*, 448 U.S. 607, 645–46 (1980) (plurality opinion); *National Cable Television Assn. v. United States*, 415 U.S. 336, 341–43 (1974).

Second, the abandonment of constitutional limits on delegation has been offset by the rapid growth of judicial review of agency action for conformity to statutory purposes. According to one prominent scholar, "[b]road delegations of power to regulatory agencies, questionable in light of the grant of legislative power to Congress in Article I of the Constitution, have been allowed largely on the assumption that courts would be available to ensure agency fidelity to whatever statutory directives have been issued."[3] Most of this review takes place under the Administrative Procedure Act (APA) and is the subject matter of the course in Administrative Law. This sort of review occurs in several different forms:

- Substantive Review of Legal Questions: Courts review whether actions taken and regulations issued are consistent with the terms of the underlying statutes delegating authority to the agency. This review is qualified by the *Chevron* doctrine counseling deference to agency interpretations of ambiguities in the statutes they administer.

- Substantive Review of Fact & Policy Questions: Courts conduct very deferential review of such questions under the "arbitrary and capricious" standard.

- Procedural Review: Courts also review whether agency decisionmaking satisfies procedural requirements in the APA, such as public "notice and comment" for certain forms of rulemaking.

The second half of the *American Trucking* opinion illustrates statutory review under the APA. Note the difference from the constitutional nondelegation principle: Whereas the constitutional principle prohibits *Congress* from enacting statutes that delegate too broadly, statutory review constrains the *agency* to follow whatever statutory constraints Congress does enact. Hence the *American Trucking* court strikes down the agency's rule because it rests on an incorrect interpretation of the Clean Air Act. What are the advantages of such statutory review over constitutional review under the classical nondelegation doctrine? Is statutory review an adequate substitute from the standpoint of the constitutional interests in keeping Congress accountable for legislative choices?

7.   APA review of agency action will often overlap with issues concerning the President's ability to act unilaterally under *Youngstown*. This overlap was evident in recent litigation over President Obama's effort to reform federal immigration policy by executive action. After efforts to reform the nation's immigration laws stalled in Congress, the Obama administration promulgated a directive in 2014 entitled Deferred Action for Parents of Americans and Lawful Permanent Residents (DAPA). DAPA offered "deferred action"—a promise not detain or deport—to a large class of about four million aliens who were not lawfully present in the United States. It made this status available to unlawful aliens who (1) had a child who was either a citizen or a legal permanent resident, (2) had been in the country

---

[3]   CASS R. SUNSTEIN, AFTER THE RIGHTS REVOLUTION: RECONCEIVING THE REGULATORY STATE 143 (1990).

since January 1, 2010, (3) did not fall into three categories that had been designated high-priority for immigration enforcement, and (4) did not present any other factors that would make deferred action inappropriate. The result of deferred action was to make previously unlawful aliens "lawfully present in the United States" and eligible for work authorization and participation in other federal and state programs.[4] In a press conference shortly after DAPA issued, President Obama stated that, because Congress had failed to act, "I just took an action to change the law."[5]

The Obama administration grounded DAPA in the Immigration and Nationality Act (INA), which charges the Secretary of Homeland Security "with the administration and enforcement of th[e INA] and all other laws relating to the immigration and naturalization of aliens." 8 U.S.C. § 1103(a)(1). That INA authorizes the Secretary to "establish such regulations; . . . issue such instructions; and perform such other acts as he deems necessary," 8 U.S.C. § 1103(a)(2). Congress has likewise tasked the Secretary with "[e]stablishing national immigration enforcement policies and priorities." 6 U.S.C. § 202(5). In essence, the Administration justified DAPA as an exercise of prosecutorial discretion, reflecting a reasonable judgment that aliens meeting the DAPA criteria should be a low priority for deportation.

The State of Texas, joined by 25 other states, challenged DAPA on the grounds that it was inconsistent with the underlying federal immigration statutes, that it violated the President's Article II obligation to "take care" that those laws "be faithfully executed," and that it violated the APA's procedural requirements because it had been issued without an opportunity for notice and comment. The U.S. District Court for the Southern District of Texas granted the plaintiffs' request for a preliminary injunction preventing DAPA from going into effect, finding that the plaintiffs were likely to prevail on their claims on the merits. In particular, the district court determined that "[t]he DAPA program clearly represents a substantive change in immigration policy. It is a program instituted to give a certain, newly-adopted class of 4.3 million illegal immigrants not only 'legal presence' in the United States, but also the right to work legally and the right to receive a myriad of governmental benefits to which they would not otherwise be entitled. It does more than 'supplement' the statute; if anything, it contradicts the INA. It is, in effect, a new law."[6] The Fifth Circuit affirmed the District Court's grant of the preliminary injunction, and the Supreme Court affirmed by an equally-divided court[7]—thereby preventing DAPA from going into effect prior to the end of President Obama's presidency.

---

[4] Memorandum from Jeh Johnson, Sec'y, Dep't of Homeland Sec., to Leon Rodriguez, Dir., USCIS, et al. 2 (Nov. 20, 2014), https://www.dhs.gov/sites/default/files/publications/14_1120_memo_deferred_action.pdf.

[5] Press Release, Remarks by the President on Immigration—Chicago, IL, The White House Office of the Press Secretary (Nov. 25, 2014), available at https://obamawhitehouse.archives.gov/the-press-office/2014/11/25/remarks-president-immigration-chicago-il.

[6] *Texas v. United States*, 86 F. Supp. 3d 591, 670 (S.D. Tex. 2015).

[7] *United States v. Texas*, 136 S. Ct. 2271 (2016).

The DAPA litigation illustrates the complexity of contemporary challenges to exercises of executive authority. One might think of such cases under *Youngstown*, so that the question is whether the President is acting consistent with Congressional pronouncements (Justice Jackson's first category) or contrary to them (Jackson's third category). But this sort of litigation will often be brought as a claim for statutory review under the APA, inquiring both whether executive action is permissible under the relevant statutory delegations of authority and whether that action satisfies the APA's procedural requirement. Either way, the ultimate question is whether Congress has authorized the President to do what he did. As the DAPA litigation also illustrates, that question will often be difficult to resolve, given the breadth of the President's delegated authority in many areas of the law.

How should the Supreme Court have ruled in the DAPA case? Given the practical impossibility of deporting all unlawful aliens, isn't it inevitable that the Executive must prioritize certain categories of such aliens over others? At that point, isn't it simple decency to notify persons *not* prioritized for enforcement that they need not live in fear of deportation? Should it matter that Congress had failed to approve proposals similar to DAPA, and that the President himself had characterized DAPA as an effort to "change the law"? If DAPA was constitutional, is there any limit on the President's ability to liberalize the immigration laws—or other statutory regimes—simply by de-prioritizing certain classes of persons or activities for enforcement?

8.   Scholars have devoted a great deal of energy to explaining and justifying the administrative state. Administrative theory attempts to explain the purpose of agencies and how they should operate. It must justify their legitimacy in a constitutional democracy even though they are not mentioned in the Constitution or directly politically accountable to the People. Administrative theory in particular must resolve agencies' place in the constitutional government and explain their relationship with all three branches. For legal scholars and practitioners, such theory especially must tell courts when and how to review agency decisions. Several different theoretical paradigms have developed to meet these challenges:

- *The "transmission belt" model*: Traditional administrative law viewed agencies as merely carrying out clear statements of congressional law and policy, without exercising any independent discretion. Judicial review served to ensure that agencies did follow Congress's instruction without involving judges in policy questions. The transmission belt model also explained how agencies should operate; any agency policy or procedure should focus on effectuating Congress's instructions. Finally, agencies derived their democratic authority and accountability from Congress. But as Congress gave agencies extremely broad discretion after the New Deal, the transmission belt theory became unrealistic.

- *The expertise model*: Many New Dealers responded to unprecedented economic crisis by concluding that professional experts rather than politicians should direct policy. The agencies' legitimacy thus derived from their expertise rather than their connection to Congress. Concerns about agency discretion were minimized by the view that agency experts were restrained by their own professional judgment. This technocratic model soon came under attack, however. Critics argued that "expert" administrators actually harbored their own biases and that, more broadly, technocratic judgments were in fact political.

- *The process theory model*: Concerns about agency discretion led to the Administrative Procedure Act, which provided some guidance for agency decisionmaking and judicial review. Continuing scholarly criticism led many courts to impose even more procedural requirements on agencies; courts began examining the factual basis of agency decisions and demanding that agencies provide reasoned explanations for their policies. This model was part of the larger process theory movement, which saw the responsibility of courts as protecting democratic processes rather than imposing courts' substantive preferences. Note that this model retained the basic idea that agency administrators were experts who could make policy independent of Congress—it merely reformed how those administrators reached their final decisions.

- *The interest group representation model*: By the 1970s, scholars realized that even experts could not reach one definitive answer to problems—for example, even economists disagree over how to run the national economy. Pluralist politics replaced the New Deal's faith that experts had all the answers. The interest group representation model focused administrative law on giving all interested parties a voice in decisionmaking and forcing agencies to reflect those interests in their final judgments. The agencies thus derived democratic legitimacy not from their connection to an elected Congress or President, but from the opportunities for popular participation in the agency's own decisionmaking procedures. Agencies struggled, however, to consider all possible conflicting interests, and critics argued that regulated interests were effectively able to "capture" particular agencies.

- *The presidential control model*: Whereas the transmission belt model justified agencies based on congressional control, later scholars defended agencies as arms of another elected representative: the president.[8] Under this model, statutes may give agencies broad discretion because the president directs their policy goals and monitors their decisions; it assumes that the president is accountable to the public for agency decisions and that the president acts reasonably when directing policy. Of course, emphasizing presidential control may heighten concerns about the accretion of presidential

---

[8] *See, e.g.*, Elena Kagan, *Presidential Administration*, 114 HARV. L. REV. 2245 (2001).

authority, and it hardly solves the basic nondelegation issue with transferring lawmaking authority outside the legislative branch.

Which, if any, of these theories do you find persuasive? Does the existence of so many different theoretical efforts to satisfy concerns about agency legitimacy suggest that a single, coherent theory of administrative law will prove elusive? Does the Constitution require that we have such a theory?

See also: The seminal discussion of how administrative law has addressed the dilemmas of delegation is Richard Stewart, *The Reformation of American Administrative Law*, 88 HARV. L. REV. 1667 (1975). For a useful contemporary overview of administrative law paradigms, see Lisa Schultz Bressman, *Beyond Accountability: Arbitrariness and Legitimacy in the Administrative State*, 78 N.Y.U. L. REV. 461, 469–91 (2003). Although most contemporary academics accept the demise of the nondelegation doctrine, a forceful argument in favor of reviving it appears in DAVID SCHOENBROD, POWER WITHOUT RESPONSIBILITY: HOW CONGRESS ABUSES THE PEOPLE THROUGH DELEGATION (1993). For an argument that the doctrine is alive and well and living in the rules of statutory construction, see Cass R. Sunstein, *Nondelegation Canons*, 67 U. CHI. L. REV. 315 (2000).

SECTION 13.2 ALTERING THE LEGISLATIVE PROCESS

As the national government has grown larger and more complex, Congress has frequently enacted statutes that alter, in various respects, traditional institutional arrangements. The cases in this unit deal with efforts to alter the legislative process itself. *INS v. Chadha* concerns the legislative veto, which allowed Congress to overrule actions taken by executive officials without needing to enact a new statute overturning such action. *Clinton v. New York* deals with the line-item veto, which authorized the President to veto particular provisions of omnibus taxing and spending legislation rather than having to accept or reject the entire package. In both cases, the Court invalidated these innovations as impermissible departures from the legislative procedure set forth in Article I.

Just like the cases in the preceding unit, *Chadha* and *Clinton v. New York* are both cases about delegation. As Justice White's dissent in *Chadha* explains, the legislative veto was a response to Congress's need to delegate vast areas of legislative authority to executive agencies. By reserving the right to "veto" executive actions taken pursuant to these broad delegations, Congress could retain oversight authority without having to overcome the burdens of inertia that impede new legislation. The legislative veto was also an instance of *self*-delegation: Congress delegated the authority to act to a subset of itself—a single house, or even a single committee—rather than requiring the concurrence of both houses and presentment to the President.

The initial challenge to the line-item veto in *Clinton v. New York* was framed as an Article I, § 7 challenge along *Chadha*'s lines, but the opinions quickly devolved into a debate about delegation. As the majority implicitly conceded, the heart of the case is not whether Congress may authorize the President not to spend funds or not to enforce particular aspects of legislation under certain circumstances, but whether Congress had imposed sufficient constraints upon the President's discretion in this regard. By holding that Congress had not, the majority arguably struck down a federal statute on delegation grounds for the first time since 1935.

Both of these cases raise the more fundamental issue of whether the separation of powers set forth in the Constitution's formal provisions, which have not been altered in any relevant way since 1789, still makes sense for a Twenty-first Century government. Alternately, the question is whether so many departures from the original separation of powers— e.g., vast delegations of lawmaking authority creating an immense administrative state—have *already* occurred that strict adherence to formal provisions like Article I, § 7 should not be required. In this vein, one might consider both the legislative and line-item vetoes as "compensating adjustments," meant to maintain overall balance in a system that has already been much altered by institutional developments over the past century. As you read, consider whether the Court should be more sympathetic to such compensating adjustments.

Immigration and Naturalization Service v. Chadha
462 U.S. 919 (1983)

■ **CHIEF JUSTICE BURGER delivered the opinion of the Court.**

. . . Each [of these cases] presents a challenge to the constitutionality of the provision in § 244(c)(2) of the Immigration and Nationality Act, authorizing one House of Congress, by resolution, to invalidate the decision of the Executive Branch, pursuant to authority delegated by Congress to the Attorney General of the United States, to allow a particular deportable alien to remain in the United States.

I

Chadha is an East Indian who was born in Kenya and holds a British passport. He was lawfully admitted to the United States in 1966 on a nonimmigrant student visa. His visa expired on June 30, 1972. On October 11, 1973, the District Director of the Immigration and Naturalization Service ordered Chadha to show cause why he should not be deported for having "remained in the United States for a longer time than permitted." . . . Chadha conceded that he was deportable for overstaying his visa and the hearing was adjourned to enable him to file an application for suspension of deportation under § 244(a)(1) of the Act. Section 244(a)(1), at the time in question, provided:

> [T]he Attorney General may, in his discretion, suspend deportation and adjust the status to that of an alien lawfully admitted for permanent residence, in the case of an alien who

applies to the Attorney General for suspension of deportation and—

(1) is deportable under any law of the United States . . .; has been physically present in the United States for a continuous period of not less than seven years immediately preceding the date of such application, and proves that during all of such period he was and is a person of good moral character; and is a person whose deportation would, in the opinion of the Attorney General, result in extreme hardship to the alien or to his spouse, parent, or child, who is a citizen of the United States or an alien lawfully admitted for permanent residence.[1]

. . . On the basis of evidence adduced at the hearing, affidavits submitted with the application, and the results of a character investigation conducted by the INS, the Immigration Judge, on June 25, 1974, ordered that Chadha's deportation be suspended. The Immigration Judge found that Chadha met the requirements of § 244(a)(1): he had resided continuously in the United States for over seven years, was of good moral character, and would suffer "extreme hardship" if deported.

Pursuant to § 244(c)(1) of the Act, the Immigration Judge suspended Chadha's deportation and a report of the suspension was transmitted to Congress. Section 244(c)(1) provides:

Upon application by any alien who is found by the Attorney General to meet the requirements of subsection (a) of this section the Attorney General may in his discretion suspend deportation of such alien. If the deportation of any alien is suspended under the provisions of this subsection, a complete and detailed statement of the facts and pertinent provisions of law in the case shall be reported to the Congress with the reasons for such suspension. Such reports shall be submitted on the first day of each calendar month in which Congress is in session.

Once the Attorney General's recommendation for suspension of Chadha's deportation was conveyed to Congress, Congress had the power under § 244(c)(2) of the Act, to veto the Attorney General's determination that Chadha should not be deported. Section 244(c)(2) provides:

(2) In the case of an alien specified in paragraph (1) of subsection (a) of this subsection—

if during the session of the Congress at which a case is reported, or prior to the close of the session of the Congress next following the session at which a case is reported, either the Senate or the House of Representatives passes a resolution stating in substance that it does not favor the suspension of such

---

[1] Congress delegated the major responsibilities for enforcement of the Immigration and Nationality Act to the Attorney General. The Attorney General discharges his responsibilities through the Immigration and Naturalization Service, a division of the Department of Justice.

deportation, the Attorney General shall thereupon deport such alien . . . . If, within the time above specified, neither the Senate nor the House of Representatives shall pass such a resolution, the Attorney General shall cancel deportation proceedings.

. . . On December 12, 1975, Representative Eilberg, Chairman of the Judiciary Subcommittee on Immigration, Citizenship, and International Law, introduced a resolution opposing "the granting of permanent residence in the United States to [six] aliens," including Chadha. . . . [T]he House consideration of the resolution was based on Representative Eilberg's statement from the floor that

> [it] was the feeling of the committee, after reviewing 340 cases, that the aliens contained in the resolution [Chadha and five others] did not meet these statutory requirements, particularly as it relates to hardship; and it is the opinion of the committee that their deportation should not be suspended.

The resolution was passed without debate or recorded vote. . . . [T]he resolution was not treated as an Art. I legislative act; it was not submitted to the Senate or presented to the President for his action.

. . . On November 8, 1976, Chadha was ordered deported pursuant to the House action. . . . Chadha filed a petition for review. . . . The Immigration and Naturalization Service agreed with Chadha's position before the Court of Appeals and joined him in arguing that § 244(c)(2) is unconstitutional. . . .

[T]he Court of Appeals held that the House was without constitutional authority to order Chadha's deportation. . . . We . . . now affirm. . . .

III

A

. . . [T]he fact that a given law or procedure is efficient, convenient, and useful in facilitating functions of government, standing alone, will not save it if it is contrary to the Constitution. Convenience and efficiency are not the primary objectives—or the hallmarks—of democratic government and our inquiry is sharpened rather than blunted by the fact that congressional veto provisions are appearing with increasing frequency in statutes which delegate authority to executive and independent agencies. . . .

JUSTICE WHITE undertakes to make a case for the proposition that the one-House veto is a useful "political invention," and we need not challenge that assertion. . . . But policy arguments supporting even useful "political inventions" are subject to the demands of the Constitution which defines powers and, with respect to this subject, sets out just how those powers are to be exercised.

Explicit and unambiguous provisions of the Constitution prescribe and define the respective functions of the Congress and of the Executive in the legislative process. . . . Article I provides:

All legislative Powers herein granted shall be vested in a Congress of the United States, which shall consist of a Senate *and* House of Representatives. Art. I, § 1.

Every Bill which shall have passed the House of Representatives *and* the Senate, *shall*, before it becomes a law, be presented to the President of the United States. . . . Art. I, § 7, cl. 2.

Every Order, Resolution, or Vote to which the Concurrence of the Senate and House of Representatives may be necessary (except on a question of Adjournment) *shall be* presented to the President of the United States; and before the Same shall take Effect, *shall be* approved by him, or being disapproved by him, *shall be* repassed by two thirds of the Senate and House of Representatives, according to the Rules and Limitations prescribed in the Case of a Bill. Art. I, § 7, cl. 3.

These provisions of Art. I are integral parts of the constitutional design for the separation of powers. . . . [T]he purposes underlying the Presentment Clauses, Art. I, § 7, cls. 2, 3, and the bicameral requirement of Art. I, § 1, and § 7, cl. 2, guide our resolution of the important question presented in these cases. . . .

B

The Presentment Clauses

The records of the Constitutional Convention reveal that the requirement that all legislation be presented to the President before becoming law was uniformly accepted by the Framers. . . .

The decision to provide the President with a limited and qualified power to nullify proposed legislation by veto was based on the profound conviction of the Framers that the powers conferred on Congress were the powers to be most carefully circumscribed. It is beyond doubt that lawmaking was a power to be shared by both Houses and the President. In The Federalist No. 73, Hamilton focused on the President's role in making laws:

If even no propensity had ever discovered itself in the legislative body to invade the rights of the Executive, the rules of just reasoning and theoretic propriety would of themselves teach us that the one ought not to be left to the mercy of the other, but ought to possess a constitutional and effectual power of self-defence. . . .

The President's role in the lawmaking process also reflects the Framers' careful efforts to check whatever propensity a particular Congress might have to enact oppressive, improvident, or ill-considered measures. The President's veto . . . was described later during public debate on ratification:

> It establishes a salutary check upon the legislative body, calculated to guard the community against the effects of faction, precipitancy, or of any impulse unfriendly to the public good, which may happen to influence a majority of that body. . . . The primary inducement to conferring the power in question upon the Executive is, to enable him to defend himself; the secondary one is to increase the chances in favor of the community against the passing of bad laws, through haste, inadvertence, or design.

. . . [T]he Presentment Clauses serve the important purpose of assuring that a "national" perspective is grafted on the legislative process:

> The President is a representative of the people just as the members of the Senate and of the House are, and it may be, at some times, on some subjects, that the President elected by all the people is rather more representative of them all than are the members of either body of the Legislature whose constituencies are local and not countrywide. . . .

Myers v. United States, 272 U.S. 52 (1926).

C

Bicameralism

The bicameral requirement of Art. I, §§ 1, 7, was of scarcely less concern to the Framers than was the Presidential veto and indeed the two concepts are interdependent. By providing that no law could take effect without the concurrence of the prescribed majority of the Members of both Houses, the Framers reemphasized their belief . . . that legislation should not be enacted unless it has been carefully and fully considered by the Nation's elected officials. In the Constitutional Convention debates on the need for a bicameral legislature, James Wilson . . . commented:

> . . . If the Legislative authority be not restrained, there can be neither liberty nor stability; and it can only be restrained by dividing it within itself, into distinct and independent branches. In a single house there is no check, but the inadequate one, of the virtue & good sense of those who compose it.

Hamilton argued that a Congress comprised of a single House was antithetical to the very purposes of the Constitution. Were the Nation to adopt a Constitution providing for only one legislative organ, he warned:

> [We] shall finally accumulate, in a single body, all the most important prerogatives of sovereignty, and thus entail upon our posterity one of the most execrable forms of government that human infatuation ever contrived. Thus we should create in reality that very tyranny which the adversaries of the new Constitution either are, or affect to be, solicitous to avert.

. . . However familiar, it is useful to recall that apart from their fear that special interests could be favored at the expense of public needs, the Framers were also concerned, although not of one mind, over the apprehensions of the smaller states. . . . [T]he Great Compromise, under which one House was viewed as representing the people and the other the states, allayed the fears of both the large and small states.

We see therefore that the Framers were acutely conscious that the bicameral requirement and the Presentment Clauses would serve essential constitutional functions. The President's participation in the legislative process was to protect the Executive Branch from Congress and to protect the whole people from improvident laws. The division of the Congress into two distinctive bodies assures that the legislative power would be exercised only after opportunity for full study and debate in separate settings. The President's unilateral veto power, in turn, was limited by the power of two-thirds of both Houses of Congress to overrule a veto thereby precluding final arbitrary action of one person. . . . [T]he prescription for legislative action in Art. I, §§ 1, 7, represents the Framers' decision that the legislative power of the Federal Government be exercised in accord with a single, finely wrought and exhaustively considered, procedure.

IV

The Constitution sought to divide the delegated powers of the new Federal Government into three defined categories, Legislative, Executive, and Judicial, to assure, as nearly as possible, that each branch of government would confine itself to its assigned responsibility. The hydraulic pressure inherent within each of the separate Branches to exceed the outer limits of its power, even to accomplish desirable objectives, must be resisted.

Although not "hermetically" sealed from one another, the powers delegated to the three Branches are functionally identifiable. When any Branch acts, it is presumptively exercising the power the Constitution has delegated to it. When the Executive acts, he presumptively acts in an executive or administrative capacity as defined in Art. II. And when, as here, one House of Congress purports to act, it is presumptively acting within its assigned sphere.

Beginning with this presumption, we must nevertheless establish that the challenged action under § 244(c)(2) is of the kind to which the procedural requirements of Art. I, § 7, apply. Not every action taken by either House is subject to the bicameralism and presentment requirements of Art. I. Whether actions taken by either House are, in law and fact, an exercise of legislative power depends not on their form but upon "whether they contain matter which is properly to be regarded as legislative in its character and effect." . . .

In purporting to exercise power defined in Art. I, § 8, cl. 4, to "establish an uniform Rule of Naturalization," the House took action that had the purpose and effect of altering the legal rights, duties, and relations of persons, including the Attorney General, Executive Branch officials and Chadha, all outside the Legislative Branch. Section 244(c)(2) purports to authorize one House of Congress to require the Attorney General to deport an individual alien whose deportation otherwise would be canceled under § 244. The one-House veto operated in these cases to overrule the Attorney General and mandate Chadha's deportation; absent the House action, Chadha would remain in the United States. Congress has *acted* and its action has altered Chadha's status.

The legislative character of the one-House veto in these cases is confirmed by the character of the congressional action it supplants. Neither the House of Representatives nor the Senate contends that, absent the veto provision in § 244(c)(2), either of them, or both of them acting together, could effectively require the Attorney General to deport an alien once the Attorney General, in the exercise of legislatively delegated authority,[16] had determined the alien should remain in the United States. Without the challenged provision in § 244(c)(2), this could have been achieved, if at all, only by legislation requiring deportation. Similarly, a veto by one House of Congress under § 244(c)(2) cannot be justified as an attempt at amending the standards set out in § 244(a)(1), or as a repeal of § 244 as applied to Chadha. Amendment and repeal of statutes, no less than enactment, must conform with Art. I.

The nature of the decision implemented by the one-House veto in these cases further manifests its legislative character. After long experience with the clumsy, time-consuming private bill procedure, Congress made a deliberate choice to delegate to the Executive Branch, and specifically to the Attorney General, the authority to allow deportable aliens to remain in this country in certain specified circumstances. It is not disputed that this choice to delegate authority is precisely the kind of decision that can be implemented only in accordance with the procedures set out in Art. I. Disagreement with the Attorney General's decision on Chadha's deportation—that is, Congress' decision to deport Chadha—no less than Congress' original choice to delegate to the Attorney General the authority to make that decision, involves determinations of policy that Congress can implement in only one way;

---

[16] Congress protests that affirming the Court of Appeals in these cases will sanction "lawmaking by the Attorney General. . . . Why is the Attorney General exempt from submitting his proposed changes in the law to the full bicameral process?" To be sure, some administrative agency action—rulemaking, for example—may resemble "lawmaking." See 5 U. S. C. § 551(4), which defines an agency's "rule" as "the whole or part of an agency statement of general or particular applicability and future effect designed to implement, interpret, or prescribe *law* or policy. . . ." . . . Clearly, however . . . "the President's power to see that the laws are faithfully executed refutes the idea that he is to be a lawmaker." *Youngstown Sheet & Tube Co.* v. *Sawyer.* When the Attorney General performs his duties pursuant to § 244, he does not exercise "legislative" power. The bicameral process is not necessary as a check on the Executive's administration of the laws because his administrative activity cannot reach beyond the limits of the statute that created it—a statute duly enacted pursuant to Art. I, §§ 1, 7. The constitutionality of the Attorney General's execution of the authority delegated to him by § 244 involves only a question of delegation doctrine. . . .

bicameral passage followed by presentment to the President. Congress must abide by its delegation of authority until that delegation is legislatively altered or revoked.[19]

Finally . . . when the Framers intended to authorize either House of Congress to act alone and outside of its prescribed bicameral legislative role, they narrowly and precisely defined the procedure for such action. There are four provisions in the Constitution, explicit and unambiguous, by which one House may act alone with the unreviewable force of law, not subject to the President's veto:

(a) The House of Representatives alone was given the power to initiate impeachments. Art. I, § 2, cl. 5;

(b) The Senate alone was given the power to conduct trials following impeachment on charges initiated by the House and to convict following trial. Art. I, § 3, cl. 6;

(c) The Senate alone was given final unreviewable power to approve or to disapprove Presidential appointments. Art. II, § 2, cl. 2;

(d) The Senate alone was given unreviewable power to ratify treaties negotiated by the President. Art. II, § 2, cl. 2.

Clearly, when the Draftsmen sought to confer special powers on one House, independent of the other House, or of the President, they did so in explicit, unambiguous terms.[21] . . . These exceptions are narrow, explicit, and separately justified; none of them authorize the action challenged here. . . .

Since it is clear that the action by the House under § 244(c)(2) was not within any of the express constitutional exceptions authorizing one House to act alone, and equally clear that it was an exercise of legislative power, that action was subject to the standards prescribed in Art. I.[22] . . .

---

[19] . . . The Constitution provides Congress with abundant means to oversee and control its administrative creatures. Beyond the obvious fact that Congress ultimately controls administrative agencies in the legislation that creates them, other means of control, such as durational limits on authorizations and formal reporting requirements, lie well within Congress' constitutional power.

[21] . . . One might also include another "exception" to the rule that congressional action having the force of law be subject to the bicameral requirement and the Presentment Clauses. Each House has the power to act alone in determining specified internal matters. Art. I, § 7, cls. 2, 3, and § 5, cl. 2. However, this "exception" only empowers Congress to bind itself and . . . further indicates the Framers' intent that Congress not act in any legally binding manner outside a closely circumscribed legislative arena, except in specific and enumerated instances. . . .

[22] JUSTICE POWELL's position is that the one-House veto in this case is a *judicial* act and therefore unconstitutional as beyond the authority vested in Congress by the Constitution. We agree that there is a sense in which one-House action pursuant to § 244(c)(2) has a judicial cast, since it purports to "review" Executive action. In this case, for example, the sponsor of the resolution vetoing the suspension of Chadha's deportation argued that Chadha "did not meet [the] statutory requirements" for suspension of deportation. To be sure, it is normally up to the courts to decide whether an agency has complied with its statutory mandate. But the attempted analogy between judicial action and the one-House veto is less than perfect. Federal courts do not enjoy a roving mandate to correct alleged excesses of administrative agencies; we are limited by Art. III to hearing cases and controversies and no justiciable case or controversy was presented by the Attorney General's decision to allow Chadha to remain in this country. We are

To accomplish what has been attempted by one House of Congress in this case requires action in conformity with the express procedures of the Constitution's prescription for legislative action: passage by a majority of both Houses and presentment to the President.[23] . . .

The choices we discern as having been made in the Constitutional Convention impose burdens on governmental processes that often seem clumsy, inefficient, even unworkable, but those hard choices were consciously made by men who had lived under a form of government that permitted arbitrary governmental acts to go unchecked. There is no support in the Constitution or decisions of this Court for the proposition that the cumbersomeness and delays often encountered in complying with explicit constitutional standards may be avoided, either by the Congress or by the President. See *Youngstown Sheet & Tube Co. v. Sawyer.*

With all the obvious flaws of delay, untidiness, and potential for abuse, we have not yet found a better way to preserve freedom than by making the exercise of power subject to the carefully crafted restraints spelled out in the Constitution.

V

We hold that the congressional veto provision in § 244(c)(2) is . . . unconstitutional. Accordingly, the judgment of the Court of Appeals is *Affirmed.*

■ JUSTICE POWELL, concurring in the judgment.

The Court's decision, based on the Presentment Clauses, Art. I, § 7, cls. 2 and 3, apparently will invalidate every use of the legislative veto. The breadth of this holding gives one pause. Congress has included the veto in literally hundreds of statutes, dating back to the 1930's. Congress clearly views this procedure as essential to controlling the delegation of power to administrative agencies. . . . In my view, the cases may be decided on a narrower ground. When Congress finds that a particular person does not satisfy the statutory criteria for permanent residence in this country it has assumed a judicial function in violation of the principle of separation of powers. Accordingly, I concur only in the judgment.

---

aware of no decision . . . where a federal court has reviewed a decision of the Attorney General suspending deportation of an alien pursuant to the standards set out in § 244(a)(1). . . .

[23] . . . JUSTICE WHITE suggests that the Attorney General's action . . . suspending deportation is equivalent to a *proposal* for legislation and that because congressional approval is indicated "by the failure to veto, the one-House veto satisfies the requirement of bicameral approval." . . . Even if it were clear that Congress entertained such an arcane theory when it enacted § 244(c)(2), which JUSTICE WHITE does not suggest, this would amount to nothing less than an amending of Art. I. . . . But the steps required by Art. I, §§ 1, 7, make certain that there is an opportunity for deliberation and debate. To allow Congress to evade the strictures of the Constitution and in effect enact Executive proposals into law by mere silence cannot be squared with Art. I.

I

A

The Framers perceived that "[the] accumulation of all powers legislative, executive and judiciary in the same hands, whether of one, a few or many, and whether hereditary, self appointed, or elective, may justly be pronounced the very definition of tyranny." The Federalist No. 47, p. 324 (J. Cooke ed. 1961) (J. Madison). Theirs was not a baseless fear. Under British rule, the Colonies suffered the abuses of unchecked executive power that were attributed, at least popularly, to a hereditary monarchy. During the Confederation, the States reacted by removing power from the executive and placing it in the hands of elected legislators. But many legislators proved to be little better than the Crown. "The supremacy of legislatures came to be recognized as the supremacy of faction and the tyranny of shifting majorities. The legislatures confiscated property, erected paper money schemes, [and] suspended the ordinary means of collecting debts." Levi, *Some Aspects of Separation of Powers*, 76 Colum.L.Rev. 369, 374–75 (1976)

One abuse that was prevalent during the Confederation was the exercise of judicial power by the state legislatures. The Framers were well acquainted with the danger of subjecting the determination of the rights of one person to the "tyranny of shifting majorities." Jefferson observed that members of the General Assembly in his native Virginia had not been prevented from assuming judicial power, and "[they] have accordingly *in many* instances *decided rights* which should have been left to *judiciary controversy*." The same concern also was evident in the reports of the Council of the Censors, a body that was charged with determining whether the Pennsylvania Legislature had complied with the State Constitution. The Council found that during this period "[the] constitutional trial by jury had been violated; and powers assumed, which had not been delegated by the Constitution. . . . [Cases] belonging to the judiciary department, frequently [had been] drawn within legislative cognizance and determination."

It was to prevent the recurrence of such abuses that the Framers vested the executive, legislative, and judicial powers in separate branches. Their concern that a legislature should not be able unilaterally to impose a substantial deprivation on one person was expressed not only in this general allocation of power, but also in more specific provisions, such as the Bill of Attainder Clause, Art. I, § 9, cl. 3. . . . This Clause, and the separation-of-powers doctrine generally, reflect the Framers' concern that trial by a legislature lacks the safeguards necessary to prevent the abuse of power.

B

The Constitution does not establish three branches with precisely defined boundaries. . . . But where one branch has impaired or sought to assume a power central to another branch, the Court has not hesitated to enforce the doctrine. Functionally, the doctrine may be violated in two ways. One branch may interfere impermissibly with the other's performance of its constitutionally assigned function. Alternatively, the doctrine may be violated when one branch assumes a function that more properly is entrusted to another. These cases present the latter situation.

II

... On its face, the House's action appears clearly adjudicatory.[7] The House did not enact a general rule; rather it made its own determination that six specific persons did not comply with certain statutory criteria. It thus undertook the type of decision that traditionally has been left to other branches. Even if the House ... simply reviewed the Immigration and Naturalization Service's findings, it still assumed a function ordinarily entrusted to the federal courts.[8] See *Foti v. INS,* 375 U.S. 217 (1963) (holding that courts of appeals have jurisdiction to review INS decisions denying suspension of deportation). ...

The impropriety of the House's assumption of this function is confirmed by the fact that its action raises the very danger the Framers sought to avoid—the exercise of unchecked power. In deciding whether Chadha deserves to be deported, Congress is not subject to any internal constraints that prevent it from arbitrarily depriving him of the right to remain in this country. Unlike the judiciary or an administrative agency, Congress is not bound by established substantive rules. Nor is it subject to the procedural safeguards, such as the right to counsel and a hearing before an impartial tribunal, that are present when a court or an agency adjudicates individual rights. The only effective constraint on Congress' power is political, but Congress is most accountable politically when it prescribes rules of general applicability. When it decides rights of specific persons, those rights are subject to "the tyranny of a shifting majority."

... I would not reach the broader question whether legislative vetoes are invalid under the Presentment Clauses.

■ JUSTICE WHITE, dissenting.

Today the Court not only invalidates § 244(c)(2) of the Immigration and Nationality Act, but also sounds the death knell for nearly 200 other statutory provisions in which Congress has reserved a "legislative veto." ...

---

[7]   [T]he fact that the House's action alters an individual's legal status [does not] indicate, as the Court reasons, that the action is legislative rather than adjudicative in nature.... [R]easonable minds may disagree over the character of an act, and the more helpful inquiry, in my view, is whether the act in question raises the dangers the Framers sought to avoid.

[8]   The Court reasons ... that the one-House veto exercised in this case was not judicial in nature because the decision of the [INS] did not present a justiciable issue that could have been reviewed by a court on appeal.... Even if review of the particular decision to suspend deportation is not committed to the courts, the House ... in effect acted as an appellate court by overruling the Service's application of established law to Chadha. And unlike a court or an administrative agency, it did not provide Chadha with the right to counsel or a hearing before acting. ...

The prominence of the legislative veto mechanism in our contemporary political system and its importance to Congress can hardly be overstated. It has become a central means by which Congress secures the accountability of executive and independent agencies. Without the legislative veto, Congress is faced with a Hobson's choice: either to refrain from delegating the necessary authority, leaving itself with a hopeless task of writing laws with the requisite specificity to cover endless special circumstances across the entire policy landscape, or in the alternative, to abdicate its law-making function to the Executive Branch and independent agencies. . . . Accordingly . . . [t]he device is known in every field of governmental concern: reorganization, budgets, foreign affairs, war powers, and regulation of trade, safety, energy, the environment, and the economy.

I

The legislative veto developed initially in response to the problems of reorganizing the sprawling Government structure created in response to the Depression. The Reorganization Acts established the chief model for the legislative veto. When President Hoover requested authority to reorganize the Government in 1929, he coupled his request that the "Congress be willing to delegate its authority over the problem (subject to defined principles) to the Executive" with a proposal for legislative review. . . . Congress followed President Hoover's suggestion and authorized reorganization subject to legislative review. . . . Over the years, the provision was used extensively. . . .

Congress and the President applied the legislative veto procedure to resolve the delegation problem for national security and foreign affairs. World War II occasioned the need to transfer greater authority to the President in these areas. The legislative veto offered the means by which Congress could confer additional authority while preserving its own constitutional role. During World War II, Congress enacted over 30 statutes conferring powers on the Executive with legislative veto provisions. President Roosevelt accepted the veto as the necessary price for obtaining exceptional authority. . . .

During the 1970's the legislative veto was important in resolving a series of major constitutional disputes between the President and Congress over claims of the President to broad impoundment, war, and national emergency powers. The key provision of the War Powers Resolution, 50 U.S.C. § 1544(c), authorizes the termination by concurrent resolution of the use of armed forces in hostilities. A similar measure resolved the problem posed by Presidential claims of inherent power to impound appropriations. . . . These statutes were followed by others resolving similar problems: the National Emergencies Act, § 202, resolving the longstanding problems with unchecked Executive emergency power; the International Security Assistance and Arms Export Control Act, resolving the problem of foreign arms sales; and the

Nuclear Non-Proliferation Act of 1978, resolving the problem of exports of nuclear technology.

In the energy field, the legislative veto served to balance broad delegations in legislation emerging from the energy crisis of the 1970's. In the educational field, it was found that fragmented and narrow grant programs "inevitably lead to Executive-Legislative confrontations" because they inaptly limited the Commissioner of Education's authority. The response was to grant the Commissioner of Education rulemaking authority, subject to a legislative veto. In the trade regulation area, the veto preserved congressional authority over the Federal Trade Commission's broad mandate to make rules to prevent businesses from engaging in "unfair or deceptive acts or practices in commerce."

Even this brief review suffices to demonstrate that the legislative veto is more than "efficient, convenient, and useful." It is an important if not indispensable political invention that allows the President and Congress to resolve major constitutional and policy differences, assures the accountability of independent regulatory agencies, and preserves Congress' control over lawmaking. Perhaps there are other means of accommodation and accountability, but the increasing reliance of Congress upon the legislative veto suggests that the alternatives to which Congress must now turn are not entirely satisfactory.[10]

The history of the legislative veto also makes clear that it has not been a sword with which Congress has struck out to aggrandize itself at the expense of the other branches—the concerns of Madison and Hamilton. Rather, the veto has been a means of defense, a reservation of ultimate authority necessary if Congress is to fulfill its designated role under Art. I as the Nation's lawmaker. While the President has often

---

[10] While Congress could write certain statutes with greater specificity, it is unlikely that this is a realistic or even desirable substitute for the legislative veto. The controversial nature of many issues would prevent Congress from reaching agreement on many major problems if specificity were required in their enactments. For example, in the deportation context, the solution is not for Congress to create more refined categorizations of the deportable aliens whose status should be subject to change. In 1979, the [INS] proposed regulations setting forth factors to be considered in the exercise of discretion under numerous provisions of the Act, but not including § 244, to ensure "fair and uniform" adjudication "under appropriate discretionary criteria." The proposed rule was canceled in 1981, because . . . "[i]t is impossible to list or foresee all of the adverse or favorable factors which may be present in a given set of circumstances."

Oversight hearings and congressional investigations have their purpose, but unless Congress is to be rendered a think tank or debating society, they are no substitute for the exercise of actual authority. The "delaying" procedure . . . while satisfactory for certain measures, has its own shortcomings. Because a new law must be passed to restrain administrative action, Congress must delegate authority without the certain ability of being able to check its exercise.

Finally, the passage of corrective legislation after agency regulations take effect or Executive Branch officials have acted entails the drawbacks endemic to a retroactive response. "Post hoc substantive revision of legislation, the only available corrective mechanism in the absence of postenactment review could have serious prejudicial consequences; if Congress retroactively tampered with a price control system after prices have been set, the economy could be damaged and private rights seriously impaired; if Congress rescinded the sale of arms to a foreign country, our relations with that country would be severely strained; and if Congress reshuffled the bureaucracy after a President's reorganization proposal had taken effect, the results could be chaotic."

objected to particular legislative vetoes . . . the Executive has more often agreed to legislative review as the price for a broad delegation of authority. . . .

II

For all these reasons, the apparent sweep of the Court's decision today is regrettable. The Court's Art. I analysis appears to invalidate all legislative vetoes irrespective of form or subject. Because the legislative veto is commonly found as a check upon rulemaking by administrative agencies and upon broad-based policy decisions of the Executive Branch, it is particularly unfortunate that the Court reaches its decision in cases involving the exercise of a veto over deportation decisions regarding particular individuals. . . . [T]o strike an entire class of statutes based on consideration of a somewhat atypical and more readily indictable exemplar of the class is irresponsible. . . .

The reality of the situation is that the constitutional question posed today is one of immense difficulty over which the Executive and Legislative Branches—as well as scholars and judges—have understandably disagreed. That disagreement stems from the silence of the Constitution on the precise question. . . . Thus, our task should be to determine whether the legislative veto is consistent with the purposes of Art. I and the principles of separation of powers which are reflected in that Article and throughout the Constitution. We should not find the lack of a specific constitutional authorization for the legislative veto surprising, and I would not infer disapproval of the mechanism from its absence. . . . Only within the last half century has the complexity and size of the Federal Government's responsibilities grown so greatly that the Congress must rely on the legislative veto as the most effective if not the only means to insure its role as the Nation's lawmaker. But the wisdom of the Framers was to anticipate that the Nation would grow and new problems of governance would require different solutions. . . .

III

The Court holds that the disapproval of a suspension of deportation by the resolution of one House of Congress is an exercise of legislative power without compliance with the prerequisites for lawmaking set forth in Art. I of the Constitution. . . .

[T]he Court's truismatic exposition of these Clauses . . . does not . . . answer the constitutional question before us. The power to exercise a legislative veto is not the power to write new law without bicameral approval or Presidential consideration. The veto must be authorized by statute and may only negative what an Executive department or independent agency has proposed. On its face, the legislative veto no more allows one House of Congress to make law than does the Presidential veto confer such power upon the President. . . .

A

The terms of the Presentment Clauses suggest only that bills and their equivalent are subject to the requirements of bicameral passage and presentment to the President. . . . Although the Clause does not specify the actions for which the concurrence of both Houses is "necessary," the proceedings at the Philadelphia Convention suggest its purpose was to prevent Congress from circumventing the presentation requirement in the making of new legislation. . . . There is no record that the Convention contemplated, let alone intended, that these Art. I requirements would someday be invoked to restrain the scope of congressional authority pursuant to duly enacted law.

When the Convention did turn its attention to the scope of Congress' lawmaking power, the Framers were expansive. The Necessary and Proper Clause, Art. I, § 8, cl. 18, vests Congress with the power "[to] make all Laws which shall be necessary and proper for carrying into Execution the foregoing Powers [the enumerated powers of § 8] and all other Powers vested by this Constitution in the Government of the United States, or in any Department or Officer thereof." It is long settled that Congress may "exercise its best judgment in the selection of measures, to carry into execution the constitutional powers of the government," and "avail itself of experience, to exercise its reason, and to accommodate its legislation to circumstances." *McCulloch v. Maryland.*

B

The Court heeded this counsel in approving the modern administrative state. The Court's holding today that all legislative-type action must be enacted through the lawmaking process ignores that legislative authority is routinely delegated to the Executive Branch, to the independent regulatory agencies, and to private individuals and groups. "The rise of administrative bodies probably has been the most significant legal trend of the last century. . . . They have become a veritable fourth branch of the Government, which has deranged our three-branch legal theories. . . ." *FTC v. Ruberoid Co.,* 343 U.S. 470 (1952) (Jackson, J. dissenting). This Court's decisions sanctioning such delegations make clear that Art. I does not require all action with the effect of legislation to be passed as a law.

Theoretically, agencies and officials were asked only to "fill up the details," and the rule was that Congress cannot delegate any part of its legislative power except under the limitation of a prescribed standard. . . . In practice, however, restrictions on the scope of the power that could be delegated diminished and all but disappeared. In only two instances did the Court find an unconstitutional delegation. *Panama Refining Co. v. Ryan*; *A.L.A. Schechter Poultry Corp. v. United States.* In other cases, the "intelligible principle" through which agencies have attained enormous control over the economic affairs of the country was held to include such formulations as "just and reasonable," *Tagg Bros. & Moorhead v. United States,* 280 U.S. 420 (1930); "public interest," *New*

York Central Securities Corp. v. United States, 287 U.S. 12 (1932); "public convenience, interest, or necessity," *Federal Radio Comm'n v. Nelson Bros. Bond & Mortgage Co.,* 289 U.S. 266 (1933); and "unfair methods of competition." *FTC v. Gratz,* 253 U.S. 421 (1920).

The wisdom and the constitutionality of these broad delegations are matters that still have not been put to rest. But for present purposes, these cases establish that by virtue of congressional delegation, legislative power can be exercised by independent agencies and Executive departments without the passage of new legislation. For some time, the sheer amount of law—the substantive rules that regulate private conduct and direct the operation of government—made by the agencies has far outnumbered the lawmaking engaged in by Congress through the traditional process. There is no question but that agency rulemaking is lawmaking in any functional or realistic sense of the term. . . . These regulations bind courts and officers of the Federal Government, may pre-empt state law, and grant rights to and impose obligations on the public. In sum, they have the force of law.

If Congress may delegate lawmaking power to independent and Executive agencies, it is most difficult to understand Art. I as prohibiting Congress from also reserving a check on legislative power for itself. Absent the veto, the agencies receiving delegations of legislative or quasi-legislative power may issue regulations having the force of law without bicameral approval and without the President's signature. It is thus not apparent why the reservation of a veto over the exercise of that legislative power must be subject to a more exacting test. In both cases, it is enough that the initial statutory authorizations comply with the Art. I requirements. . . . [R]ules and adjudications by the agencies meet the Court's own definition of legislative action for they "[alter] the legal rights, duties, and relations of persons . . . outside the Legislative Branch," and involve "determinations of policy." . . . If the effective functioning of a complex modern government requires the delegation of vast authority which, by virtue of its breadth, is legislative or "quasi-legislative" in character, I cannot accept that Art. I—which is, after all, the source of the nondelegation doctrine—should forbid Congress to qualify that grant with a legislative veto.[21]

C

2

The central concern of the presentment and bicameralism requirements of Art. I is that when a departure from the legal status quo

---

[21] . . . The Court also argues that the legislative character of the challenged action of one House is confirmed by the fact that "when the Framers intended to authorize either House of Congress to act alone and outside of its prescribed bicameral legislative role, they narrowly and precisely defined the procedure for such action." . . . [T]he short answer is that all of these carefully defined exceptions to the presentment and bicameralism strictures do not involve action of the Congress pursuant to a duly enacted statute. Indeed, for the most part these powers—those of impeachment, review of appointments, and treaty ratification—are not legislative powers at all. . . .

is undertaken, it is done with the approval of the President and both Houses of Congress—or, in the event of a Presidential veto, a two-thirds majority in both Houses. This interest is fully satisfied by the operation of § 244(c)(2). The President's approval is found in the Attorney General's action in recommending to Congress that the deportation order for a given alien be suspended. The House and the Senate indicate their approval of the Executive's action by not passing a resolution of disapproval within the statutory period. Thus, a change in the legal status quo—the deportability of the alien—is consummated only with the approval of each of the three relevant actors. The disagreement of any one of the three maintains the alien's pre-existing status: the Executive may choose not to recommend suspension; the House and Senate may each veto the recommendation. . . .

[I]t may be objected that Congress cannot indicate its approval of legislative change by inaction. In the Court of Appeals' view, inaction by Congress "could equally imply endorsement, acquiescence, passivity, indecision, or indifference," and the Court appears to echo this concern. This objection appears more properly directed at the wisdom of the legislative veto than its constitutionality. The Constitution does not and cannot guarantee that legislators will carefully scrutinize legislation and deliberate before acting. In a democracy it is the electorate that holds the legislators accountable for the wisdom of their choices . . .

IV

[T]he history of the separation-of-powers doctrine is also a history of accommodation and practicality. . . . Our decisions reflect this judgment. . . . The separation-of-powers doctrine has heretofore led to the invalidation of Government action only when the challenged action violated some express provision in the Constitution. In *Buckley v. Valeo* and *Myers v. United States,* congressional action compromised the appointment power of the President. In *United States v. Klein,* 13 Wall. 128 (1872), an Act of Congress was struck for encroaching upon judicial power, but the Court found that the Act also impinged upon the Executive's exclusive pardon power. Because we must have a workable efficient Government, this is as it should be. . . .

Section 244(c)(2) survives this test. The legislative veto provision does not "[prevent] the Executive Branch from accomplishing its constitutionally assigned functions." First, it is clear that the Executive Branch has no "constitutionally assigned" function of suspending the deportation of aliens. . . . Moreover, the Court believes that the legislative veto we consider today is best characterized as an exercise of legislative or quasi-legislative authority. Under this characterization, the practice does not, even on the surface, constitute an infringement of executive or judicial prerogative. The Attorney General's suspension of deportation is equivalent to a proposal for legislation. The nature of the Attorney General's role as recommendatory is not altered because § 244 provides for congressional action through disapproval rather than by ratification. In comparison to private bills, which must be initiated in the Congress and which allow a Presidential veto to be overriden by a two-thirds majority in both Houses of Congress, § 244 augments rather than reduces the Executive Branch's authority. So understood, congressional review does not undermine, as the Court of Appeals thought, the "weight and dignity" that attends the decisions of the Executive Branch.

Nor does § 244 infringe on the judicial power, as JUSTICE POWELL would hold. Section 244 makes clear that Congress has reserved its own judgment as part of the statutory process. Congressional action does not substitute for judicial review of the Attorney General's decisions. . . .

I do not suggest that all legislative vetoes are necessarily consistent with separation-of-powers principles. A legislative check on an inherently executive function, for example, that of initiating prosecutions, poses an entirely different question. But the legislative veto device here—and in many other settings—is far from an instance of legislative tyranny over the Executive. It is a necessary check on the unavoidably expanding power of the agencies, both Executive and independent, as they engage in exercising authority delegated by Congress.

V

. . . Today's decision strikes down in one fell swoop provisions in more laws enacted by Congress than the Court has cumulatively invalidated in its history. I fear it will now be more difficult to "[insure] that the fundamental policy decisions in our society will be made not by an appointed official but by the body immediately responsible to the people." I must dissent.

Clinton v. City of New York
524 U.S. 417 (1998)

■ JUSTICE STEVENS delivered the opinion of the Court.

The Line Item Veto Act was enacted in April 1996 and became effective on January 1, 1997. . . . [T]he President exercised his authority to cancel one provision in the Balanced Budget Act of 1997, and two provisions in the Taxpayer Relief Act of 1997. Appellees, claiming that they had been injured by two of those cancellations, filed these cases in the District Court. That Court . . . held the statute invalid, and we . . . expedited our review. [W]e agree that the cancellation procedures set forth in the Act violate the Presentment Clause, Art. I, § 7, cl. 2, of the Constitution.

I

We begin by reviewing the canceled items that are at issue in these cases.

Section 4722(c) of the Balanced Budget Act

Title XIX of the Social Security Act, as amended, authorizes the Federal Government to transfer huge sums of money to the States to help finance medical care for the indigent. In 1991, Congress directed that those federal subsidies be reduced by the amount of certain taxes levied by the States on health care providers. In 1994, the Department of Health and Human Services (HHS) notified the State of New York that 15 of its taxes were covered by the 1991 Act, and that as of June 30, 1994, the statute therefore required New York to return $955 million to the United States. The notice advised the State that it could apply for a waiver on certain statutory grounds. New York did request a waiver for those tax programs, as well as for a number of others, but HHS has not formally acted on any of those waiver requests. New York has estimated that the amount at issue for the period from October 1992 through March 1997 is as high as $2.6 billion.

Because HHS had not taken any action on the waiver requests, New York turned to Congress for relief. On August 5, 1997, Congress enacted a law that resolved the issue in New York's favor. Section 4722(c) of the Balanced Budget Act of 1997 identifies the disputed taxes and provides that they "are deemed to be permissible health care related taxes and in compliance with the requirements" of the relevant provisions of the 1991 statute.

On August 11, 1997, the President sent identical notices to the Senate and to the House of Representatives canceling "one item of new direct spending," specifying § 4722(c) as that item, and stating that he had determined that "this cancellation will reduce the Federal budget deficit." He explained that § 4722(c) would have permitted New York "to continue relying upon impermissible provider taxes to finance its Medicaid program" and that "this preferential treatment would have increased Medicaid costs, would have treated New York differently from all other States, and would have established a costly precedent for other States to request comparable treatment."

Section 968 of the Taxpayer Relief Act

A person who realizes a profit from the sale of securities is generally subject to a capital gains tax. Under existing law, however, an ordinary business corporation can acquire a corporation, including a food processing or refining company, in a merger or stock-for-stock transaction in which no gain is recognized to the seller; the seller's tax payment, therefore, is deferred. If, however, the purchaser is a farmers' cooperative, the parties cannot structure such a transaction because the stock of the cooperative may be held only by its members; thus, a seller dealing with a farmers' cooperative cannot obtain the benefits of tax deferral.

In § 968 of the Taxpayer Relief Act of 1997, Congress amended § 1042 of the Internal Revenue Code to permit owners of certain food refiners and processors to defer the recognition of gain if they sell their stock to eligible farmers' cooperatives. The purpose of the amendment, as repeatedly explained by its sponsors, was "to facilitate the transfer of refiners and processors to farmers' cooperatives." The amendment to § 1042 was one of the 79 "limited tax benefits" authorized by the Taxpayer Relief Act of 1997 and specifically identified in Title XVII of that Act as "subject to [the] line item veto."

On the same date that he canceled the "item of new direct spending" involving New York's health care programs, the President also canceled this limited tax benefit. In his explanation of that action, the President endorsed the objective of encouraging "value-added farming through the purchase by farmers' cooperatives of refiners or processors of agricultural goods," but concluded that the provision lacked safeguards and also "failed to target its benefits to small-and-medium-size cooperatives."

II

Appellees filed two separate actions against the President and other federal officials challenging these two cancellations. The plaintiffs in the first case are the City of New York, two hospital associations, one hospital, and two unions representing health care employees. The plaintiffs in the second are a farmers' cooperative consisting of about 30 potato growers in Idaho and an individual farmer who is a member and officer of the cooperative. The District Court consolidated the two cases. . . .

IV

The Line Item Veto Act gives the President the power to "cancel in whole" three types of provisions that have been signed into law: "(1) any dollar amount of discretionary budget authority; (2) any item of new direct spending; or (3) any limited tax benefit." It is undisputed that the New York case involves an "item of new direct spending" and that the Snake River case involves a "limited tax benefit" as those terms are defined in the Act. It is also undisputed that each of those provisions had been signed into law pursuant to Article I, § 7, of the Constitution before it was canceled.

The Act requires the President to adhere to precise procedures whenever he exercises his cancellation authority. In identifying items for cancellation he must consider the legislative history, the purposes, and other relevant information about the items. He must determine, with respect to each cancellation, that it will "(i) reduce the Federal budget deficit; (ii) not impair any essential Government functions; and (iii) not harm the national interest." Moreover, he must transmit a special message to Congress notifying it of each cancellation within five calendar days (excluding Sundays) after the enactment of the canceled provision. It is undisputed that the President meticulously followed these procedures in these cases.

A cancellation takes effect upon receipt by Congress of the special message from the President. If, however, a "disapproval bill" pertaining to a special message is enacted into law, the cancellations set forth in that message become "null and void." The Act sets forth a detailed expedited procedure for the consideration of a "disapproval bill," but no such bill was passed for either of the cancellations involved in these cases.[24] A majority vote of both Houses is sufficient to enact a disapproval bill. The Act does not grant the President the authority to cancel a disapproval bill, but he does, of course, retain his constitutional authority to veto such a bill.

. . . With respect to both an item of new direct spending and a limited tax benefit, the cancellation prevents the item "from having legal force or effect." Thus, under the plain text of the statute, the two actions of the President that are challenged in these cases prevented one section of the Balanced Budget Act of 1997 and one section of the Taxpayer Relief Act of 1997 "from having legal force or effect." The remaining provisions of those statutes, with the exception of the second canceled item in the latter, continue to have the same force and effect as they had when signed into law.

In both legal and practical effect, the President has amended two Acts of Congress by repealing a portion of each. "Repeal of statutes, no less than enactment, must conform with Art. I." *INS v. Chadha,* 462 U.S. 919 (1983). There is no provision in the Constitution that authorizes the President to enact, to amend, or to repeal statutes. Both Article I and Article II assign responsibilities to the President that directly relate to the lawmaking process, but neither addresses the issue presented by these cases. The President "shall from time to time give to the Congress Information on the State of the Union, and recommend to their Consideration such Measures as he shall judge necessary and expedient. . . ." Art. II, § 3. Thus, he may initiate and influence legislative proposals. Moreover, after a bill has passed both Houses of Congress, but "before it becomes a Law," it must be presented to the President. If he approves it, "he shall sign it, but if not he shall return it, with his Objections to that House in which it shall have originated, who shall enter the Objections at large on their Journal, and proceed to reconsider it." Art. I, § 7, cl. 2. His "return" of a bill, which is usually described as a "veto," is subject to being overridden by a two-thirds vote in each House.

There are important differences between the President's "return" of a bill pursuant to Article I, § 7, and the exercise of the President's cancellation authority pursuant to the Line Item Veto Act. The constitutional return takes place *before* the bill becomes law; the

---

[24] Congress failed to act upon proposed legislation to disapprove these cancellations. Indeed, despite the fact that the President has canceled at least 82 items since the Act was passed, Congress has enacted only one law, over a Presidential veto, disapproving *any* cancellation, see Pub. L. 105–159 (1998) (disapproving the cancellation of 38 military construction spending items).

statutory cancellation occurs *after* the bill becomes law. The constitutional return is of the entire bill; the statutory cancellation is of only a part. Although the Constitution expressly authorizes the President to play a role in the process of enacting statutes, it is silent on the subject of unilateral Presidential action that either repeals or amends parts of duly enacted statutes.

There are powerful reasons for construing constitutional silence on this profoundly important issue as equivalent to an express prohibition. The procedures governing the enactment of statutes set forth in the text of Article I were the product of the great debates and compromises that produced the Constitution itself. Familiar historical materials provide abundant support for the conclusion that the power to enact statutes may only "be exercised in accord with a single, finely wrought and exhaustively considered, procedure." *Chadha.* Our first President understood the text of the Presentment Clause as requiring that he either "approve all the parts of a Bill, or reject it in toto." What has emerged in these cases from the President's exercise of his statutory cancellation powers, however, are truncated versions of two bills that passed both Houses of Congress. They are not the product of the "finely wrought" procedure that the Framers designed. . . .

V

The Government advances two related arguments . . . . First, relying primarily on *Field v. Clark,* 143 U.S. 649 (1892), the Government contends that the cancellations were merely exercises of discretionary authority granted to the President by the Balanced Budget Act and the Taxpayer Relief Act read in light of the previously enacted Line Item Veto Act. Second, the Government submits that the substance of the authority to cancel tax and spending items "is, in practical effect, no more and no less than the power to 'decline to spend' specified sums of money, or to 'decline to implement' specified tax measures." Neither argument is persuasive.

In *Field v. Clark*, the Court upheld the constitutionality of the Tariff Act of 1890. That statute contained a "free list" of almost 300 specific articles that were exempted from import duties "unless otherwise specially provided for in this act." Section 3 was a special provision that directed the President to suspend that exemption for sugar, molasses, coffee, tea, and hides "whenever, and so often" as he should be satisfied that any country producing and exporting those products imposed duties on the agricultural products of the United States that he deemed to be "reciprocally unequal and unreasonable. . . ." The section then specified the duties to be imposed on those products during any such suspension. The Court provided this explanation for its conclusion that § 3 had not delegated legislative power to the President:

> Nothing involving the expediency or the just operation of such legislation was left to the determination of the President. . . . When he ascertained the fact that duties and exactions,

reciprocally unequal and unreasonable, were imposed upon the agricultural or other products of the United States by a country producing and exporting sugar, molasses, coffee, tea or hides, it became his duty to issue a proclamation declaring the suspension, as to that country, which Congress had determined should occur. He had no discretion in the premises except in respect to the duration of the suspension so ordered. But that related only to the enforcement of the policy established by Congress. As the suspension was absolutely required when the President ascertained the existence of a particular fact, it cannot be said that in ascertaining that fact and in issuing his proclamation . . . he exercised the function of making laws. . . .

This passage identifies three critical differences between the power to suspend the exemption from import duties and the power to cancel portions of a duly enacted statute. First, the exercise of the suspension power was contingent upon a condition that did not exist when the Tariff Act was passed: the imposition of "reciprocally unequal and unreasonable" import duties by other countries. In contrast, the exercise of the cancellation power within five days after the enactment of the Balanced Budget and Tax Reform Acts necessarily was based on the same conditions that Congress evaluated when it passed those statutes. Second, under the Tariff Act, when the President determined that the contingency had arisen, he had a duty to suspend; in contrast, while it is true that the President was required by the Act to make three determinations before he canceled a provision, those determinations did not qualify his discretion to cancel or not to cancel. Finally, whenever the President suspended an exemption under the Tariff Act, he was executing the policy that Congress had embodied in the statute. In contrast, whenever the President cancels an item of new direct spending or a limited tax benefit he is rejecting the policy judgment made by Congress and relying on his own policy judgment. . . .

[W]hen enacting the statutes discussed in *Field*, Congress itself made the decision to suspend or repeal the particular provisions at issue upon the occurrence of particular events subsequent to enactment, and it left only the determination of whether such events occurred up to the President. The Line Item Veto Act authorizes the President himself to effect the repeal of laws, for his own policy reasons, without observing the procedures set out in Article I, § 7. The fact that Congress intended such a result is of no moment. Although Congress presumably anticipated that the President might cancel some of the items in the Balanced Budget Act and in the Taxpayer Relief Act, Congress cannot alter the procedures set out in Article I, § 7, without amending the Constitution.

Neither are we persuaded by the Government's contention that the President's authority to cancel new direct spending and tax benefit items is no greater than his traditional authority to decline to spend appropriated funds. The Government has reviewed in some detail the series of statutes in which Congress has given the Executive broad discretion over the expenditure of appropriated funds. For example, the First Congress appropriated "sums not exceeding" specified amounts to be spent on various Government operations. In those statutes, as in later years, the President was given wide discretion with respect to both the amounts to be spent and how the money would be allocated among different functions. It is argued that the Line Item Veto Act merely confers comparable discretionary authority over the expenditure of appropriated funds. The critical difference between this statute and all of its predecessors, however, is that unlike any of them, this Act gives the President the unilateral power to change the text of duly enacted statutes. None of the Act's predecessors could even arguably have been construed to authorize such a change.

VI

Although they are implicit in what we have already written, the profound importance of these cases makes it appropriate to emphasize three points.

First, we express no opinion about the wisdom of the procedures authorized by the Line Item Veto Act. . . .

Second, although appellees challenge the validity of the Act on alternative grounds, the only issue we address concerns the "finely wrought" procedure commanded by the Constitution. . . . Thus, because we conclude that the Act's cancellation provisions violate Article I, § 7, of the Constitution, we find it unnecessary to consider the District Court's alternative holding that the Act "impermissibly disrupts the balance of powers among the three branches of government."

Third, our decision rests on the narrow ground that the procedures authorized by the Line Item Veto Act are not authorized by the Constitution. The Balanced Budget Act of 1997 is a 500-page document that became "Public Law 105–33" after three procedural steps were taken: (1) a bill containing its exact text was approved by a majority of the Members of the House of Representatives; (2) the Senate approved precisely the same text; and (3) that text was signed into law by the President. The Constitution explicitly requires that each of those three steps be taken before a bill may "become a law." Art. I, § 7. If one paragraph of that text had been omitted at any one of those three stages, Public Law 105–33 would not have been validly enacted. If the Line Item Veto Act were valid, it would authorize the President to create a different law—one whose text was not voted on by either House of Congress or presented to the President for signature. Something that might be known as "Public Law 105–33 as modified by the President" may or may not be desirable, but it is surely not a document that may "become a law" pursuant to the procedures designed by the Framers of Article I, § 7, of the Constitution.

If there is to be a new procedure in which the President will play a different role in determining the final text of what may "become a law," such change must come not by legislation but through the amendment procedures set forth in Article V of the Constitution.

The judgment of the District Court is affirmed.

■ JUSTICE KENNEDY, concurring.

A nation cannot plunder its own treasury without putting its Constitution and its survival in peril. The statute before us, then, is of first importance, for it seems undeniable the Act will tend to restrain persistent excessive spending. Nevertheless, for the reasons given by JUSTICE STEVENS in the opinion for the Court, the statute must be found invalid. Failure of political will does not justify unconstitutional remedies.

I write to respond to my colleague JUSTICE BREYER, who observes that the statute does not threaten the liberties of individual citizens, a point on which I disagree. The argument is related to his earlier suggestion that our role is lessened here because the two political branches are adjusting their own powers between themselves. . . .

Separation of powers was designed to implement a fundamental insight: concentration of power in the hands of a single branch is a threat to liberty. The Federalist states the axiom in these explicit terms: "The accumulation of all powers, legislative, executive, and judiciary, in the same hands . . . may justly be pronounced the very definition of tyranny." The Federalist No. 47. . . .

In recent years, perhaps, we have come to think of liberty as defined by that word in the Fifth and Fourteenth Amendments and as illuminated by the other provisions of the Bill of Rights. The conception of liberty embraced by the Framers was not so confined. They used the principles of separation of powers and federalism to secure liberty in the fundamental political sense of the term, quite in addition to the idea of freedom from intrusive governmental acts. The idea and the promise were that when the people delegate some degree of control to a remote central authority, one branch of government ought not possess the power to shape their destiny without a sufficient check from the other two. In this vision, liberty demands limits on the ability of any one branch to influence basic political decisions. . . .

It follows that if a citizen who is taxed has the measure of the tax or the decision to spend determined by the Executive alone, without adequate control by the citizen's Representatives in Congress, liberty is threatened. Money is the instrument of policy and policy affects the lives of citizens. The individual loses liberty in a real sense if that instrument is not subject to traditional constitutional constraints. . . .

The Constitution is not bereft of controls over improvident spending. Federalism is one safeguard, for political accountability is easier to enforce within the States than nationwide. The other principal mechanism, of course, is control of the political branches by an informed and responsible electorate. Whether or not federalism and control by the electorate are adequate for the problem at hand, they are two of the structures the Framers designed for the problem the statute strives to confront. The Framers of the Constitution could not command statesmanship. They could simply provide structures from which it might emerge. The fact that these mechanisms, plus the proper functioning of the separation of powers itself, are not employed, or that they prove insufficient, cannot validate an otherwise unconstitutional device. With these observations, I join the opinion of the Court.

■ **JUSTICE BREYER, with whom JUSTICE O'CONNOR and JUSTICE SCALIA join as to Part III, dissenting.**

II

I approach the constitutional question before us with three general considerations in mind. *First*, the Act represents a legislative effort to provide the President with the power to give effect to some, but not to all, of the expenditure and revenue-diminishing provisions contained in a single massive appropriations bill. And this objective is constitutionally proper.

When our Nation was founded, Congress could easily have provided the President with this kind of power. In that time period, our population was less than four million, federal employees numbered fewer than 5,000, annual federal budget outlays totaled approximately $4 million, and the entire operative text of Congress's first general appropriations law read as follows:

> Be it enacted . . . that there be appropriated for the service of the present year, to be paid out of the monies which arise, either from the requisitions heretofore made upon the several states, or from the duties on import and tonnage, the following sums, viz. A sum not exceeding two hundred and sixteen thousand dollars for defraying the expenses of the civil list, under the late and present government; a sum not exceeding one hundred and thirty-seven thousand dollars for defraying the expenses of the department of war; a sum not exceeding one hundred and ninety thousand dollars for discharging the warrants issued by the late board of treasury, and remaining unsatisfied; and a sum not exceeding ninety-six thousand dollars for paying the pensions to invalids.

At that time, a Congress, wishing to give a President the power to select among appropriations, could simply have embodied each appropriation in a separate bill, each bill subject to a separate Presidential veto.

Today, however, our population is about 250 million, the Federal Government employs more than four million people, the annual federal budget is $1.5 trillion, and a typical budget appropriations bill may have a dozen titles, hundreds of sections, and spread across more than 500 pages of the Statutes at Large. Congress cannot divide such a bill into thousands, or tens of thousands, of separate appropriations bills, each one of which the President would have to sign, or to veto, separately. Thus, the question is whether the Constitution permits Congress to choose a particular novel *means* to achieve this same, constitutionally legitimate, *end*.

Second, the case in part requires us to focus upon the Constitution's generally phrased structural provisions, provisions that delegate all "legislative" power to Congress and vest all "executive" power in the President. The Court, when applying these provisions, has interpreted them generously in terms of the institutional arrangements that they permit. See, *e.g.*, *Mistretta v. United States*, 488 U.S. 361 (1989) (upholding delegation of authority to Sentencing Commission to promulgate Sentencing Guidelines); *Crowell v. Benson*, 285 U.S. 22 (1932) (permitting non-Article III commission to adjudicate factual disputes arising under federal dock workers' compensation statute). . . .

Third, we need not here referee a dispute among the other two branches. . . . Cf. *Youngstown Sheet and Tube Co.*, 343 U.S. at 635 (Jackson, J., concurring) ("Presidential powers are not fixed but fluctuate, depending on their disjunction or conjunction with those of Congress . . . [and when] the President acts pursuant to an express or implied authorization of Congress, his authority is at its maximum").

These three background circumstances mean that, when one measures the *literal* words of the Act against the Constitution's *literal* commands, the fact that the Act may closely resemble a different, literally unconstitutional, arrangement is beside the point. . . . The background circumstances also mean that we are to interpret nonliteral Separation of Powers principles in light of the need for "workable government." If we apply those principles in light of that objective, as this Court has applied them in the past, the Act is constitutional.

III

The Court believes that the Act violates the literal text of the Constitution. A simple syllogism captures its basic reasoning:

Major Premise: The Constitution sets forth an exclusive method for enacting, repealing, or amending laws.

Minor Premise: The Act authorizes the President to "repeal or amend" laws in a different way, namely by announcing a cancellation of a portion of a previously enacted law.

Conclusion: The Act is inconsistent with the Constitution.

I find this syllogism unconvincing, however, because its Minor Premise is faulty. When the President "canceled" the two appropriation measures now before us, he did not *repeal* any law nor did he *amend* any law. He simply *followed* the law, leaving the statutes, as they are literally written, intact.

To understand why one cannot say, *literally speaking*, that the President has repealed or amended any law, imagine how the provisions of law before us might have been, but were not, written. Imagine that the canceled New York health care tax provision at issue here, had instead said the following:

> Section One. Taxes . . . that were collected by the State of New York from a health care provider before June 1, 1997 and for which a waiver of provisions [requiring payment] have been sought . . . are deemed to be permissible health care related taxes . . . *provided however that the President may prevent the just-mentioned provision from having legal force or effect if he determines x, y and z.* (Assume x, y and z to be the same determinations required by the Line Item Veto Act).

. . . One could not say that a President who "prevents" the deeming language from "having legal force or effect" has either *repealed* or *amended* this particular hypothetical statute. Rather, the President has *followed* that law to the letter. He has exercised the power it explicitly delegates to him. He has executed the law, not repealed it.

It could make no significant difference to this linguistic point were the italicized proviso to appear, not as part of what I have called Section One, but, instead, at the bottom of the statute page, say referenced by an asterisk, with a statement that it applies to every spending provision in the act next to which a similar asterisk appears. And that being so, it could make no difference if that proviso appeared, instead, in a different, earlier-enacted law, along with legal language that makes it applicable to every future spending provision picked out according to a specified formula.

But, of course, this last-mentioned possibility is this very case. The earlier law, namely, the Line Item Veto Act, says that "the President may . . . prevent such [future] budget authority from having legal force or effect." Its definitional sections make clear that it applies to the 1997 New York health care provision, just as they give a special legal meaning to the word "cancel". For that reason, one cannot dispose of this case through a purely literal analysis as the majority does. Literally speaking, the President has not "repealed" or "amended" anything. He has simply *executed* a power conferred upon him by Congress, which power is contained in laws that were enacted in compliance with the exclusive method set forth in the Constitution.

Nor can one dismiss this literal compliance as some kind of formal quibble, as if it were somehow "obvious" that what the President has done "amounts to," "comes close to," or is "analogous to" the repeal or amendment of a previously enacted law. That is because the power the Act grants the President (to render designated appropriations items without "legal force or effect") also "amounts to," "comes close to," or is "analogous to" a different legal animal, the delegation of a power to choose one legal path as opposed to another. . . .

This is not the first time that Congress has delegated to the President or to others this kind of power—a contingent power to deny effect to certain statutory language. See, *e.g.*, Pub. L. 95–384, § 13(a) ("Section 620(x) of the Foreign Assistance Act of 1961 *shall be of no further force and effect* upon the President's determination and certification to the Congress that the resumption of full military cooperation with Turkey is in the national interest of the United States and [other criteria]") (emphasis added); 41 U.S.C. § 405b (subsection (a) requires the Office of Federal Procurement Policy to issue "government-wide regulations" setting forth a variety of conflict of interest standards, but subsection (e) says that "if the President determines" that the regulations "would have a significantly adverse effect on the accomplishment of the mission" of government agencies, "the requirement [to promulgate] the regulations . . . *shall be null and void*") (emphasis added); Gramm-Rudman-Hollings Act, § 252(a)(4) (authorizing the President to issue a "final order" that has the effect of "*permanently cancelling*" sequestered amounts in spending statutes in order to achieve budget compliance) (emphasis added); Pub. L. 104–208 ("Public Law 89–732 [dealing with immigration from Cuba] *is repealed* . . . upon a determination by the President . . . that a democratically elected government in Cuba is in power") (emphasis added).

All of these examples, like the Act, delegate a power to take action that will render statutory provisions "without force or effect." Every one of these examples, like the present Act, delegates the power to choose between alternatives, each of which the statute spells out in some detail. None of these examples delegates a power to "repeal" or "amend" a statute, or to "make" a new law. Nor does the Act. Rather, the delegated power to nullify statutory language was *itself* created and defined by Congress, and included in the statute books on an equal footing with (indeed, as a component part of) the sections that are potentially subject to nullification. . . .

Because one cannot say that the President's exercise of the power the Act grants is, literally speaking, a "repeal" or "amendment," the fact that the Act's procedures differ from the Constitution's exclusive procedures for enacting (or repealing) legislation is beside the point. The Act *itself* was enacted in accordance with these procedures, and its failure to require the President to satisfy those procedures does not make the Act unconstitutional.

IV

Because I disagree with the Court's holding of literal violation, I must consider whether the Act nonetheless violates Separation of Powers principles—principles that arise out of the Constitution's vesting of the "executive Power" in "a President," U.S. Const., Art. II, § 1, and "all legislative Powers" in "a Congress," Art. I, § 1. There are three relevant Separation of Powers questions here: (1) Has Congress given the President the wrong kind of power, *i.e.*, "non-Executive" power? (2) Has

Congress given the President the power to "encroach" upon Congress' own constitutionally reserved territory? (3) Has Congress given the President too much power, violating the doctrine of "nondelegation?" These three limitations help assure "adequate control by the citizen's representatives in Congress," upon which JUSTICE KENNEDY properly insists. And with respect to *this* Act, the answer to all these questions is "no."

A

Viewed conceptually, the power the Act conveys is the right kind of power. It is "executive." As explained above, an exercise of that power "executes" the Act. Conceptually speaking, it closely resembles the kind of delegated authority—to spend or not to spend appropriations, to change or not to change tariff rates—that Congress has frequently granted the President, any differences being differences in degree, not kind.

The fact that one could also characterize this kind of power as "legislative," say, if Congress itself (by amending the appropriations bill) prevented a provision from taking effect, is beside the point. This Court has frequently found that the exercise of a particular power, such as the power to make rules of broad applicability, or to adjudicate claims, can fall within the constitutional purview of more than one branch of Government. The Court does not "carry out the distinction between legislative and executive action with mathematical precision" or "divide the branches into watertight compartments," for, as others have said, the Constitution "blends" as well as "separates" powers in order to create a workable government.

The Court has upheld congressional delegation of rulemaking power and adjudicatory power to federal agencies, guideline-writing power to a Sentencing Commission, and prosecutor-appointment power to judges. It is far easier *conceptually* to reconcile the power at issue here with the relevant constitutional description ("executive") than in many of these cases. And cases in which the Court may have found a delegated power and the basic constitutional function of another branch conceptually irreconcilable are yet more distant. . . .

B

The Act does not undermine what this Court has often described as the principal function of the Separation of Powers, which is to maintain the tripartite structure of the Federal Government—and thereby protect individual liberty—by providing a safeguard against the encroachment or aggrandizement of one branch at the expense of the other. *See* The Federalist No. 51. . . .

[O]ne cannot say that the Act "encroaches" upon Congress' power, when Congress retained the power to insert, by simple majority, into any future appropriations bill, into any section of any such bill, or into any phrase of any section, a provision that says the Act will not apply.

Congress also retained the power to "disapprove," and thereby reinstate, any of the President's cancellations. And it is Congress that drafts and enacts the appropriations statutes that are subject to the Act in the first place—and thereby defines the outer limits of the President's cancellation authority. Thus *this* Act is not the sort of delegation "without . . . sufficient check" that concerns JUSTICE KENNEDY. Indeed, the President acts only in response to, and on the terms set by, the Congress.

Nor can one say that the Act's basic substantive objective is constitutionally improper, for the earliest Congresses could have, and often did, confer on the President this sort of discretionary authority over spending. And, if an individual Member of Congress, who say, favors aid to Country A but not to Country B, objects to the Act on the ground that the President may "rewrite" an appropriations law to do the opposite, one can respond, "But a majority of Congress voted that he have that power; you may vote to exempt the relevant appropriations provision from the Act; and if you command a majority, your appropriation is safe." Where the burden of overcoming legislative inertia lies is within the power of Congress to determine by rule. Where is the encroachment?

Nor can one say the Act's grant of power "aggrandizes" the Presidential office. The grant is limited to the context of the budget. It is limited to the power to spend, or not to spend, particular appropriated items, and the power to permit, or not to permit, specific limited exemptions from generally applicable tax law from taking effect. These powers, as I will explain in detail, resemble those the President has exercised in the past on other occasions. The delegation of those powers to the President may strengthen the Presidency, but any such change in Executive Branch authority seems minute when compared with the changes worked by delegations of other kinds of authority that the Court in the past has upheld.

C

The "nondelegation" doctrine represents an added constitutional check upon Congress' authority to delegate power to the Executive Branch. And it raises a more serious constitutional obstacle here. The Constitution permits Congress to "seek assistance from another branch" of Government, the "extent and character" of that assistance to be fixed "according to common sense and the inherent necessities of the governmental co-ordination." *J. W. Hampton, Jr., & Co. v. United States*, 276 U.S. 394, 406 (1928). But there are limits on the way in which Congress can obtain such assistance; it cannot delegate any part of its legislative power except under the limitation of a prescribed standard. Or, in Chief Justice Taft's more familiar words, the Constitution permits only those delegations where Congress "shall lay down by legislative act an *intelligible principle* to which the person or body authorized to [act] is directed to conform." *Id.* at 409.

The Act before us seeks to create such a principle in three ways. The first is procedural. The Act tells the President that, in "identifying dollar amounts [or] . . . items . . . for cancellation" (which I take to refer to his selection of the amounts or items he will "prevent from having legal force or effect"), he is to "consider," among other things,

> the legislative history, construction, and purposes of the law which contains [those amounts or items, and] . . . any specific sources of information referenced in such law or . . . the best available information. . . .

The second is purposive. The clear purpose behind the Act, confirmed by its legislative history, is to promote "greater fiscal accountability" and to "eliminate wasteful federal spending and . . . special tax breaks."

The third is substantive. The President must determine that, to "prevent" the item or amount "from having legal force or effect" will "reduce the Federal budget deficit; . . . not impair any essential Government functions; and . . . not harm the national interest."

The resulting standards are broad. But this Court has upheld standards that are equally broad, or broader. See, *e.g.*, *National Broadcasting Co.* v. *United States,* 319 U.S. 190 (1943) (upholding delegation to Federal Communications Commission to regulate broadcast licensing as "public interest, convenience, or necessity" require). . . .

The case before us . . . is limited to one area of government, the budget, and it seeks to give the President the power, in one portion of that budget, to tailor spending and special tax relief to what he concludes are the demands of fiscal responsibility. Nor is the standard that governs his judgment, though broad, any broader than the standard that currently governs the award of television licenses, namely "public convenience, interest, *or* necessity." To the contrary, (a) the broadly phrased limitations in the Act, together with (b) its evident deficit reduction purpose, and (c) a procedure that guarantees Presidential awareness of the reasons for including a particular provision in a budget bill, taken together, guide the President's exercise of his discretionary powers. . . .

■ JUSTICE SCALIA, with whom JUSTICE O'CONNOR joins, and with whom JUSTICE BREYER joins as to Part III, concurring in part and dissenting in part.

III

. . . . Unlike the Court . . . I do not believe that Executive cancellation of this item of direct spending violates the Presentment Clause. . . .

[T]he Court's problem with the Act is not that it authorizes the President to veto parts of a bill and sign others into law, but rather that it authorizes him to "cancel"—prevent from "having legal force or effect"—certain parts of duly enacted statutes.

Article I, § 7 of the Constitution obviously prevents the President from cancelling a law that Congress has not authorized him to cancel. . . . But that is not this case. It was certainly arguable, as an original matter, that Art. I, § 7 also prevents the President from cancelling a law which itself *authorizes* the President to cancel it. But as the Court acknowledges, that argument has long since been made and rejected. . . . The Tariff Act of 1890 authorized the President to "suspend, by proclamation to that effect" certain of its provisions if he determined that other countries were imposing "reciprocally unequal and unreasonable" duties. This Court upheld the constitutionality of that Act in *Field v. Clark,* 143 U.S. 649 (1892), reciting the history since 1798 of statutes conferring upon the President the power to, *inter alia,* "discontinue the prohibitions and restraints hereby enacted and declared," "suspend the operation of the aforesaid act," and "declare the provisions of this act to be inoperative."

. . . Art. I, § 7, therefore . . . does not demand the result the Court reaches. It no more categorically prohibits the Executive *reduction* of congressional dispositions in the course of implementing statutes that authorize such reduction, than it categorically prohibits the Executive *augmentation* of congressional dispositions in the course of implementing statutes that authorize such augmentation—generally known as substantive rulemaking. There are, to be sure, limits upon the former just as there are limits upon the latter—and I am prepared to acknowledge that the limits upon the former may be much more severe. Those limits are established, however, not by some categorical prohibition of Art. I, § 7, which our cases conclusively disprove, but by what has come to be known as the doctrine of unconstitutional delegation of legislative authority . . . .

It is this doctrine, and not the Presentment Clause, that was discussed in the *Field* opinion, and it is this doctrine, and not the Presentment Clause, that is the issue presented by the statute before us here. That is why the Court is correct to distinguish prior authorizations of Executive cancellation, such as the one involved in *Field,* on the ground that they were contingent upon an Executive finding of fact, and on the ground that they related to the field of foreign affairs, an area where the President has a special "degree of discretion and freedom." These distinctions have nothing to do with whether the details of Art. I, § 7 have been complied with, but everything to do with whether the authorizations went too far by transferring to the Executive a degree of political, law-making power that our traditions demand be retained by the Legislative Branch.

I turn, then, to the crux of the matter: whether Congress's authorizing the President to cancel an item of spending gives him a power that our history and traditions show must reside exclusively in the Legislative Branch. . . .

Insofar as the degree of political, "law-making" power conferred upon the Executive is concerned, there is not a dime's worth of difference between Congress's authorizing the President to *cancel* a spending item, and Congress's authorizing money to be spent on a particular item at the President's discretion. And the latter has been done since the Founding of the Nation. From 1789–1791, the First Congress made lump-sum appropriations for the entire Government—"sums not exceeding" specified amounts for broad purposes. From a very early date Congress also made permissive individual appropriations, leaving the decision whether to spend the money to the President's unfettered discretion. In 1803, it appropriated $50,000 for the President to build "not exceeding fifteen gun boats, to be armed, manned and fitted out, and employed for such purposes as in his opinion the public service may require." President Jefferson reported that "the sum of fifty thousand dollars appropriated by Congress for providing gun boats remains unexpended. The favorable and peaceable turn of affairs on the Mississippi rendered an immediate execution of that law unnecessary." Examples of appropriations committed to the discretion of the President abound in our history. . . .

Certain Presidents have claimed Executive authority to withhold appropriated funds even *absent* an express conferral of discretion to do so. In 1876, for example, President Grant reported to Congress that he would not spend money appropriated for certain harbor and river improvements, because "under no circumstances [would he] allow expenditures upon works not clearly national," and in his view, the appropriations were for "works of purely private or local interest, in no sense national." President Franklin D. Roosevelt impounded funds appropriated for a flood control reservoir and levee in Oklahoma. President Truman ordered the impoundment of hundreds of millions of dollars that had been appropriated for military aircraft. President Nixon, the Mahatma Ghandi of all impounders, asserted at a press conference in 1973 that his "constitutional right" to impound appropriated funds was "absolutely clear." Our decision two years later in *Train v. City of New York,* 420 U.S. 35 (1975), proved him wrong, but it implicitly confirmed that Congress may confer discretion upon the executive to withhold appropriated funds, even funds appropriated for a specific purpose. . . .

The short of the matter is this: Had the Line Item Veto Act authorized the President to "decline to spend" any item of spending contained in the Balanced Budget Act of 1997, there is not the slightest doubt that authorization would have been constitutional. What the Line Item Veto Act does instead—authorizing the President to "cancel" an item of spending—is technically different. But the technical difference does *not* relate to the technicalities of the Presentment Clause, which have been fully complied with; and the doctrine of unconstitutional delegation, which *is* at issue here, is preeminently *not* a doctrine of technicalities. The title of the Line Item Veto Act, which was perhaps designed to simplify for public comprehension, or perhaps merely to comply with the terms of a campaign pledge, has succeeded in faking out the Supreme Court. The President's action it authorizes in fact is not a line-item veto and thus does not offend Art. I, § 7; and insofar as the substance of that action is concerned, it is no different from what Congress has permitted the President to do since the formation of the Union. . . .

For the foregoing reasons, I respectfully dissent.

NOTE ON THE LEGISLATIVE PROCESS CASES

1.   Would it be fair to say that the majority opinions in *Chadha* and *Clinton v. New York* boil down to a more learned version of the Schoolhouse Rock cartoon, *I'm Just a Bill*? If they did, would there be anything wrong with that? In both cases, the majority's claim is that the lawmaking process set forth in the constitutional text is quite specific: a bill goes to both houses of Congress, and if it passes it goes to the President, who either signs or vetoes it. Both the legislative and line-item vetoes purport to alter this procedure, and such alterations are impermissible. Given how unclear or open-ended many provisions of the Constitution are, isn't the Court's urge to strictly enforce provisions that *do* seem clear understandable?

2.   On the other hand, isn't Justice White correct in *Chadha* that the legislative process has *already* been altered—almost beyond recognition—by the prevalence of lawmaking by administrative agencies, which takes place outside the Art. I process altogether? Given that reality, doesn't the legislative veto serve a valuable function by reclaiming a meaningful role for Congress in the administrative lawmaking process? Doesn't the legislative veto thus take us *closer* to the Founders' original vision?

This sort of argument typically defends an innovation like the legislative veto as a "compensating adjustment"—a further departure from the original textual scheme, but one which offsets an earlier departure.[9] Critics often decry this as a "two wrongs make a right" approach to constitutional interpretation.[10] What do you think? Are compensating adjustments legitimate?

3.   These opinions, as well as the delegation opinions in the previous section, illustrate two distinct types of formalist separation of powers claims. Delegation claims are "mixing" claims—they argue that one branch (the executive) is exercising powers belonging to a different branch (the legislative).[11] *Chadha*, by contrast, is about whether a branch (Congress) can exercise *its* power (legislation) in a way that avoids the textual strictures on action by that branch. It is not, in other words, a case about the wrong

---

[9]   *See, e.g.,* Peter B. McCutchen, *Mistakes, Precedent, and the Rise of the Administrative State: Toward a Constitutional Theory of the Second Best,* 80 CORNELL L. REV. 1 (1994).

[10]   For a more general critique, see Michael Klarman, *Antifidelity,* 70 S. CAL. L. REV. 381 (1997).

[11]   *See also Bowsher v. Synar,* 478 U.S. 714 (1986) (striking down a statute delegating certain budgetary powers to the Comptroller General, on the ground that the Comptroller was part of the legislative branch but exercised executive authority under the statute).

branch exercising a power, but rather about a branch exercising the right power in the wrong way.[12] Which kind of claim is at issue in *Clinton v. New York*?

4.   The legislative veto is a means by which Congress can exercise supervisory control over agency actions taken pursuant to delegated authority. A number of other mechanisms may also serve this purpose:

- *Report and Wait*: Congress can require that rules be submitted to Congress and become effective only after a period of, say, 60 days. This would give Congress time to pass a statutory restriction if it really wanted to.

- *Sunset Provisions*: Congress can provide that agency authority lapses after a few years, requiring renewal through a new statute.

- *Joint Resolutions*: Congress can provide that agency action becomes effective only if approved by both Houses of Congress through a joint resolution, which can be vetoed by the President. One could require a joint resolution of *approval* or *disapproval*.

- *Informal Agreements*: Congress can refuse to grant agency authority to act unless the agency informally agrees not to do certain things without the approval of, say, its supervising committee. These agreements aren't legally binding, but the committee is in a position to punish the agency—for instance, by cutting its funds—if it reneges.

- *Appropriations Rules*: Congress can provide, by internal rule, that appropriations for a particular action will not be approved by the appropriations committee without a resolution by the authorizing committee approving the action.

To what extent would these options serve the same ends as the legislative veto? Are any of them constitutionally problematic under *Chadha*? Note that Congress has often simply continued to enact (hundreds of) legislative vetoes notwithstanding *Chadha*. How is this possible? And what does it tell you about the efficacy of judicial review in this area?

5.   As a former law professor, Justice Breyer is fond of spinning hypotheticals. In his dissent in *Clinton v. New York*, he contrasts three different ways of achieving the same end, some of which would be constitutional under the majority's approach and some of which would not be. The following three cases flesh out his example:

Case 1:   § 101. Hospitals meeting certain qualifications in New York shall be exempt from federal taxes. The President may prevent this provision from having legal force or effect if he determines that so doing will (i) reduce the

---

[12] *See generally Metropolitan Washington Airports Auth. v. Citizens for Abatement of Aircraft Noise, Inc.*, 510 U.S. 252, 274–77 (1991) (discussing these two distinct separation of powers constraints).

federal budget deficit; (ii) not impair any essential government functions; and (iii) not harm the national interest.

Case 2:　§ 101. Hospitals meeting certain qualifications in New York shall be exempt from federal taxes.*

§ 102.　Gas stations selling ethanol shall receive a federal tax credit on all such sales.*

§ 103.　The federal government shall spend $50 million to build a new dam in Idaho.*

* The President may prevent this provision from having legal force or effect if he determines that so doing will (i) reduce the federal budget deficit; (ii) not impair any essential government functions; and (iii) not harm the national interest.

Case 3:　*1996 Statute:* The President may prevent any tax or spending provision in a federal law from having legal force or effect if he determines that so doing will (i) reduce the federal budget deficit; (ii) not impair any essential government functions; and (iii) not harm the national interest.

1999 Statute: Hospitals meeting certain qualifications in New York shall be exempt from federal taxes.

Is there a meaningful difference between these three cases? To what extent should the form of enactment make a *constitutional* difference?

6.　What is the significance of the extended debate in *Clinton v. NY* about the Court's prior decision in *Field v. Clark*? In *Field*, a federal statute created certain exemptions from the tariff on imports, but also allowed the President to suspend those exemptions—that is, subject the countries in question to the tariff—if those countries were imposing duties on American products. In effect, the statute authorized the President to suspend the effect of a federal law. The Court upheld the law on the ground that all the President was really doing was finding whether certain factual conditions, such as whether other countries were trading with us on reasonable terms, were met.

Significantly, *Field* was a case about the nondelegation doctrine, not about the Art. I, § 7 process. Is *Clinton v. New York* really a nondelegation case? If so, should people be more excited about it?

7.　Should the majority in *Clinton v. New York* have made an encroachment argument? The effect of the line-item veto, after all, is to significantly increase the leverage of the President in budgetary negotiations by foreclosing Congress from offering a "take it or leave it" package. Is that sufficient to throw the branches out of balance, even for a functionalist?

SECTION 13.3   EXECUTIVE PRIVILEGES AND IMMUNITIES

Much of separation of powers law concerns the powers and structure of the Executive branch. We have already considered the demise of the nondelegation doctrine, which makes the modern Executive branch possible. In this section, we deal with the President himself—in particular, his amenability to judicial process. Although in many respects the scope of the President's authority has expanded massively in the Twentieth Century, the President has arguably become more accountable for his exercise of that authority as well. The next case dramatically illustrates that development.

United States v. Nixon
418 U.S. 683 (1974)

■ MR. CHIEF JUSTICE BURGER delivered the opinion of the Court.

This litigation presents for review the denial of a motion, filed in the District Court on behalf of the President of the United States, in the case of *United States v. Mitchell* (D.C. Crim. No. 74–110), to quash a third-party subpoena *duces tecum* issued by the United States District Court for the District of Columbia, pursuant to Fed. Rule Crim. Proc. 17(c). The subpoena directed the President to produce certain tape recordings and documents relating to his conversations with aides and advisers. The court rejected the President's claims of absolute executive privilege, of lack of jurisdiction, and of failure to satisfy the requirements of Rule 17(c). The President appealed to the Court of Appeals. We granted both the United States' petition for certiorari before judgment, and also the President's cross-petition for certiorari before judgment, because of the public importance of the issues presented and the need for their prompt resolution.

On March 1, 1974, a grand jury of the United States District Court for the District of Columbia returned an indictment charging seven named individuals[3] with various offenses, including conspiracy to defraud the United States and to obstruct justice. Although he was not designated as such in the indictment, the grand jury named the President, among others, as an unindicted coconspirator. On April 18, 1974, upon motion of the Special Prosecutor, a subpoena *duces tecum* was issued pursuant to Rule 17(c) to the President by the United States District Court and made returnable on May 2, 1974. This subpoena required the production, in advance of the September 9 trial date, of certain tapes, memoranda, papers, transcripts, or other writings relating to certain precisely identified meetings between the President and

---

[3]   The seven defendants were John N. Mitchell, H. R. Haldeman, John D. Ehrlichman, Charles W. Colson, Robert C. Mardian, Kenneth W. Parkinson, and Gordon Strachan. Each has occupied either a position of responsibility on the White House Staff or a position with the Committee for the Re-election of the President. Colson entered a guilty plea on another charge, and is no longer a defendant.

others. The Special Prosecutor was able to fix the time, place, and persons present at these discussions because the White House daily logs and appointment records had been delivered to him. On April 30, the President publicly released edited transcripts of 43 conversations; portions of 20 conversations subject to subpoena in the present case were included. On May 1, 1974, the President's counsel filed a "special appearance" and a motion to quash the subpoena under Rule 17(c). This motion was accompanied by a formal claim of privilege. At a subsequent hearing, further motions to expunge the grand jury's action naming the President as an unindicted coconspirator and for protective orders against the disclosure of that information were filed or raised orally by counsel for the President.

On May 20, 1974, the District Court denied the motion to quash and the motions to expunge and for protective orders. It further ordered "the President or any subordinate officer, official, or employee with custody or control of the documents or objects subpoenaed" to deliver to the District Court, on or before May 31, 1974, the originals of all subpoenaed items, as well as an index and analysis of those items, together with tape copies of those portions of the subpoenaed recordings for which transcripts had been released to the public by the President on April 30. The District Court rejected jurisdictional challenges based on a contention that the dispute was nonjusticiable because it was between the Special Prosecutor and the Chief Executive and hence "intra-executive" in character; it also rejected the contention that the Judiciary was without authority to review an assertion of executive privilege by the President. . . .

The District Court held that the judiciary, not the President, was the final arbiter of a claim of executive privilege. The court concluded that, under the circumstances of this case, the presumptive privilege was overcome by the Special Prosecutor's *prima facie* "demonstration of need sufficiently compelling to warrant judicial examination in chambers." . . .

II. JUSTICIABILITY

In the District Court, the President's counsel argued that the court lacked jurisdiction to issue the subpoena because the matter was an intra-branch dispute between a subordinate and superior officer of the Executive Branch, and hence not subject to judicial resolution. That argument has been renewed in this Court with emphasis on the contention that the dispute does not present a "case" or "controversy" which can be adjudicated in the federal courts. The President's counsel argues that the federal courts should not intrude into areas committed to the other branches of Government. He views the present dispute as essentially a "jurisdictional" dispute within the Executive Branch which he analogizes to a dispute between two congressional committees. Since the Executive Branch has exclusive authority and absolute discretion to decide whether to prosecute a case, it is contended that a President's decision is final in determining what evidence is to be used in a given criminal case. Although his counsel concedes that the President has delegated certain specific powers to the Special Prosecutor, he has not waived nor delegated to the Special Prosecutor the President's duty to claim privilege as to all materials . . . which fall within the President's inherent authority to refuse to disclose to any executive officer. The Special Prosecutor's demand for the items therefore presents, in the view of the President's counsel, a political question under *Baker v. Carr,* since it involves a "textually demonstrable" grant of power under Art. II.

The mere assertion of a claim of an "intra-branch dispute," without more, has never operated to defeat federal jurisdiction; justiciability does not depend on such a surface inquiry. . . . Our starting point is the nature of the proceeding for which the evidence is sought—here, a pending criminal prosecution. It is a judicial proceeding in a federal court alleging violation of federal laws, and is brought in the name of the United States as sovereign. Under the authority of Art. II, § 2, Congress has vested in the Attorney General the power to conduct the criminal litigation of the United States Government. It has also vested in him the power to appoint subordinate officers to assist him in the discharge of his duties. Acting pursuant to those statutes, the Attorney General has delegated the authority to represent the United States in these particular matters to a Special Prosecutor with unique authority and tenure.[8] The regulation gives the Special Prosecutor explicit power to contest the invocation of executive privilege in the process of seeking evidence deemed relevant to the performance of these specially delegated duties.

So long as this regulation is extant, it has the force of law. . . . [I]t is theoretically possible for the Attorney General to amend or revoke the regulation defining the Special Prosecutor's authority. But he has not done so. So long as this regulation remains in force, the Executive Branch

---

[8]　The regulation issued by the Attorney General pursuant to his statutory authority, vests in the Special Prosecutor plenary authority to control the course of investigations and litigation related to

> all offenses arising out of the 1972 Presidential Election for which the Special Prosecutor deems it necessary and appropriate to assume responsibility, allegations involving the President, members of the White House staff, or Presidential appointees, and any other matters which he consents to have assigned to him by the Attorney General.

In particular, the Special Prosecutor was given full authority, *inter alia,* "to contest the assertion of 'Executive Privilege' . . . and handl[e] all aspects of any cases within his jurisdiction." The regulation then goes on to provide:

> In exercising this authority, the Special Prosecutor will have the greatest degree of independence that is consistent with the Attorney General's statutory accountability for all matters falling within the jurisdiction of the Department of Justice. The Attorney General will not countermand or interfere with the Special Prosecutor's decisions or actions. The Special Prosecutor will determine whether and to what extent he will inform or consult with the Attorney General about the conduct of his duties and responsibilities. In accordance with assurances given by the President to the Attorney General that the President will not exercise his Constitutional powers to effect the discharge of the Special Prosecutor or to limit the independence that he is hereby given, the Special Prosecutor will not be removed from his duties except for extraordinary improprieties on his part and without the President's first consulting the Majority and the Minority Leaders and Chairmen and ranking Minority Members of the Judiciary Committees of the Senate and House of Representatives and ascertaining that their consensus is in accord with his proposed action.

is bound by it, and indeed the United States, as the sovereign composed of the three branches, is bound to respect and to enforce it. . . .

The demands of and the resistance to the subpoena present an obvious controversy in the ordinary sense, but that alone is not sufficient to meet constitutional standards. In the constitutional sense, controversy means more than disagreement and conflict; rather it means the kind of controversy courts traditionally resolve. Here at issue is the production or nonproduction of specified evidence deemed by the Special Prosecutor to be relevant and admissible in a pending criminal case. It is sought by one official of the Executive Branch within the scope of his express authority; it is resisted by the Chief Executive on the ground of his duty to preserve the confidentiality of the communications of the President. Whatever the correct answer on the merits, these issues are "of a type which are traditionally justiciable." . . . This setting assures there is that concrete adverseness which sharpens the presentation of issues upon which the court so largely depends for illumination of difficult constitutional questions. Moreover, since the matter is one arising in the regular course of a federal criminal prosecution, it is within the traditional scope of Art. III power.

In light of the uniqueness of the setting in which the conflict arises, the fact that both parties are officers of the Executive Branch cannot be viewed as a barrier to justiciability. It would be inconsistent with the applicable law and regulation, and the unique facts of this case, to conclude other than that the Special Prosecutor has standing to bring this action, and that a justiciable controversy is presented for decision. . . .

IV. THE CLAIM OF PRIVILEGE

A

. . . [W]e turn to the claim that the subpoena should be quashed because it demands "confidential conversations between a President and his close advisors that it would be inconsistent with the public interest to produce." The first contention is a broad claim that the separation of powers doctrine precludes judicial review of a President's claim of privilege. The second contention is that, if he does not prevail on the claim of absolute privilege, the court should hold as a matter of constitutional law that the privilege prevails over the subpoena *duces tecum*.

In the performance of assigned constitutional duties, each branch of the Government must initially interpret the Constitution, and the interpretation of its powers by any branch is due great respect from the others. The President's counsel, as we have noted, reads the Constitution as providing an absolute privilege of confidentiality for all Presidential communications. Many decisions of this Court, however, have unequivocally reaffirmed the holding of *Marbury v. Madison* that "[i]t is emphatically the province and duty of the judicial department to say what the law is." . . . In a series of cases, the Court interpreted the explicit immunity conferred by express provisions of the Constitution on Members of the House and Senate by the Speech or Debate Clause, U.S. Const. Art. I, § 6. . . .

Notwithstanding the deference each branch must accord the others, the "judicial Power of the United States" vested in the federal courts by Art. III, § 1, of the Constitution can no more be shared with the Executive Branch than the Chief Executive, for example, can share with the Judiciary the veto power, or the Congress share with the Judiciary the power to override a Presidential veto. Any other conclusion would be contrary to the basic concept of separation of powers and the checks and balances that flow from the scheme of a tripartite government. We therefore reaffirm that it is the province and duty of this Court "to say what the law is" with respect to the claim of privilege presented in this case. *Marbury v. Madison.*

B

In support of his claim of absolute privilege, the President's counsel urges two grounds, one of which is common to all governments and one of which is peculiar to our system of separation of powers. The first ground is the valid need for protection of communications between high Government officials and those who advise and assist them in the performance of their manifold duties; the importance of this confidentiality is too plain to require further discussion. Human experience teaches that those who expect public dissemination of their remarks may well temper candor with a concern for appearances and for their own interests to the detriment of the decisionmaking process. Whatever the nature of the privilege of confidentiality of Presidential communications in the exercise of Art. II powers, the privilege can be said to derive from the supremacy of each branch within its own assigned area of constitutional duties. Certain powers and privileges flow from the nature of enumerated powers;[16] the protection of the confidentiality of Presidential communications has similar constitutional underpinnings.

The second ground asserted by the President's counsel in support of the claim of absolute privilege rests on the doctrine of separation of powers. Here it is argued that the independence of the Executive Branch within its own sphere insulates a President from a judicial subpoena in

---

[16] The Special Prosecutor argues that there is no provision in the Constitution for a Presidential privilege as to the President's communications corresponding to the privilege of Members of Congress under the Speech or Debate Clause. But the silence of the Constitution on this score is not dispositive.

> The rule of constitutional interpretation announced in *McCulloch v. Maryland* that that which was reasonably appropriate and relevant to the exercise of a granted power was to be considered as accompanying the grant, has been so universally applied that it suffices merely to state it.

Marshall v. Gordon, 243 U.S. 521 (1917).

an ongoing criminal prosecution, and thereby protects confidential Presidential communications.

However, neither the doctrine of separation of powers nor the need for confidentiality of high-level communications, without more, can sustain an absolute, unqualified Presidential privilege of immunity from judicial process under all circumstances. The President's need for complete candor and objectivity from advisers calls for great deference from the courts. However, when the privilege depends solely on the broad, undifferentiated claim of public interest in the confidentiality of such conversations, a confrontation with other values arises. Absent a claim of need to protect military, diplomatic, or sensitive national security secrets, we find it difficult to accept the argument that even the very important interest in confidentiality of Presidential communications is significantly diminished by production of such material for *in camera* inspection with all the protection that a district court will be obliged to provide.

The impediment that an absolute, unqualified privilege would place in the way of the primary constitutional duty of the Judicial Branch to do justice in criminal prosecutions would plainly conflict with the function of the courts under Art. III. In designing the structure of our Government and dividing and allocating the sovereign power among three co-equal branches, the Framers of the Constitution sought to provide a comprehensive system, but the separate powers were not intended to operate with absolute independence. . . . To read the Art. II powers of the President as providing an absolute privilege as against a subpoena essential to enforcement of criminal statutes on no more than a generalized claim of the public interest in confidentiality of nonmilitary and nondiplomatic discussions would upset the constitutional balance of "a workable government" and gravely impair the role of the courts under Art. III.

C

Since we conclude that the legitimate needs of the judicial process may outweigh Presidential privilege, it is necessary to resolve those competing interests in a manner that preserves the essential functions of each branch. The right and indeed the duty to resolve that question does not free the Judiciary from according high respect to the representations made on behalf of the President. . . .

A President and those who assist him must be free to explore alternatives in the process of shaping policies and making decisions, and to do so in a way many would be unwilling to express except privately. These are the considerations justifying a presumptive privilege for Presidential communications. The privilege is fundamental to the operation of Government, and inextricably rooted in the separation of powers under the Constitution. In *Nixon v. Sirica*, 487 F.2d 700 (D.C. Cir. 1973), the Court of Appeals held that such Presidential communications are "presumptively privileged," and this position is accepted by both parties in the present litigation. We agree with Mr. Chief Justice Marshall's observation, therefore, that "[i]n no case of this kind would a court be required to proceed against the president as against an ordinary individual." *United States v. Burr*, 25 F.Cas. pp. 187, 190, 192 (No. 14,694) (CCVa.1807).

But this presumptive privilege must be considered in light of our historic commitment to the rule of law. This is nowhere more profoundly manifest than, in our view, that the twofold aim [of criminal justice] is that guilt shall not escape or innocence suffer. We have elected to employ an adversary system of criminal justice in which the parties contest all issues before a court of law. The need to develop all relevant facts in the adversary system is both fundamental and comprehensive. The ends of criminal justice would be defeated if judgments were to be founded on a partial or speculative presentation of the facts. The very integrity of the judicial system and public confidence in the system depend on full disclosure of all the facts, within the framework of the rules of evidence. To ensure that justice is done, it is imperative to the function of courts that compulsory process be available for the production of evidence needed either by the prosecution or by the defense.

Only recently the Court restated the ancient proposition of law, albeit in the context of a grand jury inquiry, rather than a trial, that "the public . . . has a right to every man's evidence," except for those persons protected by a constitutional, common law, or statutory privilege. *Branzburg v. Hayes*, 408 U.S. 665 (1972). . . . [T]hese exceptions to the demand for every man's evidence are not lightly created nor expansively construed, for they are in derogation of the search for truth.

In this case, the President challenges a subpoena served on him as a third party requiring the production of materials for use in a criminal prosecution; he does so on the claim that he has a privilege against disclosure of confidential communications. He does not place his claim of privilege on the ground they are military or diplomatic secrets. As to these areas of Art. II duties, the courts have traditionally shown the utmost deference to Presidential responsibilities. . . . No case of the Court, however, has extended this high degree of deference to a President's generalized interest in confidentiality. Nowhere in the Constitution, as we have noted earlier, is there any explicit reference to a privilege of confidentiality, yet to the extent this interest relates to the effective discharge of a President's powers, it is constitutionally based.

The right to the production of all evidence at a criminal trial similarly has constitutional dimensions. The Sixth Amendment explicitly confers upon every defendant in a criminal trial the right "to be confronted with the witnesses against him" and "to have compulsory process for obtaining witnesses in his favor." Moreover, the Fifth Amendment also guarantees that no person shall be deprived of liberty without due process of law. It is the manifest duty of the courts to vindicate those guarantees, and to accomplish that it is essential that all relevant and admissible evidence be produced.

In this case, we must weigh the importance of the general privilege of confidentiality of Presidential communications in performance of the President's responsibilities against the inroads of such a privilege on the fair administration of criminal justice.[19] The interest in preserving confidentiality is weighty indeed, and entitled to great respect. However, we cannot conclude that advisers will be moved to temper the candor of their remarks by the infrequent occasions of disclosure because of the possibility that such conversations will be called for in the context of a criminal prosecution.

On the other hand, the allowance of the privilege to withhold evidence that is demonstrably relevant in a criminal trial would cut deeply into the guarantee of due process of law and gravely impair the basic function of the court. A President's acknowledged need for confidentiality in the communications of his office is general in nature, whereas the constitutional need for production of relevant evidence in a criminal proceeding is specific and central to the fair adjudication of a particular criminal case in the administration of justice. Without access to specific facts, a criminal prosecution may be totally frustrated. The President's broad interest in confidentiality of communications will not be vitiated by disclosure of a limited number of conversations preliminarily shown to have some bearing on the pending criminal cases.

We conclude that, when the ground for asserting privilege as to subpoenaed materials sought for use in a criminal trial is based only on the generalized interest in confidentiality, it cannot prevail over the fundamental demands of due process of law in the fair administration of criminal justice. The generalized assertion of privilege must yield to the demonstrated, specific need for evidence in a pending criminal trial. . . .

E

Enforcement of the subpoena *duces tecum* was stayed pending this Court's resolution of the issues raised by the petitions for certiorari. Those issues now having been disposed of, the matter of implementation will rest with the District Court. . . . Statements that meet the test of admissibility and relevance must be isolated; all other material must be excised. . . . It is elementary that *in camera* inspection of evidence is always a procedure calling for scrupulous protection against any release or publication of material not found by the court, at that stage, probably admissible in evidence and relevant to the issues of the trial for which it is sought. That being true of an ordinary situation, it is obvious that the District Court has a very heavy responsibility to see to it that

---

[19] We are not here concerned with the balance between the President's generalized interest in confidentiality and the need for relevant evidence in civil litigation, nor with that between the confidentiality interest and congressional demands for information, nor with the President's interest in preserving state secrets. . . .

Presidential conversations, which are either not relevant or not admissible, are accorded that high degree of respect due the President of the United States. Mr. Chief Justice Marshall, sitting as a trial judge in the *Burr* case, was extraordinarily careful to point out that "[i]n no case of this kind would a court be required to proceed against the president as against an ordinary individual." Marshall's statement cannot be read to mean in any sense that a President is above the law, but relates to the singularly unique role under Art. II of a President's communications and activities, related to the performance of duties under that Article. Moreover, a President's communications and activities encompass a vastly wider range of sensitive material than would be true of any "ordinary individual." It is therefore necessary in the public interest to afford Presidential confidentiality the greatest protection consistent with the fair administration of justice. . . . We have no doubt that the District Judge will at all times accord to Presidential records that high degree of deference suggested in *United States v. Burr* and will discharge his responsibility to see to it that until released to the Special Prosecutor no *in camera* material is revealed to anyone. . . .

Affirmed.

■ MR. JUSTICE REHNQUIST took no part in the consideration or decision of these cases.

NOTE ON EXECUTIVE PRIVILEGES AND IMMUNITIES

1.   Why did President Nixon comply with the Supreme Court's order in the Watergate tapes case? Recall that, in *Marbury v. Madison*, nearly everyone assumes President Jefferson would *not* have complied with an order from the Court to confirm Marbury's appointment. What changed in the intervening 171 years? Can you imagine any situation in which an American president would defy a Supreme Court order today?

2.   Although the Court's decision in *Nixon* is famous for ordering the President to turn over the tapes, it is also important for explicitly endorsing the notion of Executive Privilege. Where does this privilege come from? The "penumbra" of Article II? What do you make of the reference to McCulloch in footnote 16? Isn't that a case about *Congress*'s powers?

Presidents have typically grounded the privilege, as the Court did in *Nixon*, in functional arguments that the Executive branch would be unable to function without it. Can similar arguments be made about other branches? Could Congress, for example, subpoena the bench memos that law clerks write for their justices at the Supreme Court?

3.   The executive privilege invoked in *Nixon* is only one of a variety of privileges that presidents have invoked to contest disclosure of sensitive communications and information. There is also a "state secrets" privilege, originally recognized by the Supreme Court in *United States v. Reynolds*, 345 U.S. 1 (1953), which permits the government to block the release of any information that, if disclosed, would "expose military matters which, in the interest of national security, should not be divulged." The privilege must be

formally invoked by the head of the relevant government department and "actually personally considered" by him. [13] In recent years, terrorism litigation has brought the state secret doctrine back to the forefront of the public discourse.[14] President Bush invoked the doctrine frequently during his time in office, and was often vehemently criticized for doing so. One of the most vocal critics was Senator Barack Obama; as President, however, Obama has been considerably more willing to invoke the privilege.[15] How rigorously should a court review the President's invocation of the state secrets privilege?

4.   Other important privileges include the traditional attorney-client privilege for communications with White House legal staff and Department of Justice attorneys. In the governmental context, attorney-client privilege raises complex questions concerning the precise identity of a government lawyer's "client."[16] Consider, for instance, a White House counsel advising the President as to the legality of a contemplated course of action; is the client the President, the Executive Branch, the United States government, or the American people? The answer to that question may matter greatly if, for example, access to such communications is sought by a congressional investigative committee.

In recent years, Presidents have asserted more adventurous claims to privilege. During the Monica Lewinsky scandal, for example, President Bill Clinton asserted a "protective function privilege" to prevent access to Secret Service records concerning visitors to the White House. The United States Court of Appeals for the D.C. Circuit rejected that claim, and the Supreme Court denied certiorari.[17] How willing should courts be to extend the scope of the privilege recognized in *Nixon*?

5.   *United States v. Nixon* concerned the obligation of the President to turn over information needed to resolve the criminal prosecution of another; eight years later, the Court considered whether the President could actually be sued. *Nixon v. Fitzgerald*, 457 U.S. 731 (1982), involved a suit by a "whistleblower" who claimed to have lost his job with the Department of the Air Force in retaliation for testimony before a congressional subcommittee about government waste. The Court held that President Nixon was

---

[13]   *See generally* Rita Glasionov, *In Furtherance of Transparency and Litigants' Rights: Reforming the State Secrets Privilege*, 77 GEO. WASH. L. REV. 458, 466 (2009).

[14]   *See Developments in the Law—Access to Courts, Compensating Victims of Wrongful Detention, Torture and Abuse in the U.S. War on Terror*, 122 HARV. L. REV. 1158, 1163 (2009) (discussing the use of the state secrets doctrine in terrorism cases and noting that the courts have been "manifestly deferential" when the doctrine has been invoked).

[15]   *See* John Schwartz, *Obama Backs off a Reversal on Secrets*, N.Y. TIMES (Feb. 9, 2009). President Obama has since revised the Department of Justice Policy on State Secrets, putting in place a new policy which would require approval by the Attorney General in order to invoke the privilege. *See* Charlie Savage, *Justice Dept. to Limit Use of State Secrets Privilege*, N.Y. TIMES (Sep. 22, 2009); Jonathan Adler, *Narrowing the State Secrets Privilege*, THE VOLOKH CONSPIRACY (Sept. 23, 2009, 8:16 am), http://volokh.com/posts/1253708168. It is not clear what ramifications this change in policy will have for the application of the privilege in practice.

[16]   *See, e.g., In re Lindsey*, 158 F.3d 1263, 1271–78 (D.C. Cir. 1998) (exploring the differences between the government attorney-client privilege and the traditional privilege in private practice).

[17]   *See In re Sealed Case*, 148 F.3d 1073 (D.C. Cir. 1998).

"absolutely immune from civil damages liability for his official acts." In so holding, the majority stressed the President's "unique position in the constitutional scheme" and the concern that the threat of civil liability might render him "unduly cautious in the discharge of his official duties." In dissent, Justice White warned that the majority's decision "places the President above the law. It is a reversion to the old notion that the King can do no wrong." Do you agree? Is impeachment an adequate remedy for a president's official misconduct?

In a companion case, however, the Court held that the President's absolute immunity did not extend to cover his subordinate officers; such officers generally enjoy only a "qualified immunity" that shields them from liability unless they violated "clearly established law."[18] Since the President typically acts through subordinates, does their potential liability mitigate the immunity of the Chief Executive himself?

6.   The Court proved more sympathetic to arguments that the President must be subject to law in *Clinton v. Jones*, 520 U.S. 681 (1997), which involved a civil suit against the President for his *un*official acts. Paula Jones alleged that, while Governor of Arkansas, Bill Clinton sexually harassed her. Justice Stevens' opinion for eight justices pointed out that the absolute immunity of the President in *Fitzgerald*, as well as similar immunities that courts have recognized for prosecutors, legislators, and judges, "serves the public interest in enabling such officials to perform their designated functions effectively without fear that a particular decision may give rise to personal liability." He noted, however, that "[t]his reasoning provides no support for an immunity for unofficial conduct." In response to concerns that the course of litigation could interfere with the performance of the President's duties, Justice Stevens pointed out that district courts retain a great deal of discretion over the course of proceedings, and that they could be expected to exercise that discretion in such a way as to protect the President's ability to do his job.

In *Jones*, the Court dismissed concerns that allowing civil suits "will generate a large volume of politically motivated harassing and frivolous litigation." How does the Court's decision look in light of the subsequent course of events? Testifying in his deposition in the *Jones* litigation, President Clinton gave a famously untruthful answer that led to his impeachment by the House on charges of perjury and obstruction of justice. Although Clinton was ultimately acquitted by the Senate, the proceedings arguably paralyzed his presidency. Does that suggest that presidents should not be subject to civil suits *at all*? That such suits should be held in abeyance until the President is out of office? Or that presidents should not lie at their depositions?

---

[18]   *See Harlow v. Fitzgerald*, 457 U.S. 800 (1982).

SECTION 13.4 APPOINTMENTS AND THE UNITARY EXECUTIVE

The vast majority of federal employees—tens of thousands of persons—work for the Executive branch, and yet the Constitution generally refers to the Executive as if it were a single person. There is thus considerable tension between the fact that much of the Executive branch is created by statute—statutes creating and, frequently, reorganizing the various executive agencies, for example—and Article II, section one's proclamation that "[t]he executive Power shall be vested in a President." The principle of the *unitary* executive is that whatever additional executive institutions and officers are created, all of those persons ultimately work for, and are accountable to, the single President.

This concept has been frequently misunderstood. Justice Samuel Alito offered a helpful clarification at his confirmation hearing:

> Seated at the witness table, [Judge Alito] went on, "I think it's important to draw a distinction between two very different ideas. One is the scope of Executive power . . . . [W]e might think of that as how big is this table, the extent of the Executive power." That was distinct from a second question, "[W]hen you have a power that is within the prerogative of the Executive, who controls [it]?" In his earlier discussions of the unitary executive, he had been talking about the second question. "[T]he concept of [the] unitary Executive doesn't have to do with the scope of Executive power," Justice Alito clarified. "It has to do with who within the Executive branch controls the exercise of Executive power, and the theory is the Constitution says the Executive power is conferred on the President."[19]

This arrangement is necessary both to maximize the President's freedom and initiative and because the President is the only executive official elected by and accountable to the People. There is considerable debate about whether this unitary principle is absolute or whether it admits of exceptions—such as nominally "independent" agencies like the Federal Trade Commission. But even if there may be exceptions, most agree that unitariness is the norm at the federal level.

Not all executive branches are structured this way. Most state constitutions elect a number of important executive officers separately from the Governor. In Texas, for example, the Lieutenant Governor and Attorney General are separately elected and do not "work for" the Governor in any strong sense; likewise, local District Attorneys are elected separately and not answerable to the state Attorney general. This willingness to weaken the executive at the state level may be attributable to the fact that state governors lack military and foreign policy functions;

---

[19] John Harrison, *The Unitary Executive and the Scope of Executive Power*, 126 YALE L.J. F.   374   (2016),   www.yalelawjournal.org/forum/the-unitary-executive-and-the-scope-of-executive-power (quoting Justice Alito's testimony).

it is those functions, after all, that strongly influenced the Framers in favor of an undivided national executive.

Although "unitariness" may serve as a general shorthand reference to the integrity of the Executive branch, it refers primarily to the President's control over his officers. Three variables are critical: the power to appoint an officer, to control his or her actions, and to remove that officer. The second of these variables—control over the officer's actions—may seem the most important, but it is almost always achieved indirectly through the power to appoint or, more importantly, to remove. Appointments issues are generally resolved under the Appointments Clause, which provides that "principal" officers must be appointed by the President himself (and confirmed by the Senate) while Congress may arrange for "inferior" officers to be appointed by other persons or entities. The constitutional text does not speak directly to removal, and the issue whether Congress may limit the President's removal power has been contentious for much of our history. A dispute over removal of executive officers was, for example, one of the issues that led to President Andrew Johnson's impeachment during Reconstruction.

Both appointment and removal—as well as more general questions about the "mixing" of governmental powers and "encroachment" on the functions of the Executive—were at issue in the landmark case of *Morrison v. Olson*.

Morrison v. Olson
487 U.S. 654 (1988)

■ **CHIEF JUSTICE REHNQUIST delivered the opinion of the Court.**

This case presents us with a challenge to the independent counsel provisions of the Ethics in Government Act of 1978. We hold today that these provisions of the Act do not violate the Appointments Clause of the Constitution, Art. II, § 2, cl. 2, or the limitations of Article III, nor do they impermissibly interfere with the President's authority under Article II in violation of the constitutional principle of separation of powers.

I

Briefly stated, Title VI of the Ethics in Government Act[1] allows for the appointment of an "independent counsel" to investigate and, if appropriate, prosecute certain high ranking Government officials for violations of federal criminal laws.[2] The Act requires the Attorney

---

[1]   The Act was first enacted by Congress in 1978, and has been twice reenacted, with amendments. The current version of the statute states that . . . it shall "cease to be effective five years after the date of the enactment of the Independent Counsel Reauthorization Act of 1987."

[2]   [T]he statute applies to violations of "any Federal criminal law other than a violation classified as a Class B or C misdemeanor or an infraction." Section 591(b) sets forth the individuals who may be the target of an investigation by the Attorney General, including the President and Vice President, Cabinet level officials, certain high ranking officials in the Executive Office of the President and the Justice Department, the Director and Deputy Director of Central Intelligence, the Commissioner of Internal Revenue, and certain officials involved in

General, upon receipt of information that he determines is "sufficient to constitute grounds to investigate whether any person [covered by the Act] may have violated any Federal criminal law," to conduct a preliminary investigation of the matter. When the Attorney General has completed this investigation, or 90 days has elapsed, he is required to report to a special court (the Special Division) created by the Act "for the purpose of appointing independent counsels."[3] . . . If . . . the Attorney General has determined that there are "reasonable grounds to believe that further investigation or prosecution is warranted," then he "shall apply to the division of the court for the appointment of an independent counsel." . . . Upon receiving this application, the Special Division "shall appoint an appropriate independent counsel and shall define that independent counsel's prosecutorial jurisdiction."[5]

With respect to all matters within the independent counsel's jurisdiction, the Act grants the counsel "full power and independent authority to exercise all investigative and prosecutorial functions and powers of the Department of Justice, the Attorney General, and any other officer or employee of the Department of Justice." The functions of the independent counsel include conducting grand jury proceedings and other investigations, participating in civil and criminal court proceedings and litigation, and appealing any decision in any case in which the counsel participates in an official capacity. [T]he counsel's powers include "initiating and conducting prosecutions in any court of competent jurisdiction, framing and signing indictments, filing informations, and handling all aspects of any case, in the name of the United States." The counsel may appoint employees, may request and obtain assistance from the Department of Justice, and may accept referral of matters from the Attorney General if the matter falls within the counsel's jurisdiction as defined by the Special Division. The Act also states that an independent counsel "shall, except where not possible, comply with the written or other established policies of the Department of Justice respecting enforcement of the criminal laws." In addition, whenever a matter has been referred to an independent counsel under the Act, the Attorney General and the Justice Department are required to suspend all investigations and proceedings regarding the matter. An independent counsel has "full authority to dismiss matters within [his or her] prosecutorial jurisdiction without conducting an investigation or at any

---

the President's national political campaign. [T]he Attorney General may also conduct a preliminary investigation of persons not named in § 591(b) if an investigation by the Attorney General or other Department of Justice official "may result in a personal, financial, or political conflict of interest."

[3]   The Special Division is a division of the United States Court of Appeals for the District of Columbia Circuit. The court consists of three circuit court judges or justices appointed by the Chief Justice of the United States. . . .

[5]   Upon request of the Attorney General, in lieu of appointing an independent counsel the Special Division may "expand the prosecutorial jurisdiction of an independent counsel." Section 593 also authorizes the Special Division to fill vacancies arising because of the death, resignation, or removal of an independent counsel. . . .

subsequent time before prosecution, if to do so would be consistent" with Department of Justice policy.[7]

Two statutory provisions govern the length of an independent counsel's tenure in office. The first defines the procedure for removing an independent counsel. Section 596(a)(1) provides:

> An independent counsel appointed under this chapter may be removed from office, other than by impeachment and conviction, only by the personal action of the Attorney General and only for good cause, physical disability, mental incapacity, or any other condition that substantially impairs the performance of such independent counsel's duties.

If an independent counsel is removed pursuant to this section, the Attorney General is required to submit a report to both the Special Division and the Judiciary Committees of the Senate and the House "specifying the facts found and the ultimate grounds for such removal." Under the current version of the Act, an independent counsel can obtain judicial review of the Attorney General's action by filing a civil action in the United States District Court for the District of Columbia. Members of the Special Division "may not hear or determine any such civil action or any appeal of a decision in any such civil action." The reviewing court is authorized to grant reinstatement or "other appropriate relief."

The other provision governing the tenure of the independent counsel defines the procedures for "terminating" the counsel's office. Under § 596(b)(1), the office of an independent counsel terminates when he or she notifies the Attorney General that he or she has completed or substantially completed any investigations or prosecutions undertaken pursuant to the Act. In addition, the Special Division, acting either on its own or on the suggestion of the Attorney General, may terminate the office of an independent counsel at any time if it finds that "the investigation of all matters within the prosecutorial jurisdiction of such independent counsel . . . have been completed or so substantially completed that it would be appropriate for the Department of Justice to complete such investigations and prosecutions."

Finally, the Act provides for congressional oversight of the activities of independent counsel. An independent counsel may from time to time send Congress statements or reports on his or her activities. The "appropriate committees of the Congress" are given oversight jurisdiction in regard to the official conduct of an independent counsel, and the counsel is required by the Act to cooperate with Congress in the exercise of this jurisdiction. The counsel is required to inform the House of Representatives of "substantial and credible information which [the

---

[7]   The 1987 amendments to the Act specify that the Department of Justice "shall pay all costs relating to the establishment and operation of any office of independent counsel." The Attorney General must report to Congress regarding the amount expended on investigations and prosecutions by independent counsel. In addition, the independent counsel must also file a report of major expenses with the Special Division every six months.

counsel] receives . . . that may constitute grounds for an impeachment." In addition, the Act gives certain congressional committee members the power to "request in writing that the Attorney General apply for the appointment of an independent counsel." The Attorney General is required to respond to this request within a specified time but is not required to accede to the request.

The proceedings in this case provide an example of how the Act works in practice. In 1982, two Subcommittees of the House of Representatives issued subpoenas directing the Environmental Protection Agency (EPA) to produce certain documents relating to the efforts of the EPA and the Land and Natural Resources Division of the Justice Department to enforce the "Superfund Law." At that time, appellee Olson was the Assistant Attorney General for the Office of Legal Counsel (OLC), appellee Schmults was Deputy Attorney General, and appellee Dinkins was the Assistant Attorney General for the Land and Natural Resources Division. Acting on the advice of the Justice Department, the President ordered the Administrator of EPA to invoke executive privilege to withhold certain of the documents on the ground that they contained "enforcement sensitive information." The Administrator obeyed this order and withheld the documents. In response, the House voted to hold the Administrator in contempt, after which the Administrator and the United States together filed a lawsuit against the House. The conflict abated in March 1983, when the administration agreed to give the House Subcommittees limited access to the documents.

The following year, the House Judiciary Committee began an investigation into the Justice Department's role in the controversy over the EPA documents. During this investigation, appellee Olson testified before a House Subcommittee on March 10, 1983. . . . In 1985, the majority members of the Judiciary Committee published a lengthy report . . . suggest[ing] that . . . Olson had given false and misleading testimony to the Subcommittee on March 10, 1983, and that appellees Schmults and Dinkins had wrongfully withheld certain documents from the Committee, thus obstructing the Committee's investigation. The Chairman of the Judiciary Committee forwarded a copy of the report to the Attorney General with a request . . . that he seek the appointment of an independent counsel to investigate the allegations against Olson, Schmults, and Dinkins. . . .

The Attorney General . . . requested appointment of an independent counsel to investigate whether Olson's March 10, 1983, testimony "regarding the completeness of [OLC's] response to the Judiciary Committee's request for OLC documents, and regarding his knowledge of EPA's willingness to turn over certain disputed documents to Congress, violated 18 U. S. C. § 1505, § 1001, or any other provision of federal criminal law." . . .

On April 23, 1986, the Special Division appointed James C. McKay as independent counsel to investigate "whether the testimony of . . . Olson and his revision of such testimony on March 10, 1983, violated either 18 U. S. C. § 1505 or § 1001, or any other provision of federal law." . . . McKay later resigned as independent counsel, and on May 29, 1986, the Division appointed appellant Morrison as his replacement, with the same jurisdiction. . . .

[I]n May and June 1987, appellant caused a grand jury to issue and serve subpoenas *ad testificandum* and *duces tecum* on appellees. All three appellees moved to quash the subpoenas, claiming, among other things, that the independent counsel provisions of the Act were unconstitutional and that appellant accordingly had no authority to proceed. On July 20, 1987, the District Court upheld the constitutionality of the Act and denied the motions to quash. The court subsequently ordered that appellees be held in contempt . . . for continuing to refuse to comply with the subpoenas. . . .

A divided Court of Appeals reversed. The majority ruled first that an independent counsel is not an "inferior Officer" of the United States for purposes of the Appointments Clause. Accordingly, the court found the Act invalid because it does not provide for the independent counsel to be nominated by the President and confirmed by the Senate, as the Clause requires for "principal" officers. The court then went on to consider several alternative grounds for its conclusion that the statute was unconstitutional. In the majority's view, the Act also violates the Appointments Clause insofar as it empowers a court of law to appoint an "inferior" officer who performs core executive functions; the Act's delegation of various powers to the Special Division violates the limitations of Article III; the Act's restrictions on the Attorney General's power to remove an independent counsel violate the separation of powers; and finally, the Act interferes with the Executive Branch's prerogative to "take care that the Laws be faithfully executed," Art. II, § 3. . . . We now reverse. . . .

III

The Appointments Clause of Article II reads as follows:

> [The President] shall nominate, and by and with the Advice and Consent of the Senate, shall appoint Ambassadors, other public Ministers and Consuls, Judges of the supreme Court, and all other Officers of the United States, whose Appointments are not herein otherwise provided for, and which shall be established by Law: but the Congress may by Law vest the Appointment of such inferior Officers, as they think proper, in the President alone, in the Courts of Law, or in the Heads of Departments. U.S. Const., Art. II, § 2, cl. 2.

The parties do not dispute that [t]he Constitution for purposes of appointment . . . divides all its officers into two classes. . . . Principal officers are selected by the President with the advice and consent of the Senate. Inferior officers Congress may allow to be appointed by the President alone, by the heads of departments, or by the Judiciary. The initial question is, accordingly, whether appellant is an "inferior" or a "principal" officer.[12] If she is the latter . . . then the Act is in violation of the Appointments Clause.

The line between "inferior" and "principal" officers is one that is far from clear, and the Framers provided little guidance into where it should be drawn. We need not attempt here to decide exactly where the line falls between the two types of officers, because in our view appellant clearly falls on the "inferior officer" side of that line. Several factors lead to this conclusion.

First, appellant is subject to removal by a higher Executive Branch official. Although appellant may not be "subordinate" to the Attorney General (and the President) insofar as she possesses a degree of independent discretion to exercise the powers delegated to her under the Act, the fact that she can be removed by the Attorney General indicates that she is to some degree "inferior" in rank and authority. Second, appellant is empowered by the Act to perform only certain, limited duties. An independent counsel's role is restricted primarily to investigation and, if appropriate, prosecution for certain federal crimes. Admittedly, the Act delegates to appellant "full power and independent authority to exercise all investigative and prosecutorial functions and powers of the Department of Justice," but this grant of authority does not include any authority to formulate policy for the Government or the Executive Branch, nor does it give appellant any administrative duties outside of those necessary to operate her office. The Act specifically provides that in policy matters appellant is to comply to the extent possible with the policies of the Department.

Third, appellant's office is limited in jurisdiction. Not only is the Act itself restricted in applicability to certain federal officials suspected of certain serious federal crimes, but an independent counsel can only act within the scope of the jurisdiction that has been granted by the Special Division pursuant to a request by the Attorney General. Finally, appellant's office is limited in tenure. There is concededly no time limit on the appointment of a particular counsel. Nonetheless, the office of independent counsel is "temporary" in the sense that an independent counsel is appointed essentially to accomplish a single task, and when that task is over the office is terminated, either by the counsel herself or by action of the Special Division. Unlike other prosecutors, appellant has no ongoing responsibilities that extend beyond the accomplishment of the mission that she was appointed for and authorized by the Special Division to undertake. In our view, these factors relating to the "ideas of tenure, duration . . . and duties" of the independent counsel are sufficient

---

[12] It is clear that appellant is an "officer" of the United States, not an "employee."

to establish that appellant is an "inferior" officer in the constitutional sense. . . .

This does not, however, end our inquiry under the Appointments Clause. Appellees argue that even if appellant is an "inferior" officer, the Clause does not empower Congress to place the power to appoint such an officer outside the Executive Branch. They contend that the Clause does not contemplate congressional authorization of "interbranch appointments," in which an officer of one branch is appointed by officers of another branch. The relevant language of the Appointments Clause is worth repeating. It reads: ". . . but the Congress may by Law vest the Appointment of such inferior Officers, as they think proper, in the President alone, in the courts of Law, or in the Heads of Departments." On its face, the language of this "excepting clause" admits of no limitation on interbranch appointments. Indeed, the inclusion of "as they think proper" seems clearly to give Congress significant discretion to determine whether it is "proper" to vest the appointment of . . . executive officials in the "courts of Law." . . .

[T]he history of the Clause provides no support for appellees' position. . . . [T]here was little or no debate on the question whether the Clause empowers Congress to provide for interbranch appointments, and there is nothing to suggest that the Framers intended to prevent Congress from having that power.

We do not mean to say that Congress' power to provide for interbranch appointments of "inferior officers" is unlimited. In addition to separation-of-powers concerns, which would arise if such provisions for appointment had the potential to impair the constitutional functions assigned to one of the branches . . . Congress' decision to vest the appointment power in the courts would be improper if there was some "incongruity" between the functions normally performed by the courts and the performance of their duty to appoint. In this case, however, we do not think it impermissible for Congress to vest the power to appoint independent counsel in a specially created federal court. We thus disagree with the Court of Appeals' conclusion that there is an inherent incongruity about a court having the power to appoint prosecutorial officers.[13] We have recognized that courts may appoint private attorneys to act as prosecutor for judicial contempt judgments. . . .[14] Congress, of course, was concerned when it created the office of independent counsel with the conflicts of interest that could arise in situations when the Executive Branch is called upon to investigate its own high-ranking officers. If it were to remove the appointing authority from the Executive Branch, the most logical place to put it was in the Judicial Branch. In the

---

[13] Indeed, in light of judicial experience with prosecutors in criminal cases, it could be said that courts are especially well qualified to appoint prosecutors. . . .

[14] We note also the longstanding judicial practice of appointing defense attorneys for individuals who are unable to afford representation, notwithstanding the possibility that the appointed attorney may appear in court before the judge who appointed him.

light of the Act's provision making the judges of the Special Division ineligible to participate in any matters relating to an independent counsel they have appointed, we do not think that appointment of the independent counsel by the court runs afoul of the constitutional limitation on "incongruous" interbranch appointments.

IV

Appellees next contend that the powers vested in the Special Division . . . conflict with Article III of the Constitution. We have long recognized that by the express provision of Article III, the judicial power of the United States is limited to "Cases" and "Controversies." As a general rule, we have broadly stated that "executive or administrative duties of a nonjudicial nature may not be imposed on judges holding office under Art. III of the Constitution." The purpose of this limitation is to help ensure the independence of the Judicial Branch and to prevent the Judiciary from encroaching into areas reserved for the other branches. . . .

Most importantly, the Act vests in the Special Division the power to choose who will serve as independent counsel and the power to define his or her jurisdiction. Clearly, once it is accepted that the Appointments Clause gives Congress the power to vest the appointment of officials such as the independent counsel in the "courts of Law," there can be no Article III objection to the Special Division's exercise of that power, as the power itself derives from the Appointments Clause. . . . Appellees contend, however, that the Division's Appointments Clause powers do not encompass the power to define the independent counsel's jurisdiction. We disagree. In our view, Congress' power under the Clause to vest the "Appointment" of inferior officers in the courts may, in certain circumstances, allow Congress to give the courts some discretion in defining the nature and scope of the appointed official's authority. Particularly when, as here, Congress creates a temporary "office" the nature and duties of which will by necessity vary with the factual circumstances giving rise to the need for an appointment in the first place, it may vest the power to define the scope of the office in the court as an incident to the appointment of the officer pursuant to the Appointments Clause. . . .

The Act also vests in the Special Division various powers and duties in relation to the independent counsel that, because they do not involve appointing the counsel or defining his or her jurisdiction, cannot be said to derive from the Division's Appointments Clause authority. These duties include granting extensions for the Attorney General's preliminary investigation; receiving the report of the Attorney General at the conclusion of his preliminary investigation; referring matters to the counsel upon request; receiving reports from the counsel regarding expenses incurred; receiving a report from the Attorney General following the removal of an independent counsel; granting attorney's fees upon request to individuals who were investigated but not indicted by an independent counsel; receiving a final report from the counsel; deciding whether to release the counsel's final report to Congress or the public and determining whether any protective orders should be issued; and terminating an independent counsel when his or her task is completed.

Leaving aside for the moment the Division's power to terminate an independent counsel, we do not think that Article III absolutely prevents Congress from vesting these other miscellaneous powers in the Special Division pursuant to the Act. As we observed above, one purpose of the broad prohibition upon the courts' exercise of "executive or administrative duties of a nonjudicial nature," is to maintain the separation between the Judiciary and the other branches of the Federal Government by ensuring that judges do not encroach upon executive or legislative authority or undertake tasks that are more properly accomplished by those branches. In this case, the miscellaneous powers described above do not impermissibly trespass upon the authority of the Executive Branch. Some of these allegedly "supervisory" powers conferred on the court are passive: the Division merely "receives" reports from the counsel or the Attorney General, it is not entitled to act on them or to specifically approve or disapprove of their contents. Other provisions of the Act do require the court to exercise some judgment and discretion, but the powers granted by these provisions are themselves essentially ministerial. The Act simply does not give the Division the power to "supervise" the independent counsel in the exercise of his or her investigative or prosecutorial authority. And, the functions that the Special Division is empowered to perform are not inherently "Executive"; indeed, they are directly analogous to functions that federal judges perform in other contexts, such as deciding whether to allow disclosure of matters occurring before a grand jury, deciding to extend a grand jury investigation, or awarding attorney's fees.

We are more doubtful about the Special Division's power to terminate the office of the independent counsel. . . . [T]he power to terminate, especially when exercised by the Division on its own motion, is "administrative" to the extent that it requires the Special Division to monitor the progress of proceedings of the independent counsel and come to a decision as to whether the counsel's job is "completed." It also is not a power that could be considered typically "judicial," as it has few analogues among the court's more traditional powers. Nonetheless, we do not . . . view this provision as a significant judicial encroachment upon executive power or upon the prosecutorial discretion of the independent counsel.

. . . [I]t is the duty of federal courts to construe a statute in order to save it from constitutional infirmities, and to that end we think a narrow construction is appropriate here. The termination provisions of the Act do not give the Special Division anything approaching the power to *remove* the counsel while an investigation or court proceeding is still underway—this power is vested solely in the Attorney General. As we see it, "termination" may occur only when the duties of the counsel are truly "completed" or "so substantially completed" that there remains no need for any continuing action by the independent counsel. It is basically a device for removing from the public payroll an independent counsel who has served his or her purpose, but is unwilling to acknowledge the fact. So construed, the Special Division's power to terminate does not pose a sufficient threat of judicial intrusion into matters that are more properly within the Executive's authority to require that the Act be invalidated as inconsistent with Article III.

Nor do we believe . . . that the Special Division's exercise of the various powers specifically granted to it under the Act poses any threat to the "impartial and independent federal adjudication of claims within the judicial power of the United States." . . . First, the Act as it currently stands gives the Special Division itself no power to review any of the actions of the independent counsel or any of the actions of the Attorney General with regard to the counsel. Accordingly, there is no risk of partisan or biased adjudication of claims regarding the independent counsel by that court. Second, the Act prevents members of the Special Division from participating in "*any* judicial proceeding concerning a matter which involves such independent counsel while such independent counsel is serving in that office or which involves the exercise of such independent counsel's official duties, regardless of whether such independent counsel is still serving in that office." We think both the special court and its judges are sufficiently isolated by these statutory provisions from the review of the activities of the independent counsel so as to avoid any taint of the independence of the Judiciary such as would render the Act invalid under Article III. . . .

V

We now turn to consider whether the Act is invalid under the constitutional principle of separation of powers. Two related issues must be addressed: The first is whether the provision of the Act restricting the Attorney General's power to remove the independent counsel to only those instances in which he can show "good cause," taken by itself, impermissibly interferes with the President's exercise of his constitutionally appointed functions. The second is whether, taken as a whole, the Act violates the separation of powers by reducing the President's ability to control the prosecutorial powers wielded by the independent counsel.

A

Two Terms ago we had occasion to consider whether it was consistent with the separation of powers for Congress to pass a statute that authorized a Government official who is removable only by Congress to participate in what we found to be "executive powers." *Bowsher v. Synar,* 478 U.S. 714 (1986). We held in *Bowsher* that "Congress cannot reserve for itself the power of removal of an officer charged with the execution of the laws except by impeachment." A primary antecedent for this ruling was our 1926 decision in *Myers v. United States,* 272 U.S. 52. *Myers* had considered the propriety of a federal statute by which certain postmasters of the United States could be removed by the President only "by and with the advice and consent of the Senate." There too, Congress' attempt to involve itself in the removal of an executive official was found to be sufficient grounds to render the statute invalid. As we observed in *Bowsher,* the essence of the decision in *Myers* was the judgment that the Constitution prevents Congress from "draw[ing] to itself . . . the power to remove or the right to participate in the exercise of that power. . . ."

Unlike both *Bowsher* and *Myers,* this case does not involve an attempt by Congress itself to gain a role in the removal of executive officials other than its established powers of impeachment and conviction. The Act instead puts the removal power squarely in the hands of the Executive Branch; an independent counsel may be removed from office, "only by the personal action of the Attorney General, and only for good cause." There is no requirement of congressional approval of the Attorney General's removal decision, though the decision is subject to judicial review. In our view, the removal provisions of the Act make this case more analogous to *Humphrey's Executor v. United States,* 295 U.S. 602 (1935), and *Wiener v. United States,* 357 U.S. 349 (1958), than to *Myers* or *Bowsher.*

In *Humphrey's Executor,* the issue was whether a statute restricting the President's power to remove the Commissioners of the Federal Trade Commission (FTC) only for "inefficiency, neglect of duty, or malfeasance in office" was consistent with the Constitution. We stated that whether Congress can "condition the [President's power of removal] by fixing a definite term and precluding a removal except for cause, will depend upon the character of the office." Contrary to the implication of some dicta in *Myers,* the President's power to remove Government officials simply was not "all-inclusive in respect of civil officers with the exception of the judiciary provided for by the Constitution." At least in regard to "quasi-legislative" and "quasi-judicial" agencies such as the FTC,[25] "[t]he authority of Congress, in creating [such] agencies, to require them to act in discharge of their duties independently of executive control . . . includes, as an appropriate incident, power to fix the period during which they shall continue in office, and to forbid their removal except for cause in the meantime." In *Humphrey's Executor,* we found it "plain" that the Constitution did not give the President "illimitable power of removal" over the officers of independent agencies. Were the President to have the power to remove FTC Commissioners at will, the "coercive influence" of

---

[25] We described the FTC as "an administrative body created by Congress to carry into effect legislative policies embodied in the statute in accordance with the legislative standard therein prescribed, and to perform other specified duties as a legislative or as a judicial aid." Such an agency was not "an arm or an eye of the executive," and the commissioners were intended to perform their duties "without executive leave and . . . free from executive control." As we put it at the time, the powers of the FTC were not "purely" executive, but were "quasi-legislative or quasi-judicial."

the removal power would "threate[n] the independence of [the] commission."

Similarly, in *Wiener* we considered whether the President had unfettered discretion to remove a member of the War Claims Commission, which had been established by Congress in the War Claims Act of 1948. The Commission's function was to receive and adjudicate certain claims for compensation from those who had suffered personal injury or property damage at the hands of the enemy during World War II. Commissioners were appointed by the President, with the advice and consent of the Senate, but the statute made no provision for the removal of officers, perhaps because the Commission itself was to have a limited existence. As in *Humphrey's Executor*, however, the Commissioners were entrusted by Congress with adjudicatory powers that were to be exercised free from executive control. In this context, "Congress did not wish to have hang over the Commission the Damocles' sword of removal by the President for no reason other than that he preferred to have on that Commission men of his own choosing." Accordingly, we rejected the President's attempt to remove a Commissioner "merely because he wanted his own appointees on [the] Commission," stating that "no such power is given to the President directly by the Constitution, and none is impliedly conferred upon him by statute."

Appellees contend that *Humphrey's Executor* and *Wiener* are distinguishable from this case because they did not involve officials who performed a "core executive function." They argue that our decision in *Humphrey's Executor* rests on a distinction between "purely executive" officials and officials who exercise "quasi-legislative" and "quasi-judicial" powers. In their view, when a "purely executive" official is involved, the governing precedent is *Myers*, not *Humphrey's Executor*. And, under *Myers*, the President must have absolute discretion to discharge "purely" executive officials at will.

We undoubtedly did rely on the terms "quasi-legislative" and "quasi-judicial" to distinguish the officials involved in *Humphrey's Executor* and *Wiener* from those in *Myers*, but our present considered view is that the determination of whether the Constitution allows Congress to impose a "good cause"-type restriction on the President's power to remove an official cannot be made to turn on whether or not that official is classified as "purely executive."[27] The analysis contained in our removal cases is designed not to define rigid categories of those officials who may or may not be removed at will by the President,[28] but to ensure that Congress

---

[27] Indeed, this Court has never held that the Constitution prevents Congress from imposing limitations on the President's power to remove *all* executive officials simply because they wield "executive" power. . . .

[28] The difficulty of defining such categories of "executive" or "quasi-legislative" officials is illustrated by a comparison of our decisions in cases such as *Humphrey's Executor, Buckley v. Valeo,* 424 U.S. 1 (1976), and *Bowsher.* In *Buckley,* we indicated that the functions of the Federal Election Commission are "administrative," and "more legislative and judicial in nature," and are "of kinds usually performed by independent regulatory agencies or by some department in

does not interfere with the President's exercise of the "executive power" and his constitutionally appointed duty to "take care that the laws be faithfully executed" under Article II. *Myers* was undoubtedly correct in its holding, and in its broader suggestion that there are some "purely executive" officials who must be removable by the President at will if he is to be able to accomplish his constitutional role.[29] . . . At the other end of the spectrum from *Myers*, the characterization of the agencies in *Humphrey's Executor* and *Wiener* as "quasi-legislative" or "quasi-judicial" in large part reflected our judgment that it was not essential to the President's proper execution of his Article II powers that these agencies be headed up by individuals who were removable at will. We do not mean to suggest that an analysis of the functions served by the officials at issue is irrelevant. But the real question is whether the removal restrictions are of such a nature that they impede the President's ability to perform his constitutional duty. . . .

[W]e cannot say that the imposition of a "good cause" standard for removal by itself unduly trammels on executive authority. There is no real dispute that the functions performed by the independent counsel are "executive" in the sense that they are law enforcement functions that typically have been undertaken by officials within the Executive Branch. As we noted above, however, the independent counsel is an inferior officer under the Appointments Clause, with limited jurisdiction and tenure and lacking policymaking or significant administrative authority. Although the counsel exercises no small amount of discretion and judgment in deciding how to carry out his or her duties under the Act, we simply do not see how the President's need to control the exercise of that discretion is so central to the functioning of the Executive Branch as to require as a matter of constitutional law that the counsel be terminable at will by the President.[31]

---

the Executive Branch under the direction of an Act of Congress." In *Bowsher*, we found that the functions of the Comptroller General were "executive" in nature, in that he was required to "exercise judgment concerning facts that affect the application of the Act," and he must "interpret the provisions of the Act to determine precisely what budgetary calculations are required." Compare this with the description of the FTC's powers in *Humphrey's Executor*, which we stated "occupie[d] no place in the executive department": "The [FTC] is an administrative body created by Congress to carry into effect legislative policies embodied in the statute in accordance with the legislative standard therein prescribed, and to perform other specified duties as a legislative or as a judicial aid." [I]t is hard to dispute that the powers of the FTC at the time of *Humphrey's Executor* would at the present time be considered "executive," at least to some degree.

[29] The dissent says that the language of Article II vesting the executive power of the United States in the President requires that every officer of the United States exercising any part of that power must serve at the pleasure of the President and be removable by him at will. This rigid demarcation—a demarcation incapable of being altered by law in the slightest degree, and applicable to tens of thousands of holders of offices neither known nor foreseen by the Framers—depends upon an extrapolation from general constitutional language which we think is more than the text will bear. . . .

[31] We note by way of comparison that various federal agencies whose officers are covered by "good cause" removal restrictions exercise civil enforcement powers that are analogous to the prosecutorial powers wielded by an independent counsel. See, e. g., 15 U. S. C. § 45(m) (giving the FTC the authority to bring civil actions to recover civil penalties for the violations of rules

Nor do we think that the "good cause" removal provision at issue here impermissibly burdens the President's power to control or supervise the independent counsel, as an executive official, in the execution of his or her duties under the Act. This is not a case in which the power to remove an executive official has been completely stripped from the President, thus providing no means for the President to ensure the "faithful execution" of the laws. Rather, because the independent counsel may be terminated for "good cause," the Executive, through the Attorney General, retains ample authority to assure that the counsel is competently performing his or her statutory responsibilities in a manner that comports with the provisions of the Act. Although we need not decide in this case exactly what is encompassed within the term "good cause" under the Act, the legislative history of the removal provision also makes clear that the Attorney General may remove an independent counsel for "misconduct." Here, as with the provision of the Act conferring the appointment authority of the independent counsel on the special court, the congressional determination to limit the removal power of the Attorney General was essential, in the view of Congress, to establish the necessary independence of the office. We do not think that this limitation as it presently stands sufficiently deprives the President of control over the independent counsel to interfere impermissibly with his constitutional obligation to ensure the faithful execution of the laws.

B

The final question to be addressed is whether the Act, taken as a whole, violates the principle of separation of powers by unduly interfering with the role of the Executive Branch. . . . [W]e have never held that the Constitution requires that the three branches of Government "operate with absolute independence." . . .

We observe first that this case does not involve an attempt by Congress to increase its own powers at the expense of the Executive Branch. Unlike some of our previous cases, . . . this case simply does not pose a "dange[r] of congressional usurpation of Executive Branch functions." Indeed, with the exception of the power of impeachment— which applies to all officers of the United States—Congress retained for itself no powers of control or supervision over an independent counsel. . . . Congress' role under the Act is limited to receiving reports or other information and oversight of the independent counsel's activities, functions that we have recognized generally as being incidental to the legislative function of Congress.

Similarly, we do not think that the Act works any *judicial* usurpation of properly executive functions. . . . [T]he Special Division has no power to appoint an independent counsel *sua sponte*; it may only do so

---

respecting unfair competition); 15 U. S. C. §§ 2061, 2071, 2076(b)(7)(A) (giving the Consumer Product Safety Commission the authority to obtain injunctions and apply for seizure of hazardous products).

upon the specific request of the Attorney General, and the courts are specifically prevented from reviewing the Attorney General's decision not to seek appointment. In addition, once the court has appointed a counsel and defined his or her jurisdiction, it has no power to supervise or control the activities of the counsel. . . .

Finally, we do not think that the Act "impermissibly undermine[s]" the powers of the Executive Branch, or "disrupts the proper balance between the coordinate branches [by] prevent[ing] the Executive Branch from accomplishing its constitutionally assigned functions." It is undeniable that the Act reduces the amount of control or supervision that the Attorney General and, through him, the President exercises over the investigation and prosecution of a certain class of alleged criminal activity. . . . Nonetheless, the Act does give the Attorney General several means of supervising or controlling the prosecutorial powers that may be wielded by an independent counsel. Most importantly, the Attorney General retains the power to remove the counsel for "good cause" . . . No independent counsel may be appointed without a specific request by the Attorney General, and the Attorney General's decision not to request appointment if he finds "no reasonable grounds to believe that further investigation is warranted" is committed to his unreviewable discretion. The Act thus gives the Executive a degree of control over the power to initiate an investigation by the independent counsel. In addition, the jurisdiction of the independent counsel is defined with reference to the facts submitted by the Attorney General, and once a counsel is appointed, the Act requires that the counsel abide by Justice Department policy unless it is not "possible" to do so. Notwithstanding the fact that the counsel is to some degree "independent" and free from executive supervision to a greater extent than other federal prosecutors, in our view these features of the Act give the Executive Branch sufficient control over the independent counsel to ensure that the President is able to perform his constitutionally assigned duties.

VI

In sum, we conclude today that it does not violate the Appointments Clause for Congress to vest the appointment of independent counsel in the Special Division; that the powers exercised by the Special Division under the Act do not violate Article III; and that the Act does not violate the separation-of-powers principle by impermissibly interfering with the functions of the Executive Branch. The decision of the Court of Appeals is therefore

Reversed.

■ **JUSTICE SCALIA, dissenting.**

. . . The Framers of the Federal Constitution . . . viewed the principle of separation of powers as the absolutely central guarantee of a just Government. . . . The principle . . . is expressed in our Constitution in the first section of each of the first three Articles. . . . [T]he provision at issue here, Art. II, § 1, cl. 1, provides that "[t]he executive Power shall be vested in a President of the United States of America." . . . [T]he Founders conspicuously and very consciously declined to sap the Executive's strength in the same way they had weakened the Legislature: by dividing the executive power. Proposals to have multiple executives, or a council of advisers with separate authority were rejected. Thus, while "[a]ll legislative Powers herein granted shall be vested in a Congress of the United States, which shall consist of a Senate *and* House of Representatives," U.S. Const., Art. I, § 1 (emphasis added), "[t]he executive Power shall be vested in *a President of the United States*," Art. II, § 1, cl. 1 (emphasis added).

That is what this suit is about. Power. The allocation of power among Congress, the President, and the courts in such fashion as to preserve the equilibrium the Constitution sought to establish—so that "a gradual concentration of the several powers in the same department," Federalist No. 51 (J. Madison), can effectively be resisted. Frequently an issue of this sort will come before the Court clad, so to speak, in sheep's clothing: the potential of the asserted principle to effect important change in the equilibrium of power is not immediately evident, and must be discerned by a careful and perceptive analysis. But this wolf comes as a wolf. . . .

II

. . . To repeat, Article II, § 1, cl. 1, of the Constitution provides: "The executive Power shall be vested in a President of the United States." [T]his does not mean *some of* the executive power, but *all of* the executive power. It seems to me, therefore, that the decision of the Court of Appeals invalidating the present statute must be upheld on fundamental separation-of-powers principles if the following two questions are answered affirmatively: (1) Is the conduct of a criminal prosecution (and of an investigation to decide whether to prosecute) the exercise of purely executive power? (2) Does the statute deprive the President of the United States of exclusive control over the exercise of that power? Surprising to say, the Court appears to concede an affirmative answer to both questions. . . .

The Court concedes that "[t]here is no real dispute that the functions performed by the independent counsel are 'executive',," though it qualifies that concession by adding "in the sense that they are law enforcement functions that typically have been undertaken by officials within the Executive Branch." The qualifier adds nothing but atmosphere. In what *other* sense can one identify "the executive Power" that is supposed to be vested in the President . . . *except* by reference to what has always and everywhere—if conducted by government at all—been conducted never by the legislature, never by the courts, and always by the executive. There is no possible doubt that the independent counsel's functions fit this description. She is vested with the "full power and independent authority to exercise all *investigative and prosecutorial* functions and powers of the Department of Justice [and] the Attorney General."

Governmental investigation and prosecution of crimes is a quintessentially executive function.

As for the second question, whether the statute before us deprives the President of exclusive control over that quintessentially executive activity: The Court does not, and could not possibly, assert that it does not. That is indeed the whole object of the statute. Instead, the Court points out that the President, through his Attorney General, has at least *some* control. [T]he Court greatly exaggerates the extent of that "some" Presidential control. "Most importan[t]" among these controls, the Court asserts, is the Attorney General's "power to remove the counsel for 'good cause.' " This is somewhat like referring to shackles as an effective means of locomotion. As we recognized in *Humphrey's Executor v. United States,* 295 U.S. 602 (1935)—indeed, what *Humphrey's Executor* was all about— limiting removal power to "good cause" is an impediment to, not an effective grant of, Presidential control. . . . Congress, of course, operated under no such illusion when it enacted this statute, describing the "good cause" limitation as "protecting the independent counsel's ability to act independently of the President's direct control" since it permits removal only for "misconduct."

Moving on . . . the Court notes that no independent counsel may be appointed without a specific request from the Attorney General. [T]he condition that renders such a request mandatory (inability to find "no reasonable grounds to believe" that further investigation is warranted) is so insubstantial that the Attorney General's discretion is severely confined. And once the referral is made, it is for the Special Division to determine the scope and duration of the investigation. And in any event, the limited power over referral is irrelevant to the question whether, *once appointed*, the independent counsel exercises executive power free from the President's control. Finally, the Court points out that the Act directs the independent counsel to abide by general Justice Department policy, except when not "possible." The exception alone shows this to be an empty promise. Even without that, however, one would be hard put to come up with many investigative or prosecutorial "policies" . . . that are absolute. Almost all investigative and prosecutorial decisions—including the ultimate decision whether, after a technical violation of the law has been found, prosecution is warranted—involve the balancing of innumerable legal and practical considerations. . . . In sum, the balancing of various legal, practical, and political considerations, none of which is absolute, is the very essence of prosecutorial discretion. To take this away is to remove the core of the prosecutorial function, and not merely "some" Presidential control.

[I]t is ultimately irrelevant *how much* the statute reduces Presidential control. The case is over when the Court acknowledges, as it must, that "[i]t is undeniable that the Act reduces the amount of control or supervision that the Attorney General and, through him, the President exercises over the investigation and prosecution of a certain class of alleged criminal activity." It effects a revolution in our constitutional jurisprudence for the Court, once it has determined that (1) purely executive functions are at issue here, and (2) those functions have been given to a person whose actions are not fully within the supervision and control of the President, nonetheless to proceed further to sit in judgment of whether "the President's need to control the exercise of [the independent counsel's] discretion is *so central* to the functioning of the Executive Branch" as to require complete control, whether the conferral of his powers upon someone else "*sufficiently* deprives the President of control over the independent counsel to interfere impermissibly with [his] constitutional obligation to ensure the faithful execution of the laws," and whether "the Act give[s] the Executive Branch *sufficient* control over the independent counsel to ensure that the President is able to perform his constitutionally assigned duties." It is not for us to determine, and we have never presumed to determine, how much of the purely executive powers of government must be within the full control of the President. The Constitution prescribes that they *all* are. . . .

Is it unthinkable that the President should have such exclusive power, even when alleged crimes by him or his close associates are at issue? No more so than that Congress should have the exclusive power of legislation, even when what is at issue is its own exemption from the burdens of certain laws. See Civil Rights Act of 1964, Title VII (prohibiting "employers," not defined to include the United States, from discriminating on the basis of race, color, religion, sex, or national origin). No more so than that this Court should have the exclusive power to pronounce the final decision on justiciable cases and controversies, even those pertaining to the constitutionality of a statute reducing the salaries of the Justices. See *United States v. Will,* 449 U.S. 200 (1980). A system of separate and coordinate powers necessarily involves an acceptance of exclusive power that can theoretically be abused. . . . The checks against any branch's abuse of its exclusive powers are twofold: First, retaliation by one of the other branch's use of *its* exclusive powers: Congress, for example, can impeach the executive who willfully fails to enforce the laws. . . . Second, and ultimately, there is the political check that the people will replace those in the political branches . . . who are guilty of abuse. Political pressures produced special prosecutors—for Teapot Dome and for Watergate, for example—long before this statute created the independent counsel.

The Court has, nonetheless, replaced the clear constitutional prescription that the executive power belongs to the President with a "balancing test." What are the standards to determine how the balance is to be struck, that is, how much removal of Presidential power is too much? . . . Once we depart from the text of the Constitution, just where short of that do we stop? . . . Having abandoned as the basis for our decisionmaking the text of Article II that "the executive Power" must be vested in the President, the Court does not even attempt to craft a *substitute* criterion . . . that today governs, and in the future will govern, the decision of such questions. Evidently, the governing standard is to be what might be called the unfettered wisdom of a majority of this Court, revealed to an obedient people on a case-by-case basis. This is not only not the government of laws that the Constitution established; it is not a government of laws at all.

[E]ven as an ad hoc, standardless judgment the Court's conclusion must be wrong. Before this statute was passed, the President, in taking action disagreeable to the Congress, or an executive officer giving advice to the President or testifying before Congress concerning one of those many matters on which the two branches are from time to time at odds, could be assured that his acts and motives would be adjudged—insofar as the decision whether to conduct a criminal investigation and to prosecute is concerned—in the Executive Branch, that is, in a forum attuned to the interests and the policies of the Presidency. That was one of the natural advantages the Constitution gave to the Presidency, just as it gave Members of Congress (and their staffs) the advantage of not being prosecutable for anything said or done in their legislative capacities. See U.S. Const., Art. I, § 6, cl. 1. It is the very object of this legislation to eliminate that assurance of a sympathetic forum. . . . Perhaps the boldness of the President himself will not be affected—though I am not even sure of that. . . . But as for the President's high-level assistants, who typically have no political base of support, it is as utterly unrealistic to think that they will not be intimidated by this prospect, and that their advice to him and their advocacy of his interests before a hostile Congress will not be affected, as it would be to think that the Members of Congress and their staffs would be unaffected by replacing the Speech or Debate Clause with a similar provision. It deeply wounds the President, by substantially reducing the President's ability to protect himself and his staff. That is the whole object of the law, of course, and I cannot imagine why the Court believes it does not succeed.

Besides weakening the Presidency by reducing the zeal of his staff . . . the institution of the independent counsel enfeebles him more directly in his constant confrontations with Congress, by eroding his public support. Nothing is so politically effective as the ability to charge that one's opponent and his associates are not merely wrongheaded, naive, ineffective, but, in all probability, "crooks." And nothing so effectively gives an appearance of validity to such charges as a Justice Department investigation. . . . The present statute provides ample means for that sort of attack. . . . Thus, in the 10 years since the institution of the independent counsel was established by law, there have been nine highly publicized investigations, a source of constant political damage to two administrations. That they could not remotely be described as merely the application of "normal" investigatory and prosecutory standards is demonstrated by . . . the following facts: Congress appropriates approximately $50 million annually for general legal activities, salaries, and expenses of the Criminal Division of the Department of Justice. . . . By comparison, between May 1986 and August 1987, four independent counsel . . . spent almost $5 million (one-tenth of the amount annually appropriated to the entire Criminal Division). . . . For fiscal year 1989, the Department of Justice has requested $52 million for the entire Criminal Division, and $7 million to support the activities of independent counsel. . . .

III

[T]he basic separation-of-powers principles I have discussed are what give life and content to our jurisprudence concerning the President's power to appoint and remove officers. . . . Because appellant . . . was not appointed by the President with the advice and consent of the Senate, but rather by the Special Division of the United States Court of Appeals, her appointment is constitutional only if (1) she is an "inferior" officer within the meaning of the above Clause, and (2) Congress may vest her appointment in a court of law.

As to the first of these inquiries, the Court does not attempt to "decide exactly" what establishes the line between principal and "inferior" officers, but is confident that, whatever the line may be, appellant "clearly falls on the 'inferior officer' side" of it. The Court gives three reasons: *First*, she "is subject to removal by a higher Executive Branch official," namely, the Attorney General. *Second*, she is "empowered by the Act to perform only certain, limited duties." *Third*, her office is "limited in jurisdiction" and "limited in tenure."

The first of these lends no support to the view that appellant is an inferior officer. Appellant is removable only for "good cause" or physical or mental incapacity. By contrast, most (if not all) *principal* officers in the Executive Branch may be removed by the President *at will*. I fail to see how the fact that appellant is more difficult to remove than most principal officers helps to establish that she is an inferior officer. . . .

The second reason offered by the Court—that appellant performs only certain, limited duties—may be relevant to whether she is an inferior officer, but it mischaracterizes the extent of her powers. As the Court states: "Admittedly, the Act delegates to appellant [the] '*full power and independent authority to exercise all investigative and prosecutorial functions and powers of the Department of Justice.*'" Moreover, in addition to this general grant of power she is given a broad range of specifically enumerated powers. . . . Once all of this is "admitted," it seems to me impossible to maintain that appellant's authority is so "limited" as to render her an inferior officer. . . .

The final set of reasons given by the Court for why the independent counsel clearly is an inferior officer emphasizes the limited nature of her jurisdiction and tenure. Taking the latter first, I find nothing unusually limited about the independent counsel's tenure. To the contrary, unlike most high ranking Executive Branch officials, she continues to serve until she (or the Special Division) decides that her work is substantially completed. This particular independent prosecutor has already served more than two years, which is at least as long as many Cabinet officials. As to the scope of her jurisdiction, there can be no doubt that is small (though far from unimportant). But within it she exercises more than the full power of the Attorney General. The Ambassador to Luxembourg is not anything less than a principal officer, simply because Luxembourg is small. And the federal judge who sits in a small district is not for that reason "inferior in rank and authority." . . .

I think it preferable to look to the text of the Constitution and the division of power that it establishes. These demonstrate, I think, that the independent counsel is not an inferior officer because she is not *subordinate* to any officer in the Executive Branch (indeed, not even to the President). Dictionaries in use at the time of the Constitutional Convention gave the word "inferiour" two meanings which it still bears today: (1) "[l]ower in place, . . . station, . . . rank of life, . . . value or excellency," and (2) "[s]ubordinate." S. Johnson, Dictionary of the English Language (6th ed. 1785). . . . If what was meant was merely "lower in station or rank," one would use instead a term such as "lesser officers." At the only other point in the Constitution at which the word "inferior" appears, it plainly connotes a relationship of subordination. Article III vests the judicial power of the United States in "one supreme Court, and in such *inferior* Courts as the Congress may from time to time ordain and establish." U.S. Const., Art. III, § 1 (emphasis added). In Federalist No. 81, Hamilton pauses to describe the "inferior" courts authorized by Article III as inferior in the sense that they are "subordinate" to the Supreme Court.

That "inferior" means "subordinate" is also consistent with what little we know about the evolution of the Appointments Clause. . . . It is perfectly obvious . . . both from the relative brevity of the discussion this addition received, and from the content of that discussion, that it was intended merely to make clear . . . that those officers appointed by the President with Senate approval could on their own appoint their subordinates, who would, of course, by chain of command still be under the direct control of the President.

This interpretation is, moreover, consistent with our admittedly sketchy precedent in this area. . . . To be sure, it is not a *sufficient* condition for "inferior" officer status that one be subordinate to a principal officer. Even an officer who is subordinate to a department head can be a principal officer. . . . But it is surely a *necessary* condition for inferior officer status that the officer be subordinate to another officer.

The independent counsel is not even subordinate to the President. . . . Because appellant is not subordinate to another officer, she is not an "inferior" officer and her appointment other than by the President with the advice and consent of the Senate is unconstitutional.

IV

I will not discuss at any length why the restrictions upon the removal of the independent counsel also violate our established precedent dealing with that specific subject. . . . I cannot avoid commenting, however, about the essence of what the Court has done to our removal jurisprudence today.

There is, of course, no provision in the Constitution stating who may remove executive officers, except the provisions for removal by impeachment. Before the present decision it was established, however, (1) that the President's power to remove principal officers who exercise purely executive powers could not be restricted, see *Myers v. United States,* 272 U.S. 52 (1926), and (2) that his power to remove inferior officers who exercise purely executive powers, and whose appointment Congress had removed from the usual procedure of Presidential appointment with Senate consent, could be restricted, at least where the appointment had been made by an officer of the Executive Branch.[4] . . .

Since our 1935 decision in *Humphrey's Executor v. United States*—which was considered by many at the time the product of an activist, anti-New Deal Court bent on reducing the power of President Franklin Roosevelt—it has been established that the line of permissible restriction upon removal of principal officers lies at the point at which the powers exercised by those officers are no longer purely executive. Thus, removal restrictions have been generally regarded as lawful for so-called "independent regulatory agencies," such as the Federal Trade Commission, the Interstate Commerce Commission, and the Consumer Product Safety Commission, which engage substantially in what has been called the "quasi-legislative activity" of rulemaking, and for members of Article I courts, such as the Court of Military Appeals, who engage in the "quasi-judicial" function of adjudication. It has often been observed, correctly in my view, that the line between "purely executive" functions and "quasi-legislative" or "quasi-judicial" functions is not a clear one or even a rational one. But at least it permitted the identification of certain officers, and certain agencies, whose functions were entirely within the control of the President. . . . Today, however, *Humphrey's Executor* is swept into the dustbin of repudiated constitutional principles. . . .

---

[4] The Court misunderstands my opinion to say that "every officer of the United States exercising any part of [the executive] power must serve at the pleasure of the President and be removable by him at will." Of course, as my discussion here demonstrates, that has never been the law and I do not assert otherwise. What I *do* assert—and what the Constitution seems plainly to prescribe—is that the President must have control over all exercises of the executive power. That requires that he have plenary power to remove principal officers such as the independent counsel, but it does not require that he have plenary power to remove inferior officers. Since the latter are, as I have described, subordinate to, *i. e.*, subject to the supervision of, principal officers who (being removable at will) have the President's complete confidence, it is enough—at least if they have been appointed by the President or by a principal officer—that they be removable *for cause*, which would include, of course, the failure to accept supervision. . . .

One can hardly grieve for the shoddy treatment given today to *Humphrey's Executor*. . . . But one must grieve for the Constitution. *Humphrey's Executor* at least had the decency formally to observe the constitutional principle that the President had to be the repository of *all* executive power, which . . . necessarily means that he must be able to discharge those who do not perform executive functions according to his liking. [O]nce an officer is appointed "it is only the authority that can remove him, and not the authority that appointed him, that he must fear and, in the performance of his functions, obey." . . . There are now no lines. If the removal of a prosecutor, the virtual embodiment of the power to "take care that the laws be faithfully executed," can be restricted, what officer's removal cannot? . . . [I]t is now open season upon the President's removal power for all executive officers. . . . The Court essentially says to the President: "Trust us. We will make sure that you are able to accomplish your constitutional role." I think the Constitution gives the President—and the people—more protection than that.

V

The purpose of the separation and equilibration of powers in general, and of the unitary Executive in particular, was not merely to assure effective government but to preserve individual freedom. Those who hold or have held offices covered by the Ethics in Government Act are entitled to that protection as much as the rest of us, and I conclude my discussion by considering the effect of the Act upon the fairness of the process they receive.

Only someone who has worked in the field of law enforcement can fully appreciate the vast power and the immense discretion that are placed in the hands of a prosecutor with respect to the objects of his investigation. Justice Robert Jackson, when he was Attorney General under President Franklin Roosevelt, described it . . . as follows:

> One of the greatest difficulties of the position of prosecutor is that he must pick his cases, because no prosecutor can even investigate all of the cases in which he receives complaints. . . . What every prosecutor is practically required to do is to select the cases for prosecution and to select those in which the offense is the most flagrant, the public harm the greatest, and the proof the most certain.

> If the prosecutor is obliged to choose his case, it follows that he can choose his defendants. Therein is the most dangerous power of the prosecutor: that he will pick people that he thinks he should get, rather than cases that need to be prosecuted. With the law books filled with a great assortment of crimes, a prosecutor stands a fair chance of finding at least a technical violation of some act on the part of almost anyone. In such a case, it is not a question of discovering the commission of a crime and then looking for the man who has committed it, it is a

question of picking the man and then searching the law books,
or putting investigators to work, to pin some offense on him.

Under our system of government, the primary check against
prosecutorial abuse is a political one. The prosecutors who exercise this
awesome discretion are selected and can be removed by a President,
whom the people have trusted enough to elect. Moreover, when crimes
are not investigated and prosecuted fairly, nonselectively, with a
reasonable sense of proportion, the President pays the cost in political
damage to his administration. . . . That result . . . was precisely what the
Founders had in mind when they provided that all executive powers
would be exercised by a *single* Chief Executive. As Hamilton put it, "[t]he
ingredients which constitute safety in the republican sense are a due
dependence on the people, and a due responsibility." The President is
directly dependent on the people, and since there is only *one* President,
he is responsible. The people know whom to blame, whereas "one of the
weightiest objections to a plurality in the executive . . . is that it tends to
conceal faults and destroy responsibility." Federalist No. 70.

That is the system of justice the rest of us are entitled to, but what
of that select class consisting of present or former high-level Executive
Branch officials? If an allegation is made against them of any violation of
any federal criminal law . . . the Attorney General must give it his
attention. That in itself is not objectionable. But if . . . the Attorney
General is unable to say that there are "no reasonable grounds to believe"
that further investigation is warranted, a process is set in motion that is
not in the full control of persons "dependent on the people," and whose
flaws cannot be blamed on the President. An independent counsel is
selected, and the scope of his or her authority prescribed, by a panel of
judges. What if they are politically partisan, as judges have been known
to be, and select a prosecutor antagonistic to the administration, or even
to the particular individual who has been selected for this special
treatment? There is no remedy for that, not even a political one. . . . The
independent counsel thus selected proceeds to assemble a staff. . . . One
thing is certain, however: it involves investigating and perhaps
prosecuting a particular individual. . . . What would be the reaction if, in
an area not covered by this statute, the Justice Department posted a
public notice inviting applicants to assist in an investigation and possible
prosecution of a certain prominent person? Does this not invite what
Justice Jackson described as "picking the man and then searching the
law books, or putting investigators to work, to pin some offense on him"?
. . . It seems to me not conducive to fairness. But even if it were entirely
evident that unfairness was in fact the result—the judges hostile to the
administration, the independent counsel an old foe of the President, the
staff refugees from the recently defeated administration—*there would be
no one accountable to the public to whom the blame could be assigned.*

I do not mean to suggest that anything of this sort . . . occurred in
the present case. I know and have the highest regard for the judges on

the Special Division, and the independent counsel herself is a woman of accomplishment, impartiality, and integrity. But the fairness of a process must be adjudged on the basis of what it permits to happen. . . . It is true, of course, that a similar list of horribles could be attributed to an ordinary Justice Department prosecution—a vindictive prosecutor, an antagonistic staff, etc. But the difference is the difference that the Founders envisioned when they established a single Chief Executive accountable to the people: the blame can be assigned to someone who can be punished.

The above described possibilities of irresponsible conduct . . . will rarely occur, and in the average case the threat to fairness is quite different. As described in the brief filed on behalf of three ex-Attorneys General from each of the last three administrations:

> The problem is less spectacular but much more worrisome. It is that the institutional environment of the Independent Counsel—specifically, her isolation from the Executive Branch and the internal checks and balances it supplies—is designed to heighten, not to check, all of the occupational hazards of the dedicated prosecutor; the danger of too narrow a focus, of the loss of perspective, of preoccupation with the pursuit of one alleged suspect to the exclusion of other interests.

It is, in other words, an additional advantage of the unitary Executive that it can achieve a more uniform application of the law. . . . The mini-Executive that is the independent counsel, however, operating in an area where so little is law and so much is discretion, is intentionally cut off from the unifying influence of the Justice Department, and from the perspective that multiple responsibilities provide. What would normally be regarded as a technical violation . . . may in his or her small world assume the proportions of an indictable offense. What would normally be regarded as an investigation that has reached the level of pursuing such picayune matters that it should be concluded, may to him or her be an investigation that ought to go on for another year. How frightening it must be to have your own independent counsel and staff appointed, with nothing else to do but to investigate you until investigation is no longer worthwhile—with whether it is worthwhile not depending upon what such judgments usually hinge on, competing responsibilities. And to have that counsel and staff decide, with no basis for comparison, whether what you have done is bad enough, willful enough, and provable enough, to warrant an indictment. . . .

The notion that every violation of law should be prosecuted, including . . . every violation by those in high places, is an attractive one. . . . *Fiat justitia, ruat coelum.* Let justice be done, though the heavens may fall. The reality is, however, that it is not an absolutely overriding value. . . . I cannot imagine that there are not many thoughtful men and women in Congress who realize that the benefits of this legislation are far outweighed by its harmful effect upon our system of government. . . . But it is difficult to vote not to enact, and even more difficult to vote to repeal, a statute called, appropriately enough, the Ethics in Government Act. . . . By its shortsighted action today, I fear the Court has permanently encumbered the Republic with an institution that will do it great harm.

Worse than what it has done, however, is the manner in which it has done it. A government of laws means a government of rules. Today's decision on the basic issue of fragmentation of executive power is ungoverned by rule, and hence ungoverned by law. It extends into the very heart of our most significant constitutional function the "totality of the circumstances" mode of analysis that this Court has in recent years become fond of. Taking all things into account, we conclude that the power taken away from the President here is not really *too* much. The next time executive power is assigned to someone other than the President we may conclude, taking all things into account, that it *is* too much. That opinion, like this one, will not be confined by any rule. We will describe . . . the effects of the provision in question, and will authoritatively announce: "The President's need to control the exercise of the [subject officer's] discretion *is* so central to the functioning of the Executive Branch as to require complete control." This is not analysis; it is ad hoc judgment. . . .

The ad hoc approach to constitutional adjudication has real attraction, even apart from its work-saving potential. It is guaranteed to produce a result, in every case, that will make a majority of the Court happy with the law. The law is, by definition, precisely what the majority thinks, taking all things into account, it *ought* to be. I prefer to rely upon the judgment of the wise men who constructed our system, and of the people who approved it, and of two centuries of history that have shown it to be sound. Like it or not, that judgment says, quite plainly, that "[t]he executive Power shall be vested in a President of the United States."

NOTE ON THE INDEPENDENT COUNSEL AND THE UNITARY EXECUTIVE

1.   It is important to keep straight the various challenges to the independent counsel statute in *Morrison*. The executive officials challenging the law argued that

- the independent counsel was improperly appointed by someone *other than the President*;

- even if Congress could vest authority to appoint the independent counsel in another official, it could not vest that authority in *another branch* of government;

- the statute improperly restricted the President's power to *remove* the independent counsel;

- more generally, the independent counsel exercised executive authority but was *not subject to the control of the President*; and

- the independent counsel statute *altered the balance of power* between Congress and the Executive.

How would you characterize each of these claims in the typology of separation of powers arguments that we have developed thus far? Which is the most persuasive?

2.   Is the majority's analysis in *Morrison* functional or formal? Is it consistent with the approach that the Court took in *Chadha* and *Clinton v. NY*? If not, can you explain the divergence? Is Justice Scalia right to criticize not only the result in *Morrison* but also the Court's methodology? What is the central point of his criticism?

3.   What are the advantages and disadvantages of unitariness in the executive? Especially during the George W. Bush Administration, the term "unitary executive" sometimes came to stand for a broad set of claims about executive power, such as the claim that certain executive functions, such as the interrogation of enemy combatants, are not subject to congressional control. These sorts of claims should not distract us from the more traditional principle of the unitary executive, which focuses on the President's right to control executive officers. This principle, while still somewhat controversial, has been embraced by scholars from a variety of ideological perspectives.[20] Do you agree that every executive official should be subject to presidential control? To a large extent, these questions depend on whether you think the best check on Executive power is accountability of all officials through a politically-responsible president, on the one hand, or checks and balances *within* the executive branch, on the other. What do you think?

4.   Two prior cases are important to understanding presidential authority to *remove* executive officials. *Myers v. United States*, 272 U.S. 52 (1926), struck down a statute that purported to limit the President's authority to remove federal postmasters. *Humphrey's Executor v. United States*, 295 U.S. 602 (1935), on the other hand, upheld Congress's authority to limit the President's removal power over commissioners of the Federal Trade Commission. The latter case upheld the notion of "independent agencies"—that is, federal administrative agencies not under the direct control of the President. The Court relied heavily on the notion that such agencies exercise "quasi-legislative" and "quasi-judicial" powers. Prior to *Morrison*, most observers had understood the removal of officials exercising purely *executive* functions to be governed by *Myers*, rather than *Humphrey's Executor*. Was the Court right to abandon this dividing line in *Morrison*?

5.   Justice Scalia's dissent was a lonely one in *Morrison*, and Scalia remained *vox clamantis in deserto* on this issue for many years afterwards. He gained a great many new adherents, however, in the wake of Kenneth Starr's independent counsel investigation of President Bill Clinton in the

---

[20] *See, e.g.*, Lawrence Lessig & Cass R. Sunstein, *The President and the Administration*, 94 COLUM. L. REV. 1 (1994) (agreeing that "[a] strongly unitary executive can promote important values of accountability, coordination, and uniformity in the execution of the laws").

Monica Lewinsky matter. Did the Starr investigation prove Justice Scalia right?

6. The independent counsel statute has always contained a "sunset" provision—meaning that it expires if not renewed through new legislation by Congress. Following the Starr investigation of President Clinton, the statute was allowed to expire in 1999 and has not been revived since. Is this a good or a bad thing? Various institutional alternatives to the statute have been proposed:

- *No Statute:* As Justice Scalia points out, an independent counsel was appointed in Watergate by the Justice Department, even in the absence of a statute. That independent counsel was removable by the President, and President Nixon in fact did remove him—but at great political cost, and Nixon felt obliged to appoint a replacement to continue the investigation.

- *Congressional Investigation:* Congressional committees can investigate anyone they like, including the President. (It was such an investigation that sparked the initial controversy in *Morrison*.) They have broad subpoena powers and can hold non-cooperating persons in contempt of Congress.

- *Civil Service:* Some commentators proposed that independent counsel-type investigations should be conducted by a special division of the Justice Department composed of only civil service people, not political appointees. The office would have a limited budget and would be subject to supervision by the Attorney General, who could be required to recuse herself if she, the President, or the Vice-President were being investigated.

What do you think of these alternatives?

7. The Supreme Court's most recent encounter with the Appointments Clause occurred in *Free Enterprise Fund v. Public Company Accounting Oversight Board*, 561 U.S. 477 (2010). The Court again emphasized the importance of the President's power to remove inferior officers, this time in the context of the Public Company Accounting Oversight Board, a hybrid entity created by the Sarbanes-Oxley Act.

Congress enacted the Sarbanes-Oxley Act in 2002 in reaction to a "series of celebrated accounting debacles," including the Enron scandal. The Act included a number of measures meant to increase transparency and accountability in the financial sector, including the creation of the Public Company Accounting Oversight Board. Under the Act, the Board enjoyed broad power to investigate public accounting firms, impose sanctions, and establish auditing, quality control, ethics, and other standards for the entire accounting industry. Congress labeled the Board as a "nonprofit corporation," thus giving the Board the power to pay salaries much higher than the government pay scale would allow. But unlike private self-regulatory bodies, the Board was created by the government and composed of members appointed by the Securities and Exchange Commission.

While the Court noted the unique nature of the Board's composition and position in the industry, it ultimately held that the removal process, rather than the Board itself, was unconstitutional. The Act provided that Board members could be removed only for good cause, which was to be determined by members of the Securities and Exchange Commission; those Commissioners, moreover, were themselves removable only for cause. Although the Court acknowledged that each individual layer of tenure would be permitted under *Humphrey's Executor*, the Court found that the two layers combined did not "merely add to the Board's independence, but transform[ed] it." The President would not be able to control the Board, and the chain of command would be such that no elected official could be held publicly accountable for the Board's actions. The two-tiered removal procedure was therefore an unconstitutional limit on the executive power.

Writing for a four-justice minority, Justice Breyer argued for a functional analysis, contending that neither the Constitution nor precedent provides any clear answers in this area. In his view, the need for technical expertise and political insulation justified the two-tier tenure system for the Board. Moreover, Justice Breyer's calculated that there are presently at least 573 government officials who are removable only by heads of agencies who themselves are removable only for cause. While the *PCAOB* decision does not strike a serious blow to the Sarbanes-Oxley Act, it may have broader implications for the structure of government agencies as well as the manner in which inferior officers perform their jobs.[21] If *PCAOB* represents a trend toward greater formalism in such matters, *contra Morrison*, would that be a good thing?

8.   The Recess Appointments Clause confers on the President the power "to fill up all Vacancies that may happen during the Recess of the Senate, by granting Commissions which shall expire at the End of their next Session." Art. II, § 2, cl. 3. This power has become important in an era of divided government, as presidents may use it to circumvent (at least for a time) a hostile Senate's refusal to confirm their nominees to judgeships and executive offices. In *National Labor Relations Board v. Noel Canning*, 134 S. Ct. 2550 (2014), the Court explored three questions concerning recess appointments: (1) what counts as a "recess" (i.e., only breaks between formal sessions of Congress, or the more frequent intra-session recesses)? (2) Does "vacancies that may happen" refer only to vacancies that originate during a recess, or to all vacancies that exist during a recess? And (3) If only recesses of significant length trigger the appointments power, should length of a recess be calculated with regard to *pro forma* sessions that transact no business? The last question concerned whether the Senate could effectively stave off presidential appointments by technically convening during periods of inactivity.

---

[21] *See* Richard H. Pildes, Free Enterprise Fund, *Boundary-Enforcing Decisions, and the Unitary Executive Branch Theory of Government Administration*, 2 DUKE J. CONST. L. & PUB. POL'Y SPECIAL ISSUE 1, 1 (2010) (arguing that the *PCAOB* decision "presents the most expansive vision of presidential power over the structure of administrative agencies in perhaps ninety years").

In an opinion by Justice Breyer, the Court accepted the President's position that intra-session recesses count and that "vacancies" includes pre-existing ones. It held, however, that recesses under ten days would presumptively not support a recess appointment and that pro-forma sessions must be considered in calculating that time. As a result, the appointments to the NLRB in question were unconstitutional. Justice Scalia (joined by Roberts, Thomas, and Alito) concurred in the judgment. They would have adopted the stricter reading on the first two questions.

The decision in *Noel Canning* has considerable practical significance, both because it invalidated a significant number of past recess appointments (and therefore cast doubt on official actions by those appointees) and because it affects the leverage of the President vis-à-vis the Senate. But the case was also interesting methodologically, because in the absence of any textual elaboration the Court relied extensively on the historical practice of the political branches to discern the Constitution's meaning. With regard to the second question, for example, Justice Breyer observed that "the President has consistently and frequently interpreted the Recess Appointments Clause to apply to vacancies that initially occur before, but continue to exist during, a recess of the Senate. The Senate as a body has not countered this practice for nearly three-quarters of a century, perhaps longer. The tradition is long enough to entitle the practice to great regard in determining the true construction of the constitutional provision." Justice Scalia, in turn, objected that "the political branches cannot by agreement alter the constitutional structure. Plainly, then, a self-aggrandizing practice adopted by one branch well after the founding, often challenged, and never before blessed by this Court—in other words, the sort of practice on which the majority relies in this case—does not relieve us of our duty to interpret the Constitution in light of its text, structure, and original understanding."

How heavily should the Court rely on past practice and the political branches' interpretation of their own powers? Did *Noel Canning* recognize a form of constitutional "adverse possession"? Is the Constitution's text specific enough to do without this sort of "historical gloss"?[22]

---

[22] *See generally* Curtis A. Bradley & Neil Siegel, After Recess: Historical Practice, Textual Ambiguity, and Constitutional Adverse Possession, 2014 Sup. Ct. Rev. 1 (2015).

CHAPTER FOURTEEN

MILITARY AND FOREIGN AFFAIRS POWERS

James Madison predicted in Federalist 45 that "times of war and danger" would "probably bear a small proportion" to "times of peace and security," but that has not been the story of the Twentieth and early Twenty-first Centuries. Danger, if not war, has been a constant condition at least since 1914, and the need for a vigilant and nimble foreign policy has proven unrelenting over the past century. Nor does "peace and security" describe the actual situation of the Early Republic. The young United States was a weak state in a world of great power conflict. Hence, one of the primary reasons that the Framers opted for a strong, unitary executive was the perceived need for initiative, speed, and secrecy in dealing with a complex and dangerous international environment. At the same time, the Framers retained a suspicion of executive aggrandizement that they had learned from the example of George III. They thus created a strong President with important foreign affairs powers, but they likewise rejected the notion that checks and balances should stop at the water's edge. This chapter surveys the meaning of such checks and balances in the field of foreign and military affairs.

The first section of this Chapter deals with the general power of the national Executive in foreign affairs. It surveys three alternate conceptions of the origins and scope of that power: the theory that Article II vests a general "executive power" in the President that includes significant unenumerated foreign affairs powers; the notion that such powers are "inherent in national sovereignty" and thus need not be grounded in the Constitution at all; and the *Youngstown* principle, derived from Justice Jackson's concurrence, that presidential authority is primarily a function of congressional authorization and prohibition. These alternative theories have broad implications for a variety of separation of powers problems arising in both military and civilian contexts. Section 14.2 thus considers what happens when congressional and presidential directives concerning foreign affairs come into conflict.

The remaining two sections turn to military matters. Section 14.3 concerns the constitutional allocation of authority to use military force—that is, the boundary between the President's "Commander in Chief" power and the Congress's authority to declare war. We will consider both a trio of litigated cases from the Nineteenth Century and more modern interpretations of the war power by both the President and Congress. Section 14.4 addresses powers incident to the conduct of war, such as the power to suspend the writ of *habeas corpus* and the power to detain suspected terrorists and try them before military commissions. Although recent years have seen relatively little conflict between the branches over the use of force itself—both Presidents Bush sought authorization from Congress before taking the nation to war in Kuwait, Afghanistan, and Iraq—executive actions incident to war have become highly controversial in the wake of the War on Terror.

SECTION 14.1   SOURCES OF PRESIDENTIAL POWER IN FOREIGN AFFAIRS

It has long been said—if only imperfectly achieved—that the nation speaks with "one voice" in foreign affairs. Madison wrote in Federalist 42, for example, that "[i]f we are to be one nation in any respect, it clearly ought to be in respect to other nations." As it has turned out, that "one voice" is most often the President's. That said, it is hard to ignore the fact that the Constitution contains no reference to a general "foreign affairs" power, and the specifically enumerated foreign affairs powers granted to the President in Article II (e.g., to receive ambassadors and act as Commander in Chief) pale beside those granted to Congress in Article I (e.g., to declare war, to define and punish offenses against international law, and to regulate foreign commerce). Edward Corwin summed up the situation by pronouncing that "[t]he Constitution is an invitation to struggle for the privilege of directing American foreign policy. The power to determine the substantive content of American foreign policy is a divided power, with the lion's share falling usually, though by no means always, to the President."[1]

The materials in this Chapter present three distinct theories of executive power in foreign affairs. The first is the Hamiltonian or "Vesting Clause" theory, which holds that Article II vests in the President not simply the enumerated executive powers delineated in that article, but also all residual powers that would have been considered "executive" in nature at the Founding and that are not specifically reserved to Congress. This residual authority would include important foreign affairs powers. The second approach, illustrated in the *Curtiss-Wright* case, argues that foreign affairs powers are "inherent in sovereignty" and thus stem from sources outside the constitutional text. While an inherent powers theory does not in itself speak to which branch of the national government enjoys which powers, *Curtiss-Wright* locates those powers in the President. Finally, a third approach follows Justice Jackson's *Youngstown* concurrence by supposing that presidential foreign affairs powers are largely a function of congressional authorization and prohibition. That approach seemed ascendant in the late twentieth century.[2] However, the *Zivotofsky* case—considered in the next section—permitted the President to disregard a direct statutory requirement for

---

[1]   EDWARD S. CORWIN, THE PRESIDENT: OFFICE AND POWERS, 1787–1984, at 201 (Randall W. Bland et al. eds., 5th ed. 1984).

[2]   *See, e.g., Dames & Moore v. Regan*, 453 U.S. 654 (1981).

the first time. At the time of this writing, the only thing one can say for sure is that controversy over the scope of executive power in foreign affairs is certain to continue.

We begin with the controversy over President George Washington's declaration of neutrality in the global conflict between Britain and France. War broke out between those two great powers shortly after the French Revolution in 1789. Although much of that conflict played out in Europe, extensive fighting took place in the North American colonial possessions of the belligerents and their allies, as well as on the high seas. Because of extensive historical and commercial ties, some Americans (especially Federalists and New Englanders) were inclined to favor Britain; on the other hand, gratitude for French support in the American Revolution and ideological enthusiasm for the French Revolution led many other Americans (especially Republicans) to support the French. Complicating this political disorder were a number of treaty obligations binding the U.S. to both Britain (in the Jay treaty ending the Revolutionary War) and France (in treaties of friendship and mutual assistance arising out of that war).[3] Fearing that his young and weak nation would be trampled among the clashing great powers, President Washington was desperate to remain neutral notwithstanding American sympathies and obligations. His proclamation of neutrality, reprinted below, was controversial because it was not authorized by Congress. Alexander Hamilton's essays under the pseudonym "Pacificus," were written to defend the legitimacy of Washington's proclamation.

Proclamation of Neutrality, April 22, 1793 (George Washington)

By the President of the United States of America: A Proclamation

Whereas it appears that a state of war exists between Austria, Prussia, Sardinia, Great Britain, and the United Netherlands, of the one part, and France on the other; and the duty and interest of the United States require, that they should with sincerity and good faith adopt and pursue a conduct friendly and impartial towards the belligerent Powers:

I have therefore thought fit by these presents to declare the disposition of the United States to observe the conduct aforesaid towards those Powers respectively; and to exhort and warn the citizens of the United States carefully to avoid all acts and proceedings whatsoever, which may in any manner tend to contravene such disposition.

And I hereby also make known, that whosoever of the citizens of the United States shall render himself liable to punishment or forfeiture under the law of nations, by committing, aiding, or abetting hostilities against any of the said Powers, or by carrying to any of them those

---

[3] These treaty obligations were the subject of Secretary of State Thomas Jefferson's inquiry in the *Correspondence of the Justices* back in Chapter Two.

articles which are deemed contraband by the *modern* usage of nations, will not receive the protection of the United States, against such punishment or forfeiture; and further, that I have given instructions to those officers, to whom it belongs, to cause prosecutions to be instituted against all persons, who shall, within the cognizance of the courts of the United States, violate the law of nations, with respect to the Powers at war, or any of them.

"Pacificus" No. 1 (Alexander Hamilton)
Philadelphia, June 29, 1793

It will not be disputed that the management of the affairs of this country with foreign nations is confided to the Government of the [United States]. . . . The inquiry then is—what department of the Government of the [United States] is the proper one to make a declaration of Neutrality. . . .

A correct and well informed mind will discern at once that it can belong neither to the Legislative nor Judicial Department and of course must belong to the Executive.

The Legislative Department is not the *organ* of intercourse between the [United States] and foreign Nations. It is charged neither with *making* nor *interpreting* Treaties. It is therefore not naturally that Organ of the Government which is to pronounce the existing condition of the Nation, with regard to foreign Powers, or to admonish the Citizens of their obligations and duties as founded upon that condition of things. Still less is it charged with enforcing the execution and observance of these obligations and those duties.

It is equally obvious that the act in question is foreign to the Judiciary Department of the Government. The province of that Department is to decide litigations in particular cases. It is indeed charged with the interpretation of treaties; but it exercises this function only in the litigated cases; that is where contending parties bring before it a specific controversy. It has no concern with pronouncing upon the external political relations of Treaties between Government and Government. . . .

It must then of necessity belong to the Executive Department to exercise the function in Question—when a proper case for the exercise of it occurs.

It appears to be connected with that department in various capacities, as the *organ* of intercourse between the Nation and foreign Nations—as the interpreter of the National Treaties in those cases in which the Judiciary is not competent, that is in the cases between Government and Government—as that Power, which is charged with the Execution of the Laws, of which Treaties form a part—as that Power which is charged with the command and application of the Public Force.

This view of the subject is so natural and obvious—so analogous to general theory and practice—that no doubt can be entertained of its justness, unless such doubt can be deduced from particular provisions of the Constitution of the [United States].

Let us see then if cause for such doubt is to be found in that constitution.

The second Article of the Constitution of the [United States], section 1st, establishes this general Proposition, that "The Executive Power shall be vested in a President of the United States of America."

The same article in a succeeding Section proceeds to designate particular cases of Executive Power. It declares among other things that the President shall be Commander in Chief of the army and navy of the [United States] and of the Militia of the several states when called into the actual service of the [United States], that he shall have power by and with the advice of the senate to make treaties; that it shall be his duty to receive ambassadors and other public Ministers and to take care that the laws be faithfully executed.

It would not consist with the rules of sound construction to consider this enumeration of particular authorities as derogating from the more comprehensive grant contained in the general clause, further than as it may be coupled with express restrictions or qualifications; as in regard to the cooperation of the Senate in the appointment of Officers and the making of treaties; which are qualifications of the general executive powers of appointing officers and making treaties: Because the difficulty of a complete and perfect specification of all the cases of Executive authority would naturally dictate the use of general terms—and would render it improbable that a specification of certain particulars was designed as a substitute for those terms, when antecedently used. The different mode of expression employed in the constitution in regard to the two powers the Legislative and the Executive serves to confirm this inference. In the article which grants the legislative powers of the Govern[ment] the expressions are—"*All Legislative powers herein granted shall be vested in a Congress of the [United States]*"; in that which grants the Executive Power the expressions are, as already quoted "The Executive Power shall be vested in a President of the [United States] of America."

The enumeration ought rather therefore to be considered as intended by way of greater caution, to specify and regulate the principal articles implied in the definition of Executive Power; leaving the rest to flow from the general grant of that power, interpreted in conformity to other parts of the constitution and to the principles of free government.

The general doctrine then of our constitution is, that the Executive Power of the Nation is vested in the President; subject only to the *exceptions* and *qu[a]lifications* which are expressed in the instrument.

Two of these have been already noticed—the participation of the Senate in the appointment of Officers and the making of Treaties. A third remains to be mentioned the right of the Legislature "to declare war and grant letters of marque and reprisal."

With these exceptions the Executive Power of the Union is completely lodged in the President. . . .

And since upon general principles for reasons already given, the issuing of a proclamation of neutrality is merely an Executive Act; since also the general Executive Power of the Union is vested in the President, the conclusion is, that the step, which has been taken by him, is liable to no just exception on the score of authority.

It may be observed that this Inference would be just if the power of declaring war had not been vested in the Legislature, but that this power naturally includes the right of judging whether the Nation is under obligations to make war or not.

The answer to this is, that however true it may be, that the right of the Legislature to declare war includes the right of judging whether the Nation be under obligations to make War or not—it will not follow that the Executive is in any case excluded from a similar right of Judgment, in the execution of its own functions.

If the Legislature have a right to make war on the one hand—it is on the other the duty of the Executive to preserve Peace till war is declared; and in fulfilling that duty, it must necessarily possess a right of judging what is the nature of the obligations which the treaties of the Country impose on the Government; and when in pursuance of this right it has concluded that there is nothing in them inconsistent with a *state* of neutrality, it becomes both its province and its duty to enforce the laws incident to that state of the Nation. The Executive is charged with the execution of all laws, the laws of Nations as well as the Municipal law, which recognises and adopts those laws. It is consequently bound, by faithfully executing the laws of neutrality, when that is the state of the Nation, to avoid giving a cause of war to foreign Powers. . . .

It deserves to be remarked, that as the participation of the senate in the making of Treaties and the power of the Legislature to declare war are exceptions out of the general "Executive Power" vested in the President, they are to be construed strictly—and ought to be extended no further than is essential to their execution.

While therefore the Legislature can alone declare war, can alone actually transfer the nation from a state of Peace to a state of War—it belongs to the "Executive Power," to do whatever else the laws of Nations cooperating with the Treaties of the Country enjoin, in the intercourse of the [United States] with foreign Powers.

In this distribution of powers the wisdom of our constitution is manifested. It is the province and duty of the Executive to preserve to the

Nation the blessings of peace. The Legislature alone can interrupt those blessings, by placing the Nation in a state of War.

But though it has been thought advisable to vindicate the authority of the Executive on this broad and comprehensive ground—it was not absolutely necessary to do so. That clause of the constitution which makes it his duty to "take care that the laws be faithfully executed" might alone have been relied upon, and this simple process of argument pursued.

The President is the constitutional Executor of the laws. Our Treaties and the laws of Nations form a part of the law of the land. He who is to execute the laws must first judge for himself of their meaning. In order to the observance of that conduct, which the laws of nations combined with our treaties prescribed to this country, in reference to the present War in Europe, it was necessary for the President to judge for himself whether there was any thing in our treaties incompatible with an adherence to neutrality. Having judged that there was not, he had a right, and if in his opinion the interests of the Nation required it, it was his duty, as Executor of the laws, to proclaim the neutrality of the Nation, to exhort all persons to observe it, and to warn them of the penalties which would attend its non observance.

The Proclamation has been represented as enacting some new law. This is a view of it entirely erroneous. It only proclaims a *fact* with regard to the *existing state* of the Nation, informs the citizens of what the laws previously established require of them in that state, & warns them that these laws will be put in execution against the Infractors of them.

United States v. Curtiss-Wright Export Corp.
299 U.S. 304 (1936)

[The challenged legislation in this case arose out of the Chaco War, a devastating conflict between Bolivia and Paraguay from 1932 to 1935. The war was fought over the Gran Chaco region, an area believed to be rich in oil. In response to the increasingly hostile fighting and massive bloodshed, Congress passed, and President Roosevelt signed into law, House Joint Resolution 347. The legislation provided that the President, if he made a finding that the "prohibition of the sale of arms and munitions of war in the United States to those countries now engaged in armed conflict in the Chaco" might "contribute to the reestablishment of peace between those countries," he could issue a "proclamation to that effect" and prohibit the sale of such objects in the United States. President Roosevelt issued such a proclamation on May 28, 1934, and Curtiss-Wright Export Corporation was indicted for violating the resolution soon after.

The Chaco War claimed about 100,000 lives, and caused countries on both sides to lose great amounts of wealth and natural resources. Attempts at peace negotiations proved successful in 1935, and the subsequent peace conference in Buenos Aires resulted in the Treaty of Buenos Aires of 1938, which awarded most of the contested region to Paraguay. The Gran Chaco, thought to be rich in oil reserves, turned out to have no oil at all.]

■ **MR. JUSTICE SUTHERLAND delivered the opinion of the Court.**

On January 27, 1936, an indictment was returned in the court below, the first count of which charges that appellees . . . conspired to sell in the United States certain arms of war, namely fifteen machine guns, to Bolivia, a country then engaged in armed conflict in the Chaco, in violation of the Joint Resolution of Congress approved May 28, 1934, and the provisions of a proclamation issued on the same day by the President of the United States pursuant to authority conferred by § 1 of the resolution. . . . The Joint Resolution follows:

> *Resolved by the Senate and House of Representatives of the United States of America in Congress assembled*, That if the President finds that the prohibition of the sale of arms and munitions of war in the United States to those countries now engaged in armed conflict in the Chaco may contribute to the reestablishment of peace between those countries, and if after consultation with the governments of other American Republics and with their cooperation, as well as that of such other governments as he may deem necessary, he makes proclamation to that effect, it shall be unlawful to sell, except under such limitations and exceptions as the President prescribes, any arms or munitions of war in any place in the United States to the countries now engaged in that armed conflict, or to any person, company, or association acting in the interest of either country, until otherwise ordered by the President or by Congress.

> Sec. 2. Whoever sells any arms or munitions of war in violation of section 1 shall, on conviction, be punished by a fine not exceeding $10,000 or by imprisonment not exceeding two years, or both.

The President's proclamation, after reciting the terms of the Joint Resolution, declares:

> Now, therefore, I, Franklin D. Roosevelt, President of the United States of America, acting under and by virtue of the authority conferred in me by the said joint resolution of Congress, do hereby declare and proclaim that I have found that the prohibition of the sale of arms and munitions of war in the United States to those countries now engaged in armed conflict in the Chaco may contribute to the reestablishment of peace between those countries, and that I have consulted with the governments of other American Republics and have been assured of the cooperation of such governments as I have

deemed necessary as contemplated by the said joint resolution; and I do hereby admonish all citizens of the United States and every person to abstain from every violation of the provisions of the joint resolution above set forth, hereby made applicable to Bolivia and Paraguay, and I do hereby warn them that all violations of such provisions will be rigorously prosecuted.

And I do hereby enjoin upon all officers of the United States charged with the execution of the laws thereof, the utmost diligence in preventing violations of the said joint resolution and this my proclamation issued thereunder, and in bringing to trial and punishment any offenders against the same.

And I do hereby delegate to the Secretary of State the power of prescribing exceptions and limitations to the application of the said joint resolution of May 28, 1934, as made effective by this my proclamation issued thereunder.

. . . Appellees severally demurred to the first count of the indictment on the grounds (1) that it did not charge facts sufficient to show the commission by appellees of any offense against any law of the United States; . . . The points urged in support of the demurrers were, first, that the joint resolution effects an invalid delegation of legislative power to the executive. . . . The court below sustained the demurrers upon the first point. . . .

First. It is contended that by the Joint Resolution, the going into effect and continued operation of the resolution was conditioned (a) upon the President's judgment as to its beneficial effect upon the reestablishment of peace between the countries engaged in armed conflict in the Chaco; (b) upon the making of a proclamation, which was left to his unfettered discretion, thus constituting an attempted substitution of the President's will for that of Congress; (c) upon the making of a proclamation putting an end to the operation of the resolution, which again was left to the President's unfettered discretion; and (d) further, that the extent of its operation in particular cases was subject to limitation and exception by the President, controlled by no standard. In each of these particulars, appellees urge that Congress abdicated its essential functions and delegated them to the Executive.

Whether, if the Joint Resolution had related solely to internal affairs it would be open to the challenge that it constituted an unlawful delegation of legislative power to the Executive, we find it unnecessary to determine. The whole aim of the resolution is to affect a situation entirely external to the United States, and falling within the category of foreign affairs. The determination which we are called to make, therefore, is whether the Joint Resolution, as applied to that situation, is vulnerable to attack under the rule that forbids a delegation of the law-making power. In other words, assuming (but not deciding) that the challenged delegation, if it were confined to internal affairs, would be invalid, may it nevertheless be sustained on the ground that its exclusive aim is to afford a remedy for a hurtful condition within foreign territory?

It will contribute to the elucidation of the question if we first consider the differences between the powers of the federal government in respect of foreign or external affairs and those in respect of domestic or internal affairs. That there are differences between them, and that these differences are fundamental, may not be doubted.

The two classes of powers are different, both in respect of their origin and their nature. The broad statement that the federal government can exercise no powers except those specifically enumerated in the Constitution, and such implied powers as are necessary and proper to carry into effect the enumerated powers, is categorically true only in respect of our internal affairs. In that field, the primary purpose of the Constitution was to carve from the general mass of legislative powers *then possessed by the states* such portions as it was thought desirable to vest in the federal government, leaving those not included in the enumeration still in the states. That this doctrine applies only to powers which the states had, is self evident. And since the states severally never possessed international powers, such powers could not have been carved from the mass of state powers but obviously were transmitted to the United States from some other source. During the colonial period, those powers were possessed exclusively by and were entirely under the control of the Crown. By the Declaration of Independence, "the Representatives of the United States of America" declared the United [not the several] Colonies to be free and independent states, and as such to have "full Power to levy War, conclude Peace, contract Alliances, establish Commerce and to do all other Acts and Things which Independent States may of right do."

As a result of the separation from Great Britain by the colonies acting as a unit, the powers of external sovereignty passed from the Crown not to the colonies severally, but to the colonies in their collective and corporate capacity as the United States of America. Even before the Declaration, the colonies were a unit in foreign affairs, acting through a common agency—namely the Continental Congress, composed of delegates from the thirteen colonies. That agency exercised the powers of war and peace, raised an army, created a navy, and finally adopted the Declaration of Independence. Rulers come and go; governments end and forms of government change; but sovereignty survives. A political society cannot endure without a supreme will somewhere. Sovereignty is never held in suspense. When, therefore, the external sovereignty of Great Britain in respect of the colonies ceased, it immediately passed to the Union. That fact was given practical application almost at once. The treaty of peace, made on September 23, 1783, was concluded between his Brittanic Majesty and the "United States of America."

The Union existed before the Constitution, which was ordained and established among other things to form "a more perfect Union." Prior to that event, it is clear that the Union, declared by the Articles of Confederation to be "perpetual," was the sole possessor of external sovereignty and in the Union it remained without change save in so far as the Constitution in express terms qualified its exercise. The Framers' Convention was called and exerted its powers upon the irrefutable postulate that though the states were several their people in respect of foreign affairs were one. In that convention, the entire absence of state power to deal with those affairs was thus forcefully stated by Rufus King:

> The states were not 'sovereigns' in the sense contended for by some. They did not possess the peculiar features of sovereignty—they could not make war, nor peace, nor alliances, nor treaties. Considering them as political beings, they were dumb, for they could not speak to any foreign sovereign whatever. They were deaf, for they could not hear any propositions from such sovereign. They had not even the organs or faculties of defence or offence, for they could not of themselves raise troops, or equip vessels, for war.

It results that the investment of the federal government with the powers of external sovereignty did not depend upon the affirmative grants of the Constitution. The powers to declare and wage war, to conclude peace, to make treaties, to maintain diplomatic relations with other sovereignties, if they had never been mentioned in the Constitution, would have vested in the federal government as necessary concomitants of nationality. Neither the Constitution nor the laws passed in pursuance of it have any force in foreign territory unless in respect of our own citizens; and operations of the nation in such territory must be governed by treaties, international understandings and compacts, and the principles of international law. As a member of the family of nations, the right and power of the United States in that field are equal to the right and power of the other members of the international family. Otherwise, the United States is not completely sovereign. The power to acquire territory by discovery and occupation, the power to expel undesirable aliens, the power to make such international agreements as do not constitute treaties in the constitutional sense, none of which is expressly affirmed by the Constitution, nevertheless exist as inherently inseparable from the conception of nationality. This the court recognized, and in each of the cases cited found the warrant for its conclusions not in the provisions of the Constitution, but in the law of nations.

In *Burnet v. Brooks,* 288 U.S. 378 (1933), we said, "As a nation with all the attributes of sovereignty, the United States is vested with all the powers of government necessary to maintain an effective control of international relations."

Not only, as we have shown, is the federal power over external affairs in origin and essential character different from that over internal affairs, but participation in the exercise of the power is significantly limited. In this vast external realm, with its important, complicated, delicate and manifold problems, the President alone has the power to speak or listen as a representative of the nation. He *makes* treaties with the advice and consent of the Senate; but he alone negotiates. Into the field of negotiation the Senate cannot intrude; and Congress itself is powerless to invade it. As Marshall said in his great argument of March 7, 1800, in the House of Representatives, "The President is the sole organ of the nation in its external relations, and its sole representative with foreign nations." The Senate Committee on Foreign Relations at a very early day in our history (February 15, 1816), reported to the Senate, among other things, as follows:

> The President is the constitutional representative of the United States with regard to foreign nations. He manages our concerns with foreign nations and must necessarily be most competent to determine when, how, and upon what subjects negotiation may be urged with the greatest prospect of success. For his conduct he is responsible to the Constitution. The committee consider this responsibility the surest pledge for the faithful discharge of his duty. They think the interference of the Senate in the direction of foreign negotiations calculated to diminish that responsibility and thereby to impair the best security for the national safety. The nature of transactions with foreign nations, moreover, requires caution and unity of design, and their success frequently depends on secrecy and dispatch.

It is important to bear in mind that we are here dealing not alone with an authority vested in the President by an exertion of legislative power, but with such an authority plus the very delicate, plenary and exclusive power of the President as the sole organ of the federal government in the field of international relations—a power which does not require as a basis for its exercise an act of Congress, but which, of course, like every other governmental power, must be exercised in subordination to the applicable provisions of the Constitution. It is quite apparent that if, in the maintenance of our international relations, embarrassment—perhaps serious embarrassment—is to be avoided and success for our aims achieved, congressional legislation which is to be made effective through negotiation and inquiry within the international field must often accord to the President a degree of discretion and freedom from statutory restriction which would not be admissible were domestic affairs alone involved. Moreover, he, not Congress, has the better opportunity of knowing the conditions which prevail in foreign countries, and especially is this true in time of war. He has his confidential sources of information. He has his agents in the form of diplomatic, consular and other officials. Secrecy in respect of information gathered by them may be highly necessary, and the premature disclosure of it productive of harmful results. Indeed, so clearly is this true that the first President refused to accede to a request to lay before the House of Representatives the instructions, correspondence and documents relating to the negotiation of the Jay Treaty—a refusal the wisdom of which was recognized by the House itself and has never since been doubted. In his reply to the request, President Washington said:

> The nature of foreign negotiations requires caution, and their success must often depend on secrecy; and even when brought to a conclusion a full disclosure of all the measures, demands, or eventual concessions which may have been proposed or contemplated would be extremely impolitic; for this might have a pernicious influence on future negotiations, or produce immediate inconveniences, perhaps danger and mischief, in relation to other powers. The necessity of such caution and secrecy was one cogent reason for vesting the power of making treaties in the President, with the advice and consent of the Senate, the principle on which that body was formed confining it to a small number of members. To admit, then, a right in the House of Representatives to demand and to have as a matter of course all the papers respecting a negotiation with a foreign power would be to establish a dangerous precedent. . . .

When the President is to be authorized by legislation to act in respect of a matter intended to affect a situation in foreign territory, the legislator properly bears in mind the important consideration that the form of the President's action—or, indeed, whether he shall act at all— may well depend, among other things, upon the nature of the confidential information which he has or may thereafter receive, or upon the effect which his action may have upon our foreign relations. This consideration, in connection with what we have already said on the subject, discloses the unwisdom of requiring Congress in this field of governmental power to lay down narrowly definite standards by which the President is to be governed. . . . "As a government, the United States is invested with all the attributes of sovereignty. As it has the character of nationality it has the powers of nationality, especially those which concern its relations and intercourse with other countries. *We should hesitate long before limiting or embarrassing such powers.*"

In the light of the foregoing observations, it is evident that this court should not be in haste to apply a general rule which will have the effect of condemning legislation like that under review as constituting an unlawful delegation of legislative power. The principles which justify such legislation find overwhelming support in the unbroken legislative practice which has prevailed almost from the inception of the national government to the present day. . . .

Practically every volume of the United States Statutes contains one or more acts or joint resolutions of Congress authorizing action by the President in respect of subjects affecting foreign relations, which either leave the exercise of the power to his unrestricted judgment, or provide a standard far more general than that which has always been considered requisite with regard to domestic affairs . . .

The result of holding that the joint resolution here under attack is void and unenforceable as constituting an unlawful delegation of legislative power would be to stamp this multitude of comparable acts and resolutions as likewise invalid. And while this court may not, and should not, hesitate to declare acts of Congress, however many times repeated, to be unconstitutional if beyond all rational doubt it finds them to be so, an impressive array of legislation such as we have just set forth, enacted by nearly every Congress from the beginning of our national existence to the present day, must be given unusual weight in the process of reaching a correct determination of the problem. A legislative practice such as we have here, evidenced not by only occasional instances, but marked by the movement of a steady stream for a century and a half of time, goes a long way in the direction of proving the presence of unassailable ground for the constitutionality of the practice, to be found in the origin and history of the power involved, or in its nature, or in both combined. . . .

The uniform, long-continued and undisputed legislative practice just disclosed rests upon an admissible view of the Constitution which, even if the practice found far less support in principle than we think it does, we should not feel at liberty at this late day to disturb.

. . . [W]e conclude there is sufficient warrant for the broad discretion vested in the President to determine whether the enforcement of the statute will have a beneficial effect upon the reestablishment of peace in the affected countries; whether he shall make proclamation to bring the resolution into operation; whether and when the resolution shall cease to operate and to make proclamation accordingly; and to prescribe limitations and exceptions to which the enforcement of the resolution shall be subject. . . .

Reversed.

■ MR. JUSTICE MCREYNOLDS **does not agree.** He is of opinion that the court below reached the right conclusion and its judgment ought to be affirmed.

■ MR. JUSTICE STONE took no part in the consideration or decision of this case.

NOTE ON THE SOURCES OF PRESIDENTIAL POWER IN FOREIGN AFFAIRS

1.   President Washington's Neutrality Proclamation did three things: (a) it proclaimed U.S. neutrality in the conflict between Britain and France; (b) it announced that the U.S. government would not seek to *protect* Americans who violated that neutrality; and (c) it threatened to prosecute Americans who violated the neutrality policy. Is there anything problematic about (a) and (b)? With respect to (c), much depends, does it not, on Hamilton's last paragraph, which asserts that the Proclamation did not change the pre-existing law or create any new legal obligations? Would the

President have had the power to create a new federal legal obligation, punishable by criminal sanctions?

2.   Article II of the Constitution confers relatively few enumerated powers on the President. Those powers include:

- To be Commander in Chief of the armed forces;
- To require written opinions from the heads of departments;
- To grant reprieves and pardons for federal crimes;
- To make treaties (with advice and consent of the Senate);
- To appoint various federal officers;
- To convene Congress;
- To receive Ambassadors; and
- To take care that the laws be faithfully executed.

It is instructive to compare this modest list to what the President actually *does* in our system of government. In the area of foreign affairs, Louis Henkin has identified a number of "missing" powers—that is, powers that presidents have long exercised without specific enumerations in Article II:

- To acquire or cede territory;
- To recognize foreign governments;
- To grant or withhold foreign aid;
- To set up consulates and maintain the whole apparatus of foreign policy;
- To establish "doctrines" to guide U.S. foreign and defense policy, such as the Monroe Doctrine or the recent doctrine of preemption;
- To terminate treaties, as opposed to make them; and
- To deal with immigration and the rights of aliens.

According to Professor Henkin, "[t]hese 'missing' powers, and a host of others, were clearly intended for, and have always been exercised by, the federal government, but where does the Constitution say that it shall be so?"[4] Some of these powers may be inferred from textual provisions; some may be necessary and proper to other, enumerated powers. But the relative weakness of the President's enumerated authority poses a central question for this section: How can the Presidency be so weak on paper and so strong in practice?

3.   One answer to the preceding question is Alexander Hamilton's argument that the Vesting Clause of Article II confers a general "executive" power on the President. James Madison wrote a series of essays responding to "Pacificus" under the pen name "Helvidius." Madison's chief argument was that the power to proclaim neutrality was, in this case, most closely related to the powers to declare war and make treaties—both of which belong

---

⁴   LOUIS HENKIN, FOREIGN AFFAIRS AND THE UNITED STATES CONSTITUTION 14–15 (2d ed. 1996).

(in whole or in part) to Congress. He also argued that Hamilton's view of general executive authority was modeled on the British monarchy, which Americans had definitively rejected in 1776.[5]

Saikrishna Prakash and Michael Ramsey have offered a modern version of Hamilton's argument. They contend that "foreign affairs powers are presidential . . . from the ordinary eighteenth-century meaning of executive power":

> [T]he President's executive foreign affairs power is residual, encompassing only those executive foreign affairs powers not allocated elsewhere by the Constitution's text. The Constitution's allocation of specific foreign affairs powers or roles to Congress or the Senate are properly read as assignments away from the President. . . . [O]nce the drafting was complete, the President had a greatly diminished foreign affairs power as compared to the English monarchy. But the President retained a residual power— that is, the President, as the possessor of "the executive Power," had those executive foreign affairs powers not allocated elsewhere by the text. In short, far from suffering from huge gaps, the Constitution has a simple default rule. . . . Foreign affairs powers not assigned elsewhere belong to the President, by virtue of the President's executive power; while foreign affairs powers specifically allocated elsewhere are not presidential powers, in spite of the President's executive power.[6]

Other scholars have disputed this reading, however, on both textual and historical grounds. Curtis Bradley and Martin Flaherty have argued, for example, that the Hamiltonian view "cannot explain some of Article II's specific grants of foreign affairs authority, and it sits uneasily with the Constitution's enumerated powers structure." They also dispute the historical support for the Hamiltonian position:

> [The] historical narrative . . . has two central features. First, it is a story of continuity, whereby European political theory is carried forward, relatively unblemished, into American constitutional design and practice. Second, the narrative relies on what could be called "executive power essentialism"—the proposition that the Founders had in mind, and intended the Constitution to reflect, a conception of what is "naturally" or "essentially" within the executive power. We argue that this historical narrative is wrong on both counts. Among other things, the narrative fails to take account of complexity within eighteenth-century political theory, the experience of state constitutionalism before 1787, and the Founders' self-conscious rejection of the British model of government. The narrative also understates the degree to which the constitutional Founders were functionalists, willing to deviate

---

[5]   For the complete collection of Hamilton's "Pacificus" essays, as well as Madison's "Helvidius" essays in response, see The Online Library of Liberty, at http://oll.libertyfund.org/index.php?option=com_staticxt&staticfile=show.php%3Ftitle=1910&Itemid=27.

[6]   Saikrishna B. Prakash & Michael D. Ramsey, *The Executive Power over Foreign Affairs*, 111 YALE L. J. 231, 254 (2001).

from pure political theory and essentialist categories in order to design an effective government.[7]

Surveying earlier versions of this debate, Professor Henkin remarked that "the constitutional lawyer will have the hard choice between the theory that the conduct of foreign affairs, undefined, was indeed 'granted in bulk' to the President as executive power, and the need to scrounge among, and stretch, spare constitutional clauses to eke out full powers which the President has in fact commanded and many of which he was probably intended to have."[8] Which "hard choice" seems more plausible to you?

4.   A second account of presidential power holds that it is not grounded in "residual" executive authority but rather inherit in the sovereignty of the United States. Justice Sutherland's opinion in *Curtiss-Wright* is the primary source cited by advocates of broad executive authority in international affairs. Sutherland argued that foreign affairs powers are "powers of external sovereignty" that exist separately from the powers granted in the Constitution. These powers, originally held by the Crown, passed to the Union after Great Britain's dominion over the colonies ceased. The opinion raises as many questions as it answers, however. First, does Justice Sutherland's account of sovereignty hold up on its own terms? After all, sovereignty did not pass directly from Britain to the national government, but rather descended through the Articles of Confederation, under which the *states* were sovereign. And even under the 1789 Constitution, isn't it the *People* who are sovereign, not the national government? *See, e.g.,* the discussion of sovereignty in the *Term Limits* case in Chapter Eight.

More importantly, what does the extended discussion of why the national government must have inherent foreign affairs powers have to do with the actual issue in the case, which concerns the allocation of those powers between Congress and the President? Sutherland argues that these powers are vested in the President, as he is the "sole organ of the nation" who "alone has the power to speak or listen as a representative of the nation."[9] Sutherland bases this conclusion on the fact that the president alone is granted the authority, in the Constitution, to negotiate treaties with foreign countries (though he makes them with the advice and consent of the Senate). Are you convinced by this argument?

Can Justice Sutherland's assertion that the President is the "sole organ" of the nation in foreign affairs be squared with the extensive foreign affairs powers that the text grants to Congress? After all, Congress has the power to declare war, regulate commerce with foreign nations, and take several other actions relating to foreign affairs. In any event, why must foreign

---

[7]   Curtis A. Bradley & Martin S. Flaherty, *Executive Power Essentialism and Foreign Affairs*, 102 MICH. L. REV. 545 (2004).

[8]   HENKIN, *supra* note 3, at 40.

[9]   The "sole organ" language comes from John Marshall's declaration, made during a debate in the House of Representatives in 1800, that "[t]he president is the sole organ of the nation in its external relations, and its sole representative with foreign nations." Many have taken issue with Justice Sutherland's use of this quotation, arguing that the quote is taken out of context because Marshall's speech dealt exclusively with the president's role in implementing treaties. Does this criticism affect your view of Sutherland's opinion?

affairs powers lie exclusively in one body? Would it be possible for the different branches of government to exercise concurrent authority? Could the powers be divided among the branches?

Alongside his political theory treatise in Curtiss-Wright, Justice Sutherland offered some practical reasons for executive primacy in foreign affairs. These arguments rest on the practical necessity of wide presidential discretion to deal with quickly evolving situations, his ability to act with secrecy, and the President's unique access to information regarding conditions abroad. Do these pragmatic arguments provide a better basis for the holding?

5.   *Curtiss-Wright* is the most prominent of an important line of cases claiming that the foreign affairs powers of the national government stem not from the Constitution itself, but rather from the mere existence of the United States as a sovereign and independent nation. This approach—that is, relying on *powers inherent in sovereignty*—grounds foreign affairs powers in the nature of nationhood and in international law. Under this theory, government action need not be based on enumerated power grants; it is generally not subject to much judicial review by courts; and it is often not restricted by affirmative constitutional guarantees.[10]

This notion is perhaps best accepted in immigration law, where it forms the basis of the "plenary power" doctrine. In the *Chinese Exclusion Case*,[11] for example, the Court upheld Congress's right to exclude aliens from the United States retroactively. Chae Chan Ping was a Chinese citizen who had resided in the U.S. for 12 years in 1887, when he departed to visit his homeland. He took with him a customs certificate, issued by the federal government, indicating that he was a lawful U.S. resident and had a right to return. Mr. Ping arrived back in San Francisco harbor six days after passage of the Scott Act, which barred all Chinese nationals from entering the country regardless of whether they had a certificate. Having been precluded even from retrieving his property in the U.S., Ping filed suit, arguing that Scott Act was outside Congress's power to enact and that it deprived him of liberty and property without due process of law.

The Court rejected Ping's arguments. It rested Congress's power to exclude aliens from the United States on the government's inherent authority, reasoning that "[T]he United States, in their relation to foreign countries and their subjects or citizens are one nation, invested with powers which belong to independent nations, the exercise of which can be invoked for the maintenance of its absolute independence and security throughout its entire territory."[12] The nation's inherent powers included the right "[t]o preserve its independence . . . against foreign aggression and encroachment . . . whether from the foreign nation acting in its national

---

[10]   *See generally* Sarah H. Cleveland, *Powers Inherent in Sovereignty: Indians, Aliens, Territories, and the Nineteenth Century Origins of Plenary Power over Foreign Affairs*, 81 TEXAS L. REV. 1 (2002).

[11]   *See, e.g.*, Chae Chan Ping v. United States, 130 U.S. 581 (1889).

[12]   *Id.* at 604.

character or from vast hordes of its people crowding in upon us."[13] And although the Court seemed to acknowledge that these inherent powers could be limited by "the constitution itself," the Court ignored Ping's due process claim and suggested that the government's decision was not subject to judicial review. "The government," Justice Field wrote, "is clothed with authority to determine the occasion on which the powers shall be called forth; and its determinations, so far as the subjects affected are concerned, are necessarily conclusive upon all its departments and officers."[14]

In an 1892 case involving a Japanese national seeking admission to the U.S. for the first time, the Court went even further in suggesting that where aliens are concerned, decisions of the political branches simply are not subject to constitutional constraint:

> It is not within the province of the judiciary to order that foreigners who have never been naturalized, nor acquired any domicil or residence within the United States, nor even been admitted into the country pursuant to law, shall be permitted to enter, in opposition to the constitutional and lawful measures of the legislative and executive branches of the national government. As to such persons, the decisions of the executive [and Congress], are due process of law.[15]

Although this plenary power doctrine has been qualified in a variety of ways, it has never been overruled. Do you agree with the Court that governmental foreign affairs powers can be derived an extra-constitutional source, such as sovereignty? Would it have been impossible to derive congressional power to regulate immigration from Article I? If immigration powers *are* derived from sovereignty, does it follow that they are less subject to constitutional limitations like due process? That their exercise is less subject to judicial review?

6. A third theory holds that most of the President's authority in foreign affairs (and generally) derives from Congress. This was the view of Justices Jackson and Frankfurter in *Youngstown*, who saw presidential power as generally a function of either congressional authorization or prohibition. Similarly, Dean Harold Koh has written that America's "national security constitution" is composed primarily of "framework statutes" that delegate important foreign affairs powers to the President.[16] One example would be the International Emergency Economic Powers Act, 50 U.S.C. §§ 1701–1706, which delegates authority to take certain actions to settle economic disputes with foreign nations.[17] But there are many, many other examples of extensive congressional delegations of authority to the President to take action on behalf of the nation.

---

[13] *Id.* at 606.

[14] *Id. See also* Cleveland, *supra* note 10, at 124–34.

[15] *Nishimiura Ekiu v. United States*, 142 U.S. 651, 660 (1892).

[16] *See* HAROLD HONGJU KOH, THE NATIONAL SECURITY CONSTITUTION: SHARING POWER AFTER THE IRAN-CONTRA AFFAIR (1990).

[17] *See Dames & Moore v. Regan*, 453 U.S. 654 (1981) (construing the IEEPA).

Does the congressional delegation theory provide a more plausible account of executive power in foreign affairs? Does it leave the President too dependent on Congress?

7.   How do the different sources of presidential power bear on recent presidential orders restricting entry of nationals from certain Muslim countries into the United States? On January 27, 2017, President Donald Trump issued an executive order that, *inter alia*, barred aliens from seven majority-Muslim countries from entering the United States for a period of 90 days and suspended the U.S. refugee admission program for 120 days. The order was widely criticized, and several lawsuits were immediately filed to challenge it on a variety of grounds.

To what extent does the plenary power doctrine support President Trump's authority to issue his immigration order? Professor Cleveland recounts that "[t]he doctrine of plenary power over immigration was reinvigorated by the cold war immigration cases of the early 1950s, in which the Court combined the doctrine with *Curtiss-Wright* to uphold an inherent executive power over immigration."[18] Even if one believes in plenary immigration powers derived from sovereignty, isn't it more plausible to ascribe them to *Congress* than to the executive? In any event, do you think a Court that decided cases like *Lopez* (insisting that our government is one of enumerated powers) and *American Trucking* (requiring that executive agency action must conform to underlying statutory grants of authority)— not to mention all the cases expanding judicial review in individual rights cases since the Second World War—would uphold the reasoning in *Chae Chan Ping* or *Curtiss-Wright* today?

If one views the Trump order through *Youngstown*'s delegated powers model, one must nevertheless come to grips with some broad delegations in the immigration area. In particular, a provision enacted as part of the Immigration and Naturalization Act in 1952 provides:

> Whenever the President finds that the entry of any aliens or of any class of aliens into the United States would be detrimental to the interests of the United States, he may by proclamation, and for such period as he shall deem necessary, suspend the entry of all aliens or any class of aliens as immigrants or nonimmigrants, or impose on the entry of aliens any restrictions he may deem to be appropriate.[19]

It is possible that later legislation, such as the statute setting up the U.S. refugee program, may qualify the breadth of this language; moreover, past practice under this provision suggests it is meant to facilitate narrower exclusions than the present order. And the President's exercise of authority under the INA may still be subject to attack under various individual rights provisions of the Constitution. Nonetheless, does this provision suggest that

---

[18]   Cleveland, *supra* note 10, at 159–60.

[19]   8 U.S.C. 1182(f). For a helpful analysis, see Kate M. Manuel, *Executive Authority to Exclude Aliens: In Brief*, Congressional Research Service, Jan. 23, 2017, available at https://fas. org/sgp/crs/homesec/R44743.pdf.

critics of President Trump's order should direct at least some of their fire at Congress's willingness to delegate very broad powers to the Executive?

SECTION 14.2   CONGRESS VS. THE PRESIDENT IN FOREIGN AFFAIRS

Although advocates of broad presidential powers not subject to congressional control often rely on *Curtiss-Wright*, it is important to recall that that case involved an express delegation of authority from Congress to the President. Indeed, the constitutional question in the case was whether Congress's delegation was *too broad* and thus offended the nondelegation doctrine. Any suggestion that the President's powers were not subject to congressional control were thus plainly dictum in *Curtiss-Wright*.

In any event, *Youngstown*'s model—that presidential power is largely a function of congressional authorization and prohibition— seemed to become dominant. In the late twentieth and early twenty-first century. A majority of the Court adopted Justice Jackson's three categories in *Dames & Moore v. Regan*,[20] and in *Medellin v. Texas*[21] the Court struck down President George W. Bush's order to a state supreme court on the ground that it fell in the disfavored third category. Debate persisted, however, concerning whether any executive actions might stand in the face of congressional prohibition. The Court finally confronted that question in the *Zivotofsky* case.

Zivotofsky v. Kerry
135 S. Ct. 2076 (2015)

■ JUSTICE KENNEDY delivered the opinion of the Court.

A delicate subject lies in the background of this case. That subject is Jerusalem. Questions touching upon the history of the ancient city and its present legal and international status are among the most difficult and complex in international affairs. In our constitutional system these matters are committed to the Legislature and the Executive, not the Judiciary. As a result, in this opinion the Court does no more, and must do no more, than note the existence of international debate and tensions respecting Jerusalem. Those matters are for Congress and the President to discuss and consider as they seek to shape the Nation's foreign policies.

The Court addresses two questions to resolve the interbranch dispute now before it. First, it must determine whether the President has the exclusive power to grant formal recognition to a foreign sovereign. Second, if he has that power, the Court must determine whether Congress can command the President and his Secretary of State to issue

---

[20]   453 U.S. 654 (1981).
[21]   552 U.S. 491 (2008).

a formal statement that contradicts the earlier recognition. The statement in question here is a congressional mandate that allows a United States citizen born in Jerusalem to direct the President and Secretary of State, when issuing his passport, to state that his place of birth is "Israel."

I

A

Jerusalem's political standing has long been, and remains, one of the most sensitive issues in American foreign policy, and indeed it is one of the most delicate issues in current international affairs. In 1948, President Truman formally recognized Israel in a signed statement of "recognition." That statement did not recognize Israeli sovereignty over Jerusalem. Over the last 60 years, various actors have sought to assert full or partial sovereignty over the city, including Israel, Jordan, and the Palestinians. Yet, in contrast to a consistent policy of formal recognition of Israel, neither President Truman nor any later United States President has issued an official statement or declaration acknowledging any country's sovereignty over Jerusalem. Instead, the Executive Branch has maintained that " 'the status of Jerusalem . . . should be decided not unilaterally but in consultation with all concerned.' " In a letter to Congress then-Secretary of State Warren Christopher expressed the Executive's concern that "[t]here is no issue related to the Arab-Israeli negotiations that is more sensitive than Jerusalem." He further noted the Executive's opinion that "any effort . . . to bring it to the forefront" could be "very damaging to the success of the peace process."

The President's position on Jerusalem is reflected in State Department policy regarding passports and consular reports of birth abroad. Understanding that passports will be construed as reflections of American policy, the State Department's Foreign Affairs Manual instructs its employees, in general, to record the place of birth on a passport as the "country [having] present sovereignty over the actual area of birth." If a citizen objects to the country listed as sovereign by the State Department, he or she may list the city or town of birth rather than the country. The FAM, however, does not allow citizens to list a sovereign that conflicts with Executive Branch policy. Because the United States does not recognize any country as having sovereignty over Jerusalem, the FAM instructs employees to record the place of birth for citizens born there as "Jerusalem."

In 2002, Congress passed the Act at issue here, the Foreign Relations Authorization Act, Fiscal Year 2003, 116 Stat. 1350. Section 214 of the Act is titled "United States Policy with Respect to Jerusalem as the Capital of Israel." The subsection that lies at the heart of this case, § 214(d), addresses passports. That subsection seeks to override the FAM by allowing citizens born in Jerusalem to list their place of birth as "Israel." Titled "Record of Place of Birth as Israel for Passport Purposes," § 214(d) states "[f]or purposes of the registration of birth, certification of nationality, or issuance of a passport of a United States citizen born in the city of Jerusalem, the Secretary shall, upon the request of the citizen or the citizen's legal guardian, record the place of birth as Israel."

When he signed the Act into law, President George W. Bush issued a statement declaring his position that § 214 would, "if construed as mandatory rather than advisory, impermissibly interfere with the President's constitutional authority to formulate the position of the United States, speak for the Nation in international affairs, and determine the terms on which recognition is given to foreign states." The President concluded, "U.S. policy regarding Jerusalem has not changed."

Some parties were not reassured by the President's statement. A cable from the United States Consulate in Jerusalem noted that the Palestine Liberation Organization Executive Committee, Fatah Central Committee, and the Palestinian Authority Cabinet had all issued statements claiming that the Act " 'undermines the role of the U.S. as a sponsor of the peace process.' " In the Gaza Strip and elsewhere residents marched in protest.

In response the Secretary of State advised diplomats to express their understanding of "Jerusalem's importance to both sides and to many others around the world." He noted his belief that America's "policy towards Jerusalem" had not changed.

B

In 2002, petitioner Menachem Binyamin Zivotofsky was born to United States citizens living in Jerusalem. In December 2002, Zivotofsky's mother visited the American Embassy in Tel Aviv to request both a passport and a consular report of birth abroad for her son. She asked that his place of birth be listed as " 'Jerusalem, Israel.' " The Embassy clerks explained that, pursuant to State Department policy, the passport would list only "Jerusalem." Zivotofsky's parents objected and, as his guardians, brought suit on his behalf in the United States District Court for the District of Columbia, seeking to enforce § 214(d). . . .

After Zivotofsky brought suit, the District Court dismissed his case, reasoning that it presented a nonjusticiable political question and that Zivotofsky lacked standing. The Court of Appeals for the District of Columbia Circuit reversed on the standing issue, but later affirmed the District Court's political question determination.

This Court granted certiorari, vacated the judgment, and remanded the case. Whether § 214(d) is constitutional, the Court held, is not a question reserved for the political branches. In reference to Zivotofsky's claim the Court observed "the Judiciary must decide if Zivotofsky's interpretation of the statute is correct, and whether the statute is constitutional"—not whether Jerusalem is, in fact, part of Israel.

On remand the Court of Appeals held the statute unconstitutional. It determined that "the President exclusively holds the power to determine whether to recognize a foreign sovereign," and that "section

214(d) directly contradicts a carefully considered exercise of the Executive branch's recognition power."

This Court again granted certiorari.

II

In considering claims of Presidential power this Court refers to Justice Jackson's familiar tripartite framework from *Youngstown Sheet & Tube Co. v. Sawyer,* 343 U.S. 579, 635–638 (1952) (concurring opinion). The framework divides exercises of Presidential power into three categories: First, when "the President acts pursuant to an express or implied authorization of Congress, his authority is at its maximum, for it includes all that he possesses in his own right plus all that Congress can delegate." Second, "in absence of either a congressional grant or denial of authority" there is a "zone of twilight in which he and Congress may have concurrent authority," and where "congressional inertia, indifference or quiescence may" invite the exercise of executive power. Finally, when "the President takes measures incompatible with the expressed or implied will of Congress . . . he can rely only upon his own constitutional powers minus any constitutional powers of Congress over the matter." To succeed in this third category, the President's asserted power must be both "exclusive" and "conclusive" on the issue.

In this case the Secretary contends that § 214(d) infringes on the President's exclusive recognition power by "requiring the President to contradict his recognition position regarding Jerusalem in official communications with foreign sovereigns." In so doing the Secretary acknowledges the President's power is "at its lowest ebb." *Youngstown.* Because the President's refusal to implement § 214(d) falls into Justice Jackson's third category, his claim must be "scrutinized with caution," and he may rely solely on powers the Constitution grants to him alone.

To determine whether the President possesses the exclusive power of recognition the Court examines the Constitution's text and structure, as well as precedent and history bearing on the question.

A

Recognition is a "formal acknowledgement" that a particular "entity possesses the qualifications for statehood" or "that a particular regime is the effective government of a state." Restatement (Third) of Foreign Relations Law of the United States § 203, Comment *a*, p. 84 (1986). It may also involve the determination of a state's territorial bounds. Recognition is often effected by an express written or oral declaration. It may also be implied—for example, by concluding a bilateral treaty or by sending or receiving diplomatic agents.

Legal consequences follow formal recognition. Recognized sovereigns may sue in United States courts and may benefit from sovereign immunity when they are sued. The actions of a recognized sovereign committed within its own territory also receive deference in domestic courts under the act of state doctrine. Recognition at international law, furthermore, is a precondition of regular diplomatic relations. Recognition is thus useful, even necessary, to the existence of a state.

Despite the importance of the recognition power in foreign relations, the Constitution does not use the term "recognition," either in Article II or elsewhere. The Secretary asserts that the President exercises the recognition power based on the Reception Clause, which directs that the President "shall receive Ambassadors and other public Ministers." Art. II, § 3. As Zivotofsky notes, the Reception Clause received little attention at the Constitutional Convention. In fact, during the ratification debates, Alexander Hamilton claimed that the power to receive ambassadors was "more a matter of dignity than of authority," a ministerial duty largely "without consequence." The Federalist No. 69, p. 420 (C. Rossiter ed. 1961).

At the time of the founding, however, prominent international scholars suggested that receiving an ambassador was tantamount to recognizing the sovereignty of the sending state. See E. DE VATTEL, THE LAW OF NATIONS § 78, p. 461 (1758) (J. Chitty ed. 1853). It is a logical and proper inference, then, that a Clause directing the President alone to receive ambassadors would be understood to acknowledge his power to recognize other nations.

This in fact occurred early in the Nation's history when President Washington recognized the French Revolutionary Government by receiving its ambassador. See A. Hamilton, Pacificus No. 1, in The Letters of Pacificus and Helvidius 5, 13–14 (1845) (reprint 1976) (President "acknowledged the republic of France, by the reception of its minister"). After this incident the import of the Reception Clause became clear—causing Hamilton to change his earlier view. He wrote that the Reception Clause "includes th[e power] of judging, in the case of a revolution of government in a foreign country, whether the new rulers are competent organs of the national will, and ought to be recognised, or not." See also 3 J. Story, Commentaries on the Constitution of the United States § 1560, p. 416 (1833) ("If the executive receives an ambassador, or other minister, as the representative of a new nation . . . it is an acknowledgment of the sovereign authority *de facto* of such new nation, or party"). As a result, the Reception Clause provides support, although not the sole authority, for the President's power to recognize other nations.

The inference that the President exercises the recognition power is further supported by his additional Article II powers. It is for the President, "by and with the Advice and Consent of the Senate," to "make Treaties, provided two thirds of the Senators present concur." Art. II, § 2, cl. 2. In addition, "he shall nominate, and by and with the Advice and Consent of the Senate, shall appoint Ambassadors" as well as "other public Ministers and Consuls." *Ibid.*

As a matter of constitutional structure, these additional powers give the President control over recognition decisions. At international law, recognition may be effected by different means, but each means is dependent upon Presidential power. In addition to receiving an ambassador, recognition may occur on "the conclusion of a bilateral treaty," or the "formal initiation of diplomatic relations," including the dispatch of an ambassador. The President has the sole power to negotiate treaties, and the Senate may not conclude or ratify a treaty without Presidential action. The President, too, nominates the Nation's ambassadors and dispatches other diplomatic agents. Congress may not send an ambassador without his involvement. Beyond that, the President himself has the power to open diplomatic channels simply by engaging in direct diplomacy with foreign heads of state and their ministers. The Constitution thus assigns the President means to effect recognition on his own initiative. Congress, by contrast, has no constitutional power that would enable it to initiate diplomatic relations with a foreign nation. Because these specific Clauses confer the recognition power on the President, the Court need not consider whether or to what extent the Vesting Clause, which provides that the "executive Power" shall be vested in the President, provides further support for the President's action here. Art. II, § 1, cl. 1.

The text and structure of the Constitution grant the President the power to recognize foreign nations and governments. The question then becomes whether that power is exclusive. The various ways in which the President may unilaterally effect recognition—and the lack of any similar power vested in Congress—suggest that it is. So, too, do functional considerations. Put simply, the Nation must have a single policy regarding which governments are legitimate in the eyes of the United States and which are not. Foreign countries need to know, before entering into diplomatic relations or commerce with the United States, whether their ambassadors will be received; whether their officials will be immune from suit in federal court; and whether they may initiate lawsuits here to vindicate their rights. These assurances cannot be equivocal.

Recognition is a topic on which the Nation must 'speak . . . with one voice.' That voice must be the President's. Between the two political branches, only the Executive has the characteristic of unity at all times. And with unity comes the ability to exercise, to a greater degree, "[d]ecision, activity, secrecy, and dispatch." The Federalist No. 70, p. 424 (A. Hamilton). The President is capable, in ways Congress is not, of engaging in the delicate and often secret diplomatic contacts that may lead to a decision on recognition. He is also better positioned to take the decisive, unequivocal action necessary to recognize other states at international law. . . .

[T]he President since the founding has exercised this unilateral power to recognize new states—and the Court has endorsed the practice. Texts and treatises on international law treat the President's word as the final word on recognition. See, *e.g.,* Restatement (Third) of Foreign

Relations Law § 204, at 89 ("Under the Constitution of the United States the President has exclusive authority to recognize or not to recognize a foreign state or government"). . . .

It remains true, of course, that many decisions affecting foreign relations—including decisions that may determine the course of our relations with recognized countries—require congressional action. Congress may "regulate Commerce with foreign Nations," "establish an uniform Rule of Naturalization," "define and punish Piracies and Felonies committed on the high Seas, and Offences against the Law of Nations," "declare War," "grant Letters of Marque and Reprisal," and "make Rules for the Government and Regulation of the land and naval Forces." U.S. Const., Art. I, § 8. In addition, the President cannot make a treaty or appoint an ambassador without the approval of the Senate. Art. II, § 2, cl. 2. The President, furthermore, could not build an American Embassy abroad without congressional appropriation of the necessary funds. Art. I, § 8, cl. 1. Under basic separation-of-powers principles, it is for the Congress to enact the laws, including "all Laws which shall be necessary and proper for carrying into Execution" the powers of the Federal Government. § 8, cl. 18.

In foreign affairs, as in the domestic realm, the Constitution "enjoins upon its branches separateness but interdependence, autonomy but reciprocity." *Youngstown,* 343 U.S., at 635 (Jackson, J., concurring). Although the President alone effects the formal act of recognition, Congress' powers, and its central role in making laws, give it substantial authority regarding many of the policy determinations that precede and follow the act of recognition itself. If Congress disagrees with the President's recognition policy, there may be consequences. Formal recognition may seem a hollow act if it is not accompanied by the dispatch of an ambassador, the easing of trade restrictions, and the conclusion of treaties. And those decisions require action by the Senate or the whole Congress.

In practice, then, the President's recognition determination is just one part of a political process that may require Congress to make laws. The President's exclusive recognition power encompasses the authority to acknowledge, in a formal sense, the legitimacy of other states and governments, including their territorial bounds. Albeit limited, the exclusive recognition power is essential to the conduct of Presidential duties. The formal act of recognition is an executive power that Congress may not qualify. If the President is to be effective in negotiations over a formal recognition determination, it must be evident to his counterparts abroad that he speaks for the Nation on that precise question. . . .

B

No single precedent resolves the question whether the President has exclusive recognition authority and, if so, how far that power extends. In part that is because, until today, the political branches have resolved their disputes over questions of recognition. . . . In the end, however, a fair reading of the cases shows that the President's role in the recognition process is both central and exclusive.

During the administration of President Van Buren, in a case involving a dispute over the status of the Falkland Islands, the Court noted that "when the executive branch of the government" assumes "a fact in regard to the sovereignty of any island or country, it is conclusive on the judicial department." *Williams v. Suffolk Ins. Co.,* 13 Pet. 415, 420 (1839). Once the President has made his determination, it "is enough to know, that in the exercise of his constitutional functions, he has decided the question. Having done this under the responsibilities which belong to him, it is obligatory on the people and government of the Union."

Later, during the 1930's and 1940's, the Court addressed issues surrounding President Roosevelt's decision to recognize the Soviet Government of Russia. In *United States v. Belmont,* 301 U.S. 324 (1937), and *United States v. Pink,* 315 U.S. 203 (1942), New York state courts declined to give full effect to the terms of executive agreements the President had concluded in negotiations over recognition of the Soviet regime. In particular the state courts, based on New York public policy, did not treat assets that had been seized by the Soviet Government as property of Russia and declined to turn those assets over to the United States. The Court stated that it "may not be doubted" that "recognition, establishment of diplomatic relations . . . and agreements with respect thereto" are "within the competence of the President." *Belmont,* 301 U.S., at 330. In these matters, "the Executive ha[s] authority to speak as the sole organ of th [e] government." The Court added that the President's authority "is not limited to a determination of the government to be recognized. It includes the power to determine the policy which is to govern the question of recognition." *Pink, supra,* at 229. Thus, New York state courts were required to respect the executive agreements.

It is true, of course, that *Belmont* and *Pink* are not direct holdings that the recognition power is exclusive. Those cases considered the validity of executive agreements, not the initial act of recognition. The President's determination in those cases did not contradict an Act of Congress. And the primary issue was whether the executive agreements could supersede state law. Still, the language in *Pink* and *Belmont,* which confirms the President's competence to determine questions of recognition, is strong support for the conclusion that it is for the President alone to determine which foreign governments are legitimate.

Banco Nacional de Cuba contains even stronger statements regarding the President's authority over recognition. There, the status of Cuba's Government and its acts as a sovereign were at issue. As the Court explained, "Political recognition is exclusively a function of the Executive." Because the Executive had recognized the Cuban Government, the Court held that it should be treated as sovereign and could benefit from the "act of state" doctrine. As these cases illustrate, the Court has long considered recognition to be the exclusive prerogative of the Executive.

The Secretary now urges the Court to define the executive power over foreign relations in even broader terms. He contends that under the Court's precedent the President has "exclusive authority to conduct diplomatic relations," along with "the bulk of foreign-affairs powers." In support of his submission that the President has broad, undefined powers over foreign affairs, the Secretary quotes *United States v. Curtiss-Wright Export Corp.,* which described the President as "the sole organ of the federal government in the field of international relations." This Court declines to acknowledge that unbounded power. A formulation broader than the rule that the President alone determines what nations to formally recognize as legitimate—and that he consequently controls his statements on matters of recognition—presents different issues and is unnecessary to the resolution of this case.

The *Curtiss-Wright* case does not extend so far as the Secretary suggests. In *Curtiss-Wright,* the Court considered whether a congressional delegation of power to the President was constitutional. Congress had passed a joint resolution giving the President the discretion to prohibit arms sales to certain militant powers in South America. The resolution provided criminal penalties for violation of those orders. The Court held that the delegation was constitutional, reasoning that Congress may grant the President substantial authority and discretion in the field of foreign affairs. Describing why such broad delegation may be appropriate, the opinion stated:

> In this vast external realm, with its important, complicated, delicate and manifold problems, the President alone has the power to speak or listen as a representative of the nation. He *makes* treaties with the advice and consent of the Senate; but he alone negotiates. Into the field of negotiation the Senate cannot intrude; and Congress itself is powerless to invade it. As Marshall said in his great argument of March 7, 1800, in the House of Representatives, 'The President is the sole organ of the nation in its external relations, and its sole representative with foreign nations.'

This description of the President's exclusive power was not necessary to the holding of *Curtiss-Wright*—which, after all, dealt with congressionally authorized action, not a unilateral Presidential determination. Indeed, *Curtiss-Wright* did not hold that the President is free from Congress' lawmaking power in the field of international relations. The President does have a unique role in communicating with foreign governments, as then-Congressman John Marshall acknowledged. But whether the realm is foreign or domestic, it is still the Legislative Branch, not the Executive Branch, that makes the law.

In a world that is ever more compressed and interdependent, it is essential the congressional role in foreign affairs be understood and respected. For it is Congress that makes laws, and in countless ways its laws will and should shape the Nation's course. The Executive is not free from the ordinary controls and checks of Congress merely because foreign affairs are at issue. See, *e.g., Medellín v. Texas,* 552 U.S. 491, 523–532 (2008); *Youngstown,* 343 U.S., at 589, 72 S.Ct. 863; *Little v. Barreme,* 2 Cranch 170, 177–179 (1804). It is not for the President alone to determine the whole content of the Nation's foreign policy.

That said, judicial precedent and historical practice teach that it is for the President alone to make the specific decision of what foreign power he will recognize as legitimate, both for the Nation as a whole and for the purpose of making his own position clear within the context of recognition in discussions and negotiations with foreign nations. Recognition is an act with immediate and powerful significance for international relations, so the President's position must be clear. Congress cannot require him to contradict his own statement regarding a determination of formal recognition. . . .

C

Having examined the Constitution's text and this Court's precedent, it is appropriate to turn to accepted understandings and practice. In separation-of-powers cases this Court has often "put significant weight upon historical practice." *NLRB v. Noel Canning,* 134 S.Ct. 2550, 2559 (2014). Here, history is not all on one side, but on balance it provides strong support for the conclusion that the recognition power is the President's alone. As Zivotofsky argues, certain historical incidents can be interpreted to support the position that recognition is a shared power. But the weight of historical evidence supports the opposite view, which is that the formal determination of recognition is a power to be exercised only by the President. . . .

From the first Administration forward, the President has claimed unilateral authority to recognize foreign sovereigns. For the most part, Congress has acquiesced in the Executive's exercise of the recognition power. On occasion, the President has chosen, as may often be prudent, to consult and coordinate with Congress. As Judge Tatel noted in this case, however, "the most striking thing" about the history of recognition "is what is absent from it: a situation like this one," where Congress has enacted a statute contrary to the President's formal and considered statement concerning recognition.

The first debate over the recognition power arose in 1793, after France had been torn by revolution. Once the Revolutionary Government was established, Secretary of State Jefferson and President Washington, without consulting Congress, authorized the American Ambassador to resume relations with the new regime. Soon thereafter, the new French Government proposed to send an ambassador, Citizen Genet, to the United States. Members of the President's Cabinet agreed that receiving Genet would be a binding and public act of recognition. They decided, however, both that Genet should be received and that consultation with

Congress was not necessary. Congress expressed no disagreement with this position, and Genet's reception marked the Nation's first act of recognition—one made by the President alone.

The recognition power again became relevant when yet another revolution took place—this time, in South America, as several colonies rose against Spain. In 1818, Speaker of the House Henry Clay announced he "intended moving the recognition of Buenos Ayres and probably of Chile." Clay thus sought to appropriate money " '[f]or one year's salary' " for " 'a Minister' " to present-day Argentina. President Monroe, however, did not share that view. Although Clay gave "one of the most remarkable speeches of his career," his proposed bill was defeated. That action has been attributed, in part, to the fact that Congress agreed the recognition power rested solely with the President. Four years later, after the President had decided to recognize the South American republics, Congress did pass a resolution, on his request, appropriating funds for "such missions to the independent nations on the American continent, as the President of the United States may deem proper."

A decade later, President Jackson faced a recognition crisis over Texas. In 1835, Texas rebelled against Mexico and formed its own government. But the President feared that recognizing the new government could ignite a war. After Congress urged him to recognize Texas, the President delivered a message to the Legislature. He concluded there had not been a "deliberate inquiry" into whether the President or Congress possessed the recognition power. He stated, however, "on the ground of expediency, I am disposed to concur" with Congress' preference regarding Texas. In response Congress appropriated funds for a "diplomatic agent to be sent to the Republic of Texas, whenever the President of the United States . . . shall deem it expedient to appoint such minister." Thus, although he cooperated with Congress, the President was left to execute the formal act of recognition.

President Lincoln, too, sought to coordinate with Congress when he requested support for his recognition of Liberia and Haiti. In his first annual message to Congress he said he could see no reason "why we should persevere longer in withholding our recognition of the independence and sovereignty of Hayti and Liberia." Nonetheless, he was "[u]nwilling" to "inaugurate a novel policy in regard to them without the approbation of Congress." In response Congress concurred in the President's recognition determination and enacted a law appropriating funds to appoint diplomatic representatives to the two countries—leaving, as usual, the actual dispatch of ambassadors and formal statement of recognition to the President.

Three decades later, the branches again were able to reach an accord, this time with regard to Cuba. In 1898, an insurgency against the Spanish colonial government was raging in Cuba. President McKinley determined to ask Congress for authorization to send armed forces to Cuba to help quell the violence. Although McKinley thought Spain was to blame for the strife, he opposed recognizing either Cuba or its insurgent government. At first, the House proposed a resolution consistent with McKinley's wishes. The Senate countered with a resolution that authorized the use of force but that did recognize both Cuban independence and the insurgent government. When the Senate's version reached the House, the House again rejected the language recognizing Cuban independence. The resolution went to Conference, which, after debate, reached a compromise. The final resolution stated "the people of the Island of Cuba are, and of right ought to be, free and independent," but made no mention of recognizing a new Cuban Government. Accepting the compromise, the President signed the joint resolution.

For the next 80 years, Presidents consistently recognized new states and governments without any serious opposition from, or activity in, Congress. The next debate over recognition did not occur until the late 1970's. It concerned China.

President Carter recognized the People's Republic of China (PRC) as the government of China, and derecognized the Republic of China, located on Taiwan. As to the status of Taiwan, the President "acknowledge[d] the Chinese position" that "Taiwan is part of China," but he did not accept that claim. The President proposed a new law defining how the United States would conduct business with Taiwan. The Act (in a simplified summary) treated Taiwan as if it were a legally distinct entity from China—an entity with which the United States intended to maintain strong ties.

Throughout the legislative process, however, no one raised a serious question regarding the President's exclusive authority to recognize the PRC—or to decline to grant formal recognition to Taiwan. Rather, Congress accepted the President's recognition determination as a completed, lawful act; and it proceeded to outline the trade and policy provisions that, in its judgment, were appropriate in light of that decision.

This history confirms the Court's conclusion in the instant case that the power to recognize or decline to recognize a foreign state and its territorial bounds resides in the President alone. For the most part, Congress has respected the Executive's policies and positions as to formal recognition. At times, Congress itself has defended the President's constitutional prerogative. Over the last 100 years, there has been scarcely any debate over the President's power to recognize foreign states. In this respect the Legislature, in the narrow context of recognition, on balance has acknowledged the importance of speaking "with one voice." The weight of historical evidence indicates Congress has accepted that the power to recognize foreign states and governments and their territorial bounds is exclusive to the Presidency.

III

As the power to recognize foreign states resides in the President alone, the question becomes whether § 214(d) infringes on the Executive's consistent decision to withhold recognition with respect to Jerusalem. See *Nixon v. Administrator of General Services,* 433 U.S. 425, 443 (1977) (action unlawful when it "prevents the Executive Branch from accomplishing its constitutionally assigned functions").

Section 214(d) requires that, in a passport or consular report of birth abroad, "the Secretary shall, upon the request of the citizen or the citizen's legal guardian, record the place of birth as Israel" for a "United States citizen born in the city of Jerusalem." That is, § 214(d) requires the President, through the Secretary, to identify citizens born in Jerusalem who so request as being born in Israel. But according to the President, those citizens were not born in Israel. As a matter of United States policy, neither Israel nor any other country is acknowledged as having sovereignty over Jerusalem. In this way, § 214(d) directly contradicts the carefully calibrated and longstanding Executive branch policy of neutrality toward Jerusalem.

If the power over recognition is to mean anything, it must mean that the President not only makes the initial, formal recognition determination but also that he may maintain that determination in his and his agent's statements. This conclusion is a matter of both common sense and necessity. If Congress could command the President to state a recognition position inconsistent with his own, Congress could override the President's recognition determination. Under international law, recognition may be effected by written or oral declaration of the recognizing state. In addition an act of recognition must leave no doubt as to the intention to grant it. Thus, if Congress could alter the President's statements on matters of recognition or force him to contradict them, Congress in effect would exercise the recognition power.

As Justice Jackson wrote in *Youngstown,* when a Presidential power is "exclusive," it "disabl[es] the Congress from acting upon the subject." Here, the subject is quite narrow: The Executive's exclusive power extends no further than his formal recognition determination. But as to that determination, Congress may not enact a law that directly contradicts it. This is not to say Congress may not express its disagreement with the President in myriad ways. For example, it may enact an embargo, decline to confirm an ambassador, or even declare war. But none of these acts would alter the President's recognition decision.

If Congress may not pass a law, speaking in its own voice, that effects formal recognition, then it follows that it may not force the President himself to contradict his earlier statement. That congressional command would not only prevent the Nation from speaking with one voice but also prevent the Executive itself from doing so in conducting foreign relations.

Although the statement required by § 214(d) would not itself constitute a formal act of recognition, it is a mandate that the Executive contradict his prior recognition determination in an official document issued by the Secretary of State. As a result, it is unconstitutional. This is all the more clear in light of the longstanding treatment of a passport's place-of-birth section as an official executive statement implicating recognition. The Secretary's position on this point has been consistent: He will not place information in the place-of-birth section of a passport that contradicts the President's recognition policy. If a citizen objects to the country listed as sovereign over his place of birth, then the Secretary will accommodate him by listing the city or town of birth rather than the country. But the Secretary will not list a sovereign that contradicts the President's recognition policy in a passport. Thus, the Secretary will not list "Israel" in a passport as the country containing Jerusalem.

The flaw in § 214(d) is further underscored by the undoubted fact that the purpose of the statute was to infringe on the recognition power—a power the Court now holds is the sole prerogative of the President. The statute is titled "United States Policy with Respect to Jerusalem as the Capital of Israel." The House Conference Report proclaimed that § 214 "contains four provisions related to the recognition of Jerusalem as Israel's capital." And, indeed, observers interpreted § 214 as altering United States policy regarding Jerusalem—which led to protests across the region. From the face of § 214, from the legislative history, and from its reception, it is clear that Congress wanted to express its displeasure with the President's policy by, among other things, commanding the Executive to contradict his own, earlier stated position on Jerusalem. This Congress may not do.

It is true, as Zivotofsky notes, that Congress has substantial authority over passports. The Court does not question the power of Congress to enact passport legislation of wide scope. In *Kent v. Dulles,* 357 U.S. 116 (1958), for example, the Court held that if a person's " 'liberty' " to travel "is to be regulated" through a passport, "it must be pursuant to the law-making functions of the Congress." Later cases . . . also proceeded on the assumption that Congress must authorize the grounds on which passports may be approved or denied. This is consistent with the extensive lawmaking power the Constitution vests in Congress over the Nation's foreign affairs.

The problem with § 214(d), however, lies in how Congress exercised its authority over passports. It was an improper act for Congress to "aggrandiz[e] its power at the expense of another branch" by requiring the President to contradict an earlier recognition determination in an official document issued by the Executive Branch. To allow Congress to control the President's communication in the context of a formal recognition determination is to allow Congress to exercise that exclusive power itself. As a result, the statute is unconstitutional.

* * *

In holding § 214(d) invalid the Court does not question the substantial powers of Congress over foreign affairs in general or passports in particular. This case is confined solely to the exclusive power of the President to control recognition determinations, including formal statements by the Executive Branch acknowledging the legitimacy of a state or government and its territorial bounds. Congress cannot command the President to contradict an earlier recognition determination in the issuance of passports.

The judgment of the Court of Appeals for the District of Columbia Circuit is

Affirmed.

■ **JUSTICE THOMAS, concurring in the judgment in part and dissenting in part.**

Our Constitution allocates the powers of the Federal Government over foreign affairs in two ways. First, it expressly identifies certain foreign affairs powers and vests them in particular branches, either individually or jointly. Second, it vests the residual foreign affairs powers of the Federal Government—*i.e.,* those not specifically enumerated in the Constitution—in the President by way of Article II's Vesting Clause.

Section 214(d) of the Foreign Relations Authorization Act, Fiscal Year 2003, ignores that constitutional allocation of power insofar as it directs the President, contrary to his wishes, to list "Israel" as the place of birth of Jerusalem-born citizens on their passports. The President has long regulated passports under his residual foreign affairs power, and this portion of § 214(d) does not fall within any of Congress' enumerated powers.

By contrast, § 214(d) poses no such problem insofar as it regulates consular reports of birth abroad. Unlike passports, these reports were developed to effectuate the naturalization laws, and they continue to serve the role of identifying persons who need not be naturalized to obtain U.S. citizenship. The regulation of these reports does not fall within the President's foreign affairs powers, but within Congress' enumerated powers under the Naturalization and Necessary and Proper Clauses.

Rather than adhere to the Constitution's division of powers, the Court relies on a distortion of the President's recognition power to hold both of these parts of § 214(d) unconstitutional. Because I cannot join this faulty analysis, I concur only in the portion of the Court's judgment holding § 214(d) unconstitutional as applied to passports. I respectfully dissent from the remainder of the Court's judgment.

I

A

The Constitution specifies a number of foreign affairs powers and divides them between the political branches. Among others, Article I allocates to Congress the powers "[t]o regulate Commerce with foreign Nations," "[t]o establish an uniform Rule of Naturalization," "[t]o define and punish Piracies and Felonies committed on the high Seas, and Offenses against the Law of Nations," and "[t]o declare War, grant Letters of Marque and Reprisal, and make Rules concerning Captures on Land and Water." Art. I, § 8. For his part, the President has certain express powers relating to foreign affairs, including the powers, "by and with the Advice and Consent of the Senate," to "appoint Ambassadors," and "to make Treaties, provided two thirds of the Senators present concur." Art. II, § 2. He is also assigned certain duties with respect to foreign affairs, including serving as "Commander in Chief of the Army and Navy of the United States," *ibid.*, and "receiv[ing] Ambassadors and other public Ministers," Art. II, § 3.

These specific allocations, however, cannot account for the entirety of the foreign affairs powers exercised by the Federal Government. Neither of the political branches is expressly authorized, for instance, to communicate with foreign ministers, to issue passports, or to repel sudden attacks. Yet the President has engaged in such conduct, with the support of Congress, since the earliest days of the Republic. Prakash & Ramsey, The Executive Power Over Foreign Affairs, 111 Yale L.J. 231, 298–346 (2001).

The President's longstanding practice of exercising unenumerated foreign affairs powers reflects a constitutional directive that "the President ha[s] primary responsibility—along with the necessary power—to protect the national security and to conduct the Nation's foreign relations." *Hamdi v. Rumsfeld,* 542 U.S. 507, 580 (2004) (THOMAS, J., dissenting). Specifically, the Vesting Clause of Article II provides that "[t]he executive Power shall be vested in a President of the United States." Art. II, § 1. This Clause is notably different from the Vesting Clause of Article I, which provides only that "[a]ll legislative Powers *herein granted* shall be vested in a Congress of the United States," Art. I, § 1 (emphasis added). By omitting the words "herein granted" in Article II, the Constitution indicates that the "executive Power" vested in the President is not confined to those powers expressly identified in the document. Instead, it includes all powers originally understood as falling within the "executive Power" of the Federal Government.

B

Founding-era evidence reveals that the "executive Power" included the foreign affairs powers of a sovereign State. John Locke's 17th-century writings laid the groundwork for this understanding of executive power.

Locke described foreign affairs powers—including the powers of "war and peace, leagues and alliances, and all the transactions with all persons and communities without the commonwealth"—as "federative" power. SECOND TREATISE OF CIVIL GOVERNMENT § 146, p. 73 (J. Gough ed. 1947). He defined the "executive" power as "comprehending the execution of the municipal laws of the society within itself upon all that are parts of it." Importantly, however, Locke explained that the federative and executive powers must be lodged together, lest "disorder and ruin" erupt from the division of the "force of the public."

Subsequent thinkers began to refer to both of these powers as aspects of "executive power." William Blackstone, for example, described the executive power in England as including foreign affairs powers, such as the "power of sending embassadors to foreign states, and receiving embassadors at home"; making "treaties, leagues, and alliances with foreign states and princes"; "making war and peace"; and "issu[ing] letters of marque and reprisal." 1 COMMENTARIES ON THE LAWS OF ENGLAND 245, 249, 250, 242–252 (1765). Baron de Montesquieu similarly described executive power as including the power to "mak[e] peace or war, sen[d] or receiv[e] embassies, establis[h] the public security, and provid[e] against invasions." THE SPIRIT OF THE LAWS bk. XI, ch. 6, p. 151 (O. Piest ed., T. Nugent transl. 1949). In fact, most writers of Montesquieu's time were inclined to think of the executive branch of government as being concerned nearly entirely with foreign affairs.

That understanding of executive power prevailed in America. Following independence, Congress assumed control over foreign affairs under the Articles of Confederation. At that time, many understood that control to be an exercise of executive power. . . . This view of executive power was widespread at the time of the framing of the Constitution. Thomas Rutherforth's Institutes of Natural Law—a treatise routinely cited by the Founders—explained that "external executive power" includes "not only what is properly called military power, but the power likewise of making war or peace, the power of engaging in alliances for an encrease of strength, . . . the power of entering into treaties, and of making leagues to restore peace . . . and the power of adjusting the rights of a nation in respect of navigation, trade, etc." During the ratification debates, James Wilson likewise referred to the "executive powers of government" as including the external powers of a nation. And Alexander Hamilton, writing as Publius, asserted that "[t]he actual conduct of foreign negotiations," "the arrangement of the army and navy, the directions of the operations of war . . . and other matters of a like nature" are "executive details" that "fal[l] peculiarly within the province of the executive department." The Federalist No. 72, pp. 435–436 (C. Rossiter ed. 1961).

Given this pervasive view of executive power, it is unsurprising that those who ratified the Constitution understood the "executive Power" vested by Article II to include those foreign affairs powers not otherwise allocated in the Constitution. James Iredell, for example, told the North Carolina ratifying convention that, under the new Constitution, the President would "regulate all intercourse with foreign powers" and act as the "primary agent" of the United States, though no specific allocation of foreign affairs powers in the document so provided. . . .

C

Early practice of the founding generation also supports this understanding of the "executive Power." Upon taking office, President Washington assumed the role of chief diplomat; began to direct the Secretary of Foreign Affairs who, under the Articles of Confederation, had reported to the Congress; and established the foreign policy of the United States. At the same time, he respected Congress' prerogatives to declare war, regulate foreign commerce, and appropriate funds.

For its part, Congress recognized a broad Presidential role in foreign affairs. It created an "Executive department" called the "Department of Foreign Affairs," with a Secretary wholly subordinate to the President. . . . Subsequent interactions between President Washington and Congress indicated that the parties involved believed the Constitution vested the President with authority to regulate dealings with foreign nations. In his first State of the Union Address, President Washington told Congress that "[t]he interests of the United States require, that our intercourse with other nations should be facilitated by such provisions as will enable me to fulfil my duty in that respect." To that end, he asked for compensation for employees and a fund designated for "defraying the expenses incident to the conduct of our foreign affairs." Congress responded by passing "An Act providing the means of intercourse between the United States and foreign nations."

During the congressional debate over that bill, the President sought an opinion from Thomas Jefferson—at that time, Secretary of State— about the scope of the Senate's power in this area. Jefferson responded that "[t]he transaction of business with foreign nations is executive altogether." Opinion on the Powers of the Senate (Apr. 24, 1790), in 5 WRITINGS OF THOMAS JEFFERSON 161 (P. Ford ed. 1895). As such, Jefferson concluded that it properly belonged "to the head" of the executive department, "except as to such portions of it as are specially submitted to the senate." According to Washington's diaries, he received similar advice from John Jay and James Madison about "the propriety of consulting the Senate on the places to which it would be necessary to send persons in the Diplomatic line, and Consuls." All agreed that the Senate lacked a "Constitutional right to interfere with either, & that it might be impolitic to draw it into a precedent their powers extending no farther than to an approbation or disapprobation of the person nominated by the President all the rest being Executive and vested in the President by the Constitution."

Washington followed this advice. He corresponded directly with U.S. ministers, moved them among countries, and removed them from their positions at will. He also corresponded with foreign leaders, representing that his role as the "supreme executive authority" authorized him to receive and respond to their letters on behalf of the United States. When foreign ministers addressed their communications to Congress, he informed them of their error.

Washington's control over foreign affairs extended beyond communications with other governments. When confronted with the question whether to recognize the French Republic as the lawful government of France, he received the French Republic's emissary without the involvement of Congress. When he later concluded that the emissary had acted inappropriately, he again acted without the involvement of Congress to ask the French executive to recall him. Washington also declared neutrality on behalf of the United States during the war between England and France in 1793, an action Hamilton pseudonymously defended as a proper exercise of the power vested in the President by the "general grant" of executive power in the Vesting Clause. Pacificus No. 1 (June 29, 1793), LETTERS OF PACIFICUS AND HELVIDIUS 10 (1845). For its part, Congress applauded the President's decision.

In short, the practices of the Washington administration and First Congress confirm that Article II's Vesting Clause was originally understood to include a grant of residual foreign affairs power to the Executive.

II

The statutory provision at issue implicates the President's residual foreign affairs power. Section 214(d) instructs the Secretary of State, upon request of a citizen born in Jerusalem (or that citizen's legal guardian), to list that citizen's place of birth as Israel on his passport and consular report of birth abroad, even though it is the undisputed position of the United States that Jerusalem is not a part of Israel. The President argues that this provision violates his foreign affairs powers generally and his recognition power specifically. Zivotofsky rejoins that Congress passed § 214(d) pursuant to its enumerated powers and its action must therefore take precedence.

Neither has it quite right. The President is not constitutionally compelled to implement § 214(d) as it applies to passports because passport regulation falls squarely within his residual foreign affairs power and Zivotofsky has identified no source of congressional power to require the President to list Israel as the place of birth for a citizen born in Jerusalem on that citizen's passport. Section 214(d) can, however, be constitutionally applied to consular reports of birth abroad because those documents do not fall within the President's foreign affairs authority but do fall within Congress' enumerated powers over naturalization.

A

1

In the Anglo-American legal tradition, passports have consistently been issued and controlled by the body exercising executive power—in England, by the King; in the colonies, by the Continental Congress; and in the United States, by President Washington and every President since. . . .

After the ratification of the Constitution, President Washington immediately took responsibility for issuing passports. Although " '[p]ast practice does not, by itself, create power,' " "a governmental practice [that] has been open, widespread, and unchallenged since the early days of the Republic . . . should guide our interpretation of an ambiguous constitutional provision." *NLRB v. Noel Canning,* 134 S.Ct. 2550, 2594 (2014) (SCALIA, J., concurring in judgment). The history of the President's passport regulation in this country is one such practice. From the ratification until the end of the Civil War, the President issued passports without any authorization from Congress. . . . Congress acted in support of that authority by criminalizing the "violat[ion] [of] any safe-conduct or passport duly obtained and issued under the authority of the United States." . . . The President has continued to designate and prescribe the rules for passports ever since.

2

That the President has the power to regulate passports under his residual foreign affairs powers does not, however, end the matter, for Congress has repeatedly legislated on the subject of passports. These laws have always been narrow in scope. For example, Congress enacted laws prohibiting the issuance of passports to noncitizens, created an exception to that rule for "persons liable to military duty," and then eliminated that exception. It passed laws regulating the fees that the State Department should impose for issuance of the passports. It also enacted legislation addressing the duration for which passports may remain valid. And it passed laws imposing criminal penalties for false statements made when applying for passports, along with misuse of passports and counterfeiting or forgery of them.

As with any congressional action, however, such legislation is constitutionally permissible only insofar as it is promulgated pursuant to one of Congress' enumerated powers. I must therefore address whether Congress had constitutional authority to enact § 214(d)'s regulation of passports. . . . The Constitution contains no Passport Clause, nor does it explicitly vest Congress with "plenary authority over passports." Because our Government is one of enumerated powers, Congress has no power to act unless the Constitution authorizes it to do so. And the Constitution plainly sets forth the 'few and defined' powers that Congress may exercise. A "passport power" is not one of them.

Section 214(d)'s passport directive fares no better under those powers actually included in Article I. To start, it does not fall within the power "[t]o regulate Commerce with foreign Nations." "At the time the original Constitution was ratified, 'commerce' consisted of selling, buying, and bartering, as well as transporting for these purposes." *United States v. Lopez,* 514 U.S. 549, 585 (1995) (THOMAS, J., concurring). The listing of the place of birth of an applicant—whether born in Jerusalem or not—does not involve selling, buying, bartering, or transporting for those purposes. Cf. *United States v. Morrison,* 529 U.S. 598, 613 (2000).

True, a passport is frequently used by persons who may intend to engage in commerce abroad, but that use is insufficient to bring § 214(d)'s passport directive within the scope of this power. The specific conduct at issue here—the listing of the birthplace of a U.S. citizen born in Jerusalem on a passport by the President—is not a commercial activity. Any commercial activities subsequently undertaken by the bearer of a passport are yet further removed from that regulation.

The power "[t]o establish an uniform Rule of Naturalization" is similarly unavailing. At the founding, the word "naturalization" meant "[t]he act of investing aliens with the privileges of native subjects." 2 S. JOHNSON, A DICTIONARY OF THE ENGLISH LANGUAGE 1293 (4th ed. 1773). A passport has never been issued as part of the naturalization process. It is—and has always been—a "travel document," DEPT. OF STATE, 7 FOREIGN AFFAIRS MANUAL (or FAM) § 1311(b) (2013), issued for the same purpose it has always served: a request from one sovereign to another for the protection of the bearer.

For similar reasons, the Necessary and Proper Clause gives Congress no authority here. . . . The Clause is not a warrant to Congress to enact any law that bears some conceivable connection to the exercise of an enumerated power. Instead, there must be a necessary and proper fit between the 'means' (the federal law) and the 'end' (the enumerated power or powers) it is designed to serve. . . . At most, [a passport] bears a tertiary relationship to an activity Congress is permitted to regulate: It directs the President's formulation of a document, which, in turn, may be used to facilitate travel, which, in turn, may facilitate foreign commerce. And the distinctive history of the passport as a travel rather than citizenship document makes its connection to naturalization even more tenuous.

Nor can this aspect of § 214(d) be justified as an exercise of Congress' power to enact laws to carry into execution the President's residual foreign affairs powers. . . . To be "proper" . . . a law "must be consistent with principles of separation of powers, principles of federalism, and individual rights." Lawson & Granger, *The "Proper" Scope of Federal Power: A Jurisdictional Interpretation of the Sweeping Clause,* 43 Duke L.J. 267, 291, 297 (1993). . . .

First, a law could be "improper" if it purports to direct another branch's exercise of its power. See Calabresi & Prakash, *The President's*

Power to Execute the Laws, 104 Yale L.J. 541, 591 (1994) ("[T]he Clause . . . does [not] allow Congress to tell constitutionally empowered actors how they can implement their exclusive powers"). Second, a law could be "improper" if it takes one of those actions *and* the branch to which the power is allocated objects to the action. *See* Prakash & Ramsey 255–256.

[T]he application of § 214(d) to passports would be improper under either approach. . . . Section 214(d) directs the President to exercise his power to issue and regulate the content of passports in a particular way, and the President has objected to that direction. . . .

Justice SCALIA would locate Congress' power to enact the passport directive of § 214(d) in Congress' power under the Necessary and Proper Clause to bring into effect its enumerated power over naturalization. As an initial matter, he asserts that "[t]he naturalization power . . . enables Congress to furnish the people it makes citizens with papers verifying their citizenship," yet offers no support for this interpretation of a clause that, by its terms, grants Congress only the "Power . . . To establish an uniform Rule of Naturalization," U.S. Const., Art. I, § 8, cl. 4. He then concludes that, if Congress can grant such documents, "it may also require these [documents] to record his birthplace as 'Israel' " pursuant to its power under the Necessary and Proper Clause. But this theory does not account for the President's power to act in this area, nor does it confront difficult questions about the application of the Necessary and Proper Clause in the case of conflict among the branches.

Justice SCALIA disapproves of my "assertion of broad, unenumerated 'residual powers' in the President," but offers no response to my interpretation of the words "executive Power" in the Constitution. . . .

Justice SCALIA's dissent *does* at least answer how, in his view, the Constitution would resolve a conflict between the political branches, each acting pursuant to the powers granted them under the Constitution. He believes that congressional power should trump in any such conflict. I see nothing in the Constitution that clearly mandates that solution to a difficult separation-of-powers question . . . .

* * *

Because the President has residual foreign affairs authority to regulate passports and because there appears to be no congressional power that justifies § 214(d)'s application to passports, Zivotofsky's challenge to the Executive's designation of his place of birth on his passport must fail.

B

Although the consular report of birth abroad shares some features with a passport, it is historically associated with naturalization, not foreign affairs. In order to establish a "uniform Rule of Naturalization," Congress must be able to identify the categories of persons who are eligible for naturalization, along with the rules for that process. Congress thus has always regulated the acquisition of citizenship by being born abroad of American parents . . . in the exercise of the power conferred by the Constitution to establish a uniform rule of naturalization. It has determined that children born abroad to U.S. parents, subject to some exceptions, are natural-born citizens who do not need to go through the naturalization process. 8 U.S.C. §§ 1401(c), (d), (g).

The consular report of birth abroad is well suited to carrying into execution the power conferred on Congress in the Naturalization Clause. The report developed in response to Congress' requirement that children born abroad to U.S. citizens register with the consulate or lose their citizenship. And it continues to certify the acquisition of U.S. citizenship at birth by a person born abroad to a U.S. citizen. . . .

[A]lthough registration is no longer required to maintain birthright citizenship, the consular report of birth abroad remains the primary means by which children born abroad may obtain official acknowledgement of their citizenship. Once acknowledged as U.S. citizens, they need not pursue the naturalization process to obtain the rights and privileges of citizenship in this country. Regulation of the report is thus "appropriate" and "plainly adapted" to the exercise of the naturalization power.

By contrast, regulation of the report bears no relationship to the President's residual foreign affairs power. It has no historical pedigree uniquely associated with the President, contains no communication directed at a foreign power, and is primarily used for domestic purposes. To the extent that a citizen born abroad seeks a document to use as evidence of his citizenship abroad, he must obtain a passport.

Because regulation of the consular report of birth abroad is justified as an exercise of Congress' powers under the Naturalization and Necessary and Proper Clauses and does not fall within the President's foreign affairs powers, § 214(d)'s treatment of that document is constitutional.[8]

III

The majority does not perform this analysis, but instead relies on a variation of the recognition power. That power is among the foreign affairs powers vested in the President by Article II's Vesting Clause, as is confirmed by Article II's express assignment to the President of the duty of receiving foreign Ambassadors, Art. II, § 3. But I cannot join the majority's analysis because no act of recognition is implicated here. . . .

Perhaps recognizing that a formal recognition is not implicated here, the majority reasons that, if the Executive's exclusive recognition power "is to mean anything, it must mean that the President not only makes the initial, formal recognition determination but also that he may

---

[8] As the issue is not presented, I need not decide how a direct conflict between action pursuant to an enumerated power of Congress and action pursuant to the residual foreign affairs power of the President should be resolved.

maintain that determination in his and his agent's statements." By "alter[ing] the President's statements on matters of recognition or forc[ing] him to contradict them," the majority reasons, "Congress in effect would exercise the recognition power." This argument stretches the recognition power beyond all recognition. Listing a Jerusalem-born citizen's place of birth as "Israel" cannot amount to recognition because the United States already recognizes Israel as an international person. Rather than adopt a novel definition of the recognition power, the majority should have looked to other foreign affairs powers in the Constitution to resolve this dispute.

* * *

Adhering to the Constitution's allocation of powers leads me to reach a different conclusion in this case from my colleagues: Section 214(d) can be constitutionally applied to consular reports of birth abroad, but not passports. I therefore respectfully concur in the judgment in part and dissent in part.

■ **CHIEF JUSTICE ROBERTS, with whom JUSTICE ALITO joins, dissenting.**

Today's decision is a first: Never before has this Court accepted a President's direct defiance of an Act of Congress in the field of foreign affairs. We have instead stressed that the President's power reaches "its lowest ebb" when he contravenes the express will of Congress, "for what is at stake is the equilibrium established by our constitutional system." *Youngstown Sheet & Tube Co. v. Sawyer,* 343 U.S. 579, 637–638 (1952) (Jackson, J., concurring).

Justice SCALIA's principal dissent, which I join in full, refutes the majority's unprecedented holding in detail. I write separately to underscore the stark nature of the Court's error on a basic question of separation of powers.

The first principles in this area are firmly established. The Constitution allocates some foreign policy powers to the Executive, grants some to the Legislature, and enjoins the President to "take Care that the Laws be faithfully executed." Art. II, § 3. The Executive may disregard "the expressed or implied will of Congress" only if the Constitution grants him a power "at once so conclusive and preclusive" as to "disabl[e] the Congress from acting upon the subject." *Youngstown* (Jackson, J., concurring).

Assertions of exclusive and preclusive power leave the Executive "in the least favorable of possible constitutional postures," and such claims have been "scrutinized with caution" throughout this Court's history. *Id.,* For our first 225 years, no President prevailed when contradicting a statute in the field of foreign affairs. See *Medellín v. Texas,* 552 U.S. 491 (2008); *Hamdan v. Rumsfeld,* 548 U.S. 557 (2006); *Youngstown; Little v. Barreme,* 2 Cranch 170 (1804).

In this case, the President claims the exclusive and preclusive power to recognize foreign sovereigns. The Court devotes much of its analysis to accepting the Executive's contention. I have serious doubts about that position. The majority places great weight on the Reception Clause, which directs that the Executive "shall receive Ambassadors and other public Ministers." Art. II, § 3. But that provision, framed as an obligation rather than an authorization, appears alongside the *duties* imposed on the President by Article II, Section 3, not the *powers* granted to him by Article II, Section 2. Indeed, the People ratified the Constitution with Alexander Hamilton's assurance that executive reception of ambassadors "is more a matter of dignity than of authority" and "will be without consequence in the administration of the government." The Federalist No. 69, p. 420 (C. Rossiter ed. 1961). In short, at the time of the founding, "there was no reason to view the reception clause as a source of discretionary authority for the president." Adler, *The President's Recognition Power: Ministerial or Discretionary?* 25 Presidential Studies Q. 267, 269 (1995).

The majority's other asserted textual bases are even more tenuous. The President does have power to make treaties and appoint ambassadors. Art. II, § 2. But those authorities are *shared* with Congress, so they hardly support an inference that the recognition power is *exclusive*.

Precedent and history lend no more weight to the Court's position. The majority cites dicta suggesting an exclusive executive recognition power, but acknowledges contrary dicta suggesting that the power is shared. See, *e.g., United States v. Palmer,* 3 Wheat. 610, 643, 4 L.Ed. 471 (1818) ("the courts of the union must view [a] newly constituted government as it is viewed by *the legislative and executive departments* of the government of the United States" (emphasis added)). When the best you can muster is conflicting dicta, precedent can hardly be said to support your side.

As for history, the majority admits that it too points in both directions. Some Presidents have claimed an exclusive recognition power, but others have expressed uncertainty about whether such preclusive authority exists. Those in the skeptical camp include Andrew Jackson and Abraham Lincoln, leaders not generally known for their cramped conceptions of Presidential power. Congress has also asserted its authority over recognition determinations at numerous points in history. The majority therefore falls short of demonstrating that "Congress has accepted" the President's exclusive recognition power. In any event, we have held that congressional acquiescence is only "pertinent" when the President acts in the absence of express congressional authorization, not when he asserts power to disregard a statute, as the Executive does here. *Medellín,* 552 U.S., at 528.

In sum, although the President has authority over recognition, I am not convinced that the Constitution provides the "conclusive and preclusive" power required to justify defiance of an express legislative mandate. *Youngstown* (Jackson, J., concurring). As the leading scholar on this issue has concluded, the "text, original understanding, post-ratification history, and structure of the Constitution do not support the . . . expansive claim that this executive power is plenary." Reinstein, *Is the President's Recognition Power Exclusive?* 86 Temp. L. Rev. 1, 60 (2013).

But even if the President does have exclusive recognition power, he still cannot prevail in this case, because the statute at issue *does not implicate recognition.* The relevant provision, § 214(d), simply gives an American citizen born in Jerusalem the option to designate his place of birth as Israel "[f]or purposes of" passports and other documents. The State Department itself has explained that "identification"—not recognition—"is the principal reason that U.S. passports require 'place of birth.'" Congress has not disputed the Executive's assurances that § 214(d) does not alter the longstanding United States position on Jerusalem. And the annals of diplomatic history record no examples of official recognition accomplished via optional passport designation.

The majority acknowledges both that the "Executive's exclusive power extends no further than his formal recognition determination" and that § 214(d) does "not itself constitute a formal act of recognition." Taken together, these statements come close to a confession of error. The majority attempts to reconcile its position by reconceiving § 214(d) as a "mandate that the Executive contradict his prior recognition determination in an official document issued by the Secretary of State." But as just noted, neither Congress nor the Executive Branch regards § 214(d) as a recognition determination, so it is hard to see how the statute could contradict any such determination.

At most, the majority worries that there may be a *perceived* contradiction based on a *mistaken* understanding of the effect of § 214(d), insisting that some "observers interpreted § 214 as altering United States policy regarding Jerusalem." To afford controlling weight to such impressions, however, is essentially to subject a duly enacted statute to an international heckler's veto.

Moreover, expanding the President's purportedly exclusive recognition power to include authority to avoid potential misunderstandings of legislative enactments proves far too much. Congress could validly exercise its enumerated powers in countless ways that would create more severe perceived contradictions with Presidential recognition decisions than does § 214(d). If, for example, the President recognized a particular country in opposition to Congress's wishes, Congress could declare war or impose a trade embargo on that country. A neutral observer might well conclude that these legislative actions had, to put it mildly, created a perceived contradiction with the President's recognition decision. And yet each of them would undoubtedly be constitutional. So too would statements by nonlegislative actors that might be seen to contradict the President's recognition positions, such as the declaration in a political party platform that "Jerusalem is and will remain the capital of Israel." Landler, *Pushed by Obama, Democrats Alter Platform Over Jerusalem*, N.Y. Times, Sept. 6, 2012, p. A14.

Ultimately, the only power that could support the President's position is the one the majority purports to reject: the "exclusive authority to conduct diplomatic relations." The Government offers a single citation for this allegedly exclusive power: *United States v. Curtiss-Wright Export Corp.*, 299 U.S. 304, 319–320 (1936). But as the majority rightly acknowledges, *Curtiss-Wright* did not involve a claim that the Executive could contravene a statute; it held only that he could act pursuant to a legislative delegation.

The expansive language in *Curtiss-Wright* casting the President as the "sole organ" of the Nation in foreign affairs certainly has attraction for members of the Executive Branch. The Solicitor General invokes the case no fewer than ten times in his brief. But our precedents have never accepted such a sweeping understanding of executive power. See *Hamdan*, 548 U.S., at 591–592; *Dames & Moore*, 453 U.S., at 661–662; *Youngstown*, 343 U.S., at 587 (majority opinion); *id.*, at 635, n. 2 (Jackson, J., concurring); cf. *Little*, 2 Cranch, at 179 (Marshall, C.J.) ("I confess the first bias of my mind was very strong in favour of . . . the executive . . . [b]ut I have been convinced that I was mistaken.").

Just a few Terms ago, this Court rejected the President's argument that a broad foreign relations power allowed him to override a state court decision that contradicted U.S. international law obligations. *Medellín*, 552 U.S., at 523–532. If the President's so-called general foreign relations authority does not permit him to countermand a State's lawful action, it surely does not authorize him to disregard an express statutory directive enacted by Congress, which—unlike the States—has extensive foreign relations powers of its own. Unfortunately, despite its protest to the contrary, the majority today allows the Executive to do just that.

Resolving the status of Jerusalem may be vexing, but resolving this case is not. Whatever recognition power the President may have, exclusive or otherwise, is not implicated by § 214(d). It has not been necessary over the past 225 years to definitively resolve a dispute between Congress and the President over the recognition power. Perhaps we could have waited another 225 years. But instead the majority strains to reach the question based on the mere possibility that observers overseas might misperceive the significance of the birthplace designation at issue in this case. And in the process, the Court takes the perilous step—for the first time in our history—of allowing the President to defy an Act of Congress in the field of foreign affairs.

I respectfully dissent.

■ JUSTICE SCALIA, with whom THE CHIEF JUSTICE and JUSTICE ALITO join, dissenting.

Before this country declared independence, the law of England entrusted the King with the exclusive care of his kingdom's foreign affairs. The royal prerogative included the "sole power of sending ambassadors to foreign states, and receiving them at home," the sole authority to "make treaties, leagues, and alliances with foreign states and princes," "the sole prerogative of making war and peace," and the "sole power of raising and regulating fleets and armies." 1 W. Blackstone, Commentaries *253, *257, *262. The People of the United States had other ideas when they organized our Government. They considered a sound structure of balanced powers essential to the preservation of just government, and international relations formed no exception to that principle.

The People therefore adopted a Constitution that divides responsibility for the Nation's foreign concerns between the legislative and executive departments. The Constitution gave the President the "executive Power," authority to send and responsibility to receive ambassadors, power to make treaties, and command of the Army and Navy—though they qualified some of these powers by requiring consent of the Senate. Art. II, §§ 1–3. At the same time, they gave Congress powers over war, foreign commerce, naturalization, and more. Art. I, § 8. "Fully eleven of the powers that Article I, § 8 grants Congress deal in some way with foreign affairs." L. Tribe, American Constitutional Law, § 5–18, p. 965.

This case arises out of a dispute between the Executive and Legislative Branches about whether the United States should treat Jerusalem as a part of Israel. The Constitution contemplates that the political branches will make policy about the territorial claims of foreign nations the same way they make policy about other international matters: The President will exercise his powers on the basis of his views, Congress its powers on the basis of its views. That is just what has happened here.

I

. . . Before turning to Presidential power under Article II, I think it well to establish the statute's basis in congressional power under Article I. Congress's power to "establish an uniform Rule of Naturalization," Art. I, § 8, cl. 4, enables it to grant American citizenship to someone born abroad. The naturalization power also enables Congress to furnish the people it makes citizens with papers verifying their citizenship—say a consular report of birth abroad (which certifies citizenship of an American born outside the United States) or a passport (which certifies citizenship for purposes of international travel). As the Necessary and Proper Clause confirms, every congressional power "carries with it all those incidental powers which are necessary to its complete and effectual execution." *Cohens v. Virginia,* 6 Wheat. 264, 429 (1821). Even on a miserly understanding of Congress's incidental authority, Congress may make grants of citizenship "effectual" by providing for the issuance of certificates authenticating them.

One would think that if Congress may grant Zivotofsky a passport and a birth report, it may also require these papers to record his birthplace as "Israel." The birthplace specification promotes the document's citizenship-authenticating function by identifying the bearer, distinguishing people with similar names but different birthplaces from each other, helping authorities uncover identity fraud, and facilitating retrieval of the Government's citizenship records. To be sure, recording Zivotofsky's birthplace as "Jerusalem" rather than "Israel" would fulfill these objectives, but when faced with alternative ways to carry its powers into execution, Congress has the "discretion" to choose the one it deems "most beneficial to the people." *McCulloch v. Maryland,* 4 Wheat. 316, 421 (1819). It thus has the right to decide that recording birthplaces as "Israel" makes for better foreign policy. Or that regardless of international politics, a passport or birth report should respect its bearer's conscientious belief that Jerusalem belongs to Israel.

No doubt congressional discretion in executing legislative powers has its limits; Congress's chosen approach must be not only "necessary" to carrying its powers into execution, but also "proper." Congress thus may not transcend boundaries upon legislative authority stated or implied elsewhere in the Constitution. But as we shall see, § 214(d) does not transgress any such restriction.

II

The Court frames this case as a debate about recognition. Recognition is a sovereign's official acceptance of a status under international law. A sovereign might recognize a foreign entity as a state, a regime as the other state's government, a place as part of the other state's territory, rebel forces in the other state as a belligerent power, and so on. President Truman recognized Israel as a state in 1948, but Presidents have consistently declined to recognize Jerusalem as a part of Israel's (or any other state's) sovereign territory.

The Court holds that the Constitution makes the President alone responsible for recognition and that § 214(d) invades this exclusive power. I agree that the Constitution *empowers* the President to extend recognition on behalf of the United States, but I find it a much harder question whether it makes that power exclusive. The Court tells us that "the weight of historical evidence" supports exclusive executive authority over "the formal determination of recognition." But even with its attention confined to formal recognition, the Court is forced to admit that "history is not all on one side." To take a stark example, Congress legislated in 1934 to grant independence to the Philippines, which were then an American colony. In the course of doing so, Congress directed the President to "recognize the independence of the Philippine Islands as a separate and self-governing nation" and to "acknowledge the authority and control over the same of the government instituted by the people thereof." Constitutional? And if Congress may control recognition when exercising its power "to dispose of . . . the Territory or other Property belonging to the United States," Art. IV, § 3, cl. 2, why not when exercising other enumerated powers? Neither text nor history nor precedent yields a clear answer to these questions. Fortunately, I have no need to confront these matters today—nor does the Court—because § 214(d) plainly does not concern recognition.

Recognition is more than an announcement of a policy. Like the ratification of an international agreement or the termination of a treaty, it is a formal legal act with effects under international law. It signifies acceptance of an international status, and it makes a commitment to continued acceptance of that status and respect for any attendant rights. See, *e.g.*, Convention on the Rights and Duties of States, Art. 6, Dec. 26, 1933, 49 Stat. 3100, T.S. No. 881. "Its legal effect is to create an estoppel. . . . That act can consist of an express conferral of recognition, or one of a handful of acts that by international custom imply recognition—chiefly, entering into a bilateral treaty, and sending or receiving an ambassador.

To know all this is to realize at once that § 214(d) has nothing to do with recognition. Section 214(d) does not require the Secretary to make a formal declaration about Israel's sovereignty over Jerusalem. And nobody suggests that international custom infers acceptance of sovereignty from the birthplace designation on a passport or birth report, as it does from bilateral treaties or exchanges of ambassadors. Recognition would preclude the United States (as a matter of international law) from later contesting Israeli sovereignty over Jerusalem. But making a notation in a passport or birth report does not encumber the Republic with any international obligations. It leaves the Nation free (so far as international law is concerned) to change its mind in the future. That would be true even if the statute required *all* passports to list "Israel." But in fact it requires only those passports to list "Israel" for which the citizen (or his guardian) *requests* "Israel"; all the rest, under the Secretary's policy, list "Jerusalem." It is utterly impossible for this deference to private requests to constitute an act that unequivocally manifests an intention to grant recognition.

Section 214(d) performs a more prosaic function than extending recognition. Just as foreign countries care about what our Government has to say about their borders, so too American citizens often care about what our Government has to say about their identities. The State Department does not grant or deny recognition in order to accommodate these individuals, but it does make exceptions to its rules about how it records birthplaces. Although normal protocol requires specifying the bearer's country of birth in his passport, the State Department will, if the bearer protests, specify the city of birth instead—so that an Irish nationalist may have his birthplace recorded as "Belfast" rather than

"United Kingdom." And although normal protocol requires specifying the country with *present* sovereignty over the bearer's place of birth, a special exception allows a bearer born before 1948 in what was then Palestine to have his birthplace listed as "Palestine." Section 214(d) requires the State Department to make a further accommodation. Even though the Department normally refuses to specify a country that lacks recognized sovereignty over the bearer's birthplace, it must suspend that policy upon the request of an American citizen born in Jerusalem. Granting a request to specify "Israel" rather than "Jerusalem" does not recognize Israel's sovereignty over Jerusalem, just as granting a request to specify "Belfast" rather than "United Kingdom" does not derecognize the United Kingdom's sovereignty over Northern Ireland. . . .

Section 214(d), by the way, expressly directs the Secretary to "record the place of birth as Israel" "*[f]or purposes of* the registration of birth, certification of nationality, or issuance of a passport." (Emphasis added.) And the law bears the caption, "Record of Place of Birth as Israel *for Passport Purposes.*" (Emphasis added.) Finding recognition in this provision is rather like finding admission to the Union in a provision that treats American Samoa as a State for purposes of a federal highway safety program, 23 U.S.C. § 401.

III

The Court complains that § 214(d) requires the Secretary of State to issue official documents implying that Jerusalem is a part of Israel; that it appears in a section of the statute bearing the title "United States Policy with Respect to Jerusalem as the Capital of Israel"; and that foreign "observers interpreted [it] as altering United States policy regarding Jerusalem." But these features do not show that § 214(d) recognizes Israel's sovereignty over Jerusalem. They show only that the law displays symbolic support for Israel's territorial claim. That symbolism may have tremendous significance as a matter of international diplomacy, but it makes no difference as a matter of constitutional law.

Even if the Constitution gives the President sole power to extend recognition, it does not give him sole power to make all decisions relating to foreign disputes over sovereignty. To the contrary, a fair reading of Article I allows Congress to decide for itself how its laws should handle these controversies. Read naturally, power to "regulate Commerce with foreign Nations," § 8, cl. 3, includes power to regulate imports from Gibraltar as British goods or as Spanish goods. Read naturally, power to "regulate the Value . . . of foreign Coin," § 8, cl. 5, includes power to honor (or not) currency issued by Taiwan. And so on for the other enumerated powers. These are not airy hypotheticals. A trade statute from 1800, for example, provided that "the whole of the island of Hispaniola"—whose status was then in controversy—"shall for purposes of [the] act be considered as a dependency of the French Republic." § 7, 2 Stat. 10. In 1938, Congress allowed admission of the Vatican City's public records in federal courts, decades before the United States extended formal recognition. ch. 682, 52 Stat. 1163. The Taiwan Relations Act of 1979 grants Taiwan capacity to sue and be sued, even though the United States does not recognize it as a state. 22 U.S.C. § 3303(b)(7). Section 214(d) continues in the same tradition.

The Constitution likewise does not give the President exclusive power to determine which claims to statehood and territory "are legitimate in the eyes of the United States." Congress may express its own views about these matters by declaring war, restricting trade, denying foreign aid, and much else besides. To take just one example, in 1991, Congress responded to Iraq's invasion of Kuwait by enacting a resolution authorizing use of military force. No doubt the resolution reflected Congress's views about the legitimacy of Iraq's territorial claim. The preamble referred to Iraq's "illegal occupation" and stated that "the international community has demanded . . . that Kuwait's independence and legitimate government be restored." These statements are far more categorical than the caption "United States Policy with Respect to Jerusalem as the Capital of Israel." Does it follow that the authorization of the use of military force invaded the President's exclusive powers? Or that it would have done so had the President recognized Iraqi sovereignty over Kuwait?

History does not even support an exclusive Presidential power to make what the Court calls "formal statements" about "the legitimacy of a state or government and its territorial bounds." For a long time, the Houses of Congress have made formal statements announcing their own positions on these issues, again without provoking constitutional objections. A recent resolution expressed the House of Representatives' "strong support for the legitimate, democratically-elected Government of Lebanon" and condemned an "illegitimate" and "unjustifiable" insurrection by "the terrorist group Hizballah." An earlier enactment declared "the sense of the Congress that . . . Tibet . . . is an occupied country under the established principles of international law" and that "Tibet's true representatives are the Dalai Lama and the Tibetan Government in exile." After Texas won independence from Mexico, the Senate resolved that "the State of Texas having established and maintained an independent Government, . . . it is expedient and proper . . . that the independent political existence of the said State be acknowledged by the Government of the United States."

In the final analysis, the Constitution may well deny Congress power to recognize—the power to make an international commitment accepting a foreign entity as a state, a regime as its government, a place as a part of its territory, and so on. But whatever else § 214(d) may do, it plainly does not make (or require the President to make) a commitment accepting Israel's sovereignty over Jerusalem.

IV

. . . The Court . . . announces a rule that is blatantly gerrymandered to the facts of this case. It concludes that, in addition to the exclusive power to make the "formal recognition determination," the President holds an ancillary exclusive power "to control . . . formal statements by the Executive Branch acknowledging the legitimacy of a state or government and its territorial bounds." It follows, the Court explains, that Congress may not "requir[e] the President to contradict an earlier recognition determination in an official document issued by the Executive Branch." So requiring imports from Jerusalem to be taxed like goods from Israel is fine, but requiring Customs to issue an official invoice to that effect is not? Nonsense. . . .

At times, the Court seems concerned with the possibility of congressional interference with the President's ability to extend or withhold legal recognition. The Court concedes, as it must, that the notation required by § 214(d) "would not itself constitute a formal act of recognition." It still frets, however, that Congress *could* try to regulate the President's "statements" in a way that "override[s] the President's recognition determination." But "[t]he circumstance, that . . . [a] power may be abused, is no answer. All powers may be abused." 2 J. STORY, COMMENTARIES ON THE CONSTITUTION OF THE UNITED STATES § 921, p. 386 (1833). What matters is whether *this* law interferes with the President's ability to withhold recognition. It would be comical to claim that it does. The Court identifies no reason to believe that the United States—or indeed any other country—uses the place-of-birth field in passports and birth reports as a forum for performing the act of recognition. That is why nobody thinks the United States withdraws recognition from Canada when it accommodates a Quebec nationalist's request to have his birthplace recorded as "Montreal."

To the extent doubts linger about whether the United States recognizes Israel's sovereignty over Jerusalem, § 214(d) leaves the President free to dispel them by issuing a disclaimer of intent to recognize. A disclaimer always suffices to prevent an act from effecting recognition. Restatement (Second) of Foreign Relations Law of the United States § 104(1) (1962). Recall that an earlier law grants citizens born in Taiwan the right to have their birthplaces recorded as "Taiwan." The State Department has complied with the law, but states in its Foreign Affairs Manual: "The United States does not officially recognize Taiwan as a 'state' or 'country,' although passport issuing officers may enter 'Taiwan' as a place of birth." Nothing stops a similar disclaimer here.

At other times, the Court seems concerned with Congress's failure to give effect to a recognition decision that the President has already made. The Court protests, for instance, that § 214(d) "directly contradicts" the President's refusal to recognize Israel's sovereignty over Jerusalem. But even if the Constitution empowers the President alone to extend recognition, it nowhere obliges Congress to align its laws with the President's recognition decisions. Because the President and Congress are "perfectly co-ordinate by the terms of their common commission," The Federalist No. 49, p. 314 (C. Rossiter ed. 1961) (Madison), the President's use of the recognition power does not constrain Congress's use of its legislative powers.

Congress has legislated without regard to recognition for a long time and in a range of settings. . . . Federal law today prohibits murdering a foreign government's officials, 18 U.S.C. § 1116, counterfeiting a foreign government's bonds, § 478, and using American vessels to smuggle goods in violation of a foreign government's laws, § 546—all "irrespective of recognition by the United States," §§ 11, 1116. Just as Congress may legislate independently of recognition in all of those areas, so too may it legislate independently of recognition when regulating the recording of birthplaces.

The Court elsewhere objects that § 214(d) interferes with the autonomy and unity of the Executive Branch, setting the branch against itself. The Court suggests, for instance, that the law prevents the President from maintaining his neutrality about Jerusalem in "his and his agent's statements." That is of no constitutional significance. As just shown, Congress has power to legislate without regard to recognition, and where Congress has the power to legislate, the President has a duty to "take Care" that its legislation "be faithfully executed," Art. II, § 3. . . . The Executive's involvement in carrying out this law does not affect its constitutionality; the Executive carries out every law.

The Court's error could be made more apparent by applying its reasoning to the President's power "to make Treaties," Art. II, § 2, cl. 2. There is no question that Congress may, if it wishes, pass laws that openly flout treaties made by the President. *Head Money Cases,* 112 U.S. 580, 597 (1884). Would anyone have dreamt that the President may refuse to carry out such laws—or, to bring the point closer to home, refuse to execute federal courts' judgments under such laws—so that the Executive may "speak with one voice" about the country's international obligations? To ask is to answer. . . .

In the end, the Court's decision does not rest on text or history or precedent. It instead comes down to "functional considerations"— principally the Court's perception that the Nation "must speak with one voice" about the status of Jerusalem. The vices of this mode of analysis go beyond mere lack of footing in the Constitution. Functionalism of the sort the Court practices today will *systematically* favor the unitary President over the plural Congress in disputes involving foreign affairs. It is possible that this approach will make for more effective foreign policy, perhaps as effective as that of a monarchy. It is certain that, in the long run, it will erode the structure of separated powers that the People established for the protection of their liberty.

V

Justice THOMAS's concurrence deems § 214(d) constitutional to the extent it regulates birth reports, but unconstitutional to the extent it regulates passports. The concurrence finds no congressional power that would extend to the issuance or contents of passports. Including the power to regulate foreign commerce—even though passports facilitate the transportation of passengers, "a part of our commerce with foreign nations," *Henderson v. Mayor of New York,* 92 U.S. 259, 270 (1876). Including the power over naturalization—even though passports issued to citizens, like birth reports, "have the same force and effect as proof of United States citizenship as certificates of naturalization," 22 U.S.C. § 2705. Including the power to enforce the Fourteenth Amendment's guarantee that "[a]ll persons born or naturalized in the United States . . . are citizens of the United States"—even though a passport provides evidence of citizenship and so helps enforce this guarantee abroad. Including the power to exclude persons from the territory of the United States, see Art. I, § 9, cl. 1—even though passports are the principal means of identifying citizens entitled to entry. Including the powers under which Congress has restricted the ability of various people to leave the country (fugitives from justice, for example, see 18 U.S.C. § 1073)— even though passports are the principal means of controlling exit. Including the power to "make all needful Rules and Regulations respecting the Territory or other Property belonging to the United States," Art. IV, § 3, cl. 2—even though "[a] passport remains at all times the property of the United States," 7 FAM § 1317 (2013). The concurrence's stingy interpretation of the enumerated powers forgets that the Constitution does not "partake of the prolixity of a legal code," that "only its great outlines [are] marked, its important objects designated, and the minor ingredients which compose those objects [left to] be deduced from the nature of the objects themselves." *McCulloch,* 4 Wheat., at 407. It forgets, in other words, "that it is a *constitution* we are expounding." . . .

Returning to this side of the Atlantic, the concurrence says that passports have a "historical pedigree uniquely associated with the President." This statement overlooks the reality that, until Congress restricted the issuance of passports to the State Department in 1856, "passports were also issued by governors, mayors, and even . . . notaries public." Assn. of the Bar of the City of New York, Special Committee to Study Passport Procedures, Freedom to Travel 6 (1958). To be sure, early Presidents granted passports without express congressional authorization. But this point establishes Presidential authority over passports in the face of congressional *silence,* not Presidential authority in the face of congressional *opposition.* . . . Congress has made laws about eligibility to receive passports, the duration for which passports remain valid, and even the type of paper used to manufacture passports. . . . History and precedent thus refute any suggestion that the Constitution disables Congress from regulating the President's issuance and formulation of passports. . . .

That brings me, in analytic crescendo, to the concurrence's suggestion that *even if* Congress's enumerated powers otherwise encompass § 214(d), and *even if* the President's power to regulate the contents of passports is not exclusive, the law might *still* violate the Constitution, because it "conflict[s]" with the President's passport policy. It turns the Constitution upside-down to suggest that in areas of shared authority, it is the executive policy that preempts the law, rather than the other way around. Congress *may* make laws necessary and proper for carrying into execution the President's powers, Art. I, § 8, cl. 18, but the President *must* "take Care" that Congress's legislation "be faithfully executed," Art. II, § 3. And Acts of Congress made in pursuance of the Constitution are the "supreme Law of the Land"; acts of the President (apart from treaties) are not. Art. VI, cl. 2. That is why Chief Justice Marshall was right to think that a law prohibiting the seizure of foreign ships trumped a military order requiring it. *Little v. Barreme,* 2 Cranch 170, 178–179 (1804). It is why Justice Jackson was right to think that a President who "takes measures incompatible with the expressed or implied will of Congress" may "rely only upon his own constitutional powers *minus any constitutional powers of Congress over the matter.*" *Youngstown Sheet & Tube Co. v. Sawyer,* 343 U.S. 579, 637 (1952) (concurring opinion) (emphasis added). And it is why Justice THOMAS is wrong to think that even if § 214(d) operates in a field of shared authority the President might still prevail.

Whereas the Court's analysis threatens congressional power over foreign affairs with gradual erosion, the concurrence's approach shatters it in one stroke. The combination of (a) the concurrence's assertion of broad, unenumerated "residual powers" in the President; (b) its parsimonious interpretation of Congress's enumerated powers; and (c) its even more parsimonious interpretation of Congress's authority to enact laws "necessary and proper for carrying into Execution" the President's executive powers; produces (d) a presidency more reminiscent of George III than George Washington.

* * *

International disputes about statehood and territory are neither rare nor obscure. Leading foreign debates during the 19th century concerned how the United States should respond to revolutions in Latin America, Texas, Mexico, Hawaii, Cuba. During the 20th century, attitudes toward Communist governments in Russia and China became conspicuous subjects of agitation. Disagreements about Taiwan, Kashmir, and Crimea remain prominent today. A President empowered to decide all questions relating to these matters, immune from laws embodying congressional disagreement with his position, would have uncontrolled mastery of a vast share of the Nation's foreign affairs.

That is not the chief magistrate under which the American People agreed to live when they adopted the national charter. They believed that "[t]he accumulation of all powers, legislative, executive, and judiciary, in the same hands, . . . may justly be pronounced the very definition of tyranny." The Federalist No. 47, p. 301 (Madison). For this reason, they did not entrust either the President or Congress with sole power to adopt uncontradictable policies about *any* subject—foreign-sovereignty disputes included. They instead gave each political department its own powers, and with that the freedom to contradict the other's policies. Under the Constitution they approved, Congress may require Zivotofsky's passport and birth report to record his birthplace as Israel, even if that requirement clashes with the President's preference for neutrality about the status of Jerusalem.

I dissent.

NOTE ON *ZIVOTOFSKY* AND THE EXTENT OF PRESIDENTIAL POWER AT ITS "LOWEST EBB"

1.   *Zivotofsky* is the first case to uphold presidential action despite it having been forbidden by Congress. In *Youngstown*, Justice Jackson said that presidential power is at its "lowest ebb" in this situation. The *Zivotofsky* majority appears to accept Jackson's principle that the President may act in such a way only if he is exercising an *exclusive* power—that is, if Congress's prohibitory act is unconstitutional. Why was § 214(d) unconstitutional? Was it because, as Justice Thomas suggested, Congress lacked any enumerated power to regulate passports? Doesn't that require an awfully narrow reading of Congress's "necessary and proper" authority to implement, say, its power to regulate international commerce? Was the problem that § 214(d) was an act of diplomatic recognition, and that power is exclusively vested in the President? Or is it because Congress cannot exercise its enumerated power in such a way as to functionally interfere with the President's exercise of *his* power?

If you read the majority as adopting the third theory, what does that mean, exactly? Does the Court reject the notion, adopted by the dissenters and seemingly implicit in *Youngstown*, that in the event of overlapping powers Congress's action must prevail? Is rejecting that principle consistent with the Supremacy Clause? After all, purely executive actions are *not* identified as "supreme law" in Article VI. On the other hand, does Justice Scalia mean to say that a congressional enactment, as long as it is within Congress's enumerated powers, *always* trumps executive action? Given the breadth of Congress's powers, couldn't this swallow up the President's independent authority? Could Congress, in the exercise of its enumerated powers to regulate the armed forces, set specific limits on military operations during wartime (e.g., "Don't bomb North Vietnam")?

2.   What are the boundaries of functional "interference"? Does the majority's result depend on its suggestion that Congress was not exercising any affirmative power that clearly belonged to it? Suppose that, rather than directly regulating passports, Congress takes other measures that

undermine the foreign policy expressed in a Presidential recognition decision. What would happen, for instance, if the President chose to recognize Israel's claim to Jerusalem and to signify this by opening a consulate there; in that scenario, could Congress nonetheless cut off funds for such a project? Could it require U.S. trade officials to treat goods originating in Jerusalem as being from Israel, in the event that this made a difference under U.S. trade laws? Could it issue a declaration of war against the Palestinian authority for refusing to acknowledge Israeli sovereignty over the City? If you think some of these measures would be problematic, is the calculus a legal one based on the clarity with which the Constitution grants the relevant power to Congress? Or is it one of policy, based on the degree to which the particular action would undermine the Executive's preferred foreign policy?

Would it be fair to say that Justice Kennedy's opinion in *Zivotofsky* reflects the same sort of pragmatic sense of fair play that one sees in his opinions on affirmative action or gay rights? Is this sort of open-ended moderation equally appropriate in the separation of powers context?

3.   One central consideration in *Zivotofsky* is the notion that United States should "speak with one voice" in foreign affairs. How realistic is that, given our constitutional structure? As Professor Cleveland has pointed out, "it is clear that the Framers guaranteed, as a matter of constitutional design, that the United States would not 'speak with one voice' in foreign relations. The foreign affairs powers are carefully divided among the three branches of the national government, with Article I of the Constitution bestowing the bulk of the foreign affairs powers on Congress."[22] "This structural division," she explains, "has yielded a number of memorable conflicts. The Senate may refuse to consent to international agreements that the President has negotiated and signed, as in the infamous case of the Versailles Treaty. This tension has manifested itself more recently with the Senate's refusal to ratify many human rights treaties."[23] Likewise, "Congress may adopt legislation, with the President's signature, that is opposed by the Executive and that exposes the United States to international controversy. Recent examples include Congress' refusal to appropriate funds for United Nations dues and Congress' imposition of restrictions on U.S. foreign assistance for international family planning organizations."[24] A recent example is the Justice Against Sponsors of Terrorism Act,[25] which permitted families of persons killed in the September 11, 2001 terrorist attacks to sue Saudi Arabia for allegedly aiding those attacks. President Obama vetoed the bill on the ground that it would undermine U.S. relations with a valued ally, but Congress overrode that veto by overwhelming votes in both houses.

Should the Constitution be read to allow the President to formulate a coherent foreign policy to present to the world? Is that even possible in our

---

[22]   Sarah H. Cleveland, Crosby *and the 'One Voice' Myth in U.S. Foreign Relations*, 46 VILL. L. REV. 975, 984 (2001).

[23]   *Id.* at 985.

[24]   *Id.* at 987.

[25]   Pub. L. 114–222 (Sept. 28, 2016).

contemporary political circumstances? [26] Is the *Zivotofsky* majority suggesting that congressional action differing from public positions taken by the President in foreign affairs is unconstitutional? Could Congress, for example, pass a nonbinding resolution stating its belief that "Jerusalem is part of the sovereign state of Israel"?

4.   Although *Zivotofsky* is the first Supreme Court decision to strike down a congressional statute regulating the President's own constitutional powers, the argument is not new. A prominent example occurred in controversial memoranda issued by the George W. Bush Justice Department's Office of Legal Consel concerning the use of torture to interrogate suspected terrorists. Congress had prohibited the use of torture by statute,[27] but the memorandum argued that Executive branch officials could ignore the statute because it unconstitutionally infringed the President's powers as Commander in Chief.[28]

Does *Zivotofsky* support the memorandum's argument? Does it matter that Congress has its own textually-enumerated powers to "make Rules for the Government and Regulation of the land and naval Forces," Art. I, § 8, cl. 14, as well as to "define and punish . . . Offenses against the Law of Nations," Art. I, § 8, cl. 10?

5.   How big a victory is *Zivotofsky* for the President in areas other than passport control? Nearly all of the opinions cast cold water on the President's perennial citation to *Curtiss-Wright* for the proposition that he is the "sole organ" of the nation in foreign affairs, with the exclusive right to conduct foreign policy. Only one justice (Thomas) adopted the residual view of the Executive power described by Professors Prakash and Ramsey. And the justices that most observers would have expected to be most solidly pro-Executive power—Chief Justice Roberts and Justice Scalia—both came out resoundingly against the President in this case and seemed to commit themselves to a fairly narrow view of executive authority for future cases. Do you think *Zivotofsky* heralds an expansion or contraction of Executive power?

SECTION 14.3   THE POWER TO USE MILITARY FORCE

War powers are obviously among the most important topics in separation of powers law, yet they also remain among the most controversial and mysterious. One reason is that contemporary courts rarely hear war powers cases, so that we have few judicial opinions explicating the relevant constitutional principles. Modern courts tend to duck war powers controversies by finding them non-justiciable for

---

[26]   Achieving coherence may be difficult even within the Executive Branch. *See, e.g.*, Max Fisher, *The State Department's Dissent Memo on Syria: An Explanation*, N.Y. TIMES, June 22, 2016, available at https://www.nytimes.com/2016/06/23/world/middleeast/syria-assad-obama-diplomats-memo.html?_r=0 (describing a leaked memorandum from 51 State Department officials criticizing the Obama Administration's Syria policy).

[27]   *See* 18 U.S.C. § 2340A.

[28]   *See* Memorandum for Alberto R. Gonzales, Counsel to the President, from Jay S. Bybee, Assistant Attorney General, re *Standards of Conduct for Interrogations under 18 U.S.C. §§ 2340–2340A*, August 1, 2002, at pp. 36 39, available at http://news.findlaw.com/nytimes/docs/doj/bybee80102mem.pdf.

reasons of standing or ripeness or by invoking the political question doctrine. Many of the cases that we do have thus come from the nineteenth century, when federal courts occasionally resolved questions of war powers in connection with *prize* cases—that is, cases concerning the sale of enemy ships lawfully captured pursuant to the laws of war.

A lack of judicial opinions does not, of course, mean that the Constitution does not speak to the issue. Indeed, war powers disputes present an excellent example of constitutional interpretation by the executive and legislative branches of the government. The War Powers Resolution, for instance, represents an effort by Congress to codify its understanding of the allocation of war powers; President Nixon's veto message (the Resolution passed over that veto) presents what largely continues to be the Executive's response. Although the Resolution dates from the Vietnam era, the 2011 dispute over President Obama's use of military force in Libya attests to the continuing relevance of this debate.

This section concerns the use of military force *per se*, while the following one concerns additional powers incident to the use of force. Most prominently, the latter powers include power to detain persons interfering with the war effort or violating the laws of war. The Constitution divides the Congress's power to "declare war" from the President's powers as "commander in chief." For centuries, partisans of the respective branches have vehemently disagreed about the respective scope of these two powers. The first set of cases in this section plays out these issues in a series of nineteenth century controversies, but the excerpt that immediately follows from President Bush's 2002 statement on the National Security Strategy should help you assess how these old cases might bear on the modern security environment. The materials that comprise the remainder of this section assess Congress's efforts to regulate the President's use of military force.

Little v. Barreme
6 U.S. 170 (1804)

■ MARSHALL, CHIEF JUSTICE, now delivered the opinion of the Court.

The Flying-Fish, a Danish vessel having on board Danish and neutral property, was captured on the 2d of December 1799, on a voyage from Jeremie to St. Thomas, by the United States frigate Boston, commanded by Captain Little, and brought into the port of Boston, where she was libelled as an American vessel that had violated the non-intercourse law.

The judge before whom the cause was tried, directed a restoration of the vessel and cargo as neutral property, but refused to award damages for the capture and detention, because in his opinion, there was probable cause to suspect the vessel to be American.

On an appeal to the circuit court this sentence was reversed, because the Flying-Fish was on a voyage from, not to, a French port, and was therefore, had she even been an American vessel, not liable to capture on the high seas.

During the hostilities between the United States and France, an act for the suspension of all intercourse between the two nations was annually passed. That under which the Flying-Fish was condemned, declared every vessel, owned, hired or employed wholly or in part by an American, which should be employed in any traffic or commerce with or for any person resident within the jurisdiction or under the authority of the French republic, to be forfeited together with her cargo; the one half to accrue to the United States, and the other to any person or persons, citizens of the United States, who will inform and prosecute for the same.

The 5th section of this act authorises the president of the United States, to instruct the commanders of armed vessels, "to stop and examine any ship or vessel of the United States on the high sea, which there may be reason to suspect to be engaged in any traffic or commerce contrary to the true tenor of the act, and if upon examination it should appear that such ship or vessel is bound or sailing to any port or place within the territory of the French republic or her dependencies, it is rendered lawful to seize such vessel, and send her into the United States for adjudication."

It is by no means clear that the president of the United States whose high duty it is to "take care that the laws be faithfully executed," and who is commander in chief of the armies and navies of the United States, might not, without any special authority for that purpose, in the then existing state of things, have empowered the officers commanding the armed vessels of the United States, to seize and send into port for adjudication, American vessels which were forfeited by being engaged in this illicit commerce. But when it is observed that the general clause of the first section of the "act, which declares that such vessels may be seized, and may be prosecuted in any district or circuit court, which shall be holden within or for the district where the seizure shall be made," obviously contemplates a seizure within the United States; and that the 5th section gives a special authority to seize on the high seas, and limits that authority to the seizure of vessels bound or sailing to a French port, the legislature seem to have prescribed that the manner in which this law shall be carried into execution, was to exclude a seizure of any vessel not bound to a French port. Of consequence, however strong the circumstances might be, which induced captain Little to suspect the Flying-Fish to be an American vessel, they could not excuse the detention of her, since he would not have been authorised to detain her had she been really American.

It was so obvious, that if only vessels sailing to a French port could be seized on the high seas, that the law would be very often evaded, that this act of congress appears to have received a different construction from the executive of the United States; a construction much better calculated to give it effect.

A copy of this act was transmitted by the secretary of the navy, to the captains of the armed vessels, who were ordered to consider the 5th section as a part of their instructions. The same letter contained the following clause. "A proper discharge of the important duties enjoined on you, arising out of this act, will require the exercise of a sound and an impartial judgment. You are not only to do all that in you lies, to prevent all intercourse, whether direct or circuitous, between the ports of the United States, and those of France or her dependencies, where the vessels are apparently as well as really American, and protected by American papers only, but you are to be vigilant that vessels or cargoes really American, but covered by Danish or other foreign papers, and bound to or from French ports, do not escape you."

These orders given by the executive under the construction of the act of congress made by the department to which its execution was assigned, enjoin the seizure of American vessels sailing from a French port. Is the officer who obeys them liable for damages sustained by this misconstruction of the act, or will his orders excuse him? If his instructions afford him no protection, then the law must take its course, and he must pay such damages as are legally awarded against him; if they excuse an act not otherwise excusable, it would then be necessary to inquire whether this is a case in which the probable cause which existed to induce a suspicion that the vessel was American, would excuse the captor from damages when the vessel appeared in fact to be neutral.

I confess the first bias of my mind was very strong in favour of the opinion that though the instructions of the executive could not give a right, they might yet excuse from damages. I was much inclined to think that a distinction ought to be taken between acts of civil and those of military officers; and between proceedings within the body of the country and those on the high seas. That implicit obedience which military men usually pay to the orders of their superiors, which indeed is indispensably necessary to every military system, appeared to me strongly to imply the principle that those orders, if not to perform a prohibited act, ought to justify the person whose general duty it is to obey them, and who is placed by the laws of his country in a situation which in general requires that he should obey them. I was strongly inclined to think that where, in consequence of orders from the legitimate authority, a vessel is seized with pure intention, the claim of the injured party for damages would be against that government from which the orders proceeded, and would be a proper subject for negotiation. But I have been convinced that I was mistaken, and I have receded from this first opinion. I acquiesce in that of my brethren, which is, that the instructions cannot change the nature of the transaction, or legalize an act which without those instructions would have been a plain trespass.

It becomes therefore unnecessary to inquire whether the probable cause afforded by the conduct of the Flying-Fish to suspect her of being an American, would excuse Captain Little from damages for having seized and sent her into port, since had she actually been an American, the seizure would have been unlawful.

Captain Little then must be answerable in damages to the owner of this neutral vessel. . . . There appears then to be no error in the judgment of the circuit court, and it must be affirmed with costs.

The Prize Cases
67 U.S. 635 (1863)

These were cases in which the vessels named, together with their cargoes, were severally captured and brought in as prizes by public ships of the United States. The libels were filed by the proper District Attorneys, on behalf of the United States and on behalf of the officers and crews of the ships, by which the captures were respectively made. In each case the District Court pronounced a decree of condemnation, from which the claimants took an appeal.

■ **MR. JUSTICE GRIER.** There are certain propositions of law which must necessarily affect the ultimate decision of these cases. . . . They are, 1st. Had the President a right to institute a blockade of ports in possession of persons in armed rebellion against the Government, on the principles of international law, as known and acknowledged among civilized States? . . .

I.   Neutrals have a right to challenge the existence of a blockade de facto, and also the authority of the party exercising the right to institute it. They have a right to enter the ports of a friendly nation for the purposes of trade and commerce, but are bound to recognize the rights of a belligerent engaged in actual war, to use this mode of coercion, for the purpose of subduing the enemy.

That a blockade de facto actually existed, and was formally declared and notified by the President on the 27th and 30th of April, 1861, is an admitted fact in these cases.

That the President, as the Executive Chief of the Government and Commander-in-chief of the Army and Navy, was the proper person to make such notification, has not been, and cannot be disputed.

The right of prize and capture has its origin in the "jus belli," and is governed and adjudged under the law of nations. To legitimate the capture of a neutral vessel or property on the high seas, a war must exist de facto, and the neutral must have a knowledge or notice of the intention of one of the parties belligerent to use this mode of coercion against a port, city, or territory, in possession of the other. Let us enquire whether, at the time this blockade was instituted, a state of war existed which would justify a resort to these means of subduing the hostile force.

War has been well defined to be, "That state in which a nation prosecutes its right by force." The parties belligerent in a public war are independent nations. But it is not necessary to constitute war, that both parties should be acknowledged as independent nations or sovereign States. A war may exist where one of the belligerents claims sovereign rights as against the other.

Insurrection against a government may or may not culminate in an organized rebellion, but a civil war always begins by insurrection against the lawful authority of the Government. A civil war is never solemnly declared; it becomes such by its accidents—the number, power, and organization of the persons who originate and carry it on. When the party in rebellion occupy and hold in a hostile manner a certain portion of territory; have declared their independence; have cast off their allegiance; have organized armies; have commenced hostilities against their former sovereign, the world acknowledges them as belligerents, and the contest a war. They claim to be in arms to establish their liberty and independence, in order to become a sovereign State, while the sovereign party treats them as insurgents and rebels who owe allegiance, and who should be punished with death for their treason.

The laws of war, as established among nations, have their foundation in reason, and all tend to mitigate the cruelties and misery produced by the scourge of war. Hence the parties to a civil war usually concede to each other belligerent rights. They exchange prisoners, and adopt the other courtesies and rules common to public or national wars.

"A civil war," says Vattel, "breaks the bands of society and government, or at least suspends their force and effect; it produces in the nation two independent parties, who consider each other as enemies, and acknowledge no common judge. Those two parties, therefore, must necessarily be considered as constituting, at least for a time, two separate bodies, two distinct societies. Having no common superior to judge between them, they stand in precisely the same predicament as two nations who engage in a contest and have recourse to arms.

"This being the case, it is very evident that the common laws of war—those maxims of humanity, moderation, and honor—ought to be observed by both parties in every civil war. Should the sovereign conceive he has a right to hang up his prisoners as rebels, the opposite party will make reprisals, & c., & c.; the war will become cruel, horrible, and every day more destructive to the nation."

As a civil war is never publicly proclaimed, *eo nomine* against insurgents, its actual existence is a fact in our domestic history which the Court is bound to notice and to know. The true test of its existence, as found in the writing of the sages of the common law, may be thus summarily stated: "When the regular course of justice is interrupted by revolt, rebellion, or insurrection, so that the Courts of Justice cannot be kept open, civil war exists and hostilities may be prosecuted on the same footing as if those opposing the Government were foreign enemies invading the land."

By the Constitution, Congress alone has the power to declare a national or foreign war. It cannot declare war against a State, or any number of States, by virtue of any clause in the Constitution. The Constitution confers on the President the whole Executive power. He is bound to take care that the laws be faithfully executed. He is Commander-in-chief of the Army and Navy of the United States, and of the militia of the several States when called into the actual service of the United States. He has no power to initiate or declare a war either against a foreign nation or a domestic State. But by the Acts of Congress of February 28th, 1795, and 3d of March, 1807, he is authorized to call out the militia and use the military and naval forces of the United States in case of invasion by foreign nations, and to suppress insurrection against the government of a State or of the United States.

If a war be made by invasion of a foreign nation, the President is not only authorized but bound to resist force by force. He does not initiate the war, but is bound to accept the challenge without waiting for any special legislative authority. And whether the hostile party be a foreign invader, or States organized in rebellion, it is none the less a war, although the declaration of it be "unilateral." Lord Stowell observes, "It is not the less a war on that account, for war may exist without a declaration on either side. It is so laid down by the best writers on the law of nations. A declaration of war by one country only, is not a mere challenge to be accepted or refused at pleasure by the other."

The battles of Palo Alto and Resaca de la Palma had been fought before the passage of the Act of Congress of May 13th, 1846, which recognized "a state of war as existing by the act of the Republic of Mexico." This act not only provided for the future prosecution of the war, but was itself a vindication and ratification of the Act of the President in accepting the challenge without a previous formal declaration of war by Congress.

This greatest of civil wars was not gradually developed by popular commotion, tumultuous assemblies, or local unorganized insurrections. However long may have been its previous conception, it nevertheless sprung forth suddenly from the parent brain, a Minerva in the full panoply of war. The President was bound to meet it in the shape it presented itself, without waiting for Congress to baptize it with a name; and no name given to it by him or them could change the fact. . . .

As soon as the news of the attack on Fort Sumter, and the organization of a government by the seceding States, assuming to act as belligerents, could become known in Europe, to wit, on the 13th of May, 1861, the Queen of England issued her proclamation of neutrality, "recognizing hostilities as existing between the Government of the United States of America and certain States styling themselves the Confederate States of America." This was immediately followed by similar declarations or silent acquiescence by other nations. After such an official recognition by the sovereign, a citizen of a foreign State is estopped to deny the existence of a war with all its consequences as regards neutrals. . . .

The law of nations is also called the law of nature; it is founded on the common consent as well as the common sense of the world. It contains no such anomalous doctrine as that which this Court are now for the first time desired to pronounce, to wit: That insurgents who have risen in rebellion against their sovereign, expelled her Courts, established a revolutionary government, organized armies, and commenced hostilities, are not enemies because they are traitors; and a war levied on the Government by traitors, in order to dismember and destroy it, is not a war because it is an "insurrection."

Whether the President in fulfilling his duties, as Commander in-chief, in suppressing an insurrection, has met with such armed hostile resistance, and a civil war of such alarming proportions as will compel him to accord to them the character of belligerents, is a question to be decided by him, and this Court must be governed by the decisions and acts of the political department of the Government to which this power was entrusted. "He must determine what degree of force the crisis demands." The proclamation of blockade is itself official and conclusive evidence to the Court that a state of war existed which demanded and authorized a recourse to such a measure. . . .

If it were necessary to the technical existence of a war, that it should have a legislative sanction, we find it in almost every act passed at the extraordinary session of the Legislature of 1861, which was wholly employed in enacting laws to enable the Government to prosecute the war with vigor and efficiency. And finally, in 1861, we find Congress "ex major cautela" and in anticipation of such astute objections, passing an act "approving, legalizing, and making valid all the acts, proclamations, and orders of the President, & c., as if they had been issued and done under the previous express authority and direction of the Congress of the United States."

Without admitting that such an act was necessary under the circumstances, it is plain that if the President had in any manner assumed powers which it was necessary should have the authority or sanction of Congress, that . . . this ratification has operated to perfectly cure the defect. . . .

The objection made to this act of ratification, that it is ex post facto, and therefore unconstitutional and void, might possibly have some weight on the trial of an indictment in a criminal Court. But precedents from that source cannot be received as authoritative in a tribunal administering public and international law.

On this first question therefore we are of the opinion that the President had a right, jure belli, to institute a blockade of ports in possession of the States in rebellion, which neutrals are bound to regard. . . .

■ **MR. JUSTICE NELSON, dissenting.**

. . . Another objection taken to the seizure of this vessel and cargo is, that there was no existing war between the United States and the States in insurrection within the meaning of the law of nations, which drew after it the consequences of a public or civil war. A contest by force between independent sovereign States is called a public war; and, when duly commenced by proclamation or otherwise, it entitles both of the belligerent parties to all the rights of war against each other, and as respects neutral nations. Chancellor Kent observes, "Though a solemn declaration, or previous notice to the enemy, be now laid aside, it is essential that some formal public act, proceeding directly from the competent source, should announce to the people at home their new relations and duties growing out of a state of war, and which should equally apprize neutral nations of the fact, to enable them to conform their conduct to the rights belonging to the new state of things." "Such an official act operates from its date to legalize all hostile acts, in like manner as a treaty of peace operates from its date to annul them." He further observes, "as war cannot lawfully be commenced on the part of the United States without an act of Congress, such act is, of course, a formal notice to all the world, and equivalent to the most solemn declaration."

The legal consequences resulting from a state of war between two countries at this day are well understood, and will be found described in every approved work on the subject of international law. The people of the two countries become immediately the enemies of each other—all intercourse commercial or otherwise between then unlawful—all contracts existing at the commencement of the war suspended, and all made during its existence utterly void. The insurance of enemies' property, the drawing of bills of exchange or purchase on the enemies' country, the remission of bills or money to it are illegal and void. Existing partnerships between citizens or subjects of the two countries are dissolved, and, in fine, interdiction of trade and intercourse direct or indirect is absolute and complete by the mere force and effect of war itself. All the property of the people of the two countries on land or sea are subject to capture and confiscation by the adverse party as enemies' property, with certain qualifications as it respects property on land, all treaties between the belligerent parties are annulled. The ports of the respective countries may be blockaded, and letters of marque and reprisal granted as rights of war, and the law of prizes as defined by the law of nations comes into full and complete operation, resulting from maritime captures, jur belli. War also effects a change in the mutual relations of all States or countries, not directly, as in the case of the belligerents, but immediately and indirectly, though they take no part in the contest, but remain neutral. . . .

By our Constitution this power is lodged in Congress. Congress shall have power "to declare war, grant letters of marque and reprisal, and make rules concerning captures on land and water." . . .

In the case of a rebellion . . . there is no doubt, if in its progress and enlargement the government thus sought to be overthrown sees fit, it may by the competent power recognize, or declare the existence of a state of civil war, which will draw after it all the consequences and rights of war between the contending parties as in the case of a public war. . . . It is not to be denied, therefor, that if a civil war existed between that portion of the people in organized insurrection to overthrow this Government at the time this vessel and cargo were seized, and if she was guilty of a violation of the blockade, she would be lawful prize of war. But before this insurrection against the established Government can be dealt with on the footing of a civil war . . . it must be recognized or declared by the war-making power of the Government. No power short of this can change the legal status of the Government or the relations of its citizens from that of peace to a state of war, or bring into existence all those duties and obligations to neutral third parties growing out of a state of war. . . . There is no difference in this respect between a civil or a public war. . . .

An idea seemed to be entertained that all that was necessary to constitute a war was organized hostility in the district of country in a state of rebellion—that conflicts on land and on sea—the taking of towns and capture of fleets—in fine, the magnitude and dimensions of the resistance against the Government—constituted war with all the belligerent rights belonging to civil war. . . .

Now, in one sense, no doubt this is war, and may be a war of the most extensive and threatening dimensions and effects, but it is a statement simply of its existence in a material sense, and has no relevancy or weight when the question is what constitutes war in a legal sense, in the sense of the law of nations, and of the Constitution of the United States? . . . But we are asked, what would become of the peace and integrity of the Union in case of an insurrection at home or invasion from abroad if this power could not be exercised by the President in the recess of Congress, and until that body could be assembled? . . .

[A]mple provision has been made under the Constitution and laws against any sudden and unexpected disturbance of the public peace from insurrection at home or invasion from abroad. The whole military and naval power of the country is put under the control of the President to meet the emergency. He may call out a force in proportion to its necessities, one regiment or fifty, one ship-of-war or any number at his discretion. . . . But whatever its numbers, whether great or small . . . the nature of the power is the same. It is the exercise of a power under the municipal laws of the country and not under the law of nations; and, as we see, furnishes the most ample means of repelling attacks from abroad or suppressing disturbances at home until the assembling of Congress, who can, if it be deemed necessary, bring into operation the war power, and thus change the nature and character of the contest. Then, instead of being carried on under the municipal law of 1795, it would be under the law of nations, and the Acts of Congress as war measures with all the rights of war. . . .

The Acts of 1795 and 1807 did not, and could not under the Constitution, confer on the President the power of declaring war against a State of this Union, or of deciding that war existed, and upon that ground authorize the capture and confiscation of the property of every citizen of the State whenever it was found on the waters. . . . This great power over the business and property of the citizen is reserved to the legislative department by the express words of the Constitution. It cannot be delegated or surrendered to the Executive. Congress alone can determine whether war exists or should be declared; and until they have acted, no citizen of the State can be punished in his person or property, unless he had committed some offence against a law of Congress passed before the act was committed, which made it a crime, and defined the punishment. The penalty of confiscation for the acts of others with which he had no concern cannot lawfully be inflicted. . . .

Congress assembled on the call for an extra session the 4th of July, 1861, and among the first acts passed was one in which the President was authorized by proclamation to interdict all trade and intercourse between all the inhabitants of States in insurrection and the rest of the United States, subjecting vessel and cargo to capture and condemnation as prize. . . . This Act of Congress, we think, recognized a state of civil war between the Government and the Confederate States, and made it territorial. . . .

Congress on the 6th of August, 1862, passed an Act confirming all acts, proclamations, and orders of the President, after the 4th of March, 1861, respecting the army and navy, and legalizing them, so far as was competent for that body, and it has been suggested, but scarcely argued, that this legislation on the subject had the effect to bring into existence an ex post facto civil war with all the rights of capture and confiscation, jure belli, from the date referred to. An ex post facto law is defined, when, after an action, indifferent in itself, or lawful, is committed, the Legislature then, for the first time, declares it to have been a crime and inflicts punishment upon the person who committed it. . . .

Here the captures were without any Constitutional authority, and void; and, on principle, no subsequent ratification could make them valid.

Upon the whole . . . I am compelled to the conclusion that no civil war existed between this Government and the States in insurrection till recognized by the Act of Congress 13th of July, 1861; that the President does not possess the power under the Constitution to declare war or recognize its existence within the meaning of the law of nations, which carries with it belligerent rights, and thus change the country and all its citizens from a state of peace to a state of war; that this power belongs exclusively to the Congress of the United States, and, consequently, that the President had no power to set on foot a blockade under the law of nations, and that the capture of the vessel and cargo in this case, and in all cases before us in which the capture occurred before the 13th of July, 1861, for breach of blockade, or as enemies' property, are illegal and void, and that the decrees of condemnation should be reversed and the vessel and cargo restored.

■ MR. CHIEF JUSTICE TANEY, MR. JUSTICE CATRON and MR. JUSTICE CLIFFORD, concurred in the dissenting opinion of MR. JUSTICE NELSON.

Durand v. Hollins
8 F. Cas. 111 (C.C.S.D.N.Y. 1860)

[In 1854, Captain George Hollins, of the U.S.S. *Cyane*, ordered the bombardment of Greytown, Nicaragua, in response to the theft and destruction of American property and an attack on an American minister. Durand, an American citizen living in Greytown, sued Hollins for destruction of his property caused by the bombardment. In defense, Hollins argued that his actions had been authorized by the Secretary of the Navy.]

■ NELSON, CIRCUIT JUSTICE.

The principal ground of objection to the pleas, as a defence of the action, is, that neither the president nor the secretary of the navy had authority to give the orders relied on to the defendant, and, hence, that they afford no ground of justification.

The executive power, under the constitution, is vested in the president of the United States (article 2, § 1). He is commander-in-chief of the army and navy, (*Id.* § 2), and has imposed upon him the duty to "take care that the laws be faithfully executed" (*Id.* § 3). . . .

As the executive head of the nation, the president is made the only legitimate organ of the general government, to open and carry on correspondence or negotiations with foreign nations, in matters concerning the interests of the country or of its citizens. It is to him, also, the citizens abroad must look for protection of person and of property, and for the faithful execution of the laws existing and intended for their protection. For this purpose, the whole executive power of the country is placed in his hands, under the constitution, and the laws passed in pursuance thereof; and different departments of government have been organized, through which this power may be most conveniently executed, whether by negotiation or by force—a department of state and a department of the navy.

Now, as it respects the interposition of the executive abroad, for the protection of the lives or property of the citizen, the duty must, of necessity, rest in the discretion of the president. Acts of lawless violence, or of threatened violence to the citizen or his property, cannot be anticipated and provided for; and the protection, to be effectual or of any avail, may, not unfrequently, require the most prompt and decided action. Under our system of government, the citizen abroad is as much entitled to protection as the citizen at home. The great object and duty of government is the protection of the lives, liberty, and property of the people composing it, whether abroad or at home; and any government failing in the accomplishment of the object, or the performance of the duty, is not worth preserving.

I have said, that the interposition of the president abroad, for the protection of the citizen, must necessarily rest in his discretion; and it is quite clear that, in all cases where a public act or order rests in executive discretion neither he nor his authorized agent is personally civilly responsible for the consequences. As was observed by Chief Justice Marshall, in *Marbury v. Madison*: "By the constitution of the United States, the president is invested with certain important political powers, in the exercise of which he is to use his own discretion, and is accountable only to his country in his political character, and to his own conscience. To aid him in the performance of these duties, he is authorized to appoint certain officers, who act by his authority, and in conformity with his orders. In such cases, their acts are his acts, and, whatever opinion may be entertained of the manner in which executive discretion may be used, still there exists, and can exist, no power to control that discretion. The subjects are political. They respect the nation, not individual rights, and, being intrusted to the executive, the decision of the executive is conclusive." This is a sound principle, and governs the present case. The question whether it was the duty of the president to interpose for the protection of the citizens at Greytown against an irresponsible and marauding community that had established itself there, was a public political question, in which the government, as well as the citizens whose interests were involved, was concerned, and which belonged to the executive to determine; and his decision is final and conclusive, and justified the defendant in the execution of his orders given through the secretary of the navy.

Judgment for defendant.

National Security Council, The National Security Strategy of the United States of America (September 2002)

The gravest danger to freedom lies at the crossroads of radicalism and technology. When the spread of chemical and biological and nuclear weapons, along with ballistic missile technology—when that occurs, even weak states and small groups could attain a catastrophic power to strike great nations. Our enemies have declared this very intention, and have been caught seeking these terrible weapons. They want the capability to blackmail us, or to harm us, or to harm our friends—and we will oppose them with all our power.

President Bush, West Point, New York, June 1, 2002

The nature of the Cold War threat required the United States—with our allies and friends—to emphasize deterrence of the enemy's use of force, producing a grim strategy of mutual assured destruction. With the collapse of the Soviet Union and the end of the Cold War, our security environment has undergone profound transformation.

Having moved from confrontation to cooperation as the hallmark of our relationship with Russia, the dividends are evident: an end to the balance of terror that divided us; an historic reduction in the nuclear arsenals on both sides; and cooperation in areas such as counterterrorism and missile defense that until recently were inconceivable.

But new deadly challenges have emerged from rogue states and terrorists. None of these contemporary threats rival the sheer destructive power that was arrayed against us by the Soviet Union. However, the nature and motivations of these new adversaries, their determination to obtain destructive powers hitherto available only to the world's strongest states, and the greater likelihood that they will use weapons of mass destruction against us, make today's security environment more complex and dangerous.

In the 1990s we witnessed the emergence of a small number of rogue states that, while different in important ways, share a number of attributes. These states:

- brutalize their own people and squander their national resources for the personal gain of the rulers;

- display no regard for international law, threaten their neighbors, and callously violate international treaties to which they are party;

- are determined to acquire weapons of mass destruction, along with other advanced military technology, to be used as threats or offensively to achieve the aggressive designs of these regimes;

- sponsor terrorism around the globe; and

- reject basic human values and hate the United States and everything for which it stands.

At the time of the Gulf War, we acquired irrefutable proof that Iraq's designs were not limited to the chemical weapons it had used against Iran and its own people, but also extended to the acquisition of nuclear weapons and biological agents. In the past decade North Korea has become the world's principal purveyor of ballistic missiles, and has tested increasingly capable missiles while developing its own WMD arsenal. Other rogue regimes seek nuclear, biological, and chemical weapons as well. These states' pursuit of, and global trade in, such weapons has become a looming threat to all nations.

We must be prepared to stop rogue states and their terrorist clients before they are able to threaten or use weapons of mass destruction against the United States and our allies and friends. Our response must take full advantage of strengthened alliances, the establishment of new partnerships with former adversaries, innovation in the use of military forces, modern technologies, including the development of an effective missile defense system, and increased emphasis on intelligence collection and analysis.

Our comprehensive strategy to combat WMD includes:

- *Proactive counterproliferation efforts.* We must deter and defend against the threat before it is unleashed. We must ensure that key capabilities—detection, active and passive defenses, and counterforce capabilities—are integrated into our defense transformation and our homeland security systems. . . .

- *Strengthened nonproliferation efforts to prevent rogue states and terrorists from acquiring the materials, technologies, and expertise necessary for weapons of mass destruction.* We will enhance diplomacy, arms control, multilateral export controls, and threat reduction assistance that impede states and terrorists seeking WMD, and when necessary, interdict enabling technologies and materials. . . .

- *Effective consequence management to respond to the effects of WMD use, whether by terrorists or hostile states.* Minimizing the effects of WMD use against our people will help deter those who possess such weapons and dissuade those who seek to acquire them by persuading enemies that they cannot attain their desired ends. The United States must also be prepared to respond to the effects of WMD use against our forces abroad, and to help friends and allies if they are attacked.

It has taken almost a decade for us to comprehend the true nature of this new threat. Given the goals of rogue states and terrorists, the United States can no longer solely rely on a reactive posture as we have in the past. The inability to deter a potential attacker, the immediacy of today's threats, and the magnitude of potential harm that could be caused by our adversaries' choice of weapons, do not permit that option. We cannot let our enemies strike first.

In the Cold War, especially following the Cuban missile crisis, we faced a generally status quo, risk-averse adversary. Deterrence was an effective defense. But deterrence based only upon the threat of retaliation is less likely to work against leaders of rogue states more willing to take risks, gambling with the lives of their people, and the wealth of their nations.

- In the Cold War, weapons of mass destruction were considered weapons of last resort whose use risked the destruction of those who used them. Today, our enemies see weapons of mass destruction as weapons of choice. For rogue states these weapons are tools of intimidation and military aggression against their neighbors. These weapons may also allow these states to attempt to blackmail the United States and our allies to prevent us from deterring or repelling the aggressive behavior of rogue states. Such states also see these weapons as their best means of overcoming the conventional superiority of the United States.

- Traditional concepts of deterrence will not work against a terrorist enemy whose avowed tactics are wanton destruction and the targeting of innocents; whose so-called soldiers seek martyrdom in death and whose most potent protection is statelessness. The overlap between states that sponsor terror and those that pursue WMD compels us to action.

For centuries, international law recognized that nations need not suffer an attack before they can lawfully take action to defend themselves against forces that present an imminent danger of attack. Legal scholars and international jurists often conditioned the legitimacy of preemption on the existence of an imminent threat—most often a visible mobilization of armies, navies, and air forces preparing to attack.

We must adapt the concept of imminent threat to the capabilities and objectives of today's adversaries. Rogue states and terrorists do not seek to attack us using conventional means. They know such attacks would fail. Instead, they rely on acts of terror and, potentially, the use of weapons of mass destruction—weapons that can be easily concealed, delivered covertly, and used without warning.

The targets of these attacks are our military forces and our civilian population, in direct violation of one of the principal norms of the law of warfare. As was demonstrated by the losses on September 11, 2001, mass civilian casualties is the specific objective of terrorists and these losses would be exponentially more severe if terrorists acquired and used weapons of mass destruction.

The United States has long maintained the option of preemptive actions to counter a sufficient threat to our national security. The greater the threat, the greater is the risk of inaction—and the more compelling the case for taking anticipatory action to defend ourselves, even if uncertainty remains as to the time and place of the enemy's attack. To forestall or prevent such hostile acts by our adversaries, the United States will, if necessary, act preemptively.

The United States will not use force in all cases to preempt emerging threats, nor should nations use preemption as a pretext for aggression. Yet in an age where the enemies of civilization openly and actively seek the world's most destructive technologies, the United States cannot remain idle while dangers gather. We will always proceed deliberately, weighing the consequences of our actions. To support preemptive options, we will:

- build better, more integrated intelligence capabilities to provide timely, accurate information on threats, wherever they may emerge;

- coordinate closely with allies to form a common assessment of the most dangerous threats; and

- continue to transform our military forces to ensure our ability to conduct rapid and precise operations to achieve decisive results.

The purpose of our actions will always be to eliminate a specific threat to the United States or our allies and friends. The reasons for our actions will be clear, the force measured, and the cause just.

Michael D. Ramsey, Textualism and War Powers[*]

The contemporary debate over the constitutional allocation of war powers offers an unsatisfactory choice between ignoring the Constitution's text and ignoring what the Framers said about it. Those who would give comprehensive war powers to Congress point to an array of quotations from leading Framers and other political leaders stating or heavily implying that the decision to go to war lies with the legislative body. Those who favor presidential war powers reply that Congress has the constitutional power "to declare War," not the power to authorize the use of military force; and since few in the eighteenth century would have thought that a formal declaration of war was required before using military force, Congress's power cannot be so broad.[4] Congressional advocates have no persuasive answer to the textual point, save to say that the text cannot be taken literally in light of the Framers' later statements. Presidential advocates have no persuasive response to the

---

[*]   Excerpted from 69 U. CHI. L. REV. 1543, 1543–47 (2002).

[4]   In claiming a presidential power to use military force based on the text of the Constitution, presidential advocates rely on Article II, Section 1, which states that "the executive Power" of the United States is vested in the President. As recent scholarship has shown, in the eighteenth century the ordinary understanding of the phrase "executive power" included substantial power over foreign affairs, including war powers. *See* Saikrishna B. Prakash and Michael D. Ramsey, *The Executive Power over Foreign Affairs*, 111 YALE L. J. 231, 265–72 (2001) (referring to the ideas of Locke, Montesquieu, Blackstone, and others). Thus, unless the Constitution specifically allocates it elsewhere, the power to begin military hostilities would seem to lie with the President.

Framers' post-drafting commentary, save to say that the Framers' commentary cannot be taken literally in light of the plain text.

As we confront complex questions about the constitutional allocation of war powers in modern conflicts, this impasse at the level of first principles presents a serious difficulty. If we cannot establish how the Constitution originally made the basic allocation of war powers, there seems to be little hope of consensus regarding its application to complicated modern events.[5] The roles of the President and Congress in recent conflicts such as the Gulf War, Bosnia, and Kosovo, and in the ongoing response to the recent terrorist attacks, have been much debated. But it is hard to see much progress being made in this regard, if both the case for the President and the case for Congress are subject to such fundamental objections.

This Article describes a textual allocation of war powers that avoids the difficulties of both sides in the current debate. The problem, I argue, is that neither side has paid sufficient attention to the eighteenth-century meaning of declaring war. At present, essentially everyone in the war powers debate assumes that this phrase means issuing a formal declaration of war, in keeping with its most common modern meaning. Thus presidential advocates argue that the phrase should be given its literal meaning in Article I, Section 8, so that Congress's power does not extend to "undeclared" conflicts; congressional advocates counter that we must move beyond the literal meaning of the text to give effect to a broader "Framers' intent," since the Framers, despite what they wrote, could not have meant to limit Congress's role to issuance or nonissuance of a formal declaration.

I argue . . . that the eighteenth-century meaning of declaring war was not limited to formal declarations, as has commonly been supposed. Instead, "declaring war" meant initiating a state of war by a public act, and it was understood that this could be done either by a formal declaration or by commencing armed hostilities. In the words of Emmerich de Vattel, perhaps the leading international law scholar of the time, "when one nation takes up arms against another, she from that moment declares herself an enemy to all the individuals of the latter." Or as John Locke earlier wrote, war may be declared "by Word or Action."

---

[5] To raise a few modern problems: If the United States is attacked, as it was on September 11, 2001, may the President respond not only against the attackers, but against their allies and supporters? May the President respond against state supporters of terrorism more generally, even those not directly complicit in the September 11 attacks? What if a U.S. ally is attacked, or U.S. strategic interests are threatened by aggression, as occurred prior to the Gulf War? What if the U.S. military campaign is of limited scope to achieve a narrow objective, as was the air campaign during the Kosovo crisis; or what of a U.S. peacekeeping deployment into an area fraught with hostilities but not directly opposed by any hostile power, as in Bosnia? And if congressional involvement is required in any of these actions, must it actually take the form of a formal declaration of war, or may something less definitive suffice? Without an agreed textual starting point, we cannot begin to answer these questions. Even scholars who generally agree that Congress has most of the war-initiation powers are divided upon the proper outcome in specific cases.

Applying this definition reveals a textual division of war powers between the President and Congress. Because war can be declared by commencing hostilities as well as by formal announcement, it should be clear from the text that Congress has power over both sorts of declarations, and the President does not. The President's possession of "the executive Power" does not alter this conclusion, even if the executive power is read, in keeping with modern textualist scholarship, to include foreign affairs power. Though previously included within the traditional executive power of eighteenth-century political thought, the power to declare war by hostilities or formal announcement is assigned to Congress by the Constitution's text, and thereby denied to the President.

This conclusion is not, however, a complete vindication of Congress, for eighteenth-century usage suggests two substantial presidential war powers. First, a nation under direct attack did not need to "declare" war. Because self-defense in the face of hostile attack was considered an absolute right that a nation would always exercise, one did not need to look for a public manifestation of an intent to do so—rather, it was assumed. Thus "declaring" war by action indicated an initiation of armed hostilities in a time of peace, not a response to an attack where the peace had already been breached by the other side. If this is correct, Congress's declare-war power does not limit the President's power to respond to an attack, which remains part of the "executive Power" of Article II, Section 1. And the response, in eighteenth-century terms, did not have to be limited to defensive or proportionate measures. Thus an attack in itself gives the President the authority to respond and carry the conflict to its conclusion.

Second, the declare-war power extends only to war. Eighteenth-century usage is clear that not all military deployments are "war" (although the distinction did not turn on the presence or absence of a formal declaration). Moreover, threatening or provocative acts, while sometimes giving a just cause for war, were not declarations of war in themselves. Again, as these matters were not conveyed to Congress as part of the declare-war power, they remain part of the President's executive power over foreign affairs. . . .

NOTE ON THE CONSTITUTIONAL ALLOCATION OF WAR POWERS

1. Just as the Constitution contains no reference to a general "foreign affairs power," so too there is no general "war power." Instead, the Constitution recognizes several different war powers and divides them between Congress and the President.

Article I grants power to Congress

- to declare War,
- to grant Letters of Marque and Reprisal, and make Rules concerning Captures on Land and Water,
- to raise and support Armies,

- to provide and maintain a Navy,

- to make Rules for the Government and Regulation of the land and naval Forces,

- to provide for calling forth the Militia to execute the Laws of the Union, suppress Insurrections and repel Invasions, and

- to provide for organizing, arming, and disciplining, the Militia.

Article II, on the other hand, grants important military powers to the President by declaring that he or she "shall be Commander in Chief of the Army and Navy of the United States, and of the Militia of the several States, when called into the actual Service of the United States."

Finally, some powers are expressly prohibited to the States:

- To engage in war (unless invaded or in imminent danger); and

- To keep troops or ships of war during peacetime.

These prohibitions are in keeping with the Constitution's historical concern for monopolizing powers of war and peace in the Federal Government. But it's interesting, isn't it, that neither of these prohibitions is absolute?

2. Although the Founding-era material on the meaning of constitutional war powers is somewhat sparse, some discussions occurred at the Convention and more extensive exchanges took place among the Founding Generation during the Neutrality Controversy shortly after ratification. Much of the evidence can be condensed into three key points:

First, the Founding-era debate evinces considerable distrust of the Executive. Alexander Hamilton was at pains in the Federalist to show how much *less* power the President is given than the King of England had—another instance of constitutional meaning being shaped by what the Founders were reacting *against*. And James Madison warned in his Helvidius essay that "[w]ar is in fact the true nurse of executive aggrandizement." This warning prefigured Justice Jackson's concern in *Youngstown* that the Executive will create military conflicts as a pretext for expanding his own powers.

Second, a great deal of the early commentary indicates that the Founders did not want the President to be able to *start* a war. James Wilson, for example, told the Pennsylvania ratifying convention that "[i]t will not be in the power of a single man . . . to involve us in such distress [war], for the important power of declaring war is vested in the legislature at large."

At the same time, however, the Founders also largely agreed that the President should have sole charge of actual military operations. They thus wished to gain the advantages of unitary initiative and efficiency for the prosecution of wars, while assigning the instigation of conflict to the more deliberative and inertia-bound body of the legislature. As Professor Ramsey's discussion indicates, however, this strong strand of the historical commentary is only imperfectly reflected in the actual text.

3. Lawyers and scholars have long divided into two rough "camps" concerning the constitutional allocation of war powers. The Congress people say that the history just discussed makes clear that the Founders didn't want

to be able to commit troops without congressional authorization, outside a very narrow exception for responding to sudden attacks. The Executive people, on the other hand, say either (1) the power to declare war was intended to be very narrow, so that its only consequence was to trigger certain legal conditions incident to wartime; or (2) that we just shouldn't be originalists on this because the world has changed.

Professor Ramsey's article, of which a brief excerpt appears above, purports to offer something of a middle ground. He argues that Congress must authorize any action that explicitly or by action initiates a state of war with another nation. But the President may:

- Take military actions short of creating a state of war;

- Respond to an attack that initiates a state of war and prosecute the war to its conclusion; and

- Take actions, like deploying troops or severing diplomatic relations, that are likely to *provoke* an attack.

Does this position make sense? Does it persuasively harmonize the text and what the Framers said about it?

4.   What is the relationship between the President's Commander in Chief power and Congress's Declare War power in *Little*? How does that relation compare to Justice Jackson's concurrence in *Youngstown*? Should Justice Jackson have cited *Little*? Does *Zivotofsky* cast any doubt on *Little*?

5.   Should we require Congressional action before the President can respond to sudden attacks? How do the *Prize Cases* bear on that question? How much weight should we place on Congress's retroactive authorization of President Lincoln's actions? Was that authorization necessary, once an attack on the U.S. had created a state of war? Would Justice Nelson's dissent have denied the President this power to respond? If not, then what point is Justice Nelson making?

Does an attack have to be on U.S. territory to trigger the President's Commander in Chief power? Or do attacks on Americans abroad, as in *Durand*, count the same as attacks on the nation itself? Would an attack on American tourists in Iran, for instance, justify an invasion by U.S. forces without Congressional approval? What about an attack on a U.S. ally? Would it make a difference if the ally in question had signed a mutual defense treaty with the United States—such as the NATO treaty—committing the U.S. to treat an attack on the ally as an attack on the U.S.? In such a circumstance, should Senate ratification of the treaty count as congressional authorization to go to war on the ally's behalf?

6.   Does the notion that the President may respond to sudden attacks hold true even if the President *provokes* the attack? Consider the events leading up to the Mexican-American war in 1846, which arose out of a boundary dispute concerning the border between Texas and Mexico. [29] Mexico had moved its army to the south bank of the Rio Grande (the

---

[29]   For a good account of the Mexican conflict, see DANIEL WALKER HOWE, WHAT HATH GOD WROUGHT: THE TRANSFORMATION OF AMERICA, 1815–1848, at 744–91 (2007).

boundary claimed by the U.S.); in June 1845, President James K. Polk ordered American troops to the north bank—within the disputed territory—where they blockaded the river and aimed their cannons at the other side. Unsurprisingly, military incidents occurred in which at least some Mexican troops come across the river into what was claimed to be U.S. territory. Polk used this "attack" as grounds to request a declaration of war from Congress, which Congress duly provided. But if Mexico had truly attacked us, was such a declaration even necessary? After the war's conclusion, the House of Representatives adopted a resolution stating that the Mexican-American War was "a war unnecessarily and unconstitutionally begun by the President of the United States."[30] In what sense was the war "unconstitutional"?

If we accept *arguendo* that the Mexican incursions were attacks to which the President was entitled to respond, how far do his powers go? Ought he to be limited to fending off the attacks? Or do the attacks create a state of war, obviating Congress's declaration power and placing us in the realm of the Commander in Chief power? In other words, may the President then prosecute the war all the way to its conclusion? Was Polk entitled to prosecute the Mexican War all the way, as the Marines' Hymn puts it, "to the Halls of Montezuma"?

7.   The National Security Strategy is an effort by the National Security Council to expound and justify basic aspects of American foreign and military policy. Note that the excerpt printed above purports to extend the "sudden attacks" rationale to justify preemptive military operations against certain threats, especially weapons of mass destruction. Can this be squared with the constitutional scheme?

More generally, do the changes in the American security environment suggest that our eighteenth century security framework is obsolete? Given the threats the nation now faces, is Professor John Yoo right to suggest that "it certainly is no longer clear that the constitutional system ought to be fixed so as to make it difficult to use force"?[31] Does Congress's ability to confer certain additional powers by statute over time mitigate this problem? Could Congress delegate its authority to authorize the use of military force to the President?

8.   Under Justice Jackson's approach, Executive authority is largely a function of congressional action. The following statute reflects Congress's effort to codify the allocation of war powers:

War Powers Resolution

50 U.S.C. § 1541 *et seq.*

§ 1541. Purpose and policy

(a) Congressional declaration. It is the purpose of this joint resolution to fulfill the intent of the framers of the Constitution of the United States

---

[30] Cong. Globe, 30th Cong., 1st Sess. (1848).

[31] JOHN C. YOO, THE POWERS OF WAR AND PEACE: THE CONSTITUTION AND FOREIGN AFFAIRS AFTER 9/11 ix (2005).

and insure that the collective judgment of both the Congress and the President will apply to the introduction of United States Armed Forces into hostilities, or into situations where imminent involvement in hostilities is clearly indicated by the circumstances, and to the continued use of such forces in hostilities or in such situations.

(b) Congressional legislative power under necessary and proper clause. Under article I, section 8, of the Constitution, it is specifically provided that the Congress shall have the power to make all laws necessary and proper for carrying into execution, not only its own powers but also all other powers vested by the Constitution in the Government of the United States, or in any department or officer thereof.

(c) Presidential executive power as Commander-in-Chief; limitation. The constitutional powers of the President as Commander-in-Chief to introduce United States Armed Forces into hostilities, or into situations where imminent involvement in hostilities is clearly indicated by the circumstances, are exercised only pursuant to (1) a declaration of war, (2) specific statutory authorization, or (3) a national emergency created by attack upon the United States, its territories or possessions, or its armed forces.

§ 1542. Consultation; initial and regular consultations

The President in every possible instance shall consult with Congress before introducing United States Armed Forces into hostilities or into situations where imminent involvement in hostilities is clearly indicated by the circumstances, and after every such introduction shall consult regularly with the Congress until United States Armed Forces are no longer engaged in hostilities or have been removed from such situations.

§ 1543. Reporting requirement

(a) Written report; time of submission; circumstances necessitating submission; information reported. In the absence of a declaration of war, in any case in which United States Armed Forces are introduced—

(1) into hostilities or into situations where imminent involvement in hostilities is clearly indicated by the circumstances;

(2) into the territory, airspace or waters of a foreign nation, while equipped for combat, except for deployments which relate solely to supply, replacement, repair, or training of such forces; or

(3) in numbers which substantially enlarge United States Armed Forces equipped for combat already located in a foreign nation;

the President shall submit within 48 hours to the Speaker of the House of Representatives and to the President pro tempore of the Senate a report, in writing, setting forth—

(A) the circumstances necessitating the introduction of United States Armed Forces;

(B) the constitutional and legislative authority under which such introduction took place; and

(C) the estimated scope and duration of the hostilities or involvement.

(b) Other information reported. The President shall provide such other information as the Congress may request in the fulfillment of its constitutional responsibilities with respect to committing the Nation to war and to the use of United States Armed Forces abroad.

(c) Periodic reports; semiannual requirement. Whenever United States Armed Forces are introduced into hostilities or into any situation described in subsection (a) of this section, the President shall, so long as such armed forces continue to be engaged in such hostilities or situation, report to the Congress periodically on the status of such hostilities or situation as well as on the scope and duration of such hostilities or situation, but in no event shall he report to the Congress less often than once every six months.

§ 1544. Congressional action

(a) Transmittal of report and referral to Congressional Committees; joint request for convening Congress. Each report submitted pursuant to [§ 1543(a)(1)] shall be transmitted to the Speaker of the House of Representatives and to the President pro tempore of the Senate on the same calendar day. Each report so transmitted shall be referred to the Committee on Foreign Affairs of the House of Representatives and to the Committee on Foreign Relations of the Senate for appropriate action. If, when the report is transmitted, the Congress has adjourned sine die or has adjourned for any period in excess of three calendar days, the Speaker of the House of Representatives and the President pro tempore of the Senate, if they deem it advisable (or if petitioned by at least 30 percent of the membership of their respective Houses) shall jointly request the President to convene Congress in order that it may consider the report and take appropriate action pursuant to this section.

(b) Termination of use of United States Armed Forces; exceptions; extension period. Within sixty calendar days after a report is submitted or is required to be submitted pursuant to [§ 1543(a)(1)], whichever is earlier, the President shall terminate any use of United States Armed Forces with respect to which such report was submitted (or required to be submitted), unless the Congress (1) has declared war or has enacted a specific authorization for such use of United States Armed Forces, (2) has extended by law such sixty-day period, or (3) is physically unable to meet as a result of an armed attack upon the United States. Such sixty-day period shall be extended for not more than an additional thirty days if the President determines and certifies to the Congress in writing that unavoidable military necessity respecting the safety of United States Armed Forces requires the continued use of such armed forces in the course of bringing about a prompt removal of such forces.

(c) Concurrent resolution for removal by President of United States Armed Forces. Notwithstanding subsection (b), at any time that United States Armed Forces are engaged in hostilities outside the territory of the United States, its possession and territories without a declaration of war or specific statutory authorization, such forces shall be removed by the President if the Congress so directs by concurrent resolution.

§ 1547. Interpretation of joint resolution

(a) Inferences from any law or treaty. Authority to introduce United States Armed Forces into hostilities or into situations wherein involvement in hostilities is clearly indicated by the circumstances shall not be inferred—

(1) from any provision of law (whether or not in effect before the date of the enactment of this joint resolution), including any provision contained in any appropriation Act, unless such provision specifically authorizes the introduction of United States Armed Forces into hostilities or into such situations and states that it is intended to constitute specific statutory authorization within the meaning of this joint resolution; or

(2) from any treaty heretofore or hereafter ratified unless such treaty is implemented by legislation specifically authorizing the introduction of United States Armed Forces into hostilities or into such situations and stating that it is intended to constitute specific statutory authorization within the meaning of this joint resolution.

(b) Joint headquarters operations of high-level military commands. Nothing in this joint resolution shall be construed to require any further specific statutory authorization to permit members of United States Armed Forces to participate jointly with members of the armed forces of one or more foreign countries in the headquarters operations of high-level military commands which were established prior to the date of enactment of this joint resolution and pursuant to the United Nations Charter or any treaty ratified by the United States prior to such date.

(c) Introduction of United States Armed Forces. For purposes of this joint resolution, the term "introduction of United States Armed Forces" includes the assignment of members of such armed forces to command, coordinate, participate in the movement of, or accompany the regular or irregular military forces of any foreign country or government when such military forces are engaged, or there exists an imminent threat that such forces will become engaged, in hostilities.

(d) Constitutional authorities or existing treaties unaffected; construction against grant of Presidential authority respecting use of United States Armed Forces. Nothing in this joint resolution—

(1) is intended to alter the constitutional authority of the Congress or of the President, or the provisions of existing treaties; or

(2) shall be construed as granting any authority to the President with respect to the introduction of United States Armed Forces into hostilities or into situations wherein involvement in hostilities is clearly indicated by the circumstances which authority he would not have had in the absence of this joint resolution.

§ 1548. Separability of provisions

If any provision of this joint resolution or the application thereof to any person or circumstance is held invalid, the remainder of the joint resolution and the application of such provision to any other person or circumstance shall not be affected thereby.

Richard Nixon, Veto Message on the War Powers Resolution
October 24, 1973

To the House of Representatives:

I hereby return without my approval House Joint Resolution 542—the War Powers Resolution. While I am in accord with the desire of the Congress to assert its proper role in the conduct of our foreign affairs, the restrictions which this resolution would impose upon the authority of the President are both unconstitutional and dangerous to the best interests of our Nation.

The proper roles of the Congress and the Executive in the conduct of foreign affairs have been debated since the founding of our country. Only recently, however, has there been a serious challenge to the wisdom of the Founding Fathers in choosing not to draw a precise and detailed line of demarcation between the foreign policy powers of the two branches.

The Founding Fathers understood the impossibility of foreseeing every contingency that might arise in this complex area. They acknowledged the need for flexibility in responding to changing circumstances. They recognized that foreign policy decisions must be made through close cooperation between the two branches and not through rigidly codified procedures.

These principles remain as valid today as they were when our Constitution was written. Yet House Joint Resolution 542 would violate those principles by defining the President's powers in ways which would strictly limit his constitutional authority.

Clearly Unconstitutional

House Joint Resolution 542 would attempt to take away, by a mere legislative act, authorities which the President has properly exercised under the Constitution for almost 200 years. One of its provisions would automatically cut off certain authorities after sixty days unless the Congress extended them. Another would allow the Congress to eliminate certain authorities merely by the passage of a concurrent resolution—an action which does not normally have the force of law, since it denies the President his constitutional role in approving legislation.

I believe that both these provisions are unconstitutional. The only way in which the constitutional powers of a branch of the Government can be altered is by amending the Constitution—and any attempt to make such alterations by legislation alone is clearly without force.

Undermining Our Foreign Policy

While I firmly believe that a veto of House Joint Resolution 542 is warranted solely on constitutional grounds, I am also deeply disturbed by the practical consequences of this resolution. For it would seriously undermine this Nation's ability to act decisively and convincingly in times of international crisis. As a result, the confidence of our allies in our ability to assist them could be diminished and the respect of our adversaries for our deterrent posture could decline. A permanent and substantial element of unpredictability would be injected into the world's assessment of American behavior, further increasing the likelihood of miscalculation and war.

If this resolution had been in operation, America's effective response to a variety of challenges in recent years would have been vastly complicated or even made impossible. We may well have been unable to respond in the way we did during the Berlin crisis of 1961, the Cuban missile crisis of 1962, the Congo rescue operation in 1964, and the Jordanian crisis of 1970—to mention just a few examples. In addition, our recent actions to bring about a peaceful settlement of the hostilities in the Middle East would have been seriously impaired if this resolution had been in force.

While all the specific consequences of House Joint Resolution 542 cannot yet be predicted, it is clear that it would undercut the ability of the United States to act as an effective influence for peace. For example, the provision automatically cutting off certain authorities after 60 days unless they are extended by the Congress could work to prolong or intensify a crisis. Until the Congress suspended the deadline, there would be at least a chance of United States withdrawal and an adversary would be tempted therefore to postpone serious negotiations until the 60 days were up. Only after the Congress acted would there be a strong incentive for an adversary to negotiate. In addition, the very existence of a deadline could lead to an escalation of hostilities in order to achieve certain objectives before the 60 days expired.

The measure would jeopardize our role as a force for peace in other ways as well. It would, for example, strike from the President's hand a wide range of important peace-keeping tools by eliminating his ability to exercise quiet diplomacy backed by subtle shifts in our military deployments. It would also cast into doubt authorities which Presidents have used to undertake certain humanitarian relief missions in conflict areas, to protect fishing boats from seizure, to deal with ship or aircraft hijackings, and to respond to threats of attack. Not the least of the adverse consequences of this resolution would be the prohibition contained in section 8 against fulfilling our obligations under the NATO treaty as ratified by the Senate. Finally, since the bill is somewhat vague as to when the 60 day rule would apply, it could lead to extreme confusion and dangerous disagreements concerning the prerogatives of the two branches, seriously damaging our ability to respond to international crises.

Failure to Require Positive Congressional Action

I am particularly disturbed by the fact that certain of the President's constitutional powers as Commander in Chief of the Armed Forces would terminate automatically under this resolution 60 days after they were invoked. No overt Congressional action would be required to cut off these powers—they would disappear automatically unless the Congress extended them. In effect, the Congress is here attempting to increase its policy-making role through a provision which requires it to take absolutely no action at all.

In my view, the proper way for the Congress to make known its will on such foreign policy questions is through a positive action, with full debate on the merits of the issue and with each member taking the responsibility of casting a yes or no vote after considering those merits. The authorization and appropriations process represents one of the ways in which such influence can be exercised. I do not, however, believe that the Congress can responsibly contribute its considered, collective judgment on such grave questions without full debate and without a yes or no vote. Yet this is precisely what the joint resolution would allow. It would give every future Congress the ability to handcuff every future President merely by doing nothing and sitting still. In my view, one cannot become a responsible partner unless one is prepared to take responsible action. . . .

RICHARD NIXON

Joint Resolution, Sept. 18, 2001

107 P.L. 40; 115 Stat. 224

To authorize the use of United States Armed Forces against those responsible for the recent attacks launched against the United States.

Whereas, on September 11, 2001, acts of treacherous violence were committed against the United States and its citizens; and

Whereas, such acts render it both necessary and appropriate that the United States exercise its rights to self-defense and to protect United States citizens both at home and abroad; and

Whereas, in light of the threat to the national security and foreign policy of the United States posed by these grave acts of violence; and

Whereas, such acts continue to pose an unusual and extraordinary threat to the national security and foreign policy of the United States; and

Whereas, the President has authority under the Constitution to take action to deter and prevent acts of international terrorism against the United States: Now, therefore, be it

Resolved by the Senate and House of Representatives of the United States of America in Congress assembled,

SECTION 1.   SHORT TITLE.

This joint resolution may be cited as the "Authorization for Use of Military Force".

SEC. 2.   AUTHORIZATION FOR USE OF UNITED STATES ARMED FORCES.

(a) In General.—That the President is authorized to use all necessary and appropriate force against those nations, organizations, or persons he determines planned, authorized, committed, or aided the terrorist attacks that occurred on September 11, 2001, or harbored such organizations or persons, in order to prevent any future acts of international terrorism against the United States by such nations, organizations or persons.

(b) War Powers Resolution Requirements.—

(1) Specific statutory authorization.—Consistent with section 8(a)(1) of the War Powers Resolution, the Congress declares that this section is intended to constitute specific statutory authorization within the meaning of section 5(b) of the War Powers Resolution.

(2) Applicability of other requirements.—Nothing in this resolution supercedes any requirement of the War Powers Resolution.

Joint Resolution, Oct. 16, 2002
107 P.L. 243; 116 Stat. 1498

To authorize the use of United States Armed Forces against Iraq.

Whereas in 1990 in response to Iraq's war of aggression against and illegal occupation of Kuwait, the United States forged a coalition of nations to liberate Kuwait and its people in order to defend the national security of the United States and enforce United Nations Security Council resolutions relating to Iraq;

Whereas after the liberation of Kuwait in 1991, Iraq entered into a United Nations sponsored cease-fire agreement pursuant to which Iraq unequivocally agreed, among other things, to eliminate its nuclear, biological, and chemical weapons programs and the means to deliver and develop them, and to end its support for international terrorism;

Whereas the efforts of international weapons inspectors, United States intelligence agencies, and Iraqi defectors led to the discovery that

Iraq had large stockpiles of chemical weapons and a large scale biological weapons program, and that Iraq had an advanced nuclear weapons development program that was much closer to producing a nuclear weapon than intelligence reporting had previously indicated;

Whereas Iraq, in direct and flagrant violation of the cease-fire, attempted to thwart the efforts of weapons inspectors to identify and destroy Iraq's weapons of mass destruction stockpiles and development capabilities, which finally resulted in the withdrawal of inspectors from Iraq on October 31, 1998;

Whereas in Public Law 105–235 (August 14, 1998), Congress concluded that Iraq's continuing weapons of mass destruction programs threatened vital United States interests and international peace and security, declared Iraq to be in "material and unacceptable breach of its international obligations" and urged the President "to take appropriate action, in accordance with the Constitution and relevant laws of the United States, to bring Iraq into compliance with its international obligations";

Whereas Iraq both poses a continuing threat to the national security of the United States and international peace and security in the Persian Gulf region and remains in material and unacceptable breach of its international obligations by, among other things, continuing to possess and develop a significant chemical and biological weapons capability, actively seeking a nuclear weapons capability, and supporting and harboring terrorist organizations;

Whereas Iraq persists in violating resolution of the United Nations Security Council by continuing to engage in brutal repression of its civilian population thereby threatening international peace and security in the region, by refusing to release, repatriate, or account for non-Iraqi citizens wrongfully detained by Iraq, including an American serviceman, and by failing to return property wrongfully seized by Iraq from Kuwait;

Whereas the current Iraqi regime has demonstrated its capability and willingness to use weapons of mass destruction against other nations and its own people;

Whereas the current Iraqi regime has demonstrated its continuing hostility toward, and willingness to attack, the United States, including by attempting in 1993 to assassinate former President Bush and by firing on many thousands of occasions on United States and Coalition Armed Forces engaged in enforcing the resolutions of the United Nations Security Council;

Whereas members of al Qaida, an organization bearing responsibility for attacks on the United States, its citizens, and interests, including the attacks that occurred on September 11, 2001, are known to be in Iraq;

Whereas Iraq continues to aid and harbor other international terrorist organizations, including organizations that threaten the lives and safety of United States citizens;

Whereas the attacks on the United States of September 11, 2001, underscored the gravity of the threat posed by the acquisition of weapons of mass destruction by international terrorist organizations;

Whereas Iraq's demonstrated capability and willingness to use weapons of mass destruction, the risk that the current Iraqi regime will either employ those weapons to launch a surprise attack against the United States or its Armed Forces or provide them to international terrorists who would do so, and the extreme magnitude of harm that would result to the United States and its citizens from such an attack, combine to justify action by the United States to defend itself;

Whereas United Nations Security Council Resolution 678 (1990) authorizes the use of all necessary means to enforce United Nations Security Council Resolution 660 (1990) and subsequent relevant resolutions and to compel Iraq to cease certain activities that threaten international peace and security, including the development of weapons of mass destruction and refusal or obstruction of United Nations weapons inspections in violation of United Nations Security Council Resolution 687 (1991), repression of its civilian population in violation of United Nations Security Council Resolution 688 (1991), and threatening its neighbors or United Nations operations in Iraq in violation of United Nations Security Council Resolution 949 (1994);

Whereas in the Authorization for Use of Military Force Against Iraq Resolution (Public Law 102–1), Congress has authorized the President "to use United States Armed Forces pursuant to United Nations Security Council Resolution 678 (1990) in order to achieve implementation of Security Council Resolution 660, 661, 662, 664, 665, 666, 667, 669, 670, 674, and 677";

Whereas in December 1991, Congress expressed its sense that it "supports the use of all necessary means to achieve the goals of United Nations Security Council Resolution 687 as being consistent with the Authorization of Use of Military Force Against Iraq Resolution (Public Law 102–1)," that Iraq's repression of its civilian population violates United Nations Security Council Resolution 688 and "constitutes a continuing threat to the peace, security, and stability of the Persian Gulf region," and that Congress, "supports the use of all necessary means to achieve the goals of United Nations Security Council Resolution 688";

Whereas the Iraq Liberation Act of 1998 (Public Law 105–338) expressed the sense of Congress that it should be the policy of the United States to support efforts to remove from power the current Iraqi regime and promote the emergence of a democratic government to replace that regime;

Whereas on September 12, 2002, President Bush committed the United States to "work with the United Nations Security Council to meet our common challenge" posed by Iraq and to "work for the necessary resolutions," while also making clear that "the Security Council resolutions will be enforced, and the just demands of peace and security will be met, or action will be unavoidable";

Whereas the United States is determined to prosecute the war on terrorism and Iraq's ongoing support for international terrorist groups combined with its development of weapons of mass destruction in direct violation of its obligations under the 1991 cease-fire and other United Nations Security Council resolutions make clear that it is in the national security interests of the United States and in furtherance of the war on terrorism that all relevant United Nations Security Council resolutions be enforced, including through the use of force if necessary;

Whereas Congress has taken steps to pursue vigorously the war on terrorism through the provision of authorities and funding requested by the President to take the necessary actions against international terrorists and terrorist organizations, including those nations, organizations, or persons who planned, authorized, committed, or aided the terrorist attacks that occurred on September 11, 2001, or harbored such persons or organizations;

Whereas the President and Congress are determined to continue to take all appropriate actions against international terrorists and terrorist organizations, including those nations, organizations, or persons who planned, authorized, committed, or aided the terrorist attacks that occurred on September 11, 2001, or harbored such persons or organizations;

Whereas the President has authority under the Constitution to take action in order to deter and prevent acts of international terrorism against the United States, as Congress recognized in the joint resolution on Authorization for Use of Military Force (Public Law 107–40); and

Whereas it is in the national security interests of the United States to restore international peace and security to the Persian Gulf region: Now, therefore, be it

Resolved by the Senate and House of Representatives of the United States of America in Congress assembled,

SEC. 1.   SHORT TITLE.

This joint resolution may be cited as the "Authorization for Use of Military Force Against Iraq Resolution of 2002".

SEC. 2.   SUPPORT FOR UNITED STATES DIPLOMATIC EFFORTS.

The Congress of the United States supports the efforts by the President to—

(1) strictly enforce through the United Nations Security Council all relevant Security Council resolutions regarding Iraq and encourages him in those efforts; and

(2) obtain prompt and decisive action by the Security Council to ensure that Iraq abandons its strategy of delay, evasion and noncompliance and promptly and strictly complies with all relevant Security Council resolutions regarding Iraq.

SEC. 3.   AUTHORIZATION FOR USE OF UNITED STATES ARMED FORCES.

(a) Authorization.—The President is authorized to use the Armed Forces of the United States as he determines to be necessary and appropriate in order to—

(1) defend the national security of the United States against the continuing threat posed by Iraq; and

(2) enforce all relevant United Nations Security Council resolutions regarding Iraq.

(b) Presidential Determination.—In connection with the exercise of the authority granted in subsection (a) to use force the President shall, prior to such exercise or as soon thereafter as may be feasible, but no later than 48 hours after exercising such authority, make available to the Speaker of the House of Representatives and the President pro tempore of the Senate his determination that—

(1) reliance by the United States on further diplomatic or other peaceful means alone either (A) will not adequately protect the national security of the United States against the continuing threat posed by Iraq or (B) is not likely to lead to enforcement of all relevant United Nations Security Council resolutions regarding Iraq; and

(2) acting pursuant to this joint resolution is consistent with the United States and other countries continuing to take the necessary actions against international terrorist and terrorist organizations, including those nations, organizations, or persons who planned, authorized, committed or aided the terrorist attacks that occurred on September 11, 2001.

(c) War Powers Resolution Requirements.—

(1) Specific statutory authorization.—Consistent with section 8(a)(1) of the War Powers Resolution, the Congress declares that this section is intended to constitute specific statutory authorization within the meaning of section 5(b) of the War Powers Resolution.

(2) Applicability of other requirements.—Nothing in this joint resolution supersedes any requirement of the War Powers Resolution.

SEC. 4.   REPORTS TO CONGRESS.

(a) Reports.—The President shall, at least once every 60 days, submit to the Congress a report on matters relevant to this joint resolution, including actions taken pursuant to the exercise of authority granted in section 3 and the status of planning for efforts that are expected to be required after such actions are completed, including those actions described in section 7 of the Iraq Liberation Act of 1998 (Public Law 105–338).

(b) Single Consolidated Report.—To the extent that the submission of any report described in subsection (a) coincides with the submission of any other report on matters relevant to this joint resolution otherwise required to be submitted to Congress pursuant to the reporting requirements of the War Powers Resolution (Public Law 93–148), all such reports may be submitted as a single consolidated report to the Congress.

(c) Rule of Construction.—To the extent that the information required by section 3 of the Authorization for Use of Military Force Against Iraq Resolution (Public Law 102–1) is included in the report required by this section, such report shall be considered as meeting the requirements of section 3 of such resolution.

NOTE ON DECLARATIONS, AUTHORIZATIONS, AND RESOLUTIONS

1.   There has been a lot of fighting in American history, but only 5 declarations of war by Congress:

- the War of 1812
- the Mexican-American War of 1846–48
- the Spanish-American War of 1898
- World War I
- World War II

One study, on the other hand, counts 234 uses of force by the United States. Some of these were authorized by Congress without a declaration of war:

- Barbary Pirates (1802)
- Civil War (1861)
- Gulf of Tonkin Resolution (1964)
- Both Gulf Wars (1991 & 2003)

When Congress issues such authorizations, the question becomes one of scope. Scope questions were a particular problem, for example, with the Gulf of Tonkin Resolution authorizing the Vietnam War. Note also that sometimes authorization comes retroactively, as in the case of the Civil War. On innumerable occasions, of course, U.S. military forces have gone into combat without either a declaration or an authorization.

2.   What was Congress trying to achieve in the War Powers Resolution? How much does it actually constrain the President? Could it be made more effective? Was President Nixon right to veto it on constitutional grounds? On policy grounds?

3.   Is the War Powers Resolution enforceable? In particular, could it be enforced by a court? Many decisions in the lower courts have declared

efforts to enforce aspects of the Resolution non-justiciable under the political question doctrine. Looking back to the discussion of that doctrine in *Baker v. Carr*, are war powers questions properly nonjusticiable? Is there a textual commitment of these questions to some other branch? A lack of judicially manageable standards?

4. Presidents generally insist that they do not need authorization to initiate military hostilities. The elder President Bush, for example, famously asserted that "I didn't have to get permission from some old goat in Congress to kick Saddam Hussein out of Kuwait." However, in each of the major recent conflicts—the Gulf War, Afghanistan, and Iraq—the President has sought such authorization anyway. Why do Presidents do this?

That trend changed with the Obama Administration. In March of 2011, United States air and naval forces intervened—as part of a NATO-led multilateral force—in the Libyan civil. Although the operation was supported by a United Nations Security Council Resolution, President Obama did not seek Congress's authorization for the mission. Rather, the President took the position that the military's actions did not amount to "hostilities" within the meaning of the War Powers Resolution. Harold Koh, the Legal Advisor to the State Department and a prominent international and foreign relations law scholar at Yale Law School, defended this conclusion in testimony before Congress:

> [A]s everyone recognizes, the legal trigger for the [War Powers Resolution's] automatic pullout clock, "hostilities" is an ambiguous term of art that is defined nowhere in the statute.... [T]he historical practice . . . suggests that when U.S. forces engage in a limited military mission that involves limited exposure for U.S. troops and limited risk of serious escalation and employs limited military means, we are not in hostilities of the kind envisioned by the War Powers Resolution.[32]

In response to this testimony, Senator Richard Lugar noted that "United States war planes have reportedly struck Libya air defenses some 60 times since NATO assumed the lead role in the Libya campaign. Predator drones reportedly have fired missiles on some 30 occasions. Most significantly, the broader range of airstrikes being carried out by other NATO forces depend on the essential support functions provided by the United States." [33] Similarly, Senator Richard Durbin—a Democrat generally supportive of the Administration—objected that "[h]ostilities by remote control are still hostilities. We are killing with drones what we would otherwise be killing with fighter planes. And we are engaged in hostilities in Libya."[34]

Was Professor Koh's argument that sustained naval and air and air attacks on a foreign nation did not constitute "hostilities" plausible? If the

---

[32] S. Hrg. 112–89, *Libya and War Powers*, Senate Committee on Foreign Relations, June 28, 2011 (Statement of Harold Koh).

[33] *Id.* (Statement of Senator Lugar).

[34] David A. Fahrenthold, *Obama's Negation of 'Hostilities' in Libya Draws Criticism*, WASH. POST, June 20, 2011, available at https://www.washingtonpost.com/politics/obamas-negation-of-hostilities-in-libya-draws-criticism/2011/06/20/AGV2zTdH_story.html?utm_term=4b4a33a4389b.

language of the War Powers Resolution is really this flexible, can it serve as any kind of constraint on the President? Would it have been better for President Obama to simply reaffirm President Nixon's position that the Resolution is unconstitutional and therefore not binding on the Executive? If President Obama's refusal to seek authorization for the 2011 Libya operation represents a change in executive practice, would that be a bad thing?

5.   The 9/11 Authorization and the Iraq Authorization, although quite close together in time, are very different documents. Two differences stand out. First, the Iraq resolution spends a great deal of space laying out the factual case for war, based primarily on the risk that Iraq was in the process of obtaining weapons of mass destruction. Does this suggest that authorizations serve a dual purpose—not only conferring legal authority on the president, but also helping to build popular support for the war effort? Second, the Iraq authorization also makes a *legal* case for war as a matter of international law. Relatedly, seems to oblige the President to undertake diplomatic efforts to resolve the conflict before resorting to war and to attempt to pursue action Iraq through multilateral means. Are these aspects of the authorization legally binding on the President? To what extent to they reflect an increased integration of world opinion and international law into American debates about the use of military force?

6.   Once Congress authorizes the President to use military force, can it retract that authorization? Legislation proposed by Senators Robert Byrd and Hillary Clinton, for example, would have repealed the 2002 authorization for the Iraq War. Would such an action be an exercise of the Declare War power or the Commander in Chief power?

Even if Congress may not retract an authorization once given, it has important other levers for controlling military policy. Most important, it can withhold funding for continued military operations, as several Members of Congress proposed with respect to operations in Iraq. How viable an option is this, really?

7.   How broadly should authorizations to use force be construed? In *Hamdi v. Rumsfeld*, 542 U.S. 507 (2004), the Supreme Court construed the Sept. 18, 2001 resolution as including an authorization to detain suspected "enemy combatants" captured in Afghanistan. Does the authorization say anything about detaining people? We explore questions of detention incident to military operations further in the next section.

SECTION 14.4   POWERS INCIDENT TO THE CONDUCT OF WAR

War is hell, and not just for the immediate combatants. As the *Steel Seizure Case* illustrated, governments often invoke military hostilities as grounds for all sorts of measures intended to help the war effort, including extensive regulation of the home front. War may also put significant strain on the domestic system for maintaining order. The *Hamdan* case in this section deals with ongoing efforts to adapt our existing legal categories—which distinguish sharply between war and criminal justice—to a "war on terrorism." The *Merryman* decision, however, demonstrates that these supposedly "cutting edge" problems of internal order and executive detention have been with us for a very long time.

Merryman concerns the constitutional power, noted in Article I, to suspend the writ of *habeas corpus*. The Latin phrase "habeas corpus" translates loosely to "produce the body." The writ of *habeas corpus* was a common law procedural vehicle by which someone who had been imprisoned or otherwise detained could require the government to appear in court and establish the legal basis for the detention to a judge's satisfaction. As such, *habeas* was a critical limitation on arbitrary detention of persons, especially by executive authority. *Suspension* of the writ, as in *Merryman*, allows the Executive to restrict the liberty of persons without any judicial check. It thus becomes critical to determine whether the President can exercise this power himself, or whether only Congress can suspend the writ. In assessing President Lincoln's actions in *Merryman*, however, consider the dire emergency outlined in Justice Rehnquist's account of the circumstances behind the case.

Today, the principal use of *habeas* is quite different from that in *Merryman*; primarily, it affords *federal* courts an opportunity to determine whether *state* courts are respecting federal rights in the context of ordinary criminal trials. But the War on Terror, and its concomitant detention of suspected terrorists by the Executive, has revived the older use of *habeas* as a vehicle to test the legality of executive detention in the absence of a judicial trial. In the *Hamdan* case, a detainee at Guantanamo Bay filed *habeas* petitions in order to challenge the Government's right to try him for violations of the law of war before a military commission rather than an Article III court. *Hamdan* demonstrates not only the continuing importance of judicial review by *habeas corpus* as a limit on executive authority, but also the extent to which presidential power remains a function of congressional action.

Ex parte Merryman

17 F. Cas. 144 (1861)

■ TANEY, CIRCUIT JUSTICE.

The application in this case for a writ of habeas corpus is made to me under the 14th section of the judiciary act of 1789, which renders effectual for the citizen the constitutional privilege of the writ of habeas corpus. That act gives to the courts of the United States, as well as to each justice of the supreme court, and to every district judge, power to grant writs of habeas corpus for the purpose of an inquiry into the cause of commitment. The petition was presented to me, at Washington, under the impression that I would order the prisoner to be brought before me there, but as he was confined in Fort McHenry, in the city of Baltimore, which is in my circuit, I resolved to hear it in the latter city, as obedience to the writ, under such circumstances, would not withdraw General Cadwalader, who had him in charge, from the limits of his military command.

The petition presents the following case: The petitioner resides in Maryland, in Baltimore county; while peaceably in his own house, with his family, it was at two o'clock on the morning of the 25th of May 1861, entered by an armed force, professing to act under military orders; he was then compelled to rise from his bed, taken into custody, and conveyed to Fort McHenry, where he is imprisoned by the commanding officer, without warrant from any lawful authority.

The commander of the fort, General George Cadwalader, by whom he is detained in confinement, in his return to the writ, does not deny any of the facts alleged in the petition. He states that the prisoner was arrested by order of General Keim, of Pennsylvania, and conducted as aforesaid to Fort McHenry, by his order, and placed in his (General Cadwalader's) custody, to be there detained by him as a prisoner.

A copy of the warrant or order under which the prisoner was arrested was demanded by his counsel, and refused: and it is not alleged in the return, that any specific act, constituting any offence against the laws of the United States, has been charged against him upon oath, but he appears to have been arrested upon general charges of treason and rebellion, without proof, and without giving the names of the witnesses, or specifying the acts which, in the judgment of the military officer, constituted these crimes. Having the prisoner thus in custody upon these vague and unsupported accusations, he refuses to obey the writ of habeas corpus, upon the ground that he is duly authorized by the president to suspend it.

The case, then, is simply this: a military officer, residing in Pennsylvania, issues an order to arrest a citizen of Maryland, upon vague and indefinite charges, without any proof, so far as appears; under this order, his house is entered in the night, he is seized as a prisoner, and conveyed to Fort McHenry, and there kept in close confinement; and when a habeas corpus is served on the commanding officer, requiring him to produce the prisoner before a justice of the supreme court, in order that he may examine into the legality of the imprisonment, the answer of the officer, is that he is authorized by the president to suspend the writ of habeas corpus at his discretion, and in the exercise of that discretion, suspends it in this case, and on that ground refuses obedience to the writ.

As the case comes before me, therefore, I understand that the president not only claims the right to suspend the writ of habeas corpus himself, at his discretion, but to delegate that discretionary power to a military officer, and to leave it to him to determine whether he will or will not obey judicial process that may be served upon him. No official notice has been given to the courts of justice, or to the public, by proclamation or otherwise, that the president claimed this power, and had exercised it in the manner stated in the return. And I certainly listened to it with some surprise, for I had supposed it to be one of those points of constitutional law upon which there was no difference of opinion, and that it was admitted on all hands, that the privilege of the writ could not be suspended, except by act of congress.

When the conspiracy of which Aaron Burr was the head, became so formidable, and was so extensively ramified, as to justify, in Mr. Jefferson's opinion, the suspension of the writ, he claimed, on his part, no power to suspend it, but communicated his opinion to congress, with all the proofs in his possession, in order that congress might exercise its discretion upon the subject, and determine whether the public safety required it. And in the debate which took place upon the subject, no one suggested that Mr. Jefferson might exercise the power himself, if, in his opinion, the public safety demanded it. . . .

The clause of the constitution, which authorizes the suspension of the privilege of the writ of habeas corpus, is in the 9th section of the first article. This article is devoted to the legislative department of the United States, and has not the slightest reference to the executive department. It begins by providing "that all legislative powers therein granted, shall be vested in a congress of the United States, which shall consist of a senate and house of representatives." And after prescribing the manner in which these two branches of the legislative department shall be chosen, it proceeds to enumerate specifically the legislative powers which it thereby grants [and legislative powers which it expressly prohibits]; and at the conclusion of this specification, a clause is inserted giving congress "the power to make all laws which shall be necessary and proper for carrying into execution the foregoing powers, and all other powers vested by this constitution in the government of the United States, or in any department or officer thereof."

The power of legislation granted by this latter clause is, by its words, carefully confined to the specific objects before enumerated. But as this limitation was unavoidably somewhat indefinite, it was deemed necessary to guard more effectually certain great cardinal principles, essential to the liberty of the citizen, and to the rights and equality of the states, by denying to congress, in express terms, any power of legislation over them. It was apprehended, it seems, that such legislation might be attempted, under the pretext that it was necessary and proper to carry into execution the powers granted; and it was determined, that there should be no room to doubt, where rights of such vital importance were concerned; and accordingly, this clause is immediately followed by an enumeration of certain subjects, to which the powers of legislation shall not extend. The great importance which the framers of the constitution attached to the privilege of the writ of habeas corpus, to protect the liberty of the citizen, is proved by the fact, that its suspension, except in cases of invasion or rebellion, is first in the list of prohibited powers; and even in these cases the power is denied, and its exercise prohibited, unless the public safety shall require it.

It is true, that in the cases mentioned, congress is, of necessity, the judge of whether the public safety does or does not require it; and their judgment is conclusive. But the introduction of these words is a standing admonition to the legislative body of the danger of suspending it, and of the extreme caution they should exercise, before they give the government of the United States such power over the liberty of a citizen.

It is the second article of the constitution that provides for the organization of the executive department, enumerates the powers conferred on it, and prescribes its duties. And if the high power over the liberty of the citizen now claimed, was intended to be conferred on the president, it would undoubtedly be found in plain words in this article; but there is not a word in it that can furnish the slightest ground to justify the exercise of the power. . . .

The only power . . . which the president possesses, where the "life, liberty or property" of a private citizen is concerned, is the power and duty prescribed in the third section of the second article, which requires "that he shall take care that the laws shall be faithfully executed." He is not authorized to execute them himself, or through agents or officers, civil or military, appointed by himself, but he is to take care that they be faithfully carried into execution, as they are expounded and adjudged by the co-ordinate branch of the government to which that duty is assigned by the constitution. It is thus made his duty to come in aid of the judicial authority, if it shall be resisted by a force too strong to be overcome without the assistance of the executive arm; but in exercising this power he acts in subordination to judicial authority, assisting it to execute its process and enforce its judgments.

With such provisions in the constitution, expressed in language too clear to be misunderstood by any one, I can see no ground whatever for supposing that the president, in any emergency, or in any state of things, can authorize the suspension of the privilege of the writ of habeas corpus, or the arrest of a citizen, except in aid of the judicial power. He certainly does not faithfully execute the laws, if he takes upon himself legislative power, by suspending the writ of habeas corpus, and the judicial power also, by arresting and imprisoning a person without due process of law.

Nor can any argument be drawn from the nature of sovereignty, or the necessity of government, for self-defence in times of tumult and danger. The government of the United States is one of delegated and limited powers; it derives its existence and authority altogether from the constitution, and neither of its branches, executive, legislative or judicial, can exercise any of the powers of government beyond those specified and granted; for the tenth article of the amendments to the constitution, in express terms, provides that "the powers not delegated to the United States by the constitution, nor prohibited by it to the states, are reserved to the states, respectively, or to the people."

Indeed, the security against imprisonment by executive authority, provided for in the fifth article of the amendments to the constitution, which I have before quoted, is nothing more than a copy of a like provision in the English constitution, which had been firmly established before the declaration of independence. Blackstone states it in the following words: "To make imprisonment lawful, it must be either by process of law from the courts of judicature, or by warrant from some legal officer having authority to commit to prison."

The people of the United Colonies, who had themselves lived under its protection, while they were British subjects, were well aware of the necessity of this safeguard for their personal liberty. And no one can believe that, in framing a government intended to guard still more efficiently the rights and liberties of the citizen, against executive encroachment and oppression, they would have conferred on the president a power which the history of England had proved to be dangerous and oppressive in the hands of the crown; and which the people of England had compelled it to surrender, after a long and obstinate struggle on the part of the English executive to usurp and retain it.

The right of the subject to the benefit of the writ of habeas corpus, it must be recollected, was one of the great points in controversy, during the long struggle in England between arbitrary government and free institutions, and must therefore have strongly attracted the attention of the statesmen engaged in framing a new and, as they supposed, a freer government than the one which they had thrown off by the revolution. From the earliest history of the common law, if a person were imprisoned, no matter by what authority, he had a right to the writ of habeas corpus, to bring his case before the king's bench; if no specific offence were charged against him in the warrant of commitment, he was entitled to be forthwith discharged; and if an offence were charged which was bailable in its character, the court was bound to set him at liberty on bail. The most exciting contests between the crown and the people of England, for the time of Magna Charta, were in relation to the privilege of this writ, and they continued until the passage of . . . the great habeas corpus act.

This statute put an end to the struggle, and finally and firmly secured the liberty of the subject against the usurpation and oppression of the executive branch of the government. . . .

And Chief Justice Marshall, in . . . *Ex parte Bollman,* uses this decisive language: "It may be worthy of remark, that this act (speaking of the one under which I am proceeding) was passed by the first congress of the United States, sitting under a constitution which had declared 'that the privilege of the writ of habeas corpus should not be suspended, unless when, in cases of rebellion or invasion, the public safety may require it.' Acting under the immediate influence of this injunction, they must have felt, with peculiar force, the obligation of providing efficient means, by which this great constitutional privilege should receive life and activity; for if the means be not in existence, the privilege itself would be lost, although no law for its suspension should be enacted. Under the impression of this obligation, they give to all the courts the power of awarding writs of habeas corpus." And again on page 101: "If at any time, the public safety should require the suspension of the powers vested by this act in the courts of the United States, it is for the legislature to say so. That question depends on political considerations, on which the legislature is to decide; until the legislative will be expressed, this court can only see its duty, and must obey the laws." I can add nothing to these clear and emphatic words of my great predecessor.

But the documents before me show, that the military authority in this case has gone far beyond the mere suspension of the privilege of the writ of habeas corpus. It has, by force of arms, thrust aside the judicial authorities and officers to whom the constitution has confided the power and duty of interpreting and administering the laws, and substituted a military government in its place, to be administered and executed by military officers. For, at the time these proceedings were had against John Merryman, the district judge of Maryland, the commissioner appointed under the act of congress, the district attorney and the marshal, all resided in the city of Baltimore, a few miles only from the home of the prisoner. Up to that time, there had never been the slightest resistance or obstruction to the process of any court or judicial officer of the United States, in Maryland, except by the military authority. And if a military officer, or any other person, had reason to believe that the prisoner had committed any offence against the laws of the United States, it was his duty to give information of the fact and the evidence to support it, to the district attorney; it would then have become the duty of that officer to bring the matter before the district judge or commissioner, and if there was sufficient legal evidence to justify his arrest, the judge or commissioner would have issued his warrant to the marshal to arrest him; and upon the hearing of the case, would have held him to bail, or committed him for trial, according to the character of the offence, as it appeared in the testimony, or would have discharged him immediately, if there was not sufficient evidence to support the accusation. There was no danger of any obstruction or resistance to the action of the civil authorities, and therefore no reason whatever for the interposition of the military.

Yet, under these circumstances, a military officer, stationed in Pennsylvania, without giving any information to the district attorney, and without any application to the judicial authorities, assumes to himself the judicial power in the district of Maryland; undertakes to decide what constitutes the crime of treason or rebellion; what evidence (if indeed he required any) is sufficient to support the accusation and justify the commitment; and commits the party, without a hearing, even before himself, to close custody, in a strongly garrisoned fort, to be there held, it would seem, during the pleasure of those who committed him.

The constitution provides, as I have before said, that "no person shall be deprived of life, liberty or property, without due process of law." It declares that "the right of the people to be secure in their persons, houses, papers and effects, against unreasonable searches and seizures, shall not be violated; and no warrant shall issue, but upon probable cause, supported by oath or affirmation, and particularly describing the place to be searched, and the persons or things to be seized." It provides that the party accused shall be entitled to a speedy trial in a court of justice.

These great and fundamental laws, which congress itself could not suspend, have been disregarded and suspended, like the writ of habeas corpus, by a military order, supported by force of arms. Such is the case now before me, and I can only say that if the authority which the constitution has confided to the judiciary department and judicial officers, may thus, upon any pretext or under any circumstances, be usurped by the military power, at its discretion, the people of the United States are no longer living under a government of laws, but every citizen holds life, liberty and property at the will and pleasure of the army officer in whose military district he may happen to be found.

In such a case, my duty was too plain to be mistaken. I have exercised all the power which the constitution and laws confer upon me, but that power has been resisted by a force too strong for me to overcome. It is possible that the officer who has incurred this grave responsibility may have misunderstood his instructions, and exceeded the authority intended to be given him; I shall, therefore, order all the proceedings in this case, with my opinion, to be filed and recorded in the circuit court of the United States for the district of Maryland, and direct the clerk to transmit a copy, under seal, to the president of the United States. It will then remain for that high officer, in fulfilment of his constitutional obligation to "take care that the laws be faithfully executed," to determine what measures he will take to cause the civil process of the United States to be respected and enforced.

William H. Rehnquist, All the Laws but One[*]

Lincoln Suspends Habeas Corpus

[President Lincoln made his first call for troops on April 15, 1861. The northern states responded with enthusiastic celebrations.] The reaction of the Upper South and border states was quite different. Six of the seven governors responded to Lincoln's call for troops with defiant refusals, characterizing his request as unconstitutional and, indeed, wicked. Two days after Lincoln's call, the Virginia convention, which had been in continuous session since February but without a majority for secession, voted eighty-five to fifty-five to secede. . . .

---

[*] Excerpted from WILLIAM H. REHNQUIST, ALL THE LAWS BUT ONE: CIVIL LIBERTIES IN WARTIME ch. 2 (1998).

Fear was rampant in the nation's capital:

In the eyes of the North, Washington was a cherished symbol of the nation's power, to be held and defended at all costs. To the South, the capital was a great prize whose capture would enhance the prestige of the rebellious government, and surely bring its recognition by foreign powers. The Confederate Secretary of War publicly boasted that before the first of May the Stars and Bars would float over the dome of the Federal capital. Richmond secessionists were panting for the attack, and the Enquirer called on Virginia volunteers to be ready to join the march of a southern army on Washington. The confidence of the disloyal residents of the capital increased the impression that the danger was imminent and acute.

. . . On the evening of April 18, the first dribbling of troops responding to Lincoln's call reached Washington: one company of regulars from Minnesota, and some four hundred volunteers from Pennsylvania. They had been stoned and harassed as they passed through Baltimore. The following day, there was news of a full-scale riot there, in which citizens had stoned Northern troops and the troops had fired back.

Baltimore was an absolutely critical rail junction for the purpose of bringing troops from the north or west into Washington, because the railroad coming down the coast from New York and Philadelphia, as well as the line from Harrisburg, ran through that city. The Baltimore & Ohio Railroad from the west joined the Baltimore—Washington line a few miles southwest of Baltimore at Relay House. This strategic location, plus the substantial degree of secessionist sympathy in Baltimore, made the city the Achilles' heel of the early efforts to bring federal troops to defend Washington. And the status of Maryland as a border state, whose adherence to the Union was problematic, exacerbated this difficulty. Maryland teetered both geographically and ideologically between North and South. If the secessionists were to gain the upper hand, the Union war effort could be seriously compromised.

Though small in area, Maryland comprises a remarkable diversity of geography, stretching from the Atlantic Ocean on the east to the summit of the Appalachians on the west. . . . The early English settlers along Chesapeake Bay developed a plantation system of agriculture whose primary crop was tobacco, supplemented by corn and wheat. Slaves were extensively used in the tobacco economy. But the part of the state west of Baltimore—with its small cities such as Frederick, Hagerstown, and Cumberland—was settled by Scotch-Irish and then Germans who had landed primarily in Philadelphia and spread out along the Cumberland Valley in Pennsylvania and the Shenandoah Valley in Virginia.

Baltimore lay between these two groups of very diverse settlers. . . . Work had begun on the Baltimore & Ohio Railroad, linking Baltimore with the west, in 1830, and by 1853 that line had reached the Ohio River.

The Baltimore & Susquehanna Railroad, leading to Harrisburg and beyond, was begun in 1829, and the rail link between Baltimore and Washington was completed in 1834.

Riots such as those that took place with the passage of Union troops on April 19 were not new to Baltimore. Indeed, it was known colloquially by then as "Mob City." In 1853, there had been a melee among city firemen; in 1856, a riot between Democrats and Know-nothings after the election of that year; and in 1857, a pitched battle between the city militia and strikers against the Baltimore & Ohio Railroad.

The Governor of Maryland in 1861 was Thomas Hicks, a cautious Union sympathizer very much aware of the delicate balance of opinion in his state. Responding to Lincoln's call for troops, he requested from Secretary Cameron a guarantee that Maryland's militia would be used only in that state or in the District of Columbia. Having received it, he issued a proclamation counseling restraint to the citizens of the state, and agreed to furnish troops on the conditions stated.

But the citizens of Baltimore did not heed the Governor's counsel. Four days after Lincoln issued his call for volunteers, a Massachusetts regiment arrived from Philadelphia at Baltimore's President Street Station. Instead of having the troops march the mile-and-a-half route from there to the Camden Station, where they would board the train for Washington, it was decided that the railroad cars themselves, with the troops aboard, would be drawn through the city by horses. Ten cars carried the first contingent, and eight of them successfully passed a gathering mob on Gay Street. But the ninth car stopped momentarily, and in a trice all of its windows were broken by flying rocks and stones. Other cars were now assailed, and the troops sought shelter on the floors of their cars. Nine cars finally made it to Camden Station, but the tenth didn't. The mob placed rocks and sand on the horse-car tracks, and the soldiers alighted and fell back to the station whence they had come.

Five hundred men of the Massachusetts regiment were now at Camden Station, ready to depart for Washington; 350 were at President Street Station. Between them was a mob of twenty thousand Confederate sympathizers. The troops decided to fight their way through on foot, and the mob closed in behind as they marched. The Baltimore police tried to form an escort, but the mob got between them and the soldiers. Mayor George Brown attempted to quiet the crowd by marching with the troops for a short way.

Soon the crowd loosed a volley of paving stones at the soldiers, who finally turned and fired their rifles into the crowd. People in the mob fired back. Two soldiers and four civilians were killed. The troops eventually made it to Camden Station, where the train immediately headed for Washington. Just as it did so, members of the crowd gave a cheer for Jefferson Davis; a soldier fired from the train and killed a prominent Baltimore merchant. In the final tally, sixteen people were killed, four soldiers and twelve civilians.

A mass meeting was called for 5 p.m. in Baltimore's Monument Square. Mayor Brown and Governor Hicks were among the speakers who urged the citizens of Baltimore to rise up and fight the "invasion." The next day's edition of the *New York Times*—Saturday, April 20, 1861— carried this headline on its front page:

STARTING FROM BALTIMORE

The Northern Troops Mobbed and Fired Upon—The Troops Return the Fire—Four Massachusetts Volunteers Killed and Several Wounded—Several of the Rioters Killed.

That night, Hicks, who was spending the night at Brown's home, was awakened by the Mayor and Marshal Thomas Kane, Chief of the Baltimore police, who urged him to order that railroad bridges north of Baltimore be burned in order to prevent more federal troops from entering the city. Hicks reluctantly agreed, and several spans on both the Harrisburg and Philadelphia lines were burned that night.

Several times in the next week, delegations of Baltimore officials either met with or wrote to Lincoln and Seward. First, they urged that no more federal troops be sent through the city; the administration agreed to this because General Winfield Scott thought that another route would do: The troops could detrain at Perryville, north of Baltimore on Chesapeake Bay, and go by ship from there to Annapolis, and from Annapolis by land to Washington. But a few days later, the Baltimore delegations were demanding that no troops go through Maryland at all, and that Lord Lyons, the British Minister, be asked to mediate the conflict between the North and the South. To this Lincoln replied that "our men are not moles, who can tunnel under the ground."

During the week following the Baltimore riots, the city of Washington seemed virtually cut off from the rest of the North. Not only were no troops arriving, but the telegraph lines had been cut and mail deliveries from the north were irregular. It was feared that ships would be unable to come up the Potomac because of a Confederate blockade on the lower part of the river.

Lincoln, by nature and habit so calm, so equable, so undemonstrative, nevertheless passed this period of interrupted communication and isolation from the North in the state of nervous tension which put all his great powers of mental and physical endurance to their severest trial. General Scott's reports, though invariably expressing his confidence and successful defense, frankly admitted the evident danger; and the President, with his acuteness of observation and his rapidity and correctness of inference, lost no single one of the external indications of doubt and apprehension. Day after day prediction failed and hope was deferred; troops did not come, ships did not arrive, railroads remained broken, messengers failed to reach their destination. . . .

In others' society [Lincoln] gave no sign of these inner emotions. But once, on the afternoon of the twenty-third, the business of the day being over, the Executive Office deserted, after walking the floor alone in silent thought for nearly an hour, he stopped and gazed long and wistfully out of the window down the Potomac in the direction of the expected ships; and unconscious of other presence in the room, at length broke out with irrepressible anguish in the repeated exclamation, "Why don't they come! Why don't they come!"

It was during this period of deep uneasiness in the capital following the Baltimore riots and bridge-burnings that Lincoln began to consider the possibility of suspending the writ of *habeas corpus* along the rail routes from the north. *Habeas corpus,* an important safeguard of personal liberty derived from English common law, was a right available to anyone arrested or detained by the government. The writ was directed to the official who had custody of the prisoner, and required that official to explain to the court issuing the writ the basis for holding the prisoner. The court would then determine whether the prisoner should be released or remanded to official custody.

Seward, reminiscing many years later, said to F. B. Carpenter, who was then in Auburn to paint his portrait:

There were two points in the administration . . . upon which all subsequent events hinged. One was the suspension of the Habeas Corpus Act. . . . The Habeas Corpus Act had not been suspended because of Mr. Lincoln's extreme reluctance at that period to assume such a responsibility. Those to whom he looked for advice, almost to a man, opposed this action.

On Sunday morning I went to the White House alone, and told the President that this step could no longer be delayed. He still argued against it. I told him emphatically that perdition was the sure penalty of further hesitation. He sat for some time in silence, then took up his pen and said: 'It shall be so!' The next day the proclamation suspending the Habeas Corpus Act was issued.

Among those whom Lincoln consulted about the suspension of the writ was Attorney General Edward Bates, a cautious Missourian who had been born and raised in Virginia. Bates compiled what there was of legal precedent on the question. Governor Hicks decided to call the Maryland legislature into session on April 26—not in Annapolis, which had been occupied by federal troops, but in Frederick, in western Maryland. The selection of the site was not inadvertent; most of the people in western Maryland were Unionists, and there would be no gangs of rowdies in the streets or in the galleries. The Governor urged the legislature to preserve its "neutral position" between the North and the South, and after some debate the legislature agreed. It refused to call a state convention to adopt an ordinance of secession but named committees to visit both Lincoln and Davis with a view to making peace.

When Lincoln first learned of Hicks's plan to convene the legislature, he considered arresting the legislators in order to prevent them from meeting. The matter was discussed in the Cabinet. But cooler heads prevailed, and Lincoln outlined his position in a formal directive to General Scott:

Washington, April 25. 1861

Lieutenant-General Scott.

My Dear Sir: The Maryland legislature assembles tomorrow at Annapolis, and not improbably will take action to arm the people of that State against the United States. The question has been submitted to and considered by me whether it would not be justifiable, upon the ground of necessary defense, for you, as General in Chief of the United States Army, to arrest or disperse the members of that body. I think it would not be justifiable nor efficient for the desired object.

First. They have clearly legal right to assemble, and we can not know in advance that their action will not be lawful and peaceful, and if we wait until they shall have acted their arrest or dispersion will not lessen the effect of their action.

Secondly. We can not permanently prevent their action. If we arrest them, we can not long hold them as prisoners, and when liberated they will immediately reassemble and take their action; and precisely the same if we simply disperse them—they will immediately reassemble in some other place.

I therefore conclude that it is only left to the Commanding General to watch and await their action, which, if it shall be to arm their people against the United States, he is to adopt the most prompt and efficient means to counteract, even, if necessary to the bombardment of their cities and, in the extremest necessity, the suspension of the writ of *habeas corpus*

Your obedient servant,

ABRAHAM LINCOLN

But Lincoln decided that more than watchful waiting was required with respect to the rioting and bridge-burning in Baltimore. Finally convinced of the wisdom of Seward's advice, he sent the following order to General Scott on April 27:

The Commanding General of the Army of the United States:

You are engaged in suppressing an insurrection against the laws of the United States. If at any point on or in the vicinity of any military line which is now or which shall be used between the city of Philadelphia and the city of Washington you find resistance which renders it necessary to suspend the writ of *habeas corpus* for the public safety, you personally, or through the officer in command at the point where resistance occurs, are authorized to suspend the writ.

Given under my hand and the seal of the United States, at the city of Washington, this 27th day of April, 1861, and of the Independence of the United States the eighty-fifth.

ABRAHAM LINCOLN

Hamdan v. Rumsfeld
548 U.S. 557 (2006)

■ JUSTICE STEVENS **announced the judgment of the Court and delivered the opinion of the Court with respect to Parts I through IV, Parts VI through VI-D-iii, Part VI-D-v, and Part VII, and an opinion with respect to Parts V and VI-D-iv, in which** JUSTICE SOUTER, JUSTICE GINSBURG, **and** JUSTICE BREYER **join.**

Petitioner Salim Ahmed Hamdan, a Yemeni national, is in custody at an American prison in Guantanamo Bay, Cuba. In November 2001, during hostilities between the United States and the Taliban (which then governed Afghanistan), Hamdan was captured by militia forces and turned over to the U. S. military. In June 2002, he was transported to Guantanamo Bay. Over a year later, the President deemed him eligible for trial by military commission for then-unspecified crimes. After another year had passed, Hamdan was charged with one count of conspiracy "to commit . . . offenses triable by military commission."

Hamdan filed petitions for writs of habeas corpus and mandamus to challenge the Executive Branch's intended means of prosecuting this charge. He concedes that a court-martial constituted in accordance with the Uniform Code of Military Justice (UCMJ), 10 U.S.C. § 801 et seq., would have authority to try him. His objection is that the military commission the President has convened lacks such authority, for two principal reasons: First, neither congressional Act nor the common law of war supports trial by this commission for the crime of conspiracy—an offense that, Hamdan says, is not a violation of the law of war. Second, Hamdan contends, the procedures that the President has adopted to try him violate the most basic tenets of military and international law, including the principle that a defendant must be permitted to see and hear the evidence against him.

The District Court granted Hamdan's request for a writ of habeas corpus. The Court of Appeals for the District of Columbia Circuit reversed. Recognizing . . . that trial by military commission is an extraordinary measure raising important questions about the balance of powers in our constitutional structure, we granted certiorari.

For the reasons that follow, we conclude that the military commission convened to try Hamdan lacks power to proceed because its structure and procedures violate both the UCMJ and the Geneva Conventions. Four of us also conclude, see Part V, *infra*, that the offense with which Hamdan has been charged is not an "offens[e] that by . . . the law of war may be tried by military commissions." 10 U.S.C. § 821.

I

On September 11, 2001, agents of the al Qaeda terrorist organization hijacked commercial airplanes and attacked the World Trade Center in New York City and the national headquarters of the Department of Defense in Arlington, Virginia. Americans will never forget the devastation wrought by these acts. Nearly 3,000 civilians were killed.

Congress responded by adopting a Joint Resolution authorizing the President to "use all necessary and appropriate force against those nations, organizations, or persons he determines planned, authorized, committed, or aided the terrorist attacks . . . in order to prevent any future acts of international terrorism against the United States by such nations, organizations or persons." Authorization for Use of Military Force (AUMF). Acting pursuant to the AUMF, and having determined that the Taliban regime had supported al Qaeda, the President ordered the Armed Forces of the United States to invade Afghanistan. In the ensuing hostilities, hundreds of individuals, Hamdan among them, were captured and eventually detained at Guantanamo Bay.

On November 13, 2001, while the United States was still engaged in active combat with the Taliban, the President issued a comprehensive military order intended to govern the "Detention, Treatment, and Trial of Certain Non-Citizens in the War Against Terrorism." Those subject to the November 13 Order include any noncitizen for whom the President determines "there is reason to believe" that he or she (1) "is or was" a member of al Qaeda or (2) has engaged or participated in terrorist activities aimed at or harmful to the United States. Any such individual "shall, when tried, be tried by military commission for any and all offenses triable by military commission that such individual is alleged to have committed, and may be punished in accordance with the penalties provided under applicable law, including imprisonment or death." . . .

On July 3, 2003, the President announced his determination that Hamdan and five other detainees at Guantanamo Bay were subject to the November 13 Order and thus triable by military commission. In December 2003, military counsel was appointed to represent Hamdan. Two months later, counsel filed demands for charges and for a speedy trial pursuant to Article 10 of the UCMJ. On February 23, 2004, the legal adviser to the Appointing Authority denied the applications, ruling that Hamdan was not entitled to any of the protections of the UCMJ. Not until July 13, 2004, after Hamdan had commenced this action in the United States District Court for the Western District of Washington, did the

Government finally charge him with the offense for which, a year earlier, he had been deemed eligible for trial by military commission.

The charging document, which is unsigned, contains 13 numbered paragraphs. The first two paragraphs recite the asserted bases for the military commission's jurisdiction—namely, the November 13 Order and the President's July 3, 2003, declaration that Hamdan is eligible for trial by military commission. The next nine paragraphs, collectively entitled "General Allegations," describe al Qaeda's activities from its inception in 1989 through 2001 and identify Osama bin Laden as the group's leader. Hamdan is not mentioned in these paragraphs.

Only the final two paragraphs, entitled "Charge: Conspiracy," contain allegations against Hamdan. Paragraph 12 charges that "from on or about February 1996 to on or about November 24, 2001," Hamdan "willfully and knowingly joined an enterprise of persons who shared a common criminal purpose and conspired and agreed with [named members of al Qaeda] to commit the following offenses triable by military commission: attacking civilians; attacking civilian objects; murder by an unprivileged belligerent; and terrorism." There is no allegation that Hamdan had any command responsibilities, played a leadership role, or participated in the planning of any activity.

Paragraph 13 lists four "overt acts" that Hamdan is alleged to have committed sometime between 1996 and November 2001 in furtherance of the "enterprise and conspiracy": (1) he acted as Osama bin Laden's "bodyguard and personal driver," "believ[ing]" all the while that bin Laden "and his associates were involved in" terrorist acts prior to and including the attacks of September 11, 2001; (2) he arranged for transportation of, and actually transported, weapons used by al Qaeda members and by bin Laden's bodyguards (Hamdan among them); (3) he "drove or accompanied [O]sama bin Laden to various al Qaida-sponsored training camps, press conferences, or lectures," at which bin Laden encouraged attacks against Americans; and (4) he received weapons training at al Qaeda-sponsored camps.

After this formal charge was filed, the United States District Court for the Western District of Washington transferred Hamdan's habeas and mandamus petitions to the United States District Court for the District of Columbia. Meanwhile, a Combatant Status Review Tribunal (CSRT) convened pursuant to a military order issued on July 7, 2004, decided that Hamdan's continued detention at Guantanamo Bay was warranted because he was an "enemy combatant."[1] Separately, proceedings before the military commission commenced.

On November 8, 2004, however, the District Court granted Hamdan's petition for habeas corpus and stayed the commission's

---

[1] An "enemy combatant" is defined by the military order as "an individual who was part of or supporting Taliban or al Qaeda forces, or associated forces that are engaged in hostilities against the United States or its coalition partners."

proceedings. . . . The Court of Appeals for the District of Columbia Circuit reversed. . . . On November 7, 2005, we granted certiorari to decide whether the military commission convened to try Hamdan has authority to do so, and whether Hamdan may rely on the Geneva Conventions in these proceedings.

IV

The military commission, a tribunal neither mentioned in the Constitution nor created by statute, was born of military necessity. Though foreshadowed in some respects by earlier tribunals like the Board of General Officers that General Washington convened to try British Major John Andre for spying during the Revolutionary War, the commission "as such" was inaugurated in 1847. As commander of occupied Mexican territory, and having available to him no other tribunal, General Winfield Scott that year ordered the establishment of both "military commissions" to try ordinary crimes committed in the occupied territory and a "council of war" to try offenses against the law of war.

When the exigencies of war next gave rise to a need for use of military commissions, during the Civil War, the dual system favored by General Scott was not adopted. Instead, a single tribunal often took jurisdiction over ordinary crimes, war crimes, and breaches of military orders alike. As further discussed below, each aspect of that seemingly broad jurisdiction was in fact supported by a separate military exigency. Generally, though, the need for military commissions during this period—as during the Mexican War—was driven largely by the then very limited jurisdiction of courts-martial: "The occasion for the military commission arises principally from the fact that the jurisdiction of the court-martial proper, in our law, is restricted by statute almost exclusively to members of the military force and to certain specific offences defined in a written code."

Exigency alone, of course, will not justify the establishment and use of penal tribunals not contemplated by Article I, § 8 and Article III, § 1 of the Constitution unless some other part of that document authorizes a response to the felt need. See *Ex parte Milligan*, 71 U.S. 2 (1866) ("Certainly no part of the judicial power of the country was conferred on [military commissions]"). And that authority, if it exists, can derive only from the powers granted jointly to the President and Congress in time of war.

The Constitution makes the President the "Commander in Chief" of the Armed Forces, Art. II, § 2, cl. 1, but vests in Congress the powers to "declare War . . . and make Rules concerning Captures on Land and Water," Art. I, § 8, cl. 11, to "raise and support Armies," *id.*, cl. 12, to "define and punish . . . Offences against the Law of Nations," *id.*, cl. 10, and "To make Rules for the Government and Regulation of the land and naval Forces," *id.*, cl. 14. The interplay between these powers was described by Chief Justice Chase in the seminal case of *Ex parte*

Milligan: . . . Congress cannot direct the conduct of campaigns, nor can the President, or any commander under him, without the sanction of Congress, institute tribunals for the trial and punishment of offences, either of soldiers or civilians, unless in cases of a controlling necessity, which justifies what it compels, or at least insures acts of indemnity from the justice of the legislature.

Whether Chief Justice Chase was correct in suggesting that the President may constitutionally convene military commissions "without the sanction of Congress" in cases of "controlling necessity" is a question this Court has not answered definitively, and need not answer today. For we held in *Ex Parte Quirin,* 317 U.S. 1 (1942), that Congress had, through Article of War 15, sanctioned the use of military commissions in such circumstances. Article 21 of the UCMJ, the language of which is substantially identical to the old Article 15 and was preserved by Congress after World War II,[22] reads as follows:

> Jurisdiction of courts-martial not exclusive.

> The provisions of this code conferring jurisdiction upon courts-martial shall not be construed as depriving military commissions, provost courts, or other military tribunals of concurrent jurisdiction in respect of offenders or offenses that by statute or by the law of war may be tried by such military commissions, provost courts, or other military tribunals.

We have no occasion to revisit *Quirin*'s controversial characterization of Article of War 15 as congressional authorization for military commissions. Contrary to the Government's assertion, however, even *Quirin* did not view the authorization as a sweeping mandate for the President to "invoke military commissions when he deems them necessary." Rather, the *Quirin* Court recognized that Congress had simply preserved what power, under the Constitution and the common law of war, the President had had before 1916 to convene military commissions—with the express condition that the President and those under his command comply with the law of war.[23] . . .

The Government would have us dispense with the inquiry [into the law of war] and find in either the AUMF or the [Detainee Treatment Act of 2005 (DTA)] specific, overriding authorization for the very commission that has been convened to try Hamdan. Neither of these congressional Acts, however, expands the President's authority to convene military commissions. First, while we assume that the AUMF activated the President's war powers and that those powers include the authority to

---

[22] Article 15 was first adopted as part of the Articles of War in 1916. When the Articles of War were codified and re-enacted as the UCMJ in 1950, Congress determined to retain Article 15 because it had been "construed by the Supreme Court [in *Quirin*]." S. Rep. No. 486 (1949).

[23] Whether or not the President has independent power, absent congressional authorization, to convene military commissions, he may not disregard limitations that Congress has, in proper exercise of its own war powers, placed on his powers. See *Youngstown Sheet & Tube Co. v. Sawyer* (Jackson, J., concurring). The Government does not argue otherwise.

convene military commissions in appropriate circumstances, there is nothing in the text or legislative history of the AUMF even hinting that Congress intended to expand or alter the authorization set forth in Article 21 of the UCMJ.

Likewise, the DTA cannot be read to authorize this commission. Although the DTA, unlike either Article 21 or the AUMF, was enacted after the President had convened Hamdan's commission, it contains no language authorizing that tribunal or any other at Guantanamo Bay. The DTA obviously "recognize[s]" the existence of the Guantanamo Bay commissions in the weakest sense, because it references some of the military orders governing them and creates limited judicial review of their "final decision[s]." But the statute also pointedly reserves judgment on whether "the Constitution and laws of the United States are applicable" in reviewing such decisions and whether, if they are, the "standards and procedures" used to try Hamdan and other detainees actually violate the "Constitution and laws."

Together, the UCMJ, the AUMF, and the DTA at most acknowledge a general Presidential authority to convene military commissions in circumstances where justified under the "Constitution and laws," including the law of war. Absent a more specific congressional authorization, the task of this Court is . . . to decide whether Hamdan's military commission is so justified. . . .

V

The common law governing military commissions may be gleaned from past practice and what sparse legal precedent exists. Commissions historically have been used in three situations. First, they have substituted for civilian courts at times and in places where martial law has been declared. Their use in these circumstances has raised constitutional questions but is well recognized.[25] Second, commissions have been established to try civilians as part of a temporary military government over occupied enemy territory or territory regained from an enemy where civilian government cannot and does not function. Illustrative of this second kind of commission is the one that was established, with jurisdiction to apply the German Criminal Code, in occupied Germany following the end of World War II.

The third type of commission, convened as an "incident to the conduct of war" when there is a need "to seize and subject to disciplinary

---

[25] The justification for, and limitations on, these commissions were summarized in *Milligan:* "If, in foreign invasion or civil war, the courts are actually closed, and it is impossible to administer criminal justice according to law, *then*, on the theatre of active military operations, where war really prevails, there is a necessity to furnish a substitute for the civil authority, thus overthrown, to preserve the safety of the army and society; and as no power is left but the military, it is allowed to govern by martial rule until the laws can have their free course. As necessity creates the rule, so it limits its duration; for, if this government is continued *after* the courts are reinstated, it is a gross usurpation of power. Martial rule can never exist where the courts are open, and in the proper and unobstructed exercise of their jurisdiction. It is also confined to the locality of actual war."

measures those enemies who in their attempt to thwart or impede our military effort have violated the law of war," has been described as "utterly different" from the other two. Not only is its jurisdiction limited to offenses cognizable during time of war, but its role is primarily a factfinding one—to determine, typically on the battlefield itself, whether the defendant has violated the law of war. The last time the U. S. Armed Forces used the law-of-war military commission was during World War II. In *Quirin*, this Court sanctioned President Roosevelt's use of such a tribunal to try Nazi saboteurs captured on American soil during the War. And in *Yamashita*, we held that a military commission had jurisdiction to try a Japanese commander for failing to prevent troops under his command from committing atrocities in the Philippines. 327 U.S. 1 (1946).

Quirin is the model the Government invokes most frequently to defend the commission convened to try Hamdan. . . . Since Guantanamo Bay is neither enemy-occupied territory nor under martial law, the law-of-war commission is the only model available. . . . *Quirin* represents the high-water mark of military power to try enemy combatants for war crimes.

The classic treatise penned by Colonel William Winthrop . . . describes at least four preconditions for exercise of jurisdiction by a tribunal of the type convened to try Hamdan. First, "[a] military commission, (except where otherwise authorized by statute), can legally assume jurisdiction only of offenses committed within the field of the command of the convening commander." W. Winthrop, Military Law and Precedents 831, 836 (rev. 2d ed.1920). The "field of command" in these circumstances means the "theatre of war." Second, the offense charged "must have been committed within the period of the war." No jurisdiction exists to try offenses "committed either before or after the war." Third, a military commission not established pursuant to martial law or an occupation may try only "[i]ndividuals of the enemy's army who have been guilty of illegitimate warfare or other offences in violation of the laws of war" and members of one's own army "who, in time of war, become chargeable with crimes or offences not cognizable, or triable, by the criminal courts or under the Articles of war." Finally, a law-of-war commission has jurisdiction to try only two kinds of offense: "Violations of the laws and usages of war cognizable by military tribunals only," and "[b]reaches of military orders or regulations for which offenders are not legally triable by court-martial under the Articles of war."

All parties agree that Colonel Winthrop's treatise accurately describes the common law governing military commissions, and that the jurisdictional limitations he identifies were incorporated in Article of War 15 and, later, Article 21 of the UCMJ. It also is undisputed that Hamdan's commission lacks jurisdiction to try him unless the charge "properly set[s] forth, not only the details of the act charged, but the circumstances conferring jurisdiction." The question is whether the preconditions designed to ensure that a military necessity exists to justify the use of this extraordinary tribunal have been satisfied here.

The charge against Hamdan . . . alleges a conspiracy extending over a number of years, from 1996 to November 2001. . . . [T]he most serious defect of this charge [is that the] offense it alleges is not triable by law-of-war military commission. [The plurality went on to survey at length evidence that conspiracy is not a crime against the laws of war.]

VI

Whether or not the Government has charged Hamdan with an offense against the law of war cognizable by military commission, the commission lacks power to proceed. The UCMJ conditions the President's use of military commissions on compliance not only with the American common law of war, but also with the rest of the UCMJ itself, insofar as applicable, and with the "rules and precepts of the law of nations"—including, *inter alia*, the four Geneva Conventions signed in 1949. The procedures that the Government has decreed will govern Hamdan's trial by commission violate these laws.

A

The commission's procedures are set forth in Commission Order No. 1, which was amended most recently on August 31, 2005—after Hamdan's trial had already begun. Every commission established pursuant to Commission Order No. 1 must have a presiding officer and at least three other members, all of whom must be commissioned officers. The presiding officer's job is to rule on questions of law and other evidentiary and interlocutory issues; the other members make findings and, if applicable, sentencing decisions. The accused is entitled to appointed military counsel and may hire civilian counsel at his own expense so long as such counsel is a U. S. citizen with security clearance "at the level SECRET or higher."

The accused also is entitled to a copy of the charge(s) against him, both in English and his own language (if different), to a presumption of innocence, and to certain other rights typically afforded criminal defendants in civilian courts and courts-martial. These rights are subject, however, to one glaring condition: The accused and his civilian counsel may be excluded from, and precluded from ever learning what evidence was presented during, any part of the proceeding that either the Appointing Authority or the presiding officer decides to "close." Grounds for such closure "include the protection of information classified or classifiable . . . ; information protected by law or rule from unauthorized disclosure; the physical safety of participants in Commission proceedings, including prospective witnesses; intelligence and law enforcement sources, methods, or activities; and other national security interests." Appointed military defense counsel must be privy to these closed sessions, but may, at the presiding officer's discretion, be forbidden to reveal to his or her client what took place therein.

Another striking feature of the rules governing Hamdan's commission is that they permit the admission of *any* evidence that, in the opinion of the presiding officer, "would have probative value to a reasonable person." Under this test, not only is testimonial hearsay and evidence obtained through coercion fully admissible, but neither live testimony nor witnesses' written statements need be sworn. Moreover, the accused and his civilian counsel may be denied access to evidence in the form of "protected information" (which includes classified information as well as "information protected by law or rule from unauthorized disclosure" and "information concerning other national security interests"), so long as the presiding officer concludes that the evidence is "probative" . . . and that its admission without the accused's knowledge would not "result in the denial of a full and fair trial."[43] Finally, a presiding officer's determination that evidence "would not have probative value to a reasonable person" may be overridden by a majority of the other commission members.

Once all the evidence is in, the commission members (not including the presiding officer) must vote on the accused's guilt. A two-thirds vote will suffice for both a verdict of guilty and for imposition of any sentence not including death (the imposition of which requires a unanimous vote). Any appeal is taken to a three-member review panel composed of military officers and designated by the Secretary of Defense, only one member of which need have experience as a judge. The review panel is directed to "disregard any variance from procedures specified in this Order or elsewhere that would not materially have affected the outcome of the trial before the Commission." Once the panel makes its recommendation to the Secretary of Defense, the Secretary can either remand for further proceedings or forward the record to the President with his recommendation as to final disposition. The President then, unless he has delegated the task to the Secretary, makes the "final decision." He may change the commission's findings or sentence only in a manner favorable to the accused.

B

Hamdan raises both general and particular objections to the procedures set forth in Commission Order No. 1. His general objection is that the procedures' admitted deviation from those governing courts-martial itself renders the commission illegal. Chief among his particular objections are that he may, under the Commission Order, be convicted based on evidence he has not seen or heard, and that any evidence admitted against him need not comply with the admissibility or

---

[43] As the District Court observed, this section apparently permits reception of testimony from a confidential informant in circumstances where "Hamdan will not be permitted to hear the testimony, see the witness's face, or learn his name. If the government has information developed by interrogation of witnesses in Afghanistan or elsewhere, it can offer such evidence in transcript form, or even as summaries of transcripts."

relevance rules typically applicable in criminal trials and court-martial proceedings. . . .

C

In part because the difference between military commissions and courts-martial originally was a difference of jurisdiction alone, and in part to protect against abuse and ensure evenhandedness under the pressures of war, the procedures governing trials by military commission historically have been the same as those governing courts-martial. Accounts of commentators from Winthrop through General Crowder—who drafted Article of War 15 and whose views have been deemed "authoritative" by this Court—confirm as much. As recently as the Korean and Vietnam wars, during which use of military commissions was contemplated but never made, the principle of procedural parity was espoused as a background assumption.

There is a glaring historical exception to this general rule. The procedures and evidentiary rules used to try General Yamashita near the end of World War II deviated in significant respects from those then governing courts-martial. The force of that precedent, however, has been seriously undermined by post-World War II developments. . . . At least partially in response to subsequent criticism of General Yamashita's trial, the UCMJ's codification of the Articles of War after World War II expanded the category of persons subject thereto to include defendants in Yamashita's (and Hamdan's) position, and the Third Geneva Convention of 1949 extended prisoner-of-war protections to individuals tried for crimes committed before their capture. . . .

The uniformity principle is not an inflexible one; it does not preclude all departures from the procedures dictated for use by courts-martial. But any departure must be tailored to the exigency that necessitates it. That understanding is reflected in Article 36 of the UCMJ, which provides:

> (a) The procedure, including modes of proof, in cases before courts-martial, courts of inquiry, military commissions, and other military tribunals may be prescribed by the President by regulations which shall, so far as he considers practicable, apply the principles of law and the rules of evidence generally recognized in the trial of criminal cases in the United States district courts, but which may not be contrary to or inconsistent with this chapter.
>
> (b) All rules and regulations made under this article shall be uniform insofar as practicable and shall be reported to Congress.

Article 36 places two restrictions on the President's power to promulgate rules of procedure for courts-martial and military commissions alike. First, no procedural rule he adopts may be "contrary to or inconsistent with" the UCMJ—however practical it may seem. Second, the rules adopted must be "uniform insofar as practicable." That is, the rules applied to military commissions must be the same as those applied to courts-martial unless such uniformity proves impracticable.

Hamdan argues that Commission Order No. 1 violates both of these restrictions; he maintains that the procedures described in the Commission Order are inconsistent with the UCMJ and that the Government has offered no explanation for their deviation from the procedures governing courts-martial, which are set forth in the Manual for Courts-Martial, United States (2005 ed.). Among the inconsistencies Hamdan identifies is that between § 6 of the Commission Order, which permits exclusion of the accused from proceedings and denial of his access to evidence in certain circumstances, and the UCMJ's requirement that "[a]ll . . . proceedings" other than votes and deliberations by courts-martial "shall be made a part of the record and shall be in the presence of the accused." Hamdan also observes that the Commission Order dispenses with virtually all evidentiary rules applicable in courts-martial.

The Government has three responses. First, it argues, only 9 of the UCMJ's 158 Articles—the ones that expressly mention "military commissions"—actually apply to commissions, and Commission Order No. 1 sets forth no procedure that is "contrary to or inconsistent with" those 9 provisions. Second, the Government contends, military commissions would be of no use if the President were hamstrung by those provisions of the UCMJ that govern courts-martial. Finally, the President's determination that "the danger to the safety of the United States and the nature of international terrorism" renders it impracticable "to apply in military commissions . . . the principles of law and rules of evidence generally recognized in the trial of criminal cases in the United States district courts," is, in the Government's view, explanation enough for any deviation from court-martial procedures.

Hamdan has the better of this argument. Without reaching the question whether any provision of Commission Order No. 1 is strictly "contrary to or inconsistent with" other provisions of the UCMJ, we conclude that the "practicability" determination the President has made is insufficient to justify variances from the procedures governing courts-martial. Subsection (b) of Article 36 was added after World War II, and requires a different showing of impracticability from the one required by subsection (a). Subsection (a) requires that the rules the President promulgates for courts-martial, provost courts, and military commissions alike conform to those that govern procedures in Article III courts, "so far as *he considers* practicable." Subsection (b), by contrast, demands that the rules applied in courts-martial, provost courts, and military commissions—whether or not they conform with the Federal Rules of Evidence—be "uniform *insofar as practicable*." Under the latter provision, then, the rules set forth in the Manual for Courts-Martial must apply to military commissions unless impracticable.

The President here has determined, pursuant to subsection (a), that it is impracticable to apply the rules and principles of law that govern "the trial of criminal cases in the United States district courts" to Hamdan's commission. We assume that complete deference is owed that determination. The President has not, however, made a similar official determination that it is impracticable to apply the rules for courts-martial.[51] And even if subsection (b)'s requirements may be satisfied without such an official determination, the requirements of that subsection are not satisfied here.

Nothing in the record before us demonstrates that it would be impracticable to apply court-martial rules in this case. There is no suggestion, for example, of any logistical difficulty in securing properly sworn and authenticated evidence or in applying the usual principles of relevance and admissibility. Assuming *arguendo* that the reasons articulated in the President's Article 36(a) determination ought to be considered in evaluating the impracticability of applying court-martial rules, the only reason offered in support of that determination is the danger posed by international terrorism. Without for one moment underestimating that danger, it is not evident to us why it should require, in the case of Hamdan's trial, any variance from the rules that govern courts-martial.

The absence of any showing of impracticability is particularly disturbing when considered in light of the clear and admitted failure to apply one of the most fundamental protections afforded not just by the Manual for Courts-Martial but also by the UCMJ itself: the right to be present. Whether or not that departure technically is "contrary to or inconsistent with" the terms of the UCMJ, the jettisoning of so basic a right cannot lightly be excused as "practicable."

Under the circumstances, then, the rules applicable in courts-martial must apply. Since it is undisputed that Commission Order No. 1 deviates in many significant respects from those rules, it necessarily violates Article 36(b).

The Government's objection that requiring compliance with the court-martial rules imposes an undue burden both ignores the plain meaning of Article 36(b) and misunderstands the purpose and the history of military commissions. The military commission was not born of a desire to dispense a more summary form of justice than is afforded by courts-martial; it developed, rather, as a tribunal of necessity to be employed when courts-martial lacked jurisdiction over either the accused or the subject matter. Exigency lent the commission its legitimacy, but did not further justify the wholesale jettisoning of procedural protections. That history explains why the military commission's procedures typically

---

[51] We may assume that such a determination would be entitled to a measure of deference. For the reasons given by Justice Kennedy, however, the level of deference accorded to a determination made under subsection (b) presumably would not be as high as that accorded to a determination under subsection (a).

have been the ones used by courts-martial. . . . Article 21 did not transform the military commission from a tribunal of true exigency into a more convenient adjudicatory tool. Article 36, confirming as much, strikes a careful balance between uniform procedure and the need to accommodate exigencies that may sometimes arise in a theater of war. That Article not having been complied with here, the rules specified for Hamdan's trial are illegal.

D

[The Court concluded that "the procedures adopted to try Hamdan also violate the Geneva Conventions."]

VII

We have assumed, as we must, that the allegations made in the Government's charge against Hamdan are true. We have assumed, moreover, the truth of the message implicit in that charge—viz., that Hamdan is a dangerous individual whose beliefs, if acted upon, would cause great harm and even death to innocent civilians, and who would act upon those beliefs if given the opportunity. It bears emphasizing that Hamdan does not challenge, and we do not today address, the Government's power to detain him for the duration of active hostilities in order to prevent such harm. But in undertaking to try Hamdan and subject him to criminal punishment, the Executive is bound to comply with the Rule of Law that prevails in this jurisdiction.

The judgment of the Court of Appeals is reversed, and the case is remanded for further proceedings.

It is so ordered.

■ The CHIEF JUSTICE took no part in the consideration or decision of this case.

■ JUSTICE BREYER, with whom JUSTICE KENNEDY, JUSTICE SOUTER, and JUSTICE GINSBURG join, concurring.

. . . The Court's conclusion ultimately rests upon a single ground: Congress has not issued the Executive a "blank check." Indeed, Congress has denied the President the legislative authority to create military commissions of the kind at issue here. Nothing prevents the President from returning to Congress to seek the authority he believes necessary.

Where, as here, no emergency prevents consultation with Congress, judicial insistence upon that consultation does not weaken our Nation's ability to deal with danger. To the contrary, that insistence strengthens the Nation's ability to determine—through democratic means—how best to do so. The Constitution places its faith in those democratic means. Our Court today simply does the same.

■ JUSTICE KENNEDY, with whom JUSTICE SOUTER, JUSTICE GINSBURG, and JUSTICE BREYER join as to Parts I and II, concurring in part.

Military Commission Order No. 1, which governs the military commission established to try petitioner Salim Hamdan for war crimes, exceeds limits that certain statutes, duly enacted by Congress, have placed on the President's authority to convene military courts. This is not a case, then, where the Executive can assert some unilateral authority to fill a void left by congressional inaction. It is a case where Congress, in the proper exercise of its powers as an independent branch of government, and as part of a long tradition of legislative involvement in matters of military justice, has considered the subject of military tribunals and set limits on the President's authority. Where a statute provides the conditions for the exercise of governmental power, its requirements are the result of a deliberative and reflective process engaging both of the political branches. Respect for laws derived from the customary operation of the Executive and Legislative Branches gives some assurance of stability in time of crisis. The Constitution is best preserved by reliance on standards tested over time and insulated from the pressures of the moment.

These principles seem vindicated here, for a case that may be of extraordinary importance is resolved by ordinary rules. The rules of most relevance here are those pertaining to the authority of Congress and the interpretation of its enactments.

It seems appropriate to recite these rather fundamental points because the Court refers, as it should in its exposition of the case, to the requirement of the Geneva Conventions of 1949 that military tribunals be "regularly constituted"—a requirement that controls here, if for no other reason, because Congress requires that military commissions like the ones at issue conform to the "law of war," 10 U.S.C. § 821. Whatever the substance and content of the term "regularly constituted" as interpreted in this and any later cases, there seems little doubt that it relies upon the importance of standards deliberated upon and chosen in advance of crisis, under a system where the single power of the Executive is checked by other constitutional mechanisms. All of which returns us to the point of beginning—that domestic statutes control this case. If Congress, after due consideration, deems it appropriate to change the controlling statutes, in conformance with the Constitution and other laws, it has the power and prerogative to do so.

I join the Court's opinion, save Parts V and VI-D-iv. . . .

I

Trial by military commission raises separation-of-powers concerns of the highest order. Located within a single branch, these courts carry the risk that offenses will be defined, prosecuted, and adjudicated by executive officials without independent review. Concentration of power puts personal liberty in peril of arbitrary action by officials, an incursion the Constitution's three-part system is designed to avoid. It is imperative, then, that when military tribunals are established, full and proper authority exists for the Presidential directive.

The proper framework for assessing whether Executive actions are authorized is the three-part scheme used by Justice Jackson in his opinion in *Youngstown Sheet & Tube Co. v. Sawyer.* "When the President acts pursuant to an express or implied authorization of Congress, his authority is at its maximum, for it includes all that he possesses in his own right plus all that Congress can delegate." "When the President acts in absence of either a congressional grant or denial of authority, he can only rely upon his own independent powers, but there is a zone of twilight in which he and Congress may have concurrent authority, or in which its distribution is uncertain." And "[w]hen the President takes measures incompatible with the expressed or implied will of Congress, his power is at its lowest ebb."

In this case, as the Court observes, the President has acted in a field with a history of congressional participation and regulation. In the Uniform Code of Military Justice, which Congress enacted, building on earlier statutes, in 1950 and later amended, Congress has set forth governing principles for military courts. The UCMJ as a whole establishes an intricate system of military justice. It authorizes courts-martial in various forms; it regulates the organization and procedure of those courts; it defines offenses and rights for the accused; and it provides mechanisms for appellate review. As explained below, the statute further recognizes that special military commissions may be convened to try war crimes. While these laws provide authority for certain forms of military courts, they also impose limitations, at least two of which control this case. If the President has exceeded these limits, this becomes a case of conflict between Presidential and congressional action—a case within Justice Jackson's third category, not the second or first. . . .

III

In light of the conclusion that the military commission here is unauthorized under the UCMJ, I see no need to consider several further issues addressed in the plurality opinion by Justice Stevens and the dissent by Justice Thomas.

First, I would not decide whether Common Article 3's standard . . . necessarily requires that the accused have the right to be present at all stages of a criminal trial. I likewise see no need to address the validity of the conspiracy charge against Hamdan—an issue addressed at length in Part V of Justice Stevens' opinion and in Part II-C of Justice Thomas' dissent. In light of the conclusion that the military commissions at issue are unauthorized Congress may choose to provide further guidance in this area. Congress, not the Court, is the branch in the better position to undertake the "sensitive task of establishing a principle not inconsistent with the national interest or international justice." . . .

With these observations I join the Court's opinion with the exception of Parts V and VI-D-iv.

■ JUSTICE SCALIA, with whom JUSTICE THOMAS and JUSTICE ALITO join, dissenting.

[Justice Scalia argued that, by enacting the Detainee Treatment Act of 2005, Congress had stripped the federal courts of jurisdiction to hear Hamdan's case.]

■ JUSTICE THOMAS, with whom JUSTICE SCALIA joins, and with whom JUSTICE ALITO joins in all but Parts I, II-C-1, and III-B-2, dissenting.

. . . [T]he Court's opinion openly flouts our well-established duty to respect the Executive's judgment in matters of military operations and foreign affairs. The Court's evident belief that *it* is qualified to pass on the "[m]ilitary necessity" of the Commander in Chief's decision to employ a particular form of force against our enemies is so antithetical to our constitutional structure that it simply cannot go unanswered. I respectfully dissent.

I

Our review of petitioner's claims arises in the context of the President's wartime exercise of his commander-in-chief authority in conjunction with the complete support of Congress. Accordingly, it is important to take measure of the respective roles the Constitution assigns to the three branches of our Government in the conduct of war.

[T]he structural advantages attendant to the Executive Branch— namely, the decisiveness, " 'activity, secrecy, and dispatch' " that flow from the Executive's " 'unity' " (quoting The Federalist No. 70 (A. Hamilton))—led the Founders to conclude that the "President ha[s] primary responsibility—along with the necessary power—to protect the national security and to conduct the Nation's foreign relations." Consistent with this conclusion, the Constitution vests in the President "[t]he executive Power," Art. II, § 1, provides that he "shall be Commander in Chief" of the Armed Forces, § 2, and places in him the power to recognize foreign governments, § 3. This Court has observed that these provisions confer upon the President broad constitutional authority to protect the Nation's security in the manner he deems fit. *See, e.g., Prize Cases.*

Congress, to be sure, has a substantial and essential role in both foreign affairs and national security. But "Congress cannot anticipate and legislate with regard to every possible action the President may find it necessary to take or every possible situation in which he might act," and "[s]uch failure of Congress . . . does not, 'especially . . . in the areas of foreign policy and national security,' imply 'congressional disapproval' of action taken by the Executive." *Dames & Moore v. Regan.* Rather, in these domains, the fact that Congress has provided the President with broad authorities does not imply—and the Judicial Branch should not infer—that Congress intended to deprive him of particular powers not specifically enumerated. See *Dames & Moore.*

When "the President acts pursuant to an express or implied authorization from Congress," his actions are " 'supported by the strongest of presumptions and the widest latitude of judicial interpretation, and the burden of persuasion . . . rest[s] heavily upon any who might attack it.' " Accordingly, in the very context that we address today, this Court has concluded that "the detention and trial of petitioners—ordered by the President in the declared exercise of his powers as Commander in Chief of the Army in time of war and of grave public danger—are not to be set aside by the courts without the clear conviction that they are in conflict with the Constitution or laws of Congress constitutionally enacted."

Under this framework, the President's decision to try Hamdan before a military commission for his involvement with al Qaeda is entitled to a heavy measure of deference. In the present conflict, Congress has authorized the President "to use all necessary and appropriate force against those nations, organizations, or persons *he determines* planned, authorized, committed, or aided the terrorist attacks that occurred on September 11, 2001 . . . in order to prevent any future acts of international terrorism against the United States by such nations, organizations or persons." Authorization for Use of Military Force. As a plurality of the Court observed in *Hamdi*, the "capture, detention, and *trial* of unlawful combatants, by 'universal agreement and practice,' are 'important incident[s] of war,' " and are therefore "an exercise of the 'necessary and appropriate force' Congress has authorized the President to use." *Hamdi*'s observation that military commissions are included within the AUMF's authorization is supported by this Court's previous recognition that "[a]n important incident to the conduct of war is the adoption of measures by the military commander, not only to repel and defeat the enemy, but to seize and subject to disciplinary measures those enemies who, in their attempt to thwart or impede our military effort, have violated the law of war." *In re Yamashita,* 327 U.S. 1 (1946).

Although the Court concedes the legitimacy of the President's use of military commissions in certain circumstances, it suggests that the AUMF has no bearing on the scope of the President's power to utilize military commissions in the present conflict. Instead, the Court determines the scope of this power based exclusively on Article 21 of the Uniform Code of Military Justice, the successor to Article 15 of the Articles of War, which *Quirin* held "authorized trial of offenses against the law of war before [military] commissions." As I shall discuss below, Article 21 alone supports the use of commissions here. Nothing in the language of Article 21, however, suggests that it outlines the entire reach of congressional authorization of military commissions in all conflicts— quite the contrary, the language of Article 21 presupposes the existence of military commissions under an independent basis of authorization.[1]

---

[1]   As previously noted, Article 15 of the Articles of War was the predecessor of Article 21 of the UCMJ. Article 21 provides as follows: "The provisions of this chapter conferring

Indeed, consistent with *Hamdi*'s conclusion that the AUMF itself authorizes the trial of unlawful combatants, the original sanction for military commissions historically derived from congressional authorization of "the initiation of war" with its attendant authorization of "the employment of all necessary and proper agencies for its due prosecution." Accordingly, congressional authorization for military commissions pertaining to the instant conflict derives not only from Article 21 of the UCMJ, but also from the more recent, and broader, authorization contained in the AUMF.[2]

I note the Court's error respecting the AUMF not because it is necessary to my resolution of this case—Hamdan's military commission can plainly be sustained solely under Article 21—but to emphasize the complete congressional sanction of the President's exercise of his commander-in-chief authority to conduct the present war. In such circumstances, as previously noted, our duty to defer to the Executive's military and foreign policy judgment is at its zenith; it does not countenance the kind of second-guessing the Court repeatedly engages in today. Military and foreign policy judgments

> are and should be undertaken only by those directly responsible to the people whose welfare they advance or imperil. They are decisions of a kind for which the Judiciary has neither aptitude, facilities nor responsibility and which has long been held to belong in the domain of political power not subject to judicial intrusion or inquiry. *Chicago & Southern Air Lines, Inc. v. Waterman S.S. Corp.*, 333 U.S. 103, 111 (1948).

It is within this framework that the lawfulness of Hamdan's commission should be examined. . . .

III

The Court holds that even if "the Government has charged Hamdan with an offense against the law of war cognizable by military commission, the commission lacks power to proceed" because of its failure to comply with the terms of the UCMJ and the four Geneva Conventions signed in 1949. This position is untenable.

A

As with the jurisdiction of military commissions, the procedure of such commissions "has [not] been prescribed by statute," but "has been adapted in each instance to the need that called it forth." *Madsen v. Kinsella*, 343 U.S. 341, 347–48 (1952). Indeed, this Court has concluded

---

jurisdiction upon courts-martial do not deprive military commissions, provost courts, or other military tribunals of concurrent jurisdiction with respect to offenders or offenses that by statute or by the law of war may be tried by military commissions, provost courts, or other military tribunals."

[2] Although the President very well may have inherent authority to try unlawful combatants for violations of the law of war before military commissions, we need not decide that question because Congress has authorized the President to do so.

that "[i]n the absence of attempts by Congress to limit the President's power, it appears that, as Commander-in-Chief of the Army and Navy of the United States, he may, in time of war, establish and prescribe the jurisdiction and procedure of military commissions." *Id.,* at 348. This conclusion is consistent with this Court's understanding that military commissions are "our common-law war courts." *Id.,* at 346–347.[15] As such, "[s]hould the conduct of those who compose martial-law tribunals become [a] matter of judicial determination subsequently before the civil courts, those courts will give great weight to the opinions of the officers as to what the customs of war in any case justify and render necessary." Birkhimer 534.

The Court nevertheless concludes that at least one provision of the UCMJ amounts to an attempt by Congress to limit the President's power. This conclusion is not only contrary to the text and structure of the UCMJ, but it is also inconsistent with precedent of this Court. Consistent with *Madsen's* conclusion pertaining to the common-law nature of military commissions and the President's discretion to prescribe their procedures, Article 36 of the UCMJ authorizes the President to establish procedures for military commissions "which shall, *so far as he considers practicable,* apply the principles of law and the rules of evidence generally recognized in the trial of criminal cases in the United States district courts, but which may not be contrary to or inconsistent with this chapter." 10 U.S.C. § 836(a) (emphasis added). Far from constraining the President's authority, Article 36 recognizes the President's prerogative to depart from the procedures applicable in criminal cases whenever *he alone* does not deem such procedures "practicable." While the procedural regulations promulgated by the Executive must not be "contrary to" the UCMJ, only a few provisions of the UCMJ mention "military commissions," and there is no suggestion that the procedures to be employed by Hamdan's commission implicate any of those provisions.

Notwithstanding the foregoing, the Court concludes that Article 36(b) of the UCMJ, 10 U.S.C. § 836(b), which provides that "[a]ll rules and regulations made under this article shall be uniform insofar as practicable," requires the President to employ the same rules and

---

[15] [T]he Court maintains that, as a "general rule," "the procedures governing trials by military commission historically have been the same as those governing courts-martial." While it is undoubtedly true that military commissions have invariably employed most of the procedures employed by courts-martial, that is not a requirement. See Winthrop at 841 ("[M]ilitary commissions . . . are commonly conducted according to the rules and forms governing courts-martial. These war-courts are indeed more summary in their action than are the courts held under the Articles of war, and . . . their proceedings . . . will not be rendered *illegal* by the omission of details required upon trials by courts-martial" (emphasis in original; footnotes omitted)). Moreover, such a requirement would conflict with the settled understanding of the flexible and responsive nature of military commissions and the President's wartime authority to employ such tribunals as he sees fit. See W. Birkhimer, Military Government and Martial Law 536, 537–538 (3d rev.ed.1914) ("[M]ilitary commissions may so vary their procedure as to adapt it to any situation, and may extend their powers to any necessary degree . . . . The military commander decides upon the character of the military tribunal which is suited to the occasion . . . and his decision is final").

procedures in military commissions as are employed by courts-martial "insofar as practicable". The Court further concludes that Hamdan's commission is unlawful because the President has not explained why it is not practicable to apply the same rules and procedures to Hamdan's commission as would be applied in a trial by court-martial.

This interpretation of § 836(b) is unconvincing. As an initial matter, the Court fails to account for our cases interpreting the predecessor to Article 21 of the UCMJ—Article 15 of the Articles of War—which provides crucial context that bears directly on the proper interpretation of Article 36(b). Article 15 of the Articles of War provided that:

> The provisions of these articles conferring jurisdiction upon courts-martial shall not be construed as depriving military commissions, provost courts, or other military tribunals of concurrent jurisdiction in respect of offenders or offenses that by statute or by the law of war may be triable by such military commissions, provost courts, or other military tribunals. 41 Stat. 790.

In *Yamashita,* this Court concluded that Article 15 of the Articles of War preserved the President's unfettered authority to prescribe military commission procedure. . . . And this Court recognized that Article 15's preservation of military commissions as common-law war courts preserved the President's Commander in Chief authority to both "establish" military commissions and to "prescribe [their] procedure[s]." *Madsen,* 343 U.S., at 348. . . .

Nothing in the text of Article 36(b) supports the Court's sweeping conclusion that it represents an unprecedented congressional effort to change the nature of military commissions from common-law war courts to tribunals that must presumptively function like courts-martial. And such an interpretation would be strange indeed. The vision of uniformity that motivated the adoption of the UCMJ, embodied specifically in Article 36(b), is nothing more than uniformity across the separate branches of the armed services. *See* Act of May 5, 1950, ch. 169, 64 Stat. 107 (preamble to the UCMJ explaining that the UCMJ is an Act "[t]o unify, consolidate, revise, and codify the Articles of War, the Articles for the Government of the Navy, and the disciplinary laws of the Coast Guard"). There is no indication that the UCMJ was intended to require uniformity in procedure between courts-martial and military commissions, tribunals that the UCMJ itself recognizes are different. To the contrary, the UCMJ expressly recognizes that different tribunals will be constituted in different manners and employ different procedures. *See* 10 U.S.C. § 866 (providing for three different types of courts-martial—general, special, and summary—constituted in different manners and employing different procedures). . . .

Even if Article 36(b) could be construed to require procedural uniformity among the various tribunals contemplated by the UCMJ, Hamdan would not be entitled to relief. Under the Court's reading, the

President is entitled to prescribe different rules for military commissions than for courts-martial when he determines that it is not "practicable" to prescribe uniform rules. The Court does not resolve the level of deference such determinations would be owed, however, because, in its view, "[t]he President has not . . . [determined] that it is impracticable to apply the rules for courts-martial." This is simply not the case. On the same day that the President issued Military Commission Order No. 1, the Secretary of Defense explained that "the president decided to establish military commissions because he wanted the option of a process that is different from those processes which we already have, namely, the federal court system . . . and the military court system," Dept. of Defense News Briefing on Military Commissions (Mar. 21, 2002) (remarks of Donald Rumsfeld), and that "[t]he commissions are intended to be different . . . because the [P]resident recognized that there had to be differences to deal with the unusual situation we face and that a different approach was needed." *Ibid.* The President reached this conclusion because

> we're in the middle of a war, and . . . had to design a procedure that would allow us to pursue justice for these individuals while at the same time prosecuting the war most effectively. And that means setting rules that would allow us to preserve our intelligence secrets, develop more information about terrorist activities that might be planned for the future so that we can take action to prevent terrorist attacks against the United States. . . . [T]here was a constant balancing of the requirements of our war policy and the importance of providing justice for the individuals . . . and *each* deviation from the standard kinds of rules that we have in our criminal courts was motivated by the desire to strike this balance between individual justice and the broader war policy. *Ibid.* (remarks of Douglas J. Feith, Under Secretary of Defense for Policy (emphasis added)).

The Court provides no explanation why the President's determination that employing court-martial procedures in the military commissions established pursuant to Military Commission Order No. 1 would hamper our war effort is in any way inadequate to satisfy its newly minted "practicability" requirement. . . . And, in the context of the present conflict, it is exactly the kind of determination Congress countenanced when it authorized the President to use all necessary and appropriate force against our enemies. Accordingly, the President's determination is sufficient to satisfy any practicability requirement imposed by Article 36(b).

The Court further contends that Hamdan's commission is unlawful because it fails to provide him the right to be present at his trial, as recognized in 10 U.S.C. § 839(c) (2000 ed., Supp.V). But § 839(c) applies to courts-martial, not military commissions. It provides:

When the members of a court-martial deliberate or vote, only the members may be present. All other proceedings, including any other consultation of the members of the court with counsel or the military judge, shall be made a part of the record and shall be in the presence of the accused, the defense counsel, the trial counsel, and, in cases in which a military judge has been detailed to the court, the military judge.

In context, "all other proceedings" plainly refers exclusively to "other proceedings" pertaining to a court-martial.[18] This is confirmed by the provision's subsequent reference to "members of the *court* " and to "cases in which a military judge has been detailed to the *court*." It is also confirmed by the other provisions of § 839, which refer only to courts-martial. Section 839(c) simply does not address the procedural requirements of military commissions. . . .

For these reasons, I would affirm the judgment of the Court of Appeals.

■ **JUSTICE ALITO, with whom JUSTICE SCALIA and JUSTICE THOMAS join in Parts I-III, dissenting.**

[Justice Alito rejected the Court's holding that trying Hamdan by military commission violated the Geneva Convention.]

NOTE ON PRESIDENTIAL POWER AND EXECUTIVE DETENTION AND TRIAL

1.   Chief Justice Taney heard the *Merryman* case in his capacity as a trial judge sitting on circuit, and his decision was never reviewed by the Supreme Court. How persuasive is Taney's construction of the Suspension Clause as empowering only Congress to suspend the writ? Note that the Clause is phrased as a *limit* on government power, not a power grant—much like the *ex post facto* clause. Would we presume that, because the *ex post facto* prohibition is placed in Article I, that the clause does not bind the whole government—for example, that an administrative agency could impose *ex post facto* penalties for violating administrative regulations? And if the restriction on suspensions binds the whole government, does that imply that the *power* to suspend likewise belongs to the whole government? Are there any structural benefits to a reading that permits suspensions but only at the behest of Congress?

2.   Chief Justice Rehnquist's book, which provides valuable background as to why President Lincoln felt it necessary to suspend *habeas corpus*, draws its title from Lincoln's response to critics in an address to Congress on July 4, 1861:

---

[18] In addition to being foreclosed by the text of the provision, the Court's suggestion that 10 U.S.C. § 839(c) (2000 ed., Supp.V) applies to military commissions is untenable because it would require, in military commission proceedings, that the accused be present when the members of the commission voted on his guilt or innocence.

[T]he legality and propriety [of the suspension] are questioned [on the ground that] one who is sworn to 'take care that the laws be faithfully executed,' should not himself violate them. . . . The whole of the laws which were required to be faithfully executed, were being resisted, and failing of execution, in nearly one-third of the States. Must they be allowed to finally fail of execution, even had it been perfectly clear, that by the use of the means necessary to their execution, some single law [the statute authorizing writs of habeas corpus], made in such extreme tenderness of the citizen's liberty, that practically it relieves more of the guilty, than of the innocent, should, to a very limited extent, be violated? To state the question more directly, are all the laws, *but one*, to go unexecuted, and the government itself go to pieces, lest that one be violated?"[35]

In general, President Lincoln was a believer in, and practitioner of, emergency powers; the Emancipation Proclamation, for example, was justified as an exercise of emergency powers in support of the war effort. Did Lincoln take executive emergency powers too far? If one is sympathetic with President Lincoln's actions during the Civil War, is the majority opinion in *Hamdan* tenable?

3. The debate over military commissions has actually focused on three crucial issues:

- The power of the government to use military commissions as a substitute for trial of suspected evildoers in the ordinary civilian justice system;

- The power of the *President* to employ such commissions without specific authorization from Congress; and

- The extent to which such commissions must be subject to review and oversight by Article III federal courts.

Hamdan discusses the first issue in laying out the two circumstances in which use of the military justice system is appropriate: a) to substitute for the civilian justice system for all crimes and defendants when the civilian justice system is unavailable (e.g., in occupied territory); and b) to try prosecutions for war crimes even if the civilian courts are open. (A third instance concerns the use of ordinary military courts—courts martial—to try crimes by servicemen.) Why do you think the President was so keen on using military commissions to try suspected terrorists? Are those reasons legitimate?

4. The second issue identified in the previous note is the central question in *Hamdan*. The Court approaches that question through the lens of Justice Jackson's framework from *Youngstown*. Some proponents of the President's military commission order had suggested that the President had inherent executive power to establish such commission, wholly independent of Congress and perhaps not even subject to congressional prohibition. But

---

[35] Message to Congress in Special Session of July 4, 1861, in 4 THE COLLECTED WORKS OF ABRAHAM LINCOLN 421, 429—30 (Roy P. Basler, ed., 1953).

the Administration did not press that position in the Supreme Court. Did *Zivotofsky* revive that view?

The central debate under *Youngstown* concerns not the meaning of the *constitutional* separation of powers, but rather the extent of congressional authorization in the Uniform Code of Military Justice and the Authorization to Use Military Force. As Justice Breyer makes clear, the Court's finding that authorization was wanting left it open to Congress to provide such authorization later on, and Congress in fact did so in the Military Commissions Act of 2006 (MCA). The MCA is a complex statute, and its full import will not be clear until it has been authoritatively construed by the courts. Basically, it a) authorizes the use of military commissions to try suspected terrorists; b) provides specific procedural rules for those commissions, including several significant protections for the accused; and c) significantly restricts judicial review of executive detention of suspected terrorists by the federal courts.[36] Should passage of the MCA be considered a congressional "override" of the Supreme Court's decision in *Hamdan*? Does it make the decision unimportant? Indeed, what good does it do to invalidate the President's military commissions while at the same time stating that Congress could achieve the same thing by statute?

5.   The third issue—judicial review of military commission proceedings and of the status of detainees more generally—was at issue in *Hamdan* to an extent but has been omitted from the excerpts reproduced here. The constitutional question concerns the power of the political branches to prevent the federal courts from hearing federal claims— particularly claims that federal constitutional rights have been violated. The Court returned to this question in *Boumediene v. Bush*, 553 U.S. 723 (2008), holding (in a 5–4 decision authored by Justice Kennedy) that Congress's effort to restrict review of the status of the Guantanamo detainees by Article III courts violated the Suspension Clause. This gloriously complicated question—concerning Congress's ability to check judicial review by restricting federal court jurisdiction—is a central focus in courses on Federal Courts; it is, alas, outside the scope of *this* course.

6.   A final question in *Hamdan* concerns the extent to which *international* law constrains the exercise of the President's war powers. The content of international law governing the treatment of detainees and suspected war criminals is, of course, a question most directly addressed in courses on international law. But the matter of international law's effect in the domestic legal sphere is itself a question of domestic constitutional law. How does international law enter into the debate in *Hamdan*? If a military commission would be consistent with the federal constitutional guarantee of Due Process, should international law be interpreted to add anything to that requirement?

7.   Like *Bush v. Gore* (discussed in Section 2.3) and *United States v. Nixon* (Section 13.3), *Hamdan v. Rumsfeld* is a good case for assessing the Supreme Court's role over two centuries after *Marbury v. Madison*. In *Bush*

---

[36] For the full text of the MCA, see http://www.washingtonpost.com/wp-srv/politics/documents/cheney/military_commissions_act.pdf.

v. Gore, the Court settled a disputed presidential election; in *Nixon*, it intruded into the President's confidential communications; now, in *Hamdan*, the Court interposes itself in a key area of military policy during wartime. Each of these cases suggest that the American federal judiciary has made enormous gains in strength and independence over the course of two centuries.

Consider, however, the extent to which *Hamdan* may support three additional propositions:

- The judiciary is on strongest ground when it does not seek to impose an ultimate answer, but when it requires the political branches to deliberate further (*Gregory*) or work together (*Hamdan*);

- The Constitution both requires and allows considerable institutional flexibility, so that many key questions—e.g., the means of conducting elections (Voting Rights Act), investigating misconduct (*Morrison*), or conducting trials (*Hamdan*)—can and must be fleshed out through statutes and regulations; and

- Questions that initially seem to most directly implicate individual rights—such as who can be deported (*Chadha*), what conduct may be criminalized (*Lopez*), or how an accused war criminal may be tried (*Hamdan*)—will often turn on issues of constitutional structure.

Are these propositions true? If so, are they consistent with your expectations when you started this course?

PART FOUR

LIBERTY AND EQUALITY

If history has confirmed the wisdom of the Framers' focus on structural arrangements in the original Constitution, it has also validated the Antifederalists' insistence on a Bill of Rights. Despite the Federalists' assurances that the structural safeguards built into the Philadelphia draft left the new national government without power to invade civil liberties, that was rather plainly not true. Consider, for example, a ban on interstate shipment of newspapers critical of the government. Such a ban would clearly fall within Congress's commerce power, and without a specific guarantee of freedom of the press such measures might have proven a highly effective means of suppressing dissent. Although that particular measure was never undertaken, our history demonstrates that *both* structural and rights provisions are crucial to preserving American freedom.

This final Part thus turns from constitutional structure to rights. Our coverage is necessarily selective; the First Amendment's Speech and Religion Clauses typically need a course of their own, and they are accordingly omitted here. Rather the focus is on the Equal Protection and Due Process Clauses of the Fourteenth Amendment, along with their parallel requirements for federal action in the Fifth Amendment. Chapters Fifteen and Sixteen in this Part build on the historical foundation in Part II, providing an overview of contemporary doctrine concerning, respectively, equal protection and due process. These two concepts often intertwine, however, and viewing each in isolation presents a necessarily incomplete picture of their potential. Chapter Seventeen thus focuses on a particular case study—the spectacular flowering of gay rights over the course of just a few decades—that illustrates how due process and equal protection may act in combination.

Although rights jurisprudence has proven a powerful weapon against various forms of oppression, it also has the potential to disrupt settled social arrangements and mores or to override democratic choices about policy and values. The materials in this Part thus continue the conversation running throughout this book about the institutional role of constitutional principles and judicial review in a democratic society. It would be hard to exaggerate the degree to which that role has expanded since 1789. As you read these materials, you should ask yourself whether the contemporary Supreme Court simply reflects the increasing polarization of American society or offers a hope of common ground.

CHAPTER FIFTEEN

EQUAL PROTECTION

Section One of the Fourteenth Amendment forbids any State "to deny to any person within its jurisdiction the equal protection of the laws." In many ways, this principle is the direct descendant of the Declaration of Independence's "self-evident" truth that "all men are created equal." That truth found no explicit mention in the Bill of Rights, however—perhaps because the Framers had relatively little concern that the new federal government would threaten equality, or perhaps because the Framers were not all that egalitarian. Textual recognition came only belatedly in the Fourteenth Amendment, which not only ensured that the Constitution's equality principle would be inextricably bound up with race but also necessitated some awkward doctrinal gymnastics in *Bolling v. Sharpe*[1] to ensure that it would apply "equally" to the national government. The can be little doubt, however, that the Fourteenth Amendment's promise of equality is right at the heart of contemporary hopes for—and debates about—American constitutionalism.

Chapters Four and Six tracked the Court's development of this principle in the Reconstruction and Civil Rights periods; the present chapter undertakes a general assessment of contemporary equal protection doctrine. That doctrine—unlike the *Brown* decisions—has been centrally concerned with standards of review. Current law incorporates the "double standard" of judicial review discussed in Chapter Five, distinguishing sharply between certain forms of differential treatment triggering "strict scrutiny" and reserving a far more deferential form of review for other government classifications. Strict scrutiny has been applied primarily to racial classifications, and Section 15.1 focuses on the nature and limits of that scrutiny. Section 15.2 turns to gender classifications, which generally get "intermediate" scrutiny. Section 15.3 explores the criteria for applying these forms of heightened scrutiny to classifications based on other characteristics, such as age or disability.

The last two sections deal with complications to this general structure. Section 15.4 addresses the controversial topic of "benign" discrimination or "affirmative action"—that is, governmental classifications intended to benefit groups that have previously suffered from social and/or legal discrimination. The central question here is whether the same non-deferential scrutiny that applies to "malign" discrimination should apply to "benign" classifications based on the same characteristic, such as race or gender. (Critics question the very possibility that any form of discrimination based on race or gender can

---

[1]   347 U.S. 497 (1954). *See* Section 6.1, *supra.*

be "benign.") Although the Court generally has applied heightened scrutiny to benign discrimination, its application of those stricter standards to well-intentioned laws has tended to undermine the distinction between deferential and non-deferential review.

Section 15.5 addresses a different route to strict scrutiny, based on government discrimination that implicates a "fundamental right." This is a potentially far-reaching concept, but its application has been controversial and under-developed, primarily because it tends to blur the conceptual divide between equal protection and due process.

Section 15.1 Race After *Brown*

As the Court noted in the *Slaughter-House Cases*, the Fourteenth Amendment's central purpose was "the freedom of the slave race . . . and the protection of the newly-made freeman and citizen from the oppressions of those who had formerly exercised unlimited dominion over him."[2] This purpose likely accounts for the Equal Protection Clause's somewhat odd phrasing. The Framers of the Fourteenth Amendment aimed not simply at laws that imposed unique burdens on African Americans—like slavery itself—but also at the pervasive denial to the freedmen of the benefits of a state's generally-applicable legal regime. Black people frequently found themselves unable, for example, to enforce contractual claims and property rights, obtain police and fire protection, or exercise other rights generally available to citizens. The most basic Fourteenth Amendment problem, then, was the denial to African Americans of the "equal protection" of these generally-applicable legal entitlements.

Loving v. Virginia
388 U.S. 1 (1967)

■ **Mr. Chief Justice Warren delivered the opinion of the Court.**

This case presents a constitutional question never addressed by this Court: whether a statutory scheme adopted by the State of Virginia to prevent marriages between persons solely on the basis of racial classifications violates the Equal Protection and Due Process Clauses of the Fourteenth Amendment. For reasons which seem to us to reflect the central meaning of those constitutional commands, we conclude that these statutes cannot stand consistently with the Fourteenth Amendment.

In June 1958, two residents of Virginia, Mildred Jeter, a Negro woman, and Richard Loving, a white man, were married in the District of Columbia pursuant to its laws. Shortly after their marriage, the Lovings returned to Virginia and established their marital abode in

---

[2]   83 U.S. (16 Wall.) 36, 71 (1872).

Caroline County. At the October Term, 1958, of the Circuit Court Caroline County, a grand jury issued an indictment charging the Lovings with violating Virginia's ban on interracial marriages. On January 6, 1959, the Lovings pleaded guilty to the charge and were sentenced to one year in jail; however, the trial judge suspended the sentence for a period of 25 years on the condition that the Lovings leave the State and not return to Virginia together for 25 years. He stated in an opinion that:

> 'Almighty God created the races white, black, yellow, malay and red, and he placed them on separate continents. And but for the interference with his arrangement there would be no cause for such marriages. The fact that he separated the races shows that he did not intend for the races to mix.'

After their convictions, the Lovings took up residence in the District of Columbia. On November 6, 1963, they filed a motion in the state trial court to vacate the judgment and set aside the sentence on the ground that the statutes which they had violated were repugnant to the Fourteenth Amendment. The motion not having been decided by October 28, 1964, the Lovings instituted a class action in the United States District Court for the Eastern District of Virginia requesting that a three-judge court be convened to declare the Virginia antimiscegenation statutes unconstitutional and to enjoin state officials from enforcing their convictions. On January 22, 1965, the state trial judge denied the motion to vacate the sentences, and the Lovings perfected an appeal to the Supreme Court of Appeals of Virginia. On February 11, 1965, the three-judge District Court continued the case to allow the Lovings to present their constitutional claims to the highest state court.

The Supreme Court of Appeals upheld the constitutionality of the antimiscegenation statutes and, after modifying the sentence, affirmed the convictions. The Lovings appealed this decision, and we noted probable jurisdiction on December 12, 1966.

The two statutes under which appellants were convicted and sentenced are part of a comprehensive statutory scheme aimed at prohibiting and punishing interracial marriages. The Lovings were convicted of violating s 20—58 of the Virginia Code:

> 'Leaving State to evade law.—If any white person and colored person shall go out of this State, for the purpose of being married, and with the intention of returning, and be married out of it, and afterwards return to and reside in it, cohabiting as man and wife, they shall be punished as provided in s 20—59, and the marriage shall be governed by the same law as if it had been solemnized in this State. The fact of their cohabitation here as man and wife shall be evidence of their marriage.'

Section 20—59, which defines the penalty for miscegenation, provides:

> 'Punishment for marriage.—If any white person intermarry with a colored person, or any colored person intermarry with a

white person, he shall be guilty of a felony and shall be punished by confinement in the penitentiary for not less than one nor more than five years.'

Other central provisions in the Virginia statutory scheme are § 20—57, which automatically voids all marriages between 'a white person and a colored person' without any judicial proceeding, and §§ 20—54 and 1—14 which, respectively, define 'white persons' and 'colored persons and Indians' for purposes of the statutory prohibitions. The Lovings have never disputed in the course of this litigation that Mrs. Loving is a 'colored person' or that Mr. Loving is a 'white person' within the meanings given those terms by the Virginia statutes.

Virginia is now one of 16 States which prohibit and punish marriages on the basis of racial classifications. Penalties for miscegenation arose as an incident to slavery and have been common in Virginia since the colonial period. The present statutory scheme dates from the adoption of the Racial Integrity Act of 1924, passed during the period of extreme nativism which followed the end of the First World War. The central features of this Act, and current Virginia law, are the absolute prohibition of a 'white person' marrying other than another 'white person,' a prohibition against issuing marriage licenses until the issuing official is satisfied that the applicants' statements as to their race are correct, certificates of 'racial composition' to be kept by both local and state registrars, and the carrying forward of earlier prohibitions against racial intermarriage.

I

In upholding the constitutionality of these provisions in the decision below, the Supreme Court of Appeals of Virginia . . . concluded that the State's legitimate purposes were 'to preserve the racial integrity of its citizens,' and to prevent 'the corruption of blood,' 'a mongrel breed of citizens,' and 'the obliteration of racial pride,' obviously an endorsement of the doctrine of White Supremacy. The court also reasoned that marriage has traditionally been subject to state regulation without federal intervention, and, consequently, the regulation of marriage should be left to exclusive state control by the Tenth Amendment.

While the state court is no doubt correct in asserting that marriage is a social relation subject to the State's police power, the State does not contend in its argument before this Court that its powers to regulate marriage are unlimited notwithstanding the commands of the Fourteenth Amendment. Nor could it do so . . . . Instead, the State argues that the meaning of the Equal Protection Clause, as illuminated by the statements of the Framers, is only that state penal laws containing an interracial element as part of the definition of the offense must apply equally to whites and Negroes in the sense that members of each race are punished to the same degree. Thus, the State contends that, because its miscegenation statutes punish equally both the white and the Negro participants in an interracial marriage, these statutes, despite their reliance on racial classifications do not constitute an invidious discrimination based upon race. The second argument advanced by the State assumes the validity of its equal application theory. The argument is that, if the Equal Protection Clause does not outlaw miscegenation statutes because of their reliance on racial classifications, the question of constitutionality would thus become whether there was any rational basis for a State to treat interracial marriages differently from other marriages. On this question, the State argues, the scientific evidence is substantially in doubt and, consequently, this Court should defer to the wisdom of the state legislature in adopting its policy of discouraging interracial marriages.

Because we reject the notion that the mere 'equal application' of a statute containing racial classifications is enough to remove the classifications from the Fourteenth Amendment's proscription of all invidious racial discriminations, we do not accept the State's contention that these statutes should be upheld if there is any possible basis for concluding that they serve a rational purpose. The mere fact of equal application does not mean that our analysis of these statutes should follow the approach we have taken in cases involving no racial discrimination where the Equal Protection Clause has been arrayed against a statute discriminating between the kinds of advertising which may be displayed on trucks in New York City, *Railway Express Agency, Inc. v. People of State of New York*, 336 U.S. 106 (1949), or an exemption in Ohio's ad valorem tax for merchandise owned by a non-resident in a storage warehouse, *Allied Stores of Ohio, Inc. v. Bowers*, 358 U.S. 522 (1959). In these cases, involving distinctions not drawn according to race, the Court has merely asked whether there is any rational foundation for the discriminations, and has deferred to the wisdom of the state legislatures. In the case at bar, however, we deal with statutes containing racial classifications, and the fact of equal application does not immunize the statute from the very heavy burden of justification which the Fourteenth Amendment has traditionally required of state statutes drawn according to race.

The State argues that statements in the Thirty-ninth Congress about the time of the passage of the Fourteenth Amendment indicate that the Framers did not intend the Amendment to make unconstitutional state miscegenation laws.... [W]e have said ... that although these historical sources 'cast some light' they are not sufficient to resolve the problem; '(a)t best, they are inconclusive. The most avid proponents of the post-War Amendments undoubtedly intended them to remove all legal distinctions among 'all persons born or naturalized in the United States.' Their opponents, just as certainly, were antagonistic to both the letter and the spirit of the Amendments and wished them to have the most limited effect.' *Brown v. Board of Education of Topeka*, 347 U.S. 483, 489 (1954). We have rejected the proposition that the debates in the Thirty-ninth Congress or in the state legislatures which ratified the

Fourteenth Amendment supported the theory advanced by the State, that the requirement of equal protection of the laws is satisfied by penal laws defining offenses based on racial classifications so long as white and Negro participants in the offense were similarly punished. *McLaughlin v. State of Florida*, 379 U.S. 184 (1964)....

The Equal Protection Clause requires the consideration of whether the classifications drawn by any statute constitute an arbitrary and invidious discrimination. The clear and central purpose of the Fourteenth Amendment was to eliminate all official state sources of invidious racial discrimination in the States. *Slaughter-House Cases*, 16 Wall. 36, 71 (1873); *Strauder v. State of West Virginia*, 100 U.S. 303, 307–308 (1880).

There can be no question but that Virginia's miscegenation statutes rest solely upon distinctions drawn according to race. The statutes proscribe generally accepted conduct if engaged in by members of different races. Over the years, this Court has consistently repudiated '(d)istinctions between citizens solely because of their ancestry' as being 'odious to a free people whose institutions are founded upon the doctrine of equality.' *Hirabayashi v. United States*, 320 U.S. 81, 100 (1943). At the very least, the Equal Protection Clause demands that racial classifications, especially suspect in criminal statutes, be subjected to the 'most rigid scrutiny,' *Korematsu v. United States*, 323 U.S. 214, 216 (1944), and, if they are ever to be upheld, they must be shown to be necessary to the accomplishment of some permissible state objective, independent of the racial discrimination which it was the object of the Fourteenth Amendment to eliminate....

There is patently no legitimate overriding purpose independent of invidious racial discrimination which justifies this classification. The fact that Virginia prohibits only interracial marriages involving white persons demonstrates that the racial classifications must stand on their own justification, as measures designed to maintain White Supremacy. We have consistently denied the constitutionality of measures which restrict the rights of citizens on account of race. There can be no doubt that restricting the freedom to marry solely because of racial classifications violates the central meaning of the Equal Protection Clause.

II

These statutes also deprive the Lovings of liberty without due process of law in violation of the Due Process Clause of the Fourteenth Amendment. The freedom to marry has long been recognized as one of the vital personal rights essential to the orderly pursuit of happiness by free men.

Marriage is one of the 'basic civil rights of man,' fundamental to our very existence and survival. *Skinner v. State of Oklahoma*, 316 U.S. 535, 541 (1942). To deny this fundamental freedom on so unsupportable a basis as the racial classifications embodied in these statutes, classifications so directly subversive of the principle of equality at the heart of the Fourteenth Amendment, is surely to deprive all the State's citizens of liberty without due process of law. The Fourteenth Amendment requires that the freedom of choice to marry not be restricted by invidious racial discriminations. Under our Constitution, the freedom to marry or not marry, a person of another race resides with the individual and cannot be infringed by the State. . . .

Reversed.

■ MR. JUSTICE STEWART, concurring.

I have previously expressed the belief that 'it is simply not possible for a state law to be valid under our Constitution which makes the criminality of an act depend upon the race of the actor.' *McLaughlin v. State of Florida*, 379 U.S. 184, 198 (1964) (concurring opinion). Because I adhere to that belief, I concur in the judgment of the Court.

NOTE ON INTERRACIAL MARRIAGE AND STRICT SCRUTINY FOR RACIAL CLASSIFICATIONS

1. Can the law in *Loving* be struck down on the same rationale that the Court articulated in *Brown*? The latter opinion placed a great deal of weight on the importance of education, which is not implicated here. And surely one would not say that "separate can never be equal" with respect to marriage; there are of course many good marriages between two black persons and between two white persons. Does the argument that *legal* separation necessarily fosters inequality nonetheless have some purchase in this context?

2. The leading race cases in Chapter Six, such as *Brown*, did not adopt or discuss a specific standard of review. *Loving*, however, states that while ordinary governmental classifications should receive rational basis, racial classifications bear a "very heavy burden of justification." This language is now understood to require "strict scrutiny"—that is, the racial classification must be supported by a compelling state interest, and the classification must be narrowly tailored to further that interest.[3] What sort of interests should be judged sufficiently compelling to satisfy this standard? The Court's citation of *Korematsu v. United States*, 323 U.S. 214, 216 (1944), suggests that the interests should be truly fundamental—for instance, preventing an imminent Japanese invasion of California. Should the bar be that high? Or should more prosaic interests, such as promoting diversity in higher education, suffice?

The Court's invocation of *Korematsu* also highlights—perhaps inadvertently—a second aspect of strict scrutiny. That case, of course, *upheld* the Roosevelt Administration's decision to intern thousands of Japanese-Americans in camps during World War II. There is now a widespread historical consensus "that there could have been no reasonable military

---

[3] The Court would not actually formulate strict scrutiny in these canonical terms until *Shapiro v. Thompson*, 394 U.S. 618, 638 (1969). *See infra* Section 15.5.

assessment of an emergency at the time, that the orders were based upon racial stereotypes, and that the orders caused needless suffering and shame for thousands of American citizens."[4] The judgment of history thus confirms the need for courts not only to demand a "compelling" justification for racial discrimination, but also to look behind the government's own assessment of the facts supporting such an interest. Modern strict scrutiny cases thus supplement the "compelling interest" requirement with rigorous review of the "fit" between the racial classification and that interest, informed by an independent judicial judgment of the underlying facts.

3.   What is the significance of Part II of the Court's opinion, which holds that Virginia's anti-miscegenation statute violates the Due Process Clause of the Fourteenth Amendment? Is the Court saying that marriage is a fundamental right as a matter of substantive due process, so that *any* restriction on who may marry would violate the Due Process Clause, even in the absence of a racial classification? Many states, for example, prohibit marriage by persons within a certain degree of consanguity—e.g., first cousins may not wed in some states. Do such laws have to pass strict scrutiny? If, as the Court's opinion suggests, *racial* discrimination is essential to its analysis, then what work is Part II doing?

Washington v. Davis

426 U.S. 229 (1976)

■ **MR. JUSTICE WHITE delivered the opinion of the Court.**

This case involves the validity of a qualifying test administered to applicants for positions as police officers in the District of Columbia Metropolitan Police Department. The test was sustained by the District Court but invalidated by the Court of Appeals. We are in agreement with the District Court and hence reverse the judgment of the Court of Appeals.

I

This action began on April 10, 1970, when two Negro police officers filed suit against the then Commissioner of the District of Columbia, the Chief of the District's Metropolitan Police Department, and the Commissioners of the United States Civil Service Commission. An amended complaint ... alleged that the promotion policies of the Department were racially discriminatory and sought a declaratory judgment and an injunction. The respondents Harley and Sellers were permitted to intervene, their amended complaint asserting that their applications to become officers in the Department had been rejected, and that the Department's recruiting procedures discriminated on the basis of race against black applicants by a series of practices including, but not limited to, a written personnel test which excluded a disproportionately high number of Negro applicants.... Respondents then filed a motion

---

[4]   *Hirabayashi v. United States*, 828 F.2d 591, 593 (9th Cir 1987) (vacating Hirabayashi's convictions, over four decades later, for violating the orders upheld in *Korematsu*) .

for partial summary judgment with respect to the recruiting phase of the case, seeking a declaration that the test administered to those applying to become police officers is "unlawfully discriminatory and thereby in violation of the due process clause of the Fifth Amendment . . . ." The District of Columbia defendants, petitioners here, and the federal parties also filed motions for summary judgment with respect to the recruiting aspects of the case, asserting that respondents were entitled to relief on neither constitutional nor statutory grounds. The District Court granted petitioners' and denied respondents' motions.

According to the findings and conclusions of the District Court, to be accepted by the Department and to enter an intensive 17-week training program, the police recruit was required to satisfy certain physical and character standards, to be a high school graduate or its equivalent, and to receive a grade of at least 40 out of 80 on "Test 21," which is "an examination that is used generally throughout the federal service," which "was developed by the Civil Service Commission, not the Police Department," and which was "designed to test verbal ability, vocabulary, reading and comprehension."

The validity of Test 21 was the sole issue before the court on the motions for summary judgment. The District Court noted that there was no claim of "an intentional discrimination or purposeful discriminatory acts" but only a claim that Test 21 bore no relationship to job performance and "has a highly discriminatory impact in screening out black candidates." Respondents' evidence, the District Court said, warranted three conclusions: "(a) The number of black police officers, while substantial, is not proportionate to the population mix of the city. (b) A higher percentage of blacks fail the Test than whites. (c) The Test has not been validated to establish its reliability for measuring subsequent job performance." This showing was deemed sufficient to shift the burden of proof to the defendants in the action, petitioners here; but the court nevertheless concluded that on the undisputed facts respondents were not entitled to relief. The District Court relied on several factors. Since August 1969, 44% of new police force recruits had been black; that figure also represented the proportion of blacks on the total force and was roughly equivalent to 20- to 29-year-old blacks in the 50-mile radius in which the recruiting efforts of the Police Department had been concentrated. It was undisputed that the Department had systematically and affirmatively sought to enroll black officers many of whom passed the test but failed to report for duty. The District Court rejected the assertion that Test 21 was culturally slanted to favor whites and was "satisfied that the undisputable facts prove the test to be reasonably and directly related to the requirements of the police recruit training program and that it is neither so designed nor operates (sic) to discriminate against otherwise qualified blacks'. It was thus not necessary to show that Test 21 was not only a useful indicator of training school performance but had also been validated in terms of job performance—

"The lack of job performance validation does not defeat the Test, given its direct relationship to recruiting and the valid part it plays in this process." The District Court ultimately concluded that "(t)he proof is wholly lacking that a police officer qualifies on the color of his skin rather than ability" and that the Department "should not be required on this showing to lower standards or to abandon efforts to achieve excellence."

Having lost on both constitutional and statutory issues in the District Court, respondents brought the case to the Court of Appeals claiming that their summary judgment motion, which rested on purely constitutional grounds, should have been granted. The tendered constitutional issue was whether the use of Test 21 invidiously discriminated against Negroes and hence denied them due process of law contrary to the commands of the Fifth Amendment. The Court of Appeals, addressing that issue, announced that it would be guided by *Griggs v. Duke Power Co.*, 401 U.S. 424 (1971), a case involving the interpretation and application of Title VII of the Civil Rights Act of 1964, and held that the statutory standards elucidated in that case were to govern the due process question tendered in this one. The court went on to declare that lack of discriminatory intent in designing and administering Test 21 was irrelevant; the critical fact was rather that a far greater proportion of blacks four times as many failed the test than did whites. This disproportionate impact, standing alone and without regard to whether it indicated a discriminatory purpose, was held sufficient to establish a constitutional violation, absent proof by petitioners that the test was an adequate measure of job performance in addition to being an indicator of probable success in the training program, a burden which the court ruled petitioners had failed to discharge. That the Department had made substantial efforts to recruit blacks was held beside the point and the fact that the racial distribution of recent hirings and of the Department itself might be roughly equivalent to the racial makeup of the surrounding community, broadly conceived, was put aside as a "comparison (not) material to this appeal." The Court of Appeals, over a dissent, accordingly reversed the judgment of the District Court and directed that respondents' motion for partial summary judgment be granted. We granted the petition for certiorari, filed by the District of Columbia officials.

II

Because the Court of Appeals erroneously applied the legal standards applicable to Title VII cases in resolving the constitutional issue before it, we reverse its judgment in respondents' favor. . . .

As the Court of Appeals understood Title VII, employees or applicants proceeding under it need not concern themselves with the employer's possibly discriminatory purpose but instead may focus solely on the racially differential impact of the challenged hiring or promotion practices. This is not the constitutional rule. We have never held that the constitutional standard for adjudicating claims of invidious racial discrimination is identical to the standards applicable under Title VII, and we decline to do so today.

The central purpose of the Equal Protection Clause of the Fourteenth Amendment is the prevention of official conduct discriminating on the basis of race. It is also true that the Due Process Clause of the Fifth Amendment contains an equal protection component prohibiting the United States from invidiously discriminating between individuals or groups. *Bolling v. Sharpe*, 347 U.S. 497 (1954). But our cases have not embraced the proposition that a law or other official act, without regard to whether it reflects a racially discriminatory purpose, is unconstitutional solely because it has a racially disproportionate impact.

Almost 100 years ago, *Strauder v. West Virginia*, 100 U.S. 303 (1880), established that the exclusion of Negroes from grand and petit juries in criminal proceedings violated the Equal Protection Clause, but the fact that a particular jury or a series of juries does not statistically reflect the racial composition of the community does not in itself make out an invidious discrimination forbidden by the Clause. "A purpose to discriminate must be present which may be proven by systematic exclusion of eligible jurymen of the proscribed race or by unequal application of the law to such an extent as to show intentional discrimination." *Akins v. Texas*, 325 U.S. 398, 403–404 (1945). A defendant in a criminal case is entitled "to require that the State not deliberately and systematically deny to members of his race the right to participate as jurors in the administration of justice." *Alexander v. Louisiana*, 405 U.S. 625, 628–629 (1972). . . .

The school desegregation cases have also adhered to the basic equal protection principle that the invidious quality of a law claimed to be racially discriminatory must ultimately be traced to a racially discriminatory purpose. That there are both predominantly black and predominantly white schools in a community is not alone violative of the Equal Protection Clause. The essential element of de jure segregation is "a current condition of segregation resulting from intentional state action. *Keyes v. School Dist. No. 1*, 413 U.S. 189, 205 (1973). The differentiating factor between de jure segregation and so-called de facto segregation . . . is purpose or intent to segregate." The Court has also recently rejected allegations of racial discrimination based solely on the statistically disproportionate racial impact of various provisions of the Social Security Act because "(t)he acceptance of appellants' constitutional theory would render suspect each difference in treatment among the grant classes, however lacking in racial motivation and however otherwise rational the treatment might be." *Jefferson v. Hackney*, 406 U.S. 535, 548 (1972).

This is not to say that the necessary discriminatory racial purpose must be express or appear on the face of the statute, or that a law's disproportionate impact is irrelevant in cases involving Constitution-based claims of racial discrimination. A statute, otherwise neutral on its face, must not be applied so as invidiously to discriminate on the basis of race. *Yick Wo v. Hopkins*, 118 U.S. 356 (1886). It is also clear from the cases dealing with racial discrimination in the selection of juries that the systematic exclusion of Negroes is itself such an "unequal application of the law . . . as to show intentional discrimination." *Akins v. Texas*, 325 U.S. at 404. . . .

Necessarily, an invidious discriminatory purpose may often be inferred from the totality of the relevant facts, including the fact, if it is true, that the law bears more heavily on one race than another. It is also not infrequently true that the discriminatory impact in the jury cases for example, the total or seriously disproportionate exclusion of Negroes from jury venires may for all practical purposes demonstrate unconstitutionality because in various circumstances the discrimination is very difficult to explain on nonracial grounds. Nevertheless, we have not held that a law, neutral on its face and serving ends otherwise within the power of government to pursue, is invalid under the Equal Protection Clause simply because it may affect a greater proportion of one race than of another. Disproportionate impact is not irrelevant, but it is not the sole touchstone of an invidious racial discrimination forbidden by the Constitution. Standing alone, it does not trigger the rule that racial classifications are to be subjected to the strictest scrutiny and are justifiable only by the weightiest of considerations. . . .

As an initial matter, we have difficulty understanding how a law establishing a racially neutral qualification for employment is nevertheless racially discriminatory and denies "any person . . . equal protection of the laws" simply because a greater proportion of Negroes fail to qualify than members of other racial or ethnic groups. Had respondents, along with all others who had failed Test 21, whether white or black, brought an action claiming that the test denied each of them equal protection of the laws as compared with those who had passed with high enough scores to qualify them as police recruits, it is most unlikely that their challenge would have been sustained. Test 21, which is administered generally to prospective Government employees, concededly seeks to ascertain whether those who take it have acquired a particular level of verbal skill; and it is untenable that the Constitution prevents the Government from seeking modestly to upgrade the communicative abilities of its employees rather than to be satisfied with some lower level of competence, particularly where the job requires special ability to communicate orally and in writing. Respondents, as Negroes, could no more successfully claim that the test denied them equal protection than could white applicants who also failed. The conclusion would not be different in the face of proof that more Negroes than whites had been disqualified by Test 21. That other Negroes also failed to score well would, alone, not demonstrate that respondents individually were being denied equal protection of the laws by the application of an otherwise valid qualifying test being administered to prospective police recruits.

Nor on the facts of the case before us would the disproportionate impact of Test 21 warrant the conclusion that it is a purposeful device to discriminate against Negroes and hence an infringement of the constitutional rights of respondents as well as other black applicants. As we have said, the test is neutral on its face and rationally may be said to serve a purpose the Government is constitutionally empowered to pursue. Even agreeing with the District Court that the differential racial effect of Test 21 called for further inquiry, we think the District Court correctly held that the affirmative efforts of the Metropolitan Police Department to recruit black officers, the changing racial composition of the recruit classes and of the force in general, and the relationship of the test to the training program negated any inference that the Department discriminated on the basis of race or that "a police officer qualifies on the color of his skin rather than ability."

Under Title VII, Congress provided that when hiring and promotion practices disqualifying substantially disproportionate numbers of blacks are challenged, discriminatory purpose need not be proved, and that it is an insufficient response to demonstrate some rational basis for the challenged practices. It is necessary, in addition, that they be "validated" in terms of job performance in any one of several ways, perhaps by ascertaining the minimum skill, ability, or potential necessary for the position at issue and determining whether the qualifying tests are appropriate for the selection of qualified applicants for the job in question. However this process proceeds, it involves a more probing judicial review of, and less deference to, the seemingly reasonable acts of administrators and executives than is appropriate under the Constitution where special racial impact, without discriminatory purpose, is claimed. We are not disposed to adopt this more rigorous standard for the purposes of applying the Fifth and the Fourteenth Amendments in cases such as this.

A rule that a statute designed to serve neutral ends is nevertheless invalid, absent compelling justification, if in practice it benefits or burdens one race more than another would be far-reaching and would raise serious questions about, and perhaps invalidate, a whole range of tax, welfare, public service, regulatory, and licensing statutes that may be more burdensome to the poor and to the average black than to the more affluent white. . . .

As we have indicated, it was error to direct summary judgment for respondents based on the Fifth Amendment. . . .

The judgment of the Court of Appeals accordingly is reversed.

So ordered.

■ MR. JUSTICE STEWART joins Parts I and II of the Court's opinion.

■ **MR. JUSTICE STEVENS, concurring.**

While I agree with the Court's disposition of this case, I add these comments on the constitutional issue discussed in Part II and the statutory issue discussed in Part III of the Court's opinion.

The requirement of purposeful discrimination is a common thread running through the cases summarized in Part II. These cases include criminal convictions which were set aside because blacks were excluded from the grand jury, a reapportionment case in which political boundaries were obviously influenced to some extent by racial considerations, a school desegregation case, and a case involving the unequal administration of an ordinance purporting to prohibit the operation of laundries in frame buildings. Although it may be proper to use the same language to describe the constitutional claim in each of these contexts, the burden of proving a prima facie case may well involve differing evidentiary considerations. The extent of deference that one pays to the trial court's determination of the factual issue, and indeed, the extent to which one characterizes the intent issue as a question of fact or a question of law, will vary in different contexts.

Frequently the most probative evidence of intent will be objective evidence of what actually happened rather than evidence describing the subjective state of mind of the actor. For normally the actor is presumed to have intended the natural consequences of his deeds. This is particularly true in the case of governmental action which is frequently the product of compromise, of collective decisionmaking, and of mixed motivation. It is unrealistic, on the one hand, to require the victim of alleged discrimination to uncover the actual subjective intent of the decisionmaker or, conversely, to invalidate otherwise legitimate action simply because an improper motive affected the deliberation of a participant in the decisional process. A law conscripting clerics should not be invalidated because an atheist voted for it.

My point in making this observation is to suggest that the line between discriminatory purpose and discriminatory impact is not nearly as bright, and perhaps not quite as critical, as the reader of the Court's opinion might assume. I agree, of course, that a constitutional issue does not arise every time some disproportionate impact is shown. On the other hand, when the disproportion is as dramatic as in *Gomillion v. Lightfoot*, 364 U.S. 339 (1960), or *Yick Wo v. Hopkins*, 118 U.S. 356 (1886), it really does not matter whether the standard is phrased in terms of purpose or effect. Therefore, although I accept the statement of the general rule in the Court's opinion, I am not yet prepared to indicate how that standard should be applied in the many cases which have formulated the governing standard in different language. . . .

[Justice Brennan, joined by Justice Marshall, dissented on statutory grounds without discussing the constitutional question.]

NOTE ON DISCRIMINATORY PURPOSE AND DISPARATE IMPACTS

1.   How realistic is it to expect discrimination plaintiffs to prove discriminatory intent? Won't government officials always claim to have some nondiscriminatory reason for adopting a policy that tends to exclude members of minority groups? Does the Court sufficiently guard against this possibility in *Davis*?

2.   Purpose tests often make lawyers and judges nervous, but they occur throughout the law nonetheless. Imagine that a different federal agency, the Federal Emergency Management Association (FEMA), adopted Test 21 as a requirement for all its employees engaged in disaster relief efforts. Imagine further that minutes of a high-level meeting among FEMA administrators divulged that the agency had adopted the test deliberately as a means of excluding racial minorities from the agency. Would this bad motive make the test unconstitutional, even though an attack on the *same policy* was rejected in *Davis*?

Or consider the problem of collective intent. Consider a state legislature with one hundred members that approves a state policy by a vote of 55 to 45. Fifteen members can be shown to have adopted the proposal for racially discriminatory reasons—not a majority of the legislature or of the coalition voting for the measure, but votes that were essential for the measure to pass. Should a court find discriminatory purpose in that scenario? What if it can be shown that the racist legislatures would have supported the measure anyway, even if it had lacked a racial impact?

On the other hand, legal consequences turn on purpose all the time. In the criminal law, intent to kill spells the difference between murder and manslaughter. Under the First Amendment, government may often restrict speech for reasons unrelated to its content, but faces a significantly higher burden of justification if its purpose stems from opposition to the speaker's message. *See, e.g., United States v. O'Brien*, 391 U.S. 367 (1968). It may not be possible entirely to avoid purpose-based tests. Should the Court's nonetheless avoid them where possible? Does it matter whether purpose is being treated as a necessary or a sufficient condition for establishing unlawful discrimination? For instance, in a situation inverse to *Davis*, should a plaintiff be able to establish that a policy with *no* disparate effects is nonetheless unlawful if motivated by a racially discriminatory purpose?

3.   The court of appeals in *Davis* thought that constitutional challenges to government action under the Equal Protection Clause (or, in the case of actions by federal authorities, the equal protection "component" of the Fifth Amendment's Due Process Clause) should be governed by the same standard as suits brought under Title VII of the 1964 Civil Rights Act. Title VII, which is the primary statutory provision governing employment discrimination by both private and government actors, forbids employers "to fail or refuse to hire or to discharge any individual, or otherwise to discriminate against any individual with respect to his compensation, terms, conditions, or privileges of employment, because of such individual's race, color, religion, sex, or national origin; or (2) to limit, segregate, or classify his employees or applicants for employment in any way which would deprive or

tend to deprive any individual of employment opportunities or otherwise adversely affect his status as an employee, because of such individual's race, color, religion, sex, or national origin." 42 U.S.C. § 2000e–2.

In *Griggs v. Duke Power Co.*, 401 U.S. 424 (1971), the Court held that Title VII "proscribes not only overt discrimination but also practices that are fair in form, but discriminatory in operation." It thus held unlawful an employer's policy requiring a high school education for employment in most departments of its business, because that policy was shown to have a disparate impact on African-Americans. The Court acknowledged the company's "lack of discriminatory intent," but held that "Congress directed the thrust of the Act to the consequences of employment practices, not simply the motivation." Read in light of *Davis*, *Griggs* seems to go significantly beyond what the Constitution requires. Is that a good thing or a bad thing? Is it desirable that Congress should be able to regulate by statute behavior that the Equal Protection Clause would not reach, even if it were undertaken by a state actor?

In answering this question, does it matter that an employer found to have engaged in a discriminatory practice under Title VII based on a showing of disparate impact may nonetheless sustain that practice by showing that it is related to the job in question? That standard seems significantly more permissive than the strict scrutiny applied to racial classifications under the Equal Protection Clause. And the Court has recently suggested that such limitations on disparate impact liability are necessary to "avoid the serious constitutional questions that might arise under the [Federal Housing Act], for instance, if such liability were imposed based solely on a showing of a statistical disparity." *Texas Department of Housing and Community Affairs v. Inclusive Communities Project, Inc.*, 135 S. Ct. 2507, 2522 (2015). Would combining Title VII's test for what counts as discriminatory treatment with the Constitution's test for when such treatment is permissible result in an approach much stricter than Title VII itself? What are the "serious constitutional questions" to which Justice Kennedy referred in *Inclusive Communities*?

4.   How one assesses *Washington v. Davis* may depend, at least in part, on what one thinks is the aim of equal protection jurisprudence. If the Equal Protection and Due Process Clauses are directed toward preventing and rooting out wrongful government conduct, then it may be plausible to say that only purposeful discrimination is really wrongful. If, on the other hand, these Clauses are directed toward achieving a broadly equal society, then it might be necessary to go further and foreclose practices that stand in the way of that goal, even if they are not intrinsically rooted in prejudice. Which of these approaches is a more plausible account of the intent of the Fourteenth Amendment's framers? Which is more appealing on normative grounds?

Even if one accepts that only purposeful discrimination counts as a constitutional "wrong," might one nonetheless conclude that evidence of disparate impact is often the only way to "smoke out" such bad motives? Does the opinion in *Davis* foreclose this?

SECTION 15.2 GENDER DISCRIMINATION

Writing in 1972, Gerald Gunther noted that "[a]t the beginning of the 1960's, judicial intervention under the banner of equal protection was virtually unknown outside racial discrimination cases."[5] In 1971, the Supreme Court held for the first time, in *Reed v. Reed*,[6] that a law discriminating against women violated the Equal Protection Clause of the Fourteenth Amendment. The winning brief in that case was written by a youngish Rutgers law professor named Ruth Bader Ginsburg. Professor Ginsburg founded the American Civil Liberties Union's Women's Rights Project a year later and litigated a series of landmark cases broadening constitutional protections against gender discrimination. Following her appointment to the Supreme Court in 1993, Justice Ginsburg would give those protections their strictest statement to date in *United States v. Virginia*.

Craig v. Boren

429 U.S. 190 (1976)

■ MR. JUSTICE BRENNAN delivered the opinion of the Court.

The interaction of two sections of an Oklahoma statute, Okla.Stat., Tit. 37, §§ 241 and 245,[1] prohibits the sale of "nonintoxicating" 3.2% beer to males under the age of 21 and to females under the age of 18. The question to be decided is whether such a gender-based differential constitutes a denial to males 18–20 years of age of the equal protection of the laws in violation of the Fourteenth Amendment.

This action was brought in the District Court for the Western District of Oklahoma on December 20, 1972, by appellant Craig, a male then between 18 and 21 years of age, and by appellant Whitener, a licensed vendor of 3.2% beer. The complaint sought declaratory and injunctive relief against enforcement of the gender-based differential on the ground that it constituted invidious discrimination against males 18–20 years of age. A three-judge court convened under 28 U.S.C. § 2281 sustained the constitutionality of the statutory differential and dismissed the action. . . . We reverse.

---

[5] *Gerald Gunther, The Supreme Court, 1971 Term—Foreword: In Search of Evolving Doctrine on a Changing Court: A Model for a Newer Equal Protection*, 86 Harv. L. Rev. 1, 8 (1972).

[6] 404 U.S. 71 (1971).

[1] Sections 241 and 245 provide in pertinent part:

§ 241. "It shall be unlawful for any person who holds a license to sell and dispense beer . . . to sell, barter or give to any minor any beverage containing more than one-half of one per cent of alcohol measured by volume and not more than three and two-tenths (3.2) per cent of alcohol measured by weight.

§ 245. "A 'minor,' for the purposes of Section . . . 241 . . . is defined as a female under the age of eighteen (18) years, and a male under the age of twenty-one (21) years."

II

A

Before 1972, Oklahoma defined the commencement of civil majority at age 18 for females and age 21 for males. In contrast, females were held criminally responsible as adults at age 18 and males at age 16. After the Court of Appeals for the Tenth Circuit held in 1972, on the authority of *Reed v. Reed*, 404 U.S. 71 (1971), that the age distinction was unconstitutional for purposes of establishing criminal responsibility as adults, the Oklahoma Legislature fixed age 18 as applicable to both males and females. In 1972, 18 also was established as the age of majority for males and females in civil matters, except that §§ 241 and 245 of the 3.2% beer statute were simultaneously codified to create an exception to the gender-free rule.

Analysis may appropriately begin with the reminder that *Reed* emphasized that statutory classifications that distinguish between males and females are "subject to scrutiny under the Equal Protection Clause." 404 U.S., at 75. To withstand constitutional challenge, previous cases establish that classifications by gender must serve important governmental objectives and must be substantially related to achievement of those objectives. Thus, in *Reed*, the objectives of "reducing the workload on probate courts" and "avoiding intrafamily controversy" were deemed of insufficient importance to sustain use of an overt gender criterion in the appointment of administrators of intestate decedents' estates. Decisions following *Reed* similarly have rejected administrative ease and convenience as sufficiently important objectives to justify gender-based classifications. And only two Terms ago, *Stanton v. Stanton*, 421 U.S. 7 (1975) . . . held that *Reed* required invalidation of a Utah differential age-of-majority statute, notwithstanding the statute's coincidence with and furtherance of the State's purpose of fostering "old notions" of role typing and preparing boys for their expected performance in the economic and political worlds.[6]

Reed v. Reed has also provided the underpinning for decisions that have invalidated statutes employing gender as an inaccurate proxy for other, more germane bases of classification. Hence, "archaic and overbroad" generalizations concerning the financial position of servicewomen, *Frontiero v. Richardson*, 411 U.S. 677, 689 n. 23 (1973), and working women, *Weinberger v. Wiesenfeld*, 420 U.S. 636, 643 (1975), could not justify use of a gender line in determining eligibility for certain governmental entitlements. Similarly, increasingly outdated misconceptions concerning the role of females in the home rather than in

---

[6] *Kahn v. Shevin*, 416 U.S. 351 (1974) and *Schlesinger v. Ballard*, 419 U.S. 498 (1975), upholding the use of gender-based classifications, rested upon the Court's perception of the laudatory purposes of those laws as remedying disadvantageous conditions suffered by women in economic and military life. Needless to say, in this case Oklahoma does not suggest that the age-sex differential was enacted to ensure the availability of 3.2% beer for women as compensation for previous deprivations.

the "marketplace and world of ideas" were rejected as loose-fitting characterizations incapable of supporting state statutory schemes that were premised upon their accuracy. In light of the weak congruence between gender and the characteristic or trait that gender purported to represent, it was necessary that the legislatures choose either to realign their substantive laws in a gender-neutral fashion, or to adopt procedures for identifying those instances where the sex-centered generalization actually comported with fact.

In this case, too, *Reed*, we feel is controlling. We turn then to the question whether, under *Reed*, the difference between males and females with respect to the purchase of 3.2% beer warrants the differential in age drawn by the Oklahoma statute. We conclude that it does not.

B

The District Court . . . found the requisite important governmental objective in the traffic-safety goal proffered by the Oklahoma Attorney General. It then concluded that the statistics introduced by the appellees established that the gender-based distinction was substantially related to achievement of that goal.

C

We accept for purposes of discussion the District Court's identification of the objective underlying §§ 241 and 245 as the enhancement of traffic safety.[7] Clearly, the protection of public health and safety represents an important function of state and local governments. However, appellees' statistics in our view cannot support the conclusion that the gender-based distinction closely serves to achieve that objective and therefore the distinction cannot under Reed withstand equal protection challenge.

The appellees introduced a variety of statistical surveys. First, an analysis of arrest statistics for 1973 demonstrated that 18–20-year-old male arrests for "driving under the influence" and "drunkenness" substantially exceeded female arrests for that same age period.[8]

---

[7] That this was the true purpose is not at all self-evident. The purpose is not apparent from the face of the statute and the Oklahoma Legislature does not preserve statutory history materials capable of clarifying the objectives served by its legislative enactments. The District Court acknowledged the nonexistence of materials necessary "to reveal what the actual purpose of the legislature was," but concluded that "we feel it apparent that a major purpose of the legislature was to promote the safety of the young persons affected and the public generally." Similarly, the attorney for Oklahoma, while proposing traffic safety as a legitimate rationale for the 3.2% beer law, candidly acknowledged at oral argument that he is unable to assert that traffic safety is "indeed the reason" for the gender line contained in § 245. For this appeal we find adequate the appellee's representation of legislative purpose, leaving for another day consideration of whether the statement of the State's Assistant Attorney General should suffice to inform this Court of the legislature's objectives, or whether the Court must determine if the litigant simply is selecting a convenient, but false, post hoc rationalization.

[8] The disparities in 18–20-year-old male-female arrests were substantial for both categories of offenses: 427 versus 24 for driving under the influence of alcohol, and 966 versus 102 for drunkenness. Even if we assume that a legislature may rely on such arrest data in some situations, these figures do not offer support for a differential age line, for the disproportionate

Similarly, youths aged 17–21 were found to be overrepresented among those killed or injured in traffic accidents, with males again numerically exceeding females in this regard. Third, a random roadside survey in Oklahoma City revealed that young males were more inclined to drive and drink beer than were their female counterparts. Fourth, Federal Bureau of Investigation nationwide statistics exhibited a notable increase in arrests for "driving under the influence."[11] Finally, statistical evidence gathered in other jurisdictions, particularly Minnesota and Michigan, was offered to corroborate Oklahoma's experience by indicating the pervasiveness of youthful participation in motor vehicle accidents following the imbibing of alcohol. Conceding that "the case is not free from doubt," the District Court nonetheless concluded that this statistical showing substantiated "a rational basis for the legislative judgment underlying the challenged classification."

Even were this statistical evidence accepted as accurate, it nevertheless offers only a weak answer to the equal protection question presented here. The most focused and relevant of the statistical surveys, arrests of 18–20-year-olds for alcohol-related driving offenses, exemplifies the ultimate unpersuasiveness of this evidentiary record. Viewed in terms of the correlation between sex and the actual activity that Oklahoma seeks to regulate driving while under the influence of alcohol the statistics broadly establish that .18% of females and 2% of males in that age group were arrested for that offense. While such a disparity is not trivial in a statistical sense, it hardly can form the basis for employment of a gender line as a classifying device. Certainly if maleness is to serve as a proxy for drinking and driving, a correlation of 2% must be considered an unduly tenuous "fit." Indeed, prior cases have consistently rejected the use of sex as a decisionmaking factor even though the statutes in question certainly rested on far more predictive empirical relationships than this.[13]

Moreover, the statistics exhibit a variety of other shortcomings that seriously impugn their value to equal protection analysis. Setting aside the obvious methodological problems,[14] the surveys do not adequately

---

arrests of males persisted at older ages; indeed, in the case of arrests for drunkenness, the figures for all ages indicated even more male involvement in such arrests at later ages.

[11] The FBI made no attempt to relate these arrest figures either to beer drinking or to an 18–21 age differential, but rather found that male arrests for all ages exceeded 90% of the total.

[13] For example, we can conjecture that in *Reed*, Idaho's apparent premise that women lacked experience in formal business matters (particularly compared to men) would have proved to be accurate in substantially more than 2% of all cases. And in both *Frontiero* and *Wiesenfeld*, we expressly found appellees' empirical defense of mandatory dependency tests for men but not women to be unsatisfactory, even though we recognized that husbands are still far less likely to be dependent on their wives than vice versa.

[14] The very social stereotypes that find reflection in age-differential laws, see Stanton v. Stanton, 421 U.S. 7, 14–15 (1975), are likely substantially to distort the accuracy of these comparative statistics. Hence "reckless" young men who drink and drive are transformed into arrest statistics, whereas their female counterparts are chivalrously escorted home. See, e. g., W. Reckless & B. Kay, *The Female Offender* 4, 7, 13, 16–17 (Report to Presidential Commission on Law Enforcement and Administration of Justice, 1967). . . .

justify the salient features of Oklahoma's gender-based traffic-safety law. None purports to measure the use and dangerousness of 3.2% beer as opposed to alcohol generally, a detail that is of particular importance since, in light of its low alcohol level, Oklahoma apparently considers the 3.2% beverage to be "nonintoxicating." Moreover, many of the studies, while graphically documenting the unfortunate increase in driving while under the influence of alcohol, make no effort to relate their findings to age-sex differentials as involved here. . . .

There is no reason to belabor this line of analysis. It is unrealistic to expect either members of the judiciary or state officials to be well versed in the rigors of experimental or statistical technique. But this merely illustrates that proving broad sociological propositions by statistics is a dubious business, and one that inevitably is in tension with the normative philosophy that underlies the Equal Protection Clause. Suffice to say that the showing offered by the appellees does not satisfy us that sex represents a legitimate, accurate proxy for the regulation of drinking and driving. In fact, when it is further recognized that Oklahoma's statute prohibits only the selling of 3.2% beer to young males and not their drinking the beverage once acquired (even after purchase by their 18–20-year-old female companions), the relationship between gender and traffic safety becomes far too tenuous to satisfy *Reed*'s requirement that the gender-based difference be substantially related to achievement of the statutory objective. . . .

We conclude that the gender-based differential contained in Okla.Stat., Tit. 37, § 245 constitutes a denial of the equal protection of the laws to males aged 18–20 and reverse the judgment of the District Court.

It is so ordered.

■ MR. JUSTICE STEVENS, concurring.

There is only one Equal Protection Clause. It requires every State to govern impartially. It does not direct the courts to apply one standard of review in some cases and a different standard in other cases. Whatever criticism may be leveled at a judicial opinion implying that there are at least three such standards applies with the same force to a double standard.

I am inclined to believe that what has become known as the two-tiered analysis of equal protection claims does not describe a completely logical method of deciding cases, but rather is a method the Court has employed to explain decisions that actually apply a single standard in a reasonably consistent fashion. I also suspect that a careful explanation of the reasons motivating particular decisions may contribute more to an identification of that standard than an attempt to articulate it in all-encompassing terms. It may therefore be appropriate for me to state the principal reasons which persuaded me to join the Court's opinion.

In this case, the classification is not as obnoxious as some the Court has condemned,[1] nor as inoffensive as some the Court has accepted. It is objectionable because it is based on an accident of birth,[2] because it is a mere remnant of the now almost universally rejected tradition of discriminating against males in this age bracket,[3] and because, to the extent it reflects any physical difference between males and females, it is actually perverse.[4] The question then is whether the traffic safety justification put forward by the State is sufficient to make an otherwise offensive classification acceptable.

The classification is not totally irrational. For the evidence does indicate that there are more males than females in this age bracket who drive and also more who drink. Nevertheless, there are several reasons why I regard the justification as unacceptable. It is difficult to believe that the statute was actually intended to cope with the problem of traffic safety,[5] since it has only a minimal effect on access to a not very intoxicating beverage and does not prohibit its consumption. Moreover, the empirical data submitted by the State accentuate the unfairness of treating all 18–21-year-old males as inferior to their female counterparts. The legislation imposes a restraint on 100% of the males in the class allegedly because about 2% of them have probably violated one or more laws relating to the consumption of alcoholic beverages. It is unlikely that this law will have a significant deterrent effect either on that 2% or on the law-abiding 98%. But even assuming some such slight benefit, it does not seem to me that an insult to all of the young men of the State can be justified by visiting the sins of the 2% on the 98%.

■ MR. CHIEF JUSTICE BURGER, dissenting.

. . . On the merits, we have only recently recognized that our duty is not "to create substantive constitutional rights in the name of guaranteeing equal protection of the laws." *San Antonio School Dist. v. Rodriguez*, 411 U.S. 1, 33 (1973). Thus, even interests of such importance in our society as public education and housing do not qualify as "fundamental rights" for equal protection purposes because they have no textually independent constitutional status. *See id.*, at 29–39 (education);

---

[1] Men as a general class have not been the victims of the kind of historic, pervasive discrimination that has disadvantaged other groups.

[2] "(S)ince sex, like race and national origin, is an immutable characteristic determined solely by the accident of birth, the imposition of special disabilities upon the members of a particular sex because of their sex would seem to violate the basic concept of our system that legal burdens should bear some relationship to individual responsibility." *Frontiero v. Richardson*, 411 U.S. 677, 686 (1973).

[3] Apparently Oklahoma is the only State to permit this narrow discrimination to survive the elimination of the disparity between the age of majority for males and females.

[4] Because males are generally heavier than females, they have a greater capacity to consume alcohol without impairing their driving ability than do females.

[5] There is no legislative history to indicate that this was the purpose, and several features of the statutory scheme indicate the contrary. . . . I would not be surprised if it represented nothing more than the perpetuation of a stereotyped attitude about the relative maturity of the members of the two sexes in this age bracket. . . .

Lindsey v. Normet, 405 U.S. 56 (1972) (housing). Though today's decision does not go so far as to make gender-based classifications "suspect," it makes gender a disfavored classification. Without an independent constitutional basis supporting the right asserted or disfavoring the classification adopted, I can justify no substantive constitutional protection other than the normal protection afforded by the Equal Protection Clause.

The means employed by the Oklahoma Legislature to achieve the objectives sought may not be agreeable to some judges, but since eight Members of the Court think the means not irrational, I see no basis for striking down the statute as violative of the Constitution simply because we find it unwise, unneeded, or possibly even a bit foolish. . . .

■ **MR. JUSTICE REHNQUIST, dissenting.**

The Court's disposition of this case is objectionable on two grounds. First is its conclusion that men challenging a gender-based statute which treats them less favorably than women may invoke a more stringent standard of judicial review than pertains to most other types of classifications. Second is the Court's enunciation of this standard, without citation to any source, as being that "classifications by gender must serve important governmental objectives and must be substantially related to achievement of those objectives." The only redeeming feature of the Court's opinion, to my mind, is that it apparently signals a retreat by those who joined the plurality opinion in *Frontiero v. Richardson*, 411 U.S. 677 (1973), from their view that sex is a "suspect" classification for purposes of equal protection analysis. I think the Oklahoma statute challenged here need pass only the "rational basis" equal protection analysis expounded in cases such as *McGowan v. Maryland*, 366 U.S. 420 (1961), and *Williamson v. Lee Optical Co.*, 348 U.S. 483 (1955), and I believe that it is constitutional under that analysis.

I

In *Frontiero v. Richardson, supra*, the opinion for the plurality sets forth the reasons of four Justices for concluding that sex should be regarded as a suspect classification for purposes of equal protection analysis. These reasons center on our Nation's "long and unfortunate history of sex discrimination," which has been reflected in a whole range of restrictions on the legal rights of women, not the least of which have concerned the ownership of property and participation in the electoral process. Noting that the pervasive and persistent nature of the discrimination experienced by women is in part the result of their ready identifiability, the plurality rested its invocation of strict scrutiny largely upon the fact that "statutory distinctions between the sexes often have the effect of invidiously relegating the entire class of females to inferior legal status without regard to the actual capabilities of its individual members."

Subsequent to *Frontiero*, the Court has declined to hold that sex is a suspect class, *Stanton v. Stanton*, 421 U.S. 7, 13 (1975), and no such holding is imported by the Court's resolution of this case. However, the Court's application here of an elevated or "intermediate" level scrutiny, like that invoked in cases dealing with discrimination against females, raises the question of why the statute here should be treated any differently from countless legislative classifications unrelated to sex which have been upheld under a minimum rationality standard.

Most obviously unavailable to support any kind of special scrutiny in this case, is a history or pattern of past discrimination, such as was relied on by the plurality in *Frontiero* to support its invocation of strict scrutiny. There is no suggestion in the Court's opinion that males in this age group are in any way peculiarly disadvantaged, subject to systematic discriminatory treatment, or otherwise in need of special solicitude from the courts.

The Court does not discuss the nature of the right involved, and there is no reason to believe that it sees the purchase of 3.2% beer as implicating any important interest, let alone one that is "fundamental" in the constitutional sense of invoking strict scrutiny. Indeed, the Court's accurate observation that the statute affects the selling but not the drinking of 3.2% beer further emphasizes the limited effect that it has on even those persons in the age group involved. There is, in sum, nothing about the statutory classification involved here to suggest that it affects an interest, or works against a group, which can claim under the Equal Protection Clause that it is entitled to special judicial protection.

It is true that a number of our opinions contain broadly phrased dicta implying that the same test should be applied to all classifications based on sex, whether affecting females or males. E. g., *Frontiero v. Richardson*, *supra*, 411 U.S., at 688; *Reed v. Reed*, 404 U.S. 71, 76 (1971). However, before today, no decision of this Court has applied an elevated level of scrutiny to invalidate a statutory discrimination harmful to males, except where the statute impaired an important personal interest protected by the Constitution.[1] There being no such interest here, and there being no plausible argument that this is a discrimination against

---

[1]   In *Stanley v. Illinois*, 405 U.S. 645 (1972), the Court struck down a statute allowing separation of illegitimate children from a surviving father but not a surviving mother, without any showing of parental unfitness. The Court stated that "the interest of a parent in the companionship, care, custody, and management of his or her children 'come(s) to this Court with a momentum for respect lacking when appeal is made to liberties which derive merely from shifting economic arrangements.'"

In *Kahn v. Shevin*, 416 U.S. 351 (1974), the Court upheld Florida's $500 property tax exemption for widows only. The opinion of the Court appears to apply a rational-basis test, and is so understood by the dissenters.

In *Weinberger v. Wiesenfeld*, 420 U.S. 636 (1975), the Court invalidated § 202(g) of the Social Security Act, which allowed benefits to mothers but not fathers of minor children, who survive the wage earner. This statute was treated, in the opinion of the Court, as a discrimination against female wage earners, on the ground that it minimizes the financial security which their work efforts provide for their families.

females,[2] the Court's reliance on our previous sex-discrimination cases is ill-founded. It treats gender classification as a talisman which without regard to the rights involved or the persons affected calls into effect a heavier burden of judicial review.

The Court's conclusion that a law which treats males less favorably than females "must serve important governmental objectives and must be substantially related to achievement of those objectives" apparently comes out of thin air. The Equal Protection Clause contains no such language, and none of our previous cases adopt that standard. I would think we have had enough difficulty with the two standards of review which our cases have recognized the norm of "rational basis," and the "compelling state interest" required where a "suspect classification" is involved so as to counsel weightily against the insertion of still another "standard" between those two. How is this Court to divine what objectives are important? How is it to determine whether a particular law is "substantially" related to the achievement of such objective, rather than related in some other way to its achievement? Both of the phrases used are so diaphanous and elastic as to invite subjective judicial preferences or prejudices relating to particular types of legislation, masquerading as judgments whether such legislation is directed at "important" objectives or, whether the relationship to those objectives is "substantial" enough.

I would have thought that if this Court were to leave anything to decision by the popularly elected branches of the Government, where no constitutional claim other than that of equal protection is invoked, it would be the decision as to what governmental objectives to be achieved by law are "important," and which are not. As for the second part of the Court's new test, the Judicial Branch is probably in no worse position than the Legislative or Executive Branches to determine if there is any rational relationship between a classification and the purpose which it might be thought to serve. But the introduction of the adverb "substantially" requires courts to make subjective judgments as to operational effects, for which neither their expertise nor their access to data fits them. And even if we manage to avoid both confusion and the mirroring of our own preferences in the development of this new doctrine, the thousands of judges in other courts who must interpret the Equal Protection Clause may not be so fortunate.

II

The applicable rational-basis test is one which "permits the States a wide scope of discretion in enacting laws which affect some groups of

---

[2]   I am not unaware of the argument from time to time advanced, that all discriminations between the sexes ultimately redound to the detriment of females, because they tend to reinforce "old notions" restricting the roles and opportunities of women. As a general proposition applying equally to all sex categorizations, I believe that this argument was implicitly found to carry little weight in our decisions upholding gender-based differences. See *Schlesinger v. Ballard*, 419 U.S. 498 (1975); *Kahn v. Shevin*, 416 U.S. 351 (1974). Seeing no assertion that it has special applicability to the situation at hand, I believe it can be dismissed as an insubstantial consideration.

citizens differently than others. The constitutional safeguard is offended only if the classification rests on grounds wholly irrelevant to the achievement of the State's objective. State legislatures are presumed to have acted within their constitutional power despite the fact that, in practice, their laws result in some inequality. A statutory discrimination will not be set aside if any state of facts reasonably may be conceived to justify it." *McGowan v. Maryland*, 366 U.S., at 425–426.

Our decisions indicate that application of the Equal Protection Clause in a context not justifying an elevated level of scrutiny does nor demand "mathematical nicety" or the elimination of all inequality. Those cases recognize that the practical problems of government may require rough accommodations of interests, and hold that such accommodations should be respected unless no reasonable basis can be found to support them. Whether the same ends might have been better or more precisely served by a different approach is no part of the judicial inquiry under the traditional minimum rationality approach.

The Court "accept(s) for purposes of discussion" the District Court's finding that the purpose of the provisions in question was traffic safety, and proceeds to examine the statistical evidence in the record in order to decide if "the gender-based distinction closely serves to achieve that objective." . . . I believe that a more traditional type of scrutiny is appropriate in this case, and I think that the Court would have done well here to heed its own warning that "(i)t is unrealistic to expect . . . members of the judiciary . . . to be well versed in the rigors of experimental or statistical technique." One need not immerse oneself in the fine points of statistical analysis, however, in order to see the weaknesses in the Court's attempted denigration of the evidence at hand.

One survey of arrest statistics assembled in 1973 indicated that males in the 18–20 age group were arrested for "driving under the influence" almost 18 times as often as their female counterparts, and for "drunkenness" in a ratio of almost 10 to 1. Accepting, as the Court does, appellants' comparison of the total figures with 1973 Oklahoma census data, this survey indicates a 2% arrest rate among males in the age group, as compared to a .18% rate among females.

Other surveys indicated (1) that over the five-year period from 1967 to 1972, nationwide arrests among those under 18 for drunken driving increased 138%, and that 93% of all persons arrested for drunken driving were male; (2) that youths in the 17–21 age group were overrepresented among those killed or injured in Oklahoma traffic accidents, that male casualties substantially exceeded female, and that deaths in this age group continued to rise while overall traffic deaths declined; (3) that over three-fourths of the drivers under 20 in the Oklahoma City area are males, and that each of them, on average, drives half again as many miles per year as their female counterparts; (4) that four-fifths of male drivers under 20 in the Oklahoma City area state a drink preference for beer, while about three-fifths of female drivers of that age state the same preference; and (5) that the percentage of male drivers under 20 admitting to drinking within two hours of driving was half again larger than the percentage for females, and that the percentage of male drivers of that age group with a blood alcohol content greater than .01% was almost half again larger than for female drivers.

The Court's criticism of the statistics relied on by the District Court conveys the impression that a legislature in enacting a new law is to be subjected to the judicial equivalent of a doctoral examination in statistics. Legislatures are not held to any rules of evidence such as those which may govern courts or other administrative bodies, and are entitled to draw factual conclusions on the basis of the determination of probable cause which an arrest by a police officer normally represents. In this situation, they could reasonably infer that the incidence of drunk driving is a good deal higher than the incidence of arrest.

And while, as the Court observes, relying on a report to a Presidential Commission which it cites in a footnote, such statistics may be distorted as a result of stereotyping, the legislature is not required to prove before a court that its statistics are perfect. In any event, if stereotypes are as pervasive as the Court suggests, they may in turn influence the conduct of the men and women in question, and cause the young men to conform to the wild and reckless image which is their stereotype.

The Court also complains of insufficient integration of the various surveys on several counts that the injury and death figures are in no way directly correlated with intoxication; that the national arrest figures for drunk driving contain no breakdown for the 18 to 21-year-old group; and that the arrest records for intoxication are not tied to the consumption of 3.2% beer. But the State of Oklahoma and certainly this Court for purposes of equal protection review can surely take notice of the fact that drunkenness is a significant cause of traffic casualties, and that youthful offenders have participated in the increase of the drunk-driving problem. On this latter point, the survey data indicating increased driving casualties among 18–21-year-olds, while overall casualties dropped, are not irrelevant.

Nor is it unreasonable to conclude from the expressed preference for beer by four-fifths of the age-group males that that beverage was a predominant source of their intoxication-related arrests. Taking that as the predicate, the State could reasonably bar those males from any purchases of alcoholic beer, including that of the 3.2% variety. This Court lacks the expertise or the data to evaluate the intoxicating properties of that beverage, and in that posture our only appropriate course is to defer to the reasonable inference supporting the statute that taken in sufficient quantity this beer has the same effect as any alcoholic beverage.

Quite apart from these alleged methodological deficiencies in the statistical evidence, the Court appears to hold that that evidence, on its face, fails to support the distinction drawn in the statute. The Court notes that only 2% of males (as against .18% of females) in the age group were arrested for drunk driving, and that this very low figure establishes "an unduly tenuous 'fit' " between maleness and drunk driving in the 18 to 20-year-old group. On this point the Court misconceives the nature of the equal protection inquiry.

The rationality of a statutory classification for equal protection purposes does not depend upon the statistical "fit" between the class and the trait sought to be singled out. It turns on whether there may be a sufficiently higher incidence of the trait within the included class than in the excluded class to justify different treatment. Therefore the present equal protection challenge to this gender-based discrimination poses only the question whether the incidence of drunk driving among young men is sufficiently greater than among young women to justify differential treatment. Notwithstanding the Court's critique of the statistical evidence, that evidence suggests clear differences between the drinking and driving habits of young men and women. Those differences are grounds enough for the State reasonably to conclude that young males pose by far the greater drunk-driving hazard, both in terms of sheer numbers and in terms of hazard on a per-driver basis. The gender-based difference in treatment in this case is therefore not irrational.

The Court's argument that a 2% correlation between maleness and drunk driving is constitutionally insufficient therefore does not pose an equal protection issue concerning discrimination between males and females. The clearest demonstration of this is the fact that the precise argument made by the Court would be equally applicable to a flat bar on such purchases by anyone, male or female, in the 18–20 age group; in fact it would apply a fortiori in that case given the even more "tenuous 'fit' " between drunk-driving arrests and femaleness. The statistics indicate that about 1% of the age group population as a whole is arrested. What the Court's argument is relevant to is not equal protection, but due process whether there are enough persons in the category who drive while drunk to justify a bar against purchases by all members of the group.

Cast in those terms, the argument carries little weight, in light of our decisions indicating that such questions call for a balance of the State's interest against the harm resulting from any overinclusiveness or underinclusiveness. The personal interest harmed here is very minor: the present legislation implicates only the right to purchase 3.2% beer, certainly a far cry from the important personal interests which have on occasion supported this Court's invalidation of statutes on similar reasoning. And the state interest involved is significant: the prevention of injury and death on the highways.

This is not a case where the classification can only be justified on grounds of administrative convenience. There being no apparent way to single out persons likely to drink and drive, it seems plain that the legislature was faced here with the not atypical legislative problem of legislating in terms of broad categories with regard to the purchase and consumption of alcohol. I trust . . . that there would be no due process violation if no one in this age group were allowed to purchase 3.2% beer. Since males drink and drive at a higher rate than the age group as a whole, I fail to see how a statutory bar with regard only to them can create any due process problem.

The Oklahoma Legislature could have believed that 18–20-year-old males drive substantially more, and tend more often to be intoxicated than their female counterparts; that they prefer beer and admit to drinking and driving at a higher rate than females; and that they suffer traffic injuries out of proportion to the part they make up of the population. Under the appropriate rational-basis test for equal protection, it is neither irrational nor arbitrary to bar them from making purchases of 3.2% beer, which purchases might in many cases be made by a young man who immediately returns to his vehicle with the beverage in his possession. The record does not give any good indication of the true proportion of males in the age group who drink and drive (except that it is no doubt greater than the 2% who are arrested), but whatever it may be I cannot see that the mere purchase right involved could conceivably raise a due process question. There being no violation of either equal protection or due process, the statute should accordingly be upheld.

United States v. Virginia
518 U.S. 515 (1996)

■ JUSTICE GINSBURG delivered the opinion of the Court.

Virginia's public institutions of higher learning include an incomparable military college, Virginia Military Institute (VMI). The United States maintains that the Constitution's equal protection guarantee precludes Virginia from reserving exclusively to men the unique educational opportunities VMI affords. We agree.

I

Founded in 1839, VMI is today the sole single-sex school among Virginia's 15 public institutions of higher learning. VMI's distinctive mission is to produce "citizen-soldiers," men prepared for leadership in civilian life and in military service. VMI pursues this mission through pervasive training of a kind not available anywhere else in Virginia. Assigning prime place to character development, VMI uses an "adversative method" modeled on English public schools and once characteristic of military instruction. VMI constantly endeavors to instill physical and mental discipline in its cadets and impart to them a strong moral code. The school's graduates leave VMI with heightened comprehension of their capacity to deal with duress and stress, and a large sense of accomplishment for completing the hazardous course.

VMI has notably succeeded in its mission to produce leaders; among its alumni are military generals, Members of Congress, and business executives. The school's alumni overwhelmingly perceive that their VMI training helped them to realize their personal goals. VMI's endowment reflects the loyalty of its graduates; VMI has the largest per-student endowment of all public undergraduate institutions in the Nation.

Neither the goal of producing citizen-soldiers nor VMI's implementing methodology is inherently unsuitable to women. And the school's impressive record in producing leaders has made admission desirable to some women. Nevertheless, Virginia has elected to preserve exclusively for men the advantages and opportunities a VMI education affords.

II

A

From its establishment in 1839 as one of the Nation's first state military colleges, VMI has remained financially supported by Virginia and "subject to the control of the [Virginia] General Assembly." First southern college to teach engineering and industrial chemistry, VMI once provided teachers for the Commonwealth's schools. Civil War strife threatened the school's vitality, but a resourceful superintendent regained legislative support by highlighting "VMI's great potential[,] through its technical know-how," to advance Virginia's postwar recovery.

VMI today enrolls about 1,300 men as cadets. Its academic offerings in the liberal arts, sciences, and engineering are also available at other public colleges and universities in Virginia. But VMI's mission is special. It is the mission of the school

> 'to produce educated and honorable men, prepared for the varied work of civil life, imbued with love of learning, confident in the functions and attitudes of leadership, possessing a high sense of public service, advocates of the American democracy and free enterprise system, and ready as citizen-soldiers to defend their country in time of national peril.' 766 F.Supp. 1407, 1425 (W.D.Va.1991) (quoting Mission Study Committee of the VMI Board of Visitors, Report, May 16, 1986).

In contrast to the federal service academies, institutions maintained to prepare cadets for career service in the armed forces, VMI's program is directed at preparation for both military and civilian life; only about 15% of VMI cadets enter career military service.

VMI produces its "citizen-soldiers" through an adversative, or doubting, model of education which features physical rigor, mental stress, absolute equality of treatment, absence of privacy, minute regulation of behavior, and indoctrination in desirable values. As one Commandant of Cadets described it, the adversative method "dissects the young student," and makes him aware of his "limits and capabilities," so that he knows "how far he can go with his anger . . . how much he can take under stress ... exactly what he can do when he is physically exhausted."

VMI cadets live in spartan barracks where surveillance is constant and privacy nonexistent; they wear uniforms, eat together in the mess hall, and regularly participate in drills. Entering students are incessantly exposed to the rat line, an extreme form of the adversative model, comparable in intensity to Marine Corps boot camp. Tormenting and punishing, the rat line bonds new cadets to their fellow sufferers and, when they have completed the 7-month experience, to their former tormentors.

VMI's "adversative model" is further characterized by a hierarchical "class system" of privileges and responsibilities, a "dyke system" for assigning a senior class mentor to each entering class "rat," and a stringently enforced "honor code," which prescribes that a cadet "does not lie, cheat, steal nor tolerate those who do."

VMI attracts some applicants because of its reputation as an extraordinarily challenging military school, and because its alumni are exceptionally close to the school. Women have no opportunity anywhere to gain the benefits of the system of education at VMI.

B

In 1990, prompted by a complaint filed with the Attorney General by a female high-school student seeking admission to VMI, the United States sued the Commonwealth of Virginia and VMI, alleging that VMI's exclusively male admission policy violated the Equal Protection Clause of the Fourteenth Amendment. Trial of the action consumed six days and involved an array of expert witnesses on each side.

In the two years preceding the lawsuit, the District Court noted, VMI had received inquiries from 347 women, but had responded to none of them. "[S]ome women, at least," the court said, "would want to attend the school if they had the opportunity." The court further recognized that, with recruitment, VMI could "achieve at least 10% female enrollment"— "a sufficient 'critical mass' to provide the female cadets with a positive educational experience." And it was also established that "some women are capable of all of the individual activities required of VMI cadets." In addition, experts agreed that if VMI admitted women, "the VMI ROTC experience would become a better training program from the perspective of the armed forces, because it would provide training in dealing with a mixed-gender army."

The District Court ruled in favor of VMI, however, and rejected the equal protection challenge pressed by the United States. . . . [It] reasoned that education in "a single-gender environment, be it male or female," yields substantial benefits. . . . If single-gender education for males ranks as an important governmental objective, it becomes obvious, the District Court concluded, that the *only* means of achieving the objective "is to exclude women from the all-male institution—VMI."

"Women are [indeed] denied a unique educational opportunity that is available only at VMI," the District Court acknowledged. But "[VMI's] single-sex status would be lost, and some aspects of the [school's] distinctive method would be altered," if women were admitted . . . . Thus, "sufficient constitutional justification" had been shown, the District Court held, "for continuing [VMI's] single-sex policy."

The Court of Appeals for the Fourth Circuit disagreed and vacated the District Court's judgment. The appellate court held: "The Commonwealth of Virginia has not . . . advanced any state policy by which it can justify its determination, under an announced policy of diversity, to afford VMI's unique type of program to men and not to women." . . . Remanding the case, the appeals court assigned to Virginia, in the first instance, responsibility for selecting a remedial course. . . .

C

In response to the Fourth Circuit's ruling, Virginia proposed a parallel program for women: Virginia Women's Institute for Leadership (VWIL). The 4-year, state-sponsored undergraduate program would be located at Mary Baldwin College, a private liberal arts school for women, and would be open, initially, to about 25 to 30 students. Although VWIL would share VMI's mission—to produce "citizen-soldiers"—the VWIL program would differ, as does Mary Baldwin College, from VMI in academic offerings, methods of education, and financial resources.

The average combined SAT score of entrants at Mary Baldwin is about 100 points lower than the score for VMI freshmen. Mary Baldwin's faculty holds significantly fewer Ph.D.'s than the faculty at VMI and receives significantly lower salaries. While VMI offers degrees in liberal arts, the sciences, and engineering, Mary Baldwin, at the time of trial, offered only bachelor of arts degrees. A VWIL student seeking to earn an engineering degree could gain one, without public support, by attending Washington University in St. Louis, Missouri, for two years, paying the required private tuition.

Experts in educating women at the college level composed the Task Force charged with designing the VWIL program; Task Force members were drawn from Mary Baldwin's own faculty and staff. Training its attention on methods of instruction appropriate for "most women," the Task Force determined that a military model would be "wholly inappropriate" for VWIL.

VWIL students would participate in ROTC programs and a newly established, "largely ceremonial" Virginia Corps of Cadets, but the VWIL House would not have a military format and VWIL would not require its students to eat meals together or to wear uniforms during the schoolday. In lieu of VMI's adversarial method, the VWIL Task Force favored "a cooperative method which reinforces self-esteem." In addition to the standard bachelor of arts program offered at Mary Baldwin, VWIL students would take courses in leadership, complete an off-campus leadership externship, participate in community service projects, and assist in arranging a speaker series.

Virginia represented that it will provide equal financial support for in-state VWIL students and VMI cadets, and the VMI Foundation agreed to supply a $5.4625 million endowment for the VWIL program Mary Baldwin's own endowment is about $19 million; VMI's is $131 million. Mary Baldwin will add $35 million to its endowment based on future commitments; VMI will add $220 million. The VMI Alumni Association has developed a network of employers interested in hiring VMI graduates. The Association has agreed to open its network to VWIL graduates, but those graduates will not have the advantage afforded by a VMI degree.

D

Virginia returned to the District Court seeking approval of its proposed remedial plan, and the court decided the plan met the requirements of the Equal Protection Clause. . . . [T]he "controlling legal principles," the District Court decided, "do not require the Commonwealth to provide a mirror image VMI for women." The court anticipated that the two schools would "achieve substantially similar outcomes." . . .

A divided Court of Appeals affirmed the District Court's judgment. . . . "[P]roviding the option of a single-gender college education may be considered a legitimate and important aspect of a public system of higher education," the appeals court observed; that objective, the court added, is "not pernicious." . . . [T]he adversative method vital to a VMI education . . . "was not designed to exclude women," the court noted, but women could not be accommodated in the VMI program, the court believed, for female participation in VMI's adversative training "would destroy . . . any sense of decency that still permeates the relationship between the sexes."

Having determined, deferentially, the legitimacy of Virginia's purpose, the court considered the question of means. Exclusion of "men at Mary Baldwin College and women at VMI," the court said, was essential to Virginia's purpose, for without such exclusion, the Commonwealth could not "accomplish [its] objective of providing single-gender education." . . .

The key question, the court said, was whether men at VMI and women at VWIL would obtain "substantively comparable benefits at their institution or through other means offered by the [S]tate." Although the appeals court recognized that the VWIL degree "lacks the historical benefit and prestige" of a VMI degree, it nevertheless found the educational opportunities at the two schools "sufficiently comparable." . . .

III

The cross-petitions in this suit present two ultimate issues. First, does Virginia's exclusion of women from the educational opportunities provided by VMI—extraordinary opportunities for military training and civilian leadership development—deny to women capable of all of the individual activities required of VMI cadets the equal protection of the laws guaranteed by the Fourteenth Amendment? Second, if VMI's "unique" situation—as Virginia's sole single-sex public institution of higher education—offends the Constitution's equal protection principle, what is the remedial requirement?

IV

We note, once again, the core instruction of this Court's pathmarking decisions in *J.E.B. v. Alabama ex rel. T. B.*, 511 U.S. 127, 136–137, and n. 6 (1994), and *Mississippi Univ. for Women v. Hogan*, 458 U.S. 718, 724 (1982): Parties who seek to defend gender-based government action must demonstrate an "exceedingly persuasive justification" for that action.

Today's skeptical scrutiny of official action denying rights or opportunities based on sex responds to volumes of history. As a plurality of this Court acknowledged a generation ago, "our Nation has had a long and unfortunate history of sex discrimination." *Frontiero v. Richardson,* 411 U.S. 677, 684 (1973). Through a century plus three decades and more of that history, women did not count among voters composing "We the People";[5] not until 1920 did women gain a constitutional right to the franchise. And for a half century thereafter, it remained the prevailing doctrine that government, both federal and state, could withhold from women opportunities accorded men so long as any "basis in reason" could be conceived for the discrimination.

In 1971, for the first time in our Nation's history, this Court ruled in favor of a woman who complained that her State had denied her the equal protection of its laws. *Reed v. Reed,* 404 U.S. 71, 73 (holding unconstitutional Idaho Code prescription that, among " 'several persons claiming and equally entitled to administer [a decedent's estate], males must be preferred to females' "). Since *Reed,* the Court has repeatedly recognized that neither federal nor state government acts compatibly with the equal protection principle when a law or official policy denies to women, simply because they are women, full citizenship stature—equal opportunity to aspire, achieve, participate in and contribute to society based on their individual talents and capacities. See, *e.g., Kirchberg v. Feenstra,* 450 U.S. 455, 462–463 (1981) (affirming invalidity of Louisiana law that made husband "head and master" of property jointly owned with

---

[5]   As Thomas Jefferson stated the view prevailing when the Constitution was new: "Were our State a pure democracy . . . there would yet be excluded from their deliberations . . . [w]omen, who, to prevent depravation of morals and ambiguity of issue, could not mix promiscuously in the public meetings of men." Letter from Thomas Jefferson to Samuel Kercheval (Sept. 5, 1816), in 10 Writings of Thomas Jefferson 45–46, n. 1 (P. Ford ed. 1899).

his wife, giving him unilateral right to dispose of such property without his wife's consent); *Stanton v. Stanton,* 421 U.S. 7 (1975) (invalidating Utah requirement that parents support boys until age 21, girls only until age 18).

Without equating gender classifications, for all purposes, to classifications based on race or national origin, the Court, in post-*Reed* decisions, has carefully inspected official action that closes a door or denies opportunity to women (or to men). To summarize the Court's current directions for cases of official classification based on gender: Focusing on the differential treatment for denial of opportunity for which relief is sought, the reviewing court must determine whether the proffered justification is "exceedingly persuasive." The burden of justification is demanding and it rests entirely on the State. The State must show "at least that the [challenged] classification serves 'important governmental objectives and that the discriminatory means employed' are 'substantially related to the achievement of those objectives.'" *Mississippi Univ. for Women,* 458 U.S., at 724. The justification must be genuine, not hypothesized or invented *post hoc* in response to litigation. And it must not rely on overbroad generalizations about the different talents, capacities, or preferences of males and females. See *Weinberger v. Wiesenfeld,* 420 U.S. 636, 643, 648 (1975).

The heightened review standard our precedent establishes does not make sex a proscribed classification. Supposed "inherent differences" are no longer accepted as a ground for race or national origin classifications. Physical differences between men and women, however, are enduring: "[T]he two sexes are not fungible; a community made up exclusively of one [sex] is different from a community composed of both." *Ballard v. United States,* 329 U.S. 187, 193 (1946).

"Inherent differences" between men and women, we have come to appreciate, remain cause for celebration, but not for denigration of the members of either sex or for artificial constraints on an individual's opportunity. Sex classifications may be used to compensate women "for particular economic disabilities [they have] suffered," *Califano v. Webster,* 430 U.S. 313, 320 (1977) *(per curiam),* to "promot[e] equal employment opportunity," see *California Fed. Sav. & Loan Assn. v. Guerra,* 479 U.S. 272, 289 (1987), to advance full development of the talent and capacities of our Nation's people.[7] But such classifications may

---

[7]   Several *amici* have urged that diversity in educational opportunities is an altogether appropriate governmental pursuit and that single-sex schools can contribute importantly to such diversity. Indeed, it is the mission of some single-sex schools "to dissipate, rather than perpetuate, traditional gender classifications." See Brief for Twenty-six Private Women's Colleges as *Amici Curiae* 5. We do not question the Commonwealth's prerogative evenhandedly to support diverse educational opportunities. We address specifically and only an educational opportunity recognized by the District Court and the Court of Appeals as "unique," an opportunity available only at Virginia's premier military institute, the Commonwealth's sole single-sex public university or college.

not be used, as they once were, to create or perpetuate the legal, social, and economic inferiority of women.

Measuring the record in this case against the review standard just described, we conclude that Virginia has shown no "exceedingly persuasive justification" for excluding all women from the citizen-soldier training afforded by VMI. We therefore affirm the Fourth Circuit's initial judgment, which held that Virginia had violated the Fourteenth Amendment's Equal Protection Clause. Because the remedy proffered by Virginia—the Mary Baldwin VWIL program—does not cure the constitutional violation, *i.e.,* it does not provide equal opportunity, we reverse the Fourth Circuit's final judgment in this case.

V

... Virginia ... asserts two justifications in defense of VMI's exclusion of women. First, the Commonwealth contends, "single-sex education provides important educational benefits," and the option of single-sex education contributes to "diversity in educational approaches." Second, the Commonwealth argues, "the unique VMI method of character development and leadership training," the school's adversative approach, would have to be modified were VMI to admit women. We consider these two justifications in turn.

A

Single-sex education affords pedagogical benefits to at least some students, Virginia emphasizes, and that reality is uncontested in this litigation. Similarly, it is not disputed that diversity among public educational institutions can serve the public good. But Virginia has not shown that VMI was established, or has been maintained, with a view to diversifying, by its categorical exclusion of women, educational opportunities within the Commonwealth. In cases of this genre, our precedent instructs that "benign" justifications proffered in defense of categorical exclusions will not be accepted automatically; a tenable justification must describe actual state purposes, not rationalizations for actions in fact differently grounded.

Mississippi Univ. for Women is immediately in point. There the State asserted, in justification of its exclusion of men from a nursing school, that it was engaging in "educational affirmative action" by "compensat[ing] for discrimination against women." Undertaking a "searching analysis," the Court found no close resemblance between "the alleged objective" and "the actual purpose underlying the discriminatory classification." Pursuing a similar inquiry here, we reach the same conclusion.

Neither recent nor distant history bears out Virginia's alleged pursuit of diversity through single-sex educational options. In 1839, when the Commonwealth established VMI, a range of educational opportunities for men and women was scarcely contemplated. Higher education at the time was considered dangerous for women;[9] reflecting widely held views about women's proper place, the Nation's first universities and colleges—for example, Harvard in Massachusetts, William and Mary in Virginia—admitted only men. VMI was not at all novel in this respect: In admitting no women, VMI followed the lead of the Commonwealth's flagship school, the University of Virginia, founded in 1819.

"[N]o struggle for the admission of women to a state university," a historian has recounted, "was longer drawn out, or developed more bitterness, than that at the University of Virginia." In 1879, the State Senate resolved to look into the possibility of higher education for women . . . . Virginia eventually provided for several women's seminaries and colleges. Farmville Female Seminary became a public institution in 1884. Two women's schools, Mary Washington College and James Madison University, were founded in 1908; another, Radford University, was founded in 1910. By the mid-1970's, all four schools had become coeducational.

Debate concerning women's admission as undergraduates at the main university continued well past the century's midpoint. Familiar arguments were rehearsed. If women were admitted, it was feared, they "would encroach on the rights of men; there would be new problems of government, perhaps scandals; the old honor system would have to be changed; standards would be lowered to those of other coeducational schools; and the glorious reputation of the university, as a school for men, would be trailed in the dust."

Ultimately, in 1970, "the most prestigious institution of higher education in Virginia," the University of Virginia, introduced coeducation and, in 1972, began to admit women on an equal basis with men. . . .

Virginia describes the current absence of public single-sex higher education for women as "an historical anomaly." But the historical record indicates action more deliberate than anomalous: First, protection of women against higher education; next, schools for women far from equal in resources and stature to schools for men; finally, conversion of the separate schools to coeducation. The state legislature, prior to the advent of this controversy, had repealed "[a]ll Virginia statutes requiring individual institutions to admit only men or women." And in 1990, an official commission, "legislatively established to chart the future goals of higher education in Virginia," reaffirmed the policy " 'of affording broad

---

[9] Dr. Edward H. Clarke of Harvard Medical School, whose influential book, Sex in Education, went through 17 editions, was perhaps the most well-known speaker from the medical community opposing higher education for women. He maintained that the physiological effects of hard study and academic competition with boys would interfere with the development of girls' reproductive organs. See E. Clarke, Sex in Education 38–39, 62–63 (1873); see also C. Meigs, Females and Their Diseases 350 (1848) (after five or six weeks of "mental and educational discipline," a healthy woman would "lose . . . the habit of menstruation" and suffer numerous ills as a result of depriving her body for the sake of her mind).

access' " while maintaining " 'autonomy and diversity.' " Significantly, the commission reported:

> Because colleges and universities provide opportunities for students to develop values and learn from role models, it is extremely important that they deal with faculty, staff, and students without regard to sex, race, or ethnic origin.

This statement, the Court of Appeals observed, "is the only explicit one that we have found in the record in which the Commonwealth has expressed itself with respect to gender distinctions." . . .

In sum, we find no persuasive evidence in this record that VMI's male-only admission policy is in furtherance of a state policy of 'diversity.' No such policy, the Fourth Circuit observed, can be discerned from the movement of all other public colleges and universities in Virginia away from single-sex education. . . . A purpose genuinely to advance an array of educational options, as the Court of Appeals recognized, is not served by VMI's historic and constant plan—a plan to "affor[d] a unique educational benefit only to males." However "liberally" this plan serves the Commonwealth's sons, it makes no provision whatever for her daughters. That is not *equal* protection.

B

Virginia next argues that VMI's adversative method of training provides educational benefits that cannot be made available, unmodified, to women. Alterations to accommodate women would necessarily be "radical," so "drastic," Virginia asserts, as to transform, indeed "destroy," VMI's program. Neither sex would be favored by the transformation, Virginia maintains: Men would be deprived of the unique opportunity currently available to them; women would not gain that opportunity because their participation would "eliminat[e] the very aspects of [the] program that distinguish [VMI] from . . . other institutions of higher education in Virginia."

The District Court forecast from expert witness testimony, and the Court of Appeals accepted, that coeducation would materially affect "at least these three aspects of VMI's program—physical training, the absence of privacy, and the adversative approach." And it is uncontested that women's admission would require accommodations, primarily in arranging housing assignments and physical training programs for female cadets. It is also undisputed, however, that "the VMI methodology could be used to educate women." . . . "[S]ome women, at least, would want to attend [VMI] if they had the opportunity," the District Court recognized, and "some women," the expert testimony established, "are capable of all of the individual activities required of VMI cadets." The parties, furthermore, agree that "*some* women can meet the physical standards [VMI] now impose[s] on men." In sum, as the Court of Appeals stated, "neither the goal of producing citizen soldiers," VMI's *raison d'être,* "nor VMI's implementing methodology is inherently unsuitable to women."

In support of its initial judgment for Virginia . . . the District Court made "findings" on "gender-based developmental differences." These "findings" restate the opinions of Virginia's expert witnesses, opinions about typically male or typically female "tendencies." For example, "[m]ales tend to need an atmosphere of adversativeness," while "[f]emales tend to thrive in a cooperative atmosphere." "I'm not saying that some women don't do well under [the] adversative model," VMI's expert on educational institutions testified, "undoubtedly there are some [women] who do"; but educational experiences must be designed "around the rule," this expert maintained, and not "around the exception."

The United States does not challenge any expert witness estimation on average capacities or preferences of men and women. Instead, the United States emphasizes that time and again since this Court's turning point decision in *Reed v. Reed,* 404 U.S. 71 (1971), we have cautioned reviewing courts to take a "hard look" at generalizations or "tendencies" of the kind pressed by Virginia, and relied upon by the District Court. State actors controlling gates to opportunity, we have instructed, may not exclude qualified individuals based on "fixed notions concerning the roles and abilities of males and females." *Mississippi Univ. for Women,* 458 U.S., at 725.

It may be assumed, for purposes of this decision, that most women would not choose VMI's adversative method. . . . [I]t is also probable that many men would not want to be educated in such an environment. . . . Education, to be sure, is not a "one size fits all" business. The issue, however, is not whether "women—or men—should be forced to attend VMI"; rather, the question is whether the Commonwealth can constitutionally deny to women who have the will and capacity, the training and attendant opportunities that VMI uniquely affords.

The notion that admission of women would downgrade VMI's stature, destroy the adversative system and, with it, even the school,[11] is a judgment hardly proved, a prediction hardly different from other self-fulfilling prophecies, once routinely used to deny rights or opportunities. When women first sought admission to the bar and access to legal education, concerns of the same order were expressed. For example, in 1876, the Court of Common Pleas of Hennepin County, Minnesota, explained why women were thought ineligible for the practice of law. Women train and educate the young, the court said, which

> forbids that they shall bestow that time (early and late) and labor, so essential in attaining to the eminence to which the true

---

[11] Forecasts of the same kind were made regarding admission of women to the federal military academies. See, *e.g.,* Hearings on H.R. 9832 et al. before Subcommittee No. 2 of the House Committee on Armed Services, 93d Cong., 2d Sess., 137 (1975) (statement of Lt. Gen. A.P. Clark, Superintendent of U.S. Air Force Academy) ("It is my considered judgment that the introduction of female cadets will inevitably erode this vital atmosphere.").

lawyer should ever aspire. . . . [T]he opposition of courts to the admission of females to practice . . . arises rather from a comprehension of the magnitude of the responsibilities connected with the successful practice of law, and a desire to *grade up* the profession.

. . . Medical faculties similarly resisted men and women as partners in the study of medicine. More recently, women seeking careers in policing encountered resistance based on fears that their presence would "undermine male solidarity"; deprive male partners of adequate assistance; and lead to sexual misconduct. Field studies did not confirm these fears.

Women's successful entry into the federal military academies,[13] and their participation in the Nation's military forces, indicate that Virginia's fears for the future of VMI may not be solidly grounded. The Commonwealth's justification for excluding all women from "citizen-soldier" training for which some are qualified, in any event, cannot rank as "exceedingly persuasive," as we have explained and applied that standard.

Virginia and VMI trained their argument on "means" rather than "end," and thus misperceived our precedent. Single-sex education at VMI serves an "important governmental objective," they maintained, and exclusion of women is not only "substantially related," it is essential to that objective. . . . The Commonwealth's misunderstanding and, in turn, the District Court's, is apparent from VMI's mission: to produce "citizen-soldiers," individuals

> imbued with love of learning, confident in the functions and attitudes of leadership, possessing a high sense of public service, advocates of the American democracy and free enterprise system, and ready. . . to defend their country in time of national peril. Mission Study Committee of the VMI Board of Visitors, Report, May 16, 1986.

Surely that goal is great enough to accommodate women, who today count as citizens in our American democracy equal in stature to men. Just as surely, the Commonwealth's great goal is not substantially advanced by women's categorical exclusion, in total disregard of their individual merit, from the Commonwealth's premier "citizen-soldier" corps.[16] Virginia, in sum, has fallen far short of establishing the

---

[13] Women cadets have graduated at the top of their class at every federal military academy. See Brief for Lieutenant Colonel Rhonda Cornum et al. as *Amici Curiae* 11, n. 25; cf. Defense Advisory Committee on Women in the Services, Report on the Integration and Performance of Women at West Point 64 (1992).

[16] VMI has successfully managed another notable change. The school admitted its first African-American cadets in 1968. See The VMI Story 347–349 (students no longer sing "Dixie," salute the Confederate flag or the tomb of General Robert E. Lee at ceremonies and sports events). As the District Court noted, VMI established a program on "retention of black cadets" designed to offer academic and social-cultural support to "minority members of a dominantly white and tradition-oriented student body."

'exceedingly persuasive justification, that must be the solid base for any gender-defined classification.

VI

In the second phase of the litigation, Virginia presented its remedial plan—maintain VMI as a male-only college and create VWIL as a separate program for women. . . . Inspecting the VMI and VWIL educational programs to determine whether they "afford[ed] to both genders benefits comparable in substance, [if] not in form and detail," the Court of Appeals concluded that Virginia had arranged for men and women opportunities "sufficiently comparable" to survive equal protection evaluation. The United States challenges this "remedial" ruling as pervasively misguided.

A

A remedial decree, this Court has said, must closely fit the constitutional violation; it must be shaped to place persons unconstitutionally denied an opportunity or advantage in "the position they would have occupied in the absence of [discrimination]." See *Milliken v. Bradley,* 433 U.S. 267, 280 (1977). The constitutional violation in this suit is the categorical exclusion of women from an extraordinary educational opportunity afforded men. A proper remedy for an unconstitutional exclusion, we have explained, aims to "eliminate [so far as possible] the discriminatory effects of the past" and to "bar like discrimination in the future." *Louisiana v. United States,* 380 U.S. 145, 154 (1965).

Virginia chose not to eliminate, but to leave untouched, VMI's exclusionary policy. For women only, however, Virginia proposed a separate program, different in kind from VMI and unequal in tangible and intangible facilities. Having violated the Constitution's equal protection requirement, Virginia was obliged to show that its remedial proposal directly addressed and related to the violation, *i.e.,* the equal protection denied to women ready, willing, and able to benefit from educational opportunities of the kind VMI offers. Virginia described VWIL as a "parallel program," and asserted that VWIL shares VMI's mission of producing "citizen-soldiers" and VMI's goals of providing "education, military training, mental and physical discipline, character . . . and leadership development." If the VWIL program could not eliminate the discriminatory effects of the past, could it at least bar like discrimination in the future? A comparison of the programs said to be "parallel" informs our answer. . . .

VWIL affords women no opportunity to experience the rigorous military training for which VMI is famed. Instead, the VWIL program deemphasizes military education and uses a "cooperative method" of education "which reinforces self-esteem."

VWIL students participate in ROTC and a "largely ceremonial" Virginia Corps of Cadets, but Virginia deliberately did not make VWIL a military institute. The VWIL House is not a military-style residence and VWIL students need not live together throughout the 4-year program, eat meals together, or wear uniforms during the schoolday. VWIL students thus do not experience the "barracks" life crucial to the VMI experience, the spartan living arrangements designed to foster an "egalitarian ethic." "[T]he most important aspects of the VMI educational experience occur in the barracks," the District Court found, yet Virginia deemed that core experience nonessential, indeed inappropriate, for training its female citizen-soldiers.

VWIL students receive their "leadership training" in seminars, externships, and speaker series, episodes and encounters lacking the "[p]hysical rigor, mental stress, . . . minute regulation of behavior, and indoctrination in desirable values" made hallmarks of VMI's citizen-soldier training. Kept away from the pressures, hazards, and psychological bonding characteristic of VMI's adversative training, VWIL students will not know the "feeling of tremendous accomplishment" commonly experienced by VMI's successful cadets.

Virginia maintains that these methodological differences are "justified pedagogically," based on "important differences between men and women in learning and developmental needs," "psychological and sociological differences" Virginia describes as "real" and "not stereotypes." The Task Force charged with developing the leadership program for women, drawn from the staff and faculty at Mary Baldwin College, "determined that a military model and, especially VMI's adversative method, would be wholly inappropriate for educating and training *most women*." . . .

As earlier stated, generalizations about "the way women are," estimates of what is appropriate for *most women,* no longer justify denying opportunity to women whose talent and capacity place them outside the average description. Notably, Virginia never asserted that VMI's method of education suits *most men.* . . .

In contrast to the generalizations about women on which Virginia rests, we note again these dispositive realities [found by the courts below]: VMI's "implementing methodology" is not "inherently unsuitable to women"; "some women . . . do well under [the] adversative model"; "some women, at least, would want to attend [VMI] if they had the opportunity"; "some women are capable of all of the individual activities required of VMI cadets," and "can meet the physical standards [VMI] now impose[s] on men." It is on behalf of these women that the United States has instituted this suit, and it is for them that a remedy must be crafted,[19] a remedy that will end their exclusion from a state-supplied

---

[19] Admitting women to VMI would undoubtedly require alterations necessary to afford members of each sex privacy from the other sex in living arrangements, and to adjust aspects of the physical training programs. Experience shows such adjustments are manageable. See U.S. Military Academy, A. Vitters, N. Kinzer, & J. Adams, Report of Admission of Women (Project Athena I–IV) (1977–1980) (4-year longitudinal study of the admission of women to West

educational opportunity for which they are fit, a decree that will bar like discrimination in the future.

B

In myriad respects other than military training, VWIL does not qualify as VMI's equal. VWIL's student body, faculty, course offerings, and facilities hardly match VMI's. Nor can the VWIL graduate anticipate the benefits associated with VMI's 157-year history, the school's prestige, and its influential alumni network. . . .

Mary Baldwin does not offer a VWIL student the range of curricular choices available to a VMI cadet. . . . VWIL students attend a school that does not have a math and science focus; they cannot take at Mary Baldwin any courses in engineering or the advanced math and physics courses VMI offers.

For physical training, Mary Baldwin has "two multi-purpose fields" and "[o]ne gymnasium." VMI has "an NCAA competition level indoor track and field facility; a number of multi-purpose fields; baseball, soccer and lacrosse fields; an obstacle course; large boxing, wrestling and martial arts facilities; an 11-laps-to-the-mile indoor running course; an indoor pool; indoor and outdoor rifle ranges; and a football stadium that also contains a practice field and outdoor track."

Although Virginia has represented that it will provide equal financial support for in-state VWIL students and VMI cadets, and the VMI Foundation has agreed to endow VWIL with $5.4625 million, the difference between the two schools' financial reserves is pronounced. . . .

The VWIL student does not graduate with the advantage of a VMI degree. Her diploma does not unite her with the legions of VMI "graduates [who] have distinguished themselves" in military and civilian life. . . . A VWIL graduate cannot assume that the "network of business owners, corporations, VMI graduates and non-graduate employers . . . interested in hiring VMI graduates" will be equally responsive to her search for employment.

Virginia, in sum, while maintaining VMI for men only, has failed to provide any "comparable single-gender women's institution." Instead, the Commonwealth has created a VWIL program fairly appraised as a "pale shadow" of VMI in terms of the range of curricular choices and faculty stature, funding, prestige, alumni support and influence. . . .

[W]e rule here that Virginia has not shown substantial equality in the separate educational opportunities the Commonwealth supports at VWIL and VMI.

Point); Defense Advisory Committee on Women in the Services, Report on the Integration and Performance of Women at West Point 17–18 (1992).

C

. . . The Fourth Circuit plainly erred in exposing Virginia's VWIL plan to a deferential analysis, for all gender-based classifications today warrant "heightened scrutiny." Valuable as VWIL may prove for students who seek the program offered, Virginia's remedy affords no cure at all for the opportunities and advantages withheld from women who want a VMI education and can make the grade.[20] In sum, Virginia's remedy does not match the constitutional violation; the Commonwealth has shown no "exceedingly persuasive justification" for withholding from women qualified for the experience premier training of the kind VMI affords.

VII

. . . A prime part of the history of our Constitution . . . is the story of the extension of constitutional rights and protections to people once ignored or excluded. VMI's story continued as our comprehension of "We the People" expanded. There is no reason to believe that the admission of women capable of all the activities required of VMI cadets would destroy the Institute rather than enhance its capacity to serve the "more perfect Union."

For the reasons stated, the initial judgment of the Court of Appeals is affirmed, the final judgment of the Court of Appeals is reversed, and the case is remanded for further proceedings consistent with this opinion.

It is so ordered.

■ JUSTICE THOMAS **took no part in the consideration or decision of these cases.**

■ CHIEF JUSTICE REHNQUIST, **concurring in the judgment.**

The Court holds first that Virginia violates the Equal Protection Clause by maintaining the Virginia Military Institute's (VMI's) all-male admissions policy, and second that establishing the Virginia Women's Institute for Leadership (VWIL) program does not remedy that violation. While I agree with these conclusions, I disagree with the Court's analysis and so I write separately.

I

Two decades ago in *Craig v. Boren*, 429 U.S. 190, 197 (1976), we announced that "[t]o withstand constitutional challenge, . . . classifications by gender must serve important governmental objectives and must be substantially related to achievement of those objectives." We

---

[20] Virginia's prime concern, it appears, is that "plac[ing] men and women into the adversarial relationship inherent in the VMI program . . . would destroy, at least for that period of the adversarial training, any sense of decency that still permeates the relationship between the sexes." It is an ancient and familiar fear. *See, e.g., In re Lavinia Goodell,* 39 Wis. 232, 246 (1875) (denying female applicant's motion for admission to the bar of its court, Wisconsin Supreme Court explained: "Discussions are habitually necessary in courts of justice, which are unfit for female ears. The habitual presence of women at these would tend to relax the public sense of decency and propriety.").

have adhered to that standard of scrutiny ever since. While the majority adheres to this test today, it also says that the Commonwealth must demonstrate an " 'exceedingly persuasive justification' " to support a gender-based classification. It is unfortunate that the Court thereby introduces an element of uncertainty respecting the appropriate test. . . .

[T]he phrase "exceedingly persuasive justification" . . . is best confined, as it was first used, as an observation on the difficulty of meeting the applicable test, not as a formulation of the test itself. To avoid introducing potential confusion, I would have adhered more closely to our traditional, "firmly established" standard that a gender-based classification "must bear a close and substantial relationship to important governmental objectives."

Our cases dealing with gender discrimination also require that the proffered purpose for the challenged law be the actual purpose. It is on this ground that the Court rejects the first of two justifications Virginia offers for VMI's single-sex admissions policy, namely, the goal of diversity among its public educational institutions. While I ultimately agree that the Commonwealth has not carried the day with this justification, I disagree with the Court's method of analyzing the issue.

VMI was founded in 1839, and, as the Court notes, admission was limited to men because under the then-prevailing view men, not women, were destined for higher education. However misguided this point of view may be by present-day standards, it surely was not unconstitutional in 1839. The adoption of the Fourteenth Amendment, with its Equal Protection Clause, was nearly 30 years in the future. . . . Long after the adoption of the Fourteenth Amendment, and well into this century, legal distinctions between men and women were thought to raise no question under the Equal Protection Clause. . . . Then, in 1971, we decided *Reed v. Reed*, 404 U.S. 71, which the Court correctly refers to as a seminal case. But its facts have nothing to do with admissions to any sort of educational institution. . . . Even at the time of our decision in *Reed v. Reed,* therefore, Virginia and VMI were scarcely on notice that its holding would be extended across the constitutional board. . . . In *Mississippi Univ. for Women v. Hogan,* a case actually involving a single-sex admissions policy in higher education, the Court held that the exclusion of men from a nursing program violated the Equal Protection Clause. This holding did place Virginia on notice that VMI's men-only admissions policy was open to serious question. . . .

Before this Court, Virginia has sought to justify VMI's single-sex admissions policy primarily on the basis that diversity in education is desirable, and that while most of the public institutions of higher learning in the Commonwealth are coeducational, there should also be room for single-sex institutions. I agree with the Court that there is scant evidence in the record that this was the real reason that Virginia decided to maintain VMI as men only. But, unlike the majority, I would consider only evidence that postdates our decision in *Hogan,* and would draw no negative inferences from the Commonwealth's actions before that time. I think that after *Hogan,* the Commonwealth was entitled to reconsider its policy with respect to VMI, and not to have earlier justifications, or lack thereof, held against it.

Even if diversity in educational opportunity were the Commonwealth's actual objective, the Commonwealth's position would still be problematic. The difficulty with its position is that the diversity benefited only one sex; there was single-sex public education available for men at VMI, but no corresponding single-sex public education available for women. When *Hogan* placed Virginia on notice that VMI's admissions policy possibly was unconstitutional, VMI could have dealt with the problem by admitting women; but its governing body felt strongly that the admission of women would have seriously harmed the institution's educational approach. Was there something else the Commonwealth could have done to avoid an equal protection violation? Since the Commonwealth did nothing, we do not have to definitively answer that question.

I do not think, however, that the Commonwealth's options were as limited as the majority may imply. The Court cites, without expressly approving it, a statement from the opinion of the dissenting judge in the Court of Appeals, to the effect that the Commonwealth could have "simultaneously opened single-gender undergraduate institutions having substantially comparable curricular and extracurricular programs, funding, physical plant, administration and support services, and faculty and library resources." If this statement is thought to exclude other possibilities, it is too stringent a requirement. VMI had been in operation for over a century and a half, and had an established, successful, and devoted group of alumni. No legislative wand could instantly call into existence a similar institution for women; and it would be a tremendous loss to scrap VMI's history and tradition. . . . Had Virginia made a genuine effort to devote comparable public resources to a facility for women, and followed through on such a plan, it might well have avoided an equal protection violation. . . .

But, as I have noted, neither the governing board of VMI nor the Commonwealth took any action after 1982. If diversity in the form of single-sex, as well as coeducational, institutions of higher learning were to be available to Virginians, that diversity had to be available to women as well as to men. . . .

Virginia offers a second justification for the single-sex admissions policy: maintenance of the adversative method. I agree with the Court that this justification does not serve an important governmental objective. A State does not have substantial interest in the adversative methodology unless it is pedagogically beneficial. While considerable evidence shows that a single-sex education is pedagogically beneficial for some students, and hence a State may have a valid interest in promoting that methodology, there is no similar evidence in the record that an adversative method is pedagogically beneficial or is any more likely to produce character traits than other methodologies.

II

The Court defines the constitutional violation in these cases as "the categorical exclusion of women from an extraordinary educational opportunity afforded to men." By defining the violation in this way, and by emphasizing that a remedy for a constitutional violation must place the victims of discrimination in " 'the position they would have occupied in the absence of [discrimination],' " the Court necessarily implies that the only adequate remedy would be the admission of women to the all-male institution. As the foregoing discussion suggests, I would not define the violation in this way; it is not the "exclusion of women" that violates the Equal Protection Clause, but the maintenance of an all-men school without providing any—much less a comparable—institution for women.

Accordingly, the remedy should not necessarily require either the admission of women to VMI or the creation of a VMI clone for women. An adequate remedy in my opinion might be a demonstration by Virginia that its interest in educating men in a single-sex environment is matched by its interest in educating women in a single-sex institution. . . . It would be a sufficient remedy, I think, if the two institutions offered the same quality of education and were of the same overall caliber.

If a State decides to create single-sex programs, the State would, I expect, consider the public's interest and demand in designing curricula. And rightfully so. But the State should avoid assuming demand based on stereotypes; it must not assume *a priori,* without evidence, that there would be no interest in a women's school of civil engineering, or in a men's school of nursing.

In the end, the women's institution Virginia proposes, VWIL, fails as a remedy, because it is distinctly inferior to the existing men's institution and will continue to be for the foreseeable future. VWIL simply is not, in any sense, the institution that VMI is. . . . I therefore ultimately agree with the Court that Virginia has not provided an adequate remedy.

■ **JUSTICE SCALIA, dissenting.**

Today the Court shuts down an institution that has served the people of the Commonwealth of Virginia with pride and distinction for over a century and a half. To achieve that desired result, it rejects (contrary to our established practice) the factual findings of two courts below, sweeps aside the precedents of this Court, and ignores the history of our people. As to facts: It explicitly rejects the finding that there exist "gender-based developmental differences" supporting Virginia's restriction of the "adversative" method to only a men's institution, and the finding that the all-male composition of the Virginia Military Institute (VMI) is essential to that institution's character. As to precedent: It drastically revises our established standards for reviewing sex-based classifications. And as to history: It counts for nothing the long tradition, enduring down to the present, of men's military colleges supported by both States and the Federal Government.

Much of the Court's opinion is devoted to deprecating the closed-mindedness of our forebears with regard to women's education, and even with regard to the treatment of women in areas that have nothing to do with education. Closed-minded they were—as every age is, including our own, with regard to matters it cannot guess, because it simply does not consider them debatable. The virtue of a democratic system with a First Amendment is that it readily enables the people, over time, to be persuaded that what they took for granted is not so, and to change their laws accordingly. . . . The same cannot be said of this most illiberal Court, which has embarked on a course of inscribing one after another of the current preferences of the society (and in some cases only the counter-majoritarian preferences of the society's law-trained elite) into our Basic Law. . . . I dissent.

I

I shall devote most of my analysis to evaluating the Court's opinion on the basis of our current equal protection jurisprudence, which regards this Court as free to evaluate everything under the sun by applying one of three tests: "rational basis" scrutiny, intermediate scrutiny, or strict scrutiny. . . . I have no problem with a system of abstract tests such as rational basis, intermediate, and strict scrutiny (though I think we can do better than applying strict scrutiny and intermediate scrutiny whenever we feel like it). Such formulas are essential to evaluating whether the new restrictions that a changing society constantly imposes upon private conduct comport with that "equal protection" our society has always accorded in the past. But in my view the function of this Court is to *preserve* our society's values regarding (among other things) equal protection, not to *revise* them; to prevent backsliding from the degree of restriction the Constitution imposed upon democratic government, not to prescribe, on our own authority, progressively higher degrees. For that reason it is my view that, whatever abstract tests we may choose to devise, they cannot supersede—and indeed ought to be crafted *so as to reflect*—those constant and unbroken national traditions that embody the people's understanding of ambiguous constitutional texts. More specifically, it is my view that when a practice not expressly prohibited by the text of the Bill of Rights bears the endorsement of a long tradition of open, widespread, and unchallenged use that dates back to the beginning of the Republic, we have no proper basis for striking it down. The same applies, *mutatis mutandis,* to a practice asserted to be in violation of the post-Civil War Fourteenth Amendment.

The all-male constitution of VMI comes squarely within such a governing tradition. Founded by the Commonwealth of Virginia in 1839 and continuously maintained by it since, VMI has always admitted only men. And in that regard it has not been unusual. For almost all of VMI's more than a century and a half of existence, its single-sex status reflected the uniform practice for government-supported military colleges. Another famous Southern institution, The Citadel, has existed as a state-funded school of South Carolina since 1842. And all the federal military colleges—West Point, the Naval Academy at Annapolis, and even the Air Force Academy, which was not established until 1954—admitted only males for most of their history. Their admission of women in 1976 (upon which the Court today relies) came not by court decree, but because the people, through their elected representatives, decreed a change. In other words, the tradition of having government-funded military schools for men is as well rooted in the traditions of this country as the tradition of sending only men into military combat. . . .

And the same applies, more broadly, to single-sex education in general, which, as I shall discuss, is threatened by today's decision with the cutoff of all state and federal support. Government-run *non*military educational institutions for the two sexes have until very recently also been part of our national tradition. "[It is] [c]oeducation, historically, [that] is a novel educational theory. From grade school through high school, college, and graduate and professional training, much of the Nation's population during much of our history has been educated in sexually segregated classrooms." *Mississippi Univ. for Women v. Hogan,* 458 U.S. 718, 736 (1982) (Powell, J., dissenting). These traditions may of course be changed by the democratic decisions of the people, as they largely have been.

Today, however, change is forced upon Virginia, and reversion to single-sex education is prohibited nationwide, not by democratic processes but by order of this Court. Even while bemoaning the sorry, bygone days of "fixed notions" concerning women's education, the Court favors current notions so fixedly that it is willing to write them into the Constitution of the United States by application of custom-built "tests." This is not the interpretation of a Constitution, but the creation of one.

II

To reject the Court's disposition today, however, it is not necessary to accept my view that the Court's made-up tests cannot displace longstanding national traditions as the primary determinant of what the Constitution means. It is only necessary to apply honestly the test the Court has been applying to sex-based classifications for the past two decades. It is well settled, as Justice O'CONNOR stated some time ago for a unanimous Court, that we evaluate a statutory classification based on sex under a standard that lies "[b]etween th [e] extremes of rational basis review and strict scrutiny." *Clark v. Jeter,* 486 U.S. 456, 461 (1988). We have denominated this standard "intermediate scrutiny" and under it have inquired whether the statutory classification is "substantially related to an important governmental objective."

Before I proceed to apply this standard to VMI, I must comment upon the manner in which the Court *avoids* doing so. Notwithstanding our above-described precedents and their firmly established principles, the United States urged us to hold in this litigation "that strict scrutiny is the correct constitutional standard for evaluating classifications that deny opportunities to individuals based on their sex." . . . The Court, while making no reference to the Government's argument, effectively accepts it.

Although the Court in two places recites the test as stated in *Hogan,* which asks whether the State has demonstrated "that the classification serves important governmental objectives and that the discriminatory means employed are substantially related to the achievement of those objectives," the Court never answers the question presented in anything resembling that form. When it engages in analysis, the Court instead prefers the phrase "exceedingly persuasive justification" from *Hogan.* . . . [T]the Court proceeds to interpret "exceedingly persuasive justification" in a fashion that contradicts the reasoning of *Hogan* and our other precedents.

That is essential to the Court's result, which can only be achieved by establishing that intermediate scrutiny is not survived if there are *some* women interested in attending VMI, capable of undertaking its activities, and able to meet its physical demands. . . . Similarly, the Court states that "[t]he Commonwealth's justification for excluding all women from 'citizen-soldier' training for which some are qualified . . . cannot rank as 'exceedingly persuasive'. . . ."

Only the amorphous "exceedingly persuasive justification" phrase, and not the standard elaboration of intermediate scrutiny, can be made to yield this conclusion that VMI's single-sex composition is unconstitutional because there exist several women (or, one would have to conclude under the Court's reasoning, a single woman) willing and able to undertake VMI's program. Intermediate scrutiny has never required a least-restrictive-means analysis, but only a "substantial relation" between the classification and the state interests that it serves. Thus, in *Califano v. Webster,* 430 U.S. 313 (1977) *(per curiam),* we upheld a congressional statute that provided higher Social Security benefits for women than for men. We reasoned that "women . . . as such have been unfairly hindered from earning as much as men," but we did not require proof that each woman so benefited had suffered discrimination or that each disadvantaged man had not; it was sufficient that even under the former congressional scheme "women *on the average* received lower retirement benefits than men." The reasoning in our other intermediate-scrutiny cases has similarly required only a substantial relation between end and means, not a perfect fit. In *Rostker v. Goldberg,* 453 U.S. 57 (1981), we held that selective-service registration could constitutionally exclude women, because even "assuming that a small number of women could be drafted for noncombat roles, Congress simply did not consider it worth the added burdens of including women in draft and registration plans." In *Metro Broadcasting, Inc. v. FCC,* 497 U.S. 547, 579, 582–583 (1990), overruled on other grounds, *Adarand Constructors, Inc. v. Peña,*

515 U.S. 200, 227, 115 S.Ct. 2097, 2112–2113, 132 L.Ed.2d 158 (1995), we held that a classification need not be accurate "in every case" to survive intermediate scrutiny so long as, "in the aggregate," it advances the underlying objective. There is simply no support in our cases for the notion that a sex-based classification is invalid unless it relates to characteristics that hold true in every instance.

Not content to execute a *de facto* abandonment of the intermediate scrutiny that has been our standard for sex-based classifications for some two decades, the Court purports to reserve the question whether, even in principle, a higher standard (*i.e.,* strict scrutiny) should apply. "The Court has," it says, "*thus far* reserved most stringent judicial scrutiny for classifications based on race or national origin . . ."; and it describes our earlier cases as having done no more than decline to "equat[e] gender classifications, *for all purposes,* to classifications based on race or national origin." The wonderful thing about these statements is that they are not actually false—just as it would not be actually false to say that "our cases have thus far reserved the 'beyond a reasonable doubt' standard of proof for criminal cases," or that "we have not equated tort actions, for all purposes, to criminal prosecutions." But the statements are misleading, insofar as they suggest that we have not already categorically *held* strict scrutiny to be inapplicable to sex-based classifications. See, *e.g., Heckler v. Mathews,* 465 U.S. 728 (1984) (*upholding* state action after applying *only* intermediate scrutiny); *Michael M. v. Superior Court of Sonoma Cty.,* 450 U.S. 464 (1981) (plurality and both concurring opinions) (same); *Califano v. Webster, supra, (per curiam)* (same). And the statements are irresponsible, insofar as they are calculated to destabilize current law. Our task is to clarify the law—not to muddy the waters, and not to exact overcompliance by intimidation. The States and the Federal Government are entitled to know *before they act* the standard to which they will be held, rather than be compelled to guess about the outcome of Supreme Court peek-a-boo.

The Court's intimations are particularly out of place because it is perfectly clear that, if the question of the applicable standard of review for sex-based classifications were to be regarded as an appropriate subject for reconsideration, the stronger argument would be not for elevating the standard to strict scrutiny, but for reducing it to rational-basis review. The latter certainly has a firmer foundation in our past jurisprudence: Whereas no majority of the Court has ever applied strict scrutiny in a case involving sex-based classifications, we routinely applied rational-basis review until the 1970's, see, *e.g., Hoyt v. Florida,* 368 U.S. 57 (1961). And of course normal, rational-basis review of sex-based classifications would be much more in accord with the genesis of heightened standards of judicial review, the famous footnote in *United States v. Carolene Products Co.,* 304 U.S. 144 (1938), which said (intimatingly) that we did not have to inquire in the case at hand whether prejudice against discrete and insular minorities may be a special condition, which tends seriously to curtail the operation of those political processes ordinarily to be relied upon to protect minorities, and which may call for a correspondingly more searching judicial inquiry.

It is hard to consider women a "discrete and insular minorit[y]" unable to employ the "political processes ordinarily to be relied upon," when they constitute a majority of the electorate. And the suggestion that they are incapable of exerting that political power smacks of the same paternalism that the Court so roundly condemns. Moreover, a long list of legislation proves the proposition false. See, *e.g.,* Equal Pay Act of 1963, 29 U.S.C. § 206(d); Title VII of the Civil Rights Act of 1964, 42 U.S.C. § 2000e–2; Title IX of the Education Amendments of 1972, 20 U.S.C. § 1681; Women's Business Ownership Act of 1988, Pub.L. 100–533, 102 Stat. 2689; Violence Against Women Act of 1994, Pub.L. 103–322, Title IV, 108 Stat. 1902.

III

A

It is beyond question that Virginia has an important state interest in providing effective college education for its citizens. That single-sex instruction is an approach substantially related to that interest should be evident enough from the long and continuing history in this country of men's and women's colleges. But beyond that, as the Court of Appeals here stated: "That single-gender education at the college level is beneficial to both sexes is a *fact established in this case.*"

The evidence establishing that fact was overwhelming—indeed, "virtually uncontradicted" in the words of the court that received the evidence. As an initial matter, Virginia demonstrated at trial that "[a] substantial body of contemporary scholarship and research supports the proposition that, although males and females have significant areas of developmental overlap, they also have differing developmental needs that are deep-seated." While no one questioned that for many students a coeducational environment was nonetheless not inappropriate, that could not obscure the demonstrated benefits of single-sex colleges. For example, the District Court stated as follows:

> One empirical study in evidence, not questioned by any expert, demonstrates that single-sex colleges provide better educational experiences than coeducational institutions. Students of both sexes become more academically involved, interact with faculty frequently, show larger increases in intellectual self-esteem and are more satisfied with practically all aspects of college experience (the sole exception is social life) compared with their counterparts in coeducational institutions. Attendance at an all-male college substantially increases the likelihood that a student will carry out career plans in law, business and college

teaching, and also has a substantial positive effect on starting salaries in business. Women's colleges increase the chances that those who attend will obtain positions of leadership, complete the baccalaureate degree, and aspire to higher degrees.

"[I]n the light of this very substantial authority favoring single-sex education," the District Court concluded that "the VMI Board's decision to maintain an all-male institution is fully justified even without taking into consideration the other unique features of VMI's teaching and training." This finding alone, which even this Court cannot dispute, should be sufficient to demonstrate the constitutionality of VMI's all-male composition.

But besides its single-sex constitution, VMI is different from other colleges in another way. It employs a "distinctive educational method," sometimes referred to as the "adversative, or doubting, model of education." "Physical rigor, mental stress, absolute equality of treatment, absence of privacy, minute regulation of behavior, and indoctrination in desirable values are the salient attributes of the VMI educational experience." No one contends that this method is appropriate for all individuals; education is not a "one size fits all" business. Just as a State may wish to support junior colleges, vocational institutes, or a law school that emphasizes case practice instead of classroom study, so too a State's decision to maintain within its system one school that provides the adversative method is "substantially related" to its goal of good education. Moreover, it was uncontested that "if the state were to establish a women's VMI-type [*i.e.,* adversative] program, the program would attract an insufficient number of participants to make the program work"; and it was found by the District Court that if Virginia were to include women in VMI, the school "would eventually find it necessary to drop the adversative system altogether." Thus, Virginia's options were an adversative method that excludes women or no adversative method at all.

There can be no serious dispute that, as the District Court found, single-sex education and a distinctive educational method "represent legitimate contributions to diversity in the Virginia higher education system." As a theoretical matter, Virginia's educational interest would have been *best* served (insofar as the two factors we have mentioned are concerned) by six different types of public colleges—an all-men's, an all-women's, and a coeducational college run in the "adversative method," and an all-men's, an all-women's, and a coeducational college run in the "traditional method." But as a practical matter, of course, Virginia's financial resources, like any State's, are not limitless, and the Commonwealth must select among the available options. Virginia thus has decided to fund, in addition to some 14 coeducational 4-year colleges, one college that is run as an all-male school on the adversative model: the Virginia Military Institute.

Virginia did not make this determination regarding the make-up of its public college system on the unrealistic assumption that no other colleges exist. Substantial evidence in the District Court demonstrated that the Commonwealth has long proceeded on the principle that " '[h]igher education resources should be viewed as a whole—public and private' "—because such an approach enhances diversity and because " 'it is academic and economic waste to permit unwarranted duplication.' " It is thus significant that, whereas there are "four all-female private [colleges] in Virginia," there is only "one private all-male college," which "indicates that the private sector is providing for th[e] [former] form of education to a much greater extent that it provides for all-male education." In these circumstances, Virginia's election to fund one public all-male institution and one on the adversative model—and to concentrate its resources in a single entity that serves both these interests in diversity—is substantially related to the Commonwealth's important educational interests.

B

The Court today has no adequate response to this clear demonstration of the conclusion produced by application of intermediate scrutiny. . . . The Court suggests that Virginia's claimed purpose in maintaining VMI as an all-male institution—its asserted interest in promoting diversity of educational options—is not "genuin[e]," but is a pretext for discriminating against women. . . . That is wrong on numerous grounds. First and foremost, in its implication that such an explicit statement of "actual purposes" is needed. . . . Each state decision to adopt or maintain a governmental policy need not be accompanied—in anticipation of litigation and on pain of being found to lack a relevant state interest—by a lawyer's contemporaneous recitation of the State's purposes. The Constitution is not some giant Administrative Procedure Act, which imposes upon the States the obligation to set forth a "statement of basis and purpose" for their sovereign Acts, see 5 U.S.C. § 553(c). . . .

It is, moreover, not true that Virginia's contemporary reasons for maintaining VMI are not explicitly recorded. It is hard to imagine a more authoritative source on this subject than the 1990 Report of the Virginia Commission on the University of the 21st Century (1990 Report). As the parties stipulated, that report "notes that the hallmarks of Virginia's educational policy are 'diversity and autonomy.' " It said: "The formal system of higher education in Virginia includes a great array of institutions: state-supported and independent, two-year and senior, research and highly specialized, traditionally black *and single-sex.*" . . .

The Court contends that "[a] purpose genuinely to advance an array of educational options . . . is not served" by VMI. It relies on the fact that all of Virginia's *other* public colleges have become coeducational. The apparent theory of this argument is that unless Virginia pursues a great deal of diversity, its pursuit of some diversity must be a sham. This fails to take account of the fact that Virginia's resources cannot support all possible permutations of schools, and of the fact that Virginia coordinates its public educational offerings with the offerings of in-state private educational institutions that the Commonwealth provides money for its residents to attend and otherwise assists—which include four women's colleges.[3] . . .

In addition to disparaging Virginia's claim that VMI's single-sex status serves a state interest in diversity, the Court finds fault with Virginia's failure to offer education based on the adversative training method to women. It dismisses the District Court's " 'findings' on 'gender-based developmental differences' " on the ground that "[t]hese 'findings' restate the opinions of Virginia's expert witnesses, opinions about typically male or typically female 'tendencies.' " How remarkable to criticize the District Court on the ground that its findings rest on the evidence (*i.e.,* the testimony of Virginia's witnesses)! . . .

It is not too much to say that this approach to the litigation has rendered the trial a sham. But treating the evidence as irrelevant is absolutely necessary for the Court to reach its conclusion. Not a single witness contested, for example, Virginia's "substantial body of 'exceedingly persuasive' evidence . . . that some students, both male and female, benefit from attending a single-sex college" and "[that] [f]or those students, the opportunity to attend a single-sex college is a valuable one, likely to lead to better academic and professional achievement." . . .

The Court contends that Virginia, and the District Court, erred, and "misperceived our precedent," by "train[ing] their argument on 'means' rather than 'end.' " The Court focuses on "VMI's mission," which is to produce individuals "imbued with love of learning, confident in the functions and attitudes of leadership, possessing a high sense of public service, advocates of the American democracy and free enterprise system, and ready . . . to defend their country in time of national peril." "Surely," the Court says, "that goal is great enough to accommodate women." . . .

The Court's analysis at least has the benefit of producing foreseeable results. Applied generally, it means that whenever a State's ultimate objective is "great enough to accommodate women" (as it always will be), then the State will be held to have violated the Equal Protection Clause if it restricts to men even one means by which it pursues that objective— no matter how few women are interested in pursuing the objective by that means, no matter how much the single-sex program will have to be

---

[3] The Commonwealth provides tuition assistance, scholarship grants, guaranteed loans, and work-study funds for residents of Virginia who attend private colleges in the Commonwealth. These programs involve substantial expenditures. . . . In addition, as the parties stipulated in the District Court, the Commonwealth provides other financial support and assistance to private institutions—including single-sex colleges—through low-cost building loans, state-funded services contracts, and other programs. The State Council of Higher Education for Virginia, in a 1989 document . . . has described these various programs as a "means by which the Commonwealth can provide funding to its independent institutions, thereby helping to maintain a diverse system of higher education."

changed if both sexes are admitted, and no matter how beneficial that program has theretofore been to its participants.

The Court argues that VMI would not have to change very much if it were to admit women. The principal response to that argument is that it is irrelevant: If VMI's single-sex status is substantially related to the government's important educational objectives . . . that concludes the inquiry. . . .

But if such a debate were relevant, the Court would certainly be on the losing side. The District Court found as follows: "[T]he evidence establishes that key elements of the adversative VMI educational system, with its focus on barracks life, would be fundamentally altered, and the distinctive ends of the system would be thwarted, if VMI were forced to admit females and to make changes necessary to accommodate their needs and interests." . . . As the Court of Appeals summarized it, "the record supports the district court's findings that at least these three aspects of VMI's program—physical training, the absence of privacy, and the adversative approach—would be materially affected by coeducation, leading to a substantial change in the egalitarian ethos that is a critical aspect of VMI's training."

In the face of these findings by two courts below, amply supported by the evidence, and resulting in the conclusion that VMI would be fundamentally altered if it admitted women, this Court simply pronounces that "[t]he notion that admission of women would downgrade VMI's stature, destroy the adversative system and, with it, even the school, is a judgment hardly proved." . . . [5]

Finally, the absence of a precise "all-women's analogue" to VMI is irrelevant. In *Mississippi Univ. for Women v. Hogan*, 458 U.S. 718 (1982), we attached no constitutional significance to the absence of an all-male nursing school. As Virginia notes, if a program restricted to one sex is necessarily unconstitutional unless there is a parallel program restricted to the other sex, "the opinion in *Hogan* could have ended with its first footnote, which observed that 'Mississippi maintains no other single-sex public university or college.' "

Although there is no precise female-only analogue to VMI, Virginia has created during this litigation the Virginia Women's Institute for Leadership (VWIL), a state-funded all-women's program run by Mary Baldwin College. I have thus far said nothing about VWIL because it is, under our established test, irrelevant, so long as *VMI* 's all-male character is "substantially related" to an important state goal. But VWIL

---

[5]   The Court's do-it-yourself approach to factfinding, which throughout is contrary to our well-settled rule that we will not "undertake to review concurrent findings of fact by two courts below in the absence of a very obvious and exceptional showing of error," *Graver Tank & Mfg. Co. v. Linde Air Products Co.*, 336 U.S. 271, 275 (1949), is exemplified by its invocation of the experience of the federal military academies to prove that not much change would occur. In fact, the District Court noted that "the West Point experience" *supported* the theory that a coeducational VMI would have to "adopt a [different] system," for West Point found it necessary upon becoming coeducational to "move away" from its adversative system.

now exists, and the Court's treatment of it shows how far reaching today's decision is.

VWIL was carefully designed by professional educators who have long experience in educating young women. The program *rejects* the proposition that there is a "difference in the respective spheres and destinies of man and woman," *Bradwell v. State,* 16 Wall. 130, 141 (1873), and is designed to "provide an all-female program that will achieve substantially similar outcomes [to VMI's] in an all-female environment." After holding a trial where voluminous evidence was submitted and making detailed findings of fact, the District Court concluded that "there is a legitimate pedagogical basis for the different means employed [by VMI and VWIL] to achieve the substantially similar ends." The Court of Appeals undertook a detailed review of the record and affirmed.[6] . . . It is worth noting that none of the United States' own experts in the remedial phase of this litigation was willing to testify that VMI's adversative method was an appropriate methodology for educating women. This Court, however, does not care. Even though VWIL was carefully designed by professional educators who have tremendous experience in the area, and survived the test of adversarial litigation, the Court simply declares, with no basis in the evidence, that these professionals acted on " 'overbroad' generalizations."

C

. . . [T]he concurrence dismisses out of hand what it calls Virginia's "second justification for the single-sex admissions policy: maintenance of the adversative method." The concurrence reasons that "this justification does not serve an important governmental objective" because, whatever the record may show about the pedagogical benefits of *single-sex* education, "there is no similar evidence in the record that an adversative method is pedagogically beneficial or is any more likely to produce character traits than other methodologies." That is simply wrong. See, *e.g.,* 766 F.Supp., at 1426 (factual findings concerning character traits produced by VMI's adversative methodology); *id.,* at 1434 (factual findings concerning benefits for many college-age men of an adversative approach in general). In reality, the pedagogical benefits of VMI's adversative approach were not only proved, but were a *given* in this litigation. The reason the woman applicant who prompted this suit wanted to enter VMI was assuredly not that she wanted to go to an all-male school; it would cease being all-male as soon as she entered. She wanted the distinctive adversative education that VMI provided, and the battle was joined (in the main) over whether VMI had a basis for

---

6   The Court is incorrect in suggesting that the Court of Appeals applied a "deferential" "brand of review inconsistent with the more exacting standard our precedent requires." That court "inquir[ed] (1) whether the state's objective is 'legitimate and important,' and (2) whether 'the requisite direct, substantial relationship between objective and means is present,' " 44 F.3d, at 1235 (quoting *Mississippi Univ. for Women v. Hogan,* 458 U.S. 718, 725 (1982)). To be sure, such review is "deferential" to a degree that the Court's new standard is not, *for it is intermediate scrutiny.* . . .

excluding women from that approach. The Court's opinion recognizes this, and devotes much of its opinion to demonstrating that " 'some women . . . do well under [the] adversative model' " and that "[i]t is on behalf of these women that the United States has instituted this suit." . . .

IV

A

Under the constitutional principles announced and applied today, single-sex public education is unconstitutional. By going through the motions of applying a balancing test—asking whether the State has adduced an "exceedingly persuasive justification" for its sex-based classification—the Court creates the illusion that government officials in some future case will have a clear shot at justifying some sort of single-sex public education. . . . [But] the rationale of today's decision is sweeping: for sex-based classifications, a redefinition of intermediate scrutiny that makes it indistinguishable from strict scrutiny. Indeed, the Court indicates that if any program restricted to one sex is "uniqu[e]," it must be opened to members of the opposite sex "who have the will and capacity" to participate in it. I suggest that the single-sex program that will not be capable of being characterized as "unique" is not only unique but nonexistent.[8]

In any event, regardless of whether the Court's rationale leaves some small amount of room for lawyers to argue, it ensures that single-sex public education is functionally dead. The costs of litigating the constitutionality of a single-sex education program, and the risks of ultimately losing that litigation, are simply too high to be embraced by public officials. . . .

This is especially regrettable because, as the District Court here determined, educational experts in recent years have increasingly come to "suppor[t] [the] view that substantial educational benefits flow from a single-gender environment, be it male or female, *that cannot be replicated in a coeducational setting.*" "The evidence in th[is] case," for example, "is virtually uncontradicted" to that effect. Until quite recently, some public officials have attempted to institute new single-sex programs, at least as experiments. In 1991, for example, the Detroit Board of Education announced a program to establish three boys-only schools for inner-city youth; it was met with a lawsuit, a preliminary injunction was swiftly entered by a District Court that purported to rely on *Hogan,* and the Detroit Board of Education voted to abandon the litigation and thus abandon the plan. Today's opinion assures that no such experiment will be tried again.

---

[8]   In this regard, I note that the Court . . . provides no example of a program that *would* pass muster under its reasoning today: not even, for example, a football or wrestling program. On the Court's theory, any woman ready, willing, and physically able to participate in such a program would, *as a constitutional matter,* be entitled to do so.

B

There are few extant single-sex public educational programs. The potential of today's decision for widespread disruption of existing institutions lies in its application to *private* single-sex education. Government support is immensely important to private educational institutions. Mary Baldwin College—which designed and runs VWIL—notes that private institutions of higher education in the 1990–1991 school year derived approximately 19 percent of their budgets from federal, state, and local government funds, *not including financial aid to students.* Charitable status under the tax laws is also highly significant for private educational institutions, and it is certainly not beyond the Court that rendered today's decision to hold that a donation to a single-sex college should be deemed contrary to public policy and therefore not deductible if the college discriminates on the basis of sex. See *Bob Jones Univ. v. United States,* 461 U.S. 574 (1983).

The Court adverts to private single-sex education only briefly . . . . The Government, in its briefs to this Court, at least purports to address the consequences of its attack on VMI for public support of private single-sex education. It contends that private colleges that are the direct or indirect beneficiaries of government funding are not thereby necessarily converted into state actors to which the Equal Protection Clause is then applicable. That is true. It is also virtually meaningless.

The issue will be not whether government assistance turns private colleges into state actors, but whether the government *itself* would be violating the Constitution by providing state support to single-sex colleges. For example, in *Norwood v. Harrison,* 413 U.S. 455 (1973), we saw no room to distinguish between state operation of racially segregated schools and state support of privately run segregated schools. "Racial discrimination in state-operated schools is barred by the Constitution and '[i]t is also axiomatic that a state may not induce, encourage or promote private persons to accomplish what it is constitutionally forbidden to accomplish.' " . . .

Justice Brandeis said it is "one of the happy incidents of the federal system that a single courageous State may, if its citizens choose, serve as a laboratory; and try novel social and economic experiments without risk to the rest of the country." *New State Ice Co. v. Liebmann,* 285 U.S. 262, 311 (1932) (dissenting opinion). But it is one of the unhappy incidents of the federal system that a self-righteous Supreme Court, acting on its Members' personal view of what would make a " 'more perfect Union,' " . . . can impose its own favored social and economic dispositions nationwide. As today's disposition . . . show[s], this places it beyond the power of a "single courageous State," not only to introduce novel dispositions that the Court frowns upon, but to reintroduce, or indeed even adhere to, disfavored dispositions that are centuries old. . . . The sphere of self-government reserved to the people of the Republic is progressively narrowed. . . .

Today's decision does not leave VMI without honor; no court opinion can do that. In an odd sort of way, it is precisely VMI's attachment to such old-fashioned concepts as manly "honor" that has made it, and the system it represents, the target of those who today succeed in abolishing public single-sex education. The record contains a booklet that all first-year VMI students (the so-called "rats") were required to keep in their possession at all times. Near the end there appears the following period piece, entitled "The Code of a Gentleman":

> Without a strict observance of the fundamental Code of Honor, no man, no matter how 'polished,' can be considered a gentleman. The honor of a gentleman demands the inviolability of his word, and the incorruptibility of his principles. He is the descendant of the knight, the crusader; he is the defender of the defenseless and the champion of justice . . . or he is not a Gentleman.
>
> A Gentleman . . .
>
> Does not discuss his family affairs in public or with acquaintances.
>
> Does not speak more than casually about his girl friend.
>
> Does not go to a lady's house if he is affected by alcohol. He is temperate in the use of alcohol.
>
> Does not lose his temper; nor exhibit anger, fear, hate, embarrassment, ardor or hilarity in public. . . .
>
> A gentleman never discusses the merits or demerits of a lady.
>
> Does not mention names exactly as he avoids the mention of what things cost. . . .
>
> Does not display his wealth, money or possessions.
>
> Does not put his manners on and off, whether in the club or in a ballroom. He treats people with courtesy, no matter what their social position may be.
>
> Does not slap strangers on the back nor so much as lay a finger on a lady.
>
> Does not 'lick the boots of those above' nor 'kick the face of those below him on the social ladder.'
>
> Does not take advantage of another's helplessness or ignorance and assumes that no gentleman will take advantage of him. . . .

I do not know whether the men of VMI lived by this code; perhaps not. But it is powerfully impressive that a public institution of higher education still in existence sought to have them do so. I do not think any of us, women included, will be better off for its destruction.

NOTE ON EQUAL PROTECTION AND GENDER

1. If the Fourteenth Amendment was directed at "the freedom of the slave race," as the Court observed in the *Slaughter-House Cases*, then what is the basis for applying heightened scrutiny to gender classifications as well? As the justices note in *United States v. Virginia*, the Court did not do so for over a century after ratification of the Equal Protection Clause. Can an originalist support heightened scrutiny for gender classifications?

Even on a more evolutionary view of constitutional meaning, should gender classifications be treated as suspect or "quasi"-suspect? As explored in Section 15.3, *infra*, heightened scrutiny has generally depended on notions that a particular characteristic is generally irrelevant to legitimate government interests and that the group in question is a politically-powerless minority. Is gender generally irrelevant in the way that race is now thought to be? Should the law ignore, for example, the biological fact that only women can become pregnant? Are women—not a minority, after all—nonetheless politically powerless? Does classifying them as such promote the very paternalism that the Court has sought to undermine?

In Footnote 4 of *Carolene Products*, the Court referred to "discrete and insular minorities" as needing special judicial protection. The idea seems to have been that minorities that are "insular"—that is, that tend to live apart from other groups in society—are less likely to elicit the sympathy of, and thus to form effective political coalitions with, other groups. Is it thus important that unlike racial minorities, forced by segregation and prejudice to live apart from the white majority, women and men generally live in close proximity throughout society, and familial bonds may encourage one gender to be aware of and sympathetic to the needs of the other? Or does the long history of gender discrimination suggest that "insularity" is hardly a necessary condition for prejudice?

2. *Craig v. Boren* is one of a surprising number of gender cases in which the challenged discrimination seems to work in favor of women and against men. Why do you think advocates for women's equality targeted so many of these statutes in the early days of the campaign for equal treatment? More generally, would you agree that the discrimination in *Craig* is really "benign" from a woman's perspective? Does the state's assumption that women will be more responsible about alcohol and driving actually help perpetuate gender stereotypes that, in other contexts, may be harmful to women? Is the very notion that women and men differ along such lines harmful?

3. Many have long pressed for a specific constitutional amendment to protect rights to gender equality. Suffragist leaders originally introduced the Equal Rights Amendment in Congress in 1923, and in 1972 Congress passed and submitted to the States a version that provided as follows:

Section 1. Equality of rights under the law shall not be denied or abridged by the United States or by any State on account of sex.

Section 2. The Congress shall have the power to enforce, by appropriate legislation, the provisions of this article.

Section 3. This amendment shall take effect two years after the date of ratification.

The original deadline for ratification was 1979, by which time 35 of the necessary 38 states had ratified the proposal. Although Congress purported to extend that deadline to 1982, no additional states ratified and five states purported to rescind their ratifications.

Many observers have suggested that the Supreme Court's decisions invalidating many forms of gender discrimination under the Equal Protection Clause took the wind out of the ERA's sails, basically by achieving much of the ERA's purpose without a new amendment. Would it have been better to have a specific amendment dealing with gender discrimination? Would the cases in this section have been easier if they'd been litigated under the ERA?

4.   Did Justice Ginsburg try to change the standard of review for gender classifications in *United States v. Virginia*? Is requiring an "exceedingly persuasive justification" for the state's classification the same as traditional intermediate scrutiny? Would VMI's policy have stood up under the traditional standard?

How should the constitutional standard bear on the factual disputes in the case? Intermediate scrutiny, unlike both strict scrutiny and rational basis review, can go either way in application; the choice of a standard does not, as in the other two cases, largely predetermine the ultimate result. That means that the facts of particular cases matter to a considerably greater degree than in many of the contexts we have seen. And unlike many constitutional cases, *United States v. Virginia* featured a full-dress trial, complete with extensive expert testimony and factual findings by the district court. Ordinarily, such findings are reviewed only for "clear error." Fed. R. Civ. P. 52(a)(6). On the other hand, is that standard appropriate when constitutional rights are at stake, and the appellate court may fear that the lower court's findings reflect the same sorts of stereotypes as the challenged policy?

5.   Does *United States v. Virginia* effectively make state-sponsored single-sex education impossible, as Justice Scalia suggests? The answer may depend on the relative weight of three strands in Justice Ginsburg's majority opinion. One strand emphasizes that *any* differential treatment of the genders must provide an "exceedingly persuasive justification"—a standard that may simply deter states from trying. A second suggests that any "unique" opportunity afforded to one sex must be afforded to the other, which will at least complicate any effort to tailor single-sex education to characteristics of a particular gender. But the third strand simply emphasized how implausible the VWIL program was as a substitute for VMI. Is the principle really that "separate but equal" is acceptable for gender, but the government must simply do a better job of making sure that separate is plausibly equal?

6.   What do you make of Justice Scalia's inclusion, in his dissent, of VMI's "Code of a Gentleman"? Do these values remain appropriate in the twenty-first century? Would they lose their power if promoted in a less-

gendered way? Do courts have the tools to evaluate the relationship between gendered codes and practices of this kind and ends—such as decency and honest behavior—that the State has a legitimate interest in promoting?

SECTION 15.3   OTHER CLASSIFICATIONS

The Equal Protection Clause does not, of course, mention either race or gender; it simply forbids state governments to deny "the equal protection of the laws." In principle, *all* government acts that distinguish among persons are subject to review under this provision. The problem, of course, is that nearly all laws and government actions treat some persons differently from others. The cases in this section thus deal with two distinct problems. First, how should courts approach government policies that draw distinctions among persons without implicating a "suspect" basis for classification like race or gender? Second, how should courts evaluate new candidates for suspect-ness, such as classifications based on disability or sexual orientation?

New York City Transit Authority v. Beazer
440 U.S. 568 (1979)

■ **MR. JUSTICE STEVENS delivered the opinion of the Court.**

The New York City Transit Authority refuses to employ persons who use methadone. The District Court found that this policy violates the Equal Protection Clause of the Fourteenth Amendment. . . . The Court of Appeals affirmed . . . . We now reverse.

The Transit Authority (TA) operates the subway system and certain bus lines in New York City. It employs about 47,000 persons, of whom many—perhaps most—are employed in positions that involve danger to themselves or to the public. For example, some 12,300 are subway motormen, towermen, conductors, or bus operators. The District Court found that these jobs are attended by unusual hazards and must be performed by "persons of maximum alertness and competence." Certain other jobs, such as operating cranes and handling high-voltage equipment, are also considered "critical" or "safety sensitive," while still others, though classified as "noncritical," have a potentially important impact on the overall operation of the transportation system.

TA enforces a general policy against employing persons who use narcotic drugs. The policy is reflected in Rule 11(b) of TA's Rules and Regulations.

> Employees must not use, or have in their possession, narcotics, tranquilizers, drugs of the Amphetamine group or barbiturate derivatives or paraphernalia used to administer narcotics or barbiturate derivatives, except with the written permission of the Medical Director—Chief Surgeon of the System.

Methadone is regarded as a narcotic within the meaning of Rule 11(b). No written permission has ever been given by TA's medical director for the employment of a person using methadone.

The District Court found that methadone is a synthetic narcotic and a central nervous system depressant. If injected into the bloodstream with a needle, it produces essentially the same effects as heroin. Methadone has been used legitimately in at least three ways—as a pain killer, in "detoxification units" of hospitals as an immediate means of taking addicts off of heroin, and in long-range "methadone maintenance programs" as part of an intended cure for heroin addiction. In such programs the methadone is taken orally in regular doses for a prolonged period. As so administered, it does not produce euphoria or any pleasurable effects associated with heroin; on the contrary, it prevents users from experiencing those effects when they inject heroin, and also alleviates the severe and prolonged discomfort otherwise associated with an addict's discontinuance of the use of heroin.

About 40,000 persons receive methadone maintenance treatment in New York City, of whom about 26,000 participate in the five major public or semipublic programs, and 14,000 are involved in about 25 private programs. The sole purpose of all these programs is to treat the addiction of persons who have been using heroin for at least two years.

Methadone maintenance treatment in New York is largely governed by regulations promulgated by the New York State Drug Abuse Control Commission. Under the regulations, the newly accepted addict must first be detoxified, normally in a hospital. A controlled daily dosage of methadone is then prescribed. The regulations require that six doses a week be administered at a clinic, while the seventh day's dose may be taken at home. If progress is satisfactory for three months, additional doses may be taken away from the clinic, although throughout most of the program, which often lasts for several years, there is a minimum requirement of three clinic appearances a week. During these visits, the patient not only receives his doses but is also counseled and tested for illicit use of drugs.

The evidence indicates that methadone is an effective cure for the physical aspects of heroin addiction. But the District Court also found "that many persons attempting to overcome heroin addiction have psychological or life-style problems which reach beyond what can be cured by the physical taking of doses of methadone." The crucial indicator of successful methadone maintenance is the patient's abstinence from the illegal or excessive use of drugs and alcohol. The District Court found that the risk of reversion to drug or alcohol abuse declines dramatically after the first few months of treatment. Indeed, "the strong majority" of patients who have been on methadone maintenance for at least a year are free from illicit drug use. But a significant number are not. On this critical point, the evidence relied upon by the District Court reveals that even among participants with more than 12 months' tenure in methadone maintenance programs, the incidence of drug and alcohol abuse may often approach and even exceed 25%.

This litigation was brought by the four respondents as a class action on behalf of all persons who have been, or would in the future be, subject to discharge or rejection as employees of TA by reason of participation in a methadone maintenance program. Two of the respondents are former employees of TA who were dismissed while they were receiving methadone treatment. The other two were refused employment by TA, one both shortly before and shortly after the successful conclusion of his methadone treatment, and the other while he was taking methadone. Their complaint alleged that TA's blanket exclusion of all former heroin addicts receiving methadone treatment was illegal under . . . the Equal Protection Clause of the Fourteenth Amendment.

The trial record contains extensive evidence concerning the success of methadone maintenance programs, the employability of persons taking methadone, and the ability of prospective employers to detect drug abuse or other undesirable characteristics of methadone users. In general, the District Court concluded that there are substantial numbers of methadone users who are just as employable as other members of the general population and that normal personnel-screening procedures—at least if augmented by some method of obtaining information from the staffs of methadone programs—would enable TA to identify the unqualified applicants on an individual basis. On the other hand, the District Court recognized that at least one-third of the persons receiving methadone treatment—and probably a good many more—would unquestionably be classified as unemployable.

After extensively reviewing the evidence, the District Court briefly stated its conclusion that TA's methadone policy is unconstitutional. The conclusion rested on the legal proposition that a public entity "cannot bar persons from employment on the basis of criteria which have no rational relation to the demands of the jobs to be performed." Because it is clear that substantial numbers of methadone users are capable of performing many of the jobs at TA, the court held that the Constitution will not tolerate a blanket exclusion of all users from all jobs.

The District Court enjoined TA from denying employment to any person solely because of participation in a methadone maintenance program. Recognizing, however, the special responsibility for public safety borne by certain TA employees and the correlation between longevity in a methadone maintenance program and performance capability, the injunction authorized TA to exclude methadone users from specific categories of safety-sensitive positions and also to condition eligibility on satisfactory performance in a methadone program for at least a year. In other words, the court held that TA could lawfully adopt general rules excluding all methadone users from some jobs and a large number of methadone users from all jobs. . . . The Court of Appeals affirmed the District Court's constitutional holding. . . .

The Equal Protection Clause of the Fourteenth Amendment provides that no State shall "deny to any person within its jurisdiction the equal protection of the laws." The Clause announces a fundamental principle: the State must govern impartially. General rules that apply evenhandedly to all persons within the jurisdiction unquestionably comply with this principle. Only when a governmental unit adopts a rule that has a special impact on less than all the persons subject to its jurisdiction does the question whether this principle is violated arise.

In this case, TA's Rule 11(b) places a meaningful restriction on all of its employees and job applicants; in that sense the rule is one of general applicability and satisfies the equal protection principle without further inquiry. The District Court, however, interpreted the rule as applicable to the limited class of persons who regularly use narcotic drugs, including methadone. As so interpreted, we are necessarily confronted with the question whether the rule reflects an impermissible bias against a special class.

Respondents have never questioned the validity of a special rule for all users of narcotics. Rather, they originally contended that persons receiving methadone should not be covered by that rule; in other words, they should not be included within a class that is otherwise unobjectionable. Their constitutional claim was that methadone users are entitled to be treated like most other employees and applicants rather than like other users of narcotics. But the District Court's findings unequivocally establish that there are relevant differences between persons using methadone regularly and persons who use no narcotics of any kind.[32]

Respondents no longer question the need, or at least the justification, for special rules for methadone users. Indeed, they vigorously defend the District Court's opinion which expressly held that it would be permissible for TA to have a special rule denying methadone users any employment unless they had been undergoing treatment for at least a year, and another special rule denying even the most senior and reliable methadone users any of the more dangerous jobs in the system.

---

[32] The District Court found that methadone is a narcotic. Moreover, every member of the class of methadone users was formerly addicted to the use of heroin. None is completely cured; otherwise, there would be no continuing need for treatment. All require some measure of special supervision, and all must structure their weekly routines around mandatory appearances at methadone clinics. The clinics make periodic checks as long as the treatment continues in order to detect evidence of drug abuse. Employers must review, and sometimes verify, these checks; since the record indicates that the information supplied by treatment centers is not uniformly reliable, the employer has a special and continuing responsibility to review the condition of these persons.

In addition, a substantial percentage of persons taking methadone will not successfully complete the treatment program. The findings do not indicate with any precision the number who drop out, or the number who can fairly be classified as unemployable, but the evidence indicates that it may well be a majority of those taking methadone at any given time.

The constitutional defect in TA's employment policies, according to the District Court, is not that TA has special rules for methadone users, but rather that *some* members of the class should have been exempted from *some* requirements of the special rules. Left intact by its holding are rules requiring special supervision of methadone users to detect evidence of drug abuse, and excluding them from high-risk employment. Accepting those rules, the District Court nonetheless concluded that employment in nonsensitive jobs could not be denied to methadone users who had progressed satisfactorily with their treatment for one year, and who, when examined individually, satisfied TA's employment criteria. In short, having recognized that disparate treatment of methadone users simply because they are methadone users is permissible—and having excused TA from an across-the-board requirement of individual consideration of such persons—the District Court construed the Equal Protection Clause as requiring TA to adopt additional and more precise special rules for that special class. . . .

At its simplest, the District Court's conclusion was that TA's rule is broader than necessary to exclude those methadone users who are not actually qualified to work for TA. We may assume not only that this conclusion is correct but also that it is probably unwise for a large employer like TA to rely on a general rule instead of individualized consideration of every job applicant. But these assumptions concern matters of personnel policy that do not implicate the principle safeguarded by the Equal Protection Clause. As the District Court recognized, the special classification created by TA's rule serves the general objectives of safety and efficiency.[39] Moreover, the exclusionary line challenged by respondents "is not one which is directed 'against' any individual or category of persons, but rather it represents a policy choice . . . made by that branch of Government vested with the power to make such choices." *Marshall v. United States*, 414 U.S. 417, 428 (1974). Because it does not circumscribe a class of persons characterized by some unpopular trait or affiliation, it does not create or reflect any special likelihood of bias on the part of the ruling majority.[40] Under these

---

[39] "[L]egislative classifications are valid unless they bear no rational relationship to the State's objectives. State legislation 'does not violate the Equal Protection Clause merely because the classifications it makes are imperfect. *Washington v. Confederated Bands & Tribes of the Yakima Indian Nation*, 439 U.S. 463, 501–502 (1979). See also *Vance v. Bradley*, 440 U.S. 93, 108 (1979) ("Even if the classification involved here is to some extent both underinclusive and overinclusive, and hence the line drawn by Congress imperfect, it is nevertheless the rule that in a case like this perfection is by no means required.").

[40] Since *Barbier v. Connolly*, 113 U.S. 27 (1885), the Court's equal protection cases have recognized a distinction between "invidious discrimination"—i. e., classifications drawn "with an evil eye and an unequal hand" or motivated by "a feeling of antipathy" against, a specific group of residents, *Yick Wo v. Hopkins*, 118 U.S. 356, 373–374 (1886)—and those special rules that "are often necessary for general benefits [such as] supplying water, preventing fires, lighting districts, cleaning streets, opening parks, and many other objects." *Barbier, supra*, 113 U.S., at 31. See also *Washington v. Davis*, 426 U.S. 229, 239–241 (1976). Quite plainly, TA's Rule 11(b) was motivated by TA's interest in operating a safe and efficient transportation system rather than by any special animus against a specific group of persons. Respondents recognize this valid general motivation, as did the District Court, and for that reason neither challenges TA's rule as it applies to all narcotic users, or even to all methadone users. Because respondents

circumstances, it is of no constitutional significance that the degree of rationality is not as great with respect to certain ill-defined subparts of the classification as it is with respect to the classification as a whole.[41]

No matter how unwise it may be for TA to refuse employment to individual car cleaners, track repairmen, or bus drivers simply because they are receiving methadone treatment, the Constitution does not authorize a federal court to interfere in that policy decision. The judgment of the Court of Appeals is

Reversed.

■ MR. JUSTICE WHITE, with whom MR. JUSTICE MARSHALL joins, dissenting.

Although the Court purports to apply settled principles to unique facts, the result reached does not square with . . . the Equal Protection Clause. Accordingly, but respectfully, I dissent. . . .

The District Court found that the evidence conclusively established that petitioners exclude from employment all persons who are successfully on methadone maintenance—that is, those who after one year are "free of the use of heroin, other illicit drugs, and problem drinking"—and those who have graduated from methadone programs and remain drug free for less than five years; that past or present successful methadone maintenance is not a meaningful predictor of poor performance or conduct in most job categories; that petitioners could use their normal employee-screening mechanisms to separate the successfully maintained users from the unsuccessful; and that petitioners do exactly that for other groups that common sense indicates might also be suspect employees.[9] Petitioners did not challenge these factual conclusions in the Court of Appeals, but that court nonetheless

---

merely challenge the rule insofar as it applies to some methadone users that challenge does not even raise the question whether the rule falls on the "invidious" side of the *Barbier* distinction. Accordingly, there is nothing to give rise to a presumption of illegality and to warrant our especially "attentive judgment."

[41] "When a legal distinction is determined, as no one doubts that it may be, between night and day, childhood and maturity, or any other extremes, a point has to be fixed or a line has to be drawn, or gradually picked out by successive decisions, to mark where the change takes place. Looked at by itself without regard to the necessity behind it the line or point seems arbitrary. It might as well or nearly as well be a little more to one side or the other. But when it is seen that a line or point there must be, and that there is no mathematical or logical way of fixing it precisely, the decision of the legislature must be accepted unless we can say that it is very wide of any reasonable mark." *Louisville Gas & Electric Co. v. Coleman*, 277 U.S. 32, 41, 48 S.Ct. 423, 426, 72 L.Ed. 770 (Holmes, J., dissenting).

[9] Respondents presented numerous top experts in this field and large employers experienced with former heroin users treated with methadone. Both sides rested after six days of trial, but the District Court demanded nine more days of further factual development, and an 8-hour inspection of petitioners' facilities, because it did not believe that the evidence could do so one-sidedly in respondents' favor. The court correctly realized its responsibility in a public-law case of this type to demand the whole story before making a constitutional ruling. See Chayes, The Role of the Judge in Public Law Litigation, 89 HARV.L.REV. 1281 (1976). The District Court called six witnesses of its own, and it chose them primarily because they had written articles on methadone maintenance that petitioners asserted had shown the unreliability of that method of dealing with heroin addiction. It also correctly expressed its refusal to base its judgment on shifting medical opinions.

reviewed the evidence and found that it overwhelmingly supported the District Court's findings. It bears repeating, then, that both the District Court and the Court of Appeals found that those who have been maintained on methadone for at least a year and who are free from the use of illicit drugs and alcohol can easily be identified through normal personnel procedures and, for a great many jobs, are as employable as and present no more risk than applicants from the general population.

Though petitioners' argument here is primarily an attack upon the factfinding below, the Court does not directly accept that thesis. Instead, it concludes that the District Court and the Court of Appeals both misapplied the Equal Protection Clause. On the facts as found, however, one can reach the Court's result only if that Clause imposes no real constraint at all in this situation.

The question before us is the rationality of placing successfully maintained or recently cured persons in the same category as those just attempting to escape heroin addiction or who have failed to escape it, rather than in with the general population. The asserted justification for the challenged classification is the objective of a capable and reliable work force, and thus the characteristic in question is employability. "Employability," in this regard, does not mean that any particular applicant, much less every member of a given group of applicants, will turn out to be a model worker. Nor does it mean that no such applicant will ever become or be discovered to be a malingerer, thief, alcoholic, or even heroin addict. All employers take such risks. Employability, as the District Court used it in reference to successfully maintained methadone users, means only that the employer is no more likely to find a member of that group to be an unsatisfactory employee than he would an employee chosen from the general population.

Petitioners had every opportunity, but presented nothing to negative the employability of successfully maintained methadone users as distinguished from those who were unsuccessful. Instead, petitioners, like the Court, dwell on the methadone failures—those who quit the programs or who remain but turn to illicit drug use. The Court, for instance, makes much of the drug use of many of those in methadone programs, including those who have been in such programs for more than one year. But this has little force since those persons are not "successful," can be and have been identified as such,[11] and . . . are not within the protection of the District Court's injunction. That 20% to 30% are unsuccessful after one year in a methadone program tells us nothing about the employability of the successful group, and it is the latter category of applicants that the District Court and the Court of Appeals

---

[11] The evidence indicates that poor risks will shake out of a methadone maintenance program within six months. It is a measure of the District Court's caution that it set a 1-year standard.

held to be unconstitutionally burdened by the blanket rule disqualifying them from employment.

The District Court and the Court of Appeals were therefore fully justified in finding that petitioners could not reasonably have concluded that the protected group is less employable than the general population and that excluding it "[has] no rational relation to the demands of the jobs to be performed."[12] In fact, the Court assumes that petitioners' policy is unnecessarily broad in excluding the successfully maintained and the recently cured and that a member of that group can be selected with adequate precision. Despite this, the validity of the exclusion is upheld on the rational basis of the uninvolved portion of the rule, that is, that the rule excludes many who are less employable. But petitioners must justify the distinction between groups, not just the policy to which they have attached the classification. The purpose of the rule as a whole is relevant only if the classification within the rule serves the purpose, but the majority's assumption admits that is not so. . . .

Of course, the District Court's order permitting total exclusion of all methadone users maintained for less than one year, whether successfully or not, would still exclude some employables and would to this extent be overinclusive. "Overinclusiveness" as to the primary objective of employability is accepted for less successful methadone users because it fulfills a secondary purpose and thus is not "overinclusive" at all. Although many of those who have not been successfully maintained for a year are employable, as a class they, unlike the protected group, are not as employable as the general population. Thus, even assuming the bad risks could be identified, serving the end of employability would require unusual efforts to determine those more likely to revert. But that legitimate secondary goal is not fulfilled by excluding the protected class: The District Court found that the fact of successful participation for one year could be discovered through petitioners' normal screening process without additional effort and, I repeat, that those who meet that criterion are no more likely than the average applicant to turn out to be poor employees. Accordingly, the rule's classification of successfully maintained persons as dispositively different from the general population is left without any justification and, with its irrationality and invidiousness thus uncovered, must fall before the Equal Protection Clause.[15]

---

[12] A major sponsor of the recent amendments to the Rehabilitation Act described the congressional determination behind them as being that a public employer "cannot assume that a history of alcoholism or drug addiction, including a past addiction currently treated by methadone maintenance, poses sufficient danger in and of itself to justify exclusion [from employment]. Such an assumption would have no basis in fact . . . ." 124 Cong.Rec. 37510 (1978) (Sen. Williams).

[15] I have difficulty also with the Court's easy conclusion that the challenged rule was "[q]uite plainly" not motivated "by any special animus against a specific group of persons." Heroin addiction is a special problem of the poor, and the addict population is composed largely of racial minorities that the Court has previously recognized as politically powerless and historical subjects of majoritarian neglect. Persons on methadone maintenance have few

Finally, even were the District Court wrong, and even were successfully maintained persons marginally less employable than the average applicant,[16] the blanket exclusion of only these people, when but a few are actually unemployable and when many other groups have varying numbers of unemployable members, is arbitrary and unconstitutional. Many persons now suffer from or may again suffer from some handicap related to employability.[17] But petitioners have singled out respondents—unlike ex-offenders, former alcoholics and mental patients, diabetics, epileptics, and those currently using tranquilizers, for example—for sacrifice to this at best ethereal and likely nonexistent risk of increased unemployability. Such an arbitrary assignment of burdens

---

interests in common with members of the majority, and thus are unlikely to have their interests protected, or even considered, in governmental decisionmaking. Indeed, petitioners stipulated that "[o]ne of the reasons for the . . . drug policy is the fact that [petitioners] fee[l] an adverse public reaction would result if it were generally known that [petitioners] employed persons with a prior history of drug abuse, including persons participating in methadone maintenance programs." It is hard for me to reconcile that stipulation of animus against former addicts with our past holdings that "a bare . . . desire to harm a politically unpopular group cannot constitute a *legitimate* governmental interest." *United States Dept. of Agriculture v. Moreno*, 413 U.S. 528, 534 (1973). On the other hand, the afflictions to which petitioners are more sympathetic, such as alcoholism and mental illness, are shared by both white and black, rich and poor.

Some weight should also be given to the history of the rule. See *Arlington Heights v. Metropolitan Housing Dev. Corp.*, 429 U.S. 252, 267–268 (1977). Petitioners admit that it was not the result of a reasoned policy decision and stipulated that they had never studied the ability of those on methadone maintenance to perform petitioners' jobs. Petitioners are not directly accountable to the public, are not the type of official body that normally makes legislative judgments of fact such as those relied upon by the majority today, and are by nature more concerned with business efficiency than with other public policies for which they have no direct responsibility. Cf. *Hampton v. Mow Sun Wong*, 426 U.S. 88, 103 (1976). Both the State and City of New York, which do exhibit those democratic characteristics, hire persons in methadone programs for similar jobs.

These factors together strongly point to a conclusion of invidious discrimination. The Court, however, refuses to view this rule as one "circumscrib[ing] a class of persons characterized by some unpopular trait or affiliation," because it is admittedly justified as applied to many current and former heroin addicts. Because the challenged classification unfairly burdens only a portion of all heroin addicts, the Court reasons that it cannot possibly have been spurred by animus by the "ruling majority." All that shows, however, is that the characteristic in question is a legitimate basis of distinction in some circumstances; heroin addiction is a serious affliction that will often affect employability. But sometimes antipathy extends beyond the facts that may have given rise to it, and when that happens the "stereotyped reaction may have no rational relationship—other than pure prejudicial discrimination—to the stated purpose for which the classification is being made." *Mathews v. Lucas*, 427 U.S. 495, 520–521 (1976) (STEVENS, J., dissenting). That is the case here.

[16] The District Court found that the only common physical effects of methadone maintenance are increases in sweating, insomnia, and constipation, and a decrease in sex drive. Those disabilities are unfortunate but are hardly related to inability to be a subway janitor. This Court hints that the employability of even those successfully being maintained on methadone might be reduced by their obligation to appear at their clinics three times a week. But all employees have outside obligations, and petitioners have neither argued nor proved that this particular duty would interfere with work.

The District Court did find that a possible but rare effect of methadone is minor impairment of abilities "required for the performance of potentially hazardous tasks, such as driving a car or operating machinery," and the court exempted from the relief ordered such positions as subway motorman, which require "unique sensitivity." . But this does not make rational the blanket exclusion from all jobs, regardless of the qualifications required.

[17] The District Court found, and petitioners have not challenged, that current problem drinkers present more of an employment risk than do respondents. Petitioners do not automatically discharge employees who are found to have a drinking problem.

among classes that are similarly situated with respect to the proffered objectives is the type of invidious choice forbidden by the Equal Protection Clause.

City of Cleburne v. Cleburne Living Center
473 U.S. 432 (1985)

■ JUSTICE WHITE delivered the opinion of the Court.

A Texas city denied a special use permit for the operation of a group home for the mentally retarded, acting pursuant to a municipal zoning ordinance requiring permits for such homes. The Court of Appeals for the Fifth Circuit held that mental retardation is a "quasi-suspect" classification and that the ordinance violated the Equal Protection Clause because it did not substantially further an important governmental purpose. We hold that a lesser standard of scrutiny is appropriate, but conclude that under that standard the ordinance is invalid as applied in this case.

I

In July 1980, respondent Jan Hannah purchased a building at 201 Featherston Street in the city of Cleburne, Texas, with the intention of leasing it to Cleburne Living Center, Inc. (CLC), for the operation of a group home for the mentally retarded. It was anticipated that the home would house 13 retarded men and women, who would be under the constant supervision of CLC staff members. . . .

[U]nder the zoning regulations applicable to the site, a special use permit, renewable annually, was required for the construction of "[h]ospitals for the insane or feeble-minded, or alcoholic [sic] or drug addicts, or penal or correctional institutions." The city had determined that the proposed group home should be classified as a "hospital for the feebleminded." After holding a public hearing on CLC's application, the City Council voted 3 to 1 to deny a special use permit.

CLC then filed suit in Federal District Court against the city and a number of its officials, alleging, *inter alia,* that the zoning ordinance was invalid on its face and as applied because it discriminated against the mentally retarded in violation of the equal protection rights of CLC and its potential residents. The District Court found that "[i]f the potential residents of the Featherston Street home were not mentally retarded, but the home was the same in all other respects, its use would be permitted under the city's zoning ordinance," and that the City Council's decision "was motivated primarily by the fact that the residents of the home would be persons who are mentally retarded." Even so, the District Court held the ordinance and its application constitutional. Concluding that no fundamental right was implicated and that mental retardation was neither a suspect nor a quasi-suspect classification, the court employed the minimum level of judicial scrutiny applicable to equal protection claims. The court deemed the ordinance, as written and applied, to be rationally related to the city's legitimate interests in "the legal responsibility of CLC and its residents ... the safety and fears of residents in the adjoining neighborhood," and the number of people to be housed in the home.

The Court of Appeals for the Fifth Circuit reversed, determining that mental retardation was a quasi-suspect classification and that it should assess the validity of the ordinance under intermediate-level scrutiny. Because mental retardation was in fact relevant to many legislative actions, strict scrutiny was not appropriate. But in light of the history of "unfair and often grotesque mistreatment" of the retarded, discrimination against them was "likely to reflect deep-seated prejudice." In addition, the mentally retarded lacked political power, and their condition was immutable. The court considered heightened scrutiny to be particularly appropriate in this case, because the city's ordinance withheld a benefit which, although not fundamental, was very important to the mentally retarded. Without group homes, the court stated, the retarded could never hope to integrate themselves into the community.[6] Applying the test that it considered appropriate, the court held that the ordinance was invalid on its face because it did not substantially further any important governmental interests. ... We granted certiorari.

II

The Equal Protection Clause of the Fourteenth Amendment commands that no State shall "deny to any person within its jurisdiction the equal protection of the laws," which is essentially a direction that all persons similarly situated should be treated alike. Section 5 of the Amendment empowers Congress to enforce this mandate, but absent controlling congressional direction, the courts have themselves devised standards for determining the validity of state legislation or other official action that is challenged as denying equal protection. The general rule is that legislation is presumed to be valid and will be sustained if the classification drawn by the statute is rationally related to a legitimate state interest. When social or economic legislation is at issue, the Equal Protection Clause allows the States wide latitude, and the Constitution presumes that even improvident decisions will eventually be rectified by the democratic processes.

The general rule gives way, however, when a statute classifies by race, alienage, or national origin. These factors are so seldom relevant to the achievement of any legitimate state interest that laws grounded in such considerations are deemed to reflect prejudice and antipathy-a view

---

[6]   The District Court had found:

"Group homes currently are the principal community living alternatives for persons who are mentally retarded. The availability of such a home in communities is an essential ingredient of normal living patterns for persons who are mentally retarded, and each factor that makes such group homes harder to establish operates to exclude persons who are mentally retarded from the community."

that those in the burdened class are not as worthy or deserving as others. For these reasons and because such discrimination is unlikely to be soon rectified by legislative means, these laws are subjected to strict scrutiny and will be sustained only if they are suitably tailored to serve a compelling state interest. Similar oversight by the courts is due when state laws impinge on personal rights protected by the Constitution.

Legislative classifications based on gender also call for a heightened standard of review. That factor generally provides no sensible ground for differential treatment. "[W]hat differentiates sex from such nonsuspect statuses as intelligence or physical disability ... is that the sex characteristic frequently bears no relation to ability to perform or contribute to society." *Frontiero v. Richardson,* 411 U.S. 677, 686 (1973) (plurality opinion). Rather than resting on meaningful considerations, statutes distributing benefits and burdens between the sexes in different ways very likely reflect outmoded notions of the relative capabilities of men and women. A gender classification fails unless it is substantially related to a sufficiently important governmental interest. *Craig v. Boren,* 429 U.S. 190 (1976). Because illegitimacy is beyond the individual's control and bears "no relation to the individual's ability to participate in and contribute to society," *Mathews v. Lucas,* 427 U.S. 495, 505 (1976), official discriminations resting on that characteristic are also subject to somewhat heightened review. Those restrictions "will survive equal protection scrutiny to the extent they are substantially related to a legitimate state interest." *Mills v. Habluetzel,* 456 U.S. 91, 99 (1982).

We have declined, however, to extend heightened review to differential treatment based on age:

> While the treatment of the aged in this Nation has not been wholly free of discrimination, such persons, unlike, say, those who have been discriminated against on the basis of race or national origin, have not experienced a 'history of purposeful unequal treatment' or been subjected to unique disabilities on the basis of stereotyped characteristics not truly indicative of their abilities. *Massachusetts Board of Retirement v. Murgia,* 427 U.S. 307, 313 (1976).

The lesson of *Murgia* is that where individuals in the group affected by a law have distinguishing characteristics relevant to interests the State has the authority to implement, the courts have been very reluctant, as they should be in our federal system and with our respect for the separation of powers, to closely scrutinize legislative choices as to whether, how, and to what extent those interests should be pursued. In such cases, the Equal Protection Clause requires only a rational means to serve a legitimate end.

III

Against this background, we conclude for several reasons that the Court of Appeals erred in holding mental retardation a quasi-suspect classification calling for a more exacting standard of judicial review than is normally accorded economic and social legislation. First, it is undeniable, and it is not argued otherwise here, that those who are mentally retarded have a reduced ability to cope with and function in the everyday world. Nor are they all cut from the same pattern: as the testimony in this record indicates, they range from those whose disability is not immediately evident to those who must be constantly cared for.[9] They are thus different, immutably so, in relevant respects, and the States' interest in dealing with and providing for them is plainly a legitimate one.[10] How this large and diversified group is to be treated under the law is a difficult and often a technical matter, very much a task for legislators guided by qualified professionals and not by the perhaps ill-informed opinions of the judiciary. Heightened scrutiny inevitably involves substantive judgments about legislative decisions, and we doubt that the predicate for such judicial oversight is present where the classification deals with mental retardation.

Second, the distinctive legislative response, both national and state, to the plight of those who are mentally retarded demonstrates not only that they have unique problems, but also that the lawmakers have been addressing their difficulties in a manner that belies a continuing antipathy or prejudice and a corresponding need for more intrusive oversight by the judiciary. Thus, the Federal Government has not only outlawed discrimination against the mentally retarded in federally funded programs, see § 504 of the Rehabilitation Act of 1973, 29 U.S.C. § 794, but it has also provided the retarded with the right to receive "appropriate treatment, services, and habilitation" in a setting that is "least restrictive of [their] personal liberty." Developmental Disabilities Assistance and Bill of Rights Act, 42 U.S.C. §§ 6010(1), (2). In addition, the Government has conditioned federal education funds on a State's

---

[9] Mentally retarded individuals fall into four distinct categories. The vast majority— approximately 89%—are classified as "mildly" retarded, meaning that their IQ is between 50 and 70. Approximately 6% are "moderately" retarded, with IQs between 35 and 50. The remaining two categories are "severe" (IQs of 20 to 35) and "profound" (IQs below 20). These last two categories together account for about 5% of the mentally retarded population.

Mental retardation is not defined by reference to intelligence or IQ alone, however. The American Association on Mental Deficiency (AAMD) has defined mental retardation as " 'significantly subaverage general intellectual functioning existing concurrently with deficits in adaptive behavior and manifested during the developmental period.' " "Deficits in adaptive behavior" are limitations on general ability to meet the standards of maturation, learning, personal independence, and social responsibility expected for an individual's age level and cultural group. Mental retardation is caused by a variety of factors, some genetic, some environmental, and some unknown.

[10] As Dean Ely has observed:

"Surely one has to feel sorry for a person disabled by something he or she can't do anything about, but I'm not aware of any reason to suppose that elected officials are unusually unlikely to share that feeling. Moreover, classifications based on physical disability and intelligence are typically accepted as legitimate, even by judges and commentators who assert that immutability is relevant. The explanation, when one is given, is that *those* characteristics (unlike the one the commentator is trying to render suspect) are often relevant to legitimate purposes. At that point there's not much left of the immutability theory, is there?" J. Ely, Democracy and Distrust 150 (1980).

assurance that retarded children will enjoy an education that, "to the maximum extent appropriate," is integrated with that of nonmentally retarded children. Education of the Handicapped Act, 20 U.S.C. § 1412(5)(B). The Government has also facilitated the hiring of the mentally retarded into the federal civil service by exempting them from the requirement of competitive examination. See 5 CFR § 213.3102(t) (1984). The State of Texas has similarly enacted legislation that acknowledges the special status of the mentally retarded by conferring certain rights upon them, such as "the right to live in the least restrictive setting appropriate to [their] individual needs and abilities," including "the right to live . . . in a group home." Mentally Retarded Persons Act of 1977, Tex.Rev.Civ.Stat.Ann., Art. 5547–300, § 7 (Vernon Supp.1985).[11]

Such legislation thus singling out the retarded for special treatment reflects the real and undeniable differences between the retarded and others. That a civilized and decent society expects and approves such legislation indicates that governmental consideration of those differences in the vast majority of situations is not only legitimate but also desirable. It may be, as CLC contends, that legislation designed to benefit, rather than disadvantage, the retarded would generally withstand examination under a test of heightened scrutiny. The relevant inquiry, however, is whether heightened scrutiny is constitutionally mandated in the first instance. Even assuming that many of these laws could be shown to be substantially related to an important governmental purpose, merely requiring the legislature to justify its efforts in these terms may lead it to refrain from acting at all. Much recent legislation intended to benefit the retarded also assumes the need for measures that might be perceived to disadvantage them. The Education of the Handicapped Act, for example, requires an "appropriate" education, not one that is equal in all respects to the education of nonretarded children; clearly, admission to a class that exceeded the abilities of a retarded child would not be appropriate. Similarly, the Developmental Disabilities Assistance Act and the Texas Act give the retarded the right to live only in the "least restrictive setting" appropriate to their abilities, implicitly assuming the need for at least some restrictions that would not be imposed on others. Especially given the wide variation in the abilities and needs of the retarded themselves, governmental bodies must have a certain amount of flexibility and freedom from judicial oversight in shaping and limiting their remedial efforts.

Third, the legislative response, which could hardly have occurred and survived without public support, negates any claim that the mentally retarded are politically powerless in the sense that they have no ability to attract the attention of the lawmakers. Any minority can be said to be

---

[11] . . . A number of States have passed legislation prohibiting zoning that excludes the retarded. See, *e.g.*, Cal.Health & Safety Code Ann. § 1566 *et seq.* (West 1979 and Supp.1985); Conn.Gen.Stat. § 8–3e (Supp.1985); N.D.Cent.Code § 25–16–14(2) (Supp.1983); R.I.Gen.Laws, § 45–24–22 (1980). See also Md.Health Code Ann. § 7–102 (Supp.1984).

powerless to assert direct control over the legislature, but if that were a criterion for higher level scrutiny by the courts, much economic and social legislation would now be suspect.

Fourth, if the large and amorphous class of the mentally retarded were deemed quasi-suspect for the reasons given by the Court of Appeals, it would be difficult to find a principled way to distinguish a variety of other groups who have perhaps immutable disabilities setting them off from others, who cannot themselves mandate the desired legislative responses, and who can claim some degree of prejudice from at least part of the public at large. One need mention in this respect only the aging, the disabled, the mentally ill, and the infirm. We are reluctant to set out on that course, and we decline to do so.

Doubtless, there have been and there will continue to be instances of discrimination against the retarded that are in fact invidious, and that are properly subject to judicial correction under constitutional norms. But the appropriate method of reaching such instances is not to create a new quasi-suspect classification and subject all governmental action based on that classification to more searching evaluation. Rather, we should look to the likelihood that governmental action premised on a particular classification is valid as a general matter, not merely to the specifics of the case before us. Because mental retardation is a characteristic that the government may legitimately take into account in a wide range of decisions, and because both State and Federal Governments have recently committed themselves to assisting the retarded, we will not presume that any given legislative action, even one that disadvantages retarded individuals, is rooted in considerations that the Constitution will not tolerate.

Our refusal to recognize the retarded as a quasi-suspect class does not leave them entirely unprotected from invidious discrimination. To withstand equal protection review, legislation that distinguishes between the mentally retarded and others must be rationally related to a legitimate governmental purpose. This standard, we believe, affords government the latitude necessary both to pursue policies designed to assist the retarded in realizing their full potential, and to freely and efficiently engage in activities that burden the retarded in what is essentially an incidental manner. The State may not rely on a classification whose relationship to an asserted goal is so attenuated as to render the distinction arbitrary or irrational. See *United States Dept. of Agriculture v. Moreno,* 413 U.S. 528, 535 (1973). Furthermore, some objectives-such as "a bare ... desire to harm a politically unpopular group," *id.,* at 534, are not legitimate state interests. Beyond that, the mentally retarded, like others, have and retain their substantive constitutional rights in addition to the right to be treated equally by the law.

IV

We turn to the issue of the validity of the zoning ordinance insofar as it requires a special use permit for homes for the mentally retarded. . . . The city does not require a special use permit in an R–3 zone for apartment houses, multiple dwellings, boarding and lodging houses, fraternity or sorority houses, dormitories, apartment hotels, hospitals, sanitariums, nursing homes for convalescents or the aged (other than for the insane or feebleminded or alcoholics or drug addicts), private clubs or fraternal orders, and other specified uses. It does, however, insist on a special permit for the Featherston home, and it does so, as the District Court found, because it would be a facility for the mentally retarded. May the city require the permit for this facility when other care and multiple-dwelling facilities are freely permitted?

It is true, as already pointed out, that the mentally retarded as a group are indeed different from others not sharing their misfortune, and in this respect they may be different from those who would occupy other facilities that would be permitted in an R–3 zone without a special permit. But this difference is largely irrelevant unless the Featherston home and those who would occupy it would threaten legitimate interests of the city in a way that other permitted uses such as boarding houses and hospitals would not. Because in our view the record does not reveal any rational basis for believing that the Featherston home would pose any special threat to the city's legitimate interests, we affirm the judgment below insofar as it holds the ordinance invalid as applied in this case.

The District Court found that the City Council's insistence on the permit rested on several factors. First, the Council was concerned with the negative attitude of the majority of property owners located within 200 feet of the Featherston facility, as well as with the fears of elderly residents of the neighborhood. But mere negative attitudes, or fear, unsubstantiated by factors which are properly cognizable in a zoning proceeding, are not permissible bases for treating a home for the mentally retarded differently from apartment houses, multiple dwellings, and the like. It is plain that the electorate as a whole, whether by referendum or otherwise, could not order city action violative of the Equal Protection Clause, and the City may not avoid the strictures of that Clause by deferring to the wishes or objections of some fraction of the body politic. "Private biases may be outside the reach of the law, but the law cannot, directly or indirectly, give them effect." *Palmore v. Sidoti*, 466 U.S. 429, 433 (1984).

Second, the Council had two objections to the location of the facility. It was concerned that the facility was across the street from a junior high school, and it feared that the students might harass the occupants of the Featherston home. But the school itself is attended by about 30 mentally retarded students, and denying a permit based on such vague, undifferentiated fears is again permitting some portion of the community to validate what would otherwise be an equal protection violation. The other objection to the home's location was that it was located on "a five hundred year flood plain." This concern with the possibility of a flood, however, can hardly be based on a distinction between the Featherston home and, for example, nursing homes, homes for convalescents or the aged, or sanitariums or hospitals, any of which could be located on the Featherston site without obtaining a special use permit. The same may be said of another concern of the Council-doubts about the legal responsibility for actions which the mentally retarded might take. If there is no concern about legal responsibility with respect to other uses that would be permitted in the area, such as boarding and fraternity houses, it is difficult to believe that the groups of mildly or moderately mentally retarded individuals who would live at 201 Featherston would present any different or special hazard.

Fourth, the Council was concerned with the size of the home and the number of people that would occupy it. The District Court found, and the Court of Appeals repeated, that "[i]f the potential residents of the Featherston Street home were not mentally retarded, but the home was the same in all other respects, its use would be permitted under the city's zoning ordinance." Given this finding, there would be no restrictions on the number of people who could occupy this home as a boarding house, nursing home, family dwelling, fraternity house, or dormitory. The question is whether it is rational to treat the mentally retarded differently. It is true that they suffer disability not shared by others; but why this difference warrants a density regulation that others need not observe is not at all apparent. At least this record does not clarify how, in this connection, the characteristics of the intended occupants of the Featherston home rationally justify denying to those occupants what would be permitted to groups occupying the same site for different purposes. Those who would live in the Featherston home are the type of individuals who, with supporting staff, satisfy federal and state standards for group housing in the community; and there is no dispute that the home would meet the federal square-footage-per-resident requirement for facilities of this type. In the words of the Court of Appeals, "[t]he City never justifies its apparent view that other people can live under such 'crowded' conditions when mentally retarded persons cannot."

In the courts below the city also urged that the ordinance is aimed at avoiding concentration of population and at lessening congestion of the streets. These concerns obviously fail to explain why apartment houses, fraternity and sorority houses, hospitals and the like, may freely locate in the area without a permit. So, too, the expressed worry about fire hazards, the serenity of the neighborhood, and the avoidance of danger to other residents fail rationally to justify singling out a home such as 201 Featherston for the special use permit, yet imposing no such restrictions on the many other uses freely permitted in the neighborhood.

The short of it is that requiring the permit in this case appears to us to rest on an irrational prejudice against the mentally retarded, including those who would occupy the Featherston facility and who would live under the closely supervised and highly regulated conditions expressly provided for by state and federal law.

The judgment of the Court of Appeals is affirmed insofar as it invalidates the zoning ordinance as applied to the Featherston home. The judgment is otherwise vacated, and the case is remanded.

It is so ordered.

■ JUSTICE STEVENS, with whom THE CHIEF JUSTICE joins, concurring.

The Court of Appeals disposed of this case as if a critical question to be decided were which of three clearly defined standards of equal protection review should be applied to a legislative classification discriminating against the mentally retarded. In fact, our cases have not delineated three-or even one or two-such well-defined standards. Rather, our cases reflect a continuum of judgmental responses to differing classifications which have been explained in opinions by terms ranging from "strict scrutiny" at one extreme to "rational basis" at the other. I have never been persuaded that these so-called "standards" adequately explain the decisional process. Cases involving classifications based on alienage, illegal residency, illegitimacy, gender, age, or-as in this case-mental retardation, do not fit well into sharply defined classifications. . . .

In my own approach to these cases, I have always asked myself whether I could find a "rational basis" for the classification at issue. The term "rational," of course, includes a requirement that an impartial lawmaker could logically believe that the classification would serve a legitimate public purpose that transcends the harm to the members of the disadvantaged class. Thus, the word "rational"-for me at least-includes elements of legitimacy and neutrality that must always characterize the performance of the sovereign's duty to govern impartially.

The rational-basis test, properly understood, adequately explains why a law that deprives a person of the right to vote because his skin has a different pigmentation than that of other voters violates the Equal Protection Clause. It would be utterly irrational to limit the franchise on the basis of height or weight; it is equally invalid to limit it on the basis of skin color. None of these attributes has any bearing at all on the citizen's willingness or ability to exercise that civil right. We do not need to apply a special standard, or to apply "strict scrutiny," or even "heightened scrutiny," to decide such cases.

In every equal protection case, we have to ask certain basic questions. What class is harmed by the legislation, and has it been subjected to a "tradition of disfavor" by our laws?[6] What is the public purpose that is being served by the law? What is the characteristic of the disadvantaged class that justifies the disparate treatment? In most cases the answer to these questions will tell us whether the statute has a "rational basis." The answers will result in the virtually automatic invalidation of racial classifications and in the validation of most economic classifications, but they will provide differing results in cases involving classifications based on alienage, gender, or illegitimacy. But that is not because we apply an "intermediate standard of review" in these cases; rather it is because the characteristics of these groups are sometimes relevant and sometimes irrelevant to a valid public purpose, or, more specifically, to the purpose that the challenged laws purportedly intended to serve. . . .

The discrimination against the mentally retarded that is at issue in this case is the city's decision to require an annual special use permit before property in an apartment house district may be used as a group home for persons who are mildly retarded. The record convinces me that this permit was required because of the irrational fears of neighboring property owners, rather than for the protection of the mentally retarded persons who would reside in respondent's home. . . .

Accordingly, I join the opinion of the Court.

■ **JUSTICE MARSHALL, with whom JUSTICE BRENNAN and JUSTICE BLACKMUN join, concurring in the judgment in part and dissenting in part.**

The Court holds that all retarded individuals cannot be grouped together as the "feebleminded" and deemed presumptively unfit to live in a community. Underlying this holding is the principle that mental retardation *per se* cannot be a proxy for depriving retarded people of their rights and interests without regard to variations in individual ability. With this holding and principle I agree. The Equal Protection Clause requires attention to the capacities and needs of retarded people as individuals.

I cannot agree, however, with the way in which the Court reaches its result or with the narrow, as-applied remedy it provides for the city of Cleburne's equal protection violation. The Court holds the ordinance invalid on rational-basis grounds and disclaims that anything special, in the form of heightened scrutiny, is taking place. Yet Cleburne's ordinance surely would be valid under the traditional rational-basis test applicable

---

[6]   The Court must be especially vigilant in evaluating the rationality of any classification involving a group that has been subjected to a "tradition of disfavor [for] a traditional classification is more likely to be used without pausing to consider its justification than is a newly created classification. Habit, rather than analysis, makes it seem acceptable and natural to distinguish between male and female, alien and citizen, legitimate and illegitimate; for too much of our history there was the same inertia in distinguishing between black and white. But that sort of stereotyped reaction may have no rational relationship-other than pure prejudicial discrimination-to the stated purpose for which the classification is being made." *Mathews v. Lucas,* 427 U.S. 495, 520–521 (1976) (STEVENS, J., dissenting).

to economic and commercial regulation. In my view, it is important to articulate, as the Court does not, the facts and principles that justify subjecting this zoning ordinance to the searching review-the heightened scrutiny-that actually leads to its invalidation. Moreover, in invalidating Cleburne's exclusion of the "feebleminded" only as applied to respondents, rather than on its face, the Court radically departs from our equal protection precedents. Because I dissent from this novel and truncated remedy, and because I cannot accept the Court's disclaimer that no "more exacting standard" than ordinary rational-basis review is being applied, I write separately.

I

At the outset, two curious and paradoxical aspects of the Court's opinion must be noted. First, because the Court invalidates Cleburne's zoning ordinance on rational-basis grounds, the Court's wide-ranging discussion of heightened scrutiny is wholly superfluous to the decision of this case. . . .

Second, the Court's heightened-scrutiny discussion is even more puzzling given that Cleburne's ordinance is invalidated only after being subjected to precisely the sort of probing inquiry associated with heightened scrutiny. To be sure, the Court does not label its handiwork heightened scrutiny, and perhaps the method employed must hereafter be called "second order" rational-basis review rather than "heightened scrutiny." But however labeled, the rational basis test invoked today is most assuredly not the rational-basis test of *Williamson v. Lee Optical of Oklahoma, Inc.,* 348 U.S. 483 (1955) . . . .

The Court, for example, concludes that legitimate concerns for fire hazards or the serenity of the neighborhood do not justify singling out respondents to bear the burdens of these concerns, for analogous permitted uses appear to pose similar threats. Yet under the traditional and most minimal version of the rational-basis test, "reform may take one step at a time, addressing itself to the phase of the problem which seems most acute to the legislative mind." *Williamson v. Lee Optical of Oklahoma, Inc., supra,* 348 U.S., at 489. The "record" is said not to support the ordinance's classifications, but under the traditional standard we do not sift through the record to determine whether policy decisions are squarely supported by a firm factual foundation. Finally, the Court further finds it "difficult to believe" that the retarded present different or special hazards inapplicable to other groups. In normal circumstances, the burden is not on the legislature to convince the Court that the lines it has drawn are sensible; legislation is presumptively constitutional, and a State "is not required to resort to close distinctions or to maintain a precise, scientific uniformity with reference" to its goals.

I share the Court's criticisms of the overly broad lines that Cleburne's zoning ordinance has drawn. But if the ordinance is to be invalidated for its imprecise classifications, it must be pursuant to more powerful scrutiny than the minimal rational-basis test used to review classifications affecting only economic and commercial matters. The same imprecision in a similar ordinance that required opticians but not optometrists to be licensed to practice, see *Williamson v. Lee Optical of Oklahoma, Inc., supra* . . . would hardly be fatal to the statutory scheme.

The refusal to acknowledge that something more than minimum rationality review is at work here is, in my view, unfortunate in at least two respects.[4] The suggestion that the traditional rational-basis test allows this sort of searching inquiry creates precedent for this Court and lower courts to subject economic and commercial classifications to similar and searching "ordinary" rational-basis review—a small and regrettable step back toward the days of *Lochner v. New York,* 198 U.S. 45 (1905). Moreover, by failing to articulate the factors that justify today's "second order" rational-basis review, the Court provides no principled foundation for determining when more searching inquiry is to be invoked. Lower courts are thus left in the dark on this important question, and this Court remains unaccountable for its decisions employing, or refusing to employ, particularly searching scrutiny. Candor requires me to acknowledge the particular factors that justify invalidating Cleburne's zoning ordinance under the careful scrutiny it today receives.

II

I have long believed the level of scrutiny employed in an equal protection case should vary with "the constitutional and societal importance of the interest adversely affected and the recognized invidiousness of the basis upon which the particular classification is drawn." *San Antonio Independent School District v. Rodriguez,* 411 U.S. 1, 99 (1973) (MARSHALL, J., dissenting). When a zoning ordinance works to exclude the retarded from all residential districts in a community, these two considerations require that the ordinance be convincingly justified as substantially furthering legitimate and important purposes.

First, the interest of the retarded in establishing group homes is substantial. The right to "establish a home" has long been cherished as one of the fundamental liberties embraced by the Due Process Clause. See *Meyer v. Nebraska,* 262 U.S. 390, 399 (1923). For retarded adults, this right means living together in group homes, for as deinstitutionalization has progressed, group homes have become the primary means by which retarded adults can enter life in the community. . . . Excluding group homes deprives the retarded of much of what makes for human freedom and fulfillment-the ability to form bonds and take part in the life of a community.

---

[4] The two cases the Court cites in its rational-basis discussion, *Zobel v. Williams,* 457 U.S. 55 (1982), and *United States Dept. of Agriculture v. Moreno,* 413 U.S. 528 (1973), expose the special nature of the rational-basis test employed today. As two of only a handful of modern equal protection cases striking down legislation under what purports to be a rational-basis standard, these cases must be and generally have been viewed as intermediate review decisions masquerading in rational-basis language.

Second, the mentally retarded have been subject to a lengthy and tragic history of segregation and discrimination that can only be called grotesque. During much of the 19th century, mental retardation was viewed as neither curable nor dangerous and the retarded were largely left to their own devices. By the latter part of the century and during the first decades of the new one, however, social views of the retarded underwent a radical transformation. Fueled by the rising tide of Social Darwinism, the "science" of eugenics, and the extreme xenophobia of those years, leading medical authorities and others began to portray the "feeble-minded" as a "menace to society and civilization . . . responsible in a large degree for many, if not all, of our social problems." A regime of state-mandated segregation and degradation soon emerged that in its virulence and bigotry rivaled, and indeed paralleled, the worst excesses of Jim Crow. Massive custodial institutions were built to warehouse the retarded for life; the aim was to halt reproduction of the retarded and "nearly extinguish their race." Retarded children were categorically excluded from public schools, based on the false stereotype that all were ineducable and on the purported need to protect nonretarded children from them. State laws deemed the retarded "unfit for citizenship." . . .

Prejudice, once let loose, is not easily cabined. As of 1979, most States still categorically disqualified "idiots" from voting, without regard to individual capacity and with discretion to exclude left in the hands of low-level election officials. Not until Congress enacted the Education of the Handicapped Act, 84 Stat. 175, as amended, *20 U.S.C. § 1400 et seq.,* were "the door[s] of public education" opened wide to handicapped children. But most important, lengthy and continuing isolation of the retarded has perpetuated the ignorance, irrational fears, and stereotyping that long have plagued them.

In light of the importance of the interest at stake and the history of discrimination the retarded have suffered, the Equal Protection Clause requires us to do more than review the distinctions drawn by Cleburne's zoning ordinance as if they appeared in a taxing statute or in economic or commercial legislation. The searching scrutiny I would give to restrictions on the ability of the retarded to establish community group homes leads me to conclude that Cleburne's vague generalizations for classifying the "feeble-minded" with drug addicts, alcoholics, and the insane, and excluding them where the elderly, the ill, the boarder, and the transient are allowed, are not substantial or important enough to overcome the suspicion that the ordinance rests on impermissible assumptions or outmoded and perhaps invidious stereotypes.

III

In its effort to show that Cleburne's ordinance can be struck down under no "more exacting standard . . . than is normally accorded economic and social legislation," the Court offers several justifications as to why the retarded do not warrant heightened judicial solicitude. These justifications, however, find no support in our heightened-scrutiny precedents and cannot withstand logical analysis.

The Court downplays the lengthy "history of purposeful unequal treatment" of the retarded, by pointing to recent legislative action that is said to "beli[e] a continuing antipathy or prejudice." Building on this point, the Court similarly concludes that the retarded are not "politically powerless" and deserve no greater judicial protection than "[a]ny minority" that wins some political battles and loses others. The import of these conclusions, it seems, is that . . . [o]nce society begins to recognize certain practices as discriminatory, in part because previously stigmatized groups have mobilized politically to lift this stigma, the Court would refrain from approaching such practices with the added skepticism of heightened scrutiny.

Courts, however, do not sit or act in a social vacuum. Moral philosophers may debate whether certain inequalities are absolute wrongs, but history makes clear that constitutional principles of equality, like constitutional principles of liberty, property, and due process, evolve over time; what once was a "natural" and "self-evident" ordering later comes to be seen as an artificial and invidious constraint on human potential and freedom. Shifting cultural, political, and social patterns at times come to make past practices appear inconsistent with fundamental principles upon which American society rests, an inconsistency legally cognizable under the Equal Protection Clause. It is natural that evolving standards of equality come to be embodied in legislation. When that occurs, courts should look to the fact of such change as a source of guidance on evolving principles of equality. In an analysis the Court today ignores, the Court reached this very conclusion when it extended heightened scrutiny to gender classifications and drew on parallel legislative developments to support that extension: . . .

Moreover, even when judicial action *has* catalyzed legislative change, that change certainly does not eviscerate the underlying constitutional principle. The Court, for example, has never suggested that race-based classifications became any less suspect once extensive legislation had been enacted on the subject.

For the retarded, just as for Negroes and women, much has changed in recent years, but much remains the same; out-dated statutes are still on the books, and irrational fears or ignorance, traceable to the prolonged social and cultural isolation of the retarded, continue to stymie recognition of the dignity and individuality of retarded people. Heightened judicial scrutiny of action appearing to impose unnecessary barriers to the retarded is required in light of increasing recognition that such barriers are inconsistent with evolving principles of equality embedded in the Fourteenth Amendment.

The Court also offers a more general view of heightened scrutiny, a view focused primarily on when heightened scrutiny does *not* apply as opposed to when it does apply. Two principles appear central to the

Court's theory. First, heightened scrutiny is said to be inapplicable where *individuals* in a group have distinguishing characteristics that legislatures properly may take into account in some circumstances. Heightened scrutiny is also purportedly inappropriate when many legislative classifications affecting the *group* are likely to be valid. We must, so the Court says, "look to the likelihood that governmental action premised on a particular classification is valid as a general matter, not merely to the specifics of the case before us," in deciding whether to apply heightened scrutiny.

If the Court's first principle were sound, heightened scrutiny would have to await a day when people could be cut from a cookie mold. Women are hardly alike in all their characteristics, but heightened scrutiny applies to them because legislatures can rarely use gender itself as a proxy for these other characteristics. Permissible distinctions between persons must bear a reasonable relationship to their *relevant* characteristics, and gender *per se* is almost never relevant. Similarly, that some retarded people have reduced capacities in some areas does not justify using retardation as a proxy for reduced capacity in areas where relevant individual variations in capacity do exist.

The Court's second assertion-that the standard of review must be fixed with reference to the number of classifications to which a characteristic would validly be relevant-is similarly flawed. Certainly the assertion is not a logical one; that a characteristic may be relevant under some or even many circumstances does not suggest any reason to presume it relevant under other circumstances where there is reason to suspect it is not. A sign that says "men only" looks very different on a bathroom door than a courthouse door.

Our heightened-scrutiny precedents belie the claim that a characteristic must virtually always be irrelevant to warrant heightened scrutiny. . . . Heightened but not strict scrutiny is considered appropriate in areas such as gender, illegitimacy, or alienage[20] because the Court views the trait as relevant under some circumstances but not others. That view-indeed the very concept of heightened, as opposed to strict, scrutiny-is flatly inconsistent with the notion that heightened scrutiny should not apply to the retarded because "mental retardation is a characteristic that the government may legitimately take into account in a wide range of decisions." Because the government also may not take this characteristic into account in many circumstances, such as those presented here, careful review is required to separate the permissible from the invalid in classifications relying on retardation.

The fact that retardation may be deemed a constitutional irrelevancy in *some* circumstances is enough, given the history of

---

[20] Alienage classifications present a related variant, for strict scrutiny is applied to such classifications in the economic and social area, but only heightened scrutiny is applied when the classification relates to "political functions." . . .

discrimination the retarded have suffered, to require careful judicial review of classifications singling out the retarded for special burdens. . . .

Discrimination, in the Fourteenth Amendment sense, connotes a substantive constitutional judgment that two individuals or groups are entitled to be treated equally with respect to something. With regard to economic and commercial matters, no basis for such a conclusion exists, for as Justice Holmes urged the *Lochner* Court, the Fourteenth Amendment was not "intended to embody a particular economic theory. . . ." *Lochner v. New York,* 198 U.S., at 75 (dissenting). As a matter of substantive policy, therefore, government is free to move in any direction, or to change directions, in the economic and commercial sphere. The structure of economic and commercial life is a matter of political compromise, not constitutional principle, and no norm of equality requires that there be as many opticians as optometrists, see *Williamson v. Lee Optical of Oklahoma, Inc.,* 348 U.S. 483 (1955). . . .

But the Fourteenth Amendment does prohibit other results under virtually all circumstances, such as castes created by law along racial or ethnic lines, and significantly constrains the range of permissible government choices where gender or illegitimacy, for example, are concerned. Where such constraints, derived from the Fourteenth Amendment, are present, and where history teaches that they have systemically been ignored, a "more searching judicial inquiry" is required. *United States v. Carolene Products Co.,* 304 U.S. 144, 153, n. 4 (1938).

That more searching inquiry, be it called heightened scrutiny or "second order" rational-basis review, is a method of approaching certain classifications skeptically, with judgment suspended until the facts are in and the evidence considered. The government must establish that the classification is substantially related to important and legitimate objectives, see, *e.g., Craig v. Boren,* 429 U.S. 190 (1976), so that valid and sufficiently weighty policies actually justify the departure from equality. Heightened scrutiny does not allow courts to second-guess reasoned legislative or professional judgments tailored to the unique needs of a group like the retarded, but it does seek to assure that the hostility or thoughtlessness with which there is reason to be concerned has not carried the day. By invoking heightened scrutiny, the Court recognizes, and compels lower courts to recognize, that a group may well be the target of the sort of prejudiced, thoughtless, or stereotyped action that offends principles of equality found in the Fourteenth Amendment. Where classifications based on a particular characteristic have done so in the past, and the threat that they may do so remains, heightened scrutiny is appropriate.[24]

---

[24] No single talisman can define those groups likely to be the target of classifications offensive to the Fourteenth Amendment and therefore warranting heightened or strict scrutiny; experience, not abstract logic, must be the primary guide. The "political powerlessness" of a group may be relevant, but that factor is neither necessary, as the gender cases demonstrate,

As the history of discrimination against the retarded and its continuing legacy amply attest, the mentally retarded have been, and in some areas may still be, the targets of action the Equal Protection Clause condemns. . . . [H]eightened scrutiny is surely appropriate. . . .

NOTE ON RATIONAL BASIS REVIEW AND THE IDENTIFICATION OF SUSPECT CLASSIFICATIONS

1.   As we saw at the end of Chapter Five, the deferential "rational basis" standard applied in cases like *Beazer* reflects the New Deal Court's turn away from intrusive judicial review of economic and social legislation after 1937. With some important exceptions, rational basis review under the Equal Protection Clause has generally been equally deferential as such review under the Due Process Clause. Is it obvious that this should be so? Part of the problem in cases like *Lochner v. New York*—which the rational basis standard may be seen as a reaction against—was the nonobvious connection between the Fourteenth Amendment's textual guarantee of "due process of law" and the operative doctrine of "freedom of contract." Isn't the more searching review undertaken by the lower courts in *Beazer* a good deal closer to the textual mandate of ensuring "equal protection of the laws"? Should courts be less deferential when asking whether distinctions among similarly-situated persons can be justified under the Equal Protection Clause than when it is asked to protect unenumerated and concededly non-fundamental rights under the Due Process Clause?

2.   Most bright-line rules—such as "no methadone users in the Transit Authority"—are subject to the criticism that they are either over- or under-inclusive (or both) with respect to the underlying policy interests that the rule is meant to vindicate. In *Beazer*, the District Court concluded after

---

nor sufficient, as the example of minors illustrates. Minors cannot vote and thus might be considered politically powerless to an extreme degree. Nonetheless, we see few statutes reflecting prejudice or indifference to minors, and I am not aware of any suggestion that legislation affecting them be viewed with the suspicion of heightened scrutiny. Similarly, immutability of the trait at issue may be relevant, but many immutable characteristics, such as height or blindness, are valid bases of governmental action and classifications under a variety of circumstances.

The political powerlessness of a group and the immutability of its defining trait are relevant insofar as they point to a social and cultural isolation that gives the majority little reason to respect or be concerned with that group's interests and needs. Statutes discriminating against the young have not been common nor need be feared because those who do vote and legislate were once themselves young, typically have children of their own, and certainly interact regularly with minors. Their social integration means that minors, unlike discrete and insular minorities, tend to be treated in legislative arenas with full concern and respect, despite their formal and complete exclusion from the electoral process.

The discreteness and insularity warranting a "more searching judicial inquiry," *United States v. Carolene Products Co.*, 304 U.S. 144, 153, n. 4 (1938), must therefore be viewed from a social and cultural perspective as well as a political one. To this task judges are well suited, for the lessons of history and experience are surely the best guide as to when, and with respect to what interests, society is likely to stigmatize individuals as members of an inferior caste or view them as not belonging to the community. Because prejudice spawns prejudice, and stereotypes produce limitations that confirm the stereotype on which they are based, a history of unequal treatment requires sensitivity to the prospect that its vestiges endure. In separating those groups that are discrete and insular from those that are not, as in many important legal distinctions, "a page of history is worth a volume of logic." *New York Trust Co. v. Eisner*, 256 U.S. 345, 349 (1921) (Holmes, J.).

hearing extensive evidence that the Transit Authority's legitimate interests in safety and efficiency could be satisfied by a more nuanced rule permitting employment only of methadone users who had successfully completed a year of treatment and excluding even those users from safety-sensitive positions. The Authority's categorical exclusion of users from the program, in other words, was over-inclusive. Does the Supreme Court question that conclusion? Or is the point simply that the Equal Protection Clause does not require that degree of nuance? Is the latter view defensible?

Wasn't the Authority's rule also *under*-inclusive? As Justice White's dissent pointed out, the District Court also made an unchallenged finding that "problem drinkers" posed more of a risk than methadone users, and yet were not automatically discharged from employment. Doesn't this undercut the Authority's categorical exclusion of methadone users?

3. One important function of arguments about over and underinclusiveness is to smoke out unstated biases and prejudices: If the law or policy poorly fits its articulated rationale, then perhaps the reason is that the policy in fact stems from some unarticulated prejudice. Justice White noted in his *Beazer* dissent that "[h]eroin addiction is a special problem of the poor, and the addict population is composed largely of racial minorities that the Court has previously recognized as politically powerless and historical subjects of majoritarian neglect." To what extend should the worry that imprecise classifications may stem from a disregard of the interests of disfavored groups justify more searching review under the Equal Protection Clause? Does this concern help explain the way the Court examined the local ordinance in *Cleburne*?

4. Rational basis review is often justified as a means of deference to the democratic process; by deferring to the judgments of elected officials, courts respect the deliberative processes of political institutions and allow the people to govern themselves. But Justice White's dissent in *Beazer* objected that the methadone policy "was not the result of a reasoned policy decision and [the Transit Authority] stipulated that they had never studied the ability of those on methadone maintenance to perform petitioners' jobs." Moreover, he observed that the Authority was "not directly accountable to the public." Should these sorts of facts matter in calibrating the standard of review? In other words, should rational basis review apply to all government actions that do not employ a suspect or quasi-suspect classification, or should it be available only when the policy in question has in fact been adopted by a politically-accountable body through open and deliberative processes?

5. Why didn't the Court accept the mentally disabled as a suspect class in *Cleburne*? The Court has suggested that a variety of factors are relevant to suspect class status: whether the group has a history of oppression; whether the characteristic that defines the class is generally a relevant and legitimate basis for distinctive treatment; whether the subject is "immutable"; and whether the group is "politically powerless." As both the *Cleburne* majority opinion and Justice Brennan's dissent make clear, these factors form more of a rough guide than a checklist of necessary conditions. Does mental disability warrant treatment as a suspect classification based on these factors? Can you think of other classifications that might?

The Court rejected suspect class treatment for the aged in *Massachusetts Board of Retirement v. Murgia,* 427 U.S. 307 (1976), based on reasoning similar to that in *Cleburne.* Lower courts and commentators have debated whether sexual orientation should be considered a suspect classification, and the Obama Administration took the position that it should in refusing to defend the constitutionality of the Defense of Marriage Act.[7] As you will see in Chapter Seventeen, the Supreme Court has largely sidestepped that question. A final prominent, but unsuccessful, candidate for suspect class status has been the poor. Although the Court has on several occasions struck down access charges to both criminal and civil litigants on the ground that they excluded indigent persons,[8] it has never held that wealth-based classifications are inherently suspect.[9] Should it?[10]

6.   Is the rational basis review that the Court purported to apply in *Cleburne* really the same as that applied in *Beazer*? Many commentators have suggested that the *Cleburne* court applied a "covert" form of heightened scrutiny.[11] If that is true, shouldn't the Court have acknowledged what it was doing and articulated the criteria for when this sort of heightened scrutiny will apply in the future? Based on the *Cleburne* opinion, what do you think those criteria are?

SECTION 15.4 AFFIRMATIVE ACTION AND "BENIGN" RACIAL CLASSIFICATIONS

The paradigm case of equal protection review involves a scenario like *Brown v. Board of Education*, in which a classification drawn on racial lines works to disadvantage black people. These sorts of "malign" racial classifications rarely reach the Supreme Court these days, as the strong presumption that they are invalid is well-established. The principal debate concerning racial classifications, rather, involves classifications that are arguably "benign"—that is, designed to benefit racial minorities that have historically been subject to widespread discrimination and prejudice. This is the controversy over "affirmative action" programs that take note of race in order to work toward a more equal society generally.

The affirmative action debate implicates a basic disagreement over the meaning of the Equal Protection Clause. Recall that in *Plessy v. Ferguson,*

---

[7]   *See Letter from the Attorney General to Congress on Litigation Involving the Defense of Marriage Act,* Feb. 23, 2011, available at http://www.justice.gov/opa/pr/letter-attorney-general-congress-litigation-involving-defense-marriage-act.

[8]   *See Boddie v. Connecticut,* 401 U.S. 371 (1971) (striking down filing fees in divorce cases as applied to indigent persons); *Griffin v. Illinois,* 351 U.S. 12 (1956) (holding that denial of an appeal to an indigent criminal defendant who could not afford a trial transcript denied equal protection of the laws).

[9]   *See, e.g., Harris v. McRae,* 448 U.S. 297, 323 (1980) (observing that "this Court has held repeatedly that poverty, standing alone, is not a suspect classification"); *but see generally* Henry Rose, *The Poor as a Suspect Class Under the Equal Protection Clause: An Open Constitutional Question,* 34 NOVA L. REV. 407 (2010) (arguing that the question remains open).

[10]   For further discussion of this question, see *San Antonio Independent School Dist v. Rodriguez* in Section 15.5, *infra.*

[11]   *See, e.g.,* LAURENCE H. TRIBE, AMERICAN CONSTITUTIONAL LAW, §§ 16–3, 16–31 (2d ed. 1988).

the elder Justice Harlan's dissent asserted that "[o]ur Constitution is color-blind, and neither knows nor tolerates classes among citizens. . . . The law regards man as man, and takes no account of . . . his color when his civil rights as guaranteed by the supreme law of the land are involved." Colorblindness provided a sufficient basis to attack *de jure* segregation and other legal disadvantages imposed on African-Americans because of their race. Chief Justice John Roberts summed up the colorblind perspective for the current Court when he stated, in *Parents Involved in Community Schools v. Seattle School District No. 1*, that "[t]he way to stop discrimination on the basis of race is to stop discriminating on the basis of race."

But it is far from clear that ending *de jure* discrimination can erase the effects of centuries of slavery and discrimination. Abundant evidence exists that racial bias persists in our society. As Justice Ruth Bader Ginsburg put it in *Adarand Constructors, Inc. v. Pena*, "[b]ias both conscious and unconscious, reflecting traditional and unexamined habits of thought, keeps up barriers that must come down if equal opportunity and nondiscrimination are ever genuinely to become this country's law and practice." Hence, the anti-subordination reading of equal protection insists that government must sometimes take account of race in order to raise up disadvantaged groups. This perspective supports a variety of race-conscious remedies for discrimination, including affirmative action in hiring, contracting, and school admissions.

Even if one accepts the anti-subordination reading of the Equal Protection Clause, however, significant complexities remain. Gender cases like *Craig v. Boren*, for example, have often proceeded on the assumption that even classifications that disadvantage men—the historically favored group—may perpetuate gender stereotypes that, in the long run, tend to subordinate women. In the race-based affirmative action cases that follow, Justice Clarence Thomas and others have likewise contended that racial preferences may work to undermine the disadvantaged groups they seek to protect. These sorts of arguments question whether one can really distinguish between "benign" and "malign" discrimination at all.

The cases that follow depict a Court grappling both with fundamental disagreements of principle and considerable empirical uncertainty. The number, complexity, and vehemence of the opinions reflect deep divisions in the broader society. In other comparably intractable areas of constitutional controversy, such as the freedom of contract cases in the *Lochner* era, one can make a plausible argument that the Court should simply leave the key issues to political resolution. The text and history of the Equal Protection Clause make that considerably more difficult here. But it is equally difficult to see how the Court is likely to achieve a settled resolution of these debates about race and equality anytime soon.

Adarand Constructors, Inc. v. Peña

515 U.S. 200 (1995)

■ JUSTICE O'CONNOR announced the judgment of the Court and delivered an opinion with respect to Parts I, II, III-A, III-B, III-D, and IV, which is for the Court except insofar as it might be inconsistent with the views expressed in JUSTICE SCALIA'S concurrence, and an opinion with respect to Part III-C in which JUSTICE KENNEDY joins.

Petitioner Adarand Constructors, Inc., claims that the Federal Government's practice of giving general contractors on Government projects a financial incentive to hire subcontractors controlled by "socially and economically disadvantaged individuals," and in particular, the Government's use of race-based presumptions in identifying such individuals, violates the equal protection component of the Fifth Amendment's Due Process Clause. The Court of Appeals rejected Adarand's claim. We conclude, however, that courts should analyze cases of this kind under a different standard of review than the one the Court of Appeals applied. We therefore vacate the Court of Appeals' judgment and remand the case for further proceedings.

I

In 1989, the Central Federal Lands Highway Division (CFLHD), which is part of the United States Department of Transportation (DOT), awarded the prime contract for a highway construction project in Colorado to Mountain Gravel & Construction Company. Mountain Gravel then solicited bids from subcontractors for the guardrail portion of the contract. Adarand, a Colorado-based highway construction company specializing in guardrail work, submitted the low bid. Gonzales Construction Company also submitted a bid.

The prime contract's terms provide that Mountain Gravel would receive additional compensation if it hired subcontractors certified as small businesses controlled by "socially and economically disadvantaged individuals." Gonzales is certified as such a business; Adarand is not. Mountain Gravel awarded the subcontract to Gonzales, despite Adarand's low bid, and Mountain Gravel's Chief Estimator has submitted an affidavit stating that Mountain Gravel would have accepted Adarand's bid, had it not been for the additional payment it received by hiring Gonzales instead. Federal law requires that a subcontracting clause similar to the one used here must appear in most federal agency contracts, and it also requires the clause to state that "[t]he contractor shall presume that socially and economically disadvantaged individuals include Black Americans, Hispanic Americans, Native Americans, Asian Pacific Americans, and other minorities, or any other individual found to be disadvantaged by the [Small Business] Administration pursuant to section 8(a) of the Small Business Act." 15 U.S.C. §§ 637(d)(2), (3). Adarand claims that the presumption set forth in that statute discriminates on the basis of race in violation of the Federal Government's Fifth Amendment obligation not to deny anyone equal protection of the laws.

These fairly straightforward facts implicate a complex scheme of federal statutes and regulations, to which we now turn. The Small Business Act (Act), 72 Stat. 384, as amended, 15 U.S.C. § 631 *et seq.*, declares it to be "the policy of the United States that small business concerns, [and] small business concerns owned and controlled by socially and economically disadvantaged individuals, . . . shall have the maximum practicable opportunity to participate in the performance of contracts let by any Federal agency." § 8(d)(1), 15 U.S.C. § 637(d)(1). The Act defines "socially disadvantaged individuals" as "those who have been subjected to racial or ethnic prejudice or cultural bias because of their identity as a member of a group without regard to their individual qualities," § 8(a)(5), 15 U.S.C. § 637(a)(5), and it defines "economically disadvantaged individuals" as "those socially disadvantaged individuals whose ability to compete in the free enterprise system has been impaired due to diminished capital and credit opportunities as compared to others in the same business area who are not socially disadvantaged." § 8(a)(6)(A), 15 U.S.C. § 637(a)(6)(A). . . .

The Small Business Administration (SBA) has implemented these statutory directives in a variety of ways, two of which are relevant here. One is the "8(a) program," which is available to small businesses controlled by socially and economically disadvantaged individuals as the SBA has defined those terms. The 8(a) program confers a wide range of benefits on participating businesses . . . one of which is automatic eligibility for subcontractor compensation provisions of the kind at issue in this case. . . . The other SBA program relevant to this case is the "8(d) subcontracting program," which unlike the 8(a) program is limited to eligibility for subcontracting provisions like the one at issue here. . . . [I]n both the 8(a) and the 8(d) programs, the presumptions of disadvantage are rebuttable if a third party comes forward with evidence suggesting that the participant is not, in fact, either economically or socially disadvantaged. 13 CFR §§ 124.111(c)–(d), 124.601–124.609 (1994). . . .

The operative clause in the contract in this case reads as follows:

Subcontracting. This subsection is supplemented to include a Disadvantaged Business Enterprise (DBE) Development and Subcontracting Provision as follows:

Monetary compensation is offered for awarding subcontracts to small business concerns owned and controlled by socially and economically disadvantaged individuals. . . .

The Contractor will be paid an amount computed as follows:

1. If a subcontract is awarded to one DBE, 10 percent of the final amount of the approved DBE subcontract, not to exceed 1.5 percent of the original contract amount.

2. If subcontracts are awarded to two or more DBEs, 10 percent of the final amount of the approved DBE subcontracts, not to exceed 2 percent of the original contract amount.

To benefit from this clause, Mountain Gravel had to hire a subcontractor who had been certified as a small disadvantaged business by the SBA, a state highway agency, or some other certifying authority acceptable to the contracting officer. . . .

After losing the guardrail subcontract to Gonzales, Adarand filed suit against various federal officials in the United States District Court for the District of Colorado, claiming that the race-based presumptions involved in the use of subcontracting compensation clauses violate Adarand's right to equal protection. The District Court granted the Government's motion for summary judgment. It understood our decision in *Fullilove v. Klutznick,* 448 U.S. 448 (1980), to have adopted "a lenient standard, resembling intermediate scrutiny, in assessing" the constitutionality of federal race-based action. Applying that "lenient standard," as further developed in *Metro Broadcasting, Inc. v. FCC,* 497 U.S. 547 (1990), the Court of Appeals upheld the use of subcontractor compensation clauses. . . .

III

Respondents urge that "[t]he Subcontracting Compensation Clause program is . . . a program based on *disadvantage,* not on race," and thus that it is subject only to "the most relaxed judicial scrutiny." To the extent that the statutes and regulations involved in this case are race neutral, we agree. Respondents concede, however, that "the race-based rebuttable presumption used in some certification determinations under the Subcontracting Compensation Clause" is subject to some heightened level of scrutiny. The parties disagree as to what that level should be. . . .

Adarand's claim arises under the Fifth Amendment to the Constitution, which provides that "No person shall . . . be deprived of life, liberty, or property, without due process of law." Although this Court has always understood that Clause to provide some measure of protection against *arbitrary* treatment by the Federal Government, it is not as explicit a guarantee of *equal* treatment as the Fourteenth Amendment, which provides that "No *State* shall . . . deny to any person within its jurisdiction the equal protection of the laws" (emphasis added). Our cases have accorded varying degrees of significance to the difference in the language of those two Clauses. We think it necessary to revisit the issue here.

A

Through the 1940's, this Court had routinely taken the view in non-race-related cases that, "[u]nlike the Fourteenth Amendment, the Fifth contains no equal protection clause and it provides no guaranty against discriminatory legislation by Congress." *Detroit Bank v. United States,* 317 U.S. 329, 337 (1943). . . . In *Bolling v. Sharpe,* 347 U.S. 497 (1954), the Court for the first time explicitly questioned the existence of any difference between the obligations of the Federal Government and the States to avoid racial classifications. . . . *Bolling*'s facts concerned school desegregation, but its reasoning was not so limited. The Court's observations that "[d]istinctions between citizens solely because of their ancestry are by their very nature odious," *Hirabayashi v. United States,* 320 U.S. 320, 100 (1943), and that "all legal restrictions which curtail the civil rights of a single racial group are immediately suspect," *Korematsu v. United States,* 323 U.S. 214, 216 (1944), carry no less force in the context of federal action than in the context of action by the States—indeed, they first appeared in cases concerning action by the Federal Government. *Bolling* relied on those observations and reiterated " 'that the Constitution of the United States, in its present form, forbids, so far as civil and political rights are concerned, discrimination *by the General Government, or by the States,* against any citizen because of his race.' "

. . .

Later cases in contexts other than school desegregation did not distinguish between the duties of the States and the Federal Government to avoid racial classifications. . . . [O]ne commentator observed that "[i]n case after case, fifth amendment equal protection problems are discussed on the assumption that fourteenth amendment precedents are controlling." Karst, The Fifth Amendment's Guarantee of Equal Protection, 55 N.C.L.Rev. 541, 554 (1977). . . . We do not understand a few contrary suggestions appearing in cases in which we found special deference to the political branches of the Federal Government to be appropriate, *e.g., Hampton v. Mow Sun Wong,* 426 U.S. 88, 100, 101–102 n. 21 (1976) (federal power over immigration), to detract from this general rule.

B

Most of the cases discussed above involved classifications burdening groups that have suffered discrimination in our society. In 1978, the Court confronted the question whether race-based governmental action designed to *benefit* such groups should also be subject to "the most rigid scrutiny." *Regents of Univ. of Cal. v. Bakke,* 438 U.S. 265, involved an equal protection challenge to a state-run medical school's practice of reserving a number of spaces in its entering class for minority students. The petitioners argued that "strict scrutiny" should apply only to "classifications that disadvantage 'discrete and insular minorities.' " *Bakke* did not produce an opinion for the Court, but Justice Powell's opinion announcing the Court's judgment rejected the argument. In a passage joined by Justice White, Justice Powell wrote that "[t]he guarantee of equal protection cannot mean one thing when applied to one individual and something else when applied to a person of another color." He concluded that "[r]acial and ethnic distinctions of any sort are inherently suspect and thus call for the most exacting judicial examination." On the other hand, four Justices in *Bakke* would have applied a less stringent standard of review to racial classifications "designed to further remedial purposes," see *id.,* at 359 (Brennan, White, Marshall, and Blackmun, JJ., concurring in judgment in part and dissenting in part). And four Justices thought the case should be decided on statutory grounds. *Id.,* at 411–412, 421 (STEVENS, J., joined by Burger, C.J., and Stewart and REHNQUIST, JJ., concurring in judgment in part and dissenting in part).

Two years after Bakke, the Court faced another challenge to remedial race-based action, this time involving action undertaken by the Federal Government. In *Fullilove v. Klutznick*, 448 U.S. 448 (1980), the Court upheld Congress' inclusion of a 10% set-aside for minority-owned businesses in the Public Works Employment Act of 1977. As in *Bakke*, there was no opinion for the Court. Chief Justice Burger, in an opinion joined by Justices White and Powell, observed that "[a]ny preference based on racial or ethnic criteria must necessarily receive a most searching examination to make sure that it does not conflict with constitutional guarantees." . . . It then upheld the program under that test . . . . Justice Powell wrote separately to express his view that the plurality opinion had essentially applied "strict scrutiny" as described in his *Bakke* opinion—i.e., it had determined that the set-aside was "a necessary means of advancing a compelling governmental interest"—and had done so correctly. Justice Stewart (joined by then-Justice REHNQUIST) dissented, arguing that the Constitution required the Federal Government to meet the same strict standard as the States when enacting racial classifications, and that the program before the Court failed that standard. Justice STEVENS also dissented, arguing that "[r]acial classifications are simply too pernicious to permit any but the most exact connection between justification and classification," and that the program before the Court could not be characterized "as a 'narrowly tailored' remedial measure." Justice Marshall (joined by Justices Brennan and Blackmun) concurred in the judgment, reiterating . . . that any race-based governmental action designed to "remed[y] the present effects of past racial discrimination" should be upheld if it was "substantially related" to the achievement of an "important governmental objective"—i.e., such action should be subjected only to what we now call "intermediate scrutiny."

In *Wygant v. Jackson Bd. of Ed.*, 476 U.S. 267 (1986), the Court considered a Fourteenth Amendment challenge to another form of remedial racial classification. The issue in *Wygant* was whether a school board could adopt race-based preferences in determining which teachers to lay off. Justice Powell's plurality opinion observed that "the level of scrutiny does not change merely because the challenged classification operates against a group that historically has not been subject to governmental discrimination," and stated the two-part inquiry as "whether the layoff provision is supported by a compelling state purpose and whether the means chosen to accomplish that purpose are narrowly tailored." In other words, "racial classifications of any sort must be subjected to 'strict scrutiny.'" *Id.*, at 285 (O'CONNOR, J., concurring in part and concurring in judgment). The plurality then concluded that the school board's interest in "providing minority role models for its minority students, as an attempt to alleviate the effects of societal discrimination" was not a compelling interest that could justify the use of a racial classification. It added that "[s]ocietal discrimination, without more, is too amorphous a basis for imposing a racially classified remedy" and insisted instead that "a public employer . . . must ensure that, before it embarks on an affirmative-action program, it has convincing evidence that remedial action is warranted. That is, it must have sufficient evidence to justify the conclusion that there has been prior discrimination." Justice White concurred only in the judgment, although he agreed that the school board's asserted interests could not, "singly or together, justify this racially discriminatory layoff policy." Four Justices dissented, three of whom again argued for intermediate scrutiny of remedial race-based government action. *Id.*, at 301–302 (Marshall, J., joined by Brennan and Blackmun, JJ., dissenting).

The Court's failure to produce a majority opinion in *Bakke, Fullilove,* and *Wygant* left unresolved the proper analysis for remedial race-based governmental action. The Court resolved the issue, at least in part, in 1989. *Richmond v. J.A. Croson Co.*, 488 U.S. 469 (1989), concerned a city's determination that 30% of its contracting work should go to minority-owned businesses. A majority of the Court in *Croson* held that "the standard of review under the Equal Protection Clause is not dependent on the race of those burdened or benefited by a particular classification," and that the single standard of review for racial classifications should be "strict scrutiny." Id., at 493–494 (opinion of O'CONNOR, J., joined by REHNQUIST, C.J., and White and KENNEDY, JJ.); id., at 520 (SCALIA, J., concurring in judgment). As to the classification before the Court, the plurality agreed that "a state or local subdivision . . . has the authority to eradicate the effects of private discrimination within its own legislative jurisdiction," but the Court thought that the city had not acted with "a 'strong basis in evidence for its conclusion that remedial action was necessary.'" The Court also thought it "obvious that [the] program is not narrowly tailored to remedy the effects of prior discrimination."

With *Croson*, the Court finally agreed that the Fourteenth Amendment requires strict scrutiny of all race-based action by state and local governments. But *Croson* of course had no occasion to declare what standard of review the Fifth Amendment requires for such action taken by the Federal Government. . . . Despite lingering uncertainty in the details, however, the Court's cases through *Croson* had established three general propositions with respect to governmental racial classifications. First, skepticism: "'Any preference based on racial or ethnic criteria must necessarily receive a most searching examination,'" *Wygant*, 476

U.S., at 273 (plurality opinion of Powell, J.). Second, consistency: "[T]he standard of review under the Equal Protection Clause is not dependent on the race of those burdened or benefited by a particular classification," *Croson*, 488 U.S., at 494 (plurality opinion), i.e., all racial classifications reviewable under the Equal Protection Clause must be strictly scrutinized. And third, congruence: "Equal protection analysis in the Fifth Amendment area is the same as that under the Fourteenth Amendment," *Buckley v. Valeo*, 424 U.S. 1, 93 (1976). Taken together, these three propositions lead to the conclusion that any person, of whatever race, has the right to demand that any governmental actor subject to the Constitution justify any racial classification subjecting that person to unequal treatment under the strictest judicial scrutiny. . . .

A year later, however, the Court took a surprising turn. *Metro Broadcasting, Inc. v. FCC*, 497 U.S. 547 (1990), involved a Fifth Amendment challenge to two race-based policies of the Federal Communications Commission (FCC). In *Metro Broadcasting,* the Court repudiated the long-held notion that "it would be unthinkable that the same Constitution would impose a lesser duty on the Federal Government" than it does on a State to afford equal protection of the laws, *Bolling, supra,* at 500. It did so by holding that "benign" federal racial classifications need only satisfy intermediate scrutiny, even though *Croson* had recently concluded that such classifications enacted by a State must satisfy strict scrutiny. "[B]enign" federal racial classifications, the Court said, "—even if those measures are not 'remedial' in the sense of being designed to compensate victims of past governmental or societal discrimination—are constitutionally permissible to the extent that they serve *important* governmental objectives within the power of Congress and are *substantially related* to achievement of those objectives." The Court did not explain how to tell whether a racial classification should be deemed "benign," other than to express "confiden[ce] that an 'examination of the legislative scheme and its history' will separate benign measures from other types of racial classifications."

Applying this test, the Court first noted that the FCC policies at issue did not serve as a remedy for past discrimination. Proceeding on the assumption that the policies were nonetheless "benign," it concluded that they served the "important governmental objective" of "enhancing broadcast diversity," and that they were "substantially related" to that objective. It therefore upheld the policies.

By adopting intermediate scrutiny as the standard of review for congressionally mandated "benign" racial classifications, *Metro Broadcasting* departed from prior cases in two significant respects. First, it turned its back on *Croson*'s explanation of why strict scrutiny of all governmental racial classifications is essential:

> Absent searching judicial inquiry into the justification for such race-based measures, there is simply no way of determining

> what classifications are 'benign' or 'remedial' and what
> classifications are in fact motivated by illegitimate notions of
> racial inferiority or simple racial politics. Indeed, the purpose of
> strict scrutiny is to 'smoke out' illegitimate uses of race by
> assuring that the legislative body is pursuing a goal important
> enough to warrant use of a highly suspect tool. The test also
> ensures that the means chosen 'fit' this compelling goal so
> closely that there is little or no possibility that the motive for
> the classification was illegitimate racial prejudice or stereotype.
>
> *Croson, supra,* at 493 (plurality opinion of O'CONNOR, J.).

We adhere to that view today, despite the surface appeal of holding
"benign" racial classifications to a lower standard, because "it may not
always be clear that a so-called preference is in fact benign," *Bakke,
supra,* at 298 (opinion of Powell, J.). . . .

Second, *Metro Broadcasting* squarely rejected one of the three
propositions established by the Court's earlier equal protection cases,
namely, congruence between the standards applicable to federal and
state racial classifications, and in so doing also undermined the other
two—skepticism of all racial classifications and consistency of treatment
irrespective of the race of the burdened or benefited group. Under *Metro
Broadcasting,* certain racial classifications ("benign" ones enacted by the
Federal Government) should be treated less skeptically than others; and
the race of the benefited group is critical to the determination of which
standard of review to apply. *Metro Broadcasting* was thus a significant
departure from much of what had come before it.

The three propositions undermined by Metro Broadcasting all derive
from the basic principle that the Fifth and Fourteenth Amendments to
the Constitution protect *persons,* not *groups.* It follows from that
principle that all governmental action based on race—a *group*
classification long recognized as "in most circumstances irrelevant and
therefore prohibited," *Hirabayashi,* 320 U.S., at 100—should be
subjected to detailed judicial inquiry to ensure that the *personal* right to
equal protection of the laws has not been infringed. These ideas have long
been central to this Court's understanding of equal protection, and
holding "benign" state and federal racial classifications to different
standards does not square with them. "[A] free people whose institutions
are founded upon the doctrine of equality," *ibid.,* should tolerate no
retreat from the principle that government may treat people differently
because of their race only for the most compelling reasons. Accordingly,
we hold today that all racial classifications, imposed by whatever federal,
state, or local governmental actor, must be analyzed by a reviewing court
under strict scrutiny. In other words, such classifications are
constitutional only if they are narrowly tailored measures that further
compelling governmental interests. To the extent that *Metro
Broadcasting* is inconsistent with that holding, it is overruled. . . .

C

"Although adherence to precedent is not rigidly required in constitutional cases, any departure from the doctrine of *stare decisis* demands special justification." *Arizona v. Rumsey,* 467 U.S. 203, 212 (1984). . . . *Metro Broadcasting* undermined important principles of this Court's equal protection jurisprudence, established in a line of cases stretching back over 50 years. Those principles together stood for an "embracing" and "intrinsically soun[d]" understanding of equal protection "verified by experience," namely, that the Constitution imposes upon federal, state, and local governmental actors the same obligation to respect the personal right to equal protection of the laws. . . . We cannot adhere to our most recent decision without colliding with an accepted and established doctrine. . . .

It is worth pointing out the difference between the applications of *stare decisis* in this case and in *Planned Parenthood of Southeastern Pa. v. Casey,* 505 U.S. 833 (1992). *Casey* explained how considerations of *stare decisis* inform the decision whether to overrule a long-established precedent that has become integrated into the fabric of the law. Overruling precedent of that kind naturally may have consequences for "the ideal of the rule of law." In addition, such precedent is likely to have engendered substantial reliance, as was true in *Casey* itself. But in this case, as we have explained, we do not face a precedent of that kind, because *Metro Broadcasting* itself *departed* from our prior cases—and did so quite recently. By refusing to follow *Metro Broadcasting,* then, we do not depart from the fabric of the law; we restore it. We also note that reliance on a case that has recently departed from precedent is likely to be minimal, particularly where, as here, the rule set forth in that case is unlikely to affect primary conduct in any event. . . .

"The real problem," Justice Frankfurter explained, "is whether a principle shall prevail over its later misapplications." *Helvering v. Hallock,* 309 U.S 106, 122 (1940). *Metro Broadcasting's* untenable distinction between state and federal racial classifications lacks support in our precedent, and undermines the fundamental principle of equal protection as a personal right. In this case, as between that principle and "its later misapplications," the principle must prevail.

D

. . . Some have questioned the importance of debating the proper standard of review of race-based legislation. But we agree with Justice STEVENS that, "[b]ecause racial characteristics so seldom provide a relevant basis for disparate treatment, and because classifications based on race are potentially so harmful to the entire body politic, it is especially important that the reasons for any such classification be clearly identified and unquestionably legitimate," and that "[r]acial classifications are simply too pernicious to permit any but the most exact connection between justification and classification." *Fullilove, supra,* at 533–535, 537 (dissenting opinion). We think that requiring strict scrutiny is the best way to ensure that courts will consistently give racial classifications that kind of detailed examination, both as to ends and as to means. *Korematsu* demonstrates vividly that even "the most rigid scrutiny" can sometimes fail to detect an illegitimate racial classification. Any retreat from the most searching judicial inquiry can only increase the risk of another such error occurring in the future.

Finally, we wish to dispel the notion that strict scrutiny is "strict in theory, but fatal in fact." *Fullilove, supra,* at 519 (Marshall, J., concurring in judgment). The unhappy persistence of both the practice and the lingering effects of racial discrimination against minority groups in this country is an unfortunate reality, and government is not disqualified from acting in response to it. As recently as 1987, for example, every Justice of this Court agreed that the Alabama Department of Public Safety's "pervasive, systematic, and obstinate discriminatory conduct" justified a narrowly tailored race-based remedy. See *United States v. Paradise,* 480 U.S. 149 (1987). When race-based action is necessary to further a compelling interest, such action is within constitutional constraints if it satisfies the "narrow tailoring" test this Court has set out in previous cases.

IV

Because our decision today alters the playing field in some important respects, we think it best to remand the case to the lower courts for further consideration in light of the principles we have announced.... Accordingly, the judgment of the Court of Appeals is vacated, and the case is remanded for further proceedings consistent with this opinion.

It is so ordered.

■ **JUSTICE SCALIA, concurring in part and concurring in the judgment.**

I join the opinion of the Court, except Part III-C, and except insofar as it may be inconsistent with the following: In my view, government can never have a "compelling interest" in discriminating on the basis of race in order to "make up" for past racial discrimination in the opposite direction. Individuals who have been wronged by unlawful racial discrimination should be made whole; but under our Constitution there can be no such thing as either a creditor or a debtor race. That concept is alien to the Constitution's focus upon the individual, see Amdt. 14, § 1 ("[N]or shall any State . . . deny *to any person*" the equal protection of the laws) (emphasis added), and its rejection of dispositions based on race, see Amdt. 15, § 1 (prohibiting abridgment of the right to vote "on account of race"), or based on blood, see Art. III, § 3 ("[N]o Attainder of Treason shall work Corruption of Blood"); Art. I, § 9, cl. 8 ("No Title of Nobility shall be granted by the United States"). To pursue the concept of racial entitlement—even for the most admirable and benign of purposes—is to reinforce and preserve for future mischief the way of thinking that produced race slavery, race privilege and race hatred. In the eyes of government, we are just one race here. It is American.

It is unlikely, if not impossible, that the challenged program would survive under this understanding of strict scrutiny, but I am content to leave that to be decided on remand.

■ **JUSTICE THOMAS, concurring in part and concurring in the judgment.**

I agree with the majority's conclusion that strict scrutiny applies to *all* government classifications based on race. I write separately, however, to express my disagreement with the premise underlying Justice STEVENS' and Justice GINSBURG's dissents: that there is a racial paternalism exception to the principle of equal protection. I believe that there is a "moral [and] constitutional equivalence" between laws designed to subjugate a race and those that distribute benefits on the basis of race in order to foster some current notion of equality. Government cannot make us equal; it can only recognize, respect, and protect us as equal before the law.

That these programs may have been motivated, in part, by good intentions cannot provide refuge from the principle that under our Constitution, the government may not make distinctions on the basis of race. As far as the Constitution is concerned, it is irrelevant whether a government's racial classifications are drawn by those who wish to oppress a race or by those who have a sincere desire to help those thought to be disadvantaged. There can be no doubt that the paternalism that appears to lie at the heart of this program is at war with the principle of inherent equality that underlies and infuses our Constitution.

These programs not only raise grave constitutional questions, they also undermine the moral basis of the equal protection principle. Purchased at the price of immeasurable human suffering, the equal protection principle reflects our Nation's understanding that such classifications ultimately have a destructive impact on the individual and our society. Unquestionably, "[i]nvidious [racial] discrimination is an engine of oppression," *post* (STEVENS, J., dissenting). It is also true that "[r]emedial" racial preferences may reflect "a desire to foster equality in society," *ibid.* But there can be no doubt that racial paternalism and its unintended consequences can be as poisonous and pernicious as any other form of discrimination. So-called "benign" discrimination teaches many that because of chronic and apparently immutable handicaps, minorities cannot compete with them without their patronizing indulgence. Inevitably, such programs engender attitudes of superiority or, alternatively, provoke resentment among those who believe that they have been wronged by the government's use of race. These programs stamp minorities with a badge of inferiority and may cause them to develop dependencies or to adopt an attitude that they are "entitled" to preferences. . . .

In my mind, government-sponsored racial discrimination based on benign prejudice is just as noxious as discrimination inspired by malicious prejudice.* In each instance, it is racial discrimination, plain and simple.

■ **JUSTICE STEVENS, with whom JUSTICE GINSBURG joins, dissenting.**

I

The Court's concept of skepticism is, at least in principle, a good statement of law and of common sense. Undoubtedly, a court should be wary of a governmental decision that relies upon a racial classification. . . . But . . . substantial agreement on the standard to be applied in deciding difficult cases does not necessarily lead to agreement on how those cases actually should or will be resolved. . . .

II

The Court's concept of "consistency" assumes that there is no significant difference between a decision by the majority to impose a special burden on the members of a minority race and a decision by the majority to provide a benefit to certain members of that minority notwithstanding its incidental burden on some members of the majority. In my opinion that assumption is untenable. There is no moral or constitutional equivalence between a policy that is designed to perpetuate a caste system and one that seeks to eradicate racial subordination. Invidious discrimination is an engine of oppression, subjugating a disfavored group to enhance or maintain the power of the majority. Remedial race-based preferences reflect the opposite impulse: a desire to foster equality in society. No sensible conception of the Government's constitutional obligation to govern impartially should ignore this distinction.[1] . . .

The consistency that the Court espouses would disregard the difference between a "No Trespassing" sign and a welcome mat. It would treat a Dixiecrat Senator's decision to vote against Thurgood Marshall's confirmation in order to keep African-Americans off the Supreme Court as on a par with President Johnson's evaluation of his nominee's race as a positive factor. It would equate a law that made black citizens ineligible

---

*   It should be obvious that every racial classification helps, in a narrow sense, some races and hurts others. As to the races benefited, the classification could surely be called "benign." Accordingly, whether a law relying upon racial taxonomy is "benign" or "malign" either turns on "whose ox is gored," or on distinctions found only in the eye of the beholder.

[1]   [T]he majority's "flexible" approach to "strict scrutiny" may well take into account differences between benign and invidious programs. . . . Even if this is so, however, I think it is unfortunate that the majority insists on applying the label "strict scrutiny" to benign race-based programs. That label has usually been understood to spell the death of any governmental action to which a court may apply it. The Court suggests today that "strict scrutiny" means something different—something less strict—when applied to benign racial classifications. Although I agree that benign programs deserve different treatment than invidious programs, there is a danger that the fatal language of "strict scrutiny" will skew the analysis and place well-crafted benign programs at unnecessary risk.

for military service with a program aimed at recruiting black soldiers. An attempt by the majority to exclude members of a minority race from a regulated market is fundamentally different from a subsidy that enables a relatively small group of newcomers to enter that market. An interest in "consistency" does not justify treating differences as though they were similarities.

The Court's explanation for treating dissimilar race-based decisions as though they were equally objectionable is a supposed inability to differentiate between "invidious" and "benign" discrimination. But the term "affirmative action" is common and well understood. Its presence in everyday parlance shows that people understand the difference between good intentions and bad. As with any legal concept, some cases may be difficult to classify,[4] but our equal protection jurisprudence has identified a critical difference between state action that imposes burdens on a disfavored few and state action that benefits the few "in spite of" its adverse effects on the many.

Indeed, our jurisprudence has made the standard to be applied in cases of invidious discrimination turn on whether the discrimination is "intentional," or whether, by contrast, it merely has a discriminatory "effect." *Washington v. Davis,* 426 U.S. 229 (1976). Surely this distinction is at least as subtle, and at least as difficult to apply as the usually obvious distinction between a measure intended to benefit members of a particular minority race and a measure intended to burden a minority race. . . .

Nothing is inherently wrong with applying a single standard to fundamentally different situations, as long as that standard takes relevant differences into account. For example, if the Court in all equal protection cases were to insist that differential treatment be justified by relevant characteristics of the members of the favored and disfavored classes that provide a legitimate basis for disparate treatment, such a standard would treat dissimilar cases differently while still recognizing that there is, after all, only one Equal Protection Clause. See *Cleburne v. Cleburne Living Center, Inc.,* 473 U.S. 432, 451–455 (1985) (STEVENS, J., concurring); *San Antonio Independent School Dist. v. Rodriguez,* 411 U.S. 1, 98–110 (1973) (Marshall, J., dissenting). Under such a standard, subsidies for disadvantaged businesses may be constitutional though special taxes on such businesses would be invalid. But a single standard that purports to equate remedial preferences with invidious discrimination cannot be defended in the name of "equal protection."

Moreover, the Court may find that its new "consistency" approach to race-based classifications is difficult to square with its insistence upon rigidly separate categories for discrimination against different classes of

---

[4]   For example, in *Richmond v. J.A. Croson Co.,* 488 U.S. 469 (1989), a majority of the members of the city council that enacted the race-based set-aside were of the same race as its beneficiaries.

individuals. For example, as the law currently stands, the Court will apply "intermediate scrutiny" to cases of invidious gender discrimination and "strict scrutiny" to cases of invidious race discrimination, while applying the same standard for benign classifications as for invidious ones. If this remains the law, then today's lecture about "consistency" will produce the anomalous result that the Government can more easily enact affirmative-action programs to remedy discrimination against women than it can enact affirmative-action programs to remedy discrimination against African-Americans—even though the primary purpose of the Equal Protection Clause was to end discrimination against the former slaves. See *Associated General Contractors of Cal., Inc. v. San Francisco*, 813 F.2d 922 (CA9 1987) (striking down racial preference under strict scrutiny while upholding gender preference under intermediate scrutiny). When a court becomes preoccupied with abstract standards, it risks sacrificing common sense at the altar of formal consistency.

As a matter of constitutional and democratic principle, a decision by representatives of the majority to discriminate against the members of a minority race is fundamentally different from those same representatives' decision to impose incidental costs on the majority of their constituents in order to provide a benefit to a disadvantaged minority.[5] Indeed . . . the former is virtually always repugnant to the principles of a free and democratic society, whereas the latter is, in some circumstances, entirely consistent with the ideal of equality. . . .

III

The Court's concept of "congruence" assumes that there is no significant difference between a decision by the Congress of the United States to adopt an affirmative-action program and such a decision by a State or a municipality. In my opinion that assumption is untenable. It

---

[5]   In his concurrence, Justice THOMAS argues that the most significant cost associated with an affirmative-action program is its adverse stigmatic effect on its intended beneficiaries. Although I agree that this cost may be more significant than many people realize, I do not think it applies to the facts of this case. First, this is not an argument that petitioner Adarand, a white-owned business, has standing to advance. No beneficiaries of the specific program under attack today have challenged its constitutionality—perhaps because they do not find the preferences stigmatizing, or perhaps because their ability to opt out of the program provides them all the relief they would need. Second, even if the petitioner in this case were a minority-owned business challenging the stigmatizing effect of this program, I would not find Justice THOMAS' extreme proposition—that there is a moral and constitutional equivalence between an attempt to subjugate and an attempt to redress the effects of a caste system—at all persuasive. It is one thing to question the wisdom of affirmative-action programs: There are many responsible arguments against them, including the one based upon stigma that Congress might find persuasive when it decides whether to enact or retain race-based preferences. It is another thing altogether to equate the many well-meaning and intelligent lawmakers and their constituents—whether members of majority or minority races—who have supported affirmative action over the years, to segregationists and bigots.

Finally, although Justice THOMAS is more concerned about the potential effects of these programs than the intent of those who enacted them (a proposition at odds with this Court's jurisprudence, see *Washington v. Davis,* 426 U.S. 229 (1976), but not without a strong element of common sense, I am not persuaded that the psychological damage brought on by affirmative action is as severe as that engendered by racial subordination. That, in any event, is a judgment the political branches can be trusted to make. . . .

ignores important practical and legal differences between federal and state or local decisionmakers.

These differences have been identified repeatedly and consistently both in opinions of the Court and in separate opinions authored by Members of today's majority. Thus, in *Metro Broadcasting, Inc. v. FCC*, 497 U.S. 547 (1990), in which we upheld a federal program designed to foster racial diversity in broadcasting, we identified the special "institutional competence" of our National Legislature. "It is of overriding significance in these cases," we were careful to emphasize, "that the FCC's minority ownership programs have been specifically approved— indeed, mandated—by Congress." We recalled the several opinions in *Fullilove* that admonished this Court to " 'approach our task with appropriate deference to the Congress, a co-equal branch charged by the Constitution with the power to "provide for the . . . general Welfare of the United States" and "to enforce, by appropriate legislation," the equal protection guarantees of the Fourteenth Amendment.' 448 U.S., at 472. . . .

In his separate opinion in *Richmond v. J.A. Croson Co.,* 488 U.S. 469, 520–524 (1989), Justice SCALIA discussed the basis for this distinction [between federal and state programs]. He observed that "it is one thing to permit racially based conduct by the Federal Government—whose legislative powers concerning matters of race were explicitly enhanced by the Fourteenth Amendment, see U.S. Const., Amdt. 14, § 5—and quite another to permit it by the precise entities against whose conduct in matters of race that Amendment was specifically directed, see Amdt. 14, § 1." Continuing, Justice SCALIA explained why a "sound distinction between federal and state (or local) action based on race rests not only upon the substance of the Civil War Amendments, but upon social reality and governmental theory."

> What the record shows, in other words, is that racial discrimination against any group finds a more ready expression at the state and local than at the federal level. To the children of the Founding Fathers, this should come as no surprise. An acute awareness of the heightened danger of oppression from political factions in small, rather than large, political units dates to the very beginning of our national history. As James Madison observed in support of the proposed Constitution's enhancement of national powers:

> 'The smaller the society, the fewer probably will be the distinct parties and interests composing it; the fewer the distinct parties and interests, the more frequently will a majority be found of the same party; and the smaller the number of individuals composing a majority, and the smaller the compass within which they are placed, the more easily will they concert and execute their plan of oppression. Extend the sphere and you take in a greater variety of parties and interests; you make it

less probable that a majority of the whole will have a common motive to invade the rights of other citizens; or if such a common motive exists, it will be more difficult for all who feel it to discover their own strength and to act in unison with each other.' The Federalist No. 10, pp. 82–84 (C. Rossiter ed. 1961).

In her plurality opinion in *Croson*, Justice O'CONNOR also emphasized the importance of this distinction when she responded to the city's argument that *Fullilove* was controlling. . . .

Presumably, the majority is now satisfied that its theory of "congruence" between the substantive rights provided by the Fifth and Fourteenth Amendments disposes of the objection based upon divided constitutional powers. But it is one thing to say (as no one seems to dispute) that the Fifth Amendment encompasses a general guarantee of equal protection as broad as that contained within the Fourteenth Amendment. It is another thing entirely to say that Congress' institutional competence and constitutional authority entitles it to no greater deference when it enacts a program designed to foster equality than the deference due a state legislature. . . .

The Fourteenth Amendment directly empowers Congress at the same time it expressly limits the States. This is no accident. It represents our Nation's consensus, achieved after hard experience throughout our sorry history of race relations, that the Federal Government must be the primary defender of racial minorities against the States, some of which may be inclined to oppress such minorities. A rule of "congruence" that ignores a purposeful "incongruity" so fundamental to our system of government is unacceptable.

In my judgment, the Court's novel doctrine of "congruence" is seriously misguided. Congressional deliberations about a matter as important as affirmative action should be accorded far greater deference than those of a State or municipality. . . .

■ **JUSTICE GINSBURG, with whom JUSTICE BREYER joins, dissenting.**

. . . I write separately to underscore not the differences the several opinions in this case display, but the considerable field of agreement— the common understandings and concerns—revealed in opinions that together speak for a majority of the Court.

I

. . . The divisions in this difficult case should not obscure the Court's recognition of the persistence of racial inequality and a majority's acknowledgment of Congress' authority to act affirmatively, not only to end discrimination, but also to counteract discrimination's lingering effects. Those effects, reflective of a system of racial caste only recently ended, are evident in our workplaces, markets, and neighborhoods. Job applicants with identical resumés, qualifications, and interview styles still experience different receptions, depending on their race.[3] White and African-American consumers still encounter different deals.[4] People of color looking for housing still face discriminatory treatment by landlords, real estate agents, and mortgage lenders.[5] Minority entrepreneurs sometimes fail to gain contracts though they are the low bidders, and they are sometimes refused work even after winning contracts.[6] Bias both conscious and unconscious, reflecting traditional and unexamined habits of thought, keeps up barriers that must come down if equal opportunity and nondiscrimination are ever genuinely to become this country's law and practice.

Given this history and its practical consequences, Congress surely can conclude that a carefully designed affirmative action program may help to realize, finally, the "equal protection of the laws" the Fourteenth Amendment has promised since 1868.[8]

II

The lead opinion uses one term, "strict scrutiny," to describe the standard of judicial review for all governmental classifications by race. But that opinion's elaboration strongly suggests that the strict standard

---

[3]   See, e.g., H. Cross, G. Kennedy, J. Mell, & W. Zimmermann, Employer Hiring Practices: Differential Treatment of Hispanic and Anglo Job Seekers 42 (Urban Institute Report 90–4, 1990) (e.g., Anglo applicants sent out by investigators received 52% more job offers than matched Hispanics); M. Turner, M. Fix, & R. Struyk, Opportunities Denied, Opportunities Diminished: Racial Discrimination in Hiring xi (Urban Institute Report 91–9, 1991) ("In one out of five audits, the white applicant was able to advance farther through the hiring process than his black counterpart. In one out of eight audits, the white was offered a job although his equally qualified black partner was not. In contrast, black auditors advanced farther than their white counterparts only 7 percent of the time, and received job offers while their white partners did not in 5 percent of the audits.").

[4]   See, e.g., Ayres, Fair Driving: Gender and Race Discrimination in Retail Car Negotiations, 104 HARV.L.REV. 817, 821–822, 819, 828 (1991) ("blacks and women simply cannot buy the same car for the same price as can white men using identical bargaining strategies"; the final offers given white female testers reflected 40 percent higher markups than those given white male testers; final offer markups for black male testers were twice as high, and for black female testers three times as high as for white male testers).

[5]   See, e.g., A Common Destiny: Blacks and American Society 50 (G. Jaynes & R. Williams eds. 1989) ("[I]n many metropolitan areas one-quarter to one-half of all [housing] inquiries by blacks are met by clearly discriminatory responses."); M. Turner, R. Struyk, & J. Yinger, U.S. Dept. of Housing and Urban Development, Housing Discrimination Study: Synthesis i–vii (Sept. 1991) (1989 audit study of housing searches in 25 metropolitan areas; over half of African-American and Hispanic testers seeking to rent or buy experienced some form of unfavorable treatment compared to paired white testers); Leahy, Are Racial Factors Important for the Allocation of Mortgage Money?, 44 AM.J.ECON. & SOC. 185, 193 (1985) (controlling for socioeconomic factors, and concluding that "even when neighborhoods appear to be similar on every major mortgage-lending criterion except race, mortgage-lending outcomes are still unequal").

[6]   See, e.g., Associated General Contractors v. Coalition for Economic Equity, 950 F.2d 1401, 1415 (CA9 1991) (detailing examples in San Francisco).

[8]   On the differences between laws designed to benefit a historically disfavored group and laws designed to burden such a group, see, e.g., Carter, When Victims Happen To Be Black, 97 YALE L.J. 420, 433–434 (1988) ("[W]hatever the source of racism, to count it the same as racialism, to say that two centuries of struggle for the most basic of civil rights have been mostly about freedom from racial categorization rather than freedom from racial oppression, is to trivialize the lives and deaths of those who have suffered under racism. To pretend . . . that the issue presented in Bakke was the same as the issue in Brown is to pretend that history never happened and that the present doesn't exist.").

announced is indeed "fatal" for classifications burdening groups that have suffered discrimination in our society. That seems to me, and, I believe, to the Court, the enduring lesson one should draw from *Korematsu v. United States,* 323 U.S. 214 (1944); for in that case, scrutiny the Court described as "most rigid" nonetheless yielded a pass for an odious, gravely injurious racial classification. See *ante,* at 2106 (lead opinion). A *Korematsu*-type classification, as I read the opinions in this case, will never again survive scrutiny: Such a classification, history and precedent instruct, properly ranks as prohibited.

[H]owever, the lead opinion has dispelled the notion that "strict scrutiny" is " 'fatal in fact.' " Properly, a majority of the Court calls for review that is searching, in order to ferret out classifications in reality malign, but masquerading as benign. The Court's once lax review of sex-based classifications demonstrates the need for such suspicion. See, *e.g., Hoyt v. Florida,* 368 U.S. 57, 60 (1961) (upholding women's "privilege" of automatic exemption from jury service). Today's decision thus usefully reiterates that the purpose of strict scrutiny "is precisely to distinguish legitimate from illegitimate uses of race in governmental decisionmaking," "to 'differentiate between' permissible and impermissible governmental use of race," to distinguish " 'between a "No Trespassing" sign and a welcome mat.' "

Close review also is in order for this further reason. . . . [A]s this very case shows, some members of the historically favored race can be hurt by catchup mechanisms designed to cope with the lingering effects of entrenched racial subjugation. Court review can ensure that preferences are not so large as to trammel unduly upon the opportunities of others or interfere too harshly with legitimate expectations of persons in once-preferred groups. . . .

While I would not disturb the programs challenged in this case, and would leave their improvement to the political branches, I see today's decision as one that allows our precedent to evolve, still to be informed by and responsive to changing conditions.

NOTE ON "BENIGN" AND "MALIGN" DISCRIMINATION

1.   One theme running through the cases in this section is the difficulty of drawing a clear line between instances of "malign" and "benign" discrimination. In emphasizing this difficulty, the *Adarand* majority invokes *Richmond v. J.A. Croson Co.,* 488 U.S. 469 (1989), which struck down a minority set-aside program for awarding construction contracts with the City of Richmond. Noting that "blacks constitute approximately 50% of the population of the City of Richmond," and that "[f]ive of the nine seats on the city council are held by blacks," the Court pointed out that the set-aside program benefited the more politically-powerful group within the relevant jurisdiction. On these facts, was the racial classification in *Croson* "malign" or "benign"? On the other hand, is the factual setting of *Croson* so atypical

as to make the case irrelevant to a case like *Adarand*, which involved a federal program administered across the entire United States?

The more fundamental argument that "malign" and "benign" classifications are indistinguishable stems from the belief, reflected in Justice Thomas's opinion in *Adarand*, that treating persons differently based on their race is always wrong and counterproductive. Hence, in *Croson*, Justice O'Connor objected that a more lenient standard of review for "benign" racial classifications "effectively assures that race will always be relevant in American life, and that the ultimate goal of eliminating entirely from governmental decisionmaking such irrelevant factors as a human being's race will never be achieved." This theme will reappear in the cases throughout this section. Do you find it persuasive?

2. *Adarand* overruled the Court's prior decision in *Metro Broadcasting, Inc. v. FCC*, 497 U.S. 547 (1990), which upheld a federal program promoting minority ownership of radio and television stations. Although the Court had adopted strict scrutiny for "benign" racial classifications employed by state and local governments in *Croson*, *Metro Broadcasting* nonetheless held that *federal* affirmative action programs were subject only to intermediate review. Was this distinction—which several of the justices in the *Adarand* majority had accepted in *Croson*—tenable? Was the Court wrong to overrule it in *Adarand*?

3. Why didn't the Court actually decide the validity of the set-aside program in *Adarand*? And what did the Court mean in seeking "to dispel the notion that strict scrutiny is strict in theory, but fatal in fact"? The latter question implicates an important distinction between "categorization" and "balancing" in constitutional doctrine. Professor Kathleen Sullivan explained the difference:

> Categorization is the taxonomist's style—a job of classification and labeling. When categorical formulas operate, all the important work in litigation is done at the outset. Once the relevant right and mode of infringement have been described, the outcome follows, without any explicit judicial balancing of the claimed right against the government's justification for the infringement. Balancing is more like grocer's work (or Justice's)—the judge's job is to place competing rights and interests on a scale and weigh them against each other. Here the outcome is not determined at the outset, but depends on the relative strength of a multitude of factors. These two styles have competed endlessly in contemporary constitutional law; neither has ever entirely eclipsed the other.[12]

As Sullivan explains, the tiers of scrutiny in equal protection and other areas of doctrine have represented a form of categorization:

> True, the standard formulations of these tests require a court to go through the motions of balancing a right against a legitimate or compelling interest. But this is not real balancing. If the standard

---

[12] Kathleen M. Sullivan, *Post-Liberal Judging: The Roles of Categorization and Balancing*, 63 U. COLO. L. REV. 293, 293–94 (1992).

is rationality, the government is supposed to win-and any lawyer who hires expert witnesses to dispute the empirical basis for legislation under this standard of review is wasting the client's money. If strict scrutiny is applied, the challenged law is never supposed to survive . . . . Hence Professor Gerald Gunther's pithy aphorism: "strict in theory and fatal in fact."[13]

In rejecting the notion that strict scrutiny should always be fatal, *Adarand* seems to suggest that strict scrutiny should, in fact, involve meaningful balancing; as a result, the categorization step (determining the level of scrutiny) would no longer be dispositive. The *Cleburne* case in the last section did much the same thing at the other end of the spectrum, effectively rejecting the notion that rational basis review should always come out in favor of the government.

You will see similar arguments that strict scrutiny should not always be "fatal in fact" in *Grutter* and *Parents Involved*. Irrespective of whether you think the racial classifications at issue in *Adarand* and in those later cases should be upheld, do you agree with this move away from categorization toward balancing in framing the doctrine? Does that move threaten to undermine the determinacy of the general presumption against race-based classifications? Or does it simply shift that indeterminacy from the first step (determining the level of scrutiny) to the second (applying it to the classification at issue)?

Grutter v. Bollinger

539 U.S. 306 (2003)

■ JUSTICE O'CONNOR delivered the opinion of the Court.

This case requires us to decide whether the use of race as a factor in student admissions by the University of Michigan Law School (Law School) is unlawful.

I

A

The Law School ranks among the Nation's top law schools. It receives more than 3,500 applications each year for a class of around 350 students. Seeking to "admit a group of students who individually and collectively are among the most capable," the Law School looks for individuals with "substantial promise for success in law school" and "a strong likelihood of succeeding in the practice of law and contributing in diverse ways to the well-being of others." More broadly, the Law School seeks "a mix of students with varying backgrounds and experiences who will respect and learn from each other." . . .

The hallmark of [the Law's School's admissions] policy is its focus on academic ability coupled with a flexible assessment of applicants' talents,

---

[13] *Id.* at 296 (quoting Gerald Gunther, *Foreword: In Search of Evolving Doctrine on a Changing Court: A Model for a Newer Equal Protection*, 86 HARV. L. REV. 1, 8 (1972).

experiences, and potential "to contribute to the learning of those around them." The policy requires admissions officials to evaluate each applicant based on all the information available in the file, including a personal statement, letters of recommendation, and an essay describing the ways in which the applicant will contribute to the life and diversity of the Law School. In reviewing an applicant's file, admissions officials must consider the applicant's undergraduate grade point average (GPA) and Law School Admission Test (LSAT) score because they are important (if imperfect) predictors of academic success in law school. The policy stresses that "no applicant should be admitted unless we expect that applicant to do well enough to graduate with no serious academic problems."

The policy makes clear, however, that even the highest possible score does not guarantee admission to the Law School. Nor does a low score automatically disqualify an applicant. Rather, the policy requires admissions officials to look beyond grades and test scores to other criteria that are important to the Law School's educational objectives. So-called " 'soft' variables" such as "the enthusiasm of recommenders, the quality of the undergraduate institution, the quality of the applicant's essay, and the areas and difficulty of undergraduate course selection" are all brought to bear in assessing an "applicant's likely contributions to the intellectual and social life of the institution."

The policy aspires to "achieve that diversity which has the potential to enrich everyone's education and thus make a law school class stronger than the sum of its parts." The policy does not restrict the types of diversity contributions eligible for "substantial weight" in the admissions process . . . . [It] does, however, reaffirm the Law School's longstanding commitment to "one particular type of diversity," that is, "racial and ethnic diversity with special reference to the inclusion of students from groups which have been historically discriminated against, like African-Americans, Hispanics and Native Americans, who without this commitment might not be represented in our student body in meaningful numbers." By enrolling a " 'critical mass' of [underrepresented] minority students," the Law School seeks to "ensur[e] their ability to make unique contributions to the character of the Law School."

The policy does not define diversity "solely in terms of racial and ethnic status." Nor is the policy "insensitive to the competition among all students for admission to the [L]aw [S]chool." Rather, the policy seeks to guide admissions officers in "producing classes both diverse and academically outstanding, classes made up of students who promise to continue the tradition of outstanding contribution by Michigan Graduates to the legal profession."

B

Petitioner Barbara Grutter is a white Michigan resident who applied to the Law School in 1996 with a 3.8 GPA and 161 LSAT score. The Law School initially placed petitioner on a waiting list, but subsequently rejected her application. In December 1997, petitioner filed suit in the United States District Court for the Eastern District of Michigan against the Law School, the Regents of the University of Michigan, Lee Bollinger (Dean of the Law School from 1987 to 1994, and President of the University of Michigan from 1996 to 2002), Jeffrey Lehman (Dean of the Law School), and Dennis Shields (Director of Admissions at the Law School from 1991 until 1998). Petitioner alleged that respondents discriminated against her on the basis of race in violation of the Fourteenth Amendment; Title VI of the Civil Rights Act of 1964, 78 Stat. 252, 42 U.S.C. § 2000d; and Rev. Stat. § 1977, as amended, 42 U.S.C. § 1981.

Petitioner further alleged that her application was rejected because the Law School uses race as a "predominant" factor, giving applicants who belong to certain minority groups "a significantly greater chance of admission than students with similar credentials from disfavored racial groups." Petitioner also alleged that respondents "had no compelling interest to justify their use of race in the admissions process." Petitioner requested compensatory and punitive damages, an order requiring the Law School to offer her admission, and an injunction prohibiting the Law School from continuing to discriminate on the basis of race. . . .

The District Court granted petitioner's motion for class certification and for bifurcation of the trial into liability and damages phases. The class was defined as " 'all persons who (A) applied for and were not granted admission to the University of Michigan Law School for the academic years since (and including) 1995 until the time that judgment is entered herein; and (B) were members of those racial or ethnic groups, including Caucasian, that Defendants treated less favorably in considering their applications for admission to the Law School.' " . . .

During the 15-day bench trial, the parties introduced extensive evidence concerning the Law School's use of race in the admissions process. Dennis Shields, Director of Admissions when petitioner applied to the Law School, testified that he did not direct his staff to admit a particular percentage or number of minority students, but rather to consider an applicant's race along with all other factors. Shields testified that at the height of the admissions season, he would frequently consult the so-called "daily reports" that kept track of the racial and ethnic composition of the class (along with other information such as residency status and gender). This was done, Shields testified, to ensure that a critical mass of underrepresented minority students would be reached so as to realize the educational benefits of a diverse student body. . . .

Erica Munzel, who succeeded Shields as Director of Admissions, testified that " 'critical mass' " means " 'meaningful numbers' " or " 'meaningful representation,' " which she understood to mean a number that encourages underrepresented minority students to participate in the classroom and not feel isolated. Munzel stated there is no number [or] percentage . . . that constitute critical mass. Munzel also asserted that she must consider the race of applicants because a critical mass of underrepresented minority students could not be enrolled if admissions decisions were based primarily on undergraduate GPAs and LSAT scores.

The current Dean of the Law School, Jeffrey Lehman, also testified. Like the other Law School witnesses, Lehman did not quantify critical mass in terms of numbers or percentages. He indicated that critical mass means numbers such that underrepresented minority students do not feel isolated or like spokespersons for their race. When asked about the extent to which race is considered in admissions, Lehman testified that it varies from one applicant to another. In some cases, according to Lehman's testimony, an applicant's race may play no role, while in others it may be a " 'determinative' " factor.

The District Court heard extensive testimony from Professor Richard Lempert, who chaired the faculty committee that drafted the 1992 policy. Lempert emphasized that the Law School seeks students with diverse interests and backgrounds to enhance classroom discussion and the educational experience both inside and outside the classroom. When asked about the policy's " 'commitment to racial and ethnic diversity with special reference to the inclusion of students from groups which have been historically discriminated against, " Lempert explained that this language did not purport to remedy past discrimination, but rather to include students who may bring to the Law School a perspective different from that of members of groups which have not been the victims of such discrimination. Lempert acknowledged that other groups, such as Asians and Jews, have experienced discrimination, but explained they were not mentioned in the policy because individuals who are members of those groups were already being admitted to the Law School in significant numbers.

Kent Syverud . . . a professor at the Law School when the 1992 admissions policy was adopted and . . . now Dean of Vanderbilt Law School . . . submitted several expert reports on the educational benefits of diversity. Syverud's testimony indicated that when a critical mass of underrepresented minority students is present, racial stereotypes lose their force because nonminority students learn there is no " 'minority viewpoint' " but rather a variety of viewpoints among minority students.

In an attempt to quantify the extent to which the Law School actually considers race in making admissions decisions, the parties introduced voluminous evidence at trial. Relying on data obtained from the Law School, petitioner's expert, Dr. Kinley Larntz, generated and analyzed "admissions grids" for the years in question (1995–2000). . . . Dr. Larntz made " 'cell-by-cell' " comparisons between applicants of different races to determine whether a statistically significant relationship existed between race and admission rates. He concluded that membership in certain minority groups " 'is an extremely strong factor in the decision for acceptance,' " and that applicants from these minority groups " 'are given an extremely large allowance for admission' " as compared to applicants who are members of nonfavored groups. Dr. Larntz conceded, however, that race is not the predominant factor in the Law School's admissions calculus.

Dr. Stephen Raudenbush, the Law School's expert, focused on the predicted effect of eliminating race as a factor in the Law School's admission process. In Dr. Raudenbush's view, a race-blind admissions system would have a " 'very dramatic,' " negative effect on underrepresented minority admissions. He testified that in 2000, 35 percent of underrepresented minority applicants were admitted. Dr. Raudenbush predicted that if race were not considered, only 10 percent of those applicants would have been admitted. Under this scenario, underrepresented minority students would have constituted 4 percent of the entering class in 2000 instead of the actual figure of 14.5 percent.

In the end, the District Court concluded that the Law School's use of race as a factor in admissions decisions was unlawful. Applying strict scrutiny, the District Court determined that the Law School's asserted interest in assembling a diverse student body was not compelling because "the attainment of a racially diverse class . . . was not recognized as such by *Bakke* and it is not a remedy for past discrimination." The District Court went on to hold that even if diversity were compelling, the Law School had not narrowly tailored its use of race to further that interest. The District Court granted petitioner's request for declaratory relief and enjoined the Law School from using race as a factor in its admissions decisions. . . .

Sitting en banc, the Court of Appeals reversed the District Court's judgment and vacated the injunction. . . . We granted certiorari to resolve the disagreement among the Courts of Appeals on a question of national importance: Whether diversity is a compelling interest that can justify the narrowly tailored use of race in selecting applicants for admission to public universities. Compare *Hopwood v. Texas,* 78 F.3d 932 (C.A.5 1996) *(Hopwood I)* (holding that diversity is not a compelling state interest), with *Smith v. University of Wash. Law School,* 233 F.3d 1188 (C.A.9 2000) (holding that it is).

II

A

We last addressed the use of race in public higher education over 25 years ago. In the landmark *Bakke* case, we reviewed a racial set-aside program that reserved 16 out of 100 seats in a medical school class for members of certain minority groups. 438 U.S. 265 (1978). The decision produced six separate opinions, none of which commanded a majority of the Court. Four Justices would have upheld the program against all attack on the ground that the government can use race to "remedy disadvantages cast on minorities by past racial prejudice." *Id.,* at 325 (joint opinion of Brennan, White, Marshall, and Blackmun, JJ., concurring in judgment in part and dissenting in part). Four other Justices avoided the constitutional question altogether and struck down the program on statutory grounds. *Id.,* at 408 (opinion of STEVENS, J., joined by Burger, C. J., and Stewart and REHNQUIST, JJ., concurring in judgment in part and dissenting in part). Justice Powell provided a fifth vote not only for invalidating the set-aside program, but also for reversing the state court's injunction against any use of race whatsoever. The only holding for the Court in *Bakke* was that a "State has a substantial interest that legitimately may be served by a properly devised admissions program involving the competitive consideration of race and ethnic origin." Thus, we reversed that part of the lower court's judgment that enjoined the university "from any consideration of the race of any applicant."

Since this Court's splintered decision in *Bakke,* Justice Powell's opinion announcing the judgment of the Court has served as the touchstone for constitutional analysis of race-conscious admissions policies. Public and private universities across the Nation have modeled their own admissions programs on Justice Powell's views on permissible race-conscious policies. . . . Justice Powell began by stating that "[t]he guarantee of equal protection cannot mean one thing when applied to one individual and something else when applied to a person of another color. If both are not accorded the same protection, then it is not equal." In Justice Powell's view, when governmental decisions "touch upon an individual's race or ethnic background, he is entitled to a judicial determination that the burden he is asked to bear on that basis is precisely tailored to serve a compelling governmental interest." Under this exacting standard, only one of the interests asserted by the university survived Justice Powell's scrutiny.

First, Justice Powell rejected an interest in " 'reducing the historic deficit of traditionally disfavored minorities in medical schools and in the medical profession' " as an unlawful interest in racial balancing. Second, Justice Powell rejected an interest in remedying societal discrimination because such measures would risk placing unnecessary burdens on innocent third parties "who bear no responsibility for whatever harm the beneficiaries of the special admissions program are thought to have suffered." Third, Justice Powell rejected an interest in "increasing the number of physicians who will practice in communities currently underserved," concluding that even if such an interest could be compelling in some circumstances the program under review was not "geared to promote that goal."

Justice Powell approved the university's use of race to further only one interest: "the attainment of a diverse student body." With the important proviso that "constitutional limitations protecting individual rights may not be disregarded," Justice Powell grounded his analysis in the academic freedom that "long has been viewed as a special concern of the First Amendment." Justice Powell emphasized that nothing less than the "'nation's future depends upon leaders trained through wide exposure' to the ideas and mores of students as diverse as this Nation of many peoples." In seeking the "right to select those students who will contribute the most to the 'robust exchange of ideas,' " a university seeks "to achieve a goal that is of paramount importance in the fulfillment of its mission." Both "tradition and experience lend support to the view that the contribution of diversity is substantial."

Justice Powell was, however, careful to emphasize that in his view race "is only one element in a range of factors a university properly may consider in attaining the goal of a heterogeneous student body." For Justice Powell, "[i]t is not an interest in simple ethnic diversity, in which a specified percentage of the student body is in effect guaranteed to be members of selected ethnic groups," that can justify the use of race. Rather, "[t]he diversity that furthers a compelling state interest encompasses a far broader array of qualifications and characteristics of which racial or ethnic origin is but a single though important element."

In the wake of our fractured decision in *Bakke,* courts have struggled to discern whether Justice Powell's diversity rationale, set forth in part of the opinion joined by no other Justice, is nonetheless binding precedent under *Marks v. United States*, 430 U.S. 188 (1977). In that case, we explained that "[w]hen a fragmented Court decides a case and no single rationale explaining the result enjoys the assent of five Justices, the holding of the Court may be viewed as that position taken by those Members who concurred in the judgments on the narrowest grounds." As the divergent opinions of the lower courts demonstrate, however, "[t]his test is more easily stated than applied to the various opinions supporting the result in *[Bakke]*."

We do not find it necessary to decide whether Justice Powell's opinion is binding under *Marks*. . . . [F]or the reasons set out below, today we endorse Justice Powell's view that student body diversity is a compelling state interest that can justify the use of race in university admissions.

B

The Equal Protection Clause provides that no State shall "deny to any person within its jurisdiction the equal protection of the laws." U.S. Const., Amdt. 14, § 2. Because the Fourteenth Amendment "protect[s] *persons,* not *groups,*" all "governmental action based on race—a *group* classification long recognized as in most circumstances irrelevant and therefore prohibited—should be subjected to detailed judicial inquiry to ensure that the *personal* right to equal protection of the laws has not been infringed." *Adarand Constructors, Inc. v. Peña,* 515 U.S. 200, 227 (1995). . . . It follows . . . that "government may treat people differently because of their race only for the most compelling reasons." *Adarand,* 515 U.S., at 227.

We have held that all racial classifications imposed by government "must be analyzed by a reviewing court under strict scrutiny." *Ibid.* This means that such classifications are constitutional only if they are narrowly tailored to further compelling governmental interests. "Absent searching judicial inquiry into the justification for such race-based measures," we have no way to determine what "classifications are 'benign' or 'remedial' and what classifications are in fact motivated by illegitimate notions of racial inferiority or simple racial politics." *Richmond v. J.A. Croson Co.,* 488 U.S. 469, 493 (1989) (plurality opinion). We apply strict scrutiny to all racial classifications to " 'smoke out' illegitimate uses of race by assuring that [government] is pursuing a goal important enough to warrant use of a highly suspect tool." *Ibid.*

Strict scrutiny is not "strict in theory, but fatal in fact." *Adarand, supra,* at 237. . . . Context matters when reviewing race-based governmental action under the Equal Protection Clause. In *Adarand Constructors, Inc. v. Peña,* we made clear that strict scrutiny must take " 'relevant differences' into account." Indeed, as we explained, that is its "fundamental purpose." Not every decision influenced by race is equally objectionable, and strict scrutiny is designed to provide a framework for carefully examining the importance and the sincerity of the reasons advanced by the governmental decisionmaker for the use of race in that particular context.

III

A

With these principles in mind, we turn to the question whether the Law School's use of race is justified by a compelling state interest. . . . [R]espondents assert only one justification for their use of race in the admissions process: obtaining "the educational benefits that flow from a diverse student body." In other words, the Law School asks us to recognize, in the context of higher education, a compelling state interest in student body diversity. . . .

[W]e have never held that the only governmental use of race that can survive strict scrutiny is remedying past discrimination. Nor, since *Bakke,* have we directly addressed the use of race in the context of public higher education. Today, we hold that the Law School has a compelling interest in attaining a diverse student body.

The Law School's educational judgment that such diversity is essential to its educational mission is one to which we defer. The Law School's assessment that diversity will, in fact, yield educational benefits is substantiated by respondents and their *amici.* Our scrutiny of the interest asserted by the Law School is no less strict for taking into account complex educational judgments in an area that lies primarily within the expertise of the university. . . .

We have long recognized that, given the important purpose of public education and the expansive freedoms of speech and thought associated with the university environment, universities occupy a special niche in our constitutional tradition. . . . Justice Powell reasoned that by claiming "the right to select those students who will contribute the most to the 'robust exchange of ideas,' " a university "seek[s] to achieve a goal that is of paramount importance in the fulfillment of its mission." Our conclusion that the Law School has a compelling interest in a diverse student body is informed by our view that attaining a diverse student body is at the heart of the Law School's proper institutional mission, and that "good faith" on the part of a university is "presumed" absent "a showing to the contrary."

As part of its goal of "assembling a class that is both exceptionally academically qualified and broadly diverse," the Law School seeks to "enroll a 'critical mass' of minority students." The Law School's interest is not simply to assure within its student body some specified percentage of a particular group merely because of its race or ethnic origin. That would amount to outright racial balancing, which is patently unconstitutional. *Freeman v. Pitts,* 503 U.S. 467, 494 (1992) ("Racial balance is not to be achieved for its own sake"). Rather, the Law School's concept of critical mass is defined by reference to the educational benefits that diversity is designed to produce.

These benefits are substantial. As the District Court emphasized, the Law School's admissions policy promotes "cross-racial understanding," helps to break down racial stereotypes, and "enables [students] to better understand persons of different races." . . . "[C]lassroom discussion is livelier, more spirited, and simply more enlightening and interesting" when the students have "the greatest possible variety of backgrounds." . . . [N]umerous studies show that student body diversity promotes learning outcomes, and "better prepares students for an increasingly diverse workforce and society, and better prepares them as professionals." Brief for American Educational Research Association et al. as *Amici Curiae* 3; see, *e.g.,* W. Bowen & D. Bok, The Shape of the River (1998).

These benefits are not theoretical but real, as major American businesses have made clear that the skills needed in today's increasingly global marketplace can only be developed through exposure to widely diverse people, cultures, ideas, and viewpoints. Brief for 3M et al. as *Amici Curiae* 5; Brief for General Motors Corp. as *Amicus Curiae* 3–4. What is more, high-ranking retired officers and civilian leaders of the United States military assert that, "[b]ased on [their] decades of experience," a "highly qualified, racially diverse officer corps . . . is essential to the military's ability to fulfill its principle mission to provide national security." Brief for Julius W. Becton, Jr., et al. as *Amici Curiae* 5. The primary sources for the Nation's officer corps are the service academies and the Reserve Officers Training Corps (ROTC), the latter comprising students already admitted to participating colleges and universities. At present, "the military cannot achieve an officer corps that is *both* highly qualified *and* racially diverse unless the service academies and the ROTC used limited race-conscious recruiting and admissions policies." . . .

This Court has long recognized that "education . . . is the very foundation of good citizenship." *Brown v. Board of Education,* 347 U.S. 483, 493 (1954). For this reason, the diffusion of knowledge and opportunity through public institutions of higher education must be accessible to all individuals regardless of race or ethnicity. The United States, as *amicus curiae,* affirms that "[e]nsuring that public institutions are open and available to all segments of American society, including people of all races and ethnicities, represents a paramount government objective." And, "[n]owhere is the importance of such openness more acute than in the context of higher education." Effective participation by members of all racial and ethnic groups in the civic life of our Nation is essential if the dream of one Nation, indivisible, is to be realized.

Moreover, universities, and in particular, law schools, represent the training ground for a large number of our Nation's leaders. *Sweatt v. Painter,* 339 U.S. 629, 634 (1950). Individuals with law degrees occupy roughly half the state governorships, more than half the seats in the United States Senate, and more than a third of the seats in the United States House of Representatives. The pattern is even more striking when it comes to highly selective law schools. . . .

In order to cultivate a set of leaders with legitimacy in the eyes of the citizenry, it is necessary that the path to leadership be visibly open to talented and qualified individuals of every race and ethnicity. All members of our heterogeneous society must have confidence in the openness and integrity of the educational institutions that provide this training. . . . Access to legal education (and thus the legal profession) must be inclusive of talented and qualified individuals of every race and ethnicity, so that all members of our heterogeneous society may participate in the educational institutions that provide the training and education necessary to succeed in America. . . .

B

Even in the limited circumstance when drawing racial distinctions is permissible to further a compelling state interest, government is still "constrained in how it may pursue that end: [T]he means chosen to accomplish the [government's] asserted purpose must be specifically and narrowly framed to accomplish that purpose." *Shaw v. Hunt,* 517 U.S. 899, 908 (1996). The purpose of the narrow tailoring requirement is to ensure that "the means chosen 'fit' th[e] compelling goal so closely that there is little or no possibility that the motive for the classification was illegitimate racial prejudice or stereotype." *Croson,* 488 U.S., at 493 (plurality opinion). . . . That inquiry must be calibrated to fit the distinct issues raised by the use of race to achieve student body diversity in public higher education. Contrary to Justice KENNEDY's assertions, we do not "abando[n] strict scrutiny." Rather . . . we adhere to *Adarand's* teaching that the very purpose of strict scrutiny is to take such "relevant differences into account."

To be narrowly tailored, a race-conscious admissions program cannot use a quota system—it cannot "insulat[e] each category of applicants with certain desired qualifications from competition with all other applicants." *Bakke,* 438 U.S., at 315 (opinion of Powell, J.). Instead, a university may consider race or ethnicity only as a " 'plus' in a particular applicant's file," without "insulat[ing] the individual from comparison with all other candidates for the available seats." In other words, an admissions program must be "flexible enough to consider all pertinent elements of diversity in light of the particular qualifications of each applicant, and to place them on the same footing for consideration, although not necessarily according them the same weight."

We find that the Law School's admissions program bears the hallmarks of a narrowly tailored plan. As Justice Powell made clear in *Bakke,* truly individualized consideration demands that race be used in a flexible, nonmechanical way. It follows from this mandate that universities cannot establish quotas for members of certain racial groups or put members of those groups on separate admissions tracks. Nor can universities insulate applicants who belong to certain racial or ethnic groups from the competition for admission. Universities can, however, consider race or ethnicity more flexibly as a "plus" factor in the context of individualized consideration of each and every applicant.

We are satisfied that the Law School's admissions program . . . does not operate as a quota. Properly understood, a "quota" is a program in which a certain fixed number or proportion of opportunities are "reserved exclusively for certain minority groups." *Croson, supra,* at 496 (plurality opinion). Quotas . . . "insulate the individual from comparison with all other candidates for the available seats," *Bakke, supra,* at 317 (opinion of Powell, J.). In contrast, a permissible goal requires only a good-faith effort to come within a range demarcated by the goal itself, and permits consideration of race as a "plus" factor in any given case while still ensuring that each candidate competes with all other qualified applicants. . . .

The Law School's goal of attaining a critical mass of underrepresented minority students does not transform its program into a quota. Some attention to numbers, without more, does not transform a flexible admissions system into a rigid quota. Nor, as Justice KENNEDY posits, does the Law School's consultation of the "daily reports," which keep track of the racial and ethnic composition of the class (as well as of residency and gender), "sugges[t] there was no further attempt at individual review save for race itself" during the final stages of the admissions process. To the contrary, the Law School's admissions officers testified without contradiction that they never gave race any more or less weight based on the information contained in these reports. Moreover . . . between 1993 and 1998, the number of African-American, Latino, and

Native-American students in each class at the Law School varied from 13.5 to 20.1 percent, a range inconsistent with a quota.

THE CHIEF JUSTICE believes that the Law School's policy conceals an attempt to achieve racial balancing, and cites admissions data to contend that the Law School discriminates among different groups within the critical mass. But, as THE CHIEF JUSTICE concedes, the number of underrepresented minority students who ultimately enroll in the Law School differs substantially from their representation in the applicant pool and varies considerably for each group from year to year. . . .

Here, the Law School engages in a highly individualized, holistic review of each applicant's file, giving serious consideration to all the ways an applicant might contribute to a diverse educational environment. The Law School affords this individualized consideration to applicants of all races. There is no policy, either *de jure* or *de facto,* of automatic acceptance or rejection based on any single "soft" variable. Unlike the program at issue in *Gratz v. Bollinger,* 539 U.S. 244 (2003), the Law School awards no mechanical, predetermined diversity "bonuses" based on race or ethnicity. Like the Harvard plan, the Law School's admissions policy "is flexible enough to consider all pertinent elements of diversity in light of the particular qualifications of each applicant, and to place them on the same footing for consideration, although not necessarily according them the same weight." *Bakke, supra,* at 317 (opinion of Powell, J.). . . .

The Law School does not . . . limit in any way the broad range of qualities and experiences that may be considered valuable contributions to student body diversity. To the contrary, the 1992 policy makes clear "[t]here are many possible bases for diversity admissions," and provides examples of admittees who have lived or traveled widely abroad, are fluent in several languages, have overcome personal adversity and family hardship, have exceptional records of extensive community service, and have had successful careers in other fields. The Law School seriously considers each "applicant's promise of making a notable contribution to the class by way of a particular strength, attainment, or characteristic— *e.g.,* an unusual intellectual achievement, employment experience, nonacademic performance, or personal background." All applicants have the opportunity to highlight their own potential diversity contributions through the submission of a personal statement, letters of recommendation, and an essay describing the ways in which the applicant will contribute to the life and diversity of the Law School.

What is more, the Law School actually gives substantial weight to diversity factors besides race. The Law School frequently accepts nonminority applicants with grades and test scores lower than underrepresented minority applicants (and other nonminority applicants) who are rejected. This shows that the Law School seriously weighs many other diversity factors besides race that can make a real and dispositive difference for nonminority applicants as well. . . .

Petitioner and the United States argue that the Law School's plan is not narrowly tailored because race-neutral means exist to obtain the educational benefits of student body diversity that the Law School seeks. We disagree. Narrow tailoring does not require exhaustion of every conceivable race-neutral alternative. Nor does it require a university to choose between maintaining a reputation for excellence or fulfilling a commitment to provide educational opportunities to members of all racial groups. See *Wygant v. Jackson Bd. of Ed.,* 476 U.S. 267, 280, n. 6 (1986) (alternatives must serve the interest " 'about as well' "). Narrow tailoring does, however, require serious, good faith consideration of workable race-neutral alternatives that will achieve the diversity the university seeks.

We agree with the Court of Appeals that the Law School sufficiently considered workable race-neutral alternatives. The District Court took the Law School to task for failing to consider race-neutral alternatives such as "using a lottery system" or "decreasing the emphasis for all applicants on undergraduate GPA and LSAT scores." But these alternatives would require a dramatic sacrifice of diversity, the academic quality of all admitted students, or both. . . .

Because a lottery would make . . . nuanced judgment impossible, it would effectively sacrifice all other educational values, not to mention every other kind of diversity. So too with the suggestion that the Law School simply lower admissions standards for all students, a drastic remedy that would require the Law School to become a much different institution and sacrifice a vital component of its educational mission. The United States advocates "percentage plans," recently adopted by public undergraduate institutions in Texas, Florida, and California, to guarantee admission to all students above a certain class-rank threshold in every high school in the State. The United States does not, however, explain how such plans could work for graduate and professional schools. Moreover, even assuming such plans are race-neutral, they may preclude the university from conducting the individualized assessments necessary to assemble a student body that is not just racially diverse, but diverse along all the qualities valued by the university. We are satisfied that the Law School adequately considered race-neutral alternatives currently capable of producing a critical mass without forcing the Law School to abandon the academic selectivity that is the cornerstone of its educational mission.

We acknowledge that "there are serious problems of justice connected with the idea of preference itself." *Bakke,* 438 U.S., at 298 (opinion of Powell, J.). Narrow tailoring, therefore, requires that a race-conscious admissions program not unduly harm members of any racial group. . . . We are satisfied that the Law School's admissions program does not. . . . As Justice Powell recognized in *Bakke,* so long as a race-conscious admissions program uses race as a "plus" factor in the context of individualized consideration, a rejected applicant

> will not have been foreclosed from all consideration for that seat simply because he was not the right color or had the wrong surname. . . . His qualifications would have been weighed fairly and competitively, and he would have no basis to complain of unequal treatment under the Fourteenth Amendment.

We agree that, in the context of its individualized inquiry into the possible diversity contributions of all applicants, the Law School's race-conscious admissions program does not unduly harm nonminority applicants.

We are mindful, however, that "[a] core purpose of the Fourteenth Amendment was to do away with all governmentally imposed discrimination based on race." *Palmore v. Sidoti,* 466 U.S. 429, 432 (1984). Accordingly, race-conscious admissions policies must be limited in time. This requirement reflects that racial classifications, however compelling their goals, are potentially so dangerous that they may be employed no more broadly than the interest demands. Enshrining a permanent justification for racial preferences would offend this fundamental equal protection principle. We see no reason to exempt race-conscious admissions programs from the requirement that all governmental use of race must have a logical end point. . . .

In the context of higher education, the durational requirement can be met by sunset provisions in race-conscious admissions policies and periodic reviews to determine whether racial preferences are still necessary to achieve student body diversity. Universities in California, Florida, and Washington State, where racial preferences in admissions are prohibited by state law, are currently engaged in experimenting with a wide variety of alternative approaches. Universities in other States can and should draw on the most promising aspects of these race-neutral alternatives as they develop. Cf. *United States v. Lopez,* 514 U.S. 549, 581 (1995) (KENNEDY, J., concurring) ("[T]he States may perform their role as laboratories for experimentation to devise various solutions where the best solution is far from clear"). . . .

We take the Law School at its word that it would "like nothing better than to find a race-neutral admissions formula" and will terminate its race-conscious admissions program as soon as practicable. It has been 25 years since Justice Powell first approved the use of race to further an interest in student body diversity in the context of public higher education. Since that time, the number of minority applicants with high grades and test scores has indeed increased. We expect that 25 years from now, the use of racial preferences will no longer be necessary to further the interest approved today.

IV

In summary, the Equal Protection Clause does not prohibit the Law School's narrowly tailored use of race in admissions decisions to further a compelling interest in obtaining the educational benefits that flow from a diverse student body. . . . The judgment of the Court of Appeals for the Sixth Circuit, accordingly, is affirmed.

It is so ordered.

■ **JUSTICE GINSBURG, with whom JUSTICE BREYER joins, concurring.**

. . . It is well documented that conscious and unconscious race bias, even rank discrimination based on race, remain alive in our land, impeding realization of our highest values and ideals. . . . However strong the public's desire for improved education systems may be, it remains the current reality that many minority students encounter markedly inadequate and unequal educational opportunities. Despite these inequalities, some minority students are able to meet the high threshold requirements set for admission to the country's finest undergraduate and graduate educational institutions. As lower school education in minority communities improves, an increase in the number of such students may be anticipated. From today's vantage point, one may hope, but not firmly forecast, that over the next generation's span, progress toward nondiscrimination and genuinely equal opportunity will make it safe to sunset affirmative action.*

■ **JUSTICE SCALIA, with whom JUSTICE THOMAS joins, concurring in part and dissenting in part.**

. . . The "educational benefit" that the University of Michigan seeks to achieve by racial discrimination consists, according to the Court, of " 'cross-racial understanding,' " and " 'better prepar[ation of] students for an increasingly diverse workforce and society,' " all of which is necessary not only for work, but also for good "citizenship." . . . If properly considered an "educational benefit" at all, it is surely not one that is either uniquely relevant to law school or uniquely "teachable" in a formal educational setting. *And therefore:* If it is appropriate for the University of Michigan Law School to use racial discrimination for the purpose of putting together a "critical mass" that will convey generic lessons in socialization and good citizenship, surely it is no less appropriate—

---

* As the Court explains, the admissions policy challenged here survives review under the standards stated in *Adarand Constructors, Inc. v. Peña*, 515 U.S. 200 (1995), *Richmond v. J.A. Croson Co.*, 488 U.S. 469 (1989), and Justice Powell's opinion in *Regents of Univ. of Cal. v. Bakke*, 438 U.S. 265 (1978). This case therefore does not require the Court to revisit whether all governmental classifications by race, whether designed to benefit or to burden a historically disadvantaged group, should be subject to the same standard of judicial review. Cf. *Gratz, post*, 539 U.S., at 301–302 (GINSBURG, J., dissenting); *Adarand*, 515 U.S., at 274, n. 8 (GINSBURG, J., dissenting). Nor does this case necessitate reconsideration whether interests other than "student body diversity," ante, at 2337, rank as sufficiently important to justify a race-conscious government program. Cf. *Gratz, post*, 539 U.S., at 301–302, (GINSBURG, J., dissenting); *Adarand*, 515 U.S., at 273–274 (GINSBURG, J., dissenting).

indeed, *particularly* appropriate—for the civil service system of the State of Michigan to do so. There, also, those exposed to "critical masses" of certain races will presumably become better Americans, better Michiganders, better civil servants. And surely private employers cannot be criticized—indeed, should be praised—if they also "teach" good citizenship to their adult employees through a patriotic, all-American system of racial discrimination in hiring. . . .

Unlike a clear constitutional holding that racial preferences in state educational institutions are impermissible, or even a clear anticonstitutional holding that racial preferences in state educational institutions are OK, today's *Grutter-Gratz* split double header seems perversely designed to prolong the controversy and the litigation. . . .

■ JUSTICE THOMAS, with whom JUSTICE SCALIA joins as to Parts I–VII, concurring in part and dissenting in part.

Frederick Douglass, speaking to a group of abolitionists almost 140 years ago, delivered a message lost on today's majority:

> [I]n regard to the colored people, there is always more that is benevolent, I perceive, than just, manifested towards us. What I ask for the negro is not benevolence, not pity, not sympathy, but simply *justice*. The American people have always been anxious to know what they shall do with us. . . . I have had but one answer from the beginning. Do nothing with us! Your doing with us has already played the mischief with us. Do nothing with us! If the apples will not remain on the tree of their own strength, if they are worm-eaten at the core, if they are early ripe and disposed to fall, let them fall! . . . And if the negro cannot stand on his own legs, let him fall also. All I ask is, give him a chance to stand on his own legs! Let him alone! . . . [Y]our interference is doing him positive injury. What the Black Man Wants: An Address Delivered in Boston, Massachusetts, on 26 January 1865, reprinted in 4 The Frederick Douglass Papers 59, 68 (J. Blassingame & J. McKivigan eds.1991).

Like Douglass, I believe blacks can achieve in every avenue of American life without the meddling of university administrators. Because I wish to see all students succeed whatever their color, I share, in some respect, the sympathies of those who sponsor the type of discrimination advanced by the University of Michigan Law School (Law School). The Constitution does not, however, tolerate institutional devotion to the status quo in admissions policies when such devotion ripens into racial discrimination. Nor does the Constitution countenance the unprecedented deference the Court gives to the Law School, an approach inconsistent with the very concept of "strict scrutiny."

No one would argue that a university could set up a lower general admissions standard and then impose heightened requirements only on black applicants. Similarly, a university may not maintain a high admissions standard and grant exemptions to favored races. The Law School, of its own choosing, and for its own purposes, maintains an exclusionary admissions system that it knows produces racially disproportionate results. Racial discrimination is not a permissible solution to the self-inflicted wounds of this elitist admissions policy.

The majority upholds the Law School's racial discrimination not by interpreting the people's Constitution, but by responding to a faddish slogan of the cognoscenti. Nevertheless, I concur in part in the Court's opinion. First, I agree with the Court insofar as its decision, which approves of only one racial classification, confirms that further use of race in admissions remains unlawful. Second, I agree with the Court's holding that racial discrimination in higher education admissions will be illegal in 25 years. I respectfully dissent from the remainder of the Court's opinion and the judgment, however, because I believe that the Law School's current use of race violates the Equal Protection Clause and that the Constitution means the same thing today as it will in 300 months.

I

. . . The strict scrutiny standard that the Court purports to apply in this case was first enunciated in *Korematsu v. United States*, 323 U.S. 214 (1944). . . . A majority of the Court has validated only two circumstances where "pressing public necessity" or a "compelling state interest" can possibly justify racial discrimination by state actors. First, the lesson of *Korematsu* is that national security constitutes a "pressing public necessity," though the government's use of race to advance that objective must be narrowly tailored. Second, the Court has recognized as a compelling state interest a government's effort to remedy past discrimination for which it is responsible. *Richmond v. J.A. Croson Co.*, 488 U.S. 469, 504 (1989).

The contours of "pressing public necessity" can be further discerned from those interests the Court has rejected as bases for racial discrimination. For example, *Wygant v. Jackson Bd. of Ed.*, 476 U.S. 267 (1986), found unconstitutional a collective-bargaining agreement between a school board and a teachers' union that favored certain minority races. The school board defended the policy on the grounds that minority teachers provided "role models" for minority students and that a racially "diverse" faculty would improve the education of all students. Nevertheless, the Court found that the use of race violated the Equal Protection Clause, deeming both asserted state interests insufficiently compelling.

An even greater governmental interest involves the sensitive role of courts in child custody determinations. In *Palmore v. Sidoti*, 466 U.S. 429 (1984), the Court held that even the best interests of a child did not constitute a compelling state interest that would allow a state court to award custody to the father because the mother was in a mixed-race marriage. Finally, the Court has rejected an interest in remedying general societal discrimination as a justification for race discrimination. See *Croson*, 488 U.S., at 496–498 (plurality opinion); id., at 520–521 (SCALIA, J., concurring in judgment). . . .

The Constitution abhors classifications based on race, not only because those classifications can harm favored races or are based on illegitimate motives, but also because every time the government places citizens on racial registers and makes race relevant to the provision of burdens or benefits, it demeans us all.

II

Unlike the majority, I seek to define with precision the interest being asserted by the Law School before determining whether that interest is so compelling as to justify racial discrimination. The Law School maintains that it wishes to obtain "educational benefits that flow from student body diversity." . . . Undoubtedly there are other ways to "better" the education of law students aside from ensuring that the student body contains a "critical mass" of underrepresented minority students. Attaining "diversity," whatever it means,[3] is the mechanism by which the Law School obtains educational benefits, not an end of itself. The Law School, however, apparently believes that only a racially mixed student body can lead to the educational benefits it seeks. How, then, is the Law School's interest in these allegedly unique educational "benefits" *not* simply the forbidden interest in "racial balancing," that the majority expressly rejects? . . .

One must also consider the Law School's refusal to entertain changes to its current admissions system that might produce the same educational benefits. The Law School adamantly disclaims any race-neutral alternative that would reduce "academic selectivity," which would in turn "require the Law School to become a very different institution, and to sacrifice a core part of its educational mission." In other words, the Law School seeks to improve marginally the education it offers without sacrificing too much of its exclusivity and elite status.[4]

The proffered interest that the majority vindicates today, then, is not simply "diversity." Instead the Court upholds the use of racial

---

[3]   "[D]iversity," for all of its devotees, is more a fashionable catchphrase than it is a useful term, especially when something as serious as racial discrimination is at issue. Because the Equal Protection Clause renders the color of one's skin constitutionally irrelevant to the Law School's mission, I refer to the Law School's interest as an "aesthetic." . . . I also use the term "aesthetic" because I believe it underlines the ineffectiveness of racially discriminatory admissions in actually helping those who are truly underprivileged. It must be remembered that the Law School's racial discrimination does nothing for those too poor or uneducated to participate in elite higher education and therefore presents only an illusory solution to the challenges facing our Nation.

[4]   The Law School believes both that the educational benefits of a racially engineered student body are large and that adjusting its overall admissions standards to achieve the same racial mix would require it to sacrifice its elite status. If the Law School is correct that the educational benefits of "diversity" are so great, then achieving them by altering admissions standards should not compromise its elite status. The Law School's reluctance to do this suggests that the educational benefits it alleges are not significant or do not exist at all.

discrimination as a tool to advance the Law School's interest in offering a marginally superior education while maintaining an elite institution. Unless each constituent part of this state interest is of pressing public necessity, the Law School's use of race is unconstitutional. . . .

III

A

A close reading of the Court's opinion reveals that all of its legal work is done through one conclusory statement: The Law School has a "compelling interest in securing the educational benefits of a diverse student body." . . . Justice Powell's opinion in *Bakke* and the Court's decision today rest on the fundamentally flawed proposition that racial discrimination can be contextualized so that a goal, such as classroom aesthetics, can be compelling in one context but not in another. This "we know it when we see it" approach to evaluating state interests is not capable of judicial application. Today, the Court insists on radically expanding the range of permissible uses of race to something as trivial (by comparison) as the assembling of a law school class. . . .

B

Under the proper standard, there is no pressing public necessity in maintaining a public law school at all and, it follows, certainly not an elite law school. Likewise, marginal improvements in legal education do not qualify as a compelling state interest.

1

While legal education at a public university may be good policy or otherwise laudable, it is obviously not a pressing public necessity when the correct legal standard is applied. Additionally, circumstantial evidence as to whether a state activity is of pressing public necessity can be obtained by asking whether all States feel compelled to engage in that activity. . . . In this sense, the absence of a public, American Bar Association (ABA) accredited, law school in Alaska, Delaware, Massachusetts, New Hampshire, and Rhode Island, provides further evidence that Michigan's maintenance of the Law School does not constitute a compelling state interest.

2

. . . [E]ven assuming that a State may, under appropriate circumstances, demonstrate a cognizable interest in having an elite law school, Michigan has failed to do so here.

This Court has limited the scope of equal protection review to interests and activities that occur within that State's jurisdiction. The Court held in *Missouri ex rel. Gaines v. Canada,* 305 U.S. 337 (1938), that Missouri could not satisfy the demands of "separate but equal" by paying for legal training of blacks at neighboring state law schools, while maintaining a segregated law school within the State. . . . The Equal Protection Clause, as interpreted by the Court in *Gaines,* does not permit

States to justify racial discrimination on the basis of what the rest of the Nation "may do or fail to do." The only interests that can satisfy the Equal Protection Clause's demands are those found within a State's jurisdiction.

The only cognizable state interests vindicated by operating a public law school are, therefore, the education of that State's citizens and the training of that State's lawyers. . . . The Law School today, however, does precious little training of those attorneys who will serve the citizens of Michigan. In 2002, graduates of the Law School made up less than 6% of applicants to the Michigan bar, even though the Law School's graduates constitute nearly 30% of all law students graduating in Michigan. Less than 16% of the Law School's graduating class elects to stay in Michigan after law school. Thus, while a mere 27% of the Law School's 2002 entering class is from Michigan, only half of these, it appears, will stay in Michigan.

In sum, the Law School trains few Michigan residents and overwhelmingly serves students, who, as lawyers, leave the State of Michigan. By contrast, Michigan's other public law school, Wayne State University Law School, sends 88% of its graduates on to serve the people of Michigan. It does not take a social scientist to conclude that it is precisely the Law School's status as an elite institution that causes it to be a waystation for the rest of the country's lawyers, rather than a training ground for those who will remain in Michigan. The Law School's decision to be an elite institution does little to advance the welfare of the people of Michigan or any cognizable interest of the State of Michigan.

Again, the fact that few States choose to maintain elite law schools raises a strong inference that there is nothing compelling about elite status. Arguably, only the public law schools of the University of Texas, the University of California, Berkeley (Boalt Hall), and the University of Virginia maintain the same reputation for excellence as the Law School.[5]
. . .

IV

The interest in remaining elite and exclusive that the majority thinks so obviously critical requires the use of admissions "standards" that, in turn, create the Law School's "need" to discriminate on the basis of race. . . . The majority errs, however, because race-neutral alternatives must only be "workable" and do "about as well" *in vindicating the compelling state interest*. The Court never explicitly holds that the Law School's desire to retain the status quo in "academic selectivity" is itself a compelling state interest, and, as I have demonstrated, it is not. Therefore, the Law School should be forced to choose between its classroom aesthetic and its exclusionary admissions system—it cannot have it both ways.

---

[5]   Cf. U.S. News & World Report, America's Best Graduate Schools 28 (2004 ed.) (placing these schools in the uppermost 15 in the Nation).

With the adoption of different admissions methods, such as accepting all students who meet minimum qualifications, the Law School could achieve its vision of the racially aesthetic student body without the use of racial discrimination. The Law School concedes this, but the Court holds, implicitly and under the guise of narrow tailoring, that the Law School has a compelling state interest in doing what it wants to do. I cannot agree. First, under strict scrutiny, the Law School's assessment of the benefits of racial discrimination and devotion to the admissions status quo are not entitled to any sort of deference, grounded in the First Amendment or anywhere else. Second, even if its "academic selectivity" must be maintained at all costs along with racial discrimination, the Court ignores the fact that other top law schools have succeeded in meeting their aesthetic demands without racial discrimination.

A

The Court bases its unprecedented deference to the Law School—a deference antithetical to strict scrutiny—on an idea of "educational autonomy" grounded in the First Amendment. In my view, there is no basis for a right of public universities to do what would otherwise violate the Equal Protection Clause.

The constitutionalization of "academic freedom" began with the concurring opinion of Justice Frankfurter in *Sweezy v. New Hampshire*, 354 U.S. 234 (1957). Sweezy, a Marxist economist, was investigated by the Attorney General of New Hampshire on suspicion of being a subversive. The prosecution sought, inter alia, the contents of a lecture Sweezy had given at the University of New Hampshire. The Court held that the investigation violated due process.

Justice Frankfurter went further, however, reasoning that the First Amendment created a right of academic freedom that prohibited the investigation. *Id.*, at 256–267 (opinion concurring in result). Much of the rhetoric in Justice Frankfurter's opinion was devoted to the personal right of Sweezy to free speech. . . . I doubt that when Justice Frankfurter spoke of governmental intrusions into the independence of universities, he was thinking of the Constitution's ban on racial discrimination. The majority's broad deference to both the Law School's judgment that racial aesthetics leads to educational benefits and its stubborn refusal to alter the status quo in admissions methods finds no basis in the Constitution or decisions of this Court.

B

1

The Court's deference to the Law School's conclusion that its racial experimentation leads to educational benefits will, if adhered to, have serious collateral consequences. The Court relies heavily on social science evidence to justify its deference. But see also Rothman, Lipset, & Nevitte, Racial Diversity Reconsidered, 151 Public Interest 25 (2003) (finding that the racial mix of a student body produced by racial discrimination of the type practiced by the Law School in fact hinders students' perception of academic quality). The Court never acknowledges, however, the growing evidence that racial (and other sorts) of heterogeneity actually impairs learning among black students. See, *e.g.,* Flowers & Pascarella, Cognitive Effects of College Racial Composition on African American Students After 3 Years of College, 40 J. of College Student Development 669, 674 (1999) (concluding that black students experience superior cognitive development at Historically Black Colleges (HBCs) and that, even among blacks, "a substantial diversity moderates the cognitive effects of attending an HBC"). . . .

The majority grants deference to the Law School's "assessment that diversity will, in fact, yield educational benefits." It follows, therefore . . . [a]n HBC's rejection of white applicants in order to maintain racial homogeneity seems permissible, therefore, under the majority's view of the Equal Protection Clause. . . .

2

Moreover one would think, in light of the Court's decision in *United States v. Virginia*, 518 U.S. 515 (1996), that before being given license to use racial discrimination, the Law School would be required to radically reshape its admissions process, even to the point of sacrificing some elements of its character. In *Virginia*, a majority of the Court, without a word about academic freedom, accepted the all-male Virginia Military Institute's (VMI) representation that some changes in its "adversative" method of education would be required with the admission of women, but did not defer to VMI's judgment that these changes would be too great. Instead, the Court concluded that they were "manageable." That case involved sex discrimination, which is subjected to intermediate, not strict, scrutiny. So in *Virginia*, where the standard of review dictated that greater flexibility be granted to VMI's educational policies than the Law School deserves here, this Court gave no deference. Apparently where the status quo being defended is that of the elite establishment—here the Law School—rather than a less fashionable Southern military institution, the Court will defer without serious inquiry and without regard to the applicable legal standard.

C

. . . [T]he majority ignores the "experience" of those institutions that have been forced to abandon explicit racial discrimination in admissions. The sky has not fallen at Boalt Hall at the University of California, Berkeley, for example. Prior to Proposition 209's adoption of Cal. Const., Art. 1, § 31(a), which bars the State from "grant[ing] preferential treatment . . . on the basis of race . . . in the operation of . . . public education," Boalt Hall enrolled 20 blacks and 28 Hispanics in its first-year class for 1996. In 2002, without deploying express racial discrimination in admissions, Boalt's entering class enrolled 14 blacks and 36 Hispanics. Total underrepresented minority student enrollment at Boalt Hall now exceeds 1996 levels. Apparently the Law School cannot be counted on to be as resourceful. . . .

V

[T]here is much to be said for the view that the use of tests and other measures to "predict" academic performance is a poor substitute for a system that gives every applicant a chance to prove he can succeed in the study of law. The rallying cry that in the absence of racial discrimination in admissions there would be a true meritocracy ignores the fact that the entire process is poisoned by numerous exceptions to "merit." For example . . . elite institutions utilize a so-called "legacy" preference to give the children of alumni an advantage in admissions. . . . The Equal Protection Clause does not, however, prohibit the use of unseemly legacy preferences or many other kinds of arbitrary admissions procedures. What the Equal Protection Clause does prohibit are classifications made on the basis of race. . . .

In any event, there is nothing ancient, honorable, or constitutionally protected about "selective" admissions. The University of Michigan should be well aware that alternative methods have historically been used for the admission of students, for it brought to this country the German certificate system in the late-19th century. Under this system, a secondary school was certified by a university so that any graduate who completed the course offered by the school was offered admission to the university. . . . The facially race-neutral "percent plans" now used in Texas, California, and Florida are in many ways the descendents of the certificate system.

Certification was replaced by selective admissions in the beginning of the 20th century, as universities sought to exercise more control over the composition of their student bodies. Since its inception, selective admissions has been the vehicle for racial, ethnic, and religious tinkering and experimentation by university administrators. . . . Columbia, Harvard, and others infamously determined that they had "too many" Jews, just as today the Law School argues it would have "too many" whites if it could not discriminate in its admissions process. . . .

Columbia employed intelligence tests precisely because Jewish applicants, who were predominantly immigrants, scored worse on such tests. . . . Similarly no modern law school can claim ignorance of the poor performance of blacks, relatively speaking, on the Law School Admission Test (LSAT). Nevertheless, law schools continue to use the test and then attempt to "correct" for black underperformance by using racial discrimination in admissions so as to obtain their aesthetic student body. The Law School's continued adherence to measures it knows produce racially skewed results is not entitled to deference by this Court. . . .

The Court will not even deign to make the Law School try other methods, however, preferring instead to grant a 25-year license to violate the Constitution. And the same Court that had the courage to order the desegregation of all public schools in the South now fears, on the basis of platitudes rather than principle, to force the Law School to abandon a decidedly imperfect admissions regime that provides the basis for racial discrimination.

VI

The absence of any articulated legal principle supporting the majority's principal holding suggests another rationale. I believe what lies beneath the Court's decision today are the benighted notions that one can tell when racial discrimination benefits (rather than hurts) minority groups and that racial discrimination is necessary to remedy general societal ills. This Court's precedents supposedly settled both issues, but clearly the majority still cannot commit to the principle that racial classifications are *per se* harmful and that almost no amount of benefit in the eye of the beholder can justify such classifications.

Putting aside what I take to be the Court's implicit rejection of *Adarand's* holding that beneficial and burdensome racial classifications are equally invalid, I must contest the notion that the Law School's discrimination benefits those admitted as a result of it. . . . [N]owhere in any of the filings in this Court is any evidence that the purported "beneficiaries" of this racial discrimination prove themselves by performing at (or even near) the same level as those students who receive no preferences.

The silence in this case is deafening to those of us who view higher education's purpose as imparting knowledge and skills to students, rather than a communal, rubber-stamp, credentialing process. The Law School is not looking for those students who, despite a lower LSAT score or undergraduate grade point average, will succeed in the study of law. The Law School seeks only a facade—it is sufficient that the class looks right, even if it does not perform right.

The Law School tantalizes unprepared students with the promise of a University of Michigan degree and all of the opportunities that it offers. These overmatched students take the bait, only to find that they cannot succeed in the cauldron of competition. And this mismatch crisis is not restricted to elite institutions. See T. Sowell, Race and Culture 176–177 (1994) ("Even if most minority students are able to meet the normal standards at the 'average' range of colleges and universities, the systematic mismatching of minority students begun at the top can mean that such students are generally overmatched throughout all levels of higher education"). Indeed, to cover the tracks of the aestheticists, this cruel farce of racial discrimination must continue—in selection for the Michigan Law Review, see University of Michigan Law School Student Handbook 2002–2003, pp. 39–40 (noting the presence of a "diversity plan" for admission to the review), and in hiring at law firms and for judicial clerkships—until the "beneficiaries" are no longer tolerated. While these students may graduate with law degrees, there is no evidence that they have received a qualitatively better legal education (or become better lawyers) than if they had gone to a less "elite" law school for which they were better prepared. And the aestheticists will never address the real problems facing "underrepresented minorities,"[11] instead continuing their social experiments on other people's children.

Beyond the harm the Law School's racial discrimination visits upon its test subjects, no social science has disproved the notion that this discrimination engenders attitudes of superiority or, alternatively, provokes resentment among those who believe that they have been wronged by the government's use of race. These programs stamp minorities with a badge of inferiority and may cause them to develop dependencies or to adopt an attitude that they are 'entitled' to preferences.

It is uncontested that each year, the Law School admits a handful of blacks who would be admitted in the absence of racial discrimination. . . . The majority of blacks are admitted to the Law School because of discrimination, and because of this policy all are tarred as undeserving. . . . When blacks take positions in the highest places of government, industry, or academia, it is an open question today whether their skin color played a part in their advancement. The question itself is the stigma—because either racial discrimination did play a role, in which case the person may be deemed "otherwise unqualified," or it did not, in which case asking the question itself unfairly marks those blacks who would succeed without discrimination. . . .

* * *

[T]he majority has placed its *imprimatur* on a practice that can only weaken the principle of equality embodied in the Declaration of Independence and the Equal Protection Clause. "Our Constitution is color-blind, and neither knows nor tolerates classes among citizens." *Plessy v. Ferguson,* 163 U.S. 537, 559 (1896) (Harlan, J., dissenting). It has been nearly 140 years since Frederick Douglass asked the intellectual ancestors of the Law School to "[d]o nothing with us!" and the Nation adopted the Fourteenth Amendment. Now we must wait another 25 years to see this principle of equality vindicated. I therefore respectfully dissent from the remainder of the Court's opinion and the judgment.

■ CHIEF JUSTICE REHNQUIST, with whom JUSTICE SCALIA, JUSTICE KENNEDY, and JUSTICE THOMAS join, dissenting.

I agree with the Court that, "in the limited circumstance when drawing racial distinctions is permissible," the government must ensure

---

[11] For example, there is no recognition by the Law School in this case that even with their racial discrimination in place, black *men* are "underrepresented" at the Law School. See ABA-LSAC Guide 426 (reporting that the Law School has 46 black women and 28 black men). Why does the Law School not also discriminate in favor of black men over black women, given this underrepresentation? The answer is, again, that all the Law School cares about is its own image among know-it-all elites, not solving real problems like the crisis of black male underperformance.

that its means are narrowly tailored to achieve a compelling state interest. . . . The Law School claims it must take the steps it does to achieve a " 'critical mass' " of underrepresented minority students. But its actual program bears no relation to this asserted goal. Stripped of its "critical mass" veil, the Law School's program is revealed as a naked effort to achieve racial balancing. . . .

Although the Court recites the language of our strict scrutiny analysis, its application of that review is unprecedented in its deference. . . .

In practice, the Law School's program bears little or no relation to its asserted goal of achieving "critical mass." Respondents explain that the Law School seeks to accumulate a "critical mass" of *each* underrepresented minority group. But the record demonstrates that the Law School's admissions practices with respect to these groups differ dramatically and cannot be defended under any consistent use of the term "critical mass."

From 1995 through 2000, the Law School admitted between 1,130 and 1,310 students. Of those, between 13 and 19 were Native American, between 91 and 108 were African-American, and between 47 and 56 were Hispanic. If the Law School is admitting between 91 and 108 African-Americans in order to achieve "critical mass," thereby preventing African-American students from feeling "isolated or like spokespersons for their race," one would think that a number of the same order of magnitude would be necessary to accomplish the same purpose for Hispanics and Native Americans. . . .

These different numbers, moreover, come only as a result of substantially different treatment among the three underrepresented minority groups . . . . The school asserts that it "frequently accepts nonminority applicants with grades and test scores lower than underrepresented minority applicants (and other nonminority applicants) who are rejected." Specifically, the Law School states that "[s]ixty-nine minority applicants were rejected between 1995 and 2000 with at least a 3.5 [Grade Point Average (GPA)] and a [score of] 159 or higher on the [Law School Admission Test (LSAT)]" while a number of Caucasian and Asian-American applicants with similar or lower scores were admitted.

Review of the record reveals only 67 such individuals. Of these 67 individuals, *56* were Hispanic, while only 6 were African-American, and only 5 were Native American. This discrepancy reflects a consistent practice. . . .

Respondents have *never* offered any race-specific arguments explaining why significantly more individuals from one underrepresented minority group are needed in order to achieve "critical mass" or further student body diversity. They certainly have not explained why Hispanics, who they have said are among "the groups most isolated by racial barriers in our country," should have their admission capped out in this manner. . . .

Only when the "critical mass" label is discarded does a likely explanation for these numbers emerge. The Court states that the Law School's goal of attaining a "critical mass" of underrepresented minority students is not an interest in merely " 'assur[ing] within its student body some specified percentage of a particular group merely because of its race or ethnic origin.' " The Court recognizes that such an interest "would amount to outright racial balancing, which is patently unconstitutional."

But the correlation between the percentage of the Law School's pool of applicants who are members of the three minority groups and the percentage of the admitted applicants who are members of these same groups is far too precise . . . . For example, in 1995, when 9.7% of the applicant pool was African-American, 9.4% of the admitted class was African-American. By 2000, only 7.5% of the applicant pool was African-American, and 7.3% of the admitted class was African-American. . . . The tight correlation between the percentage of applicants and admittees of a given race, therefore, must result from careful race based planning by the Law School.

I do not believe that the Constitution gives the Law School such free rein in the use of race. [T]his is precisely the type of racial balancing that the Court itself calls "patently unconstitutional."

Finally, I believe that the Law School's program fails strict scrutiny because it is devoid of any reasonably precise time limit on the Law School's use of race in admissions. . . . Our previous cases have required some limit on the duration of programs such as this because discrimination on the basis of race is invidious.

The Court suggests a possible 25-year limitation on the Law School's current program. Respondents, on the other hand, remain more ambiguous, explaining that "[t]he Law School of course recognizes that race-conscious programs must have reasonable durational limits, and the Sixth Circuit properly found such a limit in the Law School's resolve to cease considering race when genuine race-neutral alternatives become available." These discussions of a time limit are the vaguest of assurances. In truth, they permit the Law School's use of racial preferences on a seemingly permanent basis. . . .

■ **JUSTICE KENNEDY, dissenting.**

The separate opinion by Justice Powell in *Regents of Univ. of Cal. v. Bakke*, 438 U.S. 265 (1978) . . . in my view, states the correct rule for resolving this case. The Court, however, does not apply strict scrutiny. By trying to say otherwise, it undermines both the test and its own controlling precedents. . . .

Having approved the use of race as a factor in the admissions process, the majority proceeds to nullify the essential safeguard Justice Powell insisted upon as the precondition of the approval. The safeguard was rigorous judicial review, with strict scrutiny as the controlling standard. . . . The Court confuses deference to a university's definition of its educational objective with deference to the implementation of this goal. In the context of university admissions the objective of racial diversity can be accepted based on empirical data known to us, but deference is not to be given with respect to the methods by which it is pursued. Preferment by race, when resorted to by the State, can be the most divisive of all policies, containing within it the potential to destroy confidence in the Constitution and in the idea of equality. . . .

To be constitutional, a university's compelling interest in a diverse student body must be achieved by a system where individual assessment is safeguarded through the entire process. There is no constitutional objection to the goal of considering race as one modest factor among many others to achieve diversity, but an educational institution must ensure, through sufficient procedures, that each applicant receives individual consideration and that race does not become a predominant factor in the admissions decisionmaking. The Law School failed to comply with this requirement, and by no means has it carried its burden to show otherwise by the test of strict scrutiny.

The Court's refusal to apply meaningful strict scrutiny will lead to serious consequences. . . . Dean Allan Stillwagon, who directed the Law School's Office of Admissions from 1979 to 1990 . . . testified that faculty members were "breathtakingly cynical" in deciding who would qualify as a member of underrepresented minorities. An example he offered was faculty debate as to whether Cubans should be counted as Hispanics: One professor objected on the grounds that Cubans were Republicans. Many academics at other law schools who are "affirmative action's more forthright defenders readily concede that diversity is merely the current rationale of convenience for a policy that they prefer to justify on other grounds." Schuck, Affirmative Action: Past, Present, and Future, 20 Yale L. & Pol'y Rev. 1, 34 (2002) (citing Levinson, Diversity, 2 U. Pa. J. Const. L. 573, 577–578 (2000); Rubenfeld, Affirmative Action, 107 Yale L.J. 427, 471 (1997)). This is not to suggest the faculty at Michigan or other law schools do not pursue aspirations they consider laudable and consistent with our constitutional traditions. It is but further evidence of the necessity for scrutiny that is real, not feigned, where the corrosive category of race is a factor in decisionmaking. . . .

If universities are given the latitude to administer programs that are tantamount to quotas, they will have few incentives to make the existing minority admissions schemes transparent and protective of individual review. The unhappy consequence will be to perpetuate the hostilities that proper consideration of race is designed to avoid. The perpetuation, of course, would be the worst of all outcomes. Other programs do exist which will be more effective in bringing about the harmony and mutual respect among all citizens that our constitutional tradition has always sought. They, and not the program under review here, should be the model, even if the Court defaults by not demanding it.

It is regrettable the Court's important holding allowing racial minorities to have their special circumstances considered in order to improve their educational opportunities is accompanied by a suspension of the strict scrutiny which was the predicate of allowing race to be considered in the first place. If the Court abdicates its constitutional duty to give strict scrutiny to the use of race in university admissions, it negates my authority to approve the use of race in pursuit of student diversity. The Constitution cannot confer the right to classify on the basis of race even in this special context absent searching judicial review. For these reasons, though I reiterate my approval of giving appropriate consideration to race in this one context, I must dissent in the present case.

NOTE ON AFFIRMATIVE ACTION IN HIGHER EDUCATION

1.   One cannot help but be struck by the influence of Justice Lewis Powell's opinion in *Regents of the University of California v. Bakke*, 438 U.S. 265 (1978)—an opinion that on much of its crucial reasoning garnered exactly *one* vote. Alan Bakke, a white male, applied to the University of California at Davis medical school in both 1973 and 1974, only to be rejected. He sued the university, complaining that he had been excluded from a "special admissions program" that reserved a number of class seats for racial minorities. Bakke convinced the California Supreme Court to hold the special program unlawful, order his admission to the medical school, and enjoin the university from considering race in its admissions program. On appeal, the U.S. Supreme Court affirmed the first two holding, but reversed the injunction forbidding consideration of race in any form.

The only person who agreed with all aspects of this disposition was Justice Powell. Four justices (Burger, Stewart, Rehnquist, and Stevens) thought the university's policy violated Title VI of the Civil Rights Act of 1964 and thus did not reach the constitutional question, although it seems clear that several of these justices would have held the policy unconstitutional if they had needed to decide that question. Four other justices (Brennan, Marshall, White, and Blackmun) rejected both the statutory and constitutional claims, taking a broad view of the government's authority to engage in affirmative action. Justice Powell, however, thought affirmative action subject to strict scrutiny but acknowledged that a university might legitimately pursue a compelling interest in a diverse student body. In doing so, he insisted, the university must eschew racial quotas and guarantee each applicant individualized consideration.

The controlling influence of Justice Powell's opinion, as illustrated in both *Adarand* and *Grutter*, testifies to the power of the "median justice"— that is, the justice or justices that occupy a central position on a divided court. Is it appropriate that the resolution of such weighty constitutional and political issues should consistently—and not just in particular cases—come down to the views of one or two justices? Some critics suggest that these dynamics confirm that the Court is a "political" institution, but is the position taken by Justice Powell in *Bakke* (or Justice O'Connor in *Grutter*) any less "legal" in nature than the views of the other justices?

2.   The Court's adoption of Justice Powell's distinction between quotas and individualized consideration led to a split result for the University of Michigan. On the same day that the University saw its law school admissions policy upheld in *Grutter* but had its *undergraduate* admissions policy struck down in *Gratz v. Bollinger*, 539 U.S. 244 (2003). Michigan's undergraduate policy employed a point system to evaluate applicants, with applicants needing at least 100 (out of 150 possible) points for admission. The affirmative action policy automatically awarded 20 points to each applicant who was an "underrepresented" minority (African-Americans, Hispanics, and Native Americans); by comparison, the policy would provide at most 5 points for "extraordinary artistic talent." Hence, the Court found that Michigan's policy "makes race a decisive factor for virtually every minimally qualified underrepresented minority applicant." As a result, Chief Justice Rehnquist's majority opinion (joined by O'Connor, Kennedy, Scalia, and Thomas) found that the policy was not narrowly tailored to the State's compelling interest in diversity because if failed to provide the sort of meaningful individualized review demanded by Justice Powell's analysis in *Bakke*. Justice O'Connor, the author of *Grutter*, joined the Court's opinion and concurred to underscore the lack of individualized review. Justice Breyer issued a curious opinion concurring in the judgment, which said without explanation that "I join Justice O'CONNOR's opinion except insofar as it joins that of the Court."

Justices Stevens, Souter, and Ginsburg dissented, arguing for an approach that distinguishes benign from malign discrimination and contending that no one was really harmed by Michigan's policy. Given that these justices joined the majority in *Grutter*, should they have made more of an effort to demonstrate that the undergraduate policy met *Grutter*'s standard? Could they have? On the other hand, keep in mind that while Michigan runs a relatively small law school (1001 JD students enrolled in fall 2014), the undergraduate institution is massive (over 28,000 in fall 2014). Is the sort of individualized review that *Grutter* demands practical on that scale?

3.   In *Grutter*, Justice Thomas accused the majority of mischaracterizing the Law School's interests. That interest, he argued, could not have simply been in having a diverse student body, because that could have been achieved through open admissions or a lottery. The interest, rather, was in achieving racial diversity *while maintaining status as a highly selective, "elite" law school.* Is that a fair characterization? If so, to what extent is maintaining an elite law school a compelling interest? Should it make a difference that few states actually do so? That graduates of the Law School make up a relatively small proportion of lawyers serving the state?

Justice Thomas's question points to one of the most difficult aspects of means/ends review: The government's end can almost always be achieved through some other means, but changing the means usually will entail some sacrifice in efficiency or the degree to which the end is met, and collateral values may have to be sacrificed as well. The degree of "narrow tailoring" required at the various levels of scrutiny generally reflects the degree to which the Constitution requires the government to accept those sacrifices. Does the Court's acceptance of the Law School's formulation of its interest in *Grutter* reflect a watering-down of the strict scrutiny standard in this regard?

4.   *Grutter* also departed from ordinary principles of strict scrutiny in deferring to the University's judgments about not only the value of diversity but also the means necessary to reach that goal. Was that appropriate? Certainly there are good reasons to defer to experts about difficult questions of educational policy, much as courts generally defer to expert administrative agencies on complex questions of regulatory policy. But the general notion behind strict scrutiny has been that deference is *not* appropriate when the government impinges on fundamental rights or employs suspect classifications? Has the Court's imposition of strict scrutiny in affirmative action cases come at the cost of watering down the strictness of the scrutiny imposed? If so, is that a positive or negative development?

5.   The Michigan affirmative action story took a somewhat surprising turn in 2006, when the state's voters adopted a state constitutional amendment prohibiting state and local government entities in Michigan from granting race-based preferences in a wide range of decisions. That amendment provided, *inter alia*, that "[t]he state shall not discriminate against, or grant preferential treatment to, any individual or group on the basis of race, sex, color, ethnicity, or national origin in the operation of public employment, public education, or public contracting." Mich. Const. art. I, § 26. A variety of plaintiffs, including proponents of affirmative action as well as students, faculty, and prospective applicants to Michigan public universities, challenged the new provision. Although the district court upheld § 26, the Sixth Circuit (sitting en banc) held the amendment unconstitutional under the Equal Protection Clause.

A divided Supreme Court reversed in *Schuette v. Coalition to Defend Affirmative Action, Integration and Immigrant Rights and Fight for Equality by any Means Necessary (BAMN)*, 134 S. Ct. 1623 (2014). The plaintiffs, and the Sixth Circuit, had relied on cases dealing with government action altering the political channels open to racial minorities for securing policies in their interests. In *Washington v. Seattle Sch. Dist. No. 1*, 458 U.S. 457 (1982), for example, voters opposed to the Seattle School Board's busing plan passed a state initiative barring busing to desegregate schools. The Court found this unconstitutional because "explicitly us[ed] the racial nature of a decision to determine the decisionmaking process."[14] In *Schuette*, however, the Court rejected any broad reading of this "political process doctrine." Justice Kennedy's plurality opinion (joined by Roberts and Alito) read the cases narrowly, suggesting they stand only "for the unremarkable principle that the State may not alter the procedures of government to target racial

---

[14]   *See also Hunter v. Erickson*, 393 U.S. 385 (1969) (striking down an amendment to the Akron city charter requiring any antidiscrimination housing ordinances to be approved by referendum); *Reitman v. Mulkey*, 387 U.S. 369 (1967) (striking down an amendment to the California constitution prohibiting state regulation of private discrimination in housing).

minorities." And Justice Scalia (joined by Thomas) concurred in the judgment on the ground that Seattle and the other "political process" cases should be overruled.

In dissent, Justice Sotomayor (joined by Ginsburg) argued for vigorous adherence to the political process doctrine. As she framed that doctrine, "governmental action deprives minority groups of equal protection when it (1) has a racial focus, targeting a policy or program that inures primarily to the benefit of the minority, and (2) alters the political process in a manner that uniquely burdens racial minorities' ability to achieve their goals through that process." Would it violate this principle for Congress to enact a statute preempting state and local set-asides for minority contractors, because reinstatement of those benefits to minorities would now require an Act of Congress? Doesn't enactment of any federal statute "alter the political process" in a way that makes life more difficult for opponents of the policy that the statute embodies? Would the political process doctrine mean that issues of great concern to racial minorities must always be decided at the lowest possible level of government?

6.   Justice Thomas's dissent in *Grutter* raises difficult and emotionally-fraught issues about the impact of affirmative action on minority students, those students' place in the law school community, and more generally whether affirmative action is good or bad for black people. Frank discussion of those issues in the classroom setting is difficult. It may be easier, however, to address these questions at one remove by asking, "Who decides?" Courts can hear expert evidence on the sociological and educational impact of affirmative action, and—as they do in cases ranging from privacy to punitive damages to the Eighth Amendment—they can apply their own sense of fairness. Electorates may, as they later did in amending the Michigan Constitution, make their own judgments reflecting the popular well. University administrators—at both public institutions and private ones not bound by the Equal Protection Clause—may bring their own expertise and experience to bear. Is diversity also a value here—in the sense that we might better proceed by allowing a diverse group of decisionmakers to make different decisions in different settings?

The answer to this question has implications for a range of issues. They include: whether to formulate the doctrine on benign discrimination as a "rule" (requiring the same outcome in all cases) or a "standard" (allowing cases-by-case judgments); whether to treat public institutions as unique or apply the same rules to private ones through federal statutory requirements and the state action doctrine; and whether to recognize, *contra* the Sixth Circuit in *Schuette*, a zone where some forms of affirmative action are permissible but not required. The continuing division in the Court's opinions on these issues, and the power of the arguments on both sides, suggests that we are a long way from consensus on the right answers to the legitimacy of affirmative action. Given that reality, should the law aim to foster a diversity of responses for the time being?

7.   One plausible reaction to *Grutter* and *Gratz* would be to note the irony of debating basic questions of social justice in the context of admissions to elite law schools. Most observers seem to agree that tweaking such policies

is unlikely to address the real wellsprings of inequality. The last case in this sequence returns us to the context of *Brown* itself: primary and secondary schooling.

Parents Involved in Community Schools
v. Seattle School District No. 1
551 U.S. 701 (2007)

■ Chief JUSTICE ROBERTS announced the judgment of the Court, and delivered the opinion of the Court with respect to Parts I, II, III-A, and III-C, and an opinion with respect to Parts III-B and IV, in which JUSTICE SCALIA, JUSTICE THOMAS, and JUSTICE ALITO join.

The school districts in these cases voluntarily adopted student assignment plans that rely upon race to determine which public schools certain children may attend. The Seattle school district classifies children as white or nonwhite; the Jefferson County school district as black or "other." In Seattle, this racial classification is used to allocate slots in oversubscribed high schools. In Jefferson County, it is used to make certain elementary school assignments and to rule on transfer requests. In each case, the school district relies upon an individual student's race in assigning that student to a particular school, so that the racial balance at the school falls within a predetermined range based on the racial composition of the school district as a whole. Parents of students denied assignment to particular schools under these plans solely because of their race brought suit, contending that allocating children to different public schools on the basis of race violated the Fourteenth Amendment guarantee of equal protection. The Courts of Appeals below upheld the plans. We granted certiorari, and now reverse.

I

Both cases present the same underlying legal question—whether a public school that had not operated legally segregated schools or has been found to be unitary may choose to classify students by race and rely upon that classification in making school assignments. Although we examine the plans under the same legal framework, the specifics of the two plans, and the circumstances surrounding their adoption, are in some respects quite different.

A

Seattle School District No. 1 operates 10 regular public high schools. In 1998, it adopted the plan at issue in this case for assigning students to these schools. The plan allows incoming ninth graders to choose from among any of the district's high schools, ranking however many schools they wish in order of preference.

Some schools are more popular than others. If too many students list the same school as their first choice, the district employs a series of "tiebreakers" to determine who will fill the open slots at the oversubscribed school. The first tiebreaker selects for admission students who have a sibling currently enrolled in the chosen school. The next tiebreaker depends upon the racial composition of the particular school and the race of the individual student. In the district's public schools approximately 41 percent of enrolled students are white; the remaining 59 percent, comprising all other racial groups, are classified by Seattle for assignment purposes as nonwhite.[2] If an oversubscribed school is not within 10 percentage points of the district's overall white/nonwhite racial balance, it is what the district calls "integration positive," and the district employs a tiebreaker that selects for assignment students whose race "will serve to bring the school into balance." If it is still necessary to select students for the school after using the racial tiebreaker, the next tiebreaker is the geographic proximity of the school to the student's residence.

Seattle has never operated segregated schools—legally separate schools for students of different races—nor has it ever been subject to court-ordered desegregation. It nonetheless employs the racial tiebreaker in an attempt to address the effects of racially identifiable housing patterns on school assignments. Most white students live in the northern part of Seattle, most students of other racial backgrounds in the southern part. Four of Seattle's high schools are located in the north—Ballard, Nathan Hale, Ingraham, and Roosevelt—and five in the south—Rainier Beach, Cleveland, West Seattle, Chief Sealth, and Franklin. One school—Garfield—is more or less in the center of Seattle.

For the 2000–2001 school year, five of these schools were oversubscribed—Ballard, Nathan Hale, Roosevelt, Garfield, and Franklin—so much so that 82 percent of incoming ninth graders ranked one of these schools as their first choice. Three of the oversubscribed schools were "integration positive" because the school's white enrollment the previous school year was greater than 51 percent—Ballard, Nathan Hale, and Roosevelt. Thus, more nonwhite students (107, 27, and 82, respectively) who selected one of these three schools as a top choice received placement at the school than would have been the case had race not been considered, and proximity been the next tiebreaker. Franklin was "integration positive" because its nonwhite enrollment the previous school year was greater than 69 percent; 89 more white students were assigned to Franklin by operation of the racial tiebreaker in the 2000–2001 school year than otherwise would have been. Garfield was the only oversubscribed school whose composition during the 1999–2000 school year was within the racial guidelines, although in previous years Garfield's enrollment had been predominantly nonwhite, and the racial tiebreaker had been used to give preference to white students.

---

[2] The racial breakdown of this nonwhite group is approximately 23.8 percent Asian-American, 23.1 percent African-American, 10.3 percent Latino, and 2.8 percent Native-American.

Petitioner Parents Involved in Community Schools (Parents Involved) is a nonprofit corporation comprising the parents of children who have been or may be denied assignment to their chosen high school in the district because of their race. The concerns of Parents Involved are illustrated by Jill Kurfirst, who sought to enroll her ninth-grade son, Andy Meeks, in Ballard High School's special Biotechnology Career Academy. Andy suffered from attention deficit hyperactivity disorder and dyslexia, but had made good progress with hands-on instruction, and his mother and middle school teachers thought that the smaller biotechnology program held the most promise for his continued success. Andy was accepted into this selective program but, because of the racial tiebreaker, was denied assignment to Ballard High School. Parents Involved commenced this suit in the Western District of Washington, alleging that Seattle's use of race in assignments violated the Equal Protection Clause of the Fourteenth Amendment . . . .

The District Court granted summary judgment to the school district. . . . A panel of the Ninth Circuit then . . . reversed the District Court . . . determin[ing] that while achieving racial diversity and avoiding racial isolation are compelling government interests, Seattle's use of the racial tiebreaker was not narrowly tailored to achieve these interests. The Ninth Circuit granted rehearing en banc and overruled the panel decision, affirming the District Court's determination that Seattle's plan was narrowly tailored to serve a compelling government interest. We granted certiorari.

B

Jefferson County Public Schools operates the public school system in metropolitan Louisville, Kentucky. In 1973 a federal court found that Jefferson County had maintained a segregated school system, and in 1975 the District Court entered a desegregation decree. Jefferson County operated under this decree until 2000, when the District Court dissolved the decree after finding that the district had achieved unitary status by eliminating "[t]o the greatest extent practicable" the vestiges of its prior policy of segregation.

In 2001, after the decree had been dissolved, Jefferson County adopted the voluntary student assignment plan at issue in this case. Approximately 34 percent of the district's 97,000 students are black; most of the remaining 66 percent are white. The plan requires all nonmagnet schools to maintain a minimum black enrollment of 15 percent, and a maximum black enrollment of 50 percent.

At the elementary school level, based on his or her address, each student is designated a "resides" school to which students within a specific geographic area are assigned; elementary resides schools are "grouped into clusters in order to facilitate integration." The district assigns students to nonmagnet schools in one of two ways: Parents of kindergartners, first graders, and students new to the district may submit an application indicating a first and second choice among the schools within their cluster; students who do not submit such an application are assigned within the cluster by the district. Decisions to assign students to schools within each cluster are based on available space within the schools and the racial guidelines in the District's current student assignment plan. If a school has reached the "extremes of the racial guidelines," a student whose race would contribute to the school's racial imbalance will not be assigned there. After assignment, students at all grade levels are permitted to apply to transfer between nonmagnet schools in the district. Transfers may be requested for any number of reasons, and may be denied because of lack of available space or on the basis of the racial guidelines.

When petitioner Crystal Meredith moved into the school district in August 2002, she sought to enroll her son, Joshua McDonald, in kindergarten for the 2002–2003 school year. His resides school was only a mile from his new home, but it had no available space—assignments had been made in May, and the class was full. Jefferson County assigned Joshua to another elementary school in his cluster, Young Elementary. This school was 10 miles from home, and Meredith sought to transfer Joshua to a school in a different cluster, Bloom Elementary, which—like his resides school—was only a mile from home. Space was available at Bloom, and intercluster transfers are allowed, but Joshua's transfer was nonetheless denied because, in the words of Jefferson County, "[t]he transfer would have an adverse effect on desegregation compliance" of Young.

Meredith brought suit in the Western District of Kentucky, alleging violations of the Equal Protection Clause of the Fourteenth Amendment. The District Court found that Jefferson County had asserted a compelling interest in maintaining racially diverse schools, and that the assignment plan was . . . narrowly tailored to serve that compelling interest. The Sixth Circuit affirmed . . . .

III

A

It is well established that when the government distributes burdens or benefits on the basis of individual racial classifications, that action is reviewed under strict scrutiny. *Grutter v. Bollinger*; Adarand Constructors, Inc. v. Pena . . . . In order to satisfy this searching standard of review, the school districts must demonstrate that the use of individual racial classifications in the assignment plans here under review is "narrowly tailored" to achieve a "compelling" government interest.

[O]ur prior cases, in evaluating the use of racial classifications in the school context, have recognized two interests that qualify as compelling. The first is the compelling interest of remedying the effects of past intentional discrimination. See *Freeman v. Pitts,* 503 U.S. 467, 494 (1992). Yet the Seattle public schools have not shown that they were ever segregated by law, and were not subject to court-ordered desegregation decrees. The Jefferson County public schools were previously segregated by law and were subject to a desegregation decree entered in 1975. In 2000, the District Court that entered that decree dissolved it, finding that Jefferson County had "eliminated the vestiges associated with the former policy of segregation and its pernicious effects," and thus had achieved "unitary" status. Jefferson County accordingly does not rely upon an interest in remedying the effects of past intentional discrimination in defending its present use of race in assigning students.

Nor could it. We have emphasized that the harm being remedied by mandatory desegregation plans is the harm that is traceable to segregation, and that "the Constitution is not violated by racial imbalance in the schools, without more." *Milliken v. Bradley,* 433 U.S. 267, 280 n. 14 (1977). Once Jefferson County achieved unitary status, it had remedied the constitutional wrong that allowed race-based assignments. Any continued use of race must be justified on some other basis.

The second government interest we have recognized as compelling for purposes of strict scrutiny is the interest in diversity in higher education upheld in *Grutter.* The specific interest found compelling in *Grutter* was student body diversity "in the context of higher education." The diversity interest was not focused on race alone but encompassed "all factors that may contribute to student body diversity." . . .

The Court quoted the articulation of diversity from Justice Powell's opinion in *Regents of Univ. of Cal. v. Bakke,* 438 U.S. 265 (1978), noting that "it is not an interest in simple ethnic diversity, in which a specified percentage of the student body is in effect guaranteed to be members of selected ethnic groups, that can justify the use of race." Instead, what was upheld in *Grutter* was consideration of "a far broader array of qualifications and characteristics of which racial or ethnic origin is but a single though important element."

The entire gist of the analysis in *Grutter* was that the admissions program at issue there focused on each applicant as an individual, and not simply as a member of a particular racial group. The classification of applicants by race upheld in *Grutter* was only as part of a "highly individualized, holistic review." . . . The point of the narrow tailoring analysis in which the *Grutter* Court engaged was to ensure that the use of racial classifications was indeed part of a broader assessment of diversity, and not simply an effort to achieve racial balance, which the Court explained would be "patently unconstitutional."

In the present cases, by contrast, race is not considered as part of a broader effort to achieve "exposure to widely diverse people, cultures, ideas, and viewpoints"; race, for some students, is determinative standing alone. The districts argue that other factors, such as student preferences, affect assignment decisions under their plans, but under each plan when race comes into play, it is decisive by itself. It is not simply one factor weighed with others in reaching a decision, as in

Grutter; it is *the* factor. Like the University of Michigan undergraduate plan struck down in *Gratz,* the plans here "do not provide for a meaningful individualized review of applicants" but instead rely on racial classifications in a "nonindividualized, mechanical" way.

Even when it comes to race, the plans here employ only a limited notion of diversity, viewing race exclusively in white/nonwhite terms in Seattle and black/"other" terms in Jefferson County. The Seattle "Board Statement Reaffirming Diversity Rationale" speaks of the "inherent educational value" in "[p]roviding students the opportunity to attend schools with diverse student enrollment." But under the Seattle plan, a school with 50 percent Asian-American students and 50 percent white students but no African-American, Native-American, or Latino students would qualify as balanced, while a school with 30 percent Asian-American, 25 percent African-American, 25 percent Latino, and 20 percent white students would not. It is hard to understand how a plan that could allow these results can be viewed as being concerned with achieving enrollment that is "broadly diverse." . . .

B

[B]oth school districts assert additional interests. . . . to justify their race-based assignments. . . . Seattle contends that its use of race helps to reduce racial concentration in schools and to ensure that racially concentrated housing patterns do not prevent nonwhite students from having access to the most desirable schools. Jefferson County has articulated a similar goal, phrasing its interest in terms of educating its students "in a racially integrated environment." Each school district argues that educational and broader socialization benefits flow from a racially diverse learning environment, and each contends that because the diversity they seek is racial diversity—not the broader diversity at issue in *Grutter*—it makes sense to promote that interest directly by relying on race alone.

The parties and their amici dispute whether racial diversity in schools in fact has a marked impact on test scores and other objective yardsticks or achieves intangible socialization benefits. The debate is not one we need to resolve, however, because it is clear that the racial classifications employed by the districts are not narrowly tailored to the goal of achieving the educational and social benefits asserted to flow from racial diversity. In design and operation, the plans are directed only to racial balance, pure and simple, an objective this Court has repeatedly condemned as illegitimate.

The plans are tied to each district's specific racial demographics, rather than to any pedagogic concept of the level of diversity needed to obtain the asserted educational benefits. In Seattle, the district seeks white enrollment of between 31 and 51 percent (within 10 percent of "the district white average" of 41 percent), and nonwhite enrollment of between 49 and 69 percent (within 10 percent of "the district minority average" of 59 percent). In Jefferson County, by contrast, the district seeks black enrollment of no less than 15 or more than 50 percent, a range designed to be "equally above and below Black student enrollment systemwide," based on the objective of achieving at "all schools . . . an African-American enrollment equivalent to the average district-wide African-American enrollment" of 34 percent. . . . The districts offer no evidence that the level of racial diversity necessary to achieve the asserted educational benefits happens to coincide with the racial demographics of the respective school districts. . . .

In fact, in each case the extreme measure of relying on race in assignments is unnecessary to achieve the stated goals, even as defined by the districts. For example, at Franklin High School in Seattle, the racial tiebreaker was applied because nonwhite enrollment exceeded 69 percent, and resulted in an incoming ninth-grade class in 2000–2001 that was 30.3 percent Asian-American, 21.9 percent African-American, 6.8 percent Latino, 0.5 percent Native-American, and 40.5 percent Caucasian. Without the racial tiebreaker, the class would have been 39.6 percent Asian-American, 30.2 percent African-American, 8.3 percent Latino, 1.1 percent Native-American, and 20.8 percent Caucasian. When the actual racial breakdown is considered, enrolling students without regard to their race yields a substantially diverse student body under any definition of diversity. . . .

[W]orking backward to achieve a particular type of racial balance, rather than working forward from some demonstration of the level of diversity that provides the purported benefits, is a fatal flaw under our existing precedent. We have many times over reaffirmed that "[r]acial balance is not to be achieved for its own sake." *Freeman,* 503 U.S., at 494. *Grutter* itself reiterated that "outright racial balancing" is "patently unconstitutional." 539 U.S., at 330.

Accepting racial balancing as a compelling state interest would justify the imposition of racial proportionality throughout American society, contrary to our repeated recognition that "[a]t the heart of the Constitution's guarantee of equal protection lies the simple command that the Government must treat citizens as individuals, not as simply components of a racial, religious, sexual or national class." *Miller v. Johnson,* 515 U.S. 900, 911 (1995).[14] . . .

The validity of our concern that racial balancing has no logical stopping point is demonstrated here by the degree to which the districts tie their racial guidelines to their demographics. As the districts' demographics shift, so too will their definition of racial diversity. . . .

---

[14] In contrast, Seattle's Web site formerly described "emphasizing individualism as opposed to a more collective ideology" as a form of "cultural racism," and currently states that the district has no intention " 'to hold onto unsuccessful concepts such as [a] . . . colorblind mentality.' " Compare *Plessy v. Ferguson,* 163 U.S. 537, 559 (1896) (Harlan, J., dissenting) ("Our Constitution is color-blind, and neither knows nor tolerates classes among citizens. In respect of civil rights, all citizens are equal before the law").

Jefferson County phrases its interest as "racial integration," but integration certainly does not require the sort of racial proportionality reflected in its plan. . . .

To the extent the objective is sufficient diversity so that students see fellow students as individuals rather than solely as members of a racial group, using means that treat students solely as members of a racial group is fundamentally at cross-purposes with that end.

C

The districts assert, as they must, that the way in which they have employed individual racial classifications is necessary to achieve their stated ends. The minimal effect these classifications have on student assignments, however, suggests that other means would be effective. Seattle's racial tiebreaker results, in the end, only in shifting a small number of students between schools. . . .

As the panel majority in [the Court of Appeals] concluded:

> [T]he tiebreaker's annual effect is thus merely to shuffle a few handfuls of different minority students between a few schools— about a dozen additional Latinos into Ballard, a dozen black students into Nathan Hale, perhaps two dozen Asians into Roosevelt, and so on. The District has not met its burden of proving these marginal changes . . . outweigh the cost of subjecting hundreds of students to disparate treatment based solely upon the color of their skin.

Similarly, Jefferson County's use of racial classifications has only a minimal effect on the assignment of students. . . . Jefferson County estimates that the racial guidelines account for only 3 percent of assignments. As Jefferson County explains, "the racial guidelines have minimal impact in this process, because they mostly influence student assignment in subtle and indirect ways."

While we do not suggest that *greater* use of race would be preferable, the minimal impact of the districts' racial classifications on school enrollment casts doubt on the necessity of using racial classifications. . . . The districts have also failed to show that they considered methods other than explicit racial classifications to achieve their stated goals. Narrow tailoring requires serious, good faith consideration of workable race-neutral alternatives, and yet in Seattle several alternative assignment plans—many of which would not have used express racial classifications—were rejected with little or no consideration. Jefferson County has failed to present any evidence that it considered alternatives, even though the district already claims that its goals are achieved primarily through means other than the racial classifications.

IV

. . . Justice BREYER seeks to justify the plans at issue under our precedents recognizing the compelling interest in remedying past intentional discrimination. Not even the school districts go this far, and for good reason. The distinction between segregation by state action and racial imbalance caused by other factors has been central to our jurisprudence in this area for generations. The dissent elides this distinction between *de jure* and *de facto* segregation, casually intimates that Seattle's school attendance patterns reflect illegal segregation,[15] and fails to credit the judicial determination—under the most rigorous standard—that Jefferson County had eliminated the vestiges of prior segregation. The dissent thus alters in fundamental ways not only the facts presented here but the established law.

Justice BREYER's reliance on *McDaniel v. Barresi*, 402 U.S. 39 (1971), highlights how far removed the discussion in the dissent is from the question actually presented in these cases. *McDaniel* concerned a Georgia school system that had been segregated by law. There was no doubt that the county had operated a "dual school system," and no one questions that the obligation to disestablish a school system segregated by law can include race-conscious remedies—whether or not a court had issued an order to that effect. The present cases are before us, however, because the Seattle school district was never segregated by law, and the Jefferson County district has been found to be unitary, having eliminated the vestiges of its prior dual status. The justification for race-conscious remedies in *McDaniel* is therefore not applicable here. . . .

Justice BREYER's dissent next relies heavily on dicta from *Swann v. Charlotte-Mecklenburg Bd. of Ed.*, 402 U.S. 1, 16 (1970)—far more heavily than the school districts themselves. The dissent acknowledges that the two-sentence discussion in *Swann* was pure dicta, but nonetheless asserts that it demonstrates a "basic principle of constitutional law" that provides "authoritative legal guidance." Initially, as the Court explained just last Term, "we are not bound to follow our dicta in a prior case in which the point now at issue was not fully debated." *Central Va. Community College v. Katz*, 546 U.S. 356, 363 (2006). That is particularly true given that, when *Swann* was decided, this Court had not yet confirmed that strict scrutiny applies to racial classifications like those before us. . . .

Justice BREYER would not only put such extraordinary weight on admitted dicta, but relies on the statement for something it does not remotely say. *Swann* addresses only a possible state objective; it says nothing of the permissible *means*—race conscious or otherwise—that a school district might employ to achieve that objective. The reason for this

---

[15] Justice BREYER makes much of the fact that in 1978 Seattle "settled" an NAACP complaint alleging illegal segregation with the federal Office for Civil Rights (OCR). The memorandum of agreement between Seattle and OCR, of course, contains no admission by Seattle that such segregation ever existed or was ongoing at the time of the agreement, and simply reflects a "desire to avoid the incovenience [*sic*] and expense of a formal OCR investigation," which OCR was obligated under law to initiate upon the filing of such a complaint.

omission is clear enough, since the case did not involve any voluntary means adopted by a school district. . . .

Further, for all the lower court cases Justice BREYER cites as evidence of the "prevailing legal assumption," embodied by *Swann,* very few are pertinent. Most are not. For example, the dissent features *Tometz v. Board of Ed., Waukegan City School Dist. No. 61,* 39 Ill.2d 593, 597– 598, 237 N.E.2d 498, 501 (1968), as evidence that "state and federal courts had considered the matter settled and uncontroversial." But *Tometz* addressed a challenge to a statute requiring race-consciousness in drawing school attendance boundaries—an issue well beyond the scope of the question presented in these cases. Importantly, it considered that issue only under rational-basis review, which even the dissent grudgingly recognizes is an improper standard for evaluating express racial classifications. Other cases cited are similarly inapplicable. See, *e.g., Citizens for Better Ed. v. Goose Creek Consol. Independent School Dist.,* 719 S.W.2d 350, 352–353 (Tex.App.1986) (upholding rezoning plan under rational-basis review).[16] . . .

Justice BREYER's dissent also asserts that these cases are controlled by *Grutter,* claiming that the existence of a compelling interest in these cases "follows a fortiori " from *Grutter,* and accusing us of tacitly overruling that case. The dissent overreads *Grutter,* however, in suggesting that it renders pure racial balancing a constitutionally compelling interest; *Grutter* itself recognized that using race simply to achieve racial balance would be "patently unconstitutional." The Court was exceedingly careful in describing the interest furthered in *Grutter* as "not an interest in simple ethnic diversity" but rather a "far broader array of qualifications and characteristics" in which race was but a single element. We take the *Grutter* Court at its word. . . .

Justice BREYER's dissent candidly dismisses the significance of this Court's repeated *holdings* that all racial classifications must be reviewed under strict scrutiny, arguing that a different standard of review should be applied because the districts use race for beneficent rather than malicious purposes.

This Court has recently reiterated, however, that " '*all* racial classifications [imposed by government] . . . must be analyzed by a reviewing court under strict scrutiny.' " *Johnson v. California,* 543 U.S. 499, 505 (2005). Justice BREYER nonetheless relies on the good intentions and motives of the school districts, stating that he has found "no case that . . . repudiated this constitutional asymmetry between that which seeks to *exclude* and that which seeks to *include* members of

---

[16] In fact, all the cases Justice BREYER's dissent cites as evidence of the "prevailing legal assumption" were decided before this Court definitively determined that "all racial classifications . . . must be analyzed by a reviewing court under strict scrutiny." *Adarand Constructors, Inc. v. Peña,* 515 U.S. 200, 227 (1995). Many proceeded under the now-rejected view that classifications seeking to benefit a disadvantaged racial group should be held to a lesser standard of review. . . .

minority races." We have found many. Our cases clearly reject the argument that motives affect the strict scrutiny analysis. See *Johnson, supra,* at 505 ("We have insisted on strict scrutiny in every context, even for so-called 'benign' racial classifications"); *Adarand, supra,* at 227 (rejecting idea that " 'benign' " racial classifications may be held to "different standards"); *Croson,* 488 U.S., at 500 ("Racial classifications are suspect, and that means that simple legislative assurances of good intention cannot suffice"). . . .

The reasons for rejecting a motives test for racial classifications are clear enough. "The Court's emphasis on 'benign racial classifications' suggests confidence in its ability to distinguish good from harmful governmental uses of racial criteria. History should teach greater humility . . . .

Justice BREYER speaks of bringing "the races" together . . . as the justification for excluding individuals on the basis of their race. Again, this approach to racial classifications is fundamentally at odds with our precedent, which makes clear that the Equal Protection Clause protect[s] *persons,* not *groups.* This fundamental principle goes back, in this context, to *Brown* itself. See *Brown v. Board of Education,* 349 U.S. 294, 300 (1955) (*Brown II*) ("At stake is the *personal* interest of the plaintiffs in admission to public schools . . . on a nondiscriminatory basis" (emphasis added)). . . .

Justice BREYER's position comes down to a familiar claim: The end justifies the means. . . . Our established strict scrutiny test for racial classifications, however, insists on detailed examination, both as to ends *and* as to means. Simply because the school districts may seek a worthy goal does not mean they are free to discriminate on the basis of race to achieve it, or that their racial classifications should be subject to less exacting scrutiny.

Despite his argument that these cases should be evaluated under a "standard of review that is not 'strict' in the traditional sense of that word," Justice BREYER still purports to apply strict scrutiny to these cases. It is evident, however, that Justice BREYER's brand of narrow tailoring is quite unlike anything found in our precedents. Without any detailed discussion of the operation of the plans, the students who are affected, or the districts' failure to consider race-neutral alternatives, the dissent concludes that the districts have shown that these racial classifications are necessary to achieve the districts' stated goals. . . .

In keeping with his view that strict scrutiny should not apply, Justice BREYER repeatedly urges deference to local school boards on these issues. Such deference is fundamentally at odds with our equal protection jurisprudence. We put the burden on state actors to demonstrate that their race-based policies are justified.

Justice BREYER's dissent ends on an unjustified note of alarm. It predicts that today's decision "threaten[s]" the validity of "[h]undreds of state and federal statutes and regulations." But the examples the dissent mentions—for example, a provision of the No Child Left Behind Act of 2001 that requires States to set measurable objectives to track the achievement of students from major racial and ethnic groups, 20 U.S.C. § 6311(b)(2)(C)(v) (2000 ed., Supp. IV)—have nothing to do with the pertinent issues in these cases.

Justice BREYER also suggests that other means for achieving greater racial diversity in schools are necessarily unconstitutional if the racial classifications at issue in these cases cannot survive strict scrutiny. These other means—*e.g.,* where to construct new schools, how to allocate resources among schools, and which academic offerings to provide to attract students to certain schools—implicate different considerations than the explicit racial classifications at issue in these cases, and we express no opinion on their validity—not even in dicta. . . .

* * *

If the need for the racial classifications embraced by the school districts is unclear, even on the districts' own terms, the costs are undeniable. . . . Government action dividing us by race is inherently suspect because such classifications promote "notions of racial inferiority and lead to a politics of racial hostility," *Croson,* 488 U.S., at 493 (plurality opinion), "reinforce the belief, held by too many for too much of our history, that individuals should be judged by the color of their skin," *Shaw v. Reno,* 509 U.S. 630, 657 (1993), and "endorse race-based reasoning and the conception of a Nation divided into racial blocs, thus contributing to an escalation of racial hostility and conflict." *Metro Broadcasting,* 497 U.S., at 603 (O'Connor, J., dissenting). As the Court explained in *Rice v. Cayetano,* 528 U.S. 495, 517 (2000), "[o]ne of the principal reasons race is treated as a forbidden classification is that it demeans the dignity and worth of a person to be judged by ancestry instead of by his or her own merit and essential qualities."

All this is true enough in the contexts in which these statements were made—government contracting, voting districts, allocation of broadcast licenses, and electing state officers—but when it comes to using race to assign children to schools, history will be heard. In *Brown v. Board of Education,* 347 U.S. 483 (1954) (*Brown I*), we held that segregation deprived black children of equal educational opportunities regardless of whether school facilities and other tangible factors were equal, because government classification and separation on grounds of race themselves denoted inferiority. It was not the inequality of the facilities but the fact of legally separating children on the basis of race on which the Court relied to find a constitutional violation in 1954. The next Term, we accordingly stated that "full compliance" with *Brown I* required school districts "to achieve a system of determining admission to the public schools *on a nonracial basis.*" *Brown II,* 349 U.S., at 300–301 (emphasis added).

The parties and their *amici* debate which side is more faithful to the heritage of *Brown,* but the position of the plaintiffs in *Brown* was spelled out in their brief and could not have been clearer: "[T]he Fourteenth Amendment prevents states from according differential treatment to American children on the basis of their color or race." What do the racial classifications at issue here do, if not accord differential treatment on the basis of race? As counsel who appeared before this Court for the plaintiffs in *Brown* put it: "We have one fundamental contention which we will seek to develop in the course of this argument, and that contention is that no State has any authority under the equal-protection clause of the Fourteenth Amendment to use race as a factor in affording educational opportunities among its citizens." Tr. of Oral Arg. in *Brown I,* O.T. 1952, No. 8, p. 7 (Robert L. Carter, Dec. 9, 1952). There is no ambiguity in that statement. And it was that position that prevailed in this Court . . . .

Before *Brown,* schoolchildren were told where they could and could not go to school based on the color of their skin. The school districts in these cases have not carried the heavy burden of demonstrating that we should allow this once again—even for very different reasons. For schools that never segregated on the basis of race, such as Seattle, or that have removed the vestiges of past segregation, such as Jefferson County, the way "to achieve a system of determining admission to the public schools on a nonracial basis," *Brown II, supra,* at 300–301, is to stop assigning students on a racial basis. The way to stop discrimination on the basis of race is to stop discriminating on the basis of race.

The judgments of the Courts of Appeals for the Sixth and Ninth Circuits are reversed, and the cases are remanded for further proceedings.

It is so ordered.

■ JUSTICE THOMAS, concurring.

Today, the Court holds that state entities may not experiment with race-based means to achieve ends they deem socially desirable. I wholly concur in THE CHIEF JUSTICE's opinion. I write separately to address several of the contentions in Justice BREYER's dissent. Contrary to the dissent's arguments, resegregation is not occurring in Seattle or Louisville; these school boards have no present interest in remedying past segregation; and these race-based student-assignment programs do not serve any compelling state interest. Accordingly, the plans are unconstitutional. Disfavoring a colorblind interpretation of the Constitution, the dissent would give school boards a free hand to make decisions on the basis of race—an approach reminiscent of that advocated by the segregationists in *Brown v. Board of Education,* 347 U.S. 483 (1954). This approach is just as wrong today as it was a half century ago. . . .

I

A

Because this Court has authorized and required race-based remedial measures to address *de jure* segregation, it is important to define segregation clearly and to distinguish it from racial imbalance. In the context of public schooling, segregation is the deliberate operation of a school system to "carry out a governmental policy to separate pupils in schools solely on the basis of race." *Swann v. Charlotte-Mecklenburg Bd. of Ed.,* 402 U.S. 1, 6 (1971). . . . Racial imbalance is the failure of a school district's individual schools to match or approximate the demographic makeup of the student population at large. Racial imbalance is not segregation. Although presently observed racial imbalance might result from past *de jure* segregation, racial imbalance can also result from any number of innocent private decisions, including voluntary housing choices. . . . Because racial imbalance is not inevitably linked to unconstitutional segregation, it is not unconstitutional in and of itself.

Although there is arguably a danger of racial imbalance in schools in Seattle and Louisville, there is no danger of resegregation. No one contends that Seattle has established or that Louisville has reestablished a dual school system that separates students on the basis of race. . . .

C

. . . . [A] school cannot "remedy" racial imbalance in the same way that it can remedy segregation. Remediation of past *de jure* segregation is a one-time process involving the redress of a discrete legal injury inflicted by an identified entity. At some point, the discrete injury will be remedied, and the school district will be declared unitary. Unlike *de jure* segregation, there is no ultimate remedy for racial imbalance. Individual schools will fall in and out of balance in the natural course, and the appropriate balance itself will shift with a school district's changing demographics. Thus, racial balancing will have to take place on an indefinite basis—a continuous process with no identifiable culpable party and no discernable end point. In part for those reasons, the Court has never permitted outright racial balancing solely for the purpose of achieving a particular racial balance.

II

A

. . . Even supposing it mattered to the constitutional analysis, the race-based student-assignment programs before us are not as benign as the dissent believes. [R]acial paternalism and its unintended consequences can be as poisonous and pernicious as any other form of discrimination. As these programs demonstrate, every time the government uses racial criteria to "bring the races together," someone gets excluded, and the person excluded suffers an injury solely because of his or her race. The petitioner in the Louisville case received a letter from the school board informing her that her *kindergartner* would not be allowed to attend the school of petitioner's choosing because of the child's race. Doubtless, hundreds of letters like this went out from both school boards every year these race-based assignment plans were in operation. This type of exclusion, solely on the basis of race, is precisely the sort of government action that pits the races against one another, exacerbates racial tension, and provokes resentment among those who believe that they have been wronged by the government's use of race. . . .

B

Though the dissent admits to discomfort in applying strict scrutiny to these plans, it claims to have nonetheless applied that exacting standard. But in its search for a compelling interest, the dissent casually accepts even the most tenuous interests asserted on behalf of the plans, grouping them all under the term "integration." "[I]ntegration," we are told, has "three essential elements." None of these elements is compelling. . . .

1

According to the dissent, integration involves "an interest in setting right the consequences of prior conditions of segregation." . . . [T]he school boards have no interest in remedying the sundry consequences of prior segregation unrelated to schooling, such as "housing patterns, employment practices, economic conditions, and social attitudes." General claims that past school segregation affected such varied societal trends are "too amorphous a basis for imposing a racially classified remedy," *Wygant,* 476 U.S., at 276 (plurality opinion), because "[i]t is sheer speculation" how decades-past segregation in the school system might have affected these trends, see *Croson,* 488 U.S., at 499. Consequently, school boards seeking to remedy those societal problems with race-based measures in schools today would have no way to gauge the proper scope of the remedy. Indeed, remedial measures geared toward such broad and unrelated societal ills have " 'no logical stopping point,' " *ibid.,* and threaten to become "ageless in their reach into the past, and timeless in their ability to affect the future," *Wygant, supra,* at 276 (plurality opinion). . . .

2

Next, the dissent argues that . . . racially balanced schools improve educational outcomes for black children. In support, the dissent unquestioningly cites certain social science research to support propositions that are hotly disputed among social scientists. In reality, it is far from apparent that coerced racial mixing has any educational benefits, much less that integration is necessary to black achievement.

Scholars have differing opinions as to whether educational benefits arise from racial balancing. Some have concluded that black students receive genuine educational benefits. See, *e.g.,* Crain & Mahard, Desegregation and Black Achievement: A Review of the Research, 42 Law & Contemp. Prob. 17, 48 (Summer 1978). Others have been more circumspect. See, *e.g.,* Henderson, Greenberg, Schneider, Uribe, & Verdugo, High-Quality Schooling for African American Students, in Beyond Desegregation 162, 166 (M. Shujaa ed. 1996) ("Perhaps desegregation does not have a single effect, positive or negative, on the academic achievement of African American students, but rather some strategies help, some hurt, and still others make no difference whatsoever. It is clear to us that focusing simply on demographic issues detracts from focusing on improving schools"). And some have concluded that there are no demonstrable educational benefits. See, *e.g.,* Armor & Rossell, Desegregation and Resegregation in the Public Schools, in Beyond the Color Line: New Perspectives on Race and Ethnicity in America 219, 239, 251 (A. Thernstrom & S. Thernstrom eds. 2002). The *amicus* briefs in the cases before us mirror this divergence of opinion. . . .

Add to the inconclusive social science the fact of black achievement in "racially isolated" environments. See T. Sowell, Education: Assumptions Versus History 7–38 (1986). Before *Brown,* the most prominent example of an exemplary black school was Dunbar High School. Dunbar is by no means an isolated example. Even after *Brown,* some schools with predominantly black enrollments have achieved outstanding educational results. There is also evidence that black students attending historically black colleges achieve better academic results than those attending predominantly white colleges.

The Seattle School Board itself must believe that racial mixing is not necessary to black achievement. Seattle operates a K–8 "African-American Academy," which has a "nonwhite" enrollment of 99%. That school was founded in 1990 as part of the school board's effort to "increase academic achievement." According to the school's most recent annual report, "[a]cademic excellence" is its "primary goal." This racially imbalanced environment has reportedly produced test scores "higher across all grade levels in reading, writing and math." Contrary to what the dissent would have predicted, the children in Seattle's African American Academy have shown gains when placed in a "highly segregated" environment.

Given this tenuous relationship between forced racial mixing and improved educational results for black children, the dissent cannot plausibly maintain that an educational element supports the integration interest, let alone makes it compelling.

Perhaps recognizing as much, the dissent argues that the social science evidence is "strong enough to permit a democratically elected school board reasonably to determine that this interest is a compelling one." This assertion is inexplicable. It is not up to the school boards—the very government entities whose race-based practices we must strictly scrutinize—to determine what interests qualify as compelling under the Fourteenth Amendment to the United States Constitution. Rather, this Court must assess independently the nature of the interest asserted and the evidence to support it in order to determine whether it qualifies as compelling under our precedents. In making such a determination, we have deferred to state authorities only once, see *Grutter,* 539 U.S., at 328–330, and that deference was prompted by factors uniquely relevant to higher education. The dissent's proposed test—whether sufficient social science evidence supports a government unit's conclusion that the interest it asserts is compelling—calls to mind the rational-basis standard of review the dissent purports not to apply. See *Williamson v. Lee Optical of Okla., Inc.,* 348 U.S. 483, 488 (1955). Furthermore, it would leave our equal protection jurisprudence at the mercy of elected government officials evaluating the evanescent views of a handful of social scientists. To adopt the dissent's deferential approach would be to abdicate our constitutional responsibilities.

3

Finally, the dissent asserts a "democratic element" to the integration interest. It defines the "democratic element" as "an interest in producing an educational environment that reflects the 'pluralistic society' in which our children will live." Environmental reflection, though, is just another way to say racial balancing. And "[p]referring members of any one group for no reason other than race or ethnic origin is discrimination for its own sake." *Bakke,* 438 U.S., at 307 (opinion of Powell, J.). This the Constitution forbids. . . .

By the dissent's account, improvements in racial attitudes depend upon the increased contact between black and white students thought to occur in more racially balanced schools. There is no guarantee, however, that students of different races in the same school will actually spend time with one another. Schools frequently group students by academic ability as an aid to efficient instruction, but such groupings often result in classrooms with high concentrations of one race or another. See, *e.g.,* Yonezawa, Wells, & Serna, Choosing Tracks: "Freedom of Choice" in Detracking Schools, 39 Am. Ed. Research J. 37, 38 (2002); Mickelson, Subverting Swann: First- and Second-Generation Segregation in the Charlotte-Mecklenburg Schools, 38 Am. Ed. Research J. 215, 233–234 (2001) (describing this effect in schools in Charlotte, North Carolina). In addition to classroom separation, students of different races within the same school may separate themselves socially. See Hallinan & Williams, Interracial Friendship Choices in Secondary Schools, 54 Am. Sociological Rev. 67, 72–76 (1989). Therefore, even supposing interracial contact leads directly to improvements in racial attitudes and race relations, a program that assigns students of different races to the same schools might not capture those benefits. Simply putting students together under the same roof does not necessarily mean that the students will learn together or even interact.

Furthermore, it is unclear whether increased interracial contact improves racial attitudes and relations.[17] One researcher has stated that "the reviews of desegregation and intergroup relations were unable to come to any conclusion about what the probable effects of desegregation were . . . [;]virtually all of the reviewers determined that few, if any, firm conclusions about the impact of desegregation on intergroup relations could be drawn." Schofield, School Desegregation and Intergroup Relations: A Review of the Literature, in 17 Review of Research in Education 335, 356 (G. Grant ed.1991). Some studies have even found that a deterioration in racial attitudes seems to result from racial mixing in schools. See N. St. John, School Desegregation Outcomes for Children 67–68 (1975) ("A glance at [the data] shows that for either race positive findings are less common than negative findings"); Stephan, The Effects of School Desegregation: An Evaluation 30 Years After *Brown*, in 3 Advances in Applied Social Psychology 181, 183–186 (M. Saks & L. Saxe eds.1986). Therefore, it is not nearly as apparent as the dissent suggests that increased interracial exposure automatically leads to improved racial attitudes or race relations.

Given our case law and the paucity of evidence supporting the dissent's belief that these plans improve race relations, no democratic element can support the integration interest. . . .

C

[O]nly those measures the State must take to provide a bulwark against anarchy . . . or to prevent violence and a government's effort to remedy past discrimination for which it is responsible constitute compelling interests. Neither of the parties has argued—nor could they— that race-based student assignment is necessary to provide a bulwark against anarchy or to prevent violence. . . .

III

Most of the dissent's criticisms of today's result can be traced to its rejection of the colorblind Constitution. The dissent attempts to marginalize the notion of a colorblind Constitution by consigning it to me and Members of today's plurality.[19] But I am quite comfortable in the

---

[17] Outside the school context, this Court's cases reflect the fact that racial mixing does not always lead to harmony and understanding. In *Johnson v. California*, 543 U.S. 499 (2005), this Court considered a California prison policy that separated inmates racially. That policy was necessary because of "numerous incidents of racial violence." As a result of this Court's insistence on strict scrutiny of that policy, inmates in the California prisons were killed. See *Beard v. Banks*, 548 U.S. 521, 536–537 (2006) (THOMAS, J., concurring in judgment) (noting that two were killed and hundreds were injured in race rioting subsequent to this Court's decision in *Johnson*).

[19] The dissent halfheartedly attacks the historical underpinnings of the colorblind Constitution. I have no quarrel with the proposition that the Fourteenth Amendment sought to bring former slaves into American society as full members. What the dissent fails to understand, however, is that the colorblind Constitution does not bar the government from taking measures to remedy past state-sponsored discrimination—indeed, it requires that such measures be taken in certain circumstances. Race-based government measures during the 1860's and 1870's to remedy *state-enforced slavery* were therefore not inconsistent with the colorblind Constitution.

company I keep. My view of the Constitution is Justice Harlan's view in *Plessy:* "Our Constitution is color-blind, and neither knows nor tolerates classes among citizens." *Plessy v. Ferguson,* 163 U.S. 537, 559 (1896) (dissenting opinion). And my view was the rallying cry for the lawyers who litigated *Brown.* See, *e.g.,* Brief for Appellants in Nos. 1, 2, and 4, and for Respondents in No. 10 on Reargument in *Brown v. Board of Education,* O.T.1953, p. 65 ("That the Constitution is color blind is our dedicated belief"); Brief for Appellants in *Brown v. Board of Education,* O.T.1952, No. 8, p. 5 ("The Fourteenth Amendment precludes a state from imposing distinctions or classifications based upon race and color alone.").

The dissent appears to pin its interpretation of the Equal Protection Clause to current societal practice and expectations, deference to local officials, likely practical consequences, and reliance on previous statements from this and other courts. Such a view was ascendant in this Court's jurisprudence for several decades. It first appeared in *Plessy,* where the Court asked whether a state law providing for segregated railway cars was "a reasonable regulation." The Court deferred to local authorities in making its determination, noting that in inquiring into reasonableness "there must necessarily be a large discretion on the part of the legislature." The Court likewise paid heed to societal practices, local expectations, and practical consequences by looking to "the established usages, customs and traditions of the people, and with a view to the promotion of their comfort, and the preservation of the public peace and good order." Guided by these principles, the Court concluded: "[W]e cannot say that a law which authorizes or even requires the separation of the two races in public conveyances is unreasonable, or more obnoxious to the Fourteenth Amendment than the acts of Congress requiring separate schools for colored children in the District of Columbia."

The segregationists in *Brown* embraced the arguments the Court endorsed in *Plessy.* Though *Brown* decisively rejected those arguments, today's dissent replicates them to a distressing extent. Thus, the dissent argues that "[e]ach plan embodies the results of local experience and community consultation." Similarly, the segregationists made repeated appeals to societal practice and expectation. The dissent argues that "weight [must be given] to a local school board's knowledge, expertise, and concerns," and with equal vigor, the segregationists argued for deference to local authorities. The dissent argues that today's decision "threatens to substitute for present calm a disruptive round of race-related litigation," and claims that today's decision "risks serious harm to the law and for the Nation." The segregationists also relied upon the likely practical consequences of ending the state-imposed system of racial separation. . . .

The similarities between the dissent's arguments and the segregationists' arguments do not stop there. Like the dissent, the segregationists repeatedly cautioned the Court to consider practicalities and not to embrace too theoretical a view of the Fourteenth Amendment. And just as the dissent argues that the need for these programs will lessen over time, the segregationists claimed that reliance on segregation was lessening and might eventually end.

What was wrong in 1954 cannot be right today.[27] . . .

* * *

The plans before us base school assignment decisions on students' race. Because "[o]ur Constitution is color-blind, and neither knows nor tolerates classes among citizens," such race-based decisionmaking is unconstitutional. *Plessy, supra,* at 559 (Harlan, J., dissenting). I concur in THE CHIEF JUSTICE's opinion so holding.

■ JUSTICE KENNEDY, concurring in part and concurring in the judgment.

. . . [I] join Parts I and II of the Court's opinion. I also join Parts III-A and III-C for reasons provided below. My views do not allow me to join the balance of the opinion by THE CHIEF JUSTICE, which seems to me to be inconsistent in both its approach and its implications with the history, meaning, and reach of the Equal Protection Clause. Justice BREYER's dissenting opinion, on the other hand, rests on what in my respectful submission is a misuse and mistaken interpretation of our precedents. . . .

I

The plurality . . . does not acknowledge that the school districts have identified a compelling interest here. For this reason, among others, I do not join Parts III-B and IV. Diversity, depending on its meaning and definition, is a compelling educational goal a school district may pursue.

It is well established that when a governmental policy is subjected to strict scrutiny, the government has the burden of proving that racial classifications "are narrowly tailored measures that further compelling governmental interests." *Adarand Constructors, Inc. v. Peña,* 515 U.S. 200, 227 (1995). "Absent searching judicial inquiry into the justification for such race-based measures, there is simply no way of determining what classifications are 'benign' or 'remedial' and what classifications are in fact motivated by illegitimate notions of racial inferiority or simple racial politics." *Richmond v. J.A. Croson Co.,* 488 U.S. 469, 493 (1989) (plurality opinion). And the inquiry into less restrictive alternatives demanded by the narrow tailoring analysis requires in many cases a thorough understanding of how a plan works. The government bears the

---

[27] It is no answer to say that . . . *Brown* involved invidious racial classifications whereas the racial classifications here are benign. . . . The segregationists in *Brown* argued that their racial classifications were benign, not invidious. See Tr. of Oral Arg. in *Briggs v. Elliott,* et al., O.T.1953, No. 2 etc., at 83 ("It [South Carolina] is confident of its good faith and intention to produce equality for all of its children of whatever race or color. It is convinced that the happiness, the progress and the welfare of these children is best promoted in segregated schools"). . . .

burden of justifying its use of individual racial classifications. As part of that burden it must establish, in detail, how decisions based on an individual student's race are made in a challenged governmental program. . . .

Jefferson County in its briefing has explained how and when it employs these classifications only in terms so broad and imprecise that they cannot withstand strict scrutiny. While it acknowledges that racial classifications are used to make certain assignment decisions, it fails to make clear, for example, who makes the decisions; what if any oversight is employed; the precise circumstances in which an assignment decision will or will not be made on the basis of race; or how it is determined which of two similarly situated children will be subjected to a given race-based decision. . . .When a court subjects governmental action to strict scrutiny, it cannot construe ambiguities in favor of the State.

As for the Seattle case, the school district has gone further in describing the methods and criteria used to determine assignment decisions on the basis of individual racial classifications. The district, nevertheless, has failed to make an adequate showing in at least one respect. It has failed to explain why, in a district composed of a diversity of races, with fewer than half of the students classified as "white," it has employed the crude racial categories of "white" and "non-white" as the basis for its assignment decisions.

The district has identified its purposes as follows: "(1) to promote the educational benefits of diverse school enrollments; (2) to reduce the potentially harmful effects of racial isolation by allowing students the opportunity to opt out of racially isolated schools; and (3) to make sure that racially segregated housing patterns did not prevent non-white students from having equitable access to the most popular over-subscribed schools." Yet the school district does not explain how, in the context of its diverse student population, a blunt distinction between "white" and "non-white" furthers these goals. . . . As the district fails to account for the classification system it has chosen, despite what appears to be its ill fit, Seattle has not shown its plan to be narrowly tailored to achieve its own ends; and thus it fails to pass strict scrutiny.

II

Our Nation from the inception has sought to preserve and expand the promise of liberty and equality on which it was founded. . . . The enduring hope is that race should not matter; the reality is that too often it does.

This is by way of preface to my respectful submission that parts of the opinion by THE CHIEF JUSTICE imply an all-too-unyielding insistence that race cannot be a factor in instances when, in my view, it may be taken into account. The plurality opinion is too dismissive of the legitimate interest government has in ensuring all people have equal opportunity regardless of their race. The plurality's postulate that "[t]he way to stop discrimination on the basis of race is to stop discriminating on the basis of race" is not sufficient to decide these cases. Fifty years of experience since *Brown v. Board of Education,* 347 U.S. 483 (1954), should teach us that the problem before us defies so easy a solution. School districts can seek to reach *Brown*'s objective of equal educational opportunity. The plurality opinion is at least open to the interpretation that the Constitution requires school districts to ignore the problem of *de facto* resegregation in schooling. I cannot endorse that conclusion. . . .

The statement by Justice Harlan that "[o]ur Constitution is color-blind" was most certainly justified in the context of his dissent in *Plessy v. Ferguson,* 163 U.S. 537, 559 (1896). . . . And, as an aspiration, Justice Harlan's axiom must command our assent. In the real world, it is regrettable to say, it cannot be a universal constitutional principle.

In the administration of public schools by the state and local authorities it is permissible to consider the racial makeup of schools and to adopt general policies to encourage a diverse student body, one aspect of which is its racial composition. Cf. *Grutter v. Bollinger,* 539 U.S. 306 (2003). If school authorities are concerned that the student-body compositions of certain schools interfere with the objective of offering an equal educational opportunity to all of their students, they are free to devise race-conscious measures to address the problem in a general way and without treating each student in different fashion solely on the basis of a systematic, individual typing by race.

School boards may pursue the goal of bringing together students of diverse backgrounds and races through other means, including strategic site selection of new schools; drawing attendance zones with general recognition of the demographics of neighborhoods; allocating resources for special programs; recruiting students and faculty in a targeted fashion; and tracking enrollments, performance, and other statistics by race. These mechanisms are race conscious but do not lead to different treatment based on a classification that tells each student he or she is to be defined by race, so it is unlikely any of them would demand strict scrutiny to be found permissible. Executive and legislative branches, which for generations now have considered these types of policies and procedures, should be permitted to employ them with candor and with confidence that a constitutional violation does not occur whenever a decisionmaker considers the impact a given approach might have on students of different races. Assigning to each student a personal designation according to a crude system of individual racial classifications is quite a different matter; and the legal analysis changes accordingly.

Each respondent has asserted that its assignment of individual students by race is permissible because there is no other way to avoid racial isolation in the school districts. Yet, as explained, each has failed to provide the support necessary for that proposition. And individual racial classifications employed in this manner may be considered legitimate only if they are a last resort to achieve a compelling interest.

In the cases before us it is noteworthy that the number of students whose assignment depends on express racial classifications is limited. I join Part III-C of the Court's opinion because I agree that in the context of these plans, the small number of assignments affected suggests that the schools could have achieved their stated ends through different means. These include the facially race-neutral means set forth above or, if necessary, a more nuanced, individual evaluation of school needs and student characteristics that might include race as a component. The latter approach would be informed by *Grutter,* though of course the criteria relevant to student placement would differ based on the age of the students, the needs of the parents, and the role of the schools.

III

The dissent rests on the assumptions that these sweeping race-based classifications of persons are permitted by existing precedents; that its confident endorsement of race categories for each child in a large segment of the community presents no danger to individual freedom in other, prospective realms of governmental regulation; and that the racial classifications used here cause no hurt or anger of the type the Constitution prevents. Each of these premises is, in my respectful view, incorrect.

A

The dissent's reliance on this Court's precedents to justify the explicit, sweeping, classwide racial classifications at issue here is a misreading of our authorities that, it appears to me, tends to undermine well-accepted principles needed to guard our freedom. And in his critique of that analysis, I am in many respects in agreement with THE CHIEF JUSTICE. The conclusions he has set forth in Part III-A of the Court's opinion are correct, in my view, because the compelling interests implicated in the cases before us are distinct from the interests the Court has recognized in remedying the effects of past intentional discrimination and in increasing diversity in higher education. As the Court notes, we recognized the compelling nature of the interest in remedying past intentional discrimination in *Freeman v. Pitts,* 503 U.S. 467, 494 (1992), and of the interest in diversity in higher education in *Grutter.* At the same time, these compelling interests, in my view, do help inform the present inquiry. And to the extent the plurality opinion can be interpreted to foreclose consideration of these interests, I disagree with that reasoning.

As to the dissent, the general conclusions upon which it relies have no principled limit and would result in the broad acceptance of governmental racial classifications in areas far afield from schooling. The dissent's permissive strict scrutiny (which bears more than a passing resemblance to rational-basis review) could invite widespread governmental deployment of racial classifications. There is every reason to think that, if the dissent's rationale were accepted, Congress, assuming an otherwise proper exercise of its spending authority or commerce power, could mandate either the Seattle or the Jefferson County plans nationwide. There seems to be no principled rule, moreover, to limit the dissent's rationale to the context of public schools. . . .

This brings us to the dissent's reliance on the Court's opinions in *Gratz v. Bollinger*, 539 U.S. 244 (2003), and *Grutter*, 539 U.S. 306 (2003). If today's dissent said it was adhering to the views expressed in the separate opinions in *Gratz* and *Grutter*, that would be understandable, and likely within the tradition—to be invoked, in my view, in rare instances—that permits us to maintain our own positions in the face of stare decisis when fundamental points of doctrine are at stake. To say, however, that we must ratify the racial classifications here at issue based on the majority opinions in *Gratz* and *Grutter* is, with all respect, simply baffling.

Gratz involved a system where race was not the entire classification. The procedures in *Gratz* placed much less reliance on race than do the plans at issue here. The issue in *Gratz* arose, moreover, in the context of college admissions where students had other choices and precedent supported the proposition that First Amendment interests give universities particular latitude in defining diversity. Even so the race factor was found to be invalid. If *Gratz* is to be the measure, the racial classification systems here are a fortiori invalid. . . .

The same must be said for the controlling opinion in *Grutter*. There the Court sustained a system that, it found, was flexible enough to take into account "all pertinent elements of diversity" and considered race as only one factor among many. Seattle's plan, by contrast, relies upon a mechanical formula that has denied hundreds of students their preferred schools on the basis of three rigid criteria: placement of siblings, distance from schools, and race. If those students were considered for a whole range of their talents and school needs with race as just one consideration, *Grutter* would have some application. That, though, is not the case. . . .

B

To uphold these programs the Court is asked to brush aside two concepts of central importance for determining the validity of laws and decrees designed to alleviate the hurt and adverse consequences resulting from race discrimination. The first is the difference between *de jure* and *de facto* segregation; the second, the presumptive invalidity of a State's use of racial classifications to differentiate its treatment of individuals. . . .

The distinction between government and private action . . . can be amorphous . . . . Yet, like so many other legal categories that can overlap in some instances, the constitutional distinction between *de jure* and *de facto* segregation has been thought to be an important one.... Where there has been *de jure* segregation, there is a cognizable legal wrong, and the courts and legislatures have broad power to remedy it. The remedy, though, was limited in time and limited to the wrong. The Court has allowed school districts to remedy their prior *de jure* segregation by classifying individual students based on their race. See *North Carolina Bd. of Ed. v. Swann,* 402 U.S. 43, 45–46 (1971). The limitation of this power to instances where there has been *de jure* segregation serves to confine the nature, extent, and duration of governmental reliance on individual racial classifications.

The cases here were argued upon the assumption, and come to us on the premise, that the discrimination in question did not result from *de jure* actions. And when *de facto* discrimination is at issue our tradition has been that the remedial rules are different. The State must seek alternatives to the classification and differential treatment of individuals by race, at least absent some extraordinary showing not present here.

C

The dissent refers to an opinion filed by Judge Kozinski in one of the cases now before us, and that opinion relied upon an opinion filed by Chief Judge Boudin in a case presenting an issue similar to the one here. See *Parents Involved VII,* 426 F.3d 1162, 1193–1196 (C.A.9 2005) (concurring opinion), in turn citing *Comfort v. Lynn School Comm.,* 418 F.3d 1, 27, 29 (C.A.1 2005) (Boudin, C. J., concurring)). Though this may oversimplify the matter a bit, one of the main concerns underlying those opinions was this: If it is legitimate for school authorities to work to avoid racial isolation in their schools, must they do so only by indirection and general policies? Does the Constitution mandate this inefficient result? Why may the authorities not recognize the problem in candid fashion and solve it altogether through resort to direct assignments based on student racial classifications? So, the argument proceeds, if race is the problem, then perhaps race is the solution.

The argument ignores the dangers presented by individual classifications, dangers that are not as pressing when the same ends are achieved by more indirect means. When the government classifies an individual by race, it must first define what it means to be of a race. Who exactly is white and who is nonwhite? To be forced to live under a state-mandated racial label is inconsistent with the dignity of individuals in our society. And it is a label that an individual is powerless to change. Governmental classifications that command people to march in different directions based on racial typologies can cause a new divisiveness. The practice can lead to corrosive discourse, where race serves not as an element of our diverse heritage but instead as a bargaining chip in the political process. On the other hand race-conscious measures that do not rely on differential treatment based on individual classifications present these problems to a lesser degree.

The idea that if race is the problem, race is the instrument with which to solve it cannot be accepted as an analytical leap forward. And if this is a frustrating duality of the Equal Protection Clause it simply reflects the duality of our history and our attempts to promote freedom in a world that sometimes seems set against it. Under our Constitution the individual, child or adult, can find his own identity, can define her own persona, without state intervention that classifies on the basis of his race or the color of her skin. . . .

With this explanation I concur in the judgment of the Court.

■ JUSTICE BREYER, with whom JUSTICE STEVENS, JUSTICE SOUTER, and JUSTICE GINSBURG join, dissenting.

These cases consider the longstanding efforts of two local school boards to integrate their public schools. The school board plans before us resemble many others adopted in the last 50 years by primary and secondary schools throughout the Nation. All of those plans represent local efforts to bring about the kind of racially integrated education that *Brown v. Board of Education,* 347 U.S. 483 (1954), long ago promised—efforts that this Court has repeatedly required, permitted, and encouraged local authorities to undertake. This Court has recognized that the public interests at stake in such cases are "compelling." We have approved of "narrowly tailored" plans that are no less race conscious than the plans before us. And we have understood that the Constitution *permits* local communities to adopt desegregation plans even where it does not *require* them to do so.

The plurality . . . threatens to substitute for present calm a disruptive round of race-related litigation, and it undermines *Brown's* promise of integrated primary and secondary education that local communities have sought to make a reality. This cannot be justified in the name of the Equal Protection Clause.

I

Facts

. . . In *Brown,* this Court held that the government's segregation of schoolchildren by race violates the Constitution's promise of equal protection. The Court emphasized that "education is perhaps the most important function of state and local governments." . . . In dozens of subsequent cases, this Court told school districts previously segregated by law what they must do at a minimum to comply with *Brown's* constitutional holding. The measures required by those cases often included race-conscious practices, such as mandatory busing and race-based restrictions on voluntary transfers. Beyond those minimum requirements, the Court left much of the determination of how to achieve integration to the judgment of local communities. . . .

As a result, different districts . . . adopted, modified, and experimented with hosts of different kinds of plans, including race-conscious plans, all with a similar objective: greater racial integration of public schools. . . . Overall these efforts brought about considerable racial integration. More recently, however, progress has stalled. Between 1968 and 1980, the number of black children attending a school where minority children constituted more than half of the school fell from 77% to 63% in the Nation (from 81% to 57% in the South) but then reversed direction by the year 2000, rising from 63% to 72% in the Nation (from 57% to 69% in the South). Similarly, between 1968 and 1980, the number of black children attending schools that were more than 90% minority fell from 64% to 33% in the Nation (from 78% to 23% in the South), but that too reversed direction, rising by the year 2000 from 33% to 37% in the Nation (from 23% to 31% in the South). As of 2002, almost 2.4 million students, or over 5% of all public school enrollment, attended schools with a white population of less than 1%. . . . Today, more than one in six black children attend a school that is 99%–100% minority. In light of the evident risk of a return to school systems that are in fact (though not in law) resegregated, many school districts have felt a need to maintain or to extend their integration efforts.

The upshot is that myriad school districts operating in myriad circumstances have devised myriad plans, often with race-conscious elements, all for the sake of eradicating earlier school segregation, bringing about integration, or preventing retrogression. Seattle and Louisville are two such districts, and the histories of their present plans set forth typical school integration stories.

I describe those histories at length in order to highlight three important features of these cases. First, the school districts' plans serve "compelling interests" and are "narrowly tailored" on any reasonable definition of those terms. Second, the distinction between *de jure* segregation (caused by school systems) and *de facto* segregation (caused, *e.g.,* by housing patterns or generalized societal discrimination) is meaningless in the present context, thereby dooming the plurality's endeavor to find support for its views in that distinction. Third, real-world efforts to substitute racially diverse for racially segregated schools (however caused) are complex, to the point where the Constitution cannot plausibly be interpreted to rule out categorically all local efforts to use means that are "conscious" of the race of individuals.

In both Seattle and Louisville, the local school districts began with schools that were highly segregated in fact. In both cities, plaintiffs filed lawsuits claiming unconstitutional segregation. In Louisville, a Federal District Court found that school segregation reflected pre-*Brown* state laws separating the races. In Seattle, the plaintiffs alleged that school segregation unconstitutionally reflected not only generalized societal discrimination and residential housing patterns, but also *school board policies and actions* that had helped to create, maintain, and aggravate racial segregation. In Louisville, a federal court entered a remedial decree. In Seattle, the parties settled after the school district pledged to undertake a desegregation plan. In both cities, the school boards adopted plans designed to achieve integration by bringing about more racially diverse schools. In each city, the school board modified its plan several times in light of, for example, hostility to busing, the threat of resegregation, and the desirability of introducing greater student choice. And in each city, the school boards' plans have evolved over time in ways that progressively *diminish* the plans' use of explicit race-conscious criteria. . . .

The histories I have set forth describe the extensive and ongoing efforts of two school districts to bring about greater racial integration of their public schools. In both cases the efforts were in part remedial. Louisville began its integration efforts in earnest when a federal court in 1975 entered a school desegregation order. Seattle undertook its integration efforts in response to the filing of a federal lawsuit and as a result of its settlement of a segregation complaint filed with the federal OCR. . . .

When formulating the plans under review, both districts drew upon their considerable experience with earlier plans, having revised their policies periodically in light of that experience. Both districts rethought their methods over time and explored a wide range of other means, including non-race-conscious policies. Both districts also considered elaborate studies and consulted widely within their communities.

Both districts sought greater racial integration for educational and democratic, as well as for remedial, reasons. Both sought to achieve these objectives while preserving their commitment to other educational goals, *e.g.,* district wide commitment to high quality public schools, increased pupil assignment to neighborhood schools, diminished use of busing, greater student choice, reduced risk of white flight, and so forth. Consequently, the present plans expand student choice; they limit the burdens (including busing) that earlier plans had imposed upon students and their families; and they use race-conscious criteria in limited and gradually diminishing ways. In particular, they use race-conscious criteria only to mark the outer bounds of broad population-related ranges.

The histories also make clear the futility of looking simply to whether earlier school segregation was *de jure* or *de facto* in order to draw firm lines separating the constitutionally permissible from the constitutionally forbidden use of "race-conscious" criteria. . . . No one here disputes that Louisville's segregation was *de jure*. But what about Seattle's? Was it *de facto? De jure?* A mixture? Opinions differed. Or is it that a prior federal court had not adjudicated the matter? Does that make a difference? . . .

A court finding of *de jure* segregation cannot be the crucial variable. After all, a number of school districts in the South that the Government or private plaintiffs challenged as segregated *by law* voluntarily desegregated their schools *without a court order*—just as Seattle did. . . .

Moreover, Louisville's history makes clear that a community under a court order to desegregate might submit a race-conscious remedial plan *before* the court dissolved the order, but with every intention of following that plan even *after* dissolution. How could such a plan be lawful the day before dissolution but then become unlawful the very next day? . . .

The histories also indicate the complexity of the tasks and the practical difficulties that local school boards face when they seek to achieve greater racial integration. . . .

These facts and circumstances help explain why in this context, as to means, the law often leaves legislatures, city councils, school boards, and voters with a broad range of choice, thereby giving "different communities" the opportunity to "try different solutions to common problems and gravitate toward those that prove most successful or seem to them best to suit their individual needs." *Comfort v. Lynn School Comm.,* 418 F.3d 1, 28 (C.A.1 2005) (Boudin, C. J., concurring) (citing *United States v. Lopez,* 514 U.S. 549, 581 (1995) (KENNEDY, J., concurring)). . . .

II

The Legal Standard

A longstanding and unbroken line of legal authority tells us that the Equal Protection Clause permits local school boards to use race-conscious criteria to achieve positive race-related goals, even when the Constitution does not compel it. Because of its importance, I shall repeat what this Court said about the matter in *Swann.* . . .

> School authorities are traditionally charged with broad power to formulate and implement educational policy and might well conclude, for example, that in order to prepare students to live in a pluralistic society each school should have a prescribed ratio of Negro to white students reflecting the proportion for the district as a whole. *To do this as an educational policy is within the broad discretionary powers of school authorities. Swann v. Charlotte-Mecklenburg Bd. of Ed.,* 402 U.S. 1, 16 (1971) (emphasis added).

The statement was not a technical holding in the case. But the Court set forth in *Swann* a basic principle of constitutional law—a principle of law that has found wide acceptance in the legal culture. . . .

These statements nowhere suggest that this freedom is limited to school districts where court-ordered desegregation measures are also in effect. Indeed, in *McDaniel v. Barresi,* 402 U.S. 39 (1971), a case decided the same day as *Swann,* a group of parents challenged a race-conscious student assignment plan that the Clarke County School Board had *voluntarily* adopted as a remedy without a court order (though under federal agency pressure—pressure Seattle also encountered). The plan required that each elementary school in the district maintain 20% to 40% enrollment of African-American students, corresponding to the racial composition of the district. This Court upheld the plan, rejecting the parents' argument that "a person may not be *included* or *excluded* solely because he is a Negro or because he is white."

Federal authorities had claimed—as the NAACP and the [federal Department of Health, Education & Welfare] did in Seattle—that Clarke County schools were segregated in law, not just in fact. The plurality's claim that Seattle was "never segregated by law" is simply not accurate. The plurality could validly claim that *no court* ever found that Seattle schools were segregated in law. But that is also true of the Clarke County schools in *McDaniel*. Unless we believe that the Constitution enforces one legal standard for the South and another for the North, this Court should grant Seattle the permission it granted Clarke County, Georgia.

This Court has also held that school districts may be required by federal statute to undertake race-conscious desegregation efforts even when there is no likelihood that *de jure* segregation can be shown. In *Board of Ed. of City School Dist. of New York v. Harris,* 444 U.S. 130, 148–149 (1979), the Court concluded that a federal statute required school districts receiving certain federal funds to remedy faculty segregation, even though in this Court's view the racial disparities in the affected schools were purely *de facto* and would not have been actionable under the Equal Protection Clause. Not even the dissenters thought the race-conscious remedial program posed a *constitutional* problem.

Lower state and federal courts had considered the matter settled and uncontroversial even before this Court decided *Swann*. Indeed, in 1968, the Illinois Supreme Court rejected an equal protection challenge to a race-conscious state law seeking to undo *de facto* segregation. [See *Tometz v. Board of Ed., Waukegan School Dist. No. 61*, 39 Ill.2d 593, 597–598, 237 N.E.2d 498, 501.] . . . If there were doubts before *Swann* was decided, they did not survive this Court's decision. Numerous state and federal courts explicitly relied upon *Swann*'s guidance for decades to follow. For instance, a Texas appeals court in 1986 rejected a Fourteenth Amendment challenge to a voluntary integration plan by explaining:

> [T]he absence of a court order to desegregate does not mean that a school board cannot exceed minimum requirements in order to promote school integration. School authorities are traditionally given broad discretionary powers to formulate and implement educational policy and may properly decide to ensure to their students the value of an integrated school experience. *Citizens for Better Ed. v. Goose Creek Consol. Independent School Dist.*, 719 S.W.2d 350, 352–353 (Tex. App. 1987).

. . . These decisions illustrate well how lower courts understood and followed *Swann*'s enunciation of the relevant legal principle.

Courts are not alone in accepting as constitutionally valid the legal principle that *Swann* enunciated—*i.e.*, that the government may voluntarily adopt race-conscious measures to improve conditions of race even when it is not under a constitutional obligation to do so. That principle has been accepted by every branch of government and is rooted in the history of the Equal Protection Clause itself. Thus, Congress has enacted numerous race-conscious statutes that illustrate that principle or rely upon its validity. See, *e.g.,* No Child Left Behind Act of 2001, 20 U.S.C. § 6311(b)(2)(C)(v) (2000 ed., Supp. IV); § 1067 *et seq.* (authorizing aid to minority institutions). In fact, without being exhaustive, I have counted 51 federal statutes that use racial classifications. I have counted well over 100 state statutes that similarly employ racial classifications. Presidential administrations for the past half century have used and supported various race-conscious measures. And during the same time, hundreds of local school districts have adopted student assignment plans that use race-conscious criteria.

That *Swann*'s legal statement should find such broad acceptance is not surprising. For *Swann* is predicated upon a well-established legal view of the Fourteenth Amendment. That view understands the basic objective of those who wrote the Equal Protection Clause as forbidding practices that lead to racial exclusion. The Amendment sought to bring into American society as full members those whom the Nation had previously held in slavery.

There is reason to believe that those who drafted an Amendment with this basic purpose in mind would have understood the legal and practical difference between the use of race-conscious criteria in defiance of that purpose, namely to keep the races apart, and the use of race-conscious criteria to further that purpose, namely to bring the races together. Although the Constitution almost always forbids the former, it is significantly more lenient in respect to the latter. See *Gratz v. Bollinger,* 539 U.S. 244, 301 (2003) (GINSBURG, J., dissenting); *Adarand Constructors, Inc. v. Peña,* 515 U.S. 200, 243 (1995) (STEVENS, J., dissenting).

Sometimes Members of this Court have disagreed about the degree of leniency that the Clause affords to programs designed to include. But I can find no case in which this Court has followed Justice THOMAS' "color-blind" approach. And I have found no case that otherwise repudiated this constitutional asymmetry between that which seeks to *exclude* and that which seeks to *include* members of minority races.

What does the plurality say in response? First, it seeks to distinguish *Swann* and other similar cases on the ground that those cases involved remedial plans in response to *judicial findings* of *de jure* segregation. As *McDaniel* and *Harris* show, that is historically untrue. Many school districts in the South adopted segregation remedies (to which *Swann* clearly applies) without any such federal order. . . . And, in any event, the histories of Seattle and Louisville make clear that this distinction— between court-ordered and voluntary desegregation—seeks a line that sensibly cannot be drawn.

Second, the plurality downplays the importance of *Swann* and related cases by frequently describing their relevant statements as "dicta." These criticisms, however, miss the main point.... The constitutional principle enunciated in *Swann,* reiterated in subsequent cases, and relied upon over many years, provides, and has widely been thought to provide, authoritative legal guidance....

Third, a more important response is the plurality's claim that later cases—in particular *Johnson v. California,* 543 U.S. 499 (2005), *Adarand, supra,* and *Grutter v. Bollinger,* 539 U.S. 306 (2003)— supplanted Swann. The plurality says that cases such as Swann and the others I have described all "were decided before this Court definitively determined that 'all racial classifications ... must be analyzed by a reviewing court under strict scrutiny.'"...

Several of these cases were significantly more restrictive than *Swann* in respect to the degree of leniency the Fourteenth Amendment grants to programs designed to *include* people of all races. But that legal circumstance cannot make a critical difference here for two separate reasons.

First, no case—not *Adarand, Gratz, Grutter,* or any other—has ever held that the test of "strict scrutiny" means that all racial classifications—no matter whether they seek to include or exclude—must in practice be treated the same. The Court did not say in *Adarand* or in *Johnson* or in *Grutter* that it was overturning *Swann* or its central constitutional principle.

Indeed, in its more recent opinions, the Court recognized that the "fundamental purpose" of strict scrutiny review is to "take relevant differences" between "fundamentally different situations ... into account." *Adarand,* 515 U.S., at 228. The Court made clear that "[s]trict scrutiny does not trea[t] dissimilar race-based decisions as though they were equally objectionable." ... And the Court ... sought to "*dispel the notion* that strict scrutiny" is as likely to condemn *inclusive* uses of "race-conscious" criteria as it is to invalidate *exclusionary* uses. That is, it is *not* in all circumstances "'strict in theory, but fatal in fact.'" *Id.,* at 237.... The Court's holding in *Grutter* demonstrates that the Court meant what it said, for the Court upheld an elite law school's race-conscious admissions program.

The upshot is that the cases to which the plurality refers, though all applying strict scrutiny, do not treat exclusive and inclusive uses the same. Rather, they apply the strict scrutiny test in a manner that is "fatal in fact" only to racial classifications that harmfully *exclude;* they apply the test in a manner that is *not* fatal in fact to racial classifications that seek to *include....*

Second, as *Grutter* specified, "[c]ontext matters when reviewing race-based governmental action under the Equal Protection Clause." ... Here, the context is one in which school districts seek to advance or to maintain racial integration in primary and secondary schools. It is a context, as *Swann* makes clear, where history has required special administrative remedies. And it is a context in which the school boards' plans simply set race-conscious limits at the outer boundaries of a broad range.

This context is *not* a context that involves the use of race to decide who will receive goods or services that are normally distributed on the basis of merit and which are in short supply. It is not one in which race-conscious limits stigmatize or exclude; the limits at issue do not pit the races against each other or otherwise significantly exacerbate racial tensions. . . . The context here is one of racial limits that seek, not to keep the races apart, but to bring them together. . . .

If one examines the context more specifically, one finds that the districts' plans reflect efforts to overcome a history of segregation, embody the results of broad experience and community consultation, seek to expand student choice while reducing the need for mandatory busing, and use race-conscious criteria in highly limited ways that diminish the use of race compared to preceding integration efforts. They do not seek to award a scarce commodity on the basis of merit, for they are not magnet schools; rather, by design and in practice, they offer substantially equivalent academic programs and electives. Although some parents or children prefer some schools over others, school popularity has varied significantly over the years. . . .

These and related considerations convinced one Ninth Circuit judge in the Seattle case to apply a standard of constitutionality review that is less than "strict," and to conclude that this Court's precedents do not require the contrary. See 426 F.3d 1162, 1193–1194 (2005) (*Parents Involved VII*) (Kozinski, J., concurring) ("That a student is denied the school of his choice may be disappointing, but it carries no racial stigma and says nothing at all about that individual's aptitude or ability"). That judge is not alone. Cf. *Gratz, supra,* at 301 (GINSBURG, J., dissenting); *Adarand, supra,* at 243 (STEVENS, J., dissenting). . . .

In my view, this contextual approach to scrutiny is altogether fitting. I believe that the law requires application here of a standard of review that is not "strict" in the traditional sense of that word, although it does require the careful review I have just described. See *Gratz, supra,* at 301 (GINSBURG, J., joined by SOUTER, J., dissenting); *Adarand, supra,* at 242–249 (STEVENS, J., joined by GINSBURG, J., dissenting). . . .

Nonetheless, in light of *Grutter* and other precedents, see, e.g., *Bakke, supra,* at 290 (opinion of Powell, J.), . . . I shall apply the version of strict scrutiny that those cases embody. I shall consequently ask whether the school boards in Seattle and Louisville adopted these plans to serve a "compelling governmental interest" and, if so, whether the plans are "narrowly tailored" to achieve that interest. . . .

III

Applying the Legal Standard

A

Compelling Interest

The principal interest advanced in these cases to justify the use of race-based criteria [is] an interest in promoting or preserving greater racial "integration" of public schools. By this term, I mean the school districts' interest in eliminating school-by-school racial isolation and increasing the degree to which racial mixture characterizes each of the district's schools and each individual student's public school experience.

Regardless of its name ... the interest at stake possesses three essential elements. First, there is a historical and remedial element: an interest in setting right the consequences of prior conditions of segregation. ... It is an interest in continuing to combat the remnants of segregation caused in whole or in part by these school-related policies, which have often affected not only schools, but also housing patterns, employment practices, economic conditions, and social attitudes. It is an interest in maintaining hard-won gains. And it has its roots in preventing what gradually may become the *de facto* resegregation of America's public schools.

Second, there is an educational element: an interest in overcoming the adverse educational effects produced by and associated with highly segregated schools. Studies suggest that children taken from those schools and placed in integrated settings often show positive academic gains. ... Other studies reach different conclusions. But the evidence supporting an educational interest in racially integrated schools is well established and strong enough to permit a democratically elected school board reasonably to determine that this interest is a compelling one.

Research suggests, for example, that black children from segregated educational environments significantly increase their achievement levels once they are placed in a more integrated setting. ... One commentator, reviewing dozens of studies of the educational benefits of desegregated schooling, found that the studies have provided "remarkably consistent" results, showing that: (1) black students' educational achievement is improved in integrated schools as compared to racially isolated schools, (2) black students' educational achievement is improved in integrated classes, and (3) the earlier that black students are removed from racial isolation, the better their educational outcomes. See Hallinan, *Diversity Effects on Student Outcomes: Social Science Evidence*, 59 Ohio St. L. J. 733, 741–742 (1998). Multiple studies also indicate that black alumni of integrated schools are more likely to move into occupations traditionally closed to African-Americans, and to earn more money in those fields. Cf. W. BOWEN & D. BOK, THE SHAPE OF THE RIVER 118 (1998).

Third, there is a democratic element: an interest in producing an educational environment that reflects the pluralistic society in which our children will live. It is an interest in helping our children learn to work and play together with children of different racial backgrounds. It is an interest in teaching children to engage in the kind of cooperation among Americans of all races that is necessary to make a land of 300 million people one Nation.

Again, data support this insight. See, *e.g.,* Hallinan 745; Quillian & Campbell, *Beyond Black and White: The Present and Future of Multiracial Friendship Segregation*, 68 Am. Sociological Rev. 540, 541 (2003); Dawkins & Braddock, *The Continuing Significance of Desegregation: School Racial Composition and African American Inclusion in American Society*, 63 J. Negro Educ. 394, 401–403 (1994); Wells & Crain, *Perpetuation Theory and the Long-Term Effects of School Desegregation*, 64 Rev. Educ. Research 531, 550 (1994). There are again studies that offer contrary conclusions. . . . Again, however, the evidence supporting a democratic interest in racially integrated schools is firmly established and sufficiently strong to permit a school board to determine, as this Court has itself often found, that this interest is compelling.

For example, one study documented that "black and white students in desegregated schools are less racially prejudiced than those in segregated schools," and that "interracial contact in desegregated schools leads to an increase in interracial sociability and friendship." Hallinan 745. Other studies have found that both black and white students who attend integrated schools are more likely to work in desegregated companies after graduation than students who attended racially isolated schools. . . . Cities that have implemented successful school desegregation plans have witnessed increased interracial contact and neighborhoods that tend to become less racially segregated. These effects not only reinforce the prior gains of integrated primary and secondary education; they also foresee a time when there is less need to use race-conscious criteria.

[T]his Court from *Swann* to *Grutter* has treated these civic effects as an important virtue of racially diverse education. In *Grutter*, in the context of law school admissions, we found that these types of interests were, constitutionally speaking, "compelling." In light of this Court's conclusions in *Grutter*, the "compelling" nature of these interests in the context of primary and secondary public education follows here *a fortiori*. Primary and secondary schools are where the education of this Nation's children begins, where each of us begins to absorb those values we carry with us to the end of our days. As Justice Marshall said, "unless our children begin to learn together, there is little hope that our people will ever learn to live together." *Milliken v. Bradley*, 418 U.S. 717, 783 (1974) (dissenting opinion). . . .

The plurality tries to draw a distinction by reference to the well-established conceptual difference between *de jure* segregation ("segregation by state action") and *de facto* segregation ("racial imbalance caused by other factors"). But that distinction concerns what the

Constitution *requires* school boards to do, not what it *permits* them to do. . . . As to what is *permitted,* nothing in our equal protection law suggests that a State may right only those wrongs that it committed. No case of this Court has ever relied upon the *de jure/de facto* distinction in order to limit what a school district is voluntarily allowed to do. . . . Nor does any precedent indicate, as the plurality suggests with respect to Louisville, that remedial interests vanish the day after a federal court declares that a district is "unitary." . . . I do not understand why this Court's cases, which rest the significance of a "unitary" finding in part upon the wisdom and desirability of returning schools to local control, should deprive those local officials of legal *permission* to use means they once found necessary to combat persisting injustices. . . .

B

Narrow Tailoring

. . . Several factors, taken together . . . lead me to conclude that the boards' use of race-conscious criteria in these plans passes even the strictest "tailoring" test.

First, the race-conscious criteria at issue only help set the outer bounds of *broad* ranges. They constitute but one part of plans that depend primarily upon other, nonracial elements. To use race in this way is not to set a forbidden "quota." In fact, the defining feature of both plans is greater emphasis upon student choice. In Seattle, for example, in more than 80% of all cases, that choice alone determines which high schools Seattle's ninth graders will attend. . . . Indeed, the race-conscious ranges at issue in these cases often have no effect, either because the particular school is not oversubscribed in the year in question, or because the racial makeup of the school falls within the broad range, or because the student is a transfer applicant or has a sibling at the school. In these respects, the broad ranges are less like a quota and more like the kinds of "useful starting points" that this Court has consistently found permissible . . . .

Second, broad-range limits on voluntary school choice plans are less burdensome, and hence more narrowly tailored, than other race-conscious restrictions this Court has previously approved. Indeed, the plans before us are more narrowly tailored than the race-conscious admission plans that this Court approved in *Grutter.* Here, race becomes a factor only in a fraction of students' non-merit-based assignments—not in large numbers of students' merit-based applications. Moreover, the effect of applying race-conscious criteria here affects potentially disadvantaged students less severely, not more severely, than the criteria at issue in *Grutter.* Disappointed students are not rejected from a State's flagship graduate program; they simply attend a different one of the district's many public schools, which in aspiration and in fact are substantially equal. . . .

Third, the manner in which the school boards developed these plans itself reflects "narrow tailoring." . . . The school boards' widespread consultation, their experimentation with numerous other plans, indeed, the 40-year history that Part I sets forth, make clear that plans that are less explicitly race-based are unlikely to achieve the boards' "compelling" objectives. . . . Both cities once tried to achieve more integrated schools by relying solely upon measures such as redrawn district boundaries, new school building construction, and unrestricted voluntary transfers. In neither city did these prior attempts prove sufficient to achieve the city's integration goals.

Moreover, giving some degree of weight to a local school board's knowledge, expertise, and concerns in these particular matters is not inconsistent with rigorous judicial scrutiny. It simply recognizes that judges are not well suited to act as school administrators. Indeed, in the context of school desegregation, this Court has repeatedly stressed the importance of acknowledging that local school boards better understand their own communities and have a better knowledge of what in practice will best meet the educational needs of their pupils. . . .

Having looked at dozens of *amicus* briefs, public reports, news stories, and the records in many of this Court's prior cases, which together span 50 years of desegregation history in school districts across the Nation, I have discovered many examples of districts that sought integration through explicitly race-conscious methods, including mandatory busing. Yet, I have found *no* example or model that would permit this Court to say to Seattle and to Louisville: "Here is an instance of a desegregation plan that is likely to achieve your objectives and also makes less use of race-conscious criteria than your plans." And, if the plurality cannot suggest such a model—and it cannot—then it seeks to impose a "narrow tailoring" requirement that in practice would never be met. . . .

The upshot is that these plans' specific features—(1) their limited and historically diminishing use of race, (2) their strong reliance upon other non-race-conscious elements, (3) their history and the manner in which the districts developed and modified their approach, (4) the comparison with prior plans, and (5) the lack of reasonably evident alternatives—together show that the districts' plans are "narrowly tailored" to achieve their "compelling" goals. In sum, the districts' race-conscious plans satisfy "strict scrutiny" and are therefore lawful.

V

Consequences

The Founders meant the Constitution as a practical document that would transmit its basic values to future generations through principles that remained workable over time. Hence it is important to consider the potential consequences of the plurality's approach, as measured against the Constitution's objectives. To do so provides further reason to believe that the plurality's approach is legally unsound. . . .

The districts' past and current plans are not unique. They resemble other plans, promulgated by hundreds of local school boards, which have attempted a variety of desegregation methods that have evolved over time in light of experience. . . . A majority of these desegregation techniques explicitly considered a student's race. . . .

At a minimum, the plurality's views would threaten a surge of race-based litigation. Hundreds of state and federal statutes and regulations use racial classifications for educational or other purposes. In many such instances, the contentious force of legal challenges to these classifications, meritorious or not, would displace earlier calm.

The wide variety of different integration plans that school districts use throughout the Nation suggests that the problem of racial segregation in schools, including *de facto* segregation, is difficult to solve. The fact that many such plans have used explicitly racial criteria suggests that such criteria have an important, sometimes necessary, role to play. The fact that the controlling opinion would make a school district's use of such criteria often unlawful (and the plurality's "colorblind" view would make such use always unlawful) suggests that today's opinion will require setting aside the laws of several States and many local communities.

As I have pointed out, *de facto* resegregation is on the rise. It is reasonable to conclude that such resegregation can create serious educational, social, and civic problems. Given the conditions in which school boards work to set policy, they may need all of the means presently at their disposal to combat those problems. Yet the plurality would deprive them of at least one tool that some districts now consider vital—the limited use of broad race-conscious student population ranges.

I use the words "may need" here deliberately. The plurality, or at least those who follow Justice THOMAS' "color-blind" approach, may feel confident that, to end invidious discrimination, one must end *all* governmental use of race-conscious criteria including those with inclusive objectives. By way of contrast, I do not claim to know how best to stop harmful discrimination; how best to create a society that includes all Americans; how best to overcome our serious problems of increasing *de facto* segregation, troubled inner-city schooling, and poverty correlated with race. But, as a judge, I do know that the Constitution does not authorize judges to dictate solutions to these problems. Rather, the Constitution creates a democratic political system through which the people themselves must together find answers. And it is for them to debate how best to educate the Nation's children and how best to administer America's schools to achieve that aim. The Court should leave them to their work. . . .

VI

. . . The last half century has witnessed great strides toward racial equality, but we have not yet realized the promise of *Brown*. To invalidate the plans under review is to threaten the promise of *Brown*. The plurality's position, I fear, would break that promise. This is a decision that the Court and the Nation will come to regret.

I must dissent.

CONCLUDING NOTE ON AFFIRMATIVE ACTION

1.   The majority, concurrences, and dissents in *Parents Involved* fought bitterly over who was entitled to claim the mantle of *Brown v. Board of Education*. Who was most persuasive on that score? Sixty years after *Brown*, should that case continue to define the Constitution's promise of equal protection in the context of race?

2.   The Court has long held that the right at stake in cases like *Brown* and *Parents Involved* is an *individual* right—not a right attaching to racial minorities as a group. Does this make sense? Does how you answer this question influence how you think about the legitimacy of "benign" racial classifications? Isn't it more powerful, for instance, to say that everyone has the right to be treated as an individual without regard to race than it is, in light of our history, to say that discrimination against white people is just as bad as discrimination against black people? Our law, in general, has resisted the concept of group rights and injuries.[15] Has that undermined our efforts to resolve the problem of race in our society? Or does our focus on the individual help prevent balkanization of society into a war of competing identity groups?

3.   The Court fractured badly in *Parents Involved*, as in the other affirmative action cases. Who won what? It may help to break down the issues into at least the following:

- What is the level of scrutiny?

- Does the government have a compelling interest?

- Are the pupil reassignment programs narrowly tailored to that interest?

- How much deference should the school districts get, and on what points?

Is it possible to articulate a "holding of the Court" on each question? Do those holdings fit together coherently? If you were the district judge in the next pupil assignment case, would you know what the Supremes wanted you to do?

4.   Justice Kennedy notes that the *Parents Involved* dissenters seem to be holding to their previous views—which also did not prevail in *Adarand* or *Grutter*—that "benign" racial classifications are not subject to strict scrutiny. Why do you think the dissenters refuse to accept the Court's prior rulings on this issue? Is it appropriate, on a multi-member court, to refuse to

---

[15] For a rare exception, see *Beauharnais v. Illinois*, 343 U.S. 250 (1952) (upholding an Illinois law banning publications portraying the "depravity, criminality, unchastity, or lack of virtue of a class of citizens of any race, color, creed or religion" against a First Amendment challenge, on the theory that the state could legitimately prohibit "group libel").

be bound by majority decisions in prior cases where you dissented?[16] (On the other hand, could one accuse the plurality, or at least Justice Thomas, of not having accepted that the prior decisions permit a broader use of race in the "benign" context than a "colorblind" approach would allow?)

An interesting counter-example to this sort of "perpetual dissent" is John Marshall Harlan (the younger), who frequently found himself in dissent on the Warren Court. After he had lost on a particular issue, however, Harlan frequently treated that prior decision as governing law in future cases, even though he might continue to criticize the prior decision in his opinions.[17] Should contemporary justices be criticized for failing to follow Harlan's example? Are they "pursuing a sort of 'self stare decisis'—elevating [the justice's] commitment to an internally consistent personal jurisprudence over a commitment to adhere faithfully to the Court's precedents"?[18] Or would a justice, by acquiescing in a prior ruling she believes to be incorrect, be subordinating what she believes to be the actual meaning of the Constitution to what a majority of justices have said about it?

5.   Near the end of his *Parents Involved* dissent, Justice Breyer urged that "as a judge, I do know that the Constitution does not authorize judges to dictate solutions to these problems. Rather, the Constitution creates a democratic political system through which the people themselves must together find answers. And it is for them to debate how best to educate the Nation's children and how best to administer America's schools to achieve that aim. The Court should leave them to their work." It is hard to imagine a more thoughtful and pragmatic case for deference to local school boards than Justice Breyer's dissent, which illustrates the myriad considerations that local administrators must juggle. But is such deference appropriate under strict scrutiny? Is it consistent with the role the Court played in *Brown*? Would deferring here, while purporting to apply strict scrutiny, undermine the rigor of strict or heightened scrutiny in other contexts? For example, should political liberals who agree with Justice Breyer be willing to accept judicial deference to legislatures who seek to regulate abortion in various ways?[19]

6.   Would the *Parents Involved* plurality's approach require the government simply to ignore race? Would *Grutter* survive under that approach? On the other hand, isn't it fair to say that Justice Breyer "did not identify any constitutional limits on the use of race in making assignments

---

[16] For examples outside the race context, see *American Tradition Partnership, Inc. v. Bullock*, 132 S. Ct. 2490, 2491 (2012) (Breyer, J., dissenting) (refusing to accept the Court's prior decision in *Citizens United v. Federal Election Comm'n*, 558 U.S. 310 (2010), in which the *American Tradition* dissenters had also dissented); *Planned Parenthood of Southeastern Pennsylvania v. Casey*, 505 U.S. 833, 953–55 (1992) (Rehnquist, C.J., concurring in part and in the judgment and dissenting in part) (refusing to accept *Roe v. Wade*, in which he had dissented).

[17] *See* Allison Orr Larsen, *Perpetual Dissents*, 15 Geo. Mason L. Rev. 447, 452 (2008).

[18] *Id.* at 449. For a somewhat more approving view of perpetual dissent, see Jon C. Heintz, *Note, Sustained Dissent and the Extended Deliberative Process*, 88 NOTRE DAME L. REV. 1939 (2013).

[19] *Cf. Whole Woman's Health v. Hellerstedt*, 136 S. Ct. 2292 (2016) (seeming to *increase* the rigor of scrutiny applied to abortion regulation under the "undue burden" standard and refusing to defer to judgments of legislators).

that he would be prepared to enforce"?[20] Was Justice Kennedy right to find both the plurality and dissent too extreme in dealing with a sensitive situation?

A number of incidents in recent years, especially a string of police shootings of young black males, seem to reveal a marked deterioration of race relations in contemporary America. What would be the social consequences of a Supreme Court decision outlawing affirmative action across the board and insisting that "colorblindness" is sufficient to remedy racial injustice? How do these sorts of considerations bear on the *judges'* responsibility in a case like *Parents Involved*? Neil Siegel has observed that Justice Kennedy's concurrence "apprehended both the potentially balkanizing and stigmatizing consequences of government inaction in the face of widespread residential segregation and the potentially balkanizing and stigmatizing consequences of race-conscious state action aimed at ameliorating the problem." [21] Professor Siegel thus concludes that "Kennedy's opinion may fairly be characterized as a statesmanlike effort to express social values inclusively and to sustain social solidarity in the face of irreconcilable yet reasonable value conflict."[22] Do you agree? Is there an appropriate role for judicial "statesmanship" that is distinct from, and sometimes may come in conflict with, simply getting cases right on the law?

7.   For all the profound rhetoric in *Parents Involved*, everyone seems to agree that in the particular student assignment plans at issue, consideration of race actually made very little practical difference. Which way does that cut? Does it suggest that the school districts could not show their plans were narrowly tailored to their compelling interests? Or does it show that the plans in fact did not harm?

8.   The Court's most recent word on affirmative action came in *Fisher v. University of Texas at Austin*, 136 S. Ct. 2198 (2016). The *Fisher* litigation, involving consideration of race in admissions to the undergraduate program at the University of Texas, made two visits to the Supreme Court. Initially, the U.S. Court of Appeals for the Fifth Circuit had upheld the University's race-based affirmative action plan, reasoning that *Grutter* required the court to give substantial deference to the University both in the definition of the compelling interest in diversity and in evaluating whether the University's plan was narrowly tailored to that interest. The Supreme Court reversed in *Fisher I*, holding that the court of appeals had failed to apply strict scrutiny with sufficient rigor.[23] But rather than decide whether the University's plan was constitutional, the Court remanded to the court of appeals to apply the correct standard.

On remand, the court of appeals purported to apply strict scrutiny but once again upheld the University's affirmative action plan. The Supreme Court again granted *certiorari*. But this time the Court affirmed the Fifth

---

[20] Neil Siegel, *The Virtue of Judicial Statesmanship*, 86 TEXAS L. REV. 959, 1004–05 (2008).

[21] *Id.* at 1009.

[22] *Id.* at 1010.

[23] *Fisher v. University of Texas at Austin*, 133 S. Ct. 2411 (2013).

Circuit in a 4–3 decision,[24] with Justice Kennedy again writing for the majority. His relatively brief opinion in *Fisher II* expressed dissatisfaction with the parties' framing of the issues and the state of the evidentiary record, and he suggested that these problems "may limit [this case's] value for prospective guidance." On the merits, the Court's opinion insisted that strict scrutiny remains the appropriate standard, but it applied that standard in a way that seemed remarkably deferential to the University.

More than anything, *Fisher II* made clear that the divisions on the Court we have seen throughout this section still persist. What should the Court do about that going forward? Should it continue with the sort of review represented by *Grutter* and Justice Kennedy's opinion in *Parents Involved*? Or should it adopt one of the more categorical positions, either applying traditional strict scrutiny or adopting a more deferential standard for "benign" discrimination? How optimistic are you that the Court can find an approach that commands a majority?

SECTION 15.5 EQUAL PROTECTION AND FUNDAMENTAL RIGHTS

One could be forgiven for thinking that constitutional protections for equality are complicated enough without throwing in the element of unenumerated personal rights. But that is exactly what the Warren Court did in decisions like *Shapiro v. Thompson*. The cases in this section make clear that there are two paths to strict scrutiny under the Equal Protection Clause. The first and more familiar path is to show that the government has employed a suspect classification. But the second, illustrated in this section, is to demonstrate that the government has discriminated with respect to a "fundamental" right.

The fundamental rights prong of equal protection doctrine achieved its greatest prominence in the late 1960s and early 1970s. As Professor Gerald Gunther noted, the fundamental rights prong had the same "open-ended" and "freewheeling" quality as the Court's search for unenumerated rights to sexual privacy and similar interests;[25] indeed, some scholars referred to this line of doctrine as "substantive equal protection."[26] Unsurprisingly, as the *Rodriguez* case indicates, the more conservative Burger Court was less enthusiastic about this aspect of equal protection. But *Shapiro* and similar cases have never been overruled, and recent debates and decisions concerning same-sex marriage (discussed in Chapter Seventeen) illustrate the continuing importance of this form of equal protection analysis.

---

[24] Justice Antonin Scalia had died between argument and decision in the case, and Justice Elena Kagan was recused because she had participated in earlier proceedings as U.S. Solicitor General.

[25] Gunther, *supra* note 5, at 8.

[26] *See, e.g.*, Kenneth L. Karst & Harold W. Horowitz, Reitman v. Mulkey: *A Telophase of Substantive Equal Protection*, 1967 SUP. CT. REV. 39.

Shapiro v. Thompson

394 U.S. 618 (1969)

■ MR. JUSTICE BRENNAN delivered the opinion of the Court.

These thee appeals [are each] an appeal from a decision of a three-judge District Court holding unconstitutional a State or District of Columbia statutory provision which denies welfare assistance to residents of the State or District who have not resided within their jurisdictions for at least one year immediately preceding their applications for such assistance. We affirm the judgments of the District Courts in the three cases.

I

In No. 9, the Connecticut Welfare Department invoked § 17–2d of the Connecticut General Statutes to deny the application of appellee Vivian Marie Thompson for assistance under the program for Aid to Families with Dependent Children (AFDC). She was a 19-year-old unwed mother of one child and pregnant with her second child when she changed her residence in June 1966 from Dorchester, Massachusetts, to Hartford, Connecticut, to live with her mother, a Hartford resident. . . . Her application for AFDC assistance, filed in August, was denied in November solely on the ground that, as required by § 17–2d, she had not lived in the State for a year before her application was filed. She brought this action in the District Court for the District of Connecticut where a three-judge court, one judge dissenting, declared § 17–2d unconstitutional. . . . We noted probable jurisdiction.

In No. 33, there are four appellees. Three of them—appellees Harrell, Brown, and Legrant—applied for and were denied AFDC aid. The fourth, appellee Barley, applied for and was denied benefits under the program for Aid to the Permanently and Totally Disabled. The denial in each case was on the ground that the applicant had not resided in the District of Columbia for one year immediately preceding the filing of her application, as required by § 3–203 of the District of Columbia Code. . . .

The several cases were consolidated for trial, and a three-judge District Court was convened. The court, one judge dissenting, held § 3–203 unconstitutional. . . . We noted probable jurisdiction.

In No. 34, there are two appellees, Smith and Foster, who were denied AFDC aid on the sole ground that they had not been residents of Pennsylvania for a year prior to their applications as required by § 432(6) of the Pennsylvania Welfare Code. . . . A three-judge District Court for the Eastern District of Pennsylvania, one judge dissenting, declared § 432(6) unconstitutional. . . . We noted probable jurisdiction.

II

There is no dispute that the effect of the waiting-period requirement in each case is to create two classes of needy resident families indistinguishable from each other except that one is composed of residents who have resided a year or more, and the second of residents who have resided less than a year, in the jurisdiction. On the basis of this sole difference the first class is granted and the second class is denied welfare aid upon which may depend the ability of the families to obtain the very means to subsist—food, shelter, and other necessities of life. In each case, the District Court found that appellees met the test for residence in their jurisdictions, as well as all other eligibility requirements except the requirement of residence for a full year prior to their applications. On reargument, appellees' central contention is that the statutory prohibition of benefits to residents of less than a year creates a classification which constitutes an invidious discrimination denying them equal protection of the laws.[6] We agree. . . .

Primarily, appellants justify the waiting-period requirement as a protective device to preserve the fiscal integrity of state public assistance programs. It is asserted that people who require welfare assistance during their first year of residence in a State are likely to become continuing burdens on state welfare programs. Therefore, the argument runs, if such people can be deterred from entering the jurisdiction by denying them welfare benefits during the first year, state programs to assist long-time residents will not be impaired by a substantial influx of indigent newcomers.[7]

There is weighty evidence that exclusion from the jurisdiction of the poor who need or may need relief was the specific objective of these provisions. In the Congress, sponsors of federal legislation to eliminate all residence requirements have been consistently opposed by representatives of state and local welfare agencies who have stressed the fears of the States that elimination of the requirements would result in a heavy influx of individuals into States providing the most generous benefits. The sponsor of the Connecticut requirement said in its support: 'I doubt that Connecticut can and should continue to allow unlimited migration into the state on the basis of offering instant money and permanent income to all who can make their way to the state regardless of their ability to contribute to the economy.' H.B. 82, Connecticut General Assembly House Proceedings, February Special Session, 1965,

---

[6] This constitutional challenge cannot be answered by the argument that public assistance benefits are a 'privilege' and not a 'right.' See *Sherbert v. Verner*, 374 U.S. 398, 404 (1963).

[7] The waiting-period requirement has its antecedents in laws prevalent in England and the American Colonies centuries ago which permitted the ejection of individuals and families if local authorities thought they might become public charges. For example, the preamble of the English Law of Settlement and Removal of 1662 expressly recited the concern, also said to justify the three statutes before us, that large numbers of the poor were moving to parishes where more liberal relief policies were in effect. The 1662 law and the earlier Elizabethan Poor Law of 1601 were the models adopted by the American Colonies. Newcomers to a city, town, or county who might become public charges were 'warned out' or 'passed on' to the next locality. Initially, the funds for welfare payments were raised by local taxes, and the controversy as to responsibility for particular indigents was between localities in the same State. As States—first alone and then with federal grants—assumed the major responsibility, the contest of nonresponsibility became interstate.

Vol. II, pt. 7, p. 3504. In Pennsylvania, shortly after the enactment of the one-year requirement, the Attorney General issued an opinion construing the one-year requirement strictly because '(a)ny other conclusion would tend to attract the dependents of other states to our Commonwealth.' 1937–1938 Official Opinions of the Attorney General, No. 240, p. 110. In the District of Columbia case, the constitutionality of § 3–203 was frankly defended in the District Court and in this Court on the ground that it is designed to protect the jurisdiction from an influx of persons seeking more generous public assistance than might be available elsewhere.

We do not doubt that the one-year waiting period device is well suited to discourage the influx of poor families in need of assistance. An indigent who desires to migrate, resettle, find a new job, and start a new life will doubtless hesitate if he knows that he must risk making the move without the possibility of falling back on state welfare assistance during his first year of residence, when his need may be most acute. But the purpose of inhibiting migration by needy persons into the State is constitutionally impermissible.

This Court long ago recognized that the nature of our Federal Union and our constitutional concepts of personal liberty unite to require that all citizens be free to travel throughout the length and breadth of our land uninhibited by statutes, rules, or regulations which unreasonably burden or restrict this movement. That proposition was early stated by Chief Justice Taney in the *Passenger Cases*, 7 How. 283, 492 (1849):

> For all the great purposes for which the Federal government was formed, we are one people, with one common country. We are all citizens of the United States; and, as members of the same community, must have the right to pass and repass through every part of it without interruption, as freely as in our own States.

We have no occasion to ascribe the source of this right to travel interstate to a particular constitutional provision.[8] It suffices that, as Mr. Justice Stewart said for the Court in *United States v. Guest*, 383 U.S. 745, 757–758 (1966):

> The constitutional right to travel from one State to another . . . occupies a position fundamental to the concept of our Federal

---

[8] In *Corfield v. Coryell*, 6 Fed.Cas. pp. 546, 552 (No. 3230) (C.C.E.D.Pa.1825), *Paul v. Virginia*, 8 Wall. (75 U.S.) 168, 180 (1869), and *Ward v. Maryland*, 12 Wall. (79 U.S.) 418, 430 (1871), the right to travel interstate was grounded upon the Privileges and Immunities Clause of Art. IV, § 2. See also *Slaughter-House Cases*, 16 Wall. 36, 79 (1873); *Twining v. New Jersey*, 211 U.S. 78, 97 (1908). In *Edwards v. California*, 314 U.S. 160, 181, 183–185 (1941) (Douglas and Jackson, JJ., concurring), and *Twining v. New Jersey*, *supra*, reliance was placed on the Privileges and Immunities Clause of the Fourteenth Amendment. See also *Crandall v. Nevada*, 6 Wall. (73 U.S.) 35 (1868). In *Edwards v. California*, *supra*, a Commerce Clause approach was employed. See also the *Passenger Cases*, 7 How. 283 (1849), a Commerce Clause approach was employed. See also *Kent v. Dulles*, 357 U.S. 116, 125 (1958); *Aptheker v. Secretary of State*, 378 U.S. 500, 505–506 (1964); *Zemel v. Rusk*, 381 U.S. 1, 14 (1965), where the freedom of Americans to travel outside the country was grounded upon the Due Process Clause of the Fifth Amendment.

Union. It is a right that has been firmly established and repeatedly recognized. . . . (The) right finds no explicit mention in the Constitution. The reason, it has been suggested, is that a right so elementary was conceived from the beginning to be a necessary concomitant of the stronger Union the Constitution created. In any event, freedom to travel throughout the United States has long been recognized as a basic right under the Constitution.

Thus, the purpose of deterring the in-migration of indigents cannot serve as justification for the classification created by the one-year waiting period, since that purpose is constitutionally impermissible. If a law has 'no other purpose . . . than to chill the assertion of constitutional rights by penalizing those who choose to exercise them, then it (is) patently unconstitutional.' *United States v. Jackson*, 390 U.S. 570, 581 (1968).

Alternatively, appellants argue that even if it is impermissible for a State to attempt to deter the entry of all indigents, the challenged classification may be justified as a permissible state attempt to discourage those indigents who would enter the State solely to obtain larger benefits. We observe first that none of the statutes before us is tailored to serve that objective. Rather, the class of barred newcomers is all-inclusive, lumping the great majority who come to the State for other purposes with those who come for the sole purpose of collecting higher benefits. . . .

More fundamentally, a State may no more try to fence out those indigents who seek higher welfare benefits than it may try to fence out indigents generally. Implicit in any such distinction is the notion that indigents who enter a State with the hope of securing higher welfare benefits are somehow less deserving than indigents who do not take this consideration into account. But we do not perceive why a mother who is seeking to make a new life for herself and her children should be regarded as less deserving because she considers, among others factors, the level of a State's public assistance. Surely such a mother is no less deserving than a mother who moves into a particular State in order to take advantage of its better educational facilities.

Appellants argue further that the challenged classification may be sustained as an attempt to distinguish between new and old residents on the basis of the contribution they have made to the community through the payment of taxes. We have difficulty seeing how long-term residents who qualify for welfare are making a greater present contribution to the State in taxes than indigent residents who have recently arrived. . . . Appellants' reasoning would logically permit the State to bar new residents from schools, parks, and libraries or deprive them of police and fire protection. Indeed it would permit the State to apportion all benefits and services according to the past tax contributions of its citizens. The Equal Protection Clause prohibits such an apportionment of state services.

We recognize that a State has a valid interest in preserving the fiscal integrity of its programs. It may legitimately attempt to limit its expenditures, whether for public assistance, public education, or any other program. But a State may not accomplish such a purpose by invidious distinctions between classes of its citizens. It could not, for example, reduce expenditures for education by barring indigent children from its schools. Similarly, in the cases before us, appellants must do more than show that denying welfare benefits to new residents saves money. The saving of welfare costs cannot justify an otherwise invidious classification.

In sum, neither deterrence of indigents from migrating to the State nor limitation of welfare benefits to those regarded as contributing to the State is a constitutionally permissible state objective.

IV

Appellants next advance as justification certain administrative and related governmental objectives allegedly served by the waiting-period requirement. They argue that the requirement (1) facilitates the planning of the welfare budget; (2) provides an objective test of residency; (3) minimizes the opportunity for recipients fraudulently to receive payments from more than one jurisdiction; and (4) encourages early entry of new residents into the labor force.

At the outset, we reject appellants' argument that a mere showing of a rational relationship between the waiting period and these four admittedly permissible state objectives will suffice to justify the classification. The waiting-period provision denies welfare benefits to otherwise eligible applicants solely because they have recently moved into the jurisdiction. But in moving from State to State or to the District of Columbia appellees were exercising a constitutional right, and any classification which serves to penalize the exercise of that right, unless shown to be necessary to promote a compelling governmental interest, is unconstitutional. Cf. *Skinner v. Oklahoma*, 316 U.S. 535, 541 (1942); *Korematsu v. United States*, 323 U.S. 214, 216 (1944).

The argument that the waiting-period requirement facilitates budget predictability is wholly unfounded. The records in all three cases are utterly devoid of evidence that either State or the District of Columbia in fact uses the one-year requirement as a means to predict the number of people who will require assistance in the budget year. None of the appellants takes a census of new residents or collects any other data that would reveal the number of newcomers in the State less than a year. . . . Finally, the claim that a one-year waiting requirement is used for planning purposes is plainly belied by the fact that the requirement is not also imposed on applicants who are long-term residents, the group that receives the bulk of welfare payments. In short, the States rely on methods other than the one-year requirement to make budget estimates. . . .

The argument that the waiting period serves as an administratively efficient rule of thumb for determining residency similarly will not withstand scrutiny. The residence requirement and the one-year waiting-period requirement are distinct and independent prerequisites for assistance under these three statutes, and the facts relevant to the determination of each are directly examined by the welfare authorities. Before granting an application, the welfare authorities investigate the applicant's employment, housing, and family situation and in the course of the inquiry necessarily learn the facts upon which to determine whether the applicant is a resident.

Similarly, there is no need for a State to use the one-year waiting period as a safeguard against fraudulent receipt of benefits; for less drastic means are available, and are employed, to minimize that hazard. Of course, a State has a valid interest in preventing fraud by any applicant, whether a newcomer or a long-time resident. It is not denied, however, that the investigations now conducted entail inquiries into facts relevant to that subject. In addition, cooperation among state welfare departments is common. . . .

We conclude therefore that appellants in these cases do not use and have no need to use the one-year requirement for the governmental purposes suggested. Thus, even under traditional equal protection tests a classification of welfare applicants according to whether they have lived in the State for one year would seem irrational and unconstitutional. But, of course, the traditional criteria do not apply in these cases. Since the classification here touches on the fundamental right of interstate movement, its constitutionality must be judged by the stricter standard of whether it promotes a compelling state interest. Under this standard, the waiting-period requirement clearly violates the Equal Protection Clause.[21]

V

Connecticut and Pennsylvania argue, however, that the constitutional challenge to the waiting-period requirements must fail because Congress expressly approved the imposition of the requirement by the States as part of the jointly funded AFDC program.

Section 402(b) of the Social Security Act of 1935, as amended, 42 U.S.C. § 602(b), provides that:

> The Secretary shall approve any (state assistance) plan which fulfills the conditions specified in subsection (a) of this section, except that he shall not approve any plan which imposes as a condition of eligibility for aid to families with dependent

---

[21] We imply no view of the validity of waiting-period or residence requirements determining eligibility to vote, eligibility for tuition-free education, to obtain a license to practice a profession, to hunt or fish, and so forth. Such requirements may promote compelling state interests on the one hand, or, on the other, may not be penalties upon the exercise of the constitutional right of interstate travel.

children, a residence requirement which denies aid with respect to any child residing in the State (1) who has resided in the State for one year immediately preceding the application for such aid, or (2) who was born within one year immediately preceding the application, if the parent or other relative with whom the child is living has resided in the State for one year immediately preceding the birth.

On its face, the statute does not approve, much less prescribe, a one-year requirement. . . . [The legislative] history discloses that Congress enacted the directive to curb hardships resulting from lengthy residence requirements. Rather than constituting an approval or a prescription of the requirement in state plans, the directive was the means chosen by Congress to deny federal funding to any State which persisted in stipulating excessive residence requirements as a condition of the payment of benefits. . . .

But even if we were to assume, arguendo, that Congress did approve the imposition of a one-year waiting period, it is the responsive state legislation which infringes constitutional rights. By itself § 402(b) has absolutely no restrictive effect. . . . Finally . . . it follows from what we have said that the provision, insofar as it permits the one-year waiting-period requirement, would be unconstitutional. Congress may not authorize the States to violate the Equal Protection Clause. Perhaps Congress could induce wider state participation in school construction if it authorized the use of joint funds for the building of segregated schools. But could it seriously be contended that Congress would be constitutionally justified in such authorization by the need to secure state cooperation? Congress is without power to enlist state cooperation in a joint federal-state program by legislation which authorizes the States to violate the Equal Protection Clause. *Katzenbach v. Morgan*, 384 U.S. 641, 651 n. 10 (1966).

VI

. . . For the reasons we have stated in invalidating the Pennsylvania and Connecticut provisions, the District of Columbia provision is also invalid—the Due Process Clause of the Fifth Amendment prohibits Congress from denying public assistance to poor persons otherwise eligible solely on the ground that they have not been residents of the District of Columbia for one year at the time their applications are filed. . . .

Affirmed.

■ **MR. JUSTICE STEWART, concurring.**

In joining the opinion of the Court, I add a word in response to the dissent of my Brother HARLAN, who, I think, has quite misapprehended what the Court's opinion says.

The Court today does not "pick out particular human activities, characterize them as 'fundamental,' and give them added protection." To the contrary, the Court simply recognizes, as it must, an established constitutional right, and gives to that right no less protection than the Constitution itself demands.

"The constitutional right to travel from one State to another . . . has been firmly established and repeatedly recognized." *United States v. Guest*, 383 U.S. 745, 757 (1966). This constitutional right, which, of course, includes the right of "entering and abiding in any state in the Union," *Truax v. Raich*, 239 U.S. 33, 39 (1915), is not a mere conditional liberty subject to regulation and control under conventional due process or equal protection standards.[1] "(T)he right to travel freely from State to State finds constitutional protection that is quite independent of the Fourteenth Amendment." *Guest, supra*, at 760 n. 17. . . . Like the right of association, *NAACP v. Alabama*, 357 U.S. 449 (1958), it is a virtually unconditional personal right, guaranteed by the Constitution to us all.

It follows, as the Court says, that 'the purpose of deterring the in-migration of indigents cannot serve as justification for the classification created by the one-year waiting period, since that purpose is constitutionally impermissible.' And it further follows, as the Court says, that any other purposes offered in support of a law that so clearly impinges upon the constitutional right of interstate travel must be shown to reflect a compelling governmental interest. This is necessarily true whether the impinging law be a classification statute to be tested against the Equal Protection Clause, or a state of federal regulatory law, to be tested against the Due Process Clause of the Fourteenth or Fifth Amendment. . . . The Court today, therefore, is not 'contriving new constitutional principles.' It is deciding these cases under the aegis of established constitutional law.

■ MR. CHIEF JUSTICE WARREN, with whom MR. JUSTICE BLACK joins, dissenting.

In my opinion the issue before us can be simply stated: May Congress, acting under one of its enumerated powers, impose minimal nationwide residence requirements or authorize the States to do so? Since I believe that Congress does have this power and has constitutionally exercised it in these cases, I must dissent. . . .

The Court insists that § 402(b) of the Social Security Act 'does not approve, much less prescribe, a one-year requirement.' From its reading of the legislative history it concludes that Congress did not intend to authorize the States to impose residence requirements. An examination of the relevant legislative materials compels, in my view, the opposite

---

[1]   By contrast, the 'right' of international travel has been considered to be no more than an aspect of the 'liberty' protected by the Due Process Clause of the Fifth Amendment. *Kent v. Dulles*, 357 U.S. 116, 125 (1958); *Aptheker v. Secretary of State*, 378 U.S. 500, 505–506 (1964). As such, this 'right,' the Court has held, can be regulated within the bounds of due process. *Zemel v. Rusk*, 381 U.S. 1 (1965).

conclusion, i.e., Congress intended to authorize state residence requirements of up to one year. . . .

Congress, pursuant to its commerce power, has enacted a variety of restrictions upon interstate travel. It has taxed air and rail fares and the gasoline needed to power cars and trucks which move interstate. Many of the federal safety regulations of common carriers which cross state lines burden the right to travel. And Congress has prohibited by criminal statute interstate travel for certain purposes. Although these restrictions operate as a limitation upon free interstate movement of persons, their constitutionality appears well settled. . . .

The Court's right-to-travel cases lend little support to the view that congressional action is invalid merely because it burdens the right to travel. . . . The insubstantiality of the restriction imposed by residence requirements must then be evaluated in light of the possible congressional reasons for such requirements. One fact which does emerge with clarity from the legislative history is Congress' belief that a program of cooperative federalism combining federal aid with enhanced state participation would result in an increase in the scope of welfare programs and level of benefits. Given the apprehensions of many States that an increase in benefits without minimal residence requirements would result in an inability to provide an adequate welfare system, Congress deliberately adopted the intermediate course of a cooperative program. Such a program, Congress believed, would encourage the States to assume greater welfare responsibilities and would give the States the necessary financial support for such an undertaking. Our cases require only that Congress have a rational basis for finding that a chosen regulatory scheme is necessary to the furtherance of interstate commerce. See, e.g., *Katzenbach v. McClung*, 379 U.S. 294 (1964); *Wickard v. Filburn*, 317 U.S. 111 (1942). . . .

The era is long past when this Court under the rubric of due process has reviewed the wisdom of a congressional decision that interstate commerce will be fostered by the enactment of certain regulations. Compare *Adkins v. Children's Hospital*, 261 U.S. 525 (1923), with *United States v. Darby*, 312 U.S. 100 (1941). . . . I am convinced that Congress does have power to enact residence requirements of reasonable duration or to authorize the States to do so and that it has exercised this power.

The Court's decision reveals only the top of the iceberg. Lurking beneath are the multitude of situations in which States have imposed residence requirements including eligibility to vote, to engage in certain professions or occupations or to attend a state-supported university. Although the Court takes pains to avoid acknowledging the ramifications of its decision, its implications cannot be ignored. I dissent.

■ **MR. JUSTICE HARLAN, dissenting.**

The Court today holds unconstitutional Connecticut, Pennsylvania, and District of Columbia statutes which restrict certain kinds of welfare benefits to persons who have lived within the jurisdiction for at least one year immediately preceding their applications. The Court has accomplished this result by an expansion of the comparatively new constitutional doctrine that some state statutes will be deemed to deny equal protection of the laws unless justified by a 'compelling' governmental interest, and by holding that the Fifth Amendment's Due Process Clause imposes a similar limitation on federal enactments. Having decided that the 'compelling interest' principle is applicable, the Court then finds that the governmental interests here asserted are either wholly impermissible or are not 'compelling.' For reasons which follow, I disagree both with the Court's result and with its reasoning.

I

These three cases present two separate but related questions for decision. The first, arising from the District of Columbia appeal, is whether Congress may condition the right to receive Aid to Families with Dependent Children (AFDC) and aid to the permanently and totally disabled in the District of Columbia upon the recipient's having resided in the District for the preceding year. The second, presented in the Pennsylvania and Connecticut appeals, is whether a State may, with the approval of Congress, impose the same conditions with respect to eligibility for AFDC assistance. In each instance, the welfare residence requirements are alleged to be unconstitutional on two grounds: first, because they impose an undue burden upon the constitutional right of welfare applicants to travel interstate; second, because they deny to persons who have recently moved interstate and would otherwise be eligible for welfare assistance the equal protection of the laws assured by the Fourteenth Amendment (in the state cases) or the analogous protection afforded by the Fifth Amendment (in the District of Columbia case). Since the Court basically relies upon the equal protection ground, I shall discuss it first.

II

In upholding the equal protection argument, the Court has applied an equal protection doctrine of relatively recent vintage: the rule that statutory classifications which either are based upon certain 'suspect' criteria or affect 'fundamental rights' will be held to deny equal protection unless justified by a 'compelling' governmental interest.

The 'compelling interest' doctrine, which today is articulated more explicitly than ever before, constitutes an increasingly significant exception to the long established rule that a statute does not deny equal protection if it is rationally related to a legitimate governmental objective. The 'compelling interest' doctrine has two branches. The branch which requires that classifications based upon 'suspect' criteria be supported by a compelling interest apparently had its genesis in cases involving racial classifications, which have, at least since *Korematsu v. United States*, 323 U.S. 214, 216 (1944), been regarded as inherently 'suspect.'[5] . . . Today the list apparently has been further enlarged to include classifications based upon recent interstate movement, and perhaps those based upon the exercise of any constitutional right . . . .

I think that this branch of the 'compelling interest' doctrine is sound when applied to racial classifications, for historically the Equal Protection Clause was largely a product of the desire to eradicate legal distinctions founded upon race. However, I believe that the more recent extensions have been unwise. . . . [W]hen, as in . . . the present case, a classification is based upon the exercise of rights guaranteed against state infringement by the Federal Constitution, then there is no need for any resort to the Equal Protection Clause; in such instances, this Court may properly and straightforwardly invalidate any undue burden upon those rights under the Fourteenth Amendment's Due Process Clause. . . .

The second branch of the 'compelling interest' principle is even more troublesome. For it has been held that a statutory classification is subject to the 'compelling interest' test if the result of the classification may be to affect a 'fundamental right,' regardless of the basis of the classification. This rule was foreshadowed in *Skinner v. Oklahoma*, 316 U.S. 535, 541 (1942), in which an Oklahoma statute providing for compulsory sterilization of 'habitual criminals' was held subject to 'strict scrutiny' mainly because it affected 'one of the basic civil rights.' After a long hiatus, the principle re-emerged in *Reynolds v. Sims*, 377 U.S. 533, 561–562 (1964), in which state apportionment statutes were subjected to an unusually stringent test because "any alleged infringement of the right of citizens to vote must be carefully and meticulously scrutinized."[9] . . . It has reappeared today in the Court's cryptic suggestion that the 'compelling interest' test is applicable merely because the result of the classification may be to deny the appellees "food, shelter, and other necessities of life," as well as in the Court's statement that "(s)ince the classification here touches on the fundamental right of interstate movement, its constitutionality must be judged by the stricter standard of whether it promotes a compelling state interest."

I think this branch of the 'compelling interest' doctrine particularly unfortunate and unnecessary. It is unfortunate because it creates an exception which threatens to swallow the standard equal protection rule. Virtually every state statute affects important rights. This Court has repeatedly held, for example, that the traditional equal protection

---

[5] See *Loving v. Virginia*, 388 U.S. 1, 11 (1967); cf. *Bolling v. Sharpe*, 347 U.S. 497, 499 (1954). See also *Hirabayashi v. United States*, 320 U.S. 81, 100 (1943); *Yick Wo v. Hopkins*, 118 U.S. 356 (1886).

[9] Analysis is complicated when the statutory classification is grounded upon the exercise of a 'fundamental' right. For then the statute may come within the first branch of the 'compelling interest' doctrine because exercise of the right is deemed a 'suspect' criterion and also within the second because the statute is considered to affect the right by deterring its exercise. . . . The present case is another instance, insofar as welfare residence statutes both deter interstate movement and distinguish among welfare applicants on the basis of such movement. Consequently, I have not attempted to specify the branch of the doctrine upon which these decisions rest.

standard is applicable to statutory classifications affecting such fundamental matters as the right to pursue a particular occupation,[11] the right to receive greater or smaller wages[12] or to work more or less hours,[13] and the right to inherit property.[14] Rights such as these are in principle indistinguishable from those involved here, and to extend the 'compelling interest' rule to all cases in which such rights are affected would go far toward making this Court a 'super-legislature.' This branch of the doctrine is also unnecessary. When the right affected is one assured by the Federal Constitution, any infringement can be dealt with under the Due Process Clause. But when a statute affects only matters not mentioned in the Federal Constitution and is not arbitrary or irrational, I must reiterate that I know of nothing which entitles this Court to pick out particular human activities, characterize them as 'fundamental,' and give them added protection under an unusually stringent equal protection test.

I shall consider in the next section whether welfare residence requirements deny due process by unduly burdening the right of interstate travel. If the issue is regarded purely as one of equal protection, then, for the reasons just set forth, this nonracial classification should be judged by ordinary equal protection standards. The applicable criteria are familiar and well established. A legislative measure will be found to deny equal protection only if "it is without any reasonable basis, and therefore is purely arbitrary." *Lindsley v. Natural Carbonic Gas Co.*, 220 U.S. 61, 78 (1911). . . .

For reasons hereafter set forth, a legislature might rationally find that the imposition of a welfare residence requirement would aid in the accomplishment of at least four valid governmental objectives. It might also find that residence requirements have advantages not shared by other methods of achieving the same goals. In light of this undeniable relation of residence requirements to valid legislative aims, it cannot be said that the requirements are 'arbitrary' or 'lacking in rational justification.' Hence, I can find no objection to these residence requirements under the Equal Protection Clause of the Fourteenth Amendment or under the analogous standard embodied in the Due Process Clause of the Fifth Amendment.

III

The next issue, which I think requires fuller analysis than that deemed necessary by the Court under its equal protection rationale, is whether a one-year welfare residence requirement amounts to an undue burden upon the right of interstate travel. Four considerations are relevant: First, what is the constitutional source and nature of the right

---

[11] See, e.g., *Williamson v. Lee Optical Co.*, 348 U.S. 483 (1955).

[12] See, e.g., *Bunting v. Oregon*, 243 U.S. 426 (1917).

[13] See, e.g., *Miller v. Wilson*, 236 U.S. 373 (1915).

[14] See, e.g., *Ferry v. Spokane, P. & S.R. Co.*, 258 U.S. 314 (1922).

to travel which is relied upon? Second, what is the extent of the interference with that right? Third, what governmental interests are served by welfare residence requirements? Fourth, how should the balance of the competing considerations be struck?

The initial problem is to identify the source of the right to travel asserted by the appellees. Congress enacted the welfare residence requirement in the District of Columbia, so the right to travel which is invoked in that case must be enforceable against congressional action. The residence requirements challenged in the Pennsylvania and Connecticut appeals were authorized by Congress in 42 U.S.C. § 602(b), so the right to travel relied upon in those cases must be enforceable against the States even though they have acted with congressional approval.

In my view, it is playing ducks and drakes with the statute to argue, as the Court does, that Congress did not mean to approve these state residence requirements. In 42 U.S.C. § 602(b) . . . Congress directed that:

> (t)he Secretary shall approve any (state assistance) plan which fulfills the conditions specified in subsection (a) of this section, except that he shall not approve any plan which imposes as a condition of eligibility for (AFDC aid) a residence requirement (equal to or greater than one year).

I think that by any fair reading this section must be regarded as conferring congressional approval upon any plan containing a residence requirement of up to one year.

If any reinforcement is needed for taking this statutory language at face value, the overall scheme of the AFDC program and the context in which it was enacted suggest strong reasons why Congress would have wished to approve limited state residence requirements. Congress determined to enlist state assistance in financing the AFDC program, and to administer the program primarily through the States. A previous Congress had already enacted a one-year residence requirement with respect to aid for dependent children in the District of Columbia. In these circumstances, I think it only sensible to conclude that in allowing the States to impose limited residence conditions despite their possible impact on persons who wished to move interstate, Congress was motivated by a desire to encourage state participation in the AFDC program, as well as by a feeling that the States should at least be permitted to impose residence requirements as strict as that already authorized for the District of Columbia. Congress therefore had a genuine federal purpose in allowing the States to use residence tests. And I fully agree with THE CHIEF JUSTICE that this purpose would render § 602(b) a permissible exercise of Congress' power under the Commerce Clause, unless Congress were prohibited from acting by another provision of the Constitution. . . .

Opinions of this Court and of individual Justices have suggested four provisions of the Constitution as possible sources of a right to travel enforceable against the federal or state governments: the Commerce Clause;[20] the Privileges and Immunities Clause of Art. IV, § 2;[21] the Privileges and Immunities Clause of the Fourteenth Amendment;[22] and the Due Process Clause of the Fifth Amendment.[23] The Commerce Clause can be of no assistance to these appellees, since that clause grants plenary power to Congress,[24] and Congress either enacted or approved all of the residence requirements here challenged. The Privileges and Immunities Clause of Art. IV, § 2, is irrelevant, for it appears settled that this clause neither limits federal power nor prevents a State from distinguishing among its own citizens, but simply "prevents a state from discriminating against citizens of other states in favor of its own." *Hague v. CIO*, 307 U.S. 496, 511 (1939) (opinion of Roberts, J.); see *Slaughter-House Cases*, 16 Wall. 36, 77 (1873). Since Congress enacted the District of Columbia residence statute, and since the Pennsylvania and Connecticut appellees were residents and therefore citizens of those States when they sought welfare, the clause can have no application in any of these cases.

The Privileges and Immunities Clause of the Fourteenth Amendment provides that: 'No State shall make or enforce any law which shall abridge the privileges or immunities of citizens of the United States.' It is evident that this clause cannot be applicable in the District of Columbia appeal, since it is limited in terms to instances of state action. In the Pennsylvania and Connecticut cases, . . . [t]he fact of congressional approval, together with this Court's past statements about the nature of the Fourteenth Amendment Privileges and Immunities Clause, leads me to believe that the clause affords no additional help to these appellees, and that the decisive issue is whether Congress itself may impose such requirements. The view of the Privileges and Immunities Clause which has most often been adopted by the Court and by individual Justices is that it extends only to those 'privileges and immunities' which "arise or grow out of the relationship of United States citizens to the national government." *Hague v. CIO*, 307 U.S. 496, 520 (1939) (opinion of Stone, J.).[26] On the authority of *Crandall v. Nevada*, 6 Wall. 35 (1868), those privileges and immunities have repeatedly been

---

[20] See, e.g., *Edwards v. California*, 314 U.S. 160 (1941); the *Passenger Cases*, 7 How. 283 (1849).

[21] See, e.g., *Corfield v. Coryell*, 6 Fed.Cas. p. 546 (No. 3230) (1825) (Mr. Justice Washington).

[22] See, e.g., *Edwards v. California*, 314 U.S. 160, 177, 181 (1941) (Douglas and Jackson, JJ., concurring); *Twining v. New Jersey*, 211 U.S. 78, 97 (1908) (dictum).

[23] See, e.g., *Kent v. Dulles*, 357 U.S. 116, 125–127 (1958); *Aptheker v. Secretary of State*, 378 U.S. 500, 505–506 (1964).

[24] See, e.g., *Prudential Ins. Co. v. Benjamin*, 328 U.S. 408, 423 (1946). See also *Maryland v. Wirtz*, 392 U.S. 183, 193–199 (1968).

[26] See *Slaughter-House Cases*, 16 Wall. 36, 79 (1873).

said to include the right to travel from State to State,[27] presumably for the reason assigned in *Crandall*: that state restrictions on travel might interfere with intercourse between the Federal Government and its citizens.[28] This kind of objection to state welfare residence requirements would seem necessarily to vanish in the face of congressional authorization, for except in those instances when its authority is limited by a constitutional provision binding upon it (as the Fourteenth Amendment is not), Congress has full power to define the relationship between citizens and the Federal Government.

Some Justices, notably the dissenters in the *Slaughter-House Cases*, 16 Wall. 36, 83, 111, 124 (1873) (Field, Bradley, and Swayne, JJ., dissenting), and the concurring Justices in *Edwards v. California*, 314 U.S. 160, 177, 181 (1941) (Douglas and Jackson, JJ., concurring), have gone further and . . . suggested that the privileges and immunities of national citizenship, including freedom to travel, were those natural rights 'which of right belong to the citizens of all free governments,' 16 Wall., at 98 (Field, J.). However, since such rights are 'the rights of citizens of any free government,' id., at 114 (Bradley, J.), it would appear that they must be immune from national as well as state abridgement. To the extent that they may be validly limited by Congress, there would seem to be no reason why they may not be similarly abridged by States acting with congressional approval.

The concurring Justices in *Edwards* laid emphasis not upon natural rights but upon a generalized concern for the functioning of the federal system, stressing that to allow a State to curtail "the rights of national citizenship would be to contravene every conception of national unity," 314 U.S., at 181 (Douglas, J.), and that "(i)f national citizenship means less than (the right to move interstate) it means nothing." *Id.*, at 183 (Jackson, J.). However . . . Mr. Justice Jackson explicitly recognized in Edwards that: 'The right of the citizen to migrate from state to state . . . (is) subject to all constitutional limitations imposed by the federal government,' id., at 184. And nothing in the nature of federalism would seem to prevent Congress from authorizing the States to do what Congress might validly do itself. Indeed, this Court has held, for example, that Congress may empower the States to undertake regulations of commerce which would otherwise be prohibited by the negative implications of the Commerce Clause. See *Prudential Ins. Co. v. Benjamin*, 328 U.S. 408 (1946). Hence, as has already been suggested, the decisive question is whether Congress may legitimately enact welfare residence requirements, and the Fourteenth Amendment Privileges and Immunities Clause adds no extra force to the appellees' attack on the requirements.

---

[27] See, e.g., *Slaughter-House Cases*, *supra*, at 79; *Twining v. New Jersey*, *supra*, at 97.

[28] The *Crandall* Court stressed the 'right' of a citizen to come to the national capital, to have access to federal officials, and to travel to seaports. Of course, *Crandall* was decided before the enactment of the Fourteenth Amendment.

The last possible source of a right to travel is one which does operate against the Federal Government: the Due Process Clause of the Fifth Amendment. It is now settled that freedom to travel is an element of the 'liberty' secured by that clause. In *Kent v. Dulles*, 357 U.S. 116, 125–126 (1958), the Court said:

> The right to travel is a part of the 'liberty' of which the citizen cannot be deprived without due process of law under the Fifth Amendment. . . . Freedom of movement across frontiers . . . and inside frontiers as well, was a part of our heritage.

The Court echoed these remarks in *Aptheker v. Secretary of State*, 378 U.S. 500, 505–506 (1964) . . . . However, in *Zemel v. Rusk*, 381 U.S. 1 (1965), the First Amendment cast of the *Aptheker* opinion was explained as having stemmed from the fact that Aptheker was forbidden to travel because of 'expression or association on his part.' The Court noted that Zemel was 'not being forced to choose between membership in an organization and freedom to travel,' ibid., and held that the mere circumstance that Zemel's proposed journey to Cuba might be used to collect information of political and social significance was not enough to bring the case within the First Amendment category.

Finally, in *United States v. Guest*, 383 U.S. 745 (1966), the Court again had occasion to consider the right of interstate travel. Without specifying the source of that right, the Court said:

> The constitutional right to travel from one State to another * * * occupies a position fundamental to the concept of our Federal Union. It is a right that has been firmly established and repeatedly recognized. * * * (The) right finds no explicit mention in the Constitution. The reason, it has been suggested, is that a right so elementary was conceived from the beginning to be a necessary concomitant of the stronger Union the Constitution created. In any event, freedom to travel throughout the United States has long been recognized as a basic right under the Constitution.

I therefore conclude that the right to travel interstate is a 'fundamental' right which, for present purposes, should be regarded as having its source in the Due Process Clause of the Fifth Amendment.

The next questions are: (1) To what extent does a one-year residence condition upon welfare eligibility interfere with this right to travel?; and (2) What are the governmental interests supporting such a condition? The consequence of the residence requirements is that persons who contemplate interstate changes of residence, and who believe that they otherwise would qualify for welfare payments, must take into account the fact that such assistance will not be available for a year after arrival. The number or proportion of persons who are actually deterred from changing residence by the existence of these provisions is unknown. If one accepts evidence put forward by the appellees, to the effect that there would be only a minuscule increase in the number of welfare applicants were existing residence requirements to be done away with, it follows that the requirements do not deter an appreciable number of persons from moving interstate.

Against this indirect impact on the right to travel must be set the interests of the States, and of Congress with respect to the District of Columbia, in imposing residence conditions. There appear to be four such interests. First, it is evident that a primary concern of Congress and the Pennsylvania and Connecticut Legislatures was to deny welfare benefits to persons who moved into the jurisdiction primarily in order to collect those benefits. This seems to me an entirely legitimate objective. A legislature is certainly not obliged to furnish welfare assistance to every inhabitant of the jurisdiction, and it is entirely rational to deny benefits to those who enter primarily in order to receive them, since this will make more funds available for those whom the legislature deems more worthy of subsidy.

A second possible purpose of residence requirements is the prevention of fraud. A residence requirement provides an objective and workable means of determining that an applicant intends to remain indefinitely within the jurisdiction. It therefore may aid in eliminating fraudulent collection of benefits by nonresidents and persons already receiving assistance in other States. There can be no doubt that prevention of fraud is a valid legislative goal. Third, the requirement of a fixed period of residence may help in predicting the budgetary amount which will be needed for public assistance in the future. While none of the appellant jurisdictions appears to keep data sufficient to permit the making of detailed budgetary predictions in consequence of the requirement, it is probable that in the event of a very large increase or decrease in the number of indigent newcomers the waiting period would give the legislature time to make needed adjustments in the welfare laws. Obviously, this is a proper objective. Fourth, the residence requirements conceivably may have been predicated upon a legislative desire to restrict welfare payments financed in part by state tax funds to persons who have recently made some contribution to the State's economy, through having been employed, having paid taxes, or having spent money in the State. This too would appear to be a legitimate purpose.

The next question is the decisive one: whether the governmental interests served by residence requirements outweigh the burden imposed upon the right to travel. In my view, a number of considerations militate in favor of constitutionality. First, as just shown, four separate, legitimate governmental interests are furthered by residence requirements. Second, the impact of the requirements upon the freedom of individuals to travel interstate is indirect and, according to evidence put forward by the appellees themselves, insubstantial. Third, these are not cases in which a State or States, acting alone, have attempted to interfere with the right of citizens to travel, but one in which the States have acted within the terms of a limited authorization by the National Government, and in which Congress itself has laid down a like rule for the District of Columbia. Fourth, the legislatures which enacted these statutes have been fully exposed to the arguments of the appellees as to why these residence requirements are unwise, and have rejected them. This is not, therefore, an instance in which legislatures have acted without mature deliberation.

Fifth, and of longer-range importance, the field of welfare assistance is one in which there is a widely recognized need for fresh solutions and consequently for experimentation. Invalidation of welfare residence requirements might have the unfortunate consequence of discouraging the Federal and State Governments from establishing unusually generous welfare programs in particular areas on an experimental basis, because of fears that the program would cause an influx of persons seeking higher welfare payments. Sixth and finally, a strong presumption of constitutionality attaches to statutes of the types now before us. Congressional enactments come to this Court with an extremely heavy presumption of validity. See, e.g., *Brown v. Maryland*, 12 Wheat. 419, 436 (1827). A similar presumption of constitutionality attaches to state statutes, particularly when, as here, a State has acted upon a specific authorization from Congress. See, e.g., *Powell v. Pennsylvania*, 127 U.S. 678, 684–685 (1888). . . .

Today's decision, it seems to me, reflects to an unusual degree the current notion that this Court possesses a peculiar wisdom all its own whose capacity to lead this Nation out of its present troubles is contained only by the limits of judicial ingenuity in contriving new constitutional principles to meet each problem as it arises. For anyone who, like myself, believes that it is an essential function of this Court to maintain the constitutional divisions between state and federal authority and among the three branches of the Federal Government, today's decision is a step in the wrong direction. This resurgence of the expansive view of 'equal protection' carries the seeds of more judicial interference with the state and federal legislative process, much more indeed than does the judicial application of 'due process' according to traditional concepts . . . .

San Antonio Independent School District v. Rodriguez
411 U.S. 1 (1973)

■ MR. JUSTICE POWELL delivered the opinion of the Court.

This suit attacking the Texas system of financing public education was initiated by Mexican-American parents whose children attend the elementary and secondary schools in the Edgewood Independent School District, an urban school district in San Antonio, Texas. They brought a class action on behalf of schoolchildren throughout the State who are members of minority groups or who are poor and reside in school districts having a low property tax base. Named as defendants were the State Board of Education, the Commissioner of Education, the State Attorney General, and the Bexar County (San Antonio) Board of Trustees. The complaint was filed in the summer of 1968 and a three-judge court was impaneled in January 1969. In December 1971 the panel rendered its judgment in a per curiam opinion holding the Texas school finance system unconstitutional under the Equal Protection Clause of the Fourteenth Amendment. The State appealed, and we noted probable jurisdiction to consider the far-reaching constitutional questions presented. For the reasons stated in this opinion, we reverse the decision of the District Court.

I

The first Texas State Constitution, promulgated upon Texas' entry into the Union in 1845, provided for the establishment of a system of free schools. Early in its history, Texas adopted a dual approach to the financing of its schools, relying on mutual participation by the local school districts and the State. As early as 1883, the state constitution was amended to provide for the creation of local school districts empowered to levy ad valorem taxes with the consent of local taxpayers for the 'erection . . . of school buildings' and for the 'further maintenance of public free schools.' Such local funds as were raised were supplemented by funds distributed to each district from the State's Permanent and Available School Funds. The Permanent School Fund, its predecessor established in 1854 with $2,000,000 realized from an annexation settlement, was thereafter endowed with millions of acres of public land set aside to assure a continued source of income for school support. The Available School Fund, which received income from the Permanent School Fund as well as from a state ad valorem property tax and other designated taxes, served as the disbursing arm for most state educational funds throughout the late 1800's and first half of this century. Additionally, in 1918 an increase in state property taxes was used to finance a program providing free textbooks throughout the State.

Until recent times, Texas was a predominantly rural State and its population and property wealth were spread relatively evenly across the State. Sizable differences in the value of assessable property between local school districts became increasingly evident as the State became more industrialized and as rural-to-urban population shifts became more pronounced. The location of commercial and industrial property began to play a significant role in determining the amount of tax resources available to each school district. These growing disparities in population and taxable property between districts were responsible in part for increasingly notable differences in levels of local expenditure for education.

In due time it became apparent to those concerned with financing public education that contributions from the Available School Fund were not sufficient to ameliorate these disparities. Prior to 1939, the Available

School Fund contributed money to every school district at a rate of $17.50 per school-age child. Although the amount was increased several times in the early 1940's, the Fund was providing only $46 per student by 1945.

Recognizing the need for increased state funding to help offset disparities in local spending and to meet Texas' changing educational requirements, the state legislature in the late 1940's undertook a thorough evaluation of public education with an eye toward major reform. In 1947, an 18-member committee, composed of educators and legislators, was appointed to explore alternative systems in other States and to propose a funding scheme that would guarantee a minimum or basic educational offering to each child and that would help overcome interdistrict disparities in taxable resources. The Committee's efforts led to the passage of the Gilmer-Aikin bills, named for the Committee's co-chairmen, establishing the Texas Minimum Foundation School Program. Today, this Program accounts for approximately half of the total educational expenditures in Texas.

The Program calls for state and local contributions to a fund earmarked specifically for teacher salaries, operating expenses, and transportation costs. The State, supplying funds from its general revenues, finances approximately 80% of the Program, and the school districts are responsible—as a unit—for providing the remaining 20%. The districts' share, known as the Local Fund Assignment, is apportioned among the school districts under a formula designed to reflect each district's relative taxpaying ability. The Assignment is first divided among Texas' 254 counties pursuant to a complicated economic index that takes into account the relative value of each county's contribution to the State's total income from manufacturing, mining, and agricultural activities. It also considers each county's relative share of all payrolls paid within the State and, to a lesser extent, considers each county's share of all property in the State. Each county's assignment is then divided among its school districts on the basis of each district's share of assessable property within the county. The district, in turn, finances its share of the Assignment out of revenues from local property taxation.

The design of this complex system was twofold. First, it was an attempt to assure that the Foundation Program would have an equalizing influence on expenditure levels between school districts by placing the heaviest burden on the school districts most capable of paying. Second, the Program's architects sought to establish a Local Fund Assignment that would force every school district to contribute to the education of its children but that would not by itself exhaust any district's resources. Today every school district does impose a property tax from which it derives locally expendable funds in excess of the amount necessary to satisfy its Local Fund Assignment under the Foundation Program.

In the years since this program went into operation in 1949, expenditures for education—from state as well as local sources—have increased steadily. Between 1949 and 1967, expenditures increased approximately 500%. In the last decade alone the total public school budget rose from $750 million to $2.1 billion and these increases have been reflected in consistently rising per pupil expenditures throughout the State. Teacher salaries, by far the largest item in any school's budget, have increased dramatically—the state-supported minimum salary for teachers possessing college degrees has risen from $2,400 to $6,000 over the last 20 years.

The school district in which appellees reside, the Edgewood Independent School District, has been compared throughout this litigation with the Alamo Heights Independent School District. This comparison between the least and most affluent districts in the San Antonio area serves to illustrate the manner in which the dual system of finance operates and to indicate the extent to which substantial disparities exist despite the State's impressive progress in recent years. Edgewood is one of seven public school districts in the metropolitan area. Approximately 22,000 students are enrolled in its 25 elementary and secondary schools. The district is situated in the core-city sector of San Antonio in a residential neighborhood that has little commercial or industrial property. The residents are predominantly of Mexican-American descent: approximately 90% of the student population is Mexican-American and over 6% is Negro. The average assessed property value per pupil is $5,960—the lowest in the metropolitan area—and the median family income ($4,686) is also the lowest. At an equalized tax rate of $1.05 per $100 of assessed property—the highest in the metropolitan area—the district contributed $26 to the education of each child for the 1967—1968 school year above its Local Fund Assignment for the Minimum Foundation Program. The Foundation Program contributed $222 per pupil for a state-local total of $248. Federal funds added another $108 for a total of $356 per pupil.

Alamo Heights is the most affluent school district in San Antonio. Its six schools, housing approximately 5,000 students, are situated in a residential community quite unlike the Edgewood District. The school population is predominantly 'Anglo,' having only 18% Mexican-Americans and less than 1% Negroes. The assessed property value per pupil exceeds $49,000,[33] and the median family income is $8,001. In 1967—1968 the local tax rate of $.85 per $100 of valuation yielded $333 per pupil over and above its contribution to the Foundation Program. Coupled with the $225 provided from that Program, the district was able

---

[33] A map of Bexar County included in the record shows that Edgewood and Alamo Heights are among the smallest districts in the county and are of approximately equal size. Yet, as the figures above indicate, Edgewood's student population is more than four times that of Alamo Heights. This factor obviously accounts for a significant percentage of the differences between the two districts in per-pupil property values and expenditures. If Alamo Heights had as many students to educate as Edgewood does (22,000) its per pupil assessed property value would be approximately $11,100 rather than $49,000, and its per-pupil expenditures would therefore have been considerably lower.

to supply $558 per student. Supplemented by a $36 per-pupil grant from federal sources, Alamo Heights spent $594 per pupil.

Although the 1967—1968 school year figures provide the only complete statistical breakdown for each category of aid, more recent partial statistics indicate that the previously noted trend of increasing state aid has been significant. For the 1970—1971 school year, the Foundation School Program allotment for Edgewood was $356 per pupil, a 62% increase over the 1967—68 school year. Indeed, state aid alone in 1970—1971 equaled Edgewood's entire 1967—1968 school budget from local, state, and federal sources. Alamo Heights enjoyed a similar increase under the Foundation Program, netting $491 per pupil in 1970—1971. These recent figures also reveal the extent to which these two districts' allotments were funded from their own required contributions to the Local Fund Assignment. Alamo Heights, because of its relative wealth, was required to contribute out of its local property tax collections approximately $100 per pupil, or about 20% of its Foundation grant. Edgewood, on the other hand, paid only $8.46 per pupil, which is about 2.4% of its grant. It appears then that, at least as to these two districts, the Local Fund Assignment does reflect a rough approximation of the relative taxpaying potential of each.

Despite these recent increases, substantial interdistrict disparities in school expenditures found by the District Court to prevail in San Antonio and in varying degrees throughout the State still exist. And it was these disparities, largely attributable to differences in the amounts of money collected through local property taxation, that led the District Court to conclude that Texas' dual system of public school financing violated the Equal Protection Clause. The District Court held that the Texas system discriminates on the basis of wealth in the manner in which education is provided for its people. Finding that wealth is a 'suspect' classification and that education is a 'fundamental' interest, the District Court held that the Texas system could be sustained only if the State could show that it was premised upon some compelling state interest. On this issue the court concluded that '(n)ot only are defendants unable to demonstrate compelling state interests . . . they fail even to establish a reasonable basis for these classifications.'

Texas virtually concedes that its historically rooted dual system of financing education could not withstanding the strict judicial scrutiny that this Court has found appropriate in reviewing legislative judgments that interfere with fundamental constitutional rights or that involve suspect classifications. If, as previous decisions have indicated, strict scrutiny means that the State's system is not entitled to the usual presumption of validity, that the State rather than the complainants must carry a 'heavy burden of justification,' that the State must demonstrate that its educational system has been structured with 'precision,' and is 'tailored' narrowly to serve legitimate objectives and that it has selected the 'less drastic means' for effectuating its objectives, the Texas financing system and its counterpart in virtually every other State will not pass muster. The State candidly admits that '(n)o one familiar with the Texas system would contend that it has yet achieved perfection.' Apart from its concession that educational financing in Texas has 'defects' and 'imperfections,' the State defends the system's rationality with vigor and disputes the District Court's finding that it lacks a 'reasonable basis.'

This, then, establishes the framework for our analysis. We must decide, first, whether the Texas system of financing public education operates to the disadvantage of some suspect class or impinges upon a fundamental right explicitly or implicitly protected by the Constitution, thereby requiring strict judicial scrutiny. If so, the judgment of the District Court should be affirmed. If not, the Texas scheme must still be examined to determine whether it rationally furthers some legitimate, articulated state purpose and therefore does not constitute an invidious discrimination in violation of the Equal Protection Clause of the Fourteenth Amendment.

II

The District Court's opinion does not reflect the novelty and complexity of the constitutional questions posed by appellees' challenge to Texas' system of school financing. In concluding that strict judicial scrutiny was required, that court relied on decisions dealing with the rights of indigents to equal treatment in the criminal trial and appellate processes,[45] and on cases disapproving wealth restrictions on the right to vote.[46] Those cases, the District Court concluded, established wealth as a suspect classification. Finding that the local property tax system discriminated on the basis of wealth, it regarded those precedents as controlling. It then reasoned, based on decisions of this Court affirming the undeniable importance of education, that there is a fundamental right to education and that, absent some compelling state justification, the Texas system could not stand.

We are unable to agree that this case, which in significant aspects is sui generis, may be so neatly fitted into the conventional mosaic of constitutional analysis under the Equal Protection Clause. Indeed, for the several reasons that follow, we find neither the suspect-classification not the fundamental-interest analysis persuasive.

A

The wealth discrimination discovered by the District Court in this case, and by several other courts that have recently struck down school-financing laws in other States, is quite unlike any of the forms of wealth discrimination heretofore reviewed by this Court. . . .

---

[45]　E.g., Griffin v. Illinois, 351 U.S. 12 (1956); Douglas v. California, 372 U.S. 353 (1963).

[46]　Harper v. Virginia Bd. of Elections, 383 U.S. 663 (1966); McDonald v. Board of Election Com'rs, 394 U.S. 802 (1969); Bullock v. Carter, 405 U.S. 134 (1972); Goosby v. Osser, 409 U.S. 512 (1973).

The case comes to us with no definitive description of the classifying facts or delineation of the disfavored class. . . . The Texas system of school financing might be regarded as discriminating (1) against 'poor' persons whose incomes fall below some identifiable level of poverty or who might be characterized as functionally 'indigent,' or (2) against those who are relatively poorer than others, or (3) against all those who, irrespective of their personal incomes, happen to reside in relatively poorer school districts. Our task must be to ascertain whether, in fact, the Texas system has been shown to discriminate on any of these possible bases and, if so, whether the resulting classification may be regarded as suspect.

The precedents of this Court provide the proper starting point. The individuals, or groups of individuals, who constituted the class discriminated against in our prior cases shared two distinguishing characteristics: because of their impecunity they were completely unable to pay for some desired benefit, and as a consequence, they sustained an absolute deprivation of a meaningful opportunity to enjoy that benefit. In *Griffin v. Illinois*, 351 U.S. 12 (1956), and its progeny, the Court invalidated state laws that prevented an indigent criminal defendant from acquiring a transcript, or an adequate substitute for a transcript, for use at several stages of the trial and appeal process. The payment requirements in each case were found to occasion de facto discrimination against those who, because of their indigency, were totally unable to pay for transcripts. And the Court in each case emphasized that no constitutional violation would have been shown if the State had provided some 'adequate substitute' for a full stenographic transcript.

Likewise, in *Douglas v. California*, 372 U.S. 353 (1963), a decision establishing an indigent defendant's right to court-appointed counsel on direct appeal, the Court dealt only with defendants who could not pay for counsel from their own resources and who had no other way of gaining representation. *Douglas* provides no relief for those on whom the burdens of paying for a criminal defense are relatively speaking, great but not insurmountable. Nor does it deal with relative differences in the quality of counsel acquired by the less wealthy. . . .

Finally, in *Bullock v. Carter*, 405 U.S. 134 (1972), the Court invalidated the Texas filing-fee requirement for primary elections. Both of the relevant classifying facts found in the previous cases were present there. The size of the fee, often running into the thousands of dollars and, in at least one case, as high as $8,900, effectively barred all potential candidates who were unable to pay the required fee. As the system provided 'no reasonable alternative means of access to the ballot,' inability to pay occasioned an absolute denial of a position on the primary ballot.

Only appellees' first possible basis for describing the class disadvantaged by the Texas school-financing system—discrimination against a class of definably 'poor' persons—might arguably meet the criteria established in these prior cases. Even a cursory examination, however, demonstrates that neither of the two distinguishing characteristics of wealth classifications can be found here. First ... appellees have made no effort to demonstrate that it operates to the peculiar disadvantage of any class fairly definable as indigent, or as composed of persons whose incomes are beneath any designated poverty level. Indeed, there is reason to believe that the poorest families are not necessarily clustered in the poorest property districts. . . .

Second ... unlike each of the foregoing cases, lack of personal resources has not occasioned an absolute deprivation of the desired benefit. The argument here is not that the children in districts having relatively low assessable property values are receiving no public education; rather, it is that they are receiving a poorer quality education than that available to children in districts having more assessable wealth. Apart from the unsettled and disputed question whether the quality of education may be determined by the amount of money expended for it,[56] a sufficient answer to appellees' argument is that, at least where wealth is involved, the Equal Protection Clause does not require absolute equality or precisely equal advantages. Nor indeed, in view of the infinite variables affecting the educational process, can any system assure equal quality of education except in the most relative sense. Texas asserts that the Minimum Foundation Program provides an 'adequate' education for all children in the State. . . . No proof was offered at trial persuasively discrediting or refuting the State's assertion.

For these two reasons—the absence of any evidence that the financing system discriminates against any definable category of 'poor' people or that it results in the absolute deprivation of education—the disadvantaged class is not susceptible of identification in traditional terms.

As suggested above, appellees and the District Court may have embraced a second or third approach, the second of which might be characterized as a theory of relative or comparative discrimination based on family income. Appellees sought to prove that a direct correlation exists between the wealth of families within each district and the expenditures therein for education. That is, along a continuum, the poorer the family the lower the dollar amount of education received by the family's children.

The principal evidence adduced in support of this comparative-discrimination claim is an affidavit submitted by Professor Joele S. Berke of Syracuse University's Educational Finance Policy Institute. The District Court, relying in major part upon this affidavit and apparently

---

[56] Each of appellees' possible theories of wealth discrimination is founded on the assumption that the quality of education varies directly with the amount of funds expended on it and that, therefore, the difference in quality between two schools can be determined simplistically by looking at the difference in per-pupil expenditures. This is a matter of considerable dispute among educators and commentators.

accepting the substance of appellees' theory, noted, first, a positive correlation between the wealth of school districts, measured in terms of assessable property per pupil, and their levels of per-pupil expenditures. Second, the court found a similar correlation between district wealth and the personal wealth of its residents, measured in terms of median family income.

If, in fact, these correlations could be sustained, then it might be argued that expenditures on education—equated by appellees to the quality of education—are dependent on personal wealth. Appellees' comparative-discrimination theory would still face serious unanswered questions, including whether a bare positive correlation or some higher degree of correlation is necessary to provide a basis for concluding that the financing system is designed to operate to the peculiar disadvantage of the comparatively poor, and whether a class of this size and diversity could ever claim the special protection accorded 'suspect' classes. These questions need not be addressed in this case, however, since appellees' proof fails to support their allegations or the District Court's conclusions.

Professor Berke's affidavit is based on a survey of approximately 10% of the school districts in Texas. His findings, previously set out in the margin, show only that the wealthiest few districts in the sample have the highest median family incomes and spend the most on education, and that the several poorest districts have the lowest family incomes and devote the least amount of money to education. For the remainder of the districts—96 districts composing almost 90% of the sample—the correlation is inverted, i.e., the districts that spend next to the most money on education are populated by families having next to the lowest median family incomes while the districts spending the least have the highest median family incomes. It is evident that, even if the conceptual questions were answered favorably to appellees, no factual basis exists upon which to found a claim of comparative wealth discrimination.[64]

This brings us, then, to the third way in which the classification scheme might be defined—district wealth discrimination. Since the only correlation indicated by the evidence is between district property wealth and expenditures, it may be argued that discrimination might be found without regard to the individual income characteristics of district residents. Assuming a perfect correlation between district property wealth and expenditures from top to bottom, the disadvantaged class might be viewed as encompassing every child in every district except the district that has the most assessable wealth and spends the most on education. Alternatively, as suggested in Mr. Justice MARSHALL's dissenting opinion, the class might be defined more restrictively to include children in districts with assessable property which falls below

---

[64] Studies in other States have also questioned the existence of any dependable correlation between a district's wealth measured in terms of assessable property and the collective wealth of families residing in the district measured in terms of median family income.

the statewide average, or median, or below some other artificially defined level.

However described, it is clear that appellees' suit asks this Court to extend its most exacting scrutiny to review a system that allegedly discriminates against a large, diverse, and amorphous class, unified only by the common factor of residence in districts that happen to have less taxable wealth than other districts. The system of alleged discrimination and the class it defines have none of the traditional indicia of suspectness: the class is not saddled with such disabilities, or subjected to such a history of purposeful unequal treatment, or relegated to such a position of political powerlessness as to command extraordinary protection from the majoritarian political process.

We thus conclude that the Texas system does not operate to the peculiar disadvantage of any suspect class. But in recognition of the fact that this Court has never heretofore held that wealth discrimination alone provides an adequate basis for invoking strict scrutiny, appellees have not relied solely on this contention. They also assert that the State's system impermissibly interferes with the exercise of a 'fundamental' right and that accordingly the prior decisions of this Court require the application of the strict standard of judicial review. *Shapiro v. Thompson*, 394 U.S. 618 (1969). It is this question—whether education is a fundamental right, in the sense that it is among the rights and liberties protected by the Constitution—which has so consumed the attention of courts and commentators in recent years.

B

In *Brown v. Board of Education*, 347 U.S. 483 (1954), a unanimous Court recognized that 'education is perhaps the most important function of state and local governments.' . . .

Nothing this Court holds today in any way detracts from our historic dedication to public education. . . . But the importance of a service performed by the State does not determine whether it must be regarded as fundamental for purposes of examination under the Equal Protection Clause. Mr. Justice Harlan, dissenting from the Court's application of strict scrutiny to a law impinging upon the right of interstate travel, admonished that '(v)irtually every state statute affects important rights.' *Shapiro*, 394 U.S., at 661. . . .

Lindsey v. Normet, 405 U.S. 56 (1972), decided only last Term, firmly reiterates that social importance is not the critical determinant for subjecting state legislation to strict scrutiny. The complainants in that case, involving a challenge to the procedural limitations imposed on tenants in suits brought by landlords under Oregon's Forcible Entry and Wrongful Detainer Law, urged the Court to examine the operation of the statute under 'a more stringent standard than mere rationality.' The tenants argued that the statutory limitations implicated 'fundamental interests which are particularly important to the poor,' such as the "need for decent shelter" and the "right to retain peaceful possession of one's home." Mr. Justice White's analysis, in his opinion for the Court is instructive:

> We do not denigrate the importance of decent, safe and sanitary housing. But the Constitution does not provide judicial remedies for every social and economic ill. We are unable to perceive in that document any constitutional guarantee of access to dwellings of a particular quality or any recognition of the right of a tenant to occupy the real property of his landlord beyond the term of his lease, without the payment of rent . . . . Absent constitutional mandate, the assurance of adequate housing and the definition of landlord-tenant relationships are legislative, not judicial, functions.

Similarly, in *Dandridge v. Williams*, 397 U.S. 471 (1970), the Court's explicit recognition of the fact that the 'administration of public welfare assistance . . . involves the most basic economic needs of impoverished human beings,' provided no basis for departing from the settled mode of constitutional analysis of legislative classifications involving questions of economic and social policy. As in the case of housing, the central importance of welfare benefits to the poor was not an adequate foundation for requiring the State to justify its law by showing some compelling state interest.

The lesson of these cases in addressing the question now before the Court is plain. It is not the province of this Court to create substantive constitutional rights in the name of guaranteeing equal protection of the laws. Thus, the key to discovering whether education is 'fundamental' is not to be found in comparisons of the relative societal significance of education as opposed to subsistence or housing. Nor is it to be found by weighing whether education is as important as the right to travel. Rather, the answer lies in assessing whether there is a right to education explicitly or implicitly guaranteed by the Constitution.

Education, of course, is not among the rights afforded explicit protection under our Federal Constitution. . . . It is appellees' contention, however, that education is distinguishable from other services and benefits provided by the State because it bears a peculiarly close relationship to other rights and liberties accorded protection under the Constitution. Specifically, they insist that education is itself a fundamental personal right because it is essential to the effective exercise of First Amendment freedoms and to intelligent utilization of the right to vote. In asserting a nexus between speech and education, appellees urge that the right to speak is meaningless unless the speaker is capable of articulating his thoughts intelligently and persuasively. The 'marketplace of ideas' is an empty forum for those lacking basic communicative tools. Likewise, they argue that the corollary right to receive information becomes little more than a hollow privilege when the recipient has not been taught to read, assimilate, and utilize available knowledge.

A similar line of reasoning is pursued with respect to the right to vote.[78] Exercise of the franchise, it is contended, cannot be divorced from the educational foundation of the voter. The electoral process, if reality is to conform to the democratic ideal, depends on an informed electorate: a voter cannot cast his ballot intelligently unless his reading skills and thought processes have been adequately developed.

We need not dispute any of these propositions. The Court has long afforded zealous protection against unjustifiable governmental interference with the individual's rights to speak and to vote. Yet we have never presumed to possess either the ability or the authority to guarantee to the citizenry the most effective speech or the most informed electoral choice. That these may be desirable goals of a system of freedom of expression and of a representative form of government is not to be doubted. . . . But they are not values to be implemented by judicial instruction into otherwise legitimate state activities.

Even if it were conceded that some identifiable quantum of education is a constitutionally protected prerequisite to the meaningful exercise of either right, we have no indication that the present levels of educational expenditures in Texas provide an education that falls short. Whatever merit appellees' argument might have if a State's financing system occasioned an absolute denial of educational opportunities to any of its children, that argument provides no basis for finding an interference with fundamental rights where only relative differences in spending levels are involved and where—as is true in the present case—no charge fairly could be made that the system fails to provide each child with an opportunity to acquire the basic minimal skills necessary for the enjoyment of the rights of speech and of full participation in the political process.

Furthermore, the logical limitations on appellees' nexus theory are difficult to perceive. How, for instance, is education to be distinguished from the significant personal interests in the basics of decent food and shelter? Empirical examination might well buttress an assumption that the ill-fed, ill-clothed, and ill-housed are among the most ineffective participants in the political process, and that they derive the least enjoyment from the benefits of the First Amendment. If so, appellees' thesis would cast serious doubt on the authority of *Dandridge v. Williams, supra* and *Lindsey v. Normet, supra*. . . .

---

[78] Since the right to vote, per se, is not a constitutionally protected right, we assume that appellees' references to that right are simply shorthand references to the protected right, implicit in our constitutional system, to participate in state elections on an equal basis with other qualified voters whenever the State has adopted an elective process for determining who will represent any segment of the State's population.

C

[T]his is not a case in which the challenged state action must be subjected to the searching judicial scrutiny reserved for laws that create suspect classifications or impinge upon constitutionally protected rights.

We need not rest our decision, however, solely on the inappropriateness of the strict-scrutiny test. A century of Supreme Court adjudication under the Equal Protection Clause affirmatively supports the application of the traditional standard of review, which requires only that the State's system be shown to bear some rational relationship to legitimate state purposes. This case represents far more than a challenge to the manner in which Texas provides for the education of its children. We have here nothing less than a direct attack on the way in which Texas has chosen to raise and disburse state and local tax revenues. We are asked to condemn the State's judgment in conferring on political subdivisions the power to tax local property to supply revenues for local interests. In so doing, appellees would have the Court intrude in an area in which it has traditionally deferred to state legislatures. This Court has often admonished against such interferences with the State's fiscal policies under the Equal Protection Clause. . . .

Thus, we stand on familiar grounds when we continue to acknowledge that the Justices of this Court lack both the expertise and the familiarity with local problems so necessary to the making of wise decisions with respect to the raising and disposition of public revenues. . . . No scheme of taxation, whether the tax is imposed on property, income, or purchases of goods and services, has yet been devised which is free of all discriminatory impact. In such a complex arena in which no perfect alternatives exist, the Court does well not to impose too rigorous a standard of scrutiny lest all local fiscal schemes become subjects of criticism under the Equal Protection Clause.

In addition to matters of fiscal policy, this case also involves the most persistent and difficult questions of educational policy, another area in which this Court's lack of specialized knowledge and experience counsels against premature interference with the informed judgments made at the state and local levels. . . . On even the most basic questions in this area the scholars and educational experts are divided. Indeed, one of the major sources of controversy concerns the extent to which there is a demonstrable correlation between educational expenditures and the quality of education. . . . Related to the questioned relationship between cost and quality is the equally unsettled controversy as to the proper goals of a system of public education. And the question regarding the most effective relationship between state boards of education and local school boards, in terms of their respective responsibilities and degrees of control, is now undergoing searching re-examination. . . . In such circumstances, the judiciary is well advised to refrain from imposing on the States inflexible constitutional restraints that could circumscribe or handicap the continued research and experimentation so vital to finding even partial solutions to educational problems and to keeping abreast of ever-changing conditions.

It must be remembered, also, that every claim arising under the Equal Protection Clause has implications for the relationship between national and state power under our federal system. Questions of federalism are always inherent in the process of determining whether a State's laws are to be accorded the traditional presumption of constitutionality, or are to be subjected instead to rigorous judicial scrutiny. While the maintenance of the principles of federalism is a foremost consideration in interpreting any of the pertinent constitutional provisions under which this Court examines state action, it would be difficult to imagine a case having a greater potential impact on our federal system than the one now before us, in which we are urged to abrogate systems of financing public education presently in existence in virtually every State. . . .

The foregoing considerations buttress our conclusion that Texas' system of public school finance is an inappropriate candidate for strict judicial scrutiny. These same considerations are relevant to the determination whether that system, with its conceded imperfections, nevertheless bears some rational relationship to a legitimate state purpose. It is to this question that we next turn our attention.

III

. . . The District Court found that the State had failed even 'to establish a reasonable basis' for a system that results in different levels of per-pupil expenditure. We disagree.

In its reliance on state as well as local resources, the Texas system is comparable to the systems employed in virtually every other State. The power to tax local property for educational purposes has been recognized in Texas at least since 1883. When the growth of commercial and industrial centers and accompanying shifts in population began to create disparities in local resources, Texas undertook a program calling for a considerable investment of state funds.

The 'foundation grant' theory upon which Texas legislators and educators based the Gilmer-Aikin bills . . . represented an accommodation between . . . two competing forces: . . . the desire by members of society to have educational opportunity for all children, and the desire of each family to provide the best education it can afford for its own children. The Texas system of school finance is responsive to these two forces. While assuring a basis education for every child in the State, it permits and encourages a large measure of participation in and control of each district's schools at the local level. In an era that has witnessed a consistent trend toward centralization of the functions of government, local sharing of responsibility for public education has survived. . . .

The persistence of attachment to government at the lowest level where education is concerned reflects the depth of commitment of its supporters. In part, local control means . . . the freedom to devote more money to the education of one's children. Equally important, however, is the opportunity it offers for participation in the decisionmaking process that determines how those local tax dollars will be spent. Each locality is free to tailor local programs to local needs. Pluralism also affords some opportunity for experimentation, innovation, and a healthy competition for educational excellence. An analogy to the Nation-State relationship in our federal system seems uniquely appropriate. Mr. Justice Brandeis identified as one of the peculiar strengths of our form of government each State's freedom to 'serve as a laboratory; and try novel social and economic experiments.'[106] No area of social concern stands to profit more from a multiplicity of viewpoints and from a diversity of approaches than does public education.

Appellees do not question the propriety of Texas' dedication to local control of education. To the contrary, they attack the school-financing system precisely because, in their view, it does not provide the same level of local control and fiscal flexibility in all districts. Appellees suggest that local control could be preserved and promoted under other financing systems that resulted in more equality in education expenditures. While it is no doubt true that reliance on local property taxation for school revenues provides less freedom of choice with respect to expenditures for some districts than for others, the existence of 'some inequality' in the manner in which the State's rationale is achieved is not alone a sufficient basis for striking down the entire system. It may not be condemned simply because it imperfectly effectuates the State's goals. Nor must the financing system fail because, as appellees suggest, other methods of satisfying the State's interest, which occasion 'less drastic' disparities in expenditures, might be conceived. Only where state action impinges on the exercise of fundamental constitutional rights or liberties must it be found to have chosen the least restrictive alternative. It is also well to remember that even those districts that have reduced ability to make free decisions with respect to how much they spend on education still retain under the present system a large measure of authority as to how available funds will be allocated. They further enjoy the power to make numerous other decisions with respect to the operation of the schools. The people of Texas may be justified in believing that other systems of school financing, which place more of the financial responsibility in the hands of the State, will result in a comparable lessening of desired local autonomy. . . .

Appellees further urge that the Texas system is unconstitutionally arbitrary because it allows the availability of local taxable resources to turn on 'happenstance.' They see no justification for a system that allows, as they contend, the quality of education to fluctuate on the basis of the fortuitous positioning of the boundary lines of political subdivisions and

---

[106] *New State Ice Co. v. Liebmann*, 285 U.S. 262, 280, 311 (1932) (Brandeis, J., dissenting).

the location of valuable commercial and industrial property. But any scheme of local taxation—indeed the very existence of identifiable local governmental units—requires the establishment of jurisdictional boundaries that are inevitably arbitrary. It is equally inevitable that some localities are going to be blessed with more taxable assets than others.[110] Nor is local wealth a static quantity. . . .

Moreover, if local taxation for local expenditures were an unconstitutional method of providing for education then it might be an equally impermissible means of providing other necessary services customarily financed largely from local property taxes, including local police and fire protection, public health and hospitals, and public utility facilities of various kinds. We perceive no justification for such a severe denigration of local property taxation and control as would follow from appellees' contentions. It has simply never been within the constitutional prerogative of this Court to nullify statewide measures for financing public services merely because the burdens or benefits thereof fall unevenly depending upon the relative wealth of the political subdivisions in which citizens live.

In sum, to the extent that the Texas system of school financing results in unequal expenditures between children who happen to reside in different districts, we cannot say that such disparities are the product of a system that is so irrational as to be invidiously discriminatory. Texas has acknowledged its shortcomings and has persistently endeavored— not without some success—to ameliorate the differences in levels of expenditures without sacrificing the benefits of local participation. The Texas plan is not the result of hurried, ill-conceived legislation. It certainly is not the product of purposeful discrimination against any group or class. On the contrary, it is rooted in decades of experience in Texas and elsewhere, and in major part is the product of responsible studies by qualified people. In giving substance to the presumption of validity to which the Texas system is entitled, it is important to remember that at every stage of its development it has constituted a 'rough accommodation' of interests in an effort to arrive at practical and workable solutions. One also must remember that the system here challenged is not peculiar to Texas or to any other State. In its essential characteristics, the Texas plan for financing public education reflects what many educators for a half century have thought was an enlightened approach to a problem for which there is no perfect solution. We are unwilling to assume for ourselves a level of wisdom superior to that of legislators, scholars, and educational authorities in 50 States, especially where the alternatives proposed are only recently conceived and nowhere yet tested. The constitutional standard under the Equal Protection Clause is whether the challenged state action rationally furthers a

---

[110] This Court has never doubted the propriety of maintaining political subdivisions within the States and has never found in the Equal Protection Clause any per se rule of 'territorial uniformity.' *McGowan v. Maryland*, 366 U.S. 420, 427 (1961).

legitimate state purpose or interest. We hold that the Texas plan abundantly satisfies this standard. . . .

Reversed.

■ MR. JUSTICE MARSHALL, with whom MR. JUSTICE DOUGLAS concurs, dissenting.*

The Court today decides, in effect, that a State may constitutionally vary the quality of education which it offers its children in accordance with the amount of taxable wealth located in the school districts within which they reside. The majority's decision represents an abrupt departure from the mainstream of recent state and federal court decisions concerning the unconstitutionality of state educational financing schemes dependent upon taxable local wealth. More unfortunately, though, the majority's holding can only be seen as a retreat from our historic commitment to equality of educational opportunity and as unsupportable acquiescence in a system which deprives children in their earliest years of the chance to reach their full potential as citizens. The Court does this despite the absence of any substantial justification for a scheme which arbitrarily channels educational resources in accordance with the fortuity of the amount of taxable wealth within each district.

In my judgment, the right of every American to an equal start in life, so far as the provision of a state service as important as education is concerned, is far too vital to permit state discrimination on grounds as tenuous as those presented by this record. Nor can I accept the notion that it is sufficient to remit these appellees to the vagaries of the political process which, contrary to the majority's suggestion, has proved singularly unsuited to the task of providing a remedy for this discrimination.[2] I, for one, am unsatisfied with the hope of an ultimate 'political' solution sometime in the indefinite future while, in the meantime, countless children unjustifiably receive inferior educations that may 'affect their hearts and minds in a way unlikely ever to be undone.' *Brown v. Board of Education*, 347 U.S. 483, 494 (1954). I must therefore respectfully dissent.

I

. . . The appellants do not deny the disparities in educational funding caused by variations in taxable district property wealth. They do contend, however, that whatever the differences in per-pupil spending among

---

*   Justices Brennan and White also dissented on narrower grounds concerning the operation of the Texas tax scheme. [Editor's Note]

2   The District Court in this case postponed decision for some two years in the hope that the Texas Legislature would remedy the gross disparities in treatment inherent in the Texas financing scheme. It was only after the legislature failed to act in its 1971 Regular Session that the District Court, apparently recognizing the lack of hope for self-initiated legislative reform, rendered its decision. The strong vested interest of property-rich districts in the existing property tax scheme poses a substantial barrier to self-initiated legislative reform in educational financing.

Texas districts, there are no discriminatory consequences for the children of the disadvantaged districts. They recognize that what is at stake in this case is the quality of the public education provided Texas children in the districts in which they live. But appellants reject the suggestion that the quality of education in any particular district is determined by money—beyond some minimal level of funding which they believe to be assured every Texas district by the Minimum Foundation School Program. In their view, there is simply no denial of equal educational opportunity to any Texas school children as a result of the widely varying per-pupil spending power provided districts under the current financing scheme.

In my view, though, even an unadorned restatement of this contention is sufficient to reveal its absurdity. Authorities concerned with educational quality no doubt disagree as to the significance of variations in per-pupil spending. Indeed, conflicting expert testimony was presented to the District Court in this case concerning the effect of spending variations on educational achievement. We sit, however, not to resolve disputes over educational theory but to enforce our Constitution. It is an inescapable fact that if one district has more funds available per pupil than another district, the former will have greater choice in educational planning than will the latter. In this regard, I believe the question of discrimination in educational quality must be deemed to be an objective one that looks to what the State provides its children, not to what the children are able to do with what they receive. That a child forced to attend an underfunded school with poorer physical facilities, less experienced teachers, larger classes, and a narrower range of courses than a school with substantially more funds—and thus with greater choice in educational planning—may nevertheless excel is to the credit of the child, not the State. Indeed, who can ever measure for such a child the opportunities lost and the talents wasted for want of a broader, more enriched education? Discrimination in the opportunity to learn that is afforded a child must be our standard.

Hence, even before this Court recognized its duty to tear down the barriers of state-enforced racial segregation in public education, it acknowledged that inequality in the educational facilities provided to students may be discriminatory state action as contemplated by the Equal Protection Clause. As a basis for striking down state-enforced segregation of a law school, the Court in *Sweatt v. Painter*, 339 U.S. 629, 633–634 (1950), stated:

> (W)e cannot find substantial equality in the educational opportunities offered white and Negro law students by the State. In terms of number of the faculty, variety of courses and opportunity for specialization, size of the student body, scope of the library, availability of law review and similar activities, the (whites only) Law School is superior. . . . It is difficult to believe

that one who had a free choice between these law schools would consider the question close.

Likewise, it is difficult to believe that if the children of Texas had a free choice, they would choose to be educated in districts with fewer resources, and hence with more antiquated plants, less experienced teachers, and a less diversified curriculum. . . .

The consequences, in terms of objective educational input, of the variations in district funding caused by the Texas financing scheme are apparent from the data introduced before the District Court. For example, in 1968–1969, 100% of the teachers in the property-rich Alamo Heights School District had college degrees. By contrast, during the same school year only 80.02% of the teachers had college degrees in the property poor Edgewood Independent School District. . . . This is undoubtedly a reflection of the fact that the top of Edgewood's teacher salary scale was approximately 80% of Alamo Heights. And, not surprisingly, the teacher-student ratio varies significantly between the two districts. In other words, as might be expected, a difference in the funds available to districts results in a difference in educational inputs available for a child's public education in Texas. . . .

At the very least, in view of the substantial interdistrict disparities in funding and in resulting educational inputs shown by appellees to exist under the Texas financing scheme, the burden of proving that these disparities do not in fact affect the quality of children's education must fall upon the appellants. . . .

[T]he appellants and the majority may believe that the Equal Protection Clause cannot be offended by substantially unequal state treatment of persons who are similarly situated so long as the State provides everyone with some unspecified amount of education which evidently is 'enough.' The basis for such a novel view is far from clear. It is, of course, true that the Constitution does not require precise equality in the treatment of all persons. . . . But this Court has never suggested that because some 'adequate' level of benefits is provided to all, discrimination in the provision of services is therefore constitutionally excusable. The Equal Protection Clause is not addressed to the minimal sufficiency but rather to the unjustifiable inequalities of state action. It mandates nothing less than that 'all persons similarly circumstanced shall be treated alike.' *F. S. Royster Guano Co. v. Virginia*, 253 U.S. 412, 415 (1920).

Even if the Equal Protection Clause encompassed some theory of constitutional adequacy, discrimination in the provision of educational opportunity would certainly seem to be a poor candidate for its application. Neither the majority nor appellants inform us how judicially manageable standards are to be derived for determining how much education is 'enough' to excuse constitutional discrimination. . . . Certainly appellants' mere assertion before this Court of the adequacy of the education guaranteed by the Minimum Foundation School Program cannot obscure the constitutional implications of the discrimination in educational funding and objective educational inputs resulting from the local property tax—particularly since the appellees offered substantial uncontroverted evidence before the District Court impugning the now much touted 'adequacy' of the education guaranteed by the Foundation Program.

In my view, then, it is inequality—not some notion of gross inadequacy—of educational opportunity that raises a question of denial of equal protection of the laws. . . . Here, appellees have made a substantial showing of wide variations in educational funding and the resulting educational opportunity afforded to the schoolchildren of Texas. This discrimination is, in large measure, attributable to significant disparities in the taxable wealth of local Texas school districts. This is a sufficient showing to raise a substantial question of discriminatory state action in violation of the Equal Protection Clause. . . .

Despite the evident discriminatory effect of the Texas financing scheme, both the appellants and the majority raise substantial questions concerning the precise character of the disadvantaged class in this case. The District Court concluded that the Texas financing scheme draws 'distinction between groups of citizens depending upon the wealth of the district in which they live' and thus creates a disadvantaged class composed of persons living in property-poor districts. In light of the data introduced before the District Court, the conclusion that the schoolchildren of property-poor districts constitute a sufficient class for our purposes seems indisputable to me. . . .

[T]his Court has consistently recognized that where there is in fact discrimination against individual interests, the constitutional guarantee of equal protection of the laws is not inapplicable simply because the discrimination is based upon some group characteristic such as geographic location. . . . [H]aving established public education for its citizens, the State, as a direct consequence of the variations in local property wealth endemic to Texas' financing scheme, has provided some Texas schoolchildren with substantially less resources for their education than others. Thus, while on its face the Texas scheme may merely discriminate between local districts, the impact of that discrimination falls directly upon the children whose educational opportunity is dependent upon where they happen to live. . . .

II

. . . This Court has repeatedly held that state discrimination which either adversely affects a 'fundamental interest' or is based on a distinction of a suspect character must be carefully scrutinized to ensure that the scheme is necessary to promote a substantial, legitimate state interest. The majority today concludes, however, that the Texas scheme is not subject to such a strict standard of review under the Equal Protection Clause. . . . I cannot accept such an emasculation of the Equal Protection Clause in the context of this case.

A

To begin, I must once more voice my disagreement with the Court's rigidified approach to equal protection analysis. . . . A principled reading of what this Court has done reveals that it has applied a spectrum of standards in reviewing discrimination allegedly violative of the Equal Protection Clause. . . .

I therefore cannot accept the majority's labored efforts to demonstrate that fundamental interests, which call for strict scrutiny of the challenged classification, encompass only established rights which we are somehow bound to recognize from the text of the Constitution itself. To be sure, some interests which the Court has deemed to be fundamental for purposes of equal protection analysis are themselves constitutionally protected rights. Thus, discrimination against the guaranteed right of freedom of speech has called for strict judicial scrutiny. See *Police Dept. of City of Chicago v. Mosley*, 408 U.S. 92 (1972). . . . But it will not do to suggest that the 'answer' to whether an interest is fundamental for purposes of equal protection analysis is always determined by whether that interest 'is a right . . . explicitly or implicitly guaranteed by the Constitution.'[59]

I would like to know where the Constitution guarantees the right to procreate, *Skinner v. Oklahoma*, 316 U.S. 535, 541 (1942), or the right to vote in state elections, e.g., *Reynolds v. Sims*, 377 U.S. 533 (1964), or the right to an appeal from a criminal conviction, e.g., *Griffin v. Illinois*, 351 U.S. 12 (1956). These are instances in which, due to the importance of the interests at stake, the Court has displayed a strong concern with the existence of discriminatory state treatment. But the Court has never said or indicated that these are interests which independently enjoy fullblown constitutional protection. . . .

The majority is, of course, correct when it suggests that the process of determining which interests are fundamental is a difficult one. But I do not think the problem is insurmountable. And I certainly do not accept the view that the process need necessarily degenerate into an unprincipled, subjective 'picking-and-choosing' between various interests . . . . The task in every case should be to determine the extent to which constitutionally guaranteed rights are dependent on interests not mentioned in the Constitution. As the nexus between the specific constitutional guarantee and the nonconstitutional interest draws closer, the nonconstitutional interest becomes more fundamental and the degree of judicial scrutiny applied when the interest is infringed on a discriminatory basis must be adjusted accordingly. Thus, it cannot be denied that interests such as procreation, the exercise of the state franchise, and access to criminal appellate processes are not fully

---

[59] Indeed, the Court's theory would render the established concept of fundamental interests in the context of equal protection analysis superfluous, for the substantive constitutional right itself requires that this Court strictly scrutinize any asserted state interest for restricting or denying access to any particular guaranteed right.

guaranteed to the citizen by our Constitution. But these interests have nonetheless been afforded special judicial consideration in the face of discrimination because they are, to some extent, interrelated with constitutional guarantees. Procreation is now understood to be important because of its interaction with the established constitutional right of privacy. The exercise of the state franchise is closely tied to basic civil and political rights inherent in the First Amendment. And access to criminal appellate processes enhances the integrity of the range of rights implicit in the Fourteenth Amendment guarantee of due process of law. Only if we closely protect the related interests from state discrimination do we ultimately ensure the integrity of the constitutional guarantee itself. . . .

B

. . . It is true that this Court has never deemed the provision of free public education to be required by the Constitution. . . . Nevertheless, the fundamental importance of education is amply indicated by the prior decisions of this Court, by the unique status accorded public education by our society, and by the close relationship between education and some of our most basic constitutional values. . . .

Undoubtedly, this Court's most famous statement on the subject is that contained in *Brown v. Board of Education*, 347 U.S., at 493:

> Today, education is perhaps the most important function of state and local governments. Compulsory school attendance laws and the great expenditures for education both demonstrate our recognition of the importance of education to our democratic society. It is required in the performance of our most basic public responsibilities, even service in the armed forces. It is the very foundation of good citizenship. Today it is a principal instrument in awakening the child to cultural values, in preparing him for later professional training, and in helping him to adjust normally to his environment. . . .

Only last Term, the Court recognized that '(p)roviding public schools ranks at the very apex of the function of a State.' *Wisconsin v. Yoder*, 406 U.S. 205, 213 (1972). This is clearly borne out by the fact that in 48 of our 50 States the provision of public education is mandated by the state constitution. No other state function is so uniformly recognized as an essential element of our society's well-being. In large measure, the explanation for the special importance attached to education must rest, as the Court recognized in *Yoder*, on the facts that 'some degree of education is necessary to prepare citizens to participate effectively and intelligently in our open political system . . . ,' and that 'education prepares individuals to be self-reliant and self-sufficient participants in society.' . . .

Education directly affects the ability of a child to exercise his First Amendment rights, both as a source and as a receiver of information and ideas, whatever interests he may pursue in life. This Court's decision in *Sweezy v. New Hampshire*, 354 U.S. 234, 250 (1957), speaks of the right of students 'to inquire, to study and to evaluate, to gain new maturity and understanding . . .' Of particular importance is the relationship between education and the political process. 'Americans regard the public schools as a most vital civic institution for the preservation of a democratic system of government.' *School District of Abington Township v. Schempp*, 374 U.S. 203, 230 (1963) (Brennan, J., concurring). . . .

While ultimately disputing little of this, the majority seeks refuge in the fact that the Court has 'never presumed to possess either the ability or the authority to guarantee to the citizenry the most effective speech or the most informed electoral choice.' This serves only to blur what is in fact at stake. . . . Appellees do not now seek the best education Texas might provide. They do seek, however, an end to state discrimination resulting from the unequal distribution of taxable district property wealth that directly impairs the ability of some districts to provide the same educational opportunity that other districts can provide with the same or even substantially less tax effort. . . . [T]he precise question here is what importance should attach to education for purposes of equal protection analysis of that discrimination. As this Court held in *Brown v. Board of Education*, 347 U.S., at 493, the opportunity of education, 'where the state has undertaken to provide it, is a right which must be made available to all on equal terms.' The factors just considered, including the relationship between education and the social and political interests enshrined within the Constitution, compel us to recognize the fundamentality of education and to scrutinize with appropriate care the bases for state discrimination affecting equality of educational opportunity in Texas' school districts[75]—a conclusion which is only strengthened when we consider the character of the classification in this case.

C

The District Court found that in discriminating between Texas schoolchildren on the basis of the amount of taxable property wealth located in the district in which they live, the Texas financing scheme created a form of wealth discrimination. This Court has frequently recognized that discrimination on the basis of wealth may create a classification of a suspect character and thereby call for exacting judicial scrutiny. See, e.g., *Griffin v. Illinois*, 351 U.S. 12 (1956); *Douglas v. California*, 372 U.S. 353 (1963). The majority, however, considers any

---

[75] The majority's reliance on this Court's traditional deference to legislative bodies in matters of taxation falls wide of the mark in the context of this particular case. The decisions on which the Court relies were simply taxpayer suits challenging the constitutionality of a tax burden in the face of exemptions or differential taxation afforded to others. . . . But in this case we are presented with a claim of discrimination of an entirely different nature—a claim that the revenue-producing mechanism directly discriminates against the interests of some of the intended beneficiaries; and, in contrast to the taxpayer suits, the interest adversely affected is of substantial constitutional and societal importance. . . .

wealth classification in this case to lack certain essential characteristics which it contends are common to the instances of wealth discrimination that this Court has heretofore recognized. We are told that in every prior case involving a wealth classification, the members of the disadvantaged class have 'shared two distinguishing characteristics: because of their impecunity they were completely unable to pay for some desired benefit, and as a consequence, they sustained an absolute deprivation of a meaningful opportunity to enjoy that benefit.' I cannot agree. . . .

In *Harper v. Virginia Board of Elections*, 383 U.S. 663 (1966), the Court struck down as violative of the Equal Protection Clause an annual Virginia poll tax of $1.50, payment of which by persons over the age of 21 was a prerequisite to voting in Virginia elections. In part, the Court relied on the fact that the poll tax interfered with a fundamental interest—the exercise of the state franchise. In addition, though, the Court emphasized that '(l)ines drawn on the basis of wealth or property . . . are traditionally disfavored.' Under the first part of the theory announced by the majority, the disadvantaged class in *Harper*, in terms of a wealth analysis, should have consisted only of those too poor to afford the $1.50 necessary to vote. But the *Harper* Court did not see it that way. In its view, the Equal Protection Clause 'bars a system which excludes (from the franchise) those unable to pay a fee to vote or who fail to pay.' So far as the Court was concerned, the 'degree of the discrimination (was) irrelevant.' Thus, the Court struck down the poll tax in toto; it did not order merely that those too poor to pay the tax be exempted. . . .

Similarly, *Griffin* and *Douglas* refute the majority's contention that we have in the past required an absolute deprivation before subjecting wealth classifications to strict scrutiny. The Court characterizes *Griffin* as a case concerned simply with the denial of a transcript or an adequate substitute therefor, and *Douglas* as involving the denial of counsel. But in both cases the question was in fact whether 'a State that (grants) appellate review can do so in a way that discriminates against some convicted defendants on account of their poverty.' *Griffin*, 351 U.S., at 18. In that regard, the Court concluded that . . . 'the type of an appeal a person is afforded . . . hinges upon whether or not he can pay for the assistance of counsel,' *Douglas*, 372 U.S., at 355—356. The right of appeal itself was not absolutely denied to those too poor to pay; but because of the cost of a transcript and of counsel, the appeal was a substantially less meaningful right for the poor than for the rich. . . .[77]

---

[77] Even if I put side the Court's misreading of *Griffin* and *Douglas*, the Court fails to offer any reasoned constitutional basis for restricting cases involving wealth discrimination to instances in which there is an absolute deprivation of the interest affected. As I have already discussed, the Equal Protection Clause guarantees equality of treatment of those persons who are similarly situated; it does not merely bar some form of excessive discrimination between such persons. Outside the context of wealth discrimination, the Court's reapportionment decisions clearly indicate that relative discrimination is within the purview of the Equal Protection Clause. . . .

This is not to say that the form of wealth classification in this case does not differ significantly from those recognized in the previous decisions of this Court. Our prior cases have dealt essentially with discrimination on the basis of personal wealth. Here, by contrast, the children of the disadvantaged Texas school districts are being discriminated against not necessarily because of their personal wealth or the wealth of their families, but because of the taxable property wealth of the residents of the district in which they happen to live. The appropriate question, then, is whether the same degree of judicial solicitude and scrutiny that has previously been afforded wealth classifications is warranted here.

As the Court points out, no previous decision has deemed the presence of just a wealth classification to be sufficient basis to call forth rigorous judicial scrutiny of allegedly discriminatory state action. That wealth classifications alone have not necessarily been considered to bear the same high degree of suspectness as have classifications based on, for instance, race or alienage may be explainable on a number of grounds. The 'poor' may not be seen as politically powerless as certain discrete and insular minority groups. Personal poverty may entail much the same social stigma as historically attached to certain racial or ethnic groups. But personal poverty is not a permanent disability; its shackles may be escaped. Perhaps most importantly, though, personal wealth may not necessarily share the general irrelevance as a basis for legislative action that race or nationality is recognized to have. While the 'poor' have frequently been a legally disadvantaged group, it cannot be ignored that social legislation must frequently take cognizance of the economic status of our citizens. Thus, we have generally gauged the invidiousness of wealth classifications with an awareness of the importance of the interests being affected and the relevance of personal wealth to those interests.

When evaluated with these considerations in mind, it seems to me that discrimination on the basis of group wealth in this case likewise calls for careful judicial scrutiny. First, it must be recognized that while local district wealth may serve other interests, it bears no relationship whatsoever to the interest of Texas schoolchildren in the educational opportunity afforded them by the State of Texas. . . .

The disability of the disadvantaged class in this case extends as well into the political processes upon which we ordinarily rely as adequate for the protection and promotion of all interests. Here legislative reallocation of the State's property wealth must be sought in the face of inevitable opposition from significantly advantaged districts that have a strong vested interest in the preservation of the status quo, a problem not completely dissimilar to that faced by underrepresented districts prior to the Court's intervention in the process of reapportionment, see *Baker v. Carr*, 369 U.S. 186, 191—192 (1962).

Nor can we ignore the extent to which, in contrast to our prior decisions, the State is responsible for the wealth discrimination in this instance. . . . The means for financing public education in Texas are selected and specified by the State. It is the State that has created local school districts, and tied educational funding to the local property tax and thereby to local district wealth. At the same time, governmentally imposed land use controls have undoubtedly encouraged and rigidified natural trends in the allocation of particular areas for residential or commercial use, and thus determined each district's amount of taxable property wealth. In short, this case, in contrast to the Court's previous wealth discrimination decisions, can only be seen as 'unusual in the extent to which governmental action is the cause of the wealth classifications.'

In the final analysis, then the invidious characteristics of the group wealth classification present in this case merely serve to emphasize the need for careful judicial scrutiny of the State's justifications for the resulting interdistrict discrimination in the educational opportunity afforded to the schoolchildren of Texas.

D

The nature of our inquiry into the justifications for state discrimination is essentially the same in all equal protection cases: We must consider the substantiality of the state interests sought to be served, and we must scrutinize the reasonableness of the means by which the State has sought to advance its interests. . . .

The only justification offered by appellants to sustain the discrimination in educational opportunity caused by the Texas financing scheme is local educational control. . . . At the outset, I do not question that local control of public education, as an abstract matter, constitutes a very substantial state interest. . . . But I need not now decide how I might ultimately strike the balance were we confronted with a situation where the State's sincere concern for local control inevitably produced educational inequality. For, on this record, it is apparent that the State's purported concern with local control is offered primarily as an excuse rather than as a justification for interdistrict inequality.

In Texas, statewide laws regulate in fact the most minute details of local public education. For example, the State prescribes required courses. All textbooks must be submitted for state approval, and only approved textbooks may be used. The State has established the qualifications necessary for teaching in Texas public schools and the procedures for obtaining certification. The State has even legislated on the length of the school day. . . .

Moreover, even if we accept Texas' general dedication to local control in educational matters, it is difficult to find any evidence of such dedication with respect to fiscal matters. It ignores reality to suggest—as the Court does—that the local property tax element of the Texas financing scheme reflects a conscious legislative effort to provide school districts with local fiscal control. If Texas had a system truly dedicated to local fiscal control, one would expect the quality of the educational opportunity provided in each district to vary with the decision of the voters in that district as to the level of sacrifice they wish to make for public education. In fact, the Texas scheme produces precisely the opposite result. Local school districts cannot choose to have the best education in the State by imposing the highest tax rate. Instead, the quality of the educational opportunity offered by any particular district is largely determined by the amount of taxable property located in the district—a factor over which local voters can exercise no control. . . .

In my judgment, any substantial degree of scrutiny of the operation of the Texas financing scheme reveals that the State has selected means wholly inappropriate to secure its purported interest in assuring its school districts local fiscal control. At the same time, appellees have pointed out a variety of alternative financing schemes which may serve the State's purported interest in local control as well as, if not better than, the present scheme without the current impairment of the educational opportunity of vast numbers of Texas schoolchildren. . . .

III

In conclusion, it is essential to recognize that an end to the wide variations in taxable district property wealth inherent in the Texas financing scheme would entail none of the untoward consequences suggested by the Court or by the appellants.

First, affirmance of the District Court's decisions would hardly sound the death knell for local control of education. . . . Clearly, this suit has nothing to do with local decisionmaking with respect to educational policy or even educational spending. It involves only a narrow aspect of local control—namely, local control over the raising of educational funds. . . .

Nor does the District Court's decision even necessarily eliminate local control of educational funding. The District Court struck down nothing more than the continued interdistrict wealth discrimination inherent in the present property tax. Both centralized and decentralized plans for educational funding not involving such interdistrict discrimination have been put forward. The choice among these or other alternatives would remain with the State, not with the federal courts. . . .

The Court seeks solace for its action today in the possibility of legislative reform. The Court's suggestions of legislative redress and experimentation will doubtless be of great comfort to the schoolchildren of Texas' disadvantaged districts, but considering the vested interests of wealthy school districts in the preservation of the status quo, they are worth little more. The possibility of legislative action is, in all events, no answer to this Court's duty under the Constitution to eliminate unjustified state discrimination. . . . Thus, I believe that the wide disparities in taxable district property wealth inherent in the local property tax element of the Texas financing scheme render that scheme violative of the Equal Protection Clause.[100]

I would therefore affirm the judgment of the District Court.

NOTE ON THE FUNDAMENTAL RIGHTS PRONG OF EQUAL PROTECTION DOCTRINE

1. Justice Harlan's dissent in *Shapiro* criticized the majority for creating a new and, in his view, superfluous form of constitutional scrutiny. He pointed out that in any case that implicates a fundamental right, such as the right to travel, the fundamental nature of that right will itself trigger strict scrutiny of any government restriction. Was Harlan right to suggest that analyzing such cases in equal protection terms adds nothing to the analysis?

On the other hand, Justice Marshall's dissent in *Rodriguez* highlights what equal protection may add. There, Texas argued that there could be no constitutional violation because the plaintiffs had neither pleaded nor proved that their particular school districts failed to provide an adequate education. This might well be a winning answer if the plaintiffs were arguing simply that their school districts had violated their fundamental right to education (assuming that such a right existed). Analysis grounded in a restriction on a personal right focuses simply on the relationship between the government and the individual plaintiff. But equal protection scrutiny focuses on the *relative* disparity between how government treats one person or group and how it treats another. This is just as true under the fundamental rights prong as under the suspect classification prong. Hence, the question in *Rodriguez* was not whether the schooling that Texas provided plaintiffs violated their rights in an absolute sense, but rather whether Texas could justify the fact that its funding scheme provided a better education to some people than it did to others. The fundamental rights prong of equal protection, in other words, shifts the focus of strict scrutiny from the way the government treats the plaintiff, viewed in isolation, to the differences between how the government treats the plaintiff and how it treats other similarly situated persons.

Does this suggest Justice Marshall was wrong to assert that the fundamental rights prong of equal protection would be meaningless if the class of rights were limited to established rights, like free speech? Won't it generally be much harder for the government to justify disparities in treatment than to justify actions directed at particular persons in isolation?

2. Under the Court's cases, governmental action implicating a fundamental right appears to trigger strict equal protection scrutiny in two conceptually distinct ways. First, a government classification may

---

[100] Of course, nothing in the Court's decision today should inhibit further review of state educational funding schemes under state constitutional provisions. See *Milliken v. Green*, 389 Mich. 1, 203 N.W.2d 457 (1972), rehearing granted, Jan. 1973; *Robinson v. Cahill*, 118 N.J. Super. 223, 287 A.2d 187; 119 N.J.Super. 40, 289 A.2d 569 (1972); cf. *Serrano v. Priest*, 5 Cal.3d 584, 96 Cal.Rptr. 601, 487 P.2d 1241 (1971).

discriminate in the *allocation of or access to* a fundamental right. *Skinner v. Oklahoma* was such a case. There, the state's "three strikes and you're sterilized" law deprived criminals of their fundamental right to procreate—but only when they had committed some crimes and not others. Likewise, *Rodriguez* involved classifications that resulted in the differential provision of public education, to which the plaintiffs asserted they had a fundamental right. Second, a classification may discriminate between persons in a way that *burdens* the exercise of a fundamental right. In *Shapiro*, for instance, the government discriminated with respect to state-administered welfare benefits. No one said they had a fundamental right to those benefits, but the plaintiffs argued that denial of benefits to persons who had recently moved to the state effectively penalized those persons' exercise of their fundamental right to travel.

This distinction is certainly not air-tight, and it will not always be possible to draw sharp lines between the two sorts of cases. But nothing turns doctrinally on which sort of classification is at issue; both sorts of state action trigger strict scrutiny of the underlying classification. The point is simply that government action may implicate fundamental rights in multiple ways, and it is helpful to identify with some precision the way that a governmental classification bears on those rights in order to make or evaluate an equal protection claim.

3.   One important difference between the two sorts of cases discussed in the previous note is that the second category will typically implicate not only the fundamental rights principle but also the doctrine of unconstitutional conditions. Under that doctrine, the Constitution limits the government's ability to require individuals (or other right-holders) to waive constitutional rights as a condition on the receipt of government benefits, even if one has no right to the benefit itself.[27] One can frame *Shapiro*, for example, as an unconstitutional condition (giving up the right to travel) on the receipt of government welfare benefits. Justice Brennan alluded to this problem in footnote 6 of his opinion, noting only that Thompson's and the other plaintiffs' claims could not be dismissed on the ground that welfare is a "privilege," not a "right."

Unfortunately, an analytically clean approach to unconstitutional conditions problems has eluded both courts and scholars.[28] Virtually any unconstitutional conditions case could be analyzed as an equal protection problem like *Shapiro*. For example, Justice Brennan cited *Sherbert v. Verner*, 374 U.S. 398 (1963), a free exercise of religion case in which the plaintiff argued that she had unconstitutionally been denied unemployment benefits on account of her refusal to work on her Sabbath. Although *Sherbert* was decided under the Free Exercise Clause, one could frame her claim similarly to *Shapiro*: The state violated the Equal Protection Clause by imposing a burden (the denial of unemployment benefits) on persons exercising a fundamental right (religious exercise) but providing those benefits to those

[27]   *See* Section 16.1, *infra*.

[28]   *See, e.g.,* Cass R. Sunstein, *Why the Unconstitutional Conditions Doctrine is an Anachronism (With Particular Reference to Religion, Speech, and Abortion)*, 70 B.U. L. Rev. 593 (1990); Kathleen M. Sullivan, *Unconstitutional Conditions*, 102 HARV. L. REV. 1413 (1989).

who did not exercise that right. It is not at all clear that turning cases like *Sherbert* into equal protection problems makes them any easier. Should the Court have analyzed *Shapiro* as a straight-up case about the right to travel and left the Equal Protection Clause out of it?

4.   *Shapiro* involved discrimination against persons who have recently moved into a state from a different state. As we saw in Chapter Eleven, state laws discriminating against out-of-staters are ordinarily subject to strict scrutiny under the Dormant Commerce Clause. Would it have made more sense in *Shapiro* to treat the one-year residency requirements as a form of discrimination against out-of-staters?

Thinking of *Shapiro* as a quasi-Dormant Commerce Clause case helps explain the debate between the majority and Chief Justice Warren, who emphasized Congress's approval of one-year residency requirements in § 402(b) of the Social Security Act. Congress, after all, may authorize discrimination against out-of-staters that would otherwise violate the Dormant Commerce Clause. Would it vitiate that principle if the out-of-staters could argue that even authorized discrimination burdened their right to travel and thus denied equal protection of the laws? Alternatively, should Congressional approval matter on grounds similar to those advanced by the dissenters in *Adarand*, who argued that racial discrimination by the federal government should be subject to a lower standard of review than discrimination by state governments?

5.   *Rodriguez* involved both suspect classification and fundamental rights arguments. As we saw in Section 15.3, *supra*, the Court flirted for a time with the notion that wealth classifications deserve some form of higher scrutiny, but ultimately refused to declare them categorically suspect. The *Rodriguez* majority thus found that school financing claims did not fall within the ambiguously-defined but clearly narrow class of situations in which such classifications are impermissible—and that, because school funding does not turn on the wealth of particular individuals, it is not a wealth classification at all. Was the Court wrong to be more concerned about relatively small-scale impositions, like the charge for a trial transcript in *Griffin v. Illinois*, 351 U.S. 12 (1956), than the large-scale but less personal inequalities created by government policies like the school funding regime in *Rodriguez*?

If the Court ultimately shied away from holding all wealth classifications suspect because those classifications are pervasive in society, doesn't the fundamental rights prong of equal protection offer a good solution to that problem? The *Rodriguez* plaintiffs argued that wealth classifications are particularly damaging when they implicate a fundamental interest like the education of children. Should the Court have been more receptive to this theory?

6.   Our Constitution protects fundamental rights to own a gun,[29] dance in the nude,[30] and prevent military personnel from staying overnight

---

[29] *District of Columbia v. Heller*, 554 U.S. 570 (2008).

[30] *Barnes v. Glen Theatre, Inc.*, 501 U.S. 560 (1991).

in your house.[31] Isn't education at least as important as these protected interests? And isn't it as central to personal autonomy as the interests protected—despite their lack of textual enumeration—in cases like *Griswold* and *Roe*? Should the Court have been more sympathetic to the argument that education is a fundamental right in *Rodriguez*?

The Court seems to have shied away from recognizing education as fundamental for reasons similar to the ones that made it reluctant to recognize mental disability as a suspect classification in *Cleburne*. Notwithstanding the affirmative action cases, strict scrutiny is most often "fatal in fact." It works best in areas where society is generally willing to live entirely without a particular sort of regulation, such as regulations of political speech. But as the Court noted in *Cleburne*, society's need to care for the disabled legitimately requires a great deal of government intervention and regulation, and strict scrutiny of any law or program treating the disabled differently from the able would make such a regime largely impossible. Similarly, the *Rodriguez* majority was unwilling to introduce strict scrutiny into what it saw as a delicate realm of legitimate and complex school financing decisions. Was Justice Powell correct to worry that recognizing education as a fundamental right would have disrupted state provision of public schooling? Do the defects identified in the democratic process governing such decisions by Justice Marshall's dissent warrant a greater judicial role?

7.   Justice Marshall's dissent in *Rodriguez* closed by noting that "nothing in the Court's decision today should inhibit further review of state educational funding schemes under state constitutional provisions." As Emily Zackin has illustrated, many state constitutions have protected rights to public education since the nineteenth century.[32] After the Supreme Court's decision in *Rodriguez*, school funding litigation shifted largely to the state courts. Professor Zackin notes that "[b]y 2007, state high courts had considered the constitutionality of state systems of public school financing in all but seven states, and the challenges to state financing for education prevailed in twenty-six of these cases."[33] It is thus critical to remember that the federal constitution is not the only source of rights in our legal system. States remain free to provide more extensive protections, and they have done so in many critical areas. Should this make the U.S. Supreme Court more willing to interpret the national constitution narrowly? Or should the states' willingness to go further encourage the Court to do likewise?

The latest round of the Texas litigation may offer a cautionary tale about the prospects of judicial review in the education realm. In 2014, a state district judge struck down the state's school financing system in a massive suit filed by more than 600 school districts. On appeal, the Texas Supreme Court issued a massive opinion that was highly critical of the state school system's efficiency and fairness, stating that the State's children "deserve

---

[31]   U.S. Constitution, amdt. III.

[32]   EMILY ZACKIN, LOOKING FOR RIGHTS IN ALL THE WRONG PLACES: WHY STATE CONSTITUTIONS CONTAIN AMERICA'S POSITIVE RIGHTS 67–105 (2013).

[33]   *Id.* at 102.

transformational, top-to-bottom reforms that amount to more than Band-Aid on top of Band-Aid." The Court reversed the trial judge, however, noting that "our lenient standard of review in this policy-laden area counsels modesty. The judicial role is not to second-guess whether our system is optimal, but whether it is constitutional."[34] Does this outcome and reasoning suggest that judicial review is unlikely to accomplish much in this area?

8. The most basic question about fundamental rights analysis under the Equal Protection Clause is whether it adds anything to substantive due process—or whether it simply injects all the difficulties appertaining to the latter principle into equal protection jurisprudence as well. As noted already, *Shapiro* involved a right already recognized under other constitutional provisions, raising the question whether the case should have simply been decided as a right-to-travel case, not an equal protection case. *Rodriguez*, on the other hand, refused to recognize an unenumerated right to public education for many of the same reasons of judicial restraint that have constrained the Court's substantive due process jurisprudence. We turn to that jurisprudence in the next chapter. Nonetheless, as Chapter Seventeen shows, the equality principle may yet have an independent contribution to make to fundamental rights jurisprudence.

---

[34] *Morath v. The Texas Taxpayer and Student Fairness Coalition*, 490 S.W.3d 826, 833, 886 (Tex. 2016).

CHAPTER SIXTEEN

DUE PROCESS

This chapter addresses three aspects of contemporary due process doctrine. The first concerns efforts to identify new rights, such as previously unprotected aspects of family privacy as well as rights to make other sensitive personal decisions, such as physician-assisted suicide for terminally ill patients. These cases also raise two pervasive theoretical problems, concerning the level of generality at which rights should be defined and the problem of "unconstitutional conditions," by which certain conditions on the receipt of government benefits may be treated as a restriction on constitutionally-protected liberties.

The middle section of this chapter addresses *procedural* due process. The textual language of "due *process*" does, after all, suggest a focus on procedure rather than substance. Courses in Civil and Criminal Procedure cover much of this ground, of course. But procedural due process also plays an important substantive role by providing some degree of protection to liberty and property interests that have not been recognized as "fundamental" in the Court's substantive due process jurisprudence.

Finally, the last section addresses a limited but potentially significant revival of the Supreme Court's concern with economic rights. As we saw in Chapter Five, the Court largely abandoned freedom of contract and similar notions of economic substantive due process as part of the "switch in time" in 1937, and the revival of substantive due process in the privacy arena has largely steered clear of restricting economic regulation. But in certain limited areas, such as punitive damages in civil cases and retroactive legislation imposing economic burdens, the Court has begun to assert itself once more.

The most fascinating developments in contemporary due process have occurred in the field of gay rights. But because those cases intertwine principles of due process and equal protection (with a smattering of federalism thrown in for good measure) we treat gay rights in its own chapter immediately following this one.

SECTION 16.1 IDENTIFYING SUBSTANTIVE RIGHTS AND BURDENS

Since *Griswold v. Connecticut*, litigants have invited the federal courts to recognize a wide variety of interests as fundamental rights under the Due Process Clause. The Court seemed to swear off the enterprise of recognizing new fundamental rights in *Bowers v.*

Hardwick,[1] which rejected a substantive due process challenge to a state law barring sodomy. Writing for the majority, Justice Byron White refused "to take a more expansive view of our authority to discover new fundamental rights imbedded in the Due Process Clause":

> The Court is most vulnerable and comes nearest to illegitimacy when it deals with judge-made constitutional law having little or no cognizable roots in the language or design of the Constitution. That this is so was painfully demonstrated by the face-off between the Executive and the Court in the 1930's, which resulted in the repudiation of much of the substantive gloss that the Court had placed on the Due Process Clauses of the Fifth and Fourteenth Amendments. There should be, therefore, great resistance to expand the substantive reach of those Clauses, particularly if it requires redefining the category of rights deemed to be fundamental. Otherwise, the Judiciary necessarily takes to itself further authority to govern the country without express constitutional authority.[2]

This resolution did not entirely stick, however. The Court has continued to recognize fundamental rights under the Due Process Clause in a variety of contexts, although it continues also to refer to the cautions Justice White expressed in *Bowers*.

This section explores the Court's approach to evaluating fundamental personal rights under the Due Process Clause. The principal cases here explore important methodological questions concerning the assessment of such claims. Although the cases in this section each rejects the asserted right, the Court's analysis has proven open-ended enough to recognize fundamental rights to choose homosexual relationships[3] and new aspects of family privacy, such as parents' right to control access to their children.[4] This section also addresses the modern expansion of what it means to *burden* a personal right. Most of the rights cases in this book have concerned outright government restrictions on the exercise of those rights. As the modern welfare state has developed a pervasive role in the provision of government benefits, however, the law has come to accept that conditions on the receipt of those benefits can also function as restrictions on the exercise of individual rights. The first section of this chapter thus concludes with an exploration of the "unconstitutional conditions" problem, which has become a ubiquitous but confusing aspect of contemporary constitutional law.

---

[1]   478 U.S. 186 (1986).

[2]   *Id.* at 194–95.

[3]   *See* Lawrence v. Texas, 593 U.S. 558 (2003); *see also* Chapter Seventeen, *infra*.

[4]   *See* Troxel v. Granville, 530 U.S. 57 (2000).

Michael H. v. Gerald D.

491 U.S. 110 (1989)

■ JUSTICE SCALIA announced the judgment of the Court and delivered an opinion, in which THE CHIEF JUSTICE joins, and in all but footnote 6 of which JUSTICE O'CONNOR and JUSTICE KENNEDY join.

Under California law, a child born to a married woman living with her husband is presumed to be a child of the marriage. Cal.Evid.Code Ann. § 621. The presumption of legitimacy may be rebutted only by the husband or wife, and then only in limited circumstances. The instant appeal presents the claim that this presumption infringes upon the due process rights of a man who wishes to establish his paternity of a child born to the wife of another man, and the claim that it infringes upon the constitutional right of the child to maintain a relationship with her natural father.

I

The facts of this case are, we must hope, extraordinary. On May 9, 1976, in Las Vegas, Nevada, Carole D., an international model, and Gerald D., a top executive in a French oil company, were married. The couple established a home in Playa del Rey, California, in which they resided as husband and wife when one or the other was not out of the country on business. In the summer of 1978, Carole became involved in an adulterous affair with a neighbor, Michael H. In September 1980, she conceived a child, Victoria D., who was born on May 11, 1981. Gerald was listed as father on the birth certificate and has always held Victoria out to the world as his daughter. Soon after delivery of the child, however, Carole informed Michael that she believed he might be the father.

In the first three years of her life, Victoria remained always with Carole, but found herself within a variety of quasi-family units. In October 1981, Gerald moved to New York City to pursue his business interests, but Carole chose to remain in California. At the end of that month, Carole and Michael had blood tests of themselves and Victoria, which showed a 98.07% probability that Michael was Victoria's father. In January 1982, Carole visited Michael in St. Thomas, where his primary business interests were based. There Michael held Victoria out as his child. In March, however, Carole left Michael and returned to California, where she took up residence with yet another man, Scott K. Later that spring, and again in the summer, Carole and Victoria spent time with Gerald in New York City, as well as on vacation in Europe. In the fall, they returned to Scott in California.

In November 1982, rebuffed in his attempts to visit Victoria, Michael filed a filiation action in California Superior Court to establish his paternity and right to visitation. In March 1983, the court appointed an attorney and guardian ad litem to represent Victoria's interests. Victoria then filed a cross-complaint asserting that if she had more than one psychological or *de facto* father, she was entitled to maintain her filial relationship, with all of the attendant rights, duties, and obligations, with both. In May 1983, Carole filed a motion for summary judgment. During this period, from March through July 1983, Carole was again living with Gerald in New York. In August, however, she returned to California, became involved once again with Michael, and instructed her attorneys to remove the summary judgment motion from the calendar.

For the ensuing eight months, when Michael was not in St. Thomas he lived with Carole and Victoria in Carole's apartment in Los Angeles and held Victoria out as his daughter. In April 1984, Carole and Michael signed a stipulation that Michael was Victoria's natural father. Carole left Michael the next month, however, and instructed her attorneys not to file the stipulation. In June 1984, Carole reconciled with Gerald and joined him in New York, where they now live with Victoria and two other children since born into the marriage.

In May 1984, Michael and Victoria, through her guardian ad litem, sought visitation rights for Michael *pendente lite*. To assist in determining whether visitation would be in Victoria's best interests, the Superior Court appointed a psychologist to evaluate Victoria, Gerald, Michael, and Carole. The psychologist recommended that Carole retain sole custody, but that Michael be allowed continued contact with Victoria pursuant to a restricted visitation schedule. The court concurred and ordered that Michael be provided with limited visitation privileges *pendente lite*.

On October 19, 1984, Gerald, who had intervened in the action, moved for summary judgment on the ground that under Cal.Evid.Code § 621 there were no triable issues of fact as to Victoria's paternity. This law provides that "the issue of a wife cohabiting with her husband, who is not impotent or sterile, is conclusively presumed to be a child of the marriage." The presumption may be rebutted by blood tests, but only if a motion for such tests is made, within two years from the date of the child's birth, either by the husband or, if the natural father has filed an affidavit acknowledging paternity, by the wife.

On January 28, 1985, having found that affidavits submitted by Carole and Gerald sufficed to demonstrate that the two were cohabiting at conception and birth and that Gerald was neither sterile nor impotent, the Superior Court granted Gerald's motion for summary judgment, rejecting Michael's and Victoria's challenges to the constitutionality of § 621. The court also denied their motions for continued visitation pending the appeal under Cal.Civ.Code § 4601, which provides that a court may, in its discretion, grant "reasonable visitation rights . . . to any . . . person having an interest in the welfare of the child." It found that allowing such visitation would "violat[e] the intention of the Legislature by impugning the integrity of the family unit."

On appeal, Michael asserted, *inter alia*, that the Superior Court's application of § 621 had violated his procedural and substantive due process rights. Victoria also raised a due process challenge to the statute, seeking to preserve her *de facto* relationship with Michael as well as with Gerald. She contended, in addition, that as § 621 allows the husband and, at least to a limited extent, the mother, but not the child, to rebut the presumption of legitimacy, it violates the child's right to equal protection. Finally, she asserted a right to continued visitation with Michael under § 4601. After submission of briefs and a hearing, the California Court of Appeal affirmed the judgment of the Superior Court and upheld the constitutionality of the statute. . . .

Before us, Michael and Victoria both raise equal protection and due process challenges. We do not reach Michael's equal protection claim, however, as it was neither raised nor passed upon below.

II

The California statute that is the subject of this litigation is, in substance, more than a century old. California Code of Civ.Proc. § 1962(5), enacted in 1872, provided that "[t]he issue of a wife cohabiting with her husband, who is not impotent, is indisputably presumed to be legitimate." . . . In their present form, the substantive provisions of the statute are as follows:

§ 621. Child of the marriage; notice of motion for blood tests

(a) Except as provided in subdivision (b), the issue of a wife cohabiting with her husband, who is not impotent or sterile, is conclusively presumed to be a child of the marriage.

(b) Notwithstanding the provisions of subdivision (a), if the court finds that the conclusions of all the experts, as disclosed by the evidence based upon blood tests . . . are that the husband is not the father of the child, the question of paternity of the husband shall be resolved accordingly.

(c) The notice of motion for blood tests under subdivision (b) may be raised by the husband not later than two years from the child's date of birth.

(d) The notice of motion for blood tests under subdivision (b) may be raised by the mother of the child not later than two years from the child's date of birth if the child's biological father has filed an affidavit with the court acknowledging paternity of the child.

(e) The provisions of subdivision (b) shall not apply to any case coming within the provisions of Section 7005 of the Civil Code [dealing with artificial insemination] or to any case in which the wife, with the consent of the husband, conceived by means of a surgical procedure.

III

We address first the claims of Michael. At the outset, it is necessary to clarify what he sought and what he was denied. California law, like nature itself, makes no provision for dual fatherhood. Michael was seeking to be declared *the* father of Victoria. The immediate benefit he evidently sought to obtain from that status was visitation rights. But if Michael were successful in being declared the father, other rights would follow—most importantly, the right to be considered as the parent who should have custody, a status which "embrace[s] the sum of parental rights with respect to the rearing of a child, including the child's care; the right to the child's services and earnings; the right to direct the child's activities; the right to make decisions regarding the control, education, and health of the child; and the right, as well as the duty, to prepare the child for additional obligations, which includes the teaching of moral standards, religious beliefs, and elements of good citizenship." 4 California Family Law § 60.02[1][b]. All parental rights, including visitation, were automatically denied by denying Michael status as the father. While Cal.Civ.Code Ann. § 4601 places it within the discretionary power of a court to award visitation rights to a nonparent, the Superior Court here, affirmed by the Court of Appeal, held that California law denies visitation, against the wishes of the mother, to a putative father who has been prevented by § 621 from establishing his paternity.

Michael raises two related challenges to the constitutionality of § 621. First, he asserts that requirements of procedural due process prevent the State from terminating his liberty interest in his relationship with his child without affording him an opportunity to demonstrate his paternity in an evidentiary hearing. We believe this claim derives from a fundamental misconception of the nature of the California statute. While § 621 is phrased in terms of a presumption, that rule of evidence is the implementation of a substantive rule of law. California declares it to be, except in limited circumstances, *irrelevant* for paternity purposes whether a child conceived during, and born into, an existing marriage was begotten by someone other than the husband and had a prior relationship with him. As the Court of Appeal phrased it:

> The conclusive presumption is actually a substantive rule of law based upon a determination by the Legislature as a matter of overriding social policy, that given a certain relationship between the husband and wife, the husband is to be held responsible for the child, and that the integrity of the family unit should not be impugned.

Of course the conclusive presumption not only expresses the State's substantive policy but also furthers it, excluding inquiries into the child's paternity that would be destructive of family integrity and privacy. . . .

We therefore reject Michael's procedural due process challenge and proceed to his substantive claim.

Michael contends as a matter of substantive due process that, because he has established a parental relationship with Victoria, protection of Gerald's and Carole's marital union is an insufficient state interest to support termination of that relationship. This argument is, of course, predicated on the assertion that Michael has a constitutionally protected liberty interest in his relationship with Victoria.

It is an established part of our constitutional jurisprudence that the term "liberty" in the Due Process Clause extends beyond freedom from physical restraint. Without that core textual meaning as a limitation, defining the scope of the Due Process Clause "has at times been a treacherous field for this Court," giving "reason for concern lest the only limits to . . . judicial intervention become the predilections of those who happen at the time to be Members of this Court." *Moore v. East Cleveland*, 431 U.S. 494, 502 (1977). The need for restraint has been cogently expressed by Justice WHITE:

> That the Court has ample precedent for the creation of new constitutional rights should not lead it to repeat the process at will. The Judiciary, including this Court, is the most vulnerable and comes nearest to illegitimacy when it deals with judge-made constitutional law having little or no cognizable roots in the language or even the design of the Constitution. Realizing that the present construction of the Due Process Clause represents a major judicial gloss on its terms, as well as on the anticipation of the Framers . . . the Court should be extremely reluctant to breathe still further substantive content into the Due Process Clause so as to strike down legislation adopted by a State or city to promote its welfare. Whenever the Judiciary does so, it unavoidably pre-empts for itself another part of the governance of the country without express constitutional authority. *Moore, supra,* at 544 (dissenting opinion).

In an attempt to limit and guide interpretation of the Clause, we have insisted not merely that the interest denominated as a "liberty" be "fundamental" (a concept that, in isolation, is hard to objectify), but also that it be an interest traditionally protected by our society.[2] As we have put it, the Due Process Clause affords only those protections "so rooted in the traditions and conscience of our people as to be ranked as fundamental." *Snyder v. Massachusetts,* 291 U.S. 97, 105 (1934) (Cardozo, J.). Our cases reflect "continual insistence upon respect for the teachings of history [and] solid recognition of the basic values that underlie our society. . . ." *Griswold v. Connecticut,* 381 U.S. 479, 501 (1965) (Harlan, J., concurring in judgment).

This insistence that the asserted liberty interest be rooted in history and tradition is evident, as elsewhere, in our cases according

---

[2] We do not understand what Justice BRENNAN has in mind by an interest "that society traditionally has thought important . . . without protecting it." The protection need not take the form of an explicit constitutional provision or statutory guarantee, but it must at least exclude (all that is necessary to decide the present case) a societal tradition of enacting laws *denying* the interest. Nor do we understand why our practice of limiting the Due Process Clause to traditionally protected interests turns the Clause "into a redundancy." Its purpose is to prevent future generations from lightly casting aside important traditional values—not to enable this Court to invent new ones.

constitutional protection to certain parental rights. Michael reads the landmark case of *Stanley v. Illinois,* 405 U.S. 645 (1972), and . . . subsequent cases . . . as establishing that a liberty interest is created by biological fatherhood plus an established parental relationship—factors that exist in the present case as well. We think that distorts the rationale of those cases. As we view them, they rest not upon such isolated factors but upon the historic respect—indeed, sanctity would not be too strong a term—traditionally accorded to the relationships that develop within the unitary family.[3] In *Stanley,* for example, we forbade the destruction of such a family when, upon the death of the mother, the State had sought to remove children from the custody of a father who had lived with and supported them and their mother for 18 years. As Justice Powell stated for the plurality in *Moore v. East Cleveland, supra,* 431 U.S., at 503: "Our decisions establish that the Constitution protects the sanctity of the family precisely because the institution of the family is deeply rooted in this Nation's history and tradition."

Thus, the legal issue in the present case reduces to whether the relationship between persons in the situation of Michael and Victoria has been treated as a protected family unit under the historic practices of our society, or whether on any other basis it has been accorded special protection. We think it impossible to find that it has. In fact, quite to the contrary, our traditions have protected the marital family (Gerald, Carole, and the child they acknowledge to be theirs) against the sort of claim Michael asserts.[4]

The presumption of legitimacy was a fundamental principle of the common law. Traditionally, that presumption could be rebutted only by proof that a husband was incapable of procreation or had had no access to his wife during the relevant period. As explained by Blackstone, nonaccess could only be proved "if the husband be out of the kingdom of England (or, as the law somewhat loosely phrases it, *extra quatuor maria* [beyond the four seas]) for above nine months. . . ." 1 Blackstone's Commentaries 456 (J. Chitty ed. 1826). And, under the common law both

---

[3]   Justice BRENNAN asserts that only a "pinched conception of 'the family'" would exclude Michael, Carole, and Victoria from protection. We disagree. The family unit accorded traditional respect in our society, which we have referred to as the "unitary family," is typified, of course, by the marital family, but also includes the household of unmarried parents and their children. Perhaps the concept can be expanded even beyond this, but it will bear no resemblance to traditionally respected relationships—and will thus cease to have any constitutional significance—if it is stretched so far as to include the relationship established between a married woman, her lover, and their child, during a 3-month sojourn in St. Thomas, or during a subsequent 8-month period when, if he happened to be in Los Angeles, he stayed with her and the child.

[4]   Justice BRENNAN insists that in determining whether a liberty interest exists we must look at Michael's relationship with Victoria in isolation, without reference to the circumstance that Victoria's mother was married to someone else when the child was conceived, and that that woman and her husband wish to raise the child as their own. We cannot imagine what compels this strange procedure of looking at the act which is assertedly the subject of a liberty interest in isolation from its effect upon other people—rather like inquiring whether there is a liberty interest in firing a gun where the case at hand happens to involve its discharge into another person's body. . . .

in England and here, neither husband nor wife could be a witness to prove access or nonaccess. The primary policy rationale underlying the common law's severe restrictions on rebuttal of the presumption appears to have been an aversion to declaring children illegitimate, thereby depriving them of rights of inheritance and succession and likely making them wards of the state. A secondary policy concern was the interest in promoting the "peace and tranquillity of States and families," a goal that is obviously impaired by facilitating suits against husband and wife asserting that their children are illegitimate. Even though, as bastardy laws became less harsh, judges in both England and the United States gradually widened the acceptable range of evidence that could be offered by spouses, and placed restraints on the 'four seas rule,' the law retained a strong bias against ruling the children of married women illegitimate.

We have found nothing in the older sources, nor in the older cases, addressing specifically the power of the natural father to assert parental rights over a child born into a woman's existing marriage with another man. Since it is Michael's burden to establish that such a power (at least where the natural father has established a relationship with the child) is so deeply embedded within our traditions as to be a fundamental right, the lack of evidence alone might defeat his case. But the evidence shows that even in modern times—when, as we have noted, the rigid protection of the marital family has in other respects been relaxed—the ability of a person in Michael's position to claim paternity has not been generally acknowledged. For example, a 1957 annotation on the subject: "Who may dispute presumption of legitimacy of child conceived or born during wedlock," 53 A.L.R.2d 572, shows three States (including California) with statutes limiting standing to the husband or wife and their descendants, one State (Louisiana) with a statute limiting it to the husband, two States (Florida and Texas) with judicial decisions limiting standing to the husband, and two States (Illinois and New York) with judicial decisions denying standing even to the mother. Not a single decision is set forth specifically according standing to the natural father, and "express indications of the nonexistence of any . . . limitation" upon standing were found only "in a few jurisdictions."

Moreover, even if it were clear that one in Michael's position generally possesses, and has generally always possessed, standing to challenge the marital child's legitimacy, that would still not establish Michael's case. As noted earlier, what is at issue here is not entitlement to a state pronouncement that Victoria was begotten by Michael. It is no conceivable denial of constitutional right for a State to decline to declare facts unless some legal consequence hinges upon the requested declaration. What Michael asserts here is a right to have himself declared the natural father *and thereby to obtain parental prerogatives.*[5] What he

---

[5]   According to Justice BRENNAN, Michael does not claim—and in order to prevail here need not claim—a substantive right to maintain a parental relationship with Victoria, but merely the right to "a hearing on the issue" of his paternity. *Post,* at 2359, n. 12. "Michael's

must establish, therefore, is not that our society has traditionally allowed a natural father in his circumstances to establish paternity, but that it has traditionally accorded such a father parental rights, or at least has not traditionally denied them. Even if the law in all States had always been that the entire world could challenge the marital presumption and obtain a declaration as to who was the natural father, that would not advance Michael's claim. Thus, it is ultimately irrelevant, even for purposes of determining *current* social attitudes towards the alleged substantive right Michael asserts, that the present law in a number of States appears to allow the natural father—including the natural father who has not established a relationship with the child—the theoretical power to rebut the marital presumption. What counts is whether the States in fact award substantive parental rights to the natural father of a child conceived within, and born into, an extant marital union that wishes to embrace the child. We are not aware of a single case, old or new, that has done so. This is not the stuff of which fundamental rights qualifying as liberty interests are made.[6]

---

challenge . . . does not depend," we are told, "on his ability ultimately to obtain visitation rights." *Post,* at 2354. To be sure it does not depend upon his ability ultimately to *obtain* those rights, but it surely depends upon his *asserting a claim* to those rights, which is precisely what Justice BRENNAN denies. We cannot grasp the concept of a "right to a hearing" on the part of a person who claims no substantive entitlement that the hearing will assertedly vindicate.

[6]   Justice BRENNAN criticizes our methodology in using historical traditions specifically relating to the rights of an adulterous natural father, rather than inquiring more generally "whether parenthood is an interest that historically has received our attention and protection." There seems to us no basis for the contention that this methodology is "nove[l]." For example, in *Bowers v. Hardwick,* 478 U.S. 186 (1986), we noted that at the time the Fourteenth Amendment was ratified all but 5 of the 37 States had criminal sodomy laws, that all 50 of the States had such laws prior to 1961, and that 24 States and the District of Columbia continued to have them; and we concluded from that record, regarding that very specific aspect of sexual conduct, that "to claim that a right to engage in such conduct is 'deeply rooted in this Nation's history and tradition' or 'implicit in the concept of ordered liberty' is, at best, facetious." In *Roe v. Wade,* 410 U.S. 113 (1973), we spent about a fifth of our opinion negating the proposition that there was a longstanding tradition of laws proscribing abortion.

We do not understand why, having rejected our focus upon the societal tradition regarding the natural father's rights vis-à-vis a child whose mother is married to another man, Justice BRENNAN would choose to focus instead upon "parenthood." Why should the relevant category not be even more general—perhaps "family relationships"; or "personal relationships"; or even "emotional attachments in general"? Though the dissent has no basis for the level of generality it would select, we do: We refer to the most specific level at which a relevant tradition protecting, or denying protection to, the asserted right can be identified. If, for example, there were no societal tradition, either way, regarding the rights of the natural father of a child adulterously conceived, we would have to consult, and (if possible) reason from, the traditions regarding natural fathers in general. But there is such a more specific tradition, and it unqualifiedly denies protection to such a parent.

One would think that Justice BRENNAN would appreciate the value of consulting the most specific tradition available, since he acknowledges that "[e]ven if we can agree . . . that 'family' and 'parenthood' are part of the good life, it is absurd to assume that we can agree on the content of those terms and destructive to pretend that we do." Because such general traditions provide such imprecise guidance, they permit judges to dictate rather than discern the society's views. The need, if arbitrary decisionmaking is to be avoided, to adopt the most specific tradition as the point of reference—or at least to announce, as Justice BRENNAN declines to do, some other criterion for selecting among the innumerable relevant traditions that could be consulted—is well enough exemplified by the fact that in the present case Justice BRENNAN's opinion and Justice O'CONNOR's opinion, which disapproves this footnote, *both* appeal to tradition, but on the basis of the tradition they select reach opposite results. Although assuredly having the

In *Lehr v. Robertson,* 463 U.S. 248 (1983), a case involving a natural father's attempt to block his child's adoption by the unwed mother's new husband, we observed that "[t]he significance of the biological connection is that it offers the natural father an opportunity that no other male possesses to develop a relationship with his offspring," and we assumed that the Constitution might require some protection of that opportunity. Where, however, the child is born into an extant marital family, the natural father's unique opportunity conflicts with the similarly unique opportunity of the husband of the marriage; and it is not unconstitutional for the State to give categorical preference to the latter. . . . In accord with our traditions, a limit is also imposed by the circumstance that the mother is, at the time of the child's conception and birth, married to, and cohabitating with, another man, both of whom wish to raise the child as the offspring of their union. It is a question of legislative policy and not constitutional law whether California will allow the presumed parenthood of a couple desiring to retain a child conceived within and born into their marriage to be rebutted.

We do not accept Justice BRENNAN's criticism that this result "squashes" the liberty that consists of "the freedom not to conform." It seems to us that reflects the erroneous view that there is only one side to this controversy—that one disposition can expand a "liberty" of sorts without contracting an equivalent "liberty" on the other side. Such a happy choice is rarely available. Here, to *provide* protection to an adulterous natural father is to *deny* protection to a marital father, and vice versa. If Michael has a "freedom not to conform" (whatever that means), Gerald must equivalently have a "freedom to conform." One of them will pay a price for asserting that "freedom"—Michael by being unable to act as father of the child he has adulterously begotten, or Gerald by being unable to preserve the integrity of the traditional family unit he and Victoria have established. Our disposition does not choose between these two "freedoms," but leaves that to the people of California. Justice BRENNAN's approach chooses one of them as the constitutional imperative, on no apparent basis except that the unconventional is to be preferred.

IV

We have never had occasion to decide whether a child has a liberty interest, symmetrical with that of her parent, in maintaining her filial

---

virtue (if it be that) of leaving judges free to decide as they think best when the unanticipated occurs, a rule of law that binds neither by text nor by any particular, identifiable tradition is no rule of law at all.

Finally, we may note that this analysis is not inconsistent with the result in cases such as *Griswold v. Connecticut,* 381 U.S. 479 (1965), or *Eisenstadt v. Baird,* 405 U.S. 438 (1972). None of those cases acknowledged a longstanding and still extant societal tradition withholding the very right pronounced to be the subject of a liberty interest and then rejected it. Justice BRENNAN must do so here. In this case, the existence of such a tradition, continuing to the present day, refutes any possible contention that the alleged right is "so rooted in the traditions and conscience of our people as to be ranked as fundamental" or "implicit in the concept of ordered liberty."

relationship. We need not do so here because, even assuming that such a right exists, Victoria's claim must fail. Victoria's due process challenge is, if anything, weaker than Michael's. Her basic claim is not that California has erred in preventing her from establishing that Michael, not Gerald, should stand as her legal father. Rather, she claims a due process right to maintain filial relationships with both Michael and Gerald. This assertion merits little discussion, for, whatever the merits of the guardian ad litem's belief that such an arrangement can be of great psychological benefit to a child, the claim that a State must recognize multiple fatherhood has no support in the history or traditions of this country. Moreover, even if we were to construe Victoria's argument as forwarding the lesser proposition that, whatever her status vis-à-vis Gerald, she has a liberty interest in maintaining a filial relationship with her natural father, Michael, we find that, at best, her claim is the obverse of Michael's and fails for the same reasons. . . .

The judgment of the California Court of Appeal is

Affirmed.

■ JUSTICE O'CONNOR, with whom JUSTICE KENNEDY joins, concurring in part.*

I concur in all but footnote 6 of Justice SCALIA's opinion. This footnote sketches a mode of historical analysis to be used when identifying liberty interests protected by the Due Process Clause of the Fourteenth Amendment that may be somewhat inconsistent with our past decisions in this area. See *Griswold v. Connecticut,* 381 U.S. 479 (1965); *Eisenstadt v. Baird,* 405 U.S. 438 (1972). On occasion the Court has characterized relevant traditions protecting asserted rights at levels of generality that might not be "the most specific level" available. See *Loving v. Virginia,* 388 U.S. 1, 12 (1967). I would not foreclose the unanticipated by the prior imposition of a single mode of historical analysis. *Poe v. Ullman,* 367 U.S. 497, 542, 544 (1961) (Harlan, J., dissenting).

■ JUSTICE BRENNAN, with whom JUSTICE MARSHALL and JUSTICE BLACKMUN join, dissenting.

In a case that has yielded so many opinions as has this one, it is fruitful to begin by emphasizing the common ground shared by a majority of this Court. Five Members of the Court refuse to foreclose "the possibility that a natural father might ever have a constitutionally protected interest in his relationship with a child whose mother was married to, and cohabiting with, another man at the time of the child's conception and birth." *Ante* (STEVENS, J., concurring in judgment); *post* (WHITE, J., dissenting). Five Justices agree that the flaw inhering in a conclusive presumption that terminates a constitutionally protected

---

* Justice Stevens also concurred in the judgment on the ground that, as he read the California statute, it did allow Michael H. a fair opportunity to seek visitation rights. [Editor's Note]

interest without any hearing whatsoever is a *procedural* one. See *post* (WHITE, J., dissenting); *ante* (STEVENS, J., concurring in judgment). Four Members of the Court agree that Michael H. has a liberty interest in his relationship with Victoria, see *post* (WHITE, J., dissenting), and one assumes for purposes of this case that he does, see *ante* (STEVENS, J., concurring in judgment).

In contrast, only one other Member of the Court fully endorses Justice SCALIA's view of the proper method of analyzing questions arising under the Due Process Clause. Nevertheless, because the plurality opinion's exclusively historical analysis portends a significant and unfortunate departure from our prior cases and from sound constitutional decisionmaking, I devote a substantial portion of my discussion to it.

I

Once we recognized that the "liberty" protected by the Due Process Clause of the Fourteenth Amendment encompasses more than freedom from bodily restraint, today's plurality opinion emphasizes, the concept was cut loose from one natural limitation on its meaning. This innovation paved the way, so the plurality hints, for judges to substitute their own preferences for those of elected officials. Dissatisfied with this supposedly unbridled and uncertain state of affairs, the plurality casts about for another limitation on the concept of liberty.

It finds this limitation in "tradition." Apparently oblivious to the fact that this concept can be as malleable and as elusive as "liberty" itself, the plurality pretends that tradition places a discernible border around the Constitution. The pretense is seductive; it would be comforting to believe that a search for "tradition" involves nothing more idiosyncratic or complicated than poring through dusty volumes on American history. Yet, as Justice WHITE observed in his dissent in *Moore v. East Cleveland,* 431 U.S. 494, 549 (1977): "What the deeply rooted traditions of the country are is arguable." Indeed, wherever I would begin to look for an interest "deeply rooted in the country's traditions," one thing is certain: I would not stop (as does the plurality) at Bracton, or Blackstone, or Kent, or even the American Law Reports in conducting my search. Because reasonable people can disagree about the content of particular traditions, and because they can disagree even about which traditions are relevant to the definition of "liberty," the plurality has not found the objective boundary that it seeks.

Even if we could agree, moreover, on the content and significance of particular traditions, we still would be forced to identify the point at which a tradition becomes firm enough to be relevant to our definition of liberty and the moment at which it becomes too obsolete to be relevant any longer. The plurality supplies no objective means by which we might make these determinations. Indeed, as soon as the plurality sees signs that the tradition upon which it bases its decision (the laws denying putative fathers like Michael standing to assert paternity) is crumbling, it shifts ground and says that the case has nothing to do with that tradition, after all. "[W]hat is at issue here," the plurality asserts after canvassing the law on paternity suits, "is not entitlement to a state pronouncement that Victoria was begotten by Michael." But that is precisely what is at issue here, and the plurality's last-minute denial of this fact dramatically illustrates the subjectivity of its own analysis.

It is ironic that an approach so utterly dependent on tradition is so indifferent to our precedents. Citing barely a handful of this Court's numerous decisions defining the scope of the liberty protected by the Due Process Clause to support its reliance on tradition, the plurality acts as though English legal treatises and the American Law Reports always have provided the sole source for our constitutional principles. They have not. Just as common-law notions no longer define the "property" that the Constitution protects, see *Goldberg v. Kelly,* 397 U.S. 254 (1970), neither do they circumscribe the "liberty" that it guarantees. On the contrary, " '[l]iberty' and 'property' are broad and majestic terms. They are among the '[g]reat [constitutional] concepts . . . purposely left to gather meaning from experience. . . . [T]hey relate to the whole domain of social and economic fact, and the statesmen who founded this Nation knew too well that only a stagnant society remains unchanged.' " *Board of Regents of State Colleges v. Roth,* 408 U.S. 564, 571 (1972).

It is not that tradition has been irrelevant to our prior decisions. Throughout our decisionmaking in this important area runs the theme that certain interests and practices—freedom from physical restraint, marriage, childbearing, childrearing, and others—form the core of our definition of "liberty." Our solicitude for these interests is partly the result of the fact that the Due Process Clause would seem an empty promise if it did not protect them, and partly the result of the historical and traditional importance of these interests in our society. In deciding cases arising under the Due Process Clause, therefore, we have considered whether the concrete limitation under consideration impermissibly impinges upon one of these more generalized interests.

Today's plurality, however, does not ask whether parenthood is an interest that historically has received our attention and protection; the answer to that question is too clear for dispute. Instead, the plurality asks whether the specific variety of parenthood under consideration—a natural father's relationship with a child whose mother is married to another man—has enjoyed such protection.

If we had looked to tradition with such specificity in past cases, many a decision would have reached a different result. Surely the use of contraceptives by unmarried couples, *Eisenstadt v. Baird,* 405 U.S. 438 (1972), or even by married couples, *Griswold v. Connecticut,* 381 U.S. 479 (1965); the freedom from corporal punishment in schools, *Ingraham v. Wright,* 430 U.S. 651 (1977); the freedom from an arbitrary transfer from a prison to a psychiatric institution, *Vitek v. Jones,* 445 U.S. 480 (1980); and even the right to raise one's natural but illegitimate children, *Stanley v. Illinois,* 405 U.S. 645 (1972), were not "interest[s] traditionally protected by our society," at the time of their consideration by this Court. If we had asked, therefore, in *Eisenstadt, Griswold, Ingraham, Vitek,* or *Stanley* itself whether the specific interest under consideration had been traditionally protected, the answer would have been a resounding "no." That we did not ask this question in those cases highlights the novelty of the interpretive method that the plurality opinion employs today.

The plurality's interpretive method is more than novel; it is misguided. It ignores the good reasons for limiting the role of "tradition" in interpreting the Constitution's deliberately capacious language. In the plurality's constitutional universe, we may not take notice of the fact that the original reasons for the conclusive presumption of paternity are out of place in a world in which blood tests can prove virtually beyond a shadow of a doubt who sired a particular child and in which the fact of illegitimacy no longer plays the burdensome and stigmatizing role it once did. Nor, in the plurality's world, may we deny "tradition" its full scope by pointing out that the rationale for the conventional rule has changed over the years, as has the rationale for Cal.Evid.Code Ann. § 621;[1] instead, our task is simply to identify a rule denying the asserted interest and not to ask whether the basis for that rule—which is the true reflection of the values undergirding it—has changed too often or too recently to call the rule embodying that rationale a "tradition." Moreover, by describing the decisive question as whether Michael's and Victoria's interest is one that has been "traditionally *protected by* our society," rather than one that society traditionally has thought important (with or without protecting it), and by suggesting that our sole function is to "*discern* the society's views," the plurality acts as if the only purpose of the Due Process Clause is to confirm the importance of interests already protected by a majority of the States. Transforming the protection afforded by the Due Process Clause into a redundancy mocks those who, with care and purpose, wrote the Fourteenth Amendment.

In construing the Fourteenth Amendment to offer shelter only to those interests specifically protected by historical practice, moreover, the plurality ignores the kind of society in which our Constitution exists. We are not an assimilative, homogeneous society, but a facilitative, pluralistic one, in which we must be willing to abide someone else's unfamiliar or even repellent practice because the same tolerant impulse protects our own idiosyncrasies. Even if we can agree, therefore, that "family" and "parenthood" are part of the good life, it is absurd to assume that we can agree on the content of those terms and destructive to pretend that we do. In a community such as ours, "liberty" must include the freedom not to conform. The plurality today squashes this freedom

---

[1]   *See In re Marriage of Sharyne and Stephen B.,* 124 Cal.App.3d 524, 528–531, 177 Cal.Rptr. 429, 431–433 (1981) (noting that California courts initially justified conclusive presumption of paternity on the ground that biological paternity was impossible to prove, but that the preservation of family integrity became the rule's paramount justification when paternity tests became reliable).

by requiring specific approval from history before protecting anything in the name of liberty.

The document that the plurality construes today is unfamiliar to me. It is not the living charter that I have taken to be our Constitution; it is instead a stagnant, archaic, hidebound document steeped in the prejudices and superstitions of a time long past. *This* Constitution does not recognize that times change, does not see that sometimes a practice or rule outlives its foundations. I cannot accept an interpretive method that does such violence to the charter that I am bound by oath to uphold.

II

The plurality's reworking of our interpretive approach is all the more troubling because it is unnecessary. This is not a case in which we face a "new" kind of interest, one that requires us to consider for the first time whether the Constitution protects it. On the contrary, we confront an interest—that of a parent and child in their relationship with each other—that was among the first that this Court acknowledged in its cases defining the "liberty" protected by the Constitution, see, *e.g., Meyer v. Nebraska,* 262 U.S. 390, 399 (1923); *Skinner v. Oklahoma,* 316 U.S. 535, 541 (1942), and I think I am safe in saying that no one doubts the wisdom or validity of those decisions. Where the interest under consideration is a parent-child relationship, we need not ask, over and over again, whether that interest is one that society traditionally protects.

Thus, to describe the issue in this case as whether the relationship existing between Michael and Victoria "has been treated as a protected family unit under the historic practices of our society, or whether on any other basis it has been accorded special protection," is to reinvent the wheel. The better approach—indeed, the one commanded by our prior cases and by common sense—is to ask whether the specific parent-child relationship under consideration is close enough to the interests that we already have protected to be deemed an aspect of "liberty" as well. On the facts before us, therefore, the question is not what "level of generality" should be used to describe the relationship between Michael and Victoria, but whether the relationship under consideration is sufficiently substantial to qualify as a liberty interest under our prior cases.

On four prior occasions, we have considered whether unwed fathers have a constitutionally protected interest in their relationships with their children. See *Stanley v. Illinois,* 405 U.S. 645 (1972); *Quilloin v. Walcott,* 434 U.S. 246 (1978); *Caban v. Mohammed,* 441 U.S. 380 (1979); and *Lehr v. Robertson,* 463 U.S. 248 (1983). Though different in factual and legal circumstances, these cases have produced a unifying theme: although an unwed father's biological link to his child does not, in and of itself, guarantee him a constitutional stake in his relationship with that child, such a link combined with a substantial parent-child relationship will do so. "When an unwed father demonstrates a full commitment to the responsibilities of parenthood by com [ing] forward to participate in the rearing of his child,' . . . his interest in personal contact with his child acquires substantial protection under the Due Process Clause. At that point it may be said that he 'act[s] as a father toward his children." *Lehr v. Robertson, supra,* at 261. This commitment is why Mr. Stanley and Mr. Caban won; why Mr. Quilloin and Mr. Lehr lost; and why Michael H. should prevail today. Michael H. is almost certainly Victoria D.'s natural father, has lived with her as her father, has contributed to her support, and has from the beginning sought to strengthen and maintain his relationship with her.

Claiming that the intent of these cases was to protect the "unitary family," the plurality waves *Stanley, Quilloin, Caban,* and *Lehr* aside. In evaluating the plurality's dismissal of these precedents, it is essential to identify its conception of the "unitary family." If, by acknowledging that *Stanley* et al. sought to protect "the relationships that develop within the unitary family," the plurality meant only to describe the kinds of relationships that develop when parents and children live together (formally or informally) as a family, then the plurality's vision of these cases would be correct. But that is not the plurality's message. Though it pays lipservice to the idea that marriage is not the crucial fact in denying constitutional protection to the relationship between Michael and Victoria, the plurality cannot mean what it says.

The evidence is undisputed that Michael, Victoria, and Carole did live together as a family; that is, they shared the same household, Victoria called Michael "Daddy," Michael contributed to Victoria's support, and he is eager to continue his relationship with her. Yet they are not, in the plurality's view, a "unitary family," whereas Gerald, Carole, and Victoria do compose such a family. The only difference between these two sets of relationships, however, is the fact of marriage. The plurality, indeed, expressly recognizes that marriage is the critical fact in denying Michael a constitutionally protected stake in his relationship with Victoria: no fewer than six times, the plurality refers to Michael as the "*adulterous* natural father" or the like.[3] However, the very premise of *Stanley* and the cases following it is that marriage is not decisive in answering the question whether the Constitution protects the parental relationship under consideration. These cases are, after all, important precisely because they involve the rights of *unwed* fathers. It is important to remember, moreover, that in *Quilloin, Caban,* and *Lehr,* the putative father's demands would have disrupted a "unitary family" as the plurality defines it; in each case, the husband of the child's mother sought to adopt the child over the objections of the natural father. Significantly, our decisions in those cases in no way relied on the need to protect the marital family. Hence the plurality's claim that *Stanley,*

---

[3] In one place, the plurality opinion appears to suggest that the length of time that Michael and Victoria lived together is relevant to the question whether they have a liberty interest in their relationship with each other. The point is not pursued, however, and in any event I am unable to find in the traditions on which the plurality otherwise exclusively relies any emphasis on the duration of the relationship between the putative father and child.

Quilloin, Caban, and *Lehr* were about the "unitary family," as that family is defined by today's plurality, is surprising indeed.

The plurality's exclusive rather than inclusive definition of the "unitary family" is out of step with other decisions as well. This pinched conception of "the family," crucial as it is in rejecting Michael's and Victoria's claims of a liberty interest, is jarring in light of our many cases preventing the States from denying important interests or statuses to those whose situations do not fit the government's narrow view of the family. [See, e.g.] *Loving v. Virginia,* 388 U.S. 1 (1967). . . .

The plurality's focus on the "unitary family" is misdirected for another reason. It conflates the question whether a liberty interest exists with the question what procedures may be used to terminate or curtail it. It is no coincidence that we never before have looked at the relationship that the unwed father seeks to disrupt, rather than the one he seeks to preserve, in determining whether he has a liberty interest in his relationship with his child. To do otherwise is to allow the State's interest in terminating the relationship to play a role in defining the "liberty" that is protected by the Constitution. According to our established framework under the Due Process Clause, however, we first ask whether the person claiming constitutional protection has an interest that the Constitution recognizes; if we find that he or she does, we next consider the State's interest in limiting the extent of the procedures that will attend the deprivation of that interest. By stressing the need to preserve the "unitary family" and by focusing not just on the relationship between Michael and Victoria but on their "situation" as well, today's plurality opinion takes both of these steps at once.

The plurality's premature consideration of California's interests is evident from its careful limitation of its holding to those cases in which "the mother is, at the time of the child's conception and birth, married to, and cohabitating with, another man, *both of whom wish to raise the child as the offspring of their union.*" The highlighted language suggests that if Carole or Gerald alone wished to raise Victoria, or if both were dead and the State wished to raise her, Michael and Victoria might be found to have a liberty interest in their relationship with each other. But that would be to say that whether Michael and Victoria have a liberty interest varies with the State's interest in recognizing that interest, for it is the State's interest in protecting the marital family—and not Michael and Victoria's interest in their relationship with each other—that varies with the status of Carole and Gerald's relationship. It is a bad day for due process when the State's interest in terminating a parent-child relationship is reason to conclude that that relationship is not part of the "liberty" protected by the Fourteenth Amendment.

The plurality has wedged itself between a rock and a hard place. If it limits its holding to those situations in which a wife and husband wish to raise the child together, then it necessarily takes the State's interest into account in defining "liberty"; yet if it extends that approach to circumstances in which the marital union already has been dissolved, then it may no longer rely on the State's asserted interest in protecting the "unitary family" in denying that Michael and Victoria have been deprived of liberty.

The plurality's confusion about the proper analysis of claims involving procedural due process also becomes obvious when one examines the plurality's shift in emphasis from the putative father's standing to his ability to obtain parental prerogatives. In announcing that what matters is not the father's ability to claim paternity, but his ability to obtain "substantive parental rights," the plurality turns procedural due process upside down. Michael's challenge in this Court does not depend on his ability ultimately to obtain visitation rights; it would be strange indeed if, before one could be granted a hearing, one were required to prove that one would prevail on the merits. The point of procedural due process is to give the litigant a fair chance at prevailing, not to ensure a particular substantive outcome. Nor does Michael's challenge depend on the success of fathers like him in obtaining parental rights in past cases; procedural due process is, by and large, an individual guarantee, not one that should depend on the success or failure of prior cases having little or nothing to do with the claimant's own suit.

III

Because the plurality decides that Michael and Victoria have no liberty interest in their relationship with each other, it need consider neither the effect of § 621 on their relationship nor the State's interest in bringing about that effect. It is obvious, however, that the effect of § 621 is to terminate the relationship between Michael and Victoria before affording any hearing whatsoever on the issue whether Michael is Victoria's father. This refusal to hold a hearing is properly analyzed under our procedural due process cases, which instruct us to consider the State's interest in curtailing the procedures accompanying the termination of a constitutionally protected interest. California's interest, minute in comparison with a father's interest in his relationship with his child, cannot justify its refusal to hear Michael out on his claim that he is Victoria's father. . . .

■ **JUSTICE WHITE, with whom JUSTICE BRENNAN joins, dissenting.**

. . . Like Justices BRENNAN, MARSHALL, BLACKMUN, and STEVENS, I do not agree with the plurality opinion's conclusion that a natural father can never "have a constitutionally protected interest in his relationship with a child whose mother was married to, and cohabiting with, another man at the time of the child's conception and birth." Prior cases here have recognized the liberty interest of a father in his relationship with his child. In none of these cases did we indicate that the father's rights were dependent on the marital status of the mother or biological father. The basic principle enunciated in the Court's unwed father cases is that an unwed father who has demonstrated a sufficient commitment to his paternity by way of personal, financial, or custodial responsibilities has a protected liberty interest in a relationship with his child.

We have not before faced the question of a biological father's relationship with his child when the child was born while the mother was married to another man. On several occasions however, we have considered whether a biological father has a constitutionally cognizable interest in an opportunity to establish paternity. *Stanley v. Illinois,* 405 U.S. 645 (1972), recognized the biological father's right to a legal relationship with his illegitimate child, holding that the Due Process Clause of the Fourteenth Amendment entitled the biological father to a hearing on his fitness before his illegitimate children could be removed from his custody. We rejected the State's treatment of Stanley "not as a parent but as a stranger to his children." . . .

I fail to see the fairness in the process established by the State of California and endorsed by the Court today. Michael has evidence which demonstrates that he is the father of young Victoria. Yet he is blocked by the State from presenting that evidence to a court. As a result, he is foreclosed from establishing his paternity and is ultimately precluded, by the State, from developing a relationship with his child. "A fundamental requirement of due process is the opportunity to be heard. It is an opportunity which must be granted at a meaningful time and in a meaningful manner." *Armstrong v. Manzo,* 380 U.S. 545, 552 (1965). I fail to see how Michael was granted any meaningful opportunity to be heard when he was precluded at the very outset from introducing evidence which would support his assertion of paternity. Michael has never been afforded an opportunity to present his case in any meaningful manner. . . .

NOTE ON *MICHAEL H.* AND THE LEVEL OF GENERALITY PROBLEM

1.   The justices in *Michael H.* disagreed, to at least some extent, as to whether Michael's claim sounded in substantive or procedural due process. Was the plurality right to frame the claim as a substantive one, rather than a claim for the denial of fair procedure? Although Justice Brennan claimed to be arguing for a procedural right only, much of his analysis also seemed substantive, with the result that it is not altogether clear which characterization was adopted by a majority of the Court.

This chapter will consider both substantive and procedural due process, although we will emphasize the former. In the modern era, substantive due process jurisprudence has been concerned with the identification of "fundamental" rights, with the state being required to justify any infringement of those rights by overcoming strict scrutiny. Procedural due process claims, on the other hand, generally involve interests in liberty or property that need not necessarily rise to the "fundamental" level, but which entitle individuals to certain procedural protections before the state may deprive them of that interest.[5]

Many situations will implicate both procedural and substantive due process arguments. In *Michael H.*, the California statute was framed as an evidentiary presumption, with restrictions on who has standing to rebut that presumption. But the intent and practical effect of that statute, as the majority emphasized, was simply to deny to unwed fathers any parental rights when a child is born into an intact marriage. Under those circumstances, wasn't Michael necessarily asserting a substantive entitlement to establish a relationship with Victoria if he were, in fact, her biological father? On the other hand, even under the plurality's analysis, Michael would nonetheless have had a procedural due process right to have a judge determine whether the facts necessary to trigger § 621's presumption—for instance, whether Carole and Gerald were in fact married and living together when Victoria was born—were true.

2.   Michael H. raised an equal protection challenge to the California statute in the Supreme Court, but the Court did not reach that issue because it had not been argued in the courts below. He might have claimed that the right to establish and maintain a relationship with one's biological child is fundamental, and that any discrimination in the allocation of that right— here, between Carole and Gerald, who both had standing to determine paternity under California law, and Michael, who did not—is subject to strict scrutiny under cases like *Shapiro v. Thompson* and *Skinner v. Oklahoma*. Do you think Michael could have prevailed on such an argument if the Court had reached it? What are the pros and cons of framing a claim like Michael's under the Due Process or Equal Protection Clauses?

3.   Although footnote 4 of *Carolene Products* is indisputably the most famous footnote in constitutional law,[6] footnote 6 of Justice Scalia's plurality opinion in *Michael H.* has a plausible claim to second place. It proposes a solution to what is known as the "level of generality problem" in the definition of unenumerated fundamental rights. In an important article commenting on *Michael H.*, Laurence Tribe and Michael Dorf framed that problem as follows:

Even when prior cases explicitly designate a right [as fundamental], limitations of space as well as the institutional limitations embodied in Article III's case or controversy requirement will mean that those prior cases have not spelled out the precise contours of the right. The question then becomes: *at what level of generality should the Court describe the right previously protected and the right currently claimed?* The more abstractly one states the already-protected right, the more likely it becomes that the claimed right will fall within its protection. For instance, did the Court in *Griswold v. Connecticut* recognize the narrow right to use contraception or the broader right to make a variety of procreative decisions? Obviously, the

---

[5]   *See infra* Section 16.2.

[6]   *See* Section 5.4, *supra.*

descriptive choice will affect the Court's decisions in other cases, such as those involving abortion.[7]

This problem arises in a wide variety of doctrinal contexts, but it has been most vexing with respect to substantive due process. If judges are to apply the law rather than simply imposing their own values, they must be able to ground their choice of an appropriate level of generality for describing protected rights in something other than their own inclinations.

Justice Scalia argued in *Michael H.* that unenumerated rights must be grounded in tradition, but he acknowledged that reliance on social and legal traditions raises the same level of generality problem that Professors Tribe and Dorf discussed with respect to precedents. This problem, he argued, should be resolved by relying on the most specific possible level of generality in evaluating the tradition. One problem with Justice Scalia's approach, however, is that even he arguably did not select the most specific possible level of generality in *Michael H.* As Jack Balkin has pointed out,

> [T]here has been no established tradition in California for protecting Justice Scalia's own rights to visit his children, since there is no tradition of affording protection to fathers who are children of Italian immigrants and who graduated from Ivy League law schools before 1965, were appointed to the United States Supreme Court by former governors of the state of California and have more than two children but less than thirteen. Indeed, the question has hardly ever come up.[8]

Professor Balkin's formulation of the relevant tradition is obviously more specific than Justice Scalia's; it is also patently absurd. The point, of course, is simply that courts cannot simply always go with the most specific possible formulation, but rather must choose a level of generality that makes sense under the circumstances. But is there any general principle that can guide the court in making that determination? If not, are you worried that courts will simply manipulate the level of generality in order to justify a result reached on other, unacknowledged grounds?

Washington v. Glucksberg

521 U.S. 702 (1997)

■ **CHIEF JUSTICE REHNQUIST delivered the opinion of the Court.**

The question presented in this case is whether Washington's prohibition against "caus[ing]" or "aid[ing]" a suicide offends the Fourteenth Amendment to the United States Constitution. We hold that it does not.

It has always been a crime to assist a suicide in the State of Washington. In 1854, Washington's first Territorial Legislature

---

[7]   Laurence H. Tribe & Michael C. Dorf, *Levels of Generality in the Definition of Rights*, 57 U. CHI. L. REV. 1057, 1058 (1990).

[8]   J.M. Balkin, *Tradition, Betrayal, and the Politics of Deconstruction*, 11 CARDOZO L. REV. 1613, 1615 (1990).

outlawed "assisting another in the commission of self murder." Today, Washington law provides: "A person is guilty of promoting a suicide attempt when he knowingly causes or aids another person to attempt suicide." Wash. Rev. Code 9A.36.060(1). "Promoting a suicide attempt" is a felony, punishable by up to five years' imprisonment and up to a $10,000 fine. At the same time, Washington's Natural Death Act, enacted in 1979, states that the "withholding or withdrawal of life sustaining treatment" at a patient's direction "shall not, for any purpose, constitute a suicide."

Petitioners in this case are the State of Washington and its Attorney General. Respondents Harold Glucksberg, M.D., Abigail Halperin, M.D., Thomas A. Preston, M.D., and Peter Shalit, M.D., are physicians who practice in Washington. These doctors occasionally treat terminally ill, suffering patients, and declare that they would assist these patients in ending their lives if not for Washington's assisted suicide ban. In January 1994, respondents, along with three gravely ill, pseudonymous plaintiffs who have since died and Compassion in Dying, a nonprofit organization that counsels people considering physician assisted suicide, sued in the United States District Court, seeking a declaration that Wash Rev. Code 9A.36.060(1) is, on its face, unconstitutional.

The plaintiffs asserted "the existence of a liberty interest protected by the Fourteenth Amendment which extends to a personal choice by a mentally competent, terminally ill adult to commit physician assisted suicide." Relying primarily on *Planned Parenthood v. Casey* and *Cruzan v. Director, Missouri Dept. of Health*, 497 U.S. 261 (1990), the District Court agreed and concluded that Washington's assisted suicide ban is unconstitutional because it "places an undue burden on the exercise of [that] constitutionally protected liberty interest." The District Court also decided that the Washington statute violated the Equal Protection Clause's requirement that " 'all persons similarly situated . . . be treated alike.' "

A panel of the Court of Appeals for the Ninth Circuit reversed, emphasizing that "[i]n the two hundred and five years of our existence no constitutional right to aid in killing oneself has ever been asserted and upheld by a court of final jurisdiction." The Ninth Circuit reheard the case en banc, reversed the panel's decision, and affirmed the District Court. Like the District Court, the en banc Court of Appeals emphasized our *Casey* and *Cruzan* decisions. The court also discussed what it described as "historical" and "current societal attitudes" toward suicide and assisted suicide and concluded that "the Constitution encompasses a due process liberty interest in controlling the time and manner of one's death—that there is, in short, a constitutionally recognized 'right to die.' " . . . We granted certiorari, and now reverse.

I

We begin, as we do in all due process cases, by examining our Nation's history, legal traditions, and practices. In almost every State—

indeed, in almost every western democracy—it is a crime to assist a suicide. The States' assisted suicide bans are not innovations. Rather, they are longstanding expressions of the States' commitment to the protection and preservation of all human life. Indeed, opposition to and condemnation of suicide—and, therefore, of assisting suicide—are consistent and enduring themes of our philosophical, legal, and cultural heritages. *See generally* New York State Task Force on Life and the Law, *When Death is Sought: Assisted Suicide and Euthanasia in the Medical Context* 77–82 (May 1994).

More specifically, for over 700 years, the Anglo American common law tradition has punished or otherwise disapproved of both suicide and assisting suicide. . . . Sir William Blackstone, whose *Commentaries on the Laws of England* not only provided a definitive summary of the common law but was also a primary legal authority for 18th and 19th century American lawyers, referred to suicide as "self murder". . . . Blackstone emphasized that "the law has . . . ranked [suicide] among the highest crimes," although, anticipating later developments, he conceded that the harsh and shameful punishments imposed for suicide "borde[r] a little upon severity."

For the most part, the early American colonies adopted the common law approach. . . . Over time, however, the American colonies abolished these harsh common law penalties. . . . [H]owever, . . . the movement away from the common law's harsh sanctions did not represent an acceptance of suicide; rather, as Chief Justice Swift [of Connecticut] observed, this change reflected the growing consensus that it was unfair to punish the suicide's family for his wrongdoing. . . .

That suicide remained a grievous, though nonfelonious, wrong is confirmed by the fact that colonial and early state legislatures and courts did not retreat from prohibiting assisting suicide. Swift, in his early 19th century treatise on the laws of Connecticut, stated that "[i]f one counsels another to commit suicide, and the other by reason of the advice kills himself, the advisor is guilty of murder as principal." This was the well established common law view. And the prohibitions against assisting suicide never contained exceptions for those who were near death. . . .

The earliest American statute explicitly to outlaw assisting suicide was enacted in New York in 1828, and many of the new States and Territories followed New York's example. . . . By the time the Fourteenth Amendment was ratified, it was a crime in most States to assist a suicide. . . . In this century, the Model Penal Code also prohibited "aiding" suicide, prompting many States to enact or revise their assisted suicide bans.

Though deeply rooted, the States' assisted suicide bans have in recent years been reexamined and, generally, reaffirmed. Because of advances in medicine and technology, Americans today are increasingly likely to die in institutions, from chronic illnesses. Public concern and democratic action are therefore sharply focused on how best to protect dignity and independence at the end of life, with the result that there have been many significant changes in state laws and in the attitudes these laws reflect. Many States, for example, now permit "living wills," surrogate health care decisionmaking, and the withdrawal or refusal of life sustaining medical treatment. At the same time, however, voters and legislators continue for the most part to reaffirm their States' prohibitions on assisting suicide.

The Washington statute at issue in this case was enacted in 1975 as part of a revision of that State's criminal code. Four years later, Washington passed its Natural Death Act, which specifically stated that the "withholding or withdrawal of life sustaining treatment . . . shall not, for any purpose, constitute a suicide" and that "[n]othing in this chapter shall be construed to condone, authorize, or approve mercy killing. . . ." In 1991, Washington voters rejected a ballot initiative which, had it passed, would have permitted a form of physician assisted suicide. Washington then added a provision to the Natural Death Act expressly excluding physician assisted suicide.

California voters rejected an assisted suicide initiative similar to Washington's in 1993. On the other hand, in 1994, voters in Oregon enacted, also through ballot initiative, that State's "Death With Dignity Act," which legalized physician assisted suicide for competent, terminally ill adults. Since the Oregon vote, many proposals to legalize assisted suicide have been and continue to be introduced in the States' legislatures, but none has been enacted. And just last year, Iowa and Rhode Island joined the overwhelming majority of States explicitly prohibiting assisted suicide. Also, on April 30, 1997, President Clinton signed the Federal Assisted Suicide Funding Restriction Act of 1997, which prohibits the use of federal funds in support of physician assisted suicide.

Thus, the States are currently engaged in serious, thoughtful examinations of physician assisted suicide and other similar issues. For example, New York State's Task Force on Life and the Law—an ongoing, blue ribbon commission composed of doctors, ethicists, lawyers, religious leaders, and interested laymen—was convened in 1984 and commissioned with "a broad mandate to recommend public policy on issues raised by medical advances." Over the past decade, the Task Force has recommended laws relating to end of life decisions, surrogate pregnancy, and organ donation. After studying physician assisted suicide, however, the Task Force unanimously concluded that "[l]egalizing assisted suicide and euthanasia would pose profound risks to many individuals who are ill and vulnerable. . . . [T]he potential dangers of this dramatic change in public policy would outweigh any benefit that might be achieved."

Attitudes toward suicide itself have changed since Bracton, but our laws have consistently condemned, and continue to prohibit, assisting suicide. Despite changes in medical technology and notwithstanding an increased emphasis on the importance of end of life decisionmaking, we have not retreated from this prohibition. Against this backdrop of history, tradition, and practice, we now turn to respondents' constitutional claim.

II

The Due Process Clause guarantees more than fair process, and the "liberty" it protects includes more than the absence of physical restraint. The Clause also provides heightened protection against government interference with certain fundamental rights and liberty interests. In a long line of cases, we have held that, in addition to the specific freedoms protected by the Bill of Rights, the "liberty" specially protected by the Due Process Clause includes the rights to marry, *Loving v. Virginia*, 388 U.S. 1 (1967); to have children, *Skinner v. Oklahoma ex rel. Williamson*, 316 U.S. 535 (1942); to direct the education and upbringing of one's children, *Meyer v. Nebraska*, 262 U.S. 390 (1923); *Pierce v. Society of Sisters*, 268 U.S. 510 (1925); to marital privacy, *Griswold v. Connecticut*; to use contraception, *ibid*; Eisenstadt v. Baird; to bodily integrity, *Rochin v. California*, 342 U.S. 165 (1952), and to abortion, *Casey*. We have also assumed, and strongly suggested, that the Due Process Clause protects the traditional right to refuse unwanted lifesaving medical treatment. *Cruzan*.

But we "ha[ve] always been reluctant to expand the concept of substantive due process because guideposts for responsible decisionmaking in this unchartered area are scarce and open ended." By extending constitutional protection to an asserted right or liberty interest, we, to a great extent, place the matter outside the arena of public debate and legislative action. We must therefore "exercise the utmost care whenever we are asked to break new ground in this field," lest the liberty protected by the Due Process Clause be subtly transformed into the policy preferences of the members of this Court.

Our established method of substantive due process analysis has two primary features: First, we have regularly observed that the Due Process Clause specially protects those fundamental rights and liberties which are, objectively, "deeply rooted in this Nation's history and tradition." Second, we have required in substantive due process cases a "careful description" of the asserted fundamental liberty interest. Our Nation's history, legal traditions, and practices thus provide the crucial "guideposts for responsible decisionmaking" that direct and restrain our exposition of the Due Process Clause. . . .

Justice Souter, relying on Justice Harlan's dissenting opinion in *Poe v. Ullman*, would largely abandon this restrained methodology, and instead ask "whether [Washington's] statute sets up one of those 'arbitrary impositions' or 'purposeless restraints' at odds with the Due Process Clause of the Fourteenth Amendment." In our view, however, the development of this Court's substantive due process jurisprudence, described briefly above, has been a process whereby the outlines of the "liberty" specially protected by the Fourteenth Amendment—never fully clarified, to be sure, and perhaps not capable of being fully clarified— have at least been carefully refined by concrete examples involving fundamental rights found to be deeply rooted in our legal tradition. This approach tends to rein in the subjective elements that are necessarily present in due process judicial review. In addition, by establishing a threshold requirement—that a challenged state action implicate a fundamental right—before requiring more than a reasonable relation to a legitimate state interest to justify the action, it avoids the need for complex balancing of competing interests in every case.

. . . [R]espondents assert a "liberty to choose how to die" and a right to "control of one's final days," and describe the asserted liberty as "the right to choose a humane, dignified death" and "the liberty to shape death." As noted above, we have a tradition of carefully formulating the interest at stake in substantive due process cases. For example, although *Cruzan* is often described as a "right to die" case, we were, in fact, more precise: we assumed that the Constitution granted competent persons a "constitutionally protected right to refuse lifesaving hydration and nutrition." The Washington statute at issue in this case prohibits "aid[ing] another person to attempt suicide," and, thus, the question before us is whether the "liberty" specially protected by the Due Process Clause includes a right to commit suicide which itself includes a right to assistance in doing so.

We now inquire whether this asserted right has any place in our Nation's traditions. Here, as discussed above, we are confronted with a consistent and almost universal tradition that has long rejected the asserted right, and continues explicitly to reject it today, even for terminally ill, mentally competent adults. To hold for respondents, we would have to reverse centuries of legal doctrine and practice, and strike down the considered policy choice of almost every State.

Respondents contend, however, that the liberty interest they assert is consistent with this Court's substantive due process line of cases, if not with this Nation's history and practice. Pointing to *Casey* and *Cruzan*, respondents read our jurisprudence in this area as reflecting a general tradition of "self sovereignty" and as teaching that the "liberty" protected by the Due Process Clause includes "basic and intimate exercises of personal autonomy." According to respondents, our liberty jurisprudence, and the broad, individualistic principles it reflects, protects the "liberty of competent, terminally ill adults to make end of life decisions free of undue government interference." . . .

In *Cruzan*, we considered whether Nancy Beth Cruzan, who had been severely injured in an automobile accident and was in a persistive vegetative state, "ha[d] a right under the United States Constitution which would require the hospital to withdraw life sustaining treatment" at her parents' request. We began with the observation that "[a]t common law, even the touching of one person by another without consent and without legal justification was a battery." We then discussed the related rule that "informed consent is generally required for medical treatment." After reviewing a long line of relevant state cases, we concluded that "the common law doctrine of informed consent is viewed as generally encompassing the right of a competent individual to refuse medical treatment." Next, we reviewed our own cases on the subject, and stated that "[t]he principle that a competent person has a constitutionally protected liberty interest in refusing unwanted medical treatment may be inferred from our prior decisions." Therefore, "for purposes of [that] case, we assume[d] that the United States Constitution would grant a competent person a constitutionally protected right to refuse lifesaving hydration and nutrition." We concluded that, notwithstanding this right, the Constitution permitted Missouri to require clear and convincing evidence of an incompetent patient's wishes concerning the withdrawal of life sustaining treatment.

Respondents contend . . . that "the constitutional principle behind recognizing the patient's liberty to direct the withdrawal of artificial life support applies at least as strongly to the choice to hasten impending death by consuming lethal medication." . . . The right assumed in *Cruzan*, however, was not simply deduced from abstract concepts of personal autonomy. . . . The decision to commit suicide with the assistance of another may be just as personal and profound as the decision to refuse unwanted medical treatment, but it has never enjoyed similar legal protection. Indeed, the two acts are widely and reasonably regarded as quite distinct. In *Cruzan* itself, we recognized that most States outlawed assisted suicide—and even more do today—and we certainly gave no intimation that the right to refuse unwanted medical treatment could be somehow transmuted into a right to assistance in committing suicide.

Respondents also rely on *Casey*. . . . [They] emphasize the statement in *Casey* that "[a]t the heart of liberty is the right to define one's own concept of existence, of meaning, of the universe, and of the mystery of human life. Beliefs about these matters could not define the attributes of personhood were they formed under compulsion of the State." By choosing this language, the Court's opinion in *Casey* described, in a general way and in light of our prior cases, those personal activities and decisions that this Court has identified as so deeply rooted in our history and traditions, or so fundamental to our concept of constitutionally ordered liberty, that they are protected by the Fourteenth Amendment. . . . That many of the rights and liberties protected by the Due Process Clause sound in personal autonomy does not warrant the sweeping conclusion that any and all important, intimate, and personal decisions are so protected, and *Casey* did not suggest otherwise.

The history of the law's treatment of assisted suicide in this country has been and continues to be one of the rejection of nearly all efforts to permit it. That being the case, our decisions lead us to conclude that the asserted "right" to assistance in committing suicide is not a fundamental liberty interest protected by the Due Process Clause. The Constitution also requires, however, that Washington's assisted suicide ban be rationally related to legitimate government interests. This requirement is unquestionably met here. As the court below recognized, Washington's assisted suicide ban implicates a number of state interests.

First, Washington has an "unqualified interest in the preservation of human life." The State's prohibition on assisted suicide, like all homicide laws, both reflects and advances its commitment to this interest. . . .

The State also has an interest in protecting the integrity and ethics of the medical profession. . . . [T]he American Medical Association, like many other medical and physicians' groups, has concluded that "[p]hysician assisted suicide is fundamentally incompatible with the physician's role as healer." . . .

Next, the State has an interest in protecting vulnerable groups— including the poor, the elderly, and disabled persons—from abuse, neglect, and mistakes. . . . We have recognized . . . the real risk of subtle coercion and undue influence in end of life situations. . . . The State's interest here goes beyond protecting the vulnerable from coercion; it extends to protecting disabled and terminally ill people from prejudice, negative and inaccurate stereotypes, and "societal indifference." The State's assisted suicide ban reflects and reinforces its policy that the lives of terminally ill, disabled, and elderly people must be no less valued than the lives of the young and healthy, and that a seriously disabled person's suicidal impulses should be interpreted and treated the same way as anyone else's.

Finally, the State may fear that permitting assisted suicide will start it down the path to voluntary and perhaps even involuntary euthanasia. . . . If suicide is protected as a matter of constitutional right, it is argued, "every man and woman in the United States must enjoy it." . . . Thus, it turns out that what is couched as a limited right to "physician assisted suicide" is likely, in effect, a much broader license, which could prove extremely difficult to police and contain. Washington's ban on assisting suicide prevents such erosion.

This concern is further supported by evidence about the practice of euthanasia in the Netherlands. The Dutch government's own study revealed that in 1990, there were 2,300 cases of voluntary euthanasia (defined as "the deliberate termination of another's life at his request"), 400 cases of assisted suicide, and more than 1,000 cases of euthanasia without an explicit request. In addition to these latter 1,000 cases, the study found an additional 4,941 cases where physicians administered lethal morphine overdoses without the patients' explicit consent. This study suggests that, despite the existence of various reporting procedures, euthanasia in the Netherlands has not been limited to competent, terminally ill adults who are enduring physical suffering, and that regulation of the practice may not have prevented abuses in cases involving vulnerable persons, including severely disabled neonates and elderly persons suffering from dementia. . . . Washington, like most other States, reasonably ensures against this risk by banning, rather than regulating, assisting suicide.

We need not weigh exactingly the relative strengths of these various interests. They are unquestionably important and legitimate, and Washington's ban on assisted suicide is at least reasonably related to their promotion and protection. We therefore hold that Wash. Rev. Code § 9A.36.060(1) does not violate the Fourteenth Amendment, either on its face or "as applied to competent, terminally ill adults who wish to hasten their deaths by obtaining medication prescribed by their doctors."

* * *

Throughout the Nation, Americans are engaged in an earnest and profound debate about the morality, legality, and practicality of physician assisted suicide. Our holding permits this debate to continue, as it should in a democratic society. The decision of the en banc Court of Appeals is reversed, and the case is remanded for further proceedings consistent with this opinion.

■ JUSTICE O'CONNOR, concurring.*

. . . I join the Court's opinions because I agree that there is no generalized right to "commit suicide." But respondents urge us to address the narrower question whether a mentally competent person who is experiencing great suffering has a constitutionally cognizable interest in controlling the circumstances of his or her imminent death. I see no need to reach that question in the context of the facial challenges to the New York and Washington laws at issue here. The parties and *amici* agree that in these States a patient who is suffering from a terminal illness and who is experiencing great pain has no legal barriers to obtaining medication, from qualified physicians, to alleviate that suffering, even to the point of causing unconsciousness and hastening death. In this light, even assuming that we would recognize such an interest, I agree that the State's interests in protecting those who are not truly competent or facing imminent death, or those whose decisions to hasten death would not truly be voluntary, are sufficiently weighty to justify a prohibition against physician assisted suicide.

Every one of us at some point may be affected by our own or a family member's terminal illness. There is no reason to think the democratic process will not strike the proper balance between the interests of terminally ill, mentally competent individuals who would seek to end their suffering and the State's interests in protecting those who might seek to end life mistakenly or under pressure. As the Court recognizes,

---

* JUSTICE GINSBURG concurs in the Court's judgments substantially for the reasons stated in this opinion. JUSTICE BREYER joins this opinion except insofar as it joins the opinions of the Court.

States are presently undertaking extensive and serious evaluation of physician assisted suicide and other related issues. In such circumstances, "the . . . challenging task of crafting appropriate procedures for safeguarding . . . liberty interests is entrusted to the 'laboratory' of the States . . . in the first instance." . . .

■ **JUSTICE STEVENS, concurring in the judgments.**

The Court ends its opinion with the important observation that our holding today is fully consistent with a continuation of the vigorous debate about the "morality, legality, and practicality of physician assisted suicide" in a democratic society. I write separately to make it clear that there is also room for further debate about the limits that the Constitution places on the power of the States to punish the practice. . . .

Today, the Court decides that Washington's statute prohibiting assisted suicide is not invalid "on its face," that is to say, in all or most cases in which it might be applied. That holding, however, does not foreclose the possibility that some applications of the statute might well be invalid.

As originally filed, this case presented a challenge to the Washington statute on its face and as it applied to three terminally ill, mentally competent patients and to four physicians who treat terminally ill patients. After the District Court issued its opinion holding that the statute placed an undue burden on the right to commit physician assisted suicide, the three patients died. Although the Court of Appeals considered the constitutionality of the statute "as applied to the prescription of life ending medication for use by terminally ill, competent adult patients who wish to hasten their deaths," the court did not have before it any individual plaintiff seeking to hasten her death or any doctor who was threatened with prosecution for assisting in the suicide of a particular patient; its analysis and eventual holding that the statute was unconstitutional was not limited to a particular set of plaintiffs before it.

The appropriate standard to be applied in cases making facial challenges to state statutes has been the subject of debate within this Court. . . . [T]he Court does conceive of respondents' claim as a facial challenge—addressing not the application of the statute to a particular set of plaintiffs before it, but the constitutionality of the statute's categorical prohibition against "aid[ing] another person to attempt suicide." Accordingly, the Court requires the plaintiffs to show that the interest in liberty protected by the Fourteenth Amendment "includes a right to commit suicide which itself includes a right to assistance in doing so."

History and tradition provide ample support for refusing to recognize an open ended constitutional right to commit suicide. . . . Thus, I fully agree with the Court that the "liberty" protected by the Due Process

Clause does not include a categorical "right to commit suicide which itself includes a right to assistance in doing so."

But just as our conclusion that capital punishment is not always unconstitutional did not preclude later decisions holding that it is sometimes impermissibly cruel, so is it equally clear that a decision upholding a general statutory prohibition of assisted suicide does not mean that every possible application of the statute would be valid. A State, like Washington, that has authorized the death penalty and thereby has concluded that the sanctity of human life does not require that it always be preserved, must acknowledge that there are situations in which an interest in hastening death is legitimate. Indeed, not only is that interest sometimes legitimate, I am also convinced that there are times when it is entitled to constitutional protection. . . .

The state interests supporting a general rule banning the practice of physician assisted suicide do not have the same force in all cases. . . . As the New York State Task Force on Life and the Law recognized, a State's prohibition of assisted suicide is justified by the fact that the " 'ideal' " case in which "patients would be screened for depression and offered treatment, effective pain medication would be available, and all patients would have a supportive committed family and doctor" is not the usual case. Although, as the Court concludes today, these potential harms are sufficient to support the State's general public policy against assisted suicide, they will not always outweigh the individual liberty interest of a particular patient. Unlike the Court of Appeals, I would not say as a categorical matter that these state interests are invalid as to the entire class of terminally ill, mentally competent patients. I do not, however, foreclose the possibility that an individual plaintiff seeking to hasten her death, or a doctor whose assistance was sought, could prevail in a more particularized challenge. Future cases will determine whether such a challenge may succeed. . . .

There remains room for vigorous debate about the outcome of particular cases that are not necessarily resolved by the opinions announced today. How such cases may be decided will depend on their specific facts. In my judgment, however, it is clear that the so called "unqualified interest in the preservation of human life," is not itself sufficient to outweigh the interest in liberty that may justify the only possible means of preserving a dying patient's dignity and alleviating her intolerable suffering.

■ JUSTICE SOUTER, concurring in the judgment.

. . . The question is whether the statute sets up one of those "arbitrary impositions" or "purposeless restraints" at odds with the Due Process Clause of the Fourteenth Amendment. *Poe v. Ullman*, 367 U.S. 497 (1961) (Harlan, J., dissenting). I conclude that the statute's application to the doctors has not been shown to be unconstitutional, but I write separately to give my reasons for analyzing the substantive due process claims as I do, and for rejecting this one. . . .

The case reaches us on an order granting summary judgment, and we must take as true the undisputed allegations that each of the patients was mentally competent and terminally ill, and that each made a knowing and voluntary choice to ask a doctor to prescribe "medications . . . to be self administered for the purpose of hastening . . . death." The State does not dispute that each faced a passage to death more agonizing both mentally and physically, and more protracted over time, than death by suicide with a physician's help, or that each would have chosen such a suicide for the sake of personal dignity, apart even from relief from pain. Each doctor in this case claims to encounter patients like the original plaintiffs who have died, that is, mentally competent, terminally ill, and seeking medical help in "the voluntary self termination of life". While there may be no unanimity on the physician's professional obligation in such circumstances, I accept here respondents' representation that providing such patients with prescriptions for drugs that go beyond pain relief to hasten death would, in these circumstances, be consistent with standards of medical practice. Hence, I take it to be true, as respondents say, that the Washington statute prevents the exercise of a physician's "best professional judgment to prescribe medications to [such] patients in dosages that would enable them to act to hasten their own deaths."

In their brief to this Court, the doctors claim not that they ought to have a right generally to hasten patients' imminent deaths, but only to help patients who have made "personal decisions regarding their own bodies, medical care, and, fundamentally, the future course of their lives," and who have concluded responsibly and with substantial justification that the brief and anguished remainders of their lives have lost virtually all value to them. Respondents fully embrace the notion that the State must be free to impose reasonable regulations on such physician assistance to ensure that the patients they assist are indeed among the competent and terminally ill and that each has made a free and informed choice in seeking to obtain and use a fatal drug.

In response, the State argues that the interest asserted by the doctors is beyond constitutional recognition because it has no deep roots in our history and traditions. But even aside from that, without disputing that the patients here were competent and terminally ill, the State insists that recognizing the legitimacy of doctors' assistance of their patients as contemplated here would entail a number of adverse consequences that the Washington Legislature was entitled to forestall. The nub of this part of the State's argument is not that such patients are constitutionally undeserving of relief on their own account, but that any attempt to confine a right of physician assistance to the circumstances presented by these doctors is likely to fail.

First, the State argues that the right could not be confined to the terminally ill. Even assuming a fixed definition of that term, the State observes that it is not always possible to say with certainty how long a person may live. It asserts that "[t]here is no principled basis on which [the right] can be limited to the prescription of medication for terminally ill patients to administer to themselves" when the right's justifying principle is as broad as "merciful termination of suffering." Second, the State argues that the right could not be confined to the mentally competent, observing that a person's competence cannot always be assessed with certainty, and suggesting further that no principled distinction is possible between a competent patient acting independently and a patient acting through a duly appointed and competent surrogate. Next, according to the State, such a right might entail a right to or at least merge in practice into "other forms of life ending assistance," such as euthanasia. Finally, the State believes that a right to physician assistance could not easily be distinguished from a right to assistance from others, such as friends, family, and other health care workers. The State thus argues that recognition of the substantive due process right at issue here would jeopardize the lives of others outside the class defined by the doctors' claim, creating risks of irresponsible suicides and euthanasia, whose dangers are concededly within the State's authority to address.

When the physicians claim that the Washington law deprives them of a right falling within the scope of liberty that the Fourteenth Amendment guarantees against denial without due process of law, they are not claiming some sort of procedural defect in the process through which the statute has been enacted or is administered. Their claim, rather, is that the State has no substantively adequate justification for barring the assistance sought by the patient and sought to be offered by the physician. Thus, we are dealing with a claim to one of those rights sometimes described as rights of substantive due process and sometimes as unenumerated rights, in view of the breadth and indeterminacy of the "due process" serving as the claim's textual basis. The doctors accordingly arouse the skepticism of those who find the Due Process Clause an unduly vague or oxymoronic warrant for judicial review of substantive state law, just as they also invoke two centuries of American constitutional practice in recognizing unenumerated, substantive limits on governmental action. Although this practice has neither rested on any single textual basis nor expressed a consistent theory . . . a brief overview of its history is instructive on two counts. The persistence of substantive due process in our cases points to the legitimacy of the modern justification for such judicial review found in Justice Harlan's dissent in *Poe*, on which I will dwell further on, while the acknowledged failures of some of these cases point with caution to the difficulty raised by the present claim.

Before the ratification of the Fourteenth Amendment, substantive constitutional review resting on a theory of unenumerated rights occurred largely in the state courts applying state constitutions that commonly contained either due process clauses like that of the Fifth

Amendment (and later the Fourteenth) or the textual antecedents of such clauses, repeating Magna Carta's guarantee of "the law of the land." On the basis of such clauses, or of general principles untethered to specific constitutional language, state courts evaluated the constitutionality of a wide range of statutes.

Thus, a Connecticut court approved a statute legitimating a class of previous illegitimate marriages, as falling within the terms of the "social compact," while making clear its power to review constitutionality in those terms. *Goshen v. Stonington*, 4 Conn. 209 (1822). In the same period, a specialized court of equity . . . found its own authorization unconstitutional as "partial" legislation violating the state constitution's "law of the land" clause. *Bank of the State v. Cooper*, 2 Yerg. 599 (Tenn. 1831). And the middle of the 19th century brought the famous *Wynehamer* case, invalidating a statute purporting to render possession of liquor immediately illegal except when kept for narrow, specified purposes, the state court finding the statute inconsistent with the state's due process clause. *Wynehamer v. People*, 13 N.Y. 378 (1856). The statute was deemed an excessive threat to the "fundamental rights of the citizen" to property.

Even in this early period, however, this Court . . . [made] it clear on several occasions that it too had no doubt of the judiciary's power to strike down legislation that conflicted with important but unenumerated principles of American government. In most such instances, after declaring its power to invalidate what it might find inconsistent with rights of liberty and property, the Court nevertheless went on to uphold the legislative acts under review. See, e.g., *Wilkinson v. Leland*, 2 Pet. 627 (1829); *Calder v. Bull*, 3 Dall. 386 (1798) (opinion of Chase, J.); see also *Corfield v. Coryell*, 6 F. Cas. 546 (No. 3,230) (1823). But in *Fletcher v. Peck*, 6 Cranch 87 (1810), the Court went further. It struck down an act of the Georgia legislature that purported to rescind a sale of public land ab initio and reclaim title for the State, and so deprive subsequent, good faith purchasers of property conveyed by the original grantees. The Court rested the invalidation on alternative sources of authority: the specific prohibitions against bills of attainder, ex post-facto laws, laws impairing contracts in Article I, § 10 of the Constitution; and "general principles which are common to our free institutions," by which Chief Justice Marshall meant that a simple deprivation of property by the State could not be an authentically "legislative" act.

Fletcher was not, though, the most telling early example of such review. For its most salient instance in this Court before the adoption of the Fourteenth Amendment was, of course, the case that the Amendment would in due course overturn, *Dred Scott v. Sandford*, 19 How. 393 (1857). Unlike *Fletcher*, *Dred Scott* was textually based on a due process clause (in the Fifth Amendment, applicable to the national government), and it was in reliance on that clause's protection of property that the Court invalidated the Missouri Compromise. This substantive protection of an owner's property in a slave taken to the territories was traced to the absence of any enumerated power to affect that property granted to the Congress by Article I of the Constitution, the implication being that the government had no legitimate interest that could support the earlier congressional compromise. The ensuing judgment of history needs no recounting here.

After the ratification of the Fourteenth Amendment, with its guarantee of due process protection against the States, interpretation of the words "liberty" and "property" as used in due process clauses became a sustained enterprise, with the Court generally describing the due process criterion in converse terms of reasonableness or arbitrariness. That standard is fairly traceable to Justice Bradley's dissent in the *Slaughter House Cases*, in which he said that a person's right to choose a calling was an element of liberty (as the calling, once chosen, was an aspect of property) and declared that the liberty and property protected by due process are not truly recognized if such rights may be "arbitrarily assailed."[6] After that, opinions comparable to those that preceded *Dred Scott* expressed willingness to review legislative action for consistency with the Due Process Clause even as they upheld the laws in question. See, e.g., *Munn v. Illinois*, 94 U.S. 113 (1877); *Mugler v. Kansas*, 123 U.S. 623 (1887).

The theory became serious, however, beginning with *Allgeyer v. Louisiana*, 165 U.S. 578 (1897), where the Court invalidated a Louisiana statute for excessive interference with Fourteenth Amendment liberty to contract and offered a substantive interpretation of "liberty," that in the aftermath of the so called *Lochner* Era has been scaled back in some respects, but expanded in others, and never repudiated in principle. The Court said that Fourteenth Amendment liberty includes "the right of the citizen to be free in the enjoyment of all his faculties; to be free to use them in all lawful ways; to live and work where he will; to earn his livelihood by any lawful calling; to pursue any livelihood or avocation; and for that purpose to enter into all contracts which may be proper, necessary and essential to his carrying out to a successful conclusion the purposes above mentioned." "[W]e do not intend to hold that in no such case can the State exercise its police power," the Court added, but "[w]hen and how far such power may be legitimately exercised with regard to these subjects must be left for determination to each case as it arises."

Although this principle was unobjectionable, what followed for a season was, in the realm of economic legislation, the echo of *Dred Scott*. *Allgeyer* was succeeded within a decade by *Lochner v. New York*, and the era to which that case gave its name, famous now for striking down as arbitrary various sorts of economic regulations that post-New Deal courts

---

6 The *Slaughter House Cases* are important, of course, for their holding that the Privileges or Immunities Clause was no source of any but a specific handful of substantive rights. To a degree, then, that decision may have led the Court to look to the Due Process Clause as a source of substantive rights.

have uniformly thought constitutionally sound. [W]hile the cases in the *Lochner* line routinely invoked a correct standard of constitutional arbitrariness review, they harbored the spirit of *Dred Scott* in their absolutist implementation of the standard they espoused.

Even before the deviant economic due process cases had been repudiated, however, the more durable precursors of modern substantive due process were reaffirming this Court's obligation to conduct arbitrariness review, beginning with *Meyer v. Nebraska*, 262 U.S. 390 (1923). Without referring to any specific guarantee of the Bill of Rights, the Court invoked precedents from the *Slaughter House Cases* through *Adkins* to declare that the Fourteenth Amendment protected "the right of the individual to contract, to engage in any of the common occupations of life, to acquire useful knowledge, to marry, establish a home and bring up children, to worship God according to the dictates of his own conscience, and generally to enjoy those privileges long recognized at common law as essential to the orderly pursuit of happiness by free men." The Court then held that the same Fourteenth Amendment liberty included a teacher's right to teach and the rights of parents to direct their children's education without unreasonable interference by the States, with the result that Nebraska's prohibition on the teaching of foreign languages in the lower grades was, "arbitrary and without reasonable relation to any end within the competency of the State."

After *Meyer* and *Pierce*, two further opinions took the major steps that lead to the modern law. The first was not even in a due process case but one about equal protection, *Skinner v. Oklahoma*, 316 U.S. 535 (1942), where the Court emphasized the "fundamental" nature of individual choice about procreation and so foreshadowed not only the later prominence of procreation as a subject of liberty protection, but the corresponding standard of "strict scrutiny," in this Court's Fourteenth Amendment law. *Skinner*, that is, added decisions regarding procreation to the list of liberties recognized in *Meyer* and *Pierce* and loosely suggested, as a gloss on their standard of arbitrariness, a judicial obligation to scrutinize any impingement on such an important interest with heightened care. In so doing, it suggested a point that Justice Harlan would develop, that the kind and degree of justification that a sensitive judge would demand of a State would depend on the importance of the interest being asserted by the individual.

The second major opinion leading to the modern doctrine was Justice Harlan's *Poe* dissent just cited, the conclusion of which was adopted in *Griswold v. Connecticut*, and the authority of which was acknowledged in *Planned Parenthood of Southeastern Pa. v. Casey*. The dissent is important for three things that point to our responsibilities today. The first is Justice Harlan's respect for the tradition of substantive due process review itself, and his acknowledgement of the Judiciary's obligation to carry it on. For two centuries American courts, and for much of that time this Court, have thought it necessary to provide some degree of review over the substantive content of legislation under constitutional standards of textual breadth. The obligation was understood before *Dred Scott* and has continued after the repudiation of *Lochner*'s progeny, most notably on the subjects of segregation in public education, *Bolling v. Sharpe*, interracial marriage, *Loving v. Virginia*, 388 U.S. 1 (1967), marital privacy and contraception, *Carey v. Population Services Int'l*, 431 U.S. 678 (1977), abortion, *Planned Parenthood of Southeastern Pa. v. Casey*, *Roe v. Wade*, and physical confinement, *Foucha v. Louisiana*, 504 U.S. 71 (1992). This enduring tradition of American constitutional practice is, in Justice Harlan's view, nothing more than what is required by the judicial authority and obligation to construe constitutional text and review legislation for conformity to that text. See *Marbury v. Madison*. Like many judges who preceded him and many who followed, he found it impossible to construe the text of due process without recognizing substantive, and not merely procedural, limitations. "Were due process merely a procedural safeguard it would fail to reach those situations where the deprivation of life, liberty or property was accomplished by legislation which by operating in the future could, given even the fairest possible procedure in application to individuals, nevertheless destroy the enjoyment of all three." The text of the Due Process Clause thus imposes nothing less than an obligation to give substantive content to the words "liberty" and "due process of law."

Following the first point of the *Poe* dissent, on the necessity to engage in the sort of examination we conduct today, the dissent's second and third implicitly address those cases, already noted, that are now condemned with virtual unanimity as disastrous mistakes of substantive due process review. The second of the dissent's lessons is a reminder that the business of such review is not the identification of extratextual absolutes but scrutiny of a legislative resolution (perhaps unconscious) of clashing principles, each quite possibly worthy in and of itself, but each to be weighed within the history of our values as a people. It is a comparison of the relative strengths of opposing claims that informs the judicial task, not a deduction from some first premise. Thus informed, judicial review still has no warrant to substitute one reasonable resolution of the contending positions for another, but authority to supplant the balance already struck between the contenders only when it falls outside the realm of the reasonable. Part III, below, deals with this second point, and also with the dissent's third, which takes the form of an object lesson in the explicit attention to detail that is no less essential to the intellectual discipline of substantive due process review than an understanding of the basic need to account for the two sides in the controversy and to respect legislation within the zone of reasonableness.

My understanding of unenumerated rights in the wake of the *Poe* dissent and subsequent cases avoids the absolutist failing of many older cases without embracing the opposite pole of equating reasonableness with past practice described at a very specific level. That understanding begins with a concept of "ordered liberty":

> Due Process has not been reduced to any formula; its content cannot be determined by reference to any code. The best that can be said is that through the course of this Court's decisions it has represented the balance which our Nation, built upon postulates of respect for the liberty of the individual, has struck between that liberty and the demands of organized society. If the supplying of content to this Constitutional concept has of necessity been a rational process, it certainly has not been one where judges have felt free to roam where unguided speculation might take them. The balance of which I speak is the balance struck by this country, having regard to what history teaches are the traditions from which it developed as well as the traditions from which it broke. That tradition is a living thing. A decision of this Court which radically departs from it could not long survive, while a decision which builds on what has survived is likely to be sound. No formula could serve as a substitute, in this area, for judgment and restraint.

After the *Poe* dissent, as before it, this enforceable concept of liberty would bar statutory impositions even at relatively trivial levels when governmental restraints are undeniably irrational as unsupported by any imaginable rationale. See, e.g., *United States v. Carolene Products Co.* Such instances are suitably rare. The claims of arbitrariness that mark almost all instances of unenumerated substantive rights are those resting on certain interests requir[ing] particularly careful scrutiny of the state needs asserted to justify their abridgment. In the face of an interest this powerful a State may not rest on threshold rationality or a presumption of constitutionality, but may prevail only on the ground of an interest sufficiently compelling to place within the realm of the reasonable a refusal to recognize the individual right asserted.

This approach calls for a court to assess the relative "weights" or dignities of the contending interests, and to this extent the judicial method is familiar to the common law. Common law method is subject, however, to two important constraints in the hands of a court engaged in substantive due process review. First, such a court is bound to confine the values that it recognizes to those truly deserving constitutional stature, either to those expressed in constitutional text, or those exemplified by "the traditions from which [the Nation] developed," or revealed by contrast with "the traditions from which it broke." "We may not draw on our merely personal and private notions and disregard the limits . . . derived from considerations that are fused in the whole nature of our judicial process . . . [,] considerations deeply rooted in reason and in the compelling traditions of the legal profession."

The second constraint, again, simply reflects the fact that constitutional review, not judicial lawmaking, is a court's business here.

The weighing or valuing of contending interests in this sphere is only the first step, forming the basis for determining whether the statute in question falls inside or outside the zone of what is reasonable in the way it resolves the conflict between the interests of state and individual. It is no justification for judicial intervention merely to identify a reasonable resolution of contending values that differs from the terms of the legislation under review. It is only when the legislation's justifying principle, critically valued, is so far from being commensurate with the individual interest as to be arbitrarily or pointlessly applied that the statute must give way. Only if this standard points against the statute can the individual claimant be said to have a constitutional right.

The *Poe* dissent thus reminds us of the nature of review for reasonableness or arbitrariness and the limitations entailed by it. But the opinion cautions against the repetition of past error in another way as well, more by its example than by any particular statement of constitutional method: it reminds us that the process of substantive review by reasoned judgment is one of close criticism going to the details of the opposing interests and to their relationships with the historically recognized principles that lend them weight or value.

Although the *Poe* dissent disclaims the possibility of any general formula for due process analysis (beyond the basic analytic structure just described), Justice Harlan of course assumed that adjudication under the Due Process Clauses is like any other instance of judgment dependent on common law method, being more or less persuasive according to the usual canons of critical discourse. When identifying and assessing the competing interests of liberty and authority, for example, the breadth of expression that a litigant or a judge selects in stating the competing principles will have much to do with the outcome and may be dispositive. As in any process of rational argumentation, we recognize that when a generally accepted principle is challenged, the broader the attack the less likely it is to succeed. . . .

Just as results in substantive due process cases are tied to the selections of statements of the competing interests, the acceptability of the results is a function of the good reasons for the selections made. It is here that the value of common law method becomes apparent, for the usual thinking of the common law is suspicious of the all or nothing analysis that tends to produce legal petrification instead of an evolving boundary between the domains of old principles. Common law method tends to pay respect instead to detail, seeking to understand old principles afresh by new examples and new counterexamples. The "tradition is a living thing," albeit one that moves by moderate steps carefully taken. . . . Exact analysis and characterization of any due process claim is critical to the method and to the result. . . .

The argument supporting respondents' position . . . progresses through three steps of increasing forcefulness. First, it emphasizes the decriminalization of suicide. Reliance on this fact is sanctioned under the standard that looks not only to the tradition retained, but to society's occasional choices to reject traditions of the legal past. While the common law prohibited both suicide and aiding a suicide, with the prohibition on aiding largely justified by the primary prohibition on self inflicted death itself, the State's rejection of the traditional treatment of the one leaves the criminality of the other open to questioning that previously would not have been appropriate. The second step in the argument is to emphasize that the State's own act of decriminalization gives a freedom of choice much like the individual's option in recognized instances of bodily autonomy. One of these, abortion, is a legal right to choose in spite of the interest a State may legitimately invoke in discouraging the practice, just as suicide is now subject to choice, despite a state interest in discouraging it. The third step is to emphasize that respondents claim a right to assistance not on the basis of some broad principle that would be subject to exceptions if that continuing interest of the State's in discouraging suicide were to be recognized at all. Respondents base their claim on the traditional right to medical care and counsel, subject to the limiting conditions of informed, responsible choice when death is imminent, conditions that support a strong analogy to rights of care in other situations in which medical counsel and assistance have been available as a matter of course. There can be no stronger claim to a physician's assistance than at the time when death is imminent, a moral judgment implied by the State's own recognition of the legitimacy of medical procedures necessarily hastening the moment of impending death.

In my judgment, the importance of the individual interest here, as within that class of "certain interests" demanding careful scrutiny of the State's contrary claim, cannot be gainsaid. Whether that interest might in some circumstances, or at some time, be seen as "fundamental" to the degree entitled to prevail is not, however, a conclusion that I need draw here, for I am satisfied that the State's interests described in the following section are sufficiently serious to defeat the present claim that its law is arbitrary or purposeless.

The State has put forward several interests to justify the Washington law as applied to physicians treating terminally ill patients, even those competent to make responsible choices: protecting life generally, discouraging suicide even if knowing and voluntary, and protecting terminally ill patients from involuntary suicide and euthanasia, both voluntary and nonvoluntary.

It is not necessary to discuss the exact strengths of the first two claims of justification in the present circumstances, for the third is dispositive for me. That third justification is different from the first two, for it addresses specific features of respondents' claim, and it opposes that claim not with a moral judgment contrary to respondents', but with a recognized state interest in the protection of nonresponsible individuals and those who do not stand in relation either to death or to their physicians as do the patients whom respondents describe. The State claims interests in protecting patients from mistakenly and involuntarily deciding to end their lives, and in guarding against both voluntary and involuntary euthanasia. Leaving aside any difficulties in coming to a clear concept of imminent death, mistaken decisions may result from inadequate palliative care or a terminal prognosis that turns out to be error; coercion and abuse may stem from the large medical bills that family members cannot bear or unreimbursed hospitals decline to shoulder. Voluntary and involuntary euthanasia may result once doctors are authorized to prescribe lethal medication in the first instance, for they might find it pointless to distinguish between patients who administer their own fatal drugs and those who wish not to, and their compassion for those who suffer may obscure the distinction between those who ask for death and those who may be unable to request it. The argument is that a progression would occur, obscuring the line between the ill and the dying, and between the responsible and the unduly influenced, until ultimately doctors and perhaps others would abuse a limited freedom to aid suicides by yielding to the impulse to end another's suffering under conditions going beyond the narrow limits the respondents propose. The State thus argues, essentially, that respondents' claim is not as narrow as it sounds, simply because no recognition of the interest they assert could be limited to vindicating those interests and affecting no others. The State says that the claim, in practical effect, would entail consequences that the State could, without doubt, legitimately act to prevent.

The mere assertion that the terminally sick might be pressured into suicide decisions by close friends and family members would not alone be very telling. Of course that is possible, not only because the costs of care might be more than family members could bear but simply because they might naturally wish to see an end of suffering for someone they love. But one of the points of restricting any right of assistance to physicians, would be to condition the right on an exercise of judgment by someone qualified to assess the patient's responsible capacity and detect the influence of those outside the medical relationship.

The State, however, goes further, to argue that dependence on the vigilance of physicians will not be enough. First, the lines proposed here (particularly the requirement of a knowing and voluntary decision by the patient) would be more difficult to draw than the lines that have limited other recently recognized due process rights. . . . Second, this difficulty could become the greater by combining with another fact within the realm of plausibility, that physicians simply would not be assiduous to preserve the line. They have compassion, and those who would be willing to assist in suicide at all might be the most susceptible to the wishes of a patient, whether the patient were technically quite responsible or not. Physicians, and their hospitals, have their own financial incentives, too, in this new age of managed care. Whether acting from compassion or under some other influence, a physician who would provide a drug for a patient to administer might well go the further step of administering the drug himself; so, the barrier between assisted suicide and euthanasia could become porous, and the line between voluntary and involuntary euthanasia as well. The case for the slippery slope is fairly made out here, not because recognizing one due process right would leave a court with no principled basis to avoid recognizing another, but because there is a plausible case that the right claimed would not be readily containable by reference to facts about the mind that are matters of difficult judgment, or by gatekeepers who are subject to temptation, noble or not.

Respondents propose an answer to all this, the answer of state regulation with teeth. Legislation proposed in several States, for example, would authorize physician assisted suicide but require two qualified physicians to confirm the patient's diagnosis, prognosis, and competence; and would mandate that the patient make repeated requests witnessed by at least two others over a specified time span; and would impose reporting requirements and criminal penalties for various acts of coercion.

But at least at this moment there are reasons for caution in predicting the effectiveness of the teeth proposed. Respondents' proposals, as it turns out, sound much like the guidelines now in place in the Netherlands, the only place where experience with physician assisted suicide and euthanasia has yielded empirical evidence about how such regulations might affect actual practice. Dutch physicians must engage in consultation before proceeding, and must decide whether the patient's decision is voluntary, well considered, and stable, whether the request to die is enduring and made more than once, and whether the patient's future will involve unacceptable suffering. There is, however, a substantial dispute today about what the Dutch experience shows. Some commentators marshall evidence that the Dutch guidelines have in practice failed to protect patients from involuntary euthanasia and have been violated with impunity. This evidence is contested. The day may come when we can say with some assurance which side is right, but for now it is the substantiality of the factual disagreement, and the alternatives for resolving it, that matter. They are, for me, dispositive of the due process claim at this time.

I take it that the basic concept of judicial review with its possible displacement of legislative judgment bars any finding that a legislature has acted arbitrarily when the following conditions are met: there is a serious factual controversy over the feasibility of recognizing the claimed right without at the same time making it impossible for the State to engage in an undoubtedly legitimate exercise of power; facts necessary to resolve the controversy are not readily ascertainable through the judicial process; but they are more readily subject to discovery through legislative factfinding and experimentation. It is assumed in this case, and must be, that a State's interest in protecting those unable to make responsible decisions and those who make no decisions at all entitles the State to bar aid to any but a knowing and responsible person intending suicide, and to prohibit euthanasia. How, and how far, a State should act in that interest are judgments for the State, but the legitimacy of its action to deny a physician the option to aid any but the knowing and responsible is beyond question.

The capacity of the State to protect the others if respondents were to prevail is, however, subject to some genuine question, underscored by the responsible disagreement over the basic facts of the Dutch experience. This factual controversy is not open to a judicial resolution with any substantial degree of assurance at this time. It is not, of course, that any controversy about the factual predicate of a due process claim disqualifies a court from resolving it. Courts can recognize captiousness, and most factual issues can be settled in a trial court. At this point, however, the factual issue at the heart of this case does not appear to be one of those. The principal enquiry at the moment is into the Dutch experience, and I question whether an independent front line investigation into the facts of a foreign country's legal administration can be soundly undertaken through American courtroom litigation. While an extensive literature on any subject can raise the hopes for judicial understanding, the literature on this subject is only nascent. Since there is little experience directly bearing on the issue, the most that can be said is that whichever way the Court might rule today, events could overtake its assumptions, as experimentation in some jurisdictions confirmed or discredited the concerns about progression from assisted suicide to euthanasia.

Legislatures, on the other hand, have superior opportunities to obtain the facts necessary for a judgment about the present controversy. Not only do they have more flexible mechanisms for factfinding than the Judiciary, but their mechanisms include the power to experiment, moving forward and pulling back as facts emerge within their own jurisdictions. There is, indeed, good reason to suppose that in the absence of a judgment for respondents here, just such experimentation will be attempted in some of the States. See, e.g., Ore. Rev. Stat. Ann. §§ 127.800 et seq.

I do not decide here what the significance might be of legislative foot dragging in ascertaining the facts going to the State's argument that the right in question could not be confined as claimed. Sometimes a court may be bound to act regardless of the institutional preferability of the political branches as forums for addressing constitutional claims. See, e.g., *Bolling v. Sharpe*. Now, it is enough to say that our examination of legislative reasonableness should consider the fact that the Legislature of the State of Washington is no more obviously at fault than this Court is in being uncertain about what would happen if respondents prevailed today. We therefore have a clear question about which institution, a legislature or a court, is relatively more competent to deal with an emerging issue as to which facts currently unknown could be dispositive. The answer has to be, for the reasons already stated, that the legislative process is to be preferred. There is a closely related further reason as well.

One must bear in mind that the nature of the right claimed, if recognized as one constitutionally required, would differ in no essential way from other constitutional rights guaranteed by enumeration or derived from some more definite textual source than "due process." An unenumerated right should not therefore be recognized, with the effect of displacing the legislative ordering of things, without the assurance that its recognition would prove as durable as the recognition of those other rights differently derived. To recognize a right of lesser promise would simply create a constitutional regime too uncertain to bring with it the expectation of finality that is one of this Court's central obligations in making constitutional decisions.

Legislatures, however, are not so constrained. The experimentation that should be out of the question in constitutional adjudication displacing legislative judgments is entirely proper, as well as highly desirable, when the legislative power addresses an emerging issue like assisted suicide. The Court should accordingly stay its hand to allow reasonable legislative consideration. While I do not decide for all time that respondents' claim should not be recognized, I acknowledge the legislative institutional competence as the better one to deal with that claim at this time.

NOTE ON *GLUCKSBERG* AND THE NATURE OF SUBSTANTIVE DUE PROCESS REVIEW

1.   The Court in *Glucksberg* was unanimous in refusing to strike down the Washington statute by recognizing a broad and fundamental right to physician-assisted suicide. Was the Court correct in refusing to extend *Casey, Griswold*, and the other privacy cases to this situation? Can we really say that the choice faced by a terminal cancer patient is any less profound than the decision of a couple to use contraception? Or is the Court saying rather that it is not in as good a position to make these sorts of judgments as a state legislature?

2.   Justice Stevens' concurrence in *Glucksberg* relies on the distinction that draws between a "facial" and an "as-applied" challenge to the Washington law.[9] Recall that a facial challenge requires the plaintiff to demonstrate that the law in question has very few, if any, constitutional applications; an as-applied challenge requires only a showing that the law is unconstitutional in application to the particular circumstances before the court.

As Justice Stevens notes, the Justices have sometimes disagreed as to the proper standard to apply to facial challenges. But all agree that facial challenges are more difficult to win than as-applied ones. Hence, while Justice Stevens is unwilling to say that the Washington statute is

---

[9]   *See also* Section 9.1, *supra*.

unconstitutional on its face, he reserves the possibility that it might be unconstitutional as applied in certain circumstances. What circumstances do you think would suffice to render the statute unconstitutional? Is Justice O'Connor right in assuming that, by allowing terminal patients to take palliative drugs even though those drugs may hasten death, the statute actually does not apply to most circumstances that might implicate a patient's fundamental rights?

3. Justice Souter's concurrence in *Glucksberg* features a useful summary of the history of substantive due process. That account serves two primary purposes (other than providing an excellent review of much of this course). First, it connects the textual guarantee of "due process of law" with not only the practice of the state courts and the U.S. Supreme Court in the early Republic, but also the English law principle that government may act only "by the law of the land." This effectively provides an *originalist* pedigree for substantive due process that had been lacking in earlier cases. Is it persuasive?

Second, the origins of substantive due process in judicial invalidation of arbitrary or irrational governmental action help shape the modern contours of substantive due process review. For Justice Souter, the "tiers of scrutiny" in modern doctrine simply crystallize a more fundamental reasonableness analysis; applying "strict scrutiny" to infringements of "fundamental rights," in other words, simply reflects a judicial judgment that, in that particular context, government restrictions are unlikely to be reasonable.

Is the majority in *Glucksberg* right to reject Justice Souter's suggestion that substantive due process ultimately boils down to a question of reasonableness in all cases? Does the fine-grained analysis that Souter undertakes of the physician-assisted suicide question repose too much faith in that ability of judicial judgment to constrain itself? Consider this issue in relation to the similar debate, in the last chapter, between Justices Stevens and Marshall and the rest of the Court as to the utility of tiers of scrutiny in equal protection analysis.

4. Notwithstanding *Glucksberg*'s cautious approach to recognizing new rights, the Rehnquist Court proved willing to expand the scope of substantive due process along a number of dimensions. The most prominent examples involved rights of family and sexual privacy; in particular, the Court decided a string of important cases protecting the rights of gays and lesbians.[10] It also revived, to at least some extent, the Court's traditional concern for economic liberty.[11] Alongside the identification of new rights, however, the Court also confronted a stream of cases concerning what it means to *restrict* a right. The next case addresses that question.

---

[10] *See infra* Chapter Seventeen. *See also* Troxel v. Granville, 530 U.S. 57 (2000) (striking down a state law permitting courts to confer visitation rights on grandparents notwithstanding parental objections as an interference with the fundamental right of parents to raise their children).

[11] *See infra* Section 16.3.

Rust v. Sullivan

500 U.S. 173 (1991)

■ CHIEF JUSTICE REHNQUIST delivered the opinion of the Court.

These cases concern a facial challenge to Department of Health and Human Services (HHS) regulations which limit the ability of Title X fund recipients to engage in abortion-related activities. The United States Court of Appeals for the Second Circuit upheld the regulations, finding them to be a permissible construction of the statute as well as consistent with the First and Fifth Amendments to the Constitution. . . . We affirm.

I

A

In 1970, Congress enacted Title X of the Public Health Service Act (Act), 84 Stat. 1506, as amended, 42 U.S.C. §§ 300 to 300a–6, which provides federal funding for family-planning services. The Act authorizes the Secretary to "make grants to and enter into contracts with public or nonprofit private entities to assist in the establishment and operation of voluntary family planning projects which shall offer a broad range of acceptable and effective family planning methods and services." § 300(a). Grants and contracts under Title X must "be made in accordance with such regulations as the Secretary may promulgate." § 300a–4(a). Section 1008 of the Act, however, provides that "[n]one of the funds appropriated under this subchapter shall be used in programs where abortion is a method of family planning." 42 U.S.C. § 300a–6. That restriction was intended to ensure that Title X funds would "be used only to support preventive family planning services, population research, infertility services, and other related medical, informational, and educational activities." H.R.Conf.Rep. No. 91–1667, p. 8 (1970).

In 1988, the Secretary promulgated new regulations designed to provide " 'clear and operational guidance' to grantees about how to preserve the distinction between Title X The regulations clarify, through the definition of the term "family planning," that Congress intended Title X funds "to be used only to support *preventive* family planning services." H.R.Conf.Rep. No. 91–1667, p. 8. Accordingly, Title X services are limited to "preconceptional counseling, education, and general reproductive health care," and expressly exclude "pregnancy care (including obstetric or prenatal care)." 42 CFR § 59.2 (1989).[2] The regulations "focus the emphasis of the Title X program on its traditional mission: The provision of preventive family planning services specifically designed to enable individuals to determine the number and spacing of their children, while clarifying that pregnant women must be referred to appropriate prenatal care services." 53 Fed.Reg. 2925 (1988).

---

[2] "Most clients of title X-sponsored clinics are not pregnant and generally receive only physical examinations, education on contraceptive methods, and services related to birth control." General Accounting Office Report.

The regulations attach three principal conditions on the grant of federal funds for Title X projects. First, the regulations specify that a "Title X project may not provide counseling concerning the use of abortion as a method of family planning or provide referral for abortion as a method of family planning." 42 CFR § 59.8(a)(1) (1989). Because Title X is limited to preconceptional services, the program does not furnish services related to childbirth. Only in the context of a referral out of the Title X program is a pregnant woman given transitional information. § 59.8(a)(2). Title X projects must refer every pregnant client "for appropriate prenatal and/or social services by furnishing a list of available providers that promote the welfare of mother and unborn child." The list may not be used indirectly to encourage or promote abortion, "such as by weighing the list of referrals in favor of health care providers which perform abortions, by including on the list of referral providers health care providers whose principal business is the provision of abortions, by excluding available providers who do not provide abortions, or by 'steering' clients to providers who offer abortion as a method of family planning." § 59.8(a)(3). The Title X project is expressly prohibited from referring a pregnant woman to an abortion provider, even upon specific request. One permissible response to such an inquiry is that "the project does not consider abortion an appropriate method of family planning and therefore does not counsel or refer for abortion." § 59.8(b)(5).

Second, the regulations broadly prohibit a Title X project from engaging in activities that "encourage, promote or advocate abortion as a method of family planning." § 59.10(a). Forbidden activities include lobbying for legislation that would increase the availability of abortion as a method of family planning, developing or disseminating materials advocating abortion as a method of family planning, providing speakers to promote abortion as a method of family planning, using legal action to make abortion available in any way as a method of family planning, and paying dues to any group that advocates abortion as a method of family planning as a substantial part of its activities.

Third, the regulations require that Title X projects be organized so that they are "physically and financially separate" from prohibited abortion activities. § 59.9. To be deemed physically and financially separate, "a Title X project must have an objective integrity and independence from prohibited activities. Mere bookkeeping separation of Title X funds from other monies is not sufficient." The regulations provide a list of nonexclusive factors for the Secretary to consider in conducting a case-by-case determination of objective integrity and independence, such as the existence of separate accounting records and separate personnel, and the degree of physical separation of the project from facilities for prohibited activities.

B

Petitioners are Title X grantees and doctors who supervise Title X funds suing on behalf of themselves and their patients. Respondent is the Secretary of HHS. After the regulations had been promulgated, but before they had been applied, petitioners filed two separate actions, later consolidated, challenging the facial validity of the regulations and seeking declaratory and injunctive relief to prevent implementation of the regulations. Petitioners challenged the regulations on the grounds that they were not authorized by Title X and that they violate the First and Fifth Amendment rights of Title X clients and the First Amendment rights of Title X health providers. After initially granting petitioners a preliminary injunction, the District Court rejected petitioners' statutory and constitutional challenges to the regulations and granted summary judgment in favor of the Secretary.

A panel of the Court of Appeals for the Second Circuit affirmed. . . . [It] rejected petitioners' Fifth Amendment challenge. It held that the regulations do not impermissibly burden a woman's right to an abortion because the "government may validly choose to favor childbirth over abortion and to implement that choice by funding medical services relating to childbirth but not those relating to abortion." Finding that the prohibition on the performance of abortions upheld by the Court in *Webster v. Reproductive Health Services,* 492 U.S. 490 (1989), was "substantially greater in impact than the regulations challenged in the instant matter," the court concluded that the regulations "create[d] no affirmative legal barriers to access to abortion."

The court likewise found that the "Secretary's implementation of Congress's decision not to fund abortion counseling, referral or advocacy also does not, under applicable Supreme Court precedent, constitute a facial violation of the First Amendment rights of health care providers or of women." . . .

II

We begin by pointing out the posture of the cases before us. Petitioners are challenging the *facial* validity of the regulations. Thus, we are concerned only with the question whether, on their face, the regulations are both authorized by the Act and can be construed in such a manner that they can be applied to a set of individuals without infringing upon constitutionally protected rights. Petitioners face a heavy burden in seeking to have the regulations invalidated as facially unconstitutional. "A facial challenge to a legislative Act is, of course, the most difficult challenge to mount successfully, since the challenger must establish that no set of circumstances exists under which the Act would be valid. The fact that [the regulations] might operate unconstitutionally under some conceivable set of circumstances is insufficient to render [them] wholly invalid." *United States v. Salerno,* 481 U.S. 739, 745 (1987).

[The Court rejected petitioners' contention that the regulations exceed the Secretary's authority under Title X and are arbitrary and capricious.]

III

Petitioners contend that the regulations violate the First Amendment by impermissibly discriminating based on viewpoint because they prohibit "all discussion about abortion as a lawful option— including counseling, referral, and the provision of neutral and accurate information about ending a pregnancy—while compelling the clinic or counselor to provide information that promotes continuing a pregnancy to term." They assert that the regulations violate the "free speech rights of private health care organizations that receive Title X funds, of their staff, and of their patients" by impermissibly imposing "viewpoint-discriminatory conditions on government subsidies" and thus "penaliz[e] speech funded with non-Title X monies." Because "Title X continues to fund speech ancillary to pregnancy testing in a manner that is not evenhanded with respect to views and information about abortion, it invidiously discriminates on the basis of viewpoint." Relying on *Regan v. Taxation with Representation of Wash.,* 461 U.S. 540 (1983) . . . petitioners also assert that while the Government may place certain conditions on the receipt of federal subsidies, it may not "discriminate invidiously in its subsidies in such a way as to 'ai[m] at the suppression of dangerous ideas.'" *Regan, supra,* 461 U.S., at 548.

There is no question but that the statutory prohibition contained in § 1008 is constitutional. In *Maher v. Roe,* 432 U.S. 464 (1977), we upheld a state welfare regulation under which Medicaid recipients received payments for services related to childbirth, but not for nontherapeutic abortions. The Court rejected the claim that this unequal subsidization worked a violation of the Constitution. We held that the government may "make a value judgment favoring childbirth over abortion, and . . . implement that judgment by the allocation of public funds." Here the Government is exercising the authority it possesses under *Maher* and *Harris v. McRae,* 448 U.S. 297 (1980), to subsidize family planning services which will lead to conception and childbirth, and declining to "promote or encourage abortion." The Government can, without violating the Constitution, selectively fund a program to encourage certain activities it believes to be in the public interest, without at the same time funding an alternative program which seeks to deal with the problem in another way. In so doing, the Government has not discriminated on the basis of viewpoint; it has merely chosen to fund one activity to the exclusion of the other. "[A] legislature's decision not to subsidize the exercise of a fundamental right does not infringe the right." *Regan, supra,* 461 U.S., at 549. "A refusal to fund protected activity, without more, cannot be equated with the imposition of a 'penalty' on that activity." *McRae, supra,* 448 U.S., at 317, n. 19. "There is a basic difference between direct state interference with a protected activity and state encouragement of an alternative activity consonant with legislative policy." *Maher, supra,* 432 U.S., at 475.

The challenged regulations implement the statutory prohibition by prohibiting counseling, referral, and the provision of information regarding abortion as a method of family planning. They are designed to ensure that the limits of the federal program are observed. The Title X program is designed not for prenatal care, but to encourage family planning. A doctor who wished to offer prenatal care to a project patient who became pregnant could properly be prohibited from doing so because such service is outside the scope of the federally funded program. The regulations prohibiting abortion counseling and referral are of the same ilk; "no funds appropriated for the project may be used in programs where abortion is a method of family planning," and a doctor employed by the project may be prohibited in the course of his project duties from counseling abortion or referring for abortion. This is not a case of the Government "suppressing a dangerous idea," but of a prohibition on a project grantee or its employees from engaging in activities outside of the project's scope.

To hold that the Government unconstitutionally discriminates on the basis of viewpoint when it chooses to fund a program dedicated to advance certain permissible goals, because the program in advancing those goals necessarily discourages alternative goals, would render numerous Government programs constitutionally suspect. When Congress established a National Endowment for Democracy to encourage other countries to adopt democratic principles, 22 U.S.C. § 4411(b), it was not constitutionally required to fund a program to encourage competing lines of political philosophy such as communism and fascism. Petitioners' assertions ultimately boil down to the position that if the government chooses to subsidize one protected right, it must subsidize analogous counterpart rights. But the Court has soundly rejected that proposition. *Regan v. Taxation with Representation of Wash., supra; Maher v. Roe, supra; Harris v. McRae, supra.* Within far broader limits than petitioners are willing to concede, when the Government appropriates public funds to establish a program it is entitled to define the limits of that program. . . .

Petitioners rely heavily on their claim that the regulations would not, in the circumstance of a medical emergency, permit a Title X project to refer a woman whose pregnancy places her life in imminent peril to a provider of abortions or abortion-related services. These cases, of course, involve only a facial challenge to the regulations, and we do not have before us any application by the Secretary to a specific fact situation. On their face, we do not read the regulations to bar abortion referral or counseling in such circumstances. Abortion counseling as a "method of family planning" is prohibited, and it does not seem that a medically necessitated abortion in such circumstances would be the equivalent of its use as a "method of family planning." Neither § 1008 nor the specific restrictions of the regulations would apply. Moreover, the regulations themselves contemplate that a Title X project would be permitted to engage in otherwise-prohibited abortion-related, activity in such circumstances. Section 59.8(a)(2) provides a specific exemption for emergency care and requires Title X recipients "to refer the client immediately to an appropriate provider of emergency medical services." Section 59.5(b)(1) also requires Title X projects to provide "necessary referral to other medical facilities when medically indicated."[4]

Petitioners also contend that the restrictions on the subsidization of abortion-related speech contained in the regulations are impermissible because they condition the receipt of a benefit, in these cases Title X funding, on the relinquishment of a constitutional right, the right to engage in abortion advocacy and counseling. Relying on *Perry v. Sindermann,* 408 U.S. 593, 597 (1972), and *FCC v. League of Women Voters of Cal.,* 468 U.S. 364 (1984), petitioners argue that "even though the government may deny [a] . . . benefit for any number of reasons, there are some reasons upon which the government may not rely. It may not deny a benefit to a person on a basis that infringes his constitutionally protected interests—especially, his interest in freedom of speech." *Perry, supra,* 408 U.S., at 597.

Petitioners' reliance on these cases is unavailing, however, because here the Government is not denying a benefit to anyone, but is instead simply insisting that public funds be spent for the purposes for which they were authorized. The Secretary's regulations do not force the Title X grantee to give up abortion-related speech; they merely require that the grantee keep such activities separate and distinct from Title X activities. Title X expressly distinguishes between a Title X *grantee* and a Title X *project.* The grantee, which normally is a health-care organization, may receive funds from a variety of sources for a variety of purposes. The grantee receives Title X funds, however, for the specific and limited purpose of establishing and operating a Title X project. The regulations govern the scope of the Title X *project's* activities, and leave the grantee unfettered in its other activities. The Title X *grantee* can continue to perform abortions, provide abortion-related services, and engage in abortion advocacy; it simply is required to conduct those activities through programs that are separate and independent from the project that receives Title X funds.

---

[4] We also find that, on their face, the regulations are narrowly tailored to fit Congress' intent in Title X that federal funds not be used to "promote or advocate" abortion as a "method of family planning." The regulations are designed to ensure compliance with the prohibition of § 1008 that none of the funds appropriated under Title X be used in a program where abortion is a method of family planning. We have recognized that Congress' power to allocate funds for public purposes includes an ancillary power to ensure that those funds are properly applied to the prescribed use. See *South Dakota v. Dole,* 483 U.S. 203, 207–209 (1987) (upholding against Tenth Amendment challenge requirement that States raise drinking age as condition to receipt of federal highway funds).

In contrast, our "unconstitutional conditions" cases involve situations in which the Government has placed a condition on the *recipient* of the subsidy rather than on a particular program or service, thus effectively prohibiting the recipient from engaging in the protected conduct outside the scope of the federally funded program. In *FCC v. League of Women Voters of Cal.,* we invalidated a federal law providing that noncommercial television and radio stations that receive federal grants may not "engage in editorializing." Under that law, a recipient of federal funds was "barred absolutely from all editorializing" because it "is not able to segregate its activities according to the source of its funding" and thus "has no way of limiting the use of its federal funds to all noneditorializing activities." The effect of the law was that "a noncommercial educational station that receives only 1% of its overall income from [federal] grants is barred absolutely from all editorializing" and "barred from using even wholly private funds to finance its editorial activity." We expressly recognized, however, that were Congress to permit the recipient stations to "establish 'affiliate' organizations which could then use the station's facilities to editorialize with nonfederal funds, such a statutory mechanism would plainly be valid." Such a scheme would permit the station "to make known its views on matters of public importance through its nonfederally funded, editorializing affiliate without losing federal grants for its noneditorializing broadcast activities."

Similarly, in *Regan* we held that Congress could, in the exercise of its spending power, reasonably refuse to subsidize the lobbying activities of tax-exempt charitable organizations by prohibiting such organizations from using tax-deductible contributions to support their lobbying efforts. In so holding, we explained that such organizations remained free "to receive deductible contributions to support . . . nonlobbying activit[ies]." Thus, a charitable organization could create, under § 501(c)(3) of the Internal Revenue Code of 1954, an affiliate to conduct its nonlobbying activities using tax-deductible contributions, and at the same time establish, under § 501(c)(4), a separate affiliate to pursue its lobbying efforts without such contributions. Given that alternative, the Court concluded that "Congress has not infringed any First Amendment rights or regulated any First Amendment activity[; it] has simply chosen not to pay for [appellee's] lobbying." We also noted that appellee "would, of course, have to ensure that the § 501(c)(3) organization did not subsidize the § 501(c)(4) organization; otherwise, public funds might be spent on an activity Congress chose not to subsidize." The condition that federal funds will be used only to further the purposes of a grant does not violate constitutional rights. "Congress could, for example, grant funds to an organization dedicated to combating teenage drug abuse, but condition the grant by providing that none of the money received from Congress should be used to lobby state legislatures."

By requiring that the Title X grantee engage in abortion-related activity separately from activity receiving federal funding, Congress has, consistent with our teachings in *League of Women Voters* and *Regan,* not denied it the right to engage in abortion-related activities. Congress has merely refused to fund such activities out of the public fisc, and the Secretary has simply required a certain degree of separation from the Title X project in order to ensure the integrity of the federally funded program.

The same principles apply to petitioners' claim that the regulations abridge the free speech rights of the grantee's staff. . . .

This is not to suggest that funding by the Government, even when coupled with the freedom of the fund recipients to speak outside the scope of the Government-funded project, is invariably sufficient to justify Government control over the content of expression. For example, this Court has recognized that the existence of a Government "subsidy," in the form of Government-owned property, does not justify the restriction of speech in areas that have been traditionally open to the public for expressive activity or have been expressly dedicated to speech activity. . . .

IV

We turn now to petitioners' argument that the regulations violate a woman's Fifth Amendment right to choose whether to terminate her pregnancy. We recently reaffirmed the long-recognized principle that "the Due Process Clauses generally confer no affirmative right to governmental aid, even where such aid may be necessary to secure life, liberty, or property interests of which the government itself may not deprive the individual." *Webster v. Reproductive Health Services,* 492 U.S. 490, 507 (1989). The Government has no constitutional duty to subsidize an activity merely because the activity is constitutionally protected and may validly choose to fund childbirth over abortion and " 'implement that judgment by the allocation of public funds' " for medical services relating to childbirth but not to those relating to abortion. The Government has no affirmative duty to "commit any resources to facilitating abortions," and its decision to fund childbirth but not abortion "places no governmental obstacle in the path of a woman who chooses to terminate her pregnancy, but rather, by means of unequal subsidization of abortion and other medical services, encourages alternative activity deemed in the public interest." *Harris v. McRae,* 448 U.S. 297, 315 (1980).

That the regulations do not impermissibly burden a woman's Fifth Amendment rights is evident from the line of cases beginning with Maher and McRae and culminating in our most recent decision in *Webster.* Just as Congress' refusal to fund abortions in *McRae* left "an indigent woman with at least the same range of choice in deciding whether to obtain a medically necessary abortion as she would have had if Congress had chosen to subsidize no health care costs at all," 448 U.S., at 317, and "Missouri's refusal to allow public employees to perform abortions in public hospitals leaves a pregnant woman with the same choices as if the State had chosen not to operate any public hospitals," *Webster, supra,* 492 U.S., at 509, Congress' refusal to fund abortion counseling and advocacy leaves a pregnant woman with the same choices as if the Government had chosen not to fund family-planning services at all. The difficulty that a woman encounters when a Title X project does not provide abortion counseling or referral leaves her in no different position than she would have been if the Government had not enacted Title X.

In *Webster,* we stated that "[h]aving held that the State's refusal [in *Maher*] to fund abortions does not violate *Roe v. Wade,* it strains logic to reach a contrary result for the use of public facilities and employees." It similarly would strain logic, in light of the more extreme restrictions in those cases, to find that the mere decision to exclude abortion-related services from a federally funded *preconceptional* family planning program is unconstitutional. . . .

Petitioners contend, however, that most Title X clients are effectively precluded by indigency and poverty from seeing a health-care provider who will provide abortion-related services. But once again, even these Title X clients are in no worse position than if Congress had never enacted Title X. "The financial constraints that restrict an indigent woman's ability to enjoy the full range of constitutionally protected freedom of choice are the product not of governmental restrictions on access to abortion, but rather of her indigency." *McRae, supra,* 448 U.S., at 316.

The Secretary's regulations are a permissible construction of Title X and do not violate either the First or Fifth Amendments to the Constitution. Accordingly, the judgment of the Court of Appeals is

Affirmed.

■ JUSTICE BLACKMUN, with whom JUSTICE MARSHALL joins, with whom JUSTICE STEVENS joins as to Parts II and III, and with whom JUSTICE O'CONNOR joins as to Part I, dissenting.

. . . I conclude that the Secretary's regulation of referral, advocacy, and counseling activities exceeds his statutory authority, and, also, that the regulations violate the First and Fifth Amendments of our Constitution. Accordingly, I dissent . . . .

Until today, the Court never has upheld viewpoint-based suppression of speech simply because that suppression was a condition upon the acceptance of public funds. Whatever may be the Government's power to condition the receipt of its largess upon the relinquishment of constitutional rights, it surely does not extend to a condition that suppresses the recipient's cherished freedom of speech based solely upon the content or viewpoint of that speech. This rule is a sound one, for, as the Court often has noted: " 'A regulation of speech that is motivated by nothing more than a desire to curtail expression of a particular point of view on controversial issues of general interest is the purest example of a "law . . . abridging the freedom of speech, or of the press." ' " *League of Women Voters,* 468 U.S., at 383–384. . . .

Nothing in the Court's opinion in *Regan v. Taxation with Representation of Washington,* 461 U.S. 540 (1983), can be said to challenge this long-settled understanding. . . . [T]he Court explained: "The case would be different if Congress were to discriminate invidiously in its subsidies in such a way as to aim at the suppression of dangerous ideas. . . . We find no indication that the statute was intended to suppress any ideas or any demonstration that it has had that effect." . . .

It cannot seriously be disputed that the counseling and referral provisions at issue in the present cases constitute content-based regulation of speech. Title X grantees may provide counseling and referral regarding any of a wide range of family planning and other topics, save abortion. . . .

The regulations are also clearly viewpoint based. While suppressing speech favorable to abortion with one hand, the Secretary compels antiabortion speech with the other. . . .

By far the most disturbing aspect of today's ruling is the effect it will have on the Fifth Amendment rights of the women who, supposedly, are beneficiaries of Title X programs. The majority rejects petitioners' Fifth Amendment claims summarily. It relies primarily upon the decisions in *Harris v. McRae,* 448 U.S. 297 (1980), and *Webster v. Reproductive Health Services,* 492 U.S. 490 (1989). There were dissents in those cases, and we continue to believe that they were wrongly and unfortunately decided. Be that as it may, even if one accepts as valid the Court's theorizing in those cases, the majority's reasoning in the present cases is flawed.

Until today, the Court has allowed to stand only those restrictions upon reproductive freedom that, while limiting the availability of abortion, have left intact a woman's ability to decide without coercion whether she will continue her pregnancy to term. *Maher v. Roe, McRae,* and *Webster* are all to this effect. Today's decision abandons that principle, and with disastrous results.

Contrary to the majority's characterization, this is not a situation in which individuals seek Government aid in exercising their fundamental rights. The Fifth Amendment right asserted by petitioners is the right of a pregnant woman to be free from affirmative governmental *interference* in her decision. *Roe v. Wade,* 410 U.S. 113 (1973), and its progeny are not so much about a medical procedure as they are about a woman's fundamental right to self-determination. Those cases serve to vindicate the idea that "liberty," if it means anything, must entail freedom from governmental domination in making the most intimate and personal of decisions. See, *e.g., Akron v. Akron Center for Reproductive Health, Inc.,* 462 U.S. 416, 444 (1983) (governmental interest in ensuring that pregnant women receive medically relevant information "will not justify abortion regulations designed to influence the woman's informed choice between abortion or childbirth"). By suppressing medically pertinent information and injecting a restrictive ideological message unrelated to considerations of maternal health, the Government places formidable obstacles in the path of Title X clients' freedom of choice and thereby violates their Fifth Amendment rights.

It is crystal clear that the aim of the challenged provisions—an aim the majority cannot escape noticing—is not simply to ensure that federal funds are not used to perform abortions, but to "reduce the incidence of abortion." 42 CFR § 59.2 (1990) (in definition of "family planning"). As recounted above, the regulations require Title X physicians and counselors to provide information pertaining only to childbirth, to refer a pregnant woman for prenatal care irrespective of her medical situation, and, upon direct inquiry, to respond that abortion is not an "appropriate method" of family planning.

The undeniable message conveyed by this forced speech, and the one that the Title X client will draw from it, is that abortion nearly always is an improper medical option. Although her physician's words, in fact, are strictly controlled by the Government and wholly unrelated to her particular medical situation, the Title X client will reasonably construe them as professional advice to forgo her right to obtain an abortion. As would most rational patients, many of these women will follow that perceived advice and carry their pregnancy to term, despite their needs to the contrary and despite the safety of the abortion procedure for the vast majority of them. Others, delayed by the regulations' mandatory prenatal referral, will be prevented from acquiring abortions during the period in which the process is medically sound and constitutionally protected.

In view of the inevitable effect of the regulations, the majority's conclusion that "[t]he difficulty that a woman encounters when a Title X project does not provide abortion counseling or referral leaves her in no different position than she would have been if the Government had not enacted Title X," is insensitive and contrary to common human experience. Both the purpose and result of the challenged regulations are to deny women the ability voluntarily to decide their procreative destiny. For these women, the Government will have obliterated the freedom to choose as surely as if it had banned abortions outright. The denial of this freedom is not a consequence of poverty but of the Government's ill-intentioned distortion of information it has chosen to provide. . . .

While technically leaving intact the fundamental right protected by *Roe v. Wade,* the Court, "through a relentlessly formalistic catechism," *McRae,* 448 U.S., at 341 (MARSHALL, J., dissenting), once again has rendered the right's substance nugatory. This is a course nearly as noxious as overruling *Roe* directly, for if a right is found to be unenforceable, even against flagrant attempts by government to circumvent it, then it ceases to be a right at all. This, I fear, may be the effect of today's decision.

■ **Justice Stevens, dissenting.**

. . . Because I am convinced that the 1970 Act did not authorize the Secretary to censor the speech of grant recipients or their employees, I would hold the challenged regulations invalid and reverse the judgment of the Court of Appeals.

Even if I thought the statute were ambiguous, however, I would reach the same result for the reasons stated in Justice O'CONNOR's dissenting opinion. As she also explains, if a majority of the Court had reached this result, it would be improper to comment on the constitutional issues that the parties have debated. Because the majority has reached out to decide the constitutional questions, however, I am persuaded that Justice BLACKMUN is correct in concluding that the majority's arguments merit a response. I am also persuaded that Justice BLACKMUN has correctly analyzed these issues. I have therefore joined Parts II and III of his opinion.

■ **Justice O'Connor, dissenting.**

. . . In these cases, we need only tell the Secretary that his regulations are not a reasonable interpretation of the statute; we need not tell Congress that it cannot pass such legislation. If we rule solely on statutory grounds, Congress retains the power to force the constitutional question by legislating more explicitly. It may instead choose to do nothing. That decision should be left to Congress; we should not tell Congress what it cannot do before it has chosen to do it. It is enough in this litigation to conclude that neither the language nor the history of § 1008 compels the Secretary's interpretation, and that the interpretation raises serious First Amendment concerns. On this basis alone, I would reverse the judgment of the Court of Appeals and invalidate the challenged regulations.

Note on Individual Rights and Unconstitutional Conditions

1. *Rust v. Sullivan* is an example of the "unconstitutional condition" problem; it asks whether, although providers of family-planning services have no constitutional right to federal funding, the Constitution nonetheless restricts the government's ability to condition that funding on the providers' agreement forego their right, under the First Amendment, to counsel their patients regarding abortion options. We first encountered the unconstitutional conditions doctrine in Chapter Nine in connection with the Spending Clause. In that context, the question is when Congress may condition federal funds on a *state*'s consent to federal requirements that, under the anti-commandeering doctrine, Congress could not impose directly. The unconstitutional conditions doctrine has not been particularly strict in

the federalism context. Should it be more rigorous when individual rights are at stake?

2.   The unconstitutional conditions problem often raises the question whether government must provide funds to facilitate the exercise of fundamental rights. As an example of the latter question, the Title X grantees in *Rust* also argued that the regulations violated their counselees' right to an abortion under the Due Process Clause. This argument was largely foreclosed by the Court's previous decision in *Harris v. McRae*, 448 U.S. 297 (1980). The *Harris* plaintiffs challenged the Hyde Amendment, which forbade federal funding of abortions under Medicaid. The Court rejected the argument that, because Medicaid provided funds for childbirth but not for abortion, the Hyde Amendment effectively deprived indigent women of any real choice whether to terminate their pregnancies: "[A]lthough government may not place obstacles in the path of a woman's exercise of her freedom of choice," the Court said, "it need not remove those not of its own creation. Indigency falls in the latter category." Hence, the Due Process Clause "does not confer an entitlement to such funds as may be necessary to realize all the advantages of that freedom [to choose]."

This public funding question occurs in a variety of contexts in constitutional law, and it often cuts across ideological lines. In a classic article, for example, Michael McConnell argued that the abortion funding question in *Harris* and disputes over entitlement to government funding for religious schools "seem to pose the same question of constitutional law: when is the government's refusal to fund a constitutionally protected choice an impermissible 'burden' on the exercise of the right?"[12] He explained:

> In both cases, the Constitution protects the right to decide for oneself—whether to have an abortion or to carry the child to term, and whether to obtain a religious or a secular education for one's children. And in both cases, the government funds one alternative and not the other: the Hyde Amendment to the Medicaid Act prohibits the use of federal funds to perform abortions, and a series of Supreme Court decisions, of which *Lemon v. Kurtzman*[13] is the most prominent, effectively prohibit the use of government funds for religious schools.

> More interestingly, the arguments made by proponents of abortion funding and religious education funding are essentially the same.[14]

Professor McConnell illustrated this congruence by paraphrasing Justice Brennan's dissent in *Harris* as it would look if the argument were instead for funding of religious education:

> A poor woman [with school-age children] confronts two alternatives: she may elect either to [send them to secular schools] or to [send them to religious schools]. In the abstract, of course, this

---

[12] Michael W. McConnell, *The Selective Funding Problem: Abortions and Religious Schools*, 104 HARV. L. REV. 989, 989 (1991).

[13] 403 U.S. 602 (1971).

[14] McConnell, *supra* note 12, at 989–90.

choice is hers alone, and the Court rightly observes that [*Lemon*] "places no governmental obstacle in the path of a woman who chooses to [send her children to religious school]." But the reality of the situation is that [*Lemon*] has effectively removed this choice from the indigent woman's hands. By funding all of the expenses associated with [secular education] and none of the expenses incurred in [religious education], the Government literally makes an offer that the indigent woman cannot afford to refuse. . . . [M]any poverty-stricken women will choose to [send their children to secular schools] simply because the Government provides funds for [this], even though these same women would have chosen [religious schools] if the Government had also paid for that option, or indeed if the Government has stayed out of the picture altogether and had defrayed the costs of neither . . . .[15]

As Professor McConnell notes, Justice Brennan and other liberals would surely reject this argument for funding religious school, just as most conservatives who favor such funding nonetheless endorse *Harris*'s holding denying funding for abortions. Arguments like McConnell's can help keep us honest: If you think the Constitution requires government funding in one context but not the other, can you make a principled argument explaining why?[16]

3.   Courts and scholars have approached the unconstitutional conditions problem in a variety of ways.[17] Justice Oliver Wendell Holmes, for instance, viewed the unconstitutional conditions "problem" as no problem at all; for him, the greater power to deny a benefit included the lesser power to condition that benefit on waiver of a constitutional right.[18] Modern courts and scholars typically acknowledge that such conditions do pose a problem. Many analyses emphasize one or the other of the following themes:

Subsidy/Penalty: Cases like *Harris* distinguish between a policy choice not to subsidize a particular activity (e.g., subsidizing childbirth but not abortion), and the imposition of penalties on constitutionally-protected activity. Hence, *Shapiro v. Thompson* in the last chapter viewed the denial of welfare benefits to new arrivals in a state not as a refusal to subsidize those persons, but rather as a penalty on the exercise of their protected right to interstate travel. Distinguishing between subsidies and penalties requires establishing some baseline of "normal" government treatment; once established, benefits that rise above the baseline are gratuitous subsidies, and denials of reasonably-expected benefits are penalties. The trouble, as Cass Sunstein has observed, is that "generating the appropriate baselines

---

[15]   *Id.* at 990. Bracketed text reflects McConnell's alterations to 448 U.S. at 333–34 (Brennan, J., dissenting).

[16]   One possible ground of distinction would rest on *Lemon*'s holding that public funding of religious education violates the Establishment Clause of the First Amendment. But that broad holding is no longer good law. *See Zelman v. Simmons-Harris*, 536 U.S. 639 (2002).

[17]   *See, e.g.*, Kathleen Sullivan, *Unconstitutional Conditions*, 102 HARV. L. REV. 1413 (1989); Richard Epstein, *Foreword: Unconstitutional Conditions, State Power and the Limits of Consent*, 102 HARV. L. REV. 4 (1988).

[18]   *See* Section 9.3, *supra* (discussing Holmes's view in *McAuliffe v. Mayor of New Bedford*, 155 Mass. 216, 220 (1892)).

from which to distinguish subsidies from penalties is exceptionally difficult."[19] For instance, in *Rust* and *Harris*, is the baseline that modern government subsidizes all reproductive healthcare (and counseling regarding such care), including abortion? Or is it, as the Court apparently thought, that private individuals are ordinarily on their own?

Germaneness/Nexus: Other approaches have examined the relation between the condition on a government benefit and the reason for providing that benefit in the first place. In *Nollan v. California Coastal Comm'n*, 483 U.S. 825 (1987), for example, the Court considered whether a state-imposed condition on a development permit effected a taking of property without just compensation in violation. The Nollans wished to replace their beachfront bungalow with a larger home, for which they needed a permit from the Commission. The Commission, however, conditioned the grant of the permit (to which the Nollans had no constitutional entitlement) on their surrender of an easement to the public to pass over their property along the beach (a requirement that would have been a taking if simply imposed by the state without the Nollans' consent). The Court found the condition unconstitutional because although the Commission could legitimately have withheld the development permit based on its interest in preserving views of the beach, the beachfront pedestrian easement that the Commission had required did not further that interest. Instead, the Commission had simply used their control over the development permit as leverage to extract a different benefit that the Commission desired, but had no right to take without compensation. The lack of a "nexus" between the government benefit and the condition imposed on that benefit thus required the Court to treat the condition as an outright requirement, which violated the Takings Clause.[20] Was there really no plausible nexus between the Commission's two purposes in *Nollan*? Are courts employing this approach likely to reach predictable and determinate results?

Coercion: An unconstitutional condition is, like a proposition from the Godfather, an "offer you can't refuse." Many government conditions are thus analyzed in terms of whether they are "coercive." Sometimes the coercion analysis parallels the approaches already discussed, but sometimes it simply assesses whether the "benefit" is so significant, or the recipients circumstances so desperate, that the recipient has no real choice. Hence, *National Federation of Business v. Sebelius*, 567 U.S. 519 (2012), emphasized that Medicaid funding to the states is simply so massive that no state could afford to forfeit that funding by refusing to participate in the Affordable Care Act's Medicaid Expansion.[21] *NFIB* may have been an easy case because the dollar amounts were so great, but how are courts to assess coercion in closer cases? Generally speaking, courts have been reluctant to draw lines between

---

[19] Cass R. Sunstein, *Why the Unconstitutional Conditions Doctrine is an Anachronism (with Particular Reference to Religion, Speech, and Abortion)*, 70 B.U. L. REV. 593, 602 (1990).

[20] *See also South Dakota v. Dole*, 483 U.S. 203 (1987) (inquiring, *inter alia*, whether the federal government's condition on highway funds, requiring raising the drinking age, was "germane" to the government's underlying interest in funding highway construction); Section 9.3, *supra* (discussing *Dole*).

[21] *See supra* Section 9.3.

coercion and voluntary acceptance of a condition in the unconstitutional conditions context. Do you think a workable doctrine can be fashioned on this basis?

4.   The unconstitutional conditions doctrine is an analytical tool for determining when a purportedly voluntary condition offered by the government should be treated as an outright restriction on constitutional rights. It follows that a condition on a government benefit cannot be unconstitutional if the government could constitutionally impose that condition as a direct requirement or restriction. The Court provided a reminder of this point in *Rumsfeld v. Forum for Academic and Institutional Rights, Inc. (FAIR)*, 547 U.S. 47 (2006). That case involved a free speech challenge to the Solomon Amendment, which denied federal funding to institutions of higher education that denied access to military recruiters. FAIR argued that this condition on federal funding unconstitutionally burdened their First Amendment right to protest the military's "don't ask, don't tell" policy on gay and lesbian military personnel by forbidding military recruiting on campus. The Court, however, did not reach the question whether the funding condition was unconstitutional as a condition, because it determined that the First Amendment would not foreclose Congress from simply requiring military access to campus directly. Such a requirement, the Court found, did not require universities to endorse the military's position on homosexuality or foreclose them from protesting that position during the recruiting process. The crucial point for purposes is simply that "a funding condition cannot be unconstitutional if it could be constitutionally imposed directly." *Id.* at 59–60. Don't forget to ask that question before you analyze the more thorny issues addressed in this section.

5.   Finally, it is worth asking whether there really *is* a single "unconstitutional conditions doctrine" that applies in a wide variety of constitutional contexts and is governed by a consistent set of rules. Professor Sunstein has argued that "[i]nstead of a general unconstitutional conditions doctrine asking whether there has been 'coercion' or 'penalty,' what is necessary is a highly particular, constitutionally-centered model of reasons: an approach that asks whether, under the provision at issue, the government has constitutionally sufficient justifications for affecting constitutionally protected interests."[22] In other words, conditions affecting free speech rights of individuals might be governed by quite different rules from conditions affecting the sovereignty and autonomy of state governments under the Tenth Amendment. Do you think the various unconstitutional conditions problems surveyed in this section and in other parts of this course are sufficiently similar in their structure that they ought to be governed by a common set of principles?

SECTION 16.2   PROCEDURAL DUE PROCESS

Discussion of the Due Process Clause in this book has focused on "substantive" due process, even though John Hart Ely aptly described that

---

[22]   Sunstein, *supra* note 19, at 595.

concept as "a contradiction in terms—sort of like "green pastel redness."[23] The primary thrust of due process is, of course, *procedural*. Even when the government is not prohibited outright from depriving individuals of a protected interest, it may be obligated to certain procedures—such as offering notice, a hearing, or a statement of reasons for the government's decision.

Other courses, such as civil and criminal procedure, explore this aspect of due process in far more detail than this book can offer. But procedural due process often does provide some degree of protection for substantive interests that may not rise to the level of fundamental rights, including property interests in public entitlements and liberty interests in making certain medical decisions. This sort of protection forms an important backstop to the more limited scope of substantive due process.

The following cases offer a brief introduction to this vast body of law. *Roth* and *Perry* focus on the identification of protected property or liberty interests. When such an interest exists, *Matthews* is the leading case on determining what process is due. Finally, *Cruzan* presents a roughly similar end-of-life scenario to *Glucksberg*, except that the Court analyzes it in procedural rather than substantive terms. That case thus provides an instructive contrast on the protections offered by substantive and procedural approaches.

Board of Regents of State Colleges v. Roth
408 U.S. 564 (1972)

■ **MR. JUSTICE STEWART delivered the opinion of the Court.**

In 1968 the respondent, David Roth, was hired for his first teaching job as assistant professor of political science at Wisconsin State University-Oshkosh. He was hired for a fixed term of one academic year. The notice of his faculty appointment specified that his employment would begin on September 1, 1968, and would end on June 30, 1969.[1] The respondent completed that term. But he was informed that he would not be rehired for the next academic year.

The respondent had no tenure rights to continued employment. Under Wisconsin statutory law a state university teacher can acquire tenure as a 'permanent' employee only after four years of year-to-year employment. Having acquired tenure, a teacher is entitled to continued

---

[23] JOHN HART ELY, DEMOCRACY AND DISTRUST: A THEORY OF JUDICIAL REVIEW 18 (1980).

[1] The respondent had no contract of employment. Rather, his formal notice of appointment was the equivalent of an employment contract.

The notice of his appointment provided that: 'David F. Roth is hereby appointed to the faculty of the Wisconsin State University Position number 0262. (Location:) Oshkosh as (Rank:) Assistant Professor of (Department:) Political Science this (Date:) first day of (Month:) September (Year:) 1968.' The notice went on to specify that the respondent's 'appointment basis' was for the 'academic year.' And it provided that '(r)egulations governing tenure are in accord with Chapter 37.31, Wisconsin Statutes. The employment of any staff member for an academic year shall not be for a term beyond June 30th of the fiscal year in which the appointment is made.' See n. 2, infra.

employment 'during efficiency and good behavior.' A relatively new teacher without tenure, however, is under Wisconsin law entitled to nothing beyond his one-year appointment.[2] There are no statutory or administrative standards defining eligibility for re-employment. State law thus clearly leaves the decision whether to rehire a nontenured teacher for another year to the unfettered discretion of university officials.

The procedural protection afforded a Wisconsin State University teacher before he is separated from the University corresponds to his job security. As a matter of statutory law, a tenured teacher cannot be 'discharged except for cause upon written charges' and pursuant to certain procedures.[3] A nontenured teacher, similarly, is protected to some extent during his one-year term. Rules promulgated by the Board of Regents provide that a nontenured teacher 'dismissed' before the end of the year may have some opportunity for review of the 'dismissal.' But the Rules provide no real protection for a nontenured teacher who simply is not re-employed for the next year. He must be informed by February 1 'concerning retention or non-retention for the ensuing year.' But 'no reason for non-retention need be given. No review or appeal is provided in such case.'[4]

In conformance with these Rules, the President of Wisconsin State University-Oshkosh informed the respondent before February 1, 1969, that he would not be rehired for the 1969–1970 academic year. He gave

---

[2]   Wis.Stat. s 37.31(1) (1967), in force at the time, provided in pertinent part that:

'All teachers in any state university shall initially be employed on probation. The employment shall be permanent, during efficiency and good behavior after 4 years of continuous service in the state university system as a teacher.'

[3]   Wis.Stat. s 37.31(1) further provided that:

'No teacher who has become permanently employed as herein provided shall be discharged except for cause upon written charges. Within 30 days of receiving the written charges, such teacher may appeal the discharge by a written notice to the president of the board of regents of state colleges. The board shall cause the charges to be investigated, hear the case and provide such teacher with a written statement as to their decision.'

[4]   The Rules, promulgated by the Board of Regents in 1967, provide:

'RULE I—February first is established throughout the State University system as the deadline for written notification of non-tenured faculty concerning retention or non-retention for the ensuing year. The President of each University shall give such notice each year on or before this date.'

'RULE II—During the time a faculty member is on probation, no reason for non-retention need be given. No review or appeal is provided in such case.'

'RULE III—'Dismissal' as opposed to 'Non-Retention' means termination of responsibilities during an academic year. When a non-tenure faculty member is dismissed he has no right under Wisconsin Statutes to a review of his case or to appeal. The President may, however, in his discretion, grant a request for a review within the institution, either by a faculty committee or by the President, or both. Any such review would be informal in nature and would be advisory only.'

'RULE IV—When a non-tenure faculty member is dismissed he may request a review by or hearing before the Board of Regents. Each such request will be considered separately and the Board will, in its discretion, grant or deny same in each individual case.'

the respondent no reason for the decision and no opportunity to challenge it at any sort of hearing.

The respondent then brought this action in Federal District Court alleging that the decision not to rehire him for the next year infringed his Fourteenth Amendment rights. He attacked the decision both in substance and procedure. First, he alleged that the true reason for the decision was to punish him for certain statements critical of the University administration, and that it therefore violated his right to freedom of speech.[5] Second, he alleged that the failure of University officials to give him notice of any reason for nonretention and an opportunity for a hearing violated his right to procedural due process of law.

The District Court granted summary judgment for the respondent on the procedural issue, ordering the University officials to provide him with reasons and a hearing. The Court of Appeals, with one judge dissenting, affirmed this partial summary judgment. We granted certiorari. The only question presented to us at this stage in the case is whether the respondent had a constitutional right to a statement of reasons and a hearing on the University's decision not to rehire him for another year. We hold that he did not.

I

The requirements of procedural due process apply only to the deprivation of interests encompassed by the Fourteenth Amendment's protection of liberty and property. When protected interests are implicated, the right to some kind of prior hearing is paramount.[7] But the range of interests protected by procedural due process is not infinite.

The District Court decided that procedural due process guarantees apply in this case by assessing and balancing the weights of the particular interests involved. It concluded that the respondent's interest in re-employment at Wisconsin State University-Oshkosh outweighed the University's interest in denying him re-employment summarily. Undeniably, the respondent's re-employment prospects were of major concern to him—concern that we surely cannot say was insignificant. And a weighing process has long been a part of any determination of the

---

[5]   While the respondent alleged that he was not rehired because of his exercise of free speech, the petitioners insisted that the non-retention decision was based on other, constitutionally valid grounds. The District Court came to no conclusion whatever regarding the true reason for the University President's decision. 'In the present case,' it stated, 'it appears that a determination as to the actual bases of (the) decision must await amplification of the facts at trial. . . . Summary judgment is inappropriate.'

[7]   Before a person is deprived of a protected interest, he must be afforded opportunity for some kind of a hearing, 'except for extraordinary situations where some valid governmental interest is at stake that justifies postponing the hearing until after the event.' *Boddie v. Connecticut*, 401 U.S. 371, 379 (1971). 'While '(m)any controversies have raged about . . . the Due Process Clause,' . . . it is fundamental that except in emergency situations (and this is not one) due process requires that when a State seeks to terminate (a protected) interest . . . , it must afford 'notice and opportunity for hearing appropriate to the nature of the case' before the termination becomes effective.' *Bell v. Burson*, 402 U.S. 535, 542 (1971). . . .

form of hearing required in particular situations by procedural due process. But, to determine whether due process requirements apply in the first place, we must look not to the 'weight' but to the nature of the interest at stake. We must look to see if the interest is within the Fourteenth Amendment's protection of liberty and property.

'Liberty' and 'property' are broad and majestic terms. They are among the '(g)reat (constitutional) concepts . . . purposely left to gather meaning from experience. . . . (T)hey relate to the whole domain of social and economic fact, and the statesmen who founded this Nation knew too well that only a stagnant society remains unchanged.' *National Mutual Ins. Co. v. Tidewater Transfer Co.*, 337 U.S. 582, 646 (1949) (Frankfurter, J., dissenting). For that reason, the Court has fully and finally rejected the wooden distinction between 'rights' and 'privileges' that once seemed to govern the applicability of procedural due process rights. The Court has also made clear that the property interests protected by procedural due process extend well beyond actual ownership of real estate, chattels, or money. By the same token, the Court has required due process protection for deprivations of liberty beyond the sort of formal constraints imposed by the criminal process.

Yet, while the Court has eschewed rigid or formalistic limitations on the protection of procedural due process, it has at the same time observed certain boundaries. For the words 'liberty' and 'property' in the Due Process Clause of the Fourteenth Amendment must be given some meaning.

II

'While this court has not attempted to define with exactness the liberty . . . guaranteed (by the Fourteenth Amendment), the term has received much consideration and some of the included things have been definitely stated. Without doubt, it denotes not merely freedom from bodily restraint but also the right of the individual to contract, to engage in any of the common occupations of life, to acquire useful knowledge, to marry, establish a home and bring up children, to worship God according to the dictates of his own conscience, and generally to enjoy those privileges long recognized . . . as essential to the orderly pursuit of happiness by free men.' *Meyer v. Nebraska*, 262 U.S. 390, 399 (1923). In a Constitution for a free people, there can be no doubt that the meaning of 'liberty' must be broad indeed.

There might be cases in which a State refused to re-employ a person under such circumstances that interests in liberty would be implicated. But this is not such a case. The State, in declining to rehire the respondent, did not make any charge against him that might seriously damage his standing and associations in his community. It did not base the nonrenewal of his contract on a charge, for example, that he had been guilty of dishonesty, or immorality. Had it done so, this would be a different case. For '(w)here a person's good name, reputation, honor, or integrity is at stake because of what the government is doing to him, notice and an opportunity to be heard are essential.' *Wisconsin v. Constantineau*, 400 U.S. 433, 437 (1971). In such a case, due process would accord an opportunity to refute the charge before University officials. In the present case, however, there is no suggestion whatever that the respondent's 'good name, reputation, honor, or integrity' is at stake.

Similarly, there is no suggestion that the State, in declining to reemploy the respondent, imposed on him a stigma or other disability that foreclosed his freedom to take advantage of other employment opportunities. The State, for example, did not invoke any regulations to bar the respondent from all other public employment in state universities. Had it done so, this, again, would be a different case. For '(t)o be deprived not only of present government employment but of future opportunity for it certainly is no small injury . . . .' *Joint Anti-Fascist Refugee Committee v. McGrath*, 341 U.S.123, 185 (1951) (Jackson, J., concurring). . . . In the present case, however, this principle does not come into play.[13]

To be sure, the respondent has alleged that the nonrenewal of his contract was based on his exercise of his right to freedom of speech. But this allegation is not now before us. The District Court stayed proceedings on this issue, and the respondent has yet to prove that the decision not to rehire him was, in fact, based on his free speech activities.

Hence, on the record before us, all that clearly appears is that the respondent was not rehired for one year at one university. It stretches the concept too far to suggest that a person is deprived of 'liberty' when he simply is not rehired in one job but remains as free as before to seek another.

III

The Fourteenth Amendment's procedural protection of property is a safeguard of the security of interests that a person has already acquired in specific benefits. These interests—property interests—may take many forms.

Thus, the Court has held that a person receiving welfare benefits under statutory and administrative standards defining eligibility for them has an interest in continued receipt of those benefits that is

---

[13] The District Court made an assumption 'that non-retention by one university or college creates concrete and practical difficulties for a professor in his subsequent academic career.' And the Court of Appeals based its affirmance of the summary judgment largely on the premise that 'the substantial adverse effect non-retention is likely to have upon the career interests of an individual professor' amounts to a limitation on future employment opportunities sufficient invoke procedural due process guarantees. But even assuming, arguendo, that such a 'substantial adverse effect' under these circumstances would constitute a state-imposed restriction on liberty, the record contains no support for these assumptions. There is no suggestion of how nonretention might affect the respondent's future employment prospects. Mere proof, for example, that his record of nonretention in one job, taken alone, might make him somewhat less attractive to some other employers would hardly establish the kind of foreclosure of opportunities amounting to a deprivation of 'liberty.'

safeguarded by procedural due process. *Goldberg v. Kelly*, 397 U.S. 254 (1970). Similarly, in the area of public employment, the Court has held that a public college professor dismissed from an office held under tenure provisions, and college professors and staff members dismissed during the terms of their contracts, have interests in continued employment that are safeguarded by due process. Only last year, the Court held that this principle 'proscribing summary dismissal from public employment without hearing or inquiry required by due process' also applied to a teacher recently hired without tenure or a formal contract, but nonetheless with a clearly implied promise of continued employment.

Certain attributes of 'property' interests protected by procedural due process emerge from these decisions. To have a property interest in a benefit, a person clearly must have more than an abstract need or desire for it. He must have more than a unilateral expectation of it. He must, instead, have a legitimate claim of entitlement to it. It is a purpose of the ancient institution of property to protect those claims upon which people rely in their daily lives, reliance that must not be arbitrarily undermined. It is a purpose of the constitutional right to a hearing to provide an opportunity for a person to vindicate those claims.

Property interests, of course, are not created by the Constitution. Rather they are created and their dimensions are defined by existing rules or understandings that stem from an independent source such as state law—rules or understandings that secure certain benefits and that support claims of entitlement to those benefits. Thus, the welfare recipients in *Goldberg v. Kelly*, supra, had a claim of entitlement to welfare payments that was grounded in the statute defining eligibility for them. The recipients had not yet shown that they were, in fact, within the statutory terms of eligibility. But we held that they had a right to a hearing at which they might attempt to do so.

Just as the welfare recipients' 'property' interest in welfare payments was created and defined by statutory terms, so the respondent's 'property' interest in employment at Wisconsin State University-Oshkosh was created and defined by the terms of his appointment. Those terms secured his interest in employment up to June 30, 1969. But the important fact in this case is that they specifically provided that the respondent's employment was to terminate on June 30. They did not provide for contract renewal absent 'sufficient cause.' Indeed, they made no provision for renewal whatsoever.

Thus, the terms of the respondent's appointment secured absolutely no interest in re-employment for the next year. They supported absolutely no possible claim of entitlement to re-employment. Nor, significantly, was there any state statute or University rule or policy that secured his interest in re-employment or that created any legitimate claim to it.[16] In these circumstances, the respondent surely had an abstract concern in being rehired, but he did not have a property interest sufficient to require the University authorities to give him a hearing when they declined to renew his contract of employment.

IV

Our analysis of the respondent's constitutional rights in this case in no way indicates a view that an opportunity for a hearing or a statement of reasons for nonretention would, or would not, be appropriate or wise in public colleges and universities. For it is a written Constitution that we apply. Our role is confined to interpretation of that Constitution.

We must conclude that the summary judgment for the respondent should not have been granted, since the respondent has not shown that he was deprived of liberty or property protected by the Fourteenth Amendment. The judgment of the Court of Appeals, accordingly, is reversed and the case is remanded for further proceedings consistent with this opinion.

It is so ordered.

Reversed and remanded.

■ MR. JUSTICE POWELL took no part in the decision of this case.

■ MR. JUSTICE MARSHALL, dissenting.*

. . . While I agree with Part I of the Court's opinion, setting forth the proper framework for consideration of the issue presented, and also with those portions of Parts II and III of the Court's opinion that assert that a public employee is entitled to procedural due process whenever a State stigmatizes him by denying employment, or injures his future employment prospects severely, or whenever the State deprives him of a property interest. I would go further than the Court does in defining the terms 'liberty' and 'property.'

The prior decisions of this Court, discussed at length in the opinion of the Court, establish a principle that is as obvious as it is compelling— i.e., federal and state governments and governmental agencies are restrained by the Constitution from acting arbitrarily with respect to employment opportunities that they either offer or control. Hence, it is now firmly established that whether or not a private employer is free to act capriciously or unreasonably with respect to employment practices, at least absent statutory or contractual controls, a government employer is different. The government may only act fairly and reasonably.

---

[16] To be sure, the respondent does suggest that most teachers hired on a year-to-year basis by Wisconsin State University-Oshkosh are, in fact, rehired. But the District Court has not found that there is anything approaching a 'common law' of re-employment, see *Perry v. Sindermann*, 408 U.S. 593, 602 (1972), so strong as to require University officials to give the respondent a statement of reasons and a hearing on their decision not to rehire him.

* Justice Douglas also dissented, primarily on First Amendment grounds. [Editor's Note]

This Court has long maintained that 'the right to work for a living in the common occupations of the community is of the very essence of the personal freedom and opportunity that it was the purpose of the (Fourteenth) Amendment to secure.' *Truax v. Raich*, 239 U.S. 33, 41 (1915) (Hughes, J). It has also established that the fact that an employee has no contract guaranteeing work for a specific future period does not mean that as the result of action by the government he may be discharged at any time, for any reason or for no reason.

In my view, every citizen who applies for a government job is entitled to it unless the government can establish some reason for denying the employment. This is the 'property' right that I believe is protected by the Fourteenth Amendment and that cannot be denied 'without due process of law.' And it is also liberty—liberty to work—which is the 'very essence of the personal freedom and opportunity' secured by the Fourteenth Amendment.

This Court has often had occasion to note that the denial of public employment is a serious blow to any citizen. Thus, when an application for public employment is denied or the contract of a government employee is not renewed, the government must say why, for it is only when the reasons underlying government action are known that citizens feel secure and protected against arbitrary government action.

Employment is one of the greatest, if not the greatest, benefits that governments offer in modern-day life. When something as valuable as the opportunity to work is at stake, the government may not reward some citizens and not others without demonstrating that its actions are fair and equitable. And it is procedural due process that is our fundamental guarantee of fairness, our protection against arbitrary, capricious, and unreasonable government action.

Mr. Justice Douglas has written that:

'It is not without significance that most of the provisions of the Bill of Rights are procedural. It is procedure that spells much of the difference between rule by law and rule by whim or caprice. Steadfast adherence to strict procedural safeguards is our main assurance that there will be equal justice under law.' *Joint Anti-Fascist Refugee Committee v. McGrath*, supra, 341 U.S., at 179 (concurring opinion).

And Mr. Justice Frankfurter has said that '(t)he history of American freedom is, in no small measure, the history of procedure.' *Malinski v. New York*, 324 U.S. 401, 414 (1945) (separate opinion). With respect to occupations controlled by the government, one lower court has said that '(t)he public has the right to expect its officers . . . to make adjudications on the basis of merit. The first step toward insuring that these expectations are realized is to require adherence to the standards of due process; absolute and uncontrolled discretion invites abuse.' *Hornsby v. Allen*, 326 F.2d 605, 610 (CA5 1964).

We have often noted that procedural due process means many different things in the numerous contexts in which it applies. See, e.g., *Goldberg v. Kelly*, 397 U.S. 254 (1970). Prior decisions have held that an applicant for admission to practice as an attorney before the United States Board of Tax Appeals may not be rejected without a statement of reasons and a chance for a hearing on disputed issues of fact;[4] that a tenured teacher could not be summarily dismissed without notice of the reasons and a hearing;[5] that an applicant for admission to a state bar could not be denied the opportunity to practice law without notice of the reasons for the rejection of his application and a hearing;[6] and even that a substitute teacher who had been employed only two months could not be dismissed merely because she refused to take a loyalty oath without an inquiry into the specific facts of her case and a hearing on those in dispute.[7] I would follow these cases and hold that respondent was denied due process when his contract was not renewed and he was not informed of the reasons and given an opportunity to respond.

It may be argued that to provide procedural due process to all public employees or prospective employees would place an intolerable burden on the machinery of government. The short answer to that argument is that it is not burdensome to give reasons when reasons exist. Whenever an application for employment is denied, an employee is discharged, or a decision not to rehire an employee is made, there should be some reason for the decision. It can scarcely be argued that government would be crippled by a requirement that the reason be communicated to the person most directly affected by the government's action.

Where there are numerous applicants for jobs, it is likely that few will choose to demand reasons for not being hired. But, if the demand for reasons is exceptionally great, summary procedures can be devised that would provide fair and adequate information to all persons. As long as the government has a good reason for its actions it need not fear disclosure. It is only where the government acts improperly that procedural due process is truly burdensome. And that is precisely when it is most necessary.

It might also be argued that to require a hearing and a statement of reasons is to require a useless act, because a government bent on denying employment to one or more persons will do so regardless of the procedural hurdles that are placed in its path. Perhaps this is so, but a requirement of procedural regularity at least renders arbitrary action more difficult. Moreover, proper procedures will surely eliminate some of the arbitrariness that results, not from malice, but from innocent error. 'Experience teaches ... that the affording of procedural safeguards, which by their nature serve to illuminate the underlying facts, in itself

---

[4]   *Goldsmith v. United States Board of Tax Appeals*, 270 U.S. 117 (1926).

[5]   *Slochower v. Board of Higher Education*, 350 U.S. 551 (1956).

[6]   *Willner v. Committee on Character*, 373 U.S. 96 (1963).

[7]   *Connell v. Higginbotham*, 403 U.S. 207 (1971).

often operates to prevent erroneous decisions on the merits from occurring.' *Silver v. New York Stock Exchange*, 373 U.S. 341, 366 (1963). When the government knows it may have to justify its decisions with sound reasons, its conduct is likely to be more cautious, careful, and correct.

Professor Gellhorn put the argument well:

'In my judgment, there is no basic division of interest between the citizenry on the one hand and officialdom on the other. Both should be interested equally in the quest for procedural safeguards. I echo the late Justice Jackson in saying: 'Let it not be overlooked that due process of law is not for the sole benefit of an accused. It is the best insurance for the Government itself against those blunders which leave lasting stains on a system of justice'—blunders which are likely to occur when reasons need not be given and when the reasonableness and indeed legality of judgments need not be subjected to any appraisal other than one's own. . . .' Summary of Colloquy on Administrative Law, 6 J. Soc. Pub. Teachers of Law, 70, 73 (1961).

Accordingly, I dissent.

Perry v. Sindermann
408 U.S. 593 (1972)

■ **MR. JUSTICE STEWART delivered the opinion of the Court.**

From 1959 to 1969 the respondent, Robert Sindermann, was a teacher in the state college system of the State of Texas. After teaching for two years at the University of Texas and for four years at San Antonio Junior College, he became a professor of Government and Social Science at Odessa Junior College in 1965. He was employed at the college for four successive years, under a series of one-year contracts. He was successful enough to be appointed, for a time, the cochairman of his department.

During the 1968—1969 academic year, however, controversy arose between the respondent and the college administration. The respondent was elected president of the Texas Junior College Teachers Association. In this capacity, he left his teaching duties on several occasions to testify before committees of the Texas Legislature, and he became involved in public disagreements with the policies of the college's Board of Regents. In particular, he aligned himself with a group advocating the elevation of the college to four-year status—a change opposed by the Regents. And, on one occasion, a newspaper advertisement appeared over his name that was highly critical of the Regents.

Finally, in May 1969, the respondent's one-year employment contract terminated and the Board of Regents voted not to offer him a new contract for the next academic year. The Regents issued a press release setting forth allegations of the respondent's insubordination. But they provided him no official statement of the reasons for the nonrenewal of his contract. And they allowed him no opportunity for a hearing to challenge the basis of the nonrenewal.

The respondent then brought this action in Federal District Court. He alleged primarily that the Regents' decision not to rehire him was based on his public criticism of the policies of the college administration and thus infringed his right to freedom of speech. He also alleged that their failure to provide him an opportunity for a hearing violated the Fourteenth Amendment's guarantee of procedural due process. The petitioners—members of the Board of Regents and the president of the college—denied that their decision was made in retaliation for the respondent's public criticism and argued that they had no obligation to provide a hearing.[2] On the basis of these bare pleadings and three brief affidavits filed by the respondent, the District Court granted summary judgment for the petitioners. It concluded that the respondent had 'no cause of action against the (petitioners) since his contract of employment terminated May 31, 1969, and Odessa Junior College has not adopted the tenure system.'

The Court of Appeals reversed the judgment of the District Court. First, it held that, despite the respondent's lack of tenure, the nonrenewal of his contract would violate the Fourteenth Amendment if it in fact was based on his protected free speech. Since the actual reason for the Regents' decision was 'in total dispute' in the pleadings, the court remanded the case for a full hearing on this contested issue of fact. Second, the Court of Appeals held that, despite the respondent's lack of tenure, the failure to allow him an opportunity for a hearing would violate the constitutional guarantee of procedural due process if the respondent could show that he had an 'expectancy' of re-employment. It, therefore, ordered that this issue of fact also be aired upon remand. We granted a writ of certiorari, and we have considered this case along with *Board of Regents v. Roth*, 408 U.S. 564 (1972).

I

The first question presented is whether the respondent's lack of a contractual or tenure right to re-employment, taken alone, defeats his claim that the nonrenewal of his contract violated the First and Fourteenth Amendments. We hold that it does not.

For at least a quarter-century, this Court has made clear that even though a person has no 'right' to a valuable governmental benefit and even though the government may deny him the benefit for any number of reasons, there are some reasons upon which the government may not rely. It may not deny a benefit to a person on a basis that infringes his constitutionally protected interests—especially, his interest in freedom of speech. For if the government could deny a benefit to a person because

---

[2] The petitioners claimed, in their motion for summary judgment, that the decision not to retain the respondent was really based on his insubordinate conduct.

of his constitutionally protected speech or associations, his exercise of those freedoms would in effect be penalized and inhibited. This would allow the government to 'produce a result which (it) could not command directly.' *Speiser v. Randall*, 357 U.S. 513, 526 (1972). Such interference with constitutional rights is impermissible.

We have applied this general principle to denials of tax exemptions, *Speiser v. Randall*, supra, unemployment benefits, *Sherbert v. Verner*, 374 U.S. 398, 404—405 (1963), and welfare payments, *Shapiro v. Thompson*, 394 U.S. 618, 627, n. 6 (1969). But, most often, we have applied the principle to denials of public employment. *United Public Workers v. Mitchell*, 330 U.S. 75, 100 (1947). We have applied the principle regardless of the public employee's contractual or other claim to a job.

Thus, the respondent's lack of a contractual or tenure 'right' to re-employment for the 1969–1970 academic year is immaterial to his free speech claim. Indeed, twice before, this Court has specifically held that the nonrenewal of a nontenured public school teacher's one-year contract may not be predicated on his exercise of First and Fourteenth Amendment rights. We reaffirm those holdings here.

In this case, of course, the respondent has yet to show that the decision not to renew his contract was, in fact, made in retaliation for his exercise of the constitutional right of free speech. The District Court foreclosed any opportunity to make this showing when it granted summary judgment. Hence, we cannot now hold that the Board of Regents' action was invalid.

But we agree with the Court of Appeals that there is a genuine dispute as to 'whether the college refused to renew the teaching contract on an impermissible basis—as a reprisal for the exercise of constitutionally protected rights.' The respondent has alleged that his nonretention was based on his testimony before legislative committees and his other public statements critical of the Regents' policies. And he has alleged that this public criticism was within the First and Fourteenth Amendments' protection of freedom of speech. Plainly, these allegations present a bona fide constitutional claim. For this Court has held that a teacher's public criticism of his superiors on matters of public concern may be constitutionally protected and may, therefore, be an impermissible basis for termination of his employment. *Pickering v. Board of Education*, 391 U.S. 563 (1968).

For this reason we hold that the grant of summary judgment against the respondent, without full exploration of this issue, was improper.

II

The respondent's lack of formal contractual or tenure security in continued employment at Odessa Junior College, though irrelevant to his free speech claim, is highly relevant to his procedural due process claim. But it may not be entirely dispositive.

We have held today in *Board of Regents v. Roth*, 408 U.S. 564 (1972), that the Constitution does not require opportunity for a hearing before the nonrenewal of a nontenured teacher's contract, unless he can show that the decision not to rehire him somehow deprived him of an interest in 'liberty' or that he had a 'property' interest in continued employment, despite the lack of tenure or a formal contract. In Roth the teacher had not made a showing on either point to justify summary judgment in his favor.

Similarly, the respondent here has yet to show that he has been deprived of an interest that could invoke procedural due process protection. As in *Roth*, the mere showing that he was not rehired in one particular job, without more, did not amount to a showing of a loss of liberty.[5] Nor did it amount to a showing of a loss of property.

But the respondent's allegations—which we must construe most favorably to the respondent at this stage of the litigation—do raise a genuine issue as to his interest in continued employment at Odessa Junior College. He alleged that this interest, though not secured by a formal contractual tenure provision, was secured by a no less binding understanding fostered by the college administration. In particular, the respondent alleged that the college had a de facto tenure program, and that he had tenure under that program. He claimed that he and others legitimately relied upon an unusual provision that had been in the college's official Faculty Guide for many years:

> Teacher Tenure: Odessa College has no tenure system. The Administration of the College wishes the faculty member to feel that he has permanent tenure as long as his teaching services are satisfactory and as long as he displays a cooperative attitude toward his co-workers and his superiors, and as long as he is happy in his work.

Moreover, the respondent claimed legitimate reliance upon guidelines promulgated by the Coordinating Board of the Texas College and University System that provided that a person, like himself, who had been employed as a teacher in the state college and university system for seven years or more has some form of job tenure. Thus, the respondent offered to prove that a teacher with his long period of service at this particular State College had no less a 'property' interest in continued employment than a formally tenured teacher at other colleges, and had no less a procedural due process right to a statement of reasons and a hearing before college officials upon their decision not to retain him.

We have made clear in *Roth*, supra, at 577, that 'property' interests subject to procedural due process protection are not limited by a few rigid,

---

[5] The Court of Appeals suggested that the respondent might have a due process right to some kind of hearing simply if he asserts to college officials that their decision was based on his constitutionally protected conduct. We have rejected this approach in *Board of Regents v. Roth*, supra, 408 U.S., at 575, n. 14.

technical forms. Rather, 'property' denotes a broad range of interests that are secured by 'existing rules or understandings.' A person's interest in a benefit is a 'property' interest for due process purposes if there are such rules or mutually explicit understandings that support his claim of entitlement to the benefit and that he may invoke at a hearing.

A written contract with an explicit tenure provision clearly is evidence of a formal understanding that supports a teacher's claim of entitlement to continued employment unless sufficient 'cause' is shown. Yet absence of such an explicit contractual provision may not always foreclose the possibility that a teacher has a 'property' interest in reemployment. For example, the law of contracts in most, if not all, jurisdictions long has employed a process by which agreements, though not formalized in writing, may be 'implied.' 3 A. Corbin on Contracts ss 561—572A (1960). Explicit contractual provisions may be supplemented by other agreements implied from 'the promisor's words and conduct in the light of the surrounding circumstances.' And, '(t)he meaning of (the promisor's) words and acts is found by relating them to the usage of the past.'

A teacher, like the respondent, who has held his position for a number of years, might be able to show from the circumstances of this service—and from other relevant facts—that he has a legitimate claim of entitlement to job tenure. Just as this Court has found there to be a common law of a particular industry or of a particular plant that may supplement a collective-bargaining agreement, so there may be an unwritten 'common law' in a particular university that certain employees shall have the equivalent of tenure. This is particularly likely in a college or university, like Odessa Junior College, that has no explicit tenure system even for senior members of its faculty, but that nonetheless may have created such a system in practice.[7]

In this case, the respondent has alleged the existence of rules and understandings, promulgated and fostered by state officials, that may justify his legitimate claim of entitlement to continued employment absent 'sufficient cause.' We disagree with the Court of Appeals insofar as it held that a mere subjective 'expectancy' is protected by procedural due process, but we agree that the respondent must be given an opportunity to prove the legitimacy of his claim of such entitlement in light of 'the policies and practices of the institution.' Proof of such a property interest would not, of course, entitle him to reinstatement. But such proof would obligate college officials to grant a hearing at his

---

[7]   We do not now hold that the respondent has any such legitimate claim of entitlement to job tenure. For '(p)roperty interests . . . are not created by the Constitution. Rather, they are created and their dimensions are defined by existing rules or understandings that stem from an independent source such as state law . . . .' *Board of Regents v. Roth*, supra, 408 U.S., at 577 (1972). If it is the law of Texas that a teacher in the respondent's position has no contractual or other claim to job tenure, the respondent's claim would be defeated.

request, where he could be informed of the grounds for his nonretention and challenge their sufficiency.

Therefore, while we do not wholly agree with the opinion of the Court of Appeals, its judgment remanding this case to the District Court is affirmed.

■ MR. JUSTICE POWELL took no part in the decision of this case.

■ MR. JUSTICE MARSHALL, dissenting in part.*

. . . I agree with Part I of the Court's opinion holding that respondent has presented a bona fide First Amendment claim that should be considered fully by the District Court. But, for the reasons stated in my dissenting opinion in *Board of Regents v. Roth*, 408 U.S. 564, at 587, I would modify the judgment of the Court of Appeals to direct the District Court to enter summary judgment for respondent entitling him to a statement of reasons why his contract was not renewed and a hearing on disputed issues of fact.

■ MR. CHIEF JUSTICE BURGER, concurring [in both *Roth* and *Perry*].

I concur in the Court's judgments and opinions in *Perry* and *Sindermann* but there is one central point in both decisions that I would like to underscore since it may have been obscured in the comprehensive discussion of the cases. That point is that the relationship between a state institution and one of its teachers is essentially a matter of state concern and state law. The Court holds today only that a state-employed teacher who has a right to re-employment under state law, arising from either an express or implied contract, has, in turn, a right guaranteed by the Fourteenth Amendment to some form of prior administrative or academic hearing on the cause for nonrenewal of his contract. Thus, whether a particular teacher in a particular context has any right to such administrative hearing hinges on a question of state law. . . .

If relevant state contract law is unclear, a federal court should, in my view, abstain from deciding whether he is constitutionally entitled to a prior hearing, and the teacher should be left to resort to state courts on the questions arising under state law.

Matthews v. Eldridge
424 U.S. 319 (1976)

■ MR. JUSTICE POWELL delivered the opinion of the Court.

The issue in this case is whether the Due Process Clause of the Fifth Amendment requires that prior to the termination of Social Security disability benefit payments the recipient be afforded an opportunity for an evidentiary hearing.

---

*   Justice Brennan, joined by Justice Douglas, also agreed with Justice Marshall's opinion. [Editor's Note]

I

Cash benefits are provided to workers during periods in which they are completely disabled under the disability insurance benefits program created by the 1956 amendments to Title II of the Social Security Act. 70 Stat. 815, 42 U.S.C. § 423.[1] Respondent Eldridge was first awarded benefits in June 1968. In March 1972, he received a questionnaire from the state agency charged with monitoring his medical condition. Eldridge completed the questionnaire, indicating that his condition had not improved and identifying the medical sources, including physicians, from whom he had received treatment recently. The state agency then obtained reports from his physician and a psychiatric consultant. After considering these reports and other information in his file the agency informed Eldridge by letter that it had made a tentative determination that his disability had ceased in May 1972. The letter included a statement of reasons for the proposed termination of benefits, and advised Eldridge that he might request reasonable time in which to obtain and submit additional information pertaining to his condition.

In his written response, Eldridge disputed one characterization of his medical condition and indicated that the agency already had enough evidence to establish his disability.[2] The state agency then made its final determination that he had ceased to be disabled in May 1972. This determination was accepted by the Social Security Administration (SSA), which notified Eldridge in July that his benefits would terminate after that month. The notification also advised him of his right to seek reconsideration by the state agency of this initial determination within six months.

Instead of requesting reconsideration Eldridge commenced this action challenging the constitutional validity of the administrative procedures established by the Secretary of Health, Education, and Welfare for assessing whether there exists a continuing disability. He sought an immediate reinstatement of benefits pending a hearing on the issue of his disability. The Secretary moved to dismiss on the grounds that Eldridge's benefits had been terminated in accordance with valid administrative regulations and procedures and that he had failed to exhaust available remedies. In support of his contention that due process

---

[1]   The program is financed by revenues derived from employee and employer payroll taxes. It provides monthly benefits to disabled persons who have worked sufficiently long to have an insured status, and who have had substantial work experience in a specified interval directly preceding the onset of disability. Benefits also are provided to the worker's dependents under specified circumstances. When the recipient reaches age 65 his disability benefits are automatically converted to retirement benefits. In fiscal 1974 approximately 3,700,000 persons received assistance under the program.

[2]   Eldridge originally was disabled due to chronic anxiety and back strain. He subsequently was found to have diabetes. The tentative determination letter indicated that aid would be terminated because available medical evidence indicated that his diabetes was under control, that there existed no limitations on his back movements which would impose severe functional restrictions, and that he no longer suffered emotional problems that would preclude him from all work for which he was qualified. In his reply letter he claimed to have arthritis of the spine rather than a strained back.

requires a pretermination hearing, Eldridge relied exclusively upon this Court's decision in *Goldberg v. Kelly*, 397 U.S. 254 (1970), which established a right to an "evidentiary hearing" prior to termination of welfare benefits.[4] The Secretary contended that *Goldberg* was not controlling since eligibility for disability benefits, unlike eligibility for welfare benefits, is not based on financial need and since issues of credibility and veracity do not play a significant role in the disability entitlement decision, which turns primarily on medical evidence.

The District Court concluded that the administrative procedures pursuant to which the Secretary had terminated Eldridge's benefits abridged his right to procedural due process. . . . [T]he Court of Appeals for the Fourth Circuit affirmed the injunction barring termination of Eldridge's benefits prior to an evidentiary hearing. We reverse. . . .

III

A

Procedural due process imposes constraints on governmental decisions which deprive individuals of "liberty" or "property" interests within the meaning of the Due Process Clause of the Fifth or Fourteenth Amendment. The Secretary does not contend that procedural due process is inapplicable to terminations of Social Security disability benefits. He recognizes, as has been implicit in our prior decisions, that the interest of an individual in continued receipt of these benefits is a statutorily created "property" interest protected by the Fifth Amendment. Cf. *Board of Regents v. Roth*, 408 U.S. 564, 576–578 (1972). Rather, the Secretary contends that the existing administrative procedures, detailed below, provide all the process that is constitutionally due before a recipient can be deprived of that interest.

This Court consistently has held that some form of hearing is required before an individual is finally deprived of a property interest. The "right to be heard before being condemned to suffer grievous loss of any kind, even though it may not involve the stigma and hardships of a criminal conviction, is a principle basic to our society." *Joint Anti-Fascist Comm. v. McGrath*, 341 U.S. 123, 168 (1951) (Frankfurter, J., concurring). The fundamental requirement of due process is the opportunity to be heard "at a meaningful time and in a meaningful manner." *Armstrong v. Manzo*, 380 U.S. 545, 552 (1965). Eldridge agrees that the review procedures available to a claimant before the initial determination of ineligibility becomes final would be adequate if disability benefits were not terminated until after the evidentiary hearing stage of the administrative process. The dispute centers upon

---

[4] In *Goldberg* the Court held that the pretermination hearing must include the following elements: (1) "timely and adequate notice detailing the reasons for a proposed termination"; (2) "an effective opportunity (for the recipient) to defend by confronting any adverse witnesses and by presenting his own arguments and evidence orally"; (3) retained counsel, if desired; (4) an "impartial" decisionmaker; (5) a decision resting "solely on the legal rules and evidence adduced at the hearing"; (6) a statement of reasons for the decision and the evidence relied on. . . .

what process is due prior to the initial termination of benefits, pending review.

In recent years this Court increasingly has had occasion to consider the extent to which due process requires an evidentiary hearing prior to the deprivation of some type of property interest even if such a hearing is provided thereafter. In only one case, *Goldberg v. Kelly*, has the Court held that a hearing closely approximating a judicial trial is necessary. In other cases requiring some type of pretermination hearing as a matter of constitutional right the Court has spoken sparingly about the requisite procedures. . . . In *Fuentes v. Shevin*, 407 U.S. 67, 96–97 (1972), the Court said only that in a replevin suit between two private parties the initial determination required something more than an ex parte proceeding before a court clerk. Similarly, *Bell v. Burson*, 402 U.S. 535, 540 (1971), held, in the context of the revocation of a state-granted driver's license, that due process required only that the prerevocation hearing involve a probable-cause determination as to the fault of the licensee, noting that the hearing "need not take the form of a full adjudication of the question of liability." More recently, in *Arnett v. Kennedy*, 416 U.S. 134, 142–146 (1974), we sustained the validity of procedures by which a federal employee could be dismissed for cause. They included notice of the action sought, a copy of the charge, reasonable time for filing a written response, and an opportunity for an oral appearance. Following dismissal, an evidentiary hearing was provided.

These decisions underscore the truism that due process, unlike some legal rules, is not a technical conception with a fixed content unrelated to time, place and circumstances. Due process is flexible and calls for such procedural protections as the particular situation demands. Accordingly, resolution of the issue whether the administrative procedures provided here are constitutionally sufficient requires analysis of the governmental and private interests that are affected. More precisely, our prior decisions indicate that identification of the specific dictates of due process generally requires consideration of three distinct factors: First, the private interest that will be affected by the official action; second, the risk of an erroneous deprivation of such interest through the procedures used, and the probable value, if any, of additional or substitute procedural safeguards; and finally, the Government's interest, including the function involved and the fiscal and administrative burdens that the additional or substitute procedural requirement would entail.

We turn first to a description of the procedures for the termination of Social Security disability benefits and thereafter consider the factors bearing upon the constitutional adequacy of these procedures.

B

The disability insurance program is administered jointly by state and federal agencies. State agencies make the initial determination whether a disability exists, when it began, and when it ceased. The standards applied and the procedures followed are prescribed by the Secretary, who has delegated his responsibilities and powers under the Act to the SSA.

In order to establish initial and continued entitlement to disability benefits a worker must demonstrate that he is unable

> to engage in any substantial gainful activity by reason of any medically determinable physical or mental impairment which can be expected to result in death or which has lasted or can be expected to last for a continuous period of not less than 12 months . . . . 42 U.S.C. § 423(d)(1)(A).

To satisfy this test the worker bears a continuing burden of showing, by means of "medically acceptable clinical and laboratory diagnostic techniques," that he has a physical or mental impairment of such severity that "he is not only unable to do his previous work but cannot, considering his age, education, and work experience, engage in any other kind of substantial gainful work which exists in the national economy, regardless of whether such work exists in the immediate area in which he lives, or whether a specific job vacancy exists for him, or whether he would be hired if he applied for work."

The principal reasons for benefits terminations are that the worker is no longer disabled or has returned to work. As Eldridge's benefits were terminated because he was determined to be no longer disabled, we consider only the sufficiency of the procedures involved in such cases.

The continuing-eligibility investigation is made by a state agency acting through a "team" consisting of a physician and a nonmedical person trained in disability evaluation. The agency periodically communicates with the disabled worker, usually by mail in which case he is sent a detailed questionnaire or by telephone, and requests information concerning his present condition, including current medical restrictions and sources of treatment, and any additional information that he considers relevant to his continued entitlement to benefits.

Information regarding the recipient's current condition is also obtained from his sources of medical treatment. If there is a conflict between the information provided by the beneficiary and that obtained from medical sources such as his physician, or between two sources of treatment, the agency may arrange for an examination by an independent consulting physician. Whenever the agency's tentative assessment of the beneficiary's condition differs from his own assessment, the beneficiary is informed that benefits may be terminated, provided a summary of the evidence upon which the proposed determination to terminate is based, and afforded an opportunity to review the medical reports and other evidence in his case file. He also may respond in writing and submit additional evidence.

The state agency then makes its final determination, which is reviewed by an examiner in the SSA Bureau of Disability Insurance. If, as is usually the case, the SSA accepts the agency determination it notifies the recipient in writing, informing him of the reasons for the decision, and of his right to seek de novo reconsideration by the state agency. Upon acceptance by the SSA, benefits are terminated effective two months after the month in which medical recovery is found to have occurred.

If the recipient seeks reconsideration by the state agency and the determination is adverse, the SSA reviews the reconsideration determination and notifies the recipient of the decision. He then has a right to an evidentiary hearing before an SSA administrative law judge. The hearing is nonadversary, and the SSA is not represented by counsel. As at all prior and subsequent stages of the administrative process, however, the claimant may be represented by counsel or other spokesmen. If this hearing results in an adverse decision, the claimant is entitled to request discretionary review by the SSA Appeals Council and finally may obtain judicial review.[21]

Should it be determined at any point after termination of benefits, that the claimant's disability extended beyond the date of cessation initially established, the worker is entitled to retroactive payments. If, on the other hand, a beneficiary receives any payments to which he is later determined not to be entitled, the statute authorizes the Secretary to attempt to recoup these funds in specified circumstances.

C

Despite the elaborate character of the administrative procedures provided by the Secretary, the courts below held them to be constitutionally inadequate, concluding that due process requires an evidentiary hearing prior to termination. In light of the private and governmental interests at stake here and the nature of the existing procedures, we think this was error.

Since a recipient whose benefits are terminated is awarded full retroactive relief if he ultimately prevails, his sole interest is in the uninterrupted receipt of this source of income pending final administrative decision on his claim. . . . Only in *Goldberg* has the Court held that due process requires an evidentiary hearing prior to a temporary deprivation. It was emphasized there that welfare assistance is given to persons on the very margin of subsistence:

> The crucial factor in this context a factor not present in the case of . . . virtually anyone else whose governmental entitlements are ended is that termination of aid pending resolution of a controversy over eligibility may deprive an eligible recipient of the very means by which to live while he waits.

---

[21] Unlike all prior levels of review, which are de novo, the district court is required to treat findings of fact as conclusive if supported by substantial evidence. 42 U.S.C. § 405(g).

Eligibility for disability benefits, in contrast, is not based upon financial need. Indeed, it is wholly unrelated to the worker's income or support from many other sources, such as earnings of other family members, workmen's compensation awards, tort claims awards, savings, private insurance, public or private pensions, veterans' benefits, food stamps, public assistance, or the many other important programs, both public and private, which contain provisions for disability payments affecting a substantial portion of the work force

As *Goldberg* illustrates, the degree of potential deprivation that may be created by a particular decision is a factor to be considered in assessing the validity of any administrative decisionmaking process. The potential deprivation here is generally likely to be less than in Goldberg, although the degree of difference can be overstated. As the District Court emphasized, to remain eligible for benefits a recipient must be "unable to engage in substantial gainful activity. Thus . . . there is little possibility that the terminated recipient will be able to find even temporary employment to ameliorate the interim loss.

As we recognized last Term in *Fusari v. Steinberg*, 419 U.S. 379, 389 (1975), "the possible length of wrongful deprivation of . . . benefits (also) is an important factor in assessing the impact of official action on the private interests." The Secretary concedes that the delay between a request for a hearing before an administrative law judge and a decision on the claim is currently between 10 and 11 months. Since a terminated recipient must first obtain a reconsideration decision as a prerequisite to invoking his right to an evidentiary hearing, the delay between the actual cutoff of benefits and final decision after a hearing exceeds one year.

In view of the torpidity of this administrative review process, and the typically modest resources of the family unit of the physically disabled worker,[26] the hardship imposed upon the erroneously terminated disability recipient may be significant. Still, the disabled worker's need is likely to be less than that of a welfare recipient. In addition to the possibility of access to private resources, other forms of government assistance will become available where the termination of disability benefits places a worker or his family below the subsistence level. In view of these potential sources of temporary income, there is less reason here than in *Goldberg* to depart from the ordinary principle, established by our decisions, that something less than an evidentiary hearing is sufficient prior to adverse administrative action.

D

An additional factor to be considered here is the fairness and reliability of the existing pretermination procedures, and the probable

---

[26] Amici cite statistics compiled by the Secretary which indicate that in 1965 the mean income of the family unit of a disabled worker was $3,803, while the median income for the unit was $2,836. The mean liquid assets i. e., cash, stocks, bonds of these family units was $4,862; the median was $940. These statistics do not take into account the family unit's nonliquid assets i.e., automobile, real estate, and the like.

value, if any, of additional procedural safeguards. Central to the evaluation of any administrative process is the nature of the relevant inquiry. In order to remain eligible for benefits the disabled worker must demonstrate by means of "medically acceptable clinical and laboratory diagnostic techniques" that he is unable "to engage in any substantial gainful activity by reason of any medically determinable physical or mental impairment . . . ." In short, a medical assessment of the worker's physical or mental condition is required. This is a more sharply focused and easily documented decision than the typical determination of welfare entitlement. In the latter case, a wide variety of information may be deemed relevant, and issues of witness credibility and veracity often are critical to the decisionmaking process. *Goldberg* noted that in such circumstances "written submissions are a wholly unsatisfactory basis for decision."

By contrast, the decision whether to discontinue disability benefits will turn, in most cases, upon "routine, standard, and unbiased medical reports by physician specialists" concerning a subject whom they have personally examined.[28] . . . To be sure, credibility and veracity may be a factor in the ultimate disability assessment in some cases. But procedural due process rules are shaped by the risk of error inherent in the truthfinding process as applied to the generality of cases, not the rare exceptions. The potential value of an evidentiary hearing, or even oral presentation to the decisionmaker, is substantially less in this context than in *Goldberg*.

The decision in Goldberg also was based on the Court's conclusion that written submissions were an inadequate substitute for oral presentation because they did not provide an effective means for the recipient to communicate his case to the decisionmaker. Written submissions were viewed as an unrealistic option, for most recipients lacked the "educational attainment necessary to write effectively" and could not afford professional assistance. In addition, such submissions would not provide the "flexibility of oral presentations" or "permit the recipient to mold his argument to the issues the decision maker appears to regard as important." In the context of the disability-benefits-entitlement assessment the administrative procedures under review here fully answer these objections.

---

[28] The decision is not purely a question of the accuracy of a medical diagnosis since the ultimate issue which the state agency must resolve is whether in light of the particular worker's "age, education, and work experience" he cannot "engage in any . . . substantial gainful work which exists in the national economy . . . ." Yet information concerning each of these worker characteristics is amenable to effective written presentation. The value of an evidentiary hearing, or even a limited oral presentation, to an accurate presentation of those factors to the decisionmaker does not appear substantial. Similarly, resolution of the inquiry as to the types of employment opportunities that exist in the national economy for a physically impaired worker with a particular set of skills would not necessarily be advanced by an evidentiary hearing. The statistical information relevant to this judgment is more amenable to written than to oral presentation.

The detailed questionnaire which the state agency periodically sends the recipient identifies with particularity the information relevant to the entitlement decision, and the recipient is invited to obtain assistance from the local SSA office in completing the questionnaire. More important, the information critical to the entitlement decision usually is derived from medical sources, such as the treating physician. Such sources are likely to be able to communicate more effectively through written documents than are welfare recipients or the lay witnesses supporting their cause. The conclusions of physicians often are supported by X-rays and the results of clinical or laboratory tests, information typically more amenable to written than to oral presentation.

A further safeguard against mistake is the policy of allowing the disability recipient's representative full access to all information relied upon by the state agency. In addition, prior to the cutoff of benefits the agency informs the recipient of its tentative assessment, the reasons therefor, and provides a summary of the evidence that it considers most relevant. Opportunity is then afforded the recipient to submit additional evidence or arguments, enabling him to challenge directly the accuracy of information in his file as well as the correctness of the agency's tentative conclusions. These procedures, again as contrasted with those before the Court in *Goldberg*, enable the recipient to "mold" his argument to respond to the precise issues which the decisionmaker regards as crucial.

Despite these carefully structured procedures, amici point to the significant reversal rate for appealed cases as clear evidence that the current process is inadequate. Depending upon the base selected and the line of analysis followed, the relevant reversal rates urged by the contending parties vary from a high of 58.6% for appealed reconsideration decisions to an overall reversal rate of only 3.3%. Bare statistics rarely provide a satisfactory measure of the fairness of a decisionmaking process. Their adequacy is especially suspect here since the administrative review system is operated on an open-file basis. A recipient may always submit new evidence, and such submissions may result in additional medical examinations. Such fresh examinations were held in approximately 30% to 40% of the appealed cases, in fiscal 1973, either at the reconsideration or evidentiary hearing stage of the administrative process. In this context, the value of reversal rate statistics as one means of evaluating the adequacy of the pretermination process is diminished. Thus, although we view such information as relevant, it is certainly not controlling in this case.

E

In striking the appropriate due process balance the final factor to be assessed is the public interest. This includes the administrative burden and other societal costs that would be associated with requiring, as a matter of constitutional right, an evidentiary hearing upon demand in all cases prior to the termination of disability benefits. The most visible burden would be the incremental cost resulting from the increased number of hearings and the expense of providing benefits to ineligible recipients pending decision. No one can predict the extent of the increase, but the fact that full benefits would continue until after such hearings would assure the exhaustion in most cases of this attractive option. Nor would the theoretical right of the Secretary to recover undeserved benefits result, as a practical matter, in any substantial offset to the added outlay of public funds. The parties submit widely varying estimates of the probable additional financial cost. We only need say that experience with the constitutionalizing of government procedures suggests that the ultimate additional cost in terms of money and administrative burden would not be insubstantial.

Financial cost alone is not a controlling weight in determining whether due process requires a particular procedural safeguard prior to some administrative decision. But the Government's interest, and hence that of the public, in conserving scarce fiscal and administrative resources is a factor that must be weighed. At some point the benefit of an additional safeguard to the individual affected by the administrative action and to society in terms of increased assurance that the action is just, may be outweighed by the cost. Significantly, the cost of protecting those whom the preliminary administrative process has identified as likely to be found undeserving may in the end come out of the pockets of the deserving since resources available for any particular program of social welfare are not unlimited.

But more is implicated in cases of this type than ad hoc weighing of fiscal and administrative burdens against the interests of a particular category of claimants. The ultimate balance involves a determination as to when, under our constitutional system, judicial-type procedures must be imposed upon administrative action to assure fairness. We reiterate the wise admonishment of Mr. Justice Frankfurter that differences in the origin and function of administrative agencies "preclude wholesale transplantation of the rules of procedure, trial and review which have evolved from the history and experience of courts." *FCC v. Pottsville Broadcasting Co.*, 309 U.S. 134, 143 (1940). The judicial model of an evidentiary hearing is neither a required, nor even the most effective, method of decisionmaking in all circumstances. The essence of due process is the requirement that "a person in jeopardy of serious loss (be given) notice of the case against him and opportunity to meet it." *Joint Anti-Fascist Comm. v. McGrath*, 341 U.S., at 171–172 (Frankfurter, J., concurring). All that is necessary is that the procedures be tailored, in light of the decision to be made, to "the capacities and circumstances of those who are to be heard," *Goldberg v. Kelly*, 397 U.S., at 268–269, to insure that they are given a meaningful opportunity to present their case. In assessing what process is due in this case, substantial weight must be given to the good-faith judgments of the individuals charged by Congress with the administration of social welfare programs that the procedures they have provided assure fair consideration of the entitlement claims of individuals. This is especially so where, as here, the prescribed procedures not only provide the claimant with an effective process for asserting his claim prior to any administrative action, but also assure a right to an evidentiary hearing, as well as to subsequent judicial review, before the denial of his claim becomes final.

We conclude that an evidentiary hearing is not required prior to the termination of disability benefits and that the present administrative procedures fully comport with due process.

The judgment of the Court of Appeals is

Reversed.

■ MR. JUSTICE STEVENS **took no part in the consideration or decision of this case.**

■ MR. JUSTICE BRENNAN, **with whom** MR. JUSTICE MARSHALL **concurs, dissenting.**

. . . I agree with the District Court and the Court of Appeals that, prior to termination of benefits, Eldridge must be afforded an evidentiary hearing of the type required for welfare beneficiaries under Title IV of the Social Security Act, 42 U.S.C. s 601 et seq. See *Goldberg v. Kelly*, 397 U.S. 254 (1970). I would add that the Court's consideration that a discontinuance of disability benefits may cause the recipient to suffer only a limited deprivation is no argument. It is speculative. Moreover, the very legislative determination to provide disability benefits, without any prerequisite determination of need in fact, presumes a need by the recipient which is not this Court's function to denigrate. Indeed, in the present case, it is indicated that because disability benefits were terminated there was a foreclosure upon the Eldridge home and the family's furniture was repossessed, forcing Eldridge, his wife, and their children to sleep in one bed. Finally, it is also no argument that a worker, who has been placed in the untenable position of having been denied disability benefits, may still seek other forms of public assistance.

Cruzan by Cruzan v. Director, Missouri Dept. of Public Health
497 U.S. 261 (1990)

■ CHIEF JUSTICE REHNQUIST **delivered the opinion of the Court.**

Petitioner Nancy Beth Cruzan was rendered incompetent as a result of severe injuries sustained during an automobile accident. Copetitioners Lester and Joyce Cruzan, Nancy's parents and coguardians, sought a court order directing the withdrawal of their daughter's artificial feeding and hydration equipment after it became apparent that she had virtually no chance of recovering her cognitive faculties. The Supreme Court of Missouri held that because there was no clear and convincing evidence of Nancy's desire to have life-sustaining treatment withdrawn under such circumstances, her parents lacked authority to effectuate such a request. We granted certiorari, and now affirm.

On the night of January 11, 1983, Nancy Cruzan lost control of her car as she traveled down Elm Road in Jasper County, Missouri. The vehicle overturned, and Cruzan was discovered lying face down in a ditch without detectable respiratory or cardiac function. Paramedics were able to restore her breathing and heartbeat at the accident site, and she was transported to a hospital in an unconscious state. An attending neurosurgeon diagnosed her as having sustained probable cerebral contusions compounded by significant anoxia (lack of oxygen). The Missouri trial court in this case found that permanent brain damage generally results after 6 minutes in an anoxic state; it was estimated that Cruzan was deprived of oxygen from 12 to 14 minutes. She remained in a coma for approximately three weeks and then progressed to an unconscious state in which she was able to orally ingest some nutrition. In order to ease feeding and further the recovery, surgeons implanted a gastrostomy feeding and hydration tube in Cruzan with the consent of her then husband. Subsequent rehabilitative efforts proved unavailing. She now lies in a Missouri state hospital in what is commonly referred to as a persistent vegetative state: generally, a condition in which a person exhibits motor reflexes but evinces no indications of significant cognitive function.[1] The State of Missouri is bearing the cost of her care.

---

[1]   The State Supreme Court, adopting much of the trial court's findings, described Nancy Cruzan's medical condition as follows:

". . . (1) [H]er respiration and circulation are not artificially maintained and are within the normal limits of a thirty-year-old female; (2) she is oblivious to her environment except for reflexive responses to sound and perhaps painful stimuli; (3) she suffered anoxia of the brain resulting in a massive enlargement of the ventricles filling with cerebrospinal fluid in the area where the brain has degenerated and [her] cerebral cortical atrophy is irreversible, permanent, progressive and ongoing; (4) her highest cognitive brain function is exhibited by her grimacing perhaps in recognition of ordinarily painful stimuli, indicating the experience of pain and apparent response to sound; (5) she is a spastic quadriplegic; (6) her four extremities are contracted with irreversible muscular and tendon damage to all extremities; (7) she has no cognitive or reflexive ability to swallow food or water to maintain her daily essential needs and . . . she will never recover her ability to swallow sufficient [sic] to satisfy her needs. In sum, Nancy is diagnosed as in a persistent vegetative state. She is not dead. She is not terminally ill. Medical experts testified that she could live another thirty years." Cruzan v. Harmon, 760 S.W.2d 408, 411 (Mo.1988) (en banc).

In observing that Cruzan was not dead, the court referred to the following Missouri statute:

"For all legal purposes, the occurrence of human death shall be determined in accordance with the usual and customary standards of medical practice, provided that death shall not be determined to have occurred unless the following minimal conditions have been met:

"(1) When respiration and circulation are not artificially maintained, there is an irreversible cessation of spontaneous respiration and circulation; or

"(2) When respiration and circulation are artificially maintained, and there is total and irreversible cessation of all brain function, including the brain stem and that such determination is made by a licensed physician." Mo.Rev.Stat. § 194.005 (1986).

Since Cruzan's respiration and circulation were not being artificially maintained, she obviously fit within the first proviso of the statute.

After it had become apparent that Nancy Cruzan had virtually no chance of regaining her mental faculties, her parents asked hospital employees to terminate the artificial nutrition and hydration procedures. All agree that such a removal would cause her death. The employees refused to honor the request without court approval. The parents then sought and received authorization from the state trial court for termination. The court found that a person in Nancy's condition had a fundamental right under the State and Federal Constitutions to refuse or direct the withdrawal of "death prolonging procedures." The court also found that Nancy's "expressed thoughts at age twenty-five in somewhat serious conversation with a housemate friend that if sick or injured she would not wish to continue her life unless she could live at least halfway normally suggests that given her present condition she would not wish to continue on with her nutrition and hydration."

The Supreme Court of Missouri reversed by a divided vote. The court recognized a right to refuse treatment embodied in the common-law doctrine of informed consent, but expressed skepticism about the application of that doctrine in the circumstances of this case. The court also declined to read a broad right of privacy into the State Constitution which would "support the right of a person to refuse medical treatment in every circumstance," and expressed doubt as to whether such a right existed under the United States Constitution. It then decided that the Missouri Living Will statute, Mo.Rev.Stat. § 459.010 *et seq.*, embodied a state policy strongly favoring the preservation of life. The court found that Cruzan's statements to her roommate regarding her desire to live or die under certain conditions were "unreliable for the purpose of determining her intent," "and thus insufficient to support the co-guardians['] claim to exercise substituted judgment on Nancy's behalf." It rejected the argument that Cruzan's parents were entitled to order the termination of her medical treatment, concluding that "no person can assume that choice for an incompetent in the absence of the formalities required under Missouri's Living Will statutes or the clear and convincing, inherently reliable evidence absent here." The court also expressed its view that "[b]road policy questions bearing on life and death are more properly addressed by representative assemblies" than judicial bodies.

We granted certiorari to consider the question whether Cruzan has a right under the United States Constitution which would require the

---

Dr. Fred Plum, the creator of the term "persistent vegetative state" and a renowned expert on the subject, has described the "vegetative state" in the following terms:

"'Vegetative state describes a body which is functioning entirely in terms of its internal controls. It maintains temperature. It maintains heart beat and pulmonary ventilation. It maintains digestive activity. It maintains reflex activity of muscles and nerves for low level conditioned responses. But there is no behavioral evidence of either self-awareness or awareness of the surroundings in a learned manner.'" *In re Jobes,* 108 N.J. 394, 403, 529 A.2d 434, 438 (1987).

hospital to withdraw life-sustaining treatment from her under these circumstances.

At common law, even the touching of one person by another without consent and without legal justification was a battery. Before the turn of the century, this Court observed that "[n]o right is held more sacred, or is more carefully guarded, by the common law, than the right of every individual to the possession and control of his own person, free from all restraint or interference of others, unless by clear and unquestionable authority of law." *Union Pacific R. Co. v. Botsford,* 141 U.S. 250, 251 (1891). This notion of bodily integrity has been embodied in the requirement that informed consent is generally required for medical treatment. Justice Cardozo, while on the Court of Appeals of New York, aptly described this doctrine: "Every human being of adult years and sound mind has a right to determine what shall be done with his own body; and a surgeon who performs an operation without his patient's consent commits an assault, for which he is liable in damages." *Schloendorff v. Society of New York Hospital,* 211 N.Y. 125, 129–130, 105 N.E. 92, 93 (1914). The informed consent doctrine has become firmly entrenched in American tort law.

The logical corollary of the doctrine of informed consent is that the patient generally possesses the right not to consent, that is, to refuse treatment. Until about 15 years ago and the seminal decision in *In re Quinlan,* 70 N.J. 10, 355 A.2d 647 (1976), the number of right-to-refuse-treatment decisions was relatively few. Most of the earlier cases involved patients who refused medical treatment forbidden by their religious beliefs, thus implicating First Amendment rights as well as common-law rights of self-determination. More recently, however, with the advance of medical technology capable of sustaining life well past the point where natural forces would have brought certain death in earlier times, cases involving the right to refuse life-sustaining treatment have burgeoned.

In the *Quinlan* case, young Karen Quinlan suffered severe brain damage as the result of anoxia and entered a persistent vegetative state. Karen's father sought judicial approval to disconnect his daughter's respirator. The New Jersey Supreme Court granted the relief, holding that Karen had a right of privacy grounded in the Federal Constitution to terminate treatment. Recognizing that this right was not absolute, however, the court balanced it against asserted state interests. Noting that the State's interest "weakens and the individual's right to privacy grows as the degree of bodily invasion increases and the prognosis dims," the court concluded that the state interests had to give way in that case. The court also concluded that the "only practical way" to prevent the loss of Karen's privacy right due to her incompetence was to allow her guardian and family to decide "whether she would exercise it in these circumstances."

After *Quinlan,* however, most courts have based a right to refuse treatment either solely on the common-law right to informed consent or on both the common-law right and a constitutional privacy right. . . . Other courts have found state statutory law relevant to the resolution of these issues. . . . As these cases demonstrate, the common-law doctrine of informed consent is viewed as generally encompassing the right of a competent individual to refuse medical treatment. Beyond that, these cases demonstrate both similarity and diversity in their approaches to decision of what all agree is a perplexing question with unusually strong moral and ethical overtones. State courts have available to them for decision a number of sources-state constitutions, statutes, and common law-which are not available to us. In this Court, the question is simply and starkly whether the United States Constitution prohibits Missouri from choosing the rule of decision which it did. This is the first case in which we have been squarely presented with the issue whether the United States Constitution grants what is in common parlance referred to as a "right to die." . . .

The Fourteenth Amendment provides that no State shall "deprive any person of life, liberty, or property, without due process of law." The principle that a competent person has a constitutionally protected liberty interest in refusing unwanted medical treatment may be inferred from our prior decisions. In *Jacobson v. Massachusetts,* 197 U.S. 11, 24–30 (1905), for instance, the Court balanced an individual's liberty interest in declining an unwanted smallpox vaccine against the State's interest in preventing disease. Decisions prior to the incorporation of the Fourth Amendment into the Fourteenth Amendment analyzed searches and seizures involving the body under the Due Process Clause and were thought to implicate substantial liberty interests.

Just this Term, in the course of holding that a State's procedures for administering antipsychotic medication to prisoners were sufficient to satisfy due process concerns, we recognized that prisoners possess "a significant liberty interest in avoiding the unwanted administration of antipsychotic drugs under the Due Process Clause of the Fourteenth Amendment." *Washington v. Harper,* 494 U.S. 210, 221–222 (1990). Still other cases support the recognition of a general liberty interest in refusing medical treatment. *Vitek v. Jones,* 445 U.S. 480, 494 (1980) (transfer to mental hospital coupled with mandatory behavior modification treatment implicated liberty interests); *Parham v. J.R.,* 442 U.S. 584, 600 (1979) ("[A] child, in common with adults, has a substantial liberty interest in not being confined unnecessarily for medical treatment").

But determining that a person has a "liberty interest" under the Due Process Clause does not end the inquiry;[7] "whether respondent's constitutional rights have been violated must be determined by

---

[7] Although many state courts have held that a right to refuse treatment is encompassed by a generalized constitutional right of privacy, we have never so held. We believe this issue is more properly analyzed in terms of a Fourteenth Amendment liberty interest. See *Bowers v. Hardwick,* 478 U.S. 186, 194–195 (1986).

balancing his liberty interests against the relevant state interests." *Youngberg v. Romeo,* 457 U.S. 307, 321 (1982).

Petitioners insist that under the general holdings of our cases, the forced administration of life-sustaining medical treatment, and even of artificially delivered food and water essential to life, would implicate a competent person's liberty interest. Although we think the logic of the cases discussed above would embrace such a liberty interest, the dramatic consequences involved in refusal of such treatment would inform the inquiry as to whether the deprivation of that interest is constitutionally permissible. But for purposes of this case, we assume that the United States Constitution would grant a competent person a constitutionally protected right to refuse lifesaving hydration and nutrition.

Petitioners go on to assert that an incompetent person should possess the same right in this respect as is possessed by a competent person. They rely primarily on our decisions in *Parham v. J.R., supra,* and *Youngberg v. Romeo, supra.* In *Parham,* we held that a mentally disturbed minor child had a liberty interest in "not being confined unnecessarily for medical treatment," but we certainly did not intimate that such a minor child, after commitment, would have a liberty interest in refusing treatment. In *Youngberg,* we held that a seriously retarded adult had a liberty interest in safety and freedom from bodily restraint. *Youngberg,* however, did not deal with decisions to administer or withhold medical treatment.

The difficulty with petitioners' claim is that in a sense it begs the question: An incompetent person is not able to make an informed and voluntary choice to exercise a hypothetical right to refuse treatment or any other right. Such a "right" must be exercised for her, if at all, by some sort of surrogate. Here, Missouri has in effect recognized that under certain circumstances a surrogate may act for the patient in electing to have hydration and nutrition withdrawn in such a way as to cause death, but it has established a procedural safeguard to assure that the action of the surrogate conforms as best it may to the wishes expressed by the patient while competent. Missouri requires that evidence of the incompetent's wishes as to the withdrawal of treatment be proved by clear and convincing evidence. The question, then, is whether the United States Constitution forbids the establishment of this procedural requirement by the State. We hold that it does not.

Whether or not Missouri's clear and convincing evidence requirement comports with the United States Constitution depends in part on what interests the State may properly seek to protect in this situation. Missouri relies on its interest in the protection and preservation of human life, and there can be no gainsaying this interest. As a general matter, the States-indeed, all civilized nations-demonstrate their commitment to life by treating homicide as a serious crime. Moreover, the majority of States in this country have laws imposing criminal penalties on one who assists another to commit suicide. We do not think a State is required to remain neutral in the face of an informed and voluntary decision by a physically able adult to starve to death.

But in the context presented here, a State has more particular interests at stake. The choice between life and death is a deeply personal decision of obvious and overwhelming finality. We believe Missouri may legitimately seek to safeguard the personal element of this choice through the imposition of heightened evidentiary requirements. It cannot be disputed that the Due Process Clause protects an interest in life as well as an interest in refusing life-sustaining medical treatment. Not all incompetent patients will have loved ones available to serve as surrogate decisionmakers. And even where family members are present, "[t]here will, of course, be some unfortunate situations in which family members will not act to protect a patient." *In re Jobes,* 108 N.J. 394, 419, 529 A.2d 434, 447 (1987). A State is entitled to guard against potential abuses in such situations. Similarly, a State is entitled to consider that a judicial proceeding to make a determination regarding an incompetent's wishes may very well not be an adversarial one, with the added guarantee of accurate factfinding that the adversary process brings with it.[9] Finally, we think a State may properly decline to make judgments about the "quality" of life that a particular individual may enjoy, and simply assert an unqualified interest in the preservation of human life to be weighed against the constitutionally protected interests of the individual.

In our view, Missouri has permissibly sought to advance these interests through the adoption of a "clear and convincing" standard of proof to govern such proceedings. "The function of a standard of proof, as that concept is embodied in the Due Process Clause and in the realm of factfinding, is to instruct the factfinder concerning the degree of confidence our society thinks he should have in the correctness of factual conclusions for a particular type of adjudication." *Addington v. Texas,* 441 U.S. 418, 423 (1979). "This Court has mandated an intermediate standard of proof—'clear and convincing evidence'—when the individual interests at stake in a state proceeding are both particularly important and more substantial than mere loss of money." *Santosky v. Kramer,* 455

---

[9] Since Cruzan was a patient at a state hospital when this litigation commenced, the State has been involved as an adversary from the beginning. However, it can be expected that many disputes of this type will arise in private institutions, where a guardian *ad litem* or similar party will have been appointed as the sole representative of the incompetent individual in the litigation. In such cases, a guardian may act in entire good faith, and yet not maintain a position truly adversarial to that of the family. Indeed, as noted by the court below, "[t]he guardian *ad litem* [in this case] finds himself in the predicament of believing that it is in Nancy's 'best interest to have the tube feeding discontinued,' but 'feeling that an appeal should be made because our responsibility to her as attorneys and guardians *ad litem* was to pursue this matter to the highest court in the state in view of the fact that this is a case of first impression in the State of Missouri.'" Cruzan's guardian ad litem has also filed a brief in this Court urging reversal of the Missouri Supreme Court's decision. None of this is intended to suggest that the guardian acted the least bit improperly in this proceeding. It is only meant to illustrate the limits which may obtain on the adversarial nature of this type of litigation.

U.S. 745, 756 (1982). Thus, such a standard has been required in deportation proceedings, in denaturalization proceedings, in civil commitment proceedings, and in proceedings for the termination of parental rights. Further, this level of proof, "or an even higher one, has traditionally been imposed in cases involving allegations of civil fraud, and in a variety of other kinds of civil cases involving such issues as . . . lost wills, oral contracts to make bequests, and the like." *Woodby v. INS,* 385 U.S. 276, 285, n. 18 (1966).

We think it self-evident that the interests at stake in the instant proceedings are more substantial, both on an individual and societal level, than those involved in a run-of-the-mine civil dispute. But not only does the standard of proof reflect the importance of a particular adjudication, it also serves as "a societal judgment about how the risk of error should be distributed between the litigants." *Santosky, supra,* 455 U.S. at 755. The more stringent the burden of proof a party must bear, the more that party bears the risk of an erroneous decision. We believe that Missouri may permissibly place an increased risk of an erroneous decision on those seeking to terminate an incompetent individual's life-sustaining treatment. An erroneous decision not to terminate results in a maintenance of the status quo; the possibility of subsequent developments such as advancements in medical science, the discovery of new evidence regarding the patient's intent, changes in the law, or simply the unexpected death of the patient despite the administration of life-sustaining treatment at least create the potential that a wrong decision will eventually be corrected or its impact mitigated. An erroneous decision to withdraw life-sustaining treatment, however, is not susceptible of correction. In *Santosky,* one of the factors which led the Court to require proof by clear and convincing evidence in a proceeding to terminate parental rights was that a decision in such a case was final and irrevocable. The same must surely be said of the decision to discontinue hydration and nutrition of a patient such as Nancy Cruzan, which all agree will result in her death.

It is also worth noting that most, if not all, States simply forbid oral testimony entirely in determining the wishes of parties in transactions which, while important, simply do not have the consequences that a decision to terminate a person's life does. At common law and by statute in most States, the parol evidence rule prevents the variations of the terms of a written contract by oral testimony. The statute of frauds makes unenforceable oral contracts to leave property by will, and statutes regulating the making of wills universally require that those instruments be in writing. There is no doubt that statutes requiring wills to be in writing, and statutes of frauds which require that a contract to make a will be in writing, on occasion frustrate the effectuation of the intent of a particular decedent, just as Missouri's requirement of proof in this case may have frustrated the effectuation of the not-fully-expressed desires of Nancy Cruzan. But the Constitution does not require general rules to work faultlessly; no general rule can.

In sum, we conclude that a State may apply a clear and convincing evidence standard in proceedings where a guardian seeks to discontinue nutrition and hydration of a person diagnosed to be in a persistent vegetative state. We note that many courts which have adopted some sort of substituted judgment procedure in situations like this, whether they limit consideration of evidence to the prior expressed wishes of the incompetent individual, or whether they allow more general proof of what the individual's decision would have been, require a clear and convincing standard of proof for such evidence.

The Supreme Court of Missouri held that in this case the testimony adduced at trial did not amount to clear and convincing proof of the patient's desire to have hydration and nutrition withdrawn. In so doing, it reversed a decision of the Missouri trial court which had found that the evidence "suggest [ed]" Nancy Cruzan would not have desired to continue such measures, but which had not adopted the standard of "clear and convincing evidence" enunciated by the Supreme Court. The testimony adduced at trial consisted primarily of Nancy Cruzan's statements made to a housemate about a year before her accident that she would not want to live should she face life as a "vegetable," and other observations to the same effect. The observations did not deal in terms with withdrawal of medical treatment or of hydration and nutrition. We cannot say that the Supreme Court of Missouri committed constitutional error in reaching the conclusion that it did.[11]

Petitioners alternatively contend that Missouri must accept the "substituted judgment" of close family members even in the absence of substantial proof that their views reflect the views of the patient. They rely primarily upon our decisions in *Michael H. v. Gerald D.,* 491 U.S. 110 (1989), and *Parham v. J.R.,* 442 U.S. 584 (1979). But we do not think these cases support their claim. In *Michael H.,* we *upheld* the constitutionality of California's favored treatment of traditional family relationships; such a holding may not be turned around into a constitutional requirement that a State *must* recognize the primacy of those relationships in a situation like this. And in *Parham,* where the patient was a minor, we also *upheld* the constitutionality of a state scheme in which parents made certain decisions for mentally ill minors.

---

[11] The clear and convincing standard of proof has been variously defined in this context as "proof sufficient to persuade the trier of fact that the patient held a firm and settled commitment to the termination of life supports under the circumstances like those presented," *In re Westchester County Medical Center on Behalf of O'Connor,* 72 N.Y.2d 517, 531, 534 N.Y.S.2d 886, 892 (1988), and as evidence which "produces in the mind of the trier of fact a firm belief or conviction as to the truth of the allegations sought to be established, evidence so clear, direct and weighty and convincing as to enable [the factfinder] to come to a clear conviction, without hesitancy, of the truth of the precise facts in issue." *In re Jobes,* 108 N.J., at 407–408. In both of these cases the evidence of the patient's intent to refuse medical treatment was arguably stronger than that presented here. The New York Court of Appeals and the Supreme Court of New Jersey, respectively, held that the proof failed to meet a clear and convincing threshold.

Here again petitioners would seek to turn a decision which allowed a State to rely on family decisionmaking into a constitutional requirement that the State recognize such decisionmaking. But constitutional law does not work that way.

No doubt is engendered by anything in this record but that Nancy Cruzan's mother and father are loving and caring parents. If the State were required by the United States Constitution to repose a right of "substituted judgment" with anyone, the Cruzans would surely qualify. But we do not think the Due Process Clause requires the State to repose judgment on these matters with anyone but the patient herself. Close family members may have a strong feeling-a feeling not at all ignoble or unworthy, but not entirely disinterested, either-that they do not wish to witness the continuation of the life of a loved one which they regard as hopeless, meaningless, and even degrading. But there is no automatic assurance that the view of close family members will necessarily be the same as the patient's would have been had she been confronted with the prospect of her situation while competent. All of the reasons previously discussed for allowing Missouri to require clear and convincing evidence of the patient's wishes lead us to conclude that the State may choose to defer only to those wishes, rather than confide the decision to close family members.[12]

The judgment of the Supreme Court of Missouri is

Affirmed.

■ JUSTICE O'CONNOR, concurring.

. . . Today's decision, holding only that the Constitution permits a State to require clear and convincing evidence of Nancy Cruzan's desire to have artificial hydration and nutrition withdrawn, does not preclude a future determination that the Constitution requires the States to implement the decisions of a patient's duly appointed surrogate. Nor does it prevent States from developing other approaches for protecting an incompetent individual's liberty interest in refusing medical treatment. As is evident from the Court's survey of state court decisions, no national consensus has yet emerged on the best solution for this difficult and sensitive problem. Today we decide only that one State's practice does not violate the Constitution; the more challenging task of crafting appropriate procedures for safeguarding incompetents' liberty interests is entrusted to the "laboratory" of the States, *New State Ice Co. v. Liebmann,* 285 U.S. 262, 311 (1932) (Brandeis, J., dissenting), in the first instance.

---

[12] We are not faced in this case with the question whether a State might be required to defer to the decision of a surrogate if competent and probative evidence established that the patient herself had expressed a desire that the decision to terminate life-sustaining treatment be made for her by that individual. . . .

■ JUSTICE SCALIA, concurring.

The various opinions in this case portray quite clearly the difficult, indeed agonizing, questions that are presented by the constantly increasing power of science to keep the human body alive for longer than any reasonable person would want to inhabit it. The States have begun to grapple with these problems through legislation. I am concerned, from the tenor of today's opinions, that we are poised to confuse that enterprise as successfully as we have confused the enterprise of legislating concerning abortion-requiring it to be conducted against a background of federal constitutional imperatives that are unknown because they are being newly crafted from Term to Term. That would be a great misfortune.

While I agree with the Court's analysis today, and therefore join in its opinion, I would have preferred that we announce, clearly and promptly, that the federal courts have no business in this field; that American law has always accorded the State the power to prevent, by force if necessary, suicide-including suicide by refusing to take appropriate measures necessary to preserve one's life; that the point at which life becomes "worthless," and the point at which the means necessary to preserve it become "extraordinary" or "inappropriate," are neither set forth in the Constitution nor known to the nine Justices of this Court any better than they are known to nine people picked at random from the Kansas City telephone directory; and hence, that even when it *is* demonstrated by clear and convincing evidence that a patient no longer wishes certain measures to be taken to preserve his or her life, it is up to the citizens of Missouri to decide, through their elected representatives, whether that wish will be honored. It is quite impossible (because the Constitution says nothing about the matter) that those citizens will decide upon a line less lawful than the one we would choose; and it is unlikely (because we know no more about "life and death" than they do) that they will decide upon a line less reasonable.

The text of the Due Process Clause does not protect individuals against deprivations of liberty *simpliciter*. It protects them against deprivations of liberty "without due process of law." To determine that such a deprivation would not occur if Nancy Cruzan were forced to take nourishment against her will, it is unnecessary to reopen the historically recurrent debate over whether "due process" includes substantive restrictions. It is at least true that no "substantive due process" claim can be maintained unless the claimant demonstrates that the State has deprived him of a right historically and traditionally protected against state interference. *Michael H. v. Gerald D.,* 491 U.S. 110, 122 (1989) (plurality opinion). That cannot possibly be established here.

At common law in England, a suicide-defined as one who "deliberately puts an end to his own existence, or commits any unlawful malicious act, the consequence of which is his own death," 4 W. Blackstone, Commentaries *189—was criminally liable. Although the

States abolished the penalties imposed by the common law (*i.e.,* forfeiture and ignominious burial), they did so to spare the innocent family and not to legitimize the act. Case law at the time of the adoption of the Fourteenth Amendment generally held that assisting suicide was a criminal offense. And most States that did not explicitly prohibit assisted suicide in 1868 recognized, when the issue arose in the 50 years following the Fourteenth Amendment's ratification, that assisted and (in some cases) attempted suicide were unlawful. Thus, there is no significant support for the claim that a right to suicide is so rooted in our tradition that it may be deemed 'fundamental' or 'implicit in the concept of ordered liberty.'

Petitioners rely on three distinctions to separate Nancy Cruzan's case from ordinary suicide: (1) that she is permanently incapacitated and in pain; (2) that she would bring on her death not by any affirmative act but by merely declining treatment that provides nourishment; and (3) that preventing her from effectuating her presumed wish to die requires violation of her bodily integrity. None of these suffices. Suicide was not excused even when committed "to avoid those ills which [persons] had not the fortitude to endure." 4 Blackstone, *supra,* at *189. . . .The second asserted distinction-suggested by the recent cases canvassed by the Court concerning the right to refuse treatment, relies on the dichotomy between action and inaction. Suicide, it is said, consists of an affirmative act to end one's life; refusing treatment is not an affirmative act "causing" death, but merely a passive acceptance of the natural process of dying. I readily acknowledge that the distinction between action and inaction has some bearing upon the legislative judgment of what ought to be prevented as suicide-though even there it would seem to me unreasonable to draw the line precisely between action and inaction, rather than between various forms of inaction. It would not make much sense to say that one may not kill oneself by walking into the sea, but may sit on the beach until submerged by the incoming tide; or that one may not intentionally lock oneself into a cold storage locker, but may refrain from coming indoors when the temperature drops below freezing. Even as a legislative matter, in other words, the intelligent line does not fall between action and inaction but between those forms of inaction that consist of abstaining from "ordinary" care and those that consist of abstaining from "excessive" or "heroic" measures. Unlike action versus inaction, that is not a line to be discerned by logic or legal analysis, and we should not pretend that it is.

But to return to the principal point for present purposes: the irrelevance of the action-inaction distinction. Starving oneself to death is no different from putting a gun to one's temple as far as the common-law definition of suicide is concerned; the cause of death in both cases is the suicide's conscious decision to "pu[t] an end to his own existence." 4 Blackstone, *supra,* at *189. Of course the common law rejected the action-inaction distinction in other contexts involving the taking of human life as well. . . .

The third asserted basis of distinction-that frustrating Nancy Cruzan's wish to die in the present case requires interference with her bodily integrity-is likewise inadequate, because such interference is impermissible only if one begs the question whether her refusal to undergo the treatment on her own is suicide. It has always been lawful not only for the State, but even for private citizens, to interfere with bodily integrity to prevent a felony. That general rule has of course been applied to suicide. At common law, even a private person's use of force to prevent suicide was privileged. It is not even reasonable, much less required by the Constitution, to maintain that although the State has the right to prevent a person from slashing his wrists, it does not have the power to apply physical force to prevent him from doing so, nor the power, should he succeed, to apply, coercively if necessary, medical measures to stop the flow of blood. The state-run hospital, I am certain, is not liable under 42 U.S.C. § 1983 for violation of constitutional rights, nor the private hospital liable under general tort law, if, in a State where suicide is unlawful, it pumps out the stomach of a person who has intentionally taken an overdose of barbiturates, despite that person's wishes to the contrary. . . .

What I have said above is not meant to suggest that I would think it desirable, if we were sure that Nancy Cruzan wanted to die, to keep her alive by the means at issue here. I assert only that the Constitution has nothing to say about the subject. . . . Are there, then, no reasonable and humane limits that ought not to be exceeded in requiring an individual to preserve his own life? There obviously are, but they are not set forth in the Due Process Clause. What assures us that those limits will not be exceeded is the same constitutional guarantee that is the source of most of our protection-what protects us, for example, from being assessed a tax of 100% of our income above the subsistence level, from being forbidden to drive cars, or from being required to send our children to school for 10 hours a day, none of which horribles are categorically prohibited by the Constitution. Our salvation is the Equal Protection Clause, which requires the democratic majority to accept for themselves and their loved ones what they impose on you and me. This Court need not, and has no authority to, inject itself into every field of human activity where irrationality and oppression may theoretically occur, and if it tries to do so it will destroy itself.

■ JUSTICE BRENNAN, with whom JUSTICE MARSHALL and JUSTICE BLACKMUN join, dissenting.

. . . Because I believe that Nancy Cruzan has a fundamental right to be free of unwanted artificial nutrition and hydration, which right is not outweighed by any interests of the State, and because I find that the improperly biased procedural obstacles imposed by the Missouri

Supreme Court impermissibly burden that right, I respectfully dissent. Nancy Cruzan is entitled to choose to die with dignity.

I

A

"[T]he timing of death-once a matter of fate-is now a matter of human choice." Office of Technology Assessment Task Force, Life Sustaining Technologies and the Elderly 41 (1988). Of the approximately 2 million people who die each year, 80% die in hospitals and long-term care institutions, and perhaps 70% of those after a decision to forgo life-sustaining treatment has been made. Nearly every death involves a decision whether to undertake some medical procedure that could prolong the process of dying. Such decisions are difficult and personal. They must be made on the basis of individual values, informed by medical realities, yet within a framework governed by law. The role of the courts is confined to defining that framework, delineating the ways in which government may and may not participate in such decisions.

The question before this Court is a relatively narrow one: whether the Due Process Clause allows Missouri to require a now-incompetent patient in an irreversible persistent vegetative state to remain on life support absent rigorously clear and convincing evidence that avoiding the treatment represents the patient's prior, express choice. If a fundamental right is at issue, Missouri's rule of decision must be scrutinized under the standards this Court has always applied in such circumstances. As we said in *Zablocki v. Redhail,* 434 U.S. 374, 388 (1978), if a requirement imposed by a State "significantly interferes with the exercise of a fundamental right, it cannot be upheld unless it is supported by sufficiently important state interests and is closely tailored to effectuate only those interests." . . . An evidentiary rule, just as a substantive prohibition, must meet these standards if it significantly burdens a fundamental liberty interest. . . .

B

The starting point for our legal analysis must be whether a competent person has a constitutional right to avoid unwanted medical care. Earlier this Term, this Court held that the Due Process Clause of the Fourteenth Amendment confers a significant liberty interest in avoiding unwanted medical treatment. *Washington v. Harper,* 494 U.S. 210, 221–222 (1990). Today, the Court concedes that our prior decisions "support the recognition of a general liberty interest in refusing medical treatment." The Court, however, avoids discussing either the measure of that liberty interest or its application by assuming, for purposes of this case only, that a competent person has a constitutionally protected liberty interest in being free of unwanted artificial nutrition and hydration. . . .

But if a competent person has a liberty interest to be free of unwanted medical treatment, as both the majority and Justice

O'CONNOR concede, it must be fundamental. "We are dealing here with [a decision] which involves one of the basic civil rights of man." *Skinner v. Oklahoma ex rel. Williamson,* 316 U.S. 535, 541 (1942). Whatever other liberties protected by the Due Process Clause are fundamental, those liberties that are 'deeply rooted in this Nation's history and tradition' are among them. . . .

The right to be free from medical attention without consent, to determine what shall be done with one's own body, *is* deeply rooted in this Nation's traditions, as the majority acknowledges. This right has long been "firmly entrenched in American tort law" and is securely grounded in the earliest common law. . . . Thus, freedom from unwanted medical attention is unquestionably among those principles "so rooted in the traditions and conscience of our people as to be ranked as fundamental." *Snyder v. Massachusetts,* 291 U.S. 97, 105 (1934).

That there may be serious consequences involved in refusal of the medical treatment at issue here does not vitiate the right under our common-law tradition of medical self-determination. It is "a well-established rule of general law . . . that it is the patient, not the physician, who ultimately decides if treatment-any treatment-is to be given at all. . . . The rule has never been qualified in its application by either the nature or purpose of the treatment, or the gravity of the consequences of acceding to or foregoing it." *Tune v. Walter Reed Army Medical Hospital,* 602 F.Supp. 1452, 1455 (DC 1985).[6]

No material distinction can be drawn between the treatment to which Nancy Cruzan continues to be subject-artificial nutrition and hydration-and any other medical treatment. The artificial delivery of nutrition and hydration is undoubtedly medical treatment. The technique to which Nancy Cruzan is subject-artificial feeding through a gastrostomy tube-involves a tube implanted surgically into her stomach through incisions in her abdominal wall. It may obstruct the intestinal tract, erode and pierce the stomach wall, or cause leakage of the stomach's contents into the abdominal cavity. . . . The patient must be monitored daily by medical personnel as to weight, fluid intake, and fluid output; blood tests must be done weekly. . . .

Nor does the fact that Nancy Cruzan is now incompetent deprive her of her fundamental rights. See *Youngberg v. Romeo,* 457 U.S. 307, 315–316, 319 (1982) (holding that severely retarded man's liberty interests in safety, freedom from bodily restraint, and reasonable training survive involuntary commitment); *Parham v. J.R.,* 442 U.S. 584, 600 (1979) (recognizing a child's substantial liberty interest in not being confined

---

[6]   Under traditional tort law, exceptions have been found only to protect dependent children. *See Cruzan v. Harmon,* 760 S.W.2d 408, 422, n. 17 (Mo.1988) (citing cases where Missouri courts have ordered blood transfusions for children over the religious objection of parents); *see also Winthrop University Hospital v. Hess,* 128 Misc.2d 804, 490 N.Y.S.2d 996 (Sup.Ct. Nassau Cty. 1985) (court ordered blood transfusion for religious objector because she was the mother of an infant and had explained that her objection was to the signing of the consent, not the transfusion itself).

unnecessarily for medical treatment). As the majority recognizes, the question is not whether an incompetent has constitutional rights, but how such rights may be exercised. . . .

II

. . . Although the right to be free of unwanted medical intervention, like other constitutionally protected interests, may not be absolute,[12] no state interest could outweigh the rights of an individual in Nancy Cruzan's position. Whatever a State's possible interests in mandating life-support treatment under other circumstances, there is no good to be obtained here by Missouri's insistence that Nancy Cruzan remain on life-support systems if it is indeed her wish not to do so. Missouri does not claim, nor could it, that society as a whole will be benefited by Nancy's receiving medical treatment. No third party's situation will be improved and no harm to others will be averted.[13]

The only state interest asserted here is a general interest in the preservation of life. But the State has no legitimate general interest in someone's life, completely abstracted from the interest of the person living that life, that could outweigh the person's choice to avoid medical treatment. "[T]he regulation of constitutionally protected decisions . . . must be predicated on legitimate state concerns *other than* disagreement with the choice the individual has made. . . . Otherwise, the interest in liberty protected by the Due Process Clause would be a nullity." *Hodgson v. Minnesota,* 497 U.S. 417, 435 (1990) (opinion of STEVENS, J.). Thus, the State's general interest in life must accede to Nancy Cruzan's particularized and intense interest in self-determination in her choice of medical treatment. There is simply nothing legitimately within the State's purview to be gained by superseding her decision.

Moreover, there may be considerable danger that Missouri's rule of decision would impair rather than serve any interest the State does have in sustaining life. Current medical practice recommends use of heroic measures if there is a scintilla of a chance that the patient will recover, on the assumption that the measures will be discontinued should the patient improve. When the President's Commission in 1982 approved the withdrawal of life-support equipment from irreversibly vegetative

---

[12] See *Jacobson v. Massachusetts,* 197 U.S. 11, 26–27 (1905) (upholding a Massachusetts law imposing fines or imprisonment on those refusing to be vaccinated as "of paramount necessity" to that State's fight against a smallpox epidemic).

[13] Were such interests at stake, however, I would find that the Due Process Clause places limits on what invasive medical procedures could be forced on an unwilling comatose patient in pursuit of the interests of a third party. If Missouri were correct that its interests outweigh Nancy's interest in avoiding medical procedures as long as she is free of pain and physical discomfort, it is not apparent why a State could not choose to remove one of her kidneys without consent on the ground that society would be better off if the recipient of that kidney were saved from renal poisoning. Nancy cannot feel surgical pain. Nor would removal of one kidney be expected to shorten her life expectancy. . . . Indeed, why could the State not perform medical experiments on her body, experiments that might save countless lives, and would cause her no greater burden than she already bears by being fed through the gastrostomy tube? This would be too brave a new world for me and, I submit, for our Constitution.

patients, it explained that "[a]n even more troubling wrong occurs when a treatment that might save life or improve health is not started because the health care personnel are afraid that they will find it very difficult to stop the treatment if, as is fairly likely, it proves to be of little benefit and greatly burdens the patient." A New Jersey court recognized that families as well as doctors might be discouraged by an inability to stop life-support measures from "even attempting certain types of care [which] could thereby force them into hasty and premature decisions to allow a patient to die." *In re Conroy,* 98 N.J. 321, 370, 486 A.2d 1209, 1234 (1985).[15]

III

This is not to say that the State has no legitimate interests to assert here. As the majority recognizes, Missouri has a *parens patriae* interest in providing Nancy Cruzan, now incompetent, with as accurate as possible a determination of how she would exercise her rights under these circumstances. Second, if and when it is determined that Nancy Cruzan would want to continue treatment, the State may legitimately assert an interest in providing that treatment. But *until* Nancy's wishes have been determined the only state interest that may be asserted is an interest in safe-guarding the accuracy of that determination.

Accuracy, therefore, must be our touchstone. Missouri may constitutionally impose only those procedural requirements that serve to enhance the accuracy of a determination of Nancy Cruzan's wishes or are at least consistent with an accurate determination. The Missouri "safeguard" that the Court upholds today does not meet that standard. The determination needed in this context is whether the incompetent person would choose to live in a persistent vegetative state on life support or to avoid this medical treatment. Missouri's rule of decision imposes a markedly asymmetrical evidentiary burden. Only evidence of specific statements of treatment choice made by the patient when competent is admissible to support a finding that the patient, now in a persistent vegetative state, would wish to avoid further medical treatment. Moreover, this evidence must be clear and convincing. No proof is required to support a finding that the incompetent person would wish to continue treatment.

---

[15] In any event, the state interest identified by the Missouri Supreme Court-a comprehensive and "unqualified" interest in preserving life-is not even well supported by that State's own enactments. In the first place, Missouri has no law requiring every person to procure any needed medical care nor a state health insurance program to underwrite such care. Second, as the state court admitted, Missouri has a living will statute which specifically "allows and encourages the pre-planned termination of life." The fact that Missouri actively provides for its citizens to choose a natural death under certain circumstances suggests that the State's interest in life is not so unqualified as the court below suggests. It is true that this particular statute does not apply to nonterminal patients and does not include artificial nutrition and hydration as one of the measures that may be declined. Nonetheless, Missouri has also not chosen to require court review of every decision to withhold or withdraw life support made on behalf of an incompetent patient. Such decisions are made every day, without state participation. . . .

A

The majority offers several justifications for Missouri's heightened evidentiary standard. First, the majority explains that the State may constitutionally adopt this rule to govern determinations of an incompetent's wishes in order to advance the State's substantive interests, including its unqualified interest in the preservation of human life. Missouri's evidentiary standard, however, cannot rest on the State's own interest in a particular substantive result. To be sure, courts have long erected clear and convincing evidence standards to place the greater risk of erroneous decisions on those bringing disfavored claims. In such cases, however, the choice to discourage certain claims was a legitimate, constitutional policy choice. In contrast, Missouri has no such power to disfavor a choice by Nancy Cruzan to avoid medical treatment, because Missouri has no legitimate interest in providing Nancy with treatment until it is established that this represents her choice. Just as a State may not override Nancy's choice directly, it may not do so indirectly through the imposition of a procedural rule.

Second, the majority offers two explanations for why Missouri's clear and convincing evidence standard is a means of enhancing accuracy, but neither is persuasive. The majority initially argues that a clear and convincing evidence standard is necessary to compensate for the possibility that such proceedings will lack the "guarantee of accurate factfinding that the adversary process brings with it." . . . An adversarial proceeding is of particular importance when one side has a strong personal interest which needs to be counterbalanced to assure the court that the questions will be fully explored. A minor who has a strong interest in obtaining permission for an abortion without notifying her parents may come forward whether or not society would be satisfied that she has made the decision with the seasoned judgment of an adult. The proceeding here is of a different nature. Barring venal motives, which a trial court has the means of ferreting out, the decision to come forward to request a judicial order to stop treatment represents a slowly and carefully considered resolution by at least one adult and more frequently several adults that discontinuation of treatment is the patient's wish. . . .

In a hearing to determine the treatment preferences of an incompetent person, a court is not limited to adjusting burdens of proof as its only means of protecting against a possible imbalance. Indeed, any concern that those who come forward will present a one-sided view would be better addressed by appointing a guardian ad litem, who could use the State's powers of discovery to gather and present evidence regarding the patient's wishes. A guardian ad litem's task is to uncover any conflicts of interest and ensure that each party likely to have relevant evidence is consulted and brought forward-for example, other members of the family, friends, clergy, and doctors Missouri's heightened evidentiary standard attempts to achieve balance by discounting evidence; the guardian ad litem technique achieves balance by probing for additional evidence.

Where, as here, the family members, friends, doctors, and guardian ad litem agree, it is not because the process has failed, as the majority suggests. It is because there is no genuine dispute as to Nancy's preference.

The majority next argues that where, as here, important individual rights are at stake, a clear and convincing evidence standard has long been held to be an appropriate means of enhancing accuracy, citing decisions concerning what process an individual is due before he can be deprived of a liberty interest. In those cases, however, this Court imposed a clear and convincing standard as a constitutional minimum on the basis of its evaluation that one side's interests clearly outweighed the second side's interests and therefore the second side should bear the risk of error. See *Santosky v. Kramer,* 455 U.S. 745, 753, 766–767 (1982) (requiring a clear and convincing evidence standard for termination of parental rights because the parent's interest is fundamental but the State has no legitimate interest in termination unless the parent is unfit, and finding that the State's interest in finding the best home for the child does not arise until the parent has been found unfit); *Addington v. Texas,* 441 U.S. 418, 426–427 (1979) (requiring clear and convincing evidence in an involuntary commitment hearing because the interest of the individual far outweighs that of a State, which has no legitimate interest in confining individuals who are not mentally ill and do not pose a danger to themselves or others). Moreover, we have always recognized that shifting the risk of error reduces the likelihood of errors in one direction at the cost of increasing the likelihood of errors in the other. In the cases cited by the majority, the imbalance imposed by a heightened evidentiary standard was not only acceptable but required because the standard was deployed to protect an individual's exercise of a fundamental right, as the majority admits, In contrast, the Missouri court imposed a clear and convincing evidence standard as an obstacle to the exercise of a fundamental right.

The majority claims that the allocation of the risk of error is justified because it is more important not to terminate life support for someone who would wish it continued than to honor the wishes of someone who would not. An erroneous decision to terminate life support is irrevocable, says the majority, while an erroneous decision not to terminate "results in a maintenance of the status quo."[17] But, from the point of view of the

---

[17] The majority's definition of the "status quo," of course, begs the question. Artificial delivery of nutrition and hydration represents the "status quo" only if the State has chosen to permit doctors and hospitals to keep a patient on life-support systems over the protests of his family or guardian. The "status quo" absent that state interference would be the natural result of his accident or illness (and the family's decision). The majority's definition of status quo, however, is "to a large extent a predictable, yet accidental confluence of technology, psyche, and inertia. The general citizenry . . . never said that it favored the creation of coma wards where permanently unconscious patients would be tended for years and years. Nor did the populace as a whole authorize the preeminence of doctors over families in making treatment decisions for incompetent patients." Rhoden, Litigating Life and Death, 102 Harv.L.Rev. 375, 433–434 (1988).

patient, an erroneous decision in either direction is irrevocable. An erroneous decision to terminate artificial nutrition and hydration, to be sure, will lead to failure of that last remnant of physiological life, the brain stem, and result in complete brain death. An erroneous decision not to terminate life support, however, robs a patient of the very qualities protected by the right to avoid unwanted medical treatment. His own degraded existence is perpetuated; his family's suffering is protracted; the memory he leaves behind becomes more and more distorted.

Even a later decision to grant him his wish cannot undo the intervening harm. But a later decision is unlikely in any event. . . .

B

Even more than its heightened evidentiary standard, the Missouri court's categorical exclusion of relevant evidence dispenses with any semblance of accurate factfinding. The court adverted to no evidence supporting its decision, but held that no clear and convincing, inherently reliable evidence had been presented to show that Nancy would want to avoid further treatment. In doing so, the court failed to consider statements Nancy had made to family members and a close friend.[19] The court also failed to consider testimony from Nancy's mother and sister that they were certain that Nancy would want to discontinue artificial nutrition and hydration,[20] even after the court found that Nancy's family

---

[19] The trial court had relied on the testimony of Athena Comer, a long-time friend, co-worker, and housemate for several months, as sufficient to show that Nancy Cruzan would wish to be free of medical treatment under her present circumstances. Ms. Comer described a conversation she and Nancy had while living together, concerning Ms. Comer's sister who had become ill suddenly and died during the night. The Comer family had been told that if she had lived through the night, she would have been in a vegetative state. Nancy had lost a grandmother a few months before. Ms. Comer testified: "Nancy said she would never want to live [in a vegetative state] because if she couldn't be normal or even, you know, like half way, and do things for yourself, because Nancy always did, that she didn't want to live . . . and we talked about it a lot." She said "several times" that "she wouldn't want to live that way because if she was going to live, she wanted to be able to live, not to just lay in a bed and not be able to move because you can't do anything for yourself." "[S]he said that she hoped that [all the] people in her family knew that she wouldn't want to live [in a vegetative state] because she knew it was usually up to the family whether you lived that way or not."

The conversation took place approximately a year before Nancy's accident and was described by Ms. Comer as a "very serious" conversation that continued for approximately half an hour without interruption. The Missouri Supreme Court dismissed Nancy's statement as "unreliable" on the ground that it was an informally expressed reaction to other people's medical conditions.

The Missouri Supreme Court did not refer to other evidence of Nancy's wishes or explain why it was rejected. Nancy's sister Christy, to whom she was very close, testified that she and Nancy had had two very serious conversations about a year and a half before the accident. A day or two after their niece was stillborn (but would have been badly damaged if she had lived), Nancy had said that maybe it was part of a "greater plan" that the baby had been stillborn and did not have to face "the possible life of mere existence." A month later, after their grandmother had died after a long battle with heart problems, Nancy said that "it was better for my grandmother not to be kind of brought back and forth [by] medical [treatment], brought back from a critical near point of death. . . ."

[20] Nancy's sister Christy, Nancy's mother, and another of Nancy's friends testified that Nancy would want to discontinue the hydration and nutrition. Christy said that "Nancy would be horrified at the state she is in." She would also "want to take that burden away from [her family]." Based on "a lifetime of experience [I know Nancy's wishes] are to discontinue the hydration and the nutrition." Nancy's mother testified: "Nancy would not want to be like she is

was loving and without malignant motive. The court also failed to consider the conclusions of the guardian ad litem, appointed by the trial court, that there was clear and convincing evidence that Nancy would want to discontinue medical treatment and that this was in her best interests. The court did not specifically define what kind of evidence it would consider clear and convincing, but its general discussion suggests that only a living will or equivalently formal directive from the patient when competent would meet this standard.

Too few people execute living wills or equivalently formal directives for such an evidentiary rule to ensure adequately that the wishes of incompetent persons will be honored.[21] While it might be a wise social policy to encourage people to furnish such instructions, no general conclusion about a patient's choice can be drawn from the absence of formalities. . . .

The testimony of close friends and family members, on the other hand, may often be the best evidence available of what the patient's choice would be. It is they with whom the patient most likely will have discussed such questions and they who know the patient best. . . . The Missouri court's decision to ignore this whole category of testimony is also at odds with the practices of other States.

The Missouri court's disdain for Nancy's statements in serious conversations not long before her accident, for the opinions of Nancy's family and friends as to her values, beliefs and certain choice, and even for the opinion of an outside objective factfinder appointed by the State evinces a disdain for Nancy Cruzan's own right to choose. The rules by which an incompetent person's wishes are determined must represent every effort to determine those wishes. The rule that the Missouri court adopted and that this Court upholds, however, skews the result away from a determination that as accurately as possible reflects the individual's own preferences and beliefs. It is a rule that transforms human beings into passive subjects of medical technology. . . .

C

I do not suggest that States must sit by helplessly if the choices of incompetent patients are in danger of being ignored. . . . [N]othing in the Constitution prevents States from reviewing the advisability of a family

---

now. [I]f it were me up there or Christy or any of us, she would be doing for us what we are trying to do for her. I know she would, . . . as her mother."

21 Surveys show that the overwhelming majority of Americans have not executed such written instructions. See Emmanuel & Emmanuel, The Medical Directive: A New Comprehensive Advance Care Document, 261 JAMA 3288 (1989) (only 9% of Americans execute advance directives about how they would wish treatment decisions to be handled if they became incompetent); American Medical Association Surveys of Physician and Public Opinion on Health Care Issues 29–30 (1988) (only 15% of those surveyed had executed living wills); 2 President's Commission for the Study of Ethical Problems in Medicine and Biomedical and Behavioral Research, Making Health Care Decisions 241–242 (1982) (23% of those surveyed said that they had put treatment instructions in writing).

decision, by requiring a court proceeding or by appointing an impartial guardian ad litem.

There are various approaches to determining an incompetent patient's treatment choice in use by the several States today, and there may be advantages and disadvantages to each and other approaches not yet envisioned. The choice, in largest part, is and should be left to the States, so long as each State is seeking, in a reliable manner, to discover what the patient would want. But with such momentous interests in the balance, States must avoid procedures that will prejudice the decision. "To err either way-to keep a person alive under circumstances under which he would rather have been allowed to die, or to allow that person to die when he would have chosen to cling to life-would be deeply unfortunate." *In re Conroy,* 98 N.J., at 343, 486 A.2d, at 1220.

D

Finally, I cannot agree with the majority that where it is not possible to determine what choice an incompetent patient would make, a State's role as *parens patriae* permits the State automatically to make that choice itself. . . . A State's legitimate interest in safeguarding a patient's choice cannot be furthered by simply appropriating it. . . .

A State's inability to discern an incompetent patient's choice still need not mean that a State is rendered powerless to protect that choice. But I would find that the Due Process Clause prohibits a State from doing more than that. A State may ensure that the person who makes the decision on the patient's behalf is the one whom the patient himself would have selected to make that choice for him. And a State may exclude from consideration anyone having improper motives. But a State generally must either repose the choice with the person whom the patient himself would most likely have chosen as proxy or leave the decision to the patient's family.[23]

IV

. . . Missouri and this Court have displaced Nancy's own assessment of the processes associated with dying. They have discarded evidence of her will, ignored her values, and deprived her of the right to a decision as closely approximating her own choice as humanly possible. They have done so disingenuously in her name and openly in Missouri's own. That Missouri and this Court may truly be motivated only by concern for incompetent patients makes no matter. As one of our most prominent jurists warned us decades ago: "Experience should teach us to be most on our guard to protect liberty when the government's purposes are beneficent. . . . The greatest dangers to liberty lurk in insidious encroachment by men of zeal, well meaning but without understanding."

---

[23] Only in the exceedingly rare case where the State cannot find any family member or friend who can be trusted to endeavor genuinely to make the treatment choice the patient would have made does the State become the legitimate surrogate decisionmaker.

Olmstead v. United States, 277 U.S. 438, 479 (1928) (Brandeis, J., dissenting).

I respectfully dissent.

■ **JUSTICE STEVENS, dissenting.**

Our Constitution is born of the proposition that all legitimate governments must secure the equal right of every person to "Life, Liberty, and the pursuit of Happiness." In the ordinary case we quite naturally assume that these three ends are compatible, mutually enhancing, and perhaps even coincident.

The Court would make an exception here. It permits the State's abstract, undifferentiated interest in the preservation of life to overwhelm the best interests of Nancy Beth Cruzan, interests which would, according to an undisputed finding, be served by allowing her guardians to exercise her constitutional right to discontinue medical treatment. Ironically, the Court reaches this conclusion despite endorsing three significant propositions which should save it from any such dilemma. First, a competent individual's decision to refuse life-sustaining medical procedures is an aspect of liberty protected by the Due Process Clause of the Fourteenth Amendment. Second, upon a proper evidentiary showing, a qualified guardian may make that decision on behalf of an incompetent ward. Third, in answering the important question presented by this tragic case, it is wise " 'not to attempt, by any general statement, to cover every possible phase of the subject.' " Together, these considerations suggest that Nancy Cruzan's liberty to be free from medical treatment must be understood in light of the facts and circumstances particular to her.

I would so hold: In my view, the Constitution requires the State to care for Nancy Cruzan's life in a way that gives appropriate respect to her own best interests. . . .

This case is the first in which we consider whether, and how, the Constitution protects the liberty of seriously ill patients to be free from life-sustaining medical treatment. So put, the question is both general and profound. We need not, however, resolve the question in the abstract. Our responsibility as judges both enables and compels us to treat the problem as it is illuminated by the facts of the controversy before us.

The most important of those facts are these: "Clear and convincing evidence" established that Nancy Cruzan is "oblivious to her environment except for reflexive responses to sound and perhaps to painful stimuli"; that "she has no cognitive or reflexive ability to swallow food or water"; that "she will never recover" these abilities; and that her "cerebral cortical atrophy is irreversible, permanent, progressive and ongoing." App. to Pet. for Cert. A94–A95. Recovery and consciousness are impossible; the highest cognitive brain function that can be hoped for is a grimace in "recognition of ordinarily painful stimuli" or an "apparent response to sound." . . .

To be constitutionally permissible, Missouri's intrusion upon these fundamental liberties must, at a minimum, bear a reasonable relationship to a legitimate state end. See, *e.g., Meyer v. Nebraska,* 262 U.S., at 400; *Doe v. Bolton,* 410 U.S. 179, 194–195, 199 (1973). Missouri asserts that its policy is related to a state interest in the protection of life. In my view, however, it is an effort to define life, rather than to protect it, that is the heart of Missouri's policy. Missouri insists, without regard to Nancy Cruzan's own interests, upon equating her life with the biological persistence of her bodily functions. Nancy Cruzan, it must be remembered, is not now simply incompetent. She is in a persistent vegetative state and has been so for seven years. The trial court found, and no party contested, that Nancy has no possibility of recovery and no consciousness.

It seems to me that the Court errs insofar as it characterizes this case as involving "judgments about the 'quality' of life that a particular individual may enjoy," Nancy Cruzan is obviously *"alive"* in a physiological sense. But for patients like Nancy Cruzan, who have no consciousness and no chance of recovery, there is a serious question as to whether the mere persistence of their bodies is *"life"* as that word is commonly understood, or as it is used in both the Constitution and the Declaration of Independence. The State's unflagging determination to perpetuate Nancy Cruzan's physical existence is comprehensible only as an effort to define life's meaning, not as an attempt to preserve its sanctity. . . .

In short, there is no reasonable ground for believing that Nancy Beth Cruzan has any *personal* interest in the perpetuation of what the State has decided is her life. As I have already suggested, it would be possible to hypothesize such an interest on the basis of theological or philosophical conjecture. But even to posit such a basis for the State's action is to condemn it. It is not within the province of secular government to circumscribe the liberties of the people by regulations designed wholly for the purpose of establishing a sectarian definition of life. See *Webster v. Reproductive Health Services,* 492 U.S. 490, 566–572 (1989) (STEVENS, J., dissenting).

My disagreement with the Court is thus unrelated to its endorsement of the clear and convincing standard of proof for cases of this kind. Indeed, I agree that the controlling facts must be established with unmistakable clarity. The critical question, however, is not how to prove the controlling facts but rather what proven facts should be controlling. In my view, the constitutional answer is clear: The best interests of the individual, especially when buttressed by the interests of all related third parties, must prevail over any general state policy that simply ignores those interests. . . .

I respectfully dissent.

NOTE ON PROCEDURAL DUE PROCESS

1.   The procedural due process cases are an example of federal constitutional protection for interests that the Constitution does not itself create. In *Roth* and *Perry*, for example, the relevant property interests in state employment were created by *state* law. Most property interests are created and defined by state law. *Matthews*, on the other hand, involved a property interest in federal welfare benefits created by federal law; other examples would include property interests in a federal patent on an invention or in land secured by grant from the United States. But even in the latter cases, the federal property interest is not created by the Constitution itself, but rather by operation of a federal statute.

Procedural due process protection thus depends on the creation of an underlying interest in liberty or property by some other form of law. This situation also arises under other constitutional provisions, such as the Takings Clause of the Fifth Amendment (which protects preexisting property interests), Article I, § 10's Contract Clause (which protects contractual rights), and the Full Faith and Credit Clause in Article IV (which protects judgments entered in the courts of another state). The underlying law—typically *state* law—will define the protected interests, which federal law defines the form and extent of the protection that the Constitution provides for those interests. Hence, as *Matthews* illustrates, once some other form of law creates a property interest, federal constitutional doctrine determine the procedural protections that due process demands before a person may be deprived of that interest.

The relationship between state and federal law in these sorts of cases gives rise to interesting questions concerning the allocation of authority between state and federal courts. State courts, after all, are the last word on the content of state law, but the U.S. Supreme Court has jurisdiction to review the federal question of whether a state has deprived a person of a property interest without due process or impaired the obligation of a contract, even though the underlying interests are grounded in the law of a state.[24] These issues are explored in the upper level Federal Courts course.

2.   Although state law creates the underlying entitlements in most procedural due process cases, it is a federal question whether the interest that state law creates is sufficiently definite to trigger federal due process protection. Why did the Court find no protected interest in *Roth*, but that such an interest might exist in *Perry*? And what difference did it make in these cases whether one analyzes the protected interest as one of liberty or property?

Sometimes, however, federal due process protections attach to certain interests whether or not they are also recognized and protected by state law. *Cruzan* illustrates this phenomenon. The Court found that Nancy Cruzan had a protected liberty interest in refusing life-sustaining medical treatment based on prior decisions recognizing a protected liberty interest in various

---

[24] *See, e.g., Indiana ex rel. Anderson v. Brand*, 303 U.S. 95 (1938) (reviewing appeal from state supreme court in a Contracts Clause case).

forms of bodily integrity. This interest stemmed not from state law—although state law also protects that interest in a variety of ways—but from the basic importance of bodily integrity to personal autonomy its traditional protection in our law.

Is the recognition of a protected liberty interest in *Cruzan* just a second-best form of substantive due process? Is the Court saying that the Due Process Clause protects a range of substantive interests—not just fundamental rights like privacy and abortion, but also less fundamental interests that nonetheless trigger procedural protection? Would such a hybrid form of procedural/substantive due process be useful? Legitimate?

3.   Procedural due process may often work in relation to other constitutional theories. In *Roth* and *Perry*, for example, the plaintiffs had both also made First Amendment claims that they had been dismissed in retaliation for their protected speech. Hence, one important effect of recognizing a protected liberty or property interest under the Due Process Clause would thus be to give them a procedural opportunity to develop evidence to support their First Amendment claims.

In *Cruzan*, on the other hand, procedural due process served as a way of providing partial protection to an interest—in ending a life that had become unlivable due to illness or injury—that fell just short of recognition as a fundamental right in *Glucksberg*. Is procedural protection for a person's right to make this choice, as in *Cruzan*, a better way to protect the autonomy interest than what the *Glucksberg* plaintiffs sought—that is, as a fundamental substantive due process right? Procedural protection would be unhelpful, however, if Missouri simply eliminated any opportunity to refuse life-sustaining medical treatment. In that event, do you think *Glucksberg* would foreclose any due process challenge to the prohibition?

SECTION 16.3   THE REVIVAL OF ECONOMIC SUBSTANTIVE DUE PROCESS?

In *Ferguson v. Skrupa*, the Court reaffirmed that it had "abandon[ed] . . . the use of the 'vague contours' of the Due Process Clause to nullify laws which a majority of the Court believed to be economically unwise."[25] That remains largely true, despite the significant revival of substantive due process in the non-economic sphere. But as we have already discussed,[26] the economic/non-economic distinction is quite ambiguous—it would make little sense to many contemporary economists, who tend to view economic principles as applicable to the whole range of human behavior.[27] Perhaps for that reason, the revival of substantive due process in "non-economic" cases has begun to bleed over into more traditionally economic contexts. This section considers two

---

[25]   372 U.S. 726, 731 (1963).

[26]   *See supra* Section 5.4.

[27]   *See, e.g.,* STEVEN D. LEVITT & STEPHEN J. DUBNER, FREAKONOMICS: A ROGUE ECONOMIST EXPLORES THE HIDDEN SIDE OF EVERYTHING (2009).

instances of this movement, involving punitive damages and retroactive regulatory legislation.

BMW of North America, Inc. v. Gore

517 U.S. 559 (1996)

■ **JUSTICE STEVENS delivered the opinion of the Court.**

The Due Process Clause of the Fourteenth Amendment prohibits a State from imposing a " 'grossly excessive' " punishment on a tortfeasor. *TXO Production Corp. v. Alliance Resources Corp.,* 509 U.S. 443, 454 (1993). The wrongdoing involved in this case was the decision by a national distributor of automobiles not to advise its dealers, and hence their customers, of predelivery damage to new cars when the cost of repair amounted to less than 3 percent of the car's suggested retail price. The question presented is whether a $2 million punitive damages award to the purchaser of one of these cars exceeds the constitutional limit.

I

In January 1990, Dr. Ira Gore, Jr. (respondent), purchased a black BMW sports sedan for $40,750.88 from an authorized BMW dealer in Birmingham, Alabama. After driving the car for approximately nine months, and without noticing any flaws in its appearance, Dr. Gore took the car to "Slick Finish," an independent detailer, to make it look " 'snazzier than it normally would appear.' " Mr. Slick, the proprietor, detected evidence that the car had been repainted.[1] Convinced that he had been cheated, Dr. Gore brought suit against petitioner BMW of North America (BMW), the American distributor of BMW automobiles. Dr. Gore alleged, *inter alia,* that the failure to disclose that the car had been repainted constituted suppression of a material fact.[3] The complaint prayed for $500,000 in compensatory and punitive damages, and costs.

At trial, BMW acknowledged that it had adopted a nationwide policy in 1983 concerning cars that were damaged in the course of manufacture or transportation. If the cost of repairing the damage exceeded 3 percent of the car's suggested retail price, the car was placed in company service for a period of time and then sold as used. If the repair cost did not exceed 3 percent of the suggested retail price, however, the car was sold as new without advising the dealer that any repairs had been made. Because the $601.37 cost of repainting Dr. Gore's car was only about 1.5 percent of its

---

[1]   The top, hood, trunk, and quarter panels of Dr. Gore's car were repainted at BMW's vehicle preparation center in Brunswick, Georgia. The parties presumed that the damage was caused by exposure to acid rain during transit between the manufacturing plant in Germany and the preparation center.

[3]   Alabama codified its common-law cause of action for fraud in a 1907 statute that is still in effect. The statute provides: "Suppression of a material fact which the party is under an obligation to communicate constitutes fraud. The obligation to communicate may arise from the confidential relations of the parties or from the particular circumstances of the case." Ala.Code § 6–5–102.

suggested retail price, BMW did not disclose the damage or repair to the Birmingham dealer.

Dr. Gore asserted that his repainted car was worth less than a car that had not been refinished. To prove his actual damages of $4,000, he relied on the testimony of a former BMW dealer, who estimated that the value of a repainted BMW was approximately 10 percent less than the value of a new car that had not been damaged and repaired. To support his claim for punitive damages, Dr. Gore introduced evidence that since 1983 BMW had sold 983 refinished cars as new, including 14 in Alabama, without disclosing that the cars had been repainted before sale at a cost of more than $300 per vehicle. Using the actual damage estimate of $4,000 per vehicle, Dr. Gore argued that a punitive award of $4 million would provide an appropriate penalty for selling approximately 1,000 cars for more than they were worth.

In defense of its disclosure policy, BMW argued that it was under no obligation to disclose repairs of minor damage to new cars and that Dr. Gore's car was as good as a car with the original factory finish. It disputed Dr. Gore's assertion that the value of the car was impaired by the repainting and argued that this good-faith belief made a punitive award inappropriate. BMW also maintained that transactions in jurisdictions other than Alabama had no relevance to Dr. Gore's claim.

The jury returned a verdict finding BMW liable for compensatory damages of $4,000. In addition, the jury assessed $4 million in punitive damages, based on a determination that the nondisclosure policy constituted "gross, oppressive or malicious" fraud. See Ala.Code §§ 6–11–20, 6–11–21.

BMW filed a post-trial motion to set aside the punitive damages award. The company introduced evidence to establish that its nondisclosure policy was consistent with the laws of roughly 25 States defining the disclosure obligations of automobile manufacturers, distributors, and dealers. The most stringent of these statutes required disclosure of repairs costing more than 3 percent of the suggested retail price; none mandated disclosure of less costly repairs.[7] Relying on these statutes, BMW contended that its conduct was lawful in these States and therefore could not provide the basis for an award of punitive damages.

BMW also drew the court's attention to the fact that its nondisclosure policy had never been adjudged unlawful before this action was filed. Just months before Dr. Gore's case went to trial, the jury in a similar lawsuit filed by another Alabama BMW purchaser found that BMW's failure to disclose paint repair constituted fraud. *Yates v. BMW of North America, Inc.*, 642 So.2d 937 (Ala.1993).[8] Before the judgment

---

[7]   BMW acknowledged that a Georgia statute enacted *after* Dr. Gore purchased his car would require disclosure of similar repairs to a car before it was sold in Georgia. Ga.Code Ann. §§ 40–1–5(b)–(e) (1994).

[8]   While awarding a comparable amount of compensatory damages, the *Yates* jury awarded no punitive damages at all. In *Yates*, the plaintiff also relied on the 1983 nondisclosure

in this case, BMW changed its policy by taking steps to avoid the sale of any refinished vehicles in Alabama and two other States. When the $4 million verdict was returned in this case, BMW promptly instituted a nationwide policy of full disclosure of all repairs, no matter how minor.

In response to BMW's arguments, Dr. Gore asserted that the policy change demonstrated the efficacy of the punitive damages award. He noted that while no jury had held the policy unlawful, BMW had received a number of customer complaints relating to undisclosed repairs and had settled some lawsuits.[9] Finally, he maintained that the disclosure statutes of other States were irrelevant because BMW had failed to offer any evidence that the disclosure statutes supplanted, rather than supplemented, existing causes of action for common-law fraud.

The trial judge denied BMW's post-trial motion, holding, *inter alia,* that the award was not excessive. On appeal, the Alabama Supreme Court also rejected BMW's claim that the award exceeded the constitutionally permissible amount. The court's excessiveness inquiry applied the factors articulated in *Green Oil Co. v. Hornsby,* 539 So.2d 218, 223–224 (Ala.1989), and approved in *Pacific Mut. Life Ins. Co. v. Haslip,* 499 U.S. 1, 21–22 (1991). Based on its analysis, the court concluded that BMW's conduct was "reprehensible"; the nondisclosure was profitable for the company; the judgment "would not have a substantial impact upon [BMW's] financial position"; the litigation had been expensive; no criminal sanctions had been imposed on BMW for the same conduct; the award of *no* punitive damages in *Yates* reflected "the inherent uncertainty of the trial process"; and the punitive award bore a "reasonable relationship" to "the harm that was likely to occur from [BMW's] conduct as well as . . . the harm that actually occurred."

The Alabama Supreme Court did, however, rule in BMW's favor on one critical point: The court found that the jury improperly computed the amount of punitive damages by multiplying Dr. Gore's compensatory damages by the number of similar sales in other jurisdictions. Having found the verdict tainted, the court held that "a constitutionally reasonable punitive damages award in this case is $2,000,000," and therefore ordered a remittitur in that amount. The court's discussion of the amount of its remitted award expressly disclaimed any reliance on "acts that occurred in other jurisdictions"; instead, the court explained that it had used a "comparative analysis" that considered Alabama cases, "along with cases from other jurisdictions, involving the sale of an

---

policy, but instead of offering evidence of 983 repairs costing more than $300 each, he introduced a bulk exhibit containing 5,856 repair bills to show that petitioner had sold over 5,800 new BMW vehicles without disclosing that they had been repaired.

9   Prior to the lawsuits filed by Dr. Yates and Dr. Gore, BMW and various BMW dealers had been sued 14 times concerning presale paint or damage repair. According to the testimony of BMW's in-house counsel at the postjudgment hearing on damages, only one of the suits concerned a car repainted by BMW.

automobile where the seller misrepresented the condition of the vehicle and the jury awarded punitive damages to the purchaser."[11]

Because we believed that a review of this case would help to illuminate "the character of the standard that will identify unconstitutionally excessive awards" of punitive damages, see *Honda Motor Co. v. Oberg,* 512 U.S. 415, 420 (1994), we granted certiorari.

II

Punitive damages may properly be imposed to further a State's legitimate interests in punishing unlawful conduct and deterring its repetition. In our federal system, States necessarily have considerable flexibility in determining the level of punitive damages that they will allow in different classes of cases and in any particular case. Most States that authorize exemplary damages afford the jury similar latitude, requiring only that the damages awarded be reasonably necessary to vindicate the State's legitimate interests in punishment and deterrence. Only when an award can fairly be categorized as "grossly excessive" in relation to these interests does it enter the zone of arbitrariness that violates the Due Process Clause of the Fourteenth Amendment. For that reason, the federal excessiveness inquiry appropriately begins with an identification of the state interests that a punitive award is designed to serve. We therefore focus our attention first on the scope of Alabama's legitimate interests in punishing BMW and deterring it from future misconduct.

No one doubts that a State may protect its citizens by prohibiting deceptive trade practices and by requiring automobile distributors to disclose presale repairs that affect the value of a new car. But the States need not, and in fact do not, provide such protection in a uniform manner. Some States rely on the judicial process to formulate and enforce an appropriate disclosure requirement by applying principles of contract and tort law. Other States have enacted various forms of legislation that define the disclosure obligations of automobile manufacturers, distributors, and dealers. The result is a patchwork of rules representing the diverse policy judgments of lawmakers in 50 States.

That diversity demonstrates that reasonable people may disagree about the value of a full disclosure requirement. Some legislatures may conclude that affirmative disclosure requirements are unnecessary because the self-interest of those involved in the automobile trade in

---

[11] Other than *Yates v. BMW of North America, Inc.,* 642 So.2d 937 (Ala.1993), in which no punitive damages were awarded, the Alabama Supreme Court cited no such cases. In another portion of its opinion, the court did cite five Alabama cases, none of which involved either a dispute arising out of the purchase of an automobile or an award of punitive damages. All of these cases support the proposition that appellate courts in Alabama presume that jury verdicts are correct. In light of the Alabama Supreme Court's conclusion that (1) the jury had computed its award by multiplying $4,000 by the number of refinished vehicles sold in the United States and (2) that the award should have been based on Alabama conduct, respect for the error-free portion of the jury verdict would seem to produce an award of $56,000 ($4,000 multiplied by 14, the number of repainted vehicles sold in Alabama).

developing and maintaining the goodwill of their customers will motivate them to make voluntary disclosures or to refrain from selling cars that do not comply with self-imposed standards. Those legislatures that do adopt affirmative disclosure obligations may take into account the cost of government regulation, choosing to draw a line exempting minor repairs from such a requirement. In formulating a disclosure standard, States may also consider other goals, such as providing a "safe harbor" for automobile manufacturers, distributors, and dealers against lawsuits over minor repairs.

We may assume, *arguendo,* that it would be wise for every State to adopt Dr. Gore's preferred rule, requiring full disclosure of every presale repair to a car, no matter how trivial and regardless of its actual impact on the value of the car. But while we do not doubt that Congress has ample authority to enact such a policy for the entire Nation, it is clear that no single State could do so, or even impose its own policy choice on neighboring States. See *Bonaparte v. Tax Court,* 104 U.S. 592, 594 (1881) ("No State can legislate except with reference to its own jurisdiction. . . . Each State is independent of all the others in this particular").[16] Similarly, one State's power to impose burdens on the interstate market for automobiles is not only subordinate to the federal power over interstate commerce, *Gibbons v. Ogden,* 9 Wheat. 1, 194–196 (1824), but is also constrained by the need to respect the interests of other States, see, *e.g., Healy v. Beer Institute,* 491 U.S. 324, 335–336 (1989) (the Constitution has a "special concern both with the maintenance of a national economic union unfettered by state-imposed limitations on interstate commerce and with the autonomy of the individual States within their respective spheres").

We think it follows from these principles of state sovereignty and comity that a State may not impose economic sanctions on violators of its laws with the intent of changing the tortfeasors' lawful conduct in other States.[17] Before this Court Dr. Gore argued that the large punitive damages award was necessary to induce BMW to change the nationwide policy that it adopted in 1983. But by attempting to alter BMW's

---

[16] See also *Bigelow v. Virginia,* 421 U.S. 809, 824 (1975) ("A State does not acquire power or supervision over the internal affairs of another State merely because the welfare and health of its own citizens may be affected when they travel to that State"); *New York Life Ins. Co. v. Head,* 234 U.S. 149, 161 (1914) ("[I]t would be impossible to permit the statutes of Missouri to operate beyond the jurisdiction of that State . . . without throwing down the constitutional barriers by which all the States are restricted within the orbits of their lawful authority and upon the preservation of which the Government under the Constitution depends. This is so obviously the necessary result of the Constitution that it has rarely been called in question and hence authorities directly dealing with it do not abound"); *Huntington v. Attrill,* 146 U.S. 657, 669 (1892) ("Laws have no force of themselves beyond the jurisdiction of the State which enacts them, and can have extra-territorial effect only by the comity of other States").

[17] State power may be exercised as much by a jury's application of a state rule of law in a civil lawsuit as by a statute. See *New York Times Co. v. Sullivan,* 376 U.S. 254, 265 (1964) ("The test is not the form in which state power has been applied but, whatever the form, whether such power has in fact been exercised"); *San Diego Building Trades Council v. Garmon,* 359 U.S. 236, 247 (1959) ("[R]egulation can be as effectively exerted through an award of damages as through some form of preventive relief").

nationwide policy, Alabama would be infringing on the policy choices of other States. To avoid such encroachment, the economic penalties that a State such as Alabama inflicts on those who transgress its laws, whether the penalties take the form of legislatively authorized fines or judicially imposed punitive damages, must be supported by the State's interest in protecting its own consumers and its own economy. Alabama may insist that BMW adhere to a particular disclosure policy in that State. Alabama does not have the power, however, to punish BMW for conduct that was lawful where it occurred and that had no impact on Alabama or its residents.[19] Nor may Alabama impose sanctions on BMW in order to deter conduct that is lawful in other jurisdictions.

In this case, we accept the Alabama Supreme Court's interpretation of the jury verdict as reflecting a computation of the amount of punitive damages "based in large part on conduct that happened in other jurisdictions." As the Alabama Supreme Court noted, neither the jury nor the trial court was presented with evidence that any of BMW's out-of-state conduct was unlawful. "The only testimony touching the issue showed that approximately 60% of the vehicles that were refinished were sold in states where failure to disclose the repair was not an unfair trade practice."[20] The Alabama Supreme Court therefore properly eschewed reliance on BMW's out-of-state conduct and based its remitted award solely on conduct that occurred within Alabama.[21] The award must be analyzed in the light of the same conduct, with consideration given only to the interests of Alabama consumers, rather than those of the entire Nation. When the scope of the interest in punishment and deterrence that an Alabama court may appropriately consider is properly limited, it is apparent—for reasons that we shall now address—that this award is grossly excessive.

III

Elementary notions of fairness enshrined in our constitutional jurisprudence dictate that a person receive fair notice not only of the conduct that will subject him to punishment, but also of the severity of

---

[19] See *Bordenkircher v. Hayes,* 434 U.S. 357, 363 (1978) ("To punish a person because he has done what the law plainly allows him to do is a due process violation of the most basic sort"). Our cases concerning recidivist statutes are not to the contrary. Habitual offender statutes permit the sentencing court to enhance a defendant's punishment for a crime in light of prior convictions, including convictions in foreign jurisdictions. A sentencing judge may even consider past criminal behavior which did not result in a conviction and lawful conduct that bears on the defendant's character and prospects for rehabilitation. *Williams v. New York,* 337 U.S. 241 (1949). But we have never held that a sentencing court could properly *punish* lawful conduct. This distinction is precisely the one we draw here.

[20] Given that the verdict was based in part on out-of-state conduct that was lawful where it occurred, we need not consider whether one State may properly attempt to change a tortfeasor's *unlawful* conduct in another State.

[21] Of course, the fact that the Alabama Supreme Court correctly concluded that it was error for the jury to use the number of sales in other States as a multiplier in computing the amount of its punitive sanction does not mean that evidence describing out-of-state transactions is irrelevant in a case of this kind. To the contrary, as we stated in *TXO Production Corp. v. Alliance Resources Corp.,* 509 U.S. 443, 462, n. 28 (1993), such evidence may be relevant to the determination of the degree of reprehensibility of the defendant's conduct.

the penalty that a State may impose.[22] Three guideposts, each of which indicates that BMW did not receive adequate notice of the magnitude of the sanction that Alabama might impose for adhering to the nondisclosure policy adopted in 1983, lead us to the conclusion that the $2 million award against BMW is grossly excessive: the degree of reprehensibility of the nondisclosure; the disparity between the harm or potential harm suffered by Dr. Gore and his punitive damages award; and the difference between this remedy and the civil penalties authorized or imposed in comparable cases. We discuss these considerations in turn.

Degree of Reprehensibility

Perhaps the most important indicium of the reasonableness of a punitive damages award is the degree of reprehensibility of the defendant's conduct. As the Court stated nearly 150 years ago, exemplary damages imposed on a defendant should reflect "the enormity of his offense." *Day v. Woodworth,* 13 How. 363, 371 (1852).[24] This principle reflects the accepted view that some wrongs are more blameworthy than others. Thus, we have said that "nonviolent crimes are less serious than crimes marked by violence or the threat of violence." *Solem v. Helm,* 463 U.S. 277, 292–293 (1983). Similarly, "trickery and deceit," *TXO,* 509 U.S., at 462, are more reprehensible than negligence. In *TXO,* both the West Virginia Supreme Court and the Justices of this Court placed special emphasis on the principle that punitive damages may not be "grossly out of proportion to the severity of the offense." Indeed, for Justice KENNEDY, the defendant's intentional malice was the decisive element in a "close and difficult" case.

In this case, none of the aggravating factors associated with particularly reprehensible conduct is present. The harm BMW inflicted on Dr. Gore was purely economic in nature. The presale refinishing of the car had no effect on its performance or safety features, or even its appearance for at least nine months after his purchase. BMW's conduct evinced no indifference to or reckless disregard for the health and safety of others. To be sure, infliction of economic injury, especially when done intentionally through affirmative acts of misconduct, or when the target is financially vulnerable, can warrant a substantial penalty. But this observation does not convert all acts that cause economic harm into torts

---

[22] See *Miller v. Florida,* 482 U.S. 423 (1987) (*Ex Post Facto* Clause violated by retroactive imposition of revised sentencing guidelines that provided longer sentence for defendant's crime); *Bouie v. City of Columbia,* 378 U.S. 347 (1964) (retroactive application of new construction of statute violated due process); *Lankford v. Idaho,* 500 U.S. 110 (1991) (due process violated because defendant and his counsel did not have adequate notice that judge might impose death sentence). The strict constitutional safeguards afforded to criminal defendants are not applicable to civil cases, but the basic protection against "judgments without notice" afforded by the Due Process Clause, *Shaffer v. Heitner,* 433 U.S. 186, 217 (1977) (STEVENS, J., concurring in judgment), is implicated by civil *penalties.*

[24] The principle that punishment should fit the crime "is deeply rooted and frequently repeated in common-law jurisprudence." *Solem v. Helm,* 463 U.S. 277, 284 (1983).

that are sufficiently reprehensible to justify a significant sanction in addition to compensatory damages.

Dr. Gore contends that BMW's conduct was particularly reprehensible because nondisclosure of the repairs to his car formed part of a nationwide pattern of tortious conduct. Certainly, evidence that a defendant has repeatedly engaged in prohibited conduct while knowing or suspecting that it was unlawful would provide relevant support for an argument that strong medicine is required to cure the defendant's disrespect for the law. Our holdings that a recidivist may be punished more severely than a first offender recognize that repeated misconduct is more reprehensible than an individual instance of malfeasance. . . .

We do not think it can be disputed that there may exist minor imperfections in the finish of a new car that can be repaired (or indeed, left unrepaired) without materially affecting the car's value.[30] There is no evidence that BMW acted in bad faith when it sought to establish the appropriate line between presumptively minor damage and damage requiring disclosure to purchasers. For this purpose, BMW could reasonably rely on state disclosure statutes for guidance. In this regard, it is also significant that there is no evidence that BMW persisted in a course of conduct after it had been adjudged unlawful on even one occasion, let alone repeated occasions.[31]

Finally, the record in this case discloses no deliberate false statements, acts of affirmative misconduct, or concealment of evidence of improper motive, such as were present in *Haslip* and *TXO*. We accept, of course, the jury's finding that BMW suppressed a material fact which Alabama law obligated it to communicate to prospective purchasers of repainted cars in that State. But the omission of a material fact may be less reprehensible than a deliberate false statement, particularly when there is a good-faith basis for believing that no duty to disclose exists.

That conduct is sufficiently reprehensible to give rise to tort liability, and even a modest award of exemplary damages does not establish the high degree of culpability that warrants a substantial punitive damages award. Because this case exhibits none of the circumstances ordinarily associated with egregiously improper conduct, we are persuaded that BMW's conduct was not sufficiently reprehensible to warrant imposition of a $2 million exemplary damages award.

Ratio

The second and perhaps most commonly cited indicium of an unreasonable or excessive punitive damages award is its ratio to the

---

[30] The Alabama Supreme Court has held that a car may be considered "new" as a matter of law even if its finish contains minor cosmetic flaws. *Wilburn v. Larry Savage Chevrolet, Inc.*, 477 So.2d 384 (1985). . . .

[31] Before the verdict in this case, BMW had changed its policy with respect to Alabama and two other States. Five days after the jury award, BMW altered its nationwide policy to one of full disclosure.

actual harm inflicted on the plaintiff. See *TXO,* 509 U.S., at 459. The principle that exemplary damages must bear a "reasonable relationship" to compensatory damages has a long pedigree. Scholars have identified a number of early English statutes authorizing the award of multiple damages for particular wrongs. Some 65 different enactments during the period between 1275 and 1753 provided for double, treble, or quadruple damages. Our decisions in both *Haslip* and *TXO* endorsed the proposition that a comparison between the compensatory award and the punitive award is significant.

In *Haslip* we concluded that even though a punitive damages award of "more than 4 times the amount of compensatory damages" might be "close to the line," it did not "cross the line into the area of constitutional impropriety." *TXO,* following dicta in *Haslip,* refined this analysis by confirming that the proper inquiry is "whether there is a reasonable relationship between the punitive damages award and *the harm likely to result from the defendant's conduct* as well as the harm that actually has occurred." Thus, in upholding the $10 million award in *TXO,* we relied on the difference between that figure and the harm to the victim that would have ensued if the tortious plan had succeeded. That difference suggested that the relevant ratio was not more than 10 to 1.

The $2 million in punitive damages awarded to Dr. Gore by the Alabama Supreme Court is 500 times the amount of his actual harm as determined by the jury.[35] Moreover, there is no suggestion that Dr. Gore or any other BMW purchaser was threatened with any additional potential harm by BMW's nondisclosure policy. The disparity in this case is thus dramatically greater than those considered in *Haslip* and *TXO.*

Of course, we have consistently rejected the notion that the constitutional line is marked by a simple mathematical formula, even one that compares actual *and potential* damages to the punitive award. Indeed, low awards of compensatory damages may properly support a higher ratio than high compensatory awards, if, for example, a particularly egregious act has resulted in only a small amount of economic damages. A higher ratio may also be justified in cases in which the injury is hard to detect or the monetary value of noneconomic harm might have been difficult to determine. It is appropriate, therefore, to reiterate our rejection of a categorical approach. Once again, we return to what we said . . . in *Haslip:* "We need not, and indeed we cannot, draw a mathematical bright line between the constitutionally acceptable and the constitutionally unacceptable that would fit every case. We can say, however, that [a] general concer[n] of reasonableness . . . properly enter[s] into the constitutional calculus." In most cases, the ratio will be within a constitutionally acceptable range, and remittitur will not be justified on this basis. When the ratio is a breathtaking 500 to 1, however,

---

[35] Even assuming each repainted BMW suffers a diminution in value of approximately $4,000, the award is 35 times greater than the total damages of all 14 Alabama consumers who purchased repainted BMW's.

the award must surely "raise a suspicious judicial eyebrow." *TXO,* 509 U.S., at 481 (O'CONNOR, J., dissenting).

Sanctions for Comparable Misconduct

Comparing the punitive damages award and the civil or criminal penalties that could be imposed for comparable misconduct provides a third indicium of excessiveness. As Justice O'CONNOR has correctly observed, a reviewing court engaged in determining whether an award of punitive damages is excessive should "accord 'substantial deference' to legislative judgments concerning appropriate sanctions for the conduct at issue." *Browning-Ferris Industries of Vt., Inc. v. Kelco Disposal, Inc.,* 492 U.S. 257, 301 (1989) (opinion concurring in part and dissenting in part). In *Haslip,* the Court noted that although the exemplary award was "much in excess of the fine that could be imposed," imprisonment was also authorized in the criminal context. In this case the $2 million economic sanction imposed on BMW is substantially greater than the statutory fines available in Alabama and elsewhere for similar malfeasance.

The maximum civil penalty authorized by the Alabama Legislature for a violation of its Deceptive Trade Practices Act is $2,000; other States authorize more severe sanctions, with the maxima ranging from $5,000 to $10,000. . . .

The sanction imposed in this case cannot be justified on the ground that it was necessary to deter future misconduct without considering whether less drastic remedies could be expected to achieve that goal. The fact that a multimillion dollar penalty prompted a change in policy sheds no light on the question whether a lesser deterrent would have adequately protected the interests of Alabama consumers. In the absence of a history of noncompliance with known statutory requirements, there is no basis for assuming that a more modest sanction would not have been sufficient to motivate full compliance with the disclosure requirement imposed by the Alabama Supreme Court in this case.

IV

We assume, as the juries in this case and in the *Yates* case found, that the undisclosed damage to the new BMW's affected their actual value. Notwithstanding the evidence adduced by BMW in an effort to prove that the repainted cars conformed to the same quality standards as its other cars, we also assume that it knew, or should have known, that as time passed the repainted cars would lose their attractive appearance more rapidly than other BMW's. Moreover, we of course accept the Alabama courts' view that the state interest in protecting its citizens from deceptive trade practices justifies a sanction in addition to the recovery of compensatory damages. We cannot, however, accept the conclusion of the Alabama Supreme Court that BMW's conduct was sufficiently egregious to justify a punitive sanction that is tantamount to a severe criminal penalty.

The fact that BMW is a large corporation rather than an impecunious individual does not diminish its entitlement to fair notice of the demands that the several States impose on the conduct of its business. Indeed, its status as an active participant in the national economy implicates the federal interest in preventing individual States from imposing undue burdens on interstate commerce. While each State has ample power to protect its own consumers, none may use the punitive damages deterrent as a means of imposing its regulatory policies on the entire Nation.

As in *Haslip*, we are not prepared to draw a bright line marking the limits of a constitutionally acceptable punitive damages award. Unlike that case, however, we are fully convinced that the grossly excessive award imposed in this case transcends the constitutional limit.[41] Whether the appropriate remedy requires a new trial or merely an independent determination by the Alabama Supreme Court of the award necessary to vindicate the economic interests of Alabama consumers is a matter that should be addressed by the state court in the first instance.

The judgment is reversed, and the case is remanded for further proceedings not inconsistent with this opinion.

It is so ordered.

■ **JUSTICE BREYER, with whom JUSTICE O'CONNOR and JUSTICE SOUTER join, concurring.**

The Alabama state courts have assessed the defendant $2 million in "punitive damages" for having knowingly failed to tell a BMW automobile buyer that, at a cost of $600, it had repainted portions of his new $40,000 car, thereby lowering its potential resale value by about 10%. The Court's opinion, which I join, explains why we have concluded that this award, in this case, was "grossly excessive" in relation to legitimate punitive damages objectives, and hence an arbitrary deprivation of life, liberty, or property in violation of the Due Process Clause. Members of this Court have generally thought, however, that if "fair procedures were followed, a judgment that is a product of that process is entitled to a strong presumption of validity." *TXO Production Corp. v. Alliance Resources Corp.*, 509 U.S. 443, 457 (1993). And the Court also has found that punitive damages procedures very similar to those followed here were not, by themselves, fundamentally unfair. Thus, I believe it important to explain why this presumption of validity is overcome in this instance.

The reason flows from the Court's emphasis in *Haslip* upon the constitutional importance of legal standards that provide "reasonable constraints" within which "discretion is exercised," that assure

---

[41] Justice GINSBURG expresses concern that we are "the *only* federal court policing" this limit. The small number of punitive damages questions that we have reviewed in recent years, together with the fact that this is the first case in decades in which we have found that a punitive damages award exceeds the constitutional limit, indicates that this concern is at best premature. In any event, this consideration surely does not justify an abdication of our responsibility to enforce constitutional protections in an extraordinary case such as this one.

"meaningful and adequate review by the trial court whenever a jury has fixed the punitive damages," and permit "appellate review [that] makes certain that the punitive damages are reasonable in their amount and rational in light of their purpose to punish what has occurred and to deter its repetition."

This constitutional concern, itself harkening back to the Magna Carta, arises out of the basic unfairness of depriving citizens of life, liberty, or property, through the application, not of law and legal processes, but of arbitrary coercion. Requiring the application of law, rather than a decisionmaker's caprice, does more than simply provide citizens notice of what actions may subject them to punishment; it also helps to assure the uniform general treatment of similarly situated persons that is the essence of law itself. See *Railway Express Agency, Inc. v. New York,* 336 U.S. 106, 112 (1949) (Jackson, J., concurring) ("[T]here is no more effective practical guaranty against arbitrary and unreasonable government than to require that the principles of law which officials would impose upon a minority must be imposed generally").

Legal standards need not be precise in order to satisfy this constitutional concern. See *Haslip, supra,* at 20 (comparing punitive damages standards to such legal standards as "reasonable care," "due diligence," and "best interests of the child"). But they must offer some kind of constraint upon a jury or court's discretion, and thus protection against purely arbitrary behavior. The standards the Alabama courts applied here are vague and open ended to the point where they risk arbitrary results. In my view, although the vagueness of those standards does not, by itself, violate due process, it does invite the kind of scrutiny the Court has given the particular verdict before us. This is because the standards, as the Alabama Supreme Court authoritatively interpreted them here, provided no significant constraints or protection against arbitrary results.

First, the Alabama statute that permits punitive damages does not itself contain a standard that readily distinguishes between conduct warranting very small, and conduct warranting very large, punitive damages awards. That statute permits punitive damages in cases of "oppression, fraud, wantonness, or malice." But the statute goes on to define those terms broadly, to encompass far more than the egregious conduct that those terms, at first reading, might seem to imply. An intentional misrepresentation, made through a statement or silence, can easily amount to "fraud" sufficient to warrant punitive damages. The statute thereby authorizes punitive damages for the most serious kinds of misrepresentations, say, tricking the elderly out of their life savings, for much less serious conduct, such as the failure to disclose repainting a car, at issue here, and for a vast range of conduct in between.

Second, the Alabama courts, in this case, have applied the "factors" intended to constrain punitive damages awards in a way that belies that purpose. *Green Oil Co. v. Hornsby,* 539 So.2d 218 (Ala.1989), sets forth seven factors that appellate courts use to determine whether or not a jury award was "grossly excessive" and which, in principle, might make up for the lack of significant constraint in the statute. But, as the Alabama courts have authoritatively interpreted them, and as their application in this case illustrates, they impose little actual constraint.

(a) *Green Oil* requires that a punitive damages award "bear a reasonable relationship to the harm that is likely to occur from the defendant's conduct as well as to the harm that actually has occurred." But this standard does little to guide a determination of what counts as a "reasonable" relationship, as this case illustrates.... For reasons explored by the majority in greater depth, the relationship between this award and the underlying conduct seems well beyond the bounds of the "reasonable." To find a "reasonable relationship" between purely economic harm totaling $56,000, without significant evidence of future repetition, and a punitive award of $2 million is to empty the "reasonable relationship" test of meaningful content. . . .

(b) *Green Oil*'s second factor is the "degree of reprehensibility" of the defendant's conduct. Like the "reasonable relationship" test, this factor provides little guidance on how to relate culpability to the size of an award. . . . [F]or the reasons discussed by the majority, I do not see how the Alabama courts could find conduct that (they assumed) caused $56,000 of relevant economic harm *especially or unusually* reprehensible enough to warrant $2 million in punitive damages, or a significant portion of that award. To find to the contrary, as the Alabama courts did, is not simply unreasonable; it is to make "reprehensibility" a concept without constraining force, i.e., to deprive the concept of its constraining power to protect against serious and capricious deprivations.

(c) *Green Oil* 's third factor requires "punitive damages" to "remove the profit" of the illegal activity and "be in excess of the profit, so that the defendant recognizes a loss." This factor has the ability to limit awards to a fixed, rational amount. But as applied, that concept's potential was not realized, for the court did not limit the award to anywhere near the $56,000 in profits evidenced in the record. . . .

(d) *Green Oil*'s fourth factor is the "financial position" of the defendant. Since a fixed dollar award will punish a poor person more than a wealthy one, one can understand the relevance of this factor to the State's interest in retribution (though not necessarily to its interest in deterrence, given the more distant relation between a defendant's wealth and its responses to economic incentives). This factor, however, is not necessarily intended to act as a significant *constraint* on punitive awards. Rather, it provides an open-ended basis for inflating awards when the defendant is wealthy, as this case may illustrate. That does not make its use unlawful or inappropriate; it simply means that this factor cannot make up for the failure of other factors, such as "reprehensibility," to constrain significantly an award that purports to punish a defendant's conduct.

(e) *Green Oil*'s fifth factor is the "costs of litigation" and the State's desire "to encourage plaintiffs to bring wrongdoers to trial." This standard provides meaningful constraint to the extent that the enhancement it authorized is linked to a fixed, ascertainable amount approximating actual costs, even when defined generously to reflect the contingent nature of plaintiffs' victories. But as this case shows, the factor cannot operate as a constraint when an award much in excess of costs is approved for other reasons. An additional aspect of the standard—the need to "encourage plaintiffs to bring wrongdoers to trial"—is a factor that does not constrain, but enhances, discretionary power—especially when unsupported by evidence of a *special* need to encourage litigation (which the Alabama courts here did not mention).

(f) *Green Oil*'s sixth factor is whether or not "criminal sanctions have been imposed on the defendant for his conduct." This factor did not apply here.

(g) *Green Oil*'s seventh factor requires that "other civil actions" filed "against the same defendant, based on the same conduct," be considered in mitigation. That factor did not apply here.

Thus, the first, second, and third *Green Oil* factors, in principle, might sometimes act as constraints on arbitrary behavior. But *as the Alabama courts interpreted those standards in this case*, even taking those three factors together, they could not have significantly constrained the court system's ability to impose "grossly excessive" awards.

Third, the state courts neither referred to, nor made any effort to find, nor enunciated any other standard that either directly, or indirectly as background, might have supplied the constraining legal force that the statute and *Green Oil* standards (as interpreted here) lack. Dr. Gore did argue to the jury an economic theory based on the need to offset the totality of the harm that the defendant's conduct caused. Some theory of that general kind might have provided a significant constraint on arbitrary awards . . . . Some economists, for example, have argued for a standard that would deter illegal activity causing solely economic harm through the use of punitive damages awards that, as a whole, would take from a wrongdoer the total cost of the harm caused. My understanding of the intuitive essence of some of those theories, which I put in crude form (leaving out various qualifications), is that they could permit juries to calculate punitive damages by making a rough estimate of global harm, dividing that estimate by a similarly rough estimate of the number of successful lawsuits that would likely be brought, and adding generous attorney's fees and other costs. Smaller damages would not sufficiently discourage firms from engaging in the harmful conduct, while larger damages would "over-deter" by leading potential defendants to spend more to prevent the activity that causes the economic harm, say, through employee training, than the cost of the harm itself. Larger damages might also "double count" by including in the punitive damages award some of the compensatory, or punitive, damages that subsequent plaintiffs would also recover.

The record before us, however, contains nothing suggesting that the Alabama Supreme Court, when determining the allowable award, applied *any* "economic" theory that might explain the $2 million recovery. And courts properly tend to judge the rationality of judicial actions in terms of the reasons that were given, and the facts that were before the court, not those that might have been given on the basis of some conceivable set of facts (unlike the rationality of economic statutes enacted by legislatures subject to the public's control through the ballot box, see, *e.g., FCC v. Beach Communications, Inc.,* 508 U.S. 307, 315 (1993)). Therefore, reference to a constraining "economic" theory, which might have counseled more deferential review by this Court, is lacking in this case.

Fourth, I cannot find any community understanding or historic practice that this award might exemplify and which, therefore, would provide background standards constraining arbitrary behavior and excessive awards. A punitive damages award of $2 million for intentional misrepresentation causing $56,000 of harm is extraordinary by historical standards, and, as far as I am aware, finds no analogue until relatively recent times. . . . And, as the majority opinion makes clear, the record contains nothing to suggest that the extraordinary size of the award in this case is explained by the extraordinary wrongfulness of the defendant's behavior, measured by historical or community standards, rather than arbitrariness or caprice.

Fifth, there are no other legislative enactments here that classify awards and impose quantitative limits that would significantly cabin the fairly unbounded discretion created by the absence of constraining legal standards. Cf., *e.g.,* Tex. Civ. Prac. & Rem.Code Ann. § 41.008 (punitive damages generally limited to greater of double damages, or $200,000, except cap does not apply to suits arising from certain serious criminal acts enumerated in the statute); Conn. Gen.Stat. § 52–240b (punitive damages may not exceed double compensatory damages in product liability cases); Fla. Stat. § 768.73(1) (punitive damages in certain actions limited to treble compensatory damages); Ga.Code Ann. § 51–12–5.1(g) ($250,000 cap in certain actions).

The upshot is that the rules that purport to channel discretion in this kind of case, here did not do so in fact. That means that the award in this case was both (a) the product of a system of standards that did not significantly constrain a court's, and hence a jury's, discretion in making that award; and (b) grossly excessive in light of the State's legitimate punitive damages objectives.

The first of these reasons has special importance where courts review a jury-determined punitive damages award. That is because one cannot expect to direct jurors like legislators through the ballot box; nor can one expect those jurors to interpret law like judges, who work within a discipline and hierarchical organization that normally promotes roughly uniform interpretation and application of the law. Yet here Alabama expects jurors to act, at least a little, like legislators or judges, for it permits them, to a certain extent, to create public policy and to apply that policy, not to compensate a victim, but to achieve a policy-related objective outside the confines of the particular case.

To the extent that neither clear legal principles nor fairly obvious historical or community-based standards (defining, say, especially egregious behavior) significantly constrain punitive damages awards, is there not a substantial risk of outcomes so arbitrary that they become difficult to square with the Constitution's assurance, to every citizen, of the law's protection? The standards here, as authoritatively interpreted, in my view, make this threat real and not theoretical. And, in these unusual circumstances, where legal standards offer virtually no constraint, I believe that this lack of constraining standards warrants this Court's detailed examination of the award.

The second reason—the severe disproportionality between the award and the legitimate punitive damages objectives—reflects a judgment about a matter of degree. I recognize that it is often difficult to determine just when a punitive award exceeds an amount reasonably related to a State's legitimate interests, or when that excess is so great as to amount to a matter of constitutional concern. Yet whatever the difficulties of drawing a precise line, once we examine the award in this case, it is not difficult to say that this award lies on the line's far side. The severe lack of proportionality between the size of the award and the underlying punitive damages objectives shows that the award falls into the category of "gross excessiveness" set forth in this Court's prior cases.

These two reasons *taken together* overcome what would otherwise amount to a "strong presumption of validity." *TXO*, 509 U.S., at 457. And, for those two reasons, I conclude that the award in this unusual case violates the basic guarantee of nonarbitrary governmental behavior that the Due Process Clause provides.

■ JUSTICE SCALIA, with whom JUSTICE THOMAS joins, dissenting.

Today we see the latest manifestation of this Court's recent and increasingly insistent "concern about punitive damages that 'run wild.'" *Pacific Mut. Life Ins. Co. v. Haslip,* 499 U.S. 1, 18 (1991). Since the Constitution does not make that concern any of our business, the Court's activities in this area are an unjustified incursion into the province of state governments.

In earlier cases that were the prelude to this decision, I set forth my view that a state trial procedure that commits the decision whether to impose punitive damages, and the amount, to the discretion of the jury, subject to some judicial review for "reasonableness," furnishes a defendant with all the process that is "due." I do not regard the

Fourteenth Amendment's Due Process Clause as a secret repository of substantive guarantees against "unfairness"—neither the unfairness of an excessive civil compensatory award, nor the unfairness of an "unreasonable" punitive award. What the Fourteenth Amendment's procedural guarantee assures is an opportunity to contest the reasonableness of a damages judgment in state court; but there is no federal guarantee a damages award actually *be* reasonable.

This view, which adheres to the text of the Due *Process* Clause, has not prevailed in our punitive damages cases. When, however, a constitutional doctrine adopted by the Court is not only mistaken but also insusceptible of principled application, I do not feel bound to give it *stare decisis* effect—indeed, I do not feel justified in doing so. Our punitive damages jurisprudence compels such a response. The Constitution provides no warrant for federalizing yet another aspect of our Nation's legal culture (no matter how much in need of correction it may be), and the application of the Court's new rule of constitutional law is constrained by no principle other than the Justices' subjective assessment of the "reasonableness" of the award in relation to the conduct for which it was assessed.

Because today's judgment represents the first instance of this Court's invalidation of a state-court punitive assessment as simply unreasonably large, I think it a proper occasion to discuss these points at some length.

I

The most significant aspects of today's decision—the identification of a "substantive due process" right against a "grossly excessive" award, and the concomitant assumption of ultimate authority to decide anew a matter of "reasonableness" resolved in lower court proceedings—are of course not new. *Haslip* and *TXO* revived the notion, moribund since its appearance in the first years of this century, that the measure of civil punishment poses a question of constitutional dimension to be answered by this Court. Neither of those cases, however, nor any of the precedents upon which they relied, actually took the step of declaring a punitive award unconstitutional simply because it was "too big."

At the time of adoption of the Fourteenth Amendment, it was well understood that punitive damages represent the assessment by the jury, as the voice of the community, of the measure of punishment the defendant deserved. Today's decision, though dressed up as a legal opinion, is really no more than a disagreement with the community's sense of indignation or outrage expressed in the punitive award of the Alabama jury, as reduced by the State Supreme Court. It reflects not merely, as the concurrence candidly acknowledges, "a judgment about a matter of degree," but a judgment about the appropriate degree of indignation or outrage, which is hardly an analytical determination.

There is no precedential warrant for giving our judgment priority over the judgment of state courts and juries on this matter. The only support for the Court's position is to be found in a handful of errant federal cases, bunched within a few years of one other, which invented the notion that an unfairly severe civil sanction amounts to a violation of constitutional liberties. . . . The only case relied upon in which the Court actually invalidated a civil sanction does not even support constitutional review for excessiveness, since it really concerned the validity, as a matter of *procedural* due process, of state legislation that imposed a significant penalty on a common carrier which lacked the means of determining the legality of its actions before the penalty was imposed. See *Southwestern Telegraph & Telephone Co. v. Danaher,* 238 U.S. 482, 489–491 (1915). The *amount* of the penalty was not a subject of independent scrutiny. . . . More importantly, this latter group of cases—which again are the *sole* precedential foundation put forward for the rule of constitutional law espoused by today's Court—simply fabricated the "substantive due process" right at issue. . . .

II

One might understand the Court's eagerness to enter this field, rather than leave it with the state legislatures, if it had something useful to say. In fact, however, its opinion provides virtually no guidance to legislatures, and to state and federal courts, as to what a "constitutionally proper" level of punitive damages might be.

We are instructed at the outset of Part II of the Court's opinion—the beginning of its substantive analysis—that "the federal excessiveness inquiry . . . begins with an identification of the state interests that a punitive award is designed to serve." On first reading this, one is faced with the prospect that federal punitive damages law (the new field created by today's decision) will be beset by the sort of "interest analysis" that has laid waste the formerly comprehensible field of conflict of laws. The thought that each assessment of punitive damages, as to each offense, must be examined to determine the precise "state interests" pursued, is most unsettling. Moreover, if those "interests" are the most fundamental determinant of an award, one would think that due process would require the assessing jury to be *instructed* about them.

It appears, however (and I certainly hope), that all this is a false alarm. As Part II of the Court's opinion unfolds, it turns out to be directed, not to the question "How much punishment is too much?" but rather to the question "Which acts can be punished?" "Alabama does not have the power," the Court says, "to punish BMW for conduct that was lawful where it occurred and that had no impact on Alabama or its residents." That may be true, though only in the narrow sense that a person cannot be *held liable to be punished* on the basis of a lawful act. But if a person has been held subject to punishment because he committed an *un*lawful act, the *degree* of his punishment assuredly *can* be increased on the basis of any other conduct of his that displays his wickedness, unlawful or not. Criminal sentences can be computed, we have said, on the basis of "information concerning every aspect of a defendant's life," *Williams v. New York,* 337 U.S. 241, 250–252 (1949). The Court at one point seems to acknowledge this, observing that, although a sentencing court "[cannot] properly *punish* lawful conduct," it may in assessing the penalty "consider . . . lawful conduct that bears on the defendant's character." That concession is quite incompatible, however, with the later assertion that, since "neither the jury nor the trial court was presented with evidence that any of BMW's out-of-state conduct was unlawful," the Alabama Supreme Court "therefore properly eschewed reliance on BMW's out-of-state conduct, . . . and based its remitted award solely on conduct that occurred within Alabama." Why could the Supreme Court of Alabama not consider lawful (but disreputable) conduct, both inside and outside Alabama, for the purpose of assessing just how bad an actor BMW was?

The Court follows up its statement that "Alabama does not have the power . . . to punish BMW for conduct that was lawful where it occurred" with the statement: "Nor may Alabama impose sanctions on BMW in order to deter conduct that is lawful in other jurisdictions." The Court provides us no citation of authority to support this proposition—other than the barely analogous cases cited earlier in the opinion—and I know of none.

These significant issues pronounced upon by the Court are not remotely presented for resolution in the present case. There is no basis for believing that Alabama has sought to control conduct elsewhere. The statutes at issue merely permit civil juries to treat conduct such as petitioner's as fraud, and authorize an award of appropriate punitive damages in the event the fraud is found to be "gross, oppressive, or malicious." To be sure, respondent did invite the jury to consider out-of-state conduct in its calculation of damages, but any increase in the jury's initial award based on that consideration is not a component of the remitted judgment before us. As the Court several times recognizes, in computing the amount of the remitted award the Alabama Supreme Court—whether it was constitutionally required to or not—"expressly disclaimed any reliance on acts that occurred in other jurisdictions." Thus, the only question presented by this case is whether that award, limited to petitioner's Alabama conduct and viewed in light of the factors identified as properly informing the inquiry, is excessive. The Court's sweeping (and largely unsupported) statements regarding the relationship of punitive awards to lawful or unlawful out-of-state conduct are the purest dicta.

III

In Part III of its opinion, the Court identifies "[t]hree guideposts" that lead it to the conclusion that the award in this case is excessive: degree of reprehensibility, ratio between punitive award and plaintiff's actual harm, and legislative sanctions provided for comparable misconduct. The legal significance of these "guideposts" is nowhere explored, but their necessary effect is to establish federal standards governing the hitherto exclusively state law of damages. Apparently (though it is by no means clear) all three federal "guideposts" can be overridden if "necessary to deter future misconduct"—a loophole that will encourage state reviewing courts to uphold awards as necessary for the "adequat[e] protect[ion]" of state consumers, *ibid*. By effectively requiring state reviewing courts to concoct rationalizations—whether within the "guideposts" or through the loophole—to justify the intuitive punitive reactions of state juries, the Court accords neither category of institution the respect it deserves.

Of course it will not be easy for the States to comply with this new federal law of damages, no matter how willing they are to do so. In truth, the "guideposts" mark a road to nowhere; they provide no real guidance at all. As to "degree of reprehensibility" of the defendant's conduct, we learn that "nonviolent crimes are less serious than crimes marked by violence or the threat of violence," and that "trickery and deceit" are "more reprehensible than negligence." As to the ratio of punitive to compensatory damages, we are told that a "general concer[n] of reasonableness . . . enter[s] into the constitutional calculus,"—though even "a breathtaking 500 to 1" will not necessarily do anything more than " 'raise a suspicious judicial eyebrow,' " (quoting *TXO, supra,* at 481 (O'CONNOR, J., dissenting), an opinion which, when confronted with that "breathtaking" ratio, approved it). And as to legislative sanctions provided for comparable misconduct, they should be accorded "substantial deference." One expects the Court to conclude: "To thine own self be true."

These crisscrossing platitudes yield no real answers in no real cases. And it must be noted that the Court nowhere says that these three "guideposts" are the *only* guideposts; indeed, it makes very clear that they are not—explaining away the earlier opinions that do not really follow these "guideposts" on the basis of *additional* factors, thereby "reiterat[ing] our rejection of a categorical approach." In other words, even these utter platitudes, if they should ever happen to produce an answer, may be overridden by other unnamed considerations. The Court has constructed a framework that does not genuinely constrain, that does not inform state legislatures and lower courts—that does nothing at all except confer an artificial air of doctrinal analysis upon its essentially ad hoc determination that this particular award of punitive damages was not "fair."

The Court distinguishes today's result from *Haslip* and *TXO* partly on the ground that "the record in this case discloses no deliberate false statements, acts of affirmative misconduct, or concealment of evidence of improper motive, such as were present in *Haslip* and *TXO*." This seemingly rejects the findings necessarily made by the jury—that petitioner had committed a fraud that was "gross, oppressive, or malicious," Ala.Code § 6–11–20(b)(1). Perhaps that rejection is intentional; the Court does not say.

The relationship between judicial application of the new "guideposts" and jury findings poses a real problem for the Court, since as a matter of logic there is no more justification for ignoring the jury's determination as to *how* reprehensible petitioner's conduct was (*i.e.,* how much it deserves to be punished), than there is for ignoring its determination that it was reprehensible *at all* (*i.e.,* that the wrong was willful and punitive damages are therefore recoverable). That the issue has been framed in terms of a constitutional right against unreasonably *excessive* awards should not obscure the fact that the logical and necessary consequence of the Court's approach is the recognition of a constitutional right against unreasonably *imposed* awards as well. The elevation of "fairness" in punishment to a principle of "substantive due process" means that every punitive award unreasonably imposed is unconstitutional; such an award is by definition excessive, since it attaches a penalty to conduct undeserving of punishment. Indeed, if the Court is correct, it must be that every claim that a state jury's award of *compensatory* damages is "unreasonable" (because not supported by the evidence) amounts to an assertion of constitutional injury. And the same would be true for determinations of liability. By today's logic, *every* dispute as to evidentiary sufficiency in a state civil suit poses a question of constitutional moment, subject to review in this Court. That is a stupefying proposition.

For the foregoing reasons, I respectfully dissent.

■ **JUSTICE GINSBURG, with whom THE CHIEF JUSTICE joins, dissenting.**

The Court, I am convinced, unnecessarily and unwisely ventures into territory traditionally within the States' domain, and does so in the face of reform measures recently adopted or currently under consideration in legislative arenas. The Alabama Supreme Court, in this case, endeavored to follow this Court's prior instructions; and, more recently, Alabama's highest court has installed further controls on awards of punitive damages. I would therefore leave the state court's judgment undisturbed, and resist unnecessary intrusion into an area dominantly of state concern.

I

The respect due the Alabama Supreme Court requires that we strip from this case a false issue: No impermissible "extraterritoriality" infects the judgment before us; the excessiveness of the award is the sole issue genuinely presented. The Court ultimately so recognizes, but further clarification is in order.

Dr. Gore's experience was not unprecedented among customers who bought BMW vehicles sold as flawless and brand-new. In addition to his own encounter, Gore showed, through paint repair orders introduced at trial, that on 983 other occasions since 1983, BMW had shipped new vehicles to dealers without disclosing paint repairs costing at least $300; at least 14 of the repainted vehicles, the evidence also showed, were sold as new and undamaged to consumers in Alabama. Sales nationwide, Alabama's Supreme Court said, were admissible "as to the issue of a 'pattern and practice' of such acts." There was "no error," the court reiterated, "in the admission of the evidence that showed how pervasive the nondisclosure policy was and the intent behind BMW NA's adoption of it." That determination comports with this Court's expositions.

Alabama's highest court next declared that the

> jury could not use the number of similar acts that a defendant has committed in other jurisdictions as a multiplier when determining the *dollar amount* of a punitive damages award. Such evidence may not be considered in setting the size of the civil penalty, because neither the jury nor the trial court had evidence before it showing in which states the conduct was wrongful.

Because the Alabama Supreme Court provided this clear statement of the State's law, the multiplier problem encountered in Gore's case is not likely to occur again. Now, as a matter of Alabama law, it is plainly impermissible to assess punitive damages by multiplication based on out-of-state events not shown to be unlawful.

No Alabama authority, it bears emphasis—no statute, judicial decision, or trial judge instruction—ever countenanced the jury's multiplication of the $4,000 diminution in value estimated for each refinished car by the number of such cars (approximately 1,000) shown to have been sold nationwide. . . .

In brief, Gore's case is idiosyncratic. The jury's improper multiplication, tardily featured by petitioner, is unlikely to recur in Alabama and does not call for error correction by this Court.

Because the jury apparently (and erroneously) had used acts in other States as a multiplier to arrive at a $4 million sum for punitive damages, the Alabama Supreme Court itself determined "the maximum amount that a properly functioning jury could have awarded." The *per curiam* opinion emphasized that in arriving at $2 million as "the *amount of punitive damages* to be awarded in this case, [the court did] not consider those acts that occurred in other jurisdictions." . . . In sum, the Alabama Supreme Court left standing the jury's decision that the facts warranted *an award* of punitive damages—a determination not contested in this Court—and the state court concluded that, considering only acts in Alabama, $2 million was "a constitutionally reasonable punitive damages award."

II

A

Alabama's Supreme Court reports that it "thoroughly and painstakingly" reviewed the jury's award, according to principles set out in its own pathmarking decisions and in this Court's opinions in *TXO* and *Haslip*. The Alabama court said it gave weight to several factors, including BMW's deliberate ("reprehensible") presentation of refinished cars as new and undamaged, without disclosing that the value of those cars had been reduced by an estimated 10%, the financial position of the defendant, and the costs of litigation. These standards, we previously held, "impos[e] a sufficiently definite and meaningful constraint on the discretion of Alabama factfinders in awarding punitive damages." *Haslip*, 499 U.S., at 22. Alabama's highest court could have displayed its labor pains more visibly, but its judgment is nonetheless entitled to a presumption of legitimacy. See *Rowan v. Runnels*, 5 How. 134, 139 (1847) ("[T]his court will always feel itself bound to respect the decisions of the State courts, and from the time they are made will regard them as conclusive in all cases upon the construction of their own constitution and laws.").

We accept, of course, that Alabama's Supreme Court applied the State's own law correctly. Under that law, the State's objectives— "punishment and deterrence"—guide punitive damages awards. Nor should we be quick to find a constitutional infirmity when the highest state court endeavored a corrective for one counsel's slip and the other's oversight—counsel for plaintiff's excess in summation, unobjected to by counsel for defendant—and when the state court did so intending to follow the process approved in our *Haslip* and *TXO* decisions.

B

The Court finds Alabama's $2 million award not simply excessive, but grossly so, and therefore unconstitutional. The decision leads us further into territory traditionally within the States' domain,[3] and commits the Court, now and again, to correct "misapplication of a properly stated rule of law." But cf. this Court's Rule 10 ("A petition for a writ of certiorari is rarely granted when the asserted error consists of erroneous factual findings or the misapplication of a properly stated rule of law."). The Court is not well equipped for this mission. Tellingly, the Court repeats that it brings to the task no "mathematical formula," no "categorical approach," no "bright line." It has only a vague concept of substantive due process, a "raised eyebrow" test, as its ultimate guide.[5]

---

[3] See *Browning-Ferris Industries of Vt., Inc. v. Kelco Disposal, Inc.*, 492 U.S. 257, 278 (1989) (In any "lawsuit where state law provides the basis of decision, the propriety of an award of punitive damages for the conduct in question, and the factors the jury may consider in determining their amount, are questions of state law."); *Silkwood v. Kerr-McGee Corp.*, 464 U.S. 238, 255 (1984) ("Punitive damages have long been a part of traditional state tort law.").

[5] Justice BREYER's concurring opinion offers nothing more solid. Under *Pacific Mut. Life Ins. Co. v. Haslip*, 499 U.S. 1 (1991), he acknowledges, Alabama's standards for punitive

In contrast to habeas corpus review under 28 U.S.C. § 2254, the Court will work at this business alone. It will not be aided by the federal district courts and courts of appeals. It will be the only federal court policing the area. The Court's readiness to superintend state-court punitive damages awards is all the more puzzling in view of the Court's longstanding reluctance to countenance review, even by courts of appeals, of the size of verdicts returned by juries in federal district court proceedings. And the reexamination prominent in state courts[6] and in legislative arenas[*] serves to underscore why the Court's enterprise is undue.

For the reasons stated, I dissent from this Court's disturbance of the judgment the Alabama Supreme Court has made.

Eastern Enterprises v. Apfel
524 U.S. 498 (1998)

■ JUSTICE O'CONNOR announced the judgment of the Court and delivered an opinion, in which THE CHIEF JUSTICE, JUSTICE SCALIA, and JUSTICE THOMAS join.

In this case, the Court considers a challenge under the Due Process and Takings Clauses of the Constitution to the Coal Industry Retiree

---

damages, standing alone, do not violate due process. But they "invit[e] the kind of scrutiny the Court has given the particular verdict before us." Pursuing that invitation, Justice BREYER concludes that, matching the particular facts of this case to Alabama's "legitimate punitive damages objectives," the award was " 'gross[ly] excessiv[e].' " The exercise is engaging, but ultimately tells us only this: too big will be judged unfair. What is the Court's measure of too big? Not a cap of the kind a legislature could order, or a mathematical test this Court can divine and impose. Too big is, in the end, the amount at which five Members of the Court bridle.

[6]   See, *e.g., Distinctive Printing and Packaging Co. v. Cox,* 232 Neb. 846, 857, 443 N.W.2d 566, 574 (1989) (*per curiam*) ("[P]unitive, vindictive, or exemplary damages contravene Neb. Const. art. VII, § 5, and thus are not allowed in this jurisdiction."); *Santana v. Registrars of Voters of Worcester,* 398 Mass. 862, 502 N.E.2d 132 (1986) (punitive damages are not permitted, unless expressly authorized by statute); *Fisher Properties, Inc. v. Arden-Mayfair, Inc.,* 106 Wash.2d 826, 852, 726 P.2d 8, 23 (1986) (en banc) (same).

In *Life Ins. Co. of Georgia v. Johnson,* No. 1940357 (Nov. 17, 1995), the Alabama Supreme Court revised the State's regime for assessments of punitive damages. Henceforth, trials will be bifurcated. Initially, juries will be instructed to determine liability and the amount of compensatory damages, if any; also, the jury is to return a special verdict on the question whether a punitive damages award is warranted. If the jury answers yes to the punitive damages question, the trial will be resumed for the presentation of evidence and instructions relevant to the amount appropriate to award as punitive damages.

After postverdict trial court review and subsequent appellate review, the amount of the final punitive damages judgment will be paid into the trial court. The trial court will then order payment of litigation expenses, including the plaintiff's attorney's fees, and instruct the clerk to divide the remainder equally between the plaintiff and the State General Fund. The provision for payment to the State General Fund is applicable to all judgments not yet satisfied, and therefore would apply to the judgment in Gore's case.

[*]   In an appendix, Justice Ginsburg noted that "[a]t least one state legislature has prohibited punitive damages altogether, unless explicitly provided by statute," see N.H.Rev.Stat. Ann. § 507:16 (1994), and she surveyed "some of the several controls enacted or under consideration in the States" including " (1) caps on awards; (2) provisions for payment of sums to state agencies rather than to plaintiffs; and (3) mandatory bifurcated trials with separate proceedings for punitive damages determinations." [Editor's Note]

Health Benefit Act of 1992 (Coal Act or Act), 26 U.S.C. §§ 9701–9722 (1994 ed. and Supp. II), which establishes a mechanism for funding health care benefits for retirees from the coal industry and their dependents. We conclude that the Coal Act, as applied to petitioner Eastern Enterprises, effects an unconstitutional taking.

I

[Congress enacted the Coal Industry Retiree Health Benefit Act of 1992 (Coal Act) to provide a comprehensive solution to the breakdown of private efforts to supply healthcare to coal miners and their families. The United Mine Workers of America began negotiating with the mining industry to improve healthcare for miners in the late 1930s. After a series of strikes, the federal government brokered a series of industry-wide National Bituminous Coal Wage Agreements (NBCWAs) between 1949 and 1971. These agreements created a common fund, financed by contributions from all companies in the industry, to provide health benefits to miners and their dependents. The funds did not provide fixed levels of benefits or, by their terms, guarantee lifetime healthcare. The 1974 NBCWA broadened coverage and, for the first time, explicitly provided health benefits to retirees. The funds encountered financial problems, however, and many coal companies began to withdraw from the industry. Ultimately, Congress enacted the Coal Act to create a Combined Benefit Fund financed by annual premiums assessed against "signatory coal operators"—that is, any coal company that signed any NBCWA requiring contributions to the 1950 or 1974 benefit plans. This included "related persons," such as successors in interest to those companies or corporations under common control, even if those companies were no longer in the coal industry.]

II

A

Eastern was organized as a Massachusetts business trust in 1929, under the name Eastern Gas and Fuel Associates. Its current holdings include Boston Gas Company and a barge operator. Therefore, although Eastern is no longer involved in the coal industry, it is "in business" within the meaning of the Coal Act. Until 1965, Eastern conducted extensive coal mining operations centered in West Virginia and Pennsylvania. As a signatory to each NBCWA executed between 1947 and 1964, Eastern made contributions of over $60 million to the 1947 and 1950 [Welfare and Retirement] Funds.

In 1963, Eastern decided to transfer its coal-related operations to a subsidiary, Eastern Associated Coal Corp. (EACC). The transfer was completed by the end of 1965, and was described in Eastern's federal income tax return as an agreement by EACC to assume all of Eastern's liabilities arising out of coal mining and marketing operations in exchange for Eastern's receipt of EACC's stock. EACC made similar representations in Security and Exchange Commission filings, describing itself as the successor to Eastern's coal business.

Eastern retained its stock interest in EACC through a subsidiary corporation, Coal Properties Corp. (CPC), until 1987, and it received dividends of more than $100 million from EACC during that period. In 1987, Eastern sold its interest in CPC to respondent Peabody Holding Company, Inc. (Peabody). Under the terms of the agreement effecting the transfer, Peabody, CPC, and EACC assumed responsibility for payments to certain benefit plans, including the "Benefit Plan for UMWA Represented Employees of EACC and Subs." As of June 30, 1987, the 1950 and 1974 Benefit Plans reported surplus assets, totaling over $33 million.

B

Following enactment of the Coal Act, the Commissioner assigned to Eastern the obligation for Combined Fund premiums respecting over 1,000 retired miners who had worked for the company before 1966, based on Eastern's status as the pre-1978 signatory operator for whom the miners had worked for the longest period of time. Eastern's premium for a 12-month period exceeded $5 million.

Eastern responded by suing the Commissioner, as well as the Combined Fund and its trustees, in the United States District Court for the District of Massachusetts. Eastern asserted that the Coal Act, either on its face or as applied, violates substantive due process and constitutes a taking of its property in violation of the Fifth Amendment. Eastern also challenged the Commissioner's interpretation of the Coal Act. The District Court granted summary judgment for respondents on all claims, upholding both the Commissioner's interpretation of the Coal Act and the Act's constitutionality.

The Court of Appeals for the First Circuit affirmed. . . . Other Courts of Appeals have also upheld the Coal Act against constitutional challenges. In view of the importance of the issues raised in this case, we granted certiorari. . . .

IV

A

The Takings Clause of the Fifth Amendment provides: "[N]or shall private property be taken for public use, without just compensation." The aim of the Clause is to prevent the government "from forcing some people alone to bear public burdens which, in all fairness and justice, should be borne by the public as a whole." *Armstrong v. United States*, 364 U.S. 40, 49 (1960).

This case does not present the "classi[c] taking" in which the government directly appropriates private property for its own use. Although takings problems are more commonly presented when "the interference with property can be characterized as a physical invasion by government, than when interference arises from some public program adjusting the benefits and burdens of economic life to promote the common good," *Penn Central Transp. Co. v. New York City,* 438 U.S. 104, 124 (1978), economic regulation such as the Coal Act may nonetheless effect a taking, see *Security Industrial Bank, supra,* at 78. See also *Calder v. Bull,* 3 Dall. 386, 388 (1798) (opinion of Chase, J.) ("It is against all reason and justice" to presume that the legislature has been entrusted with the power to enact "a law that takes *property* from A. and gives it to B"). By operation of the Act, Eastern is permanently deprived of those assets necessary to satisfy its statutory obligation, not to the Government, but to the Combined Fund, and "a strong public desire to improve the public condition is not enough to warrant achieving the desire by a shorter cut than the constitutional way of paying for the change," *Pennsylvania Coal Co. v. Mahon,* 260 U.S. 393, 416 (1922).

Of course, a party challenging governmental action as an unconstitutional taking bears a substantial burden. Government regulation often "curtails some potential for the use or economic exploitation of private property," *Andrus v. Allard,* 444 U.S. 51, 65 (1979), and "not every destruction or injury to property by governmental action has been held to be a 'taking' in the constitutional sense," *Armstrong, supra,* at 48. In light of that understanding, the process for evaluating a regulation's constitutionality involves an examination of the "justice and fairness" of the governmental action. That inquiry, by its nature, does not lend itself to any set formula, and the determination whether " 'justice and fairness' require that economic injuries caused by public action [must] be compensated by the government, rather than remain disproportionately concentrated on a few persons," is essentially ad hoc and fact intensive, *Kaiser Aetna v. United States,* 444 U.S. 164, 175 (1979). We have identified several factors, however, that have particular significance: "[T]he economic impact of the regulation, its interference with reasonable investment backed expectations, and the character of the governmental action." *Ibid.*

B

Our analysis in this case is informed by previous decisions considering the constitutionality of somewhat similar legislative schemes. In *Usery v. Turner Elkhorn Mining Co.,* 428 U.S. 1 (1976), we had occasion to review provisions of the Black Lung Benefits Act of 1972, 30 U.S.C. § 901 *et seq.,* which required coal operators to compensate certain miners and their survivors for death or disability due to black lung disease caused by employment coal mines. Coal operators challenged the provisions of the Act relating to miners who were no longer employed in the industry, arguing that those provisions violated substantive due process by imposing "an unexpected liability for past, completed acts that were legally proper and, at least in part, unknown to be dangerous at the time."

In rejecting the operators' challenge, we explained that "legislative Acts adjusting the burdens and benefits of economic life come to the Court with a presumption of constitutionality, and . . . the burden is on one complaining of a due process violation to establish that the legislature has acted in an arbitrary and irrational way." We observed that stricter limits may apply to Congress' authority when legislation operates in a retroactive manner, but concluded that the assignment of liability for black lung benefits was "justified as a rational measure to spread the costs of the employees' disabilities to those who have profited from the fruits of their labor."

Several years later, we confronted a due process challenge to the Multiemployer Pension Plan Amendments Act of 1980 (MPPAA). See *Pension Benefit Guaranty Corporation v. R.A. Gray & Co.,* 467 U.S. 717 (1984). The MPPAA was enacted to supplement ERISA, 29 U.S.C. § 1001 *et seq.,* which established the Pension Benefit Guaranty Corporation (PBGC) to administer an insurance program for vested pension benefits. For a temporary period, the PBGC had discretionary authority to pay benefits upon the termination of multiemployer pension plans, after which insurance coverage would become mandatory. If the PBGC exercised that authority, employers who had contributed to the plan during the five years before its termination faced liability for an amount proportional to their share of contributions to the plan during that period.

Despite Congress' effort to insure multiemployer plan benefits through ERISA, many multiemployer plans were in a precarious financial position as the date for mandatory coverage approached. After a series of hearings and debates, Congress passed the MPPAA, which imposed a payment obligation upon any employer withdrawing from a multiemployer pension plan, the amount of which depended on the employer's share of the plan's unfunded vested benefits. The MPPAA applied retroactively to withdrawals within the five months preceding the statute's enactment.

In *Gray,* an employer that had participated in a multiemployer pension plan brought a due process challenge to the statutory liability stemming from its withdrawal from the plan four months before the MPPAA was enacted. Relying on our decision in *Turner Elkhorn,* we rejected the employer's claim. It was rational, we determined, for Congress to impose retroactive liability "to prevent employers from taking advantage of a lengthy legislative process [by] withdrawing while Congress debated necessary revisions in the statute." In addition, we explained, "as the [MPPAA] progressed through the legislative process, Congress advanced the effective date chosen so that it would encompass only that retroactive time period that Congress believed would be necessary to accomplish its purposes." Accordingly, we concluded that the MPPAA exemplified the "customary congressional practice" of enacting "retroactive statutes confined to short and limited periods required by the practicalities of producing national legislation."

This Court again considered the constitutionality of the MPPAA in *Connolly v. Pension Benefit Guaranty Corporation,* 475 U.S. 211 (1986), which presented the question whether the MPPAA withdrawal liability provisions effected an unconstitutional taking. The action was brought by trustees of a multiemployer pension plan that, under collective bargaining agreements, received contributions from employers on the basis of the hours worked by their employees. We agreed that the liability imposed by the MPPAA constituted a permanent deprivation of assets, but we rejected the notion that "such a statutory liability to a private party always constitutes an uncompensated taking prohibited by the Fifth Amendment." "In the course of regulating commercial and other human affairs," we explained, "Congress routinely creates burdens for some that directly benefit others." Consistent with our decisions in *Gray* and *Turner Elkhorn,* we reasoned that legislation is not unlawful solely because it upsets otherwise settled expectations.

Moreover, given our holding in *Gray* that the MPPAA did not violate due process, we concluded that "it would be surprising indeed to discover" that the statute effected a taking. Although the employers in *Connolly* had contractual agreements expressly limiting their contributions to the multiemployer plan, we observed that "[c]ontracts, however express, cannot fetter the constitutional authority of Congress" and "the fact that legislation disregards or destroys existing contractual rights does not always transform the regulation into an illegal taking." Focusing on the three factors of "particular significance"—the economic impact of the regulation, the extent to which the regulation interferes with investment-backed expectations, and the character of the governmental action—we determined that the MPPAA did not violate the Takings Clause.

The governmental action at issue in *Connolly* was not a physical invasion of employers' assets; rather, it "safeguard[ed] the participants in multiemployer pension plans by requiring a withdrawing employer to fund its share of the plan obligations incurred during its association with the plan." In addition, although the amounts assessed under the MPPAA were substantial, we found it important that "[t]he assessment of withdrawal liability [was] not made in a vacuum . . . but directly depend[ed] on the relationship between the employer and the plan to which it had made contributions." Further, "a significant number of provisions in the Act . . . moderate[d] and mitigate[d] the economic impact of an individual employer's liability." Accordingly, we found "nothing to show that the withdrawal liability actually imposed on an employer w[ould] always be out of proportion to its experience with the plan." Nor did the MPPAA interfere with employers' reasonable investment-backed expectations, for, by the time of the MPPAA's enactment, "[p]rudent employers . . . had more than sufficient notice not only that pension plans were currently regulated, but also that withdrawal itself might trigger additional financial obligations." For those reasons, we determined that "fairness and justice" did not require anyone other than the withdrawing employers and the remaining parties to the pension agreements to bear the burden of funding employees' vested benefits.

We once more faced challenges to the MPPAA under the Due Process and Takings Clauses in *Concrete Pipe & Products of Cal., Inc. v. Construction Laborers Pension Trust for Southern Cal.,* 508 U.S. 602 (1993). In that case, the employer focused on the fact that its contractual commitment to the multiemployer plan did not impose withdrawal liability. We first rejected the employer's substantive due process challenge based on our decisions in *Gray* and *Turner Elkhorn,* notwithstanding the employer's argument that the MPPAA imposed upon it a higher liability than its contract contemplated. The claim under the Takings Clause, meanwhile, was resolved by *Connolly.* We explained that, as in that case, the Government had not occupied or destroyed the employer's property. As to the severity of the MPPAA's impact, we concluded that the employer had not shown that its withdrawal liability was " 'out of proportion to its experience with the plan' " Turning to the employer's reasonable investment-backed expectations, we repeated our observation in *Connolly* that "pension plans had long been subject to federal regulation." Moreover, although the employer's liability under the MPPAA exceeded ERISA's original cap on withdrawal liability, we found that there was "no reasonable basis to expect that [ERISA's] legislative ceiling would never be lifted." In sum, as in *Connolly,* the employer "voluntarily negotiated and maintained a pension plan which was determined to be within the strictures of ERISA," making the burden the MPPAA imposed upon it neither unfair nor unjust.

Our opinions in *Turner Elkhorn, Connolly,* and *Concrete Pipe* make clear that Congress has considerable leeway to fashion economic legislation, including the power to affect contractual commitments between private parties. Congress also may impose retroactive liability to some degree, particularly where it is "confined to short and limited periods required by the practicalities of producing national legislation." *Gray,* 467 U.S., at 731. Our decisions, however, have left open the possibility that legislation might be unconstitutional if it imposes severe retroactive liability on a limited class of parties that could not have anticipated the liability, and the extent of that liability is substantially disproportionate to the parties' experience.

C

We believe that the Coal Act's allocation scheme, as applied to Eastern, presents such a case. We reach that conclusion by applying the three factors that traditionally have informed our regulatory takings analysis. Although Justice KENNEDY and Justice BREYER would pursue a different course in evaluating the constitutionality of the Coal Act, they acknowledge that this Court's opinions in *Connolly* and

Concrete Pipe indicate that the regulatory takings framework is germane to legislation of this sort.

As to the first factor relevant in assessing whether a regulatory taking has occurred, economic impact, there is no doubt that the Coal Act has forced a considerable financial burden upon Eastern. The parties estimate that Eastern's cumulative payments under the Act will be on the order of $50 to $100 million. Eastern's liability is thus substantial, and the company is clearly deprived of the amounts it must pay the Combined Fund. The fact that the Federal Government has not specified the assets that Eastern must use to satisfy its obligation does not negate that impact. . . .

That liability is not, of course, a permanent physical occupation of Eastern's property of the kind that we have viewed as a *per se* taking. See *Loretto v. Teleprompter Manhattan CATV Corp.*, 458 U.S. 419, 441 (1982). But our decisions upholding the MPPAA suggest that an employer's statutory liability for multiemployer plan benefits should reflect some "proportion[ality] to its experience with the plan." *Concrete Pipe,* 508 U.S., at 645. In *Concrete Pipe* and *Connolly,* the employers had voluntarily negotiated and maintained a pension plan which was determined to be within the strictures of ERISA and consequently, the statutory liability was linked to the employers' conduct.

Here, however, while Eastern contributed to the 1947 and 1950 W&R Funds, it ceased its coal mining operations in 1965 and neither participated in negotiations nor agreed to make contributions in connection with the Benefit Plans under the 1974, 1978, or subsequent NBCWA's. It is the latter agreements that first suggest an industry commitment to the funding of lifetime health benefits for both retirees and their family members. Although EACC continued mining coal until 1987 as a subsidiary of Eastern, Eastern's liability under the Act bears no relationship to its ownership of EACC; the Act assigns Eastern responsibility for benefits relating to miners that Eastern itself, not EACC, employed, while EACC would be assigned the responsibility for any miners that it had employed. Thus, the Act does not purport, as Justice BREYER suggests, to assign liability to Eastern based on the " 'last man out' problem" that developed after benefits were significantly expanded in 1974. During the years in which Eastern employed miners, retirement and health benefits were far less extensive than under the 1974 NBCWA, were unvested, and were fully subject to alteration or termination. Before 1974, as Justice BREYER notes, Eastern could not have contemplated liability for the provision of lifetime benefits to the widows of deceased miners, a beneficiary class that is likely to be substantial. Although Eastern at one time employed the Combined Fund beneficiaries that it has been assigned under the Coal Act, the correlation between Eastern and its liability to the Combined Fund is tenuous, and the amount assessed against Eastern resembles a calculation made in a vacuum. The company's obligations under the Act depend solely on its roster of employees some 30 to 50 years before the statute's enactment, without any regard to responsibilities that Eastern accepted under any benefit plan the company itself adopted.

It is true that Eastern may be able to seek indemnification from EACC or Peabody. But although the Act preserves Eastern's right to pursue indemnification, it does not confer any right of reimbursement. Moreover, the possibility of indemnification does not alter the fact that Eastern has been assessed over $5 million in Combined Fund premiums and that its liability under the Coal Act will continue for many years. To the extent that Eastern may have entered into contractual arrangements to insure itself against liabilities arising out of its former coal operations, that indemnity is neither enhanced nor supplanted by the Coal Act and does not affect the availability of the declaratory relief Eastern seeks.

We are also not persuaded by respondents' argument that the Coal Act "moderate[s] and mitigate[s] the economic impact" upon Eastern. Although Eastern is not assigned the premiums for former employees who later worked for companies that signed the 1978 NBCWA, Eastern had no control over the activities of its former employees subsequent to its departure from the coal industry in 1965. By contrast, the provisions of the MPPAA that we identified as potentially moderating the employer's liability in *Connolly* were generally within the employer's control. The mere fact that Eastern is not forced to bear the burden of lifetime benefits respecting *all* of its former employees does not mean that the company's liability for some of those employees is not a significant economic burden.

For similar reasons, the Coal Act substantially interferes with Eastern's reasonable investment-backed expectations. The Act's beneficiary allocation scheme reaches back 30 to 50 years to impose liability against Eastern based on the company's activities between 1946 and 1965. Thus, even though the Act mandates only the payment of future health benefits, it nonetheless attaches new legal consequences to an employment relationship completed before its enactment.

Retroactivity is generally disfavored in the law, in accordance with fundamental notions of justice that have been recognized throughout history. In his Commentaries on the Constitution, Justice Story reasoned: "Retrospective laws are, indeed, generally unjust; and, as has been forcibly said, neither accord with sound legislation nor with the fundamental principles of the social compact." 2 J. Story, Commentaries on the Constitution § 1398 (5th ed. 1891). A similar principle abounds in the laws of other nations. See, *e.g., Gustavson Drilling (1964) Ltd. v. Minister of National Revenue,* 66 D.L.R.3d 449, 462 (Can. 1975) (discussing rule that statutes should not be construed in a manner that would impair existing property rights); The French Civil Code, Preliminary Title, Art. 2, p. 2 ("Legislation only provides for the future; it has no retroactive effect") (J. Crabb transl., rev. ed. 1995). "Retroactive legislation," we have explained, "presents problems of unfairness that are more serious than those posed by prospective legislation, because it can deprive citizens of legitimate expectations and upset settled transactions." *General Motors Corp. v. Romein,* 503 U.S. 181, 191 (1992).

Our Constitution expresses concern with retroactive laws through several of its provisions, including the *Ex Post Facto* and Takings Clauses. In *Calder v. Bull,* 3 Dall. 386 (1798), this Court held that the *Ex Post Facto* Clause is directed at the retroactivity of penal legislation, while suggesting that the Takings Clause provides a similar safeguard against retrospective legislation concerning property rights. See *id.,* 3 U.S., at 394 (opinion of Chase, J.) ("The restraint against making any *ex post facto laws* was not considered, by the framers of the constitution, as extending to prohibit the depriving a citizen even of a *vested right to property;* or the provision, 'that *private* property should not be taken for public use, without just compensation,' was unnecessary"). In *Security Industrial Bank,* we considered a Takings Clause challenge to a Bankruptcy Code provision permitting debtors to avoid certain liens, possibly including those predating the statute's enactment. We expressed "substantial doubt whether the retroactive destruction of the appellees' liens . . . comport[ed] with the Fifth Amendment," and therefore construed the statute as applying only to lien interests vesting after the legislation took effect. Similar concerns led this Court to strike down a bankruptcy provision as an unconstitutional taking where it affected substantive rights acquired before the provision was adopted. *Louisville Joint Stock Land Bank v. Radford,* 295 U.S. 555, 601–602 (1935).

Like those provisions, the Coal Act operates retroactively, divesting Eastern of property long after the company believed its liabilities under the 1950 W&R Fund to have been settled. And the extent of Eastern's retroactive liability is substantial and particularly far reaching. Even in areas in which retroactivity is generally tolerated, such as tax legislation, some limits have been suggested. See, *e.g., United States v. Darusmont,* 449 U.S. 292, 296–297 (1981) *(per curiam)* (noting Congress' practice of confining retroactive application of tax provisions to "short and limited periods"). The distance into the past that the Act reaches back to impose a liability on Eastern and the magnitude of that liability raise substantial questions of fairness. See *Landgraf v. USI Film Products,* 511 U.S. 244, 265 (1994) ("Elementary considerations of fairness dictate that individuals should have an opportunity to know what the law is and to conform their conduct accordingly; settled expectations should not be lightly disrupted").

Respondents and their *amici curiae* assert that the extent of retroactive liability is justified because there was an implicit, industry wide agreement during the time that Eastern was involved in the coal industry to fund lifetime health benefits for qualifying miners and their dependents. That contention, however, is not supported by the pre-1974 NBCWA's. . . . Moreover, even though retirees received medical benefits before 1974, and perhaps developed a corresponding expectation that those benefits would continue, the Coal Act imposes liability respecting a much broader range of beneficiaries. In any event, the question is not whether miners had an expectation of lifetime benefits, but whether Eastern should bear the cost of those benefits as to miners it employed before 1966.

Eastern only participated in the 1947 and 1950 W&R Funds, which operated on a pay-as-you-go basis, and under which the degree of benefits and the classes of beneficiaries were subject to the trustees' discretion. Not until 1974, when ERISA forced revisions to the 1950 W&R Fund, could lifetime medical benefits under the multiemployer agreement have been viewed as promised. Eastern was no longer in the industry when the evergreen and guarantee clauses of the 1978 and subsequent NBCWA's shifted the 1950 and 1974 Benefit Plans from a defined contribution framework to a guarantee of defined benefits, at least for the life of the agreements. Thus, unlike the pension withdrawal liability upheld in *Concrete Pipe* and *Connolly,* the Coal Act's scheme for allocation of Combined Fund premiums is not calibrated either to Eastern's past actions or to any agreement—implicit or otherwise—by the company. Nor would the pattern of the Federal Government's involvement in the coal industry have given Eastern sufficient notice that lifetime health benefits might be guaranteed to retirees several decades later.

Eastern's liability also differs from coal operators' responsibility for benefits under the Black Lung Benefits Act of 1972. That legislation merely imposed "liability for the effects of disabilities bred in the past [that] is justified as a rational measure to spread the costs of the employees' disabilities to those who have profited from the fruits of their labor." *Turner Elkhorn,* 428 U.S., at 18. Likewise, Eastern might be responsible for employment-related health problems of all former employees whether or not the cost was foreseen at the time of employment, but there is no such connection here. There is no doubt that many coal miners sacrificed their health on behalf of this country's industrial development, and we do not dispute that some members of the industry promised lifetime medical benefits to miners and their dependents during the 1970's. Nor do we, as Justice STEVENS suggests, question Congress' policy decision that the miners are entitled to relief. But the Constitution does not permit a solution to the problem of funding miners' benefits that imposes such a disproportionate and severely retroactive burden upon Eastern.

Finally, the nature of the governmental action in this case is quite unusual. That Congress sought a legislative remedy for what it perceived to be a grave problem in the funding of retired coal miners' health benefits is understandable; complex problems of that sort typically call for a legislative solution. When, however, that solution singles out certain employers to bear a burden that is substantial in amount, based on the employers' conduct far in the past, and unrelated to any commitment that the employers made or to any injury they caused, the governmental action implicates fundamental principles of fairness underlying the Takings Clause. Eastern cannot be forced to bear the expense of lifetime health benefits for miners based on its activities decades before those benefits were promised. Accordingly, in the specific circumstances of this case, we conclude that the Coal Act's application to Eastern effects an unconstitutional taking.

D

Eastern also claims that the manner in which the Coal Act imposes liability upon it violates substantive due process. To succeed, Eastern would be required to establish that its liability under the Act is "arbitrary and irrational." *Turner Elkhorn, supra,* at 15. Our analysis of legislation under the Takings and Due Process Clauses is correlated to some extent, and there is a question whether the Coal Act violates due process in light of the Act's severely retroactive impact. At the same time, this Court has expressed concerns about using the Due Process Clause to invalidate economic legislation. See *Ferguson v. Skrupa,* 372 U.S. 726, 731 (1963) (noting "our abandonment of the use of the 'vague contours' of the Due Process Clause to nullify laws which a majority of the Court believ[e] to be economically unwise"); see also *Williamson v. Lee Optical of Okla., Inc.,* 348 U.S. 483, 488 (1955) ("The day is gone when this Court uses the Due Process Clause . . . to strike down . . . laws, regulatory of business and industrial conditions, because they may be unwise, improvident, or out of harmony with a particular school of thought"). Because we have determined that the third tier of the Coal Act's allocation scheme violates the Takings Clause as applied to Eastern, we need not address Eastern's due process claim. . . .

V

In enacting the Coal Act, Congress was responding to a serious problem with the funding of health benefits for retired coal miners. While we do not question Congress' power to address that problem, the solution it crafted improperly places a severe, disproportionate, and extremely retroactive burden on Eastern. Accordingly, we conclude that the Coal Act's allocation of liability to Eastern violates the Takings Clause, and that 26 U.S.C. § 9706(a)(3) should be enjoined as applied to Eastern. The judgment of the Court of Appeals is reversed, and the case is remanded for further proceedings.

It is so ordered.

■ JUSTICE THOMAS, concurring.

Justice O'CONNOR'S opinion correctly concludes that the Coal Act's imposition of retroactive liability on petitioner violates the Takings Clause. I write separately to emphasize that the *Ex Post Facto* Clause of the Constitution, Art. I, § 9, cl. 3, even more clearly reflects the principle that "[r]etrospective laws are, indeed, generally unjust." 2 J. Story, Commentaries on the Constitution § 1398, p. 272 (5th ed. 1891). Since

Calder v. Bull, 3 Dall. 386 (1798), however, this Court has considered the *Ex Post Facto* Clause to apply only in the criminal context. I have never been convinced of the soundness of this limitation, which in *Calder* was principally justified because a contrary interpretation would render the Takings Clause unnecessary. In an appropriate case, therefore, I would be willing to reconsider *Calder* and its progeny to determine whether a retroactive civil law that passes muster under our current Takings Clause jurisprudence is nonetheless unconstitutional under the *Ex Post Facto* Clause. Today's case, however, does present an unconstitutional taking, and I join Justice O'CONNOR's well-reasoned opinion in full.

■ JUSTICE KENNEDY, concurring in the judgment and dissenting in part.

The plurality's careful assessment of the history and purpose of the statute in question demonstrates the necessity to hold it arbitrary and beyond the legitimate authority of the Government to enact. In my view, which is in full accord with many of the plurality's conclusions, the relevant portions of the Coal Industry Retiree Health Benefit Act of 1992 (Coal Act) must be invalidated as contrary to essential due process principles, without regard to the Takings Clause of the Fifth Amendment. I concur in the judgment holding the Coal Act unconstitutional but disagree with the plurality's Takings Clause analysis, which, it is submitted, is incorrect and quite unnecessary for decision of the case. I must record my respectful dissent on this issue.

I

. . . Our cases do not support the plurality's conclusion that the Coal Act takes property. The Coal Act imposes a staggering financial burden on the petitioner, Eastern Enterprises, but it regulates the former mine owner without regard to property. It does not operate upon or alter an identified property interest, and it is not applicable to or measured by a property interest. The Coal Act does not appropriate, transfer, or encumber an estate in land (*e.g.,* a lien on a particular piece of property), a valuable interest in an intangible (*e.g.,* intellectual property), or even a bank account or accrued interest. The law simply imposes an obligation to perform an act, the payment of benefits. The statute is indifferent as to how the regulated entity elects to comply or the property it uses to do so. To the extent it affects property interests, it does so in a manner similar to many laws; but until today, none were thought to constitute takings. To call this sort of governmental action a taking as a matter of constitutional interpretation is both imprecise and, with all due respect, unwise.

As the role of Government expanded, our experience taught that a strict line between a taking and a regulation is difficult to discern or to maintain. This led the Court in *Pennsylvania Coal Co. v. Mahon,* 260 U.S. 393 (1922), to try to span the two concepts when specific property was subjected to what the owner alleged to be excessive regulation. "The general rule at least is, that while property may be regulated to a certain extent, if regulation goes too far it will be recognized as a taking." The quoted sentence is, of course, the genesis of the so-called regulatory takings doctrine. See *Lucas v. South Carolina Coastal Council,* 505 U.S. 1003, 1014 (1992) ("Prior to Justice Holmes's exposition in *Pennsylvania Coal Co. v. Mahon,* it was generally thought that the Takings Clause reached only a 'direct appropriation' of property or the functional equivalent of a 'practical ouster of [the owner's] possession' "). Without denigrating the importance the regulatory takings concept has assumed in our law, it is fair to say it has proved difficult to explain in theory and to implement in practice. Cases attempting to decide when a regulation becomes a taking are among the most litigated and perplexing in current law. See *Penn Central Transp. Co. v. New York City,* 438 U.S. 104, 123 (1978) ("The question of what constitutes a 'taking' for purposes of the Fifth Amendment has proved to be a problem of considerable difficulty").

Until today, however, one constant limitation has been that in all of the cases where the regulatory taking analysis has been employed, a specific property right or interest has been at stake. After the decision in *Pennsylvania Coal Co. v. Mahon, supra,* we confronted cases where specific and identified properties or property rights were alleged to come within the regulatory takings prohibition: air rights for high-rise buildings, *Penn Central, supra;* zoning on parcels of real property, *e.g., Agins v. City of Tiburon,* 447 U.S. 255 (1980); trade secrets, *Ruckelshaus v. Monsanto Co.,* 467 U.S. 986 (1984); right of access to property, *e.g., PruneYard Shopping Center v. Robins,* 447 U.S. 74 (1980); right to affix on structures, *Loretto v. Teleprompter Manhattan CATV Corp.,* 458 U.S. 419 (1982); right to transfer property by devise or intestacy, *e.g., Hodel v. Irving,* 481 U.S. 704 (1987); creation of an easement, *Nollan v. California Coastal Comm'n,* 483 U.S. 825 (1987); right to build or improve, *Lucas, supra;* liens on real property, *Armstrong v. United States,* 364 U.S. 40 (1960); right to mine coal, *Keystone Bituminous Coal Assn. v. DeBenedictis,* 480 U.S. 470 (1987); right to sell personal property, *Andrus v. Allard,* 444 U.S. 51 (1979); and the right to extract mineral deposits, *Goldblatt v. Hempstead,* 369 U.S. 590 (1962). The regulations in the cited cases were challenged as being so excessive as to destroy, or take, a specific property interest. The plurality's opinion disregards this requirement and, by removing this constant characteristic from takings analysis, would expand an already difficult and uncertain rule to a vast category of cases not deemed, in our law, to implicate the Takings Clause.

The difficulties in determining whether there is a taking or a regulation even where a property right or interest is identified ought to counsel against extending the regulatory takings doctrine to cases lacking this specificity. The existence of at least this outer boundary for application of the regulatory takings rule provides some necessary predictability for governmental entities. Our definition of a taking, after all, is binding on all of the States as well as the Federal Government. The plurality opinion would throw one of the most difficult and litigated areas of the law into confusion, subjecting States and municipalities to the potential of new and unforeseen claims in vast amounts. The existing category of cases involving specific property interests ought not to be obliterated by extending regulatory takings analysis to the amorphous class of cases embraced by the plurality's opinion today.

True, the burden imposed by the Coal Act may be just as great if the Government had appropriated one of Eastern's plants, but the mechanism by which the Government injures Eastern is so unlike the act of taking specific property that it is incongruous to call the Coal Act a taking, even as that concept has been expanded by the regulatory takings principle. In the terminology of our regulatory takings analysis, the character of the governmental action renders the Coal Act not a taking of property. While the usual taking occurs when the government physically acquires property for itself, our regulatory takings analysis recognizes a taking may occur when property is not appropriated by the government or is transferred to other private parties. See, *e.g., Loretto, supra* (transfer of physical space from landlords to cable companies).

As the range of governmental conduct subjected to takings analysis has expanded, however, we have been careful not to lose sight of the importance of identifying the property allegedly taken, lest all governmental action be subjected to examination under the constitutional prohibition against taking without just compensation, with the attendant potential for money damages. We have asked how the challenged governmental action is implemented with particular emphasis on the extent to which a specific property right is affected. See *id.,* at 432 (physical invasion "is a government action of such a unique character that it is a taking without regard to other factors"); *Penn Central, supra,* at 124 ("A 'taking' may more readily be found when the interference with property can be characterized as a physical invasion by government, than when interference arises from some public program adjusting the benefits and burdens of economic life to promote the common good"). The Coal Act neither targets a specific property interest nor depends upon any particular property for the operation of its statutory mechanisms. The liability imposed on Eastern no doubt will reduce its net worth and its total value, but this can be said of any law which has an adverse economic effect.

The circumstance that the statute does not take money for the Government but instead makes it payable to third persons is not a factor I rely upon to show the lack of a taking. While there are instances where the Government's self-enrichment may make it all the more evident a taking has occurred, the Government ought not to have the capacity to give itself immunity from a takings claim by the device of requiring the transfer of property from one private owner directly to another. At the same time, the Government's imposition of an obligation between private parties, or destruction of an existing obligation, must relate to a specific property interest to implicate the Takings Clause. . . .

If the plurality is adopting its novel and expansive concept of a taking in order to avoid making a normative judgment about the Coal Act, it fails in the attempt; for it must make the normative judgment in all events. The imprecision of our regulatory takings doctrine does open the door to normative considerations about the wisdom of government decisions. See, *e.g., Agins v. City of Tiburon,* 447 U.S., at 260 (zoning constitutes a taking if it does not "substantially advance legitimate state interests"). This sort of analysis is in uneasy tension with our basic understanding of the Takings Clause, which has not been understood to be a substantive or absolute limit on the government's power to act. The Clause operates as a conditional limitation, permitting the government to do what it wants so long as it pays the charge. The Clause presupposes what the government intends to do is otherwise constitutional:

> As its language indicates, and as the Court has frequently noted, [the Takings Clause] does not prohibit the taking of private property, but instead places a condition on the exercise of that power. This basic understanding of the Amendment makes clear that it is designed not to limit the governmental interference with property rights per se, but rather to secure compensation in the event of otherwise proper interference amounting to a taking. *First English Evangelical Lutheran Church of Glendale v. County of Los Angeles,* 482 U.S. 304, 314–315 (1987).

Given that the constitutionality of the Coal Act appears to turn on the legitimacy of Congress' judgment rather than on the availability of compensation, the more appropriate constitutional analysis arises under general due process principles rather than under the Takings Clause.

It should be acknowledged that there are passages in some of our cases on the imposition of retroactive liability for an employer's withdrawal from a pension plan which might give some support to the plurality's discussion of the Takings Clause. See *Connolly v. Pension Benefit Guaranty Corporation,* 475 U.S. 211, 223 (1986); *Concrete Pipe & Products of Cal., Inc. v. Construction Laborers Pension Trust for Southern Cal.,* 508 U.S. 602, 641 (1993). . . . My reading of *Connolly,* and *Concrete Pipe,* is that we should proceed first to general due process principles, reserving takings analysis for cases where the governmental action is otherwise permissible. . . .

II

When the constitutionality of the Coal Act is tested under the Due Process Clause, it must be invalidated. Accepted principles forbidding retroactive legislation of this type are sufficient to dispose of the case.

Although we have been hesitant to subject economic legislation to due process scrutiny as a general matter, the Court has given careful consideration to due process challenges to legislation with retroactive effects. As today's plurality opinion notes, for centuries our law has harbored a singular distrust of retroactive statutes. In the words of Chancellor Kent: "A retroactive statute would partake in its character of the mischiefs of an *ex post facto* law . . . ; and in every other case relating to contracts or property, it would be against every sound principle." 1 J. Kent, Commentaries on American Law *455. Justice Story reached a similar conclusion: "Retrospective laws are, indeed, generally unjust; and, as has been forcibly said, neither accord with sound legislation nor with the fundamental principles of the social compact." 2 J. Story, Commentaries on the Constitution § 1398 (5th ed. 1891).

The Court's due process jurisprudence reflects this distrust. For example, in *Usery v. Turner Elkhorn Mining Co.,* 428 U.S. 1, 15 (1976), the Court held due process requires an inquiry into whether in enacting the retroactive law the legislature acted in an arbitrary and irrational way. Even though prospective economic legislation carries with it the presumption of constitutionality, "[i]t does not follow . . . that what Congress can legislate prospectively it can legislate retrospectively. The retrospective aspects of [economic] legislation, as well as the prospective aspects, must meet the test of due process, and the justifications for the latter may not suffice for the former." We have repeated this formulation in numerous recent decisions and given serious consideration to retroactivity-based due process challenges, all without questioning the validity of the underlying due process principle. *United States v. Carlton,* 512 U.S. 26, 31 (1994); *Concrete Pipe, supra,* at 636–641; *General Motors Corp. v. Romein,* 503 U.S. 181, 191 (1992); *United States v. Sperry Corp.,* 493 U.S. 52, 64 (1989); *Pension Benefit Guaranty Corporation v. R.A. Gray & Co.,* 467 U.S. 717, 729–730 (1984). These decisions treat due process challenges based on the retroactive character of the statutes in question as serious and meritorious, thus confirming the vitality of our legal tradition's disfavor of retroactive economic legislation. Indeed, it is no accident that the primary retroactivity precedents upon which today's plurality opinion relies in its takings analysis were grounded in due process. *Ante* (citing *Turner Elkhorn, R.A. Gray,* and *Concrete Pipe*).

These cases reflect our recognition that retroactive lawmaking is a particular concern for the courts because of the legislative "tempt[ation] to use retroactive legislation as a means of retribution against unpopular groups or individuals." *Landgraf v. USI Film Products,* 511 U.S. 244, 266 (1994); see also Hochman, The Supreme Court and the Constitutionality of Retroactive Legislation, 73 Harv. L.Rev. 692, 693 (1960) (a retroactive law "may be passed with an exact knowledge of who will benefit from it"). If retroactive laws change the legal consequences of transactions long closed, the change can destroy the reasonable certainty and security which are the very objects of property ownership. As a consequence, due process protection for property must be understood to incorporate our settled tradition against retroactive laws of great severity. Groups targeted by retroactive laws, were they to be denied all protection, would have a justified fear that a government once formed to protect expectations now can destroy them. Both stability of investment and confidence in the constitutional system, then, are secured by due process restrictions against severe retroactive legislation.

The case before us represents one of the rare instances where the Legislature has exceeded the limits imposed by due process. The plurality opinion demonstrates in convincing fashion that the remedy created by the Coal Act bears no legitimate relation to the interest which the Government asserts in support of the statute. In our tradition, the degree of retroactive effect is a significant determinant in the constitutionality of a statute. *United States v. Carlton, supra,* at 32; see also *Dunbar v. Boston & P.R. Corp.,* 181 Mass. 383, 386, 63 N.E. 916, 917 (1902) (Holmes, C. J.). As the plurality explains today, in creating liability for events which occurred 35 years ago the Coal Act has a retroactive effect of unprecedented scope.

While we have upheld the imposition of liability on former employers based on past employment relationships, the statutes at issue were remedial, designed to impose an "actual, measurable cost of [the employer's] business" which the employer had been able to avoid in the past. As Chancellor Kent noted: "Such statutes have been held valid when clearly just and reasonable, and conducive to the general welfare, even though they might operate in a degree upon existing rights." 1 Kent, Commentaries on American Law, at *455–*456. The Coal Act, however, does not serve this purpose. Eastern was once in the coal business and employed many of the beneficiaries, but it was not responsible for their expectation of lifetime health benefits or for the perilous financial condition of the 1950 and 1974 plans which put the benefits in jeopardy. As the plurality opinion discusses in detail, the expectation was created by promises and agreements made long after Eastern left the coal business. Eastern was not responsible for the resulting chaos in the funding mechanism caused by other coal companies leaving the framework of the National Bituminous Coal Wage Agreement. This case is far outside the bounds of retroactivity permissible under our law.

Finding a due process violation in this case is consistent with the principle that "under the deferential standard of review applied in substantive due process challenges to economic legislation there is no need for mathematical precision in the fit between justification and means." *Concrete Pipe, supra,* at 639. Statutes may be invalidated on due process grounds only under the most egregious of circumstances. This case represents one of the rare instances in which even such a permissive standard has been violated.

Application of the Coal Act to Eastern would violate the proper bounds of settled due process principles, and I concur in the plurality's conclusion that the judgment of the Court of Appeals must be reversed.

■ JUSTICE BREYER, with whom JUSTICE STEVENS, JUSTICE SOUTER, and JUSTICE GINSBURG join, dissenting.

We must decide whether it is fundamentally unfair for Congress to require Eastern Enterprises to pay the health care costs of retired miners who worked for Eastern before 1965, when Eastern stopped mining coal. For many years Eastern benefited from the labor of those miners. Eastern helped to create conditions that led the miners to expect continued health care benefits for themselves and their families after they retired. And Eastern, until 1987, continued to draw sizable profits from the coal industry through a wholly owned subsidiary. For these reasons, I believe that Congress did not act unreasonably or otherwise unjustly in imposing these health care costs upon Eastern. Consequently, in my view, the statute before us is constitutional.

I

As a preliminary matter, I agree with Justice KENNEDY that the plurality views this case through the wrong legal lens. The Constitution's Takings Clause does not apply. That Clause refers to the taking of "private property . . . for public use, without just compensation." U.S. Const., Amdt. 5. As this language suggests, at the heart of the Clause lies a concern, not with preventing arbitrary or unfair government action, but with providing *compensation* for legitimate government action that takes "private property" to serve the "public" good.

The "private property" upon which the Clause traditionally has focused is a specific interest in physical or intellectual property. It requires compensation when the government takes that property for a public purpose. This case involves not an interest in physical or intellectual property, but an ordinary liability to pay money, and not to the Government, but to third parties.

This Court has not directly held that the Takings Clause applies to the creation of this kind of liability. The Court has made clear that not only seizures through eminent domain but also certain "takings" through regulation can require "compensation" under the Clause. See, *e.g.*, *Pennsylvania Coal Co. v. Mahon,* 260 U.S. 393, 415 (1922) ("[W]hile property may be regulated to a certain extent, if regulation goes too far it will be recognized as a taking"); *Lucas v. South Carolina Coastal Council,* 505 U.S. 1003 (1992) (land-use regulation that deprives owner of all economically beneficial use of property constitutes taking). But these precedents concern the taking of interests in *physical* property.

The Court has also made clear that the Clause can apply to monetary interest generated from a fund into which a private individual has paid money. *Webb's Fabulous Pharmacies, Inc. v. Beckwith,* 449 U.S. 155 (1980). But the monetary interest at issue there arose out of the operation of a specific, separately identifiable fund of money. And the government took that interest for itself. Here there is no specific fund of money; there is only a general liability; and that liability runs not to the Government, but to third parties.

The Court in two cases has arguably acted *as if* the Takings Clause might apply to the creation of a general liability. *Connolly, supra*; *Concrete Pipe & Products of Cal., Inc. v. Construction Laborers Pension Trust for Southern Cal.*, 508 U.S. 602 (1993). But in the first of those cases, the Court said that the Takings Clause had not been violated, in part because "the Government does not physically invade or permanently appropriate any . . . assets for its own use." It also rejected the position that a taking occurs "whenever legislation requires one person to use his or her assets for the benefit of another." The second case basically followed the analysis of the first case. *Concrete Pipe*, 508 U.S., at 641–647. And both cases rejected the claim of a Takings Clause violation.

The dearth of Takings Clause authority is not surprising, for application of the Takings Clause here bristles with conceptual difficulties. If the Clause applies when the government simply orders A to pay B, why does it not apply when the government simply orders A to pay the government, *i.e.*, when it assesses a tax? Would that Clause apply to some or to all statutes and rules that "routinely creat[e] burdens for some that directly benefit others"? *Connolly, supra*, at 223. Regardless, could a court apply the same kind of Takings Clause analysis when violation means the law's invalidation, rather than simply the payment of "compensation?" See *First English Evangelical Lutheran Church of Glendale v. County of Los Angeles*, 482 U.S. 304, 315 (1987) ("[The Takings Clause] is designed not to limit the governmental interference with property rights *per se*, but rather to secure *compensation* in the event of otherwise proper interference amounting to a taking").

We need not face these difficulties, however, for there is no need to torture the Takings Clause to fit this case. The question involved—the potential unfairness of retroactive liability—finds a natural home in the Due Process Clause, a Fifth Amendment neighbor. That Clause . . . safeguards citizens from arbitrary or irrational legislation. And the Due Process Clause can offer protection against legislation that is unfairly retroactive at least as readily as the Takings Clause might, for as courts have sometimes suggested, a law that is fundamentally unfair because of its retroactivity is a law that is basically arbitrary.

Nor does application of the Due Process Clause automatically trigger the Takings Clause, just because the word "property" appears in both. That word appears in the midst of different phrases with somewhat different objectives, thereby permitting differences in the way in which the term is interpreted.

Insofar as the plurality avoids reliance upon the Due Process Clause for fear of resurrecting *Lochner v. New York*, 198 U.S. 45 (1905), and related doctrines of "substantive due process," that fear is misplaced. As the plurality points out, an unfair retroactive assessment of liability upsets settled expectations, and it thereby undermines a basic objective of law itself. See, *e.g., Fletcher v. Peck,* 6 Cranch 87, 143 (1810) (Johnson, J., concurring) (suggesting that retroactive legislation is invalid because it offends principles of natural law).

To find that the Due Process Clause protects against this kind of fundamental unfairness—that it protects against an unfair allocation of public burdens through this kind of specially arbitrary retroactive means—is to read the Clause in light of a basic purpose: the *fair application of law,* which purpose hearkens back to the Magna Carta. It is not to resurrect long-discredited substantive notions of "freedom of contract."

Thus, like the plurality I would inquire if the law before us is fundamentally unfair or unjust. But I would ask this question because, like Justice KENNEDY, I believe that, *if so,* the Coal Act would "deprive" Eastern of "property, without due process of law." U.S. Const., Amdt. 14, § 1.

II

The substantive question before us is whether or not it is fundamentally unfair to require Eastern to make *future* payments for health care costs of retired miners and their families, on the basis of Eastern's *past* association with these miners. Congress might have assessed all those who now use coal, or the taxpayer, in order to pay for those retired coal miners' health benefits. But Congress, instead, imposed this liability on Eastern. The "fairness" question is, why Eastern?

The answer cannot lie in a contractual promise to pay, for Eastern made no such contractual promise. Nor did Eastern participate in any benefit plan that made such a contractual promise, prior to its departure from the coal industry in 1965. But, as Justice STEVENS points out, this case is not a civil law suit for breach of contract. It is a constitutional challenge to Congress' decision to assess a new future liability on the basis of an old employment relationship. Unless it is fundamentally unfair and unjust, in terms of Eastern's reasonable reliance and settled expectations, to impose that liability, the Coal Act's "reachback" provision meets that challenge.

I believe several features of this case demonstrate that the relationship between Eastern and the payments demanded by the Coal Act is special enough to pass the Constitution's fundamental fairness test. That is, even though Eastern left the coal industry in 1965, the historical circumstances, taken together, prevent Eastern from showing that the Coal Act's "reachback" liability provision so frustrates Eastern's reasonable settled expectations as to impose an unconstitutional liability.

For one thing, the liability that the statute imposes upon Eastern extends only to miners whom Eastern itself employed. See 26 U.S.C. § 9706(a) (imposing "reachback" liability only where no presently operating coal firm which ratified 1978 or subsequent bargaining agreement ever employed the retiree, and Eastern employed the retiree longer than any other "reachback" firm). They are miners whose labor benefited Eastern when they were younger and healthier. Insofar as working conditions created a risk of future health problems for those miners, Eastern created those conditions. And these factors help to distinguish Eastern from others with respect to a later obligation to pay the health care costs that inevitably arise in old age

Congress has sometimes imposed liability, even "retroactive" liability, designed to prevent degradation of a natural resource, upon those who have used and benefited from it. See, *e.g.,* Comprehensive Environmental Response, Compensation, and Liability Act of 1980, 42 U.S.C. § 9601 *et seq.* (1994 ed. and Supp. I). That analogy, while imperfect, calls attention to the special tie between a firm and its former employee, a human resource, that helps to explain the special retroactive liability. That connection, while not by itself justifying retroactive liability here, helps to distinguish a firm like Eastern, which employed a miner but no longer makes coal, from other funding sources, say, current coal producers or coal consumers, who now make or use coal but who have never employed that miner or benefited from his work.

More importantly, the record demonstrates that Eastern, before 1965, contributed to the making of an important "promise" to the miners. That "promise," even if not contractually enforceable, led the miners to "develo[p]" a reasonable "expectation" that they would continue to receive "[retiree] medical benefits." The relevant history, outlined below, shows that industry action (including action by Eastern), combined with Federal Government action and the miners' own forbearance, produced circumstances that made it natural for the miners to believe that either industry or Government (or both) would make every effort to see that they received health benefits after they retired—regardless of what terms were explicitly included in previously signed bargaining agreements. . . .

Others have reached similar conclusions. The Coal Commission more recently said:

> Retired coal miners have legitimate expectations of health care benefits for life; that was the promise they received during their working lives and that is how they planned their retirement years. That commitment should be honored. Coal Comm'n Report 1, App. (CA1) 1332.

And numerous supporters of the present law read the history as showing, for example, that the "miners went to work each day under the assumption that their health benefits would be there when they retired." 138 Cong. Rec. 20121 (1992) (Sen. Wofford).

Further, the Federal Government played a significant role in developing the expectations that these "promises" created. In 1946, as mentioned above, during a strike related to health and pension benefits, the Government seized the mines and imposed the "Krug-Lewis Agreement," which established the basic health benefits framework. In 1948, during a strike related to pension benefits, the Government again intervened In later years, but before 1965, Congress provided the W&R Fund with special tax benefits, helped the Fund to build hospitals, and established health and safety standards. . . .

I repeat that the Federal Government's words and deeds, along with those of the pre-1965 industry, did not necessarily create contractually binding promises (which, had they existed, might have eliminated the need for this legislation). But in labor relations, as in human relations, one can create promises and understandings which, even in the absence of a legally enforceable contract, others reasonably expect will be honored. Indeed, in labor relations such industrywide understandings may spell the difference between labor war and labor peace, for the parties may look to a strike, not to a court, for enforcement. It is that kind of important, mutual understanding that is at issue here. For the record shows that pre-1965 statements and other conduct led management to understand, and labor legitimately to expect, that health care benefits for retirees and their dependents would continue to be provided.

Finally, Eastern continued to obtain profits from the coal mining industry long after 1965, for it operated a wholly owned coal-mining subsidiary, Eastern Associated Coal Corp. (hereinafter EACC), until the late 1980's. Between 1966 and 1987, Eastern effectively ran EACC, sharing officers, supervising management, and receiving 100% of EACC's approximately $100 million in dividends. Eastern officials, in their role as EACC directors, ratified the post-1965 bargaining agreements, and must have remained aware of the W&R Fund's deepening financial crisis.

Taken together, these circumstances explain why it is not fundamentally unfair for Congress to impose upon Eastern liability for the future health care costs of miners whom it long ago employed—rather than imposing that liability, for example, upon the present industry, coal consumers, or taxpayers. Each diminishes the reasonableness of Eastern's expectation that, by leaving the industry, it could fall within the Constitution's protection against unfairly retroactive liability.

These circumstances, as elaborated by the record, mean that Eastern knew of the potential funding problems that arise in any multiemployer benefit plan before it left the industry. Eastern knew or should have known that, in light of the structure of the benefit plan and the frequency with which coal operators went out of business, a "last man out" problem could exacerbate the health plan's funding difficulties. Eastern also knew or should have known that because of prior federal involvement, future federal intervention to solve any such problem was a serious possibility. Eastern knew, by the very nature of the problem, that any legislative effort to solve such a problem could well occur many years into the future. And, most importantly, Eastern played a significant role in creating the miners' expectations that led to this legislation. Add to these circumstances the two others I have mentioned—that Eastern had benefited from the labor of the miners for whose future health care it must provide, and that Eastern remained in the industry, drawing from it substantial profits (though doing business through a subsidiary, which usually, *but not always,* insulates an owner from liability).

The upshot, if I follow the form of analysis this Court used in *Connolly,* is that I cannot say the Government's regulation has unfairly interfered with Eastern's "distinct investment-backed expectations." . . . And the fact that the statute here narrows Eastern's liability to those whom it employed, while explicitly preserving Eastern's rights to indemnification from others (thereby helping Eastern spread the risk of this liability), 26 U.S.C. § 9706(f)(6), helps to diminish the Coal Act's "economic impact" upon Eastern as well.

I would put the matter more directly, however. The law imposes upon Eastern the burden of showing that the statute, because of its retroactive effect, is fundamentally unfair or unjust. The circumstances I have mentioned convince me that Eastern cannot show a sufficiently reasonable expectation that it would remain free of future health care cost liability for the workers whom it employed. Eastern has therefore failed to show that the law unfairly upset its legitimately settled expectations. Because, in my view, Eastern has not met its burden, I would uphold the "reachback" provision of the Coal Act as constitutional.

NOTE ON THE (POSSIBLE) REVIVAL OF ECONOMIC SUBSTANTIVE DUE PROCESS

1.   Was Justice Scalia, dissenting in *BMW*, right to be wary about recognizing economic rights under the Due Process Clause? Is the right to be free from an "excessive" civil punishment (in the form of a punitive damages award) meaningfully distinguishable from the right to be free from unreasonable regulation that the Court enforced in *Lochner*? Does *BMW* represent a weakening of the traditional post-1937 "double standard" that purported to protect "personal" (whatever that means) rights but not "economic" ones?

The lineup of justices in *BMW* did not reflect the usual ideological divide. Justices O'Connor, Kennedy, Souter, and Breyer joined Justice Stevens's majority opinion, while Chief Justice Rehnquist and Justices Scalia, Thomas, and Ginsburg dissented. Why do you think the punitive damages issue split the typical coalitions in this way? Can you see why justices of varying ideological perspectives would be worried about a revival of substantive due process in the economic sphere?

2.   The justices in *Eastern Enterprises* divided over whether the plaintiffs' challenge to the Coal Act was best understood in terms of the Due Process Clause or the Takings Clause. Although the plurality, who supplied

four of the five votes invalidating the Act's retrospective liability provisions, would have rested on the Takings Clause, Justice Kennedy's critical concurrence in the judgment agreed with the four dissenters that the case should be evaluated in terms of substantive due process. The case thus appears to stand for the proposition that the Due Process Clause prohibits at least some forms of retroactive economic legislation.

On the other hand, did the dissenters employ a sufficiently similar analysis to Justice Kennedy's that we can say *Eastern Enterprises* adopted a particular approach to due process scrutiny of retroactive legislation? Or does the case simply stand for the more general proposition that retroactive imposition of burdens on private parties is constitutionally problematic, with the precise doctrinal test for such legislation remaining to be worked out in future cases?

3.   More generally, is it really possible to distinguish sharply between the sorts of cases in which the Court has revived strong substantive due process cases and the "economic" contexts in which legislatures supposedly should get more deference? For instance, if Congress enacted a federal statute regulating abortion, would that statute not withstand Commerce Clause scrutiny on the ground that abortion is an "economic" activity that involves the purchase and sale of a medical service? If that is true, then how is state regulation of abortion not "economic" in nature and deserving of rational basis review? Is there any justification for reviewing regulation of the safety of contraceptives under a higher standard than applies to the regulation of other medical drugs and devices?

To say that economic and non-economic activities are hard to distinguish, of course, is not to say what a more unitary standard for substantive due process review should look like. Do you agree that an across-the-board approach would be better? If so, should it be strict or deferential? Or should the Court adopt some other basis for distinguishing when strict or deferential review is appropriate.

CHAPTER SEVENTEEN

GAY RIGHTS AND THE RELATION BETWEEN LIBERTY AND EQUALITY

The Supreme Court's broad recognition of rights for gays and lesbians is one of the most striking developments in modern constitutional law. This chapter examines that development as a case study in the relationship between the Due Process and Equal Protection Clauses. Notions of fundamental rights and equal treatment have each played an important role in advancing the cause of gay rights. These cases thus provide a valuable illustration of the ways in which these principles differ, as well as the ways in which they may complement one another. And as with the commerce clause and freedom of contract cases during the *Lochner*, it would be difficult to understand one doctrinal strand without also taking account of the other.

The gay rights cases have also prompted vigorous debate about the role of the Supreme Court in American society. This is especially true of the two cases at the end of the chapter, *United States v. Windsor* and *Obergefell v. Hodges*, which both struck down restrictions on same-sex marriage. This chapter thus revisits the issues raised in Chapter Six regarding the Court's ability to promote social change. The dynamic in these cases is different, however, with the Court not so much leading the way as protecting social innovations launched in the States and ratifying a remarkable sea change in public opinion.

SECTION 17.1 INITIAL SKEPTICISM

Gay rights did not get off to a good start in the Supreme Court. The first major opinion is *Bowers v. Hardwick*, which rejected a substantive due process challenge to Georgia's sodomy. The Court's opinion seemed to reflect something of a backlash against the wave of expansive privacy decisions that began in *Griswold* and culminated in *Roe*. In *Hardwick*, Justice White's majority opinion tried to draw a line in the sand.

Bowers v. Hardwick

478 U.S. 186 (1986)

■ **JUSTICE WHITE delivered the opinion of the Court.**

In August 1982, respondent Hardwick (hereafter respondent) was charged with violating the Georgia statute criminalizing sodomy[1] by committing that act with another adult male in the bedroom of respondent's home. After a preliminary hearing, the District Attorney decided not to present the matter to the grand jury unless further evidence developed.

Respondent then brought suit in the Federal District Court, challenging the constitutionality of the statute insofar as it criminalized consensual sodomy.[2] He asserted that he was a practicing homosexual, that the Georgia sodomy statute, as administered by the defendants, placed him in imminent danger of arrest, and that the statute for several reasons violates the Federal Constitution. The District Court granted the defendants' motion to dismiss for failure to state a claim . . . .

A divided panel of the Court of Appeals for the Eleventh Circuit reversed. . . . Relying on our decisions in *Griswold v. Connecticut,* 381 U.S. 479 (1965); *Eisenstadt v. Baird,* 405 U.S. 438 (1972); *Stanley v. Georgia,* 394 U.S. 557 (1969); and *Roe v. Wade,* 410 U.S. 113 (1973), the court went on to hold that the Georgia statute violated respondent's fundamental rights because his homosexual activity is a private and intimate association that is beyond the reach of state regulation by reason of the Ninth Amendment and the Due Process Clause of the Fourteenth Amendment. The case was remanded for trial, at which, to prevail, the State would have to prove that the statute is supported by a compelling interest and is the most narrowly drawn means of achieving that end.

Because other Courts of Appeals have arrived at judgments contrary to that of the Eleventh Circuit in this case, we granted the Attorney General's petition for certiorari questioning the holding that the sodomy statute violates the fundamental rights of homosexuals. We agree with

---

[1]   Georgia Code Ann. § 16–6–2 (1984) provides, in pertinent part, as follows:

"(a) A person commits the offense of sodomy when he performs or submits to any sexual act involving the sex organs of one person and the mouth or anus of another. . . .

"(b) A person convicted of the offense of sodomy shall be punished by imprisonment for not less than one nor more than 20 years. . . ."

[2]   John and Mary Doe were also plaintiffs in the action. They alleged that they wished to engage in sexual activity proscribed by § 16–6–2 in the privacy of their home and that they had been "chilled and deterred" from engaging in such activity by both the existence of the statute and Hardwick's arrest. The District Court held, however, that because they had neither sustained, nor were in immediate danger of sustaining, any direct injury from the enforcement of the statute, they did not have proper standing to maintain the action. The Court of Appeals affirmed the District Court's judgment dismissing the Does' claim for lack of standing, and the Does do not challenge that holding in this Court.

The only claim properly before the Court, therefore, is Hardwick's challenge to the Georgia statute as applied to consensual homosexual sodomy. We express no opinion on the constitutionality of the Georgia statute as applied to other acts of sodomy.

petitioner that the Court of Appeals erred, and hence reverse its judgment.

This case does not require a judgment on whether laws against sodomy between consenting adults in general, or between homosexuals in particular, are wise or desirable. It raises no question about the right or propriety of state legislative decisions to repeal their laws that criminalize homosexual sodomy, or of state-court decisions invalidating those laws on state constitutional grounds. The issue presented is whether the Federal Constitution confers a fundamental right upon homosexuals to engage in sodomy and hence invalidates the laws of the many States that still make such conduct illegal and have done so for a very long time. The case also calls for some judgment about the limits of the Court's role in carrying out its constitutional mandate.

We first register our disagreement with the Court of Appeals and with respondent that the Court's prior cases have construed the Constitution to confer a right of privacy that extends to homosexual sodomy and for all intents and purposes have decided this case. The reach of this line of cases was sketched in *Carey v. Population Services International*, 431 U.S. 678, 685 (1977). *Pierce v. Society of Sisters*, 268 U.S. 510 (1925), and *Meyer v. Nebraska*, 262 U.S. 390 (1923), were described as dealing with child rearing and education; *Prince v. Massachusetts*, 321 U.S. 158 (1944), with family relationships; *Skinner v. Oklahoma ex rel. Williamson*, 316 U.S. 535 (1942), with procreation; *Loving v. Virginia*, 388 U.S. 1 (1967), with marriage; *Griswold v. Connecticut, supra,* and *Eisenstadt v. Baird, supra,* with contraception; and *Roe v. Wade*, 410 U.S. 113 (1973), with abortion. The latter three cases were interpreted as construing the Due Process Clause of the Fourteenth Amendment to confer a fundamental individual right to decide whether or not to beget or bear a child. *Carey v. Population Services International, supra,* 431 U.S., at 688–689.

Accepting the decisions in these cases and the above description of them, we think it evident that none of the rights announced in those cases bears any resemblance to the claimed constitutional right of homosexuals to engage in acts of sodomy that is asserted in this case. No connection between family, marriage, or procreation on the one hand and homosexual activity on the other has been demonstrated, either by the Court of Appeals or by respondent. Moreover, any claim that these cases nevertheless stand for the proposition that any kind of private sexual conduct between consenting adults is constitutionally insulated from state proscription is unsupportable. Indeed, the Court's opinion in *Carey* twice asserted that the privacy right, which the *Griswold* line of cases found to be one of the protections provided by the Due Process Clause, did not reach so far.

Precedent aside, however, respondent would have us announce, as the Court of Appeals did, a fundamental right to engage in homosexual sodomy. This we are quite unwilling to do. It is true that despite the language of the Due Process Clauses of the Fifth and Fourteenth Amendments, which appears to focus only on the processes by which life, liberty, or property is taken, the cases are legion in which those Clauses have been interpreted to have substantive content, subsuming rights that to a great extent are immune from federal or state regulation or proscription. Among such cases are those recognizing rights that have little or no textual support in the constitutional language. *Meyer, Prince,* and *Pierce* fall in this category, as do the privacy cases from *Griswold* to *Carey.*

Striving to assure itself and the public that announcing rights not readily identifiable in the Constitution's text involves much more than the imposition of the Justices' own choice of values on the States and the Federal Government, the Court has sought to identify the nature of the rights qualifying for heightened judicial protection. In *Palko v. Connecticut,* 302 U.S. 319, 325, 326 (1937), it was said that this category includes those fundamental liberties that are "implicit in the concept of ordered liberty," such that "neither liberty nor justice would exist if [they] were sacrificed." A different description of fundamental liberties appeared in *Moore v. East Cleveland,* 431 U.S. 494, 503 (1977) (opinion of POWELL, J.), where they are characterized as those liberties that are "deeply rooted in this Nation's history and tradition."

It is obvious to us that neither of these formulations would extend a fundamental right to homosexuals to engage in acts of consensual sodomy. Proscriptions against that conduct have ancient roots. Sodomy was a criminal offense at common law and was forbidden by the laws of the original thirteen States when they ratified the Bill of Rights. In 1868, when the Fourteenth Amendment was ratified, all but 5 of the 37 States in the Union had criminal sodomy laws. In fact, until 1961,[7] all 50 States outlawed sodomy, and today, 24 States and the District of Columbia continue to provide criminal penalties for sodomy performed in private and between consenting adults. Against this background, to claim that a right to engage in such conduct is "deeply rooted in this Nation's history and tradition" or "implicit in the concept of ordered liberty" is, at best, facetious.

Nor are we inclined to take a more expansive view of our authority to discover new fundamental rights imbedded in the Due Process Clause. The Court is most vulnerable and comes nearest to illegitimacy when it deals with judge-made constitutional law having little or no cognizable roots in the language or design of the Constitution. That this is so was painfully demonstrated by the face-off between the Executive and the Court in the 1930's, which resulted in the repudiation of much of the substantive gloss that the Court had placed on the Due Process Clauses

---

[7] In 1961, Illinois adopted the American Law Institute's Model Penal Code, which decriminalized adult, consensual, private, sexual conduct. Criminal Code of 1961, §§ 11–2, 11–3, 1961 Ill. Laws, pp. 1985, 2006. See American Law Institute, Model Penal Code § 213.2 (Proposed Official Draft 1962).

of the Fifth and Fourteenth Amendments. There should be, therefore, great resistance to expand the substantive reach of those Clauses, particularly if it requires redefining the category of rights deemed to be fundamental. Otherwise, the Judiciary necessarily takes to itself further authority to govern the country without express constitutional authority. The claimed right pressed on us today falls far short of overcoming this resistance.

Respondent, however, asserts that the result should be different where the homosexual conduct occurs in the privacy of the home. He relies on *Stanley v. Georgia,* 394 U.S. 557 (1969), where the Court held that the First Amendment prevents conviction for possessing and reading obscene material in the privacy of one's home: "If the First Amendment means anything, it means that a State has no business telling a man, sitting alone in his house, what books he may read or what films he may watch.

Stanley did protect conduct that would not have been protected outside the home, and it partially prevented the enforcement of state obscenity laws; but the decision was firmly grounded in the First Amendment. The right pressed upon us here has no similar support in the text of the Constitution, and it does not qualify for recognition under the prevailing principles for construing the Fourteenth Amendment. Its limits are also difficult to discern. Plainly enough, otherwise illegal conduct is not always immunized whenever it occurs in the home. Victimless crimes, such as the possession and use of illegal drugs, do not escape the law where they are committed at home. *Stanley* itself recognized that its holding offered no protection for the possession in the home of drugs, firearms, or stolen goods. And if respondent's submission is limited to the voluntary sexual conduct between consenting adults, it would be difficult, except by fiat, to limit the claimed right to homosexual conduct while leaving exposed to prosecution adultery, incest, and other sexual crimes even though they are committed in the home. We are unwilling to start down that road.

Even if the conduct at issue here is not a fundamental right, respondent asserts that there must be a rational basis for the law and that there is none in this case other than the presumed belief of a majority of the electorate in Georgia that homosexual sodomy is immoral and unacceptable. This is said to be an inadequate rationale to support the law. The law, however, is constantly based on notions of morality, and if all laws representing essentially moral choices are to be invalidated under the Due Process Clause, the courts will be very busy indeed. Even respondent makes no such claim, but insists that majority sentiments about the morality of homosexuality should be declared inadequate. We do not agree, and are unpersuaded that the sodomy laws of some 25 States should be invalidated on this basis.[8]

Accordingly, the judgment of the Court of Appeals is

Reversed.

■ CHIEF JUSTICE BURGER, concurring.

I join the Court's opinion, but I write separately to underscore my view that in constitutional terms there is no such thing as a fundamental right to commit homosexual sodomy.

As the Court notes, the proscriptions against sodomy have very "ancient roots." Decisions of individuals relating to homosexual conduct have been subject to state intervention throughout the history of Western civilization. Condemnation of those practices is firmly rooted in Judeo-Christian moral and ethical standards. Homosexual sodomy was a capital crime under Roman law. See Code Theod. 9.7.6; Code Just. 9.9.31. During the English Reformation when powers of the ecclesiastical courts were transferred to the King's Courts, the first English statute criminalizing sodomy was passed. 25 Hen. VIII, ch. 6. Blackstone described "the infamous *crime against nature*" as an offense of "deeper malignity" than rape, a heinous act "the very mention of which is a disgrace to human nature," and "a crime not fit to be named." 4 W. Blackstone, Commentaries *215. The common law of England, including its prohibition of sodomy, became the received law of Georgia and the other Colonies. In 1816 the Georgia Legislature passed the statute at issue here, and that statute has been continuously in force in one form or another since that time. To hold that the act of homosexual sodomy is somehow protected as a fundamental right would be to cast aside millennia of moral teaching.

This is essentially not a question of personal "preferences" but rather of the legislative authority of the State. I find nothing in the Constitution depriving a State of the power to enact the statute challenged here.

■ JUSTICE POWELL, concurring.

I join the opinion of the Court. I agree with the Court that there is no fundamental right—*i.e.,* no substantive right under the Due Process Clause—such as that claimed by respondent Hardwick, and found to exist by the Court of Appeals. This is not to suggest, however, that respondent may not be protected by the Eighth Amendment of the Constitution. The Georgia statute at issue in this case, Ga.Code Ann. § 16–6–2 (1984), authorizes a court to imprison a person for up to 20 years for a single private, consensual act of sodomy. In my view, a prison sentence for such conduct—certainly a sentence of long duration—would create a serious Eighth Amendment issue. Under the Georgia statute a single act of sodomy, even in the private setting of a home, is a felony

---

[8]   Respondent does not defend the judgment below based on the Ninth Amendment, the Equal Protection Clause, or the Eighth Amendment.

comparable in terms of the possible sentence imposed to serious felonies such as aggravated battery, § 16–5–24, first-degree arson, § 16–7–60, and robbery, § 16–8–40.

In this case, however, respondent has not been tried, much less convicted and sentenced.[2] Moreover, respondent has not raised the Eighth Amendment issue below. For these reasons this constitutional argument is not before us.

■ JUSTICE BLACKMUN, with whom JUSTICE BRENNAN, JUSTICE MARSHALL, and JUSTICE STEVENS join, dissenting.

This case is no more about "a fundamental right to engage in homosexual sodomy," as the Court purports to declare, than *Stanley v. Georgia,* 394 U.S. 557 (1969), was about a fundamental right to watch obscene movies, or *Katz v. United States,* 389 U.S. 347 (1967), was about a fundamental right to place interstate bets from a telephone booth. Rather, this case is about "the most comprehensive of rights and the right most valued by civilized men," namely, "the right to be let alone." *Olmstead v. United States,* 277 U.S. 438, 478 (1928) (Brandeis, J., dissenting).

The statute at issue, Ga.Code Ann. § 16–6–2, denies individuals the right to decide for themselves whether to engage in particular forms of private, consensual sexual activity. The Court concludes that § 16–6–2 is valid essentially because "the laws of . . . many States . . . still make such conduct illegal and have done so for a very long time." But the fact that the moral judgments expressed by statutes like § 16–6–2 may be " 'natural and familiar . . . ought not to conclude our judgment upon the question whether statutes embodying them conflict with the Constitution of the United States.' " *Roe v. Wade,* 410 U.S. 113, 117 (1973). Like Justice Holmes, I believe that "[i]t is revolting to have no better reason for a rule of law than that so it was laid down in the time of Henry IV. It is still more revolting if the grounds upon which it was laid down have vanished long since, and the rule simply persists from blind imitation of the past." Holmes, The Path of the Law, 10 Harv. L. Rev. 457, 469 (1897). I believe we must analyze Hardwick's claim in the light of the values that underlie the constitutional right to privacy. If that right means anything, it means that, before Georgia can prosecute its citizens for making choices about the most intimate aspects of their lives, it must do more than assert that the choice they have made is an " 'abominable crime not

---

[2]   It was conceded at oral argument that, prior to the complaint against respondent Hardwick, there had been no reported decision involving prosecution for private homosexual sodomy under this statute for several decades. See *Thompson v. Aldredge,* 187 Ga. 467, 200 S.E. 799 (1939). Moreover, the State has declined to present the criminal charge against Hardwick to a grand jury, and this is a suit for declaratory judgment brought by respondents challenging the validity of the statute. The history of nonenforcement suggests the moribund character today of laws criminalizing this type of private, consensual conduct. Some 26 States have repealed similar statutes. But the constitutional validity of the Georgia statute was put in issue by respondents, and for the reasons stated by the Court, I cannot say that conduct condemned for hundreds of years has now become a fundamental right.

fit to be named among Christians.' " *Herring v. State,* 119 Ga. 709, 721, 46 S.E. 876, 882 (1904).

I

In its haste to reverse the Court of Appeals and hold that the Constitution does not "confe[r] a fundamental right upon homosexuals to engage in sodomy," the Court relegates the actual statute being challenged to a footnote and ignores the procedural posture of the case before it. A fair reading of the statute and of the complaint clearly reveals that the majority has distorted the question this case presents.

First, the Court's almost obsessive focus on homosexual activity is particularly hard to justify in light of the broad language Georgia has used. Unlike the Court, the Georgia Legislature has not proceeded on the assumption that homosexuals are so different from other citizens that their lives may be controlled in a way that would not be tolerated if it limited the choices of those other citizens. Rather, Georgia has provided that "[a] person commits the offense of sodomy when he performs or submits to any sexual act involving the sex organs of one person and the mouth or anus of another." Ga.Code Ann. § 16–6–2(a). The sex or status of the persons who engage in the act is irrelevant as a matter of state law. In fact, to the extent I can discern a legislative purpose for Georgia's 1968 enactment of § 16–6–2, that purpose seems to have been to broaden the coverage of the law to reach heterosexual as well as homosexual activity.[1] I therefore see no basis for the Court's decision to treat this case as an "as applied" challenge to § 16–6–2, or for Georgia's attempt, both in its brief and at oral argument, to defend § 16–6–2 solely on the grounds that it prohibits homosexual activity. Michael Hardwick's standing may rest in significant part on Georgia's apparent willingness to enforce against homosexuals a law it seems not to have any desire to enforce against heterosexuals. But his claim that § 16–6–2 involves an unconstitutional intrusion into his privacy and his right of intimate association does not depend in any way on his sexual orientation. . . .

II

"Our cases long have recognized that the Constitution embodies a promise that a certain private sphere of individual liberty will be kept largely beyond the reach of government." *Thornburgh v. American College of Obstetricians & Gynecologists,* 476 U.S. 747, 772 (1986). In construing the right to privacy, the Court has proceeded along two somewhat distinct, albeit complementary, lines. First, it has recognized a privacy interest with reference to certain *decisions* that are properly for

---

[1] Until 1968, Georgia defined sodomy as "the carnal knowledge and connection against the order of nature, by man with man, or in the same unnatural manner with woman." Ga.Crim.Code § 26–5901 (1933). In *Thompson v. Aldredge,* 187 Ga. 467, 200 S.E. 799 (1939), the Georgia Supreme Court held that § 26–5901 did not prohibit lesbian activity. And in *Riley v. Garrett,* 219 Ga. 345, 133 S.E.2d 367 (1963), the Georgia Supreme Court held that § 26–5901 did not prohibit heterosexual cunnilingus. Georgia passed the act-specific statute currently in force "perhaps in response to the restrictive court decisions such as *Riley,*" Note, The Crimes Against Nature, 16 J.Pub.L. 159, 167, n. 47 (1967).

the individual to make. *E.g., Roe v. Wade,* 410 U.S. 113 (1973); *Pierce v. Society of Sisters,* 268 U.S. 510 (1925). Second, it has recognized a privacy interest with reference to certain *places* without regard for the particular activities in which the individuals who occupy them are engaged. *E.g., United States v. Karo,* 468 U.S. 705 (1984); *Payton v. New York,* 445 U.S. 573 (1980); *Rios v. United States,* 364 U.S. 253 (1960). The case before us implicates both the decisional and the spatial aspects of the right to privacy.

A

The Court concludes today that none of our prior cases dealing with various decisions that individuals are entitled to make free of governmental interference "bears any resemblance to the claimed constitutional right of homosexuals to engage in acts of sodomy that is asserted in this case." While it is true that these cases may be characterized by their connection to protection of the family, the Court's conclusion that they extend no further than this boundary ignores the warning in *Moore v. East Cleveland,* 431 U.S. 494, 501 (1977) (plurality opinion), against "clos[ing] our eyes to the basic reasons why certain rights associated with the family have been accorded shelter under the Fourteenth Amendment's Due Process Clause." We protect those rights not because they contribute, in some direct and material way, to the general public welfare, but because they form so central a part of an individual's life. "[T]he concept of privacy embodies the moral fact that a person belongs to himself and not others nor to society as a whole." *Thornburgh,* 476 U.S., at 777, n. 5, (STEVENS, J., concurring). And so we protect the decision whether to marry precisely because marriage "is an association that promotes a way of life, not causes; a harmony in living, not political faiths; a bilateral loyalty, not commercial or social projects." *Griswold,* 381 U.S., at 486. We protect the decision whether to have a child because parenthood alters so dramatically an individual's self-definition, not because of demographic considerations or the Bible's command to be fruitful and multiply. And we protect the family because it contributes so powerfully to the happiness of individuals, not because of a preference for stereotypical households. The Court recognized in *Roberts,* 468 U.S., at 619, that the "ability independently to define one's identity that is central to any concept of liberty" cannot truly be exercised in a vacuum; we all depend on the "emotional enrichment from close ties with others."

Only the most willful blindness could obscure the fact that sexual intimacy is "a sensitive, key relationship of human existence, central to family life, community welfare, and the development of human personality," *Paris Adult Theatre I v. Slaton,* 413 U.S. 49, 63 (1973). The fact that individuals define themselves in a significant way through their intimate sexual relationships with others suggests, in a Nation as diverse as ours, that there may be many "right" ways of conducting those relationships, and that much of the richness of a relationship will come from the freedom an individual has to *choose* the form and nature of these intensely personal bonds.

In a variety of circumstances we have recognized that a necessary corollary of giving individuals freedom to choose how to conduct their lives is acceptance of the fact that different individuals will make different choices. For example, in holding that the clearly important state interest in public education should give way to a competing claim by the Amish to the effect that extended formal schooling threatened their way of life, the Court declared: "There can be no assumption that today's majority is 'right' and the Amish and others like them are 'wrong.' A way of life that is odd or even erratic but interferes with no rights or interests of others is not to be condemned because it is different." *Wisconsin v. Yoder,* 406 U.S. 205, 223–224 (1972). The Court claims that its decision today merely refuses to recognize a fundamental right to engage in homosexual sodomy; what the Court really has refused to recognize is the fundamental interest all individuals have in controlling the nature of their intimate associations with others.

B

The behavior for which Hardwick faces prosecution occurred in his own home, a place to which the Fourth Amendment attaches special significance. The Court's treatment of this aspect of the case is symptomatic of its overall refusal to consider the broad principles that have informed our treatment of privacy in specific cases. Just as the right to privacy is more than the mere aggregation of a number of entitlements to engage in specific behavior, so too, protecting the physical integrity of the home is more than merely a means of protecting specific activities that often take place there. Even when our understanding of the contours of the right to privacy depends on "reference to a 'place,' " *Katz v. United States,* 389 U.S., at 361 (Harlan, J., concurring), "the essence of a Fourth Amendment violation is not the breaking of [a person's] doors, and the rummaging of his drawers, but rather is the invasion of his indefeasible right of personal security, personal liberty and private property." *California v. Ciraolo,* 476 U.S. 207, 226 (1986) (POWELL, J., dissenting).

The Court's interpretation of the pivotal case of *Stanley v. Georgia,* 394 U.S. 557 (1969), is entirely unconvincing. *Stanley* held that Georgia's undoubted power to punish the public distribution of constitutionally unprotected, obscene material did not permit the State to punish the private possession of such material. According to the majority here, *Stanley* relied entirely on the First Amendment, and thus, it is claimed, sheds no light on cases not involving printed materials. But that is not what *Stanley* said. Rather, the *Stanley* Court anchored its holding in the Fourth Amendment's special protection for the individual in his home . . . . Indeed, the right of an individual to conduct intimate relationships in the intimacy of his or her own home seems to me to be the heart of the Constitution's protection of privacy.

III

The Court's failure to comprehend the magnitude of the liberty interests at stake in this case leads it to slight the question whether petitioner, on behalf of the State, has justified Georgia's infringement on these interests. I believe that neither of the two general justifications for § 16–6–2 that petitioner has advanced warrants dismissing respondent's challenge for failure to state a claim.

First, petitioner asserts that the acts made criminal by the statute may have serious adverse consequences for "the general public health and welfare," such as spreading communicable diseases or fostering other criminal activity. Inasmuch as this case was dismissed by the District Court on the pleadings, it is not surprising that the record before us is barren of any evidence to support petitioner's claim. In light of the state of the record, I see no justification for the Court's attempt to equate the private, consensual sexual activity at issue here with the "possession in the home of drugs, firearms, or stolen goods" to which *Stanley* refused to extend its protection. None of the behavior so mentioned in *Stanley* can properly be viewed as "[v]ictimless": drugs and weapons are inherently dangerous, and for property to be "stolen," someone must have been wrongfully deprived of it. Nothing in the record before the Court provides any justification for finding the activity forbidden by § 16–6–2 to be physically dangerous, either to the persons engaged in it or to others.[4]

The core of petitioner's defense of § 16–6–2, however, is that respondent and others who engage in the conduct prohibited by § 16–6–2 interfere with Georgia's exercise of the " 'right of the Nation and of the States to maintain a decent society,' " *Paris Adult Theatre I v. Slaton,* 413 U.S., at 59–60. Essentially, petitioner argues, and the Court agrees, that the fact that the acts described in § 16–6–2 "for hundreds of years, if not thousands, have been uniformly condemned as immoral" is a sufficient reason to permit a State to ban them today.

I cannot agree that either the length of time a majority has held its convictions or the passions with which it defends them can withdraw legislation from this Court's scrutiny. See, *e.g., Roe v. Wade,* 410 U.S. 113 (1973); *Loving v. Virginia,* 388 U.S. 1 (1967); *Brown v. Board of*

---

[4] Although I do not think it necessary to decide today issues that are not even remotely before us, it does seem to me that a court could find simple, analytically sound distinctions between certain private, consensual sexual conduct, on the one hand, and adultery and incest (the only two vaguely specific "sexual crimes" to which the majority points), on the other. For example, marriage, in addition to its spiritual aspects, is a civil contract that entitles the contracting parties to a variety of governmentally provided benefits. A State might define the contractual commitment necessary to become eligible for these benefits to include a commitment of fidelity and then punish individuals for breaching that contract. Moreover, a State might conclude that adultery is likely to injure third persons, in particular, spouses and children of persons who engage in extramarital affairs. With respect to incest, a court might well agree with respondent that the nature of familial relationships renders true consent to incestuous activity sufficiently problematical that a blanket prohibition of such activity is warranted. Notably, the Court makes no effort to explain why it has chosen to group private, consensual homosexual activity with adultery and incest rather than with private, consensual heterosexual activity by unmarried persons or, indeed, with oral or anal sex within marriage.

Education, 347 U.S. 483 (1954).[5] As Justice Jackson wrote so eloquently for the Court in *West Virginia Board of Education v. Barnette,* 319 U.S. 624, 641–642 (1943), "we apply the limitations of the Constitution with no fear that freedom to be intellectually and spiritually diverse or even contrary will disintegrate the social organization. . . . [F]reedom to differ is not limited to things that do not matter much. That would be a mere shadow of freedom. The test of its substance is the right to differ as to things that touch the heart of the existing order." It is precisely because the issue raised by this case touches the heart of what makes individuals what they are that we should be especially sensitive to the rights of those whose choices upset the majority.

The assertion that "traditional Judeo-Christian values proscribe" the conduct involved cannot provide an adequate justification for § 16–6–2. That certain, but by no means all, religious groups condemn the behavior at issue gives the State no license to impose their judgments on the entire citizenry. The legitimacy of secular legislation depends instead on whether the State can advance some justification for its law beyond its conformity to religious doctrine. Thus, far from buttressing his case, petitioner's invocation of Leviticus, Romans, St. Thomas Aquinas, and sodomy's heretical status during the Middle Ages undermines his suggestion that § 16–6–2 represents a legitimate use of secular coercive power.[6] A State can no more punish private behavior because of religious intolerance than it can punish such behavior because of racial animus. "The Constitution cannot control such prejudices, but neither can it tolerate them. Private biases may be outside the reach of the law, but the law cannot, directly or indirectly, give them effect." *Palmore v. Sidoti,* 466 U.S. 429, 433 (1984). No matter how uncomfortable a certain group may make the majority of this Court, we have held that "[m]ere public intolerance or animosity cannot constitutionally justify the deprivation of a person's physical liberty." *O'Connor v. Donaldson,* 422 U.S. 563, 575

---

[5]   The parallel between *Loving* and this case is almost uncanny. There, too, the State relied on a religious justification for its law. There, too, defenders of the challenged statute relied heavily on the fact that when the Fourteenth Amendment was ratified, most of the States had similar prohibitions. There, too, at the time the case came before the Court, many of the States still had criminal statutes concerning the conduct at issue. Yet the Court held, not only that the invidious racism of Virginia's law violated the Equal Protection Clause, but also that the law deprived the Lovings of due process by denying them the "freedom of choice to marry" that had "long been recognized as one of the vital personal rights essential to the orderly pursuit of happiness by free men."

[6]   The theological nature of the origin of Anglo-American antisodomy statutes is patent. It was not until 1533 that sodomy was made a secular offense in England. 25 Hen. VIII, ch. 6. Until that time, the offense was, in Sir James Stephen's words, "merely ecclesiastical." 2 J. Stephen, A History of the Criminal Law of England 429–430 (1883). Pollock and Maitland similarly observed that "[t]he crime against nature. . . was so closely connected with heresy that the vulgar had but one name for both." 2 F. Pollock & F. Maitland, The History of English Law 554 (1895). The transfer of jurisdiction over prosecutions for sodomy to the secular courts seems primarily due to the alteration of ecclesiastical jurisdiction attendant on England's break with the Roman Catholic Church, rather than to any new understanding of the sovereign's interest in preventing or punishing the behavior involved. Cf. 6 E. Coke, Institutes, ch. 10 (4th ed. 1797).

(1975). See also *United States Dept. of Agriculture v. Moreno,* 413 U.S. 528, 534 (1973).

Nor can § 16–6–2 be justified as a "morally neutral" exercise of Georgia's power to "protect the public environment," *Paris Adult Theatre I,* 413 U.S., at 68–69. Certainly, some private behavior can affect the fabric of society as a whole. Reasonable people may differ about whether particular sexual acts are moral or immoral, but "we have ample evidence for believing that people will not abandon morality, will not think any better of murder, cruelty and dishonesty, merely because some private sexual practice which they abominate is not punished by the law." H.L.A. Hart, Immorality and Treason, reprinted in The Law as Literature 220, 225 (L. Blom-Cooper ed. 1961). Petitioner and the Court fail to see the difference between laws that protect public sensibilities and those that enforce private morality. Statutes banning public sexual activity are entirely consistent with protecting the individual's liberty interest in decisions concerning sexual relations: the same recognition that those decisions are intensely private which justifies protecting them from governmental interference can justify protecting individuals from unwilling exposure to the sexual activities of others. But the mere fact that intimate behavior may be punished when it takes place in public cannot dictate how States can regulate intimate behavior that occurs in intimate places.

This case involves no real interference with the rights of others, for the mere knowledge that other individuals do not adhere to one's value system cannot be a legally cognizable interest, let alone an interest that can justify invading the houses, hearts, and minds of citizens who choose to live their lives differently.

IV

It took but three years for the Court to see the error in its analysis in *Minersville School District v. Gobitis,* 310 U.S. 586 (1940), and to recognize that the threat to national cohesion posed by a refusal to salute the flag was vastly outweighed by the threat to those same values posed by compelling such a salute. See *West Virginia Board of Education v. Barnette,* 319 U.S. 624 (1943). I can only hope that here, too, the Court soon will reconsider its analysis and conclude that depriving individuals of the right to choose for themselves how to conduct their intimate relationships poses a far greater threat to the values most deeply rooted in our Nation's history than tolerance of nonconformity could ever do. Because I think the Court today betrays those values, I dissent.

■ **JUSTICE STEVENS, with whom JUSTICE BRENNAN and JUSTICE MARSHALL join, dissenting.**

Like the statute that is challenged in this case, the rationale of the Court's opinion applies equally to the prohibited conduct regardless of whether the parties who engage in it are married or unmarried, or are of the same or different sexes.[2] Sodomy was condemned as an odious and sinful type of behavior during the formative period of the common law. That condemnation was equally damning for heterosexual and homosexual sodomy. Moreover, it provided no special exemption for married couples.[5] The license to cohabit and to produce legitimate offspring simply did not include any permission to engage in sexual conduct that was considered a "crime against nature."

The history of the Georgia statute before us clearly reveals this traditional prohibition of heterosexual, as well as homosexual, sodomy.[6] Indeed, at one point in the 20th century, Georgia's law was construed to permit certain sexual conduct between homosexual women even though such conduct was prohibited between heterosexuals. The history of the statutes cited by the majority as proof for the proposition that sodomy is not constitutionally protected similarly reveals a prohibition on heterosexual, as well as homosexual, sodomy.[8]

Because the Georgia statute expresses the traditional view that sodomy is an immoral kind of conduct regardless of the identity of the persons who engage in it, I believe that a proper analysis of its constitutionality requires consideration of two questions: First, may a State totally prohibit the described conduct by means of a neutral law applying without exception to all persons subject to its jurisdiction? If not, may the State save the statute by announcing that it will only enforce the law against homosexuals? The two questions merit separate discussion.

I

Our prior cases make two propositions abundantly clear. First, the fact that the governing majority in a State has traditionally viewed a particular practice as immoral is not a sufficient reason for upholding a law prohibiting the practice; neither history nor tradition could save a

---

[2] The Court states that the "issue presented is whether the Federal Constitution confers a fundamental right upon homosexuals to engage in sodomy and hence invalidates the laws of the many States that still make such conduct illegal and have done so for a very long time." In reality, however, it is the indiscriminate prohibition of sodomy, heterosexual as well as homosexual, that has been present "for a very long time." Moreover, the reasoning the Court employs would provide the same support for the statute as it is written as it does for the statute as it is narrowly construed by the Court.

[5] See J. May, The Law of Crimes § 203 (2d ed. 1893) ("Sodomy, otherwise called buggery, bestiality, and the crime against nature, is the unnatural copulation of two persons with each other, or of a human being with a beast. . . . It may be committed by a man with a man, by a man with a beast, or by a woman with a beast, or by a man with a woman—his wife, in which case, if she consent, she is an accomplice").

[6] The predecessor of the current Georgia statute provided: "Sodomy is the carnal knowledge and connection against the order of nature, by man with man, or in the same unnatural manner with woman." Ga.Code, Tit. 1, Pt. 4, § 4251 (1861). This prohibition of heterosexual sodomy was not purely hortatory. See, *e.g., Comer v. State,* 21 Ga.App. 306, 94 S.E. 314 (1917) (affirming prosecution for consensual heterosexual sodomy).

[8] A review of the statutes cited by the majority discloses that, in 1791, in 1868, and today, the vast majority of sodomy statutes do not differentiate between homosexual and heterosexual sodomy.

law prohibiting miscegenation from constitutional attack.[9] Second, individual decisions by married persons, concerning the intimacies of their physical relationship, even when not intended to produce offspring, are a form of "liberty" protected by the Due Process Clause of the Fourteenth Amendment. *Griswold v. Connecticut,* 381 U.S. 479 (1965). Moreover, this protection extends to intimate choices by unmarried as well as married persons. *Carey v. Population Services International,* 431 U.S. 678 (1977); *Eisenstadt v. Baird,* 405 U.S. 438 (1972). . . .

Society has every right to encourage its individual members to follow particular traditions in expressing affection for one another and in gratifying their personal desires. It, of course, may prohibit an individual from imposing his will on another to satisfy his own selfish interests. It also may prevent an individual from interfering with, or violating, a legally sanctioned and protected relationship, such as marriage. And it may explain the relative advantages and disadvantages of different forms of intimate expression. But when individual married couples are isolated from observation by others, the way in which they voluntarily choose to conduct their intimate relations is a matter for them—not the State—to decide.[10] The essential "liberty" that animated the development of the law in cases like *Griswold, Eisenstadt,* and *Carey* surely embraces the right to engage in nonreproductive, sexual conduct that others may consider offensive or immoral.

Paradoxical as it may seem, our prior cases thus establish that a State may not prohibit sodomy within "the sacred precincts of marital bedrooms," *Griswold,* 381 U.S., at 485, or, indeed, between unmarried heterosexual adults. *Eisenstadt,* 405 U.S., at 453. In all events, it is perfectly clear that the State of Georgia may not totally prohibit the conduct proscribed by § 16–6–2 of the Georgia Criminal Code.

II

If the Georgia statute cannot be enforced as it is written—if the conduct it seeks to prohibit is a protected form of liberty for the vast majority of Georgia's citizens—the State must assume the burden of justifying a selective application of its law. Either the persons to whom Georgia seeks to apply its statute do not have the same interest in "liberty" that others have, or there must be a reason why the State may be permitted to apply a generally applicable law to certain persons that it does not apply to others.

The first possibility is plainly unacceptable. Although the meaning of the principle that "all men are created equal" is not always clear, it surely must mean that every free citizen has the same interest in "liberty" that the members of the majority share. From the standpoint of

---

[9] See *Loving v. Virginia,* 388 U.S. 1 (1967). Interestingly, miscegenation was once treated as a crime similar to sodomy.

[10] Indeed, the Georgia Attorney General concedes that Georgia's statute would be unconstitutional if applied to a married couple. Significantly, Georgia passed the current statute three years after the Court's decision in *Griswold.*

the individual, the homosexual and the heterosexual have the same interest in deciding how he will live his own life, and, more narrowly, how he will conduct himself in his personal and voluntary associations with his companions. State intrusion into the private conduct of either is equally burdensome.

The second possibility is similarly unacceptable. A policy of selective application must be supported by a neutral and legitimate interest—something more substantial than a habitual dislike for, or ignorance about, the disfavored group. Neither the State nor the Court has identified any such interest in this case. The Court has posited as a justification for the Georgia statute "the presumed belief of a majority of the electorate in Georgia that homosexual sodomy is immoral and unacceptable." But the Georgia electorate has expressed no such belief—instead, its representatives enacted a law that presumably reflects the belief that *all sodomy* is immoral and unacceptable. Unless the Court is prepared to conclude that such a law is constitutional, it may not rely on the work product of the Georgia Legislature to support its holding. For the Georgia statute does not single out homosexuals as a separate class meriting special disfavored treatment.

Nor, indeed, does the Georgia prosecutor even believe that all homosexuals who violate this statute should be punished. This conclusion is evident from the fact that the respondent in this very case has formally acknowledged in his complaint and in court that he has engaged, and intends to continue to engage, in the prohibited conduct, yet the State has elected not to process criminal charges against him. As Justice POWELL points out, moreover, Georgia's prohibition on private, consensual sodomy has not been enforced for decades. The record of nonenforcement, in this case and in the last several decades, belies the Attorney General's representations about the importance of the State's selective application of its generally applicable law.[12]

Both the Georgia statute and the Georgia prosecutor thus completely fail to provide the Court with any support for the conclusion that homosexual sodomy, *simpliciter,* is considered unacceptable conduct in that State, and that the burden of justifying a selective application of the generally applicable law has been met.

III

The Court orders the dismissal of respondent's complaint even though the State's statute prohibits all sodomy; even though that prohibition is concededly unconstitutional with respect to heterosexuals; and even though the State's *post hoc* explanations for selective application are belied by the State's own actions. At the very least, I think

---

[12] It is, of course, possible to argue that a statute has a purely symbolic role. Since the Georgia Attorney General does not even defend the statute as written, however, see n. 10, *supra,* the State cannot possibly rest on the notion that the statute may be defended for its symbolic message.

it clear at this early stage of the litigation that respondent has alleged a constitutional claim sufficient to withstand a motion to dismiss.

I respectfully dissent.

NOTE ON GAY RIGHTS, DUE PROCESS, AND EQUAL PROTECTION

1. *Bowers v. Hardwick* illustrates the pervasive importance in constitutional law of "framing" the issue presented.[1] To begin with, we might frame the case as being about either the right to make certain decisions about sexual intimacy, or as about individuals' right to privacy concerning activities conducted in their own home. In his petition for rehearing in *Hardwick*, for example, Professor Laurence Tribe (who had argued the case on Hardwick's behalf) asserted that "[t]he question before the Court is not what Respondent Michael Hardwick was doing in the privacy of his bedroom, but what the State of Georgia was doing there."[2] From this standpoint, doesn't *Hardwick* seem rather close to *Griswold*'s concern with keeping the state out of the marital bedroom? Does the traditional right to a private space in the home really disappear when the marital element drops out?

Framed as a question of sexual autonomy, on the other hand, *Hardwick* presents a classic level of generality problem.[3] Writing for the majority, Justice White said that "[t]he issue presented is whether the Federal Constitution confers a fundamental right upon homosexuals to engage in sodomy"—a question that, to his mind, practically answered itself. On the other hand, Justice Blackmun's dissent quoted Justice Brandeis in arguing that "this case is about 'the most comprehensive of rights and the right most valued by civilized men,' namely, 'the right to be let alone.' " Both of these descriptions are, on some level, plainly correct. But they plainly point in different directions. It is hard to imagine that the framers of either the Fifth or the Fourteenth Amendment were especially interested in protecting homosexuals, and none of the Court's prior precedents had extended any protection to homosexual activity. But the more general notion of sexual privacy has solid roots in *Griswold*, *Eisenstadt*, and *Roe*. How you frame the question, in other words, takes you a long way toward the answer.

Three years after *Hardwick*, Justice Scalia argued in *Michael H. v. Gerald D.* that courts should always assess rights claims at the most specific possible level of generality. That is basically what Justice White did in *Hardwick*. Do you agree that this was the correct approach? Does the *Michael H.* principle explain why the Court framed *Hardwick* as a case about sex rather than the privacy of the home?

2. Michael Hardwick did not make an equal protection argument in *Hardwick*. Was this a mistake? Consider the following description by Cass Sunstein of the respective roles of due process and equal protection:

---

[1] *See generally* Daryl J. Levinson, *Framing Transactions in Constitutional Law*, 111 YALE L. J. 1311 (2002).

[2] Petition for Rehearing for Respondent in No. 85–140, *Bowers v. Hardwick* (1986).

[3] *See* Section 16.1, *supra*.

From its inception, the Due Process Clause has been interpreted largely (though not exclusively) to protect traditional practices against short-run departures. The clause has therefore been associated with a particular conception of judicial review, one that sees the courts as safeguards against novel developments brought about by temporary majorities who are insufficiently sensitive to the claims of history.

The Equal Protection Clause, by contrast, has been understood as an attempt to protect disadvantaged groups from discriminatory practices, however deeply engrained and longstanding. The Due Process Clause often looks backward; it is highly relevant to the Due Process issue whether an existing or time-honored convention, described at the appropriate level of generality, is violated by the practice under attack. By contrast, the Equal Protection Clause looks forward, serving to invalidate practices that were widespread at the time of its ratification and that were expected to endure. The two clauses therefore operate along different tracks.[4]

Does Professor Sunstein's account suggest that equal protection would have been a more promising line of argument in *Hardwick*?

3.   After *Bowers*, several federal courts of appeal held that classifications based on sexual orientation are not suspect—and therefore not subject to heightened scrutiny—under the Equal Protection Clause. Writing for the D.C. Circuit in *Padula v. Webster*, 822 F.2d 97 (D.C. Cir. 1987), Judge Robert Bork reasoned that even though *Bowers* did not involve an equal protection claim, its result foreclosed recognition of gays and lesbians as a suspect class:

It would be quite anomalous . . . to declare status defined by conduct that states may constitutionally criminalize as deserving of strict scrutiny under the equal protection clause. More importantly, in all those cases in which the Supreme Court has accorded suspect or quasi-suspect status to a class, the Court's holding was predicated on an unarticulated, but necessarily implicit, notion that it is plainly unjustifiable (in accordance with standards not altogether clear to us) to discriminate invidiously against the particular class. If the Court was unwilling to object to state laws that criminalize the behavior that defines the class, it is hardly open to a lower court to conclude that state sponsored discrimination against the class is invidious. After all, there can hardly be more palpable discrimination against a class than making the conduct that defines the class criminal.

Padula involved a challenge to the FBI's policy disfavoring employment of homosexuals. The court of appeals found that policy rationally related to a legitimate government interest, because FBI agents would have to work in many states that had criminalized

---

4   Cass R. Sunstein, *Sexual Orientation and the Constitution: A Note on the Relationship Between Due Process and Equal Protection*, 55 U. CHI. L. REV. 1161, 1163 (1988).

homosexual conduct and because homosexuals are more vulnerable to blackmail.

Not all circuit courts accepted *Padula*'s reasoning. In *Watkins v. U.S. Army*, 837 F.2d 1428 (9th Cir. 1988), the U.S. Court of Appeals for the Ninth Circuit recognized sexual orientation as a suspect classification. The court observed that "[w]hile it is not our role to question *Hardwick*'s concerns about substantive due process and specifically the right to privacy, these concerns have little relevance to equal protection doctrine." The court went on to find that gays and lesbians satisfied the criteria for suspect class status: (1) they had "suffered a history of purposeful discrimination"; (2) sexual orientation "plainly has no relevance to a person's ability to perform or contribute to society"; (3) it is an "immutable" characteristic; and (4) the "general animus towards homosexuality" in society renders gays and lesbians a politically powerless group.

Does *Padula* or *Watkins* have the better of the argument on suspect class status for gays and lesbians?

SECTION 17.2   THE TIDE TURNS—AND THE TIERS BREAK DOWN

A decade after *Bowers v. Hardwick*, the Court's decision in *Romer v. Evans* seemed to signal a new direction on gay rights. *Romer* struck down a Colorado state constitutional amendment, adopted by a popular referendum, that was primarily directed toward keeping particular progressive enclaves like Aspen or Boulder from adopting ordinances prohibiting discrimination against gays and lesbians. *Romer* did not directly challenge *Hardwick*; it was an equal protection case, and it purported to apply rational basis review. But both the result and Justice Kennedy's passionate opinion—a far cry from Chief Justice Burger's reference to homosexuality as "a crime not fit to be named"—seemed to mark a sea change in the Court's perspective on gay rights.

The Court confirmed this shift in *Lawrence v. Texas*, which struck down the Texas sodomy statute and overruled *Hardwick* outright. Unlike *Romer*, *Lawrence* rested on due process rather than equal protection. But like *Romer*, *Lawrence* was cagey about the standard of review, speaking in general terms of "liberty" and eschewing any specification of the level of scrutiny. Both these cases thus contributed to a tendency that we saw in Chapter Fifteen—that is, the Court's steady retreat from definitive tiers of scrutiny.

Romer v. Evans
517 U.S. 620 (1996)

■ **JUSTICE KENNEDY delivered the opinion of the Court.**

One century ago, the first Justice Harlan admonished this Court that the Constitution "neither knows nor tolerates classes among citizens." *Plessy v. Ferguson,* 163 U.S. 537, 559 (1896) (dissenting opinion). Unheeded then, those words now are understood to state a commitment to the law's neutrality where the rights of persons are at stake. The Equal Protection Clause enforces this principle and today requires us to hold invalid a provision of Colorado's Constitution.

I

The enactment challenged in this case is an amendment to the Constitution of the State of Colorado, adopted in a 1992 statewide referendum. The parties and the state courts refer to it as "Amendment 2," its designation when submitted to the voters. The impetus for the amendment and the contentious campaign that preceded its adoption came in large part from ordinances that had been passed in various Colorado municipalities. For example, the cities of Aspen and Boulder and the city and County of Denver each had enacted ordinances which banned discrimination in many transactions and activities, including housing, employment, education, public accommodations, and health and welfare services. What gave rise to the statewide controversy was the protection the ordinances afforded to persons discriminated against by reason of their sexual orientation. See Boulder Rev. Code § 12–1–1 (defining "sexual orientation" as "the choice of sexual partners, i.e., bisexual, homosexual or heterosexual"); Denver Rev. Municipal Code, Art. IV, § 28–92 (defining "sexual orientation" as "[t]he status of an individual as to his or her heterosexuality, homosexuality or bisexuality"). Amendment 2 repeals these ordinances to the extent they prohibit discrimination on the basis of "homosexual, lesbian or bisexual orientation, conduct, practices or relationships." Colo. Const., Art. II, § 30b.

Yet Amendment 2, in explicit terms, does more than repeal or rescind these provisions. It prohibits all legislative, executive or judicial action at any level of state or local government designed to protect the named class, a class we shall refer to as homosexual persons or gays and lesbians. The amendment reads:

> No Protected Status Based on Homosexual, Lesbian or Bisexual Orientation. Neither the State of Colorado, through any of its branches or departments, nor any of its agencies, political subdivisions, municipalities or school districts, shall enact, adopt or enforce any statute, regulation, ordinance or policy whereby homosexual, lesbian or bisexual orientation, conduct, practices or relationships shall constitute or otherwise be the basis of or entitle any person or class of persons to have or claim any minority status, quota preferences, protected status or claim of discrimination. This Section of the Constitution shall be in all respects self-executing.

Soon after Amendment 2 was adopted, this litigation to declare its invalidity and enjoin its enforcement was commenced in the District Court for the City and County of Denver. Among the plaintiffs (respondents here) were homosexual persons, some of them government employees. They alleged that enforcement of Amendment 2 would subject them to immediate and substantial risk of discrimination on the basis of their sexual orientation. Other plaintiffs (also respondents here) included the three municipalities whose ordinances we have cited and certain other governmental entities which had acted earlier to protect homosexuals from discrimination but would be prevented by Amendment 2 from continuing to do so. Although Governor Romer had been on record opposing the adoption of Amendment 2, he was named in his official capacity as a defendant, together with the Colorado Attorney General and the State of Colorado.

The trial court granted a preliminary injunction to stay enforcement of Amendment 2, and an appeal was taken to the Supreme Court of Colorado. Sustaining the interim injunction and remanding the case for further proceedings, the State Supreme Court held that Amendment 2 was subject to strict scrutiny under the Fourteenth Amendment because it infringed the fundamental right of gays and lesbians to participate in the political process. . . . On remand, the State advanced various arguments in an effort to show that Amendment 2 was narrowly tailored to serve compelling interests, but the trial court found none sufficient. It enjoined enforcement of Amendment 2, and the Supreme Court of Colorado, in a second opinion, affirmed the ruling. We granted certiorari and now affirm the judgment, but on a rationale different from that adopted by the State Supreme Court.

II

The State's principal argument in defense of Amendment 2 is that it puts gays and lesbians in the same position as all other persons. So, the State says, the measure does no more than deny homosexuals special rights. This reading of the amendment's language is implausible. We rely not upon our own interpretation of the amendment but upon the authoritative construction of Colorado's Supreme Court. The state court, deeming it unnecessary to determine the full extent of the amendment's reach, found it invalid even on a modest reading of its implications. The critical discussion of the amendment . . . is as follows:

> The immediate objective of Amendment 2 is, at a minimum, to repeal existing statutes, regulations, ordinances, and policies of state and local entities that barred discrimination based on sexual orientation. *See* Aspen, Colo., Mun. Code § 13–98 (1977) (prohibiting discrimination in employment, housing and public accommodations on the basis of sexual orientation); Boulder, Colo., Rev. Code §§ 12–1–2 to –4 (1987) (same); Denver, Colo., Rev. Mun. Code art. IV, §§ 28–91 to –116 (1991) (same); Executive Order No. D0035 (December 10, 1990) (prohibiting employment discrimination for 'all state employees, classified and exempt' on the basis of sexual orientation); Colorado Insurance Code, § 10–3–1104, 4A C.R.S. (1992 Supp.) (forbidding health insurance providers from determining

insurability and premiums based on an applicant's, a beneficiary's, or an insured's sexual orientation); and various provisions prohibiting discrimination based on sexual orientation at state colleges.

The 'ultimate effect' of Amendment 2 is to prohibit any governmental entity from adopting similar, or more protective statutes, regulations, ordinances, or policies in the future unless the state constitution is first amended to permit such measures.[*]

Sweeping and comprehensive is the change in legal status effected by this law. So much is evident from the ordinances the Colorado Supreme Court declared would be void by operation of Amendment 2. Homosexuals, by state decree, are put in a solitary class with respect to transactions and relations in both the private and governmental spheres. The amendment withdraws from homosexuals, but no others, specific legal protection from the injuries caused by discrimination, and it forbids reinstatement of these laws and policies.

The change Amendment 2 works in the legal status of gays and lesbians in the private sphere is far reaching, both on its own terms and when considered in light of the structure and operation of modern anti-discrimination laws. That structure is well illustrated by contemporary statutes and ordinances prohibiting discrimination by providers of public accommodations. "At common law, innkeepers, smiths, and others who 'made profession of a public employment,' were prohibited from refusing, without good reason, to serve a customer." *Hurley v. Irish-American Gay, Lesbian and Bisexual Group of Boston, Inc.,* 515 U.S. 557, 571 (1995). The duty was a general one and did not specify protection for particular groups. The common-law rules, however, proved insufficient in many instances, and it was settled early that the Fourteenth Amendment did not give Congress a general power to prohibit discrimination in public accommodations, *Civil Rights Cases,* 109 U.S. 3, 25 (1883). In consequence, most States have chosen to counter discrimination by enacting detailed statutory schemes. See, *e.g.,* S.D. Codified Laws §§ 20–13–10, 20–13–22, 20–13–23; Iowa Code §§ 216.6–216.8; Okla. Stat., Tit. 25, §§ 1302, 1402; 43 Pa. Cons. Stat. §§ 953, 955; N.J. Stat. Ann. §§ 10:5–3, 10:5–4; N.H. Rev. Stat. Ann. §§ 354–A:7, 354–A:10, 354–A:17; Minn. Stat. § 363.03.

Colorado's state and municipal laws typify this emerging tradition of statutory protection and follow a consistent pattern. The laws first enumerate the persons or entities subject to a duty not to discriminate. The list goes well beyond the entities covered by the common law. The Boulder ordinance, for example, has a comprehensive definition of entities deemed places of "public accommodation." They include "any place of business engaged in any sales to the general public and any place

---

[*]   *Evans v. Romer,* 854 P.2d 1270, 1284–85 (Colo. 1993) [Editor's Note].

that offers services, facilities, privileges, or advantages to the general public or that receives financial support through solicitation of the general public or through governmental subsidy of any kind." Boulder Rev. Code § 12–1–1(j) (1987). The Denver ordinance is of similar breadth, applying, for example, to hotels, restaurants, hospitals, dental clinics, theaters, banks, common carriers, travel and insurance agencies, and "shops and stores dealing with goods or services of any kind," Denver Rev. Municipal Code, Art. IV, § 28–92 (1991).

These statutes and ordinances also depart from the common law by enumerating the groups or persons within their ambit of protection. Enumeration is the essential device used to make the duty not to discriminate concrete and to provide guidance for those who must comply. In following this approach, Colorado's state and local governments have not limited antidiscrimination laws to groups that have so far been given the protection of heightened equal protection scrutiny under our cases. Rather, they set forth an extensive catalog of traits which cannot be the basis for discrimination, including age, military status, marital status, pregnancy, parenthood, custody of a minor child, political affiliation, physical or mental disability of an individual or of his or her associates—and, in recent times, sexual orientation. Aspen Municipal Code § 13–98(a)(1) (1977); Boulder Rev. Code §§ 12–1–1 to 12–1–4 (1987); Denver Rev. Municipal Code, Art. IV, §§ 28–92 to 28–119 (1991); Colo. Rev. Stat. §§ 24–34–401 to 24–34–707 (1988 and Supp.1995).

Amendment 2 bars homosexuals from securing protection against the injuries that these public-accommodations laws address. That in itself is a severe consequence, but there is more. Amendment 2, in addition, nullifies specific legal protections for this targeted class in all transactions in housing, sale of real estate, insurance, health and welfare services, private education, and employment. See, *e.g.*, Aspen Municipal Code §§ 13–98(b), (c) (1977); Boulder Rev. Code §§ 12–1–2, 12–1–3 (1987); Denver Rev. Municipal Code, Art. IV, §§ 28–93 to 28–95, 28–97 (1991).

Not confined to the private sphere, Amendment 2 also operates to repeal and forbid all laws or policies providing specific protection for gays or lesbians from discrimination by every level of Colorado government. The State Supreme Court cited two examples of protections in the governmental sphere that are now rescinded and may not be reintroduced. The first is Colorado Executive Order D0035 (1990), which forbids employment discrimination against " 'all state employees, classified and exempt' on the basis of sexual orientation." Also repealed, and now forbidden, are "various provisions prohibiting discrimination based on sexual orientation at state colleges." The repeal of these measures and the prohibition against their future reenactment demonstrate that Amendment 2 has the same force and effect in

Colorado's governmental sector as it does elsewhere and that it applies to policies as well as ordinary legislation.

Amendment 2's reach may not be limited to specific laws passed for the benefit of gays and lesbians. It is a fair, if not necessary, inference from the broad language of the amendment that it deprives gays and lesbians even of the protection of general laws and policies that prohibit arbitrary discrimination in governmental and private settings. See, *e.g.,* Colo. Rev. Stat. § 24–4–106(7) (1988) (agency action subject to judicial review under arbitrary and capricious standard); § 18–8–405 (making it a criminal offense for a public servant knowingly, arbitrarily, or capriciously to refrain from performing a duty imposed on him by law); § 10–3–1104(1)(f) (prohibiting "unfair discrimination" in insurance); 4 Colo. Code of Regulations 801–1, Policy 11–1 (1983) (prohibiting discrimination in state employment on grounds of specified traits or "other non-merit factor"). At some point in the systematic administration of these laws, an official must determine whether homosexuality is an arbitrary and, thus, forbidden basis for decision. Yet a decision to that effect would itself amount to a policy prohibiting discrimination on the basis of homosexuality, and so would appear to be no more valid under Amendment 2 than the specific prohibitions against discrimination the state court held invalid.

If this consequence follows from Amendment 2, as its broad language suggests, it would compound the constitutional difficulties the law creates. The state court did not decide whether the amendment has this effect, however, and neither need we. In the course of rejecting the argument that Amendment 2 is intended to conserve resources to fight discrimination against suspect classes, the Colorado Supreme Court made the limited observation that the amendment is not intended to affect many anti-discrimination laws protecting nonsuspect classes. In our view that does not resolve the issue. In any event, even if, as we doubt, homosexuals could find some safe harbor in laws of general application, we cannot accept the view that Amendment 2's prohibition on specific legal protections does no more than deprive homosexuals of special rights. To the contrary, the amendment imposes a special disability upon those persons alone. Homosexuals are forbidden the safeguards that others enjoy or may seek without constraint. They can obtain specific protection against discrimination only by enlisting the citizenry of Colorado to amend the State Constitution or perhaps, on the State's view, by trying to pass helpful laws of general applicability. This is so no matter how local or discrete the harm, no matter how public and widespread the injury. We find nothing special in the protections Amendment 2 withholds. These are protections taken for granted by most people either because they already have them or do not need them; these are protections against exclusion from an almost limitless number of transactions and endeavors that constitute ordinary civic life in a free society.

III

The Fourteenth Amendment's promise that no person shall be denied the equal protection of the laws must coexist with the practical necessity that most legislation classifies for one purpose or another, with resulting disadvantage to various groups or persons. We have attempted to reconcile the principle with the reality by stating that, if a law neither burdens a fundamental right nor targets a suspect class, we will uphold the legislative classification so long as it bears a rational relation to some legitimate end. See, *e.g., Heller v. Doe,* 509 U.S. 312, 319–320 (1993).

Amendment 2 fails, indeed defies, even this conventional inquiry. First, the amendment has the peculiar property of imposing a broad and undifferentiated disability on a single named group, an exceptional and, as we shall explain, invalid form of legislation. Second, its sheer breadth is so discontinuous with the reasons offered for it that the amendment seems inexplicable by anything but animus toward the class it affects; it lacks a rational relationship to legitimate state interests.

Taking the first point, even in the ordinary equal protection case calling for the most deferential of standards, we insist on knowing the relation between the classification adopted and the object to be attained. The search for the link between classification and objective gives substance to the Equal Protection Clause; it provides guidance and discipline for the legislature, which is entitled to know what sorts of laws it can pass; and it marks the limits of our own authority. In the ordinary case, a law will be sustained if it can be said to advance a legitimate government interest, even if the law seems unwise or works to the disadvantage of a particular group, or if the rationale for it seems tenuous. See *New Orleans v. Dukes,* 427 U.S. 297 (1976) (tourism benefits justified classification favoring pushcart vendors of certain longevity); *Williamson v. Lee Optical of Okla., Inc.,* 348 U.S. 483 (1955) (assumed health concerns justified law favoring optometrists over opticians); *Railway Express Agency, Inc. v. New York,* 336 U.S. 106 (1949) (potential traffic hazards justified exemption of vehicles advertising the owner's products from general advertising ban); *Kotch v. Board of River Port Pilot Comm'rs for Port of New Orleans,* 330 U.S. 552 (1947) (licensing scheme that disfavored persons unrelated to current river boat pilots justified by possible efficiency and safety benefits of a closely knit pilotage system). The laws challenged in the cases just cited were narrow enough in scope and grounded in a sufficient factual context for us to ascertain some relation between the classification and the purpose it served. By requiring that the classification bear a rational relationship to an independent and legitimate legislative end, we ensure that classifications are not drawn for the purpose of disadvantaging the group burdened by the law. *See Railroad Retirement Bd. v. Fritz,* 449 U.S. 166, 181 (1980) (STEVENS, J., concurring) ("If the adverse impact on the disfavored class is an apparent aim of the legislature, its impartiality would be suspect").

Amendment 2 confounds this normal process of judicial review. It is at once too narrow and too broad. It identifies persons by a single trait and then denies them protection across the board. The resulting disqualification of a class of persons from the right to seek specific protection from the law is unprecedented in our jurisprudence. The absence of precedent for Amendment 2 is itself instructive; "[d]iscriminations of an unusual character especially suggest careful consideration to determine whether they are obnoxious to the constitutional provision." *Louisville Gas & Elec. Co. v. Coleman,* 277 U.S. 32, 37–38 (1928).

It is not within our constitutional tradition to enact laws of this sort. Central both to the idea of the rule of law and to our own Constitution's guarantee of equal protection is the principle that government and each of its parts remain open on impartial terms to all who seek its assistance. " 'Equal protection of the laws is not achieved through indiscriminate imposition of inequalities.' " *Sweatt v. Painter,* 339 U.S. 629, 635 (1950). Respect for this principle explains why laws singling out a certain class of citizens for disfavored legal status or general hardships are rare. A law declaring that in general it shall be more difficult for one group of citizens than for all others to seek aid from the government is itself a denial of equal protection of the laws in the most literal sense. "The guaranty of 'equal protection of the laws is a pledge of the protection of equal laws.' " *Skinner v. Oklahoma ex rel. Williamson,* 316 U.S. 535, 541 (1942).

Davis v. Beason, 133 U.S. 333 (1890), not cited by the parties but relied upon by the dissent, is not evidence that Amendment 2 is within our constitutional tradition, and any reliance upon it as authority for sustaining the amendment is misplaced. In *Davis,* the Court approved an Idaho territorial statute denying Mormons, polygamists, and advocates of polygamy the right to vote and to hold office because, as the Court construed the statute, it "simply excludes from the privilege of voting, or of holding any office of honor, trust or profit, those who have been convicted of certain offences, and those who advocate a practical resistance to the laws of the Territory and justify and approve the commission of crimes forbidden by it." To the extent Davis held that persons advocating a certain practice may be denied the right to vote, it is no longer good law. *Brandenburg v. Ohio,* 395 U.S. 444 (1969) (per curiam). To the extent it held that the groups designated in the statute may be deprived of the right to vote because of their status, its ruling could not stand without surviving strict scrutiny, a most doubtful outcome. To the extent *Davis* held that a convicted felon may be denied the right to vote, its holding is not implicated by our decision and is unexceptionable. See *Richardson v. Ramirez,* 418 U.S. 24 (1974).

A second and related point is that laws of the kind now before us raise the inevitable inference that the disadvantage imposed is born of animosity toward the class of persons affected. "[I]f the constitutional conception of 'equal protection of the laws' means anything, it must at the very least mean that a bare . . . desire to harm a politically unpopular group cannot constitute a *legitimate* governmental interest." *Department of Agriculture v. Moreno,* 413 U.S. 528, 534 (1973). Even laws enacted for broad and ambitious purposes often can be explained by reference to legitimate public policies which justify the incidental disadvantages they impose on certain persons. Amendment 2, however, in making a general announcement that gays and lesbians shall not have any particular protections from the law, inflicts on them immediate, continuing, and real injuries that outrun and belie any legitimate justifications that may be claimed for it. We conclude that, in addition to the far-reaching deficiencies of Amendment 2 that we have noted, the principles it offends, in another sense, are conventional and venerable; a law must bear a rational relationship to a legitimate governmental purpose, and Amendment 2 does not.

The primary rationale the State offers for Amendment 2 is respect for other citizens' freedom of association, and in particular the liberties of landlords or employers who have personal or religious objections to homosexuality. Colorado also cites its interest in conserving resources to fight discrimination against other groups. The breadth of the amendment is so far removed from these particular justifications that we find it impossible to credit them. We cannot say that Amendment 2 is directed to any identifiable legitimate purpose or discrete objective. It is a status-based enactment divorced from any factual context from which we could discern a relationship to legitimate state interests; it is a classification of persons undertaken for its own sake, something the Equal Protection Clause does not permit. "[C]lass legislation . . . [is] obnoxious to the prohibitions of the Fourteenth Amendment. . . ." *Civil Rights Cases,* 109 U.S., at 24.

We must conclude that Amendment 2 classifies homosexuals not to further a proper legislative end but to make them unequal to everyone else. This Colorado cannot do. A State cannot so deem a class of persons a stranger to its laws. Amendment 2 violates the Equal Protection Clause, and the judgment of the Supreme Court of Colorado is affirmed.

It is so ordered.

■ JUSTICE SCALIA, with whom THE CHIEF JUSTICE and JUSTICE THOMAS join, dissenting.

The Court has mistaken a Kulturkampf for a fit of spite. The constitutional amendment before us here is not the manifestation of a " 'bare . . . desire to harm' " homosexuals, but is rather a modest attempt by seemingly tolerant Coloradans to preserve traditional sexual mores against the efforts of a politically powerful minority to revise those mores through use of the laws. That objective, and the means chosen to achieve it, are not only unimpeachable under any constitutional doctrine hitherto pronounced (hence the opinion's heavy reliance upon principles of righteousness rather than judicial holdings); they have been specifically approved by the Congress of the United States and by this Court.

In holding that homosexuality cannot be singled out for disfavorable treatment, the Court contradicts a decision, unchallenged here, pronounced only 10 years ago, see *Bowers v. Hardwick,* 478 U.S. 186 (1986), and places the prestige of this institution behind the proposition that opposition to homosexuality is as reprehensible as racial or religious bias. Whether it is or not is *precisely* the cultural debate that gave rise to the Colorado constitutional amendment (and to the preferential laws against which the amendment was directed). Since the Constitution of the United States says nothing about this subject, it is left to be resolved by normal democratic means, including the democratic adoption of provisions in state constitutions. This Court has no business imposing upon all Americans the resolution favored by the elite class from which the Members of this institution are selected, pronouncing that "animosity" toward homosexuality is evil. I vigorously dissent.

I

Let me first discuss Part II of the Court's opinion, its longest section, which is devoted to rejecting the State's arguments that Amendment 2 "puts gays and lesbians in the same position as all other persons," and "does no more than deny homosexuals special rights." The Court concludes that this reading of Amendment 2's language is "implausible" under the "authoritative construction" given Amendment 2 by the Supreme Court of Colorado.

In reaching this conclusion, the Court considers it unnecessary to decide the validity of the State's argument that Amendment 2 does not deprive homosexuals of the "protection [afforded by] general laws and policies that prohibit arbitrary discrimination in governmental and private settings." I agree that we need not resolve that dispute, because the Supreme Court of Colorado has resolved it for us. In the case below, the Colorado court stated:

> [I]t is significant to note that Colorado law currently proscribes discrimination against persons who are not suspect classes, including discrimination based on age, § 24–34–402(1)(a), 10A C.R.S. (1994 Supp.); marital or family status, § 24–34–502(1)(a), 10A C.R.S. (1994 Supp.); veterans' status, § 28–3–506, 11B C.R.S. (1989); and for any legal, off-duty conduct such as smoking tobacco, § 24–34–402.5, 10A C. R.S. (1994 Supp.). *Of course Amendment 2 is not intended to have any effect on this legislation, but seeks only to prevent the adoption of antidiscrimination laws intended to protect gays, lesbians, and bisexuals.*" (emphasis added).

The Court utterly fails to distinguish this portion of the Colorado court's opinion. Colorado Rev. Stat. § 24–34–402.5, which this passage authoritatively declares not to be affected by Amendment 2, was respondents' primary example of a generally applicable law whose protections would be unavailable to homosexuals under Amendment 2. The clear import of the Colorado court's conclusion that it is not affected is that "general laws and policies that prohibit arbitrary discrimination" would continue to prohibit discrimination on the basis of homosexual conduct as well. This analysis, which is fully in accord with (indeed, follows inescapably from) the text of the constitutional provision, lays to rest such horribles, raised in the course of oral argument, as the prospect that assaults upon homosexuals could not be prosecuted. The amendment prohibits special treatment of homosexuals, and nothing more. It would not affect, for example, a requirement of state law that pensions be paid to all retiring state employees with a certain length of service; homosexual employees, as well as others, would be entitled to that benefit. But it would prevent the State or any municipality from making death-benefit payments to the "life partner" of a homosexual when it does not make such payments to the long-time roommate of a nonhomosexual employee. Or again, it does not affect the requirement of the State's general insurance laws that customers be afforded coverage without discrimination unrelated to anticipated risk. Thus, homosexuals could not be denied coverage, or charged a greater premium, with respect to auto collision insurance; but neither the State nor any municipality could require that distinctive health insurance risks associated with homosexuality (if there are any) be ignored.

Despite all of its hand wringing about the potential effect of Amendment 2 on general antidiscrimination laws, the Court's opinion ultimately does not dispute all this, but assumes it to be true. The only denial of equal treatment it contends homosexuals have suffered is this: They may not obtain *preferential* treatment without amending the State Constitution. That is to say, the principle underlying the Court's opinion is that one who is accorded equal treatment under the laws, but cannot as readily as others obtain *preferential* treatment under the laws, has been denied equal protection of the laws. If merely stating this alleged "equal protection" violation does not suffice to refute it, our constitutional jurisprudence has achieved terminal silliness.

The central thesis of the Court's reasoning is that any group is denied equal protection when, to obtain advantage (or, presumably, to avoid disadvantage), it must have recourse to a more general and hence more difficult level of political decisionmaking than others. The world has never heard of such a principle, which is why the Court's opinion is so long on emotive utterance and so short on relevant legal citation. And it seems to me most unlikely that any multilevel democracy can function under such a principle. For *whenever* a disadvantage is imposed, or conferral of a benefit is prohibited, at one of the higher levels of democratic decisionmaking (*i.e.,* by the state legislature rather than local government, or by the people at large in the state constitution rather than the legislature), the affected group has (under this theory) been denied equal protection. To take the simplest of examples, consider a state law prohibiting the award of municipal contracts to relatives of mayors or city councilmen. Once such a law is passed, the group composed of such relatives must, in order to get the benefit of city contracts, persuade the state legislature—unlike all other citizens, who need only persuade the municipality. It is ridiculous to consider this a denial of equal protection, which is why the Court's theory is unheard of.

The Court might reply that the example I have given is *not* a denial of equal protection only because the same "rational basis" (avoidance of corruption) which renders constitutional the *substantive discrimination* against relatives (*i.e.,* the fact that they alone cannot obtain city contracts) also automatically suffices to sustain what might be called the *electoral-procedural discrimination* against them (*i.e.,* the fact that they must go to the state level to get this changed). This is of course a perfectly reasonable response, and would explain why "electoral-procedural discrimination" has not hitherto been heard of: A law that is valid in its substance is automatically valid in its level of enactment. But the Court cannot afford to make this argument, for as I shall discuss next, there is no doubt of a rational basis for the substance of the prohibition at issue here. The Court's entire novel theory rests upon the proposition that there is something *special*—something that cannot be justified by normal "rational basis" analysis—in making a disadvantaged group (or a nonpreferred group) resort to a higher decisionmaking level. That proposition finds no support in law or logic.

II

I turn next to whether there was a legitimate rational basis for the substance of the constitutional amendment—for the prohibition of special protection for homosexuals.[1] It is unsurprising that the Court avoids discussion of this question, since the answer is so obviously yes. The case most relevant to the issue before us today is not even mentioned in the Court's opinion: In *Bowers v. Hardwick,* 478 U.S. 186 (1986), we held that the Constitution does not prohibit what virtually all States had done from the founding of the Republic until very recent years—making homosexual conduct a crime. That holding is unassailable, except by those who think that the Constitution changes to suit current fashions. But in any event it is a given in the present case: Respondents' briefs did not urge overruling *Bowers,* and at oral argument respondents' counsel expressly disavowed any intent to seek such overruling. If it is constitutionally permissible for a State to make homosexual conduct criminal, surely it is constitutionally permissible for a State to enact other laws merely *disfavoring* homosexual conduct. (As the Court of Appeals for the District of Columbia Circuit has aptly put it: "If the Court

---

[1]   The Court evidently agrees that "rational basis"—the normal test for compliance with the Equal Protection Clause—is the governing standard. The trial court rejected respondents' argument that homosexuals constitute a "suspect" or "quasi suspect" class, and respondents elected not to appeal that ruling to the Supreme Court of Colorado. See *Evans* v. *Romer,* 882 P. 2d 1335, 1341, n. 3 (1994). And the Court implicitly rejects the Supreme Court of Colorado's holding, see *Evans* v. *Romer,* 854 P. 2d 1270, 1282 (1993), that Amendment 2 infringes upon a "fundamental right" of "independently identifiable class[es]" to "participate equally in the political process." *Ante,* at 4.

[in *Bowers*] was unwilling to object to state laws that criminalize the behavior that defines the class, it is hardly open . . . to conclude that state sponsored discrimination against the class is invidious. After all, there can hardly be more palpable discrimination against a class than making the conduct that defines the class criminal." *Padula v. Webster,* 822 F.2d 97, 103 (1987).) And *a fortiori* it is constitutionally permissible for a State to adopt a provision *not even* disfavoring homosexual conduct, but merely prohibiting all levels of state government from bestowing *special protections* upon homosexual conduct. Respondents (who, unlike the Court, cannot afford the luxury of ignoring inconvenient precedent) counter *Bowers* with the argument that a greater-includes-the-lesser rationale cannot justify Amendment 2's application to individuals who do not engage in homosexual acts, but are merely of homosexual "orientation." Some Courts of Appeals have concluded that, with respect to laws of this sort at least, that is a distinction without a difference. See *Equality Foundation of Greater Cincinnati, Inc. v. Cincinnati,* 54 F.3d 261, 267 (C.A.6 1995) ("[F]or purposes of these proceedings, it is virtually impossible to distinguish or separate individuals of a particular *orientation* which predisposes them toward a particular sexual conduct from those who actually *engage* in that particular type of sexual conduct"); *Steffan v. Perry,* 41 F.3d 677, 689–690 (C.A.D.C.1994). The Supreme Court of Colorado itself appears to be of this view. See 882 P.2d, at 1349–1350 ("Amendment 2 targets this class of persons based on four characteristics: sexual orientation; conduct; practices, and relationships. Each characteristic provides a potentially different way of identifying that class of persons who are gay, lesbian, or bisexual. These four characteristics are not truly severable from one another because each provides nothing more than a different way of identifying *the same class of persons*") (emphasis added).

But assuming that, in Amendment 2, a person of homosexual "orientation" is someone who does not engage in homosexual conduct but merely has a tendency or desire to do so, *Bowers* still suffices to establish a rational basis for the provision. If it is rational to criminalize the conduct, surely it is rational to deny special favor and protection to those with a self-avowed tendency or desire to engage in the conduct. Indeed, where criminal sanctions are not involved, homosexual "orientation" is an acceptable stand-in for homosexual conduct. A State "does not violate the Equal Protection Clause merely because the classifications made by its laws are imperfect," *Dandridge v. Williams,* 397 U.S. 471, 485 (1970). Just as a policy barring the hiring of methadone users as transit employees does not violate equal protection simply because *some* methadone users pose no threat to passenger safety, see *New York City Transit Authority v. Beazer,* 440 U.S. 568 (1979), and just as a mandatory retirement age of 50 for police officers does not violate equal protection even though it prematurely ends the careers of many policemen over 50 who still have the capacity to do the job, see *Massachusetts Bd. of Retirement v. Murgia,* 427 U.S. 307 (1976) *(per curiam),* Amendment 2 is not constitutionally invalid simply because it could have been drawn more precisely so as to withdraw special antidiscrimination protections only from those of homosexual "orientation" who actually engage in homosexual conduct. As Justice KENNEDY wrote, when he was on the Court of Appeals, in a case involving discharge of homosexuals from the Navy: "Nearly any statute which classifies people may be irrational as applied in particular cases. Discharge of the particular plaintiffs before us would be rational, under minimal scrutiny, not because their particular cases present the dangers which justify Navy policy, but instead because the general policy of discharging all homosexuals is rational." *Beller v. Middendorf,* 632 F.2d 788, 808–809, n. 20 (C.A.9 1980).

Moreover, even if the provision regarding homosexual "orientation" *were* invalid, respondents' challenge to Amendment 2—which is a facial challenge—must fail. "A facial challenge to a legislative Act is, of course, the most difficult challenge to mount successfully, since the challenger must establish that no set of circumstances exists under which the Act would be valid." *United States v. Salerno,* 481 U.S. 739, 745 (1987). It would not be enough for respondents to establish (if they could) that Amendment 2 is unconstitutional as applied to those of homosexual "orientation"; since, under *Bowers,* Amendment 2 is unquestionably constitutional as applied to those who engage in homosexual conduct, the facial challenge cannot succeed. Some individuals of homosexual "orientation" who do not engage in homosexual acts might successfully bring an as-applied challenge to Amendment 2, but so far as the record indicates, none of the respondents is such a person.

III

The foregoing suffices to establish what the Court's failure to cite any case remotely in point would lead one to suspect: No principle set forth in the Constitution, nor even any imagined by this Court in the past 200 years, prohibits what Colorado has done here. But the case for Colorado is much stronger than that. What it has done is not only unprohibited, but eminently reasonable, with close, congressionally approved precedent in earlier constitutional practice.

First, as to its eminent reasonableness. The Court's opinion contains grim, disapproving hints that Coloradans have been guilty of "animus" or "animosity" toward homosexuality, as though that has been established as un-American. Of course it is our moral heritage that one should not hate any human being or class of human beings. But I had thought that one could consider certain conduct reprehensible—murder, for example, or polygamy, or cruelty to animals—and could exhibit even "animus" toward such conduct. Surely that is the only sort of "animus" at issue here: moral disapproval of homosexual conduct, the same sort of moral disapproval that produced the centuries-old criminal laws that we held constitutional in *Bowers.* The Colorado amendment does not, to speak entirely precisely, prohibit giving favored status to people who are *homosexuals;* they can be favored for many reasons—for example, because they are senior citizens or members of racial minorities. But it prohibits giving them favored status *because of their homosexual conduct*—that is, it prohibits favored status *for homosexuality.*

But though Coloradans are, as I say, *entitled* to be hostile toward homosexual conduct, the fact is that the degree of hostility reflected by Amendment 2 is the smallest conceivable. The Court's portrayal of Coloradans as a society fallen victim to pointless, hate-filled "gay-bashing" is so false as to be comical. Colorado not only is one of the 25 States that have repealed their antisodomy laws, but was among the first to do so. See 1971 Colo. Sess. Laws, ch. 121, § 1. But the society that eliminates criminal punishment for homosexual acts does not necessarily abandon the view that homosexuality is morally wrong and socially harmful; often, abolition simply reflects the view that enforcement of such criminal laws involves unseemly intrusion into the intimate lives of citizens. Cf. Brief for Lambda Legal Defense and Education Fund, Inc., et al. as *Amici Curiae* in *Bowers v. Hardwick,* O.T. 1985, No. 85–140, p. 25, n. 21 (antisodomy statutes are "unenforceable by any but the most offensive snooping and wasteful allocation of law enforcement resources"); Kadish, The Crisis of Overcriminalization, 374 The Annals of the American Academy of Political and Social Science 157, 161 (1967) ("To obtain evidence [in sodomy cases], police are obliged to resort to behavior which tends to degrade and demean both themselves personally and law enforcement as an institution").

There is a problem, however, which arises when criminal sanction of homosexuality is eliminated but moral and social disapprobation of homosexuality is meant to be retained. The Court cannot be unaware of that problem; it is evident in many cities of the country, and occasionally bubbles to the surface of the news, in heated political disputes over such matters as the introduction into local schools of books teaching that homosexuality is an optional and fully acceptable "alternative life style." The problem (a problem, that is, for those who wish to retain social disapprobation of homosexuality) is that, because those who engage in homosexual conduct tend to reside in disproportionate numbers in certain communities, have high disposable income, and, of course, care about homosexual-rights issues much more ardently than the public at large, they possess political power much greater than their numbers, both locally and statewide. Quite understandably, they devote this political power to achieving not merely a grudging social toleration, but full social acceptance, of homosexuality.

By the time Coloradans were asked to vote on Amendment 2, their exposure to homosexuals' quest for social endorsement was not limited to newspaper accounts of happenings in places such as New York, Los Angeles, San Francisco, and Key West. Three Colorado cities—Aspen, Boulder, and Denver—had enacted ordinances that listed "sexual orientation" as an impermissible ground for discrimination, equating the moral disapproval of homosexual conduct with racial and religious bigotry. The phenomenon had even appeared statewide: The Governor of Colorado had signed an executive order pronouncing that "in the State of Colorado we recognize the diversity in our pluralistic society and strive to bring an end to discrimination in any form," and directing state agency-heads to "ensure non-discrimination" in hiring and promotion based on, among other things, "sexual orientation." do not mean to be critical of these legislative successes; homosexuals are as entitled to use the legal system for reinforcement of their moral sentiments as is the rest of society. But they are subject to being countered by lawful, democratic countermeasures as well.

That is where Amendment 2 came in. It sought to counter both the geographic concentration and the disproportionate political power of homosexuals by (1) resolving the controversy at the statewide level, and (2) making the election a single-issue contest for both sides. It put directly, to all the citizens of the State, the question: Should homosexuality be given special protection? They answered no. The Court today asserts that this most democratic of procedures is unconstitutional. Lacking any cases to establish that facially absurd proposition, it simply asserts that it *must* be unconstitutional, because it has never happened before.

> [Amendment 2] identifies persons by a single trait and then denies them protection across the board. The resulting disqualification of a class of persons from the right to seek specific protection from the law is unprecedented in our jurisprudence. The absence of precedent for Amendment 2 is itself instructive. . . .
>
> It is not within our constitutional tradition to enact laws of this sort. Central both to the idea of the rule of law and to our own Constitution's guarantee of equal protection is the principle that government and each of its parts remain open on impartial terms to all who seek its assistance.

As I have noted above, this is proved false every time a state law prohibiting or disfavoring certain conduct is passed, because such a law prevents the adversely affected group—whether drug addicts, or smokers, or gun owners, or motorcyclists—from changing the policy thus established in "each of [the] parts" of the State. What the Court says is even demonstrably false at the constitutional level. The Eighteenth Amendment to Federal Constitution, for example, deprived those who drank alcohol not only of the power to alter the policy of prohibition *locally* or through *state legislation,* but even of the power to alter it through *state constitutional amendment* or *federal legislation.* The Establishment Clause of the First Amendment prevents theocrats from having their way by converting their fellow citizens at the local, state, or federal statutory level; as does the Republican Form of Government Clause prevent monarchists.

But there is a much closer analogy, one that involves precisely the effort by the majority of citizens to preserve its view of sexual morality statewide, against the efforts of a geographically concentrated and politically powerful minority to undermine it. The Constitutions of the States of Arizona, Idaho, New Mexico, Oklahoma, and Utah *to this day* contain provisions stating that polygamy is "forever prohibited." See Ariz. Const., Art. XX, par. 2; Idaho Const., Art. I, § 4; N.M. Const., Art. XXI, § 1; Okla. Const., Art. I, § 2; Utah Const., Art. III, § 1. Polygamists, and those who have a polygamous "orientation," have been "singled out" by these provisions for much more severe treatment than merely denial of favored status; and that treatment can only be changed by achieving amendment of the state constitutions. The Court's disposition today suggests that these provisions are unconstitutional, and that polygamy must be permitted in these States on a state-legislated, or perhaps even local-option, basis—unless, of course, polygamists for some reason have fewer constitutional rights than homosexuals.

The United States Congress, by the way, *required* the inclusion of these antipolygamy provisions in the Constitutions of Arizona, New Mexico, Oklahoma, and Utah, as a condition of their admission to statehood. See Arizona Enabling Act, 36 Stat. 569; New Mexico Enabling Act, 36 Stat. 558; Oklahoma Enabling Act, 34 Stat. 269; Utah Enabling Act, 28 Stat. 108. (For Arizona, New Mexico, and Utah, moreover, the Enabling Acts required that the antipolygamy provisions be "irrevocable without the consent of the United States and the people of said State"— so that not only were "each of [the] parts" of these States not "open on impartial terms" to polygamists, but even the States as a whole were not; polygamists would have to persuade the whole country to their way of thinking.) Idaho adopted the constitutional provision on its own, but the 51st Congress, which admitted Idaho into the Union, found its Constitution to be "republican in form *and . . . in conformity with the Constitution of the United States.*" Act of Admission of Idaho, 26 Stat. 215 (emphasis added). Thus, this "singling out" of the sexual practices of a single group for statewide, democratic vote—so utterly alien to our constitutional system, the Court would have us believe—has not only happened, but has received the explicit approval of the United States Congress.

I cannot say that this Court has explicitly approved any of these state constitutional provisions; but it has approved a territorial statutory provision that went even further, depriving polygamists of the ability even to achieve a constitutional amendment, by depriving them of the power to vote. In *Davis v. Beason,* 133 U.S. 333 (1890), Justice Field wrote for a unanimous Court:

> In our judgment, § 501 of the Revised Statutes of Idaho Territory, which provides that 'no person . . . who is a bigamist or polygamist or who teaches, advises, counsels, or encourages any person or persons to become bigamists or polygamists, or to

commit any other crime defined by law, or to enter into what is known as plural or celestial marriage, or who is a member of any order, organization or association which teaches, advises, counsels, or encourages its members or devotees or any other persons to commit the crime of bigamy or polygamy, or any other crime defined by law . . . is permitted to vote at any election, or to hold any position or office of honor, trust, or profit within this Territory,' *is not open to any constitutional or legal objection.*

To the extent, if any, that this opinion permits the imposition of adverse consequences upon mere abstract advocacy of polygamy, it has, of course, been overruled by later cases. See *Brandenburg v. Ohio,* 395 U.S. 444 (1969) *(per curiam).* But the proposition that polygamy can be criminalized, and those engaging in that crime deprived of the vote, remains good law. See *Richardson v. Ramirez,* 418 U.S. 24, 53 (1974). *Beason* rejected the argument that such discrimination is a denial of the equal protection of the laws. Among the Justices joining in that rejection were the two whose views in other cases the Court today treats as equal protection lodestars—Justice Harlan, who was to proclaim in *Plessy v. Ferguson,* 163 U.S. 537, 559 (1896) (dissenting opinion), that the Constitution "neither knows nor tolerates classes among citizens," and Justice Bradley, who had earlier declared that "class legislation . . . [is] obnoxious to the prohibitions of the Fourteenth Amendment," *Civil Rights Cases,* 109 U.S. 3, 24 (1883).[3]

This Court cited *Beason* with approval as recently as 1993, in an opinion authored by the same Justice who writes for the Court today. That opinion said: "[A]dverse impact will not always lead to a finding of impermissible targeting. For example, a social harm may have been a legitimate concern of government for reasons quite apart from discrimination. . . . See, e.g., . . . *Davis v. Beason,* 133 U.S. 333 (1890)." *Church of Lukumi Babalu Aye, Inc. v. Hialeah,* 508 U.S. 520, 535 (1993). It remains to be explained how § 501 of the Idaho Revised Statutes was

---

[3]   The Court labors mightily to get around *Beason,* see *ante,* at 12–13, but cannot escape the central fact that this Court found the statute at issue—which went much further than Amendment 2, denying polygamists not merely special treatment but the right *to vote*—"not open to any constitutional or legal objection," rejecting the appellant's argument (much like the argument of respondents today) that the statute impermissibly "single[d] him out," Brief for Appellant in *Davis* v. *Beason,* O. T. 1889, No. 1261, p. 41. The Court adopts my conclusions that (a) insofar as *Beason* permits the imposition of adverse consequences based upon mere advocacy, it has been overruled by subsequent cases, and (b) insofar as *Beason* holds that convicted felons may be denied the right to vote, it remains good law. To these conclusions, it adds something new: the claim that "[t]o the extent [*Beason*] held that the groups designated in the statute may be deprived of the right to vote because of their status, its ruling could not stand without surviving strict scrutiny, a most doubtful outcome." *Ante,* at 12–13. But if that is so, it is only because we have declared the right *to vote* to be a "fundamental political right," see, *e.g., Dunn* v. *Blumstein,* 405 U.S. 330, 336 (1972), deprivation of which triggers strict scrutiny. Amendment 2, of course, does not deny the fundamental right to vote, and the Court rejects the Colorado court's view that there exists a fundamental right to participate in the political process. Strict scrutiny is thus not in play here. See *ante,* at 10. Finally, the Court's suggestion that § 501 of the Revised Statutes of Idaho, and Amendment 2, deny rights on account of "status" (rather than conduct) opens up a broader debate involving the significance of *Bowers* to this case, a debate which the Court is otherwise unwilling to join.

not an "impermissible targeting" of polygamists, but (the much more mild) Amendment 2 is an "impermissible targeting" of homosexuals. Has the Court concluded that the perceived social harm of polygamy is a "legitimate concern of government," and the perceived social harm of homosexuality is not?

IV

I strongly suspect that the answer to the last question is yes, which leads me to the last point I wish to make: The Court today, announcing that Amendment 2 "defies . . . conventional [constitutional] inquiry" and "confounds [the] normal process of judicial review" employs a constitutional theory heretofore unknown to frustrate Colorado's reasonable effort to preserve traditional American moral values. The Court's stern disapproval of "animosity" towards homosexuality might be compared with what an earlier Court (including the revered Justices Harlan and Bradley) said in *Murphy v. Ramsey,* 114 U.S. 15 (1885), rejecting a constitutional challenge to a United States statute that denied the franchise in federal territories to those who engaged in polygamous cohabitation:

> [C]ertainly no legislation can be supposed more wholesome and necessary in the founding of a free, self-governing commonwealth, fit to take rank as one of the co-ordinate States of the Union, than that which seeks to establish it on the basis of the idea of the family, as consisting in and springing from the union for life of one man and one woman in the holy estate of matrimony; the sure foundation of all that is stable and noble in our civilization; the best guaranty of that reverent morality which is the source of all beneficent progress in social and political improvement.

I would not myself indulge in such official praise for heterosexual monogamy, because I think it no business of the courts (as opposed to the political branches) to take sides in this culture war.

But the Court today has done so, not only by inventing a novel and extravagant constitutional doctrine to take the victory away from traditional forces, but even by verbally disparaging as bigotry adherence to traditional attitudes. To suggest, for example, that this constitutional amendment springs from nothing more than " 'a bare . . . desire to harm a politically unpopular group,' " is nothing short of insulting. (It is also nothing short of preposterous to call "politically unpopular" a group which enjoys enormous influence in American media and politics, and which, as the trial court here noted, though composing no more than 4% of the population had the support of 46% of the voters on Amendment 2.)

When the Court takes sides in the culture wars, it tends to be with the knights rather than the villeins—and more specifically with the Templars, reflecting the views and values of the lawyer class from which the Court's Members are drawn. How that class feels about homosexuality will be evident to anyone who wishes to interview job applicants at virtually any of the Nation's law schools. The interviewer may refuse to offer a job because the applicant is a Republican; because he is an adulterer; because he went to the wrong prep school or belongs to the wrong country club; because he eats snails; because he is a womanizer; because she wears real-animal fur; or even because he hates the Chicago Cubs. But if the interviewer should wish not to be an associate or partner of an applicant because he disapproves of the applicant's homosexuality, *then* he will have violated the pledge which the Association of American Law Schools requires all its member schools to exact from job interviewers: "assurance of the employer's willingness" to hire homosexuals. Bylaws of the Association of American Law Schools, Inc. § 6–4(b). This law-school view of what "prejudices" must be stamped out may be contrasted with the more plebeian attitudes that apparently still prevail in the United States Congress, which has been unresponsive to repeated attempts to extend to homosexuals the protections of federal civil rights laws, see, *e.g.,* Employment Non-Discrimination Act of 1994, S. 2238, 103d Cong., 2d Sess. (1994); Civil Rights Amendments of 1975, H.R. 5452, 94th Cong., 1st Sess. (1975), and which took the pains to exclude them specifically from the Americans with Disabilities Act of 1990, see 42 U.S.C. § 12211(a) (1988 ed., Supp. V).

* * *

Today's opinion has no foundation in American constitutional law, and barely pretends to. The people of Colorado have adopted an entirely reasonable provision which does not even disfavor homosexuals in any substantive sense, but merely denies them preferential treatment. Amendment 2 is designed to prevent piecemeal deterioration of the sexual morality favored by a majority of Coloradans, and is not only an appropriate means to that legitimate end, but a means that Americans have employed before. Striking it down is an act, not of judicial judgment, but of political will. I dissent.

Lawrence v. Texas

539 U.S. 558 (2003)

■ **JUSTICE KENNEDY delivered the opinion of the Court.**

Liberty protects the person from unwarranted government intrusions into a dwelling or other private places. In our tradition the State is not omnipresent in the home. And there are other spheres of our lives and existence, outside the home, where the State should not be a dominant presence. Freedom extends beyond spatial bounds. Liberty presumes an autonomy of self that includes freedom of thought, belief, expression, and certain intimate conduct. The instant case involves liberty of the person both in its spatial and more transcendent dimensions.

I

The question before the Court is the validity of a Texas statute making it a crime for two persons of the same sex to engage in certain intimate sexual conduct.

In Houston, Texas, officers of the Harris County Police Department were dispatched to a private residence in response to a reported weapons disturbance. They entered an apartment where one of the petitioners, John Geddes Lawrence, resided. The right of the police to enter does not seem to have been questioned. The officers observed Lawrence and another man, Tyron Garner, engaging in a sexual act. The two petitioners were arrested, held in custody over night, and charged and convicted before a Justice of the Peace.

The complaints described their crime as "deviate sexual intercourse, namely anal sex, with a member of the same sex (man)." The applicable state law . . . provides: "A person commits an offense if he engages in deviate sexual intercourse with another individual of the same sex." The statute defines "[d]eviate sexual intercourse" as follows:

(A) any contact between any part of the genitals of one person and the mouth or anus of another person; or

(B) the penetration of the genitals or the anus of another person with an object.

The petitioners . . . challenged the statute as a violation of the Equal Protection Clause of the Fourteenth Amendment and of a like provision of the Texas Constitution. Those contentions were rejected. The petitioners, having entered a plea of *nolo contendere*, were each fined $200 and assessed court costs of $141.25.

The Court of Appeals for the Texas Fourteenth District . . . rejected the constitutional arguments and affirmed the convictions. [T]he Court of Appeals considered our decision in *Bowers v. Hardwick*, 478 U.S. 186 (1986), to be controlling on the federal due process aspect of the case. . . .

The petitioners were adults at the time of the alleged offense. Their conduct was in private and consensual.

II

We conclude the case should be resolved by determining whether the petitioners were free as adults to engage in the private conduct in the exercise of their liberty under the Due Process Clause of the Fourteenth Amendment to the Constitution. For this inquiry we deem it necessary to reconsider the Court's holding in *Bowers*.

In [*Griswold v. Connecticut*], the Court invalidated a state law prohibiting the use of drugs or devices of contraception and counseling or aiding and abetting the use of contraceptives. The Court described the protected interest as a right to privacy and placed emphasis on the marriage relation and the protected space of the marital bedroom.

After *Griswold* it was established that the right to make certain decisions regarding sexual conduct extends beyond the marital relationship. In *Eisenstadt v. Baird,* 405 U.S. 438 (1972), the Court invalidated a law prohibiting the distribution of contraceptives to unmarried persons. . . . The opinions in *Griswold* and *Eisenstadt* were part of the background for the decision in *Roe v. Wade.* . . . Although the Court held the woman's rights were not absolute, her right to elect an abortion did have real and substantial protection as an exercise of her liberty under the Due Process Clause. The Court cited cases that protect spatial freedom and cases that go well beyond it. *Roe* recognized the right of a woman to make certain fundamental decisions affecting her destiny and confirmed once more that the protection of liberty under the Due Process Clause has a substantive dimension of fundamental significance in defining the rights of the person.

In *Carey v. Population Services Int'l*, 431 U.S. 678 (1977), the Court confronted a New York law forbidding sale or distribution of contraceptive devices to persons under 16 years of age. Although there was no single opinion for the Court, the law was invalidated. Both *Eisenstadt* and *Carey*, as well as the holding and rationale in *Roe*, confirmed that the reasoning of *Griswold* could not be confined to the protection of rights of married adults. . . .

The facts in *Bowers* had some similarities to the instant case. A police officer, whose right to enter seems not to have been in question, observed Hardwick, in his own bedroom, engaging in intimate sexual conduct with another adult male. The conduct was in violation of a Georgia statute making it a criminal offense to engage in sodomy. One difference between the two cases is that the Georgia statute prohibited the conduct whether or not the participants were of the same sex, while the Texas statute, as we have seen, applies only to participants of the same sex. Hardwick was not prosecuted, but he brought an action in federal court to declare the state statute invalid. He alleged he was a practicing homosexual and that the criminal prohibition violated rights guaranteed to him by the Constitution. The Court, in an opinion by Justice White, sustained the Georgia law. Chief Justice Burger and Justice Powell joined the opinion of the Court and filed separate, concurring opinions. Four Justices dissented.

The Court began its substantive discussion in *Bowers* as follows: "The issue presented is whether the Federal Constitution confers a fundamental right upon homosexuals to engage in sodomy and hence invalidates the laws of the many States that still make such conduct illegal and have done so for a very long time." That statement, we now conclude, discloses the Court's own failure to appreciate the extent of the liberty at stake. To say that the issue in *Bowers* was simply the right to engage in certain sexual conduct demeans the claim the individual put forward, just as it would demean a married couple were it to be said marriage is simply about the right to have sexual intercourse. The laws involved in *Bowers* and here . . . have more far-reaching consequences, touching upon the most private human conduct, sexual behavior, and in the most private of places, the home. The statutes do seek to control a personal relationship that, whether or not entitled to formal recognition in the law, is within the liberty of persons to choose without being punished as criminals.

This, as a general rule, should counsel against attempts by the State, or a court, to define the meaning of the relationship or to set its boundaries absent injury to a person or abuse of an institution the law protects. It suffices for us to acknowledge that adults may choose to enter upon this relationship in the confines of their homes and their own private lives and still retain their dignity as free persons. When sexuality finds overt expression in intimate conduct with another person, the conduct can be but one element in a personal bond that is more enduring. The liberty protected by the Constitution allows homosexual persons the right to make this choice.

Having misapprehended the claim of liberty there presented to it, and thus stating the claim to be whether there is a fundamental right to engage in consensual sodomy, the *Bowers* Court said: "Proscriptions against that conduct have ancient roots." . . . At the outset it should be noted that there is no longstanding history in this country of laws directed at homosexual conduct as a distinct matter. . . . The English prohibition was understood to include relations between men and women as well as relations between men and men. Nineteenth-century commentators similarly read American sodomy, buggery, and crime-against-nature statutes as criminalizing certain relations between men and women and between men and men. . . . Thus early American sodomy laws were not directed at homosexuals as such but instead sought to prohibit nonprocreative sexual activity more generally. This does not suggest approval of homosexual conduct. It does tend to show that this particular form of conduct was not thought of as a separate category from like conduct between heterosexual persons.

Laws prohibiting sodomy do not seem to have been enforced against consenting adults acting in private. A substantial number of sodomy prosecutions and convictions for which there are surviving records were for predatory acts against those who could not or did not consent, as in the case of a minor or the victim of an assault. As to these, one purpose for the prohibitions was to ensure there would be no lack of coverage if a predator committed a sexual assault that did not constitute rape as defined by the criminal law. . . .

To the extent that there were any prosecutions for the acts in question, 19th-century evidence rules imposed a burden that would make a conviction more difficult to obtain even taking into account the problems always inherent in prosecuting consensual acts committed in private. . . . The rule may explain in part the infrequency of these prosecutions. In all events that infrequency makes it difficult to say that society approved of a rigorous and systematic punishment of the consensual acts committed in private and by adults. . . . It was not until the 1970's that any State singled out same-sex relations for criminal prosecution, and only nine States have done so. Post-*Bowers* even some of these States did not adhere to the policy of suppressing homosexual conduct. Over the course of the last decades, States with same-sex prohibitions have moved toward abolishing them.

In summary, the historical grounds relied upon in *Bowers* are more complex than the majority opinion and the concurring opinion by Chief Justice Burger indicate. Their historical premises are not without doubt and, at the very least, are overstated.

It must be acknowledged, of course, that the Court in *Bowers* was making the broader point that for centuries there have been powerful voices to condemn homosexual conduct as immoral. The condemnation has been shaped by religious beliefs, conceptions of right and acceptable behavior, and respect for the traditional family. For many persons these are not trivial concerns but profound and deep convictions accepted as ethical and moral principles to which they aspire and which thus determine the course of their lives. These considerations do not answer the question before us, however. The issue is whether the majority may use the power of the State to enforce these views on the whole society through operation of the criminal law.

Chief Justice Burger joined the opinion for the Court in *Bowers* and further explained his views as follows: "Decisions of individuals relating to homosexual conduct have been subject to state intervention throughout the history of Western civilization. Condemnation of those practices is firmly rooted in Judeao-Christian moral and ethical standards." . . . [W]e think that our laws and traditions in the past half century . . . show an emerging awareness that liberty gives substantial protection to adult persons in deciding how to conduct their private lives in matters pertaining to sex. "[H]istory and tradition are the starting point but not in all cases the ending point of the substantive due process inquiry."

This emerging recognition should have been apparent when *Bowers* was decided. In 1955 the American Law Institute promulgated the Model Penal Code and made clear that it did not recommend or provide for "criminal penalties for consensual sexual relations conducted in private." It justified its decision on three grounds: (1) The prohibitions undermined respect for the law by penalizing conduct many people engaged in; (2) the statutes regulated private conduct not harmful to others; and (3) the laws were arbitrarily enforced and thus invited the danger of blackmail. In 1961 Illinois changed its laws to conform to the Model Penal Code. Other States soon followed.

In *Bowers* the Court referred to the fact that before 1961 all 50 States had outlawed sodomy, and that at the time of the Court's decision 24 States and the District of Columbia had sodomy laws. Justice Powell pointed out that these prohibitions often were being ignored, however. Georgia, for instance, had not sought to enforce its law for decades.

The sweeping references by Chief Justice Burger to the history of Western civilization and to Judeo-Christian moral and ethical standards did not take account of other authorities pointing in an opposite direction. A committee advising the British Parliament recommended in 1957 repeal of laws punishing homosexual conduct. Parliament enacted the substance of those recommendations 10 years later.

Of even more importance, almost five years before *Bowers* was decided the European Court of Human Rights considered a case with parallels to *Bowers* and to today's case. An adult male resident in Northern Ireland alleged he was a practicing homosexual who desired to engage in consensual homosexual conduct. The laws of Northern Ireland forbade him that right. He alleged that he had been questioned, his home had been searched, and he feared criminal prosecution. The court held that the laws proscribing the conduct were invalid under the European Convention on Human Rights. *Dudgeon v. United Kingdom*, 45 Eur. Ct. H. R. (1981) ¶ *52*. Authoritative in all countries that are members of the Council of Europe (21 nations then, 45 nations now), the decision is at odds with the premise in *Bowers* that the claim put forward was insubstantial in our Western civilization.

In our own constitutional system the deficiencies in *Bowers* became even more apparent in the years following its announcement. The 25 States with laws prohibiting the relevant conduct referenced in the *Bowers* decision are reduced now to 13, of which 4 enforce their laws only against homosexual conduct. In those States where sodomy is still proscribed, whether for same-sex or heterosexual conduct, there is a pattern of nonenforcement with respect to consenting adults acting in private. The State of Texas admitted in 1994 that as of that date it had not prosecuted anyone under those circumstances.

Two principal cases decided after *Bowers* cast its holding into even more doubt. In *Planned Parenthood of Southeastern Pa. v. Casey*, the Court reaffirmed the substantive force of the liberty protected by the Due Process Clause. . . . In explaining the respect the Constitution demands for the autonomy of the person in making these choices, we stated as follows:

> These matters, involving the most intimate and personal choices a person may make in a lifetime, choices central to personal dignity and autonomy, are central to the liberty protected by the Fourteenth Amendment. At the heart of liberty is the right to define one's own concept of existence, of meaning, of the universe, and of the mystery of human life. Beliefs about these matters could not define the attributes of personhood were they formed under compulsion of the State.

Persons in a homosexual relationship may seek autonomy for these purposes, just as heterosexual persons do. The decision in *Bowers* would deny them this right.

The second post-*Bowers* case of principal relevance is *Romer v. Evans,* 517 U.S. 620 (1996). There the Court struck down class-based legislation directed at homosexuals as a violation of the Equal Protection Clause. *Romer* invalidated an amendment to Colorado's constitution which named as a solitary class persons who were homosexuals, lesbians, or bisexual either by "orientation, conduct, practices or relationships," and deprived them of protection under state antidiscrimination laws. We concluded that the provision was "born of animosity toward the class of persons affected" and further that it had no rational relation to a legitimate governmental purpose.

As an alternative argument in this case, counsel for the petitioners and some *amici* contend that *Romer* provides the basis for declaring the Texas statute invalid under the Equal Protection Clause. That is a tenable argument, but we conclude the instant case requires us to address whether *Bowers* itself has continuing validity. Were we to hold the statute invalid under the Equal Protection Clause some might question whether a prohibition would be valid if drawn differently, say, to prohibit the conduct both between same-sex and different-sex participants.

Equality of treatment and the due process right to demand respect for conduct protected by the substantive guarantee of liberty are linked in important respects, and a decision on the latter point advances both interests. If protected conduct is made criminal and the law which does so remains unexamined for its substantive validity, its stigma might remain even if it were not enforceable as drawn for equal protection reasons. When homosexual conduct is made criminal by the law of the State, that declaration in and of itself is an invitation to subject homosexual persons to discrimination both in the public and in the private spheres. The central holding of *Bowers* has been brought in question by this case, and it should be addressed. Its continuance as precedent demeans the lives of homosexual persons.

The stigma this criminal statute imposes, moreover, is not trivial. The offense, to be sure, is but a class C misdemeanor, a minor offense in the Texas legal system. Still, it remains a criminal offense with all that imports for the dignity of the persons charged. The petitioners will bear on their record the history of their criminal convictions. . . .

The foundations of *Bowers* have sustained serious erosion from our recent decisions in *Casey* and *Romer*. When our precedent has been thus weakened, criticism from other sources is of greater significance. In the United States criticism of *Bowers* has been substantial and continuing, disapproving of its reasoning in all respects, not just as to its historical assumptions. The courts of five different States have declined to follow it in interpreting provisions in their own state constitutions parallel to the Due Process Clause of the Fourteenth Amendment.

To the extent *Bowers* relied on values we share with a wider civilization, it should be noted that the reasoning and holding in *Bowers* have been rejected elsewhere. The European Court of Human Rights has followed not *Bowers* but its own decision in *Dudgeon v. United Kingdom.* See *P.G. & J.H. v. United Kingdom*, App. No. 00044787/98, ¶ *56* (Eur. Ct. *H.R.,* Sept. 25, 2001); *Modinos v. Cyprus*, 259 Eur. Ct. *H.R.* (1993); *Norris v. Ireland*, 142 Eur. Ct. *H.R.* (1988). Other nations, too, have taken action consistent with an affirmation of the protected right of homosexual adults to engage in intimate, consensual conduct. The right the petitioners seek in this case has been accepted as an integral part of human freedom in many other countries. There has been no showing that in this country the governmental interest in circumscribing personal choice is somehow more legitimate or urgent.

The doctrine of *stare decisis* is essential to the respect accorded to the judgments of the Court and to the stability of the law. It is not, however, an inexorable command. . . . [T]here has been no individual or societal reliance on *Bowers* of the sort that could counsel against overturning its holding once there are compelling reasons to do so. *Bowers* itself causes uncertainty, for the precedents before and after its issuance contradict its central holding. . . .

Bowers was not correct when it was decided, and it is not correct today. It ought not to remain binding precedent. *Bowers v. Hardwick* should be and now is overruled.

The present case does not involve minors. It does not involve persons who might be injured or coerced or who are situated in relationships where consent might not easily be refused. It does not involve public conduct or prostitution. It does not involve whether the government must give formal recognition to any relationship that homosexual persons seek to enter. The case does involve two adults who, with full and mutual consent from each other, engaged in sexual practices common to a homosexual lifestyle. The petitioners are entitled to respect for their private lives. The State cannot demean their existence or control their destiny by making their private sexual conduct a crime. Their right to liberty under the Due Process Clause gives them the full right to engage in their conduct without intervention of the government. "It is a promise of the Constitution that there is a realm of personal liberty which the government may not enter." The Texas statute furthers no legitimate state interest which can justify its intrusion into the personal and private life of the individual.

Had those who drew and ratified the Due Process Clauses of the Fifth Amendment or the Fourteenth Amendment known the components of liberty in its manifold possibilities, they might have been more specific. They did not presume to have this insight. They knew times can blind us to certain truths and later generations can see that laws once thought necessary and proper in fact serve only to oppress. As the Constitution endures, persons in every generation can invoke its principles in their own search for greater freedom.

The judgment of the Court of Appeals for the Texas Fourteenth District is reversed, and the case is remanded for further proceedings not inconsistent with this opinion.

■ JUSTICE O'CONNOR, concurring in the judgment.

. . . I joined *Bowers*, and do not join the Court in overruling it. Nevertheless, I agree with the Court that Texas' statute banning same-sex sodomy is unconstitutional. Rather than relying on the substantive component of the Fourteenth Amendment's Due Process Clause, as the Court does, I base my conclusion on the Fourteenth Amendment's Equal Protection Clause.

The Equal Protection Clause of the Fourteenth Amendment "is essentially a direction that all persons similarly situated should be treated alike." Under our rational basis standard of review, "legislation is presumed to be valid and will be sustained if the classification drawn by the statute is rationally related to a legitimate state interest."

Laws such as economic or tax legislation that are scrutinized under rational basis review normally pass constitutional muster, since "the Constitution presumes that even improvident decisions will eventually be rectified by the democratic processes." We have consistently held, however, that some objectives, such as "a bare . . . desire to harm a politically unpopular group," are not legitimate state interests. When a law exhibits such a desire to harm a politically unpopular group, we have applied a more searching form of rational basis review to strike down such laws under the Equal Protection Clause.

We have been most likely to apply rational basis review to hold a law unconstitutional under the Equal Protection Clause where, as here, the challenged legislation inhibits personal relationships. In *Department of Agriculture v. Moreno*, 413 U.S. 528 (1973), for example, we held that a law preventing those households containing an individual unrelated to any other member of the household from receiving food stamps violated equal protection because the purpose of the law was to " 'discriminate against hippies.' " The asserted governmental interest in preventing food stamp fraud was not deemed sufficient to satisfy rational basis review. In *Eisenstadt v. Baird*, we refused to sanction a law that discriminated between married and unmarried persons by prohibiting the distribution of contraceptives to single persons. Likewise, in *Cleburne v. Cleburne Living Center*, 473 U.S. 432 (1985), we held that it was irrational for a State to require a home for the mentally disabled to obtain a special use permit when other residences—like fraternity houses and apartment buildings—did not have to obtain such a permit. And in *Romer v. Evans*, we disallowed a state statute that "impos[ed] a broad and undifferentiated disability on a single named group"—specifically, homosexuals. . . .

The statute at issue here makes sodomy a crime only if a person "engages in deviate sexual intercourse with another individual of the same sex." Sodomy between opposite-sex partners, however, is not a crime in Texas. That is, Texas treats the same conduct differently based solely on the participants. Those harmed by this law are people who have a same-sex sexual orientation and thus are more likely to engage in behavior prohibited by § 21.06.

The Texas statute makes homosexuals unequal in the eyes of the law by making particular conduct—and only that conduct—subject to criminal sanction. It appears that prosecutions under Texas' sodomy law are rare. This case shows, however, that prosecutions under § 21.06 *do* occur. And while the penalty imposed on petitioners in this case was relatively minor, the consequences of conviction are not. As the Court notes, petitioners' convictions, if upheld, would disqualify them from or restrict their ability to engage in a variety of professions, including medicine, athletic training, and interior design. Indeed, were petitioners to move to one of four States, their convictions would require them to register as sex offenders to local law enforcement.

And the effect of Texas' sodomy law is not just limited to the threat of prosecution or consequence of conviction. Texas' sodomy law brands all homosexuals as criminals, thereby making it more difficult for homosexuals to be treated in the same manner as everyone else. Indeed, Texas itself has previously acknowledged the collateral effects of the law, stipulating in a prior challenge to this action that the law "legally sanctions discrimination against [homosexuals] in a variety of ways unrelated to the criminal law," including in the areas of "employment, family issues, and housing."

Texas attempts to justify its law, and the effects of the law, by arguing that the statute satisfies rational basis review because it furthers the legitimate governmental interest of the promotion of morality. . . . This case raises a different issue than *Bowers*: whether, under the Equal Protection Clause, moral disapproval is a legitimate state interest to justify by itself a statute that bans homosexual sodomy, but not heterosexual sodomy. It is not. Moral disapproval of this group, like a bare desire to harm the group, is an interest that is insufficient to satisfy rational basis review under the Equal Protection Clause. . . .

Moral disapproval of a group cannot be a legitimate governmental interest under the Equal Protection Clause because legal classifications must not be "drawn for the purpose of disadvantaging the group burdened by the law." Texas' invocation of moral disapproval as a legitimate state interest proves nothing more than Texas' desire to criminalize homosexual sodomy. But the Equal Protection Clause prevents a State from creating "a classification of persons undertaken for its own sake." And because Texas so rarely enforces its sodomy law as applied to private, consensual acts, the law serves more as a statement of dislike and disapproval against homosexuals than as a tool to stop criminal behavior. The Texas sodomy law "raise[s] the inevitable inference that the disadvantage imposed is born of animosity toward the class of persons affected."

Texas argues, however, that the sodomy law does not discriminate against homosexual persons. Instead, the State maintains that the law discriminates only against homosexual conduct. While it is true that the law applies only to conduct, the conduct targeted by this law is conduct that is closely correlated with being homosexual. Under such circumstances, Texas' sodomy law is targeted at more than conduct. It is instead directed toward gay persons as a class. "After all, there can hardly be more palpable discrimination against a class than making the conduct that defines the class criminal." When a State makes homosexual conduct criminal, and not "deviate sexual intercourse" committed by persons of different sexes, "that declaration in and of itself is an invitation to subject homosexual persons to discrimination both in the public and in the private spheres." . . .

A State can of course assign certain consequences to a violation of its criminal law. But the State cannot single out one identifiable class of citizens for punishment that does not apply to everyone else, with moral disapproval as the only asserted state interest for the law. The Texas sodomy statute subjects homosexuals to "a lifelong penalty and stigma. A legislative classification that threatens the creation of an underclass . . . cannot be reconciled with" the Equal Protection Clause.

Whether a sodomy law that is neutral both in effect and application would violate the substantive component of the Due Process Clause is an issue that need not be decided today. I am confident, however, that so long as the Equal Protection Clause requires a sodomy law to apply equally to the private consensual conduct of homosexuals and heterosexuals alike, such a law would not long stand in our democratic society. In the words of Justice Jackson:

> The framers of the Constitution knew, and we should not forget today, that there is no more effective practical guaranty against arbitrary and unreasonable government than to require that the principles of law which officials would impose upon a minority be imposed generally. Conversely, nothing opens the door to arbitrary action so effectively as to allow those officials to pick and choose only a few to whom they will apply legislation and thus to escape the political retribution that might be visited upon them if larger numbers were affected. *Railway Express Agency, Inc. v. New York*, 336 U.S. 106 (1949) (concurring opinion).

That this law as applied to private, consensual conduct is unconstitutional under the Equal Protection Clause does not mean that other laws distinguishing between heterosexuals and homosexuals would similarly fail under rational basis review. Texas cannot assert any legitimate state interest here, such as national security or preserving the traditional institution of marriage. Unlike the moral disapproval of same-sex relations—the asserted state interest in this case—other reasons exist to promote the institution of marriage beyond mere moral disapproval of an excluded group. . . .

■ JUSTICE SCALIA, with whom THE CHIEF JUSTICE and JUSTICE THOMAS join, dissenting.

"Liberty finds no refuge in a jurisprudence of doubt." That was the Court's sententious response, barely more than a decade ago, to those seeking to overrule *Roe v. Wade*. The Court's response today, to those who have engaged in a 17-year crusade to overrule *Bowers v. Hardwick*, is very different. The need for stability and certainty presents no barrier.

Most of the rest of today's opinion has no relevance to its actual holding—that the Texas statute "furthers no legitimate state interest which can justify" its application to petitioners under rational-basis review. Though there is discussion of "fundamental proposition[s]" and "fundamental decisions," nowhere does the Court's opinion declare that homosexual sodomy is a "fundamental right" under the Due Process Clause; nor does it subject the Texas law to the standard of review that would be appropriate (strict scrutiny) if homosexual sodomy *were* a "fundamental right." Thus, while overruling the *outcome* of *Bowers*, the Court leaves strangely untouched its central legal conclusion: "[R]espondent would have us announce . . . a fundamental right to engage in homosexual sodomy. This we are quite unwilling to do." Instead the Court simply describes petitioners' conduct as "an exercise of their liberty"—which it undoubtedly is—and proceeds to apply an unheard-of form of rational-basis review that will have far-reaching implications beyond this case.

I

I begin with the Court's surprising readiness to reconsider a decision rendered a mere 17 years ago in *Bowers v. Hardwick*. I do not myself believe in rigid adherence to *stare decisis* in constitutional cases; but I do believe that we should be consistent rather than manipulative in invoking the doctrine. Today's opinions in support of reversal do not bother to distinguish—or indeed, even bother to mention—the paean to *stare decisis* coauthored by three Members of today's majority in *Planned Parenthood v. Casey*. There, when *stare decisis* meant preservation of judicially invented abortion rights, the widespread criticism of *Roe* was strong reason to *reaffirm* it:

> Where, in the performance of its judicial duties, the Court decides a case in such a way as to resolve the sort of intensely divisive controversy reflected in *Roe*[,] . . . its decision has a dimension that the resolution of the normal case does not carry . . . . [T]o overrule under fire in the absence of the most

compelling reason ... would subvert the Court's legitimacy beyond any serious question.

Today, however, the widespread opposition to *Bowers*, a decision resolving an issue as "intensely divisive" as the issue in *Roe*, is offered as a reason in favor of *overruling* it. Gone, too, is any "enquiry" (of the sort conducted in *Casey*) into whether the decision sought to be overruled has "proven 'unworkable.' "

Today's approach to *stare decisis* invites us to overrule an erroneously decided precedent ... *if:* (1) its foundations have been "eroded" by subsequent decisions; (2) it has been subject to "substantial and continuing" criticism; and (3) it has not induced "individual or societal reliance" that counsels against overturning. The problem is that *Roe* itself—which today's majority surely has no disposition to overrule—satisfies these conditions to at least the same degree as *Bowers*. ...

I do not quarrel with the Court's claim that *Romer v. Evans* "eroded" the "foundations" of *Bowers'* rational-basis holding. But *Roe* and *Casey* have been equally "eroded" by *Washington v. Glucksberg*, which held that *only* fundamental rights which are "deeply rooted in this Nation's history and tradition" qualify for anything other than rational basis scrutiny under the doctrine of "substantive due process." *Roe* and *Casey*, of course, subjected the restriction of abortion to heightened scrutiny without even attempting to establish that the freedom to abort *was* rooted in this Nation's tradition.

Bowers, the Court says, has been subject to "substantial and continuing [criticism]. . . ." Of course, *Roe* too (and by extension *Casey*) had been (and still is) subject to unrelenting criticism, including criticism from the two commentators cited by the Court today.

That leaves, to distinguish the rock-solid, unamendable disposition of *Roe* from the readily overrulable *Bowers*, only the third factor. . . . It seems to me that the "societal reliance" on the principles confirmed in *Bowers* and discarded today has been overwhelming. Countless judicial decisions and legislative enactments have relied on the ancient proposition that a governing majority's belief that certain sexual behavior is "immoral and unacceptable" constitutes a rational basis for regulation. . . . State laws against bigamy, same-sex marriage, adult incest, prostitution, masturbation, adultery, fornication, bestiality, and obscenity are likewise sustainable only in light of *Bowers'* validation of laws based on moral choices. Every single one of these laws is called into question by today's decision. . . . The impossibility of distinguishing homosexuality from other traditional "morals" offenses is precisely why *Bowers* rejected the rational-basis challenge. "The law," it said, "is constantly based on notions of morality, and if all laws representing essentially moral choices are to be invalidated under the Due Process Clause, the courts will be very busy indeed."

What a massive disruption of the current social order, therefore, the overruling of *Bowers* entails. Not so the overruling of *Roe*, which would simply have restored the regime that existed for centuries before 1973, in which the permissibility of and restrictions upon abortion were determined legislatively State-by-State. . . . To tell the truth, it does not surprise me, and should surprise no one, that the Court has chosen today to revise the standards of *stare decisis* set forth in *Casey*. It has thereby exposed *Casey*'s extraordinary deference to precedent for the result-oriented expedient that it is.

II

Having decided that it need not adhere to *stare decisis*, the Court still must establish that *Bowers* was wrongly decided and that the Texas statute, as applied to petitioners, is unconstitutional.

Texas Penal Code Ann. § 21.06(a) undoubtedly imposes constraints on liberty. So do laws prohibiting prostitution, recreational use of heroin, and, for that matter, working more than 60 hours per week in a bakery. But there is no right to "liberty" under the Due Process Clause, though today's opinion repeatedly makes that claim. The Fourteenth Amendment *expressly allows* States to deprive their citizens of "liberty," so long as "due process of law" is provided. . . .

Our opinions applying the doctrine known as "substantive due process" hold that the Due Process Clause prohibits States from infringing *fundamental* liberty interests, unless the infringement is narrowly tailored to serve a compelling state interest. We have held repeatedly, in cases the Court today does not overrule, that *only* fundamental rights qualify for this so-called "heightened scrutiny" protection—that is, rights which are " 'deeply rooted in this Nation's history and tradition.' " All other liberty interests may be abridged or abrogated pursuant to a validly enacted state law if that law is rationally related to a legitimate state interest.

Bowers held, first, that criminal prohibitions of homosexual sodomy are not subject to heightened scrutiny because they do not implicate a "fundamental right" under the Due Process Clause. . . .

III

The Court's description of "the state of the law" at the time of *Bowers* only confirms that *Bowers* was right. The Court points to *Griswold v. Connecticut*. But that case *expressly disclaimed* any reliance on the doctrine of "substantive due process," and grounded the so-called "right to privacy" in penumbras of constitutional provisions *other than* the Due Process Clause. *Eisenstadt v. Baird* likewise had nothing to do with "substantive due process"; it invalidated a Massachusetts law prohibiting the distribution of contraceptives to unmarried persons solely on the basis of the Equal Protection Clause. . . .

Roe v. Wade recognized that the right to abort an unborn child was a "fundamental right" protected by the Due Process Clause. The *Roe*

Court, however, made no attempt to establish that this right was " 'deeply rooted in this Nation's history and tradition' "; instead, it based its conclusion that "the Fourteenth Amendment's concept of personal liberty . . . is broad enough to encompass a woman's decision whether or not to terminate her pregnancy" on its own normative judgment that anti-abortion laws were undesirable. We have since rejected *Roe*'s holding that regulations of abortion must be narrowly tailored to serve a compelling state interest, see *Planned Parenthood v. Casey*—and thus, by logical implication, *Roe*'s holding that the right to abort an unborn child is a "fundamental right."

After discussing the history of antisodomy laws, the Court proclaims that, "it should be noted that there is no longstanding history in this country of laws directed at homosexual conduct as a distinct matter." This observation in no way casts into doubt the "definitive [historical] conclusion" on which *Bowers* relied: that our Nation has a longstanding history of laws prohibiting *sodomy in general*—regardless of whether it was performed by same-sex or opposite-sex couples. . . . It is (as *Bowers* recognized) entirely irrelevant whether the laws in our long national tradition criminalizing homosexual sodomy were "directed at homosexual conduct as a distinct matter." . . .

Next the Court makes the claim, again unsupported by any citations, that "[l]aws prohibiting sodomy do not seem to have been enforced against consenting adults acting in private." The key qualifier here is "acting in private"—since the Court admits that sodomy laws *were* enforced against consenting adults. . . . If all the Court means by "acting in private" is "on private premises, with the doors closed and windows covered," it is entirely unsurprising that evidence of enforcement would be hard to come by. . . . Surely that lack of evidence would not sustain the proposition that consensual sodomy on private premises with the doors closed and windows covered was regarded as a "fundamental right," even though all other consensual sodomy was criminalized. . . . *Bowers'* conclusion that homosexual sodomy is not a fundamental right "deeply rooted in this Nation's history and tradition" is utterly unassailable.

Realizing that fact, the Court instead says: "[W]e think that our laws and traditions in the past . . . show *an emerging awareness* that liberty gives substantial protection to adult persons in deciding how to conduct their private lives *in matters pertaining to sex*." Apart from the fact that such an "emerging awareness" does not establish a "fundamental right," the statement is factually false. States continue to prosecute all sorts of crimes by adults "in matters pertaining to sex": prostitution, adult incest, adultery, obscenity, and child pornography. Sodomy laws, too, have been enforced "in the past half century," in which there have been 134 reported cases involving prosecutions for consensual, adult, homosexual sodomy. In relying, for evidence of an "emerging recognition," upon the American Law Institute's 1955 recommendation not to criminalize " 'consensual sexual relations conducted in private,' " the Court ignores the fact that this recommendation was "a point of resistance in most of the states that considered adopting the Model Penal Code."

In any event, an "emerging awareness" is by definition not "deeply rooted in this Nation's history and tradition[s]," as we have said "fundamental right" status requires. Constitutional entitlements do not spring into existence because some States choose to lessen or eliminate criminal sanctions on certain behavior. Much less do they spring into existence, as the Court seems to believe, because *foreign nations* decriminalize conduct. The *Bowers* majority opinion *never* relied on "values we share with a wider civilization," but rather rejected the claimed right to sodomy on the ground that such a right was not " 'deeply rooted in *this Nation's* history and tradition.' " . . . The Court's discussion of these foreign views (ignoring, of course, the many countries that have retained criminal prohibitions on sodomy) is therefore meaningless dicta. Dangerous dicta, however, since "this Court . . . should not impose foreign moods, fads, or fashions on Americans."

IV

I turn now to the ground on which the Court squarely rests its holding: the contention that there is no rational basis for the law here under attack. . . . The Texas statute undeniably seeks to further the belief of its citizens that certain forms of sexual behavior are "immoral and unacceptable"—the same interest furthered by criminal laws against fornication, bigamy, adultery, adult incest, bestiality, and obscenity. *Bowers* held that this *was* a legitimate state interest. The Court today reaches the opposite conclusion. The Texas statute, it says, "furthers *no legitimate state interest* which can justify its intrusion into the personal and private life of the individual." The Court embraces instead Justice Stevens' declaration in his *Bowers* dissent, that "the fact that the governing majority in a State has traditionally viewed a particular practice as immoral is not a sufficient reason for upholding a law prohibiting the practice." This effectively decrees the end of all morals legislation. If, as the Court asserts, the promotion of majoritarian sexual morality is not even a *legitimate* state interest, none of the above-mentioned laws can survive rational-basis review.

V

Finally, I turn to petitioners' equal-protection challenge, which no Member of the Court save Justice O'Connor embraces: On its face § 21.06(a) applies equally to all persons. Men and women, heterosexuals and homosexuals, are all subject to its prohibition of deviate sexual intercourse with someone of the same sex. To be sure, § 21.06 does distinguish between the sexes insofar as concerns the partner with whom the sexual acts are performed: men can violate the law only with other men, and women only with other women. But this cannot itself be a denial of equal protection, since it is precisely the same distinction regarding partner that is drawn in state laws prohibiting marriage with someone of the same sex while permitting marriage with someone of the opposite sex.

The objection is made, however, that the antimiscegenation laws invalidated in *Loving v. Virginia*, 388 U.S. 1 (1967), similarly were applicable to whites and blacks alike, and only distinguished between the races insofar as the *partner* was concerned. In *Loving*, however, we correctly applied heightened scrutiny, rather than the usual rational-basis review, because the Virginia statute was "designed to maintain White Supremacy." A racially discriminatory purpose is always sufficient to subject a law to strict scrutiny, even a facially neutral law that makes no mention of race. No purpose to discriminate against men or women as a class can be gleaned from the Texas law, so rational-basis review applies. That review is readily satisfied here by the same rational basis that satisfied it in *Bowers*—society's belief that certain forms of sexual behavior are "immoral and unacceptable." . . .

Justice O'Connor argues that the discrimination in this law which must be justified is not its discrimination with regard to the sex of the partner but its discrimination with regard to the sexual proclivity of the principal actor. . . . Of course the same could be said of any law. A law against public nudity targets "the conduct that is closely correlated with being a nudist," and hence "is targeted at more than conduct"; it is "directed toward nudists as a class." But be that as it may. Even if the Texas law *does* deny equal protection to "homosexuals as a class," that denial *still* does not need to be justified by anything more than a rational basis, which our cases show is satisfied by the enforcement of traditional notions of sexual morality.

Justice O'Connor simply decrees application of "a more searching form of rational basis review" to the Texas statute. The cases she cites do not recognize such a standard, and reach their conclusions only after finding, as required by conventional rational-basis analysis, that no conceivable legitimate state interest supports the classification at issue. Nor does Justice O'Connor explain precisely what her "more searching form" of rational-basis review consists of. It must at least mean, however, that laws exhibiting " 'a . . . desire to harm a politically unpopular group,' " are invalid *even though* there may be a conceivable rational basis to support them.

This reasoning leaves on pretty shaky grounds state laws limiting marriage to opposite-sex couples. Justice O'Connor seeks to preserve them by the conclusory statement that "preserving the traditional institution of marriage" is a legitimate state interest. But "preserving the traditional institution of marriage" is just a kinder way of describing the State's *moral disapproval* of same-sex couples. Texas's interest in § 21.06 could be recast in similarly euphemistic terms: "preserving the traditional sexual mores of our society." In the jurisprudence Justice O'Connor has seemingly created, judges can validate laws by characterizing them as "preserving the traditions of society" (good); or invalidate them by characterizing them as "expressing moral disapproval" (bad).

* * *

Today's opinion is the product of a Court, which is the product of a law-profession culture, that has largely signed on to the so-called homosexual agenda, by which I mean the agenda promoted by some homosexual activists directed at eliminating the moral opprobrium that has traditionally attached to homosexual conduct. I noted in an earlier opinion the fact that the American Association of Law Schools (to which any reputable law school *must* seek to belong) excludes from membership any school that refuses to ban from its job-interview facilities a law firm (no matter how small) that does not wish to hire as a prospective partner a person who openly engages in homosexual conduct.

One of the most revealing statements in today's opinion is the Court's grim warning that the criminalization of homosexual conduct is "an invitation to subject homosexual persons to discrimination both in the public and in the private spheres." It is clear from this that the Court has taken sides in the culture war, departing from its role of assuring, as neutral observer, that the democratic rules of engagement are observed. Many Americans do not want persons who openly engage in homosexual conduct as partners in their business, as scoutmasters for their children, as teachers in their children's schools, or as boarders in their home. They view this as protecting themselves and their families from a lifestyle that they believe to be immoral and destructive. The Court views it as "discrimination" which it is the function of our judgments to deter. So imbued is the Court with the law profession's anti-anti-homosexual culture, that it is seemingly unaware that the attitudes of that culture are not obviously "mainstream"; that in most States what the Court calls "discrimination" against those who engage in homosexual acts is perfectly legal; that proposals to ban such "discrimination" under Title VII have repeatedly been rejected by Congress; that in some cases such "discrimination" is *mandated* by federal statute, see 10 U.S.C. § 654(b)(1) (mandating discharge from the armed forces of any service member who engages in or intends to engage in homosexual acts); and that in some cases such "discrimination" is a constitutional right, see *Boy Scouts of America v. Dale*, 530 U.S. 640 (2000).

Let me be clear that I have nothing against homosexuals, or any other group, promoting their agenda through normal democratic means. Social perceptions of sexual and other morality change over time, and every group has the right to persuade its fellow citizens that its view of such matters is the best. That homosexuals have achieved some success in that enterprise is attested to by the fact that Texas is one of the few remaining States that criminalize private, consensual homosexual acts. But persuading one's fellow citizens is one thing, and imposing one's views in absence of democratic majority will is something else. I would no more *require* a State to criminalize homosexual acts—or, for that matter, display *any* moral disapprobation of them—than I would *forbid* it to do so. . . .

One of the benefits of leaving regulation of this matter to the people rather than to the courts is that the people, unlike judges, need not carry things to their logical conclusion. The people may feel that their disapprobation of homosexual conduct is strong enough to disallow homosexual marriage, but not strong enough to criminalize private homosexual acts—and may legislate accordingly. The Court today pretends that it possesses a similar freedom of action, so that we need not fear judicial imposition of homosexual marriage, as has recently occurred in Canada. . . . See *Halpern v. Toronto*, 2003 WL 34950 (Ontario Ct. App.). At the end of its opinion . . . the Court says that the present case "does not involve whether the government must give formal recognition to any relationship that homosexual persons seek to enter." Do not believe it. More illuminating than this bald, unreasoned disclaimer is the progression of thought displayed by an earlier passage in the Court's opinion, which notes the constitutional protections afforded to "personal decisions relating to *marriage*, procreation, contraception, family relationships, child rearing, and education," and then declares that "[p]ersons in a homosexual relationship may seek autonomy for these purposes, just as heterosexual persons do." Today's opinion dismantles the structure of constitutional law that has permitted a distinction to be made between heterosexual and homosexual unions, insofar as formal recognition in marriage is concerned. If moral disapprobation of homosexual conduct is "no legitimate state interest" for purposes of proscribing that conduct . . . what justification could there possibly be for denying the benefits of marriage to homosexual couples exercising "[t]he liberty protected by the Constitution"? . . .

The matters appropriate for this Court's resolution are only three: Texas's prohibition of sodomy neither infringes a "fundamental right" (which the Court does not dispute), nor is unsupported by a rational relation to what the Constitution considers a legitimate state interest, nor denies the equal protection of the laws. I dissent.

NOTE ON GAY RIGHTS, DUE PROCESS, AND EQUAL PROTECTION

1.   Many observers have had a hard time taking Justice Kennedy's opinion in *Romer* at face value. Recall that, under traditional formulations of rational basis review, legislation may be significantly over- and under-inclusive with respect to the interest served. Moreover, courts generally do not second-guess the government's factual or policy judgments. And even if the government does not provide a rationale for the legislation, the courts have generally been willing to formulate a hypothetical rationale if one can plausibly be imagined.[5] Can Amendment 2 really not be sustained at this level of review? Consider, for example, that every new anti-discrimination

---

[5]   *See* Section 5.4, *supra*.

statute or ordinance generates both compliance and litigation costs. Avoiding costs is always a legitimate governmental interest (if one all too frequently ignored). And prohibiting localities from enacting new anti-discrimination rules saves those costs for both private and public actors. Why isn't that a sufficient rationale to uphold the amendment?

2. *Romer* is most plausibly read as applying some form of heightened scrutiny. The Court, for example, holds Colorado to the rationales that it actually argued in support of Amendment 2, rather than formulating better rationales that the referendum's proponents might have had in mind. Given the breadth of the amendment and the relatively weak rationales offered in its support, the Court did not need to apply strict or intermediate scrutiny in *Romer*, but surely it did not apply the sort of rubber stamp employed in cases like *Williamson v. Lee Optical* in Section 5.4.

Why did the Court apply a heightened form of review? Several accounts are possible:

- The Court stressed that "the amendment seems inexplicable by anything but animus toward the class it affects," and the Court has sometimes emphasized animosity toward particular groups as a trigger for heightened rational review. *See, e.g., Department of Agriculture v. Moreno*, 413 U.S. 528, 534 (1973) (stating that "a bare . . . desire to harm a politically unpopular group cannot constitute a *legitimate* governmental interest").

- A prominent *amicus* brief filed by Harvard Law Professor Laurence Tribe and signed by an all-star cast of constitutional law academics argued that the Fourteenth Amendment's "command is violated when a state's constitution renders some persons ineligible for "the . . . protection of the laws" from an entire category of mistreatment—here, the mistreatment of discrimination, however invidious and unwarranted." This meant, in their view, that "Amendment 2 constitutes a per se violation of the Equal Protection Clause."[6] The Court seemed to echo this theory when it said that "[a] State cannot . . . deem a class of persons a stranger to its laws."

- Rational basis review is generally justified as a form of deference to the democratic pedigree and deliberative capacity of the legislature. Amendment 2, however, was not adopted by the Colorado legislature—it was a popular referendum, adopted after a sometimes-ugly anti-gay campaign. It may be that the Court felt a law adopted through this extraordinary process deserved less deference.[7]

- In *Cleburne*, the Court seemed to apply a heightened form of rationality review—perhaps because the mentally disabled fit

---

[6]   *See* Brief of Laurence H. Tribe, John Hart Ely, Gerald Gunther, Philip B. Kurland, and Kathleen M. Sullivan as *Amici Curiae* in Support of Respondents in No. 94–1039, *Romer v. Evans* (June 9, 1995).

[7]   *See, e.g.,* Robin Charlow, *Judicial Review, Equal Protection and the Problem with Plebiscites*, 79 Cornell L. Rev. 527 (1994) (arguing for stricter judicial review of referenda).

several of the indicia for suspect class status even if the Court was ultimately unwilling to go that far. Similarly, in *Romer*, the Court was unwilling to declare sexual orientation classifications suspect, but it may have been influenced by the strength of the case for that status in this instance.

The latter two rationales find little support in the Court's opinion, but they may capture part of the underlying dynamics of the case. Are any of these rationales persuasive?

Is the right recognized in *Lawrence* a fair extrapolation from the Court's earlier privacy cases? The joint opinion in *Casey* described the earlier privacy decisions as protecting "personal decisions relating to marriage, procreation, contraception, family relationships, child rearing, and education," and all of them involved the conception or raising of children. Does *Lawrence* extend the privacy right to sex generally? Does the reasoning of the prior cases support that extension?

3.   What do you make of the appeals to history and evolving social mores in *Lawrence*? Does it matter, as Justice Kennedy argues, that longstanding legal prohibitions on sodomy were directed at all persons, without singling out homosexuals as a class? Could one argue that characterizing the matter this way actually masks the age-old persecution of homosexuals, and that a stronger argument would frankly acknowledge that history and demand redress? In considering this question, note the arguably different nature of due process and equal protection arguments described by Professor Sunstein in Section 17.1, *supra*.

Justice Kennedy suggests that the most relevant history is the evolving toleration of homosexuality in contemporary America. How settled does a change in social mores have to be before the Court can rely on it to inform its interpretation of the Due Process Clause? Can we really say that we have reached consensus on issues of gay rights in this country? Or is it appropriate for the Justices' own morality to inform their resolution of contested moral questions? Is Justice Scalia right to say that "the Court has taken sides in the culture war"? On the other hand, isn't that what the Court did in *Brown*?

Finally, was it appropriate, in considering evolving standards of morality, to consider the views of other countries? Did the majority explain why it found the views of Western European countries relevant, as opposed to countries in the Islamic world that are less tolerant of homosexuals? Is the *Lawrence* Court's use of foreign authority any different from the reliance of many of the opinions in *Glucksberg* on Denmark's experience with physician-assisted suicide?

4.   Does the *Lawrence* majority faithfully apply the doctrine of *stare decisis* that the joint opinion extolled in *Casey*? Recall that *Casey* said courts should generally consider four factors: (a) the workability and coherence of the prior legal rule; (b) reliance on the prior rule; (c) changes in the surrounding law; and (d) changes in the relevant facts. The Court also suggested that, when the Court resolves a divisive social issue, its rulings should take on extraordinary precedential force. How does *Bowers v. Hardwick*, 478 U.S. 186 (1986), which upheld Georgia's sodomy statute

against a due process challenge and which the Court overrules in *Lawrence*,
fare under these criteria?

5.   What standard of review did the Court apply in *Lawrence*? The
"blackletter" framework in this area had been that laws infringing
"fundamental" rights are subject to strict scrutiny under the Due Process
Clause, and that all other governmental actions are subject only to rational
basis review. Hence, *Bowers* found that no fundamental right to sodomy
existed and applied the rational basis test. *Casey* complicated this
framework somewhat by holding that some due process rights must be
analyzed under an "undue burden" test, which seems to connote a form of
intermediate scrutiny for rights in areas where some forms of regulation may
be necessary for those rights' effective vindication (e.g., *bona fide* health and
safety regulation of abortion services).

How does *Lawrence* fit into this framework? Is Justice Scalia right to
characterize the majority as deciding the case under a rational basis
standard? If he is, then it is a far different rationality standard than we saw
in cases like *Williamson v. Lee Optical*.[8] Should we instead think of
Lawrence as applying a form of heightened review, but without expressly
invoking the tiers of scrutiny found in the prior caselaw? Doesn't the Court's
ambiguity on this point only sow confusion in an important area of the law?
Can you think of any reason why the Court would not have wanted simply
to declare a fundamental right of gay persons to have sex?

6.   Justice O'Connor's concurrence in *Lawrence* rejected the majority's
due process rationale, but argued that the Texas law should be struck down
under the Equal Protection Clause. Would that have been a more appealing
justification for the result in the case? Should *Lawrence* have built more
directly on the foundation of *Romer*? Should it have addressed straight-on
the standard of equal protection scrutiny for classifications based on sexual
orientation?

Note that *Lawrence* raises both a narrow and a broad equal protection
argument. The narrow argument stems from the fact that the Texas statute
treats same-sex couples differently from different-sex couples performing the
same sex acts. If that argument were to succeed, it would have no bearing on
state laws that ban sodomy without regard to who commits it. The broad
argument, on the other hand, would say that bans on "sodomy" inherently
discriminate against same-sex couples by criminalizing the primary form of
sex available to them—whether or not such bans also apply to different-sex
couples. Which argument do you understand Justice O'Connor to be making
in *Lawrence*? Which would provide the better basis for a decision striking
down the Texas sodomy law?

SECTION 17.3   THE MARRIAGE OF EQUALITY AND DUE PROCESS (AND FEDERALISM?)

The majority and dissent sparred in *Lawrence* as to whether the result
in that case committed the Court to strike down laws prohibiting same-sex

---

[8]   *See supra* Section 5.4.

marriage. That issue came to the Court relatively quickly. It came first, however, in the form of the federal Defense of Marriage Act (DOMA),[9] a federal statute adopted by large congressional majorities and signed by President Bill Clinton in the mid-1990s, in response to state court decisions suggesting that a right to same-sex marriage might be recognized under some state constitutions. DOMA did two things: (1) it provided that "marriage" would be defined for purposes of *federal* law as existing only between a man and a woman; and (2) it absolved individual states of any obligation to recognize same-sex marriages solemnized in another state. The Court struck down the DOMA in *United States v. Windsor*, relying on an equal protection argument that also incorporated significant elements of federalism.[10]

Windsor purported to leave open, however, the question whether a *state* might prohibit same-sex marriage. The lower courts tended to read *Windsor* as effectively answering that question, however, and several different district and circuit courts promptly struck down state same-sex marriage bans around the country. The Court thus had little choice but to hear the issue in *Obergefell v. Hodges*, only two years after *Windsor*. The *Obergefell* decision striking down same-sex marriage bans in Michigan, Ohio, Kentucky, and Tennessee represented a culmination—at least for now—of the movement begun in *Romer*. The Court's decision also sparked serious criticism of the Court for usurping the role of the democratic process in defining basic family relationships.

United States v. Windsor
133 S. Ct. 2675 (2013)

■ **JUSTICE KENNEDY delivered the opinion of the Court.**

Two women then resident in New York were married in a lawful ceremony in Ontario, Canada, in 2007. Edith Windsor and Thea Spyer returned to their home in New York City. When Spyer died in 2009, she left her entire estate to Windsor. Windsor sought to claim the estate tax exemption for surviving spouses. She was barred from doing so, however, by a federal law, the Defense of Marriage Act, which excludes a same-sex partner from the definition of "spouse" as that term is used in federal statutes. Windsor paid the taxes but filed suit to challenge the constitutionality of this provision. The United States District Court and the Court of Appeals ruled that this portion of the statute is unconstitutional and ordered the United States to pay Windsor a refund. This Court granted certiorari and now affirms the judgment in Windsor's favor.

---

[9] 2 Pub L No 104–199, 110 Stat 2419 (1996).

[10] A second marriage case in the same term, *Hollingsworth v. Perry*, 133 S. Ct. 2652 (2013), involved California's state constitutional amendment, adopted by public initiative as "Proposition 8," prohibiting same-sex marriage. The Governor and Attorney General of California declined to defend Proposition 8, however, and the Supreme Court held that the initiative's proponents lacked standing to appeal the case following a district court decision striking the initiative down.

I

In 1996, as some States were beginning to consider the concept of same-sex marriage, see, *e.g., Baehr v. Lewin,* 74 Haw. 530, 852 P.2d 44 (1993), and before any State had acted to permit it, Congress enacted the Defense of Marriage Act (DOMA), 110 Stat. 2419. DOMA contains two operative sections: Section 2, which has not been challenged here, allows States to refuse to recognize same-sex marriages performed under the laws of other States. See 28 U.S.C. § 1738C.

Section 3 is at issue here. It amends the Dictionary Act in Title 1, § 7, of the United States Code to provide a federal definition of "marriage" and "spouse." Section 3 of DOMA provides as follows:

> In determining the meaning of any Act of Congress, or of any ruling, regulation, or interpretation of the various administrative bureaus and agencies of the United States, the word 'marriage' means only a legal union between one man and one woman as husband and wife, and the word 'spouse' refers only to a person of the opposite sex who is a husband or a wife.
> 1 U.S.C. § 7.

The definitional provision does not by its terms forbid States from enacting laws permitting same-sex marriages or civil unions or providing state benefits to residents in that status. The enactment's comprehensive definition of marriage for purposes of all federal statutes and other regulations or directives covered by its terms, however, does control over 1,000 federal laws in which marital or spousal status is addressed as a matter of federal law. See GAO, D. Shah, Defense of Marriage Act: Update to Prior Report 1 (GAO–04–353R, 2004).

Edith Windsor and Thea Spyer met in New York City in 1963 and began a long-term relationship. Windsor and Spyer registered as domestic partners when New York City gave that right to same-sex couples in 1993. Concerned about Spyer's health, the couple made the 2007 trip to Canada for their marriage, but they continued to reside in New York City. The State of New York deems their Ontario marriage to be a valid one.

Spyer died in February 2009, and left her entire estate to Windsor. Because DOMA denies federal recognition to same-sex spouses, Windsor did not qualify for the marital exemption from the federal estate tax, which excludes from taxation "any interest in property which passes or has passed from the decedent to his surviving spouse." 26 U.S.C. § 2056(a). Windsor paid $363,053 in estate taxes and sought a refund. The Internal Revenue Service denied the refund, concluding that, under DOMA, Windsor was not a "surviving spouse." Windsor commenced this refund suit in the United States District Court for the Southern District of New York. She contended that DOMA violates the guarantee of equal protection, as applied to the Federal Government through the Fifth Amendment.

While the tax refund suit was pending, the Attorney General of the United States notified the Speaker of the House of Representatives, pursuant to 28 U.S.C. § 530D, that the Department of Justice would no longer defend the constitutionality of DOMA's § 3. Noting that "the Department has previously defended DOMA against . . . challenges involving legally married same-sex couples," the Attorney General informed Congress that "the President has concluded that given a number of factors, including a documented history of discrimination, classifications based on sexual orientation should be subject to a heightened standard of scrutiny." The Department of Justice has submitted many § 530D letters over the years refusing to defend laws it deems unconstitutional, when, for instance, a federal court has rejected the Government's defense of a statute and has issued a judgment against it. This case is unusual, however, because the § 530D letter was not preceded by an adverse judgment. The letter instead reflected the Executive's own conclusion, relying on a definition still being debated and considered in the courts, that heightened equal protection scrutiny should apply to laws that classify on the basis of sexual orientation.

Although "the President . . . instructed the Department not to defend the statute in *Windsor*," he also decided "that Section 3 will continue to be enforced by the Executive Branch" and that the United States had an "interest in providing Congress a full and fair opportunity to participate in the litigation of those cases." The stated rationale for this dual-track procedure (determination of unconstitutionality coupled with ongoing enforcement) was to "recogniz[e] the judiciary as the final arbiter of the constitutional claims raised."

In response to the notice from the Attorney General, the Bipartisan Legal Advisory Group (BLAG) of the House of Representatives voted to intervene in the litigation to defend the constitutionality of § 3 of DOMA. The Department of Justice did not oppose limited intervention by BLAG. The District Court denied BLAG's motion to enter the suit as of right, on the rationale that the United States already was represented by the Department of Justice. The District Court, however, did grant intervention by BLAG as an interested party. See Fed. Rule Civ. Proc. 24(a)(2).

On the merits of the tax refund suit, the District Court ruled against the United States. It held that § 3 of DOMA is unconstitutional and ordered the Treasury to refund the tax with interest. Both the Justice Department and BLAG filed notices of appeal, and the Solicitor General filed a petition for certiorari before judgment. Before this Court acted on the petition, the Court of Appeals for the Second Circuit affirmed the District Court's judgment. It applied heightened scrutiny to classifications based on sexual orientation, as both the Department and Windsor had urged. The United States has not complied with the judgment. Windsor has not received her refund, and the Executive Branch continues to enforce § 3 of DOMA. . . .

III

When at first Windsor and Spyer longed to marry, neither New York nor any other State granted them that right. After waiting some years, in 2007 they traveled to Ontario to be married there. It seems fair to conclude that, until recent years, many citizens had not even considered the possibility that two persons of the same sex might aspire to occupy the same status and dignity as that of a man and woman in lawful marriage. For marriage between a man and a woman no doubt had been thought of by most people as essential to the very definition of that term and to its role and function throughout the history of civilization. That belief, for many who long have held it, became even more urgent, more cherished when challenged. For others, however, came the beginnings of a new perspective, a new insight. Accordingly some States concluded that same-sex marriage ought to be given recognition and validity in the law for those same-sex couples who wish to define themselves by their commitment to each other. The limitation of lawful marriage to heterosexual couples, which for centuries had been deemed both necessary and fundamental, came to be seen in New York and certain other States as an unjust exclusion.

Slowly at first and then in rapid course, the laws of New York came to acknowledge the urgency of this issue for same-sex couples who wanted to affirm their commitment to one another before their children, their family, their friends, and their community. And so New York recognized same-sex marriages performed elsewhere; and then it later amended its own marriage laws to permit same-sex marriage. New York, in common with, as of this writing, 11 other States and the District of Columbia, decided that same-sex couples should have the right to marry and so live with pride in themselves and their union and in a status of equality with all other married persons. After a statewide deliberative process that enabled its citizens to discuss and weigh arguments for and against same-sex marriage, New York acted to enlarge the definition of marriage to correct what its citizens and elected representatives perceived to be an injustice that they had not earlier known or understood. See Marriage Equality Act, 2011 N.Y. Laws 749.

Against this background of lawful same-sex marriage in some States, the design, purpose, and effect of DOMA should be considered as the beginning point in deciding whether it is valid under the Constitution. By history and tradition the definition and regulation of marriage, as will be discussed in more detail, has been treated as being within the authority and realm of the separate States. Yet it is further established that Congress, in enacting discrete statutes, can make determinations that bear on marital rights and privileges. Just this Term the Court upheld the authority of the Congress to pre-empt state laws, allowing a former spouse to retain life insurance proceeds under a federal program that gave her priority, because of formal beneficiary designation rules, over the wife by a second marriage who survived the husband.

Hillman v. Maretta, 569 U.S. ___, 133 S.Ct. 1943 (2013). This is one example of the general principle that when the Federal Government acts in the exercise of its own proper authority, it has a wide choice of the mechanisms and means to adopt. See *McCulloch v. Maryland,* 4 Wheat. 316, 421 (1819). Congress has the power both to ensure efficiency in the administration of its programs and to choose what larger goals and policies to pursue.

Other precedents involving congressional statutes which affect marriages and family status further illustrate this point. In addressing the interaction of state domestic relations and federal immigration law Congress determined that marriages "entered into for the purpose of procuring an alien's admission [to the United States] as an immigrant" will not qualify the noncitizen for that status, even if the noncitizen's marriage is valid and proper for state-law purposes. 8 U.S.C. § 1186a(b)(1). And in establishing income-based criteria for Social Security benefits, Congress decided that although state law would determine in general who qualifies as an applicant's spouse, common-law marriages also should be recognized, regardless of any particular State's view on these relationships. 42 U.S.C. § 1382c(d)(2).

Though these discrete examples establish the constitutionality of limited federal laws that regulate the meaning of marriage in order to further federal policy, DOMA has a far greater reach; for it enacts a directive applicable to over 1,000 federal statutes and the whole realm of federal regulations. And its operation is directed to a class of persons that the laws of New York, and of 11 other States, have sought to protect. See *Goodridge v. Department of Public Health,* 440 Mass. 309, 798 N.E.2d 941 (2003); An Act Implementing the Guarantee of Equal Protection Under the Constitution of the State for Same Sex Couples, 2009 Conn. Pub. Acts no. 09–13; *Varnum v. Brien,* 763 N.W.2d 862 (Iowa 2009); Vt. Stat. Ann., Tit. 15, § 8 (2010); N.H.Rev.Stat. Ann. § 457:1–a (West Supp.2012); Religious Freedom and Civil Marriage Equality Amendment Act of 2009, 57 D.C. Reg. 27 (Dec. 18, 2009); N.Y. Dom. Rel. Law Ann. § 10–a (West Supp. 2013); Wash. Rev.Code § 26.04.010 (2012); Citizen Initiative, Same-Sex Marriage, Question 1 (Me. 2012); Md. Fam. Law Code Ann. § 2–201 (Lexis 2012); An Act to Amend Title 13 of the Delaware Code Relating to Domestic Relations to Provide for Same-Gender Civil Marriage and to Convert Existing Civil Unions to Civil Marriages, 79 Del. Laws ch. 19 (2013); An act relating to marriage; providing for civil marriage between two persons; providing for exemptions and protections based on religious association, 2013 Minn. Laws ch. 74; An Act Relating to Domestic Relations—Persons Eligible to Marry, 2013 R. I. Laws ch. 4.

In order to assess the validity of that intervention it is necessary to discuss the extent of the state power and authority over marriage as a matter of history and tradition. State laws defining and regulating marriage, of course, must respect the constitutional rights of persons, see, *e.g., Loving v. Virginia,* 388 U.S. 1 (1967); but, subject to those guarantees, "regulation of domestic relations" is "an area that has long been regarded as a virtually exclusive province of the States." *Sosna v. Iowa,* 419 U.S. 393, 404 (1975).

The recognition of civil marriages is central to state domestic relations law applicable to its residents and citizens. See *Williams v. North Carolina,* 317 U.S. 287, 298 (1942) ("Each state as a sovereign has a rightful and legitimate concern in the marital status of persons domiciled within its borders"). The definition of marriage is the foundation of the State's broader authority to regulate the subject of domestic relations with respect to the "[p]rotection of offspring, property interests, and the enforcement of marital responsibilities." *Ibid.* "[T]he states, at the time of the adoption of the Constitution, possessed full power over the subject of marriage and divorce . . . [and] the Constitution delegated no authority to the Government of the United States on the subject of marriage and divorce." *Haddock v. Haddock,* 201 U.S. 562, 575 (1906); see also *In re Burrus,* 136 U.S. 586, 593–594 (1890) ("The whole subject of the domestic relations of husband and wife, parent and child, belongs to the laws of the States and not to the laws of the United States").

Consistent with this allocation of authority, the Federal Government, through our history, has deferred to state-law policy decisions with respect to domestic relations. In *De Sylva v. Ballentine,* 351 U.S. 570 (1956), for example, the Court held that, "[t]o decide who is the widow or widower of a deceased author, or who are his executors or next of kin," under the Copyright Act "requires a reference to the law of the State which created those legal relationships" because "there is no federal law of domestic relations." In order to respect this principle, the federal courts, as a general rule, do not adjudicate issues of marital status even when there might otherwise be a basis for federal jurisdiction. See *Ankenbrandt v. Richards,* 504 U.S. 689, 703 (1992). Federal courts will not hear divorce and custody cases even if they arise in diversity because of "the virtually exclusive primacy . . . of the States in the regulation of domestic relations." *Id.,* at 714 (Blackmun, J., concurring in judgment).

The significance of state responsibilities for the definition and regulation of marriage dates to the Nation's beginning; for "when the Constitution was adopted the common understanding was that the domestic relations of husband and wife and parent and child were matters reserved to the States." *Ohio ex rel. Popovici v. Agler,* 280 U.S. 379, 383–384 (1930). Marriage laws vary in some respects from State to State. For example, the required minimum age is 16 in Vermont, but only 13 in New Hampshire. Likewise the permissible degree of consanguinity can vary (most States permit first cousins to marry, but a handful—such as Iowa and Washington—prohibit the practice). But these rules are in every event consistent within each State.

Against this background DOMA rejects the long-established precept that the incidents, benefits, and obligations of marriage are uniform for all married couples within each State, though they may vary, subject to constitutional guarantees, from one State to the next. Despite these considerations, it is unnecessary to decide whether this federal intrusion on state power is a violation of the Constitution because it disrupts the federal balance. The State's power in defining the marital relation is of central relevance in this case quite apart from principles of federalism. Here the State's decision to give this class of persons the right to marry conferred upon them a dignity and status of immense import. When the State used its historic and essential authority to define the marital relation in this way, its role and its power in making the decision enhanced the recognition, dignity, and protection of the class in their own community. DOMA, because of its reach and extent, departs from this history and tradition of reliance on state law to define marriage. " '[D]iscriminations of an unusual character especially suggest careful consideration to determine whether they are obnoxious to the constitutional provision.' " *Romer v. Evans,* 517 U.S. 620, 633 (1996).

The Federal Government uses this state-defined class for the opposite purpose—to impose restrictions and disabilities. That result requires this Court now to address whether the resulting injury and indignity is a deprivation of an essential part of the liberty protected by the Fifth Amendment. What the State of New York treats as alike the federal law deems unlike by a law designed to injure the same class the State seeks to protect.

In acting first to recognize and then to allow same-sex marriages, New York was responding "to the initiative of those who [sought] a voice in shaping the destiny of their own times." *Bond v. United States,* 564 U.S.___, ___, 131 S.Ct. 2355, 2359 (2011). These actions were without doubt a proper exercise of its sovereign authority within our federal system, all in the way that the Framers of the Constitution intended. The dynamics of state government in the federal system are to allow the formation of consensus respecting the way the members of a discrete community treat each other in their daily contact and constant interaction with each other.

The States' interest in defining and regulating the marital relation, subject to constitutional guarantees, stems from the understanding that marriage is more than a routine classification for purposes of certain statutory benefits. Private, consensual sexual intimacy between two adult persons of the same sex may not be punished by the State, and it can form "but one element in a personal bond that is more enduring." *Lawrence v. Texas,* 539 U.S. 558, 567 (2003). By its recognition of the validity of same-sex marriages performed in other jurisdictions and then by authorizing same-sex unions and same-sex marriages, New York sought to give further protection and dignity to that bond. For same-sex couples who wished to be married, the State acted to give their lawful conduct a lawful status. This status is a far-reaching legal acknowledgment of the intimate relationship between two people, a relationship deemed by the State worthy of dignity in the community equal with all other marriages. It reflects both the community's considered perspective on the historical roots of the institution of marriage and its evolving understanding of the meaning of equality.

IV

DOMA seeks to injure the very class New York seeks to protect. By doing so it violates basic due process and equal protection principles applicable to the Federal Government. See U.S. Const., Amdt. 5; *Bolling v. Sharpe,* 347 U.S. 497 (1954). The Constitution's guarantee of equality "must at the very least mean that a bare congressional desire to harm a politically unpopular group cannot" justify disparate treatment of that group. *Department of Agriculture v. Moreno,* 413 U.S. 528, 534–535 (1973). In determining whether a law is motived by an improper animus or purpose, "discriminations of an unusual character" especially require careful consideration. DOMA cannot survive under these principles. The responsibility of the States for the regulation of domestic relations is an important indicator of the substantial societal impact the State's classifications have in the daily lives and customs of its people. DOMA's unusual deviation from the usual tradition of recognizing and accepting state definitions of marriage here operates to deprive same-sex couples of the benefits and responsibilities that come with the federal recognition of their marriages. This is strong evidence of a law having the purpose and effect of disapproval of that class. The avowed purpose and practical effect of the law here in question are to impose a disadvantage, a separate status, and so a stigma upon all who enter into same-sex marriages made lawful by the unquestioned authority of the States.

The history of DOMA's enactment and its own text demonstrate that interference with the equal dignity of same-sex marriages, a dignity conferred by the States in the exercise of their sovereign power, was more than an incidental effect of the federal statute. It was its essence. The House Report announced its conclusion that "it is both appropriate and necessary for Congress to do what it can to defend the institution of traditional heterosexual marriage. . . . H.R. 3396 is appropriately entitled the 'Defense of Marriage Act.' The effort to redefine 'marriage' to extend to homosexual couples is a truly radical proposal that would fundamentally alter the institution of marriage." H.R.Rep. No. 104–664, pp. 12–13 (1996). The House concluded that DOMA expresses "both moral disapproval of homosexuality, and a moral conviction that heterosexuality better comports with traditional (especially Judeo-Christian) morality." The stated purpose of the law was to promote an "interest in protecting the traditional moral teachings reflected in heterosexual-only marriage laws." Were there any doubt of this far-reaching purpose, the title of the Act confirms it: The Defense of Marriage.

The arguments put forward by BLAG are just as candid about the congressional purpose to influence or interfere with state sovereign choices about who may be married. As the title and dynamics of the bill indicate, its purpose is to discourage enactment of state same-sex marriage laws and to restrict the freedom and choice of couples married under those laws if they are enacted. The congressional goal was "to put a thumb on the scales and influence a state's decision as to how to shape its own marriage laws." *Massachusetts v. U.S. Dept. of Health & Human Servs.*, 682 F.3d 1, 12–13 (CA1 2012). The Act's demonstrated purpose is to ensure that if any State decides to recognize same-sex marriages, those unions will be treated as second-class marriages for purposes of federal law. This raises a most serious question under the Constitution's Fifth Amendment.

DOMA's operation in practice confirms this purpose. When New York adopted a law to permit same-sex marriage, it sought to eliminate inequality; but DOMA frustrates that objective through a system-wide enactment with no identified connection to any particular area of federal law. DOMA writes inequality into the entire United States Code. The particular case at hand concerns the estate tax, but DOMA is more than a simple determination of what should or should not be allowed as an estate tax refund. Among the over 1,000 statutes and numerous federal regulations that DOMA controls are laws pertaining to Social Security, housing, taxes, criminal sanctions, copyright, and veterans' benefits.

DOMA's principal effect is to identify a subset of state-sanctioned marriages and make them unequal. The principal purpose is to impose inequality, not for other reasons like governmental efficiency. Responsibilities, as well as rights, enhance the dignity and integrity of the person. And DOMA contrives to deprive some couples married under the laws of their State, but not other couples, of both rights and responsibilities. By creating two contradictory marriage regimes within the same State, DOMA forces same-sex couples to live as married for the purpose of state law but unmarried for the purpose of federal law, thus diminishing the stability and predictability of basic personal relations the State has found it proper to acknowledge and protect. By this dynamic DOMA undermines both the public and private significance of state-sanctioned same-sex marriages; for it tells those couples, and all the world, that their otherwise valid marriages are unworthy of federal recognition. This places same-sex couples in an unstable position of being in a second-tier marriage. The differentiation demeans the couple, whose moral and sexual choices the Constitution protects, see *Lawrence,* 539 U.S. 558, and whose relationship the State has sought to dignify. And it humiliates tens of thousands of children now being raised by same-sex couples. The law in question makes it even more difficult for the children to understand the integrity and closeness of their own family and its concord with other families in their community and in their daily lives.

Under DOMA, same-sex married couples have their lives burdened, by reason of government decree, in visible and public ways. By its great reach, DOMA touches many aspects of married and family life, from the mundane to the profound. It prevents same-sex married couples from obtaining government healthcare benefits they would otherwise receive. See 5 U.S.C. §§ 8901(5), 8905. It deprives them of the Bankruptcy Code's special protections for domestic-support obligations. See 11 U.S.C. §§ 101(14A), 507(a)(1)(A), 523(a)(5), 523(a)(15). It forces them to follow a complicated procedure to file their state and federal taxes jointly. Technical Bulletin TB–55, 2010 Vt. Tax LEXIS 6 (Oct. 7, 2010); Brief for Federalism Scholars as *Amici Curiae* 34. It prohibits them from being buried together in veterans' cemeteries. National Cemetery Administration Directive 3210/1, p. 37 (June 4, 2008).

For certain married couples, DOMA's unequal effects are even more serious. The federal penal code makes it a crime to "assaul[t], kidna[p], or murde[r] . . . a member of the immediate family" of "a United States official, a United States judge, [or] a Federal law enforcement officer," 18 U.S.C. § 115(a)(1)(A), with the intent to influence or retaliate against that official, § 115(a)(1). Although a "spouse" qualifies as a member of the officer's "immediate family," § 115(c)(2), DOMA makes this protection inapplicable to same-sex spouses.

DOMA also brings financial harm to children of same-sex couples. It raises the cost of health care for families by taxing health benefits provided by employers to their workers' same-sex spouses. See 26 U.S.C. § 106; Treas. Reg. § 1.106–1, 26 CFR § 1.106–1 (2012); IRS Private Letter Ruling 9850011 (Sept. 10, 1998). And it denies or reduces benefits allowed to families upon the loss of a spouse and parent, benefits that are an integral part of family security. See Social Security Administration, Social Security Survivors Benefits 5 (2012) (benefits available to a surviving spouse caring for the couple's child), online at http://www.ssa.gov/pubs/EN–05–10084.pdf.

DOMA divests married same-sex couples of the duties and responsibilities that are an essential part of married life and that they in most cases would be honored to accept were DOMA not in force. For instance, because it is expected that spouses will support each other as they pursue educational opportunities, federal law takes into consideration a spouse's income in calculating a student's federal financial aid eligibility. See 20 U.S.C. § 1087nn(b). Same-sex married couples are exempt from this requirement. The same is true with respect to federal ethics rules. Federal executive and agency officials are prohibited from "participat[ing] personally and substantially" in matters as to which they or their spouses have a financial interest. 18 U.S.C. § 208(a). A similar statute prohibits Senators, Senate employees, and their spouses from accepting high-value gifts from certain sources, see 2 U.S.C. § 31–2(a)(1), and another mandates detailed financial disclosures by numerous high-ranking officials and their spouses. See 5 U.S.C.App.

§§ 102(a), (e). Under DOMA, however, these Government-integrity rules do not apply to same-sex spouses.

* * *

The power the Constitution grants it also restrains. And though Congress has great authority to design laws to fit its own conception of sound national policy, it cannot deny the liberty protected by the Due Process Clause of the Fifth Amendment.

What has been explained to this point should more than suffice to establish that the principal purpose and the necessary effect of this law are to demean those persons who are in a lawful same-sex marriage. This requires the Court to hold, as it now does, that DOMA is unconstitutional as a deprivation of the liberty of the person protected by the Fifth Amendment of the Constitution.

The liberty protected by the Fifth Amendment's Due Process Clause contains within it the prohibition against denying to any person the equal protection of the laws. See *Bolling,* 347 U.S., at 499–500. While the Fifth Amendment itself withdraws from Government the power to degrade or demean in the way this law does, the equal protection guarantee of the Fourteenth Amendment makes that Fifth Amendment right all the more specific and all the better understood and preserved.

The class to which DOMA directs its restrictions and restraints are those persons who are joined in same-sex marriages made lawful by the State. DOMA singles out a class of persons deemed by a State entitled to recognition and protection to enhance their own liberty. It imposes a disability on the class by refusing to acknowledge a status the State finds to be dignified and proper. DOMA instructs all federal officials, and indeed all persons with whom same-sex couples interact, including their own children, that their marriage is less worthy than the marriages of others. The federal statute is invalid, for no legitimate purpose overcomes the purpose and effect to disparage and to injure those whom the State, by its marriage laws, sought to protect in personhood and dignity. By seeking to displace this protection and treating those persons as living in marriages less respected than others, the federal statute is in violation of the Fifth Amendment. This opinion and its holding are confined to those lawful marriages.

The judgment of the Court of Appeals for the Second Circuit is affirmed.

It is so ordered.

■ CHIEF JUSTICE ROBERTS, dissenting.

I agree with Justice SCALIA that this Court lacks jurisdiction to review the decisions of the courts below. On the merits of the constitutional dispute the Court decides to decide, I also agree with Justice SCALIA that Congress acted constitutionally in passing the Defense of Marriage Act (DOMA). Interests in uniformity and stability amply justified Congress's decision to retain the definition of marriage that, at that point, had been adopted by every State in our Nation, and every nation in the world.

The majority sees a more sinister motive, pointing out that the Federal Government has generally (though not uniformly) deferred to state definitions of marriage in the past. That is true, of course, but none of those prior state-by-state variations had involved differences over something—as the majority puts it—"thought of by most people as essential to the very definition of [marriage] and to its role and function throughout the history of civilization." That the Federal Government treated this fundamental question differently than it treated variations over consanguinity or minimum age is hardly surprising—and hardly enough to support a conclusion that the "principal purpose" of the 342 Representatives and 85 Senators who voted for it, and the President who signed it, was a bare desire to harm. Nor do the snippets of legislative history and the banal title of the Act to which the majority points suffice to make such a showing. At least without some more convincing evidence that the Act's principal purpose was to codify malice, and that it furthered *no* legitimate government interests, I would not tar the political branches with the brush of bigotry.

But while I disagree with the result to which the majority's analysis leads it in this case, I think it more important to point out that its analysis leads no further. The Court does not have before it, and the logic of its opinion does not decide, the distinct question whether the States, in the exercise of their "historic and essential authority to define the marital relation," may continue to utilize the traditional definition of marriage.

The majority goes out of its way to make this explicit in the penultimate sentence of its opinion. It states that "[t]his opinion and its holding are confined to those lawful marriages"—referring to same-sex marriages that a State has already recognized as a result of the local "community's considered perspective on the historical roots of the institution of marriage and its evolving understanding of the meaning of equality." Justice SCALIA believes this is a " 'bald, unreasoned disclaime[r].' " In my view, though, the disclaimer is a logical and necessary consequence of the argument the majority has chosen to adopt. The dominant theme of the majority opinion is that the Federal Government's intrusion into an area "central to state domestic relations law applicable to its residents and citizens" is sufficiently "unusual" to set off alarm bells. I think the majority goes off course, as I have said, but it is undeniable that its judgment is based on federalism.

The majority extensively chronicles DOMA's departure from the normal allocation of responsibility between State and Federal Governments, emphasizing that DOMA "rejects the long-established precept that the incidents, benefits, and obligations of marriage are uniform for all married couples within each State." But there is no such departure when one State adopts or keeps a definition of marriage that differs from that of its neighbor, for it is entirely expected that state definitions would "vary, subject to constitutional guarantees, from one State to the next." Thus, while "[t]he State's power in defining the marital relation is of central relevance" to the majority's decision to strike down DOMA here, that power will come into play on the other side of the board in future cases about the constitutionality of state marriage definitions. So too will the concerns for state diversity and sovereignty that weigh against DOMA's constitutionality in this case.

It is not just this central feature of the majority's analysis that is unique to DOMA, but many considerations on the periphery as well. For example, the majority focuses on the legislative history and title of this particular Act; those statute-specific considerations will, of course, be irrelevant in future cases about different statutes. The majority emphasizes that DOMA was a "systemwide enactment with no identified connection to any particular area of federal law," but a State's definition of marriage "is the foundation of the State's broader authority to regulate the subject of domestic relations with respect to the '[p]rotection of offspring, property interests, and the enforcement of marital responsibilities.'" And the federal decision undermined (in the majority's view) the "dignity [already] conferred by the States in the exercise of their sovereign power," whereas a State's decision whether to expand the definition of marriage from its traditional contours involves no similar concern.

We may in the future have to resolve challenges to state marriage definitions affecting same-sex couples. That issue, however, is not before us in this case. . . . I write only to highlight the limits of the majority's holding and reasoning today, lest its opinion be taken to resolve not only a question that I believe is not properly before us—DOMA's constitutionality—but also a question that all agree, and the Court explicitly acknowledges, is not at issue.

■ JUSTICE SCALIA, with whom JUSTICE THOMAS joins, and with whom THE CHIEF JUSTICE joins as to Part I, dissenting.

This case is about power in several respects. It is about the power of our people to govern themselves, and the power of this Court to pronounce the law. Today's opinion aggrandizes the latter, with the predictable consequence of diminishing the former. We have no power to decide this case. And even if we did, we have no power under the Constitution to invalidate this democratically adopted legislation. The Court's errors on both points spring forth from the same diseased root: an exalted conception of the role of this institution in America. . . .

II

For the reasons above, I think that this Court has, and the Court of Appeals had, no power to decide this suit. We should vacate the decision below and remand to the Court of Appeals for the Second Circuit, with instructions to dismiss the appeal. Given that the majority has volunteered its view of the merits, however, I proceed to discuss that as well.

A

There are many remarkable things about the majority's merits holding. The first is how rootless and shifting its justifications are. For example, the opinion starts with seven full pages about the traditional power of States to define domestic relations—initially fooling many readers, I am sure, into thinking that this is a federalism opinion. But we are eventually told that "it is unnecessary to decide whether this federal intrusion on state power is a violation of the Constitution," and that "[t]he State's power in defining the marital relation is of central relevance in this case quite apart from principles of federalism" because "the State's decision to give this class of persons the right to marry conferred upon them a dignity and status of immense import." But no one questions the power of the States to define marriage (with the concomitant conferral of dignity and status), so what is the point of devoting seven pages to describing how long and well established that power is? Even after the opinion has formally disclaimed reliance upon principles of federalism, mentions of "the usual tradition of recognizing and accepting state definitions of marriage" continue. What to make of this? The opinion never explains. My guess is that the majority, while reluctant to suggest that defining the meaning of "marriage" in federal statutes is unsupported by any of the Federal Government's enumerated powers,[4] nonetheless needs some rhetorical basis to support its pretense that today's prohibition of laws excluding same-sex marriage is confined to the Federal Government (leaving the second, state-law shoe to be dropped later, maybe next Term). But I am only guessing.

Equally perplexing are the opinion's references to "the Constitution's guarantee of equality." Near the end of the opinion, we are told that although the "equal protection guarantee of the Fourteenth Amendment makes [the] Fifth Amendment [due process] right all the more specific and all the better understood and preserved"—what can *that* mean?— "the Fifth Amendment itself withdraws from Government the power to degrade or demean in the way this law does." The only possible interpretation of this statement is that the Equal Protection Clause, even the Equal Protection Clause as incorporated in the Due Process Clause, is not the basis for today's holding. But the portion of the majority opinion that explains why DOMA is unconstitutional (Part IV) begins by citing *Bolling v. Sharpe,* 347 U.S. 497 (1954), *Department of Agriculture v. Moreno,* 413 U.S. 528 (1973), and *Romer v. Evans,* 517 U.S. 620 (1996)—

---

[4]   Such a suggestion would be impossible, given the Federal Government's long history of making pronouncements regarding marriage—for example, conditioning Utah's entry into the Union upon its prohibition of polygamy. See Act of July 16, 1894, ch. 138, § 3, 28 Stat. 108 ("The constitution [of Utah]" must provide "perfect toleration of religious sentiment," "*Provided,* That polygamous or plural marriages are forever prohibited").

all of which are equal-protection cases.[5] And those three cases are the *only* authorities that the Court cites in Part IV about the Constitution's meaning, except for its citation of *Lawrence v. Texas,* 539 U.S. 558 (2003) (not an equal-protection case) to support its passing assertion that the Constitution protects the "moral and sexual choices" of same-sex couples.

Moreover, if this is meant to be an equal-protection opinion, it is a confusing one. The opinion does not resolve and indeed does not even mention what had been the central question in this litigation: whether, under the Equal Protection Clause, laws restricting marriage to a man and a woman are reviewed for more than mere rationality. That is the issue that divided the parties and the court below, compare Brief for Respondent Bipartisan Legal Advisory Group of U.S. House of Representatives (merits) 24–28 (no), with Brief for Respondent Windsor (merits) 17–31 and Brief for United States (merits) 18–36 (yes); and compare 699 F.3d 169, 180–185 (C.A.2 2012) (yes), with *id.,* at 208–211 (Straub, J., dissenting in part and concurring in part) (no). In accord with my previously expressed skepticism about the Court's "tiers of scrutiny" approach, I would review this classification only for its rationality. As nearly as I can tell, the Court agrees with that; its opinion does not apply strict scrutiny, and its central propositions are taken from rational-basis cases like *Moreno.* But the Court certainly does not *apply* anything that resembles that deferential framework. See *Heller v. Doe,* 509 U.S. 312, 320 (1993) (a classification " 'must be upheld . . . if there is any reasonably conceivable state of facts' " that could justify it).

The majority opinion need not get into the strict-vs.-rational-basis scrutiny question, and need not justify its holding under either, because it says that DOMA is unconstitutional as "a deprivation of the liberty of the person protected by the Fifth Amendment of the Constitution"; that it violates "basic due process" principles; and that it inflicts an "injury and indignity" of a kind that denies "an essential part of the liberty protected by the Fifth Amendment." The majority never utters the dread words "substantive due process," perhaps sensing the disrepute into which that doctrine has fallen, but that is what those statements mean. Yet the opinion does not argue that same-sex marriage is "deeply rooted in this Nation's history and tradition," *Washington v. Glucksberg,* 521 U.S. 702, 720–721 (1997), a claim that would of course be quite absurd. So would the further suggestion (also necessary, under our substantive-due-process precedents) that a world in which DOMA exists is one bereft of " 'ordered liberty.' " *Id.,* at 721 (quoting *Palko v. Connecticut,* 302 U.S. 319, 325 (1937)).

Some might conclude that this loaf could have used a while longer in the oven. But that would be wrong; it is already overcooked. The most expert care in preparation cannot redeem a bad recipe. The sum of all the

---

[5]   Since the Equal Protection Clause technically applies only against the States, see U.S. Const., Amdt. 14, *Bolling* and *Moreno,* dealing with federal action, relied upon "the equal protection component of the Due Process Clause of the Fifth Amendment."

Court's nonspecific hand-waving is that this law is invalid (maybe on equal-protection grounds, maybe on substantive-due-process grounds, and perhaps with some amorphous federalism component playing a role) because it is motivated by a " 'bare . . . desire to harm' " couples in same-sex marriages. It is this proposition with which I will therefore engage.

B

As I have observed before, the Constitution does not forbid the government to enforce traditional moral and sexual norms. See *Lawrence v. Texas,* 539 U.S. 558, 599 (2003) (SCALIA, J., dissenting). I will not swell the U.S. Reports with restatements of that point. It is enough to say that the Constitution neither requires nor forbids our society to approve of same-sex marriage, much as it neither requires nor forbids us to approve of no-fault divorce, polygamy, or the consumption of alcohol.

However, even setting aside traditional moral disapproval of same-sex marriage (or indeed same-sex sex), there are many perfectly valid—indeed, downright boring—justifying rationales for this legislation. Their existence ought to be the end of this case. For they give the lie to the Court's conclusion that only those with hateful hearts could have voted "aye" on this Act. And more importantly, they serve to make the contents of the legislators' hearts quite irrelevant: "It is a familiar principle of constitutional law that this Court will not strike down an otherwise constitutional statute on the basis of an alleged illicit legislative motive." *United States v. O'Brien,* 391 U.S. 367, 383 (1968). Or at least it *was* a familiar principle. By holding to the contrary, the majority has declared open season on any law that (in the opinion of the law's opponents and any panel of like-minded federal judges) can be characterized as mean-spirited.

The majority concludes that the only motive for this Act was the "bare . . . desire to harm a politically unpopular group." Bear in mind that the object of this condemnation is not the legislature of some once-Confederate Southern state (familiar objects of the Court's scorn), but our respected coordinate branches, the Congress and Presidency of the United States. Laying such a charge against them should require the most extraordinary evidence, and I would have thought that every attempt would be made to indulge a more anodyne explanation for the statute. The majority does the opposite—affirmatively concealing from the reader the arguments that exist in justification. It makes only a passing mention of the "arguments put forward" by the Act's defenders, and does not even trouble to paraphrase or describe them. I imagine that this is because it is harder to maintain the illusion of the Act's supporters as unhinged members of a wild-eyed lynch mob when one first describes their views as *they* see them.

To choose just one of these defenders' arguments, DOMA avoids difficult choice-of-law issues that will now arise absent a uniform federal definition of marriage. Imagine a pair of women who marry in Albany and then move to Alabama, which does not "recognize as valid any marriage of parties of the same sex." Ala.Code § 30–1–19(e) (2011). When the couple files their next federal tax return, may it be a joint one? Which State's law controls, for federal-law purposes: their State of celebration (which recognizes the marriage) or their State of domicile (which does not)? (Does the answer depend on whether they were just visiting in Albany?) Are these questions to be answered as a matter of federal common law, or perhaps by borrowing a State's choice-of-law rules? If so, *which* State's? And what about States where the status of an out-of-state same-sex marriage is an unsettled question under local law? DOMA avoided all of this uncertainty by specifying which marriages would be recognized for federal purposes. That is a classic purpose for a definitional provision.

Further, DOMA preserves the intended effects of prior legislation against then-unforeseen changes in circumstance. When Congress provided (for example) that a special estate-tax exemption would exist for spouses, this exemption reached only *opposite-sex* spouses—those being the only sort that were recognized in *any* State at the time of DOMA's passage. When it became clear that changes in state law might one day alter that balance, DOMA's definitional section was enacted to ensure that state-level experimentation did not automatically alter the basic operation of federal law, unless and until Congress made the further judgment to do so on its own. That is not animus—just stabilizing prudence. Congress has hardly demonstrated itself unwilling to make such further, revising judgments upon due deliberation. See, *e.g.,* Don't Ask, Don't Tell Repeal Act of 2010, 124 Stat. 3515.

The Court mentions none of this. Instead, it accuses the Congress that enacted this law and the President who signed it of something much worse than, for example, having acted in excess of enumerated federal powers—or even having drawn distinctions that prove to be irrational. Those legal errors may be made in good faith, errors though they are. But the majority says that the supporters of this Act acted with *malice*—with *the "purpose"* "to disparage and to injure" same-sex couples. It says that the motivation for DOMA was to "demean," to "impose inequality," to "impose . . . a stigma," to deny people "equal dignity," to brand gay people as "unworthy," and to "*humiliat*[e]" their children.

I am sure these accusations are quite untrue. To be sure (as the majority points out), the legislation is called the Defense of Marriage Act. But to defend traditional marriage is not to condemn, demean, or humiliate those who would prefer other arrangements, any more than to defend the Constitution of the United States is to condemn, demean, or humiliate other constitutions. To hurl such accusations so casually demeans *this institution*. In the majority's judgment, any resistance to its holding is beyond the pale of reasoned disagreement. To question its high-handed invalidation of a presumptively valid statute is to act (the majority is sure) with *the purpose* to "disparage," "injure," "degrade," "demean," and "humiliate" our fellow human beings, our fellow citizens, who are homosexual. All that, simply for supporting an Act that did no more than codify an aspect of marriage that had been unquestioned in our society for most of its existence—indeed, had been unquestioned in virtually all societies for virtually all of human history. It is one thing for a society to elect change; it is another for a court of law to impose change by adjudging those who oppose it *hostes humani generis,* enemies of the human race.

* * *

The penultimate sentence of the majority's opinion is a naked declaration that "[t]his opinion and its holding are confined" to those couples "joined in same-sex marriages made lawful by the State." I have heard such "bald, unreasoned disclaimer[s]" before. When the Court declared a constitutional right to homosexual sodomy, we were assured that the case had nothing, nothing at all to do with "whether the government must give formal recognition to any relationship that homosexual persons seek to enter." *Lawrence,* 539 U.S. at 578. Now we are told that DOMA is invalid because it "demeans the couple, whose moral and sexual choices the Constitution protects"—with an accompanying citation of *Lawrence.* It takes real cheek for today's majority to assure us, as it is going out the door, that a constitutional requirement to give formal recognition to same-sex marriage is not at issue here—when what has preceded that assurance is a lecture on how superior the majority's moral judgment in favor of same-sex marriage is to the Congress's hateful moral judgment against it. I promise you this: The only thing that will "confine" the Court's holding is its sense of what it can get away with.

I do not mean to suggest disagreement with THE CHIEF JUSTICE's view, that lower federal courts and state courts can distinguish today's case when the issue before them is state denial of marital status to same-sex couples—or even that this Court could *theoretically* do so. Lord, an opinion with such scatter-shot rationales as this one (federalism noises among them) can be distinguished in many ways. And deserves to be. State and lower federal courts should take the Court at its word and distinguish away.

In my opinion, however, the view that *this* Court will take of state prohibition of same-sex marriage is indicated beyond mistaking by today's opinion. As I have said, the real rationale of today's opinion, whatever disappearing trail of its legalistic argle-bargle one chooses to follow, is that DOMA is motivated by " 'bare . . . desire to harm' " couples in same-sex marriages. . . . In sum, that Court which finds it so horrific that Congress irrationally and hatefully robbed same-sex couples of the "personhood and dignity" which state legislatures conferred upon them, will of a certitude be similarly appalled by state legislatures' irrational and hateful failure to acknowledge that "personhood and dignity" in the first place. As far as this Court is concerned, no one should be fooled; it is just a matter of listening and waiting for the other shoe. . . .

As to that debate: Few public controversies touch an institution so central to the lives of so many, and few inspire such attendant passion by good people on all sides. Few public controversies will ever demonstrate so vividly the beauty of what our Framers gave us, a gift the Court pawns today to buy its stolen moment in the spotlight: a system of government that permits us to rule *ourselves*. Since DOMA's passage, citizens on all sides of the question have seen victories and they have seen defeats. There have been plebiscites, legislation, persuasion, and loud voices—in other words, democracy. Victories in one place for some, see North Carolina Const., Amdt. 1 (providing that "[m]arriage between one man and one woman is the only domestic legal union that shall be valid or recognized in this State") (approved by a popular vote, 61% to 39% on May 8, 2012), are offset by victories in other places for others, see Maryland Question 6 (establishing "that Maryland's civil marriage laws allow gay and lesbian couples to obtain a civil marriage license") (approved by a popular vote, 52% to 48%, on November 6, 2012). Even in a *single State*, the question has come out differently on different occasions. Compare Maine Question 1 (permitting "the State of Maine to issue marriage licenses to same-sex couples") (approved by a popular vote, 53% to 47%, on November 6, 2012) with Maine Question 1 (rejecting "the new law that lets same-sex couples marry") (approved by a popular vote, 53% to 47%, on November 3, 2009).

In the majority's telling, this story is black-and-white: Hate your neighbor or come along with us. The truth is more complicated. It is hard to admit that one's political opponents are not monsters, especially in a struggle like this one, and the challenge in the end proves more than today's Court can handle. Too bad. A reminder that disagreement over something so fundamental as marriage can still be politically legitimate would have been a fit task for what in earlier times was called the judicial temperament. We might have covered ourselves with honor today, by promising all sides of this debate that it was theirs to settle and that we would respect their resolution. We might have let the People decide.

But that the majority will not do. Some will rejoice in today's decision, and some will despair at it; that is the nature of a controversy that matters so much to so many. But the Court has cheated both sides, robbing the winners of an honest victory, and the losers of the peace that comes from a fair defeat. We owed both of them better. I dissent.

■ **JUSTICE ALITO, with whom JUSTICE THOMAS joins as to Parts II and III, dissenting.**

Our Nation is engaged in a heated debate about same-sex marriage. That debate is, at bottom, about the nature of the institution of marriage. Respondent Edith Windsor, supported by the United States, asks this Court to intervene in that debate, and although she couches her argument in different terms, what she seeks is a holding that enshrines in the Constitution a particular understanding of marriage under which the sex of the partners makes no difference. The Constitution, however, does not dictate that choice. It leaves the choice to the people, acting through their elected representatives at both the federal and state levels. I would therefore hold that Congress did not violate Windsor's constitutional rights by enacting § 3 of the Defense of Marriage Act (DOMA), 110 Stat. 2419, which defines the meaning of marriage under federal statutes that either confer upon married persons certain federal benefits or impose upon them certain federal obligations. . . .

II

. . . Same-sex marriage presents a highly emotional and important question of public policy—but not a difficult question of constitutional law. The Constitution does not guarantee the right to enter into a same-sex marriage. Indeed, no provision of the Constitution speaks to the issue.

The Court has sometimes found the Due Process Clauses to have a substantive component that guarantees liberties beyond the absence of physical restraint. And the Court's holding that "DOMA is unconstitutional as a deprivation of the liberty of the person protected by the Fifth Amendment of the Constitution" suggests that substantive due process may partially underlie the Court's decision today. But it is well established that any "substantive" component to the Due Process Clause protects only "those fundamental rights and liberties which are, objectively, 'deeply rooted in this Nation's history and tradition,' " as well as " 'implicit in the concept of ordered liberty,' such that 'neither liberty nor justice would exist if they were sacrificed.' " *Washington v. Glucksberg,* 521 U.S. 702, 720–721 (1997).

It is beyond dispute that the right to same-sex marriage is not deeply rooted in this Nation's history and tradition. In this country, no State permitted same-sex marriage until the Massachusetts Supreme Judicial Court held in 2003 that limiting marriage to opposite-sex couples violated the State Constitution. See *Goodridge v. Department of Public Health,* 440 Mass. 309, 798 N.E.2d 941. Nor is the right to same-sex marriage deeply rooted in the traditions of other nations. No country allowed same-sex couples to marry until the Netherlands did so in 2000.

What Windsor and the United States seek, therefore, is not the protection of a deeply rooted right but the recognition of a very new right, and they seek this innovation not from a legislative body elected by the people, but from unelected judges. Faced with such a request, judges have cause for both caution and humility.

The family is an ancient and universal human institution. Family structure reflects the characteristics of a civilization, and changes in family structure and in the popular understanding of marriage and the family can have profound effects. Past changes in the understanding of marriage—for example, the gradual ascendance of the idea that romantic love is a prerequisite to marriage—have had far-reaching consequences. But the process by which such consequences come about is complex, involving the interaction of numerous factors, and tends to occur over an extended period of time.

We can expect something similar to take place if same-sex marriage becomes widely accepted. The long-term consequences of this change are not now known and are unlikely to be ascertainable for some time to come.[5] There are those who think that allowing same-sex marriage will seriously undermine the institution of marriage. See, *e.g.,* S. Girgis, R. Anderson, & R. George, What is Marriage? Man and Woman: A Defense 53–58 (2012); Finnis, Marriage: A Basic and Exigent Good, 91 The Monist 388, 398 (2008). Others think that recognition of same-sex marriage will fortify a now-shaky institution. See, *e.g.,* A. Sullivan, Virtually Normal: An Argument About Homosexuality 202–203 (1996); J. Rauch, Gay Marriage: Why It Is Good for Gays, Good for Straights, and Good for America 94 (2004).

At present, no one—including social scientists, philosophers, and historians—can predict with any certainty what the long-term ramifications of widespread acceptance of same-sex marriage will be. And judges are certainly not equipped to make such an assessment. The Members of this Court have the authority and the responsibility to interpret and apply the Constitution. Thus, if the Constitution contained a provision guaranteeing the right to marry a person of the same sex, it would be our duty to enforce that right. But the Constitution simply does not speak to the issue of same-sex marriage. In our system of government, ultimate sovereignty rests with the people, and the people have the right to control their own destiny. Any change on a question so fundamental should be made by the people through their elected officials.

III

Perhaps because they cannot show that same-sex marriage is a fundamental right under our Constitution, Windsor and the United States couch their arguments in equal protection terms. They argue that § 3 of DOMA discriminates on the basis of sexual orientation, that classifications based on sexual orientation should trigger a form of "heightened" scrutiny, and that § 3 cannot survive such scrutiny. They further maintain that the governmental interests that § 3 purports to serve are not sufficiently important and that it has not been adequately shown that § 3 serves those interests very well. The Court's holding, too, seems to rest on "the equal protection guarantee of the Fourteenth Amendment"—although the Court is careful not to adopt most of Windsor's and the United States' argument.

In my view, the approach that Windsor and the United States advocate is misguided. Our equal protection framework, upon which

---

[5] As sociologists have documented, it sometimes takes decades to document the effects of social changes—like the sharp rise in divorce rates following the advent of no-fault divorce—on children and society. See generally J. Wallerstein, J. Lewis, & S. Blakeslee, The Unexpected Legacy of Divorce: The 25 Year Landmark Study (2000).

Windsor and the United States rely, is a judicial construct that provides a useful mechanism for analyzing a certain universe of equal protection cases. But that framework is ill suited for use in evaluating the constitutionality of laws based on the traditional understanding of marriage, which fundamentally turn on what marriage is.

Underlying our equal protection jurisprudence is the central notion that "[a] classification 'must be reasonable, not arbitrary, and must rest upon some ground of difference having a fair and substantial relation to the object of the legislation, so that all persons similarly circumstanced shall be treated alike.'" *Reed v. Reed,* 404 U.S. 71, 76 (1971). The modern tiers of scrutiny—on which Windsor and the United States rely so heavily—are a heuristic to help judges determine when classifications have that "fair and substantial relation to the object of the legislation."

So, for example, those classifications subject to strict scrutiny—*i.e.,* classifications that must be narrowly tailored to achieve a compelling government interest,—are those that are "so seldom relevant to the achievement of any legitimate state interest that laws grounded in such considerations are deemed to reflect prejudice and antipathy." *Cleburne v. Cleburne Living Center, Inc.,* 473 U.S. 432, 440 (1985).

In contrast, those characteristics subject to so-called intermediate scrutiny—*i.e.,* those classifications that must be substantially related to the achievement of important governmental objectives—are those that are *sometimes* relevant considerations to be taken into account by legislators, but "generally provid[e] no sensible ground for different treatment," *Cleburne, supra,* at 440. For example, the Court has held that statutory rape laws that criminalize sexual intercourse with a woman under the age of 18 years, but place no similar liability on partners of underage men, are grounded in the very real distinction that "young men and young women are not similarly situated with respect to the problems and the risks of sexual intercourse." *Michael M. v. Superior Court, Sonoma Cty.,* 450 U.S. 464, 471 (1981) (plurality opinion). The plurality reasoned that "[o]nly women may become pregnant, and they suffer disproportionately the profound physical, emotional, and psychological consequences of sexual activity." In other contexts, however, the Court has found that classifications based on gender are "arbitrary," *Reed, supra,* at 76, and based on "outmoded notions of the relative capabilities of men and women," *Cleburne, supra,* at 441, as when a State provides that a man must always be preferred to an equally qualified woman when both seek to administer the estate of a deceased party, see *Reed, supra,* at 76–77.

Finally, so-called rational-basis review applies to classifications based on "distinguishing characteristics relevant to interests the State has the authority to implement." *Cleburne, supra,* at 441. We have long recognized that "the equal protection of the laws must coexist with the practical necessity that most legislation classifies for one purpose or another, with resulting disadvantages to various groups or persons." *Romer v. Evans,* 517 U.S. 620, 631 (1996). . . .

In asking the Court to determine that § 3 of DOMA is subject to and violates heightened scrutiny, Windsor and the United States thus ask us to rule that the presence of two members of the opposite sex is as rationally related to marriage as white skin is to voting or a Y-chromosome is to the ability to administer an estate. That is a striking request and one that unelected judges should pause before granting. Acceptance of the argument would cast all those who cling to traditional beliefs about the nature of marriage in the role of bigots or superstitious fools.

By asking the Court to strike down DOMA as not satisfying some form of heightened scrutiny, Windsor and the United States are really seeking to have the Court resolve a debate between two competing views of marriage.

The first and older view, which I will call the "traditional" or "conjugal" view, sees marriage as an intrinsically opposite-sex institution. BLAG notes that virtually every culture, including many not influenced by the Abrahamic religions, has limited marriage to people of the opposite sex. And BLAG attempts to explain this phenomenon by arguing that the institution of marriage was created for the purpose of channeling heterosexual intercourse into a structure that supports child rearing. Others explain the basis for the institution in more philosophical terms. They argue that marriage is essentially the solemnizing of a comprehensive, exclusive, permanent union that is intrinsically ordered to producing new life, even if it does not always do so. While modern cultural changes have weakened the link between marriage and procreation in the popular mind, there is no doubt that, throughout human history and across many cultures, marriage has been viewed as an exclusively opposite-sex institution and as one inextricably linked to procreation and biological kinship.

The other, newer view is what I will call the "consent-based" vision of marriage, a vision that primarily defines marriage as the solemnization of mutual commitment—marked by strong emotional attachment and sexual attraction—between two persons. At least as it applies to heterosexual couples, this view of marriage now plays a very prominent role in the popular understanding of the institution. Indeed, our popular culture is infused with this understanding of marriage. Proponents of same-sex marriage argue that because gender differentiation is not relevant to this vision, the exclusion of same-sex couples from the institution of marriage is rank discrimination.

The Constitution does not codify either of these views of marriage (although I suspect it would have been hard at the time of the adoption of the Constitution or the Fifth Amendment to find Americans who did not take the traditional view for granted). The silence of the Constitution on this question should be enough to end the matter as far as the judiciary is concerned. Yet, Windsor and the United States implicitly ask us to endorse the consent-based view of marriage and to reject the traditional view, thereby arrogating to ourselves the power to decide a question that philosophers, historians, social scientists, and theologians are better qualified to explore.[7] Because our constitutional order assigns the resolution of questions of this nature to the people, I would not presume to enshrine either vision of marriage in our constitutional jurisprudence.

Legislatures, however, have little choice but to decide between the two views. We have long made clear that neither the political branches of the Federal Government nor state governments are required to be neutral between competing visions of the good, provided that the vision of the good that they adopt is not countermanded by the Constitution. See, *e.g., Rust v. Sullivan,* 500 U.S. 173, 192 (1991) ("[T]he government may make a value judgment favoring childbirth over abortion"). Accordingly, both Congress and the States are entitled to enact laws recognizing either of the two understandings of marriage. And given the size of government and the degree to which it now regulates daily life, it seems unlikely that either Congress or the States could maintain complete neutrality even if they tried assiduously to do so.

Rather than fully embracing the arguments made by Windsor and the United States, the Court strikes down § 3 of DOMA as a classification not properly supported by its objectives. The Court reaches this conclusion in part because it believes that § 3 encroaches upon the States' sovereign prerogative to define marriage. . . . To the extent that the Court takes the position that the question of same-sex marriage should be resolved primarily at the state level, I wholeheartedly agree. I hope

---

7 The degree to which this question is intractable to typical judicial processes of decisionmaking was highlighted by the trial in *Hollingsworth v. Perry,* 558 U.S. 183 (2010). In that case, the trial judge, after receiving testimony from some expert witnesses, purported to make "findings of fact" on such questions as why marriage came to be, *Perry v. Schwarzenegger,* 704 F.Supp.2d 921, 958 (N.D.Cal.2010) (finding of fact no. 27) ("Marriage between a man and a woman was traditionally organized based on presumptions of division of labor along gender lines. Men were seen as suited for certain types of work and women for others. Women were seen as suited to raise children and men were seen as suited to provide for the family"), what marriage is, *id.,* at 961 (finding of fact no. 34) ("Marriage is the state recognition and approval of a couple's choice to live with each other, to remain committed to one another and to form a household based on their own feelings about one another and to join in an economic partnership and support one another and any dependents"), and the effect legalizing same-sex marriage would have on opposite-sex marriage, *id.,* at 972 (finding of fact no. 55) ("Permitting same-sex couples to marry will not affect the number of opposite-sex couples who marry, divorce, cohabit, have children outside of marriage or otherwise affect the stability of opposite-sex marriages").

At times, the trial reached the heights of parody, as when the trial judge questioned his ability to take into account the views of great thinkers of the past because they were unavailable to testify in person in his courtroom. See 13 Tr. in No. C 09–2292 VRW (ND Cal.), pp. 3038–3039.

And, if this spectacle were not enough, some professors of constitutional law have argued that we are bound to accept the trial judge's findings—including those on major philosophical questions and predictions about the future—unless they are "clearly erroneous." See Brief for Constitutional Law and Civil Procedure Professors as *Amici Curiae* in *Hollingsworth v. Perry,* O.T. 2012, No. 12–144, pp. 2–3. Only an arrogant legal culture that has lost all appreciation of its own limitations could take such a suggestion seriously.

that the Court will ultimately permit the people of each State to decide this question for themselves. Unless the Court is willing to allow this to occur, the whiffs of federalism in the today's opinion of the Court will soon be scattered to the wind.

In any event, § 3 of DOMA, in my view, does not encroach on the prerogatives of the States, assuming of course that the many federal statutes affected by DOMA have not already done so. Section 3 does not prevent any State from recognizing same-sex marriage or from extending to same-sex couples any right, privilege, benefit, or obligation stemming from state law. All that § 3 does is to define a class of persons to whom federal law extends certain special benefits and upon whom federal law imposes certain special burdens. In these provisions, Congress used marital status as a way of defining this class—in part, I assume, because it viewed marriage as a valuable institution to be fostered and in part because it viewed married couples as comprising a unique type of economic unit that merits special regulatory treatment. Assuming that Congress has the power under the Constitution to enact the laws affected by § 3, Congress has the power to define the category of persons to whom those laws apply.

* * *

For these reasons, I would hold that § 3 of DOMA does not violate the Fifth Amendment. I respectfully dissent.

Obergefell v. Hodges
135 S. Ct. 2584 (2015)

■ JUSTICE KENNEDY delivered the opinion of the Court.

The Constitution promises liberty to all within its reach, a liberty that includes certain specific rights that allow persons, within a lawful realm, to define and express their identity. The petitioners in these cases seek to find that liberty by marrying someone of the same sex and having their marriages deemed lawful on the same terms and conditions as marriages between persons of the opposite sex.

I

These cases come from Michigan, Kentucky, Ohio, and Tennessee, States that define marriage as a union between one man and one woman. See, *e.g.*, Mich. Const., Art. I, § 25; Ky. Const. § 233A; Ohio Rev.Code Ann. § 3101.01; Tenn. Const., Art. XI, § 18. The petitioners are 14 same-sex couples and two men whose same-sex partners are deceased. The respondents are state officials responsible for enforcing the laws in question. The petitioners claim the respondents violate the Fourteenth Amendment by denying them the right to marry or to have their marriages, lawfully performed in another State, given full recognition.

Petitioners filed these suits in United States District Courts in their home States. Each District Court ruled in their favor. . . . [The] United

States Court of Appeals for the Sixth Circuit . . . consolidated the cases and reversed the judgments of the District Courts. The Court of Appeals held that a State has no constitutional obligation to license same-sex marriages or to recognize same-sex marriages performed out of State. . . .

This Court granted review, limited to two questions. The first, presented by the cases from Michigan and Kentucky, is whether the Fourteenth Amendment requires a State to license a marriage between two people of the same sex. The second, presented by the cases from Ohio, Tennessee, and, again, Kentucky, is whether the Fourteenth Amendment requires a State to recognize a same-sex marriage licensed and performed in a State which does grant that right. . . .

II

A

From their beginning to their most recent page, the annals of human history reveal the transcendent importance of marriage. The lifelong union of a man and a woman always has promised nobility and dignity to all persons, without regard to their station in life. Marriage is sacred to those who live by their religions and offers unique fulfillment to those who find meaning in the secular realm. Its dynamic allows two people to find a life that could not be found alone, for a marriage becomes greater than just the two persons. Rising from the most basic human needs, marriage is essential to our most profound hopes and aspirations.

The centrality of marriage to the human condition makes it unsurprising that the institution has existed for millennia and across civilizations. Since the dawn of history, marriage has transformed strangers into relatives, binding families and societies together. Confucius taught that marriage lies at the foundation of government. This wisdom was echoed centuries later and half a world away by Cicero, who wrote, "The first bond of society is marriage; next, children; and then the family." There are untold references to the beauty of marriage in religious and philosophical texts spanning time, cultures, and faiths, as well as in art and literature in all their forms. It is fair and necessary to say these references were based on the understanding that marriage is a union between two persons of the opposite sex.

That history is the beginning of these cases. The respondents say it should be the end as well. To them, it would demean a timeless institution if the concept and lawful status of marriage were extended to two persons of the same sex. Marriage, in their view, is by its nature a gender-differentiated union of man and woman. This view long has been held—and continues to be held—in good faith by reasonable and sincere people here and throughout the world.

The petitioners acknowledge this history but contend that these cases cannot end there. Were their intent to demean the revered idea and reality of marriage, the petitioners' claims would be of a different order. But that is neither their purpose nor their submission. To the contrary, it is the enduring importance of marriage that underlies the petitioners' contentions. This, they say, is their whole point. Far from seeking to devalue marriage, the petitioners seek it for themselves because of their respect—and need—for its privileges and responsibilities. And their immutable nature dictates that same-sex marriage is their only real path to this profound commitment.

Recounting the circumstances of three of these cases illustrates the urgency of the petitioners' cause from their perspective. Petitioner James Obergefell, a plaintiff in the Ohio case, met John Arthur over two decades ago. They fell in love and started a life together, establishing a lasting, committed relation. In 2011, however, Arthur was diagnosed with amyotrophic lateral sclerosis, or ALS. This debilitating disease is progressive, with no known cure. Two years ago, Obergefell and Arthur decided to commit to one another, resolving to marry before Arthur died. To fulfill their mutual promise, they traveled from Ohio to Maryland, where same-sex marriage was legal. It was difficult for Arthur to move, and so the couple were wed inside a medical transport plane as it remained on the tarmac in Baltimore. Three months later, Arthur died. Ohio law does not permit Obergefell to be listed as the surviving spouse on Arthur's death certificate. By statute, they must remain strangers even in death, a state-imposed separation Obergefell deems "hurtful for the rest of time." He brought suit to be shown as the surviving spouse on Arthur's death certificate.

April DeBoer and Jayne Rowse are co-plaintiffs in the case from Michigan. They celebrated a commitment ceremony to honor their permanent relation in 2007. They both work as nurses, DeBoer in a neonatal unit and Rowse in an emergency unit. In 2009, DeBoer and Rowse fostered and then adopted a baby boy. Later that same year, they welcomed another son into their family. The new baby, born prematurely and abandoned by his biological mother, required around-the-clock care. The next year, a baby girl with special needs joined their family. Michigan, however, permits only opposite-sex married couples or single individuals to adopt, so each child can have only one woman as his or her legal parent. If an emergency were to arise, schools and hospitals may treat the three children as if they had only one parent. And, were tragedy to befall either DeBoer or Rowse, the other would have no legal rights over the children she had not been permitted to adopt. This couple seeks relief from the continuing uncertainty their unmarried status creates in their lives.

Army Reserve Sergeant First Class Ijpe DeKoe and his partner Thomas Kostura, co-plaintiffs in the Tennessee case, fell in love. In 2011, DeKoe received orders to deploy to Afghanistan. Before leaving, he and Kostura married in New York. A week later, DeKoe began his deployment, which lasted for almost a year. When he returned, the two settled in Tennessee, where DeKoe works full-time for the Army Reserve. Their lawful marriage is stripped from them whenever they reside in

Tennessee, returning and disappearing as they travel across state lines. DeKoe, who served this Nation to preserve the freedom the Constitution protects, must endure a substantial burden. . . .

B

The ancient origins of marriage confirm its centrality, but it has not stood in isolation from developments in law and society. The history of marriage is one of both continuity and change. That institution—even as confined to opposite-sex relations—has evolved over time.

For example, marriage was once viewed as an arrangement by the couple's parents based on political, religious, and financial concerns; but by the time of the Nation's founding it was understood to be a voluntary contract between a man and a woman. As the role and status of women changed, the institution further evolved. Under the centuries-old doctrine of coverture, a married man and woman were treated by the State as a single, male-dominated legal entity. As women gained legal, political, and property rights, and as society began to understand that women have their own equal dignity, the law of coverture was abandoned. These and other developments in the institution of marriage over the past centuries were not mere superficial changes. Rather, they worked deep transformations in its structure, affecting aspects of marriage long viewed by many as essential.

These new insights have strengthened, not weakened, the institution of marriage. Indeed, changed understandings of marriage are characteristic of a Nation where new dimensions of freedom become apparent to new generations, often through perspectives that begin in pleas or protests and then are considered in the political sphere and the judicial process.

This dynamic can be seen in the Nation's experiences with the rights of gays and lesbians. Until the mid-20th century, same-sex intimacy long had been condemned as immoral by the state itself in most Western nations, a belief often embodied in the criminal law. For this reason, among others, many persons did not deem homosexuals to have dignity in their own distinct identity. A truthful declaration by same-sex couples of what was in their hearts had to remain unspoken. Even when a greater awareness of the humanity and integrity of homosexual persons came in the period after World War II, the argument that gays and lesbians had a just claim to dignity was in conflict with both law and widespread social conventions. Same-sex intimacy remained a crime in many States. Gays and lesbians were prohibited from most government employment, barred from military service, excluded under immigration laws, targeted by police, and burdened in their rights to associate.

For much of the 20th century, moreover, homosexuality was treated as an illness. When the American Psychiatric Association published the first Diagnostic and Statistical Manual of Mental Disorders in 1952, homosexuality was classified as a mental disorder, a position adhered to until 1973. Only in more recent years have psychiatrists and others recognized that sexual orientation is both a normal expression of human sexuality and immutable.

In the late 20th century, following substantial cultural and political developments, same-sex couples began to lead more open and public lives and to establish families. This development was followed by a quite extensive discussion of the issue in both governmental and private sectors and by a shift in public attitudes toward greater tolerance. As a result, questions about the rights of gays and lesbians soon reached the courts . . . .

This Court first gave detailed consideration to the legal status of homosexuals in *Bowers v. Hardwick*, 478 U.S. 186 (1986). There it upheld the constitutionality of a Georgia law deemed to criminalize certain homosexual acts. Ten years later, in *Romer v. Evans*, 517 U.S. 620 (1996), the Court invalidated an amendment to Colorado's Constitution that sought to foreclose any branch or political subdivision of the State from protecting persons against discrimination based on sexual orientation. Then, in 2003, the Court overruled *Bowers*, holding that laws making same-sex intimacy a crime "demea[n] the lives of homosexual persons." *Lawrence v. Texas*, 539 U.S. 558, 575 (2003).

Against this background, the legal question of same-sex marriage arose. In 1993, the Hawaii Supreme Court held Hawaii's law restricting marriage to opposite-sex couples constituted a classification on the basis of sex and was therefore subject to strict scrutiny under the Hawaii Constitution. *Baehr v. Lewin,* 74 Haw. 530, 852 P.2d 44. Although this decision did not mandate that same-sex marriage be allowed, some States were concerned by its implications and reaffirmed in their laws that marriage is defined as a union between opposite-sex partners. So too in 1996, Congress passed the Defense of Marriage Act (DOMA), defining marriage for all federal-law purposes as "only a legal union between one man and one woman as husband and wife." 1 U.S.C. § 7.

The new and widespread discussion of the subject led other States to a different conclusion. In 2003, the Supreme Judicial Court of Massachusetts held the State's Constitution guaranteed same-sex couples the right to marry. See *Goodridge v. Department of Public Health,* 440 Mass. 309, 798 N.E.2d 941 (2003). After that ruling, some additional States granted marriage rights to same-sex couples, either through judicial or legislative processes. . . . Two Terms ago, in *United States v. Windsor,* 133 S.Ct. 2675 (2013), this Court invalidated DOMA to the extent it barred the Federal Government from treating same-sex marriages as valid even when they were lawful in the State where they were licensed. DOMA, the Court held, impermissibly disparaged those same-sex couples "who wanted to affirm their commitment to one another before their children, their family, their friends, and their community."

Numerous cases about same-sex marriage have reached the United States Courts of Appeals in recent years. With the exception of the opinion here under review and one other, see *Citizens for Equal Protection v. Bruning,* 455 F.3d 859, 864–868 (C.A.8 2006), the Courts of Appeals have held that excluding same-sex couples from marriage violates the Constitution. . . . [M]ost [district courts], too, have concluded same-sex couples must be allowed to marry. In addition the highest courts of many States have contributed to this ongoing dialogue in decisions interpreting their own State Constitutions.

After years of litigation, legislation, referenda, and the discussions that attended these public acts, the States are now divided on the issue of same-sex marriage.

III

Under the Due Process Clause of the Fourteenth Amendment, no State shall "deprive any person of life, liberty, or property, without due process of law." The fundamental liberties protected by this Clause . . . extend to certain personal choices central to individual dignity and autonomy, including intimate choices that define personal identity and beliefs. See, *e.g., Eisenstadt v. Baird,* 405 U.S. 438, 453 (1972); *Griswold v. Connecticut,* 381 U.S. 479, 484–486 (1965).

The identification and protection of fundamental rights is an enduring part of the judicial duty to interpret the Constitution. That responsibility, however, "has not been reduced to any formula." *Poe v. Ullman,* 367 U.S. 497, 542 (1961) (Harlan, J., dissenting). Rather, it requires courts to exercise reasoned judgment in identifying interests of the person so fundamental that the State must accord them its respect. That process is guided by many of the same considerations relevant to analysis of other constitutional provisions that set forth broad principles rather than specific requirements. History and tradition guide and discipline this inquiry but do not set its outer boundaries. . . .

The nature of injustice is that we may not always see it in our own times. The generations that wrote and ratified the Bill of Rights and the Fourteenth Amendment did not presume to know the extent of freedom in all of its dimensions, and so they entrusted to future generations a charter protecting the right of all persons to enjoy liberty as we learn its meaning. When new insight reveals discord between the Constitution's central protections and a received legal stricture, a claim to liberty must be addressed.

Applying these established tenets, the Court has long held the right to marry is protected by the Constitution. In *Loving v. Virginia,* 388 U.S. 1, 12 (1967), which invalidated bans on interracial unions, a unanimous Court held marriage is "one of the vital personal rights essential to the orderly pursuit of happiness by free men." The Court reaffirmed that holding in *Zablocki v. Redhail,* 434 U.S. 374, 384 (1978), which held the right to marry was burdened by a law prohibiting fathers who were behind on child support from marrying. The Court again applied this principle in *Turner v. Safley,* 482 U.S. 78, 95 (1987), which held the right to marry was abridged by regulations limiting the privilege of prison inmates to marry. Over time and in other contexts, the Court has reiterated that the right to marry is fundamental under the Due Process Clause. See, e.g., *Griswold, supra*, at 486; *Skinner v. Oklahoma*, 316 U.S. 535, 541 (1942); *Meyer v. Nebraska*, 262 U.S. 390, 399 (1923).

It cannot be denied that this Court's cases describing the right to marry presumed a relationship involving opposite-sex partners. The Court, like many institutions, has made assumptions defined by the world and time of which it is a part. This was evident in *Baker v. Nelson*, 409 U.S. 810, a one-line summary decision issued in 1972, holding the exclusion of same-sex couples from marriage did not present a substantial federal question.

Still, there are other, more instructive precedents. . . . A first premise of the Court's relevant precedents is that the right to personal choice regarding marriage is inherent in the concept of individual autonomy. This abiding connection between marriage and liberty is why *Loving* invalidated interracial marriage bans under the Due Process Clause. Like choices concerning contraception, family relationships, procreation, and childrearing, all of which are protected by the Constitution, decisions concerning marriage are among the most intimate that an individual can make. Indeed, the Court has noted it would be contradictory "to recognize a right of privacy with respect to other matters of family life and not with respect to the decision to enter the relationship that is the foundation of the family in our society." *Zablocki, supra,* at 386.

Choices about marriage shape an individual's destiny. As the Supreme Judicial Court of Massachusetts has explained, because "it fulfils yearnings for security, safe haven, and connection that express our common humanity, civil marriage is an esteemed institution, and the decision whether and whom to marry is among life's momentous acts of self-definition." *Goodridge,* 440 Mass., at 322, 798 N.E.2d, at 955.

The nature of marriage is that, through its enduring bond, two persons together can find other freedoms, such as expression, intimacy, and spirituality. This is true for all persons, whatever their sexual orientation. There is dignity in the bond between two men or two women who seek to marry and in their autonomy to make such profound choices.

A second principle in this Court's jurisprudence is that the right to marry is fundamental because it supports a two-person union unlike any other in its importance to the committed individuals. This point was central to *Griswold v. Connecticut,* which held the Constitution protects the right of married couples to use contraception. . . .

The right to marry thus dignifies couples who "wish to define themselves by their commitment to each other." Marriage responds to the universal fear that a lonely person might call out only to find no one there. It offers the hope of companionship and understanding and assurance that while both still live there will be someone to care for the other.

As this Court held in *Lawrence,* same-sex couples have the same right as opposite-sex couples to enjoy intimate association. *Lawrence* invalidated laws that made same-sex intimacy a criminal act. And it acknowledged that "[w]hen sexuality finds overt expression in intimate conduct with another person, the conduct can be but one element in a personal bond that is more enduring." But while *Lawrence* confirmed a dimension of freedom that allows individuals to engage in intimate association without criminal liability, it does not follow that freedom stops there. Outlaw to outcast may be a step forward, but it does not achieve the full promise of liberty.

A third basis for protecting the right to marry is that it safeguards children and families and thus draws meaning from related rights of childrearing, procreation, and education. See *Pierce v. Society of Sisters,* 268 U.S. 510 (1925); *Meyer,* 262 U.S., at 399. The Court has recognized these connections by describing the varied rights as a unified whole: "[T]he right to 'marry, establish a home and bring up children' is a central part of the liberty protected by the Due Process Clause." *Zablocki,* 434 U.S., at 384. Under the laws of the several States, some of marriage's protections for children and families are material. But marriage also confers more profound benefits. By giving recognition and legal structure to their parents' relationship, marriage allows children "to understand the integrity and closeness of their own family and its concord with other families in their community and in their daily lives." *Windsor, supra,* 133 S.Ct., at 2694–2695. Marriage also affords the permanency and stability important to children's best interests.

As all parties agree, many same-sex couples provide loving and nurturing homes to their children, whether biological or adopted. And hundreds of thousands of children are presently being raised by such couples. Most States have allowed gays and lesbians to adopt, either as individuals or as couples, and many adopted and foster children have same-sex parents. This provides powerful confirmation from the law itself that gays and lesbians can create loving, supportive families.

Excluding same-sex couples from marriage thus conflicts with a central premise of the right to marry. Without the recognition, stability, and predictability marriage offers, their children suffer the stigma of knowing their families are somehow lesser. They also suffer the significant material costs of being raised by unmarried parents, relegated through no fault of their own to a more difficult and uncertain family life. The marriage laws at issue here thus harm and humiliate the children of same-sex couples.

That is not to say the right to marry is less meaningful for those who do not or cannot have children. An ability, desire, or promise to procreate is not and has not been a prerequisite for a valid marriage in any State. In light of precedent protecting the right of a married couple not to procreate, it cannot be said the Court or the States have conditioned the right to marry on the capacity or commitment to procreate. The constitutional marriage right has many aspects, of which childbearing is only one.

Fourth and finally, this Court's cases and the Nation's traditions make clear that marriage is a keystone of our social order. Alexis de Tocqueville recognized this truth on his travels through the United States almost two centuries ago:

> There is certainly no country in the world where the tie of marriage is so much respected as in America . . . [W]hen the American retires from the turmoil of public life to the bosom of his family, he finds in it the image of order and of peace. . . . [H]e afterwards carries [that image] with him into public affairs. 1 Democracy in America 309 (H. Reeve transl., rev. ed. 1990).

In *Maynard v. Hill*, 125 U.S. 190, 211 (1888), the Court echoed de Tocqueville, explaining that marriage is "the foundation of the family and of society, without which there would be neither civilization nor progress." Marriage, the *Maynard* Court said, has long been " 'a great public institution, giving character to our whole civil polity.' " This idea has been reiterated even as the institution has evolved in substantial ways over time, superseding rules related to parental consent, gender, and race once thought by many to be essential. Marriage remains a building block of our national community.

For that reason, just as a couple vows to support each other, so does society pledge to support the couple, offering symbolic recognition and material benefits to protect and nourish the union. Indeed, while the States are in general free to vary the benefits they confer on all married couples, they have throughout our history made marriage the basis for an expanding list of governmental rights, benefits, and responsibilities. These aspects of marital status include: taxation; inheritance and property rights; rules of intestate succession; spousal privilege in the law of evidence; hospital access; medical decisionmaking authority; adoption rights; the rights and benefits of survivors; birth and death certificates; professional ethics rules; campaign finance restrictions; workers' compensation benefits; health insurance; and child custody, support, and visitation rules. Valid marriage under state law is also a significant status for over a thousand provisions of federal law. The States have contributed to the fundamental character of the marriage right by placing that institution at the center of so many facets of the legal and social order.

There is no difference between same- and opposite-sex couples with respect to this principle. Yet by virtue of their exclusion from that institution, same-sex couples are denied the constellation of benefits that the States have linked to marriage. This harm results in more than just material burdens. Same-sex couples are consigned to an instability many opposite-sex couples would deem intolerable in their own lives. As the

State itself makes marriage all the more precious by the significance it attaches to it, exclusion from that status has the effect of teaching that gays and lesbians are unequal in important respects. It demeans gays and lesbians for the State to lock them out of a central institution of the Nation's society. Same-sex couples, too, may aspire to the transcendent purposes of marriage and seek fulfillment in its highest meaning.

The limitation of marriage to opposite-sex couples may long have seemed natural and just, but its inconsistency with the central meaning of the fundamental right to marry is now manifest. With that knowledge must come the recognition that laws excluding same-sex couples from the marriage right impose stigma and injury of the kind prohibited by our basic charter.

Objecting that this does not reflect an appropriate framing of the issue, the respondents refer to *Washington v. Glucksberg*, 521 U.S. 702, 721 (1997), which called for a " 'careful description' " of fundamental rights. They assert the petitioners do not seek to exercise the right to marry but rather a new and nonexistent "right to same-sex marriage." *Glucksberg* did insist that liberty under the Due Process Clause must be defined in a most circumscribed manner, with central reference to specific historical practices. Yet while that approach may have been appropriate for the asserted right there involved (physician-assisted suicide), it is inconsistent with the approach this Court has used in discussing other fundamental rights, including marriage and intimacy. Loving did not ask about a "right to interracial marriage"; *Turner* did not ask about a "right of inmates to marry"; and *Zablocki* did not ask about a "right of fathers with unpaid child support duties to marry." Rather, each case inquired about the right to marry in its comprehensive sense, asking if there was a sufficient justification for excluding the relevant class from the right.

That principle applies here. If rights were defined by who exercised them in the past, then received practices could serve as their own continued justification and new groups could not invoke rights once denied. This Court has rejected that approach, both with respect to the right to marry and the rights of gays and lesbians. See *Loving,* 388 U.S., at 12; *Lawrence,* 539 U.S., at 566–567.

The right to marry is fundamental as a matter of history and tradition, but rights come not from ancient sources alone. They rise, too, from a better informed understanding of how constitutional imperatives define a liberty that remains urgent in our own era. Many who deem same-sex marriage to be wrong reach that conclusion based on decent and honorable religious or philosophical premises, and neither they nor their beliefs are disparaged here. But when that sincere, personal opposition becomes enacted law and public policy, the necessary consequence is to put the imprimatur of the State itself on an exclusion that soon demeans or stigmatizes those whose own liberty is then denied. Under the Constitution, same-sex couples seek in marriage the same legal treatment as opposite-sex couples, and it would disparage their choices and diminish their personhood to deny them this right.

The right of same-sex couples to marry that is part of the liberty promised by the Fourteenth Amendment is derived, too, from that Amendment's guarantee of the equal protection of the laws. The Due Process Clause and the Equal Protection Clause are connected in a profound way, though they set forth independent principles. Rights implicit in liberty and rights secured by equal protection may rest on different precepts and are not always co-extensive, yet in some instances each may be instructive as to the meaning and reach of the other. . . .

In *Loving* the Court invalidated a prohibition on interracial marriage under both the Equal Protection Clause and the Due Process Clause. . . . The synergy between the two protections is illustrated further in *Zablocki*. There the Court invoked the Equal Protection Clause as its basis for invalidating the challenged law, which, as already noted, barred fathers who were behind on child-support payments from marrying without judicial approval. The equal protection analysis depended in central part on the Court's holding that the law burdened a right "of fundamental importance." It was the essential nature of the marriage right that made apparent the law's incompatibility with requirements of equality. . . .

In *Lawrence* the Court acknowledged the interlocking nature of these constitutional safeguards in the context of the legal treatment of gays and lesbians. Although *Lawrence* elaborated its holding under the Due Process Clause, it acknowledged, and sought to remedy, the continuing inequality that resulted from laws making intimacy in the lives of gays and lesbians a crime against the State. . . .

This dynamic also applies to same-sex marriage. . . . [T]he marriage laws enforced by the respondents are in essence unequal: same-sex couples are denied all the benefits afforded to opposite-sex couples and are barred from exercising a fundamental right. Especially against a long history of disapproval of their relationships, this denial to same-sex couples of the right to marry works a grave and continuing harm. The imposition of this disability on gays and lesbians serves to disrespect and subordinate them. And the Equal Protection Clause, like the Due Process Clause, prohibits this unjustified infringement of the fundamental right to marry.

These considerations lead to the conclusion that the right to marry is a fundamental right inherent in the liberty of the person, and under the Due Process and Equal Protection Clauses of the Fourteenth Amendment couples of the same-sex may not be deprived of that right and that liberty. . . . *Baker v. Nelson* must be and now is overruled, and the State laws challenged by Petitioners in these cases are now held invalid to the extent they exclude same-sex couples from civil marriage on the same terms and conditions as opposite-sex couples.

IV

There may be an initial inclination in these cases to proceed with caution—to await further legislation, litigation, and debate. The respondents warn there has been insufficient democratic discourse before deciding an issue so basic as the definition of marriage. In its ruling on the cases now before this Court, the majority opinion for the Court of Appeals made a cogent argument that it would be appropriate for the respondents' States to await further public discussion and political measures before licensing same-sex marriages.

Yet there has been far more deliberation than this argument acknowledges. There have been referenda, legislative debates, and grassroots campaigns, as well as countless studies, papers, books, and other popular and scholarly writings. There has been extensive litigation in state and federal courts. Judicial opinions addressing the issue have been informed by the contentions of parties and counsel, which, in turn, reflect the more general, societal discussion of same-sex marriage and its meaning that has occurred over the past decades. As more than 100 *amici* make clear in their filings, many of the central institutions in American life—state and local governments, the military, large and small businesses, labor unions, religious organizations, law enforcement, civic groups, professional organizations, and universities—have devoted substantial attention to the question. This has led to an enhanced understanding of the issue—an understanding reflected in the arguments now presented for resolution as a matter of constitutional law.

Of course, the Constitution contemplates that democracy is the appropriate process for change, so long as that process does not abridge fundamental rights. Last Term, a plurality of this Court reaffirmed the importance of the democratic principle in *Schuette v. BAMN,* 134 S.Ct. 1623 (2014), noting the "right of citizens to debate so they can learn and decide and then, through the political process, act in concert to try to shape the course of their own times." . . . But as *Schuette* also said, "[t]he freedom secured by the Constitution consists, in one of its essential dimensions, of the right of the individual not to be injured by the unlawful exercise of governmental power." Thus, when the rights of persons are violated, "the Constitution requires redress by the courts," notwithstanding the more general value of democratic decisionmaking. This holds true even when protecting individual rights affects issues of the utmost importance and sensitivity.

The dynamic of our constitutional system is that individuals need not await legislative action before asserting a fundamental right. The Nation's courts are open to injured individuals who come to them to vindicate their own direct, personal stake in our basic charter. An individual can invoke a right to constitutional protection when he or she is harmed, even if the broader public disagrees and even if the legislature refuses to act. The idea of the Constitution "was to withdraw certain subjects from the vicissitudes of political controversy, to place them beyond the reach of majorities and officials and to establish them as legal principles to be applied by the courts." *West Virginia Bd. of Ed. v. Barnette,* 319 U.S. 624, 638 (1943). This is why "fundamental rights may not be submitted to a vote; they depend on the outcome of no elections." *Ibid.* It is of no moment whether advocates of same-sex marriage now enjoy or lack momentum in the democratic process. The issue before the Court here is the legal question whether the Constitution protects the right of same-sex couples to marry.

This is not the first time the Court has been asked to adopt a cautious approach to recognizing and protecting fundamental rights. In *Bowers,* a bare majority upheld a law criminalizing same-sex intimacy. . . . Although *Bowers* was eventually repudiated in *Lawrence,* men and women were harmed in the interim, and the substantial effects of these injuries no doubt lingered long after *Bowers* was overruled. . . .

A ruling against same-sex couples would have the same effect . . . . The petitioners' stories make clear the urgency of the issue they present to the Court. James Obergefell now asks whether Ohio can erase his marriage to John Arthur for all time. April DeBoer and Jayne Rowse now ask whether Michigan may continue to deny them the certainty and stability all mothers desire to protect their children, and for them and their children the childhood years will pass all too soon. Ijpe DeKoe and Thomas Kostura now ask whether Tennessee can deny to one who has served this Nation the basic dignity of recognizing his New York marriage. Properly presented with the petitioners' cases, the Court has a duty to address these claims and answer these questions. . . .

The respondents also argue allowing same-sex couples to wed will harm marriage as an institution by leading to fewer opposite-sex marriages. This may occur, the respondents contend, because licensing same-sex marriage severs the connection between natural procreation and marriage. That argument, however, rests on a counterintuitive view of opposite-sex couple's decisionmaking processes regarding marriage and parenthood. Decisions about whether to marry and raise children are based on many personal, romantic, and practical considerations; and it is unrealistic to conclude that an opposite-sex couple would choose not to marry simply because same-sex couples may do so. The respondents have not shown a foundation for the conclusion that allowing same-sex marriage will cause the harmful outcomes they describe. . . . [T]hese cases involve only the rights of two consenting adults whose marriages would pose no risk of harm to themselves or third parties.

Finally, it must be emphasized that religions, and those who adhere to religious doctrines, may continue to advocate with utmost, sincere conviction that, by divine precepts, same-sex marriage should not be condoned. The First Amendment ensures that religious organizations and persons are given proper protection as they seek to teach the principles that are so fulfilling and so central to their lives and faiths, and to their own deep aspirations to continue the family structure they have long revered. . . . The Constitution, however, does not permit the State to bar same-sex couples from marriage on the same terms as accorded to couples of the opposite sex.

V

These cases also present the question whether the Constitution requires States to recognize same-sex marriages validly performed out of State. . . . Being married in one State but having that valid marriage denied in another is one of the most perplexing and distressing complications in the law of domestic relations. Leaving the current state of affairs in place would maintain and promote instability and uncertainty. For some couples, even an ordinary drive into a neighboring State to visit family or friends risks causing severe hardship in the event of a spouse's hospitalization while across state lines. In light of the fact that many States already allow same-sex marriage—and hundreds of thousands of these marriages already have occurred—the disruption caused by the recognition bans is significant and ever-growing.

As counsel for the respondents acknowledged at argument, if States are required by the Constitution to issue marriage licenses to same-sex couples, the justifications for refusing to recognize those marriages performed elsewhere are undermined. The Court, in this decision, holds same-sex couples may exercise the fundamental right to marry in all States. It follows . . . that there is no lawful basis for a State to refuse to recognize a lawful same-sex marriage performed in another State on the ground of its same-sex character.

No union is more profound than marriage, for it embodies the highest ideals of love, fidelity, devotion, sacrifice, and family. In forming a marital union, two people become something greater than once they were. As some of the petitioners in these cases demonstrate, marriage embodies a love that may endure even past death. It would misunderstand these men and women to say they disrespect the idea of marriage. Their plea is that they do respect it, respect it so deeply that they seek to find its fulfillment for themselves. Their hope is not to be condemned to live in loneliness, excluded from one of civilization's oldest institutions. They ask for equal dignity in the eyes of the law. The Constitution grants them that right.

The judgment of the Court of Appeals for the Sixth Circuit is reversed.

It is so ordered.

■ **CHIEF JUSTICE ROBERTS, with whom JUSTICE SCALIA and JUSTICE THOMAS join, dissenting.**

Petitioners make strong arguments rooted in social policy and considerations of fairness. They contend that same-sex couples should be allowed to affirm their love and commitment through marriage, just like opposite-sex couples. That position has undeniable appeal; over the past six years, voters and legislators in eleven States and the District of

Columbia have revised their laws to allow marriage between two people of the same sex.

But this Court is not a legislature. Whether same-sex marriage is a good idea should be of no concern to us. Under the Constitution, judges have power to say what the law is, not what it should be. The people who ratified the Constitution authorized courts to exercise "neither force nor will but merely judgment." The Federalist No. 78, p. 465 (C. Rossiter ed. 1961) (A. Hamilton).

Although the policy arguments for extending marriage to same-sex couples may be compelling, the legal arguments for requiring such an extension are not. The fundamental right to marry does not include a right to make a State change its definition of marriage. And a State's decision to maintain the meaning of marriage that has persisted in every culture throughout human history can hardly be called irrational. In short, our Constitution does not enact any one theory of marriage. The people of a State are free to expand marriage to include same-sex couples, or to retain the historic definition.

Today, however, the Court takes the extraordinary step of ordering every State to license and recognize same-sex marriage. Many people will rejoice at this decision, and I begrudge none their celebration. But for those who believe in a government of laws, not of men, the majority's approach is deeply disheartening. Supporters of same-sex marriage have achieved considerable success persuading their fellow citizens—through the democratic process—to adopt their view. That ends today. Five lawyers have closed the debate and enacted their own vision of marriage as a matter of constitutional law. Stealing this issue from the people will for many cast a cloud over same-sex marriage, making a dramatic social change that much more difficult to accept.

The majority's decision is an act of will, not legal judgment. The right it announces has no basis in the Constitution or this Court's precedent. The majority expressly disclaims judicial "caution" and omits even a pretense of humility, openly relying on its desire to remake society according to its own "new insight" into the "nature of injustice." As a result, the Court invalidates the marriage laws of more than half the States and orders the transformation of a social institution that has formed the basis of human society for millennia, for the Kalahari Bushmen and the Han Chinese, the Carthaginians and the Aztecs. Just who do we think we are?

It can be tempting for judges to confuse our own preferences with the requirements of the law. But as this Court has been reminded throughout our history, the Constitution "is made for people of fundamentally differing views." *Lochner v. New York,* 198 U.S. 45, 76 (1905) (Holmes, J., dissenting). Accordingly, "courts are not concerned with the wisdom or policy of legislation." *Id.,* at 69 (Harlan, J., dissenting). The majority today neglects that restrained conception of the judicial role. It seizes for itself a question the Constitution leaves to the people, at a time when the people are engaged in a vibrant debate on that question. And it answers that question based not on neutral principles of constitutional law, but on its own "understanding of what freedom is and must become." I have no choice but to dissent.

Understand well what this dissent is about: It is not about whether, in my judgment, the institution of marriage should be changed to include same-sex couples. It is instead about whether, in our democratic republic, that decision should rest with the people acting through their elected representatives, or with five lawyers who happen to hold commissions authorizing them to resolve legal disputes according to law. The Constitution leaves no doubt about the answer.

I

Petitioners and their *amici* base their arguments on the "right to marry" and the imperative of "marriage equality." There is no serious dispute that, under our precedents, the Constitution protects a right to marry and requires States to apply their marriage laws equally. The real question in these cases is what constitutes "marriage," or—more precisely—*who decides* what constitutes "marriage"?

The majority largely ignores these questions, relegating ages of human experience with marriage to a paragraph or two. Even if history and precedent are not "the end" of these cases, I would not "sweep away what has so long been settled" without showing greater respect for all that preceded us.

A

As the majority acknowledges, marriage "has existed for millennia and across civilizations." For all those millennia, across all those civilizations, "marriage" referred to only one relationship: the union of a man and a woman. Tr. of Oral Arg. on Question 1, p. 12 (petitioners conceding that they are not aware of any society that permitted same-sex marriage before 2001). As the Court explained two Terms ago, "until recent years, . . . marriage between a man and a woman no doubt had been thought of by most people as essential to the very definition of that term and to its role and function throughout the history of civilization." *United States v. Windsor*, 133 S.Ct. 2675, 2689 (2013).

This universal definition of marriage as the union of a man and a woman is no historical coincidence. Marriage did not come about as a result of a political movement, discovery, disease, war, religious doctrine, or any other moving force of world history—and certainly not as a result of a prehistoric decision to exclude gays and lesbians. It arose in the nature of things to meet a vital need: ensuring that children are conceived by a mother and father committed to raising them in the stable conditions of a lifelong relationship.

The premises supporting this concept of marriage are so fundamental that they rarely require articulation. The human race must procreate to survive. Procreation occurs through sexual relations between a man and a woman. When sexual relations result in the conception of a child, that child's prospects are generally better if the mother and father stay together rather than going their separate ways. Therefore, for the good of children and society, sexual relations that can lead to procreation should occur only between a man and a woman committed to a lasting bond.

Society has recognized that bond as marriage. And by bestowing a respected status and material benefits on married couples, society encourages men and women to conduct sexual relations within marriage rather than without. As one prominent scholar put it, "Marriage is a socially arranged solution for the problem of getting people to stay together and care for children that the mere desire for children, and the sex that makes children possible, does not solve." J.Q. Wilson, The Marriage Problem 41 (2002).

This singular understanding of marriage has prevailed in the United States throughout our history. . . . Early Americans drew heavily on legal scholars like William Blackstone, who regarded marriage between "husband and wife" as one of the "great relations in private life," and philosophers like John Locke, who described marriage as "a voluntary compact between man and woman" centered on "its chief end, procreation" and the "nourishment and support" of children. 1 W. Blackstone, Commentaries *410; J. Locke, Second Treatise of Civil Government §§ 78–79, p. 39 (J. Gough ed. 1947). To those who drafted and ratified the Constitution, this conception of marriage and family "was a given: its structure, its stability, roles, and values accepted by all." Forte, The Framers' Idea of Marriage and Family, in The Meaning of Marriage 100, 102 (R. George & J. Elshtain eds. 2006).

The Constitution itself says nothing about marriage, and the Framers thereby entrusted the States with "[t]he whole subject of the domestic relations of husband and wife." *Windsor,* 133 S.Ct., at 2691. There is no dispute that every State at the founding—and every State throughout our history until a dozen years ago—defined marriage in the traditional, biologically rooted way. . . .

In his first American dictionary, Noah Webster defined marriage as "the legal union of a man and woman for life," which served the purposes of "preventing the promiscuous intercourse of the sexes, . . . promoting domestic felicity, and . . . securing the maintenance and education of children." 1 An American Dictionary of the English Language (1828). An influential 19th-century treatise defined marriage as "a civil status, existing in one man and one woman legally united for life for those civil and social purposes which are based in the distinction of sex." J. Bishop, Commentaries on the Law of Marriage and Divorce 25 (1852). The first edition of Black's Law Dictionary defined marriage as "the civil status of one man and one woman united in law for life." Black's Law Dictionary 756 (1891). The dictionary maintained essentially that same definition for the next century.

This Court's precedents have repeatedly described marriage in ways that are consistent only with its traditional meaning. . . . More recent cases have directly connected the right to marry with the "right to procreate." *Zablocki v. Redhail,* 434 U.S. 374, 386 (1978).

As the majority notes, some aspects of marriage have changed over time. Arranged marriages have largely given way to pairings based on romantic love. States have replaced coverture, the doctrine by which a married man and woman became a single legal entity, with laws that respect each participant's separate status. Racial restrictions on marriage, which "arose as an incident to slavery" to promote "White Supremacy," were repealed by many States and ultimately struck down by this Court.

. . . [T]hese developments . . . did not, however, work any transformation in the core structure of marriage as the union between a man and a woman. If you had asked a person on the street how marriage was defined, no one would ever have said, "Marriage is the union of a man and a woman, where the woman is subject to coverture." The majority may be right that the "history of marriage is one of both continuity and change," but the core meaning of marriage has endured.

B

Shortly after this Court struck down racial restrictions on marriage in *Loving,* a gay couple in Minnesota sought a marriage license. They argued that the Constitution required States to allow marriage between people of the same sex for the same reasons that it requires States to allow marriage between people of different races. The Minnesota Supreme Court rejected their analogy to *Loving,* and this Court summarily dismissed an appeal. *Baker v. Nelson,* 409 U.S. 810 (1972).

In the decades after *Baker,* greater numbers of gays and lesbians began living openly, and many expressed a desire to have their relationships recognized as marriages. Over time, more people came to see marriage in a way that could be extended to such couples. Until recently, this new view of marriage remained a minority position. After the Massachusetts Supreme Judicial Court in 2003 interpreted its State Constitution to require recognition of same-sex marriage, many States— including the four at issue here—enacted constitutional amendments formally adopting the longstanding definition of marriage.

Over the last few years, public opinion on marriage has shifted rapidly. . . . In all, voters and legislators in eleven States and the District of Columbia have changed their definitions of marriage to include same-sex couples. The highest courts of five States have decreed that same result under their own Constitutions. The remainder of the States retain the traditional definition of marriage. . . .

In a carefully reasoned decision, the Court of Appeals acknowledged the democratic "momentum" in favor of "expand[ing] the definition of marriage to include gay couples," but concluded that petitioners had not made "the case for constitutionalizing the definition of marriage and for removing the issue from the place it has been since the founding: in the hands of state voters." That decision interpreted the Constitution correctly, and I would affirm.

II

Petitioners first contend that the marriage laws of their States violate the Due Process Clause. The Solicitor General of the United States, appearing in support of petitioners, expressly disowned that position before this Court. The majority nevertheless resolves these cases for petitioners based almost entirely on the Due Process Clause. . . .

[T]he majority's approach has no basis in principle or tradition, except for the unprincipled tradition of judicial policymaking that characterized discredited decisions such as *Lochner v. New York,* 198 U.S. 45 (1905). Stripped of its shiny rhetorical gloss, the majority's argument is that the Due Process Clause gives same-sex couples a fundamental right to marry because it will be good for them and for society. If I were a legislator, I would certainly consider that view as a matter of social policy. But as a judge, I find the majority's position indefensible as a matter of constitutional law.

A

Petitioners' "fundamental right" claim falls into the most sensitive category of constitutional adjudication. Petitioners do not contend that their States' marriage laws violate an *enumerated* constitutional right, such as the freedom of speech protected by the First Amendment. There is, after all, no "Companionship and Understanding" or "Nobility and Dignity" Clause in the Constitution. . . .

Allowing unelected federal judges to select which unenumerated rights rank as "fundamental"—and to strike down state laws on the basis of that determination—raises obvious concerns about the judicial role. Our precedents have accordingly insisted that judges "exercise the utmost care" in identifying implied fundamental rights, "lest the liberty protected by the Due Process Clause be subtly transformed into the policy preferences of the Members of this Court." *Washington v. Glucksberg,* 521 U.S. 702, 720 (1997).

The need for restraint in administering the strong medicine of substantive due process is a lesson this Court has learned the hard way. The Court first applied substantive due process to strike down a statute in *Dred Scott v. Sandford,* 19 How. 393 (1857). There the Court invalidated the Missouri Compromise on the ground that legislation restricting the institution of slavery violated the implied rights of slaveholders. The Court relied on its own conception of liberty and property in doing so. In a dissent that has outlasted the majority opinion, Justice Curtis explained that when the "fixed rules which govern the interpretation of laws [are] abandoned, and the theoretical opinions of individuals are allowed to control" the Constitution's meaning, "we have no longer a Constitution; we are under the government of individual men, who for the time being have power to declare what the Constitution is, according to their own views of what it ought to mean."

Dred Scott 's holding was overruled on the battlefields of the Civil War and by constitutional amendment after Appomattox, but its approach to the Due Process Clause reappeared. In a series of early 20th-century cases, most prominently *Lochner v. New York,* this Court invalidated state statutes that presented "meddlesome interferences with the rights of the individual," and "undue interference with liberty of person and freedom of contract."

The dissenting Justices in *Lochner* explained that the New York law could be viewed as a reasonable response to legislative concern about the health of bakery employees, an issue on which there was at least "room for debate and for an honest difference of opinion." *Id.,* at 72 (opinion of Harlan, J.). The majority's contrary conclusion required adopting as constitutional law "an economic theory which a large part of the country does not entertain." *Id.,* at 75 (opinion of Holmes, J.). As Justice Holmes memorably put it, "The Fourteenth Amendment does not enact Mr. Herbert Spencer's Social Statics," a leading work on the philosophy of Social Darwinism. The Constitution "is not intended to embody a particular economic theory. . . . It is made for people of fundamentally differing views, and the accident of our finding certain opinions natural and familiar or novel and even shocking ought not to conclude our judgment upon the question whether statutes embodying them conflict with the Constitution." . . .

By empowering judges to elevate their own policy judgments to the status of constitutionally protected "liberty," the *Lochner* line of cases left "no alternative to regarding the court as a . . . legislative chamber." L. Hand, The Bill of Rights 42 (1958).

Eventually, the Court recognized its error and vowed not to repeat it. "The doctrine that . . . due process authorizes courts to hold laws unconstitutional when they believe the legislature has acted unwisely," we later explained, "has long since been discarded. We have returned to the original constitutional proposition that courts do not substitute their social and economic beliefs for the judgment of legislative bodies, who are elected to pass laws." *Ferguson v. Skrupa,* 372 U.S. 726, 730 (1963). Thus, it has become an accepted rule that the Court will not hold laws unconstitutional simply because we find them "unwise, improvident, or out of harmony with a particular school of thought." *Williamson v. Lee Optical of Okla., Inc.,* 348 U.S. 483, 488 (1955).

Rejecting *Lochner* does not require disavowing the doctrine of implied fundamental rights, and this Court has not done so. But to avoid repeating *Lochner's* error of converting personal preferences into constitutional mandates, our modern substantive due process cases have stressed the need for "judicial self-restraint." Our precedents have required that implied fundamental rights be "objectively, deeply rooted in this Nation's history and tradition," and "implicit in the concept of ordered liberty, such that neither liberty nor justice would exist if they were sacrificed." *Glucksberg,* 521 U.S., at 720–721. . . .

Proper reliance on history and tradition of course requires looking beyond the individual law being challenged, so that every restriction on liberty does not supply its own constitutional justification. The Court is right about that. But given the few guideposts for responsible decisionmaking in this unchartered area, an approach grounded in history imposes limits on the judiciary that are more meaningful than any based on an abstract formula. Expanding a right suddenly and dramatically is likely to require tearing it up from its roots. Even a sincere profession of "discipline" in identifying fundamental rights does not provide a meaningful constraint on a judge, for "what he is really likely to be 'discovering,' whether or not he is fully aware of it, are his own values," J. Ely, Democracy and Distrust 44 (1980). The only way to ensure restraint in this delicate enterprise is "continual insistence upon respect for the teachings of history, solid recognition of the basic values that underlie our society, and wise appreciation of the great roles [of] the doctrines of federalism and separation of powers." *Griswold v. Connecticut,* 381 U.S. 479, 501 510 (1965) (Harlan, J., concurring in judgment).

B

The majority['s] . . . aggressive application of substantive due process breaks sharply with decades of precedent and returns the Court to the unprincipled approach of *Lochner*.

1

The majority's driving themes are that marriage is desirable and petitioners desire it. The opinion describes the "transcendent importance" of marriage and repeatedly insists that petitioners do not seek to "demean," "devalue," "denigrate," or "disrespect" the institution. Nobody disputes those points. Indeed, the compelling personal accounts of petitioners and others like them are likely a primary reason why many Americans have changed their minds about whether same-sex couples should be allowed to marry. As a matter of constitutional law, however, the sincerity of petitioners' wishes is not relevant.

When the majority turns to the law, it relies primarily on precedents discussing the fundamental "right to marry." *Turner v. Safley,* 482 U.S. 78, 95 (1987); *Zablocki,* 434 U.S., at 383; see *Loving,* 388 U.S., at 12. . . . None of the laws at issue in those cases purported to change the core definition of marriage as the union of a man and a woman. . . . Removing racial barriers to marriage therefore did not change what a marriage was any more than integrating schools changed what a school was. As the majority admits, the institution of "marriage" discussed in every one of these cases "presumed a relationship involving opposite-sex partners."

In short, the "right to marry" cases stand for the important but limited proposition that particular restrictions on access to marriage *as traditionally defined* violate due process. These precedents say nothing at all about a right to make a State change its definition of marriage, which is the right petitioners actually seek here. Neither petitioners nor the majority cites a single case or other legal source providing any basis for such a constitutional right. . . .

2

The majority suggests that "there are other, more instructive precedents" informing the right to marry. Although not entirely clear, this reference seems to correspond to a line of cases discussing an implied fundamental "right of privacy." *Griswold,* 381 U.S., at 486. In the first of those cases, the Court invalidated a criminal law that banned the use of contraceptives. The Court stressed the invasive nature of the ban, which threatened the intrusion of "the police to search the sacred precincts of marital bedrooms." In the Court's view, such laws infringed the right to privacy in its most basic sense: the "right to be let alone."

The Court also invoked the right to privacy in *Lawrence v. Texas,* 539 U.S. 558 (2003), which struck down a Texas statute criminalizing homosexual sodomy. Lawrence relied on the position that criminal sodomy laws, like bans on contraceptives, invaded privacy by inviting "unwarranted government intrusions" that "touc[h] upon the most private human conduct, sexual behavior . . . in the most private of places, the home."

Neither *Lawrence* nor any other precedent in the privacy line of cases supports the right that petitioners assert here. Unlike criminal laws banning contraceptives and sodomy, the marriage laws at issue here involve no government intrusion. They create no crime and impose no punishment. Same-sex couples remain free to live together, to engage in intimate conduct, and to raise their families as they see fit. No one is "condemned to live in loneliness" by the laws challenged in these cases— no one. . . .

The majority also relies on Justice Harlan's influential dissenting opinion in *Poe v. Ullman,* 367 U.S. 497 (1961). As the majority recounts, that opinion states that "[d]ue process has not been reduced to any formula." But far from conferring the broad interpretive discretion that the majority discerns, Justice Harlan's opinion makes clear that courts implying fundamental rights are not "free to roam where unguided speculation might take them." They must instead have "regard to what history teaches" and exercise not only "judgment" but "restraint." Of particular relevance, Justice Harlan explained that "laws regarding marriage which provide both when the sexual powers may be used and the legal and societal context in which children are born and brought up . . . form a pattern so deeply pressed into the substance of our social life that any Constitutional doctrine in this area must build upon that basis."

In sum, the privacy cases provide no support for the majority's position, because petitioners do not seek privacy. Quite the opposite, they seek public recognition of their relationships, along with corresponding government benefits. Our cases have consistently refused to allow litigants to convert the shield provided by constitutional liberties into a sword to demand positive entitlements from the State. See *DeShaney v. Winnebago County Dept. of Social Servs.*, 489 U.S. 189, 196 (1989); Thus, although the right to privacy recognized by our precedents certainly plays a role in protecting the intimate conduct of same-sex couples, it provides no affirmative right to redefine marriage and no basis for striking down the laws at issue here.

3

Perhaps recognizing how little support it can derive from precedent, the majority goes out of its way to jettison the "careful" approach to implied fundamental rights taken by this Court in *Glucksberg*. It is revealing that the majority's position requires it to effectively overrule *Glucksberg*, the leading modern case setting the bounds of substantive due process. At least this part of the majority opinion has the virtue of candor. Nobody could rightly accuse the majority of taking a careful approach.

Ultimately, only one precedent offers any support for the majority's methodology: *Lochner v. New York*, 198 U.S. 45. The majority opens its opinion by announcing petitioners' right to "define and express their identity." The majority later explains that "the right to personal choice regarding marriage is inherent in the concept of individual autonomy." This freewheeling notion of individual autonomy echoes nothing so much as "the general right of an individual to be free in his person and in his power to contract in relation to his own labor." *Lochner*, 198 U.S., at 58.

To be fair, the majority does not suggest that its individual autonomy right is entirely unconstrained. The constraints it sets are precisely those that accord with its own "reasoned judgment," informed by its "new insight" into the "nature of injustice," which was invisible to all who came before but has become clear "as we learn [the] meaning" of liberty. The truth is that today's decision rests on nothing more than the majority's own conviction that same-sex couples should be allowed to marry because they want to, and that "it would disparage their choices and diminish their personhood to deny them this right." Whatever force that belief may have as a matter of moral philosophy, it has no more basis in the Constitution than did the naked policy preferences adopted in *Lochner*. . . .

One immediate question invited by the majority's position is whether States may retain the definition of marriage as a union of two people. Cf. *Brown v. Buhman*, 947 F.Supp.2d 1170 (Utah 2013), appeal pending, No. 14–4117 (CA10). Although the majority randomly inserts the adjective "two" in various places, it offers no reason at all why the two-person element of the core definition of marriage may be preserved while the man-woman element may not. Indeed, from the standpoint of history and tradition, a leap from opposite-sex marriage to same-sex marriage is much greater than one from a two-person union to plural unions, which have deep roots in some cultures around the world. If the majority is willing to take the big leap, it is hard to see how it can say no to the shorter one.

It is striking how much of the majority's reasoning would apply with equal force to the claim of a fundamental right to plural marriage. If "[t]here is dignity in the bond between two men or two women who seek to marry and in their autonomy to make such profound choices," why would there be any less dignity in the bond between three people who, in exercising their autonomy, seek to make the profound choice to marry? If a same-sex couple has the constitutional right to marry because their children would otherwise "suffer the stigma of knowing their families are somehow lesser," why wouldn't the same reasoning apply to a family of three or more persons raising children? If not having the opportunity to marry "serves to disrespect and subordinate" gay and lesbian couples, why wouldn't the same "imposition of this disability," serve to disrespect and subordinate people who find fulfillment in polyamorous relationships? See Bennett, Polyamory: The Next Sexual Revolution? Newsweek, July 28, 2009 (estimating 500,000 polyamorous families in the United States); Li, Married Lesbian "Throuple" Expecting First Child, N.Y. Post, Apr. 23, 2014; Otter, Three May Not Be a Crowd: The Case for a Constitutional Right to Plural Marriage, 64 Emory L.J. 1977 (2015).

I do not mean to equate marriage between same-sex couples with plural marriages in all respects. There may well be relevant differences that compel different legal analysis. But if there are, petitioners have not pointed to any. . . .

4

Near the end of its opinion, the majority offers perhaps the clearest insight into its decision. Expanding marriage to include same-sex couples, the majority insists, would "pose no risk of harm to themselves or third parties." This argument again echoes *Lochner,* which relied on its assessment that "we think that a law like the one before us involves neither the safety, the morals nor the welfare of the public, and that the interest of the public is not in the slightest degree affected by such an act."

Then and now, this assertion of the "harm principle" sounds more in philosophy than law. The elevation of the fullest individual self-realization over the constraints that society has expressed in law may or may not be attractive moral philosophy. But a Justice's commission does not confer any special moral, philosophical, or social insight sufficient to justify imposing those perceptions on fellow citizens under the pretense of "due process." There is indeed a process due the people on issues of this sort—the democratic process. Respecting that understanding requires the Court to be guided by law, not any particular school of social thought. As Judge Henry Friendly once put it, echoing Justice Holmes's dissent in *Lochner,* the Fourteenth Amendment does not enact John Stuart Mill's On Liberty any more than it enacts Herbert Spencer's Social Statics. And it certainly does not enact any one concept of marriage.

The majority's understanding of due process lays out a tantalizing vision of the future for Members of this Court: If an unvarying social institution enduring over all of recorded history cannot inhibit judicial policymaking, what can? But this approach is dangerous for the rule of law. The purpose of insisting that implied fundamental rights have roots in the history and tradition of our people is to ensure that when unelected judges strike down democratically enacted laws, they do so based on something more than their own beliefs. The Court today not only overlooks our country's entire history and tradition but actively repudiates it, preferring to live only in the heady days of the here and now. I agree with the majority that the "nature of injustice is that we may not always see it in our own times." As petitioners put it, "times can blind." But to blind yourself to history is both prideful and unwise. "The past is never dead. It's not even past." W. Faulkner, Requiem for a Nun 92 (1951).

III

In addition to their due process argument, petitioners contend that the Equal Protection Clause requires their States to license and recognize same-sex marriages. The majority does not seriously engage with this claim. Its discussion is, quite frankly, difficult to follow. The central point seems to be that there is a "synergy between" the Equal Protection Clause and the Due Process Clause, and that some precedents relying on one Clause have also relied on the other. Absent from this portion of the opinion, however, is anything resembling our usual framework for deciding equal protection cases. It is casebook doctrine that the "modern Supreme Court's treatment of equal protection claims has used a means-ends methodology in which judges ask whether the classification the government is using is sufficiently related to the goals it is pursuing." G. Stone, L. Seidman, C. Sunstein, M. Tushnet, & P. Karlan, Constitutional Law 453 (7th ed. 2013). The majority's approach today is different:

> Rights implicit in liberty and rights secured by equal protection may rest on different precepts and are not always co-extensive, yet in some instances each may be instructive as to the meaning and reach of the other. In any particular case one Clause may be thought to capture the essence of the right in a more accurate and comprehensive way, even as the two Clauses may converge in the identification and definition of the right.

The majority goes on to assert in conclusory fashion that the Equal Protection Clause provides an alternative basis for its holding. Yet the majority fails to provide even a single sentence explaining how the Equal

Protection Clause supplies independent weight for its position, nor does it attempt to justify its gratuitous violation of the canon against unnecessarily resolving constitutional questions. In any event, the marriage laws at issue here do not violate the Equal Protection Clause, because distinguishing between opposite-sex and same-sex couples is rationally related to the States' "legitimate state interest" in "preserving the traditional institution of marriage." *Lawrence,* 539 U.S., at 585 (O'Connor, J., concurring in judgment).

It is important to note with precision which laws petitioners have challenged. Although they discuss some of the ancillary legal benefits that accompany marriage, such as hospital visitation rights and recognition of spousal status on official documents, petitioners' lawsuits target the laws defining marriage generally rather than those allocating benefits specifically. The equal protection analysis might be different, in my view, if we were confronted with a more focused challenge to the denial of certain tangible benefits. Of course, those more selective claims will not arise now that the Court has taken the drastic step of requiring every State to license and recognize marriages between same-sex couples.

IV

The legitimacy of this Court ultimately rests upon the respect accorded to its judgments. That respect flows from the perception—and reality—that we exercise humility and restraint in deciding cases according to the Constitution and law. The role of the Court envisioned by the majority today, however, is anything but humble or restrained. Over and over, the majority exalts the role of the judiciary in delivering social change. In the majority's telling, it is the courts, not the people, who are responsible for making "new dimensions of freedom . . . apparent to new generations," for providing "formal discourse" on social issues, and for ensuring "neutral discussions, without scornful or disparaging commentary."

Nowhere is the majority's extravagant conception of judicial supremacy more evident than in its description—and dismissal—of the public debate regarding same-sex marriage. Yes, the majority concedes, on one side are thousands of years of human history in every society known to have populated the planet. But on the other side, there has been "extensive litigation," "many thoughtful District Court decisions," "countless studies, papers, books, and other popular and scholarly writings," and "more than 100" *amicus* briefs in these cases alone. What would be the point of allowing the democratic process to go on? It is high time for the Court to decide the meaning of marriage, based on five lawyers' "better informed understanding" of "a liberty that remains urgent in our own era." The answer is surely there in one of those *amicus* briefs or studies.

Those who founded our country would not recognize the majority's conception of the judicial role. They after all risked their lives and fortunes for the precious right to govern themselves. They would never have imagined yielding that right on a question of social policy to unaccountable and unelected judges. And they certainly would not have been satisfied by a system empowering judges to override policy judgments so long as they do so after "a quite extensive discussion." In our democracy, debate about the content of the law is not an exhaustion requirement to be checked off before courts can impose their will. "Surely the Constitution does not put either the legislative branch or the executive branch in the position of a television quiz show contestant so that when a given period of time has elapsed and a problem remains unresolved by them, the federal judiciary may press a buzzer and take its turn at fashioning a solution." Rehnquist, The Notion of a Living Constitution, 54 Texas L. Rev. 693, 700 (1976). As a plurality of this Court explained just last year, "It is demeaning to the democratic process to presume that voters are not capable of deciding an issue of this sensitivity on decent and rational grounds." *Schuette v. BAMN*, 134 S.Ct. 1623, 1637 (2014).

The Court's accumulation of power does not occur in a vacuum. It comes at the expense of the people. And they know it. Here and abroad, people are in the midst of a serious and thoughtful public debate on the issue of same-sex marriage. They see voters carefully considering same-sex marriage, casting ballots in favor or opposed, and sometimes changing their minds. They see political leaders similarly reexamining their positions, and either reversing course or explaining adherence to old convictions confirmed anew. They see governments and businesses modifying policies and practices with respect to same-sex couples, and participating actively in the civic discourse. They see countries overseas democratically accepting profound social change, or declining to do so. This deliberative process is making people take seriously questions that they may not have even regarded as questions before.

When decisions are reached through democratic means, some people will inevitably be disappointed with the results. But those whose views do not prevail at least know that they have had their say, and accordingly are—in the tradition of our political culture—reconciled to the result of a fair and honest debate. In addition, they can gear up to raise the issue later, hoping to persuade enough on the winning side to think again. . . .

But today the Court puts a stop to all that. By deciding this question under the Constitution, the Court removes it from the realm of democratic decision. There will be consequences to shutting down the political process on an issue of such profound public significance. Closing debate tends to close minds. People denied a voice are less likely to accept the ruling of a court on an issue that does not seem to be the sort of thing courts usually decide. As a thoughtful commentator observed about another issue, "The political process was moving . . . , not swiftly enough for advocates of quick, complete change, but majoritarian institutions were listening and acting. Heavy-handed judicial intervention was

difficult to justify and appears to have provoked, not resolved, conflict."
Ginsburg, Some Thoughts on Autonomy and Equality in Relation to *Roe
v. Wade,* 63 N.C. L. Rev. 375, 385–386 (1985). Indeed, however heartened
the proponents of same-sex marriage might be on this day, it is worth
acknowledging what they have lost, and lost forever: the opportunity to
win the true acceptance that comes from persuading their fellow citizens
of the justice of their cause. And they lose this just when the winds of
change were freshening at their backs.

Federal courts are blunt instruments when it comes to creating
rights. They have constitutional power only to resolve concrete cases or
controversies; they do not have the flexibility of legislatures to address
concerns of parties not before the court or to anticipate problems that
may arise from the exercise of a new right. Today's decision, for example,
creates serious questions about religious liberty. Many good and decent
people oppose same-sex marriage as a tenet of faith, and their freedom to
exercise religion is—unlike the right imagined by the majority—actually
spelled out in the Constitution. Amdt. 1.

Respect for sincere religious conviction has led voters and legislators
in every State that has adopted same-sex marriage democratically to
include accommodations for religious practice. The majority's decision
imposing same-sex marriage cannot, of course, create any such
accommodations. . . .

Hard questions arise when people of faith exercise religion in ways
that may be seen to conflict with the new right to same-sex marriage—
when, for example, a religious college provides married student housing
only to opposite-sex married couples, or a religious adoption agency
declines to place children with same-sex married couples. Indeed, the
Solicitor General candidly acknowledged that the tax exemptions of some
religious institutions would be in question if they opposed same-sex
marriage. There is little doubt that these and similar questions will soon
be before this Court. Unfortunately, people of faith can take no comfort
in the treatment they receive from the majority today.

Perhaps the most discouraging aspect of today's decision is the
extent to which the majority feels compelled to sully those on the other
side of the debate. The majority offers a cursory assurance that it does
not intend to disparage people who, as a matter of conscience, cannot
accept same-sex marriage. That disclaimer is hard to square with the
very next sentence, in which the majority explains that "the necessary
consequence" of laws codifying the traditional definition of marriage is to
"demea[n] or stigmatiz[e]" same-sex couples. The majority reiterates
such characterizations over and over. By the majority's account,
Americans who did nothing more than follow the understanding of
marriage that has existed for our entire history—in particular, the tens
of millions of people who voted to reaffirm their States' enduring
definition of marriage—have acted to "lock . . . out," "disparage,"
"disrespect and subordinate," and inflict "[d]ignitary wounds" upon their

gay and lesbian neighbors. These apparent assaults on the character of fairminded people will have an effect, in society and in court. Moreover, they are entirely gratuitous. It is one thing for the majority to conclude that the Constitution protects a right to same-sex marriage; it is something else to portray everyone who does not share the majority's "better informed understanding" as bigoted.

In the face of all this, a much different view of the Court's role is possible. That view is more modest and restrained. It is more skeptical that the legal abilities of judges also reflect insight into moral and philosophical issues. It is more sensitive to the fact that judges are unelected and unaccountable, and that the legitimacy of their power depends on confining it to the exercise of legal judgment. It is more attuned to the lessons of history, and what it has meant for the country and Court when Justices have exceeded their proper bounds. And it is less pretentious than to suppose that while people around the world have viewed an institution in a particular way for thousands of years, the present generation and the present Court are the ones chosen to burst the bonds of that history and tradition.

If you are among the many Americans—of whatever sexual orientation—who favor expanding same-sex marriage, by all means celebrate today's decision. Celebrate the achievement of a desired goal. Celebrate the opportunity for a new expression of commitment to a partner. Celebrate the availability of new benefits. But do not celebrate the Constitution. It had nothing to do with it.

I respectfully dissent.

■ **JUSTICE SCALIA, with whom JUSTICE THOMAS joins, dissenting.**

I join THE CHIEF JUSTICE's opinion in full. I write separately to call attention to this Court's threat to American democracy.

The substance of today's decree is not of immense personal importance to me. The law can recognize as marriage whatever sexual attachments and living arrangements it wishes, and can accord them favorable civil consequences, from tax treatment to rights of inheritance. Those civil consequences—and the public approval that conferring the name of marriage evidences—can perhaps have adverse social effects, but no more adverse than the effects of many other controversial laws. So it is not of special importance to me what the law says about marriage. It is of overwhelming importance, however, who it is that rules me. Today's decree says that my Ruler, and the Ruler of 320 million Americans coast-to-coast, is a majority of the nine lawyers on the Supreme Court. . . .

Until the courts put a stop to it, public debate over same-sex marriage displayed American democracy at its best. Individuals on both sides of the issue passionately, but respectfully, attempted to persuade their fellow citizens to accept their views. Americans considered the arguments and put the question to a vote. The electorates of 11 States, either directly or through their representatives, chose to expand the traditional definition of marriage. Many more decided not to. Win or lose, advocates for both sides continued pressing their cases, secure in the knowledge that an electoral loss can be negated by a later electoral win. That is exactly how our system of government is supposed to work.

The Constitution places some constraints on self-rule—constraints adopted *by the People themselves* when they ratified the Constitution and its Amendments. . . . These cases ask us to decide whether the Fourteenth Amendment contains a limitation that requires the States to license and recognize marriages between two people of the same sex. Does it remove *that* issue from the political process?

Of course not. It would be surprising to find a prescription regarding marriage in the Federal Constitution since, as the author of today's opinion reminded us only two years ago (in an opinion joined by the same Justices who join him today): "[R]egulation of domestic relations is an area that has long been regarded as a virtually exclusive province of the States." *United States v. Windsor*, 133 S.Ct. 2675, 2691 (2013). . . . But we need not speculate. When the Fourteenth Amendment was ratified in 1868, every State limited marriage to one man and one woman, and no one doubted the constitutionality of doing so. That resolves these cases. When it comes to determining the meaning of a vague constitutional provision—such as "due process of law" or "equal protection of the laws"—it is unquestionable that the People who ratified that provision did not understand it to prohibit a practice that remained both universal and uncontroversial in the years after ratification. We have no basis for striking down a practice that is not expressly prohibited by the Fourteenth Amendment's text, and that bears the endorsement of a long tradition of open, widespread, and unchallenged use dating back to the Amendment's ratification. Since there is no doubt whatever that the People never decided to prohibit the limitation of marriage to opposite-sex couples, the public debate over same-sex marriage must be allowed to continue.

But the Court ends this debate, in an opinion lacking even a thin veneer of law. Buried beneath the mummeries and straining-to-be-memorable passages of the opinion is a candid and startling assertion: No matter *what* it was the People ratified, the Fourteenth Amendment protects those rights that the Judiciary, in its "reasoned judgment," thinks the Fourteenth Amendment ought to protect. That is so because "[t]he generations that wrote and ratified the Bill of Rights and the Fourteenth Amendment did not presume to know the extent of freedom in all of its dimensions. . . ." One would think that sentence would continue: ". . . and therefore they provided for a means by which the People could amend the Constitution," or perhaps ". . . and therefore they left the creation of additional liberties, such as the freedom to marry someone of the same sex, to the People, through the never-ending process of legislation." But no. What logically follows, in the majority's judge-empowering estimation, is: "and so they entrusted to future generations a charter protecting the right of all persons to enjoy liberty as we learn its meaning." The "we," needless to say, is the nine of us. . . .

This is a naked judicial claim to legislative—indeed, *super*-legislative—power; a claim fundamentally at odds with our system of government. . . . A system of government that makes the People subordinate to a committee of nine unelected lawyers does not deserve to be called a democracy.

Judges are selected precisely for their skill as lawyers; whether they reflect the policy views of a particular constituency is not (or should not be) relevant. Not surprisingly then, the Federal Judiciary is hardly a cross-section of America. Take, for example, this Court, which consists of only nine men and women, all of them successful lawyers who studied at Harvard or Yale Law School. Four of the nine are natives of New York City. Eight of them grew up in east- and west-coast States. Only one hails from the vast expanse in-between. Not a single Southwesterner or even, to tell the truth, a genuine Westerner (California does not count). Not a single evangelical Christian (a group that comprises about one quarter of Americans), or even a Protestant of any denomination. The strikingly unrepresentative character of the body voting on today's social upheaval would be irrelevant if they were functioning as *judges,* answering the legal question whether the American people had ever ratified a constitutional provision that was understood to proscribe the traditional definition of marriage. But of course the Justices in today's majority are not voting on that basis; *they say they are not.* And to allow the policy question of same-sex marriage to be considered and resolved by a select, patrician, highly unrepresentative panel of nine is to violate a principle even more fundamental than no taxation without representation: no social transformation without representation. . . .

■ **JUSTICE THOMAS, with whom JUSTICE SCALIA joins, dissenting.**

. . . [T]he majority invokes our Constitution in the name of a "liberty" that the Framers would not have recognized, to the detriment of the liberty they sought to protect. Along the way, it rejects the idea—captured in our Declaration of Independence—that human dignity is innate and suggests instead that it comes from the Government. This distortion of our Constitution not only ignores the text, it inverts the relationship between the individual and the state in our Republic. I cannot agree with it. . . .

Even if the doctrine of substantive due process were somehow defensible—it is not—petitioners still would not have a claim. To invoke the protection of the Due Process Clause at all—whether under a theory of "substantive" or "procedural" due process—a party must first identify a deprivation of "life, liberty, or property." The majority claims these state laws deprive petitioners of "liberty," but the concept of "liberty" it conjures up bears no resemblance to any plausible meaning of that word as it is used in the Due Process Clauses.

A

1

As used in the Due Process Clauses, "liberty" most likely refers to "the power of locomotion, of changing situation, or removing one's person to whatsoever place one's own inclination may direct; without imprisonment or restraint, unless by due course of law." 1 W. Blackstone, Commentaries on the Laws of England 130 (1769) (Blackstone). That definition is drawn from the historical roots of the Clauses and is consistent with our Constitution's text and structure.

Both of the Constitution's Due Process Clauses reach back to Magna Carta. Chapter 39 of the original Magna Carta provided, "No free man shall be taken, imprisoned, disseised, outlawed, banished, or in any way destroyed, nor will We proceed against or prosecute him, except by the lawful judgment of his peers and by the law of the land." Magna Carta, ch. 39, in A. Howard, Magna Carta: Text and Commentary 43 (1964). . . . In his influential commentary on the provision many years later, Sir Edward Coke interpreted the words "by the law of the land" to mean the same thing as "by due process of the common law."

After Magna Carta became subject to renewed interest in the 17th century, William Blackstone referred to this provision as protecting the "absolute rights of every Englishman." And he formulated those absolute rights as "the right of personal security," which included the right to life; "the right of personal liberty"; and "the right of private property." He defined "the right of personal liberty" as "the power of locomotion, of changing situation, or removing one's person to whatsoever place one's own inclination may direct; without imprisonment or restraint, unless by due course of law."

The Framers drew heavily upon Blackstone's formulation, adopting provisions in early State Constitutions that replicated Magna Carta's language, but were modified to refer specifically to "life, liberty, or property." State decisions interpreting these provisions between the founding and the ratification of the Fourteenth Amendment almost uniformly construed the word "liberty" to refer only to freedom from physical restraint.

In enacting the Fifth Amendment's Due Process Clause, the Framers similarly chose to employ the "life, liberty, or property" formulation, though they otherwise deviated substantially from the States' use of Magna Carta's language in the Clause. When read in light of the history of that formulation, it is hard to see how the "liberty" protected by the Clause could be interpreted to include anything broader than freedom from physical restraint. That was the consistent usage of the time when "liberty" was paired with "life" and "property." And that usage avoids rendering superfluous those protections for "life" and "property."

If the Fifth Amendment uses "liberty" in this narrow sense, then the Fourteenth Amendment likely does as well. Indeed, this Court has previously commented, "The conclusion is . . . irresistible, that when the same phrase was employed in the Fourteenth Amendment [as was used in the Fifth Amendment], it was used in the same sense and with no greater extent." *Hurtado v. California,* 110 U.S. 516, 534–535 (1884). And this Court's earliest Fourteenth Amendment decisions appear to interpret the Clause as using "liberty" to mean freedom from physical restraint. . . . That the Court appears to have lost its way in more recent years does not justify deviating from the original meaning of the Clauses.

2

Even assuming that the "liberty" in those Clauses encompasses something more than freedom from physical restraint, it would not include the types of rights claimed by the majority. In the American legal tradition, liberty has long been understood as individual freedom *from* governmental action, not as a right *to* a particular governmental entitlement.

The founding-era understanding of liberty was heavily influenced by John Locke, whose writings "on natural rights and on the social and governmental contract" were cited "[i]n pamphlet after pamphlet" by American writers. B. Bailyn, The Ideological Origins of the American Revolution 27 (1967). Locke described men as existing in a state of nature, possessed of the "perfect freedom to order their actions and dispose of their possessions and persons as they think fit, within the bounds of the law of nature, without asking leave, or depending upon the will of any other man." J. Locke, Second Treatise of Civil Government, § 4, p. 4 (J. Gough ed. 1947) (Locke). Because that state of nature left men insecure in their persons and property, they entered civil society, trading a portion of their natural liberty for an increase in their security. Upon consenting to that order, men obtained civil liberty, or the freedom "to be under no other legislative power but that established by consent in the commonwealth; nor under the dominion of any will or restraint of any law, but what that legislative shall enact according to the trust put in it."

This philosophy permeated the 18th-century political scene in America. . . . The founding-era idea of civil liberty as natural liberty constrained by human law necessarily involved only those freedoms that existed *outside of* government. As one later commentator observed, "[L]iberty in the eighteenth century was thought of much more in relation to 'negative liberty'; that is, freedom *from,* not freedom *to,* freedom from a number of social and political evils, including arbitrary government power." J. Reid, The Concept of Liberty in the Age of the American Revolution 56 (1988). Or as one scholar put it in 1776, "[T]he common idea of liberty is merely negative, and is only the *absence of restraint.*" R. Hey, Observations on the Nature of Civil Liberty and the Principles of Government § 13, p. 8 (1776) . . . .

B

Whether we define "liberty" as locomotion or freedom from governmental action more broadly, petitioners have in no way been deprived of it.

Petitioners cannot claim, under the most plausible definition of "liberty," that they have been imprisoned or physically restrained by the States for participating in same-sex relationships. To the contrary, they have been able to cohabitate and raise their children in peace. They have been able to hold civil marriage ceremonies in States that recognize same-sex marriages and private religious ceremonies in all States. They have been able to travel freely around the country, making their homes where they please. Far from being incarcerated or physically restrained, petitioners have been left alone to order their lives as they see fit.

Nor, under the broader definition, can they claim that the States have restricted their ability to go about their daily lives as they would be able to absent governmental restrictions. Petitioners do not ask this Court to order the States to stop restricting their ability to enter same-sex relationships, to engage in intimate behavior, to make vows to their partners in public ceremonies, to engage in religious wedding ceremonies, to hold themselves out as married, or to raise children. The States have imposed no such restrictions. Nor have the States prevented petitioners from approximating a number of incidents of marriage through private legal means, such as wills, trusts, and powers of attorney.

Instead, the States have refused to grant them governmental entitlements. Petitioners claim that as a matter of "liberty," they are entitled to access privileges and benefits that exist solely *because of* the government. They want, for example, to receive the State's *imprimatur* on their marriages—on state issued marriage licenses, death certificates, or other official forms. And they want to receive various monetary benefits, including reduced inheritance taxes upon the death of a spouse, compensation if a spouse dies as a result of a work-related injury, or loss of consortium damages in tort suits. But receiving governmental recognition and benefits has nothing to do with any understanding of "liberty" that the Framers would have recognized.

To the extent that the Framers would have recognized a natural right to marriage that fell within the broader definition of liberty, it would not have included a right to governmental recognition and benefits. Instead, it would have included a right to engage in the very same activities that petitioners have been left free to engage in—making vows, holding religious ceremonies celebrating those vows, raising children, and otherwise enjoying the society of one's spouse—without governmental interference. . . .

Petitioners' misconception of liberty carries over into their discussion of our precedents identifying a right to marry, not one of which has expanded the concept of "liberty" beyond the concept of negative liberty. Those precedents all involved absolute prohibitions on private actions associated with marriage. *Loving v. Virginia,* 388 U.S. 1 (1967), for example, involved a couple who was criminally prosecuted for marrying in the District of Columbia and cohabiting in Virginia.[5] They were each sentenced to a year of imprisonment, suspended for a term of 25 years on the condition that they not reenter the Commonwealth together during that time.[6] In a similar vein, *Zablocki v. Redhail,* 434 U.S. 374 (1978), involved a man who was prohibited, on pain of criminal penalty, from "marry[ing] in Wisconsin or elsewhere" because of his outstanding child-support obligations. And *Turner v. Safley,* 482 U.S. 78 (1987), involved state inmates who were prohibited from entering marriages without the permission of the superintendent of the prison, permission that could not be granted absent compelling reasons. In *none* of those cases were individuals denied solely governmental recognition and benefits associated with marriage.

In a concession to petitioners' misconception of liberty, the majority characterizes petitioners' suit as a quest to "find . . . liberty by marrying someone of the same sex and having their marriages deemed lawful on the same terms and conditions as marriages between persons of the opposite sex." But "liberty" is not lost, nor can it be found in the way petitioners seek. As a philosophical matter, liberty is only freedom from governmental action, not an entitlement to governmental benefits. And as a constitutional matter, it is likely even narrower than that, encompassing only freedom from physical restraint and imprisonment. The majority's "better informed understanding of how constitutional imperatives define . . . liberty,"—better informed, we must assume, than that of the people who ratified the Fourteenth Amendment—runs headlong into the reality that our Constitution is a "collection of 'Thou

---

[5]   The suggestion of petitioners and their *amici* that antimiscegenation laws are akin to laws defining marriage as between one man and one woman is both offensive and inaccurate. "America's earliest laws against interracial sex and marriage were spawned by slavery." P. Pascoe, What Comes Naturally: Miscegenation Law and the Making of Race in America 19 (2009). For instance, Maryland's 1664 law prohibiting marriages between " 'freeborne English women' " and " 'Negro Sla[v]es' " was passed as part of the very act that authorized lifelong slavery in the colony. Virginia's antimiscegenation laws likewise were passed in a 1691 resolution entitled "An act for suppressing outlying Slaves." Act of Apr. 1691, Ch. XVI, 3 Va. Stat. 86 (W. Hening ed. 1823) (reprint 1969). "It was not until the Civil War threw the future of slavery into doubt that lawyers, legislators, and judges began to develop the elaborate justifications that signified the emergence of miscegenation law and made restrictions on interracial marriage the foundation of post-Civil War white supremacy."

Laws defining marriage as between one man and one woman do not share this sordid history. The traditional definition of marriage has prevailed in every society that has recognized marriage throughout history. Brief for Scholars of History and Related Disciplines as *Amici Curiae* 1. It arose not out of a desire to shore up an invidious institution like slavery, but out of a desire "to increase the likelihood that children will be born and raised in stable and enduring family units by both the mothers and the fathers who brought them into this world." *Id.,* at 8. And it has existed in civilizations containing all manner of views on homosexuality.

[6]   The prohibition extended so far as to forbid even religious ceremonies, thus raising a serious question under the First Amendment's Free Exercise Clause . . . .

shalt nots,'" *Reid v. Covert,* 354 U.S. 1, 9 (1957) (plurality opinion), not
"Thou shalt provides."

III

The majority's inversion of the original meaning of liberty will likely
cause collateral damage to other aspects of our constitutional order that
protect liberty.

A

The majority apparently disregards the political process as a
protection for liberty. . . . As a general matter, when the States act
through their representative governments or by popular vote, the liberty
of their residents is fully vindicated. This is no less true when some
residents disagree with the result; indeed, it seems difficult to imagine
any law on which all residents of a State would agree. What matters is
that the process established by those who created the society has been
honored.

That process has been honored here. The definition of marriage has
been the subject of heated debate in the States. Legislatures have
repeatedly taken up the matter on behalf of the People, and 35 States
have put the question to the People themselves. In 32 of those 35 States,
the People have opted to retain the traditional definition of marriage.
That petitioners disagree with the result of that process does not make it
any less legitimate. Their civil liberty has been vindicated.

B

Aside from undermining the political processes that protect our
liberty, the majority's decision threatens the religious liberty our Nation
has long sought to protect. . . .

Numerous *amici*—even some not supporting the States—have
cautioned the Court that its decision here will "have unavoidable and
wide-ranging implications for religious liberty." In our society, marriage
is not simply a governmental institution; it is a religious institution as
well. Today's decision might change the former, but it cannot change the
latter. It appears all but inevitable that the two will come into conflict,
particularly as individuals and churches are confronted with demands to
participate in and endorse civil marriages between same-sex couples.

The majority appears unmoved by that inevitability. It makes only
a weak gesture toward religious liberty in a single paragraph. And even
that gesture indicates a misunderstanding of religious liberty in our
Nation's tradition. Religious liberty is about more than just the
protection for "religious organizations and persons . . . as they seek to
teach the principles that are so fulfilling and so central to their lives and
faiths." Religious liberty is about freedom of action in matters of religion
generally, and the scope of that liberty is directly correlated to the civil
restraints placed upon religious practice.

Although our Constitution provides some protection against such governmental restrictions on religious practices, the People have long elected to afford broader protections than this Court's constitutional precedents mandate. Had the majority allowed the definition of marriage to be left to the political process—as the Constitution requires—the People could have considered the religious liberty implications of deviating from the traditional definition as part of their deliberative process. Instead, the majority's decision short-circuits that process, with potentially ruinous consequences for religious liberty.

IV

Perhaps recognizing that these cases do not actually involve liberty as it has been understood, the majority goes to great lengths to assert that its decision will advance the "dignity" of same-sex couples. The flaw in that reasoning, of course, is that the Constitution contains no "dignity" Clause, and even if it did, the government would be incapable of bestowing dignity.

Human dignity has long been understood in this country to be innate. When the Framers proclaimed in the Declaration of Independence that "all men are created equal" and "endowed by their Creator with certain unalienable Rights," they referred to a vision of mankind in which all humans are created in the image of God and therefore of inherent worth. That vision is the foundation upon which this Nation was built.

The corollary of that principle is that human dignity cannot be taken away by the government. Slaves did not lose their dignity (any more than they lost their humanity) because the government allowed them to be enslaved. Those held in internment camps did not lose their dignity because the government confined them. And those denied governmental benefits certainly do not lose their dignity because the government denies them those benefits. The government cannot bestow dignity, and it cannot take it away. . . .

Our Constitution—like the Declaration of Independence before it—was predicated on a simple truth: One's liberty, not to mention one's dignity, was something to be shielded from—not provided by—the State. Today's decision casts that truth aside. In its haste to reach a desired result, the majority misapplies a clause focused on "due process" to afford substantive rights, disregards the most plausible understanding of the "liberty" protected by that clause, and distorts the principles on which this Nation was founded. Its decision will have inestimable consequences for our Constitution and our society. I respectfully dissent.

■ **JUSTICE ALITO, with whom JUSTICE SCALIA and JUSTICE THOMAS join, dissenting.**

. . . Attempting to circumvent the problem presented by the newness of the right found in these cases, the majority claims that the issue is the right to equal treatment. Noting that marriage is a fundamental right, the majority argues that a State has no valid reason for denying that right to same-sex couples. This reasoning is dependent upon a particular understanding of the purpose of civil marriage. Although the Court expresses the point in loftier terms, its argument is that the fundamental purpose of marriage is to promote the well-being of those who choose to marry. Marriage provides emotional fulfillment and the promise of support in times of need. And by benefiting persons who choose to wed, marriage indirectly benefits society because persons who live in stable, fulfilling, and supportive relationships make better citizens. It is for these reasons, the argument goes, that States encourage and formalize marriage, confer special benefits on married persons, and also impose some special obligations. This understanding of the States' reasons for recognizing marriage enables the majority to argue that same-sex marriage serves the States' objectives in the same way as opposite-sex marriage.

This understanding of marriage, which focuses almost entirely on the happiness of persons who choose to marry, is shared by many people today, but it is not the traditional one. For millennia, marriage was inextricably linked to the one thing that only an opposite-sex couple can do: procreate.

Adherents to different schools of philosophy use different terms to explain why society should formalize marriage and attach special benefits and obligations to persons who marry. Here, the States defending their adherence to the traditional understanding of marriage have explained their position using the pragmatic vocabulary that characterizes most American political discourse. Their basic argument is that States formalize and promote marriage, unlike other fulfilling human relationships, in order to encourage potentially procreative conduct to take place within a lasting unit that has long been thought to provide the best atmosphere for raising children. They thus argue that there are reasonable secular grounds for restricting marriage to opposite-sex couples.

If this traditional understanding of the purpose of marriage does not ring true to all ears today, that is probably because the tie between marriage and procreation has frayed. Today, for instance, more than 40% of all children in this country are born to unmarried women. This development undoubtedly is both a cause and a result of changes in our society's understanding of marriage.

While, for many, the attributes of marriage in 21st-century America have changed, those States that do not want to recognize same-sex marriage have not yet given up on the traditional understanding. They worry that by officially abandoning the older understanding, they may contribute to marriage's further decay. It is far beyond the outer reaches of this Court's authority to say that a State may not adhere to the understanding of marriage that has long prevailed, not just in this country and others with similar cultural roots, but also in a great variety of countries and cultures all around the globe. . . .

III

Today's decision usurps the constitutional right of the people to decide whether to keep or alter the traditional understanding of marriage. The decision will also have other important consequences.

It will be used to vilify Americans who are unwilling to assent to the new orthodoxy. In the course of its opinion, the majority compares traditional marriage laws to laws that denied equal treatment for African-Americans and women. The implications of this analogy will be exploited by those who are determined to stamp out every vestige of dissent.

Perhaps recognizing how its reasoning may be used, the majority attempts, toward the end of its opinion, to reassure those who oppose same-sex marriage that their rights of conscience will be protected. We will soon see whether this proves to be true. I assume that those who cling to old beliefs will be able to whisper their thoughts in the recesses of their homes, but if they repeat those views in public, they will risk being labeled as bigots and treated as such by governments, employers, and schools.

The system of federalism established by our Constitution provides a way for people with different beliefs to live together in a single nation. If the issue of same-sex marriage had been left to the people of the States, it is likely that some States would recognize same-sex marriage and others would not. It is also possible that some States would tie recognition to protection for conscience rights. The majority today makes that impossible. By imposing its own views on the entire country, the majority facilitates the marginalization of the many Americans who have traditional ideas. Recalling the harsh treatment of gays and lesbians in the past, some may think that turnabout is fair play. But if that sentiment prevails, the Nation will experience bitter and lasting wounds.

Today's decision will also have a fundamental effect on this Court and its ability to uphold the rule of law. If a bare majority of Justices can invent a new right and impose that right on the rest of the country, the only real limit on what future majorities will be able to do is their own sense of what those with political power and cultural influence are willing to tolerate. Even enthusiastic supporters of same-sex marriage should worry about the scope of the power that today's majority claims.

Today's decision shows that decades of attempts to restrain this Court's abuse of its authority have failed. A lesson that some will take from today's decision is that preaching about the proper method of interpreting the Constitution or the virtues of judicial self-restraint and humility cannot compete with the temptation to achieve what is viewed as a noble end by any practicable means. I do not doubt that my colleagues in the majority sincerely see in the Constitution a vision of liberty that happens to coincide with their own. But this sincerity is cause for concern, not comfort. What it evidences is the deep and perhaps irremediable corruption of our legal culture's conception of constitutional interpretation.

Most Americans—understandably—will cheer or lament today's decision because of their views on the issue of same-sex marriage. But all Americans, whatever their thinking on that issue, should worry about what the majority's claim of power portends.

NOTE ON EQUALITY, LIBERTY, AND FEDERALISM IN THE RECOGNITION OF SAME-SEX MARRIAGE

1. The Obama Administration declined to defend DOMA's constitutionality in *Windsor* on account of its view that classifications based on sexual orientation are suspect and subject to intermediate scrutiny under the Equal Protection Clause.[11] At the time, there was no precedential support for that proposition other than the Ninth Circuit's decision in *Watkins*, and that decision had been subsequently withdrawn by the *en banc* court.[12] Should the President be able to decline to defend a statute's constitutionality under these circumstances? In your own view, was the pre-*Windsor* law so clearly against DOMA that a President could not defend it in good faith? On the other hand, the President does take his own oath to defend the Constitution; isn't it important to allow him to employ his own judgment as a further check on unconstitutional action by Congress?

In addressing these questions, keep in mind that a decision not to defend is likely to lead to a statute's invalidation. This may function, in practice, as a sort of Presidential "super veto," since it may be applied to statutes that became law before the President took office and cannot be overridden by Congress. If you agree with President Obama's decision not to defend the DOMA, would you also agree that the next Republican president could have declined to defend the Affordable Care Act against a constitutional challenge? If you do think that there should be constraints on Presidential decisions not to defend, where would you draw the line?[13]

2. What was the Court's rationale in *Windsor*? An *amicus* brief had argued that Congress lacked any enumerated power to enact the DOMA,[14]

---

[11] *See Letter from the Attorney General to Congress on Litigation Involving the Defense of Marriage Act*, Feb. 23, 2011, available at http://www.justice.gov/opa/pr/2011/February/11-ag-223.html. The administration continued, however, to *enforce* the statute notwithstanding its view that the DOMA was unconstitutional. This meant that the IRS collected $363,053 from Edith Windsor under a statute that the President had concluded was so clearly unconstitutional that he could not defend it in court. Is this behavior with the President's oath to support the Constitution? Shouldn't the President have to either abandon the statute entirely—neither enforcing nor defending it—or enforce *and* defend it?

[12] *See Watkins v. U.S. Army*, 875 F.2d 699, 711 (9th Cir. 1989) (*en banc*) (ruling for Watkins on other grounds).

[13] On these questions, *see generally* Daniel J. Meltzer, *Executive Defense of Congressional Acts*, 61 DUKE L. J. 1183 (2012).

[14] *See* Brief of Federalism Scholars as Amici Curiae in Support of Respondent Windsor, *United States v. Windsor*, No 12–307 (filed March 2013), available at http://scholarship.law.duke.edu/faculty_scholarship/2858/.

and the Court began its analysis with an extensive discussion of the primacy of the states with respect to marriage. But Justice Kennedy ultimately found it "unnecessary to decide whether [DOMA's] federal intrusion on state power is a violation of the Constitution because it disrupts the federal balance." Instead, the Court's holding plainly rested on equal protection. As in *Romer*, Justice Kennedy purported to find DOMA unconstitutional under rational basis review. But wasn't Justice Scalia right, in dissent, to say that "the Court certainly does not *apply* anything that resembles that deferential framework"?

If *Windsor* did apply some form of heightened scrutiny, how did it get there? The majority does not appear to hold that classifications based on sexual orientation are inherently suspect, as the President had concluded in his decision not to defend DOMA. But what about the fundamental rights prong of equal protection analysis? As we saw in Chapter Fifteen, the Court declared marriage a fundamental right for equal protection purposes in *Loving v. Virginia*, 388 U.S. 1 (1967).[15] But controversy has raged over whether "marriage" is inherently between a man and a woman, or whether it is simply a general notion of commitment that any sort of couple could enter into. Proponents of the former view have stressed the procreative function of marriage, arguing that marriage inherently has to do with childbirth and childrearing, and that same-sex couples simply cannot have that sort of relationship. Same-sex marriage proponents, on the other hand, have argued for a romantic conception of marriage based on the loving commitment of any two persons. But how is a court to choose between the procreative and the romantic vision of marriage in order to determine whether same-sex and different-sex couples are similarly situated for equal protection purposes? Is there any objective constitutional basis for such a judgment?

Justice Kennedy's *Windsor* opinion seems to have used federalism to escape this dilemma. He did not have to choose between procreation and romance because *New York* had already made that choice, opting for the broader definition of marriage when it decided to recognize same-sex unions. Hence, the Court wrote that

> The class to which DOMA directs its restrictions and restraints are those persons who are joined in same-sex marriages made lawful by the State. DOMA singles out a class of persons deemed by a State entitled to recognition and protection to enhance their own liberty. It imposes a disability on the class by refusing to acknowledge a status the State finds to be dignified and proper.

DOMA thus denied Edith Windsor the equal protection of the laws *of New York* by imposing a distinction between same-sex and different-sex couples that New York itself had rejected.[16]

---

[15] *Loving* was, in a sense, overdetermined. The Court rested strict scrutiny in that case on the presence of race discrimination as well as a fundamental right. But surely if contraception and abortion are fundamental rights, *marriage*—with a far stronger pedigree in law and tradition—is also fundamental.

[16] For elaboration of this reading of *Windsor*, see Ernest A. Young & Erin C. Blondel, *Federalism, Liberty, and Equality in* United States v. Windsor, 2012 CATO SUP. CT. REV. 117

Does this incorporation of federalism into the equal protection analysis make sense? Or does it make better sense of *Windsor* to read it as simply holding that the Equal Protection Clause requires equal access to marriage for same-sex couples, full stop?

3.   Federalism has also played a broader role in the same-sex marriage debate. In 1996, when DOMA was enacted, only 27 percent of Americans supported same-sex marriage, while 68 percent opposed it.[17] Pollsters have found a remarkable—and remarkably steady—increase in support for same-sex marriage over the past two decades. Three years ago, *uber*-pollster Nate Silver projected that, by 2020, majorities in all but six states would favor same-sex marriage in a ballot initiative, with four more states extremely close to the tipping point by that date and the last two not so far behind.[18] National polling in 2015, just before the Court's decision in *Obergefell*, showed 60 percent in favor and 37 percent against.[19]

Consistent with early disapproval of same-sex marriage, 40 states had either constitutional or statutory prohibitions on same-sex marriage by the end of 2000.[20] But proponents and opponents of same-sex marriage were not evenly distributed geographically, and in some states proponents were able to secure state laws recognizing civil unions for gay couples or full-fledged same-sex marriages. The initial changes were ordered by state supreme courts construing their state constitutions, but beginning with Connecticut in 2005 some state legislatures began recognizing same-sex unions by statute.[21]

Although we presently lack much empirical work on the causes of this sea change in American opinion and law, it seems plausible that the dynamics of federalism had much to do with it. Adoption of a policy by one jurisdiction has an important demonstrative effect. Hence, advocates of same-sex marriage can point to Vermont, an early adopter, for an example of what a world with same-sex marriage would look like. Some evidence suggests support for gay rights is closely linked to familiarity with gay individuals.[22] While that research assesses the impact of person-to-person interactions, a more diffuse form of familiarity effect might exist as well.

(2013); Ernest A. Young, United States v. Windsor *and the Role of State Law in Defining Rights Claims*, 99 VA. L. REV. ONLINE 39 (2013). For a somewhat different view, emphasizing *Windsor*'s anti-animus strand, see Dale Carpenter, *Windsor Products: Equal Protection from Animus*, 2013 Sup. Ct. Rev. 183 (2014).

[17] *Marriage*, Gallup.com, http://www.gallup.com/poll/117328/marriage.aspx (last visited Feb. 1, 2016).

[18] Nate Silver, *How Opinion on Same-Sex marriage is Changing, and What It Means*, FiveThirtyEight, N.Y. TIMES, March 26, 2013, available at http://fivethirtyeight.blogs.nytimes.com/2013/03/26/how-opinion-on-same-sex-marriage-is-changing-and-what-it-means/?_r=0.

[19] *Marriage, supra* note 17.

[20] *Same Sex Marriage Laws*, Nat'l Conf. of State Legislatures, http://www.ncsl.org/research/human-services/same-sex-marriage-laws.aspx#2 (visited Feb. 1, 2016).

[21] *See id.*

[22] See, e.g., Shawn Neidorf & Rich Morin, *Four-in-Ten Americans Have Close Friends or Relatives Who are Gay*, PEW RES. CTR. (May 22, 2007), http://www.pewresearch.org/2007/05/22/fourinten-americans-have-close-friends-or-relatives-who-are-gay/ (reporting poll findings that "[people who have a close gay friend or family member are more likely to support gay marriage and they are also significantly less likely to favor allowing schools to fire gay teachers than are those with little or no personal contact with gays").

Americans know that the sky has not fallen in Vermont since the state recognized same-sex marriages in 2009, and no one has turned into a pillar of salt. By 2013, when the Court decided *Windsor*, almost 40 percent of the United States population lived in a jurisdiction that recognized same-sex marriages. Under those circumstances, it becomes more difficult to portray those marriages as weird or un-American.[23] But without the initial example of a few states experimenting with reform, it is hard to know whether this revolution would have gotten off the ground.[24]

Not all states used their autonomy to legalize same-sex marriage in this period, of course; in fact, most states went out of their way to prohibit it. Does that suggest that the federal structure was a net negative for marriage reform? Or is it more important, in the long run, to have the potential for a few significant experiments even if most states initially reject reform?

4.   *Obergefell* posed the question that *Windsor* seemed to reserve: Can a *state* validly prohibit same-sex marriage? And in resolving this question, the Court was forced to decide for itself what conception of marriage best fits our traditions, practices, and mores. Is *Obergefell* primarily a decision about due process or equal protection? Is the Court's rationale (a) that everyone has a fundamental right to marry the person of their choice? (b) that marriage is a fundamental right, and therefore it may not be denied to same-sex couples without compelling justification? Or (c) that denial of equal rights to marry is a form of discrimination based on sexual orientation that cannot pass muster under the applicable level of scrutiny? Do any of these traditional doctrinal formulae really fit the Court's opinion? Or does *Obergefell* signify the further weakening of traditional doctrinal categories (similar to *Lawrence*'s undifferentiated appeal to "liberty")?

5.   Given the polling discussed in note (3), *supra*, there is every reason to believe that (a) the Court's action in *Obergefell* was largely consistent with the evolving state of American public opinion, and (b) recognition of same-sex marriage would have come about through political action within the reasonably foreseeable future even absent the Court's ruling. Should this make any difference? Which way would it cut? Does it show that the Court gauged the *zeitgeist* correctly, or that the Court's intervention was unnecessary? If the correct interpretation of the Constitution is that same-sex couples have a right to marry, on what ground could one urge them to await a democratic resolution of this controversy?

6.   Unlike *Windsor*, *Obergefell* imposed a uniform national answer to the question whether same-sex marriages should be recognized. In dissent,

---

[23] Eliana Dockterman, *These are the Next Gay-Marriage Battlegrounds*, Time, Nov. 10, 2013,   http://nation.time.com/2013/11/10/these-are-the-next-gay-marriage-battlegrounds/ ("With Illinois, we have 37% of American people living in a freedom-to-marry state . . . .") (quoting Alan Wolfson of Freedom to Marry).

[24] *See generally* Heather K. Gerken, *Dissenting by Deciding*, 57 STAN. L. REV. 1745 (2005) (arguing that where national minorities constitute a majority within a particular state, they can not only express their dissenting views, but actually enact them into law and therefore more effectively demonstrate the virtues of their position); Ernest A. Young, *Exit, Voice, and Loyalty as Federalism Strategies: Lessons from the Same-Sex Marriage Debate*, 85 U. COLO. L. REV. 1133 (2014) (discussing the influence of federalist dynamics on the evolution of law and opinion on same-sex marriage).

Justice Alito pointed out that "[t]he system of federalism established by our Constitution provides a way for people with different beliefs to live together in a single nation." Under *Windsor*, for example, one might (at least in principle) defend New York's right to recognize same-sex marriage without impugning the motives of states refusing such recognition. Under the Court's due process/equality rationale in *Obergefell*, on the other hand, isn't it hard to say that recognition of same-sex is constitutionally *required* without questioning whether people who would deny such recognition are people of good will? That hardly means, of course, that the *Obergefell* majority's reasoning is incorrect—but it does raise the stakes of constitutional debate. Is there any way remaining, in *Obergefell*'s wake, to say that reasonable people may disagree on these questions? If not, how do we help the millions of Americans who celebrate the Court's ruling "live together in a single nation" with the millions of Americans who are not yet convinced?

7.   A final question takes us back to the origins of judicial review in *Marbury v. Madison*: In that case, Chief Justice Marshall had to walk on a knife edge between defiance and possible retaliation from the political branches, on the one hand, and institutional irrelevance on the other. Just over two centuries later, in *Obergefell*, the Court asserted—with complete confidence that the rest of the nation would comply—its authority to redefine one of the most basic relationships in American society. What explains this astounding transformation in the Court's role and authority? Does it mean, as the dissenters suggested, that We the People have lost the authority to govern ourselves? Or does it reflect a historically remarkable common commitment of Americans to the rule of law?

INDEX